ENCYCLOPEDIA OF
RELIGION
SECOND EDITION

ENCYCLOPEDIA OF RELIGION

SECOND EDITION

1

AARON
•
ATTENTION

LINDSAY JONES
EDITOR IN CHIEF

MACMILLAN REFERENCE USA
An imprint of Thomson Gale, a part of The Thomson Corporation

THOMSON
GALE

Detroit • New York • San Francisco • San Diego • New Haven, Conn. • Waterville, Maine • London • Munich

THOMSON
GALE

Encyclopedia of Religion, Second Edition
Lindsay Jones, Editor in Chief

For more information, contact
Macmillan Reference USA
An imprint of Thomson Gale
27500 Drake Rd.
Farmington, Hills, MI 48331-3535
Or you can visit our Internet site at
http://www.gale.com

LIBRARY OF CONGRESS CATALOGING-IN-PUBLICATION DATA

Encyclopedia of religion / Lindsay Jones, editor in chief.— 2nd ed.
p. cm.
Includes bibliographical references and index.
ISBN 0-02-865733-0 (SET HARDCOVER : ALK. PAPER) —
ISBN 0-02-865734-9 (V. 1) — ISBN 0-02-865735-7 (v. 2) —
ISBN 0-02-865736-5 (v. 3) — ISBN 0-02-865737-3 (v. 4) —
ISBN 0-02-865738-1 (v. 5) — ISBN 0-02-865739-X (v. 6) —
ISBN 0-02-865740-3 (v. 7) — ISBN 0-02-865741-1 (v. 8) —
ISBN 0-02-865742-X (v. 9) — ISBN 0-02-865743-8 (v. 10)
— ISBN 0-02-865980-5 (v. 11) — ISBN 0-02-865981-3 (v.
12) — ISBN 0-02-865982-1 (v. 13) — ISBN 0-02-865983-X
(v. 14) — ISBN 0-02-865984-8 (v. 15)
1. RELIGION—ENCYCLOPEDIAS. I. JONES, LINDSAY,
1954-

BL31.E46 2005
200'.3—dc22 2004017052

This title is also available as an e-book.
ISBN 0-02-865997-X
Contact your Thomson Gale representative for ordering information.

Printed in the United States of America
10 9 8 7 6 5 4 3 2 1

EDITORS AND CONSULTANTS

Harvard Forum on Religion and Ecology
Ecology and Religion

JOSEPH HARRIS
Francis Lee Higginson Professor of English Literature and Professor of Folklore, Harvard University
Germanic Religions

URSULA KING
Professor Emerita, Senior Research Fellow and Associate Member of the Institute for Advanced Studies, University of Bristol, England, and Professorial Research Associate, Centre for Gender and Religions Research, School of Oriental and African Studies, University of London
Gender and Religion

DAVID MORGAN
Duesenberg Professor of Christianity and the Arts, and Professor of Humanities and Art History, Valparaiso University
Color Inserts and Essays

JOSEPH F. NAGY
Professor, Department of English, University of California, Los Angeles
Celtic Religion

MATTHEW OJO
Obafemi Awolowo University
African Religions

JUHA PENTIKÄINEN
Professor of Comparative Religion, The University of Helsinki, Member of Academia Scientiarum Fennica, Finland
Arctic Religions and Uralic Religions

TED PETERS
Professor of Systematic Theology, Pacific Lutheran Theological Seminary and the Center for Theology and the Natural Sciences at the Graduate Theological Union, Berkeley, California
Science and Religion

FRANK E. REYNOLDS
Professor of the History of Religions and Buddhist Studies in the Divinity School and the Department of South Asian Languages and Civilizations, Emeritus, University of Chicago
History of Religions

GONZALO RUBIO
Assistant Professor, Department of Classics and Ancient Mediterranean Studies and Department of History and Religious Studies, Pennsylvania State University
Ancient Near Eastern Religions

SUSAN SERED
Director of Research, Religion, Health and Healing Initiative, Center for the Study of World Religions, Harvard University, and Senior Research Associate, Center for Women's Health and Human Rights, Suffolk University
Healing, Medicine, and Religion

LAWRENCE E. SULLIVAN
Professor, Department of Theology, University of Notre Dame
History of Religions

WINNIFRED FALLERS SULLIVAN
Dean of Students and Senior Lecturer in the Anthropology and Sociology of Religion, University of Chicago
Law and Religion

TOD SWANSON
Associate Professor of Religious Studies, and Director, Center for Latin American Studies, Arizona State University
South American Religions

MARY EVELYN TUCKER
Professor of Religion, Bucknell University, Founder and Coordinator, Harvard Forum on Religion and Ecology, Research Fellow, Harvard Yenching Institute, Research Associate, Harvard Reischauer Institute of Japanese Studies
Ecology and Religion

HUGH URBAN
Associate Professor, Department of Comparative Studies, Ohio State University
Politics and Religion

CATHERINE WESSINGER
Professor of the History of Religions and Women's Studies, Loyola University New Orleans
New Religious Movements

ROBERT A. YELLE
Mellon Postdoctoral Fellow, University of Toronto
Law and Religion

ERIC ZIOLKOWSKI
Charles A. Dana Professor of Religious Studies, Lafayette College
Literature and Religion

EDITORIAL AND PRODUCTION STAFF

PUBLISHER
Frank Menchaca

PUBLISHING DIRECTOR
Hélène Potter

PROJECT EDITORS
Deirdre S. Blanchfield, Dawn Cavalieri, Joann Cerrito, Stephen Cusack, Deirdre Graves, Alan Hedblad, Anjanelle Klisz

CONTRIBUTING PROJECT EDITORS
Katy Balcer, Shawn Corridor, Mark Drouillard, Melissa Hill, Jane Malonis, Kate Millson, Jenai Mynatt, Jaime E. Noce, Carol Schwartz, Christine Slovey, Ken Wachsberger, Nicole Watkins

EDITORIAL TECHNICAL SUPPORT
Mark Springer

ADMINISTRATIVE SUPPORT
Cheryl Poloni

MANUSCRIPT EDITORS
Kari Bethel, Carol Brennan, Sheryl A. Ciccarelli, Judith A. Clinebell, Tony Coulter, Judith Culligan, Andrew Cunningham, Anne C. Davidson, Michael R. Fischbach, Rebecca J. Frey, Paul R. Greenland, Ellen Hawley, Peter Jaskowiak, Jean Fortune Kaplan, Eric B. Lagergren, Michael L. Levine, Steven M. Long, Eric Lowenkron, Matthew May, Andrew H. Miller, Michael J. O'Neal, Janet Patterson, Kathleen A. Roy, Mary H. Russell, Amy Loerch Strumolo, Karen Akins Swartz, Alan Thwaits, Visual Education Group

PROOFREADERS
Dorothy Bauhoff, Judith Culligan, Laurie DiMauro, Jennifer Gariepy, Kevin S. Hile, Carol Holmes, Thomas F. McMahon, Melodie Monahan, Amy L. Unterburger, Thomas Wiloch

BIBLIOGRAPHY RESEARCHERS
Warner Belanger, Erin Colihan, Brian Collins, Mary V. Dearborn, Daniela Dumbrava, Dina Ripsman Eylon, Anthony P. Johnson, Arthur McKeown, Laura Morelli, Chiara Ombretta Tommasi

TRANSLATORS
Names of translators appear throughout the body of the encyclopedia, at the end of each article that has been rendered into English.

INDEXER
Coughlin Indexing Services, Inc.

PRODUCT DESIGN
Michelle DiMercurio, Tracey Rowens

IMAGING
Randy Bassett, Lezlie Light, Michael Logusz, Dan Newell, Christine O'Bryan, Denay Wilding

GRAPHIC ART
Mark A. Berger

RIGHTS ACQUISITION AND MANAGEMENT
Lori Hines, Mari Masalin-Cooper, Shalice Shah-Caldwell

TYPESETTER
Datapage Technologies International, Inc.

COMPOSITION
Evi Seoud, Mary Beth Trimper

MANUFACTURING
Wendy Blurton, Dorothy Maki

TABLE OF CONTENTS

*Volume 15 includes Appendix, Synoptic Outline of
Contents, and Index*

PREFACE TO THE SECOND EDITION

To participate in a revision of Mircea Eliade's *Encyclopedia of Religion,* first published in 1987, is an occasion of intense humility, but also a grand opportunity. Though not without its critics, the first edition was suitably heralded as the standard reference work in the field, a truly landmark achievement. The work of revision has, at nearly every turn, amplified rather than diminished appreciation for the accomplishment of those original volumes. Dealing firsthand with the conceptual and organizational challenges, coupled with the logistical labors of coordinating the efforts of countless scholars and editors, redoubles a sense of admiration, respect, and gratitude for the makers of the original version of this encyclopedia.

If the making of that original set posed innumerable theoretical, organizational, and practical challenges, the revision of such a work evokes no fewer questions of balance and compromise. On the one hand, the building and remodeling of a work of this wide scope is a preeminently collaborative enterprise. It is born of a vast community of scholars, together participating in an immensely collective project; the interactivity among editors, consultants, and contributors has indeed provided perhaps the most rewarding aspects of this project. Yet, on the other hand, such a large and multifaceted undertaking has a deeply impersonal, even anonymous, quality. Face-to-face meetings among participants are few, schedules fast, authors and editors far-spaced. By engaging the talents of so many people from so many places, large encyclopedias, and even more so their revisions, perpetuate the pretense of anonymous, objective, and interchangeable authors; numerous hands touch every piece, and the target of responsibility either for credit or for blame is not always easy to locate.

Such an encyclopedia requires, in one respect, a large measure of consensus among contributors as to what religion is and what academic students of religion ought to and ought not to circumscribe within their view. But, in another respect, it is a scholarly consensus of a very broad and pliant sort. Careful reading reveals enormous diversity of perspective among first-edition contributors, far more than is often assumed; and for the revision, even among the principal decision makers, and positively among the contributors, there is a very wide spectrum of opinions as to the most serviceable definitions of religion and the most worthy purview for the field of religious studies.

On the one hand, encyclopedias seem by nature vehicles of convention, destined to simplify, reify, essentialize, and provide falsely stabilized views of dynamic historical eras, religious traditions, doctrines, and practices. Yet, on the other hand, a large percentage of the contributors to this project understand their academic calling to be primarily one of disruption and destabilization; many have explicitly dedicated their careers to complicating and calling to question conventional wisdoms about religion and things religious. Thus in order to capitalize on their talents, contributors were provided explicit instructions, tidy scope descriptions, and specific word allotments, but they were also provided a fair measure of space for improvisation and flexibility. One member of the editorial board framed the balance this way:

> The letters to all contributors should include a general statement that we wish to respect their judgment in defining the general contours of each article, and the scope descriptions are meant only to be suggestive, although of course we do hope that we will be taken seriously. Also that we are looking for entries that reflect the current state of the field and that we are hoping that each entry will not gloss over problems of evidence or conceptualization in the current state of the field but will instead frankly acknowledge such problems and make them key parts of the entry in a bid to make the [second edition of the *Encyclopedia of Religion*] look to the future and help to shape things to come.

The intellectual challenges are likewise reflected in more practical tensions and balancing acts. Perhaps most onerous-ly, the recruitment of literally hundreds of qualified scholars, available and willing to deliver their work in a timely manner, is no mean task. For some, participation in an encyclopedia of this stature is a high calling, a fortuitous opportunity to engage a uniquely wide readership; others, however, admit far less enthusiasm about undertaking assignments construed as diversions from their more technical research, more public service than privilege. Once aboard, contributors had to balance the standards of accuracy, sophistication, and scholarly nuance that would satisfy themselves and their academic peers with the encyclopedia's incentive to reach a far more broad, less specialized audience.

The balancing of word counts is likewise a constant concern, and the space allotted to various topics is, to some real extent, a telling indicator as to the relative importance of those topics, at least in the eyes of the editorial board. Yet, equations of article length and significance, a familiar assumption among reviewers, are invariably too simple, too little aware of the practical exigencies of accepted and declined invitations, met and missed deadlines, obeyed and ignored editorial recommendations. The most well considered intentions and the clearest of visions are, not infrequently, causalities in the stiff competition for the time of twenty-first century academics. In fact, it is both noteworthy and deeply disappointing that several dozen additional new articles were conceived but never successfully assigned, and also that at least three dozen promised articles had not arrived by the production deadline, and thus had to be omitted from the revision. Gaps and asymmetries in coverage could, therefore, have innumerable explanations.

Be that as it may, perhaps the most vexing acts of balance and compromise are built into the very notion of "revision" itself. Neither defense nor attack, revision demands commingled attitudes of respect for and discontent with the original. To revise requires, on the one side, that a goodly portion of the previous work will remain intact; this editorial board was not afforded a fully fresh point of departure. Yet, on the other side, the initiative of revising does afford, even necessitates, changes, reconceptualizations, and wholly new additions that respond both to recent events and to recent trends in scholarship. Revision is, by nature and by design, a balancing and a juxtaposition of old and new elements.

This complex intermingling of first-edition and new components enriches but also greatly complicates the critical use and assessment of these volumes. The synoptic outline of contents, the alphabetical list of entries, and the index provide usefully comprehensive guides, but to discover all that is new and different between the second edition and its precedent can, nonetheless, pose a difficult challenge. The remainder of this preface works, therefore, to direct attention (1) to some of the most prominent new elements of this revision; (2) to the decision-making processes that put those adjustments in place; and (3) to the conventions in this edition that can assist in ascertaining the precise status of individual entries.

Assessments, Adjustments, and Conventions

The initial step in the revision process was a comprehensive evaluation of every one of the 2,750 first-edition entries. As though dealing out an enormous deck of cards, each of the original articles was assigned to suitable members of the thirteen-person board of associate editors or the slate of some two dozen consultants. Parity did not apply insofar as a sturdy few were taxed with assessing hundreds of articles, others with only a handful. In the subsequent entry-by-entry review, a relatively small number of articles were completely jettisoned while the huge remainder was assigned to one of three categories.

A first category of entries is composed of those approved to be reprinted with few or no changes. Though roughly 1,800 articles in this set were to remain largely or fully intact, attempts were made to reach the authors of those first-edition entries both with an invitation to modify or update their contribution in ways that they saw fit and with a request that they augment the bibliography with relevant sources that had appeared in the interim. Of course, many of those scholars were no longer active in the profession; others did not reply; and others declined to make any alterations to their original articles. Articles that were, therefore, reprinted essentially unchanged have a designation of "(1987)" following the author's name. In numerous instances, however, first-edition authors did take the occasion to adjust their own articles in small or large ways. For these articles, the attribution of authorship is followed by two dates, for example, Eleanor Zelliot (1987 and 2005). Additionally, where original authors of articles in this set were unavailable or nonresponsive, many of the respective bibliographies were nonetheless supplemented with relevant new sources; this accounts for those bylines that include the designation "Revised Bibliography," which signals that a "New Sources" section is appended to the bibliography.

A second category of entries comprises those judged to need significant revision or updating. These articles are perhaps most properly worthy of the title "revised" insofar as they both retain a substantial portion of the original work and introduce substantially new information and/or new conceptual formulations. This sort of revision took one of three forms. In some cases, original authors were enlisted to rework and update their own articles; those articles (not unlike those in which authors voluntarily revised their original articles) are consequently attributed to a sole author but with two dates, for example, Davíd Carrasco (1987 and 2005). In many other cases, the revision was undertaken by a different scholar, which accounts for those articles that are attributed to two authors, for example, Robertson Davies (1987) and Eric Ziolkowski (2005). Irrespective of whether the modifications were completed by the original author or by someone else, the revisions are, in some instances, modest, perhaps addressing recent events or attending to an important new publication on the topic; but, in other cases, the adjustments and reconceptualizations are more thoroughgoing. All of the revisions and "updates" of these sorts do, however, eventuate in entries that are, at once, old and new.

A third variation on this revision theme—and one of the more distinctive features of the second edition of *Encyclopedia of Religion*—is a consequence of those situations in which the original article was assessed as a still-valuable exposition of the topic, worthy of reprinting, but not a treatment that could any longer be represented as state-of-the-art. In many of these instances, the first-edition entry provided a seminal statement on the subject, but was distinctive, or sometimes idiosyncratic, in ways that precluded revision or updating per se. Thus, instead of reworking the original, it was more suitable to retain the integrity of that article by reprinting it unchanged and then augmenting it with a kind of supplementary addendum. For instance, Mircea Eliade wrote the first-edition entry "Sexuality: An Overview," which articulates a prominent, still-important exposition of the topic, but not one that can be regarded as current in a field of study where there has been enormous activity in the past two decades. The original entry is, therefore, allowed to stand with the parenthetical designation "[First Edition]" and then is complemented by a completely new entry titled "Sexuality: An Overview [Further Considerations]," which focuses attention on research and perspectives that have emerged since the first edition. This pairing of prominent but now dated first-edition entries with new complementary pieces—there are roughly fifty of these juxtapositions of old and new—adds a special texture to the revision; it facilitates a kind of historical, even archaeological, appreciation of the unfolding succession of ideas on a topic. But the same editorial tactic also places a special burden on readers. Accordingly, as a cautionary note, it would, in principle, never be suitable to rely on one of these "First Edition" pieces without reading ahead also to its complimentary, sometimes quite critical, "Further Considerations" counterpart.

In any case, the initial article-by-article assessment of the first edition eventuated also in a third category constituted of those entries for which a topic and title were retained but the actual article was completely replaced. There are well over three hundred of these new renditions of already-standing topics. As a rule, authors of these replacement articles were invited to employ the original entry as a resource but not necessarily a model, that is, to compose an essentially new treatment of the existing topic. Not surprisingly, one can find instances in which there is considerable continuity between the original and present articles while, in other cases, the first-edition article and its new, second-edition iteration share little beyond the title. That is to say, the great majority of these so-termed replacement articles are, for all practical purposes, thoroughly new entries. Consequently, author attribution for these articles includes a parenthetical date precisely like other new articles, for example, Mary MacDonald (2005).

New Features and Configurations

In addition to these various layers of revision and replacement, the second edition introduces entries on nearly six hundred topics that did not appear in the first edition. New topics and titles are added to almost every portion of the revision, but especially noteworthy are those that appear in related sets of articles—or so-termed composite entries. Many of these composite sets, which were also a very prominent feature of the first edition, provide a means of surveying the geographical distribution of a large tradition: The "Buddhism" composite entry, for example, is composed of articles that treat, in succession, "Buddhism in India," "Buddhism in Southeast Asia," "Buddhism in Central Asia," and so on. In many other cases, however, these composite sets are trained on a broad topic or theme such as "Pilgrimage," "Iconography," "Music," or "Soul," which is then addressed in a cross-culturally comparative fashion. In the main, these thematically configured composites open with a broad overview article, which is then followed by a series of articles that explore that large theme either in different contexts and/or from different angles of view. And, although every sort of composite entry enjoys a measure of revision, it is these thematically linked sets that are subject to the most venturesome innovation and growth. Several permutations and outstanding examples deserve quick comment.

In numerous instances, thematic composite entries that appeared in the original edition were reworked and very substantially expanded. For example, the first-edition "Afterlife" composite entry included an overview and only two area-specific articles, one on Jewish concepts of the afterlife and another on Chinese concepts. In the new edition, however, that pair is complemented by completely new entries on African conceptions of the afterlife, as well as Australian, Oceanic, Mesoamerican, Christian, Islamic, Greek and Roman, and Germanic concepts. The first-edition "Cosmology" composite is similarly expanded with thoroughly new entries on the cosmologies of Africa, indigenous Australia, Oceania, indigenous North America and Mesoamerica, South America, Islam, and finally, so-termed "Scientific Cosmologies." Or, to cite just one more such example of the enhancement of a standing composite entry, the original cluster of entries under the rubric of "Rites of Passage," which had included entries solely on Hindu, Jewish, and Muslim rites, is fleshed out to include new articles on African, Oceanic, Mesoamerican, and Neopagan rites of passage.

Other second-edition composite entries—article sets that provide some of the most notable new contributions to the revision—result from cases in which a topic that had received fairly limited coverage in the first edition becomes the subject of a much more extensive block of new articles. For instance, where the original edition had modest-length and broadly-framed articles devoted to "Healing," "Medicine," and "Diseases and Cures," the revision explores those themes far more fully via a composite entry that opens with "Healing and Medicine: An Overview," which is then followed by fourteen completely new articles trained on healing practices in various regions and traditions, for example, in Africa, in the African diaspora, in the Ancient Near East, in Judaism, in Islamic texts and traditions, in the popular healing practices of Middle Eastern cultures, in Greece and Rome, and so on. A sole first-edition entry on "Ecology" is supplanted by a full constellation of "Ecology and Religion" articles that includes eleven new tradition-specific articles on various ways of conceiving the interrelations between humans, the earth, and the cosmos, as well as thematic entries on environmental ethics and on science, religion, and ecology. "Law and Religion" is also much expanded and fully reconfigured in a set of thirteen articles that address the topic in six different regions or traditions and then in relation to six different sorts of themes, such as law and religion in connection with literature, with critical theory, with human rights, with morality, with new religious movements and, finally, with punishment. And, by the same token, the free-standing entry on "Politics and Religion" in the first edition is replaced by a ten-part composite entry that begins with a broad overview of the topic and then engages intersections of religion and politics in each of several traditions.

Additional composite entries are completely new insofar as they have no direct counterpart in the first edition. The treatment of literature, for instance, an enormous and multi-faceted topic that streams through countless sections of the encyclopedia, was reconfigured in ways that issued in a completely new ten-part composite entry on fiction and religion in various guises. In that case, a lead entry titled "Fiction: History of the Novel" is complemented by all new entries that survey connections between religion and the Western novel, Latin American fiction, Chinese fiction, Japanese fiction, Southeast Asian fiction, Australian fiction, Oceanic fiction, African fiction, and Native American fiction. Another fully new composite entry under the rubric of "Transculturation and Religion" opens with an overview that situates "the problem of religion" within the context of the making of the modern world; subsequent elements of the set address the role of religion in the formation of, respectively, modern Canada, the modern Caribbean, modern Japan, modern India, and modern Oceania. Other innovative new composite entries, though on somewhat more modest scales, engage such topics as "Orgy," "Sociobiology and Evolutionary Psychology," and "Humor and Religion."

Particularly notable among new composite entries is the twenty-one-part "Gender and Religion," a wholly new set that deserves special mention not only as the largest such grouping in the revision, but also as part of a three-tiered initiative to engage the abundance of important work that has appeared in that field since the original version. At one level, the instructions to authors of *every* article for this edition, whether revised or completely new, included an incitement to consider seriously, and to make explicit, the gendered dynamics of the religious doctrines, practices, and institutions under consideration. A second level of revision focused on individual entries: standing articles like "Women's Studies," "Human Body," and "Spirit Possession" were revisited, then replaced or heavily reworked in light of contemporary approaches to gender and religion. Space was opened also for numerous new topical entries such as "Beauty," "Gynocentrism," "Lesbianism," "Men's Studies in Religion," "Patriarchy and Matriarchy," and "Thealogy"; for several midsized composite entries on "Feminism," "Feminist Theology," and "Nuns"; and for numerous new biographical entries on women. Finally, at a third and especially ambitious level, the completely new "Gender and Religion" composite entry employs the familiar pattern of an overview article, followed by a succession of region- or tradition-specific articles; but this set is unique in its scale of execution.

New religious movements is yet another area of major growth and reconceptualization. In fact, no segment of the encyclopedia enjoys quite such extensive enlargement. The original five-part composite entry is replaced by an eleven-part set that includes not only a revamped overview and new or reworked area-specific articles on the United States, Europe, Japan, and Latin America, but also thematic and comparative articles on the scriptures of new religious movements and on new religious movements in relation to women, to children, to millennialism, and to violence. Where the first-edition synoptic outline listed a couple dozen supporting articles under the heading of "New Religions and Modern Movements," the revision includes nearly three times that many. Among the wealth of new topical entries are "Anticult Movements," "Brainwashing (Debate)," and "Deprogramming"; "Neopaganism" and "Wicca"; "Swedenborgianism," "Rastafarianism," "UFO Religions," "Heaven's Gate," "Aum Shinrikyō," and "Falun Gong." Similarly abundant new biographical articles address figures ranging from Aleister Crowley, Daddy Grace, Matilda Joslyn Gage, Emma Curtis Hopkins, and L. Ron Hubbard to Jim Jones and David Koresh, to mention just a few.

An innovative new composite entry under the rubric of "Study of Religion" is one of several components designed to engage matters of theory, method, and intellectual history, concerns that were very important for the first edition and remained a priority for the second. Where the original edition had entries focused primarily on the emergence and development of religious studies in Western Europe and the United States, this new "Study of Religion" grouping works to survey ways in which the nature and study of "religion" have been conceptualized and institutionalized also in Eastern Europe, Japan, North Africa and the Middle East, sub-Saharan Africa, and South Asia. Also in a methodological realm, most of the eighteen first-edition "History of Study" entries (e.g., "Australian Religions: History of Study"; "Chinese Religion: History of Study"; "Egyptian Religion: History of Study"; etc.) were substantially updated or replaced, and entirely new entries were added to address the history of the study of African American religions, Baltic religion, Celtic religions,

Confucianism, and Germanic religions, along with new entries on the history of the study of gender and religion, of Gnosticism, and of new religious movements. Numerous of the "Methods of Study" entries were revised, and wholly new offerings include "Ethology of Religion," "Literature: Critical Theory and Religious Studies," "Subaltern Studies," and a two-part set on "Sociobiology and Evolutionary Psychology." Of more than one hundred first-edition entries listed in the synoptic outline under so-called "Scholarly Terms," very few were deleted; some are substantially revised (e.g., "Conversion," "Dualism," and "Tradition"); some prominent terms are augmented with "Further Considerations" pieces (e.g., "Mysticism," "Ritual," "Religion," "Sacrifice," and "Syncretism"); and many others are replaced with essentially new entries (e.g., "Charisma," "Folklore," "Religious Experience," and "Sacred Time"). Completely new offerings under that heading include "Colonialism and Post-colonialism," "Creolization," "Globalization and Religion," "Implicit Religion," "Invisible Religion," "Orientalism," "Spirituality," and "World Religions." And with respect to "Scholars of Religion," another area of special distinction for *Encyclopedia of Religion,* we retained the policy of separate biographical entries only for scholars who are deceased, but nonetheless added more than fifty new names to the list.

The enumeration of important new articles and features could, as they say, go on and on. In the Judaism section, nearly all of the principal articles, the main "Judaism: An Overview" included, are thoroughly rewritten and more than thirty new topics were added. Among the articles on Islam, a high percentage both of the large geographical survey entries and the dozens of shorter supporting articles are revised in variously minor and major ways, and numerous wholly new topics have been introduced. The treatment of Buddhism, including the several composite configurations devoted to that tradition, received especially thoroughgoing reconceptualizations, as well as the introduction of more than two dozen completely new topics, numerous of them focused on Tibet. North American Indian religions was also a zone of especially extensive revision and expansion in ways that reflect the tumultuous changes in that field over the past two decades and the emergence of a generation of native scholars whose presence was largely absent from the first edition. The large lists under "Art and Religion" and, even more, "Science and Religion" were areas of considerable growth and innovation. Yes, the enumeration of new and reworked features could go on and on. It is, to be sure, only via direct engagement of the entries themselves that one can really begin to appreciate all that is new and different between the second edition and its precedent.

In sum, then, it is important to note that the associate editors and consultants—all of whom deserve enormous credit for their expertise, insight, and endurance—worked without any fixed quota as to how much would change and how much remain the same. This open policy proved a proverbial mixed blessing—both an ample benefit and what became a heavy burden insofar as, it is safe to say, the extent of revision and enlargement far exceeded anyone's expectation. The final tally of new and essentially new entries, in fact, exceeds by fourfold the initial projections, which were only whispered at the outset of the process. Were there anticipation in the beginning that this revised second edition would include, as it does, well over five hundred new topics, nearly one thousand completely new articles, and 1.5 million more words than the original *Encyclopedia of Religion* perhaps fewer would have agreed to participate in the editorial initiative.

The fortuitous result is, nevertheless, a scholarly resource too large and layered for anyone to master or even appreciate fully; no one can attain that vantage that affords a view of the whole. Instead—and happily—individual readers will inevitably be drawn to those parts that appeal to their distinct interests and serve their special purposes. This encyclopedia is, in an important sense, many encyclopedias, each of which emerges in dynamic relations with the persons who read and use it. Moreover, time and again, searching and serendipity blend so that an entry simply happened upon, an article or aspect other than that which you are seeking, evokes the strongest excitement and provides the most satisfying reward. Even those of us with much invested in this revision, continue to read, reread, and experience these volumes with a sense of discovery. It is our sincere hope, moreover, that this new edition can provide other readers that same ongoing sense of exploration and evocation of interest.

LINDSAY JONES
Ohio State University, September 2004

VISUAL ESSAYS: RATIONALE

Without exception, religions around the world and throughout time have included a vital visual dimension—whether it is icons to contemplate, sacred diagrams used in ritual, powerful objects charged with the capacity to protect or heal, the creation of sacred spaces, or the use of clothing, vestments, or liturgical objects in worship. Because human beings rely heavily on sight for information about their worlds, images of different kinds have always played an important role in the design of religious spaces and rites and in the daily practices of the devout. Art historians, anthropologists, archeologists, and historians of religion have long noted the significance of images in religious life.

The fourteen visual essays included in the second edition of *Encyclopedia of Religion* seek to demonstrate how pervasively visual culture permeates religion. Each of the essays is organized around a practice or theme common to many different religions. Since the goal was to explore the relevance and power of the visual culture of religion, the task in each case has been to show how images and visual practices participate in the lived experience of religion. This approach contrasts with the passive use of images sometimes used by scholars and reference works merely to illustrate religious practice or doctrine. In no instance does an image appear here in that capacity. Images are not used in these essays to recall or exemplify religious ideas or topics, but to provide concrete examples of how religions happen visually, that is, how images are put to use in visual practices that are the substance and experience of religious belief. Thus, the emphasis has been consistently on what images do.

The fourteen themes have been selected in order to show the great variety of ways in which images, objects, and spaces make religious practice take the form it does. Broadly speaking, images accomplish at least five operations:

1. They create a sense of time.
2. They create a sense of space.
3. They structure relations with other persons, beings, and communities.
4. They shape one's state of mind and body for ritual and devotional experience.
5. They visualize sacred texts, intermingling word and image or transforming them into one another.

Of course, a single image may do several or even all of these. But for the sake of clarity, selections for each essay focus on one function.

I do not suppose that any of these operations is unique to imagery. One might make the same points regarding food, dress, dance, or any of the arts regarding most, if not all, of the functions. But images will operate in different terms from other media. The larger point here is to show by means of example and comparison how images and visual practices provide rich evidence for the study and understanding of religion as a lived and visually engaging experience.

VISUAL ESSAY THEMES

The fourteen essays are organized under the five broad rubrics outlined above. It is important to underscore the fact that any given image might be classified simultaneously under several of the themes and rubrics. In fact, categories such as "space" and "time" are only extricated and regarded *in abstracto* since, in practice, they are often collapsed into a single domain of experience, as several examples of the sacred diagrams in the third essay will show. Moreover, images that perform such acts as healing or protection, or images that help one to remember or convey information, do so within the cultural contexts of their users. An image is not an autonomous entity, but is embedded in a life-world and a history, and charged with meaning and purpose within its society and civilization, deprived of which its function and power to signify and operate to purpose are necessarily compromised. Like any cultural artifact, images are not things in themselves, but organic components of an operating whole. But in order to convey as clearly as possible the individual functions of images, the fourteen themes are placed under discrete rubrics.

To remove images and visual practices from one habitat and history, as often happens through migration, colonization, warfare, and trade, means to inaugurate new cultural and historical meanings. The ability of images to transcend one context, to synthesize different systems of meaning, to help invent new traditions of practice and thought, and to lead many lives beyond those originally ascribed to them are all part of the power of images that will be explored visually in these essays.

The operative question posed throughout the organization of these themes and the examples gathered under each has been: what do images do in religious life? Images are not used identically in various religions, though there are many striking parallels. And images often mark and remember the boundary of one tradition and another. Not all of the categories listed below apply to every religious tradition. Not every religion in human history is represented. Indeed, far from it. The task was not universal coverage, but rather an attempt to register some of the most important things that images do, things that belong at the heart of any study of religious practice and history. Students and scholars should find in these categories and their examples a prompt for the visual investigation of virtually any religious group, behavior, or idea.

I. Time

1. Sacred Time—the creation of time in ritual, memory, prophecy, or dream time; that is, remembering, looking ahead, and stepping out of time.
2. Visual Narrative—the visual means of storytelling.
3. Cosmic Visions—maps, calendars, *maṇḍalas, yantras,* astrological charts, and sacred diagrams.

II. Space

4. Sacred Matter—the use of images and objects such as relics, reliquaries, amulets, or liturgical objects in religious practice.
5. Sacred Space—the role of images in creating shrines, monuments, gardens, temples, mosques, churches, and pilgrimage sites.

III. Structuring Social Relations

6. Community—imaging clan, tribe, ancestor, family, nation, congregation, ethnicity, and race.
7. Commerce of Images—the role that images play in the metaphysical as well as social economies of the sacred.
8. Appropriation and Identity—the manner in which images facilitate transformation, migration, and evolution of religious ideas and practices.
9. Efficacious Images—images that heal, protect, or enable their users to benefit or harm others.
10. Portraits—images of ancestors, teachers, saints, or deities that enable veneration, adoration, or union.

IV. Shaping Mind and Body

11. Sacred Gaze—images that assist meditation, visualization, memory, and aesthetic contemplation.
12. The True Image—visual traditions in certain religions that seek nonhumanly created images of a deity, founder, or saint.
13. Images and the Body—how images are used to condition the body, affect its operation, and control it.

V. Imaging Sacred Text

14. Word and Image—artifacts involving the integration of text and image in order to intensify the artifact's meaning and effect or evade taboos against pictorial representation.

DAVID MORGAN
Valparaiso University, September 2004

PREFACE TO THE FIRST EDITION

Such an encyclopedia as this has long been overdue. In all areas of religious studies—in the historical religious traditions as well as in nonliterate ("primitive") religious systems—the "information explosion" of recent decades has demanded a new presentation of available materials. Further, in the last half century, new methodological approaches and more adequate hermeneutics have enhanced our knowledge of the existential value, the social function, and the cultural creativity of religions throughout history. We understand better now the mind and the behavior of *homo religious* ("religious man"), and we know much more about the beginnings, the growth, and the crises of different religions of the world.

These impressive advances in information and understanding have helped to eradicate the cliches, highly popular in the nineteenth century, concerning the mental capacity of nonliterate peoples and the poverty and provincialism of non-Western cultures. To realize the radical change of perspective, it suffices to compare, for instance, the current interpretations of an Australian Aboriginal ritual, a traditional African mythology, an Inner Asian shamanistic seance, or such complex phenomena as yoga and alchemy with the evaluations *en vogue* a few generations ago. Perhaps for the first time in history we recognize today not only the unity of human races but also the spiritual values and cultural significance of their religious creations.

I shall not here attempt to survey all the decisive contributions of recent research to a more correct appreciation of the dialectics of the sacred and of so many ethnic and historical religious systems. A few examples will serve to underscore my point.

In some areas of religious studies, unexpected and astonishing consequences of recent archaeological or textual discoveries have become almost immediately apparent. Excavations at Mohenjo-Daro and Harappa, for instance, have revealed the grandiose proto-historical urban civilization of the Indus Valley, and discoveries of the library of gnostic writings at Nag Hammadi in Upper Egypt and of a great number of Essene manuscripts at Qumran, near the Dead Sea, have given us documents of immeasurable value. Although publication and translation are not yet completed, much light has already been thrown on two problems that were extremely controversial until a generation ago.

A specific characteristic of the last several decades' activities has been the amazing number of Asian religious texts that have been edited and, in many cases, translated for the first time into a European language. This editorial enterprise has been accompanied by the publication of a series of monographs spanning a range of scholarship difficult to imagine a few generations ago. The significance of such works is enormous, and the consequences of their publication are far-reaching.

The esoteric and occult traditions, misunderstood or neglected by former generations of scholars born and brought up in a positivistic milieu, constitute but one area of study on which recent research has cast new light. Here, much that was once obscure has been illuminated by, for instance, the classic monographs of Gershom Scholem on Qabbalah and on Jewish gnostic and mystical systems. Scholem's erudition and insight have disclosed to us a coherent and profound world of meaning in texts that had earlier been generally dismissed as mere magic and superstition. Likewise, our understanding of Islamic mysticism has been radically improved by Louis Massignon's works, while Henry Corbin and his disciples have revealed the neglected dimensions of Ismā'īlī esoteric tradition.

Also, in the past forty years we have witnessed a more correct and comprehensive appraisal of Chinese, Indian, and Western alchemies. Until recently, alchemy was regarded either as a proto-chemistry—that is, as an embryonic, naive, or prescientific discipline—or as a mass of superstitious rubbish that was culturally irrelevant. The investigations of Joseph Needham and Nathan Sivin have proved that Chinese alchemy has a holistic structure, that it is a traditional science *sui generis,* not intelligible without its cosmologies and its ethical and, so to say, "existential" presuppositions and soteriological implications. And it is significant that in China alchemy was intimately related to secret Taoist practices, that in India it was a part of Tantric Yoga, and that, in the West, Greco-Egyptian and Renaissance alchemy was usually connected with gnosticism and Hermetism—all of which are secret, "occult" traditions.

A most surprising result of contemporary scholarship has been the discovery of the important role that alchemy and Hermetic esotericism have played in Western thought, not only in the Italian Renaissance but also in the triumph of Copernicus's new astronomy, in the heliocentric theory of the solar system. Frances A. Yates has brilliantly analyzed the deep implications of the passionate interest in Hermetism in this period. For almost two centuries, Egyptian magic, alchemy, and esotericism have obsessed innumerable theologians and philosophers, believers as well as skeptics and cryptoatheists. Yet, only recently has the importance of alchemy in Newton's thinking, for example, been revealed. Betty J. T. Dobbs has pointed out that Newton probed in his laboratory "the whole vast literature of the older alchemy as it has never been probed before or since." In fact, Newton sought in alchemy the structure of the small world to match his cosmological system.

Among many other examples of the progress realized in the last several decades, I may also recall the reevaluation of European popular traditions. Until the 1930s, the religious systems of Australian Aborigines and North American Indians were more seriously investigated, and were better understood, than were European folk traditions. On the one hand, researchers were interested mainly in folk literature; on the other hand, their interpretations of rituals and "popular mythologies" usually followed one of the fashionable theorists, such as Wilhelm Mannhardt or James G. Frazer. Furthermore, many scholars, in both eastern and western Europe, considered rural traditions as fragmentary and debased survivals from a superior layer of culture, from that, say, represented by the feudal aristocracy or that derived from church literature. In sum, taking into account the powerful influences of the church and of urban culture, one was inclined to doubt the authenticity or the archaism of rural religious traditions in Europe.

Recent and more rigorous studies have revealed a quite different situation. The Austrian ethnologist Leopold Schmidt, for example, has shown that certain mythico-ritual scenarios that were still current among peasants of central and southeastern Europe at the beginning of the twentieth century preserved mythological fragments and rituals that had disappeared in ancient Greece before the time of Homer. Other scholars have concluded that Romanian and Balkan folklore preserves Homeric and pre-Homeric themes and motifs. According to the American linguist and anthropologist Paul Friedrich, "The attitudes of contemporary Greek peasants toward the Virgin Mary might bear in some way on our understanding of the Classical Demeter." And the archaeologist Marija Gimbutas has pointed out that the pre-Christian layer in Baltic folklore "is so ancient that it undoubtedly reaches back to prehistoric times—at least to the Iron Age or in the case of some elements even several millennia deeper." As to the archaism of Irish popular traditions, recent studies have demonstrated numerous analogies with ancient Indian ideas and customs.

Even more important, popular traditions around the globe reveal a specific originality in their reinterpretation of the Christian message. In many cultures, peasants practice what can be called a "cosmic Christianity," which, in a "total" history of Christendom, ought to have a place, for it represents a new type of religious creativity. Thus, parallel to the different Christian theologies constructed both on Hebrew scriptures and on Greek metaphysics, one must also set the "popular theology" that assimilated and christianized many archaic traditions, from Neolithic to Oriental and Hellenistic religions. In this way, the religious history of Christian Europe will be deprovincialized and its universal values will become more evident.

I may also recall some of the results of contemporary work on the religious meaning—or function—of oral, and even written, literature. Some years ago, a number of scholars pointed out the initiatory symbols and motifs of certain categories of fairy tale. Significantly, almost at the same time many critics in Europe as well as in the United States began to investigate the patterns of initiation recognizable in various literary works. In both types of narrative, oral and written, we are led into an imaginary world, and in both we meet characters who undergo a series of initiatory ordeals, a common plot structure that is generally presented more or less transparently. The difference is that, while some fairy tales can be regarded as reflecting the remembrance of actual initiation rites practiced in the past, such is not true of modern literary works.

Specialists have also identified initiatory elements in such classical sources as the sixth book of Vergil's *Aeneid,* in a number of scenarios and personages of the Arthurian legends, in the neo-Greek epic *Digenis Akritas,* in Tibetan epic poetry, and elsewhere. Most probably, these elements are ghostly souvenirs of the distant past, memories, vaguely recalled, of ancient initiatory rituals. But such cannot be so with initiatory structures found in modern literature from Coleridge's *The Rime of the Ancient Mariner* and Eliot's *The Waste Land* to the many novels of James Fenimore Cooper, Jules Verne, Mark Twain, and William Faulkner. Nevertheless, these facts are relevant for an understanding of modern Western man. Indeed, in a desacralized world such as ours, the "sacred" is present and active chiefly in imaginary universes. But imaginary experiences are part of the total human being. This means that nostalgia for initiatory trials and scenarios, nostalgia deciphered in so many literary and artistic works (including the cinema), reveals modern man's longing for a *renovation* capable of radically changing his existence.

Of course, this is only an example of the unconscious reaction against the desacralization of modern Western societies, in some regards a phenomenon parallel to the acculturation of many traditional ("primitive") cultures. This complex and delicate problem warrants far more attention then I can give it here, but I do wish to note that what has been called the "occult explosion" in contemporary North America belongs to the same desperate effort to react against the growing desacralization of the modern world, specifically the almost general crisis of the Christian churches.

The most significant advance in religious studies of the past several decades has been realized in our understanding of primal religions—that is, the religious systems of "primitive," nonliterate peoples. There is no doubt that improvement of fieldwork methods and the growing interest of anthropologists in depth psychology, linguistics, and historiographical methodology have contributed to this success. Especially the researches, hypotheses, and controversies in relation to myths and mythological thinking have played a decisive role. The once-popular theories of the intellectual inferiority of "savages," or of their "pre-logical mentality," have been obsolete for some time. Anthropologists and sociologists as well as historians of religions nowadays emphasize the structural coherence of "primitive" religious beliefs and ideas. Although, as is always true in humanistic disciplines, no general theory on the "primitive mind" has been universally accepted, one methodological presupposition seems to be shared by the majority of today's scholars: namely, the "normality" and, consequently, the creativity of the primal religions.

Indeed, it has been repeatedly pointed out that the archaic mind has never been stagnant, that some nonliterate peoples have made important technological discoveries and that some others have had a certain sense of history. Such radical modification of our former understanding and evaluation of nonliterate religious traditions has been in part a consequence of growing interest in the structure and the morphology of the sacred—that is, in religious experience and in its ritual and symbolic expressions.

Progressively, scholars have realized the necessity of trying to discover the meanings given by nonliterate peoples to their own religious activities. W. E. H. Stanner, who dedicated his life to the study of Australian Aborigines, emphatically asserted that their religion must be approached "*as* religion and not as a mirror of something else." Stanner repeatedly criticized the fallacious presupposition "that the social order is primary and in some cases causal, and the religious order secondary and in some sense consequential." Equally significant is the affirmation of the British Africanist E. E. Evans-Pritchard that knowledge of Christian theology, exegesis, symbolic thought, and ritual better enables the anthropologist to understand "primitive" ideas and practices.

An obvious corollary may thence be drawn: that knowledge of the religious ideas and practices of other traditions better enables anyone to understand his or her own. The history of religions is the story of the human encounter with the sacred—a universal phenomenon made evident in myriad ways.

These, then, are some of the themes and topics that the interested reader will find in the hundreds of articles that constitute this encyclopedia. In planning it, the editors and the staff have aimed at a concise, clear, and objective description of the totality of human experiences of the sacred. We have, we hope, paid due attention to traditions both great and small, to the historical religions as well as to the primal religions, to the religious systems of the East as well as to those of the West. Wishing particularly to avoid reductionism and Western cultural bias, we have given far greater space to the religions of non-Western areas than have earlier reference books on religion. Finally, and in conformity with the international design of our encyclopedia, we have invited scholars from five continents to contribute articles related to their specific areas of research.

Our encyclopedia was not conceived as a dictionary, with entries covering the entire vocabulary in every field of religious studies. Rather, it was conceived as a system of articles on important ideas, beliefs, rituals, myths, symbols, and persons that have played a role in the universal history of religions from Paleolithic times to the present day. Thus, the reader will not find here entries on all the popes or on all the patriarchs of the Eastern churches, nor on all the saints, mystics, and minor figures of the various religious traditions. Instead, here is a great network of historical and descriptive articles, synthetical discussions, and interpretive essays that make available contemporary insight into the long and multifaceted history of religious man.

Here, among many others, are articles devoted to recent archaeological and textual discoveries and, particularly important, articles devoted to the reevaluation of facts and systems of thought ignored or neglected until a few decades ago: for instance, the history of Hermetism and of alchemy, the occult revival in our time, the creativity of "popular" religions, the millenaristic movements among contemporary "primitive" societies, and the religious dimensions of the arts. A more rigorous study of such themes not only illuminates their meanings but, in some cases, opens new perspectives on the evaluation of other cultural phenomena.

By consulting various entries in the encyclopedia, the reader will learn the latest results of anthropological research and the current evaluation of various primal religions. These, in turn, have led to the burgeoning contemporary interest in the structure, meaning, and functions of myth and of religious symbols. A number of articles herein are devoted to these subjects, which are equally important, I might add, for recent Western philosophical inquiry. As a matter of fact, the exegesis of mythical thinking has played a central role in the works of many distinguished modern philosophers and linguists. Similarly, a more adequate understanding of symbolic thinking has contributed to the systematic study of religious symbols, and, thus, to a reevaluation of the central role of religious symbolism.

I need not list here other examples of recent methodological progress that has made possible our present comprehension of religious structures and creations. It suffices to say that the researches of the last half century concern not only the historian of religions, the anthropologist, and the sociologist but also the political scientist, the social historian, the psychologist, and the philosopher. To know the great variety of worldviews assumed by religious man, to comprehend the expanse of his spiritual universe, is, finally, to advance our general knowledge of humankind. It is true that most of the worldviews of primal societies and archaic civilizations have long since been left behind by history. But they have not vanished without a trace. They have contributed toward making us what we are today, and so, after all, they are part of our own history.

MIRCEA ELIADE
Chicago, March 1986

FOREWORD TO THE FIRST EDITION

Mircea Eliade, the editor in chief of this encyclopedia, died in April 1986, shortly after drafting his preface. The publisher wisely chose to leave his preface substantially as he had composed it, and it was suggested that I spell out in a foreword what might be called the encyclopedia's "angle of vision," to supplement what had already been said by its editor in chief.

Needless to say, it would be virtually impossible for an encyclopedia of this sort to cover adequately every religious idea, practice, and phenomenon known to the human race. At the same time, the publisher, the editors, and our many advisers wished to produce not a dictionary but a genuine encyclopedia that would introduce educated, nonspecialist readers to important ideas, practices, and persons in the religious experience of humankind from the Paleolithic past to our day.

The present work has much in common with another major English-language encyclopedia produced earlier in this century, namely, the thirteen-volume *Encyclopaedia of Religion and Ethics,* edited by James Hastings with assistance from John A. Selbie, Louis H. Gray, and others (Edinburgh, 1908–1926; reprint, New York, 1955; hereafter designated *ERE*). Both came into being at times when knowledge about the various religions had grown to such a degree that without an encyclopedic work of some sort, it would not be possible, as the architects of the *ERE* put it, "to have at our command the vast stores of learning which have accumulated."

The planners of both encyclopedias attempted to solicit contributions from the most advanced scholars at work in the various fields of study; they asked their contributors for the most up-to-date information available, to be sure, but also for histories of interpretation and the most current interpretive schemas. That much of what was said in the *ERE* has now gone out of date and that all of it reflects the scholarship of the time in which it was produced are melancholy reminders that any encyclopedia, including this one, begins to grow obsolete almost before it is published.

Readers will notice, of course, some basic differences between these two encyclopedias. Joachim Wach (1898–1955) often reminded us that religion usually has three "expressions" (his term) or dimensions, namely, the theoretical (e.g., doctrines, dogmas, myths, theologies, ethics), the practical (e.g., cults, sacraments, meditations), and the sociological (e.g., religious groupings, ecclesiastical forms). Our encyclopedia tries to do justice as much as possible to these three dimensions of religion, in contradistinction to the *ERE,* which focused primarily on the theoretical aspect to the exclusion of the practical and the sociological. Admittedly, the division of human experience into various compartments—religion, philosophy, ethics, art, and so on—is largely a Western convention; and historically, in the West, theology (cognitive attempts to systematize religious teachings) has occupied a conspicuously important place in defining religion, which in turn has enjoyed a traditionally ambiguous but close relationship with ethics and the philosophy of religion. Thus it is not surprising that the *ERE* was primarily concerned with theologies and philosophies of religion and with ethics, for it was the underlying theological and philosophical interest of the planners of the *ERE* that led them to look for normativeness in religion and ethics. In this sense, the *ERE* and the present encyclopedia are very different.

It is important to appreciate the difference between the mental world of the planners of the *ERE* and our own mental world. Unconsciously if not consciously, the planners of the *ERE* viewed non-Western peoples, histories, cultures, and religions primarily from the Western perspective. It was doubtless true that politically, socially, culturally, religiously, economically, and militarily the power of Western colonial nations reached its zenith during the nineteenth century, and that the most important events of the modern world occurred through the impetus and initiative of the West. Moreover, as has been aptly remarked, the ethos of the nineteenth century lasted rather longer than the actual calendar end of the century; and furthermore, although World War I undeniably weakened the unity and cohesiveness of the European family of nations, a persistent carryover of the vitality of the Western powers, Western civilization, and Western learning remained even in Asia and Africa until the end of World War II.

To many non-Western peoples, the year 1945 marked a significant line of demarcation between two worlds of experience. In their eyes, the Western colonial powers—even when they meant well—had acted in the manner of parents who refuse to allow their children to grow up by making all the important decisions for them. The years after World War II witnessed not only the emergence of many new and inexperienced nations but, more important, a redefinition on a global scale of the dignity, value, and freedom of human beings, including non-Western peoples. While knowledgeable Western scholars of the nineteenth and early twentieth centuries saw non-Western peoples only as sources of religious and cultural data for Western scholars to analyze within their own (i.e., Western) methodologies and frameworks, after World War II these same non-Western peoples rightly began to insist on participating in the global effort to develop adequate interpretive schemes for apprehending the entire religious experience of humankind, past and present, prehistoric to modern. Accordingly, the present encyclopedia has attempted to enlarge the mental world of contemporary scholarship by drawing a large number of contributors from the non-Western world. This has turned out to be a far more difficult approach—but a far more rewarding one—than a primarily Western-based compendium modeled on the *ERE* would have been.

During the early twentieth century, three major areas of "scholarly" or "scientific" study of religion(s)—often called "comparative religion" or the "comparative study of religions"—were taken for granted. The first comprised a narrow historical and ethnological survey of a short series of particular religions, conceived as the simple collection of "raw" religious data—beliefs, practices, feelings, moods, attitudes—often colored by an evolutionary ideology. Scholars were keenly aware, however, of the personal and corporate aspects and the immanental and transcendental dimensions of religions. The second area aimed to classify religious data according to what Stanley A. Cook in the *ERE* called "certain persistent and prevalent notions of the 'evolution' of thought and … practices … in the history of culture" (*ERE,* vol. 10, p. 664). The third area was usually reserved for the philosophy of religion or sometimes for theology. In all three areas, scholars were conscious of the virtues of the comparative method of inquiry—"the unbiased co-ordination of all comparable data irrespective of context or age"—which aims to break down "racial, social, intellectual, and psychical boundaries, and to bring into relation all classes and races of men" (ibid.). They were careful to point out, however, that "similar practices can have different meanings or motives, and similar ideas and beliefs can be differently expressed … [so that] confusion has often been caused by naive comparisons and rash inferences" (ibid.). A rational scheme of interpretation of religious ideas, usually a philosophy of religion although sometimes a theology, was brought in to introduce order and to adjudicate nebulous, confusing, and competing religious claims. The following statement succinctly expresses the main concern of the *ERE*:

> Whenever the ethical or moral value of activities or conditions is questioned, the value of religion is involved; and all deep-stirring experiences invariably compel a reconsideration of the most fundamental ideas, whether they are explicitly religious or not. Ultimately there arise problems of justice, human destiny, God, and the universe; and these in turn involve problems of the relation between 'religious' and other ideas, the validity of ordinary knowledge, and practicable conceptions of 'experience' and 'reality.' (ibid., p. 662)

Undeniably the *ERE* was an important embodiment of the deep concerns of informed Western theologians and philosophers with religion and ethics in the early twentieth century, and it represented a high standard, with contributions from many of the most erudite scholars of comparative religion at the time.

Clearly, our encyclopedia of religion is the product of a different time and a different sort of scholarship. The multidimensional scholarly style of Mircea Eliade, our editor in chief, might best exemplify the character of our encyclopedia. Born in Romania, Eliade early aspired to be a physical scientist but was lured into the study of the philosophy of the Italian Renaissance during his college days. He studied Indian philosophy and Yoga at the University of Calcutta and in the Himalayas. Once back in Romania, he taught at the University of Bucharest and also established his reputation as a creative writer. After serving as a cultural attache in both London and Lisbon, he taught and wrote in Paris as a self-styled refugee. In 1956 he was invited to teach at the University of Chicago, and there he spent the next thirty years, until his death in 1986. While he taught the history of religions in the Divinity School and in the Committee of Social Thought, he also collaborated often with philosopher Paul Ricoeur and theologian Paul Tillich. His numerous writings include systematic works; historical studies; monographs on yoga, shamanism, folk religion, and alchemy; autobiographies; drama; stories of the occult; and novels.

Eliade hoped that the present encyclopedia would implement his lifelong vision of a "total hermeneutics," a coherent interpretive framework for the entire human experience (called once by Wach "integral understanding"). Eliade's total hermeneutics was based on his understanding of the general scientific study of religions (*allgemeine Religionswissenschaft*), known as the "history of religions" to the international association of scholars of the discipline, and was dependent as well on various social, physical, and biological sciences; law; humanistic disciplines, especially the arts and literature; philosophy (more particularly the philosophy of religion); and theologies. It was Eliade's conviction that all of these disciplines in combination must attempt to decipher the meaning of human experience in this mysterious universe. Indeed, from the dawn of history, human beings have been working, discovering, and religious beings simultaneously.

The editors agreed with Eliade that the basic methodology underlying our encyclopedia should be that of the history of religions (*Religionswissenschaft*), which consists of two dimensions, historical and systematic. In this framework, the historical dimension depends upon a mutual interaction between histories of individual religions—any of the prehistoric, early historic, historic, premodern, modern, or contemporary "primitive" religions—and the history of *religion-myths,* symbols, rituals, and so on. The systematic task consists of phenomenological, comparative, sociological, and psychological studies of religions. (Eliade's particular contribution here has been termed the "morphological" study of religion.)

Eliade and the editors were convinced that with the combination of the history of religions and all the other disciplines mentioned previously it would be possible to arrive at certain disciplined generalizations about the nature of religion, as well as a structuring of religious data, which would increase our understanding of the meaning of human experience or the mode of being human in this universe. Accordingly, in the early planning stage, at least, we created three categories of articles. Our first broad category was planned to include historical and descriptive essays on particular religious communities and traditions, both the "great" traditions (Hinduism, Buddhism, Judaism, Christianity, Islam) and the "small" (traditional African societies, Australian Aboriginal groups, Mesoamerican cultures, and others). Our second broad category was slated to cover topics in the history of religion (e.g., "afterlife," "alchemy," "myth," "ritual," "symbol," and so on). Finally, our third broad category was planned to include examinations of the relationships between religion and other areas of culture (e.g., law, science, the arts, and others).

Inevitably, there were bound to be duplications among topics in different categories, as in the case of "ritual," "ritual studies," and the rituals of individual religious traditions. There are also, we found, some religious phenomena that defy easy categorization. Thus, our three categories were merely the framework on which we based our plans; we expanded and embellished it as need arose.

In editing an encyclopedia on "religion," we have had to face many problems that editors of encyclopedias on other subjects might easily avoid. One such problem involves what H. Richard Niebuhr called the "inner" and the "outer" meanings of religious phenomena. Wilfred Cantwell Smith once remarked that to outsiders Islam is a religion of the Muslims but to the Muslims Islam is a religion of truth. Our encyclopedia has made a serious effort on this account to balance the inner, theological, soteriological meanings and the outer, historical, sociological, anthropological, historical, and cultural meanings; but it is doubtful that our efforts will completely satisfy those partisans who seek only the "inner" or the "outer" meanings of religious phenomena. There are surely some people who think that their religious tradition alone encompasses the whole and final truth. It is beyond the scope of our encyclopedia to address this issue.

Readers should, however, know what our stance toward religion(s) is. We have assumed that there is no such thing as a purely religious phenomenon. A religious phenomenon is a human phenomenon and thus is not only religious but also social, cultural, psychological, biological, and so on. Yet as Eliade rightly said, "To try to grasp the essence of such a phenomenon by means of physiology, psychology, sociology, economics, linguistics, art or any other study is false; it misses the one unique and irreducible element in it—the element of the sacred" (*Patterns in Comparative Religion,* London, 1958, p. xi). Thus, throughout this encyclopedia we have made every effort to avoid "reductionist" interpretations of religion.

By the same token, we have avoided the currently fashionable theory of dividing history into a simplistic formula of tradition versus modern. We recall that from the time of the Enlightenment in Europe many scholars sought the "origin" of religion in order to understand the meaning of religions. In their inquiry, they paid scant attention to the historical dimensions of religions because to them, history signified primarily the accretions of time and the process of degeneration, presumably from the origin of religion. On the other hand, many scholars today are preoccupied with the contemporary manifestations of religions without adequate appreciation of the historical processes that impinge on the present. They often equate the traditional with an inherited culture long identified with a stagnating society, and thus to them what is not modern has the derogatory connotation of tradition. It is our intention, therefore, to avoid both such a facile use of history and the formula of tradition versus modern.

Our editor in chief sincerely appreciated the dedication of the editors and the staff members who, over the years, created entries; wrote up descriptions for articles; solicited consultants, advisers, and contributors; read the submitted articles; made suggestions for revisions; and much more. Among the editors, Charles J. Adams and Annemarie Schimmel made important contributions in the history of religion in addition to their original assignment in the histories of religions, Islam. Martin E. Marty, Richard P. McBrien, and Robert M. Seltzer handled not only their original assignments of Protestantism, Catholicism, and Judaism, respectively, but were also indispensable in formulating theories and frameworks. Seltzer's assignment also included Israelite religion as well as other religions of the ancient Near East.

Jacob Needleman undertook the formidable task of relating religion to other areas of life. Eliade himself not only functioned as our editor in chief but also acted as a supervising editor for archaic, primal religions (with Victor Turner and Lawrence E. Sullivan, our associate editor) and for Hinduism (helped by William K. Mahony, our assistant editor). Turner, of course, covered the vast area of anthropology, folklores, and folk religions; and I, besides collaborating on the history of religion, was in charge of Chinese, Korean, and Japanese religions and of Buddhism. Sullivan worked with Eliade on the history of religion and with Turner on primal religions; Mahoney worked with Eliade on Hinduism and with me on Buddhism. All of us enjoyed the help of the project editors on the Macmillan staff.

We all witnessed Eliade's deep grief at the news of Victor Turner's death in 1983. Turner had at one time chaired the Committee on Social Thought at the University of Chicago, a committee on which Eliade served for many years. In him were combined abundant energy and multidimensional interests and a broad learning, all of which he freely offered to the encyclopedia. His death was a great blow to us all.

Eliade wished to acknowledge publicly all the formal and informal consultants, advisers, and contributors, many of whom were friends, colleagues, and former students of the editors. This is an appropriate place to express our gratitude to Franklin I. Gamwell, dean of the Divinity School of the University of Chicago, and to Bernard McGinn, program coordinator of the Institute for the Advanced Study of Religion in the Divinity School, for providing facilities for editorial meetings of the encyclopedia. We also wish to thank Wendy D. O'Flaherty (on the study of Hinduism especially), other Chicago colleagues, and Gregory D. Alles and Peter Chemery, who served as Eliade's research assistants, for generously offering their scholarship, their time, and their labor.

All of the editors share Eliade's sentiment, often expressed at various meetings, in recognizing the initiative of Jeremiah Kaplan, president of Macmillan Publishing Company, and of Charles E. Smith, vice-president and publisher, for undertaking this gigantic and expensive enterprise, and the efficiency and effectiveness of the project editors on the publisher's staff in bringing this undertaking to a successful conclusion.

Of course, everyone involved in the realization of *The Encyclopedia of Religion*—editors, consultants, contributors, and staff—laments the untimely death of Mircea Eliade. But we should recall the epitaph of Sir Christopher Wren at Saint Paul's in London: "If you seek his monument, look around you." In like vein, we can say about Mircea Eliade, who passed away before his encyclopedia came to full fruition, "If you seek his monument, look in these volumes." This encyclopedia was his final undertaking, and he will remain alive in the minds of its readers for decades to come.

I consider it a great privilege to have known and worked with Mircea Eliade for more than three decades. I wish to express my personal gratitude to the Macmillan staff, to fellow advisers, and to the contributors who made this encyclopedia possible. Although the foregoing statement is largely mine, I hope that it expresses as well something of the sentiments of my colleagues on the board of editors.

JOSEPH M. KITAGAWA
Chicago, August 1986

INTRODUCTION TO THE FIRST EDITION

During the early days of the development of this encyclopedia, the board of editors and the senior members of the staff met often, both formally and informally, to exchange ideas, to decide editorial policies, and to discuss plans for the contents of the work we had undertaken to produce. At first, given the enormous scope of our topic, and the great variety of religious traditions and fields of study that it includes, it seemed impossible that any coherent system of articles could be devised that would limn the entire circle of current learning on religion and that would, further, serve the purposes both of the general reader and of specialists in various areas of religious studies. Soon, however, it became apparent that the conceptual scheme mapped out by Mircea Eliade, our editor in chief, and the editorial formats and systems used by Macmillan were extremely compatible. Indeed, quite early in our planning stage, we realized the possibilities of creating a work that would be both truly encyclopedic and widely useful. At the conclusion of the editorial meeting in which we had reached this happy consensus, Victor Turner remarked, with evident delight, "And so, then, we shall let a thousand flowers bloom."

As usual, Turner's metaphor was apt. Not only did his horticultural image echo Eliade's particular interest in vegetative symbolism—from the Goethean notion of the primordial plant to the widespread image of the cosmic tree—but it suggested a correspondence between editing and gardening that I have long known to be true.

The editor and the gardener do, in fact, have much in common. The one, just as the other, must know taxonomy, and he must plan his garden with care. He must consider the genera and species of vegetal materials he wishes to include, the size and shape of his plot, the number and arrangement of plants, their growing season and their heights and textures and colors. Then the soil must be prepared, stones removed, seeds sown and nourished. After a while, germination occurs and plants emerge. With an eye toward the planned appearance of the garden at maturity, individual plants must be tended and encouraged to grow; some must be pinched back to improve their shape, propped up to permit their development, or given extra nutriments to build their strength. Attention must constantly be paid, and the garden must be rid of noxious weeds and pernicious pests. This all done, and given favorable atmospheric conditions, a garden may grow and flourish.

The end result may be much as the gardener had planned, forming the orderly patterns of the original design and exhibiting the structural symmetries, pleasing contrasts, and pretty juxtapositions that the gardener had first imagined. But there will surely be some surprises along the way. Some seeds may fail to sprout; others may yield proliferous growth. A natural balance seems to obtain. Just as a few seedlings may be undersized, weak, and thin, some few early blossoms of disappointingly pallid hue, other plants may foliate and flower with unexpected vigor and splendor. For all a gardener's careful planning, a garden grows as it will.

Yet, if the conceptual scheme of a garden has been judiciously and imaginatively wrought and if the gardener works with skill and patience and knowledge of the needs of the various plants, the garden may, in the end, be a wondrous thing. A thousand flowers may indeed one day bloom, to enchant the eye, engage the mind, and enrich the spirit.

The present encyclopedia is a garden of nearly three thousand flowers, grown from seeds sown in scholarly fields around the globe and transplanted here to form this great collection of articles. The board of editors and the Macmillan staff have gladly labored in this large and elaborate plot during the seven years of its planning and cultivation, sharing our chores with uncommon congeniality and good will. Now that the season of bloom is upon us, it falls to me, as the senior project editor on the Macmillan staff, to recapitulate some of the editorial policies we established, some of the editorial decisions we made, and some of the editorial practices we followed in making our garden grow.

To cover the vast territory outlined by our editor in chief in his general plan for the encyclopedia, the editors undertook to develop specific plans for articles in their various areas of specialization. Governed only by a general word allotment and suggestions for certain patterns of coverage, each editor was given free rein to determine the number, kind, and length of articles for the area(s) assigned to him or her. Staff members assigned to corresponding areas coordinated and supplemented the editors' plans for coverage but did not substantially alter them. Some parts of our plans were assigned to project editors on the Macmillan staff and were developed by them on the expert advice of special consultants. Consequently, in the final conceptual scheme of things, selection and arrangement of materials on the various religious traditions and fields of study turned out to be generally similar but particularly diverse, reflecting not only the different states of current scholarship in different fields but also the personal judgments and emphases of the various supervising editors.

Entries in the encyclopedia, it was early decided, would be alphabetically arranged. To avoid the dilemma of "alphabetization versus systematization," however, we also planned to follow the admirable practice of earlier Macmillan encyclopedias in using "composite entries" to group two or more articles under one heading, thus permitting systematic discussion of various aspects of broad topics. As an aid to the reader, we planned to put a headnote to each composite entry to explain its organization and, where appropriate, to offer a rationale for its partition. In developing composite entries, I should note, we did not always strive for exhaustive systematization; instead, we sometimes allowed ourselves to design pairs or groups of articles reflecting the idiosyncracies of current scholarly interest in various topics.

Once our plans were laid, and details of the several parts of our conceptual scheme began to fall into place, contributors selected from the international community of scholars were invited to undertake assignments in their special fields of study. For each article, a length was specified and a brief scope description was suggested. Except in terms of length, however, contributors were not restricted. On the contrary, as experts in their fields, they were encouraged to develop their articles according to their best judgment. We requested that a selected bibliography accompany each article, to call attention to some of the most useful publications on the topics discussed, to make recommendations for further reading, and to indicate bibliographic resources. Our general aim was to procure fresh, original articles from the best writers and thinkers and scholars in the world, forming a collection that would accurately reflect what we currently know—or, as one distinguished contributor put it, what we think we know—about the particular histories of religions past and present, great and small, as well as of the general history of religion viewed on a universal scale.

Our reach, we believe, did not exceed our grasp. The response to our invitations was overwhelmingly affirmative, and as manuscripts began to arrive in our offices from all the four corners of the earth, we soon saw that our encyclopedia would fulfill its promise. Our garden flourished from the very beginning; almost every seed sprouted, and there were remarkably few weeds.

There were, however, many gardening tasks to be done. The arrival of manuscripts brought us finally and squarely face to face with certain editorial problems of writing style that we had earlier anticipated, and with a few that we had not. We were confronted, of course, by problems of translation, transliteration, and romanization of many foreign languages, which, given the international tenor of our contributors and the pandemic scope of our project, we had fully expected. But we were also confronted by some surprisingly thorny problems of vocabulary and orthography that arose from the need to coordinate various conventions employed in different areas of religious studies and the need to establish standards of writing style that would be both acceptable to scholars and intelligible to nonspecialists.

Given that we had set out to produce an English-language encyclopedia and that we had decided to invite contributions from leading scholars around the globe, regardless of their native languages, the specter of translation loomed large and early. Contributors who preferred to write their articles in languages other than English were encouraged to enlist the aid of a trusted colleague as translator. Many of them did so, and submitted their articles to us in English. Many more did not, and submitted their articles to us in a great variety of European and Asian languages. Drawing upon the talents of translators both here and abroad, as well as upon the language skills of staff members, we undertook to put all these articles into clear and accurate English. We hope that we have successfully avoided an equation that Italians make—"Traduttore a traditore" (roughly, "Translation is treachery")—and that we have everywhere been faithful to our contributors' meanings. Translators are credited at the end of each article that has been rendered into English.

Translation of prose does not, of course, lay to rest all editorial problems with foreign languages. Many linguistic issues hovered over us, awaiting resolution. As a general policy, we had decided to restrict ourselves to the Latin alphabet, not venturing into such other alphabets as those of Sanskrit, Hebrew, Greek, or Arabic or into such other writing systems as those used to transcribe spoken Chinese, Japanese, or Korean. Yet all these languages, and many more, are the stuff of religious studies, and we were obliged to deal with them sensibly within an English context. A multitude of names and technical terms in all the world's languages, couched in various alphabets and writing systems, demanded to be appropriately spelled via transliteration or romanization into the Latin alphabet of English.

Generally, we agreed to prefer the modern, scholarly spellings that most closely approximate the orthography and/or pronunciation of the original language. Thus we decided to follow the transliteration and romanization systems used by the United States Library of Congress. These, by and large, are the traditional systems of scholarship in the English-speaking world and are thus to be found in the majority of secondary sources in Western libraries.

For languages for which the Library of Congress has issued no romanization table and for which no scholarly consensus has yet clearly emerged, we have made decisions on romanization based on the most expert advice we could secure. The languages of many indigenous peoples of Africa, the Americas, Australia, and Oceania, for example, have long been spoken but only recently written. For those for which standard systems of romanization have been established (e.g., Khoisan, Navajo), we have used them; for others, we have followed traditional practices. For languages for which scholarly practices of romanization vary widely—as in transcription of the languages of the ancient Near East—we have generally preferred the simplest system commonly used. For languages on which scholarly preference seems to be about equally divided between two standard systems of romanization (e.g., Tibetan), we have, realizing the impossibility of pleasing everyone, chosen to please ourselves. Gardeners' choice, as it were.

The spelling systems we have followed employ a moderate range of diacritical marks to indicate pronunciation in various languages. In addition to standard diacritics (e.g., the acute accent, the grave accent, the macron, the circumflex, the tilde, et al.), we decided to use an apostrophe (ʾ) to represent the hamzah in Arabic and the alef in Hebrew, a reversed apostrophe (ʿ) to represent ʿayn in Arabic and ʿayin in Hebrew, and a single quotation mark (') to indicate voiced consonants in Chinese. Besides these, we have used a few special characters (e.g., the thorn, the edh, et al.) in spelling Old English and Middle English, venerable ancestors of our modern language, and Old Norse, its ancient Germanic cousin.

Having made all these decisions regarding our preferences for scholarly usage of foreign languages, we found that personal names, both mythic and historical, continued to give us editorial trouble. We wished, wherever possible, to spell names according to the transliteration and romanization systems we had chosen, thus establishing a harmonious editorial consistency and, at the same time, restoring a certain linguistic and cultural integrity to names whose origins had, in Western scholarship, generally been englished or latinized or grecized beyond recognition. We wished, in short, to name Greeks in Greek, Chinese in Chinese, Arabs in Arabic, and so on.

To a certain degree we have been successful in our attempts to spell proper names "properly." Where our spellings differ markedly from those to which English readers may be accustomed, we have usually given traditional forms in parentheses: Ibn Sīnā (Avicenna), Meng-tzu (Mencius), Óđinn (Odin), Zarathushtra (Zoroaster). For historical figures who habitually spoke or wrote more than one language, we have transliterated their names from the language of their major works. Appropriate spelling of the names of Jewish scholars—polyglots all, it seems—has involved some particularly fine decisions, but, faced with several choices, we have generally preferred to give them in Hebrew.

Common sense, of course, frequently overruled all our editorial principles. Many names are too firmly embedded in the English language to bear alteration to more scholarly forms. Consequently, we have used latinized forms of most ancient Greek names (e.g., *Athena, Plato,* and *Phidias,* not *Athēnē, Platon,* and *Pheidias*), and we have invariably used englished names of biblical figures (e.g., *Moses, Jeremiah,* and *Jesus,* not *Mosheh, Yirmiyahu,* and *Yeshuah*). Otherwise, we have used commonly latinized or grecized names (e.g., *Confucius, Maimonides*) followed by more accurate forms in parentheses. Widely known place-names are given in englished forms (e.g., *Tokyo, Vienna,* and *Rome,* not *Tōkyō, Wien,* and *Roma*); less well known places are named in the language of the locale.

Appropriate spelling of names and terms in foreign languages was thus among our major editorial concerns, but no less so, and perhaps more so, was appropriate use of English terms. In devising our plans for the contents of the encyclopedia, and especially in choosing the terms under which articles would be entered into the overall alphabetical order, we endeavored to be constantly attuned to the nuances of meaning, and to the limits of meaning, of the terms that we chose to employ. We have used English words, of course, as headings for many articles planned to present cross-cultural perspectives of broad topics. But in all instances where genuine doubts about the suitability of an entry term could legitimately be raised with respect to a particular religious tradition, we planned to present a separate discussion under the idiom employed by the tradition itself. In all articles on cross-cultural topics, we encouraged contributors to speculate on the usefulness of the entry term as an organizing principle in the study of religion. We often urged them, too, to venture beyond their customary range of specialization and to take the broadest possible view of their topics, thus developing rare hybrids of unusual texture and variegation.

The plants in our garden, then, are named by terms both English and non-English, and they are arranged in the order of the Latin alphabet, strictly letter by letter. Throughout the alphabetical order, articles are located under the terms that we hope will be first consulted by most readers, both specialists and nonspecialists. Entries under *alternative* spellings and synonyms give cross-references to the actual location of articles. In addition, an extensive system of cross-references within articles has been employed to direct the reader to discussions of related topics. As final aids to the reader, a synoptic outline of contents and a thorough topical index appear in volume 16, and it is there that curious researchers should turn for systematic references to the names, the terms, and the topics they seek.

Like mushrooms after rain, other issues of appropriate use of language sprang up all over our garden. Perhaps nowhere more than in religious studies are conventions of writing style so bewilderingly diverse and thus so challenging to editors intent on stylistic consistency. In establishing principles of capitalization, italicization, and other such minutiae of editorial style, we tried always to remain flexible, observing the scholarly shibboleths of various religious traditions and, wherever we could without generating confusion, accommodating contributors' preferences. We have striven for consistency, to be sure, but we have always let context be our guide, varying details of style to suit content wherever necessary. Our chief aim in all our decisions has been to make meaning clear.

By no means, however, did we abandon all standards of writing style and let chaos reign. Editing, like all creative acts, is a messy business, but, like gardening, it is also both an orderly process and a process of establishing order.

Order, engendering clarity, is a consummation we have devoutly wished. Through use of standard forms of names and parenthetical notations of alternate forms, we have tried to make sure that all persons and places mentioned are clearly identified. We have standardized year dates to those of the Gregorian calendar, generally cited in terms of the common era, but we have also given dates by other systems of chronology wherever context demanded them. We have kept abbreviations to a minimum, and we have listed those we have used in the front of each of our volumes. In devising bibliographies, we offered our contributors two standard formats, prose and list, and allowed them to choose the more appropriate to their articles. Regardless of format, our researchers have verified the accuracy of all bibliographic data, and we have taken pains to ensure that English-language editions are cited if they exist.

All these editorial concerns, among numerous others, have entered into the care of our garden. We are happy at last to see it in full flower, and we believe that it presents a splendid array of great variety, worth, and interest. We trust that Victor Turner would have been pleased.

Thanks due from the Macmillan staff to the many people who aided us in our gardening chores are expressed in a special section of acknowledgments in volume 16. I cannot close this introduction, however, without making a general acknowledgment of our gratitude to the contributors, whose ready cooperation greatly eased our efforts; to the consultants, who lent us the conceptual tools and technical devices that we needed; and to the board of editors, who shared our labors and became our friends. Most of all, we are grateful to have known and worked with Mircea Eliade, our editor in chief. In all his dealings with us, his generosity of spirit was boundless, his sweetness, kindness, and gentleness never failing. His genius is represented in these volumes, and through them it will live, in the words of Ben Jonson, as long as "we have wits to read, and praise to give."

CLAUDE CONYERS
New York, October 1986

LIST OF ARTICLES

Articles included in the Encyclopedia are listed below in alphabetic order. Contributors' names follow the article title; first-edition contributors are indicated by (1987) and second-edition contributors are noted as (2005). Articles updated or revised for the second edition have both dates listed. *Revised Bibliography* indicates that only the bibliography was updated for this edition.

A

AARON
Edward L. Greenstein (1987)

ABBAHU
Robert Goldenberg (1987)
Revised Bibliography

ABBAYE
Baruch M. Bokser (1987)
Revised Bibliography

'ABD AL-JABBĀR
Alnoor Dhanani (2005)

'ABD AL-RĀZIQ, 'ALĪ
Ibrahim I. Ibrahim (1987)

'ABDUH, MUḤAMMAD
Ali E. Hillal Dessouki (1987)

ABELARD, PETER
Eileen F. Kearney (1987)

ABHINAVAGUPTA
Alexis Sanderson (1987)
Revised Bibliography

ABLUTIONS
Han J. W. Drijvers (1987)
Revised Bibliography

ABRAHAM
John Van Seters (1987)
Revised Bibliography

ABRAVANEL, ISAAC
Norbert M. Samuelson (1987)
Revised Bibliography

ABŪ AL-HUDHAYL AL-'ALL ĀF
R. M. Frank (1987)

ABŪ BAKR
M. A. Zaki Badawi (2005)

ABŪ ḤANĪFAH
Zafar Ishaq Ansari (1987)

ABULAFIA, ME'IR
Bernard Septimus (1987)
Revised Bibliography

ABŪ YŪSUF
Jeanette A. Wakin (1987)

ACEHNESE RELIGION
James T. Siegel (1987)
Revised Bibliography

ADAD
Edward Lipiński (2005)

ADAM
Michael Fishbane (1987)

ADAMS, HANNAH
Thomas A. Tweed (2005)

ĀDI GRANTH
Surindar Singh Kohli (1987)

ADLER, FELIX
Benny Kraut (1987)

ADONIS
Edward Lipiński (2005)

ADRET, SHELOMOH BEN AVRAHAM
Marc Saperstein (1987)
Revised Bibliography

AEGEAN RELIGIONS
Olivier Pelon (1987)
Nanno Marinatos (2005)

AESTHETICS: PHILOSOPHICAL AESTHETICS
James Alfred Martin, Jr. (1987 and 2005)

AESTHETICS: VISUAL AESTHTICS
Rudolf Arnheim (1987)

AFFLICTION: AFRICAN CULTS OF AFFLICTION
John M. Janzen (1987 and 2005)

AFFLICTION: AN OVERVIEW
Vieda Skultans (1987)
Revised Bibliography

AFGHĀNĪ, JAMĀL AL-DĪN AL-
Albert Hourani (1987)

AFRICAN AMERICAN RELIGIONS: AN OVERVIEW
James Anthony Noel (2005)

AFRICAN AMERICAN RELIGIONS: HISTORY OF STUDY
Tracey E. Hucks (2005)
Dianne M. Stewart (2005)

AFRICAN AMERICAN RELIGIONS: MUSLIM MOVEMENTS
Albert J. Raboteau (1987)
Revised Bibliography

AFRICAN RELIGIONS: AN OVERVIEW
Benjamin C. Ray (1987)

C

CAMPBELL, ALEXANDER
David Edwin Harrell, Jr. (1987)

CAMPBELL, JOSEPH
Mark W. MacWilliams (2005)

CANAANITE RELIGION: AN OVERVIEW
Alan M. Cooper (1987)
Revised Bibliography

CANAANITE RELIGION: THE LITERATURE
Michael D. Coogan (1987 and 2005)

CANDRAKĪRTI
Mimaki Katsumi (1987)
Revised Bibliography

CANISIUS, PETER
Jill Raitt (1987)

CANNIBALISM
Paula Brown (1987)
Beth A. Conklin (2005)

CANON
Gerald T. Sheppard (1987)
Revised Bibliography

CAO DAI
Robert S. Ellwood (1987 and 2005)

CAPPS, WALTER
David Chidester (2005)

CARDS
Richard W. Thurn (1987)
Revised Bibliography

CARGO CULTS [FIRST EDITION]
Peter Lawrence (1987)

CARGO CULTS [FURTHER CONSIDERATIONS]
Martha Kaplan (2005)

CARIBBEAN RELIGIONS: AFRO-CARIBBEAN RELIGIONS
George Eaton Simpson (1987)

CARIBBEAN RELIGIONS: PRE-COLUMBIAN RELIGIONS
Stephen D. Glazier (1987)

CARNIVAL
Maria Julia Goldwasser (1987)
Revised Bibliography

CARROLL, JOHN
Thomas O'Brien Hanley (1987)

CĀRVĀKA
Bimal Krishna Matilal (1987)

CASSIAN, JOHN
Panagiotis C. Christou (1987)

CASSIRER, ERNST
Donald Phillip Verene (1987)
Revised Bibliography

CASTRATION
Dario M. Cosi (1987 and 2005)

CASTRÉN, MATTHIAS ALEXANDER
Juha Pentikäinen (2005)

CASUISTRY
Albert R. Jonsen (1987)
Revised Bibliography

CATHARI
Gordon Leff (1987)

CATHARSIS
Robert Turcan (1987 and 2005)

CATHERINE OF SIENA
Suzanne Noffke (1987)

CATS
Annemarie Schimmel (1987)
Revised Bibliography

CATTLE
Bruce Lincoln (1987)
Revised Bibliography

CAVES
Doris Heyden (1987)
Revised Bibliography

CAYCE, EDGAR
Robert S. Ellwood (2005)

CELIBACY
Daniel Gold (1987 and 2005)

CELTIC RELIGION: AN OVERVIEW
Proinsias Mac Cana (1987 and 2005)

CELTIC RELIGION: HISTORY OF STUDY
Joseph F. Nagy (2005)

CENTER OF THE WORLD
Mircea Eliade (1987)
Lawrence E. Sullivan (1987)
Revised Bibliography

CENTRAL BANTU RELIGIONS
Elizabeth Colson (1987)
Revised Bibliography

CEREMONY
Bobby C. Alexander (1987 and 2005)

CERULARIOS, MICHAEL
John Travis (1987)

CHAN
John R. McRae (2005)

CHANCE
Michiko Yusa (1987 and 2005)

CHANNING, WILLIAM ELLERY,
John C. Godbey (1987)

CHANTEPIE DE LA SAUSSAYE, P. D.
Jacques Waardenburg (1987)
Revised Bibliography

CHANTING
Johanna Spector (1987)
Revised Bibliography

CHAOS
Norman J. Girardot (1987)

CHAOS THEORY
John Polkinghorne (2005)

CHARISMA
George L. Scheper (2005)

CHARITY
Demetrios J. Constantelos (1987 and 2005)

CHARLEMAGNE
Donald A. Bullough (1987)

CHASTITY
Kate Cooper (2005)

CHENG HAO
Deborah Sommer (1987 and 2005)

CHENG YI
Deborah Sommer (1987 and 2005)

CHEROKEE RELIGIOUS TRADITIONS
Michelene E. Pesantubbee (2005)

CHILD
Wallace B. Clift (1987)

CHILD, LYDIA MARIA
Lori Kenschaft (2005)

CHINESE PHILOSOPHY
David S. Nivison (1987 and 2005)

CHINESE RELIGION: AN OVERVIEW
Daniel L. Overmyer (1987)
Joseph A. Adler (2005)

CHINESE RELIGION: HISTORY OF STUDY
Norman J. Girardot (1987)
Terry F. Kleeman (2005)

CHINESE RELIGION: MYTHIC THEMES
Norman J. Girardot (1987)
Revised Bibliography

CHINESE RELIGION: POPULAR RELIGION
Vincent Goossaert (2005)

CHINESE RELIGIOUS YEAR
Laurence G. Thompson (1987)
Revised Bibliography

D

E

G

J

K

KNOX, JOHN
John H. Leith (1987)

KŌBEN
Leo M. Pruden (1987)

KOHLER, KAUFMANN
Benny Kraut (1987)

KOKUGAKU
Ishida Ichirō (1987)
Peter Nosco (2005)

KOMI RELIGION
Nikolai Konakov (2005)

KONGO RELIGION
John M. Janzen (1987)
Revised Bibliography

KONG SPRUL BLO GROS MTHA' YAS (KONGTRUL LODRO TAYE)
E. Gene Smith (2005)

KONKŌKYŌ
Helen Hardacre (1987)

KOOK, AVRAHAM YITSḤAQ
Benjamin Ish-Shalom (2005)

KOREAN RELIGION
Francisca Cho (2005)

KORESH, DAVID
James D. Tabor (2005)

KOSMAS AITOLOS
Nomikos Michael Vaporis (1987)

KOTLER, AHARON
Shaul Stampfer (1987)
Revised Bibliography

KOU QIANZHI
Richard B. Mather (1987)

KRAEMER, HENDRIK
Willem A. Bijlefeld (1987)
Revised Bibliography

KRAMRISCH, STELLA
Michael W. Meister (2005)

KRISHNAMURTI, JIDDU
Charles S. J. White (1987 and 2005)

KRISTENSEN, W. BREDE
John B. Carman (1987)
Revised Bibliography

KROCHMAL, NAḤMAN
Robert M. Seltzer (1987)
Revised Bibliography

KṚṢṆA
John Stratton Hawley (1987 and 2005)

KṚṢṆAISM
Friedhelm E. Hardy (1987)
Revised Bibliography

KṢITIGARBHA
Miriam Levering (1987)
Revised Bibliography

KUBRĀ, NAJM AL-DĪN
Muhammadisa Waley (2005)

KUIJI
Alan Sponberg (1987)
Revised Bibliography

KULTURKREISELEHRE
Kurt Rudolph (1987)
Alessandra Ciattini (2005)

KUMĀRAJĪVA
Dale Todaro (1987)

KUMAZAWA BANZAN
I. J. McMullen (1987)

KUMBHA MELĀ
William S. Sax (1987)
Revised Bibliography

KUṆḌALINĪ
Hugh B. Urban (2005)

KUROZUMIKYŌ
Hirota Masaki (1987)
Revised Bibliography

KURUKṢETRA
Alf Hiltebeitel (1987)

KUSHITE RELIGION
William Y. Adams (1987)
Revised Bibliography

KŪYA
Edward Kamens (1987 and 2005)

L

LABYRINTH
Lima de Freitas (1987)
Revised Bibliography

LADY OF THE ANIMALS
Carol P. Christ (1987 and 2005)

LAESTADIUS, LARS LEVI
Juha Pentikäinen (2005)

LĀHORĪ, MUḤAMMAD ʿALĪ
Sajida S. Alvi (1987 and 2005)

LAIMA
Haralds Biezais (1987)
Revised Bibliography

LAITY
F. Stanley Lusby (1987)
Revised Bibliography

LAKES
Richard F. Townsend (1987)
Revised Bibliography

LAKOTA RELIGIOUS TRADITIONS
William K. Powers (1987)
James Garrett (2005)
Kathleen J. Martin (2005)

LAMOTTE, ÉTIENNE
Hubert Durt (1987 and 2005)

LANDVÆTTIR
John Lindow (1987 and 2005)

LANG, ANDREW
Benjamin C. Ray (1987)
Revised Bibliography

LANGER, SUSANNE
Arabella Lyon (2005)

LANGUAGE: BUDDHIST VIEWS OF LANGUAGE
Luis O. Gómez (1987)
Revised Bibliography

LANGUAGE: SACRED LANGUAGE
Wade T. Wheelock (1987)

LAO RELIGION
Georges Condominas (1987)
Revised Bibliography

LAOZI
Judith Magee Boltz (1987)

LARES
Attilio Mastrocinque (2005)

LAS CASAS, BARTOLOMÉ DE
Sidney H. Rooy (1987)

LA VALLÉE POUSSIN, LOUIS DE
Hubert Durt (1987)
Revised Bibliography

LAW, WILLIAM
Erwin P. Rudolph (1987)

LAW AND RELIGION: AN OVERVIEW
Winnifred Fallers Sullivan (2005)
Robert A. Yelle (2005)

LAW AND RELIGION: LAW AND NEW RELIGIOUS MOVEMENTS
James T. Richardson (2005)

LAW AND RELIGION: LAW AND RELIGION IN BUDDHISM
Rebecca R. French (2005)

LAW AND RELIGION: LAW AND RELIGION IN CHINESE RELIGIONS
Laura A. Skosey (2005)

LAW AND RELIGION: LAW AND RELIGION IN HINDUISM
Richard W. Lariviere (2005)

LOGICAL POSITIVISM
Frederick Ferré (1987)
Revised Bibliography

LOGOS
Jean Pépin (1987)
Revised Bibliography

LOISY, ALFRED
Richard J. Resch (1987)
Revised Bibliography

LOKI
John Lindow (2005)

LONERGAN, BERNARD
Frederick E. Crowe (1987 and 2005)

LÖNNROT, ELIAS
Felix J. Oinas (1987)
Revised Bibliography

LORD OF THE ANIMALS
Otto Zerries (1987)

LORD'S PRAYER
Geoffrey Wainwright (1987 and 2005)

LOTUS
Joel P. Brereton (1987)

LÖW, YEHUDAH BEN BETSAL'EL OF PRAGUE
Byron L. Sherwin (1987)
Revised Bibliography

LOWIE, ROBERT H.
Raymond D. Fogelson (1987)

LUBA RELIGION
J. A. Theuws (1987)
Revised Bibliography

LUDI SAECULARES
John Scheid (1987)
Revised Bibliography

LUGBARA RELIGION
John Middleton (1987)
Revised Bibliography

LUGH
Elizabeth A. Gray (2005)

LUKE THE EVANGELIST
D. Moody Smith (1987 and 2005)

LULL, RAMÓN
Annemarie Schimmel (1987)

LUPERCALIA
Robert Schilling (1987)
Revised Bibliography

LURIA, ISAAC
Lawrence Fine (1987)
Revised Bibliography

LURIA, SHELOMOH
Michael Stanislawski (1987)
Revised Bibliography

LUSTRATIO
John Scheid (1987)
Revised Bibliography

LUTHER, MARTIN
Hans J. Hillerbrand (1987)

LUTHERANISM
Eric W. Gritsch (1987)
Revised Bibliography

LU XIUJING
Catherine M. Bell (1987)
Revised Bibliography

LU XIANGSHAN
On-cho Ng (2005)

M

MABINOGION
Brynley F. Roberts (1987 and 2005)

MADHHAB
M. Hashim Kamali (1987)

MADHVA
Karl H. Potter (1987)

MĀDHYAMIKA
Kajiyama Yūichi (1987)
Revised Bibliography

MADRASAH
Richard W. Bulliet (1987)

MA GCIG LAB SGRON (MACHIG LABDRON)
Janet Gyatso (2005)

MAGEN DAVID
Joseph Gutmann (1987)
Revised Bibliography

MAGI
Albert de Jong (2005)

MAGIC: MAGIC IN EAST ASIA
Donald Harper (1987)

MAGIC: MAGIC IN EASTERN EUROPE
Ionna Andreesco-Miereanu (1987)
Revised Bibliography

MAGIC: MAGIC IN GRECO-ROMAN ANTIQUITY
Hans Dieter Betz (1987)

MAGIC: MAGIC IN INDIGENOUS SOCIETIES
Donald R. Hill (1987)

MAGIC: MAGIC IN ISLAM
Toufic Fahd (1987)

MAGIC: MAGIC IN MEDIEVAL AND RENAISSANCE EUROPE
Richard Kieckhefer (2005)

MAGIC: MAGIC IN SOUTH ASIA
Ariel Glucklich (2005)

MAGIC: THEORIES OF MAGIC
John Middleton (1987 and 2005)

MAHĀBHĀRATA
Alf Hiltebeitel (1987)
Revised Bibliography

MAHĀMUDRĀ
Roger R. Jackson (2005)

MAHĀSĀṂGHIKA
Luis O. Gómez (1987)
Revised Bibliography

MAHĀSIDDHAS
Reginald Ray (1987)
Revised Bibliography

MAHĀVAIROCANA
Charles D. Orzech (1987)
Revised Bibliography

MAHĀVĪRA
Colette Caillat (1987)

MAID OF LUDMIR
Ada Rapoport-Albert (2005)

MAIMONIDES, ABRAHAM
Paul B. Fenton (2005)

MAIMONIDES, MOSES
Isadore Twersky (1987)
Revised Bibliography

MAITREYA
Lewis R. Lancaster (1987)
Revised Bibliography

MAJLISĪ, AL-
Etan Kohlberg (1987)

MAKARIOS OF EGYPT
Theodore Zissis (1987)

MALALASEKERA, G. P.
N. A. Jayawickrama (1987)
Revised Bibliography

MALBIM
A. Stanley Dreyfus (1987)

MALCOLM X
Lawrence H. Mamiya (1987)

MĀLIK IBN ANAS
Susan A. Spectorsky (1987)
Devin J. Stewart (2005)

MALINOWSKI, BRONISLAW
Michael A. Baenen (1987)
Revised Bibliography

MATRES
Françoise le Roux (1987)
Christian-J. Guyonvarc'h (1987)

MATTHEW THE EVANGELIST
D. Moody Smith (1987 and 2005)

MĀTURĪDĪ, AL-
R. Marston Speight (1987)
Ibrahim Kalin (2005)

MĀUI
Katharine Luomala (1987)

MAURICE, FREDERICK DENISON
Olive J. Brose (1987)

MAUSS, MARCEL
Marcel Fournier (2005)

MĀWARDĪ, AL-
Donald P. Little (1987)

MAWDŪDĪ, SAYYID ABŪ AL-A'LĀ
Sheila McDonough (1987)

MAWLID
Dale F. Eickelman (1987)

MAWU-LISA
James S. Thayer (1987)

MAXIMÓN
Vincent Stanzione (2005)

MAXIMOS THE CONFESSOR
Nicholas Karazafiris (1987)

MĀYĀ
Teun Goudriaan (1987)

MAYA RELIGION
David Stuart (2005)

MAZDAKISM
Ehsan Yarshater (2005)

MBONA
J. Matthew Schoffeleers (1987)
Revised Bibliography

MCPHERSON, AIMEE SEMPLE
Robert Mapes Anderson (1987)

MEAD, MARGARET
Paul Shankman (2005)

MEDIA AND RELIGION
Stewart M. Hoover (2005)

MEDICAL ETHICS
Lisa Soleymani Lehmann (2005)

MEDITATION
Frederic B. Underwood (1987)

MEGALITHIC RELIGION: HISTORICAL CULTURES
J. Stephen Lansing (1987)
Revised Bibliography

MEGALITHIC RELIGION: PREHISTORIC EVIDENCE
Marija Gimbutas (1987)

MEHER BABA
Charles C. Haynes (1987 and 2005)

ME'IR
Tzvee Zahavy (1987)
Revised Bibliography

ME'IR BEN BARUKH OF ROTHENBURG
Gerald J. Blidstein (1987)

MELANCHTHON, PHILIPP
Clyde L. Manschreck (1987)

MELANESIAN RELIGIONS: AN OVERVIEW
Ann Chowning (1987)
Revised Bibliography

MELANESIAN RELIGIONS: MYTHIC THEMES
Fitz John Porter Poole (1987)
Revised Bibliography

MELQART
Corinne Bonnet (2005)

MEMORIZATION
Phillipe Borgeaud (1987 and 2005)

MENDELSSOHN, MOSES
Robert M. Seltzer (1987)
Revised Bibliography

MENDICANCY
Rosemary Rader (1987)
Revised Bibliography

MENGZI
Philip J. Ivanhoe (2005)

MENNONITES
Cornelius J. Dyck (1987)
Revised Bibliography

MEN'S STUDIES IN RELIGION
Björn Krondorfer (2005)
Philip Culbertson (2005)

MENSTRUATION
Melissa Raphael (2005)

MERCIER, DÉSIRÉ JOSEPH
Gary Lease (1987)

MEREZHKOVSKII, DMITRII
Bernice Glatzer Rosenthal (1987 and 2005)

MERIT: AN OVERVIEW
Michael Pye (1987)
Revised Bibliography

MERIT: BUDDHIST CONCEPTS
John S. Strong (1987)
Revised Bibliography

MERIT: CHRISTIAN CONCEPTS
Michael Pye (1987)
Revised Bibliography

MERLIN
Brynley F. Roberts (1987 and 2005)

MERTON, THOMAS
Anthony Padovano (1987)

MESOAMERICAN RELIGIONS: CLASSIC CULTURES
Doris Heyden (1987)

MESOAMERICAN RELIGIONS: COLONIAL CULTURES
Veronica Gutiérrez (2005)
Matthew Restall (2005)

MESOAMERICAN RELIGIONS: CONTEMPORARY CULTURES
Robert S. Carlsen (2005)

MESOAMERICAN RELIGIONS: FORMATIVE CULTURES
Hasso von Winning (1987)

MESOAMERICAN RELIGIONS: HISTORY OF STUDY
Yolotl González Torres (1987 and 2005)

MESOAMERICAN RELIGIONS: MYTHIC THEMES
Doris Heyden (1987)
Yolotl González Torres (2005)
Davíd Carrasco (2005)

MESOAMERICAN RELIGIONS: POSTCLASSIC CULTURES
H. B. Nicholson (1987 and 2005)

MESOAMERICAN RELIGIONS: PRE-COLUMBIAN RELIGIONS
Miguel Léon-Portilla (1987 and 2005)

MESOPOTAMIAN RELIGIONS: AN OVERVIEW [FIRST EDITION]
Thorkild Jacobsen (1987)

MESOPOTAMIAN RELIGIONS: AN OVERVIEW [FURTHER CONSIDERATIONS]
Giovanni Pettinato (2005)

MESOPOTAMIAN RELIGIONS: HISTORY OF STUDY
Thorkild Jacobsen (1987)
Pietro Mander (2005)

MONTAGU, LILY
Ellen M. Umansky (1987)
Revised Bibliography

MONTANISM
Kurt Aland (1987)

MONTANUS
Kurt Aland (1987)

MOODY, DWIGHT L.
James F. Findlay (1987)

MOON
Jean Rhys Bram (1987)
Revised Bibliography

MOORE, GEORGE FOOT
F. Stanley Lusby (1987)
Steven Fine (2005)

MORALITY AND RELIGION
Ronald M. Green (1987)
Revised Bibliography

MORAVIANS
David A. Schattschneider (1987)
Revised Bibliography

MORMONISM
Klaus J. Hansen (1987 and 2005)

MORRISON, ROBERT
Paul V. Martinson (1987)

MORTIFICATION
Dario Sabbatucci (1987)
Revised Bibliography

MOSES
John Van Seters (1987)

MOSQUE: ARCHITECTURAL ASPECTS
Hasan-Uddin Khan (2005)

MOSQUE: HISTORY AND TRADITION
Syed Gulzar Haider (2005)

MOTOORI NORINAGA
Ueda Kenji (1987)
Revised Bibliography

MOUNTAINS
Diana L. Eck (1987)

MOVEMENT FOR THE RESTORATION OF THE TEN COMMANDMENTS OF GOD
Massimo Introvigne (2005)

MOZI
John Makeham (2005)

MUDRĀ
Sanjukta Gupta (2005)

MUḤAMMAD
Karen Armstrong (2005)

MUḤAMMAD AḤMAD
John O. Hunwick (1987)

MUISCA RELIGION
Pita Kelekna (1987)
Revised Bibliography

MULLĀ ṢADRĀ
Fazlur Rahman (1987)
Revised Bibliography

MÜLLER, F. MAX
Jon R. Stone (2005)

MÜLLER, KARL O.
Burton Feldman (1987)
Revised Bibliography

MÜNTZER, THOMAS
Eric W. Gritsch (1987)

MŪRTI
Gary Michael Tartakov (1987)

MURUKAṈ
Fred W. Clothey (1987 and 2005)

MUSAR MOVEMENT
Gershon C. Bacon (1987 and 2005)

MUSES
Jeannie Carlier (1987)
Silvia Milanezi (1987)
Revised Bibliography

MUSEUMS AND RELIGION
Crispin Paine (2005)

MUSIC: MUSIC AND RELIGION
Ter Ellingson (1987)
Revised Bibliography

MUSIC: MUSIC AND RELIGION IN CHINA, KOREA, AND TIBET
Isabel Wong (1987)

MUSIC: MUSIC AND RELIGION IN GREECE, ROME, AND BYZANTIUM
Eric Werner (1987)
Revised Bibliography

MUSIC: MUSIC AND RELIGION IN INDIA
Philip V. Bohlman (2005)

MUSIC: MUSIC AND RELIGION IN INDIGENOUS AUSTRALIA
Elizabeth Mackinlay (2005)
John J. Bradley (2005)

MUSIC: MUSIC AND RELIGION IN JAPAN
Kishibe Shigeo (1987)
Ogi Mitsuo (2005)

MUSIC: MUSIC AND RELIGION IN MESOAMERICA
Arnd Adje Both (2005)

MUSIC: MUSIC AND RELIGION IN OCEANIA
Richard M. Moyle (2005)

MUSIC: MUSIC AND RELIGION IN SOUTH AMERICA
Acácio Tadeu de Camargo Piedade (2005)
Deise Lucy Oliveira Montardo (2005)

MUSIC: MUSIC AND RELIGION IN SOUTHEAST ASIA
David Harnish (2005)

MUSIC: MUSIC AND RELIGION IN SUB-SAHARAN AFRICA
J. H. Kwabena Nketia (1987)
Revised Bibliography

MUSIC: MUSIC AND RELIGION IN THE MIDDLE EAST
Amnon Shiloah (1987)

MUSIC: RELIGIOUS MUSIC IN THE WEST
Frank Burch Brown (2005)

MUSLIM BROTHERHOOD
Afaf Lutfi al-Sayyud Marsot (1987)

MUSŌ SŌSEKI
Martin Collcutt (1987)

MUʿTAZILAH
Josef van Ess (1987)

MYERHOFF, BARBARA G.
Riv-Ellen Prell (1987 and 2005)

MYSTERY RELIGIONS
Kurt Rudolph (1987)
Revised Bibliography

MYSTICAL UNION IN JUDAISM, CHRISTIANITY, AND ISLAM
Bernard McGinn (2005)

MYSTICISM [FIRST EDITION]
Louis Dupré (1987)

MYSTICISM [FURTHER CONSIDERATIONS]
Peter Moore (2005)

MYTH: AN OVERVIEW
Kees W. Bolle (1987 and 2005)

MYTH: MYTH AND HISTORY
Paul Ricoeur (1987)
Revised Bibliography

MYTH AND RITUAL SCHOOL
Walter Harrelson (1987 and 2005)

N

NABATEAN RELIGION
John F. Healey (2005)

NABU
Tikva Frymer-Kensky (1987)
Revised Bibliography

O

Q

R

RAVA'
Baruch M. Bokser (1987)
Revised Bibliography

RĀWẒAH-KHVĀNĪ
Peter Chelkowski (1987)

RĀZĪ, FAKHR AL-DĪN AL-
Feras Q. Hamza (2005)

RE
Leonard H. Lesko (1987)

REBECCA
Frederick E. Greenspahn (1987 and 2005)

RECONSTRUCTIONIST JUDAISM
Rebecca T. Alpert (2005)

REDEMPTION
Ileana Marcoulesco (1987)
Revised Bibliography

REFERENCE WORKS
Edgar Krentz (1987)
Martha S. Alt (2005)
Roberta A. Schaafsma (2005)

REFLEXIVITY
Barbara A. Babcock (1987)
Revised Bibliography

REFORM
Joseph L. Blau (1987)
Revised Bibliography

REFORMATION
Hans J. Hillerbrand (1987)
Revised Bibliography

REFORM JUDAISM
Michael A. Meyer (1987 and 2005)

REGULY, ANTAL
Vilmos Voigt (2005)

REIMARUS, HERMANN SAMUEL
Charles H. Talbert (1987)

REINACH, SALOMON
Willem A. Bijlefeld (1987)
Revised Bibliography

REINCARNATION
J. Bruce Long (1987)
Revised Bibliography

REINES, YITSḤAQ YA'AQOV
David Biale (1987)
Revised Bibliography

REIYŪKAI KYŌDAN
Helen Hardacre (1987)

REJUVENATION
Wallace B. Clift (1987)

RELATIVISM
Richard H. Popkin (1987)
Revised Bibliography

RELICS
John S. Strong (1987 and 2005)

RELIGION [FIRST EDITION]
Winston L. King (1987)

RELIGION [FURTHER CONSIDERATIONS]
Gregory D. Alles (2005)

RELIGIONSGESCHICHTLICHE SCHULE
Kurt Rudolph (1987)
Revised Bibliography

RELIGIOUS BROADCASTING
Gregor T. Goethals (1987)
Phillip Charles Lucas (2005)

RELIGIOUS COMMUNITIES: CHRISTIAN RELIGIOUS ORDERS
Nathan D. Mitchell (1987)
Revised Bibliography

RELIGIOUS COMMUNITIES: RELIGION, COMMUNITY, AND SOCIETY
Joseph M. Kitagawa (1987)

RELIGIOUS DIVERSITY
Shmuel N. Eisenstadt (1987)
Revised Bibliography

RELIGIOUS EDUCATION
J. Mark Halstead (2005)

RELIGIOUS EXPERIENCE
Ann Taves (2005)

RENAN, ERNEST
Richard J. Resch (1987)
Revised Bibliography

REN AND YI
Kwong-loi Shun (2005)

RENNYO
Kenshi Kusano (2005)

RENOU, LOUIS
Marie-Simone Renou (1987)
Revised Bibliography

REPENTANCE
David E. Aune (1987)
Revised Bibliography

RESHEF
Edward Lipiński (2005)

RESURRECTION
Helmer Ringgren (1987)
Revised Bibliography

RETREAT
Juan Manuel Lozano (1987)

REVEL, BERNARD
Aaron Rakeffet-Rothkoff (1987)
Revised Bibliography

REVELATION
Johannes Deninger (1987)

REVENGE AND RETRIBUTION
Elmar Klinger (1987)

REVIVAL AND RENEWAL
Kenelm Burridge (1987)
Revised Bibliography

REVOLUTION
Guenter Lewy (1987)
Revised Bibliography

RICCI, MATTEO
Julia Ching (1987)

RICHARDSON, CYRIL C.
David W. Lotz (1987)

RISSHŌ KŌSEIKAI
Morioka Kiyomi (1987)
Revised Bibliography

RITES OF PASSAGE: AFRICAN RITES
James L. Cox (2005)

RITES OF PASSAGE: AN OVERVIEW [FIRST EDITION]
Linda A. Camino (1987)
Barbara G. Myerhoff (1987)
Edith Turner (2005)

RITES OF PASSAGE: AN OVERVIEW [FURTHER CONSIDERATIONS]
Barry Stephenson (2005)

RITES OF PASSAGE: HINDU RITES
Patrick Olivelle (1987 and 2005)

RITES OF PASSAGE: JEWISH RITES
Harvey E. Goldberg (2005)

RITES OF PASSAGE: MESOAMERICAN RITES
Kay A. Read (2005)

RITES OF PASSAGE: MUSLIM RITES
Dale F. Eickelman (1987)

RITES OF PASSAGE: NEOPAGAN RITES
Sarah Pike (2005)

RITES OF PASSAGE: OCEANIC RITES
Philip Gibbs (2005)

RITSCHL, ALBRECHT
David W. Lotz (1987)

RITUAL [FIRST EDITION]
Evan M. Zuesse (1987)

RITUAL [FURTHER CONSIDERATIONS]
Catherine M. Bell (2005)

S

SAMĀ'
Khaliq Aḥmad Nizami (1987)
Revised Bibliography

SAMĀDHI
Georg Feuerstein (1987)
Revised Bibliography

SAMARITANS
Reinhard Pummer (2005)

SAṂGHA: AN OVERVIEW
Heinz Bechert (1987 and 2005)

SAṂGHA: SAṂGHA AND SOCIETY IN SOUTH AND SOUTHEAST ASIA
H. L. Seneviratne (1987)

SAṂGHA: SAṂGHA AND SOCIETY IN TIBET
Georges Dreyfus (2005)

SAMI RELIGION
Louise Bäckman (1987)
Juha Pentikäinen (2005)

SĀṂKHYA
Edeltraud Harzer (1987 and 2005)

SAṂNYĀSA
Patrick Olivelle (1987 and 2005)

SAMOYED RELIGION
Robert Austerlitz (1987)
Juha Pentikäinen (2005)

SAṂSĀRA
Brian K. Smith (1987)
Revised Bibliography

SAMSON
Edward L. Greenstein (1987 and 2005)

SAMUEL
John Van Seters (1987)
Revised Bibliography

SANCTUARY
Gregory D. Alles (1987)
Revised Bibliography

SANHEDRIN
David Goodblatt (1987)
Revised Bibliography

ŚAṄKARA
David N. Lorenzen (1987)
Revised Bibliography

ŚĀNTARAKṢITA
Sara L. McClintock (2005)

SANTERÍA
Joseph M. Murphy (1987)

ŚĀNTIDEVA
Susanne Mrozik (2005)

SAOSHYANT
Gherardo Gnoli (1987)

ŚĀRADĀ DEVĪ
Neelima Shukla-Bhatt (2005)

SARAH
Frederick E. Greenspahn (2005)

SARASVATĪ
Donna Marie Wulff (1987)

SARMATIAN RELIGION
D. S. Raevskii (1987)
Revised Bibliography

SARTRE, JEAN-PAUL
Maurice Natanson (1987)
Revised Bibliography

SARVĀSTIVĀDA
Luis O. Gómez (1987)
Revised Bibliography

ŚĀSTRA LITERATURE
Ludo Rocher (1987)
Revised Bibliography

SATAN
Arvind Sharma (1987 and 2005)

SATANISM
David G. Bromley (2005)

SATI
Julia Leslie (2005)

SAUL
John Van Seters (1987)
Revised Bibliography

SAULE
Vaira Vīķe-Freiberga (2005)

SAURA HINDUISM
Thomas J. Hopkins (1987)
Revised Bibliography

SAUTRĀNTIKA
Tadeusz Skorupski (1987)
Revised Bibliography

SAVONAROLA, GIROLAMO
Donald Weinstein (1987)

ṢAWM
Zafar Ishaq Ansari (1987)

SAXO GRAMMATICUS
John Weinstock (1987 and 2005)

SAYERS, DOROTHY L.
Ann Loades (2005)

SCAPEGOAT
Jan N. Bremmer (2005)

SCHECHTER, SOLOMON
Ismar Schorsch (1987)
Revised Bibliography

SCHELER, MAX
Manfred S. Frings (1987)

SCHELLING, FRIEDRICH
Thomas F. O'Meara (1987 and 2005)

SCHENIRER, SARAH
Blu Greenberg (1987)
Revised Bibliography

SCHIMMEL, ANNEMARIE
Peter Antes (2005)

SCHISM: AN OVERVIEW
Nancy T. Ammerman (1987)
Revised Bibliography

SCHISM: CHRISTIAN SCHISM
John Lawrence Boojamra (1987)
Revised Bibliography

SCHLEGEL, FRIEDRICH
Hans J. Klimkeit (1987)
Revised Bibliography

SCHLEIERMACHER, FRIEDRICH
B. A. Gerrish (1987)
Sergio Sorrentino (2005)

SCHMIDT, WILHELM
Joseph Henninger (1987)
Alessandra Ciattini (2005)

SCHNEERSON, MENACHEM M.
Naftali Loewenthal (2005)

SCHOLARIOS, GENNADIOS
Nomikos Michael Vaporis (1987)

SCHOLASTICISM
James A. Weisheipl (1987)
Revised Bibliography

SCHOLEM, GERSHOM
David Biale (1987)
Revised Bibliography

SCHWEITZER, ALBERT
Martin E. Marty (1987)
Revised Bibliography

SCIENCE AND RELIGION
Ted Peters (2005)

SCIENTOLOGY
J. Gordon Melton (2005)

SCRIPTURE
William A. Graham (1987 and 2005)

SCYTHIAN RELIGION
D. S. Raevskii (1987)
Revised Bibliography

SEASONAL CEREMONIES
Theodor H. Gaster (1987)
Revised Bibliography

SHINTŌ
Brian Bocking (2005)

SHNE'UR ZALMAN OF LYADY
Arthur Green (1987)
Revised Bibliography

SHONA RELIGION
M. F. C. Bourdillon (1987)

SHOTOKU TAISHI
Miyamoto Youtaro (2005)

SHRINES
Paul B. Courtright (1987 and 2005)

SHUGENDŌ
H. Byron Earhart (1987)
Revised Bibliography

SHUGS LDAN (SHUGDEN)
Georges Dreyfus (2005)

SIBYLLINE ORACLES
Arnaldo Momigliano (1987)
Emilio Suárez de la Torre (2005)

SIDDUR AND MAḤZOR
Lawrence A. Hoffman (1987)
Revised Bibliography

SÍDH
Proinsias Mac Cana (1987 and 2005)

SIKHISM
Nikky-Guninder Kaur Singh (2005)

ŚĪLABHADRA
Mimaki Katsumi (1987)

SIMA CHENGZHEN
Franciscus Verellen (2005)

SIMONS, MENNO
Cornelius J. Dyck (1987)

SIN AND GUILT
André LaCocque (1987)
Revised Bibliography

SINGH, GOBIND
Khushwant Singh (1987)
Revised Bibliography

SINHALA RELIGION
Gananath Obeyesekere (1987)
Revised Bibliography

SIRHINDĪ, AḤMAD
Yohanan Friedmann (1987 and 2005)

ŚIVA [FIRST EDITION]
Stella Kramrisch (1987)

ŚIVA [FURTHER CONSIDERATIONS]
Karen Pechilis (2005)

SKEPTICS AND SKEPTICISM
Richard H. Popkin (1987)
Revised Bibliography

SKOBTSOVA, MARIA
Sergei Hackel (2005)

SKY: THE HEAVENS AS HIEROPHANY
Ioan Petru Culianu (1987)
Revised Bibliography

SKY: MYTHS AND SYMBOLISM
Anthony F. Aveni (2005)

SLAVIC RELIGION
Marija Gimbutas (1987)
Revised Bibliography

SLEEP
Jonathan Z. Smith (1987)

SMART, NINIAN
Ursula King (2005)

SMITH, HANNAH WHITALL
Melvin E. Dieter (2005)

SMITH, JOSEPH
Klaus J. Hansen (1987 and 2005)

SMITH, MORTON
Joseph Sievers (2005)

SMITH, WILFRED CANTWELL
Peter Slater (2005)

SMITH, W. ROBERTSON
T. O. Beidelman (1987)
Robert A. Segal (2005)

SMOKING
Francis Robicsek (1987)

SNAKES
Manfred Lurker (1987)
Revised Bibliography

SNORRI STURLUSON
John Weinstock (1987 and 2005)

SNOUCK HURGRONJE, CHRISTIAAN
Dale F. Eickelman (1987)
Revised Bibliography

SOCIETY AND RELIGION [FIRST EDITION]
Walter H. Capps (1987)

SOCIETY AND RELIGION [FURTHER CONSIDERATIONS]
Wade Clark Roof (2005)

SOCIOBIOLOGY AND EVOLUTIONARY PSYCHOLOGY: AN OVERVIEW
Holmes Rolston III (2005)

SOCIOBIOLOGY AND EVOLUTIONARY PSYCHOLOGY: DARWINISM AND RELIGION
Mikael Stenmark (2005)

SOCIOLOGY: SOCIOLOGY AND RELIGION [FIRST EDITION]
Robert Nisbet (1987)

SOCIOLOGY: SOCIOLOGY AND RELIGION [FURTHER CONSIDERATIONS]
Robert A. Segal (2005)

SOCIOLOGY: SOCIOLOGY OF RELIGION [FIRST EDITION]
Winston Davis (1987)

SOCIOLOGY: SOCIOLOGY OF RELIGION [FURTHER CONSIDERATIONS]
Robert A. Segal (2005)

SOCRATES
Alessandro Stavru (2005)

SÖDERBLOM, NATHAN
Charles J. Adams (1987)
Revised Bibliography

SOFER, MOSHEH
Steven M. Lowenstein (1987)
Revised Bibliography

SOHM, RUDOLF
James Luther Adams (1987)
Revised Bibliography

SŌKA GAKKAI
Shimazono Susumu (2005)

SŎ KYŎNGDŎK
Michael C. Kalton (1987)
Revised Bibliography

SOL INVICTUS
J. Rufus Fears (1987)

SÖLLE, DOROTHEE
Nancy C. Ring (2005)

SOLOMON
John Van Seters (1987)
Revised Bibliography

SOLOMON ISLANDS RELIGIONS
Roger M. Keesing (1987)
Pierre Maranda (2005)

SOLOVEITCHIK, JOSEPH BAER
Moshe Sokol (2005)

SOLOV'EV, VLADIMIR
Bernice Glatzer Rosenthal (1987 and 2005)

SOMA
Joel P. Brereton (2005)

THEALOGY
Melissa Raphael (2005)

THECLA
Stephen J. Davis (2005)

THEISM
Peter A. Bertocci (1987)
Revised Bibliography

THEOCRACY
Dewey D. Wallace, Jr. (1987 and 2005)

THEODICY
Ronald M. Green (1987)
Revised Bibliography

THEODORE OF MOPSUESTIA
Panagiotis C. Christou (1987)

THEODORE OF STUDIOS
Demetrios J. Constantelos (1987)
Revised Bibliography

THEODORET OF CYRRHUS
Theodore Zissis (1987)

THEODOSIUS
Noel Q. King (1987 and 2005)

THEOLOGY: CHRISTIAN THEOLOGY
Yves Congar (1987)
Revised Bibliography

THEOLOGY: COMPARATIVE THEOLOGY
David Tracy (1987)
Revised Bibliography

THEOSOPHICAL SOCIETY
John Algeo (2005)

THERAVĀDA
Frank E. Reynolds (1987)
Regina T. Clifford (1987)
Revised Bibliography

THÉRÈSE OF LISIEUX
Peter T. Rohrbach (1987)

THERIANTHROPISM
Stanley Walens (1987)

THESMOPHORIA
M. L. West (1987)
Revised Bibliography

THEURGY
Richard A. Norris (1987)
Revised Bibliography

THIASOI
Klaus-Peter Köpping (1987)
Revised Bibliography

THOMAS À KEMPIS
Howard G. Hageman (1987)

THOMAS AQUINAS
James A. Weisheipl (1987)

THOR
Edgar C. Polomé (1987)
Joseph Harris (2005)

THOTH
Leonard H. Lesko (1987)

THRACIAN RELIGION
Ioan Petru Culianu (1987)
Cicerone Poghirc (1987)
Revised Bibliography

THRACIAN RIDER
Ioan Petru Culianu (1987)
Cicerone Poghirc (1987)
Revised Bibliography

TIAN
Laurence G. Thompson (1987)

TIANTAI
Leo M. Pruden (1987)

TIBETAN RELIGIONS: AN OVERVIEW
Per Kvaerne (1987 and 2005)

TIBETAN RELIGIONS: HISTORY OF STUDY
Michael L. Walter (1987)
Françoise Pommaret (2005)

TIELE, C. P.
Jacques Waardenburg (1987)
Revised Bibliography

TIKHON
James W. Cunningham (1987)

TIKHON OF ZADONSK
Thomas Hopko (1987)

TIKOPIA RELIGION
Raymond Firth (1987)
Judith Macdonald (2005)

TILAK, BAL GANGADHAR
Ainslie T. Embree (1987 and 2005)

TILĀWAH
Richard C. Martin (1987)

TILLICH, PAUL JOHANNES
Robert P. Scharlemann (1987 and 2005)

TIMOTHY AILUROS
Demetrios J. Constantelos (1987)

TINGLEY, KATHERINE
W. Michael Ashcraft (2005)

TĪRTHAṂKARAS
Colette Caillat (1987 and 2005)

TITHES
Walter Harrelson (1987 and 2005)

TIV RELIGION
Paul Bohannan (1987)
Revised Bibliography

TJURUNGAS
John E. Stanton (1987)

TLALOC
Philip P. Arnold (2005)

TLAXCALAN RELIGION
Hugo G. Nutini (1987 and 2005)

TOBACCO
Peter T. Furst (2005)

TOLSTOY, LEO
Sylvia Juran (1987)

TOLTEC RELIGION
Hanns J. Prem (1987)
Revised Bibliography

TOMBS
Peter Metcalf (2005)

TOMOL
Dennis F. Kelley (2005)

TÖNNIES, FERDINAND
James Luther Adams (1987)
Revised Bibliography

TORAH
Martin S. Jaffee (2005)

TORAJA RELIGION
Hetty Nooy-Palm (1987)
Revised Bibliography

TORQUEMADA, TOMÁS DE
Marvin R. O'Connell (1987)

TOSAFOT [FIRST EDITION]
E. E. Urbach (1987)

TOSAFOT [FURTHER CONSIDERATIONS]
Ephraim Kanarfogel (2005)

TOTEMISM
Roy Wagner (1987)
Revised Bibliography

TOTONAC RELIGION
Roberto Williams-Garcia (1987)
Revised Bibliography

TOUCHING
Geoffrey Parrinder (1987)

TOURISM AND RELIGION
Thomas S. Bremer (2005)

TOWERS
Jeffrey F. Meyer (2005)
J. Daniel White (2005)

TRADITION
Paul Valliere (1987 and 2005)

U

WISE, ISAAC M.
S. D. Temkin (1987)
Revised Bibliography

WISE, JOHN
Edwin S. Gaustad (1987 and 2005)

WISE, STEPHEN S.
Abraham J. Karp (1987)
Revised Bibliography

WISSOWA, GEORG
Henry Jay Watkin (1987)
Revised Bibliography

WITCHCRAFT: AFRICAN WITCHCRAFT
Maxwell Gay Marwick (1987)
Revised Bibliography

WITCHCRAFT: CONCEPTS OF WITCHCRAFT
Jeffrey Burton Russell (1987)
Sabina Magliocco (2005)

WITTGENSTEIN, LUDWIG
Henry Le Roy Finch (1987)

WOLFF, CHRISTIAN
Charles A. Corr (1987 and 2005)

WOLVES
Ann Dunnigan (1987)
Revised Bibliography

WOMEN'S STUDIES IN RELIGION
Julie Clague (2005)

WŎNHYO
Robert Evans Buswell, Jr. (1987 and 2005)

WORK
Karen Ready (1987)
Revised Bibliography

WORLD RELIGIONS
Tomoko Masuzawa (2005)

WORLD'S PARLIAMENT OF RELIGIONS
Robert S. Ellwood (1987 and 2005)

WORSHIP AND DEVOTIONAL LIFE: BUDDHIST DEVOTIONAL LIFE IN EAST ASIA
Richard K. Payne (2005)

WORSHIP AND DEVOTIONAL LIFE: BUDDHIST DEVOTIONAL LIFE IN SOUTHEAST ASIA
Peter Skilling (2005)

WORSHIP AND DEVOTIONAL LIFE: BUDDHIST DEVOTIONAL LIFE IN TIBET
Françoise Pommaret (2005)

WORSHIP AND DEVOTIONAL LIFE: CHRISTIAN WORSHIP
Thomas J. Talley (1987)
Revised Bibliography

WORSHIP AND DEVOTIONAL LIFE: DAOIST DEVOTIONAL LIFE
John Lagerwey (1987 and 2005)

WORSHIP AND DEVOTIONAL LIFE: HINDU DEVOTIONAL LIFE
Paul B. Courtright (1987)
Revised Bibliography

WORSHIP AND DEVOTIONAL LIFE: JEWISH WORSHIP
Ruth Langer (2005)

WORSHIP AND DEVOTIONAL LIFE: MUSLIM WORSHIP
Vernon James Schubel (2005)

WOVOKA
John A. Grim (1987)

WUNDT, WILHELM
Wallace B. Clift (1987)
Revised Bibliography

WYCLIF, JOHN
Massey H. Shepherd, Jr. (1987)

X

XAVIER, FRANCIS
John F. Broderick (1987)

XENOPHANES
Giovanni Casadio (2005)

XIAN
John Lagerwey (2005)

XIAO
Keith Knapp (2005)

XIAO BAOZHEN
Kubo Noritada (1987)
Revised Bibliography

XINXING
Miyakawa Hisayuki (1987)
Revised Bibliography

XI WANG MU
Michael Loewe (1987)

XUANZANG
Alan Sponberg (1987)
Revised Bibliography

XUNZI
Aaron Stalnaker (2005)

Y

YA'AQOV BEN ASHER
Bernard Septimus (1987)
Revised Bibliography

YAKUT RELIGION
Laurence Delaby (1987)

YAMA
Sukumari Bhattacharji (1987)
Revised Bibliography

YAMAGA SOKŌ
Samuel Hideo Yamashita (1987)

YAMATO TAKERU
Isomae Jun'ichi (2005)

YAMAZAKI ANSAI
Kate Wildman Nakai (1987 and 2005)

YĀMUNA
Walter G. Neevel, Jr. (1987 and 2005)

YANTRA
Madhu Khanna (1987)
Revised Bibliography

YAO AND SHUN
Sarah Allan (1987 and 2005)

YATES, FRANCES AMELIA
J. B. Trapp (2005)

YAZATAS
Gherardo Gnoli (1987)

YEHOSHU'A BEN ḤANANYAH
Tzvee Zahavy (1987)
Revised Bibliography

YEHOSHU'A BEN LEVI
Robert Goldenberg (1987)
Revised Bibliography

YEHUDAH BAR IL'AI
Tzvee Zahavy (1987)
Revised Bibliography

YEHUDAH BAR YEḤEZQE'L
Baruch M. Bokser (1987)
Revised Bibliography

YEHUDAH HA-LEVI
Barry S. Kogan (1987)
Revised Bibliography

YEHUDAH HA-NASI'
Gary G. Porton (1987 and 2005)

YE SHES MTSHO RGYAL (YESHE TSOGYAL)
Janet Gyatso (2005)

YESHIVAH
Shaul Stampfer (1987)
Revised Bibliography

LIST OF CONTRIBUTORS

Contributors to the Encyclopedia are listed below in alphabetic order followed by their academic affiliations and the article(s) they contributed. Articles reprinted from the first edition are indicated by (1987) following the article name. Affiliations provided for these authors are their 1987 affiliations. New or updated articles are indicated by (2005) and include current affiliations for the authors.

Robert Ackerman
Montclair, New Jersey
FRAZER, JAMES G. (1987)

Joyce Ackroyd
University of Queensland
BUSHIDŌ (1987)

Charles J. Adams
Institute of Islamic Studies, McGill University
CORBIN, HENRY (1987)
JAMĀ'AT-I ISLĀMĪ (1987)
SÖDERBLOM, NATHAN (1987)

James Luther Adams
Harvard University
LEGITIMATION (1987)
SOHM, RUDOLF (1987)
TÖNNIES, FERDINAND (1987)

William Y. Adams
University of Kentucky
AKSUMITE RELIGION (1987)
KUSHITE RELIGION (1987)

A. W. H. Adkins
University of Chicago
EVANS, ARTHUR (1987)
HARRISON, JANE E. (1987)

Joseph A. Adler
Kenyon College
CHINESE RELIGION: AN OVERVIEW (2005)

Asma Afsaruddin
University of Notre Dame
FĀṬIMAH BINT MUḤAMMAD (2005)
FREE WILL AND PREDESTINATION: ISLAMIC CONCEPTS (2005)

Kamran Scot Aghaie
University of Texas at Austin
MESSIANISM: MESSIANISM IN THE MUSLIM TRADITION (2005)

Akintunde E. Akinade
High Point University
CHRISTIANITY: CHRISTIANITY IN SUB-SAHARAN AFRICA [FURTHER CONSIDERATIONS] (2005)

Shirin Akiner
University of London
ISLAM: ISLAM IN CENTRAL ASIA (2005)

Hirakawa Akira
Waseda University
STUPA WORSHIP (1987)

Kurt Aland
Westfälische Wilhelms-Universität Münster
MONTANISM (1987)
MONTANUS (1987)

Azra Alavi
Aligarh Muslim University, Aligarh, India
NIẒĀM AL-DĪN AWLIYĀ' (2005)

Catherine L. Albanese
Wright State University
CHRISTIANITY: CHRISTIANITY IN NORTH AMERICA (1987)

Shalom Albeck
Bar Ilan University
TAM, YA'AQOV BEN ME'IR (1987)

Ezio Albrile
Torino, Italy
GNOSTICISM: HISTORY OF STUDY (2005)
MANDAEAN RELIGION (2005)

Gerardo Aldana
University of California, Santa Barbara
COSMOLOGY: INDIGENOUS NORTH AND MESOAMERICAN COSMOLOGIES (2005)

Bobby C. Alexander
University of Texas at Dallas
CEREMONY (1987 AND 2005)

Hilarion Alfeyev
Bishop of Vienna and Austria, Russian Orthodox Church
RUSSIAN ORTHODOX CHURCH (2005)

Hamid Algar
University of California, Berkeley
'ULAMĀ' (1987)

John Algeo
University of Georgia (emeritus)
THEOSOPHICAL SOCIETY (2005)

M. Athar Ali
Aligarh Muslim University
HUJWĪRĪ, AL- (1987)

Sarah Allan
Dartmouth College
YAO AND SHUN (1987 AND 2005)

Douglas Allen
University of Maine
HUSSERL, EDMUND (1987 AND 2005)
PHENOMENOLOGY OF RELIGION (1987 AND 2005)

James P. Allen
Metropolitan Museum of Art
AKHENATON (2005)

Michael Allen
University of Sydney
VANUATU RELIGIONS (1987)

Gregory D. Alles
McDaniel College
DYNAMISM (1987)
HOMO RELIGIOSUS (1987)
OTTO, RUDOLF (2005)
RELIGION [FURTHER CONSIDERATIONS] (2005)
SANCTUARY (1987)
STUDY OF RELIGION: AN OVERVIEW (2005)

C. Fitzsimons Allison
Episcopal Diocese of South Carolina
PUSEY, EDWARD BOUVERIE (1987)

Dale C. Allison, Jr.
Pittsburgh Theological Seminary
BIBLICAL LITERATURE: NEW TESTAMENT (2005)
JESUS (2005)

Adel Allouche
Yale University
ARABIAN RELIGIONS (1987 AND 2005)

Rebecca T. Alpert
Temple University
RECONSTRUCTIONIST JUDAISM (2005)

Martha S. Alt
Ohio State University
REFERENCE WORKS (2005)

Josef L. Altholz
University of Minnesota, Twin Cities
ULTRAMONTANISM (1987)

David Altshuler
George Washington University
JOSEPHUS FLAVIUS (1987)

Sajida S. Alvi
McGill University
LĀHORĪ, MUḤAMMAD ʿALĪ (1987 AND 2005)
WALĪ ALLĀH, SHĀH (2005)

Mehdi Aminrazavi
University of Mary Washington
SUHRAWARDĪ, SHIHĀB AL-DĪN YAḤYĀ (2005)

Nancy T. Ammerman
Emory University
SCHISM: AN OVERVIEW (1987)

Albert Ampe
Universiteit Antwerpen
RUUSBROEC, JAN VAN (1987)

Darrel W. Amundsen
Western Washington University
HEALING AND MEDICINE: HEALING AND MEDICINE IN CHRISTIANITY (2005)
HEALING AND MEDICINE: HEALING AND MEDICINE IN GREECE AND ROME (2005)
SPURGEON, CHARLES HADDON (1987)

Georges C. Anawati
Institut Dominicain d'Etudes Orientales, Cairo
ATTRIBUTES OF GOD: ISLAMIC CONCEPTS (1987)
KALĀM (1987)

Carol S. Anderson
Kalamazoo College
LESBIANISM (2005)

Pamela Sue Anderson
University of Oxford
BEAUTY (2005)

Robert Mapes Anderson
Wagner College
MCPHERSON, AIMEE SEMPLE (1987)
PENTECOSTAL AND CHARISMATIC CHRISTIANITY (1987 AND 2005)

Ionna Andreesco-Miereanu
Centre National de la Recherche Scientifique, Paris
MAGIC: MAGIC IN EASTERN EUROPE (1987)

Allan A. Andrews
University of Vermont
GENSHIN (1987)
HŌNEN (1987)

Pietro Angelini
L'Università Orientale di Napoli
DE MARTINO, ERNESTO (2005)

Sigma Ankrava
University of Latvia
BALTIC RELIGION: AN OVERVIEW (2005)

Zafar Ishaq Ansari
International Islamic University, Islamabad
ABŪ ḤANĪFAH (1987)
ṢAWM (1987)

Peter Antes
University of Hannover
NEW YEAR FESTIVALS (2005)
SCHIMMEL, ANNEMARIE (2005)

Veikko Anttonen
School of Cultural Research, University of Turku, Finland
HARVA, UNO (2005)

Michiko Yamaguchi Aoki
Roger Williams College
ŌKUNINUSHI NO MIKOTO (1987)

Frédérique Apffel-Marglin
Smith College
HIERODOULEIA (1987 AND 2005)
YONI (1987 AND 2005)

Diane Apostolos-Cappadona
Center for Muslim-Christian Understanding, Georgetown University
ART AND RELIGION (2005)
DANCE: POPULAR AND FOLK DANCE [FURTHER CONSIDERATIONS] (2005)
DANCE: THEATRICAL AND LITURGICAL DANCE [FURTHER CONSIDERATIONS] (2005)
HUMAN BODY: HUMAN BODIES, RELIGION, AND ART (2005)
ICONOCLASM: AN OVERVIEW (2005)
ICONOGRAPHY: ICONOGRAPHY AS VISIBLE RELIGION [FURTHER CONSIDERATIONS] (2005)

Arjun Appadurai
University of Pennsylvania
INDIAN RELIGIONS: HISTORY OF STUDY (1987)

Nazir Arabzoda
University of Dushanbe
NĀṢIR-I KHUSRAW (2005)

Francis A. Arinze
Secretariat for Non-Christians, Vatican City
IGBO RELIGION (1987)

Brian G. Armstrong
Georgia State University (emeritus)
CALVIN, JOHN (1987)

Karen Armstrong
London, England
MUḤAMMAD (2005)

Roger Arnaldez
Université de Paris IV (Paris-Sorbonne) (emeritus)
IBN ḤAZM (1987)

Rudolf Arnheim
University of Michigan, Ann Arbor
AESTHETICS: VISUAL AESTHETICS (1987)

Philip P. Arnold
Syracuse University
COLORS (2005)
TLALOC (2005)

Linda B. Arthur
Washington State University
CLOTHING: DRESS AND RELIGION IN AMERICA'S SECTARIAN COMMUNITIES (2005)

Avak Asadourian
Armenian Diocese of Iraq
GREGORY OF DATEV (1987)
GREGORY OF NAREK (1987)
NERSĒS OF CLA (1987)

Ali S. Asani
Harvard University
AGA KHAN (1987)
GINĀN (1987)
ISLAM: ISLAM IN SOUTH ASIA (2005)
POETRY: ISLAMIC POETRY (2005)

W. Michael Ashcraft
Truman State University
POINT LOMA THEOSOPHICAL COMMUNITY (2005)
TINGLEY, KATHERINE (2005)

Jes P. Asmussen
Københavns Universitet
CHRISTENSEN, ARTHUR (1987)
LEHMANN, EDVARD (1987)

Prapod Assavavirulhakarn
Chulalongkorn University
BLESSING (2005)

Aziz Suryal Atiya
University of Utah
CHRISTIANITY: CHRISTIANITY IN NORTH AFRICA (1987)
COPTIC CHURCH (1987)

Christopher P. Atwood
Indiana University
BUDDHISM: BUDDHISM IN MONGOLIA (2005)

Roger Aubert
Université Catholique de Louvain-la-Neuve
PIUS IX (1987)
VATICAN COUNCILS: VATICAN I (1987)

David E. Aune
University of Notre Dame
CIRCLE (2005)
ORACLES (1987)
REPENTANCE (1987)

Robert Austerlitz
Columbia University
NUM (1987)
SAMOYED RELIGION (1987)

Harry Aveling
Ohio University
FICTION: SOUTHEAST ASIAN FICTION AND RELIGION (2005)

Anthony F. Aveni
Colgate University
CALENDARS: MESOAMERICAN CALENDARS (2005)
SKY: MYTHS AND SYMBOLISM (2005)

Peter J. Awn
Columbia University
SUFISM (1987)

Mahmoud M. Ayoub
University of Toronto
'ĀSHŪRĀ' (1987)
ḤILLĪ, AL- (1987)
QUR'ĀN: ITS ROLE IN MUSLIM PRACTICE AND LIFE (1987)

Th. P. van Baaren
Rijksuniversiteit te Groningen
AFTERLIFE: GEOGRAPHIES OF DEATH (1987)

Barbara A. Babcock
University of Arizona
REFLEXIVITY (1987)

Louise Bäckman
Stockholms Universitet
NUM-TŪREM (1987)
SAMI RELIGION (1987)

Gershon C. Bacon
Bar-Ilan University
AGUDAT YISRA'EL (1987 AND 2005)
MUSAR MOVEMENT (1987 AND 2005)
SALANTER, YISRA'EL (1987 AND 2005)

S. J. Badakhchani
Institute of Ismaili Studies, London
ṬŪSĪ, NAṢĪR AL-DĪN (2005)

M. A. Zaki Badawi
Muslim College, London
ABŪ BAKR (2005)

Michael A. Baenen
Somerville, Massachusetts
MALINOWSKI, BRONISLAW (1987)

Marc David Baer
University of California, Irvine
DÖNMEH (2005)

Serge Bahuchet
Centre National de la Recherche Scientifique, Paris
PYGMY RELIGIONS (1987)

Constantina Bailly
New York, New York
PATAÑJALI THE GRAMMARIAN (1987)

William Sims Bainbridge
National Science Foundation
FAMILY, THE (2005)

Frank Baker
Duke University
ASBURY, FRANCIS (1987)
COKE, THOMAS (1987)
METHODIST CHURCHES (1987)
WESLEY BROTHERS (1987)

David L. Balás
University of Dallas
BASIL OF CAESAREA (1987)

Nalini Balbir
University of Paris
GENDER AND RELIGION: GENDER AND JAINISM (2005)

Robert W. Balch
University of Montana
HEAVEN'S GATE (2005)

Ximena Chávez Balderas
Templo Mayor Museum, Mexico City
AFTERLIFE: MESOAMERICAN CONCEPTS (2005)
FUNERAL RITES: MESOAMERICAN FUNERAL RITES (2005)

John F. Baldovin
Jesuit School of Theology, Berkeley
CHRISTMAS (1987)
EASTER (1987)
EPIPHANY (1987)

Bando Shōjun
Otani University
BENCHŌ (1987)

Carl Bangs
Saint Paul School of Theology, Kansas City
ARMINIUS, JACOBUS (1987)

Moshe Barasch
Hebrew University of Jerusalem
ICONOGRAPHY: JEWISH ICONOGRAPHY [FIRST EDITION] (1987)

Beatriz Barba de Piña Chán
Instituto Nacional de Antropologia e Historia, Mexico City
SPELLS (1987)

Charles Barber
University of Notre Dame
ICONOCLASM: ICONOCLASM IN THE BYZANTINE TRADITION (2005)

Hugh Barbour
Earlham College
FOX, GEORGE (1987)
QUAKERS (1987)

John D. Barbour
St. Olaf College
AUTOBIOGRAPHY (2005)

André Bareau
Collège de France
BUDDHISM, SCHOOLS OF: EARLY DOCTRINAL SCHOOLS OF BUDDHISM (1987)

Eileen Barker
London School of Economics
NEW RELIGIOUS MOVEMENTS: NEW RELIGIOUS MOVEMENTS IN EUROPE (1987 AND 2005)
UNIFICATION CHURCH (1987 AND 2005)

John Barker
University of British Columbia
POLITICS AND RELIGION: POLITICS AND OCEANIC RELIGIONS (2005)

Michael Barkun
Maxwell School, Syracuse University
CHRISTIAN IDENTITY MOVEMENT (2005)

James Barr
Christ Church, University of Oxford
DELITZSCH, FRIEDRICH (1987)

T. H. Barrett
School of Oriental and African Studies, University of London
DAOISM: HISTORY OF STUDY (1987 AND 2005)
GE HONG (1987)
LI SHAOJUN (1987)

Anne Llewellyn Barstow
State University of New York, College at Old Westbury
JOAN OF ARC (1987)

J. Robert Barth
Boston College
COLERIDGE, SAMUEL TAYLOR (1987 AND 2005)

R. K. Barz
Australian National University
VALLABHA (1987)

Jacques Barzun
Columbia University (emeritus)
JAMES, WILLIAM (1987)

A. L. Basham
(deceased)
ĀJĪVIKAS (1987)

Judith R. Baskin
University of Oregon
MIQVEH (2005)

Joseph W. Bastien
University of Texas at Arlington
ATAHUALLPA (1987 AND 2005)
SOUTH AMERICAN INDIANS: INDIANS OF THE MODERN ANDES (1987)

Martine Batchelor
La Sauve, France
NUNS: BUDDHIST NUNS (2005)

Emery J. Battis
Washington, D.C.
HUTCHINSON, ANNE (1987)

Robert M. Baum
Iowa State University
AFRICAN RELIGIONS: HISTORY OF STUDY (2005)
ALINESITOUE (2005)
DIOLA RELIGION (1987)
PROPHECY: AFRICAN PROPHETISM (2005)

Martin Baumann
University of Lucerne, Switzerland
BUDDHISM: BUDDHISM IN THE WEST (2005)

John Beattie
Linacre College, University of Oxford
INTERLACUSTRINE BANTU RELIGIONS (1987)

Tina Beattie
Roehampton University
FEMINIST THEOLOGY: CHRISTIAN FEMINIST THEOLOGY (2005)
GENDER AND RELIGION: GENDER AND CHRISTIANITY (2005)
MARY: FEMINIST PERSPECTIVES (2005)

George S. Bebis
Holy Cross Greek Orthodox School of Theology, Brookline, Massachusetts
APOLLINARIS OF LAODICEA (1987)
GREGORY OF SINAI (1987)
IGNATIUS OF ANTIOCH (1987)
NIKODIMOS OF THE HOLY MOUNTAIN (1987)

Heinz Bechert
Georg-August-Universitat zu Gottingen
SAṂGHA: AN OVERVIEW (1987 AND 2005)

Brenda E. F. Beck
University of British Columbia
DOMESTIC OBSERVANCES: HINDU PRACTICES (1987)

Guy L. Beck
Tulane University
FREEMASONS (2005)

Mary Farrell Bednarowski
United Theological Seminary of the Twin Cities
NEW RELIGIOUS MOVEMENTS: NEW RELIGIOUS MOVEMENTS AND WOMEN (2005)

Susan Fitzpatrick Behrens
California State University, Northridge
GENDER AND RELIGION: GENDER AND SOUTH AMERICAN RELIGIONS (2005)

T. O. Beidelman
New York University
CIRCUMCISION (1987 AND 2005)
SMITH, W. ROBERTSON (1987)

Benjamin Beit-Hallahmi
Haifa University
LEUBA, JAMES H. (1987)
STARBUCK, E. D. (1987)

Nicole Belayche
École Pratique des Hautes-Études, Paris, France
IUPITER DOLICHENUS (2005)

Catherine M. Bell
Santa Clara University
LU XIUJING (1987)
RITUAL [FURTHER CONSIDERATIONS] (2005)

Diane Bell
George Washington University
BERNDT, CATHERINE H. (2005)
DREAMING, THE (2005)
GENDER AND RELIGION: GENDER AND AUSTRALIAN INDIGENOUS RELIGIONS (2005)

Nicole Belmont
Collège de France
GENNEP, ARNOLD VAN (1987)

Jack Bemporad
Temple Sinai of Bergen County, Tenafly, New Jersey
SOUL: JEWISH CONCEPT (1987)
SUFFERING (1987)

Paula Ben-Amos
Indiana University, Bloomington
EDO RELIGION (1987)

Dagmar Benner
Cambridge University
HEALING AND MEDICINE: HEALING AND MEDICINE IN ĀYURVEDA AND SOUTH ASIA (2005)

Alexandre Bennigsen
École Pratique des Hautes Études, Collège de France
ISLAM: ISLAM IN THE CAUCASUS AND THE MIDDLE VOLGA (1987)

Elizabeth P. Benson
Institute of Andean Studies, Los Angeles
BOCHICA (1987)
INTI (1987)
MANCO CAPAC AND MAMA OCLLO (1987)
VIRACOCHA (1987)

David Berger
Brooklyn College, City University of New York
POLEMICS: JEWISH-CHRISTIAN POLEMICS (1987)
NAHMANIDES, MOSES (1987)

Stephen E. Berk
California State University, Long Beach
DWIGHT, TIMOTHY (1987)

Niyazi Berkes
McGill University (emeritus)
GÖKALP, ZİYAM [FIRST EDITION] (1987)

Judith A. Berling
Indiana University, Bloomington
DAI ZHEN (1987)
GU YANWU (1987)
ORTHOPRAXY (1987)

John Bern
University of Newcastle, Australia
NGUKURR RELIGION (1987)

Alberto Bernabé
Universidad Complutense, Madrid, Spain
HURRIAN RELIGION (2005)
ORPHEUS (2005)

Paul Bernabeo
New York, New York
APOLOGETICS (1987)

Catherine H. Berndt
University of Western Australia
AUSTRALIAN INDIGENOUS RELIGIONS: MYTHIC THEMES [FIRST EDITION] (1987)
RAINBOW SNAKE (1987)
WAWALAG (1987)
YULUNGGUL SNAKE (1987)

Ronald M. Berndt
University of Western Australia
DJAN'KAWU (1987)
GADJERI (1987)

Peter A. Bertocci
Boston University (emeritus)
THEISM (1987)

Eberhard Bethge
Wachtberg-Villiprott, West Germany
BONHOEFFER, DIETRICH (1987)

Anne H. Betteridge
University of Arizona
DOMESTIC OBSERVANCES: MUSLIM PRACTICES (1987)

Hans Dieter Betz
University of Chicago
APOSTLES (1987)
LIBATION (1987)
MAGIC: MAGIC IN GRECO-ROMAN ANTIQUITY (1987)

Peter Beyer
University of Ottawa
GLOBALIZATION AND RELIGION (2005)

Sukumari Bhattacharji
Jadavpur University
RUDRA (1987)
VARUṆA (1987)
YAMA (1987)

Thanissaro Bhikkhu
Metta Forest Monastery, Valley Center, California
EIGHTFOLD PATH (2005)

David Biale
University of California, Davis
ALKALAI, YEHUDAH BEN SHELOMOH (1987)
BAR-ILAN, ME'IR (1987)
MOHILEVER, SHEMU'EL (1987)
REINES, YITSḤAQ YA'AQOV (1987)
SCHOLEM, GERSHOM (1987)
ZIONISM (1987 AND 2005)

Ugo Bianchi
Università degli Studi, Rome
BRELICH, ANGELO (1987)
CONFESSION OF SINS (1987)
DEMIURGE (1987)
DUALISM (1987)
HISTORY OF RELIGIONS (1987)
TWINS: AN OVERVIEW (1987)

Daniel P. Biebuyck
University of Delaware
DRAMA: AFRICAN RELIGIOUS DRAMA (1987)

Haralds Biezais
Uppsala Universitet
BALTIC RELIGION: AN OVERVIEW (1987)
DAINAS (1987)
LAIMA (1987)
PĒRKONS (1987)
ZEME (1987)

Willem A. Bijlefeld
Hartford Seminary
BETH, KARL (1987)
KRAEMER, HENDRIK (1987)
NILSSON, MARTIN P. (1987)
REINACH, SALOMON (1987)
ROHDE, ERWIN (1987)

Purushottama Bilimoria
Deakin University of Melbourne, Stony Brook
AVIDYĀ (2005)

Jon-Christian Billigmeier
University of California, Santa Barbara
ALPHABETS (1987 AND 2005)

Norman Birnbaum
Georgetown University
WEBER, MAX (1987)

Raoul Birnbaum
Harvard University
AVALOKITEŚVARA (1987)

BHAIṢAJYAGURU (1987)
MAÑJUŚRĪ (1987)

Barbara Bishop
Schola Contemplationis, Pfafftown, North Carolina
JULIAN OF NORWICH (1987)

Joseph L. Blau
Columbia University (emeritus)
REFORM (1987)

Gerald J. Blidstein
Ben-Gurion University of the Negev
ALFASI, YITSḤAQ BEN YA'AQOV (1987)
GERSHOM BEN YEHUDAH (1987)
H'AI GAON (1987)
HALAKHAH: HISTORY OF HALAKHAH (1987)
ME'IR BEN BARUKH OF ROTHENBURG (1987)
SHERIRA'GAON (1987)

Raymond Bloch
Académie des Inscriptions et Belles Lettres, Paris
PORTENTS AND PRODIGIES (1987)

Alfred Bloom
University of Hawaii, Manoa
SHINRAN (1987)

Lowell W. Bloss
Hobart and William Smith Colleges
NĀGAS AND YAKṢAS (1987 AND 2005)

Brian Bocking
School of Oriental and African Studies, University of London
SHINTŌ (2005)

William M. Bodiford
University of California, Los Angeles
DŌGEN (2005)
KEIZAN (2005)

Herbert L. Bodman, Jr.
University of North Carolina at Chapel Hill
CALIPHATE (1987)

Martha Bohachevsky-Chomiak
Manhattanville College
TRUBETSKOI, EVGENII (1987)
TRUBETSKOI, SERGEI (1987)

Paul Bohannan
University of Southern California
TIV RELIGION (1987)

Philip V. Bohlman
University of Chicago
MUSIC: MUSIC AND RELIGION IN INDIA (2005)

Stephen R. Bokenkamp
Indiana University
DAOISM: AN OVERVIEW (2005)

Baruch M. Bokser
Jewish Theological Seminary of America
ABBAYE (1987)
AMORAIM (1987)
ASHI (1987)
HUNA' (1987)
RABBAH BAR NAHMANI (1987)
RAV (1987)
RAVA' (1987)
SHEMU'EL THE AMORA (1987)
YEHUDAH BAR YEḤEZQE'L (1987)

Kees W. Bolle
University of California, Los Angeles (emeritus)
ANIMISM AND ANIMATISM (1987)
COSMOLOGY: AN OVERVIEW (1987 AND 2005)
EUHEMERUS AND EUHEMERISM (2005)
FATE (1987 AND 2005)
HIEROS GAMOS (1987)
MYTH: AN OVERVIEW (1987 AND 2005)
VRIES, JAN DE (1987)

Judith Magee Boltz
University of Washington
DAOISM: DAOIST LITERATURE (1987 AND 2005)
LAOZI (1987)

George Clement Bond
Teachers College, Columbia University
LENSHINA, ALICE (1987)

George D. Bond
Northwestern University
DEVĀNAṂPIYATISSA (1987)
MOGGALIPUTTATISSA (1987)
PERFECTIBILITY (1987 AND 2005)

Corinne Bonnet
Universite de Toulouse II - Le Mirail
CUMONT, FRANZ (2005)
ESHMUN (2005)
MELQART (2005)

John Lawrence Boojamra
Saint Vladimir's Orthodox Theological Seminary, Crestwood, New York
SCHISM: CHRISTIAN SCHISM (1987)

James A. Boon
Princeton University
ANTHROPOLOGY, ETHNOLOGY, AND RELIGION (1987 AND 2005)
DRAMA: BALINESE DANCE AND DANCE DRAMA (1987)

Phillipe Borgeaud
Université de Genève
MEMORIZATION (1987 AND 2005)
PAN (1987 AND 2005)

Arnd Adje Both
International Study Group on Music Archaeology
MUSIC: MUSIC AND RELIGION IN MESOAMERICA (2005)

Larry D. Bouchard
University of Virginia
LITERATURE: LITERATURE AND RELIGION (2005)

Issa J. Boullata
Institute of Islamic Studies, McGill University
IBN AL-FĀRIḌ (1987 AND 2005)
I'JĀZ (1987)

M. F. C. Bourdillon
University of Zimbabwe
SHONA RELIGION (1987)

Erika Bourguignon
Ohio State University
GEOMANCY (1987)
NECROMANCY (1987 AND 2005)

Henry Warner Bowden
Rutgers University
TEKAKWITHA, KATERI (1987 AND 2005)

Gerhard Böwering
Fairfield University
KALĀBĀDHĪ, AL- (1987)
MI'RĀJ (1987)
SHABISTARĪ, AL- (1987)

Faubion Bowers
New York, New York
CALLIGRAPHY: CHINESE AND JAPANESE CALLIGRAPHY (1987)

Fiona Bowie
University of Bristol
GENDER ROLES (2005)
HILDEGARD OF BINGEN (2005)

John J. Bradley
University of Queensland
AFTERLIFE: AUSTRALIAN INDIGENOUS CONCEPTS (2005)
COSMOLOGY: AUSTRALIAN INDIGENOUS COSMOLOGY (2005)
MUSIC: MUSIC AND RELIGION IN INDIGENOUS AUSTRALIA (2005)

David Brakke
Indiana University
NAG HAMMADI (2005)

Jean Rhys Bram
Hunter College, City University of New York
MOON (1987)
SUN (1987)

James R. Brandon
University of Hawaii, Manoa
DRAMA: EAST ASIAN DANCE AND THEATER (1987)

Monica Brătulescu
Hebrew University of Jerusalem
WINTER SOLSTICE SONGS (1987)

Ernst Breisach
Western Michigan University
HISTORIOGRAPHY: AN OVERVIEW (1987)

Francis J. Bremer
Millersville State College
PURITANISM (1987)

Thomas S. Bremer
Rhodes College, Memphis, Tennessee
TOURISM AND RELIGION (2005)

Jan N. Bremmer
Rijksuniversiteit Groningen, The Netherlands
AGŌGĒ (1987 AND 2005)
DELPHI (1987 AND 2005)
GREEK RELIGION [FURTHER CONSIDERATIONS] (2005)
HADES (2005)
HERA (2005)
POSEIDON (1987 AND 2005)
SCAPEGOAT (2005)
SOUL: GREEK AND HELLENISTIC CONCEPTS (1987)
TRANSMIGRATION (2005)

Frederick E. Brenk
Pontifical Biblical Institute, Rome
PLUTARCH (2005)

Michael Brenner
University of Munich
JEWISH STUDIES: JEWISH STUDIES SINCE 1919 (2005)

Joel P. Brereton
University of Texas at Austin
LOTUS (1987)
SACRED SPACE (1987)
SOMA (2005)

Dominique Briquel
Université de Paris-Sorbonne, France
ETRUSCAN RELIGION (2005)
QUIRINUS (2005)

Luc Brisson
CNRS, Paris
PLATO (2005)

John F. Broderick
Campion Center, Weston, Massachusetts
IGNATIUS LOYOLA (1987)
JESUITS (1987)
XAVIER, FRANCIS (1987)

Raymond Brodeur
Université Laval, Québec
MARIE DE L'INCARNATION (2005)

David G. Bromley
Virginia Commonwealth University
BRAINWASHING (DEBATE) (2005)
NEW RELIGIOUS MOVEMENTS: NEW RELIGIOUS MOVEMENTS AND VIOLENCE (2005)
SATANISM (2005)

Olive J. Brose
Westbrook, Connecticut
MAURICE, FREDERICK DENISON (1987)

Alexandra R. Brown
Washington and Lee University
WISDOM LITERATURE: THEORETICAL PERSPECTIVES (1987 AND 2005)

Colin Brown
University of Canterbury (emeritus)
CHRISTIANITY: CHRISTIANITY IN AUSTRALIA AND NEW ZEALAND (1987 AND 2005)

Delmer M. Brown
Inter-University Center for Japanese Language Studies, Tokyo
JIEN (1987)

Frank Burch Brown
Christian Theological Seminary, Indianapolis, Indiana
MUSIC: RELIGIOUS MUSIC IN THE WEST (2005)
POETRY: POETRY AND RELIGION (2005)

John Pairman Brown
Northern California Ecumenical Council, Berkeley
KINGDOM OF GOD (1987)

Joseph Epes Brown
University of Montana
BLACK ELK (1987)
SUN DANCE [FIRST EDITION] (1987)

Karen McCarthy Brown
Drew University
HEALING AND MEDICINE: HEALING AND MEDICINE IN THE AFRICAN DIASPORA (2005)
VODOU (1987 AND 2005)

Paula Brown
State University of New York at Stony Brook
CANNIBALISM (1987)

Robert McAfee Brown
Pacific School of Religion, Berkeley
ECUMENICAL MOVEMENT (1987)

Christopher R. Browning
University of North Carolina at Chapel Hill
HOLOCAUST, THE: HISTORY (1987 AND 2005)

Fanny E. Bryan
Urbana, Illinois
ISLAM: ISLAM IN THE CAUCASUS AND THE MIDDLE VOLGA (1987)

Raymond J. Bucher
Curia Generalizia dei Frati Minori, Rome
FRANCIS OF ASSISI (1987)

John Buckler
University of Illinois, Urbana-Champaign
JEROME (1987)

Jorunn Jacobsen Buckley
University of North Carolina at Greensboro
GINZA (1987)
MANDA D'HIIA (1987)
MANDAEAN RELIGION (1987)

Thomas Buckley
University of Massachusetts, Boston
NORTH AMERICAN INDIANS: INDIANS OF CALIFORNIA AND THE INTERMOUNTAIN REGION (1987)

John B. Buescher
Tibetan Broadcast Service of the Voice of America, Washington, D.C.
SPIRITUALISM (2005)

Katia Buffetrille
École Pratique des Hautes-Études, Paris, France
PILGRIMAGE: TIBETAN PILGRIMAGE (2005)

Gudrun Bühnemann
University of Wisconsin—Madison

MAṆḌALAS: BUDDHIST MAṆḌALAS (2005)

Richard W. Bulliet
Columbia University
MADRASAH (1987)

Donald A. Bullough
University of Saint Andrews
ALCUIN (1987)
CHARLEMAGNE (1987)

Grace G. Burford
Prescott College, Prescott, Arizona
HORNER, I. B. (2005)
PALI TEXT SOCIETY (2005)

Craig A. Burgdoff
Capital University, Columbus
SACRILEGE (2005)

Ronald Burke
University of Nebraska at Omaha
DÖLLINGER, JOHANN (1987)

Walter Burkert
Universitat Zurich
OMOPHAGIA (1987)

Pamela J. Burnham
Santa Cruz, California
ALPHABETS (2005)

Kenelm Burridge
University of British Colombia
REVIVAL AND RENEWAL (1987)

John P. Burris
Rollins College
COMPARATIVE-HISTORICAL METHOD [FURTHER CONSIDERATIONS] (2005)

Robert Evans Buswell, Jr.
University of California, Los Angeles
BUDDHISM: BUDDHISM IN KOREA (1987 AND 2005)
CHINUL (1987 AND 2005)
ŬICH'ŎN (1987 AND 2005)
ŬISANG (1987 AND 2005)
WŎNHYO (1987 AND 2005)

Jonathan M. Butler
University of California, Riverside
SEVENTH-DAY ADVENTISM (1987)

José Ignacio Cabezón
University of California, Santa Barbara
TSONG KHA PA (2005)

Nancy Caciola
University of California, San Diego
EXORCISM (2005)

Colette Caillat
Membre de l'Académie des Inscriptions et Belles-Lettres, Institut de France, Paris
AHIṂSĀ (1987 AND 2005)
GOŚĀLA (1987 AND 2005)
MAHĀVĪRA (1987)
TĪRTHAṂKARAS (1987 AND 2005)

Geneviève Calame-Griaule
Centre National de la Recherche Scientifique, Paris
DOGON RELIGION (1987)

Carnegie Samuel Calian
Pittsburgh Theological Seminary
BERDIAEV, NIKOLAI (1987)

Mario Califano
Centro Argentino de Etnológia Americana, Buenos Aires
SOUTH AMERICAN INDIANS: INDIANS OF THE GRAN CHACO (1987)

J. Baird Callicott
Yale University
ECOLOGY AND RELIGION: ENVIRONMENTAL ETHICS, WORLD RELIGIONS, AND ECOLOGY (2005)

Linda A. Camino
University of Virginia
RITES OF PASSAGE: AN OVERVIEW [FIRST EDITION] (1987)

Claudia V. Camp
Texas Christian University
ḤOKHMAH (2005)

Alberto Camplani
University of Rome "La Sapienza"
BARDAISAN (2005)

Virgil Cândea
Asociația "România," Bucharest
ICONS (1987)

Walter H. Capps
University of California, Santa Barbara
SOCIETY AND RELIGION [FIRST EDITION] (1987)

John D. Caputo
Villanova University
DECONSTRUCTION (2005)

Francine Cardman
Weston Jesuit School of Theology
PRIESTHOOD: CHRISTIAN PRIESTHOOD (2005)

Jeannie Carlier
École des Hautes Études en Sciences Sociales, Collège de France
MUSES (1987)

Robert S. Carlsen
University of Colorado at Denver
MESOAMERICAN RELIGIONS: CONTEMPORARY CULTURES (2005)

P. Allan Carlsson
Virginia Military Institute
BUTLER, JOSEPH (1987)

John B. Carman
Harvard University
BHAKTI (1987)
KRISTENSEN, W. BREDE (1987)
RĀMĀNUJA (1987)
ŚRĪ VAIṢṆAVAS (1987)

Shalom Carmy
Yeshiva University
BIBLICAL EXEGESIS: JEWISH VIEWS (1987)
ZEKHUT AVOT (2005)

David Carpenter
St. Joseph's University
GOLD AND SILVER (1987)
INSPIRATION (1987)
JADE (1987)
MONEY (1987)

Davíd Carrasco
Harvard University
AZTEC RELIGION (1987)
COATLICUE (1987)
HUITZILOPOCHTLI (1987)
HUMAN SACRIFICE: AZTEC RITES (1987 AND 2005)
KINGSHIP: KINGSHIP IN MESOAMERICA AND SOUTH AMERICA (1987 AND 2005)
MESOAMERICAN RELIGIONS: MYTHIC THEMES (2005)
QUETZALCOATL (1987)
SACRIFICE [FURTHER CONSIDERATIONS] (2005)
TEZCATLIPOCA (1987)
WHEATLEY, PAUL (2005)

E. Gerhard Carroll
University of Notre Dame
FÉNELON, FRANÇOIS (1987)

James P. Carse
New York University
SHAPE SHIFTING (1987)

John Ross Carter
Colgate University

BUDDHAGHOSA (1987)
FOUR NOBLE TRUTHS (1987)

Giovanni Casadio
Università degli Studi di Salerno
AION (2005)
BIANCHI, UGO (2005)
HISTORIOGRAPHY: WESTERN STUDIES [FURTHER CONSIDERATIONS] (2005)
XENOPHANES (2005)

Phillip Cash Cash
University of Arizona
NEZ PERCE (NIIMÍIPUU) RELIGIOUS TRADITIONS (2005)

Victoria Cass
University of Colorado at Boulder
GENDER AND RELIGION: GENDER AND CHINESE RELIGIONS (2005)

Maria Catalina
Global Unified Earth Systems Studies
NATIVE AMERICAN SCIENCE (2005)

Eleonora Cavallini
University of Bologna
EROS (2005)

Paola Ceccarelli
Università dell'Aquila
ATHENA (2005)

Ursula-Angelika Cedzich
DePaul University
ICONOGRAPHY: DAOIST ICONOGRAPHY (2005)

Bruno Centrone
Università di Pisa, Italy
PYTHAGORAS (2005)

Giovanni Cerri
Rome, Italy
PARMENIDES (2005)

J. H. Chajes
University of Haifa
DYBBUK (2005)

Kisor K. Chakrabarti
Calcutta, India
VAIŚEṢIKA (1987)

Duane Champagne
University of California
NORTH AMERICAN INDIAN RELIGIONS: NEW RELIGIOUS MOVEMENTS (2005)

Claire Champollion
Université de Haute Bretagne
TAULER, JOHANNES (1987)

Abdin Chande
Adelphi University
ISLAM: ISLAM IN SUB-SAHARAN AFRICA (2005)

Stuart Chandler
Indiana University of Pennsylvania
FOGUANGSHAN (2005)

Hao Chang
Hong Kong University of Science and Technology
KANG YUWEI (1987 AND 2005)

Anne Chapman
Centre National de la Recherche Scientifique, Paris
SELK'NAM RELIGION (1987)

David W. Chappell
University of Hawaii (emeritus)
DAOCHUO (1987 AND 2005)
JINGTU (1987 AND 2005)

Christopher Key Chapple
Loyola Marymount University
ECOLOGY AND RELIGION: ECOLOGY AND JAINISM (2005)

James H. Charlesworth
Princeton Theological Seminary
BIBLICAL LITERATURE: APOCRYPHA AND PSEUDEPIGRAPHA (1987)

Leon Chartrand
University of Toronto
BEARS (2005)

Robert Chazan
New York University
ANTI-SEMITISM (2005)
PERSECUTION: JEWISH EXPERIENCE (1987 AND 2005)

Peter Chelkowski
New York University
RĀWẒAH-KHVĀNĪ (1987)
TA'ZIYAH (1987)

Peter C. Chemery
Chicago, Illinois
METEOROLOGICAL BEINGS (1987)
VEGETATION (1987)

Jack W. Chen
Wellesley College
POLITICS AND RELIGION: POLITICS AND CHINESE RELIGION (2005)

Richard S. Y. Chi
(deceased)
DHARMAPĀLA (1987)

Boris Chichlo
Centre National de la Recherche Scientifique, Paris
DOLGAN RELIGION (1987 AND 2005)
TUNGUZ RELIGION (1987 AND 2005)

David Chidester
University of Cape Town
CAPPS, WALTER (2005)
COLONIALISM AND POSTCOLONIALISM (2005)
JONESTOWN AND PEOPLES TEMPLE (2005)

Julia Ching
Victoria College, University of Toronto
CONFUCIUS (1987)
RICCI, MATTEO (1987)

Silvia Maria Chiodi
Consiglio Nazionale delle Ricerche (CNR), Roma, Italy
AN (2005)

Ezra Chitando
University of Zimbabwe
STUDY OF RELIGION: THE ACADEMIC STUDY OF RELIGION IN SUB-SAHARAN AFRICA (2005)

William C. Chittick
State University of New York at Stony Brook
DHIKR (1987)

Francisca Cho
Georgetown University
KOREAN RELIGION (2005)

Jamsheed K. Choksy
Indiana University
ATESHGAH (2005)
GENDER AND RELIGION: GENDER AND ZOROASTRIANISM (2005)
PARSIS (2005)
ZOROASTRIANISM (2005)
ZURVANISM (2005)

Youssef M. Choueiri
University of Exeter
QUTB, SAYYID (2005)

Ann Chowning
Victoria University of Wellington
MELANESIAN RELIGIONS: AN OVERVIEW (1987)

Carol P. Christ
Ariadne Institute for the Study of Myth and Ritual
LADY OF THE ANIMALS (1987 AND 2005)

William A. Christian, Jr.
Hamden, Connecticut
FOLK RELIGION: AN OVERVIEW (1987 AND 2005)

Panagiotis C. Christou
Patriarchal Institute for Patristic Studies, Thessaloniki
CABASILAS, NICHOLAS (1987)
CASSIAN, JOHN (1987)
CYPRIAN (1987)
CYRIL OF JERUSALEM (1987)
MARK OF EPHESUS (1987)
THEODORE OF MOPSUESTIA (1987)

Malcolm Nāea Chun
University of Hawaii, Manoa
HAWAIIAN RELIGION (2005)

Mary C. Churchill
University of Iowa
WHITE BUFFALO CALF WOMAN (2005)

Alessandra Ciattini
University of Rome
JENSEN, ADOLF E. (2005)
KULTURKREISELEHRE (2005)
SCHMIDT, WILHELM (2005)

Eugen Ciurtin
University of Bucharest
CULIANU, IOAN PETRU (2005)
WIDENGREN, GEO (2005)

Beverley Clack
Oxford Brookes University
HUMAN BODY: HUMAN BODIES, RELIGION, AND GENDER (2005)

Julie Clague
University of Glasgow
WOMEN'S STUDIES IN RELIGION (2005)

Elizabeth A. Clark
Duke University
CLEMENT OF ALEXANDRIA (1987 AND 2005)

Lynn Schofield Clark
University of Colorado
POPULAR CULTURE (2005)

Mary T. Clark
Manhattanville College (emeritus)
NEOPLATONISM (1987 AND 2005)
PLOTINUS (1987 AND 2005)

Matthew Clark
East Sussex, United Kingdom
SĀDHUS AND SĀDHVĪS (2005)

Anne Clarke
New York, New York
GROTIUS, HUGO (1987)

L. Clarke
Concordia University, Montreal
'IṢMAH (2005)

Peter B. Clarke
Oxford University
AFRICAN RELIGIONS: NEW RELIGIOUS MOVEMENTS (2005)

Thomas Cleary
Kyoto, Japan
LINJI (1987)

James Clifford
University of California, Santa Cruz
LEENHARDT, MAURICE (1987)

Michael D. Clifford
New York, New York
PSYCHOLOGY: PSYCHOTHERAPY AND RELIGION (1987 AND 2005)

Regina T. Clifford
Chicago, Illinois
THERAVĀDA (1987)

Wallace B. Clift
University of Denver
CHILD (1987)
REJUVENATION (1987)
VIERKANDT, ALFRED (1987)
WUNDT, WILHELM (1987)

Fred W. Clothey
University of Pittsburgh
MURUKAṈ (1987 AND 2005)
TAMIL RELIGIONS (1987)

John B. Cobb, Jr.
Claremont School of Theology (emeritus)
ECOLOGY AND RELIGION: ECOLOGY AND CHRISTIANITY (2005)
GOD: GOD IN POSTBIBLICAL CHRISTIANITY (1987)
WHITEHEAD, ALFRED NORTH (1987)

Mark R. Cohen
Princeton University
JUDAISM: JUDAISM IN THE MIDDLE EAST AND NORTH AFRICA TO 1492 (1987)

Robert L. Cohn
Northwestern University
SAINTHOOD (1987)

Douglas Cole
Simon Fraser University
BOAS, FRANZ (1987)

Martin Collcutt
Princeton University
EISAI (1987)
GOZAN ZEN (1987)
MUSŌ SŌSEKI (1987)

John J. Collins
Yale University
APOCALYPSE: AN OVERVIEW (1987 AND 2005)
APOCALYPSE: JEWISH APOCALYPTICISM TO THE RABBINIC PERIOD (2005)

Raymond F. Collins
Katholieke Universiteit Leuven
GOSPEL (1987)

Steven Collins
Bristol University
SOUL: BUDDHIST CONCEPTS (1987)

Louise Collis
London, England
KEMPE, MARGERY (1987)

Dominique Collon
British Museum, London
ICONOGRAPHY: MESOPOTAMIAN ICONOGRAPHY (1987)

Carsten Colpe
Freie Universität Berlin
SACRED AND THE PROFANE, THE (1987)
SYNCRETISM [FIRST EDITION] (1987)

Elizabeth Colson
University of California, Berkeley
CENTRAL BANTU RELIGIONS (1987)

W. Richard Comstock
University of California, Santa Barbara
DOCTRINE (1987)

Georges Condominas
École des Hautes Études en Sciences Sociales, Collège de France
LAO RELIGION (1987)
VIETNAMESE RELIGION (1987)

Yves Congar
Couvent Saint-Jacques, Paris
THEOLOGY: CHRISTIAN THEOLOGY (1987)

Beth A. Conklin
Vanderbilt University
CANNIBALISM (2005)

Demetrios J. Constantelos
Stockton State College

CHARITY (1987 AND 2005)
EVAGRIOS OF PONTUS (1987)
JULIAN OF HALICARNASSUS (1987)
NIKEPHOROS KALLISTOS (1987)
TARASIOS (1987)
THEODORE OF STUDIOS (1987)
TIMOTHY AILUROS (1987)

Michael D. Coogan
Stonehill College
CANAANITE RELIGION: THE LITERATURE (1987 AND 2005)

John W. Cook
Yale University (emeritus) and Henry Luce Foundation, President Emeritus
ICONOGRAPHY: CHRISTIAN ICONOGRAPHY (1987 AND 2005)

Scott Cook
Grinnell College
HAN FEI ZI (2005)

Alan M. Cooper
Hebrew Union College–Jewish Institute of Religion, Cincinnati
CANAANITE RELIGION: AN OVERVIEW (1987)
PHOENICIAN RELIGION [FIRST EDITION] (1987)

Kate Cooper
University of Manchester
CHASTITY (2005)

Roger J. Corless
Duke University (emeritus)
TANLUAN (1987)

Vincent J. Cornell
University of Arkansas
GOD: GOD IN ISLAM (2005)
QUR'ĀN: ITS ROLE IN MUSLIM PRACTICE AND LIFE (2005)

Catherine Cornille
Boston College
GURŪ (2005)

Charles A. Corr
Southern Illinois University, Edwardsville (emeritus)
WOLFF, CHRISTIAN (1987 AND 2005)

John E. Cort
Denison University
IMAGES: IMAGES, ICONS, AND IDOLS (2005)

Dario M. Cosi
University of Bologna, Italy
CASTRATION (1987 AND 2005)

Allison Coudert
State University of New York, College at Oneonta
ALCHEMY: RENAISSANCE ALCHEMY (1987)
ELIXIR (1987)
FAUST (1987)
HORNS (1987)
PARACELSUS (1987)

Paul B. Courtright
Emory University
GĀṆAPATYAS (1987)
GAṆEŚA (1987)
SHRINES (1987 AND 2005)
WORSHIP AND DEVOTIONAL LIFE: HINDU DEVOTIONAL LIFE (1987)

James L. Cox
University of Edinburgh
RITES OF PASSAGE: AFRICAN RITES (2005)

Kenneth Cragg
Anglican Diocese of Oxford
SHAHĀDAH (1987)

Vincent Crapanzano
Queens College, City University of New York
FRENZY (1987)
SPIRIT POSSESSION: AN OVERVIEW (1987)

I. M. Crawford
Western Australian Museum, Perth
WANDJINA (1987)

Suzanne J. Crawford
Pacific Lutheran University, Tacoma, Washington
BLACK ELK (2005)

James L. Crenshaw
Vanderbilt University
WISDOM LITERATURE: BIBLICAL BOOKS [FIRST EDITION] (1987)

Donald A. Crosby
Colorado State University (emeritus)
BUSHNELL, HORACE (1987 AND 2005)

Richard Crouter
Carleton College
AMBROSE (1987)

Henri Crouzel
Institut Catholique de Toulouse
ORIGEN (1987)

Douglas S. Crow
Fordham University, Bronx
GHAYBAH (1987)

Frederick E. Crowe
Lonergan Research Institute of Regis College, Toronto
LONERGAN, BERNARD (1987 AND 2005)

Mark Csikszentmihalyi
University of Wisconsin—Madison
CONFUCIANISM: AN OVERVIEW (2005)
CONFUCIANISM: THE CLASSICAL CANON (2005)

Mihaly Csikszentmihalyi
University of Chicago
FLOW EXPERIENCE (1987)

Bryan J. Cuevas
Florida State University
VAJRASATTVA (2005)

Philip Culbertson
Auckland Consortium of Theological Education, Remuera, Auckland
MEN'S STUDIES IN RELIGION (2005)

Ioan Petru Culianu
Rijksuniversiteit te Groningen
ASTROLOGY (1987)
BENDIS (1987)
DACIAN RIDERS (1987)
GETO-DACIAN RELIGION (1987)
SABAZIOS (1987)
SACRILEGE (1987)
SEXUALITY: SEXUAL RITES IN EUROPE (1987)
SKY: THE HEAVENS AS HIEROPHANY (1987)
THRACIAN RELIGION (1987)
THRACIAN RIDER (1987)
ZALMOXIS (1987)

Mark D. Cummings
New York, New York
DAO'AN (1987)
DAOSHENG (1987)

James W. Cunningham
College of Saint Catherine, Saint Paul, Minnesota
POBEDONOSTSEV, KONSTANTIN (1987)
PROKOPOVICH, FEOFAN (1987)
SERGII (1987)
TIKHON (1987)

Lawrence S. Cunningham
Florida State University
ANTHONY OF PADUA (1987)

Charles E. Curran
Southern Methodist University
CHRISTIAN ETHICS (1987 AND 2005)

Brian E. Daley
Weston School of Theology, Cambridge, Massachusetts
COUNCILS: CHRISTIAN COUNCILS (1987)

Marie W. Dallam
Temple University
DADDY GRACE (2005)

Joseph Dan
Hebrew University of Jerusalem
BA'AL SHEM TOV (1987 AND 2005)
HASIDISM: AN OVERVIEW (1987)
JEWISH THOUGHT AND PHILOSOPHY: JEWISH ETHICAL LITERATURE (1987)

R. N. Dandekar
Bhandarkar Oriental Research Institute, Poona
VAIṢṆAVISM: AN OVERVIEW (1987)
VEDĀNTA (1987)
VEDAS (1987)

Norman Daniel
Institute Dominicain d'Études Orientales, Cairo
POLEMICS: CHRISTIAN-MUSLIM POLEMICS [FIRST EDITION] (1987)

David Daniell
University College, London
TYNDALE, WILLIAM (2005)

Victor Danner
Indiana University, Bloomington
IBN 'AṬĀ' ALLĀH (1987)

Eugene G. d'Aquili
University of Pennsylvania
NEUROSCIENCE AND RELIGION: NEUROEPISTEMOLOGY (1987)

Adolf Darlap
Leopold-Franzens Universität Innsbruck
DOGMA (1987)
VATICAN COUNCILS: VATICAN II [FIRST EDITION] (1987)

William R. Darrow
Williams College
PRATT, JAMES B. (2005)

Clifford Davidson
Western Michigan University
DRAMA: EUROPEAN RELIGIOUS DRAMA [FURTHER CONSIDERATIONS] (2005)

Hilda R. Ellis Davidson
University of Cambridge
GRIMM BROTHERS (1987)

Alan Davies
Victoria College, University of Toronto
ANTI-SEMITISM (1987)

J. G. Davies
University of Birmingham
ARCHITECTURE (1987)
BASILICA, CATHEDRAL, AND CHURCH (1987)

Oliver Davies
King's College London
HILDEGARD OF BINGEN (2005)

Robertson Davies
Massey College, University of Toronto
FICTION: THE WESTERN NOVEL AND RELIGION (1987)

Richard H. Davis
Bard College
IMAGES: VENERATION OF IMAGES (2005)

Scott Davis
Miyazaki International College
HUMOR AND RELIGION: HUMOR AND RELIGION IN EAST ASIAN CONTEXTS (2005)

Stephen J. Davis
Yale University
THECLA (2005)

Winston Davis
Southwestern University, Georgetown, Texas
SOCIOLOGY: SOCIOLOGY OF RELIGION [FIRST EDITION] (1987)
WEALTH (1987)

Dell deChant
University of South Florida
FILLMORE, CHARLES AND MYRTLE (2005)
NEW THOUGHT MOVEMENT (2005)
UNITY (2005)

Hubert Decleer
School for International Training
MAR PA (2005)

Laurence Delaby
Musée de l'Homme, Paris
YAKUT RELIGION (1987)

Roland A. Delattre
University of Minnesota, Twin Cities
DESIRE (1987)

Vine Deloria, Jr.
University of Colorado
POLITICS AND RELIGION: POLITICS AND NATIVE AMERICAN RELIGIOUS TRADITIONS (2005)

Raymond J. DeMallie
Indiana University
DELORIA, ELLA CARA (2005)
WALKER, JAMES R. (2005)

Arthur Andrew Demarest
Vanderbilt University
ARCHAEOLOGY AND RELIGION (1987)

William A. Dembski
Baylor University
INTELLIGENT DESIGN (2005)

David E. Demson
Emmanuel College, University of Toronto (emeritus)
ZWINGLI, HULDRYCH (1987 AND 2005)

Robert D. Denham
Roanoke College
FRYE, NORTHROP (2005)

Johannes Deninger
Johann Wolfgang Goethe-Universität Frankfurt
REVELATION (1987)

Mark Dennis
St. Paul, Minnesota
BUDDHISM, SCHOOLS OF: EAST ASIAN BUDDHISM (2005)

Frederick Mathewson Denny
University of Colorado at Boulder
DA'WAH (1987)
HANDS (1987)
KNEES (1987)
NAMES AND NAMING (1987)
POSTURES AND GESTURES (1987)

Philip Denwood
School of Oriental and African Studies, University of London
TEMPLE: BUDDHIST TEMPLE COMPOUNDS IN TIBET (2005)

Karen Derris
University of Redlands
BUDDHAS AND BODHISATTVAS: ETHICAL PRACTICES ASSOCIATED WITH BUDDHAS AND BODHISATTVAS (2005)

Shlomo Deshen
Bar-Ilan University
DOMESTIC OBSERVANCES: JEWISH PRACTICES (1987)

Leslie G. Desmangles
Trinity College
CREOLIZATION (2005)

Michel Despland
Concordia University
CONSCIENCE (1987)
SUPERNATURAL, THE (1987)

Ali E. Hillal Dessouki
University of Cairo
ʿABDUH, MUḤAMMAD (1987)

Marcel Detienne
École Pratique des Hautes Études, Collège de France
DIONYSOS (1987)
ORPHEUS (1987)

Eliot Deutsch
University of Hawaii, Manoa
BHAGAVADGĪTĀ (1987)

Rex Deverell
McMaster Divinity College, Ontario, Canada
DRAMA: MODERN WESTERN THEATER (2005)

Alnoor Dhanani
Harvard University
ʿABD AL-JABBĀR (2005)

Mariasusai Dhavamony
Pontificia Universitas Gregoriana
ŚAIVISM: ŚAIVA SIDDHĀNTA (1987)

Stanley Diamond
New School for Social Research, New York
RADIN, PAUL (1987)

Manuel C. Díaz y Díaz
Universidad de Compostela (emeritus)
ISIDORE OF SEVILLE (1987 AND 2005)

Richard A. Diehl
University of Missouri, Columbia
OLMEC RELIGION (1987)

Melvin E. Dieter
Asbury Theological Seminary, Wilmore, Kentucky
HOLINESS MOVEMENT (2005)
SMITH, HANNAH WHITALL (2005)

Michael Dillon
University of Durham
ISLAM: ISLAM IN CHINA (2005)

Devorah Dimant
University of Haifa
PESHER (2005)

Jay Dobbin
Colonia, Yap
MICRONESIAN RELIGIONS: AN OVERVIEW (2005)

James C. Dobbins
Oberlin College
GANJIN (1987)

Federico Kauffmann Doig
Lima, Peru
SOUTH AMERICAN INDIANS: INDIANS OF THE ANDES IN THE PRE-INCA PERIOD (1987)

Wendy Doniger
University of Chicago
ANDROGYNES (1987)
BRAHMĀ (1987)
HORSES (1987)
INDIAN RELIGIONS: MYTHIC THEMES (1987)
INDRA (1987)
PRALAYA (1987)
VṚTRA (1987)

Neal Donner
Los Angeles, California
ZHIYI (1987)

Maureen H. Donovan
Ohio State University
JAPANESE RELIGIONS: RELIGIOUS DOCUMENTS (2005)

Margaret Anne Doody
University of Notre Dame
FICTION: HISTORY OF THE NOVEL (2005)

Nelly van Doorn-Harder
Valparaiso University
GENDER AND RELIGION: GENDER AND ISLAM (2005)

Christine Downing
San Diego State University
ATHENA (1987)
HESTIA (1987)

A. Stanley Dreyfus
Hebrew Union College–Jewish Institute of Religion, New York
MALBIM (1987)

Georges Dreyfus
Williams College
SAṂGHA: SAṂGHA AND SOCIETY IN TIBET (2005)
SHUGS LDAN (SHUGDEN) (2005)

Han J. W. Drijvers
Rijksuniversiteit te Groningen
ABLUTIONS (1987)
VIRGINITY (1987)
VOCATION (1987)

Tom F. Driver
Union Theological Seminary, New York
DRAMA: MODERN WESTERN THEATER (1987)

Saurabh Dube
El Colegio de México
UNTOUCHABLES, RELIGIONS OF (2005)

Jacques Duchesne-Guillemin
Université de Liège (emeritus)
CUMONT, FRANZ (1987)
GOBLET D'ALVIELLA, EUGÈNE (1987)
KNOWLEDGE AND IGNORANCE (1987)

Donald F. Duclow
Gwynedd-Mercy College
DIONYSIUS THE AREOPAGITE (1987)
NICHOLAS OF CUSA (1987 AND 2005)

Kathleen Dugan
New Milford, Connecticut
GENDER AND RELIGION: GENDER AND NORTH AMERICAN INDIAN RELIGIOUS TRADITIONS (2005)

Avery Dulles
Catholic University of America
CHURCH (1987 AND 2005)

Paul Dundas
University of Edinburgh
COSMOLOGY: JAIN COSMOLOGY (2005)
JAINISM (2005)

James D. G. Dunn
University of Durham
ENTHUSIASM (1987)

John D. Dunne
University of Wisconsin—Madison
BUDDHISM, SCHOOLS OF: MAHĀYĀNA PHILOSOPHICAL SCHOOLS OF BUDDHISM (2005)
NĀGĀRJUNA (2005)

Ann Dunnigan
New York, New York
FISH (1987)
OWLS (1987)
RAIN (1987)
SWANS (1987)
WOLVES (1987)

Madeline Duntley
The College of Wooster
RITUAL STUDIES (2005)

Louis Dupré
Yale University
MARX, KARL (1987)
MYSTICISM [FIRST EDITION] (1987)

Hubert Durt
École Française d'Extrême-Orient, Kyoto
FOUCHER, ALFRED (1987)
LAMOTTE, ÉTIENNE (1987 AND 2005)
LA VALLÉE POUSSIN, LOUIS DE (1987)

Françoise Dussart
University of Connecticut
WARLPIRI RELIGION (2005)

Pierre Duviols
Universite d'Aix-Marseille I
INCA RELIGION (1987)

Cornelius J. Dyck
Associated Mennonite Biblical Seminary, Elkhart, Indiana
ANABAPTISM (1987)
MENNONITES (1987)
SIMONS, MENNO (1987)

John W. Eadie
University of Michigan, Ann Arbor
CONSTANTINE (1987)

H. Byron Earhart
Western Michigan University
KITAGAWA, JOSEPH M. (2005)
SHUGENDŌ (1987)

Christine Eber
New Mexico State University
GENDER AND RELIGION: GENDER AND MESOAMERICAN RELIGIONS (2005)

Gary L. Ebersole
University of Missouri—Kansas City
DEATH (2005)
JAPANESE RELIGIONS: AN OVERVIEW (2005)
POETRY: JAPANESE RELIGIOUS POETRY (2005)
TEARS (2005)

Diana L. Eck
Harvard University
BANARAS (1987)
CIRCUMAMBULATION (1987)
MOUNTAINS (1987)
RIVERS (1987)

Malcolm David Eckel
Boston University
BUDDHIST PHILOSOPHY (2005)

Carl-Martin Edsman
Uppsala Universitet
ALTAR (1987)
BOATS (1987)
BRIDGES (1987)
STONES (1987)

Mary Edwardsen
New York, New York
EVOLUTION: EVOLUTIONISM (1987)
PREHISTORIC RELIGIONS: AN OVERVIEW (1987)

Franz-Karl Ehrhard
University of Munich
BUDDHISM, SCHOOLS OF: HIMALAYAN BUDDHISM (2005)

Ute Eickelkamp
Charles Darwin University and Macquarie University
AUSTRALIAN INDIGENOUS RELIGIONS: MYTHIC THEMES [FURTHER CONSIDERATIONS] (2005)

Dale F. Eickelman
New York University
MAWLID (1987)
RITES OF PASSAGE: MUSLIM RITES (1987)
SNOUCK HURGRONJE, CHRISTIAAN (1987)

Shmuel N. Eisenstadt
Hebrew University of Jerusalem
RELIGIOUS DIVERSITY (1987)

George R. Elder
Hunter College, City University of New York
CROSSROADS (1987)
QUATERNITY (1987)

Mircea Eliade
(deceased)
ALCHEMY: AN OVERVIEW (1987)
ANDROGYNES (1987)
CENTER OF THE WORLD (1987)
DEUS OTIOSUS (1987)
EARTH (1987)
HIEROPHANY (1987)
INITIATION: AN OVERVIEW (1987)
METALS AND METALLURGY (1987)
ORIENTATION (1987)
SEXUALITY: AN OVERVIEW [FIRST EDITION] (1987)
SHAMANISM: AN OVERVIEW [FIRST EDITION] (1987)
YOGA (1987)

David Ellenson
Hebrew Union College–Jewish Institute of Religion, Los Angeles
GEIGER, ABRAHAM (1987)
HILDESHEIMER, ESRIEL (1987)
HIRSCH, SAMSON RAPHAEL (1987)
HOFFMANN, DAVID (1987)
HOLDHEIM, SAMUEL (1987)
SPEKTOR, YITSḤAQ ELḤANAN (1987)

Ter Ellingson
University of Washington
DRUMS (1987)
MUSIC: MUSIC AND RELIGION (1987)

Robert S. Ellwood
University of Southern California
BLAVATSKY, H. P. (2005)
CAO DAI (1987 AND 2005)
CAYCE, EDGAR (2005)
NEW RELIGIOUS MOVEMENTS: NEW RELIGIOUS MOVEMENTS IN JAPAN (1987)
WORLD'S PARLIAMENT OF RELIGIONS (1987 AND 2005)

Mohammad Jafar Elmi
Islamic College for Advanced Studies, London
ṬABĀṬABĀʾĪ, ʿALLĀMA (2005)

Christoph Elsas
Freie Universität Berlin
CLEMEN, CARL (1987)

Constance W. Elsberg
Northern Virginia Community College
HEALTHY, HAPPY, HOLY ORGANIZATION (3HO) (2005)

Ainslie T. Embree
Columbia University
AKBAR (1987 AND 2005)
SEN, KESHAB CHANDRA (1987 AND 2005)
TILAK, BAL GANGADHAR (1987 AND 2005)

Stephen Emmel
Westfälische Wilhelms-Universität Münster
SHENOUTE (2005)

Kirk Endicott
Dartmouth College
NEGRITO RELIGIONS: AN OVERVIEW (1987 AND 2005)
NEGRITO RELIGIONS: NEGRITOS OF THE MALAY PENINSULA (1987)

Melvin B. Endy, Jr.
Hamilton College
PENN, WILLIAM (1987)

Shifra Epstein
Israel Museum, Jerusalem
PURIM PLAYS (1987)

Peter C. Erb
Wilfrid Laurier University
BOEHME, JAKOB (1987)

Carl W. Ernst
Pomona College
BLASPHEMY: ISLAMIC CONCEPT (1987)

A. M. Esnoul
Paris, France
MOKṢA (1987)
OṂ (1987)

John L. Esposito
Georgetown University
POLITICS AND RELIGION: POLITICS AND ISLAM (2005)

Josef van Ess
Eberhard-Karls-Universität Tübingen
IJĪ, ʿAḌUD AL-DĪN AL- (1987)
MUʿTAZILAH (1987)

David B. Evans
Saint John's University, Jamaica, New York
LEONTIUS OF BYZANTIUM (1987)

George Every
Oscott College, Sutton Coldfield, England
JUSTINIAN I (1987)

Toufic Fahd
Université de Strasbourg II
MAGIC: MAGIC IN ISLAM (1987)

Antoine Faivre
Sorbonne
ESOTERICISM (1987 AND 2005)
HERMETISM (1987 AND 2005)
NATURE: RELIGIOUS AND PHILOSOPHICAL SPECULATIONS (1987 AND 2005)
OCCULTISM (1987 AND 2005)

Majid Fakhry
American University of Beirut; Georgetown University
IBN RUSHD (2005)
OCCASIONALISM (1987)

Nancy Auer Falk
Western Michigan University
FEMININE SACRALITY (1987 AND 2005)
PŪJĀ: HINDU PŪJĀ (1987 AND 2005)

Paul Lawrence Farber
Oregon State University
EVOLUTION: EVOLUTIONARY ETHICS (2005)

Charles E. Farhadian
Westmont College
CONVERSION (2005)

Roberto Farneti
University of Bologna
HOBBES, THOMAS (2005)

Phyllis Ann Fast
University of Alaska Fairbanks
ATHAPASKAN RELIGIOUS TRADITIONS: AN OVERVIEW (2005)
NORTH AMERICAN INDIANS: INDIANS OF THE FAR NORTH (2005)

Bernard Faure
Cornell University
BODHIDHARMA (1987)

J. Rufus Fears
Indiana University, Bloomington
AUGUSTUS (1987)
DEA DIA (1987)
EMPEROR'S CULT (1987)
SOL INVICTUS (1987)

Anne Feldhaus
Arizona State University
MARATHI RELIGIONS (1987 AND 2005)

Burton Feldman
University of Denver
CREUZER, G. F. (1987)
GÖRRES, JOSEPH VON (1987)
MÜLLER, KARL O. (1987)
USENER, HERMANN (1987)

Seymour Feldman
Rutgers, The State University of New Jersey, New Brunswick Campus
ARISTOTELIANISM (1987)
ARISTOTLE (1987)
JEWISH THOUGHT AND PHILOSOPHY: PREMODERN PHILOSOPHY (1987)

Paul B. Fenton
Paris, France
MAIMONIDES, ABRAHAM (2005)

Sirarpi Feredjian-Aivazian
Fairlawn, New Jersey
PILGRIMAGE: EASTERN CHRISTIAN PILGRIMAGE (1987)

Deane Fergie
Adelaide University
AUSTRALIAN INDIGENOUS RELIGIONS: AN OVERVIEW (2005)

Gary B. Ferngren
Oregon State University
GALEN (1987)
HEALING AND MEDICINE: HEALING AND MEDICINE IN CHRISTIANITY (2005)
HEALING AND MEDICINE: HEALING AND MEDICINE IN GREECE AND ROME (2005)
HIPPOCRATES (1987 AND 2005)

Franco Ferrari
University of Salerno
ARISTOTLE (2005)

Frederick Ferré
University of Georgia
ANALYTIC PHILOSOPHY (1987)
LOGICAL POSITIVISM (1987)

Georg Feuerstein
Johannine Daist Communion, Clearlake, California
PRĀṆA (1987)
SAMĀDHI (1987)

Maribel Fierro
Consejo Superior de Investigaciones Científicas
ISLAM: ISLAM IN ANDALUSIA (2005)

Robert E. Fierstien
Temple Beth Or, Brick, New Jersey
RABBINATE: THE RABBINATE IN MODERN JUDAISM (2005)

Abdou Filali-Ansary
Aga Khan University
ISLAM: AN OVERVIEW [FURTHER CONSIDERATIONS](2005)

Henry Le Roy Finch
Hunter College, City University of New York
EPISTEMOLOGY (1987)
WITTGENSTEIN, LUDWIG (1987)

James F. Findlay
University of Rhode Island
MOODY, DWIGHT L. (1987)

Ellison Banks Findly
Trinity College
AGNI (1987 AND 2005)
BREATH AND BREATHING (1987 AND 2005)

Lawrence Fine
Indiana University, Bloomington
APOCALYPSE: MEDIEVAL JEWISH APOCALYPTIC LITERATURE (1987)
CORDOVERO, MOSHEH (1987)
LURIA, ISAAC (1987)
VITAL, ḤAYYIM (1987)

Steven Fine
University of Cincinnati
ICONOGRAPHY: JEWISH ICONOGRAPHY [FURTHER CONSIDERATIONS] (2005)
MOORE, GEORGE FOOT (2005)
SYNAGOGUE (2005)

Reuven Firestone
Hebrew Union College–Jewish Institute of Religion, Los Angeles
JERUSALEM: JERUSALEM IN JUDAISM, CHRISTIANITY, AND ISLAM (2005)

Raymond Firth
University of London (emeritus)
TIKOPIA RELIGION (1987)

Michael Fishbane
Brandeis University
ADAM (1987)
CAIN AND ABEL (1987)
DANIEL (1987)
ESTHER (1987)
EVE (1987)
JONAH (1987)
NOAH (1987)

Joseph Fitzer
St. John's University, Jamaica, New York
MÖHLER, JOHANN ADAM (1987)

Thomas E. FitzGerald
Holy Cross Greek Orthodox School of Theology, Brookline, Massachusetts
EASTERN CHRISTIANITY (2005)

James H. Foard
Arizona State University
IPPEN (1987 AND 2005)

Harry Wells Fogarty
New York, New York
ROSICRUCIANS (1987)

Raymond D. Fogelson
University of Chicago
LOWIE, ROBERT H. (1987)
NORTH AMERICAN [INDIAN] RELIGIONS: HISTORY OF STUDY [FIRST EDITION] (1987)

Richard C. Foltz
University of Florida
ECOLOGY AND RELIGION: ECOLOGY AND ISLAM (2005)

Charlotte Elisheva Fonrobert
Stanford University
PURIFICATION: PURIFICATION IN JUDAISM (2005)

Charles W. Forman
Yale University
CHRISTIANITY: CHRISTIANITY IN THE PACIFIC ISLANDS [FIRST EDITION] (1987)

Douglas A. Foster
Abilene Christian University
CHURCHES OF CHRIST (2005)

Lawrence Foster
Georgia Institute of Technology
LEE, ANN (1987 AND 2005)
NOYES, JOHN HUMPHREY (1987 AND 2005)
SHAKERS (1987)

Marcel Fournier
Montreal University
MAUSS, MARCEL (2005)

James J. Fox
Australian National University
SOUTHEAST ASIAN RELIGIONS: INSULAR CULTURES (1987)

Steven D. Fraade
Yale University
ENOCH (1987)

Daniel Frank
Ohio State University
KARAITES (2005)

R. M. Frank
Catholic University of America
ABŪ AL-HUDHAYL AL-ʿALLĀF (1987)
ASHʿARĪ AL- (1987)
ASHʿARĪYAH (1987)

David L. Freeman
Temple Israel, Boston
HEALING AND MEDICINE: HEALING AND MEDICINE IN JUDAISM (2005)

Lima de Freitas
Instituto de Arte, Lisbon
LABYRINTH (1987)

Rebecca R. French
State University of New York at Buffalo
LAW AND RELIGION: LAW AND RELIGION IN BUDDHISM (2005)

W. H. C. Frend
University of Glasgow (emeritus)
DONATISM (1987)
MONOPHYSITISM (1987)
PERSECUTION: CHRISTIAN EXPERIENCE (1987)

Pamela R. Frese
College of Wooster
FLOWERS (1987)
MARRIAGE (1987)
TREES (1987)

Gérard Freyburger
Université de Haute Alsace
FIDES (1987)

LeeEllen Friedland
Philadelphia, Pennsylvania
DANCE: POPULAR AND FOLK DANCE [FIRST EDITION] (1987)

Yohanan Friedmann
Hebrew University of Jerusalem
AḤMADIYAH (2005)
SIRHINDĪ, AḤMAD (1987 AND 2005)

Paul Friedrich
University of Chicago
TARASCAN RELIGION (1987 AND 2005)

Manfred S. Frings
DePaul University
SCHELER, MAX (1987)

Karlfried Froehlich
Princeton Theological Seminary
CRUSADES: CHRISTIAN PERSPECTIVE (1987)

Tikva Frymer-Kensky
University of Michigan, Ann Arbor
ASHUR (1987)
ENUMA ELISH (1987)
ISRAELITE LAW: PERSONAL STATUS AND FAMILY LAW (1987)
ISRAELITE LAW: STATE AND JUDICIARY LAW (1987)
MARDUK (1987)
NABU (1987)
UTU (1987)

Bruce Fudge
New York University
BUKHĀRĪ, AL- (2005)

Fujita Kōtatsu
Hokkaido University
PURE AND IMPURE LANDS (1987)

Fujiwara Ryōsetsu
Ryukoku University (emeritus)
NIANFO (1987)
SHANDAO (1987)

Sakoto Fujiwara
Taisho University
STUDY OF RELIGION: THE ACADEMIC STUDY OF RELIGION IN JAPAN (2005)

Fujiyoshi Jikai
Kyoto, Japan
JŌDOSHŪ (1987)

William J. Fulco
Jesuits at Loyola University, Los Angeles
HURRIAN RELIGION (1987)

Reginald H. Fuller
Protestants Episcopal Theological Seminary in Virginia (emeritus)
GOD: GOD IN THE NEW TESTAMENT (1987 AND 2005)

Robert C. Fuller
Bradley University
HEALING AND MEDICINE: ALTERNATIVE MEDICINE IN THE NEW AGE (2005)

Peter T. Furst
University of Pennsylvania Museum of Archaeology and Anthropology, and Museum of Indian Arts & Culture
HUICHOL RELIGION (1987 AND 2005)
SHAMANISM: SOUTH AMERICAN SHAMANISM (1987 AND 2005)
TOBACCO (2005)

Nagao Gadjin
Otani University
VASUBANDHU (1987 AND 2005)

Peter Gaeffke
University of Pennsylvania
MAṆḌALAS: HINDU MAṆḌALAS (1987)

Mügé Galin
Ohio State University
WALDMAN, MARILYN ROBINSON (2005)

Jacques Galinier
Université de Bordeaux III
OTOMÍ RELIGION (1987)

Eugene V. Gallagher
Connecticut College
BRANCH DAVIDIANS (2005)
NEW RELIGIOUS MOVEMENTS: SCRIPTURES OF NEW RELIGIOUS MOVEMENTS (2005)

Nancy Gallagher
University of California, Santa Barbara
HEALING AND MEDICINE: HEALING AND MEDICINE IN ISLAMIC TEXTS AND TRADITIONS (2005)

Mario Gandini
Biblioteca comunale "G.C. Croce" San Giovanni in Persiceto (Bologna, Italy)
PETTAZZONI, RAFFAELE (2005)

Pranab Ganguly
Anthropological Survey of India, Calcutta
NEGRITO RELIGIONS: NEGRITOS OF THE ANDAMAN ISLANDS (1987)

Peter Gardella
Manhattanville College
FOOD (2005)

Iain Gardner
University of Sydney
DOCETISM (2005)

Richard A. Gardner
Sophia University
HUMOR AND RELIGION: AN OVERVIEW (2005)
HUMOR AND RELIGION: HUMOR AND RELIGION IN EAST ASIAN CONTEXTS (2005)

James Garrett
Kiksapa Consultants
LAKOTA RELIGIOUS TRADITIONS (2005)

Giulia Sfameni Gasparro
University of Messina
DEMETER AND PERSEPHONE (2005)
GODDESS WORSHIP: GODDESS WORSHIP IN THE HELLENISTIC WORLD (2005)

Theodor H. Gaster
Barnard College, Columbia University (emeritus)
AMULETS AND TALISMANS (1987)
DRAMA: ANCIENT NEAR EASTERN RITUAL DRAMA [FIRST EDITION] (1987)
MONSTERS (1987)
SEASONAL CEREMONIES (1987)

Albertine Gaur
British Library
CALLIGRAPHY: AN OVERVIEW (2005)

Edwin S. Gaustad
University of California, Riverside
BAPTIST CHURCHES (1987)
WHITEFIELD, GEORGE (1987 AND 2005)
WISE, JOHN (1987 AND 2005)

Liam Gearon
Centre for Research in Human Rights, Roehampton University
HUMAN RIGHTS AND RELIGION (2005)

Patrick J. Geary
University of Florida
CULT OF SAINTS (1987)

Armin W. Geertz
Aarhus Universitet
ICONOGRAPHY: NATIVE NORTH AMERICAN ICONOGRAPHY (1987)

Jay Geller
Vanderbilt Divinity School
FETISHISM (2005)

Paul Gendrop
Mexico City
PYRAMIDS: AN OVERVIEW (1987)
TEMPLE: MESOAMERICAN TEMPLES (1987)

Joachim Gentz
University of Goettingen
DONG ZHONGSHU (2005)

Jane S. Gerber
Graduate School and University Center, City University of New York
JUDAISM: JUDAISM IN THE MIDDLE EAST AND NORTH AFRICA SINCE 1492 (1987 AND 2005)

David Germano
University of Virginia
BUDDHIST MEDITATION: TIBETAN BUDDHIST MEDITATION (2005)
DZOGCHEN (2005)
KLONG CHEN RAB 'BYAMS PA (LONGCHENPA) (2005)

Edwn Gerow
University of Chicago
BĀDARĀYAṆA (1987)

B. A. Gerrish
University of Chicago
BAUR, F. C. (1987)
CREEDS: CHRISTIAN CREEDS (1987)
ERASMUS, DESIDERIUS (1987)
SCHLEIERMACHER, FRIEDRICH (1987)

Alan Gewirth
University of Chicago
MARSILIUS OF PADUA (1987)

Philip Gibbs
Melanesian Institute, Papua New Guinea
OCEANIC RELIGIONS: NEW RELIGIOUS MOVEMENTS (2005)
RITES OF PASSAGE: OCEANIC RITES (2005)

Michelle Gilbert
Peabody Museum of Natural History, New Haven
AKAN RELIGION (1987)
FON AND EWE RELIGION (1987)

Sam D. Gill
University of Colorado at Boulder
PRAYER (1987)
SHAMANISM: NORTH AMERICAN SHAMANISM (1987)

Marija Gimbutas
University of California, Los Angeles
BABA YAGA (1987)
DAZHBOG (1987)
DOUBLENESS (1987)
MEGALITHIC RELIGION: PREHISTORIC EVIDENCE (1987)
MOKOSH (1987)
PERUN (1987)
PREHISTORIC RELIGIONS: OLD EUROPE (1987)
SLAVIC RELIGION (1987)
SVENTOVIT (1987)
TRIGLAV (1987)
VELES-VOLOS (1987)

Robert M. Gimello
University of Arizona
HUAYAN (1987)

Jean-Louis Girard
Université de Strasbourg II
MINERVA (1987)

Norman J. Girardot
Lehigh University
CHAOS (1987)
CHINESE RELIGION: HISTORY OF STUDY (1987)
CHINESE RELIGION: MYTHIC THEMES (1987)
GRANET, MARCEL (1987)
VISUAL CULTURE AND RELIGION: OUTSIDER ART (2005)

Yehoshua Gitay
Ben-Gurion University of the Negev
AMOS (1987)
HOSEA (1987)
ISAIAH (1987)
MICAH (1987)

Stephen D. Glazier
Westmont College
CARIBBEAN RELIGIONS: PRE-COLUMBIAN RELIGIONS (1987)

Elisabeth G. Gleason
University of San Francisco
CONTARINI, GASPARO (1987)

Rod M. Glogower
Georgetown Synagogue, Washington, D.C.
FEINSTEIN, MOSHE (1987)

Ariel Glucklich
Georgetown University
DHARMA: HINDU DHARMA (2005)
MAGIC: MAGIC IN SOUTH ASIA (2005)
PAIN (2005)

Gherardo Gnoli
Instituto Italiano per il Medio ed Estremo Oriente, Rome
AHURAS (1987)
AIRYANA VAĒJAH (1987)
AMESHA SPENTAS (1987)
ANĀHITĀ (1987)
AVESTA (1987)
CHINVAT BRIDGE (1987)
DAIVAS (1987)
DAKHMA (1987)
FRASHŌKERETI (1987)
FRAVASHIS (1987)
HAOMA (1987)
IRANIAN RELIGIONS (1987)
KHVARENAH (1987)
MANICHAEISM: AN OVERVIEW (1987)
MITHRA (1987)
SAOSHYANT (1987)
TUCCI, GIUSEPPE (1987)
YAZATAS (1987)

John C. Godbey
Meadville/Lombard Theological Seminary, Chicago
CHANNING, WILLIAM ELLERY, (1987)
HUS, JAN (1987)
SERVETUS, MICHAEL (1987)
SOZZINI, FAUSTO PAVOLO (1987)
UNITARIAN UNIVERSALIST ASSOCIATION (1987)

John D. Godsey
Wesley Theological Seminary, Washington, D.C.
NEOORTHODOXY (1987)

Gregor T. Goethals
Rhode Island School of Design
RELIGIOUS BROADCASTING (1987)

William E. Gohlman
State University of New York, College at Genesco
IBN SĪNĀ (1987 AND 2005)

Daniel Gold
Cornell University
CELIBACY (1987 AND 2005)
CONSECRATION (1987 AND 2005)

Harvey E. Goldberg
Hebrew University of Jerusalem
RITES OF PASSAGE: JEWISH RITES (2005)

Robert Goldenberg
State University of New York at Stony Brook
ABBAHU (1987)
EL'AZAR BEN PEDAT (1987)
SHIM'ON BEN LAQISH (1987)
TALMUD (1987 AND 2005)
YEHOSHU'A BEN LEVI (1987)
YOḤANAN BAR NAPPAḤA' (1987)

Judah Goldin
University of Pennsylvania
MIDRASH AND AGGADAH [FIRST EDITION] (1987)

Matt Goldish
Ohio State University
SHABBETAI TSEVI [FURTHER CONSIDERATIONS] (2005)

Irving Goldman
New School for Social Research, New York
GENEALOGY (1987)

Marion S. Goldman
Professor of Sociology and Religious tudies, University of Oregon
RAJNEESH (2005)

Maria Julia Goldwasser
Museu Historico da Circade do Rio de Janeiro
CARNIVAL (1987)

Luis O. Gómez
University of Michigan, Ann Arbor
BUDDHISM: BUDDHISM IN INDIA (1987)
BUDDHIST BOOKS AND TEXTS: EXEGESIS AND HERMENEUTICS (1987 AND 2005)
LANGUAGE: BUDDHIST VIEWS OF LANGUAGE (1987)
MAHĀSĀṂGHIKA (1987)
SARVĀSTIVĀDA (1987)

Jan Gonda
Rijksuniversiteit te Utrecht
INDIAN RELIGIONS: AN OVERVIEW (1987)
VIṢṆU (1987)

Michelle A. Gonzalez
Loyola Marymount University, Los Angeles
JUANA INÉS DE LA CRUZ DE ASBAJE Y RAMIREZ (2005)

David Goodblatt
University of Maryland at College Park
SANHEDRIN (1987)

Felicitas D. Goodman
Cuyamungue Institute, Columbus, Ohio
GLOSSOLALIA (1987)
VISIONS (1987)

L. E. Goodman
University of Hawaii, Manoa
IBN BĀJJAH (1987)

H. McKennie Goodpasture
Union Theological Seminary, Richmond, Virginia
AUGUSTINE OF CANTERBURY (1987)
CLOTILDA (1987)
CYRIL AND METHODIUS (1987)
PATRICK (1987)

Peter Goodrich
Cardozo School of Law, New York
LAW AND RELIGION: LAW, RELIGION, AND CRITICAL THEORY (2005)

Vincent Goossaert
Centre National de la Recherche Scientifique, Paris
CHINESE RELIGION: POPULAR RELIGION (2005)

Richard Gordon
Ilmmünster, Germany
MITHRAISM (2005)

René Gothóni
University of Helsinki
CONFESSION OF SINS (2005)
SUNDÉN, HJALMAR (2005)

Stephen Gottschalk
Wellesley, Massachusetts
CHRISTIAN SCIENCE (1987)

Teun Goudriaan
Rijksuniversiteit te Utrecht
MĀYĀ (1987)

Friedrich Wilhelm Graf
Ludwig-Maximilians-Universität München
TROELTSCH, ERNST (1987)

Fritz Graf
Ohio State University
APOLLO (2005)
ARTEMIS (2005)
ELEUSINIAN MYSTERIES (1987)
EMPEDOCLES (2005)
HERAKLES (2005)
HOMER (2005)
SYNCRETISM [FURTHER CONSIDERATIONS] (2005)
VIOLENCE (2005)
ZEUS (2005)

William A. Graham
Harvard University
SCRIPTURE (1987 AND 2005)

Patrick Granfield
Catholic University of America
PAPACY (1987 AND 2005)

Robert M. Grant
University of Chicago
EUSEBIUS (1987)
GOODENOUGH, ERWIN R. (1987)
NOCK, ARTHUR DARBY (1987)

Allan G. Grapard
East-West Center, Honolulu, Hawaii
ENCHIN (1987)
HONJISUIJAKU (1987)

William Grassie
Metanexus Institute, Philadelphia
ECOLOGY AND RELIGION: SCIENCE, RELIGION, AND ECOLOGY (2005)

David B. Gray
Rice University
CAKRASAMVARA (2005)
GUHYASAMĀJA (2005)
HEVAJRA (2005)

Elizabeth A. Gray
Harvard University
FOMHOIRE (2005)
LUGH (2005)
TUATHA DÉ DANANN (2005)

S. J. M. Gray
College of Wooster
EAGLES AND HAWKS (1987)
TREES (1987)

Richard L. Greaves
Florida State University
BUNYAN, JOHN (1987)

Arthur Green
Reconstructionist Rabbinical College
DOV BER OF MEZHIRICH (1987)
ELIMELEKH OF LIZHENSK (1987)
HASIDISM: HABAD HASIDISM (1987)
HASIDISM: SATMAR HASIDISM (1987)
LEVI YITSḤAQ OF BERDICHEV (1987)
NAḤMAN OF BRATSLAV (1987)
SHNE'UR ZALMAN OF LYADY (1987)

Garrett Green
Connecticut College
FICHTE, JOHANN GOTTLIEB (1987)

Ronald M. Green
Dartmouth College
MORALITY AND RELIGION (1987)
THEODICY (1987)

Tamara M. Green
Hunter College, City University of New York
ICONOGRAPHY: GRECO-ROMAN ICONOGRAPHY (1987)

Blu Greenberg
Riverdale, New York
SCHENIRER, SARAH (1987)

Moshe Greenberg
Hebrew University of Jerusalem
EZEKIEL (1987)

Samuel Greengus
Hebrew Union College-Jewish Institute of Religion, Cincinnati
ISRAELITE LAW: CRIMINAL LAW (1987)

Frederick E. Greenspahn
Florida Atlantic University
ISAAC (1987 AND 2005)
ISHMAEL (1987 AND 2005)
JACOB (1987 AND 2005)
JOSEPH (1987 AND 2005)
RACHEL AND LEAH (1987 AND 2005)
REBECCA (1987 AND 2005)
SARAH (2005)

Edward L. Greenstein
Tel Aviv University
AARON (1987)
CYRUS II (1987 AND 2005)
JOSHUA (1987 AND 2005)
MIRIAM (1987 AND 2005)
PSALMS (1987 AND 2005)
SAMSON (1987 AND 2005)

Peter N. Gregory
University of Illinois, Urbana-Champaign
ZONGMI (1987)

J. Gwyn Griffiths
University College of Swansea
HELLENISTIC RELIGIONS (1987)

Laura S. Grillo
Pacifica Graduate Institute, Carpinteria, California
GRIAULE, MARCEL (2005)
DIETERLEN, GERMAINE (2005)

John A. Grim
Bucknell University
ECOLOGY AND RELIGION: AN OVERVIEW (2005)

ECOLOGY AND RELIGION: ECOLOGY AND INDIGENOUS TRADITIONS (2005)
NORTH AMERICAN INDIANS: INDIANS OF THE NORTHEAST WOODLANDS (1987 AND 2005)
WOVOKA (1987)

Ronald L. Grimes
Wilfrid Laurier University
PORTALS (1987)
PROCESSION (1987)

Eric W. Gritsch
Lutheran Theological Seminary, Gettysburg, Pennsylvania
LUTHERANISM (1987)
MÜNTZER, THOMAS (1987)

Paul Groner
University of Virginia
SAICHŌ (1987 AND 2005)
TENDAISHŪ (2005)

Claudia Gross
University of Auckland
KINSHIP (2005)

Lawrence W. Gross
Iowa State University
ANISHINAABE RELIGIOUS TRADITIONS (2005)

Rita M. Gross
University of Wisconsin—Eau Claire
BIRTH (1987 AND 2005)
COUVADE (1987)
FEMINIST THEOLOGY: AN OVERVIEW (2005)
GENDER AND RELIGION: GENDER AND BUDDHISM (2005)

Cristiano Grottanelli
Università degli studi, Rome
AGRICULTURE (1987)
DRAGONS (1987)
KINGSHIP: KINGSHIP IN THE ANCIENT MEDITERRANEAN WORLD (1987)

Vinigi Grottanelli
Università degli Studi, Rome
AFRICAN RELIGIONS: HISTORY OF STUDY (1987)

Jean Guiart
Musée de l'Homme, Paris
NEW CALEDONIA RELIGION (1987)
OCEANIC RELIGIONS: AN OVERVIEW (2005)
OCEANIC RELIGIONS: MISSIONARY MOVEMENTS (1987 AND 2005)

Charles Guittard
University of Paris X-Nanterre
FORTUNA (2005)
JUPITER (2005)
MARS (2005)
VESTA (2005)

Natalie Gummer
Beloit College
BUDDHIST BOOKS AND TEXTS: RITUAL USES OF BOOKS (2005)
BUDDHIST BOOKS AND TEXTS: TRANSLATION (2005)

Sanjukta Gupta
Oxford University
HINDU TANTRIC LITERATURE (1987 AND 2005)
JĪVANMUKTI (1987)
MUDRĀ (2005)

Veronica Gutiérrez
Pennsylvania State University
MESOAMERICAN RELIGIONS: COLONIAL CULTURES (2005)

Joseph Gutmann
Wayne State University
MAGEN DAVID (1987)
SYNAGOGUE (1987)

Christian-J. Guyonvarc'h
Université de Haute Bretagne
EPONA (1987)
MAPONOS (1987)
MATRES (1987)

Janet Gyatso
Harvard University
MA GCIG LAB SGRON (MACHIG LABDRON) (2005)
TREASURE TRADITION (2005)
YE SHES MTSHO RGYAL (YESHE TSOGYAL) (2005)

David L. Haberman
University of Arizona
ROY, RAM MOHAN (1987)
VṚNDĀVANA (1987)

JaHyun Kim Haboush
University of Illinois, Urbana-Champaign
CONFUCIANISM IN KOREA (1987)
YI T'OEGYE (1987)
YI YULGOK (1987)

Sergei Hackel
University of Sussex
AKSAKOV, IVAN (1987)
AVVAKUM (1987)
DOSTOEVSKY, FYODOR (1987)
FILARET OF MOSCOW (1987)
JOSEPH OF VOLOKOLAMSK (1987)
KHOMIAKOV, ALEKSEI (1987)
KIREEVSKII, IVAN (1987)
NIKON (1987)
SERGII OF RADONEZH (1987)
SKOBTSOVA, MARIA (2005)
SORSKII, NIL (1987)

Rosalind I. J. Hackett
University of Tennessee, Knoxville
LAW AND RELIGION: LAW, RELIGION, AND HUMAN RIGHTS (2005)

Wadi Z. Haddad
Hartford Seminary
TAFTĀZĀNĪ, AL- (1987)

Haga Noboru
University of Tsukuba
ISHIDA BAIGAN (1987)
KAMO NO MABUCHI (1987)

Howard G. Hageman
New Brunswick Theological Seminary, New Brunswick, New Jersey
THOMAS À KEMPIS (1987)

Syed Gulzar Haider
Carleton University, Ottawa, Canada
MOSQUE: HISTORY AND TRADITION (2005)

Getatchew Haile
Saint John's University, Collegeville, Minnesota
ETHIOPIAN CHURCH (1987)

Hamid Haji
Institute of Ismaili Studies, London
QĀḌĪ AL-NU'MĀN (2005)

Hans Thomas Hakl
Graz, Austria
EVOLA, JULIUS (2005)
SEXUALITY: SEXUAL RITES IN EUROPE (2005)

Wilhelm Halbfass
University of Pennsylvania
INDIAN RELIGIONS: HISTORY OF STUDY (1987)

Bruce Cameron Hall
University of Michigan, Ann Arbor
STCHERBATSKY, THEODORE (1987)

Nathan J. Hallanger
Graduate Theological Union
EUGENICS (2005)

Barry Hallen
Morehouse College and Du Bois Institute, Harvard University

COSMOLOGY: AFRICAN COSMOLOGIES (2005)

Charles Hallisey
University of Wisconsin—Madison
BUDDHA (1987)
BUDDHISM: AN OVERVIEW (1987)
DUṬṬHAGĀMAṆĪ (1987)
PĀRAMITĀS (1987)

Christopher R. Hallpike
Dalhousie University
HAIR (1987)

J. Mark Halstead
University of Plymouth, United Kingdom
RELIGIOUS EDUCATION (2005)

Roberte Hamayon
École Pratique des Hautes Études, Collège de France
BURIAT RELIGION (1987)
ONGON (1987)
SOUTHERN SIBERIAN RELIGIONS (1987)

Charles H. Hambrick
Vanderbilt University
OKINAWAN RELIGION (1987)

Feras Q. Hamza
Institute of Ismaili Studies, London
AFTERLIFE: ISLAMIC CONCEPTS (2005)
RĀZĪ, FAKHR AL-DĪN AL- (2005)

William L. Hanaway, Jr.
University of Pennsylvania
DRAMA: MIDDLE EASTERN NARRATIVE TRADITIONS (1987)

Don Handelman
Hebrew University of Jerusalem
CLOWNS (1987 AND 2005)
PLAY (1987 AND 2005)

Robert T. Handy
Union Theological Seminary, New York (emeritus)
WILLIAMS, ROGER (1987)

Wouter J. Hanegraaff
University of Amsterdam
NEW AGE MOVEMENT (2005)

Thomas O'Brien Hanley
Loyola College in Maryland
CARROLL, JOHN (1987)

Judith Lynne Hanna
University of Maryland, College Park
DANCE: DANCE AND RELIGION (1987 AND 2005)

Anne Hansen
University of Wisconsin—Milwaukee
KHMER RELIGION (2005)

Klaus J. Hansen
Queen's University, Canada
MORMONISM (1987 AND 2005)
SMITH, JOSEPH (1987 AND 2005)

F. Allan Hanson
University of Kansas
MAORI RELIGION [FIRST EDITION] (1987)
POLYNESIAN RELIGIONS: AN OVERVIEW (1987)

S. Nomanul Haq
Philadelphia, Pennsylvania
FĀRĀBĪ, AL- (2005)

Stanley Samuel Harakas
Holy Cross Greek Orthodox School of Theology, Brookline, Massachusetts (emeritus)
BULGAKOV, SERGEI (1987)
CHRISTIANITY: CHRISTIANITY IN EASTERN EUROPE (1987 AND 2005)
GREEK ORTHODOX CHURCH (1987)
JOHN OF DAMASCUS (1987)

Helen Hardacre
Princeton University
ANCESTORS: ANCESTOR WORSHIP (1987)
KONKŌKYŌ (1987)
REIYŪKAI KYŌDAN (1987)

Rachel E. Harding
Iliff School of Theology, Denver, Colorado
AFRO-BRAZILIAN RELIGIONS (2005)

O. B. Hardison, Jr.
Folger Shakespeare Library, Washington, D.C.
DRAMA: EUROPEAN RELIGIOUS DRAMA [FIRST EDITION] (1987)

Charlotte E. Hardman
University of Durham
NEW RELIGIOUS MOVEMENTS: NEW RELIGIOUS MOVEMENTS AND CHILDREN (2005)

Friedhelm E. Hardy
King's College, University of London
ĀḺVĀRS (1987)
KṚṢṆAISM (1987)

Bernhard Häring
Pontificia Universitas Lateranensis
TEMPTATION (1987)

Gail M. Harley
University of South Florida, Tampa, Florida
FILLMORE, CHARLES AND MYRTLE (2005)
HOPKINS, EMMA CURTIS (2005)
UNITY (2005)

David Harnish
Bowling Green State University
MUSIC: MUSIC AND RELIGION IN SOUTHEAST ASIA (2005)

Donald Harper
Stanford University
MAGIC: MAGIC IN EAST ASIA (1987)

Marilyn J. Harran
Chapman College
SUICIDE (1987)

Stevan Harrell
University of Washington
DOMESTIC OBSERVANCES: CHINESE PRACTICES (1987)

David Edwin Harrell, Jr.
University of Arkansas
CAMPBELL, ALEXANDER (1987)
DISCIPLES OF CHRIST (1987)

Walter Harrelson
Vanderbilt University (emeritus)
MYTH AND RITUAL SCHOOL (1987 AND 2005)
TEN COMMANDMENTS (1987)
TITHES (1987 AND 2005)

Amanda Nolacea Harris
University of Illinois, Urbana-Champaign
ZAPATISMO AND INDIGENOUS RESISTANCE (2005)

Ishwar C. Harris
College of Wooster
BHAVE, VINOBA (1987)

Joseph Harris
Harvard University
THOR (2005)

Kevin Hart
University of Notre Dame
FICTION: OCEANIC FICTION AND RELIGION (2005)
LITERATURE: RELIGIOUS DIMENSIONS OF MODERN WESTERN LITERATURE [FURTHER CONSIDERATIONS] (2005)

Jens-Uwe Hartmann
Institut für Indologie und Iranistik, Munich

BUDDHISM: BUDDHISM IN CENTRAL ASIA (2005)

Charles Hartshorne
University of Texas at Austin (emeritus)
PANTHEISM AND PANENTHEISM (1987)
TRANSCENDENCE AND IMMANENCE (1987)

Van A. Harvey
Stanford University
BAUER, BRUNO (1987 AND 2005)
FEUERBACH, LUDWIG (1987 AND 2005)
HERMENEUTICS (1987 AND 2005)
STRAUSS, DAVID FRIEDRICH (1987 AND 2005)

Warren Zev Harvey
Hebrew University of Jerusalem
CRESCAS, ḤASDAI (1987 AND 2005)

Edeltraud Harzer
University of Texas at Austin
PRAKṚTI (1987 AND 2005)
PURUṢA (1987 AND 2005)
SĀṂKHYA (1987 AND 2005)

Hase Shōtō
Kyoto University
JŌDO SHINSHŪ (1987)

Adrian Hastings
University of Leeds
CHRISTIANITY: CHRISTIANITY IN SUB-SAHARAN AFRICA [FIRST EDITION] (1987)

Sachiko Hatanaka
Chubu University
TANGAROA (1987)

Brian A. Hatcher
Illinois Wesleyan University
RAMAKRISHNA (2005)
VIVEKANANDA (2005)

Hattori Masaaki
Professor Emeritus, Kyoto University
ASAṄGA (1987)
DIGNĀGA (1987)
YOGĀCĀRA (1987 AND 2005)

Hanna Havnevik
University of Oslo
ANI LOCHEN (2005)

Peter S. Hawkins
Yale University
DANTE ALIGHIERI (1987)
POETRY: CHRISTIAN POETRY (1987)

John Stratton Hawley
Barnard College, Columbia University
HINDI RELIGIOUS TRADITIONS (1987 AND 2005)
KṚṢṆA (1987 AND 2005)
SŪRDĀS (2005)

Sîan Hawthorne
University of London
FEMINISM: FEMINISM, GENDER STUDIES, AND RELIGION (2005)
GENDER AND RELIGION: HISTORY OF STUDY (2005)
GYNOCENTRISM (2005)

Perwaiz Hayat
Concordia University, Montreal
DĀRĀ SHIKŌH, MUḤAMMAD (2005)

Zachary Hayes
Catholic Theological Union, Chicago, Illinois
BONAVENTURE (1987)

Charles C. Haynes
First Amendment Center
MEHER BABA (1987 AND 2005)

Jeffrey Haynes
London Metropolitan University
POLITICS AND RELIGION: POLITICS AND AFRICAN RELIGIOUS TRADITIONS (2005)

Thomas N. Headland
University of Hawaii, Manoa
NEGRITO RELIGIONS: NEGRITOS OF THE PHILIPPINE ISLANDS (1987)

John F. Healey
University of Manchester
NABATEAN RELIGION (2005)

John J. Heaney
Fordham University, Bronx (emeritus)
HÜGEL, FRIEDRICH VON (1987 AND 2005)

Jan C. Heesterman
Rijksuniversiteit te Leiden
BRAHMAN (1987)
BRĀHMAṆAS AND ĀRAṆYAKAS (1987)
VEDISM AND BRAHMANISM (1987)

Synnøve Heggem
University of Oslo
GRUNDTVIG, NIKOLAI FREDERIK SEVERIN (2005)

Samuel C. Heilman
Queens College City University of New York
ORTHODOX JUDAISM: FURTHER CONSIDERATIONS (2005)

Maria Heim
Amherst College
ALMSGIVING (2005)
BUDDHIST ETHICS (2005)

Norvin Hein
Yale University
LĪLĀ (1987)

Steven Heine
Florida International University
ZEN (2005)

Walther Heissig
Rheinische Friedrich-Wilhelms-Universität Bonn
MONGOL RELIGIONS (1987)

James Heitzman
Georgia State University
CITIES (2005)

Natasha Heller
Harvard University
POLITICS AND RELIGION: POLITICS AND CHINESE RELIGION (2005)

Monika K. Hellwig
Georgetown University
EUCHARIST (1987)
SACRAMENT: CHRISTIAN SACRAMENTS (1987)

Ronald S. Hendel
University of California, Berkeley
ISRAELITE RELIGION (2005)

Joseph Henninger
Anthropos-Institut, Sankt Augustin, West Germany
GRAEBNER, FRITZ (1987)
NEW YEAR FESTIVALS (1987)
SACRIFICE [FIRST EDITION] (1987)
SCHMIDT, WILHELM (1987)

Robert G. Henricks
Dartmouth College
DEMIÉVILLE, PAUL (1987)
GROOT, J. J. M. DE (1987)

William E. Herbrechtsmeier
Los Angeles, California
PROPHECY: AN OVERVIEW (1987)

Gilbert Herdt
University of Chicago
HOMOSEXUALITY (1987)

Nimachia Hernandez
University of California, Berkeley
BLACKFEET RELIGIOUS TRADITIONS (2005)

Noreen L. Herzfeld
St. John's University, Collegeville, Minnesota
ARTIFICIAL INTELLIGENCE (2005)
CYBERNETICS (2005)

Linda Hess
Radcliffe College
POETRY: INDIAN RELIGIOUS POETRY (1987)

Peter M. J. Hess
Berkeley, California
COPERNICUS, NICOLAUS (2005)
TWO BOOKS, THE (2005)

Luc de Heusch
Université Libre de Bruxelles
SOUTHERN AFRICAN RELIGIONS: SOUTHERN BANTU RELIGIONS (1987)

Julia Cuervo Hewitt
Pennsylvania State University
FICTION: LATIN AMERICAN FICTION AND RELIGION (2005)

Martinez Hewlett
Dominican School of Philosophy and Theology
EVOLUTION: EVOLUTIONISM (2005)
EVOLUTION: THE CONTROVERSY WITH CREATIONISM (2005)

Doris Heyden
Instituto Nacional de Antropología e Historia, Mexico City
CAVES (1987)
MESOAMERICAN RELIGIONS: CLASSIC CULTURES (1987)
MESOAMERICAN RELIGIONS: MYTHIC THEMES (1987)

John C. Higgins-Biddle
University of Conneticut Health Center
LOCKE, JOHN (1987 AND 2005)

Donald R. Hill
State University of New York, College at Oneonta
MAGIC: MAGIC IN INDIGENOUS SOCIETIES (1987)

William J. Hill
Catholic University of America
ATTRIBUTES OF GOD: CHRISTIAN CONCEPTS (1987)
PROOFS FOR THE EXISTENCE OF GOD (1987)

Hans J. Hillerbrand
Southern Methodist University
LUTHER, MARTIN (1987)
REFORMATION (1987)

Gregory A. Hillis
University of California, Santa Barbara
BUDDHIST MEDITATION: TIBETAN BUDDHIST MEDITATION
KLONG CHEN RAB 'BYAMS PA (LONGCHENPA) (2005)

Alf Hiltebeitel
George Washington University
ARJUNA (1987)
GAMBLING (1987)
HINDUISM (1987)
INDUS VALLEY RELIGION (1987)
KURUKṢETRA (1987)
MAHĀBHĀRATA (1987)

Teresia Mbari Hinga
DePaul University
AFTERLIFE: AFRICAN CONCEPTS (2005)

Melinda Hinkson
Australian National University
STANNER, W. E. H. (2005)

TJ Hinrichs
Harvard University
HEALING AND MEDICINE: HEALING AND MEDICINE IN CHINA (2005)

E. Glenn Hinson
Southern Baptist Theological Seminary
CONSTANTINIANISM (1987)
IRENAEUS (1987)
JUSTIN MARTYR (1987)
TERTULLIAN (1987)

Almut Hintze
School of Oriental and African Studies, University of London
AHURA MAZDĀ AND ANGRA MAINYU (2005)

Dennis Hirota
Ryukoku University, Kyoto, Japan
KARMAN: BUDDHIST CONCEPTS (2005)

Hirota Masaki
Okayama University
KUROZUMIKYŌ (1987)

Stephen Hirtenstein
Oxford, United Kingdom
IBN AL-'ARABĪ (2005)

Mervyn Hiskett
Kent, England
DAN FODIO, USUMAN (1987)

Miriam Hoexter
Hebrew University of Jerusalem
WAQF (2005)

Lawrence A. Hoffman
Hebrew Union College–Jewish Institute of Religion, New York
LITURGY (2005)
SIDDUR AND MAḤZOR (1987)

Harry A. Hoffner, Jr.
University of Chicago
HITTITE RELIGION (1987)
TESHUB (1987)

W. Hofstee
Leiden University, The Netherlands
BAAL, JAN VAN (2005)

Eugene W. Holland
Ohio State University
PSYCHOLOGY: SCHIZOANALYSIS AND RELIGION (2005)

Tawny L. Holm
University of Pennsylvania
ASTARTE (2005)
DAVID [FURTHER CONSIDERATIONS] (2005)
MOABITE RELIGION (2005)
PHOENICIAN RELIGION [FURTHER CONSIDERATIONS] (2005)
WISDOM LITERATURE: BIBLICAL BOOKS [FURTHER CONSIDERATIONS] (2005)

John Clifford Holt
Bowdoin College
PRIESTHOOD: BUDDHIST PRIESTHOOD (1987 AND 2005)

Peter Homans
University of Chicago
FREUD, SIGMUND (1987 AND 2005)
JUNG, C. G. (1987)

Lauri Honko
Turun Yliopisto
FINNO-UGRIC RELIGIONS: AN OVERVIEW (1987)

Walter Hooper
Oxford, England
LEWIS, C. S. (1987)

Stewart M. Hoover
University of Colorado at Boulder
MEDIA AND RELIGION (2005)

Paul Jeffrey Hopkins
University of Virginia
DGE LUGS PA (1987 AND 2005)

Thomas J. Hopkins
Franklin and Marshall College
ĀRYA SAMĀJ (1987)
BRĀHMO SAMĀJ (1987)
DAYANANDA SARASVATI (1987)
INDUS VALLEY RELIGION (1987)
SAURA HINDUISM (1987)
VIVEKANANDA (1987)

Thomas Hopko
Saint Vladimir's Orthodox Theological Seminary, Crestwood, New York
FLORENSKII, PAVEL (1987)
IOANN OF KRONSTADT (1987)
RUSSIAN ORTHODOX CHURCH (1987)
TIKHON OF ZADONSK (1987)
VLADIMIR I (1987)

Mihály Hoppál
Magyar Tudományos Akadémia, Budapest
FINNO-UGRIC RELIGIONS: HISTORY OF STUDY (1987)

Bretislav Horyna
Masaryk-University Brno, Czech Republic
STUDY OF RELIGION: THE ACADEMIC STUDY OF RELIGION IN EASTERN EUROPE AND RUSSIA (2005)

Hoshino Eiki
Taisho University
PILGRIMAGE: BUDDHIST PILGRIMAGE IN EAST ASIA (1987)

Albert Hourani
University of Oxford (emeritus)
AFGHĀNĪ, JAMĀL AL-DĪN AL- (1987)
RASHĪD RIḌĀ, MUḤAMMAD (1987)

John F. Howes
University of British Columbia
KAGAWA TOYOHIKO (1987)
UCHIMURA KANZŌ (1987)

C. Julia Huang
National Tsing Hua University, Taiwan
CIJI (2005)

Tracey E. Hucks
Haverford, Pennsylvania
AFRICAN AMERICAN RELIGIONS: HISTORY OF STUDY (2005)

Clarke Hudson
Indiana University
BUDDHIST MEDITATION: EAST ASIAN BUDDHIST MEDITATION (2005)

D. Dennis Hudson
Smith College
PIḶḶAI LOKĀCĀRYA (1987)

Winthrop S. Hudson
University of North Carolina at Chapel Hill
DENOMINATIONALISM (1987)

R. I. G. Hughes
Yale University
BACON, FRANCIS (1987)

Stephen Hugh-Jones
University of Cambridge
YURUPARY (1987)

Åke Hultkrantz
Stockholms Universitet
ARCTIC RELIGIONS: AN OVERVIEW (1987)
ARCTIC RELIGIONS: HISTORY OF STUDY (1987)
GHOST DANCE (1987)
NORTH AMERICAN [INDIAN] RELIGIONS: AN OVERVIEW (1987)

S. C. Humphreys
University of Michigan, Ann Arbor
FUSTEL DE COULANGES, N. D. (1987)

John O. Hunwick
Northwestern University
MUḤAMMAD AḤMAD (1987)

Manfred Hutter
University of Bonn, Germany
BĀBĪS (2005)
BAHĀʾĪS (2005)
MANICHAEISM: MANICHAEISM IN IRAN (2005)

Kathryn Hutton
New York, New York
LIONS (1987)

Syed Akbar Hyder
University of Texas at Austin
KARBALA (2005)

Ibrahim I. Ibrahim
Georgetown University
ʿABD AL-RĀZIQ, ʿALĪ (1987)

Moshe Idel
Hebrew University of Jerusalem
QABBALAH (1987)
SEFER YETSIRAH (1987)
ZOHAR (1987)

John M. Ingham
University of Minnesota, Twin Cities
NAHUATL RELIGION (1987)

Marcia C. Inhorn
University of Michigan, Ann Arbor
HEALING AND MEDICINE: POPULAR HEALING PRACTICES IN MIDDLE EASTERN CULTURES (2005)

Massimo Introvigne
Center for Studies in New Religions, Torino, Italy
CULTS AND SECTS (2005)
MOVEMENT FOR THE RESTORATION OF THE TEN COMMANDMENTS OF GOD (2005)
TEMPLE SOLAIRE (2005)

Ishida Ichirō
Tohoku University
AME NO KOYANE (1987)
KOKUGAKU (1987)

Benjamin Ish-Shalom
Bar Ilan University, Beit Morasha of Jerusalem, and Institute for Jewish Studies
KOOK, AVRAHAM YITSḤAQ (2005)

Isomae Jun'ichi
Japan Women's University
ANESAKI MASAHARU (2005)
JAPANESE RELIGIONS: THE STUDY OF MYTHS (2005)
YAMATO TAKERU (2005)

Philip J. Ivanhoe
Boston University
MENGZI (2005)

Julia Iwersen
Hamburg, Germany
GIMBUTAS, MARIJA (2005)
GNOSTICISM: GNOSTICISM FROM THE MIDDLE AGES TO THE PRESENT (2005)
LIGHT AND DARKNESS (2005)
VIRGIN GODDESS (2005)

Fahir İz
Boğaziçi Üniversitesi
YUNUS EMRE (1987)

Toshihiko Izutsu
Keio University
ISHRĀQĪYAH (1987)

Roger R. Jackson
Carleton College
MAHĀMUDRĀ (2005)
SGAM PO PA (GAMPOPA) (2005)

Louis Jacobs
Leo Baeck College, London (emeritus)
ATTRIBUTES OF GOD: JEWISH CONCEPTS (1987)

GOD: GOD IN POSTBIBLICAL JUDAISM (1987 AND 2005)
ḤANUKKAH (1987)
JEWISH RELIGIOUS YEAR (1987)
PASSOVER (1987)
PURIM (1987)
RO'SH HA-SHANAH AND YOM KIPPUR (1987)
SHABBAT (1987)
SHAVU'OT (1987)
SUKKOT (1987)

Thorkild Jacobsen
Harvard University (emeritus)
FRANKFORT, HENRI (1987)
MESOPOTAMIAN RELIGIONS: AN OVERVIEW [FIRST EDITION] (1987)
MESOPOTAMIAN RELIGIONS: HISTORY OF STUDY (1987)
NINHURSAGA (1987)

David C. Jacobson
Brown University
AGNON, SHEMU'EL YOSEF (2005)

Martin S. Jaffee
University of Washington
DISCIPLESHIP (2005)
ORAL TORAH (2005)
TORAH (2005)

George Alfred James
University of North Texas
ATHEISM (1987 AND 2005)
SALUTATIONS (1987 AND 2005)

John M. Janzen
University of Kansas
AFFLICTION: AFRICAN CULTS OF AFFLICTION (1987 AND 2005)
KONGO RELIGION (1987)

E. H. Rick Jarow
Vassar College
PURĀṆAS (2005)

David Jasper
University of Glasgow
LITERATURE: CRITICAL THEORY AND RELIGIOUS STUDIES (2005)

Pupul Jayakar
Government of India, Department of Culture, New Delhi
INDIAN RELIGIONS: RURAL TRADITIONS (1987)

N. A. Jayawickrama
Buddhist and Pali University of Sri Lanka
MALALASEKERA, G. P. (1987)

James B. Jeffries
Colgate University
MANITOU (2005)

Daniel Jenkins
London, England
BROWNE, ROBERT (1987)
CONGREGATIONALISM (1987)

Theodore W. Jennings, Jr.
Seminario Metodista de México, Mexico City
SACRAMENT: AN OVERVIEW (1987)

Jeppe Sinding Jensen
University of Aarhus, Aarhus, Denmark
STRUCTURALISM [FURTHER CONSIDERATIONS] (2005)

Lionel M. Jensen
University of Notre Dame
CONFUCIANISM: HISTORY OF STUDY (2005)

Robert Jewett
Garrett-Evangelical Theological Seminary, Evanston, Illinois
PAUL THE APOSTLE (1987)

Ren Jiyu
Chinese Academy of Social Sciences, Peking
TANG YONGTONG (1987 AND 2005)

Darrell Jodock
Gustavus Adolphus College
BERGSON, HENRI (1987 AND 2005)

A. H. Johns
Australian National University
ISLAM: ISLAM IN SOUTHEAST ASIA (1987 AND 2005)
ṬARĪQAH (1987)

Greg Johnson
Franklin and Marshall College
LAW AND RELIGION: LAW AND RELIGION IN INDIGENOUS CULTURES (2005)

Paul Christopher Johnson
University of Michigan, Ann Arbor
GARIFUNA RELIGION (2005)
TRANSCULTURATION AND RELIGION: RELIGION IN THE FORMATION OF THE MODERN CARIBBEAN (2005)

Matthew V. Johnson, Sr.
Wake Forest University
BLACK THEOLOGY (2005)

Patricia A. Johnston
Brandeis University
VERGIL (2005)

Sarah Iles Johnston
Ohio State University
AFTERLIFE: GREEK AND ROMAN CONCEPTS (2005)
HEKATE (2005)
DIVINATION: GREEK AND ROMAN DIVINATION (2005)
ORPHIC GOLD TABLETS (2005)

Alan Jones
University of Oxford
IBĀḌIYYA (2005)

Albert de Jong
Leiden University
MAGI (2005)
ZARATHUSHTRA (2005)

Albert R. Jonsen
University of California, San Francisco
CASUISTRY (1987)

Dan W. Jorgensen
University of Western Ontario
OCEANIC RELIGIONS: HISTORY OF STUDY [FIRST EDITION] (1987)

George Joseph
Hobart and William Smith Colleges
FICTION: AFRICAN FICTION AND RELIGION (2005)

Mark Juergensmeyer
University of California, Santa Barbara
GANDHI, MOHANDAS (1987 AND 2005)
NONVIOLENCE (1987 AND 2005)

Bennetta Jules-Rosette
University of California, San Diego
KIMBANGU, SIMON (1987)
MARANKE, JOHN (1987)

Sylvia Juran
New York, New York
TOLSTOY, LEO (1987)

Lutz Kaelber
University of Vermont
MONASTICISM: CHRISTIAN MONASTICISM (2005)

Walter O. Kaelber
Wagner College
ASCETICISM (1987)
INITIATION: MEN'S INITIATION (1987)

Adrienne L. Kaeppler
Smithsonian Institution

POLYNESIAN RELIGIONS: MYTHIC THEMES (1987 AND 2005)

Henry Kahane
University of Illinois, Urbana-Champaign
ALCHEMY: HELLENISTIC AND MEDIEVAL ALCHEMY (1987)
GRAIL, THE (1987)

Renée Kahane
University of Illinois, Urbana-Champaign
ALCHEMY: HELLENISTIC AND MEDIEVAL ALCHEMY (1987)
GRAIL, THE (1987)

Kajiyama Yūichi
Kyoto University
MĀDHYAMIKA (1987)

Kakubayashi Fumio
Massey University
AMATERASU ŌMIKAMI (1987 AND 2005)
JIMMU (1987 AND 2005)
SUSANO-O NO MIKOTO (1987 AND 2005)

Ibrahim Kalin
College of the Holy Cross
MĀTURĪDĪ, AL- (2005)

Menachem Kallus
Bar Ilan University
TSADDIQ (2005)

Michael C. Kalton
Kansas State University
CHŎNG YAGYONG (1987)
SŎ KYŎNGDŎK (1987)

Ogbu Kalu
McCormick Theological Seminary
IGBO RELIGION (2005)

David J. Kalupahana
University of Hawaii, Manoa
PRATĪTYA-SAMUTPĀDA (1987)

Janet Kalven
Union Institute of Cincinnati
GRAIL MOVEMENT (2005)

Mohammad Hashim Kamali
Institute of Islamic Studies, McGill University
ḤADĪTH (2005)
ISLAMIC LAW: PERSONAL LAW (1987)
MADHHAB (1987)
QIYĀS (1987)

Edward Kamens
Yale University
KŪYA (1987 AND 2005)
ONMYŌDŌ (1987)

J. H. Kamstra
Universiteit van Amsterdam
EN NO GYŌJA (1987)
GYŌGI (1987)
HIJIRI (1987)
JINGŌ (1987)

Ephraim Kanarfogel
Yeshiva University
RABBINATE: THE RABBINATE IN PRE-MODERN JUDAISM (2005)
TOSAFOT [FURTHER CONSIDERATIONS] (2005)

Charles Kannengiesser
University of Notre Dame
ARIANISM (1987)
ATHANASIUS (1987)
ATHENAGORAS (1987)
CYRIL OF ALEXANDRIA (1987)

Flora Edouwaye S. Kaplan
New York University
EDO RELIGION (2005)

Martha Kaplan
Vassar College
CARGO CULTS [FURTHER CONSIDERATIONS] (2005)

Steven Kaplan
Hebrew University of Jerusalem
JUDAISM: JUDAISM IN NORTHEAST AFRICA (2005)

Matthew T. Kapstein
Paris, France
BUDDHISM: BUDDHISM IN TIBET (2005)
BUDDHISM, SCHOOLS OF: TANTRIC RITUAL SCHOOLS OF BUDDHISM [FURTHER CONSIDERATIONS] (2005)
BUDDHISM, SCHOOLS OF: TIBETAN AND MONGOLIAN BUDDHISM (2005)
PADMASAMBHAVA (2005)
RNYING MA PA (NYINGMAPA) SCHOOL (2005)
SAKYA PAṆḌITA (SA SKYA PAṆḌITA) (2005)

George Karahalios
Holy Cross Greek Orthodox School of Theology, Brookline, Massachusetts
PSELLUS, MICHAEL (1987)

Nicholas Karazafiris
Thessaloniki, Greece
MAXIMOS THE CONFESSOR (1987)

Abraham J. Karp
University of Rochester
LEESER, ISAAC (1987)
WISE, STEPHEN S. (1987)

Tazim R. Kassam
Syracuse University
ṢALĀT (2005)

Thomas P. Kasulis
Northland College, Ashland, Wisconsin
NIRVĀṆA (1987)

Nathan Katz
Florida International University
BHĀVAVIVEKA (1987)
JUDAISM: JUDAISM IN ASIA (2005)

Paul R. Katz
Academia Sinica
TAIWANESE RELIGIONS (2005)

Steven T. Katz
Cornell University
HOLOCAUST, THE: JEWISH THEOLOGICAL RESPONSES (1987)

Leslie S. Kawamura
University of Calgary
ATĪŚA (1987)
TĀRĀ (1987 AND 2005)

Eileen F. Kearney
University of Notre Dame
ABELARD, PETER (1987)
PETER LOMBARD (1987)

Ian Keen
Australian National University
DJAN'KAWU (2005)

Roger M. Keesing
Australian National University
SOLOMON ISLANDS RELIGIONS (1987)

Charles W. Kegley
California State College, Bakersfield
BRUNNER, EMIL (1987)

Pita Kelekna
Fordham University, Lincoln Center
MUISCA RELIGION (1987)

Mary L. Keller
University of Wyoming
SPIRIT POSSESSION: WOMEN AND POSSESSION (2005)

Dennis F. Kelley
University of Missouri, Columbia
NORTH AMERICAN INDIAN RELIGIONS: MYTHIC THEMES (2005)
TOMOL (2005)

Morton Kelsey
University of Notre Dame
MIRACLES: MODERN PERSPECTIVES (1987)
OTHERWORLD (1987)

Carolyn Bereznak Kenny
University of California, Santa Barbara
HAIDA RELIGIOUS TRADITIONS (2005)

Lori Kenschaft
Arlington, Massachusetts
CHILD, LYDIA MARIA (2005)

William M. Kephart
University of Pennsylvania
HUTTERIAN BRETHREN (1987)

Michael A. Kerze
California State University, Northridge
EUCLID (1987)
NUMBERS: BINARY SYMBOLISM (1987)
PTOLEMY (1987)

Veselin Kesich
Saint Vladimir's Orthodox Theological Seminary, Crestwood, New York
VIA NEGATIVA (1987)

Michael Kessler
University of Chicago Divinity School
LAW AND RELIGION: LAW, RELIGION, AND MORALITY (2005)

Charles F. Keyes
University of Washington
THAI RELIGION (1987)
PILGRIMAGE: BUDDHIST PILGRIMAGE IN SOUTH AND SOUTHEAST ASIA (1987)
SOUTHEAST ASIAN RELIGIONS: MAINLAND CULTURES (1987)

Majid Khadduri
Johns Hopkins University
SHĀFIʿĪ, AL- (1987)

Abrahim H. Khan
Trinity College, University of Toronto
STUDY OF RELIGION: THE ACADEMIC STUDY OF RELIGION IN SOUTH ASIA (2005)

Hasan-Uddin Khan
Roger Williams University
MOSQUE: ARCHITECTURAL ASPECTS (2005)

Madhu Khanna
Wolfson College, University of Oxford
YANTRA (1987)

Saleem Kidwai
Aligarh Muslim University
KHUSRAW, AMĪR (1987)

Richard Kieckhefer
Northwestern University
MAGIC: MAGIC IN MEDIEVAL AND RENAISSANCE EUROPE (2005)

Hanna H. Kim
New York University
SWAMINARAYAN MOVEMENT (2005)

Yong-choon Kim
University of Rhode Island
CH'ŎNDOGYO (1987)

Noel Q. King
University of California, Santa Cruz and Guru Nanak Dev University, Amritsar, India
THEODOSIUS (1987 AND 2005)

Ursula King
University of Bristol
GENDER AND RELIGION: AN OVERVIEW (2005)
NUNS: AN OVERVIEW (2005)
PETRE, MAUDE DOMINICA (2005)
SMART, NINIAN (2005)
TEILHARD DE CHARDIN, PIERRE (2005)

Winston L. King
Vanderbilt University (emeritus)
RELIGION [FIRST EDITION] (1987)
SUZUKI SHŌSAN (1987)

Karen Kingsley
Tulane University
MONASTERY (1987)

Jacob N. Kinnard
James Madison University
ICONOGRAPHY: BUDDHIST ICONOGRAPHY (2005)

David Kinsley
McMaster University
AVATĀRA (1987)
DEVOTION (1987)

Hans Kippenberg
University of Bremen
APOSTASY (1987 AND 2005)
CODES AND CODIFICATION (1987)
ICONOGRAPHY: ICONOGRAPHY AS VISIBLE RELIGION [FIRST EDITION] (1987)
LAW AND RELIGION: LAW AND RELIGION IN THE ANCIENT MEDITERRANEAN WORLD (2005)

Kishibe Shigeo
Tokyo
MUSIC: MUSIC AND RELIGION IN JAPAN (1987)

Joseph M. Kitagawa
University of Chicago (emeritus)
ELIADE, MIRCEA [FIRST EDITION] (1987)
JAPANESE RELIGIONS: AN OVERVIEW (1987)
RELIGIOUS COMMUNITIES: RELIGION, COMMUNITY, AND SOCIETY (1987)
WACH, JOACHIM [FIRST EDITION] (1987)

James M. Kittelson
Ohio State University
BUCER, MARTIN (1987)

Kimura Kiyotaka
University of Tokyo
DUSHUN (1987 AND 2005)
FAZANG (1987)
ZHIYAN (1987)

M. H. Klaiman
Maplewood, Minnesota
MASCULINE SACRALITY (1987)

Samuel Z. Klausner
University of Pennsylvania
MARTYRDOM (1987)

Terry F. Kleeman
University of Colorado at Boulder
CHINESE RELIGION: HISTORY OF STUDY (2005)

Inge Kleivan
Københavns Universitet
INUIT RELIGIOUS TRADITIONS (1987)
SEDNA (1987)

Hans J. Klimkeit
Rheinische Friedrich-Wilhelms-Universität Bonn
SCHLEGEL, FRIEDRICH (1987)

Elmar Klinger
Bayerische-Julius-Maximilians-Universität Würzburg
REVENGE AND RETRIBUTION (1987)
VOWS AND OATHS (1987)

W. Randolph Kloetzli
Washington, D.C.
COSMOLOGY: BUDDHIST COSMOLOGY (1987)

COSMOLOGY: HINDU COSMOLOGY (1987)

Keith Knapp
The Citadel
XIAO (2005)

David M. Knipe
University of Wisconsin—Madison
EPICS (1987)
FIRE (2005)
PRAJĀPATI (1987)
PRIESTHOOD: HINDU PRIESTHOOD (1987)
TAPAS (1987)

Alexander Knysh
University of Michigan, Ann Arbor
JUNAYD, AL- (2005)

Harold G. Koenig
Duke University Medical Center, Durham, North Carolina
HEALTH AND RELIGION (2005)

John Koenig
General Theological Seminary, New York, New York
HOSPITALITY (1987 AND 2005)

R. M. Koentjaraningrat
Universitas Indonesia
JAVANESE RELIGION (1987)

Barry S. Kogan
Hebrew Union College–Jewish Institute of Religion, Cincinnati
SAʿADYAH GAON (1987)
YEHUDAH HA-LEVI (1987)

Etan Kohlberg
Hebrew University of Jerusalem
IBN BĀBAWAYHI (1987)
MAJLISĪ, AL- (1987)

Surindar Singh Kohli
Panjab University (emeritus)
ĀDI GRANTH (1987)

Livia Kohn
Boston University
DAO AND DE (2005)
PRIESTHOOD: DAOIST PRIESTHOOD (2005)

Leszek Kolakowski
All Souls College, University of Oxford, and University of Chicago
DESCARTES, RENÉ (1987)
GOOD, THE (1987)
JASPERS, KARL (1987)
PASCAL, BLAISE (1987)
QUIETISM (1987)

Robert Kolb
Concordia College, Saint Paul, Minnesota
FLACIUS, MATTHIAS (1987)

Nikolai Konakov
Russian Academy of Science
KOMI RELIGION (2005)

David Konstan
Wesleyan University
OCEANS (1987)

David Kopf
Minneapolis, Minnesota
TRANSCULTURATION AND RELIGION: RELIGION IN THE FORMATION OF MODERN INDIA (2005)

Klaus-Peter Köpping
University of Heidelberg
ANAMNESIS (1987)
BULL-ROARERS (1987)
PANATHENAIA (1987)
PROMETHEUS (1987 AND 2005)
THIASOI (1987)

Aaron K. Koseki
University of Illinois, Urbana-Champaign
JIZANG (1987)
SENGZHAO (1987)

Christine Kovic
University of Houston—Clear Lake
GENDER AND RELIGION: GENDER AND MESOAMERICAN RELIGIONS (2005)

Martin Kraatz
Philipps-Universität Marburg (retired)
FRICK, HEINRICH (1987 AND 2005)

David Kraemer
Jewish Theological Seminary of America
ELʿAZAR BEN ʿAZARYAH (1987)
ELIʿEZER BEN HYRCANUS (1987)
GAMLIʾEL OF YAVNEH (1987)
TANNAIM (1987)

Stella Kramrisch
Philadelphia Museum of Art
ICONOGRAPHY: HINDU ICONOGRAPHY (1987)
ŚIVA [FIRST EDITION] (1987)

Benny Kraut
University of Cincinnati
ADLER, FELIX (1987)
ETHICAL CULTURE (1987)
KOHLER, KAUFMANN (1987)

Howard Kreisel
Ben-Gurion University of the Negev
PROPHECY: PROPHECY IN POST-BIBLICAL JUDAISM (2005)

Angèle Kremer-Marietti
Rosny-sous-Bois, France
COMTE, AUGUSTE (1987)
POSITIVISM (1987)

Edgar Krentz
Lutheran School of Theology at Chicago
REFERENCE WORKS (1987)

Jeffrey J. Kripal
Rice University
PHALLUS AND VAGINA (2005)
SEXUALITY: AN OVERVIEW [FURTHER CONSIDERATIONS] (2005)

Björn Krondorfer
St. Mary's College of Maryland
MEN'S STUDIES IN RELIGION (2005)

John D. Krugler
Marquette University
CALVERT, GEORGE (1987)

Kubo Noritada
Rikkyo University
LIU DEREN [FIRST EDITION] (1987)
WANG ZHE (1987)
XIAO BAOZHEN (1987)

Hilda Kuper
University of California, Los Angeles (emeritus)
SWAZI RELIGION (1987)

Janīna Kursīte
University of Latvia
BALTIC RELIGION: HISTORY OF STUDY (2005)
BALTIC SANCTUARIES (2005)
MĀRA (AND GREAT MOTHERS) (2005)
TWINS: BALTIC TWIN DEITIES (2005)

Kenshi Kusano
Otani University
RENNYO (2005)

Matti Kuusi
Helsingin Yliopisto
ILMARINEN (1987)
LEMMINKÄINEN (1987)
VÄINÄMÖINEN (1987)

Per Kvaerne
Universiteit i Oslo
BON (1987 AND 2005)
TIBETAN RELIGIONS: AN OVERVIEW (1987 AND 2005)

André LaCocque
Chicago Theological Seminary
SIN AND GUILT (1987)

Catherine Mowry LaCugna
University of Notre Dame
TRINITY (1987)

William R. LaFleur
University of California, Los Angeles
BIOGRAPHY (1987)

John Lagerwey
École Française d'Extrême-Orient, Paris
DAOISM: THE DAOIST RELIGIOUS COMMUNITY (1987)
PRIESTHOOD: DAOIST PRIESTHOOD (1987)
WORSHIP AND DEVOTIONAL LIFE: DAOIST DEVOTIONAL LIFE (1987 AND 2005)
XIAN (2005)
ZHENREN (1987 AND 2005)

Arzina R. Lalani
Institute of Ismaili Studies, London
JAʿFAR AL-ṢĀDIQ (2005)

Louise Lamphere
Brown University
NAVAJO RELIGIOUS TRADITIONS (1987)

Lewis R. Lancaster
University of California, Berkeley (emeritus); President, University of the West
BUDDHIST BOOKS AND TEXTS: CANON AND CANONIZATION (1987 AND 2005)
MAITREYA (1987)

Günter Lanczkowski
Ruprecht-Karl-Universität Heidelberg
BERTHOLET, ALFRED (1987)

Gary G. Land
Andrews University, Berrien Springs, Michigan
SEVENTH-DAY ADVENTISM (2005)

Hermann Landolt
Institute of Islamic Studies, McGill University
WALĀYAH (1987)

David Christopher Lane
Mount San Antonio College
ECKANKAR (2005)

Ruth Langer
Boston College
WORSHIP AND DEVOTIONAL LIFE: JEWISH WORSHIP (2005)

J. Stephen Lansing
University of Southern California
BALINESE RELIGION (1987)
MEGALITHIC RELIGION: HISTORICAL CULTURES (1987)

Richard W. Lariviere
University of Texas at Austin
LAW AND RELIGION: LAW AND RELIGION IN HINDUISM (2005)

AbdAllāh Laroui
Université Mohammed V, Rabat
ISLAM: ISLAM IN NORTH AFRICA (1987)

Amado J. Láscar
Ohio University
ZAPATISMO AND INDIGENOUS RESISTANCE (2005)

Daniel J. Lasker
Ben-Gurion University of the Negev
ALBO, YOSEF (1987)
BLASPHEMY: JEWISH CONCEPT (2005)

James E. Latham
American College in Paris
BREAD (1987)
FOOD (1987)
LEAVEN (1987)
SALT (1987)

Quentin Lauer
Fordham University, Bronx
HEGEL, G. W. F. (1987)

Jean-Pierre Laurant
Centre National de la Recherche Scientifique, Paris
BURCKHARDT, TITUS (2005)

Bruce B. Lawrence
Duke University
BĪRŪNĪ, AL- (1987)
KHĀNAGĀH (1987)
NUBŪWAH (2005)
SHAHRASTĀNĪ, AL- (1987)
SHAHRASTĀNĪ, AL- (1987)

Frederick G. Lawrence
Boston College
POLITICAL THEOLOGY (1987)

Peter Lawrence
University of Sydney
CARGO CULTS [FIRST EDITION] (1987)
NEW GUINEA RELIGIONS [FIRST EDITION] (1987)

Edmund Leach
University of Cambridge (emeritus)
STRUCTURALISM [FIRST EDITION] (1987)

Gary Lease
University of California, Santa Cruz
MERCIER, DÉSIRÉ JOSEPH (1987)

Miguel C. Leatham
Texas Christian University
NEW RELIGIOUS MOVEMENTS: NEW RELIGIOUS MOVEMENTS IN LATIN AMERICA (2005)

Jean Leclercq
Abbaye Saint-Maurice, Clervaux
BERNARD OF CLAIRVAUX (1987)

David Adams Leeming
University of Connecticut, Storrs
QUESTS (1987 AND 2005)

Gordon Leff
University of York
CATHARI (1987)
WALDENSIANS (1987 AND 2005)
WILLIAM OF OCKHAM (1987 AND 2005)

Frederic K. Lehman (Chit Hlaing)
University of Illinois, Urbana-Champaign
BURMESE RELIGION (1987)

Lisa Soleymani Lehmann
Harvard Medical School and Brigham and Women's Hospital
MEDICAL ETHICS (2005)

John H. Leith
Union Theological Seminary, Richmond
FAREL, GUILLAUME (1987)
KNOX, JOHN (1987)
PRESBYTERIANISM, REFORMED (1987)

Mary Joan Winn Leith
Stonehill College
GENDER AND RELIGION: GENDER AND ANCIENT NEAR EASTERN RELIGIONS (2005)

David Lelyveld
University of Minnesota, Twin Cities
AMEER ALI, SYED (1987)

Harris Lenowitz
University of Utah
DÖNMEH (2005)
FRANK, JACOB (2005)

Bill Leonard
Wake Forest University
BAPTIST CHURCHES (2005)

Miguel León-Portilla
Universidad Nacional Autónoma de México
MESOAMERICAN RELIGIONS: PRE-COLUMBIAN RELIGIONS (1987 AND 2005)

Françoise Le Roux
Université de Haute Bretagne
EPONA (1987)
MAPONOS (1987)
MATRES (1987)

Leonard H. Lesko
Brown University
AMUN (1987)
ATUM (1987)
EGYPTIAN RELIGION: AN OVERVIEW (1987)
HATHOR (1987)
HORUS (1987)
OSIRIS (1987)
PTAH (1987)
RE (1987)
SETH (1987)
THOTH (1987)

Julia Leslie
(deceased)
GENDER AND RELIGION: GENDER AND HINDUISM (2005)
SATI (2005)

William A. Lessa
University of California, Los Angeles (emeritus)
MICRONESIAN RELIGIONS: AN OVERVIEW (1987)

Rebecca M. Lesses
Ithaca College
LILITH (2005)

Miriam Levering
University of Tennessee, Knoxville
KṢITIGARBHA (1987)

Baruch A. Levine
New York University
BIBLICAL TEMPLE (1987)
LEVITES (1987)
PRIESTHOOD: JEWISH PRIESTHOOD (1987)

Lee I. Levine
Hebrew University of Jerusalem
PATRIARCHATE (2005)

Nehemia Levtzion
Hebrew University of Jerusalem
ISLAM: ISLAM IN SUB-SAHARAN AFRICA (1987)

Leonard W. Levy
Claremont Graduate School
BLASPHEMY: CHRISTIAN CONCEPT (1987)

F. D. Lewis
Emory University
ṬARĪQAH (2005)

Leonard Lewisohn
Institute of Ismaili Studies, London
ʿAṬṬĀR, FARĪD AL-DĪN (2005)
BISṬĀMĪ, ABŪ YAZĪD AL- (2005)

Guenter Lewy
University of Massachusetts, Amherst
REVOLUTION (1987)

Richard L. Libowitz
Saint Joseph's University
KAPLAN, MORDECAI (1987 AND 2005)

Murray H. Lichtenstein
Hunter College, City University of New York
ḤOKHMAH (1987)

Charles S. Liebman
Bar-Ilan University
ORTHODOX JUDAISM [FIRST EDITION] (1987)

Samuel N. C. Lieu
Macquarie University, Sydney
MANICHAEISM: MANICHAEISM IN CENTRAL ASIA AND CHINA (2005)
MANICHAEISM: MANICHAEISM IN THE ROMAN EMPIRE (2005)

Bruce Lincoln
University of Minnesota, Twin Cities
BEVERAGES (1987)
CATTLE (1987)
DISMEMBERMENT (1987)
HUMAN BODY: MYTHS AND SYMBOLISM (1987)
INDO-EUROPEAN RELIGIONS: AN OVERVIEW (1987)
INITIATION: WOMEN'S INITIATION (1987)
WAR AND WARRIORS: AN OVERVIEW (1987)

David C. Lindberg
University of Wisconsin—Madison
PECHAM, JOHN (1987)

John Lindow
University of California, Berkeley
BALDR (2005)
BERSERKERS (1987 AND 2005)
FYLGJUR (1987 AND 2005)
LANDVÆTTIR (1987 AND 2005)
LOKI (2005)
VALHǪLL (1987 AND 2005)
VALKYRIES (1987 AND 2005)

Galina Lindquist
University of Stockholm
SHAMANISM: NEOSHAMANISM (2005)

Elaine Lindsay
DeKalb, Illinois
FICTION: AUSTRALIAN FICTION AND RELIGION (2005)

Gillian Lindt
Columbia University
LEADERSHIP (1987)

Edward Lipiński
Catholic University of Leuven, Belgium
ADAD (2005)
ADONIS (2005)
ATHIRAT (2005)
RESHEF (2005)

John Lippitt
University of Hertfordshire
HUMOR AND RELIGION: HUMOR, IRONY, AND THE COMIC IN WESTERN THEOLOGY AND PHILOSOPHY (2005)

Roger Lipsey
New York, New York
COOMARASWAMY, ANANDA (1987)

Donald P. Little
Institute of Islamic Studies, McGill University
CRUSADES: MUSLIM PERSPECTIVE (1987)
MĀWARDĪ, AL- (1987)

C. Scott Littleton
Occidental College
DUMÉZIL, GEORGES (2005)
INDO-EUROPEAN RELIGIONS: HISTORY OF STUDY (1987 AND 2005)
WAR AND WARRIORS: INDO-EUROPEAN BELIEFS AND PRACTICES (1987 AND 2005)

B. A. Litvinskii
Academy of Sciences of the U.S.S.R., Moscow
PREHISTORIC RELIGIONS: THE EURASIAN STEPPES AND INNER ASIA (1987)
SHEEP AND GOATS (1987)

James J. Y. Liu
Stanford University

POETRY: CHINESE RELIGIOUS POETRY (1987)

James C. Livingston
College of William and Mary
MARITAIN, JACQUES (1987)

Ann Loades
University of Durham, United Kingdom
SAYERS, DOROTHY L. (2005)

Michael Loewe
University of Cambridge
XI WANG MU (1987)

Naftali Loewenthal
University College London
SCHNEERSON, MENACHEM M. (2005)

Roger Ivar Lohmann
Trent University
CULTURE (2005)

Charles H. Long
University of California, Santa Barbara (emeritus)
ANCESTORS: MYTHIC ANCESTORS (1987)
COSMOGONY (1987)
POPULAR RELIGION (1987)
TRANSCULTURATION AND RELIGION: AN OVERVIEW (2005)

J. Bruce Long
Claremont Graduate School
LIFE (1987)
REINCARNATION (1987)
UNDERWORLD (1987)
WEBS AND NETS (1987)

Jerome H. Long
Wesleyan University
CULTURE HEROES (1987)

Donald Lopez
University of Michigan, Ann Arbor
BUDDHIST STUDIES (2005)

David N. Lorenzen
Universidad Nacional Autónoma de México
DURGĀ HINDUISM (1987)
GORĀKHNĀTH (1987)
HAṬHAYOGA (1987)
ŚAIVISM: AN OVERVIEW (1987)
ŚAIVISM: KĀPĀLIKAS (1987)
ŚAIVISM: PĀŚUPATAS (1987)
ŚAṄKARA (1987)

David W. Lotz
Union Theological Seminary, New York
HARNACK, ADOLF VON (1987)
PAUCK, WILHELM (1987)
RICHARDSON, CYRIL C. (1987)
RITSCHL, ALBRECHT (1987)

Steven M. Lowenstein
University of Judaism, Los Angeles
SOFER, MOSHEH (1987)

Juan Manuel Lozano
Claret House, Chicago
EREMITISM (1987)
RETREAT (1987)

Phillip Charles Lucas
Stetson University
ASSOCIATION FOR RESEARCH AND ENLIGHTENMENT (2005)
CHURCH UNIVERSAL AND TRIUMPHANT (2005)
HOLY ORDER OF MANS (2005)
PROPHET, MARK AND ELIZABETH CLARE (2005)
RELIGIOUS BROADCASTING (2005)

Rodney Lucas
Adelaide University
AUSTRALIAN INDIGENOUS RELIGIONS: HISTORY OF STUDY [FURTHER CONSIDERATIONS] (2005)

Theodore M. Ludwig
Valparaiso University
GODS AND GODDESSES (1987 AND 2005)
INCANTATION (1987)
MONOTHEISM (1987 AND 2005)
ORDINATION (1987 AND 2005)

Katharine Luomala
University of Hawaii, Manoa (emeritus)
HAWAIIAN RELIGION (1987)
MICRONESIAN RELIGIONS: MYTHIC THEMES (1987)
MĀUI (1987)

Manfred Lurker
Forschungskreis für Symbolik, Salzburg
SNAKES (1987)

F. Stanley Lusby
University of Tennessee, Knoxville
HASTINGS, JAMES (1987)
HAYDON, A. EUSTACE (1987)
HEAVEN AND HELL (1987)
LAITY (1987)
MOORE, GEORGE FOOT (1987)

Philip Lutgendorf
University of Iowa
MONKEYS (2005)

John E. Lynch
Catholic University of America
CHURCH: CHURCH POLITY (1987 AND 2005)

Arabella Lyon
State University of New York at Buffalo
LANGER, SUSANNE (2005)

John J. MacAloon
University of Chicago
GAMES (1987)

Proinsias Mac Cana
(deceased)
CELTIC RELIGION: AN OVERVIEW (1987 AND 2005)
CONALL CERNACH (1987 AND 2005)
FERGHUS MAC ROICH (1987 AND 2005)
HEAD: THE CELTIC HEAD CULT (1987 AND 2005)
SÍDH (1987 AND 2005)
TÁIN BÓ CUAILNGE (1987 AND 2005)

Carol P. MacCormack
London School of Hygiene and Tropical Medicine, University of London
CLITORIDECTOMY (1987)

Judith Macdonald
University of Waikato, New Zealand
ATUA (2005)
FIRTH, RAYMOND (2005)
TIKOPIA RELIGION (2005)

Mary N. MacDonald
Le Moyne College, Syracuse, New York
GARDENS: GARDENS IN INDIGENOUS TRADITIONS (2005)
GENDER AND RELIGION: GENDER AND OCEANIC RELIGIONS (2005)
LAWRENCE, PETER (2005)
NEW GUINEA RELIGIONS [FURTHER CONSIDERATIONS] (2005)
SPIRITUALITY (2005)

Wyatt MacGaffey
Haverford College
KINGSHIP: KINGSHIP IN SUB-SAHARAN AFRICA (1987 AND 2005)

Geddes MacGregor
University of Southern California
DOUBT AND BELIEF (1987)
SOUL: CHRISTIAN CONCEPTS (1987)

Elizabeth Mackinlay
University of Queensland
MUSIC: MUSIC AND RELIGION IN INDIGENOUS AUSTRALIA (2005)

Sam Mackintosh
Saint Joseph's University
DOMESTIC OBSERVANCES: CHRISTIAN PRACTICES (1987)

John Macquarrie
Christ Church, University of Oxford
EXISTENTIALISM (1987)

Mark W. MacWilliams
St. Lawrence University
CAMPBELL, JOSEPH (2005)
NAKAYAMA MIKI (2005)

Kenneth Maddock
Macquarie University
ALL-FATHER (1987)
AUSTRALIAN INDIGENOUS RELIGIONS: HISTORY OF STUDY [FIRST EDITION] (1987)
HARTLAND, E. SIDNEY (1987)
HOWITT, A. W. (1987)

Wilfred Madelung
Oriental Institute, University of Oxford
IMAMATE (1987)
SHIISM: AN OVERVIEW (1987)
SHIISM: ISMĀʿĪLĪYAH (1987)

Enrique Maestas
Cuelgahen Nde Lipan Apache of Texas
APACHE RELIGIOUS TRADITIONS (2005)

Michel Maffesoli
Université Sorbonne Paris V
ORGY: AN OVERVIEW (2005)

Elaine Magalis
New York, New York
ANCHOR (1987)
CROWN (1987)
DIAMOND (1987)
FEET (1987)
KEYS (1987)
NIMBUS (1987)

Shaul Magid
Indiana University
HASIDISM: HABAD HASIDISM (2005)
JEWISH RENEWAL MOVEMENT (2005)

Sabina Magliocco
California State University, Northridge
WITCHCRAFT: CONCEPTS OF WITCHCRAFT (2005)

Aldo Magris
University of Trieste
GNOSTICISM: GNOSTICISM FROM ITS ORIGINS TO THE MIDDLE AGES [FURTHER CONSIDERATIONS] (2005)
KERÉNYI, KÁROLY (2005)
STOICISM (2005)

Jean-Pierre Mahé
Université de Paris III (Sorbonne-Nouvelle)
HERMES TRISMEGISTOS (1987)

William K. Mahony
Davidson College
CAKRAVARTIN (1987)
ENLIGHTENMENT (1987 AND 2005)
FLIGHT (1987)
KARMAN: HINDU AND JAIN CONCEPTS (1987)
ṚTA (1987)
SPIRITUAL DISCIPLINE (1987)
UPANIṢADS (1987)

Bernhard Maier
University of Bonn
DRUIDS (2005)

John S. Major
Asia Society, New York
QI (1987)
SHANGDI (1987)

George Makdisi
University of Pennsylvania
ḤANĀBILAH (1987)
IBN TAYMĪYAH (1987)

John Makeham
University of Adelaide
MOZI (2005)

John Makransky
Boston College
TATHĀGATA (2005)

Krikor H. Maksoudian
Arlington, Massachusetts
GREGORY THE ILLUMINATOR (1987)
MASHTOTSʿ, MESROP (1987)
NERSĒS THE GREAT (1987)
SAHAK PARTHEV (1987)

Michael Maliszewski
University of Chicago
MARTIAL ARTS: AN OVERVIEW (1987)

George A. Maloney
Saint Patrick's Novitiate, Midway City, California
SYMEON THE NEW THEOLOGIAN (1987)

Lawrence H. Mamiya
Vassar College
ELIJAH MUHAMMAD (1987 AND 2005)
MALCOLM X (1987)

Peter Manchester
State University of New York at Stony Brook
ETERNITY (1987)

Pietro Mander
Universita' di Napoli "L'Orientale," Italy
ASHUR (2005)
DUMUZI (2005)
HEALING AND MEDICINE: HEALING AND MEDICINE IN THE ANCIENT NEAR EAST (2005)
KINGSHIP: KINGSHIP IN THE ANCIENT MEDITERRANEAN WORLD (2005)
MESOPOTAMIAN RELIGIONS: HISTORY OF STUDY (2005)
SOUL: ANCIENT NEAR EASTERN CONCEPTS (2005)
UTU (2005)

Clyde L. Manschreck
Rice University
MELANCHTHON, PHILIPP (1987)

Georgios I. Mantzaridis
Aristotelian University of Thessaloniki
GREGORY PALAMAS (1987)

Pierre Maranda
Université Laval, Québec
SOLOMON ISLANDS RELIGIONS (2005)

Grazia Marchianò
University of Siena, Arezzo
ZOLLA, ELÉMIRE (2005)

Clemente Marconi
Columbia University
TEMPLE: ANCIENT NEAR EASTERN AND MEDITERRANEAN TEMPLES (2005)

Ileana Marcoulesco
International Circle for Research in Philosophy, Houston
FREE WILL AND DETERMINISM (1987)
INTUITION (1987)
REDEMPTION (1987)

David Marcus
Jewish Theological Seminary of America
ENLIL (1987)
ISRAELITE LAW: PROPERTY LAW (1987)
NANNA (1987)
NERGAL (1987)

Ivan G. Marcus
Jewish Theological Seminary of America
ASHKENAZIC HASIDISM (1987)
JUDAISM: JUDAISM IN NORTHERN AND EASTERN EUROPE TO 1500 (1987)
RASHI (1987)

Nanno Marinatos
University of Illinois
AEGEAN RELIGIONS (2005)

Michael E. Marmura
University of Toronto
FALSAFAH (1987)
SOUL: ISLAMIC CONCEPTS (1987)

George M. Marsden
University of Notre Dame
EVANGELICAL AND FUNDAMENTAL CHRISTIANITY (1987 AND 2005)

Afaf Lutfi al-Sayyud Marsot
University of California, Los Angeles
MUSLIM BROTHERHOOD (1987)

Dale B. Martin
Yale University
ANGLICANISM (2005)

Joel W. Martin
Temecula, California
TECUMSEH (2005)

James Alfred Martin, Jr.
Wake Forest University (emeritus); Columbia University (emeritus)
AESTHETICS: PHILOSOPHICAL AESTHETICS (1987 AND 2005)

Judith G. Martin
University of Dayton
ASHRAM (2005)

Kathleen J. Martin
California Polytechnic State University
LAKOTA RELIGIOUS TRADITIONS (2005)
NORTH AMERICAN INDIANS: INDIANS OF THE PLAINS (2005)

Nancy M. Martin
Chapman University
MIRABAI (2005)

R. M. Martin
(deceased)
LOGIC (1987)
SEMANTICS (1987)

Richard C. Martin
Arizona State University
LEFT AND RIGHT (1987)
PILGRIMAGE: MUSLIM PILGRIMAGE (1987)
TILĀWAH (1987)

Paul V. Martinson
Lutheran Northwestern Seminary, Saint Paul, Minnesota
MORRISON, ROBERT (1987)

Martin E. Marty
University of Chicago
PAUL VI (1987)
PROTESTANTISM (1987)
SCHWEITZER, ALBERT (1987)

Maxwell Gay Marwick
Chipping Norton, England
WITCHCRAFT: AFRICAN WITCHCRAFT (1987)

Attilio Mastrocinque
University of Verona
HERMES (2005)
LARES (2005)
OSIRIS (2005)

Tomoko Masuzawa
University of Michigan, Ann Arbor
WORLD RELIGIONS (2005)

Richard B. Mather
University of Minnesota, Twin Cities
KOU QIANZHI (1987)

Bimal Krishna Matilal
All Souls College, University of Oxford
CĀRVĀKA (1987)
GAUḌAPĀDA (1987)
JÑĀNA (1987)
MĪMĀṂSĀ (1987)
NIMBĀRKA (1987)
VIJÑĀNABHIKṢU (1987)

Matsumae Takeshi
Ritsumeikan University
IZANAGI AND IZANAMI (1987)

Bruce Matthews
Acadia University
POLITICS AND RELIGION: POLITICS AND BUDDHISM (2005)

Walter Harding Maurer
University of Hawaii, Manoa
PAÑCATANTRA (1987)

Laurent Mayali
University of California, Berkeley
LAW AND RELIGION: LAW AND RELIGION IN MEDIEVAL EUROPE (2005)

Mayeda Sengaku
University of Tokyo
NANJŌ BUNYŪ (1987)

Ann Elizabeth Mayer
Wharton School of the University of Pennsylvania
ISLAMIC LAW: SHARĪʿAH (1987 AND 2005)

Michel M. Mazzaoui
University of Utah
ʿALAWĪYŪN (1987)

Jane Dammen McAuliffe
Emory University
ʿĀʾISHAH BINT ABĪ BAKR (1987)

William Leon McBride
Purdue University
ROUSSEAU, JEAN-JACQUES (1987)

Richard P. McBrien
University of Notre Dame
ROMAN CATHOLICISM [FIRST EDITION] (1987)

Ernest G. McClain
Brooklyn College, City University of New York (emeritus)
GEOMETRY (1987)

Sara L. McClintock
Oxford University
KAMALAŚĪLA (2005)
ŚĀNTARAKṢITA (2005)

Aminah Beverly McCloud
DePaul University
ISLAM: ISLAM IN THE AMERICAS (2005)

James F. McCue
University of Iowa
CLEMENT OF ROME (1987)
PETER THE APOSTLE (1987)

Rachel Fell McDermott
Barnard College
BENGALI RELIGIONS (2005)
GODDESS WORSHIP: THE HINDU GODDESS (2005)

Robert A. McDermott
Bernard M. Baruch College, City University of New York
ANTHROPOSOPHY (1987 AND 2005)
MONISM (1987)
RADHAKRISHNAN, SARVEPALLI (1987)
STEINER, RUDOLF (1987 AND 2005)

Heather McDonald
Australian Institute of Aboriginal and Torres Strait Islander Studies

AUSTRALIAN INDIGENOUS RELIGIONS: NEW RELIGIOUS MOVEMENTS (2005)

Sheila McDonough
Concordia University
MAWDŪDĪ, SAYYID ABŪ AL-AʿLĀ (1987)
ORTHODOXY AND HETERODOXY (1987)

Ian A. McFarland
University of Aberdeen
JUSTIFICATION (2005)

Bernard McGinn
University of Chicago
ANTICHRIST (1987 AND 2005)
MYSTICAL UNION IN JUDAISM, CHRISTIANITY, AND ISLAM (2005)

Thomas McGonigle
Dominican Motherhouse, Sinsinawa, Wisconsin
DOMINIC (1987)
DOMINICANS (1987)

William McGuire
Princeton University Press
KERÉNYI, KÁROLY (1987)
NEUMANN, ERICH (1987)

C. T. McIntire
University of Toronto
FREE WILL AND PREDESTINATION: CHRISTIAN CONCEPTS (1987 AND 2005)
HISTORY: CHRISTIAN VIEWS (1987 AND 2005)

Catherine McKenna
City University of New York
BRIGHID (2005)

Alyce M. McKenzie
Southern Methodist University, Dallas, Texas
PARABLES AND PROVERBS (2005)

Edward H. McKinley
Asbury College
BOOTH, WILLIAM (1987 AND 2005)
SALVATION ARMY (1987 AND 2005)

Ian McMorran
Oriental Institute, University of Oxford
WANG FUZHI (1987)

I. J. McMullen
Oriental Institute, University of Oxford
KUMAZAWA BANZAN (1987)

Ernan McMullin
University of Notre Dame
MATERIALISM (1987)

Michael D. McNally
Carleton College
NATIVE AMERICAN CHRISTIANITIES (2005)

William H. McNeill
Colebrook, Connecticut
MIGRATION AND RELIGION (1987)

James Kale McNeley
Diné College
ATHAPASKAN RELIGIOUS TRADITIONS: ATHAPASKAN CONCEPTS OF WIND AND POWER (2005)

John R. McRae
Indiana University
BUDDHISM, SCHOOLS OF: CHINESE BUDDHISM (2005)
CHAN (2005)
HUINENG (2005)

Joseph M. McShane
Le Moyne College
GIBBONS, JAMES (1987)
LEO XIII (1987)

C. A. Meier
Eidgenössische Technische Hochschule, Zurich
ASKLEPIOS (1987)

Michael W. Meister
University of Pennsylvania
KRAMRISCH, STELLA (2005)
TEMPLE: BUDDHIST TEMPLE COMPOUNDS IN SOUTH ASIA (2005)
TEMPLE: HINDU TEMPLES (1987)

Renée Levine Melammed
Schechter Institute of Jewish Studies, Jerusalem
MARRANOS (2005)

Sabine Melchior-Bonnet
Collège de France
MIRRORS (2005)

J. Gordon Melton
Institute for the Study of American Religion
HUBBARD, L. RON (2005)
I AM (2005)
NEW RELIGIOUS MOVEMENTS: HISTORY OF STUDY (2005)
NUWAUBIANS (2005)
SCIENTOLOGY (2005)

Annabelle M. Melville
Bridgewater, Massachusetts
SETON, ELIZABETH (1987)

Paul R. Mendes-Flohr
Hewbrew University of Jerusalem
JEWISH THOUGHT AND PHILOSOPHY: MODERN THOUGHT (1987 AND 2005)

Ruth I. Meserve
Indiana University, Bloomington
INNER ASIAN RELIGIONS (1987)

Michel Meslin
Université de Paris IV (Paris-Sorbonne)
BAPTISM (1987)
EYE (1987)
HEAD: SYMBOLISM AND RITUAL USE (1987)
HEART (1987)

Ellen Messer
George Washington University
RAPPAPORT, ROY A. (2005)

Peter Metcalf
University of Virginia
BORNEAN RELIGIONS (1987)
TOMBS (2005)

Jeffrey F. Meyer
University of North Carolina at Charlotte
TOWERS (2005)

Michael A. Meyer
Hebrew Union College-Jewish Institute of Religion, Cincinnati
REFORM JUDAISM (1987 AND 2005)

Paul Meyvaert
Medieval Academy of America, Cambridge, Massachusetts
BEDE (1987)
GREGORY I (1987)
HINCMAR (1987)
INNOCENT I (1987)

Susan O. Michelman
University of Kentucky
CLOTHING: CLOTHING AND RELIGION IN THE WEST (2005)

Michio Araki
University of Tsukuba
BUDDHISM, SCHOOLS OF: JAPANESE BUDDHISM (1987)
KAMI (2005)
TRANSCULTURATION AND RELIGION: RELIGION IN THE FORMATION OF MODERN JAPAN (2005)

Robert Middlekauff
Huntington Library, San Marino, California
MATHER FAMILY (1987)

John Middleton
Yale University
EAST AFRICAN RELIGIONS: AN OVERVIEW (1987)
EVANS-PRITCHARD, E. E. (1987)
LUGBARA RELIGION (1987)
MAGIC: THEORIES OF MAGIC (1987 AND 2005)
NUER AND DINKA RELIGION (1987)

Thomas Mikelson
Cambridge, Massachusetts
LEGITIMATION (1987)

Silvia Milanezi
École des Hautes Études en Sciences Sociales, Collège de France
MUSES (1987)

Alan L. Miller
Miami University, Oxford, Ohio (emeritus)
JAPANESE RELIGIONS: POPULAR RELIGION (1987 AND 2005)
POWER (1987 AND 2005)

Barbara Stoler Miller
Barnard College, Columbia University
JAYADEVA (1987)

James Miller
Queen's University, Canada
ECOLOGY AND RELIGION: ECOLOGY AND DAOISM (2005)

Stuart S. Miller
University of Connecticut
BEIT HILLEL AND BEIT SHAMMAI (1987)
GAMLI'EL THE ELDER (1987 AND 2005)
HILLEL (1987 AND 2005)

Timothy Miller
University of Kansas
NEW RELIGIOUS MOVEMENTS: NEW RELIGIOUS MOVEMENTS IN THE UNITED STATES (2005)

William D. Miller
Lloyd, Florida
DAY, DOROTHY (1987)
WEIL, SIMONE (1987)

Kenneth Mills
University of Toronto
SOUTH AMERICAN INDIANS: INDIANS OF THE COLONIAL ANDES (2005)

Margaret A. Mills
Ohio State University
FOLK RELIGION: FOLK ISLAM (2005)
ORAL TRADITION (1987)

Mimaki Katsumi
Kyoto University
ĀRYADEVA (1987)
BUDDHAPĀLITA (1987)
CANDRAKĪRTI (1987)
ŚĪLABHADRA (1987)

Paul M. Minus
Methodist Theological School in Ohio (retired)
RAUSCHENBUSCH, WALTER (1987 AND 2005)

Nathan D. Mitchell
Dallas, Texas
RELIGIOUS COMMUNITIES: CHRISTIAN RELIGIOUS ORDERS (1987)

Ogi Mitsuo
Niigata University, Japan
MUSIC: MUSIC AND RELIGION IN JAPAN (2005)

Miyakawa Hisayuki
Kanagawa, Japan
LIANG WUDI (1987)
PARAMĀRTHA (1987)
TANYAO (1987)
XINXING (1987)

Judith S. Modell
Carnegie-Mellon University
BENEDICT, RUTH (1987)

A. George Molland
University of Aberdeen
BACON, ROGER (1987)

Arnaldo Momigliano
(deceased)
FORTUNA (1987)
HISTORIOGRAPHY: WESTERN STUDIES [FIRST EDITION] (1987)
PENATES (1987)
ROMAN RELIGION: THE IMPERIAL PERIOD (1987)
SIBYLLINE ORACLES (1987)

Bruce W. Monserud
University of Florida
BENNETT, JOHN G. (2005)

Deise Lucy Oliveira Montardo
Anthropology Museum of the Federal University of Santa Catarina
MUSIC: MUSIC AND RELIGION IN SOUTH AMERICA (2005)

William Monter
Northwestern University (emeritus)
INQUISITION, THE: THE INQUISITION IN THE OLD WORLD (2005)

Dominic V. Monti
St. Bonaventure University
FRANCISCANS (1987 AND 2005)

Joseph N. Moody
Boston College, Saint John's Seminary
GALLICANISM (1987)

Beverly Moon
New York, New York
ARCHETYPES (1987)
PEARL (1987)

Catherine M. Mooney
Weston Jesuit School of Theology
NUNS: CHRISTIAN NUNS AND SISTERS (2005)

Alexander Moore
University of California, Los Angeles
CUNA RELIGION (1987)

Peter Moore
University of Kent
MYSTICISM [FURTHER CONSIDERATIONS] (2005)

Rebecca Moore
San Diego State University
JONES, JIM (2005)

Walter L. Moore
Florida State University
ECK, JOHANN (1987)

Matti Moosa
Gannon University
NESTORIAN CHURCH (1987)

Claudio Moreschini
University of Pisa
PLATONISM (2005)

David Morgan
Valparaiso University
VISUAL CULTURE AND RELIGION: AN OVERVIEW (2005)

Michael L. Morgan
Indiana University
FACKENHEIM, EMIL (2005)

Morioka Kiyomi
Seijo University
RISSHŌ KŌSEIKAI (1987)

Howard Morphy
Centre for Cross-Cultural Research, Australian National University

ICONOGRAPHY: AUSTRALIAN ABORIGINAL ICONOGRAPHY (1987 AND 2005)

James Winston Morris
Institute of Ismaili Studies, Paris
TAQĪYAH (1987)

Lawrence P. Morris
Fitzwilliam College
AFTERLIFE: GERMANIC CONCEPTS (2005)

John Morton
La Trobe University, Melbourne
GILLEN, FRANCIS JAMES, AND BALDWIN SPENCER (2005)
RÓHEIM, GÉZA (2005)

Lotte Motz
Hunter College, City University of New York
DVERGAR (1987)

Richard M. Moyle
University of Auckland, New Zealand
MUSIC: MUSIC AND RELIGION IN OCEANIA (2005)

Susanne Mrozik
Mount Holyoke College
ŚĀNTIDEVA (2005)

Lewis S. Mudge
San Francisco Theological Seminary
CHURCH: ECCLESIOLOGY (2005)

Rūta Muktupāvela
Latvian Academy of Culture
ANCESTORS: BALTIC CULT OF ANCESTORS (2005)

Valdis Muktupāvels
University of Latvia
BALTIC RELIGION: NEW RELIGIOUS MOVEMENTS (2005)

Patrick B. Mullen
Ohio State University
FOLKLORE (2005)

Werner Muller
Eberhard-Karls-Universität Tübingen (emeritus)
NORTH AMERICAN INDIANS: INDIANS OF THE FAR NORTH (1987)

Mark Mullins
Sophia University
CHRISTIANITY: CHRISTIANITY IN ASIA (2005)

Hasan Qasim Murad
University of Karachi
ḤASAN AL-BAṢRĪ (1987)

Murakami Shigeyoshi
Tokyo
ŌMOTOKYŌ (1987)

Murano Senchu
Nichiren Sect Mission of Hawaii
NIKKŌ (1987)

Francis X. Murphy
Holy Redeemer College, Washington D.C.
JOHN XXIII (1987)

Joseph M. Murphy
Georgetown University
SANTERÍA (1987)

Barbara G. Myerhoff
(deceased)
RITES OF PASSAGE: AN OVERVIEW [FIRST EDITION] (1987)

Jody Elizabeth Myers
California State University, Northridge
KALISCHER, TSEVI HIRSCH (1987 AND 2005)

Karol Mysliwiec
Polska Akademia Nauk, Warsaw
ICONOGRAPHY: EGYPTIAN ICONOGRAPHY (1987)

Eden Naby
Harvard University
ʿALĪ SHĪR NAVĀʾĪ (1987)

Pamela S. Nadell
American University
CONSERVATIVE JUDAISM (2005)

Joseph Nagy
University of California, Los Angeles
CELTIC RELIGION: HISTORY OF STUDY (2005)

Kate Wildman Nakai
Sophia University
FUJIWARA SEIKA (1987)
HAYASHI RAZAN (1987 AND 2005)
YAMAZAKI ANSAI (1987 AND 2005)

Azim Nanji
Institute of Ismaili Studies, London
ASSASSINS (1987)
GARDENS: ISLAMIC GARDENS (2005)
ISLAM: AN OVERVIEW [FURTHER CONSIDERATIONS] (2005)
ISLAMIC STUDIES [FURTHER CONSIDERATIONS] (2005)
ZAKĀT (2005)

Vasudha Narayanan
University of Florida
DEVOTION (2005)
ECOLOGY AND RELIGION: ECOLOGY AND HINDUISM (2005)
HINDUISM IN SOUTHEAST ASIA (2005)

Karl J. Narr
Westfälische Wilhelms-Universität Münster
PALEOLITHIC RELIGION (1987)

Kathleen S. Nash
Le Moyne College, Syracuse, New York
KENYON, KATHLEEN (2005)

Manning Nash
University of Chicago
NATS (1987)

Seyyed Hossein Nasr
George Washington University
DARWĪSH (1987 AND 2005)
GUÉNON, RENÉ (1987 AND 2005)
SHIISM: ITHNĀ ʿASHARĪYAH (1987 AND 2005)

Maurice Natanson
Yale University
SARTRE, JEAN-PAUL (1987)

Walter G. Neevel, Jr.
University of Wisconsin—Madison
RAMAKRISHNA (1987)
YĀMUNA (1987 AND 2005)

Lisias Noguera Negrão
Universidade de São Paulo
KARDECISM (1987)

Stephen C. Neill
(deceased)
BONIFACE (1987)
CHRISTIANITY: CHRISTIANITY IN ASIA (1987)
MISSIONS: CHRISTIAN MISSIONS (1987)
WILLIBRORD (1987)

John K. Nelson
University of San Francisco
POLITICS AND RELIGION: POLITICS AND JAPANESE RELIGIONS (2005)

Leon Nemoy
Annenberg Research Institute, Philadelphia
ʿANAN BEN DAVID (1987)
KARAITES (1987)

Tiran Nersoyan
New York, New York
ARMENIAN CHURCH (1987)

Eleanor Nesbitt
Cheylesmore, United Kingdom
GURŪ GRANTH SĀHIB (2005)

Arnaldo Nesti
International Center for Studies on Contemporary Religions, Siena
IMPLICIT RELIGION (2005)

Jacob Neusner
Brown University
MISHNAH AND TOSEFTA (1987)
RABBINIC JUDAISM IN LATE ANTIQUITY (1987)
YOḤANAN BEN ZAKK'AI (1987)

Venetia Newall
University College, University of London
EGG (1987)
FAIRIES (1987)

Andrew B. Newberg
University of Pennsylvania Health System
NEUROSCIENCE AND RELIGION: NEUROEPISTEMOLOGY (2005)
NEUROSCIENCE AND RELIGION: NEUROTHEOLOGY (2005)

Gordon D. Newby
Emory University
KA'BAH (2005)

John W. Newman
Earlham College
HALL, G. STANLEY (1987)

Carol A. Newsom
Emory University
ECCLESIASTES (2005)
JOB (2005)

On-cho Ng
Pennsylvania State University
LU XIANGSHAN (2005)

Cuong Tu Nguyen
George Mason University
STHIRAMATI (2005)

H. B. Nicholson
University of California, Los Angeles (emeritus)
ICONOGRAPHY: MESOAMERICAN ICONOGRAPHY (1987)
MESOAMERICAN RELIGIONS: POSTCLASSIC CULTURES (1987 AND 2005)

Jorgen S. Nielsen
University of Birmingham
ISLAM: ISLAM IN MODERN EUROPE (2005)

Paul K. Nietupski
John Carroll University, Cleveland, Ohio
BUDDHIST BOOKS AND TEXTS: CANON AND CANONIZATION—VINAYA (2005)
MONASTICISM: BUDDHIST MONASTICISM (2005)

Robert Nisbet
Columbia University
SOCIOLOGY: SOCIOLOGY AND RELIGION [FIRST EDITION] (1987)

David S. Nivison
Stanford University
CHINESE PHILOSOPHY (1987 AND 2005)
LI (1987)
ZHANG XUECHENG (1987)

Khaliq Aḥmad Nizami
Aligarh Muslim University, Aligarh, India
SAMĀ' (1987)
ṢUḤBAH (1987)

J. H. Kwabena Nketia
University of Pittsburgh
MUSIC: MUSIC AND RELIGION IN SUB-SAHARAN AFRICA (1987)

James Anthony Noel
San Francisco Theological Seminary
AFRICAN-AMERICAN RELIGIONS: AN OVERVIEW (2005)
ALLEN, RICHARD (2005)
CRUMMELL, ALEXANDER (2005)
GARVEY, MARCUS (2005)
JONES, ABSALOM (2005)
LIELE, GEORGE (2005)
SEYMOUR, WILLIAM (2005)
TURNER, HENRY MCNEAL (2005)

Suzanne Noffke
Sisters of Saint Dominic, Middleton, Wisconsin
CATHERINE OF SIENA (1987)

Mary Lee Nolan
Oregon State University
PILGRIMAGE: ROMAN CATHOLIC PILGRIMAGE IN THE NEW WORLD (1987)

Hetty Nooy-Palm
Koninklijk Instituut voor de Tropen, Amsterdam
TORAJA RELIGION (1987)

Kawahashi Noriko
Nagoya Institute of Technology
GENDER AND RELIGION: GENDER AND JAPANESE RELIGIONS (2005)

Richard A. Norris
Union Theological Seminary, New York
GREGORY OF NYSSA (1987)
ONTOLOGY (1987)
THEURGY (1987)

Richard North
University College, London
PAGANISM, ANGLO-SAXON (2005)

Peter Nosco
University of British Columbia
CONFUCIANISM IN JAPAN (1987 AND 2005)
KOKUGAKU (2005)

David Novak
University of Toronto
HALAKHAH: STRUCTURE OF HALAKHAH (1987)
KASHRUT (1987 AND 2005)

Philip Novak
Dominican University of California
ATTENTION (1987 AND 2005)

Ronald L. Numbers
University of Wisconsin—Madison
SEVENTH-DAY ADVENTISM (1987)
WHITE, ELLEN GOULD (1987)

Hugo G. Nutini
University of Pittsburgh
DAY OF THE DEAD (2005)
TLAXCALAN RELIGION (1987 AND 2005)

Guy Oakes
Monmouth College, West Long Branch, New Jersey
DILTHEY, WILHELM (1987)

Francis Oakley
Williams College
BONIFACE VIII (1987)

Hiroshi Obayashi
Rutgers University
AFTERLIFE: CHRISTIAN CONCEPTS (2005)

Gananath Obeyesekere
Princeton University
SINHALA RELIGION (1987)

Susan O'Brien
Margaret Beaufort Institute of Theology, Cambridge, United Kingdom
WARD, MARY (2005)

Joseph T. O'Connell
University of Toronto
CAITANYA (2005)

Marvin R. O'Connell
University of Notre Dame
BELLARMINO, ROBERTO (1987)
BORROMEO, CARLO (1987)
SUÁREZ, FRANCISCO (1987)
TORQUEMADA, TOMÁS DE (1987)
TRENT, COUNCIL OF (1987)

June O'Connor
University of California, Riverside
AUROBINDO GHOSE (1987)

Leo J. O'Donovan
Society of Jesus, Maryland Province
RAHNER, KARL (1987)

Schubert M. Ogden
Southern Methodist University
BULTMANN, RUDOLF (1987)

David Ògúngbilé
University, Ile-Ife, Nigeria
GOD: AFRICAN SUPREME BEINGS (2005)

Emiko Ohnuki-Tierney
University of Wisconsin—Madison
AINU RELIGION (1987)
HEALING AND MEDICINE: HEALING AND MEDICINE IN JAPAN (2005)

Felix J. Oinas
Indiana University, Bloomington
LÖNNROT, ELIAS (1987)
TUONELA (1987)

Oyeronke Olajubu
University of Ilorin, Ilorin, Nigeria
GENDER AND RELIGION: GENDER AND AFRICAN RELIGIOUS TRADITIONS (2005)

Jennifer Oldstone-Moore
Wittenberg University
SEIDEL, ANNA KATHARINA (2005)

Maurice Olender
École Pratique des Hautes Études, Collège de France
BAUBO (1987)
PRIAPUS (1987)

Patrick Olivelle
University of Texas at Austin
RITES OF PASSAGE: HINDU RITES (1987 AND 2005)
SAṂNYĀSA (1987 AND 2005)

Miguel Angel Olivera
Buenos Aires
MAPUCHE RELIGION (1987)

Carl Olson
Allegheny College
TRANSCENDENTAL MEDITATION (2005)

John J. O'Meara
University College, Dublin, National University of Ireland
ERIUGENA, JOHN SCOTTUS (1987)

Thomas F. O'Meara
University of Notre Dame
ECKHART, JOHANNES (1987)
GRACE (1987)
SCHELLING, FRIEDRICH (1987 AND 2005)

Mary R. O'Neil
University of Washington
SUPERSTITION (1987)

Isabelle Onians
University of Oxford
VAJRADHARA (2005)
VAJRAPĀṆI (2005)

Johannes van Oort
University of Utrecht / University of Nijmegen
MANICHAEISM: MANICHAEISM AND CHRISTIANITY (2005)

Eric M. Orlin
University of Puget Sound
POLITICS AND RELIGION: POLITICS AND ANCIENT MEDITERRANEAN RELIGIONS (2005)

Heather S. Orr
Western State College of Colorado
BALLGAMES: MESOAMERICAN BALLGAMES (2005)

Charles D. Orzech
University of North Carolina at Greensboro
AMOGHAVAJRA (1987)
MAHĀVAIROCANA (1987)
ŚUBHĀKARASIṂHA (1987)
VAJRABODHI (1987)
ZHENYAN (1987)

Juan M. Ossio
Pontificia Universidad Católica del Perú
MESSIANISM: SOUTH AMERICAN MESSIANISM (2005)

Eckart Otto
University of Munich
COVENANT (2005)
ISRAELITE LAW: AN OVERVIEW (2005)

Daniel L. Overmyer
University of British Columbia
CHINESE RELIGION: AN OVERVIEW (1987)

David Ownby
Université de Montréal
FALUN GONG (2005)

Willard G. Oxtoby
Trinity College, University of Toronto
HOLY, IDEA OF THE (1987)
PRIESTHOOD: AN OVERVIEW (1987)

Andrea Pacini
Edoardo Agnelli Centre for Comparative Religious Studies, Turin, Italy
CHRISTIANITY: CHRISTIANITY IN THE MIDDLE EAST (2005)

William E. Paden
University of Vermont
COMPARATIVE RELIGION (2005)

André Padoux
Centre National de la Recherche Scientifique, Paris
CAKRAS (1987)
ŚAIVISM: PRATYABHIJÑĀ (1987)
ŚAIVISM: VĪRAŚAIVAS (1987)

Anthony Padovano
Ramapo College of New Jersey
MERTON, THOMAS (1987)

Crispin Paine
University College Chichester
MUSEUMS AND RELIGION (2005)

Susan J. Palmer
Dawson College
RAËLIANS (2005)
TWELVE TRIBES (2005)

Raimundo Panikkar
University of California, Santa Barbara (emeritus)
DEITY (1987)

Geoffrey Parrinder
University of London
GHOSTS (1987)
PEACE (1987)
TOUCHING (1987)
TRIADS (1987)

William B. Parsons
Rice University

PSYCHOLOGY: PSYCHOLOGY OF RELIGION (2005)

Harry B. Partin
Duke University
CLASSIFICATION OF RELIGIONS (1987)
PARADISE (1987)
PINARD DE LA BOULLAYE, HENRI (1987)

Raphael Patai
Forest Hills, New York
FOLK RELIGION: FOLK JUDAISM (1987)

Anne Pattel-Gray
Tauondi Incorporated
AUSTRALIAN INDIGENOUS RELIGIONS: ABORIGINAL CHRISTIANITY (2005)

Laurie Louise Patton
Emory University
COSMOLOGY: HINDU COSMOLOGY (2005)
LIFE (2005)
SUBALTERN STUDIES (2005)

Robert S. Paul
Austin Presbyterian Theological Seminary
MINISTRY (1987)

Richard K. Payne
Institute of Buddhist Studies
FUDŌ (2005)
SHINGONSHŪ (2005)
WORSHIP AND DEVOTIONAL LIFE: BUDDHIST DEVOTIONAL LIFE IN EAST ASIA (2005)

James L. Peacock
University of North Carolina at Chapel Hill
DRAMA: JAVANESE WAYANG (1987 AND 2005)
SOUTHEAST ASIAN RELIGIONS: NEW RELIGIOUS MOVEMENTS IN INSULAR CULTURES (1987 AND 2005)

Birger A. Pearson
University of California, Santa Barbara
HYPOSTASIS (1987)

Joanne E. Pearson
Cardiff University
WICCA (2005)

Karen Pechilis
Drew University
ŚIVA [FURTHER CONSIDERATIONS] (2005)
SOUL: INDIAN CONCEPTS (2005)

Jaroslav Pelikan
Yale University
CHRISTIANITY: AN OVERVIEW (1987)
CHRISTIANITY: CHRISTIANITY IN WESTERN EUROPE (1987)
FAITH (1987)

Olivier Pelon
Université Lyon II
AEGEAN RELIGIONS (1987)

Christian Pelras
Centre National de la Recherche Scientifique, Paris
BUGIS RELIGION (1987)

Robert D. Pelton
Madonna House, Combemere, Canada
TRICKSTERS: AFRICAN TRICKSTERS (1987)

John Pemberton III
Amherst College
ICONOGRAPHY: TRADITIONAL AFRICAN ICONOGRAPHY (1987 AND 2005)
YORUBA RELIGION (1987)

Kenneth Pennington
Syracuse University
INNOCENT III (1987)

M. Basil Pennington
St. Joseph's Abbey, Spencer, Massachusetts
CISTERCIANS (1987)

Juha Pentikäinen
Helsingin Yliopisto (University of Helsinki)
BATHS (2005)
CASTRÉN, MATTHIAS ALEXANDER (2005)
DONNER, KAI (2005)
FINNISH RELIGIONS (2005)
FINNO-UGRIC RELIGIONS: AN OVERVIEW (2005)
FINNO-UGRIC RELIGIONS: HISTORY OF STUDY (2005)
HAAVIO, MARTTI (2005)
HONKO, LAURI (2005)
KARELIAN RELIGION (2005)
LAESTADIUS, LARS LEVI (2005)
MARI AND MORDVIN RELIGION (1987)
SAMI RELIGION (2005)
SAMOYED RELIGION (2005)
TUONELA (2005)

Jean Pépin
Centre National de la Recherche Scientifique, Paris
LOGOS (1987)

Andrés Alejandro Pérez Diez
Centro Argentino de Etnológia Americana, Buenos Aires
WARAO RELIGION (1987)

Pheme Perkins
Boston College
GNOSTICISM: GNOSTICISM AS A CHRISTIAN HERESY (1987)

James W. Perkinson
Marygrove College and Ecumenical Theological Seminary
PERCUSSION AND NOISE (2005)

Bernard C. Perley
University of Wisconsin—Milwaukee
NORTH AMERICAN INDIANS: INDIANS OF THE NORTHWEST COAST [FURTHER CONSIDERATIONS] (2005)
TRICKSTERS: NORTH AMERICAN TRICKSTERS [FURTHER CONSIDERATIONS] (2005)

Moshe Perlmann
University of California, Los Angeles
POLEMICS: MUSLIM-JEWISH POLEMICS (1987)

Henry Pernet
Carpinteria, California
MASKS (2005)

Michelene E. Pesantubbee
University of Iowa
CHEROKEE RELIGIOUS TRADITIONS (2005)

F. E. Peters
New York University
JERUSALEM: AN OVERVIEW (1987)

Rudolph Peters
Nederlands Instituut voor Archaeologie en Arabische Studien, Cairo
JIHĀD (1987)

Ted Peters
Pacific Lutheran Theological Seminary
SCIENCE AND RELIGION (2005)

Gregory R. Peterson
South Dakota State University
NEUROSCIENCE AND RELIGION: AN OVERVIEW (2005)

Indira Viswanathan Peterson
Mount Holyoke College

GANGES RIVER (1987)
ŚAIVISM: NĀYAṈĀRS (1987)

Giovanni Pettinato
Università degli Studi di Roma "La Sapienza"
AKITU (2005)
ATRAHASIS (2005)
EBLAITE RELIGION (2005)
ENKI (2005)
ENLIL (2005)
ENUMA ELISH (2005)
GILGAMESH (2005)
INANNA (2005)
MESOPOTAMIAN RELIGIONS: AN OVERVIEW [FURTHER CONSIDERATIONS] (2005)
NERGAL (2005)
NINHURSAGA (2005)
NINURTA (2005)

Lloyd W. Pflueger
Truman State University
ĪŚVARA (2005)

Giulia Piccaluga
Università degli Studi, Rome
BINDING (1987)
CALENDARS: AN OVERVIEW (1987)
CHRONOLOGY (1987)
KNOTS (1987)

Acácio Tadeu de Camargo Piedade
Universidade do Estado de Santa Catarina
MUSIC: MUSIC AND RELIGION IN SOUTH AMERICA (2005)

Nelson Pike
University of California, Irvine
EMPIRICISM (1987)
HUME, DAVID (1987)

Sarah Pike
California State University, Chico
NEOPAGANISM (2005)
RITES OF PASSAGE: NEOPAGAN RITES (2005)

Anthony B. Pinn
Rice University
NATION OF ISLAM (2005)

Andrea Piras
University of Bologna
ANGELS (2005)
MANI (2005)

Vinciane Pirenne-Delforge
Université de Liège, Belgium
APHRODITE (2005)

Andrew H. Plaks
Princeton University; Hebrew University of Jerusalem
GOLDEN RULE (2005)

Xavier De Planhol
Université de Paris IV (Paris-Sorbonne)
DESERTS (1987)

S. Brent Plate
Texas Christian University
FILM AND RELIGION (2005)

Cicerone Poghirc
Centre Roumain de Recherches, Paris
BENDIS (1987)
DACIAN RIDERS (1987)
GETO-DACIAN RELIGION (1987)
SABAZIOS (1987)
THRACIAN RELIGION (1987)
THRACIAN RIDER (1987)
ZALMOXIS (1987)

John Polkinghorne
Queens' College, Cambridge
CHAOS THEORY (2005)
COSMOLOGY: SCIENTIFIC COSMOLOGIES (2005)

Edgar C. Polomé
University of Texas at Austin
FREYJA (1987)
FREYR (1987)
GERMANIC RELIGION: AN OVERVIEW (1987)
HEIMDALLR (1987)
NJǪRÐR (1987)
THOR (1987)

Françoise Pommaret
Centre National de la Recherche Scientifique, Paris
TIBETAN RELIGIONS: HISTORY OF STUDY (2005)
WORSHIP AND DEVOTIONAL LIFE: BUDDHIST DEVOTIONAL LIFE IN TIBET (2005)

Mu-chou Poo
Institute of History and Philology, Academia Sinica, Taipei, Taiwan
AFTERLIFE: CHINESE CONCEPTS (2005)

Deborah A. Poole
Johns Hopkins University
SOUTH AMERICAN INDIAN RELIGIONS: HISTORY OF STUDY (1987 AND 2005)

Fitz John Porter Poole
University of California, San Diego
MELANESIAN RELIGIONS: MYTHIC THEMES (1987)

Ismail K. Poonawala
University of California, Los Angeles
AL-AZHAR (2005)
IKHWĀN AL-ṢAFĀʾ (1987)
QARĀMIṬAH (1987)

Richard H. Popkin
Washington University, Saint Louis
RELATIVISM (1987)
SKEPTICS AND SKEPTICISM (1987)

Gregory F. Porter
San Francisco, California
UNDERHILL, EVELYN (1987)

Gary G. Porton
University of Illinois, Urbana-Champaign
ʿAQIVAʾ BEN YOSEF (1987)
ELISHAʿ BEN AVUYAH (1987 AND 2005)
YEHUDAH HA-NASIʾ (1987 AND 2005)
YISHMAʿEʾL BEN ELISHAʿ (1987)

Stephen G. Post
Case Western Reserve University
SOROKIN, PITIRIM ALEKSANDROVICH (2005)

Karl H. Potter
Universtiy of Washington
GUṆAS (1987)
MADHVA (1987)

Robert Potter
University of California, Santa Barbara
HROTSVIT (2005)

William K. Powers
Rutgers, The State University of New Jersey, New Brunswick Campus
DRAMA: NORTH AMERICAN INDIAN DANCE AND DRAMA (1987)
LAKOTA RELIGIOUS TRADITIONS (1987)
NORTH AMERICAN INDIANS: INDIANS OF THE PLAINS (1987)

Judith L. Poxon
California State University, Sacramento
FEMINISM: FRENCH FEMINISTS ON RELIGION (2005)

Carlo Prandi
University of Parma
INVISIBLE RELIGION (2005)

Charles S. Prebish
Pennsylvania State University

COUNCILS: BUDDHIST COUNCILS (1987)

Riv-Ellen Prell
University of Minnesota, Twin Cities
MYERHOFF, BARBARA G. (1987 AND 2005)

Hanns J. Prem
Ludwig-Maximilians-Universität München
TOLTEC RELIGION (1987)

John Prest
Balliol College, University of Oxford
GARDENS: AN OVERVIEW (1987 AND 2005)

James J. Preston
State University of New York, College at Oneonta
GODDESS WORSHIP: AN OVERVIEW (1987)
GODDESS WORSHIP: THEORETICAL PERSPECTIVES (1987)
PURIFICATION: AN OVERVIEW (1987)

Eleanor M. Preston-Whyte
University of Natal
ZULU RELIGION (1987)

Richard Price
Johns Hopkins University
AFRO-SURINAMESE RELIGIONS (1987)

Simon Price
University of Oxford
ROMAN RELIGION: THE IMPERIAL PERIOD (2005)

Anne Primavesi
University of London
GAIA (2005)

Leonard Norman Primiano
University of Pennsylvania
ALL FOOLS' DAY (1987)
HALLOWEEN (1987)

Stephen Prothero
Boston University
OLCOTT, HENRY STEEL (2005)

Wayne Proudfoot
Columbia University
PHILOSOPHY: PHILOSOPHY OF RELIGION (1987)

James H. Provost
Catholic University of America
EXCOMMUNICATION (1987)

Leo M. Pruden
American University of Oriental Studies, Los Angeles
KŌBEN (1987)
TIANTAI (1987)

Michael J. Puett
Harvard University
BONES (2005)

Reinhard Pummer
University of Ottawa
SAMARITANS (2005)

Michael Pye
Philipps-Universität Marburg
MERIT: AN OVERVIEW (1987)
MERIT: CHRISTIAN CONCEPTS (1987)
UPĀYA (1987)

Christopher S. Queen
Harvard University
ENGAGED BUDDHISM (2005)

Andrew Quintman
University of Michigan, Ann Arbor
MI LA RAS PA (2005)

Gilles Quispel
Rijksuniversiteit te Utrecht
GNOSTICISM: GNOSTICISM FROM ITS ORIGINS TO THE MIDDLE AGES [FIRST EDITION] (1987)
SOPHIA (1987)

B. Tahera Qutbuddin
University of Chicago
ZAYNAB BINT ʿALĪ (2005)

Albert J. Raboteau
Princeton University
AFRICAN AMERICAN RELIGIONS: MUSLIM MOVEMENTS (1987)
KING, MARTIN LUTHER, JR. (1987)

Kathryn Allen Rabuzzi
Syracuse University
FAMILY (1987)
HOME (1987)

Friedhelm K. Radandt
King's College, Briarcliff Manor, New York
HERDER, JOHANN GOTTFRIED (1987 AND 2005)

Rosemary Rader
St. Paul's Priory, Saint Paul, Minnesota
FASTING (1987)
MENDICANCY (1987)

D. S. Raevskii
Academy of Sciences of the U.S.S.R., Moscow
SARMATIAN RELIGION (1987)
SCYTHIAN RELIGION (1987)

Habibeh Rahim
Hunter College, City University of New York
ALCHEMY: ISLAMIC ALCHEMY (1987)
INCENSE (1987)

Fazlur Rahman
University of Chicago
IQBAL, MUHAMMAD (1987)
ISLAM: AN OVERVIEW [FIRST EDITION] (1987)
MULLĀ ṢADRĀ (1987)

Karl Rahner
(deceased)
DOGMA (1987)
VATICAN COUNCILS: VATICAN II [FIRST EDITION] (1987)

Jill Raitt
University of Missouri, Columbia
BEZA, THEODORE (1987)
CANISIUS, PETER (1987)
POLITICS AND RELIGION: POLITICS AND CHRISTIANITY (2005)

Aaron Rakeffet-Rothkoff
Michlala, Jerusalem
REVEL, BERNARD (1987)

Lewis R. Rambo
San Francisco Theological Seminary
CONVERSION (1987 AND 2005)

Velcheru Narayana Rao
University of Wisconsin—Madison
BALARĀMA (1987)
HANUMĀN (1987)
RĀMA (1987)
RĀMĀYAṆA (1987)
TULSĪDĀS (1987)
VĀLMĪKI (1987)

Melissa Raphael
University of Gloucestershire
GENDER AND RELIGION: GENDER AND JUDAISM (2005)
MENSTRUATION (2005)
PATRIARCHY AND MATRIARCHY (2005)
THEALOGY (2005)

Ada Rapoport-Albert
University College London
MAID OF LUDMIR (2005)

Ravi Ravindra
Dalhousie University
EINSTEIN, ALBERT (1987)
GALILEO GALILEI (1987)
KEPLER, JOHANNES (1987)
NEWTON, ISAAC (1987)

Benjamin C. Ray
University of Virginia
AFRICAN RELIGIONS: AN OVERVIEW (1987)
EAST AFRICAN RELIGIONS: NORTHEAST BANTU RELIGIONS (1987)
LANG, ANDREW (1987)
TURNER, VICTOR (1987)

J. D. Ray
University of Cambridge
PYRAMIDS: EGYPTIAN PYRAMIDS (1987)

Reginald Ray
The Naropa Institute, Boulder
MAHĀSIDDHAS (1987)
NĀ RO PA (1987)

Kay A. Read
DePaul University
HUMAN SACRIFICE: AN OVERVIEW (1987 AND 2005)
RITES OF PASSAGE: MESOAMERICAN RITES (2005)

Karen Ready
New York, New York
WORK (1987)

Bernard M. G. Reardon
University of Newcastle upon Tyne
MODERNISM: CHRISTIAN MODERNISM (1987 AND 2005)

Donald B. Redford
University of Toronto
EGYPTIAN RELIGION: THE LITERATURE (1987)

Anthony Redmond
The Australian National University, Canberra, Australia
UNGARINYIN RELIGION (2005)

Marjorie E. Reeves
Oxford, England
JOACHIM OF FIORE (1987)

Janice Reid
University of Western Sydney, Australia
HEALING AND MEDICINE: HEALING AND MEDICINE IN INDIGENOUS AUSTRALIA (2005)

Jennifer I. M. Reid
University of Maine, Framington
TRANSCULTURATION AND RELIGION: RELIGION IN THE FORMATION OF MODERN CANADA (2005)

Marie-Louise Reiniche
École des Hautes Études en Sciences Sociales, Collège de France
DĪVĀLĪ (1987)
HINDU RELIGIOUS YEAR (1987)
HOLĪ (1987)
NAVARĀTRI (1987)

Bryan S. Rennie
Westminster College
ELIADE, MIRCEA [FURTHER CONSIDERATIONS] (2005)

Marie-Simone Renou
Paris, France
RENOU, LOUIS (1987)

Richard J. Resch
Loras College
LOISY, ALFRED (1987)
RENAN, ERNEST (1987)

Matthew Restall
Pennsylvania State University
MESOAMERICAN RELIGIONS: COLONIAL CULTURES (2005)

John Reumann
Lutheran Theological Seminary at Philadelphia (emeritus)
MARY: AN OVERVIEW (1987 AND 2005)

Frank E. Reynolds
University of Chicago
BUDDHA (1987)
BUDDHISM: AN OVERVIEW (1987)
DUṬṬHAGĀMAṆĪ (1987)
MONGKUT (1987)
THERAVĀDA (1987)

David M. Rhoads
Lutheran School of Theology at Chicago
ZEALOTS (1987 AND 2005)

Alfred Ribi
C. G. Jung-Institut Küsnacht/Zürich
DEMONS: PSYCHOLOGICAL PERSPECTIVES (1987)

Gaetano Riccardo
Istituto Universitario Orientale, Naples, Italy
KINGSHIP: AN OVERVIEW (2005)

Audrey I. Richards
(deceased)
BEMBA RELIGION (1987)

James T. Richardson
University of Nevada, Reno
JESUS MOVEMENT (2005)
LAW AND RELIGION: LAW AND NEW RELIGIOUS MOVEMENTS (2005)

Mac Linscott Ricketts
Louisburg College, Emeritus Professor of Religion
LEACH, EDMUND (2005)
TRICKSTERS: NORTH AMERICAN TRICKSTERS [FIRST EDITION] (1987)

Paul Ricoeur
Université de Paris IV (Paris-Sorbonne) and University of Chicago (emeritus)
EVIL (1987)
MYTH: MYTH AND HISTORY (1987)

Julien Ries
Université Catholique de Louvain-la-Neuve
FALL, THE (1987)
IDOLATRY (1987)

Nancy C. Ring
Le Moyne College, Syracuse, New York
SÖLLE, DOROTHEE (2005)
VATICAN COUNCILS: VATICAN II [FURTHER CONSIDERATIONS] (2005)

Helmer Ringgren
Uppsala Universitet
COMPARATIVE MYTHOLOGY (1987)
JUDGMENT OF THE DEAD (1987)
MESSIANISM: AN OVERVIEW (1987)
RESURRECTION (1987)

Marlene Dobkin de Rios
University of California, Irvine; emerita, California State University, Fullerton
PSYCHEDELIC DRUGS (2005)

Andrew Rippin
University of Victoria
BAYḌĀWĪ, AL- (1987)
ṬABARĪ, AL- (2005)
TAFSĪR (1987)
ZAMAKHSHARĪ, AL- (1987)

Claude Rivière
Université de Paris V, Sorbonne
LÉVY-BRUHL, LUCIEN (1987)
SOUL: CONCEPTS IN INDIGENOUS RELIGIONS (1987 AND 2005)

Sajjad H. Rizvi
University of Bristol
ḤUSAYN IBN ʿALĪ, AL- (2005)
SHAYKHĪYAH (2005)

Ronald G. Roberson
United States Conference of Catholic Bishops, Washington, D.C.

SYRIAC ORTHODOX CHURCH OF ANTIOCH (2005)

Brynley F. Roberts
Cardiff University (Honorary Professor)
ANNWN (1987 AND 2005)
ARTHUR (1987 AND 2005)
MABINOGION (1987 AND 2005)
MERLIN (1987 AND 2005)
TALIESIN (1987 AND 2005)

Noel Robertson
Brock University
ANTHESTERIA (2005)

Roland Robertson
University of Pittsburgh
ECONOMICS AND RELIGION (1987)
FUNCTIONALISM (1987)
RADCLIFFE-BROWN, A. R. (1987)

Francis Robicsek
Sanger Clinic, P.A., Charlotte, North Carolina
SMOKING (1987)

Françoise Robin
Institut National des Langues et Civilisations Orientales, Paris
GESAR (2005)

Isabelle Robinet
Institut des Langues Orientales, Valpuiseaux, France
GUO XIANG (1987)
ZHANG DAOLING (1987)
ZHANG JUE (1987)
ZHANG LU (1987)

David Robinson
Michigan State University
FULBE RELIGION (1987)
ʿUMAR TĀL (1987)

Thomas A. Robinson
University of Lethbridge
HERESY: CHRISTIAN CONCEPTS (2005)

Ludo Rocher
University of Pennsylvania
MANU (1987)
ŚĀSTRA LITERATURE (1987)
SŪTRA LITERATURE (1987)

E. Burke Rochford, Jr.
Middlebury College
PRABHUPADA, A. C. BHAKTIVEDANTA. (2005)

Susan Rodgers
Ohio University
BATAK RELIGION (1987)

Peter T. Rohrbach
Potomac, Maryland
TERESA OF ÁVILA (1987)
THÉRÈSE OF LISIEUX (1987)

Lynn E. Roller
University of California, Davis
CYBELE (2005)

Holmes Rolston III
Colorado State University
SOCIOBIOLOGY AND EVOLUTIONARY PSYCHOLOGY: AN OVERVIEW (2005)

András Róna-Tas
Budapest
CHUVASH RELIGION (1987)

Annmari Ronnberg
Archive for Research in Archetypal Symbolism, New York
SPITTLE AND SPITTING (1987)

Wayne R. Rood
Pacific School of Religion, Berkeley
COMENIUS, JOHANNES AMOS (1987)

Wade Clark Roof
University of California, Santa Barbara
SOCIETY AND RELIGION [FURTHER CONSIDERATIONS] (2005)

Sidney H. Rooy
Educación Teológica, Buenos Aires
CHRISTIANITY: CHRISTIANITY IN LATIN AMERICA (1987)
LAS CASAS, BARTOLOMÉ DE (1987)

Miriam Rosen
New York, New York
CALLIGRAPHY: HEBREW MICROGRAPHY (1987)

Jean E. Rosenfeld
University of California, Los Angeles
MAORI RELIGION [FURTHER CONSIDERATIONS] (2005)

Richard A. Rosengarten
University of Chicago
LAW AND RELIGION: LAW, RELIGION, AND LITERATURE (2005)

Bernice Glatzer Rosenthal
Fordham University
MEREZHKOVSKII, DMITRII (1987 AND 2005)
SOLOVʾEV, VLADIMIR (1987 AND 2005)

Franz Rosenthal
Yale University (emeritus)
IBN KHALDŪN (1987)

Harold D. Roth
University of Toronto
FANGSHI (1987 AND 2005)
LIU AN (1987 AND 2005)
ZHUANGZI (2005)

Fritz A. Rothschild
Jewish Theological Seminary of America
HESCHEL, ABRAHAM JOSHUA (1987)

Leroy S. Rouner
Boston University
HOCKING, WILLIAM ERNEST (1987)
IDEALISM (1987)

Jean-Paul Roux
École du Louvre, Paris
BLOOD (1987)
TENGRI (1987)
TURKIC RELIGIONS (1987)

Elizabeth Ashman Rowe
Somerville, Massachusetts
ÁLFAR (2005)
DVERGAR (2005)
EDDAS (2005)
FREYJA (2005)
FREYR (2005)
GERMANIC RELIGION: AN OVERVIEW (2005)
GERMANIC RELIGION: HISTORY OF STUDY (2005)
HEIMDALLR (2005)
JÖTNAR (2005)
NJǪRÐR (2005)
ÓÐINN (2005)
RUNES [FURTHER CONSIDERATIONS] (2005)
SAGAS (2005)
TÝR (2005)

Christopher Rowland
University of Oxford
BIBLICAL EXEGESIS: CHRISTIAN VIEWS (2005)

Gonzalo Rubio
Pennsylvania State University
DAGAN (2005)
DRAMA: ANCIENT NEAR EASTERN RITUAL DRAMA [FURTHER CONSIDERATIONS] (2005)
PHILISTINE RELIGION (2005)

Jean Rudhardt
Université de Genève
FLOOD, THE (1987)
WATER (1987)

Erwin P. Rudolph
Wheaton College, Illinois
LAW, WILLIAM (1987)

Kurt Rudolph
Phillipps-Universität Marburg
HERESY: AN OVERVIEW (1987)
KULTURKREISELEHRE (1987)
MYSTERY RELIGIONS (1987)
RELIGIONSGESCHICHTLICHE SCHULE (1987)
WELLHAUSEN, JULIUS (1987)
WISDOM (1987)

Rosemary Radford Ruether
Garrett-Evangelical Theological Seminary, Evanston, Illinois
ANDROCENTRISM (1987)

Jeffrey C. Ruff
Marshall University
STUDY OF RELIGION: THE ACADEMIC STUDY OF RELIGION IN NORTH AMERICA (2005)

Frithiof Rundgren
Uppsala Universitet
NYBERG, H. S. (1987)

Jörg Rüpke
University of Erfurt
FASTI (2005)
ROMAN RELIGION: THE EARLY PERIOD (2005)

Brian O. Ruppert
University of Illinois, Urbana-Champaign
BUDDHISM: BUDDHISM IN JAPAN (2005)

J. R. Russell
Columbia University
ARMENIAN RELIGION (1987)

Jeffrey Burton Russell
University of California, Santa Barbara
WITCHCRAFT: CONCEPTS OF WITCHCRAFT (1987)

T. C. Russell
University of Manitoba
TAO HONGJING (2005)

J. Joseph Ryan
(deceased)
DAMIAN, PETER (1987)

Jennifer Rycenga
San Jose State University
STANTON, ELIZABETH CADY (2005)

Michael A. Rynkiewich
Asbury Theological Seminary, Wilmore, Kentucky
MICRONESIAN RELIGIONS: MYTHIC THEMES (2005)

Dario Sabbatucci
Università degli Studi, Rome
MORTIFICATION (1987)
ORDEAL (1987)

Thomas F. Sable
University of Scranton
UNIATE CHURCHES (1987 AND 2005)

Abdullah Saeed
University of Melbourne
QUR'ĀN: TRADITION OF SCHOLARSHIP AND INTERPRETATION (2005)

Omid Safi
Colgate University
MODERNISM: ISLAMIC MODERNISM (2005)

Klaus Sagaster
Rheinische Friedrich-Wilhelms-Universität Bonn
CHINGGIS KHAN (1987)
ERLIK (1987)
ÜLGEN (1987)

Donald P. St. John
Moravian College
HANDSOME LAKE (1987)
IROQUOIS RELIGIOUS TRADITIONS (1987)
NEOLIN (1987 AND 2005)
NORTH AMERICAN INDIANS: INDIANS OF THE NORTHEAST WOODLANDS (1987 AND 2005)

John A. Saliba
University of Detroit Mercy
UFO RELIGIONS (2005)

Richard C. Salter
Hobart and William Smith Colleges
RASTAFARIANISM (2005)

Judy D. Saltzman
California Polytechnic State University
GURDJIEFF, G. I. (2005)
JUDGE, WILLIAM Q. (2005)
OUSPENSKY, P. D. (2005)

Geoffrey Samuel
Cardiff University
HEALING AND MEDICINE: HEALING AND MEDICINE IN TIBET (2005)

Norbert M. Samuelson
Arizona State University
ABRAVANEL, ISAAC (1987)
GERSONIDES (1987 AND 2005)
IBN DAUD, AVRAHAM (1987)
IBN GABIROL, SHELOMOH (1987 AND 2005)

Alexis Sanderson
Oriental Institute, University of Oxford
ABHINAVAGUPTA (1987)
ŚAIVISM: KRAMA ŚAIVISM (1987)
ŚAIVISM: ŚAIVISM IN KASHMIR (1987)
ŚAIVISM: TRIKA ŚAIVISM (1987)

James Hugh Sanford
University of North Carolina at Chapel Hill
IKKYŪ SŌJUN (1987)

Marc Saperstein
George Washington University
ADRET, SHELOMOH BEN AVRAHAM (1987)
ASHER BEN YEḤIʾEL (1987)
IBN ʿEZRAʾ, AVRAHAM (1987 AND 2005)

Jonathan D. Sarna
Hebrew Union College–Jewish Institute of Religion, Cincinnati
SZOLD, HENRIETTA (1987)

Nahum M. Sarna
Brandeis University
BIBLICAL LITERATURE: HEBREW SCRIPTURES (1987)

David Sassian
New York, New York
EMERSON, RALPH WALDO (1987)

Nicholas J. Saunders
University College London
JAGUARS (2005)

Deborah F. Sawyer
Lancaster University
GENDER AND RELIGION: GENDER AND ANCIENT MEDITERRANEAN RELIGIONS (2005)

William S. Sax
South Asia Institute, University of Heidelberg
KUMBHA MELĀ (1987)
PILGRIMAGE: HINDU PILGRIMAGE (2005)

Roberta A. Schaafsma
Santa Fe, New Mexico
REFERENCE WORKS (2005)

Richard Schacht
University of Illinois, Urbana-Champaign
NIETZSCHE, FRIEDRICH (1987)

Kurtis R. Schaeffer
University of Alabama
KARMA PAS (2005)

Robert P. Scharlemann
University of Virginia (retired)
TILLICH, PAUL JOHANNES (1987 AND 2005)

David A. Schattschneider
Moravian Theological Seminary
MORAVIANS (1987)
ZINZENDORF, NIKOLAUS (1987 AND 2005)

Richard Schechner
New York University
PERFORMANCE AND RITUAL (1987 AND 2005)

Bernhard Scheid
Austrian Academy of Sciences
ECOLOGY AND RELIGION: ECOLOGY AND SHINTŌ (2005)

John Scheid
Collège de France
ARVAL BROTHERS (1987 AND 2005)
DEA DIA (2005)
FASTI (1987)
LUDI SAECULARES (1987)
LUSTRATIO (1987)

Raymond P. Scheindlin
Jewish Theological Seminary of America
BAḤYE IBN PAQUDA (1987 AND 2005)

George L. Scheper
Professor emeritus, Humanities Community College of Baltimore County, Essex
CHARISMA (2005)
CURSING (2005)

Lawrence H. Schiffman
New York University
ESSENES (1987)
DEAD SEA SCROLLS (1987)
SADDUCEES (2005)

Robert Schilling
École Pratique des Hautes Études, Collège de France, and Université de Strasbourg II
DIANA (1987)
JANUS (1987)
JUNO (1987)
JUPITER (1987)
LUPERCALIA (1987)
MARS (1987)
NUMEN (1987)
PARENTALIA (1987)
PONTIFEX (1987)
ROMAN RELIGION: THE EARLY PERIOD (1987)
VENUS (1987)
VESTA (1987)

Annemarie Schimmel
Harvard University
ANDRAE, TOR (1987)
CALLIGRAPHY: ISLAMIC CALLIGRAPHY (1987)
CATS (1987)
ḤALLĀJ, AL- (1987)
HEILER, FRIEDRICH (1987)
ICONOGRAPHY: ISLAMIC ICONOGRAPHY (1987)
ISLAMIC RELIGIOUS YEAR (1987)
LULL, RAMÓN (1987)
NUMBERS: AN OVERVIEW (1987)
NŪR MUḤAMMAD (1987)
QURRAT AL-ʿAYN ṬĀHIRAH (1987)
RĀBIʿAH AL-ʿADAWĪYAH (1987)
RŪMĪ, JALĀL AL-DĪN (1987)

Robert S. Schine
Middlebury College
COHEN, HERMANN (2005)

Conrad Schirokauer
City College, City University of New York
ZHU XI (1987 AND 2005)

Eva Schmidt
Magyar Tudományos Akadémia, Budapest
KHANTY AND MANSI RELIGION (1987)

Sandra M. Schneiders
Jesuit School of Theology, Berkeley
JOHN OF THE CROSS (1987 AND 2005)

Juliane Schober
Arizona State University
U NU (2005)

J. Matthew Schoffeleers
Vrije Universiteit, Amsterdam
MBONA (1987)

Steven Scholl
Kalimat Press, Los Angeles
SHAYKHĪYAH (1987)

Karine Schomer
University of California, Berkeley
SŪRDĀS (1987)

Ismar Schorsch
Jewish Theological Seminary of America
FRANKEL, ZACHARIAS (1987)
JEWISH STUDIES: JEWISH STUDIES FROM 1818 TO 1919 (1987)
SCHECHTER, SOLOMON (1987)

Vernon James Schubel
Kenyon College
WORSHIP AND DEVOTIONAL LIFE: MUSLIM WORSHIP (2005)

Michael J. Schuck
Loyola University
ROMAN CATHOLICISM [FURTHER CONSIDERATIONS] (2005)

David G. Schultenover
Creighton University
TYRRELL, GEORGE (1987)

Hillel Schwartz
University of California, San Diego
MILLENARIANISM: AN OVERVIEW (1987)
SACRED TIME (2005)

Steven S. Schwarzschild
Washington University, Saint Louis
COHEN, HERMANN (1987)
ROSENZWEIG, FRANZ (1987)

Nathan A. Scott, Jr.
University of Virginia
LITERATURE: RELIGIOUS DIMENSIONS OF MODERN WESTERN LITERATURE [FIRST EDITION] (1987)

R. Kevin Seasoltz
Saint Anselm's Abbey, Washington, D.C.
BENEDICTINES (1987)
BENEDICT OF NURSIA (1987)

Anthony Seeger
Indiana University, Bloomington
GE MYTHOLOGY (1987)

Robert A. Segal
University of Lancaster, United Kingdom
GASTER, THEODOR H. (2005)
HEROES (2005)
JUNG, C. G. (2005)
SMITH, W. ROBERTSON (2005)
SOCIOLOGY: SOCIOLOGY AND RELIGION [FURTHER CONSIDERATIONS] (2005)
SOCIOLOGY: SOCIOLOGY OF RELIGION [FURTHER CONSIDERATIONS] (2005)

Anna Seidel
École Française d'Extrême-Orient, Kyoto
HUANGDI (1987)
MASPERO, HENRI (1987)
TAIPING (1987)
YU (1987)
YUHUANG (1987)

Robert M. Seltzer
Hunter College and the Graduate School, City University of New York
HISTORY: JEWISH VIEWS (1987)
JEWISH PEOPLE (1987 AND 2005)
KROCHMAL, NAḤMAN (1987)
MENDELSSOHN, MOSES (1987)

H. L. Seneviratne
University of Virginia
SAṂGHA: SAṂGHA AND SOCIETY IN SOUTH AND SOUTHEAST ASIA (1987)

Bernard Septimus
Harvard University
ABULAFIA, ME'IR (1987)
YA'AQOV BEN ASHER (1987)

Susan Sered
Harvard University
HEALING AND MEDICINE: AN OVERVIEW (2005)

R. B. Serjeant
University of Saint Andrews
ḤARAM AND ḤAWṬAH (1987)

Scott Sessions
Amherst College
INQUISITION, THE: THE INQUISITION IN THE NEW WORLD (2005)

T. K. Seung
University of Texas at Austin
KANT, IMMANUEL (1987 AND 2005)

William A. Shack
University of California, Berkeley
EAST AFRICAN RELIGIONS: ETHIOPIAN RELIGIONS (1987)

Meir Shahar
Tel Aviv University
MARTIAL ARTS: CHINESE MARTIAL ARTS (2005)

Reza Shah-Kazemi
Institute of Ismaili Studies, London
'ALĪ IBN ABĪ ṬĀLIB (2005)
ṬABĀṬABĀ'Ī, 'ALLĀMA (2005)

Muhammad Kazem Shaker
Qom University
HAWZAH (2005)

Paul Shankman
University of Colorado at Boulder
MEAD, MARGARET (2005)

Thomas A. Shannon
Worcester Polytechnic Institute
BIOETHICS (2005)

Robert H. Sharf
University of California, Berkeley
SUZUKI, D. T. (2005)

Arvind Sharma
McGill University
DEVILS (1987)
ECSTASY (1987)
OBEDIENCE (1987 AND 2005)
SATAN (1987 AND 2005)

Eric J. Sharpe
University of Sydney
BRANDON, S. G. F. (1987)
DIALOGUE OF RELIGIONS (1987)
JAMES, E. O. (1987)
MANISM (1987)
MANNHARDT, WILHELM (1987)
MARETT, R. R. (1987)
PREANIMISM (1987)
TYLOR, E. B. (1987)

Richard Shek
California State University, Sacramento
MILLENARIANISM: CHINESE MILLENARIAN MOVEMENTS (1987 AND 2005)

Massey H. Shepherd, Jr.
Church Divinity School of the Pacific, Berkeley
ANGLICANISM (1987)
CRANMER, THOMAS (1987)
HOOKER, RICHARD (1987)
WYCLIF, JOHN (1987)

Gerald T. Sheppard
Emmanuel College, University of Toronto
CANON (1987)
PROPHECY: AN OVERVIEW (1987)

Byron L. Sherwin
Spertus College of Judaica
LÖW, YEHUDAH BEN BETSAL'EL OF PRAGUE (1987)

Amnon Shiloah
Hebrew University of Jerusalem
MUSIC: MUSIC AND RELIGION IN THE MIDDLE EAST (1987)

Edward Shils
University of Chicago
INTELLECTUALS (1987)

Shimazono Susumu
University of Tokyo
NEW RELIGIOUS MOVEMENTS: NEW RELIGIOUS MOVEMENTS IN JAPAN (2005)
ŌMOTOKYŌ (2005)
SŌKA GAKKAI (2005)

Larry D. Shinn
Berea College
INTERNATIONAL SOCIETY FOR KRISHNA CONSCIOUSNESS (1987 AND 2005)

Roger Lincoln Shinn
University of Chicago
NIEBUHR, REINHOLD (1987 AND 2005)

Jan Shipps
Purdue University
YOUNG, BRIGHAM (1987)

Moshe Shokeid
Tel-Aviv University
PILGRIMAGE: CONTEMPORARY JEWISH PILGRIMAGE (1987 AND 2005)

Frank Shuffelton
University of Rochester
HOOKER, THOMAS (1987)

Neelima Shukla-Bhatt
University of Edinburgh (emeritus)
ĀNANDAMAYĪ MĀ (2005)
ŚĀRĀDA DEVĪ (2005)

Kwong-loi Shun
University of Toronto
REN AND YI (2005)

Anson Shupe
Indiana University-Purdue University, Fort Wayne
ANTICULT MOVEMENTS (2005)
DEPROGRAMMING (2005)

Muzammil H. Siddiqi
Islamic Society, Garden Grove, California
ṢALĀT (1987)

James T. Siegel
Cornell University
ACEHNESE RELIGION (1987)

Lee Siegel
University of Hawaii, Manoa
BHAGAVADGĪTĀ (1987)

Joseph Sievers
Pontifical Biblical Institute
SMITH, MORTON (2005)

Alejandra Siffredi
Universidad de Buenos Aires
TEHUELCHE RELIGION (1987)

Pierre André Sigal
Université de Montpellier III (Paul Valéry)
PILGRIMAGE: ROMAN CATHOLIC PILGRIMAGE IN EUROPE (1987)

Anna-Leena Siikala
Helsingin Yliopisto
DESCENT INTO THE UNDERWORLD (1987)
SHAMANISM: SIBERIAN AND INNER ASIAN SHAMANISM (1987)
UKKO (1987)

Laurence J. Silberstein
Lehigh University
BUBER, MARTIN (1987 AND 2005)
KAUFMANN, YEḤEZKEL (1987)

Francisco Marco Simón
Universidad de Zaragoza
FLAMEN (2005)
IBERIAN RELIGION (2005)

George Eaton Simpson
Oberlin College
CARIBBEAN RELIGIONS: AFRO-CARIBBEAN RELIGIONS (1987)
CHRISTIANITY: CHRISTIANITY IN THE CARIBBEAN REGION (1987)

Khushwant Singh
Bombay, India
SINGH, GOBIND (1987)

Nikky-Guninder Kaur Singh
Colby College
DASAM GRANTH (2005)
GENDER AND RELIGION: GENDER AND SIKHISM (2005)
NĀNAK (2005)
SIKHISM (2005)

Denis Sinor
Indiana University
HUN RELIGION (1987)
UMAI (1987)

Nathan Sivin
University of Pennsylvania
ALCHEMY: CHINESE ALCHEMY (1987 AND 2005)

Peter Skilling
Lumbini International Research Institute
WORSHIP AND DEVOTIONAL LIFE: BUDDHIST DEVOTIONAL LIFE IN SOUTHEAST ASIA (2005)

Tadeusz Skorupski
School of Oriental and African Studies, University of London
PRAJÑĀ (1987)
DHARMA: BUDDHIST DHARMA AND DHARMAS (1987)
SAUTRĀNTIKA (1987)
TATHATĀ (1987)

Laura A. Skosey
University of Chicago
LAW AND RELIGION: LAW AND RELIGION IN CHINESE RELIGIONS (2005)

Vieda Skultans
University of Bristol
AFFLICTION: AN OVERVIEW (1987)

Peter Slater
Trinity College, University of Toronto
BAKHTIN, M. M. (2005)
HOPE (1987)
SMITH, WILFRED CANTWELL (2005)

R. C. Sleigh, Jr.
University of Massachusetts, Amherst
LEIBNIZ, GOTTFRIED WILHELM (1987)

Ninian Smart
University of Lancaster, United Kingdom and University of California, Santa Barbara
COMPARATIVE-HISTORICAL METHOD [FIRST EDITION] (1987)
SOTERIOLOGY (1987)

Brian K. Smith
University of California, Riverside
SAṂSĀRA (1987)
TANTRISM: HINDU TANTRISM (2005)
VARṆA AND JĀTI (2005)
VEDĀṄGAS (2005)

D. Moody Smith
Duke University
JOHN THE EVANGELIST (1987 AND 2005)
LUKE THE EVANGELIST (1987 AND 2005)
MARK THE EVANGELIST (1987 AND 2005)
MATTHEW THE EVANGELIST (1987 AND 2005)

E. Gene Smith
Tibetan Buddhist Resource Center
KONG SPRUL BLO GROS MTHA' YAS (KONGTRUL LODRO TAYE) (2005)

Frederick M. Smith
University of Iowa
MANTRA (2005)

Jane I. Smith
Harvard University
AFTERLIFE: AN OVERVIEW (1987)
ĪMĀN AND ISLĀM (1987)

John E. Smith
Yale University
PHILOSOPHY: PHILOSOPHY AND RELIGION (1987)

Jonathan Z. Smith
University of Chicago
AGES OF THE WORLD (1987)
DYING AND RISING GODS (1987)
GOLDEN AGE (1987)
SLEEP (1987)

Robert J. Smith
Cornell University
DOMESTIC OBSERVANCES: JAPANESE PRACTICES (1987)

Warren Thomas Smith
Interdenominational Theological Center, Atlanta
AUGUSTINE OF HIPPO (1987)

Stuart W. Smithers
San Francisco, California
SPIRITUAL GUIDE (1987)

David L. Snellgrove
School of Oriental and African Studies, University of London (emeritus)
BUDDHAS AND BODHISATTVAS: CELESTIAL BUDDHAS AND BODHISATTVAS (1987)

Moshe Sokol
Lander College for Men, Touro College
SOLOVEITCHIK, JOSEPH BAER (2005)

Robert Somerville
Columbia University
GREGORY VII (1987 AND 2005)
LEO I (1987)

Deborah Sommer
Gettysburg College
CHENG HAO (1987 AND 2005)
CHENG YI (1987 AND 2005)
ICONOGRAPHY: CONFUCIAN ICONOGRAPHY (2005)

Sergio Sorrentino
University of Salerno
SCHLEIERMACHER, FRIEDRICH (2005)

Aidan Southall
University of Wisconsin—Madison
TSWANA RELIGION (1987)

Susanna W. Southard
Vanderbilt University
RUTH AND NAOMI (2005)

Joseph J. Spae
Oud-Heverlee, Belgium
ITŌ JINSAI (1987)

Johanna Spector
Jewish Theological Seminary of America
CHANTING (1987)

Susan A. Spectorsky
Queens College, City University of New York
MĀLIK IBN ANAS (1987)
MAṢLAḤAH (1987)

R. Marston Speight
Hartford Seminary
CREEDS: AN OVERVIEW (1987)
MĀTURĪDĪ, AL- (1987)

S. David Sperling
Hebrew Union College–Jewish Institute of Religion, New York
GOD: GOD IN THE HEBREW SCRIPTURES (1987 AND 2005)
JEREMIAH (1987)

Lewis W. Spitz
Stanford University
BRUNO, GIORDANO (1987)
FICINO, MARSILIO (1987)
HUMANISM (1987)
PICO DELLA MIRANDOLA, GIOVANNI (1987)

Alan Sponberg
Princeton University
KUIJI (1987)
XUANZANG (1987)

Dragoslav Srejović
Univerzitet u Beogradu
NEOLITHIC RELIGION (1987)

Smriti Srinivas
University of California, Davis
CITIES (2005)
SAI BABA MOVEMENT (2005)

Max L. Stackhouse
Princeton Theological Seminary
CHRISTIAN SOCIAL MOVEMENTS (1987 AND 2005)
MISSIONS: MISSIONARY ACTIVITY (1987 AND 2005)

Aaron Stalnaker
Indiana University
XUNZI (2005)

Joan Stambaugh
Hunter College, City University of New York
PHILOSOPHY: AN OVERVIEW (1987)

James J. Stamoolis
International Fellowship of Evangelical Students, Jeannette, Pennsylvania
INNOKENTII VENIAMINOV (1987)

Shaul Stampfer
Hebrew University of Jerusalem
KAGAN, YISRA'EL ME'IR (1987)
KOTLER, AHARON (1987)
YESHIVAH (1987)

Michael Stanislawski
Columbia University
ELIYYAHU BEN SHELOMOH ZALMAN (1987)
ISSERLES, MOSHEH (1987)
LURIA, SHELOMOH (1987)

John E. Stanton
University of Western Australia
BERNDT, RONALD (2005)
TJURUNGAS (1987)

Vincent Stanzione
Moses Mesoamerican Archive, Peabody Museum
MAXIMÓN (2005)

Michael Stausberg
University of Bergen
KLIMKEIT, HANS-JOACHIM (2005)

Alessandro Stavru
Università degli Studi di Napoli "L'Orientale"
BACHOFEN, J. J. (2005)
OTTO, WALTER F. (2005)
SOCRATES (2005)

Stephen J. Stein
Indiana University, Bloomington
EDWARDS, JONATHAN (1987)

Nancy Shatzman Steinhardt
University of Pennsylvania
TEMPLE: BUDDHIST TEMPLE COMPOUNDS IN EAST ASIA (2005)
TEMPLE: CONFUCIAN TEMPLE COMPOUNDS (1987 AND 2005)
TEMPLE: DAOIST TEMPLE COMPOUNDS (1987 AND 2005)

Ernst Steinkellner
Universität Wien
DHARMAKĪRTI (1987)

William H. Stemper, Jr.
Forum for Corporate Responsibility, New York
FREEMASONS (1987)

Mikael Stenmark
Uppsala University
SOCIOBIOLOGY AND EVOLUTIONARY PSYCHOLOGY: DARWINISM AND RELIGION (2005)

Walter Stephens
Johns Hopkins University
DEMONS: AN OVERVIEW (2005)

Barry Stephenson
University of Calgary
RITES OF PASSAGE: AN OVERVIEW [FURTHER CONSIDERATIONS] (2005)

David Stern
University of Pennsylvania
AFTERLIFE: JEWISH CONCEPTS (1987)
COHEN, ARTHUR A. (2005)

Carole Lynn Stewart
University of Calgary
CIVIL RELIGION (2005)

Devin J. Stewart
Emory University
MĀLIK IBN ANAS (2005)

Dianne M. Stewart
Emory University
AFRICAN AMERICAN RELIGIONS: HISTORY OF STUDY (2005)

Norman A. Stillman
State University of New York at Binghamton
BERBER RELIGION (1987)

Elettra Stimilli
Dipartimento di Filosofia, Univerità di Salerno, Italy
TAUBES, JAKOB (2005)

George W. Stocking, Jr.
University of Chicago
CODRINGTON, R. H. (1987 AND 2005)

F. Ernest Stoeffler
Temple University
FRANCKE, AUGUST HERMANN (1987)
PIETISM (1987)
SPENER, PHILIPP JAKOB (1987)

Jacqueline I. Stone
Princeton University
NICHIRENSHŪ (2005)

Jon R. Stone
California State University, Long Beach
MÜLLER, F. MAX (2005)

Jeffrey Stout
Princeton University
NATURALISM (1987)

Yuri Stoyanov
University of London
DUALISM (2005)

Frederick J. Streng
Southern Methodist University
ŚŪNYAM AND ŚŪNYATĀ (1987)
TRUTH (1987)

Ivan Strenski
University of California, Riverside
DURKHEIM, ÉMILE (2005)

John S. Strong
Bates College
MĀRA (2005)
MERIT: BUDDHIST CONCEPTS (1987)
PRZYLUSKI, JEAN (2005)
RELICS (1987 AND 2005)

Peter T. Struck
University of Pennsylvania
SYMBOL AND SYMBOLISM (2005)

David Stuart
Harvard University
MAYA RELIGION (2005)

Kocku von Stuckrad
University of Amsterdam
ENCYCLOPEDIAS (2005)
FESTSCHRIFTEN (2005)

Theodore Stylianopoulos
Holy Cross Greek Orthodox School of Theology, Brookline, Massachusetts
EPHRAEM OF SYRIA (1987)
ISAAC THE SYRIAN (1987)
SERAFIM OF SAROV (1987)

Sharada Sugirtharajah
University of Birmingham, United Kingdom
RAMABAI, PANDITA (2005)

Lawrence E. Sullivan
University of Notre Dame
AXIS MUNDI (1987)
CENTER OF THE WORLD (1987)
DEUS OTIOSUS (1987)
EARTH (1987)
HEALING AND MEDICINE: AN OVERVIEW (2005)
HIEROPHANY (1987)
NATURE: WORSHIP OF NATURE (1987)
ORIENTATION (1987)
SUPREME BEINGS (1987)
TRICKSTERS: AN OVERVIEW (1987)
TRICKSTERS: MESOAMERICAN AND SOUTH AMERICAN TRICKSTERS (1987)

Winnifred Fallers Sullivan
University of Chicago
LAW AND RELIGION: AN OVERVIEW (2005)

Bengt Sundkler
Uppsala Universitet
SHEMBE, ISAIAH (1987)

Kenneth Surin
Duke University
LIBERATION (2005)

A. Rand Sutherland
Florida Southern College
BOETHIUS (1987)

William L. Svelmoe
St. Mary's College, Notre Dame
EVANGELICAL AND FUNDAMENTAL CHRISTIANITY (2005)

Mark N. Swanson
Luther Seminary, St. Paul, Minnesota
COPTIC CHURCH (2005)

Paul L. Swanson
Nanzan Institute of Religion and Culture, Nagoya, Japan
ENNIN (1987)

Michael Swartz
Ohio State University
JUDAISM: AN OVERVIEW (2005)

Samy Swayd
San Diego State University
DRUZE (2005)

Donald K. Swearer
Swarthmore College (emeritus); Harvard Divinity School
ARHAT (1987)
BUDDHADĀSA (2005)
BUDDHISM: BUDDHISM IN SOUTHEAST ASIA (1987)
BUDDHIST RELIGIOUS YEAR (1987)
ECOLOGY AND RELIGION: ECOLOGY AND BUDDHISM (2005)
FOLK RELIGION: FOLK BUDDHISM (1987)

Daniel M. Swetschinski
University of Arizona
MARRANOS (1987)

Laura Furlan Szanto
University of California, Santa Barbara
FICTION: NATIVE AMERICAN FICTION AND RELIGION (2005)
POETRY: NATIVE AMERICAN POETRY AND RELIGION (2005)

James D. Tabor
University of North Carolina at Chapel Hill
KORESH, DAVID (2005)

Ikael Tafari
University of the West Indies
RASTAFARIANISM (2005)

Sunao Taira
Tsukuba University
OKINAWAN RELIGION (2005)

Suha Taji-Farouki
University of Exeter
QUTB, SAYYID (2005)

Sarolta A. Takács
Rutgers, the State University of New Jersey
ISIS (2005)

Charles H. Talbert
Wake Forest University
REIMARUS, HERMANN SAMUEL (1987)

Thomas J. Talley
General Theological Seminary, New York
CHRISTIAN LITURGICAL YEAR (1987)
WORSHIP AND DEVOTIONAL LIFE: CHRISTIAN WORSHIP (1987)

Frank Talmage
University of Toronto
KIMḤI, DAVID (1987)

Elsa Tamez
Universidad Bíblica Latinoamericana, Costa Rica
LIBERATION THEOLOGY (2005)

Kenneth Tanaka
Albany, California
HUIYUAN (1987)

Gary Michael Tartakov
Iowa State University
MŪRTI (1987)

Karl Taube
University of California, Riverside

DRAMA: MESOAMERICAN DANCE AND DRAMA (2005)
JADE (2005)

Rhonda Taube
University of California, San Diego
DRAMA: MESOAMERICAN DANCE AND DRAMA (2005)

Ann Taves
Claremont School of Theology and Claremont Graduate University
JAMES, WILLIAM (2005)
RELIGIOUS EXPERIENCE (2005)

Bron Taylor
University of Florida
EARTH FIRST! (2005)
ECOLOGY AND RELIGION: ECOLOGY AND NATURE RELIGIONS (2005)

Eugene Taylor
Harvard University
CONSCIOUSNESS, STATES OF (2005)

Mark C. Taylor
Williams College
KIERKEGAARD, SØREN (1987)

Rodney L. Taylor
University of Colorado at Boulder
ZHANG ZAI (1987 AND 2005)
ZHOU DUNYI (1987 AND 2005)

Barbara Tedlock
State University of New York at Buffalo
DREAMS (1987 AND 2005)

Stephen F. Teiser
Arizona State University
BUDDHISM: BUDDHISM IN CHINA (2005)

Javier Teixidor
Centre National de la Recherche Scientifique, Paris
ARAMEAN RELIGION (1987)

S. D. Temkin
University of Miami
WISE, ISAAC M. (1987)

James S. Thayer
Oklahoma State University
MAWU-LISA (1987)
UNKULUNKULU (1987)

J. A. Theuws
Vaalbeck, Belgium
LUBA RELIGION (1987)

Jacqueline M. C. Thomas
Centre National de la Recherche Scientifique, Paris
PYGMY RELIGIONS (1987)

Louis-Vincent Thomas
Universite de Paris V (Rene Descartes)
FUNERAL RITES: AN OVERVIEW (1987)

Laurence G. Thompson
University of Southern California
CHINESE RELIGIOUS YEAR (1987)
JIAO (1987)
TIAN (1987)

Linus J. Thro
Saint Louis University
GILSON, ÉTIENNE (1987)

Robert A. F. Thurman
Amherst College
TATHĀGATA-GARBHA (1987)

Richard W. Thurn
New York, New York
ASHES (1987)
BLADES (1987)
CARDS (1987)
FOUNTAIN (1987)

Antoine Tibesar
Academy of American Franciscan History, West Bethesda, Maryland
SERRA, JUNIPERO (1987)

Mihaela Timus
Center for the History of Religions, University of Bucharest, Romania
WIKANDER, STIG (2005)

Tink Tinker
Iliff School of Theology, Denver, Colorado
OSAGE RELIGIOUS TRADITIONS (2005)
SUN DANCE [FURTHER CONSIDERATIONS] (2005)
VISION QUEST (2005)

Hava Tirosh-Samuelson
Arizona State University
ECOLOGY AND RELIGION: ECOLOGY AND JUDAISM (2005)

Francis V. Tiso
Institute of Noetic Sciences, Petaluma, California
ORGY: ORGY IN ASIA (2005)

Linda M. Tober
University of Tennessee, Knoxville
HEAVEN AND HELL (1987)

Dale Todaro
New York, New York
KUMĀRAJĪVA (1987)

Brian M. du Toit
University of Florida
HEALING AND MEDICINE: HEALING AND MEDICINE IN AFRICA (2005)

Toki Masanori
Kokugakuin University
PRIESTHOOD: SHINTŌ PRIESTHOOD (1987)

R. A. Tomlinson
University of Birmingham
TEMPLE: ANCIENT NEAR EASTERN AND MEDITERRANEAN TEMPLES (1987)

Chiara Ombretta Tommasi
Università degli Studi di Pisa
APOTHEOSIS (2005)
ASCENSION (2005)
ORGY: ORGY IN MEDIEVAL AND MODERN EUROPE (2005)
ORGY: ORGY IN THE ANCIENT MEDITERRANEAN WORLD (2005)

Robert Tonkinson
University of Western Australia
MARDU RELIGION (1987 AND 2005)

James B. Torrance
University of Aberdeen
BARTH, KARL (1987)

Emilio Suárez de la Torre
University of Valladolid
PINDAR (2005)
SIBYLLINE ORACLES (2005)

Yolotl González Torres
Instituto Nacional de Antropología e Historia
MESOAMERICAN RELIGIONS: HISTORY OF STUDY (1987 AND 2005)
MESOAMERICAN RELIGIONS: MYTHIC THEMES (2005)

Sandy Toussaint
University of Western Australia
KABERRY, PHYLLIS M. (2005)

Richard F. Townsend
Art Institute of Chicago
GEOGRAPHY (1987)
LAKES (1987)

David Tracy
University of Chicago
THEOLOGY: COMPARATIVE THEOLOGY (1987)

J. B. Trapp
Warburg Institute, University of London
YATES, FRANCES AMELIA (2005)

John Travis
Holy Cross Greek Orthodox School of Theology, Brookline, Massachusetts
CERULARIOS, MICHAEL (1987)
GREGORY OF CYPRUS (1987)
NIKEPHOROS (1987)

Diane Treacy-Cole
University of Bristol
EDDY, MARY BAKER (2005)
MARY MAGDALENE (2005)

Lucio Troiani
Università di Pavia
CICERO (2005)

Christian W. Troll
Vidyajyoti Institute, Delhi
AHMAD KHAN, SAYYID (1987)

Garry W. Trompf
University of Sydney
CHRISTIANITY: CHRISTIANITY IN THE PACIFIC ISLANDS [FURTHER CONSIDERATIONS] (2005)
COSMOLOGY: OCEANIC COSMOLOGIES (2005)
JEVONS, F. B. (1987)
OCEANIC RELIGIONS: HISTORY OF STUDY [FURTHER CONSIDERATIONS] (2005)
SHARPE, ERIC J. (2005)
SPENCER, HERBERT (1987)
STUDY OF RELIGION: THE ACADEMIC STUDY OF RELIGION IN AUSTRALIA AND OCEANIA (2005)
TRANSCULTURATION AND RELIGION: RELIGION IN THE FORMATION OF MODERN OCEANIA (2005)
UTOPIA (1987)

Mary Evelyn Tucker
Bucknell University
ECOLOGY AND RELIGION: AN OVERVIEW (2005)
ECOLOGY AND RELIGION: ECOLOGY AND CONFUCIANISM (2005)
KAIBARA EKKEN (1987)
NAKAE TŌJU (1987)

William Tuladhar-Douglas
Oxford Centre for Buddhist Studies
PŪJĀ: BUDDHIST PŪJĀ (2005)

Diana G. Tumminia
California State University, Sacramento
UNARIUS ACADEMY OF SCIENCE (2005)

Robert Turcan
Université Lyon III (Jean Moulin)
AGNŌSTOS THEOS (1987 AND 2005)
APOCATASTASIS (1987)
APOTHEOSIS (1987)
CATHARSIS (1987 AND 2005)
DEIFICATION (1987)
DIETERICH, ALBRECHT (1987)

Edith Turner
University of Virginia
BODILY MARKS (2005)
LIMINALITY (2005)
MARRIAGE (1987)
NDEMBU RELIGION (1987)
PILGRIMAGE: AN OVERVIEW (1987 AND 2005)
RITES OF PASSAGE: AN OVERVIEW [FIRST EDITION] (2005)

Karen Turner
Holy Cross College
LEGALISM (2005)

Victor Turner
(deceased)
BODILY MARKS (1987)

Thomas A. Tweed
University of North Carolina at Chapel Hill
ADAMS, HANNAH (2005)

Isadore Twersky
Harvard University
AVRAHAM BEN DAVID OF POSQUIÈRES (1987)
MAIMONIDES, MOSES (1987)

Ruel W. Tyson, Jr.
University of North Carolina at Chapel Hill
JOURNALISM AND RELIGION (1987)

Ueda Kenji
Kokugakuin University
HIRATA ATSUTANE (1987)
MOTOORI NORINAGA (1987)
NORITO (1987)

Uehara Toyoaki
Indiana University, Bloomington
TENRIKYŌ (1987)

Ellen M. Umansky
Fairfield University
ELECTION (1987)
EXILE (1987 AND 2005)
MONTAGU, LILY (1987)

Frederic B. Underwood
Upperco, Maryland
MEDITATION (1987)

Taitetsu Unno
Smith College
KARUṆĀ (1987)
MAPPŌ (1987)

E. E. Urbach
Israel Academy of Sciences and Humanities, Jerusalem
TOSAFOT [FIRST EDITION] (1987)

Hugh Urban
Ohio State University
CAKRAS (2005)
CROWLEY, ALEISTER (2005)
KUṆḌALINĪ (2005)
POLITICS AND RELIGION: AN OVERVIEW (2005)
TAGORE, RABINDRANATH (1987 AND 2005)

Gary Urton
Harvard University
ETHNOASTRONOMY (1987 AND 2005)

Paul Valliere
Butler University
TRADITION (1987 AND 2005)

F. Van Ommeslaeghe
Société des Bollandistes, Brussels
CHRYSOSTOM (1987)

John Van Seters
University of North Carolina at Chapel Hill
ABRAHAM (1987)
DAVID [FIRST EDITION] (1987)
ELIJAH (1987)
ELISHA (1987)
EZRA (1987)
JOSIAH (1987)
MOSES (1987)
NATHAN (1987)
NEHEMIAH (1987)
SAMUEL (1987)
SAUL (1987)
SOLOMON (1987)

Nomikos Michael Vaporis
Holy Cross Greek Orthodox School of Theology, Brookline, Massachusetts
KOSMAS AITOLOS (1987)
SCHOLARIOS, GENNADIOS (1987)

H. Paul Varley
Columbia University
JAPANESE RELIGIONS: RELIGIOUS DOCUMENTS (1987)

Kapila Vatsyayan
Government of India, Department of Culture, New Delhi
DRAMA: INDIAN DANCE AND DANCE DRAMA (1987)

Charlotte Vaudeville
Université de Paris III (Sorbonne-Nouvelle) and École Pratique des Hautes Études, Collège de France
KABĪR (1987)

Juan Adolfo Vázquez
University of Pittsburgh
SOUTH AMERICAN INDIAN RELIGIONS: MYTHIC THEMES (1987)

Anuradha Veeravalli
Delhi University
INDIAN PHILOSOPHIES (2005)
NYĀYA (2005)

Francisco Diez de Velasco
Universidad de La Laguna, Canary Islands, Spain
DESCENT INTO THE UNDERWORLD (2005)

Franciscus Verellen
Institute of Chinese Studies
DU GUANGTING (2005)
SIMA CHENGZHEN (2005)

Donald Phillip Verene
Emory University
CASSIRER, ERNST (1987)
VICO, GIOVANNI BATTISTA (1987)

Jean-Pierre Vernant
Collège de France
GREEK RELIGION [FIRST EDITION] (1987)

Marilyn Notah Verney
University of California, Santa Barbara
NAVAJO RELIGIOUS TRADITIONS (2005)

Alec Vidler
Friars of the Sack, Rye, England
BLONDEL, MAURICE (1987)

Vaira Vīķe-Freiberga
President of the Republic of Latvia
SAULE (2005)

Shafique N. Virani
Harvard University
AHL AL-BAYT (2005)

David R. Vishanoff
Emory University
NAẒẒĀM, AL- (2005)

Burton L. Visotzky
Jewish Theological Seminary
MIDRASH AND AGGADAH [FURTHER CONSIDERATONS] (2005)

Vilmos Voigt
Eötvös Loránd Tudományegyetem, Budapest (Institute of Ethnography)
DÖMÖTÖR, TEKLA (2005)
HUNGARIAN RELIGION (2005)
REGULY, ANTAL (2005)

John O. Voll
Georgetown University
IBN ʿABD AL-WAHHĀB, MUḤAMMAD (1987 AND 2005)
WAHHĀBĪYAH (1987 AND 2005)

John E. Vollmer
New York, New York
CLOTHING: CLOTHING AND RELIGION IN THE EAST (2005)
TEXTILES (1987 AND 2005)

M. Heerma van Voss
University of Amsterdam (emeritus)
ANUBIS (1987 AND 2005)
BLEEKER, C. JOUCO (1987)

Hent de Vries
Johns Hopkins University
ORIENTALISM (2005)

Jacques Waardenburg
Rijksuniversiteit te Utrecht
BREUIL, HENRI (1987)
CHANTEPIE DE LA SAUSSAYE, P. D. (1987)
GOLDZIHER, IGNÁCZ (1987)
ISLAMIC STUDIES [FIRST EDITION] (1987)
LEEUW, GERARDUS VAN DER (1987)
MASSIGNON, LOUIS (1987)
TIELE, C. P. (1987)
WENSINCK, A. J. (1987)

Roy Wagner
University of Virginia
AFTERLIFE: OCEANIC CONCEPTS (2005)
GOLDENWEISER, ALEXANDER A. (1987)
MANA (2005)
TABOO (1987)
TOTEMISM (1987)

Rudolf G. Wagner
University of Heidelberg
WANG BI (1987 AND 2005)

Sally Roesch Wagner
Matilda Joslyn Gage Foundation, Fayetteville, New York
GAGE, MATILDA JOSLYN (2005)

Erik Wahlgren
University of California, Los Angeles (emeritus)
RUNES [FIRST EDITION] (1987)

Manabu Waida
University of Alberta
AUTHORITY (1987)
BIRDS (1987)
COCKS (1987)
ELEPHANTS (1987)
FOXES (1987)
FROGS AND TOADS (1987)
HEDGEHOGS (1987)
INCARNATION (1987)
INSECTS (1987)
KINGSHIP: KINGSHIP IN EAST ASIA (1987)
MIRACLES: AN OVERVIEW (1987)
PIGS (1987)
RABBITS (1987)
TURTLES AND TORTOISES (1987)

David Waines
University of Lancaster, United Kingdom
ʿUMAR IBN AL-KHAṬṬĀB (1987)

Geoffrey Wainwright
Duke University
BERENGAR OF TOURS (1987 AND 2005)
LORD'S PRAYER (1987 AND 2005)

Jeanette A. Wakin
Columbia University
ABŪ YŪSUF (1987)

Paul Waldau
Tufts University
ANIMALS (2005)

Marilyn Robinson Waldman
Ohio State University
ESCHATOLOGY: ISLAMIC ESCHATOLOGY (1987)
NUBŪWAH (1987)
SUNNAH (1987)

William S. Waldron
Middlebury College
ĀLAYA-VIJÑĀNA (2005)

Stanley Walens
University of California, San Diego
NORTH AMERICAN INDIANS: INDIANS OF THE NORTHWEST COAST [FIRST EDITION] (1987)
POTLATCH (1987)
THERIANTHROPISM (1987)

Muhammadisa Waley
The British Library, London
KUBRĀ, NAJM AL-DĪN (2005)

J. H. Walgrave
(deceased)
NEWMAN, JOHN HENRY (1987)

Sheila S. Walker
University of California, Berkeley
HARRIS, WILLIAM WADE (1987)

Vesna A. Wallace
University of California, Santa Barbara
KĀLACAKRA (2005)

Dewey D. Wallace, Jr.
Professor of Religion, George Washington University
FREE WILL AND PREDESTINATION: AN OVERVIEW (1987 AND 2005)
THEOCRACY (1987 AND 2005)

James Waller
New York, New York
EVOLUTION: EVOLUTIONISM (1987)
PREHISTORIC RELIGIONS: AN OVERVIEW (1987)

Glenn Wallis
University of Georgia
GLASENAPP, HELMUTH VON (2005)

Neal H. Walls
University of Edinburgh (emeritus)
ANAT (2005)
BAAL (2005)
EL (2005)

Michael L. Walter
Indiana University Libraries, Bloomington
TIBETAN RELIGIONS: HISTORY OF STUDY (1987)

Jonathan S. Walters
Whitman College
AŚOKA (2005)
MISSIONS: BUDDHIST MISSIONS (2005)

Aihe Wang
University of Hong Kong
YINYANG WUXING (2005)

Richard G. Wang
University of Florida
FICTION: CHINESE FICTION AND RELIGION (2005)

Kallistos Ware
Pembroke College, University of Oxford
CYRIL I (1987)
PETR MOGHILA (1987)

Watanabe Hōyō
Rissho University
NICHIREN (1987)

Manabu Watanabe
Nanzan University
AUM SHINRIKYŌ (2005)

Henry Jay Watkin
New York, New York
WISSOWA, GEORG (1987)

W. Montgomery Watt
University of Edinburgh
CREEDS: ISLAMIC CREEDS (1987)
FREE WILL AND PREDESTINATION: ISLAMIC CONCEPTS (1987)
GHAZĀLI, ABŪ ḤĀMID AL- (1987)

Alex Wayman
Columbia University
BUDDHISM, SCHOOLS OF: TANTRIC RITUAL SCHOOLS OF BUDDHISM [FIRST EDITION] (1987)

R. K. Webb
University of Maryland, Baltimore County
MARTINEAU, JAMES (1987)

Val Webb
Augsburg College, Minnesota
NIGHTINGALE, FLORENCE (2005)

Sabra J. Webber
Ohio State University
HUMOR AND RELIGION: HUMOR AND ISLAM (2005)

Timothy P. Weber
Denver Conservative Baptist Seminary
IRVING, EDWARD (1987)

George Weckman
Ohio University
COMMUNITY (1987)
MONASTICISM: AN OVERVIEW (1987)
SECRET SOCIETIES (1987 AND 2005)

David L. Weddle
Colorado College
JEHOVAH'S WITNESSES (2005)

Kirk Wegter-McNelly
Boston University
PHYSICS AND RELIGION (2005)

Tu Wei-ming
Harvard University
SOUL: CHINESE CONCEPTS (1987)
TAIJI (1987)
WANG YANGMING (1987)

Donald Weinstein
University of Arizona
SAVONAROLA, GIROLAMO (1987)

John Weinstock
University of Texas at Austin
OLAF THE HOLY (1987)
SAXO GRAMMATICUS (1987 AND 2005)
SNORRI STURLUSON (1987 AND 2005)

Robert Weisbrot
Colby College, Waterville, Maine
FATHER DIVINE (2005)

James A. Weisheipl
(deceased)
ALBERTUS MAGNUS (1987)
ANSELM (1987)
NOMINALISM (1987)
SCHOLASTICISM (1987)
THOMAS AQUINAS (1987)

Bernard G. Weiss
University of Utah
IJMĀʿ (1987)
IJTIH ĀD (1987)
QĀḌĪ (1987)
UṢŪL AL-FIQH (1987)

Mitchell G. Weiss
Harvard University
ĀYURVEDA (1987)

Chava Weissler
Lehigh University
TEKHINES (2005)

G. R. Welbon
University of Pennsylvania
BURNOUF, EUGÈNE (1987 AND 2005)
LÉVI, SYLVAIN (1987 AND 2005)
OLDENBERG, HERMANN (1987 AND 2005)
VAIKHĀNASAS (1987 AND 2005)
VAṢṆAVISM: BHĀGAVATAS (1987 AND 2005)
VAṢṆAVISM: PĀÑCARĀTRAS (1987 AND 2005)
ZAEHNER, R. C. (1987)
ZIMMER, HEINRICH ROBERT (1987 AND 2005)

Mary Wellemeyer
Unitarian Universalist Church, Manchester, New Hampshire
SERVETUS, MICHAEL (2005)

Willeke Wendrich
University of California, Los Angeles
EGYPTIAN RELIGION: HISTORY OF STUDY (2005)

R. J. Zwi Werblowsky
Hebrew University of Jerusalem
ANTHROPOMORPHISM (1987)
ESCHATOLOGY: AN OVERVIEW (1987)
KARO, YOSEF (1987)
LIGHT AND DARKNESS (1987)
MESSIANISM: JEWISH MESSIANISM (1987)
POLYTHEISM (1987)
SHABBETAI TSEVI [FIRST EDITION] (1987)
TRANSMIGRATION (1987)

Eric Werner
New York, New York
MUSIC: MUSIC AND RELIGION IN GREECE, ROME, AND BYZANTIUM (1987)

Jack Wertheimer
Jewish Theological Seminary of America
BAECK, LEO (1987)

L. P. Wessell, Jr.
University of Colorado
LESSING, G. E. (1987)

Robert Wessing
Nothern Illinois University
SUNDANESE RELIGION (1987)

Catherine Wessinger
Loyola University, New Orleans
BESANT, ANNIE (2005)
NEW RELIGIOUS MOVEMENTS: AN OVERVIEW (2005)
NEW RELIGIOUS MOVEMENTS: NEW RELIGIOUS MOVEMENTS AND MILLENNIALISM (2005)
YOGANANDA (2005)

Cornel West
Yale University
METAPHYSICS (1987)

M. L. West
Royal Holloway College and Bedford College, University of London
EROS (1987)
HESIOD (1987)
THESMOPHORIA (1987)

Joan Goodnick Westenholz
Bible Lands Museum Jerusalem
GODDESS WORSHIP: GODDESS WORSHIP IN THE ANCIENT NEAR EAST (2005)

E. J. Westlake
University of Michigan, Ann Arbor
DRAMA: DRAMA AND RELIGION (2005)

Brannon Wheeler
University of Washington
STUDY OF RELIGION: THE ACADEMIC STUDY OF RELIGION IN NORTH AFRICA AND THE MIDDLE EAST (2005)
UMMAH (2005)

Wade T. Wheelock
James Madison University
LANGUAGE: SACRED LANGUAGE (1987)

Charles S. J. White
American University, Washington, D.C.
ELIXIR (2005)
GIFT GIVING (1987 AND 2005)
KRISHNAMURTI, JIDDU (1987 AND 2005)

David Gordon White
University of California, Santa Barbara
ALCHEMY: INDIAN ALCHEMY (1987 AND 2005)
DOGS (2005)
TANTRISM: AN OVERVIEW (2005)

J. Daniel White
University of North Carolina at Charlotte
TOWERS (2005)

Peter M. Whiteley
Sarah Lawrence College
NORTH AMERICAN INDIANS: INDIANS OF THE SOUTHWEST (1987)

Norman E. Whitten, Jr.
University of Illinois, Urbana-Champaign
AMAZONIAN QUECHUA RELIGIONS (1987)

G. M. Wickens
University of Toronto
ḤĀFIẒ SHĪRĀZĪ (1987)
SAʿDĪ (1987)

Kathleen O'Brien Wicker
Scripps College
MAMI WATA (2005)

Christian Wiese
McGill University
JONAS, HANS (2005)

James B. Wiggins
Syracuse University
EXPULSION (2005)

Robert L. Wilken
University of Notre Dame
EBIONITES (1987)
MARCION (1987)
MARCIONISM (1987)
NESTORIANISM (1987)
NESTORIUS (1987)
PELAGIANISM (1987)
PELAGIUS (1987)

John Alden Williams
University of Texas at Austin
KHĀRIJĪS (1987)

Paul Williams
University of Bristol
BODHISATTVA PATH (2005)

Roberto Williams-Garcia
Universidad Veracruzana
TOTONAC RELIGION (1987)

Jane Williams-Hogan
Bryn Athyn College
SWEDENBORG, EMANUEL (2005)
SWEDENBORGIANISM (2005)

Janice D. Willis
Wesleyan University
BU STON (1987)

Edwin N. Wilmsen
Boston University
KHOI AND SAN RELIGION (1987)

Bryan R. Wilson
All Souls College, University of Oxford
SECULARIZATION (1987)

John F. Wilson
Princeton University
MODERNITY (1987)

Liz Wilson
Miami University
NUDITY (2005)

Monica Wilson
(deceased)
NYAKYUSA RELIGION (1987)
SOUTHERN AFRICAN RELIGIONS: AN OVERVIEW (1987)

Robert R. Wilson
Yale University
PROPHECY: BIBLICAL PROPHECY (1987)

Thomas A. Wilson
Hamilton College
CONFUCIANISM: THE IMPERIAL CULT (2005)

Walter Wink
Auburn Theological Seminary
JOHN THE BAPTIST (1987)

Michael Winkelman
Arizona State University
SHAMANISM: AN OVERVIEW [FURTHER CONSIDERATIONS] (2005)

Hasso von Winning
Southwest Museum, Los Angeles, California
MESOAMERICAN RELIGIONS: FORMATIVE CULTURES (1987)

Donald F. Winslow
Episcopal Divinity School, Cambridge, Massachusetts
GREGORY OF NAZIANZUS (1987)

David Winston
Graduate Theological Union, Berkeley (emeritus)
PHILO JUDAEUS (1987 AND 2005)
SPINOZA, BARUCH (2005)

William J. Wolf
Episcopal Divinity School, Cambridge, Massachusetts (emeritus)
ATONEMENT: CHRISTIAN CONCEPTS (1987)

Elliot R. Wolfson
New York University
SHEKHINAH (2005)

Allan B. Wolter
Catholic University of America (emeritus)
DUNS SCOTUS, JOHN (1987)

Mari Womack
San Pedro, California
SPORTS AND RELIGION (2005)

Isabel Wong
University of Illinois, Urbana-Champaign
MUSIC: MUSIC AND RELIGION IN CHINA, KOREA, AND TIBET (1987)

Allen W. Wood
Cornell University
DEISM (1987)
ENLIGHTENMENT, THE (1987)

Juliette Wood
Cardiff University
GENDER AND RELIGION: GENDER AND CELTIC RELIGIONS (2005)

Hiram Woodward
Walters Art Museum
TEMPLE: BUDDHIST TEMPLE COMPOUNDS IN SOUTHEAST ASIA (2005)

Mark R. Woodward
Arizona State University
SOUTHEAST ASIAN RELIGIONS: HISTORY OF STUDY (2005)

Marcia Wright
Columbia University
KINJIKITILE (1987)

Robin M. Wright
State University of Campinas
COSMOLOGY: SOUTH AMERICAN COSMOLOGIES (2005)
SOUTH AMERICAN INDIANS: INDIANS OF THE CENTRAL AND EASTERN AMAZON (2005)
SOUTH AMERICAN INDIANS: INDIANS OF THE NORTHWEST AMAZON (2005)

Donna Marie Wulff
Brown University
RĀDHĀ (1987)
SARASVATĪ (1987)

Ina Wunn
University of Hannover
ETHOLOGY OF RELIGION (2005)
WARBURG, ABY (2005)

Walter S. Wurzburger
Congregation Shaaray Tefila, Lawrence, New York
ATONEMENT: JEWISH CONCEPTS (1987)

Turrell V. Wylie
(deceased)
DALAI LAMA (1987)

Teri Shaffer Yamada
California State University, Long Beach
FICTION: SOUTHEAST ASIAN FICTION AND RELIGION (2005)

Samuel Hideo Yamashita
Pomona College
OGYŪ SORAI (1987)
YAMAGA SOKŌŌ (1987)

Philip Yampolsky
Columbia University
HAKUIN (1987)
HUINENG (1987)

Ehsan Yarshater
Columbia University
MAZDAKISM (2005)
NOWRŪZ (1987 AND 2005)

Neguin Yavari
Columbia University
NIẒĀM AL-MULK (2005)

Sabino Perea Yébenes
Universidad de Murcia, Spain
DIANA (2005)

Robert A. Yelle
University of Toronto
LAW AND RELIGION: AN OVERVIEW (2005)
LAW AND RELIGION: LAW, RELIGION, AND PUNISHMENT (2005)

Vasileios Yioultsis
Aristotelian University of Thessaloniki
PHOTIOS (1987)

Angela Yiu
Sophia University
FICTION: JAPANESE FICTION AND RELIGION (2005)

Glenn E. Yocum
Whittier College
MĀṆIKKAVĀCAKAR (1987)
MEYKAṆṬĀR (1987)
UMĀPATI ŚIVĀCĀRYA (1987)

Serinity Young
Hunter College, City University of New York
STARS (1987)

Suzanne Youngerman
Laban-Bartenieff Institute of Movement Studies, New York, New York
DANCE: THEATRICAL AND LITURGICAL DANCE [FIRST EDITION] (1987)

Miyamoto Youtaro
Kansai University
SHOTOKU TAISHI (2005)

Anthony C. Yu
University of Chicago
LITERATURE: LITERATURE AND RELIGION (1987)

Chun-fang Yü
Rutgers, The State University of New Jersey, New Brunswick Campus
ZHUHONG (1987)

Yü Ying-shih
Yale University
WANG CHONG (1987)

Jan Yün-hua
McMaster University
FAXIAN (1987)
TAIXU (1987)
YIJING (1987)

Michiko Yusa
Western Washington University
CHANCE (1987 AND 2005)
HENOTHEISM (1987 AND 2005)
NISHIDA KITARŌ (2005)
PARADOX AND RIDDLES (1987 AND 2005)

Dario Zadra
Pontificia Universitas Gregoriana
SYMBOLIC TIME (1987)

Dominique Zahan
Université de Paris V (René Descartes)
BAMBARA RELIGION (1987)
WEST AFRICAN RELIGIONS (1987)

Tzvee Zahavy
University of Minnesota, Twin Cities
BERURYAH (1987)
ME'IR (1987)
SHIM'ON BAR YOḤ'AI (1987)
SHIM'ON BEN GAMLI'EL II (1987)
ṬARFON (1987)
YEHOSHU'A BEN ḤANANYAH (1987)
YEHUDAH BAR IL'AI (1987)
YOSE BEN ḤALAFTA' (1987)

Shamoon Zamir
King's College London
SAID, EDWARD W. (2005)

Edwin Zehner
DeKalb, Illinois
DHAMMAKĀYA MOVEMENT (2005)

Eleanor Zelliot
Carleton College
AMBEDKAR, B. R. (1987 AND 2005)
MARATHI RELIGIONS (1987 AND 2005)

Otto Zerries
Ludwig-Maximilians-Universität München
FROBENIUS, LEO (1987)
JENSEN, ADOLF E. (1987)
LORD OF THE ANIMALS (1987)
PREUSS, KONRAD T. (1987)
SOUTH AMERICAN INDIAN RELIGIONS: AN OVERVIEW (1987)

Madeline C. Zilfi
University of Maryland at College Park
SHAYKH AL-ISLĀM (1987)

Michael E. Zimmerman
Tulane University
HEIDEGGER, MARTIN (1987)

Grover A. Zinn, Jr.
Oberlin College
HUGH OF SAINT-VICTOR (1987)

Eric Ziolkowski
Lafayette College
FICTION: THE WESTERN NOVEL AND RELIGION (2005)
WACH, JOACHIM [FURTHER CONSIDERATIONS] (2005)

Steven J. Zipperstein
Wolfson College, University of Oxford
GINZBERG, ASHER (2005)
JUDAISM: JUDAISM IN NORTHERN AND EASTERN EUROPE SINCE 1500 (1987)

Theodore Zissis
Aristotelian University of Thessaloniki
BARLAAM OF CALABRIA (1987)
EUTYCHES (1987)
JEREMIAS II (1987)
MAKARIOS OF EGYPT (1987)
PACHOMIUS (1987)
SEVERUS OF ANTIOCH (1987)
THEODORET OF CYRRHUS (1987)

Michael J. Zogry
University of Kansas
BALLGAMES: NORTH AMERICAN INDIAN BALLGAMES (2005)
NORTH AMERICAN INDIANS: INDIANS OF THE SOUTHEAST WOODLANDS (2005)

Laurie Zoloth
Northwestern University
GENETICS AND RELIGION (2005)

Evan M. Zuesse
South Australian College of Advanced Education
AFRICAN RELIGIONS: MYTHIC THEMES (1987)
DIVINATION: AN OVERVIEW (1987)
RITUAL [FIRST EDITION] (1987)

R. Tom Zuidema
University of Illinois, Urbana-Champaign
CALENDARS: SOUTH AMERICAN CALENDARS (1987)

Erik Zürcher
Rijksuniversiteit te Leiden
AMITĀBHA (1987)

ABBREVIATIONS AND SYMBOLS USED IN THIS WORK

abbr. abbreviated; abbreviation
abr. abridged; abridgment
AD *anno Domini,* in the year of the (our) Lord
Afrik. Afrikaans
AH *anno Hegirae,* in the year of the Hijrah
Akk. Akkadian
Ala. Alabama
Alb. Albanian
Am. *Amos*
AM *ante meridiem,* before noon
amend. amended; amendment
annot. annotated; annotation
Ap. *Apocalypse*
Apn. *Apocryphon*
app. appendix
Arab. Arabic
ʿArakh. *ʿArakhin*
Aram. Aramaic
Ariz. Arizona
Ark. Arkansas
Arm. Armenian
art. article (pl., arts.)
AS Anglo-Saxon
Asm. Mos. *Assumption of Moses*
Assyr. Assyrian
A.S.S.R. Autonomous Soviet Socialist Republic
Av. Avestan
ʿA.Z. *ʿAvodah zarah*
b. born
Bab. Babylonian
Ban. Bantu
1 Bar. *1 Baruch*
2 Bar. *2 Baruch*
3 Bar. *3 Baruch*
4 Bar. *4 Baruch*
B.B. *Bavaʾ batraʾ*
BBC British Broadcasting Corporation
BC before Christ
BCE before the common era
B.D. Bachelor of Divinity
Beits. *Beitsah*
Bekh. *Bekhorot*
Beng. Bengali
Ber. *Berakhot*
Berb. Berber
Bik. *Bikkurim*
bk. book (pl., bks.)
B.M. *Bavaʾ metsiʿaʾ*
BP before the present
B.Q. *Bavaʾ qammaʾ*
Brāh. *Brāhmaṇa*
Bret. Breton
B.T. Babylonian Talmud
Bulg. Bulgarian
Burm. Burmese
c. *circa,* about, approximately
Calif. California
Can. Canaanite
Catal. Catalan
CE of the common era
Celt. Celtic
cf. *confer,* compare
Chald. Chaldean
chap. chapter (pl., chaps.)
Chin. Chinese
C.H.M. Community of the Holy Myrrhbearers
1 Chr. *1 Chronicles*
2 Chr. *2 Chronicles*
Ch. Slav. Church Slavic
cm centimeters
col. column (pl., cols.)
Col. *Colossians*
Colo. Colorado
comp. compiler (pl., comps.)
Conn. Connecticut
cont. continued
Copt. Coptic
1 Cor. *1 Corinthians*
2 Cor. *2 Corinthians*
corr. corrected
C.S.P. Congregatio Sancti Pauli, Congregation of Saint Paul (Paulists)
d. died
D Deuteronomic (source of the Pentateuch)
Dan. Danish
D.B. Divinitatis Baccalaureus, Bachelor of Divinity
D.C. District of Columbia
D.D. Divinitatis Doctor, Doctor of Divinity
Del. Delaware
Dem. *Demaʾi*
dim. diminutive
diss. dissertation
Dn. *Daniel*
D.Phil. Doctor of Philosophy
Dt. *Deuteronomy*
Du. Dutch
E Elohist (source of the Pentateuch)
Eccl. *Ecclesiastes*
ed. editor (pl., eds.); edition; edited by

'Eduy. *'Eduyyot*
e.g. *exempli gratia,* for example
Egyp. Egyptian
1 En. *1 Enoch*
2 En. *2 Enoch*
3 En. *3 Enoch*
Eng. English
enl. enlarged
Eph. *Ephesians*
'Eruv. *'Eruvin*
1 Esd. *1 Esdras*
2 Esd. *2 Esdras*
3 Esd. *3 Esdras*
4 Esd. *4 Esdras*
esp. especially
Est. Estonian
Est. *Esther*
et al. *et alii,* and others
etc. *et cetera,* and so forth
Eth. Ethiopic
EV English version
Ex. *Exodus*
exp. expanded
Ez. *Ezekiel*
Ezr. *Ezra*
2 Ezr. *2 Ezra*
4 Ezr. *4 Ezra*
f. feminine; and following (pl., ff.)
fasc. fascicle (pl., fascs.)
fig. figure (pl., figs.)
Finn. Finnish
fl. *floruit,* flourished
Fla. Florida
Fr. French
frag. fragment
ft. feet
Ga. Georgia
Gal. *Galatians*
Gaul. Gaulish
Ger. German
Giṭ. *Giṭṭin*
Gn. *Genesis*
Gr. Greek
Ḥag. *Ḥagigah*
Ḥal. *Ḥallah*
Hau. Hausa
Hb. *Habakkuk*
Heb. Hebrew
Heb. *Hebrews*
Hg. *Haggai*
Hitt. Hittite
Hor. *Horayot*
Hos. *Hosea*
Ḥul. *Ḥullin*
Hung. Hungarian
ibid. *ibidem,* in the same place (as the one immediately preceding)
Icel. Icelandic
i.e. *id est,* that is
IE Indo-European
Ill. Illinois
Ind. Indiana
intro. introduction
Ir. Gael. Irish Gaelic
Iran. Iranian
Is. *Isaiah*
Ital. Italian
J Yahvist (source of the Pentateuch)
Jas. *James*
Jav. Javanese
Jb. *Job*
Jdt. *Judith*
Jer. *Jeremiah*
Jgs. *Judges*
Jl. *Joel*
Jn. *John*
1 Jn. *1 John*
2 Jn. *2 John*
3 Jn. *3 John*
Jon. *Jonah*
Jos. *Joshua*
Jpn. Japanese
JPS Jewish Publication Society translation (1985) of the Hebrew Bible
J.T. Jerusalem Talmud
Jub. *Jubilees*
Kans. Kansas
Kel. *Kelim*
Ker. *Keritot*
Ket. *Ketubbot*
1 Kgs. *1 Kings*
2 Kgs. *2 Kings*
Khois. Khoisan
Kil. *Kil'ayim*
km kilometers
Kor. Korean
Ky. Kentucky
l. line (pl., ll.)
La. Louisiana
Lam. *Lamentations*
Lat. Latin
Latv. Latvian
L. en Th. Licencié en Théologie, Licentiate in Theology
L. ès L. Licencié ès Lettres, Licentiate in Literature
Let. Jer. *Letter of Jeremiah*
lit. literally
Lith. Lithuanian
Lk. *Luke*
LL Late Latin
LL.D. Legum Doctor, Doctor of Laws
Lv. *Leviticus*
m meters
m. masculine
M.A. Master of Arts
Ma 'as. *Ma'aserot*
Ma 'as. Sh. *Ma' aser sheni*
Mak. *Makkot*
Makh. *Makhshirin*
Mal. *Malachi*
Mar. Marathi
Mass. Massachusetts
1 Mc. *1 Maccabees*
2 Mc. *2 Maccabees*
3 Mc. *3 Maccabees*
4 Mc. *4 Maccabees*
Md. Maryland
M.D. Medicinae Doctor, Doctor of Medicine
ME Middle English
Meg. *Megillah*
Me 'il. *Me'ilah*
Men. *Menaḥot*
MHG Middle High German
mi. miles
Mi. *Micah*
Mich. Michigan
Mid. *Middot*
Minn. Minnesota
Miq. *Miqva'ot*
MIran. Middle Iranian
Miss. Mississippi
Mk. *Mark*
Mo. Missouri
Mo'ed Q. *Mo'ed qaṭan*
Mont. Montana
MPers. Middle Persian
MS. *manuscriptum,* manuscript (pl., MSS)
Mt. *Matthew*
MT Masoretic text
n. note
Na. *Nahum*
Nah. Nahuatl
Naz. *Nazir*
N.B. *nota bene,* take careful note
N.C. North Carolina
n.d. no date
N.Dak. North Dakota
NEB New English Bible
Nebr. Nebraska

Ned. *Nedarim*
Neg. *Negaʿim*
Neh. *Nehemiah*
Nev. Nevada
N.H. New Hampshire
Nid. *Niddah*
N.J. New Jersey
Nm. *Numbers*
N.Mex. New Mexico
no. number (pl., nos.)
Nor. Norwegian
n.p. no place
n.s. new series
N.Y. New York
Ob. *Obadiah*
O.Cist. Ordo Cisterciencium, Order of Cîteaux (Cistercians)
OCS Old Church Slavonic
OE Old English
O.F.M. Ordo Fratrum Minorum, Order of Friars Minor (Franciscans)
OFr. Old French
Ohal. *Ohalot*
OHG Old High German
OIr. Old Irish
OIran. Old Iranian
Okla. Oklahoma
ON Old Norse
O.P. Ordo Praedicatorum, Order of Preachers (Dominicans)
OPers. Old Persian
op. cit. *opere citato,* in the work cited
OPrus. Old Prussian
Oreg. Oregon
ʿOrl. *ʿOrlah*
O.S.B. Ordo Sancti Benedicti, Order of Saint Benedict (Benedictines)
p. page (pl., pp.)
P Priestly (source of the Pentateuch)
Pa. Pennsylvania
Pahl. Pahlavi
Par. *Parah*
para. paragraph (pl., paras.)
Pers. Persian
Pes. *Pesahim*
Ph.D. Philosophiae Doctor, Doctor of Philosophy
Phil. *Philippians*
Phlm. *Philemon*
Phoen. Phoenician
pl. plural; plate (pl., pls.)
PM *post meridiem,* after noon
Pol. Polish
pop. population
Port. Portuguese
Prv. *Proverbs*
Ps. *Psalms*
Ps. 151 *Psalm 151*
Ps. Sol. *Psalms of Solomon*
pt. part (pl., pts.)
1Pt. *1 Peter*
2 Pt. *2 Peter*
Pth. Parthian
Q hypothetical source of the synoptic Gospels
Qid. *Qiddushin*
Qin. *Qinnim*
r. reigned; ruled
Rab. *Rabbah*
rev. revised
R. ha-Sh. *Roʾsh ha-shanah*
R.I. Rhode Island
Rom. Romanian
Rom. *Romans*
R.S.C.J. Societas Sacratissimi Cordis Jesu, Religious of the Sacred Heart
RSV Revised Standard Version of the Bible
Ru. *Ruth*
Rus. Russian
Rv. *Revelation*
Rv. Ezr. *Revelation of Ezra*
San. *Sanhedrin*
S.C. South Carolina
Scot. Gael. Scottish Gaelic
S.Dak. South Dakota
sec. section (pl., secs.)
Sem. Semitic
ser. series
sg. singular
Sg. *Song of Songs*
Sg. of 3 *Prayer of Azariah and the Song of the Three Young Men*
Shab. *Shabbat*
Shav. *Shavuʿot*
Sheq. *Sheqalim*
Sib. Or. *Sibylline Oracles*
Sind. Sindhi
Sinh. Sinhala
Sir. *Ben Sira*
S.J. Societas Jesu, Society of Jesus (Jesuits)
Skt. Sanskrit
1 Sm. *1 Samuel*
2 Sm. *2 Samuel*
Sogd. Sogdian
Soṭ. *Soṭah*
sp. species (pl., spp.)
Span. Spanish
sq. square
S.S.R. Soviet Socialist Republic
st. stanza (pl., ss.)
S.T.M. Sacrae Theologiae Magister, Master of Sacred Theology
Suk. *Sukkah*
Sum. Sumerian
supp. supplement; supplementary
Sus. *Susanna*
s.v. *sub verbo,* under the word (pl., s.v.v.)
Swed. Swedish
Syr. Syriac
Syr. Men. *Syriac Menander*
Taʿan. *Taʿanit*
Tam. Tamil
Tam. *Tamid*
Tb. *Tobit*
T.D. *Taishō shinshū daizōkyō,* edited by Takakusu Junjirō et al. (Tokyo,1922–1934)
Tem. *Temurah*
Tenn. Tennessee
Ter. Terumot
Ṭev. Y. *Ṭevul yom*
Tex. Texas
Th.D. Theologicae Doctor, Doctor of Theology
1 Thes. *1 Thessalonians*
2 Thes. *2 Thessalonians*
Thrac. Thracian
Ti. *Titus*
Tib. Tibetan
1 Tm. *1 Timothy*
2 Tm. *2 Timothy*
T. of 12 *Testaments of the Twelve Patriarchs*
Ṭoh. *ṭohorot*
Tong. Tongan
trans. translator, translators; translated by; translation
Turk. Turkish
Ukr. Ukrainian
Upan. *Upaniṣad*
U.S. United States
U.S.S.R. Union of Soviet Socialist Republics
Uqts. *Uqtsin*
v. verse (pl., vv.)
Va. Virginia
var. variant; variation
Viet. Vietnamese

viz. *videlicet,* namely
vol. volume (pl., vols.)
Vt. Vermont
Wash. Washington
Wel. Welsh
Wis. Wisconsin
Wis. *Wisdom of Solomon*
W.Va. West Virginia
Wyo. Wyoming

Yad. *Yadayim*
Yev. *Yevamot*
Yi. Yiddish
Yor. Yoruba
Zav. *Zavim*
Zec. *Zechariah*
Zep. *Zephaniah*
Zev. *Zevaḥim*

* hypothetical
? uncertain; possibly; perhaps
° degrees
+ plus
– minus
= equals; is equivalent to
× by; multiplied by
→ yields

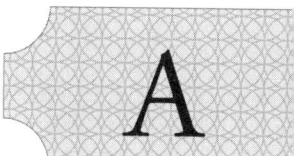

A

AARON, or, in Hebrew, Aharon; Israelite leader and priest who flourished, according to tradition, in the thirteenth century BCE. In its redacted form, the Pentateuch provides a fairly complete biography of Aaron, the first priest in the biblical tradition. Born to Amram and Jochebed of the Levite tribe when the Israelites were slaves in Egypt, he was the elder brother by three years of the great prophet-leader Moses, and he assisted Moses in liberating the Israelites and leading them through the Sinai wilderness to the Promised Land of Israel. Israel's God, YHVH, instructed Moses to appoint Aaron and his sons as the exclusive priests of the people, and Aaron ministered in the capacity of chief priest until he died, in the last year of the journey.

Most Bible scholars, however, regard this unified picture of the life and role of Aaron as a relatively late invention of the so-called Priestly school (the P source). Biblical traditions concerning Aaron present diverse views. In addition to the Priestly representation, in which the functions of Aaron and his sons establish precedents for the official priests of all succeeding generations (see, for example, *Exodus* 30:10, 40:15, and *Leviticus* 6:11), Aaron is remembered as a military-political leader who acts as a lieutenant of Moses in the Israelites' battle against the Amalekites (*Ex.* 17:12) and who serves as a magistrate in Moses' absence (*Ex.* 24:14). Aaron is cited as a leader of the Exodus in *Micah* 6:4 and in *Psalms* 77:21.

Aaron also fulfills an apparently prophetic role. He serves as Moses' spokesman to the Israelites and to the pharaoh of Egypt, performing magical feats by the power of YHVH. In *Numbers* 12, Aaron and his sister Miriam challenge Moses' unique prophetic status, claiming revelation for themselves as well, but YHVH rebukes them.

Two Pentateuchal narratives revolve around the legitimacy of Aaron's priesthood. In *Numbers* 17:16ff. Moses vindicates Aaron: he inscribes the names of the tribes on twelve poles, but only the pole of the Levite tribe, bearing Aaron's name, sprouts blossoms. In *Exodus* 32 Aaron succumbs to the people's plea to construct a physical image of God and makes a golden calf. The Pentateuch (*Ex.* 32:35, *Dt.* 9:20) condemns Aaron

---

CLOCKWISE FROM TOP LEFT CORNER. Fourteenth-century BCE terra-cotta hedgehog of Aegean Rhyton, from Ugarit, Syria. Louvre, Paris. *[©Erich Lessing/Art Resource, N.Y.]*; Facsimile of prehistoric paintings in Lascaux Cave in southwestern France. Musée des Antiquites Nationales, France. *[©Réunion des Musées Nationaux/Art Resource, N.Y.]*; Ancient Egyptian underworld god Anubis. Cairo Museum. *[©Roger Wood/Corbis]*; Pyramid of the Sun at Teotihuacan, Mexico. *[©Charles & Josette Lenars/Corbis]*; Late-nineteenth-century brass Altar of the Hand shrine from Benin. British Museum, London. *[©HIP/Scala/Art Resource, N.Y.]*.

for this apostasy and appears to favor those Levites associated with Moses over the priests represented by Aaron.

Aaron's golden calf is generally associated with the calves set up centuries later by King Jeroboam I (r. 928–907 BCE) in the far northern town of Dan and in the central town of Bethel after the northern tribes of Israel seceded from the Israelite empire circa 920 BCE. On the basis of this, and of the connection of Aaronite priests to Bethel mentioned in *Judges* 20:26–28, some scholars have concluded that Aaron was the founder of the northern priesthood, which was later assimilated into the Jerusalem priesthood. Others believe that the Aaronites originated in the south and because of their traditional legitimacy were appointed to positions in the northern cult.

As the various traditions were combined in the Pentateuch, Aaron became the paradigm of the priest and Moses of the prophet, but Aaron's role was clearly subordinated to that of his younger brother.

See Also Levites; Priesthood, article on Jewish Priesthood.

Bibliography

The most commonly held reconstruction of the history of the Israelite priesthood and the place of Aaron and the Aaronites in it is Aelred Cody's *A History of Old Testament Priesthood* (Rome, 1969), which also contains a comprehensive bibliography. An important revision of the common theory is Frank Moore Cross's *Canaanite Myth and Hebrew Epic: Essays in the History of the Religion of Israel* (Cambridge, Mass., 1973), pp. 195–215. For the view that Aaron was the founder of the northern Israelite priesthood, see Theophile J. Meek's *Hebrew Origins* (1936; reprint, New York, 1960), pp. 31–33, 119–147. Extensive analyses of the Aaron passages in the Pentateuch can be found in Hugo Gressmann's *Mose und seine Zeit: Ein Kommentar zu den Mose-sagen* (Göttingen, 1913), pp. 199–218, 264–283, 338–344. The most comprehensive history of the scholarly debate, with a detailed literary-historical analysis of the pertinent biblical passages, is Heinrich Valentin's *Aaron: Eine Studie zur vorpriesterschriftlichen Aaron-Überlieferung* (Göttingen, 1978).

Edward L. Greenstein (1987)

ABBAHU

ABBAHU (fl. toward the turn of the fourth century CE), Palestinian amora. Abbahu was the younger contemporary of both Shimʿon ben Laqish ("Resh Laqish") and Elʿazar ben Pedat, with whom he studied, but his main teacher was Yoḥanan bar Nappaḥaʾ. Abbahu eventually settled in Caesarea, where he became head of the rabbinic academy. Because of the cosmopolitan nature of that city he had frequent contacts with Christians, Samaritans, and other "heretics"; surviving reports suggest that Abbahu engaged in frequent polemics against these rivals.

Among the reports of these polemics are an exegesis attributed to Abbahu in which *Isaiah* 44:6 is taken to be God's explicit denial of a father or a brother or a son (*Ex. Rab.* 29.4) and a remark ascribed to Abbahu to the effect that "if a man tells you 'I am God' he is lying" (J.T., *Taʿan.* 2.1, 65b). Abbahu is also said to have brought about a change in the legal status of the Samaritans in the Jewish community so that now they were to be considered Gentiles in all respects (J.T., *ʿA. Z.* 5.4, 44d).

Abbahu engaged in secular studies and, to his colleagues' consternation, taught his daughter Greek (J.T., *Shab.* 6.1, 7d). His familiarity with the surrounding culture gave him relatively easy access to the Roman authorities, a privilege that he used to intercede for his brethren when the occasion demanded (B.T., *Ket.* 17a). This combination of openness to the surrounding culture and willingness to combat rival religious movements made Abbahu an effective advocate of the rabbinic viewpoint. He was able to insist on the exclusive legitimacy of rabbinic teachings without seeming to demand that Jews live in isolation from their surroundings or that they abjure any interest in the activities of their neighbors.

Some of Abbahu's ritual enactments, most notably concerning the sounding of the ram's horn on Roʾsh ha-Shanah, the New Year festival (B.T., *R. ha-Sh.* 34a), became normative practice in Jewish life. Despite his polemical activities, he was remembered within his own community as a peacemaker and a man of modesty (B.T., *Sot.* 40a). He was said to have been a man of wealth and good looks. His disciples included leading scholars of the next generation.

Bibliography

Hyman, Aaron. *Toledot tannaʾim ve-amoraʾim* (1910). Reprint, Jerusalem, 1964.

Levine, Lee I. "R. Abbahu of Caesarea." In *Christianity, Judaism and Other Greco-Roman Cults,* edited by Jacob Neusner, vol. 4, pp. 56–76. Leiden, 1975.

New Sources

Lachs, Samuel Tobias. "Rabbi Abbahu and the Minim." *Jewish Quarterly Review* 60 (1970): 197–212.

Robert Goldenberg (1987)
Revised Bibliography

ABBAYE

ABBAYE (d. c. 338), a leading fourth-generation Babylonian amora. Abbaye, who studied with his uncle Rabbah bar Nahmani and with Yosef bar Ḥiyyaʾ of Pumbedita, drew on teachings both from Babylonia and, indirectly, from Palestine; his teachings relay his erudition and subtle analytic ability. At Yosef's death (c. 323), Abbaye became the leading teacher in Pumbedita, where he taught legal, aggadic, and exegetical subjects to students individually and, in *pirqaʾ* gatherings held on sabbaths and special occasions, to the public at large. He applied rabbinic law in his role as judge of the local Jewish court and supervisor of the market's weights and measures.

With an independent mind, he evaluated both sides of issues and reportedly even resorted to curses to support or oppose a given opinion (B.T., *Ber.* 29a). Like Rava', Yosef's son, he used terminology to conceptualize the Mishnah's literary characteristics and taught *baraitot,* his own versions of formulated law that might dispute the Mishnah. Rava' and Abbaye compared earlier teachings and assayed their underlying logic and relation to the Mishnah. The Talmud's records of these discussions may, however, have been shaped by postamoraic authorities. Because Abbaye refused to harmonize disparities between the Mishnah and other sources, he limited the Mishnah, saying its ruling did not apply to all cases, or admitted the inconsistency between the sources. This sensitivity to the text is likewise seen in his interest in assessing what are appropriate interpretations of scripture (B.T., *Ḥul.* 133a).

Stories about Abbaye portray him as humble; dedicated to Torah study, even when poor (B.T., *Git.* 60b); solicitous of students (B.T., *Shab.* 118b–119a), the elderly, and gentiles (B.T., *Ber.* 17a); and a doer of good works (B.T., *R. ha-Sh.* 18a). This reputation is reflected in his dictum that "to love the Lord your God" requires a person to make God's name become beloved by others, for people will attribute one's good deeds to one's devotion to God (B.T., *Yoma'* 86a). Related teachings of Abbaye assert that whoever follows the sages' teaching is called a saint, and Torah study and good deeds bring divine blessings and protection against evil. Reportedly exhibiting an awareness of God from his youth (B.T., *Ber.* 48a), he lectured on creation and the manifestation of the divine in the world as well as on sin and redemption, and taught that the divine presence is found in synagogues, though he elevated the piety of Torah study over that of prayer.

More supernatural stories circulated about Abbaye and Rava' than about others in their generation, and in them he has contact with the divine realm even more frequently than Rava'. People believed that Abbaye was protected from demons, a recipient of divine communications, a source of practical good advice, and, like some other ancient holy individuals, a juggler (B.T., *Suk.* 53a). On the other hand, later circles declared that the law follows Rava' and not Abbaye in all but six cases (B.T., *B.M.* 22b).

See Also Amoraim; Rava'.

Bibliography

A comprehensive treatment and bibliography of Abbaye and his teachings may be found in Jacob Neusner's *A History of the Jews in Babylonia,* 5 vols. (Leiden, 1966–1970), esp. vol. 4, passim. Note in particular Jacob N. Epstein's *Mavo' le-nusah ha-Mishnah,* 2 vols. (1948; reprint, Jerusalem, 1964), pp. 369–381, on Abbaye's attitude to the Mishnah; and Raphael Loewe's "The 'Plain' Meaning of Scripture in Early Jewish Exegesis," *Papers of the Institute of Jewish Studies* (London) 1 (1964): 160–165, on his attitude to scripture. See also David M. Goodblatt's *Rabbinic Instruction in Sasanian Babylonia* (Leiden, 1975).

New Sources

Schwartz, Howard. *Reimagining the Bible: The Storytelling of the Rabbis.* New York, 1998.

Baruch M. Bokser (1987)
Revised Bibliography

ʿABD AL-JABBĀR.

ʿABD AL-JABBĀR. Beginning his discussion of the eleventh generation of the Mu'tazilah, the biographer of al-Jushamī al-Bayhaqī (d. 494/1100) states:

> Belonging to this generation, and in fact the foremost of them and the leader of them with regards to his excellence, is Chief Judge Abū al-Ḥasan ʿAbd al-Jabbār ibn Aḥmad ibn ʿAbd Allāh ʿAbd al-Jabbār al-Hamadhānī. . . . I cannot conceive of any expression which will convey his status regarding his excellence or his elevated rank in [this] discipline [namely *kalām*]. He is the one who tore *kalām* open and spread it out, producing its major works as a result of which *kalām* spread far and wide reaching the East and the West. In these works, he put down the detailed arguments (*daqīq*) as well as the major theses (*jalīl*) of *kalām* in an entirely novel manner. (*Sharḥ al-'uyūn,* 365)

Life. ʿAbd al-Jabbār (Abū al-Ḥasan ʿAbd al-Jabbār ibn Aḥmad al-Hamadhānī, Qāḍī al-Quḍāt) was born in the town of Asadābād in the district of Hamadhān around 320/932. He began his study of the *ḥadīth* (traditions of the Prophet), *fiqh* (religious law) and other religious sciences with local scholars in Asadābād and Qazwīn. In 340/951 he departed for Hamadhān and five years later went to Isfahan to study there. Soon afterwards he moved to the intellectual center of Basra, where he participated in debates and study-circles as an Ash'arī *mutakallim* and adherent of the Shāfi'ī legal school. According to al-Jushamī, he subsequently "recognized the truth and was guided," that is to say, he abandoned Ash'arī *kalām* and embraced Mu'tazilī *kalām,* becoming a student of Abū Isḥāq ibn ʿAyyāsh (his dates are not known). He later moved to Baghdad to study under Abū ʿAbd Allāh al-Baṣrī (d. 369/979) who, like Abū Isḥāq ibn ʿAyyāsh had studied under the famous Mu'tazilī master, Abū Hāshim al-Jubbā'ī (d. 321/933), the leader of the Bahshamīya (namely the Mu'tazilīs who inclined towards the views of Abū Hāshim). After several years of study during which he also taught and compiled several works, ʿAbd al-Jabbār took leave of Abū ʿAbd Allāh al-Baṣrī in 360/970, departing for Rāmhurmuz where he began to teach and to dictate his *magnum opus—al-Mughnī fī uṣūl al-dīn.* Soon after, he joined the retinue of the Mu'tazilī-leaning Būyid official al-Ṣāḥib ibn al-'Abbād. In 367/977, al-Ṣāḥib ibn al-'Abbād became vizier to the Būyid ruler Mu'ayyad al-Dawla and then appointed his protégé, ʿAbd al-Jabbār, to the position of Chief Judge (*qāḍī al-quḍāt*) of Rayy and its environs. Intellectually curious, and himself a poet and scholar, al-Ṣāḥib ibn al-'Abbād had collected a vast library and gathered a distinguished group of philosophers, theologians, and literatteurs to his court in Rayy. ʿAbd al-Jabbār implies at the end of *al-Mughnī* that he profited from his participation at al-Ṣāḥib ibn al-'Abbād's court gatherings. ʿAbd al-Jabbār held the position of Chief Judge until the death of his patron in 385/995. Subsequently, the Būyid ruler Fakhr al-Dawla seized al-Ṣāḥib's property, dismissed his appointees, and confiscated their properties. Fakhr al-Dawla had ʿAbd al- Jabbār arrested, allegedly because of his refusal to recite the funeral prayer for al-Ṣāḥib ibn ʿAbbād. It is likely that ʿAbd al-Jabbār was released shortly afterwards. After the death of Fakhr al-Dawla in 387/997, Rayy was nominally ruled by his minor son Majd al-Dawla (actual control was wielded by his regent mother al-Sayyida). ʿAbd al-Jabbār was on good terms with Majd al-Dawla and wrote his *Kitāb al-Majd* for him. In 389/999 he went to Mecca on pilgrimage and was greeted with honor during his passage through Baghdad. This was due not only to his prestige as judge and author but also because ʿAbd al-Jabbār was considered the leader of the Bahshamīya Mu'tazilah after the death of his teacher Abū ʿAbdallāh al-Baṣrī in 369/979. On his return, he taught in Baghdad for some time and also in Qazwīn. During his later years in Rayy, ʿAbd al-Jabbār may have had the opportunity to meet Ibn Sīnā during the philosopher's stay there in 403–405/1013–1015. The majority of historical sources state that ʿAbd al- Jabbār died in 415/1024.

As a result of his longevity, ʿAbd al-Jabbār was a teacher to many students in Rayy and other locations. Some students were Imāmī or Zaydī Shīʿah, indicative of the spread of Mu'tazilism among these Muslim denominations. Among the more prominent of his students were Abū Rashīd al-Nisābūrī (his death year is not known), who studied with him in Rayy and assumed the leadership of the Bahshamīya on ʿAbd al-Jabbār's death; the Shīʿī Imāmī scholar al-Sharīf al-Murtaḍā (d. 436/1044), who studied ʿAbd al-Jabbār during his stay in Baghdād in 389/999; Abū Muḥammad al-Ḥusayn ibn Aḥmad ibn Mattawayh (dates unknown), Abū al-Ḥusayn al-Baṣrı (d. 432/1040), the Zaydī scholar Aḥmad Abū Hāshim al-Ḥusaynī also known as Mānakdīm Shishdev (d. 425/1034), and the Zaydī imām al-Mu'ayyad billāh Aḥmad ibn al-Ḥusayn al-Āmilī (d. 411/1020)

WRITINGS. ʿAbd al-Jabbār scholarship extends over several of the Islamic religious sciences: Qurʾān commentary *(tafsīr)*, prophetic tradition *(ḥadīth)*, biography, theology (kalām), principles of jurisprudence (uṣul al-fiqh), and law. Most of his works have not survived. As a result of the Zaydī embrace of Mu'tazilism, Mu'tazilī texts continued to be studied in Yemen, where they held sway, resulting in the preservation of some of the works of ʿAbd al-Jabbār and his students. These works were rediscovered in the late 1950s and many of them have been published.

The most significant of these is ʿAbd al-Jabbār's *al-Mughnī fī abwāb al-tawḥīd wa l-'adl*, which may be translated as "What one needs to know regarding God's unity and justice." Fourteen of the twenty volumes of *al-Mughnī* have been recovered. It is the most comprehensive text on classical Mu'tazilī *kalām* and preserves the doctrines, discussions, and differences of earlier generations, most significantly Abū ʿAlī al-Jubbāʾī and his son Abū Hāshim al-Jubbāʾī. The work is divided into two sections: the first discusses God's unicity *(tawḥīd)*, namely, a detailed presentation of the argument that the world is temporally created by an eternal Creator-God, the attributes of this Deity, and a refutation of the views of non-monotheists.

The second section treats God's justice (*ʿadl*), explaining that God's acts cannot be evil; that the Qurʾān is God's created speech; that persons of sound mind have free will and are under obligation *(taklīf)* to God to fulfill duties that can generally be known by reason and that, as acts of kindness *(luṭf)*, God has specified in the guidance He has provided to human beings in revelation through the institution of prophecy and teachings of prophets; that this guidance, as well as the endowment of reason and free will are necessary in order for God to be just; that by fulfilling these obligations human beings have the opportunity to earn a reward, namely Paradise, or by rejecting them to be condemned to Hell; that pain and suffering in the world which is not the result of human action is created purposefully by God in order to remind human beings of their obligations and thereby prevent the extreme harm of being condemned to Hell—in this sense they also constitute acts of kindness; and, that God will compensate minors and mentally incompetent individuals, and generally any person who is incapable of fulfilling obligations placed on them.

In the *Mughnī*, the section on God's justice also includes the remainder of the "five principles of the Mu'tazila," including, "the promise and the threat," "the intermediate position," and the "command to enjoin established and commonly-known virtuous action and to prohibit reprehensible action" which is the basis of the institution of post-prophetic leadership and political authority (*imāma*).

BIBLIOGRAPHY

The only comprehensive biography of ʿAbd al-Jabbār is ʿAbd al-Karīm ʿUthmān's *Qāḍī l-Quḍāt ʿAbd al-Jabbār b. Aḥmad al-Hamādhānī*. Beirut, 1968. Al-Jushamī's *Sharḥ al-'uyūn*, a biographical dictionary of the Mu'tazila, is an important source of information about ʿAbd al-Jabbār and his students. Al-Jushamī's text is published in al-Balkhī, Abū l-Qāsim; ʿAbd al-Jabbār, Qāḍī; al-Jushamī, al-Ḥākim's *Faḍl al-i'tizāl wa ṭabāqāt al-mu'tazila*, edited by Fu'ād Sayyid, Tunis, 1974. The intellectual and social environment at the Būyid court is the subject of Joel L. Kraemer's *Humanism in the Renaissance of Islam: The Cultural Revival during the Buyid Age*, Leiden, 1992. ʿAbd al-Jabbār's short treatise on the five principles of the Mu'tazila (*Kitāb uṣul al-khamsa*) is available in English translation in Richard C. Martin, Mark R. Woodward, and Dwi S. Atmaja's *Defenders of Reason in Islam: Mu'tazilism from Medieval School to Modern Symbol*, Oxford, 1978. For a general overview of the Basrian Mu'tazilı worldview see Richard M. Frank's "Several Fundamental Assumptions of the Baṣra School of the Mu'tazila," *Studia Islamica* 33 (1971): 5–18. ʿAbd al-Jabbār's rationalist ethics is the subject of George F. Hourani's *Islamic Rationalism: the Ethics of 'Abd al-Jabbār,* Oxford, 1971. 'Abd al-Jabbār's views on the nature of the Qur'ān, namely the Mu'tazilī perspective that it is created rather than eternal, is discussed in J.R.T.M. Peters's *God's Created Speech: A Study in the Speculative Theology of the Mu'tazilī Qāḍī l-Quḍāt Abū 1-Ḥasan 'Abd al-Jabbār ibn Aḥmad al-Hamadhānī,* Leiden, 1976. 'Abd al-Jabbār's epistemology is the subject of Marie Bernard's *Le problème de la connaissance d'après le Mugnı du cadi 'Abd al-Jabbār.* Algiers, 1982. 'Abd al-Jabbār's views on man's obligation, suffering, God's kindness, reward, and compensation are discussed in Margaretha Heemskerk's *Suffering in the Mu'tazilite Theology: 'Abd al-Jabbār's Teaching on Pain and Divine Justice,* Leiden, 2000.

ALNOOR DHANANI (2005)

'ABD AL-RĀZĪQ, 'ALĪ (1888–1966), Muslim jurist and author. Born in a village of Middle Egypt, 'Abd al-Rāzīq studied Islamic law at al-Azhar in Cairo, from which he was graduated in 1911. In 1912, he went to Oxford to study politics and economics, remaining there until the outbreak of World War I. In 1915, he was appointed a judge in the *sharī'ah* courts in Alexandria and other provincial towns. The publication of his book *Al-Islām wa-uṣūl al-ḥukm* (Islam and the fundamentals of authority) in 1925 aroused violent uproar. 'Abd al-Rāzīq was formally condemned by a council of twenty-four leading *'ulamā'* (Muslim scholars) of al-Azhar, with the rector at their head. Dismissed from his appointment and declared unfit to hold public office, he lived the rest of his life privately.

Al-Islām wa-uṣūl al-ḥukm, published only one year after Atatürk's abolition of the caliphate, is a treatise on the theory of government and the source of authority in Islam. 'Abd al-Rāzīq's main argument is that there is no such thing as an Islamic system of government. Neither the Qur'ān nor *ḥadīth* (tradition) stipulates the existence of the caliphate or the combination of temporal and religious powers. *Ijmā'* (Islamic consensus) also provides no basis for the caliphate's legitimacy. In fact, historically the caliphate was based on power and coercion and is not, therefore, a necessary part of the religion of Islam.

'Abd al-Rāzīq's most radical theory had to do with the prophecy of Muḥammad. His view was that, like other prophets, Muḥammad had a spiritual mission: he was sent to reveal a truth about God and to guide men to a virtuous life; he was not sent to exercise political authority. Thus, 'Abd al-Rāzīq denied any constitutional implications in *sharī'ah* (Islamic law). Herein lies his revolutionary departure from the orthodox position on Muḥammad's prophecy and the *sharī'ah,* and hence the violent opposition of the *'ulamā'.*

Muslim theologians had always taught that Islam was unique because it was at once a religious and political community. 'Abd al-Rāzīq disclaimed any political foundation in the *sharī'ah.* Condemned by the *'ulamā',* his ideas were nevertheless accepted by the ruling elites in Egypt and later in most Arab countries. Western-modeled constitutions were inaugurated, and the secular nation-state finally emerged in the world of Islam.

BIBLIOGRAPHY

'Abd al-Rāzīq, 'Alī. *Al-Islām wa-uṣūl al-ḥukm.* Cairo, 1925. A French translation by Léon Bercher, "L'Islam et les bases du pouvoir," appeared in the *Revue des études islamiques* 7 (1933): 353–390 and 8 (1934): 163–222.

Adams, Charles C. *Islam and Modernism in Egypt* (1933). Reprint, New York, 1968. This book remains a valuable study of the Islamic reform movement in Egypt's history. Chapter 10 is particularly important for the emergence of nonorthodox ideas.

Hourani, Albert. *Arabic Thought in the Liberal Age, 1798–1939.* 2d ed. Cambridge U.K., 1983. The best single work on Arabic thought in the nineteenth and early twentieth centuries. Chapter 7, "Abduh's Egyptian Disciples: Islam and Modern Civilization," is an excellent study of 'Abd al-Rāzīq's work in particular and other Muslim reformers in general.

Rosenthal, E. I. J. *Islam in the Modern National State.* Cambridge U.K., 1965. A general work on the crisis of Islam and the emergence of the secular nation-state in the Islamic world. Chapter 4, "For and against the Caliphate," is a comprehensive review of the debate that took place in the 1920s.

IBRAHIM I. IBRAHIM (1987)

'ABD AL-WAHHĀB SEE IBN 'ABD AL-WAHHĀB, MUḤAMMAD

'ABDUH, MUḤAMMAD (AH 1266–1322/1849–1905 CE), Egyptian intellectual regarded as the architect of Islamic modernism and one of the most prominent Islamic reformers of the nineteenth and twentieth centuries. He was born into a well-to-do family in a village of the Nile Delta. At the age of thirteen he went to study at the Aḥmadī Mosque in Ṭanṭa and continued his education at al-Azhar, the renowned university in Cairo, where he studied logic, philosophy, and mysticism. For a time he came under the influence of the pan-Islamic reformer Jamāl al-Dīn al-Afghānī and became involved in the 'Urābī revolt against the British (1881–1882). Exiled for six years after the revolt was put down, he worked in Lebanon to establish an Islamic school system and collaborated with al-Afghānī in Paris on a number of activities, including the publication of a popular journal, *Al-'urwah al-wuthqā* (The firmest bond). The tone of the paper was radical and agitational, reflecting the revolutionary spirit of Afghānī rather than the reformist one of 'Abduh. Although it was naturally banned in Islamic countries under British occupation, its eighteen issues were smuggled in and widely followed by Muslim intellectuals. The two men also established an association under the same name working for Muslim unity and social reform. In the course of these activities, ʿAbduh traveled to Britain and Tunis and reportedly entered Egypt in disguise.

During his career ʿAbduh held a number of important positions. In 1880, he became the editor of *Al-waqāʾī al-misrīyah*, the official gazette. In 1889 he was appointed judge and ten years later, he became the mufti of Egypt, the highest authority on the interpretation of Muslim law. As mufti he initiated reform of the religious courts and the administration of *awqāf* (religious endowments).

ʿAbduh's writings include *Risālat al-wāridāt* (Treatise consisting of mystical inspirations), *Risālat al-tawḥīd* (translated in English as *The Theology of Unity*), and the interpretation of Qurʾān known as *Tafsīr al-manār*. In these writings, one finds traces of different Islamic influences: mysticism, Muʿtazilī theology, activism, and orthodoxy. *Risālat al-tawḥīd* was intended to be a brief and simple statement on theological issues. Distinguishing between the essentials and inessentials of religion, ʿAbduh argued that major source of the Muslim decline was their inability to make this distinction. Revelation and reason are complementary ways to reach truth, since reason is the power that enables the Muslim to distinguish truth from falsehood. Freedom of will also depends on human knowledge or reason.

ʿAbduh considered Islam the cornerstone of private and public life. Yet he was struck by the decay of Islamic societies, which he saw as the main problem that all Muslim thinkers had to face. He sought to regenerate the religion and purify it of what he believed were alien accretions from the past. The aim of his life, as he defined it, was to free the minds of Muslims from the shackles of *taqlīd* (blind acceptance of tradition) and to demonstrate the compatibility of Islam with modernity. For him, the cure for the ills of Muslim societies lay in a return to true Islam through the recovery of its essentials in the Qurʾān and *sunnah* (traditions of the Prophet) and the interpretation of these texts in the light of modern times.

The best method to achieve these goals, ʿAbduh believed, was through *ijtihād* (the exercise of individual judgment) and the establishment of links between certain traditional concepts and the ideas of the modern age. Thus, *maṣlaḥah*, the public interest, became utility, and *shūrā*, the coliph's council, became a consultative assembly. He maintained that there was no incompatibility between Islam and reason or between revelation and science. Islam encouraged reason, condemned blind imitation, attacked fatalism, and affirmed the exercise of free will. The influence of Muʿtazilī ideas upon his thought is most evident at this point. He argued that Islam was in harmony with and tolerant of all rational inquiry and science. Thus, the scientific achievements of the West, to which the Muslims had contributed in their classical age, should be adopted without fear or hesitation. Failure to do so would lead either to stagnation and further underdevelopment or to the indiscriminate importation of Western ideas, resulting in a loss of Islamic values.

Concrete reform and social change were ʿAbduh's primary concerns. Like other reformers of his time, he addressed himself primarily to political issues rather than the rethinking of basic religious positions. He believed that the legal system was a crucial factor in the prosperity of countries and that laws should change according to circumstances. The reform of Islamic law requires that the principle of *maṣlaḥah* be upheld and that jurists exercise *talfīq* ("piecing together") to synthesize judgments from the four Sunnī legal schools. Stressing the need for social and political reform, he underlined the importance of education and attacked despotic rulers; for him the true Muslim leader was once bound by law and obliged to consult with the people.

The essence of ʿAbduh's legacy, then, is his attempt to conduct a dialogue between Islam and the modern world; by so doing, he, perhaps more than any other Muslim thinker, contributed to the development of modernist and reformist trends in Islam, especially in the Arab countries and Indonesia. Ultimately ʿAbduh owes his prominence to his search for an indigenous Islamic philosophy for modern times. He developed criteria by which the impact of Western civilization could be differentiated and controlled and elaborated a synthesis of Islam and modernity with which Muslims could remain committed to their religion while actively engaged in modern society. His synthesis was subject to criticism, but the approach has left a marked impact on modern Islamic thought and society.

BIBLIOGRAPHY

The classic work on Muḥammad ʿAbduh is Charles C. Adams's *Islam and Modernism in Egypt* (1933, reprint, New York, 1968), which includes a detailed analysis of his career and views. Another important early contribution by an Egyptian professor of philosophy is Osman Amin's *Muhammad Abduh*, translated by Charles Wendell (Washington, D.C., 1953). A lengthy analysis of his political views appears in Malcolm Kerr's *Islamic Reform: The Political and Legal Theories of Muhammad Abduh and Rashid Rida* (Berkeley, 1966). Important analyses and evaluations of his view and influence are found in Albert Hourani's *Arabic Thought in the Liberal Age, 1798–1939*, 2d ed. (Cambridge U.K., 1983); Kenneth Cragg's *Counsels in Contemporary Islam* (Edinburgh, 1965); and particularly, Zaki Badawi's *The Reformers of Egypt: A Critique of Al-Afghani, Abduh and Ridha* (London, 1978). For critical evaluation, see Elie Kedourie's *Afghani and Abduh: An Essay on Religious Unbelief and Political Activism in Modern Islam* (London, 1966).

ALI E. HILLAL DESSOUKI (1987)

ABEL SEE CAIN AND ABEL

ABELARD, PETER (1079–1142), logician and Christian theologian. Peter Abelard was born at Le Pallet, outside of Nantes (Brittany). He chose to pursue the study and teaching of logic and journeyed to hear the lectures of Roscelin of Compiègne at Loches (Anjou); he later went to Paris to attend classes with the renowned dialectician William of Champeaux. His celebrated controversy with William on the question of universals revealed the persuasiveness of Abelard's quick mind and penetrating insight. Abelard's own teaching career began in Melun and Corbeil to the south of Paris, but he soon returned to Paris, teaching at Nôtre-Dame and at Mont-Sainte-Geneviève, just across the Seine from the capital.

Abelard's interest in applying twelfth-century methods of dialectical inquiry to Christian doctrine led him to study theology at Laon (c. 1113) with Anselm of Laon, who was recognized for his lectures on patristic teaching and for his role in the formation of a standardized biblical commentary (*Glossa ordinaria*). Abelard's return to Paris before he completed the course of studies was influenced by several factors. He was indeed disenchanted with Anselm's method, which, although it organized information in a systematic fashion, relied more on repeating past authority than on any personal critique. The work at Laon was a formidable accomplishment, but Peter wanted more. He was determined to bring a fresh approach to theology.

It was at this time that Abelard met Héloïse, the niece of Fulbert, a canon of Nôtre-Dame. Peter became her tutor, friend, and lover. Much of their early relationship—the love affair, the birth of their son Astrolabe, a secret marriage followed by the punitive castration of Abelard ordered by Fulbert—is recorded by Peter in *The Story of My Misfortunes.* After the tragedy and his loss of prestige as a teacher, Abelard insisted that Héloïse enter religious life at the convent of Argenteuil (c. 1119) while he made profession at the royal Abbey of Saint-Denis. Peter Abelard was officially affiliated with Saint-Denis for almost four years. During this time he studied the sources of the Christian tradition. The brilliant mind that had once captured the imagination of students of logic was now applied to sorting out a coherent presentation of doctrine from a nearly unintelligible accretion of teachings. The task was awesome. Abelard's *Sic et non* (Yes and No) faced the problem directly by arranging conflicting patristic opinions around key doctrinal issues. The work was timely and challenging. Students, armed with the exegetical principles enunciated in the prologue, were eager to resolve the 158 questions. Abelard's second theological work from this time was a discussion of the Trinity structured within dialectical analysis (*Theologia "Summi boni"*) and was not favorably received. The text was in fact condemned at a public trial in Soissons (1121). His treatise was burned, and Peter was temporarily confined to the nearby Abbey of Saint-Medard. He returned to Saint-Denis but only briefly; in 1122, Abelard was released from the obligation of residency there.

Humiliated at the turn of events in his life, Peter sought solitude. When he was given land along the banks of the Ardusson at Quincy (Troyes), he built an oratory and dedicated it to the Paraclete. Within a short time, however, students came to his retreat. In his teaching, he began to modify his approach in his discussion of the Trinity, and he composed the first draft of his second major theological treatise, *Christian Theology.* Abelard then accepted election as abbot of Saint-Guildas, a monastery near Vannes (Brittany), and unsuccessfully attempted monastic reform (c. 1127).

Little is known of Abelard's public activities after this. But in 1129, Suger, then abbot of Saint-Denis, reclaimed the lands of Argenteuil from Héloïse's community. She turned to Peter for assistance, and he gave them the oratory he had built. When the foundation was confirmed by Innocent II and the bishop of Troyes (1131), Héloïse became the first prioress. As cofounder with Héloïse, Abelard was considerably involved in the formation of the ideals that would shape the community's life. Héloïse's critique of the Benedictine rule (letter 6 of the published correspondence of Héloïse and Abelard), for example, elicited two doctrinal letters from Abelard: *On the Origin of Nuns* and *Rule of Life* (letters 7 and 8). Abelard also replied to forty-two questions on problematic scriptural texts sent by Héloïse (*Problemata Heloissae*) and commented extensively on the opening chapters of *Genesis* (*Expositio in Hexaemeron*). He prepared a collection of sermons, prayers, a breviary, and 143 hymns as well. His recommendations about the study of biblical languages (letter 9) and his instruction on reading scripture gave Héloïse extraordinary directives concerning the relationship of study to understanding the scriptures.

This work with the Paraclete was, however, only one aspect of Abelard's achievement. From 1135 onward, he was engaged in the composition of his *Ethics,* in expounding Paul's *Letter to the Romans,* and in drafting a new study on the Trinity (*Theologia "Scholarium"*). Several doctrinal letters and *Dialogue of a Philosopher with a Jew and with a Christian* are also the work of these fruitful years. But the newness of Abelard's ideas and the rigor with which he upheld the primacy of dialectics for a true theology threatened many. William of Saint-Thierry and Bernard of Clairvaux were among Peter's opponents, and through their efforts there was a second condemnation of Abelard by the Council of Sens (1140). Peter insisted that his teaching was misunderstood and intended to appeal his case with the pope. Ill health made a journey to Rome impossible, however, and Abelard retired to Cluny, where he was befriended by its abbot, Peter the Venerable. The final writings, *Apology* and *Confession of Faith,* reflect Abelard's sincerity and doctrinal orthodoxy. Abelard ultimately left Cluny for Saint-Marcel-sur-Saône, a smaller priory, where he died, probably in 1142.

Although Abelard's initial fame rested on his success as a teacher of logic, within a few decades his commentaries on logic (the *Introductiones parvulum* and the *Logica ingredientibus*), as well as his own treatise, the *Dialectica,* were replaced by the metaphysics of Aristotle. In the theological arena, Abelard exercised unusual leadership as a teacher during the formative years in the developing theology of the schools.

His students were numerous, and a few school works, such as the *Sentences of Hermann* (*Epitome theologiae Christianae*) or the considerable exposition of Pauline writings (*Commentaria Cantabrigiensis*), rely heavily on Abelard's teaching. Several well-known masters also turned to Abelard as a significant thinker. Perhaps the most important of these is Peter Lombard, whose *Book of Sentences,* modeled on Abelard's *Sic et non,* contains many of Abelard's opinions and became the primary text for training theologians during the next four hundred years. However, the most lasting influence Peter held was with the community of the Paraclete. Until its dissolution during the French Revolution (1792), the monastery held its own as the special foundation of Héloïse and Master Peter, preserving Abelardian manuscripts and conserving the finer points of his teachings.

The literary legacy of Abelard records the genius of a probing, mature, and experienced teacher. He expounded texts vigorously and forged seminal ideas for the development of Christian thought. He opposed Augustinian views on several counts, denying for example that the guilt of Adam was transmitted to humanity. Abelard created a more precise language to describe the interior character of sin and moral culpability and considered consent as the single factor that could render human behavior sinful. He also believed that the redemption theories that expressed the notion of a price or ransom imposed on God were unacceptable. Instead, Abelard held that Christ's redemptive work as the incarnate Word, in life as in death, was the supreme expression and fulfillment of God's creative love. Finally, Abelard's approach to theology was part of a new mode of thought that brought questions, debate, and systematization to the fore as the science of sacred doctrine. Abelard did this with bravado, drawing upon the best in these procedures, creating a few himself, and integrating both method and doctrine through the filter of his penetrating intelligence.

BIBLIOGRAPHY

In the nineteenth century, scholarly research on the twelfth century as a locus for monastic reform and the rise of the schools fostered a renaissance in Abelardian studies. The nineteenth-century editions of Abelard's theological writings remain invaluable: volume 178 of the *Patrologia Latina,* edited by J.-P. Migne (Paris, 1885), and *Petri Abaelardi opera,* 2 vols., edited by Victor Cousin (Paris, 1849–1859). More recent critical editions and major studies of Abelard's works are listed below, in chronological order.

Texts and Studies

Buytaert, Eligius M., ed. *Petri Abelardi opera theologica.* 2 vols. In *Corpus Christianorum, Continuatio Mediaevalis,* vols. 11 and 12. Turnhout, 1969. Includes a comprehensive bibliography up to 1967.

Jolivet, Jean. *Arts du langage et théologie chez Abélard.* Études de philosophie mediévale, no. 57. Paris, 1969.

Luscombe, David E. *The School of Peter Abelard.* Cambridge Studies in Medieval Life and Thought, n.s. no. 14. Cambridge, 1969.

Luscombe, David E. *Peter Abelard.* The Historical Association, General Series, no. 95. London, 1979. Includes an excellent updated bibliography, a list of English translations of Abelard's works, a summary of the best scholarly articles, and a critique of the most significant studies on Abelard.

Peppermüller, Rolf. *Abaelards Auslegung des Römerbriefes.* Beiträge zur Geschichte der Philosophie und der Theologie des Mittelalters, n.s. no. 10. Münster, 1972.

Weingart, Richard E. *The Logic of Divine Love: A Critical Analysis of the Soteriology of Peter Abailard.* Oxford, 1970.

Essay Collections

Peter Abelard. Edited by Eligius M. Buytaert. Proceedings of the International Conference, Louvain, 10–12 May 1971. Mediaevalia Lovanensia, series I, studia II. Louvain, 1974.

Pierre Abélard, Pierre le Vénérable: Les courants philosophiques, littéraires et artistiques en occident au milieu du douzième siècle. Abbaye de Cluny, 2–9 July 1972. Colloques internationaux du Centre National de la Recherche Scientifique, no. 546. Paris, 1975.

Petrus Abaelardus (1079–1142): Person, Werk und Wirkung. Proceedings of the International Colloquium, Trier, 17–19 April 1979. Edited by Rudolph Thomas, David E. Luscombe, et al. Trier theologische Studien, no. 18. Trier, Germany, 1981.

EILEEN F. KEARNEY (1987)

ABHINAVAGUPTA (fl. c. 975–1025 CE), Kashmirian Śaiva theologian. Descended from Atrigupta, a brahman scholar brought to Kashmir from the Doab by King Lalitāditya (c. 724–760 CE), Abhinavagupta was the son, conceived in Kaula ritual, of Vimalā and Narasiṃhagupta. He lost his mother in early childhood—a circumstance that he saw as the start of his spiritual progress—and was trained by his learned Śaiva father in grammar, logic and hermeneutics. Later, when immersed in the study of the poetic arts, he became intoxicated with devotion to Śiva, and, giving up all thoughts of marriage and family, pursued the life of a student in the homes of numerous exponents of the various Śaiva traditions and their opponents.

Abhinavagupta's major works fall into four groups, treating the Trika, the Krama, the Pratyabhijñā, and aesthetics. In the field of the Trika his main effort went into the exegesis of the *Mālinīvijayottara Tantra,* which he saw not only as the fundamental scripture of the Trika but also as the essence of the entire Śaiva revelation in all its branches. In the *Mālinīvijayavārttika* he elaborated this claim, arguing for a "supreme nondualism" (*paramādvayavāda*) that attributed to the Absolute as autonomous consciousness the power to contain both plurality and unity as the modes of its self-representation, and thereby demonstrated that the Trika, as the embodiment in revelation of this Absolute, transcends and contains the dichotomy between the orthodox (dualist) and heterodox (nondualist) directions in Saivism then confronting each other.

The monumental *Tantrāloka,* composed later, expounded all aspects of the Trika, theoretical, yogic, and ritual, while seeking to integrate within the catholic authority of the *Mālinīvijayottara Tantra* later, more heterodox developments, particularly the Krama-based cult of Kālī. Between these two works he composed the *Parātriṃśikāvivaraṇa*, in which he focused on the elite Kaula practices of the Trika. The Krama, strongly present in the Trika of *Tantrāloka*, was the object of independent study in his commentary on the *Kramastotra* (Krama Hymn) of the lineage of Jñānanetranātha. This either has not survived or has not yet come to light. Of Abhinavagupta's work on the Krama we have only his short *Kramastotra* and a quotation from an unnamed work in which he follows the Krama worship of the *Devīpañcaśataka*.

In the philosophical tradition of the Pratyabhijñā we have two masterly commentaries, the *Īśvarapratyabhijñāvimarśini* on the *Pratyabhijñākārikā* of his teacher's teacher Utpaladeva, and the *Īśvarapratyabhijñāvivṛtivimarśinī* on that author's lost auto-commentary on the same. Through the profound philosophical scholarship of these works the nondualistic tradition was fully equipped to justify its rejection of the dualism of the Śaiva Siddhānta, the illusionism of the Vedānta, and the lack of the concept of transcendental synthesis in the nondualistic idealism of the Yogācāra Buddhists, while seeing these positions as approximations to its own.

In the field of aesthetics Abhinavagupta achieved pan-Indian recognition for his commentaries on the *Dhvanyāloka* of Ānandavardhana, fortifying the latter's doctrine of the primacy of suggestion (*dhvani*) in poetry, and on the *Bharatanāṭyaśāstra*. This second commentary, the *Abhinavabhāratī*, exhibits vast learning in the arts of drama, dance, and music, and is justly famous for its subtle theory on the nature of aesthetic experience as a distinct mode of cognition between worldly, appetitive awareness and the blissful interiority of enlightened consciousness. The study of aesthetics was traditional among the Śaivas of Kashmir, reflecting the importance of dance and music in their liturgies and the aestheticism of the Kaula mystical cults, which saw enlightenment not in withdrawal from extroverted cognition but in its contemplation as the spontaneous radiance of the self.

Abhinavagupta profoundly influenced the subsequent history of Śaivism in Kashmir, both directly and indirectly, through the simpler and more formulaic works of popularization produced by his pupil Kṣemarāja. The nondualistic doctrine which they expounded permanently colonized the cult of Svacchandabhairava, which was the basic Śaivism of the valley of Kashmir, and later it formed the basis of the Kashmirian cult of the goddess Tripurasundarī. This influence was not confined to Kashmir: Abhinavagupta's lineage established this tradition in Tamil Nadu, particularly at the great Śaiva center of Cidambaram, propagating the belief that Abhinavagupta was no mortal but an incarnation of Śiva himself. Many Sanskrit works by Tamils on the Trika, Krama, Pratyabhijñā, and Śrīvidyā (e.g. Kṛṣṇadāsa's *Śivasūtravārttika* and *Parātriṃśikālaghuvṛttivimarśinī*, the anonymous *Īśvarapratyabhijñāvimarśinīvyākhyā*, Maheśvarānanda's *Mahārthamañjarīparimala*, Tejānandanātha's *Ānandakalpalatikā*, Śivānanda's *Nityāṣoḍaśikārṇavarjuvimarśini*, Amṛtānanda's *Yoginīhṛ-dayadīpikā*, and Śrīnivāsa's *Tripurārahasyajñānakhaṇḍavyākhyā*) maintained this tradition from the eleventh to the nineteenth century. Outside the Tantric Śaiva milieu the works of Abhinavagupta and Kṣemarāja provided the metaphysical infrastructure of the *Ahirbudhnya Saṃhitā* and *Lakṣmī Tantra* of the Pañcarātra Vaiṣṇnavas and inspired the Śaiva Vedānta of Śrīkaṇṭha, devotee of Śiva at Cidambaram.

SEE ALSO Śaivism, articles on Krama Śaivism, Pratyabhijñā, Śaivism in Kashmir, Trika Śaivism.

BIBLIOGRAPHY

Gnoli, Raniero, ed. *The Aesthetic Experience according to Abhinavagupta.* 2d rev. ed. Varanasi, 1968.

Pandey, Kanti Chandra. *Abhinavagupta: An Historical and Philosophical Study.* 2d ed., rev. & enl. Varanasi, 1963.

New Sources

Isaeva, N. V. *From Early Vedanta to Kashmir Shaivism: Gaudapada, Bhartrhari, and Abhinavagupta.* Albany, 1995.

Muller-Ortega, Paul Eduardo. *The Triadic Heart of Siva: Kaula Tantricism of Abhinavagupta in the Non-dual Shaivism of Kashmir.* Albany, 1989.

ALEXIS SANDERSON (1987)
Revised Bibliography

ABLUTIONS are ceremonial washings of the human body or particular parts of it; of objects that come into close contact with the human body, such as cooking utensils or food; and sometimes of such special religious items as statues of deities or saints. Ablutions can be performed through washing with water, through immersion, or through sprinkling. And, instead of pure water, water mixed with salt, cow dung, sand, or urine can be used. Ablutions are symbolic actions meant not to create physical cleanness but to remove ritual uncleanness or pollution. Therefore, they should be interpreted not as forms of magical belief, manifestations of primitive hygiene, or expressions of savage psychology but above all as ritual acts performed to create order and abolish disorder in social reality.

Ablutions and related symbolic behaviors are carried out in societies that are characterized by well-defined and clearly marked distinctions between the phases of human life, ranging from birth through puberty and marriage to death. Ablutions are performed as well in relation to the different social roles of the sexes and to the various roles that a person can play in society. Carried out at transitional stages, ablutions are ritual and symbolic actions designed to avert the dangers inherent in those particular stages, where social forms are fluid. Ablutions mark transitions from one phase to another or from one area of society to another. They therefore belong, at least in part, to the category of rites of passage.

Ablutions that mark the transition from the profane sector of society to the sacred one are well known. The Babylonian high priest performed ablutions in water from the Tigris or the Euphrates before he carried out his daily functions. For ablutions and ritual sprinklings a special building, the *bit rimki* ("washing house") was constructed next to the priest's house or the temple. There, the life-giving water from *apsu* (the primeval deep of sweet waters) was used for all kinds of ablutions. Water, the creative element *par excellence*, was used to create order wherever and whenever this order was threatened, intentionally or not. In traditional Chinese religion, preparation for a sacrificial ceremony occupied three days and involved bathing and wearing of clean raiment. Before the pharaoh in ancient Egypt could participate in any religious ceremony his body had to be purified by a sprinkling with water and natron. The water, called "water of life and good fortune," was brought from the sacred pool that belonged to every Egyptian temple. The priests of Israel were subjected to very strict rules of purity (*Lv.* 21:22) and were not permitted to eat of the holy offerings unless they had washed their whole body with water (*Lv.* 22:6). Before entering the temple to perform their duties, priests in Israel had to wash their hands and feet in the "laver of brass . . . that they die not" (*Ex.* 30:17 ff.). Similar rites are observed in other religions.

Islam, a religion without a true priesthood, requires every believer to wash before the act of prayer (*ṣalāt*, performed five times a day facing toward Mecca) according to the prescriptions of the Qur'ān: "O believers, when ye come to fulfill the prayer, wash your faces, and your hands as far as the elbows; and rub your heads, and your feet unto the ankles, and if ye be polluted then purify yourselves" (5:9). *Sūrah* 4:46 allows the use of sand instead of water: "Wash yourselves; but if you be sick, or upon a journey, or one of you come from the privy or have touched a woman, and ye find no water, then take pure earth and rub your faces and hands therewith." This ritual ablution is performed at a tank or a reservoir provided with spouts that is to be found in or near the courtyard of every mosque. The water must be pure; therefore, rainwater is preferred, although water from other sources may be used. The rite is elaborately described in the *ḥadīth*. Muḥammad derived this purificatory rite, like other elements of Islam, from Jewish and Christian sources. In the latter religion the use of water for purificatory purposes, in particular by a person entering a church or by a priest before the beginning of mass, is another example of a partial ablution in the transition from profane to sacred territory.

As human beings undergo ablution before contact with the sacred, so the gods sometimes wash before exposure to ordinary people. In the highly elaborate daily ritual of an Egyptian temple, the cult statue was purified with water, natron, and incense every morning. In Indian Jainism the statues representing the gods are bathed every morning, and a man can worship in a temple only after he has taken a bath and doned clean clothes. Even offerings are ritually purified with water before they are presented to the gods. In ancient Egypt this was accomplished by pouring libations over them. The *Records of the Ritual and Music of the Holy Temple of Chinese Confucianism*, the latest edition of which was published in 1887, gives exact rules for purificatory rites in the Confucian ceremonial. Fifteen days before the sacrificial ceremony, the custodian of the temple and his assistants go to a park in which animals are kept and select unblemished ones. These animals are ceremonially washed with warm water that day and every day thereafter until the time for the sacrifice arrives. In all of the instances mentioned, ablution is not a removal of uncleanness or dirt but a symbolic action performed by man in order to prepare himself for and adapt himself to the crossing of a sociocultural frontier. The transition between two social forms in an ambiguous event, therefore, unclean and in need of purification.

Where social forms have been attacked, pollution looms, and purification, often in the form of ablution, is requisite. Ablution is consequently often a set element in puberty rites, in which the transition from childhood to full adult life is symbolically performed and marked. On the Fiji Islands, at the close of the ceremonies for entering adulthood all the initiates went to the river and washed off the black paint (the color of death!) with which they had been smeared. Ablution is here the mark of entering a new phase of life, a kind of death-and-renewal ritual. The Bathonga nubility customs for girls required a period of seclusion at the appearance of the menses. Girls undergoing this transition were covered each morning with a cloth and led to a pool in which they were immersed to the neck. Afterward they were imprisoned in a hut, where they received instruction about the behavior and duties of a grown woman. Bathonga boys likewise experienced a period of seclusion during which they received instruction and were smeared with white paint or white clay as a sign that they had abandoned the darkness of childhood. At the end of their period of seclusion, all the paraphernalia of the school were destroyed, and the boys were led to a stream, where they washed off the white, cut their hair, and put on new clothes.

The initiation rite is a symbolic death and revival often expressed through immersion in water. Jewish proselytes, for example, had to undergo immersion before entering their new life as believing Jews. In the same way, Christian baptism is an initiation rite incorporating all the symbolism of death and resurrection to mark the transition from the world to the church, from sin to grace, from the polluted earth to the pure kingdom of God.

Childbirth and death, entrance to and departure from the world of the living, are fundamental transitory phases, and therefore dangerous. In many cultures, the period after childbirth is one of uncleanness for women, in which they may pollute those, particularly men, who come into contact with them. Therefore, they must be ritually purified (i.e., must perform ablutions) before they regain their normal state and can return to their normal tasks. Among the Inuit

(Eskimo) a pregnant woman is separated from her husband and must leave her usual dwelling place since she may otherwise pollute the food. Immediately after the birth she must wash from head to foot, and after the first night following the birth she must make herself new clothes. Following this she is readmitted into society. In ancient Egypt the same customs were followed. During and after childbirth, women usually remained secluded in a special house, called the "birthhouse" or "house of purification," where for fourteen days they purified themselves through ablutions and fumigation with incense. When this purification was complete, they could resume their household duties. Judaism still has very strict rules for the purification of women after childbirth, detailed in *Leviticus* 12:1–8. The period of uncleanness varies according to whether a boy or a girl is born. After the birth of a boy the period of uncleanness is forty days; after that of a girl this period is doubled. During these days "she [the mother] shall touch no hallowed thing, nor come into the sanctuary." At the expiration of the period of uncleanness she has to offer a lamb and a young pigeon or turtledove.

Contact with a corpse also requires purificatory ablutions, in particular for those persons who handle the body, prepare the grave, and take care of the burial. Their activities are situated in the intermediary zone between death and life and are, therefore, especially dangerous and polluting. Among Indian tribes of the Northwest Coast of North America, the duty of disposing of the body is performed by gravediggers (never members of the family) who thus become unclean and, in addition to following special restrictions regarding food and sexual relations, must undergo ablutions. Among the Bathonga the men who dig the grave—again, a task not performed by relatives—must undergo a rite of ablution after the burial and, with their wives, are subjected to steam baths. These men and women use special spoons for five days and are not allowed to eat from the common plate. The purification is extended even to the hut in which a person dies. Among the Thompson Indians the hut in which a death takes place is washed with water.

Often widows and widowers share in the pollution that death causes. Among the various tribes of the Dene and Salish, for example, widows are regarded as particularly unclean. They must retire to the woods for a year, performing purificatory rites, bathing in streams, and taking sweat-baths. Participants in the worship of ancestors are often required to undergo purification rites, since they can be regarded as having had special contact with the dead. In China both husband and wife have to hold vigil, observe fasting regulations, and wash their heads and bodies before bringing a sacrifice to the ancestors. In ancient Egypt, frequent ablutions were part of a ritual performed by the dead or by the gods to secure entrance into a new life. In the "place of purification" (i.e., the embalmer's workshop), the dead body was washed with water and other liquids in order to preserve its integrity in the intermediary state between old and new life. The extensive and complicated purificatory rules of ancient Israel included the prescript that "every soul that eateth that which died of itself, or that which was torn with beasts, whether it be one of your own country, or a stranger, he shall both wash his clothes, and bathe himself in water, and be unclean until the even" (*Lv.* 17:15).

Among the Amba in East Africa the funeral almost always occurs on the same day a person dies and is usually not performed by close relatives of the dead. The first ceremony after death is the most important mortuary rite. At dawn on the morning of the fourth day after the death all the men and women of the residential group take a bath and, after bathing, shave their heads. Following that, a long mortuary ceremony starts. Ablution and shaving are necessary to undo the dangers and the pollution that are inherent in the sphere between life and death.

Marriage is another rite of passage and, therefore, ablution rites often belong to its preliminaries. In Attica, in Classical Greece, the bride was purified by ablution with water from the sacred spring in preparation for the marriage ceremony. In the Southern Celebes the bridegroom bathes in holy water, whereas the bride is fumigated. In all Muslim countries purifying the bride with water and painting her with henna are the most important preliminaries to the wedding rite. The bath usually takes place a day or two before the bride's departure for the groom's house.

Extensive ablutions remain an essential part of the highly ritualistic life of the Mandaeans, a Gnostic sect that dates back to antiquity and whose present adherents live in Baghdad and in some regions in southern Iraq. Ablution undoes the pollution that is considered to manifest itself in various marginal situations in Mandaean social life. As all powers that are part of a given social system express it, so powers of pollution are inherent in the structure of ideas. To understand the function of ablutions in such societies a definition of pollution is requisite. It is a punishment or "a symbolic breaking of that which should be joined or joining of that which should be separate" (Douglas, 1966, p. 113). Concepts of pollution and ablution rites occur; therefore, only in cultures in which social and cosmic lines of structure are clearly defined and strictly maintained.

The Mandaeans are bearers of such a culture, which they, as a minority group, try by all means to keep intact. Since the human body functions as a symbol of society, the boundaries of the physical body symbolize those of the body social. Especially among minorities, rituals give expression to a deep anxiety about the body's refuse; this symbolizes a care to protect the unity of the group and its well-defined confines. The same phenomenon can be detected in the many purificatory rules of the ancient Israelites, also a religious minority. The Mandaeans follow an elaborate system of ablutions, in particular for birth, marriage, sexual contact, and death, that is, aspects of human life in which the orifices of the body are clearly important or bodily boundaries are transgressed. Birth, death, marriage, and coition pollute those involved, who are then segregated from their fellows until they have been purified through ablution, in this case, by immersion in living water. When the time of her giving birth approaches, a woman washes herself and prepares a place apart from the household. As soon as the child has come into the world, the midwife washes it, and the mother has to immerse herself three times in the river. The woman remains segregated for a time, and even pots and plates used by her receive ritual ablution. Mother and child have to undergo several ablutions and immersions before they can reenter normal life. If during these rites, which take place in the open air and in the often cold water of the river, the child soils or wets the clothing of the serving priest, the priest continues the ceremony as though nothing has happened. However, he must afterward go through a complete ablution at the hands of another priest. It often happens that during this rigorous ordeal the newborn baby dies. The ceremony is then continued with a dummy of dough in the place of the child in order to ensure the safe journey of the dead baby's soul to the world of light. The officiating priest, however, becomes defiled through contact with the dead and must undergo triple immersion and be provided with new clothes and new priestly paraphernalia before he is allowed to resume his duties. This illustrates the polluting power of the dead. A dying man is not permitted to die in his lay clothes. As death approaches, water is brought from the river, the sick man's clothes are removed, and he is doused three times from head to foot. Then he is lifted, placed on clean bedding facing the North Star, and clothed in new ceremonial dress. In this way the dying man is given his place in the cosmic order and crosses the border between life and death. Needless to say, the actual funeral is accompanied by the elaborate ablution of attendants and cult objects.

At marriage, the bride and bridegroom must undergo two immersions in water in the ceremonial cult hut, or *mandi;* they are then given new ceremonial dresses. The wedding ceremony has a clear cosmic symbolism that relates the social order to the cosmic one. Immersions and ablutions are an element of daily Mandaean practice that gives protection and the promise of everlasting life, since water is the life-fluid *par excellence.* Immersions and ablutions are also purificatory, undoing the pollution in marginal situations. The Mandaeans perform three kinds of ceremonial ablutions. The first is enacted by each Mandaean individually and daily just before sunrise, in other words, at the border between dark and light. The second ablution is a triple immersion in the river, done by a woman after menstruation and after childbirth, after touching a dead body, after coition, after nocturnal pollution, or after contact with a defiled person, since impurity is contagious. The third ablution, called *masbuta* ("baptism"), is performed by a priest and should take place every Sunday after major defilements. Not only the human body and its orifices but also vegetables and food need ablution and are, therefore, three times immersed in the river before being eaten. Pots and pans must at certain times be baptized, too. The ritual cleaning of food by immersion was also practiced in the Christian community of Elcasaite baptists in which Mani, the founder of Manichaeism, grew up. This ablution was a main point of controversy between Mani and other members of the sect, however, since Mani wished to emphasize not ritual cleaning but purity through asceticism. Food, in particular, enters the body by being eaten, and, therefore, ritual cleanness of food is especially important among minority groups, for whom the external borders of the social system are under constant pressure. The Israelites, the Mandaeans, and the Hindus provide examples of such purity and ablution systems. Hindu society consists of a range of castes, or cultural subunits, between which strict borderlines are maintained through purity rules, since each caste is like a minority group in relation to the whole. The higher the caste, the purer it must be. The body social is, therefore, like a human body: the high castes do the mental work; the lowest castes cut hair, carry away waste matter, and bury corpses. But the object of these purity rules is not one of hygiene but to keep the social system clean. Because belonging to a certain caste and, consequently, to a certain place in the hierarchy of purity is biologically determined, sexual purity, in particular of women, is strictly guarded. After sexual contact a woman has to perform ablutions. The most effective ritual purification is a bath in the Ganges (though the Ganges is one of the dirtiest rivers in the world!) or in another *tīrtha* ("ford"). In this context ablutions and immersions are clearly not hygienic activities, rather, they are ritual manipulations of the human body that symbolize social cleanness, which maintains the various social boundary lines.

See Also Baptism; Birth; Death; Purification; Rites of Passage; Water.

Bibliography

For a basic understanding of ritual washings and their socioreligious meanings, see Mary Douglas's *Purity and Danger: An Analysis of Concepts of Pollution and Taboo* (New York, 1966) and her *Natural Symbols: Explorations in Cosmology* (New York, 1970). Much material can be found under the entry "Purification" in the *Encyclopaedia of Religion and Ethics,* edited by James Hastings, vol. 10 (Edinburgh, 1918), although interpretations offered there should be treated with caution. For ancient Greece, see Louis Moulinier's *Le pur et l'impur dans la pensée des Grecs d'Homère à Aristote,* a special issue of *Études et commentaires,* no. 11 (Paris, 1952). The Mandaean rituals have been described by Ethel S. Drower in *The Mandaeans of Iraq and Iran: Their Cults, Customs, Magic, Legends and Folklore* (1937; reprint, Leiden, 1962). For Muslim practices, see A. J. Wensinck's "Die Entstehung der muslimischen Reinheitsgesetzgebung," *Der Islam* 5 (1914): 62–80, and the entry "Ablution" in the *Dictionary of Islam,* 2d ed. (London, 1896). For India, see M. N. Srinivas's *Religion and Society among the Coorgs of South India* (Oxford, 1952) and Nur Yalman's "On the Purity of Women in the Castes of Ceylon and Malabar," *Journal of the Royal Anthropological Institute* 93 (January–June 1963): 25–58.

New Sources

For ablutions in general see Bernhard Maier, "Reinheit. I: Religionsgeschichtlich," in *Theologische Realenziklopädie,* vol. 28

(1997), pp. 473–477, with bibliography. See also, as far as the Greco-Roman world is concerned: René Ginouvès, *Balaneutike. Recherches sur le bain dans l'antiquité grecque* (Paris, 1962); Eva Keuls, *The Water Carriers in Hades. A Study of Catharsis through Toil in Classical Antiquity* (Amsterdam, 1974); Robert Parker, *Miasma. Pollution and Purification in Egypt, Greece and Rome* (Oxford, 1983); R. A. Wild, *Water in the Cultic Worship of Isis and Sarapis* (Leiden, 1981); Georges Roux, "L'eau et la divination dans le sanctuaire de Delphes," in *L'homme et l'eau en Méditerranée et au Proche Orient, I: Séminaire de recherche 1979–1980*, pp. 155–159 (Lyon, 1981); Susan Cole-Guettel, "The Uses of Water in Greek Sanctuaries," in *Early Greek Cult Practice. Proceedings of the Fifth International Symposium at the Swedish Institute at Athens, 26–29 June 1986*, edited by Robin Hägg, Nanno Marinatos, and Gullög C. Nordquist, pp. 161–165 (Stockholm, 1988); Alan Peatfield, "Water, Fertility, and Purification in Minoan Religion," in *Klados: Essays in Honour of J. N. Coldstream*, edited by Christine E. Morris, pp. 217–227 (London, 1995).

Ablutions in connection with baptismal ceremonies in Gnostic communities are investigated by Eric Segelberg, *Masbuta: Studies in the Ritual of the Mandean Baptism* (Uppsala, 1958), and Jorunn Jacobsen Buckley, *The Mandeans* (Oxford, 2002), pp. 59–86.

For the various purificatory rituals in Islamism, besides the general introduction by Andrew Rippin, *Muslims: Their Religious Beliefs and Practices* (London, 2001), see G. H. Bousquet, "Ghusl" (general ablution of the whole body, prescribed after any sexual intercourse, before the daily prayers and for the corpses) in *Encyclopédie de l'Islam*, vol. 2, coll. 1130–1131 (Leiden, 1965); E. Chaumont, "Wuḍū," (minor or "simple" ablution of face, feet, and hands, obligatory before a ritual act, such as prayer or handling the Qur'ān) in *Encyclopédie de l'Islam*, vol. 11, coll. 237–238 (Leiden, 2004); A. J. Wensinck and A. K. Reinhart, "Tayammum" (ablution with sand) in *Encyclopédie de l'Islam*, vol. 10, coll. 428–429 (Leiden, 2002); G. H. Bousquet, "La pureté rituelle en Islam," *Revue de l'Histoire des Religions* 138 (1950): 53–71; A. K. Reinhart "Impurity/ No Danger," *History of Religions* 30 (1990): 1–24. For the ablutions prescribed to the *shaihd* (Islamic martyr) before the suicide attack see the document published by David Cook, "Suicide Attacks or Martyrdom Operations in Contemporary Jihad Literature," *Nova Religio. The Journal of Alternative and Emergent Religion* 6, no. 1 (2002): 7–44.

Ablution practice in Hinduism is investigated by Diana Eck, *Banaras: City of Light* (New York, 1982).

HAN J. W. DRIJVERS (1987)
Revised Bibliography

ABORIGINAL RELIGIONS SEE AUSTRALIAN INDIGENOUS RELIGIONS, *ARTICLE ON* ABORIGINAL CHRISTIANITY

ABRAHAM,

or, in Hebrew, Avraham; the ancestor of the Hebrews through the line of Isaac and Jacob and of the Arabs through Ishmael.

ABRAHAM IN THE WORLD OF THE NEAR EAST. The ancestors of Israel are portrayed in the Bible as living a nomadic or pastoral life among the older population of Palestine before the time of the Israelite settlement (c. thirteenth century BCE). With the great increase in knowledge about the ancient Near East during the past century, scholars have attempted to fit Abraham and his family into the background of Near Eastern culture in the second millennium BCE. Comparisons are made with the personal names of the ancestors; the names of peoples and places; social customs having to do with marriage, childbearing, and inheritance rights; and types of nomadism in the various stories in order to establish the background and social milieu out of which the ancestors came. The effort to place the patriarchs in the second millennium BCE has been unsuccessful, however, because all of the features in the stories can be attested to in sources of the first millennium BCE, and some of the items in the stories, such as the domestication of the camel or reference to Philistines, Arameans, and Arabs, belong to a much later time. The special effort to fit the war between Abraham and the kings of the east (*Gn.* 14) into the history of the second millennium by trying to identify the various kings and nations involved has failed to yield plausible proposals. The four eastern kingdoms, Elam, Babylonia, Assyria, and that of the Hittites, referred to cryptically in this text, never formed an alliance, nor did they ever control Palestine either collectively or individually during the second millennium BCE. The whole account is historically impossible, and the story is very likely a late addition to *Genesis.*

ABRAHAM AND TRADITION-HISTORY. Another method of approaching the Abraham stories is through tradition-history, which attempts to identify the individual stories as legends ("sagas") and to regard them as separate units of tradition with their original setting in the nomadic life of the tribes during their earliest contacts with the indigenous population. The common concern of a number of the stories is the quest for land and progeny, which reflects the urge of the land-hungry nomads to gain a foothold in the land where they had temporary pasturage. The stories thus portray a process of gradual peaceful settlement by separate groups, each represented by a different patriarch. The combination of the traditions reflects the subsequent amalgamation of the groups with their traditions, which led to the creation of the genealogical chain of Abraham, Isaac, and Jacob. This whole process of tradition development is viewed as taking place at the oral tradition stage, before it reached the written form.

This approach has not gone unchallenged (Van Seters, 1975). The degree to which the stories of Abraham reflect a long process of oral tradition is debatable. For instance, the tradition of Beersheba as a cult place cannot belong to the premonarchy period because the excavations carried out under the direction of Yohanan Aharoni show that the city was a new foundation of the Judean monarchy. While some of the individual stories may reflect traditions of varying degrees of antiquity, the process of collecting and arranging the stories is still best explained as reflecting literary activity.

RELIGION OF ABRAHAM. The traditio-historical approach to the patriarchal stories has led to the view that the tradition reflects a nomadic form of personal religion in which the "god of the fathers" is the patron god of the clan. He is associated with a specific person, such as Abraham, who experiences a theophany and receives the divine promises of land and progeny. Also belonging to this "primitive" level of Israelite religion are the references to sacred trees and stones and the setting up of numerous altars. The frequent references to El in the patriarchal stories reflect either the encounter of the nomadic religion with the Canaanite religion of the land, with its high god El, or the original identity of the "god of the fathers."

The problem with these reconstructions of Israel's early religion is that the emphasis upon Yahveh as the God of Abraham, Isaac, and Jacob and the identifying of Yahveh with El are attested only in exilic sources. Furthermore, the themes of the divine promise of land and numerous progeny cannot be shown in a single instance to belong to the oral stage of the tradition's development. One must conclude therefore that the religion of Abraham is the religion of the authors of the present form of the tradition.

ABRAHAM IN THE WRITTEN SOURCES. Scholars have long recognized that the story of Abraham is not a unity but combines the works of more than one author. The literary analysis of the Pentateuch, established by Julius Wellhausen and others in the nineteenth century, recognizes three independent sources. The earliest of these, the Yahvist (J), is dated to the united monarchy (c. 950 BCE) and is viewed as using the Abraham tradition to support the claims of the Davidic empire. The Elohist (E) in *Genesis* 20–22 is dated to the time of the prophets (c. eighth century BCE). The Priestly (P) source is of postexilic date (c. 400 BCE) and is found only in the episodes of *Genesis* 17 and 23 and in a few chronological notices.

While this literary analysis has long held sway, some scholars have begun to dispute the dates given to the sources and to understand their relationship to each other in quite a different way. In this view some of the early J stories (*Gn.* 12:10–20, 16, 18:1, 18:10–14, 21:2, 21:6–7) and the so-called E source were used by the J author along with his own material to shape the biblical story of Abraham as a major national tradition in the exilic period. The P writer made a few additions to this tradition in the postexilic period, while the story about the kings of the east in *Genesis* 14 was the latest addition in the Hellenistic period.

THE ABRAHAM TRADITION IN GENESIS. A distinctive feature of the Abraham tradition is that it contains a number of short stories that are not linked in a continuous narrative. This has fostered the view that they reflect a stage of oral tradition before their collection into a literary work. Furthermore, the fact that a number of stories appear as doublets has suggested that tradition variants found their way into separate literary sources. The doublets, however, are actually carefully composed literary modifications of the earlier stories meant to put forward the author's own point of view and religious concerns.

The twice-told tales. There are two stories about how the patriarch's wife was passed off as his sister in order to protect himself in a foreign land. The first one (*Gn.* 12:10–20) is simply an entertaining folktale whereby Abraham appears to outsmart the Egyptians and come away with both wealth and wife. The second version (chap. 20) seeks to exonerate the patriarch of any moral wrongdoing. Abraham did not lie, because Sarah actually was his half sister, and God was not unjust in his treatment of the king but actually recognized his innocence and provided him with a way out of his dilemma. The whole matter is resolved amicably. Yet a third version of the story is found in the Isaac tradition (26:1–11), which makes use of elements from both of the earlier stories but with the emphasis here on God's guidance and providence. The account of Hagar's flight (chap. 16) and her later expulsion with Ishmael (21:8–21) are also doublets. The first is an ethnographic etiology on the origin and nature of the Ishmaelites, while the second transforms this theme into an aspect of the divine promises to Abraham, since Ishmael is also his offspring.

In none of these cases does the later version constitute an independent variant of the tradition. Instead, it is an attempt by a later author to modify the way one understands the earlier story in terms of a later attitude on morals and piety, as in the case of *Genesis* 20, or a later use of the Abraham tradition to emphasize ethnic identity and destiny.

Abraham and Lot. The inclusion of Lot in the Abraham tradition affords a contrast between the forefather of the Ammonites and the Moabites and the forefather of the Hebrews. When they go their separate ways (*Gn.* 13), Lot appears to gain the better territory by his choice of the fertile valley in the region of Sodom, while Abraham is left with the land of Canaan. But this merely anticipates the story of the destruction of Sodom and Gomorrah (chaps. 18–19) and Lot's ultimate location in the eastern highlands.

The story of Sodom and Gomorrah follows a familiar classical theme, as in the story of Baucis and Philemon (Ovid, *Metamorphoses* 8.616ff.), in which the gods send emissaries in the guise of strangers to investigate violence and corruption on earth. The strangers are ill treated by the population, except for an old couple who offer them hospitality and are rewarded while the rest of the population is destroyed. In the Bible, Abraham's hospitality is rewarded by the promise of Isaac's birth (18:1–15). Lot also entertains the two angels and protects them from the cities' inhabitants, who try to abuse them. This leads to the judgment on Sodom and Gomorrah, but Lot and his family are rescued, except for Lot's wife, who looks back and becomes a pillar of salt. The story also serves as the context for a discussion of the possible fate of the righteous along with sinners when God makes a judgment upon the wicked (18:16–33).

Abraham and Isaac. The account of Isaac's birth (*Gn.* 18:1, 18:10–14, 21:2, 21:6–7) was originally told as a single story quite separate from the story of Sodom and Gomorrah with which it is now combined. It emphasized the wonder of the birth of the child to the aged couple and played upon the meaning of Isaac's name, "laughter." The *ʿaqedah,* or "binding," of Isaac (chap. 22) became very important in the later development of the tradition. The frequent suggestion that the story arose as a protest against child sacrifice is speculative and has little support in the present text. The author makes clear at the outset that the command to sacrifice Isaac is a divine testing. While the sacrifice is stayed by divine intervention and a ram substituted in Isaac's place, Abraham's obedience is commended and the divine promises renewed. The matchmaking of chapter 24 recounts how Abraham sent his servant to Harran, the land of his kinsmen, to find a wife for Isaac, and how through divine guidance the servant was led to the house of Rebecca. The story stresses the providence of God in the destiny of Abraham's descendants. It also raises the theme of ethnic purity—a matter of some concern in the exilic period.

Covenant of Abraham. The Yahvist who brought together the diverse elements of the Abraham tradition created a sense of unity in the collection by means of the themes of the divine promises of numerous progeny and the gift of the land of Canaan. J begins with God's call to Abraham to leave his homeland for a new land and his promise of nationhood and divine blessing (*Gn.* 12:1–3). As soon as Abraham reaches the land of Canaan, God gives it to him as an inheritance (12:7). The promises are again repeated after Abraham's separation from Lot (13:14–17). The promise theme reaches its climax in chapter 15, in which God assures Abraham again of numerous descendants and makes a covenant with him according to which he gives him the region from the river of Egypt to the Euphrates. Thereafter the promises are again mentioned in a number of other stories about Abraham (16:10, 18:18, 21:13, 21:18, 22:15–18, 24:7) as well as in those of Isaac and Jacob. Unlike the covenant of Sinai, the Abrahamic covenant is not conditioned by law since the promises have already been guaranteed by Abraham's obedience (22:15–18, 26:3–5).

The Priestly writer's treatment of the covenant (chap. 17) builds directly upon J's version but introduces a number of modifications. First, God appears to Abraham as El Shaddai (17:1) instead of as Yahveh (15:7). This change is explained by P in *Exodus* 6:2–3 in the suggestion that the patriarchs knew God only by the name El Shaddai, whereas the name Yahveh was first revealed to Moses. Second, the writer marks the covenant by a change of names from Abram and Sarai to Abraham and Sarah and modifies the tradition accordingly. Third, the covenant with its promises includes the sign of circumcision. Only through this rite may Israelites of a later day be participants in the destiny of the covenant community. This is an ecclesial conception of identity most appropriate to those living in the Diaspora communities.

Burial of Sarah. In the account of Sarah's burial in chapter 23 (P), Abraham is portrayed as striking a bargain with the inhabitants of Hebron to purchase a piece of land and a cave in which to bury his wife. This becomes the special burial site for Abraham himself and for most of the other patriarchs. What is remarkable about the account is its lack of any religious treatment of the burial or of any reference to the deity in the story. The author's intention may have been to frustrate any ancestral veneration by such a "secular" account, but if so, it was not successful since the supposed location of the burial site in Hebron is regarded as a holy place by Jews, Christians, and Muslims down to the present day.

ABRAHAM IN OTHER BOOKS OF THE BIBLE. In the Pentateuch and the historical books mention is made of the promises to the patriarchs as the basis for God's mercy toward Israel in his rescue of the people from Egypt, in his forgiveness of their disobedience in the wilderness, in his gift to them of the land of Canaan, and finally in his rescue of Israel from Aramean domination. Abraham is not mentioned in preexilic prophecy. It is only with the crisis of the exile that the figure of Abraham becomes a paradigm of hope for the restoration of nationhood and Israel's return to the land of its forefathers. It is especially in "Second Isaiah" (*Is.* 41:8–10, 51:1–2) that Abraham is the focus of Israelite identity and destiny. So too in the exilic Psalm 105 Israel's identity is based upon the election and covenant of Abraham. The Sinai covenant is passed over in silence.

ABRAHAM IN POSTBIBLICAL JUDAISM. One use of the Abraham tradition in postbiblical times can be seen in the anti-Hellenistic work of the Maccabean period known as *Jubilees,* or the *Little Genesis* (chaps. 12–23). There Abraham becomes the model of appropriate Jewish piety. The book tells how Abraham, while still in Chaldea, came to a knowledge of the true God, learned the divine language of Hebrew, and repudiated the idolatry of his native land. After receiving the divine call he went to the land of Canaan. One significant amplification of the biblical tradition of Abraham is the emphasis on Abraham's observance of many of the Mosaic laws and of his giving instruction in these laws to Isaac his son and even to his grandson Jacob. Special emphasis is also given to the covenant of Abraham as the covenant of circumcision and a warning to those Jews who neglect this practice (see 15:9–14, 15:25–34, 16:14). The theme of Abraham's testing by God is more nearly paralleled to that of Job by including in the Abraham story the figure of Mastema (Satan), who becomes responsible for instigating the trials. Abraham endures ten trials, the climax of which is the divine command to sacrifice Isaac (17:15–18, 18:1–13; see also *Avot* 5.3, *Judith* 8:25f.).

Josephus Flavius, the Jewish historian of Roman times who was writing for a Gentile audience, presents Abraham in a much more apologetic tone—as a pious philosopher of great learning (*Jewish Antiquities* 1.7–17). He states that Abraham was the first to reason to a knowledge of God, creator of the universe, by his observations of the heavens. Abraham was, however, forced to leave Babylonia because of religious persecution (see also *Judith* 5:8). He took with him the Babylonian sciences of astronomy and mathematics, which he taught to the Egyptians during his sojourn in their country, and in this way the knowledge of such sciences eventually came to the Greeks. (See also the Hellenistic-Jewish fragments in Eusebius's *Praeparatio evangelica,* 9.17ff., where Abraham teaches the Phoenicians as well.) Josephus places little emphasis upon the distinctively Jewish features of the Abraham tradition. He even passes rather lightly over the episode of his circumcision and defers to another place a discussion of the law of circumcision.

Philo Judaeus of Alexandria devotes two treatises to Abraham: *On Abraham,* part of his *Exposition of the Law* (directed to Gentiles), and *On the Migration of Abraham,* part of his *Allegory of the Jewish Law* (directed to Jewish readers). The first work is primarily a Hellenistic biography to demonstrate Abraham's piety and wisdom and the Greek virtues of justice, courage, and moderation, to which, in place of prudence, the author adds faith. Abraham also observes the law, not, however, the Law of Moses (as in *Jubilees*) but the law of nature. The life of Abraham is further interpreted allegorically, especially in the second work, as the mystical journey of the sage who reaches perfection through education. From Chaldean idolatry, astrology, and sense perception the soul progresses through reason and philosophy to a knowledge of God. The outlook here is a form of moral and mystical Greek philosophy.

The rabbinic *aggadah* on Abraham is well represented by the *midrash Genesis Rabbah,* 39–62. For the rabbis, also, Abraham was the first man to recognize the existence of God while in Chaldea amongst the idolatry there. Abraham's call to go to an unknown land was the beginning of his trials of faith, of which the binding of Isaac was the climax and by which his rewards, blessing, and merit on behalf of others would be all the greater. The rabbinic tradition is very insistent that Abraham kept all the Mosaic commandments, both the written and unwritten law (see also B.T., *Yoma'* 28b; B.T., *Qiddushin* 82a; *Midrash Tehillim* 112; *Numbers Rabbah* 12). Abraham is also viewed as a prophet, primarily in the sense that he received revelations from God about the future and the unseen world. And Abraham is a priest whose priesthood is somehow linked with that of Melchizedek and whose sacrifice on Mount Moriah was at the site of the future Temple.

ABRAHAM IN CHRISTIANITY. The figure of Abraham plays a special role in the New Testament, especially in the thought of the apostle Paul. In *Romans* 4 Paul argues that Abraham was justified by faith in God prior to his being circumcised and therefore prior to any works of the law, so the law is not necessary for justification—that is, for being considered righteous before God. Abraham becomes the father of the faithful, and the election of Abraham is thus extended to all who have faith. Nevertheless, Paul is not willing to give up God's special election of the Jews and so argues for their ultimate salvation as well. In *Galatians* 3:6–9 and 3:15–18 Paul uses a somewhat different argument by suggesting that salvation came to the Gentiles through Abraham's blessing; this blessing was transmitted through Abraham's "seed," which Paul identifies with Jesus.

The *Letter to the Hebrews* (11:8–12, 11:17–19) uses Abraham as an example of faith, recounting his response to God's call to sojourn in the land of promise, his belief with Sarah in the promise of offspring, and his testing through the sacrifice of Isaac. All of these are made to reflect faith in God beyond the limitations of this life, a heavenly abode, and the belief in future resurrection of the dead. By contrast, *James* 2:20–24 uses the sacrifice of Isaac as an example of Abraham's being justified by works and not just by faith alone.

ABRAHAM IN ISLAM. Abraham is mentioned more frequently in the Qur'ān than is any other biblical figure. He is regarded as the first prophet because he was the first to convert to the true God and to preach against the idolatry of his people (*sūrahs* 19:41ff., 21:51ff., 26:69ff., 37:83ff.). He was also the first Muslim because he practiced *islam*—submission to absolute obedience to God—when he was tested by the command to sacrifice his son (2:124ff., 37:102ff.). Abraham, with the aid of his son Ishmael, the father of the Arabs, was responsible for the founding of the Ka'bah in Mecca, the first sanctuary of God (2:125, 2:127). Muḥammad viewed himself as the reviver of this ancient faith, which he regarded as older than both Judaism and Christianity (3:65). Following Jewish tradition, he also regarded Abraham as the first recipient of the divine revelation of the book (2:129).

BIBLIOGRAPHY

It is difficult in a brief bibliography to do justice to the broad spectrum of scholarly opinion about the Abraham tradition. On matters of the history of the patriarchal age, John Bright's *A History of Israel,* 3d ed. (Philadelphia, 1981), may be said to represent an American school of thought, while Siegfried Herrmann's *Geschichte Israels in alttestamentlicher Zeit* (Munich, 1973), translated by John Bowden as *A History of Israel in Old Testament Times,* 2d ed. (Philadelphia, 1981), presents an approach favored by many German biblical scholars. A mediating position is that found in Roland de Vaux's *Histoire ancienne d'Israël: Des origines à l'installation en Canaan* (Paris, 1971), translated by David Smith as *The Early History of Israel* (Philadelphia, 1978).

On the religion of Abraham, see Albrecht Alt's *Der Gott der Väter: Ein Beitrag zur Vorgeschichte der Israelitischen Religion* (Stuttgart, 1929), translated by R. A. Wilson as "The God of the Fathers," in *Essays on Old Testament History and Religion* (Oxford, 1966), pp. 1–77; and Frank Moore Cross's *Canaanite Myth and Hebrew Epic: Essays in the History of the Religion of Israel* (Cambridge, Mass., 1973), pp. 3–75.

On the literary development of the tradition, see Hermann Gunkel's *Genesis* (Göttingen, 1901). The introduction to this work was translated and edited by William H. Carruth as *The Legends of Genesis* (Chicago, 1901) and reissued with an introduction by William F. Albright (New York, 1964). See also the commentary in Gerhard von Rad's *Das erste Buch Mose, Genesis,* 3 vols. (Göttingen, 1949–1953), translated by John H. Marks as *Genesis: A Commentary,* 3 vols. (Philadelphia, 1961). A commentary that reflects the American school is the one in Nahum M. Sarna's *Understanding Genesis* (New York, 1966).

Critical reappraisals of the historicity of the Abraham tradition can be found in Thomas L. Thompson's *The Historicity of the Patriarchal Narratives: The Quest for the Historical Abraham* (New York, 1974), and in my *Abraham in History and Tradition* (New Haven, Conn., 1975). The latter work also contains a critical discussion of the literary tradition of Abraham.

Recent surveys of the present state of scholarship on Abraham are represented by William G. Denver and W. Malcolm Clark in "The Patriarchal Traditions," chapter 2 of *Israelite and Judaean History,* edited by John H. Hayes and J. Maxwell Miller (Philadelphia, 1977), pp. 70–148; and Claus Westermann's *Genesis,* pt. 2, "Biblischer Kommentar Altes Testament," vol. 1, no. 2 (Neukirchen-Vluyn, 1981). This latter work contains an extensive bibliography.

For a treatment of Abraham in later Jewish sources, see Samuel Sandmel's *Philo's Place in Judaism: A Study of Conceptions of Abraham in Jewish Literature* (Cincinnati, 1955). See also the article "Abraham" in *Theologische Realenzyklopädie,* vol. 1 (New York, 1977).

New Sources

Brodsky, Harold. "Did Abram Wage a Just War?" *Jewish Bible Quarterly* 31 (2003): 167–173.

Cohen, Jeffrey M. "Displacement in the Matriarchal Home: A Psychological Study of the Abraham-Sarah Marriage." *Jewish Bible Quarterly* 30 (2002): 90–96.

Fleishman, Joseph. "On the Significance of a Name Change and Circumcision in *Genesis* 17." *Journal of the Ancient Near Eastern Society* 28 (2002): 19–32.

Kahn, Pinchas. "The Mission of Abraham: *Genesis* 18:17–22:19." *Jewish Bible Quarterly* 30 (2002): 155–163.

Kaltner, John. "Abraham's Sons: How the Bible and Qur'an See the Same Story Differently." *Bible Review* 18 (2002): 16–23, 45–46.

Lee, Jung H. "Abraham in a Different Voice: Rereading 'Fear and Trembling' with Care." *Religious Studies* 36 (2000): 377–400.

Levenson, Jon Douglas. "The Conversion of Abraham to Judaism, Christianity, and Islam." In *The Idea of Biblical Interpretation,* edited by Hindy Najman and Judith H. Newman, pp. 3–40. Leiden and Boston, 2004.

Noegel, Scott B. "Abraham's Ten Trials and a Biblical Numerical Convention." *Jewish Bible Quarterly* 31 (2003): 73–83.

JOHN VAN SETERS (1987)
Revised Bibliography

ABRAHAM BEN DAVID OF POSQUIÈRES

SEE AVRAHAM BEN DAVID OF POSQUIÈRES

ABRAVANEL, ISAAC (1437–1508), known as Abravanel, Abrabanel, and Abarbanel; Spanish-Portuguese biblical commentator, theologian, and philosopher. Born in Lisbon into a wealthy Jewish family from Seville, Isaac ben Judah Abravanel succeeded his father as the treasurer to Alfonso V, king of Aragon, but in 1483 for political reasons he had to flee to Castille, where he remained in the service of Ferdinand and Isabella until the expulsion of the Jews on May 31, 1492. He then moved to Naples in the service of King Ferrante I until a French invasion forced him to flee with the king to Messina in 1494. Isaac resided in Corfu until 1496; then moved to Monopoli (Apulia), and in 1503 settled in Venice, where he spent the last years of his life.

Isaac's earliest work, composed when he was in his teens, was *Tsurot ha-yesodot* (Forms of the elements). His next, completed around 1465, was *'Ateret zeqenim* (Crown of the ancients). The first deals with ontology; the second covers divine providence and the nature of prophecy. Between 1483 and 1505 Isaac wrote commentaries on the Pentateuch, *Joshua, Judges, Samuel, Kings, Isaiah, Jeremiah, Ezekiel,* and the twelve minor prophets. In 1496 he completed a commentary on *Deuteronomy* titled *Mirkevet ha-mishneh* (The second chariot); another on the Passover Haggadah, *Zevah pesah* (The sacrifice of Passover); and a third on the tractate *Avot* in the Mishnah, *Nahalot avot* (Paternal inheritance).

Between 1496 and 1498 Isaac composed a set of three books known as "The Tower of Salvation." The first, *Ma'yenei ha-yeshu'ah* (The fountains of salvation), is a commentary on the *Book of Daniel.* The second, *Yeshu'ot meshiho* (The salvation of his anointed), is a study of *midrashim* and passages from the Talmud that deal with the Messiah and the messianic age. The third, *Mashmi'a yeshu'ah* (Announcing salvation), is a commentary on the messianic prophecies found in all of the books of the prophets.

Isaac wrote three books that deal specifically with the philosophy of Maimonides (Mosheh ben Maimon, 1135/8–1204): *Ro'sh amanah* (The principles of faith; 1494), a detailed commentary (1505) on Maimonides' *Guide of the Perplexed,* and the *Ma'amar qatser* (Short treaties; 1505), which discusses at length what Isaac considered to be the most difficult problems in the *Guide.* In 1505 Isaac also completed two works on creation, *Shamayim hadashim* (The new heavens) and *Mif'alot Elohim* (The works of God).

Isaac's last written works were answers to questions raised by Sha'ul ha-Kohen of Candia. These *responsa* refer to two lost books: *The Inheritance of the Prophets,* an essay against Maimonides' theory of prophecy, and *The Justice of the Universe,* which deals with divine providence.

The dominant theme of Isaac's writings is his opposition to what he considered to be the excessive rationalism of the Jewish Aristotelians who followed Maimonides, particularly Gersonides (Levi ben Gershom). Isaac was motivated by the fear that this kind of sophisticated Jewish thought, given the threats to Jewish survival present in the exile, would undermine the faith of the simple Jew. Isaac rejected the claims of both Hasdai Crescas and Yosef Albo that it is possible to single out fundamental principles of Judaism. Isaac argued that Judaism has no conceptual axioms; every law and every belief in the Torah is equally fundamental.

Isaac opposed naturalistic interpretations of prophecy. He argued that all prophecy is produced directly by God and that the events reported in prophetic visions actually occurred in the physical world. Furthermore, prophetic knowledge differs qualitatively from natural knowledge. Natural knowledge at best yields claims that are merely probable, whereas revealed knowledge is necessarily true.

Isaac drew his political theory from the political structures of ancient Rome, the Venice of his day, and the Torah. He claimed that a political state is required only because of the human imperfection that resulted from the sin of Adam. Consequently, no political state is perfect. The best political order is that of theocracy; the next best is a monarchy, limited by the national laws of a superior court or Sanhedrin and the local laws of elected municipal lower courts.

Two cosmological judgments underlie Isaac's view of history. One is his rejection of the Aristotelian conception of the spheres as living entities. The other is his affirmation of a literal understanding of the doctrine of creation out of nothing. What philosophers mistakenly believe to be natural law is God's will made manifest through the actions of angels (God's agents for rewarding human beings) and demons (God's agents for punishing human beings), and/or the willed choices of human beings. Nothing occurs through impersonal, natural forces.

Isaac pictured the course of human history as a circle that began when humanity separated from God and that will end when humanity returns to God. However, after Adam's initial fall that began history, there was, is, and will be continuous disintegration until the messianic age. The penultimate state of history will begin when a revived Muslim empire in alliance with the Ten Lost Tribes of Israel will conquer the Christians and retake possession of Jerusalem. Next, the Messiah, who is not Jesus of Nazareth, will appear, and the Muslims will turn over Jerusalem to him. At that time all of the Jewish people will return to the Land of Israel, and the Messiah will rule the world. Then a reign will follow during which humanity will progressively improve until, in the end, the physical, human world will give way to a spiritual world of pure souls who eternally will contemplate God's essence. The two dates that Isaac cited for the coming of the Messiah are 1503 and 1531.

See Also Messianism, article on Jewish Messianism.

Bibliography

Guttmann, Jacob. *Die religionsphilosophischen Lehren des Isaak Abravanel.* Breslau, 1916.

Heschel, Abraham Joshua. *Don Jizchak Abravanel.* Berlin, 1937.

Levy, Solomon. *Isaac Abravanel as a Theologian.* London, 1939.

Minkin, Jacob S. *Abarbanel and the Expulsion of the Jews from Spain.* New York, 1938.

Netanyahu, Benzion. *Don Isaac Abravanel.* Philadelphia, 1953.

Sarachek, Joseph. *Don Isaac Abravanel.* New York, 1938.

Schmueli, Ephraim. *Don Yitshaq Abarbanel ve-geirush Sefarad* (Don Isaac Abravanel and the expulsion of the Jews from Spain). Jerusalem, 1963.

Trend, J. B., and Herbert Loewe. *Isaac Abravanel: Six Lectures.* Cambridge, U.K., 1937.

New Sources

Attias, Jean-Christophe. "Isaac Abravanel: Between Ethnic Memory and National Memory." *Jewish Social Studies* 2 (1996): 137–156.

Feldman, Seymour. *Philosophy in a Time of Crisis: Don Isaac Abravanel, Defender of the Faith.* London and New York, 2003.

Gaon, Solomon. *The Influence of the Catholic Theologian Alfonso Tostado on the Pentateuch Commentary of Isaac Abravanel.* Library of Sephardic History and Thought, vol. 2. New York, 1993.

Norbert M. Samuelson (1987)
Revised Bibliography

ABSTINENCE

See Asceticism; Celibacy; Fasting; Spiritual Discipline

ABŪ AL-HUDHAYL AL-ʿALLĀF

(d. between AH 227 and 235, 842 and 850 CE), more fully Abū al-Hudhayl Muḥammad ibn al-Hudhayl al-ʿAllāf al-ʿAbdī; Muslim theologian of the Muʿtazilī school. Little is known of the life of Abū al-Hudhayl. He was a client (*mawlā*) of the tribe ʿAbd al-Qays and is said to have studied with a certain Uthmān al-Tawīl, an agent for the Muʿtazilī propaganda of Wāṣil ibn ʿAtaʾ (d. 748/9). About 819 he entered the court of the caliph al-Maʾmūn, where he was renowned for his skill in disputation and for his ability to quote poetry. Of his numerous theological, philosophical, apologetic, and polemic writings, none has survived. He is reported to have been more than a hundred years old at the time of his death.

The fragmentary and somewhat gnomic reports of Abū al-Hudhayl's doctrine supplied by later writers allow only a superficial view of his teaching, nor is it possible to determine the significance of several apparent parallels to earlier Christian writers. His teaching is based on a systematic analysis of the predicates attached to things, where the primary assertion is indicated by the noun subject used in the analytic paraphrase. For example, "*x* moves" is analyzed as "a motion belongs to *x*," and "*y* knows," as "a cognition belongs to *y*." Since the subject term of the analysis is taken to designate an entity, the method tended to posit many reified properties, such as "location" (*kawn*), "conjunction," or "lifelessness." Abū al-Hudhayl's conception of material beings was atomistic: bodies are composites of discrete atoms (sg., *jawhar*) in each of which subsists a set of various entitative properties (sg., *ma'nā*), categorically referred to as "accidents." The atoms and some kinds of accidents perdure over many moments of time while other accidents exist only for a single instant. Because speech consists of accidents in a material substrate, the Qur'ān as God's speech is also created; it exists originally in a celestial archetype, "The Cherished Tablet," of which there are quotations.

Analyzing the descriptions of God given in the Qur'ān, Abū al-Hudhayl taught that God has cognition, power, life, eternity, grandeur, and so forth, but each of these attributes is God himself, even though they are distinguishable as such from each other. His volitions, however, come to exist temporally "in no substrate," simultaneously with his creation of their objects, as does his creative command, "Be," the reality of which is asserted by "creates." He held also that the potential objects of God's power are finite in number and that consequently there must come a time when even the activity of the blessed in Paradise will terminate in an unalterable state of bliss. This thesis he is said to have renounced late in his life.

Whether or not Abū al-Hudhayl first introduced atomism and the analytic method into the Mu'tazilī *kalām* is uncertain; in any event, Abū 'Alī al-Jubbā'ī (d. 913) considers that it is Abū al-Hudhayl "who initiated *kalām*." His most important direct disciple was Abū Ya'qūb al-Shaḥḥām, who was in turn the master of al-Jubbā'ī. The latter basically refined the system of Abū al-Hudhayl so as to lay the immediate foundation of what later became the predominant tradition of Mu'tazilī theology. Also through al-Jubba'ī, who was the teacher of al-Ash'arī (d. 935), the teaching of Abū al-Hudhayl came to play a significant role in the formation of classical Ash'arī doctrine.

SEE ALSO Mu'tazilah.

BIBLIOGRAPHY

Frank, R. M. *The Metaphysics of Created Being According to Abū al-Hudhayl al-'Allāf.* Istanbul, 1966. Although dated, remains a useful summary.

Frank, R. M. "The Divine Attributes according to the Teaching of Abū l-Hudhayl al-'Allāf." *Le muséon* 82 (1969): 451–506. Contains a general outline of his theology with attention to several patristic parallels.

R. M. FRANK (1987)

ABŪ BAKR (c. 572–634) was the first Caliph and close companion of the Prophet and founder of the Islamic Empire. In the classical Arab tradition a person is given an *ism* (name), *kunyah* (an agnomen consisting of Abū [father] followed by the name of a son), and *laqab* (nickname or title usually of a favorable nature). Hence Abū Bakr was so called, although his name was Abd Allah, and his *laqab,* Ati Atik (freed slave), was given to him by his mother because he was spared from the death in infancy that befell all her other sons. His father was 'Uthām of the clan of Taym of the tribe of Quraysh. His mother was Salma bint Sakhr of the same clan. He was born around 572 CE. He married four times and had six children, including 'Ā'ishah, who married the Prophet and played a significant role in some of the early events in Muslim history, and who also served as a transmitter of *ḥadīth.*

Ibn Isḥāq, the author of an early biography of the Prophet, describes Abū Bakr as a kindly man popular among his contemporaries and most knowledgeable about the genealogy of the Quraysh and the values and traditions of their ancestors. The people used to call upon him for his knowledge, his experience as a merchant, and his good companionship. He lived in the same area of Mecca as Khadījah, the wife of the Prophet, which may have brought about their friendship and may have been the reason that Abū Bakr was among the first adult male Muslims. We know very little about his life before the advent of Islam; the reports concerning the details of his life are sometimes contradictory and confusing. Nevertheless a reasonable picture of his life may be glimpsed through the different traditions and reports. As a relatively wealthy merchant, Abū Bakr used his wealth and resources to support the poor among the nascent Muslim community. In particular he bought and freed Muslim slaves, among whom was Bilāl the Abyssinian, who later became well-known as a devout Muslim and as a *muezzin* (the one who gives the call to prayer).

Abū Bakr's personal influence helped bring to Islam some of the leading members of Meccan society. As a result he faced the hostility of other Meccans, but remained one of the Prophet's closest companions. When the pressure on the early Muslim community became intolerable, some of them took refuge in Abyssinia, but Abū Bakr remained with the Prophet in Mecca. It is unlikely that his comparatively minor clan was able to offer Abū Bakr protection, even though he was its chief, but it might have been that his extended friendships and acknowledged gentle demeanor deterred the Meccans from being too harsh on him.

After the Prophet had built connections among the people of Yathrib he advised those who feared Meccan hostility to emigrate there. Abū Bakr stayed behind because the Prophet wanted him as his companion on the journey to Yathrib. Abū Bakr's family supplied the food and camels and helped to thwart the efforts of the Quraysh to capture the Prophet. Later his family, except his father Abū Kuhafa and his son Abd al-Raḥmān, followed him to Yathrib. Abd al-Raḥmān eventually converted to Islam, but earlier he had engaged in fighting against Muslims in the major battles of Badr and Uḥud.

In Yathrib, which the Prophet renamed al-Madīnah (Medina), Abū Bakr had a special place within the community. He was always at the side of the Prophet and took part in all the campaigns led by the Prophet. Abū Bakr's counsel was always sought and his closeness to the Prophet made him familiar with his ideas and intentions. It is said that among the senior companions he never questioned the judgments of the Prophet. When at Ḥudaybiyah the Prophet decided to make peace with the Meccans on conditions that were seen as humiliating by many other followers, Abū Bakr stood by his leader, who was facing a serious rebellion. This agreement was a prelude to the bloodless conquest of Mecca itself.

Earlier in Mecca, when the Prophet proclaimed the account known in Muslim traditions as the "night journey" (*isrāʾ*) from Mecca to Jerusalem and back, some Meccans thought that such a claim would shake Abū Bakr's faith in the Prophet's veracity; but he affirmed his faith in the Prophet and was given the title of al-Siddiq (the firm and trustworthy believer). In Muslim literature he therefore is often referred to as al-Siddiq.

The death of the Prophet in 632 threatened the order that he had established, and created a crisis regarding succession. At the time of his death almost all of the Arabian Peninsula was under his control. Nevertheless there was a possible threat from the north by Byzantium, which encouraged the northern tribes to defect. To ward off this threat the Prophet organized an army under the leadership of young Usāmah ibn Zaid with orders to march to the borders of Syria, deter Byzantium, and subdue the northern tribes. As the army camped outside Medina awaiting the Prophet's orders the news of his death arrived.

There were rebellions among various tribes led by "prophets" who modeled themselves on the Prophet, each claiming to have received their own "Qurʾān" through an angel of revelation. They claimed equal status to his, and one of them, Musaylamah, referred to in history as the "Liar," demanded that Arabia should be divided between himself and the Prophet. In Yemen, a local leader took over from the Prophet's appointed representative of Medina. Individuals claiming to be prophets and prophetesses cropped up among several tribes. Some groups who had given allegiance to Islam reverted to their pre-Islamic religion, while others remained faithful to Islam but refused to pay *zakāt*, which the Qurʾān had promulgated, to Medina on the grounds that the duty to remit it ended with the death of the Prophet. Muslim historians have named this particular rebellion Riddah (apostasy) and the struggle to subdue them as the wars of Riddah. These were uncoordinated groups, and mostly local, without any common leader; they were all eventually subdued under Abū Bakr's leadership.

When the death of the Prophet was announced the Anṣār (the Muslim inhabitants of Medina) gathered in the *saqifa* of Banu Saʾidah to elect one of their own as successor to the Prophet. The ancient tribal rivalry between the Aws and Khazradj, the two tribes of Medina, delayed their decision to allow the Muhājirūn (the Muslim immigrants to Medina) to join the meeting. According to historical accounts ʿUmar ibn al-Khaṭṭāb and Abū Akbr succeeded in persuading the gathering to choose Abū Bakr as the new leader. Abū Bakr gathered his advisors to plan his first move. Against their advice he ordered the army to march to the north, leaving Medina exposed to attack by hostile tribes. This daring move must have impressed his enemies as a sign of self-confidence. During the absence of the army Abū Bakr was able to defeat the tribe who attacked Medina. Abū Bakr came to be known as Khalifat Rasūl Allāh, that is, the deputy or successor to the messenger of God (the Prophet).

Once the Muslim army returned after putting down an early rebellion, Abū Bakr appointed Khālid ibn al-Walid commander of the main army to put down the other major insurgencies. After subduing one of the rebels, Khālid marched towards Yamana, where Musaylamah had gathered a large army that had resisted earlier attempts to subdue him. Khālid defeated and killed Musaylamah at the Battle of al-ʿAkrabaʾ. This was the bloodiest battle of the Riddah wars; thousands lost their lives, and the place came to be called the Garden of Death. This victory was crucial in restoring control of the center of Arabia to Muslim rule. The Muslims lost a good number of reciters of the Qurʾān in this battle. This prompted Abū Bakr, according to Muslim sources, to appoint secretaries to collect the Qurʾān, relying on the already recorded material and the memories of the surviving reciters. He also sent other commanders to subdue the remaining rebel tribes and to secure other regions of the peninsula.

While the Riddah campaigns were still raging, one of the Muslim commanders had already taken control of Persian-held centers and advanced to the Euphrates, opening up the possibility of conquering Iraq. On being advised that a victory against the Persians was likely, Abū Bakr recalled Khālid from Yamama and ordered him to march towards Iraq. This marked the beginning of the conquest of Palestine and Syria. Abū Bakr sent three columns towards Palestine and Syria under Muslim commanders. After some initial success, they were driven back by the superior forces of the Byzantine army. Abū Bakr ordered Khālid to leave Iraq and reinforce the army in Palestine. Their combined forces defeated the Byzantines at the famous Battle of Ajnadayn in July 634. Abū Bakr died soon after on August 23.

The caliphate of Abū Bakr was characterized by the constant struggle to restore the authority of Medina and by direct military action against rebellions in the Arabian Peninsula and eventually against the Persian and Byzantine empires. His rule marks the first major advances in Muslim rule over Byzantine and Sassanian controlled territories.

Abū Bakr was noted for his simple and austere life. It is said that on his deathbed, he gave back all that he had received as salary to the Muslim treasury. During his short tenure as caliph, he sought to bring order at a turbulent time in Muslim history after the death of the Prophet. He did not attempt to alter dramatically the administrative organization and arrangements in Medina or in the newly conquered territories. Before his death, he appointed ʿUmar bin al-Khaṭṭāb to be his successor, believing that this choice would prevent possible strife.

BIBLIOGRAPHY

al-Balādhurī. *The Origins of the Islamic State.* Translated by Phillip Hitti. New York, 1968.

Donner, Fred. *The Early Islamic Conquests.* Princeton, N.J., 1981.

Kennedy, Hugh. *The Prophet and the Age of the Caliphates: Islamic Near East from the Sixth to the Eleventh Century.* London, 1986; 2d ed., Harlow, U.K., and New York, 2004.

Madelung, Wilferd. *The Succession to Muḥammad: A Study of the Early Caliphate.* Cambridge, U.K., 1997.

al-Ṭabarī, Abu Jahar Muḥammad. *Biographies of the Prophets, Companions, and their Successors.* Translated and annotated by Ella Landau-Tasseron. Albany, N.Y., 1998.

M. A. ZAKI BADAWI (2005)

ABŪ ḤANĪFAH (AH 80?–150/699?–767 CE), more fully Abū Ḥanīfah al-Nuʿmān ibn Thābit ibn Zūṭā; theologian, jurist, and founder of the first of the four orthodox schools of law in Sunnī Islam. As a theologian, he persuasively argued against Khārijī extremism and espoused several positions that became an integral part of the orthodox doctrine, especially the idea that sin did not render one an unbeliever. As a jurist, he reviewed the then-existing body of legal doctrines, elaborated the law by formulating views on new questions, and integrated these into a coherent system by anchoring them to an elaborate and basically consistent legal theory.

LIFE. Abū Ḥanīfah was born in Kufa, then the capital of Iraq and a major intellectual center of the Islamic world. He was of non-Arab origin: his grandfather was a freed slave from Kabul who became a client (*mawlā*) of an Arabian tribe, Taym Allāh. His father, Thābit, was certainly a Muslim, and presumably even his grandfather had converted to Islam. The family was prosperous, and Abū Ḥanīfah himself became a successful manufacturer and merchant of silk. Renowned for his honest dealings, he devoted a good part of his income to charitable purposes, especially to helping scholars in need.

Abū Ḥanīfah had a well-rounded education under a number of able scholars. Drawn to theology in his youth, he soon made his mark as a theologian through participation in theological debates. For some reason his infatuation with theology did not last long, and he turned instead to law, which occupied him for the better part of his life. His principal teacher in this realm was Hammād ibn Abī Sulaymān (d. 737), then the foremost representative of the Iraqi school of law. Abū Ḥanīfah remained his disciple for eighteen years and after his mentor's death was acknowledged as the head of the Iraqi school. He also learned from, and exchanged views with, a host of other scholars, notably Abū ʿAmr al-Shaʿbī (d. 722), ʿAṭāʾ ibn Abī Rabāḥ (d. 732), and Jaʿfar al-Ṣādiq (d. 765). Abū Ḥanīfah also benefited from constant traveling, contacts with a wide variety of people, direct involvement in business life, and exposure to the heterogeneous and dynamic society of Iraq and the materially advanced conditions there.

Because of his independent income, Abū Ḥanīfah neither needed nor cared for governmental patronage and was thus immune from governmental pressure, a situation that helped Islamic law develop independently of political authority. Likewise, owing to his disposition and academic preoccupation, Abū Ḥanīfah did not involve himself in active power politics. At the same time, he was not entirely happy with the dynasties under which he lived—the Umayyads and the Abbasids—and his sympathies lay, if at all, with the opposition. It is probably for this reason, coupled with pietistic precaution, that Abū Ḥanīfah was unwilling to be identified with either of the two regimes; he repeatedly declined to accept governmental positions, especially judgeships, and presumably even lent moral support to the ʿAlid revolt of Muḥammad, who was popularly known as al-Nafs al-Zakīyah (d. 762). These facts explain the harsh treatment meted out to Abū Ḥanīfah under both dynasties, culminating in imprisonment from the time of the revolt to his death five years later.

CONTRIBUTION TO THEOLOGY. Abū Ḥanīfah's main theological doctrines may be determined primarily from a small treatise, the *Epistle to ʿUthmān al-Battī,* which was doubtlessly written by the not-so-prolific Abū Ḥanīfah himself. A few other brief treatises, especially those called *Fiqh Akbar I* and *Fiqh absaṭ,* also represent his theological views, though they may have been written by others.

His foremost concern, as reflected in these documents, was to refute the extremist theological positions of the time, especially those of the Khārijīs. Abū Ḥanīfah vigorously refuted the Khārijī doctrine that faith and good works were inalienable and that sins cast believers out of the fold of Islam, dooming them to suffer eternally in hell. He emphasized that faith, consisting essentially of verbal confession coupled with inner conviction, did not increase or decrease. Thus by mere sinning one did not lose faith. By taking this position Abū Ḥanīfah did not wish to demean moral uprightness or to lower the quality of religious life. Rather, in the context of the Khārijī denial to believing sinners the rights of Muslims, including their lives and property, a doctrine that had caused much bloodshed and seemed to threaten the orderly existence of the Muslim community, Abū Ḥanīfah's main concern was the juridical and communal aspect, of faith as the determinant of a person's membership in the Muslim *ummah* and the resulting entitlement to certain juridical rights and privileges.

The main opponents of the Khārijīs at the time were the Murjiʾah. Abū Ḥanīfah's opposition to Khārijī doctrines understandably earned him the reputation of being a Murjiʾī, a reputation that has been accepted rather uncritically by most Western scholars. The Murjiʾah, and especially their extreme wing, held the view that if one had faith, sin would cause that person no harm. Abū Ḥanīfah's position was significantly different. In the *Epistle to ʿUthmān al-Battī* he writes: "He who obeys God in all the laws, according to us, is of the people of paradise. He who leaves both faith and works is an infidel, of the people of the [hell] fire. But one who believes but is guilty of some breach of the laws is a believing sinner, and God will do as He wishes about him: punish him if he wills, and forgive him if he wills."

On the whole, Abū Ḥanīfah's approach to theological questions is characterized by the tendency to avoid extremes and to adopt middle-of-the road positions, and by his concern for the unity and solidarity of Muslims. His catholicity is reflected in many of his doctrines, as in his rejection of the schismatic positions of both the Shīʿah (who opposed ʿUthman) and the Kharjis (who opposed both ʿUthmān and ʿAlī): "We disavow none of the companions of the apostle of God; nor do we adhere to any of them exclusively. We leave the question of ʿUthmān and ʿAlī to God, who knows the secret and hidden things."

The kernel of Abū Ḥanīfah's position on sin became the standard orthodox doctrine. Moreover, his approach initiated a powerful theological movement that contributed to the final formulations of Sunnī theological doctrines on important questions relating to free will and predestination and the attributes of God. The impact of his ideas is reflected in the works of many major theologians, including al-Ṭaḥawī (d. 933), al-Māturidī (d. 944), and al-Samarqandī (d. 993).

CONTRIBUTION TO LAW. Abū Ḥanīfah's overriding interest for the greater part of his life, however, was law, and it is upon his contribution in this field that his fame mainly rests.

By Abū Ḥanīfah's time interaction among the different centers of Islamic jurisprudence, notably Medina, Kufa, and Syria, had led to a growing awareness of disagreements on legal questions. As a result, there was a perceived need for an integrated code of legal doctrines that could be justified by reference to a set of generally recognized principles and thus be universally accepted by Muslims. Abū Ḥanīfah addressed himself almost single-mindedly to this task. In collaboration with a sizable number of his students, who were specialists in Islamic law and its related fields, he thoroughly surveyed the entire field of Islamic law, reviewed the existing doctrines, and formulated new doctrines with a view to cover all possible contingencies.

Abū Ḥanīfah did not actually compose his legal corpus; instead, he dictated his doctrines to his students. The most reliable sources for these doctrines, therefore, are the works of his students, especially Abū Yūsuf (d. 799) and al-Shaybānī (d. 804). While their works abound with Abū Ḥanīfah's legal doctrines, statements about his legal theory are few and far between, and are of a fragmentary nature. Nonetheless, the assumption that he did not have a clear legal theory is contradicted by the high degree of systematic consistency found in his doctrines. Abū Ḥanīfah's legal theory can be, and has been, deduced by a careful study of his legal doctrines. In addition, works of a later period contain a few statements ascribed to Abū Ḥanīfah regarding his legal theory (see, e.g., al-Khaṭīb al-Baghdādī, *Taʾrīkh Baghdād,* vol. 13, p. 368, and al-Makkī and al-Kardarī, *Manāqib,* vol. 1, p. 82). Whether Abū Ḥanīfah actually made those statements or not, they do seem to express broadly certain essentials of his legal theory. Likewise, later works also indicate that Abū Ḥanīfah had a set of fairly subtle and elaborate rules for interpretation of the authoritative texts, designating their relative authority and working out their legal significance.

On the whole, Abū Ḥanīfah's legal doctrines evidence a high degree of systematic consistency and seem to be the work of a brilliant albeit speculative juristic mind. Again and again, he disregards established practice and considerations of judicial and administrative convenience in favor of systematic and technical legal issues. His legal acumen and juristic strictness were such that Abū Ḥanīfah reached the highest level of legal thought for his time. Compared with the work of his contemporaries, such as the Kufan judge-jurist Ibn Abī Laylā (d. 756), the Syrian al-Awzāʿī (d. 774), and the Medinese Mālik (d. 795), his doctrines are more carefully formulated and systematically consistent and his technical legal thought more highly developed and refined.

Legal doctrines before Abū Ḥanīfah had been formulated mainly in response to actual problems; he attempted instead to formulate doctrines relating to questions that might arise sometime in the future. This method, which considerably enlarged the scope of Islamic law, further refined the already advanced legal thinking which was required for its application. It was also to lead, however, to extravagant use of imagination, and much energy was devoted to solving questions that would virtually never arise in actual life.

Abū Ḥanīfah's excessive use of analogical reasoning (*qiyās*), his wont to formulate doctrines in response to hypothetical legal questions, and above all his tendency to set aside isolated traditions (*āḥād*) if they tended to impose a restrictive interpretation on the legal import of Qurʾanic verses, earned him the reputation belonging to a group pejoratively called *ahl al-raʾy* ("people of independent opinion"), as opposed to *ahl al-ḥadīth* ("people of authoritative tradition"). This, however, was a polemical allegation rather than an objective statement of Abū Ḥanīfah's own standpoint or that of his school. More recent research has shown that there was scarcely any essential difference, in theory or practice, between the attitude of Abū Ḥanīfah and that of other legal schools regarding the use of a *raʾy* (independent opinion) on questions of religious law. As for traditions, there is ample evidence to show that Abū Ḥanīfah accepted traditions from the Prophet as well as from companions, and that he even accepted isolated traditions. He tended to disregard isolated traditions in cases involving a contradiction between those traditions and what he considered to be more authentic sources, and he did so not arbitrarily but in the light of an elaborate set of rules that he and his school had developed.

INFLUENCE. The legal doctrines of Abū Ḥanīfah were further developed by his disciples, especially Abū Yūsuf and al-Shāybanī. The resulting Ḥanafī school of law found favor with the Abbasid caliphs and a number of Muslim dynasties, especially the Ottomans, who accorded it exclusive official recognition. Today it enjoys more or less official status in most of the Arab countries that were formerly under Ottoman rule (e.g., Iraq, Jordan, Egypt, Sudan, Syria). Since large numbers of Muslims voluntarily accepted the Ḥanafī school, its adherents have become more numerous than those of any other school. They constitute a vast majority of the Muslim population of South Asia, Turkey, the Balkans, Cyprus, West and Central Asia, China, and Afghanistan and are well represented in the Arab countries, especially Syria and Iraq.

BIBLIOGRAPHY

The best bibliographical source for Abū Ḥanīfah, which far supersedes earlier works of this genre, is Fuat Sezgin's *Geschichte des arabischen Schriftums,* vol. 1 (Leiden, 1967), pp. 409–433. The only full-scale work on Abū Ḥanīfah available in any Western language is Muḥammad Shiblī Nuʿmani's *Imām Abū Ḥanīfah: Life and Work* (1889–1890), translated by M. Hadi Hussain (Lahore, 1972).

For biographical information about Abū Ḥanīfah, see the standard Muslim biographical dictionaries and also hagiographical and polemical writings relating to him. These, however, should be used critically. In the latter category, see particularly Abū al-Mu'ayyad al-Makkī and Muḥammad ibn Muḥammad al-Kardarī's *Manāqib al-imām al-aʿẓam* (Hyderabad, AH 1321); Abū ʿAbd Allāh Ḥusayn al-Ṣaymarī's *Akhbār Abī Ḥanīfah wa-aṣḥābih* (Hyderabad, 1974); and Shams al-Dīn Muḥammad ibn Yūsuf al-Ṣāliḥī al-Dimashqī al-Shāfiʿī's *ʿUqūd al-jumān fī manāqib al-imām al-aʿẓam Ab ī Ḥanīfah al-Nūʿmān* (Hyderabad, 1974). For a work that has brought together much information, and especially a vast body of negative hearsay opinion about Abū Ḥanīfah, see al-Khaṭīb al-Baghdādī's *Ta'rīkh Baghdād,* vol. 13 (Cairo, 1931), pp. 323–454. Among later works, the most useful study of Abū Ḥanīfah's life and thought is Muḥammad Abū Zahrah's *Abū Ḥanīfah,* 2d ed. (Cairo, 1960). See also Wahbī Sulaymān al-Albānī's *Abū Ḥanīfah al-Nuʿmān,* 2d ed. (Damascus, 1973). For Abū Ḥanīfah's political ideas and involvement in politics, see Manāẓir Aḥsan Gīlānī's *Imām Abū Ḥanīfah kī siyāsī zindagī,* 2d ed. (Karachi, 1957).

For the legal doctrines of Abū Ḥanīfah and his contribution to Islamic law, especially its legal theory, in addition to the works of Nuʿmānī and Abū Zahrah, see Muḥammad Yūsuf Mūsā's *Ta'rīkh al-fiqh al-islāmī,* vol. 3 (Cairo, 1956); Muḥammad ibn al-Ḥasan al-Fāsī's *Al-fikr al-sāmī fī Ta'rīkh al-fiqh al-islāmī,* 2 vols. (Cairo, 1976–1977); and Muḥammad Mukhtār al-Qāḍī's *Al-rā'y fī al-fiqh al-islāmī* (Cairo, 1949). For writings in Western languages touching on Abū Ḥanīfah's contribution to Islamic law, see Ignácz Goldziher's *The Ẓāhirīs: Their Doctrine and Their History,* translated and edited by Wolfgang Behn (Leiden, 1971); Joseph Schacht's *The Origins of Muḥammadan Jurisprudence* (Oxford, 1959) and *An Introduction to Islamic Law* (Oxford, 1964); and Ahmad Hasan's *The Early Development of Islamic Jurisprudence* (Islamabad, 1970). See also my "The Early Development of Fiqh in Kūfah: A Study of the Works of Abū Yūsuf and Al-Shaybānī" (Ph. D. diss., McGill University, 1967).

For Abū Ḥanīfah's theological views and contribution to theology, in addition to the works of Abū Zahrah and Nuʿmānī mentioned above, see A. J. Wensinck's *The Muslim Creed: Its Genesis and Historical Development* (1932; reprint, New York, 1965) and W. Montgomery Watt's *The Formative Period of Islamic Thought* (Edinburgh, 1973). See also Joseph Schacht's "An Early Murci'ite Treatise: The Kitāb al-ʿĀlim wal Mutaʿallim," *Oriens* 17 (1974): 96–117. For an important and authentic writing of Abū Ḥanīfah on theology, see "The Epistle of Abū Ḥanīfah to ʿUthmān al-Battī," in *Islam,* edited by John Alden Williams (New York, 1962), pp. 176–179. For English translations of some writings of Abū Ḥanīfah, including both authentic and questionable writings, see Wensinck's *The Muslim Creed.*

For the original sources of Abū Ḥanīfah's doctrines, see mainly the works of his two disciples, Abū Yūsuf and al-Shaybānī. Only the works dealing with financial affairs, public law, and the law of nations are available in English translation. These are *Abū Yūsuf's Kitab al-kharāj,* translated by A. Ben Shemesh, "Taxation in Islam," vol. 3 (Leiden and London, 1969), and Muḥammad ibn al-Ḥasan al-Shaybānī's *The Islamic Law of Nations,* translated by Majid Khadduri (Baltimore, 1966).

For the process of codification of law by Abū Ḥanīfah, see Muḥammad Hamidullah's "Codification of Muslim Law by Abū Ḥanīfah," in *Zeki Velidi Togan'a armağan: Symbolae in honorem Z. V. Togan* by Herbert Jansky and others (Istanbul, 1950–1955).

ZAFAR ISHAQ ANSARI (1987)

ABULAFIA, ME'IR (c. 1165–1244), known by the acronym RaMaH (Rabbi Me'ir ha-Levi). Abulafia was the first major Talmudist to appear in Spain in the period following Spanish Jewry's decisive transfer from Muslim to Christian rule in the mid-twelfth century. He was born in Burgos but moved early in his career to Toledo. His family included prominent communal leaders, some of whom served the Castilian monarchy as diplomats and administrators. Abulafia was fluent in Arabic and steeped in the culture of Spanish Jewry's "golden age"—its Hebrew linguistics and poetry, biblical exegesis, and philosophy. He was among the leading Hebrew poets of his generation, composing both secular and sacred poetry. Despite his versatility and breadth, Abulafia's religious sensibility was fundamentally conservative: his educational ideal was anchored in classical texts and his theological stance in tradition.

Abulafia's primary vocation was Talmudic studies. His detailed and highly original commentaries combine legal conceptualization with pragmatism. They also reveal the earliest traces of the northern European influence that was to transform Spanish *halakhah.* Only two of these commentaries (to the Babylonian Talmud tractates *Bava' Batra'* and *Sanhedrin*) have survived intact, but quotations from others were preserved by later authors and influenced the subsequent development of Jewish law. Abulafia was widely consulted on halakhic questions, although only a fraction of his *responsa* survive.

Abulafia also composed an important work of biblical "text criticism," *Masoret seyag la-Torah*. This study of defective and *plene* spellings in the Pentateuch has been credited with the establishment of a virtually definitive consonantal text for Torah scrolls throughout the world.

Abulafia is remembered by modern historians mostly as a critic of Maimonides (Mosheh ben Maimon, 1135/8–1204). In the first years of the thirteenth century, he attacked Maimonides' interpretation of *ʿolam ha-ba'*, "the world to come." Maimonides interpreted *ʿolam ha-ba'* along the lines of the philosophical notion of immortality. Abulafia thought this reinterpretation tantamount to a denial of the rabbinic idea of bodily resurrection and protested loudly. The ensuing controversy, which involved scholars in Catalonia, Provence, and northern France, was apparently brought to a close by the European publication of Maimonides' *Epistle on Resurrection*.

More wide-ranging and intense was the controversy that engulfed Jewish communities throughout Europe during the 1230s. Abulafia, along with Spanish colleagues like Yehudah ibn Alfakhar and Moses Nahmanides, was aligned with French traditionalists critical of Maimonidean rationalism. But unlike his French allies, Abulafia often interpreted *aggadah* (the nonlegal component of Talmudic literature) nonliterally and engaged in extra-Talmudic scientific and philosophical studies. Moreover, he admired much of Maimonides' intellectual achievement. His antirationalism focused, rather, on radical tendencies present in Spain: a stringent and all-encompassing naturalism, as well as the doctrine of salvation by philosophy and the attendant threat of antinomianism. Against philosophical naturalism, Abulafia defended the primacy of God's free will, and against a philosophical soteriology, he defended the primacy of "Torah and good deeds."

Abulafia's mature years saw the emergence of Qabbalah as a vigorous competitor of Maimonidean rationalism for the loyalty of Hispano-Jewish intellectuals. Some traditions claim that Abulafia himself was a qabbalist. His writings do not, however, support this contention. They rather reflect a militantly antimythic sensibility and a conscious renunciation of the grand quest for cosmic "secrets"—philosophical or mystical—which Abulafia considered beyond humanity's ken.

BIBLIOGRAPHY

Albeck, Shalom. "The Principles of Government in the Jewish Communities of Spain until the Thirteenth Century" (in Hebrew). *Zion* 25 (1960): 85–121.

Carmi, T., ed. and trans. *The Penguin Book of Hebrew Verse*. New York, 1981. A brief sample of Abulafia's poetry is on pages 392–394.

Septimus, Bernard. *Hispano-Jewish Culture in Transition: The Career and Controversies of Ramah*. Cambridge, Mass., 1982. Biographical information and an intellectual profile, with extensive references.

Septimus, Bernard. "Kings, Angels or Beggars: Tax Law and Spirituality in a Hispano-Jewish Responsum." In *Studies in Medieval Jewish History and Literature*, edited by Isadore Twersky, vol.2, pp. 309–336. Cambridge, Mass., 1984. Studies Abulafia's opposition to professionalized scholarship.

New Sources

Abulafia, Meir. *Yad Ramah ve-shitot kadmonim ʿal Masekhet Gittin*. Edited by Avraham Zevulun Shoshanah. Jerusalem, 1989.

Forcano, Manuel. "Rabí Xeixet Benveniste versus Rabí Meir Abulàfia (un episodi de la controvèrsia maimonidiana a Catalunya)." In *Mossé ben Nahman i el seu temps: simposi commemoratiu del vuitè centenari del seu naixement 1194–1994*, edited by Joan Boadas i Raset and Sílvia Planas i Marcé, pp. 257–266. Girona, Spain, 1994.

Novak, David. "Both Selective and Electic: [On] Bernard Septimus, 'Hispano-Jewish Culture in Tradition; the Career and Controversies of Ramah,' 1982." *Judaism* 33 (1984): 364–365.

BERNARD SEPTIMUS (1987)
Revised Bibliography

ABŪ YŪSUF (AH 113–182/731–798 CE), more fully Yaʿqūb ibn Ibrāhīm al-Anṣārī al-Kūfī; Islamic jurisconsult and, with Muhammad ibn Hasan al-Shāybanī (d. AH 189/805 CE), one of the founders of the Ḥanafī school of law. Abū Yūsuf flourished at a time of transition, when legal doctrine was still being formulated independently of the practice of the courts by groups of idealistic religious scholars in geographically determined schools. At the same time, individual scholars were appointed *qāḍīs*, or judges, by the government, especially under the Abbasids, who fostered a policy of official support for the religious law. The period also coincided with the beginning of the literary expression of technical legal thought. Abū Yūsuf's life and doctrines may be seen in the context of all these developments.

As a student and disciple of Abū Ḥanīfah, Abū Yūsuf is identified primarily with the tradition of Kufa in religious law and traditions. Born in Kufa, he was of Medinese ancestry. He is known to have studied with Mālik ibn Anas in Medina and others, but tradition states that Abū Ḥanīfah recognized the moral and intellectual excellence of the penniless young man and took him under his wing. Abū Yūsuf lived in Kufa as a practicing judge until he was appointed *qāḍī* of the capital (Baghdad), or chief judge, as his honorific (*qāḍī al-quḍāt*) indicates, by the Abbasid caliph, Hārūn al-Rashīd. The first to receive this title, Abū Yūsuf was not only consulted on the appointment and dismissal of the judiciary throughout the empire but acted as counselor to the caliph on legal and administrative matters and on financial policy. His chief extant work, the *Kitāb al-kharāj*, a treatise on taxation, public finance, and penal law, was written at the caliph's request and contains a long introduction addressed to him.

A number of works on religious law, most of which are either reasoned polemics or comparative studies of the doctrines of his contemporaries, are attributed to Abū Yūsuf, but few of these have survived. Abū Yūsuf's own doctrine can be seen within the framework of the developing technical legal thought of the Iraqi scholars, who lived in a more heterogeneous milieu and were inspired by a freer method of inquiry than that followed by the more tradition-bound Medinese. However, Abū Yūsuf tended to rely more on *ḥadīth* as the basis for legal rulings than had Abū Ḥanīfah, probably because a larger number of authoritative traditions from the Prophet had come into existence by Abū Yūsuf's time. Further, where Abū Ḥanīfah could proceed along lines of theoretical speculation and systematic consistency, Abū Yūsuf's experience as a practicing *qāḍī* caused him to mitigate his master's formalism, if often at the expense of his master's superior reasoning. In contrast to al-Shaybānī, an academic lawyer, prolific writer, and the systematizer of the school of Kufa, Abū Yūsuf was a man of affairs who made his influence felt in court circles. Since Abū Ḥanīfah himself left no writings on law, it was through the activity of these two men that the ancient school of Kufa was to become the Ḥanafī school of law.

BIBLIOGRAPHY

Abū Yūsuf's *Kitāb al-kharāj* has been translated into French by Edmond Fagnan as *Le livre de l'impôt foncier* (Paris, 1927), and partially into English by Aharon Ben Shemesh as Abū Yūsuf's *Kitāb al-kharāj* (Leiden, 1969). Ben Shemesh's translation omits the sections dealing with history, criminal justice, and administration and rearranges the order of the sections of the text on taxation; on the whole it is not so lucid a translation as Fagnan's. A systematic study of Abū Yūsuf's thought and his role in the creation of Islamic law is given by Joseph Schacht in his pathbreaking *Origins of Muhammadan Jurisprudence* (Oxford, 1950). For the historical context, see Schacht's *An Introduction to Islamic Law* (Oxford, 1964).

JEANETTE A. WAKIN (1987)

ACEHNESE RELIGION. Aceh, a province of Indonesia on the northern tip of Sumatra, is a predominantly Muslim region. More than 90 percent of the people are Acehnese speaking; other languages include Gayo, the language of people living in the central mountains, and Alas, a Batak dialect spoken by a people living south of the Gayo. Most Acehnese are currently bilingual, also speaking Indonesian, the national language. Malay was spoken by some in the coastal areas in the nineteenth century and was also the language of the Acehnese court and of the literature produced there. Acehnese, however, was both the everyday and the literary language of the countryside; religious texts are found in both Acehnese and Malay.

Aceh was once an Islamic kingdom. When Ibn Baṭṭūṭah visited Pasè, on the east coast, in 1345 CE he found Islam well established. Aceh served as a source of Islamic conversion for other parts of the Indonesian archipelago. It was also host to visiting Islamic scholars from India, Syria, and Egypt.

Aceh's early history shows marked influences from the Indian subcontinent. This, perhaps, is the source of the heterodox mysticism expounded by Ḥamzah Fanṣūrī and his successor Shams al-Dīn al-Samatrā' (d. 1630). Shams al-Dīn won the favor of Aceh's greatest ruler, Iskandar Muda, whose posthumous name was Makota ʿĀlam (r. 1607–1636). It has been suggested that Shams al-Dīn's teachings may not have been as heterodox as they were made out to be by succeeding Islamic teachers. Whatever the case, under the next king, Iskandar Thānī (r. 1636–1641), the followers of these mystics were banished from the court and their books burned. This was done after the arrival at court of the Gujarati Islamic scholar Nūr al-Dīn al-Rānīrī in 1637, presumably with the aid of another scholar, ʿAbd al-Ra'ūf al-Sinkilī.

Since that time Acehnese Islam has remained in the orthodox tradition. Mystical movements have not been as strong there as in other parts of the Indonesian archipelago. When they did arise, however, they frequently took unique forms rather than becoming part of the standard *tarekat* (Arab., *ṭāriqah*) orders, despite the fact that, particularly in the nineteenth century, many Acehnese in Mecca joined such orders, most commonly the Qādirīyah or Naqshbandīyah.

The Acehnese countryside was only nominally ruled by the court. Local nobility (*uleebelangs*) administered law with and often without the help of *kali* (judges). Their administration was frequently vigorously opposed by the *ʿulamā'* (religious scholars) who ran religious boarding schools known as *rangkangs*.

In the villages there are two locations of religious practices. The first is the *meunasah*. Today, as in the nineteenth century, the *meunasah* is a dormitory for adolescent boys and often for some adult men as well. During the fasting month it is the site of the recitation of the voluntary prayers known as *traweh* and of the men's recitation of the Qur'ān. In the nineteenth century the official in charge of the *meunasah*, the *teungku meunasah*, collected the religious taxes (*zakāt* and *fitrah*); currently a committee of village members does this. In 1906 Christiaan Snouck Hurgronje reported that the *tenungku meunasah* lived off the *zakāt* and *fitrah* he collected as well as from the proceeds from arrangements of marriages and burial fees. Today, the *zakāt* and *fitrah* are distributed to the village poor while the local branch of the National Office of Religious Affairs is in charge of the registration of marriages. The *meunasah* is often the site of elementary instruction in Qur'anic recitation, though this also takes place in the homes of teachers.

Curing rituals and rites of passage take place at the other site of religious practice, the house. A series of rituals governs the stages of life beginning with pregnancy. Snouck Hurgronje described these as practiced in the late nineteenth century; they persist today, but now as then the formalities of the rituals are unexplicated.

Such rituals nonetheless serve important functions that can best be seen by tracing the life patterns of men and women. Born into the house owned by his mother, at adolescence a boy moves into the *meunasah* to sleep. In later adolescence he is likely to leave the village altogether, moving to distant parts suitable for the growing of cash crops or offering opportunities for trade. Even after marriage he is unlikely to return home for any length of time. The house his family lives in is owned by his in-laws and later given to his wife, who is also likely to receive rice land for her maintenance. He is expected to provide money earned away from home for the care of his children. This pattern is most rigorously followed in the region of Pidie on the east coast and perhaps least prevalent on the west coast where cash crops are grown in the villages.

For the male, rites of passage mark many transition points of his movement out of his mother's house and his uneasy return to his wife's house. The negative quality of these rituals, by which is meant that they move men out of the households they are born into but never fully reestablish them in new ones, is partly responsible for the lack of Acehnese exegesis of the rituals. The male self is defined through them by movement away from women. The rituals sever connections that are to be reestablished not through ritual but through economic means. A man becomes fully a husband and father only when he provides money for his family. Even the wedding ceremony itself centers not on his relation to his wife but on his parents' relation to the parents of the bride. These ceremonies involve the negation of the signs that signify the boy's past rather than being the opportunity for their explication.

The Islamization of Aceh can best be placed within this context. Snouck Hurgronje described the religious schools ordinarily found away from the villages. The *ʿulamāʾ*, or teachers, who ran these schools were sometimes the leaders of reform movements that stressed the need for observance of the daily prayers and the fasting month, and for the combating of immoral practices. Popular response to such movements was enthusiastic but reform was never lasting. Paradoxically, the Acehnese adhered to Islam to the point, even, of willingness to die for it, as was proven by the long-lasting Acehnese War (1873–1914?), but only sporadically observed its major tenets. However the avidity for dying in a war against unbelievers, so often attested to by the Dutch who attempted to "pacify" the Acehnese, takes on a certain sense in the context of their rites of passage. The constitution of the self through the negation of its own history culminated in death in the holy war.

Even after the end of organized hostilities against the Dutch, what might be called an individual form of the holy war continued. The Dutch named the sudden and often suicidal attack on Europeans that Acehnese believed would result in their immediate entry into paradise "Acehnese murder." Such attacks occurred from the end of the Acehnese War through the 1930s. During the 1930s, however, they became considerably less frequent, probably as a result of the popular success of the Islamic reform movement. Under the leadership of the Acehnese religious scholar Daud Beureuʾeh, religious schools based on European models were established. These schools taught both religious and secular subjects and produced the leaders of Aceh during the Japanese and revolutionary periods. The other success of this reform movement was the institutionalization of *ʿibadah* (religious ritual), particularly the daily prayers.

As a result of the world economic depression during the 1930s, Acehnese men became unable to provide cash for their households as was incumbent upon them to do. It was in that context that the reform movement took permanent hold. The movement promised the construction of a new society if only men followed religious ritual. Prayer in particular was thought to put men into a state of rationality *(akal)* in which their passionate nature (*hawā nafsu*) would be contained and channeled into religiously sanctioned ends.

Reform brought with it a new interpretation of the male life pattern, according to which movement out of the household was associated with the proper channeling of *hawā nafsu.* With that came an institutionalization of Islamic belief and practice that colored the everyday relationships of men both with other men in the market and domestically with their wives and mothers.

In the lives of women also, ritual served not to integrate individuals into their roles so much as it did to separate them from influences that would prevent them from fulfilling their expected functions. In the nineteenth century, beliefs about spirits similar to those found in Java were common in Aceh. Spirits, particularly those called *burong,* which seemed to represent unfulfilled desires, were thought to disrupt life. Like curing rites, women's rites of passage prevented or ameliorated the actions of these spirits.

With the success of reformist Islam, belief in these spirits has become unimportant for men. Even for women belief in spirits has been muted by the criticism of the reformers. However, these beliefs still play an important role for women in a somewhat disguised form. Spirits are believed to bring dreams. Women, remembering their dreams, remember too that they have been visited by spirits who have, however, left them. Being free of spirits, they feel a certain competence and authority in their domestic roles.

The Acehnese War gave the *ʿulamāʾ* an importance that they had not previously attained. With the end of the war, their influence was confined to what the Dutch defined as religious matters and they were presumably depoliticized. The greatest success of the *ʿulamāʾ,* however, came with the popular acceptance of religious reform, which laid the basis for further political activity. Youth groups composed of former students of the modernist schools were the leaders of the 1945–1946 revolution, which resulted in the elimination of the Acehnese nobility. Daud Beureuʾeh himself became military governor of the province during the revolution and spent his time further consolidating modernist religious achievements. From 1953 till 1961, however, he led a rebellion against the central government; one demand of that rebellion was the acceptance of Islamic law as the law of the province. That demand was not met, and attempts to institutionalize Islamic law in the province continue as it seeks political independence from the Republic of Indonesia in a conflict that has brought great suffering and hardship to the region.

Today Aceh is the site of an Islamic university, but the form that Islam should take continues to be a major concern. The success of the reformist movement itself has aroused opposition. Mystical movements have sprung up in areas where the tendency of men to leave their villages in pursuit of a living was not so pronounced because of the possibility of raising market crops locally. The Naqshbandī *tarekat,* members of which were mainly older villagers, had great popular success in the 1950s and 1960s on the west coast of Aceh and has spread to other areas. During the 1970s, numerous heterodox mystical sects arose that have been met with vigorous opposition by the *ʿulamāʾ*.

SEE ALSO Islam, article on Islam in Southeast Asia.

BIBLIOGRAPHY

The best account of nineteenth-century Acehnese life remains Christiaan Snouck Hurgronje's *The Achehnese,* 2 vols., translated by A. W. S. O'Sullivan (Leiden, 1906). My own *The Rope of God* (Berkeley, Calif., 1969) and *Shadow and Sound: The Historical Thought of a Sumatran People* (Chicago, 1979) further trace the evolution of Acehnese religious life. M. Nur El Ibrahimy's *Teungku Muhammad Daud Beureueh* (Jakarta, 1982) is the most important source for the reform movement. An account of Acehnese textual studies can be found in Petrus J. Voorhoeve's *Critical Survey of Studies on the Languages of Sumatra* (The Hague, 1955).

New Sources

Andaya, Leonard. "The Seventeenth-Century Acehnese Model of Malay Society." In *Reading Asia: New Research in Asian Studies,* edited by Frans Husken and Dick van der Meij, pp. 83–109. Richmond, 2001.

Kraus, Werner. "Transformations of a Religious Community: The Shattariyya Sufi Brotherhood in Aceh." In *Nationalism and Cultural Revival in Southeast Asia: Perspectives from the Centre and Region,* edited by Sri Kuhnt-Saptodewo, Volker Grabowsky, and Martin Groheim, pp. 169–189. Wiesbaden, 1997.

Robinson, Kathryn. "Gender, Islam and Culture in Indonesia." In *Love, Sex and Power: Women in Southeast Asia,* edited by Susan Blackburn, pp. 17–30. Clayton, Australia, 2001.

Smith, Holly. *Aceh: Art and Culture.* Kuala Lumpur and New York, 1997.

Wieringa, Edwin. "The Drama of the King and the Holy War against the Dutch: The Koteuah of the Acehnese Epic Hikayat Prang Gompeuni." *Bulletin of the School of Oriental & African Studies* 61, no. 2 (1998): 298–308.

JAMES T. SIEGEL (1987)
Revised Bibliography

ACHUAR RELIGION SEE AMAZONIAN QUECHUA RELIGIONS

ADAD is the Old Akkadian and Assyro-Babylonian name of the ancient Middle Eastern storm god, called Adda (Addu) or Hadda (Haddu) in northwest Semitic areas and known later as Hadad, especially among the Arameans. A shortened form, Dad, occurs in personal names. Since the cuneiform sign for the "wind" (IM) was used regularly and as early as the third millennium BCE to write the divine name Adad in Mesopotamia, this is likely to have been its original meaning, just as *aḍu,* with a pharyngealized dental, means "wind" in Libyco-Berber, which is the Afro-Asiatic language closest to Semitic. The name is also related to Arabic *hadda,* "to tear down" or "to raze," a verb originally referring to a violent storm.

EXTENSION OF ADAD'S CULT. As a personification of a power of nature, Adad can bring havoc and destruction; on the other hand, he brings the rain in due season, and he causes the land to become fertile. This is why his cult plays an important role among sedentary populations in areas of rain-fed agriculture, such as northern Syria and Mesopotamia. He was not prominent in southern Babylonia, where farming was based on irrigation, and no similar Egyptian deity was worshiped in the valley and delta of the Nile, where agriculture depended on the flooding of the river. The cult of the Syrian storm god was nevertheless introduced in Egypt in the mid-second millennium BCE, and he was assimilated there with the Egyptian god Seth. The introduction of his worship in this region is probably related to the reign of the Hyksos dynasties, which were native to Canaan or Phoenicia.

CHARACTERISTICS AND RELATIONSHIP TO OTHER DEITIES. Adad is pictured on monuments and seal cylinders with lightning and the thunderbolt. In Assyro-Babylonian hymns, literary texts such as the flood story, and magic and curse formulas, the somber aspects of the god tend to predominate. For instance, the epilogue of the Laws of Hammurabi invokes Adad to bring want and hunger to the malefactor's land by depriving it of rain, and to cast thunder over his city, causing flooding. Adad is also known as Ramman, "the Thunderer," and his manifestations on mountain peaks and in the skies brought about his qualification as Baal of Heavens (i.e., Lord of Heavens, or Baal Saphon, Lord of Djebel el-Aqra) in northern Syria, thus blurring the distinction between the storm god and the mountain god. Due to the importance of his cult, he simply became Baal, "the Lord," and this antonomasia often replaced his proper name in northwest Semitic areas, at Ugarit and Emar, in Phoenicia, and in Canaan. The biblical condemnation of the cult of Baal refers likewise to the storm god.

Adad/Hadad also plays a role in entrusting royal power to kings. Hadad's prophets at Aleppo helped Zimri-Lim to regain the throne of Mari circa 1700 BCE. According to an inscription from Tel Dan from the mid-ninth century BCE, Hadad "made king" the ruler of Damascus, and in the eighth century BCE he gave "the scepter of succession" to Panamuwa II in the Aramean kingdom of Sam'al. Adad/Hadad appears sometimes as a war god, especially in Assyria and in Damascus, the Aramean capital city of which he was the chief deity.

Among his main cult centers were Aleppo and Sikkan/Guzana, biblical Gozan, in northern Syria, where he has been identified with the Hurrian storm god Teshub, and the Hittite and Luwian god Tarhunza or Tarhunt. In Anatolia, the storm god usually stood at the head of the local pantheon. His name is often concealed under the IM logogram, as it is in northern Mesopotamia and Syria. He was a heavenly god, a personification of the storm and its accompanying phenomena, such as thunder, lightning, and rain. His sacred animal was the bull.

In Syria, during the Old Babylonian period, Hadad's main sanctuary of Aleppo housed "the weapon with which he smote the Sea," regarded as a precious relic. This was a souvenir of Hadad's fight against the Sea, called Yam in Ugaritic mythological texts, which deal at length with this cosmic battle. Later Hadad became the chief god of Damascus; his temple stood at the site of the present-day Umayyad Mosque. Assyrian lexical texts identify him with Iluwer, a divine name appearing on the Aramaic stele of Zakkur, king of Hamat and Luʿash. This equation may reflect a particular syncretistic tendency of the late period and does not appear again in northwest Semitic sources. As in Anatolia, Adad's sacred animal was the bull, which symbolized might and vitality. On North Syrian stelae he is represented standing on the back of a bull, while a first-century CE stele from Dura-Europos on the Euphrates depicts him seated on a throne, with bulls on both sides.

Adad was usually accompanied by a consort, called Shala in Mesopotamia, Anat at Ugarit, and Atargatis in later periods. His father was Dagan, "the cloudy sky," and a "son of Adad," Apladda, was worshiped on the Middle Euphrates. In Greco-Roman times, Adad/Hadad was identified with Zeus, in particular at Damascus, and with Jupiter Heliopolitanus. He seems to have been identified with Jupiter Dolichenus as well, since priests attached to the latter's cult bore names such as "Son of (H)adad." Macrobius could still write circa 400 CE that "the Syrians give the name Adad to the god, which they revere as first and greatest of all." Of course, it should be made clear that we are dealing here not with a singular god, but with a name used to designate either the chief storm god of a country or a local corresponding deity, which generally had an additional qualification. The qualification usually indicated the mountain that was believed to be the abode of the deity, or a city with an important shrine. For instance, the neo-Assyrian inscription of Sargon II (r. 721–705 BCE) engraved on a stele erected in 717 BCE at Citium on Cyprus mentions "the Baal of the Mount Hurri." This is apparently the storm god of Mount Hor, present-day Ras ash-Shaqqah, which faces Cyprus and was situated on the northern border of the Holy Land according to *Numbers* 34:7–8. Ras ash-Shaqqah is one of the northern summits of the Lebanese range in the vicinity of the coast, between Byblos and Tripolis, and it was known to Greek writers as the hallowed Theouprosopon, "God's face." In the fourth century BCE, Hadad of Mabbuk was worshiped in northern Syria, in the town known later as Hierapolis, "holy city." On the obverse of a local coin, the god, horned and bearded, is represented in a long Persian-style robe. His symbols, the schematic head of a bull and a double-axe, accompany the figure. In Rome, at the time of the Empire, there was a Syrian sanctuary on Janiculum Hill, dedicated to, among others, Adad of the Lebanon.

ADAD AS VEGETATION GOD. A misinterpretation of the "beating" of the breasts as a sign of mourning, compared in *Zechariah* 12:11 with the loud rumbling of Hadad the Thunderer, led to the opinion that Adad was a dying god. The mourning alluded to by the prophet was not occasioned by Hadad's death, but by the fate of Jerusalem. As for Hadad's thundering, it was not resounding "in the valley of Megiddo," as commonly proposed in commentaries and translations of the Bible, but "in the valley of splendor." This appellation is likely to refer to the fertile Beqaʿ Valley between the Lebanon and Anti-Lebanon ranges, where the thunder of the storm god, probably Hadad of Lebanon, resounded loudly in the mountains. The word *mgdwn* of the Hebrew text is an Aramaic loanword (*migdān*), meaning "splendor," and its plural is used in *Targum Onqelos* to designate "splendid gifts," for instance in *Genesis* 24:53 and *Deuteronomy* 33:13–14.

Nonetheless, according to a mythological poem from Ugarit, when the land suffers from lack of rain, Baal/Haddu is supposed to be dead for seven years, and the prosperous state is restored only after he returns to life. The mythical scheme of seven years of famine and of seven years of great plenty is echoed not only in the story of Joseph in Egypt in *Genesis* 41 and 45:6, but also in the inscription of Idrimi, king of Alalakh in the fifteenth century BCE. This inscription refers to the seven years that Idrimi spent in exile, comparing this period with the "seven years of the storm god." This septennial motive is interwoven at Ugarit with themes reflecting a seasonal pattern. At any rate, the myth reflects a development that brought about the identification of the storm god with a vegetation god. A stele from Ugarit expresses this syncretism in a plastic way, showing the storm god who proceeds to the right above the mountains, brandishing a mace in his right hand, and holding in his left a lance with the point resting on the ground and the upper part flourishing upward in the form of a plant.

The connection between rain and the storm god was so deeply rooted that the poet could say in a mythological composition from Ugarit that "Baal rains," while Mishnaic and Talmudic texts could later call "field of Baal" or "property of Baal" a piece of ground sufficiently watered by rain and requiring no artificial irrigation. In addition, in Arabic *baʿl* is the name given to land or plants thriving on a natural water supply. The Aramaic inscription from Tell Fekherye, dedicated in the mid-ninth century BCE to Hadad of Sikkan calls him "water controller of heaven and earth, who brings down prosperity, and provides pasture and watering place for all the lands, and provides water supply and jugs to all the gods, his brothers, water controller of all the rivers, who makes all the lands luxuriant, the merciful god to whom praying is sweet."

SEE ALSO Aramean Religion; Baal; Teshub.

BIBLIOGRAPHY

Comprehensive studies of the Mesopotamian and North Syrian storm god are provided by Daniel Schwemer, *Die Wettergottgestalten Mesopotamiens und Nordsyriens im Zeitalter der Keilschriftkulturen* (Berlin, 2001), and Alberto R. W. Green, *The Storm-God in the Ancient Near East* (Winona Lake, Ind., 2003). An excellent concise presentation of the god in West Semitic areas is given by Jonas C. Greenfield, "Hadad" in *Dictionary of Deities and Demons in the Bible*, edited by Karel van der Toorn, Bob Becking, and Pieter W. van der Horst, 2d ed. (Leiden and Grand Rapids, Mich., 1999), pp. 377–382, with a bibliography. The Aramaic god Hadad is presented by Edward Lipiński, *The Aramaeans: Their Ancient History, Culture, Religion* (Louvain, Belgium, 2000), pp. 626–636.

The problem of Baal/Haddu as "dying and rising god" at Ugarit was reexamined in a convincing way by Tryggve N. D. Mettinger, *The Riddle of Resurrection: "Dying and Rising Gods" in the Ancient Near East* (Stockholm, 2001), pp. 55–81. Adad's somber aspects in Mesopotamian curses are presented by Sebastian Grätz, *Der strafende Wettergott: Erwägungen zur Traditionsgeschichte des Adad-Fluchs im Alten Orient und im Alten Testament* (Bodenheim, Germany, 1998). The iconography is reviewed and analyzed by A. Vanel, *L'iconographie du dieu de l'orage dans le Proche-Orient ancien jusqu'au VIIe siècle avant J. C.* (Paris, 1965), and A. Abou-Assaf, "Die Ikonographie des altbabylonischen Wettergottes," *Baghdader Mitteilungen* 14 (1983): 43–66. For later periods, see Michał Gawlikowski, "Hadad" in *Lexicon Iconographicum Mythologiae Classicae*, vol. 4/1, pp. 365–367, and vol. 4/2, pp. 209–210 (Zurich and Munich, 1981–1997). The North Syrian god was studied by Horst Klengel, "Der Wettergott von Halab," *Journal of Cuneiform Studies* 19 (1965): 87–95, as well as Horst and Evelyn Klengel, "The Syrian Weather-God and Trade Relations," *Annales Archéologiques Arabes Syriennes* 43 (1999): 169–177. For Anatolia, consult also Philo H. J. Houwink ten Cate, "The Hittite Storm God: His Role and His Rule according to Hittite Cuneiform Sources" in *Natural Phenomena: Their Meaning, Depiction, and Description in the Ancient Near East*, edited by D. J. W. Meijer (Amsterdam, 1992), pp. 83–148. For the iconography of Baal-Seth in Egypt, see Izak Cornelius, *The Iconography of the Canaanite Gods Reshef and Ba'al: Late Bronze and Iron Age I Periods (c. 1500–1000 BCE)* (Fribourg, Switzerland, and Göttingen, Germany, 1994).

EDWARD LIPIŃSKI (2005)

ADAM is the designation and name of the first human creature in the creation narratives found in the Hebrew scriptures (Old Testament). The word *adam* may refer to the fact that this being was an "earthling" formed from the red-hued clay of the earth (in Hebrew, *adom* means "red," *adamah* means "earth"). Significantly, this latter report is found only in *Genesis* 2:7, where the creator god enlivens him by blowing into his nostrils the breath of life. Here the first being is clearly a lone male, since the female was not yet formed from one of his ribs to be his helpmate (*'ezer ke-negdo; Gn.* 2:21–23). In the earlier textual account of *Genesis* 1:1–24a, which is generally considered to be a later version than that found in *Genesis* 2:4b–25, God first consults with his divine retinue and then makes an *adam* in his own "form and image": "in the form of God he created him; male and female he created them" (*Gn.* 1:27). If the second clause is not simply a later qualification of a simultaneous creation of a male and a female both known as *adam* (see also *Gn.* 5:1), then we may have a trace of the creation of a primordial androgyne.

Later ancient traditions responded to this version by speculating that the original unity was subsequently separated and that marriage is a social restitution of this polarity. Medieval Jewish Qabbalah, which took the expression "in the image of God" with the utmost seriousness, projected a vision of an *adam qadmon,* or "primordial Adam," as one of the configurations by which the emanation of divine potencies that constituted the simultaneous self-revelation of God and his creation could be imagined. And because Adam is both male and female according to scriptural authority, the qabbalists variously refer to a feminine aspect of the godhead that, like the feminine of the human world, must be reintegrated with its masculine counterpart through religious action and contemplation. Such a straight anthropomorphic reading of *Genesis* 1:27 was often rejected by religious philosophers especially (both Jewish and Christian), and the language of scripture was interpreted to indicate that the quality which makes the human similar to the divine is the intellect or will. Various intermediate positions have been held, and even some modern Semiticists have preferred to understand the phrase "image of God" metaphorically; that is, as referring to man as a divine "viceroy" (in the light of an Akkadian expression), and this in disregard of clearly opposing testimony in both Mesopotamian creation texts (like *Enuma elish*) and biblical language itself (cf. *Gn.* 5:1–3).

According to the first scriptural narrative, this *adam* was the crown of creation. Of his creation alone was the phrase "very good" used by God (*Gn.* 1:30f.). Moreover, this being was commissioned to rule over the nonhuman creations of the earth as a faithful steward (*Gn.* 1:29–2:9). Out of regard for the life under his domain, this being was to be a vegetarian. In the second version (where the specifying designation *ha-adam*, "the Adam," predominates; cf. *Gn.* 2:7–4:1), the creature is put into a divine garden as its caretaker and told not to eat of two trees—the tree of the knowledge of good and evil and the tree of life, that is, the two sources of knowledge and being—under pain of death (*Gn.* 2:15–17). This interdict is subsequently broken, with the result that death, pain of childbirth, and a blemished natural world were decreed for humankind (*Gn.* 3:14–19).

This primordial fault, which furthermore resulted in the banishment of Adam and his companion from the garden (*Gn.* 3:22–24), and the subsequent propagation of the human species as such (*Gn.* 4:1ff.), has been variously treated. The dominant rabbinic tradition is that the sin of Adam resulted in mortality for humankind and did not constitute a qualitative change in the nature of the species—it was not now set under the sign of sin as it was in the main Christian tradition, beginning with Paul and exemplified in the theologies of Augustine and John Calvin. For Christian theology, the innate corruption of human nature that resulted from Adam's fall was restored by the atoning death of a new Adam, Jesus (cf. *1 Cor.* 15:22). In one Christian tradition, the redemptive blood of Christ flowed onto the grave of Adam, who was buried under Calvary in the Holy Sepulcher. The typologizing of Adam in Jewish tradition often focused on him as the prototype of humankind, and so the episode in Eden was read as exemplary or allegorical of the human condition and the propensity to sin. In this light, various spiritual, moral, or even legal consequences were also drawn, particularly with respect to the unity of the human race deriving from this "one father"—a race formed, according to one legend, from different colored clays found throughout the earth. In addition, mystics, philosophical contemplatives, and Gnostics of all times saw in the life of Adam a pattern for their own religious quest of life—as, for example, the idea that the world of the first Adam was one of heavenly luminosity, subsequently diminished; the idea that Adam was originally a spiritual being, subsequently transformed into a being of flesh—his body became his "garments of shame"; or even the idea that Adam in Eden was originally sunk in deep contemplation of the divine essence but that he subsequently became distracted, with the result that he became the prisoner of the phenomenal world. For many of these traditions, the spiritual ideal was to retrieve the lost spiritual or mystical harmony Adam originally had with God and all being.

Apocryphal books about Adam and his life were produced in late antiquity and in the Middle Ages, and the theme was also quite popular in Jewish and Christian iconography, in medieval morality plays, and in Renaissance art and literature. Well known among the latter is John Milton's *Paradise Lost,* illustrated by John Dryden. Michelangelo's great *Creation of Adam* in the Sistine Chapel, the Edenic world in the imagination of the modern painter Marc Chagall, and the agonies of loss, guilt, and punishment seen in the works of Franz Kafka demonstrate the continuing power of the theme of Adam's expulsion from Eden.

See Also Eve; Fall, The; Paradise.

Bibliography

Fishbane, Michael. *Text and Texture.* New York, 1979. See pages 17–23.

Ginzberg, Louis. *The Legends of the Jews* (1909–1938). 7 vols. Translated by Henrietta Szold et al. Reprint, Philadelphia, 1937–1966. See volume 1, pages 49–102; volume 5, pages 63–131; and the index.

Le Bachelet, Xavier. "Adam." In *Dictionnaire de théologie catholique,* vol. 1, cols. 368–386. Paris, 1903.

Sarna, Nahum M. *Understanding Genesis.* New York, 1972. See pages 12–18.

Speiser, E. A. *Genesis.* Anchor Bible, vol. 1. Garden City, N.Y., 1964. See pages 3–28.

Michael Fishbane (1987)

ADAMS, HANNAH. Well known in New England during her lifetime, Hannah Adams (1755–1831) has been remembered, if at all, as the first American-born woman to earn her living by writing. However, she also has a preeminent place in the history of the study of religion. Adams wrote three theological and didactic books: *The Truth and Excellence of the Christian Religion Exhibited* (1804), which offered biographical sketches of "eminent" lay Christians; *Concise Account of the London Society for Promoting Christianity amongst the Jews* (1816), which exhorted Americans to evangelize the "lost sheep of the house of Israel"; and *Letters on the Gospels* (1824), which aimed to help young people "read the New Testament with more pleasure and advantage." As these texts indicate, Adams shared a great deal with other theological liberals during the Early National period. A Congregationalist who sided with the Unitarians, Adams favored a supernatural rationalism that endorsed both reason and revelation as sources of religious authority. She bubbled with a millennialist optimism that supported missionary outreach, but also championed "religious liberty," bemoaned sectarianism, and condemned intolerance.

Impatience with intolerance—as well as poverty and curiosity—prompted her first and most important contribution to the study of religion. She started it after becoming "disgusted by the want of candor" in Thomas Broughton's *Historical Dictionary of All Religions* (1742). In 1778, Adams began researching and writing her *Dictionary of All Religions and Religious Denominations,* a survey of religions that first appeared in 1784 (as *Alphabetical Compendium of the Various Sects*) and went through four American editions and several British editions. Scholars of U.S. Judaism have taken note of her two-volume *History of the Jews* (1812) because it drew on correspondence with Jewish leaders to offer an important account of Judaism in the United States (Adams, 1812, vol. 2, pp. 204–220). However, it was Adams's *Dictionary,* especially the fourth edition of 1817, that secured her a preeminent place in the history of the study of religion. Trying to avoid Broughton's pejorative accounts and dismissive labels, Adams not only offered a glimpse of the increasing religious diversity of Early National America, but she also provided an angle of vision on the wider religious world.

The resourceful Adams used varied sources of information. She wrote to religious leaders, including the Catholic bishop John Carroll, and visited some groups, including the Swedenborgians. She also mined depositories of official documents, as she did when researching New England history. Adams had studied Latin and Greek, but she primarily relied on secondary sources in English that she found in bookshops and libraries, including the personal library of former president John Adams, a distant relative, and the collection at the Boston Athenaeum, where Chester Harding's oil painting of her still hangs.

Using the classification scheme that predominated at the time, Adams considered four broad categories of religions: Jews, Muslims, heathens, and Christians. The latter received disproportionate attention: 85 percent of the more than seven hundred entries covered Christian ideas and groups. However, she considered other religions more fully and less dismissively than Broughton. The dictionary format itself—unlike Broughton's thematic organization—conveyed to readers that all religions were on the same footing, and Adams included a number of entries on non-Christian traditions, including eleven on Judaism, six on Islam, five on indigenous religions, and four on Zoroastrianism. She also penned eleven entries on religions in East and South Asia, including Hinduism, Sikhism, Buddhism, Confucianism, Daoism, and Shintō.

However, it is Adams's approach that seems most noteworthy. She set out four methodological "rules," guidelines that anticipated those advocated by some later interpreters of religion. First, she aimed "to avoid giving the least preference of one denomination above another." That meant, for Adams, omitting passages where authors "pass judgment" and rejecting denigrating labels such as "Heretics, Schismatics, Enthusiasts, Fanatics," and so on. Second, she resolved to let adherents speak for themselves, taking accounts of religions and sects "from their own authors." Third, she aimed to identify the "general collective sense" of each tradition, thereby avoiding descriptions that take a marginal group to represent the larger tradition. Fourth, Adams announced that she would "take the utmost care not to misrepresent the ideas" of authors.

Adams was not able to "avoid giving the least preference." As with all scholars of religion, her social location and personal convictions shaped her interpretations. In the volume's introduction, which described the religious world at the time of Jesus, she noted that the "heathens" venerated many gods. To explain that diversity, Adams recounted naturalist and euhemerist theories of the origin of religion: the gods originated in encounters with nature or in the propensity to deify heroes. Yet none of the non-Christian faiths, including Judaism, were as lofty as the tradition initiated by Jesus. "Christianity broke forth from the east like a rising sun," Adams suggested, "and dispelled the universal darkness which obscured every part of the globe" (Adams, 1992, p. 11). In this passage from the introduction, and in some entries, Adams revealed her theological commitments. She sometimes recorded, almost word for word, misleading or negative descriptions. She sometimes seemed blind to the ways a borrowed phrase violated her commitment to fair representation. Yet, to her credit, Adams never treated a religion or sect more negatively than her sources, and when a British edition added denigrating labels and phrases she deleted them in the subsequent American edition. Most important, she anticipated later developments by prescribing a critical and judicious approach to the comparative study of religion. Louis Henry Jordan, who wrote an early history of the field, listed Adams as the only American included among the "prophets and pioneers" (Jordan, 1986, pp. 146–150). Even if most subsequent histories have overlooked Adams or minimized her contributions—and those of other women—Jordan's assessment still seems appropriate. If we consider the historical context—not to mention the obstacles she faced as the first American woman to earn her living by writing—Adams's *Dictionary* seems to be "a really notable undertaking" (Jordan, 1986, p. 149).

BIBLIOGRAPHY

Adams, Hannah. *Alphabetical Compendium of the Various Sects Which Have Appeared from the Beginning of the Christian Era to the Present Day.* Boston, 1784.

Adams, Hannah. *The Truth and Excellence of the Christian Religion Exhibited.* Boston, 1804.

Adams, Hannah. *The History of the Jews from the Destruction of the Temple to the Nineteenth Century.* 2 vols. Boston, 1812.

Adams, Hannah. *A Concise Account of the London Society for Promoting Christianity amongst the Jews.* Boston, 1816.

Adams, Hannah. *Letters on the Gospels.* Cambridge, U.K., 1824.

Adams, Hannah. *A Memoir of Miss Hannah Adams, Written by Herself with Additional Notices by a Friend.* Boston, 1832.

Adams, Hannah. *A Dictionary of All Religions and Religious Denominations, Jewish, Heathen, Mahometan, and Christian, Ancient and Modern* (4th ed., 1817). Introduction by Thomas A. Tweed. Atlanta, 1992.

Broughton, Thomas. *An Historical Dictionary of All Religions from the Creation of the World to This Perfect Time.* London, 1742.

Jackson, Carl. *Oriental Religions and American Thought: Nineteenth Century Explorations.* Westport, Conn., 1981. Jackson's history of the American encounter with Asian thought from the late eighteenth century to the Parliament of Religions in 1893 includes a three-page account of Hannah Adams's work (pp. 16–19).

Jordan, Louis Henry. *Comparative Religion: Its Genesis and Growth.* Reprint, Atlanta, 1986. Originally published in Edinburgh in 1905, this was an early attempt to recount the "origin, progress, and aim of the science of Comparative Religion." The section on the field's "prophets and pioneers" offers a brief account of the significance of Hannah Adams and her work (pp. 146–150).

King, Ursula. "A Question of Identity: Women Scholars and the Study of Religion." In *Religion and Gender,* edited by Ursula

King, pp. 219–244. Oxford, 1995. An analysis of the place of women scholars in the history of the study of religion, King's chapter also notes Adams's significance for the field (pp. 222, 224).

Tweed, Thomas A. "An American Pioneer in the Study of Religion: Hannah Adams (1755–1831) and her *Dictionary of All Religions*." *Journal of the American Academy of Religion* 40 (1992): 437–464. This article offers an overview of the life and work of Hannah Adams as a scholar of religion.

Vella, Michael W. "Theology, Genre, and Gender: The Precarious Place of Hannah Adams in American Literary History." *Early American Literature* 28 (1993): 21–41. Vella's article assesses Adams's place in American literary history.

THOMAS A. TWEED (2005)

ĀDI GRANTH ("first book") is the earliest scripture of the Sikhs; the second scripture is the *Dasam Granth* ("tenth book"). The *Ādi Granth* is an anthology of medieval religious poetry, relating to the radical school of the Bhaki Movement. Those whose verses are included in it lived between the twelfth and the seventeenth century CE. The *Granth* was compiled by Gurū Arjan Dev in 1604 at Amritsar, utilizing the material already collected by Gurū Nānak, the founder of Sikhism, and Gurū Amar Dās, third *gurū* of the Sikhs, who also made several of his own additions. Bhāī Gurdās was the scribe. The scripture was installed as the *Gurū Granth Sāheb* in the Harī Mandir (Golden Temple) by the *gurū* himself; the first high priest *(granthī)* was Bābā Budhā.

The original *Granth Sāheb* is known as *Kartārpur dī bīṛ* ("the recension of Kartarpur") because it came into the possession of Dhīr Mal, a grandson of Gurū Hargobind, the sixth *gurū,* who lived at Kartarpur in Jullundur district. While this recension was being taken for binding to Lahore, the second recension was prepared by Banno and is hence known as *Bhāī Banno dī bīṛ*. His additions to the end of *Granth Sāheb* were not approved by Gurū Arjan Dev. The third and final recension was prepared in 1704 by Gurū Gobind Singh, the tenth *gurū,* at Damdamā, where he resided for some time after leaving Anandpur. The scribe was Bhāī Manī Singh. This recension is known as *Damdame Wālī bīṛ*. The hymns of Gurū Tegh Bahadur, the ninth *gurū,* were added to it. The guruship was bestowed on this final recension by the tenth *gurū,* thereby ending the line of personal guruship.

Besides the hymns of the first five and the ninth Sikh *gurūs*, the hymns of the pre-Nānak saints, including Nāmdev, Kabīr, and Ravidās, and the verses of some contemporary poets, mostly bards, are included in the *Ādi Granth*. The poetry of the scripture is musical and metrical. Except for the *japu* of Gurū Nānak in the beginning and the *sloks* and *swayyās* at the end, all the other compositions are set in various *rāgas* and *rāginīs*. These compositions include hymns of the *gurūs* in serial order, in set patterns of stanza forms and musical notations. These are followed by longer poems with special subheadings, then the *chhants* and *vārs* of the Sikh *gurūs* in serial order. At the end of each *rāga* or *rāginī* appear the hymns of the various saints in turn, beginning with Kabīr and followed by Nāmdev, Ravidās, and others. Various forms of versification, including folk song forms, are used.

Because the saints and *gurūs* represented in the *Ādi Granth* belong to different regions and social strata, the scripture is a treasury of medieval Indian languages and dialects. Besides writings in the common language, called *sant bhāṣā* ("saint language"), containing affixes and case terminations of the language of the area of the saint concerned, the *Ādi Granth* also contains poems composed in Braj Bhāṣā, Western Hindi, Eastern Punjabi, Lahndi, and Sindhi. The influence of Eastern, Western, and Southern Apabhramsas, Sanskrit, Persian, Arabic, and Marathi are discernible in various poems and hymns. The saint-poets have clothed their spiritual experiences in the imagery derived from both the world of nature and the world of man. Because of the similarity of spiritual experience, there is undoubtedly a good deal of repetition in the content of these verses, but the diverse imagery used in the hymns makes the poetry appealing and always fresh.

The saint-poets and *gurūs* represented in the *Ādi Granth* speak of the prevailing degeneration of religious life. They denounce formalism, ritualism, and symbolism. They consider ethical greatness the basis for spiritual greatness. The seekers must imbibe godly attributes and other qualities in their lives and avoid sinful acts. Prominence is given to truth, but still greater prominence to the practice of truth. The active life of a householder is considered the best life, and the division of humankind into castes and various stages is rejected. The hand and the mind both must act together to attain loftier ideals. There is a close connection in the *Ādi Granth* between the doctrine of *karman* and that of grace. Although it holds that *hukm* (the will of God) reigns supreme, the *Ādi Granth* does not deny the freedom of the individual. The reality of the world forms the basis of Sikh ethics. Though the world is transient, its existence is real.

The *Ādi Granth* opposes all distinctions of caste and color. It espouses universal brotherhood. Religious practices and outward symbols create ego, which can be overcome by remembrance of the name of the Lord, in the company of the saints *(sādh sangat)* and the grace of the true *gurū* and the Lord. We meet the true *gurū* by the grace of God and realize God by the grace of the true *gurū*. The ideal is the realization of God, and for the attainment of this ideal the disciple must seek the guidance of the true *gurū,* who has full knowledge of *brahman*. With the tenth *gurū*'s surrender of personal guruship to the *Granth* itself, the Word (Skt., *śabda*) henceforth is the *gurū*. The lotus-feet of the Lord are the only heaven for the true disciple. The state of realization is called *sahj* ("equipoise"). In this state the mind and intellect become absolutely pure.

According to the *Ādi Granth,* God *(brahman)* is one without a second. His name is Truth. He is the creator, devoid of fear and enmity. He is immortal, unborn, and self-existent. He is truth, consciousness, and bliss. He is omnipresent, omnipotent, and omniscient. He is changeless and flawless. When he wills to become many, he begins his sport like a juggler. Before the creation he is in abstract meditation and without attributes, but after the creation, he, as Īśvara, manifests himself as the treasure house of all qualities. The soul *(jīva)* is part and parcel of *brahman.* It has its own individuality, but since it comes out of *brahman* it is also immortal. The physical body decays, but the *jīva* continues forever. *Prakṛti,* or *māyā,* is not a separate ultimate reality. It has been created by God. It leads the *jīva* away from God and thus toward transmigration. When the influence of *māyā* vanishes, the *jīva* realizes *brahman.* It is wrong to delimit the creation of the infinite Lord. The Truth is immanent in the universe. The human body is its repository and an epitome of the universe. It is a microcosm.

SEE ALSO Guru Granth Sahib; Kabīr; Nānak; Singh, Gobind.

BIBLIOGRAPHY

Kohli, Surindar Singh. *Sikh Ethics.* New Delhi, 1975.

Kohli, Surindar Singh. *A Critical Study of Adi Granth.* 2d ed. Delhi, 1976.

Kohli, Surindar Singh. *Outlines of Sikh Thought.* 2d ed. New Delhi, 1978.

Singh, Pandit Tara. *Gurmat Nirṇay Sāgar.* Lahore, 1904.

Singh, Sher Gyani. *Philosophy of Sikhism.* 2d ed. Delhi, 1966.

Singh, Taran. *Srīi Gurū Grantha Sāhiba dā Sāhitika Itihāsa.* Amritsar, 1963.

SURINDAR SINGH KOHLI (1987)

ADLER, FELIX (1851–1933), social, educational, and religious reformer; founder of the New York Society for Ethical Culture. Born in Alzey, Germany, Adler came to the United States at the age of six when his father, Rabbi Samuel Adler, accepted the country's most prestigious Reform pulpit, at Temple Emanu-El in New York. By example and instruction his parents fostered his passion for social justice, religious sensibilities, and Jewish education. After graduation from Columbia College in 1870, he returned to Germany to study at the Berlin Hochschule für die Wissenschaft des Judentums with Abraham Geiger in order to prepare for a career in the Reform rabbinate. When the school's opening was delayed for almost two years, Adler immersed himself in university studies, first at Berlin and then at Heidelberg, where he received his doctorate in Semitics *summa cum laude* in 1873. His formative German experiences precipitated an intellectual break with Judaism: After his exposure to historicism, evolution, critical studies of the Bible, anthropology, and Neo-Kantianism, Adler's belief in theism and the spiritual uniqueness of Judaism was undermined. Kant's analysis of ethical imperatives lent authority to Adler's new faith in a moral law independent of a personal deity, and the German industrial order, with its attendant socioeconomic problems for labor and society, along with Friedrich Lange's proposed solutions, brought into focus the major ills of industrial society that Adler came to address in America throughout his life.

Upon his return home, it was expected that he would eventually succeed his father at Emanu-El, but his one sermon on October 11, 1873, alienated some of the established members. Adler's admirers, however, sponsored him as nonresident professor of Hebrew and Oriental literature at Cornell between 1873 and 1876, and they then served as the nucleus of a Sunday lecture movement that he inaugurated on May 15, 1876. The following February this movement was incorporated as the New York Society for Ethical Culture.

To Adler, this society represented a religious organization that transcended creeds and united people in ethical deeds; it was dedicated to the inherent worth of each individual, to personal and communal ethical growth, and to the application of an ethical perspective to every social context. Over the years, the society served as Adler's platform not only for philosophical conceptualizations but also for concrete social reforms. In the late 1870s he established the first free kindergarten in New York, the first district nursing program, and a workingman's lyceum; in 1880 he organized a workingman's school (later the Ethical Culture School), and in 1891 he founded the Summer School of Applied Ethics. Adler was also intimately involved in tenement housing reform and good-government clubs and served as chairman of the National Child Labor Committee from 1904 to 1921. He launched the Fieldston School in 1928.

As an intellectual, Adler enjoyed the esteem of his peers and accumulated impressive scholarly credentials: He founded the *International Journal of Ethics* (1890), was appointed professor of political and social ethics at Columbia (1902), and delivered Oxford's Hibbert Lectures (1923), published as *The Reconstruction of the Spiritual Ideal* (1924). Nevertheless, the fundamental intellectual effort of his last years—the philosophical justification of his ethical ideal of a spiritual universe—had negligible impact. Where this was attempted, as in *An Ethical Philosophy of Life* (1918), it was dismissed as an example of Neo-Kantian religious idealism. Indeed, his earlier, less abstruse works—*Creed and Deed* (1877), *Life and Destiny* (1903), *The Religion of Duty* (1905), *The World Crisis and Its Meaning* (1915)—were far better received.

In his day, Adler was publicly lauded as prophet, social visionary, and apostle of moral justice even by the Jewish community he had left. Yet toward the end of his life he was intellectually alienated from his own organization, and in the early twenty-first century most Ethical Culture members know him only as their movement's founder.

SEE ALSO Ethical Culture.

BIBLIOGRAPHY

The fullest biography is Horace L. Friess's *Felix Adler and Ethical Culture* (New York, 1981). Friess (Adler's son-in-law) presents the full scope of Adler's activities combined with personal memories of the man and an insightful analysis of Adler's intellectual evolution and his final ethical position. My own study *From Reform Judaism to Ethical Culture: The Religious Evolution of Felix Adler* (Cincinnati, 1979) analyzes Adler's religious departure from Judaism, its causes, and its repercussions for both Adler and the American Jewish community. It treats the Jewish reaction to Adler and to the Ethical Culture Society and uses Adler as a model by which to understand new models of Jewish apostasy in modern Jewish history. Robert S. Guttchen's *Felix Adler* (New York, 1974) presents a very useful analysis of Adler's concept of human worth and his educational philosophy. The book is prefaced with a perceptive biographical sketch of Adler by Howard B. Radest. The latter's own book, *Toward Common Ground: The Story of the Ethical Societies in the United States* (New York, 1969), furnishes further information on Adler.

BENNY KRAUT (1987)

ADONIS is a divine name coined in Greek from the northwest Semitic exclamation *ʾadōnī*, "my lord," probably shortened from the dirge *hōy ʾadōnī*, "Woe, my lord," which is echoed in Greek by *aiai, Adonin.*

ORIGINS. The Greek tradition connects Adonis with Byblos. Hence his worship must be of Byblian origin. It is unknown whether the male deity thus invoked or mourned in the first millennium BCE was initially a city god or heroic eponym, a Baal of Byblos, or a god of the countryside, as suggested by his assimilation with Tammuz and Dionysos in the Middle East, and by his characterization as a vegetation deity in later Greco-Roman tradition. The latter view is supported by Lucian's notice that Byblian women performed their mourning ritual for Adonis "through the whole countryside," and by a similar detail in the description of the Adonis festival at Seville circa 287 CE, as reported in the *Martyrology of Saints Justa and Rufina.* The center of Adonis's worship was at Aphaca in Mount Lebanon, a single day's journey from Byblos. At the site of the famous spring, the main source of the Adonis River or Nahr Ibrahim, stood a temple, where the cult of Adonis was maintained until the time of Emperor Constantine the Great, who ordered the destruction of the shrine. Although it was partially rebuilt by Julian the Apostate, little survives of the ancient buildings, except some Roman ruins.

Adonis's Semitic name or epithet *naʿmān*, "the beautiful" or "the lovely one," was preserved by *Isaiah* 17:10 and by Greek authors, especially when comparing the anemone to Adonis. Naʿmān or Naaman is a West Semitic proper name, attested from the second millennium BCE onward, and the epithet occurs frequently in literary texts from Ugarit. It implies that Adonis was conceived as a youth of remarkable beauty. Instead, he lacks any feature that would characterize him as a deity of the netherworld, except his secondary assimilation to Osiris, the king of the dead, in the Alexandrian ritual.

MYTHS. Several mythical stories are related to Adonis. According to the myth that Apollodorus cites from Panyassis of Halicarnassus, active in the early fifth century BCE, Adonis was the son of the Assyrian/Syrian king Theias by his daughter Smyrna, who by deceiving him as to her identity, conceived Adonis by him. When Theias discovered the truth he would have slain his daughter, but the gods in pity changed her into a myrrh tree. As the myrrh tree grows only in southern Arabia and in Somaliland, it is unlikely that it belongs to the original story. *Smyrna* must be a Graecized form of *šarmīna*, the evergreen cypress, which perfectly fits the Adonis myth. After ten months, according to Apollodorus, the tree burst, letting Adonis come forth. This epiphany characterizes him as a vegetation god. It is similar to the birth of Malakbēl as represented on an altar from Rome, one side of which shows the young god emerging from a cypress. This kind of epiphany is well known in the Middle East and it also occurs in Assyria. The Adonis myth uses the same theme as the story of Judah and Tamar, "the Date Palm," in *Genesis* 38. By deceiving her father-in-law as to her identity, Tamar conceived two sons by him. When Judah discovered the truth he would have slain his daughter-in-law, but Tamar made her justification by applying to the custom and duty of levirate marriage. Panyassis's fable may reflect another institution—the sacred marriage celebrated by the king with a priestess, possibly a king's daughter. Since Theias is apparently the same legendary character as Toi or Tai (Tʿy), king of Hamat (Syria), who entered the Bible in *2 Samuel* 8:9–10, the myth could be as old as the ninth century BCE, when the worship of Pahalatis, possibly the Mistress (Bʿlt) of Byblos, is attested at Hamat.

Adonis's agrarian nature of dying and rising god, like the Sumerian god Dumuzi and the Assyrian Tammuz, is implied also by Panyassis's complementary account of the seasonal split in Adonis's life between Aphrodite and Persephone, the queen of the netherworld. When Adonis was born, Aphrodite put the infant in a chest. This feature of the account parallels the case of Dionysos venerated at Delphi in a fan, but also recalls the stories of Sargon of Akkad and of Moses in *Exodus* 2:1–10. However, Aphrodite handed the child in the chest to the care of Persephone, who afterward refused to give him up. Zeus, an appeal being made to him, decided that Adonis should spend a third of the year with Persephone and a third with Aphrodite, and the remaining third at his own disposal.

Aphrodite is obviously Astarte, the mythic queen of Byblos according to Plutarch, but she is also Balthi, the great goddess or Mistress of Byblos, according to the Syriac homily of Pseudo-Meliton. As for Persephone, she probably corresponds to Sheʾol, a chthonic goddess whose name in Hebrew designates the netherworld. Zeus's verdict is a variant of a folktale, upon which Solomon's arbitration in *1 Kings* 3:16–

28 is also based. The antiquity of this particular myth of Adonis is confirmed by scenes engraved on Etruscan bronze mirrors from the fifth to third centuries BCE, showing Zeus's arbitration, the sadness of Turan (the Etruscan Venus), and her happiness when her lover Atunis rejoins her. Love scenes of Venus and Adonis also appear on mosaics, in particular at Lixus, the ancient Phoenician settlement on the Atlantic coast of Morocco. An interesting variant of these myths is represented on a Roman cameo: Adonis sleeps naked at the foot of a tree, guarded by his dog; two cupids try to wake him up, while Aphrodite waits amorously for his "awaking."

An important element in appreciating Adonis's agrarian connection is the story of the killing of Adonis by a "boar out of the wood," an animal known for ravaging the vines, as *Psalms* 80:9–14 complains. The story related to Adonis seems to be of Semitic origin as well, since Jerome's allusion to the killing of Adonis "in the month of June" must be based on Aramaic *ḥăzīr*, which in Syriac means both "boar" and "June." But its original protagonist may have been Attis, slain by a boar according to Pausanias. Adonis fighting the boar is represented as a hunter on a mosaic from Carranque near Toledo, dated to the fourth century CE.

Another version of the slaying of Adonis is preserved by Pseudo-Meliton, who calls him Tammuz. Since Balthi was in love with him, Hephaestus, her jealous husband, "slew Tammuz in Mount Lebanon, while he was clearing the land" (*šnīra burza*). Adonis was then buried at Aphaca, where Balthi also died.

CULT. The cult of Adonis was especially popular with women. Annual festivals, called Adonia, were held at Byblos and also, at least from the seventh century BCE onward, in Cyprus and at different places in Greece. Its earliest record is a fragment of a poem by Sappho, who was native to Lesbos in the Aegean. Her poem was apparently written in the form of a dialogue between a woman, possibly representing Aphrodite, and a chorus of young female attendants. It refers to "the lovely Adonis," using a Greek translation of Adonis's Semitic name or epithet *naʿmān*, and invites the young maidens to mourn for him by beating their breasts and rending their tunics. The Semitic features of the ritual are confirmed by Aristophanes' references to the Adonia being celebrated in Athens on the roof of a building by women shrieking "Woe, woe, Adonis!" and beating their breasts.

A very elaborate Alexandrian festival is described by Theocritus in the third century BCE. The rites consisted of a magnificent wedding pageant for Adonis and Aphrodite. The next day women carried Adonis's image to the seashore amid lamentations and expressed the hope of witnessing his return the following year. The Egyptian cult of Osiris most likely had a bearing on the Ptolemaic ritual and its influence could have reached Byblos, since the well-known legend of Isis finding the body of Osiris murdered by Seth localizes the mythical event at Byblos. A special feature of the festival was the "Adonis gardens," first recorded by Plato and alluded to in *Isaiah* 17:10–11. These were small pots of seeds forced to grow artificially, which rapidly faded. Egyptian origin is possible. They were similar, in fact, to the so-called beds of Osiris showing Osiris's shape; these were planted with corn seeds, the sprouting of which signified the god's resurrection.

There was perhaps considerable variation in the content of the Adonis festival and much of the original intent of the rites appears to have been forgotten. Originally, rites and mystery-plays reenacted dying and revival, disappearance and return. The mourning of Adonis is well documented in written sources, but his revival, return, or rebirth is not attested directly before Lucianus's *De dea Syria*, Origen, and Jerome. However, the "recovering of Adonis" by Venus, often depicted in Rome according to Plautus's comedy *Menaechmi* 143–145 (dated tentatively from 194 BCE), Adonis's marvelous birth from the evergreen cypress, and the division of his life between Aphrodite and Persephone all have the idea of revival, rebirth, or awakening in common and are concerned with vegetation. According to *De dea Syria*, sacred prostitution was included in the ritual at Byblos, a sacred marriage with Aphrodite took place in the Alexandrian ritual, and the cells of the temple of Adonis at Dura-Europos may have served the same purpose. Its mythical aim was probably the "rebirth" of Adonis.

According to *De dea Syria*, Adonis's revival was celebrated on the third day of the festival. The "third day" seems to have been a predestined moment for the revival, since the "finding of Osiris" by Isis took place on the third day according to Plutarch, the revival of the nation takes place on the third day according to *Hosea* 6:2, and Jesus' resurrection is dated to "the third day" in *1 Corinthians* 15:4. At any rate, the triduum has a larger application in cult and historiography.

It is difficult to answer the question whether Adonis was initially a god of vegetation in general, a vine god, a tree spirit, as is suggested by his birth from a tree, or a grain spirit. According to Ammianus Marcellinus, writing in the second half of the fourth century CE, the Adonis festival was "symbolic of the reaping of ripe fruits of the field." Origen stated one century earlier that Adonis is "the symbol of the fruits of the earth, mourned when they are sown, but causing joy when they rise." According to Jerome, the "slaying of Adonis is shown by seeds dying in the earth, and his resurrection by the crops in which dead seeds are reborn." These explanations favor the conception of Adonis as a grain spirit, the more so because a sentence from Pseudo-Meliton, usually emended and mistranslated, shows him laboring in the field. In this context Adonis's appearance as a hunter in one of the myths might signify that he was protecting the fields against wild boars.

SEE ALSO Dumuzi; Dying and Rising Gods; Eshmun.

BIBLIOGRAPHY

A comprehensive study of Adonis is provided by Tryggve N. D. Mettinger, *The Riddle of Resurrection: "Dying and Rising Gods" in the Ancient Near East* (Stockholm, 2001), in particular pp. 113–154, 175–179, and 209–212, with former literature. See also G. Piccaluga, "Adonis, i cacciatori falliti e l'avvento dell'agricoltura," in *Il mito greco: Atti del convegno internazionale*, edited by Bruno Gentili and Giuseppe Paioni (Rome, 1977), pp. 33–48; Sergio Ribichini, *Adonis: Aspetti "Orientali" di un mito greco* (Rome, 1981); and Edward Lipiński, *Dieux et déesses de l'univers phénicien et punique* (Louvain, Belgium, 1995), pp. 90–108. For Adonis in Greek literature and arts, see Wahib Atallah, *Adonis dans la littérature et l'art grecs* (Paris, 1966). For the "Adonis gardens," see the monograph by Gerhard J. Baudy, *Adonisgärten: Studien zur antiken Samensymbolik* (Frankfurt am Main, 1986), and, with prudence, Marcel Detienne, *The Gardens of Adonis: Spices in Greek Mythology*, translated by Janet Lloyd (Atlanic Highlands, N.J., 1977). The iconography is presented by B. Servais-Soyez, "Adonis," in *Lexicon Iconographicum Mythologiae Classicae* (Zurich and Munich, 1981–1997), vol. 1/1, pp. 222–229, and vol. 1/2, pp. 160–170.

EDWARD LIPIŃSKI (2005)

ADRET, SHELOMOH BEN AVRAHAM

ADRET, SHELOMOH BEN AVRAHAM (c. 1235–1310), known by the acronym RaSHBa' (Rabbi Shelomoh ben Avraham); Spanish rabbi and legal authority. Born into a leading family of Aragon, Adret studied with Yonah Gerondi and with the great Talmudist, biblical commentator, and qabbalist Moses Nahmanides (Mosheh ben Naḥman). During his four decades as rabbi of Barcelona, Adret was considered by the Aragonese kings to be the dominant Jewish figure in the realm.

Adret's scholarly reputation was established by his *novellae* (Heb., *ḥiddushim*) on many Talmudic tractates, and contemporaries recognized him as an outstanding authority on Jewish law. Rabbis of Aragon and of many distant countries submitted their formal legal inquiries to him, and his collected *responsa*, numbering in the thousands, made him one of the most prolific and influential of all Jewish legal respondents. An important source for the history of Jewish communal life, these *responsa* treat problems relating to communal self-government, fiscal administration, and institutions such as the synagogue, court, house of study, and voluntary societies.

Occasionally Adret was confronted with formal questions of a theological nature, usually flowing from problematic biblical passages or rabbinic pronouncements. Scattered through his *responsa* are significant statements on the proper role of philosophical speculation in interpreting traditional texts, the possibility of contemporary prophecy, astrology, dreams, magic and divine providence, the search for rational explanations of the commandments, the immutability of the Torah, and eschatological doctrine.

Adret strongly denounced the messianic pretensions of the eccentric mystic Abraham Abulafia and later claimed that without his firm opposition many Jews would have been deceived. He also warned Jewish communities against a Jew called the "prophet of Ávila," who maintained that a mystical work had been revealed to him by an angel.

His most controversial foray into public affairs was instigated by complaints from southern France about the destructive impact of philosophical learning upon young Jews. In 1305, after a three-year correspondence, Adret promulgated a formal ban in his Barcelona synagogue, prohibiting those less than twenty-five years old from studying books of Greek natural science or metaphysics. The writings of Maimonides were not proscribed, and the study of medicine was explicitly excluded from the prohibition.

Because of his role in this conflict, Adret was frequently depicted by nineteenth-century Jewish historians as part of a group of narrow-minded, obstinate zealots. His own work, however, especially his *novellae* on selected Talmudic *aggadot,* reveals an openness to the use of philosophical literature for exegetical purposes, although he clearly repudiated the extreme philosophical positions denying creation and individual providence. He also suggested qabbalistic interpretations of rabbinic statements. The fact that several of his disciples wrote commentaries on the Torah or explications of Nahmanides' commentary in which the mystical element was pronounced led Gershom Scholem to speak of the qabbalistic "school" of Adret.

Adret's writings include answers to Christians who used the *aggadah* to undermine the authority of the sages or to support Christian theological positions; one source describes an actual debate with a Christian thinker. Adret is also presumed to have written a *Ma'amar 'al Yishma'e'l,* published by Perles, responding to the anti-Jewish tracts of the eleventh-century Spanish Muslim intellectual Ahmad ibn Hazm. This apologetical work defends the Torah against charges of containing inconsistencies and describing repugnant behavior; it answers the claim that the original Torah had been lost and that Judaism contained perversions and distortions of God's authentic teaching.

BIBLIOGRAPHY

The biography by Joseph Perles, *R. Salomo ben Abraham ben Adereth: Sein Leben und seine Schriften* (Breslau, 1963), remains the only full-length treatment of this important figure. The best discussion of his role as communal leader in historical context is in Yitzhak F. Baer's *History of the Jews in Christian Spain,* vol. 1 (Philadelphia, 1961), pp. 278–305. Isidore Epstein's *The Responsa of Rabbi Solomon Ben Adreth of Barcelona (1235–1310) as a Source of the History of Spain* (London, 1925) is still a useful collection of passages dealing with communal organization and administration, although it overlooks some of the most important historical material. Louis Jacobs summarizes the *responsa* pertaining to problems of Jewish religious thought in *Theology in the Responsa* (London, 1975), pp. 57–79. The most extensive account of Adret's role in the conflict over the study of philosophy, in Joseph Sarachek's *Faith and Reason* (Williamsport, Pa., 1935), requires modification based on more recent studies in periodicals, such as Joseph Shatzmiller's "Bein Abba' Mari le-Rashba'," in *Meḥqarim be-toledot 'am Yisra'el ve-Erets Yisra'el* 3 (1974–1975): 121–137.

New Sources

Adang, Camilla. "A Jewish Reply to Ibn Hazm: Solomon b. Adret's Polemic against Islam." In *Judíos y musulmanes en al-Andalus y el Magreb: contactos intelectuales. Actas reunidas y presentadas por Maribel Fierro*, pp. 179–209. Madrid, 2002.

Cohen, Jonathan. "Charitable Contributions, Communal Welfare Organizations, and Allegiance to the Community according to Rashba." *HUCA* 72 (2001): 85–100.

Horwitz, David. "Rashba's Attitude towards Science and Its Limits" (in Hebrew). *Torah U-Madda Journal* 3 (1991–1992): 52–81.

MARC SAPERSTEIN (1987)
Revised Bibliography

AEGEAN RELIGIONS. The Aegean world is composed of three distinctive regions, all located at the Eastern edge of the Mediterranean: the island of Crete, the mainland of Greece, and the islands between the mainland and the coast of Anatolia. The people of the mainland, the Mycenaeans, were Greek-speaking. The inhabitants of the island of Crete were the Minoans, who spoke an as yet undeciphered language. The islanders were apparently non-Greek, and fell into the political and cultural orbit of the Minoans and later the Mycenaeans in the second millennium BCE. The Aegeans shared many cultural traits with the Near East, but retained a distinctive regional character. The Minoans and Myceneans had palace cultures shortly after 2000 BCE, but for the people of the islands, no such claim can be made.

Little is known about the religion of the islands north of Crete that are collectively called the Cyclades. Numerous marble figures and figurines have been found but most of them are without context. It is uncertain whether or not they were used for worship. Dearth of data makes a reconstruction of Cycladic religion next to impossible.

MINOAN RELIGION. The religious beliefs of the Minoans are more accessible despite the absence of decipherable texts.

The myth of the great goddess and matriarchy. If Minoan religion is popular today, this is partly due to the great mother goddess (see figure 1). This is the legacy of the excavator of Knossos, Sir Arthur Evans (1851–1941), who may be said to have invented Minoan culture at the beginning of the twentieth century. For his interpretations he relied on images represented on wall paintings, rings, and seal stones. Most of all he was impressed by several faience statuettes of bare-breasted females handling snakes that he excavated in the palace of Knossos.

In his view, the snake goddess represented one aspect of a "Great Mother Nature Goddess." She was a patroness of kings and sailors alike; she embodied fertility and motherhood; and she ruled over sky, earth, and the underworld. There was one male divinity, but he was a subordinate boy god: the son or consort of the great mother goddess. Evans underplayed the fact that the so-called boy god was an armed mature young man. He was undoubtedly influenced by theories of matriarchy that were fashionable at the turn of the century. His theories found fertile ground: one of the reasons that the concept of the mother goddess is alive today is that it appeals to contemporary feminist movements. Yet there are reasons to question the definition of matriarchy; all palace cultures of the Near East in the second millennium BCE had potent female goddesses and mothers of gods, and none was a matriarchy. Evans's matriarchal society is perhaps best viewed as a modern myth.

FIGURE 1. Snake goddess of Knossos (after Evans, 1921–1936, v. 1, fig. 362a). *Illustration courtesy of Nanno Marinatos.*

It is thus perhaps wiser to view Minoan religion in the context of other kingdoms of the Near Eastern Mediterranean in the second millennium BCE, all of which were theocracies with male kings and armies. All of them had young male warrior gods: Reshep, Baal, El, Adad, Sin, Ningirsu, and so on in the Mesopotamian and Levantine kingdoms. Egypt had its own warrior gods: Amon, Seth, Horus. All of these cultures also had powerful female deities. Some of these goddesses were even warrior-like and destructive: Anat, Ishtar, Sekhmet. Female deities could also have mother-goddess qualities: Asherah (Atrt) in Ugarit is called mother of gods; Hathor and Isis in Egypt were also mother goddesses. Most goddesses had in addition a strong sexual appeal that could be dangerous to males. The bare-breasted snake goddess of Minoan Crete (figure 1) would have been regarded as sexually alluring, but this dos not mean that she was *the* goddess. The Near Eastern frame makes it likely that Minoan Crete may have had a complex constellation of male and female deities, although the distinctive regional identity of Crete should not be lost sight of.

Yet it is difficult to go beyond theories when discussing Minoan religious mythology. This is because we lack narrative texts from the Minoan culture (Linear A is yet to be fully deciphered). On the other hand, many images exist, and they give information that is highly valuable, although it differs from the information we get from texts. An attempt to sort out the iconography and archaeological evidence was made by Martin P. Nilsson (1874–1967) in the 1920s. Although systematic, Nilsson fell into a methodological pitfall: he was more interested in Minoan religion as a precursor of Greek mythology than as a system in its own right. The striking parallels to the Near East were ignored. Thus, he was more eager to find the early forms of Athena, Rhea, and Artemis than to penetrate the nature of the deities themselves. His bias towards ancient Greek religion is evident in the title of his book: *The Minoan-Mycenaean Religion and its Survival in Greek Religion* (2d ed., 1950). It is worth noting, however, that he was unconvinced of Evans's view of the great mother goddess.

Theocracy, polytheism, and the character of Minoan gods. Nilsson argued that the Minoans had polytheism (1950, pp. 389–425), and he was proven right. Recent evidence throws new light on the issue. A golden ring, excavated in a grave at Poros near modern Herakleion on Crete shows three gods together (Dimopoulou and Rethemiotakis, 2000). The center is taken up by an impressive male god holding a scepter. He faces an equally impressive seated goddess who is flanked by large birds. A third goddess is rendered as a minute figure descending from the air. There is only one mortal worshiper in the scene at the left edge of the ring's field. He is shaking a tree invoking the gods. The ring supplies firm evidence of polytheism: a divine gathering taking place in the vicinity of a tree. Such a congregation is echoed in the Hittite text about the god Telepinu: "The gods [were gathered] in assembly under the *hatalkesnas* tree. For the *hatalkesnas* tree I have fixed long years" (Pritchard, 1969, pp. 126–128).

The characterization of the gods is important. The female goddess is seated on an invisible throne in midair; her power is expressed through enthronement. The male god, on the other hand, exudes bodily rigor by extending his arm in a gesture of command. A similar male god occurs on a ring impression found at Chania (figure 2). He looms large over a cluster of buildings, which may be conceived as a palace or town, establishing himself as the patron of this town.

Further information is supplied by another ring, the impression of which has survived in several examples found by Evans at Knossos (figure 3). Here the central figure is a goddess who stands on the top of a mountain.

She is saluted by a male figure, who is usually interpreted as a human worshiper but who may well be a king because the vision of ordinary humans would not be recorded visually on a ring in a theocratic society. Behind the goddess is a building, which can be identified as a palace because it has many stories. Here we have a sacred landscape, which includes a palace and a mountain.

FIGURE 2. Ring impression from Chania showing a male god over a town (after Hallager, 1985, p. 50, fig. 11). ***Illustration courtesy of Nanno Marintos.***

The three rings discussed above show that there existed a multiplicity of divinities and that power was not centered only around one dominant goddess; there was also a male god whose bodily vigor was evident in his standing posture. The Minoan pantheon was probably complex and must have included one or several divine couples. Moreover, gods and goddesses were associated with a multistory building that can be best defined as a divine palace. This association of god and palace supports the view of Evans that Minoan Crete was a theocracy.

Patronage of Minoan gods and gender roles. The Minoan gods probably had different spheres of power, such as hunting, war, and fertility. Most likely they also had different domains: the sea, the underworld, or the sky (in which case they would appear as stellar bodies). They also had social spheres: one of their functions must have been supervision of the raising of young people. This gender-oriented patronage is illustrated in a scene from a stone chalice found at Hagia Triada, Crete (figure 4).

A young male with a commanding gesture receives a procession of young hunters (Evans, 1921–1936, vol. 2, pp. 790–792). Although he is generally known as the "Chieftain" (thus named by Evans), his commanding gesture and posture rather suggest that he may be a god. Alternatively he is a king having assumed the identical appearance of the god. The ambiguity is revealing: gods and rulers were shown in a similar manner in Minoan art. At any rate, the god or his earthly representative acts as patron of the hunt.

FIGURE 3. Goddess on mountain and male visionary (king?) (after Evans, 1921–1936, vol. 3, fig. 323). *Illustration courtesy of Nanno Marinatos.*

FIGURE 4. A god or king receiving a procession of hunters on a stone chalice from Hagia Triada (after Evans, 1921–1936, vol. 2, combination of figs. 476 and 517). *Illustration courtesy of Nanno Marinatos.*

In the female sphere we find the same relationship: the young female goddess supervises her protégées. On a painting from Thera (Santorini), a goddess is seated on a platform and receives offerings from young women (Doumas, 1992, fig. 122). The dress and hairstyles of the worshipers reflect the divine prototype. There are many other instances as well where a goddess receives a female procession (Marinatos, 1993, pp. 147–165). This evidence suggests that there were gender specific roles for the Minoan deities. It also implies that the deities provided role models for the young. There is therefore an educational aspect to Minoan religion.

Although Minoan goddesses and gods are never depicted in the nude, the exposed breasts of the females (figure 1) and the pronounced phallus sheaths of the males (figures 2 and 4) suggest that sexuality was emphasized. The bare breasts of goddesses have a meaning equivalent to the complete nudity of Near Eastern goddesses. Female power is apparently expressed as sexuality in both cultural regions (Marinatos, 1993).

Rituals of Minoan religion: Ceremonial banqueting, sacrifice, and invocation. There can be no religion without rituals of offerings to the gods. As has been stressed by sociologists and historians of religion, the social dimension of offering is feasting. Food is a way of exchange and redistribution of wealth, especially in highly stratified societies. There is plenty of evidence for Minoan feasting in extra-urban sanctuaries and cemeteries. But the open courts in front of the palaces could also have accommodated a large number of banqueters. Most interesting evidence has been unearthed in the newly excavated palace of Galatas on Crete, which included a hearth and baking dishes (Rethemiotakis, 1999). Hittite texts from the second millennium offer us detailed descriptions of the role of the king and the queen during offering ceremonies. The royalty entered the temple and performed elaborate rituals of offering. An interesting inscription mentions that the king and queen drank from the cup of the storm god (Alp, 1983, p. 221). In this way the king and queen shared a meal with the god.

The throne room in the palace of Knossos may have been used in a similar way. The throne, flanked by griffins and palm trees, has been viewed by some scholars as the seat of a female, a queen or a priestess, because only goddesses are flanked by griffins in Minoan art (Reusch, 1958; Hägg, 1986; Niemeier, 1986). It is less frequently noticed that there was a kitchen in the adjacent complex; this kitchen shows that ceremonial banqueting may be associated with the throne room.

Animal sacrifice is a prerequisite for banqueting, but it is also a rite of invocation: the gods are invited to participate in the feast. This aspect of sacrificial ritual is depicted on a terra-cotta coffin, known as the sarcophagus from Hagia Triada. One of the long sides of this sarcophagus shows a sacrificed bull tied on a table. A long-robed woman, who may be the queen, presides over the ritual, while a male plays the flute. To the right is a second separate scene involving a priestess dressed in a hide skirt. She stands before an altar, over which are a pitcher and a basket of fruit, which are bloodless offerings. The two panels show that the Minoans made a clear distinction between the two types of altars and the two types of offerings (compare with *Exod.* 25:2 and 27:1). This distinction between bloody and bloodless offerings is also made in Greek religion.

To whom are the offerings made on the Hagia Triada sarcophagus? The shrine in front of which the offerings are made stands to the right of the priestess in the hide skirt. It is a building with a gate surmounted by the so-called horns. Above the gate a sacred tree is protruding; it evidently was the focus of the cult, taking the function of a cult statue. If the viewer walks around the sarcophagus and looks at the short side, the gods will be found as well: there are two female deities arriving in a griffin-drawn chariot. Noteworthy are two facts: (1) The tree shrine has a function equivalent to a temple; namely, it is the house of god and it is the *locus*

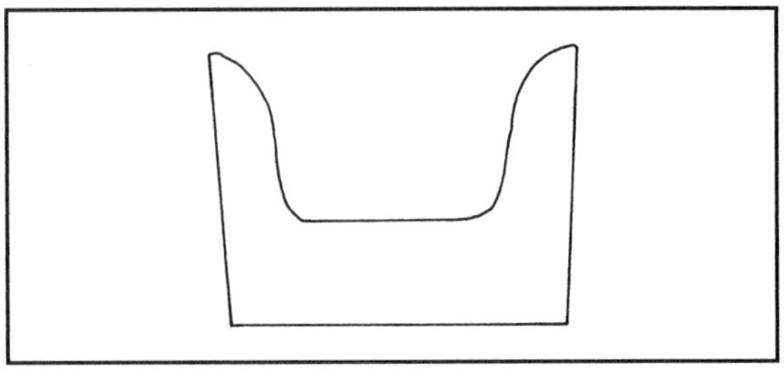

FIGURE 5A. Horns of consecration or mountain peaks. ***Illustration courtesy of Nanno Marinatos.***

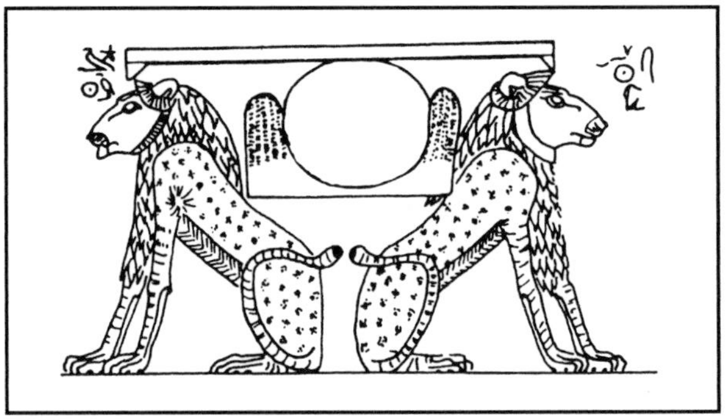

FIGURE 5B. Egyptian mountain sign with solar disk. ***Illustration courtesy of Nanno Marinatos.***

of the epiphany; (2) The goddesses are arriving at their tree shrine to partake in the sacrifice.

The sacred tree of the god or goddess was evidently also used as a medium of invocation. On certain gold rings found on both Crete and the Mycenaean mainland, we see male or female worshipers shaking or bending a tree. It was perhaps thought that frenzied movement on the part of the worshiper mobilized the gods to come. Alternatively, the tree was imagined as the abode of the deity. The invocation of the gods is depicted only on gold rings. It seems that this ritual was associated with the monopolization of religion by the upper classes.

The symbols of Minoan religion: "horns" and double axes. The Minoans surely had aniconic cults, as Evans had already surmised in a fundamental article written in 1901. Aniconic symbols, such as the double axe, loom large in Minoan imagery, but it is uncertain what they mean. At any rate, it is worth noting that cult standards with the symbols of the gods they represent are common in religions of the Near East, especially animal cult standards and standards with astral symbols.

Also common is the sign of the "horns of consecration," which occurs both as a graphic design and as a cult object (figure 5a).

The designation "horns" is due to Evans, who saw a superficial resemblance to bull's horns. But many scholars observed that there is a striking resemblance between the Minoan sign and the Egyptian symbol of the "two mountains of the horizon," the sun disk rising between twin peaks (figure 5b).

The similarity between the two symbols is too striking to be ignored. In addition, the Minoan sign is similar to its Egyptian equivalent in its framing of an object: a tree or a double axe, or sometimes other implements of cult, such as libation vessels. In view of this, it is likely that the so-called horns represent a stylized landscape of two mountains that define the east and west axis of the universe. If the horns are mountains, this would explain why in real and represented architecture, the object is always placed on top of a building (figure 3). Its function in such a case would be to allude to mountain ranges in an abstract manner.

The double axe (figure 6) is more elusive, and there is no equivalent sign in the Near East or Egypt. Evans thought that it symbolized the great goddess (Evans, 1901, p. 106; see also Pötscher, 1990, pp. 143–160).

Nilsson, who was more practically minded, considered it a simple sacrificial instrument (Nilsson, 1950, p. 226). Evans was probably more correct however: the double axe appears in contexts that suggest that it played a role in the cosmology of Minoan mythology. Noteworthy is its frequent occurrence on coffins. It seems unlikely in view of this that it was a mere tool of cult, especially since it never occurs as a sacrificial instrument in imagery. A clue may be that the axe can be conceived as a tree with sprouting leaves or even flowers. Was it a regenerative symbol as has sometimes been argued (Dietrich, 1974)? A second clue is that it occurs between the two tips of the mountain sign above (figure 5a, the so-called horns). This suggests that the double axe was perceived as an object that belonged between the edges of the two mountains of the horizon: is it a symbol of the sun or moon? This possibility is speculative but may explain the ubiquity of the sign and its centrality in Minoan religion better than the alternative theory that it is a sacrificial axe.

The palaces as cult centers. Whatever interpretation we give to the Minoan deities and their symbols the archaeological evidence is clear as to how society was organized. The cult centers were undoubtedly the palaces. They contained central courts with a multiplicity of modest shrine rooms arranged around them. Most palaces also had large west plazas where the public could gather. The walls were decorated with paintings that depicted (among other subjects) processional and ritual scenes. There is thus little doubt that they were the major cult centers of the community. To date no separate temples have been found (Rutkowski, 1986). The complete fusion of secular and religious authority points to a theocratic system.

Outside the town there were nature sanctuaries in caves or mountain peaks. These were the extra-urban sanctuaries of which Mount Juktas and Kato Syme have yielded the most impressive finds (Peatfield 1990; overview in Jones,

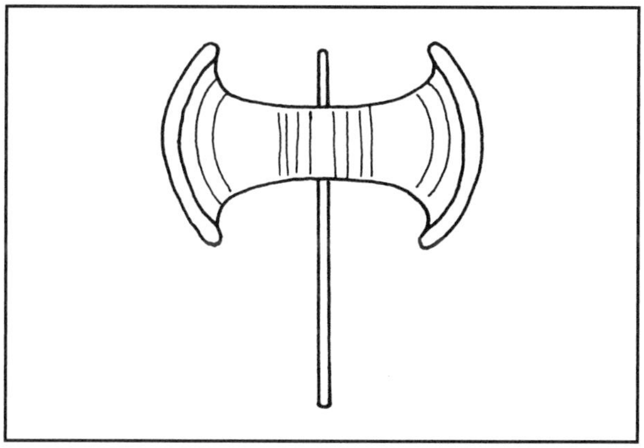

FIGURE 6. Minoan double axe. *Illustration courtesy of Nanno Marinatos.*

1999; Lebessi, 1985 and 2002). There is little doubt that the extra-urban sanctuaries were under palatial control in the middle of the second millennium BCE. Many, however, survived the end of the palatial system.

The palaces were abandoned shortly after the middle of the second millennium BCE, with the exception of Knossos that survived for another seventy-five years. The reasons are not yet completely understood, but they may have to do with social upheaval rather than a Mycenaean invasion. The end of the palaces certainly also meant the end of the theocracy.

The new era, termed *post-palatial*, takes us to the end of the second millennium. In this period, a new type of shrine was preferred: a modest room fitted with benches upon which were placed statues of goddesses, tables of offerings, and other cult implements. The type is common in the late Bronze Age and can be found on the mainland of Greece, as well as on the Levantine coast; we may speak of an East Mediterranean type of shrine or small temple. Typical of Crete are clay goddess statues with upraised arms and elaborate headdresses. Religious syncretism with the Mycenaean religion of the mainland certainly took place in all periods of Minoan Crete.

The end of the Minoan theocracy must have brought with it many changes of the social and religious structure, but the main symbols and (probably) the main gods survived into the end of the Bronze Age (c. 1200 BCE). The Greeks of later times thought of the island as one of ninety languages, multiple ethnic groups, and ninety cities (Homer, *Odyssey* 19.172–202).

MYCENAEAN RELIGION. Mycenaean religion is similar to Minoan in that it was also centered on the palaces and utilized the same symbols as Minoan Crete.

Places of worship. Mycenaean places of worship are different from those of Minoan Crete, however, the variations being detectable in the archaeological evidence (Hägg, 1998). One extra-urban mountain peak sanctuary was excavated on Mount Kinortion near classical Epidaurus, but mountain sanctuaries are not as common as on Crete. There were Minoan-type offerings there, including double axes and figurines (Lambrinoudakis, 1981).

On the whole, the similarities between Minoan and Mycenaean religion are striking. Both cultures had theocracies with palaces as centers. The Mycenaean palace seems to have played a major ceremonial role. Instead of an open central court, however, we find a roofed hall or *megaron* with a hearth. At Pylos, the wall paintings from the throne room are similar to those of Knossos (Lang, 1966, pl. 124, no. 44aH6) depicting griffins and lions flanking the throne. In addition, some of the Pylos throne room paintings show banqueting, which is compatible with the ritual inferred through the kitchen near the Knossos throne room.

In both cultures, the religious role of the king and queen is confirmed by the written records: in the Linear B tablets the word *wa-na-ka* (king) appears frequently. The queen may have been designated as *pot-ni-ja*, namely "mistress" (Laffineur and Hägg, 2001). The takeover of Minoan royal and religious symbols by the Mycenaean dynasts is here very evident. We find in the Mycenaean kingdom double axes and the mountain sign (figures 5a, 6).

Small shrines existed in addition to the palatial *megaron*. They had benches with statues on top, and hearths for offerings. Some were incorporated into the palace; others were physically independent and spread throughout the town, as in Tiryns (Kilian, 1988) and Methana (Konsolaki, 1999; Whittaker, 1997).

One shrine within the citadel of Mycenae is revealing because it included paintings above and around the bench (figure 7).

Above the bench two goddesses were painted facing each other. Between them hover two small sketchily rendered figures that probably represent souls of the dead (Marinatos, 1988). These may be two of the goddesses of Mycenaean religion. Below, on the side of the bench, is probably the queen identifiable by her tall headdress with a plume (or a minor goddess accompanied by a griffin). Although the iconography of this fresco is nowhere matched exactly on Crete, the visual vocabulary is familiar from the latter culture. The Mycenaeans borrowed the visual vocabulary of the Minoan palace culture to express their own theocratic institution.

Data from the tablets. The decipherment of the Linear B script in 1953 by Michael Ventris as a form of Greek threw a new light on Mycenaean religion by revealing a pantheon that included many names of the later Greek gods.

The tablets were made of unbaked clay and were used as scrapbooks. They were accidentally preserved because they were baked after a conflagration. They record lists and provide economic documents. Indications about religious rituals and gods are only incidental in the form of offering. Still, it is clear that a multiplicity of male and female deities are present, among whom is a male god who bears the name of the

FIGURE 7. Fresco within a Mycenaean shrine within the citadel of Mycenaeas, reconstructed by Marinatos. ***Illustration courtesy of Nanno Marinatos.***

great god of the classical Greeks: Zeus. There was also a pantheon that we recognize as the later Olympian Greek divinities: Po-si-da-jo (Poseidon), He-ra (Hera), A-ta-na Po-ti-ni-ja (Athena), Erma (Hermes), Enyalios (Ares), and Di-wo-nu-so (Dionysos). Yet the hierarchy and articulation that define the Greek divine family do not seem to characterize the Mycenaean gods. It is to be noted that Po-si-da-jo (Poseidon) played a preeminent role at Pylos, whereas A-ta-na (Athena) is attested only at Knossos. There are also gods unknown to the later Greek pantheon, such as Ma-ri-neu and Ma-ka (Palaima et al., 2001).

The Mycenaean gods constituted a divine family, although relations between them were not necessarily the same as those of later Greek religion. For example, one god, Di-ri-mi-jo, is listed on a tablet from Pylos on the Greek mainland as being the son of Zeus and Hera. This god dropped out of the later Greek pantheon. But Di-wo-nu-so (Dionysos) seems to have been a son of Zeus both in the Creto-Mycenaean tablets (attested by a tablet found at Chania, Crete, KH. Gq 5) and in Greek times.

The offerings listed were sent from the palace to the sanctuaries. This proves that the religious organization was interwoven with the palace administration. This is typical of theocracies. Offered were animals—cattle, sheep, and pigs—as well as objects of value.

One term has been variously interpreted: *wa-na-ka.* It is undeniable that it constitutes the prototype of the word *wanax,* which in the Homeric poems is usually applied to the king.

THE MINOAN AND MYCENAEAN PANTHEON AND THE NEAR EAST. Despite their differences it is a priori likely that Minoan and Mycenaean religions had many similarities in the mythologies and the personae of their gods. Both were palatial cultures that maintained close contacts with each other and with the Near East. The Mycenaean presence in Crete (whether to be explained by dynastic links and intermarriages or by conquest) is securely attested by the presence of tablets written in Linear B shortly after 1400 BCE. After that time, there was a pool of common gods, such as Poseidon, Zeus, Athena, Dionysos, Diwija, and Hermes, all of whom are attested on both Crete and the Mycenaean mainland (Palaima et al., 2001). A religious synthesis between Minoan and Mycenaean religion in the fourteenth and thirteenth centuries BCE is thus certain. It is perhaps not correct to speak of a Mycenaean religion on Crete in the post-palatial period, but rather of a synthesis of the two systems. This synthesis may be pushed back into the sixteenth century BCE, however. This is the time when Crete was at the peak of its power, and spread its influence in the Aegean. The Mycenaeans (who were developing their own palatial system) readily adopted Minoan symbols and images of gods. The adoption of such symbols as the double axes and the mountain signs (horns) implies that there were already common elements in the two religions, and it was this commonality that enabled the transmission of the Minoan religious vocabulary to the Mycenaeans. The picture that emerges is a complex one, with influences flowing in both directions at different times.

We know, moreover, that such religious equivocations between deities took place between cultural groups in the Aegean and the Near East: Akkadian Ishtar was likened to Ugaritic Astarte and Sumerian Inanna; later on she was fused with the Greek Aphrodite. The Egyptian Seth was likened to Ugaritic Baal, both being young warrior gods. Anat and Baal, a famous couple in Ugaritic myth, resemble Isis and Osiris of Egypt. It is likely that the Minoan divine couple had properties similar to its Egyptian and Near Eastern counterparts. The religious translation of one god into another in cultures of the Near East makes it a priori likely that the same happened between Minoan Crete and the mainland Mycenaean religion. It is possible to go even further and suggest that the East Mediterranean was a melting pot of religious syncretism.

The following points may be established about the Minoan-Mycenaean pantheon. The prevalent idea that there was a dominant mother goddess in Minoan Crete (figure 1) must be revised. Both Minoan and Mycenaean religions had important deities of both genders. Even the Mycenaeans, who are considered a typical patriarchal society, had female deities that are referred to in the Linear B tablets as "mistress" (*pot-ni-ja*). This word undoubtedly represents a title (compare with the epithet "*st* lady" given to Anat or Ishtar in the Near East, the Akkadian "Belet-ili" given to the mother goddess in the *Atramchasis* epic, or the Ugaritic "ra-ba-tu" given to the great goddess of the sun [Wyatt, 1998, 224]).

The divine couple is attested iconographically in both Minoan and Mycenaean art, and textually in the Linear B tablets. It can be further established that the gods were conceived as members of a divine family. In a Linear B tablet from Pylos the triad Zeus, Hera, and Di-ri-mi-jo are attested (Tn 316). At Chania, Di-wo-nu-so is associated with Zeus, who is presumably his father.

The points above suggest that the Minoan and Mycenaean pantheons were (1) similar (although not identical) to one another and (2) similar to those of the Near East. It is tempting to postulate that myths that are common to the Near East and Egypt may also have been shared by the Minoans and Mycenaeans. There are many uncertainties about Minoan and Mycenaean myths, but they obviously did exist and they were more rich and complex than the Frazerian theories of the dying god and the fertility goddess would suggest.

See Also Labyrinth.

Bibliography

Alp, Sedat. *Beiträge zur Erforschung des Hethitschen Tempels.* Ankara, Turkey, 1983.

Brandt, Elfriede. *Gruss und Gebet.* Waldsassen Bayern, Germany, 1965.

Burkert, Walter. *Structure and History in Greek Mythology and Ritual.* Berkeley, Calif., 1979.

Cain, C. D. "Deconstructing a Narrative of Epiphany on the Isopata Ring." *American Journal of Archaeology* 105 (2001): 27–49.

Cohen, Rudolph, and Yigal Israel. *On the Road to Edom.* Jerusalem, 1995.

Dietrich, Bernard C. *The Origins of Greek Religion.* Berlin and New York, 1974.

Dimopoulou, Nota, and George Rethemiotakis. "The Sacred Conversation Ring from Poros." In *Minoisch-mykenische Glyptik: Stil, Ikonographie, Funktion,* edited by Ingo Pini, pp. 39–56. Berlin, 2000.

Doumas, Christos. *The Wall-Paintings of Thera.* Athens, 1992.

Evans, Arthur J. "The Mycenaean Tree and Pillar Cult," *Journal of Hellenic Studies* 21 (1901): 99–204.

Evans, Arthur J. *The Palace of Minos: A Comparative Account of the Successive Stages of the Early Cretan Civilization as Illustrated by the Discoveries at Knossos.* 4 vols. London, 1921–1936.

French, Elizabeth B., and K. A. Wardle, eds. *Problems in Greek Prehistory.* Bristol, UK, 1988.

Gesell, Geraldine Cornelia. *Town, Palace, and House Cult in Minoan Crete.* Göteborg, Sweden, 1985.

Hägg, Robin. "Mycenaean Religion: The Helladic and the Minoan Components." In *Linear B: A 1984 Survey,* edited by Anna Morpurgo Davies and Yves Duhoux, pp. 203–225. Louvain-la-Neuve, Belgium, 1985.

Hägg, Robin. "Die göttliche Epiphanie im minoischen Ritual." *Athenische Mitteilungen* 101 (1986): 41–62.

Hägg, Robin. "Ritual in Mycenaean Greece." In *Ansichten griechischer Rituale: Geburtstags-Symposium für Walter Burkert,* edited by Fritz Graf, pp. 99–113. Stuttgart, Germany, 1998.

Hägg, Robin. "Religious Processions in Mycenaean Greece." In *Contributions to the Archaeology and History of the Bronze and Iron Ages in the Eastern Mediterranean,* edited by Peter Fischer, pp. 143–147. Vienna, 2001.

Hägg, Robin, and Nanno Marinatos, eds. *Sanctuaries and Cults in the Aegean Bronze Age.* Stockholm, 1981.

Hallager, Erik. *The Master Impression: A Clay Sealing from the Greek-Swedish Excavations at Kastelli, Khania.* Göteborg, Sweden, 1985.

Jones, Donald W. *Peak Sanctuaries and Sacred Caves in Minoan Crete.* Jonsered, Sweden, 1999.

Kaiser, Otto, ed. *Texte aus der Umwelt des Alten Testaments* (*TUAS*). Gütersloh, Germany, 1993–1995.

Keel, Othmar, and C. Uehlinger. *Göttinnen, Götter, und Gottessymbole.* Freiburg, Germany, 1992.

Kilian, K. "Mycenaeans up to Date." In *Problems in Greek Prehistory,* edited by Elizabeth B. French and K. A. Wardle, pp. 115–152. Bristol, U.K., 1988.

Konsolaki, Eleni. "The Mycenaean Sanctuary on Methana." *Bulletin of the Institute for Classical Studies* 40 (1995): 242.

Konsolaki, Eleni. "A Group of New Mycenaean Horsemen from Methana." In *Meletemata, Studies in Aegean Archaeology Presented to Malcolm H. Wiener as He Enters His 65th Year,* edited by Philip Betancourt, Vassos Karageorghis, Robert Laffineur, and Wolf-Dietrich Niemeier, vol. 2, pp. 427–433. Liège, Belgium, 1999.

Krattenmaker, Kathleen. "Palace, Peak, and Sceptre: The Iconography of Legitimacy." In *The Role of the Ruler in the Prehistoric Aegean,* edited by Paul Rehak, pp. 49–62. Liège, Belgium, 1995.

Laffineur, Robert, and Robin Hägg. *Potnia: Deities and Religion in the Aegean Bronze Age.* Liège, Belgium, 2001.

Lambrinoudakis, V. "Remains of the Mycenaean Period in the Sanctuary of Apollon Maleatas" in *Sanctuaries and Cults in the Aegean Bronze Age,* edited by Robin Hägg and Nanno Marinatos, pp. 59–65. Stockholm, 1981.

Lang, Mabel L. *The Frescoes,* vol. 2 of *The Palace of Nestor at Pylos in Western Messenia,* edited by Carl William Blegen and Marion Rawson. Princeton, N.J., 1966.

Lebessi, A. *To iero tou Erme kai tes Aphrodites sten Syme Biannou.* Athens, 1985.

Lebessi, A. *To iero tou Erme kai tis Aphrodites sten Syme Biannou III: Ta chalkina anthropomorpha eidolia.* Athens, 2002.

Marinatos, Nanno. *Art and Religion in Thera: Reconstructing a Bronze Age Society.* Athens, 1984.

Marinatos, Nanno. *Minoan Religion: Ritual, Image, and Symbol.* Columbia, S.C., 1993.

Marinatos, Nanno. "Divine Kingship in Minoan Crete?" In *The Role of the Ruler in the Prehistoric Aegean,* edited by Paul Rehak, pp. 37–47. Liège, Belgium, 1995.

Marinatos, Nanno. *The Goddess and the Warrior: The Naked Goddess and Mistress of Animals in Early Greek Religion.* London, 2000.

Matz, Friedrich. *Göttererscheinung und Kultbild im minoischen Kreta.* Mainz, Germany, 1958.

Matz, Friedrich, and Hagen Biesanta, eds. *Corpus der minoischen und mykenischen Siege: Akademie der Literatur und Wissenschaften Mainz (CMS).* Berlin 1964–.

Niemeier, Wolf-Dietrich. "Zur Deutung des Thronraumes im Palast von Knossos." *Athenische Mitteilungen* 101 (1986): 63–66.

Niemeier, Wolf-Dietrich. "Das Stuckrelief des Prinzen mit der Federkrone aus Knossos und minosche Götterdarstellungen." *Athenische Mitteilungen* 102 (1987): 65–97.

Nilsson, Martin P. *The Minoan-Mycenaean Religion and Its Survival in Greek Religion.* 2d ed. Lund, Sweden, 1950.

Palaima, Thomas, Joan Gulizio, and Kevin Pluta. "Religion in the Room of the Chariot Tablets." In *Potnia: Deities and Religion in the Aegean Bronze Age,* edited by Robert Laffineur and Robin Hägg, pp. 453–461. Liège, Belgium, 2001.

Peatfield, Alan A. D. "Minoan Peak Sanctuaries: History and Society." *Opuscula Atheniensia* 18 (1990): 117–131.

Persson, Axel W. *The Religion of Greece in Prehistoric Times.* Berkeley, Calif., 1942.

Pini, Ingo, ed. *Fragen und Probleme in der bronzezeitlchen ägaischen Glyptik.* Berlin, 1989.

Pötscher, Walter. *Aspekte und Probleme der minoischen Religion: Ein Versuch.* Hildesheim, Germany, 1990.

Pritchard, James Bennett, ed. *Ancient Near Eastern Texts Relating to the Old Testament (ANET).* 3d ed. Princeton, N.J., 1969.

Rethemiotakis, George. "The Hearths of the Minoan Palace at Galatas." In *Meletemata: Studies in Aegean Archaeology Presented to Malcolm H. Wiener as He Enters His 65th Year,* edited by Philip Betancourt, Vassos Karageorghis, Robert Laffineur, and Wolf-Dietrich Niemeier, vol. 3, pp. 721–727. Liège, Belgium, 1999.

Reusch, H. "Zum Wandschmuck des Thronsaales in Knossos." In *Minoica, Festschrift zum. 80. Geburtstag von Johannes Sundwall,* edited by E. Grumach pp. 334–558. Berlin, 1958.

Rutkowski, Bogdan. *Frühgriechische Kultdarstellungen.* Berlin, 1981.

Rutkowski, Bogdan. *The Cult Places in the Aegean.* New Haven, Conn., 1986.

Sakellarakis, Yannis, and Efī Sapouna-Sakellaraki. *Archanes: Minoan Crete in a New Light.* Athens, 1997.

Whittaker, Helène. *Mycenaean Cult Buildings: A Study of Their Architecture and Function in the Context of the Aegean and the Eastern Mediterranean.* Bergen, Norway, 1997.

Wyatt, Nicholas. *Religious Texts from Ugarit: The Words of Ilimiku and His Colleagues.* Sheffield, U.K., 1998.

OLIVIER PELON (1987)
NANNO MARINATOS (2005)

AESTHETICS

This entry consists of the following articles:

PHILOSOPHICAL AESTHETICS
VISUAL AESTHETICS

AESTHETICS: PHILOSOPHICAL AESTHETICS

Many elements appear common to aesthetic and religious experience. Both are modes of apprehending and articulating reality. Theorists of both have affirmed that aesthetic and religious insights or intuitions afford direct, nonconceptual apprehension of the real, and that they are dependent on inspiration, genius, or other forms of giftedness. Both issue in forms, objects, and activities expressive of specific visions of reality that are frequently, though not exclusively, nondiscursive. In both realms, questions and criteria of judgment entail distinctive relations of particularity to universality and of matter to form in appraisals of truth. Further, both art and religion have sometimes exemplified and sometimes countered prevailing views of reality. In each realm, protocols of style and canons of authority emerge generically, appealing to disciplines internal to experience. Thus, examining aesthetic characteristics and considering the possible relations of aesthetic insight to religious truth and beatitude proposed by a number of seminal thinkers may achieve an enhanced understanding of religion as the apprehension and expression of distinctive experience.

CLASSICAL FORMULATIONS. Aesthetics, like theory of religion, did not emerge as a discrete discipline in the West until the eighteenth century, in the wake of the Enlightenment. In the East it was largely a secondary product of the practice of art until Eastern philosophers were influenced by modern Western thought. Yet Plato (c. 428–348 or 347 BCE) is in some respects the founder of philosophical aesthetics, having developed concepts central to subsequent reflection on the aesthetic. Foremost is that of art itself—*technē,* or know-how: the recognition of an end to be aimed at and the knowledge of how best to achieve it through the skillful use of appropriate materials and means.

Poiesis, Plato's term for aesthetic making, broadly designates all craftsmanship and more narrowly refers to the making of poems, plays, pictures, or sculptures. *Poiesis* is the verb used in the Septuagint version of the Bible for the divine "making" or creation of the world proclaimed in the book of *Genesis.* Through this association of divine creativity with human creativity in received religious texts, later Western theologian-philosophers were encouraged to incorporate elements of Platonic theory into their reflections upon the nature of the good, true, and beautiful. Platonic theory thus affected Jewish, Christian, and Islamic traditions and persisted in the philosophical disciplines that emerged from the Enlightenment.

For Plato (*Philebus,* 64e), the evaluation of *poiesis* requires a sense of proper proportion of means and ends, of measure *(summetrica).* The concept of measure, or standard, became central to his thought as he sought to identify the standards of truth, justice, beauty, and goodness, which he also called the Forms, or Ideas. The concept of measure suggested the possibility of a Form of Forms, a prior source of reality and human beatitude, that could be termed "religious" and was considered such by some successors.

For Plato the highest form of art is that of the divine maker *(demiurgos)* who composes the universe as an imitation (*mimesis*) of ultimate and unchanging Forms. Practitioners of the fine arts, however, engage in imitations that are more complex and more problematic. In this *poiesis,* moral, psychological, and other factors color a more vivid rendering of reality through appearance. Plato therefore distrusted artists' claims to knowledge and was wary of the moral and political effects of epic and drama. He advocated a form of censorship by philosopher-guardians of the state and distinguished between true imitation *(eitastikē)* and false semblance *(phantastikē),* or illusion.

Plato also held that something in true art is not reducible to know-how. The poet, it appears, is inspired, and his achievement, insofar as it cannot be reduced to rules by the normal, conscious intellect, appears to be a form of madness. The poet imitates the divine *demiurgos* (Plato, *Phaedrus,* 245; *Ion,* 523–525). Plato's dialogue "Symposium" both describes and exemplifies the ascent of the soul to the vision of the Good through the allure of the Beautiful. The Beautiful is the chief propaedeutic to the Good, which is the Form of Forms, the end also of the religious quest.

Thus Plato includes concepts central to the relation of aesthetics to religion. The conviction that aesthetic vision is also religious apprehension appears in Jewish wisdom literature and in early Christian theology and is consonant with some Hindu and Buddhist accounts of salvific knowledge. Plato's emphasis on the discernment of measure and fittingness is echoed in some forms of Confucian philosophy as well. *Poiesis* is a metaphor for the relation of the divine to the world in the cosmogonies of many religious traditions. In some Hindu speculation, all that is only penultimately real is *māyā,* or illusion, and is said to be the sport or play *(līlā)* of the ultimately real *(brahman).* In many religions of archaic societies, poetic or prophetic (shamanistic) inspiration is a means to perception of the sacred, that which is foundational to and constitutive of ordinary or profane space and time and which is articulated in accounts of events *in illo tempore.*

Aristotle (384–322 BCE), like Plato, saw art as the capacity to "make," to cause the coming into being of ends set by reason. The character of the envisioned end (*telos*) determines the appropriate means for its realization. For Aristotle, however, the forms (patterns or essences of things) do not exist apart from the materials formed, except perhaps in the case of those ultimate ends, or reasons why, that reason may contemplate. It is in the capacity for such contemplation, Aristotle says in *Nichomachean Ethics,* that human beings are most godlike and, therefore, perhaps immortal. While some things in nature occur by reason of the material that constitutes them—that is, by necessity—the primary causes of all events are the ends to which they lead and for which they appear to be designed. There is a sense therefore in which for Aristotle nature is best understood as imitating art. The source of all processes is an Unmoved Mover whose ultimacy was taken by later theologians to be of religious significance.

Excellence or beauty in a work of art depends upon immanent standards: perfection of form and felicity of method, which render a work both a satisfying whole in itself and fruitful in its effects. A composition must exhibit symmetry, harmony, and definiteness. Aristotle's only surviving treatment of aesthetic issues, the fragmentary *Poetics,* focuses on one form, tragic drama. Like Plato he saw literary and dramatic *poietikē* as mimetic. Unlike Plato, however, he believed that tragic drama may be a definitive means of knowing reality through the presentation of philosophical truth and psychological insight in character, plot, and action. Tragedy arouses the emotions of fear and pity, but the well-made tragedy effects both a therapeutic purgation of these from the soul of the spectator and a resolution in the drama itself that is akin to ritual purification. Indeed it may be said that Aristotle saw in the art of tragedy the natural development of religious media that seek to negotiate the ambiguities and paradoxes of life, with their associated feelings of awe and guilt. For some who find traditional religious resolutions anachronistic, irrelevant, or superficial, expressions of the tragic in art can serve important religious purposes, as the irrational or nonrational dimensions of life are represented and lived through aesthetically.

The Aristotelian insistence on the significance of the material—the "of what" of anything that is to be explicated, what Aristotle himself called its "material cause"—is reflected in increased interest in material culture or subculture: the material objects and commodities prized in any culture or subculture. The seemingly spontaneous, natural, or transparently motivated products of material culture can be deconstructed to reveal operations of power on behalf of dominant ideologies or constituencies (races, classes, genders, religions) or to express resistance to sublimated power. This approach includes specific attention to aesthetic and religious elements of culture. Thus even Aristotle's "material cause" is subject to a hermeneutic of suspicion in pursuit of truth that frees. A major representative of this critical approach was Michel Foucault (1926–1984). Aristotle's attention to the ritual nature and effect of tragic drama is reflected in increased interest in "ritual studies" in the field of religious studies.

Plotinus (205–270 CE), in *The Enneads* (1.6, 5.8, 6.7), incorporates a Platonic vision of ascent into his understanding of contemplation as active and productive of a form of knowledge. His Neoplatonism decisively influenced the formulation of Christian doctrine and shaped mystical expression in Jewish, Christian, and Islamic traditions through the Middle Ages. Elements of his metaphysics were subsequently resurrected by Italian Renaissance humanists, by seventeenth-century Platonists of the Cambridge school, and by nineteenth-century German Romantics.

For Latin Christianity, Augustine (354–430 CE) gave the Neoplatonic tradition the form it would retain through most of the Middle Ages. Augustine saw the arts not simply as an embellishment of explicitly religious materials but as a direct means of participation in the divine. Human art, when guided by divine will, may reflect the art of the divine, as in numerical proportion, rhythm, and harmony (Augustine, *De musica; De ordine* 11–16). In keeping with his exaltation of auditory art, he exemplified and fostered a characteristically Latin attention to rhetorical forms of expression. While Greek Christianity tended to prize visual representations and look to liturgical praxis for the development of doctrine, Western theological reflection explored a multilevel textual hermeneutic in which metaphor, parable, and other narrative forms are seen as vehicles of revelation. Augustine applied that tradition not only to Scripture, in *On Christian Doctrine* (*De doctrina Christiana;* 3, 10.14, 15.23), but also, in *The Confessions,* to the life of an individual seen as an operation of divine grace. John Cassian (c. 360–c. 435 CE) formulated a fourfold distinction between levels of scriptural meaning that became standard in the Middle Ages and influenced the development of modern literary criticism.

Thomas Aquinas (1225–1274) also turned to Scripture and Christian tradition for ultimate authority, relating them, however, to the newly recovered philosophical teachings of Aristotle. Every being *(ens),* he said, is one *(unum),* true *(verum),* and good *(bonum),* terms that apply to different beings variously according to their natures. Religious language, or talk of the divine being in terms of the finite, is possible by analogy, or proportion, as the created order displays the character of its origin. Truth is the equation of thought and thing, and good is fulfillment of desire in the truly desirable beauty. Contemplation of the good as beautiful renders knowledge of the good, because in it the soul resonates with the divine form. The beautiful is marked by integrity, proportion, harmony, and clarity. Thomas's doctrine of analogy and his emphasis on the revelatory character of the created order played major roles in subsequent theological development and in Thomist and neo-Thomist accounts of the relation of aesthetics to religion (cf. Thomas Aquinas, *Summa Theologiae,* 1.13.5, 1.16.1, 1.5.4, 2.1.27.1).

ENLIGHTENMENT AND POST-ENLIGHTENMENT FORMULATIONS. Sixteenth- and seventeenth-century developments in "natural philosophy" undercut the authority not only of Western religious traditions, identified as they were with a discredited cosmology, but also of Platonic idealism and Aristotelian scientific method. In the "enlightenment" that followed, the sense-bound character of all experience became problematic in a new way; definitions and criteria had to be developed for subjective experiences that could not be quantified. Chief among these were experiences of the beautiful and of the holy. The use of such terms as *feeling* and *sensibility* and attempts to articulate the variety of subject-object transactions characterized this debate. The relation of feeling or sensibility to the good and true was explored in terms of religious theory by some and in terms of aesthetic theory by others. Still others sought to bring both art and religion under a comprehensive theory.

Although Alexander Gottlieb Baumgarten (1714–1762) coined the term *aesthetics* in 1750, Immanuel Kant (1724–1804) was the first to develop a systematic theory of aesthetics as an integral, if not foundational, part of a philosophical system. Kant set himself the task of answering three questions: "What can I know?"; "What ought I to do?"; and "For what may I hope?" In *Critique of Pure Reason* (1781) he focused on imagination, whose work he traced from basic intuition or awareness of bare sensation, localized in the forms of space and time, to the reproduction of images schematized under "the categories of the understanding": quantity, quality, relation, and modality. These categories yield determinate concepts, expressed in propositions, analytic and synthetic, in the context of the "transcendental unity of apperception" or self-world consciousness. Such is all that the faculty of understanding can supply and all one can know in a sense warranted by the regnant conception of science. Yet reason requires the "transcendental ideas," or "regulative ideals" not only of self (or soul) and world but also of God as ground of world and soul.

Turning from the data of nature to the datum of freedom, of persons as moral agents, the dictates of pure practical reason (praxis) reveal a categorical imperative: never to make an exception of oneself to the demand of moral law; to treat all persons as ends and never merely as means; to recognize the moral dignity of persons as persons. In exploring the demands of moral life in *Critique of Practical Reason* (1788), Kant asks how disinterested moral virtue is to be related to the quest for happiness, which is also a legitimate component of the supreme good. A rational answer to this question, says Kant, demands the recognition of freedom in immortality.

A basic power assumed in the first two critiques, namely judgment, operates to subsume particulars in generals, parts in wholes, and so forth. Judgment is evidenced in acts, including logical operations, and expressed in the propositions of theoretical reason and the moral determinations of practical reason. In *The Critique of Judgement* (1790), however, Kant seeks to lay bare the general power of judgment as such. Here its form is expressive of pure feeling, of pleasure or displeasure. The controlling aesthetic category, beauty, is experienced when the free play of imagination, articulated in aesthetic forms, results in a "delight in ordering" produced by the creative artist and enjoyed by persons of aesthetic sensibility and informed taste. Feeling, however, is neither its cause nor its differentiating characteristic. Feeling merely signals that aesthetic judgment is at work.

Aesthetic judgment is characterized by four "moments":

(1) In quality, the grounding experience is that of "disinterested interest." The judging subject is fully engaged, but the focus of engagement is neither the self nor the fascination of being engaged, but rather that whose worth is not a function of the act of engagement.

(2) In quantity, judgment of the beautiful is singular yet of universal import. There is no class of which all beautiful objects are members; a specific work of art is judged to be beautiful. (Religious expressions of the unqualified

singularity of the divine display a similar resistance to systematic formulation or classification.)

(3) In terms of relation, aesthetic judgment expresses "purposiveness without purpose" or "finality without use." Parts are also wholes, and wholes are parts; means are also ends, and ends are means. This suggests analogies with religious judgment concerning the integrity or wholeness of the holy.

(4) In modality, aesthetic judgments are subjective and particular, yet they are also necessary and universal. Here the judgment bespeaks a universality and necessity that its logical form as analyzed in the first critique denies to judgments of particulars. This "given" of aesthetic judgment, Kant said, may suggest a *sensus communis,* a universal structure of intersubjectivity. Some theorists of religion appear to designate a similar structure as the *sensus numinous,* a shared sense of the holy or sacred.

Kant also examined another category of aesthetic experience, the sublime. While beauty is formal, limited, and related to discursive understanding, the sublime is experienced variously as the infinite or the overpowering. It arrests attention, "performs an outrage on imagination," and seems to draw us into a supraempirical or supernatural realm. For Kant, this experience is not mystical intuition and affords no privileged access to what lies beyond the world of appearances. Some successors, however, did associate the experience of sublimity with the experience of the holy.

Friedrich Schelling (1775–1854), pursuing an aspect of Kant's thought as amended by J. G. Fichte (1762–1814), produced a philosophy of seminal influence on literary figures such as Samuel Taylor Coleridge (1772–1834) and theologians such as Paul Tillich (1886–1965). Schelling's philosophy of identity appropriated Kant's notion of aesthetic purposiveness as that which makes scientific inquiry intelligible, but whereas this was only a regulative principle for Kant, it became for Schelling the objective determining principle of reality. In *System of Transcendental Idealism* (1800) Schelling affirmed that "intellectual or rational intuition" reveals the ultimate identity of thought and being, real and ideal. In art, he said, a fleeting glimpse of this harmony or identity is made fully objective. Philosophy therefore should ultimately pass over from reflection on art to become art itself. Even art, however, cannot fully express reality as understood in Schelling's final "positive" philosophy and in his philosophy of mythology and revelation. Positive philosophy, which asserts the primacy of will, is said to be verified in the actual history of religions, which points toward an "age of the spirit" in which all is fulfilled. The function of art is thus replaced by the history of religions.

For Coleridge, as for Schelling, philosophy begins in a "realizing intuition," an act of contemplation that is both theoretical and practical, the coincidence of subject and object on which all knowledge rests and to which all knowledge aspires. Here knowing, doing, and making, science and art, are least distinguishable. Coleridge's theory of imagination is central to his understanding of this basic apprehension. Primary imagination, he says in *Biographia Literaria* (1817), is the "living power and prime agent of all human perception, and a representation in the finite mind of the eternal act of creation in the infinite I AM" (Coleridge, 1956, p. 86). Secondary imagination differs from primary only in degree and mode of operation, but it is similarly creative, seeking "to idealize and unify." From this basic characterization spring Coleridge's theories of poetry, symbol, and religion. Religion, he says, "unites in its purposes the desiderata of the speculative and practical being; its acts, including its events, are truths and objects of philosophical insight, and vice versa the truths of which it consists are to be considered the acts and manifestations of that Being who is at once Power and Truth" (p. 167).

G. W. F. Hegel (1770–1831) aspired to complete the movement of modern philosophy toward a conception of reality as Mind or Spirit. In his *Philosophy of Fine Art* (1807) he treated art and religion as authentic expressions of Spirit, whose concrete development, portrayed in his historical dialectic, would finally be superseded in true philosophy. Art, he said, is the sensuous appearance *(Schein)* of Idea, or the Real (Spirit). It seeks to give rich concreteness to unfolding reality; in it, a concept shows itself for itself. Its earliest form, Hegel thought, is the symbolic. In classical art, whose consummate form is sculpture, the divine is expressed through the perfection of the human form. Classical art, however, betrays its inadequacy for the expression of Spirit in the very concreteness of its forms. In the Romantic arts of painting, music, and poetry, Spirit is exhibited in increasing purity; in poetry, the art of sounded imaginative concepts, it achieves its most powerful artistic expression. This theme has been elaborated by poet-critics like T. S. Eliot (1888–1965) and others. Religion, thought Hegel, is a historically parallel manifestation of the Real in that it vivifies the Real as God in myth, ritual, and theology. Indeed, the God of Romantic art, he seems to suggest, is the God of Christianity. With full disclosure of the way the Real as Spirit works in the dialectic of history, the eclipse of art and religion in their historical forms had, he thought, begun.

Søren Kierkegaard (1813–1855) reacted vigorously against Hegel's views of the ultimate character of reality and of the place of the aesthetic and religious in its perception. Truth, he said, is not the objective working out of Idea, Reason, or Spirit; a logical system is possible, but there can be no logical system of personal life as it is actually lived, of existence. Truth is a matter not of what but of how one thinks, as displayed in the engaged conduct of a life. Truth is an existential grasp of "essence" arrived at not by logical conclusion but by life-committing choice.

According to Kierkegaard, three major valuations of life are open to truth-seeking choice, or the quest for authentic existence: the aesthetic, the ethical, and the religious. The grounding principle of the aesthetic, which may include all forms of human making, is enjoyment. The aesthetic is basically ahistorical because its fulfillments are only accidentally related to temporal and spatial situations. It involves less than the whole person; its criterion is that of fittingness or definition. As life orientation, the aesthetic is ironic, because it expresses only the individual as he or she is, rather than positing a task for indefinite striving. Dependent for its satisfactions on the vagaries of fortune and taste, it leads, he said, to "the despair of not willing to be oneself."

In the ethical perspective, one experiences the dignity of the whole self and the equality of persons before the moral law; the moral imperative does set a task for unending pursuit. Herein, however, lies the irony of the ethical: one can always do more than is required by or consonant with moral law, or one experiences the impossibility of complete obedience to moral law as guilt, leading to "the despair of willing to be oneself despairingly."

It is within the religious perspective, Kierkegaard thought, that authenticity is to be experienced. Christian faith, in particular, entails the most inward and passionate—and therefore the most complete—engagement of the self, because it is committed to an absurdity: that the infinite became finite, that God became a historical person. This commitment, which is also openness to divine forgiveness and grace, restores the individual to the realm of authentic finitude. For Kierkegaard, the aesthetic, like the ethical, is not abandoned or denied in the religious attitude; it is fully affirmed and enjoyed, but in its proper place and not as a way of salvation. Other modern existentialists have found something approaching religious significance in various aesthetic forms, even though for many the authenticity proclaimed therein is that of the tragic vision or of unredeemed and unredeeming absurdity.

AESTHETIC AND RELIGIOUS EXPERIENCE. Friedrich Schleiermacher (1768–1834) turned to the life of affections or feeling to identify and celebrate the religious in his *On Religion: Speeches to Its Cultured Despisers* (1893). A brilliant preacher, hermeneut, translator of Plato, and teacher, Schleiermacher was identified with the circle of German Romantic artists whose attention to the affective dominated their work. Religion, he affirmed, is not primarily a matter of beliefs or of divine undergirding of moral law; it is rooted in a distinctive feeling, which he variously designated "the feeling of absolute dependence," "the sense of the Whole," or in his later work, *The Christian Faith* (1821–1822), the sense and taste for the Infinite (Schleiermacher, 1928, p. 55). Religious apprehension is akin, he said, to the experience of the sublime as described by Kant. While for Kant, however, the experience of the sublime bespeaks finally the dignity of man, for Schleiermacher it is a key to the experience of God. In the figure of Jesus as the Christ, he said, one sees exemplary God consciousness or complete transparency to the divine.

Rudolf Otto (1869–1937), whose *Idea of the Holy* (1917) decisively influenced developments in the theory of religion, was himself strongly influenced by both Schleiermacher and aspects of Kantian philosophy. Otto's book calls attention to nonrational dimensions of the holy, which is viewed as the distinctive religious category. Rational characterizations of the holy are expressed in conceptual superlatives (supreme being, supernatural) and other conceptual absolutes. A sense of its reality, however, must be evoked rather than rationally demonstrated, just as a sense of the aesthetic must be. The aesthetic realm thus provides for Otto the chief analogies for modes of apprehending the dimension of the holy that he termed "the numinous," the "*mysterium tremendum et fascinans*." This realm of mystery is both awesomely overpowering and the source of that fascination that leads, through the history of religions, to beatitude. "Divination" (Otto's term for the discernment of the numinous), like aesthetic intuition, operates through the senses. The expressions of such discernments, like those of aesthetic intuition, may be nonconceptual or idiosyncratically conceptual ("ideograms"); they may issue directly in sound, light, darkness, or holy silence or be conveyed indirectly through music, poetry, or other art forms. The closest analogue to that which is so expressed, said Otto, is the sublime as described by Kant, though without Kant's critical restrictions.

Gerardus van der Leeuw (1890–1950), whose *Religion in Essence and Manifestation* (1933) influenced many theorists of religion, describes the phenomenological stance in terms strikingly similar to those employed by some in describing the aesthetic attitude. Phenomenology of religion, he asserts, is not philosophy of religion, insofar as it brackets questions of religion's relation to reality and truth. It is not poetry of religion, because it seeks to understand what is expressed through its poetry. The phenomenologist of religion, rather, seeks "lovingly to gaze" on that which is to be understood and, through understanding, cherished. Schleiermacher had said that the historical forms of religion are to religion as the various forms of music are to music. Leeuw sought to comprehend the temporal and cultural diversity of religious expressions through the exercise of "surrendering love," a sympathetic mode of cognition "linking old and new."

Mircea Eliade (1907–1986) frequently described his monumental work as history or science of religion, but the stance he commends is in part that of the phenomenologist. However, it is not simply a matter of "gazing at" or resonating with apparently alien religious forms. *Homo religiosus* is universal. Understanding the diversity of experience of the sacred requires trained sensitivity to the forms and functions of the sacred, many of which are explicitly aesthetic in character. Whether there is or could be in modernity a complete loss of the sense of the sacred is for him problematic; if such a loss did occur, it would be comparable to, though more fundamental than, the loss of aesthetic sensitivity or orientation in relation to works of art.

Some modern philosophers, eschewing traditional formulations of religious faith, have found an analogue in the aesthetic. George Santayana (1863–1952), poet, essayist, and novelist as well as professional philosopher, keyed his understanding of verifiable knowledge to a conception of science that, he believed, portrayed the world as an insensate, mechanical arrangement of atoms, one existing prior to human consciousness and destined to continue after human consciousness has disappeared. Spirit is unable to rearrange the forces of nature basically or permanently, or to eliminate the exigencies of life. From within the perspective of spirit, however, persons may perceive these exigencies as necessities of existence and experience a transmutation of them "under the aspect of eternity." The gifts of the spirit entail more, however, than the passive acquiescence in fortune. Imagination may envision and affirm ideal values that become goals of highest human aspiration and sources of endless delight, even though (or perhaps because) they are never fully incarnate in the realm of existence. Chief among these is beauty, which exemplifies the ideal harmony that is the good. A life conducted in the presence of these ideals is eternal because the ideals that thus constitute its essence are eternal. They are not everlasting; they are timeless. Partially embodied in aesthetic experience and vivified in the religious life, they provide for human beings another world in which to live, one that celebrates the distinctively human dimension of the real. Religion is poetry that guides life.

John Dewey (1859–1952) held a quite different understanding of scientific inquiry and its implications for life and society. Patterns of inquiry, beginning in doubt or problem and moving through experiment to resolution, are not limited to cognitively problematic situations in which we "do not know what to think." They are also exhibited in morally problematic situations, in which we "do not know what to do." The latter may be resolved through careful discrimination between the temporal ends of courses of action and the ends as goals of moral aspiration; that is, between the desired and the desirable. We are justified, Dewey thought, in choosing those ends that enlarge the range of possible fulfillments.

The aesthetic in experience is that which makes any experience an experience. In experience as aesthetic, exemplified in those experiential achievements called works of art, the continuities of form and matter and of creative initiation and aesthetic consummation are presented directly. Experience as aesthetic is consummatory and a good in itself. In the creation and enjoyment of a work of art, one gains new perspectives on and energy for the pursuit of all other forms of experience. The sense of communion generated by a work of art, says Dewey, may take on a definitely religious quality in what one interpreter has called "the religion of shared experience." In aesthetic experience thus understood, nature achieves its human culmination.

Dewey also understood the religious in experience in terms of adapting nature to human ends and accommodating human life to those aspects of it that cannot be changed. In *A Common Faith* (1934) he describes the religious in experience as expressing the deepest and most pervasive of accommodations: faith as basic confidence, which may sustain the envisagement of ideals and religious commitment to their realizations. Indeed, Dewey argues, one may use the term *God* to express the active relation of ideal to actual. The sense of belonging to a whole, he says in *Art as Experience* (1934), is "the explanation of that feeling of exquisite intelligibility and clarity which we have in the presence of an object experienced with esthetic intensity . . . it explains the religious feeling that accompanies intense esthetic perception. We are, as it were, introduced into a world beyond this world which is nevertheless the deeper reality of the world in which we live in ordinary experience. We are carried beyond ourselves to find ourselves" (Dewey, 1934, p. 195).

Between 1910 and 1913, Bertrand Russell (1872–1970) and Alfred North Whitehead (1861–1947) published their magisterial *Principia Mathematica,* foundational for later work in the logical structure of mathematics and symbolic logic. Both thinkers went on to engage in philosophical inquiry and theory in a wide range of human concerns. Whitehead eventually sought to articulate a metaphysical-cosmological view authentic "for our cosmic era." In the process he created a special vocabulary needed for the exposition of his thought. The basic ingredients of reality he called "actual occasions," "actual entities," "events," or "droplets of experience," emphasizing ongoing relatedness in the process of reality. In *reality,* each occasion incorporates a funding from the past and an "ingression" from the future. Novelty is a feature of all actual occasions, and freedom is a category. There are three formative elements in the process that is reality: Creativity, God, and Eternal Objects. Creativity is a "given," and it does not presuppose a Creator. Eternal Objects constitute the timeless realm of infinite possibility. "God," in Whitehead's term, in God's Primordial Nature timelessly envisions these Eternal Objects (cf. Santayana). Some logical possibilities are also ontological potentialities. God in God's Consequent Nature is involved in the actualization of these potentialities. God provides both "lure" and companionship.

Whitehead entitled his major work on religion, *Religion in the Making* (1926). Religions celebrate in various ways the mystery, awesomeness, and splendor of existence and its continuous coming to be or realization of actual occasions in the society of all other actual occasions in the cosmos. Whitehead's frequently quoted statement that "religion is what an individual does with his own solitariness" (Whitehead, 1926, p. 16) is sometimes construed to express an existentialist individualism. Actually, it is his way of saying that all individuals are individualizations of a reality that is inherently social, and religion itself is always "in the making." See below for why Whitehead thought the future of world faiths may lie between Christianity and Buddhism.

Whitehead never wrote a book on aesthetics as such. Perhaps he felt that he was writing about aesthetics in nearly everything he wrote. In his description of aesthetic experience he emphasized the transactional-transformative character and transfigurational effect of the experience. Beauty is the harmonious mutual adaptation of all of the elements of aesthetic experience, and beauty is the one self-justifying aim.

Martin Heidegger (1889–1976), like Whitehead, stressed the primacy of temporality in reality. (His basic work is titled *Being and Time* [1927].) But for him it is simply the "being-ness" of being that is foundational. He sought to recover for philosophy that primordial sense of being that, he believed, characterized early Greek philosophy and had been lost in Western philosophy by the attempt to dominate Being through the strategies of scientific inquiry and various patterns of technological cultural and institutional engagement.

Like Whitehead, he found that the articulation of his philosophy required a distinctive vocabulary. In the "temporalizing" of Being, Being "comes-to-light." *Dasein* is "there-being," which can question itself about its own being. It is *human* being. But *Dasein* is also transparent to various modes of unconcealments, in subjectifying and objectifying procedures. There are three "equiprimordial" elements in this unfolding. The first is *Befindlichkeit*—"feeling" or "moodness." The second is understanding—standing under or within that which comes to light. All understanding is interpretation. There is no bare uninterpreted engagement with Being. The third ingredient in Being's coming to light is discursive reasoning. *Dasein* is both being in the world—being in the "worldhood" of things—and being with others. The "thinghood" of things is first of all the thinghood of equipment—things at hand for use. Through abstraction, use relations may become theoretical relations. Being with others entails affirming and celebrating the otherness of others in their unique integrity. The ultimate future of all authentic beings as *Dasein* is death. Authentic living unto death courageously affirms death as finis and also death as telos—one affirms one's completion of being in finitude. In authentic living, thinking is thanking.

What mode of being is a work of art? It is at one level a thing as equipment. Conservation is an essential element of its being. But a work of art may also portray that form of being which is "thing" being. A work of art is also a kind of working—an artistic "creation." The work of the artist in all media is *poiein*—poetizing in a sense epitomized in Greek sensibility. In poetry Being comes to light most clearly, or as Heidegger would later say, is most clearly "heard." Does *poiein,* whether in linguistic or other form, have religious significance?

If religion celebrates a sense of transcendence, there is a sense in which others transcend self and Being transcends all beings. But Being is not a being among beings, or transcendent "Being-itself," or a degree of being—"Higher," "Supreme," or otherwise. For much of his career Heidegger seemed to emphasize the Mystery of *Being.* Later he has seemed to emphasize the *mystery* of Being. Many contemporary theologians seem to concur in this move.

EASTERN VIEWS. Eastern philosophers did not attend to the systematic development of comprehensive aesthetic theories until these were incorporated in influential Western systems. This does not mean, however, that profound reflection on aspects of aesthetic theory in relation to religious experience is not present in many classical Eastern texts. Ananda Coomaraswamy (1877–1947), a pioneer in introducing Eastern art and aesthetics to Western communities, incorporated many of these reflections in an original and influential theory that he described, in *Christian and Oriental Philosophy of Art* (1956), as a "doctrine of art intrinsic to the Philosophia Perennis." Its major themes, he thought, are expressed in Aristotelian, Neoplatonic, and other philosophies foundational to medieval Christian thought and culture and also in Indian, Buddhist, and Confucian classics. Central to his analysis is the view that all true art is iconographic; authentic art forms and objects are to be understood as media for embodying and transmitting "ideas" or spiritual meanings. Authentic experience of a work of art requires appropriate preparation of both artist and experiencer for the work and its appreciation, and it results in a transformation of the percipient. The supreme achievement of individual consciousness is to lose (or find) itself in what is both its beginning and its end. The transformation of the artifact also effects the transformation of the artist and the percipient. The object-subject of apprehension is an imaged idea that moves the will and attracts the intellect of the artist; the idea is the source of the formation expressed in and through the work of art. Universal themes and motifs or archetypes, he thought, are expressed in varying ways in great art, whether literary, plastic, or performed.

Coomaraswamy's articulation of the transactional nature of religious apprehension through aesthetic experience foreshadows later interest in general "response theory." A useful and suggestive work in this area, drawing on neuropsychological and general theories of perception, is Michael Stephan's *A Transformational Theory of Aesthetics* (1990). Stephan focuses on visual experience. He summarizes neuropsychological-evolutionary data on the sites of sensory information in lobes and modules of the brain and their paths of intercommunication, and he emphasizes the principal sites of visual experience in nondiscursive areas. Icons as unalloyed or uninterpreted visual experience are sui generis. Foundational experience, however, includes affective import that gives rise to emotional response (cf. Heidegger's *Befindlichkeit* or moodness). Psychological "item response" theories are discussed by Wim van der Linden and Ronald K. Hambleton in *Handbook of Modern Item Response Theory* (1997). A principal advocate of "reader response" theory in literary criticism is Stanley Fish, author of *Surprised by Sin: The Reader in Paradise Lost* (1998) and *Is There a Text in This Class?* (1980).

The ultimately Real is designated *brahman* in major schools of Hindu philosophy. *Brahman* is transspatial and transtemporal. The penultimately real is *māyā,* frequently defined as illusion, but it is as real as the realm of space and time. The ultimate reality in that world is *brahman* as *ātman,* usually defined as soul or self. The goal of human souls is *mokṣa* or deliverance from the realm of *māyā* through realization of (making real) the identity of *ātman* and *brahman.* The world of *māyā* is governed by *karma,* the law of cause and effect that regulates both physical and nonphysical reality.

In traditional Hindu culture the path to *moksha* leads, for souls that have been in human form for at least one lifetime, through four stages: studenthood, householderhood, forest-dweller (retreat to a life of meditation), and *saṃnyāsa,* (living in the world as one not of the world). In the householder stage one should be guided by *dharma* (religious duty), *artha* (worldly welfare), and *kāma* (sensory pleasure). The *Kāma-Sūtra* is the Hindu classic of forms of sexual pleasure. *Kāma* is an essential ingredient in the four-stage path to *moksha.*

The ideal measure of *kāma* is *rasa,* usually translated as "Beauty." But *rasa* is an elusive concept. There are at least thirty definitions in standard Sanskrit dictionaries. It is a specific blend of specified feelings and emotions, with various *rasas* assigned to various art forms. As in other theories discussed above, the experience of *rasa* incorporates all of the elements of aesthetic experience in a manner that is transactional, transforming, and transfigural. May it also be a form of religious experience? The acme of experience as *rasa* is *santarasa. Santarasa,* writes Eliot Deutsch, "is just that transcendental realization that is joy-ful and peaceful. It is grounded in the Self and is realized as a kind of self-liberation" (Deutsch, 1975, p. 19). And ultimately "*santa* is silence . . . . The art-work in the fullness of its experience as *santarasa* points to Reality and participates in it. In pure spiritual experience there is only the Real. To the enlightened—but only to the enlightened—all experience is *santarasa*" (Deutsch, 1975, p. 19).

Whitehead said that "Buddhism is the most colossal example in history of applied metaphysics . . . a metaphysics generating a religion," in contrast with Christianity, which is "a religion seeking a metaphysic" (Whitehead, 1926, p. 50). The metaphysics of Buddhism shares many affinities with the metaphysics of Whitehead. Siddhārtha Gautama (c. 563–483 BCE), known as "Śākyamuni"—"sage of the Śākya clan,"—inherited many of the basic Hindu beliefs of his culture, which were retained as basic in Buddhism. When, as a scion of a noble family, he experienced major confrontations with the facts of old age, disease, and death, he moved on to the stage of withdrawal for intense meditation on a Way that would transcend these features of life in *māyā.* He found that Way in an experience of enlightenment that made him the exemplary Buddha—Enlightened One—and that he shared with others, who became carriers of the Buddhist enlightenment, first to Southeast Asia, then to Central and East Asia, and eventually to other continents. In the process several themes were constant. One was the transitoriness of life. Another was the transitoriness of all of those elements that constitute a human self, leading to a doctrine of "no self" or "no ownership." Another was the role of *karma* in attaining the ultimate goal of beatitude: *nirvāṇa.*

As the Way spread, other concepts became important. One is that of the *bodhisattva,* one who has generated enough good *karma* to enter *nirvāṇa* but will not do so before he or she can be a means for all others to attain the goal. Much of Buddhist devotional, meditational, and aesthetic practice focuses on one of these or on enlightened masters who share their teachings with disciples through various forms of discipline.

Major forms of such schools or sects developed in Tibet, China, Korea, and Japan. They range from manifestations of faith to receive the grace of a *bodhisattva* to disciplined study and practice under the guidance of a master that can lead to *satori* or salvific enlightenment. The Chan school of China, source of the Zen school of Japan, is of the latter type. Zen practice has strongly influenced many of the arts in China and Japan. This includes that freedom and spontaneity that follows release from the hegemony of "normal" consciousness through *kōans* whose verbal form opens the way to supradiscursive insight. The pursuit of such insight may focus on complete concentration on the ingredients of a vocational activity, like that of the warrior or athlete. Or emphasis may be on the highly ritualized restraint that should characterize the work of the actor or other artist. The "spirit of Zen" may be made manifest in many forms.

In China, Buddhism encountered the indigenous Confucian tradition, which espoused the goal of harmony between "Heaven," humans, and earth, expressed aesthetically in poetry and landscape painting. The Daoist tradition emphasized spontaneity and paradox expressed in these media.

In Japan, Buddhism was related in a variety of ways to Shintō, the indigenous religion of the islands, which in itself exhibits many aesthetic elements in its practices. Donald Keene has noted several terms in shared Japanese aesthetic vocabulary. *Aware* expresses a sense of wonder at the "giveness" of things. It also means, he says, "a gentle sorrow, adding not so much a meaning as a perfume to a sentence. It bespoke the sensitive poet's awareness of a sight or sound, of its beauty and its perishability" (Keene, 1958, p. 72). *Miyabi* "was applied to the quiet pleasures which could be savored by (those) whose tastes had been educated to them—a spray of plum blossoms, the elusive perfume of a rare wood, the delicate blending of colors in a robe" (Keene, 1958, pp. 174–175). *Yugen,* says Keene, "was a word used to describe the profound, the remote, the mysterious" (Keene, 1958, pp. 174–175). *Sabi* suggested not only "the old, but the taking of pleasure in that which was old" (Keene, 1958, p. 278). It is most profoundly felt in the tea ceremony and the tea hut. It is a quality, says Keene, that is captured in many brief and allusive poems called haiku. Again attention is drawn to the impermanence of things. This is not bemoaned. As in the Buddhist Way, it is noted simply as "the way things are." This sense is further expressed in *ukiyo,* the "floating world" of wood-block prints and of the transient passions. Some followers of many religious traditions are asking anew what is "floating" and what is permanent or enduring in the realms of aesthetics and religion within the multicultural world of globalization.

SEE ALSO Aristotle; Art and Religion; Beauty; Biblical Exegesis, article on Christian Views; Icons; Images; Literature, article on Literature and Religion; Plato; Platonism; Plotinus.

BIBLIOGRAPHY

Aristotle. *Works.* Translated and edited by William D. Ross. Oxford, 1910–1937. The classic translation of the relevant Aristotelian materials. See especially *Nichomachean Ethics* and *Poetics.*

Augustine. *De doctrina Christiana.* Translated by Thérèse Sullivan. Washington, D.C., 1930.

Augustine. *Divine Providence and the Problem of Evil.* Translated and edited by Robert P. Russell. New York, 1942. Translation of *De ordine.*

Augustine. *De musica, a Synopsis.* Translated by W. F. Jackson Knight. London, 1949.

Augustine. *Later Works.* Edited by John Burnaby. Library of Christian Classics, vol. 8. Philadelphia, 1955. Includes *De Trinitate.* This and the three preceding works embody the principal themes in Augustine's treatment of the aesthetic in relation to beatitude.

Bernabeo, Paul. "With Blended Might: An Investigation into Schleiermacher's Aesthetics and the Family Resemblance between Religion and Art." Ph.D. diss., Columbia University, 1981. The significance of Schleiermacher's aesthetic theory for his theology.

Brown, Robert F. *The Later Philosophy of Schelling.* Lewisburg, Pa., 1977.

Coleridge, Samuel Taylor. *Biographia Literaria.* Edited by George Watson. London, 1956. Contains Coleridge's statements of the relation of imagination to religious and aesthetic insight.

Coomaraswamy, Ananda K. *The Transformation of Nature in Art.* Cambridge, Mass., 1934; reprint New York, 1956.

Coomaraswamy, Ananda K. *Christian and Oriental Philosophy of Art.* New York, 1956.

Coomaraswamy, Ananda K. *Coomaraswamy,* vol. 1, *Selected Papers.* Edited by Roger Lipsey. Princeton, N.J. 1977. These Coomaraswamy works are thoughtful analyses of aspects of Asian art in relation to classical Western philosophy and theology.

Deutsch, Eliot. *Studies in Comparative Aesthetics.* Honolulu, 1975.

Dewey, John. *Art as Experience.* New York, 1934.

Dewey, John. *A Common Faith.* New Haven, Conn., 1934. These two Dewey works offer a naturalistic and humanistic understanding of the relation of the aesthetic to the religious in experience.

Fish, Stanley. *Is There a Text in This Class?* Cambridge, Mass., 1980.

Fish, Stanley. *Surprised by Sin: The Reader in Paradise Lost.* Cambridge, Mass., 1998.

Foucault, Michel. *The Archaeology of Knowledge.* Translated by A. M. Sheridan Smith. London, 1972.

Hegel, G. W. F. *The Philosophy of Fine Art.* 4 vols. Translated by Francis Plumptre Beresford Osmaston. London, 1920. Sets forth Hegel's views of the relation of art to religion in his understanding of the dialectic of Spirit.

Heidegger, Martin. *Being and Time.* Translated by John Macquarrie and Edward Robinson Jr. New York, 1962.

Heidegger, Martin. *On the Way to Language.* Translated by Peter D. Hertz. New York, 1971.

Heidegger, Martin. *Poetry, Language, Thought.* Translated by Albert Hofstadter. New York, 1971.

Kant, Immanuel. *Critique of Pure Reason.* Translated by Norman Kemp Smith. New York, 1929. Presents Kant's view of theoretical knowledge.

Kant, Immanuel. *Critique of Practical Reason and Other Writings in Moral Philosophy.* Translated and edited by Lewis White Beck. Chicago, 1949. Discusses the nature and implications of moral judgment.

Kant, Immanuel. *The Critique of Judgement.* Translated by James Creed Meredith. Oxford, 1964. Shows how the nature of judgment as such is exemplified in aesthetic judgment; also contains Kant's treatment of the sublime.

Keene, Donald. "The Vocabulary of Japanese Aesthetics I." In *Sources of Japanese Tradition,* edited by William Theodore de Bary, vol. 1. New York, 1958.

Kierkegaard, Søren. *A Kierkegaard Anthology.* Edited by Robert Bretall. New York, 1959. Contains the substance of those works of Kierkegaard that set forth his understanding of the relation of the aesthetic to the ethical and religious. See especially "Stages on Life's Way," "Either/Or," "Fear and Trembling," and "Concluding Unscientific Postscript."

Leeuw, Gerardus van der. *Phänomenologie der Religion.* Tübingen, Germany, 1933. Translated by J. E. Turner as *Religion in Essence and Manifestation* (London, 1938; 2d ed., New York, 1963). Portrays a phenomenological approach to understanding religion that exhibits many similarities to aesthetic attitudes.

Martin, James Alfred, Jr. *Beauty and Holiness.* Princeton, N.J., 1990. Includes extended discussions of several topics discussed in this article.

Niebuhr, Richard R. *Schleiermacher on Christ and Religion.* New York, 1964. Schleiermacher's aesthetic theory's significance for his theology.

Otto, Rudolf. *Das Heilige,* 9th ed. Breslau, Poland, 1922. Translated by John W. Harvey as *The Idea of the Holy* (London and New York, 1923; 2d ed., London and New York, 1950). An influential theory of religion that draws heavily on analogies from aesthetics.

Plato. *Dialogues of Plato.* Translated by Benjamin Jowett. Oxford, 1871. The classic translation of the dialogues, which set forth Plato's understanding of the role of the aesthetic in philosophical and religious truth. See especially *Philebus, Phaedrus, Ion,* and *Symposium.*

Plotinus. *The Enneads.* Translated by Stephen MacKenna and revised by B. S. Page. New York, 1957. Contains the Neoplatonic formulation most influential in subsequent Jewish, Christian, and Muslim thought.

Santayana, George. *Interpretations of Poetry and Religion.* New York, 1911.

Santayana, George. "Reason in Art." In *The Philosophy of Santayana,* edited by Irwin Edman. New York, 1942.

Santayana, George. "Reason in Religion." In *The Philosophy of Santayana,* edited by Irwin Edman. New York, 1942. These works contain major statements of Santayana's humanistic and naturalistic position on art and religion.

Saxena, Sushil Kumar. *Aesthetical Essays: Studies in Aesthetic Theory, Hindustani Music, and Kathak Dance.* Delhi, 1981. Describes the emergence of aesthetics in Indian thought and its relation to philosophical and religious issues.

Schelling, Friedrich. *The Ages of the World.* Translated by Frederick de Wolfe Bolman Jr. New York, 1942.

Schelling, Friedrich. *System of Transcendental Idealism.* Translated by Peter Heath. Charlottesville, Va., 1978.

Schleiermacher, Friedrich. *On Religion: Speeches to Its Cultured Despisers.* Translated by John Oman. London, 1893; abr. ed., New York, 1955.

Schleiermacher, Friedrich. *The Christian Faith.* Edited by H. R. Mackintosh and J. S. Stewart. Edinburgh, 1928; reprint New York, 1963. These two works portray Schleiermacher's aesthetic theory.

Stephan, Michael. *A Transformational Theory of Aesthetics.* London and New York, 1990.

"Theorists and Critics: Michel Foucault." Available from http://www.popcultures.com/theorists/foucault.html. A comprehensive survey of primary and secondary works, including digitally authored resources.

Thomas Aquinas. *Basic Writings of Saint Thomas Aquinas.* 2 vols. Edited by Anton C. Pegis. New York, 1945. Contains the major statements of Thomas on aesthetic themes in relation to theology. See especially *Summa Theologiae,* 1.13.5, 1.16.1, 1.5.4, 2.1.27.1.

van der Linden, Wim J., and Ronald K. Hambleton, eds. *Handbook of Modern Item Response Theory.* New York, 1997.

Whitehead, Alfred North. *Religion in the Making.* New York, 1926.

Whitehead, Alfred North. *Process and Reality.* New York, 1929.

Whitehead, Alfred North. *Alfred North Whitehead: A Primary-Secondary Bibliography.* Edited by Barry A. Woodbridge. Bowling Green, Ky., 1977.

JAMES ALFRED MARTIN, JR. (1987 AND 2005)

AESTHETICS: VISUAL AESTHETICS

An article on the application of visual aesthetics to religion might be expected to concentrate on paintings and sculpture with religious subject matter as well as on architecture designed for religious functions. Such an article, however, would duplicate a monograph on sacred art. The following discussion undertakes in a more general way to describe some basic perceptual and cognitive aspects of visual imagery and to examine their effects on religious art. Particularly relevant to this discussion are forms of art and kinds of religion not bound to traditional legendary subject matter.

Visual imagery defines the things and events of the world by their perceptual appearance. To be sure, perceptual characteristics are supplemented by all kinds of knowledge, but since such knowledge conveys only indirect information, it is less immediately effective. Images act primarily not by what one knows but by what strikes the eyes. They speak through the properties of shape, color, space, and sometimes motion. These properties are the carriers of visual dynamics, directed forces whose configurations act as symbolical equivalents of the dynamics that determine one's own mental and physical existence. The expressiveness of pure form enables nonrepresentational art such as architecture and "abstract" painting or sculpture to make effective statements about human experience.

RELIGIOUS ART AND REALITY. When put at the service of religion, art favors embodiment; that is, it favors objects of worship taking the shapes of physical existence, such as human figures, animals and trees, buildings and mountains, water and light. Not all visual images meet the conditions of art, but for reasons to be discussed later it is all but essential for religious purposes that they do so. Some of the conditions to which works of art are subject may create difficulties for their application toward religious ends. One such condition is that images, to be effective, must adhere to what may be called a unitary reality status: they must share a common universe of discourse, whether physical or metaphysical. As long as superhuman powers are represented as differing from terrestrial life only by degree, there is no problem. The Homeric gods, for example, are stronger and more beautiful than mortals and are exempt from the laws of nature, but otherwise interact with mortals at the same level. Therefore the nature and activity of these gods pose no difficulties for the painter. The same is true for biblical subjects. Regardless of how artist and viewer conceive the ontological status of God, Michelangelo's frescoes in the Sistine Chapel can show the creator only as a human figure, albeit one endowed with superhuman powers.

Even invisibility is no obstacle to the painter as long as it is represented as a phenomenon of the visible world; but if a supernatural power were to be shown as beyond the sphere of visibility, namely as purely spiritual, the painter could solve the task only by shifting the entire theme to the spiritual realm, the qualities of which would be represented symbolically. If, for example, the Pentecostal outpouring of the Holy Spirit were depicted in the manner of the Italian futurists by stylized flames descending on a group of dark abstract shapes, this visually coherent image could work very well as a symbolical representation of an entirely spiritual event. A painter would be unable, however, to show the interaction of a spiritual, immaterial power with a material event. Marc Chagall's Bible illustrations may be cited as an example of this limitation. Meyer Schapiro observes in his *Modern Art: Nineteenth and Twentieth Centuries* (New York, 1978): "Chagall feels awe before the divinity. How can he render God, who has forbidden all images? He has given the answer in [one of his illustrations] the *Creation of Man.* God's name is inscribed here in Hebrew letters in a luminous circle in the dark sky" (p. 130). Here the qualitative difference between the immaterial and the material would seem to be indicated by the insertion of a diagrammatic sign, which can be understood intellectually but does not express visually the nature of the divine. This inherent break in aesthetic expression is circumvented in certain images created in medieval Europe and the Far East, where heaven, earth, and underworld are represented as separate entities within a continuous picture. Interaction is sacrificed, but the visual concreteness of each realm is safeguarded.

One can make a similar point by stating that visual imagery does not readily accommodate a worldview that suffers from the modern scission between what is considered accepted knowledge, especially scientific knowledge, and what is merely believed on the basis of what was held to be true in the past. In a work of art, everything is equally true, and all truth is known by one and the same means of visual evidence. The angel of the Annunciation is as real as the Virgin, and when, in a painting by Tintoretto, Christ walks on the waters of the Sea of Gennesaret, the walk is as real as the water and the boat. As far as aesthetic reality is concerned, no faith is needed where there is the certainty of sight. At the same time no picture offers scientific proof for the truth of anything it shows. A painted tree is no more real than a winged dragon. As a work of art, a painting or sculpture persuades only by the power of its visual presence. Thus it can satisfy a viewer who accepts the story as literal truth and equally one who considers it purely symbolical, but it balks at combining both views in the same image. Given its perceptual nature, visual art favors a conception of religious experience emerging from what is accepted as factually true.

KINDS OF AESTHETIC TRUTH. Works of art, then, call for the unitary reality status of everything they show and refer to. That reality status, however, is not always the same. One can distinguish the following kinds.

Iconic. What is the ontological status of an icon that is worshiped, offered gifts and sacrifices, asked for help or intercession? For believers it is clearly treated as a physically existent power residing in their world. At the same time, the admission of an image to the world of the living is rarely the result of an illusion. Typically, believers are not deceived about the reality status of the icon's body. They know that they are in the presence of an object of wood, stone, or painted canvas. A naive psychology would see here a puzzling contradiction. What counts, however, is not the biological reality of the iconic entity but the power attributed to it. As the carrier of such power, the icon is taken neither for a living creature nor for a mere representation of something active elsewhere in time and space. It is an immediately present source of active energy.

Historical. When an Egyptian sculptor made a portrait of Queen Nefertiti, or when Diego Velázquez depicted the surrender of the Dutch city of Breda to the Spanish conqueror in 1625, the artist was convinced that he was offering a likeness of someone who was actually living or had lived, or of something that actually had taken place. This conviction prevails regardless of how much or little an artist knows about the actual appearance of his or her subject. Religious images can be intended as such portraits or chronicles, that is, as representations at the same level of truthfulness as historical documentation or scientific illustration; but there is no telling by mere inspection in which cases this is in fact the artist's attitude. Certainly it would be a mistake to assume that in religious imagery the more realistic representations are necessarily the more "literally" intended ones or that, vice versa, the more stylized and abstract images are meant to be more remote from actual fact. An artist of the high Renaissance, for instance, may have depicted the repentant Mary Magdalene very realistically for the purpose of sensuous enjoyment, caring very little about the truth of the story the work was telling; whereas certain more abstract styles, which today look remote from nature, may have seemed quite lifelike to their originators and may have been inspired by a deep belief in the truthfulness of their images.

Universal. It is, however, in the nature of artistic perception that an image is seen not simply as an individual object, person, or happening, but as the representative of a whole class of things, the significance of which goes beyond that of the individual. One may know the name of a gentleman portrayed by Rembrandt, but beyond the image of the individual is seen in the painting an expression of melancholy and resignation, vigilance and thought. In fact, one of the principal virtues of a great artist is the ability to handle shapes and colors in such a way that universal validity imposes itself through the individual instance. This symbolic quality of images is entirely compatible with the belief in their historical truth. When Dante Alighieri, in his letter to Can Grande della Scala, explains that a biblical story, such as that of the departure of the children of Israel, can be understood "in more senses than one," he distinguishes the literal from the allegorical meanings. The individual story may or may not be intended or understood as historical truth. When such truth is excluded, the human validity of the presentation may be nevertheless entirely preserved. The viewer enters the aesthetic category of fiction.

RELIGIOUS SUBJECT MATTER. In fiction the historical truth of the subject matter is commonly considered irrelevant, or even an obstacle to the creative freedom of the artist. Concerning religious art there is the question of whether such an attitude toward the subject matter is acceptable. For example, can an artist who is not a believer create a convincing image? (The term *believer* may be defined for the moment in the limited sense of someone convinced of the historical truth of the depicted facts.) A telling example of an enterprise that has had considerable religious and artistic success but has also stirred up much protest is that of the Church of Nôtre-Dame-de-Toute-Grâce at Assy, France, commissioned by the Dominican fathers during the early 1940s. The story of the church, to which William S. Rubin has devoted an extensive monograph (*Modern Sacred Art and the Church of Assy,* New York, 1961), is complex. It involves the more general issue of popular aversion to modern art, but also the fact that prestigious painters and sculptors, known to be atheists, communists, or religious Jews, were called upon to design a mosaic for the facade, a tapestry for the apse, a crucifix, and other decorations. None of the artists testified to any particular difficulty with the religious subject matter, nor did they feel that the task differed in principle from the secular work to which they were accustomed. It seems safe to assume that the religious subject matter to which the artists committed themselves, the Apocalypse, the Crucifixion, the Virgin of the litany, and so forth, exerted upon them the evocative power that inheres in any great subject, whatever its origin. The impact of the universally human dimensions of the subjects upon the artists may account for the more specifically religious effectiveness of their contributions.

In a more general sense this episode raises the question of whether visual images can ever be called religious when they lack the traditional subject matter of any particular creed. One thinks immediately of representations of nature that are intended to testify to the existence and qualities of its creator. When Augustine in his *Confessions* (10.6) inquires about the nature of God, he reports:

> I asked the earth; and it answered, "I am not he"; and whatsoever are therein made the same confession. I asked the sea and the deeps, and the creeping things that lived, and they replied, "We are not thy God, seek higher than we." I asked the breezy air, and the universal air with its inhabitants answered, "Anaximenes was deceived, I am not God." I asked the heavens, the sun, moon, and stars: "Neither," say they, "are we the God whom thou seekest." And I answered unto all these things which stand about the door of my flesh, "Ye have told me concerning my God, that ye are not he; tell me something about him." And with a loud voice they exclaimed, "He has made us." My questioning was my observing of them; and their beauty was their reply.

The things of nature give their answer to Augustine's question through their "beauty" (species). When one views a painted landscape by Altdorfer or Rubens or Sesshū, one may note such qualities as power, inexhaustible abundance, variety, order, ingenuity, and mystery. The greater the artist, the more compellingly does he or she present the objects of nature as embodiments of these virtues. What the artist cannot do, however, is give them the voice by which Augustine heard them answer: "He made us." A landscape cannot do in a painting what it does in Augustine's verbal invocation; visually, cause and effect can be shown only as acting within the realm of the forces of nature themselves, as when in a romantic landscape a cataract smashes against boulders or when a blacksmith is seen striking the glowing iron. To be sure, images can be used superbly to illustrate the belief in a creator, as Augustine does with his enumeration of the things of nature, but the belief must be brought to the images as an interpretation; it is not pronounced by the images themselves.

In 1959 the Protestant theologian Paul Tillich was invited to lecture on the topic "Art and Religion" at the Museum of Modern Art in New York. Significantly, he changed the title of his lecture to "Art and Ultimate Reality," arguing that the quest for ultimate reality was an indispensable aspect of religion and also the aim of all true art. He proceeded to describe five types of stylistic elements that he considered expressive of ultimate reality—a survey suggesting the generalization that any artistic attitude whatever can meet the criterion, provided the work attains the depth that goes with aesthetic excellence. In the discussion following his lecture Tillich was willing to conclude that "ultimate reality appears in what is usually called secular painting, and the difference of what is usually called religious painting is real only insofar as so-called religious painting deals with the traditional subject matters which have appeared in the different religious traditions" (*Cross Currents,* 1960).

Even when such a thesis is accepted in a general way, it seems evident that certain kinds of secular subjects are more congenial to common forms of the religious attitude than others. Thus images of nature point more readily to supernatural powers beyond the objects of physical appearance than do images of the works of man. More generic views do better as religious images than those of specific things or episodes. Stylized presentations can more readily transcend individuality on the way to ultimate reality than realistic ones, and this makes a Byzantine mosaic look more religious than a naturalistic photograph.

The extreme case is that of nonfigurative art, where abstraction reaches a maximum. The predicament of abstract art, however, has been, from the beginning, that although it may claim, as the painter Piet Mondrian did, that it represents ultimate reality more directly than other kinds of art, its relation to concrete experience becomes so tenuous that it risks proclaiming everything and nothing. For example, Fernand Léger, in 1952, decorated the side walls of the United Nations Assembly Hall in New York with large abstractions; his two gigantic tentacled clusters might well convey the sense of consolidated forces, but this very generic meaning can be channeled into a more specific application only with the help of the architectural setting and its known significance.

The limitations of nonfigurative imagery are reinforced when the absence of narrative subject matter is combined with an ascetic parsimony of form. The grids of the late work of Mondrian were threatened by a discrepancy between what was intended and what was achieved. When the form is even more severely reduced while the suggested subject becomes more specific. An extreme case is that of the fourteen *Stations of the Cross* painted around 1960 by the American artist Barnett Newman. These paintings, limited essentially to one or two vertical stripes on a plain background, tend to transcend the boundary between the pictorial and the diagrammatic—a distinction of considerable relevance for the problems of religious imagery. A diagram is a visual symbol of an idea or set of facts. It often reflects some essential property of its subject; but although it can evoke powerful emotions in the viewer—as when someone contemplates a chart depicting the increase of nuclear warheads—it does not create these experiences through its own formal expression. It merely conveys information. Something similar is true for traditional signs, such as the national flag, the cross, or the star of David. They, too, can release powerful responses, which are based on empirical association, not on the visual expression inherent in the image.

AESTHETIC AND RELIGIOUS EXPERIENCE. The distinction between mere factual information, as given for example in scientific illustrations, and aesthetic expression points at the same time to one of two fundamental similarities between aesthetic and religious experience. It is generally acknowledged that for a religious person it does not suffice to accept certain facts, such as the existence of God, but that the forces asserted to exist must be sensed as reverberating in the believer's own mind, so that when, for example, in the *Book of Job,* the Lord answers out of the whirlwind, the reader of the Bible is to be overcome by the greatness of the creation. This heightening of information into religious experience, however, is strongly aided by the poetry of the biblical language. It does not differ in principle from what distinguishes secular aesthetic experience from the mere conveyance of factual knowledge. One may learn all there is to learn about Picasso's response to the Spanish Civil War in his painting *Guernica* and yet never experience the painting as a work of art, unless the forces of suffering, brutality, resistance, and hope come alive in the viewer's own consciousness. For this reason the purpose of religious art can be greatly enhanced when the images are of high artistic quality and thereby carry intense expression.

But is there really no difference between aesthetic and religious experience? Is it not essential for religiosity that experiencing the nature of the world into which one is born leads to a corresponding conduct of worship, of living in conformity with the demands revealed by that experience? In comparison, aesthetic contemplation may seem to be mere passive reception. Such a view of aesthetic behavior, however, is too narrow. First of all, the very fact of artistic creation is the artist's way of placing his or her most important behavior, a life's work, actively into the context of the world he or she experiences. The art historian Kurt Badt, recalling Ruskin and Nietzsche, has defined the activity of the artist as "Feiern durch Rühmung," that is, as celebration through praise (*Kunsthistorische Versuche,* Cologne, 1968). Such a definition does not turn art into religion, but it highlights the affinity of the two.

In an even broader sense, no reception of a work of art is complete unless the viewer feels impelled to live up to the intensity, purity, and wisdom of outlook reflected in it. This demand to emulate the nobility of the work of art by one's own attitude toward the world was strikingly expressed by the poet Rainer Maria Rilke when he celebrated the beautiful forms of an Archaic marble torso of Apollo. He followed his description abruptly with the admonition "Du musst dein Leben ändern" ("You must change your life").

SEE ALSO Architecture; Art and Religion; Human Body; Iconography.

BIBLIOGRAPHY

On the religious attitude of artists see, for example, Edgar Wind's article "Traditional Religion and Modern Art: Rouault and Matisse" in his *The Eloquence of Symbols* (Oxford, 1983). Vincent van Gogh in an often-cited letter of December 1889 to Émile Bernard discusses the use of religious subject matter, a topic interpreted in its broader context by Meyer Schapiro in a paper "On a Painting of van Gogh," contained in his *Modern Art: Nineteenth and Twentieth Centuries* (New York, 1978), pp. 87–99. Explicit references to "ultimate reality" occur in the writings of Piet Mondrian found in *Plastic Art and Pure Plastic Art* (New York, 1945).

For the more general aspects of visual symbolism see, for example, Margaret Miles's "Vision: The Eye of the Body and the Eye of the Mind in St. Augustine's *De Trinitate* and *Confessions,*" *Journal of Religion* 63 (April 1983): 125–142. I have also approached these issues in *Visual Thinking* (Berkeley, 1969), the chapters on "Art and Thought" and on "Models for Theory"; the essay "The Robin and the Saint," in *Toward a Psychology of Art* (Berkeley, 1966); and the chapter "Symbols through Dynamics," in *The Dynamics of Architectural Form* (Berkeley, 1977).

RUDOLF ARNHEIM (1987)

AFFLICTION

This entry consists of the following articles:

AN OVERVIEW
AFRICAN CULTS OF AFFLICTION

AFFLICTION: AN OVERVIEW

Men, but more so women, have frequently viewed themselves as the victims of unsolicited and malevolent attention from the spirit world. Sometimes such affliction is thought to come out of the blue or to result from some quite trivial misdemeanor. More often it is thought to result from disputes or transgressions committed by the victim or by a relative. The outward signs of affliction are not uniform or obvious. They range from grossly stigmatizing conditions such as leprosy or madness, through trance, to a subjective malaise or a feeling that one has not received one's just deserts. The mechanics of attack vary. Some victims are able to describe the details of the method of attack with great precision. Others show no interest either in the reason for attack or in the method deployed. In the course of fieldwork in Maharashtra this author was told, "We are all laymen where witchcraft is concerned." In other words, no one likes to admit to a familiarity with the techniques of witchcraft for fear of being suspected a witch oneself.

Affliction is thought to be the result of human agency in some cases, divine in others. Under the rubric of divine agency lies a whole gamut of gods and spirits who are thought to take an interest in human affairs. The divine agents who interfere and cause damage in human lives have been described as peripheral to the central religious concerns of the society in question. This nomenclature is more fully discussed by I. M. Lewis in *Ecstatic Religion* (1971). Children's ailments in particular tend to be attributed to possession by a deity. In Nepal, for instance, there are three deities, Hartimata, Bhat Bhateni, and Swayambuth, whose special sphere of interest and activity is the diseases of children. In India smallpox is commonly attributed to the Hindu goddesses Sitala and (in some regions) Chechak. In such cases it is important to identify the deity responsible for illness or misfortune in order that he or she may be appeased and further damage averted. This is not the case where the afflicting agent is a spirit: in such instances victims and their families express a relative indifference concerning the exact identity of their adversary.

More often, however, affliction is thought to result from the malevolent machinations of another human being. This involves either capturing a spirit and directing it to possess the victim or else attacking the victim less circuitously by magical means. In either event the afflicted feels circumscribed by malice. Social anthropologists have often advocated a distinction between sorcery and witchcraft. The basis for the alleged distinction is that sorcery involves some physical manipulations and its efficacy depends upon learning the appropriate skills or techniques to achieve its ends, whereas witchcraft depends upon the possession of appropriate powers that transform malevolent desires into reality. (For a fuller discussion of this distinction see Middleton and Winter, 1963.) In practice this distinction appears to be more important to anthropologists than to those who bear the brunt of attack by witchcraft or sorcery. Far more important in terms of the severity of the illness, its prognosis, treatment options, and eventual outcome is the source of the affliction—in other words, whether it has been wrought by divine or human agency. It is widely held that where the afflicting power is of human origin the illness is of a more serious nature and less amenable to treatment, whereas illnesses of divine origin on the whole respond more readily to treatment. The idea that humans are less tractable and less persuadable than gods may seem strange from a Western perspective. However, whereas a dialogue can be initiated with a possessing spirit, witchcraft represents an irredeemable breakdown of human relationships: One may plead with the gods but not with an angry relative. In Maharashtra women who have lost status through, for example, divorce or barrenness interpret their plight in terms of attack by witchcraft. This observation appears to be borne out by literature from other parts of the world: Where society fails to care for an individual in the sense of allocating him or her a proper place, there witchcraft is held responsible for the stigmatized circumstances of the individual.

How is spiritual affliction identified and distinguished from natural illness? In some societies certain conditions are synonymous with spiritual affliction. For example, trance is well-nigh universally held to have a spiritual etiology, madness and leprosy widely so. Other symptoms are not so easy to place. In some societies categorization is made easier by immediate recourse to a healer who makes the diagnosis on behalf of the patient. In Nepal, for instance, the bulk of the population initially consult a healer in order to determine the causation of symptoms and to ascertain whether consultation with a medical doctor would be appropriate. The healer will determine whether or not the illness is likely to respond to Western medicine and, if so, when would be an auspicious time to consult the doctor. Failure to consult at a proper time and day may jeopardize one's chances of recovery. In practice, once the healer is consulted, few patients are turned away, as the healer's province of practice is all-embracing. Where the individual alone assesses the etiology of his or her illness, criteria for distinguishing spiritually caused from naturally caused illness are less clear-cut. Spiritual affliction is suspected if Western medicine and treatment fail to make one better, or even make one worse. Sometimes the quality of a pain has a distinctive and unusual flavor that raises instant suspicions in the patient's mind. Respondents are hard put to describe the precise quality of this distinctiveness, however confident they themselves may be of identifying it correctly. In other cases it may be the circumstances, such as an earlier dispute or envious comments, that alert the patient to the possibility of a nonnatural causation of his illness. In Nepal, among people who make use of both traditional healers and of doctors, there is a tendency to take routine ailments such as fevers and diarrhea to the doctor and more unusual or serious complaints to healers. Quite how such treatment choices are made remains to be studied.

It is widely held, but only partially true, that the spiritually afflicted are predominantly women. Informants themselves, both women and men, readily acknowledge that women are more vulnerable to spirit possession. Most often reference is made to women's alleged lack of willpower and alleged emotional liability. Frequently, mention is made of the greater risks run by women during menstruation. At such times women are held to be more vulnerable to attack by spirits. Members of the spirit possession and healing cults of northeast Africa described by Lewis (1971) are, indeed, almost exclusively female. Lewis has been most explicit and influential in his exposition of a specific epidemiology peculiar to spirit possession. Briefly, he argues that deprived women in a harshly repressive masculine culture succumb to spirit possession, particularly if they are embroiled in some personal dispute with their husbands. However, there is danger in extrapolating from these *zar* cults of Muslim societies to healing cults in other parts of the world.

Much of the literature in this area has concerned itself with an interpretation of the healer's art and an exegesis of the symbolism of healing rituals. For example, Larry Peters's *Ecstasy and Healing in Nepal* (1981) provides a uniquely literal interpretation of participant observation and is written from the perspective of a shaman's apprentice in the Kathmandu Valley. As such it provides an extraordinary account of shamanistic theory and practice but conveys predictably little information on the healer's clientele. Bruce Kapferer's study (1983) of demon possession in southern Sri Lanka likewise demonstrates through analysis of symbols why healing rituals may be therapeutically efficacious. A study by the Indian psychoanalyst Sudhir Kakar (1982) suggests that while most of the patients afflicted by *bhūt* (spirit) at a healing temple in Rajasthan were young women, affliction tended to shift between different family members. In other words, the original affliction may well have affected a male member of the family and may then have been transferred to a woman in the course of her caring for the patient. Similarly, studies of illness behavior in England show that women take on the burden of care and support for the sick.This author's study of a healing temple in Maharashtra (Skultans, 1986) finds that women attended the temple in gratitude for past cures, in lieu of another family member, or to accompany an afflicted person. Some women who were themselves afflicted came unaccompanied. All of these cases contributed toward creating a female majority. Similarly, in an earlier study of Welsh spiritualists (Skultans, 1974), this author found that although the spiritually afflicted were for the most part women, the problems that beset them were common to the family. It seems, therefore, that the afflicted are giving voice to wider problems that beset the entire family.

Affliction is most often a family affair or even a community affair. Its social structure is superbly described in John M. Janzen's highly esteemed account *The Quest for Therapy in Lower Zaire* (1978). The family is important in managing the patient and his affliction (Janzen uses the term *therapy managing group*) and is also implicated in the causation of the affliction. The affliction is thus seen as being in large part the responsibility of family and community. While the onus for making major treatment decisions lies with the kin therapy group, so does the obligation to resolve interpersonal conflicts and rivalries within the group. It has become well-nigh a truism that illness—spiritual affliction in particular—provides an opportunity for demonstrating social solidarity through a reassertion of mutual loyalties and common values, and most studies appear to bear this theory out. The very act of reintegrating the afflicted individual into his social group serves as a reminder of the group's identity.

In the course of fieldwork for a Maharashtrian study the author of this article uncovered a complex web of family involvement. Although initially one particular family member would be singled out as in need of help, it would soon be found that the entire family was afflicted. The typical pattern of affliction developed thus: Mothers, or sometimes wives, would bring their psychotic or mentally handicapped sons or husbands to the temple. A short while after arrival the patient's chief caretaker, usually the mother, would start going into a state of trance. Such trance was seen as a diagnostic tool whereby a dialogue could be initiated with the possessing spirit that would provide information concerning the nature of the illness. Trance invariably revealed that the source of the sufferer's affliction was witchcraft (*karnī*) or possession by a spirit (*bhūt*). This malevolent power was directed at the whole family because of some dispute, rivalry, or envy, and the son or husband was seen as happening to be its unfortunate victim. It was thought that the original affliction might be deflected away from the first victim if the mother or some other person took over the burden of illness and that, since the family was the target of attack, any one member could substitute for another. While this belief augured well for the prognosis of individual affliction, it meant also that the individual's cure in no way signified an end to family distress. Informants cited patterns of family illness in support of this interpretation wherein affliction assumed a hydra-headed quality striking different members of the family in different ways. Sometimes one person, most often a woman, would pray that the burden of family affliction be transferred to her. If and when her prayers were thought to be answered she would begin to experience trance regularly and to decline into chronic ill health. Thus female sacrifice plays a central role in the maintenance of family health. A significant feature of this theory of affliction is the shared concern and responsibility it generates for conditions that might otherwise be perceived as extremely annoying. Typically a number of courses of action are open to the afflicted, which can be grouped under the categories of community care and specialist care.

COMMUNITY CARE. The afflicted person may join a community or cult of the afflicted. Here the emphasis is on learning to accommodate the affliction rather than removing it. Where the affliction involves trance, this means regularizing the times of trancing. The affliction is thus transformed from a sudden, unintelligible outburst into a routine and usually mild handicap carrying with it a number of secondary benefits. Foremost among these is the companionship of the similarly afflicted. Such communities do not usually offer specialist treatment, but they are run by veterans who have themselves experienced and learned to live with the full spectrum of affliction. Indeed, cults of affliction share many of the features of Western forms of group therapy.

SPECIALIST CARE. From a treatment perspective, healers can be categorized according to the amount of time they are able to devote to individual cases. Some healing rituals are lengthy affairs spanning several days. Social anthropologists have demonstrated the therapeutic goal, if not the effect, of such rituals. An important ingredient of all such rituals is the symbolic representation of internal conflicts and the process of their resolution; the rituals thus come to symbolize the newly reconstituted self. They are public and involve a large audience. Such demonic healing rituals have been particularly well described by Kapferer in the study already cited.

Most often, however, the confrontation between healer and afflicted is of a more fleeting and less intense nature. Healers who have acquired a reputation for the successful management of the afflicted attract a huge clientele. The more popular a healer becomes, the less time he is able to devote to any one patient. This results in the paradoxical situation that the elaborate healing rituals described in loving detail by social anthropologists are carried out by those healers who have relatively few patients. Such time constraints on treatment are evident in Arthur Kleinman's description of the practice of a popular Taiwanese shaman (Kleinman and Sung, 1979). This shaman is described as spending an average of five minutes with each patient and only two minutes on busy nights. No doubt such restrictions on consultation time inhibit the performance of healing rituals. Thus, it seems, the price one pays for consultation with a prestigious healer is the whittling away of healing rituals. However, the abbreviation and attenuation of contact between healer and patient do not appear to diminish the popularity of the healers or, indeed, their reputation for success in curing affliction. Perhaps, therefore, the power to alleviate the affliction lies as much in the circumstances surrounding the consultation as in the actual consultation itself. Family support for the victim, as well as an explanation of the affliction that lays the burden of responsibility on the family rather than the individual, may play a part in the recovery of the patient.

Psychiatrists have suggested various explanations of trance (the most frequent manifestation of affliction), but none is entirely satisfactory. The most commonly held view, derived from Freud, is that trance is akin to hysteria, a view that unwittingly reinforces the stereotype of trance as a female affliction. Freud himself made the much-publicized claim that he had restored dignity to patients who would in an earlier age have been branded as possessed by the devil. Certainly, there are similarities between the clinical description given of the convulsive attacks of hysterical patients and the behavior of people in certain kinds of trance. The anesthesia of hysterics and the occurrence of anesthetic and nonbleeding areas on alleged witches provide a further point of similarity. Jung views neuroses and possession states as sharing a common etiology, namely, moral conflict, which he claims derives from the impossibility of affirming the whole of one's nature. This state then gives rise either to symptoms that are in some sense foreign to the self or to possession by a foreign being. Both conditions involve an inability to express an essential part of oneself, which is thereupon suppressed and which demands alternative expression. The rudiments of this psychoanalytic approach to possession and trance have become incorporated into many later accounts. However, while having considerable explanatory power, such approaches fail to take into account the element of learning in trancing behavior. In many contexts trance is viewed in a positive, beneficial light and is consciously sought after.

Affliction has a variety of meanings. It may signal the start of a career as a religious specialist. It may usher in an entirely different lifestyle as a member of a cult of the afflicted. It may entail a round of consultations with various specialists who may or may not be able to lift the affliction. Or it may simply be a marker for one of the expected ailments of childhood or hazards of later life.

SEE ALSO Exorcism; Healing and Medicine; Spirit Possession; Witchcraft.

BIBLIOGRAPHY

Frank, Jerome D. *Persuasion and Healing: A Comparative Study of Psychotherapy.* Baltimore, 1961.

Henry, Edward O. "A North Indian Healer and the Source of His Power." *Social Science and Medicine* 11 (1977): 309–317.

Hitchcock, John T., and Rex L. Jones, eds. *Spirit Possession in the Nepal Himalayas.* New Delhi, 1976.

Janzen, John M. *The Quest for Therapy in Lower Zaire.* Berkeley, Calif., 1978.

Kakar, Sudhir. *Shamans, Mystics, and Doctors: A Psychological Inquiry into India and Its Healing Traditions.* New York, 1982.

Kapferer, Bruce. *A Celebration of Demons: Exorcism and the Aesthetics of Healing in Sri Lanka.* Bloomington, Ind., 1983.

Kleinman, Arthur, and Liliash Sung. "Why Do Indigenous Practitioners Successfully Heal?" *Social Science and Medicine* 13 (1979): 7–26.

Lévi-Strauss, Claude. *Structural Anthropology.* 2 vols. Translated by Claire Jacobson and Brooke Grundfest Schoepf. New York, 1963.

Lewis, I. M. *Ecstatic Religion: An Anthropological Study of Spirit Possession and Shamanism.* Harmondsworth, U.K., 1971.

Middleton, John, and E. H. Winter, eds. *Witchcraft and Sorcery in East Africa.* London, 1963.

Obeyesekere, Gananath. "The Ritual Drama of the Sanni Demons: Collective Representations of Disease in Ceylon." *Comparative Studies in Society and History* 11 (1969): 174–216.

Peters, Larry. *Ecstasy and Healing in Nepal.* Malibu, Calif., 1981.

Skultans, Vieda. *Intimacy and Ritual: A Study of Spiritualism, Mediums and Groups.* London, 1974.

Skultans, Vieda. "Psychiatric Community Care: A Maharasthrian Example." *Psychological Medicine* 16 (1986): 499–502.

New Sources

Albl, Martin C. "'Are Any among You Sick?' The Health Care System in the Letter of James." *Journal of Biblical Literature* 121, no. 1 (2002): 123–143.

van Dijk, R. A., R. Reis, and M. Spierenburg. *The Quest for Fruition Through Ngoma: Political Aspects of Healing in Southern Africa.* Athens, Ohio, 2000.

Dwyer, G. *The Divine and the Demonic: Supernatural Affliction and Its Treatment in North India.* New York, 2003.

Hakuin Ekaku, and Norman Waddell. "Hakuin's Yasenkanna." *Eastern Buddhist* 34, no. 1 (2002): 79–119.

Hatamilah, M. A. *Al-Andalus: al-Tarikh wa-al-Hadarah wa-al-Mihnah: Dirasah shamilah.* Amman, Jordan, 2000.

Nichols, Terence L. "Miracles in Science and Theology." *Zygon* 37, no. 3 (2002): 703–715.

Piper, J. "The Hidden Smile of God: The Fruit of Affliction in the Lives of John Bunyan, William Cowper, and David Brainerd." In *The Swans Are not Silent,* edited by J. Piper, vol. 2. Wheaton, Ill., 2001.

VIEDA SKULTANS (1987)
Revised Bibliography

AFFLICTION: AFRICAN CULTS OF AFFLICTION

An important feature of African religions, both historically and in the twenty-first century, has been the interpretation of adversity within the framework of cults, or specialized therapeutic communities. Although cults concerned with affliction and healing are widespread on the continent, the technical term *cults of affliction* has been used in scholarship specifically to describe the healing cults found among the Bantu-speaking peoples of central and southern Africa. The two major criteria of such cults are spirit possession and the initiation of the afflicted person into the cult. These cults have also been called "drums of affliction" because of the significance in their rituals of drums and rhythmic song dancing, both termed *ngoma* ("drum"), over a wide area. Also important in this context is the elongated *ngoma*-type single-membrane drum, which plays a central role in rituals throughout the region. The importance of the drum to these cults can be related to the fact that the drumming is considered to be the voice or influence of the ancestral shades and other spirits who possess the sufferer and also provide treatment.

Societies, History, and Therapeutics. Societies from the equator down to the Drakensberg Mountains and the Kalahari Desert in the south use many of the same terms and concepts to describe their cultural life (particularly in its religious and therapeutic aspects), including terms for sickness, health, and disease etiologies (especially prevalent is the notion that "words" or an ill will may cause sickness and misfortune). Equally common to these societies are various therapeutic techniques and materials, terms for the ancestors, and the concept of *ngoma* as it relates to song-dance communities and therapies. These shared characteristics occur in spite of much local and regional adaptation to a broad range of climates, widely divergent political and economic formations and colonial experiences during the seventeenth to twentieth centuries, as well as diverse responses to various diseases and stressful environments.

Many of the societies of the subcontinent were lineage-based agrarian communities, practicing some hunting and, in regions where the sleeping-sickness-carrying tsetse fly is absent, livestock tending. Especially in coastal regions, commercial cities have emerged, linking the continent to overseas mercantile centers. The region includes southern savanna matrilineal societies such as the Kongo, Lunda, Chokwe, Kimbundu, and Bemba of the Democratic Republic of the Congo, Angola, Zambia, and Malawi; patrilineal societies such as the Luba, Lozi, Nyamwezi, and others of the central region; and in the southern region, the Shona, Sotho, and Tswana and the nearby Nguni-speaking societies of the Zulu, Swazi, and Xhosa. Numerous precolonial states and empires existed in the subcontinent, including the cluster of states of the Luba, Lunda, Kimbundu, and Chokwe; on the western coast, the Kongo, Loango, Kakongo, and Ngoyo states; the states of the eastern lakes, Kitara, Busoga, Bunyoro, Buganda, and, eastward, Nyamwezi; in the Zimbabwe region, the historic state of Monomotapa; and more recently, in the early nineteenth century, the Zulu empire and the Tswana chiefdoms, and the Sotho kingdom in the southern Africa area, associated with the great disturbances known as the Mfecane.

Cults of affliction have related dynamically to these states, either by having been brought under the tutelage of government and serving to legitimate it as a sovereign power, or by serving to preserve segments of society not directly related to the state. In the absence of the state, cults of affliction have provided a format for the perpetuation of such marginalized or afflicted social groups as women, the handicapped, and those struck with misfortune in economy-related tasks such as hunting. They are also expressly concerned with women's fertility and commerce. In some settings, the model of the cult has provided the basis for normative social authority, the definition and organization of economic activity, social organization, and more esoteric religious and artistic activities.

In colonial and postcolonial Africa, the use of affliction and adversity to organize social reproduction has contributed to the perpetuation (even the proliferation) of cults of affliction, often in a way that has baffled governmental authorities and outside observers. Cults have arisen in connection with epidemics, migration and trade routes, and shifts in modes of production. They have also emerged in response to changes in social organization and the deterioration of institutions of justice. Colonialism itself generated many of the cults of affliction appearing in the twentieth-century literature on the subject.

The cults of affliction have provided African societies with a far more pervasive concept of disease and health than that which has prevailed in the Western world. Before presenting examples of the distribution of cults of affliction in several societies, it is necessary to further describe their underlying common features.

Common Features and Variations. Beneath the diversity of cults of affliction there is a characteristic worldview regarding misfortune and how it can be classified and dealt with. Adversities that are regarded to be in the natural order of things are handled through the use of straightforward, often individual and private remedies, techniques, and interventions. Extraordinary adversities, or those that are attributed to human or spiritual forces, can only be dealt with by placating these forces or by intervening in the spiritual realm. Rather than everyday problems, cults of affliction address this second level of adversity. A hunter's chronic failure to find game, an employee's chronic loss of a job or failure to find one, accidents that occur despite taking every precaution, and misfortune juxtaposed with social conflict are all examples of extraordinary adversities.

The worldview that inspires cults of affliction includes as an axiom the idea that ancestral shades and spirits, ultimately expressions of the power of God, may influence and intervene in human affairs. The shades may either be direct, identifiable lineal ancestors or more generic "human" spirits. Other spirits of the central and southern African pantheon may include more distant nature spirits, hero spirits, or alien spirits that affect human events in varying ways. Old as well as new knowledge tends to be related to the shade and spirit forces, as events are interpreted and adversities dealt with. Thus, as common social problems increasingly occur outside the domestic community, there has been a tendency for lineal ancestors to be supplanted by more generalized spirit forces in cults of affliction.

Therapeutic attention to affliction, through the form of cults, often entails the initiation of the afflicted individual into membership in the cult, ideally resulting in his or her elevation to the status of priest or healer in the group. Whether or not this happens (there are many "dropouts" in cults of affliction) depends on the novice's progress through early stages of therapy and counseling, on his or her economic means, and the extent to which the cult's resources are controlled by an elite (where they are controlled, access is restricted). Throughout the wider cult of affliction region, initiation is marked by two distinct stages: an initial therapeutic neutralization of the affliction, and, if the novice progresses through counseling and further therapy, a second stage, a graduation to the status of fully qualified priest, healer, or professional.

The efficacy of the therapy, regardless of its specific techniques, is partly assured because of the support given by the community of the fellow afflicted, who may or may not be the sufferer's kin. In most instances of prolonged sickness in African societies the diagnosis and decisions relating to the course of therapy—the "quest for therapy"—are in the hands of a lay managing group made up of kin. In the cases that come into the orbit of cults of affliction, the support community broadens to include the cult members. The quality of support shifts from ad hoc aid from kin to a permanent involvement with a network in the initiate-novice's life, corresponding to the long-term involvement of the individual with the affliction, or as a healer-priest over it.

Some cults of affliction, such as Nkita among the Kongo of the western portion of the Democratic Republic of the Congo, are situated within lineages. Nkita responds to the unique circumstances and symptoms of lineage segmentation. Appropriately, when a generation of Nkita within a lineage fragment is afflicted, the cult provides the rationale and the setting for the regeneration of the lineage organization, and the members are reaffiliated with the ancestral source of their collective authority. Most cults of affliction, however, occur outside the kin setting. Functioning as a substitute for kin relations, they give the individual lifelong ties with others along the lines of the new affliction- or occupation-specific community. This feature has led some to hypothesize that the cults may proliferate where kin-based social units are in disarray. In the urban setting of South Africa, for example, recruitment to affliction cults is prevalent among those, especially women, who carry the burden of being single-parent household heads.

The cults of affliction are concerned with problems and responses that go well beyond trying to provide an alternative community when kin relations are in disarray. An important function of all the cults is the intellectual, analytical, and diagnostic evaluation of the nature of life and the reasons for misfortune. In this connection, distinction is often drawn between divination, the intellectual analysis of a situation, and ritual therapy, the attempt to intervene in the situation to change it. This distinction accounts for some of the diversity of affliction cult types, for where social change is intense, the need for cognitive clarity increases. Thus, in eighteenth-century coastal Kongo, during the decline of the kingdoms of the area and with the increase of trade, including the slave trade, divination cults—particularly those related to adjudication and conflict resolution—were extremely abundant. In southern Africa today, the term *ngoma* is often identified with divination because of the pressing need for analysis and interpretation of life in a region adversely affected by apartheid. Closer examination, however, shows that the functions of divination and network building are complementary, with both usually present in varying degrees and ways.

Divination, or diagnosis, always accompanies cults of affliction, either independently of the healing role or as a part of the specialized techniques and paraphernalia of a particular cult. Divination must be thought of as a continual querying of the whys, whos, and wherefores begun in the family setting in the face of misfortune, but carried through by specialists with expert judgment and training. These specialists may have had their own profound individual dilemmas or have been recruited to a particular mode of ritual life or been initiated and trained to deal with the spirit world. As a technique, divination may be based on a mechanistic system of signs and interpretations, such as the southern savanna *ngombo* basket, which is filled with symbolic objects signifying human life, the bone-throwing technique of southern African Nguni society, or the recital of scriptures from the Bible or the Qurʾān. Alternatively, divination involves direct recourse to possession, in which the diviner, as medium, speaks the words of the ancestral shade or spirit in answer to the query. Recent observers suggest that this form of divination is on the increase. Some diviners, however, use a combination of both techniques. In any case, these divined diagnoses, representing a type of analysis or interpretation of daily life, are the basis for the more synthetic, ritualized follow-through of the cults of affliction.

Although they vary tremendously, the rituals of initiation, healing, and celebration have common features throughout the area. Everywhere song and dance are at the heart of the participation of the initiate or celebrant. The *ngoma* ("song dance") is the product of the initiate's personal pilgrimage, and its lyrics tell of dreams and visions, as well as mundane experiences. These songs, and their rhythms, create a framework of reality within which the affliction or condition is defined and the remedy or mode of relating to it formulated. Thus, despite the collective setting, a great deal of individualized attention is available. The moving, pulsating context of ritual celebration is conducive to cognitive dissociation and restructuring, lending affliction cults a psychotherapeutic, even conversion-like quality, although they are not sectarian or exclusive in membership. The need to define and redefine experience persists throughout the career of the initiate and priest-healer; seasoned elders continue to deal with their own dilemmas and life transitions.

Beyond these core features, the content of affliction cults varies greatly depending on the scope of issues channeled into the format. It may range, as has been seen, from treating epidemic or chronic diseases and deformities to occupational roles that require specialized knowledge or may be dangerous to the individuals yet necessary to society. In one setting the range of issues may be placed into a single ritual format; in others, issue-linked communities may grow into numerous named orders or dances. These communities may in turn be organized as a decentralized series of local cells, or overlapping networks. Alternatively, the prevailing structure may become highly hierarchical, territorially centered on a fixed shrine or central administration. Economic and political factors often play a role in shaping the structure of affliction cults. However, the taxonomy of issues addressed usually depends on the environmental conditions or on the cults' leaders, who often express their visions of solutions to human needs. The parameters of homogeneous and diversified, decentralized and centralized structures in cults of affliction may best be described by sketching several historical and contemporary settings.

SETTINGS AND SAMPLES. The cults of affliction reveal the greatest concentration of common features in the area where linguistic homogeneity among Bantu-speaking societies is greatest—in a belt across the midcontinent that ranges from Kikongo speakers in the west to Swahili speakers in the east. A brief comparison follows of turn-of-the-twentieth-century accounts of cults of affliction among the coastal Kongo, the Ndembu of Zambia, the Lunda of Zaire, and the Sukuma of the Lake Victoria region of Tanzania, all decentralized societies.

While they were associated with individual affliction in the narrow sense, cults of affliction, or orders, in these societies also related to the sacralization and organization of technical knowledge and its relationship to the legitimation and reinforcement of the social order. Divination played a role, either specific to each cult as among the Sukuma, or as a more specialized set of techniques as among the Ndembu and Kongo, both of whom practiced the *ngombo* basket technique.

Some cults related explicitly to the prevailing economic activity in each society, largely through the cultic techniques that were preferred and the types of people who became afflicted. Thus, in Ndembu and Sukuma society, hunting was the focus of several *ngoma* orders, with specific organization centered upon the mode of hunting (whether bow and arrow or gun) and the type of animal (e.g., elephant, snake, porcupine). The Sukuma snake-handling order was, and is, a prime example of a cult devoted to the control and reproduction of technical knowledge. Known for effective snakebite treatments, the snake-dance society members possess antidotes to the numerous poisonous snake venoms of western Tanzania.

In coastal Kongo several cults dealt with trade and commerce, an appropriate focus, for these important economic activities brought divisive mercantile techniques and attitudes into lineage-based societies, as well as several contagious diseases. On the Kongo coast, where formerly centralized kingdoms had featured appeal courts, the cult of affliction format emerged in the eighteenth century as the vehicle for judicial affairs and conflict resolutions. In nineteenth-century Sukumaland, antiwitchcraft medicine cults were introduced from the Kongo Basin in response to the rising social disorder that characterized the early colonial period. The Ndembu responded to early colonialism with cults of affliction focused on new illnesses, including fevers, "wasting," and "disease of the paths," and other suspiciously colonial contagious sicknesses such as malaria, tuberculosis, and venereal diseases brought in by migrant labor. Everywhere, the cults paid much attention to twin and breach births, and other dangerous or unusual conditions of reproduction.

The label "affliction cults," understood in the narrow sense often used in the post-Enlightenment West, does not adequately fit the cults of central Africa. At the beginning of the twentieth century, in the setting of early colonialism, the *ngoma* groups provided a means of buttressing and celebrating social categories of economic pursuit (land, hunting, trade), social order and justice, and the very fabric of society (marriage, authority, women's health, reproduction), as well as specified areas of sickness in the narrower sense. The celebrative, reflexive dimension of the *ngoma* needs to be emphasized, as well. In some societies, notably those of East Africa, the *ngoma* served as a means of entertainment and competition, as sport, a role that is increasingly prominent today. Indeed, in much of East Africa, the distinction is drawn between therapeutic and entertaining types of *ngoma.* Perhaps the underlying characterization of the historical *ngoma* orders would be that they ritualized key points of the social and cultural fabric that were highly charged or highly threatened. Affliction or misfortune merely served as a mode of recruitment to leadership and a means of reproducing specialized knowledge.

The picture of cults of affliction within centralized states contrasts markedly with the settings described above. In societies such as the Tswana, where historically there has been a strong chieftainship providing social continuity and material support, cults of affliction are less influential or even entirely absent. Cults are known to have provided the impetus for the emergence of centralized polities, as in the case of the Bunzi shrine of coastal Kongo. They have also emerged in the wake of historical states, picking up the aura of royal authority and the trappings of sovereignty and transforming them into the source of mystical power. A prime example of this was the Cwezi cult of the interlacustrine region of eastern central Africa, which is today a limited cult of affliction whose spirits are the royal dynasties of the ancient Cwezi kingdom of the same region.

This dynamic relationship of cults to centralized polities has been accompanied by changes in the way spirits and shades are focused in consciousness and ritual. As the scale or function of a cult expands, narrowly defined ancestor shades may give way to nature, alien, or hero spirits. In a few instances, centralized shrine cults have persisted over centuries, defining primary values and social patterns for generations of adepts. The Bunzi shrine cult of coastal Kongo, the Mbona of Malawi, and the Korekore and Chikunda in Zimbabwe are examples of well-studied cults that, though centuries old, continue into the present. Some authors have distinguished between these centralized, regional cults and the topically focused cults of affliction. But the orders, taken in their entirety, suggest more of a continuum along several axes: centralized and segmentary, inclusive and specialized, controlled by state sovereignty versus independent, or even opposed to state sovereignty. Cults have crystallized opposition to states in both precolonial and colonial settings and, to a lesser degree, in postcolonial times. Thus, the Cwezi cult channeled opposition to hierarchical structures in a number of interlacustrine states, especially Rwanda. Cult leaders organized opposition to Rhodesian labor-recruitment practices and inspired strikes in the mines in the late nineteenth century. There are other cases of tacit resistance to colonial governments inspired by cult leadership.

Through the twentiety century and into the twenty-first, cults of affliction tended to be short-term movements born out of desperation; trying to provide a panacea for society's ills, they are an expression of the pains experienced by a large segment of the populace because of chronic social problems. There has been a great deal of interpenetration between these cults and independent Christian churches and with Islamic orders in some areas such as East Africa. New permanent cults have arisen around such characteristic ills as the nuclear family or the maintenance of a household in an urban setting; epidemic diseases such as tuberculosis and how to cope with the chronic problems related to it; the divination of problems such as unemployment in a proletarian setting; and how to succeed in business or retain a job. Many cults also focus on the alienation and entrapment so common in the African urban setting.

Affliction cults in central and southern Africa have thus used the classic themes of marginality, adversity, risk, and suffering in order to cope with the ever-necessary task of renewing society in the face of the profound economic and social change that has occurred since the late nineteenth century.

See Also Central Bantu Religions; Interlacustrine Bantu Religions; Kongo Religion; Mbona; Ndembu Religion.

Bibliography

The hallmark of scholarship on cults of affliction in central and southern Africa remains the work of Victor Turner, who first gave the subject scholarly identification, in *The Drums of Affliction: A Study of Religious Processes among the Ndembu of Zambia* (Oxford, 1968), and *Revelation and Divination in Ndembu Ritual* (Ithaca, N.Y., 1975). Studies of possession cults in Africa outside the central and southern regions that have influenced research on *ngoma,* and offer comparative perspectives, include Ian M. Lewis's *Ecstatic Religion: An Anthropological Study of Spirit Possession and Shamanism* (Harmondsworth, U.K., 1971), and Janice Boddy, *Wombs and Alien Spirits* (Madison, Wis., 1989), concerning the Zar cult in Islamic Somalia and Sudan respectively; Vincent Crapazano's *The Hamadsha: An Essay in Moroccan Ethnopsychiatry* (Berkeley, Calif., 1973); and Michael Lambek, *Human Spirits: A Cultural Account of Trance in Mayotte* (Cambridge, 1981).

Noteworthy works that have described examples of cults of affliction in general ethnographies and histories, and have focused on theoretical analysis, include the following: *Regional Cults,* edited by Richard P. Werbner (New York, 1977), brings together studies on centralized "regional" cults in southern and eastern Africa, including work on Mbona in Malawi by J. Matthew Schoffeleers, on southern Africa's high-god cult by Werbner, on regional and nonregional cults of affliction in Zambia by Wim van Binsbergen, on prophets and local shrines in Zambia by Elizabeth Colson, and on disparate regional cults in Zimbabwe by Kingsley Garbet, as well as a theoretical introduction. John M. Janzen's *Lemba, 1650–1930: A Drum of Affliction in Africa and the New World* (New York, 1981), details the emergence of this cult of affliction in the context of the coastal Congo trade and slavery. Terence Ranger's *Dance and Society in Eastern Africa, 1890–1970: The Beni Ngoma* (London, 1975), describes the rise of an urban twentieth-century *ngoma* order. René Devisch, in *Weaving the Threads of Life: The Khita Gyn-Eco-Logical Healing Cult among the Yaka* (Chicago, 1993), offers a rich ethnography of a widespread Western Bantu fertility cult. Marja Liisa Swantz describes *ngoma* orders on the Swahili coast in *Ritual and Symbol in Transitional Zaramo Society* (Uppsala, 1970). John M.Janzen, Ngoma, *Discourses of Healing in Central and Southern Africa* (Berkeley, Calif., 1992), undertakes a broad comparative perspective of *ngoma* through regional field studies in Western Equatorial Africa, East Africa, the Nguni south, and the Western Cape, establishing historical connections, common features, regional variations, and theoretical perspectives. *The Social Basis of Health and Healing in Africa* (Berkeley, Calif., 1992), edited by Steven Feierman and John M. Janzen, includes cases by Gwyn Prins on the Nzila cult of Zambia, by Janzen on Lemba, and by Ellen Corin on Zebola of urban Kinshasa and *sangoma* networks of southern Africa by Harriet Ngubane. *The Quest for Fruition through Ngoma: Political Aspects of Healing in Southern Africa* (Oxford, 2000), edited by Rijk van Dijk, Ria Reis, and Marja Spierenburg, reviews and critiques Janzen's 1992 monograph within the context of the contributors' own research on *ngoma,* including those cases of its Christianization within African independent churches. Henny Blokland on Unyamwezi, Annette Drews on *ngoma* in eastern Zambia, Ria Reis on the ideology of the wounded healer in Swaziland, Marja Spierenburg on the Mhondoro cult in Zimbabwe, Matthew Schoffeleers on a Malawian story of a scapegoat king in healing, Cor Jonker on *ngoma* themes in Zionist churches in urban Zambia, Rijk van Dijk on *ngoma* and born-again fundamentalism in Malawi.

Research on *ngoma* has seen the emergence of a number of specialized perspectives. On *ngoma* as protest, Iris Berger's study of the Cwezi cults, *Religion and Resistance: East African Kingdoms in the Precolonial Period* (Tervuren, Belgium, 1981); Peter Fry, *Spirits of Protest: Spirit Mediums and the Articulation of Consensus amongst the Zezuru of S. Rhodesia (Zimbabwe)* (Cambridge, U.K., 1976); and Charles Van Onselen's *Chibaro: African Mine Labour in Southern Rhodesia, 1900–1933* (London, 1976).

On the importance of putting *ngoma* into historical perspective: David Schoenbrun, *A Green Place, A Good Place: A Social History of the Great Lakes Region, Earliest Times to the 15th Century* (Portsmouth, Maine, 1998), situates *ngoma* and related healing in deep historical context provided by historical linguistics. Boris Wastiau's *Mahamba: The Transforming Arts of Spirit Possession among the Luvale-Speaking People of the Upper Zambezi* (Fribourg, 2000), shows the constant evolution and emergence of "paradigms of healing" and the relationship of cults of affliction to states, epidemics, and broad-ranging societal changes such as long-distance trade.

Tapio Nisula, in *Everyday Spirits and Medical Interventions: Ethnographic and Historical Notes on Therapeutic Conventions in Zanzibar Town* (Helsinki, 1999), situates *ngoma* in relation to the postcolonial state.

Musical scholarship on *ngoma*—Lyn Schumaker on the Nzila cult of Zambia, and by Steven Freidson on Tumbuka cult of Malawi, and by John Janzen on *ngoma* in South Africa—and compared to musical healing in non-African settings, may be found in Penelope Gouk's edited volume *Musical Healing in Cultural Contexts* (Aldershot, U.K., 2000). Freidson's *Dancing Prophets: Musical Experience in Tumbuka Healing* (Chicago and London, 1996), and John Blacking's chapter "Movement, Dance, Music, and the Venda Girls' Initiation Cycle" in Paul Spencer, ed., *Society and the Dance* (Cambridge, U.K., 1985) offers a picture of *ngoma* in a typology of Venda music.

Spirituality and by scholars become priests and healers: Roy Willis, *Some Spirits Heal, Others Only Dance: A Journey into Human Selfhood in an African Village* (Oxford, 1999), on the Ngulu cult of northern Zambia, Wim Van Binsbergen, 1991, "Becoming a Sangoma: Religious Anthropological Field-work in Francistown, Botswana," *Journal of Religion in Africa,* 21, no. 4, pp. 309–344.

Finally, recent wars have brought out the significance of *ngoma* in the relationship of war's victims and their survivors to the perpetrators, the articulation of memory and the recovery of society from war trauma. Richard Werbner, *Tears of the Dead* (Washington, D.C., 1991) illustrates this in Kalanga communities in society following the war of independence and the civil war in Southern Zimbabwe.

JOHN M. JANZEN (1987 AND 2005)

AFGHĀNĪ, JAMĀL AL-DĪN AL- (1838/9–1897), Muslim thinker and politician. Born near Hamadhan in Iran, al-Afghānī was Iranian, in spite of his later claim to be Afghan. His own version of his early life was not always accurate, but it seems clear that he had a traditional education in Iran and then in the Shīʿī holy city of Najaf, Iraq. He spent some early years in India, where he first learned of modern Western ideas and observed British rule over a partly Muslim population. From then onward his life was one of movement and shifting fortunes: in Afghanistan, Istanbul, and Cairo, then India again, then Paris and London, then Iran, Russia, and Iran once more, and finally in Istanbul, the capital of the Ottoman empire. Through all the changes there is a recurrent pattern: everywhere he gathered around him groups of disciples; everywhere he tried to warn Muslims of the dangers of European, and particularly British, expansion; and, although he won favor with Muslim rulers, he ended by attacking them for being weak or corrupt and was several times expelled by them.

His writings are few: *Al-radd ʿalā al-dahrīyīn* (The refutation of the materialists), an attack upon certain Indian Muslims who were willing to accept British rule, and a periodical, *Al-ʿurwah al-wuthqā* (The indissoluble link), written with the Egyptian theologian Muḥammad ʿAbduh and addressed to the whole Muslim world. It is not always easy to discover what al-Afghānī really believed, for he wrote in different ways for different audiences. His main theme is clear, however: Muslims cannot acquire the strength to resist European expansion unless they understand their own religion rightly and obey it.

His understanding of Islam seems to have been that of such Islamic philosophers as Ibn Sīnā (Avicenna), reinforced by what he learned from modern Western thinkers. Human reason properly enlightened can teach people that there is a transcendent God and that they are responsible for acting in accordance with his will. Ordinary people cannot attain to such knowledge or restrain their passions, and for them prophets have embodied the truth in symbolic forms (it is not clear whether al-Afghānī believed that prophets were inspired by God or were simply practicing a human craft). The Qurʾān is one such symbolic embodiment of the truth. Properly interpreted, its message is the same as that of reason; thus, as human knowledge advances, the Qurʾān needs to be interpreted anew.

The Qurʾān, rightly understood, teaches that Muslims should act virtuously and in a spirit of solidarity. If they do this, they will have the strength to survive in the modern world. Al-Afghānī's main endeavors were to stir Muslims to such activity and solidarity, yet his hopes of finding a Muslim ruler who would accept his advice were always disappointed. In later life he appealed more to the rising pan-Islamic sentiment of the time, and his writing and activities took on a more orthodox Islamic coloring.

Al-Afghānī's personality seems to have been powerful and attractive, and wherever he went he found followers. At times he had considerable influence, although less than he claimed. In his last years in Istanbul his fame declined, but it returned after his death, and he came to be regarded as the precursor of a wide variety of Islamic movements.

BIBLIOGRAPHY

Nikki R. Keddie's *Sayyid Jamāl ad-Dīn "al-Afghānī": A Political Biography* (Berkeley, 1972) supersedes all previous works on al-Afghānī's life. Using a wide variety of sources, it corrects inaccurate versions given by his followers and, so far as possible, traces the course of his career and the development of his ideas. Elie Kedourie's *Afghani and ʿAbduh: An Essay on Religious Unbelief and Political Activism in Modern Islam* (London, 1966) goes too far in its doubts about al-Afghānī's belief in Islam and about his importance. Keddie's *An Islamic Response to Imperialism* (Berkeley, 1966) gives a full translation of *The Refutation of the Materialists* and some other writings. The weekly periodical *Al-ʿurwah al-wuthqā*, published in Paris (March 13–October 17, 1884), has been reprinted several times in Cairo and Beirut.

ALBERT HOURANI (1987)

AFRICAN AMERICAN RELIGIONS

This entry consists of the following articles:

AN OVERVIEW
MUSLIM MOVEMENTS
HISTORY OF STUDY

AFRICAN AMERICAN RELIGIONS: AN OVERVIEW

African American religions can be studied analytically and historically. Since American religion is a broad phenomenon, the term *African American religion* must be defined. Although Christianity is the predominant African American religion in the New World and blacks have joined every major Christian denomination, they also practice other faiths such as Islam, Judaism, vodoou, and Santeria. Moreover, historically and phenomenologically African Americans' religion and identity often interact. The religious traditions Africans brought to the New World have forged an African American identity, but this identity has developed through a new religious experience shaped by the conditions Africans underwent in the Americas.

Religion, as a discrete phenomenon that can be studied apart from the cultural, social, and political realms of human interaction, is a modern notion that was not held by most of the Africans who were brought to the Americas. Religion encompasses the meanings, symbols, and rituals that interpret and regulate human contacts and exchanges with other humans, the natural world, and the invisible world. Humans must conceptualize, ritualize, and determine the meaning and value of the power they experience in these contacts and exchanges. This meaning applies to African American religions within the historical and spatial context of the Atlantic World in which it arose. Atlantic World describes the world that was created through the contacts and exchanges that occurred between Africans, Europeans, and Native Americans beginning in the sixteenth century via the mechanisms of the colonization of the Americas and the slave trade. The religions of Africans and the religions of Europeans deeply and profoundly affected these exchanges. African American religions must be studied within the Atlantic World's broad geohistorical context and through a comparison with its transatlantic counterparts. African American religions demonstrate certain distinguishing features related to typology as well as to the impact of the race of its proponents within the complex formation of a religious orientation. In this world, where Africans, Europeans, and Native Americans came to inhabit the same geographic and social space, the issue and experience of power appeared in entirely new modalities of nonreciprocity that were legitimated through ingenious social classifications, customs, and mores created by those in power.

These new modalities gave rise to new religious meanings and indeed new religions. Africans discerned and exercised alternate meanings and practices that expressed their unique understanding of the world and their place in it. This practice led to an African American identity with its religious counterparts, originating in the Middle Passage and continuing through the period of slavery. These crucibles transmuted disparate African peoples and religions into an African American people endowed with a range of religious practices and beliefs that distinguished them from their European American counterparts.

AFRICAN BACKGROUND: CONTINUITY AND DISCONTINUITY. A historical treatment of African American religions must begin in West Africa and the religions practiced there; the vast majority of Africans who arrived in the New World came from this region. While African American religions can be studied in terms of their continuity with West African forms of worship, they must simultaneously be studied as religious responses to the radical discontinuity experienced by the Africans who were forced to undergo the ordeal of the Middle Passage. Moreover, these faiths also must be seen in dynamic terms, because African societies were undergoing a process of rapid change at the time of their first contact with Europeans. This contact not only intensified the speed of that change but also transformed its nature.

Unlike most Europeans, Africans came to the Americas involuntarily as chattel slaves; the involuntary nature of their journey provoked a severe crisis of meaning in the souls of the ten to fifteen million of them who survived the Middle Passage. Some of the dominant ethnic groups that comprised the slave population brought to the Americas included the Mandingo, Wolof, Fon, Fulani, Hausa, Yoruba, Akan, Ibo, and Kongo peoples; certain aspects of African American cultural and religious life originated among these ethnic groups. A significant number of Africans who were brought to the Americas from Upper Guinea had been converted to Islam, and some from the Kongo Kingdom had become Christian, but the religions practiced by the vast majority of Africans prior to enslavement are classified as traditional African religions. This term, however, is almost a misnomer because religion was inextricably interwoven with every other cultural aspect of life in most African societies. A person did not have a religious identification per se; rather, people's sense of identity was most often connected to their village and clan.

Traditional African religions were not static because African societies have continually undergone a process of rapid change through the contacts and exchanges resulting from trade, migration, and warfare. Extensive trade networks connected the fishing villages on the coast with the agricultural villages of the interior. When a dominant group settled in a host's territory, either the host group or the dominant group adopted the religion and sometimes language of the other people. Among the Ibo around the Niger Delta region, for example, the Aro society functioned in two important capacities—they performed a religio-juristic role by operating the sacred oracle, and they controlled trade. The Ibo were a stateless society, and because the Aro did not belong to any particular village, they were, at least theoretically, able to pronounce legal decisions through the oracle without partiality. The Aro's pronouncements of penalties became much more severe during the seventeenth and eighteenth centuries, however, after its traders became middlemen in the slave trade.

Creolization in the Atlantic World. A "creole" is a person of French or Spanish descent who was born in a country other than France or Spain, usually a tropical colonial territory. This definition was later extended to include the English settlers in colonial lands; thus, the English colonists living in North America before the American Revolution can also be called "creoles." Creole is much more than an issue of place of birth, however. Creole culture is the result of contact, subordination, and settlement of peoples and cultures within the Atlantic World. The term reflected this broader meaning when it was applied to persons of French and African parentage in Haiti and Louisiana. It has come to connote the result of biological as well as cultural contacts and exchanges. Creolization in this sense was something that started even before Africans were transported across the Atlantic Ocean. It occurred on the islands off the coast of Africa and on the Iberian Peninsula. Indeed, the first enslaved Africans that were imported to the New World in the early sixteenth century came from Spain and not directly from Africa. Some of the religious and cultural manifestations of their creolization established patterns of religious life that were continued by the slave population that arrived directly from Africa. Enslaved Africans in Spain's urban areas formed their own religious confraternities and mutual aid societies to assist with burials, participate in numerous saint's days associated with Iberian Christianity, and help raise funds for their member's manumission. Such organizations were replicated in the Americas and provided a structure through which Africans organized various aspects of their religious and social life. These organizations—called *cabildos*—were noted for the songs and dances they performed at fiestas and holidays according to their respective nations. Creolization is one way of understanding how African ethnic groups adapted, blended, and reinterpreted both African and non-African religious traditions. This process occurred differently in the Caribbean and in South America, however, where Africans retained much more of their ethnicity than in North America. Nevertheless, creolization, in the broader sense of the term, did happen. The first African American religious institutions in North America grew out of benevolent and self-help groups previously organized among the Africans.

North America: Slave Religion. In North America, African American slaves did not embrace Christianity in large numbers until the Great Awakening, beginning in 1740. The revivalists of this period, including the preachers George Whitfield and William Tennent, noted that blacks were among the crowds who flocked to hear them. Despite the positive response to the revivalists made by an increasing number of slaves, by the early 1800s the majority of blacks remained only minimally touched by Christianity. Scholars speculate that the religious practices of American slaves during this period were eclectic adaptations of African retentions and borrowings from their contacts with Native Americans and European Americans. The task of reaching the rural areas where the majority of the black population resided fell to the plantation missions. The growing abolitionist movement in the North put pressure on the slave owners to admit the missionaries. At the same time, however, the missions were compelled to assure the slave owners that Christian instruction would reconcile slaves to their condition. The slaves heard preaching on the Sabbath and, in many cases, at a second evening meeting during the week. Because most states had antiliteracy laws for slaves, instruction was given orally. Sermons instructed the slaves that serving their master was synonymous with serving God and that they should be content with their condition of bondage.

Most plantation owners, however, were never really at ease with the missions' rationale that Christianity would pacify the slaves and rightly so, because the slaves generated their own interpretation of the faith. Even at the risk of beatings, there were always a few who taught themselves how to read out of an earnest passion to interpret the Scriptures directly. These interpretations were communicated by slave preachers in clandestine meetings—the invisible institution—where the slaves met in secret to worship, pray, and sing. In these meetings, they heard the preaching of such leaders as Nat Turner, Denmark Vessey, and Gabriel Prosser. If slaves were caught having secret meetings, they were severely punished. Spirituals that contained coded messages announced such meetings as well as stories of escapes from bondage on the Underground Railroad. At the secret "bush arbor" meetings, slaves could plan escapes and uprisings and contemplate the eschatological message of freedom through their songs.

Categories: Invisibility, Opacity, and Double-Consciousness. W. E. B. Du Bois's *The Souls of Black Folks* was the first phenomenological study of African American religion. This compilation of essays was first published in 1901, and it confines itself to the black religious experience in the United States. What is evident in this classic is that African American religion must be approached through a phenomenology of African American consciousness. Phenomenology basically asks the question of how something appears.

Du Bois begins his book by describing how black people appear, both to themselves and to others, by introducing the concept of double-consciousness. The racial construct constituting an African American identity was seen by Du Bois in relational terms, but it was anything but ahistorical. He situated the black religious experience in the context of the Atlantic World. His doctoral dissertation, *The Suppression of the African Slave Trade*, provided early documentation for the theme the scholar Eric Williams later developed more fully in *Capitalism and Slavery*. African American religion was situated at the core of the modern world's political economy—the slave was forced to undergo modernity and African American religion was a vital component of the struggle to survive that ordeal. William Pietz has documented how, during their initial economic exchanges with Africans, the Portuguese misinterpreted African traditional religions under the category of "the fetish," thus introducing the term into European discourse. African's religions were being "fetishized" at the same time that their bodies were being "commodified."

The experience of being powerless before the absolute power wielded over the slave by the master tended to deprive the slave of agency and self-definition. While undergoing this experience, however, the slave was also intuiting a realm of power that transcended that of the master; by relating to this realm, slaves could construct a collective identity independent of the one imposed upon them by their oppressors. Several African American thinkers, such as Howard Thurman *(The Negro Speaks of Life and Death)* and Benjamin Mays *(The Negro's God)*, have noted how African American religion functioned to help them survive the ordeal of slavery. An African American identity emerged out of the encounter and perception of a God who transcended the master and was for them and with them. Their experience of God's transcendence can be discerned in the lyrics to one spiritual: "Over my head I hear music in the air, there must be a God somewhere."

African American identity was connected with and invoked through this sort of revelatory experience. In *Trabelin' On*, Marcel Sobel argues that a distinctive worldview emerged concomitant with the black religious experience. The black religious experience is something to which white people had no access, because the very nature of their power over their slaves prevented them from encountering the slave as a subject. In his book *Significations: Signs, Symbols, and Images in the Interpretation of Religion*, Charles H. Long has shown that because whites were so assured that their definitions of those they enslaved and colonized corresponded with reality, the true identity of these "empirical others" was rendered opaque. In its "opacity," black religious experience serves as the "critique of the critique," according to Long.

MODALITIES: THE HOLY SPIRIT, MOAN, AND SHOUT. In one of the spirituals, the singer exclaims: "Every time I feel the Spirit moving in my heart I will pray." The Holy Spirit and spirits play prominent roles in African and African American religions. Slaves experienced the spirit through an ecstatic mode of religious perception as a power origination from a divine source that transcended the mundane powers that held them in degradation and bondage. This mode of religious apprehension was not entirely new. Spirit possession had already been something that characterized the indigenous religions Africans practiced prior to enslavement. When spirit possession takes place, the worshipper experiences being taken over by the entity that is invoked—a nature spirit, deceased ancestor, or a god. In the Kongo Kingdom during the late eighteenth century, a Christian convert named Dona Beatrice Kimpa, who may have been a medium prior to her conversion, claimed that she was possessed by Saint Anthony's spirit and that the Holy Family was African. This cultural heritage of participation or connection with the Creator through the intermediary of a spirit or power persisted in North America where, under the influence of Christianity, the African spirits were forgotten or abandoned. Nevertheless, the modality participation and possession by the object of religious devotion did persist in the New World. The example of Dona Beatrice Kimpa demonstrates the involvement of women in the African American religion—as prophets, healers, mystics, and social activists—although they could not serve as priestesses. Additionally, the study of African and African American women's history provides innumerable examples that highlight the relationship between mystical experience and social practice.

As in Africa, Africans in America had no uniform way of experiencing the spirit in religion. In fact, as can be surmised from Bishop Daniel Payne's objection to what he regarded as "the barbaric" practice of the ring shout, many disagreed over what was appropriate conduct in Christian worship. While it is sometimes preceded by fasting, prayer, tarrying, and what Howard Thurman called the "deep hunger" of the soul, receiving the spirit is not controlled by any prescribed technique or practice. The process depends on the temperament and conceptual tools of the person who has received the gift. Thurman, for example, wrote: "As a child, the boundaries of my life spilled over into the mystery of the ocean and wonder of the dark nights and the wooing of the wind until the breath of nature and my own breath seemed to be one—it was resonant to the tonality of God. This was a part of my cosmic religious experience as I grew up." Some viewed Life Spirit as a personal being, while others regarded it as an undifferentiated power. Regardless of the understanding, however, the phenomenon of spirit is a prominent feature in African American religion. Two modalities through which the experience of the spirit may be expressed are the moan and the shout. These modalities can also be discerned in other aspects of African American culture such as the blues, gospel, jazz, black art, black oratory, and black dance.

INSTITUTIONALIZATION. African Americans organized their own voluntary associations before they developed their own churches or denominations. In 1776 Prince Hall and fourteen other blacks founded the African Lodge No. 1 in Boston, Massachusetts. The African Union Society was organized in Newport, Rhode Island, in 1780. This society worshipped in its members' homes and accepted women. Hall and seventy-five other blacks petitioned the General Court for permission to immigrate to Africa. The plans included forming "a religious society or Christian church" on the continent with "one or more blacks [to be] ordained as their pastors or bishops." African American benevolent societies supported and reached out to one another across state lines. The Newport society sent a financial contribution to Saint Thomas Church's building project in Philadelphia, Pennsylvania, just one example of what Will B. Gravely described as "the persistent symbiosis between churches and other voluntary associations in black life." African American ministers engaged in cooperative efforts aimed at social uplift and freedom across denominational lines after forming their own churches. Black ministers also often worked in cooperation with whites to oppose slavery. Black preachers who were prominent in the abolitionist movement were the African Methodist Daniel Payne; the African American Episcopal Zionists J. W. Logan and Christopher Rush; the Episcopalians Alexander Crummell, James Holly, and Peter Williams; the Congregationalists Amos Beman, J. W. C. Pennington, Charles Ray, and Samuel Ringgold Ward; and the Presbyterians Samuel Cornish, Henry Highland Garnet, James Gloucester, and Theodore Wright. During this period, African American Catholics were small in number. In Baltimore and New Orleans, however, they managed to organize religious orders for black women—the Oblate Sisters of Providence (1829) and the Holy Family Sisters (1842).

During the colonial and pre–Revolutionary War periods, the denominations most successful in attracting African Americans to their services were the Methodists and the Baptists. While discrimination caused blacks to form separate religious bodies, they also formed their own organizations to enable them to exercise the power needed to define their destinies and respond to their perception of God's claim on their life. As Gravely stated, "The sacred power that they felt, shared, and mediated could not be contained or isolated from more mundane forms of power." The formation of African American congregations was motivated more by practical and theological concerns rather than ideological—that is, black nationalist—considerations. The Methodists often organized their African American converts into separate congregations that were supervised by a white minister. In other cases, equally objectionable to the African American worshippers, the blacks were made to sit in segregated areas in the sanctuary; they could receive Communion only after the whites had been served. In 1787 Richard Allen (a former slave), Absalom Jones, and others protested the treatment they received at Saint George's Methodist Episcopal Church in Philadelphia by withdrawing from that congregation and using the already established Free African Society as the center of their religious activity. The new organization, Saint Thomas's Protestant Episcopal Church, named Absalom Jones as the first African American Episcopal priest in 1794. The Bethel Church, another outgrowth of the Free Society, became the base for organizing the African Methodist Episcopal (AME) denomination. In 1816 a Philadelphia conference established the AME Church, with Allen replacing Daniel Coker as bishop. The AME Church adopted the Methodist Episcopal Church's Book of Discipline but with more stringent antislavery strictures. AME membership grew to eight thousand people by 1839. The AME spread the gospel not only through the efforts of camp meetings and revival services but also through printed materials generated from its own publishing house. The Book Concern Department, founded in 1818, was the first African American publishing house in the United States.

African American Baptists also organized their own churches during these periods. The first African American Baptist churches were probably those organized in the 1750s on the Byrd plantation in Mecklenburg, Virginia, and in Silver Bluff, South Carolina, by George Leiles. The Silver Bluff congregation's life was disrupted during the War of Independence; the church manager and others sought their freedom with the British in Savannah, Georgia. This move resulted in the formation of the First African Church of Savannah, which joined the Georgia Association of Baptist Churches in 1790. Other African American Baptist congregations were also organized during the revolutionary and postrevolutionary periods in Virginia (1774), Kentucky (1790), Massachusetts (1805), Pennsylvania (1809), New York (1808), and New Jersey (1812). By 1813 there were forty thousand African American Baptists; the majority them, however, belonged to the same churches as their owners.

The African Methodist Episcopal Zion (AMEZ) church began around the same time as its AME counterpart and under similar circumstances. James Varick, Peter Williams, William Brown, June Scott, and others petitioned and received permission from Bishop Francis Asbury to hold their own services in New York City in 1796. This group did not declare itself to be the AMEZ Church until 1799, however, and the church was not incorporated until 1801, when it was recognized by the General Conference of the Methodist Episcopal Church. The first conference was held at Zion Church in New York City on June 21, 1821. The AMEZ Church was the first Methodist church to ordain women to perform all functions except ordination; notably, it was also the first to officially oppose slavery and include its opposition in its Book of Discipline (1820). In 1821 the AMEZ Church had a total membership of fourteen hundred members under the leadership of twenty-two ministers.

Most African American ministers did not exercise leadership beyond the level of their local congregation because they lacked either the means or the ability. Carol V. R. George points out that "while members of the clerical elite traveled, wrote books, and addressed antislavery audiences . . . their less distinguished brothers built Sunday schools, raised money, and joined or sponsored local groups responsive to the community needs, all efforts that had the effects of heightening the racial consciousness and collective identity of black people." The majority of black clergy who served individual congregations or traveled on the circuit lived a precarious economic existence. Few black congregations, whose members often consisted primarily of servants, could maintain a full-time pastor. To survive therefore black clergy had to rely on white patrons or also work as farmers, barbers, or teachers. This predicament left many ministers and their congregations with little time or energy to directly engage in abolitionist activity, even though there was no difference between their antislavery sentiments and those of their more visible counterparts. In *Black Religion and Black Radicalism,* Gayraud Wilmore asserted that, after the Civil War, African American churches became deradicalized. This impression might be justified when looking at the clergy elite, but the vast majority of clergy and churches continued to struggle to uplift their local congregations.

Religious Diversification in the Postemancipation Period. Following the Civil War, African Americans made tremendous gains in the political arena during Reconstruction (1865–1877), when newly enfranchised blacks sent numerous elected officials of their own race to state legislatures and the U.S. Congress. When Rutherford B. Hayes was elected president of the United States, the Republican Party withdrew its support of the black cause, abandoning African Americans to the local white population that quickly disenfranchised blacks through intimidation, grandfather clauses, gerrymandering, poll taxes, and other devices. Approximately three thousand blacks were lynched between 1882 and 1910. In 1883 the Supreme Court ruled that the public accommodations section of the 1875 Civil Rights Act was unconstitutional. In 1896 the Supreme Court affirmed the nation's separate-but-equal policy in the *Plessy v. Ferguson* decision.

In this broad political environment, African Americans continued to organize religiously and socially. Emancipation provided greater latitude to their organizational efforts than what was experienced during slavery. Mobility among African Americans increased dramatically after the Civil War. The black Methodist denominations increased in number and influence among African Americans. The Methodists, however, were never able to compete with the Baptists in winning African American converts to their fold. The Baptist became the major religious force in African American life following the Civil War. As early as 1867 the Consolidated American Baptist Convention was organized. This body lasted until 1880. Baptists were organizing state conventions throughout the South by the 1870s. When the consolidated body dissolved, three smaller bodies arose—the Foreign Mission Baptist Convention of the U.S.A. (1880), the American National Baptist Convention (1880), and the American National Educational Baptist Convention (1893)—that later united into the National Baptist Convention of the U.S.A. Two underlying issues that triggered these bodies were the attempt of whites to exercise control over the black coreligionists and the conflict between conservatives and progressives in the denomination. For example, the refusal of the American Baptist Publication Society to accept contributions from blacks necessitated the formation of the National Baptist Publishing House under R. H. Boyd. Some black Baptist congregations continued to use the Sunday school literature produced by the white publishing house, while others used the material produced by the black publishing house.

The type of piety practiced by slaves did not disappear with the ending of slavery, because their social and material conditions did not change substantially with emancipation. Seventy-five percent of the African American population still lived in the South as late as 1880, and most of them earned their livelihood through some form of agriculture—often tenant farming and sharecropping. As ex-Confederates returned to power and survival became more difficult due to periodic economic depressions, African Americans began to migrate to the North and West. In the West, a new form of African American Christianity appeared: Pentecostalism. African Americans remained segregated, however, regardless of where they resided. The church served as the only institution that could provide group cohesion and self-help. Black churches continued to promote education through the encouragement of Bible reading and the formation of literary societies. They also became social service agencies by establishing mission programs in poor black areas, jails, hospitals, and homes for orphans and the elderly. A Bible school, nursery school, kindergarten, gymnasium, employment agency, and school of music were organized in Atlanta, Georgia, by H. H. Proctor's Congregational church. Another Congregational church, led by W. N. De Berry in Springfield, Massachusetts, organized an employment agency, a women's welfare league, a home for working girls, a handicraft club for boys and girls, and an evening school for domestic training. These kinds of mission programs were duplicated in most urban areas. By the beginning of the twentieth century, however, the complexity and magnitude of the problems encountered by urban African Americans were beginning to outstrip the black church's resources.

By the early twentieth century, African Americans had ceased to be a monolithic entity and were experiencing greater social differentiation, although they still represented a distinct caste in American society. Religious preferences diversified among African Americans, as some blacks became educated or urbanized. Some educated urban African Americans insisted on a dignified worship experience. On the other hand, many black migrants found the formality of the urban African American churches stifling. Thus greater differentiation in African American forms of piety developed starting in the early twentieth century. Many storefront churches proliferated in black urban areas, and various religious figures, such as Father Divine (1887–1965) and Daddy Grace

(c. 1881–1960), started significant religious movements. African Americans also joined non-Christian religions, such as the Nation of Islam—founded in the 1930s by Elijah Muhammad—and various black Jewish bodies that they regarded as being more compatible with their sense of black identity.

Pentecostalism represented a new form of Christianity that emerged among the African Americans who migrated to the western part of the United States. Its historical significance, according to David D. Daniels III, lies in the fact that in this movement African Americans did not just adapt a form of Christianity to fit their needs and circumstances—as had the African American Methodists and Baptists—but instead created a new form of Christianity.

Most historians agree that Pentecostalism has its roots in the Holiness movement that started in the Methodist Church around the end of the Civil War. The roots of the Holiness movement in turn can be traced to the heritage of revivalism in American Christianity. A holiness impulse or stream seems to infuse African American Christianity. The African American Nat Turner said in his *Confession,* "I sought to obtain true holiness before the great day of judgment should appear and then I began to receive the true knowledge of faith." In Topeka, Kansas, in the early 1900s the preacher Charles F. Parham (1873–1937) promulgated the Pentecostal doctrine of a third blessing of speaking in tongues to follow the second blessing of sanctification. The African American holiness Baptist preacher William J. Seymour took Parham's doctrine of speaking in tongues to Los Angeles in 1906, where he led a revival at 312 Azusa Street, the former sanctuary of the First African Methodist Episcopal Church. Within twelve months, the movement had spread internationally. Women played—and continue to play—a very prominent role in Pentecostalism's leadership. Perhaps the greater emphasis Pentecostalism places on prayer and healing helps account for this, since that office is more closely associated with a certain type of charisma.

The emphasis on speaking in tongues, prayer, and healing did not prevent a significant number of Pentecostal organizations from starting social programs, sending missionaries to Africa, and involving themselves in the Marcus Garvey movement and later in the Civil Rights movement. In the early twenty-first century, Pentecostalism was the fastest-growing religious movement among African Americans. Due to racial integration, social class differentiation, and the increased number of black immigrants from outside the United States, however, religious diversity among African Americans has increased significantly. Apart from mainline Christianity and Pentecostalism, African Americans have also embraced Islam, Afro-Caribbean religions, Afro-Brazilian religions, Judaism, and Buddhism.

Pentecostalism in particular and religious diversity in general challenge black theologians, feminist theologians, and African American religious scholars to determine whether these trends have any continuity with the liberationist impulse Wilmore and others have traced from the period of slavery through the Civil Rights movement led by Martin Luther King Jr., a Baptist preacher and theologian. Or should Pentecostalism in its megachurch permutation be critiqued as something that ultimately works against the quest of African American religions for freedom? The Reverend Martin Luther King Jr. led African American Christians in a profound and intense theological reflection on the nature of power in the ultimate sense and in the way it manifests itself in the lack of reciprocity in the global economy. Any new religious movements that appear on the horizon of the African American historical experience will have to come to grips with this question; in fact the viability of existing African American religious bodies will depend upon how effectively this issue is addressed.

Bibliography

The problematic nature of engaging in the study of religion and the notion of the opacity of African American religion is discussed in depth in Charles H. Long's *Significations: Signs, Symbols, and Images in the Interpretation of Religion* (Philadelphia, 1986). W. E. B. Du Bois's *Souls of Black Folk* (New York, 1999; 1st ed. 1903) is the first phenomenological-historical study of black consciousness and black religion; in this classic, Du Bois introduces the notion of "double-consciousness" as a relational term descriptive of blackness in the United States. A detailed historical description of the way creolization began to occur on the African side of the Atlantic is in George E. Brooks's *Landlords and Strangers: Ecology, Society, and Trade in Western Africa, 1000–1630* ((San Francisco, 1993). See also Richard A. Lobban Jr.'s *Cape Verde: Crioulo Colony to Independent Nation* (San Francisco, 1995). The complex issue of how the term "fetish" entered into European discourse through the fetishization of traditional African religions is discussed in great detail by William Pietz in a three articles, "The Problem of the Fetish I," *Res* 9 (1985): 5–17; "The Problem of the Fetish II: The Origin of the Fetish," *Res* 13 (1987): 23–45; and "The Problem of the Fetish IIIa: Bosman's Guinea and the Enlightenment Theory of Fetishism," *Res* 16 (1988): 105–123. The way the Middle Passage and New World experiences transformed African religion is explored in depth in John Thornton's *Africa and Africans in the Making of the Atlantic World, 1400–1680* (New York, 1992).

For an overall view of the black church in the United States, see Carter G. Woodson's *The History of the Negro Church* (Washington, D. C., 1921). For an account of black religion that describes a continuity of the protest element from the slavery period through the twentieth century, see Gayraud S. Wilmore's *Black Religion and Black Radicalism,* 2d ed. (New York, 1983). For an in-depth historical and cultural analysis of the religion practiced by black slaves in the United States, see Albert Robateau's *Slave Religion: The Invisible Institution in the Antebellum South* (Oxford, 1978). For a more phenomenological treatment of slave religion, see Howard Thurman's *Jesus and the Disinherited* (New York, 1949) and *The Negro Spiritual Speaks of Life and Death* (New York, 1947). The growth of the more visible independent black churches in the North is described in Carol V. R. George's *Segregated Sabbaths: Richard Allen and the Emergence of Independent*

Black Churches (New York, 1973). The relationship between black religion and African American consciousness is documented in Mechal Sobel's *Trabelin' On: The Slave Journey to an Afro-Baptist Faith* (Westport, Conn., 1979). See also Sterling Stuckey's *Slave Culture: Nationalist Theory and the Foundations of Black America* (New York, 1987). Excellent studies of the history of the black church in the nineteenth century and early twentieth century is in David W. Wills and Richard Newman, eds., *Black Apostles at Home and Abroad: Afro-Americans and the Christian Mission from the Revolution to Reconstruction* (Boston, 1982); and Randall K. Burkett and Richard Newman, eds., *Black Apostles: Afro-American Clergy Confront the Twentieth Century* (Boston, 1978). Will B. Gravely's article "The Rise of African American Churches in America (1786–1822): Re-Examining the Contexts," in *African American Religion: Interpretive Essays in History and Culture,* edited by Timothy E. Fulop and Albert J. Raboteau (New York, 1997), details the relationship between African American voluntary associations and their churches. In the same volume see Evelyn Brooks Higginbotham's "The Black Church: A Gender Perspective," an article that employs Du Bois's notion of double-consciousness to describe the religious experience of African American women in the United States in terms of "multiple consciousness." For an overall historical treatment of African American women, see Jacqueline Jones's *Labor of Love, Labor of Sorrow: Black Women, Work, and the Family, from Slavery to the Present* (New York, 1985). Jualynne E. Dodson's "Nineteenth-Century AME Preaching Women," in *Women in New Worlds: Historical Perspectives on the Wesleyan Tradition,* edited by Hilah Thomas and Rosemary Keller (Nashville, Tenn., 1981), documents the contribution of African American women to the AME denomination.

For a sociological description and analysis of the forms African American religion assumed in the urban environment, see Arthur Huff Fauset's *Black Gods of the Metropolis* (Philadelphia, 1944). See also St. Clair Drake and Horace R. Cayton's classic sociological study of Chicago, *Black Metropolis: A Study of Negro Life in a Northern City* (New York, 1945). Although the scholarship pertaining to black Jews is wanting, a good place to begin is Howard Brotz's *The Black Jews of Harlem* (New York, 1970). For a good history of the Nation of Islam, see E. U. Essien-Udom's *Black Nationalism: A Search for an Identity in America* (Chicago, 1962). Vinson Synan's *The Holiness-Pentecostal Movement in the United States* (Grand Rapids, Mich., 1971) is an excellent survey of this movement's historical development. See also the comprehensive and detailed article by David D. Daniels III, "Pentecostalism," in *The Encyclopedia of African American Religion,* edited by Larry G. Murphy, J. Gordon Melton, and Gary L. Ward (New York 1993). For Martin Luther King Jr.'s thought, see James M. Washington, ed., *Testament of Hope: The Essential Writings of Martin Luther King, Jr.* (San Francisco, 1986). The relationship between the Civil Rights and Black Power movements and black theology can be discerned in a collection of primary documents by Gayraud S. Wilmore and James H. Cone, *Black Theology: A Documentary History, 1966–1979* (New York, 1979). For a more contemporary sociological overview of the different black religious denomination affiliations, see C. Eric Lincoln and Lawrence H. Mamiya, eds., *The Black Church in the African American Experience* (Durham, N.C., 1990).

JAMES ANTHONY NOEL (2005)

AFRICAN AMERICAN RELIGIONS: MUSLIM MOVEMENTS

The organization of African Americans into movements that identified themselves as Muslim began in 1913, but the history of Islam among black Americans is much older. Indeed, the case has been made that black Muslims, "Moors" in the company of Spanish explorers, were the first to introduce Islam to America. Muslims from Islamized areas of Africa were enslaved in British North America, and a few left narratives of their experiences. Several of these, written in Arabic, are still extant. Missionaries remarked that Muslim slaves in antebellum Georgia and South Carolina blended Islam and Christianity by identifying God with Allāh and Jesus with Muḥammad. In the 1930s descendants of these slaves still remembered how their grandparents used to pray five times daily, facing east toward Mecca. Islam was not widespread, however, among slaves in the United States, the vast majority of whom followed the traditional religions of Africa and adopted some form of Christianity.

Muslim emigration from the Middle East in the nineteenth century did not lead to extensive contact, much less religious proselytizing, between Arab Muslims and African Americans. The potential appeal of Islam for black Americans was enunciated most effectively by Edward Wilmot Blyden (1832–1912), minister for the government of Liberia, who lectured widely in the United States. In his book *Christianity, Islam, and the Negro Race* (1888) Blyden compared the racial attitudes of Christian and Muslim missionaries in Africa and came to the conclusion that Islam had a much better record of racial equality than did Christianity.

MOORISH SCIENCE. In the late nineteenth century, black intellectuals became increasingly critical of white Christians for supporting racial segregation in America and colonialism in Africa. Europeans and Americans, they charged, were in danger of turning Christianity into a "white man's religion." After the turn of the century, Timothy Drew (1886–1929), a black delivery man from North Carolina, began teaching that Christianity was a religion for whites. The true religion of black people, he announced, was Islam. In 1913, the Noble Drew Ali, as his followers called him, founded the first Moorish Science Temple in Newark, New Jersey. Knowledge of self was the key to salvation, according to Ali, and he claimed that he had been sent by Allāh to restore to African Americans the knowledge of their true identity, stolen from them by Christian Europeans. African Americans were not Negroes; they were "Asiatics." Their original home was Morocco and their true identity was Moorish-American. Possessed of their own identity and their own religion, Moorish-Americans were empowered to overcome racial and economic oppression. The doctrines of Moorish Science were explained in *The Holy Koran,* a sixty-page booklet that bore no resemblance to the Qur'ān of Islam. By 1925, Ali had founded several temples and moved his headquarters to Chicago. There he died under mysterious circumstances in 1929. His movement split into several factions, but it survived, as various groups claimed allegiance to several rivals who claimed to be "reincarnations" of Noble Drew Ali. Though heretical in the view of orthodox Muslims, the Moorish Science Temple was the first organization to spread awareness of Islam as an alternative to Christianity among black Americans.

The first missionaries of worldwide Islam to attempt to convert African Americans came from the Aḥmadiyah movement which originated in India in 1889. The Aḥmadiyah, who regarded their founder, Mirza Ghulām Aḥmad, as a reformer of Islam, sent their first missionary to the United States in 1920. During the next decade a significant proportion of his converts were black. The Aḥmadiyah influence was far exceeded, however, by a second indigenous group of black Muslims, known as the Nation of Islam.

NATION OF ISLAM. In 1930, a peddler named Wallace D. Fard (later known as Walli Farrad, Professor Ford, Farrad Mohammed, and numerous other aliases) appeared in the black community of Detroit. Fard claimed that he had come from Mecca to reveal to black Americans their true identity as Muslims of the "lost-found tribe of Shabbazz." Like the Noble Drew Ali, Fard taught that salvation for black people lay in self-knowledge. Within a few years, he organized a Temple of Islam, a "university" (actually an elementary and secondary school), a Muslim girls' training class, and a paramilitary group, the Fruit of Islam. In 1934, Fard disappeared as mysteriously as he had come. The leadership of the Nation of Islam was taken up by Fard's chief minister, Elijah Poole (1897–1975), a black laborer from Georgia, whom Fard had renamed Elijah Muhammad.

Elijah Muhammad announced to the members of the Nation that Wallace D. Fard was actually the incarnation of Allāh and that he, Elijah, was his messenger. For the next forty years, he was regarded as such by his followers, who came to be known as the Black Muslims. According to the teachings of Messenger Muhammad, as he was called, humankind was originally black, until an evil scientist created a race of white people through genetic engineering. The whites he created turned out to be devils. Their religion is Christianity, while that of the original black people is Islam. Allāh has allowed the race of white devils to rule the world for six thousand years, a period about to end with the destruction of the world, after which a new world will be ruled by a nation of righteous blacks. Instead of striving for integration, then, blacks should separate themselves from white society which is corrupt and doomed.

Elijah Muhammad elaborated a detailed program for the Nation that included establishing Black Muslim businesses in order to achieve economic independence and demanding that the federal government set aside separate land for African Americans in reparation for slavery. Black Muslims refused to vote, to participate in the armed services, or to salute the flag. The separate identity of members of the Nation of Islam was reinforced by a strict ethical code. Alcohol, drugs, tobacco, sports, movies, and cosmetics were forbidden, along with pork and other foods identified as unclean or unhealthy.

In the 1950s, Malcolm Little (1925–1965), who had converted to the Nation of Islam in prison, rose to prominence as chief spokesman for Elijah Muhammad. As Malcolm X he became one of the most articulate critics of racial injustice in the country during the civil rights period. Rejecting the nonviolent approach of Martin Luther King, Jr., he argued that separatism and self-determination were necessary if blacks were to achieve full equality. During his pilgrimage to Mecca in 1964, however, he observed the racial cosmopolitanism of Islam and concluded that the doctrine of the Nation of Islam was incompatible with his new understanding of the religion. Breaking with Elijah Muhammad, he founded his own organization, the Muslim Mosque, Inc., in New York City. Shortly thereafter, he was assassinated. The life and death of Malcolm X helped to increase interest in Islam among black Americans.

In 1975, Elijah Muhammad died, and his son Warithuddin (Wallace Deen) Muhammad succeeded to the leadership of the Nation of Islam. Rapidly, he began to move the members of the Nation of Islam toward embracing orthodox Islam. He explained that the teachings of Wallace D. Fard and his father were to be understood allegorically, not literally. He opened the Nation of Islam to white membership and encouraged his followers to participate in the civic and political life of the country. These radical changes were symbolized by changes in name, as the Nation of Islam became the World Community of Islam in the West and then the American Muslim Mission. This last name signified the close connection that Imam Warithuddin Muhammad sought to develop between African American Muslims and the worldwide community of Islam. These changes were rejected by some Black Muslims. Under the leadership of Minister Louis Farrakhan, this faction has broken with the American Muslim Mission, returned to the original teachings and ideals of Elijah Muhammad, and readopted the old name, the Nation of Islam.

Although the Moorish Science Temple and the Nation of Islam have excited the most interest in the popular and the scholarly press, increasing numbers of black Americans have converted to Islam without having gone through the channels of these heterodox movements, as orthodox Muslim societies and associations have placed them in direct contact with the Qur'ān and with the history of Muslim culture and spirituality.

SEE ALSO Elijah Muhammad; Malcolm X; Nation of Islam.

BIBLIOGRAPHY

Essien-Udom, E. U. *Black Nationalism: A Search for an Identity in America.* Chicago, 1962.

Fauset, Arthur Huff. *Black Gods of the Metropolis: Negro Religious Cults in the Urban North.* Philadelphia, 1944.

Lincoln, Charles Eric. *The Black Muslims in America.* Boston, 1961.

Malcolm X, with Alex Haley. *The Autobiography of Malcolm X.* New York, 1965.

Waugh, Earle H., Baha Abu-Laban, and Regula B. Qureshi, eds. *The Muslim Community in North America.* Edmonton, 1983.

New Sources

Austin, Allan D., ed., *African Muslims in Antebellum America: Transatlantic Stories and Spiritual Struggles.* New York, 1997.

Curtis, Edward D., IV. *Islam in Black America: Identity, Liberation and Difference in African American Islamic Thought.* Albany, N.Y., 2002.

Dannin, Robert. *Black Pilgrimage to Islam.* New York, 2002.

Diouf, Sylviane A. *Servants of Allah: African Muslims Enslaved in the Americas.* New York, 1998.

McCloud, Aminah Beverly. *African American Islam.* New York, 1995.

Turner, Richard Brent. *Islam in the African American Experience.* 2d ed. Bloomington, Ind., 2003.

ALBERT J. RABOTEAU (1987)
Revised Bibliography

AFRICAN AMERICAN RELIGIONS: HISTORY OF STUDY

The theoretical and analytical foundation of African American religious studies was initially laid by the prophetic voices of New World blacks such as Frederick Douglass (1817–1895) and David Walker, who put forth critical proclamations that challenged the spiritual integrity of "Christian Americans" while making qualitative distinctions between the "Christianity of this land" and the "Christianity of Christ." The writings of these early scholars reveal the diversity of the black religious experience, providing glimpses into African religious practices (Olaudah Equiano, 1789); the conversion power of the "Voodoo dance" (Alexander Payne, 1886); the potency of rootwork and conjure (Frederick Douglass, 1845; Henry Bibb, 1849); the liberatory praxis of black religion (Nat Turner, 1831); the exigency of black religious institutions (Richard Allen, 1833; Jarena Lee, 1836; Christopher Rush, 1843; George Liele, 1790; Andrew Bryan, 1800; Lucius Holsey, 1898); the efficacy of Islam (Job ben Solomon, Mohammed Ali ben Said, Abdul Rahahman, Edward Blyden, 1888); and the religious revaluation of Africa (Alexander Crummell, 1862; Henry McNeal Turner, 1895). These early leaders and thinkers and their writings provided the scholastic rudiments for future studies and interrogations of the complexity, plurality, and vitality of African American religious life.

W. E. B. DU BOIS AND THE STUDY OF AFRICAN AMERICAN RELIGION. At the beginning of the twentieth century the study of African American religion advanced with greater precision as early black thinkers employed the scholarly tools of historical, sociological, and ethnographic methods. At the forefront of these new interdisciplinary approaches was W. E. B. Du Bois (1868–1963) and his 1903 publications *The Souls of Black Folk* and *The Negro Church.* These groundbreaking works insightfully placed the birth, evolution, and institutionalization of black religion in direct conversation with questions of primordial origins, religious evolution, and the sociological impact of race and urbanization. Du Bois's *The Negro Church* was the first to examine the institution of religion as a valid subject for sociological investigation. Methodologically, Du Bois engaged in both qualitative and quantitative research and conducted interviews, surveys, questionnaires and participant observation. In both *The Negro Church* and *The Souls of Black Folk,* Du Bois undertook the empirical study of black religion as it related to the comprehensive constituents of black life—institutional, political, historical, economic, and aesthetic.

Initially published as a separate essay in 1900, the chapter "Of the Faith of the Fathers" in *The Souls of Black Folk* proffered a nascent theorization of black religion. In this essay, Du Bois documented three salient characterizations of African American religion— "the Preacher, the Music, and the Frenzy"—derived from the encounter between Africa and the American slave experience. Du Bois's famous tricategorization of black religion explored the complex dimensions of black religious leadership; the authenticity of black musical expression; and black somatic experiences with the transcendent. Du Bois positioned himself in these early works as the modern progenitor of intellectual discourses on African retentions, origins, and survivals. Preceding the Melville Herskovits–E. Franklin Frazier debate by several decades, it was Du Bois who first wrestled with scholarly questions of African primordialism and New World religious transformation. For authoring some of the earliest systematic discussions of "voodooism," "obeah," and "hoodoo," Du Bois stands as the forerunner for what would later become the study of African-derived religions in the United States and the Caribbean. More specifically, he provided an etymological explication of the practice of *obi* in the West Indies, arguing on behalf of its "African origin" and its possible connection to the Egyptian notion of *ob,* or divining serpent. Contemporary scholars of black religion often stress Du Bois's assertion that "the Negro church of to-day is the social centre of Negro life in the United States," while giving short shrift to his equally important claim at the end of the same sentence, that it is also "the most characteristic expression of African character" (Du Bois, 1903). The cost of this oversight to the field of black religion was that the church has been privileged as the totalizing symbol of African American religious life, and that issues of religious diversity and alternative religious meanings have been devalued.

Du Bois posited cogent categories of black religiosity that simultaneously oscillated from the African religious heritage of the slaves to their transformative innovations in the black church. A close reading of *The Negro Church* and *The Souls of Black Folk* reveals Du Bois's dual conception of the "Negro Church." Led by a "Negro Preacher" descended from African priests and medicine men, according to Du Bois the Negro Church among the enslaved "was not at first by any means Christian . . . rather it was an adaptation and mingling of heathen rites among the members of each plantation, and roughly designated as Voodooism." In his works Du Bois affirmed the intricate relationship between black religious identity in the United States and its parent traditions of Africa. Moreover, he ultimately critiqued the European categorical construction of fetishism and argued in his later works that it was "invented as a symbol of African religion" in order to reinforce the "idea of the 'barbarous Negro'"

The Negro Church. More monographs that dealt with the Negro Church followed Du Bois's, but many of them lacked the nuanced complexities and keen analytical insights of the pioneering works. Still, crucially valid in their own right, historical and sociological studies of religion such as Carter G. Woodson's *The History of the Negro Church* (1921) and *The Rural Negro* (1930) and Benjamin Elijah Mays and Joseph Nicholson's *The Negro's Church* (1933) stand as premier works in African American ecclesiology. An historian trained in social science method, Woodson provided an overview of the major denominations of the Negro Church and analyzed their development in rural and urban contexts. Along similar lines, Mays and Nicholson's *The Negro's Church,* which was commissioned by the Institute of Social and Religious Research, was a comprehensive study of 794 urban and rural churches in the early 1930s. The authors utilized ethnographic fieldwork and sociological method to examine the internal dynamics of Negro church life as it related to ministry, worship, economy, politics, and demography.

For the next thirty years, black religion and social demographic issues continued to be an important focus for scholarly study. Heralded as one of the earliest studies in urban American ethnography, Arthur Huff Fauset's *Black Gods of the Metropolis: Negro Religious Cults in the Urban North* (1944) expanded the parameters of Negro Church studies to include such religious movements as the Father Divine Peace Mission, Bishop Grace's United House of Prayer for All People, and Ida Robinson's Mount Sinai Holy Church of America, as well as Muslim and Jewish sects such as the Church of God and Noble Drew Ali's Moorish Science Temple. Published a year after Fauset's work and funded by the Works Progress Administration, Saint Clair Drake and Horace Cayton's *Black Metropolis: A Study of Negro Life in a Northern City* (1945) examined black churches in Chicago as they negotiated the social challenges of urbanization, leadership, criminal delinquency, racial discrimination, and social class. More recent studies of religion and urbanization include Milton Sernett's *Bound for the Promised Land: African American Religion and the Great Migration* (1997), James Anthony Noel's dissertation "Search for Zion: A Social-Historical Study of African American Religious Life and Church Culture in Marin City, California from the Migration Period to the Present, 1942–1996" (1999), and Wallace Best's forthcoming book *Passionately Human, No Less Divine: Religion and Culture in Black Chicago, 1915–1952.*

Published posthumously, and nearly twenty years after Drake and Cayton, E. Franklin Frazier's *The Negro Church in America* (1964) continued the sociological study of the Negro Church in the northern United States, adding an extensive discussion of the loss of both an "African cultural heritage" and a structured "social cohesion," which Frazier argued was eventually reconstituted in the institutional Negro Church. The roots of Frazier's arguments were foreshadowed in his earlier texts, *The Negro Family in the United States* (1939) and *The Negro in the United States* (1949), and were highly contested by Melville Herskovits. Often reduced to a debate in the historiography, Herskovits and Frazier were both arguing against natural and social scientific theories of innate black inferiority and social deviance. However, their responses were different. Frazier attributed black social anomalies and cultural distance from Africa to the dehumanization caused by slavery and racism. Herskovits, on the other hand, disputed notions of black racial inferiority with theories of cultural continuity between African Americans and a sophisticated African heritage.

For many social scientists, including Frazier, the sociological study of black religion centered largely around the University of Chicago and stressed the primacy of institutions, social structure, and social organization as the basis of their analytical conceptions. However, as social scientists rather than trained religionists, their conclusive findings were often drawn at the expense of religious fluidity, theological complexity, and religious meaning.

The Black Church. After Frazier, studies of the Negro Church continued as a viable area of inquiry, eventually becoming black church studies. The works of C. Eric Lincoln and others have made important strides in sustaining the broad analytical category of the "black church." Some the these studies include Hart Nelson's *The Black Church in America* (1971) and *The Black Church in the Sixties* (1975); Dolores Lefall's *The Black Church: An Annotated Bibliography* (1973); C. Eric Lincoln's *The Black Since Frazier* (1974); Lincoln and Lawrence Mamiya's *The Black Church in the African American Experience* (1990); Ida Mukenge's *The Black Church in Urban America* (1983); William Montgomery's *Under their Own Vine and Fig Tree: The African American Church in the South, 1865–1900* (1993); Clarence Taylor's *The Black Churches of Brooklyn* (1994); Andrew Billingsley's *Mighty Like a River: The Black Church and Social Reform* (1999); Janet Cornelius's *Slave Missions and the Black Church* (1999); Clyde McQueen's *Black Churches in Texas* (2000); Anthony Pinn's *The Black Church in the Post-Civil Rights Era* (2002); and R. Drew Smith's *New Day Begun: African American Churches and Civic Culture in Post-Civil Rights America* (2003).

A major thematic strand that runs through much of black church historiography is Ethiopianism. Ethiopianism was largely predicated on identifying African Americans with the biblical prophecy of *Psalms* 68:31: "Princes shall come out of Egypt; Ethiopia shall soon stretch out her hands to God." In much of the literature on Ethiopianism, Africa symbolizes for African Americans what Charles Long calls "the religious revalorization of the land," the source of "historical beginnings," and the place of "authenticated" humanity. For rich primary and secondary sources on Ethiopianism see the multiple volumes of Marcus Garvey's writings edited by Amy Jacques Garvey, John Henrick Clarke, Tony Martin, and Robert Hill. Also quite useful is Randall Burkett's *Garveyism as a Religious Movement* (1978). In addition, see St. Claire Drake's *The Redemption of Africa and Black Religion* (1970); the excellent explications of Alexander Crummell and Edward Blyden in Josiah Young's *A Pan-African Theology* (1992); Wilson Jeremiah Moses's *The Golden Age of Black Nationalism* (1978) and *Black Messiahs and Uncle Toms* (1982); and Edwin Redkey's *Black Exodus: Black Nationalist and Back to Africa Movements 1890–1910* (1969).

An additional subcategory of black church studies has been denominational histories that seek to shed light on the diversity of black Christian religiosity. For examples of these studies see Daniel Payne, *History of the African Methodist Episcopal Church* (1891, 1922); J.W. Hood, *One Hundred Years of the African Methodist Episcopal Church* (1895); David Bradley, *The History of the A.M.E. Zion Church* (1956); Mechal Sobel, *Trabelin' On: The Slave Journey to an Afro-Baptist Faith* (1979); David Wills and Richard Newman, *Black Apostles at Home and Abroad: Afro-Americans and the Christian Mission from the Revolution to Reconstruction* (1982); Hans Baer, *The Black Spiritual Movement* (1984); Leroy Fitts, *A History of Black Baptists* (1985); James Melvin Washington, *Frustrated Fellowship: The Black Baptist Quest for Social Power* (1986); Cyprian Davis, *The History of the Black Catholics in the United States* (1990); Claude Jacobs, *The Spiritual Churches of New Orleans* (1991); Evelyn Brooks Higginbotham, *Righteous Discontent: The Women's Movement in the Black Baptist Church 1880–1920* (1993); Walter F. Pitts, *Old Ship of Zion: The Afro-Baptist Ritual in the African Diaspora* (1993); Cheryl Sanders, *Saints in Exile: The Holiness-Pentecostal Experience in African American Religion and Culture* (1996); Gardiner Shattuck, *Episcopalians and Race: Civil War to Civil Rights* (2000); Cheryl Townsend Gilkes, *"If It Wasn't for the Women": Black Women's Experience and Womanist Culture in Church and Community* (2001); Jualynne Dodson, *Engendering Church: Women, Power, and the AME Church* (2002); and Raymond Sommerville, Jr., *An Ex-Colored Church: Social Activism in the C.M.E. Church 1870–1970* (2004).

Finally, although many scholars find the denominational and "black church" approaches useful to the study of African American religion, others contend that while these categories lead to important understandings of black Christian formation, they often run the risk of obfuscating black religious variety. Important essays that complicate and interrogate the denominational approach to the study of religion include Charles Long's "The Question of Denominational Histories in the United States: Dead End or Creative Beginning?"; Nancy T. Ammerman's, "Denominations: Who and What are We Studying?"; and Laurie Maffly-Kipp's "Denominationalism and the Black Church," all of which are included in Robert Bruce Mullin and Russell Richey's *Reimagining Denominationalism: Interpretive Essays* (1994).

African American Religion: A Social Science Perspective. Since the late 1920s social science scholars dominated the area of study currently known as African-derived traditions. At the forefront of these studies were noted anthropologist Melville J. Herskovits and affiliates of the Northwestern School. As the first department chair in African Studies at a U.S. university, Herskovits, along with other well-known social scientists such as William Bascom, George Eaton Simpson, Swiss scholar Alfred Metraux, and French scholar Roger Bastide, devoted their scholarly careers to the study of "syncretic cults" throughout the New World, simultaneously cultivating new theoretical paradigms of syncretism. More importantly, among them were some of the first scholars to engage in ethnographic research on the continent of Africa as a systematic way of exploring the African antecedents of the New World. This group of distinguished social science scholars produced an impressive collection of works. Leading the way was the publication of Herskovits's life-long fieldwork throughout Africa, the Americas, and the Caribbean, starting with his two-volume *Dahomey: An Ancient West African Kingdom* (1938) and continuing with *Acculturation: The Study of Culture Contact* (1938); *Myth of the Negro Past* (1941); *Rebel Destiny: Among the Bush Negroes of Dutch Guiana*; *Life in a Haitian Valley* (1937); *Trinidad Village* (1947); and *Franz Boas: The Science of Man in the Making* (1953).

Furthering the tradition of Herskovits were the works of many of his prominent students, including, by William Bascom, *The Sociological Role of the Yoruba-Cult Group* (1944), *The Yoruba of Southwestern Nigeria* (1969), an early sound recording entitled *Drums of the Yoruba of Nigeria* (1953), *Continuity and Change in African Cultures* (coedited with Melville Herskovits, 1962), *Ifa Divination* (1969), *Shango in the New World* (1972), and *Sixteen Cowries: Yoruba Divination from Africa to the New World* (1980); and, by Daniel Crowley, *I Could Talk Old-Story Good: Creativity in Bahamas Folklore* (1966) and *African Folklore in the New World*; and Johnnetta Cole's *Traditional and Wage-Earning Labor Among Tribal Liberians* (1967) and *Race Toward Equality: The End of Racial Discrimination in Cuba* (1978).

While on a postdoctoral fellowship from the Social Science Research Council, George Eaton Simpson studied with Herskovits from 1936 to 1937. Simpson is cited as the first researcher to undertake the scholarly study of Jamaican Rastafari, "Pocomania," and "Revival Zion," which he detailed in his "Personal Reflections on Rastafari in West Kingston in the Early 1950s." In addition to Jamaica, Simpson conducted extensive fieldwork in Haiti, Trinidad, St. Lucia, and Nigeria, resulting in the following publications: *The Shango Cult in Trinidad* (1965); *Religious Cults of the Caribbean: Trinidad, Jamaica, and Haiti* (1970); *Black Religions in the New World* (1978); and *Melville J. Herskovits* (1973), which examined the theoretical and methodological contributions of the late anthropologist. Translated from French in the 1960s and 1970s, the works of Roger Bastide and Alfred Metraux have also made an enormous contribution to the study of African-derived traditions in the New World. Originally published in Paris in 1960, Bastide's *The African Religions of Brazil: Toward a Sociology of the Interpenetration of Civilizations* documented Afro-Brazilian religions such as Catimbo, Xango, Candomblé, Macumba, Umbanda, and Batuques. In addition, Bastide published *Le Candomblé de Bahia* (1958) and *African Civilizations in the New World,* translated in 1971. Also essential were Alfred Metraux's *Voodoo in Haiti,* translated in 1959, and his collection of photos, *Haiti: Black Peasants and Voodoo,* compiled with Pierre Verger.

THE HIDDEN VOICES OF WOMEN: HURSTON, DUNHAM, DEREN, AND THE STUDY OF AFRICAN DIASPORIC RELIGIONS. Neglected within most historiographical literature is the fact that as early as the 1930s, women scholars have been at the forefront of expanding the study of African American religion. As trailblazers in the field of African-derived religions, Zora Neale Hurston, Katherine Dunham, and Maya Deren excavated the historically maligned traditions of Africa practiced throughout the United States and the Caribbean, and engaged them in their publications as legitimate subjects for scholarly reflection. Combining ethnography and the arts, Hurston, Dunham, and Deren rescued the study of vodou and hoodoo from the nefarious categories of African magic and sorcery, and instead represented them as sophisticated religious and philosophical systems of thought with complex ritual integrity. Also informing their exceptional studies were their unique positions as "scholar-practitioners" who were able to engage their subject matter both as skilled ethnographers and as initiates within their respective vodou traditions. With strong support and encouragement from her mentor Franz Boas at Columbia University, Hurston embarked on ethnographic fieldwork throughout Alabama, Louisiana, and Florida, collecting folklore, tales, idioms, songs, and vodou rituals, which culminated in the 1935 publication of *Mules and Men.* In 1936 Hurston received a Guggenheim Foundation Fellowship to study West Indian practices which she called "Pocomania," "African obeah," and "voodoo." Her *Tell My Horse: Voodoo and Life in Jamaica and Haiti* (1938) is one of the earliest collections of photographic images, transcribed vodou songs, sacred drum rhythms, representations of spirit possession, and thick descriptions of vodou ritual ceremonies. As Ishmael Reed points out in the foreword, *Tell My Horse* is "more than a Voodoo work" in that Hurston "writes intelligently about the botany, sociology, anthropology, geology, and politics of these nations" Moreover, in *Tell My Horse* Hurston provided a foundation for trance-possession theory as well as for a distinct gender analysis of Caribbean and American women. In a similar vein, after acquiring special field training from Melville Herskovits and receiving a Rosenwald Fellowship to study "primitive dance and ritual" in the West Indies and Brazil in 1936, renowned choreographer Katherine Dunham traveled to Haiti, Jamaica, Cuba, Trinidad, and Martinique, documenting the sacred ritual dances of African diasporic communities. The fieldwork resulted in her seminal texts *Journey to Accompong* (1946), *The Dances of Haiti* (1947), and *Island Possessed* (1969). Like Hurston and Dunham, Maya Deren is another of the early female contributors to the scholarly study of Haitian vodou. Combining the methodological tools of filmmaking and ethnography, Deren explored the intricate world of Haitian vodou, documenting its clandestine sacred rituals in more than 18,000 feet of film footage over the course of seven years. Her interest in Haitian vodou was greatly inspired by her tours and travels with the Katherine Dunham Dance Company. In 1947 she received a Guggenheim Foundation Fellowship, which led to the publication of *Divine Horsemen: The Living Gods of Haiti* (1953). Her footage, produced under the same name, became the first depiction of Haitian vodou ritual and possession on film. Ultimately, the interdisciplinary work of Deren, Hurston, and Dunham forged the way for later female theorists of trance-possession such as Sheila Walker (*Ceremonial Spirit Possession in Africa and Afro-America: Forms, Meanings and Functional Significance for Individual and Social Groups,* 1972) and Herskovits-trained Erika Bourguignon (*Trance Dance,* 1968 and *Possession,* 1976).

STUDIES IN "SLAVE RELIGION." The study of African-derived syncretic cults throughout the Americas and the Caribbean by early male and female scholars helped in many ways to complicate and to advance future scholarly studies of "slave religion." Their archival legacies of film footage, photographs, sound recordings, crude musical scores, detailed ritual documentation, ceremonial recordings, etymological speculations, and comparative methods challenged prospective scholars in the field to avoid reducing the complexities of slave religion to binary debates on retentions, and to undertake instead careful studies of religious practice, ethnicity, population distribution of enslaved Africans, linguistics, ritual, culture, orientation, and meaning. Several scholars of the slave period who attempted this approach were Melville Herskovits in *The Myth of the Negro Past* (1941); Lorenzo Turner in *Africanisms in the Gullah Dialect* (1949); Lawrence Levine in *Black Culture and Black Consciousness* (1977); Albert Raboteau in *Slave Religion* (1978); Vincent Harding in *There Is a River: The Black Struggle for Freedom in America* (1983); Sterling Stuckey in *Slave Culture* (1987); Margaret Washington Creel in *"A Peculiar People": Slave Religion and Community-Culture Among the Gullahs* (1988); Mechal Sobel in *Trabelin' On* (1988); Joseph Holloway in *Africanisms in American Culture* (1990); and Sylvia Frey in

Water From the Rock (1991). Other useful monographs and theoretical perspectives on slavery include John Blassingame, *The Slave Community* (1972); Eugene Genovese, *Roll, Jordan, Roll* (1972); Peter Wood, *Black Majority* (1974); Leon Higginbotham, *In the Matter of Color: Race and the American Legal Process, The Colonial Period* (1978); Orlando Patterson, *Slavery and Social Death* (1982); and William Piersen, *Black Yankees: The Development of an Afro-American Subculture in Eighteenth-Century New England* (1988). Recent scholars have also given greater texture and specificity to the study of slave religion by utilizing the primary resources of slave narratives and testimonials. Voices of the formerly enslaved can be found in collections such as B.A. Botkin, *Lay My Burden Down* (1945); Frederick Ramsey, Jr., *Been Here and Gone* (1960); Clifton Johnson, *God Struck Me Dead* (1969); John Blassingame, *Slave Testimony* (1977); John Gwaltney, *Drylongso* (1980); James Mellon, *Bullwhip Days* (1988); Donna Wyant Howell, *I Was a Slave* (1995); and Ira Berlin, *Remembering Slavery* (1998).

Existing alongside studies of slave religion have been important works that explore the intersecting boundaries of slavery, religion, and music. For further study in this area see W. E. B. Du Bois, "Of the Sorrow Songs" (1903); James Weldon Johnson, *The Book of American Negro Spirituals* (1925) and *The Second Book of Negro Spirituals* (1926); Zora Neale Hurston, *The Sanctified Church* (1981); Miles Mark Fisher, *Negro Slave Songs in the United States* (1953); Eileen Southern, *The Music of Black Americans* (1971); John Lovell, Jr., *Black Song: The Forge and the Crucible* (1972); Morton Marks, "Uncovering Ritual Structures in Afro-American Music," (1974); Jon Michael Spencer, *Black Hymnody: A Hymnological History of the African American Church* (1992); Cheryl Kirk Duggan, *African American Spirituals* (1993); James Abbington, *Readings in African American Church Music and Culture* (2001); and Bernice Johnson Reagon, *If You Don't Go, Don't Hinder Me: The African American Sacred Song Tradition* (2001).

EXPANDED STUDIES OF BLACK RELIGION AND THE INFLUENCE OF BLACK THEOLOGICAL DISCOURSE. As scholars outside of the field of religion expanded the corpus on African religious cultures in the diaspora, those within the fields of religious and theological studies began to author texts that gave genuine content to the term *Black religion* within the boundaries of the United States. Within the context of black male-dominated political movements of the 1950s and 1960s, new studies on black religious radicalism and militancy emerged that complemented other scholarship within the broader field of African American studies.

Broadening the corpus to include research on non-Christian traditions, C. Eric Lincoln and Joseph Washington contributed significantly to studies of black "sects and cults." C. Eric Lincoln's dissertation on the Nation of Islam was published as *Black Muslims in America* (1961). Joseph Washington authored and edited several texts that compassed diversified permutations of black religion with attention to race, social power, and theological formation, including *Black Religion: The Negro and Christianity in the United States* (1964), *Black Sects and Cults* (1972) and *Jews in Black Perspective* (1984). Both authors gave attention to black religion as a sociopolitical phenomenon. Their studies also contested the categorical association of black religious cultures with aberrancy, pathology, or social deviancy. Lincoln accomplished this by situating the Nation of Islam within its historical context and by assessing its social influence and appeal through the lenses of gender and class. Washington engaged in similar analysis with reference to his treatments of black Islamic and Jewish movements as well as marginalized traditions of Christian persuasion, such as Holiness and Pentecostal churches, black Spiritualists, and the Shrine of the Black Madonna. Washington's most provocative text, *Black Religion: The Negro and Christianity in the United States*, interpreted black Christianity as a social protest movement lacking a sophisticated tradition of theological reflection, and he blamed white Christian institutions for this apparent deficiency. Washington's interpretation of black Christianity incited a considerable response from religious and theological scholars.

By the late 1960s African American theological scholars began to shape a new school of thought called black liberation theology. Among them were thinkers who wanted to discount Washington's representation of black Christianity. They also elevated his argument against white Christianity by exposing the racism in its theology and practice. James Cone, the most radical voice among them, pioneered this scholarly project with his texts *Black Theology and Black Power* (1969) and *A Black Theology of Liberation* (1970). In these and subsequent works, Cone deconstructed the racist ideological underpinnings of dominant European and white American theological traditions while proposing a contextual rendering of theology informed by six major sources: (1) black experience, (2) black history, (3) black culture, (4) scripture, (5) revelation, and (6) tradition. J. Deotis Roberts, Cecil Cone, Gayraud Wilmore, and Major Jones joined the conversation, each offering a distinctly nuanced interpretation of the connection between black religion and black theology. The conceptual shades of difference in their scholarship would become apparent as black theologians and scholars of religion engaged in forthright discussions about theory and method.

During the 1970s a prolific debate generated comparable scholarship concerning the appropriate aims, sources, approaches, and interpretations of black liberation theology. Three major concerns emerged as themes in solidifying the conceptual and prophetic tasks of black theology: (1) liberation, reconciliation, and violence, (2) black theology, black religion, and the African heritage, and (3) black theology and black suffering. The preoccupation with liberation, reconciliation, and violence derived primarily from a discussion between Cone and J. Deotis Roberts. In *Liberation and Reconciliation: A Black Theology* (1971), Roberts argued that black theology, as a Christian theology, had to include a mature ethic of reconciliation that would account for the imperatives of liberation praxis. Cone was not convinced that this directive was possible before giving extensive attention to the relationship between racial justice, social power, and liberation for African Americans. Writing in the shadow of the assassinations of civil rights leaders and black social unrest in urban centers across the United States, Cone was uncompromising in his willingness to entertain militant social resistance in African American struggles for justice. As many white American religious thinkers and clergy solicited support from black colleagues in decrying the Black Power movement, Cone and other black theologians resisted such cooptation by identifying the imperatives of the Black Power movement with the gospel of Jesus Christ. Cone in particular anticipated that a black theology of nonviolence ran the risk of being appropriated to conceal white racist theological hypocrisy and irresponsibility during an era when brutal racial violence against both nonviolent and militant black activists remained unchecked in white American theological discourse.

Roberts's scholarly contribution is not limited to his ethical imperative of liberation and reconciliation. His extensive corpus indicates a trajectory of scholarly reflection on philosophical theology prior to the formation of academic black theology. In addition, while we might be hard pressed to find substantive data on African contributions to slave religion in Cone's works, Roberts tangentially argued for the import of African religious and philosophical concepts to black theological discourse. This locates Roberts within the conceptual vicinity of scholars such as Gayraud Wilmore, Cecil Cone, and Charles Long on the question of the relationship between black religion and black theology.

The conversation about black religion emerged from a larger discussion among black theologians and scholars of religion, where the parameters of black theological method were tested against the data of black religious experience. In his seminal text *Black Religion and Black Radicalism* (1972) Gayraud Wilmore argued for the expansion of black theological sources to incorporate black folk religion and classical African religions. Wilmore traces the principle of black religious radicalism across diverse black religious cultures and social movements, arguing that when black radicalism waned in the established black Christian churches, it was harnessed in other religious and political institutions such as the Nation of Islam, Marcus Garvey's United Negro Improvement Association, and Black Power organizations and initiatives. Wilmore further raised the question of whether black theology, especially as articulated by James Cone, was ostensibly the "Blackenization" of white theology. In *Identity Crisis in Black Theology* (1975) Cecil Cone answered that question in the affirmative as he criticized his predecessors for premising their works upon Western European doctrinal categories as opposed to organic structures of black religious experience.

Charles Long, the sole historian of religion to enter the dialogue, redefined the discussion when he questioned the merits of the entire theological project as one that ultimately belies authentic features and contents of black religion. Long argued that the suppositional starting point of black theology could never equip scholars with the apposite tools for theorizing about the nature of black religion because many of its dimensions remain outside of the domain of established Christianity (extrachurch). In several essays that were subsequently published in *Significations: Signs, Symbols, and Images in the Interpretation of Religion* (1986), Long made the compelling case for interrogating African American religious formation within the "terror of history," suggesting three conceptual and methodological foci: (1) Africa as historical reality and religious image; (2) the involuntary presence of the black community in America; and (3) the experience and symbol of God and religious experience of blacks. Long's distinct contribution was a sophisticated analysis of attenuated facets of African American religion in black cultural forms, expressions, behaviors, modalities, and meanings such as black music, dance, culinary traditions, bodily memory, and approaches to land and water. Long called on scholars to decode these and other dimensions of black experience as germane sites of religious significations.

Black theologians were apt to talk about the justice of the Christian God and the freedom guaranteed through Jesus the Black Christ of liberation. Long, however, considered the motifs of justice and liberation within a more scrupulous exploration of how alternative symbols and experiences, such as Africa and the Atlantic, convey similar religious meanings of freedom, struggle, and divine Otherness in black experience. Black theological claims about justice and liberation proved especially unconvincing to the black humanist philosopher William Jones. In his text *Is God a White Racist: A Preamble to Black Theology* (1973) Jones identified incongruities in the theodicies of influential black theologians, and concluded that their arguments for a God of the oppressed were seriously flawed in the face of historical and collective experiential data concerning the racial subjugation and dehumanization of blacks in America. Taking this data seriously, Cornel West engaged in rigorous analyses of the systemic impoverishment plaguing African American communities. His article "Black Theology and Marxist Thought" distinctly exposed the superficial attention given to class stratification in black theology, and serves as a concise example of his approach to social criticism and liberation discourse.

Cone attempted responses to Jones, Long, Cecil Cone, Wilmore, Roberts, West, and other critics in subsequent texts and articles. Nevertheless, the early debate in black theological and religious studies is echoed in the arguments and subjects of study embraced by succeeding generations of scholars. In *A Pan African Theology: Providence and the Legacies of the Ancestors* (1992), Cone's student Josiah Young placed African religious cultures and political philosophy at the center of his reflections on Black Nationalism. He also reconceived black religious radicalism and prophetic theology within a distilled analysis of the methodological and theoretical discrepancies between Cone's and Long's approaches to black religion. Since Essien Udosen Essien-Udom's, Edwin Redkey's and Gayraud Wilmore's launching of the study of black religious nationalism, Young and others such as Wilson J. Moses, Edwin Redkey, Eddie Glaude, Elias Farajaje-Jones, and Tracey Hucks have broadened our understanding of this phenomenon across diverse religious traditions in the African diaspora. Although these works largely engage expressions of nationalism within black Christianity and Islam, Hucks's text *Approaching the African God: History, Textuality, and the Re-Ownership of Africa in the African American Yoruba Movement* (2005) distinctly treats the construal of black Nationalism within an African-derived religious context.

Other scholars have revisited important themes and introduced new theoretical treatments of black religion and black identity. Anthony Pinn's black humanist texts *Why Lord: Suffering and Evil in Black Theology* (1995) and *Moral Evil and Redemptive Suffering: A History of Theodicy in African American Religious Thought* (2002), and Victor Anderson's *Beyond Ontological Blackness: An Essay on African American Religious and Cultural Criticism* (1995) forwarded closer scrutiny of unsupported assumptions about theodicy and black suffering (Pinn) and the conceptual framing of "Black experience" (Anderson) in the black theological project.

WOMANIST RELIGIOUS THOUGHT. During the late 1980s womanist scholars began introducing new methodological and theoretical priorities through their approaches to black women's religious experience. Pioneer scholars Katie Cannon (*Black Womanist Ethics*, 1988), Jacquelyn Grant (*White Women's Christ and Black Women's Jesus: Feminist Christology and Womanist Response*, 1989) and Renita Weems (*Just a Sister Away: A Womanist Vision of Women's Relationships in the Bible*, 1988) established criteria for research that would consider the multidimensional oppression of black women in theological, ethical, and biblical studies.

Since the 1980s the womanist school of thought has generated a prolific corpus of reflection around intersectional analysis of race, gender, class, culture, and sexuality. This includes radical departures from theological doctrines and categories of analysis (Delores Williams, *Sisters in the Wilderness: The Challenge of Womanist God-Talk*, 1993, Kelly Brown Douglas, *Sexuality and the Black Church: A Womanist Perspective*, 1999, and JoAnne Terrell, *Power in the Blood: The Cross in the African American Experience*, 1998); studies of prominent black female leaders and black women's praxis traditions with attention to their religious, ethical, and theological import (Marcia Riggs, *Toward a Mediating Ethic for Black Liberation: Ethical Insights of Black Female Reformers of the Nineteenth Century*, 1999, and Rosetta Ross, *Witnessing and Testifying: Black Women, Religion, and Civil Rights*, 2003); studies of literature, music, and folk traditions (Cheryl Kirk Duggan, *Exorcising Evil: A Womanist Perspective on the Spirituals*, 1997); ethics, public policy, and social reform (Emilie Townes, *Breaking the Fine Rain of Death: African American Health Issues and a Womanist Ethic of Care*, and Joan Martin, *More than Chains and Toil: A Christian Work Ethic of Enslaved Women*, 2000); focused studies of intimate violence and abuse (Traci West, *Wounds of the Spirit: Black Women, Violence, and Resistance Ethics*, 1999); expansion of womanist theology to include analyses of African-derived traditions (Dianne Stewart, *Three Eyes for the Journey: African Dimensions of the Jamaican Religious Experience*, 2004); and collaborative texts on the motifs of suffering and hope (Emilie Townes, *A Troubling in My Soul: Womanist Perspectives on Evil and Suffering*, 1993, and *Embracing the Spirit: Womanist Perspectives on Hope, Salvation, and Transformation*, 1997). Indispensable contributions from Catholic womanist thinkers include Toinette Eugene, "Moral Values and Black Womanists" (1988); M. Shawn Copeland, "Wading Through Many Sorrows: Toward a Theology of Suffering in Womanist Perspective" (1993); and Diana Hayes, *Hagar's Daughters: Womanist Ways of Being in the World* (1999). Scholars such as Cheryl Townsend Gilkes and Linda Thomas have also bridged theoretical and methodological gaps between womanist religious thought and the social sciences. Collectively, womanist scholars have adopted and contributed innovative feminist analytical strategies that challenge the erasure of black women in the intellectual canons across the disciplines and that also contest the trivialization of women's studies research, its epistemological foundations, and theoretical frameworks.

SEMINAL ANTHOLOGIES AND DOCUMENTARY HISTORIES. Since the last quarter of the twentieth century, African American religious studies has reached a point of intellectual maturity, marked by its ability to generate several seminal anthologies in black religious and theological studies. Milton Sernett's *Afro-American Religious History: A Documentary Witness* (1985) was the first comprehensive volume to assemble original writings of pivotal black religious thinkers and leaders in the United States from the 1790s to the 1970s. Anthony Pinn also edited *By These Hands: A Documentary History of African American Humanism* (2001), which gave visibility to black humanist perspectives as a category of religious thought.

James Cone and Gayraud Wilmore's widely referenced volumes of *Black Theology: A Documentary History* chronicle the historical development of black theological studies from its nascent articulation within theologically inspired political organizations during the mid 1960s to scholarly treatments of black theology in academic discourse from the late 1960s to the early 1990s. Gayraud Wilmore's *African American Religious Studies: An Interdisciplinary Anthology* (1989) addresses theological studies methods and subject areas across several domains of scholarship in black Christian studies, including biblical studies, pastoral, historical and systematic theology, and ethics. Albert Raboteau and Timothy Fulop's *African American Religion: Interpretive Essays in History and Culture* (1997) and Cornel West and Eddie Glaude's collection *African American Religious Thought* (2003) cover broader interdisciplinary approaches and subjects in African American religious studies. Marcia Riggs's volume *Can I Get a Witness?: Prophetic Religious Voices of African American Women, an Anthology* (1997) interrupts the conventional pattern of associating African American public leadership with the masculine persona.

The history of African American religious studies also encompasses authored and edited volumes on influential black religious personalities. This genre includes multidisciplinary treatments of figures such as Martin Luther King, Jr. (James Washington, *A Testament of Hope: The Essential Writings of Martin Luther King, Jr.*, 1986; Lewis Baldwin, *To Make the Wounded Whole: The Cultural Legacy of Martin Luther King, Jr.*, 1992; Michael Dyson, *I May Not Get There With You: The True Martin Luther King, Jr.*, 2000); Howard Thurman (Alton Pollard, *Mysticism and Social Change: The Social Witness of Howard Thurman,* 1992); Anna Julia Cooper (Karen Baker-Fletcher, *A Singing Something: Womanist Reflections on Anna Julia Cooper,* 1994); Amanda Berry Smith (Adrienne Israel, *Amanda Berry Smith: From Washerwoman to Evangelist,* 1998); Theophilus G. Steward (Albert G. Miller, *Elevating the Race: Theophilus G. Steward, Black Theology, and the Making of an African American Civil Society, 1865–1924,* 2003); Reverdy Ransom (Anthony Pinn, *Making the Gospel Plain: The Writings of Bishop Reverdy C. Ransom,* 1998); and Malcolm X (Michael Dyson, *Making Malcolm: The Myth and Meaning of Malcolm X,* 1995).

Comparative studies of Malcolm X and Martin Luther King by James Cone (*Martin and Malcolm and America: A Dream or a Nightmare,* 1991) and of Howard Thurman and James Cone by Carlyle Stewart (*God, Being, and Liberation: A Comparative Analysis of the Theologies and Ethics of James H. Cone and Howard Thurman,* 1989) also address sites of intellectual correspondences among salient scholars and figures. Collectively, these volumes elucidate the religious significance of these definitive personalities within U.S. society and the import of their intellectual legacies to the study of African American religion and to the wider academy.

AFRICAN AMERICAN RELIGION AND APPROACHES TO SACRED TEXTS. The evolution of textual studies in black religion has mirrored the expansive trend in the broader field. In the arena of Christian theological studies biblical scholars have worked collaboratively and independently on themes including Africa and racial and ethnic identity, slavery, gender, power, justice, and liberation. Formidable scholars have interrogated these and other motifs in critical articles and texts that challenged established methods and theoretical assumptions in the wider field of biblical studies. These include contributions from thinkers such as Cain Hope Felder, Randall Bailey, Renita Weems, Vincent Wimbush, Clarice Martin, Allen Callahan, Demetrius Williams, and Gay Byron. Robert Hood combined his training in New Testament study with cultural criticism and theological inquiry to conduct studies of early Christianity, especially the hellenization of Christianity, in *Must God Remain Greek?: Afro Culture and God-Talk* (1974), and of anti-blackness in Christian literature and the history of Christian thought (*Begrimed and Black: Christian Traditions on Blacks and Blackness,* 1994).

Vincent Wimbush's concentration on the Bible in African American religious cultures and his extensive edited volume *African Americans and the Bible: Sacred Texts and Social Textures* (2000) represent a new expansive current in African American biblical studies. Wimbush's project sponsors and engages interdisciplinary research on biblical studies and cultural studies as they relate to African American religious communities. New studies hopefully will augur a broader conversation among scholars of sacred texts across diverse African American religions. This kind of initiative would involve biblical scholars as well as scholars studying ancient African texts of relevance to African American religious communities. Wande Abimbola's *Ifá: An Exposition of Ifá Literary Corpus* (1976), already widely referenced among Yoruba religious practitioners, would be central to such a discussion. as would Maulana Karenga's works on the Husia, especially *Selections from the Husia: Sacred Wisdom of Ancient Egypt* (1984) and his more recent interpretation of Yoruba sacred texts, *Odu Ifá: The Ethical Teachings* (1999).

NEW TRENDS AND CURRENTS IN AFRICAN AMERICAN RELIGIOUS STUDIES. Since the last two decades of the twentieth century, scholars have been proposing new categories of research and new approaches to established research areas. Two growing rubrics of scholarship concern black religious diversity and black religion, aesthetics, and popular culture, and books and articles on black folk religion and African religious cultures in the diaspora have been published at an increasing rate. These include contributions from Theophus Smith, *Conjuring Culture: Biblical Formations of Black America* (1994); Donald Matthews, *Honoring the Ancestors: An African Cultural Interpretation of Black Religion and Literature* (1997); Peter Paris, *The Spirituality of African People: The Search for a Common Moral Discourse* (1995); Joseph Murphy, *Working the Spirit: Ceremonies of the African Diaspora* (1994); George Brandon, *Santeria from Africa to the New World: The Dead Sell Memories* (1993); Jacob Olupona, *African Spirituality: Forms, Meanings, and Expressions* (2000); and Elias Farajaje-Jones and Kortright Davis, *African Creative Expressions of the Divine* (1991). Salim Faraji's article "Walking Back to Go Forward" is particularly important because it examines the Kemetic deity Heru (Horus) as an important symbol of black religious pluralism and liberation praxis, and it is distinctive in connecting liberation theology to Egyptian-inspired African American religious movements.

Women especially have advanced scholarly knowledge of the breadth and influence of these orientations through archival and ethnographic studies as well as through international research. Among their published findings are Yvonne Chireau, *Black Magic: Religion and the African American Conjuring Tradition* (2003); Rachel Harding, *A Refuge in Thunder: Candomblé and Alternative Spaces of Blackness* (2000); Tracey Hucks, *Approaching the African God: History, Textuality, and the Re-Ownership of Africa in the African*

American Yoruba Movement (2005); Karen McCarthy Brown, *Mama Lola: A Vodou Priestess in Brooklyn* (1991); Jualynne Dodson's forthcoming book, *Sacred Spaces: Religious Traditions in Oriente Cuba* (2005); Kamari Clarke, *Mapping Yoruba Networks: Power and Agency in the Making of Transnational Communities* (2004); Elizabeth McAlister, *Rara!: Vodou, Power, and Performance in Haiti and Its Diaspora* (2002); and Dianne Stewart, *Three Eyes for the Journey: African Dimensions of the Jamaican Religious Experience* (2004).

Studies of African American experiences with Islam and Judaism are also enhancing scholarly interpretations of black religious formation from slavery to the present time. Although it could be argued that the nineteenth-century writings of Edward Wilmont Blyden inaugurated a serious discussion of Islam within black religious thought, a constellation of interdisciplinary scholarly works are helping to contextualize African American Islamic traditions with greater clarity and specification. Significant contributions include Allan Austin's *African Muslims in Antebellum America: A Source Book* (1984); Richard Brent Turner's *Islam in the African American Experience* (1997); Michael Gomez's *Exchanging Our Country Marks: The Transformation of African Identities in the Colonial and Antebellum South* (1998); Aminah Beverly McCloud's *African American Islam* (1995); and Lawrence Mamiya's "Islam in America: Problems of Legacy, Identity, Cooperation, and Conflict among African American and Immigrant Muslims" (1993). *Black Zion: African American Religious Encounters with Judaism* (2000), edited by Yvonne Chireau and Nathaniel Deutsch, is also an indispensable contribution to the scholarship on African American religious traditions.

Within the area of black religion, aesthetics, and popular culture, Michael Dyson has authored several texts, including *Between God and Gangsta Rap: Bearing Witness to Black Culture* (1996); *Holler if You Hear Me: Searching for Tupac Shakur* (2001); and *Mercy, Mercy Me: The Art, Loves and Demons of Marvin Gaye* (2004). Other contributors to this emerging conversation among scholars of religion include Anthony Pinn (*Noise and Spirit: The Religious and Spiritual Sensibilities of Rap Music*, 2003) and Judith Weisenfeld, who has written several pieces on religion and black representation in film, including "'My Story Begins Before I was Born': Myth, History, and Power in Julie Dash's *Daughters of the Dust*" (2003) and "For Rent, 'Cabin in the Sky': Race, Religion, and Representational Quagmires in American Film" (2003).

BIBLIOGRAPHY

For a comprehensive overview of slave religion and slave culture see Albert Raboteau, *Slave Religion: The "Invisible Institution" in the Antebellum South* (New York, 1978); Sterling Stuckey, *Slave Culture: Nationalist Theory and the Foundation of Black America* (New York, 1987); Eugene Genovese, "Book Two: The Rock and the Church" in his *Roll, Jordan, Roll: The World the Slaves Made* (New York, 1974); and Vincent Harding, *There is a River: The Black Struggle for Freedom in America* (New York, 1981). For a more concise version of the religious history of African Americans see Albert Raboteau, *A Fire in the Bones: Reflections on African American Religious History* (Boston, 1995). A discussion of the relationship between black enslavement and black music can be found in Miles Mark Fisher, *Negro Slave Songs in the United States* (New York, 1953) and in John Lovell, *Black Song: The Forge and the Flame: The Story of How the Afro-American Spiritual Was Hammered Out* (New York, 1972). Two texts that attempt to explore the complexities of slave ethnicity and culture are Lorenzo Dow Turner, *Africanisms in the Gullah Dialect* (Chicago, 1949) and Margaret Washington Creel, *"A Peculiar People": Slave Religion and Community-Culture Among the Gullahs* (New York, 1988). Important primary sources that document the experiences and narratives of former slaves include John Blassingame, *Slave Testimony: Two Centuries of Letters, Speeches, Interviews, and Autobiographies* (Baton Rouge, La., 1977); Ira Berlin, *Remembering Slavery: African Americans Talk about their Personal Experiences of Slavery and Freedom* (New York, 1998); and James Mellon, *Bullwhip Days: The Slave Remembers* (New York, 1988). For insight on the intellectual debates concerning African retentions and survivals during the slave period see Melville J. Herskovits, *The Myth of the Negro Past* (New York, 1941); E. Franklin Frazier, *The Negro Church in America* (New York, 1974); "The Debate" in Albert Raboteau, *Slave Religion: The "Invisible Institution" in the Antebellum South* (New York, 1978); and Joseph Holloway, *Africanisms in American Culture* (Bloomington, Ind., 1990).

Three monographs of African American churches in the early twentieth century remain classics: W. E. B. Du Bois, *The Negro Church* (Atlanta, 1903) and "Of the Faith of the Fathers" in *The Souls of Black Folk* (New York, 1903); Carter G. Woodson, *The History of the Negro Church* (Washington, D.C., 1921), and Benjamin E. Mays and Joseph W. Nicholson, *The Negro's Church* (New York, 1969). For more recent studies of the black church, black Christian denominations, and black membership in traditionally white denominations, see C. Eric Lincoln, *The Black Church Since Frazier* (New York, 1974); C. Eric Lincoln and Lawrence H. Mamiya, *The Black Church in the African American Experience* (Durham, N.C., 1990); Alton Pollard III and Love Henry Whelchel, Jr., *How Long this Road: The Legacy of C. Eric Lincoln* (New York, 2003); James Walker Hood, *One Hundred Years of the African Methodist Episcopal Church* (New York, 1895); Bishop William J. Walls, *The African Methodist Episcopal Zion Church* (Charlotte, N.C., 1974); Mechal Sobel, *Trabelin' On: The Slave Journey to an Afro-Baptist Faith* (Westport, Conn., 1979); James Washington, *Frustrated Fellowship: The Black Baptist Quest for Social Power* (Macon, Ga., 1986); Sandy Martin, *Black Baptist and African Missions: The Origins of a Movement, 1880–1915* (Macon, Ga., 1989); Cheryl Sanders, *The Holiness-Pentecostal Experience in African American Religion and Culture* (New York, 1996); Sylvia Frey and Betty Wood, *Shouting to Zion: African American Protestantism in the American South and the Caribbean* (Chapel Hill, N.C., 1998); Cyprian Davis, *The History of Black Catholics in the United States* (New York, 1990); and Newell Bringhurst, *Saints, Slaves, and Blacks: The Changing Place of Black People within Mormonism* (Westport, Conn., 1981). Texts on women and gender within black Christian denominations include Evelyn Brooks Higginbotham, *Righteous Discontent: The Women's Movement in the Black Baptist Church, 1880–1920* (Cambridge, Mass., 1993) and Jualynne E. Dodson, *Engendering Church: Women, Power, and the A.M.E. Church* (Lanham, Md., 2002).

Several important texts in the study of black folklore and African-derived practices in the United States include Newbell Niles Puckett, *Folk Beliefs of the Southern Negro* (Chapel Hill, N.C., 1926); Zora Neale Hurston, *Mules and Men* (Philadelphia, 1935); Harry Middleton Hyatt, *Hoodoo, Conjuration, Witchcraft, Rootwork: Beliefs Accepted by Many Negroes and White Persons, These Being Orally Recorded Among Blacks and Whites* (Hannibal, Mo., 1970–1975); Alan Dudnes, *Mother Wit from the Laughing Barrell: Readings in the Interpretation of Afro-American Folklore* (Englewood Cliffs, N.J., 1973); and Yvonne Chireau's well-documented text *Black Magic: Religion and the African American Conjuring Tradition* (Los Angeles, 2003).

Scholarship on diverse black religious traditions include C. Eric Lincoln, *Black Muslims in America* (Boston, 1961); Joseph Washington's *Black Religion: The Negro and Christianity in the United States* (Boston, 1964), *Black Sects and Cults* (New York, 1972), and *Jews in Black Perspective* (Cranbury, N.J., 1984); Allan Austin's *African Muslims in Antebellum: A Source Book* (New York, 1984); Richard Brent Turner, *Islam in the African American Experience* (Bloomington, Ind., 1997); Michael Gomez, *Exchanging Our Country Marks: The Transformation of African Identities in the Colonial and Antebellum South* (Chapel Hill, N.C., 1998); Aminah Beverly McCloud, *African American Islam* (New York, 1995); and Anthony Pinn, *Varieties of African American Religious Experience* (Minneapolis, 1998); Yvonne Chireau and Nathaniel Deutsch, *Black Zion: African American Religious Encounters with Judaism* (New York, 2000); Peter Paris, *The Spirituality of African People: The Search for a Common Moral Discourse* (Minneapolis, 1995); Joseph Murphy, *Working the Spirit: Ceremonies of the African Diaspora* (Boston, 1994); George Brandon, *Santeria From Africa to the New World: The Dead Sell Memories* (Bloomington, Ind., 1993); Elias Farajaje-Jones and Kortright Davis, eds., *African Creative Expressions of the Divine* (Washington, D.C., 2000); Elias Farajaje-Jones, *In Search of Zion: The Spiritual Significance of Africa in Black Religious Movements* (New York, 1990); Salim Faraji's "Walking Back to Go Forward," in Garth Baker-Fletcher, ed., *Black Religion After the Million Man March* (Maryknoll, N.Y., 1998); Yvonne Chireau, *Black Magic* (Berkeley, Calif., 2003); Rachel Harding, *A Refuge in Thunder: Candomblé and Alternative Spaces of Blackness*, Bloomington, Ind., 2000); Karen McCarthy Brown, *Mama Lola: A Vodou Priestess in Brooklyn* (Berkeley, Calif., 1991); Elizabeth McAlister, *Rara!: Vodou, Power, and Performance in Haiti and Its Diaspora* (Berkeley, Calif., 2002); Kamari Clarke, *Mapping Yoruba Networks: Power and Agency in the Making of Transnational Communities* (Durham, N.C., 2004); Dianne Stewart, *Three Eyes for the Journey: African Dimensions of the Jamaican Religious Experience* (New York, 2004); and Josiah Young, *Dogged Strength Within the Veil: Africana Spirituality and the Mysterious Love of God* (Harrisburg, Pa., 2003).

For substantial theoretical treatments of African American religion see Charles Long, *Significations: Signs, Symbols, and Images in the Interpretation of Religion* (Philadelphia, 1986); Theophus Smith, *Conjuring Culture: Biblical Formations of Black America* (New York, 1994); and Donald Matthews, *Honoring the Ancestors: An African Cultural Interpretation of Black Religion and Literature* (New York, 1997).

The most comprehensive introduction to black theology, including discussion of womanist theology and the debate between black theologians and scholars of religion, is James Cone and Gayraud Wilmore's *Black Theology: A Documentary History,* Volume One: *1966–1979* (Maryknoll, N.Y., 1993) and *Black Theology: A Documentary History,* Volume Two: *1980–1992* (Maryknoll, N.Y., 1993). Mark Chapman's extensive annotated bibliographies in both volumes contain many of the references cited in this essay in addition to other works covering areas such as pastoral theology and liturgical studies. For Cornel West's early contributions to African American religious studies see *Prophesy Deliverance: An Afro-American Revolutionary Christianity* (Philadelphia, 1982) and *Prophetic Fragments* (Grand Rapids, Mich., 1988).

In addition to the womanist texts and articles already cited in this essay and the ones included and cited in *Black Theology: A Documentary History,* see N. Lynn Westfield, *Dear Sister: A Womanist Practice of Hospitality* (Cleveland, Ohio, 2001); Linda Thomas, *Under the Canopy: Ritual Process and Spiritual Resilience in South Africa* (Columbia, S.C., 1999) and "Womanist Theology, Epistemology, and a New Anthropological Paradigm," *Cross Currents* 48, no. 4 (Winter 1998–1999): 488–499; Cheryl Townsend Gilkes, *If It Wasn't For the Women* (New York, 2001); Stephanie Mitchem, *Introducing Womanist Theology* (Maryknoll, N.Y., (2002).

See references listed in this essay regarding anthologies, documentary and biographical studies. Edited texts containing works of pivotal scholars in biblical studies are Cain Hope Felder, ed., *Stony the Road We Trod* (Minneapolis, 1991) and Vincent Wimbush, ed., *African Americans and the Bible: Sacred Texts and Social Textures* (New York, 2000). Also see Cain Hope Felder, *Troubling Biblical Waters: Race, Class, and Family* (Maryknoll, N.Y., 1989). On cultural approaches to sacred texts in African American religious studies see Gay Byron, *Symbolic Blackness and Ethnic Difference in Early Christian Literature* (New York, 2002); Robert Hood's *Must God Remain Greek?: Afro Culture and God-Talk* (Minneapolis, 1974) and his *Begrimed and Black: Christian Traditions on Blacks and Blackness* (Minneapolis, 1994); Wande Abimbola's *Ifa: An Exposition of Ifa Literary Corpus* (Ibadan, Nigeria, 1976); Maulana Karenga's *Selections from the Husia: Sacred Wisdom of Ancient Egypt* (Los Angeles, 1984) and *Odu Ifa: The Ethical Teachings* (Los Angeles, 1999).

For treatments of black religion and popular culture see Michael Dyson's *Between God and Gangsta Rap: Bearing Witness to Black Culture* (New York, 1996), *Holler if You Hear Me: Searching for Tupac Shakur* (New York, 2001), and *Mercy, Mercy Me: The Art, Loves and Demons of Marvin Gaye* (New York, 2004); Anthony Pinn, *Noise and Spirit: The Religious and Spiritual Sensibilities of Rap Music* (New York, 2003); and Judith Weisenfeld, "My Story Begins Before I was Born: Myth, History, and Power in Julie Dash's *Daughters of the Dust*" in *Representing Religion in World Cinema: Filmmaking, Mythmaking, Culture Making,* edited by Brent Plate (New York, 2003) and Weisenfeld's "For Rent, 'Cabin in the Sky':

Race, Religion, and Representational Quagmires in American Film," in *African American Religious Thought: An Anthology*, edited by Cornel West and Eddie Glaude (Knoxville, Tenn., 2003).

TRACEY E. HUCKS (2005)
DIANNE M. STEWART (2005)

AFRICAN RELIGIONS

This entry consists of the following articles:

AN OVERVIEW
MYTHIC THEMES
NEW RELIGIOUS MOVEMENTS
HISTORY OF STUDY

AFRICAN RELIGIONS: AN OVERVIEW

Prior to the coming of Christianity and Islam to Africa, the peoples south of the Sahara developed their own religious systems, and these formed the basis of much of their social and cultural life. At present the indigenous religions, modified by colonial and postcolonial experience, continue to exist alongside Christianity and Islam and to play an important role in daily existence.

African traditional religions are closely tied to ethnic groups. Hence it may be said that there are as many different "religions" as there are ethnic language groups, which number more than seven hundred south of the Sahara. There are, however, many similarities among the religious ideas and practices of major cultural and linguistic areas (e.g., Guinea Coast, central Bantu, Nilotes), and certain fundamental features are common to almost all African religions. Although these features are not unique to Africa, taken together they constitute a distinctively African pattern of religious thought and action.

HISTORICAL BACKGROUND. Except for the most recent colonial and precolonial past, there is little evidence concerning the early history of African religions, especially from the remote Paleolithic period. Because of the conditions of climate and habitation, archaeological remains, such as pottery, stone implements, bronze and stone figures, earthworks, and rock paintings, have been discovered at only a few places in eastern, western, and southern Africa, and the cultural contexts of these finds are largely unknown. It was once supposed that the various contemporary hunting-gathering, agricultural, and pastoral societies in Africa developed from a few basic cultural systems, or civilizations, each with its own set of linguistic, racial, religious, economic, and material cultural characteristics. Thus the early cultural and religious history of African societies was seen in terms of the interaction and intermixture of these hypothetical cultural systems, producing the more complex cultural and religious patterns of today. But it is now recognized that elements of language, race, religion, economics, and material culture are not so closely related as was assumed and that the early cultural systems were too speculatively defined. Hence historical reconstruction on these grounds has been abandoned.

Nevertheless, research has been able to bring to light important evidence concerning the early phases of religion in certain areas. The rock paintings of southern Africa, which date mostly from the nineteenth century but also from 2000 and 6000 and 26,000 BP, appear to represent a continuous tradition of shamanism practiced by the San hunters and their ancestors. Nineteenth-century and contemporary San ethnography suggest that shamanistic trance states, induced by dancing, are the subject matter of much southern African rock art. In trance states, San men experience the presence of a sacred power in their bodies, a power that also exists in certain animals, especially the eland, a large antelope. When this power enters the dancing men, they fall into a state of deep trance, or "half-death," as the !Kung San call it. Trance enables the men to perform three kinds of acts: the luring of large game animals to the hunters, the curing of illness, and the causing of rain by killing of special "rain animals." The rock art painted by the San and their ancestors shows men performing each of these tasks. The visual signs of trance that appear in the art are bleeding from the nose, perspiration, dancing, lines piercing (or extending from) the head, the wearing of caps with antelope ears, and the partial transformation of men into animals, especially antelopes. While manifesting these signs of trance, men are shown bending over people and drawing out illness, shooting rain animals, and luring game by ritual means. There is no indication that the art itself was regarded as magical; instead, the paintings depict the ritual acts and visionary experiences by which the shamans governed the relationships between human beings, animals, and the spirits of the dead. These relationships lay at the core of San society, and the rock paintings may well record practices that date from the earliest times in southern Africa.

When agriculture began to spread south of the Sahara around 1500 BCE, an important religious development accompanied the gradual change from hunting-gathering to agricultural economies. This was the emergence of territorial cults, organized around local shrines and priests related to the land, crop production, and rain. These autochthonous cults provided political and religious leadership at the local level and also at the clan and tribal level. In central Africa the oral tradition and known history of some territorial cults date back five or six centuries and have been the key to historical reconstruction of religion in this area.

When ironworking penetrated sub-Saharan Africa in 400–500 CE, it gave rise to a number of myths, rites, and symbolic forms. Ironworking was said to have been brought by a mythic culture hero, blacksmiths were regarded as a special caste subject to ritual prohibitions, and the blacksmith's forge was sometimes regarded as a sanctuary. Iron itself was thought to have sacred properties. Throughout West Africa ironmaking, hunting, and sometimes warfare formed a sacred complex of rites and symbols under the tutelage of a culture hero or deity.

In northern Nigeria more than 150 terra-cotta figures have been found dating from at least 500 BCE to 200 CE, the earliest known terra-cotta sculpture in sub-Saharan Africa. This sculpture, known as Nok sculpture after the site at which it was first found, consists of both human and animal figures. Although it is likely that these pieces had religious significance, either as grave goods or ritual objects (or both), their meaning at present is entirely unknown.

The famous bronze heads of Ife, Nigeria, date from the twelfth to fifteenth centuries and may be distantly related to Nok sculpture. The sixteen naturalistic Ife heads were found in the ground near the royal palace at Ife. The heads have holes to which beards and crowns were attached. Each head may have represented one of the founders of the sixteen city-states that owed allegiance to Ife, and each may have carried one of the sixteen crowns. Among the Yoruba, the "head" *(ori)* is the bearer of a person's destiny, and the "head" or destiny of a king was to wear the crown. The crown was the symbol of the sacred *aṣẹ,* or power of the king, which the crown or the head itself may have contained. Bronze heads were also made in the kingdom of Benin, an offshoot of Ife located to the southeast, where they served as shrines for deceased Bini kings.

In southern Africa the wall ruins of Great Zimbabwe in present-day Zimbabwe belong to a cultural complex that evolved in the early twelfth century. Great Zimbabwe was the political capital of the Shona kings for two hundred years, until 1450. The ancestors of the kingship seem to have been represented by large, eaglelike sculptures with human characteristics, and these are thought to have been the focus of the royal ancestor cult.

Wherever kingship arose in Africa during the thirteenth to fifteenth centuries, it became a dominant part of the religious system. The rulers, whether sacred or secular, generally attained total or partial control of the preexisting territorial cults above the local level. Oral tradition usually records the encounter between the conquering kings and the autochthonous cults, which sometimes put up resistance. This encounter was often memorialized in the form of annual rites that recalled the initial conquest and subsequent accommodation between the king and the autochthonous cults whose powers over the land were necessary fro the welfare of the state. For example, at Ife there is an annual ceremonial enactment of the defeat and return of the indigenous creator god Ọbatala (also known as Oriṣa-nla), and the restoration of his cult in the city. In other cases, the local cults were taken over and grafted onto the royal cult. Thus the Lundu kings took over the preroyal cults of the supreme being in Malawi, Zimbabwe, and Mozambique and incorporated their priests and prophets into the royal sphere.

Most kings were regarded as gods or as the descendants of gods and were spiritually related to the fertility of the land and to the welfare of the people. Even in Buganda in central Uganda, where they did not have such mystical powers, the kings were regarded as sacred personages. It has become recognized that the institution of sacred kingship, which was once thought to be derived from ancient Egypt because of some general similarities with sub-Saharan kingships, was independently invented in various places in the African continent, not only in Egypt.

From the seventeenth to early nineteenth centuries, there is evidence of two types of development: an increase in spirit possession and healing cults, generally known as cults of affliction, and an emphasis upon the concept of the supreme being. The emergence of popular healing cults seems to have been linked to a breakdown in local political institutions and to contact with outside forces and new diseases. The well-documented Lemba cult in the western portion of the Democratic Republic of the Congo, which dates from the seventeenth century to the early twentieth century, was but one of many *ngoma* ("drum") therapies that were, and still are, characteristic of the religions of the Bantu-speaking peoples of central and southern Africa. During the same period, the growing importance of the concept of supreme being appears to have been linked to the enlargement of political scale and to the need to explain widespread social and political changes at the most universal level.

General Characteristics. Common to most African religions is the notion of the imperfect nature of the human condition. Almost every society has a creation myth that tells about the origins of human life and death. According to this myth, the first human beings were immortal; there was no suffering, sickness, or death. This situation came to an end because of an accident or act of disobedience. Whatever the cause, the myth explains why sickness, toil, suffering, and death are fundamental to human existence.

The counterpart to this idea is the notion that the problems of human life may be alleviated through ritual action. African religions are systems of explanation and control of immediate experience. They do not promise personal salvation in the afterlife or the salvation of the world at some future time. The promise of African religions is the renewal of human affairs here and now, a this-worldly form of salvation. Through ritual action misfortunes may be overcome, sicknesses removed, and death put off. In general, bad situations may be changed into good ones, at least temporarily. The assumption is that human beings are largely responsible for their own misfortunes and that they also possess the ritual means to overcome them. The sources of suffering lie in people's misdeeds, or sins, which offend the gods and ancestors, and in the social tensions and conflicts that can cause illness. The remedy involves the consultation of a priest or priestess who discovers the sin or the social problem and prescribes the solution, for example, an offering to appease an offended deity or a ritual to settle social tensions. Belief in the perfectibility of human beings is not a part of African traditional religions. Instead, such religions provide the means for correcting certain social and spiritual relationships that are understood to be the causes of misfortune and suffering, even death. They assume that the traditional moral and social values, which the gods and ancestors uphold, are the guidelines for the good life and emphasize these rules and values in ritual performances in order to renew people's commitment to them.

At the theological level, African religions contain both monotheistic and polytheistic principles. The concept of a supreme God is widely known in tropical Africa and existed before the coming of Christianity and Islam. The idea of a supreme God expresses the element of ultimacy, fate, and destiny, which is part of most African religions. As the ultimate principle behind things, the supreme God usually has no cult, images, temples, or priesthood. These are unnecessary because he stands above reciprocal relationships with human beings, on which the lesser gods depend.

In contrast to the invisibility and remoteness of the supreme God, the lesser gods and the ancestor spirits, which often serve as the supreme being's intermediaries, are constantly involved in daily affairs. Their many shrines, images, and priesthoods make them highly visible and important features of traditional life. They are sources of both protection and harm, depending upon how faithfully they are served. People regularly attend their shrines to pray, receive advice, and make offerings, usually in the form of animal sacrifice. Thus African religions are both polytheistic and monotheistic, depending upon the context. In matters concerning the ultimate destiny and fate of individuals and groups, the supreme God may be directly involved. In matters concerning everyday affairs, the lesser gods and ancestors are more immediately involved.

From the point of view of African religion, a human being consists of social, moral, spiritual, and physical components united together; the individual is viewed as a composite totality. That is why social conflicts can make people physically ill and why moral misdeeds can cause spiritual misfortunes. Rituals that are aimed at restoring social and spiritual relationships are therefore deemed to affect people's physical health and well-being. A person's life is also seen to pass through several stages. One of the important tasks of traditional religion is to move people successfully through the major stages of life: birth, puberty, marriage, elderhood, death, ancestorhood. Each phase has its duties, and rites of passage make sure that people know their responsibilities. In this way people's lives are given shape and pattern. Important traditional offices, such as kingship, chieftancy, and priesthood, are also maintained by rites of passage. Other rituals divide the year into seasons and give the annual cycle its form and rhythm.

Ritual authorities, such as diviners, prophets, priests, and sacred kings, serve a common religious purpose: the communication between the human world and the sacred world. Shrines and temples facilitate this process by linking together the two worlds around an altar. The priest's job is to perform prayers and sacrifices that carry people's desires to the spiritual world; the priest, in turn, communicates the will of the spiritual beings to the people.

MYTHOLOGY: CREATION, HEROES, AND TRICKSTERS. African myths deal primarily with the origin of humankind and with the origin of social and ritual institutions. They explain both the structure of the world and the social and moral conditions of human life. Most creation myths posit an original state of cosmic order and unity, and they tell of a separation or division that arose between divinity and humanity, sky and earth, order and disorder, which resulted in human mortality. These myths explain why human beings are mortal by telling how they became mortal. Thus they presuppose that humanity was originally immortal and passed into a state of mortality. The myths usually say that mortality was the result of a deliberate or accidental misdeed committed by a human being, often a woman, or an animal. Although questions of human responsibility are sometimes involved, the underlying meaning is generally that death was a necessary, indeed, a natural, outcome; otherwise, human beings would not be truly human and humanity and divinity would not be properly separated.

Some myths explain the origins and significance of death by showing that it is essentially linked to the agents of human fertility and reproduction: women, food, sexuality, and marriage. The Dinka of the southern Sudan say that the first woman disobeyed the creator god who told her to plant or pound only one grain of millet a day, lest she strike the low-hanging sky with her hoe or tall pestle. When she lifted her pole to cultivate (or pound) more millet, she struck the sky, causing the sky and God to withdraw. Thenceforth, human beings suffered sickness and death and had to toil for their food. In this myth it is a woman's desire for plenty (life), which the Dinka view indulgently, that overcame the original restrictive proximity between humanity and God. The Nuer, who live near the Dinka, say that in the beginning a young girl descended from the sky with her companions to get food and that she fell in love with a young man whom she met on earth. When she told her companions that she wished to stay on earth, they ascended to the sky and spitefully cut the rope leading to the ground, thus severing the means for immortality. The myth reflects the choice that every Nuer woman must make in marriage when she leaves her childhood home and friends and goes to live with her husband. According to the Ganda of central Uganda, the first woman disobeyed her father, the sky god, which caused her brother Death to come into the world and kill some of her children. In Buganda a girl's brother is the traditional agent of marriage and has a temporary claim to one of his sister's children. The myth implies that death is viewed as a necessary counterpart to life, as the mother's brother is a necessary counterpart to marriage and a claimant to one of his sister's children.

Another widely known myth among Bantu-speaking peoples explains the origin of death in terms of a message that failed. In the beginning the creator god gave the message of life to a slow-moving animal (e.g., chameleon, sheep). Later, he grew impatient and gave the message of death to a faster animal (e.g., lizard, goat). The faster animal arrived first and delivered his message, and death became the lot of humanity. In this myth the natural slowness and quickness of the two animals determine the outcome, making death a natural and inevitable result. Other myths emphasize the similarity between death and sleep and the inability of human beings to avoid either. According to this myth, the creator god told the people to stay awake until he returned. When he came back they had fallen asleep and failed to hear his message of immortality. When they woke up he gave them the message of death.

Hero myths tell how important cultural discoveries, such as agriculture and ironmaking, originated and how major social and ritual institutions, such as marriage, village organization, kingship, priesthood, and cult groups, came into existence. Often the founding deeds of the hero are reenacted in ritual with creative and transforming effect. The hero may continue to live among the people in spiritual form through a priest or prophet and become manifest on important ritual occasions. Many African deities are said to have been heroes who died and returned in spiritual form to serve as guardians and protectors of the people. In Africa myth and history often overlap, and together they form a unified explanation of the world since the time of the beginning.

Another type of myth is the trickster story. Trickster stories range from fable-like satirical tales to accounts of world creation. The trickster may exist only as a character in stories or as an active deity. Whatever the particular form, the trickster image expresses the fundamental ambiguities of human life. The trickster is both fooler and fooled, wily and stupid, maker and unmade. A seemingly misguided culture hero, the trickster introduces both order and disorder, confusion and wisdom into the world. The trickster's comic adventures convey a widely recognized African principle: Life achieves its wholeness through the balance of opposites. The trickster's acts of disorder prepare the way for new order; death gives way to birth. According to the Dogon of central Mali, the trickster god Ogo destroyed the original perfection of the creator god's plan and could only partly restore it. Yet the trickster also helps human beings to discover the hidden dangers of life through divination. Among the Yoruba of western Nigeria, the god Ẹṣu is both the agent of social conflict and the peacekeeper of the marketplace, as well as the confuser of men and the messenger of the gods. His two-sided nature brings together the gods and human beings in a cooperative manner through divination and sacrifice, which he supervises. The Akan-Ashanti tales about Ananse the Spider in southern Ghana and the tales about the Hare in eastern and southern Africa express profound and ironic insights into the foibles and possibilities of human nature. In general, African trickster mythology expresses optimism about the paradoxes and anomalies of life, showing that cleverness and humor may prevail in a fundamentally imperfect world.

MONOTHEISM AND POLYTHEISM. African religions combine principles of unity and multiplicity, transcendence and immanence, into a single system; thus they generally contain both monotheistic and polytheistic aspects. Often there is also the concept of an impersonal power, such as the Yoruba concept of *aṣẹ* by which all things have their being. In different contexts each of these principles may come to the fore as the primary focus of religious thought and action, although each is part of the larger whole.

As ultimate principles, many supreme Gods are like African sacred kings: they reign but do not rule. They occupy the structural center of the system but are rarely seen or heard, and when they are it is only indirectly. For this reason the supreme Gods belong more to the dimension of myth than to that of ritual. However, the world would cease to exist without them, as would a kingdom without the king. Thus, in many instances the supreme God is the one, omniscient, omnipotent, transcendent, creator, father, and judge. From the time of the first contact with Muslims and Christians, Africans recognized their supreme Gods to be the same as the God of Christianity and Islam. It is not known whether African religions were more or less monotheistic than they are today, although it is certain that African concepts of God have changed over time.

DIVINITY AND EXPERIENCE. Unlike the supreme beings, which remain in the background of religious life, the lesser divinities and spirits are bound up with everyday experience. These powers are immanent, and their relation to human beings is reciprocal and interdependent. Hence they require many shrines, temples, priests, cult groups, images, rituals, and offerings to facilitate their constant interactions with people.

The gods and spirits are known through personal encounter as living agents who directly affect people's lives. Often associated with elements of nature, such as lightning, rain, rivers, wild animals, and forests, they may be understood as images or symbols of collective psychological and social realities that resemble these natural phenomena in their powerful, dangerous, and beneficial aspects. The most common form of encounter between the human and the divine is spirit possession, the temporary presence of a deity or spirit in the consciousness of a person. Spirit possession may occur in a formal ritual context or in the normal course of everyday life. In Africa, as elsewhere, possession behavior is culturally stylized and highly symbolic. It is neither extremely pathological nor physiologically uncontrollable. It is an integral part of religion and has a well-defined role within it. In some societies possession is regarded as an affliction, and the aim is to expel the intruding god or spirit so that the suffering person may resume a normal life. Once the god or spirit has made the reasons for its appearance known through the voice of the afflicted person or through divination, offerings are made and the spirit departs. Usually the cause is some misdeed or sin that must be redressed through ritual action. In other societies possession is a more desirable phenomenon. People may regularly seek to come closer to their gods, even to identify personally with them, through possession-inducing dances that have beneficial psychological and social effects.

MEDIUMS, DIVINERS, AND PROPHETS. Sometimes a divinity may wish to form a special relationship with an individual. The god usually makes his desire known through an illness. Indeed, sickness is sometimes seen as a sacred calling that is manifested in the form of a possession. The cure will take the form of apprenticeship and initiation into the service of the deity, and it will place the person in lasting debt to society. Henceforth, the chosen man or woman becomes professionally established at a shrine and becomes the god's medium, devoted to the healing of afflicted people. He or she treats illnesses and social problems through mediumship séances. Treatment begins with a payment of money and with the questioning of the client by the spirit speaking through the medium. The interrogation is skillful and focuses upon the client's social situation. The remedy usually involves moral advice, herbal prescriptions, ritual actions, and sometimes membership in a special cult group, as among the Central Bantu-speaking peoples. The client himself may already have thought of the diagnosis and of the remedies that the medium proposes, or the séance may reveal new insights and procedures. In either case, the client departs from the consultation knowing that his problem has been expertly investigated and that he has received authoritative advice.

In Africa the distinction between mediums, diviners, priests, and prophets is a fluid one, and transition from one to the other is made easily. Generally, diviners and mediums are spiritual consultants, whereas prophets are leaders of humans. Prophets may go directly to the people with programs for action and initiate religious and political movements. For this reason prophets are often sources of religious and political change. In circumstances of widespread political unrest, priestly mediums may develop prophetic powers and initiate socio-religious change. This occurred during colonial times in East Africa: traditional prophets became leaders of political resistance in parts of Sudan, Uganda, Tanzania, and Zimbabwe. In Kenya, the Mau Mau resistance movement was also significantly implemented and sustained by traditional ritual procedures.

A more indirect form of spiritual communication involves the use of divination equipment, such as cowrie shells, leather tablets, animals entrails, palm nuts, a winnowing basket, small animal bones, and animal tracks. After careful interrogation of the client, the diviner manipulates and interprets his material in order to reach a diagnosis. Such systems work according to a basic typology of human problems, aspirations, and casual factors. The diviner applies this framework to the client's case by manipulating a divination apparatus.

The most complex system of divination in Africa is Ifa. It is practiced by the Yoruba of southern Nigeria and in various forms by the Igbo, Igala, and Nupe of Nigeria, the Ewe of Togo, and the Fon of Benin. It consists of a large number of poems that are related to a set of 256 divination patterns. When one of the patterns is cast, the diviner recites the appropriate poems. The poems tell of real-life problems experienced by the gods and ancestors in the past. Without telling the diviner the problem, the client chooses the poem that best fits the situation. The client then asks more questions of the diviner, who makes additional casts of the divination chain, until the client discovers all the potential dangers and benefits destiny holds for the client, together with the ritual means of ensuring the best possible outcome. Like all systems of divination, Ifa's predictions are general and open to interpretation. The value of divination lies not in the precision of prediction but in the decision-making processes that it offers to the client. Divination procedures require the client (and often his or her family) to examine problems fully, to consider alternative courses of action, and to obtain professional guidance. The result is a course of action that is objectively based, divinely sanctioned, and socially acceptable.

Diviners and mediums employ methods of treatment that usually involve a mixture of psychological, social, medical, and ritual means. Many illnesses are regarded as uniquely African in nature and hence as untreatable by Western methods. They include cases of infertility, stomach disorders, and a variety of ailments indicative of psychological stress and anxiety. The causes of such illnesses are generally attributed to social, spiritual, or physiological factors, either separately or in some combination. Typically, a person's problems will be attributed to his or her misdeeds or to the ill will of other people because of the belief in the social source of illness and misfortune. Equally fundamental is the notion that religion concerns the total person, their physical as well as spiritual well-being.

To the extent that European Christianity relates only to spiritual matters, African societies have fashioned their own forms of Christianity whose rituals are aimed at both the physical and spiritual ills of society. These tend to be prophet-led, independent churches that utilize the power of Christian prayer and ritual to heal physiological and psychological maladies, much like the indigenous religions. Islam has been adapted along similar lines. Although Western medicine is recognized and sought after for the treatment of infectious diseases and physical injuries, ritual techniques continue to be used in both rural and urban areas because of African ideas about the social and spiritual foundation of personal health and well-being. Where the two systems are available, people often utilize both. Increased urbanization has tended to break down certain elements of traditional religions, for example, rites for ancestor spirits and nature gods, but urbanization has created its own social, psychological, and spiritual problems for which diviners and mediums have developed methods of treatment.

RITUAL: SACRIFICE AND RITES OF PASSAGE. Ritual is the foundation of African religion. To become possessed by the gods, to speak ritual words, to perform offerings and sacrifices, or to make children into adults is to shape experience according to normative patterns of meaning and thereby to control and renew the world. The ritual sphere is the sphere in which the everyday world and the spiritual world communicate with each other and blend into one reality. Almost every African ritual is therefore an occasion in which human experience is morally and spiritually transformed. The two most important forms of African ritual are animal sacrifice and rites of passage. Both follow common patterns.

The sacrifice of animals and the offering of vegetable foods accomplish a two-way transaction between the realm of divinity and the realm of humanity. The vegetable offerings and animal victims are the mediating principles. They are given to the gods and spirits in return for their favors. Animal sacrifice is especially prominent because the life of the victim and its blood are potent spiritual forces. By killing the victim, its life is released and offered to the gods for their sustenence in exchange for their blessings, especially in the case of human life that is threatened. The act of sacrifice may also transfer the illness to the animal victim, which thus serves as a scapegoat. An animal may also be sacrificed so that its blood may act as a barrier against malevolent spiritual forces. Fowl, sheep, and goats are the most common sacrificial animals; cattle are frequently sacrificed among pastoralist peoples. Animal victims usually possess certain characteristics of color, size, shape, and behavior that make them symbolically appropriate for certain spiritual beings. Through invocations, prayers, and songs, human desires are made known, sins are confessed, and spiritual powers attracted to the sacrificial scene. Generally, the ritual word performs a dual function: it says what is desired and helps to bring about the desired through the power of ritual speech.

Sacrifices are performed on a variety of occasions in seasonal, curative, life-crisis, divinatory, and other kinds of rituals, and always as isolable ritual sequences. Sacrifices that involve the sharing of the victim's flesh confirm the bond between the people and the spiritual power, to which a portion is given. Purifications may also be performed so that the participants may be cleansed of the potent sacred elements of the sacrifice. Major sacrificial rites usually have the following structure: consecration, invocation, immolation, communion, and purification. At the social level, sacrifices and offerings bring together individuals and groups and reinforce common moral bonds. Fundamentally, blood sacrifice is a reciprocal act, bringing gods and people together in a circuit of moral, spiritual, and social unity. In this way sacrifice restores moral and spiritual balance—the healthy equilibrium between person and person, group and group, human beings and spiritual powers—which permits the positive flow of life on earth. As a sacred gift of life to the gods, sacrifice atones for human misdeeds and overcomes the human impediments to the flow of life; thus it is one of the keystones of African religions.

Rites of passage possess a threefold pattern consisting of rites of separation, transition, and reincorporation. Their purpose is to create and maintain fixed and meaningful transformations in the life cycle (birth, naming, puberty, marriage, death, ancestorhood), in the ecological and temporal cycle (planting, harvest, seasonal change, lunar and solar cycles, new year), and in the accession of persons to high office. Without these rites there would be no significant pattern to traditional life and no enduring social institutions.

The important phase in these ceremonies is the middle, or liminal, period of transition. In this phase people are morally remade into "new" social beings. Newborn infants are made into human persons, children are made into adults, men and women are made into husbands and wives, adults are made into elders, princes are made into kings, deceased persons are made into ancestor spirits. Seasonal transtions are also marked and celebrated in this way. Thus the old year is made into the new and the season of drought is made into the season of rain.

This remaking of persons and time involves the symbolic destruction of the old and the creation of the new. It is a dual process of death and rebirth, involving symbols of reversal, bisexuality, disguise, nakedness, death, humility, dirt, intoxication, pain, and infantilism. These symbols of ritual liminality have both negative and positive connotations representing the paradoxical situation of the womb/tomb—the betwixt and between period when people are neither what they were nor what they will become. In the liminal stage, people are momentary anomalies, stripped of their former selves, ready to become something new. Similarly, the time between the seasons and the time between the years belongs neither to the old nor to the new but to both. The transition phase is a time out of time, when the usual order of things is reversed or suspended, ready to become reestablished and renewed. During the Apo new year's ceremony of the Ashanti, people openly express their resentments against their neighbors, chiefs, and king in order to "cool" themselves and rid society of its tensions, which may cause harm before order is restored and the new year begins.

The most fundamental rite of passage is that which initiates the young into adulthood. In this way a society not only moves its young into new social roles but also transforms them inwardly by molding their moral and mental disposition toward the world. A period of instruction may or may not be part of this process. A Nuer boy simply tells his father that he is ready to receive the marks of *gar,* six horizontal lines cut across the forehead. His socialization is already assumed. In many West African societies the rite is held in the confines of initiation groves where the initiates are given intensified moral and religious instruction. These rites may take place over a period of years and are organized into men's and women's initiation societies, such as the Poro society among the Senufo of the Ivory Coast, Mali, and Upper Volta. By means of stories, proverbs, songs, dances, games, masks, and sacred objects, the children and youths are taught the mysteries of life and the values of the adult world. The rites define the position of the intiates in relation to God, to society, to themselves, and to the world. Some form of bodily marking is usually done, and circumcision and clitoridectomy are widely practiced. The significance of bodily marking varies. Among the Gbaya of Mali, the initiates are cut slightly on the stomach with a "mortal wound" to signify their "death" to childhood. Generally, the marks indicate that the transition to adulthood is permanent, personal, and often painful and that society has successfully imprinted itself upon the individual.

PERSONS, ANCESTORS, AND ETHICS. African concepts of the person, or self, share several characteristics. Generally, the self is regarded as composite and dynamic; it consists of several aspects, social, spiritual, and physical, and admits of degrees of vitality. The self is also open to possession by divinity, and its life history may be predestined before birth. After death, the self becomes a ghost, and in the course of several generations it becomes merged with the impersonal ancestors. Each of these aspects and potentialities of the person, sometimes misleadingly described as multiple souls, is important in different contexts and receives special ritual attention.

In West African societies, the success or failure of a person's life is explained by reference to a personal destiny that is given to the individual by the creator god before birth. A person's destiny stems from a family ancestor (usually a grandparent) who is partly reborn in the person at birth and serves as a spiritual guardian throughout life. Although destinies are largely predetermined, they are also somewhat alterable for better or worse by the gods, witches, and guardian ancestors. To realize the full potential of one's destiny, frequent recourse to divination is required to discover what destiny has in store and to ensure the best outcome. Successes and failures in life are therefore attributed both to personal initiative and to inherited destiny. After death, this immortal aspect of the personality returns to the creator god, ready to be reborn in the same lineage group. In societies where the concept of destiny is absent, the most important life-determining principle is the person's inherited lineage component, and it is this that survives after death.

The human personality is also permeable by divinity. On ritual occasions the consciousness of an individual may become temporarily replaced by the presence of a spiritual being. Often the personality of the god resembles that of the individual, and professional mediums may have several gods or spirits at their command. These are said to mount "on the head" or "on the back" of the medium. Almost everyone is susceptible to spirit possession of some sort, and when controlled in a ritual manner it has therapeutic effect.

At death, new problems of social and spiritual identity arise. When a family loses one of its members, especially a senior male or female, a significant moral and social gap occurs. The family, together with other kinsmen, must close this gap through funerary procedures. At the same time the deceased must undergo spiritual adjustment if he or she is to find a secure place in the afterlife and remain in contact with the family left behind. This is accomplished by the construction of an ancestor shrine and sometimes also by the making of an ancestor mask and costume.

Almost every family and village has its ancestor shrines, and every town its heroes who founded and protected it. From the beginning, the ancestors helped to create the world; they gave birth to the people, led them to their present homeland, created agriculture, established social rules, founded kingdoms, and invented metalworking and the arts. Their deeds laid the foundations of African myth, history, and culture. Whether the ancestors lived in the remote past or in more recent times, they are regarded as immortal spirits who transcend historical time. Through spirit possession and mediumship rites, the ancestors continue to communicate with their living descendants, who seek their help in the affairs of everyday life.

The carved images of the ancestors are not intended to be representational or abstract but conceptual and evocative. By means of stylized form and symbolic details the image conveys the characteristics of the ancestor and also helps to make the spiritual reality of the ancestor present among the people. Thus the carved ancestral icon enables the world of the living and the world of the living dead to come together for the benefit of human life.

The relationship between the community of the living and the spirits of the dead, sometimes misleadingly called "ancestor worship," has powerful social and psychological dimensions and plays a vital role in almost every African society. This is especially true in small-scale stateless societies in which sociopolitical rules are almost entirely governed by a descent system. In such societies ancestors are the focus of ritual activity, not because of a special fear of the dead or because of a strong belief in the afterlife, but because of the importance of the descent system in defining social relationships. In larger polities the royal ancestors often become the gods of the state. Superior to living kings and elders, the ancestors define and regulate social and political relations. It is they who own the land and the livestock, and it is they who regulate the prosperity of the lineage groups, villages, and kingdoms. Typically, when misfortune strikes, the ancestors are consulted through divination to discover what misdeeds have aroused their anger. The ancestors are also regularly thanked at ceremonial feasts for their watchful care, upon which the welfare of the community depends.

Not everyone may become an ancestor. Only those who led families and communities in the past as founders, elders, chiefs, or kings may serve in the afterlife as the social and political guides of the future. By contrast, ordinary people become ghosts after death. Such spirits require ritual attention at their graves, but they are finally sent away to "rest in peace," while the more positive influence of the ancestors is invoked generation after generation. The more recent ancestors receive the most frequent attention, especially at family shrines. Such ancestors are not worshiped in either a devotional or idolatrous sense but are honored and prayed to as the senior leaders of the living community.

The sufferings and misfortunes brought by the gods and ancestors are punishments aimed at correcting human behavior. By contrast, the sufferings and misfortunes caused by witches and sorcerers are undeserved and socially destructive; they are unequivocally evil. The African concept of evil is that of perverse humanity: the human witch and sorcerer. The African image of the witch and sorcerer is of humanity turned against itself. Witches act only at night, they fly through the air, walk on their hands or heads, dance naked, feast on corpses, possess unsatiable and incestuous lusts (despite sexual impotence), murder their relatives, and live in the bush with wild animals. This symbolic imagery is consistent with the sociological characteristics of the witch: disagreeable, ambitious, lying, and envious.

Accusations of witchcraft and sorcerery therefore function as a means of social control. In the past accused witches and sorcerers were forced to confess or were killed or expelled from society. Witchcraft accusations also enabled quarreling members of the same lineage to separate from each other and establish their own residences, thus restoring village order. For the most part witchcraft accusations in Africa flourished in contexts where social interaction was intense but loosely defined, as between members of the same extended family or lineage group. In such cases witchcraft was sometimes thought to be an inherited power of which the individual might be unaware until accused. In other instances it existed in the form of deliberately practiced sorcery procedures, so-called black magic, which was effective at long range and across lineage groups. Whether deliberate or not, the witch and the sorcerer were regarded as fundamentally antihuman and thus as principles of evil in a world governed by fundamentally moral and social forces.

Shrines, Temples, and Religious Art. Shrines and temples serve as channels of communication with the spiritual world, and they may also serve as dwelling places of gods and spirits. Shrines may exist in purely natural forms, such as forest groves, large rocks, rivers, and trees, where gods and spirits dwell. Every African landscape has places of this kind that are the focus of ritual activity. Human-made shrines vary in form. A simple tree branch stuck into the ground is a shrine for a family ghost among the Nuer. A large rectangular building serves as the ancestor stool chapel among the Ashanti. Whatever its form, an African shrine acts as a symbolic crossroads, a place where paths of communication between the human and spiritual worlds intersect. If the shrine serves as a temple, that is, as the dwelling place of a spiritual being, it is built in houselike fashion, like the "palaces" of the royal ancestors in Buganda. Such shrines usually have tow parts: the front section, where the priest and the people gather, and the rear section, where the god or spirit dwells. An altar stands between the two and links them together.

Shrines and temples often contain carved images of gods, spirits, and ancestors; indeed, such images sometimes serve as shrines themselves. Carved figures may function as altars for communication with spiritual beings and as physical embodiments of the spirits themselves. The Baule of the Ivory Coast carve figures to represent the spiritual spouse who everyone has in the otherworld before being born into this one. The human-shaped figure becomes a shrine through which the spirit may be propitiated. The Dan-speaking peoples of Liberia and the Ivory Coast carve wooden masks to represent and to embody forest spirits so that they may appear before the people of the villages.

More generally, African ritual art, including masks, headdresses, sacred staffs, and ceremonial implements, is fashioned according to definite stylistic forms in order to express religious ideas and major social values. The carved *chi wara* antelope headdress of the Bamana of Mali represents the mythic farming animal, called Chi Wara, that originally showed the people how to cultivate, and the antelope shape of the headdress expresses the qualities of the ideal farmer: strength, industriousness, and graceful form. Male and female headdresses are danced together, while women sing songs to encourage the young men's cultivation groups to compete with each other for high agricultural achievements. The Gẹlẹdẹ masks of the Yoruba honor the spiritual power of women, collectively known as "our mothers." This power is both creative (birth) and destructive (witchcraft). The Gẹlẹdẹ mask depicts the calm and serene face of a woman and expresses the feminine virtue of patience. The face is often surmounted by elaborately carved scenes of daily activity, for the spiritual power of "the mothers" is involved in every aspect of human life.

African traditional art is primarily concerned with the human figure because of the anthropocentric and anthropomorphic character of African religions. As has been seen, religion in Africa deals with the problems of human life, the causes of which are seen to be fundamentally human in nature. Thus social conflict produces illness, human misdeeds cause the gods and ancestors to bring misfortune, and the gods themselves are essentially human in character. African thought typically conceives of the unknown and invisible forces of life by analogy with human realities that are both knowable and controllable. Hence African sculpture represents the gods, spirits, and ancestors in a basically human form.

See Also Affliction, article on African Cults of Affliction; Central Bantu Religions; Drama, article on African Religious Drama; Iconography, article on Traditional African Iconography; Khoi and San Religion; Kingship, article on Kingship in Sub-Saharan Africa; Music, article on Music and Religion in Sub-Saharan Africa; Nuer and Dinka Religion; Tricksters, article on African Tricksters; Witchcraft, article on African Witchcraft.

Bibliography

Abimbola, 'Wande. *Ifá: An Exposition of Ifá Literary Corpus.* Ibadan, 1976.

Abrahamsson, Hans. *The Origins of Death.* Uppsala, 1951.

Awolalu, J. Omosade. *Yoruba Beliefs and Sacrificial Rites.* London, 1979.

Beattie, John, and John Middleton, eds. *Spirit Mediumship and Society in Africa.* New York, 1969.

Booth, Newell S., Jr., ed. *African Religions: A Symposium.* New York, 1977.

Dammann, Ernst. *Die Religionen Afrikas.* Stuttgart, 1963. Translated into French as *Les religions de l'Afrique* (Paris, 1964).

Evans-Pritchard, E. E. *Nuer Religion.* Oxford, 1956.

Fortes, Meyer, and Robin Horton. *Oedipus and Job in West African Religion.* Cambridge, 1984.

Griaule, Marcel. *Dieu d'eau.* Paris, 1948. Translated by Robert Redfield as *Conversations with Ogotemmêli* (London, 1965).

Janzen, John M. *Lemba, 1650–1930: A Drum of Affliction in Africa and New World.* New York, 1982.

Karp, Ivan, and Charles S. Bird, eds. *Explorations in African Systems of Thought.* Bloomington, Ind., 1980.

Lewis-Williams, David. *The Rock Art of Southern Africa.* Cambridge, U.K., 1983.

Lienhardt, Godfrey. *Divinity and Experience: The Religion of the Dinka.* Oxford, 1961.

Mbiti, John S. *African Religions and Philosophy.* New York, 1969.

Parrinder, Geoffrey. *West African Religion.* 2d ed., rev. London, 1961.

Ranger, T. O., and Isaria N. Kimambo, eds. *The Historical Study of African Religion.* Berkeley, 1972.

Rattray, R. S. *Ashanti.* Oxford, 1923.

Ray, Benjamin C. *African Religions: Symbol, Ritual, and Community.* Englewood Cliffs, N.J., 1976.

Schoffeleers, J. Matthew, ed. *Guardians of the Land: Essays on Central African Territorial Cults.* Gwelo, 1979.

Temples, Placide. *La Philosophie bantoue.* Elizabethville, 1945. Translated by Margaret Mead as *Bantu Philosophy.* Paris, 1959.

Turner, Victor. *The Forest of Symbols: Aspects of Ndembu Ritual.* Ithaca, N.Y., 1967.

Vogel, Susan M., ed. *For Spirits and Kings: African Art from the Paul and Ruth Tishman Collection.* New York, 1981.

Zahan, Dominque. *Religion, spiritualité, et pensée africaines.* Paris, 1970. Translated by Kate E. Martin and Lawrence W. Martin as *The Religion, Spirituality, and Thought of Traditional Africa* (Chicago, 1979).

Zuesse, Evan M. *Ritual Cosmos: The Sanctification of Life in African Religions.* Athens, Ohio, 1979.

BENJAMIN C. RAY (1987)

AFRICAN RELIGIONS: MYTHIC THEMES

It is common to regard myth as the chief intellectual product of cultures with strong oral traditions (in analogy to philosophical and theological texts in literate civilizations). However, this would oversimplify the African situation. While African myths, as the "true dramas" explaining how the fundamental realities came to be, do often embody profound reflections, other forms of African wisdom exist that can be equally insightful and systematic or religiously significant. Ritual, for example, can often do without myth because it evokes the living experience of realities that are controlled by ritual symbols shaped over many generations. Proverbs may form the sole content of initiatic instruction, for although perhaps trivial taken one by one, their cumulative impact may transform one's vision of life and teach a poise or stance on life that may be said to be the chief fruit of religion. The more complex divinatory systems often embody a total classification of possible events in life and may ground it in a philosophy that is impersonal and elemental. The teachings of such proverbial, ritual, or divinatory systems may not be duplicated by myths. In fact, many African religions seem to function without many myths.

However, myths do provide us with a deep insight into African religions. But this is only so if it is appreciated that many, if not most, of the published myths from African cultures deal with the quasi-folkloric tales available to outsiders and children. The existence of esoteric levels of mythology in many cultures cannot be denied. Of course, one culture's initiatic myth is often, in fragmentary form, another culture's childish tale, even though the narrative itself may remain the same. What has changed is the context, the overall meaning, and the integration of this story into a larger narrative vision. In interpreting African mythology, then, that larger context and meaning must be attended to if one is to discover the vision of the sources of reality that alone defines true myth.

Not all myth directly justifies everyday cultic life or social structures. For example, the powers that are invoked in the everyday cult of the LoDagaa of Ghana (the earth, ancestors, and medicine spirits) are hardly even mentioned in the initiatic myth of Bagre (which centers on God and the bush spirits). But this is because the Bagre myth concerns the more primordial realities that lie behind and permit the concerns of the ordinary village cult and its associated spirits. In fact, it articulates the basic vision of life that animates the LoDagaa, without which they could not exist at all.

GENERAL THEMES. There exist four major sets of themes in the rich variety of African mythologies. This classification is naturally not meant to be exhaustive. The first set centers on the primordial personal encounter of humanity with God, in which human destiny—and especially the basic boundaries and limited conditions of life—is directly determined forever. The second major set of myths centers on the process of mediation, change, and renewal in the universe, focusing on the sometimes demiurgic figures who embodied this process in the beginning of time: the trickster, the smith, the diviner, and the kingly culture hero. The third major set centers on the ways in which the present universe in all its aspects is a creative equilibrium built up by such dynamic interacting opposites as male heaven and female earth (in the first phase of creation), culture hero and chthonic earth monster (or cruel ruler), sacral king and aboriginal peoples, and even competing brothers or wedded twins (in the next phase). Sexuality, battle, and sacrifice control the transformations of this mythic history. The fourth set of major themes include highly philosophical esoteric myths found in many

Sudanic and West African religions; these theosophical syntheses, known only to the highest initiates, center on concepts of the cosmic egg or the primal word, and the inner mysteries of sacrifice.

The Personal Encounter with God. Many African religions take the basic forms of the universe for granted, and their creation myths center instead on the development of the human condition. In any case, God is usually the central actor in these myths. It must be stressed that African religions universally acknowledge a supreme being, and there is often a direct cult to this being, which may be personal (prayers to God morning and night) or communal (during such crises as famine or drought). Such movements can even be formal and enacted periodically by the group as a whole. A basic trait of the African supreme being is that he determines destiny, both personal and (in the creation myths) universal human destiny. These myths turn on that assumption.

One myth, found in the Sahelian savanna region (the region of northern Africa between the Sahara and the rainy tropics that extends from the Atlantic to the Red Sea) and in coastal West Africa, explains that God once dwelt close to or on the earth (for heaven was near then) until an accidental offense against him (or actual disobedience, usually by a woman wanting more or better food) compelled God to remove the heavens far away and to break his direct link with humanity. The Ashanti (southern Ghana) say that God, Nyame (also known as Onyankopon), withdrew heaven from the earth because he was annoyed when the low floor of heaven was knocked from below by the pestle of an old woman who was pounding *fufu* (mashed yams). So he climbed up to heaven on a thread, like the Great Spider (Ananse Kokroko) that he is. Mischievous still, the old woman ordered her children to build a tower of mortars, one atop another, right to the sky. Needing one more mortar, the children took it from the bottom—and the whole edifice collapsed, killing many. The theme of the pestle knocking against heaven is surprisingly common in these myths. It would seem to link both eating and the major task of the culture, farming, to alienation from God. Among the Mbuti Pygmies of the Ituri forest, a basically similar mythic structure involves hunting instead, as the Mbuti do not farm. The first Pygmy provided food for God by hunting, and the Pygmy's two wives cooked and served the deity's meals, but were forbidden to look directly upon him. The youngest wife stole a look, and so the Pygmies were banished from heaven to earth, to hard work and death.

The Dinka (southern Sudan) say that there used to be a rope that hung down from heaven, and people could climb it when they wished to speak to God. But when the woman kept hitting the underside of heaven with her pestle, God withdrew the heavens and had the rope cut. A variant Dinka myth attributes the original split between humanity and divinity to fratricidal clan conflicts. The Nuer, a neighboring ethnic group closely related to the Dinka, say that when people grew old they would climb the rope, become young again, then come down and begin life anew. But one day the hyena (often the symbol or animal form of witches), which had been exiled from heaven, cut the rope. Since then people have not been able to renew their lives, and they die instead. The Lozi, or Rotse (northwestern Zambia), say that the arrogant, disobedient, and murderous tendencies of the first humans so irritated God that he finally sought to flee from them. But they pursued him everywhere. At a loss for a hiding place, God consulted the divining bones, which referred him to the spider. At God's order, the spider spun a thread to heaven, and God and his family ascended into the sky. The myth goes on to relate that the first ancestors tried to reach God even then by building a tower of cut trees—but the tower crashed down.

The motif of the tower built to reach heaven is very common in the versions of the separation of heaven and earth myth found among central Bantu-speaking peoples. The Luba say that humanity originally lived in the same village as God. But the creator wearied of the constant quarreling in the village and exiled humanity to earth (village quarreling is said to anger God, harm hunting and the crops, and even prevent pregnancies and increase deaths). There humans suffered hunger and cold and, for the first time, sickness and death. Following the advice of a diviner, who told them to go back to heaven to regain immortality, the people began building an enormous wooden tower, which after months of labor reached the sky. The workers at the top signaled their success by beating a drum and playing flutes, but God hated the noise and destroyed the tower, killing the musicians. The Kaonde, Lwena, Lamba, Lala, Chokwe, and other peoples date their dispersion from this event.

It is evidently dangerous to be too close to God; humanity cannot endure such powerful fusions. The human condition is only possible when God mercifully veils himself behind his creation and spirits. One example of this view is the attitude of the Bantu-speaking peoples to the rainbow being, considered a serpent spirit that is dangerous even to see. It links heaven and earth, or male and female life principles; its appearance drives away the rains and brings drought. It is considered a primary agent or, in some cases, as even a form of God.

There are many kinds of myths that explain how death entered the world. Among these is the myth of two messengers or the perverted message. According to this myth, God sent two messengers to humanity, the first with the command that humans would never die, the second with the command that they would. But the first messenger (usually the chameleon, an animal with certain resemblances to the variegated rainbow) traveled too slowly, and the second (often the lizard or hare) arrived first. The first declaration to be given fixed human nature forever. On the other hand, death may be blamed on the primordial exile from God's presence. Or it may be said that humanity was told to stay awake to await God's arrival with the declaration of human immortality, but everyone fell asleep and missed it. There is a complex irony in this story, for it turns on the view that sleep is a foretaste of death. Only if humans were already immortal would they have been able to banish sleep. Being mortal, they succumbed to sleep—and to death. The seeming arbitrariness of all of these myths of personal interaction with God masks a deeper necessity; however, when examined more closely, this necessity merely affirms that what is, is, and so is again arbitrary. The real significance of such myths, perhaps, is that finitude or arbitrary limitation is the very essence of life: only God escapes it, and he has ordained the present order.

Throughout Africa, the distinctions between social groups are explained by choices made before God in the beginning of time. The Nyoro (eastern Uganda) say that Kintu, the first human, asked God to assign the fates and names of his three sons. God therefore placed six gifts in their path. The eldest immediately seized the bundle of food and began eating, carrying off what remained with the help of the head ring, grabbing with his free hands the ax and the knife. And so he showed himself to be the ancestral peasant (*kairu*), greedy and impulsive. The second son picked up the leather thong, which was used to tie cattle, so his destiny was that of the herder (*kahuma* or *huma*). And the youngest son took the ox's head, a sign that he was the head, or ruler (*kakama*), of all.

In the countless versions of this fateful gifts myth, found everywhere in sub-Saharan Africa, it is almost always the youngest brother who gets the best fate. God is shown as the determiner of destiny par excellence. And surprisingly, the foolish ancestor who chooses the wrong gift is often the founder of the people who tell the story, an occurrence that was perhaps especially prevalent during the colonial period. In the common topical adaptations of the myth, White Man was the youngest brother, African the eldest. Sometimes cultural distinctions arise out of other kinds of events, however. The Shilluk (southern Sudan) say that when God began to create humans, God made them from light-colored clays, so that the whites emerged. Later, when God's hands were a bit soiled, the red Arabs and Turks were formed. But toward the end, God's hands were so dirty that the black-skinned Shilluk were the result. The Fang of Gabon used to say that in the beginning God lived with his three sons, White Man, Black Man, and Gorilla. But Black Man and Gorilla disobeyed God, so he withdrew to the west coast with his white son and gave all his wealth and power to him. Gorilla retreated into the forest depths, while the unhappy black people followed the sun to the west. There they found the white people, who slowly poisoned them (with malaria). As a result of this contact, they languish now, dying, and thinking of the time when they lived with God and were happy.

Mediators between Order and Disorder. Perhaps the most surprising of the mythic mediators between the primordial flux and the eventual divine order is the trickster. Certainly one part of the meaning of the African trickster is well summarized by the blunt name given him by the Nkundo: Itonde (death). Itonde has many traits linking him to the typical culture hero. Born to the first human couple, Itonde matured rapidly and soon became a ruler. However, he behaved cruelly and rapaciously (giving us a stereotypic image of the bad king); for example, he slaughtered huge numbers of the aboriginal Pygmies. But like so many African culture heroes and archetypal kings, Itonde set himself to conquer all aboriginal powers, including Indombe, the fiery (rainbow?) serpent, ruler of the forest depths and of the Pygmies. As the master of the serpent, Itonde gained possession of the land, while the serpent obediently went down into the river to control the waters and rain at Itonde's bidding.

Among Itonde's other achievements were the creation of the two staple agricultural crops, bananas and sugarcane. Sugarcane is the fruit of two murders. Indombe had killed Itonde's brother, so in revenge Itonde hunted down a surrogate of Indombe. This victim, an anonymous man of the forest, tried to escape by turning into a sugarcane, but Itonde seized him and killed and buried him. From his body sprang sugarcane plants, indicating that sacrificial death is creative.

Itonde's own death, which released his power into the world permanently, came about through the disobedient and selfish desire of a wife for food. Pregnant and gnawed by strange appetites, she demanded a certain rare fruit available only in a dangerous region. When Itonde died seeking it, the waters oozing from his body formed the first marsh rivers (evidently, Itonde and the water serpent Indombe were strangely akin). From his corpse the first maggots emerged. His wife later gave birth to all the other insects, as well as to the six ancestors of the Nkundo and related cultures and, last of all, to Lianja, the ideal king. So from Itonde, the trickster Death, come the essentials of farming culture, including the major food crops and the changing seasons, as well as the main lines of social organization and kingship, with all the suffering and joy that they imply. Human life in its entirety comes from Death.

The Banda (Central African Republic) say that God had two sons, Ngakola, who breathed life into the first human, and Tere, the spirit of excess and confusion. Tere was assigned the task of taking all the animal species and the life-giving waters down from heaven in baskets. But, like the Luba tower builders discussed above, Tere was overeager to announce his gifts to humanity and he beat his drum while still descending. The baskets slipped from his grasp and crashed to earth, scattering all the species and waters. Tere tried to recapture the animals; those he caught became the domestic species and those that escaped changed their original nature and became wild. The same happened with the plants, creating the distinctions between wild and cultivated species. Throughout the Sudanic region figures much like Tere crop up; in the eastern Sudan they sometimes even have the same name. In the area where the central Sudanic savanna merges into the forest of the Democratic Republic of the Congo, the Bandziri, Yakoma, and Azande call him Tule or

Tore; the Mangbetu speak of their trickster as Azapane and the Babua as Mba; the Manja call him Bele while the Mbuti Pygmies tell tales of Tore.

According to the Mbuti, Tore kept fire and sexuality for himself in the primordial forest; his old mother would warm herself by the fire while he swung through the forest trees like a monkey. Meanwhile the first human couple shivered in the cold, wet undergrowth. Finally, the first man stole the embers of fire from the side of the sleeping woman and raced off into the forest; Tore chased him and recovered the fire several times but at last failed. The old woman died of the cold, transforming herself into the vengeful Mother of the Forest, who ensnares solitary hunters, abducts small children, and rules the dead but who also occasionally blesses chosen hunters with exceptional luck. But Tore, enraged at the theft and the death of his mother, cursed humanity with death. He still roams the forest, especially in the form of the rainbow serpent.

Stories of Tore found among Bantu-speaking peoples may have been influenced by the Pygmy myths; the Azande say that Tore (whom they identify with the spider) gave people water by stealing it from an old woman who had hidden it. He gave them fire, too, although it was the accidental result of a visit to the smith spirits: his loincloth caught fire, and as he fled through the forest he begged the fire to leave him and pass into the trees instead. The fire did so, which is why it emerges now when sticks are rubbed together.

In general, the trickster appears most distinct in West African and Sudanic cultures, but he appears elsewhere, too: in South Africa among the Sotho and Venda as Huveane, a figure who is part god and part culture hero. Some of the San also call the creator of all life Huve; they pray to him in the hunt, and he presides over initiations. Huve may have been borrowed from their Bantu-speaking neighbors, but the Kaggen, or Cagn, of the southern San is clearly their own creator-trickster figure and shows that the basic concepts are native to them. The Bantu Huveane (little Huve) is also the hero of many trivial adventures. Growing up with startling speed, he plays many tricks on his parents and neighbors, but his parents prosper wondrously and the other villagers are beside themselves with rage and jealousy. They conspire to kill him but are constantly made to look like fools. Finally, it is said, Huveane ascended to heaven, but he will return one day to bring happiness and prosperity to humanity.

The favorite trickster of the Bantu-speaking peoples, however, has nothing to do with creation or with the primordial shaping of culture: he is the folkloric Hare (among some cultures, Jackal), prototype of Br'er Rabbit in the tales of Uncle Remus. The primordial and creative roles of the trickster in most Bantu cultures seem to have been absorbed by the general figure of the aboriginal ruler (often monstrous or serpentine) who is defeated by the archetypal king, the second, more refined culture hero, thus establishing human society.

Divination is one of the chief ways of dealing with disorder and generating order out of it. Often the trickster is the primordial diviner as well as the patron of diviners; in particular, the various spider tricksters, which exist in cultures ranging from Mali and Ghana through to the Democratic Republic of the Congo, are almost always associated with divination. The first diviner is a significant figure in many myths. There are several different versions, for example, of how the Ifa or Fa divinatory system (used by the Yoruba of Nigeria and the Fon of Benin, Togo, and Ghana) came to be. A common Yoruba account has it that the supreme being, Ọlọrun, or Olodumare, created two beings to rule the world on his behalf, Ọbatala (also called Oriṣa-nla), demiurge and royal archetype, and Ọrunmila (or Ifa), source of wisdom. *Ọrunmila* signifies "only heaven can affect salvation" and shows that Ọrunmila is, in effect, merely the mouthpiece of God. Ọbatala was killed one day by an evil slave, but Ọrunmila collected his scattered remains together, ordered them, and deposited them throughout the world; from this have arisen the cults to the many *orisha,* the divinities. Ọrunmila moved constantly between heaven and earth in those days, solving problems not only for humanity but even for the *orisha,* who also consulted him. His eight children founded the various Yoruba kingdoms. One day, insulted by one of his children, Ọrunmila withdrew to heaven, and the forces of life ceased to operate on earth: sterility and death affected the fields as well as humanity. (This works to remind that Ọrunmila's constant companion is the trickster Eṣu, a tiny man with a huge phallus, the very image of procreative powers.) The eight children of Ọrunmila came to him in a delegation, begging him to return, but he refused, giving each of them sixteen palm nuts instead. These sixteen nuts composed a person who could be consulted on all questions of life. Ọrunmila was thus present in them.

The Fon of Dahomey explain their Fa system with similar myths. Around Porto Novo, it is said that Fa was a formless or round man without members or bones, so he could not personally do anything. But all the powerful, including the vodoun (gods) revered him like a king. However, the accumulated resentments of those humans who did not like Fa's adherence to absolute truth—or, according to other accounts, the jealousy of Xevioso, the thunder god—led to Fa being sliced to pieces. Those pieces produced a sixteen-branched palm tree or the sixteen palm nuts themselves, from which the immortal Fa still speaks.

The primordial smith is one of the chief mediatory figures in African mythology. The manipulation of creative fires (often associated with the sources of sexual generation) and the working of earth substances into cultural products have often been regarded throughout Africa as a paradigm and repetition of creation. From southern Africa to the westernmost Sudan, the smith is often the presiding elder at initiation ceremonies, the traditional healer called upon to find witches and expel their influences, and the priestly repository of the deepest mysteries. In myths, he is often the chief agent of God on earth, the demiurge who shapes the world and culture, and/or the trickster.

Among the Yoruba, Ogun, the god of iron and patron of smiths, was the first to descend to the earth while it was still a marshy wasteland. He cleared the way for the other gods. But he preferred the wastelands, for there he could hunt, and there he still rules as the deity of hunters and warriors as well as of all artisans. When Ọbatala had finished molding the physical form of the first ancestors, Ogun took over and made the final details, as he did to the whole of creation. He still presides over initiations, for the finishing touches of culture, such as circumcision and the tribal markings of initiation, belong to him. Surgeons must worship him, too, as must all those who make oaths or covenants or undergo judicial ordeals.

The Fali (Cameroon) conceive of the primal ancestor as a smith who descended from heaven on a bean stalk with a chest or box, which escaped from him (much as the baskets escaped from the Banda trickster Tere) and fell to the earth, disintegrating into four triangles. These four divisions contained all the animal and plant species; the initiated know the classes still, although the fall scattered the creatures throughout the earth. Each class has twelve subdivisions. Every aspect of Fali life is ruled by these correspondences and harmonies, putting back into order what the primal smith disordered.

According to the Dogon (Mali), all of the primal spirits, or Nommo, were smiths, masters of creative fire. One of these escaped from heaven and descended to earth on the rainbow with the ark that he had stolen; it contained the fiery essences of all species, ranged in their proper categories. The first ancestors were also in this ark (which is alternately described as a basket, granary, anvil, or womb). The ark was a picture of the entire world system, which according to some Dogon was akin to a living being, a female, mate to the smith. The smith also bore with him his hammer, which represented the male element and contained the seeds of life. The descent of the smith was not an easy one: he had to fight off the other heavenly spirits, who resented his theft. The descent became uncontrolled and ended with a crash, causing the animals, plants, and human groups in the ark to scatter in the four directions, and even breaking the serpentine, flexible limbs of the smith, so that henceforth human beings would have elbows, wrists, hips, knees, and ankles, permitting them to work.

It is said that another primal spirit, in the form of a serpent, immediately engaged the thief in battle but was killed. Its body was given to humanity to eat (or was used as the model for the first cultivated field), while the head was placed under the first smithy forge. Every smithy thereafter is symbolically situated on the head of the primal Nommo-serpent. This serpent is the symbolic mate of the first smith, and the smithing process is a kind of spiritual intercourse in which the beautiful things that are shaped are the symbolic offspring. Every time the smith strikes the anvil with his hammer, generative vibrations go forth that are like the first scattering of the seeds of life; these are shaped by the smith into the forms of culture. The smith is therefore the human embodiment of the demiurge.

The smith, in these myths, has a peculiar link to disorder and the wilderness as well as to culture. He joins both. The Dogon smith is even thought to wander in the bush still, in the form of the pale fox known as Yurugu, or Ogo, the Dogon trickster and patron of divination. So it is not surprising to find that in some cultures smithing is directly revealed to humanity by the spirits of the bush. The LoDagaa (Ghana) teach their middle-level Bagre initiates that in the beginning there were two brothers who were troubled by God until Younger Brother set off to find a solution. Overcoming several obstacles, including the crossing of an impassable river, he passed into a forest where he met with the beings of the wild, the bush spirits who control hunting and fishing even today. They taught him how to be a farmer, to clear the bush and plant grain, to harvest it and to cook it. They also taught him how to make fire, how to forge metal, and even what tools to make. Finally, they revealed how to make a smelter and how to be a smith. Following this, Younger Brother, now the ancestral smith, had a vision of the primal essences of the universe engaged in generative intercourse: the rain mated with the earth. A tree was created by this intercourse, which lifted him to heaven. There God instructed him directly in the mysteries of sexuality and family life.

A major theme in the myths of mediatory figures is creative sacrifice. Such sacrifice often marks the break between the primal era of flux and the following heroic age when the basic elements of the divine order are clearly established. Fittingly, the foundation myths of kingship and other chiefly offices often include an account of how the king sacrificed his main opponent (the aboriginal ruler) or a surrogate of him and thus began his kingly office. The sacrifice equates to the determination of order out of disorder. A common variant has the hero himself sacrificed, so that his spirit may live on in those who possess his regal implements and who fulfill his role (in a kind of eternal spirit possession). So it is with the Dogon priest-chief, the *hogon*, whose career is modeled on the exemplary death and sacrifice of the first *hogon*, Lébé (whose death, in turn, mirrors the sacrifice of the serpent opponent of the first smith). Human sacrifices therefore often marked the installation of kings, and the royal candidate himself might have to go through a symbolic death and resurrection, being killed as a natural human being or aboriginal ruler so that he can be revived as primordial king made flesh. Aged or blemished kings were actually sacrificed in some cultures so that the archetypal royal spirit inhabiting them might be released and be able to take over the offered body of the candidate.

The Shilluk say that their founding king, Nyikang, left his home country and traveled to the Nile. The waters parted, and he walked across on dry land, or, as it is more usually said, a white albino slave bore him across the river (he could not touch the waters himself). The slave, tainted by this sacrilegious contact, was sacrificed on the other side, and Nyikang walked between the two halves of his body, symbolically entering into and possessing the new land. He went on to conquer the native inhabitants and to institute culture, marrying the daughter of the aboriginal chief and so becoming husband to the land she embodied. Some myths claim that Nyikang was the offspring of a waterspirit, the crocodile mother of water creatures; this is why he has control over the rains, the Nile floods, and the fertility of the land. However, when a king's generative powers begin to slacken (his watery semen cease to flow, drought occur, famine or disease spread, etc.), he must disappear and allow the spirit of Nyikang to be passed on intact and unblemished. The ritualized installation of the successor imitates the myth of Nyikang's first conquest of the land, even down to such details as the sacrifice of an albino slave.

The Dinka, neighbors to the Shilluk who share many of their cultural values, are led by spear masters (priests who own the land) and war leaders (metaphorically, younger nephews of the spear masters, their maternal uncles). The various accounts of how the spear masters first appeared agree that in the beginning there was a spirit or ancestor called Aiwel Longar (born, some say, after the river impregnated a human woman). Aiwel Longar was powerful and mischievous even as a child, and he eventually fled hostile human society to live with the river spirit for a time. After he returned, his prosperity made people jealous, for their herds were perishing in a drought. Finally, Aiwel Longar offered to lead all of them to paradisiacal pastures, but they refused and set off on their own. The crucial event of the myth then follows, alike in all versions. Aiwel Longar laid in wait for them at a river, and as they tried to cross it, metaphorically like fish, he speared them as Dinka fishermen spear fish. One leader (differing in name according to the subtribe telling the myth) placed an ox's sacrum on his head as he crossed through the reeds, and Longar's spear was deflected. A substitutionary ox sacrifice was henceforth the basis of cultic ritual. Longar confessed himself beaten and bestowed the powers of the spear masters on the leader who had outwitted him; he also established other major features of culture. In one verison, Longar was speared by God in punishment; his head and body pinned to the ground, Longar joined heaven and earth (just like the spear masters). Thus impaled, Longar promised his help to humanity and disappeared. Spear masters, his embodiments since then, are actually buried alive when they grow too old, releasing their spirits to continue their cultic mediation.

Binary Oppositions and Interchanges. Almost universal in African mythologies is a dialectical interchange between male and female elements to produce the various aspects of the world. A creation myth of the marriage of heaven and earth often lays the groundwork. The Zulu (South Africa) may serve as an example for a closer look.

There has been some controversy concerning the status of uNkulunkulu in Zulu religion, but it appears probable that he is merely a culture hero given demiurge status, while the supreme being should be identified specifically with iNkosi yeZulu, "heavenly lord" (a title rather than a proper name, for one ought not presume to name the great directly, especially within its presence). Edwin W. Smith, in his *African Ideas of God* (1961), observed that while uNkulunkulu was spoken of as creator, it is in terms of his making things below as the agent and slave of God above (p. 108). A praise name of iNkosi yeZulu indicates this priority, which, with the fate-determining power, is one of the chief characteristics of the African supreme being: uZivelele (he who came of himself into being). Prayers used to be offered to iNkosi yeZulu for rain, and when storms were too frightening, rain doctors would pray to the celestial god as follows: "Move away, thou Lord of the Lord, move away, thou greatest of friends, move away, thou . . . Irresistible One!" (Smith, 1961, p. 109). God is also too close in thunderstorms or when the mist veils the earth; then people should stay indoors, for the lightning bird, sent by God, may strike down the guilty or unfortunate.

But if iNkosi yeZulu is self-created, he is also the first-born of serpentine twins, and the earth is his female twin. The rain is likened to the semen of God (a widespread conception among Bantu-speaking peoples). Every spring the Zulu nation celebrated the nuptials of Heaven and Earth, the latter embodied in the ever-virginal uNomkhubulwana, or iNkosazana. Sometimes also called the daughter of the first-born, she is said to be everything: river on one side, forest on the other, laden with all kinds of food, and surrounded by mist. The rainbow and the python are both identified with her and are forms of her or her servants; there is a giant python said to dwell in a sacred pool, surrounded by lesser snakes, the metamorphosed ancestral spirits. The python has a special relationship with the rainmaker doctor: when rain is needed, the doctor goes out to a certain rock in the pool in the dead of night. The snake emerges, licks off the fat from sheep or goat skins covering the motionless doctor, and recharges the medicines lying about. They will be used the next day to bring rain. Similarly, diviners are initiated by entering the pool in trance and meeting the great python under water. They may find giant mating serpents ruling there.

The marriage of the mythic archetypes Heaven and Earth provides the basic framework for such beliefs and can be symbolized by the mating of twin water serpents. From this all life originally comes. The ancestors return to dwell with the python being, too. Among some central Bantu-speaking peoples, the entire creation is said to have begun with two mating serpents or from within a giant serpent womb. In any case, the marriage of Heaven and Earth explains the otherwise enigmatic Zulu myth of the origin of humanity: the first ancestral couple emerged from a reed growing in swampland. Myths of the emergence of humanity from underground, or the primeval swamp, usually via a sacred plant or tree, are very common. Initiates throughout Africa are often made to emerge from actual or symbolic underground tunnels and/or to lie gestating beneath certain trees for long periods of time. As Jacqueline Roumeguère-Eberhardt has also shown, the symbolisms of Venda and other South African initiations, in which novices are said to lie within the womb of a great serpent, are precisely repeated in the initiatic symbolisms of such distant peoples as the Fulbe of West Africa. The Dogon also conceptualize the earth as a womb from which the first ancestors emerged via a bamboo. The first couple had been nurtured by serpentine twin spirits, the Nommo, in their underground placental chamber.

Following the mythic era in which Heaven and Earth generated the first forms of life comes the epoch of the culture hero and the founding of culture. Chieftaincy and kingship are legitimated by these myths, which installation rites may reenact. Here, too, the binary oppositions are repeated. They may be represented by the struggle of the culture hero with the forces of the primeval earth. The battle is often resolved by a conquest that is symbolized by a sacrificial rite, and is stabilized by a sexual relationship. Conquest, sacrifice, and sexuality are three powerful metaphors of transformation. For example, the Korekore, a Shona people of Chakoma District (Zimbabwe), say that Nyanhehwe, the ancestral culture hero who settled this area for the Korekore, had to fight the earth serpent Dzivaguru, who ruled the region and laid it to waste. It was a battle of forceful cunning against the magic of the earth, but Dzivaguru finally conceded defeat and even offered to share his mystical powers and medicines before retiring into the mountain pool where his shrine is still located. He also taught Nyanhehwe the social laws and the proper cult for obtaining rain from him. (These events may be compared with the history of Itonde and Indombe among the Nkundo, related earlier.) The culture hero henceforth viewed the earth as his wife, although this is a reciprocally applicable symbolism, since chiefs have had to offer virgins periodically to the spirit as its wives: some maintained the shrine, and some were ritually drowned in the pool. The rainmaker priests who preside over the shrine and its sacrificial cult protect the king mystically and are feminine to him.

Luc de Heusch has shown that throughout the central Bantu-speaking area and beyond, there is a complex mythic pattern involving a culture hero's conquest of a monstrous or uncouth opponent (an elder brother, a savage earlier ruler, or even a magician who turns eventually into a water serpent and goes down to rule the dead and the rains from the depths of a river or pool). The culture hero may be the Sun, who conquers his elder or twin brother, the Moon, thus instituting the primacy of day over night and culture over nature. (Formerly the sun and moon were of equal brightness.)

The Luba explain that the first king was an egalitarian but savage ruler of Pygmies, given to coarse habits and impulsive violence. This king, Nkongolo, who now assumes the form of a rainbow serpent, had two sisters, one of whom married a refined stranger, Mbiti Kiluwe. Mbiti's aristocratic ways shamed Nkongolo, and Mbiti was finally driven away by the king. But the sister gave birth to Mbiti's son, Kalala Ilunga, whom Nkongolo hated almost from his birth; after various conflicts, the king was prevented from attacking his infant rival because the infant had managed to flee to the other side of a river that the king could not cross (many African sacred kings are prohibited from setting foot in water, lest they fuse instantaneously with their true spiritual element, change into a water being, and leave the land and the people without the fertilizing presence of their ruler). This Luba Herod was finally decapitated by Kalala Ilunga, his body placed in the river and his head in a termite mound (termite mounds are generally regarded in central Africa as residences of the dead) or in the king's ritual hut. When the rainbow rises up and unites the body with the head, humanity cannot endure: this is the time of annual summer drought. The Luba also picture the rainbow as mating serpents, Nkongolo committing incest with his sister or heaven uniting with earth. Only when Kalala Ilunga decapitates the serpent and separates the halves of the body can the mediated human order and culture arise, with the gentler fusions of controlled rains aiding the growth of life instead of overwhelming it. So it is possible to sow and reap and depend on the seasonal recapitulation of archetypal myths. The Shilluk concepts outlined earlier belong in the same framework. This is why the death of a sacral king, embodiment of the culture hero, requires the reenactment of the basic symbolisms of the hero myth and even of the primal creation to reconstitute the world and its distinct gradations.

These polar oppositions are repeated endlessly in everyday life and thought. The Ila (Zambia) believe that every human being is shaped in the fiery womb by two tiny serpentine creatures (*bapuka*), an inert male and an active female who molds the semen and menstrual blood into the infant. The Ila homestead is likened to a similar womb in which the mother and father cooperate in procreating and then molding the children. The upper frame of each doorway has two breasts modeled on it and a symbol of fire placed below them, all of which is enclosed in the figure of an undulating serpent. Every granary has the same symbols modeled on it, and a basically similar symbolism controls smithing and even the entire layout of villages.

Examples have thus far been taken primarily from Bantu cultures, but as has been hinted already, similar oppositions appear in West African religions. According to the research of Percy Amaury Talbot in *The Peoples of Southern Nigeria* (1926), the figures of a celestial, fertilizing supreme being and a chthonic generative earth mother are encountered throughout this region and in nearly every tribe. There is often a direct cult to the supreme being, but the earth mother, as the nearest intermediary to God or, indeed, even as God herself, is more emphasized. God may be addressed as male in certain spheres and female in others. The people of the Nike region among the Igbo hold Chukwu to be the maker of everything, the one who divided the cosmos into two parts: the female Earth (Ani) and the male Sky (Igwe). Both reflect Chukwu. Each is in turn divided into two parts by the east-west travel of the (male) Sun and the south-north travel of the (female) Moon, creating not only the four directions but also the four days of the Igbo week. So, as in many cultures of the region, a constantly redoubled binary opposition shapes all levels of life. Villages in the Nike region are spatially and socially divided into upper celestial indigenes and lower earthly immigrants. Some villages extend this into a quadruple division. Even the most abstract expressions of southern Nigerian thought, such as the Ifa divinatory system, are shaped out of the doubled and redoubled combinations of male and female potencies, the father and mother creating the four spirits of the cardinal points, and these children creating the rest of the sixteen primal signs. These three generations, in their further interaction, generate the total of 256 signs, each of which represents some element of reality.

R. S. Rattray, in *Tribes of the Ashanti Hinterland*, a survey of indigenous cultures in the interior of modern Ghana, found the identification of the earth with a wife of the celestial supreme being without exception in all ethnic groups of the area, and her cult is central to the religions there. Sacrifices to her at tree shrines (the forest and the earth being identified) punctuate the seasonal calendar. The dead dwell with her. These ethnic groups also have earth priests as the heads of their clans, appointed from the direct descendants of the aboriginal settlers of the region. The legitimacy of kings who have invaded and conquered local peoples rests on their ritualized good relations with the earth priests. Often, however, chieftaincy and priesthood are merged in the same person (as in the case of the Dogon *hogon*). There is also a very sharp distinction made between the spirits of the cultivated fields and those of the bush. The Ashanti themselves, with their associated cultures, distinguish between Asase Afwa, earth mother of the cultivated fields, and Asase Yaa, her jealous sister of the underworld.

Many of the myths of these cultures deal with the question of how the wilderness emerged out of the garden of the primal era and came to almost overwhelm the scattered human settlements of the present. For from the beginning God intended for the world to be a tilled garden without bloodshed, work, hunting, or sorrow.

The Bambara (Mali), a Mande people of the western Sudanic region who formerly ruled a vast empire, developed their answer in astonishing detail and profundity. Only the general outlines of their cosmogonic myth may be sketched here because it is complex and exists in many versions. In the beginning, pure consciousness, or nothingness (*yo*), sought to know itself. Two mighty efforts at this task in succession formed two androgynous demiurges. The first, Pemba, contained all potentialities in still inchoate form, while the second, Faro, brought these potentialities into clear harmony and realization. Faro designed and created the heavens and the earth and eventually created the first human couple, distinct male and female, to counter the violent and clumsy sexual dualism created by Pemba. Pemba, seeking to rule over all, had planted himself in the earth as the first tree and generated from it a feminine being, the deformed woman Mousso Koroni Koundyé. Thus Pemba wrenched from himself his female half and together with it in bloody and violent intercourse generated all plants and animals. When Faro created humans, Pemba sought to rule them too, especially lusting after the women. Mousso Koroni Koundyé went mad with frustrated longing and jealousy and roamed the wastelands (as she still does), struggling to create life all by herself with the first crude agriculture. She also circumcised and excised all humans she met so that they would share her mutilations and pain, and to spite Pemba she told them his secrets. Thus the initiation cults were founded.

When Mousso Koroni Koundyé was no longer pregnant, she menstruated, thus bequeathing this to women as well. She polluted the earth, creating the true wilderness from this pollution, and then she died, thus introducing death into the world. Faro had to intervene and restore order to the universe; he overcame Pemba and taught the proper ways of farming in order to purify the earth from Mousso Koroni Koundyé. He revealed true speech and culture and reformed the cults. Blacksmiths continue to embody him in the world and, as such, they preside over initiations. Faro dwells in the terrestial and celestial waters, purifying and fertilizing the earth. The purpose of farming and of human domestic and cultural life is to cooperate with Faro in extending purity and divine order throughout the world, regenerating and transforming it.

An oddly similar answer to the problem of wilderness, as it may be called (the African form of the problem of evil, in a way), is given by the Fali (Cameroon), a people who live far from the Bambara. They believe that the universe is the result of the energies spiraling from two cosmic eggs. One, of the female toad (a water creature, cold and wet), spun to the west, like the sun; the other, of the male tortoise (a creature of dry land) spun to the east. These were twins. Within each egg, the contents turned in the opposite direction from the shell, constituting a kind of intercourse of male seed and female moisture, the twins within each egg. When the eggs touched, they shattered and projected outward two square earths (one black, the other red), each containing a half of all plant and animal life. The Tortoise aligned and joined the two earths so that they stopped spinning and were still. The eastern sector was the human, domesticated world, but the wilderness of the west was ruled by the black dog being, the smith. Descending from heaven the smith had touched down with the dawn in the east and planted the eight main grains in the center of the world. In this he obeyed God, for hunting had been forbidden; but he loved to hunt and eventually ignored God's command. So a drought came, forcing the smith to ascend to heaven. God lowered a new ark containing the seeds of life to the earth, but the evil smith again intervened, cutting the vine stalk and causing the ark to fall into a sterile land where it shattered into four parts (as recounted in an earlier section). So the world now stands, with the wilderness surrounding the habitations of humanity everywhere.

The task of the Fali is to re-create the original harmony of the two eggs and the balances established in the ark. The society is divided into two intermarrying clans—the Tortoise and Toad—and their interrelations must be in accord with the divine plan. Relations between husband and wife are also shaped by this motive. Every house is built so as to duplicate the ark, every village is laid out with this in mind, and the slightest rules of social and political life are structured in terms of the creation myth. Despite the false start given to culture by the evil smith (who continues to govern the wild), human life is directed by the desire to limit the disintegrations of chaos.

A penetrating point made by these myths is that human culture is not only shaped by a divine order or revelation but is also the product of a divine misdirection and perversity. The very cult that humanity celebrates is in part based on falsehood, a falsehood of the spirits. The myth of the Bagre initiation cult, among the LoDagaa, actually stresses this point explicitly several times: present life and even the cult is the product of the lies and tricks of God and the bush spirits. Nonetheless it remains a (generally) effective cult, and to preserve the ancestral beauties of this pitiful human condition, it must continue. The culture hero and trickster myths are illuminated by such unsentimental and unflinching comments.

COSMIC EGG AND PRIMAL WORD: THEOSOPHICAL MYTHS. As the above accounts indicate, many Sudanic and West African religions contain astonishing speculations known only to the higher ranks of the initiated. These speculations must often be called theosophical, for they attempt to describe the inner unfolding of the divine life itself, God's internal history, which is identified often enough with the universe's own coming-to-be. In two long articles Germaine Dieterlen (1955 and 1959) tried to show that a common myth is found throughout the western Sudan, among the peoples of the Niger River and beyond (especially those influenced by the Mande cultures). It involves the evolution of the world from the cosmic egg made by God (this egg may also be likened to an infinitesimal seed of the most ritually important crop). The cosmic egg contains twins, one of which comes out of the egg prematurely (thus making of itself an inauthentic elder brother); this would-be creator makes a bad world in which confusion and passion predominate. To regenerate the world, God sacrifices the younger (but authentically elder) twin, creating out of it an elaborately structured but perfectly harmonious order. Humanity must duplicate this order in all things. These religions give prominence to water spirits and center on fishing and agriculture; hunting is viewed negatively. Some of these cultures equate the cosmic egg to the primal word or speech uttered by God, which progressively unfolds through various stages of vibration into this perceptual universe.

A massive work by Viviana Pâques, *L'arbre cosmique*, has not only given substance to Dieterlen's claim but has also extended it in surprising directions. The myths outlined by Dieterlen are discovered in a multitude of forms extending from the Niger into the Muslim world of North Africa, preserved as a kind of pagan mystery in secret black brotherhoods, among those brought as slaves into the Muslim world. In the isolated oases of the Sahara, which have gone through millennia of internal development and gradual cultural blending, these myths are held by nonblack societies as well, despite Muslim pressures. For example, on the Fezzan oasis, the pre-Muslim Garamantes lived from prehistoric times, slowly absorbing other peoples (including black Africans from the entire Sudanic savanna) while maintaining their own culture; they were also deeply affected by Egyptian influences and, perhaps shared common Saharan motifs with prehistoric Egyptian societies. Their cosmogony was suggested in the sacrifice of a ram divided into forty-eight parts (made up of two halves, each composed of four times six pieces). This sacrifice, enacted at all personal and seasonal rites, commemorated the primordial sacrifice of the ancestral smith or serpentine water spirit who brought culture to them. The reason for the multiples of four and six is that four was considered male and three female, and the world is woven of the two together. This myth presented the key to the rhythms of the heavenly bodies, the seasons of the year, clothes, territorial structures, political and social divisions, and much else.

Some Sudanic cultures in northern Ghana, Burkina Faso, and Mali have had the reputation of, in pre-colonial times, offering human sacrifices at crucial times that required enactments of the myth. Virginal girls were preferred, but albinos were also acceptable. The name of the mythic sacrificial victim in southern Tunisia is Israel, suggesting the adaptation of the myth by Berber tribes formerly converted to Judaism. When sacrificed in heaven, Israel, also known as the angel ʿAzraʾel, is reconstituted in the world below as the sacred community of the Twelve Tribes and also as the plan of the cultivated field. More Muslim versions make Israel into the bush-trickster figure, illustrating again the historical adaptations of what is apparently a fundamental Saharan mythic structure. One of the most striking authentically sub-Saharan expressions of these conceptions is the mythology of the Dogon.

DOGON MYTHOLOGY. Of all cultures in Africa, it is of the Dogon of Mali on which exists the most voluminous and profound data relating to mythic themes. In the first years spent among them, Marcel Griaule and his students merely confirmed the impression of earlier observers that the Dogon possessed a rich ritual but only an impoverished mythology. These alleged characteristics of the Dogon were consistent with other descriptions of African cultures made by Europeans. The cult was pragmatic, directed to the clan ancestors (*binu*) and the nature spirits who resided especially in the streams (Nommo). The regional priest who presided over these cults, the *hogon*, was said to be the descendant of the first ancestral chief, Lébé, who led the people to Dogon territory. The *hogon* was, in particular, the high priest to Amma, the supreme being, and he had the standing of a chief, governing the region together with the clan elders. In an early work, Dieterlen related one of the few myths collected: in the beginning Amma dwelt with humans and they served him. When a Muslim refused to get him a drink of water, Amma decided to withdraw to heaven; but because a Dogon rushed to serve him, God revealed the present cult, by which he could be reached through his servant spirits, to the Dogon. (As known, myths of this sort, recalling the personal fateful encounters with God in the beginning, are perhaps the most universal of African mythic themes and are shared even by hunter-gatherers such as the central African Pygmies.)

In 1947, however, after fifteen years of fieldwork, Griaule was approached by Ogotemmêli, a blind elder of the Dogon, and rewarded for his many years of service to the people by the revelation of a totally unexpected world of myth, a world accessible only to initiated Dogon men. Griaule recorded this revelation in *Conversations with Ogotemmêli.* The symbolic depth, complexity, and length of this mythic narrative evoked irresistible parallels to ancient Egyptian mythology and to Christianity. Griaule discovered, for example, that the Muslim-caused withdrawal of God was merely a childish fable; in fact, Amma created the earth in the beginning, in the form of a woman. He cohabited with her to produce the Nommo, who came forth as bisexual twins. Even today the rain and the watery copper rays of the sun are like heaven's semen, generating life throughout the earth. The Nommo, masters of life force and of all wisdom, continue to govern the fertility of the world from their watery residences. Their eight seeds are carried by every human being, shaping sexual procreativity. The first eight ancestors of humanity were produced by the marriage of heaven and earth and nurtured underground by the twin Nommo. However, the first Nommo to be created, Yurugu, had no twin and was not bisexual but male; his frustrated passion for completion (not stopping even at the theft of an ark, or womb of creation, and incest with Mother Earth) threatened to disorder the whole of God's creation. God therefore exiled him to the bush, where he roams still as a jackal, but, oddly, he remains the patron of divination. To cleanse the earth of the pollution introduced by the jackal trickster, God took the last of the eight created Nommo and sacrificed him in heaven; his blood fell upon the earth as a sanctifying rain, and cleansed it, permitting life to continue.

The first human, Lébé, reduplicated the cosmic sacrifice here on earth, for he was swallowed and regurgitated by a Nommo serpent being. Lébé thus established the sacred role of chieftaincy and the cultic importance of sacrifice. Everything in human culture mirrors the primal form of Lébé and the dynamic of sacrifice, which through its transformations restores the world to the ideal form of the ark and its Nommo progenitor. The parts of houses, the sections of a family compound, the layout of a village, and the relations within the clan, all mirror the primal male and female. The female twin to the eighth Nommo still regularly visits the *hogon* in the shrine, licking him all over in the dead of night so as to regenerate his sacred energies before returning, in serpentine form, to the river. Everything in life is controlled by twinness, by male and female together. The *hogon* represents the interaction of both of these principles, and that is why he is the chief and high priest.

Griaule and his students found in these astonishing myths a complete key to Dogon culture, governing even the smallest details of everyday life. However, as it turned out, there are grades of initiation in Dogon culture, and as the years passed Griaule was introduced to deeper and deeper levels. He discovered that the universe did not actually first emerge from the marriage of Heaven and Earth, as so many other African religions held, but that there was an evolution from a cosmic egg or seed, similar to the fonio seed, which is the center of so much of the agricultural ritual of the Dogon. This egg contained four twinned couples, the quintessential elements of creation. The distorted nature of Yurugu was due to his premature attempt to break out of the cosmic egg before his brothers and sisters and to make of the placental egg itself (the universal matrix) his female consort—in short, to rule the universe. To restore the disturbed harmony of the cosmos, God permitted it to be expanded via the ark into this earth. Thus by building houses and villages and plowing their fields on the model of the cosmic egg or ark, humanity regenerates the harmonies of creation. This can only be done through knowledge of the initiatic truths; wisdom and serene insight are necessary to save or sanctify the world properly. This alone is the proper service of God.

In his last, posthumously published, magnum opus on Dogon mythology (written with Dieterlen), *Le renard pâle,* Griaule revealed that the cosmic egg was not the deepest secret of creation. Beyond that the wisest Dogon taught the mysteries of the primal word spoken by Amma, from which the entire universe emanated and which the universe reproduces. The egg may be taken as a symbolism of this deeper process. The primordial word or utterance is, in fact, Amma (God). It has, when truly spoken, eight syllables or cosmic vibrations, which became the twinned Nommo. All things echo these eight vibrations: there are eight kinds of insects, plants, animals, parts of houses and of human bodies, musical tones and modes, dialects of the Dogon language, and so on. Language—and consciousness itself—is the pivot of the universe. The wisest Dogon cultivate a meditative silence, attuning themselves to the divine utterance, which continues to be spoken and to generate the universe and all details in it. Yurugu, whose true name is Ogo, whose true animal form is that of the pale fox (not the jackal)—and who is also linked to the spider—actually serves God in ceaselessly transforming things and introducing change; this brings the universe nearer to perfection. The primal sacrifice of the youngest Nommo is part of the same process. In short, the myths of lower levels of initiation are all taken up again in this most esoteric version and subsumed under it as later, more materialized stages in the cosmic history.

Because the deepest wisdom centers on speech and its vibrations within the cosmic consciousness, Dogon sages developed the essentials of a script. Each of the first eight Nommo vibrations, for example, could be represented by a shape, rather similar in form to the Arabic letters. Dogon elders could show how these flowing shapes branched, diversified, and took material form as all the actual things of this world, stage by stage. In effect, this so-called illiterate culture had a form of writing. The priests would trace words into the foundations of altars and houses before building any further; the words contained the essence, of which the material things were the less perfect form.

Ironically, the most archaic and universally distributed types of mythic themes are preserved by the Dogon as childish folk tales or exoteric, ad hoc, and topical tales (as in the story of the Muslim and God's withdrawal). Each successive level of esotericism concerns a more recent cultural synthesis. The most esoteric myths evidently represent a response to the challenge of literate civilization, but unlike the topical and episodic response on the exoteric folk level, this response is thoroughly thought through and integrated with the entirety of Dogon culture by its sages. Each challenge is treated as a kind of revelation of deeper metaphysical realities guiding the universe, demanding a whole cultural response instead of a fragmentary one. The Dogon elders have been in the forefront of harmonious and constructive change, contrary to the European view of them as unchanging conservatives. The deep functional and spiritual relevance of myth and worldview could hardly be demonstrated more dramatically than in this process.

See Also Bambara Religion; Dogon Religion; Nuer and Dinka Religion; Southern African Religions, article on Southern Bantu Religions; Tricksters, article on African Tricksters; Zulu Religion.

Bibliography

Some good, if rather superficial, surveys of African mythology are Alice Werner's "African Mythology," in volume 7 of *The Mythology of All Races* (Boston, 1925), pp. 105–359, and Geoffrey Parrinder's *African Mythology*, 2d ed. (London, 1982). Another survey to consider is Edwin W. Smith's *African Ideas of God* (London, 1961). Briefer, but reflecting more current French scholarship, and arranged by culture areas rather than topically, and so, more contextual and historical, is Roger Bastide's "Africa: Magic and Symbolism," in *Larousse World Mythology*, edited by Pierre Grimal (New York, 1965), pp. 519–545.

Excellent regional anthologies are *Myths and Legends of the Congo*, edited by Jan Knappert (Nairobi, Kenya, 1971), and *Myths and Legends of the Bantu* (1933; London, 1968) by Alice Werner, who also offers comments in topically arranged chapters. The studies of nine cultures in *African Worlds: Studies in the Cosmological Ideas and Social Values of African Peoples*, edited by Daryll Forde (London, 1954), give a good insight into the role of myth in African worldviews.

Interesting books devoted to the myths of particular cultures include Axel-Ivar Berglund's *Zulu Thought-Patterns and Symbolism* (London, 1976); Daniel P. Biebuyck's studies of the hero epics of the Nyanga of Zaire, *The Mwindo Epic from the Banyanga (Congo Republic)* (Berkeley, Calif., 1969) and *Hero and Chief: Epic Literature from the Banyanga, Zaire Republic* (Berkeley, Calif., 1978); Jack Goody's *The Myth of the Bagre* (Oxford, 1972); Marcel Griaule's *Conversations with Ogotemmêli*, translated by Robert Redfield (London, 1965), and *Le renard pâle* (Paris, 1965); Melville J. Herskovits's *Dahomey: An Ancient West African Kingdom*, 2 vols. (New York, 1938); E. Bolaji Idowu's *Olódùmarè: God in Yoruba Belief* (London, 1962); Randall M. Packard's *Chiefship and Cosmology* (Bloomington, Ind., 1981); R. S. Rattray's *Tribes of the Ashanti Hinterland* (London, 1932); Percy Amaury Talbot's *The Peoples of Southern Nigeria* (London, 1926); and Roy Willis's *A State in the Making: Myth, History and Social Transformation in Pre-Colonial Ufipa* (Bloomington, Ind., 1981).

Comparative and analytical studies of African mythology have been pursued especially by French and German scholars. A brilliant structuralist analysis of the myths of central Bantu-speaking peoples is Luc de Heusch's *The Drunken King, or The Origin of the State* (Bloomington, Ind., 1982); de Heusch extends his analysis to political myths of Rwandan kings and to southern African myths and rites in *Mythes et rites bantous*, vol. 2, *Rois nés d'un coeur de vache* (Paris, 1982). Particularly valuable for an understanding of West African mythology is Germaine Dieterlen's *Les âmes des Dogon* (Paris, 1941); her two articles in *Journal de la Société des Africanistes* concerning the common mythic structure found throughout the western Sudanic region, "Mythe et organisation au Soudan Français," vol. 25, nos. 1–2 (1955): 39–76, and "Mythe et organisation sociale en Afrique occidentale," vol. 29, nos. 1–2 (1959): 119–138, are also useful. Viviana Pâques's work *L'arbre cosmique dans la pensée populaire et dans la vie quotidienne du Nord-ouest Africain* (Paris, 1964), uses Dieterlen's analysis and applies it in interesting ways to a wider geographical region.

Somewhat outdated but still very informative historical and comparative analyses of African creation myths are two works by Hermann Baumann, *Schöpfung und Urzeit des Menschen im Mythus der afrikanischen Völker* (Berlin, 1936) and *Das Doppelte Geschlecht* (Berlin, 1955); the latter work surveys mythologies of other continents as well. Harry Tegnaeus's *Le Héros civilisateur* (Stockholm, 1950) concerns African culture heroes. Robert D. Pelton's *The Trickster in West Africa* (Berkeley, Calif., 1980) takes a phenomenological approach and primarily discusses the Ashanti, Yoruba Fon, and Dogon tricksters. Jürgen Zwernemann's *Die Erde in Vorstellungswelt und Kultpraktiken der sudanischen Völker* (Berlin, 1968) deals with the image of the earth mother and the earth spirits in Sudanic myth and cult, with a brief survey of other African cultures as well. Jacqueline Roumeguère-Eberhardt's *Pensée et société africaines* (Paris, 1963) links Sudanic and southern African myths and cultures in a fascinating study of serpent myths, initiation rites, and cosmology. A good discussion of the role of the serpent, and of other symbolic creatures, in African mythologies can be found in Bohumil Holas's *Les dieux d'Afrique noire* (Paris, 1968). Holas is also an authority on the esoteric myths of a number of the cultures of the Ivory Coast and Guinea, such as the Bété; these are discussed as well.

An elaborate analysis of African myths concerning the origin of death, focusing on specific themes or traits and their geographical dispersion, is Hans Abrahamsson's *The Origin of Death* (Uppsala, Sweden, 1951). Valuable discussions of hero myths and legends are contained in Isadore Okpewho's *The Epic in Africa* (New York, 1979) and *Myth in Africa* (London, 1983). The latter work, graced with an excellent bibliography, is really a methodological study; despite its name it does not study the myths of Africa but instead reviews modern theories of myth and African folklore, advancing its own approach using examples from African mythology. It is particularly helpful in discussing the roles and uses of myth in modern African literature and general culture.

New Sources

Pemberton, John, III, and Funso Afolayan. *Yoruba Sacred Kingship: A Power Like That of the Gods.* Washington, D.C., 1996.

Ray, Benjamin. *Myth, Ritual and Kingship in Buganda.* New York, 1991.

Verboven, Dirk. *A Paxiological Approach to Ritual Analysis: The Sigi of the Dogon.* Ghent, Belgium, 1986.

EVAN M. ZUESSE (1987)
Revised Bibliography

AFRICAN RELIGIONS: NEW RELIGIOUS MOVEMENTS

Modern African religious movements are best understood if interpreted as creative and innovative responses to the historically unprecedented levels of upheaval and change in every area of life—cultural, economic, environmental, social, political, and religious—that followed the imposition of colonial rule, beginning in the second half of the nineteenth century. The primary aim of these movements has not been to return in fundamentalist fashion to the past and remain there but rather to review critically the traditional cultural and religious processes with a view to constructive engagement with the new.

Although the focus here is on modern African movements of Christian, Muslim, and neotraditional derivation, or combinations thereof, to illustrate something of the range and variety of Africa's modern religious tapestry, there is also discussion of modern religious movements that have entered Africa from abroad including those created by African diaspora communities, neo-Hindu movements, Buddhist-Shintō healing movements from Japan, and secular religions from the West.

TYPOLOGIES. Modern African movements vary greatly doctrinally, structurally, and liturgically, and Bryan R. Wilson's (1973) system of classification is possibly the most suitable for dealing with this variety, primarily because it is free of theological, organizational, historical, and cultural bias. Wilson's typology is based on movements' responses to the world and interpretations of the sources of evil and how it is to be overcome. From this perspective modern African religious movements can be fit with one or a combination of Wilson's seven types of modern or new religious movements: These are: (1) the conversionist response, which insists that individual and collective salvation can only come about through a profound, supernaturally wrought transformation of the self; (2) the revolutionist response, which believes that evil can only be overcome and salvation assured by divine action, thus no subjective change however profound will affect the state of the world for the better; (3) the introversionist response, which seeks salvation by withdrawing to a separate, purified community set apart from what is perceived to be an irredeemably evil world; (4) the manipulationist or gnostic response, which seeks salvation and the conquest of evil though the acquisition of the right means and techniques to deal with the problems of life; (5) the thaumaturgical response, which relies chiefly on miracles and oracles to attain salvation, which is identified as something specific such as the relief from a particular illness; (6) the reformist response, which aspires under divine guidance to overcome evil and save the world by transforming existing social structures and arrangements; and (7) the utopian response, which aims to reconstruct the world according to a set of divine principles that, if correctly applied, will result in the establishment of a world without evil. The main limitations of Wilson's typology are its inability to capture the dynamics of religious change and development movements undergo and their espousal of more than one orientation simultaneously.

Harold Turner's typology (1991), which is based on different kinds of criteria (doctrinal, organizational, and historical) uses the term *neo-primal* to refer to modern movements that seek to remain close to the traditional religion—albeit in a discriminating manner by rejecting certain elements such as magic and, at the same time, making monotheism the core of their belief systems. Turner's second category is the *hebraist* movement, so defined because members believe themselves to be descendants of the ancient Israelites and place great store by biblical prophecies. His label *synthetist* covers those modern religious movements that developed from a combination of traditional and Christian elements, examples include the African Independent Churches or African Initiated Churches (AICs). The last of Turner's categories is the *deviationist,* which he applies to churches and religious movements that give the appearance of being Christian or Islamic but deviate markedly from these religions in fundamentals. Turner's system of classification has little application to non-Christian movements, and this makes it increasingly less useful as the scope of religious innovation and interaction expands to include not only increasing numbers of modern Muslim and neotraditional movements in Africa but many new Asian religions as well.

Roy Wallis's (1984) typology of modern or new religions into world-denying or world-rejecting, world-indifferent, and world-affirming types, although widely used, requires considerable refinement. The world-indifferent category is largely redundant, and the world-affirming category would make a better fit with the response to the world of the modern religions of Africa and elsewhere if replaced by world-transforming.

AICs in Southern Africa and the Democratic Republic of the Congo. AICs were as much concerned with transforming both mission church Christianity and traditional religion and culture as the preservation of the latter. A brief account of a select number of southern AICs illustrates this. However, first a word about Bengt Sundkler's (1970, pp. 52ff.) terminology. He describes the AICs of southern Africa as either Ethiopian or Zionist. The former are AICs that seceded from white mission churches chiefly on racial grounds or those that, although sharing the same concern for African-led churches, are also keenly motivated by the desire for African leadership. The term Zionist is applied by Sundkler to those AICs of southern Africa that refer to themselves as *ama-Ziyoni* (Zionist; the meaning has nothing to do with the Jewish Zionist movement), pointing to their origins in Zion City, Illinois, where the millenarian Christian Catholic Apostolic Church in Zion was founded in 1896 by John Alexander Dowie. This church teaches divine healing, baptism by triune immersion (preferably in a river), and the imminence of the second coming of Jesus and holds tenaciously to the flat Earth theory. As will be seen, Zionist and Ethiopian churches shared many common features. Both demanded greater autonomy and placed great stress on the veneration of ancestors and rituals of purification.

One of the earliest, largest, and most influential of southern Africa's AICs is the amaNazaretha (Nazareth or Nazirite Baptist Church) founded in Zululand, South Africa, in 1913. The aims and ideology of this AIC are paradigmatic of AICs in general. Its founder Mdlimawafa Mloyisa Isaiah Shembe (1867–1935), once a member of the African Native Baptist Church, which had seceded from the white-led Baptist Church, believed in the idea of continuous divine revelation and guidance through dreams and visions. He interpreted sacramental rites as essentially rites of purification (ashes were retained as purgative symbols), modeled his mission on that of the prophet John the Baptist, and forbade the use of Western medicine, believing instead in healing through faith and blessed water.

The amaNazaretha and other AICs also introduced liturgical changes. For example, the sacred wooden drum, seen by mission churches as a separatist symbol, became the main instrument in worship. Also radically changed was the import of the hymn, which was transformed from a verse about certain religious ideas into a sacred rhythm expressed through the medium of sacred dance. AICs were not simply bridge builders between the new religious culture and the old but sought to transform both. Just as the meaning of hymns was changed so was the meaning of traditional dance festivals, which were turned into major liturgical innovations both to deepen (as in the case of the Zulu) awareness of oppression and colonization and to promote greater awareness of their status as God's chosen people. The realized eschatology of the amaNazaretha emphasizes this last point by declaring that the holy mountains of Inhlangakazi, eighty miles from Durban, and Ekuphakameni (the elated place), nearer Durban, are God's most desirable earthly temples and the location of paradise on Earth.

Despite the harassment and persecution from governments, several AICs developed into highly complex organizations with considerable assets. Among the largest and most structurally complex is the Kimbanguist Church (Église de Jesus Christ sur la Terre par Le Prophète Simon Kimbangu; EJCSK), founded in 1921 in what was at the time known as Belgian Congo, later Zaire, and finally the Democratic Republic of the Congo, by Simon Kimbangu (c. 1887–1951). Kimbangu, like Shembe, was selective in his approach to tradition and preaching (e.g., against the use of traditional rituals to combat evil forces). However, unlike Shembe, he stressed the importance of monogamy and spoke of the duty to obey the government. Like AICs generally, the EJCSK lays great store in purification rituals and the use of blessed water for healing and protection. Like many churches of the western African Aladura movement (independent churches characterized by prayer, divine healing, and baptism in the Holy Spirit), the EJCSK has become a huge enterprise with schools, hospitals, factories, and commercial companies.

Although generally not overtly political, AICs often made colonial governments nervous by their wide appeal. Kimbangu's popularity and growing following were such that the colonial government decided to have him court marshaled without any defense in 1921 on charges that included sedition and hostility to whites. Found guilty, Kimbangu was sentenced to 120 lashes and death—a penalty that was commuted to life in solitary confinement in Lumumbashi, two thousand kilometers from his home in the village of Nkamba in the western region of what is now known as the Democratic Republic of the Congo. Kimbangu's remains were reinterred at Nkamba (then called Nkamba-Jerusalem), an important place of pilgrimage, in 1960. The EJCSK operated underground until 1959, six months before independence, when it received official recognition.

AICs are to be found in great numbers elsewhere in southern, central and eastern Africa. In Kenya alone there are over two hundred AICs with several million members between them; the largest of these is the African Independent Pentecostal Church, founded in 1925 and composed mostly of Gikuyu. Also predominantly Gikuyu is the African Orthodox Church, which is under the jurisdiction of the patriarch of Alexandria.

AICs in West Africa. As in southern Africa, the pursuit of independence in church matters began in West Africa as early as the late 1880s, the point in time when many of the historic or mission churches began to abandon their goal of establishing self-governing, self-supporting African churches. In the 1890s the decision to remove the Nigerian-born Anglican bishop of the Niger Delta, Samuel Ajayi Crowther, from his post fueled the drive for ecclesiastical autonomy. The investigation and subsequent dismissal by the London-based Church Missionary Society of Crowther had the psychological effect of putting on trial the capacity of a whole race to govern itself.

By this time many African Christians were already questioning the predominantly European leadership of the Christian churches—opposed at the outset by the Church Missionary Society, the missionary wing of the Anglican Church—and began to form their own denominations. In 1888 in Lagos, Nigeria, the African Baptist Church split off from American Baptist Missionary Society over the question of leadership. African spiritual and cultural identity were also pressing issues. Opposition grew over the imposition of European names at baptism, the wearing of European dress, the exclusive use of European musical instruments and the English language in worship, and to solely white icons of Christ. The West Indian Edward Wilmot Blyden, an educator and Christian pastor in Nigeria at the time, implored mission church Christianity to take a lesson from Muslims on how to adapt Christianity to Africa by, for example, respecting (at least for the foreseeable future) such important social and economic institutions as polygamy.

Also questioned was the missionary claim to be the sole guardians and defenders of immutable moral laws, including those that imposed monogamous marriages, which were perceived to amount to foreign social arrangements. A Nigerian founding member of the African Baptist Church, Mojola Agbebi (baptized David Vincent), expressed the anxieties over cultural and personal identity and the undermining of African self-esteem in his attack on the foreign character of mission church Christianity: "Hymn books, harmonium, dedications, pew constructions, surpliced (sic) choir, the white man's names, the white man's dress, are so many non-essentials, so many props and crutches affecting the religious manhood of the Christian Africans" (cited in Clarke, 1986, p. 160).

The most successful AIC in the early twentieth century in West Africa was led by the Liberian Grebo prophet William Wade Harris (c. 1850–1920). Harris's this-worldly interpretation of Christian baptism as the most effective remedy for both moral and social evil, his preaching of a gospel of prosperity, and his allowing full participation to the polygamous, thereby alleviating the social and economic distress of conversion, account for his success and made for a clear contrast with the more socially and economically disruptive approach of mission church Christianity, widely known as the "Church of children."

Mission church Christianity attempted to counter the success of Harris and other local prophets by labeling them as charlatans and sorcerers. Although he could be strongly critical of traditional customs and religious practices, Joseph William Egyanka Appiah, the founder of the Musamo Christo Disco Church (also known as Army of the Cross of Christ Church), a Ghanaian spiritist church, was dismissed as a sorcerer by the Methodist Church in Ghana. Appiah preached an apocalyptic message mostly derived from the Old Testament. Following the biblical account of *Exodus,* one of his first acts on constructing the Holy City of Mozano, where he took the name Prophet Jemisimiham, was to smear the entrances to the homes of his followers with the blood of a sacrificed animal.

Nothing was predictable and permanent about the history and development of AICs. Often they began not as sects but as movements within the mission churches only eventually to become independent. In some cases, movements that became sectarian, such as the Native Baptist Church in Nigeria, would later be reintegrated into the main body. The Aladura movement in Nigeria began within the Anglican Church at the end of World War I. Warned in a dream that the world would be ravaged by the influenza epidemic, the Nigerian Anglican pastor Joseph Shadare from St. Saviour's Church in the city of Ijebu Ode, joined with a young teacher, Sophia Adefobe Odunlami, to combat the epidemic through the means of blessed water and prayer. In 1920 they formed the Precious Stone-Faith Tabernacle prayer association, which marked the beginnings of the Aladura or prayer movement in Yorubaland.

The Aladura stress on the power of prayer to heal resonated with traditional ideas. Just as early Yoruba Christians, known as Onigbagbo, believed that faith in Jesus bestowed on them "word power" that would affect what they prayed for, traditionalists believed that the chanting of the invocations recommended by the *babalawo* (diviner) would resolve problems of health, relationships, material distress, and so on.

The Aladura movement—in most respects indistinguishable from the southern African AICs—changed the situation of believers from that of passive to engaged participants and soon became widely associated with empowerment. The principal vehicles in the spreading of the movement were local prophets, including Christianah Abiodun Emanuel (1907–198?), also known as Captain Abiodun Emmanuel, who were hailed by followers as direct evidence of the Gospel's authority. Like Kimbangu, these prophets were perceived by the colonizers as potential threats to the stability of the colonial order. Some of these prophets, such as the founder of the Church of the Lord (Aladura), Josiah Oshitelu (1902–?) were directly political and spoke out against unlawful taxation by foreign rulers and against price increases and issued warnings of the dire consequences to come if whites continued to oppress blacks.

The Aladura response to mission church Christianity and traditional religion was selective. The Aladura Cherubim and Seraphim movement, for example, retained the Anglican Book of Common Prayer, Sunday worship, and several of the sacraments. Differences were obvious in worship, however.

Aladura churches encouraged the practice of hand clapping, stamping on the ground—a way of obtaining spiritual power, prosperity and peace—drumming, and demonstrations of the efficacy of sacred words through such exclamations as hallelujah, hosanna, and *iye* (life). Few, however, went as far as the World Christian Soldiers Church, a Kenyan (mainly Luo) movement, founded in 1942, which required all members to use musical instruments in worship. With regard to traditional religion, bans were imposed on the eating of pork, the meat of an animal that had not been slaughtered, the ritual drinking of the blood of animals (a practice acceptable to traditionalists), and the use of alcohol and tobacco.

While colonialism, aided by mission church Christianity, was hastening the process of the decoupling of traditional beliefs from the traditional political, economic, and moral structures to which they had for so long lent plausibility, the rise and rapid growth of the Aladura movement and AICs generally reveal—despite each one being composed mostly of one ethnic group—a preoccupation on an Africa-wide basis with the cultural moral, social, and spiritual limitations of imposed forms of religion in a colonial context.

Political Independence and Modern Movements. New religions and churches continued to emerge in Africa as independence approached as well as since independence was achieved (between 1957 and 1973 for most countries). Started mostly by charismatic leaders or prophets, one of the more striking characteristics of many of the modern movements has been their stridently apocalyptic and millenarian preaching, which has brought them into conflict with the newly independent governments. This was the history of the Lumpa church in Zambia founded by the Bemba prophetess Alice Lenshina (c. 1919–1978) in 1954. Claiming to have been entrusted by God with the secret of success, which the whites had hidden from Africans, and to have been raised up to prepare the world for the second coming of Jesus, Lenshina built the New Zion in the village of Kasomo. A nervous government was suspicious of this burgeoning state within the state, which opposed taxation and political authority, and confrontation led to the death of around one thousand of her followers and the banning of the movement in 1964. Alice Lenshina died in 1978, claiming that the political dimensions of her message had obscured their real content, which was spiritual wholeness and integrity.

Modern Catholic-derived churches and movements also include the Legio Maria, a breakaway movement from the lay Catholic Legion of Mary association. Founded in 1963 in Kenya, the year of independence, Legio Maria's teachings and rituals display the same concerns and preoccupations present in the AICs, which are also evident in relation to traditional belief and practice. The creation of the self-proclaimed prophets Simon Ondeto and Gaudencia Aoko, the Legio Maria, while encouraging their followers to remain Catholics, offered a ministry of deliverance from the evils of witchcraft and spirit possession. Growth was rapid, especially among the Luo, rising to an estimated 100,000 members within two years, a development that the newly independent government did not welcome. Legio Maria's success is in part attributable to the wealth of ritual resources, both Catholic and traditional, which were developed to discern and overcome the forces of evil, such as witchcraft and sorcery.

A very different modern Catholic separatist movement from the Congo (Brazzaville) is the Mouvement Croix-Koma (Nailed to the Cross), which was started in 1964 by the Catholic layman of the Lari tribe, Ta (Father) Malenda. This movement opposed outright such traditional practices as witchcraft, sorcery, and magic and by 1970 had attracted an estimated 20 percent of the population of the Congo, a majority of these coming from the Congo, Lari, and Sundi ethnic groups. At first a movement within Catholicism, this church severed all ties with the Roman Catholic Church in 1976.

Violence has been a feature of a minority of modern African religions as it has been with modern religions elsewhere. The most notorious example in the African context is the Movement for the Restoration of the Ten Commandments of God (MRTCG), which grew out of a Marian apparition movement in Rwanda in the 1970s. Although visions of the Virgin Mary (many of them concerning the devastation being wrought by AIDS) were not uncommon in the Uganda and nearby Rwanda of the 1980s, two principal visionaries are closely associated with the origins and development of the MRTCG. One was the dedicated and active Catholic who was heavily involved in local politics, Joseph Kibwetere (b. 1932), and the other was Credonia Mwerinde (b. 1952), who claimed that she had been in contact with the Virgin Mary since 1984. About this time, Kibwetere, a father of sixteen, began to be considered by followers as the leader of the nascent MRTCG and allowed his farm to be used as its headquarters until in 1992 when it was moved to Kanungu where Mwerinde's family lived and where relations with villagers, but not the civil authorities, were at times tense. Even before this move, the MRTCG had begun to attract a number of clergy including Father Dominic Kitaribaabo, who had been a postgraduate student in religious studies in the United States and had begun to reject some of the liturgical reforms of the Second Vatican Council while still recognizing the authority of the pope. As MRTCG distanced itself from mainstream Catholicism and the local community, it increasingly came to resemble an introversionist movement. Moreover, this growing isolation, reinforced by the apocalyptic messages emanating from the numerous Marian apparitions that had recently occurred, reinforced the belief in the end of the world.

The MRTCG came to depict itself as the ark of salvation, the vessel that would save those who repented from the coming apocalypse and carry them to a place that would be like heaven on Earth. Its teachings, based principally on revelations received by its leaders, were set out in the document, *A Timely Message from Heaven: The End of the Present Times,* which demanded, among other things, the renunciation of material possessions, abstinence from sexual relations, and stressed the importance of silence. Sign language was to be the main means of everyday communication between the members.

According to some scholars (Mayer, 2001), the end was predicted to come in 2000; others (Levinson, 2001) gave 1999. However, on March 17, 2000, tragedy struck. The newly built church at the movement's headquarters at Kanugu served as the venue for the previous night's all-night vigil. The following morning, fire engulfed the nearby dining hall, formerly the old church, where the worshipers had gathered, and then spread throughout the headquarters, killing and destroying everything in its wake and leaving no one with any chance of escape. Different estimates have been given of the number of those who died in this tragic event and in other instances. Subsequent investigations by the Ugandan police in March and April 2000 uncovered graves in various locations around the country that contained the corpses of MRTCG members who had been murdered. According to Jean-François Mayer (2001) the Ugandan police estimated that there were 780 victims in all, whereas David Levinson gives the total number of victims as 925 adding "perhaps all were murdered" (Levinson, 2001, p. 198).

Also of Ugandan origin is the Lord's Resistance Army, which operates largely among the Acholi in northern Uganda, under the direction of the self-proclaimed mystic Joseph Kony, one-time mentor and cousin of Alice Lekwena but who, after a quarrel with the latter, symbolized the discontinuity between her movement and his by being possessed by new and different spirits. Lekwena brought together several disparate antigovernment groups in 1987 under the banner of the Holy Spirit Movement. Defeated by Kony in a power struggle, Lekwena fled to Kenya in 1987, and the former took over the leadership of these religious rebels. Kony continued on with the complex initiation and cleansing rituals introduced by Lekwena and, like her, was determined to stamp out witchcraft and to eradicate pagan spirit mediums. Prior to engaging in battle, Kony's soldiers are "armed" with *malaika* (angel; Swahili) to protect them against the enemy. For further spiritual protection, various spirits were placed in various positions of command whereas others, including spirits from other than African nations such as Korea and China, are assigned other tasks, including the direction of government forces' bullets.

Methods of recruitment of soldiers adopted by Kony have included abducting and indoctrinating children who, when trained for combat are encouraged to loot, pillage, and rape with abandon in contrast with the strict moral discipline imposed by Lakwena. The Lord's Resistance Army battle with the Uganda government—now an international conflict involving neighboring countries such as the Sudan—has led to the death of an estimated twenty-three thousand people and to the creation of over one and a half million refugees.

Although long present in many African traditional religions including Yoruba traditional religion, what appears to be an increasingly widespread trend in Africa as in the West is the appeal of the notion of reincarnation. This is evident in, among other movements, the Brotherhood of the Cross and Star, a millenarian movement founded in 1956 in Calabar, Nigeria, by Olumba Olumba Obu. This new religion, whose goal is the establishment of God's kingdom on Earth by uniting "brothers" and "sisters" in bonds of love, attaches great importance to reincarnation and the belief in the presence at meetings of the "living dead" (a term used for the ancestors whose continued influence over this-worldly affairs is acknowledged), in the sacredness of the earth, and in the all-pervasive influence of sorcery.

Contemporary Forms of Charismatic Christianity. In the 1970s a new wave of charismatic Christianity started from within the existing churches began to sweep across Africa. Essentially composed of young, educated high school and university students, this movement emphasizes baptism in the Holy Spirit, the ready availability for Christians of the gifts and fruits of the Spirit, and speaking in tongues (*glossolalia*). Among the attractions of this ecstatic, optimistic religion is the contrast it makes with the despair generated by politics that, despite the pledges, seems to be incapable of tackling radically such serious concerns as corruption in public life, managing efficiently and effectively public resources, and guaranteeing safety and basic medical facilities.

Charismatic renewal got under way at different times in different parts of the continent. In Kenya and Tanzania in East Africa, it took shape in and was spread through associations such as the Fellowship of Christian Unions (FOCUS), in the mid-1970s. Due to tighter control over students in Ethiopia and Uganda, it was the 1980s before charismatic renewal came to occupy center stage of Christian life among the young. This was also the case in Zambia in central Africa, most of French-speaking Africa, and Zimbabwe and South Africa.

Although distinctive, the charismatic renewal movement shares in common with the AICs the insistence on the need for Christianity to be enculturated. Charismatic renewal, however, is more engaged with issues of growing importance such as gender equality, the use of modern technology, and modern medicine. Although it eschews direct political action, it is not a world-indifferent movement, nor is it an apolitical movement as demonstrated by the response of charismatics and evangelicals in the election of the "born again" President Chiluba in Zambia in 1991.

Neo-Pentecostalism from abroad. Running parallel to, and sometimes overlapping with, the charismatic renewal movement in Africa is a new wave of missionary activity involving evangelicals from other parts of the world, including Korea, Brazil, and the United States. The objective is to engage in what is presented as the real, authentic conversion of Africa to Christianity, as opposed to that incomplete and harmful form accomplished by the historic churches. Moreover, in contrast to the more ecumenical and conciliatory spirit of the historic churches to other non-Christian religions, the evangelical and charismatic religions are, paradoxically, on the one hand denouncing all forms of belief and practice that diverge from their own and, on the other hand, reinforcing the traditional worldview by insisting on the power and hold of the devil and evil spirits over those involved in false religion and superstition.

The Brazilian Igreja Universal do Reino de Deus (Universal Church of the Kingdom of God) is but one of the new Pentecostal churches to enter Africa since the 1970s and is growing rapidly not only in Lusophone or Portuguese-speaking Africa but also in Anglophone and Francophone Africa, for example, in Nigeria and the Ivory Coast. Quick to adapt and employ local ministers and ready to use the local language, this church insists on the reality of the spiritual world and on its direct influence on success and failure. As is the case with many other new churches of its kind, the Universal Church gives priority in its practice to the rite of exorcism of evil spirits, which are said to block progress to the kingdom of God. This psychologically uncomfortable theology is balanced by the prosperity doctrine, not unfamiliar to African traditional religion, which promises that turning to Jesus can lead from poverty and sickness to wealth and well-being.

MODERN ISLAM-DERIVED MOVEMENTS. Modern Muslim movements vary greatly, and even within the same movement there are often what appear to be strongly opposed tendencies. The Murid *tariqa* (brotherhood), founded in Senegal in the late nineteenth century by the Wolof Muslim cleric Ahmadu Bamba (1850/1–1927) who developed his own Muslim version of prosperity theology, combined Sufism or mysticism with an unrelenting commitment to hard and continuous agricultural work. The work ethic instilled by Bamba, similar in substance to Max Weber's (1864–1920) notion of the Protestant work ethic, has produced a thriving entrepreneurial movement with considerable assets and political influence in Senegal, the Gambia, and elsewhere in Francophone West Africa, and a trading diaspora that extends to Europe and the United States.

Millenarianism, more commonly known among Muslims as mahdism, is also a feature of several modern African Muslim movements, including the eclectic Layenne movement, also of Senegal; the exclusive, scripturalist Bamidele movement founded in Ibadan in the 1930s by a former Christian, Abdul Salami Bamidele; and the Mahdiyya movement, founded in the early 1940s in Ijebu-Ode, in southwestern Nigeria, by Al-hajj Jumat Imam who, perhaps uniquely, endeavored to develop a theology that would integrate Muslims, Christians, and traditionalists.

The *zaar* cult is a largely female, international, and modern Muslim movement that flourishes in Ethiopia (from where it gets its name), Somalia, Djibouti, and the Sudan, and to a lesser extent in Egypt and the gulf states. In Ethiopia, this worship cult involves both Muslims and Christians in Ethiopia; elsewhere, only Muslims. Spirits (*zaar*) are believed to have the power to invade human bodies and to possess them. Those possessed are the marginal and the powerless and, to be placated, the possessing spirits must be given food of good quality, perfumes, and other luxuries: the spirits often articulate the concerns and grievances of those they possess.

The victims of the spirits—numerous categories exist and are constantly being expanded and updated showing the link between religion and social change—are also obliged to dance in their honor at cult group rituals that take the form of séances, which in Somalia are called "beating the *zaar*." Ioan M. Lewis (1996) suggests that this cult serves primarily to alleviate the conditions of the oppressed and, in particular, women for whom it functions as a mystical weapon in the war between the sexes. This perspective has been constructively and interestingly critiqued by a number of scholars including Janice Boddy (1989), who does not see participation in spirit possession such as *zaar* in the Sudan as primarily an oblique strategy by means of which women bid for attention but as expressing both the conflict between village women's experiences and their self-image as defined by the gender ideals of their society and their historical consciousness of relations with outsiders. Noting that mediums are often selected from the powerful and strong lineages, not from among the weak and powerless, Jean-Paul Colleyn's (1999) study of the Nya cult in Mali also rejects Lewis's narrow interpretation of the function of spirit possession as an oblique means by which the downtrodden seek to escape from humiliation.

Whereas pacifism is a distinguishing feature of most modern Muslim movements in Africa, outbreaks of violence have also occurred, one involving the Maitatsine movement. Originating in northern Cameroon, this movement spread to northern Nigeria, where it ended in catastrophe in the 1980s when an estimated six thousand people lost their lives in riots in Kano City. This was a movement of the "lonely" poor, the displaced and marginalized (the street vendors, water carriers, and so on) who had received no benefit whatsoever from the oil boom of the 1960s and 1970s and who were without any protection against dire poverty.

Not unrelated to the rise of charismatic renewal, neo-evangelical, and neo-Pentecostal movements has been the rise of Muslim reform and missionary-minded movements composed mainly of fervent young educated high school and university students, guided by Muslim scholars of considerable intellectual repute and sanctity. These movements are dedicated to the advancement of a more orthodox, more assertive Islam and have been aided in this with spiritual and financial support from elsewhere in the Muslim world.

Strong influences include the writings of the Indian Muslim reformer Abū'l A'la Mawdūdī (1903–1979), founder of the Muslim revitalization movement the Jamāʿat-i-Islāmī. Mawdūdī encouraged Muslims to consider the vexed question of the relation between Islam and Western culture and urged them to work for an Islamic state.

Prominent activists such as Sayyid Quṭb (1906–1966), a leading member of the militant Al-Ikhwan al-Moslemoon (Muslim Brotherhood), were inspired by Mawdūdī's writings, as they were by those of the Egyptian teacher and scholar Al-Imam Hassan al-Banna (1906–1949), who founded the Ikhwān al Muslimūn in 1928, which like so many modern or new Islamic movements, rather than rejecting older institutions, go beyond them. Al-Banna understood his mission to be the countering of the corruption of Islamic society and, in particular, the corruption caused by Western influence in the face of which the Muslim leaders, he believed, remained passive. Al-Banna, who rejected the use of force as a means of reform, stressed the comprehensive and inclusive nature of Islam. The doctrine of the oneness of God (*tawḥīd*), he believed, made Islam the reference point for all aspects of life and was the prime religious reason for engaging in the transformation of society. He also rejected—and on this point his influence is evident almost everywhere there are radical Muslim reformers—what he saw as blind traditionalism, which meant essentially following the opinion of medieval Muslim scholars. Instead he insisted on the need for informed independent judgment (*ijtihād*) as the basic principle of action.

Although Al-Banna was assassinated in 1949 and his movement suppressed by Egyptian President Gamel Abdul Nasser in 1954, it continued clandestinely under Quṭb whose treatise *Ma'alim fi al-Tariq* (Milestones; 1965), written in prison, called for Muslim opposition to Western decadence—a Leninist approach to an Islamic revolution that would bring down non-Islamic regimes. Although executed by Nasser, Quṭb's writings have become essential reading for the growing number of radical Muslims in North Africa, Africa south of the Sahara, and beyond.

Thus, various Muslim associations—some of them the mirror image of evangelical, neo-Pentecostal and charismatic renewal movements—strongly influenced by Muslim revivalism in the wider world, began to embark on a *daw'a* (mission), ignoring the traditional boundaries between Christian and Muslims, an attitude that was implicitly encouraged by the new context of nation-states in which, in principle, all regions were open to all faiths. In this new context, it was possible for Muslims to demand their constitutional rights, including *sharī'ah* law administered by *sharī'ah* courts.

There are a number of Muslim missionary movements from outside Africa that are well established on the continent. The Aḥmadiyah movement, founded in what is modern Pakistan by Ghulām Aḥmad (1835–1908) and regarded as heretical by mainstream Islam for its refusal to accept the prophet Muḥammad as the last of the prophets, is particularly strong in West Africa. It is a pacific, modernizing movement that promotes a balanced school curriculum of Islamic and Western subjects and accepts Western dress and conducts marriage ceremonies in the Western Christian style.

ASIAN, AFRICAN DIASPORA, AND MODERN SECULAR RELIGIONS. Although present for over 150 years, Hinduism, Jainism, and Sikhism have exercised little direct influence on African culture and spirituality. Until the late twentieth century, there were few African Hindus and even fewer Jains and Sikhs. This situation began to change with the arrival of the neo-Hindu and other modern Asian movements that demonstrate a desire for greater inclusiveness, a characteristic also in greater evidence in twenty-first century Muslim movements, such as the Daudi Boharas and the various branches of the Ismā'īlīs, which are also present in East Africa. The lay Bahā'ī faith—founded in Iran in 1853 by Mirza Husayn-Ali (1817–1892; known as Bah'u'llah) whose teachings are summarized as the unity of God, the unity of religion, and the unity of humankind—has innumerable spiritual assemblies across Africa made up of African members.

Many neo-Hindu movements are marked by their engaged, applied spirituality, inclusiveness, and insistence on the need to give technology a spiritual underpinning. Among those active in South Africa is the Divine Life Society founded by the South Indian medical doctor turned ascetic Śivāndanda Sāraswāti Māharāj (1887–1963). Although its philosophy is based on the Hindu *bhakti* (devotional) and yogic traditions, this movement, like so many other neo-Hindu movements and modern movements whatever their cultural and spiritual origin, generally seeks to promote a practical, nonsectarian form of spirituality. To this end, its teachings embrace material from the prophets of many different faiths, including Zoroaster, Moses, the Buddha, Mahāvīra (Jainism), Jesus, Muḥammad, and Nānak (1469–1539; Sikhism). The Sri Sathya Sai Baba movement, widely known for the extraordinary thaumaturgical gifts of its leader and present in Ghana among other places, is also eclectic and committed to educational and social development.

Although there is evidence of Buddhism, mainly in the form of Indian Buddhists but also some Chinese in South Africa in the early part of the twentieth century, a Buddhist *saṃgha* (community) did not emerge until the 1970s. In 1979 a Buddhist Retreat Centre and a Buddhist Institute were opened in Natal, and from that point on various Buddhist traditions—Zen, Theravāda, Mahāyāna, and Pure Land—started to open centers in all the main towns of South Africa.

Since the 1970s modern forms of mainly lay Buddhism of Japanese origin have been making an even greater impact than these older traditions on African culture and spirituality. These new movements include Sōka Gakkai (Value Creation Society), present in Nigeria and South Africa, among other places. Philosophically Buddhist but ritually Shintō, movements from Japan such as Sekai Kyusei Kyō (Church of World Messianity; SKK) entered Africa in the early 1990s via Brazil. SKK started to disseminate its message of divine healing *(johrei)* in Lusophone Africa (Angola and Mozambique) before moving into South Africa and the Democratic Republic of the Congo. Clear parallels exist at the level of belief and ritual between the African traditional religions, modern African movements, and Japanese new religions.

The Japanese movement SKK not only emphasizes the importance of dreams and visions as guides to action and the fundamental importance of pacifying the ancestors but also offers both a spiritual explanation of the causes of sickness and faith healing as a remedy. Moreover, Japanese movements act, paradoxically, as pathways to African identity. Through the SKK several African Brazilian missionaries have discovered their African roots in Angola, which Catholic Christianity in Brazil was perceived to have destroyed.

Although many of the new Japanese modern movements are unconcerned about how they are interpreted by others—if seen as a philosophy rather than a religion, more Catholic than Buddhist, it makes little difference to leaders—there are some including the lay Nichirenist movement Sōka Gakkai and the Shintō-derived movement Tenrikyō (Religion of Heavenly Wisdom) who resist adaptation at all costs. Interestingly, although Sōka Gakkai's growth appears not to be affected by its exclusive position, Tenrikyō, whose main activities are the provision of health care and spiritual healing, has made little headway. Active in the Congo since 1966, it has only attracted an estimated two hundred adherents.

Several new Korean Pentecostal churches and new religious movements are also engaged in the new plan to evangelize Africa, including the Unification Church (formally the Holy Spirit Association for the Unification of World Christianity, more popularly known as the Moonies). Founded in 1954 in Seoul, South Korea, by the Reverend Sun Myung Moon (1920–), this millenarian movement, although dedicated to mission, has attracted relatively few adherents in Africa.

Also unsuccessful in this respect have been the modern movements developed by African diaspora communities that have found their way back to Africa. These include the Rastafarian movement from the Caribbean, which has established a model of paradise at Shashamane in Ethiopia, and Candomblé, originally from the Yoruba regions of western Nigeria and the Republic of Benin, but now being carried back home by African Brazilian devotees on pilgrimage to the traditional Yoruba homelands in southwestern Nigeria and the Republic of Benin.

Modern secular religions such as Scientology also remain numerically small, despite the fact that Scientology, which became engaged in a variety of educational and social projects in Zimbabwe and other places, shares much in common with the scientific and empirical outlook of many traditional African religions and spiritualities.

NEOTRADITIONALIST MOVEMENTS. With hindsight African traditional religions have shown a remarkable capacity for survival under the impact of modernization and the spread of the Christianity and Islam. Traditional philosophies, rituals, and symbols—reconstructed or otherwise—have proved an effective and efficient means of legitimizing the social order and of garnering resistance to political cultural and economic domination, as seen in the case of the Maji-Maji and Mau-Mau uprisings and in the independence struggle in Zimbabwe. They continue to perform important cognitive, explanatory, psychological, and healing functions. Also, as Dominique Zahan (1979) has shown, they contain a deep, mystical, spiritual dimension that has great appeal but is often overlooked in explaining their persistence.

It was widely thought, nevertheless, that they would be quickly undermined by the advance of Christianity, Islam, and secularism. But the predictions of this kind have been proved entirely wrong, including the prognosis of that landmark 1910 missionary conference in Edinburgh that declared: "Most of the people will have lost their ancient faith within a generation, and will accept that culture-religion with which they first come into contact" (Groves, 1958, p. 292). The reality is that these traditional religions have remained strong and vibrant in many parts of Africa, as elsewhere, and have greatly influenced the form and, to a lesser extent, the content and ethos of Christianity and Islam. Although initially nonproselytizing and confined by their content and ritual to a specific ethnic group, in the twenty-first century they are becoming ever more diverse in their ethnic composition and international in their outreach.

Concern about the cultural, moral, and social consequences of losing contact with the past explains the central importance attached to the veneration of the ancestors in many neotraditional movements, including the Dini Ya Msambwa (Religion of Ancestral Spirits) of Kenya founded in 1944 by Elijah Masinde (1910–1987). The Karinga initiation guilds started in Kenya in the 1920s with the aim of preserving traditional rites of passage, including female circumcision, and although they have taken on the structure and appearance of a church (there are now bishops and rural deans), these remain their distinguishing characteristics. Neotraditional movements are often concerned with clarity, that is, with separating authentic tradition from its entanglement with Christian missionary culture.

This is the principal objective of the Mungiki (masses) movement, also Kenyan, which began in the 1980s as the Tent of the Living God movement for the purpose of extracting authentic Gikuyu culture from the ambiguity to which it had been reduced by Christianity. A youth movement with a minimum of 300,000 members, most of whom are between fifteen and twenty-five years old and disadvantaged, the Mungiki are greatly influenced by Mau-Mau ideology and, like the latter, proclaim that they are fighting for land, freedom, and religion.

In the 1930s a movement of Nigerian (Yoruba) Christians formed the neotraditional church of the Ijo Orunmila to ensure that core elements of their religious culture were not destroyed. Again in Nigeria in the 1960s the Arousa cult (Edo National Church; a development from Bini traditional religion) merged with the neotraditional National Church of Nigeria, to form Godianism, which focused on belief in a single God of Africa as understood in ancient Egyptian sources.

CONCLUSIONS. Modern African religions provide students of religion with abundant material for exploring theoretical and methodological issues relating to the dynamics not only of African religious culture but of religious culture in general. As sources of spiritual insight and knowledge derived from particular historical and cultural experiences, they address core issues relating to personal and cultural identity, autonomy, and independence and offer striking examples of what globalization theorists such as Roland Robertson (1992) refer to as the process of *glocalization,* that is, the domestication of globalizing religious and cultural forces and the globalization of the local. The future is likely to see more movements emerge displaying the results in form and content of interactions between African religious culture and heritage and Asian religions.

SEE ALSO New Religious Movements, articles on New Religious Movements and Millennialism, New Religious Movements and Violence, New Religious Movements in Japan; Sōka Gakkai; Tenrikyō; Unification Church.

BIBLIOGRAPHY

Boddy, Janice. *Wombs and Alien Spirits.* Madison, Wis., 1989. This volume, in contrast to I. M. Lewis's study, focuses less on the functions of spirit possession as a means used by women to command attention and as a therapeutic outlet for psychological frustration and more on its societal meaning. Using the notion developed by Geertz (1972) of "cultural text" (i.e., the idea of text being written and read by a particular society), Boddy stresses the positive social role of the *zaar* cult among in the northern Sudan.

Bromley, David G., and J. Gordon Melton, eds. *Cults, Religion and Violence.* Cambridge, U.K., 2002. A collection of essays this volume examines the both the internal and external causes of outbreaks of violence involving new religions including the MRTCG.

Clarke, Peter B. *West Africa and Christianity.* London, 1986. This study covers the development of Christianity in West Africa from the fifteenth century to the mid-1980s. Chapter 6 examines the rise and expansion of the AICs, and chapter 7 examines changes that came with independence including developments in Christian relations with Islam and with the traditional religions of Africa.

Clarke, Peter B. *Mahdism in West Africa.* London, 1995. A study of Mahdism and Islamic millenarianism—pacific and militant, historical and contemporary—in West Africa.

Colleyn, Jean-Paul. "Horse, Hunter and Messenger: Possessed Men of the Nya Cult of Mali." In *Spirit Possession: Modernity and Power in Africa,* edited by Heike Behrend and Ute Luig, pp. 68–78. Oxford, 1999. This article offers a critique of I. M. Lewis's epidemiological account of the status of those who become possessed, claiming that it is not usually the downtrodden and marginalized, at least in the case of the Nya of Mali, a largely Muslim society, in which the androgenous, predominantly female divinity Nya takes possession of anyone she wants but usually of a minority of relatively powerful men.

Geertz, Clifford. "Deep Play: Notes on a Balinese Cockfight." *Daedalus* 101 (1972): 1–37. This article develops the notion of *cultural text,* which has proved to be an extremely useful methodological concept in scholarly research of, among other areas, spirit possession.

Groves, Charles P. *The Planting of Christianity in Africa,* vol. III, London, 1958. This three-volume history contains useful historical material on the institutions and personnel that shaped the structures and strategy of the Christian missionary movement in Africa from its beginnings until World War II (1939–1945).

Hackett, Rosalind, J., ed. *New Religious Movements in Nigeria.* Lewiston, N.Y., 1987. One of a very few interdisciplinary volumes to cover a variety of types of new religions in an African context, in this case Nigeria, ranging from neotraditional to Christian- and Islamic-derived churches and movements.

Levinson, David. "Movement for the Restoration of the Ten Commandments of God." In *African and African American Religions,* edited by Stephen D. Glazier, pp. 198–199. New York, 2001. This short account contains useful information on the early history and development of the MRTCG.

Lewis, Ioan M. *Religion in Context: Cults and Charisma.* Cambridge, UK, 1996. Covers numerous aspects of charismatic religion and includes a fascinating and thought provoking, if controversial, account of the *zaar* cult as a form of embryonic feminism and a mystical weapon in the war between the sexes.

Mayer, Jean-François. "Field Notes: The Movement for the Restoration of the Ten Commandments of God." *Nova Religio: The Journal of Alternative and Emergent Religions* 5, no. 1 (2001): 203–210. Informative account of this little-understood Ugandan movement that caused about 780 deaths.

Olupona, Jacob K., and Sulayman S. Nyang, eds. *Religious Plurality in Africa,* Berlin, 1993. A *festschrift* in honor of Dr. John Mbiti, this volume provides a comprehensive overview of Africa's different religious cultures: Christian, Islamic, oriental, and traditional.

Ojo, Matthews. *The End-Time Army: Charismatic Movements in Modern Nigeria.* London, forthcoming. A detailed study based on the author's doctoral dissertation written at the School of Oriental and African Studies, University of London, of the history, social composition, distinguishing features, purposes, and underlying social, religious, and political background to the rise of charismatic renewal churches and movements as a new religious phenomenon in Africa, with special reference to Nigeria.

Peel, John D. Y. *Aladura: A Religious Movement among the Yoruba.* Oxford, 1968. Essential reading for all social science students of the Aladura movement, it provides what is widely regarded as the most convincing explanation for its rise and expansion among the Yoruba.

Robertson, Roland. *Globalization: Social Theory and Global Culture.* London, 1992. In addition to the discourse on the meaning of globalization and the outcome of its impact on local culture which is defined as *glocalization,* there is thoughtful reflection on the response of the modern religions to globalization with special reference to Japan.

Sundkler, Bengt G. M. *Bantu Prophets in South Africa.* London, 1970. A classic study of Ethiopian and Zionist churches in southern Africa. Although dated in parts by subsequent research, this volume remains indispensable reading for any serious student of modern African religious movements.

Turner, Harold W. *History of an Independent Church: The Church of the Lord.* 2 vols. Oxford, 1967. The most detailed and informative historical and theological account available of an independent church.

Turner, Harold W. "Africa." In *The Study of Religion: Traditional and New Religion,* edited by Stewart Sutherland and Peter B. Clarke, pp. 187–194. London, 1991. This chapter gives a concise summary with examples Turner's typology of African religions.

Wallis, Roy. *The Elementary Forms of the New Religious Life.* London, 1984. A highly controversial but valued and widely used study of new and modern religious movements that, on the basis of their orientation to the world, reduces them to three basic types: world-denying, world-indifferent, and world-rejecting movements.

Wilson, Bryan R. *Magic and the Millennium: A Sociological Study of Religious Movements of Protest among Tribal and Third World Peoples.* London, 1973. Consists of a critique of the Weber-Troeltsch typology of sects and new religions and subsequent sociological attempts at classification based on this model and offers, by way of a more value-free approach, a typology based on religious movements' response to the world and their perception of the problem of evil and the means they offer to overcome it. Also relevant are the detailed accounts of numerous modern African movements that are classified using this new typology.

Wilson, Bryan R. *The Social Sources of Sectarianism.* Oxford, 1990. Discusses the relation between sects and the state, sects, and the law and sectarian diffusion, appeal, and classification and provides a provocative and stimulating account of what is termed modern secularized religion.

Zahan, Dominique. *The Religion, Spirituality and Thought of Traditional Africa.* Translated by Kate Ezra Martin and Lawrence M. Martin. Chicago, 1979. Rejects a functionalist interpretation and explores the more philosophical and mystical dimensions of African traditional religions, which greatly assists attempts to understand the enduring appeal of these religions.

PETER B. CLARKE (2005)

AFRICAN RELIGIONS: HISTORY OF STUDY

In his *The Invention of Africa* (1988) the Congolese philosopher Valentin Mudimbe noted that there is a remarkable continuity in the Western representation of Africa as a place without history and without religion. These images, he argued, played a central role in the legitimization of the Atlantic slave trade and colonization. From Herodotos (c. 484–between 430 and 420 BCE) to contemporary commentators on world civilizations, these descriptions reemerge in ways that consistently marginalize Africa from the scientific study of world religions. Religious studies scholars continue to think of their departments as focused on Western religions and Eastern religions. A residual category that includes African, Native American, Australasian, and so on—until recently labeled as primitive but since replaced by more palatable terms such as primal, oral, tribal, traditional, or indigenous—remains outside this catholic division and is usually left to anthropologists and rarely included in religious studies departments.

ANCIENT CONSIDERATIONS. Ancient commentators had some familiarity with Egypt and the North African coastal areas, and these cultures provided influential deities, rituals, and cultic paraphernalia that were selectively incorporated into the religious systems of their Mediterranean and Middle Eastern neighbors. For areas further south, however, fragmentary travelers' accounts, local gossip, and writers' imaginations provided the evidence for often wild descriptions of subhuman communities. Although these images were not universally accepted, they remained extremely influential. Africans were described as exotic and as people without religion in Hesiod's (eighth century BCE) accounts of the Semicanes, Capitones, and Pygmies as well as in Alcman's (seventh century BCE) account of the Steganopodes, Aeschylus's (525–456 BCE) account of the Conicipedes, and in many others. Even reports by commentators seeking to provide informed accounts had little use. Herodotus and other Greek writers referred to the gods of the Libyans and attributed Greek names to them, but as Stéphanie Gsell remarked in *Histoire ancienne de l'Afrique du nord* (1913–1928), it is uncertain whether these gods were actual Berber deities, gods introduced by Phoenicians, or deities whose descriptions were too strongly shaded by Greek perspectives.

Although the Romans ruled the whole of North Africa for centuries, their interest in the local religions seems to have been as slight as that of the Greeks. According to the North African Latin poet Flavius Cresconius Corippus, writing in the sixth century, the Laguata, a tribe of Tripolitania, adored a god called Curzil, who was the son of Ammon and a cow and who incarnated himself as a bull. Early twentieth-century commentators were tempted to interpret these isolated examples as traces of zoolatry or of totemism.

Arabic-speaking commentators provided descriptions of sub-Saharan Africa beginning in the ninth century, but they tended to concentrate on urban trading areas where Islamic influences were strongest. In the eleventh century, al-Bakri mentioned a mountain community in southern Morocco that he claimed worshiped a ram. He also described urban settlements in Tekrur and Ghana where there were pagan and Muslim quarters, each governed by its own laws. Finally, he visited the kingdom of Mali where he witnessed unsuccessful cattle sacrifices in a rain ritual, followed by a Muslim prayer and an abundant rainfall that led to the conversion of the king. A century later al-Hamawi mentions a Sanhaja Berber group that worships the sun. However, most of these accounts offer far richer descriptions of political organization, trade, and social customs than they do about religion.

To the extent that they were aware of local traditions, they classified them as forms of unbelief, akin to the *jahilīyah* of pre-Islamic Arabia. What Islamic observers persistently demonstrate, however, is the prolonged influence of African religions within increasingly Muslim urban communities within the Sudanic region of West Africa (see Levtzion and Hopkins, 1981).

Accounts of Early Missionaries and Explorers. As the first Europeans to explore the coast of sub-Saharan Africa, Portuguese travelers offered descriptions of African religions beginning in the late fifteenth century. However, many of these accounts reflected European Christian perspectives narrowed by the long struggle against Islam that did not end within Iberia until Portuguese exploration was well under way. The earliest writings that contain some mention of African religions are by Duarte Pacheco Pereira and Valentim Fernandes, which date to the first years of the sixteenth century and focus on the coastal communities of Senegambia and Upper Guinea. Yves Person wrote:

> The people paid honour to idols carved out of wood: the chief divinity was called Kru: They also practised worship of the dead, who were embalmed before burial. "It is usual to make a memento for all those who die: if he was a notable person, an idol is made resembling him: if he was merely a commoner or a slave, the figure is made of wood and is put in a thatched house. Every year, sacrifices of chickens or goats are made to them." (Person, 1984, p. 307)

Within a decade of the arrival of Portuguese explorers at the mouth of the Congo River, Portuguese missionaries joined them and established themselves at the court of the local monarch. Although these missionaries devoted themselves to converting Africans to Christianity and were less concerned with understanding the converts' religious backgrounds, they could not help but observe the similarities and differences between them and the obstacles and the aids in conversion. As a result, they provided richer descriptions of African religious life than their more secular fellow travelers. Some of their writings became widely read and helped to shape European images of Africa and of African religions. One of the most widely read texts was Filippo Pigafetta's *Relazione del Reame di Congo* (1591), which was based on the notes of Duarte Lopes, a Portuguese merchant who had lived in Congo for many years before being appointed as a papal envoy to the Congo's newly converted king, Alvaro I. This account describes the people of Loango who "adore whatever they like, holding the greatest god to be Sun as male, and the Moon as female; for the rest, every person elects his own Idol, which he adores according to his fancy" (Pigafetta, 1978). The description of the Congo appears to be far more sensational: "Everyone worshipped whatever he most fancied without rule or measure or reason at all" (Pigafetta, 1978). When Afonso I ordered all religious objects *(nkisi)* to be collected and destroyed, it was reported that "there was found a huge quantity of Devils of strange and frightful shape. . . . Dragons with wings, Serpents of horrible appearance, Tigers and other most monstrous animals . . . Both painted and carved in wood and stone and other material" (Pigafetta, 1978). This is an unlikely collection, judging from what is known of Congo sculpture or African fauna.

By the late sixteenth century, however, one begins to find more empathetic descriptions of African religions. In 1586, for example, the Portuguese author Santos wrote of a Bantu-speaking ethnic group, the Yao of Mozambique, in more favorable terms: "They acknowledge a God who, both in this world and in the next, measures the retribution for the good or evil done in this" (cited in Lang, 1898). This focus on a supreme being who judged the living and determined their afterlife was challenged by later commentators who focused more on ancestral cults. Similarly, Giovanni Antonio Cavazzi's *Istorica descrizione de' tre' regni Congo, Matamba Angola* (1687) reflects more knowledge of central African religious systems, including an accurate form of the name for the supreme being in the region as Nzambi-a-mpungu. Even his reports, however, retain the derogatory images that suffuse these accounts:

> Before the light of the Holy Gospel dispelled superstition and idolatry from the minds of the Congolese, these unhappy people were subject to the Devil's tyranny. . . . [Apart from Nzambi] there are other gods, inferior to him, but nevertheless worthy of homage; to these too, therefore, cult and adoration are due. . . . The pagans expose a certain quantity of idols, mostly of wood, roughly sculpted, each one of which has its own name. (Cavazzi, 1687, p. XX; translated by author)

An early account of Khoi religion was given by Guy Tachard, a Jesuit priest, in *Il viaggio di Siam de'padri gesuiti mandati dal re di Francia all'Indie, e alla China.* Tachard reports:

> These people know nothing of the creation of the world, the redemption of mankind, and the mystery of the Holy Trinity. Nevertheless they adore a god, but the cognition they have of him is very confused. They kill in his honor cows and sheep, of which they offer him meat and milk in sign of gratitude toward this deity that grants them, as they believe, now rain and now fair weather, according to their needs. (Tachard, 1693; translated by author)

Eighteenth and Early Nineteenth Centuries. Throughout the eighteenth and early nineteenth centuries, information on African religions remained at these fragmentary and often misleading levels. Reports focused on the peoples of the coastal areas of West, South, and East Africa, which were the areas most visited by European travelers. Amateur observers—navigators, explorers, traders, artisans, and naturalists—wrote most of the accounts. They lacked training in ethnographic analysis, the linguistic tools to engage in religious discourse, and the interest in religious issues as the primary focus of their concerns. Christian missionaries, who stayed longer and had an obvious interests in religious matters, came to Africa to revolutionize these societies and often displayed a mixture of contempt or pity for the benighted "heathen." It cannot be emphasized enough that the first attempts at comparison and synthesis in the framework of anthropology or the history of religions were based almost exclusively on information of this kind.

As it became more common for missionaries to spend extended periods working in a particular ethnic community, their reports began to reflect greater understanding of local religious beliefs and more tolerance of local traditions. An example of this can be found in the works of the Italian abbot Giovanni Beltrame (*Il Sennaar e lo Sciangallah*, 1879, and *Il fiume bianco e i Denka*, 1881), whose work focused on his evangelization of the peoples of the upper Nile, beginning in the mid-nineteenth century. Beltrame included, both in the original language and in his translation, the creation song with which the Dinka celebrate the creation of the world by Dengdid or Dengdit (Great Rain). He also reported that the Dinka distinguish between two verbs, *cior* or *lam*, which expresses the act of praying to God, and *verg*, which indicates prayer directed toward a person. His knowledge of the language in which religious ideas were expressed allowed him to discover that verbs related to the supreme being are always used in the present tense. Hence the Christian expression "God has always been and always will be" is rendered "God is and always is"—a grammatical detail with significant theological implications. However, when he turns to the neighboring Nuer, Beltrame's knowledge is more limited: "They believe in the existence of God, but pay no cult to him" (Beltrame, 1881, pp. 191, 275).

John H. Weeks's writings on Bakongo religion also reflect this deepening understanding. Building on thirty years of mission work in the lower Congo, he describes a religion with a supreme being, Nzambi, and equates this deity with the God of Christianity. He concludes his book with a remarkable declaration of method for someone writing in 1914: "In this statement of native beliefs I have tried to reflect the native mind. It would have been possible to have left out ideas here and there, and to have arranged the rest in such a manner that they would have dove-tailed beautifully, but in so doing I should have given my view of the religious beliefs of the natives, not a faithful account of theirs" (Weeks, 1914, p. 288).

Protestant missionary Henri A. Junod provides another example of this growing body of materials in mission anthropology. Junod lived among the Thonga of coastal Mozambique beginning in 1907, and his writing reflects a growing influence of academic anthropology. By the time he collected his writings for publication in 1927, he had become broadly familiar with theoretical debates within the fields of anthropology and history of religions and had become particularly influenced by evolutionary theory and the comparative method. Having found among the Thonga the coexistence of beliefs in a sky god and in ancestral spirits, he attempted to assess the respective antiquity of these two apparently conflicting concepts. To do so, he compared Thonga religious thought with other groups of southern Bantu-speaking communities. He followed the assertion of W. Challis and Henry Callaway that the Ngoni ancestors of the Swazi and Zulu prayed to a god of the sky before they began to worship ancestor spirits. Although Junod referred to this in evolutionary terms, he was aware that this pattern was contrary to the schemas of orthodox evolutionism. In an appendix to the 1936 edition of *The Life of a South African Tribe*, he stated that the two sets of ideas could be parallel among the Bantu-speaking groups. At the same time, however, he conjectured, on the basis of psychological considerations, a chronological sequence—naturism, animism, causalism, euhemerism—that partly accepts Nathan Söderblom's hypotheses as stated in his *Das Werden des Gottesglaubens* (1916). Junod's ambiguous conclusions reflect the case of an experienced researcher trying to combine personally observed realities with the theoretical explanations that dominated the study of African religions at that time.

The decades during which missionaries, merchants, and travelers collected much of the initial information on African religions coincided with the writing of a series of ambitious comparative works that attempted to establish the logical, if not chronological, succession of religious ideas in the world. Some continued to ignore Africa altogether. Thus in *The Philosophy of History*, Georg Friedrich Hegel dismisses Africa as a land without history, without religion, where superstition reigns: "But even Herodotus called the Negroes sorcerers; now in sorcery we have not the idea of God, of a moral faith" (Hegel, 1956, p. 93). An early prototype of the attempt to include Africa in the evolution of religions was Charles de Brosse's *Du culte des dieux fétiches* (1760), which compared sub-Saharan African beliefs and rituals with those of ancient Egypt. He adapted a Portuguese term for a highly valued object and created the term *fetish* which has been applied to African ritual objects ever since. To de Brosse, Africans worshiped fetishes, objects endowed with or containing some kind of spiritual power. This became the model for a type of religion that became known as fetishism. This and other concepts were utilized in Auguste Comte's *Cours de philosophie positive* (1830–1842) in which he outlined the evolution of various human institutions, including religion. He understood both fetishism and African religions as the most primitive form of religions.

Evolutionary theory. The rise of evolutionist theories in the human sciences in the latter half of the nineteenth century coincided with a dramatic intensification of European exploration and colonization of Africa. This provided a significant increase in the availability of data from peoples encountered for the first time in addition to new reports concerning those groups known through previous literature. These examples were often used in an uncritical fashion to represent instances of the stages of religion, often referred to as primitive religion: fetishism, ancestor worship or euhemerism, animism, totemism, idolatry, polytheism, and so on. African materials were carefully selected by various armchair theorists to support their particular evolutionary schema, with African religions always assigned a lowly status. It was through these theorists' work that African religious materials became known within the field of the history of religions and among the public at large. African materials play a prominent role in John Lubbock's *Origin of Civilisation* (1870), Grant Allen's *The Evolution of the Idea of God* (1897), Robert R. Marett's *The Threshold of Religion* (1909), and in James G. Frazer's monumental work, *The Golden Bough* (1894).

Occasionally, Africa served as an example of a higher form of primitive religion. For example, Theodor Waitz's *Anthropologie der Naturvölker* (1859–1872) distinguishes between African religions and other indigenous religions. In the second of his six volumes, Waitz concludes:

> We reach the amazing conclusion that several Negro tribes . . . in the development of their religious conceptions are much further advanced than almost all other savages [Naturvölker], so far that, though we do not call them monotheists, we may still think of them as standing on the threshold of monotheism. (Waitz, 1860, p. 167)

This stands in sharp contrast to Edward B. Tylor's *Primitive Culture,* which relied on as broad a base of available sources as Waitz but which was used to support his theory of animism as the origin of religion. To provide evidence for his thesis, Tylor overlooks or underrates documents that did not support his argument. "High above the doctrine of souls, of divine manes, of local nature-spirits, of the great deities of class and element," he wrote, " there are to be discerned in savage theology shadowings, quaint or majestic, of the conception of a Supreme Deity" (Tylor, 1874, vol. 2, p. 332). Tylor quoted extensively from literature on African religions, but he was inclined to lump all "savage" peoples together, indiscriminately speaking of the "lower races" and, at one point of "the rude natives of Siberia and Guinea" (Tylor, 1874, vol. 2, p. 160).

Other evolutionists such as Lubbock and Herbert Spencer included African ethnic groups in lists of backward societies as surviving examples of a primitive atheism or as having no religious ideas whatsoever. This categorization was refuted in Gustave Roskoff's *Das Religionswesen des rohesten Naturvölker* (1880) and in Albert Réville's *Les religions des peuples non-civilisés* (1883). These authors argued that the realities of African religions are far more complex than the label *animism* would imply. Réville wrote:

> Naturism, the cult of personified natural features, sky, sun, moon, mountains, rivers, etc., is general of African soil. . . . Animism, the worship of spirits detached from nature and without a necessary link with natural phenomena, has taken a preponderant and so to speak absorbing role. Hence the Negro's fetishism, a fetishism that little by little rises to idolatry. . . . Nevertheless one should not omit, I shall not say a trait, but a certain tendency to monotheism, easily emerging from this confused mass of African religions. Undoubtedly, the African native is not insensitive to the idea of a single all-powerful God. (Réville, 1883, vol. 1, pp. 188–90)

Admissions that Africans had ideas of a supreme being who began the process of creation clearly contradicted the widespread evolutionary theories of the time, but were largely ignored in academic circles in the English-speaking world. In *The Making of Religion* Lang systematically assembled these reports and abandoned his previous support of Tylor's animist theory. His review of African, Australian, Polynesian, and American sources led him to conclude that the idea of a supreme being could not have been derived from beliefs in spirits or totems. Although Lang referred to Africans as belonging to the "low races" and as the "lowest savages," this did not prevent him from expressing the view that their traditional religion probably began "in a kind of Theism, which is then superseded, in some degree, or even corrupted, by Animism in all its varieties" (Lang, 1909, p. 304).

Lang's belief in the antiquity of African ideas of a high god ran parallel to a similar conviction within a different milieu, in the emerging notion of *Kulturkreiselehre* (doctrine of culture circles). Wilhelm Schmidt, one of the founders of this school of thought, published an early introduction to his monumental *Der Ursprung der Gottesidee* at the same time as the publication of the third edition of Lang's *The Making of Religion.* However, almost a half a century passed before the twelve-volume work appeared (1912–1955), containing three volumes focused on Africa. Schmidt's controversial thesis of a worldwide primeval monotheism that was corrupted by later trends in successive cultural cycles cannot be fully discussed here. It should be noted, however, that according to Schmidt, the remnants of the world's earliest religious ideas are to be found among people labeled as African Pygmies, whom he considered to be monotheistic and surviving representatives of the world's most archaic, or primeval, culture.

Regardless of one's evaluation of the strength of his theory, Schmidt's presentation of data contrasts sharply with that of his predecessors. Rather than an arbitrary assemblage of data from all sources according to a specific topic chosen by the author, Schmidt systematically collected and grouped data in reference to specific ethnic groups. Whenever possible, a summary of information on the culture and physical environment associated with the community were followed by separate sections devoted to beliefs, myths, sacrifices, prayers, conceptions of the soul, eschatology, ancestor worship, and other topics. Schmidt's materials remain to this day an invaluable quarry of carefully sifted and well-ordered information. The arduous field investigation of nomadic forest hunter-gatherers, including people best known as Pygmies, should also be credited to his influence. He provided strong encouragement and advice to fellow missionaries such as O. Henri Trilles, Peter Schumacher, and Paul Schebesta and kept abreast of their ongoing investigations. The final results of this research were synthesized by Schmidt in 1933 (see Schmidt, 1912–1955, vol. 3) and eventually published in Schebesta's *Die Bambuti Pygmäen vom Ituri* (1938–1950), the third volume of which is dedicated entirely to religion.

During this period in which the quest for the origins of religion dominated research, studies of African mythology began to be published. Alice Werner's *Myths and Legends of the Bantu* appeared in 1933 and was followed in 1936 by Hermann Baumann's *Schöpfung und Urzeit des Menschen im Mythus der afrikanischen Volker.* Raffaele Pettazzoni, a staunch adversary of Schmidt's theory of primeval monotheism, also made an important contribution in his four-volume *Miti e leggendem* (1948–1963). The first volume remains the fullest and most heavily annotated collection of myths drawn from the entire continent. In his last work, *L'onniscienza di Dio* (1955), Pettazzoni examines the worldwide distribution of ideas of a supreme being. Working from a nonconfessional perspective, Pettazzoni questioned the possibility that one could ever ascertain the origin of the idea of a supreme whether it was seen as a lord of the animals, a deified ancestor, or a strictly celestial being. He does conclude, however, that many African religions, even in ancient times, had a sky god, whose existence precedes any alien influences of Judaism, Christianity, or Islam.

Ethnological view. With the European colonization of Africa a new type of literature made its appearance and garnered a central place within the field: the ethnography. Based on the image of the closed society, this type of work often ignored both cross-cultural comparison and diachronic developments. It described many aspects of a single ethnic group, starting with geographical distribution, racial characteristics, and linguistic classification, and analyzed many facets of its social structure and culture, including religion. The early twentieth century produced a far more profound sense of distinctive African cultures and the role of religion within them, although they were often superficial in this area. Many of the authors served as colonial administrators or missionaries, although some were linguists or anthropologists. Not surprisingly, they often stressed the relation between religion and social structure, an approach that became known as social functionalism. The role of religion as a source of political and economic legitimation was often the primary focus. These early ethnographies relied on field research, interviews, and participation observation, although it was rare that the researcher actually spoke the language of his or her host communities. Some of the more important works include Alfred C. Hollis's *The Masai* (1905) and *The Nandi* (1909), Diedrich Westermann's *The Shilluk People* (1912), Günter Tessmann's *Die Pangwe* (1913), Alberto Pollera's *I Baria e I Cunama* (1913), Gerhard Lindblom's *The Akamba in British East Africa* (1920), Edwin W. Smith and Andrew Dale's *The Ila-speaking Peoples of Northern Rhodesia* (1920), Heinrich Vedder's two-volume *Die Berdama* (1923), John Roscoe's *The Baganda* (1911) and *The Bakitara or Banyoro* (1923), and Louis Tauxier's *Le noir du Soudan* (1912) and *Religion, moeurs et coutumes des Agnis de la Côte d'Ivoire* (1932). During this period, Belgian scholars under the direction of Cyrille van Overbergh successfully completed a large number of ethnographies, which were intended to cover the whole range of ethnic groups of the Belgian Congo.

The academic merit of these books varied dramatically. In principle, they respect a growing emphasis on treating religion as an integral part of culture. Smith suggested in *African Ideas of God: A Symposium*: "Sociologically speaking, African religion is one aspect of African culture. No one element can be exhaustively studied and understood in isolation from the rest" (Smith, 1950, p. 14). These studies also provided clear evidence that the religions of preliterate peoples were far too complex to be adequately condensed in a mere chapter of a general monograph. This problem was recognized by experienced writers such as Robert S. Rattray who, having published his classic monograph *Ashanti* in 1923, found it necessary to supplement it with *Religion and Art in Ashanti* in 1927, and E. E. Evans-Pritchard, author of *The Nuer* (1940), later devoted a separate volume, *Nuer Religion* (1956), to the study of religion.

Before World War II, researchers had been almost exclusively European. The most significant American contributions were Melville and Frances Herskovits's *An Outline of Dahomean Religious Belief* (1933) and Melville Herskovits's *The Myth of the Negro Past* (1941). The latter work used anthropological research methods to raise important issues of African influences in the religious life of African diasporas throughout the Americas. He successfully challenged the view that slavery had erased all influences from African American culture, and he brought scholarly attention to the idea that African religions had profound influences beyond Africa itself.

Before the Second World War, few African scholars had written about their own traditional religions. In *Facing Mount Kenya* (1938), Jomo Kenyatta devoted two chapters to the religion of the Kikuyu or Gikuyu, along with an attempt to explain such controversial aspects of his culture as female circumcision. Here again, however, it was within the context of an all-embracing monograph. The most significant exception was Joseph B. Danquah's *The Akan Doctrine of God* (1944), which focused entirely on the author's national group, the Ashanti. A more appropriate title for the book would be *The Ashanti Doctrine* because Danquah was only concerned with the creeds, epistemology, and ethics of his own community and paid little attention to the related, but not identical, systems of other branches of the Akan linguistic group (e.g. Anyi, Baule, Brong, Nzema). Dense with original quotations and filled with subtle and often unusual arguments and comparisons, the book struck a decidedly new note in the concert of previous literature on the subject. It left the reader unsure, however, whether the work sought to present an overview of an Ashanti system of religious thought or was more of a personal philosophical and theological reflection by the author.

POST-WORLD WAR II EVALUATIONS. In the postwar years a few scholars devised anthologies that collected condensed accounts of several African religions. Well-known examples include *African Ideas of God: A Symposium* (1950), edited by Edwin W. Smith in collaboration with a group of Protestant missionaries, and *Textes sacrés d'Afrique noire* (1965), edited by Germaine Dieterlen with a series of essays by lay ethnologists. Amadou Hampaté Ba, a leading francophone African intellectual, wrote a preface to the work. Daryl Forde, director of the International African Institute, assembled a series of essays by leading anthropologists such as Mary Douglas, Jacques Maquet, and the Ghanaian scholar and future prime minister, K. A. Busia. Meyer Fortes and Germaine Dieterlen sought to include a broad range of European scholarship in their edited volume, *African Systems of Thought* (1966).

Two of the contributors to these anthologies were French ethnologists Marcel Griaule and Germaine Dieterlen, who worked on Dogon religion and the religious systems of other Mande-speaking communities in the West African Sudanic region. The team of Africanists led by Griaule, which included Solange de Ganay and Dieterlen, had been conducting intermittent field research among the Dogon for over fifteen years. Dieterlen had produced, among other works, *Les âmes de Dogon* (1941), whereas Griaule had already published his monumental *Masques dogon* (1938) in which he examined the religious symbolism of the masks. One day in 1946 Griaule was unexpectedly summoned by a venerable blind sage called Ogotemmêli and, in the course of a month's conversations, obtained from him the revelation of a whole mythological and cosmological system. The complexity of this system far exceeded knowledge of Dogon thought that had been previously been learned by the team. The ensuing book, *Dieu d'eau* (1948), translated by Robert Redfield as *Conversations with Ogotemmêli* (1965), was received in academic circles with a mixture of bewilderment, admiration, and perplexity. Some critics argued that it was inspired by the personal speculations of a single indigenous thinker or, at best, that it was a summary of esoteric teachings that were restricted to a small minority of the initiated. Griaule had foreseen such doubts and had declared in the preface to his book that Ogotemmêli's ontological and cosmological views were understood and shared by most adult Dogon and that the rites connected with them were celebrated by the entire local population. He went further, however, under the influence of the Negritude movement, to argue that many of these concepts would prove to be pan-African and would undoubtedly be shared among the Bambara, Bozo, Kurumba, and other neighbors of the Dogon.

Although Dieterlen's *Essai sur la religion bambara* (1951) revealed a comparable wealth of symbols, proclivity to abstractions, and original systematization of the universe among the Bambara, there were significant differences between them and Dogon conceptualizations. These differences among communities of the same ethnolinguistic family have maintained independent religious systems. Dieterlen's work, like that of Griaule, demonstrates the advantages of sustained field research over a period of many years. Dieterlen's research produced strikingly different descriptions than Louis Tauxier's *La religion bambara* (1927) which was published a generation earlier. Aware that these discrepancies might cause people to question the objectivity of the various scholars or the reliability of indigenous informants to be questioned, Dieterlen defended the efforts of her predecessors. She argued, however, that the Bambara distinguish two levels of knowledge—one very public and relatively simple and one more esoteric and more complex. This was implicit in Griaule's work as well. One could use these distinctions to explain the contrasts between different field researchers' descriptions in many other cases. Studies of the Congo, Akan-Ashanti, and Yoruba are examples of what could be a long list.

The work that most stimulated a reconsideration of African creeds in the postwar years was *La philosophie bantoue* (1945), written by Belgian Franciscan friar Placide Tempels. This book did not merely offer a synthesis of religious ideas and rituals, it analyzed criteriology, ontology, wisdom, metaphysics, psychology, jurisprudence, and ethics. It stressed the idea of a vital force operating throughout the universe, originating in a supreme being and radiating to spirits, humans, animals, plants, and some natural locales. These forces could be benign or hostile and be strengthened or weakened as they constantly influence one another. The idea of the cosmos as a hierarchy of forces, although not unique to Tempels' work, originated in his mission work and in conversations with Luba elders of southeastern Zaire rather than from anthropological sources. He quotes no academic literature other than Diedrich Westermann's *Der Afrikaner heute und morgen* (1934), in which he found supportive evidence of his theory. Furthermore, Tempels was sure that these concepts were shared by all Bantu-speaking peoples. In the introduction to the French edition, he quoted several unnamed experienced colonialists who had assured him "that he had written nothing new, but rather established order in the imprecise bulk of their own ascertainments based on their practical knowledge of the black man" (Tempels, 1949, p. 25). He also reported a message from Herskovits: "I am interested that so many of the ideas Father Tempels exposes from the Belgian Congo are so close to those that I have found among the Sudanese people of the Guinea coast area" (Tempels, 1949, p. 25). Herskovits's opinion reopened a general and still unsolved question: To what extent are worldviews and fundamental religious ideas common to all African religious systems?

As the colonial occupation of Africa loosened its hold (a slow process that began in the late 1940s and reached its conclusion in 1994), African studies shed some of its colonialist origins and also showed dramatic growth in the United States. Although the study of African religions continued to be dominated by anthropologists, the social functionalist paradigms, so useful to colonial administrators, lost some of their support. The study broadened and began to include increasing number of historians of religion, African historians, and other scholars. As Evans-Pritchard noted in *Theories of Primitive Religion* (1965): "These recent researches in particular societies bring us nearer to the formulation of the problem of what is the part played by religion, and in general by what might be called non-scientific thought, in social life" (Evans-Pritchard, 1965, p. 113). In cases such as John Middleton's *Lugbara Religion* (1960) and Godfrey Lienhardt's work on the Dinka, *Divinity and Experience* (1961), religion was the central topic. In *Una società guineana: Gli Nzema* (1977–1978), Vinigi Grottanelli examined the Nzema of Ghana, the southernmost Akan group, whose religious system grew out of a sustained interaction between a newer Christianity and an older indigenous religious system. Grottanelli used what he described as microbiographical accounts to explore the impact of religion on everyday life.

As the general trend of academic interests shifted from an abstract theological to more socially grounded and psychological context, attempts to make worldwide comparisons of religions and to ascertain the relative age of religious conceptions were gradually abandoned. Increasingly, they have been replaced by detailed studies of specific symbols, rituals, or concepts. Divination, in particular, has retained the attention of anthropologists. Victor Turner's *Ndembu Divination: Its Symbolism and Techniques* (1961) as well as a number of later works and William R. Bascom's *Ifá Divination* (1969), which examines the Yoruba divination system, are valuable contributions. Philip Peek's edited anthology *African Divination Systems* (1991) brings together a number of recent studies that reflects the influence of semiotics, the anthropology of knowledge, cognitive studies, and cross-cultural psychology. New work has also focused on the idea of sacrifice, which has been the subject of five consecutive issues of the series "Systèmes de pensée en Afrique noire" (1976–1983).

Areas of Growth. One of the more popular areas of late twentieth-century growth in the study of African religions, however, comes from the domain of art history. A new emphasis on field research in that discipline encouraged the production of new studies of African art focused on the symbolic meaning and ceremonial use of masks, figurines, and other ritual accessories, which have shed an indirect light on vital aspects of African mythology and religious rites, particularly those of West and central Africa. Dominique Zahan's *Antilope du soleil* (1980), on antelope figures in the sculpture of the Mande-speaking peoples of western Sudan, is an important example. Works by the art historian Robert F. Thompson and his students have established clear linkages between African religious art and religious artifacts in the diaspora throughout the Americas. In *Art and Religion in Africa* (1996) Rosalind Hackett has presented a broad overview of the religious significance of African art within the continent.

Another area of dramatic growth has been in the works by African theologians seeking to outline the foundations of an African spirituality that engages in a sustained interaction with the relatively newer traditions of Christianity and Islam. Works by John Mbiti, such as *African Religions and Philosophy* (1969) and *African Concepts of God* (1970), have had an enormous influence among scholars, missionaries, and the general reading public. E. Bolaji Idowu's specific work *Olodumare: God in Yoruba Belief* (1962) and his overview *African Traditional Religion* (1973) have enjoyed similar influence. Both authors have emphasized ideas of a diffuse monotheism and the profound similarities between African traditional religion and the Abrahamic religions. Mbiti has suggested that African religions lack only a sense of future time and a messianic expectation, which can be met through Christian teachings.

The Ugandan poet and scholar Okot P'Bitek has been sharply critical of these approaches, however, suggesting that what these African theologians are really doing is trying to smuggle Greek metaphysical debates about monotheism and polytheism into an African religious context. P'Bitek argues in *African Religions in Western Scholarship* (1970) that debates about monotheism and polytheism are wholly irrelevant to the day-to-day religious experience of most African adherents. Rwandan scholar Alexis Kagame has applied Tempels' Bantu philosophy to neighboring communities. Kagame's *La philosophie bantu comparée* (1976) provides far more detailed references of a Bantu-speaking ontology. 'Wande Abimbola's series of books on Ifá divination among the Yoruba provide one of the very few scholarly presentations by a priest of this method of divination that is practiced in West Africa and widely within the diasporas of the Americas. His most notable work is *Ifa: An Exposition of Ifa Literary Corpus* (1970). Jacob Olupona's *Kingship, Religion and Rituals in a Nigerian Community* (1991) presents a phemenological study of ritual life in the Ondo Yoruba city-state.

One of the most dramatic developments in the study of African religions was its discovery by the burgeoning field of African history. Although African history initially focused on the history of Europeans in Africa, a form of imperial history, beginning in the 1950s an increasing number of historians turned to the history of Africans. Quickly recognizing the inadequacy of colonial archival and European traveler and missionary accounts, they used oral traditions and field research to attempt to reconstruct the history of African societies that incorporated internal perspectives. Leading this wave of a new African history was the Belgian historian and anthropologist Jan Vansina. Still, it was not until the late 1960s that African historians began to write on the subject of African religious history apart from the history of Christianity or Islam in Africa. Terence Ranger and I. Kimambo's collection of essays on African religious history, *The Historical Study of African Religion* (1972), pioneered this new field and inspired a host of other studies. Utilizing oral traditions and participant observation, historians and anthropologists began to write histories of entire religious systems, of cults of the supreme being, of healing cults, and of territorial cults. For example, Dutch anthropologist Matthew Schofeleers wrote a series of works on the history of the Mbona cult in Malawi. Douglas Johnson's *Nuer Prophets* is a history of prophetism. Johnson and David Anderson have collected a series of historical accounts of East African prophets in their edited anthology *Revealing Prophets* (1995). In *Shrines of the Slave Trade* (1999), Robert Baum relied on oral traditions and travelers' accounts to examine the history of Diola religion in southern Senegal during the era of the Atlantic slave trade. He examined the history of specific spirit shrines that were created to assist in the regulation and containment of Diola involvement in the seizure and sale of captives in the eighteenth century. He also sketches out how such involvement affected concepts of the supreme being, lesser spirits, and the nature of local priesthoods and councils of elders. Iris Berger's *Religion and Resistance* (1981) examines the history of female spirit mediums in the interlacustrine region of East Africa.

Reflecting the growing interdisciplinary nature of the study of African religions, the most important theorist to emerge in the postcolonial era was the British sociologist Robin Horton, who taught for many years at the University of Calabar in Nigeria. He wrote three seminal essays: "African Traditional Thought and Western Science," "African Conversion," and "On the Rationality of Conversion," all of which were published in the journal *Africa.* In his essay on African traditional thought, he argued that it resembled Western science in its reliance on paradigms that sought to explain the world. He argued that African systems of thought relied on a personal idiom of explaining, predicting, and controlling events in their world. By the personal, he meant spiritual beings and forces that controlled, or at least influenced, world events. He demonstrated that, like science, African traditionalists continually tested their explanatory models, finding explanations for failures and reinforcement of their tenets for their successes.

In his two essays on conversion, he argued that there was a basic African cosmology consisting of a supreme being and of lesser spirits. Furthermore, he suggested that the supreme being was primarily concerned with the macrocosm, the wider world beyond the villages of rural Africa and the natural forces that shaped the lives of everyone. The lesser spirits, on the other hand, actively intervened in the microcosm of village and family issues. He concluded that because Africa was overwhelmingly rural and local in its orientation African religions primarily focused on the microcosm. Thus, local spirits assumed dominance in ritual life and were the primary guardians of morality. Finally, he argued that European colonialism broke down this localism, creating a need for a macrocosmic focus and greater attention to the supreme being. What proved most controversial, however, was Horton's suggestion that African religions could evolve their own focus on a supreme being, although many found this focus by converting to Islam or Christianity. Other critics thought that he overstated the rural and local nature of precolonial Africa and that there was an implicit evolutionary theory in his work that suggested that polytheism was not suited to a modern, macrocosmic world. Still, his work, more than that of any other theorist, demonstrated that African religious thought was rational, systematic, and empirical and that African traditions were capable of significant internal change. Horton's theories profoundly influenced the current generation of scholarship on African religions.

In the area of African ritual studies, Victor Turner's use of structuralism, semiotics, and performance studies enriched his analysis of the ritual process among the Ndembu of Zambia. He approached African rituals as dramatic performances, structured around a series of binary oppositions that were ultimately overcome in the course of the ritual. Influenced by the field of semiotics, he discussed the multivocality or polyvalent quality of symbols, which allowed often disparate ideas to be linked and their contradictions overcome in the course of the ritual event. Building on Van Gennep's tripartite structure of initiation rituals, Turner focused on the second, or liminal phase, and the experience of what he called *communitas,* a sense of oneness among a group of initiates in which external distinctions were abandoned. This produced what he termed an *anti-structure,* which was a vital way of immersing new initiates and renewing for elders the fundamental experiences of religious life.

A new area of scholarly investigation has been the relation between African healing systems and African religions. Beginning with such pioneering works as Margaret Field's *Search for Security* (1960), researchers have sought to understand the therapeutic qualities of African healing rituals. Field compared the work of Akan priests of the *obosom* spirits in Ghana with the work of the psychotherapists of the West. In his *Man Cures, God Heals* (1981), Kofi Appiah-Kubi offers a comparative study of Akan traditional and Akan Christian healing practices. John Janzen and other anthropologists studied a shrine of affliction, known as Ngoma, which has spread throughout southern and eastern Africa. Paul Stoller has conducted similar research in the Islamic and Songhai religious milieu of Niger.

With the growing emphasis on field research in the study of African religions, it is not surprising that later twentieth-century research has shown a strong influence of reflective anthropology. This approach abandons the idea of an invisible ethnographer and recognizes that researcher and informant, researcher and host community create distinct forms of social relations that influence the types of data collected. Most field research accounts now include a description of field research methods and the way that researchers helped to create distinct fields of interaction with host individuals and communities. Works such as Paul Stoller's *In Sorcery's Shadow* (1987) and Wim van Binsbergen's "Becoming a Sangoma" (1991) crossed the traditional borders of academic scholarship and entered into the experience of practitioners of the religious rituals that they studied. By doing so, they allowed their readers unparalleled access to the lived world of African ritual by people who shared the culture and training of scholars of religion in Europe and America.

SEE ALSO Ancestors, article on Ancestor Worship; Animism and Animatism; Anthropology, Ethnology, and Religion;

Cosmology, article on African Cosmologies; Dogon Religion; Evolution, article on Evolutionism; Study of Religion, article on The Academic Study of Religion in Sub-Saharan Africa.

BIBLIOGRAPHY

Abimbola, 'Wande. *Ifá: An Exposition of Ifá Literary Corpus.* Ibadan, 1970.

Abimbola, 'Wande. *Ifá Will Mend Our Broken World: Thoughts on Yoruba Religion and Culture in Africa and the Diaspora.* Roxbury, Mass., 1997.

Anderson, David M. and Douglas H. Johnson. *Revealing Prophets.* London, 1995.

Appiah-Kubi, Kofi. *Man Cures, God Heals.* Totowa, N.J., 1981.

Bascom, William R. *Ifá Divination.* Bloomington, Ind., 1969.

Baum, Robert. *Shrines of the Slave Trade: Diola Religion and Society in Precolonial Senegambia.* New York, 1999.

Beltrame, Giovanni. *Il fiume bianco e i Denka.* Verona, Italy, 1881.

Berger, Iris. *Religion and Resistance: East African Kingdoms in the Precolonial Period.* Tervuren, Belgian, 1981.

Binsbergen, Wim van. "Becoming a Sangoma." *Journal of Religion in Africa* 21, no. 4 (1991): 309–344.

Cavazzi, Giovanni Antonio. *Istorica descrizione de' tre' regni Congo, Matamba Angola.* Bologna, Italy, 1687.

Danquah, Joseph B. *The Akan Doctrine of God.* London, 1944.

Evans-Pritchard, E. E. *The Nuer.* Oxford, 1940.

Evans-Pritchard, E. E. *Nuer Religion.* Oxford, 1956.

Evans-Pritchard, E. E. *Theories of Primitive Religion.* Oxford, 1965.

Field, Margaret. *Search for Security: An Ethno-psychiatric Study of Rural Ghana.* Evanston, Ill., 1960.

Fortes, Meyer, and Germaine Dieterlen, eds. *African Systems of Thought.* London, 1966.

Griaule, Marcel. *Conversations with Ogotemmêli.* Translated by Robert Redfield. London, 1965.

Hackett, Rosalind. *Art and Religion in Africa.* London, 1996.

Hegel, Georg Friedrich. *The Philosophy of History.* New York, 1956.

Herskovits, Melville. *The Myth of the Negro Past.* Boston, 1941; reprint, 1958.

Hollis, Alfred C. *The Masai: Their Language and Folklore* (1905). Freeport, N.Y., 1971.

Hollis, Alfred C. *The Nandi: Their Language and Folk-lore* (1909). Oxford, 1969.

Horton, Robin. "African Traditional Thought and Western Science." *Africa* 37 (1967): 50–71, 155–187.

Horton, Robin. "African Conversion." *Africa* 41 (1971): 85–108.

Horton, Robin. "On the Rationality of Conversion." *Africa* 45 (1975): 219–35, 373–99.

Johnson, Douglas. *Nuer Prophets: a History of Prophecy from the Upper Nile in the Nineteenth and Twentieth Centuries.* Oxford, 1994.

Lang, Andrew. *The Making of Religion.* London, 1898.

Lang, Andrew. *The Making of Religion.* Rev ed. London, 1909.

Levtzion, N., and J. F. P. Hopkins, eds., *Corpus of Early Arabic Sources for West African History.* Cambridge, U.K., 1981.

Lienhardt, Godfrey. *Divinity and Experience.* Oxford, 1961.

Mbiti, John. *African Religions and Philosophy.* New York, 1969.

Mbiti, John. *Concepts of God in Africa.* London, 1970.

Middleton, John. *Lugbara Religion.* London, 1960.

Mudimbe, Valentin. *The Invention of Africa: Gnosis, Philosophy, and the Order of Knowledge.* Bloomington, Ind., 1988.

Olupona, Jacob K. *Kingship, Religion and Rituals in a Nigerian Community.* Stockholm, 1991.

Peek, Philip, ed. *African Divination Systems.* Bloomington, Ind., 1991.

Person, Yves. "The Coastal Peoples." In *General History of Africa:* Volume 4. *Africa from the Twelfth to the Sixteenth Century,* edited by DjiBril Tamsir Niane. London, 1984.

Pigafetta, Filippo. *Relazione del Reame di Congo* (1591). Milan, 1978.

Ranger, Terence, and I. Kimambo, eds. *The Historical Study of African Religion.* Berkeley, Calif., 1972.

Réville, Albert. *Les religions des peuples non-civilisés.* 2 vols. Paris, 1883.

Smith, Edwin W. *African Ideas of God: A Symposium.* London, 1950.

Stoller, Paul. *In Sorcery's Shadow: A Memoir of Apprenticeship among the Songhay of Niger.* Chicago, 1987.

Tachard, Guy. *Il viaggio di Siam de'padri gesuiti mandati dal re di Francia all'Indie, e alla China.* Milan, 1693.

Turner, Victor. *Ndembu Divination: Its Symbolism and Techniques.* Manchester, U.K., 1961.

Tylor, Edward B. *Primitive Culture: Researches into the Development of Mythology, Philosophy, Religion, Language, Art, and Custom.* 2 vols. London, 1871; reprint, 1874.

Waitz, Theodor *Anthropologie der Naturvölker.* 6 vols. Leipzig, Germany, 1859–1872.

Weeks, John H. *Among The Primitive Bakongo.* London, 1914.

Werner, Alice. *Myths and Legends of the Bantu.* London, 1933; reprint, 1968.

Westermann, Diedrich. *The Shilluk People.* Berlin, 1912; reprint, Newport, Conn., 1970.

VINIGI GROTTANELLI (1987)
ROBERT M. BAUM (2005)

AFRO-BRAZILIAN RELIGIONS. The religious landscape of Brazil is rich and varied. It includes the Roman Catholicism that arrived with the Portuguese colonizers, Spiritism influenced by nineteenth-century French philosopher Allan Kardec, twentieth-century evangelical Protestant movements, and the Buddhism, Islam, and Judaism that immigrants from Asia, the Middle East, and Europe introduced to the nation. While all of these traditions have engaged and been transformed by Brazilian social realities, it is perhaps the religions of African influence that have been most strongly associated with the country's popular culture and most deeply resonant of the particularities and complexities of Brazilian national identity.

Candomblé, Umbanda, Xangô, Tambor de Mina, Tambor de Nagô, Terecô, Pajelança, Catimbó, Batuque, and Macumba are among the names by which Afro-Brazilian religions are known in various regions of the nation. Most of these traditions have roots in nineteenth-century Brazilian slave societies and are the creation of enslaved Africans and their descendants. The religions developed as part of blacks' efforts to make sense of an experience of extraordinary disjunction and to create instruments that would sustain the deepest sources of their own humanity in the midst of great personal and collective trauma.

In some places, Afro-Brazilian religious communities emerged in connection with *quilombos,* outlying fugitive slave settlements. In others, they grew in the context of danced, processional celebrations of saint's days and holy days when plantation workers were given a sorely needed respite from the intensity of their labors. Often, in cities, communities formed in the small homes and rented rooms of African religious leaders; providing a refuge for worship, communal gathering, healing, and even organizing ways to resist slavery.

ORIGINS, COMMONALTIES, AND DISTINCTIONS. There are a number of important distinctions among the traditions, but there are also significant commonalities. Afro-Brazilian religions share an emphasis on ritual and medicinal healing, cultivation of intense and intimate relationships to spiritual entities, and mutual aid. The religions are also marked by a concept of obligation and reciprocity between human beings and the ancestral/spiritual energies who are gods, saints, orixás, nkisis, voduns, caboclos, guides, and other sacred personages accommodated and celebrated within the ritual communities. Furthermore, Afro-Brazilian religions are all essentially mediumistic, where the central rite in many ceremonies is a crossing from one kind of consciousness to an ontologically different one, facilitated by sacred percussive music and dance. The occasion of possession or trance enables devotees to experience a profound closeness to the orixás who have claimed them and who accompany the initiates in their journey through life.

These religions also share, to greater or lesser extents, a combination of influences from West and Central African traditions, native Amerindian cultural and religious practices, popular Catholicism, and Spiritism (*Espiritismo*). Their uniquenesses derive from the specific combination of elements composing their rituals, orientations, and meanings—including the historical, geographic, and cultural environment in which each was formed. Candomblé, for example, formed in the late eighteenth and early to mid-nineteenth centuries in and around the northeastern port city of Salvador, Bahia. Because West Africans from the Yoruba and Dahomey kingdoms (present-day southwestern Nigeria and Benin) and their descendants were most prominent among the population of slaves, former slaves, and free people of color in the area at that time, Candomblé developed with strong elements of Yoruba and Ewe-Fon ritual organization, language, and mythology. Umbanda, a more recent phenomenon dating from the 1920s, drew heavily on Candomblé, Spiritism, Catholicism, and persistent black and Indian folk representations in popular culture. Initially based in the industrializing cities of Rio de Janeiro and São Paulo, the new religion addressed the needs of both a workforce migrating from the rural areas and a developing, self-conscious middle class.

Xangô, a religion very similar in history and appearance to Candomblé, emerged in Recife in the state of Pernambuco. Tambor de Mina shows especially strong Dahomean influence and was organized in the nineteenth century by blacks who worked in the coastal economy in the state of Maranhão. Tambor de Nagô, situated in the same area, draws from a Yoruba resource base. Terecô (also called Tambor de Mata), another Afro-Brazilian religion found in Maranhão, was created by slaves on cotton plantations of the inland area around the city of Codó and is distinguished from the Maranhense coastal traditions by the addition of Angolan and Cabindan ritual elements. A variety of Afro-Brazilian religious practices in the extreme southern state of Rio Grande do Sul and in the Amazonian region are known by the general name Batuque. Macumba is another generic term for Afro-Brazilian religions, used especially in Rio de Janeiro; though it is sometimes pejorative.

In the arid inland northeast and the Amazonian north, interactions between blacks and Indians produced a remarkable sharing of ritual and pharmacopoeic knowledge. There, more so than elsewhere in the country, Afro-Brazilian religions are inheritors of indigenous Amerindian cultural and spiritual orientations. The exchanges created a number of religions that, while incorporating elements of African traditions, are heavily dedicated to the cultivation of indigenous Amerindian spirits and particularly strongly focused on ritual healing, often using tobacco and *jurema,* a root beverage which facilitates altered states of consciousness. Among these Afro-Indigenous traditions are a black or African Pajelança (as distinguished from a more "purely" Indian Pajelança) and Catimbó. Many of the Afro-Brazilian religions use West and Central African languages as liturgical idioms. Most common are Yoruba, Kikongo, Kimbundu, and Fon, although ritual traditions with the strongest Amerindian and Catholic influence conduct rites in Portuguese.

Another important class of Afro-Brazilian religions are the black lay Catholic confraternities that historically served as mutual aid societies and provided ritual opportunity and space for blacks to venerate saints to which they felt especially drawn. One of the best-known examples is the *Irmandade da Nossa Senhora da Boa Morte* (the Sisterhood of Our Lady of the Good Death). Like others founded at various points from the seventeenth through nineteenth centuries in different regions of Brazil, this organization was dedicated to helping its members defray funereal expenses; assist each other during illness; and, when possible, purchase manumission from slavery. In the late twentieth century, a chapter in the

Bahian town of Cachoeira became renowned for its annual three-day processional feast celebrating the Virgin Mary's bodily assumption to heaven. Membership in the *irmandade* consists exclusively of Afro-Brazilian women, many of whom are priestesses of Candomblé as well as Catholic acolytes.

On the island of Itaparica, across the bay from Salvador, are ritual communities that cultivate the spirits of male ancestral dead, the Eguns. This society is distinct from Candomblé, although many members are also prominent in Candomblé rites. Like traditional Egungun cult practices in Nigeria and Benin, the ritual communities on Itaparica island periodically summon the presence of ancestors who have passed over to the *orun* (the spiritual world), honoring and remembering them, keeping their connections to current generations vital. The Egun rites, although restricted to males in both Africa and Brazil, are believed to have been created by a female orixá—Oyá, whose special responsibility is the care of spirits of the deceased.

DEMOGRAPHIC ISSUES. Most devotees of Afro-Brazilian religions are members of the Brazilian working classes. Although blacks have historically been in the majority as participants and leaders in the religions, since the 1950s people who claim no African ancestry have increasingly joined the ranks of adepts. In some parts of southeastern Brazil there are ritual communities where more than half of the members are white. There are also Asians, Europeans, other Latin Americans, and blacks from the United States and the Caribbean who are attracted to Afro-Brazilian religions and who have been integrated into its communities. The religions continue to provide devotees an alternative space for the cultivation of connections to ancestral sources of strength, healing, and mystic/ritual approaches to the resolution of the everyday problems of modern life. They also offer access to deeper, more multifaceted, and more respected personal identities, an important resource for individuals who are severely marginalized by the political, racial, and economic structures of a profoundly unequal society. This characteristic of Afro-Brazilian religions perhaps explains the notable participation of gay men and lesbians, as both initiates and leaders, in various ritual communities.

The Brazilian national census of 2000 indicates that devotees of Afro-Brazilian religions constitute 3 percent of the country's total population. Scholars of the religions, however, have calculated the figure at closer to 8 percent. They caution that the true number of devotees is to some extent hidden behind the categories Catholic and Spiritist because many individuals who practice Afro-Brazilian religions refer to themselves publicly as participants in what are often seen as more acceptable faiths. In fact, some devotees, like the members of the Boa Morte *irmandade*, are part of more than one religious tradition. This double-consciousness, so to speak, is understandable given that historically, Afro-Brazilian religions had to constitute themselves in public relationship to Catholicism in order to survive. Several early Candomblé communities were established by members of black lay Catholic confraternities. Devotees of Tambor de Mina, Candomblé, Batuque, and Xangô all created parallels between the African divinities and Catholic saints, and often organized their own liturgical calendars around the Church's feast days.

EARLY RESEARCH. The study of Afro-Brazilian religions by academics began in the last years of the nineteenth century with the work of Raimundo Nina Rodrigues, a forensic physician based in Bahia, whose specific interest was the phenomenon of possession in Candomblé as a psychological pathology. In spite of his conceptual prejudices, Rodrigues did important work to document the formation of early Candomblé communities. His pioneering investigations were followed by those of his student Arthur Ramos, who broadened the geographic focus of Afro-Brazilian religious and cultural studies beyond Bahia, and helped situate the developing discipline in the context of Brazilian anthropological and sociological debates. Another early observer of Afro-Brazilian religion was Manuel Querino, a black art professor and essayist who, in the first three decades of the twentieth century, wrote extensively about Bahian popular cultural traditions. French sociologist Roger Bastide did the first comprehensive sociohistorical examination of major Afro-Brazilian religions, bringing an acute insight into the evocative and subtle metaphysics represented in the traditions. Others who made significant early contributions include Brazilian scholars Nunes Pereira, Gonçalves Fernandes, João do Rio (Paulo Barreto), Edison Carneiro, Octavio da Costa Eduardo, and Rene Ribeiro; French photographer and anthropologist Pierre Verger; and Americans Melville Herskovitz, Ruth Landes, and Donald Pierson.

CANDOMBLÉ. Candomblé and Umbanda are the most widespread and well-known Afro-Brazilian religions. As the best documented of the older Afro-Brazilian rites (and a direct forerunner of Umbanda, the largest of the traditions), Candomblé occupies a position of some prestige. Its oldest communities in Bahia have become the standard by which many other groups are measured. From its origins in northeastern Brazil in the last century of slavery, Candomblé expanded to many areas of the nation, carried by migrating workers to the industrializing cities of south and southeast Brazil. The central features of the religion have changed little in its expansion and continue to revolve around the cultivation of orixás, nkisis, and voduns, which are recognized as divinities, elements of the natural world, and aspects of human personality.

Candomblé is a hierarchical, initiatory religion with little moral dichotomy of good versus evil but with a strong ethical sense based in African values of reciprocity and ancestral/spiritual obligation. There are six major divisions within the tradition, organized as ethnic/liturgical "nations": Ketu, Ijexá, Jêje, Angola, Congo, and Caboclo. In their initial manifestations in the nineteenth century, the African nations of Candomblé represented the Yoruba (Ketu and Ijexá), Ewe (Jêje), and Bantu (Angola and Congo) ethnic identities of many of the individuals associated with ritual communities. Over the course of the development of the religion, and as larger numbers of Brazilian-born participants entered the ceremonies, the identity of Candomblé nations became a liturgical/ritual designation and not a genetic or clan-based one.

The Caboclo Candomblé is an additional division that specifically and extensively cultivates Amerindian ancestral spirits in addition to those of African origin. It is a more recent development, dating from the early twentieth century and prominently incorporating Brazilian national symbols such as the country's flag, its green and yellow colors, and the use of Portuguese as the language of ceremony. Because of the strength and prestige of Yoruba-based candomblés, the Yoruba term *orixá* (orisha) has become the most common descriptor of African spirits cultivated in the religion. Nonetheless, in the contexts of their own rituals, the Ewe and Bantu nations of Candomblé call the spirits by other names–voduns (among the Jêje) and nkisis (among the Congo and Angola communities).

In Brazil, the most commonly cultivated orixás of the Yoruba pantheon are Exú, orixá of the crossroads who controls communication between human beings and the world of the spirits; Ogun, warrior god of metals and the forest who is the path-breaker; and Oxôssi–ancient head of the Kêtu kingdom, a hunter orixá characterized by mental acuity. Omolû or Obaluaiye is orixá of the earth and of both illness and healing. Ossâin is guardian of herbs and herbal wisdom and Oxumarê is the serpent deity associated with life cycles of renewal. Another warrior energy, Logun-Ede, is son of Oxôssi and Oxum and shares their qualities. Xangô, the much beloved ancient king of Oyo, is orixá of fire, justice, storm, and friendship. Oxum is the orixá of sweet waters, creativity, beauty, and abundance. The energetic female warrior orixá Oyá, or Iansã, is associated with storm, transformation, and the spirits of the dead. Iemanjá, patroness of salt water, is an orixá of maternal strength and protection. Obá is another river deity, also a fierce female warrior energy; and Euá, a river nymph orixá, is associated with youthful grace and a fighting spirit. An ancient female energy, Nana Burukû, is orixá of still, muddy waters. Oxalá, father of the other orixás, is the principle of peace and protection.

Candomblé ritual communities, or *terreiros,* exist in a variety of forms. Older or more prosperous communities often feature a series of buildings that include "houses" for the deities; living and cooking space for members of the community; a large hall, or *barracão,* for conducting ceremonies, and both garden and uncultivated spaces for essential plant resources. Newer and more urban *terreiros* and those with fewer material resources are often incorporated into the homes of religious leaders, where the living room may be used as the *barracão.*

Most ritual communities involve a small number of participants; generally no more than fifty, except in the case of the oldest "mother houses" of Bahia from which many Candomblé *terreiros* around the country descend. Ceremonies open to the public may attract several times the number of actual members, and nonmembers may frequent the *terreiro* for spiritual advice and ritual assistance on a wide range of matters—including physical health, psychological stability, personal relationships, financial difficulties, and employment issues. Extensive traditions of ritual and medicinal pharmacopoeia support *trabalhos* (spiritual healing works) and many new adepts, as well as clients, are attracted to the religion by the reputation of priestesses and priests for successful intervention in problematic cases.

When a *pai* or *mãe de santo* (priest or priestess) is approached, the first step is often a *consulta,* a private divinatory session, in which the religious leader will consult the orixás by means of the *jogo de búzios,* an oracle of cowrie shells. Reading and interpreting the shells, the *mãe* or *pai de santo* diagnoses the problem and, after determining if it is within the purview of the religion's resources to address it, prescribes a remedy. This may be as simple as an herb bath and an offering of flowers or food at the seashore or as complex as the eventual need for a full initiation into the priesthood.

Individuals who are to be consecrated to the service of the orixás—those who will receive the orixás into their bodies and others who will attend and assist them—are, in a sense, called to that service. Cases of persistent (and sometimes undiagnosable) illness are often seen as signs from the orixá that an individual must undergo initiation. This is understood as both a duty and a blessing; an inherited ancestral/spiritual obligation which, if respected, brings well-being to the individual, her family, and the larger *terreiro* community; and if ignored can result in increased suffering.

Most *terreiros* follow a fairly strict organization of ritual responsibilities according to gender and length of initiation. At the pinnacle of the *terreiro* leadership is the *mãe* or *pai de santo*—the head priestess or priest—whose authority is unchallenged in the context of the ritual community. Other titles for these individuals depend on the specific ritual language and tradition of each house: *iyalorixá* and *babalorixá* (mother and father of the orixás) are terms used in the Yoruba-based candomblés; *nenguankisi* and *tatankisi* (mother and father of the nkisi) are used in the Congo and Angola candomblés; and *doné* and *doté* (chief priestess and chief priest of the voduns) in Jêje candomblés. Initiated members of the communities are *filhos* and *filhas de santo* (children of the saint).

The majority of Candomblé devotees are women, and some *terreiros* have a long-standing tradition of exclusively consecrating women as supreme leaders of the community. Indeed, the place of women as utmost ritual authorities in many *terreiros* is a distinguishing characteristic of the religion. Candomblé communities have often been recognized as "privileged" women's spaces in Brazilian society.

Beyond the chief sacerdotal positions there are explicit ritual roles designated for males and others for females. In the Yoruba-based Candomblé communities, among the most common posts held by women, after that of the high priestess, are the *iyakêkere* or *mãe pequena* (small mother), the second-highest leadership role, assistant to the high priestess or priest; *ekedis,* initiated women who do not receive the orixás but who assist those who do in a variety of ritual circumstances; and *ebomis,* a general term for initiates who have celebrated seven years or more of consecration to the orixá. *Iawôs,* "wives" of the orixá, are devotees specifically consecrated to receive the deities in their bodies and become their vessels in the human community, undergoing a lengthy, obligatory process of training. *Iawôs* can be male or female, although they are overwhelmingly women in Bahia. *Abiãs,* the most junior-level members of the community, are individuals who are being prepared for initiation and who have undergone one or more fairly simple rituals of spiritual fortification, the *obi* or *bori.* Like *iawôs, abiãs* can be male or female, but again, are predominately women and girls.

Specifically male roles include *babalorixá,* or chief priest (in *terreiros* where a male is the head rather than a female); *ogãs,* initiated men who do not receive the orixá but who assist the *terreiro* community in a variety of ways, from infrastructure and physical maintenance to financial and political influence; *axogún,* ritual slaughterer of votive animals; and *alabês,* drummers. Finally, all members of the *terreiro* are considered children of the *mãe* or *pai de santo* and they are expected to relate to each other as family, including, sometimes, adherence to prohibitions against sexual relations and marriage within the ritual community.

The central rites of Candomblé are a series of initiations, periodic reinforcements of the spiritual energies of both devotees and orixás, and a cycle of annual ceremonies in honor of the orixás. Among the first rituals a new initiate experiences are the *banho de folhas* (ritual cleansing bath with herbs), *lavagem de contas* (consecration of beaded necklaces in herb mixtures sacred to the orixás), and *obí com agua,* an offering of kola nut and water to the orixá who most closely accompanies each devotee. Other rituals related more directly to the process of initiation, or *fazer santo* (literally "to make the saint"), are designed to reinforce the spiritual link between devotee and orixá as well as to prepare the new initiate to properly receive and care for the orixá that enters her body in a ceremony. The rites associated with initiation, *obrigações,* are renewed in one-, three-, and seven-year cycles.

Each *terreiro* conducts a sequence of annual celebrations for the patron orixás of the house. These *festas* are the major public ceremonies of the religion. Initiated members who receive the orixá (*iawôs* and *ebomis*) circle the *barracão* in festive ritual dress: beautiful lace and embroidered blouses, panes of cloth with stripes or lace designs wrapped around their chests, wide skirts of lush and beautiful fabrics—their fullness accentuated by starched underskirts—and the *contas,* beaded necklaces in the colors and patterns associated with the various divinities. The women dance barefoot, in a counterclockwise ring, varying their steps and gestures in accordance with the rhythms played on sacred drums, *atabaques:* a different rhythm for each orixá. The drums are accompanied by a metal bell, *agogô,* and songs calling the orixás to join their devotees in the circle of dancers.

After a while, the spirits begin to descend, temporarily occupying the bodies of their adepts. In the moments of transition, some devotees are in perceptible discomfort, clearly demonstrating that the process of sharing their physical being and consciousness with another entity is an immensely taxing effort. Others seem to make the shift almost imperceptibly; under all but the closest observation, the moment of change passes unnoticed. As the orixás arrive, they are ushered out of the *barracão* and into back rooms where they are dressed in their own ritual clothes, in colors, textures, and designs that clearly identify each: red and white for Xangô; light blue for Iemanjá; raffia palm and burlap for Omolû; white for Oxalá. They reemerge wearing beaded crowns that cover their eyes. They carry the implements associated with their dramatic and interwoven mythologies: Oxum's mirror and fan; Oyá's horsehair whisk; Ogun's sword and shield. They dance into the small hours of the morning, pausing to receive ritual greetings and to offer hugs and parental caresses (and sometimes a concise word of advice) to members of the community and guests.

The public *festas,* as well as the private internal rituals of the *terreiros,* are ceremonies whose intent is to renew the *axé,* the essential spiritual force and life force, that is believed to reside in all forms of being in the universe. In communion with the orixás and the ancestors, in the practice of reciprocal exchange—food, music, flowers, water, dance, singing, and even the ritually open bodies of devotees—the energy of life is nourished and renewed for all who depend on that energy for their own continued existence and well-being.

In Candomblé, as in most of the Afro-Brazilian religions, ritual knowledge is primarily transmitted in oral and corporeal forms. Among devotees, very little is written down and most learning happens simply by rote experience and being present. A popular saying in the religion is *"Quem pergunta no Candomblé não aprende"* (She who asks questions in Candomblé doesn't learn). Knowledge passes as much from hand to hand in the conduct of daily tasks as from mouth to ear. The appropriate comportment in ceremonial as well as everyday contexts is one of manifest, corporeal respect for elders and for the orixás. This means that devotees with fewer years of initiation should defer to those who have more. Candomblé ceremony involves an elaborate etiquette of greeting and respect for elders that, even outside of the explicitly ritual context, requires initiates to acknowledge and ask the blessing of their elders and give special prostrated reverence to the chief priestess or priest.

Outside of the hierarchy of individual *terreiros,* there is no external organizing structure that dictates standards of ritual activity for Candomblé communities. Each house is independent and the leadership answers only to the orixás and to tradition. In some states there are licensing bodies to insure "authenticity" and affirm the training of *pais* and *mães do santo,* but these do not set policy. This is true of the other Afro-Brazilian religions as well. The absence of a larger governing organization means that each ritual community is essentially autonomous. Correspondingly, there is little institutional support for the religions beyond informal (but important) networks of friendship, mutual respect, and the rumors, reports, and inter-*terreiro* conversations that serve significantly as a kind of standardizing influence, especially among communities of the same Candomblé nation.

UMBANDA. Since the 1950s, Umbanda has had the largest and most diverse participant base among the Afro-Brazilian religions. Emerging in Rio de Janeiro in the 1920s and 1930s, it quickly spread throughout the nation, attracting devotees across a range of ethnic, racial, gender, and class identities. The ability to gain such a variety of adepts was related in part to its extraordinary capacity to incorporate elements from a vast resource base of spiritual traditions. Emerging from a foundation in Congo-Angola and Caboclo candomblés, Umbanda maintained a basic structure of orixá worship with increased emphasis on Catholic and Spiritist symbolic and conceptual elements. The new religion conspicuously assimilated prayers, invocations, and veneration of Jesus, Mary, and various saints from the Catholic tradition. It also embraced philosophical aspects of Spiritism such as dualist ethics, reincarnation, karma, and the cultivation of a great many spiritual guides who assist devotees in a variety of concerns. Perhaps most significantly, among the new religion's spiritual entities were many associated with the contradictions and complexities of Brazilian modernity.

These included the *pretos velhos,* spirits of old black slaves whose long-suffering lives of labor conferred upon them a wisdom about the world that they share easily with devotees who approach them for advice and counsel. The caboclo spirits, already developing in Candomblé by the 1920s, emerge with an even vaster influence on Brazilian popular culture through their incorporation in Umbanda, where they represent the power of the untamed forest, remarkable healing capacities, courage, and a kind of romanticized essential Brazilianness of identity. Other *guias* (spiritual guides) of Umbanda further represent marginality and subalterity in relation to the occidental white standard—the Exús and Pomba Giras (female versions of Exú) associated with the unpredictability of street life and the crossroads; the Ciganos (Gypsies), Boiadeiros (Cowboys), and Marinheiros (Sailors); and an ever-increasing variety of other folk figures whose appeal arises in part from their distance from official authority and their proven ability to negotiate, resist, and survive in the face of great adversity.

In the years immediately preceding Umbanda's founding, most Afro-Brazilian religions still suffered significant persecution. Police raids with arrests and confiscation of sacred objects were not uncommon and economical and political elites waged ideological battles against the ritual practices which were seen as at best exotic nuisances, and at worst threats to the stability and enlightenment of the country. Much of the prejudice against black religions in Brazil occurred as part of a larger system of discrimination against black people and Afro-Brazilian culture as well. This was a period when an ideal of *embranquecimento* (whitening) was promulgated as a way to move the nation toward greater development and "civilization." New devotees to Umbanda were, perhaps unconsciously, looking for ways to minimize the direct association of their religion with the scourge of blackness.

Umbanda's publicly accessible altars feature symbols of Catholic saints, Indian caboclos, and *pretos velhos,* whereas the altars to the orixás are often in less obvious parts of the *terreiro* or house. Umbanda does not generally employ votive sacrifices in its rituals and the ceremonial clothing is simpler than that of Candomblé. In some *terreiros,* hand clapping and a capella singing replaces the use of drums. By the close of the twentieth century, Umbanda in large cities had developed a kind of New Age character of anonymous therapeutic support that served both middle-class and poor devotees. One view of the religion is that it operates on the border between Afro-Indigenous ritual and Christian rationalism; between modern psychological therapy and shamanism. Interestingly, since the 1980s Umbanda has been losing adepts to Candomblé and other Afro-Brazilian religions seen by some as more "authentic" and more ritually powerful because of their stronger cultivation of African spiritual energies.

INFLUENCE ON POPULAR CULTURE. The influence of Afro-Brazilian religions extends deeply into popular culture in Brazil, belying the limitations of the relatively small number of formal adepts. As elsewhere in the African diaspora, like the United States and Cuba, black religious expression in Brazil has become the foundation for many elements of national culture. Brazilian music and dance forms, culinary traditions, literary tropes, and folk icons draw heavily from Afro-Brazilian roots, where sacred and secular artistic traditions blend almost seamlessly. The characteristic palm oil–based and expertly spiced Bahian cuisine reflects central ingredients in the sacred foods of the orixás. The resonant, multitextured percussive music and movements of samba have early-twentieth-century roots in the circle dance vernacular entertainments of rural northeastern Brazil and the *favelas* (ghettos, shantytowns) of Rio de Janeiro. Those dancers and musicians were often also participants in Afro-Brazilian religious life, extending their aesthetic sensibilities across both cultural manifestations.

Afro-Brazilian religions are a distinctly New World phenomenon reflecting the history, geography, and cultural and political encounters of the nation's varied peoples. They were created from, and are continually modified by the materials participants find available to best negotiate the challenges and possibilities of life where they live it. At the opening of the twenty-first century, one of the major challenges the Afro-Brazilian religions face is a vehement aggression by some neo-Pentecostal Protestant sects. As the *terreiros,* centers, and ritual houses of Afro-Brazilian religions seek the resources to address this newest challenge to their existence and meaning, they will draw on the wellsprings of ancestral *força* and *axé* which have seen them through other days at least as difficult as this.

Bibliography

Bastide, Roger. *The African Religions of Brazil: Toward a Sociology of the Interpenetration of Civilizations.* Baltimore, 1978. Bastide's classic sociological study of Afro-Brazilian religions was the first comprehensive effort to examine the role and meaning of religions of African origin in the historical and contemporary life of Brazilian society. Bastide examines the metaphysics, central rites, and organizational structures of all major Afro-Brazilian religious traditions.

Carybé. *Os deuses africanos no candomblé da Bahia/African Gods in the Candomblé of Bahia.* 2d ed. Salvador, Brazil, 1993. An extraordinarily beautiful artbook of watercolor paintings of the ritual life of Bahian Candomblé *terreiros;* the book includes iconographic images of the orixás, sacred instruments, ceremonial clothing, and elements of the initiation process. Essays on the history of Candomblé and the characteristics of the gods are in Portuguese and English.

Dantas, Beatriz Góiz. "Repensando a pureza nagô." *Religião e Sociedade* 8 (1982): 15–20. An important essay urging the reconsideration of the idea of "Yoruba purity" as the ideal of Afro-Brazilian religions. Emphasizes the role scholars have played in privileging West African over Central and Southern African models in the religions and suggests that this influence has in turn affected oral traditions in many of the older *terreiro* communities. In Portuguese.

Eduardo, Octavio da Costa. *The Negro in Northern Brazil: A Study in Acculturation.* New York, 1948; reprint Seattle, 1966. An anthropological examination of Afro-Brazilian familial and community life in the state of Maranhão. The book focuses particularly on religious beliefs and practices and is a classic study of Tambor de Mina and other northern Brazilian religions of African influence.

Harding, Rachel E. *A Refuge in Thunder: Candomblé and Alternative Spaces of Blackness.* Bloomington, Ind., 2000. This book describes the historical development of Candomblé in the context of nineteenth-century Bahia, focusing on the role of the religion as a resource of alternative identity, community, and connection to ancestral traditions for slaves and their descendants.

Johnson, Paul. *Secrets, Gossip, and Gods: The Transformation of Brazilian Candomblé.* New York, 2002. This book examines the way that broader cultural and market forces in Brazil have precipitated changes in Candomblé. It particularly explores the role of secrets in maintaining prestige and developing foundational knowledge in the religion.

Landes, Ruth. *The City of Women.* New York, 1947; reprint, Albuquerque, 1994. This is a pioneering anthropological study of Candomblé emphasizing particularly the role of women and homosexual men in leadership and participation.

Nascimento, Abdias do. *Orixás/Orishas: Os Deuses Vivos da Africa/The Living Gods of Africa in Brazil.* Philadelphia, 1997. A collection of paintings by artist/statesman Abdias do Nascimento. The book also contains essays by several important scholars and critics of Afro-Brazilian culture and religion. In English and Portuguese.

Prandi, Reginaldo, ed. *Encantaria Brasileira: O livro dos mestres, caboclos e encantados.* Rio de Janeiro, 2001. This edited collection of essays discusses a number of lesser-known Afro-Indigenous religious traditions of Brazil with good regional representation and both sociological and anthropological perspectives. In Portuguese.

Santos, Juana Elbein dos, and M. Deoscóredes. "Ancestor Worship in Bahia: The Egun-Cult." *Journal de la Societé des Americanistes* 58 (1969): 79–108. This essay discusses shrines for the cultivation of ancestral spirits on the island of Itaparica across the bay from Salvador, Bahia.

Sodré, Muniz. *O terreiro e a cidade: A forma social negro-brasileira.* Salvador, Brazil, 2002. This book is an engaging reflection on Afro-Brazilian religious thought and practice as an influence on Brazilian popular culture and as a means of resistance against racism. In Portuguese.

Verger, Pierre. *Dieux D'Afrique: Culte des Orishas et Vodouns a L'Ancienne Cote des Esclaves en Afrique et a Bahia.* Paris, 1995. Photographic study of the cultivation of African orishas and voduns in both West Africa and Bahia by one of the major scholars of Afro-Brazilian religion. In French.

Voeks, Robert. *Sacred Leaves of Candomblé: African Magic, Medicine, and Religion in Brazil.* Austin, Tex., 1997. A scholarly examination of the role of ritual and medicinal healing in Afro-Brazilian religion; includes traditional formulas for cleansing and healing baths as well as interviews with practitioners.

Walker, Sheila. "'The Feast of the Good Death': An Afro-Catholic Emancipation Celebration in Brazil." *SAGE: A Scholarly Journal on Black Women* 3, no. 2 (1986): 27–31. The essay describes the history and development of an important black lay Catholic sodality which has close ties to Afro-Brazilian religions.

Wimberly, Fayette. "The Expansion of Afro-Bahian Religious Practices in Nineteenth-Century Cachoeira." In *Afro-Brazilian Culture and Politics: Bahia, 1790s to 1990s,* edited by Hendrik Kraay. London, 1998. A historical examination of rituals of celebration, healing, and cultivation of African deities in a plantation town in northeastern Brazil.

Rachel E. Harding (2005)

AFRO-CARIBBEAN RELIGIONS

See CARIBBEAN RELIGIONS, *article on* AFRO-CARIBBEAN RELIGIONS

AFRO-SURINAMESE RELIGIONS.

The Republic of Surinam, formerly Dutch Guiana, lies on the northeast shoulder of South America, at 2°– 6° north latitude, 54°–58° west longitude (163,266 sq km), bordered by Guyana, Brazil, French Guiana, and the Atlantic Ocean. The ethnically diverse population—numbering about 380,000 in Surinam (Du., Suriname) and another 180,000 now living in the

Netherlands—consists of approximately 38 percent "Hindustanis" (descendants of contract laborers imported from India during the late nineteenth century), 31 percent "Creoles" (descendants of African slaves), 15 percent "Javanese" (descendants of Indonesians imported as contract laborers in the early twentieth century), 10 percent "Maroons" (descendants of African slaves who escaped from plantations and formed their own communities in Surinam's forested interior), and smaller numbers of Portuguese Jews, Chinese, and Lebanese—plus the eight thousand remaining Amerindians whose ancestors were once the country's sole inhabitants. Except for the Maroons and some Amerindians, almost the whole population lives along the coastal strip, with nearly half residing in the capital, Paramaribo.

HISTORICAL BACKGROUND. The first large-scale permanent settlement of Surinam came in 1651, when one hundred Englishmen from Barbados established a plantation colony. The Dutch took over in 1667, and during the next century and a half imported more than 300,000 Africans as slaves, drawing on a remarkable diversity of African societies and language groups. All indications point to an unusually early and rapid process of "creolization," with the slaves creating new institutions (e.g., languages and religions) by combining and elaborating their various African heritages with very little reference to the world of their European masters.

SLAVE RELIGION. The new Afro-Surinamese religion created by plantation slaves during the earliest decades of settlement already contained the central features of its two main present-day variants—the religion of the coastal Creoles (often called Winti) and the religions of the various Maroon groups. Among Surinam slaves one found, for example, many forms of divination to uncover the specific causes of illness or misfortune; rituals, including complex drumming and dancing, in which individuals were possessed by the spirits of, among others, ancestors and snake gods, and by forest and river spirits; beliefs about multiple souls; ideas about the ways that social conflict can cause illness; extensive rites for twins; secret male-warrior cults; and a focus on elaborate and lengthy funerals as the most important of all ritual occasions. Even the whites, who witnessed only a tiny proportion of slave rites, depended on the Afro-Surinamese slave religion for their own well-being. One eighteenth-century report describes how, in spite of the presence of eight white physicians in the colony, the slaves "play the greatest role with their herbs and their pretended cures, both among Christians and among Jews" (Nassy, 1974, p. 156). And the most famous slave curer-diviner, the eighteenth-century Kwasi, near the end of his life became accustomed to receiving letters from abroad addressed to "The Most Honorable and Most Learned Gentleman, Master Phillipus van Quassie, Professor of Herbology in Suriname" (Price, 1983).

Afro-Surinamese slave religion, through its interlocking beliefs and rites, provided the focus of slave culture, binding individuals ritually to their ancestors, descendants, and collaterals; expressing a firm sense of community in spite of a crushingly oppressive plantation regime; and—on many occasions—serving as the inspiration and mechanism for revolt. One European described this latter aspect of a 1770s "winty-play" on a plantation:

> Sage Matrons Dancing and Whirling Round in the Middle of an Audience, till Absolutely they froath at the mouth And drop down in the middle of them; Whatever She says to be done during this fit of Madness is Sacredly Performed by the Surrounding Multitude, which makes these meetings Exceedingly dangerous Amongst the Slaves, who are often told to murder their Masters or Desert to the Woods. (Stedman, 1985, chap. 26)

COASTAL CREOLE WINTI. The folk religion of Surinam Creoles (that majority of the Afro-Surinamese population who are not Maroons) is most often referred to by outsiders as Winti (said to derive from the English *wind)* or Afkodré (from the Dutch *afgoderij,* "idolatry"). But like many folk religions (such as Haitian Voodoo), it has no special name that is used by its adherents. For them, it is simply the core of their way of life. Since emancipation in 1863, the great majority of Creoles have also been nominal Christians; the most recent figures show somewhat more than half to be Protestants (with Moravians the most numerous) and the remainder Roman Catholics. Afro-Surinamese differ from most other Afro-Americans in the extent to which their Christianity and folk religion are compartmentalized. All observers of Winti have been struck by the remarkable lack of syncretism, in a comparative context, between Christian and Afro-American beliefs and rites in Surinam. In spite of the participation of Creoles in modern, Western-style Caribbean life, Winti continues to operate in contexts that are largely untouched by Christianity. Winti also plays a major role in the lives of many of the Surinamese who now reside in the Netherlands.

Winti provides an all-encompassing but flexible design for living. The everyday visible world is complemented by a normally unseen world that is peopled by gods and spirits of tremendous variety, who interact with humans constantly. Scholars have often tried to classify the great variety of Winti gods into four "pantheons"—all ranged below an otiose, distant, West-African-type sky god—those of the air, the earth, the water, and the forest, but such classifications may well impose an inappropriate rigidity on a shifting set of beliefs and rituals that are called into play to deal with diverse and very practical everyday human needs. The major gods and spirits include a variety of *kromanti* (fierce healing spirits), *apuku* (often-malevolent forest spirits), *aisa* (localized earth spirits), *vodu* (boa constrictor spirits), *aboma* (anaconda spirits), and a great host of others. Like the spirits of the dead, who intervene constantly in the lives of the living and are the focus of much ritual activity, these nonhuman gods or spirits can speak through possessed mediums. Frequent rites, involving specialized dances, drumming, and songs, are used to honor and placate each type of spirit, and the spirits themselves appear on these occasions, through possession, to make their wishes known. Such rites are led by *bonuman* or *luku-*

man (who may be men or women), many of whom specialize in particular kinds of spirits. But Winti is a strongly participatory religion, in which every individual plays an active role, and specialization or special knowledge is widely distributed among the population.

Winti deals with everyday concerns. Typically, an illness, minor misfortune, bad dream, or portent suggests divination by a *lukuman.* Using any of a variety of techniques, he suggests the cause—for example, a particular ancestor feels neglected, a jealous neighbor has attempted sorcery, a relative's snake spirit disapproves of a proposed marriage, the person's "soul" requires a special ritual—and then prescribes an appropriate rite. During the course of a single case of illness or misfortune, large numbers of relatives and friends may need to be mobilized and considerable financial resources expended. *Bonuman* and *lukuman* are always compensated.

MAROON RELIGIONS. There are six Maroon (or "Bush Negro") groups living along rivers in the interior of the country: the Djuka and Saramaka (each numbering about twenty thousand people), the Matawai, Aluku, and Paramaka (each about two thousand people), and the Kwinti (fewer than five hundred people). Their religions, like their languages and other aspects of culture, are related to one another, with the sharpest division being between the eastern groups (Djuka, Paramaka, Aluku) and the central groups (Saramaka, Matawai, Kwinti). Descended from slaves who escaped from coastal plantations during Surinam's first century of colonization, they have lived in relative isolation from the world of the coast.

Maroons have always enjoyed an extremely rich ritual life, which is totally integrated into their matrilineally based tribal social organization. Christian missions have had differential impact on the Maroon groups: for example, the Matawai and several thousand of the Saramaka are nominally Moravians, but the great majority of Maroons continue to participate fully in religions that were forged by their ancestors, from many different African traditions, into a vibrant new synthesis. Resembling Winti in terms of many of the particular gods and spirits invoked, the Maroon religions stand apart in their more absolute integration of belief and ritual into all aspects of life. New World creations drawing on Old World ideas, these Maroon religions remain today the most "African" of all religions in the Americas.

Rituals of many kinds form a central part of everyday Maroon life. Such decisions as where to clear a garden or build a house, whether to make a trip, or how to deal with theft or adultery are made in consultation with village deities, ancestors, forest spirits, snake gods, and other such powers. Human misfortune is directly linked to other people's antisocial acts, through complex chains of causation involving gods and spirits. Any illness or other misfortune requires immediate divination and ritual action in collaboration with these spirits and others, such as warrior gods. The means of communicating with these entities vary from spirit possession and the consultation of oracle bundles carried on men's heads to the interpretation of dreams. Gods, spirits, and ancestors, who are a constant presence in daily life, are also honored and placated through frequent prayers, libations, and great feasts.

The rituals surrounding birth and other life crises are extensive, as are those relating to more mundane activities, from hunting a tapir to planting a rice field. Among Maroons, funerals constitute the single most complex ritual event, spanning a period of many months, directly involving many hundreds of people, and uniting the world of the dead with that of the living through specialized ritual action such as coffin divination, and extensive singing, dancing, and drumming. Specialized cults—such as those devoted to twins, or to finding someone lost in the forest, or to making rain—are the possessions of particular matrilineal clans, and individual Maroons may also specialize in the treatment of particular types of spiritual problems, or in particular ritual activities, such as drumming for snake-god rites. But most Maroon ritual knowledge is broadly spread; these are highly participatory religions.

BIBLIOGRAPHY

The best overview of Surinam's social history, including religion, remains R. A. J. van Lier's *Frontier Society* (The Hague, 1971). Among the several useful English-language sources for the religion of Surinam slaves are the reports by David de Isaac Cohen Nassy and others in *Historical Essay on the Colony of Surinam, 1788,* edited by Jacob R. Marcus and Stanley Chyat, translated by Simon Cohen (Cincinnati, 1974), and by Captain J. G. Stedman in his *Narrative, of a Five-Years' Expedition . . . from the Year 1772, to 1777,* new critical ed. by Richard Price and Sally Price (Minneapolis, 1985). For the study of Winti, the pioneering work is Melville J. Herskovits and Frances S. Herskovits's *Suriname Folk-Lore* (New York, 1936); the most ambitious survey is Charles J. Wooding's *Evolving Culture: A Cross-Cultural Study of Suriname, West Africa and the Caribbean* (Washington, D.C., 1981); and an analysis of its economic aspects is found in Peter Schoonheym's *Je Geld of. . . Je Leven* (Utrecht, 1980). For the study of Maroon religions, an extensive bibliographical overview can be found in Richard Price's *The Guiana Maroons* (Baltimore, 1976); the role of religion in the making of Maroon societies is covered in Price's *First Time: The Historical Vision of an Afro-American People* (Baltimore, 1983); and messianic trends and recent changes are analyzed in H. U. E. Thoden van Velzen and W. van Wetering's "Affluence, Deprivation and the Flowering of Bush Negro Religious Movements," *Bijdragen tot de Taal-, Land- en Volkenkunde* 139 (1983): 99–139.

RICHARD PRICE (1987)

AFTERLIFE

This entry consists of the following articles:

AN OVERVIEW
GEOGRAPHIES OF DEATH
AFRICAN CONCEPTS
AUSTRALIAN INDIGENOUS CONCEPTS

AFTERLIFE: AN OVERVIEW

Views of the afterlife, of expectations concerning some form of human survival after death, cannot be isolated from the totality of the understanding of the nature of the divine, the nature of humankind, time and history, and the structure of reality. Not all religious persons have addressed the same kinds of questions, nor have ideas always been formulated in a uniform way by those nurtured within any one of the many religious traditions of the world. Nonetheless, there is a certain commonality in the kinds of basic questions that have been addressed. This article is organized topically in terms of the ways in which peoples from a range of theological perspectives in different ages and religions have seen fit to respond to these questions.

The Nature of the Divine. The basic issue concerning the nature of the divine is whether God is to be considered a personal being with and to whom one can relate or is held to be reality itself, the source and ground of being in impersonal or nonpersonal form. Between these absolutes lie a myriad of possibilities, compounded and enriched by a variety of experiences that can be termed mystical. Monotheists have struggled through the ages with questions concerning the corporeality of God, including shape and dimension, and, correspondingly, whether humankind can actually come to gaze in the hereafter on the visage of God. Others have concluded not only that the divine being is not to be conceived in any anthropomorphic form but also that the divine being, in the most absolute sense, is removed from the realm of interaction and rests as the essence of nonmanifestation. Determinations about the nature of the divine have direct ramifications, as will be seen, for human understanding of life after death.

The tension between the two concepts (the God of form and God without form) has arisen in a multitude of ways for faithful persons of various traditions. Those who depersonalize the divine to the extent that they see it as pure reality in which the essence of all things participates must ultimately sacrifice the relationship of deity and devotee, whether this be understood on the model of master and servant, parent and child, or lover and beloved. This was the problem for the philosopher Rāmānuja in twelfth-century India, whose qualified nondualism was the logically problematic attempt to reconcile a philosophical monism with the overwhelming need to respond to God in loving devotion. The Andalusian Muslim mystic Muḥy al-Dīn ībn al-ʿArabī, writing about the same time, posited a series of descending levels of the godhead through which the absolute, nonmanifest divine gradually actualizes itself to the form of a Lord with whom humans can interact.

The vision of God. Those religious traditions that have articulated an understanding of the divine in polytheistic form have tended to envision the particular gods in a concrete manner, often with the implication that the dead, or at least some of the dead, will be able to see the gods visually in the afterlife. Pictorial representations from the Middle and New Kingdoms in Egypt portray the dead person being lifted out of the sarcophagus by the jackal Anubis, taken to the Hall of Double Justice and judged, and then brought into the presence of Osiris, to be led by him to the Elysian Fields.

From the earliest times, Indian thinkers have tended to conceptualize their gods in quite specifically graphic ways. In the Vedic literature, Yama, who is at once the first mortal and the god of the dead, is portrayed as sitting under a leafy bower with his two four-eyed dogs in the presence of gods and ancestors to welcome the dead into a life that is a blissful version of earthly existence. In theistic Hinduism, the devotee expects to gaze on the face of the Beloved as Rādhā beheld Kṛṣṇa in their moments of most intense passion. The faithful Buddhist to whom access to Sukhāvatī, the Pure Land, is granted will enjoy the bliss of contemplating Amitābha Buddha himself.

Vision of the divine in the afterlife is not limited to polytheistic traditions. The sight of God in the gardens of Paradise is cherished by Muslims as the culmination of a life of piety; similar expectations have been part of the hopes of many Christians. Nor is it the case that in all polytheistic traditions there is the assumption that the dead will see those gods whom they concretely portray or conceptualize. Among the ancient Mesopotamians, the gods of the lower world were viewed as cruel and vindictive and those of the upper regions as arbitrary, with humans doomed to exist as shades in the nether regions. Thus no amount of individual effort in this life could assure one of a blissful existence in the hereafter, let alone a vision of the gods.

Divine justice and judgment. Never in the Mesopotamian consideration did there seem to be any understanding that the individual who lived the good life on earth might come to an end better than that found in the cheerless underground pit of Arallu. Justice as a function of divinity never came to bear, and the hero-king Gilgamesh, in a work attributed to the second millennium BCE, could rail against the arbitrary way in which the gods meted out death to humankind while keeping life and immortality for themselves.

It is, of course, not true that justice need be a less significant factor in the consideration of the afterlife by a society that is professedly polytheistic. What often has been the case is that the concept of ethical responsibility on the part of the individual (with concomitant judgment by the deity in some form) blends with an emphasis on magic and ritual as assurance of a felicitous state in the hereafter. The ancient Egyptian view is particularly interesting in this connection. *Maat,* the conceptual form of justice, order, and stability, became personified in the Hall of Double Justice and was understood as the means by which Osiris, the lord of the kingdom of the living dead, was finally apprised of the moral character of the one brought before him in judgment. Justice was seen as an extension of a concept of order that characterized the Egyptian worldview and that, as an essential of the eschatological reality, was in direct relationship to the establishment of stability over chaos at the time of creation. And yet it is clear from the texts that as significant as were concepts of order and justice to their view of life and death, the Egyptians never completely abandoned the feeling that the gods might not really (be able to) exercise absolute justice. Thus it was necessary to rely on ritual and magical formulas, in this way assuring that the dead would always have at their fingertips the necessary knowledge and information to answer any questions that might be posed in the final court of arbitration.

Justice, as an abstract principle of order for many ancient societies, came in monotheistic communities to be translated into a quality of the godhead itself, with the immediate ramification of justice as an ethical imperative for human beings in recognition of the nature and being of God. Thus in Islam there is a clear understanding that because God is just, he requires that a person live justly, and the quality of the individual life is actually the determining factor in the final judgment.

One of the earliest perceptions of the god who embodies this kind of justice in his very being is found in the thought of Zarathushtra (Zoroaster), the Persian prophet of the first millennium BCE. He saw in Ahura Mazdā the principles of truth, righteousness, and order upheld in much the same way as the Egyptians saw them upheld and embodied by Maat. Ahura Mazdā, however, was not for Zarathushtra the personification of truth but the great advocate of it, the divine lord into whose presence the righteous are allowed to enter at the end of time. There was never in the development of Zoroastrian orthodoxy any indication that the just could expect to see the person of Ahura Mazdā in human form, but rather there was the understanding that the soul who has lived a life of justice will be given the privilege of beholding a form of pure light.

In the development of Old Testament thought, divine justice became a particularly significant issue. In the earlier conceptions, the dark and dusty She'ol as an abode for the dead seems to have been understood much as was the Mesopotamian Arallu. There Yahveh had no jurisdiction, and gloom was assured for the righteous and wicked alike. The beginnings of hope for a more felicitous end for humankind came through reflections concerning the question of God's power and justice. If God is truly almighty, his dominion must extend to all parts of the earth and to all portions of time. And if he is truly just, then it is inconsistent that the righteous as well as the wicked should be doomed to the bitter existence of She'ol. It was with regard to God's power and justice that the seeds of an idea of resurrection to an eternal reward began to grow in the Jewish consciousness, laying the ground for the later Christian understanding of the death and resurrection of Jesus.

In Hindu and Buddhist thought, the notion of *karman* presupposes a conception of justice and judgment different from that prevailing in monotheistic traditions. Rather than the subjectivity of a judging being, there is the objective and automatic working out of cause and effect. Justice in this understanding is not so much a divine quality as an inexorable law of the universe. In its simplest form the doctrine of *karman* states that what one is now is a direct result of what one has done and been in past existences, and what one does in this lifetime will, with the accumulation of past karmic debt, be the direct determinant of the state of one's future existence. Lifetime follows lifetime in whatever form of life each successive existence takes, and liberation from the round of existences is achieved not by the intervening grace of a god but through knowledge of the truth of the realization of self. In the Vedantic understanding of the Upaniṣads, the content of this knowledge is that the self (*ātman*) is indeed identical with the Self (*brahman*), the underlying reality of all that is.

The complex of religious responses that makes up the fabric of Hinduism and Buddhism, however, includes as a major component the understanding on the part of many that the godhead must be conceptualized in a personal way. In terms of sheer numbers, far more Hindus have placed their faith in the saving grace of Lord Kṛṣṇa than have ever held to a doctrine of absolute monism. And despite the automatic character of *karman* in determining rebirth, divine or quasi-divine figures do continue to play a judicative role in the religious imagination. In Mahāyāna Buddhism there are ten judges of the dead, one of whom is a holdover from the Vedic Yama, despite the fact that in strict philosophical or ontological terms it is a Buddhist tenet that there is no such thing as a god who can judge or even a soul that can be the object of judgment.

Intercession. Issues of justice give rise to questions about the possibility of intercession for the deceased on the part of human or superhuman agency. The forms of intercession are many, from the role played by the living in providing a proper burial and maintaining the mechanical artifices of the tomb to the specific intervention in the judgment process by a figure who can plead for the well-being of the soul whose fate is in the balance. Muslims traditionally have taken great comfort in the thought that the Prophet himself will be on hand to intercede for each individual believer when he comes before the awesome throne of judgment, and through the centuries Christians have relied on the assurance that Jesus Christ sits at the right hand of God to intercede. The Buddhist concept of the *bodhisattva* is, in one sense, an extension of the idea of intercession: through the dedication or transference of merit, the saving being, who needs no more merit himself, can directly pass it on to individuals who have not reached the state of enlightenment.

The role of living persons in helping to determine the fate of the dead has ranged from giving the deceased a fitting and proper interment and celebrating a communal feast in memory of the departed (often to ensure that he or she actually stays "departed" and does not return to haunt the living) to maintaining for all time, as was the Egyptian intention, the physical apparatuses of the tomb. Sometimes it is held that these responsibilities are carried out primarily for the support of the living or out of respect for the dead. Often, however, there is a conviction that the living may actually be able to influence or help determine the future condition and existence of the souls in question. Some have challenged the supposition that the fate of the soul of the deceased must rest, even in part, on the continued ministrations of those fallible individuals with whom it had a relationship while on earth. Responsibility for the dead on the part of the living has often been seen as incompatible with a belief in the justice and mercy of God. Nonetheless, some form of prayer for the deceased on the part of the living continues to be an important responsibility of pious persons in all religious traditions.

THE NATURE OF HUMANKIND. If it is essential to a vision of the afterlife to have some understanding of the nature of that divine being or reality to whom humankind returns at death, it is no less important to have some conception of what element in the human makeup is considered to do the returning. In every religious tradition, the way in which an individual is conceived to be constituted in this life directly determines the way in which he or she is thought to survive in an existence after death.

The human constitution. Conceptions of the constitution of the human being differ not only among different religious traditions but among different schools of thought within the traditions. Nevertheless, for the purpose of a comparative typology, it is possible to generalize and speak of some of the most significant of these conceptions.

The most immediately obvious distinction, and one that has been drawn in most conceptions of the afterlife, is between the physical and the nonphysical aspects of the human person. This can be understood as the body-spirit dichotomy, with a difference sometimes drawn in the latter between spirit and soul. In the Hebrew view, a person was not understood so much as having a body, something essentially different and apart from the nonphysical side of one's being, as being a body, which implies the totality of the individual and the inseparability of the life principle from the fleshly form. Spirit was said to be blown into the flesh, making it a soul, a whole person. In itself spirit was understood as a manifestation of the divine. This way of distinguishing between soul and spirit was adopted by some Islamic and Christian theologians and philosophers, although in common usage the two terms are essentially interchangeable in both traditions. When an individual is felt to be renewed in a new body in Christ, the experience is often described as spiritual; the body of the resurrection is sometimes thought of as a spiritual body different from the earthly body of flesh and soul.

The notion that an individual is, rather than has, a body is quite foreign to most Eastern thought. In Hindu Sāṃkhya, for example, the body is part of the world of nature or matter *(prakṛti)* but is absolutely distinct from the life principle or self (*puruṣa*) from which it is separated by the process of yoga. It is the very realization of the separation of these two that amounts to liberation for the individual. Advaita Vedānta, while different from the dualistic Sāṃkhya in saying that the body is only part of the world of illusion, would agree that the key to liberation from the round of rebirths is exactly the realization that the soul or self has no lasting bond with anything physical and that the soul is associated with a particular body, human or nonhuman, only temporarily, for the fleeting moments of earthly existence.

The relationship of the human to the divine. The question of what it is that lives on after death must be seen in relation to the basic issue of whether that which is real or lasting in the human person is identical with the divine reality or is essentially different from it. A position of monism is one end of a spectrum of possible responses. In Advaita Vedānta liberation from successive existences comes only with the realization of the identity of *ātman* (the individual soul) and *brahman* (the Absolute). In some of its Ṣūfī manifestations, esoteric Islam comes very close to identifying the eternal in humans with the eternal essence (*ḥaqq*), with the further understanding that death and resurrection come in the moment-by-moment realization of that identity.

A very different kind of conceptualization is that characteristic of some traditional societies in which not only is humanity seen to be totally separate from the gods but one exists after death only as a shade or a shadow of one's former self. That which divides the human and the divine in this context is the fact that the gods are immortal and humans are not. In between such alternatives is a range of possibilities suggesting that humans manifest some element of the divine enlivening principle. In most traditions, however, a felicitous hereafter means not the realization of identity of self and absolute, but rather some circumstance in which that which survives death comes to dwell in proximity to the divine.

A number of traditions have held that certain elements that make up an individual actually become manifested and real only at the time of death. The ancient Egyptian, for instance, was said to have come into his or her own only when after death the *ba,* or continuing personality, was fully realized through the joining with its counterpart, *ka,* which acted as a kind of guardian angel. The dead did not become *ka*s but were joined to and guided by them on the journey into the afterlife. Classical Zoroastrian texts describe the soul at death sitting on the headstone of the grave for three days, after which it is led through some good or bad circumstances (depending on one's character) and finally is met by a maiden who takes the form of the actions committed by that person while on earth. The good will thus meet a beautiful creature, while the unrighteous will confront an incredibly ugly hag.

Certain similarities can be seen here with Buddhist conceptions, such as the peaceful and wrathful deities met by the deceased in the after-death visions described in the Tibetan *Book of the Dead.* The great difference is that in the Tibetan understanding one does not meet the alternatives of good or bad but experiences a whole range of deities that represent both the most sublime of human feelings and the personification of one's powers of reason. The wrathful deities are actually only a different aspect of the peaceful ones. The point is that, in some sense, as in the Egyptian and Zoroastrian cases, one comes into contact in an apparently externalized form with aspects of one's own personality, thought, and consequent past action.

RESURRECTION OF THE BODY. The significance of the body as a continuing entity in the afterlife has been attested to in many traditions. The resuscitation of the corpse expected after the elaborate processes of mummification in ancient Egypt implied the hope of permanent physical survival as well as survival of the personality. In Zoroastrian eschatology, one of the clearest statements of physical resurrection comes in the description of the Frashōkereti, or ultimate rehabilitation of the world under the dominion of Ahura Mazdā. The savior Saoshyant will raise the bones of the first ancestors and then those of all humankind, and Ahura Mazdā will invest the bones with life and clothe them with flesh for all time.

In Jewish thought, the soul was first believed to be released from the body at death, but with the development of the idea of resurrection came the belief in the continued importance of the physical body. This belief is carried over to early Christianity: Augustine in the *City of God* says that the resurrected bodies, perfect amalgamations of flesh and spirit, are free to enjoy the satisfactions of food and drink should they so desire. He finds proof for this in the example of Christ consuming a meal after his own resurrection. Proceeding from the original assurance of Jesus that not a hair on the heads of those who are granted eternal life shall perish, Augustine concludes that at the time of the resurrection of the flesh, the body will appear in that size and physical condition in which it appeared at the time of youthful maturity, or would have appeared had it had time to mature. The arguments marshaled by the philosophers of Islam have done little to shake the common faith that the reward for a life of virtue will be the experience of the pleasures of the gardens of paradise in a physical as well as a spiritual way. The kinds of proofs offered by some in the Islamic community against the resurrection of the physical form have been countered rationally, and ignored emotionally, by those for whom a purely spiritual revival seems somehow to fall short of the promises of God and the world-affirming nature of Islam itself.

Continued existence as spirit. From the earliest times, characteristic of primitive societies but certainly not exclusive to them, humankind has had a seemingly natural fear of the dead. To some extent this can be explained in terms of one's own apprehension about the meaning of death for one personally, but to a much greater extent, it seems to derive from a stated or unstated feeling that the dead have some power over the living and can actually interfere with the processes of life on earth. In more extreme cases, this has led to a kind of worship of the dead, in which those who have passed into another existence have sometimes assumed the status of gods. This has been evidenced particularly in China and Japan in the long history of ancestor worship. More generally it takes the form of concern for the proper disposal and continued remembrance of the dead, in the hope that the deceased will in no way return to "haunt" or interfere with life here on earth.

Commonly held is the assumption that because a being has undergone the experience of death, it is privy to information not held by those still in the mortal condition. Echoed in much of the great religious literature of the world is the theme that if only the dead could or would return in some form, they would have much to tell the living. The vanity of this wish for information from the departed is denied by those who are convinced that the dead can and do return and have a great deal to tell about the road that everyone, sooner or later, comes to travel. In many traditions, especially the prophetic, orthodoxy has disdained talk about the reality of ghosts and spirits functioning on earth, and it has fallen to the mythology of folklore to speculate on the best ways to propitiate the spirits of the dead and to ward off those spirits who, for a variety of reasons, are felt to be evil or malicious.

The role of community. Consideration only of the destiny of the individual results in a very unbalanced picture of conceptions of the afterlife. Important to the theologies of many of the religions of the world is the relationship of each individual to other individuals, or the idea of community, whether seen from the perspective of this world (is it necessary to be a member of a community in order to reach a blessed hereafter?) or the next (is there a community of the saved, or perhaps of the damned, in a future existence?). Common to prophetic religions is the expectation that the eschaton will result in reuniting or making whole both the individual and some portion (often the totality) of the human community. It is part of Islamic eschatological tradition that on the Day of Resurrection the specific communities of all the prophets, including that of Muḥammad, will be assembled, each at its own pond, awaiting the judgment.

The notion of community, or the importance of membership in a particular group, takes on a different kind of significance when viewed from the perspective of this world. In the Hindu tradition, liberating knowledge is limited to the twice-born, although this belief is greatly modified by those to whom a devotional relationship to some aspect of the godhead implies salvation rather than liberation. The question of whether one must be a Christian to be saved has engendered among scholars and theologians of Christianity heated arguments that still have not been resolved. *Ummah,* community in the Muslim sense of a religio-political unity, is a tremendously significant element in the understanding of Islam; some contemporary Muslims still insist that one cannot be saved if one is not a Muslim, and that one cannot be Muslim outside of community.

There are some obvious instances in the history of religions in which the community of the saved is the community of the victorious in the sense of realized eschatology, that is, the establishment of a kingdom of righteousness for a specific people here on earth. This is implicit in the theme of Zionism in Jewish thought (although it is only one interpretation, or aspect, of the Zionist ideal as it has developed historically). Even Zarathushtra, if one can correctly interpret the *Gathas,* seems at first to have envisioned the victory of *asha* ("truth, righteousness") over *druj* ("falsehood, evil") as taking place in the pastoral setting of eastern Persia within the context of this-worldly time. Realized eschatology in Christian thought refers to the understanding that Christ's life and death have, in fact, established the kingdom of God on earth for those who, in faith, are part of the body of Christ; in the mysticism of the *Gospel of John,* the Parousia, or second coming of Jesus, has already taken place. Such considerations lead directly to questions of time and history as a further category for reflection on conceptions of the afterlife.

Time and History. The way in which time, its passage and its purpose, is understood in different worldviews has a direct bearing on conceptions of the afterlife. Eastern religions and philosophies generally have conceived time as revolving in cycles, within each of which are periods of creation and destruction, with each "final" cataclysm to be followed again by the entire process of generation. In the elaborate Hindu schema of the epics and Purāṇas, there are moments of creation and destruction, eschatons when the entire universe is obliterated and reabsorbed into the body of the deity, but with the implication that this very process is endless. At the other pole are those "historical" (usually prophetic) religions that postulate a creation when time is said to have begun and a final eschaton when time as humans know it will reach its conclusion. Here history is a given, a once-and-for-all process that begins with the divine initiation and is often understood as depending at each moment on the sustaining, re-creating act of the maker. Implicit is the belief that there is a plan to history, although humans may not be able to comprehend it, and that in some sense the end, when all creation will be glorified and time will give way to eternity, is already cast and determined.

Ideal time. Many religious traditions envision a certain period that can be described as ideal time. This may be an epoch that existed before the beginning of time and will be actualized again when time itself ceases, or it may be conceptualized as having occurred within the framework of history and, thus, having the potential to be realized again in time. In the ancient Egyptian view of the universe as static, ideal time was that continuing time established by the original creation, when order replaced chaos and *maat* was the stability of society as well as the individual ethic of justice and right. A similar understanding is expressed in the Australian Aboriginal concept of a sacred period during which the mythical ancestors lived, an epoch that is removed from any linear understanding of time. In that culture, in which language has no term for time in the abstract, the infinitely remote past is related to the present through the mythology of what has been called "the Dreaming."

For those traditions that emphasize a cyclical view of history, no time can be considered ideal. In one sense, time is not ultimately real, although, in another sense, its constant repetition means that it is perceived to be more plentiful than for people of historical traditions. Insofar as one has to deal with the illusions of reality in Indian thought, the best of times might be that represented by the beginning of each of the great cosmic cycles. From that point until the terrible *kaliyuga,* time (or rather the series of events and characteristics of the periods) degenerates and finally culminates in the awesome destruction of flood and fire that concludes the cycle and initiates a new beginning. For the theistic Hindu, the perfect moment is actually that eternity in which he or she is able to abide in the presence of the Lord.

In the prophetic traditions, ideal time can be understood in several ways. The ideal age in one sense is that ushered in by the eschaton, the end of time that is itself the realization of eternity. Yet for most of the prophetic religions there is a time within history, theoretical or actualized, that can be described as ideal. For some Christians, this has been understood as the time of the historical Jesus and his initiation of the continued kingdom of God on earth. There have been significant differences among Christians in interpretation of the meaning of a new heaven and a new earth. The restoration of Zion for the Jew has immediate implications; some have argued that ideal time is any time in which Jerusalem is actualized as the home of the Jews. For the Muslim, ideal time in its best historical sense was the period of the Prophet and the first four right-guided caliphs of the Islamic community, a time potentially realizable again at any moment.

Rebirth. Issues of time and history relate directly to the question of how an individual soul (or spirit or body) maintains continuity between this life and that that lies beyond death. Some traditions hold generally to the idea of one life on earth, death, some kind of resurrection or rebirth, and then continued existence on another plane. Others believe in reincarnation (metempsychosis or transmigration) with its possibilities of a series of lives on earth or elsewhere. Human imagination, or intuition, has resourcefully suggested many variations on these alternatives.

For the most part, traditions that see time as linear and progressive have rejected the idea of rebirth on this earth and relegated to the ranks of heresy those who have attempted to espouse such a theory or to combine it with the more traditional understanding of death and resurrection to propose an existence apart from the physical world. For those who hold to the idea of resurrection, final life is not automatic but is granted by the specific act of a being or beings who actually bring the dead back to life. The victory over death may be seen as occurring immediately after the demise of the individual or as coming at some final *eschaton,* as when the savior Saoshyant breathes life into the lifeless bodies of all humanity in Zoroastrian thought, or, in Islamic tradition, when the individual souls are called to the final day of judgment.

Eastern mystical thought has articulated the concept of reincarnation with some consistency, although in the Buddhist case the difficult problem arises of identifying what it is that is born in another body if there is nothing that can be called an individual soul. Buddhist thinkers have developed elaborate and complex theories for reconciling the concept of *anātman* ("no soul") with the six categories of being into which the non-soul can be reborn. Even those religions that contemplate aeons of potential rebirths, however, do project the hope of a final release from this recurring condition.

To say that one's soul is immortal is to imply that it has always existed and that it will never for a moment cease to exist. This is the basic understanding of those who postulate recurring births in a variety of incarnations, but it need not necessarily be linked to conceptions of transmigration. A great debate took place in Islam between the philosophers, whose rational directives led them to conclude that immortality was the only possibility for humans, and the theologians, whose adherence to the word of the Qurʾān dictated the necessity of belief in the specific acts of creation and resurrection from the dead. The concepts of resurrection and immortality, however, are certainly not always seen as unambiguously antithetical. Theologians have long struggled with the determination of which term is more applicable to the Christian understanding, or whether both might in some senses pertain.

Eschatology. For those who adhere to the idea of resurrection, with the implication of some form of life eternal to follow, one of the most pressing questions concerns when that resurrection is going to occur. Millenarian expectations have taken a variety of forms in both Judaism and Christianity, with the chiliastic hope in the latter for Christ's return. This kind of eschatological anticipation is generally seen in the context of the specifics of judgment. Here again, however, there is often no clearly formulated theological statement about precisely when judgment will take place or whether it is to be an individual or a universal adjudication. Some see it as happening soon after death, while others postulate a waiting period, perhaps of great length, before the eschatological events that herald a universal judgment.

In early Christianity, there was the expectation that the return of Jesus to usher in the new age would be so soon as to come within the lifetime of the community of those who had had fellowship with him. The passage of time moderated this expectation, and new theories had to be developed to account for the state of the soul in what came to be seen as a waiting period before the messianic age.

In the Persian case, Zarathushtra himself apparently had first felt that the kingdom of righteousness would be established on earth and them implied that eternal reward or punishment would instead come after death. Later, Sasanid orthodoxy, in developing its theories of three-thousand-year cycles, came to expect a kind of temporary reward or punishment lasting from death to the period of the Frashōkereti, at which momentous time a final purging through molten metal will purify all souls for their eternal habitation in the presence of Ahura Mazdā.

Other of the prophetic religions have hesitated to interpret with such exacting clarity or to understand the particulars of reward and punishment so graphically, yet in a general way have postulated a similar period between the death of the individual and the general resurrection and ushering in of the final age. The suggestions of scriptures such as the New Testament and the Qurʾān are sufficiently unsystematic that doctrines about specific aspects of life after death have often been founded on implication rather than specification.

Savior figures. Implicit in the eschatological expectation of Judaism and Christianity is the hope for a messiah or savior. For the Jews that person has not yet come. For the Christians he has come once and will return at the Parousia. The savior concept is somewhat different in Islam; it is embodied particularly in the figure of the *mahdī* and involves a rather detailed understanding of the theological distinctions between Sunnī and Shīʿī thought as well as the relationship of the *mahdī* in its eschatological framework to the restorer and final ruler of the regenerated community of Islam.

Some variation on the idea of a savior or restorer to appear at a future time is to be found in almost all of the living religious traditions, whatever their concept of the flow and structure of time. Saoshyant of the Zoroastrian or Parsi community; the Messiah of the Old and New Testaments; Kalki, the tenth incarnation of Viṣṇu, in theistic Hinduism; and Maitreya, the future Buddha—all reflect an understanding that despite the almost universal importance placed on the necessity of individual human responsibility, it is still possible to hope for the merciful assistance of some being, divine or semidivine, in the determination of one's future circumstances.

The Structure of Reality. The interrelatedness of the kinds of themes one can develop in considering an issue such as life after death is obvious. The preceding discussion has touched on much of what falls also into the category of conceptions of the structure of reality. It therefore becomes a question not of considering new material as such, but of viewing some of the same concepts from a different perspective.

The world in time and space. The eternality of the world, and its subsequent relationship to the eternality of heaven or the rehabilitated universe, has been postulated in a variety of ways in the history of religious thought. The ancient Egyptian expected that the static nature of the world and of society would mean their perpetuation eternally. In the materialistic Zoroastrian construct, the final rehabilitation of the earth implies its purification and its joining, with a purified hell, to the extension of heaven. Judaism presents an example of the constant tension between a hope for this world, renewed, and the kingdom of heaven as an otherworldly and eternal realm. In the Hindu and Buddhist conceptions, the world is not only not eternal but is in a constant process of degeneration. Even here, however, insofar as the world is constantly re-created within the realm of conditioned *saṁsāra,* it is eternal in another sense.

For many peoples, conceptions of the afterlife are directly related to the way they understand the basic divisions of the universe. The mythology of many of the ancient traditions is rich in descriptions and visual representations of the heavens, earth, and nether regions. A classic theme of religious geography has been that the heavens are located somewhere above the earth and the nether regions below, and that these have been identified to a greater or lesser extent with the location of heaven(s) and hell(s) as after-death abodes in whatever form these have been conceived. A not uncommon spatial concept is that of the land of the dead located in the west, the place of the setting sun, which is repeated in such myths as those of the jackal Anubis, lord of the Egyptian desert, and of the western kingdom of Sukhavati, the heaven of bliss of the *bodhisattva* Avalokiteśvara.

Reward and punishment. It is often in direct relation to the existing understanding of the structure of the universe that the more specific conceptions of heaven and hell arise. These parallel places of reward and punishment were not generally present in ancient thought. The Mesopotamian *Arallu* and the Hebrew *She'ol* both designated a great pit of darkness and dust under the earth that was not a hell (in the sense of any implication of judgment), but simply an abode for the unfortunate dead. Vedic thought in India, particularly as elaborated in the descriptions of Yama and the fathers of heaven in the *Ṛgveda,* was concerned primarily with the positive fate of those who performed sacrifices and good works, the rest passing into the oblivion of nonexistence. With the introduction of the importance of knowledge over sacrifice, of *karmayoga* (liberation through works) in place of ritual performance, the kingdom of Yama was elaborated into a series of heavens, and Yama himself was gradually transformed into a judge of the dead and then a god of the underworld hells, which were correspondingly enumerated.

The greatly elaborated heavens and hells, as they came to be developed in Hindu and Buddhist thought, with their graphic descriptions of the tortures of punishment and the raptures of reward, are by nature temporary (or, at least, one's stay in them is temporary). For the Buddhist, even these abodes are part of the conditioned world of *saṁsāra* and thus by definition are ultimately unreal, as all of phenomenal existence is unreal. In any case, one is reborn from these states or conditions into another state or condition, with the understanding that not until one is reborn as a human being will final release be possible.

Quite different is the basic understanding of prophetic religions, which assumes that the eschaton and judgment result in the eternality of the final abode and resting place. The question of whether or not punishment, like reward, is eternal has long perplexed theologians. In the Judeo-Christian tradition, as well as in Islam, God's justice is always understood as tempered with mercy, and the idea of the eternality of hell has been moderated to whatever extent has seemed consistent with the prevailing theological climate.

The intermediate state. Throughout the prophetic religions it has been necessary to conceive of a kind of intermediate state or place for souls before the time of final disposition. (The very temporariness of one's stay in the Hindu and Buddhist heavens and hells suggests that they fulfill the same sort of intermediate function.) This intermediate state can be a condition of waiting, often in a specified place, for the time of final judgment. Thus, Islamic tradition developed elaborate descriptions of the *barzakh* (lit., "barrier") as a place or condition in which both good and wicked souls dwell until the day of resurrection. In later Jewish tradition, *She'ol* came to refer to a temporary place for men and women to await judgment.

In another understanding, this intermediate position is often described as being for those for whom consignment to punishment or reward is not automatic. The Qur'anic *a'rāf* ("heights"), for example, has been interpreted as the temporary abode of those whose good and evil deeds more or less balance. Christianity, in some of its forms, has elaborated the distinction between Purgatory, as a place of temporary punishment and purification, and Limbo, as a waiting state where persons such as the righteous heathen and unbaptized infants are kept.

Literal and symbolic interpretations. Common to many religious traditions is continuing debate as to the nature of the future abodes of punishment and reward. Are they to be understood as places of literal recompense or as representations of states of mind? If states, are they attainable now or only in the hereafter? Are the experiences that one has in these states or places real or imaginary? Or, in a rather different dimension, are the descriptions to be seen only as allegorical and not, in fact, indicative of what is actually going to happen either objectively or subjectively?

It is in this area, perhaps, that it is most difficult to generalize within traditions. The awe- and terror-inspiring vision may well be taken with absolute literalness by one believer, while another might see that such visions are only symbolic representations of internal rather than external recompense. The Tibetan *Book of the Dead,* a set of instructions for the dying and dead that is at the same time a description of the forty-nine-day period between death and rebirth, details the experience that the soul has with karmic apparitions in the form of peaceful and wrathful deities. The great insight that comes of the *bardo,* or intermediate state experience, is that not only are the apparitions the products of one's own mind but they also assume, for the purposes of instruction, a concrete and objective reality.

Despite the variations in conceptions of what the afterlife may entail, a belief that human beings will continue to exist in some form after the experience they term death is a universal phenomenon. Skeptics have never persuaded the body of believers, whatever the specifics of their faith, that with the demise of the physical body comes the extinction of the human essence. Most people through the ages have drawn a clear connection between the quality of life lived on this earth and the expectation of what will come after death. Contemporary researchers of near-death experiences claim that they now have the beginnings of a scientific proof of the afterlife in the apparent commonality of the experiences of those proclaimed clinically dead. For most persons of faith, however, such knowledge is part of a universal mystery that by definition is veiled from the eyes of the living. They have some assurances of faith, but the details of what awaits them in "the undiscover'd country from whose bourn no traveller returns" (Shakespeare, *Hamlet* 3.1) can only be anticipated, with the certainty that such knowledge will eventually, and inevitably, be theirs.

SEE ALSO Eschatology; Eternity; Ghosts; Golden Age; Heaven and Hell; Judgment of the Dead; Merit, article on Buddhist Concepts; Reincarnation; Resurrection; Soteriology; Soul; Transmigration.

BIBLIOGRAPHY

Some of the older comparative studies of life after death in different religious traditions, such as Elias H. Sneath's *Religion and the Future Life: The Development of the Belief in Life after Death* (New York, 1922) and Kaufmann Kohler's *Heaven and Hell in Comparative Religion* (New York, 1923), are still useful, although somewhat elementary. More recent and valuable contributions to comparative studies of life after death are *The Judgement of the Dead* by S. G. F. Brandon (London, 1967) and *Religious Encounters with Death,* edited by Frank E. Reynolds and Earle H. Waugh (University Park, Pa., 1977). Christina Grof and Stanislav Grof's *Beyond Death* (New York, 1980) is a more journalistic overview of classical and contemporary afterlife beliefs, with fine color prints. For an understanding of the relationship of theories of time to afterlife concepts, Mircea Eliade's *Cosmos and History: The Myth of the Eternal Return* (New York, 1954) is excellent. A good addition to anthropological studies on attitudes and customs of non-Western cultures toward death and afterlife is *Celebrations of Death: The Anthropology of Mortuary Ritual* (Cambridge, Mass., 1979) by Richard Huntington and Peter Metcalf.

In addition to comparative works, a number of valuable studies deal with the afterlife as envisioned in particular religious traditions. *Death and Eastern Thought,* edited by Frederick H. Holck (Nashville, 1974), deals primarily with Indian beliefs, with brief chapters on China and Japan. Themes of death and resurrection in prophetic traditions are treated in such works as George W. E. Nickelsburg's *Resurrection, Immortality, and Eternal Life in InterTestamental Judaism* (Cambridge, Mass., 1972), John Hick's *Death and Eternal Life* (London, 1976), and *The Islamic Understanding of Death and Resurrection* (Albany, N. Y., 1981), which I wrote with Yvonne Haddad. Several excellent translations of mortuary texts are available, especially *The Tibetan Book of the Dead,* 2d ed., translated by Lama Kazi Dawasamdup and edited by W. Y. Evans-Wentz (Oxford, 1949); *The Egyptian Book of the Dead,* translated by E. A. Wallis Budge (New York, 1967) and presented as an interlinear translation with hieroglyphics; and *The Islamic Book of the Dead* of Imām ʿAbd al-Raḥmān al-Qāḍī, translated by ʿA'isha ʿAbd al-Raḥmān (Norfolk, England, 1977). A very good series on mythology, including myths of death and afterlife, is published by the Hamlyn Publishing Group Ltd. (1965–); it covers a broad range of literate and nonliterate societies.

A precursor in some ways to contemporary parapsychological studies is the spiritualist movement that began in the nineteenth century in Europe and the United States; it is well documented in J. Arthur Hill's *Spiritualism: Its History, Phenomena and Doctrine* (New York, 1919). Ian Stevenson's continuing research on reincarnation in cross-cultural perspective is presented in *Twenty Cases Suggestive of Reincarnation,* 2d ed. (Charlottesville, Va., 1974). Of the many recent studies of near-death experience and research, two of the best are Michael B. Sabom's *Recollections of Death: A Medical Investigation* (New York, 1981) and Kenneth Ring's *Life at Death: A Scientific Investigation of the Near-Death Experience* (New York, 1980).

New Sources

Barloewen, Constantin von, ed. *Der Tod in den Weltkulturen und Weltreligionen.* Frankfurt am Main, 2000.

Bynum, Caroline Walker. *The Resurrection of the Body in Western Christianity, 200–1336.* New York, 1995.

Davies, Jon. *Death, Burial, and Rebirth in the Religions of Antiquity.* London, 1999.

Eylon, Dina Ripsman. *Reincarnation in Jewish Mysticism and Gnosticism.* Lewiston, N.Y., 2003.

Kaplan, Steven, ed. *Concepts of Transmigration: Perspectives on Reincarnation.* Lewiston, N.Y., 1996.

Klima, Alan. *The Funeral Casino: Meditation, Massacre, and Exchange with the Dead in Thailand.* Princeton, 2002.

Obeyesekere, Gananath. *Imagining Karma: Ethical Transformation in Amerindian, Buddhist, and Greek Rebirth.* Berkeley, 2002.

Schömbucher, Elisabeth, and Claus Peter Zolle, eds. *Ways of Dying: Death and Its Meanings in South Asia.* New Delhi, 1999.

Sogyal, Rinpoche. *The Tibetan Book of Living and Dying.* London, 1998.

Zander, Helmut. *Geschichte der Seelenwanderung in Europa: Alternative Religiöse Traditionen von der Antike bis Heute.* Darmstadt, 1999.

JANE I. SMITH (1987)
Revised Bibliography

AFTERLIFE: GEOGRAPHIES OF DEATH

Belief in some kind of existence after death is one of the more common elements of religion, as history and anthropology show. While death is everywhere recognized as inevitable, it is seldom accepted as an absolute termination of human existence. Beliefs concerning the actual conditions of life after death, however, vary widely from culture to culture. This article will examine the variety of ways in which these afterlife conditions are represented, focusing in particular on their geography.

AFTERLIFE IN GENERAL. The different representations of life after death that we find in different religions are related to their respective conceptions of the structure of the cosmos and of life on earth, and to their different beliefs about the bodily and spiritual constitution of man. The Egyptians, for example, being agriculturalists, looked forward to a future life in the bountiful "Earu fields," whereas the Indians of the North American Plains, who were hunters, looked forward to the "eternal hunting grounds." In each case the actual economic conditions of life play an important role in determining how one will conceive of the afterlife. Similarly, the location and geography of the abode of the dead is in most cultures determined by the actual geographical conditions of their present world. Only occasionally is it determined primarily by cultural factors, as for instance by the traditions of migration among a number of Polynesian religions.

The conception of the soul is also an important factor. A soul that is conceived to be eternal and spiritual leads a different type of afterlife than one that is conceived as the double of the earthly body, or as something that gradually dwindles into nothingness after death, such as we find among certain northern Eurasian religions. A belief in multiple souls within a single individual makes possible a belief in the multiple destinations of these souls. Of the five souls of the Shipape (South America), for instance, only one goes to the hereafter.

There are also marked differences in the degree of interest that particular religions display in the afterlife. While central in one religion, it may be peripheral in another. Christianity, for example, along with a small number of other religions, has made the immortality of the individual central to its system of beliefs. But this centrality of the individual is by no means universally recognized. In many other religions the continuity of life after the death of the individual is of slight interest, because the stress falls firmly on life on earth. The continued existence of man after death may not be wholly denied, but neither is it considered to be of any importance. Thoughts about the conditions of the afterlife remain vague. Thus Godfrey Lienhardt quotes an Anuak man (Upper Nile) as saying simply that no one knows where the dead are, since no one has ever seen them. The inhabitants of Bellona Island (near the Solomons) seem equally unconcerned with what might happen to them after death. In accordance with this lack of interest we find cultures that not only allow the conditions of existence in the land of the dead to remain unclear, but even leave the question of its location unanswered. Rupert M. Downes has found this to be the case among the Tiv of Nigeria, for instance, where ideas about a future state remain nebulous. By contrast, some cultures develop extremely detailed descriptions of the realm of the dead. Here one thinks in particular of medieval Christianity.

Although today we tend to be conditioned to see life after death as an eternal state befitting an immortal soul, it is of some importance to make clear that there are also cultures in which the afterlife is considered to be a temporary prolongation of the present life, to be brought to an end by a second and final death. The Pangwe (southern Cameroon) believe that after death a man lives on for a long time in heaven, but in the end he dies and his corpse is thrown out with no hope of any further existence. The Egyptians too knew the fear of dying for a second time in the hereafter.

The manner of life after death is also closely related to the moral principles of selection for entrance into the country of the dead. In some cases such special principles of selection may be absent. In such a case, the implicit criteria are essentially social, all duly initiated adult members of a community sharing the same destiny. Children and slaves (where these exist) are often excluded. Exceptions exist of course. Among the Apapocúva-Guaraní (South America) dead children go to the "country without evil." About women the opinions vary. Islam, for example, originally excluded women from the heavenly paradise, arguing that women had no immortal soul. In fact, the idea of moral retribution after death is absent from a great number of religions.

Where the conception of reward or punishment according to ethical principles does occur, it is necessary to divide the abode of the dead into two or more sections that may be localized in different places: heaven(s) and hell(s), and in some instances a place in between where souls are purified before they are allowed to enter heaven: purgatory. This may be combined with the belief in reincarnation, as in Buddhism, such that neither heaven nor hell is eternal, the latter becoming a kind of purgatory and the former only a temporary state of conditioned bliss. In cultures where a belief in reincarnation is accepted, the question of the place of a soul's rebirth is understandably of no great importance and the ideas concerning it often remain vague or contradictory.

The distance between the world of the living and the abode of the dead may give rise to the conception of a journey from the one to the other. The Inuit (Eskimo) speak of the road the dead must follow, which seems to be identical with the Milky Way. The Tibetan *Book of the Dead* serves as a guide for the soul on the difficult and dangerous journey to the hereafter and offers detailed "geographical" instructions. The world of the departed may be separated from that of the living by a river (like the Styx in Greece), which must be traversed by boat, or may be crossed by means of a bridge, as the Parsis believe.

Generally the country of the dead is represented more or less as a copy of the world of the living, and life there follows in the main the same lines as life on earth. In these cases it is difficult to speak of a "geography" of death, which would be distinct from the geography of the living. An extreme example of this is the idea which the Admiralty Islanders on Manus (near New Guinea) have developed. In Manus, personality survives death in all respects, at least for a time. A man's property remains his own and even his profession, if he has one, remains unchanged. Reo F. Fortune reports in his book *Manus Religion* that if the deceased was a member of the native constabulary appointed by the Australian administration, he remains a policeman among the ghosts after death. There he receives the periodic visits of a ghostly white district officer of a ghostly white administration and collects the ghostly taxes paid by his fellow ghosts. It is clear that in this case the conception of the country of the dead is an exact double of the land of the living. The living and the dead coexist in space, having only different modes of being. Here it is hardly possible to speak of a distinct geography of death. Although this is perhaps an extreme example, many cases exist in which the dwelling places of the dead are considered to be in the immediate neighborhood of those of the living.

The Greek settlers in southern Italy considered some wild and eerie regions as parts of the underworld existing on the surface of the earth. "Lake without birds" was an appelation of the underworld, Avernus. The *facilis descensus Averno* of which the Roman poet Vergil speaks could be located next to one's own home. Even when the hereafter is conceived as a mirror image of the world of the living, the difference is not as great as it may seem. Things may be reversed, left and right, up and down, the cycle of the seasons may have changed places, but the general principles remain the same.

Where the dead are thought to remain present in the place where they are buried (the conception of the "living corpse"), a special country of the dead may be absent, or at least unimportant. The same is true when the dead are thought to change into animals living in their natural habitat. Nevertheless, the dead always remain separated from the living, at least by their different mode of being, whether or not they are further separated by the location of the realm of which they have become inhabitants. When we find the belief that human beings after death will be reunited again with the cosmos—often considered as divine—there is a transformation in the mode of being, but the question of a geography of the dead does not properly arise. This is the case, for instance, in the Indian concept of *ātman*, the self, which returns after death to *brahman*. Where the final destination of man is conceived negatively, as in the Buddhist nirvana, any attempt to "locate" this final state falls under the same negative strictures.

GEOGRAPHIES OF DEATH. In those cases where there is the elaboration of a distinct geography of death, there appear to be three main possibilities, each with minor variations. The world of the dead may be on earth, under the earth, or in heaven. Numerous examples can be given of each.

In the first case, the world of the dead is situated on earth, but at a lesser or greater distance away from the dwellings of the living. The Trobriand Islanders (New Guinea) situate the village of the dead in the direct neighborhood of their own villages. The Celtic Tirnanog is an island in the far west on the other side of the immense ocean. According to the Tasmanians (Australia) the dead travel to an island nearby where they continue their existence; in parts of the Northern Territory (Australia) the island of the dead is situated far off in the direction of the Morning Star. According to the Ewe (Togo) the country of the dead lies a long way off from that of the living on the far side of a river, and the journey to arrive there is difficult and dangerous. We also frequently find peoples having traditions of migration, and here in many cases the abode of the departed is identified with the people's original home, described in myth. Starting from Southeast Asia, we find all over the Pacific variations of the name *Java*, not only as the actual island of the living, but also as the mythic island of the dead. This "principle of return," as it has been called, often appears in the orientation of the corpse at burial that is based on the idea of the return to the country of origin.

In the second case, the realm of the dead is situated beneath the earth or under the water. The idea of an underworld as the dwelling place of the departed is probably the commonest of all concepts in this sphere. The idea of an entrance to this region through a deep hole in the ground or a cave is also widespread. The Hopi (North America) locate the village of the dead, Kotluwalawa, in the depth of a lake called "Whispering Water." When located beneath the earth, the world of the dead is usually conceived as either a realm of shadowy figures or shades, as in the case of the Israelite She'ol and the Greek Hades, or as a place of punishment. On Bellona Island, for instance, the dead are believed to live in darkness under the ground, whereas the living inhabit the world of light on the earth. The Babylonian realm of the dead, the "country of no return," is pictured in the myth of Ishtar's descent to hell in similar terms:

> The house of darkness,
> The house the inhabitants of which lack light,
> The place where dust is their food
> and excrements their nourishments,
> Where they see no light and live in darkness.

The specification of the underworld as a place of punishment is closely connected with the more general phenomenon of the differentiation of destinies after death. As noted briefly above, a number of cultures believe in such a differentiation. We may distinguish two main types: one based on the principle of social or ritual status, and one according to ethical principles. Where the main criterion at first appears to be a kind of knowledge, closer inspection reveals that this type is best understood as a subdivision of the first social or ritual one. In the first type, illustrated for instance by the Delaware and Algonquin (North America), there exists a concept of a different destiny after death for different social or ritual groups. The fate of those lacking such status remains open. They are simply excluded from the regular abode of the dead without further thought being given to the problem of where and how they continue their existence.

The most common type of differentiation, however, is based upon ethical principles, which are employed to separate those who are to be rewarded after death from those who are to be punished. Along with this notion of postmortem punishment comes the notion of hell and purgatory as the locations where such punishments take place. While it is true that not all subterranean abodes of the dead are hells, it does seem to be the case that all hells are understood to be subterranean. Realms of darkness beneath the earth beyond the reach of sun and moon, they are illuminated solely by the flames that punish the damned.

In the final case, the world of the dead may be situated in heavenly spheres. This concept is also a very common one. We find it, for instance, in Egypt as one of several ideas concerning the location of the hereafter. The belief that this country is to be sought somewhere high in the mountains is only a variation, since in many religions mountaintops symbolize heaven and the dwelling place of the gods, as, for example, Olympus did in Greece. The Dusun (North Kalimantan, Borneo) situate the abode of the dead on a high mountain. Another variation is the belief that the dead continue their existence on or among the stars.

The heavenly country of the dead is often represented as a more or less idealized replica of that of the living. The Ngaju Dayak (South Kalimantan, Borneo), for example, go to Lewu Liau after death, a village of spirits situated in a lovely and fertile country, near a river full of fish and with woods filled with game nearby. Everything that is found on earth is found there too, but it is a better world where such things as criminality are unknown. We also encounter profane versions of such heavenly paradises, such as the land of Cocagne, mentioned in fairy tales and usually located in heavenly spheres.

MULTIPLE GEOGRAPHIES: THE EXAMPLE OF ANCIENT EGYPT. Ancient Egypt offers us an example of a multiple geography of death, combining in a single religion many of the different types we have mentioned above. Although there is no reason to think that the culture of Egypt was an especially somber one, it is true that its preoccupation with death and afterlife was great. Although the Egyptians believed in a judgment of the dead by Osiris, the god of the underworld, there seems to have been no concept of hell. Those souls that could not pass the divine judgment were destined to be eaten by Ammit, "she who devours." Egypt also knew the idea of a second and definitive death in the hereafter. The *Book of Going Forth by Day* in fact relates a myth according to which the entire world will in the end return to its primal state prior to creation, to a state of chaos or nothingness.

Egyptian religion is of particular interest because of the multiple ways in which it conceived of the hereafter, called in Egyptian Duat, the zone of twilight, or heaven by night. Five distinct conceptions may be mentioned.

First, the Egyptians recognized a country of the dead, named Amentet, the West. More exactly, this term applies to the western frontier of the fertile land, the edge of the desert where the necropolises were located. The idea of the dead who live on in the grave and graveyard was also known. The realm of the dead is at times situated beneath the earth, which it more or less duplicates, and at other times it is pictured as a system of caves and passages. In both of these cases, the dead living there are believed to be visited by the sun at night. Then there are the "Earu fields," conceived as a heavenly copy of the land of Egypt, complete with a heavenly Nile, yet superior to earth in every way. Finally, the country of the dead may be located in heaven among the stars, especially in the north among the circumpolar stars, which the Egyptians called the "stars that never die."

SEE ALSO Heaven and Hell; Otherworld; Underworld.

BIBLIOGRAPHY

Cavendish, Richard. *Visions of Heaven and Hell. London.* 1977. A useful book with many illustrations and a selected bibliography.

Champdor, Albert, trans. *Le livre des morts.* Paris, 1963. An up-to-date translation of the Egyptian *Book of Going Forth by Day.* Well illustrated. Further translated by Faubion Bowers as *The Book of the Dead* (New York, 1966).

Clemen, Carl C. *Das Leben nach dem Tode im Glauben der Menschheit.* Leipzig, 1920. Still one of the best short introductions to the theme, albeit dated as regards theory.

Cumont, Franz. *Afterlife in Roman Paganism.* New York, 1959. A standard work.

Evans-Wentz, W. Y., ed. *The Tibetan Book of the Dead.* 2d ed. Translated by Kazi Dawasamdup. London, 1949. Includes a useful introduction.

Faulkner, Raymond O., trans. *The Ancient Egyptian Book of the Dead.* Rev. ed. Edited by Carol Andrews. London, 1985. A fresh translation, lavishly illustrated.

Firth, Raymond. *The Fate of the Soul: An Interpretation of Some Primitive Concepts.* Cambridge, 1955. Short but important.

Jeremias, Alfred. *Hölle und Paradies bei den Babyloniern.* Leipzig, 1900. Short treatment of the Babylonian concepts of the hereafter. Still of value.

Kees, Hermann. *Totenglauben und Jenseitsvorstellungen der alten Ägypter: Grundlagen und Entwicklung bis zum Ende des mittleren Reiches.* 2d ed. Berlin, 1956. The standard work on Egyptian concepts of the hereafter.

Pfannmüller, Gustav, ed. *Tod, Jenseits und Unsterblichkeit in der Religion, Literatur und Philosophie der Griechen und Romer.* Munich, 1953. An anthology with a useful introduction.

New Sources

Bauckham, Richard. *The Fate of the Dead: Studies on the Jewish and Christian Apocalypses.* Boston, 1996.

Bloom, Harold. *Omens of Millennium: The Gnosis of Angels, Demons, and Resurrection.* New York, 1996.

Davis, Stephen T., ed. *Death and Afterlife.* New York, 1989.

Himmelfarb, Martha. *Ascent to Heaven in Jewish and Christian Apocalypses.* New York, 1993.

MacGregor, Geddes. *Images of Afterlife: Beliefs from Antiquity to Modern Times.* New York, 1992.

Obayashi, Hiroshi, ed. *Death and Afterlife: Perspectives of World Religion.* New York, 1992.

Taylor, John H. *Death and the Afterlife in Ancient Egypt.* Chicago, 2001.

TH. P. VAN BAAREN (1987)
Revised Bibliography

AFTERLIFE: AFRICAN CONCEPTS

Discussing African notions of afterlife necessitates several preliminary and pertinent observations.

First, Africa is characterized by a tremendous ethnic and cultural diversity. There are about three thousand African ethnic groups, each boasting a distinctive common history, culture, language, and recognizable belief system. Thus, it is possible to speak of the Yoruba notions of afterlife and compare these, say, to the Igbo or Zulu concepts, noting distinctions and similarities. This article will factor in this palpable ethnic diversity in order to avoid sweeping generalizations.

Across the many ethnic groupings and cultural expressions, however, one can discern commonalities in worldviews that make it possible to speak of an "African" worldview as compared, say, to a "Hindu" one. Summarizing distinctive markers of this African worldview, Sambuli Mosha isolates four key ideas, namely: (1) the centrality of belief in God, (2) an acknowledgment of the intrinsic unity between individuals and communities, (3) viewing the universe as an interconnected, interdependent whole, (4) embracing life as a process of spiritual formation and transformation (Mosha, 2000). All these markers shape the way Africans conceptualize both this life and the hereafter. These commonalities in worldview despite cultural ethnic differences will be assumed in this article.

Secondly, African beliefs are *dynamic* rather than static. They are shaped and influenced by other belief systems that they encounter in history. While this dynamism is manifest in all aspects of belief, here we focus on concepts of the hereafter. In this regard, we note for example that ancient Egyptians held very clear eschatological ideas featuring notions of heaven and hell and a final judgment. Thus, in the Egyptian *Book of the Dead*, a text designed to be a guide for the soul as it journeyed on beyond physical death, Osiris determines the destiny of the dead. Having measured their moral worth against the feather of Maat (symbolizing truth and justice), he sends them "west," to the "abode of the righteous," or to "hell." Today, the pyramids where the pharaohs, ancient Egyptian kings believed to be immortal, were entombed remain an enduring testimony of the ancient Egyptians' preoccupation with life after death.

Two thousand years later, these Egyptian ideas of the hereafter were part of the repertoire of beliefs in circulation in the Mediterranean world as Christianity was taking shape. Later still, in the nineteenth century, through Christian missionaries these ideas found their way into sub-Saharan Africa. Here, they reinforced prior indigenous concepts of the afterlife where these already incorporated notions of a final judgment, as in the case of the Yoruba of Nigeria and LoDagaa of Ghana (Ray, 1976, pp. 143*ff*). Elsewhere, for example among the Agikuyu of Kenya, ideas of heaven and hell were introduced de novo, since this community's prior concepts of the hereafter had no such notions. Among the Gikuyu, as was typical in most indigenous African communities, though one's moral misconduct could provoke divine anger and punishment, such punishment was this-worldly rather than delayed and otherworldly. The impact of historical encounters between cultures, and the ensuing dynamism, transformation, and fluidity of ideas will be recognized and factored in this analysis.

Against this background then, and drawing examples from the vast pool of diverse African cultures, this article discusses the topic under several interrelated headings, namely:

- Afro-theism, Cosmogonies, and African Notions of Afterlife
- Concepts of the Human Person and Implications for Life After Death
- Notions of Afterlife: Clues from Mortuary and Funerary Rituals
- The Living-Dead: Corporate Identity and the Destiny of the Individual
- The Living and the Dead: The Status and Role of Ancestors
- Change, Continuity, and Contestation: The Impact of Christianity and Other Religions

AFRO-THEISM, COSMOGONIES, AND AFRICAN NOTIONS OF AFTERLIFE. The African worldview is decidedly theistic. God (named differently by various ethnic groups) is the creative force behind the origins of the universe and human beings within it, a belief that appears in many African cosmogonic myths. These myths also indicate that in God's original intentions, the world was orderly, and human beings led a happy life in a state of immortality as long as they were close to God, their creator. Somehow, this state was interrupted, and death entered the world. Ray (1976, p. 24) reports that according to a myth of original "paradise lost" held by the Tutsi of Rwanda, in the beginning, Imana, God, created two worlds, the one above and the one below. The world below was the opposite of the world above, since it lacked in beauty and prosperity. Initially, human beings lived close to the sky and were therefore near enough to the world above to enjoy its benefits without struggle and labor. Sickness was not known, and when people died, Imana brought them back to life after three days. Perhaps because of human disobedience or greed, this relationship was lost. The promise of happiness brought by proximity to God was severed and remains only a vague future possibility. According to the myth, humans continue to suffer hardships in this world, until one day when, their expiation over, they will return to the sky. It seems from this myth that the Tutsi understand happiness and immortality to be dependent on how well they maintain the link between themselves and God.

Quite different to the Tutsi myth with its promise of at least a rudimentary eschatological hope, the Nuer myth of paradise lost stipulates that in the beginning all was happiness, since the heavens, God's abode, and earth were linked by a rope, the pathway to access divine favors and bounty. According to this myth, upon death people ascended to the sky via the rope for a short period and came back rejuvenated to earth. When the rope was severed, death became a permanent feature of the human condition. The myth suggests that this group believes that immortality is gone forever and only life and death within this world remain (Ray, 1976).

CONCEPTS OF THE HUMAN PERSON AND IMPLICATIONS FOR LIFE AFTER DEATH. More clues regarding African notions of afterlife can be gleaned from an examination of African concepts of the person. Now, in some belief systems, say Hinduism, the person is defined as the soul that is contained or even imprisoned in the body. Indeed, within Hinduism, one goal of religious activity is to facilitate the ultimate separation or liberation (*moksha*) of the soul (*ātman*) breaking out of once and for all the unending and tragic cycle of reimbodiment (*saṃsāra*).

In general, within the African context, such a rigid dualism between body and soul is not found. Instead of conceiving the person as a soul that is *contained* in a body, Africans define the person as an integral whole constituting the "outer person" (the body) and the "inner self." The Yoruba call this inner person *ori-inu* (Idowu, 1994, p. 170). Symbolized by the physical head, *ori* is also connected with God, Olódùmarè, who is the source of all being and before whom one's *ori* kneels to receive one's destiny prior to being born into this world. One's *ori*, therefore, is the *essence* of one's personality as it controls and guides one's life according to the destiny received prior to birth. At the end of one's physical life, one will give an account of one's earthly conduct before Olódùmarè (God) who will determine one's postmortem existence either in the "*Orun rere*" (Paradise or good orun) or "*Orun apadi*" (hell or Orun of the Potsherds), where one suffers a wretched afterlife. According to Bolaji Idowu, life in the "good *Orun*" is but a larger and freer copy of this worldly life, minus earthly pains and tribulations. The best postmortem reward is a reunion with one's relatives who have died before, particularly ancestors, the *Ara Orun* (Idowu, 1994, p. 177). Although Idowu presented this idea of afterlife in the context of traditional Yoruba society, it is important to note that some scholars have questioned this apparently theological explication of the Yoruba notion of afterlife. The notion may be due to the strong influence of Islam and Christianity on Yoruba culture at the time Idowu collected his materials.

That a person is considered a composite and integral whole is also evident in that often, when people claim to encounter the dead through visions and dreams or when they communicate with them through ritual, they claim to have met or spoken with "so and so," a person identifiable by name, rather than the "ghost" of so and so. Given this integral relationship between the outer and inner person, then, it would seem that at death it is the person that dies rather than "the soul" leaving the body and flying away, as some Christian popular hymns indicate.

NOTIONS OF AFTERLIFE: CLUES FROM MORTUARY AND FUNERARY RITUALS. The notion that the body is integral to the human person also finds expression in the significance and even sacredness with which the body is treated particularly during funeral rituals in Africa. Such rituals and related "oratures" (myths, stories, and songs) constitute a commentary by humans on their experiences in this world and its beyond and offer significant clues regarding concepts of the afterlife.

In the oratures, the fact of dying is often described using the metaphor of a journey. Death is depicted as "saying goodbye" to the living or "saying yes" (*gwitika* in Gikuyu) to a summons by God. Many people describe death as "a going home" (in Gikuyu, *kuinuka*) or simply, a departure (Gikuyu, *guthie*). Death is also described as "sleeping" or "resting."

This use of the metaphor of a journey is related to the fact that in general, as indicated earlier, Africans view life itself as a journey. Life is an unfolding, a process of "formation and transformation" that starts before birth and does not end at physical death. During crucial moments of this life journey, special rituals (rites of passage) designed to mark, celebrate, and help the individual successfully negotiate the key turning points, including death, are performed. Thus, for example, among the Swazi, burial of the dead is only done after three days. It is said that going through the physical death process is exhausting to the sojourner and therefore the deceased needs a few days to recuperate before continuing in the next phase of the life journey. The Swazi also bury their dead with all their vital earthly belongings, thus equipping them for the next phase of their life journey, beyond physical death. (M'passou in Cox, 1998, p. 28). Furthermore, during the period between death and burial, the Swazi, as do other communities, observe a vigil both to console the bereaved and to keep the deceased person company as they transit between this world and the next (M'passou in Cox, 1998).

Rituals are also performed to prepare and equip the deceased for the journey ahead and also to "inform" those on the other side that the deceased is on the way and they should expect him or her. The Chagga of Tanzania believe that this journey to the world of ancestors takes nine days. To make the journey easier, the corpse is anointed with fat, fed with milk, and covered with a hide to protect it from the elements. A bull is also killed specifically for the deceased's grandfather to alert him so that he can await the deceased (Mbiti, 1969, p. 155).

Mortuary rituals also emphasize the integral connection between the "inner and outer person." Since the body is integral to the person, a deceased's body is treated with utmost respect. Appropriate burial and "disposal" of the body is therefore important; otherwise, the person cannot make the transition into the other world. For this reason, even when a wild beast devours a body, leaving only a few shreds or pieces, these are carefully collected and accorded a full and respectful burial. In situations where a corpse is not retrievable, say because of drowning, a burial must still be performed, and so in some societies, a surrogate is used. The Luo of Kenya, for example, use the yago fruit, which is several feet in length and is laid in the grave to represent the dead. It is also for this reason that cremation is not a preferred method of disposal of the dead in the African context.

Failure to perform burial rites properly makes the deceased unable to negotiate the postmortem phase of the life journey successfully. Such frustrated persons may have to "come back," looking for help or for some vital equipment necessary of the journey. The Luo call such restless, deceased persons *jochiende*, while the Shona call them *mashave*. Such restless and wondering spirits are said to haunt and afflict the living as they try to gain their attention.

The Living Dead: Corporate Identity and the Destiny of the Individual. Mortuary rituals also reveal that Africans consider death a paradox. On the one hand, death and burial signifies an end to one's physical life. Meticulous and proper burial signifies that Africans understand the finality of death as a marker of the end of physical life. Death is therefore frustrating because it takes way a loved one and robs people of the companionship and other gifts that such a relationship brings. This frustration is expressed though funeral dirges. For this reason, too, death is also vigorously, collectively, and publicly mourned.

Simultaneously, however, death is not an annihilation of the person. Though the deceased may be physically gone, they are still here as persons and the living can still communicate with them. Paradoxically, then, the dead are not dead, a paradox that led Mbiti to coin the phrase "the Living-Dead" (1969, p. 81).

The belief that the dead are not dead is expressed and dramatized through rituals designed to welcome and install the deceased back into the world of the living. The Luo of Kenya call this ritual *Duogo* (Ongonga in Cox, 1998, p. 236), while the Xhosa of South Africa call it *Ukubuyisa* (Pato, in Oosthuizen and Irving, 1992, p. 134). For the Shona of Zimbabwe, the ritual *is* called *Kurova Guva* and is performed by every member of the family, who must explicitly through ritual offerings and libations indicate willingness to welcome the deceased as a continuing member of the family despite physical death. The deceased is also ritually consulted to indicate his or her acceptance thus to be reintegrated into the family (Gundani in Cox, 1998, p. 201).

According to Mbiti (1969, p. 158), this continued remembrance of the Living-Dead and their sustained interaction with the living constitutes the individual's "personal immortality." One enjoys this status so long as there are people left behind to remember him or her. As a Living-Dead one continues to be involved in matters of the corporate group of family and clan and retains one's personal name and corporate identity in this context. Thus, this is a status clearly linked or even dependent on one's place in and relationship to the corporate group, particularly the family. When after a long time such individuals are no longer remembered by name, they enter a state of what Mbiti calls collective immortality as they blend into the general world of those who have gone before (Mbiti, 1969). The Swahili call this community of the dead *Mizimu*, while their abode is referred to as *Kuzimu*.

The Living and the Dead: The Status and Role of Ancestors. The installation of the deceased back into family simultaneously marks the induction of the deceased into the world of ancestors. Henceforth, the deceased person can be honored in family rituals alongside other ancestors and enjoy a privileged position both among the living and the dead. This status, however, is not automatic. Rather, it depends on how well one conducted oneself in this life as a member of the corporate group. Those who have fulfilled their corporate duties and obligations as the community defines them are honored as "ancestors," a status analogous to but not identical to that of sainthood in Christianity. Being moral exemplars, the ancestors are also considered custodians and enforcers of justice and morality among the living, and because they are considered ontologically closer to God, they function as intermediaries between God and the people. Thus, petitionary prayer is often said through them.

Ancestorhood is therefore a status of honor reserved for the exemplary dead. The Gikuyu refer to such a persons as *mwendwo ni iri* (the people's beloved). Conversely, those who fail in their worldly obligations, or those whose actions are subversive to rather than nurturing of life, are quickly forgotten and "excommunicated" after death. The Gikuyu call such persons *muimwo ni iri* (rejected by the people). To be thus rejected, excommunicated and forgotten, is truly to die in the African understanding.

Change, Continuity, and Contestation: The Impact of Christianity and Other Religions. Historically, Africa is heir to a triple heritage of religion and culture: namely African traditional religions, Islam, and Christianity. As early as the first century CE, most of North Africa was part of the Roman Empire and therefore part of Christendom. Later on, the region came under Islamic influence, and today much of North Africa is Islamic and culturally Arabic. Meanwhile, communities like those of the Swahili of East Africa present a religio-cultural hybridity a result of years of blending indigenous African cultures with Islamic ones. Needless to say, Africans who have come into contact with Islam and Christianity have been influenced by the rather sharply defined eschatological notions featuring a final judgment, heaven and hell, and final resurrection as destinies of the soul. Muslims, for example, are encouraged to persevere through earthly tribulations in view of the "day of the Resurrection" when a judgment will be made in their favor, assuming they live a righteous this-worldly life (see Qurʾān, *sūrah* III:185).

African belief systems have been most palpably influenced and shaped by the encounter with nineteenth-century missionary Christianity. This Christianity was articulated in terms of Western culture, and its introduction coincided with the colonization of Africa. Moreover, for the most part assuming a radical difference between themselves and their worldviews and the Africans and their worldviews, and convinced of the need to convert Africans from their allegedly "primitive" and therefore "inadequate" or even "wrong" beliefs, missionaries deliberately tried to erase African beliefs and practices and to replace these with ostensibly Christian ones. This process had a tremendous impact on all aspects of African beliefs, including notions of the afterlife, our immediate concern here.

For one thing, there seems in Christian discourse and practice, a literal demotion or even demonization of ancestors. Whereas in indigenous African thought ancestors were moral exemplars, enjoying a status of honor to which the living could aspire, today, ancestors are in Christian discourse depicted as evil forces of the same character with the devil. Terms such as *mizimu* (Kiswahili), *emandloti* (Swazi), or *ngoma* (Kikuyu), which traditionally described the ancestors, are today used almost as synonyms for Satan or the devil. Furthermore, the deliberate invocation of *ngoma or mizimu* and fellowship with them through libations and prayer (Gikuyu, *kurongoreria*) is in official Christian teaching outlawed because it is considered a breach of the First Commandment. Ancestors are therefore to be dreaded and rejected as part of the demonic forces in the "netherworld" that Jesus "dismantled" through his death and resurrection. Instead of celebrating their exemplary dead, then, many Christianized Africans have seemingly adopted the Christian afterlife discourse and now celebrate angels and saints that are said to populate the heavenly sphere and with whom those who die in good standing with God will live happily after death. Thus, for example, one Gikuyu Christian funeral song bids the deceased farewell and expresses the hope that the person will be met at the gates of heaven by "multitudes of God's angels" (*Kikuyu Catholic Hymnal,* 1992, hymn 101). Whereas in the past the hope was to attain personal immortality as a Living-Dead and to enjoy a status of honor among the ancestors, Christianized Africans look forward instead to joining an otherworldly/heavenly community of God and angels as defined in the Christian discourse.

A redefinition of the human person also seems to be indicated in the Christian discourse. While traditionally one's body was considered integral to one's person and was therefore considered important even after death, today Christian funeral songs depict the body as incidental if not detrimental to one's positive destiny after death. One such song exhorts the listeners to remember that "our bodies are like flowers that wither and die" and that "We shall leave our bodies right here on earth and go to heaven in/with our souls/spirits" (*mioyo*) (*Kikuyu Catholic Hymnal,* 1992, hymn 108). People are therefore encouraged to treat the body with suspicion because fleshly desires might derail their souls from the journey to heaven. The denigration of the body implicit in these songs is quite alien to indigenous understandings of the human person and the person's destiny after death.

The songs also indicate that Christianized Africans have embraced Christian eschatological ideas of heaven and hell and even a postmortem judgment. Thus, while Africans continue to see death as a "saying yes" to God's summons, this summons is a prelude to God's judgment, which determines one's final postmortem destiny in heaven or hell. Thus, as another song reminds the listener, the issue that one should worry about is not death itself, since death is inevitable. The issue of concern is whether at death one will be in a state of readiness to meet God in the final judgment (*Kikuyu Catholic Hymnal,* 1992, hymn 100).

Simultaneously, however, while many seem to have embraced these Christianized notions of the afterlife, there is evidence, even among Christianized Africans, of a marked resistance to the seeming demonization of African beliefs, particularly beliefs in ancestors. Many Christians, albeit in camouflaged or covert ways, continue to honor and remember their dead through ritual in spite of the formal doctrinal ban. The traditional rituals of reinstating the dead into the world of the living, for example, seem to reappear camouflaged in the quite prevalent Christian rituals of "unveiling the tombstone" or "unveiling the cross." Such rituals, usually performed a year after death and burial, are reminiscent of *Kurova Guva, Ukubuyisa,* or *Duogo* rituals mentioned earlier. In Catholic circles, Christianized Africans also ritually connect with deceased family members through requesting a Mass for the dead, a doctrinally legitimate practice. This is reminiscent of rituals of communion with the deceased through shared meals and libations. Such Masses for the dead are routinely "bought," particularly around November 2, the Feast of All Souls in the Catholic liturgical calendar.

Recently, recognizing that rituals to honor the dead are carried out despite the ban, and conceding that ancestors hold a key position in African traditional religions the Catholic Synod of African Bishops recommended that attempts be made to harmonize African beliefs in ancestors with Christian beliefs regarding saints (Schotte, 1992, p. 55). This recommendation finds significant support in the thought of a growing number of African theologians such as Jean Marc Ela, a Cameroonian priest, who find the demotion and demonization of African beliefs problematic. Such theologians assert the compatibility of African beliefs with Christian ones if only the latter can shed their Western garb and be clothed afresh in terms of African culture, a process called "inculturation." In this discourse of "inculturation theology" ancestors still emerge as moral exemplars, and instead of Jesus dismantling the ancestors, he is portrayed in this theology as the "ancestor par excellence."

These theologians also argue that beyond the question of the status of ancestors in the hereafter, the ban on African beliefs in ancestors has far reaching implications in the here and now. As Ela, for example, argues in his book *My Faith as An African* (1990), ancestral veneration is simultaneously an affirmation about life after death but also an affirmation of African notions of family, which includes the living, the dead, as well as the not yet born. Doctrinally, to ban ancestral veneration, then, is to demand that Africans abandon this quite viable notion of family (Ela, 1990, p. 17). Furthermore, the ban is seemingly based on Christian notions of afterlife that define salvation as a matter of the individual's disembodied soul getting to an "otherworldly heaven." These individualistic, otherworldly, and disembodied notions of salvation seem contrary to the indigenous sensibilities that focus on "embodied" and "corporate" destiny of the person both in this life and beyond.

For this reason, and in view of the many negative social ramifications of radical individualism in Africa, Ela claims that a reclamation of African beliefs in ancestors is simultaneously a reclamation of the more viable African notion of human destiny, which focus on interconnectedness and interdependence between the individual and the community. For Ela, such a reclamation is not only doctrinally valid and acceptable but would serve as one possible antidote to "this worldly" problems that thrive on radical individualism (Ela, 1990, pp. 24ff).

It would seem, then, that contemporary debates about the afterlife in Africa are simultaneously discussions about this world and this life. It would seem also that the emphasis by Africans on a this-worldly and corporate approach to salvation resonates significantly with the prior key affirmations about God and the world in the African worldview. As we recall, Africans believe that the destiny of the individual and the community are interdependent, interconnected, and intertwined. Africans also believe in a universe that is in process of formation and transformation, and therefore life means being involved in a process of becoming, together. Moreover, in the African view, to be is to participate in an ongoing dance of life propelled by God's creative and sustaining power. This dance is only interrupted, not ended, by physical death. In the African worldview, then, notions about the "afterlife" and notions of "this life" complement and flow into one another.

BIBLIOGRAPHY

Cox, James, ed. *Rites of Passage in Contemporary Africa: Interaction Between Christian and African Traditional Religions.* Cardiff, 1998. The essays discuss the contested interface between African religions and Christianity regarding rites of passage. Dennis M'passou writes on "The Continuing Tension Between Christianity and Rites of Passage in Swaziland," Paul Gundani explores "The Roman Catholic Church and the *Kurova Guva* Ritual in Zimbabwe," and Jude Ongonga writes on "The River-Lake Luo Phenomenon of Death." All these essays challenge the view that African beliefs including those regarding the afterlife are incompatible with Christianity. Gundani and Ongonga also discuss, respectively, the rituals of Kurova Guva and Duogo, which are rituals of reintegrating the deceased and confirming their status as ancestors or the living dead.

Ela, Jean Marc. *My Faith as An African.* Maryknoll, N.Y., 1990. Drawing largely on his experiences as an African Catholic priest, Ela asserts the compatibility of African beliefs with Christianity and argues for their reclamation as both doctrinally viable and socially relevant for Africans' quest for beliefs and practices that enhance and nurture life in the here and now.

Idowu, Bolaji. *Olódùmarè: God in Yoruba Belief.* Wazobia, N.Y., 1994. This is primarily an account of Yoruba notions of God. In chapters 13 and 14 Idowu discusses Yoruba notions of human nature and definition of the person. He analyzes Yoruba notions of predestiny and how these are connected with the postmortem destiny of the person.

Kenyatta, Jomo. *Facing Mount Kenya.* New York, 1965. A monograph on the beliefs and cultural system of the Agikuyu of Kenya. Chapter 10 focuses on Gikuyu religious beliefs and highlights the place of ancestors (*ngoma*) in this system. Kenyatta distinguishes between the worship of Ngai (God) and the veneration of ancestors who he portrays as mediators between God and the living.

Magesa, Laurenti. *African Religions: The Moral Traditions of Abundant Life.* Maryknoll, N.Y., 1997. Discusses indigenous African religions as ethical systems and links belief in and veneration of ancestors to these systems. Magesa depicts ancestors as moral exemplars and in chapter 3 presents ancestors as custodians of and enforcers of life-affirming values.

Mbiti, John. *African Religions and Philosophy.* Portsmouth, N.H., 1969. Drawing examples from across the continent, Mbiti offers a systematic account of African beliefs. In chapter 8 he discusses the African notions of personal immortality and the status of the living dead, while in chapter 14 he discusses African ideas of death and the hereafter and offers an exegesis of sample funeral rituals. In chapter 3, Mbiti proposes the controversial idea that African eschatological notions are insufficiently developed because Africans lack a future dimension of time, a gap which he suggests is appropriately filled by Christianity with its eschatalogy of heaven, hell, a resurrection, and a final judgement at the end of time.

Mosha, Sambuli. *The Heartbeat of Indigenous Africa.* New York, 2000. A study of indigenous education system of the Chagga from Tanzania. Mosha contextualizes this education within the African theistic worldview with its emphasis on wholeness and interconnectedness of life as well its unfolding nature. Given this worldview, Africans see the hereafter as intimately linked with the here and now.

Mugambi, Jesse, and J. B. Ojwang, eds. *The SM Otieno Case: Death and Burial in Modern Kenya.* Nairobi, Kenya, 1989. This anthology of essays discusses and contextualizes the famous 1987 controversial case regarding the burial of SM Otieno, a Kenyan Luo. The essays analyze the legal ramifications of the case as well as religio-cultural and historical roots of the controversy and suggest that the controversy was symptomatic of the seeming clash between Western and indigenous African (specifically Luo) views regarding life, death, and the hereafter.

Murphy, Joseph. *Santería: An African Religion in America.* Boston, 1988. Murphy discusses the continuity of Yoruba religion in America, specifically in Cuba, discussing, *inter alia,* Yoruba notions about God and how these are linked with concepts of the person. He also contextualizes Santería culturally and historically and suggests that Santeria is both a reconstruction of Yoruba beliefs as well as a creative response of accommodation and resistance to mental enslavement. Santería emerges as a thinly veiled reconstruction of Yoruba ancestor veneration as well as the devotion to the Yoruba divinities (*orisha*) who are now referred to with names of saints from the Christian repertoire of the memorable dead (hence the name *Santería*).

P'bitek, Okot'. *Religion of the Central Luo.* Nairobi, Kenya, 1971. Discusses in detail the belief system of the Acholi of Uganda. P'bitek notes that the Acholi approach the dead as identifiable persons rather than mere disembodied spirits (*cwiny*) or shadows (*tipo*).

Oosthuizen, G. C., and Irving Hexham, eds. *Empirical Studies of African Independent/Indigenous Churches.* Lewiston, N.Y., 1992. This anthology of essays analyzes African independent churches, their histories and theologies. One pertinent essay by D. M. Hostetter is entitled "Disarming the Emandloti: the Ancestors," and notes how, in Christian discourse, the ancestors are subordinated to Jesus who is said to disempower them. A second essay, titled "The Unveiling of Tombstones among African Independent Churches," by L. L. Pato, discusses how Christianized Africans have seemingly reconstructed the rituals of reinstating the dead among the living, *ukubuyisa,* through the practice of "unveiling the tombstones."

Ray, Benjamin. *African Religions: Symbol, Ritual and Community.* New York, 1976. This is a monograph on African belief systems. Ray discusses *inter alia* myths of "paradise lost" and the loss of "immortality."

Schotte, Jan P., ed. *African Synod: Instrumentum Laboris.* Nairobi, Kenya, 1992. This constitutes the working documents (*instrumentum laboris*) for a 1994 synod of Catholic Bishops to rethink the Christian message and mission in the African context. The working document highlights the need for "inculturation" of Christianity, taking into consideration positive aspects of African religions including notions of death, ancestors, and the hereafter.

TERESIA MBARI HINGA (2005)

AFTERLIFE: AUSTRALIAN INDIGENOUS CONCEPTS

There are no easy generalizations to be made when dealing with issues associated with ritual particular beliefs in indigenous Australia pertaining to the question of what happens to the spirits of individuals after death. This article will focus on one region of Australia to illustrate concepts involving what may loosely be called afterlife. The particular group is the Yanyuwa people of the southwest Gulf of Carpentaria in Australia's Northern Territory.

For the Yanyuwa, the body possesses two spirits: the first, *ardirri,* comes from the land of one's paternal ancestors, and begins the process of pregnancy. Upon birth, this spirit inhabits the bones of an individual, as they are considered the least corruptible body parts. The second spirit is the *na-ngawulu,* which is often translated as the "shade" or "shadow" of an individual, also the Yanyuwa word for an actual shadow. This spirit is represented in the body by the pulse or the heartbeat. There is also the *wuwarr* spirit, which upon death manifests itself as a ghost of a person. Certain ritual actions take place in the community to remove the presence of the *wuwarr* spirit, potentially dangerous and malevolent, described as jealous of its living kin. The *na-ngawulu* is said to travel east to the spirit world, where it will live in contentment in a rich environment, but speaking a new language and "having new ears so it can no longer hear its living relatives" (Dinah Norman Marrngawi, personal communication, 2004). In more recent times—since contact with Christianity—this is the spirit that is said to travel to heaven or hell.

In the past, the piercing of the nasal septum was a common practice in Yanyuwa society. This was said to open the nose so that upon death, the spirit of the deceased would be able to smell the spirit world. The body was placed on a platform until the flesh decayed, and then the bones were gathered for further ritual to take place one to two years later. Today, internment takes place in a cemetery, but the post-funeral rituals occur as in the past. These rituals are said to join the *wuwarr* spirit to the *ardirri* (creating a spirit called the *kuyara*), and to send the spirit back to its own spiritual source on the land, where it can await rebirth as another human being. In the past, this return to country was actual, with the bones of the deceased interred in a hollow log coffin decorated with powerful designs relating to the deceased individual and country of origin. Contemporary Yanyuwa people see no conflict with new systems relating to death and dealing with various spirits, and indigenous Australians are able to construct relevant understandings of what happens after death.

However, the spirits of deceased individuals are also said to remain in the country they once inhabited, constituting a community that parallels the living Yanyuwa community. These spirits of the deceased continue to hunt and travel all over the country and sea, watching the actions of their living relatives. The spirits are said to be jealous of their living kin, and to have the ability, if they choose, to cause harm and hardship. Conversely, they can help the living, appearing in dreams and assisting their relatives with the retention of information such as place names and song cycle verses.

There are times when the inhabitants of this spirit world and the land itself are seen to be one and the same. In speaking about the land and these deceased kin, people interchange the terms for land (awara) and spirits (li-ngabangaku) often colloquially as the old people (li-wankala), so that one can talk about how the country has become poor and then say that the spirits of the deceased are jealous or cheeky. Both of these comments mean the same thing. One way of dealing with a land that has spirits residing within it is by actively speaking to the land, or "talking to country." This may involve long speeches in high oratory, or may consist of a simple statement that says no more than "here I am." Senior men and women may do no more than shout to announce their presence. This is especially so if people are still often in touch with the locality they are visiting; the land and the spirits of the deceased residing there will be familiar with them. There are times when nothing needs to be said, because people are still moving through the location. When people have not visited a locality for a long period of time, or the actions of the deceased kin are said to be working against the living, speaking to country becomes one way in which a consensus is reached between the living and the dead. By the use of oratory, order is created whereby the speaker draws on the past, reaching out to the deceased kin through genealogy and relationship, and identifying a person or group of people with a locality. It also states by what authority the person is coming to the country, and in what way the person is related. This authority is conveyed by the calling of place names and the names of people who were once associated with the country. The use of names provides a key by which an understanding is given to the event as it unfolds, but the names are also echoes from the past and links with the present generation, and are important for the negotiation of entry to place. A common phrase used in these orations translates as "do not be ignorant towards me." They are also rhetorical statements of an individual's position in relation to significant others. The presentation of self and negotiation with such orations are not beyond dispute and are also the topic of conversations where they will be evaluated against the status of the individual. People can also still often have accidental interaction with these spirits; some of these interactions are seen to be alarming and potentially dangerous while others are seen to be humorous and to be expected. Either way, they become an important source of storytelling.

While there are formal means by which the spirits of deceased are to be dealt with, there is no clear-cut understanding about the ultimate nature of the spirit in Yanyuwa society and what happens at death. What is clear, however, is that a portion of a deceased person will still reside on the land and it is this spirit that involves constant negotiation. While generalizations can be misleading in relation to indigenous understanding of death and afterlife, this belief in spirits of the deceased on the land is widespread across much of Australia.

BIBLIOGRAPHY

Bradley, John. "Landscapes of the Mind, Landscapes of the Spirit: Negotiating a Sentient Landscape." In *Working on Country: Contemporary Indigenous Management of Australia's Lands and Coastal Regions*, edited by R. Baker, J. Davies, and E. Young, pp. 295–307. New York, 2001.

Morphy, Howard. *Journey to the Crocodile Nest: An Accompanying Monograph to the Film Madarpa Funeral at Gurka'wuy.* Canberra, Australia, 1984.

Myers, F. *Pintupi Country: Pintupi Self: Sentiment, Place and Politics among Western Desert Aborigines.* Canberra, Australia, 1986.

Povinelli, Elizabeth. "'Might Be Something': The Language of Indeterminancy in Australian Aboriginal Land Use." *Man* 28, no. 4 (1993).

Rose, D. *Dingo Makes Us Human: Life and Land in an Australian Aboriginal Culture.* Cambridge, U.K., 1992.

Tamisari, F. *Body, Names, and Movement: Images of Identity among the Yolngu of North-East Arnhem Land.* Ph.D. Thesis, London School of Economics and Political Science, University of London, 1995.

JOHN J. BRADLEY (2005)

AFTERLIFE: OCEANIC CONCEPTS

The idea of the temporal continuance of some aspect of the deceased is widespread, if not universal, in Oceanic cultures. In some cases, as with the Dreaming of Australia, or the redoubled "Sky World" of the Enga people of the New Guinea highlands, the condition of the dead is coeval with the life they had lived, though on a different plane of existence. More commonly, the "place" of the dead is identified with some remote or inaccessible location, beneath the ground, under the sea, or, as with the people of the Trobriand Islands, a haunted and little-visited island (Tuma).

Because death betokens an inevitable separation, never mind the "communication" that may follow, the answer to "what happens to the human essence after the body dies?" may run away with the question. It is often coincident with a more comprehensive cosmological vision. If the best one could do to describe *this present life,* here on earth, would be a matter of metaphors and analogies, then what difference if the condition of the dead were described in that way also? For many Oceanic peoples the condition of dying itself is considered to be a long, protracted process, intermingled with grieving and mortuary practices, and the bodies of the deceased, as well as their possessions, become highly charged social objects. For many Austronesian-speaking Melanesian societies, death has great power, and a highly articulated mortuary feasting complex serves as the focus for all social life.

It would be fair to say that for many Oceanic peoples the terminal condition of the deceased is coincident with social dismissal, postponed long after the body ceases to function, and that the "afterlife" is really a sort of "half-life," analogous to the radioactive decay of an element. Living persons encounter the deceased in quasi-human form, or vice-versa, and there may be as much uncertainty and doubt among the indigenous folk as to what is actually going on as among those who study them. Death "takes prisoners," as it were, and may take a long time letting them go. There are a great many peoples in Oceania who would rather not believe in ghosts.

Those who meet their deaths through violent means, in warfare or accident, belong, in many Oceanic cultures, to a special category of after-death experience. They are conceived as restless, mobile, angry spirits, eager to avenge their unfortunate plight back upon the living, and so very dangerous and threatening. The concept is similar to that of the *preta* in the Sanskritic tradition, and to other, analogous precepts found in India and Southeast Asia. It has a widespread distribution in the Pacific, in one form or another, from the divination for "happy" as against "unhappy" ghosts on the islands of Yap, in Micronesia, to the fabled (and often surprisingly real) "Night Marchers" of Hawai'i. One New Irelander, from the Bismarck archipelago, put it this way: "Just how many American and Japanese servicemen died out there in the Pacific? Some days you can see them fishing, in gigantic waterspouts, and you can see them up in the coconut trees during a thunderstorm, with fire flashing from their eyes and armpits. When the wind scoops up moisture from the sea, *bring your children into the house!*"

Found occasionally among non-Austronesian speakers as well, the idea is analogous to another, described among coastal Papuan and Torres Strait peoples and encountered by Captain Bligh in the Tahiti area. This is that those who are shipwrecked at sea become automatically strangers to the land, demons, no longer human, who *must be killed*, for reasons of safety, by anyone encountering them.

In *Beyond the Kubea* (1940) explorer Jack Hides recounted the feeling of an unidentified interior Papuan people that the spirits of the deceased become visible as "cloud-shadows on the mountains," meaning perhaps that their afterlives, or at least our inability to make sense of them, are as evanescent as the darkness playing upon the distant expanses of montane rain forest. The idea at least captures something of the feeling of the Japanese notion of "the Floating World." But it is also emblematic of the problem faced by any inquiry into the particulars of an afterlife concept, for it excludes an explicit denial.

Denial, when met with in this context, has a power of its own. A classic instance of this, easily misunderstood, is the tenet of the Daribi people of interior Papua New Guinea: "When people die, they just go into the ground; their faces disappear, and there is no such thing as a spirit or soul that survives the death." When asked what they might call such a soul or spirit, the Daribi reply, "It is called the *izibidi*." A key to what this may mean is given by a literal translation of the term: it means "die person" and not "dead person" (which would be *bidi-iziare*). More properly, then, the action of dying itself, though terminal, has a tenacious after-effect in the potentially dangerous *izibidi*, an anomalous and paradoxical condition that most people would rather deny than think about. Daribi are afraid of *izibidi* for the very fact that they ought not to exist.

Though the Daribi expression of this point (others might call it "agnostic") is somewhat unusual for the region, its practical implications are not. The expression gives a necessary deniability (as well as considerable power) to the words and actions of the spirit mediums and shamans (*sogoyezibidi*), the main spiritual agencies in Daribi life. A more general evocation of the paradox was given to the French missionary Maurice Leenhardt (1979) in New Caledonia: "We have always had the *spirit*; what you Westerners brought to us was the *body*." All the problems and paradoxes regarding afterlife in the Pacific may be said to begin from that point.

For many Melanesian peoples, at least, "afterlife" may be an aberrant approximation, based on the continuing resonance, in memory and in *habitus*, among the survivors, of a striking or powerful *personality* removed from their midst. Thomas Maschio (1994) translates this as "memory" among the Rauto of south New Britain, and the work of Steven Feld (1982) among the Kaluli, of Mount Bosavi in Papua, reveals their *Gisaro* rite as an awesome synchronicity, uniting the worlds of the living and dead through the reverberation of sound. The Gizra folk, of the Papuan south coast, trace the mythic beginnings of our world to "the Woman Kumaz, Originator of Death and Musical Instruments."

Music may or may not be the voice of the soul, but it is surely our most eloquent evocation of resonance. At all events, it would seem to be the *closeness* or near proximity of death that predominates in many of the Papuan conceptions of afterlife, whereas other Oceanic peoples emphasize the separation. It begins as a journey for many Polynesian peoples. For the New Zealand Maori, one of the most significant shades of the deceased embarks on a long journey after dying and finally comes to reside in a world beneath the sea, very much like our own. On Tahiti the ultimate destination of the deceased depends on choices made, or trials encountered, en route. A kind of paradise, identified as "Fragrant Rohutu," represents the best of these, whereas the others, according to Christian analogies developed by the missionaries who first described them, correspond to a kind of limbo and a purgatory.

Death implies a journey, as well, for the Afek religion of the Mountain Ok peoples in the Star Mountains, the geographic center of New Guinea. One of the edifices of their Telefolip ritual complex covers the entrance to the bad road into death, called "the Road of Dogs Tearing Flesh." Another, presided over by the woman Bitsanip, a near reincarnation of the creatress, guards the entrance to the good road into death, and Bitsanip advises those who die to take it.

There is, however, the danger of a false dichotomy in some of these examples, for the journey of the deceased resonates the life values left behind in death, whereas the verses of the Kaluli *Gisaro*, a most piquant instance of death-related resonance, trace the progression of an imaginary traveler across a real landscape. Kaluli call this "singing the garden-names."

What is missed most in accounts of Oceanic afterlife concepts is neither the fault of those who tell them nor of those who write them down, but most often a glitch in the art of explanation itself, which has a certain afterlife quality of its own. We tend to favor linear, cause-and-effect strategies and vivid depictions of a scenario that is hardly more than guesswork. The best we might hope for would be the kind of pragmatic understanding that combines the afterlife concepts of the peoples in question with those of our own explanatory overtures.

What happens to the *sense* of things after the *senses* have ceased to function? Is the concept of an afterlife something reserved for the living alone, or does it correspond to something that is asymbolic, existing independently of the analogies used for its recognizance? Even our commonplace words and phrases have their resonances, and a sentence is, of course, a journey. But for a number of Melanesian peoples, and perhaps others in Oceania, the question of analogy's correspondence to reality is a moot one. For those gifted with what some scholars have called a "holographic worldview,"* the differences between symbolic analogy and reality, and, perforce between life and death, are summed together automatically and canceled, in the very thinking of them. This means that what might be considered as "afterlife" is fully coterminous with life as it is lived, that what might be called "the symbolic debt" of the living is revoked, that every person becomes a completed being when the holography is engaged on their behalf.

In formal terms, holography amounts to the complete mutual occlusion of part and whole (*any* part and *any* whole) in any contingency. When properly applied, holography obviates the stepwise patterning of logical explanation, or reasoning by analogy, by the simple virtue of being its own analogy for itself. In more familiar terms, a hologram depicts a three-dimensional imagery in a two-dimensional format and obviates the sense that would guess at its depth or spatial placement. In the terms of the mortuary feasting complex of the Barok people of New Ireland, death's hologram is life, and life's hologram is death. "The child in the womb and the corpse in the ground are one and the same thing and the same conception, the ultimate containment called *Kolume.* In everything we know and do and touch, *Kolume* is intersected by *Gala,* the ultimate severance, or the cutting-that-nurtures." What would appear to be a mortuary feasting complex is simply a highly formalized and participatory confirmation, performed on behalf of every person who dies, of the elemental oneness of *Gala* and *Kolume.* Death takes no prisoners, here, and afterlife would be anticlimactic.

We have ample evidence that something of this sort, the holographic death, was the real object of ancient Egyptian mortuary practice, belief, and ritual, though we have not escaped its purely secular afterlife. But we have better evidence, historical contingencies aside, that the Barok version of it is by no means unique in the Oceanic world. Barok themselves point out that something very similar takes place on the offshore islands of Tangga, as perhaps elsewhere in the island arcs of Austronesian-speaking Melanesia. Fine examples have been found on the islands of Sabarl and Vanatinai, in the Massim area, and on the large island of New Guinea. Effective holographic imageries, or in other words asymbolic mental models, have been discovered, usually inadvertantly, by ethnographers in a number of places in Oceania.

Closely allied to these is the conception of afterlife that might be called "reflectional," often based on a radical and *highly* articulated form of duality. Among the Enga and a number of other interior New Guinea peoples, each person has a "double," a mirror duplicate that pursues a parallel existence in the sky or in a land beneath the rivers and lakes. A South Angan speaker put it this way: "The one you see in a mirror, or in a pool of water, is not you, and it is not human." For many of these peoples the idea of an afterlife is merely contingent to what amounts to a much stronger principle, that of the self-separate identity as a manifest aspect of a bifurcate cosmos. Thus, the Kaluli, mentioned above, experience afterlife in the form of an animal double living in the forest, the water, or the air. When that creature, in its turn, dies, its spiritual essence reenters the human world.

Duality and holography are neatly combined in the afterlife concepts of many Australian Aboriginal peoples, particularly those of the central desert regions. On the one hand, the everyday world of landscape or "country" is organized according to intricate permutations and combinations of the powers of two—the marriage sections and ritual moieties. On the ether hand, the dreaming ("dreamtime"), an eternally creative epoch, is purely holographic and permeates the world of the living on a separate spiritual plane. One enters the dreaming in sleep, in ritual, and necessarily in death. But, because a *part* of one's existence is always fixed in dreaming, "afterlife" describes only one aspect of something with a vast potential scope, and that would have to include such things as "forelife" as well.

Concepts such as that of "reincarnation"—reported more frequently among Australian Aboriginal cultures than elsewhere in the Oceanic region—participate in this potential as well. If the psychology of the dreaming operates in the way that the Aboriginal peoples have described it, then the daily journey of the human soul—waking and sleeping, as well as the ritual cycles of the collective multitude—amount to a complete social encompassment of the reincarnation principle that has no peer anywhere else in the world of human cultures. Asking whether such a thing as reincarnation exists, or why or how it may operate, would be completely beside the point of what these peoples know of it.

BIBLIOGRAPHY

Battaglia, Debbora. *On the Bones of the Serpent.* Chicago, 1990. A brilliant synopsis of memory as afterlife in the context of Austronesian peoples' elaborate funerary feasting.

Feld, Steven. *Sound and Sentiment.* Philadelphia, 1982. The landmark study of Oceanic music, an evocation of soundscape among the Kaluli of interior New Guinea as understood by a talented jazz musician. Human afterlife as an intrinsic function of resonance, as expressed in metaphor, dance, birdsong, and the overtoning of musical instruments.

Hides, J. G. *Beyond the Kubea.* London, 1940. A rare book, difficult to obtain, but a treasure, with insights into the afterlife concepts of previously uncontacted peoples.

Laba, Billai. "The Woman Kumaz, Originator of Death and Musical Instruments." In *Plumes from Paradise,* edited by Pamela Swadling. Boroke, New Guinea, 1996. Laba tells of his own people, the Gizra, and their legendary origin of human afterlife. Compare with the discussion in Feld, listed above.

Leenhardt, Maurice. *Do Kamo.* Chicago, 1979. A highly original account, by an early missionary, of peoples in New Caledonia with a unique conception of language and the constraints it imposes on human life and afterlife. An exception that "proves the rule."

Lepowski, Maria. *Fruit of the Motherland.* New York, 1993. Compare with Battaglia (listed above); a rich though nontheoretical account of an Austronesian island people and their pivotal, life-and-death-defining mortuary feasting complex.

Maschio, Thomas. *To Remember the Faces of the Dead.* Madison, Wis., 1994. The magnificent study of a people of New Britain, the Rauto, whose whole conception of the meaning of things (*makai*) eschews metaphor and extols memory as the sole significant factor in afterlife. (Compare with Feld and Battaglia, listed above.)

Oliver, Douglas. *Ancient Tahitian Society.* 3 vols. Honolulu, 1974. An encyclopedic survey of the concepts, beliefs, and practices of Polynesia's most abundant civilization, with considerable attention to afterlife.

Wagner, Roy. *Habu.* Chicago, 1972. The second part of this synoptic monograph on Daribi religion, titled "The Invention of Immortality," concerns the death-related shamanic and ritual concepts and practices of a people who do not believe that ghosts exist but nonetheless fear them.

Roy Wagner (2005)

AFTERLIFE: MESOAMERICAN CONCEPTS

The term *Mesoamerica* defines a broad cultural area of great sociopolitical complexity mediated by many shared religious concepts, cosmological ideas, and ritual practices related to death and the afterlife. Researchers of the Mesoamerican region have divided its history into four periods: Preclassic (2500 BCE–200 CE), Classic (200–650 CE), Epiclassic (650–900 CE) and Postclassic (900–1521 CE). The archaeological evidence and historical record combine to yield a remarkably rich array of pre-Columbian notions of death and their vital role in the daily lives of people.

Death, Seed of Life. In the midst of great cultural and regional diversity throughout Mesoamerican history, one clear notion was shared by many if not all peoples: death was more than an occasion for fear, mourning and ritual response; rather, death was perceived as a vital, generative, and creative moment in a cosmic process. In this vision of the world, the cosmos and the human body were perceived in a very particular manner: everything in the universe, in one way or another, had supernatural implications. The gods, who traveled in a helicoidal motion, could manifest themselves anywhere and in any shape. The sacred powers of the cosmos reached everywhere and the belief in a complementary dualism pervaded all beings, objects, and places as well as the symbolic systems that expressed their roles and meanings.

Death occupies a vital place in this dichotomous universe, an element that, far from fatal, possesses a renewing quality. The sacred books show that death and all beings connected to it are associated with the creation of individuals, of peoples, and of humanity as a whole. Its name was given to one of the days of the Maya calendar, *Cimi,* and had its Mexica counterpart in *Miquiztli.* Furthermore, death was closely associated with maize, which was the sustenance of the Mesoamerican peoples. Death received ritual blood offerings because it was believed that—like the sun in the sky—death, wherever it resided or manifested itself, ensured the continuity of life. Death also played a fundamental role that related it to the earth: like the soil, it received seeds and made the harvests possible. It also housed funerary bundles and, at the end of the day, it devoured the sun, causing the night to fall.

Also associated with this life-generating notion of death was the concept that life could emerge from the world of the dead, as exemplified in the myth that relates how Quetzalcoatl, god of the wind, stole from the nether region the bones with which he created the human race. Similarly, the *Popol Vuh* narrates how the "Twin Heroes" were conceived in that region, where it was possible to die and be resurrected. Despite the peculiarities of each culture, there is enough evidence from the Mesoamerican region to suggest that death was a state closely associated to life, and not a lethal element. A chronological review shows several coincidences in the development of notions of death and life in the netherworld.

Death in Motion: Early Agricultural Societies. The regenerative powers of death are shown through different kinds of motion or dynamics. First, death is part of an oscillation between death and life, in that death is a permanent partner of life. This can be traced through the archaeological record. During the middle Preclassic period (1200–400 BCE), the duality of life and death is emphasized, as exemplified in what is considered an extraordinary clay mask found in the archaeological discoveries at the village of Tlatilco, in the Central Highlands. It represents a human face, half of it corresponding to a living being, the other in skeletal form. In this geographical area the motions of the dead in the afterlife are symbolized by the burial of companions for dead humans—companions in the forms of not only funeral offerings and various goods like vessels, jewels, or tools, but the skeletal remains of dogs. We know from late ethnohistorical sources that these dogs were believed to accompany individuals, gods, and the sun in their journeys to the underworld. With time, the presence of dogs in Mesoamerican tombs becomes a trait. As for the offerings, they might correspond to materials deemed to be needed by the soul in its journey to the netherworld.

In the western regions of Mesoamerica, a broad variety of funeral rites associated with shaft tombs suggest a kind of social continuity and movement in the afterlife. Archaeologists have learned that these tombs reveal not only distinctive ways of treating the dead body, but also a strong commitment to family ties and ethnic relations. Typically, several individuals were laid to rest in each of these shaft tombs, and in some instances blood ties have been established between the individuals in one grave. The offerings of tools, which would be used by the deceased to perform his or her job in the afterlife, were common in the later periods—in the netherworld the deceased continued with the work performed while they were alive.

An important finding of the late Preclassic period (400 BCE–200 CE) is a stele found in Izapa, Chiapas, a work considered to be of unparalleled craftsmanship that depicts a seated skeleton wearing a mask on its face. It is one of the earliest representations of death as an element in motion.

DEATH IN THE EARLY CITIES. There are many archaeological examples of the funerals of dignitaries and the importance of lineage during the exequies, and of the relationship of lineage with monumental architecture. For the rest of the population, however, funeral rites seem to be associated with domestic spaces.

In Teotihuacan, the most cosmopolitan of the region's urban centers, numerous sculptural and painted images show that rain, fertility and the commitment to sustaining agricultural resources have been found. A fundamental notion of pre-Columbian thought developed in this imposing city—the ritual significance of caves and their association with life and death. These openings, whether natural or man-made, were associated with the netherworld because of their symbolic relation to a uterus, a tomb, and the jaws of the mythic "earth monster." As confirmed by some late narratives, the life of the ancestors is thought to originate in the cave and, in serving as tombs, caves are also the final destination for some individuals. In Teotihuacan, which is a sacred re-creation of the cosmos, caves were a crucial element—from them came the raw material to build the city, and rituals took place inside them that were closely associated with death.

Teotihuacan's sophisticated agricultural cosmovision and technology is evident in the astonishing colorful murals found in palaces and apartment compounds. In the eastern quadrant of the great capital, archaeologists uncovered what is known as the Tepantitla complex, and they were able to restore a series of colorful murals depicting something like a terrestrial paradise. This paradise or sacred afterlife shows richly bejeweled characters in different postures and actions, a great blooming tree with a dynamic, twisted trunk and a richly costumed deity presiding over the scene. This image has been interpreted as Tláloc's paradise, or the Tlalocan.

During this period (c. 200 CE) death by sacrifice became a common practice as evidenced by numerous stunning discoveries in the great ceremonial compound known today as the Ciudadela. At the heart of the Ciudadela stands a majestic pyramid-temple decorated with alternating images of Quetzalcoatl and, possibly, Tláloc. Recent archaeological work found 134 human skeletons with their hands tied in the back. Exceptional offerings were placed near the individuals, such as luxurious necklaces made of shell (representing human mandibles). Often, with these immolations, the people returned the sacrifices the gods had made in the original times. Thus, death became fundamental to the operation of the cosmos.

The evidence from other sites is often considered surprising. Iconographic representations engraved in walls and pottery of the Maya region depict skeletons in motion, participating in rituals or presiding over scenes. Examples from the more lavish and complex funerals, such as the tomb of Pacal, the ruler of Palenque, date to this time. The elaboration of a monolithic sarcophagus, the carving of a tombstone, and the construction of the pyramid to function as a sepulcher, are all examples of extensive planning. Together with the sacrifice of companions and the lavish offering, this evidence demonstrates the importance of the notion of an afterlife and, probably, of the journey the ruler had to undergo to reach his destination. In this imposing tomb there is also an exultation of life and death: An image of the deceased was carved on the cover of the sarcophagus, a maize plant emerging from his chest. Such magnificent royal sepulchers are common throughout the Maya region.

Oaxaca is another region where the dual notion of life and death is apparent. The evidence from mural paintings, the clay masks that show skeletal facial features, and the location of Zapotec tombs (placed under rooms, patios, and temples) all point to the importance of death in everyday life. The area of the Gulf of Mexico is not an exception. The clay figurines from Zapotal, Veracruz, are one example, as they represent skeletons that are associated with the god of the underworld.

URBAN REORGANIZATION: SYMBOLS OF SACRIFICIAL DEATH. Different notions of death and sacrifice were consolidated during the Epiclassic period. Among these, the importance of the notion of glorious death in times of war becomes common in the archaeological record. In the city of Tajín, references to sacrifice and decapitation associated with ball games are grandly carved in stone. In the Mayan region, Chichén Itzá is another clear example of the increasing importance of such rituals. Towards the end of the period, the record shows an increase in the artistic representation of death, as is the case in Tula, where a snake carved on the side wall of a temple devours a row of skeletal people. The existence of a *Tzompantli*, or wall of skulls, near the ball court is further evidence of such expanded representation, which also appears at Chichén Itzá.

THE BODY AND LIFE AFTER DEATH. During the Postclassic period, the Mexicas and other contemporary peoples of the Central Highlands believed the body held three souls. Each soul was believed to reside in a specific region that served a function in the body and, upon death, had a specific fate. The *teyolía* resided in the heart, and was indispensable for the preservation of life. The *tonalli* was located in the head; it could exit the body and, were it not to return after a certain time, its proprietor would die. The *ihíyotl* resided in the liver. It was associated with the human passions, and it, too, could exit the body. Upon the death of the individual, these souls would dissipate, and the *teyolía* would travel to the world of the dead (López Austin, 1980, 360–370). Apparently, the Maya also believed in a kind of soul that traveled to the netherworld. This can be interpreted from the colonial records that tell of the placing of a stone in the mouth of the deceased that would receive the soul at the last breath.

The destinations of the dead are true funeral geographies, as evidenced in the three more powerful groups: Mexica, Tarascan, and Maya. It was believed that these locations could be in the heavens, the water, or under the earth, and that their entrances were caves, lagoons, or nebulous places located somewhere in the earth. Dangerous locations associated with the landscape had to be traversed in order to gain access to them. In other instances, these territories combined environmental elements with supernatural traits. The three above-mentioned groups coincided in perceiving the underworld as the main realm of the deceased. Among the Mexica, this region was known as Mictlan. Friar Bernardino de Sahagún (1997) writes that it was the destination of those who died of old age or common illness, regardless of their origin.

Nine areas had to be crossed in order to reach this region, which was located under the earth. The deceased was left all necessary items for his or her journey. The route is described in the *Codice Vaticano Latino 3738* (Vatican Latin Codex 3738). The first stop was the Chiconahuapan River, where a brownish dog awaited his master to help him across. After the crossing, the deceased ascend through a region where mountains crashed into each other. Later, he or she would face the Obsidian Mountain, and then a place where the wind was so cold that it cut like a knife. The blankets given to the dead during the funeral would help in this stage. The deceased next had to cross a place where flags wave in order to reach the place where people are pierced by arrows. More dangers awaited upon his or her arrival in the place where wild animals eat human hearts. After four years, the journey was completed with the arrival at Mictlan, a dark, windowless place ruled by Mictlantecuhtli and his wife Mictecacíhuatl. The god of the underworld was a semi-skeletal being, with curly hair and a nose made of a flint knife.

Those who died of a reason related to water faced a different fate, since they traveled to Tlalocan, a place of abundance and fertility ruled by Tláloc, god of the rain. The descent into the paradise of Tláloc could be caused by an illness associated with the powers of deity. For instance, it was believed that death by drowning or a lightning strike was more than an accidental occurrence; it was the god taking possession of the person through that force. It was believed that the god chose those who died that way.

Once they reached Tlalocan, they would help the deity, who granted water for harvests and storms. These victims were buried directly into the ground, as if they were seeds. Another special place, probably located in Tlalocan, is Chichihuauhcuahco, a nursing tree that was the destination of the souls of suckling children.

It was believed that those who died in war would travel to the "House of the Sun." These deceased were considered illustrious, and their job in the netherworld would be to fight for the preservation of the universe, insuring the transit of the sun from dawn to noon. At that point, it was handed over to women who had died in childbirth, who would accompany it until dusk, before handing it over to the lords of Mictlan.

The Maya also believed in souls having different fates. Among inhabitants of the Yucatan peninsula, the underworld was known as Mitnal. The Quiché Maya called it Xibalbá, "the region of those who vanish," the lowest stratum of the underworld, which was reached by descending a road full of dangers. Such notions were recorded in the *Popol Vuh,* a sacred book written during the early colonial period.

The content of this book was broadly diffused throughout the Maya region. It was believed that the entrance to Xibalbá was in Guatemala, and that in order to reach it one had to descend a steep staircase before crossing a river with a strong current that flowed between thorny calabash trees. Along the way, the deceased encountered another river, the river of pus, and then moved toward a river of blood and another one of water. The latter was located between two steep cliffs. Soon afterward the traveler would be at the junction of four roads, and only the black one would lead to Xibalbá, where the council chamber of the lords of the underworld was located. It was also the site of a garden with birds and flowers, and of a ball court. There was also a spring that was the source of a river and six houses that were torture chambers. Hun Camé and Vucub Camé were the supreme gods of this region, although there were other lords who caused illness and death.

Recent scholarship on the *Popol Vuh* has reiterated one of the main points made here—namely, that Mesoamerican peoples understand death to be one crucial stage in a creative, regenerative process. Several mythic episodes in the *Popul Vuh* reveal that this underworld of Xibalbá was also a region closely associated with life. It was there that the mythic heroes were conceived during one of the cosmic creations. And it was in the threatening regions of Xibalbá that each mythic hero was brought back to life in order to become the Sun and the Moon. Another deity associated with death is called *God A* in the classification of Paul Schellhas (1904). This god is also known as the skeleton (*ah Puch*) or the flatulent one (*kisín*). He was represented as being a skeleton, with body blotches caused by putrefaction, emaciated arms, and a protruding abdomen. He was associated with violent sacrifices and decapitations and is depicted on a throne of bones with his eyes closed and mouth agape—or sometimes as a feminine form.

Another world of the dead mentioned by the Maya was the *Paradise of the Ceiba*, or Coral Tree, a land of plenty that was the destination of the souls of those who hanged themselves. Like Tlalocan, in this place there was a large tree under whose shade one could rest.

In Michoacán, the Tarascan believed that the underworld was under the earth and called it Cumiechúcuaro (place where one is with the moles). It was a region inhabited by deities that looked like people and animals, and it was divided in four directions, with its entrance facing the East, where the sun rises. Cumiechúcuaro was ruled by a mole named Uhcumo.

Another world of the dead was Pátzcuaro, the entrance to which was in the lake of the same name. Associated with blackness, this place was the destination of those who died by drowning and was ruled by Chupi Tiripeme, a deity of water.

As was the case in the Central Highlands, Uarichao was the "place of women" and was to the west. It was for those who had died giving birth to their first child. Thiuime (Black Squirrel) was the deity who inhabited this region. Unlike the emaciated characters of the Maya and Mexica, these gods had the shape of animals commonly associated with the fields.

Other areas show a certain unity of beliefs about life after death, although they have not been as well documented as the above cases. In Oaxaca, the Mixtec worshiped Pitao Pecelao as the god of the underworld, and they made offerings to him during times of illness or death and to counteract the effects of omens. He was associated with wealth and luck, as well as the cultivation of the nopal, or prickly pear, again showing the unavoidable relationship between life and death.

THE ENCOUNTER OF TWO VISIONS OF DEATH. The quick and violent social transformations that took place after 1521 had an immediate impact on perceptions of life and death. The imposition of Christian mores and the death toll caused by war resulted in a transformation of funerary customs. The Western concept of life in the netherworld was based on the idea of resurrection, and the allocation of the dead in the afterlife was dependent on their behavior in life, thus becoming a reward or a punishment. This view contrasts with that of Mesoamerican religions, where the immaterial element of the body played a cosmic role in the netherworld that contributed to the functioning of the universe. Death in pre-Columbian times was related to life, and the journey to the netherworld was associated with the type of death, not with behavior.

Change in the new Spanish society was gradual. The adoption of saints, the ability of some friars to indoctrinate, and the passage of time all led to Christianity's dominance. Nevertheless, it is easy today to observe beliefs and practices that reflect syncretism and cultural wealth. In some contemporary communities it is still possible to record the continuance of pre-Columbian elements mixed with the Christian religion. The offering of dogs in contemporary Lacandon Maya tombs or the Totonac belief in the underworld—with a region for those who have drowned, one for women who died giving birth, and another one for suckling children—are very clear examples.

BIBLIOGRAPHY

Becker, Marshall Joseph. "Caches as Burials; Burials as Caches: The Meaning of Ritual Deposits among the Classic Period Lowland Maya." In *Recent Studies in Pre-Columbian Archaeology*, edited by Nicholas J. Saunders and Olivier de Montmollin, vol. 1, pp. 117–139. Oxford, 1988. Discusses the complexity in the funerary and mortuary rituals among the Maya.

Benavente, Toribio (Motolinía). *Memoriales*. Mexico City, 1971.

Benson, Elizabeth, ed. *Death and the Afterlife in Pre-Columbian America*. Washington, D.C., 1975.

Brotherston, Gordon. "Huesos de muerte, huesos de vida: la compleja figura de Mictlantecuhtli." *Cuicuilco* 1 (1994): 85–99. Deals with the relation between life and death among the Nahua, considering the archaeological records and sacred books.

Cabrero, Teresa. *La muerte en el occidente del México prehispánico*. Mexico City, 1989.

Codex Chimalpopoca, History and Mythology of the Aztecs. Translated by de John Bierhorst. Tucson, Ariz., 1981.

"Codex Vaticanus Latinus 3738." In *Antigüedades de México*, edited by Lord Kingsborough. Mexico City, 1964–1967.

Furst, Jill. "Skeletonization in Mixtec Art: A Re-evaluation." In *The Art and Iconography of Late Post-Classic Central Mexico*, edited by Elizabeth Boone, pp. 207–225. Washington, D.C., 1982.

Garza, Mercedes. *El hombre en el pensamiento religioso náhuatl y maya*. Mexico City, 1990.

López Austin, Alfredo. *Breve historia de la tradición religiosa mesoamericana*. Mexico City, 1998. A notable introduction to the religion in Mesoamerica, easy to read and with significant new data.

López Austin, Alfredo. *Cuerpo humano e Ideología*. Mexico City, 1980. A classic research about the human body among the Nahua, with an emphasis on the conception of the soul and its relation with life and death.

Manzanilla, Linda, and Carlos Serrano, eds. *Prácticas funerarias en la Ciudad de los Dioses los enterramientos humanos de la antigua Teotihuacan*. Mexico City, 1990. Remarkable compilation of Teotihuacan's funerary practices. Includes new archeological findings and the analysis of human remains recovered in this sacred place.

Matos Moctezuma, Eduardo. *Muerte a filo de obsidiana*. Mexico City, 1980. A extraordinary book, focusing on the afterlife notions and funerary rituals among the Mexica.

McAnany, Patricia. *Living with the Antecessors: Kingship and Kinship in Ancient Maya Society*. Austin, Tex., 1995.

McKeever Furst, Jill. *The Natural History of the Soul in Ancient México*. New Haven, Conn., 1995.

Ruz Lhuillier, Alberto. *Costumbres funerarias de los antiguos mayas*. Mexico City, 1989. A classic book with an exceptional inventory of archaeological funerary findings, historical information, and contemporary data on Maya culture.

Sahagún, Fray Bernardino. *Historia general de las cosas de la Nueva España.* Mexico City, 1997.

Schellhas, Paul. *Representation of Deities of the Maya Manuscript.* Cambridge, Mass., 1904.

XIMENA CHÁVEZ BALDERAS (2005)
Translated from Spanish by Fernando Feliu-Moggi

AFTERLIFE: JEWISH CONCEPTS

The concept of an afterlife in Judaism took shape gradually and was rarely cast into dogmatic or systematic form. The Jewish idea of the afterlife has focused upon belief in either corporeal resurrection or the immortality of the soul. While one or the other of these conceptions, and occasionally both together, has been present in every period in the history of Judaism, it can safely be said that these ideas underwent their most significant development during the rabbinic and medieval periods.

THE BIBLICAL PERIOD. The notion of the afterlife in the Bible is decidedly vague. After death, the individual is described as going to She'ol, a kind of netherworld, from which he "will not ascend" (*Jb.* 7:9). God, however, is attributed with the power to revive the dead (*Dt.* 32:39, *1 Sm.* 2:6), and the language of resurrection is several times used in a figurative sense, as in Ezekiel's vision of the dry bones (*Ez.* 37:1–4) and in the apocalypse of Isaiah (*Is.* 26:17–19) to describe the national restoration of the people of Israel. The earliest description of an eschatological resurrection of the dead is in *Daniel* 12:1–2, an apocalyptic text composed in the midst of the Antiochian persecutions (167–164 BCE):

> There shall be a time of trouble . . . ; and at that time your people shall be delivered, every one whose name shall be found written in the book. And many of those who sleep in the dust of the earth shall awake, some to everlasting life, and some to shame and everlasting contempt.

These verses probably do not imply a universal resurrection for all men but only for the righteous and the wicked of Israel. As some modern scholars have proposed, it is likely that the prominence the idea of resurrection began to assume in this period was a result of political and religious crises in which significant numbers of Jews suffered martyrdom. In order to maintain belief in God's justice and in his promises to the righteous that they would enjoy the restoration of Israel, it became necessary to extend the doctrine of reward and punishment beyond this life to the hereafter. (For an explicit statement of this rationale, see *2 Maccabees* 12:42–45.)

THE HELLENISTIC AGE. The term *'olam ha-ba'* ("the world to come"), in contrast to *'olam ha-zeh* ("this world"), first appears in the Hebrew *Apocalypse of Enoch* (71:15), a work composed between 164 and 105 BCE, and throughout the Hellenistic period notions of an eschatological judgment and resurrection in the apocalyptic tradition begun with the *Book of Daniel* continued to develop in Palestinian Jewish literature. To be distinguished from this eschatological tradition is the conception of the immortality of the soul that was introduced into Diaspora Judaism under the influence of Greco-Roman culture. George Foot Moore succinctly characterized the difference between the two ideas of the afterlife:

> on the one side [i.e., immortality] the dualism of body and soul, on the other [i.e., resurrection] the unity of man, soul and body. To the one the final liberation of the soul from the body, its prison-house or sepulchre, was the very meaning and worth of immortality; to the other the reunion of soul and body to live again in the completeness of man's nature. (Moore, 1927, p. 295)

The idea of immortality initially appears in Hellenistic Jewish literature in the *Wisdom of Solomon* (3:1–10, 5:15–16) and is more extensively developed in the writings of Philo Judaeus (d. 45–50 CE), who describes how the souls of the righteous return after death to their native home in heaven—or, in the case of rare individuals like the patriarchs, to the intelligible world of the ideas (*Allegorical Interpretation* 1.105–108; *On Sacrifice* 2.5). Although Philo's views were immensely influential in early Christian philosophy, they had no impact upon rabbinic Jewish thought as it developed in the subsequent centuries.

RABBINIC JUDAISM. Belief in the resurrection of the dead is the cornerstone of rabbinic eschatology. Josephus Flavius (*Jewish Antiquities* 18.13–18; *The Jewish War* 2.154–165) and the *Acts of the Apostles* (23:6–9) both attribute such belief to the Pharisees, the rabbis' predecessors before 70 CE, and in one of the few dogmatic statements about the afterlife that exist in all rabbinic literature, the Mishnah explicitly states: "All Israel has a portion in the world-to-come" except "one who says, 'There is no resurrection of the dead'" (*San.* 10.1).

Rabbinic doctrine concerning reward and punishment in the hereafter is based upon belief in the reunion of the body and the soul before judgment. Although rabbinic thought was eventually influenced by Greco-Roman ideas about the existence of the soul as an independent entity, and although there exist some relatively late rabbinic opinions that attach greater culpability to the soul than to the body for a person's sins, there are no rabbinic sources that testify to belief in the immortality of the soul independent of the notion of corporeal resurrection. The unqualified importance that the latter article of faith held for the rabbis is reflected in the great exegetical efforts they made to find sources for it in the Torah (cf. *Sifrei Dt.,* ed. L. Finkelstein, Berlin, 1939, no. 306, p. 341) and in the many references to resurrection that are found in the Targums. As testimony to God's faithfulness, the rabbis also made his power to revive the dead the subject of the second benediction in the 'Amidah, the centerpiece of the Jewish liturgy, and they included several references to the resurrection in other prayers in the liturgy.

Aside from the dogma of resurrection, however, the rabbis held differing opinions about nearly every matter connected to the afterlife. In regard to retribution in the hereafter, the first-century houses of Hillel and Shammai agreed about the reward the righteous will receive and the punishment the wicked will suffer, but they disagreed about the fate of most men who are neither wholly righteous nor utterly wicked. According to the house of Shammai, the souls of these men will be immersed in purgatorial fires until they are purified; according to the house of Hillel, God in his mercy will spare them all punishment (Tosefta, *San.* 13.3). In a lengthy Talmudic discussion, some authorities propose that upon death the souls of the righteous are gathered in "a treasury beneath the throne of glory" or, alternatively, are given habitation in paradise, while the souls of the wicked are imprisoned and cast back and forth from the slings of destructive angels until they are cleansed of their sins. Still another opinion states that the soul lingers with the body even after death, "lamenting all seven days of mourning," and for the following year it ascends and descends, unable to relinquish completely its ties with the body (B.T., *Shab.* 152a–b). Other sources attribute varying degrees of consciousness to the dead (B.T., *Ber.* 18b–19a).

On such questions as whether Gentiles or the children of wicked Gentiles can enjoy a place in the world to come, second- and third-century rabbis disagreed (Tosefta, *San.* 13.1); the law was decided in the affirmative (see Maimonides' *Mishneh Torach,* Repentance 3.5).

Some rabbinic views about the afterlife reflect beliefs commonly held in the ancient world. While the rabbis stated unequivocally that every Israelite has a place in the world to come, they also believed that persons who suffered violent or otherwise untimely deaths might not be permitted to enjoy the afterlife. The rabbis did not, however, accept the pagan belief that the unburied are refused entrance to the hereafter. While there exist a number of cases in rabbinic literature in which life after death is promised in return for a pious deed, these are relatively exceptional. A statement like the one attributed to the tanna Me'ir (second century), in which he is reported to have vouchsafed a place in the world to come to any person who lives in the Land of Israel, speaks Hebrew, and recites the Shema' prayer daily (*Sifrei Dt.,* no. 333, p. 383), should be understood partly as a rhetorical expression meant to emphasize the importance of the deeds Me'ir encourages.

In general, the subject of the future world does not appear to have obsessed the rabbis or especially to have exercised their imaginations. While there must have existed among Jews many folk beliefs concerning life after death (some of which can be extrapolated from burial customs), few have been explicitly recorded. A striking exception is the view that the body will be resurrected from the *luz,* an almond-shaped bone at the top of the spine that otherwise will turn into a snake (*Gn. Rab.* 28.3). About the ecstatic pleasures or harrowing tortures awaiting the dead, rabbinic speculations were decidedly restrained. Gan 'Eden (the Garden of Eden), the rabbinic equivalent of paradise, is sometimes described as an earthly garden; at other times, as a heavenly one. Geihinnom (Gehenna), the equivalent of hell, derives its name from the valley of Ben Hinnom south of Jerusalem in which, during the time of the biblical monarchy, a pagan cult of child sacrifice was conducted, thus endowing the valley with everlasting infamy. The exact location of the eschatological Geihinnom, however, was the subject of differing opinions: some rabbis locate it in the depths of the earth (B.T., *'Eruv.* 19a), others in the heavens or beyond the "mountains of darkness" (B.T., *Tam.* 32b); and there is even an isolated opinion that altogether denies the existence of Geihinnom as a place, defining it instead as a self-consuming fire that emerges from the bodies of the wicked and destroys them.

The reticence of rabbinic tradition about these subjects is summed up in a statement of the third-century Palestinian sage Yoḥanan bar Nappaḥa': "All the prophets prophesied only about the days of the Messiah; but of the world to come, 'eye hath not seen it, O God' [*Is.* 64:4]" (B.T., *San.* 99a, *Ber.* 34b). Yoḥanan's Babylonian contemporary Rav (Abba' bar Ayyvu) gives a more detailed description of what, at the least, will not be in the hereafter: "In the world to come, there is no eating, no drinking, no begetting of children, no bargaining or hatred or jealousy or strife; rather, the righteous will sit with crowns on their heads and enjoy the effulgence of the *shekhinah,* God's presence" (B.T., *Ber.* 17a). The rabbis usually imagined the world to come as the complete realization of all the ideals they valued most in this world. Thus, the Sabbath is once characterized as one-sixtieth of the world to come (B.T., *Ber.* 57b), and the late rabbinic *midrash Seder Eliyyahu Rabbah* records the opinion that in the hereafter there will be no sin or transgression, and all will occupy themselves with the study of Torah. The *Midrash Eleh Ezkerah* (Legend of the ten martyrs) concludes with a vivid description of the future world in which the purified souls of all the righteous are said to sit in the heavenly academy on golden thrones and to listen to 'Aqiva' ben Yosef preach on the matters of the day.

THE MIDDLE AGES. Between the eighth century and the fifteenth, Jewish views about the afterlife embraced virtually every position on the spectrum of conceivable beliefs, including extreme philosophical interpretations that altogether deny the existence of corporeal resurrection. The Spanish-Jewish philosopher Moses Maimonides (Mosheh ben Maimon, 1135/8–1204), in his *Commentary on the Mishnah,* criticizes several popular views of the world to come, all of which conceive of the eschatological bliss purely in material and sensual terms. German-Jewish pietistic literature of the twelfth and thirteenth centuries records numerous accounts of encounters with dead souls, visits to the otherworld, *danses macabres,* and other folk beliefs that were, to some degree, Judaized or otherwise rationalized. It is, however, in the literature of Jewish philosophy and Qabbalah (mysticism) that the most significant developments in Jewish eschatological thinking in the Middle Ages are to be found.

Philosophical approaches. Most medieval Jewish philosophers conceived of the afterlife in terms of the immortality of the soul, which they then defined according to their individual philosophical views. For many of these philosophers, the notion of physical resurrection in the future world is clearly problematic, and although few dared to deny its status as a fundamental dogma of Jewish faith, they sometimes had to go to extreme lengths to reconcile it with their other ideas about existence in the hereafter.

Probably the most successful in doing this was the early medieval Babylonian philosopher and sage Saʿadyah Gaon (882–942), who, in *The Book of Beliefs and Opinions,* emphasizes the unity of body and soul. Saʿadyah foresees two resurrections, the first for the righteous alone at the beginning of the messianic age (when the wicked would be sufficiently punished by being left unresurrected) and the second for everyone else at the advent of the world to come. At this latter time, the wicked will be resurrected in order to be condemned to eternal suffering, while the righteous will pass into the future world, where they will enjoy a purely spiritual existence, sustained in bliss by a fine, luminous substance that will simultaneously serve as the instrument by which the wicked will be burned forever in punishment (Saʿadyah, *Beliefs and Opinions* 6.1, 6.7, 7.13).

After Saʿadyah, the eschatological doctrines of most Jewish philosophers can be categorized by their orientation as either Neoplatonic or Aristotelian. For Jewish Neoplatonists—including Yitsḥaq Yisraʾeli (d. 955/6), Shelomoh ibn Gabirol (d. 1058), Baḥye ibn Paquda (eleventh century), and Yehudah ha-Levi (d. 1141)—beatitude in the world to come was understood as the climax of the soul's ascent toward the godhead and its union with Wisdom. Some writers speak of this state of bliss as a divine gift; according to certain views, it can be attained even in this world if the philosopher can free himself from the influence of the flesh in order to devote his soul entirely to the pursuit of the knowledge of God.

In contrast, Jewish Aristotelian philosophers treated the soul as the acquired intellect and therefore defined the ultimate felicity as a state of "conjunction" between the acquired intellect of the individual philosopher and the universal Active Intellect. Immortality was understood by them mainly as the intellectual contemplation of God. Like their Muslim counterparts, the Jewish Aristotelians disagreed over such issues as whether this state of conjunction can be attained in this world or solely in the next and whether the soul in its immortal state will preserve its individual identity or lose it in the collective unity of the impersonal Active Intellect.

Maimonides, the most celebrated Jewish Aristotelian, appears to adapt conflicting opinions on these questions (*Guide of the Perplexed* 1.74 and 3.54). Although he lists the dogma of resurrection as the thirteenth fundamental of Jewish faith, he also writes that "in the world to come the body and the flesh do not exist but only the souls of the righteous alone" (*Code of Law: Repentance* 3.6). In Maimonides' own lifetime, this extreme formulation elicited much criticism and was sometimes interpreted as denying corporeal resurrection. To defend himself, Maimonides eventually wrote his *Treatise on Resurrection,* in which he distinguishes between existence in the messianic age and in the world to come. In the former, "those persons whose souls will return to their bodies will eat, drink, marry, and procreate, and then die after enjoying long lives like those characteristic of the messianic age"; in the world to come, the souls alone of the previously resurrected persons will be restored, and they will now enjoy eternal and purely spiritual existence. Maimonides' distinction between the two periods is unique, however; in fact, the notion of corporeal resurrection so poorly fits his general philosophy, with its overall emphasis upon the purely spiritual nature of true bliss, that some modern scholars have questioned whether Maimonides' repeated affirmations of dogmatic belief in resurrection were solely concessions to tradition and popular sentiment, motivated perhaps by fear of being persecuted for heresy.

A very different criticism of the Maimonidean position was put forward in the fourteenth century by the philosopher Ḥasdai Crescas in *The Light of the Lord.* Crescas criticizes Maimonides' intellectualism and proposes that salvation comes to the soul through love of God (2.6, 3.3). A century later, Yosef Albo (d. 1444) accepted the Maimonidean chronology for the afterlife but also argued with his predecessor's intellectualism, claiming that practice, not just knowledge, of God's service makes the soul immortal (*Book of Principles* 4.29–30). Still more revealing as to the changes in Jewish eschatology that occurred over the centuries is Albo's characterization of resurrection as a "dogma accepted by our nation," but not "a fundamental or a derivative principle of divine law in general or of the law of Moses in particular" (1.23).

Qabbalistic views. Unlike medieval Jewish philosophers, Jewish mystics in the Middle Ages had no difficulty with the concept of resurrection or other such aspects of eschatological doctrine. Quite the opposite, these topics were among their favorites. In voluminous writings, the mystics described the fate of the resurrected souls, imagined the precise details of their existence in the afterlife, and charted its chronology in relation to the *sefirot,* or divine emanations.

The Spanish exegete Moses Nahmanides (Mosheh ben Naḥman, c. 1194–1270) devotes considerable effort in the *Gate of the Reward* to reconciling a mystical view of the afterlife with Maimonidean eschatology. Nahmanides posits the existence of three distinct worlds that follow this one: (1) a world of souls, roughly equivalent to the rabbinic Gan ʿEden and Geihinnom, which the soul enters immediately after death to be rewarded or punished; (2) a future world that is synonymous with the messianic age and will culminate in a final judgment and resurrection; and (3) the world to come, in which "the body will become like the soul and the soul will be cleaving to knowledge of the Most High."

A second stage in the history of qabbalistic eschatology began with the appearance of the *Zohar* (completed in approximately 1300), which describes the afterlife in terms of the separate fates of the three parts of the soul, the *nefesh,* the *ruaḥ,* and the *neshamah.* Since only the first two were considered to be susceptible to sin, they alone were subject to punishment. The *neshamah* in its unsullied state was believed to be stored up after death in a special place, often called the *tseror ha-ḥayyim,* "the bundle of life" (a term borrowed from *1 Samuel* 25:29), which was sometimes identified with one of the *sefirot.* Because the doctrine of the preexistence of the soul was also widely accepted in these qabbalistic circles, the soul's final sojourn among the *sefirot* could be seen as simply a return to its birthplace.

Probably the most unusual aspect of qabbalistic eschatology is the belief in *gilgul,* or metempsychosis, the transmigration of souls after death. This belief gained increasing prominence in qabbalistic thought from the thirteenth century onward. Originally considered a unique punishment for extraordinary sins (particularly of a sexual kind), *gilgul* came to be viewed, paradoxically, as an exemplary instance of God's mercy, since the chance to be reborn gave its victims an opportunity to correct their sins and thus restore themselves as spiritual beings. As a form of punishment, however, the concept of *gilgul* conflicted with the idea of Geihinnom—a conflict that was never successfully resolved—and in later Qabbalah, the notion of *gilgul* gradually became a principle wherein everything in the world, from inorganic matter to the angels, was believed to be in a state of constant flux and metamorphosis. Thus, in order to repair the damage they had done in their earlier existence, certain souls were supposed to have been reincarnated at later moments in history that were similar to those in which they had first lived; accordingly, David, Bathsheba, and Uriah were considered to be the *gilgulim* of Adam, Eve, and the serpent; Moses and Jethro, those of Cain and Abel. In the later Middle Ages, the notion of transmigration was eventually absorbed into folk belief. By the sixteenth century, the *dibbuq (dybbuk),* which originally was simply the name for a demon, had come to represent a soul whose sins were so enormous that they could not be repaired even through *gilgul.* The poor soul consequently wandered through the world in desperate search of refuge in helpless living persons, whom it subsequently possessed and tormented.

THE MODERN PERIOD. With the change in religious temper that occurred during the Enlightenment and has deepened since then, the problem of the afterlife has lost much of its compelling urgency for Jewish theology. Orthodox Judaism, to be sure, maintains the rabbinic dogmatic belief in resurrection as part of its conception of the messianic age, and it similarly preserves the liturgical references in their original form. In contrast, the Pittsburgh Platform (1885) of the Reform movement in America expressly rejected "as ideas not rooted in Judaism the beliefs both in bodily resurrection, and in Gehenna and Eden as abodes for eternal punishment and reward." In general, when the afterlife is considered today, it is usually spoken about in terms of personal immortality, a heritage of the medieval philosophical temper, and as good an indication as any of the *gilgulim* through which the concept has passed in the course of Jewish history.

SEE ALSO Ashkenazic Hasidism; Messianism, article on Jewish Messianism.

BIBLIOGRAPHY

There exists no single book or study that treats the entire history of Jewish eschatological thought through the ages. On the notion of the afterlife in the Bible and in the apocryphal and pseudepigraphic literature, R. H. Charles's classic *A Critical History of the Doctrine of a Future Life in Israel, in Judaism, and in Christianity* (1899; reprint, New York, 1979) is still informative, but its value has largely been superseded by George W. E. Nichelsburg's *Resurrection, Immortality, and Eternal Life in InterTestamental Judaism* (Cambridge, Mass., 1972).

For early rabbinic eschatology, the clearest and most comprehensive treatment remains George Foot Moore's *Judaism in the First Centuries of the Christian Era, the Age of Annaim,* 3 vols. (Cambridge, Mass., 1927–1930). Volume 2 contains (on pages 279–395) a useful discussion of the methodological problems involved in the study of rabbinic concepts of the afterlife and their historical background as well as translations of most of the relevant sources. An indispensable complement to Moore's summary, particularly for Greco-Roman parallels to the rabbinic concepts, is Saul Lieberman's "Some Aspects of After Life in Early Rabbinic History," in *Harry Austryn Wolfson Jubilee Volume* (English Section), vol. 2 (Jerusalem, 1965). For other special aspects of rabbinic eschatology, see Arthur Marmorstein's two essays on the afterlife in his *Studies in Jewish Theology* (London, 1950) and Martha Himmelfarb's *Tours of Hell: An Apocalyptic Form in Jewish and Christian Literature.* (Philadelphia, 1983).

On medieval philosophical views, the single book to attempt a comprehensive survey is Julius Guttmann's *Philosophies of Judaism: The History of Jewish Philosophy from Biblical Times to Franz Rosenzweig,* translated by David W. Silverman (New York, 1964), in which see the index, s.v. *Afterlife.* Moses Maimonides's *Treatise on Resurrection* has been translated into English by Fred Rosner (New York, 1982), and selected essays dealing with Maimonidean eschatology and its repercussions have been helpfully collected and edited by Jacob Sienstag in *Eschatology in Maimonidean Thought: Messianism, Resurrection, and the World to Come* (New York, 1983), which also contains a bibliography.

On qabbalistic views of the afterlife, the most important discussions are those of Gershom Scholem in *Major Trends in Jewish Mysticism,* 3d ed. (New York, 1961), and *Kabbalah* (New York, 1973). For folk beliefs concerning life after death, see Joshua Trachtenberg's *Jewish Magic and Superstition* (1939; reprint, New York, 1982), pp. 61–68.

New Sources

Avery-Peck, Alan J., and Jacob Neusner, eds. *Judaism in Late Antiquity, Part Four: Death, Afterlife, and the World-to-Come.* Leiden, 2000.

Eylon Ripsman, Dina. *Reincarnation in Jewish Mysticism and Gnosticism.* Lewiston, N.Y., 2003.

Hallote, Rachel S. *Death, Burial and Afterlife in the Biblical World: How the Israelites and Their Neighbors Treated the Dead.* Chicago, 2001.

Lang, Bernhard. "Afterlife: Ancient Israel's Changing Vision of the World Beyond." *Bible Review* 4 (1988): 12–23.

Raphael, Simcha Paull. *Jewish Views of the Afterlife.* Northvale, N.J., 1994.

Scholem, Gershom Gerhard. *On the Mystical Shape of the Godhead: Basic Concepts in the Kabbalah.* Translated by Joachim Neugroschel. Edited by Jonathan Chipman. New York, 1991.

Shekalim, Rami. *Torat ha-nefesh veha-gilgul be-reshit ha-kabalah.* Tel Aviv, 1998.

Wexelman, David M. *The Jewish Concept of Reincarnation and Creation: Based on the Writings of R. Chaim Vital.* Northvale, N.J., 1999.

David Stern (1987)
Revised Bibliography

AFTERLIFE: CHRISTIAN CONCEPTS

Biblical and Ancient Concepts. Early Christians, including the authors of the New Testament books, were steeped in beliefs concerning the impending approach of the end of the world, which would occasion the resurrection of the dead and the beginning of a new aeon. For Jewish people suffering under the oppression of the Roman Empire, "the resurrection of the dead" became a rallying symbol, particularly for those who were led by Pharisaic teachers. This belief set them apart from other segments of contemporary Jewish society, most notably the Sadducees, but also the Gentiles. Belief in the resurrection of the dead also played a crucial role for the emerging circle of Christians, for to Jews *resurrection* meant belief in a hoped-for future occurrence, whereas to Christians it meant a conviction concerning that which had already occurred in the person of Jesus, guaranteeing the future resurrection of all the faithful.

Jesus himself seldom addressed the issue of resurrection, and when he did—usually in response to challenges from his listeners—he always answered with an emphasis on the present need for conversion to a God-oriented life and neighborly love. It was Paul who made resurrection the focal point of his message. Through his encounter with the "risen" Jesus, Paul became convinced that through the resurrection, Jesus, the Christ, conquered sin and death for all humanity. Paul perceived death as running counter to God's creation, which called life into being. Death could not be a part of God's creation; it had entered into human destiny as a result of sin. Sin was the real cause of death; human beings who sinned in and with Adam, the first human, were responsible for their own mortality. Jesus' rising from the dead accomplished the conquest of sin along with its wage, death. Jesus' rising, however, was not a return to the old mortal body (resuscitation); rather, it was a resurrection to a new "spiritual" body.

Coming from a Hebraic background, Paul was unswerving about the body's essentialness to human existence because he saw the body as an integral part of God's creation. Paul insisted on the resurrection of Jesus into a new "body" to conquer death. Using a metaphor familiar to the Pharisaic circle from which he came, Paul explained bodily resurrection as analogous to a grain of wheat that, planted brown into the soil, rises afresh in green the next spring (*1 Cor.* 15: 42–43). Paul's dualism was not between body and soul, the two elements comprising the human being, but between one form of life governed by the flesh and another guided by the spirit. No one who remains in the former could expect salvation and eternal life. One has to be reborn, re-created into a spiritual being—dead to the old self and raised into a new self. This, Paul was convinced, was made possible by the resurrection of Christ.

In the New Testament the *Revelation* to John is the only book that provides a clear scenario of the end times. In *Revelation* the second coming of Jesus, fervently awaited by the early Christians, is presented as the signal for one thousand years of messianic rule, during which martyred Christians will all be resurrected and Satan will be kept bound. After a thousand years of peace and messianic rule, Satan will be unleashed to be permanently defeated in a final battle with the divine forces. With Satan consigned to eternal damnation, a second resurrection will take place in order for the whole of humankind to stand in final judgment. There is no question as to the important role this book played in the life of the early church. It not only provided an inexhaustible source of comfort and encouragement for those who had lost their loved ones to, or themselves suffered the ordeal of, persecution, but it also became a constant source of inspiration to Christians throughout history by giving them images of eternal bliss for the righteous and damnation in a fiery hell for the ungodly.

Apocalyptically conceived Christianity was a movement announcing the quick end of history, and hence, necessarily, its own end. Therefore, when the Christian movement survived beyond the first century it was forced to reevaluate its own stance. It was John's gospel that formed a bridge beyond the initial apocalyptic stage for the enduring presence of Christianity in the ensuing centuries. As the final judgment began to be seen as a distant reality, Christians began thinking about salvation as attainable in the present life. The present moment in life, rather than the end of time, became the crucial point for human existence. Jesus Christ as the Logos of the universe embodies the true meaning of the world, including human life. Turning from the ungodly to a regenerated life by believing in the divine intent embodied in the Logos is the message of the *Gospel of John*, which was written around the turn of the second century CE. The eternal life that is offered by God through Christ can be attained here and now when one's life is turned to God. Eternal life in this context is not endlessness of life but the fullness of life as God had intended in creation. Life lived with God, in itself, would constitute salvation without waiting for the final judgment. In the same way, life lived without God constitutes damnation quite apart from damnation in hell. "Those who believe in him are not condemned; but those who do not believe are condemned already, because they have not believed in the name of the only Son of God" (*Jn.* 3:18).

Though Paul wrestled with the conquest of death, Christians from the outset accepted the mortality of the human being. One must fight spiritual deadness; physical death is unavoidable. Any attempt to see human beings as immortal is rebuffed by God, who alone is eternal. Created beings possess no "natural" immortality of their own. Natural immortality would be an endless life without God's blessing, as seen in a demon that does not have to die the way humans do. During the second century CE Tatian unequivocally rejected such immortality, which he believed could be nothing but a curse. Living endlessly in itself contains no delight; it is living in communion with God that makes life desirable. For this reason, according to Jaroslav Pelikan's interpretation, Christians prefer to use the expression *eternal life* in the sense of being alive in God, both now and always (Pelikan, 1961, p. 23), to avoid the vitiated implication of immortality as a meaningless prolongation of life without God. Thus, Christian faith does not preach the circumvention of death, but rather the acceptance and overcoming of death as exemplified by the cross of Jesus.

A shift in emphasis from the remote eschatological future to the present life became more pronounced on the theological level. The futuristic kingdom of God of the New Testament came increasingly to imply a sphere of influence already present and spreading, a sphere that manifested itself in the visible institution of the earthly church, though it was not identical with it. This is the manner in which Augustine of Hippo (354–430) conceived his "City of God." The City of God was the domain of influence where love of God (*amor dei*) prevailed, whereas the earthly city (*civitas terrena*) was the domain of self-love (*amore sui*). The Roman Empire was the embodiment of the latter, but of course it was not identical with it. Augustine saw the history of humankind as the process through which a drama was unfolding in the struggle between these two forces for ultimate victory. Augustine interpreted early Christian teaching according to the dictates of the changing historical situations in which Christianity had survived. He had little to say about "heaven." It was the City of God transcendent—which manifested itself in the historical unfolding of the power of God—in which Augustine invested his entire theological energy, leaving heaven and hell mostly to the popular imagination.

Medieval and Roman Catholic Concepts. The New Testament addresses the issue of salvation through the death and resurrection of Christ, rather than heaven and hell. Through the centuries, Christian theology has developed along similar lines. It was popular piety, however, which is no less important to Christian life, that fostered and kept alive beliefs about heaven, hell, and purgatory (with increasingly vivid imagery) through the Middle Ages. With the final judgment pushed considerably into the future, people's concern became sharply focused on the fate of the individual immediately after death. The dualism of the soul and the body was firmly established by the Middle Ages, and death was seen as the separation of the soul from the body.

The postmortem journey to heaven or hell became the most widely accepted pattern of understanding the destiny of departed souls. Relying heavily upon pictorial imagery, the soul was often depicted as traveling to or residing in a heaven or hell that was conceptually integrated, and often even physically located, within a three-tiered medieval universe, with heaven always up above and hell down below. For Christians the distinctive accomplishment of Christ was the conquest of death, by which he liberated all the faithful from the yoke of death for entry into heaven, where they might know and enjoy the state for which God had created them in his own image—that is, God-centered and totally free of moral imperfections. Inestimable spiritual rewards would await those who suffered unjustly in this world or toiled for justice's sake; the final truth would be revealed to those who had sought it. In heaven, souls were to be reunited with all the loved ones who had preceded them, even though, apparently, earthly relationships, such as that between husband and wife, were not supposed to be carried over into heaven. In short, ultimate blissfulness characterized this community of all souls who were in fellowship among themselves and with God. This heavenly fellowship was the model for fellowship among Christians (*communio sanctorum*) in this world.

No longer corporeal, citizens of heaven were allowed to "see" God face to face or to "know" him immediately. In this beatific vision, the knowing of God transcended the earthly epistemological gulf between the knower and the known. The blessed would know God in contemplative interpenetration with God's knowing of himself. Thomas Aquinas (1225–1274), the monumental theologian of scholasticism, was the most eloquent proponent of the theology that made this beatific vision the ultimate goal of human beings. Faced with the infinite fullness of God, the created intellect of human beings would never cease to wonder and enjoy the inexhaustible source of knowledge, God himself.

In contrast, hell, evolving from the archaic concept of the underworld called She'ol in the Hebrew scriptures, was initially the place of all the dead, regardless of their earthly deeds. Only later in Jewish history, and then in Christianity, did it become bifurcated into the realm of punishment (hell, *Gehenna*) as distinguished from heaven. Hell came to denote the underworld to which unrepentant sinners were to be consigned. Sinners were to be cast into "outer darkness," with weeping and gnashing of teeth (see *Mt.* 25:30), or they were to be thrown into "eternal" (*Mt.* 25:41) or "unquenchable fire" (*Mk.* 9:43), or even into "a lake that burns with fire and sulfur" (*Rev.* 21:8). It was not so much the New Testament as the teaching of the later church that solidified the concept of hell as a place of punitive torture in which sinners suffer unending pain. Dante's fourteenth-century masterpiece, *Divine Comedy,* is the definitive literary representation of these widespread beliefs about hell, which were established enough to find their way into the teachings of the church.

As heaven and hell were firmly established in the medieval Christian mind into two postmortem realms with such graphic details of celestial blissfulness and ghastly underworld pain, some unresolved practical problems arose in popular piety. The idea of purgatory addressed these problems.

The great majority of Christians believe that they die in a state of moral and religious imperfection, and thus not ready for heaven. For this reason, a belief has come to prevail in popular piety that there should be an intermediate realm between this world and heaven. This realm, called *purgatory,* has no direct references in the Bible, and it only gradually found its way into Christian piety. It was not until the councils of Lyons (1274) and Florence (1439) that the Roman Catholic Church gave it an official definition. In purgatory a process of cleansing and purifying was to take place through the pain of fire. Though the capital (mortal) sins led one directly to hell, venial (minor) sins were to be expurgated in purgatory so that one might be purified enough for admission to heaven.

The idea of *indulgence,* the remission of punishment for venial sins, developed concurrently with purgatory. It was punishment for venial sins that took place in purgatory, from which sinners were expected to emerge cleansed for final beatitude. The indulgence, then, was the remission of this limited punishment in purgatory, or a shortening of the stay therein. As developed by the church, the practice of indulgence involved praying, doing penance, and merit-making in preparation for death and the consequent journey through purgatory. For hundreds of years during the Middle Ages, this practice remained important for Christians in Europe. Further extending the practice, praying and merit-making by the living, not only for themselves but also on behalf of their deceased relatives, developed into a major religious practice, enough for the church to consider it an adequate basis for the institution of the "sale" of indulgences.

Purgatory and the attendant practice of indulgence presupposed several other beliefs: first, the belief in sin that called for retribution even after Christ has accomplished reconciliation (redemption and forgiveness); second, the practice of indulgence, especially the sale of it, being based on the belief in a "treasury of merit" accumulated over time from the surplus merit bequeathed to the church by all the saints throughout history, as well as by Christ himself; and finally, the belief that the church possessed the authority to administer the said treasury and dispense merits as deemed fit, with the pope holding, as it were, the key.

Protestant Concepts. It is well known that financial abuse of the belief in purgatory and indulgences and the manner in which the church raised funds using them ignited the Protestant Reformation. The sale of indulgences provoked Martin Luther (1483–1546) into uttering diatribes such as, "No doubt the majority [of the papacy] would starve to death if purgatory did not exist." "How can you," he continued, "bear on your conscience the blasphemous fraud of purgatory, by which treacherous deception they have made fools of all the world and have falsely frightened it and stolen practically all their possessions and splendor?" (Plass, 1959, vol. 1, p. 388). Luther's ninety-five theses of 1517 were a direct assault upon the sale of indulgences. Luther considered the need for sin to be further punished after redemption as undermining the meaning of the death of Jesus. Following Luther's lead, Protestant Christians rejected all teachings concerning purgatory and indulgence.

Important in all of this is the medieval Catholic frame of reference in which things were viewed in terms of "substance," with "quantity" as the predicate. This was largely due to the influence of Aristotelian philosophy during the scholastic period. In the context of indulgences, sin and grace were considered in quantitative terms. The distinction between mortal and venial sins was as much a quantitative distinction as it was a qualitative one. Thus, even within venial sins, degrees of offense were differentiated and expurgated accordingly.

For Protestants, sin amounted to consciously ignoring or distrusting God. There were no degrees of offense once one turned one's back on God. Likewise, grace, for Protestants, was God's loving acceptance of sinners, through his sacrifice and forgiveness. There were no gradations of grace. When Luther declared that salvation could be attained by grace alone (*sola gratia*), he meant that grace is the universal act of God reconciling humankind to himself, whether sinners acknowledge it or not. The Roman Catholic conception of grace, on the other hand, was thoroughly substantial, permitting the linguistic habit of referring to it as an entity capable of being, as it were, injected into sinners. Thomas Aquinas made frequent reference to this "infusion of grace." Thus, substantialized grace could be further quantified into something measurable, just as sin was measured and expiated accordingly.

Even though at the close of the sixteenth century the Council of Trent rectified, by officially condemning, the abuse of the sale of indulgences, the Roman Catholic Church did not alter its basic posture toward the belief in purgatory and indulgence. With renewed vigor the council reaffirmed the fundamental structure of Roman Catholic soteriology, along with the worldview that sustains it. The quantitative and substantial ways of viewing sin and grace were maintained as valid, and indulgence and purgatory continued to be accepted beliefs within Roman Catholic piety and theology.

Luther, who was largely responsible for the pattern of subsequent Protestant attitudes toward salvation and eternal life, considered the Pauline interpretation of salvation as "justification by faith" to be the single most important teaching of the Bible. No one devoted more energy to bringing this Pauline teaching to the center of Christian religion than

Luther, who believed that salvation lies not so much in the context of the final judgment, the bodily resurrection, and the messianic rule, as in Christian life, lived in faith, consequent to "justification." Like Augustine, Luther rebuked millenarians by arguing that "this false notion is lodged not only in the apostles (*Acts* 1:6), but also in the chiliasts, Valentinians, the Tertullians, who played the fool with the idea that before Judgment Day the Christians alone will possess the earth and that there will be no ungodly" (Plass, 1959, vol. 1, p. 284). Luther brushed aside ideas about the imminent approach of the end, particularly the way the advent—that is, the physical establishment of messianic rule on earth—was anticipated by some millenarians. Though Luther did not dismiss the last judgment, he did not lend the full weight of his theological articulation to the eschatological concept of the general resurrection. For Luther, it was the justified life that counts. Justification carries the entire weight of soteriological and eschatological significance when Luther says that "the article of justification, which is our only protection, not only against all the powers and plottings of men but also against the gates of hell, is this: by faith alone (*sola fide*) in Christ, without works, are we declared just (*pronuntiari justos*) and saved" (Plass, 1959, vol. 2, p. 701).

It is thus clear that "eternal life" was to be experienced in the reality of the justified life here and now. For Luther the ideas of immortality and heavenly blissfulness, which played such an important part in popular Christian piety, were absorbed into the significance of eternity invested in the justified life of a Christian. This remains the predominant pattern of the Protestant understanding of eternal life, at least in its normative theological sense.

BIBLIOGRAPHY

Black, C. Clifton. "Pauline Perspectives on Death and *Romans* 5–8." *Journal of Biblical Literature* 103 (1984): 413–433.

Bruce, F. F. "Paul and the Life to Come." In *Paul: Apostle of the Heart Set Free.* Grand Rapids, Mich., 1977.

Hick, John. *Death and Eternal Life.* London, 1976.

Keck, Leander. "New Testament Views of Death." In *Perspectives on Death,* edited by Liston O. Mills. Nashville, 1969.

McDannell, Colleen, and Bernhard Lang. *Heaven: A History.* London and New Haven, Conn., 1988. 2d ed., 2001.

Pelikan, Jaroslav. *The Shape of Death: Life, Death, and Immortality in the Early Fathers.* Nashville, 1961.

Plass, Ewald M., comp. and ed. *What Luther Says: An Anthology.* 3 vols. Saint Louis, Mo., 1959.

Rahner, Karl. "On the Theology of Death." In *Modern Catholic Thinkers,* edited by A. Robert Caponigri, pp. 138–176. New York, 1960.

Rist, Martin. "Millennium." In *Interpreter's Dictionary of the Bible,* vol. 3, pp. 381–382. Nashville, 1962.

Schnackenburg, Rudolf. "The Idea of Life in the Fourth Gospel." In *The Gospel according to St. John,* translated by Cecily Hastings et al., vol. 2, pp. 352–361. New York, 1982.

Setzer, Claudia. "Resurrection of the Dead as Symbol and Strategy." *Journal of the American Academy of Religion* 69, no. 1 (2001): 65–101.

Stannard, David. *The Puritan Way of Death: A Study on Religion, Culture, and Social Change.* New York, 1977.

Stendahl, Krister, ed. *Immortality and Resurrection: Four Essays.* New York, 1965.

Van de Walle, A. R. *From Darkness to the Dawn.* Mystic, Conn., 1984.

Hiroshi Obayashi (2005)

AFTERLIFE: ISLAMIC CONCEPTS

The doctrine of an afterlife is not only a frequent theme within the Qurʾanic revelation, it is also central to the way in which Muslims have understood and explained the reasons for humankind's existence in this world. In Muslim thought, the notion of an afterlife is not only seen as giving meaning to what is a short-lived stay on this earth—with all that it entails of seemingly inexplicable human suffering, loss, and death—but it also places humankind within a divine plan, which endows them with a sense of purpose and an ultimate destiny. The knowledge of a future life beyond death, the quality of which will be determined by the moral quality of one's life on earth, has served to instill in Muslims a constant awareness of both the precarious nature of this existence and the urgent need to prepare for that future one. This urgency had manifested itself from the outset, both in the revealed text of the Qurʾān, the foundation stone of all Muslim dogma and ritual, and in the formative intellectual history of the community.

Afterlife in the Qurʾān. According to Muslim tradition, the revelations of the Qurʾān—that is, the verses (*āyāt*) that make up the chapters (*sūrahs*)—are ascribed to one of two periods of Muḥammad's prophetic career, the earlier Meccan period and the later Medinan one. The apocalyptic passages and images in the Qurʾān that herald the coming of the next life belong primarily to the former. Indeed, they constitute one of the most salient features of the earlier phase of Muḥammad's preaching, testifying to the importance of the notion of an afterlife within the overall framework of the Qurʾanic message.

The apocalypse. The apocalypse, as the climax of history, is referred to variously as "the Day of Judgement" *(yawm al-dīn)*, "the Day of Resurrection" *(yawm al-qiyāma)*, "the Last Day" *(al-yawm al-ākhir)*, "the Day of Decision" *(yawm al-faṣl)*, or "the Promised Day" *(al-yawm al-mawʿūd)*. The eschatological scheme and its accompanying symbols that usher in the next world is one familiar enough from the Judeo-Christian, and to some extent the Zoroastrian, tradition. The basic elements are, in brief: The next world will arrive in the wake of the destruction of this one—at an unknown point in time, referred to as the "Hour" (*al-sāʿa*), unknown to all but God, the blowing of a cosmic trumpet(*ṣūr*) will annihilate all creatures and destroy the familiar universe; a second sounding of the trumpet will resurrect all humankind to face the final reckoning. Every soul *(nafs)* is called to contemplate its "book" (*kitāb*) of deeds, and its deeds will be weighed in "scales" (*mīzān*). A light balance will dispense a soul to hell, whereas a weighty one will merit paradise. The "wretched" (*shaqī*), their faces blackened in terror and despair, are driven like animals to their final abode, and with their hands bound in fetters to their necks they are thrust violently into the fire of hell, where they are drenched in liquid pitch, their skins are consumed by the fire, and their faces are grilled by its flames. They suffer beatings with maces of iron, gulp fetid boiling water, taste festering blood and consume a bush of bitter thorn in the midst of scorching winds and thick black smoke.

The "fortunate" (*saʿīd*), are congratulated and led away in the company of angels towards the already-opened gates of paradise, the light of divine pleasure radiating from within them and all around them. They take up their paradisiacal abodes in the "Gardens of Eden" (*jannāt ʿAdan*), each one of them in an exclusive garden, wherein they recline on jewel-encrusted beds, dressed in the finest silk, arrayed in heavy brocade, and adorned with silver bracelets; surrounded by bashful and amorous virgins (*ḥūr*) resembling hidden pearls, they are waited on by stunningly beautiful youths who serve them the purest intoxicants, bring them endless varieties of fruits, and are constantly at their service.

Eternal life and the hereafter. The Qurʾanic idea of continued existence and eternal life in the hereafter functions not only as a consolation for believers, in view of the tribulations inherent in life on earth, it is also intended as an incentive for humankind to believe, to perform good deeds, and to reap the reward. For, the "other life" (*ākhira*, lit. "final one"), as the Qurʾān tells us, is "better" and "more enduring" (Qurʾān 87:17) than this life; "the life of this world is but amusement and play; it is the life to come that is the true life" (Qurʾān 29:64). The delights of this world, according to the Qurʾān, are transient, ultimately unsatisfying, and generally adulterated in some way. The delights in the next world, however, will be eternal, endlessly enjoyed, and absolutely pure. It is the way in which the earthly quality of these familiar delights will be redefined—transformed—that is crucial. Thus, in paradise, the houris, the wide-eyed beautiful virgins, will not have been touched by either human or *jinn* (Qurʾān 55:56); the rivers will run with "water unstaling," with "milk forever fresh," with "the clearest honey," and with "wine that is a delight to the drinkers" (Qurʾān 47:15); their drink therein "will not cause their heads to throb, nor will it make them lose their reason" (Qurʾān 56:19); the cup they will pass from one to another will inspire "no idle talk, no sinful urge" (Qurʾān 52:23). Muslim tradition would later add numerous narratives to the descriptions of paradise that emphasized the pure nature of one's existence in the next world, an existence free of the vile bodily functions of this world. One early *ḥadīth* reported by ʿAbd al-Razzāq al-Ṣanʿānī (d. 827) in his compilation of traditions (*Muṣannaf*) describes the first band of those entering paradise thus: "their faces shall resemble the full moon; they will excrete no mucus, neither will they salivate or ever need to defecate."

An indication of the centrality of the afterlife within the overall Qurʾanic narrative is that almost every act forbidden or condemned by the Qurʾān, as well as every deed commended and encouraged by it, is done so with a view to the consequences of that action or behavior for a person's fate in the next life. Thus, those who violate God's covenants are described as having "purchased the life of this world at the price of the life to come" (Qurʾān 2:86 and 3:77). In contrast, it is written that "God has purchased from the believers their selves and their worldly possessions and in return has promised them Paradise" (Qurʾān 9:111). Indeed, the Qurʾān describes the "true losers" as "those who have forfeited their souls and their relatives on the Day of Resurrection" (Qurʾān 42:45), because, having offered nothing for their future life, they now find themselves in eternal hellfire.

But whereas the Qurʾān contains frequent references to scenes that will take place on the day of judgement, as well as graphic descriptions of the pleasures enjoyed by the "inhabitants of the Garden" (*aṣḥāb al-janna*) and the torments suffered by the "inhabitants of the Fire" (*aṣḥāb*, or *ahl*, *al-nār*), crucial elements of eschatology, which had significant consequences for the scheme of the afterlife, were only worked out in the wake of intra-Muslim sectarian polemics; yet even these elements had not taken long, in historical terms, to crystallize. Already within little more than a hundred years of the Prophet's death and the codification of the Qurʾān, there emerged all of the eschatological variations and modifications to the afterlife scheme, as they are known from the compositions of the classical period, and as they are familiar to Muslims today. It was at this formative stage that the second instance of "urgency," referred to at the beginning of this article, manifested itself.

THE FORMATIVE PERIOD (C. 657–800). Two civil wars that split the community definitively within a generation of the Prophet's death and resulted in major schisms that exist in modern times were fought over the question of the rightful leadership of the community. This was not only because the rightful leader (*imām*) was necessary for the overall guidance and well-being of the community, but, more importantly, because an illegitimate leader put the salvation of the entire community at risk by endangering the afterlife scheme (as understood by all early Muslims) in which the elect community of believers were a single guided community destined for Paradise.

What seemed like purely political disagreements went to the heart of religion, for, in early Islam political opponents were necessarily religious ones too: if the leadership of the elect community of believers was to be assumed by the wrong individual, who then led them astray from the path to salvation, the entire community ran the risk of being misled. Political offences, violating as they did the stipulations of the Qurʾān, prompted similar questions about the salvation status of grave sinners within the Muslim community and, paradoxically, forced Muslims to consider a formal definition of what constituted "belief" (*īmān*). In other words, given that there is a single community of believers destined for paradise, how did one remain within it, and what offenses excluded one from it?

Discussion of the consequences of serious offenses had been confined, at a primary stage, to the political arena, but more and more discussions came to focus on grave violations of the Qurʾanic stipulations for proper moral conduct. In time, an increasingly influential group of Muslim theologians, known as traditionalists (*ahl al-ḥadīth*), came up with a compromise to the simple afterlife scheme that had been assumed by the community at its birth. The compromise was both the result of protracted debates over the salvation status of political "sinners" (religious offenders) within the Muslim community, and the political reality that frequently saw Muslim pitted in battle against fellow Muslim. These traditionalist theologians modified certain aspects of the postmortem judgement to ensure that all those who professed Islam, even if they should die without having repented of their sins, would eventually end up in paradise: if they did go to hell, they would suffer only a purgatorial stay, one consonant with the severity of their neglect of religious duties.

It should be noted that the traditionalists believed that authoritative opinions (legal and theological) could only be found in the mass of traditions (reports containing words and deeds) ascribed to the Prophet and his Companions. This body of literature, authenticated (in the sense that it was believed to go back to the Prophet), but collected and transmitted from the late seventh and early to mid-eighth centuries CE, had grown to huge proportions. It was within this body of traditions that those eschatological variations, which were used to modify the scheme of the afterlife, began to appear. The traditionalists made such variations authoritative by weaving them into the exegetical narratives to certain key verses in the Qurʾān. These verses included one that was ambiguous about the eternality of hellfire punishment (Qurʾān 11:107); another that suggested that certain individuals whose evil deeds may counterbalance their good ones, and would thus merit neither paradise nor hell (Qurʾān 7:46); and finally, two verses that were interpreted as proof of the widely held belief that the Prophet will intercede for his community on the day of judgement (Qurʾān 17:79, 93:5).

By associating such extra-scriptural elements with these Qurʾanic verses, the traditionalists were able to introduce a modified scheme of the otherworldly fate of the Muslim community. The canonical manuals of *ḥadīth*, without exception, state that no Muslim will remain in hell forever. Some will be removed from hell directly through God's intervention, whereas others will exit from it because, as the manuals inform us, the Prophet will intercede for the grave sinners of his community (minor offenses were automatically forgiven by God, so long as grave ones were avoided [Qurʾān 4:31]). Neither of these two doctrines had been explicitly taught in the Qurʾān. Nevertheless, they came to represent dogma for most Muslims. In so doing, the traditionalists had succeeded in retaining, at least superficially, the early ideal of the unified community destined for paradise.

Khārijite, Murjiʾite, and Muʿtazilite thought. Of course, not all parties were convinced by the theological innovations of the traditionalists. Two religio-political parties that had emerged in the wake of the civil wars, namely, the Khārijites (the first sectarians in Islam) and the Murjiʾa (an antisectarian movement that sought to politically reunite the divided community), resisted the influx of such teachings as having no explicit foundation in the Qurʾān. In addition, Muʿtazilah (a late-eighth-century theological school that propounded the use of rational methods and made God's justice—together with the idea of human free will—the founding principles of their thought) also saw no sound basis for either the idea of a temporary hell or the Prophet's intercession (*shafaʿa*) on behalf of grave sinners. For these rationalists, both ideas violated their principle that God's justice ensured that every individual was free to chose his or her acts in this life and would be recompensed accordingly in the next.

Needless to say, it was the traditionalist doctrine that found popular appeal among the majority of Muslims, who took comfort in the knowledge that the Prophet would be at hand to ensure their salvation at the scene of the judgement. It is noteworthy that the Muʿtazila also denied the punishment of the tomb (*ʿadhāb al-qabr*) and the "vision of God" (*ruʾyat Allāh*) in the next life, both of which, judging by the *ḥadīth* material, had come to form part of the popular beliefs of Muslims from the middle of the eighth century.

THE CLASSICAL PERIOD (POST-800 CE). Most of the developments in afterlife theology that took place during the formative period made their way into the major traditions of Islam. The doctrine of temporary hell and the Prophet's intercession were accepted by almost all Sunnīs and Shīʿah. The only difference was that in the case of the latter, the privilege of intercession was also extended to the *imāms* (with the understanding that no Shīʿī will remain in hell forever). With Sufism, however, it is difficult to make similar generalizations.

Early in its development, Sufism, properly mysticism, came to assume a certain "orthodoxy" from the point of view of traditionalist Islam. The principal figures associated with its development, the likes of al-Ḥasan al-Baṣrī (d. 728), al-Ḥārith al-Muḥāsibī (d. 857), and al-Junayd b. Muḥammad (d. 910) were all considered pious Muslims by the mainstream tradition. Classical Sufism to a large extent culminated in the works and writings of al-Ghazālī (d. 1111) himself, a bastion of traditionalist Islam. And yet Sufism would later incorporate Neoplatonic and Gnostic elements, as evidenced in the works of the great Andalusian mystic Ibn al-ʿArabī (1165–1240), elements that could not be accepted by the mainstream tradition. Sufism shared with other mainstream Muslim practice an insistence on the proper observation of the law (*sharīʿah*). Indeed, it emphasized that the practice of Islam's rituals should be carried out with discipline and devotion: constant remembrance of God (*dhikr*), a quintessential Ṣūfī practice, and the awareness of impending death and resurrection was the only way to prepare oneself for the next world.

One significant development in the classical period, in part due to the influence of Neoplatonic thought as expounded principally by Avicenna (d. 1037), but already suggested at an earlier stage by some of the rationalist theologians, the Muʿtazilah—as well as by their more orthodox counterparts, the Ashʿarīs, was the question of whether the Qurʾanic descriptions of the joys of paradise and the pains of hell should be understood literally or symbolically. The rationalists, while acknowledging the explicit scriptural references to carnal pleasures and pains, preferred to understand these as metaphors for spiritual delights and torments. The spiritual aspect became key, not just for rationalist theologians but also for philosophers and certain mystics. If, indeed, the afterlife was to be a spiritual existence of the immortal soul, then humans, through their souls, could "taste" of these joys in this world.

It is in this sense that, for many mystics, elements of the eschaton and the afterlife were internalized as constituting potential experiences of the soul in the here and now. In a similar departure from the traditionalist conception of the afterlife, the philosophers saw death—and not the resurrection—as the beginning of the next life: at the point of death the soul will be freed from its bodily incarceration and able to enjoy the superior delights of the intellect. A preference for metaphorical interpretations would reemerge in twentieth-century reformist writings, such as those of Muḥammad ʿAbduh (1849–1905) and Muḥammad Rashīd Riḍā (d. 1935).

TWENTIETH-CENTURY APPROACHES. The little that is written about the afterlife in the modern day tends to be a regurgitation of ideas and narratives taken from the classical period. In this respect, many contemporary scholars adopt the traditionalist understanding of a physical resurrection together with a literalist conception of the joys and pains of the afterlife. There are exceptions, however, and these can generally be found in the interpretations of so-called liberal or progressive Muslim thinkers.

In developing a methodology that seeks to connect the revealed text and the realities of the modern world, progressive Muslim thinkers recognize the difficulty of embracing a literal conception of the Qurʾanic descriptions of the afterlife, let alone a physical resurrection of the body. One example is the Syrian thinker Mohamad Shahrour (b. 1938). In his *al-Kitāb waʾl-Qurʾān* (The book and the Qurʾān), he argues that a different physical world will come into being in the wake of the destruction of this one. This transition will also constitute a transformation of the laws governing matter. Thus, there will be a physical reconstitution of bodies in the next world. But these other laws will mean that matter will not be subject to the opposing forces inherent in the nature of matter, forces responsible for the decay and breakdown of all things: thus, in the next world, nothing will die nor will anything be born.

Another example can be seen in *Qurʾān and Woman*, the African American intellectual Amina Wadud's (b. 1952) book that stresses, "Although the detailed and graphic depictions of the Hereafter [. . .] are sometimes quite explicit, it is obvious that these descriptions are not to be taken entirely literally, [they] are the Qurʾān's way of making the ineffable effable, of making the Unseen phenomena conceivable"(p. 58).

And yet, the idea that there will be some sort of reconstitution of a material form—that is, a corporeal afterlife—has always maintained its hold on the imagination of believers.

POPULAR PIETY. Whereas remembrance of the transience of this world and reflection on the imminent arrival of the other constitute a central element in Muslim devotions across the confessional divide, nowhere is the concern with the reality of the afterlife more obvious than in the rites performed for the dying and the dead. An early Islamic Egyptian epitaph, dated to 796 CE, bears the following inscription, intended as a supplication for relief for the dead person in his tomb: "[O God] make spacious its [the tomb's] entrances and spare him [the dead person] the punishment of the tomb" (*RCEA*, no. 58). Another epitaph, from near modern-day Cairo, dated to 831 CE, asks God to make the dead person's tomb "like a garden from the gardens of Paradise" (*RCEA*, no. 204).

Awareness of the imminence of the other world, that is to say, the need to prepare for it within the brief prelude that is this life, is reflected in the symbiotic relationship that manifests itself between the living and the dead. The dying person has the Shahādah, the profession of the faith, whispered into his or her ear. At the point of burial, the dead are "instructed" (*talqīn*) by the living to give the correct answers (in the form of God's Oneness and Muḥammad's prophethood) to the questioning that they will face in their graves (*masʾalat al-qabr*) at the hands of the two angels Munkar and Nakīr (also a relic of popular belief from the classical period). Prayer manuals, Sunnī, Shīʿī, and Ṣūfī, are replete with invocations—usually performed before the dead—that articulate the awareness on the part of the living that they will soon share the fate of the former. Muslims have always said prayers for their dead in the hope that when their time comes others will say prayers for them. Inscriptions on tombs usually enjoin the passersby to recite the *fātiḥa*, the opening verse of the Qurʾān. Not only does this provide comfort for the dead, it also secures a double reward for the one reciting it: the reward for the action itself and the knowledge, supported by numerous *ḥadīths*, that the Qurʾān intercedes at the resurrection for whoever recites from it.

However one interpreted the depictions of the afterlife in the Qurʾān, whether literally, spiritually, or metaphorically, all Muslims, be they Sunnīs, Shīʿīs, Ṣūfīs or philosophers, agreed that the value of these scriptural narratives lay in emphasizing the importance of leading a "moral" life: the reward of the hereafter was too great to forfeit.

SEE ALSO Attributes of God, article on Islamic Concepts; Eschatology, article on Islamic Eschatology; Free Will and Predestination, article on Islamic Concepts; God, article on God in Islam; Imān and Islām; Islam, overview article.

BIBLIOGRAPHY

Jane Idleman Smith and Yvonne Yazbeck Haddad's *The Islamic Understanding of Death and Resurrection* (Albany, N.Y., 1981; Oxford, 2002), remains the best introduction to the general topic of the afterlife. Although it focuses mainly on the Sunnī tradition, its information on the modern understanding of the relevant themes and one interesting appendix on women and children in the afterlife is useful. However, one of the best works on Muslim piety and religious life, including contemporary practices, is Constance E. Padwick's *Muslim Devotions: A Study of Prayer-Manuals in Common Use* (Oxford, 1961; rev. ed. 1997), which examines a range of Muslim devotions and supplications (including those relating to death and the afterlife) and provides extracts from Sunnī, Shīʿī and Ṣūfī prayer manuals. The book is a unique study in this respect and is indispensable for those interested in Muslim practice as opposed to theory.

For more detailed information on the individual elements of the eschaton and themes of the afterlife, the reader is referred to the *Encyclopedia of Islam* (2d. ed. Leiden, 1954–2002), although these will require a familiarity with Arabic transliteration: see in particular, "ʿadhāb al-ḳabr" (vol. I, p. 186), "aʿrāf" (vol. I, p. 603), "barzakh" (vol. I, p. 1071), "djanna" (vol. II, p. 447), "ḳiyāma" (vol. V, p. 235), "maʿād" (vol. V, p. 892), "munkar wa-nakīr" (vol. VII, p. 576), "sāʿa" (vol. VIII, p. 654), "shafāʿa" (vol. IX, p. 177). A more accessible recent work, with the entries given in English, is the *Encyclopedia of the Qurʾān*, edited by J. D. McAuliffe et al. (Leiden, 2000–). The work is still in progress, but the following entries may now be consulted: "Eschatology," "Hell and Hellfire," "Intercession." Other projected entries are "Last Judgement," "Paradise," "Resurrection."

Unfortunately, there are to date no complete studies of the Muslim afterlife. A few translations of primary texts on this theme have appeared, most importantly al-Ghazālī's *The Remembrance of Death and the Afterlife: Kitāb dhikr al-mawt wa-mā baʿdahu,* Book XL of the *Revival of the Religious Sciences, Ihyāʾ ʿUlūm al-Dīn,* translated with an introduction and notes by T. J. Winter (Cambridge, U.K., 1989). For a study of the specific contribution of sectarian polemic to the formation of Sunnī classical doctrine on the concepts of temporary hell and intercession, with specific reference to Qurʾanic exegesis, see Feras Hamza, "To Hell and Back: A Study of the Concepts of Hell and Intercession in Early Islam" (Ph.D. diss., Oxford University, 2002).

An important work is Soubhi el-Saleh's "La vie future selon le Coran," which can be found in the journal *Études Musulmanes* no. 13 (1971), or as a separate publication (Paris, 1971). Saleh traces the various ways in which the delights of Paradise and the torments of hell were understood according to four types of Qurʾanic commentaries, roughly representing four phases of Muslim exegesis: traditionalist, rationalist, mystic, and modern; the author examines the important question of whether these aspects of the afterlife were understood as being physical or spiritual in each of the four classes of commentaries. For an exposition of the persistently "carnal" attitude towards the delights of Paradise, with a literary focus, see A. al-Azmeh, "On the Morphology of Paradisiac Narratives," *Journal of Arabic Literature* 26 (1995), pp. 215–231.

***Shiʿi* material**

Martin J. McDermott's *The Theology of al-Shaikh al-Mufīd (d. 413/1022)* (Beirut, Lebanon, 1978) provides a Twelver Shīʿī perspective on the principal elements of the eschaton; Mahmoud Ayoub has looked at the devotional aspects of Twelver practices in his *Redemptive Suffering in Islam: A Study of the Devotional Aspects of ʿĀshūrāʾ in Twelver Shīʿism* (The Hague, 1978). A useful introduction to Twelver beliefs may now be found in *Doctrines of Shiʿi Islam: A Compendium of Imami Beliefs and Practices by Ayatollah Jaʿfar Sobhani,* translated and edited by Reza Shah-Kazemi (London, 2001), esp. pp. 120–136.

A validation of the female voice in the Qurʾān, together with the consequences for understanding the scriptural depictions of the hereafter, is given by Amina Wadud, *Qurʾān and Woman* (Kuala Lumpur, 1992), esp. pp. 44–61. Fatima Mernissi's *Women in Moslem Paradise* (New Delhi, 1986) is also interesting for its female perspective.

The tomb inscriptions referred to above are taken from the *Répertoire chronologique d'epigraphie arabe* (*RCEA*), edited by Etienne Combe et al. (Cairo, 1931-1991), see vol. 1, nos. 58 and 204.

In addition, the bibliography provided under the entry "Eschatology (Islamic Eschatology)" complements the one given here.

FERAS Q. HAMZA (2005)

AFTERLIFE: GREEK AND ROMAN CONCEPTS

As is the case with other cultures, the Greeks and Romans entertained a variety of ideas about the afterlife, some of which were mutually exclusive; they called on different ideas as the situation required. Thus, they spoke of the dead as present and angry when ill luck and a guilty conscience suggested that the deceased might be wreaking vengeance; they spoke of them as potential benefactors when paying them cult; and on yet other occasions they spoke of them as if they were completely absent from the world of the living. Both because the attitudes varied and because our information for this, as well as most other aspects of Greek and Roman antiquity, is lacunose, any survey, including the one that follows, tends to impose an artificial order on what were actually complex matters.

GREECE. Although the Greeks and Romans shared many beliefs and practices concerning death, there were also significant differences between the two cultures and they must be treated separately. Greece will be considered first.

Funerary rituals. Children and other surviving kin were expected to ensure that the dead received proper funerary rites; if they did not, the deceased could not be considered truly dead and its soul might wander restlessly between the upper world and the underworld. What constituted "proper rites" varied from place to place and time to time, but honorable disposal of the corpse by burial or cremation was the very least that was required, lest the corpse otherwise become prey for scavengers. Even symbolic burial, such as Antigone performed for her brother by sprinkling dust over his body, would suffice (Sophocles, *Antigone* 254–255). If a body were irretrievable, rites might be performed for the deceased anyway, in hopes that the soul would find rest (e.g., *Odyssey* 1.290–292). People who turned up alive after having had such rites performed were called "double-fated" *(deuteropotmoi)* and had to undergo a symbolic rebirth (Plutarch, *Roman Questions* 264f–265b; cf. Euripides, *Alcestis* 1144–1146).

Ideally, the deceased's female relatives would wash the body on the same day as death had occurred and wrap it in a shroud for burial. The next day would be given over to mourning—the informal mourning of family members being supplemented with that of hired mourners when the family could afford it and the sumptuary laws of the city allowed it. Gifts would be given to the deceased, including small objects such as he or she would have used in life. On the third day, counting inclusively, the body was buried or cremated. Libations were poured into the grave where the body or ashes had been buried and were repeated periodically, usually for at least a year. Survivors might also cut their hair and lay it upon the grave; an absent survivor could dedicate hair at a later date. A marker was set up and could be decorated with ribbons and myrtle branches. Other rituals might also be performed, depending on the desires of the deceased and his or her family. People who had no family could join funerary associations that ensured all of these rites would be carried out. (On burial rites, see Kurtz and Boardman, 1971).

Ghosts. Although any soul could become a ghost—that is, return to wander among the living—the souls that lacked proper funerary rites and the souls of those who had died too early or violently were particularly likely to return in order to cause problems for people whom they blamed for their misfortunes or people whom they envied. Whole groups of people might suffer because a soul was unhappy: cities beset by famine and pestilence sometimes sought relief by paying special cult to the ghosts of local individuals whom they assumed were causing the problems. There were means of averting ghosts as well; wreaths of a thorny plant called *rhamnos* were hung on doors and windows in the belief that this would prevent ghosts from entering a house (Photius, *Lexicon* under "*rhamnos*"). In some parts of Greece, annual festivals such as the Anthesteria invited ghosts back into the world of the living and treated them well for a few days; the underlying logic seems to have been that if the ghosts were satisfied by this extra attention they would remain peaceful for the rest of the year. Even then, however, special precautions were taken to ensure that the returning ghosts did not take too many liberties while among the living, or outstay their welcome. Other festivals, such as the Genesia (a word formed on the *gen-* root, meaning "birth" in the sense of those related to one by birth), honored dead relatives, but it is unclear whether the dead were expected to actually return at these times or simply enjoyed the festival from within the underworld.

Sometimes ghosts were useful. Specialists knew how to create small lead "curse" tablets engraved with words that compelled ghosts to return to the land of the living and do their bidding. Typically, the specialist commanded the ghost to attack someone on behalf of a paying client. The ghost might be charged with imposing insomnia on a woman whom the client loved, for example, in hopes that she would acquiesce to his demands. It was not only the ghosts' victims who feared such activities; the ghosts themselves resented being called up from their rest in the underworld. For this reason, practitioners frequently focused on the ghosts of those who had died too early or unhappily, or whose bodies were unburied, because, as mentioned above, the souls of such unfortunates could not really enter the underworld, and thus they were more readily accessible (they were also, in their anger, probably more ready to injure the living). The specialists might also promise the ghost that, if it cooperated once, the specialist would protect it from ever being bothered again. The ghosts of dead heroes were considered stronger than ordinary ghosts and were expected to help the living with all sorts of problems: they helped women conceive, aided their native cities during war, and gave prophetic advice, for example. Heroic ghosts, however, could also be much more dangerous than other ghosts when angry. (On ghosts, see Johnston, 1999.)

The land of the dead. Souls might return to earth as ghosts, but most souls, most of the time, stayed in the underground kingdom called Hades, which was ruled over by a god who was also named Hades and by his queen, Persephone. In earliest times, the Greeks seem to have believed that everyone there was treated in the same way. The souls existed in a state that was neither pleasant nor unpleasant; literary portrayals, such as that in Book 11 of the *Odyssey*, suggest that the underworld was dank and dark, and that there was little to do to pass eternal time. In the *Odyssey* and elsewhere, souls usually are portrayed as looking like their former bodies (thus women who were famous beauties while alive remained attractive, and mighty warriors still wore their armor). Souls also retained the desires and grudges they held while alive: the soul of Ajax, who felt he had been cheated by Odysseus while alive, refused to return Odysseus's greeting when they met in the underworld. And yet, in spite of the other ways in which life after death replicated what went on before, the souls lacked one of the most important abilities they had while alive: they could not communicate with the living except under special circumstances. In the *Odyssey*, it is only after Odysseus pours out the blood of a ritually slaughtered ram for them to drink that the souls can chat with him (this probably is a reflection, although exaggerated, of normal funerary ritual, which includes pouring libations into the grave). Physical contact is impossible, too, because souls have no substance: Odysseus cannot embrace his mother's ghost.

A few people do suffer punishment in a special part of the underworld according to the *Odyssey* and other Greek literary texts, although it is not clear whether the Greeks considered them to be truly dead or to have been transported to the underworld while still alive. Among the most famous are Tantalos, who endures eternal thirst and hunger, and Sisyphos, who is doomed to push a boulder uphill repeatedly. But these are unusual cases of people who had done unusually wicked things; there is no indication that the average person expected to be punished after death. There are also examples, in myth, of people who get extraordinary rewards at the end of their lives, due to their special relationships with the gods. Menelaus, Helen's husband and therefore Zeus's son-in-law, knew he would be carried off to the paradisiacal Elysian Fields at the end of his life, for example, instead of dying (*Odyssey* 4.561–569).

Myth also tells of judges in the underworld. Most commonly mentioned in this role are Minos, the former king of Crete, who was renowned for his fair judgments; his brother Rhadamanthys, who had been a lawgiver in Crete; and Aeacus, who had ruled Aegina. These judges are presented as settling disputes among the dead, rather than deciding the fate of a newly arrived soul; in other words, they also continue with "life" in much the same way as they had before death (e.g., *Odyssey* 11.568–571). It is only in certain mystery cults or philosophical contexts that we hear of judgments or tests that determine the fate of the soul upon its arrival (see below). Aeacus sometimes serves as the gatekeeper for Hades instead of one of its judges. Kerberos, the many-headed dog of Hades, whom the dead souls had to distract with a piece of food in order to enter the land of the dead (and who prevented the souls from ever leaving again), and Charon, who ferried souls across the river Styx, which divided the world of the dead from the world of the living, played a similar role insofar as they also helped to mark the boundary between life and death. In doing this, they made death seem more permanent and irreversible, but they also made the transition seem more familiar, more like the transitions one encountered in life. Most of these figures are mythic only; however, it is unlikely that the Greeks really "believed" in them. Charon is the possible exception: by the Hellenistic period, people began to bury coins with their dead, with which the souls could pay for their passage across the river. The god Hermes, in his role as Psychopompos (guide of souls), was also a figure of real cult. He was expected to help the soul reach the underworld safely and also to guide it back and forth to the upper world again when necessary (for example, during the Anthesteria, when the soul's family needed its help or when a specialist called on it to harm an enemy).

In contrast to the earliest Greek beliefs, the late archaic period saw the development of a system in which the common person might expect to receive either rewards or punishments after death; this concept was fairly widespread by the classical period. In most cases, one's lot was said to depend on one's behavior while alive—things were supposed to be evened up after death. (On the underworld and punishments after death, see Johnston, 1999, and Sourvinou-Inwood, 1995.)

Preparing for the afterlife. Given this idea, preparation for death should have required nothing more than good behavior. But few people led lives of perfect virtue, and most were therefore left anxious about what awaited them. Perhaps because of this, we also find, beginning in the late archaic period, the idea that one can escape from the postmortem effects of bad behavior and even guarantee bliss after death by being initiated into one or more so-called mysteries cults while still alive (the most famous being that at Eleusis, near Athens). Initiates could expect to spend the afterlife in a meadow or other pleasant place, eating, drinking, and dancing. Non-initiates, however exemplary their conduct had been during life, would wallow in mire forever.

The flaw in this system, as its ancient critics already saw, was that once initiated, people could behave however they liked for the rest of their lives. "It would be absurd," said Diogenes the Cynic, "if Agesilaus and Epaminondas [two Spartan generals known for nobility of character] end up in the mire after death, while worthless people, simply because they have been initiated into the mysteries, dwell on the Islands of the Blest" (Diogenes Laertius, *Lives of the Eminent Philosophers* 6.39). Although a few mystery cults may have required initiates to follow certain rules of ritualized purity for the rest of their lives (e.g., not wearing wool), there does not seem to have been any expectation that they would follow a moral or ethical code.

A variation on this theme suggested that all humanity was doomed to punishment in the underworld because of its connection to the death of Persephone's son, the god Dionysos. Dionysos had been dismembered and eaten by violent gods called Titans; Zeus incinerated the Titans with a thunderbolt, and humanity arose from their smoldering remains. Persephone thereafter held each human responsible for the loss of her son. All that could save one from postmortem misery was to be initiated into mysteries sponsored by Dionysos (who had been reborn following his consumption by the Titans). The Dionysiac mysteries are particularly interesting because they gave the initiates special knowledge of underworld geography: they taught initiates which path to follow and which to avoid once they went below, and also which infernal bodies of water were safe to drink from and which would inflict forgetfulness. Forgetfulness was dangerous because the initiates had to remember to declare in front of certain underworld divinities or guardians who would judge them that they were pure and that Dionysos had released them from any need to atone for his death at the Titans' hands. Reminders of what the initiates learned while alive were engraved on tiny gold tablets that were buried with them.

Reincarnation shows up in a few texts connected with Dionysiac mysteries and in some philosophical systems influenced by Pythagoras and Plato. Although the soul still won rewards or suffered punishments in the afterlife in these systems, it eventually was sent into a new bodily life. Souls that managed to conduct themselves properly for several cycles could win release from incarnation altogether.

The eschatological aspects of mystery cults represent a novel way of thinking about the afterlife that subsequently influenced many other religious and philosophical systems in later antiquity, including Christianity. But it must be stressed that, for whatever reason, most ancient Greeks were not initiated into them. The standard expectation for the afterlife was probably, at best, a rather boring existence and, at worst, retribution for earthly deeds.

ROME. Scholars face two problems in dealing with Rome: there is little evidence for Roman beliefs and practices in early periods, and, as time went on, the Romans adopted from the Greek literary texts that they admired Greek modes of expressing ideas about death—and probably Greek beliefs and practices as well. Thus, for example, Book 6 of Vergil's *Aeneid,* where Aeneas visits the underworld, models itself closely on Book 11 of the *Odyssey.* It does add some interesting variations: Vergil adds a Limbo-like realm for the souls of infants and of those who died after falsely being accused of crimes, as well as a special area for suicides; he also seems to draw on Pythagorean ideas of reincarnation in some parts of Book 6. Whether these additions reflect actual differences between Greek and Roman beliefs or, rather, Vergil's interest in them for thematic and narrative reasons is impossible to say. We also know that the Romans were influenced by the Etruscans in their religious beliefs, and that they were highly interested in death and the afterlife—but because we can say little about the Etruscans themselves with certainty, this does not help much. Moreover, some "Greek" ideas that the Romans may have borrowed are also found in Etruscan sources, making it hard to say whether the Romans got them from the Greeks or the Etruscans—or perhaps even whether the Greeks themselves borrowed them from the Etruscans early on. Charon, who seems to be related to a figure called Charu in Etruscan sources, is a case in point. The survey that follows points out a few salient ways in which the Romans differed from the Greeks, but most of what was said above about the Greeks is generally true for the Romans as well (e.g., they particularly feared the ghosts of the unburied and thereby put a high value on funerary rites).

The funeral and care of the dead. When a person was about to die, his nearest relative bent over to kiss him, so as to catch his last breath (Seneca, *To Marcia* 3.2). The same person closed the eyes of the deceased (Vergil, *Aeneid* 9.486–487), and then all the relatives began a practice called *conclamatio,* or "calling out to" the dead, which was periodically repeated until the body was cremated (Servius on Vergil, *Aeneid* 6.218). Timing of the burial differed from the Greeks as well; Romans kept the body of the deceased within the house for up to seven days and expected family members to continue lamenting and eating only meager amounts of food during the entire period. Before cremation, a little bit of dirt was thrown on the corpse to symbolize burial, or else a small part of the body, such as a finger, was cut off to be buried. The rest of the body was burned. After the funeral pyre had consumed the corpse, survivors poured milk and wine over the ashes and bones, to feed the deceased. (Later, the bones were interred in a tomb.) For nine days following cremation, family members continued to set themselves apart from the rest of the community. During this period, a sow and a gelded ram were sacrificed and the grave was formally consecrated. (On burial rites, see Toynbee, 1971.)

As soon as a son, when sifting through the ashes of his father's funeral pyre, found a bone, he proclaimed that the father had joined the *Di Manes,* or "divine spirits"—in other words, the ancestors (Varro, in Plut., *Moralia* 267b). As in Greece, care was taken to keep these spirits happy and beneficent through funeral banquets and other graveside offerings—especially red flowers, which were offered at a festival called the "day of roses," or at another called the "day of violets." A nine-day festival called the Dies Parentes (days of the parents) was held in February and concluded with a day called the Feralia (the "carrying" of food and other gifts to tombs); this honored the dead as kindly beings who watched over their descendants. During another festival, the Lemuria, which was held for three days in May, the head of each household had to perform rituals at night to rid the family of malevolent ghosts (*lemures* or *larvae*). In particular, he had to toss black beans onto the floor with his eyes averted, while he asserted that the beans were meant to redeem himself and his family. The ghosts were expected to gather up the beans and leave contented.

The Romans asserted from an early time that certain founding fathers had become gods after their deaths—Romulus and Aeneas, for example. Starting with Julius Caesar, the Roman Senate went further, regularly deifying exceptional individuals after death, particularly emperors and members of the imperial family. The Greeks had occasionally done this as well for important rulers, starting in the Hellenistic period, but had never fully embraced the idea. (See Price, 1984.)

SEE ALSO Orphic Gold Tablets.

BIBLIOGRAPHY

Johnston, Sarah Iles. *Restless Dead: Encounters between the Living and the Dead in Ancient Greece.* Berkeley, 1999.

Kurtz, Donna C., and John Boardman. *Greek Burial Customs.* Ithaca, N.Y., 1971.

Price, S. R. F. *Rituals and Power: The Roman Imperial Cult in Asia Minor.* Cambridge, UK, 1984.

Sourvinou-Inwood, Christiane. *"Reading" Greek Death: To the End of the Classical Period.* Oxford, 1995.

Toynbee, J. M. C. *Death and Burial in the Roman World.* Baltimore, 1971; reprint, 1996.

SARAH ILES JOHNSTON (2005)

AFTERLIFE: GERMANIC CONCEPTS

The Old Norse accounts that supply most of the detailed information about pre-Christian Germanic religion picture several different kinds of afterlife. These can be simplified into two contrasting general concepts of life after death. In one view, the dead traveled to one of several halls depending upon how they died. In the other view, the dead remained very much on earth, either staying in their grave mound or else traveling out and disturbing their former neighborhood. In both understandings of the afterlife, how one died and the rituals surrounding death could determine how the dead person fared in the afterlife.

THE HALLS OF THE DEAD. The largest and most complete mythological narratives discussing the afterlife are contained in the *Prose Edda* and the *Poetic Edda.* The *Prose Edda* was written by Snorri Sturluson (1179–1241), a politically involved Icelandic nobleman who lived roughly two centuries after the conversion of Iceland to Christianity. Snorri presents a logical and clear description of many Norse beliefs, but this well-ordered narrative most likely reflects the influence of Christian systematic theology. His sources, mainly the group of poems called the *Poetic Edda,* present a much more fractured and inconsistent view of the afterlife. Germanic paganism apparently allowed multiple and contradictory understandings of death.

As portrayed in the *Prose Edda,* the dead dwelt in various halls. The virtuous deceased went to Gimlé, called simply the best house; to Brimir, which featured a copious supply of ale; or to Sindri, which was made of red gold. The wicked went to an unnamed hall on Nástrandir (Corpse Beach), which was reserved for oath breakers and murderers and whose walls were made of snakes that spat their poison into the center of the house; or to Hvergelmir, the worst house of all, in which the serpent Níðhǫggr tormented the bodies of the dead.

The basic depictions of these halls derive from the *Poetic Edda* (*Vǫlupsá,* sts. 37–39). In *Vǫluspá,* however, only the hall on Nástrandir is linked explicitly with the dead, and the halls of Sindri and Brimir (who are supernatural people, a dwarf and a giant respectively, and not just names) seem to be gathering stations for the races inimical to the Æsir gods rather than destinations for the dead. Similarly, Hvergelmir is elsewhere pictured as a spring under the roots of the world tree and not as a hall. *Vǫlupsá* does mention a hall on Gimlé, made of gold, that will house righteous rulers once the earth has been renewed after Ragnarǫk (the end of this world), and *Vǫlupsá* also notes that a monstrous wolf feeds on the flesh of the dead in Ironwood. While other accounts do not contain these named halls, a snake-filled hall does appear in the story by Saxo Grammaticus (c.1150–1204/1220) about a trip northward to a realm of the dead, and it therefore seems likely that a snake-filled hall was an image traditionally associated with death.

Another realm for the dead found in the *Eddas* is Hel. Unlike its modern cognate *hell,* Hel, while placed underground, was not viewed as a place of damnation, but rather as simply the realm of the dead, similar to the Hebrew *she'ol.* Hel's connection with the halls mentioned above is unclear, and it may represent a separate and older view of the afterlife. Knowledge of Hel was certainly more widespread than any of the above halls, since it appears in stock phrases meaning "to die," such as *fara til heljar,* literally "travel to Hel." Hel was frequently personified in skaldic poetry, however, and Snorri pictured Hel as a goddess dwelling in Niflheimr (Misty Dwelling), a region consisting of nine underworlds. According to information unique to Snorri's account, it was those who died of sickness, old age, and famine who went to Hel.

A final abode for the dead prominent in the *Eddas* is Valhǫll, popularly known today as Valhalla. Valhǫll, in the *Eddas* as elsewhere, is portrayed as the hall of Óðinn (Odin), where certain selected warriors slain on the battlefield are taken. The hall is decorated with armor and features 540 doors, through each of which eight hundred warriors can pass at the same time. According to the poem *Grímnismál,* these chosen warriors, called *einherjar,* enjoy a merry life of feasting while they await the day when they shall go out to fight alongside Óðinn against the all-devouring wolf. According to Snorri and other sources, the warriors daily fight each other in order to practice for the upcoming final battle. The people who choose which of the slain will partake of this life of martial feasting differ depending on the source, and Óðinn, Freyja, and the valkyries are all mentioned in this connection.

EARTHLY DOMICILE. While Eddic mythology focuses on Valhǫll and the halls for the dead, other literary sources suggest that some dead remained on earth and did not travel to a separate realm. Norse sagas give several colorful accounts of *draugar* (sing. *draugr*), which are revenants, or reanimated corpses. *Grettis Saga,* for example, tells of Glámr, an irreligious farmhand who was killed on Christmas Eve by an unidentified monster. Despite a makeshift burial, Glámr returned as a revenant and haunted the old farmstead by destroying property, animals, and men until the hero Grettir defeated the *draugr* in combat, decapitated the corpse, and burned the body. Only then did the haunting end, according to the narrative.

While *draugar* actively haunted this world, other corpses remained in their grave mounds and attacked only those who dared to enter them. The corpse of Kárr the Old only came to life within his *howe,* or burial mound, when Grettir attempted to remove the treasure buried there. A fight ensued, and Grettir, as usual, finally got the upper hand. The dead in the grave mounds are not always malevolent, however. When their graves are not violated, the dead are sometimes pictured as content in their *howes;* Gunnar is described as happily gazing at the full moon from his open *howe* in *Njáls Saga.* Several *howe* dwellers were in fact believed to be gods, and their cults involved sacrifices offered at the grave mound. Certain grave mounds themselves seem to have become holy as a result; there is mention of an Árhaugr (Plenty Howe) to which sacrifices were offered around Yule.

While some dead dwelt in grave mounds, some families believed that they would reside in a mountain after death. *Eyrbyggja saga* preserves an account of Þorsteinn Þorskabítr, who was welcomed into Helgafell (Holy Mountain) with much rejoicing and merrymaking when he died by drowning. Other accounts also stress the celebration that ensued when the recently deceased joined their kin in the mountains. One common thread between many of these accounts is the worship of Þórr (Thor), but it is unclear if such worship itself enabled the dead person to enter the mountain.

A final way in which the dead remained on earth is through rebirth. Accounts of rebirth are not very common, though some famous personages, such as King Olaf the Holy, were alleged to have been the reincarnations of other people. Some critics have argued that the widespread practice of naming children after recently deceased kinsmen indicates that belief in reincarnation was once common, but the surviving evidence is not conclusive.

Burial Rites. The Germanic peoples practiced both cremation and inhumation throughout their pre-Christian history. Cremation itself was generally completed by placing the ashes in an urn and burying the urn. Inhumed corpses are often found accompanied by grave goods such as armor, food, or even other corpses. The presence of grave goods is generally thought to indicate belief in an afterlife, since the goods seem designed to aid the individual's journey to or life in the next world. Other interpretations are, of course, possible. The modern Catholic custom of burying bodies with a rosary does not reflect contemporary belief that the corpse will use it for prayer, and sentimental or symbolic readings may be more accurate than literal interpretations of the archaeological evidence.

In thirteenth-century Christian accounts, however, the earlier pagans are described as believing that grave goods would help to secure a good life after death. According to *Ynglingasaga*, the Swedish cult of Óðinn held that the dead would bring to Valhǫll whatever treasures had been buried with them in the grave. The depiction of a ravenously hungry corpse in *Egils saga einhenda ok Ásmundar* further suggests that food offerings were indeed intended as provisions for the deceased. An extremely interesting and valuable account by Ahmed Ibn Fadlan (fl. 922 CE), an Arabic ambassador who spent time among the still-pagan Rus, who are thought to have been East Scandinavian traders, records that a chieftain's death rites included the sacrifice of a servant girl who would accompany him into the afterlife. A number of graves in Anglo-Saxon England in which a female corpse without grave goods has been placed over a male corpse with grave goods provides some evidence that Ibn Fadlan's account is rooted in reality and that such sacrifices were practiced across the Germanic world. In other literary narratives, it is the wife who performed this suttee-like sacrifice.

While grave goods thus helped the dead in the next life, cremation rituals could indicate how the deceased was actually received. In Ibn Fadlan's account, Viking informants explain that a quick-burning fire, driven by a stiff wind, indicated the favor of the gods and that the dead chieftain would enter paradise without delay. The strong wind presumably also carried the smoke further, and according to Snorri, the Swedes believed that the height of the smoke from a funeral pyre indicated how much honor the dead person would receive in the realm of the dead. The closing lines of *Beowulf* likewise note that "Heaven swallowed the smoke" rising from the hero's pyre.

The most famous cremations are certainly those in which the corpse was sent out to sea in a burning boat. No archaeological remains exist that can confirm this literary tradition, but several ship burials have been found in which the corpse was placed in a ship along with grave goods, with the entire ship then being buried. The very idea of a ship implies a journey, and these ship burials may be the literal reinterpretation of what was earlier merely a metaphor. This image seems to have been well rooted among the Germanic peoples, since Iron Age graves in Gotland were sometimes enclosed by upright stones in the form of a ship, although ship burials themselves were not frequent until the sixth century.

Another ceremony that may have been intended to help the fate of the departed was the funeral feast that was held either immediately after interment or a few months later. These feasts could be important for the living as well as for the dead, since an heir took possession of his father's estates by drinking a draft called *bragafull* and then ascending to his father's chair. The living also recited poems at the feast, and *Sonatorrek,* by Egill Skallagrimsson, gives an idea of what these poems may have been like. In *Sonatorrek,* Egill laments the death of his son, but he also describes his son's reception by the gods. One purpose of such poems originally may have been to ensure the departed's safe arrival in the afterlife, since *Hákonar Saga Góða* depicts men giving speeches at the king's funeral in order to direct him to Valhǫll.

Transition to Christianity. The transition to Christianity is marked in the archaeological record by the decline of cremation burials, a decrease in the number of grave goods, and an increase in Christian jewelry, such as crosses, with a concomitant decrease in pagan amulets, such as Þórr's hammers. Many non-Christian beliefs lingered on, however; one example is revenants, though such creatures were now fitted into a Christian cosmography and were often viewed as returning temporarily from purgatory to this world. A major change must have been the distinction made between body and **saiwalō,* the proto-Germanic word from which Modern English *soul* derives. Whereas pre-Christian sources do not picture any clear division between the body and the animating principle at death, Christian teaching held that the body and soul were separated, though they would rejoin at the Last Judgment. Despite this difference, the missionaries' acceptance of **saiwalō* and their decision not to use the Latin *anima* as a loanword suggests that the Germanic peoples had a concept of soul sufficiently close to the Christian, though this soul does not seem to have played a distinct part in pagan conceptions of the afterlife. Interestingly, **saiwalō* did not survive into Old Norse, and the missionaries chose to use *sála*, borrowed from West Germanic, in lieu of any native Norse term. This absence highlights the differences between the Norse and other Germanic cultures and indicates how careful one must be in stretching the Norse literary evidence about the afterlife to cover all the Germanic peoples.

SEE ALSO Eddas; Germanic Religion, overview article; Óðinn; Snorri Sturluson; Valhǫll; Valkyries.

BIBLIOGRAPHY

An excellent survey of the Norse material is Hilda Roderick Ellis Davidson, *The Road to Hel: A Study of the Conception of the Dead in Old Norse Literature* (Cambridge, U.K., 1943), although the critical comment is now out of date. Gabriel Turville-Petre has written several good introductions to Scandinavian religion, including *Myth and Religion of the North: The Religion of Ancient Scandinavia* (New York, 1964), and David Wilson explores Anglo-Saxon cultic practice in *Anglo-Saxon Paganism* (London, 1992). Those with a knowledge of German, however, will still want to consult Jan de Vries, *Altgermanische Religionsgeschichte*, 2 vols., 2d ed., (Berlin, 1956–1957). John Lindow's *Scandinavian Mythology: An Annotated Bibliography* (New York, 1988) is a good starting place for more specific research.

Archaeological aspects of death are investigated by Sam Lucy, *The Anglo-Saxon Way of Death: Burial Rites in Early England* (Stroud, U.K., 2000), while Erik Nylén and Jan Peder Lamm have produced a glossy introduction to the Gotland stones, *Stones, Ships, and Symbols: The Picture Stones of Gotland from the Viking Age and Before* (Stockholm, 1988 [Swedish, *Bildstenar*, 1978]). A good introduction to the important ship burial at Sutton Hoo can be found in Rupert Bruce-Mitford, *The Sutton Hoo Ship Burial* (3 vols., London, 1975–1983).

LAWRENCE P. MORRIS (2005)

AFTERLIFE: CHINESE CONCEPTS

It is commonly accepted that conceptions of soul and afterlife must have developed among many human societies—China included—long before the appearance of written evidence. Unsparing efforts to discover traces in archaeological remains have yielded varying degrees of success. In the case of ancient China, the position of bodies buried at the Banpo Neolithic (c. 5000–4000 BCE) cemetery near present-day Xian was often interpreted as indicating the existence of an idea of an afterlife. The evidence—a unified westward head position—was explained as the expression of a belief in the west as the world of the dead. There is, however, very little further evidence, and nothing else is known of such a belief in a world after death during this period. A parallel situation in ancient Egypt indicates that burial positions varied from cemetery to cemetery, which should be considered a warning against interpreting burial position as evidence of a concept of the netherworld.

The earliest textual evidence from China concerning an idea of an afterlife is in oracle bone inscriptions from the Shang dynasty (c. 1500–1050 BCE). Primarily divination records, the inscriptions mentioned that deceased kings dwelled in heaven together with the God on High. This was clearly a very special afterlife, available only for royalty. There is no textual evidence indicating an afterlife for commoners, though burial custom continued to develop along the model of vertical pits with wooden coffins in varying degrees of elaboration. This implies that the belief system of the society at the time was by and large homogenous. Later, during the transition from the Warring States period (c. 403–221 BCE) to the Qin (221–206 BCE) and Han (206 BCE–220 CE) dynasties, when tomb style began to change, a detectable transformation in the perception of the afterlife occurred.

Inscriptions on bronze vessels found in tombs of the Shang and Zhou (c. 1150–256 BCE) dynasties are in general commemorative in nature, and the deeds of the owners were magnified and praised. Occasionally, the "underground" is mentioned as the place where a deceased noble will serve his lord after death. This "underground" is not described in detail, but it must indicate a common conception for the destination of the dead. Evidence of human sacrifices as well as accompanying tombs of servants and concubines are found among Shang royal tombs and certain later tombs. These are corroborated by textual evidence from the *Book of Odes*, attributed to the Zhou period, which indicates that for a long time people believed that deceased kings and rulers needed their servants after death.

THE CHANGING CONCEPT OF THE NETHERWORLD: EASTERN ZHOU TO HAN. During the Eastern Zhou (770–256 BCE) and the Warring States periods, for which written documents are relatively abundant, two terms—Yellow Spring and Dark City—were used to represent the idea of a netherworld. The term *Yellow Spring* (*huangquan*) was probably a reference to underground water, which was a metaphor for the netherworld. The *Zuozhuan*, a work that relates historical events of the Eastern Zhou period, preserved a story that concerns this idea of the Yellow Spring. The duke of Zheng was angry with his unfaithful mother and vowed never to see her again in life with the expression "we shall not meet each other unless we all reach the Yellow Spring" (i.e., the netherworld). Later, when he regretted his anger, he dug an underground tunnel to meet with her, since the tunnel was supposed to have reached the Yellow Spring. The underground tunnel is clearly a substitute for a tomb or the netherworld. Exactly what there was in the Yellow Spring, however, is not specified.

The term *Dark City* (*youdu*) first appears in the *Chuci* (Songs of the south), written by the famous Chu poet Qu Yuan (c. 343–277 BCE). In a chapter titled "Summoning the Soul," which describes the soul-recalling ritual, the poet wrote: "O soul, Go not down to the City of Darkness, where the Lord Earth lies, nine-coiled, with dreadful horns on his forehead, and a great humped back and bloody thumbs, pursuing men, swift-footed: Three eyes he has in his tiger's head, and his body is like a bull's" (Hawkes, 1959, p. 105). Here the Dark City was ruled by Lord Earth (Tu Bo), a sinister-looking horned python. Such a description betrays a certain aversion toward the afterlife, as the Dark City was clearly not a desirable place for the soul of the dead to be. Again, little is known about this Dark City. Indeed, darkness is a quality often attributed to the world of the dead. The ancient Mesopotamians believed that the world of the dead was a dark and cold place, ruled by the deities Ereshkigal and Nergal. The Jewish She'ol, also a dark place, was intimately related to the ancient Mesopotamian concept of the netherworld. The ancient Greeks conceived of the netherworld as a gloomy place, where the souls of the dead exist in a pale and shadow-like form. The idea of the darkness of the Chinese netherworld, the Dark City, is retained well into the Eastern Han period (25–220 CE). An Eastern Han funerary text states that the deceased "joined the long night, without seeing the sun and the stars. His soul dwelled alone, returned down to the darkness."

Exactly how prevalent this concept of a Dark City was in the late Warring States period, when the *Chuci* was written, is uncertain. A slightly later text found in a Qin dynasty tomb in the present-day Gansu province mentioned that the deceased "lived" in his tomb and that he did not like to wear many clothes, nor did he like offerings of food soaked with sauce. In this case, the relationship between the tomb and the Dark City is not clear.

In the Western Han during the second century BCE, texts found in tombs referred to the world of the dead as simply "underground" (*dixia*) and ruled by a host of bureaucrats, including the Lord of Underworld, the Assistant Magistrate of the Underworld, the Assistant of the Dead, the Retinue of the Graves, the Minister and Magistrate of Grave Mounds, the Commander of Ordinance for the Mounds, the Neighborhood Head of the Gate of the Souls, the Police of the Grave Mounds, the Marquis of the Eastern Mound, the Count of the Western Mound, the Official of Underneath, and the Head of Five of Gaoli (i.e., the netherworld). Governing this bureaucratic establishment was an overlord, variously known as the Yellow Emperor (Huangdi), Yellow God (Huangshen), or Heavenly Emperor (Tiandi). It is unclear how the Heavenly Emperor could be involved in the affairs of the netherworld if heaven and the underground were separate regions. All the same, the picture of the underground shaped by these figures reflects what happened above ground. In other words, a conception of a bureaucratic netherworld only became possible when the world of the living was already bureaucratized. This evidence from the Han period, in its description of the bureaucratization of the netherworld, also reflects the signs of a unified empire.

On the other hand, at every locality there was always the issue of the incorporation of local traditions into the larger structure. A group of wooden slips dated to 79 CE provided a wealth of information on local religious beliefs related to the conception of the afterlife. The texts were written in the form of contracts that recorded that, when a person was about to die, the family would employ a *wu* shaman to pray and make ale and meat offerings for the dying person. When the person died, the family members would pray to a variety of deities, including the Lord Hearth, the Controller of Fate, and a number of local deities. Sacrifice to the deities was also ministered by local *wu* shamans. When the prayer was finished, the content of the prayer and the offering was written on the wooden slips, which were meant to be taken by the deceased as a kind of contract to the Heavenly Sire (*tiangong*) to testify that indeed prayers and offerings had been performed on behalf of the deceased. It is unclear who this Heavenly Sire was, though he must have been one of the important deities in charge of the deceased. This, of course, is another form of the bureaucratization of the afterworld, as official documents on earth were imitated in the world of the dead. It is particularly interesting that here the deceased was referred to as ascending to heaven and descending to the Yellow Spring at the same time when death occurred.

Similar situations can be found in the use of contracts for the purchase of land. Archaeological excavations of tombs have produced a substantial number of contracts for the purpose of buying a piece of land for the deceased as the place of the burial. It is possible that such land contracts were originally copies of real contracts that the family members of the deceased placed in the tomb in order to provide a legitimate claim to the land. Gradually, the contract became symbolic; as the piece of land became an imaginary space, the sellers became deities or immortals and the price of the land became astronomical.

Finally, the bureaucratization of the afterlife was evidenced by the fact that it was thought that the deceased had to pay taxes even in the netherworld. A text found in an Eastern Han tomb includes the following:

> Today is an auspicious day. It is for no other reason but the deceased Zhang Shujing, who unfortunately died prematurely, is scheduled to descend into the grave. The Yellow God, who produced the Five Mountains, is in charge of the roster of the deceased, recalling the *hun* and *po*, and in charge of the list of the dead. The living may build a high tower; the dead returns and is buried deeply underneath. Eyebrows and beards having fallen, they drop and became dirt and dust. Now therefore I (the Messenger of Heavenly Emperor) present the medicine for removing poll-tax and corvée conscription, so that the descendants will not die. Nine pieces of *renshen* from Shangdang substitute for the living. The lead man is intended to substitute for the dead. The soybeans and mellon-seeds are for the dead to pay for the taxation underneath. Hereby I issue a decree to remove the earthly evil, so that no disaster will occur. When this decree arrives, restrict the officer of the Underworld, and do not disturb the Zhang family again.

Doubly urgent as prescribed by the laws and ordinances. (Poo, 1998, pp. 171–172)

Not only did the deceased have to pay tax in the netherworld, they also faced the prospect of forced labor. A small lead figurine of a man, crudely made and placed in a clay jar to be buried in the tomb, was said to be able to do all sorts of errands for the deceased, including serving as a substitute laborer. It is interesting to note a similarity between this lead man and the *ushabti* of ancient Egypt; both served as substitutes for the deceased in the performance of conscripted labor in the afterlife. Spells written on the *ushabti* engaged the double to answer (the literal meaning of *ushabti*) for all the required works.

The text quoted above was actually a protective spell aimed at securing a comfortable place for the dead in the netherworld and at the same time protecting the family members. The author of this spell is unknown but presumably belonged to the class of *fangshi* magician, an early type of Daoist priest. Thus, two categories of religious personnel were involved in mediating this world and the afterlife. The *wu* shaman was responsible for the preparation and performance of sacrificial rituals, while the *fangshi* magician was mainly involved in the manipulation of secret and sacred powers by producing spells and recipes, together with certain actions, that could control various evil spirits and ghosts.

During the Eastern Han period, Mount Tai emerged as the final destination of the dead. This place was ruled by the Lord of Mount Tai, who was in charge of the dead. This does not mean that belief in an underground netherworld, or the Yellow Spring, was completely replaced by belief in Mount Tai as the abode of the dead or that people in every corner of the empire gave up their local traditions concerning the afterlife. The process through which Mount Tai gained its importance is obscure, but it might have to do with the position of Mount Tai in the state cult. The *Shujing* (Book of history) mentions that the sage-king Shun once made sacrifice at Mount Tai. Another ancient tradition has it that the Yellow Emperor performed a sacrifice to heaven at Mount Tai and became immortal. A number of classical texts testify that mountain deities were worshipped by the rulers in order to appropriate the mandate of heaven and therefore the legitimacy to rule. The first emperor of the Qin dynasty (Qin Shihuang, r. 221–210 BCE) and Emperor Wu (r. 140–87 BCE) of the Han dynasty also performed the Grand Ceremony (*fengshan*) at Mount Tai. The sacred nature of Mount Tai was therefore well established during the early Han. One can only assume that the sacredness of Mount Tai was the basis for it to become the abode of the dead. Nonetheless, it is only in the Eastern Han period that one finds funerary texts clearly indicating that Mount Tai had become the abode of ghosts. One such text reads, "The living belong to the jurisdiction of Chang'an to the west; the dead belong to the jurisdiction of Mount Tai to the east." This indicates that the capital of the living was Chang'an, the capital of Western Han, and the capital of the dead was Mount Tai. Thus, it seems that it was during the Western Han that Mount Tai gained the attribute of being the abode of the dead, although the text was found in an Eastern Han tomb. Two small mounds below Mount Tai, Liangfu and Gaoli, also became associated with this world of the dead and were often mentioned in texts of the Eastern Han and later eras.

BURIAL STYLES AND THE CONCEPTION OF AFTERLIFE. The evolution of tomb styles reveals the transformation of the conception of the afterlife from another angle. The traditional burial style in China from the Neolithic period until the Warring States period was the vertical-pit wooden-casket tomb. The degree of personal status was shown in the size of the pit and the layers of caskets provided for the deceased as well as in the elaborateness of the funerary objects. The burial place, though certainly considered the abode of the dead, was constructed to reflect the personal sociopolitical status of the deceased. The number of accompanying bronze vessels and the layers of caskets, for example, were provided in a hierarchical order.

A change gradually took place during the Warring States period with the appearance of brick tombs, indicating a shift in emphasis in the perception of the function of the tomb. In its earlier form, the brick tomb was constructed with large bricks, which replaced the wooden outer casket of the vertical-pit tomb. During the early Western Han period, this burial style gradually gained acceptance among the people, and the tomb structure began to develop into more complicated forms. The brick burial chamber grew larger and often included an antechamber, some of which included further side chambers for storing funerary objects or even symbolic kitchens and stables with surrogate kitchen utensils and carriages. The tomb was more like an underground house for the deceased. It seems that with the emergence of brick tombs and funerary objects of daily use, the afterlife was conceived in a more realist fashion.

Similar trends can also be observed in the traditional form of vertical-pit wooden-casket tombs, particularly in former Chu areas. Beginning from the late Warring States period, the caskets developed from a single-level to a double-level structure with doors, windows, and stairs that connected the upper and lower levels. Some caskets even had pigpens in the lower levels, which undoubtedly were replicas of the houses of the living. Funerary objects, such as clay models of rice paddies, boats, carriages, cattle, even chicken and fish, created a sense of a well-provided household. Some elements that earlier had indicated the political status of the tomb owner, such as bronze vessels, were missing from the scenes.

The change observed in burial styles from the Warring States to the Han reveals a change of conception toward the afterlife. Corresponding to the textual evidence, which suggests a bureaucratized netherworld emerging with the establishment of the Han empire, the change in burial style indicates a more realistic imagining of the world after death—an imagining, however, based on an imitation of the world of the living. The textual and archaeological evidence clearly suggests that by the Eastern Han period the idea that the netherworld was similar to the mundane world had become common. By making the abode after death practically identical to the normal abode, the dead (or the dying) perhaps were thought to be relieved of the dread of uncertainty.

ATTITUDES TOWARD LIFE IN THE NETHERWORLD. Attitudes toward the afterlife were ambiguous and cannot be separated from attitudes toward death and the existence of the soul after death. The early Daoist philosopher Zhuangzi (c. fourth century BCE) held a materialist and naturalist view of the essence of life, and he perceived that the physical being was merely a gathering of the *qi* ether in the universe. When a person, or indeed any life-form, died, the body decomposed and returned to the state of *qi*. There was therefore no life after death. The Confucians, on the other hand, took a conservative stand in accepting what had long existed in Chinese culture—ghosts and spirits. Yet Confucius himself did not wish to discuss the unknown world of the spirits, and he devoted little attention to the afterlife. As a consequence, the Confucian view did not reflect what was actually believed by common people regarding death and life in the netherworld. The archaeological and textual evidence described in the previous sections demonstrates that the nature of the afterlife was a constant concern of the people. The Eastern Han philosopher Wang Chong (first century CE) gave a vivid description of the popular mentality of his time:

> Thus ordinary people, on the one side, have these very doubtful arguments (about whether ghosts exist or not), and on the other they hear of Duke Du and the like, and note that the dead in their tombs arise and have intercourse with sick people whose end is near. They then believe in this, and imagine that the dead are like the living. They commiserate with them, [thinking] that in their graves they are lonely, that their souls are solitary and without companions, that their tombs and mounds are closed and devoid of grain and other things. Therefore they make dummies to serve the corpses in their coffins, and fill the latter with eatables, to gratify the spirits. This custom has become so inveterate, and has gone to such lengths, that very often people will ruin their families and use up all their property for the coffins of the dead. (Forke, 1962, vol. 2, p. 369)

An ambiguous attitude toward death and the afterlife can be seen in these diverging views. On the one hand, life hereafter could be portrayed as a state of happiness. Tomb paintings and reliefs from the Han period often portray a happy afterlife: scenes of banquets, festivals, hunting, and traveling often occupy the central position. Inscriptions on bronze mirrors found in tombs often carry eulogies about a carefree life comparable to that of the immortals. One inscription reads: "There is happiness daily, and fortune monthly. There is joy without (bad) events, fit for having wine and food. Live leisurely, free from anxiety. Accompanied by flute and zither, with contentment of heart. Years of happiness are secure and lasting" (Karlgren, 1934, no. 79). However, other texts describing taxes and corvée labor in the afterlife as well as contracts concerning prayers and offerings to the deities betray a sense of anxiety and fear. Even the elaborate funerary paraphernalia could be seen as emerging from a sense of insecurity about an uncertain future.

SEE ALSO Alchemy, article on Chinese Alchemy; Chinese Religion, overview article, article on Mythic Themes; Daoism, overview article, article on The Daoist Religious Community; Fangshi; Huangdi; Soul, article on Chinese Concepts; Tian; Xian; Xi Wang Mu; Zhenren.

BIBLIOGRAPHY

Dien, Albert E. "Chinese Beliefs in the Afterworld." In *The Quest for Eternity: Chinese Ceramic Sculptures from the People's Republic of China*, edited by Susan L. Caroselli, pp. 1–16. Los Angeles, 1987.

Forke, Alfred, trans. *Lun Heng*. 2 vols. 2d ed. New York, 1962.

Harper, Donald L. "Resurrection in Warring States Popular Religion." *Taoist Resources* 5, no. 2 (1994): 13–28.

Hawkes, David, trans. *Chu Tz'u, The Songs of the South: An Ancient Chinese Anthology*. Oxford, 1959.

Karlgren, Bernard. "Early Chinese Mirror Inscriptions." *Bulletin of the Museum of Far Eastern Art* 6 (1934): 9–79.

Kleeman, Terry F. "Land Contracts and Related Documents." In *Chūgoku no shūkyō shiso to kagaku: Makio Ryokai festschrift*, pp. 1–34. Tokyo, 1984.

Loewe, Michael. *Ways to Paradise: The Chinese Quest for Immortality*. London, 1979.

Loewe, Michael. *Chinese Ideas of Life and Death: Faith, Myth, and Reason in the Han Period (202 BC– AD 220)*. London, 1982.

Poo, Mu-chou. "Ideas concerning Death and Burial in Pre-Han and Han China." *Asia Major*, 3d ser., 3, no. 2 (1990): 25–62.

Poo, Mu-chou. *In Search of Personal Welfare: A View of Ancient Chinese Religion*. Albany, N.Y., 1998.

Seidel, Anna. "Traces of Han Religion in Funeral Texts Found in Tombs." In *Dōkyō to shūkyō bunka*, edited by Akitsuki Kan'ei, pp. 21–57. Tokyo, 1987.

Thompson, Laurence G. "On the Prehistory of Hell in China." *Journal of Chinese Religion* 17 (1989): 27–41.

Yu, Ying-shih. "O Soul Come Back! A Study in the Changing Conceptions of the Soul and Afterlife in Pre-Buddhist China." *Harvard Journal of Asiatic Studies* 47, no. 2 (1987): 363–395.

MU-CHOU POO (2005)

AGA KHAN

AGA KHAN (Pers., Āghā Khān). First conferred in 1817 on the Ismāʿīlī imam (spiritual leader) Ḥasan ʿAlī Shāh (d. 1881) by the Qajar shah of Iran, this hereditary title is now applied to the imam of the Nizārī Ismāʿīlī Muslims. As imams of a Shīʿī community, the Aga Khans have always based their claims to leadership on their descent from ʿAlī and Fāṭimah, the son-in-law and daughter of the prophet Muḥammad. Their followers, who reside mainly in various developing countries, have traditionally looked to them for guidance on religious as well as secular matters.

Intrigues at the Iranian court during the 1830s forced Aga Khan I to migrate to India, where, under British protection, he eventually established headquarters in Bombay in 1848. An important British ally during the conquest of Sind, Aga Khan I faced strong challenges to his leadership from within his community. Most of these challenges were resolved in 1866 when Sir Joseph Arnold of the Bombay High Court issued a judgment in favor of the Aga Khan. His son ʿAlī Shāh (d. 1885) became Aga Khan II; he was, after a short period, succeeded in turn by his son, Sir Sulṭān Muḥammad Shāh.

Aga Khan III (d. 1957) initiated a process of modernizing the community through the establishment of schools, dispensaries, hospitals, housing societies, welfare organizations; the creation of communal administrative structures; and the emancipation and education of Ismāʿīlī women. He also participated in a wide range of political, social, and philanthropic activities for the benefit of Muslims, particularly those of the Indian subcontinent. His important role in public life led to his election to the presidency of the League of Nations in 1937. Under his grandson, Shāh Karīm al-Ḥusaynī, Aga Khan IV (b. 1936), an international university, the Aga Khan University, was established, with its first faculty in Karachi, Pakistan. The Aga Khan Foundation, and agency founded in 1967, is actively involved in diverse humanitarian and cultural activities.

SEE ALSO Shiism, article on Ismāʿīlīyah.

BIBLIOGRAPHY

For further discussion see Willi Frischauer's *The Aga Khans* (London, 1970) and John Norman Hollister's *The Shiʿa of India* (London, 1953), p. 364ff. The memoirs of Aga Khan III are published under the title *The Memoirs of the Aga Khan: World Enough and Time* (New York, 1954.)

ALI S. ASANI (1987)

AGAPE SEE CHARITY; EUCHARIST

AGES OF THE WORLD.

The notion that the world or the cosmos, as a living thing, undergoes stages of development similar to those of a human individual is more than a poetic conceit; it is a ubiquitous belief, one that is frequently displayed in linguistic phenomena. For example, lying behind the English word *world* is an old Germanic compound, **wer-aldh*, meaning "the life, or age, of man"; in Indo-European languages, the terms for "life" or "world" and terms designating temporal periods often shade off into each other, as in the Greek *aion* or the Latin *saeculum.*

SYSTEMS OF BINARY PERIODIZATION. The simplest form of world-periodization is a binary one: *before and after, then and now, now and then.* The distinction *before and after* is most frequently expressed in historicized form but often carries with it religious evaluation. Thus, while there are commemorative base years in some chronological systems, such as 4 Ahau 8 Cumkú (3133 BCE) among the Maya, 1 Flint (1168 BCE) among the Aztec, or the Saka era (78 CE) in India, most such systems are built around events in the lives of founders. The most familiar of these systems is the division of all human history into BC (before Christ) and AD (*anno Domini,* "in the year of our Lord," i.e., after Christ), a distinction created by the Christian monk Dionysius Exiguus in the first half of the sixth century. Dionysius established the beginning of the Christian era (or the Era of the Incarnation) as 1 January 754 AUC (*anno urbis conditae,* "from the foundation of the city [of Rome]"). The system of dating by AD did not come into wide usage until the eleventh century; the negative chronology of BC gained currency only after the publication in 1681 of Jacques-Bénigne Bossuet's *Universal History.* However, Dionysius's system ultimately became so widely accepted that it formed the basis of a new system, created in the last decades of the twentieth century, that distinguished between "the common era" (CE) and "before the common era" (BCE). (The CE–BCE system was soon increasingly favored by English-language scholars and is, in fact, the system employed by this encyclopedia.)

Periodizations similar to the Christian system are found in other religious traditions: the Muslim system of dating events AH (*anno Hegirae,* "in the year of the Hijrah"), attributed to the second caliph, ʿUmar I (634–644); the Buddhist era, in use in Ceylon and Southeast Asia, which begins with the Buddha's attaining *Nirvāṇa* in 544 BCE; the Jain era, commencing with the death of Jina in 528 BCE; and the Kollam era, restricted to the Malabar Coast, associated with Parasurama, an *avatāra* of Viṣṇu.

The other modes of binary periodization—*then and now, now and then*—while sometimes found in historicized form (such as the distinction between *antediluvian* and *postdiluvian* in Sumero-Akkadian literature) are, more usually, connected to explicit mythical themes, especially those concerned with anthropogony and eschatology. They presuppose that a sharp cleavage may be described as existing between the present state of things and an anterior or posterior state. The contrast between *then* and *now* finds its most common expression as that between an ancestral time in the mythical past and the present time of human beings. This contrast may play a dominant role in an entire religious system (as does the notion of the "Dreaming" among the Australian Aborigines), or it may serve as a motif in myths of paradise, of a Golden Age, of the origin of death, of the relocation of a high god, of a deluge, or of a fall. The distinction between *now* and *then* occurs widely in apocalyptic and millenarian traditions as in the distinction between this age and the age to come, or in mythologies concerning the end of the world.

As the above suggests, the category "ages of the world" is a somewhat fluid one. At times its primary focus is on the entire universe, at times it is limited to the earth; at times it includes the gods, humans, and all living beings, at times it is centered on man, or on stages of human history. In some traditions all of these aspects are interwoven into a cosmic drama; in other traditions only one or another of these aspects will be found.

Systems of Serial Periodization. In the usual understanding of ages of the world, more than a simple binary periodization is present; there is a system of serial periodization. Three forms predominate: a tradition of world-periods, a tradition of myths of recurrence, and a system of cosmic periods.

World-periods. The simplest form of serial periodization marks out a succession of periods from creation to final destruction, from a beginning to an end.

Iranian traditions. It is exceedingly difficult to order the Iranian traditions concerning successive world-periods with any certainty due to the fact that the most elaborate mythic schema are found only in late Pahlavi books redacted no earlier than the ninth century CE. This not simply an internal problem; it affects matters of comparison as well, inasmuch as the Iranian traditions have been held by many scholars to have been influential on Greco-Roman, Israelitic, and Christian traditions of the ages of the world that predate the Pahlavi texts. Nevertheless, elements of the fully elaborated, later traditions can be found in early texts. The myth of the Golden Age of the primordial king, Yima, is a pre-Zoroastrian, Indo-Iranian tradition; the associated notion of a worldwide, catastrophic winter that will destroy terrestrial life is an archaic Indo-European motif. The important title for savior, *saoshyant,* applied in the first instance to Zarathushtra (Zoroaster), and the notion that the present age will be transformed by the prophet immediately into one that is "excellent" with yet a future age of re-creation and transformation, occur in the earliest Zoroastrian literary strata. What is more important, from Greek reports of Iranian tradition as early as the fourth century BCE, one learns of a three-thousand-year period when one god will rule over another; a three-thousand-year period when the two gods will struggle; and a third period, of unspecified length, which will be a golden age. Hades (i.e., Ahriman) will lose power, there will be universal happiness and no need for food, and the god (Ōhrmazd) who achieved these things will be at "rest" (Theopompus, quoted in Plutarch, *Isis and Osiris* 47). Armenian Christian sources, such as Eznik of Kolb (fifth century), provide the basic elements of the Zurvanist dualistic myth, according to which prior to creation the two rival deities, Ōhrmazd and Ahriman, are each assigned nine thousand years of kingship by their father, Zurwan. Finally, there is the elaborate apocalyptic portrait of the signs of the end fully developed in the Iranian *Oracle of Hystaspes* (first century BCE), well known from its citation in Greek and Latin Christian sources from the second and third centuries.

The Sasanid period (226–652 CE) was one of intense theological controversy between rival cosmologies, out of which emerged the system of dividing the ages of the world into four trimillennia as elaborated in the Pahlavi books. The system received its classic formulation in the *Bundahishn* (Book of Primordial Creation), itself a composite work containing both elements of orthodox Mazdean speculation and Zurvanist myth. In the first trimillennium, Ōhrmazd and Ahriman coexist in Infinite Time, the former in an upper realm of light, the latter in a lower realm of darkness. After becoming aware of each other and their predestined struggle, they each fashion weapons. At the close of the first trimillennium, Ahriman crosses the Void and attacks Ōhrmazd. Ōhrmazd offers peace and is rejected. Then, knowing that he is destined to win the struggle, Ohrmazd proposes a limit to their contest—a period of nine thousand years. After Ahriman accepts, Ōhrmazd begins a new stage of the battle by reciting the central Zoroastrian prayer, the Ahuna Vairya. Thereupon Ahriman falls back into darkness, where he remains for three thousand years.

During this period of Ahriman's relative impotence, Ōhrmazd brings creation into being. Creation occurrs at two complimentary levels as a series of spiritual and material creations, the latter including Gav-aēvō-dāta (the primordial ox) and Gayō-maretan (primordial man). Ahriman, in his realm, generates his own creations and, at the end of the second trimillennium, invades Ōhrmazd's world. He corrupts it and kills Gayō-maretan and Gav-aēvō-dāta, out of whose bodies humans, other living things, and metals are generated.

The third trimillennium is Ahriman's triumph, but this turns out to be a trap. Ahriman is caught in the material world. The final trimillennium is devoted to the salvation of the world, beginning with the birth of Zarathushtra. Each of the three millenniums will be marked by a savior (a descendent of Zarathushtra) until the final millennium of Saoshyant, when there will be a final judgment, the granting of immortality, and a new world. This basic myth was adapted to a variety of systems of Iranian religious thought; a further permutation occurs in the myth of the Three Epochs in Manichaeism.

Jewish traditions. There appears to be no indigenous Israelitic tradition of the ages of the world. The historicized sequence in the *Book of Daniel* (second or third century BCE), so influential on later Jewish and Christian periodizations, of four world-empires followed by a divine kingdom and symbolized by metals or beasts (*Dn.* 2:37–45, 7:2–27) is an adaptation of Iranian anti-Hellenistic propaganda. Based, perhaps, on the sabbath-week, there is a noticeable predilection for multiples of seven. Already in *Daniel* 9, history from the Babylonian exile to the End is divided into seventy weeks of years (i.e., seventy heptads). Similar periodizations recur in a variety of early Jewish works (second century BCE–second century CE). There are schemas that divide the world into seven ages of a thousand years each (*Testament of Abraham* 19) or six ages of a thousand years plus a millennium of rest (*2 Enoch* 33:1–2). The "Apocalypse of Weeks" divides history into ten weeks of unequal length: seven weeks are past history, three are the age to come (*1 Enoch* 93:1–10, 91:12–

17). The complex calculation of jubilees (seven times seven) is employed to periodize history from creation to new creation in the *Book of Jubilees* and the *Assumption of Moses.* The duration of "this world" in contradistinction to the "world to come" is frequently given as seven thousand years, less frequently six thousand, with a division into three ages: the Age of Confusion, the Age of the Torah, and the Age of the Messiah (B. T., *San.* 97b, *'A. Z.* 9b). The other numerological system, apparently borrowed from the Iranian, focused on twelve periods (*2 Bar.* 56; *T. Ab.* 7b; *Apocalypse of Abraham* 20, 28), with the most tantalizing schema presented in the brief report in *2 Esdras* 14.11 (*4 Esdras* in the Vulgate) that the age of the world is divided into twelve parts, nine parts; and half of the tenth have already passed, two parts and the second half of the tenth remain. However, the basic distinction in the Jewish rabbinic traditions remains persistently dualistic: there are two ages of the world, "this age" (*ha-'olam hazeh*) and the "age to come" (*ha-'olam ha-ba'*).

Christian traditions. The emerging Christian traditions of the ages of the world must be seen first in relation to the Jewish. The primitive Christian writings of the first century focused on the central duality of "this age" and the "age to come" (*Mt.* 12:32, *Eph.* 1:21), being convinced that "the end of the ages has come" (*1 Cor.* 10.11). In the second and third centuries, building on contemporary exegesis of *Psalms* 90:4 (i.e., that a day for the deity equals a thousand years) and Asian Christian traditions of a thousand-year earthly reign of Christ (the millennium), which will be a Golden Age (*Rv.* 20:2–7; Papias, in Eusebius, *Church History* 3.39.1–2; Justin, *Dialogue* 81.3–4; Lactantius, *Divine Institutions* 7.24), and joined to Jewish speculations on the sabbath-week, the hexameral system was developed. This system postulated that the first six days of creation, understood as a period of six thousand years, represented the history of the world; the seventh day represented the thousand-year reign of Christ or the end of the world; occasionally an eighth day would be added, signifying "the beginning of another world" (*Barnabas* 15.3–8; Irenaeus, *Against Heresies* 5.28.3; Methodius, *Banquet* 9; Victorinus of Pettau, *On the Creation of the World* 6; Hippolytus, *Commentary on Daniel* 4.23). In such a periodization, the period of the Incarnation would either be placed in the middle of the sixth millennium (that is, 5,500 years since creation, as in Theophilus, *To Autolycus* 3.28) or at its close (the year 6000, as in Pseudo-Cyprian, *Sinai and Zion* 6). The sabbath-week system at times interacted with a fourfold system of periodization loosely based on Paul in *Galatians* 3.15–26: a period before the law; the period of the law; the period of the prophets; and, equivalent to the sabbath, the period of grace or freedom.

The most influential Christian ages of the world system was that briefly sketched out in the penultimate paragraph of Augustine's *City of God* (22.30) in the first quarter of the fifth century. The first age was from Adam to the Flood, the second from the Flood to Abraham, the third from Abraham to David, the fourth from David to the Babylonian exile, the fifth from the exile to Christ, the sixth age was the present Christian era, the seventh would mark the millennium, followed by an eighth "eternal day" of repose. Although Augustine noted temporal symmetry within the first five ages, he freed the schema from its rigid chronological limitation to a total of five or six thousand years. This flexibility allowed Augustine's system to be the base of most medieval Christian theories and to be influential through the Renaissance (see Coluccio Salutati's letter to Zonari of 5 May 1379).

Over time, modifications of the Augustinian schema were introduced. The eighth age was largely ignored. Some authors, such as Philipp van Haveng in the twelfth century, introduced the notion of an alternation of good and evil ages. The most significant modification was the work of the Calabrian mystic Joachim of Fiore (1132–1202). Joachim's work was a dazzling set of interrelated schemata built around twos, threes, sixes, sevens, and twelves. Alongside the traditional notion of "age" (*aetas*), Joachim introduced the terminology of "stage" (*status*) so that each period was seen as progressive toward a historical fulfillment and as "incubating" its successor. The first five ages, as in Augustine, extended from Adam to Christ, the sixth age was the era of the church; the seventh, the time of consummation. Further schemata were superimposed on this traditional outline. Within the first four ages, the period from Abraham to the prophets was the first stage, that of the Father, with a period of germination from Adam to Jacob and of fruition from Jacob to the prophets. The second stage, that of the Son, extended from the prophets to the present (c. 1260), with a period of germination from the prophets to Christ and of fruition from Christ to Benedict of Nursia. This second portion (which corresponds to the sixth age) was divided into six smaller periods (*etatulae*) with Joachim's times at the end of the fifth period. Yet ahead was the third stage of the Holy Spirit where, following the defeat of the Antichrist at the end of the second stage, a "new people of God" would be brought into being. It will be a Golden Age without labor, heaven will descend to earth, and life will be lived in beatific ecstasy.

Such mythic schemata persist in more secular, Western historical periodizations, but they have interacted as well with non-Christian mythologies in a variety of recent nativist movements, such as the Kugu Sorta ("big candle") movement among the Mari (Cheremis) in Russia. According to this tradition, human history began with a Golden Age and will return to one at the end of time. In between are seventeen historical ages, the present being the ninth. Beginning with the tenth age, the earth will become uninhabitable except by members of the sect.

Myths of recurrence. In a second form of serial periodization, the same series is repeated through multiple cycles of creation or activity.

Babylonian traditions. It would appear that, based on their careful astronomical observations of periodicity, late Babylonian cosmologists (e.g., Berossos, third century BCE) developed the notion of a repetitive cosmic "great year" divided into two seasons: summer, when all the planets were in conjunction with Cancer, would result in world-conflagration; winter, when the planets were in conjunction with Capricorn, would produce a universal flood (Seneca, *Naturales quaestiones* 2.29.1; the schema is attributed to Aristotle in Censorinus, *De die natali* 18.11). As brought over into Greco-Roman thought, the duration of the "great year" was fixed at 12,954 ordinary years (Cicero in the *Hortensius* according to Tacitus, *Dialogus de Oratoribus* 16.7). This period was later identified by Christian authors as the life span of the phoenix (Solinus, *Collectanea rerum Memorabilium* 33.13). Berossos himself appears to have used a far larger time scale. He fixes the reign of the ten antediluvian kings as lasting 432,000 years (a number that is the same as the Indic *kaliyuga*, which was probably influenced by Babylonian speculation).

Greco-Roman traditions. Most likely influenced by the Babylonian "great year," there was a lively Greek and Roman philosophical debate over recurrence, conjoined at times to the topic of the eternity of the world or the plurality of worlds, at other times to the transformation of the Hesiod myth of the five races of men into the later myth of the five or four ages of humanity. Although foreshadowings of this debate can be found in earlier Greek writers, it was most fully developed by the Stoics, many of whom came from the hellenized Near East. This world is but the present member of a series of identical worlds. At a particular planetary conjunction, the world will be destroyed by fire (*ekpyrōsis*), and, following another conjunction, will be restored out of fire "precisely as before." The elements of the cosmos will be in their same place, each individual life will recur with exactly the same experiences. There will be no novelty; "everything is repeated down to the minutest detail," not just once, but over and over again without end (Nemesius, *On the Nature of Man* 38).

Scandinavian traditions. In the *Vǫluspá* and in Snorri's *Gylfaginning*, a myth of both the creation and eventual destruction of the world is presented what appears to be an instance of a common Indo-European pattern. A series of worlds came into being around the great world-tree, Yggdrasill. Following a series of creative acts, the gods and then humans came into existence. After a long period, there will come Ragnarǫk, the destruction of the gods and man, preceded by Fimbulvetr, the great worldwide winter (compare the Iranian myth of Yima). The Great Snake will emerge from the ocean and flood the world; demons attack Ásgarðr, the home of the gods, and the gods and demons meet in cosmic battle in which each side slays the other. Finally, the only survivor, the giant Surtr, sets off the cosmic fire that will destroy the world. There are disparate hints that this is not the final end. The world will be restored, the sons of the dead gods will return, Baldr will reemerge, the two surviving human beings (Líf and LífÞrasir, "life" and "life-holding"), having been sheltered by the world tree, will repopulate the earth, and the cycle continue. (*Voluspá* 31–58; Snorri, *Gylfaginning* 51–53; *Vafruðnismál* 44–45).

Cosmic periods of creation. The most complex form of serial periodization features a mythology containing a series of cosmic ages, related to each other, although separated from one another by catastrophes, so that each successive creation is both a new act and, in some sense, a recapitulation of its predecessors.

Indic traditions. One of the most complex systems detailing the endless repetition of cosmic ages of the world was developed in India. Although elements occur in earlier texts, the systematic elaboration appears to be a development largely of the epic and Puranic literature between the fifth and third centuries BCE. While largely indigenous in its full expression, aspects of the system reflect the considerable interaction between Near Eastern, Hellenistic, Iranian, and Indian traditions of that time as well as more archaic Indo-European motifs.

The fundamental schema is built around a complete cycle of cosmic existence (*mahāyuga*), divided into four ages (*yugas*) of unequal length and valence, each preceded and followed by a period of transition, a "dawn" or "dusk" of proportionate duration. In its most abstract form, the four ages are correlated to throws of dice: the *kṛtayuga* (4), the *tretāyuga* (3), the *dvāparayuga* (2), and the *kaliyuga* (1). This system yields various proportional measurements for the duration of each age in different traditions: 4000/3000/2000/1000 or 4800/3600/2400/1200 or 1,728,000/1,296,000/764,000/432,000 years, yielding equivalent measurements for the length of a *mahāyuga*: 10,000 or 12,000 or 4,320,000 years. In the fully elaborated system, even more extended numbers are employed. A thousand *mahāyugas* equal one *kalpa*, which corresponds to either a day or a night in the life of Brahmā (his total life is 311,040 billion human years). Within each *kalpa* are fourteen secondary cycles (*manvantaras*), each preceded by the destruction and re-creation of the world and a new manifestation of Manu, the progenitor of the human race. (For major versions of the *yuga* myth, see *Bhāgavata Purāṇa* 3.11.6–37; *Brahmāṇḍa Purāṇa* 1.7.19–63 and 1.29.4–40; *Viṣṇu Purāṇa* 1.3.1–25.)

The fully developed myth of the four *yugas* is essentially a cosmogony described in temporal language, yet it contains within it several strands of tradition well-integrated in some versions but capable of appearing independently in other texts. One such strand is a numerical tradition that elaborates the basic schema of four proportional periods into vast cosmic numbers. This numerical schema is correlated with a tradition of the decline of *dharma*. Thus the *kṛtayuga* is also known as the *satyayuga* ("age of truth") and is characterized by elements drawn from the well-developed and independent Indic mythology of a Golden Age. The *tretāyuga* is characterized by a diminution of virtue and by the introduction of death and labor into the human sphere, that is to say, by an end to the Golden Age. The *dvāparayuga* marks the transition to the degenerative half of the cycle: evil increases, and the human life span decreases. The *kaliyuga*, which is the present age, dated by some as having begun in 3102 BCE (the traditional date of the war recounted in the *Mahābhārata*), is a period of discord and disintegration wherein evil triumphs. Through this correlation, the cosmogonic structure of the *yugas* has been transformed into an anthropology. The *yuga* myth is further intertwined with the mythology of Brahmā and Viṣṇu, especially their roles in the rhythmic expansion and contraction of the cosmos. This element is especially prominent in accounts of the *mahāpralaya*, the "great dissolution" (*Matsya Purāṇa* 167.13–25). Finally, there is the royal mythology of the Manus and the *avatāras* of Visnu, expressed in the *manvantara* cycle.

With important modifications and different soteriological implications, the Indic cosmic ages were adapted by both Buddhism and Jainism. The Indic system was influential as well on Neo-Confucian speculations on the ages of the world.

Mesoamerican traditions. Among the northern Maya, there is considerable evidence for both the conception of time (*kin*) without beginning or end that allows vast chronological computations extending back four hundred million years, a duration that encompasses all past and future world cycles, and the mythic notion of a number of previous worlds, each terminated by a universal flood.

In the Aztec traditions, as exemplified by the more than twenty versions of the myth of the suns, the *Leyenda de los Soles*, and as carved on the so-called Calendar Stone, a more complex picture is presented. Superimposed on an archaic myth that, like the Maya, depicted a continuous series of cosmic creations and destructions, is a myth of five suns, each marking an age of the world as part of a cosmogonic drama involving the struggles for supremacy among the Tezcatlipocas, the sons of the androgynous supreme deity, Ometeotl. Each one would create a world only to have it destroyed by another. Four such primeval worlds are identified, each named after the mode of their destruction: the world of the first sun, 4 Jaguar, which lasted 676 years until its inhabitants were devoured by jaguars; the second sun, 4 Wind, which lasted 364 years, until winds blew away its inhabitants; the third sun, 4 Rain of Fire, which lasted 312 years, until its people were destroyed by a heavenly fire; and the fourth sun, 4 Water, which lasted 676 years and ended in a universal deluge. The fifth sun, 4 Movement, is the world that the Aztec inhabit and represents a revolution in the cycle of creation and destruction. Rather than the peripheral symbols of the four cardinal directions, with which the previous worlds are identified, the fifth sun is the world of the center, guaranteed by an agreement between the rival deities and by divine acts of self-sacrifice.

SEE ALSO Golden Age; Utopia.

BIBLIOGRAPHY

For a general orientation from a broad comparative perspective, see Mircea Eliade's *Cosmos and History: The Myth of the Eternal Return* (New York, 1954), esp. chap. 3. The articles under the heading "Ages of the World" in the *Encyclopaedia of Religion and Ethics*, edited by James Hastings, vol. 1 (Edinburgh, 1908) are badly dated in their interpretation (the article on Babylonian systems should be ignored), but they do provide a useful anthology of texts in translation from a variety of traditions. Gary W. Trompf's *The Idea of Historical Recurrence in Western Thought: From Antiquity to the Reformation* (Berkeley, Calif., 1979), albeit devoted to a parallel theme, is the best interpretative history of world-periodization in Western thought.

On Iranian traditions, R. C. Zaehner's book *The Teachings of the Magi* (London, 1956) provides a brief exposition and translated sections from the late Pahlavi books. Geo Widengren's *Mani and Manichaeism* (New York, 1965), pp. 43–73, emphasizes the Iranian elements in the Manichaean schema. Joseph Ward Swain's "The Theory of the Four Monarchies," *Classical Philology* 35 (January 1940): 1–21, remains the classic statement on the relationship of Iranian to Israelitic schema; D. S. Russell's *The Method and Message of Jewish Apocalyptic, 200 B.C.–A.D. 100* (Philadelphia, 1964), pp. 224–229, gives an adequate summary of the early Jewish materials.

Jean Daniélou's definitive article "La typologie millénariste de la semaine dans le christianisme primitif," *Vigiliae Christianae* 2 (1948): 1–16, is summarized in his *The Theology of Jewish Christianity*, edited and translated by John A. Baker (London, 1964), pp. 377–404; Auguste Luneau's *L'histoire du salut chez les Pères de l'Église: La doctrine des âges du monde* (Paris, 1964) is extremely detailed on the patristic materials. Marjorie E. Reeves's *Joachim of Fiore and the Prophetic Future* (London, 1976), pp. 1–28, provides the best brief exposition of Joachim's system.

Thomas A. Sebeok and Francis J. Ingemann's *Studies in Cheremis: The Supernatural* (New York, 1956), pp. 320–337, gives the basic information about the Kugu Sorta. On the Babylonian great year, the essential study is B. L. van der Waerden's "Das Grosse Jahr und die ewige Wiederkehr," *Hermes* 80 (1952): 129–155. The Greek materials have been well surveyed by Charles Mugler in *Deux thèmes de la cosmologie grecque: Devenir cyclique et pluralité des mondes* (Paris, 1953), although some of his interpretations are fanciful. The entire notion of recurrence is brilliantly treated in Trompf's *The Idea of Historical Recurrence in Western Thought*, cited above.

The classic study of the Scandinavian myth remains Axel Olrik's *Ragnarök: Die Sagen vom Weltuntergang* (Berlin, 1922), but see Georges Dumézil's *Gods of the Ancient Northmen*, edited by Einar Haugen (Berkeley, Calif., 1973), chap. 3, for its setting within archaic Indo-European mythology. A major text in translation, with valuable footnotes, illustrating the Indic system of *yugas* is provided by H. H. Wilson in *The Viṣṇu Purāṇa* (London, 1840), vol. 1, pp. 44–67, now available in a second edition (Calcutta, 1961). C. D. Church gives a rich bibliography in "The Myth of the Four Yugas in the Sanskrit Purāṇas," *Purāṇa* 16 (1974): 5–25. The Indic, Buddhist, and Jain traditions are interpreted in Eliade's "Time and Eternity in Indian Thought," in *Papers from the Eranos Yearbooks*, edited by Joseph Campbell, vol. 3, *Man and Time* (New York, 1957), pp. 173–200. For a translation and commentary on the Aztec myth of the suns, see Miguel León-Portilla's *Aztec Thought and Culture: A Study of the Ancient Nahuatl Mind* (Norman, Okla., 1963), pp. 35–48.

JONATHAN Z. SMITH (1987)

AGGADAH SEE MIDRASH AND AGGADAH

AGNI

AGNI is the god of fire in ancient and traditional India. Derived from an Indo-European root, the Sanskrit word *agni* ("fire") is related to such other forms as Latin *ignis* and Lithuanian *ugnis*. A cognate appears in a Hittite text found at Bogazköy in the name *Ak/gniš*, identifying a god of devastation and annihilation. Although his mythological and ritual roots are reflected in Old Irish, Roman, and Iranian sources, the peculiar development of the god of fire as Agni owes as much to the ritualizing tendencies, the priestly vision, and the strong asceticism of the Indian context as it does to the god's Indo-European heritage.

THE RITUAL CONTEXT. Fire and heat play a central role in Vedic people's understanding of themselves within the cosmos. Fire is at once the most intimate and the most universal of elements; it can simultaneously inflict pain and bring purity, and it will, in an instant, make a person blind or give him vision. Fire is most fascinating to the Aryans, however, because of its capacity for domestication: with the taming of fire (and therefore of nature at large) come both the foundations of civilization and the means for release from it.

The Vedic mastery of fire took place within the ritual context. As the solemn (*śrauta*) ritual developed, a system of correspondences was devised whereby priests could manipulate the fires and fire hearths to create and control a tripartite cosmos: Agni as the heavenly fire, or sun, resided in the western *āhavanīya* hearth with the gods; Agni as the atmospheric fire, or moon, resided in the southern *dakṣiṇāgni* hearth with the ancestors (*pitaras*); and Agni as the earthly fire or domestic flame resided in the western *gārhapatya* hearth with humans. This system of homologies also made reference to the newly emerging class system: the heavenly or offering fire represented the priest (*brāhmaṇa*), the atmospheric or protecting fire the warrior (*kṣatriya*), and the earthly or producing fire the merchant (*vaiśya*).

As the central civilizing agent, the ritual fire played a special role in the development of the domestic (*gṛhya*) liturgy, particularly in the marriage rite (Vivāha) and funeral ceremony (Antyeṣṭi). As the symbol and agent of the transformative process, fire with its heat stood midway between the coolness of celibate studenthood and restrained householdership, and between this life and the next. Marriage itself was effected by circumambulating the fire clockwise seven times, and true wifehood implied the continual presence of the cooking fire. Likewise, passage beyond death required the special translatory properties of the cremation fire, which, because it destroyed, purified, and "reconstituted" the old self into a new one, was treated cautiously by priests, who feared the potentially demonic qualities of Agni the *kravyād* ("flesh-eating one"). Furthermore, in a practice known in India at least as early as the epics and officially banned by the British in 1828, the wife as *satī* joined her husband on his funeral pyre, thereby ensuring the spiritual mutation by fire of the entire sacrificial unit (e.g., husband and wife) into the next world.

Fire was also used to test a person's truth. Because Agni was the god who presided over speech, the truth of an individual's words was demonstrated by Agni as the "defendant" walked through (or endured an assault by) fire. The best-known example of this is in the *Ramāyāṇa* where Sītā, after being released from Rāvaṇa's citadel in Lanka, is made to prove her fidelity to Rāma by publicly entering the flames.

THE MYTHOLOGY OF AGNI. The "personality" of Agni, as developed early in Vedic thought, delineates both the specific functions of the ritual and the divine models for the behavior of man. Next to Indra, Agni is the most prominent of the Ṛgvedic gods, and his anthropomorphic qualities are taken directly from the physical fire: for example, smoke-bannered, flame-haired, tawny-bearded, sharp-jawed, bright-toothed, and seven-tongued. As the mouth of the gods, Agni becomes butter backed and butter faced on receipt of his food, the sacrificial ghee (clarified butter). He has horns and bellows like a bull; he has a tail and is groomed like a horse; and he is winged like the eagle of the sky. Ever renewed in the ritual hearth, Agni is both the youngest and the oldest of the gods, and although born of Dyaus, the sky god, his real parents are the two *araṇīs* ("fire sticks"): the upper his father and the lower his mother (or, alternately, both his mothers). He is called *sūnuḥ sahasaḥ* ("son of strength"), literally, the product of powerful friction produced by the hands of the priest or, figuratively, a manifestation of a victoriously procreative cosmic power.

By far the single most significant element in Agni's personality is his priesthood. As fire he must officiate at every sacrifice; thus he is not only the divine counterpart of the human priest but also the prototype for and most eminent exemplar of all priestly activities, especially that of the *hotṛ* priest, the reciter of the liturgy. Moreover, the mediatorial nature of Agni's office charges him with the safe transport of offerings to the gods and, in return, blessings to humanity. Since successful travel as messenger (*dūta*) between earthly petitioners and heavenly benefactors is insured by priestly eloquence, a quality derived from a combination of skill in language and insight into the cosmic mysteries, Agni is not only the preeminent priest but the preeminent seer (*kavi*) as well.

Agni's personality stresses certain key functions that come to be referred to by a system of epithets. Vaiśvānara, the fire with power over all humans, for example, represents both the fire become sun during the liturgical magic of dawn and, supported by the Matarisvan myth, the ritual fire as symbol of Aryan superiority, protecting and empowering the nation against all enemies. As a civilizing agent, Vaiśvānara represents humanity's control over light, warmth, and the demarcation of time (Agni as sun) as well as his concern for national boundaries and the establishment of an unrivaled peace (Agni against the barbarians). Jātavedas, the fire in possession of the creatures, stresses Agni's function as keeper of the Vedic family and preeminent advocate of humans, for his unbroken ritual presence, his service in strengthening and uplifting the domestic community, and his role (via the cremation fire) in guaranteeing the proper transformation of the deceased into an ancestor make him the supreme guardian of the generations as well as the perpetuator of Aryan culture. Again, Apam Napat, the fire as child of the waters, stresses both the vital and procreative powers of natural water and the intoxicating and transformative powers of ritual water.

In the Brāhmaṇas, Agni's central relation is to Prajāpati, and the joint figure Agni-Prajāpati becomes the cosmic person who is projected into being through dismemberment. The various "searches" for Agni (see, for example, his flight in *Ṛgveda* 10.51) culminate in the ritual collection and reassembly of Agni (as sacrificer and cosmos) in the Agnicayana and serve to reaffirm the presence of fire in every element. Moreover, in *Śatapatha Brāhmaṇa* 1.4.1.10ff., Agni appears as Vaiśvānara and is carried in the mouth of Māthava, king of Videgha, toward the east. Jumping from the king's mouth at the mention of butter, Vaiśvānara burns his way to the Sadānīrā River, indicating by this the contemporary extent of the Brahmanic *yajña* ("worship"). In the Upaniṣads, Agni is identified with various aspects of the all-pervading *brahman,* and in the Purāṇas, notably the *Agni Purāṇa,* Agni is identified with the high god. In spite of this, however, and despite examples of known iconographical representations of Agni (particularly in stone), the extent of his worship in the later theistic context is marginal.

Heat and the Ascetic Tradition. With the shift in emphasis from sacrifice to sacrificer in the Brāhmaṇa period, the abstract qualities of the fire's "heat" (*tapas*) become interiorized: the heat of the flame, of Soma, of the priest's sweat, and of the cooked food become part of an internal sacrifice within the body (*antaryajña*) of the "patron become priest." What was in the period of the Brāhmaṇas the elaborate fire ritual (*agnihotra*) becomes in the ascetic tradition the "interiorized fire ritual" (*antaragnihotra*). As humanity itself is identified with the sacrificial process and with the cosmos, an elaborate system of correspondences is set up homologizing the microcosmic fires of the human body with the macrocosmic fires of the universe, the whole system manipulable through the asceticism of yoga. The long-haired ascetic (*muni*), first seen holding fire and riding the wind in *Ṛgveda* 10.136, now becomes the ascetic thoroughly possessed by Agni: in his head is the fire of mind and speech, in his arms the fire of sovereign power, and in his belly and loins the fire of productivity.

See Also Fire; Vedism and Brahmanism.

Bibliography

The standard and most comprehensive catalog of Agnian lore in the *Ṛgveda* remains A. A. Macdonnell's *Vedic Mythology* (New York, 1974). Macdonnell not only lists each of Agni's traits but gives textual citations as well. An important discussion of one of Agni's epithets within the larger Vedic context can be found in Jan Gonda's *Some Observations on the Relations between Gods and Powers in the Veda, à Propos of the Phrase Sunuh Sahash* (The Hague, 1957). Expanding on the detailed study of *tapas* in Chauncey J. Blair's *Heat in the Rig Veda and Atharva Veda* (New Haven, 1961) is the excellent, and most provocative, discussion in David M. Knipe's *In the Image of Fire: Vedic Experiences of Heat* (Delhi, 1975). Focusing primarily on Brahmanic sources, the latter interprets the Agnian material from the vantage of the history of religions. A comprehensive account of the performance and symbolism of the Agnicayana is *Agni: The Vedic Ritual of the Fire Altar,* 2 vols. including tapes (Berkeley, Calif., 1970, reprint 2001), by Fritz Staal in collaboration with C. V. Somayajipad and M. Itti Ravi Nambudiri. *Indian Fire Ritual,* by Musashi Tachikawa, Shrikant Bahulkar, and Madhave Kolhatkar (Delhi, 2001), explains the basic ritual of *Iṣṭi,* using original texts and photographs of sacrificial performances made in Pune, India, in 1979.

Ellison Banks Findly (1987 and 2005)

AGNON, SHEMU'EL YOSEF

AGNON, SHEMU'EL YOSEF (1888–1970), was a Hebrew prose writer and, along with the German Jewish poet Nelly Sachs, the 1966 Nobel laureate for literature. Born Shemu'el Yosef Czaczkes in the town of Buczacz in the eastern European region of Galicia, then part of the Austro-Hungarian Empire, Agnon was raised in a traditionally observant Jewish family with an openness to participating in contemporary Western culture. Under the influence of Zionism, he immigrated to Palestine in 1908. There he lived primarily in Jaffa, which at the time was the center of secular-oriented Zionist culture. He also lived for several months in Jerusalem, a stronghold of non- and anti-Zionist ultra-Orthodox Jewry. During this period he changed his original family name, Czaczkes, to Agnon, adapted from the title of the first story he published in Palestine, "*ʿAgunot.*" (*ʿAgunot* is a Jewish legal term for women unable to remarry because their husbands are missing or refuse to grant them a proper divorce, a circumstance Agnon used metaphorically to refer to psychological and spiritual alienation.)

Apparently motivated by the desire to expand his cultural horizons, Agnon left Palestine for Germany in 1912. As the product of traditional eastern European Judaism, he became an important resource for assimilated German Jews, who found in the German translations of his Hebrew writings ways to connect with the Jewish tradition from which they were distanced. While in Germany, Agnon associated with the Jewish philosophers Martin Buber (1878–1965), with whom he began to edit a collection of Hasidic tales that was not completed, and Franz Rosenzweig (1886–1929), and with the scholar of Jewish mysticism Gershom Scholem (1897–1982). In 1924 Agnon immigrated once again to Palestine with his wife Esther (née Marx), whom he had married in Germany in 1920, and their two children, settling this time in Jerusalem.

As a youth Agnon wrote in both Yiddish and Hebrew, but beginning with his first immigration to Palestine he devoted himself to prose writing in Hebrew. Agnon departed from the traditional religious practice of his upbringing during the periods of his first immigration to Palestine and his residence in Germany, in keeping with the prevailing secular cultural ethos of Zionist settlers and Jewish intellectuals at the time. Yet by the time he settled in Jerusalem in the 1920s he had returned to a traditional pattern of observance, which he maintained for the rest of his life.

The complexity of Agnon's relationship to the Jewish religious tradition is most evident in the genres in which he wrote:

1. Anthologies of traditional Jewish texts;
2. Works of fiction and adaptations of legends that portray the world of premodern Jewry;
3. Realistic social fiction;
4. Modernistic stories of a world beset by a crisis of religious faith.

The worlds Agnon presents in his prose run the gamut of Jewish experience from premodern religious traditionalism to a modernism beset by severe identity crises. The Hebrew of these works is characterized by frequent allusions to the style and content of rabbinic, medieval, and early modern religious literature. In adopting such a religiously allusive style, Agnon maintained close ties to the world of Jewish tradition, even as he explored the challenges of modernity.

Anthologies of Traditional Texts. The approach to the Jewish tradition in these anthologies is one of respect for the spiritual treasures found in biblical, rabbinic, medieval, and early modern sources. In preparing each of these anthologies, Agnon followed in the footsteps of a number of European Hebrew writers (most notably Hayyim Nahman Bialik [1873–1934], Yehoshua Hana Ravnitzky [1859–1944], and M. Y. Berdichevsky [1865–1921]) who were concerned that the textual forms in which the Jewish tradition had been transmitted had become largely inaccessible to the modern reader. In order to preserve traditional religious knowledge among Jews, they compiled anthologies written in a uniformly accessible Hebrew style and based on modern principles of thematic organization. Two anthologies edited by Agnon were published in their entirety during his lifetime: one on the Jewish High Holidays, *Yamim nora'im* (*Days of Awe*, 1937), and one on the revelation at Mount Sinai, *Attem re'item* (*Present at Sinai*, 1959). In addition, Agnon sporadically published versions of texts in two other thematic areas: the Hasidic tradition founded by Baʿal Shem Ṭov and the relationship of Jews to their sacred texts. While he published short anthologies of texts in these two areas, it was only after his death that full anthologies of these texts were published.

Works of Fiction and Adaptations of Legends. The sources for these narratives that portray the world of premodern Jewry in eastern Europe and Palestine were folktales with which Agnon was familiar as well as his youthful experience of traditional Jewish life in Buczacz and his observation of Orthodox Jewish life in Jerusalem. Some of these narratives take the form of legends transmitted by a traditional chronicler. Others are more of a blend of pious storytelling and modern fiction. In this body of literature one may discern Agnon's highly ambivalent attitude toward the world of tradition in which he had been raised, ranging from an ironic and critical distance to a nostalgic celebration of the world of tradition as a valuable spiritual resource from which even the modern Jew has much to learn. (See, for example, the novel *Hakhnasat kallah* [*The Bridal Canopy*, 1931; 1953].)

Realistic Social Fiction. In addition to works steeped in the world of Jewish tradition, Agnon wrote a variety of works of fiction that portray the various social settings in which he lived: the Buczacz of his childhood (see the novella *Sippur pashut* [*A Simple Story*, 1935]); the Zionist settlers and Orthodox Jews of Palestine during the waning years of Ottoman rule (see the novel *Temol shilshom* [*Only Yesterday*, 1945]); German Jewry during World War I (see examples of such stories in *Twenty-One Stories* and *A Book That Was Lost and Other Stories*); Buczacz in the period between the world wars, which he observed firsthand during a visit there in 1930 (see the novel *Oreaḥ natah lalun* [*A Guest for the Night*, 1939]; and Palestine of the 1930s (see the novel *Shirah*, [*Shira*, 1971]). While less overtly preoccupied with the world of religious piety than works of the first two genres, these works, to varying degrees, explore the effects of the crisis of faith and diminishing loyalty to traditional Jewish practices that Jews have experienced in a world plagued by war and torn apart by conflicting ideologies.

Modernistic Stories. Beginning in the 1930s, Agnon published a series of surrealistic short stories under the title *Sefer hamaʿasim* (The book of deeds). In many of these stories, religious observance is disturbed by nightmarish impediments, and the protagonists are tormented by their distance from traditional faith. The fact that the narrators of these stories rarely accomplish anything (in ironic contrast to the title of the series) signifies the unresolved tension within Agnon's soul between loyalty to tradition and the attractions of modernity. Some of these stories appear in the collections *Twenty-One Stories* and *A Book That Was Lost and Other Stories.*

See Also Midrash and Aggadah; Zionism.

Bibliography

Works by Agnon in English Translation

Anthologies and collections

Betrothed and Edo and Enam: Two Tales. Translated by Walter Lever. New York, 1966.

A Book That Was Lost and Other Stories. Edited by Alan Mintz and Anne Golomb Hoffman. New York, 1995.

Days of Awe. Translated by Maurice T. Galpert and Jacob Sloan. Edited by Nahum N. Glatzer. New York, 1965.

Present at Sinai: The Giving of the Law. Translated by Michael Swirsky. Philadelphia, 1994.

Twenty-One Stories. Edited by Nahum N. Glatzer. New York, 1970.

Novellas and novels
The Bridal Canopy. Translated by I. M. Lask. Garden City, N.Y., 1937.

A Guest for the Night. Translated by Misha Louvish. New York, 1968.

In the Heart of the Seas. Translated by I. M. Lask. New York, 1947.

Only Yesterday. Translated by Barbara Harshav. Princeton, N.J., 2000.

Shira. Translated by Zeva Shapiro. New York, 1989.

A Simple Story. Translated by Hillel Halkin. New York, 1985.

Works about Agnon
Aberbach, David. *At the Handles of the Lock: Themes in the Fiction of S. J. Agnon.* Oxford, 1984.

Band, Arnold J. *Nostalgia and Nightmare: A Study in the Fiction of S. Y. Agnon.* Berkeley, Calif., 1968.

Ben-Dov, Nitza. *Agnon's Art of Indirection: Uncovering Latent Content in the Fiction of S. Y. Agnon.* Leiden, 1993.

Fisch, Harold. *S. Y. Agnon.* New York, 1975.

Hochman, Baruch. *The Fiction of S. Y. Agnon.* Ithaca, N.Y., 1970.

Hoffman, Anne Golomb. *Between Exile and Return: S. Y. Agnon and the Drama of Writing.* Albany, N.Y., 1991.

Katz, Stephen. *The Centrifugal Novel: S. Y. Agnon's Poetics of Composition.* Madison, N.J., 1999.

Laor, Dan. *Haye ʿAgnon.* Jerusalem, 1998. This biography is available only in Hebrew.

Oz, Amos. *The Silence of Heaven: Agnon's Fear of God.* Translated by Barbara Harshav. Princeton, N.J., 2000.

Patterson, David, and Glenda Abramson, eds. *Tradition and Trauma: Studies in the Fiction of S. J. Agnon.* Boulder, Colo., 1994.

Shaked, Gershon. *Shmuel Yosef Agnon: A Revolutionary Traditionalist.* Translated by Jeffrey M. Green. New York, 1989.

Shaked, Gershon. *Modern Hebrew Fiction.* Translated by Yael Lotan. Bloomington, Ind., 2000.

DAVID C. JACOBSON (2005)

AGNOSTICISM SEE DOUBT AND BELIEF

AGNŌSTOS THEOS.

The phrase *agnōstōn theōn* (nominative singular, *agnōstos theos*) was found inscribed on Greek altars dedicated "to the unknown gods." The inscription had no mystical or theosophical meaning, but arose out of a concern for cultic safety: no one wanted to incur the wrath of gods whose names were unknown but who just might exist and be vexed by the lack of honors.

The meaning of the designation *agnōstos* is indeed ambiguous: it could mean "unknowable" or "unknown," depending upon the context. God could in fact be "unknown" without necessarily being "unknowable." Even from a philosophical standpoint, "unknowable" does not require an absolute or irreconcilable meaning. God can be unknowable by the ordinary means of cognition or by discursive reason yet still be knowable by means of divine grace in contemporary or mystical intuition. This semantic uncertainty beclouds our understanding of the ancient usage.

The distinguished philologist Eduard Norden (1913) attempted to show that the notion of *agnōstos theos* was foreign and even contrary to the Classical Greek spirit. The term did not appear until late in the Classical period, and then only in texts clearly under Oriental influence: Jewish, Gnostic, Neoplatonic, and Christian writings. Further, the expression would imply "a renunciation of inquiry" (p. 84) that would ill accord with Hellenic speculation.

HELLENIC AND HELLENISTIC PAGANISM. Most often, Greek gods are identified according to geographical location and function by epithets that thus remove these gods from the category of "unknown" gods. To be sure, the gods belong to a world distinct from that of men, and possess a nature—immortal and blessed—that eludes the grasp of human understanding, regardless of the anthropomorphic images that make them physically resemble their worshipers. In their cult, however, the Greeks were concerned only with the names and the spheres of action of these superior beings, for the purpose of invoking them with some degree of effectiveness. The phrase *agnōstōn theōn* was found on two altars observed by Pausanias, one at Phaleron, the other at Olympia. The apostle Paul employed the singular when citing the inscription on an Athenian altar as he argued on behalf of monotheism (Norden, 1913, pp. 55–56). Still, there is no evidence of any cult rendered to an unknown god, nor to an unknowable one. The reconstruction that Hugo Hepding propounded for an inscription found at Pergamum that supposedly dealt with "unknown gods" was rebutted by Otto Weinreich (1915, p. 29). The *Alexander Romance* 1.33 attributes to the conqueror of Asia the erection of an altar "to the unknown god," but this detail lacks historical value (ibid., p. 28).

Philosophers have raised the question of the knowability or unknowability of God. Yet the famous statement from Plato (*Timaeus* 28c), often quoted and commented upon, addresses the ineffability of the creator god, which does not rule out that one might be able to conceive of him and to know him intuitively (Plato, *Epinomis* 7.342c–d) or analogously (*Republic* 6.506e–509a). Nevertheless in *Parmenides* (142a), Plato writes of the One who is "neither named . . . nor known." The distinction between divine power that manifests itself to men and divine being that eludes them, just like the sun that one cannot look at without being blinded, is implied by Xenophon (*Memorabilia* 4.3.13–14). Further, the distinction between existence and essence, common among Stoics, originates with Aristotle and perhaps with the doctrine of the Sophists (Festugière, 1950–1954, vol. 4, p. 16), yet the expression *agnōstos theos* still does not appear in these contexts. Damascius applies it to an Orphic text that appears to be among the most ancient: it had been quoted by Eudemus of Rhodes, a disciple of Aristotle. But Damascius rewrites Orphism in his own fashion. Even though born of the Night, this ineffable and unknowable god derives from Neoplatonism.

The Platonic tradition of the imperial Roman epoch limits the experience of the first god, ineffable and accessible, to the human intellect alone. Numenius (frag. 26) attributes to Plato the idea that only the demiurge is known to men, "while the first Intellect, the one that contains the name 'Being' within itself, remains totally unknown to men." Norden (1913) and H. J. Krämer (1963) discern Gnostic influences here. However, Numenius remains faithful to the Platonic concept of the Nous as the suprarational faculty of mystical contemplation, as well as to the idea of the Good, the greatest object of knowledge.

According to Proclus (*Elements of Theology* 123), "everything divine . . . is ineffable and *agnōston*"; that is, by surpassing the range of language, the divine lies beyond the scope of discursive reasoning. Yet Proclus's entire body of work proves that he was seeking to know God. The Unknown Father of the Neoplatonist Martianus Capella corresponds to the First Intellect of Numenius and to the God of Plato. Like Albinus and Numenius, the Latin Neoplatonist seems to think that, thanks to the Mens (identical with the Greeks' Nous), the supreme god can be conceived through mystical intuition. Damascius starts by affirming the unknowability of God, yet specifies that it is necessary to empty one's intellect so that the subject can blend with the object by removing any barrier, through *aphairesis.*

In Hermetism several contradictory currents intersect. In principle, the All that is God "is perceivable and knowable only to himself" (*Asclepius* 34). Although he cannot be comprehended or defined, he wants to be known and thus makes himself known as God. It is entirely characteristic of the Good to be known and recognized, and to ignore him is impious. He becomes visible "to the intellect and the heart" through an interior illumination (Festugière, 1950–1954, vol. 4, pp. 241ff.). Indeed, one must become God in order to attain the happiness of this "gnosis," one must become "divinized" or regenerated.

HELLENISTIC JUDAISM. One of the earliest literal appearances of *agnōstos theos* is that in Josephus Flavius (*Against Apion* 2.167): Moses, he states, showed us that God is "knowable by his power, but unknowable in his essence." In saying this, Josephus was not relying directly on Jewish tradition. (The Septuagint makes no distinction between the existence of God, manifested by the created world, and his essence.) He refers instead to the "wisest of the Greeks . . . Pythagoras, Anaxagoras, Plato, the philosopher of the Portico." The distinction was common among the Stoics, who derived it from Aristotle. It was employed whenever anyone would comment on the ancient philosophers (whence the reference to Pythagoras, Anaxagoras, and Plato).

Nonetheless, the Stoics tended to put more emphasis on the god manifested through creation. Taking a different stance, Philo Judaeus stresses in several places that it is impossible for man to grasp the invisible and incorporeal essence of God. Moses, after all, halted after being blinded by the divine beams. God made himself visible to Abraham, but man has no faculty of his own for experiencing the absolute being. The inaccessibility of the *agnōstos theos* appears to be more radical in the Jewish tradition than in most developed Hellenistic speculations. It cannot be said, however, that the notion of *agnōstos theos* itself is of Oriental origin.

GNOSTICISM. The unknown god is a fundamental theme of gnosticism. During the second century CE, the teaching of philosophers upheld the divine transcendence by making a distinction between the Demiurge, perceptible in his cosmic creation, and the supreme Intellect, inaccessible to the human intellect. This distinction was furthered by the Gnostics, who perceived an opposition between the knowable and the unknowable. The transcendent god appeared to be a stranger to the universe, concealed from the creator god as well as from his creatures (Hippolytus, *Philosophuma* 6:33; *Gospel of Truth* 18.7–14). This is the Unknown Father or the *Propator* of the angels and archangels (Irenaeus, *Against Heresies* 1.19; 1.23.2). It is also the "good god" of Marcion—"naturaliter . . . ignotus" (Tertullian, *Against Marcion* 5.16.3). The Son reveals the Father whom "no one knows." According to the Valentinians, the Unknown Father makes himself known to the aeons by ways of Monogenes (his "only begotten"). In the beginning, the angels and archangels do not know who has created them, and their ignorance of the Father causes fear and terror among them (*Gospel of Truth* 17.9–16). Yet in arousing this inner crisis (which the Gnostics express in terms of a mythico-allegorical drama), this essentially forbidding transcendence of the Father forces them into a search for salvation through gnosis, through knowledge of the Unknowable (Jonas, 1963, pp. 257f., 404ff.). This gnosis of the *agnōstos* does not proceed directly by way of reason. Certain sects employed a ritual of initiation, or mystagogy (Tröger, 1971, p. 69): the Marcionites baptized neophytes "in the name of the Unknown Father." Yet in general it is God who reveals himself. Thus a Coptic hymn addresses God: "No one can know you against your will." Gnosis proceeds not from the knowing subject but from divine grace.

CHRISTIANITY. In his sermon to the Athenians (*Acts* 17:23), Paul claims that he is proclaiming to them the God whom they honor without knowing him. Paul emphasized the basic meaning of a dedication that was written in the plural (to the *agnōstōn theōn*) in a way that was consistent with his doctrine of the mystery made known to men by the Christ. In the *Clementine Homilies* (18.18), Peter interprets *Isaiah* 1:31 ("Israel has not known me") in a way that rebuts the argument of the Marcionites: the Jews ignored the justice of the known God! Clement of Alexandria (*Miscellanies* 5.12.78.1–3) comments on the unknown god of *Acts* by referring to Plato (*Timaeus* 28c). Yet the statement by Christ in *Matthew* 11:27 ("No one knows the Son except the Father, just as no one knows the Father except the Son") legitimized the Valentinian conception of the Unknown Father and might be seen as encouraging ignorance about God. Paul reproached the pagans for this ignorance, which he condemned as an unpardonable fault (*1 Cor.* 15:34, *Rom.* 1:20, *Eph.* 4:18, *Acts* 17:30). Christ had left men with no excuse for ignorance, since he was the visible image of the invisible God and the revealer of the divine mystery (*Col.* 1:15).

Nevertheless, the Fathers of the church were fond of quoting Plato in order to show that the philosopher urged pagans to seek out the unknown god. The Fathers would also set the religious knowledge of the lowliest Christian in contrast to the idle uncertainties of the learned. They also at the same time readily stressed the unknowability of God: he is known to us only through himself in all his grandeur; he is "beyond the understandable," incomprehensible, indeed beyond being in itself. Yet divine grace and the Word allow men to conceive the unknown. The patristic tradition is practically unanimous in recognizing Christ as a type of hierophant of divine mysteries.

There is, however, a line of thought of Neoplatonic inspiration that legitimizes negative theology. The hymn to God by Gregory of Nazianzus, improperly attributed to Proclus, proclaims him to be the "only unknowable" while still being the creator of all that are knowable. Synesius of Cyrene exalts the Unknown Father, unknowable to reason and ineffable. For Dionysius the Areopagite (*Mystical Theology* 2), it is a matter of knowing an "unknowing" (*agnōsia*); in his view, Paul knew God as "transcending every mode of knowledge" (*Patrologia Graeca* 3.1073a). Thus Maximus the Confessor could write, "Even when known, he remains the Unknown." He is the *Deus absconditus* who, were it otherwise, would not be God.

SEE ALSO Deification; Via Negativa.

BIBLIOGRAPHY

Boyancé, Pierre. "Fulvius Nobilior et le dieu ineffable." In *Études sur la religion romaine*, pp. 227–252. Rome, 1972.

Canet, L. "Connaissance par non-savoir." In *Lux perpetua*, by Franz Cumont, pp. 419–421. Paris, 1949.

Dodds, E. R., ed. and trans. *Elements of Theology* (1933). 2d ed. Oxford, 1963.

Festugière, A.-J. *La révélation d'Hermès Trismégiste*. 4 vols. Paris, 1950–1954.

Geffcken, Johannes. *Zwei griechische Apologeten* (1907). 2d ed. Hildesheim, 1970.

Grant, Robert M. *Gnosticism and Early Christianity*. New York, 1966.

Jonas, Hans. *The Gnostic Religion*. 2d ed., rev. Boston, 1963.

Krämer, Hans Joachim. *Der Ursprung der Geistmetaphysik*. Amsterdam, 1963.

Nilsson, Martin P. *Geschichte der griechischen Religion*, vol. 2, *Die hellenistische und römische Zeit*. 3d ed. Munich, 1974. See pages 355 and 357.

Norden, Eduard. *Agnostos Theos: Untersuchungen zur Formengeschichte religiöser Rede* (1913). 2d ed. Darmstadt, 1956.

Places, Édouard des. *La religion grecque*. Paris, 1969.

Reitzenstein, Richard. *Die hellenistischen Mysterienreligionen* (1917). 3d ed. Darmstadt, 1966. Translated by John E. Steely as *The Hellenistic Mystery Religions* (Pittsburgh, 1978).

Tröger, Karl-Wolfgang. *Mysterienglaube und Gnosis in Corpus Hermeticum XIII*. Berlin, 1971.

Van der Horst, Pieter Willem. "The Unknown God (Acts 17:23)," R. Van den Broek, T. Baarda, and J. Mansfeld, ed. *Knowledge of God in the Graeco-Roman World* (*Epro*, 112), Leiden, 1988. See pages 19–42.

Weinreich, Otto. "De dis ignotis quaestiones selectae." *Archiv für Religionswissenschaft 18* (1915): 1–52.

ROBERT TURCAN (1987 AND 2005)
Translated from French by Paul C. Duggan

AGŌGĒ, a Greek singular noun derived from the verb *agō* ("to lead"), can be used to denote the leading by the hand of horses. In human terms, *agōgē* was used by the Spartans and the inhabitants of the island of Chios to denote the process by which their youths were "domesticated." In other words, the youths were considered to be similar to wild foals and fillies and had to be "broken" before they could enter adult society. Since this view of youths was widely shared in Greece, the term *agōgē* can be usefully employed as a rubric for examination of initiatory rituals and customs in ancient Greece.

At one time, during the Archaic period (eighth–sixth centuries BCE), initiatory rituals existed all over Greece. However, by the beginning of the Classical period (fifth–fourth centuries BCE), these rites had vanished from most urbanized Greek societies or had been reduced to a few ceremonies. Only at the margin of the Greek world, on the conservative island of Crete, did men's associations still convene in men's houses and supervise proper rites of initiation—at least until the fourth century BCE. Here, young boys had to serve at the meals in the men's houses, their low status being stressed by shabby clothes and seats on the floor. After this period of informal education, sons of aristocrats recruited boys of lower social standing to form bands, which were supervised by their fathers. These bands were trained in hunting, dancing, singing, fighting, and, a modernization, letters. Having finally passed through a short homosexual affair with a more recently initiated lover, each aristocratic youth received a military suit, a special dress, and a drinking cup, the tokens of adulthood. It still took a while, however, before the youth reached unqualified adulthood (perhaps at the age of thirty), but about this period we are not informed. When the boys left the initiatory bands, they were forced to marry *en masse*.

In Sparta, similar initiatory rites took place, but here the state supervised the youths' training, which was geared completely to the purpose of controlling the Helots, Sparta's subject population. Moreover, the Spartan system, the *agōgē*, had been extended by the introduction of a long series of age-classes. (Rites of initiation can always be contracted or prolonged, depending on a given society's needs.) In Athens, the original initiatory structure had disintegrated in the course of the sixth century BCE with the decline of aristocratic power. Nevertheless, from the exploits of Theseus (which reflect the life of an Athenian initiand), from various rituals, and from the later "national service" (*ephēbeia*), we can still deduce the existence of an initiatory system comprising transvestism, trials of strength, running, pederasty, and a stay at the margin of Athenian society.

This evidence, coupled with scattered notices from other cities, suggests a picture of initiatory rituals that were once universal in Archaic Greece. These rituals were connected with a variety of divine figures such as local heroes, Hermes, Herakles, Zeus, and Poseidon. Apollo was especially important, since he supervised the final integration into adult society. The ubiquity of initiation is confirmed by Greek mythology in which initiatory themes—some no longer mentioned in the historical period—occur with astonishing frequency.

The prototype of the Greek mythological initiand was Achilles. He was educated by the centaur Chiron far from the civilized world; centaurs also figure as initiators of other Greek heroes, such as Jason. Chiron instructed Achilles in hunting, music, and medicine, and he gave him his name, his first name being Ligyron. Subsequently, Achilles spent time on the remote island of Skyros, dressed as a girl. In the Trojan War, he was the foremost Greek hero; late versions of the myth even claim that he was invulnerable. Finally, he was killed, through the intervention of Apollo. The structure of this myth clearly reflects male initiation rites: the education in the bush, the change of name, and the transvestism; further, the heroic feats combined with the theme of invulnerability suggest a kind of martial ecstasy that was also expected from youth on the brink of adulthood among other Indo-European peoples. The death through the initiatory god Apollo suggests the "death" of the initiand before his rebirth as an adult.

Other heroes' lives also display the characteristics of an initiatory scenario. Perseus travels to a marginal area to acquire a special weapon in order to kill a monster. Oedipus is educated far from home, passes the tests of the Sphinx, and then gains the hand of the queen-widow. Jason is educated by Chiron, who also gave him his name. Having collected a band of followers (cf. the Cretan rites), he performs valiant deeds with the Argonauts before returning home to become a king.

Besides these pan-Hellenic myths, there were many local heroes who served as initiatory models for youths. One example out of many: in Cretan Phaistos, it was said that Leukippos (Leucippus), although born as a girl, had changed into a man when he reached adolescence. This myth was the *aition* for the Ekdusia ("the shedding of clothes"), the festival of Leto, mother of Apollo and Artemis. Evidently, it was a festival that celebrated the end of initiation when boys shed their female clothes (dramatized in the myth as a sex change) in order to assume proper male ones. Many such local initiatory myths were recorded in Hellenistic and Roman times long after the corresponding rites had disappeared.

Whereas boys were educated to become warriors, girls were trained for marriage. In Sparta, one of the few places about which we possess a fair amount of information, scantily clad girls started their initiation at the margin of Spartan territory in the sanctuaries of Artemis, the main Greek goddess of girls' education. Here, besides physical exercises, they were instructed through music and dancing in choruses. Evidence from other cities such as Athens confirms that this was the custom all over Greece. Girls were considered to be like wild animals that had to be tamed (they were called "bears" in Athens). This is reflected in mythology where the names of girls such as the Leukippides and Hipponoe suggest that girls were compared to wild mares who had to be domesticated.

During their final training for motherhood, aristocratic girls in Sparta had to pass through a lesbian affair, as they did on the island of Lesbos, where Sappho instructed groups of aristocratic girls. In this period, special stress was laid on enhancing their physical beauty, so that their marriages would be successfully consummated. Consequently, this period was closely connected with the cult of the beautiful Helen, who was worshiped as a goddess in Sparta. In fact, in a number of Greek cities a beauty contest constituted the end of girls' initiation. The protection of Artemis lasted until the birth of the first child, for motherhood, not loss of virginity, was the definitive entry into the world of adult women.

Many details of Greek girls' training can be found in the myths concerning Artemis, even though they tend, as myths so often do, to concentrate on the most dramatic part of the story: the final entry into marriage. The "taming" of a girl is expressed in a number of myths that all circle around her resistance to "domestication." The pursuit of the Proetides, the capture of Thetis by Peleus or of Persephone by Hades, the races to win Atalante, and even the capture of Helen by Paris—all these myths are concerned with the perceived resistance of girls to enter wedlock. Greek mythology is very much a man's world.

SEE ALSO Apollo; Artemis; Poseidon.

BIBLIOGRAPHY

The pioneer study of Greek initiation is Henri Jeanmaire's *Couroi et courètes* (Lille, 1939), and the standard study is now Angelo Brelich's *Paides e parthenoi* (Rome, 1969). Both Jeanmaire and Brelich base their analyses on comparisons with the ethnological evidence. D. B. Dodd and C. A. Faraone (eds.), *Initiation in Ancient Greek Rituals and Narratives: New Critical Perspectives* (London and New York, 2003) is a not quite successful attempt at a revisionary approach. My articles "An

Enigmatic Indo-European Rite: Paederasty," *Arethusa* 13 (1980): 279–298, and "Transvestite Dionysus," in M. Padilla (ed.), *Rites of Passage in Ancient Greece* (Lewisburg, Pa., 1999), pp. 183–200 are detailed studies of the roles of pederasty and tranvestism in the initiatory rituals. Claude Calame's *Choruses of Young Women in Ancient Greece* (Lanham, Md., 1997) is a detailed study of the girls' initiation. Fritz Graf's "The Locrian Maidens," in R. Buxton (ed.), *Oxford Readings in Greek Religion* (Oxford, 2000), pp. 250–270 is an exemplary discussion of one complex of initiatory myth and ritual.

JAN N. BREMMER (1987 AND 2005)

AGRICULTURE, the cultivation of plants for food and other ends, as opposed to the use of plants as they grow naturally in man's environment, is a rather recent phenomenon if considered relative to the time scale of the development of *Homo sapiens.* Scholars now agree in dating the most ancient archaeological traces of plant cultivation to the eighth or seventh millennium BCE and in indicating not the valleys of the Tigris-Euphrates and Nile, where the most ancient urban civilizations are attested, but the higher lands lying both west and east of Mesopotamia as the original cradles of agriculture. The Natufian culture of Palestine and other similar communities and cultural complexes in Kurdistan (Zawi Chemi Shanidar) and northern Iraq (Karim Shahir) used noncultivated (wild) wheat and barley.

The first traces of agriculture proper are found in sites such as Jericho (c. 7500 BCE), Jarmo (Iraqi Kurdistan), Tepe Sarab (Iranian Kurdistan), and Çatal Hüyük (Anatolia) and can be dated to the seventh millennium at the latest; the Palestinian early agrarian culture of the Yarmuk basin and the cultures of Al-Fayyum (Egypt) and of Tepe Siyalk (Iran) probably belong to the sixth millennium. Some scholars consider the oldest agricultural communities of eastern Europe to be almost as ancient as these Asian civilizations; recently traces of very early plant cultivation (peas, beans, etc.) have been found in Thailand.

The introduction of agriculture is not an isolated phenomenon. It develops with the beginnings of animal domestication and with a growth both in the population in general and in the size of settlements (some of the early agricultural settlements of the cultures cited above, such as Jericho in Palestine, cover a wide area, are fortified, and contain towers and buildings constructed for collective, ceremonial use). The origin of agriculture is also linked to the invention of pottery and to more sophisticated techniques for making stone tools and weapons, although these last innovations are not always synchronic with the introduction of cultivation. Although the term *Neolithic revolution,* made popular by V. Gordon Childe, expresses well the enormous importance of this series of radical innovations, the process was a slow one, extending across several millennia. According to recent studies, the history of early forms of cultivation can be divided into three long phases: (1) the final phase of the gathering economy; (2) the beginnings of plant cultivation and of animal domestication; and (3) the era of efficient village agriculture.

Although the beginnings of cultivation must be identified with the process just described, which took place in a small area of Asia and Europe and involved the domestication of wild cereals, in premodern times the cultivation of plants had already spread to all continents, and the Neolithic revolution had taken place in most of the inhabited world. At the beginning of the modern era, cultivation was present in the indigenous cultures of all lands, with the exceptions of Australia, the Arctic (for obvious climatic reasons), a wide part of North America (the central Great Plains, inhabited only recently by the buffalo-hunting Plains Indians), and smaller, isolated parts of other continents (usually those areas covered with tropical or equatorial forests and inhabited by bands of hunter-gatherers). Scholars still debate whether the presence of plant cultivation throughout the globe should be considered the result of a process of diffusion from the most ancient cradle of agriculture in the Old World or the result of a series of independent inventions. However this question is approached, one should keep in mind that cultivation is far from uniform and is far from corresponding everywhere to the model of cerealiculture in Europe and western Asia. Indeed, if we leave aside the relatively recent modifications brought about by European colonization of other continents, six geographical, ecological, and cultural zones can be distinguished according to the types or groups of plants cultivated. The zones are as follows

1. wheat zone: from Europe to China; secondary cereals: barley, spelt, oats; instrument: the plow
2. rice zone: from India to Indonesia to southern China; instruments: plow and hoe
3. millet and sorghum zone: sub-Saharan Africa; instrument: hoe
4. yam and taro zone: New Guinea, Melanesia, Polynesia; secondary plants: coconut palm, sago palm; instruments: digging stick and hoe
5. maize zone: America, from eastern North America through Central America and the Andes to northern Chile and Argentina; secondary plants: in the north—beans and pumpkins; in the south—potato and quinoa; instruments; digging stick and spade
6. manioc (cassava) zone: Amazonian area and tropical America; secondary plants: peanuts, sweet potato; instruments: digging stick and spade

As for the problem of the origin of cultivation in areas outside the original western Asian-eastern European zone where cerealiculture began, there is increasing agreement on the common origin of the cultivation of cereals in the Old World (although older, more complex theories still have their followers). Specialists still disagree, however, on both the relationship between the origins of cultivation in the New and the Old World (a more recent, autonomous invention of cultivation in America seems more probable) and the relative ages of cereal and noncereal cultivation. According to some, the cultivation of noncereal plants (mainly tubers) is an impoverished imitation of cerealiculture, whereas other scholars consider the cultivation of noncereal plants to be older than cerealiculture. This last hypothesis seems more probably correct, at least in the case of some areas of the Americas. Excavations in Venezuela and in Colombia show that cassava was cultivated there long before maize; moreover, as mentioned earlier, very ancient traces of noncereal cultivation have been discovered in Thailand.

The importance of the slow technological and economic (Neolithic) revolution that led many societies from a hunting and gathering economy to plant cultivation and animal husbandry is indeed enormous; the only phenomenon we can compare it to is the great technological revolution of early modern times, which led many societies, in a much shorter timespan, into the modern industrial era. In transforming *Homo sapiens* from a mere consumer of natural goods into a producer, the development of agriculture drastically changed the role of humanity within its environment, and thus the very nature of humankind. Moreover, it permitted a vast transformation of human life and activity, involving both a demographic increase and the rise of more complex human settlements and communities. Agriculture required an increasingly greater specialization, differentiation, and stratification within societies, and made possible and indeed necessary the "urban revolution" that was to follow within three or four millennia in Mesopotamia and Egypt. The consequences of this development in the domain of religious life were far greater than can be illustrated in this article, which deals exclusively with religious phenomena directly connected to cultivation. The historical roots of complex phenomena such as polytheism, the so-called gift-sacrifice, and priesthood, to name but three examples, lie in the humus prepared by the Neolithic revolution.

Our knowledge of the religiosity of Neolithic cultures is limited not only by an obvious factor, the lack of any written evidence, but also by a less obvious one, the abundance of totally conjectural modern "reconstructions," based upon archaeological data. Even more limiting are a misconceived comparison between modern "primitive" cultivators and the peasant cultures of more complex historical societies and the generalizations of nineteenth-century scholarship. The data furnished by sites such as Jericho (Palestine) and Çatal Hüyük and Hacilar (Anatolia) point to the cult of anthropomorphic, mainly female, beings of various types and to rituals of the dead (in particular to the preservation and treatment of human skulls), as well as to the importance of animals such as birds of prey, bulls, and leopards, often depicted in wall paintings. The cult was often domestic, but shrines of various sizes and shapes have been found, richly decorated with paintings and sculptures. The first monumental sanctuaries, however, seem to belong to the later, Mesopotamian culture of Al-Ubayyid, dated from the end of the fifth to the beginning of the fourth millennium.

The Ritual Calendar and the Great Feast. Although hunter-gatherer communities also organize their lives on a seasonal basis, the yearly rhythm of labors is vital to cultivators and implies both a cyclical perception of time and the necessity of organizing the yearly sequence with a new precision. The introduction of cultivation is thus historically connected to the introduction of a calendar that responds to the technological and ritual needs of that specific form of production. The ritual aspects of cultivation and the rhythmic periodicity of that economic form, in which periods of great abundance are followed by periods of scarcity, require strong differentiations in time and the concentration of ritual actions and festive behavior in specific, recurring periods or days of the year. The yearly calendar of cultivators is thus a festive and ritual calendar.

The festive calendars of ancient societies, even though they are often connected with more complex liturgical, mythological, and even theological conceptions, as well as with "political" celebrations, easily reveal their agricultural basis. Thus, the three main Israelite feasts recorded in the Bible are a feast of the beginning of the barley harvest, a summer feast of the end of the wheat harvest (Shavuʿot), and an autumn feast of ingathering, celebrating the collecting and storing of (noncereal) cultivated fruits (Sukkot or Asif).

Likewise, the Attic calendar of Classical times included a feast preliminary to the plowing (Proerosia) immediately followed by the feast of the Boiling of Beans (Puanopsia), then by the ritual begging for gifts by children who carried a decorated branch of olive or laurel (*eiresiōnē*), and by processions of people carrying bunches of grapes hanging from their branches (Oscophoria) or other, less easily identified objects (Thesmophoria). The other main agricultural feasts of the Attic calendar were the spring festival of flowers and new wine (Anthesteria), the wine festival of Dionysos (Dionusia), the feasts of purification and offerings in preparation for harvesting (Thargelia), and the sacrifice of a plow ox at the time of harvest (Bouphonia).

The Roman archaic calendar includes a series of spring feasts dedicated to the worship of agrarian deities (in March and April: Liberalia, Consualia, Vinalia Priora, Robigalia); a series of spring purification rites, connected to the return of the dead and to the gathering of broad beans (in May: purification fields, Lemuria, Kalendae Fabariae); summer festivals connected with the harvesting and with the new wine (in August: Vinalia Rustica, feast of Opeconsiva); a series of winter feasts of the plowing season (from December 15 to 21: Consualia, Saturnalia, Opalia, Divalia, Larentalia); a winter feast for the protection of sown cereals (in January: Feriae Sementivae); and a winter month of purification of people and fields (in February).

The agricultural origin of most yearly festivals in modern, as well as in ancient, cultivating societies can just as easily be demonstrated. Here it suffices to cite the great Indian festivals of Dussehra and Dīvālī; the former marks the end of the rainy season and the beginning of agricultural labors and is concluded by a ritual quest for alms by people carrying small fresh shoots of barley plants, while the latter is a New Year-like festival celebrating the sowing of the winter crops.

The agricultural and festive calendars of cultivators outside of the wheat zone are no less rich and complex. The structure of the calendar and the types of festivals vary according to the ecological and climatic conditions, the types of plants cultivated, and the cultural and social structure of the various societies, as is shown by the following three examples.

The Arapesh of northeastern New Guinea, who now cultivate a wide range of plants of various origins, are ruled by an archaic ritual calendar that is based on the cultivation of yams and reflects a time system simpler than the one now in use for cultivation. The main feast, the Abullu, is based upon the exhibition of each cultivator's yam produce, followed by the performance of special Abullu dances and songs, which center on the most recent death of an important member of the community, and by the distribution of yams to the guests by each producer. The producer may not consume the yams himself and must be ritually purified before the feast, for he is considered to be in a state similar to that of parents immediately after childbirth.

The rice-growing Ao-Naga of northeastern India have a complex festive calendar with three main feasts. The Moatsu feast, celebrated at the end of the sowing period, is preceded by a night of sexual abstinence and consists of a ritual suspension of order (the rigid rules relative to clothing and ornaments are not enforced; no Ao-Naga can be fined for transgression) and of the renewal of the belts that hold the men's *dao* ("daggers"). The Aobi feast precedes the beginning of the agricultural labors, and marks the end of the period during which the Ao-Naga travel and trade. Its central feature is the explusion of impurities from the village, both through the disposal of the garbage collected from the various households by a priest and by the symbolic concentration of impurities on the first stranger who enters the village area. Finally, the end of the agricultural labors is marked by a feast, called Tsungremmung, mainly dedicated to the worship of beings called *tsungrem.* The greatest of the *tsungrem,* Lichaba, a creator figure, is the main recipient of the festive offerings; pieces of pork are left out for him to consume in all the dwellings that are located at the edges of the village.

The Venda of Transvaal, in South Africa, cultivate maize and other plants (sweet potatoes, beans, pumpkins, melons) of various types and origins. Their main festivals celebrate the sowing and the harvesting. Before the sowing, each cultivator sends a small amount of mixed seeds to the lineage chief, who prepares a sacred food by cooking all the seeds together; the food is then offered to the ancestors, and a rich harvest is asked of them. A similar rite takes place in the chief's field, with the participation of the whole community; on their way to the field the young girls collect firewood to cook the offering, and beat whomever they meet with rods (the rods may be a fertility symbol). The chief announces the beginning of the harvesting. There was a time when anyone who began harvesting before the announcement would be killed. The chief celebrates a private rite; a "public" rite then takes place in the chief's field, and each lineage celebrates its own rite in the lineage chief's field. The preliminary rites consist of an offering of sugar cane to the sacred animals and of preparation of beer by women. The young people then perform a sacred dance; the sacred bull and its cow are led into the chief's kraal and asperged with beer, while the *makhadzi* (the sister of the former chief) recites a prayer to the ancestors, saying: "I give you the first grains of the yearly harvest; eat and be well; but what is now still in the fields, you should leave to us." Listing all the names of ancestors she can remember, the *makhadzi* adds that the prayer is also directed to those ancestors whose names have been forgotten. The tombs and the places where the spirits of the dead dwell are then ceremoniously visited, and offerings are left in special places for the wild animals (leopards, serpents, etc.) into which the dead are believed to be transformed.

The Venda's harvest rituals are typical of the most important and widespread agricultural feast: the feast of harvesting and of first fruits. This is first of all a feast of abundance after the long months of working and of waiting, of success after the yearly risks and dangers represented by the uncertainties of rainfall and weather. Thus, it is celebrated by more or less unrestricted license and by excessive consumption. At the same time, it is a moment of great crisis, both because it causes excessive consumption and suspends productive work and because of the risk that accompanies any liminal period as, specifically, the consumption of the first products of the year's labor. The great feast of abundance and license is thus also celebrated with "protective" rituals, such as ritual consecration of first fruits, purification and renewal of the community, and offerings and sacrifices (sometimes human sacrifice, as for example among the Aztec of Mexico or the Dravidian Khond of eastern India) to various entities.

The consumption of the first part of the new harvest involves the end of a seasonal cycle of cultivation and the beginning of a new one, and thus a renewal of time: the harvest festival is a New Year feast, and the festive sacrifice is seen as a cosmogonic act. In the great feast, the whole world starts afresh, so that order is often ritually suspended, only to be reinstated, as happened at the beginning of time.

This suspension (and reinstatement) of the social and cosmic order is the profound religious meaning of an important aspect of many seasonal festivals of cultivators and, in particular, of harvest festivals: the ritual orgy. Indeed, if envisaged in this context of periodic "rebirth," the orgy is a temporary suspension of the normal order of a given society in favor of an "excessive" collective behavior (music, dance, banqueting, sexual intercourse) that is meant to sanction the festive period and to renew and reinforce the vital energies of the social group. Orgiastic behavior on special or festive occasions is attested among all societies, but orgies have a specific importance and a particular meaning for cultivators. Alimentary orgies are extremely frequent and important; they are most often a celebration of the harvest, a ritual response to the sudden and disconcerting abundance of food after the long months of efforts and risks. Sexual orgies are also frequent (they are attested among many societies of cultivators, from the Melanesian cultivators of tuberous plants to the cerealiculturalists of the Old World), and are connected with the harvest festivals (e.g., among the Fijians during the Nanga and Mbaki feast), with (spring) festivals of the growth of vegetation (e.g., in ancient China, in India during the Holī festival or during Dīvālī), and with planting or sowing (e.g., among the Pipil of Central America). Although it maintains its fundamental quality as a ritual disruption of order and as a temporal heightening of social and individual life rhythms, the sexual orgy of cultivators also reflects the solidarity between human sexuality and fecundity and the fertility of cultivated plants that constitutes one of the central beliefs of those societies; the orgy possesses the specific function of revitalizing the forces of vegetation. In this sense, it is a collective counterpart of the "hierogamy" (ritual intercourse or marriage between humans or symbolic figures to enhance vegetal reproduction and growth during critical moments of the agrarian year).

Just as all agricultural and horticultural labors have a ritual aspect or value, the festivals of cultivators, and the harvest festivals in particular, are an integral part of agricultural activities, and are organized as an aspect of the general economic activity of the social body. This is emblematically clear, to cite but one example, among the matrilinear maize cultivators of what is today New York State, the Iroquois of the Six Nations, whose agricultural economy has recently been reconstructed. Among the Iroquois, at harvesttime labor was distributed among three different groups of women. One group collected the maize ears in baskets, a second group transported the cereal produce to the storage places, where it was buried in underground pits, and a third group prepared the harvest festival. A part of the labor force employed in the harvesting was thus devoted to the preparation of the feast, in which the men also took part before leaving the village for long hunting expeditions in the forests.

The unity of productive and ritual activity, and of the seasonal-technical and the festive-ritual calendars, was thus complete in all archaic communities of cultivators. In medieval and modern times, especially in the wheat zone, this situation was increasingly modified by the development of the liturgical calendars of the great "universal" religions (notably Christianity and Islam), which were partly independent of the seasonal pattern of agriculture, and later of the "lay" festive calendars. In this area, however, a specifically agricultural perception of time continued to exist side by side with the official calendars, and interacted with them dialectically. The new religions either accepted and transformed or rejected and tried to abolish the traditional rituals and feasts. A good example of this complex situation is the traditional festive calendar of European peasants. This calendar is the result of a complex interaction of an archaic agricultural festive system and Christian liturgy.

FIGURES AND DEITIES. The offerings cited above in connection with some agrarian festivals are examples of an extremely widespread typology of sacrificial offerings, ritual acts, and propitiatory prayers directed toward extrahuman entities of various kinds that are believed to embody, or to control, the outcome of the labors of cultivation and the abundance of the harvest. Such beings or entities can be classified into four main categories: (1) nonpersonified forces or (less correctly) "spirits" that are believed to be active in the very growth and nourishing properties of cultivated plants; (2) personified beings of different kinds, believed to embody, or to cause and control, the growth of specific cultivated plants or, more generally, the produce of cultivation; (3) polytheistic gods and goddesses who, within the context of the various pantheons, are believed to control certain aspects of the agricultural economy; (4) figures who, within "universal" and "founded" (often monotheistic) religions, are believed to influence aspects of the agricultural economy or the outcome of cultivation in a context in which the total control over reality (and thus also over agriculture) is often attributed to a single principle or deity.

The last two categories are most often historically derived from the second. The polytheistic deities, however, are more completely integrated within a unified religiosity, and constitute parts of a system of specialized extrahuman personalities. They may be officially in charge of cerealiculture (e.g., the ancient Greek goddess Demeter) or of such a specific aspect as the diseases of wheat and barley plants (e.g., the Roman deity Robigo), but in all cases they are tied to all the other deities of their specific pantheon by genealogical, mythological, and ritual bonds. The entities who preside over aspects of cultivation within "founded" religions may be secondary figures of the belief system of those religions (such as angels, saints, or in some Christian contexts, the Virgin Mary), or else figures who clearly belong to a noncanonical, folkloric religiosity and resemble strikingly the entities and figures of the first and second types in our typology. Both types, however, are marginal to the central body of belief, and their diffusion is limited, both geographically (to specific rural zones within the wide diffusion areas of the "great" religions) and socially (to the peasantry).

The existence of belief in the power of cultivated vegetation (our first category) is usually deduced from a series of ritual behaviors that has been interpreted as tending to act positively upon such a power. Such is the ritual treatment of the first or last sheaf of grain among European and other cerealiculturists. In some cases, the ritually important (first or last) sheaf of the harvest is avoided by the cultivators, in others, it is eagerly sought after. In some cases, it is taken to the farm or settlement with great ritual pomp; in other cases, it is thrown away. This ambivalence, according to Mircea Eliade, is a consequence of the ambivalent meaning of the chosen sheaf, which is both dangerous and precious because it symbolically contains or embodies the power of the harvested cereal. According to peasants of northern Europe (Finland, Estonia, Germany), the ritually chosen sheaf brings good luck and blessings to the household, protects from diseases and lightning, and keeps mice away from the harvested grain. The sheaf can be used for divination of the marriages of young women (Estonia) or of the price of grain in the following year (Germany); it has magical properties in relationship to childbirth (Finland), marriage (Scotland), and next season's harvest, so that some grain from the last sheaf of the harvest is mixed with the seeds used for the next sowing (Scandinavia and Germany). The "power" of the cultivated plants is similarly enhanced by other (e.g., hierogamic) rituals.

Only very rarely, however, are beliefs and ritual behaviors of this type not connected with some specific personification of the beings believed to embody or to control the seasonal outcome of cultivation. Indeed, though the existence of the first category of our typology is generally accepted by scholars, it would be possible to reformulate that category in favor of a widened scope of and differentiation within our second category.

In any case, the second category of our typology is extremely vast and varied and includes at least three main subcategories: (a) beings connected to, and representative of, specific cultivated plants, or the growth of cultivated vegetation in general; (b) earth-mother figures; (c) spirits of the dead or ancestors.

The first subtype is the most widespread and easily recognized. It is the nearest to the first category of our typology, and the extrahuman beings classified as belonging to this subtype are often represented by harvested plants (sometimes, the first or last or most beautiful plants of the harvest), often collected and tied together in the shape of a human (most often, a female) figure, kept until the next harvesting season, and ritually treated in various ways. Figures of this type are found on all continents. One may mention the Aztec maize goddess; the Maize Mother of pre-Columbian Peruvians, represented by a female image made with the biggest maize cobs of the harvest; the analogous Quinoa Mother, Coca Mother, and Potato Mother, all similarly represented by the same Peruvians; the various maize mothers, one for each type of maize, of the Pueblo Indians of the southwestern United States. The Karen of Burma invoke a personified "spirit of the rice"; the Minangkabau of Sumatra use special rice plants to represent the rice mother Indoea Padi; and rice mothers are known to the Tomori of Sulawesi and to the rice growers of the Malay Peninsula, who ritually treat the wife of the cultivator as a pregnant woman during the first three days after the storing of the rice. The agriculturalists of the Punjab fashioned a female figure from the most beautiful cotton plant of the harvest to represent the Cotton Mother. We have seen the ritual treatment and the magico-symbolic value of the last sheaf among the agriculturists of the wheat zone: the last sheaf, or a specially fashioned anthropomorphic image made of cereal stalks or straw, is identified in the same contexts as figures variously named Old Man (Denmark, Poland, Arabia Petraea), Queen of the Grain (Bulgaria), Old Woman (Germany, Scotland). The Berbers of Morocco used straw from the harvested fields to shape a female image they dressed in a woman's clothes that represented the Bride of the Barley.

Such figures, seemingly so similar, differ widely in their specific meanings and functions, as shown by the various roles they play in the ritual contexts. They may be believed to be entities responsible for growth of cultivated plants, and thus may be the recipients of offerings and prayers (Zara Mama, the maize mother of the Peruvians, for example, fashioned in the shape of a doll from cobs and dressed elegantly, was offered sacrifices and prayers). Or they may be believed to embody and to concentrate in themselves, rather than to control, that growth; in such cases they are ritually treated in various ways, the two most frequent and meaningful of which are the "death" pattern and the "wedding" pattern. The better known is the death pattern, which can be illustrated by the treatment of the last sheaf, identified as the Queen of Grain by the Bulgarians; the sheaf is dressed in a woman's clothes, carried around in a procession, and then burned and scattered in the fields or thrown into a body of water. Such rituals are usually interpreted as dramatizing the seasonal cycle of cultivated plants, and their periodic "death" followed by their return or "rebirth" before the next harvesting—a theory shaped in the nineteenth century by James G. Frazer and Wilhelm Mannhardt. The wedding pattern is exemplified by the "marriage" of two fistfuls of rice, collected before the harvesttime, practiced on the islands of Java, Bali, and Lombok; the two fistfuls were treated like a pair of spouses, a wedding ceremony between them was celebrated, and then they were brought to the storehouse and stored there so that the rice could grow. Another example is that of the Barley Bride of the Berbers of Morocco. Groups of women competed for the honor of carrying the straw figure processionally through the ripe crops; on other occasions, the male members of the community appeared on horseback to fight for her, thus imitating scenes that were normal for Berber weddings, including a simulated abduction of the bride. In other areas, the two patterns appear together: in Denmark the female harvester dances with an image formed with the last sheaves; she cries while she dances, and is considered a "widow" because she is married to a being who is going to die.

If considered together, the various ritual treatments of the mythical figures embodying or controlling the outcome of cultivation clearly form a complex, well-structured strategic system aimed at controlling the uncertainties of the specific modes of production. The death and the wedding patterns, in particular, deal with the critical economic moment represented by the harvesting. The death pattern ritually enacts, and thus controls, the very crisis represented by the final moment of the cycle, symbolically overcome through the destruction, and ritual reintegration (by throwing it in the water or by spreading it on the fields) of the first (or last or "best") part of the produce of cultivation, which represents the cultivated plant or its "mother," "queen," "spouse," and so on. The wedding pattern ritually enacts, and thus controls, the positive outcome of the efforts and risks of cultivation, and thus performs a symbolic fecundation of the cultivated plant—and not just any fecundation, but a cultural one, sanctioned by a marriage ritual, just as the fertilization of cultivated plants is felt to be a highly cultural phenomenon. The dramatic importance of the crisis ritually enacted and controlled by the death pattern is further clarified by the fact that the death and burial of the representative of cultivated plants is often a symbolic but sometimes a real animal, or even human, ritual killing.

While the belief in "mother" figures who represent or control the reproductive power of the cultivated plants is typical of cultivator societies, belief in an earth mother is not limited to those societies. Indeed, the personification of the earth as a fecund mother, based on the simple symbolic connection between female animal (human) fecundity and the fertility of the earth from which the plants grow, is not unknown to hunter-gatherer societies. On the other hand, most of the data interpreted as pointing toward that belief are derived from beliefs and cultic practices pertaining to polytheistic religions; the goddesses interpreted as earth figures are usually complex deities, whose connection with the fertile earth is only one aspect of their personalities. Nevertheless, the earth complex, often coupled with a cult of the sky or of a sky figure as a fertilizing father (dispenser of rain) and with the equation between fecund women and the cultivated earth, is present in many cultivators' religions and survives in specific rituals (e.g., in formulaic prayers such as the Anglo-Saxon invocation to Herce or the pseudo-Homeric hymn to Gaia, a polytheistic goddess whose name means "earth," and who was invoked as a dispenser of crops). Earth-mother beliefs are especially important in the "wheat zone," where they are more central in cosmogonic and anthropogenic myths than in direct connection with agriculture. The fact that in many cultivating societies, and possibly in the distant origins of cultivation, women were in charge of the domesticated plants enhanced the association between the female sphere and the cultivated earth. A variety of female figures, whose sexuality and fecundity are strongly stressed, are usually referred to the earth mother complex; they appear in the Old World from Neolithic times to later antiquity in the form of statuettes or in paintings and reliefs on pottery and elsewhere. The most ancient and important documents pertaining to such figures may be the recently discovered paintings on the walls of a ceremonial building in the early agricultural settlement of Çatal Hüyük; but the female figures depicted in those paintings and in roughly contemporary statuettes from Çatal Hüyük and Hacilar are never clearly associated with symbols pointing to agriculture, but rather with animals such as vultures, leopards, and bulls.

In examining some examples of seasonal calendars pertaining to cultivators, we have mentioned the connection between the dead and the products of cultivation. The most meaningful and widespread example of such a connection is the belief in the return of the dead during the harvest festival or great feast among Melanesian and Polynesian yam and taro growers. The hungry dead are believed to invade the territory of the living in that festive time and are offered part of the produce. Similar connections between fertility feasts of agriculturalists and the return of the dead are not unknown to other societies of cultivators (e.g., the Christmas festivities of the northern European peasants involve both the dead and a celebration of fertility and life).

The offering of first fruits, or of parts of the produce of cultivation, to the returning dead has been interpreted by Vittorio Lanternari as a response to the periodic crisis represented by the sudden abundance of food, and by the suspension of the labors of cultivation after the harvesting. The earth, sacrilegiously tilled or dug by the cultivators, is seen as the home of the dead, who belong to a sphere that, like the virgin earth that must be "treated" by the cultivators, is foreign and uncontrolled. By offering a part of the produce to the returning dead the cultivators react to and control the seasonal crisis and risk. The dead, moreover, return collectively, because the work of the cultivators is collective; they return annually, at the end of the agrarian cycle. They enter the village because during the year the village has invaded the earth, their domain, to modify it; they are menacingly hungry because, to satiate their own hunger, the living have attacked the earth and shall attack it again the following year.

Although this is probably a correct interpretation of the widespread belief in a collective and periodical return of the dead in crucial moments of the seasonal calendar of cultivators, other data point to different views of the relationship of the dead with the cultivated plants. In particular, the strong connection between funerary, agrarian, and sexual rituals shows that the dead are often seen as active forces in the positive outcome of the labors of cultivation. The Bambara of Mali, West Africa, for example, pour water over the head of the dead person and implore him or her to send them a good harvest; the Finnish cerealiculturalists mix bones or objects belonging to the dead with the seed during the sowing and return the objects to the graveyard after the harvest, whereas German peasants similarly use soil they have dug out from a tomb. The equation between the seed or tuber, buried in the ground, and the dead, whose memory continues in the life of their progeny, is probably the basic concept underlying these and similar cases. The structure of the ancient Chinese peasant house described by Marcel Granet, with the inner section containing the stored grain, and near it the marriage bed of the couple and the burial place of the family ancestors, is the best synthetic representation of such a conception.

ORIGIN MYTHS. The beliefs discussed so far, which shape the ritual aspect of the activities of cultivators, are expressed just as clearly in the myths traditionally related to account for the origins of cultivated plants or of the various technical and economic activities of cultivators, as well as to validate their cultural systems.

Some myths stress the symbolic correspondence between the cultivated plants and human beings and between sexual fecundity and vegetal fertility, the similarity between the techniques of cultivation and those of childraising, and the "motherly" quality of the cultivated earth. Others give more attention to the (miraculous) origin of the cultivated plants or techniques of cultivation. Among these last myths, Adolf E. Jensen distinguished two main, widespread types, attributing to cultivators of tuberous plants the type of myth that connects cultivation and death, mostly by recounting the birth of the cultivated plants from the body of a slain primordial being (the Hainuwele type) and attributing to cerealiculturalists myths of the theft of the basic cultivated cereals by primeval humankind. Jensen called the latter the Prometheus type, using the name of the Greek mythic figure Prometheus, who stole elements of human culture from the gods. But this rigid distinction should be abandoned, not only because the origin of cereals is often connected to a mythic killing (echoes of this are to be found, e.g., in the Osirian mythology of the Egyptians) but also, or rather especially, because the central theme of both these types, that of the primeval guilt connected by origin myths to the beginnings of cultivation, can be shown to be more richly differentiated. This theme includes at least (1) the killing of the primeval figure (Hainuwele type); (2) the stealing of the original cultivated plant (Prometheus type); and (3) the spying upon, and thus the offending of, a primeval generous female figure to whom the first introduction of cultivated plants or food is attributed.

Two myths of the Kiwai of New Guinea are good examples of the first type we have mentioned; they stress the earth-mother and plant-child symbolism. One of these myths tells of a woman named Opae, who gave birth but, having no husband and no idea of what a baby was, abandoned the child. A bird took care of it and protected its body and arms with taro leaves; later the bird came back with some taro bark and a taro root, covered the baby's body with the bark, and tied the root to its head. The root penetrated the ground and started to grow, and the baby's body was transformed into the first cultivated taro plant. The other Kiwai myth recounts the origin of yam cultivation. A man who had no wife dug a hole in the ground and had intercourse with the earth. But under the earth a woman was hidden, Tshikaro by name. She became pregnant, and, as is done with women at childbirth, she was surrounded by an enclosure made of mats (the mythic prototype of the enclosures protecting the yam gardens of the Kiwai) and gave birth to many yam tubers.

The most famous myth that connects cultivation and death by recounting the origin of the cultivated plants from the body of a slain primordial being is the Hainuwele myth of the islanders of Ceram (Indonesia), studied by Adolf E. Jensen and used by him as a prototype of this category. Hainuwele, a young maid, was killed, her body was cut in pieces, and the pieces were buried; from the various parts of her body, the various cultivated plants were born. The killing of Hainuwele gave rise not just to the plants, but in different ways to sexuality, to death, and to many cultural institutions. Myths of this type are present in all continents. An American example is the Maya account of the origin of maize from the heart of the Maize Mother. An African one is the Nzima (Ghana) myth of the origin of that same plant. In the Nzima myth, two female figures appear: a mother, the ancestress responsible for the introduction of maize cultivation, and her daughter, sacrificed by the mother. An ancient Greek myth of cerealiculture also features a mother and her daughter. The goddess Demeter, angry because her young daughter Persephone has been abducted by the netherworld god, causes the vegetation (specifically, cereals) to wither and abandons the gods to travel among men. She is taken for an old woman and employed by a king and his wife as a nurse for their baby. Although she is spied upon and interrupted while trying to make the baby immortal by burning it, and then leaves the king's palace forever, condemning the baby to mortality, she teaches the king the Eleusinian mysteries. Finally, Persephone returns to the upper world, where she will periodically reside, and the vegetation is revived. In other versions, Demeter teaches the techniques of agriculture to a king who had helped her. This myth, in whatever version, sanctions mortality, agriculture, and the most famous of Greek mystery rites as fundamental and related aspects of known since primeval times human existence and presents a motherly figure as responsible for the origin of cultivation.

The correspondence between the female protagonists of myths of this kind and the second type of extrahuman entities described in the previous section is often explicit. However, as in the myth of the Cochiti Pueblo of New Mexico, the correspondence may be indirect. The Mother of the Indians, we are told, abandoned her children; when they sent messengers to her underground dwelling to ask for her help in a moment of crisis, she gave them the first maize "fetish" or doll, made of a maize plant adorned with feathers and buckskin strings, a prototype of the object used by the Cochiti in agrarian rituals. Clearly, the maize figure is a substitute for the Mother, and, as in the case of Demeter in the first version of her myth, it is ritual material connected with cultivation rather than cultivation itself that is given to humans by the disappearing female.

As for the theme (subtype 3) of the offended superhuman female, it is present in many myths of the "excretion" type. In a series of myths told by the Creek, Cherokee, and Natchez maize growers of the southeastern United States, the mythic woman, who sometimes appears in the shape of a maize plant or cob, gives maize (and sometimes beans) to humans. She takes care of orphans and other needy people, and for them she produces maize grains by rubbing her own body. The woman is murdered in some versions, and in others she offers herself in sacrifice; but in all versions of the myth, before dying, she instructs the people about the actions they must perform in order to let maize and beans spring forth from her body. Myths of this type are widespread. Two more examples will serve to indicate that the themes these myths have in common are not restricted to the "excretion" motif but include the motif typical of the third "subtype" of the classification given above.

In a myth of the Toraja of Sulawesi (Indonesia), a fisherman often left his wife to go on fishing expeditions; when he came back, he always found a large pot full of rice, but his wife would not tell him from whence it had come. One day, he spied on her through a fissure in the wall of their dwelling and saw that she rubbed her hands together over the pot and thus filled it with rice. Disgusted by this discovery, he reproached her for this unclean procedure; as a result of his reproaches the woman transformed herself into a rice plant, and he became a sago palm. The yam and taro growers of Melanesia and New Guinea have similar myths (in New Guinea, the myths are about Yam Woman, who miraculously produces yams from her own body), but a complex myth, very similar to the American and Indonesian myths, is to be found among the Maori of New Zealand and accounts for the origin of the *kumara* (sweet potato). The goddess Pani took care of two young orphaned nephews and nourished them with baked *kumara;* the two brothers, who loved this previously unknown food, kept asking where it came from, but Pani would not tell them. One day, one of the brothers spied on her and discovered that she drew the sweet potatoes from her own body while lying in the water. In another version, she obtained the *kumara* by rubbing her hands on her belly. The boy told his brother: "We are eating Pani's excretions." Ashamed, Pani retired to the netherworld, where one of the nephews magically reached her and found her cultivating *kumara.*

In America, Indonesia, and New Zealand a female figure is thus believed to have obtained the main cultivated plant from her own body and to have given it generously to the needy; it is further recounted that she was spied on while doing this, and that, ashamed or offended, she disappeared, having given rise to the cultivated plants and to the techiques of agriculture. The similarity between these myths and the ancient Greek myth about Demeter is striking, and points to connections between the origin myths of cerealiculturalists and those of other cultivators. The complexity of historical derivations and typological connections between the various origin myths can be illustrated by one last, paradoxical example. In mythical times, according to traditional Maya beliefs, the rain god hit with his lightning the rock in which the maize god was hidden, and the maize god was born, the answer to the prayers of primeval, needy mankind. The later, christianized culture of Guatemala and Yucatán, however, reinterpreted the ancient Maya maize god as a Christ-like, bread-of-life figure, thus introducing elements of the Hainuwele type into a traditional myth more similar to the Prometheus type.

As shown by many of these examples, the myths about the origin of cultivation point to crisis as well as to fertility. Many such myths present the cultivation of plants as an ambiguous, dangerous innovation, caused by a primeval mistake or sin. The attitude they reflect is similar to that expressed by the ritual "return of the dead" during crucial moments of the seasonal cycle. The costs and risks of cultivation are expressed mythically and ritually by societies whose well-being, contingent upon the outcome of cultivation, is perennially at stake, and must be continually reaffirmed both by technical and by ritual and ideological means. By relegating the nonagrarian life to a distant past, and by showing the positive consequences of the "sacrilegious" invading of uncontrolled nature by human endeavor, the founding myths of cultivators reinforce the cultural and economic systems that express them and protect the social body against a recurrent series of cyclical crises.

Religious and Social Values of Cultivators. In many origin myths the female responsible for the beginning of cultivation acted in favor of helpless or derelict children who did not belong to a system of family solidarity (e.g., orphans), or she is presented as a generous nourisher. This mythic trait corresponds well to the importance of hospitality among cultivators and to the periodic redistribution of the produce of cultivation on festive occasions that reach their peak in the alimentary orgy and in the offerings of first fruits to the returning dead on ritual occasions. The foundation of all these conceptions, beliefs, and behaviors is the economic life that cultivation makes possible, a stable way of life in which the relative abundance of food makes further economic and cultural changes possible, makes the redistribution of the yearly produce among the members of the community a vital task, and provides a surplus for ritual and even orgiastic consumption on given seasonal occasions.

A relatively egalitarian ideology of collective labor, festive consumption, generalized redistribution, and hospitable generosity is typical of the less complex societies of cultivators. It is replaced by an ideology of vertical concentration and redistribution in societies in which production, distribution, and consumption of agrarian produce become more complex, tasks and roles become more differentiated, and a privileged status is assumed by a group or a person, chief, or king. The cooperation and solidarity necessary to obtain and share a good harvest are identified with the ability of the rulers to organize, to judge, and to distribute the yearly produce. Harvest festivals, as happen in Africa in the Swazi kingdom, may become the occasion for ritual dramas of rebellion and reproach, enhancing and upholding the "rights" of the subjects and stressing the "duties" of the rulers. On the other hand, in societies such as these the sanctity of the (private) property of the land, and of its symbol, the boundary stone, is upheld by religious beliefs and sactions; the other face of kingly generosity, the periodic tribute of a part of the agrarian produce to the rulers, is also upheld by sacred sanctions.

Just as the importance of social solidarity for the very survival of agrarian communities is stressed by beliefs and rites based upon redistribution and consumption, other aspects of the ethos of cultivators are expressed by other religious complexes. Despite the importance of sexual license and festive license of various types in the religiosity of cultivators, the belief that the respect of social and religious rules and prohibitions, of ritual purity, and of sexual purity in particular is essential for the good functioning of cultivation is a worldwide feature. The ritual purity of the peasants of modern northern Europe is obtained by a bath and the donning of new or clean clothes before the main agricultural labors, such as plowing or sowing or reaping. The importance of virgins, old men and women, and even eunuchs in rituals and cults either directly agrarian (such as the ancient Egyptian rites performed by castrated men to ensure the yearly Nile inundation and the fertility of the fields) or linked to mother goddesses is an extreme aspect of this symbolic complex. In many hierarchical societies, the chief or king must live in a perpetual state of ritual purity. This purity is believed to have a direct influence upon the agrarian produce and is upheld by a complex series of norms and taboos.

The correct distribution of the yearly produce of cultivation and the correct functioning of ritual and social norms are thus no less important in the religious life of cultivators than sexual symbolism or the belief that extrahuman entities control or embody the growth of cultivated plants. Of equal importance is the religious aura surrounding the specific technical aspects of agrarian production; the sanctity of animals such as the plow ox in ancient Greece or of objects such as the plow among early modern Italian peasants and the agriculturists of Madagascar today are good examples. What is most meaningful, however, is the widespread sacrality of the general complex of technical knowledge and ritual lore necessary to cultivation.

Technical knowledge and ritual lore are often believed to have been learned from extrahuman beings in mythic times. Moreover, the acquiring of that knowledge is often connected with a primeval mistake or sin and is tied to the origins of the main cultural traits of the society that are expressed in myth, as well as to the beginnings of human mortality. The fact that the Eleusinian mysteries are mythically founded by a narrative tradition that also recounts the divine origin of agriculture may point to an intrinsic connection between the technical-ritual knowledge necessary for cultivation and the ritual and symbolic knowledge about the religious value of human life that was the object of what we call "mystery" cults. This point aside, the agrarian connections of the ancient mystery cults are beyond doubt, as are the connections between the eschatological and soteriological expectations the mystery cults express and the agriculturist's awareness of the perennial repetition of the agrarian cycle of the "death" and "rebirth" of plants.

See Also Calendars; Culture Heroes; Neolithic Religion; Seasonal Ceremonies; Vegetation.

Bibliography

A useful treatment of agriculture and cultivation throughout the world, with special attention to primitive societies, is Vinigi Grottaneli's *Etnologica: L'uomo e la civita*, vol. 2, *Le opere dell'uomo* (Milan, 1965); see pages 573–754. On the origin of agriculture in the Neolithic period, see Sonia Cole's *The Neolithic Revolution*, 5th ed. (London, 1970), and other studies quoted by Grottanelli and by Mircea Eliade in *A History of Religious Ideas*, vol. 1, *From the Stone Age to the Eleusinian Mysteries* (Chicago, 1978), chapter 1. On Neolithic religion, the most ambitious study is the volume on eastern European Neolithic religions by Marija Gimbutas, *The Goddesses and Gods of Old Europe, 6500–3500 B.C.*, 2d rev. ed. (Berkeley, 1982). The main works on the religiosity and cults of agriculturalists, which shaped the field for many decades, are Wilhelm Mannhardt's *Wald- und Feldkulte*, 2 vols. (1875–1877; reprint, Darmstadt, 1963), his *Mythologische Forschungen aus dem Nachlasse* (Strassburg, 1884), and James G. Frazer's *The Golden Bough*, 3d ed., rev. and enl., 12 vols. (London, 1911–1915). Within Frazer's huge work the books treating myths and rituals of agriculture more specifically are *Adonis, Attis, Osiris*, 2 vols. (London, 1914), and *Spirits of the Corn and of the Wild*, 2 vols. (London, 1912).

Other important, later contributions on agrarian rituals and beliefs, which approach the agricultural material from the viewpoint of theories based primarily on the study of cerealiculturalist peasants, include Aukusti V. Rantasalo's *Der Ackerbau in Volksaberglauben der Finnen und Esten mit entsprechenden Gebrauchen der Germanen vergleichen*, 5 vols. (Helsinki, 1919–1925), and Johann Jakob Meyer's *Trilogie altindischer Mächte und Feste der Vegetation*, 3 vols. (Zurich and Leipzig, 1937). Vladimir I. Propp's *Russkie agrarnje prazdniki* (Leningrad, 1963), an interesting study of Russian agrarian festivals, follows Frazer with some modifications. An Italian translation is available: *Feste agrarie russe* (Bari, 1978). An important criticism of the views of Mannhardt and Frazer is C. W. von Sydow's "The Mannhardtian Theories about the Last Sheaf and the Fertility Demons from a Modern Critical Point of View," *Folklore* 45 (1934): 291–309, reprinted in C. W. von Sydow's *Selected Papers on Folklore* (Copenhagen, 1948). The most important recent contribution on "agrarian" religions is Mircea Eliade's *A History of Religious Ideas*, vol. 1 (cited above), where the central ideas expressed in his *Patterns in Comparative Religion* (New York, 1958), chaps. 7–9, are developed and at times modified.

Good studies of the religiosity of cultivators outside the "wheat zone" are Marcel Granet's *Festivals and Songs of Ancient China* (1919; New York, 1932) and Bronislaw Malinowski's *Coral Gardens and Their Magic*, 2 vols. (London, 1935). The ethnographical bibliography on the religiosity of primitive cultivators is huge; a most important study of the subject is the book by Vittorio Lanternari, *"La Grande Festa": Vita rituale e sistemi di produzione nelle società tradizionali*, 2d ed. (Bari, 1976). On the beliefs and rituals of cultivators, Angelo Brelich's *Introduzione alla storia delle religioni* (Rome, 1966) is also useful.

On earth-mother figures, see Albrecht Dieterich's *Mutter Erde*, 3d ed. (Leipzig, 1925), and the criticism by Olof Pettersson,

Mother Earth: An Analysis of the Mother Earth Concepts According to Albert Dieterich (Lund, 1967). On the earth-mother figurines, see Peter J. Ucko's study *Anthropomorphic Figurines of Predynastic Egypt and Neolithic Crete* (London, 1968).

The following sources treat the origin myths: Adolf E. Jensen's *Das religiöse Welbild einer frühen Kultur*, 2d ed. (Stuttgart, 1949); Carl A. Schmitz's "Die Problematik der mythologeme 'Hainuwele' und 'Prometheus,'" *Anthropos* 55 (1960): 215–238; Atsuhiko Yoshida's "Les excrétions de la Déesse et l'origine de l'agriculture," *Annales: Économies, sociétés, civilisations* 21 (July-August 1966): 717–728; and Gudmund Hatt's "The Corn Mother in America and in Indonesia," *Anthropos* 46 (1951): 853–914.

New Sources

Baudy, Dorothea. *Römische Umgangsriten.* Berlin-New York, 1998. Interpretation of Roman agrarian rituals in ethnological perspective.

Baudy, Gerhard. *Adonisgärten. Studien zur antiken Samensymbolik.* Frankfurt am Main, 1986. The gardens of Adonis interpreted in the frame of agrarian rituality.

Baudy, Gerhard. "Cereal Diet and the Origins of man. Myths of the Eleusinia in the Context of Ancient Mediterranean Harvest-Festivals." In *Food in Antiquity*, edited by John Wilkins. Exeter, U.K., 1995, pp. 177–195.

Bausinger, Hermann. *Volkskultur in der technischen Welt.* Stuttgart, 1961, 2d edition, Frankfurt am Main, 1986. Criticism of agrarian interpretations in German folklore.

Massenzio, "Vegetationskult." In *Handbuch religionswissenschaftlicher Grundbegriffe*, vol. 5, edited by H. Cancik, B. Gladigow and K.-H. Kohl. Stuttgart, 2001. A recent synthesis on vegetation and fertility issues in comparative religious studies, though very parochial in its perspective since the discussion is based on a selection of Italian literature.

Müller, Klaus E. *Die bessere und die schlechtere Hälfte. Ethnologie des Geschlechterkonflikts.* Frankfurt-New York, 1984. Gender roles and gender conflict in agrarian primal cultures.

Müller, Klaus E. "Grundzüge der agrarischen lebens- und Weltanschauung." *Paideuma* 19–20 (1973–1974): 54–124. The most complete and updated treatment of the relationship between religion and agriculture in a cross-cultural perspective based on a culture-historical approach.

Sabbatucci, *Mistica agraria e demistificazione.* Rome, 1986. Agrarian mysticism demystified in post-modern vein.

Schlatter, Gerhard. "Agrarische Riten." In *Handbuch religionswissenschaftlicher Grundbegriffe*, vol. 2, edited by H. Cancik, B. Gladigow and M. Laubscher, pp. 417–419. Stuttgart, 1988.

Weber-Kellermann. *Erntebrauch in der ländlichen Arbeitswelt des 19. Jahrhunderts auf Grund der Mannhardtbefragung in Deutschland von 1865.* Marburg am Lahn, Germany, 1965. A reappraisal of Mannhardt's vegetation theory.

CRISTIANO GROTTANELLI (1987)
Revised Bibliography

AGUDAT YISRA'EL

AGUDAT YISRA'EL is the world movement of Orthodox Jewry, founded in 1912. The name Agudat Yisra'el, or Agudath Israel (Union of Israel), commonly abbreviated as "Agudah," is derived from a passage in Jewish High Holy Day liturgy that speaks of all creatures forming "one union" to do God's will. Established in order to preserve the traditional Jewish way of life and to counter the influence of competing secular or religious ideologies, Agudat Yisra'el nevertheless adopted a series of ideological and organizational innovations. The very act of organizing an Orthodox political party was in itself a concession to the sociopolitical exigencies of the time, which more extreme Orthodox elements opposed on principle.

HISTORY. The initiative for the formation of Agudat Yisra'el came from the separatist Orthodox communities of Germany united in the Freie Vereinigung für die Interessen des Orthodoxen Judentums. They envisioned a worldwide union of Orthodox Jewry that would enlist the great rabbinical figures of eastern Europe and the Orthodox masses there in the fight against Zionism and Reform Judaism. At about the same time (early twentieth century), some eastern European rabbis made abortive attempts at providing an Orthodox alternative to the Zionist and Jewish socialist parties. Orthodox rabbi and historian Yitsḥaq Eiziḳ ha-Levi brought together representatives of the Freie Vereinigung and the eastern European rabbinate at Bad Homburg (1909), a meeting that laid the groundwork for what became Agudat Yisra'el. The decision of the Tenth Zionist Congress (1911) to embark on a full-fledged educational and cultural program in the Diaspora gave further impetus for an Orthodox countereffort. Elements of the religious Zionist Mizraḥi movement that broke with the Zionist Organization over this decision joined the groups founding Agudat Yisra'el.

The founding conference of the world Agudat Yisra'el was held in Kattowitz, Upper Silesia (now Katowice, Poland) in May 1912, with some three hundred delegates in attendance. This conference began the delicate task of uniting under one organizational roof representatives of Orthodox communities from Germany, from Russia, Poland, and Lithuania, and from Hungary. Though these communities shared opposition to Zionism and other secular ideologies, they divided over many religious issues of both style and substance. Beginning at Kattowitz, the compromise view that prevailed granted autonomy within the framework of Agudah to each brand of Orthodoxy to follow its path on the local and regional level with no coercion on the part of other brands to accept their views. Thus the Frankfurt Orthodox allowed wide secular education, adopted German speech and dress, but demanded a separatist Orthodox community; their Polish counterparts clung to Yiddish, preferred traditional Jewish dress and education, and refused to secede from *qehillah* (Jewish community) boards, where they often constituted the largest group.

The Kattowitz Conference set up a temporary council, whose task would be to stimulate Orthodox organization in Germany and other countries, and nominated the first Mo'etset Gedolei ha-Torah (Council of Torah Sages), the rabbinical body designed to review and supervise all major decisions of the movement. Preparations began for convening in August 1914 the supreme body of the world Agudah, to be known as the Kenesiyyah Gedolah (Great Assembly, a name derived from a phrase in *Avot* 4.11, "an assembly for the sake of heaven"), an Orthodox equivalent of and answer to the Zionist congresses. The first meeting of the Great Assembly, postponed because of the outbreak of war, did not take place until 1923.

The German occupation of Poland opened up new opportunities for the organization of Orthodox Jewry in the east. Attached as advisers to the occupation authorities, representatives of the Freie Vereinigung won the trust of the Polish rabbis and Hasidic leaders and launched the substantive organization of Agudah in Poland, which would become the largest and most politically active branch of the movement. Drawing its strength mainly from the followers of the Hasidic *rebe* of Gur (Góra Kalwaria), the Polish Agudah elected deputies to the Polish parliament and numerous city councils, and it won control of many Jewish *qehillot* (community councils), including those of the two largest communities, Warsaw and Lódź.

The interwar period, punctuated by the three Great Assemblies of 1923, 1929, and 1937, witnessed the consolidation and expansion of Agudah's work on the national and international levels. The world movement established both a Qeren ha-Torah (Torah Fund) to support Orthodox educational institutions and a Qeren ha-Yishuv (Settlement Fund) to support Orthodox efforts in Palestine, which received no aid from the Zionist organizations. Through the work of Qeren ha-Torah, local communities rebuilt schools destroyed during the war and set up new schools. Agudah politicians intervened with government officials in various countries to remove bureaucratic obstacles to the maintenance of traditional education. In Poland they gained government recognition of Agudah schools, although this involved the addition of some secular subjects to the curriculum of the *ḥeder* (lit., "room"), the traditional Jewish religious school. Even more innovative was Agudah's adoption and promotion of the Beit Ya'akov schools for girls. In the eyes of Agudah leaders, the threats facing Orthodoxy justified such a step. An entire network of (generally supplementary) primary and secondary girls' schools developed, with teachers supplied by a central teachers' seminary in Cracow. The Beit Ya'akov system soon spread to other countries.

On the international level, Agudat Yisra'el endeavored to provide an independent Orthodox viewpoint on all major Jewish issues. It most vehemently reacted to matters of special concern to Orthodox Jewry, such as proposed calendar reform or attacks on Jewish ritual slaughter. It consistently denied the right of secular Jewish organizations to speak in the name of all Jewry.

Though debate flared up on occasion within Agudah ranks over the centrality of Palestine in the Agudah agenda and worldview, Agudah developed an active presence in the Land of Israel. In the 1920s and early 1930s, it strove for recognition of the separate status of the old ultra-Orthodox community and resisted inclusion in the general representative bodies of the organized Jewish community. By the mid-thirties, however, waves of Orthodox immigrants from Germany and Poland altered the balance of power in the Agudah in Palestine in favor of more participation in and cooperation with the general community. Those who supported the old separatist line in Palestine eventually broke with Agudat Yisra'el.

The destruction of most of European Jewry in the Holocaust wiped out the major centers of Agudat Yisra'el as well, and Israel and the United States became the primary locations of party activity from then on. During the war years, Agudah activists inside and outside Nazi-occupied Europe endeavored to rescue rabbis and others. On occasion, Agudah dissented from general Jewish policies by its attempts at direct financial aid to Jews in the European ghettos, despite criticism that such help aided the enemy by breaking the economic boycott of Nazi-held Europe.

In the postwar period, Agudah took immediate steps to resume the full range of activities among the survivors in the European displaced-persons camps. The depleted ranks attending the world executive council meeting in 1947 showed the great losses Agudah had suffered, but it also demonstrated the party's determination to remain a force in the Jewish world.

Israel became the major arena for Agudah activities. In the 1940s, as a Jewish state came closer to reality, Agudah made peace with the idea of a Zionist-dominated state, and it, too, issued a call for Jewish independence. Agudah thinkers even drafted a constitution for a state based on Torah. For the first time, Agudah joined the religious Zionist Mizraḥi party in a United Religious Front to press the claim for maintenance of minimal religious standards in public life, including observance of the Sabbath and dietary laws in public institutions, rabbinical control of marriage and divorce, and government support for religious education. As a member of the governing coalition, Agudah received special support for its school system, as well as exemption from military service for religious girls and *yeshivah* students. In the early 1950s, Agudah left the coalition over the issue of compulsory alternative national service for women. As an opposition force, it railed against what it considered breaches of Jewish tradition, such as overly liberal autopsy and abortion laws or the raising of pigs on Jewish farms. Electorally, Agudat Yisra'el has consistently won the votes of approximately 3 percent of the Israeli electorate (four seats in the 120-seat Knesset). In the 1984 elections, however, defections of Sefardic and some non-Hasidic Ashkenazic elements to the new Shas party halved Agudah's Knesset representation. The 1988 elections witnessed a further split in the Agudah's ranks, as tensions of long standing between Hasidic and non-Hasidic elements in the party led the latter to form the separate Degel Hatorah ("banner of Torah") party. Despite the party split, the truncated Agudah actually increased its representation to five seats, largely due to the one-time support and active campaigning by the Habad Lubavich Hasidic group. In subsequent elections, the two factions reunited in the United Torah Judaism party. Each faction, however, maintained its own rabbinic advisory council. In the sixteenth Knesset (elected 2003), United Torah Judaism held five seats.

Both in Israel and the United States, Agudat Yisraʾel has made a generally successful adjustment to its new status of representing a small minority within Jewry. In Israel, it has become a regular, accepted part of the political scene. In 1977, after a quarter century in the opposition, it joined the center-right Likud coalition, but without representation in the cabinet. In 1984, the reduced Agudah delegation participated in the national unity coalition that forms the government, this time demanding and receiving a subcabinet appointment. In the United States, Agudah began functioning effectively only during World War II. It built its strength on the transplanted remnants of Frankfurt Orthodoxy and Holocaust survivors from eastern Europe, but eventually it built a local constituency from the graduates of Agudah-affiliated educational institutions and members of Agudah-affiliated synagogues. Agudah has become the principal voice of independent Orthodoxy, being free of the "taint" of cooperation with the non-Orthodox movements in rabbinical or congregational umbrella organizations. Agudah activists have adapted to American political conditions as an effective lobbying group, with influence on the state and federal levels and a growing presence in some local Jewish federations.

Organization and Branches. In theory, the supreme body of Agudah is the Council of Torah Sages, the institutional fulfillment of Agudah's slogan, "To solve all the problems of the day according to Torah and tradition." In reality, the council has met only infrequently as a formal body, and any ongoing rabbinical supervision of party affairs has come by way of informal consultations with key rabbis. In recent decades, however, the functioning of the rabbinical council both in Israel and the United States has become more regularized and more closely approximates its original intended function. The Israeli council has, however, been paralyzed for considerable periods by differences of opinion within its ranks, which resulted in the council not being convened.

In addition to the Council of Torah Sages, the supreme deliberative body of Agudat Yisraʾel is the Great Assembly, which is convened every five years. In between Great Assemblies, a central council of one hundred elected delegates from the assembly meets annually to assess party affairs. Management of day-to-day matters rests with a small executive committee. Organization of Agudah on the national and regional level in the United States, Israel, and Europe follows the same general pattern.

Within the Agudat Yisraʾel movement there also developed a number of subsidiary and auxiliary organizations. These included organizations for youth (Tseʿirei Agudah, founded 1919), for girls (Benot Agudah, founded 1925/6), for women (Neshei Agudah, founded 1929), and for Orthodox workers (Poʿalei Agudah, founded 1923). Of these organizations Poʿalei Agudah showed the most independence in attempting to represent the interests of its declared constituency. It proved to be an almost constant source of friction within the Agudah camp, and in Israel Poʿalei Agudah eventually split with the parent body and ran independent lists of candidates. Agudah also had its own press and school systems.

Ideology. With a few notable exceptions, such as Isaac Breuer (of Germany, later Palestine), the rabbis and publicists associated with Agudat Yisraʾel offered no systematic presentations of party doctrine. Nevertheless, an examination of newspaper articles, propaganda pamphlets, party proclamations, and rabbinic writings reveals some common themes that run through Agudah thought from its beginnings to the present.

A major ideological innovation of Agudat Yisraʾel was the doctrine of *daʿat Torah* ("Torah view"). According to this doctrine, the authority of the scholars who stood at the head of the movement extended to matters of economics and politics and was not limited to strictly religious matters. In a paradoxical twist, those men totally immersed in the study of Torah and furthest removed from everyday events are proclaimed to be best able to decide matters of political and social policy. Thus Agudat Yisraʾel as a party benefited from the unerring judgment and the aura of holiness of the Torah scholars who, theoretically at least, supervised all party activities. *Daʿat Torah* is an essentially defensive doctrine, the response of an embattled traditional leadership elite to the rise of alternative leaders and doctrines.

From the beginning, Agudah rejected the ideology of secular Zionism. At the same time, though, it consistently stressed its support for increased Jewish settlement in Palestine. The point of contention was the character of the Jewish center being built there. Agudah wished to strengthen the old centers of learning and to ensure that the new settlement be based on traditional Jewish values and laws. Agudah saw solely territorial rebirth of the Jewish people as insufficient. Even in the Land of Israel, Jews could not survive without the Torah. Since the Torah stood at the center of Agudah's concerns, it could never accept the official position of the Zionist movement that religion was a private matter.

In the long run, a detailed party program and ideology have not been crucial for Agudat Yisraʾel. It has turned to its constituency not on the basis of any specific program but on the basis of the collective charisma of the Torah sages and a general desire to defend traditional Judaism at all costs.

See Also Orthodox Judaism; Schenirer, Sarah.

Bibliography

Bacon, Gershon C. *The Politics of Tradition: Agudat Yisrael in Poland, 1916–1939.* Jerusalem, 1996.

Friedenson, Joseph. "A Concise History of Agudath Israel." In *Yaakov Rosenheim Memorial Anthology*, pp. 1–64. New York, 1968.

Mendelsohn, Ezra. "The Politics of Agudas Yisroel in Inter-War Poland." *Soviet Jewish Affairs* 2 (1972): 47–60.

Mittleman, Alan. *The Politics of Torah: The Jewish Political Tradition and the Founding of Agudat Israel.* Albany, 1996.

Schiff, Gary S. *Tradition and Politics: The Religious Parties of Israel.* Detroit, 1977.

Vital, David. *A People Apart: A Politcal History of the Jews in Europe 1789–1939*, pp. 616–640, 785–789. New York, 2001.

GERSHON C. BACON (1987 AND 2005)

AHIṂSĀ. The Sanskrit term *ahiṃsā* (literally "non-injury"), often translated as "nonviolence," has been taken into Western languages as a result of the influence of Mohandas Gandhi. Gandhi explicitly associated *ahiṃsā* with chastity and the absence of possessions as well as with the conviction that one should identify with all beings; he considered *ahiṃsā* to be based on self-control, necessitating preliminary (self-)purification. He also stressed that *ahiṃsā* is a condition of truth, which in turn can be equated with God. Hence Gandhi's invitation, in the last sentence of his autobiography: "In bidding farewell to the reader . . . I ask him to join me in praying to the God of Truth that He may grant me the boon of *ahiṃsā* in mind, word and deed" (Gandhi, 1929).

Considering the traditional Hindu equation of reality with truth (*satya*), it is not surprising that Gandhi used *ahiṃsā* not only as a moral weapon but as a political one as well; in so doing he refused to separate politics and religion. He thus resorted to, and, to a certain extent, reinterpreted an ancient Indian concept.

Similar ideas were current nearly two thousand years ago in some of the oldest Upaniṣads, developing among Brahmanic *saṃnyāsins* (ascetics, mendicants) as well as among the heterodox Buddhist and Jain communities. Such views, it has been convincingly argued, were the outcome of a kind of ideological revolution that took place in India around 500 BCE. At that time, the more contemplative values of the "metaritualist" philosophers superseded earlier magico-ritualistic concepts of religion.

It can be deduced from the more ancient texts that the Vedic Indians believed in an inverted "world beyond," where one must suffer the very fate previously inflicted by him on other beings. Whereas, in order to escape the consequences of one's (cruel) deeds the Vedic brahmans succeeded in inventing elaborate rituals, they still deemed it important, in order to avoid retaliation, to abstain from injuring other beings—thus, to practice *ahiṃsā*.

With the development of the doctrine of transmigration and retribution of actions (*karman*), liberation from rebirth became the ultimate goal of the religious life, and the renouncer's way of life became the ideal behavior. Magico-ritualistic attitudes subsided in favor of ethical and mystical values: Thus the Upaniṣadic sages point to the identity of *ātman* and *brahman* and praise the one who "sees the Self in (his) self, sees the Self in everything. . . ." In this way, the traditional, magical fear of retaliation was replaced by a sense of fellow feeling towards all that lives; *ahiṃsā,* endowed with an indubitably positive value, was expanded into such concepts as "compassion" (*dayā*), a virtue that is required particularly of those who strive after liberation, regardless of the community to which they belong.

The first major vow taken by Brahmanic ascetics and by Buddhist and Jain religious mendicants alike is that life should not be destroyed, whether in mind, in words, or in deeds. The Jains especially emphasize the unique importance of this pledge (which their lay believers also take), and emphasize that all forms of violence, including the passions, destroy the soul's ability to attain ultimate perfection; in addition, that violence turns against the very person who does not refrain from it.

The observance of *ahiṃsā* naturally implies many restrictions as far as the mendicant's diet is concerned. The only acceptable food is that which can be prepared without taking another life; meat-eating is thus shunned. In a more extreme view, plants that are cultivated and then cut and destroyed to become food are also forbidden. The ideal diet, then, consists of fruits, which fall naturally from the trees. Because various penances and ascetic practices have always been based on fasting or on living only on fruits or seeds, *ahiṃsā* came to be closely associated with vegetarianism, of which the Jains soon became and remain uncompromising advocates.

The concept of noninjury, coupled with self-control or self-restraint, was rich in many potential developments. It soon became the central ethical idea in most of the philosophies and religions of India. Indeed, in some communities *ahiṃsā* was given paramount importance, and in this respect Gandhi does not deny the great influence that the revered Jain layperson Raychandbhai Mehta exerted on him. The emphasis that Gandhi laid on *ahiṃsā*, however, would have remained of no avail had it not been firmly rooted in an immemorial Indian tradition.

SEE ALSO Gandhi, Mohandas; Nonviolence; Saṃnyāsa.

BIBLIOGRAPHY

The question of *ahiṃsā* is often addressed in Indian literature as well as by scholars. Useful references will be found in Giuseppe Spera's *Notes on Ahiṃsā* (Turin, 1982). In Bansidhar Bhatt's *Ahimsa in the Early Religious Traditions of India* (Rome, 1994, Centre for Indian and Inter-religious Studies), the appendix II (a) lists the "Published Materials on the Ahimsā" [sic]: 152–176. Hanns-Peter Schmidt has done a fundamental study on the origin of *ahiṃsā* in *Mélanges d'indianisme à la mémoire de Louis Renou* (Paris, 1968). Also see, by the same author, "Ahiṃsā and Rebirth," in *Inside the*

Texts, beyond the Texts, edited by Michael Witzel, pp. 207–234 (Cambridge 1997). Details on the Jain point of view and elaboration of the *ahiṃsā* concept are included in the chapters of Padmanabh S. Jaini's *The Jaina Path of Purification* (Berkeley, Calif., 1979). The reader will find many reflections in Gandhi's autobiography: in Gujarati, Mohandas Karamcand Gandhi's *Satyanā prayogo athavā ātmakathā,* 2 vols. (Ahmedabad, 1927–1928); in English, *An Autobiography, or The Story of My Experiments with Truth,* translated by Mahadev Desai and Pyarelal Nair (1927–1929; 2d ed., Ahmedabad, 1940).

Colette Caillat (1987 and 2005)

AHL AL-BAYT. The conception of the *ahl al-bayt,* "people of the house," "family," or "household" of the prophet Muḥammad plays a vital role in Islamic thought and piety. In the *tashahhud* portion of the ritual prayers, Muslims of all persuasions supplicate daily, "O God! Bless Muḥammad and his family *(āl),* as you blessed Abraham and his family."

Qurʾanic prophetology is pregnant with the notion of a hallowed lineage. God's chosen messengers among the Israelites are believed to have been descended from one another, as the Qurʾān states: "Truly, God chose Adam, Noah, the family of Abraham, and the family of ʿImrān above all the worlds, offspring, one after the other" (III:33–34). The Qurʾān portrays the chosen among the families and descendants (*āl, ahl, qurbā,* and *dhurrīya*) of the prophets as supportive of the messengers during their missions and included in God's merciful protection. They are often the prophets' material and spiritual legatees, heirs with respect to kingship (*mulk*), rule (*ḥukm*), wisdom (*ḥikma*), the book (*kitāb*) and the imamate (IV:54, VI:84–91, XXIX:27, XXXVII:76–77, LVII:26).

As with the families of the previous prophets, Muḥammad's family is accorded a special status in the Qurʾān, the prophetic tradition (*ḥadīth*), and the schools of religious law. At the outset of Muḥammad's mission, God commands him: "Warn your nearest kin (*al-aqrabīn*), and lower your wing to the faithful who follow you" (XXVI:214–215). The Qurʾān also makes certain monetary considerations for the Prophet's relations (*dhīʾl-qurbā*) (VIII:41, LIX:7), and on account of the sanctified status of the prophetic family, Muslim legal practice dictates that Muḥammad and his clan not touch the alms of the community, lest such defilements (*awsākh*) pollute them. The purity of the family is most famously attested to in the verse known as *taṭhīr* (purification): "God desires only to remove impurity from you, O People of the House (*ahl al-bayt*), and to purify you completely" (XXXIII:33).

Muslim tradition, in accordance with the widely reported *ḥadīth al-kisāʾ* or *al-ʿabāʾ*, generally identifies Muḥammad himself; his daughter, Fāṭima; her husband and the cousin of the Prophet, ʿAlī; and the Prophet's two grandsons by this marriage, al-Ḥasan and al-Ḥusayn, as the nucleus of the "house." Shiism also allows for the *imāms* and, in a looser sense, other righteous progeny descended from ʿAlī and Fāṭima to be accounted as part of the family, while some Sunnī reports expand the term to include the Prophet's wives or the collateral branches of his relations, such as, the ʿAbbāsids or even the Umayyads. Al-Nabhānī provides a survey of reports on who is included among the *ahl al-bayt* (*al-Sharaf al-muʿabbad li-āl Muḥammad,* Cairo, 1381/1961, pp. 10–34). It is, however, in light of the *ḥadīth al-kisāʾ* or *al-ʿabāʾ*, the "tradition of the mantle," that both Shīʿī and Sunnī commentators overwhelmingly interpret the verse of *taṭhīr.* According to this account, the Prophet wrapped himself and the other four members of his family in his mantle, solemnly declaring, "O God, these are the People of my House (*ahl baytī*)!" He then recited the Qurʾanic verse of purification. Frequently this incident is connected with the episode of *mubāhala* (mutual imprecation), which relates to the visit of a delegation of Christians from Najrān in the year 631–632. The accounts relate that there was a dispute regarding Christology and it was decided to resort to the ritual of "mutual imprecation" to decide which party was in the right, that of Muḥammad or that of the Christian delegation. Thus Muḥammad is commanded in the Qurʾān III:61: "If anyone dispute with you in this matter [concerning Jesus] after the knowledge that has come to you, say: Come, let us call our sons and your sons, our women and your women, ourselves and yourselves, then let us swear an oath and place the curse of God on those who lie." Accordingly, the five members of the *ahl al-bayt* gathered for the ritual. However, the *mubāhala* is said to have been averted when the Christian side reached a conciliation with the Prophet.

In traditions recorded in both Shīʿī and Sunnī sources, the Prophet likens his family to Noah's ark, saying: "Among you, my *ahl al-bayt* is like the Ark of Noah. Whoso embarks therein is saved and whoso lags behind is drowned." In the well-known report known as the *ḥadīth al-thaqalayn* (the tradition of the two weighty things), likewise found in both Shīʿī and Sunnī sources, he is reported to have said: "Verily, I am leaving with you two weighty things, the Book of God and my progeny, my *ahl al-bayt.* So long as you cling to these two, you will never go astray. Truly, they will not be parted from each other until they join me at the fountain [in paradise]."

In the Qurʾān XLII:23, Muḥammad is commanded to address his disciples as follows, "Say: I do not ask you for any recompense for this [the apostleship] save love for the kinsfolk (*al-qurbā*)." Here, "kinsfolk" is largely understood to be the Prophet's kinsfolk, though divergent interpretations exist as well. The general attitude is well represented in a statement of al-Shāfiʿī (d. 820), the eponymous founder of one of the four predominant Sunnī schools of jurisprudence, who is quoted as saying: "O members of the House of the Prophet, love for you is a duty to God that He has revealed in the Qurʾān. With respect to your great magnificence, it suffices to say that anyone who does not invoke blessings for you has not performed the daily prayer" (al-Nabhānī, p. 184). Along the same lines, Jaʿfar al-Ṣādiq (d. 765), a descendant of the Prophet and one of the Shīʿī *imāms*, declares: "Everything has a foundation, and the foundation of Islam is loving us, the Prophet's family" (Aḥmad b. Muḥammad al-Barqī, *Kitāb al-maḥāsin*, Najaf, 1964, p. 113). Certainly primarily Shīʿī, traditions also assign a numinous role to the family. The five family members are envisioned as beings of light, existing in pre-creation, whose names are derived from God's most beautiful names (see, for example, Furāt b. Ibrāhīm b. Furāt al-Kūfī, *Tafsīr Furāt al-Kūfī*, Najaf: al-Maṭbaʿa al-Ḥaidariyya, n.d., p. 11). Such reports provided fecund material for mystical speculation. In his Gujarati composition *Muman Chitveṇī*, for example, the fourteenth-century Ismaili sage Pīr Ṣadr al-Dīn interprets this idea by describing how the Almighty placed the pole star (*quṭb*), luminous by the light of the five holy ones, in the firmament at the time of creation. Its brilliance was so overwhelming, however, that the heavens began to tremble uncontrollably. Only when the name ʿAlī was written on the corners of the universe was stability restored (*To munīvar moṭī*, Mumbai: Dhī Khojā Sindhī Chhāpākhānuṁ, 1905, p. 3).

A number of designations, roughly synonymous with the term *ahl al-bayt*, became popular in the Muslim world. In the more restrictive sense, terms such as *ahl* (or *āl*) *al-kisā'* (or *al-ʿabā'*), "the people of the mantle," or in Persian-speaking and Persian-influenced areas, *panj tan-i pāk*, "the five pure ones," are prevalent, while in the more general sense of the descendants of the Prophet, epithets such as *āl al-nabī*, *āl al-rasūl* or *āl yāsīn* are widespread.

Throughout Islamic history, the descendants of the Prophet, often styled as *sayyids* or *sharīfs*, have been the focus of particular respect. Shīʿī *imāms*, along with many Ṣūfī *shaykhs*, Sunnī political leaders and Muslim religious scholars of various persuasions, have often drawn tremendous legitimacy and authority from their illustrious descent from the Prophet. In modern times one may cite the *imām* of the Ismailis, Prince Karim Aga Khan, and the ruling families of Morocco and Jordan as cases in point. The descendants of the *ahl al-bayt* have frequently formed a distinct social class in Muslim societies, sometimes even recognizable by distinguishing forms of dress, the green turban being particularly noteworthy. At the same time, a conception exists of a spiritual *ahl al-bayt*, sometimes referred to as the *bayt al-waḥy*, "the house of prophecy," into which the devotees of the prophetic family may be initiated, while unrighteous blood relations may be excluded. Thus one has the Prophet's celebrated dictum about his Persian disciple: "Salmān is one of us, the *ahl al-bayt*."

The theme of devotion to the members of the family has touched many aspects of Islamic piety, literature, architecture, iconography, and mystical thought through the ages. For example, the great poet ʿAbd al-Raḥmān Jāmī (d. 1492), an initiate of the Naqshbandī Ṣūfī order, declares that praise of the *ahl al-bayt* ennobles the encomiast (*Mathnawīhā-yi Haft Awrang*, Tehran, 1351 S/1972, p. 145), while Sanā'ī (d. 1121), in a section of his *Ḥadīqa*, pleads for divine pardon in the name of his love for the Prophet's kinsfolk (*Ḥadīqat al-ḥaqīqa wa sharīʿat al-ṭarīqa*, ed. Mudarris Raḍawī, Tehran, 1329 S/1950, pp. 642–643). Remarkably, domestic architecture in parts of Tajikistan and Xinjiang is centered on five columns, interpreted by the inhabitants as representative of the five purified ones of the Prophet's family. In the early twenty-first century the members of the Prophet's household continue to be celebrated in songs and invoked in prayers and are even the subjects of numerous web pages on the internet.

BIBLIOGRAPHY

Scholarly research on the concept of the *ahl al-bayt* has overwhelmingly concentrated on the political implications of this term in the early Muslim community. In this connection see Moshe Sharon's *Black Banners from the East* (Leiden, 1983); "*Ahl al-bayt*—People of the House," *Jerusalem Studies in Arabic and Islam* 8, no. 2 (1986): 169–184; and "The Umayyads as *ahl al-bayt*," *Jerusalem Studies in Arabic and Islam* 14 (1991): 115–152. An earlier but widely quoted study by Rudi Paret suggested that the term *ahl al-bayt* in the Qur'ān referred to the adherents of the cult of the House, that is, the Kaʿbah. See his "Der Plan einer neuen, leicht kommentierten Koranübersetzung," in *Orientalistische Studien Enno Littmann zu seinem 60. Geburtstag*, edited by R. Paret (Leiden, 1935). Wilferd Madelung provides a meticulous and in-depth examination of previous opinion and articulates his own conclusions in *The Succession to Muḥammad* (Cambridge, U.K., 1997). Early Shīʿī traditions, including of course those related to the *ahl al-bayt*, are examined in Mohammad Ali Amir-Moezzi, *Le Guide Divin Dans Le Shiʿisme Originel*, translated as *The Divine Guide in Early Shi'ism* (Albany, N.Y., 1994); Lynda G. Clarke, "Early Doctrine of the Shiʿah, According to the Shiʿi Sources" (Ph.D. diss., McGill University, 1994); Meir M. Bar-Asher, *Scripture and Exegesis in Early Imāmī Shiism* (Leiden, 1999); and S. Husain M. Jafri, *Origins and Early Development of Shiʿa Islam* (London, 1979). The incident of the *mubāhala* is dealt with in Louis Massignon, "La Mubāhala de Medine et l'hyperdulie de Fāṭima," reproduced in *Opera Minora*, Tome I, pp. 550–572 (Beirut, Lebanon, 1963); Abdelmadjid Méziane, "Le sense de la mubāhala d'après la tradition islamique," *Islamo-christiana* 2 (1976): 59–67; and Rudolph Strothman, "Die Mubahala in Tradition und Liturgie," *Islam* 33 (1957): 5–29. Massignon's article "Salman Pak et les premices spirituelles de l'Islam Iranien," reproduced in *Opera Minora*, Tome I, pp. 443–483 (Beirut, Lebanon, 1963), discusses the role of Salmān's initiation in Islamic piety. The appearance of the *ahl al-bayt* in Persian iconography is elaborated in Maria Vittoria Fontana, "Iconografia dell'Ahl al-Bayt: immagini di arte persiana dal XII al XX secolo" (Naples, Italy, 1994) (Supplemento n. 78 agli Annali vol. 54 [1994], fasc. 1). Reference to the most important primary source materials may be found in the above-cited texts, and in the articles in this encyclopedia on ʿAlī, Ḥusayn, and Fāṭima.

SHAFIQUE N. VIRANI (2005)

AḤMADIYAH. The Aḥmadiyah (or Ahmadiyya) movement is a modern Muslim messianic movement, founded in 1889 in the Indian province of the Panjāb by Ghulām Aḥmad (1835–1908). Having been accused of rejecting the Muslim dogma asserting the finality of Muḥammad's prophethood, the movement aroused the fierce opposition of the Sunnī Muslim mainstream. During the period of British rule in India, the controversy was merely a doctrinal dispute between private individuals or voluntary organizations. However, when most Aḥmadīs moved in 1947 to the professedly Islamic state of Pakistan, the issue was transformed into a major constitutional problem. The Sunnī Muslim mainstream demanded the formal exclusion of the Aḥmadīs from the Muslim fold. This objective was attained in 1974, when, against the fierce opposition of the Aḥmadīs, the Pakistani parliament adopted a constitutional amendment declaring them non-Muslims. In 1984, within the framework of the general trend of Islamization in Pakistan, a presidential "Ordinance no. XX of 1984" transformed much of the religious observance of the Aḥmadiyah into a criminal offense, punishable by three years of imprisonment. The ordinance has since become an instrument of choice for the harassment and judicial persecution of the Aḥmadī community. Following its promulgation, the headquarters of the Aḥmadī movement moved from Rabwah (in Pakistan) to London.

The most distinctive—and controversial—aspect of Aḥmadī religious thought was Ghulām Aḥmad's persistent claim to be a divinely inspired religious thinker and reformer. As has often been the case with Muslim revivalist and messianic movements, the starting point of Ghulām Aḥmad's thought was the assertion that Muslim religion and society has deteriorated to a point where divinely inspired reforms were essential in order to arrest the process of decline and restore the pristine purity of Islam. The most acceptable definition of his spiritual claim from the Sunnī point of view was his declaration that Allāh made him the renewer (*mujaddid*) of Islam in the fourteenth century AH (November 12, 1882–November 20, 1979). More controversial was his claim to be the *mahdī* and the promised messiah (*masīḥ-i maw'ūd*), expected by the Muslim tradition at the end of days. Ghulām Aḥmad's identification as the *mahdī* was designed to counter the Christian and Muslim belief concerning the second coming of Jesus. According to Ghulām Aḥmad, this belief is groundless: whenever the Muslim tradition suggests this idea, it should be understood as indicating not the descent of Jesus himself, but rather that of a person similar to him (*mathīl-i 'Īsā*). This person is Ghulām Aḥmad.

Ghulām Aḥmad's repeated assertion that Allāh called him a prophet was the most controversial formulation of his spiritual claim. Since this assertion is contrary to the Muslim belief that all prophecy came to an end with the completion of Muḥammad's mission, it brought upon Ghulām Aḥmad and his followers the most vociferous denunciations of the Sunnī *'ulamā'* and was always the trump card in the hand of those who wanted to exclude the Aḥmadīs from the fold of Islam. Ghulām Aḥmad explained, however, that Muslim dogma concerning the finality of Muḥammad's prophethood relates only to prophethood of the legislative variety, the one that brings a new book and a new law. After the revelation of the Qur'ān, Allāh will never again reveal a new heavenly book, nor promulgate a new divine law. He maintained that the Qur'ān is the last book to be revealed and Muslim law will remain valid forever. However, a prophet who does not bring a new book and does not promulgate a new law may appear in the Muslim community at any time. Therefore, the appearance of Ghulām Aḥmad, who represents this kind of nonlegislative prophecy and calls for the full implementation of the Muslim *sharī'ah* and of Muḥammad's instructions, does not infringe upon the dogma of the finality of Muḥammad's prophethood (*khatm-i nubuwwat*). The Aḥmadī distinction between the two types of prophethood is probably inspired by the celebrated Muslim mystic Muḥyī al-Dīn ibn al-'Arabī (d. 1240).

Prophetology is the mainstay of Aḥmadī religious thought and is the principal reason for the controversy aroused by the Aḥmadī movement. In addition to it, the Aḥmadīs also have a distinctive interpretation of the idea of *jihād*. In their view, *jihād* should be waged in a way appropriate to the threat facing Islam. In the early Muslim period, nascent Islam was in danger of physical extinction and therefore military *jihād* was called for. In Ghulām Aḥmad's lifetime, Muslims faced the onslaught of Christian missionaries who engaged, according to Ghulām Aḥmad, in a campaign of slander and defamation against Islam and the prophet Muḥammad. In such a situation, the Muslims should respond in kind and defend Islam by preaching and refuting the slander of the Christian missionaries rather than by military *jihād*. Though this interpretation is specific to Ghulām Aḥmad's lifetime and to the situation of Indian Muslims under British rule, it came to be considered as an unchanging principle in the Aḥmadī worldview.

The Aḥmadī movement split in 1914 into two branches: the Qādiyānī and the Lāhōrī. The Qādiyānī branch stressed Ghulām Aḥmad's claim to prophethood, while the Lāhōrī one maintained that the movement's founder should be considered merely as a renewer *(mujaddid)* of Islam at the beginning of the fourteenth century AH.

The Aḥmadī movement has been unrivaled in its dedication to the propagation of its version of Islam. Aḥmadī mosques and missionary centers have been established not only on the Indian subcontinent, but also in numerous cities of the Western world, Africa, and Asia. The Aḥmadīs established an organizational framework and were able to sustain the activities of the movement against considerable odds for more than a century. The elected successors of the founder (in the Qādiyānī branch) bear the title "Successor of the Messiah" (*khalīfat al-masīḥ*). Masrūr Aḥmad, the fifth successor, assumed office on April 22, 2003, and directs the movement from London.

In its relationship with the non-Muslim world, the Aḥmadiyah has been engaged in depicting Islam as a liberal, humane, and progressive religion, systematically calumniated by non-Muslims. This aspect of Aḥmadī teaching is well in line with that of modernist Muslim thinkers, though in other matters, such as the seclusion of women and polygamy, the Aḥmadīs follow the traditional point of view. One of the most distinctive features of the movement is that the Aḥmadīs consider the peaceful propagation of their version of Islam among Muslims and non-Muslims alike as essential. In this they are persistent and unrelenting.

BIBLIOGRAPHY

Bashīr al-Dīn Maḥmūd Aḥmad. *Invitation to Ahmadiyyat.* Rabwah, Pakistan, 1961; reprint, London and Boston, 1980. The most comprehensive description of Aḥmadī beliefs in English, translated from the Urdu original of Ghulām Aḥmad's son and second successor.

Binder, Leonard. *Religion and Politics in Pakistan.* Berkeley and Los Angeles, 1961. See pages 259–296. The Aḥmadī controversy during the first years of Pakistan's existence.

Brush, S. E. "Ahmadiyyat in Pakistan: Rabwa and the Ahmadis." *Muslim World* 45 (1955): 145–171.

Fisher, Humphrey J. *Ahmadiyyah: A Study of Contemporary Islam on the West African Coast.* London, 1963. An excellent study of the Aḥmadiyah in an African setting.

Friedmann, Yohanan. *Prophecy Continuous: Aspects of Aḥmadī Religious Thought and Its Medieval Background.* Berkeley, 1989. A history of the Aḥmadiyah and its expansion, and an analysis of the prophetology of the Qādiyānīs and the Lāhōrīs and of Aḥmadī *jihād.* The second printing (Delhi and New York, 2003) includes a new preface by Zafrira and Yohanan Friedmann on developments since 1984.

Ghulām Aḥmad. *Jesus in India: Jesus' Escape from Death on the Cross and Journey to India.* London, 1978.

Muhammad Zafrullah Khan. *Aḥmadiyyat: The Renaissance of Islam.* London, 1978. A history of the movement from the Aḥmadī point of view.

Muhammad Zafrullah Khan, trans. *Tadhkira: English Translation of the Dreams, Visions, and Verbal Revelations Vouchsafed to the Promised Messiah on Whom Be Peace.* London, 1976.

Pakistan National Assembly's Verdict on Finality of Prophethood of Hazrat Muhammad (Peace be upon him). Islamabad, 1974.

YOHANAN FRIEDMANN (2005)

AHMAD KHAN, SAYYID

AHMAD KHAN, SAYYID (1817–1898), also known on the Indian subcontinent as Sir Sayyid; educational reformer and religious thinker. He was born in Delhi on October 17, 1817, and died at Aligarh on March 27, 1898. Raised in the house of his maternal grandfather, the Mughal noble Khwājah Farīd al-Dīn Khan (1747–1828), he received the traditional education of a Delhi gentleman, reading the Qurʾān in Arabic and Saʿdī's *Gulistān* and *Bustān* and the *dīvān* of Ḥāfiẓ of Shiraz in Persian, together with a smattering of works on mathematics, astronomy, and Greco-Arab medicine.

At the age of nineteen Ahmad Khan entered the judicial service of the East India Company, where he was to rise, in the course of his thirty-eight years of service, to the highest ranks then open to native Indians. From the 1840s onward he published a number of short scientific and religious works, but it was his historical scholarship, and especially his Urdu-language topographical work on Delhi, *Āthār al-ṣanādīd* (1846; rev. ed., 1852), that made him known internationally.

He always considered the British the legitimate rulers of India, but a major turning point in his life came with the failure of the Indian Revolution, known as the Mutiny of 1857. Only then did he become fully convinced that the best of Western civilization could and should be assimilated by the Muslims, because Islam, properly understood, the "pure" Islam taught by the Qurʾān and lived by the Prophet, was not simply unopposed to Western civilization but was in fact its ultimate source and inspiration. In the early 1860s, Ahmad Khan founded the Scientific Society, an association for the translation into Urdu and propagation of works of Western science and scholarship; after his visit to England in 1869–1870, these efforts led to the establishment of the Muhammedan Anglo-Oriental College at Aligarh, the beginning of the first secular university for Indian Muslims.

Against considerable opposition from the *ʿulamaʾ*, as well as from members of his own class, Sir Sayyid emerged in the mid-1880s as the leader of an important sector of Indian Muslims, the majority of whom in 1887 followed his advice not to join the predominantly Hindu, middle-class Indian National Congress. Parliamentary democracy demanded active participation in the process of governmental decision making, and for lack of effective political organization among Muslims he feared that such a congress would bring about the permanent subordination of Muslims to Hindus.

Besides countless editorials and aricles for the *Aligarh Institute Gazette* and for *Tahdhīb al-akhlāq* (The Muslim Reformer), two periodicals he founded, Ahmad Khan wrote a number of important religious monographs, including *Tabyīn al-kalām* (a fragmentary commentary on the Bible in three volumes, 1862–1865), *Essays on the Life of Mohammed* (1870), and a seven-volume Urdu translation and commentary on the Qurʾān up to surah 20 (1880–1904). Most of his articles and tracts, including important parts of his Qurʾān commentary, have been reedited in sixteen volumes by M. Ismāʿīl Panīpātī in *Maqālāt-i Sar Sayyid* (Lahore, 1962–1965).

In his earliest religious writings Sayyid Ahmad Khan strives to put the person and actions of the Prophet back into the center of Muslim life, and he forcefully denounces innovation. Highly conscious of the hiatus between original Muslim practice and the contemporary reality of Indian Muslim society, he stresses the ideals that should inform a corporate Muslim life and insists on the need for an interiorized ethics of the heart. These emphases point to three major influences upon his early outlook: the Naqshbandī Mujaddidī Ṣūfī order, to which Sayyid Ahmad Khan was linked intimately by his family; the theologian, mystic, and social thinker Shāh Walī Allāh (1703–1762) and his house; and the Mujahidin movement led by Sayyid Aḥmad of Rai Bareilly (1796–1836) and Sāh Ismāʿīl (1773–1831), without the political overtones of the latter's teachings and activities, however.

The political consequences of the British crushing of the 1857 "Mutiny" led Ahmad Khan to exclude from the purview of the injunctions of the holy law the whole area of culture and society on the grounds that they were "this-worldly" and not strictly religious *(dīnī)* in character. His teaching remained opaque, however, as to which basic principles of the law—as distinguished from its elaborate prescriptions—could and should inform Muslim sociocultural life with its distinctive Islamic quality.

Sayyid Ahmad Khan not only gave single theological answers to single challenges; by going back to the sources and principles of the various Islamic religious sciences, he attempted a consistent, comprehensively valid theological response. He tried to evolve a new Muslim theology on the pattern, as he saw it, of the Muslim response to Greek philosophy and science during the Abbasid renaissance. The Christian missionary attack under the British imperial aegis, in his view, could be met by accepting and interpreting the present-day scriptures of Jews and Christians as the revealed word of God. Freed from the distortions of an erroneous dogmatic interpretation, and in the light of the uniquely clear Qurʾanic message of God's unity, the gospel of Jesus continues to be relevant.

Critical studies of Muḥammad's biography and of earliest Islam by William Muir (1819–1905) and other scholars provided Ahmad Khan with the battleground for evolving, in defensive response, ever more severe canons of external and internal *ḥadīth* criticism. Taking into account the long period of oral transmission preceding the codification of the *ḥadīth*, along with the laws of the rise and growth of legends, Sir Sayyid accepts the results of post-Newtonian natural science as established truth and uses them to justify the need for metaphorical interpretation *(taʾwīl)* of biblical and Qurʾanic texts. Contemporary and later theological critics have not failed to censure Ahmad Khan for what they consider to be philological ignorance and willfulness in scriptural interpretation.

Besides the "new sciences," the plurality of religions (each claiming the exclusive possession of final, saving truth) led Sir Sayyid to postulate reason *(ʿaql)* as the ultimate criterion of the truth. And reason, for Sir Sayyid, is nothing but the "law of nature," actually, or at least potentially, accessible in full to the human rational faculty. Any happening against the "law of nature" would mean a breach of God's promise and is thus inconceivable. Such a conviction about an all-inclusive, fully determined, and closed nexus of natural law(s) implies the negation of miracles and supernatural events as well as the rejection of traditional views regarding the efficacy of prayers of petition.

In the theologically crucial area of theological epistemology Sayyid Ahmad Khan renews the teaching of classical Muslim philosophers (*falāsifah*). The gift of prophethood, as a natural trait (*malakah*) given to a person at conception, becomes part of the predetermined system of creation and is independent of divine choice. The credibility of the Qurʾān (as of any revealed scripture) is based not on miracles but on the intrinsic value of its content, in the same way that the unsurpassed and unsurpassable greatness of Muḥammad is due to the essential nature of his teaching and to his unparalleled moral effort to spread it.

However incomplete and superficial Sayyid Ahmad Khan's acquaintance with the new sciences and with Western philosophy and historical criticism may have been, and however rash he was in accepting what he thought to be their presuppositions and lasting results, it goes to his credit that before any other Muslim he saw the necessity of a radical reappraisal of Islamic religious thought with openness to modern science, scholarship, and philosophy.

BIBLIOGRAPHY

My own *Sayyid Ahmad Khan: A Reinterpretation of Muslim Theology* (New Delhi, 1978), pp. 353–366, lists the relevant printed primary and secondary source material.

The most comprehensive and substantial biography of Ahmad Khan is *Ḥayāt-i jāvīd* by Alṭāf Ḥusayn Ḥālī. The first, more strictly biographical part of it has been translated from the Urdu original into English by K. H. Qadiri and David J. Matthews as *Hayat-i-javid: A Biographical Account of Sir Syed Ahmad Khan* (Delhi, 1980). The second part of the work offers a detailed analysis of Sir Sayyid's achievements, not least in the field of religious reform and thought. The book remains fundamental, notwithstanding the author's inclination, here and there, toward hero worship and rosy retrospect. J. M. S. Baljon's pioneering study in English, *The Reforms and Religious Ideas of Sir Sayyid Aḥmad Khān*, 3d ed., rev. (Lahore, 1964), throughout deeply indebted to Hali's work, presents an overall picture of the man, subordinating Sir Sayyid's religious quest to his educational and sociocultural concerns. Bashir Ahmad Dar's *Religious Thought of Sayyid Aḥmad Khān* (1957; reprint, Lahore, 1961) is the first monograph to bring into relief Sir Sayyid's positive contribution in the sphere of religious thought, analyzing its salient features in the context of the political, cultural, and religous situation. It describes, to some extent, the classical antecedents to which Sayyid Ahmad Khan related his own seminal ideas. In the line of B. A. Dar, my own *Sayyid Ahmad Khan*, cited above, further emphasizes, by way of a genetic approach, the interplay in Ahmad Khan's religious outlook and theological work between traditional Islamic ideas and the contemporary challenges of Christian preaching, historical criticism, and the "new sciences." It presents the overall structure of his new Muslim theology and, in part 2, offers a substantial choice of texts relating to Sayyid Ahmad Khan's credo, translated from Urdu into English for the first time. In chapter 3 of his edited work, *The Rose and the Rock: Mystical and Rational Elements in the Intellectual History of South Asian Islam* (Durham, N.C., 1979), Bruce B. Lawrence throws new light on Sir Sayyid's early phase of religious practice and thought. He detects there rational elements and mystical components important enough to merit serious attention in any critical assessment of Sayyid Ahmad Khan's later contributions.

CHRISTIAN W. TROLL (1987)

AHRIMAN SEE AHURA MAZDĀ AND ANGRA MAINYU

AHURA MAZDĀ AND ANGRA MAINYU.

Ahura Mazdā (called Lord Wisdom in the Avestan [Av.] and Ōrmazd in the Pahlavi [Pahl.] texts) and Angra Mainyu (Av. Evil Spirit, Pahl. Ahreman) are the names of the two opposed primordial powers that represent good and evil in the dualism of Iran's pre-Islamic religion, Zoroastrianism. In the structural system of the oldest literature, the *Gāthās,* Angra Mainyu is the destructive force opposed not to Ahura Mazdā directly but to Spenta Mainyu, the "beneficent spirit" representing Ahura Mazdā's creative force. These creative and destructive powers form a primordial pair of mutually exclusive opposites like light and darkness. The creative force (Spenta Mainyu) is negated by the destructive one (Angra Mainyu) in the same way that Ahura Mazdā's other spiritual creations, or Bounteous Immortals (*amesha spentas*) are negated by an evil opposite: truth (*asha*) by deceit (*druj*), good mind (*vohu manah*) by evil mind (*aka manah*), and right-mindedness (*ārmaiti*) by arrogance (*tarǝ̄maiti*). This dichotomy is also reflected in the Avestan language insofar as there are special vocabularies for the good, ahuric beings on the one hand, and for the evil, daevic ones, on the other.

Through his creative force, Spenta Mainyu, Ahura Mazdā brought forth life, while the destructive force produced non-life (Y 30.4; Y 44.7). In the Old Avestan "Worship in Seven Chapters" (*Yasna Haptanghaiti*), Ahura Mazdā is praised for creating "all that is good" (Y 37.1), and in the Gathic hymn *Yasna* 44 he is presented as the author of two manifestations of perfect life. One is spiritual and includes truth and good mind, while the other is physical, entailing such phenomena as the sun, stars, moon, earth, water, wind, clouds, plants, and the daily rhythm of light and darkness, sleep and activity, dawn, midday and night. Both spiritual and physical creations were originally made perfect, without any fault or defect, and especially free from decay and death. This positive view of a good and perfect material world is unique and of fundamental importance for Zoroastrian eschatology, for at the end of time, the physical creation will be reinstated in perfection. Both spiritual and physical life were created by Ahura Mazdā for the purpose of overcoming evil, Angra Mainyu. Apart from the distinction between spiritual and physical creation, the most salient feature of Zoroastrian doctrine is its dualistic solution to the problem of evil: the latter does not come from God but has a separate origin and is antagonistic to him and his work. All evil in the world, including deceit and death, comes from that external source.

Angra Mainyu is also opposed to Spenta Mainyu in the Younger Avesta. As observed by Herman Lommel (1930, p. 29), the two mutually antagonistic forces are presented as the originators of two opposed creations, one truthful and good, the other deceitful and evil. The two powers and their respective creations are in a constant struggle with one another. But at the end of time Spenta Mainyu will emerge victorious (Yt 13.13; Y 10.16) and Angra Mainyu will retreat "powerless" (Yt 19.96). In addition, when Zarathushtra repeats the formula "O Ahura Mazdā, most bounteous spirit, creator of the physical world, truthful one" (e.g., Yt 10.73; Yt 14.1, 14.34, 14.42; Vd 2.1 and *passim*), Spenta Mainyu functions as an epithet of Ahura Mazdā. Such a usage indicates a merger between Ahura Mazdā and his creative force.

In the cosmological myth of the Pahlavi texts, Ahreman (the Middle Persian form of Angra Mainyu) is directly opposed to Ōhrmazd (the Middle Persian form of Ahura Mazdā). The most coherent accounts of this are found in the *Bundahishn* and *Wizīdagīhā ī Zādspram* and have been conveniently, though not entirely reliably, transcribed and translated by R. C. Zaehner (1955, pp. 276–321 and 339–343). According to these accounts, in the beginning Ōhrmazd existed on high in endless light, while Ahreman was abased in endless darkness, the two being separated from one another by the Void. They were thus both limitless within themselves and limited at their boundaries. Ōhrmazd, being omniscient, was aware of the existence of Ahreman, while the latter, characterized by ignorance and hindsight, did not know of his opponent.

Ōhrmazd started the course of events by bringing forth out of himself the creation in the spirit (*mēnōg*) state. When Ahreman rushed to the boundary of his darkness, he became aware of Ōhrmazd and his spiritual creation. He then crawled back into the darkness and, in order to destroy Ōhrmazd's creatures, fashioned the evil spiritual countercreation. In a preemptive move, Ōhrmazd invited Ahreman to enter an agreement according to which battle would be limited to a period of nine thousand years. Ahreman, confident that he could defeat Ōhrmazd, accepted, and from then on was bound by that contract, which he was incapable of breaking. However, as was pointed out by Shaul Shaked (1994, p. 24), the neat distinction between good and evil is blurred here, because this myth is based on the assumption that Ahreman is true to his word, an idea incompatible with the deceitful nature of evil. Thereupon, the story continues, Ōhrmazd recited the Ahunavar prayer, thus revealing to Ahreman his final defeat. Ahreman fell in stupefaction, and while he lay unconscious, Ōhrmazd created the physical (*gētīg*) world. After three thousand years, Ahreman awoke from his stupor, beheld Ōhrmazd's beautiful and perfect physical creation, and attacked it, bringing pollution, pain, illness and death into the world. Since that attack, the world has been afflicted by evil. However, this time of "mixture" (*gumezišn*) was limited to three thousand years. The birth of Zarathushtra marked the beginning of the fourth trimillennium, in the course of which three saviors are expected to arrive at intervals of one thousand years. Zarathushtra brought the Mazdā-worshiping religion to humankind, thus equipping them with the means of fighting evil successfully. This struggle is expected to be won by the third and victorious savior (*Sōšyans*), who will drive evil out of the material world. At that point, Ahreman will withdraw powerless and the world will be reinstated in perfection (*frašegird*).

While in the Avesta there is a triangular structure of Ahura Mazdā and Spenta Mainyu, on the one hand, and Angra Mainyu, on the other, in the Pahlavi texts there is a balance of two forces on each side. From a structural point of view, Ōhrmazd is opposed by Ahreman, and *spenāg mēnōg* (the Middle Persian form of Av. *spenta mainyu*) by *gannāg mēnōg*, the foul spirit, newly formed to match *spenāg mēnōg* as a negative opposite, presumably after the upgrading of Ahreman to be directly opposed to Ōhrmazd. They are contrasted with one another, for instance in *Dādestān ī Dēnīg* 1.9, "the goodness of the Holy Spirit (*spenāg mēnōg*) and the non-goodness of the Foul Spirit (*gannāg mēnōg*)." In addition, *gannāg mēnōg* is like Ahreman in denoting the opponent of Ōhrmazd, for example, "I, who am Ōhrmazd, will be the supreme ruler and the Foul Spirit (*gannāg mēnōg*) will be the ruler of nothing" (*Dādestān ī Dēnīg* 6.3). As in the Avesta, the beneficent spirit is identified with Ōhrmazd, for instance in the formula *spenāg mēnōg dādār ōhrmazd*, "the beneficent spirit, the Creator Ōhrmazd" (e.g., *Dādestān ī Dēnīg* 35.7).

While there is direct opposition between good and evil on the spiritual level, there is no such dichotomy in the material world, which was wholly good before the assault of evil. In the structural conception of Zoroastrianism, the physical creation does not have a symmetrical negative counterpart in the way that Ahura Mazdā's perfect spiritual creation does. Angra Mainyu produced a negative countercreation only on the spiritual level, not on the physical one. The reason evil is incapable of producing a material creation is given in a *Dēnkard* passage discussed by Shaul Shaked (1967, pp. 229ff.): the good, luminous *mēnōg* carries "the hot and moist power of living nature" in itself and is therefore able to become manifest in physical, *gētīg* form. In contrast, the evil, dark *mēnōg*, being the negation of life, has a "cold and dry" nature, and is therefore incapable of "reaching compounded materiality." Evil creatures such as wolves, reptiles, and "demons who rush about" are explained as "embodied creatures of luminous seed" that have been hijacked by evil *mēnōg* forms. Thus, the presence of evil in the material world is secondary and derivative, as it presupposes the ontological reality of Ahura Mazdā's material creation. The latter was devised by its creator as a battleground that evil was bound to enter as a result of its destructive nature. Evil clings to God's good physical creation in a parasitic manner and, in the words of Mary Boyce (1975, p. 201) "preys, vampire-like" on it and tries to corrupt and eventually destroy it. However, it is able to adhere only to the physical creations, not to the spiritual ones. As shown by Shaul Shaked (1971, pp. 71ff.), evil requires the physical creations to cling to in order to be present in the material world. It is for that reason that, in the Pahlavi texts, Ōhrmazd is said to exist while Ahreman does not. The connection that underlies this statement is that Ahreman exists only on the spiritual level because the physical one does not have its own evil material creation.

SEE ALSO Zurvanism.

BIBLIOGRAPHY

de Blois, François. "Dualism in Iranian and Christian Traditions." *Journal of the Royal Asiatic Society,* Series 3, 10 (2000): 1–19.

Boyce, Mary. "Ahura Mazdā." In *Encyclopaedia Iranica,* edited by Ehsan Yarshater, vol. 1, pp. 684–687. London, 1982.

Boyce, Mary. *A History of Zoroastrianism,* vol. 1. Leiden, 1975, second impression with corrections, 1989.

Duchesne-Guillemin, Jacques. "Ahriman." In *Encyclopaedia Iranica,* edited by Ehsan Yarshater, vol. 1, pp. 670–673. London, 1982.

Gershevitch, Ilya. "Zoroaster's Own Contribution." *Journal of Near Eastern Studies* 23 (1964): 12–38.

Gnoli, Gherardo. "Dualism." In *Encyclopaedia Iranica,* edited by Ehsan Yarshater, vol. 7, pp. 576–582. Costa Mesa, Calif., 1995.

Haug, Martin. *Essays on the Sacred Language, Writings and Religions of the Parsees.* 3d ed. Bombay, 1884. Reprinted London, 2000.

Henning, Walter Bruno. *Zoroaster: Politician or Witch-doctor?* (Ratanbai Katrak Lectures 1949). London, 1951.

Jaafari-Dehaghi, M. *Dādestān ī Dēnīg.* Part I. Transcription, translation and commentary. Paris, 1998.

Lommel, Herman. *Die Religion Zarathustras nach dem Awesta dargestellt.* Tübingen, Germany, 1930.

Shaked, Shaul. "Some Notes on Ahreman, the Evil Spirit, and His Creation." In *Studies in Mysticism and Religion Presented to Gershom G. Scholem,* edited by E. E. Urbach, R. J. Zwi Werblowsky, and C. H. Wirszubski, pp. 227–234. Jerusalem, 1967. Reprinted in Shaul Shaked, *From Zoroastrian Iran to Islam: Studies in Religious History and Intercultural Contacts,* Brookfield, Vt., 1995, chapter 3.

Shaked, Shaul. "The Notions *mēnôg* and *gētîg* in the Pahlavi Texts and Their Relation to Eschatology." *Acta Orientalia* 33 (1971): 59–107.

Shaked, Shaul. *Dualism in Transformation: Varieties of Religion in Sasanian Iran* (Jordan Lectures 1991). London, 1994.

Zaehner, R. C. *Zurvan: A Zoroastrian Dilemma.* Oxford, 1955. Reprinted New York, 1972.

ALMUT HINTZE (2005)

AHURAS. The Iranian term *ahura* ("lord") corresponds to the Vedic *asura.* Whereas in the Vedas *asura* is usually applied to Dyaus-Pitṛ ("father sky"), the Indian equivalent of the Roman Jupiter, in Iran and in the Zoroastrian tradition *ahura* is applied to three divinities: Ahura Mazdā, Mithra, and Apąm Napāt ("son of the waters"). Some scholars see Apąm Napāt as the Iranian counterpart of Varuṇa, the first of the *asuras*, and have called him *Vouruna Apąm Napāt in an attempt to reconstruct a unitary structure of three original Indo-Iranian *asuras*, with Ahura Mazdā corresponding to Asura *Medhā, Mithra to Mitra, and *Vouruna Apąm Napāt to Varuṇa Apām Napāt (Boyce, 1975). These arguments, however, are not very convincing. Other scholars suppose that at the summit of an ancient Indo-Iranian pantheon was a god called Asura, without further characterization, who survived in Iran to some extent in the Ahura Mazdā of Zarathushtra (Zoroaster), but who in India abandoned the field to Varuṇa (Hillebrandt, 1927; Gershevitch, 1964). This thesis, however, is also not certain.

In both Iran and India, the term *ahura/asura* designates a class of gods or, to be more exact, a class of ruling gods (Dumézil, 1977), but their fate on either side of the Indus was different. Whereas in India the *asuras* came to represent the most archaic divinities, against which the *devas*, the "young" gods, asserted themselves, in Iran it was one of the *ahuras*, Ahura Mazdā, who displaced all the *daivas*. Thus, when Zoroastrianism reached a compromise with the ancient polytheism that had originally been condemned by Zarathushtra, the other *ahuras*, such as Mithra and Apąm Napāt, were readmitted to the cult, while the *daivas*, whose nature was bellicose and violent and who were above all warrior gods (Indra, for example), were totally demonized. It is quite likely that the *ahuras* were able to maintain their privileged position in the Zoroastrian tradition thanks to their ethical nature and to their special function as guardians of *asha* (Vedic, *ṛta*), truth and order, a fundamental concept of Indo-Iranian religions in general as well as of Zoroastrianism in particular.

Bibliography

Boyce, Mary. *A History of Zoroastrianism,* vol. 1. Leiden, 1975.

Bradke, Peter von. *Dyâus Asura, Ahura Mazdā und die Asuras.* Halle, 1885.

Duchesne-Guillemin, Jacques. *Zoroastre: Étude critique avec une traduction commentée des Gâthâ.* Paris, 1948.

Dumézil, Georges. *Les dieux souverains des Indo-Européens.* Paris, 1977.

Geiger, Bernhard. *Die Ameša Spentas: Ihr Wesen und ihre ursprüngliche Bedeutung.* Vienna, 1916.

Gershevitch, Ilya. "Zoroaster's Own Contribution." *Journal of Near Eastern Studies* 23 (1964): 12–38.

Gignoux, Philippe. "Des structures imaginaires du panthéon prézoroastrien à l'existence de Baga." In *Iranica,* edited by Gherardo Gnoli and Adriano V. Rossi, pp. 365–373. Naples, 1979.

Hillebrandt, Alfred. *Vedische Mythologie,* vol. 1. Breslau, 1927.

Kellens, Jean. *Le panthéon de l'Avesta ancien.* Wiesbaden, 1994.

Molé, Marijan. *Culte, mythe et cosmologie dans l'Iran ancien.* Paris, 1963.

GHERARDO GNOLI (1987)
Translated from Italian by Roger DeGaris

AINU RELIGION.

The Ainu are a people whose traditional homeland lay in Hokkaido, southern Sakhalin, and the Kurile islands, although their territory once included southern Kamchatka and the northern part of the main Japanese island (Honshu). Scholarly controversies over their cultural, racial, and linguistic identities remain unresolved. Their hunting-gathering way of life was discontinued with the encroachment of the Russians and the Japanese during the latter half of the nineteenth century and the first half of the twentieth century. Generalizations about Ainu culture or religion are dangerous to make, since not only are there a great many intracultural variations among the Ainu of each region, but differences occur within each group as well. Because the following description is aimed, as much as possible, at the common denominators, it may not fit in toto the religion of a particular Ainu group.

An important concept in the Ainu belief system is the soul. Most beings in the Ainu universe have a soul, and its presence is most conspicuous when it leaves the body of the owner. When one dreams, one's soul frees itself from the sleeping body and travels to places where one has never been. Similarly, a deceased person appears in one's dreams, since the soul of the deceased can travel from the world of the dead to visit one. During shamanistic performances the shaman's soul travels to the world of the dead in order to snatch back the soul of a dead person, thereby reviving him or her.

This belief underlies the Ainu emphasis on the proper treatment of the dead body of human beings and all other soul-owners of the universe. The belief results in elaborate funeral customs, which range from the bear ceremony to the careful treatment of fish bones (because they represent the dead body of a fish). Without proper treatment of the dead body, its soul cannot rest in peace in the world of the dead. For this reason, illnesses serve to remind the Ainu of their misconduct. Shamans are consulted in order to obtain diagnosis and treatment for these illnesses.

When a soul has been mistreated, it exercises the power to punish. The deities, in contrast, possess the power to punish or reward the Ainu at will. Interpretations among scholars as to the identity of the deities range from those proposing that nature be equated with the deities, to those finding that only certain members of the universe are deified. The differences in opinion originate in part from the Ainu's extensive use of the term *kamuy,* their word for "deity" or "deities." An important point in regard to the Ainu concept of deities is Chiri Mashio's interpretation that the Ainu consider all the animal deities to be exactly like humans in appearance and to live just like humans in their own country. The animal deities disguise themselves when visiting the Ainu world in order to bring meat and fur as presents to the Ainu, just as Ainu guests always bring gifts. In this view, then, the bear, which is generally considered the supreme deity, is but the mountain deity in disguise.

Besides the bears, the important deities or *kamuy* include foxes, owls (which are considered to be the deity of the settlement), seals, and a number of other sea and land animals and birds. The importance of each varies from region to region. In addition, the Ainu pantheon includes the fire goddess (Iresu-Huchi), the goddess of the sun and moon (in some regions they are separate deities), the dragon deity in the sky, the deity of the house, the deity of the *nusa* (the altar with *inaw* ritual sticks), the deity of the woods, and the deity of water.

Evil spirits and demons, called variously *oyasi* or *wenkamuy* ("evil deity"), constitute another group of beings in the universe who are more powerful than humans. They may exercise their destructive power by causing misfortunes such as epidemics. (The smallpox deity is an example.) While some of them have always been demons, others are beings that have turned into demons. When a soul is mistreated after the death of its owner, for example, it becomes a demon. The Ainu pay a great deal of attention to evil spirits and demons by observing religious rules and performing exorcism rites. A major theme in the Ainu epic poems treats human combat with demons. Characteristically, the deities never directly deal with the demons; rather, they extend their aid to the Ainu, if the latter behave properly.

Of all the rituals of the Ainu, the bear ceremony is by far the most elaborate. It is the only ceremony of the Ainu that occurs in all regions and that formally involves not only all the members of the settlement but those from numerous other settlements as well, thereby facilitating the flow of people and their communication among different settlements. The bear ceremony provides a significant opportunity for male elders to display their wealth, symbolizing their political power, to those from other settlements. Most importantly, from the perspective of the Ainu, the bear ceremony is a funeral ritual for the bear. Its purpose is to send the soul of the bear through a proper ritual so that the soul will be reborn as a bear and will revisit the Ainu with gifts of meat and fur.

The entire process of the bear ceremony takes at least two years and consists of three stages. The hunters capture and raise a bear cub. In the major ceremony, the bear is ritually killed and its soul is sent back to the mountains. Among the Sakhalin Ainu a secondary ceremony follows the major ceremony after several months. A bear cub, captured alive either while still in a den or while ambling with its mother upon emerging from the den, is usually raised by the Ainu for about a year and a half. At times women nurse these newborn cubs. Although the time of the ceremony differs according to the region, it is most often held in the beginning of the cold season; for the Sakhalin Ainu, it takes place just before they move from their coastal settlement to their inland settlement for the cold season.

The ceremony combines deeply religious elements with the merriment of eating, drinking, and dancing. All the participants don their finest clothing and adornments. Prayers are offered to the fire goddess and the deity of the house, but the major focus of the ceremony is on the deity of the mountains, who is believed to have sent the bear as a gift to the humans. After the bear is taken out of the "bear house," situated southwest of the host's house, the bear is killed by the Sakhalin Ainu with two pointed arrows. The Hokkaido Ainu use blunt arrows before they fatally shoot the bear with pointed arrows; then they strangle the already dead or dying bear between two logs. Male elders skin and dress the bear, which is then placed in front of the sacred altar where treasures are hung. Ainu treasures consist primarily of trade goods from the Japanese, such as swords and lacquerware. These are considered offerings to the deities and function as status symbols for the owner. After preliminary feasting outside at the altar, the Ainu bring the dissected bear into the host's house through the sacred window and continue their feast. Among the Hokkaido Ainu, the ceremony ends when the head of the bear is placed at the altar on a pole decorated with *inaw*. The elder bids a farewell prayer while shooting an arrow toward the eastern sky—an act signifying the safe departure of the deity. The Sakhalin Ainu bring the bear skull stuffed with ritual shavings, bones, eyes, and the penis, if the bear was male, to a sacred bone pile in the mountains. They also sacrifice two carefully chosen dogs, which they consider to be servant-messengers of the bear deities. Although often mistaken as a cruel act by outsiders, the bear ceremony is a ritual whereby the Ainu express their utmost respect for their deity.

Although the bear ceremony is distinctly a male ceremony, in that the officiants are male elders and the women must leave the scene when the bear is shot and skinned, shamanism is not an exclusively male vocation. Sakhalin Ainu shamanism differs considerably from that of the Hokkaido Ainu. Among the former, cultural valuation of shamanism is high; well-regarded members of the society, both men and women, may become shamans. Although shamans sometimes perform rites for divinations of various sorts and for miracle performances, by far the great majority of rites are performed for diagnosis and cure of illnesses. When shamans are possessed by spirits, they enter a trance state, and the spirit speaks through their mouths, providing the client with necessary information, such as the diagnosis and cure of the illness or the location of a missing object. Among the Hokkaido Ainu, whose shamanistic practice is not well recorded, shamans are usually women, who collectively have lower social status than men, although some male shamans are reported to have existed. The Hokkaido Ainu shaman also enters a possession trance, but she does so only if a male elder induces it in her by offering prayers to the deities. Although she too diagnoses illnesses, her function is confined to diagnosis, after which male elders take over and engage in the healing process. Male elders must, however, consult a shaman before they make important decisions for the community.

While Ainu religion is expressed in rituals as well as in such daily routines as the disposal of fish bones, nowhere is it more articulated than in their highly developed oral tradition, which is both a primary source of knowledge about the deities and a guideline for the Ainu conducts. There are at least twenty-seven native genres of oral tradition, each having a label in Ainu. They may be classified into two types: verses, either epic or lyric, sung or chanted; and prose that is narrated. While the prose in some genres is recited in the third person, the more common genre is first person narrative, in which a protagonist tells his own story through the mouth of the narrator-singer. The mythic and heroic epics are very complex and lengthy; some heroic epics have as many as fifteen thousand verses. While the mythic epics relate the activities of deities, the heroic epics concern the culture hero, sometimes called Aynu Rakkuru, who, with the aid of the deities, fought against demons to save the Ainu, thereby becoming the founder of Ainu people. Among the Hokkaido Ainu, the culture hero descended from the world of the deities in the sky and taught the Ainu their way of life, including fishing and hunting, and the rituals and rules governing human society. His marriage, told in various versions, is another prominent theme in the epics. Some scholars interpret the battles fought by the culture hero as being the battles that the Ainu fought against invading peoples.

SEE ALSO Bears.

BIBLIOGRAPHY

Ainu minzokushi. Tokyo, 1970. Issued by Ainu Bunka Hozon Taisaku Kyogikai. See pages 723–770.

Chiri Mashio. "Ainu no shinyo." *Hoppo bunka kenkyu hokoku* (1954): 1–78.

Chiri Mashio. *Bunrui Ainugo jiten,* vol. 3. Tokyo, 1962. See pages 359–361.

Kindaichi Kyosuke. *Ainu bungaku.* Tokyo, 1933.

Kitagawa, Joseph. "Ainu Bear Festival (Iyomante)." *History of Religions* 1 (Summer 1961): 95–151.

Ohnuki-Tierney, Emiko. *The Ainu of the Northwest Coast of Southern Sakhalin* (1974). Reprint, Prospect Heights, Ill., 1984. Pages 90–97 describe the Sakhalin Ainu bear ceremony.

Ohnuki-Tierney, Emiko. "Regional Variations in Ainu Culture." *American Ethnologist* 3 (May 1976): 297–329.

Philippi, Donald L. *Songs of Gods, Songs of Humans.* Princeton and Tokyo, 1979.

EMIKO OHNUKI-TIERNEY (1987)

AION. The trajectory of Aion extends for more than a thousand years over the whole of antiquity, from Homer to Nonnus of Panopolis. Its story has been recounted several times, and many controversial issues have been almost conclusively solved. In effect, taking part in the debate on the question of Aion has turned out to be something of an ordeal for scholars of ancient religions, for it requires them to conduct a painstaking investigation of Greek and Latin literature, ancient art, and religious topics of Greece, Rome, Egypt, Iran, Syria, and Mesopotamia. Moreover, tackling the topic of Aion entails coping with the basic tenets of the leading exponents of the *Religionsgeschichtliche Schule* (Reitzenstein, Bousset, and Norden) and testing the methodology of four of the most prominent modern historians of religions: Franz Cumont (1868–1947), Martin Persson Nilsson (1874–1967), Raffaele Pettazzoni (1883–1959), and Arthur Darby Nock (1902–1963). Before settling this matter, it is important to survey the various meanings of the Greek word *aion,* first in common usage, then in a theological context, before the emergence in the first century CE of the throngs of *aiones* (in the latinized spelling, *aeones*) that came to inhabit the hierarchical Gnostic universe.

SEMANTIC DEVELOPMENTS OF THE TEMPORAL NOTION OF *AION* FROM HOMER UNTIL THE EARLY CHRISTIAN LITERATURE. Semantic analysis and linguistic comparison (cf. the Vedic Agni, a life-giving god, and Latin *iuvenis*) have proven that at its birth in the Indo-European crucible and in its early usage by Homer, *aion* meant "life," in the sense of "vitality" or "life-fluid" (also "spinal marrow" in medical texts). After Homer the physical, nontemporal value fades out and persists only in epic diction up to Nonnus of Panopolis, the poet who in the fifth century CE competes with the Homeric archetype to build up a living theology out of dead deities.

In the Greek literature of the classical age, *aion* predominantly assumes the meaning of "life" in all its nuances, from the "lifetime" to the "lifestyle" of an individual human being. A collective reference ("generation" or "age") is also found, altogether with the more impersonal significance of "time," in competition with *chronos,* but in the narrower sense of "period of time." However, at the same time and especially in Heraclitus and Pindar, it assumes mystical nuances (in connection with the Orphic tradition) converging in the spheres of *daimon* and *moira* (fate). Only Plato, either influenced by the Persian opposition between Zurvan *akarana* (time boundless) and Zurvan *daregho-chvadhata* (time of the long dominion) or simply prompted by his linguistic and mythopoeic genius, in *Timaeus* (37d–38c) confers a fundamental shift on Aion's semantic history. The demiurge creates sensible time (*chronos*) as a moving image of eternity (*aion*) immovable in the eternal present. Consequently, Aion becomes the idea of time, which is Platonically the heavenly model of earthly time, whereas for Aristotle, *aion* is transformed into the "immortal and divine" life of Heaven, lasting in eternal duration more than in an eternal present and almost identified with heaven. Philo of Alexandria weaves Plato's intuition and Aristotle's vision into a distinctly theological pattern. Aion is the *bios* of God and of the *kosmos noetos* living in an eternal present. Another devoted follower of Plato transfers his master's intuition onto an even more metaphysical level: for Plutarch, God, who does not exist in time (*chronos*), has his only real existence in eternity (*aion*), an unmoving and nontemporal state.

In Jewish and early Christian texts (especially the New Testament and the pseudo-Clementine *Homiliae*), the usage of *aion* with the sense of eternity alternates with the seemingly antithetical usage of *aion* meaning "segment of time," that is, "age." This segment of time may coincide with "the past," with "the present age" (*ho aion outos*), or with "the age to come" (*ho aion mellon*). The doctrine of the two *aeones,* the present one being dominated by the devil-kosmokrator and nearing its end, and the one to come, which is imminent and will fulfill the messianic promises of perfection, is rooted in Jewish apocalypticism. After being hinted at in the Synoptics and in Paul, this doctrine is fully developed in the pseudo-Clementine *Homiliae* with such overtly dualistic features that they seem to echo the Persian dualistic conception of the two successive kingdoms, the first in the hands of the evil Ahriman and the second under the power of the good Ōhrmazd.

AION AS COSMIC GOD. Finally, in the Hellenistic age Aion becomes a cosmic god popular in various mysterio-sophical circles and sometimes an object of a sort of henotheistic cult. As regards the character of this cult prior to the explosion of the single Aion into the *aiones* of Gnosticism, we have very little information. With respect to visual documents, the Mithraic leontocephaline, which had already been identified with Aion by G. Zoega and was later associated with Zurvan by Franz Cumont and, finally, with Ahriman by F. Legge, only vaguely reflects the personality of Aion as a cosmic god of eternity. As regards the other monuments commonly referred to the cosmic god Aion because of the presence of the wheel of the zodiac and/or of the entwined serpent, only the elderly bearded figures appearing in mosaics and reliefs dating from the end of the first century BCE up to the sixth century CE are identified by epigraphs as representations of the god Aion. Other well-known images of a youthful, cosmic god in the zodiac refer to other deities. Only a few of the coins circulated by the Roman emperors to advertise the happiness of their empire as a sign of the renewal of time and the universe can be reliably referred to the cult of Aion (see the pieces where Aion appears surrounded by the *ouroboros* or holding the Phoenix). A telling, even if nonanthropomorphic image, of aionic time eternally revolving is that of the *ouroboros,* the serpent biting its own tail. From literary evidence and inscriptions on the magical papyri and the so-called Gnostic gems, we learn that this icon, undoubtedly Egyptian in origin, was widely conceived as a fitting and living symbol of Aion. Very little can be deduced about the cult of the god Aion in Alexandria during the Hellenistic age from the celebrated passage of Epiphanius (*Panarion* 51. 22. 9–11) concerning the Aion generated by the Virgin on the night of January 5–6. It is likely that the cult of the Alexandrine Aion witnessed by the heresiologist is only a late syncretistic fruit of an indigenous cult of Osiris in special relation to the Egyptian notion of eternity (*Nhh*) as the everlasting renewal of life out of death. In Eleusis during the reign of Augustus three Roman brothers dedicated a statue of Aion "for the might of Rome and the persistence of the mysteries." This dedication shows that in the first century BCE Aion was conceived of as a personal divine entity with its own iconography, which conferred a concrete and tangible nuance to a symbol that had, until then, only been expressed through philosophical images.

In the second century CE the Nubian town of Talmis was the center for a henotheistic cult of the local deity Mandulis, which does not necessarily mean that it was a primary place of worship to the god Aion. The worshiper who had a beatific vision of his god and expressed thanksgiving in an inscription praised Mandulis as "The Sun, the all-seeing King of the universe and omnipotent Eternity (*Aion pantokrator*)." The Nubian god is identified with the Greek Helios and is endowed with the attributes of omniscience, omnipotence, and eternity. Aion appears not as another well-defined Greek deity but simply as a feature of the Sun God.

Aion plays a prominent role in the liturgies of the magical papyri, documents containing extremely heterogeneous material from the first centuries CE. Appearing roughly twenty times in the magical papyri, Aion is compared to Helios four times and, more rarely, to other deities belonging to the solar sphere: Apollo, Agathos Daimon, or the Egyptian god Ra. It is predominantly a personal god, in particular the supreme cosmic deity, the lord of the world (*kosmokrator* or *pantokrator*), but also the First Father, invisible and self-generated, above whom there is no one. As such, in order to distinguish the god from other *aiones* or lesser deities, a superlative circumlocution of clear Semitic origin is used to define him as "God of the gods," "God of the aiones," "unique and blessed among the aiones," "Aion of the aiones," and "king and lord of the aiones."

The same conception is clearly expressed in the *Oracula Chaldaica.* Aion is defined as the "light issuing from the Father," who draws on the Father's force to dispense intelligence (*nous*) to the lower beings, endowing them with a sort of perpetual motion. The Father or the Supreme Principle is thus conceived of as an agglomeration of light (a Sun) from which a luminous particle detaches as a *deuteros theos* to illuminate and oversee the activities of the lower world. Likewise, in an oracle of the *Theosophy of Tübingen* the various gods of the cult are merely particles of the all-embracing god and his angels. In this text the supreme Aion and the various *aiones* seem to hint at the Gnostic doctrine of the *aiones* in terms that can be traced back to an Orphico-Platonic matrix.

In the *Corpus Hermeticum* the theology of Aion appears as one of the mainstays of the whole system. Right from the beginning Aion appears as the front-line physical and metaphysical principle immediately after the Supreme God: "God makes Aion, Aion makes the heaven-world, the heaven-world makes time (*chronos*), time makes the *genesis*" (*C.H.* XI. 2). Finally, as Aion is spatially and temporally infinite, it becomes the archetype, the objective of mystic-ascetic practices. Clearly, in this context Aion is not simply an abstract concept (eternity or infinite space) but an active principle, the strength (*dynamis*) or wisdom (*sophia*) of God, the Soul of the World. In other words, in the Hermetic system Aion plays the role of the "Second God" (*deuteros theos*), the intermediary between the highest, unfathomable god and the world. That is to say, it plays the same role that in other Stoic and Middle Platonic contexts is played by Logos, Sophia, by a god called *deuteros* or *demiourgos*, by a personalised *pneuma*. These entities act in a hierarchical system with three (or five) levels in which the second god modeled on or by the first god is, in turn, the model for the third god identified in the cosmos.

***AION* AND *AIONES* IN GNOSTICISM.** In the Gnostic mental universe, the *aiones* are the bricks of which the higher reality is built, the only reality that per se exists eternally and of which the lower world is merely a dim shadow. From the beginning this higher reality has been a compact whole, a solitary thought reflecting onto itself. At a certain point, it is broken down into a graded series of cosmic entities, the *aiones*, which bear the sign of the primary principle from which they sprung while remaining fatally inferior to it.

The term *aiones* first appears many times in the Gnostic treatises of Nag Hammadi, indicating an undefined number of spatial segments making up the noetic and pneumatic invisible and eternal world. In his heresiological transcription, Irenaeus uses the singular *incorruptibilis Aeon* to designate the higher world formed of all the *aiones* together as it is conceived of by the Gnostics mentioned in the *Adversus Haereses*. The term *aiones* is also frequently used in several Gnostic treatises to indicate a certain number of spatial entities conceived of as segments of the intellectual cosmos, which are diversified and stratified and also endowed with a specific personality (symbols of the mental functions). In the Sethian writings Aion appears in the singular almost exclusively to indicate the entity closest to the unfathomable Father, Barbelo, the self-generated and thrice male *aion*. More rarely, *aiones* may be used to indicate lower realities existing outside the pleroma. It would appear then that *aiones* can also be applied to the archons, basically "demons," from the court of the evil god Ialdabaoth, just as it normally identifies the category of spiritual beings created from the Supreme God, basically "angels."

The current contraposition between *aiones* as the hypostasis of the higher reality and angels as creatures of the inferior god in some texts becomes so tenuous as to disappear altogether. In view of this semantic fluidity, it is no wonder that when Epiphanius had to give names to the seven sons of Ialdabaoth who combine to mold the first man Adam, he defined them as "aiones or gods or angels." The Gnostic *aiones*, being the intermediaries between the transcendent world and the earthly world, perform a function that essentially coincides with that of the angels, the mediators between god and the cosmos in the Jewish conception that underlies Christian and Islamic angelology.

The semantic shift of *aion/aiones* from the context of time to that of space, which was already latent in both pagan and Christian Hellenistic literature, becomes a fait accompli in Gnostic scriptures, even if the temporal nuance of *aion* is not completely lost. Likewise, for the Gnostics eternity is the essential characteristic of the great Aion and his descendants, the lesser *aiones*, are merely entitled to the crumbs of this inheritance of eternity, in a spatial dimension, as they are nothing more than shadows or images of the greater *aion*.

In conclusion, the tendency of Gnostic mythopoeia to give form to abstract entities by attributing them with a concrete personality perhaps underlies the extensive speculation on the *aiones*, which are at one and the same time fragments of duration and the characters of a mythical drama halfway between the real and the symbolic. The shift from the One to the multiple, from time to space, therefore seems to stem from a process within Gnostic thought itself instead of being the result of a sort of artificial insemination in Persian or Egyptian test tubes.

SEE ALSO Eternity; Gnosticism; Hellenistic Religions; Lions; Sacred Time; Snakes; Zurvanism.

BIBLIOGRAPHY

Alföldi, Andreas. "From the Aion Plutonios of the Ptolomies to the Saeculum Frugiferum of the Roman Emperors." In *Greece and the Eastern Mediterranean in Ancient History and Prehistory*, edited by K. H. Hinzl, pp. 1–30. Berlin and New York, 1977. Important analysis of monuments, especially the coins.

Belayche, Nicole. "Aiôn: Vers une Sublimation du Temps." In *Le Temps chrétien de la fin de l'Antiquité au Moyen Age: IIIe–XIIIe siècles*, edited by Jean-Marie Leroux, pp. 11–29. Paris, 1984.

Bousset, Wilhelm. "Der Gott Aion (Aus der Unveröffentlichen Nachlass, ca. 1912–1919)," in his *Religionsgeschichtliche Studien*. Leiden, 1979, pp. 192–230. A groundbreaking work for the historico-religious interpretation, with emphasis on the magical and Hermetic texts, although virtually unknown in scholarship.

Brandon, S. G. F. *History, Time and Deity. A Historical and Comparative Study of the Conception of Time in Religious Thought and Practice*. Manchester, 1965. See pp. 56 and 61 for a (debatable) solution of the problem of the relationship between the Hellenistic Aion and the Gnostic *aiones*.

Casadio, Giovanni. "From Hellenistic *Aion* to Gnostic *Aiones*." In *Religion im Wandel der Kosmologien*, edited by Dieter Zeller, pp. 175–190. Frankfurt am Main, 1999. A synthesis, with detailed presentation of the evidence, on which this article is based.

Colpe, Carsten. "Altiranische und Zoroastrische Mythologie." In *Götter und Mythen der Kaukasischen und Iranischen Völker = Wörtebuch der Mythologie*, edited by W. Haussig, pp. 161–487, vol. 4, Stuttgart, 1986. See the entry, "Aion," pp. 246–250. Reprinted in Colpe, Carsten. *Kleine Schriften*, vol. V. Berlin, 1996, pp. 147–151.

Cumont, Franz. "Mithra et l'Orphisme." *Revue de l'Histoire des Religions* 109 (1934): 63–72. Classical interpretation of the Modena bas-relief.

Degani, Enzo. *AION da Omero ad Aristotele*. Padua and Florence, 1961. Fundamental for Aion in pre-Hellenistic literature.

Degani, Enzo. *AION*. Bologna, 2001. A synthesis of the 1961 study with amplifications to comprehend the Christian literature.

Festugière, André-Jean. *La Révelation d'Hermès Trismégiste, Le Dieu Inconnu et la Gnose.* Paris, 1954. See pp. 141–199. Fundamental for the analysis of the magical papyri and the Hermetic treatises.

Foucher, Louis. "Aiôn, le Temps Absolu." *Latomus* 55 (1996): 5–30. Accurate and comprehensive analysis of monuments: mosaics, coins, reliefs, and paintings.

Jackson, H. M. "Love Makes the World Go Round. The Classical Greek Ancestry of the Youth with the Zodiacal Circle in the Late Roman Art." In *Studies in Mithraism,* edited by J. R. Hinnells, pp. 131–164. Rome, 1994. Thorough and convincing analysis of monuments.

Jung, Carl Gustav. *Aion. Untersuchungen zur Symbolgeschichte.* Zürich, 1951, Olten, 1976. See pp. 52–55 and 517. Based on a passage in the pseudo-Clementine *Homiliae,* he argues for the substantial nature of evil in the true Christian vision and its virtual inherence to God the Creator—a view overtly Gnostic.

Le Glay, Maurice. "Aion." In *Lexicon Iconographicum Mythologiae Classicae,* vol. 1, pp. 399–411. Munich and Zürich, 1981. Very valuable, all-inclusive survey of the iconography.

Levi, Doro. "Aion." *Hesperia* 13 (1944): 269–314. Discussion of monuments, especially the mosaics.

Markschies, Christoph. *Valentinus Gnosticus? Untersuchungen zur Valentinianischen Gnosis mit einem Kommentar zu den Fragmenten Valentins.* Tübingen, Germany, 1992. See pp. 157–166. Competent discussion of Aion in Valentinus, but important also for general issues.

Musso, Luisa. "Aion." In *Enciclopedia dell'arte Antica Classica e Orientale. Secondo Supplemento,* pp. 134–142. Rome, 1994. The most comprehensive and updated survey of the iconography, with rich literature.

Nock, Arthur Darby. *Essays on Religion and the Ancient World.* Cambridge, Mass., 1972. Based on a definitive explanation of the inscription of Talmis, he argues convincingly for an interpretation of Aion as a function and not as a definite divine figure.

Norden, Eduard. *Die Geburt des Kindes. Geschichte einer Religiösen Idee,* 2d ed., pp. 24–40. Leipzig, 1924.

Puech, Henri-Charles. "La Gnose et le Temps. " *Eranos-Jahrbuch* 19 (1951): 57–113. Reprinted in Puech, Henri-Charles. *En Quête de la Gnose.* Paris, 1978.

Tardieu, Michel. *Recherches sur la Formation de l'Apocalypse de Zostrien et les Sources de Marius Victorinus.* Bures-sur-Yvette, 1996. See pp. 93–98. A careful and thorough analysis of the tripartitions of the *aiones* in *Zostranios.*

Zepf, Max. "Der Gott Aion in der Hellenistischen Theologie." *Archiv für Religionswissenschaft* 25 (1927): 225–244.

Zuntz, Günther. *Aion Gott des Römerreichs.* Heidelberg, 1989.

Zuntz, Günther. *Aion in Römerreich. Die Archäologische Zeugnisse.* Heidelberg, Germany, 1991. Drastic criticism of previous interpretations.

Zuntz, Günther. *Aion in der Literatur der Kaiserzeit.* Vienna, 1992.

GIOVANNI CASADIO (2005)

AIRYANA VAĒJAH. According to Zoroastrian belief, Airyana Vaējah (Av.), or Ērān-vēz (MPers.), is the name of the homeland of followers of the Good Religion. In Iranian cosmology Airyana Vaējah is found at the center of the world, in the central region known as Khvaniratha, the first of the seven parts *(karshvar)* into which the earth is divided. Airyana Vaējah is the setting for the principal events of Zoroastrian sacred history: the history of Gayō-maretan, the first human; of Gav-aēvō-dāta, the uniquely created bull; of Yima, the first king; and later of Zarathushtra (Zoroaster) himself.

Although Airyana Vaējah (lit., "the Aryan expanse") is of a mythical and legendary nature, attempts have been made to assign it a definite location. During the Sasanid period, for instance, it was thought to be in Azerbaijan, the area from which Zarathushtra was believed to have originated. More recently, some scholars have maintained that the original Airyana Vaējah must be placed in Khorezm, but this thesis is supported only by tenuous arguments. It is probable that at the time of Zarathushtra, Airyana Vaējah corresponded, in the minds of Iranian tribesmen, to the region that they actually occupied: the Hindu Kush or the area immediately south of it, which is part of the *Airyō-shayana,* the "seat of the Airya," mentioned in the Avestan hymn to Mithra (*Yashts* 10.13–14).

Airyana Vaējah was first and foremost the home of Zarathushtra and his religion. It was accordingly the best of all lands. The first chapter of the *Vendidad* places it first in the list of the sixteen lands that were created by Ahura Mazdā and that were threatened by the countercreation of Angra Mainyu. In this text its mythical nature is evident. The fact that a cold winter in Airyana Vaējah is said to last ten months is to be explained by the mountainous nature of the land of legend and not, as some have maintained (Marquart, 1901), by the climate of Khorezm.

SEE ALSO Iranian Religions.

BIBLIOGRAPHY

Bailey, H. W. "Iranian Studies." *Bulletin of the School of Oriental and African Studies* 6 (1930–1932): 945–955.

Benveniste, Émile. "L'Ērān-vēž et l'origine légendaire des Iraniens." *Bulletin of the School of Oriental and African Studies* 7 (1933–1935): 265–274.

Christensen, Arthur. *Le premier chapitre du Vendidad et l'histoire primitive des tribus iraniennes.* Copenhagen, 1943.

Geiger, Wilhelm. *Ostiranische Kultur im Altertum.* Erlangen, 1882.

Gnoli, Gherardo. *Ricerche storiche su Sīstān antico.* Rome, 1967.

Gnoli, Gherardo. *Zoroaster's Time and Homeland.* Naples, 1980.

Gnoli, Gherardo. *The Idea of Iran.* Rome, 1989.

Herzfeld, Ernst. *Zoroaster and His World.* Princeton, 1947.

Marquart, Josef. *Ērānšahr nach der Geographie des Ps. Moses Xorenac'i.* 2 vols. Berlin, 1901.

Munshizadeh, Davud. *Topographisch-historische Studien zum iranischen Nationalepos.* Wiesbaden, 1975.

Nyberg, H. S. *Irans forntida religioner.* Stockholm, 1937. Translated as *Die Religionen des alten Iran* (1938; 2d ed., Uppsala, 1966).

Witzel, Michael. "The Home of the Aryans." In *Anusantatyai. Festschrift für Johanna Narten zum 70. Geburtstag,* edited by Almut Hintze and Eva Tichy, pp. 283–338. Dettelbach, 2000.

GHERARDO GNOLI (1987)
Translated from Italian by Roger DeGaris

ʿĀʾISHAH BINT ABĪ BAKR (d. AH 59/678 CE), child bride of the prophet Muḥammad and daughter of the first Islamic caliph, Abū Bakr. ʿAʾishah was born in Mecca several years before the community's emigration from Mecca to Medina in AH 1/622 CE. She was the second in the series of women whom Muḥammad married after the death of his first wife, Khadījah. Although the marriage was doubtless constructed to strengthen the alliance between the Prophet and his early supporter, Abū Bakr, ʿAʾishah soon became a favorite of her husband. Tales of his delight in her abound. In childhood, she spread her toys before him, and it was in her quarters that he chose to die and requested that his body be buried.

Before and after Muḥammad's death in 632, ʿAʾishah was involved, either deliberately or inadvertently, in actions of political consequence. The first was a result of youthful thoughtlessness that precipitated a crisis of honor in the Prophet's house. ʿAʾishah had accompanied her husband on his campaign against the Banū al-Muṣṭaliq in 628, when she was about fifteen years of age. During one of the stops on the return journey to Medina she went in search of a misplaced necklace and so lost herself in this quest that she failed to notice the caravan's departure. Eventually she was found by the caravan's young rear-guard scout, Ṣafwān ibn al-Muʿaṭṭal. The scandal occasioned by her return journey alone with this male escort was eagerly fed by Muḥammad's rivals and enemies. Even among the Prophet's supporters, there were those, such as his son-in-law, ʿAlī ibn Abī Ṭālib, who urged him to divorce her. (Traditional historians date the cause of ʿAʾishah's resistance against ʿAlī's eventual caliphate to this intervention.) A Qurʾanic revelation (24:11–20) finally exonerated ʿAʾishah and set the legal bounds for any charge of adultery: henceforth, those unable to produce four witnesses to such a charge would themselves be punished. (Both Sunnī and Shīʿī commentators trace the occasion of this revelation to the episode involving ʿAʾishah.)

In the years following the Prophet's death her political activism was, at times, pronounced. Left a childless widow before she was twenty, ʿAʾishah was prevented from making another marital alliance by a Qurʾanic injunction against the remarriage of Muḥammad's wives (33:53). However, both as a widow of the Prophet and as a daughter of his first successor, the caliph Abū Bakr, ʿAʾishah was a woman of considerable prominence in the early Muslim community. She used this prominence to further the growing opposition to the third caliph, ʿUthmān. ʿAʾishah's role in the events that culminated in his assassination is debated. In an effort to exculpate her of any direct role, many historians stress her absence from Medina at the time of the caliph's death. When ʿAlī ibn Abī Ṭālib, for whom her enmity was long-standing, assumed the caliphate, ʿAʾishah joined two of the Prophet's early supporters, Ṭalḥah and al-Zubayr, in armed opposition to him. Ostensibly to avenge the murder of ʿUthmān, they gathered forces in Basra (southern Iraq) and met ʿAlī in battle in December 656. ʿAlī defeated his opponents, but ʿAʾishah's camel-drawn litter, around which intense fighting raged, was immortalized in the name by which historians came to refer to this event, the Battle of the Camel.

In the two decades that passed from the time of this engagement until her death, ʿAʾishah lived in relative obscurity in Medina, only occasionally emerging into the light of history. Her memory remains alive in the Muslim community in the many anecdotes about her and in the hundreds of *ḥadīths* for which she was a transmitter.

BIBLIOGRAPHY

ʿAʾishah is one of the few women in Muslim history to have earned a full-scale biography. This gracefully written work, by the University of Chicago scholar Nabia Abbott, is entitled *Aishah, the Beloved of Mohammed* (Chicago, 1942). While based on extended research in the traditional sources, the book reads like a good historical novel. For a condensed and more prosaic treatment of the events of her life, see W. Montgomery Watt's article "ʿAʾishah bint Abī Bakr," in the new edition of *The Encyclopaedia of Islam* (Leiden, 1960–). Watt's two volumes on the life of the Prophet, *Muhammad at Mecca* (London, 1953) and *Muhammad at Medina* (London, 1956), also carry passing references to ʿAʾishah. For an account of the Battle of the Camel that emphasizes the role of ʿAʾishah, see Laura Veccia Vaglieri's "al-Djamal" in the new edition of *The Encyclopaedia of Islam* (Leiden, 1960–).

JANE DAMMEN MCAULIFFE (1987)

ĀJĪVIKAS, or Ājīvakas, an Indian heterodox sect, founded in the sixth century BCE by Makkhali Gosāla, an approximate contemporary of the Buddha, on the basis of earlier groups of unorthodox ascetics. After a period of popularity, the sect lost ground in northern India, but survived in the south until the fourteenth century or later.

THE FOUNDER. Makkhali Gosāla figures in the Pali scriptures of Theravāda Buddhism as one of six heterodox teachers frequently mentioned together as successful founders of ascetic orders. Also among these is Mahāvīra, the founder of Jainism, described under the Pali name Nigantha Nātaputta. In Buddhist Sanskrit sources, Gosāla is mentioned under the name Maskarin Gośālīputra, in the context of the six ascetics. The Śvetāmbara Jaina scriptures record his name as Gosāla Maṅkhaliputta. The Jain *Bhagavatī Sūtra* is our main source for the story of his association with Mahāvīra. Parts of this account are much elaborated by the later commentator Jinadāsa Gaṇī in his commentary (Skt., *cūrṇī*) to the *Āvaśyaka Sūtra.* From this it appears that Gosāla, a young ascetic of doubtful antecedents, encountered Mahāvīra when the latter had been an ascetic for two years. The pair spent some seven years together, wandering over the Ganges valley, after which they parted company. Then, after six months of severe penance, Gosāla is said to have acquired supernatural powers, and to have proclaimed himself a "conqueror" (*jina*, a title also given to Mahāvīra).

It appears that Gosāla quickly gained a following among many nondescript ascetics who were already known as Ājīvikas, probably implying that they took lifelong (*ājīvat*) vows. His base was the then-important city of Sāvatthi (Skt., Śrāvastī), near Ayodhyā in central Uttar Pradesh, where he made his headquarters in the workshop of a lay disciple, the potter woman Hālāhalā. Some sixteen years later, he died in the same place. According to the *Bhagavatī Sūtra*, his death took place following a confrontation with Mahāvīra, after which he contracted a high fever and became delirious, but it appears that his own followers declared that he had ended his life by voluntary starvation resulting from a penance of six months' duration. Shortly before his death he is said to have had a conference with his six leading disciples, at which the Ājīvika scriptures were codified. The date of his death cannot be determined exactly, but it appears to have occurred a year or two before the death of the Buddha, approximately 484 BCE.

THE ĀJĪVIKA ASCETIC ORDER. The naked monks who followed Gosāla appear to have subjected themselves to rigorous and painful penances. The initiation into the Ājīvika order involved pulling out the hair by the roots and grasping a heated lump, presumably of metal. Its members established regular meeting places (*sabhā*) in various towns of the Ganges plain. They seem to have been in demand among the laity as prognosticators, and they were credited with magical powers. The Ājīvika order also enlisted women ascetics, but they are only mentioned in passing and we know nothing about them. As with the Buddhists and Jains, it appears that their most important supporters were wealthy merchants and their families. The Ājīvika monks were frequently accused by their rivals of sexual laxity, and of eating large and sumptuous meals in private to compensate for their public penance and fasting. We have no means of discovering whether these accusations had any truth in them, or whether they were mere products of *odium theologicum.* The fact, however, that both the Buddhists and the Jains looked on the Ājīvikas as their most dangerous rivals is a measure of the popularity of the latter, particularly in the fifth and fourth centuries BCE, when the traditions of the heterodox sects of India were taking shape.

The Ājīvika ascetics often ended their lives voluntarily with a penance lasting six months, during which their intake of food and drink was gradually reduced until they died of hunger and thirst. This practice has something in common with the *sallekhanā* of the Jain monks, and was evidently not carried out in every case.

In the period of the Mauryan empire (fourth to second centuries BCE), or at least during the reign of Aśoka, the Ājīvikas appear to have been particularly influential in the Ganges Plain. In his Seventh Pillar Edict, Aśoka ranks them third, after the Buddhists and Brahmans, in a list of religious groups that he patronized, and before the Jains and "various other sects." This list probably represents the order of merit in the eyes of the king. The importance and popularity of the Ājīvikas at this time may also be gauged from the fact that they were the recipients of a number of artificial caves, about fifteen miles north of Gaya in modern Bihar, not far from the scene of the Buddha's enlightenment. In the Barabar Hills, two caves contain inscriptions stating that they were given to the Ājīvikas in the twelfth year after Aśoka's consecration, and a similar inscription states that a third cave was dedicated in his nineteenth year. A fourth cave, adorned with an impressive facade, contains no inscription, but appears to belong to the same period. In the nearby Nagarjuni Hill, there are three similar caves, with inscriptions to the effect that they were dedicated to the Ājīvikas as shelters during the rainy season by King Daśaratha, one of Aśoka's successors, immediately after his consecration as king—a sure indication of his favor. Taken together, these caves and inscriptions form an impressive record of the importance of the Ājīvikas at the time. The caves are probably the oldest excavations of their kind for the use of ascetics in the whole of India. Although they are not very large, their internal walls are so brilliantly polished that enough light is reflected through the low entrances to make it possible to read a newspaper with ease. These, however, are the only significant archaeological remains of the Ājīvikas to have survived.

After the Mauryan period, the Ājīvikas lost ground and, with the exception of the Tamil sources mentioned below, only a few passing references to them occur in later literature. South Indian evidence, however, shows that they survived there until the fourteenth century. Among the numerous inscriptions recording the transference of village taxes for the upkeep of local temples, at least seventeen mention the Ājīvikas, in most cases in connection with a special Ājīvika tax, presumably paid by lay Ājīvikas. This indicates that they were not looked on with favor by the local government authorities, and were at a disadvantage in comparison with the more orthodox sects, though the tax does not appear to have been heavy. Of these inscriptions, the greatest concentration is found in Karnataka state to the east and northeast of Bangalore, and in the Kolar district of Tamil Nadu. The presence of Ājīvikas is attested as far north as the district of Guntur, just south of the Krishna River in Andhra Pradesh, and as far south as Kilur, about forty miles inland from Pondicherry.

Three important Tamil religiophilosophical texts, *Maṇimēkalai*, *Nīlakēśi*, and *Śivajñānasiddhiyar*, composed by Buddhists, Jains, and Śaivites respectively, contain outlines of Ājīvika doctrines. The most useful and informative of these is *Nīlakēśi*, probably written in the ninth century

CE. In this text the heroine Nilakesi visits a number of teachers one after the other in search of the truth. Among these are the Buddha himself and Pūraṇaṉ, the leader of the Ājīvikas, a figure of great dignity dwelling in a hermitage adorned with fragrant flowers. Probably the latest surviving evidence of the Ājīvikas is to be found in the astrological text *Jātaka-pārijāta,* written toward the latter part of the fifteenth century by Vaidyanatha Dīkṣita.

DOCTRINES OF THE ĀJĪVIKAS. The teachings of Makkhali Gosāla are summarized in this passage from the Buddhist *Dīgha Nikāya:*

> There is neither cause nor basis for the sins of living beings; they become sinful without cause or basis. Neither is there cause or basis for the purity of living beings; they become pure without cause or basis. There is no deed performed by oneself or others, no human action, no strength, no courage, no human endurance or human prowess [that can affect one's future, in this life or in later ones]. All beings, all that have breath, all that are born, all that have life, are without power, strength and virtue, but are developed by destiny, chance and nature, and experience joy and sorrow in the six classes [of existence]. . . . There are . . . 8,400,000 great *kalpas* through which fool and wise alike will take their course and [ultimately] make an end of sorrow. There is no question of bringing unripe *karma* to fruition, nor of exhausting *karma* already ripened, by virtuous conduct, by vows, by penance, or by chastity. That cannot be done. *Saṃsāra* is measured as with a bushel, with its joy and sorrow and its appointed end. It can neither be lessened nor increased, nor is there any excess or deficiency of it. Just as a ball of thread will, when thrown, unwind to its full length, so fool and wise alike will take their course, and make an end of sorrow. (*Dīgha Nikāya,* vol. 1, pp. 53–54)

This eloquent passage makes clear the fundamental principle of Ājīvika philosophy, namely *niyati,* usually translated as "fate" or "destiny." The Ājīvikas were, in fact, fatalists and determinists. Buddhism, Jainism, and orthodox Hinduism, on the other hand, all emphasize the power of human effort (*puruṣakāra*) to affect human destiny. This proposition Gosāla and his followers categorically denied. Every being is impelled by *niyati* to pass through immense cycles of birth, death and rebirth, according to a rigidly fixed order until, in his last birth, he becomes an Ājīvika monk, dies after a long final penance, and enters a state which the Ājīvikas appear to have called *nirvāṉa.* Probably the Ājīvikas, like the Jains but unlike the Buddhists, believed that the final state of bliss was to be found in the complete isolation of the soul from matter and from other souls.

In any case, they believed that free will was an illusion. The criminal might imagine that he consciously chose to rob and murder, and the pious believer might think that he gave up the world and became an ascetic of his own free will; in fact, the power of *niyati* left only one course open to them. This doctrine of *niyati* seems to have been developed by the South Indian Ājīvikas into a theory suggesting that of Parmenides, that the universe was, on final analysis, completely static. "Though we may speak of moments," says the Ājīvika teacher Pūraṇaṉ in *Nīlakēśi,* "there is really no time at all." This doctrine was known as *avicalita-nityatvam,* or "unmoving permanence."

The cosmology of the Ājīvikas was evidently very complex, but it is impossible to interpret accurately the ambiguous and obscure phrases referring to this in the texts. The Ājīvikas certainly postulated an immensely large universe, which passed through an immense number of time cycles. Each soul (*jīva*) was bound to transmigrate through eighty-four *lākhs* (1 *lākh* = 100,000) of such cycles before reaching its inevitable goal of release from transmigration. For the southern Ājīvikas, however, even this desirable goal might not be final, for it appears that only a few souls were fated to remain in bliss for all eternity; the rest achieved only "cyclic release" (*maṇḍala-mokṣa*), and were ultimately compelled to return to the world and begin another cycle of transmigration.

The southern Ājīvikas appear to have absorbed the doctrine of seven atomic substances attributed by the Buddhists to another contemporary of the Buddha, Pakudha Kaccāyana. These seven substances are earth, water, fire, air, joy, sorrow, and life. According to the Pali version of Pakudha's doctrine, these seven are uncreated and unchanging, "as firm as mountains, as stable as pillars." The Tamil *Maṇimēkalai,* however, states in its treatment of Ājīvika doctrine that the atoms combine to form molecules in fixed proportions. The soul was also atomic, in the sense that it could not be divided, but in its natural disembodied state it is said to be of immense size, 500 leagues (*yojana*) in extent.

There are indications that some of the South Indian Ājīvikas made a kind of divinity out of their founder Makkhali Gosāla, called in Tamil Maṟkali; he has become a god (*tēvaṉ*) who, according to the text *Nīlakēśi,* occasionally descends to earth to stimulate the faith of his followers. For this school of Ājīvikas, the earthly teacher of the sect is Pūraṇaṉ, evidently the same as Pūraṇa Kassapa, another of the six heterodox teachers of the Pali scriptures.

Thus it appears that, at the end of their existence, one school of Ājīvikas was assimilating its teaching to that of the devotional Vaiṣṇavas, while another, closer to the original teaching of Gosāla, was slowly absorbed by the Digambara Jains. No definite survivals of Ajivikism can be traced in any branch of modern Indian religious life, but it is possible that echoes of Ājīvika determinism may be heard in some of the gnomic wisdom of South India, for instance: "Though a man exert himself over and over again, he still only gets what comes on the appointed day."

SEE ALSO Gosāla.

BIBLIOGRAPHY

The only monograph on the subject is my own *History and Doctrines of the Ājīvikas* (1951; reprint, Delhi, 1981), upon which the foregoing article is largely based. For a critical notice, see Helen M. Johnson's review in the *Journal of the American Oriental Society* 74 (1954): 63–65. The two best earlier studies are A. F. R. Hoernle's "Ājīvikas," in the *Encyclopaedia of Religion and Ethics*, edited by James Hastings, vol. 1 (London, 1908), and Benimadhav Barua's "The Ājīvikas," *Journal of the Department of Letters* (University of Calcutta) 2 (1920): 1–80.

The chief reference to the Ājīvikas in the Pali scriptures is to be found in the *Sāmañña-phala-sutta* of the *Dīgha Nikāya*, which has been translated by T. W. Rhys Davids and C. A. F. Rhys Davids as *Dīgha Nikāya: Dialogues of the Buddha*, 3 vols. (London, 1899–1921). The most important Jaina source is the *Bhagavatī Sūtra*, 3 vols. (Bombay, 1918–1921); there are other editions of this work, but, to the best of my knowledge, no English translation exists.

A. L. BASHAM (1987)

AKAN RELIGION. The Akan are a cluster of peoples numbering some five to six million, most of whom speak a language known as Twi. They occupy the mainly forested region of southern Ghana and the eastern Ivory Coast and include the coastal Fanti to the south. They are divided into over a dozen independent kingdoms, the best known of which is the Ashanti (Asante) kingdom whose capital city is Kumasi in central Ghana.

Most Akan are forest dwellers, with yams and other root crops as staples; plantains, oil palms, and other trees are important. Cocoa, palm oil, gold, and timber have long been the main exports, producing a high standard of living. The pattern of settlement is based upon towns, each town being the seat of a king or chief. Village farms are set between the towns.

The Akan are divided into eight matrilineal clans (*abusua*), branches of which are dispersed across all the Akan kingdoms; in theory exogamous, the clans are neither corporate nor political units. The local branches of clans are divided into matrilineal lineages or *houses*, the basic property-owning residential and domestic groups. Across this matrilineal organization runs that of patrilines, noncorporate groups known as *ntoro* among the Ashanti; in most areas these groupings are today of far less importance than in the past.

The Akan believe that each human being is composed of three main elements: blood (*mogya*), deriving from the matrilineal clan and giving formal social status; character, or personality, from the patriline; and soul (*kra*), which comes from God and is one's formal destiny (*nkrabea*). A spiritual bond is thought to exist between a father and his child; the *sunsum* (spirit) of the father is said to provide strength and protection from spiritual attack or danger for his child. There is a certain amount of confusion and contradiction about the meaning of the terms *sunsum* and *kra* but it is certain that they are not synonymous. The *kra* is the permanent component of the living person. It is set free to return to the land of the ancestors only after death, though it may temporarily leave during sleep or severe illness. Usually the *kra* is protective; if a person recovers from illness or an accident he may give offerings to his *kra* in order to express gratitude for his purification and ensure further prosperity. In such a rite, he will generally be accompanied by a child who shares the same *kra* day, that is, who was born on the same day of the week (those born on the same day of the week are said to have the same *kra*). A person cannot change his own destiny, though it is believed that witches and other jealous persons may try to attack a person's soul.

The Akan peoples have long been in contact with Muslims from the Sahara, but the religious impact of Islam has been rather slight. They were affected by European colonial powers moving inland from the coast from the fifteenth century onward, and by Christian missionaries from the early nineteenth century. The colonial impact was powerful, fueled especially by the desire for gold and slaves. But despite the colonial penetration, and prolonged exposure to different economic, political, educational, and religious influences, the traditional religions of the Akan peoples have persisted strongly up through the contemporary era. Although there are wide variations among the Akan kingdoms, there are many similarities in cosmology and religious practice. Mobility of whole segments of population and of ritual shrines and individual worshipers has brought about many common religious features throughout the region.

Akan religion has few important myths other than the one that explains the split between God and humankind. In this myth the supreme being, Nyame, became annoyed by the noise made by an Ashanti woman who was pounding *fufu* (mashed and pounded yams or plantains) in a wooden mortar, and he withdrew far away from humankind as a result. Another version attributes his withdrawal to the fact that the Ashanti have *fufu*-pounding sticks that are extremely long; when the women made *fufu*, the ends of their sticks hit Nyame up there in the sky, and so he went farther and farther away. There are also clan myths explaining their separate origins and thousands of proverbs and aphorisms suffused with religious referents.

HIGH GOD. The supreme being, known as Nyame, Onyankopon, Odomankama, and other names, is said to be omniscient and omnipotent, the creator of all the world, and the giver of rain and sunshine. Born on Saturday, both he and Asase Yaa, the Thursday-born Goddess of the Earth, are formally appealed to in all prayers, although in general, it is the ancestors and deities who mediate between God and humans. Nearly all Ashanti houses formerly had a small shrine dedicated to Nyame in the form of a pot placed in the fork of a certain tree (*Nyame dua*, God's tree). Similarly shaped shrines are also found in other Akan kingdoms, though presently only in the more remote villages; there, however, the bowl in the forked God's tree usually contains a protective *suman* of one kind or another (see below).

Ancestors. The ancestors (*asaman* or *asamanfo*) live together in a place variously said to be beyond a high mountain or across a river. They are believed to know what the living do on earth and may help those in need, or punish strife or wrong-doing by causing illness or even death. The ancestors of the departed heads of an ordinary lineage watch over and support members of that lineage; those of the chiefly lineage do so for both the royal lineage and for the members of the entire town.

Black stools, which are blackened with blood and other matter, function as shrines that act as temporary resting places for the ancestral spirits of a particular matrilineage when they are summoned during rituals. (Ancestors can be contacted anywhere at any time.) Royal and nonroyal black stools are similar in appearance and function; the former, however, are considered more sacred and powerful. Black stools are kept in a special stool-house within the family compound or palace. There are very elaborate funeral ceremonies for chiefs including secondary funerary observances and, formerly, mass human sacrifices.

Libations may be poured at any time by anyone to inform the ancestors of important events, but the black stool is the responsibility of the head of the lineage. Usually the royal black stools are cared for by officials who are not members of the royal lineage but are related to the king through the patriline. There are no mediums (*okomfo*) for the ancestors, though individuals do occasionally become possessed by them.

The year is divided into nine ritual units (each of forty-two days), the first day of each being called *adae*. At *adae* some deities are celebrated and ancestors are venerated through the black stool which is cleansed and then anointed. All Akan kingdoms have an annual celebration, called *Apo* or *Odwira*, among other names. A complex festival, Apo consists of a number of ritual actions including purification of the accumulated sins and defilement of the previous year, anointment of the shrines of the deities and the ancestral black stools, celebration of the first-fruits (whence the name Yam Festival), and the renewal of the power of the king and thus the kingdom.

The Deities. The Akan distinguish between two main kinds of deity: *abosom* (sg., *obosom*) and *asuman* (sg., *suman*). While essentially the same kind of power, the former are said to be large and personalized, the latter small and not personalized. Nevertheless, an *obosom* perceived to be weak may come to be classified as a *suman* and vice versa. There are also thought to be small forest beings with backward feet (*mmoatia*) and terrifying giants (*sasabonsam*).

There are hundreds of *abosom*; they may be invoked individually or as a group. They are said to be the children of God or God's messengers, and are identified with lakes, rivers, rocks, and other natural objects. Generally they are thought able to cure illness and social problems, reveal witches, and witness the truth of an event; at the same time they are dangerous to deal with because of their destructive powers and capricious ways. They are free-ranging but can be temporarily located in shrines in the form of clay pots of water, cloth-wrapped bundles, or mounds of sacred ingredients inside a brass pan. Ritual specialists who own a deity are called *osofo* or *obosomfo*. There are also mediums (*okomfo*) who become possessed by a deity and, whether priest or priestess, are considered to be its wife.

Asuman are human-made objects in which mystical power resides. They range from small non-personalized amulets that contain magical powers in themselves, to more personalized ones that resemble *abosom*. In general, *asuman* are lower in the hierarchy of deities than are *abosom* and act as their messengers. They are appealed to for day-to-day problems, and their powers are said to be more specific than those of *abosom*.

The popularity of a particular deity will rise and fall. If it does not produce results or if a shrine official dies and is not replaced, there will be a loss of patrons and the shrine will be called dry. Powerful deities, on the other hand, may attract adherents across great distances. *Aduru* refers to both Western medicine and to herbal remedies. No offerings are made to *aduru*, and they are not personalized. While there is clarity of classification in the terminology used for these entities (*abosom*, *asuman*, and *aduru*), in practice there is much overlapping and ambiguity.

In all Akan societies disease, infertility, and untimely death are of central importance. Herbalists are consulted for specific ailments and broken bones, but since illness generally involves the total moral person and is not simply seen as a physical condition, mediums are consulted to discover if the illness or repeated deaths in one family are caused by an ancestor, deity, or by other means. People of high status are especially worried about being poisoned by bad medicine. Witches are said to be mostly women who work in covens in the spiritual world; it is believed that they attack only members of their own families.

Christianity and Islam. Over the past century many anti-witchcraft movements have appeared and spread. Most notable was the Abirewa movement in the early twentieth century, followed more recently by the Tigare and other movements from the north. New Christian movements also rise and fall, attracting large numbers of followers who concurrently attend mainstream Protestant or Catholic churches (as opposed to Pentecostal or Spiritualist churches) or are adherents of traditional religious deities.

The growing influence of Christianity in the south (linked often with the expansion of Western education, cocoa production, and trade), and of Islam in the north have weakened active participation in *abosom* and *asuman* movements, and the latter have in some cases faded with the deaths of older practitioners. The law courts are now replacing the *abosom* shrines for the resolution of conflicts. Beliefs in ancestors, linked as they are to the matrilineage and to kingship, are more tenacious. It must be stressed that in no case has Christianity replaced traditional religion; rather the two coexist side by side in a complex and uneasy relationship. Because Christianity is linked in most kingdoms to education and, therefore, to wealth, it has become the prestige religion. Traditional religion continues because for most people it is perceived to be the most efficacious system of belief, one that continues to endow the world with meaning. Traditional deities are still perceived by many to be powerful and thus to affect people's moral behavior, while traditional rituals of many kinds are still deemed to be necessary. Kings, chiefs, and most palace and clan officials adhere to traditional religious practices as part of their formal political-religious roles. This is likely to continue so long as the kingship is retained even though some of the rites are condemned by the Christian churches.

BIBLIOGRAPHY

The classic works on Akan religion are R. S. Rattray's *Ashanti* (Oxford, 1923) and *Religion and Art in Ashanti* (Oxford, 1927) and J. B. Danquah's *The Akan Doctrine of God* (1944), 2d ed. (London, 1968), although they leave much to be desired in both coverage and analysis. The best sources are K. A. Busia's "The Ashanti of the Gold Coast," in *African Worlds,* edited by Daryll Forde (London, 1954), pp. 190–209; Margaret Joyce Field's *Search for Security* (London, 1960); Meyer Fortes's *Kinship and the Social Order* (Chicago, 1969); and Malcolm McLeod's "On the Spread of Anti-Witchcraft Cults in Modern Asante," in *Changing Social Structure in Ghana,* edited by Jack Goody (London, 1975), pp. 107–117.

New Sources

Ayim-Aboagye, Desmond. *The Psychology of Akan Religious Healing.* Abo, Ghana, 1997.

Braffi, Emmanuel Kingsley. *The Akan Clans: Totemism and "Nton."* Kumasi, Ghana, 1992.

Ephirim-Donkor, Anthony. *African Spirituality: On Becoming Ancestors.* Trenton, N.J., 1997.

Fisher, Robert B. *West African Religious Traditions: Focus on the Akan of Ghana.* Maryknoll, N.Y., 1998.

Owoahene-Acheampong, Stephen. *Inculturation and African Religion: Indigenous and Western Approaches to Medical Practice.* New York, 1998.

MICHELLE GILBERT (1987)
Revised Bibliography

AKBAR (1542–1605), emperor of India in the Timurid, or Mughal, dynasty. He was born on October 15, 1542, in Umarkot, Sind, where his father, Humayun, had fled after being driven from Delhi, his capital, by his Afghan rivals. Akbar was proclaimed emperor in 1556 under the tutelage of his father's military commander, Bairam Khan, but by 1560 had succeeded in asserting his own power. His reign is one of the most memorable periods of Indian history not only because of his creation of a powerful empire but also because of his apotheosis as the ideal Indian ruler. This image of Akbar owes much to the literary genius of Abū al-Faẓl ʿAllami, his trusted friend, administrator, and biographer, as well as to the admiration of the nineteenth-century British rulers, who viewed him as their own precursor as the unifier of India. Later, Indian nationalists saw him as the great exemplar of social and religious toleration, which they believed necessary for a democratic, independent India.

Akbar was a ruler of intelligence, ambition, and restless curiosity, who exhibited great skill in selecting and controlling his officials. Very early he seems to have determined to build a strong, centralized administration, while pursuing an aggressive policy of territorial expansion. His famous definition of a king, as "a light emanating from God, a ray from the world-illuminating sun," indicates his conception of his role.

Throughout his reign, Akbar was engaged in warfare with neighboring kingdoms. As soon as the central territories around Delhi and Agra were secured, he moved south and east. In 1568, he captured Chitor, a famous stronghold of the Rajput chiefs, champions of Hinduism in North India. In subsequent battles other Rajput princes submitted to him. After defeating the Rajputs, Akbar took them into his service as generals and administrators and took many of their daughters into his royal harem. His marriage alliances with these Hindu princesses have often been interpreted as signs of his religious toleration, but they were more likely acknowledgments of the submission of the Rajputs.

After the Rajput conquest, Akbar defeated the wealthy Muslim kingdom of Gujarat in 1573, and in 1575 the Muslim ruler of Bengal submitted. In all areas, frequent uprisings by military leaders against Akbar were a reminder that Mughal power was dependent on continued assertion of central authority.

It was this need for centralized control that led Akbar to reorganize the bureaucratic structure of his empire and to reform the revenue system. He built upon the work of his predecessors, particularly Sher Shah (r. 1538–1545), in carrying out new land assessments and in bringing as much territory as possible under the direct control of imperial authority.

Akbar's religious policies have been the subject of much controversy, leading to his being regarded as an apostate to Islam, a near convert to Christianity, the inventor of a new religion, and a liberal exponent of toleration. The truth seems to be that in his genuine curiosity about religion he encouraged all varieties of religious practitioners, including Hindu *yogins* and Muslim *fakīrs* as well as European Jesuits who visited his court. On the other hand, it was probably a concern for the unity of his empire that led him to abolish *jizyah,* the discriminatory tax on non-Muslims. Badāʿūnī, a contemporary historian, while he denounced Akbar as an apostate, says that he spent whole nights in praise of God and would be found "many a morning alone in prayer and meditation in a lonely spot."

Discussions of Akbar's attitude toward orthodox Islam have centered mainly on two incidents. One was his acceptance, in 1579, of a declaration by some major Islamic theologians stating that he, as a just ruler, could, in the case of disputes between *mujtāhids* (interpreters of Islamic law), decide which was the correct interpretation. Although orthodox Islamic theologians denounced his action, it was not a denial of Islamic practice, but rather an assertion of his sovereignty and his near equality with the caliph of the Ottoman empire.

The other incident was Akbar's promulgation in 1582 of the *Dīn-i-ilāhī* (The divine faith), a syncretic statement that owed much to the Ṣūfī tradition of Islam as well as to Hinduism and Zoroastrianism. Emphasizing the union of the soul with the divine, it insisted on such ethical precepts as almsgiving, chastity, vegetarianism, and kindness to all. Elsewhere, Akbar indicated that he believed in the transmigration of souls.

For orthodox Muslims, the *Dīn-i-ilāhī* made clear that Akbar intended to replace Islam with his own heresy, but in fact there is no evidence that it had any followers outside his immediate entourage. It is possible, however, that he dreamed of the "divine faith" becoming the possession of all men, thus ending "the diversity of sects and creeds" that, he once complained, was the source of strife in his kingdom.

Akbar died at Agra on October 3, 1605. His court, one of the most magnificent in the world, was a center of culture and the arts. The great Mughal achievements in painting and architecture had their beginning in his time, and music, poetry, and calligraphy were encouraged. The measure of his importance in Indian history is that the cultural achievements of his age along with his administrative structures continued to characterize the Mughal dynasty for over two centuries, even in its long period of decline in the eighteenth and early nineteenth centuries, and remained a model for later rulers.

BIBLIOGRAPHY

The most important sources of information on Akbar's reign are the writings of Abū al-Faẓl ʿAllami, especially his *Akbarnama* and his *Āʿīn-i-Akbarī*. The former has been translated by Henry Beveridge in three volumes (1907–1939; reprint, Delhi, 1977); the latter, an account of Akbar's administrative system, was translated by H. Blochmann and H. S. Jarrett in three volumes (1873–1894) and has since been revised by D. C. Phillott and Jadu Nath Sarkar (Calcutta, 1939–1949). S. R. Sharma's *The Religious Policy of the Mughal Emperors* (New York, 1972) has a good section on Akbar, and Vincent A. Smith's *Akbar, the Great Mogul, 1542–1605* (1919; 2d ed., Delhi, 1966) is, although dated, still useful for biographical details.

Three volumes in *The New Cambridge History of India* are important for an understanding of Akbar's cultural and religious influence: John F. Richards, *The Mughal Empire* (Cambridge, UK, 1993), Catherine B. Asher, *Architecture of Mughal India* (Cambridge, 1992), and Milo Beach, *Mughal and Rajput Painting* (Cambridge, 1992). Douglas E. Streusand's *The Formation of the Mughal Empire* (Delhi, 1999) has interesting material on the relation of Akbar's religion to the state.

AINSLIE T. EMBREE (1987 AND 2005)

AKHENATON (or Akhenaten) was the tenth pharaoh of Egypt's eighteenth dynasty (c. 1352–1336 BCE) and the founder of the earliest historically documented monotheistic religion. Son of Amenhotep III and the chief queen, Tiya, Akhenaton succeeded to the throne as Amenhotep IV and took a throne name meaning "the sun's ultimate perfection, unique one of the sun," reflecting the traditional Egyptian belief that the pharaoh derived his physical being, as well as his authority, from the sun god, ruler of the world. Marriage to his chief queen, Nefertiti, produced six daughters, the first and third of whom, Meritaton and Ankhesenpaaton, were to play important roles at the end of his reign and during its aftermath. In addition, a minor queen, Kiya, gave him another daughter, whose name is not known, and Akhenaton may also have fathered, by one or both queens, the two men who eventually succeeded him as the pharaohs Smenkhkare and Tutankhamen.

At the time of Akhenaton's accession, Egypt's most important deity was Amun, "king of the gods," whose chief cult center lay in the state temples of Karnak and Luxor at Thebes (modern Luxor). Amun was worshiped as the transcendental creator, existing independently of the world he had created; this characteristic is encapsulated in his name, which means "hidden." Throughout the eighteenth dynasty, Egyptian theologians wrestled with the problem of reconciling Amun's primordial and transcendent nature with the traditional Egyptian concept of the gods as the elements and forces of the world's daily existence. Their primary solution to the difficulty was the combined god Amun-Re, representing Amun as manifest and active in the created world through its major force, the sun (the Egyptian word *Re,* also used as a name of the sun god, means "sun"). This process of combining two or more gods into a single deity, known as *syncretism,* was embedded in Egyptian thought. It reflected the realization that different gods could be understood both as independent entities and as complementary manifestations of a single, larger force—in essence, much the same as the Christian concept of the Trinity.

EARLY RULE. Akhenaton's original name, Amenhotep, means "Amun is content," and the king began his reign by honoring Amun-Re on royal monuments, as his predecessors had done. Akhenaton's earliest known project, however, was a monument erected in Karnak not for Amun-Re but for a separate form of the sun god under a new name: "Harakhti, who becomes active from the Akhet in his identity as the light that is in the Aton." Harakhti, meaning "Horus of the Akhet," was one of the traditional Egyptian gods, the sun viewed as king of nature, rising into the world from the Akhet, the liminal zone between the netherworld, where

FIGURE 1. The early form of the "didactic" name (left: "The living one, *Harakhti,* who becomes active from the *Akhet*"; right: "in his identity as the light that is in the Aton"). *Drawing by J. Allen.*

the sun was thought to go at night, and the visible horizon. The remainder of the new name identified the sun's power of kingship (Horus) as the light emanating from the solar disk itself: the word *Aton,* meaning "sundisk," referred to the physical form of the sun, visible in the sky—and depicted in Egyptian art—as a disk.

The new god's name is unlike those of other Egyptian deities; it represents not so much an appellation as the manifesto of a new creed (Egyptologists commonly refer to it as the "didactic" name). Through it, Akhenaton, who identified himself as chief priest of the new god, promulgated an innovation in Egyptian theology: recognition of the physical phenomenon of light—which in ancient Egypt meant essentially sunlight—as the primary force in the universe. This concept was further emphasized by another early innovation, enclosing the god's name in a pair of oval rings, known as *cartouches,* like those surrounding two of the king's own names (see figure 1). The new god was now overtly identified as king of the universe, ruling in consort with Akhenaton as king of the living.

Early depictions of the god were modeled on traditional representations of Harakhti, symbolic images of a human body with the head of a falcon (emblem of the god Horus) bearing a sundisk. These were soon superseded, however, by a new image: that of the Aton, a solar disk with its rays extending toward earth, giving the symbol of life to the king and his family (see figure 2). Because Akhenaton's inscriptions also frequently refer to the god as "the Aton" rather than by his full didactic name, his theology has often been misunderstood as a form of sun worship. As the full didactic name makes clear, however, Akhenaton saw the Aton merely as the vehicle through which the god manifested himself in the world. Like the traditional representations of Harakhti and other Egyptian gods, the image of the Aton in Akhenaton's art was not meant to be understood literally as a depiction of the god: instead, the solar disk with its rays is nothing more than a large-scale version of the Egyptian hieroglyph for "light."

The first promulgations of Akhenaton's new theology appeared on monuments erected in Karnak. This was the chief religious center in Egypt, but it was also home to Amun-Re, "king of the gods." Akhenaton's early activities were thus a direct assault on the primacy of Amun-Re. Political considerations undoubtedly played a part in Akhenaton's policies: through the benefactions of Akhenaton's predecessors, Karnak had become an establishment whose wealth and influence rivaled that of the royal family. But Akhenaton's actions were not guided alone, or even primarily, by politics. Egyptian religion was not merely a set of beliefs but the way in which all Egyptians understood the world around them and by which they governed and interpreted their own actions. Akhenaton's new theology was first and foremost a religious revolution.

THE MOVE TO AMARNA. The second stage in this revolution occurred in Akhenaton's fifth year on the throne. Abandoning the religious center of Karnak and the seat of government at Memphis (south of modern Cairo), the king founded a new capital city on virgin land in Middle Egypt to serve as both his residence and the center of worship for his new god. The site today is known as Amarna, a name that is also used to refer to the period of Akhenaton's rule and its artistic and intellectual manifestations. Akhenaton called the new city Akhetaton, meaning "place where the Aton becomes effective." Coincident with its founding, the king changed his own name from Amenhotep to Akhenaton, which means either "he who is effective for the Aton" or "the effective form of the Aton."

As far as is known, the king spent the remainder of his seventeen-year rule within Amarna. The new city gave Akhenaton the opportunity to develop his theology and intellectual vision free of associations with Karnak or any other religious establishment. Amarna witnessed the flowering of Akhenaton's innovations not only in religion but also in architecture and art. One of these made it possible to build the new city in the space of only a few years: in place of the monumental stone blocks of traditional Egyptian architecture, which required teams of workers to maneuver and dress, Akhenaton's builders employed smaller blocks that could be handled by a single man. Known today as *talatat,* these blocks were eventually decorated with reliefs in a new style of art, to modern eyes more naturalistic than the traditional Egyptian hieroglyphic style.

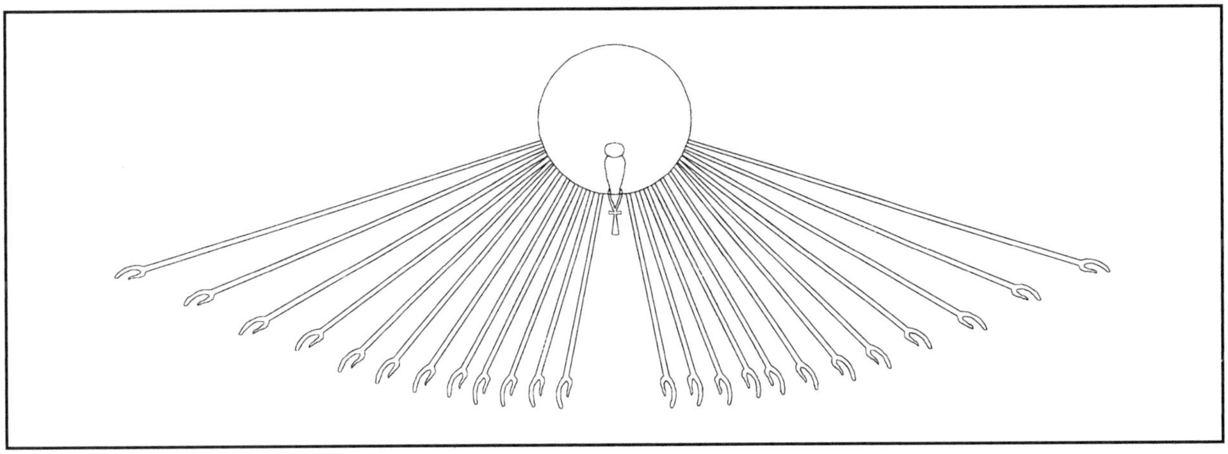

FIGURE 2. The Aton. *Drawing by J. Allen.*

Like all his innovations, Akhenaton's art and architecture were developed in the service of his new theology. They emphasized the natural world, enlivened by the power of light. Previous Egyptian temples consisted of forests of columns and dark, mysterious sanctuaries; Akhenaton's were open and airy, unroofed so as to be bathed in light. In place of the divine figures that pervaded traditional Egyptian reliefs, Amarna's monuments were decorated with scenes of nature and everyday life; private stelae and even tomb walls showed the king and his family not in heroic poses but in intimate and tender interaction with one another—all under the central hieroglyphic icon of the Aton, image of light.

The new style, however, was not entirely free of the conventions of traditional art, and one of these, employed in representations of Akhenaton and his family, has led to misplaced speculation about the king's health. The royal family was depicted in somewhat exaggerated form, with elongated heads, thin necks and waists, and large thighs. In the conventions of Egyptian art, such images were normally used for those outside the sphere of elite society: in Amarna art they reflect not physical reality but the status of the royal family as "other," unlike common human beings.

THE END OF AKHENATON'S REIGN. Amarna also witnessed the onset of the third and final stage of Akhenaton's religious revolution. Throughout his reign, the king had tolerated—and early in it, even honored—traditional Egyptian gods, though their names and images were soon banished from official reliefs. Sometime after his eleventh year of rule, however, Akhenaton's policies became more rigid. Teams were sent throughout the country to remove Amun's name and the plural word "gods" from all monuments. At the same time, the name of Akhenaton's own god was altered by replacing the name of Harakhti with "the sun," changing the word for "light" to a more neutral synonym without other divine associations, and emending the phrase "that is in the Aton" to "that comes through the Aton" (see figure 3). Besides "purifying" the name from all reference to older gods, these changes made it even clearer that the Aton was merely the god's vehicle and not the god himself.

Akhenaton seems to have died in his seventeenth year of rule. Toward the end of his reign he appointed a coregent—probably his eldest daughter, Meritaton—to rule as joint pharaoh. She may have succeeded him directly but was soon replaced by her husband, Smenkhkare. After a year or less, Smenkhkare was succeeded by his younger brother, Tutankhaton, who was married to Akhenaton's third daughter, Ankhesenpaaton. The new couple soon changed their names to Tutankhamun (or Tutankhamen) and Ankhesenamun (honoring Amun), left Amarna, and restored the traditional religion.

Tutankhamen reopened the temples and appointed all new priesthoods—the latter action an indication that his policies were not dictated by the older hierarchy. Rather than repudiate Akhenaton's theology, Tutankhamen evidently tried to integrate it into the traditionally open structure of Egyptian religion, judging by one of the thrones from his tomb, which shows him and his wife, with their new names, under the symbol of the Aton. Later kings were less lenient. Beginning with Haremhab, Tutankhamen's second successor and last king of the eighteenth dynasty, they tore down Akhenaton's monuments, defaced the royal family's names and images, and removed all the kings between Amenhotep III and Haremhab from the official register of pharaohs. Whenever it was necessary to refer to Akhenaton, he was simply called "the heretic of Akhetaton."

THE NATURE OF AKHENATON'S RELIGION. Because Akhenaton's monuments were systematically destroyed, much is still unknown about his revolution, and the significance of the evidence that has survived is often hotly debated. One of the chief points of contention is the monotheistic nature of Akhenaton's theology. With its practice of syncretism, Egyptian theology had theoretically been open to the notion of a single god behind the multiple gods of its traditional polytheism. Evidence in fact exists that some theologians had

FIGURE 3. The later form of the "didactic" name (left: "The living one, the sun, who becomes active from the Akhet"; right: "in his identity as the light that comes through the Aton"). *Drawing by J. Allen.*

discovered such a notion long before Akhenaton: essays on ethics from the Middle Kingdom (c. 1980–1780 BCE), for example, routinely use the generic term *god* instead of the name of a specific deity; since the language of these essays has no articles, this term can mean "a god," "the god," or simply "God."

Such a notion was consonant with traditional Egyptian theology, which accepted different views of divinity as equally valid (reflected, for example, in the multitude of names for the sun god). In this intellectual atmosphere, Akhenaton's new god could easily have been accommodated within the structure of Egyptian theology. Akhenaton insisted on the sole reality of his god—"unique, with no other except him," as his texts declare. Other gods had previously been given similar descriptions, but without exclusivity. Given the intellectual background from which it arose, Akhenaton's innovation was not so much the notion of a single god but his ultimate insistence on the exclusive validity of his vision. This feature qualifies Akhenaton's religion as a true monotheism. Diametrically opposed to traditional Egyptian thinking, it was probably also one of the prime factors leading to the religion's rejection by later generations.

Apart from its monotheistic nature, however, Akhenaton's theology had little in common with that of later monotheistic religions from the same part of the world. Its god was a force of nature—light—and was dependent on an element of nature—the sun—for its presence and activity in the world, far different from the transcendent sole god of Judaism and Islam. For this reason it is probably specious to speculate—as Sigmund Freud did, for example—on the possible influence of Akhenaton's thought on early Hebrew religion. With its focus on the ultimate reality of a single physical phenomenon, Akhenaton's theology has more in common with early Greek philosophy than with biblical monotheism. Like the physical elements of Greek philosophy, Akhenaton's deity is also less a personal god than a force of nature: where the traditional Egyptian gods were often shown as replying to human worship and prayer, Amarna texts and reliefs depict the Aton being adored and beseeched but never as responding in return.

The history of Jewish and Islamic monotheism, and that of Christianity as well, is marked not only by their adherents' insistence on the exclusive validity of their theology, but also by their attempt to destroy the manifestations, if not the practice, of other religions. In this too, Akhenaton's religion qualifies as truly monotheistic. His attempt to destroy the images of Amun and the notion of more than one god is the first historically documented instance of religious fanaticism.

REVELATION. Besides being the earliest recorded monotheism, Akhenaton's theology is also the first example of a revealed religion. The hymn to his god says: "there is no other who knows you except for your son, The Sun's Ultimate Perfection, Unique One of the Sun [Akhenaton's throne name], whom you have made aware of your designs and your strength." Other texts emphasize that the new religion is Akhenaton's own teaching. His courtiers say: "My lord has taught me, that I might carry out his teaching" and "How fortunate is the one who hears your teaching of life." From these and similar texts, it is clear that the new religion was revealed to Akhenaton alone. Akhenaton was the sole prophet of his new religion, just as Muḥammad and Joseph Smith were to be millennia later. Like the religions of these later prophets, Akhenaton's was also a secondary religion, one that arose in repudiation of existing beliefs.

The dominant role of the pharaoh in Egyptian society might suggest that Akhenaton's religion was imposed on his subjects and that they were forced to go along with it, even unwillingly, because he was king and his word was law. There is probably a certain amount of truth to this view. Akhenaton's religion was centered on the worship of light, but it also emphasized the divinity of the king himself—in contrast to the normal Egyptian belief that the king was the human vehicle of a divine power. One of his reliefs shows that Akhenaton himself had a priest, like traditional Egyptian gods but unlike any other pharaoh. While Akhenaton worshiped his god, other Egyptians were meant to worship not only the god but also Akhenaton himself, as the god's avatar on earth. In contrast to traditional Egyptian art, Amarna reliefs consistently show his subjects bowing low in Akhenaton's presence. The same reliefs often show the royal family surrounded by a military escort, as if in tacit recognition of possible resistance to the pharaoh's policies.

Nevertheless, it would be erroneous to conclude that the Egyptians tolerated Akhenaton's reforms only because of his position. Ancient Egypt was always ruled by one or two powerful families, and the king was their representative. He governed with their support, and if they did not share his views they could depose him: there is evidence that this happened several times in Egyptian history. It seems much more likely that Akhenaton's revelation initially swept up many of his countrymen in its enthusiasm, as history has shown with other new systems of belief—for example, in the birth of Islam, or more recently in the rise of Communism and Nazism. At first, many Egyptians were probably excited by the new vision of Akhenaton's theology and embraced it wholeheartedly.

History has also shown, however, how movements that start as enlightenment can turn to fanaticism and repression, and the same pattern is documented at Amarna—again, for the first time in history. This, in turn, usually gives rise to social unrest and disorder, and the Egyptian record indicates that this is what occurred at the end of Akhenaton's reign. In Egyptian eyes, the pharaoh's chief responsibility was the maintenance of peace and order, a concept known as *Maat.* Conversely, the absence of Maat was viewed as a sign that the king's authority was no longer legitimate. This was particularly significant in the reign of Akhenaton, who advertised himself as "living in Maat." With the new religion already on shaky ground in its opposition to traditional Egyptian thought, the disruption of Egyptian life at the end of Akhenaton's reign inevitably marked his ideas as antithetical to Maat, ultimately condemning them to the status of heresy.

SEE ALSO Monotheism.

BIBLIOGRAPHY

Aldred, Cyril. *Akhenaten, King of Egypt.* London, 1988. A standard history of the reign, somewhat outdated by more recent discoveries.

Allen, James P. "The Natural Philosophy of Akhenaten." In *Religion and Philosophy in Ancient Egypt,* edited by William Kelly Simpson, pp. 89–101. New Haven, 1989. An examination of evidence for Akhenaton's ideas as a form of natural philosophy.

Allen, James P. "The Religion of Amarna." In *The Royal Women of Amarna: Images of Beauty from Ancient Egypt,* edited by Dorothea Arnold, pp. 3–5. New York, 1996. An overview of Akhenaton's theology.

Allen, James P. "Ikhnaton." In *Collier's Encyclopedia,* edited by L. S. Bahr et al., vol. 12, p. 495. New York, 1997. A short summary of the reign and religion of Akhenaton.

Allen, James P. "Monotheism: The Egyptian Roots." *Archaeology Odyssey* 2, no. 3 (1999): 44–54. An essay on monotheistic thought in traditional Egyptian religion and Amarna theology.

Arnold, Dorothea. *The Royal Women of Amarna: Images of Beauty from Ancient Egypt.* New York, 1996. Catalog of an exhibition, including perhaps the best recent essays on Amarna art.

Assmann, Jan. *Egyptian Solar Religion in the New Kingdom: Re, Amun, and the Crisis of Polytheism,* translated by Anthony Alcock. London and New York, 1995. An in-depth analysis of the theological background to Amarna.

Assmann, Jan. *Moses the Egyptian: The Memory of Egypt in Western Monotheism.* Cambridge, Mass., 1997. An examination of the possible influence of Akhenaton's monotheism on that of Moses and later religions.

Assmann, Jan. *The Search for God in Ancient Egypt,* translated by David Lorton. Ithaca, N.Y., 2001. One of the best overall presentations of Egyptian religious thought, including a section on Amarna religion.

Assmann, Jan. *The Mind of Egypt: History and Meaning in the Time of the Pharaohs,* translated by Andrew Jenkins. New York, 2002. A study of Akhenaton's religion in the context of Egyptian thought.

Freed, Rita E., Yvonne J. Markowitz, and Sue H. D'Auria, eds. *Pharaohs of the Sun: Akhenaten, Nefertiti, Tutankhamun.* Boston, 1999. Catalogue of an exhibition of Amarna art, with studies on the art and culture of the period by several Egyptologists.

Gabolde, Marc. *D'Akhenaton à Toutânkhamoun.* Lyon and Paris, 1998. A study of the historical evidence for the end of Akhenaton's reign.

Gohary, Jocelyn. *Akhenaten's Sed-festival at Karnak.* London and New York, 1992. Presentation and discussion of Akhenaton's early monuments.

Hornung, Erik. *Akhenaten and the Religion of Light,* translated by David Lorton. Ithaca, N.Y., 1999. Incorporates much recent analysis of Akhenaton's religion and its monotheistic nature.

Montserrat, Dominic. *Akhenaten: History, Fantasy, and Ancient Egypt.* London and New York, 2000. An excellent study of modern theories and debate about the Amarna period.

Murnane, William J. *Texts from the Amarna Period in Egypt.* Atlanta, 1995. Translation of almost every known text relating to the reign of Akhenaton, with an excellent introduction to Amarna history and thought.

Redford, Donald B. *Akhenaten: The Heretic King.* Princeton, 1984. An overview by the excavator of Akhenaton's Karnak monuments, with an emphasis on the political background, generally unsympathetic in its analysis of the king's accomplishments.

Reeves, C. Nicholas. *Akhenaten: Egypt's False Prophet.* London, 2001. An overview, concerned more with history and archaeology than religion.

JAMES P. ALLEN (2005)

AKITU

AKITU. Akitu was an important Babylonian temple, located just outside the city, where the annual procession celebrating the New Year took place. The festival of the same name was celebrated in the first few days of the month of Nisan, which marked the beginning of the New Year.

The Babylonian chronicles of the first millennium include statements such as the following regarding the great Nebuchadrezzar II, who conquered Jerusalem: "In the month of April he took Bel and the son of Bel by the hand and celebrated the feast of Akitu." The following statement with the opposite meaning refers to Nabonidus, the last king of Babylon, overthrown by Cyrus the Great: "The king did not come to Babylon in the month of April, Nabu did not come to Babylon. Bel did not leave in procession. The feast of Akitu was not celebrated" (Falkenstein, 1947, p. 147). These passages reveal the importance the Babylonians attached to the celebration of the New Year, which began in April.

THE FESTIVAL. There is no doubt that for Babylonian society the feast of Akitu, named after the temple whose doors opened once at the beginning of every year, represented not only a moment of joyous celebration but also a particular moment for reflection upon their institutions, without which the New Year would begin inauspiciously. The text concerning the ritual, which is unfortunately fragmentary, indicates that the celebrations lasted eleven days, culminating with the procession of the statues of Marduk, the Babylonian supreme god, and Nabu, his son and the god of wisdom. These statues left the city temple Esagila and proceeded along the so-called Street of the Procession, its walls covered with multicolored enamel tiles, passing through the marvelous Gate of Ishtar. They sailed along the river to the temple of Akitu outside Babylon. The ritual texts describe all the ceremonies that took place during the eleven days of the celebrations, which occupied the priests day and night. Most concern the purification of the temple and its furnishings with incantations, prayers, and ablutions.

The high point was the arrival of the statue of Nabu by boat from its home city of Borsippa to take part in the procession and then the introduction of the Babylonian sovereign into the Esagila temple in order "to take the hand of Bel and his son Nabu" (Farber, 1987, p. 225). The two quotations at the beginning of this article lead to the conclusion that there was a direct link between royal legitimacy and the feast of Akitu. It seems that the festival could only be celebrated if the sovereign was present. This is certainly a limited interpretation of the action of "taking the hand of the god," however. The fact that the Assyrian kings, who aspired to the Babylonian crown, emphasized in their inscriptions that they had taken part in the festival and taken the hand of the god tends to support that this act legitimized power in Babylon.

Besides this institutional aspect, there is another equally relevant point. The sovereign, upon being introduced to the temple, was stripped of all his royal insignia, slapped, and made to kneel in front of the statue, where he recited the following confession:

> I have not failed, Lord of these lands, I have not been negligent regarding thy majesty; I have done no harm to Babylon; I have not ordained its destruction; I have not made the Esagila quake, nor have I neglected its rites; I have not smote the people who are under thy protection; I have done nothing that would make it subject to mockery; I have taken care of Babylon, I have not destroyed its walls! (Farber, 1987, p. 215)

This penitential recitation sets out the duties of the Babylonian sovereign: he must be respectful of the gods and be the careful shepherd of his people. Only after he recited these words did the sovereign once again put on his robes and receive the symbols of royal power. At this moment he was allowed to take the hands of the god Bel and the god Nabu and start the procession. When they reached the temple of Akitu, the god Marduk addressed the sovereign and his sacred city with this eagerly awaited blessing: "If you will take due care of my majesty and you will protect my people, the year now beginning will be a year of plenty for Babylon!" (Farber, 1987, p. 226). The New Year began with the procession and the final blessing, but only if the king was present at Babylon and the statue of Marduk was taken in procession were the omens for the New Year truly favorable.

INTERPRETATIONS. One further point, which certainly does not please all scholars of comparative religion and religious historians generally, who have been prone to compare the ritual of the feast of Akitu and another mythological text concerning Marduk, in which he descends to the underworld and is mistreated by the powers there before he rises to life again. Luigi Cagni collected accounts of all the theories advanced by scholars regarding the interpretation of this extremely interesting document, which has been called "Supposed 'Death' and 'Resurrection' of Marduk." Is this the description of a rite that could be compared to the death and resurrection of Christ, however distantly? The interest in such a topic by biblical scholars as well as by Orientalists and Assyriologists is understandable. In his account, Cagni quotes the views of scholars from 1918 to 1955, from Heinrich Zimmern (1862–1931) to Mario Theodoro De Liagre Böhl. The former put forward a comparison between Marduk and Jesus Christ, whereas the latter established the historical setting in which the text was written, namely the Assyria of Sennacherib, and the parodistic nature of the text itself. Cagni then proceeded to the theory of Wolfram von Soden, who categorically denied the possibility that the document implies Marduk's resurrection and instead considered it a work of parody or propaganda composed in the reign of Sennacherib, just as De Liagre Böhl proposed.

Cagni rejected von Soden's theory and put forward a mythico-cultural interpretation of the document without drawing any parallel with the death and resurrection of Christ. The text talks of the imprisonment of Marduk, which Belet-Babili and Nabu constantly seek to end. Silvia M. Chiodi (1995) showed that the death is the equivalent of a state of imprisonment, starting from a passage in the *Epic of Gilgamesh*.

As far as the end of the text is concerned, Cagni drew the following conclusion: "After detailing the apparent entry of the gods into battle against Marduk, who is shut behind the *birru* gate, the text stops at this point and is deliberately silent regarding the outcome of the struggle. If the aim of the text were political, as suggested by von Soden, it seems strange that Sennacherib's theologians, had they reached this point in the story, would have failed to mention the 'annihilation' of the power of Marduk. Nor would it have been particularly difficult for them to devise a suitable means to convey this, in a kind of anti-*Enuma Elish*" (Cagni, 1982, p. 612).

Initial studies of Babylonian civilization from about the middle of the twentieth century regarded this myth as an integral part of the ritual celebrating the New Year, but subsequent research has shown that no relation exists between the two texts. The ritual is a stand-alone text, and the myth of the suffering Marduk has no connection with the New Year celebrations. The only common aspect of the two ceremonies is the slapping: in the New Year festival the king was slapped, while in the myth the god was slapped. However, the slap the king received was meant as an act of both penitence and encouragement. The conclusion of the ritual text is interesting. The slap received by the king had to be hard enough to cause him physical pain and make him weep. Only if the king wept would the god Marduk look favorably upon his people. On such occasions, rich offerings were made to the god Marduk, as king Nabonidus confirmed: "In the month of Nisan, on the tenth day, the day on which the king of the gods, Marduk, and the gods of heaven and earth come to the E-siskur, the 'house of prayer,' in the Akitu temple of the Lord of Justice, I brought there 6,021 minas of silver, 307 minas of gold, in addition to the annual gifts, taken from votive offerings, from the wealth of the land, from the produce of the mountains, from the taxes on the villages, from the wealth of the king, from the riches which the god Marduk has bestowed upon me" (Falkenstein, 1959, p. 150).

Although the most famous festival of Akitu was held at Babylon, it should not be forgotten that Akitu was also celebrated in other cities, such as Uruk and, in Assyria, Ashur and Nineveh. The fact that the tradition is much older is shown by evidence in Sumerian documents that there were already festivals of Akitu in the pre-Sargonid period at Lagash and during the third dynasty at Ur, when it was linked to the same royal dynasty and was celebrated twice a year at Gaesh, a village near Ur. From a ritual rediscovered in Uruk it is clear that the celebration of Akitu took place twice a year, in the month of Nisan and also in the month of Tishrit. Almost nothing is known of the festival in Assyria because of a lack of relevant rituals.

The *Enuma elish* poem links the institution of kingship with the divine world. The dream of Babylon, of being the cultural and spiritual center of Mesopotamia, the overwhelming logic of which pervades the poem, became reality. A new star, the most resplendent, appeared in the mythological Mesopotamian sky. Henceforth he was recognized as the supreme god of the Babylonians and Assyrians, and in the divine Babylonian world he was known to the Greeks by his name Bel, which means "Lord." Marduk was indeed the preeminent Lord, the ruler of the gods, and Babylon was his only home. The Babylonians had no intention of forgetting their cultural heritage and celebrated the triumph of Marduk every year in the festival of the New Year. This festival, undoubtedly the most important of Babylonian festivals, could only take place in the presence of the legitimate sovereign, who led the procession after he had "taken the hand" of Bel and Nabu. The deep significance of this act, which many Assyrian kings would have willingly undertaken but were prevented from doing by the sacred defenders of authentic Babylonian tradition, is beyond question. Only a legitimate king of Babylon could take the hand of the god, so the festival was not celebrated if the king was absent.

Among the various rites of the festival, two are particularly significant. First was the annual consecration of the sovereign, subject to the penitential act followed by the slap. Second, the high priest twice raised the tablets on which the poem *Enuma elish* was written, which emphasized the direct link between the festival of the New Year and the celebration of Marduk as the supreme god of the Mesopotamian pantheon. The feast of the New Year marked the commemoration of the apotheosis of Marduk because of his victory over Tiamat and the creation of the cosmos—heaven and earth—culminating in the construction of Babylon.

These small indications clarify the central role occupied by Babylon, with its god Marduk, regarding the nation's royal line. The Babylonian sovereign ruled insofar as he was chosen by Marduk, who was made lord of the gods by the assembly of the gods. So the Babylonian king was the vicarious substitute of Marduk, not an absolute despot like the Assyrian king. Thus it is significant that in his inscriptions Nebuchadrezzar often called himself not "the king of Babylon" but "the governor of Babylon."

SEE ALSO Dying and Rising Gods; Enuma Elish; Marduk.

BIBLIOGRAPHY

Berger, Peter R. "Das Neujahrsfest nach den Köningsinschriften des ausgehenden Babylonischen Reiches." In *Actes de la XVIIe Rencontre assyriologique Internationale*, edited by André Finet, vol. 17, pp. 155–159. Ham-sur-Heure, 1970.

Black, James A. "The New Year Ceremonies in Ancient Babylon: 'Taking Bel by the Hand' and a Cultic Picnic." *Religion* 11 (January 1981): 39–59.

Cagni, Luigi M. "Misteri a Babilonia: Esempi della tematica del 'Dio in vicenda' nell'antica Mesopotamia." In *La soteriologia dei culti orientali nell'Impero romano: Atti del Colloquio Internazionale sulla soteriologia dei culti orientali nell'Impero Romano*, edited by Ugo Bianchi and Maarten J. Vermaseren, pp. 565–613. Leiden, Netherlands, 1982.

Chiodi, Silvia M. "Il prigioniero e il morto: *Epopea di Gilgamesh.* Tav. X, r. 318–320." *Oriens Antiquus Miscellanea* 2 (1995): 159–171.

Falkenstein, Adam. "Akiti-fest und Akiti-festhaus." In *Festschrift Johannes Friedrich zum 65. Geburtstag am 27. August 1958 gewidmet*, edited by Richard von Kienle, pp. 147–182. Heidelberg, 1959.

Farber, Walter. "A. Kultische Rituale. 1. Texte zum Akitu-Fest (Neujahrsrituale)." In *Rituale und Beschwörungen*, vol. 1, edited by Walter Farber, Hans Martin Kümmer, and Willem H. P. Römer, pp. 213–226. Gütersloh, Germany, 1987.

Grayson, A. K. "Chronicles and the Akitu Festival." In *Actes de la XVIIe Rencontre assyriologique Internationale*, edited by André Finet, vol. 17, pp. 160–170. Ham-sur-Heure, 1970.

Jacobsen, Thorkild. "Religious Drama in Ancient Mesopotammia." In *Unity and Diversity: Essays in the History, Literature, and Religion of the Ancient Near East*, edited by Hans Goedicke and J. J. M. Roberts, pp. 65–97. Baltimore, 1975.

Pallis, Svend Aage. *The Babylonian Akitu Festival.* Copenhagen, 1976.

Thureau-Dangin, François. *Rituels accadiens.* Paris, 1921. See pp. 192–249.

Zimmern, Heinrich. *Das babylonische Neujahrsfest.* Leipzig, Germany, 1926.

GIOVANNI PETTINATO (2005)
Translated from Italian by Paul Ellis

AKIVA BEN JOSEPH SEE 'AQIVA' BEN YOSEF

AKKADIAN RELIGION SEE MESOPOTAMIAN RELIGIONS

AKSAKOV, IVAN (1823–1886), Russian publicist, Slavophile, and pan-Slavist. Aksakov had a mixed career as civil servant, banker, and journalist. He accepted with all other Slavophiles that religion was the decisive factor in the shaping of a nation and that the essence of Russian national life (*narodnost'*) was inseparably bound up with Orthodoxy. But he was painfully aware that Orthodoxy labored under manifold constraints in his milieu; as a convinced church member he campaigned in a cogent and constructive manner for their diminution. He regretted the bureaucratization of the Russian church administration and the subjugation (often subservience) of the clergy to the state that was its result, if not its cause. Aksakov's journalism was inhibited by an official ban on his work as editor (1853). Nevertheless, he contributed regularly to such publications as *Moskovskii sbornik* (1846–1847, 1852), *Russkaia beseda* (1858–1860), and *Den'* (1860–1865).

Aksakov was less religiously oriented than the early Slavophiles. He also differed from them in his cautious appraisal of the Russian peasant (in his opinion, hardly the paragon of humility and faith as usually depicted). At the same time, he went beyond them in eventually projecting a historiographical (pan-Slavic) scheme in which the Russian people—not least because of their Orthodox heritage—would play a central role in the development (initially, the liberation) of other Slavic nations. The West, he believed, was seriously inhibited and undermined by its adherence to other creeds, whether Catholic or Protestant. Least favored of all, and viewed as renegades, were Slavic nations with a loyalty to Rome (notably Poland).

Aksakov raised funds for a Russian expeditionary force to aid the Serbs against the Turks (1876) and effectively promoted Russia's entry into war "for the faith of Christ" and in support of the Bulgarians (1877). In the aftermath of the Bulgarian episode, the climax of his career, Aksakov was even mentioned as a possible king for the newly established state.

Aksakov's appeal to the nationalism (and anti-Semitism) of his people was to persist during the last decade of his life. His funeral in 1886 was attended by several hundred thousand admirers.

BIBLIOGRAPHY

Ivan S. Aksakov's collected works were published in seven volumes as *Polnoe sobranie sochinenii I. S. Aksakova* (Moscow, 1886–1887). The fourth volume (1886) contains his principal articles on "Social Questions Related to Church Affairs" (pp. 3–358). There is a useful monograph by Stephen Lukashevich, *Ivan Aksakov, 1823–1886: A Study in Russian Thought and Politics* (Cambridge, Mass., 1965).

SERGEI HACKEL (1987)

AKSUMITE RELIGION. Civilization first appeared in the Ethiopian highlands in the fifth century before the common era. It was apparently brought by Semitic-speaking immigrants from South Arabia, who transplanted to Ethiopia many of the cultural and artistic traditions of ancient Sheba. They first established themselves in and around Yeha (formerly called Ava), near modern Adwa. In the early centuries of the common era, power shifted northward to Aksum, which remains to this day the most important religious center in Ethiopia. At the height of their power, the rulers of Aksum claimed dominion as far west as the Nile Valley and as far east as the highlands of Yemen. The kingdom of Aksum was converted to Christianity in the fourth century, long before any other region in the interior of Africa.

Comparatively little is known of the religion of pre-Christian Ethiopia. Only fragmentary information is afforded by classical authors, by the victory stelae erected by a few Aksumite rulers, and by the evidence of archaeology. Some additional details can be inferred on the basis of parallels with the better-known religions of South Arabia.

During the Yeha period, the Ethiopian religion seems to have been little different from that of Sheba. The major deities were the familiar Semitic triad of the Sun, the Moon, and Venus. In the Aksumite period a somewhat different triad emerged, consisting of Ashtar (Venus), the sea god Behr, and the earth god Medr. The sun was a female deity, called by the Sabaean name Zat-Badar. As the military power of Aksum expanded, the war god Mahram assumed increasing importance and became the special tutelary of the Aksumite rulers.

At Yeha, Aksum, and various provincial towns there were temples and altars dedicated to several of the principal deities. Temple architecture followed closely the traditions of South Arabia. The buildings stood upon an elevated, stepped platform and were approached by a monumental stairway. Very few interior details of the temples have survived, but the exterior walls were embellished with various patterns of projecting and recessed paneling. Outside the temples were votive stelae and offering tables, many of them commemorating the military victories of particular rulers. Animal and also human sacrifices were apparently a regular feature of the victory celebrations.

The most extraordinary monuments of Aksumite religious architecture are the great stone stelae erected over the tombs of many rulers. They are elaborately carved in the form of miniature skyscrapers, with a false door at the bottom and row upon row of false windows above. They are, however, devoid of inscription. Underground, the royal dead were interred in large rock-cut burial chambers, but these have been so thoroughly plundered that no offerings have ever been found in them. For this reason, and in the absence of inscriptions, it is difficult to form an impression of the part that mortuary ritual played in the religious life of the ancient Ethiopians.

BIBLIOGRAPHY

There is no general work on ancient Ethiopian religions. Very brief popular accounts can be found in Jean Doresse's *L'Empire du Prêtre-Jean,* vol. 1, *L'Éthiopie antique* (Paris, 1957), pp. 138–140, and in *Ethiopia* (London, 1959), pp. 21–27, by the same author. By far the most detailed description of ancient temples and shrines, as revealed by archaeology, is that of Daniel Krencker in his *Ältere Denkmäler nordabessiniens* (Berlin, 1913). For a brief popular description of temples and other religious monuments, see David Buxton's *The Abyssinians* (New York, 1970), pp. 86–97.

New Sources

Burstein, Stanley, ed. *Ancient African Civilizations: Kush and Axum.* Princeton, N.J., 1998.

Munro-Hay, Stuart. *Aksum: An African Civilization of Late Antiquity.* Edinburgh, 1991.

Phillipson, David W. *Ancient Ethiopia: Aksum, Its Antecedents and Successions.* London, 1998.

Phillipson, David W. *Archaeology of Aksum Ethiopia, 1993–7.* London and Oxford, 2000.

WILLIAM Y. ADAMS (1987)
Revised Bibliography

ʿALAWĪYŪN

ʿALAWĪYŪN (sg., ʿAlawī; modern English rendering, Alawis, Alawites; French, Alaouites; sometimes called Nuṣayrīyah). The Arabic word *ʿAlawī* designates, broadly speaking, a follower of ʿAlī ibn Abī Ṭālib. Next to the prophet Muḥammad, ʿAlī, Muḥammad's paternal cousin and son-in-law, is perhaps the most important personality in the religious and political history of Islam. He remains a force to contend with in the daily life of Muslims today, especially among the Shīʿah (from *shīʿat ʿAlī,* the "party" or followers of ʿAlī): "Ya ʿAlī, madad" ("O ʿAlī, help!") is a moving intercessionary expression often heard in Shīʿī circles. The word *Shīʿī* (anglicized as *Shiite*) has often been used to designate all followers of ʿAlī; but in a more restricted sense, its application is limited to the so-called Twelvers (Ithnā ʿAsharīyah) of Iran, Iraq, Lebanon, and elsewhere, while *ʿAlawī* is taken to refer exclusively to the ʿAlawī Nuṣayrīyah of northwestern Syria. The indigenous sources, past and present, do not make such clearcut distinctions, however. The other two leading Shīʿī sects, the Zaydīyah and the Ismāʿīlīyah, have had significant historical and doctrinal differences with the mainstream Twelvers. Finally, there exists a group of extremist Shīʿī sects known collectively as the Ghulāt ("exaggerators"), to which the ʿAlawī Nuṣayrīyah of Syria belong. While the Shīʿah in general hold ʿAlī and his immediate family in high esteem, the Ghulāt have gone beyond veneration, often considering ʿAlī a manifestation of the deity.

ORIGINS. The majority of Muslims, called Sunnīs, accepted the early settlement on the succession (caliphate) to the Prophet's leadership, and their religious scholars *(ʿulamāʾ)* subsequently arrived at a doctrinal position which states that "God's religion is the middle ground between exaggerated zeal [*ghulūw*] and negligence [*jafāʾ*]." It was left to the scholars to interpret God's word in the Qurʾān. The Shīʿah, on the other hand, would accept only the leadership of ʿAlī as imam par excellence, and, to satisfy the need for someone who would be specially endowed to understand the esoteric *(bāṭinī)* meaning of God's injunctions, they elevated ʿAlī to the position of *walī* of God: the "friend" of the Almighty and "custodian" of the faith. With time, the Shīʿī scholars developed an elaborate theological system which featured such concepts as *imāmah* (leadership of the Muslim community), *ʿiṣmah* (infallibility of the imam), *naṣṣ* (attested succession), *taqīyah* (religious dissimulation), and *ghaybah* (occultation). Thus the Sunnīs and the Shīʿah became two dimensions of the Islamic dispensation.

With the Ghulāt, the excessive veneration of ʿAlī took a different turn long before the ʿAlawī Nuṣayrīyah came on the scene. *Ghulūw* manifested itself in a long series of extremist movements, the earliest of which was perhaps that of al-Mukhtār (AH 66, 685/6 CE), who claimed to be an incarnation of Muḥammad ibn al-Ḥanafīyah, a son of ʿAlī by a woman from the Ḥanīfah tribe. Toward the end of the ninth century, the Qarāmiṭah offered another example of religious and social extremism; the Ismāʿīlī Shīʿī state of the Fatimids was founded on the ruins of this movement. A major phase of religious extremism appeared following the decline of Fatimid power in the eleventh century. This development coincided with the resurgence of Byzantine power south of the Taurus Mountains along the traditional limes *(thughūr, ʿawāṣim)* in the northern Syrian borderlands, the weakening position of the Shīʿī Hamdanids in Aleppo and the Buyids in Baghdad, and most of all, the influx of Crusader armies along the Syrian coastlands and their final occupation of Jerusalem in 1099.

This unsettled situation engendered three curious religious factions: the ʿAlawīyūn proper in the northwest region of Syria, the Druze sect of southern geographic Syria, and the movement of Ḥasan-i Ṣabbāḥ (the so-called Assassins) who ultimately established themselves in such mountain strongholds as Alamūt and elsewhere. While the Druze and the Assassins were direct splinters from the Ismāʿīlī Fatimids of Egypt, the ʿAlawīyūn were grounded in Twelver thought with syncretic Christian accretions.

HISTORICAL DEVELOPMENT. Almost every founder of a Shīʿī movement, including the Ghulāt sects, claimed some attachment to, or direct genealogical descent from, ʿAlī or his immediate descendants, the twelve imams. The ʿAlawī Nuṣayrīyah, though claiming no direct descent from any of the imams, believed that each of the twelve imams had a "gate" *(bāb)*, beginning with Salmān al-Fārisī, who was the "gate" of ʿAlī ibn Abī Ṭālib, and ending with Abū Shuʿayb Muḥammad ibn Nuṣayr, the "gate" to the eleventh imam, al-Ḥasan al-ʿAskarī (d. 874). The twelfth imam had no "gate"; however, Muḥammad ibn Nuṣayr continued to assume that position during the period of occultation. The ʿAlawīyūn consider the office of the *bāb* one of their basic religious institutions, and since they claim Ibn Nuṣayr as their founder, they are sometimes known as the Nuṣayrīyah. Ibn Nuṣayr was succeeded by Muḥammad ibn Jundub, then by Muḥammad al-Jinān al-Junbulānī. It was at about this time that a certain Ḥusayn ibn Ḥamdān al-Khaṣībī, originally from Egypt, was attracted to northern Syria and became the ideological leader of the movement. He was active at the courts of the Hamdanids of Aleppo and the Buyids of Baghdad. The center for ʿAlawī activity, however, moved to Latakia when these Twelver Shīʿī states succumbed to the Sunnī Seljuk Turks.

During the early Mongol period the ʿAlawī community witnessed a short revival under Emir Ḥasan al-Makzūn al-Sinjārī, "one of the greatest and most pious shaykhs of the sect, who rescued ʿAlawī authority, organized the affairs of the community, and provided his followers with a comfortable way of life" (Ṭawīl, pp. 309–310). Soon, however, the region fell under Mamluk domination. The Ḥanbalī scholar Aḥmad ibn Taymīyah (d. 1328) wrote a scathing refutation of the ʿAlawī Nuṣayrīyah *(Risālah fī al-radd ʿalā al-Nuṣayrīyah)* in which they are said to believe in the drinking of wine, the reincarnation of the soul, the antiquity of the world, and the fact that their god who created the heavens and the earth is ʿAlī ibn Abī Ṭālib, who to them is the imam in heaven and the imam on earth; and to claim that Muḥammad the prophet is only the "name" while ʿAlī is the "meaning" and essence. Condemning the ʿAlawīyūn along with other sects such as the Malahidah Assassins, the Qarāmiṭah, the Ismāʿīlīyah, and all types of *bāṭinī* esoterics, Ibn Taymīyah accuses them of *kufr* ("unbelief") worse than that of the Jews and Christians, calls them *mushrikūn* ("polytheists"), and prohibits marriage with them, partaking of their food, or allowing them to guard the frontiers of Islam. The North African traveler Ibn Baṭṭūṭah (d. 1377), who passed through Nuṣayri territory, observed that they believed in ʿAlī as their god and that they did not pray, nor did they perform ablutions or observe the fast incumbent upon all Muslims. According to Ibn Baṭṭūṭah, who was a Mālikī jurist, they used the mosques, which the Mamluk rulers had forced them to build, as stables for their animals. At one time, he reports, the sultan had ordered their extermination but was reminded by his chief minister that the Nuṣayrīyah were still needed to till the land.

In the sixteenth century, the Ottomans under Sultan Selim fought Shiism on all fronts: against a large-scale Shīʿī rebellion in Anatolia, against the Safavids of Iran, and against the ʿAlawīyūn of Syria. Once victory was attained, however, the issue was allowed to fade, and during the next four centuries the ʿAlawī communities suffered the benign neglect of Ottoman rule. They were not treated as a *millet* (autonomous religious community), and their affairs were left in the hands of their tribal chieftains. Midhat Pasha, the nineteenth-century reform-minded governor of Syria, attempted to institute a separate administration *(liwāʾ)* for the ʿAlawīyūn. Under the French Mandate after the First World War, they were treated as an "independent" state within Syria and were referred to as the "Alaouites" for the first time. The French drafted many of their young men for what came to be called the Troupes Spéciales du Levant. This special status survived into the late twentieth century with an ʿAlawī circle dominating the Syrian military government, led by President Hafiz al-Asad, himself an ʿAlawī.

RELATION TO SHIISM. Inasmuch as the ʿAlawī Nuṣayrīyah profess allegiance to ʿAlī ibn Abī Ṭālib, they share many of their beliefs and practices with the rest of the Shīʿah. Within Shiism, however, two traditions have survived: a high Islam, "orthodox," scribal tradition which has been preserved in the writings of the three main Shīʿī groups, the Twelvers, the Ismāʿīlī Seveners, and the Zaydīyah, and a folk Islam, "popular," nonscribal, secretive tradition which is the hallmark of the Ghulāt. The ʿAlawī Nuṣayrīyah of northwestern Syria belong to the latter tradition. The idea of the *bāb* as the "gate" to the imam appears to have been an attempt to preserve Twelver continuity, which the mainstream Shīʿī scholars resolved through the concept of occultation. In any case, the Shīʿī ʿAlawīyūn had no chance to further develop high Islam ideas since their patrons in Aleppo and Baghdad (the Twelver Hamdanids and Buyids respectively) had just lost their power to the ardent Sunnī Seljuks, and the ʿAlawīyūn were left essentially on their own.

At exactly the same time, moreover, the ʿAlawī lands were invaded by the Christian knights of the Crusader armies. Hence, in addition to their original extremist views about ʿAlī and the imams, the ʿAlawīyūn inherited Christian elements which they incorporated into their folk Islam beliefs (although the Islamic core remained predominant). Ideas of a trinity (a concept abhorred in official Islam) became current, with ʿAlī as the *maʿnā* (esoteric meaning and essence), Muḥammad as the *ism* (outward exoteric name), and Salmān al-Fārisī as the *bāb* (gate to ʿAlī's esoteric essence). Joined together, the three appear in a profession (Shahādah) of the faith: I testify that there is no god but ʿAlī ibn Abī Ṭālib *al-maʿbūd* ("the worshiped one"), no veil *(ḥijāb)* but Muḥammad *al-maḥmūd* ("the praised one"), and no gate but Salmān al-Fārisī *al-maqṣūd* ("the intended one"). In addition to the traditional Sunnī and Shīʿī holidays, Christian feast days such as Christmas, Epiphany, and Pentecost are celebrated. There are also several mass-type ceremonies, such as the incense mass and the *adhān* mass (for the Muslim call to prayer), during which the congregation chants hymns said to have been composed by one of the early fathers, al-Khaṣībī, although the Arabic language of the original indicates a more popular folk-literary hand. Belief in reincarnation is widespread: Muslims returning as donkeys, Christians as pigs, Jews as monkeys. This syncretic mixture of ideas has led one French authority on the ʿAlawīyūn to describe their beliefs as "a deformation of Christianity or a survival of ancient paganism" (Weulersse, 1946; p. 271). Another work, based substantially on polemical material, seems to be in partial agreement: "From an Islamic standpoint, the religious beliefs and practices of the Nuṣairīs set them off as a distinct religion, neither Islamic nor Christian nor Jewish, and it has always been the consensus of the Muslim *ʿulamāʾ*, both Sunnī and Shīʿī, that the Nusairis are *kuffār* (disbelievers, rejectors of the faith) and idolaters *(mushrikūn)*" (ʿAbd-Allāh, p. 48).

Contemporary Importance. The importance of the ʿAlawī Nuṣayri community now derives largely from the widespread contemporary revival of Islam. Their numbers have always been small: 300,000 according to Ghālib al-Ṭawīl in the 1920s; 225,000 according to Weulersse in 1943–1944; 325,311 according to Hourani in 1946; 600,000 or 700,000 according to Petran in 1972; and at most a "million or so" according to Batatu in 1981 (the last figure probably includes ʿAlawīs throughout the world). In the "independent" Alaouite state under French administration, the Representative Council of 1930, for example, included ten ʿAlawī members, two Orthodox Christians, one Maronite Christian, three Sunnīs, and one Ismāʿīlī. In more recent times, ʿAlawī leaders, both religious and secular, have been making outward attempts to gain acceptance among the rest of the (largely Sunnī) population of Syria. In 1973, for example, an official statement was issued by as many as eighty ʿAlawī religious leaders proclaiming the adherence of the community to the teachings and legal practices of Twelver Shiʿism and adding that "whatever else is attributed to them has no basis in truth and is a mere invention by their enemies and the enemies of Islam" (Batatu, p. 335). Mūsā al-Ṣadr, a politico-religious leader of Lebanon's Twelver Shīʿī community and founder of the Amal movement in the 1970s, included a number of representatives of the Lebanese ʿAlawī community in his Shīʿī Council, while a recent booklet, *Al-ʿAlawīyūn shīʿat ahl al-bayt* (a title that identifies the ʿAlawīyūn with the "party of the house of the Prophet," namely, ʿAlī and the imams), indicates a rapprochement of the community with the mainstream Twelvers. (A preface to this publication, written by a Twelver scholar, Ḥasan Mahdī Shīrāzī, avers that "the words *ʿAlawī* and *Shīʿah* are interchangeable.") Developments such as these may suggest a shift in ʿAlawī orientation from the Ghulāt to "orthodox" Twelver Shiism.

See Also Assassins; Druze; Taqiyah.

Bibliography

Older published works on the ʿAlawī Nuṣayri sect, though slightly dated, contain much useful information on the origins, beliefs, and practices of the community. See, for example, René Dussaud's *Histoire et religion des Nosairis* (Paris, 1900); Louis Massignon's "Nuṣairī," in *The Encyclopaedia of Islam* (Leiden, 1913–1934); René Basset's résumé of Dussaud's *Histoire* in the *Encyclopaedia of Religion and Ethics*, vol. 9, edited by James Hastings (Edinburgh, 1917); Samuel Lyde's *The Asian Mystery: Ansaireeh or Nusairis of Syria* (London, 1860); and Sulaymân Effendi of Adhanah's *Al-bākūrah al-Sulaymānīyah fī kashf asrār al-diyānah al-Nuṣayrīyah*, translated and partially presented by Edward E. Salisbury in the *Journal of the American Oriental Society* (1868): 227–308. Of special importance is Louis Massignon's "Esquisse d'une bibliographie nuṣayrie," in *Mélanges syriens offerts à Monsieur René Dussaud*, vol. 2 (Paris, 1939), pp. 913–922, containing a list of manuscripts on the ʿAlawīyūn which still await the specialized scholar.

More recent French works on the subject include Jacques Weulersse's *Les pays des Alaouites*, 2 vols. (Tours, 1940), his *Paysans de Syrie et du Proche-Orient* (Paris, 1946), and Munir M. Mousa's "Étude sociologique des ʿAlaouites ou Nuṣairis" (Ph.D. diss., 2 vols., Sorbonne, 1958). For important information on the ʿAlawīyūn during the thirteenth and fourteenth centuries, see Ibn Taymīyah's "Risālah fī al-radd ʿalā al-Nuṣayrīyah," in *Majmūʿ al-rasāʾil* (Cairo, 1905), pp. 94–102, and Ibn Baṭṭūṭah's *Travels*, translated by H. A. R. Gibb (London, 1962).

Special mention should be made of the first book in Arabic by a member of the ʿAlawī community, Muḥammad Amīn Ghālib al-Ṭawīl's *Taʾrīkh al-ʿAlawīyin*, originally written in Turkish and recast in Arabic (Latakia, Syria, 1921); the second edition (Beirut, 1966) contains a sixty-page critical introduction by the Twelver Shīʿī writer ʿAbd al-Raḥmān al-Khayr. Ṭawīl's work is somewhat polemical but is nevertheless full of valuable source material. Some largely unreliable statistics on the ʿAlawīyūn are found in such works as Albert Hourani's *Minorities in the Arab World* (1947; reprint, New York, 1982) and Tabitha Petran's *Syria* (New York, 1972).

Serious modern writings on the ʿAlawīyūn are scarce. See Claude Cahen's "Note sur les origines de la communauté syrienne des Nuṣayris," *Revue des études islamiques* 38 (1970): 243–249, and Hanna Batatu's "Some Observations on the Social Roots of Syria's Ruling Military Group and the Causes for Its Dominance," *Middle East Journal* 35 (1981): 331–344; also Nikolaos van Dam's *The Struggle for Power in Syria: Sectarianism, Regionalism, and Tribalism in Politics, 1961–1978* (London, 1979).

Finally, owing to contemporary attempts to rehabilitate the ʿAlawī Nuṣayrīyah within the Shīʿī fold, several works of a largely polemical nature have been produced; see, for example, ʿAbd Allāh al-Ḥusaynī's *Al-judhūr al-ta'rīkhīyah lil-Nuṣayrīyah al-ʿalawīyah* (Dubai, 1980), and ʿAbd al-Ḥusayn Mahdī al-ʿAskari's *Al-ʿAlawīyūnaw al-Nuṣayriyūn* (n.p., 1980), both of which quote extensively from the early heresiographical literature. Umar F. Abd-Allah's *The Islamic Struggle in Syria* (Berkeley, 1983), with foreword and postscript by Hamid Algar, outlines the attempt by the present ʿAlawī military regime in Syria to control the activities of the Muslim Brotherhood there.

MICHEL M. MAZZAOUI (1987)

ĀLAYA-VIJÑĀNA (Tib., *kun gzhi rnam par shes pa*; Chin., *a lai ye shi*) is the Sanskrit term denoting, roughly, "storehouse" consciousness, a conception of unconscious mental processes developed by the Yogācāra school of Indian Buddhism in the third to fifth centuries CE. *Ālaya-vijñāna* appears in such "Yogācāra" scriptures as the *Saṃdhinirmocana Sūtra* and the *Laṅkāvatāra Sūtra*, but is most systematically treated in the scholastic treatises of Asaṅga (c. 315–390) and Vasubandhu (c. mid-fourth to mid-fifth centuries). It originally addressed problems surrounding the continuity of karmic potential (*karma-upacaya*) and the latent afflictions (*anuśaya*) that had been generated by the *abhidharma* emphasis upon momentary, manifest processes of mind. How, after all, could these two essential aspects of one's samsaric existence—the potential for *karma* to ripen and for the afflictions to arise—be uninterruptedly present until their elimination far along the path to liberation if one's mind (or, more precisely, one's "mental stream," *santāna*) were comprised solely of whatever phenomena (*dharma*) were manifest at the present moment? Their manifest presence would preclude any salutary states of mind from arising, and thus prevent progress along the path, while their complete absence would be tantamount to liberation itself. The *ālaya-vijñāna* thus came to comprise the various potentialities that must continuously underlie each moment of the traditional six modes of cognitive awareness—now called manifest, arising, or functioning consciousnesses (*pravṛtti-vijñāna*) in contradistinction to the continuous yet subliminal *ālaya*, the home, base, or storehouse consciousness (*ālaya-vijñāna*).

Combining traditional analyses of consciousness (*vijñāna*) as an awareness (*not* a faculty) that arises either in dependence upon karmic formations (*saṃskārā*) or as a result of the concomitance of one's cognitive faculties and their correlative objects, *ālaya* consciousness is described in classical Yogācāra treatises as arising from moment to moment in dependence on the material sense faculties and the various cognitive and affective formations (*saṃskārā*) that constitute one's ongoing existence, as well as on its own subliminal cognitive object: an indistinct (*aparicchinna*) or imperceptible (*asaṃvidita*) apprehension of an external world (*bhājana-loka*). *Ālaya-vijñāna* is thus a complexly conditioned mode of cognitive awareness that simultaneously supports (*āśraya*) and informs all occurrences of manifest consciousness.

Also consonant with traditional characteristics of consciousness (S II 65, 101; III 54), *ālaya-vijñāna* is said in the *Saṃdhinirmocana Sūtra* to "grow, develop, and increase" due to the seeds (*bīja*) of karmic potential and the predispositions (*vāsanā*) of the afflictions that have accumulated "since beginningless time" from the karmic activities associated with the six modes of manifest cognitive awareness. The potential or "seeds" for the future arising of afflictions or of karmically resultant *dharmas*, such as sensations or consciousness itself, are thereafter "stored" in this evolving *ālaya* level of mind.

While this subliminal *ālaya* consciousness thus enjoys a simultaneous and causally reciprocal relationship with the manifest modes of cognitive awareness, it still retained, in most Indian Yogācāra treatises, its original character as the locus of accumulated karmic potential and latent afflictions, virtually defining one's samsaric existence and serving, in effect, as the "subject" of *saṃsāra* (also similar to earlier notions of *vijñāna*). Sentient beings therefore typically (mis)take *ālaya* consciousness as a substantive self (*ātmadṛṣṭi*), a form of ignorance so continuously present that it too soon came to be conceived as a distinct strata of subliminal—and karmically neutral—afflictions called "afflictive mentation" (Skt., *kliṣṭa-manas*; Tib., *nyon mongs pa can gyi yid*; Chin., *ran wu yi*), now considered a "seventh consciousness," making *ālaya-vijñāna* the eighth.

More broadly, Asaṅga's *Mahāyāna-saṃgraha* describes how the "common aspects" (*sādhāraṇa-lakṣaṇa*) of *ālaya* consciousness help to structure the arising of our common "world" (*bhājana-loka*). Our distinctively human world appears similarly to us because we have accumulated similar *karma*, which results in both our similar cognitive faculties as well as whatever cognitive and affective formations similarly condition the arising of each individual's *ālaya-vijñāna*, such as the impressions of language (*adhilāpa-vāsanā*). Together, these conditions delimit the range of stimuli that may instigate manifest consciousness, and thus also the very forms in which our common, species-specific world (*loka*) typically appear. In this way, the *ālaya-vijñāna*—"the mind with all the seeds" (*sarvabījaka-citta*) that represents our accumulated potentialities for karmic results—serves as the "common support (*samāśraya*) of all phenomenal experience (dharma)."

Although in its systematic treatments the *ālaya-vijñāna* is largely commensurate with traditional Indian Buddhist analyses of samsaric consciousness, as we have seen, the very metaphors used to describe the *ālaya-vijñāna*—an evolving "repository" form of mind (*citta*) that receives and "stores" karmic seeds and thereby serves as both support and cause (*hetu*) of all *dharmas*—invited its interpretation as a foundational mind serving as the sole basis or ground from which the entire phenomenal world arises. These tendencies were particularly pronounced in certain Chinese and Tibetan traditions, influenced no doubt by the explicit identification—in scriptures such as the *Laṅkāvatāra Sūtra* and, more importantly, the apocryphal *Awakening of Faith*—of *ālaya-vijñāna* with *tathāgatha-garbha,* the womb or matrix of the Tathāgatha. Although this identification went largely unchallenged in later Chinese Buddhism, it is not found in the classic treatises of Indian Yogācāra. The sixth-century Indian translator Paramārtha's response to this discrepancy was to preserve the *ālaya-vijñāna* as a defiled eighth consciousness, which is eliminated upon awakening, while interpolating into his translations an additional, undefiled ninth consciousness, an **amala-vijñāna,* which persists after the *ālaya-vijñāna* ceases. One of seventh-century Xuanzang's aims in retranslating Yogācāra texts was to recover the earlier, and to his mind orthodox, interpretation of *ālaya-vijñāna* as a locus of defiled consciousness unrelated to the notion of *tathāgatha-garbha.* Similar tendencies occurred in the Tibetan schools that teach "extrinsic emptiness" (*gzhan stong*), which extrapolating upon Indian Yogācāra models, posited a primordial *ālaya* wisdom (Skt., **ālaya-jñāna*; Tib., *kun gzhi ye shes*) prior to and apart from all defiled and discursive modes of consciousness (Skt., *vijñāna*; Tib., *rnam shes*), such as *ālaya-vijñāna.*

These varying notions of post- (or non-) samsaric forms of consciousness, typically expressed as transformations of *vijñāna* into *jñāna,* echo similar ideas found in the earliest Buddhist texts in which the consciousness of a buddha or arhat is no longer bound by grasping or appropriation (*anupādāna*), but is said to be "non-abiding" or "unsupported" (*appatiṭṭhita-viññāṇa*; D III 105; S I 122; S II 66, 103; S III 54).

In sum, this core Yogācāra concept touches upon some of the central concerns of Buddhist soteriology and analyses of mind, but its interpretation varies considerably depending upon which century, which school, and even which text one is investigating.

See Also Asaṅga; Dharmapāla; Soteriology; Soul, article on Buddhist Concepts; Tathāgata-garbha; Vasubandhu; Vijñāna; Yogācāra.

BIBLIOGRAPHY

Cook, Francis, trans. *Three Texts on Consciousness Only.* Berkeley, Calif., 1999. English translations from the Chinese of three Yogācāra treatises: two by Vasubandhu—the *Triṃśika* (Thirty verses) and the *Viṃśika* (Twenty verses); and one by Xuanzang—the *Cheng wei-shi lun* (Demonstration of consciousness only).

Hakamaya, Noriaki. *Yuishiki Shisō Ronkō.* Tokyo, 2001. A collection of fifty articles by a leading Japanese scholar analyzing many Yogācāra texts and concepts, including the *ālaya-vijñāna,* from a text-critical perspective.

Hakeda, Yoshito, trans. *The Awakening of Faith, Attributed to Aṣvaghosha.* New York, 1967. An apocryphal treatise immensely influential in Chinese interpretations of Yogācāra.

Keenan, John, trans. *The Scripture on the Explication of Underlying Meaning* (The *Saṃdhinirmocana Sūtra*). Berkeley, Calif., 2000. A translation of Xuanzang's Chinese rendition of this indispensable Yogācāra text.

Lamotte, Étienne, trans. *La somme du Grand Véhicle d'Asaṅga* (*Mahāyāna-saṃgraha*). Louvain, Belgium, 1938–1939. A definitive translation accompanied by extensive selections from its traditional commentaries.

Pruden, Leo, trans. *Karmasiddhiprakaraṇa: Treatise on Action by Vasubandhu.* Berkeley, Calif., 1980. An English translation of Lamotte's French translation of Vasubandhu's most abhidharmic treatment of the *ālaya-vijñāna.*

Schmithausen, Lambert. *Ālayavijñāna.* Tokyo, 1987. This groundbreaking and painstaking philological study reconstructs the initial occurrence and subsequent development of the *ālaya-vijñāna* within Indian Yogācāra texts.

Stearns, Cyrus. *The Buddha from Dolpo.* Albany, 1999. A study of the founder of the Tibetan *zhen stong* view and the theory of primordial *laya* wisdom.

Suzuki, Daisetz Teitaro, trans. *Laṅkāvatāra Sūtra.* London, 1932. A translation and study of this important Yogācāra scripture.

Waldron, William S. "Buddhist Steps to an Ecology of Mind: Thinking about 'Thoughts without a Thinker.'" *Eastern Buddhist* 34, no. 1 (2002): 1–52. Analyzes the *ālaya-vijñāna* in relation to scientific perspectives on the evolution and arising of consciousness.

Waldron, William S. *The Buddhist Unconscious: The Ālaya-vijñāna in the Context of Indian Buddhist Thought.* New York and London, 2003. Treats the antecedents to an early development of the *ālaya-vijñāna,* up to Asaṅga's *Mahāyāna-saṃgraha.*

William S. Waldron (2005)

AL-AZHAR. Literally al-Azhar means "most luminous" (an allusion to the prophet Muḥammad's daughter Fāṭima, nicknamed al-Zahrā', the eponymous ancestor of the Fāṭimids). Al-Azhar is the world's oldest mosque-university and Sunnī Islam's foremost seat of learning. Following his conquest of Egypt, Jawhar, the Sicilian commander of the army sent by the Fāṭimid caliph-*imām* al-Muʿizz li-Dīn Allāh (r. 953–975 CE) from North Africa, founded this mosque on Saturday, 24 Jumādā I 359/April 4, 970 CE, after having laid the foundations of a new capital, Cairo (*al-Qāhira,* meaning "the victorious"). Al-Azhar, situated near the royal palace at the southeast corner, was intended to serve as the official congregation mosque of the new dynasty, which was competing with the ʿAbbāsid caliphs of Baghdad for control of the Muslim world. The first Friday prayer in the mosque was inaugurated during Ramaḍān 972 CE. In addition to being a house of worship and a sanctuary like most major mosques, it soon became a place of learning. Except for the eighty-year rule of the Ayyūbids (1171–1252), who supplanted the Fāṭimids, al-Azhar has remained throughout the centuries a focal point of Islamic religious and cultural life not only for Egypt but also for the entire Muslim world.

During the early period of Islamic history, memorization of the Qurʾān, the study of *ḥadīth* (traditions of the

Prophet), and the science of jurisprudence (*fiqh*) were conducted in the mosque. The mosque was therefore the first stage in the development of the college in Islam. Al-Shāfiʿī (d. 820 CE), for example, taught various subjects in the mosque of ʿAmr b. al-ʿĀṣ. Most of those mosque-based institutions of learning became extinct over a period of time. Al-Azhar, however, continued to flourish, developed into a college, and became a university.

HISTORICAL DEVELOPMENT. Information about the curriculum in the early years of the Fāṭimids and the Mamlūks is fragmentary. However, from the available sources one could infer that Shīʿī–Ismāʿīlī law was regularly taught there. Al-Maqrīzī (d. 1442), a noted historian who had access to earlier sources and contemporary documents that are no longer extant, stated that the chief judge and chief missionary ʿAlī, the son of al-Qāḍī al-Nuʿmān, the founder of Ismāʿīlī jurisprudence, sat in al-Azhar and lectured his audience on Ismāʿīlī law. Lecturing soon became dictation when the students began to write down what was said. Subsequently ʿAlī dictated his father's *Kitāb al-Iqtiṣār*, an abridged version of Ismāʿīlī law, to a large gathering. Ibn Killis, the vizier of the Fāṭimid caliph-*imām* al-ʿAzīz (r. 975–996 CE), was the first to establish al-Azhar as a regular institution of learning where Ismāʿīlī law was taught. The vizier, who was known for his patronage of scholars, poets, and jurists, obtained a royal decree to build a large house near the mosque to provide living quarters for thirty-five jurists in addition to their salaries. On Fridays, between the midday and afternoon prayers, those jurists sat in the mosque surrounded by circles of listeners and instructed them in matters of religion and law. Describing the Fāṭimid palaces where "the sessions of wisdom" (*majālis al-ḥikma*) were held, al-Maqrīzī stated that separate sessions of wisdom for women were held in al-Azhar. In Ramaḍān 1010 the caliph-*imām* al-Ḥākim provided large endowments for the maintenance of this mosque. Al-Maqrīzī preserved the official decree with all the details. Besides endowments, rich individuals, princes, and princesses made gifts and bequests. Thus one can conclude that during the Fāṭimid rule al-Azhar had already become an important mosque and *madrasah*, a college of higher studies.

The Sunnī Ayyūbids who terminated Fāṭimid rule not only neglected al-Azhar but supplanted it by creating Sunnī *madrasahs* under their patronage to stamp out all traces of Shīʿī Fāṭimid influence. During the Mamlūk period al-Azhar regained its central place. Al-Malik al-Ẓāhir Baybars (r. 1260–1277) repaired the mosque, and the Friday sermon was resumed 1266. *Amīr* Bīlbak al-Khāzindār provided funds to support a group of jurists to teach Shāfiʿī law, a *muḥaddith* to instruct the people about proper conduct based on the traditions of the Prophet and about the spiritual doctrines of Islam, seven Qurʾān reciters (according to the seven authorized methods of recitation) to recite and teach the Qurʾān, and a *mudarris* (professor of law) for overall supervision. Women were permitted to study in the mosque.

In 1359–1360 a Qurʾanic school for orphans and a course on Ḥanafī law were initiated. Al-Maqrīzī stated that in 1415–1416 the number of indigent students, both provincial and foreign, residing in quarters around the mosque and grouped according to their provinces and nationalities (*riwāqs*), was 750. Subjects taught included the art of reciting the Qurʾān, jurisprudence of the four Sunnī schools of law, the traditions of the Prophet, exegesis of the Qurʾān, Arabic language and grammar, and preaching. At times *dhikr* sessions (literally "remembering God," a religious service common to all the mystical fraternities) were also held. The famous historian Ibn Khaldūn (d. 1406) taught at al-Azhar when he arrived in Cairo in 1383. Generous endowments and gifts from notables provided the funds for these activities.

Although the center of gravity during the Ottoman period (1517–1805) shifted to Istanbul, al-Azhar remained the preeminent seat of Arabic and Islamic learning. Probably toward the end of the seventeenth century the position of *Shaykh al-Azhar* (rector or grand *imām*) was created to preside over the affairs of al-Azhar. The position was generally filled by a leading member of the *ʿulamāʾ*. Shaykh Muḥammad ʿAbd Allāh al-Khurashī (d. 1690), a Mālikī jurist, was the first to hold this office. Al-Azhar had neither formal procedures for admissions nor grade levels, it had no required courses and no written examinations, and it did not grant official diplomas. However, a student could obtain a certificate (*ijāza*) of proficiency from his or her teacher upon completion of a prescribed course of study. Professors lectured at different corners of the mosque, and the students gathered around them. Memorization played an important part. The curriculum, in addition to Arabic language and grammar, consisted mainly of theology and law. Priorities were given to the above-mentioned religious sciences, the acquisition of which would guarantee one's success in the hereafter. Although the rational sciences were not rejected, they were neglected. Many Azharīs were also active Ṣūfīs. For them pursuing rational sciences was not conducive to cultivating a pious spiritual life. Learning and teaching therefore remained traditional.

As legal and religious authorities, Azharī scholars were greatly respected by the people, hence they exerted immense influence over the masses. At times they championed the rights of the Egyptian exploited classes and acted as mediators between the rulers and the ruled. During the French occupation of Egypt (1798–1801) al-Azhar not only acted as an intermediary between the Egyptian masses and the foreign occupiers but also became a rallying point for revolt against the French. As a result it was bombarded, occupied, and desecrated. Al-Jabartī (d. c. 1825) left a vivid description of those events.

AL-AZHAR BETWEEN REFORM AND RESISTANCE. The long campaign to subordinate al-Azhar to the state began with the rise of Muḥammad ʿAlī to power (1805–1848). He confiscated many of its endowments, fixed government stipends, and chose the rectors himself. His reforms, particularly the founding of numerous secular schools and technical institutions and the sending of missions to Europe for higher study, woke al-Azhar from its deep slumber. Government interference with the affairs of al-Azhar continued under the subsequent Khedive rulers. In 1872 Khedive Ismāʿīl installed the first non-Shāfiʿī rector in over a century and instituted a rigorous oral examination in various subjects for candidates who wished to teach at al-Azhar. In 1876 al-Azhar had 361 teachers and 10,780 students. Among the four Sunnī schools of law, Shāfiʿīs represented the largest number, followed by Mālikīs and Ḥanafīs, whereas the Ḥanbalīs were poorly represented. In 1885 a formal system of registration of students in each residential quarter was instituted. New students who had not completed certain requirements during two years of study were not eligible to receive their ration of food. Attendance was accurately recorded. During the 1890s a central library was founded with a rich collection of manuscripts, a salary scale for teachers was established, and a countrywide network of preparatory religious institutions under the care of al-Azhar was established.

During the 1930s al-Azhar became a modern university with the College of Theology, the College of Law, and the College of Arabic Language, each with a state-appointed dean. Soon all three colleges were moved to new buildings behind the mosque. The curriculum was clearly described. Postgraduate work of two to three years was established for specializations in Islamic law, preaching, and guidance. A student was required to pass written and oral examinations and present a thesis for the postgraduate degree. For the title of "professor" (*ustādh*), an equivalent of a Ph.D., more graduate work, a passing grade on a difficult examination, and a substantial thesis were required. The diploma granted at the end of four years of undergraduate study was called *shahādat al-dirāsa al-ʿāliya*, the certificate of specialization was called *al-shahāda al-ʿālimīya maʿ al-ijāza*, and the highest diploma, similar to that of a doctorate, was called *al-shahāda al-ʿālimīya maʿ darajat ustādh.*

In 1930 al-Azhar acquired its own press and started publishing a journal, the *Light of Islam*; a few years later the title was changed to *Journal of al-Azhar.* The university's Preaching and Guidance section dispatched preachers and lecturers throughout Egypt. More reforms were carried out under the reign of Jamāl ʿAbd al-Nāṣir. The Islamic Research Academy, the Department of Cultural and Islamic Missions, and the Supreme Council under the *shaykh al-Azhar* were established. The curriculum of all the colleges was revised; for example, non-*sharīʿa* law and Shīʿī-Imāmī law (called *fiqh Jaʿfarī*, after Imām Jaʿfar al-Ṣādiq) were added to the College of Law, and courses on social sciences and Western languages were added to the College of Theology. In addition to establishing the women's colleges, al-Azhar university's legislation of 1961 created new colleges of engineering, medicine, commerce, science, agriculture, and education. These new colleges were not duplicates of their counterparts in secular universities; rather they combined both the empirical as well as the religious sciences. A new campus was built in the suburb of Madīnat al-Naṣr, away from the mosque. Besides its main campus in Cairo, al-Azhar also operates several campuses throughout Egypt. Admission is open to all Muslim students who wish to study a particular academic discipline or to further and deepen their knowledge of Islam.

Outside of Egypt al-Azhar is known as a champion of Sunnī Islam and the Arabic language. Azharī professors and preachers are in demand throughout the Islamic world. The number of foreign students at al-Azhar in 1955 reached more than four thousand, while in 1990 that number peaked at six thousand, representing seventy-five countries.

Because al-Azhar shunned Islamist activists like Jamāl al-Dīn al-Afghānī, Muḥammad ʿAbduh, and Rashīd Riḍā, some people consider it a conservative institution, whereas many Islamists disparage it as subservient to the state. On the other hand, Islamists approve of al-Azhar's condemnation of controversial books. In the 1920s it stripped ʿAlī ʿAbd al-Rāziq of his Azharī degree for reinterpreting the Islamic caliphate as a secular institution. Ṭāhā Ḥusayn was forced to withdraw his provocative book on pre-Islamic poetry. A number of other books were banned or condemned. Shaykh Muḥammad Sayyid Ṭanṭāwī (b. 1928) assumed the leadership position on March 27, 1996. Prior to this appointment he served as *muftī* of Egypt from 1986 to 1996. He is known for his courage in airing his frank views on various issues confronting the Muslim world. His statement in support of the right of the French government to prohibit Muslim women from wearing the *ḥijāb* (head covering) in public schools provoked strong opposition.

BIBLIOGRAPHY

Taqī al-Dīn Ahmad al-Maqrīzī is the main source of information from al-Azhar's foundation to the Mamlūk period. Shihāb al-Dīn Ahmad al-Qalqshandī (d. 1418), a secretary in the chancery of the Mamlūk administration, citing the earlier authority Amīr Mukhtār Muḥammad al-Muṣabbiḥī (d. 1030), a court chronicler of the Fāṭimid caliph al-Ḥākim, confirms al-Maqrīzī's reports. Life at al-Azhar during the nineteenth century is vividly described by ʿAlī al-Mubārak in Arabic and by Stanley Lane-Poole and Edward Lane in English. ʿAbd al-Rahmān Jabartī, ʿAlī al-Mubārak, and later authors give a complete list of the officeholders of *shaykh al-Azhar.* ʿAbd al-Mutʿāl al-Ṣaʿīdī, who was an Azharī *shaykh* and taught in the College of Arabic Language, gives the most interesting account of reforms until 1950. An extensive bibliography of these older sources as well as new studies is provided by J. Jomier, "Al-Azhar," in *The Encyclopaedia of Islam*, new ed. (Leiden, 1960–). Al-Maqrīzī's *Ittiʿ āẓ al-ḥunafāʾ bi-akhbār al-aʾimma ʾl-Fāṭimiyyīn al-khulafāʾ*, edited by Jamāl al-Dīn al-Shayyāl and Muḥammad Ḥilmī (Cairo, 1967–1973); and George Makdisi, *The Rise of Colleges: Institutions of Learning in Islam and the West* (Edinburgh, 1981), should be consulted. For the modern period and a selected bibliography, mostly in English, see Donald M. Reid, "Al-Azhar," in *The Oxford Encyclopedia of the Modern Islamic World*, edited by John L. Esposito (New York, 1995).

ISMAIL K. POONAWALA (2005)

ALBERTUS MAGNUS (c. 1200–1280), also known as Albert the Great; German Dominican theologian and philosopher, doctor of the church, patron of natural scientists, and Christian saint. Today he is best known as the teacher of Thomas Aquinas.

Born in Lauingen on the Danube in Bavaria, Albert belonged to a distinguished military family in the service of the Hohenstaufens. While a student at Padua, he entered the mendicant Order of Preachers (Dominicans) in spring 1223, receiving the religious habit from Jordan of Saxony, successor to Dominic. Assigned to Cologne, he completed his early theological studies in 1228, then taught at Cologne, Hildesheim, Freiburg, Regensburg, and Strassburg. Around 1241 he was sent by the master general to the University of Paris for his degree in theology, which he obtained in the summer of 1245, having lectured on the *Sentences* of Peter Lombard and begun writing his *Summa parisiensis* in six parts: the sacraments, the incarnation, the resurrection, the four coevals, man, and good. In 1248 Albert returned to Cologne with Thomas Aquinas and a group of Dominican students to open a center of studies for Germany.

Toward the end of 1249, Albert acceded to the pleas of his students to explain Aristotle's philosophy. His intention was, first, to present the whole of natural science, even parts that Aristotle did not write about or that had been lost, and, second, to make all the books of Aristotle "intelligible to the Latins" by rephrasing arguments, adding new ones from his own experience, and resolving new difficulties encountered by other schools of philosophy, notably the Platonist and Epicurean schools.

From 1252 until 1279 Albert was frequently called upon to arbitrate difficult litigations on behalf of the pope or emperor. In June 1254 he was elected prior provincial of the German province of the Dominican order for three years. The most important event during Albert's term of office was the struggle for survival between the mendicant orders and the secular clergy from the University of Paris. With Bonaventure and Humbert of Romans in 1256, he represented the mendicant orders at the papal curia at Anagni against William of Saint-Amour and his colleagues from Paris. The controversy was resolved in favor of the mendicants and the condemnation of William's book on October 5, 1256. Also during Albert's term as provincial he wrote his paraphrases of Aristotle's *On the Soul* (Albert considered this paraphrase one of his most important), *On Natural Phenomena,* and *On Plants.*

Resigning as provincial in June 1257, Albert returned to teaching in Cologne, but he was appointed bishop of Regensburg by Pope Alexander IV on January 5, 1260, much against his inclinations. He was at the episcopal castle on the Danube when he wrote his commentary on book 7 of *On Animals,* but in December he set out for the papal curia at Viterbo to submit his resignation. The new pope, Urban IV, accepted his resignation around November 1261, and a successor was confirmed in May 1262. From February 1263 to October 1264 he was the official papal preacher throughout German-speaking lands for a crusade to the Holy Land. With the death of Urban IV, Albert's commission ended, and he retired to Würzburg, where he worked on paraphrases of Aristotle's *Metaphysics* and other works until 1269, when Master General John of Vercelli asked him to reside at the studium in Cologne as lector emeritus. From then until his death, Albert lived at Cologne, writing, performing para-episcopal duties, arbitrating difficult cases, and serving as an example of religious piety to all. His last will, dated January 1279, testified that he was "of sound mind and body," but from August on he seems to have become progressively senile until his death on November 15, 1280, at the age of "eighty and some."

DOCTRINE AND INFLUENCE. In recent centuries Albert has been presented as a magician or an eclectic encyclopedist with Platonic and mystical tendencies. His writings are said to defy analysis, not only because of their gigantic bulk but also because of their nature in most cases as paraphrases of mainly Aristotle's writings. Although Albert was a bishop who wrote many theological works and biblical commentaries, he was known in his own day principally as a philosopher, and his authority ranked with that of Aristotle, Ibn Sīnā (Avicenna), and Ibn Rushd (Averroës). Roger Bacon, a younger Franciscan contemporary, complained that such pretensions were unbecoming to anyone who was still living and in fact self-taught. But it was precisely to obviate such suspicions that Albert disavowed originality in his writings by referring readers back to original sources by name, to experience, and to human reason.

Albert was the only Scholastic to be called "the Great," a title that was used even before his death. His prestige continued to be recognized not only among Albertists in France and Germany in the fifteenth century, but also among philosophers of the Italian Renaissance in the sixteenth century. Among his immediate students, apart from Thomas and Ulrich, were Hugh of Strassburg, John of Freiburg, John of Lichtenburg, and Giles of Lessines. Other German Dominicans, more favorably disposed toward Platonism, developed the mystical elements in Albert's thought. These were transmitted through Theodoric of Freiberg and Berthold of Mossburg to Meister Eckhart, Johannes Tauler, Heinrich Süse, and Jan van Ruusbroec. In the early fifteenth century a distinctive school of Albertists (who opposed the Thomists) developed in Paris under Jean de Maisonneuve and was promoted by Heymerich van den Velde in Paris and Cologne. It quickly spread throughout German, Bohemian, and Polish universities; in Italian universities, however, it was the philosophical opinions of Albert himself that were kept alive.

Numerous miracles were attributed to Albert, and many spurious works—devotional, necromantic, and Scholastic—were ascribed to him. Late in the fifteenth century his cause for canonization was well advanced until charges of sorcery and magic were raised; to refute these, Peter of Prussia wrote the first really critical biography of Albert (about 1487). The

Protestant Reformation in the early sixteenth century temporarily diverted interest in Albert. He was quietly beatified by Gregory XV in 1622.

His extensive writings, occupying more than forty volumes in the critical edition (Cologne, 1951ff.), touch the whole of theology and scripture, as well as almost every branch of human knowledge in the Middle Ages, such as logic, natural science, mathematics, astronomy, ethics, and metaphysics. Ulrich of Strassburg, a Dominican disciple, described him as "a man so superior in every science that he can fittingly be called the wonder and miracle of our time." Siger of Brabant, a young contemporary of Thomas Aquinas at Paris, considered Albert and Thomas to be "the principal men in philosophy."

Albert is best known for his belief in (1) the importance of philosophy for theology and (2) the autonomy of each science in its own field by reason of proper principles and method. He paraphrased the whole of Aristotle's philosophy for beginners in theology (1249–1270); he taught and promoted philosophy in his own school of theology (1248–1260); and he chaired the Dominican commission of five masters established to draw up the first program of study in the order that made the study of philosophy mandatory (1259). He never tired of promoting secular learning for the clergy and denouncing lazy friars who did no more than criticize others. As for his view of the sciences, he defended the ability of human reason to know natural truths distinct from revelation and divine faith; he promoted and cultivated the study of the natural sciences distinct from metaphysics; and he considered mathematics an autonomous field that was simply a tool for natural science, not its organizing principle, as it was for the Platonists. In philosophy Albert was a moderate realist and fundamentally an Aristotelian, but he did not hesitate to reject certain statements when he thought Aristotle was in error, nor was he averse to incorporating into his Aristotelianism compatible truths expounded by others.

By the decree *In thesauris sapientiae* (December 15, 1931), Pius XI declared Albert a saint with the additional title of doctor. By the decree Ad Deum (December 16, 1941), Pius XII constituted him the heavenly patron of all who cultivate the natural sciences. His body is buried in Cologne, and his feast is observed on November 15.

Bibliography

Apart from numerous early printed editions of both authentic and spurious writings ascribed to Albert, two editions of his "complete works" have been published: one in twenty-one folio volumes edited by Pierre Jammy, O.P. (Lyons, 1651), the other in thirty-eight quarto volumes edited by Auguste Borgnet (Paris, 1890–1899). A third, critical edition, under the auspices of the Albertus-Magnus-Institut of Cologne, is now being issued (Münster, 1951–) and is projected at forty volumes. The only authentic work of Albert available in English is his *Book of Minerals,* translated by Dorothy Wyckoff (Oxford, 1967).

Consecutive bibliographies are provided by three complementary works: "Essai de bibliographie albertinienne," by M.-H. Laurent and Yves Congar, *Revue thomiste* 36 (1931): 422–462, covering works published up to 1930; "Bibliographie philosophique de saint Albert le Grand," by M. Schooyans, *Revista da Universidade Católica de São Paulo* 21 (1961): 36–88, covering the years from 1931 to 1960; and "Bibliographie," in *Albertus Magnus: Doctor Universalis 1280/1980,* edited by G. Meyer and A. Zimmerman (Mainz, 1980), covering the years from 1960 to 1980.

Among the basic modern studies that should be noted are Paulus von Loë's "De vita et scriptis B. Alberti Magni," *Analecta Bollandiana* 19 (1900), 20 (1901), and 21 (1902); Gilles Meersseman's *Introductio in opera omnia B. Alberti Magni* (Bruges, 1931); Franz Pelster's *Kritische Studien zum Leben und zu den Schriften Alberts des Grossen* (Freiburg, 1920); and H. C. Scheeben's *Albert der Grosse: Zur Chronologie seines Lebens* (Vechta, 1931).

English biographies and studies that can be consulted with profit are Hieronymus Wilms's *Albert the Great, Saint and Doctor of the Church* (London, 1933), Thomas M. Schwertner's *Saint Albert the Great* (New York, 1932), and Lynn Thorndike's *A History of Magic and Experimental Science,* vol. 2 (Baltimore, 1923), pp. 517–592, 692–750. Noteworthy too is *Albertus Magnus and the Sciences: Commemorative Essays, 1980,* a collection of writings edited by me (Toronto, 1980).

James A. Weisheipl (1987)

ALBIGENSIANS See CATHARI

ALBO, YOSEF

ALBO, YOSEF (fl. fifteenth century), Spanish Jewish philosopher. Albo was a student of the last major medieval Jewish philosopher, Ḥasdai Crescas (1340–1410), and a defender of Judaism in the Disputation of Tortosa (1413–1414). He is known for his *Sefer ha-ʿiqqarim* (The book of principles), which owes its popularity to an easy style (with multiple homiletical digressions) and a moderately conservative theological stance.

As its name indicates, *Sefer ha-ʿiqqarim* deals with dogmatics, a common theme in fifteenth-century Jewish thought. Albo took issue with Moses Maimonides (1135/8–1204), who had proposed thirteen principles of faith, and with Crescas, who had listed six. Apparently borrowing from his contemporary Shimʿon ben Tsemaḥ Duran (1361–1444), Albo reduced the principles of any divine religion to three: the existence of God, divine revelation, and reward and punishment. These major principles entail eight further derivative principles. The existence of God implies belief in his unity, incorporeality, independence of time, and freedom from defects. Revelation includes the principles of God's knowledge, prophecy, and the authenticity of God's messenger. Reward and punishment entail belief in individual providence. Thus, in reality, there are eleven principles of divine religion. In addition, Judaism teaches six specific articles of faith: creation ex nihilo, the superiority of Moses to other prophets, the continued validity of the Torah of Moses, the attainment of human perfection by the observance of even one of the commandments, resurrection, and the coming of the Messiah. An examination of the nature of these principles and beliefs forms the bulk of *Sefer ha-ʿiqqarim.*

Albo's work is best understood against the background of the physical and spiritual crisis of fifteenth-century Spanish Jewry. There were many Jews at that time who felt that no religion was rationally superior to another, and that loyalty to Judaism was therefore a superfluous encumbrance. Addressing himself to this attitude, Albo sets out to show that Judaism is preferable to Christianity. While reason cannot prove the truth of Judaism, it can demonstrate the falseness of Christianity; by examining the criteria that reason demands of any religion claiming to be divine, Albo attempts to demonstrate that Christianity falls short of the mark (especially in regard to God's unity and incorporeality) and hence cannot be considered a divine religion. In addition, Christians are required to hold beliefs that are logically impossible and, therefore, false. At most, Albo claims, Christianity is a conventional religion, one that promotes societal well-being but not individual immortality. Judaism, on the other hand, fits the requirements of a divine religion exactly, in that it adheres to the three principles as he has defined them. In addition, it includes no beliefs that are contrary to logic. Loyalty to Judaism is thus the reasonable course of action for the wavering Jew. Over and over, Albo subtly polemicizes against the majority religion and then, for good measure, devotes a lengthy chapter to a specific rebuttal of Christianity (which, despite its form, is not an account of an actual disputation).

In addition to its polemical value, Albo's work provides a *summa* of medieval Jewish philosophy, discussing all the major philosophical and theological issues that had been raised in the previous five hundred years. Albo was not a doctrinaire member of any particular philosophical school; he took liberally from his predecessors without fully adopting the system of any of them. On most questions Albo tends toward eclecticism and compromise. For instance, he first agrees with Maimonides that only active and negative attributes can be assigned to God, but then he switches to Crescas's view that there are some essential attributes also. Prophecy is totally dependent upon God's will (the traditional view), but the prophet must have the requisite rational faculties in order to prophesy (the philosophical view). Human perfection consists of the realization of intellectual potential (the philosophical view), but immortality depends on doing God's will as outlined in the Torah (the traditional view).

Albo's *Sefer ha-ʿiqqarim* has been published often and has maintained its popularity in traditional Jewish circles to this day.

Bibliography

Albo's major work was published in a critical edition of the Hebrew text with English translation, notes, and indexes by Isaac Husik under the title *Sefer ha-ʿIkkarim: Book of Principles,* 5 vols. (Philadelphia, 1929). Eliezer Schweid edited a condensed version of the book with a useful introduction (in Hebrew), *Sefer ha-ʿiqqarim le-Rabbi Yosef Albo* (Jerusalem, 1967), pp. 7–30. A discussion of Albo's attitude to natural law can be found in Ralph Lerner's essay "Natural Law in Albo's *Book of Roots,*" in *Ancients and Moderns,* edited by Joseph Cropsey (New York, 1964), pp. 132–148. For further analysis of Albo's thought, see my article (in Hebrew with an English summary) "Joseph Albo's Theory of Verification," *Daʿat* 5 (Summer 1980): 5–12.

New Sources

Harvey, Warren Zev. "Albo on the Reasonlessness of True Love" (in Hebrew). *Iyyun* 49 (2000): 83–86.

Rauschenbach, Sina. *Josef Albo (um 1380–1444): jüdische Philosophie und christliche Kontroverstheologie in der frühen Neuzeit.* Studies in European Judaism, vol. 3. Leiden and Boston, 2002.

Shatz, David Freedom. "Repentance and Hardening of the Hearts: Albo vs. Maimonides." *Faith and Philosophy* 14 (1997): 478–509.

Daniel J. Lasker (1987)
Revised Bibliography

ALCHEMY

This entry consists of the following articles:

AN OVERVIEW
CHINESE ALCHEMY
INDIAN ALCHEMY
HELLENISTIC AND MEDIEVAL ALCHEMY
ISLAMIC ALCHEMY
RENAISSANCE ALCHEMY

ALCHEMY: AN OVERVIEW

The vocable *alchemia* (or some alternate form such as *ars chemica*) appears in the West from the twelfth century onward in reference to the medieval quest for a means of transmuting base metals into gold, for a universal cure, and for the "elixir of immortality." The origin of the root *chem* is not yet satisfactorily explained. In Chinese, Indian, and Greek texts alchemy is referred to as "the Art," or by terms indicating radical and beneficial change, for example, *transmutation.* Until quite recently, historians of science have studied alchemy as a protochemistry, that is, an embryonic science. Indeed, like the early chemist, the practitioner of "the Art" made use of a laboratory and of certain specific instruments; more important, alchemists were the authors of a number of discoveries that later played roles in the development of the science of chemistry. To quote only a few examples: the isolation of mercury around 300 BCE; the discovery of *aqua vitae* (alcohol) and of the mineral acids, both before the thirteenth century; the preparation of vitriol and the alums.

But the methods, the ideology, and the goals of the early chemists did not prolong the alchemical heritage. The alchemists were not interested—or only subsidiarily—in the scientific study of nature. Where the early Greek mind applies itself to science it evinces an extraordinary sense of observation and argument. Yet the Greek alchemists show an inexplicable lack of interest in the physico-chemical phenomena of their work. To cite a single example, no one who has ever used sulfur could fail to observe "the curious phenomena which attend its fusion and the subsequent heating of the liquid. Now, while sulphur is mentioned hundreds of times [in Greek alchemical texts], there is no allusion to any of its characteristic properties except its action on metals" (Sherwood Taylor, quoted in Eliade, 1978, p. 147). As we shall see presently, the alchemist's quest was not scientific but spiritual.

ESOTERIC TRADITIONS AND THE IMPORTANCE OF SECRECY. In every culture where alchemy has flourished, it has always been intimately related to an esoteric or "mystical" tradition: in China to Taoism, in India to Yoga and Tantrism, in Hellenistic Egypt to *gnōsis,* in Islamic countries to Hermetic and esoteric mystical schools, in the Western Middle Ages and Renaissance to Hermetism, Christian and sectarian mysticism, and Qabbalah. In brief, all alchemists have proclaimed their art to be an esoteric technique pursuing a goal similar or comparable to that of the major esoteric and "mystical" traditions.

For this reason, great emphasis is placed by the alchemist on secrecy, that is, the esoteric transmission of alchemical doctrines and techniques. The oldest Hellenistic text, *Physikē kai mystikē* (probably written around 200 BCE), relates how this book was discovered hidden in a column of an Egyptian temple. In the prologue to one of the classical Indian alchemical treatises, *Rasārnava,* the Goddess asks Śiva for the secret of becoming a *jīvanmuleta,* that is, one "liberated in life." Śiva tells her that this secret is seldom known, even among the gods. Again, the importance of secrecy is emphasized by the most famous Chinese alchemist, Ko Hung (260–340 CE), who stated that "secrecy is thrown over the efficacious recipes. . . . The substances referred to are commonplaces which nevertheless cannot be identified without knowledge of the code concerned" (*Pao-p'u-tzu,* chap. 16). The deliberate incomprehensibility of alchemical texts for the noninitiate becomes almost a cliché in Western post-Renaissance alchemical literature. An author quoted by the fifteenth-century *Rosarium philosophorum* declares that "only he who knows how to make the Philosophers' Stone understands the words which relate to it." And the *Rosarium* warns the reader that these questions must be transmitted "mystically," just as poetry uses fables and parables. In short, we are confronted with a secret language. According to some authorities, there was even an oath not to divulge the secret in books (texts quoted in Eliade, 1978, p. 164).

The stages of the alchemical opus constitute an initiation, a series of specific experiences aimed at the radical transformation of the human condition. But the successful initiate cannot adequately express his new mode of being in a profane language. He is compelled to use a "secret language." Of course, secrecy was a general rule with almost all techniques and sciences in their early stages—from pottery, mining, and metallurgy to medicine and mathematics. The secret transmission of methods, tools, and recipes is abundantly documented in China and in India, as well as in the ancient Near East and Greece. Even so late an author as Galen warns one of his disciples that the medical knowledge that he communicates must be received as an aspirant receives the *teletē* (initiation) in the Eleusinian mysteries. As a matter of fact, being introduced into the secrets of a craft, of a technique, or of a science was tantamount to undergoing an initiation.

It is significant that the injunction to secrecy and occultation is *not* abolished by the successful accomplishment of the alchemical work. According to Ko Hung, the adepts who obtain the elixir and become "immortals" (*hsien*) continue to wander on earth, but they conceal their condition, that is, their immortality, and are recognized as such only by a few fellow alchemists. Likewise, in India there is a vast literature, both in Sanskrit and in the vernaculars, in relation to certain famous *siddhis,* yogin-alchemists who live for centuries but who seldom disclose their identity. One encounters the same belief in central and western Europe: certain Hermetists and alchemists (such as Nicolas Flamel and his wife, Pernelle) were reputed to have lived indefinitely without being recognized by their contemporaries. In the seventeenth century a similar legend circulated about the Rosicrucians and, in the following century, on a more popular level, in relation to the mysterious Comte de Saint-Germain.

ORIGINS OF ALCHEMY. The objects of the alchemical quest—namely, health and longevity, transmutation of base metals into gold, production of the elixir of immortality—have a long prehistory in the East as well as in the West. Significantly, this prehistory reveals a specific mythico-religious structure. Innumerable myths, for instance, tell of a spring, a tree, a plant, or some other substance capable of bestowing longevity, rejuvenation, or even immortality. Now, in all alchemical traditions, but particularly in Chinese alchemy, specific plants and fruits play an important role in the art of prolonging life and recovering perennial youth.

But the central aim of the alchemist was the transformation of ordinary metals into gold. This "noble" metal was imbued with sacrality. According to the Egyptians, the flesh of gods and of pharaohs was made of gold. In ancient India, a text from the eighth century BCE (*Śatapatha Brāhmaṇa* 3.8.2.27) proclaims that "gold is immortality." Interpreting alchemy as a mere technique for "turning base metals into precious ones," that is, for *imitating* gold, H. H. Dubs has suggested that the technique originated during the fourth century BCE in China, where the test for gold (which had been practiced in Mesopotamia since the fourteenth century BCE) was unknown. This hypothesis has been rejected, however, by most scholars. According to Nathan Sivin, the belief in physical immortality is documented in China by the eighth century BCE, but not until the fourth century was immortality considered attainable through the use of drugs and other techniques, and "the transformation of cinnabar into gold is not spoken of as possible, according to extant sources, before 133 BC " (Sivin, 1968, p. 25).

Mining, Metallurgy, and Alchemy. Even if the historical beginnings of alchemy are as yet obscure, parallels between certain alchemical beliefs and rituals and those of early miners and metallurgists are clear. Indeed, all these techniques reflect the idea that man can influence the temporal flux. Mineral substances, hidden in the womb of Mother Earth, shared in the sacredness attached to the goddess. Very early we are confronted with the idea that ores "grow" in the belly of the earth after the manner of embryos. Metallurgy thus takes on the character of obstetrics. The miner and metalworker intervene in the unfolding of subterranean embryology: they accelerate the rhythm of the growth of ores; they collaborate in the work of nature and assist it in giving birth more rapidly. In a word, man, with his various techniques, gradually takes the place of time: his labors replace the work of time.

With the help of fire, metalworkers transform the ores (the "embryos") into metals (the "adults"). The underlying belief is that, given enough time, the ores would have become "pure" metals in the womb of Mother Earth. Further, the "pure" metals would have become gold if they had been allowed to "grow" undisturbed for a few more thousand years. Such beliefs are well known in many traditional societies. As early as the second century BCE, Chinese alchemists declared that the "baser" minerals develop after many years into "nobler" minerals, and finally become silver or gold. Similar beliefs are shared by a number of Southeast Asian populations. For instance, the Annamites were convinced that the gold found in mines is formed slowly *in situ* over the course of centuries, and that if one had probed the earth long ago, one would have discovered bronze in the place where gold is found today.

These beliefs survived in western Europe until the industrial revolution. In the seventeenth century one Western alchemist wrote:

> If there were no exterior obstacles to the execution of her designs, Nature would always complete what she wishes to produce. . . . That is why we have to look upon the birth of imperfect metals as we would on abortions and freaks which come about only because Nature has been, as it were, misdirected or because she has encountered some fettering resistance or certain obstacles which prevent her from behaving in her accustomed way. . . . Hence although she wishes to produce only one metal, she finds herself constrained to create several. Gold and only gold is the child of her desires. Gold is her legitimate son because only gold is a genuine production of her efforts. (quoted in Eliade, 1978, p. 50)

The Alchemist Completes the Work of Nature. The transmutation of base metals into gold is tantamount to a miraculously rapid maturation. As Simone da Colonia put it: "This Art teaches us to make a remedy called the Elixir, which, being poured on imperfect metals, perfects them completely, and it is for this reason that it was invented" (quoted in Eliade, 1978, p. 166). The same idea is clearly expounded by Ben Jonson in his play *The Alchemist* (1610). One character says that "lead and other metals . . . would be gold if they had time," and another adds, "And that our Art doth further."

Moreover, the elixir is said to be capable of accelerating the temporal rhythm of all organisms and thus of quickening their growth. In a text erroneously attributed to Ramón Lull, one can read that "in Spring, by its great and marvelous heat, the Stone brings life to the plants: if thou dissolve the equivalent of a grain of salt in water, taking from this water enough to fill a nutshell, and then if thou water with it a vinestock, thy vinestock will bring forth ripe grapes in May" (quoted in Ganzenmüller, 1940, p. 159). Furthermore, Chinese as well as Islamic and Western alchemists exalted the elixir for its universal therapeutic virtues: it was said to cure all maladies, to restore youth to the old, and to prolong life by several centuries.

Alchemy and Mastery of Time. Thus it seems that the central secret of "the Art" is related to the alchemist's mastery of cosmic and human time. The early miners and metallurgists thought that, with the help of fire, they could speed up the growth of ores. The alchemists were more ambitious: they thought they could "heal" base metals and accelerate their "maturation," thereby transmuting them into nobler metals and finally into gold. But the alchemists went even further: their elixir was reputed to heal and to rejuvenate men as well, indefinitely prolonging their lives. In the alchemist's eyes, man is *creative:* he redeems nature, masters time; in sum, he perfects God's creation. The myth of alchemy is an optimistic myth; it constitutes, as it were, a "natural eschatology."

It is certainly this conception of man, as an imaginative and inexhaustibly creative being, that explains the survival of the alchemist's ideals in nineteenth-century ideology. Of course, these ideals were radically secularized in that period. Moreover, the fact that they had survived was not immediately evident at the moment when alchemy itself disappeared. Yet the triumph of experimental science did not abolish the dreams and ideals of the alchemist; on the contrary, the new ideology of the nineteenth century crystallized around the myth of infinite progress. Boosted by the development of the experimental sciences and the progress of industrialization, this ideology took up and carried forward—radical secularization notwithstanding—the millenarian dream of the alchemist. The myth of the perfection and redemption of nature has survived in camouflaged form in the Promethean program of industrialized societies, whose aim is the transformation of nature, and especially the transmutation of matter into energy. It was also in the nineteenth century that man succeeded in supplanting time. His desire to accelerate the natural tempo of organic and inorganic beings now began to be realized, as organic chemists demonstrated the possibility of accelerating and even eliminating time by preparing in laboratories and factories substances that would have taken nature thousands of years to produce. With what

SACRED TIME

Time takes many different forms, and one of the primary tasks of visual culture in religious life is to articulate and maintain particular forms of time. Tracing the descent of one's people, customs, or teachers is common. The portrait of a Tibetan lama or teacher shown here **(a)** is surrounded by a long lineage of Indian and Tibetan *gurūs*. These figures include in the center, perched above the large figure, the historical Buddha himself, the source of knowledge and spiritual authority that extends through the generations of Buddhist sages to the large figure who now assumes the pose of a buddha. The royal court of the Luba people of southeastern Democratic Republic of the Congo relies on *lukasa*, or the memory board **(b)**, to remember the stories of heroes, clan migrations, king lists, and genealogies. This item is used on ritual occasions, often to install new rulers, inscribing them into the narrative of the court and people, as well as the cosmos. By making them part of the sacred time that envelopes a people and universe, the *lukasa* and its interpreters ensure the legitimacy of the king and consecrate his reign.

Other groups rely on ritual observations to secure the collective memory of their people. Jews annually celebrate the

(a) Tibeten *thang ka* depicting Stag lung pa (Taglung Thangpa) and arhats, c. 1300 CE, distemper on canvas. *[©Réunion des Musées Nationaux/Art Resource, N.Y.]*

Passover with a ceremonial meal or Seder **(c)**, using the occasion to retell the sacred story of Israel's deliverance from bondage, as in the case of the rabbi shown here, who ritually poses historical and theological questions to a boy. Jews who came to the United States in the early twentieth century often purchased postcards, such as the one shown here **(d)**, in order to demonstrate visually the preservation of their rites to those who had remained in Eastern Europe. This visual mediation of the ritual keeping of the liturgical calendar or sacred time (the rite of Tashlikh, a prayer service held on the first day of Ro'sh

(b) LEFT. Luba chief with a memory board (*lukasa*) and staff, 1989, Democratic Republic of the Congo. *[Photograph by Mary N. Roberts and Allen F. Roberts]* **(c)** BOTTOM. A rabbi poses historical and theological questions to a Jewish boy during the Seder. *[©Roger Ressmeyer/Corbis]*

ha-Shanah) established a link that persisted in spite of distance. Other immigrants to the United States, Swedish Lutherans, invented certificates for display in the home **(e)** to commemorate such important events as marriage or confirmation in the faith. Memory is especially important for immigrants or displaced populations as a way of maintaining identity in spite of significant, even violent, change.

Another kind of reminder is the *memento mori*, or a reminder of human mortality, which may be older even

A happy New Year!
תשליך
ותשליך במצולות ים כל חטאתם
לשנה טובה תכתבו

(d) Right. A postcard depicting a Jewish Tashlikh service near the Brooklyn Bridge in New York, c. 1915. *[©Snark/Art Resource, N.Y.]* **(e)** Bottom. Swedish-American Lutheran confirmation certificate, designed by John Gast, 1902. *[Photo by Michel Raguin/Courtesy of Virginia Raguin]*

Jag vill
komma i håg
Konfirmerad

than Christianity, but was used by Christians from the Middle Ages to the modern age, as in the Dutch painting by Willem Claesz Heda **(f)**. The artist embeds in this modest still life a number of reminders of the mortal nature of human existence. The open pocket watch recalls the passing moments of life, the need for vigilance, and a dutiful attending to what is needful. The momentary freshness of the food and its frugal presentation signals the urgency and propriety of a mindful, ordered life. Remembering the transience of human existence and the caution to live in light of the inevitable end is often a message conveyed by those who construct roadside shrines like the one reproduced here **(g)**. These mark the site where

(f) Top. Willem Claesz Heda, *Breakfast Still Life*, 1629, oil on canvas. *[©Scala/Art Resource, N.Y.]* **(g)** Left. A roadside shrine for a man who was killed in an automobile accident on Highway 20 in northwest Indiana. *[Photograph by David Morgan]*

a loved one or friend died, but also warn passersby to be careful and reflective.

Images may also evoke the experience of a primordial time, one before, or outside of, or encompassing the present world. Australian Aboriginals refer to this time as *dreamtime*, which is the ancestral past and primordial age when the physical world was created as it now appears. The two most common forms of imagery associated with the portrayal of dreamtime are rock paintings and engravings, and bark painting. The rock painting **(h)** from the Australia Northern Territory shows a splayed, transparent

(h) Aboriginal rock painting of a Wanjana figure, from Nourlangie, Kakadu National Park, Northern Territory, Australia. *[©Archivo Iconografico, S.A./Corbis]*

male figure that displays its skeletal structure and prominent sexual organs in what is called x-ray style. The bark painting **(i)**, also from northern Australia, features dreamtime figures. Originally created on the portions of bark used as covering for shelters during the rainy season, bark paintings are now made by Aboriginals as fine art. Other cultures visualize the link between present time and the transcendent by capturing the shaman's transformation into totemic animals, such as in the Mochican earthenware figure from the northern coast of Peru, a deer-headed anthromorph that may represent a shaman undergoing metamorphosis **(j)**.

(i) Top. Australian Aboriginal dreamtime figures painted on bark. *[©Penny Tweedie/Corbis]* **(j) Left.** Mochican earthenware figure from Peru depicting a deer-headed anthromorph that may represent a shaman undergoing metamorphosis. *[©Werner Forman/Art Resource, N.Y.]*

(k) Twelfth-century carving of the Last Judgement adorning a tympanum above the western portal of the Church of Saint Foy in Conques, France. *[©Vanni Archive/Corbis]*

In Christian, Jewish, and Muslim religious traditions images have often visualized the future arrival of an apocalyptic figure who brings with him the end of the world. Rather than looking back to primordial moments, these images anticipate the end, as in the carving of the Last Judgment **(k)** from a twelfth-century church in France, in which the enthroned figure of Christ oversees the blessing of those chosen to enter heaven and the damnation of those (seen below) who enter the realm of eternal suffering and doom. For Shīʿī Muslims, images of a mounted Shīʿī rider portray the "hidden *imām*" or the *mahdī* (the well guided), a ninth-century leader of the

Imamite Shīʿah, Abul Qaim Muḥammad, who vanished in the tenth century and will return at the end of time to usher in justice. Such mass-produced images have a modern, Christian counterpart in two printed items from the United States (**l** and **m**), which offer a meticulous diagramming of time from biblical prophecies as millennialist Christians interpreted them in the Hebrew Bible to the second coming of Christ.

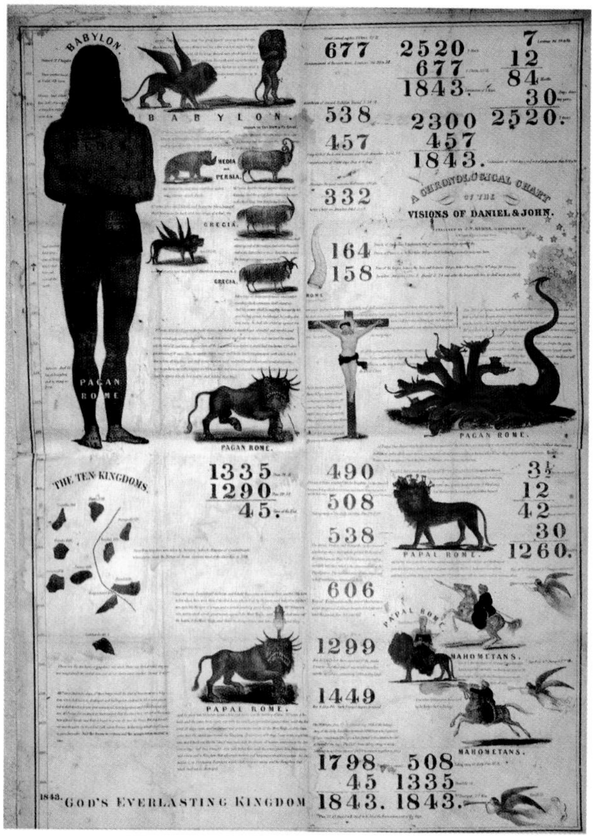

BIBLIOGRAPHY

Caruana, Wally. *Aboriginal Art.* New York, 1993; rev. ed., 2003.

Coe, Michael D., et al. *The Olmec World: Ritual and Rulership.* Princeton, 1995.

Flood, Josephine. *Rock Art of the Dreamtime: Images of Ancient Australia.* Sydney, 1997.

Pal, Pratapaditya. *Himalayas: An Aesthetic Adventure.* Chicago, 2003.

Roberts, Mary Nooter, and Allen F. Roberts, eds. *Memory: Luba Art and the Making of History.* New York and Munich, 1996.

DAVID MORGAN (2005)

(**l**) LEFT. *A Chronological Chart of the Visions of Daniel and John*, 1482, hand-tinted lithograph on cloth after an original design by Charles Fitch and Apollos Hale. *[Courtesy of James R. Nix]* (**m**) BELOW. Clarence Larkin, Dispensationalist diagram titled *The Mountain Peaks of Prophecy*, 1920. *[Used with permission of the Rev. Clarence Larkin Estate, P. O. Box 334, Glenside, Pa. 19038, U.S.A.; 215-576-5590.]*

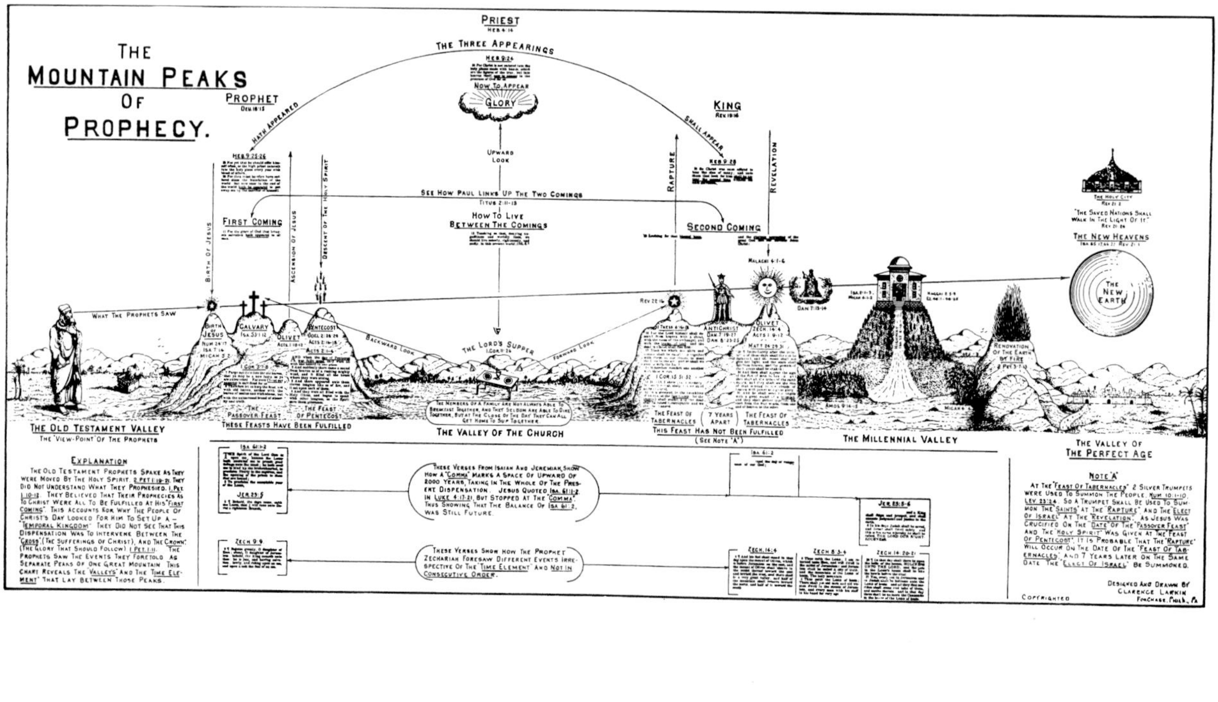

he recognizes as most essential in himself—his applied intelligence and his capacity for work—modern man takes upon himself the function of temporal duration; in other words, he takes on the role of time.

See Also Elixir; Gold and Silver; Metals and Metallurgy; Nature, article on Religious and Philosophical Speculations.

Bibliography

For the earliest relations between the rituals and mythologies of mining, metallurgy, and alchemy, see my book *The Forge and the Crucible: The Origins and Structures of Alchemy*, 2d ed. (Chicago, 1978); critical bibliographies are given therein. For a cultural history of mining, see T. A. Rickard's *Man and Metals: A History of Mining in Relation to the Development of Civilizations*, 2 vols. (New York, 1932). For the history of metallurgy, see R. J. Forbes's *Metallurgy in Antiquity: A Notebook for Archaeologists and Technologists* (Leiden, 1950) and Leslie Aitchison's *A History of Metals*, 2 vols. (London, 1960).

The origin and development of alchemy are presented from different perspectives by several authors: by Edmund von Lippmann in a three-volume work, *Entstehung und Ausbreitung der Alchemie* (Berlin, 1919–1954), of which volume 3 is indispensable; by John Reed in *Through Alchemy to Chemistry* (London, 1957); by Eric John Holmyard in *Alchemy* (Baltimore, 1957); and by Robert P. Multhauf in *The Origins of Chemistry* (London, 1966). On origins and development, see also three articles by Allan G. Debus: "The Significance of the History of Early Chemistry," *Cahiers d'histoire mondiale* 9 (1965): 39–58; "Alchemy and the Historian of Science," *History of Science* 6 (1967): 128–138; and "The Chemical Philosophers: Chemical Medicine from Paracelsus to van Helmont," *History of Science* 12 (1974): 235–259.

The works cited in this article on specific alchemical traditions are Wilhelm Ganzenmüller's *Die Alchemie im Mittelalter* (Paderborn, West Germany, 1938), translated into French as *L'alchimie au Moyen-Âge* (Paris, 1940), and Nathan Sivin's *Chinese Alchemy: Preliminary Studies* (Cambridge, Mass., 1968).

New Sources

Dobbs, Betty Jo Teeter. *The Janus Faces of Genius: The Role of Alchemy in Newton's Thought*. New York, 1991.

Heinrich, Clark. *Strange Fruit: Alchemy, Religion, and Magical Foods: A Speculative History*. London, 1995.

Marshall, Peter H. *The Philosopher's Stone: A Quest for the Secrets of Alchemy*. London, 2001.

Newman, William R. *Promethean Ambitions: Alchemy and the Quest to Perfect Nature*. Chicago, Ill., 2004.

Newman, William R., and Lawrence M. Principe. *Alchemy Tried in the Fire: Starkey, Boyle, and the Fate of Helmontian Chymistry*. Chicago, Ill., 2002.

Szulakowski, Urszula. *The Alchemy of Light: Geometry and Optics in Late Renaissance Alchemical Illustration*. Boston, 2000.

Von Martels, Z. R. W. M., ed. *Alchemy Revisited: Proceedings of the International Conference on the History of Alchemy at the University of Gronigen, 17–19 April, 1989*. New York, 1990.

Mircea Eliade (1987)
Reveised Bibliography

ALCHEMY: CHINESE ALCHEMY

Definitions of alchemy have generally been based on the experience of a single civilization—usually but not always Europe—and tend to imply that traditions that do not follow the chosen pattern are not the real thing. The sole exception is the definition of H. J. Sheppard: "Alchemy is the art of liberating parts of the Cosmos from temporal existence and achieving perfection which for metals is gold, and, for man, longevity, then immortality, and finally, redemption." This definition might be slightly qualified. Longevity and material immortality may or may not accompany salvation in a given time and place. The evolution of other substances from base materials may be more important than that of gold. In China, for instance, cinnabar was the prototype of elixir substances. Adding the specification that the alchemical art uses chemical change to symbolize the processes by which perfection is attained, one can recognize a pattern common to Hellenistic Alexandria, China, Islam, India, and early modern Europe.

The alchemy of each of the great civilizations was distinct in the knowledge on which it drew, in the symbols it created, and in the purposes for which it was used. These peculiarities depended on public structures of meaning as well as on the private discourse of the groups that took up alchemy.

Alchemy began in close alignment with popular religion, especially among educated groups in the Yangze region. It was considered one of several disciplines that could lead to individual spiritual perfection and immortality. Some Daoist movements took up its practice after about 500 CE; it influenced both Buddhist and Daoist symbolism and liturgy. The aims and means of alchemy, some important issues in its history, and its far from clear-cut relations with Daoism and with science are discussed below.

Aims and Means. Chinese ideals of individual perfection combined three ideas that would have been incompatible in Egypt or Persia. The desire for immortality, which long preceded formal philosophy or religion, was the first of these ideas. In popular culture, ideals of long life evolved into the notion that life need not end. This was not immortality of the soul in isolation, but immortality of the personality—of all that selfhood implied—within an imperishable physical body. In the most elaborate doctrines of immortality, this new physical self was nurtured within by a variety of disciplines including alchemy until, at the moment the "naked child" was fully formed, it would burst forth like a butterfly leaving behind an empty chrysalis, an almost weightless corpse.

The potent personal force that may linger on after someone dies was undifferentiated in the thought of the uneducated, but in the conceptions of specialists it was separated into ten "souls" (three *yanghun* and seven *yinpo*). Their normal postmortem dissipation could be prevented only if the body, their common site, could be made to survive with them. That, as Lu Gwei-djen and Joseph Needham have suggested, is why Chinese immortality was bound to be material.

A second implication of immortality was perfection of the spirit. Because there was no dichotomy between the spiritual and the somatic, the refining of the body was not distinct from the activity of spiritual self-cultivation. Immortality was salvation from decrepitude and death. Piety, ritual, morality, and hygiene were equally essential to the prolongation of life. Regardless of whether one considers popular views or those of Daoist, Buddhist, or Confucian initiates, all these kinds of striving were also requisite for the proper orientation of the individual toward the transcendent Way, the Dao, as each tradition defined it.

A third implication of immortality, alongside spiritual and physical perfection, was assumption into a divine hierarchy. This hierarchy was bureaucratic, a mirror of the temporal order. In fact, the bureaucratic ideal—of a symmetrical organization in which power and responsibility belonged to the post, and only temporarily to the individual who filled it—evolved more or less simultaneously in politics and religion.

There were many paths to simultaneous longevity, salvation, and celestial appointment. Meditational, devotional, and ascetic exercises carried out communally by organized religious movements or privately by individual initiates could be supplemented by physiological disciplines, sexual techniques for augmenting the vital forces, dietary regimens, or alchemy.

Why should alchemy have a part to play in this spiritual quest? To rephrase the question, what could the symbology of chemical interaction contribute? Despite the worldly implications of appointment in the divine order, this aim was reached by a mystic path, a process in which the individual attained union with the Way. This process, itself called the Way, perfectly integrated the cosmos, society, and the person.

To embody the Way one had to experience it, whether through direct illumination or through insight. This experience might begin with knowing, but deepened far beyond the limits of rational cognition. As an early alchemical poem from the *Arcane Memorandum of the Red Pine Master* (*Chisongzu xuan ji,* probably seventh century or earlier) put it,

> The Perfect Dao is a perfect emptying of heart and mind.
> Within the darkness, unknowable wonders.
> When the wise man has attained the August Source
> In time he will truly reach the clouds. (*Yun ji qi qian* 66.14a)

Adepts saw the nurturant aspect of the Way—activity that brings about perfection in the macrocosm or microcosm—in the life cycles of living things in nature. One could speak of life cycles not only in plants and animals but in minerals, which, as in Aristotle, matured from earth. Mineral evolution could transcend decay and death, for its end point was the immutable perfection of cinnabar or gold. The evolution of these two substances from base starting points was an obvious metaphor for the process that made mortals immortal. The elixir (*dan*), originally cinnabar perfected by the Way of nature, came to embody in alchemical thought the potential of humans for perfection. Thus the elixir and the art of making it came to be named for cinnabar (*dan*), even in instances when the latter was not an ingredient.

The work of the alchemist reproduced the perfecting activity of nature. As a text of circa 900 puts it, "natural cyclically transformed elixir is formed when flowing mercury, embracing [lead], becomes pregnant. . . . In 4,320 years the elixir is finished. . . . It embraces the *qi* of sun and moon, *yin* and *yang,* for 4,320 years; thus, upon repletion of its own *qi,* it becomes a cyclically transformed elixir for immortals of the highest grade and for celestial beings. When, in the world below, lead and mercury are subjected to the alchemical process for purposes of immortality, [the artificial elixir] is finished in one year. . . . What the alchemist prepares succeeds because of its correspondence on a scale of thousandths" (*Dan lun jue zhi xin jian,* p. 12b). In other words, the alchemist accomplishes in one year of 4,320 hours (12 Chinese hours per day for a round year of 360 days) what takes nature 4,320 years.

The alchemical process thus is a kind of pilot model of cosmic evolution. The seeker not only shrank time but reproduced the dimensions of the universe within the confines of his laboratory. He reduced the operation of the Way to spatial and temporal dimensions that he could encompass in contemplation, in the hope of becoming one with it.

The alchemist used a great variety of means—mainly quantitative and qualitative correspondences—to manipulate space and time in this way. His laboratory might be oriented to the cardinal directions, his furnace at the very center, both replete with uranic diagrams. The dimensions of the furnace, the emplacement of steps in its platform, the number and placement of doors for firing, all aligned it with respect to sky and earth.

Because the heat of the fire stood for the nurturant cosmic forces, recreating these forces required that he bind fire by time. He thus gradually increased and decreased the intensity of the fire in carefully timed cycles, using weighed amounts of fuel. He reproduced the seasonal cycle of warmth and cold, in the absence of thermometers, using the one precision measuring instrument readily available, the balance. Several carefully designed schedules for increasing and decreasing the weight of charcoal, and charging it into the furnace through a succession of doors, survive. They are not simple cycles, in which the end point is the same as the beginning. Successive end points slowly increase, embodying the notion of a change in the alchemical ingredients at once cyclic and progressive.

This cyclic approach to modeling was also apparent in the ingredients. The most influential early processes used two ingredients or two main ingredients that were *yin* and *yang* with respect to each other. They were conjugated and separated through one cycle after another, yielding (in the eyes of the alchemist) a series of progressively more perfect products. The mercury and lead mentioned earlier are examples; another frequently encountered pair is mercury and sulfur, which combine to form vermilion (artificial cinnabar), from which, by heating at a higher temperature, mercury can be recovered. As an alchemist about a thousand years ago phrased it, "That cinnabar should emerge from mercury and again be killed by mercury; this is the mystery within the mystery" (*Bi yu zhu sha han lin yu shu gui* of Chen Dashi, in *Zhengtong dao zang*, vol. 587). Sometimes the progressive cycle-by-cycle changes were achieved by adding additional ingredients, but in the alchemist's eyes the process remained in principle dyadic.

This does not exhaust the metaphors available to the alchemist for his use in reproducing the cyclical energetics of the Way. The figure of the cosmic egg, nurturing from the yolk the gradual differentiation of the fully formed chick, is familiar in all the great alchemical traditions. The alchemical vessel is often referred to as an egg. Persistently in China the alchemical ingredients were actually sealed inside an eggshell; the earliest detailed instructions come from the ninth century CE or somewhat later, the latest from the mid-seventeenth century. A Ming imperial prince of the early fifteenth century carried this approach to its logical conclusion by incubating his cinnabar-filled eggshell under a hen.

Cosmic process could be reenacted not only in a single room but entirely within the adept's body. Meditative techniques of self-cultivation that involve visualizing the circulation of vital energies or cosmic effluvia within the body are ambiguously documented in the fourth century BCE. By the first century CE, adepts were establishing relations with a hierarchy of gods within their bodies.

There is nothing intrinsically alchemical (or Daoist) about these exercises, but they provided a basis for internalizing the alchemical process. Metaphors were borrowed from the work of the furnace to express the union of opposites in full realization of the Way. As Farzeen Baldrian-Hussein puts it, "it is from his own body that the adept of internal alchemy (*neidan*) constructs his laboratory. In fact he finds within himself all the ingredients and apparatus of traditional alchemy: furnace, reaction vessel, mercury, cinnabar, lead, and other minerals. By a mental and physiological process he furnishes the laboratory, lights the fire of the furnace, keeps watch over the heat, brings about the marriage of the ingredients in the reaction vessel and, once the desired result has been obtained, begins the process anew on a different level" (Hussein, 1984, p. 14).

In an important scripture revealed around 300 CE, the adept controls the movement of the solar pneuma connected with cardiac functions and the lunar pneuma connected with renal functions. The first of these pneumas is called "divine elixir" and the second "liquefied gold." This interiorization of alchemy grew naturally out of the prevalent belief that the body is a microcosm, its vital processes corresponding to those of the physical world, its spirituality embodied in inner gods organized as a mirror image of the celestial and terrestrial bureaucracies.

In the pursuit of these disciplines it is not the product that matters but the process. Even some texts of external alchemy either say nothing about ingesting the elixir, or assert that immortality results from witnessing the "great work." Some descriptions of the forms and colors of the elixir when the reaction vessel is opened suggest that alchemists contemplated the product in a heightened state of consciousness.

If a protracted personal experience is the means to immunity from death, the benefits of alchemy cannot be transferable. But alchemy had other dimensions that made the transfer of elixirs highly desirable. This art could be a source of patronage, whether to underwrite its substantial expenses or to yield profit. A pre-alchemical tradition in medicine made natural drugs of the highest grade effective means to immortality (the two lower grades of drugs replenish depleted vitalities and cure illness). By a natural extension of this line of thought, many physicians studied alchemy as a source of new medicines, and alchemists adapted established drugs to their work.

Many surviving alchemical writings aim at the straightforward preparation of economically or therapeutically desirable substances. Such sources tend naturally to discuss the preparation of alchemical gold as well as elixirs related to cinnabar. Gold is a matter of relatively minor concern in the central tradition of laboratory alchemy that emphasizes individual self-cultivation.

HISTORY. This section will explore three issues pertinent to the relations of religion and alchemy: the beginnings of alchemy in China, the character of change in alchemy, and the historical relations of external and internal alchemy.

Whether alchemy originated earlier in Hellenistic Egypt or China remains uncertain. The earliest testimony from either society has not yet been rigorously dated to within a century. Differing views about Chinese origins vary largely with willingness to accept legends as historical statements.

Cinnabar and similar blood-colored compounds have been connected with ideas of death and immortality since the Neolithic period; that is how most scholars interpret the archaic custom of sprinkling red powders on corpses to be buried. The splendidly preserved corpse of the Lady of Dai (died shortly after 168 BCE, excavated 1972) contained high concentrations of mercury and lead. These elements were distributed in a way consistent with ingestion before death. Traces in the intestines include native cinnabar, frequently prescribed by physicians as an immortality drug, rather than an artificial elixir. Some historians claim that an edict dated 144 BCE against falsifying gold proves the prevalence of alchemy, but it presents no evidence that anything more was involved than artisans' use of alloys. In 133 BCE the Martial Emperor was told by an occultist that eating from plates of artificial gold would lengthen his life so that he could seek out certain immortals and, with their help, become an immortal himself by performing certain rituals. This request for patronage links gold indirectly with immortality and suggests that the direct alchemical linkage had not yet been made. As patronage increasingly became available in the decades that followed, the lore of immortals with whom patrons could be put in touch proliferated. "Medicines of immortality" were frequently mentioned, but without calling them artificial. Critical scholars find clear proof of the emergence of alchemy only in the earliest treatises on the subject: the first chapter of the *Huangdi jiuding shendan jing* (Canon of the nine-vessel divine elixir of the Yellow Lord), before the second century CE, and *Zhouyi cantong qi* (Token of the concordance of the three; the title originated by c. 140 CE, and the text after 700).

The chronological priority of East or West is not in fact a pressing issue unless the undertaking in question is substantially the same in both parts of the world. That is not the case. Needham pinpoints one significant difference when he defines Chinese alchemy as a combination of macrobiotics (the quest for material immortality through drugs) and aurifaction (the attempt to make true gold by artificial means, as distinguished from "aurifiction," in which gold is consciously faked). These definitions ignore the centrality of cinnabar. Needham notes that macrobiotics was conspicuously missing from the early occidental art, which he therefore does not consider "true" alchemy.

Other scholars evaluate not only the techniques of the alchemists but also their beliefs. The types of spiritual experience outlined above and the relation of alchemical success to appointment in a divine hierarchy are unique to China. They suggest that the alchemical quest in East Asia, as in Alexandria, cannot be adequately defined by technical goals. Both civilizations used chemical methods and metaphors for redemptive ends. The goals differed because Chinese and Hellenistic Egyptian structures of meaning and values differed. It is fitting to speak of the corresponding arts of both as "true" alchemy and to conclude that—on present knowledge—they emerged at roughly the same time.

The alchemists, unlike modern historians, did not believe that their art evolved or changed. As in any other Chinese religious or technical tradition, its practitioners assumed that its every possibility had been laid out in the archaic, divine revelations that founded it. In alchemy there were several of these seminal works, including the two already mentioned. These scriptures were to be passed down intact to those worthy to receive them, supplemented by oral explanations. Much explanation was needed, for the *Zhouyi cantong qi* was packed with metaphor and symbol, its density multilayered. In a degraded age, alchemists could grasp the inexhaustible meanings of the Sages only approximately. The issue was not progress in knowledge but regaining ancient wisdom.

Nevertheless, when a modern scientist reads them, alchemical writings over the centuries exhibit an increasingly comprehensive knowledge of chemical processes. They were also increasingly able to accommodate new impulses from popular religion. Some adepts were aware of this new content in alchemy. They attributed it to additional (but in principle timeless) revelations. It is often immortals in disguise, "remarkable men" met in strange circumstances or seen in dreams or visions, who grant them. The static ideal did not rule out change.

Current understanding suggests that, although the earliest alchemy was that of chemical processes, external and internal alchemy fused by the time of the *Zhouyi cantong qi.* This book brings an elaborate symbolism to bear on processes that can be understood equally well as external or internal to the body. The book refers not only to the internal alchemy of imaginative visualization but also to sexual disciplines that give the marriage of opposites its ultimately literal expression. Later alchemists disagree about whether sexual practices further or hinder immortality, but a number of important adepts follow the *Zhouyi cantong qi* in seeing external, internal, and sexual alchemy as aspects of a single process. In fact, the language of certain texts makes it impossible to be certain whether they are concerned with operations on mineral ingredients.

External alchemy did not retain the vitality of its internal analogue. Writings that reflect new knowledge of chemical processes became rare after about 1000. Later writers often said that only outsiders believe that alchemy is to be done—or was ever done—in the laboratory. It thus appears that innovation in the procedures of external alchemy—although not in their meanings—had largely ceased. This has been explained by a revival of Confucian ideals that discouraged educated people from doing artisanal work. Another reason may be the ascendancy of meditation and visualization over practical operations in the Daoist movements that attracted elite enthusiasts in the eleventh and twelfth centuries. Occult and manual practices, as noted above, were not mutually exclusive earlier. Another likely cause is widespread awareness that a number of emperors and high officials had died as a result of taking alchemical elixirs. To the adept the appearance of death was a sign that the perfected self had hatched out of the old body and taken office among the immortals. To secular humanists intolerant of popular beliefs, this seemed a foolish rationale for suicide.

ALCHEMY, SCIENCE, AND RELIGION. Alchemy has been studied mainly by historians of chemistry, who have shown that the Chinese art exploited the properties of many chemical substances and even incorporated considerable knowledge of quantitative relations. Scholars of medical history have demonstrated close connections between alchemy and medicine, in the substances and processes on which both drew and in the use of artificial, mainly inorganic "elixirs" by physicians to treat disease and lengthen life. Historians have tended to see alchemy as a fledgling science, a precursor of modern inorganic chemistry and iatrochemistry. Lu and Needham speak of internal alchemy as "protobiochemistry."

This view overlooks the fact that the goals of alchemy were not cognitive. They were consistently focused on spiritual cultivation and immortality, and largely concerned with reenacting cosmic process for purposes of contemplation. It is impossible to be certain that alchemists discovered any new chemical interaction or process. Because alchemists were literate and craftsmen were not, it is only to be expected that innovations by the latter would be first recorded by the former (who were almost the only members of the elite greatly interested in the chemical arts). Claims that alchemists played major roles in developing gunpowder and distillation apparatus are not supported by independent evidence about the state of contemporary industrial processes, which are still poorly explored for the first millennium CE. Similarly, too little of the medical literature has been studied to confirm that alchemists gave more to medicine than they took from it.

The idea that alchemy is Daoist by nature, or was invented by Daoists, has not survived advances since about 1970 in historical studies of Daoism. In the Celestial Master sect and other early Daoist movements drugs (including artificial preparations) were forbidden; only religious rituals and confession of sins could procure health and salvation. Upper-class initiates gradually began to use immortality drugs already fashionable in the north. As refugees after the fall of Loyang in 311 they encountered elixirs in the Yangtze region, where alchemy had long been established among popular immortality practices. The aristocratic southerners they displaced in positions of temporal power invented new religious structures to assert, by way of compensation, their spiritual superiority. Michel Strickmann has demonstrated that in doing so they adapted northern Daoist usages to local popular practices, in which immortality and alchemy were central, and in which the religious use of inorganic drugs was usual. Tao Hongjing, a man of noble southern antecedents, drew on revelations inherited from fourth-century predecessors when he founded the Supreme Purity (or Maoshan) Daoist movement under imperial patronage in about 500. Tao adapted not only old southern techniques but elaborate structures of alchemical and astral imagery. He thus formed a movement that captured upper-class allegiance, supported state power, and was supported in return for more than five centuries. He incorporated alchemical practices and symbols with Daoism—the particular Daoism that he created—for the first time. Alchemy did not originate in the Daoist milieu, and was never confined to it. Similarly, the role of alchemy in movements other than Dao's varied too greatly to constitute a fixed relationship.

See Also Dao and De; Soul, article on Chinese Concepts.

Bibliography

Primary sources are cited from the Daoist Patrology *(Zhengtong dao zang,* 1445), s.v. The most detailed modern study of Chinese alchemy is in Joseph Needham's *Science and Civilisation in China* (Cambridge, 1954-), vol. 5, pts. 2–5, but much of it is now obsolete. See the discussion of research issues in Sivin, "Research on the History of Chinese Alchemy," in *Alchemy Revisited. Proceedings of the International Conference on the History of Alchemy at the University of Groningen. 17–19 April 1989,* edited by Z.R.W.M. von Martels, pp. 3–20 (Leiden, 1990). For a comprehensive and regularly updated bibliography of recent studies see Fabrizio Pregadio, "The Golden Elixir," at http://helios.unive.it/~dsao//pregadio/index.html. The best scholarly introductions are the essays on alchemy and related topics in *Daoism Handbook,* edited by Livia Kohn (Handbuch der Orientalistik. IV. China. 14; Leiden, 2000), and the discussions of alchemy and spiritual cultivation in Lowell Skar, "Golden Elixir Alchemy: The Formation of the Southern Lineage and the Transformation of Medieval China. Asian Studies" (Ph.D. diss., University of Pennsylvania, 2003). For discussion of of internal alchemy, see Farzeen Baldrian-Hussein's *Procédés secrets au Joyau magique: Traité d'alchimie daoïste du onzième siècle* (Paris, 1984) and Skar. I discuss the symbolic structures used in alchemy at length in volume 5 of *Science and Civilisation in China,* pt. 4, pp. 210–305, summarized in more final form in "Chinese Alchemy and the Manipulation of Time," *Isis* 67 (1976): 513–526, and reprinted in *Science and Technology in East Asia,* edited by me (New York, 1977).

Pre-Daoist southern occult traditions, including alchemy, are discussed in Isabelle Robinet's "La revelation du Shangqing dans l'histoire du taoïsme" (Ph.D. diss., University of Paris, 1981). The relation between alchemy and Daoist movements has been trenchantly analyzed in Michel Strickmann's "On the Alchemy of Tao Hongjing," in *Facets of Daoism: Essays in Chinese Religion,* edited by Holmes Welch and Anna Seidel (New Haven, Conn., 1979), pp. 123–192; see also his *Le taoïsme du Maozhan: Chronique d'une révélation,* 2 vols., Mémoires de l'Institut des Hautes Études Chinoises, no. 17 (Paris, 1981).

Nathan Sivin (1987 and 2005)

ALCHEMY: INDIAN ALCHEMY

In South Asia, alchemy is inseparable from its religious contexts. Apart from Islamic alchemy, largely imported from Persia, nearly all of the documented alchemical traditions of the Indian subcontinent have been Hindu. The sole extant indigenous non-Hindu works containing significant alchemical data are the Buddhist *Kālacakra Tantra* with its eleventh-century CE *Vimalaprabhā* commentary, and an eleventh- or twelfth-century CE Jain text, the *Rasaratnasamucchaya* of Māṇikyadeva Sūri. Therefore, the focus of the present article will be Hindu alchemy.

A number of scientific subfields and disciplines, linked with a body of religious practices and techniques, comprise Hindu alchemy. These include metallurgy, traditional Indian medicine in its northern (*āyurveda*) and southern (*siddhacikitsā*) forms, iatrochemisty (*rasa śāstra*, the "science of essential substances"), rejuvenation therapy (*rasāyana*, the "path of essential substances"), sexual rehabilitation therapy (*vājīkaraṇa*), transmutational alchemy (*dhātuvāda*, the "doctrine of the elements"), elixir alchemy (*dehavāda*, the "doctrine of the body"), *haṭhayoga*, and Tantra. Although *rasa śāstra*, which persists as a subfield of Āyurveda, has incorporated many of the old alchemical formulas, apparatuses, techniques, and nomenclatures into its production of plant- and mineral-based pharmaceuticals for therapeutic use, there are no practitioners of elixir or transmutational alchemy on the Indian subcontinent today. Moreover, there are virtually no archaeological or inscriptional data related to the practice of alchemy. Therefore, any historical reconstruction of the Hindu alchemical tradition, which flourished between around 900 and 1300 CE, will of necessity be based on textual data; that is, on what may be termed the Hindu alchemical canon.

Basic Principles. The polyvalent term *rasa* is central to an understanding of Hindu alchemy. From the time of the Vedas, *rasa* has signified "fluid, juice, sap" (it is a cognate of the English "resin"). With the emergence of the alchemical tradition, the term took on a number of specialized uses, including "essential element" and "mercury." The former is a general term, applied to a group of alchemical reagents usually described as consisting of eight primary (*mahārasas*) and eight secondary (*uparasas*) elements, while the latter constitutes the supreme fluid that is quicksilver, identified by Śiva, the supreme alchemical deity, as his own essential element, i.e., his semen. (In the eleventh-century CE alchemical classic the *Rasārṇava*, Śiva reveals that "because it is the *rasa* [essential element, vital fluid] of my body, one is to call it *rasa* [mercury]" [1:36].) Mercury, purified and potentiated through its interactions with sulfur and mica—the *mahārasas* that are the mineral homologues of the female discharge (*rajas*) of Śiva's consort, the Goddess—effects the transformation of both metals and the human body into their higher essences in the Indian great chain of being. Because the universe in all its parts is constantly being regenerated out of the sexual union of the divine in its male and female hypostases, all vital animal, mineral, and vegetable substances are emanates or devolutes of divine sexual emissions; and because all participate in the same flow of the godhead, all are interchangeable, recombinatory, and perfectible. Therefore, elixir therapy, transmutation, *haṭhayoga*, and the erotico-mystical elements of Tantra are all interpenetrating and mutually reinforcing bodies of practice that fall under the general rubric of Hindu alchemy.

The theory and practice of Hindu alchemy is predicated on the concept of the perfectibility of matter, as found in both the emanationist metaphysics of Vedānta philosophy and in certain elements of dualist Sāṃkhya philosophy. According to Samkhyan metaphysics, *prakṛti*, materiality, the "stuff" of the universe, has disintegrated into twenty-five categories (*tattvas*) that can be reintegrated back into their higher evolutes. Therefore earth, the lowest of the five gross elements (*mahābhūtas*), has the potential to be reintegrated into ether, the highest element in the series, via the intermediate elements water, fire, and air. The same capacity of the higher *tattvas* of the Samkhyan hierarchies—to reintegrate their lower devolutes into themselves without themselves being modified—applies to the hierarchized elements (*dhātus*) of Hindu alchemy. In the words of the tenth-century CE *Rasahṛdaya Tantra* of Govinda, arguably the earliest systematic work on Hindu alchemy, "Woody plants are absorbed into lead; lead into tin, and tin likewise into copper. Copper [is absorbed] into silver, silver into gold, and gold is absorbed into mercury" (1:12). A parallel dynamic is observable in the *cakra* system of Hindu *haṭhayoga*, a tradition that emerged in approximately the same period.

At the heart of tantric alchemy are eighteen operations (*saṃskāras*) leading to the "perfectioning" of chemical reagents, and most especially of naturally occurring mercury, which must be purified and potentiated before it can be applied to other bodies, both metallic and human. The first sixteen of these *saṃskāras* prime mercury for the final two operations, *vedha* (transmutation: literally "penetration, piercing") and *śarīrayoga* (transubstantiation, bodily transformation: literally "body work"), in which mercury truly confounds itself with the metallic or flesh-and-blood "bodies" in question, ultimately replacing them with a mercurial or alchemical body.

The Hindu alchemical and hathayogic scriptures repeatedly invoke the goal of becoming "a second Śiva," which echoes the goal of mainstream medieval Śaiva practice as described in the Āgamas: one does not seek to become Śiva, but rather to become intimately close to Śiva, or to become *like* Śiva. Similarly, the alchemist's goal is not to become mercury, but rather, to become *like* mercury—capable of transmuting base metals into gold and human bodies into superhuman bodies—to become mercurial. It is in this way that transmutation is described in Hindu alchemical texts. Purified and potentiated mercury simultaneously penetrates and absorbs base metals into itself, causing them to become their higher evolutes, until alchemical gold is realized. At the end of the process, the transmuting mercury has itself disappeared: there is only gold, the noble, "immortal" metal, which can never be further transmuted into mercury itself. The relationship between transmutation and bodily transformation, in which the alchemist's body is itself transformed into an immortal, unaging, perfected, golden or adamantine body, is explained in the *Rasārṇava*: "As in metal, so in the body. Mercury ought always to be employed thusly. When it penetrates a metal and the body, [mercury] behaves in an identical way: first test [mercury] on a metal, then use it in the body" (17:164–165). The relationship of these processes to Śaiva metaphysics is clearly stated in the thirteenth- or fourteenth-century CE *Kulārṇava Tantra*: "Just as penetration by mercury brings about aurifaction [in metals], so the self, penetrated through initiation, attains Śiva-hood" (14:89). Ultimately, the transmutation of base metals into gold was, for the alchemist (although perhaps not for his royal clients), but a means to the higher end of bodily immortality and perfectibility, to becoming a second Śiva.

Historical Parameters. Although nearly every aspect of Indian alchemy is Hindu in its worldview and metaphysical assumptions, it remains a fact that mercury, the *materia prima* of alchemy, does not occur naturally anywhere on the subcontinent, except in trace quantities, in the form of cinnabar (mercuric sulfide) in zones of geothermal activity. Some Sanskrit terms for mercury indicate the foreign origin of the metal, which likely came to India overland or by sea from China, Tibet, or the Mediterranean world. These terms include *cīnapiṣṭa* ("Chinese powder"), *pārada* (a reference to either the Parthian or Pārada lands of Transoxiania or Baluchistan), and *mleccha* ("barbarian"). South Indian Sittar alchemy likely received its mercury through such port cities as Surat and Madras, which remain centers for the fabrication of synthetic cinnabar and calomel (mercurous chloride) from imported mercury and indigenous Indian minerals. Sittar tradition maintains that its founding alchemists Nandi and Bogar both traveled to China.

The most remarkable evidence of cultural exchanges in matters alchemical is a body of instructions for the extraction of quicksilver from the "wells" in which it naturally occurs. Virtually identical instructions are found in a fourth-century CE Syriac recension of the alchemical corpus attributed to the Greek Pseudo-Zosimus, in the twelfth- or thirteenth-century CE *Rasendracūḍāmaṇi* of Somadeva, and in the seventeenth-century CE Chinese encyclopedia, the *Ho han san cai tu hui.* In all three sources, mercury is induced to rise up out of its well when a naked maiden rides or walks past it: when the flowing metal pursues her, it is captured by alchemists and "killed" by them. Furthermore, the Chinese source identifies the land in which this mercurial well is found as *fou lin,* i.e. Syria, "far to the west." Clearly, the details of this fantastic extraction technique traveled along the same trade routes—via the Silk Road and China ships—as mercury itself. Similarities between Indian, Greek, and Chinese alchemical apparatuses and laboratory procedures are striking, but are best explained by the chemical behavior of the reagents themselves, and by the similar results of trial-and-error experiments with techniques of distillation, amalgamation, fixation, and so in the allied technologies of metallurgy, coinage, and perfumery.

The history of Indian alchemy may be broken down into three chronological phases—of magical, tantric, and Siddha alchemy. In the first of these phases, dating from about 300 to 900 CE, alchemy is the stuff of fairy tales. Transmutation and bodily immortality are its stated goals, but the means to these ends are a matter of serendipity: nowhere are laboratory techniques for the processing of mercury or the production of alchemical gold broached. Its watchword is *rasa-rasāyana*—a miraculous elixir and one of the eight supernatural powers (*siddhis*) of Gupta-age and early medieval Indian mysticism. Most often, this is an elixir or power that one wins or spirits away from gods, demigods (called Siddhas), or demons, often by traveling to their atmospheric or subterranean worlds. Alchemy of this sort becomes a staple of secular adventure and fantasy literature in this period, with kings and princes often cast in the roles of alchemical seekers.

Tantric alchemy bursts upon the scene in the tenth century, and the four hundred years that follow constitute India's alchemical "golden age." There are a number of reasons for referring to this period and its collection of alchemical classics as "tantric. " Not only are the goals of tantric alchemy consistent with those of the broader Hindu tantric tradition, but so too are the means it employs to attaining those goals. The alchemical Tantras abound in references to tantric formulae (*mantras*) and diagrams (*maṇḍalas*), as well as in descriptions of divine pantheons, yogic and meditative techniques, sexual and ritual practices, and the Śākta-Śaiva devotionalism that are the hallmarks of Hindu Tantra. Many of the major alchemical works of the period call themselves Tantras, and are cast as the revealed teachings of Śiva (often in his tantric Bhairava form) to one or another tantric form of the Goddess (Pārvatī, Kākacaṇḍeśvarī, etc.).

What truly sets tantric alchemy apart from magical alchemy is the rigor of its method and the remarkable breadth of the botanical, mineralogical, chemical, geographical, religious, and technical knowledge it mobilizes in the pursuit of its ambitious ends. While Chinese and Persian alchemical traditions no doubt interacted with tantric alchemy, the content of the Indian alchemical classics is so specifically Indian (and Hindu) as to preclude any possibility of wholesale borrowing. The roots of the revolution that was tantric alchemy may be traced back to the powerful impact of Tantra on medieval Indian technologies of power on the one hand, and to developments within the medical schools on the other. In this latter context, a gradual phasing out of the practice of surgery (*śalyatantra*)—a development some attribute to the pervasive influence of the Buddhist ideal of noninjury (*ahiṁsā*)—seems to have been compensated for by discoveries and innovations in the field of mercury- and mineral-based pharmacy.

An explanation for the near absence of South Asian Buddhist alchemical literature is in order here. Two reasons may be adduced, the first of which is historical. By the time tantric alchemy emerged in India, Buddhism was very much on the wane on the subcontinent. Two relatively early Buddhist works, the *Subāhuparipṛccha* (pre-726 CE) and Śāntideva's *Śīkṣāsamucchaya* (eighth century CE), contain short passages on magical alchemy; but apart from the second chapter of the *Kālacakra Tantra* (likely composed in twentieth-century Pakistan), the only post-tenth-century Buddhist discussions of external alchemy come from Tibet, Burma (Myanmar), or east Asia. The second reason is philosophical. Generally speaking, the focus of Buddhism is more psychological than that of Hinduism, and so it is that much of what constitutes Indo-Tibetan Buddhist alchemy is of an internal, symbolic order. Through yogic practice, mercury, identified with male Skill in Means (*upāya*), and sulfur, identified with female Wisdom (*prajñā*), are united internally, effecting a bodily transformation conceptualized as the fixing of the Thought of Enlightenment (*bodhicitta*). This is not to say that mercury-based alchemy (called "gold-making") had no place in Indo-Tibetan Buddhism: rather, because the practitioner was dependent on external elements rather than his own contemplative practice, it was deemed inferior.

In India, external, laboratory-based Hindu alchemy would also become internalized from the thirteenth century onward. No original works on the subject appear after 1300 CE, and much of elixir alchemy becomes applied to more modest therapeutic ends in the emergent field of iatrochemistry. There was, however, a final phase in the history of Indian alchemy that may be referred to as Siddha alchemy. This is most readily identified by its emphasis on combining the use of mercurial preparations with the practice of external sexual and internal yogic techniques, with the aim of attaining both an immortal, unaging body and the status or mode of being of a semi-divine Siddha. Practitioners of Siddha alchemy often referred to themselves as *Siddhas*—that is, the "Perfected Beings" they aspired to become through their practice. This two-pronged approach is already alluded to in the *Rasārṇava*: "Mercury and breath [control] are known as the Work in two parts" (1:18). Over time, the external, laboratory techniques, as well as the use of mercury-based compounds as elixirs and agents of transmutation would come to be fully internalized in the various techniques of *haṭhayoga*; however, a close examination of the terminology and dynamics of the latter tradition shows that it developed, at least in part, out of the former.

One may deduce from internal textual references, manuscript colophons, and Siddha lists that most of the authors of the major tantric alchemical works were either court physicians or members of one of the medieval Śākta-Śaiva or tantric religious orders. Many of these authors had names ending in the *-nātha* suffix, and their names figure in a number of lists of Siddhas found in both Indo-Tibetan Buddhist and Hindu sources. These include lists of the Buddhist Mahāsiddhas and of a number of Hindu groups: the Tamil Sittars of the eastern Deccan, the Māheśvara Siddhas of the western Deccan, the alchemical Rasa Siddhas, and the hathayogic Nāth Siddhas. Internal geographical references point to the Vindhya region and western Deccan as the heartland of Indian alchemical practice, in spite of the fact that the literature identifies the Himalayan region and Inner Asia as the source of many of its botanical and mineral reagents. Śrīśailam, a sacred Śaiva mountain located in the eastern Deccan, is the most frequently mentioned "paradise" of Indian alchemy, and it is here, on the outer walls of the Mallikārjuna Temple, that one finds the sole extant sculpted images of Siddha alchemists and their apparatuses. These bas-reliefs date from about 1300 to 1400 CE.

Apart from the foundational *Rasahṛdaya Tantra* and *Rasārṇava* already mentioned, the "canonical" works of Indian alchemy include the following, all from the common era: the twelfth-century *Kākacaṇḍeśvarīmata* and *Rasopaniṣat*; Gorakhnāth's *Bhūtiprakaraṇa* and Somadeva's *Rasendracūḍāmaṇi*, both from the twelfth or thirteenth century; Yaśodhara Bhaṭṭa's *Rasaprakāśasudhākara*, Nityanātha's *Rasaratnākara*, and the *Mātṛkabheda Tantra*, all from the thirteenth century; Nāgārjuna's *Rasendramaṅgala* and Vāgbhaṭṭa the Second's *Rasaratnasamucchaya*, both from the thirteenth or fourteenth century; the fourteenth-century *Ānandakanda*, and Ādinātha's *Khecarī Vidyā*, also from the fourteenth century.

SEE ALSO Āyurveda; Gorakhnāth; Nāgārjuna.

BIBLIOGRAPHY

The most comprehensive studies of Indian alchemy are David Gordon White's *The Alchemical Body: Siddha Traditions in Medieval India* (Chicago, 1996) and the rich survey of the alchemical canon found in G. Jan Meulenbeld's *A History of Indian Medical Literature*, 5 vols. (Groningen, Netherlands, 1999–2003). Several outstanding articles on Indian alchemy have been authored by Arion Roşu, among which are "Alchemy and Sacred Geography in the Medieval Deccan," *Journal of the European Ayurvedic Society* 2 (1992): 151–156, and "*Mantra* et *Yantra* dans la médecine et l'alchimie indiennes," *Journal Asiatique* 274, nos. 3–4 (1986): 205–268. A useful compendium of Indian alchemical texts in Sanskrit, with commentary and selected English-language translations, is Bhudeb Mookerji's *Rasa-jala-nidhi; or, Ocean of Indian Chemistry and Alchemy*, 5 vols. (Calcutta, 1926–1938). Excellent historical studies of Indian alchemy, in Hindi, are Satya Prakash's *Prācīn Bhārat meṃ Rasāyan kā Vikās* (Allahabad, India, 1960) and Siddhinandan Mísra's *Āyurvedīya Raśāsastra*, Jaikrishnadas Āyurveda Series no. 35 (Banaras, India, 1981).

DAVID GORDON WHITE (1987 AND 2005)

ALCHEMY: HELLENISTIC AND MEDIEVAL ALCHEMY

By the beginning of the Christian era, a change in secular and religious attitudes can be discerned. The rationalism that had guided the thinking of the elite in previous times waned, and the rise of skepticism and loss of direction led to a philosophical vacuum that stimulated a recourse to mystic intuition and divine mysteries. The area of the Roman Empire in which this process became primarily manifest was Egypt, where, after the conquest by Alexander the Great (in 332 BCE), the culture of Hellenism with its fusion of Greek and Eastern features was centered. The fashionable mystery beliefs subsumed under the names of Gnosticism and Hermetism exerted a strong attraction for practitioners of the occult sciences (astrology, magic, and medicine) as well as alchemy, the art of making gold: previously, men of science had by thought process and investigations obtained what they now expected to receive through divine revelation or supernatural inspiration. In short, science—as revealed knowledge and, for the alchemist, as a means of creating gold—turned into religion.

Such a link between alchemy and Gnosticism and Hermetism is most tangibly documented in the occult literature of Hellenistic Egypt from about the second to the fourth century. This emphasizes, first, the fact that alchemy, beyond being a craft devoted to changing matter, has a place also within the history of religions and, second, that in the alchemist's religious beliefs the general Gnostic tenets blended with his specific alchemical approach to the world. The impact of the craft can be discerned in four aspects of the cult: its doctrine, its ritual, its language, and its roots.

DOCTRINE. The soul is enchained in matter and is to be freed. Science as traditionally expounded in the schools was unable to liberate it. Only gnosis, the knowledge of God, could accomplish the task, and to convey gnosis, alchemy transformed itself into an esoteric religion. The beliefs were fantastic: visions, the chemical apparatus as a temple, the alchemical operation as a sacrificial act, mental baptism in the Hermetic vessel called the *kratēr*, and the ascension to God by means of a mystic ladder that transports the soul from the discord and suffering below to the divine order above. The doctrines of alchemy as a religion echoed the principles of alchemy as a science. These were essentially three: primal matter, sympathy, and transmutation.

Primal matter. The *opus alchimicum*, ("the alchemist's labor") centered on matter. Nobody knew, of course, what matter was, and it remained a secret of alchemy, although many chemical, mythological, and philosophical definitions were ventured in the course of time (Jung, 1953, p. 317). Thus, the *Tabula Smaragdina* (the revelation of secret alchemical teaching, of the ninth century but based on Hermetic sources) identified matter with God, because all created objects come from a single primal matter; and Comarius, an alchemist-philosopher (first century CE?) identified it with Hades, to whom the imperfect souls were chained (Jung, pp. 299, 319). Such perceptions of matter echo the alchemist's craft: his operation was, in mythical terms, a replica of divine creativity, aiming at the liberation of imprisoned matter. The inherent anthropomorphic view of matter, the "vitalist hypothesis," was going to play a fundamental role in the "sacred art," alchemy: metals, that is, matter, were considered living organisms, which are born, grow, and multiply. With the alchemist's preoccupation with matter and his belief that the divine soul is enchained in matter, he "takes upon himself the duty of carrying out the redeeming *opus*" (Jung, p. 306). Thus seen, the alchemist evolves into a priest.

Sympathy. The anthropomorphic perception of matter that assigned to the metal a human soul correlated with an occult system according to which the supposed affinity between substances expressed itself in a mutual attraction or rejection, that is, either "sympathy" or "antipathy." Such a bond linked, in particular, our world "below" to the world "above," the microcosm of man to the macrocosm of planetary divinities. The system of correspondences elaborated, for example, by the second-century astrologer Antiochus of Athens (Sheppard, *Ambix* 7, p. 46) embraced, in addition to "above" and "below," also elements, metals, and colors.

Already Maria Prophetissa (fl. early third century), also known as the "founding mother of alchemy," heralded the principle of parallelism: "Just as man results [from the association] of liquids, of solids, and of spirit, so does copper." Zosimos of Panopolis in Egypt (fl. c. 300), recognizing the identity between the behavior of matter and the events in his own (unconscious) psyche, condensed this complex insight into the formula "What is within is also without."

Transmutation. The third facet of alchemical religiosity was also linked to the alchemist's practice. A basic alchemical tenet stated that all substances could be derived through transmutation from primal matter. The technique of change consisted essentially in "coloring": the Egyptian alchemists did not intend to "make" gold but to color (*baptein*) metals and textiles through tinctures and elixirs so that they would "appear" like gold (or silver or some other metal). A "changed" metal, then, was a "new" metal. The technique of coloring evolved, in the end, into a powerful symbol of alchemical doctrine; for just as the alchemist transformed lead into silver, and silver into gold, so too he posited for matter, in his anthropomorphic view of it, a similar change, from body to spirit to soul. And in the frame of his doctrine, he identified this escalation with the renewal of man, to which he assigned the same chain of transmutations to reach the goal of redemption.

The ritual. Although the alchemist, who represented the religious bent of his profession, has been viewed as a priest, the identity of his congregation remains unknown. The sources, reading somewhat like tracts of edification, transmit no detail. Some have sensed in the texts evidence of the existence of a loosely structured brotherhood. Others, above all Festugière (1950, pp. 427–428), took the alchemical devotion (like the Hermetic) to be a cult adhered to by individuals or groups who practiced the "sacred art" and came under the spell of the mystic beliefs inherent in their work. Those nonpractitioners of alchemy who felt attracted were possibly members of the intelligentsia drawn to that particular version of modish Gnosticism.

The code that the devotee observed had various specific features. They concern the transmission of the creed, first to him and then from him, and the way of life expected of a spiritual father.

The mystagogues. The myth of transmission added the religious component to alchemical mysticism. The spokesmen invoked the authority of the supreme being, or its prophets, or the sages of old: "Behold [says Isis to her son as alchemist], the mystery has been revealed to you!" (Festugière, 1950, p. 260). Maria Prophetissa claimed that alchemical secrets were revealed to her by God. The Byzantine monk Marianus quoted alchemists saying to Maria: "The divine, hidden, and always splendid, secret is revealed to you."

With Egypt providing the setting of the cult, Egyptian mythical figures and divinities were the prime well-spring of inspiration: chiefly Thoth (Hellenized as Hermes Trismegistos), the legendary author of the Hermetica, and Isis, turned into the creators and teachers of alchemy to whom alchemical sayings and doctrines were attributed. Various Greek writings on alchemy that contained traces of Jewish monotheism were ascribed to Moses, probably in a homonymic transfer from the alchemist Moses of Alexandria. Later on, Jewish alchemical tradition evoked Enoch, the Jewish counterpart to Hermes. The Greek alchemist Pseudo-Democritus, looking in Memphis for enlightenment, conjured the ghost of the Persian Ostanes, the "Hellenized magus" of alchemy, who advised him: "The books are in the temple." Zosimos, our major source, owed his knowledge to the wisdom of Hermes.

Traditio mystica. The "sacred craft" was a secret craft. The goddess Isis instructs her son Horus: "Keep it a great secret [*megalomusterion*]." The initiated were forbidden to divulge their knowledge; they could pass it on only to their "legitimate sons" and to those who were "worthy." Alchemy, known through revelation, remained a privilege of the few, and the taboo of disclosure, well guarded through the ages, in an impressive example of *traditio mystica*, a very Hermetic feature.

Portrait of the alchemist. Just as revelation strikes the priest, so the divine mystery overwhelms the alchemist and shapes his way of life. His *opus* is not so much determined by technical knowledge and manual skill but, rather, by its true goal, redemption. His soul is to be saved. He has to strive for detachment from matter, for liberation from his passions, and for suppression of his body. He is spiritual man, alone, in search of himself, on a silent quest for God.

THE LANGUAGE OF ALCHEMY. Alchemy, like every other movement in the history of civilization, found its own forms of expression. Their pseudoscientific orientation imparted to the alchemical writings the stamp of mystery, and by displaying the "jargon of mysteries" (Festugière, 1950, p. 82) these texts produced the effect of liturgy and secured a screen against the profane. Three stylistic markers stand out:

Symbols. The alchemist, in the formulation of Wayne Shuhmaker, "did not analyze but analogized," and his own universe, metallurgy, provided the mythical imagery and stimulated new meanings. The alchemical *opus* centered on the change of matter, and transmutation of matter turned into the recurrent theme of the alchemist's cult. To him, the soul imprisoned in matter symbolized the spirit striving to purify itself from the roughage of the flesh. Matter was represented above all by metal and symbolized life and man, its growth comparable to the growth of the fetus. "The achievement of metallic transmutation became symbolic of the religious regeneration of the human soul" (Sheppard, *Ambix* 17, p. 77). With technical alchemy providing the similes that expressed Gnostic religiousity, the two-tiered semantic construct evolved that was characteristic of Hellenistic and medieval mystic language: the worldly, exoteric lexicon furnished the "surface," the *sensus litteralis*, but when applied to esoteric experience it yielded the hidden meaning, the *sensus allegoricus.*

Many lexical items were drawn into the process: thus, in the Valentinian system of Gnosticism (deriving from the second-century Egyptian Valentinus), metallurgical terms such as the following symbolized spiritual concepts. *Pneuma* signified, first, the product of natural sublimation, then, "divine spirit"; *ebullient* ("boiling up"), referring to the alchemical process of "separating the pure from the impure," was applied to wisdom; *sperma* (the "embryonic germ") yielded the "seed" of gnosis; in a similar way, such terms as *refine, filter,* and *purify* acquired spiritualized meanings. The transfer, through alchemy, from the literal to the symbolic realm contributed richly to the language of religion and, generally, abstraction. It indicates a conscious effort of the alchemist to frame his views in the terms of his craft.

Antonyms. Hellenistic alchemy tended to emphasize the varied contraries inherent in the craft: hot/cold, moist/dry, earth/air, fire/water. Antonymic structure was symbolically superimposed on matter: Maria Prophetissa distinguished metals as male and female as if they were human, and Zosimos distinguished between the metals' souls and bodies. The same antonymy, but with the focus on man himself, characterizes Gnostic dualism with its model of spiritual versus carnal man.

Aphorisms. Technical prescriptions, and in particular those that aimed at the transformation of matter, tended to be sharpened and honed so as to sound, in their lapidary style, like keys to mysteries. Such aphorisms, often bordering on the abstruse, were a favored feature of alchemical doctrine. For example, the first commandment requires secrecy and elitism: "One man to one man." Pseudo-Democritus, on the subject of liberating the imprisoned soul, declared "Transform the nature and make the spirit that is hidden inside the body come out." Maria Prophetissa said likewise, "Invert nature and you will find that which you seek."

Transmutation was tied to the law of sympathy and antipathy: "One nature rejoices in another nature; one nature triumphs over another nature; one nature masters another nature." One of Maria's axioms that subsumed a complex alchemical procedure was read by Jung (1953, p. 23) in psychological terms, according to which the even numbers signified the female principle and the odd numbers the male, the latter overwhelming the former: "One becomes two, two becomes three, and by means of the third the fourth achieves unity; thus two are but one." Maria focuses also on an analogy made between metals and humankind: "Join the male and the female, and you will find what you seek." A well-known aphorism expresses the analogy between macrocosm and microcosm: "That which is above is like to that which is below, and that which is below is like to that which is above." Several maxims rest on the principle of antonymy. The symbol of the serpent biting its tail is used to circumscribe diversity in unity: "The All is one and the All is through itself and the All goes to itself, and if it had not the All there would be no

All." The philosophers' stone is simply defined as "a stone that is not a stone."

ROOTS. The essence of the strange and complex phenomenon of alchemy is elusive, and its various interpreters were inclined to stress the feature that each considered, in genetic terms, to be its foundation. In particular, four possible sources have been isolated: classical philosophy, mystery creeds, the lore of the craft, and the workings of the unconscious.

Classical philosophy. The great cognitions of the classical tradition, from the pre-Socratics to Plato, Aristotle, and the Stoics, resurfaced in eclectic Hellenistic philosophy. Numerous doctrines prefigured crucial phases of the alchemical worldview: the concept of a primal matter; the unity of matter (seen in, say, water or fire); cosmic correspondences; the affinity of the similar; the microcosm reflecting the macrocosm; the notion of sympathy; transformation through *pneuma,* the all pervading spirit; genesis, that is, the origin of one element from another, proceding by way of opposites.

Mystery creeds. Hermetism and the alchemical cult overlap in various features. The tie between them is substantiated in the writings of Zosimos, the "divine," the "highly learned," and the outstanding representative of both creeds. The common ground consisted of "mystic reveries" (Festugière): observation and inquiry were rejected, and intuition replaced science; the "sacred craft" was revealed through divine grace; the chosen were few, bound to secrecy; and the goal was the liberation of the soul from the body.

The lore of the craft. Alchemy, hopelessly aiming at the transformation of metals into gold, has often been viewed as something like a misguided application of chemistry. Yet its significance lies, indeed lay even for its practitioners, not so much in the experimental method and the outcome of metallic transmutation as in other spheres, notably anthropology, religion, and folklore. The story has been reconstructed by Mircea Eliade: it goes back to archaic times and surfaced in Hellenistic Egypt. Its protagonist was the smith, the adept who dominated matter by transforming it. The insights deriving from his work gave rise to new meanings and symbols: matter was suffering; transmutation perfected matter; redemption was freedom from matter. In short, the primary function of alchemy, physical transmutation, escalated into metaphysical transmutation: the *opus alchimicum* became a symbol of the *opus divinum.* The title of one of the prominent alchemical works of the early post-Christian era by Pseudo-Democritus (and ascribed to Bolos from Mendes, in Egypt) stressed the dichotomy: *Phusika kai mustika* (Natural and Mystical Matters).

Depth psychology. The attribution of life to matter was the foundation of alchemical belief. Enticed by the resemblances between the dreams of his patients and alchemical symbols, C. G. Jung read this belief from his psychoanalytic standpoint as the projection of inner experience onto matter, and thus as the identification of matter with the Self. "Matter" evolved as a name for the "self." It represented an unconscious archetype, primordial images, and the alchemical *opus,* aiming at freeing, saving, and perfecting matter, and was a symbolic replica of the universal quest for the Self. Jung called it the "individuation" process.

Convergence. These four components of spiritual alchemy can be traced in Hellenistic Egypt. The craft of the goldsmith was flourishing, and metallurgy yielded the imagery while boosting, by its very nature, the identification, ever present in the human mind, of self and matter; Greek philosophy, in a stage of revival then and there, provided the basic concepts of the doctrine; and Hermetism supplied the vital climate of mystery.

Alchemy is described here as a facet of the ancient mystery religions, and this description centers on its style and manifestations in the Hellenistic period. But other cultures, tending in a similar direction, produced other varieties of spiritual alchemy. In China, it aimed at physical immortality and thus came into the orbit of medicine, with some link to the religious movement of Taoism. In India, as Eliade has shown, alchemy evolved as an analogue to the mystic discipline of yoga: that purification sought by the yogin for the body, the alchemist seeks through the purification of metals. The relationship (involving the question of polygenesis or monogenesis) between the Chinese, Indian, and Hellenic forms of spiritual alchemy is not very clear. Islamic culture, on the other hand, played a vital role in the transmission of alchemical knowledge; many of the Greek texts were translated into Arabic and through this link, reached the West during the late Middle Ages. Thus, the transmutation of matter continued, with its occult framework, into the Renaissance and beyond. But then modern science rejected ideology, and with the loss of its "exoteric" component to chemistry, alchemy was reduced to its "esoteric" questions about man's relation to the cosmos. In our day the mystic movement of the Rosicrucians, which appeared during the seventeenth century, is a typical relic—and faint echo—of the vanished Hellenistic cult.

SEE ALSO See also Gnosticism; Hermetism; Rosicrucians.

BIBLIOGRAPHY

The literature is large and rapidly growing. A comprehensive bibliography is Alan Pritchard's *Alchemy: A Bibliography of English-Language Writings* (London and Boston, 1980). The previous standard, *Collection des anciens alchimistes grecs,* edited and translated by Marcellin P. E. Berthelot and Charles-Émile Ruelle, 3 vols. (1887–1888; reprint, Osnabrück, 1967), will be superseded by *Les alchimistes grecs,* 12 vols. (1981–), a comprehensive edition of the texts, with French translations.

Good surveys, from varying standpoints and usually with bibliographical information, may be consulted in the standard cyclopedias: Wilhelm Gundel's "Alchemie," in *Reallexikon für Antike und Christentum* (Stuttgart, 1950); Franz Strunz's "Alchemie," in *Die Religion in Geschichte und Gegenwart,* 3d ed., vol. 1 (Tübingen, 1957); René Alleau's "Alchimie," in

Encyclopaedia Universalis, vol. 1 (Paris, 1968); Bernard Suler's "Alchemy," in *Encyclopaedia Judaica*, vol. 2 (Jerusalem, 1971); Manfred Ullmann's "Al-Kimiya," in *The Encyclopaedia of Islam*, new ed., vol. 5 (Leiden, 1979); and Robert P. Multhauf's "Alchemy," in *Encyclopaedia Britannica*, 15th ed., vol. 1 (Chicago, 1983).

The present overview draws, in particular, on the studies by A.-J. Festugière, *La révélation d'Hermès Trismégiste*, vol. 1 (Paris, 1950), and "Alchymica" (1939), reprinted in *Hermétisme et mystique païenne* (Paris, 1967); Mircea Eliade's *The Forge and the Crucible*, 2d ed. (Chicago, 1978); C. G. Jung's *Psychology and Alchemy*, translated by R. F. C. Hull (Princeton, 1953); and the various articles and reviews by H. J. Sheppard in the journal *Ambix*, listed in the index for volumes 1–17.

New Sources

Primary literature

Mertens, Michèle. *Les alchimistes grecs.* Paris, 1995.

Zosimos of Panopolis. *On the Letter Omega*, edited and translated by Howard M. Jackson. Missoula, Mt., 1978.

Secondary literature

Edwards, Mark J. "The Vessel of Zosimus the Alchemist." *Zeitschrift für Papyrologie und Epigraphik* 90 (1992): 55–64.

Faivre, Antoine. *The Eternal Hermes.* Grand Rapids, Mich., 1995.

Haage, Bernhard Dietrich. *Alchemie im Mittelalter.* Düsseldorf and Zürich, 1996.

Idel, Moshe. "The Origin of Alchemy according to Zosimos and a Hebrew Parallel." *Revue des Etudes Juifs* 145 (1986): 117–124.

Kahn, Didier, and Sylvain Matton, eds. *Alchimie: art, histoire et mythes. Actes du 1er colloque international de la Société d'étude de l'histoire de l'alchimie (Paris, Collège de France, 14–15–16 mars 1991).* Milan, 1995.

Matton, Sylvain. "Le commentaire dans la littérature alchimique." In *Le commentaire entre tradition et innovation. Actes du colloque international de l'Institut des traditions textuelles, Paris et Villejuif, 22–25 septembre 1999*, edited by Marie-Odile Goulet-Cazé et al., pp. 437–453. Paris, 2000.

Meinel, Christoph, ed. *Die Alchemie in der europäischen Kultur- und Wissenschaftsgeschichte.* Wiesbaden, 1986.

Von Martels, Z.R.W.N., ed. *Alchemy Revisited. Proceedings of the International Conference on the History of Alchemy at the University of Groningen. 17–19 April 1989.* Leiden, 1990.

HENRY KAHANE (1987)
RENÉE KAHANE (1987)
Revised Bibliography

ALCHEMY: ISLAMIC ALCHEMY

The Arabic term for alchemy is *al-kīmiyāʾ*. The word *kīmiyāʾ* is alternately derived from the Greek *chumeia* (or *chēmeia*), denoting the "art of transmutation," or from *kim-iya*, a South Chinese term meaning "gold-making juice." Greek and later Hellenistic writings are generally regarded as the initial impetus behind Muslim learning, thus the wide acceptance of the Greek origin of the word.

In the Islamic context, *al-kīmiyāʾ* refers to the "art" of transmuting substances, both material and spiritual, to their highest form of perfection. The word *kīmiyāʾ* also refers to the agent or catalyst that effects the transmutation and hence is used as a synonym for *al-iksīr* ("elixir") and *ḥajar al-falāsifah* ("philosopher's stone"). The search for the ideal elixir has been an ancient quest in many cultures of the world; it was supposed to transform metals to their most perfect form (gold) and minerals to their best potency and, if the correct elixir were to be found, to achieve immortality. All matter of a particular type, metals for example, were supposed to consist of the same elements. The correct *kīmiyāʾ* or *iksīr* would enable the transposition of the elements into ideal proportions and cause the metal concerned to be changed from a base form to a perfected form, for instance, copper to gold.

On another level, the philosophical theory of alchemy was used to conceptualize the purification of the soul. The terminology and procedures of alchemy were allegorized and applied to the transformation of the soul from its base, earthly, impure state to pure perfection. Elementary psychological postulations were allegorized as chemical properties. For the mystics, the *iksīr* served as a symbol of the divine truth that changed an unbeliever into a believer. In Ṣūfī literature, the spiritual master purifies the soul of the adept via various processes of spiritual alchemy. This usage of alchemical principles in the spiritual realm reflects the worldview of the ancients, including those of medieval Islam, whereby the human soul was regarded as a microcosm of the forces and principles contained in the macrocosm of the universe.

HISTORICAL BACKGROUND. In Muslim tradition, alchemy enjoys ancient roots. The cultivation of alchemy is traced back to Adam, followed by most of the major prophets and sages. This chain of transmission is then connected to the "masters" from the ancient world, including Aristotle, Galen, Socrates, Plato, and others. Muslims are considered to have received the art from these masters. In Islamic times, the prophet Muḥammad (d. 632 CE), is said to have endorsed the art, lending it grace and power; his cousin and son-in-law, ʿAlī ibn Abī Ṭālib (d. 661), is regarded as its patron. ʿAlī's descendant Jaʿfar al-Ṣādiq (d. 765) is portrayed as the next major transmitter. The Umayyad prince Khālid ibn Yazīd (660–704) is depicted as both a practitioner and a patron of alchemy who encouraged the translation of relevant Greek and Syriac texts into Arabic. Legendary tales indicate that he learned the art from a Syrian monk named Marianos, whom he sought out on long journeys to strange lands. Jābir ibn Ḥayyān (d. c. 815), who is held to be the disciple of Jaʿfar al-Ṣādiq, is credited with more than three hundred treatises on alchemy; consequently, the name of this quasi-historical figure came to imply the authority and teacher par excellence.

The Jabirian corpus. By contrast with these legendary accounts, modern scholarship places the development of Islamic alchemy in the ninth century. Jābir ibn Ḥayyān is indeed recorded as the first major alchemist, but the writings attributed to him are mainly pseudepigraphical, and many appeared as late as the tenth century. The *Book of Mercy,* the *Book of the Balances,* the *Book of One Hundred and Twelve,* the *Seventy Books,* and the *Five Hundred Books* are some of the important works in the collection. Movements such as the Ikhwān al-Ṣafā᾽ (Brethren of Purity) probably influenced or even contributed to some of the treatises in the Jabirian corpus, which forms an important source of information on alchemic techniques, equipment, materials, and attitudes.

According to the sulfur-mercury theory of metals introduced in the corpus, all metals were considered to possess these two elements, or the two principles they represent, in varying proportions, the combination of which lends each metal its peculiarities. Sulfur was responsible for the hot/dry features and mercury, the cold/moist ones. (Aristotle considered these four features to be represented by fire, earth, air, and water respectively.) Sulfur and mercury embody the positive and negative aspects of matter, also referred to as male and female properties.

The *Book of the Balances* theorizes that the metals are generated from contrary elements. Each body expresses an equilibrium of the natures composing it, and this harmony can be expressed numerically by the musical harmony that governs the heavens. The qualitative differences and degrees of intensity of the natures are analogous to the differences of tone in the musical scale. Further, each body represents a balance between internal and two external qualities, with each metal characterized by two internal and two external qualities. The transmutation of one metal into another is thus an adjustment of the ratio of the latent and manifest constituents of the first to the second, an adjustment to be brought about by an elixir. Each metal is regarded as an inversion of one of the others, and transmutation is a simple changing of qualities, which could be accomplished the same way that a physician cures by counterbalancing an excessive humor with one of contrary quality. The elixirs, in other words, were the alchemists' medicines.

According to the Jabirian corpus, there are various elixirs suitable for specific transmutations, but transmutations of every kind could be brought about by a grand or master elixir, the prime focus of the alchemists' endeavors. An important and original link between theory and practice is provided by the Jabirian author of the *Seventy Books,* who explains that material phenomena can be separated not only into their elements but into the contrary qualities by distillation. The inflammable and nonflammable vapors that are usually evolved when organic matter is subject to heat for distillation are considered to represent "fire" and "air." The condensable liquid that follows from the process is called "water," and the residue "earth." The author then attempts the division of these elements into the pair of qualities of which each was made. He claims not only that this process is applicable to organic matter but that even the hardest stones are distillable. The use of elixirs from the distillation of organic materials, which has been called a Jabirian innovation, indicates the medical orientation of alchemy. It is in their extensive pursuit of the elixir that the Jabirian treatises resemble those of al-Rāzī.

Al-Rāzī. The physician and philosopher Muḥammad ibn Zakariyā᾽ al-Rāzī (d. 925) is the next Muslim alchemist who made a major impact on the art. To the sulfur-mercury theory of the constitution of metals he added the attribute of salinity. The popular conception of alchemy with three elements—sulfur, mercury, and salt—reappeared in Europe and played an important role in Western alchemy. According to al-Rāzī, bodies were composed of invisible elements (atoms) and of empty space that lay between them. These atoms were eternal and possessed a certain size. This conception seems close to the explanation of the structure of matter in modern physics. Al-Rāzī's books, *Sirr al-asrār* (The secret of secrets) and *Madkhal al-ta῾līmī* (Instructive [or Practical] introduction), are important sources for understanding the principles and techniques of alchemy as practiced in the tenth-century Muslim world, specifically Iran. In them, he provides a systematic classification of carefully observed and verified facts regarding chemical substances, reactions, and apparatus, described in language that is free of mysticism and ambiguity. Of the voluminous Jabirian writings only the *Book of Mercy* is mentioned by al-Rāzī, perhaps because the other works were composed after his lifetime.

Other masters. Muḥammad ibn ῾Umayil (tenth century) was famous for his *Kitāb al-ma᾽ al-waraqī* (The book of the silvery water and the starry earth) and *Kitāb al῾ilm al-muktasab,* two of his main works on alchemy. The writings attributed to ῾Ali ibn Waḥshīyā᾽ (a legendary figure of the tenth century) provided encyclopedic information on the tradition of alchemy in Islam. He is an important source of information on the alchemists and their art. He also provides the views of prominent nonalchemists on the subject. Another important work compiled at this time is the *Muṣḥaf al-jamā῾ah,* known as the *Turba philosophorum* in its famous Latin translation; here the author, who has yet to be definitely identified, describes an ancient congress of alchemists chaired by Pythagoras, with Archelaus recording the doctrines expounded by nine pre-Socratic philosophers. Maslamah al-Majrīṭī (d. 1007?) was the author of the famous alchemical guide *Rutbat al-ḥakīm* (The step of the sages); his book on practical magic, *Gha῾yat al-ḥakīm* (The limit of the sages), was also very popular and was translated in the West. A notable figure in the following century is Ḥusayn ῾Ali al-Tughrā᾽i (d. 1121?), author of the important defense of alchemy *Kitāb ḥaqā῾iq al-isthishād fī-al-kīmiyā᾽* (Truths of the evidence submitted with regard to alchemy). Written in 1112, the work is a strong refutation of the negative polemics of Ibn Sīnā. Later documentation of the practice of alchemy is provided by the Egyptian Aydamir ibn ῾Alī al-Jildakī (d. 1360), whose encyclopedic works provide summaries of and commentaries upon everything that had been written on alchemy and magic before him.

Opposition to the Art. Although widespread, alchemy did not have the approval of all Muslim scholars. Thus Ibn

Sīnā (d. 1035) censured it as a futile activity and contested the assertion that humans are able to imitate nature. He asserted that the alchemists were only able to make something that externally resembles the precious metals, because the actual substance of base metals remained unchanged. The great North African historian Ibn Khaldūn (d. 1406) also made a critical assessment of Arab-Islamic alchemical activities. He characterized alchemy as the study of the properties, virtues, and temperatures of the elements used for the preparation of and search for an elixir that could transform lesser metals into gold. Elements used for the elixir included animal refuse, urine, manure, bones, feathers, blood, hair, eggs, and nails, as well as minerals. Distillation, sublimation, calcination, and other techniques were used to separate elements in the extracts used in the preparation of the elixir. Alchemists believed that if the correct elixir could be obtained by these methods, it could then be added to concocted lead, copper, or tin over fire to yield pure gold. For his part, Ibn Khaldūn rejected the alchemists' claims that their transmutations were intended to perfect the work of nature by mechanical and technical procedures. He also criticized the authenticity of works ascribed to Khālid ibn Yazīd and argued that the elaborate sciences and arts of Islam had not been developed in that early time.

Influence on the West. Islamic alchemy was brought to the West in the twelfth century, mostly through translations. The earliest extant Latin translation of an Arabic treatise on alchemy is generally considered to be Robert of Chester's work *De compositione alchemiae,* dating from 1144. Some scholars consider it as a possible later Latin forgery, but this issue is very complicated and requires further study. About the same time, Gerard of Cremona (1114–1187) translated the Jabirian *Seventy Books* into Latin; *De aluminibus et salibus* and *Liber luminis luminum* are considered his translations. Other works that seem to be translations from Arabic prior to the appearance of the first indigenous European alchemical writing (the *Ars alchemia,* c. 1225, attributed to Michael Scot, d. 1232) were the *De anima* of Ibn Sīnā, the *Turba philosophorum,* the *Emerald Tablet,* the *Secret of Creation,* and al-Rāzī's *Sirr al-asrār.* Thus it seems that the majority of celebrated Islamic alchemical works were known in Europe by the middle of the thirteenth century.

See Also Elixir.

Bibliography

For general surveys of Islamic alchemy, the following essays are useful: Salimuzzaman Siddiqi and S. Mahdihassan's "Chemistry," in *A History of Muslim Philosophy,* edited by M. M. Sharif (Wiesbaden, 1966), vol. 2, pp. 1296–1316; Seyyed Hossein Nasr's "Alchemy and Other Occult Sciences," in his *Islamic Science: An Illustrated Study* (Westerham, U.K., 1976), pp. 193–208; Eric J. Holmyard's "Alchemy in Medieval Islam," *Endeavour* 14 (July 1955): 117–125; Julius Ruska's *Turba Philosophorum: Ein Beitrag zur Geschichte der Alchemie* (Berlin, 1931); and Manfred Ullmann's "al-Kīmiyā," in *The Encyclopaedia of Islam,* new ed. (Leiden, 1960–). As yet no comprehensive critical study of the origin, development, and practices of traditional Islamic alchemy is available.

Overviews of Islamic alchemy within the context of global surveys of alchemy or chemistry can be found in Eric J. Holmyard's *Alchemy* (Baltimore, 1957), chap. 5; George Sarton's *Introduction to the History of Science,* 3 vols. in 5 (Washington, D.C., 1927–1948); Robert P. Multhauf's *The Origins of Chemistry* (London, 1966); *Studien zur Geschichte der Chemie,* edited by Julius Ruska (Berlin, 1927); and Homer H. Dub's "The Beginnings of Alchemy," *Isis* 38 (November 1947): 62–86. Dubs argues that alchemy in Islam originated in China.

Julius Ruska and Karl Garbers discuss the mutual relation of the corpus Jabirian and the writings of al-Rāzī, large alchemical works written at the end of the ninth and tenth centuries, in "Vorschriften zur Herstellung von scharfen Wässern bei Gabir und Razi," *Islam* 25 (1938): 1–35. Some of the problems surrounding these writings are studied in Ruska's *Chālid ibn Jazīd ibn Mu'āwija* and *Gā'far al-Sādiq der sechste Imām,* volumes 1 and 2 of *Arabische Alchemisten* (Heidelberg, 1924); in Paul Kraus's "Studien zu Jâbir Ibn Hayyân," *Isis* (February 1931): 7–30; and in Gerard Heym's "Al-Rāzī and Alchemy," *Ambix* 1 (March 1938): 184–191.

A valuable study of the secret names used by Arab alchemists is Julius Ruska and E. Wiedemann's "Alchemistische Decknamen," in *Sitzungsberichte der physikalisch-medicinische Sozietät* (Erlangen, 1924). Their study partially utilizes al-Tugra'ī's *Kitāb al-Jawhar al-nādir* (Book of the brilliant stone).

Habibeh Rahim (1987)

ALCHEMY: RENAISSANCE ALCHEMY

The Renaissance and post-Renaissance period marked both the high point and the turning point of alchemy in the West. During the same years in which Kepler, Galileo, Descartes, Boyle, and Newton wrote their revolutionary scientific works, more alchemical texts were published than ever before. But under the impact first of the Reformation and later of the seventeenth-century scientific revolution, alchemy was profoundly changed and ultimately discredited. The organic, qualitative theories of the alchemists were replaced by an atomistic, mechanical model of change, which eventually undermined the alchemical theory of transmutation. The balance between the spiritual and the physical, which had characterized alchemical thought throughout its long history, was shattered, and alchemy was split into two halves, theosophy and the practical laboratory science of chemistry.

The Practice of Alchemy. For the most part Renaissance alchemists accepted the theories and practices of their ancient and medieval predecessors. By the time the study of alchemy came to Europe, it was already an established discipline with a respected past. The theories upon which it was based were an integral part of ancient philosophy. Western scientists accepted these theories precisely because they provided plausible explanations for the way events were observed to occur in nature and the laboratory. Transmutation was seen to be an aspect of all forms of change. Caterpillars turn into butterflies; ice melts; food becomes flesh. Long before there were practicing alchemists, the mechanism behind these transformations was investigated. The ancients had supplied explanations that satisfied most alchemists up to the seventeenth century. By combining Aristotelian physics, Stoicism, and Hermetism, Western alchemists evolved a vitalistic philosophy that viewed all phenomena as alive and striving for perfection. Whatever is imperfect (the base metal lead, for example) will eventually become perfect (gold) in the course of time or with the help of the mysterious substance known to alchemists as the philosopher's stone.

Although transmutation appeared straightforward on a theoretical level, it proved more difficult to accomplish in practice. Thomas Norton, a famous fifteenth-century English alchemist whose *Ordinall of Alkimy* was one of the most popular alchemical works of the period, describes how frustrating the work of an alchemist could be. Just finding the appropriate raw materials was difficult enough. Norton gives a poignant portrait of an alchemist who has fallen into despair because after years of fruitless experimenting he cannot decide what to try next. Even if an alchemist was lucky enough to choose the right ingredients, there arose the additional problem of determining what to do with them.

The steps of transmutation were laid out clearly in respect to color. The work had to proceed from the black stage, during which time the alchemists believed they killed the substances in their vessels, through the white stage, during which the ingredients were purified, to the final red stage, which marked the successful fabrication of the philosopher's stone. As Norton explains, "Red is the last work in Alkimy."

Although the color sequence was well established, Renaissance alchemists could not agree on the chemical processes necessary to produce the change from black to white to red. The most optimistic practitioners said the stone was made from one substance in one vessel in one operation, but judging from pictures depicting the cluttered array of apparatus littering laboratory floors, most alchemists took a less sanguine and simplistic view of their task. Daniel Stolcius illustrates eleven chemical processes in his book on alchemical emblems (*Viridarium chymicum . . .*, 1624). Salomon Trismosin reduced the number to seven in his *Splendor Solis.* George Ripley, another respected English adept, describes twelve steps in his *Twelve Gates of Alchemy.* Dom Pernety, a French alchemist living in the eighteenth century, associates each process with one sign of the zodiac:

(1) calcination (Aries)

(2) congelation (Taurus)

(3) fixation (Gemini)

(4) dissolution (Cancer)

(5) digestion (Leo)

(6) distillation (Virgo)

(7) sublimation (Libra)

(8) separation (Scorpio)

(9) ceration (Sagittarius)

(10) fermentation (Capricorn)

(11) multiplication (Aquarius)

(12) projection (Pisces)

Alchemy had always been profoundly influenced by astrology. Since the alchemical signs of the seven metals were those of the seven planets, it seemed reasonable to assume that in their reactions they would respond to the movements of their namesakes in the heavens above.

It is not easy to describe and distinguish all the different alchemical processes. Calcination is simple enough: it involved heating a substance in an open or closed vessel and usually included oxidation and the blackening of the substance. (This process may have given alchemy one of its many names, "the black art.") Calcination was described by alchemists as "mortification," "death," or "putrefaction," and the alchemical vessel in which it occurred was the "tomb," the "coffin," even "Hades" or "Hell." Congelation and fixation consisted of making the substances solid and nonvolatile. This essential step brought the alchemist closer to gold, the most stable and "fixed" of all the metals. Dissolution and digestion were connected with the white stage and purification. Distillation and sublimation were confused by alchemists until the eighteenth century, but both processes awed them. When they saw vapors rise, condense, and revaporize, they thought they were witnessing a miraculous transformation in which the "soul" of matter separated from its "body" and reunited with it in a purer state.

Separation was an elastic term describing the filtration, decantation, or distillation of a liquid from its residue. With fermentation, multiplication, and projection, one arrives at the heart of the alchemical work of making the philosopher's stone. Through fermentation, the stone became akin to yeast and acquired the power to transmute substances. Multiplication augmented the power of the stone to such a degree that it could transmute many times its weight of base metal without losing its strength. In the final process, projection, the stone was made into a powder and thrown on whatever was to be transmuted.

Estimates about the length of time it took to make the philosopher's stone varied from one day to twelve years. The common analogy between the stone and a child (the stone was often referred to as the "royal child" or "son") explains why nine months was frequently cited. The conflicting estimates lead one to agree with Norton that for the alchemist patience was a preeminent virtue.

Another difficulty facing the alchemist was regulating the fire. Since a practical thermometer was not invented until the eighteenth century, this was an almost impossible task. Many alchemists inadvertently blew up their experiments by applying too much heat or ruined months of work by allowing the fire to die out. The problem of heat was so crucial that Norton devoted a chapter of his *Ordinall* to the subject and describes the alchemist who properly controls the fire as "a parfet Master."

The obscurity of alchemical texts provided a final and often insurmountable obstacle facing Renaissance alchemists. Alchemists were masters of metaphor. They dressed up their instructions in parables and allegories, veiled them in symbols, delighted in enigmas, and preferred to call a substance by any name other than its common one. Even the great genius Newton found himself baffled by the obscurity of alchemical literature and symbolism.

The opacity of alchemical writings was partly a response to opposition from the church, which was suspicious of the religious implications of alchemical symbolism. Alchemists were also justifiably afraid of running afoul of national laws against counterfeiting; they were afraid of being kidnapped as well. Alchemical literature is filled with stories of adepts captured by impoverished adventurers intent on wresting the secret of transmutation from them. It was therefore only prudent for alchemists to disguise their secret wisdom as well as their own identities.

Aside from the real dangers of imprisonment, excommunication, or capture, there were other reasons for the obscurity of alchemical writings. Over the centuries, the meaning of many alchemical terms changed, and the continual translation of alchemical texts (from Greek to Arabic to Latin and then into the vernaculars) compounded the confusion. The most important reason for their obscurity, however, is rooted in the nature of alchemy itself. Alchemy shared the same mystical associations that surrounded mining and metallurgy among ancient and primitive peoples. Alchemy was as much a spiritual process as a physical one, and the obscurity of alchemical language reflects its religious orientation.

ALCHEMY AS A SPIRITUAL DISCIPLINE. Mystery and religion, which were a part of alchemy from its beginnings, gained in importance from the Renaissance onward. In many cases alchemy moved out of the laboratory altogether and into the monk's cell or philosopher's study. "Our gold is not common gold," wrote the sixteenth-century author of the *Rosary of Philosophers.* The popularity of alchemy as a spiritual discipline coincided with the breakdown of religious orthodoxy and social organization during the Renaissance and the Reformation. Petrus Bonus was one of the many alchemists to emphasize the spiritual nature of alchemy. It was, he says in his work *The New Pearl of Great Price,* revealed by God, not for humanity's material comfort, but for its spiritual well-being. For these spiritual alchemists, alchemy had nothing to do with the making of gold. (They dismissed those alchemists benighted enough to think it did as "sooty empiricks" or "puffers.") All the ingredients mentioned in alchemical recipes—the minerals, metals, acids, compounds, and mixtures—were in truth only one, the alchemist, who was the base matter in need of purification by the fire; and the acid needed to accomplish this transformation came from the alchemist's own spiritual malaise and longing for wholeness and peace. The various alchemical processes had nothing to do with chemical change; they were steps in the mysterious process of spiritual regeneration. Spiritual alchemists constantly stress the moral requirements of their art. The author of *Aurora Consurgens,* for example, insists that alchemists must be humble, holy, chaste, virtuous, faithful, charitable, temperate, and obedient. These are not qualities expected of a practical chemist. That they were emphasized by spiritual alchemists demonstrates how dominant the religious aspects of alchemy had become.

The interpretation of alchemy as a spiritual discipline offended many churchmen, who viewed the combination of alchemical concepts and Christian dogma in the writings of spiritual alchemists as dangerous heresy. One of the most daring appropriations of Christian symbolism was made by Nicholas Melchior of Hermanstadt, who expounded the alchemical work in the form of a mass. Melchior had been anticipated to some extent by Norton, who had called his book an "Ordinall." Heinrich Khunrath (1560–1601) provides another example of alchemy's spiritual extremists. In his *The Amphitheatre of Eternal Wisdom,* Khunrath interprets transmutation as a mystical process occurring within the adept's soul. He calls the alchemist's laboratory a *Lab Oratorium.* Spiritual alchemists like Khunrath often identified the philosopher's stone with Christ on the grounds that both redeemed base matter. Hermann Kopp, the nineteenth-century historian of alchemy, was scandalized by the parallel drawn between Christ and the philosopher's stone, which subject took up more than fifty pages in the alchemical tract *Der Wasserstein der Weysen* (*Die Alchemie in älterer und neuer Zeit,* 1886, vol. l, p. 254). Not only did spiritual alchemists identify the philosopher's stone with Christ, but they identified themselves with both. The heresy involved is obvious. Luther was one of the few highly placed churchmen to praise alchemy both for its practical uses and for its verification of Christian doctrine.

Alchemists of the sixteenth and seventeenth centuries drew many of their ideas from Renaissance Neoplatonism and Hermetism. In all three systems, the world was seen as a single organism penetrated by spiritual forces that worked at all levels, the vegetable, animal, human, and spiritual. Frances Yates has brillantly described the "magus" mentality that evolved from these ideas and encouraged people to believe they could understand and control their environment. This state of mind is illustrated in the writings of Paracelsus (1493–1541). For Paracelsus, God was the divine alchemist, who created the world by calcinating, congealing, distilling, and sublimating the elements of chaos. Chemistry was the key to the universe, which would disclose the secrets of theology, physics, and medicine. The alchemists had only to read the reactions in their laboratories on a grand scale to fathom the mysteries of creation.

RENAISSANCE ALCHEMY AND MODERN SCIENCE. By instilling some of the grandiose ideas of spiritual alchemy into the practical study of chemical reactions, Paracelsus and his followers transformed alchemy into a universal science of matter concerned with every aspect of material change. "Chemistry is nothing else but the Art and Knowledge of Nature itself," wrote Nicolas le Fèvre in his popular book, *A Compleat Body of Chemistry* (1670). This greatly expanded vision of alchemy's role struck a responsive cord in the millenarian movements prevalent in Europe during the sixteenth and seventeenth centuries. The Rosicrucian manifestos were typical of the utopian visions in the air. Using the language and imagery of spiritual alchemy, they called for the regeneration of society and outlined in broad strokes the social, economic, political, and religious reforms necessary.

No one knows who wrote the Rosicrucian manifestos. They have been attributed to Johann Valentin Andrea (1586–1654), whose acknowledged writings contain a similar blend of utopianism and spiritual alchemy. In his most famous work, *Christianopolis,* Andrea describes an ideal society organized to promote the health, education, and welfare of its citizens. One of the institutions in this society is a "laboratory" dedicated to the investigation of nature and to the application of useful discoveries for the public good.

Francis Bacon (1561–1626) was one of the many philosophers influenced by the Rosicrucian manifestos. Bacon looked forward to what he called a "Great Instauration" of learning that would herald the return of the Golden Age. He described this in his own utopia, *The New Atlantis.*

Neither Andrea nor Bacon said much that was new or significant in terms of science. What was novel in their visions was the idea of a scientific institution whose members worked by a common method toward a common goal. The secrecy and mystery that had been such a basic part of alchemy played no role in the scientific societies each describes, although their visions had been sparked by the utopian schemes of spiritual alchemists. This was one of the most important innovations to emerge in all the utopian literature of the seventeenth century and the one that had the greatest impact on the decline of alchemy. Once alchemists openly communicated their discoveries, the stage was set for the tremendous advances that have come to be expected from the natural sciences.

In 1655 a small book was published entitled *Chymical, Medicinal, and Churgical Addresses: Made to Samuel Hartlib, Esquire.* Between the covers of this slim volume, the old and the new alchemy lie side by side. The arcane and bombastic variety of spiritual alchemy is represented by Eirenaeus Philalethes's *Ripley's Epistle to King Edward Unfolded;* but the new alchemy, dedicated to the cooperative investigation of nature for the public good, is advocated in a treatise by Boyle significantly entitled *An Invitation to a free and generous Communication of Secrets and Receits of Physick.* Boyle urged alchemists to share their secrets for the sake of common charity and scientific advancement.

The Reformation was both a cause and a consequence of a growing attitude of philosophical skepticism, which brought all the wisdom of past ages into doubt. Although skepticism was bitterly opposed by philosophers and theologians on the grounds that it undermined the very possibility of rational knowledge, it paradoxically contributed in the long run to the development of a constructive scientific method that benefited all the sciences. Observation and experiment became the shibboleths of the new science and, eventually, the cause of alchemy's undoing. As more and more negative evidence was gradually accumulated through careful laboratory experiments, the alchemical dream of transmutation faded into the recesses of history.

SEE ALSO Metals and Metallurgy.

BIBLIOGRAPHY

General accounts of the history of Renaissance alchemy and the emergence of chemistry may be found in my *Alchemy: The Philosopher's Stone* (Boulder, Colo., 1980); Allen G. Debus's *The Chemical Philosophy: Paracelsian Science and Medicine in the Sixteenth and Seventeenth Centuries,* 2 vols. (New York, 1977); Eric J. Holmyard's *Alchemy* (Baltimore, 1957); John Read's *Through Alchemy to Chemistry* (London, 1957); and J. R. Partington's *A History of Chemistry,* 4 vols. (London, 1961–1970). *Ambix: The Journal for the Society for the Study of Alchemy and Early Chemistry* (Cambridge, 1937–1979) contains important specialized articles. Maurice P. Crosland's *Historical Studies in the Language of Chemistry* (London, 1962) provides an invaluable guide to the intricacies of alchemical terminology. Betty J. Dobbs's *The Foundations of Newton's Alchemy* (Cambridge, 1975) sheds light on the period of transition from alchemy to chemistry. The best introduction to Paracelsus is Walter Pagel's *Paracelsus* (New York, 1958). Renaissance Neoplatonism, Hermetism, and the Qabbalah are brilliantly described and analyzed in Frances Yates's *Giordano Bruno and the Hermetic Tradition* (London, 1964). She discusses the Rosicrucian manifestos in *The Rosicrucian Enlightenment* (London, 1972). H. J. Sheppard has published important articles on alchemical symbolism in *Ambix.* Jacques van Lennep's *L'art et l'alchimie* (Paris, 1966) is also useful. J. W. Montgomery discusses Luther's views on alchemy in "Cross, Constellation and Crucible: Lutheran Astrology and Alchemy in the Age of Reformation," *Ambix* 11 (1963): 65–86.

There are several collections of Renaissance alchemical texts. Thomas Norton's *Ordinall* and George Ripley's *Twelve Gates* can be found in Elias Ashmole's *Theatrum Chemicum Britannicum* (1652; reprint, New York, 1967). *Theatrum Chemicum* (1659–1661) provides six volumes of alchemical writings. Another collection, the *Musaeum Hermeticum Reformatum* (Frankfurt, 1678) has been translated by Arthur E. Waite as *The Hermetic Museum,* 2 vols. (London, 1893).

New Sources

Beitchman, Philip. *Alchemy of the Word: Cabala of the Renaissance.* Albany, N.Y., 1998.

Debus, Allen G., and Michael T. Walton, eds. *Reading the Book of Nature: The Other Side of the Scientific Revolution.* Kirksville, Mo., 1998.

Dee, Arthur. *Fasciculus Chemicus.* Translated by Elias Ashmole. Edited by Lyndy Abraham. New York, 1997.

Hakansson, Hakan. "Seeing the Word: John Dee and Renaissance Occultism." Ph.D. diss., Lund University, Sweden, 2001.

Linden, Stanton J. *Darke Hierogliphicks: Alchemy in English Literature from Chaucer to the Restoration.* Lexington, 1996.

Secret, François. *Lectures on the Rosticrucian Enlightenment, the History of Alchelmy in the Renaissance, Guillaume Postel en 1981, Christian Kabbalah, Postel's Kabbaslistic Mysticism.* [Calgary], 1981.

Szulakowska, Urszula. *The Alchemy of Light: Geometry and Optics in Late Renaissance Alchemical Illustration.* Leiden and Boston, 2000.

ALLISON COUDERT (1987)
Revised Bibliography

ALCUIN (730/40–804), also known as Albinus; educator, poet, theologian, and liturgist successively at York, the Carolingian court, and Saint-Martin's, Tours. The son of a Northumbrian small landowner, Alcuin joined the York cathedral community in boyhood; he maintained a lifelong devotion to it and to its magister Ælbert, whose influence on him was rivaled only by the writings of Bede. When Ælbert was archbishop (767–778/80), the deacon Alcuin was entrusted with the teaching of adolescents (age fourteen and upward), including some attracted from other lands. His devotion to York's "saints" (e.g., its bishops) but also his concern about the failures of recent Northumbrian kings were expressed in a long poem written in the 780s. In 781, while in Italy, Alcuin met Charlemagne, who invited him to his court. By the late 780s he stood out from other clerics and scholars there because of his influence on royal administrative and other texts, and because of his qualities as a teacher. He was again in York from 790 to 793, trying to guide a weak king; and while there he was asked by Charlemagne to comment on the problem of images. Returning to Francia, he was responsible for the Synod of Frankfort's major statements against the Spanish adoptionist heresy (794).

The teaching Alcuin provided in the spelling (and pronunciation) of Latin, in grammar, rhetoric, and dialectic, was partly written down in the mid-790s. In the same period he was composing or adapting earlier prayers for private use and for new masses; the contention that he was responsible for the Supplement to the Roman Gregorian sacramentary cannot be supported. He argued strongly that conversion from paganism could only be by conviction and not imposed. Moving to Saint-Martin's as its abbot in 796/7, Alcuin engaged in an extensive correspondence with the king, fellow scholars, and former pupils; he also attracted younger scholars to Tours, in whose circle ancient logic was applied to theological problems. He produced increasingly elaborate critiques of adoptionism, drawing on a wide range of patristic and other texts; he wrote useful if hardly independent works of exegesis and a substantial work on the Trinity. He played a formative part in the preparation for the Imperial Coronation of 800, although the uniquely important part sometimes claimed for him is questionable. He supervised the production of an excellent working text of the Vulgate, widely disseminated in the ninth century by Tours scribes. One of his last works was a substantial handbook for private devotion. Much of his teaching was quickly out-of-date because his own pupils improved on it, but his personal reputation began to diminish only in the later ninth century. His pedagogic works were used by some eleventh- and twelfth-century cathedral schools, and ordinary parish priests read his work on the Trinity throughout the Middle Ages. Clergy and laity have prayed in Alcuin's words down to the present.

BIBLIOGRAPHY

Bullough, Donald A. "Alcuin and the Kingdom of Heaven: Liturgy, Theology and the Carolingian Age." In *Carolingian Essays: Andrew W. Mellon Lectures in Early Christian Studies,* edited by Uta-Renate Blumenthal, pp. 1–69. Washington, D.C., 1983. A reassessment of Alcuin's achievement on the basis of the textual and manuscript evidence.

Gaskoin, C. J. B. *Alcuin: His Life and Work* (1904). Reprint, New York, 1966. Still the best book-length biography, although in need of correction in both emphasis and detail.

Godman, Peter, ed. *Alcuin: The Bishops, Kings and Saints of York.* Oxford, 1982. A fine edition of Alcuin's longest poem with an important introduction.

Wallach, Luitpold. *Alcuin and Charlemagne: Studies in Carolingian History and Literature.* 2d ed. New York, 1968. A major contribution by a philologist and textual scholar, although at times wrongheaded. Excellent bibliography.

DONALD A. BULLOUGH (1987)

ÁLFAR (elves) are a supernatural race in Scandinavian mythology. Old Norse *álfr* corresponds to Old English *ælf* and Old High German *alp,* designating a spirit with a nature both beautiful and monstrous. Snorri Sturluson (1179–1241) divides the elves into two groups. The light elves are allied with the gods and share their dwellings in the sky (for example, the home of the god Freyr is called Álfheimr, "elf home"). A poetic circumlocution for "sun" was *álfrǫðull* (ray of the elves). Although the function of sky-dwelling elves is not specified, eddic poetry accentuates their alliance with the gods through the recurrent phrase "Æsir and elves" (e.g., *Vǫluspá,* st. 48, and *Þrymskviða,* st. 7). (The Æsir are the dominant group of gods.) An Old English charm also couples them with the Æsir, suggesting that in early times they had stood nearly on a par with the gods. The dark elves are skilled in smithcraft like the dwarves and are sometimes indistinguishable from them. Late medieval prose narratives depict the *álfar* as earth-dwelling spirits of great potency and sometimes describe female *álfar* as skilled in weaving magic cloth or as endowed with seductive beauty.

Elves were the recipients of cultic worship. The *álfablót* (sacrifice to the elves) was performed in Sweden in late autumn on individual farmsteads, according to the Icelander

Sighvatr Þórðarson, who in 1018 was traveling there on a mission for King Olaf Haraldsson of Norway. Coming to one farm, he found the housewife standing in the doorway. She told him to make off; she feared the wrath of Óðinn if he stayed, as she was holding a sacrifice to the elves. The account gives the impression that the housewife herself was conducting the sacrifice and that it was a private ceremony to which no strangers were admitted. From the tone of the poem that Sighvatr composed about the Swedes' lack of hospitality on the occasion, it appears that the *álfablót* was not performed in Christian Norway or Iceland. An earlier Norwegian king, Olaf, ruler of the district of Geirstaðir during the pagan era, was believed to bring prosperity and good harvests if sacrifices were made at his burial mound; this led to his posthumous nickname *Geirstaðaálfr* (elf of Geirstaðir). This suggests that elves, dwelling in mounds, had come to be identified with the dead.

Scholars consider the *álfar* to be forces either of sterility or death. But the *álfar* show such divergent qualities that it is not possible to obtain a clear image of their nature, although they were obviously potent forces of enduring significance. The West Germanic concept of elves began to differ from the Scandinavian one even in the early Middle Ages, and in the Anglo-Saxon area an independent tradition in folklore developed as a result of Celtic influence. But as in the Scandinavian sources, the elves are grouped with the monsters *eotenas* and *orcneas* in the Old English poem *Beowulf,* whereas other Old English texts preserve the term *ælfsciene* (beautiful as an elf).

SEE ALSO Dvergar; Germanic Religion.

BIBLIOGRAPHY

See John Lindow's *Scandinavian Mythology: An Annotated Bibliography* (New York, 1988). Among the handbooks, Hilda R. Ellis Davidson devotes a chapter to the *álfar* in *The Road to Hel: A Study of the Conception of the Dead in Old Norse Literature* (1942; reprint, New York, 1968), and the *álfar* are also discussed in Gabriel Turville-Petre's *Myth and Religion of the North* (London, 1964). The encyclopedia-style entries of Rudolf Simek's *Dictionary of Northern Mythology* (Cambridge, UK, 1993) and John Lindow's *Handbook of Norse Mythology* (Santa Barbara, Calif., 2001) are very detailed.

ELIZABETH ASHMAN ROWE (2005)

ALFASI, YITSḤAQ BEN YAʿAQOV

(1013–1103), also known by the acronym RIF (Rabbi Yitsḥaq al-Faasi); North African–Spanish Talmudist. Alfasi spent the majority of his life in North Africa, where he headed the school in Fez (Fas in Arabic, hence his name). At the age of seventy-five he was forced by political intrigues to leave for Spain, where he presided over the school at Lucena. Despite the hostility of some native scholars, the aged Alfasi gained wide recognition in his new home, attracted many disciples (among them the brilliant Yosef ibn Migash, his successor at Lucena), and was described by the twelfth-century historian Avraham ibn Daud as the leading scholar of his time. Alfasi's exposure to Spanish Jewry came at the end of his long life; he was not attracted to the philosophy and belles lettres characteristic of Spain but remained a towering Talmudist.

Alfasi's major achievement was his digest of Talmudic law, *Sefer ha-halakhot* (Book of Laws; Jerusalem, 1969), which encompassed all topics relevant to Jewish practice of his time, thus eliminating materials connected with the Temple and its system of priestly dues, sacrifices, and related purities. Coming toward the end of the geonic period, Alfasi perfected the digest form pioneered by the eighth-century *Halakhot gedolot* and others. Like them, he retains the structure of the Talmud itself, which he condenses, rather than presenting a topical discussion (for which some precedent already existed) or a code. Nonetheless, Alfasi's work overshadowed that of his predecessors completely. In essence, he managed to strike a balance between the prolix, often indecisive Talmudic discussion and the brief, intellectually unsatisfying digest of earlier authorities. Alfasi's digest provided the halakhic decision through its careful elimination and shaping of materials, yet it also retained the basic Talmudic discussion. Thus, his work satisfied the needs of authorities and students alike. Indeed, Alfasi's work was often studied in place of the Talmud, inasmuch as it presented the most significant aspects of the Talmudic discussion and guided the student toward a conclusive position on the given issue. Ibn Daud appropriately termed the digest a "miniature Talmud," and the name stuck.

The degree and nature of Alfasi's independence was already a topic of discussion in late medieval times. It would appear that Alfasi occasionally adopted a critical stance toward certain Talmudic materials, and this evaluative posture is a component of his decision-making process. This aspect of his work came to the fore when he decided on the status of various Talmudic comments, a technique apparently utilized later by Maimonides. Alfasi was a central figure in assuring the Babylonian Talmud's ascendency over the Palestinian Talmud: his statement (at the close of his digest of *ʿEruvin*) that the Babylonian Talmud, being the later work, knew and incorporated all that was valuable in the Palestinian had great circulation and influence. Nonetheless, modern scholars are divided as to the extent of Alfasi's own rejection of the Palestinian Talmud. Alfasi's attitude toward the nonlegal (aggadic) portions of the Talmud is also noteworthy: unlike his predecessors, he included moral and theological materials that bore on actual practice.

Alfasi's digest became a major force in the subsequent shaping of Jewish law. Maimonides considered himself to be in the line of Alfasian tradition, claiming that he was in basic disagreement with Alfasi on only ten issues. Yosef Karo named Alfasi as one of the three authoritative medieval sources for his *Shulḥan ʿarukh,* the basic code of Jewish law that Karo compiled in the sixteenth century.

SEE ALSO Halakhah, article on History of Halakhah.

BIBLIOGRAPHY

The best overall discussion of Alfasi remains the detailed treatment of Isaac Hirsch Weiss, *Dor dor vedorshav*, vol. 4 (Vienna, 1887), pp. 281–290. Salo W. Baron's *A Social and Religious History of the Jews*, 2d ed., rev. & enl., vol. 6 (New York, 1958), pp. 84–90, 367–370, provides an intelligent historical overview as well as an ample bibliographical survey.

GERALD J. BLIDSTEIN (1987)

ʿALĪ IBN ABĪ ṬĀLIB (c. 599–661 CE) was the cousin and son-in-law of the prophet Muḥammad through his marriage to Fāṭimah. As father of the prophet's two grandsons, al-Ḥasan and al-Ḥusayn, he was forefather of the descendants of the Prophet (known as the *shurafāʾ*, sing. *sharīf*; or *sādāt*, sing. *sayyid)*; fourth of the four "rightly guided" caliphs; and first of the *imāms* for Shīʿī Muslims—the very term *Shīʿa* being originally *shīʿat ʿAlī*, the "partisans of ʿAlī."

ʿAlī is seen within the Islamic tradition as both a heroic warrior and an eloquent saint. Accorded deep veneration by Muslims generally, ʿAlī has also elicited sharply contrasting passions: on the one hand, cursed by official decree in Umayyad mosques for decades after his death; on the other hand, divinized by his extremist followers—the *ghulāt*—to the present day. The life of this seminal figure of nascent Islam was controversial, and his influence has been, and remains, pervasive.

LIFE. ʿAlī's life can be viewed in terms of three distinct phases: the first, from his birth (c. 599) to the death of the Prophet (632); the second, from the death of the Prophet to ʿAlī's assumption of the caliphate (656); the third consists of his own brief caliphate (656–661), a period characterized by the first civil wars of Islam.

Life with the Prophet, c. 599–632. Tradition relates that ʿAlī had the unique distinction of being born in the Kaʿbah in Mecca. His mother was Fāṭimah bint Asad; and his father, Abū Ṭālib, son of ʿAbd al-Muṭṭalib, was a leading member of the clan of the Hashimites. Abū Ṭālib took care of the young orphan, Muḥammad, son of his brother ʿAbd Allāh, and he was later to be Muḥammad's chief protector when the message of Islam was openly being preached in Mecca.

When he was about five years old, ʿAlī was taken into Muḥammad's household in order to relieve Abū Ṭālib during a famine. From this time until the death of the Prophet, ʿAlī was constantly at the Prophet's side, first as a member of the household, later as a leading companion, confidant, son-in-law, and scribe. ʿAlī wrote down not only the verses of the Qurʾanic revelation at the Prophet's dictation, but also several letters and treaties. As a warrior, ʿAlī was at the forefront of nearly all the major battles fought under the Prophet's banner, and he always emerged victorious in the single combat duels with which the battles began. His courage and skill as a warrior became legendary. Frequently fighting as standard-bearer, ʿAlī's most famous military success was in the Battle of Khaybar in 629, where victory against the hitherto impregnable fortresses was achieved through his heroic leadership. The Prophet declared, when the Muslims were unable to penetrate the defenses, that he would give his standard to one who "loves God and His Messenger and is loved by God and His Messenger," and through him victory would be granted. He sent for ʿAlī, who led the Muslims to victory. It was at Khaybar that ʿAlī's strength attained legendary status: he is said to have used as a shield a gate that, after the battle, could only be lifted by eight men.

Early merits. ʿAlī is regarded as the first male to enter the religion of Islam, though he was but a youth of nine or ten years old. When the Prophet was instructed by the revelation to warn his near kin (Qurʾān 26:214), he invited the leading members of his clan to a feast, and asked who among them would be "my brother, my executor, and my successor." ʿAlī, then still only about thirteen years old, was the only one who replied, and the Prophet affirmed him in all three respects, adding "Hearken to him and obey him" (Ibn Iṣḥāq, 1968, pp. 117–118).

When in 622 the Prophet migrated from Mecca to Medina, ʿAlī offered to take the place of the Prophet, sleeping in his bed on the night the Prophet departed, thus risking his life in order to thwart an assassination attempt by the Prophet's enemies. ʿAlī then joined the Prophet and the Muslims in Medina, after having distributed to their owners in Mecca all the property held in trust by Muḥammad. In Medina, the Prophet instituted a pact of brotherhood between the emigrants from Mecca and the "helpers," the Muslims of Medina; he himself adopted ʿAlī as his brother (Ibn Iṣḥāq, 1968, p. 234),

The Prophet gave ʿAlī the honor of marrying his daughter, Fāṭimah—considered, with her mother, Muḥammad's first wife, Khadījah, as the paradigm of saintly womanhood in Islam. The Prophet's *ahl al-bayt* (people of the House), the members of which the Qurʾān refers to in 33:33 as being purified of all defilement, was indicated by the Prophet as consisting of himself, ʿAlī, Fāṭimah, and their two sons, al-Ḥasan and al-Ḥusayn. (Shīʿī sources add to this group the *imāms*, and attribute to all members of this category the status of inerrancy [*ʿiṣmah*], while certain Sunnī sources deem the Prophet's wives to be the referents of Qurʾān 33:33.) It was in his capacity as leading member of the Prophet's *ahl al-bayt* that ʿAlī was instructed to recite the *Sūrah al-Barāʾa* (The immunity, IX) to the pilgrims at Mecca in 631, even though Abū Bakr was leading the pilgrimage. It was ʿAlī who the Prophet instructed to destroy the idols in the Kaʿbah when Mecca was conquered in 629. When the Prophet died in 632, ʿAlī washed his body and led the funeral rites.

ʿAlī according to the Prophet. Numerous sayings attributed to the Prophet affirm ʿAlī's high spiritual rank. Shīʿī and Sunnī sources alike affirm the following sayings: "I am the city of knowledge, and ʿAlī is its gate" (al-Ḥākim, 2002, p. 929); "Looking at ʿAlī is an act of worship" (al-Suyūṭī,

1970, p. 97); "Verily, ʿAlī is from me, and I am from him, and he is the spiritual guardian *(walī)* of every believer after me." (al-Nasāʾī, 1998, p. 129); and "ʿAlī is with the Qurʾān and the Qurʾān is with ʿAlī" (al-Ḥākim, 2002, p. 927). The Prophet is also recorded as having said to ʿAlī the following: "You have, in relation to me, the rank of Aaron in relation to Moses—except that there is no prophet after me" (al-Nasāʾī, 1998, p. 76). Several verses of the Qurʾān were commented upon by the Prophet with reference to ʿAlī. For example, in connection with 13:7 ("Verily thou art a warner, and for every people there is a guide") the Prophet was reported as saying, "I am the warner. . .you are the guide, O ʿAlī. After me, the rightly guided shall be guided by you" (al-Suyūṭī, 1896, vol. 4, p. 45).

The most important and oft-debated prophetic saying relating to ʿAlī, however, was expressed during the sermon of Ghadīr Khumm. This was delivered after the Prophet's final pilgrimage to Mecca in 632 CE, at a pool midway between Mecca and Medina, known as Ghadīr Khumm. He assembled all the pilgrims, had a pulpit erected, and delivered an address to the thousands assembled. The address culminated in the statement: "For whomever I am the *mawlā* [guardian, master, close friend], ʿAlī is his *mawlā*." For Shīʿah, this is regarded as a clear designation (*naṣṣ*) of ʿAlī as successor to the Prophet; for Sunnīs it indicates the special proximity of ʿAlī to the Prophet, but not his nomination as successor in political terms. That the reference to ʿAlī as *mawlā* (in some versions, as *walī*) is of the highest spiritual significance, however, is not seriously disputed. The debate that continues to this day hinges on the implications of ʿAlī's spiritual authority, his *walāyah*.

The Caliphate of Abū Bakr, ʿUmar, and ʿUthmān, 632–656. ʿAlī was not consulted during the political crisis that was precipitated by the death of the Prophet and that resulted in the election of the first caliph, Abū Bakr; his absence at this crucial event set the tone for ʿAlī's role in public affairs until his own assumption of the caliphate twenty-two years later. He refrained from recognition of Abū Bakr for six months, that is, until after the death of Fāṭimah, between whom and Abū Bakr there was a major disagreement. Her claim on the orchard of Fadak as part of her inheritance from the Prophet was rejected by Abū Bakr on the basis of a saying attributed to the Prophet to the effect that the Prophets do not leave any inheritance.

This disagreement was but one overt expression of a fundamental difference of conception in regard to the spiritual and political prerogatives of the *ahl al-bayt*, a difference later to be elaborated in terms of the Sunnī-Shīʿī divergence. The earliest historical sources indicate that ʿAlī never ceased to believe that, on the basis of his kinship with the Prophet and his unique merits, he was the most appropriate person to succeed the Prophet. The relationship between ʿAlī and his predecessors in the caliphate is one of the most sensitive issues in Islamic history, and it has been subject to tendentious reporting in the sources. Sunnī works tend to overlook or downplay the disagreements between ʿAlī and the first three caliphs in the effort to present as harmonious a picture as possible of what later was to be labeled the period of the four orthodox or "rightly guided" caliphs (*al-khulafāʾ al-rāshidūn*). By contrast, Shīʿī works on the whole accuse the first three caliphs of usurping the authority granted by the Prophet to ʿAlī, and exaggerate the differences of opinion between ʿAlī and his predecessors. However, it is clear that, on the one hand, ʿAlī adopted a policy of passive acceptance of the rule of the first two caliphs, coupled with a withdrawal from public affairs—in marked contrast to his prominent role in all the major events in the Prophet's lifetime; and on the other hand, he voiced his disagreement with his predecessors over certain policies and decisions.

Such disagreement became more intense during the rule of the third caliph, ʿUthmān ibn ʿAffān, who was elected by the council or *shūrā*, which ʿUmar established shortly before his death in 644. This council was charged with the task of selecting ʿUmar's successor from six of the leading companions. At this council, evidence is given of ʿAlī's disagreement with at least certain aspects of the policies of the first two caliphs. Upon being asked by ʿAbd al-Raḥmān ibn ʿAwf, the head of the council—who had the deciding vote in case the six were equally divided—whether he was willing to assume the caliphate on the basis of the Qurʾān, the *sunnah* (conduct) of the Prophet, and the precedent of Abū Bakr and ʿUmar, ʿAlī replied by saying he would rule solely on the basis of the Qurʾān and the *sunnah* of the Prophet. When ʿUthmān was asked the same question he replied unconditionally in the affirmative and was duly appointed caliph.

The caliphate of ʿUthmān (r. 644–656) became increasingly compromised, principally by the corruption that characterized the rule of his governors—most of whom were fellow members of the Umayyad clan. ʿAlī, along with several leading companions, such as Abū Dharr al-Ghifārī, Talḥa ibn ʿUbayd Allāh, al-Zubayr ibn al-ʿAwwām, and ʿĀʾisha, had severely criticized the policies of ʿUthmān and the actions of his governors. ʿAlī played a leading role as mediator between the rebels and the caliph, indicating to the latter the just nature of many of the grievances being presented. His efforts failed, however, and opposition to ʿUthmān turned into outright revolt; the caliph was besieged in his home, and, despite the efforts of ʿAlī and his sons to protect him, ʿUthmān was killed by the rebels. ʿAlī was then prevailed upon by the rebels and other factions in Medina to assume power, which he did, albeit reluctantly according both to early reports and to his own sermons, as recorded in the *Nahj al-balāghah*.

The Caliphate of ʿAlī, 656–661. ʿAlī's short caliphate of just over five years was marked in political terms by the eruption of civil wars within the early Muslim polity; it was characterized in ethical terms by ʿAlī's unflinching adherence to strict Islamic principles, frequently at the expense of worldly success. This aspect of his rule became apparent from the very beginning. When advised by his cousin and close confidant, Ibn al-ʿAbbās, to temporarily confirm in power all of ʿUthmān's governors, and then replace them later with his own appointees when his own power was consolidated, ʿAlī adamantly refused to compromise on principles. This attitude ensured that ʿAlī's rule would be challenged by the governors whom he dismissed.

The Battle of al-Jamal. The first challenge to ʿAlī's rule arose from two senior companions of the Prophet, Ṭalḥa ibn ʿUbayd Allāh and al-Zubayr ibn al-ʿAwwām, together with ʿĀʾisha, one of the widows of the Prophet, and some of the governors ousted by ʿAlī. They accused ʿAlī of failing to punish the murderers of ʿUthmān; certain reports indicate that a charge of complicity in the murder was also made by some in this group. They mounted a revolt against him in the name of vengeance for the murdered caliph. ʿAlī reminded Ṭalḥa and al-Zubayr that they had pledged allegiance to him, and were now breaking their oaths, and he insisted that he would bring the murderers to justice as soon as he could find them. The ensuing battle, which took place near Basra on 15 Jumādā I 36 (December 8, 656), was the first civil war of Islam. It was named al-Jamal (the camel) after the camel litter of ʿĀʾisha, which became the focus of the fighting. It resulted in the victory of ʿAlī's army, the death of Ṭalḥa (killed treacherously by his own ally, Marwān ibn al-Ḥakam, who held Ṭalḥa personally responsible for the murder of the caliph), the death of al-Zubayr (killed also by one of his allies, after fleeing from the battlefield), and the surrender of ʿĀʾisha.

Muʿāwiya and the Battle of Ṣiffīn. Having defeated the Baṣran rebels, ʿAlī now turned to face the far more serious threat posed by Muʿāwiya, governor of Syria. Like Ṭalḥa and al-Zubayr, Muʿāwiya used the cry of vengeance for the murdered caliph as the pretext for his opposition to ʿAlī. In their exchange of letters, ʿAlī reminded Muʿāwiya that he was obliged to accept the election of ʿAlī, based as it was on the collective decision of the Anṣār (Medinan companions) and the Muhājirūn (Meccan companions). Muʿāwiya's response was to insist that he, as ʿUthmān's kin, had the right of retaliation prescribed in the Qurʾān (17:33). Meanwhile, in a clear indication of the real motive of his opposition, he enlisted the help of the former governor of Egypt, ʿAmr ibn al-ʿĀṣ, who had been deposed by ʿUthmān and then became the chief inciter of the rebels against the besieged caliph. Following minor skirmishes, all-out battle at Ṣiffīn began on 8 Ṣafar 37 (July 26, 657). After some days, and much bloodshed on both sides, ʿAlī's army was on the point of victory. Muʿāwiya, on the advice of ʿAmr, resorted to the strategy of hoisting copies of the Qurʾān on spears and calling for arbitration according to God's word. Though clearly a ruse, many in ʿAlī's army who were lukewarm in their support for his cause laid down their arms; led by Ashʿath ibn Qays, the most powerful tribal chief of Kūfah, they insisted on accepting this call for arbitration. ʿAlī was also compelled by the same elements within his ranks to appoint Abū Mūsā al-Ashʿarī—whose loyalty to ʿAlī was in question—as his representative in the arbitration. Muʿāwiya appointed ʿAmr as his representative.

Arbitration and the "seceders." The text of the arbitration agreement was drawn up on 15 Ṣafar 37 (August 2, 657). It called merely for the arbitrators to arrive at a decision binding on all, doing so on the basis of the Qurʾān, and to resort to the prophetic *sunnah* (conduct) if they were unable to find the necessary ruling in the Qurʾān. They were to seek peace, but apart from that, no other matter for arbitration was specifically mentioned. The arbitrators met at Dūmat al-Jandal for about three weeks in the spring of 658. This meeting was held against the background of increasing discontent in the ranks of ʿAlī's army. Many of those who had initially supported the arbitration now felt that it was not only an error to have resorted to arbitration, but a sin; it was tantamount to leaving to men a right that pertained only to God, whence their cry: "No judgment but that of God" (*Lā ḥukm illā li-Llāh*). Although ʿAlī succeeded in bringing most of the malcontents back into the fold at this stage, the seeds of a wider rebellion were sowed.

The arbitration process was almost immediately undermined by the proposal of ʿAmr that the issue of ʿUthmān's innocence of deviant innovations be decided before anything else. This effectively changed the focus of the arbitration, for once it was decided that ʿUthmān had been wrongfully killed, the legitimacy of Muʿāwiya's claim for revenge was upheld; it was thus implicit that ʿAlī was wrong in preventing this right of *lex talionis* from being exercised, and thus forfeited his right to rule. ʿAlī's representative, Abū Mūsā, failed to see through this strategy and, though the decision on ʿUthmān's innocence was supposed to be kept secret, it became widely known, resulting in the dismissal of the whole arbitration process by ʿAlī. When ʿAlī then proceeded to call his men to arms, he was confronted by the growing ranks of the "seceders" (*al-Khawārij*). Despite ʿAlī's insistence that the arbitration was now effectively abandoned, the seceders demanded that he repent of the "sin" of having accepted it in the first place. Through dialogue a large number of the seceders were reconciled, but the hard core resisted and resolved to fight to the finish.

Given the murderous tactics used by this group against ʿAlī's supporters, and their declaration that all those who opposed them were *kāfirs* (unbelievers), whose blood was licit, ʿAlī had no choice but to fight them, despite his great reluctance to engage so many of the apparently pious "Qurʾān-readers" (*al-qurrāʾ*) in their ranks. After further dialogue, which reduced their ranks considerably, the Khawārij numbered no more than 1,500 men, led by ʿAbd Allāh ibn Wahb. The resulting battle at Nahrawān (probably in Dhū al-Ḥijjah 37/May 658, but reports are contradictory; see Madelung, 1997, pp. 254–255) is said to have resulted in their all but total annihilation.

The final stage of the arbitration was held at Adhruḥ in Shaʿbān 38 (January 659). Largely irrelevant, as ʿAlī had already denounced the process and was preparing to resume hostilities, it ended in fiasco. Abū Mūsā and ʿAmr agreed to depose both their candidates and to allow a new consultative body to elect the caliph. The former held to the agreement, deposing ʿAlī, while ʿAmr simply confirmed his candidate, Muʿāwiya, as the new caliph. Although ʿAlī attempted to mount a fresh campaign against Muʿāwiya's forces, there was little enthusiasm in his ranks. Before the morning prayer of 19 Ramaḍān 40 (January 28, 661) at the congregational mosque in Kūfah, ʿAlī was struck by the poisoned sword of Ibn Muljam, one of the surviving Khawārij, who was intent on avenging his slain companions at Nahrawān. ʿAlī died two days later.

ʿALĪ AND SHIISM. ʿAlī is considered to be the first *imām* or spiritual leader of all the various branches of Shīʿī Islam—the majority Ithnāʿasharīs, the Ismāʿīlīs, the Zaydīs, and other smaller sects. Although the theologically elaborated definition of the function of the imamate came much later, this function is seen in Shiism as embodied in the person of ʿAlī. The three principal functions of the Shīʿī *imām*—spiritual guidance of the believers, interpretation of revelation and law, and political rule—were implicit or explicit in the pronouncements, attitudes, and actions of ʿAlī. Thus the later Shīʿī doctrine of the imamate can be seen as a systematic articulation, in idealized form, of the actual conduct of ʿAlī. His historic refusal to abide by the precedent of the first two caliphs, noted above, was "a cornerstone in the development of Shīʿī legal thought. . .the idea expressed by ʿAlī in the *Shūrā* took at least 50 years to become manifest in a distinguishable independent form, and was not fully developed until the imamate of Jaʿfar al-Ṣādiq" (Jafri, 1978, pp. 75–76).

There is evidence of the use of the term *shīʿat ʿAlī* in the lifetime of the Prophet. For example, in his commentary on the Qurʾān, al-Ṭabarī records that the Prophet interpreted the phrase "best of created beings" (*khayr al-bariyyah*) in 98:7 as referring to ʿAlī and his "*shīʿa*" (al-Ṭabarī, 2001, vol. 30, p. 320). Four individuals, in particular, were renowned for their attachment to ʿAlī in the lifetime of the Prophet, and might be referred to as the prototypes of later Shiism: Salmān al-Fārsī, Abū Dharr al-Ghifārī, ʿAmmār ibn Yāsir, and Miqdād ibn ʿAmr. These were the foremost members of the group that believed ʿAlī to be the legitimate successor to the Prophet. It was, however, with ʿAlī's assumption of the caliphate that more explicit reference is made to ʿAlī's status as the heir (*waṣī*) of the Prophet, and as the inheritor (*wārith*) of not only his knowledge, but also that of all the Prophets. The second oath of allegiance made to ʿAlī by his supporters in Kūfah in 658 was worded according to the *ḥadīth* of Ghadīr (Madelung, 1997, p. 253). And it was during the caliphate of ʿAlī that the term *shīʿat ʿAlī* arose, largely in contrast to the *shīʿat ʿUthmān* comprising all those who refused to recognize ʿAlī's rule, claiming instead to be following in the footsteps of the murdered caliph, revenge for whose murder was incumbent upon them. With the victory of Muʿāwiya and the establishment of the Umayyad dynasty, the political orthodoxy of the ruling "ʿUthmānī" position declared that only the caliphate of the first three caliphs was legitimate, not that of ʿAlī. This position prevailed for almost a century, and it was largely through the influence of Ibn Ḥanbal that ʿAlī's caliphate was deemed to be fully legitimate, and the definitive tenet of the four "rightly guided" caliphs gradually became incorporated thereafter within the developing religio-political orthodoxy of Sunnism (Jaʿfariyān, 2001, pp. 209–220).

Extremist Shīʿī sects. ʿAlī was the focus of various cults that attributed to him superhuman, angelic, or divine attributes. Referred to as the *ghulāt* (sing. *ghālī*) by both mainstream Shīʿīs and Sunnīs alike, these extremist sects included such groups as the Ghorābiyya, Manṣūriyya, and Rāwandiyya in the early period. In the present, such sects as the Nuṣayrīs/ʿAlawīs in Syria and Turkey and the ʿAlī Allāhīs, or Ahl-i Ḥaqq, in Iran continue to regard ʿAlī as God incarnate. Despite being regarded as heretical by majoritarian Shīʿī groups, some of the characteristic tenets espoused by these sects are also present in more mainstream Shīʿī and Ṣūfī theosophical trends, where they are given more nuanced metaphysical exposition.

SPIRITUAL AND INTELLECTUAL LEGACY. After the Qurʾān and the sayings of the Prophet, no text is more revered by the Shīʿah than the *Nahj al-balāghah*, attributed to ʿAlī. The text, comprising sermons, letters, and aphorisms, was compiled by al-Sharīf al-Raḍī (d. 1016), a renowned Shīʿī scholar of Abbasid Baghdad. In addition to providing specific ideas that served as seeds for theological elaboration in such crucial issues as the transcendence and oneness of God, the emphasis in the *Nahj* upon the importance of the intellect and knowledge greatly enhanced the receptivity of Shīʿī Islam to philosophical speculation and theosophical meditation. In terms of Arabic literature, few texts have exerted a greater influence than the *Nahj*. Important technical terms were introduced by this work into literary and philosophical Arabic, independently of the translation into Arabic of Greek texts (Corbin, 1993, p. 35). Despite doubts raised about the authenticity of the text, recent scholarship indicates that most of the sermons and sayings can in fact be traced to ʿAlī (Djebli, 1992, p. 56).

The main didactic themes of the *Nahj* include: the unfathomable nature of the divine oneness, expressed through striking paradoxes and flashes of rhetorical genius; the function and meaning of prophecy; the supreme value of the intellect; the necessity of renunciation, this being expressed in powerful imagery conveying the vanity of the life of this world; complementing this theme, the marvels of creation, all of which are so many "signs" pointing to the Creator; the dangers of falling into hypocrisy and superficiality in the performance of religious duties; and the indispensability of justice at all levels. One of the most influential letters of the *Nahj* was that written to Mālik al-Ashtar, one of ʿAlī's closest companions, appointing him governor of Egypt. It has been the subject of dozens of commentaries through the ages and is still regarded as one of the most important expressions of an ideal Islamic political constitution. A large number of profound aphorisms are also attributed to ʿAlī. Many of these sayings are contained in the eleventh-century compilation, *Ghurar al-ḥikam* (Exalted aphorisms). Several moving supplications are also attributed to ʿAlī; these have come to play a major role in the devotional life of Shīʿah, the most famous supplication being the *Duʿā Kumayl*, which is recited by devout Shīʿah every Thursday evening. A *dīwān* of poems is also attributed to ʿAlī.

ʿAlī played a fundamental role in the genesis of Islamic intellectual and spiritual culture. He is deemed to have provided impetus and content for a wide range of disciplines, including Qurʾān exegesis (*tafsīr*), theology (*kalām*), jurisprudence (*fiqh*), rhetoric (*balāghah*) and grammar (*naḥw*), and calligraphy (*khaṭṭ*), not to mention various arcane sciences, such as numerology (*jafr*) and alchemy (*al-kīmiyā*). Tales of his feats and miracles have been told and adorned by popular storytellers and poets throughout the Muslim world; his persona was thus imbued with magical and mystical elements, as well as with heroic and saintly qualities. ʿAlī was also the role-model for the chivalric orders (*futūwwa*) that emerged towards the end of the Abbasid period (twelfth to thirteenth century), being seen as the chivalric knight (*fatā*) par excellence. This association between ʿAlī and chivalry was summed up in the formula, attributed to a heavenly voice heard during the Battle of Uḥud: "No chivalric knight but ʿAlī, no sword but *dhu'l-faqār*" (*Lā fatā illā ʿAlī, lā sayf illā dhu'l-faqār*—the latter being the name of ʿAlī's sword). It is often as a knightly warrior, paragon of all virtues, that ʿAlī, one of whose honorifics was Ḥaydar ("the lion"), is portrayed in Ṣūfī poetry.

Within the Ṣūfī tradition generally, ʿAlī is almost universally affirmed as the first "Pole" (*quṭb*) of Sufism after the Prophet, an embodiment of the "perfect man" (*al-insān al-kāmil*), the "friend/saint of God" (*walī Allāh*), and as the spiritual forebear of the Ṣūfīs, standing at the head of all the "chains" (*salāsil*, sing. *silsilah*) by which the Ṣūfī orders trace their initiatic genealogy back to the Prophet. ʿAlī is regarded both as the repository of esoteric science (*maʿrifa*/*ʿirfān*/*ʿilm al-bāṭin*), and also a master of the spiritual path leading to the realization of that science, this path centering on the practice of the "remembrance of God" (*dhikr*), into which the Prophet initiated ʿAlī. According to Abu'l-Qāsim al-Junayd of Baghdad (d. 910), one of the greatest authorities of early Sufism, "ʿAlī is our Shaykh as regards the principles and as regards the endurance of affliction." This statement is recorded by ʿAlī Hujwīrī in his highly regarded Ṣūfī manual *Kashf al-maḥjūb* (Disclosure of the veiled); he sums up the attitude of the Ṣūfīs to ʿAlī in asserting that he was "the leader of the saints and the pure ones. In this Path he holds a place of tremendous honour and elevated degree." (Hujwīrī, 1997, p. 84)

ʿAlī's shrine is in Najaf, near Baghdad; it continues to attract millions of pilgrims worldwide, being regarded, after Mecca and Medina, as one of the most important pilgrimage sites for Muslims—Shīʿah and Sunnī alike—in the Islamic world.

BIBLIOGRAPHY

Āmidī, ʿAbd al-Wāḥid. *Ghurar al-ḥikam wa durar al-kalim* (Exalted aphorisms and pearls of speech). Qom, Iran, 2001. This is an eleventh-century compilation of aphorisms attributed to ʿAlī. It is a compendium of pithy, profound sayings dealing with diverse subjects of an ethical and spiritual order.

Chirri, Mohammad Jawad. *The Brother of the Prophet Mohammad (the Imam Ali): A Reconstruction of Islamic History and an Extensive Research of the Shi-ite Islamic School of Thought*. 2 vols. Detroit, 1979–1982. This nonpolemical presentation of the life of ʿAlī by a contemporary Shīʿī religious scholar remains the best single biographical source for ʿAlī in English.

Corbin, Henri. *The History of Islamic Philosophy*. Translated by Liadain Sherrard. London, 1993.

Djebli, Moktar. "Encore à propos de l'authenticité du *Nahj al-Balāgha!*" *Studia Islamica* 75 (1992): 33–56. This is an important scholarly affirmation of the authenticity of the attribution of most, if not all, of the material in the *Nahj al-balāghah* to ʿAlī.

Ḥākim, Abū ʿAbd Allāh al-. *Al-Mustadrak ʿalā'l-ṣaḥīḥayn* (Supplement to the "two sound collections"). Beirut, 2002. This important collection of *ḥadīths*, accepted as authoritative within Sunnī Islam, contains many of the most important sayings of the Prophet relating to ʿAlī, sayings that were not included in the *ṣaḥīḥayn*, that is, the "two sound collections," meaning those of Bukhārī and Muslim.

Hujwīrī, ʿAlī. *Kashf al-Maḥjūb*. Tehran, 1997. English translation by R. A. Nicholson. Cambridge, U.K., 1936.

Ibn Iṣḥāq. *The Life of Muhammad*. Translated by Alfred Guillaume. London, 1968. This fundamental text contains most of the significant historical details pertaining to ʿAlī during the lifetime of the Prophet.

Jaʿfariyān, Rasūl. *Taʾrīkh wa sīrih-yi siyāsī-yi amīr al-muʾminīn ʿAlī b. Abī Ṭālib* (The life and political history of the commander of the faithful, ʿAlī b. Abī Ṭālib). Qom, Iran, 2001. This is an excellent political biography of ʿAlī, in Persian, by one of the foremost contemporary authorities on Islamic and especially Shīʿī history in Iran.

Jafri, Seyed Muḥammad Husayn. *Origins and Early Development of Shīʿah Islam*. London, 1978. A pioneering study of the establishment of Shiism, dealing with both historical and doctrinal themes of central importance.

Kohlberg, E. "ʿAlī b. Abī Ṭāleb." In *Encyclopedia Iranica*, edited by Ehsan Yarshater, pt. 2, pp. 843–848. London and Boston, 1982.

Landolt, Hermann. "Walāyah." In *The Encyclopedia of Religion*, 1st ed., edited by Mircea Eliade, vol. 15, pp. 316–323. New York, 1987.

Madelung, Wilferd. *The Succession to Muḥammad: A Study of the Early Caliphate*. Cambridge, UK, 1997. The most comprehensive analytical account in English of ʿAlī's caliphate, drawing on the earliest sources.

Masʿūdī, Abu'l-Ḥasan al-. *Murūj al-dhahab wa maʿādin al-jawhar* (Meadows of gold and mines of jewelry). Beirut, 1965. Volume two of this important general history deals with the life of ʿAlī.

Muṭahharī, Murtaḍā. *Glimpses of the Nahj al-Balāgha.* Tehran, 1997. A good introduction and overview of the significance of the *Nahj*, with a useful and concise analysis of its principal themes.

Nasā'ī, Aḥmad ibn Shuʿayb al-. *Khaṣā'iṣ Amīr al-mu'minīn ʿAlī b. Abī Ṭālib* (Distinctive qualities of the commander of the faithful, ʿAlī b. Abī Ṭālib). Tehran, 1998. One of the most important collections of prophetic sayings on ʿAlī, by a highly respected Sunnī authority.

Poonawala, I. K. "ʿAlī b. Abī Ṭāleb." In *Encyclopedia Iranica*, edited by Ehsan Yarshater, pt. 1, pp. 838–843. Boston and London, 1982.

Raḍī, al-Sharīf al-. *Nahjul Balāghah.* Translated by Sayed Ali Reza as *The Peak of Eloquence.* New York, 1996. A complete, but not always satisfactory, translation of this seminal text.

Rashād, ʿAlī-Akbar, ed. *Dānish-nāmih-yi Imām ʿAlī.* Tehran, 2001. This is a very useful twelve-volume collection of essays in Persian on the life, thought, and influence of ʿAlī from a traditional Shīʿī point of view.

Rayshahrī, Muḥammad, ed. *Mawsūʿat al-Imām ʿAlī b. Abī Ṭālib.* Qom, Iran, 2000. A twelve-volume sourcebook on ʿAlī, consisting of primary Arabic texts pertaining to the life and thought of ʿAlī, arranged thematically, drawn mostly from traditional Shīʿī works.

Sobḥānī, Jaʿfar. *Furūgh-i wilāyat: Tārīkh-i taḥlīlī-yi zindigānī-yi Amīr al-mu'minīn ʿAlī* (The resplendence of sanctity: An analytical history of the life of the commander of the believers, ʿAlī). Tehran, 1999. The most comprehensive contemporary biography of ʿAlī in the Persian language.

Suyūṭī, Jalāl al-Dīn al-. *History of the Caliphs.* Translated by H. S. Jarrett. Amsterdam, 1970.

Suyūṭī, Jalāl al-Dīn al-. *Al-Durr al-manthūr fi'l-tafsīr bi'l-ma'thūr* (Scattered pearls of transmitted exegesis). 6 vols. Beirut, 1896. This important commentary on the Qur'ān, by one of the most eminent Sunnī authorities, records many of the Prophet's sayings relating Qur'anic verses to ʿAlī.

Ṭabarī, Abū Jaʿfar Muḥammad ibn Jarīr al-. *The History of al-Ṭabarī.* See in particular vol. 16, *The Community Divided: The Caliphate of ʿAlī I, A.D. 656–657/ A.H. 35–36.* Translated by Adrian Brockett. New York, 1997; and vol. 17, *The First Civil War: From the Battle of Ṣiffīn to the Death of ʿAlī, A.D. 656–661/ A.H. 36–40.* Translated by G. R. Hawting. New York, 1996.

Ṭabarī, Abū Jaʿfar Muḥammad ibn Jarīr al-. *Jāmiʿ al-bayān ʿan ta'wīl al-Qur'ān* (Explanatory synthesis of Qur'anic exegesis). Beirut, 2001.

Reza Shah-Kazemi (2005)

ALINESITOUE Diatta (1920–1944) was a young West African woman prophet who gained a substantial following among the Diola ethnic group of Senegambia and Guinea-Bissau during the early years of the Second World War. She also attracted followers among other ethnic groups of southern Senegal and Guinea-Bissau. The people of rural Diola work primarily as rice farmers and are often described by agronomists as the best wet rice farmers in West Africa, even though droughts are common and often result in crop failures. Prior to the time of Alinesitoue, the Diola had a long-standing tradition of direct revelation from the supreme being Emitai, yet most of these prophets had been men. (*Emitai dabognol* translates as "prophet"—an epithet meaning "whom God has sent.") Alinesitoue introduced to the Diola a series of new spirit shrines that were focused on the procurement of rain, which she claimed were given to her by Emitai. She also introduced a series of religious reforms and provided a series of teachings that were highly critical of French colonial agricultural policies. Since the time of Alinesitoue, most Diola prophets have been women who self-consciously proclaimed their prophetic calling in the tradition of Alinesitoue Diatta.

The Beginnings of a Prophet. Alinesitoue's visions began during the period of Vichy occupation of French West Africa, a particularly repressive time when Senegalese who had enjoyed the status of citizens were reduced to "native" status and when government requisitions of rice and livestock from Diola communities dramatically increased. Abandoning long-standing French traditions of secularism, the local Vichy regime supported efforts at Christian proselytization among the predominantly traditionalist (*awasena*) Diola. This, coupled with severe drought, created a spiritual crisis of conquest, in which Diola questioned a wide range of recent community borrowings from the colonial society, from conversion to Christianity or Islam, to the cultivation of peanuts as a cash crop.

Alinesitoue Diatta had her first visionary experience in 1941, while working as a maid in the French West African capital of Dakar. Walking through the crowded Sandaga market, she heard a voice calling to her, commanding her to go to a nearby beach and to dig in the sand. As water filled the hole, she realized that she had been commanded by Emitai to introduce a new series of spirit shrines (*ukine*) focused on obtaining rain to end the drought and to nurture the rice crops. Initially reluctant to teach, she returned home to the southern Senegalese township of Kabrousse. When she began to share her message, she was able to link the increasing hardships imposed by the French colonial regime, the challenges of Christian and Muslim proselytization, and the drought to the erosion of Diola communitarian values and the abandonment of traditional crops and religious practices. By introducing a new spirit shrine, *Kasila*, she renewed an emphasis on community-based ritual while underscoring the role of the supreme being and challenging the hegemony of community elders and wealthy individuals.

Alinesitoue emphatically rejected the claims of priestly groups to control ritual practice and the specialized knowledge of the shrines. She opened her shrines to full participation by women and men, young and old, rich and poor. Priests were chosen by divination; as one song of Alinesitoue described it, even an idiot could be chosen. Everyone in the community was expected to participate in the community sacrifices, feasting, and dancing for six days and nights, eating and sleeping in the public squares for the duration of the ritual. Kasila's emphasis on shared experience without the usual hierarchies based on age and gender revitalized Diola religion by creating a new structure for the renewing qualities of what Victor Turner has termed "communitas." It so happened that the rice harvest of 1942 to 1943, nurtured by abundant rainfall, was the best in years.

Alinesitoue's teachings provided more than a new ritual for the supplication of the supreme being to provide life-giving rain. She explained that the causes of the drought were rooted in Diola people's neglect of a day of rest every sixth day (*Huyaye*). Those who chose to work in the rice paddies on *Huyaye* denied the land its day of rest. Furthermore, the planting of new varieties of what were seen as European rice (actually Asian forms of *oryza sativa*) disrupted what she described as a spiritual link between rice, the land, and Emitai. While permitting the continued planting of foreign rices, Alinesitoue insisted that only Diola rice (African, *oryza glaberrima*) could be used in rituals, thus requiring continued cultivation of what was seen as a gift from Emitai.

Alinesitoue banned, however, the new cash crop of peanuts, which French agricultural agents had been pressuring Diola farmers to plant. Communities that accepted peanut cultivation found that it undermined family farmers' sexual division of labor, leading men to abandon their tasks of building dikes and irrigation systems and of doing the arduous work of plowing by hand. Whereas men concentrated on the new cash crop, women were left to do the plowing, sowing, transplanting, and harvesting. Dikes and irrigation were neglected, harvests declined, and farmers used their earnings to buy the rice that they had not planted. Alinesitoue argued that Emitai had made Diola—both men and women—plant rice, claiming that this was their central task. Furthermore, she argued that the forest land used for peanut cultivation should be left for the harvesting of palm wine and other forest products. These teachings brought her into direct conflict with the French administration.

HER LEGACY. As people flocked to Alinesitoue's community of Kabrousse, French officials worried about the possibility that she would lead a revolt. Catholic church officials saw churches emptying of catechumens and converts alike as Alinesitoue's movement gained strength. In January of 1943, a French expedition proceeded to Kabrousse and arrested her and a number of her assistants. They were taken to the state capital of Ziguinchor, tried under the Native Law Code (*Indigènat*), and sentenced to various terms of exile. Alinesitoue was exiled to the city of Timbuctou, in French Sudan, where she died of starvation in 1944. No one, not even her husband, was told of her death. It was only in 1987 that it was revealed that she had died over forty years before.

Within a few months of her arrest, two other women rose to prominence, claiming to be prophets sent by Emitai. Since then, more than thirty other prophets—mostly women—have taught about reviving rain rituals, observing the Diola day of rest, and rejecting economic dependence on external groups, be they European or Senegalese. Sixteen such prophets are active today, one of whom played the role of Alinesitoue in a play performed by a Diola theater group in Dakar (twenty years before she began to have visions herself). Another woman had a vision of a night journey to Kabrousse where she received the blessings of Alinesitoue's widower.

CONCLUSION. Although there had been prophets before the time of Alinesitoue, she gave new prominence to this tradition, insisting that Emitai was directly involved in the lives of Diola communities. She emphasized the role of Emitai in empowering the spirit shrines and a kind of covenant in which Diola farmed rice and performed the required rituals in exchange for life-giving rain from Emitai. It may well be that this prophetic tradition is a primary reason why the Diola contain the largest number of adherents of traditional religion in Senegambia. Others have sought to appropriate Alinesitoue's memory for their own causes. Senegalese officials and northern Senegalese literati have hailed her as a heroine of resistance to European colonialism. A separatist movement in the Casamance region of southern Senegal claims her as the Joan of Arc of Casamance and leader of a Diola specific resistance movement, not only against the French, but against all groups that have tried to establish political, economic, or religious control over the Diola.

SEE ALSO African Religions, overview article, and articles on Mythic Themes and New Religious Movements; Diola Religion; Gender and Religion, article on Gender and African Religious Traditions; Prophecy, article on African Prophetism.

BIBLIOGRAPHY

"Alinesitoue: A West African Woman Prophet." In *Unspoken Worlds: Women's Religious Lives*, edited by Nancy A. Falk and Rita M. Gross. Belmont, Calif, 2001.

Fall, Marouba, *Aliin Sitooye Jaata ou la Dame de Kabrus*. Dakar, Senegal, 1993.

Girard, Jean. *Genèse du pouvoir charismatique en Basse Casamance (Sénégal)*. Dakar, Senegal, 1969.

Waldman, Marilyn R. with Robert M. Baum. "Innovation as Renovation: The Prophet as an Agent of Change." In *Innovation in Religious Traditions*, edited by Michael A. Williams, et al. Berlin, 1992.

ROBERT M. BAUM (2005)

ʿALĪ SHĪR NAVĀʾĪ (AH 844–906/1441–1501 CE), more fully Mīr Niẓām al-Dīn ʿAlī Shīr Navāʾī; Central Asian poet, biographer, and patron of arts, letters, and Islamic institutions. Navāʾī was a man of versatile accomplishments who, born into the upper aristocracy of the city of Herāt (now in Afghanistan), devoted his life to public service and the arts. Honored in the eastern Islamic world, he is regarded as the greatest classical poet of the Soviet Uzbek people and a significant contributor to Persian cultural history.

The period during which Navāʾī lived saw much political conflict owing to the disintegration of rule by the descendants of Timur (Tamerlane). Small princedoms, chiefly of Turkic origin, intrigued for domination and caused much instability among the upper classes. In Navāʾī's family, changing fortunes gave the young boy opportunities to meet a variety of scholars and mystics who shaped his intellectual and religious development. For most of his adult life he was a political and personal intimate of Sultan Ḥusayn Bāyqarā (d. 1506), who provided him with further opportunity for interaction with men of letters and led to the writing of his biographical collection, *Majālis al-nafāʿis* (Gathering of spirits), composed in Chaghatai, the eastern Turkic literary language.

During this period, Herāt was not only the leading center for the arts but also a place where mysticism, and especially the Naqshbandī Ṣūfī order, flourished. Navāʾī, who has been described as a man spiritual rather than public by inclination, appears to have been an initiate into the Naqshbandī *khāngāh* (Ṣūfī hospice) headed by his friend, the great mystic poet ʿAbd al-Raḥmān Jāmī (d. 1492). Although he did not follow the ascetic path, Navāʾī never married and professed to be a dervish. Since he was a Sunnī Muslim, his lack of prejudice toward Shīʿī Muslims has led to speculation that he may have favored that sect. His friendliness toward the Shīʿah, however, probably reflects the relatively tranquil religious atmosphere of his day, particularly in contrast to the early sixteenth century, when bitter Sunnī-Shīʿī political struggles rent the natural cultural and socioeconomic relationships that had existed across the Iranian plateau.

Navāʾī's devotion to public and religious affairs is demonstrated by the fact that during his lifetime he restored and endowed about 370 mosques, *madrasahs* (Islamic colleges), caravansaries, and other pious institutions; the Mīr ʿAlī Shīr Mosque in Herāt was named for him. He wrote a total of twenty-nine literary works, mainly poetical, and some in imitation of mystical texts. Most of these are in Chaghatai, but a few are in Persian, under the pen name Fānī. Because of his position as an early champion of Chaghatai, Navāʾī has held a special place in modern Central Asian culture. His life story, embellished with apocryphal tales, has penetrated into the folk literature, theater, and opera of the Perso-Turkic culture of the region.

BIBLIOGRAPHY

The most comprehensive historical study of Navāʾī remains V. V. Barthold's Russian-language essay that appears in *Four Studies on the History of Central Asia*, vol. 3, *Mīr ʿAlī-Shīr: A History of the Turkmen People*, translated by Vladimir Minorsky and Tatiana Minorsky (Leiden, 1962). Uzbek, Russian, and Tajik literary studies of Navāʾī of more recent vintage share with Barthold's essay a reluctance to discuss the religious aspects of Navāʾī's life, focusing instead on his contributions to art, architecture, music, calligraphy, painting, and especially literature. Of these a prominent example is Evgenii E. Bertel's's *Izbrannie Trudy: Navoi i Dzhami*, 4 vols. (Moscow, 1965).

The best source for understanding Navāʾī within the cultural context of his period is Edward G. Browne's *A Literary History of Persia*, vol. 3, *The Tartar Dominion, 1265–1502* (1920; reprint, Cambridge, U.K., 1951).

EDEN NABY (1987)

ALKALAI, YEHUDAH BEN SHELOMOH

(1798–1878), rabbi and writer, one of the forerunners of modern Zionism. Born in Sarajevo and raised in Jerusalem, Alkalai became the rabbi of Semlin (modern-day Zemun), the capital of Serbia, in 1825. His interest in nationalism was probably sparked by the nationalist ferment in the Balkans in the wake of the Greek struggle for independence. He was also influenced by Yehudah ben Shemu'el Bibas, the rabbi of Corfu, who was one of the earliest nineteenth-century proponents of Jewish national settlement in the Land of Israel.

Alkalai's first nationalist writing was his 1834 pamphlet *Shemaʿ Yisraʾel* (Hear O Israel), in which he called for Jews to establish colonies in the Land of Israel as the first step in the messianic redemption. Alkalai thus argued for human initiative in a process that most religious Jews considered the province of God.

He further developed this idea in his 1839 Ladino-Hebrew textbook, *Darkhei noʿam* (Paths of peacefulness). By interpreting the word *teshuvah* ("repentance") according to its literal sense to mean "return," he turned the traditional doctrine that repentance was a necessary precondition for the messianic redemption into a requirement that the Jews first "return" to the Land of Israel.

Alkalai's nationalist thinking took on much greater urgency as a result of the Damascus Affair of 1840, when the Jews of Damascus were accused of using the blood of non-Jews for ritual purposes. Alkalai held the event to be proof that the Jews needed to regain their homeland. His first response to the Damascus Affair was the Ladino work *Shelom Yerushalayim* (The peace of Jerusalem); it was followed in 1843 by his first Hebrew work, *Minḥat Yehudah* (The offering of Judah), in which he developed his nationalist thinking in a more systematic way.

Traveling throughout Europe, Alkalai devoted the rest of his life to attempts to set up societies that would foster settlement in Palestine. These efforts bore little fruit. He also advocated the establishment of an international Jewish organization, which eventually came into being with the founding of the Alliance Israélite Universelle in 1860. Alkalai, however, played almost no role in the developments of the 1860s and 1870s that laid the groundwork for later Zionism. He died a forgotten figure in Jerusalem in 1878. Only after the establishment of the Zionist movement at the end of the nineteenth century was Alkalai remembered as a religious precursor to modern Jewish nationalism.

SEE ALSO Zionism.

BIBLIOGRAPHY

In addition to Getzel Kressel's article "Alkalai, Judah Ben Solomon Hai," in *Encyclopaedia Judaica* (Jerusalem, 1971), further biographical information as well as an example of Alkalai's writings can be found in *The Zionist Idea,* edited by Arthur Hertzberg (Philadelphia, 1959), pp. 102–107.

New Sources

Penkower, Monty Noam. "Religious Forerunners of Zionism." *Judaism* 33 (1984): 289–295.

DAVID BIALE (1987)
Revised Bibliography

ALLĀH
SEE ATTRIBUTES OF GOD, *ARTICLE ON* ISLAMIC CONCEPTS; GOD, *ARTICLE ON* GOD IN ISLAM

ALLEN, RICHARD
ALLEN, RICHARD (February 14, 1760–March 26, 1831), minister and businessperson, is regarded as the founder of the African Methodist Episcopal (AME) Church—the first African American denomination. Although he is generally regarded as the first bishop of the African Methodist Episcopal denomination, in actuality he was the second bishop. Daniel Coker was elected before Allen but was more concerned about African missions, and therefore Allen was elected as Coker's replacement.

Allen was born a slave but gained his freedom around 1781 by working during his free hours as a woodcutter, bricklayer, and wagon driver. He converted to Methodism during his late teens, and following his emancipation he began preaching during his travels around Delaware, New Jersey, and Pennsylvania while working odd jobs to support himself. In 1785 Allen was frequently assigned by Francis Ashbury to fill preach, and he also accompanied Richard Whatcoat on the Baltimore circuit.

Allen moved to Philadelphia in 1786 and began to associate with Absalom Jones (1746–1818) and other free blacks at Saint George's Methodist Church. Allen and Jones started a prayer group among the free black population and organized the Free African Society in 1787 for the purpose of mutual aid, support, and ministry to widows, orphans, and the sick. This was the first African American society organized in the United States. Philadelphia had the largest free African American population in the country, and the Free African Society was one of the major public gathering places for black people.

The success of Jones and Allen's ministry and preaching precipitated a crisis at Saint George's—what to do with the increased number of black worshippers. The white church leaders attempted to resolved the issue by segregating black worshippers in the balcony. However, on a Sunday in November 1787, after Jones seated himself in one of the front pews of the balcony, he was instructed by one of the ushers to move further to the rear of the balcony. Jones refused, and a scuffle ensued as the ushers tried to forcibly remove Jones from his seat. Jones, Allen, and the other black worshippers left the sanctuary.

Jones and Allen subsequently led regular worship services in what was called the African Church, and by 1792 their group's members were raising funds to construct a church building. The worshippers differed, however, over the choice of denominational affiliation. Most of the members voted for affiliation with the Episcopal Church. Jones went with the majority and eventually became an Episcopal priest, but Allen went with the minority that favored Methodism.

Allen reclaimed an old blacksmith's shop and renovated it into a chapel for those who preferred the Methodist style of worship. Work on the church was delayed for several months, because much of the energies of members of the Free African Society were required to help minister among the sick and tend to the dead during the yellow fever epidemic that struck Philadelphia in 1793. Bishop Ashbury dedicated Allen's chapel as Bethel Church on July 29, 1794, twelve days after Jones's Saint Thomas African Episcopal Church was dedicated.

Because Bethel was a part of the Methodist system of government, and because Allen lacked ordination, the church was still subject to white control and influence. Even though Allen was Bethel's leader, the church had to cooperate with visiting white preachers assigned to its pulpit. Allen was ordained as a deacon in 1799, but this still restricted his authority to celebrate the Lord's Supper and perform the sacrament of baptism or weddings beyond his assignment or when the ruling white elder was absent.

A number of events arising out of the contestation for power led eventually to Allen's members securing congregational autonomy through the courts. On April 7, 1816, Allen presided over the first convention that created the African Methodist Episcopal Church. He was consecrated bishop on April 11, 1816, with Absalom Jones participating in the ceremony.

Although Allen and Jones had parted ways denominationally, they continued to work closely together in many other endeavors, such as the founding of Philadelphia's African Masonic Lodge in 1798, petitioning Congress and the state legislature to end slavery in 1800, and founding of the Society for the Suppression of Vice and Immorality in 1808. In 1812 they, along with James Forten, were asked by the Vigilance Committee to organize the black Philadelphia population to help with the city defenses, and they complied by recruiting 2,500 blacks into that effort. Allen and Jones also combined their forces to organize a convention held in Philadelphia in January 1817 to oppose the goals of the American Colonization Society that had been formed to promote the emigration of blacks to Liberia.

BIBLIOGRAPHY

Allen, Richard. *The Life, Experience, and Gospel Labors of the Rt. Rev. Richard Allen.* Philadelphia, 1793; reprint, Philadelphia, 1888.

Campbell, James T. *Songs of Zion: The African Methodist Episcopal Church in the United States and South Africa.* New York, 1995.

George, Carol V. R. *Segregated Sabbaths: Richard Allen and the Emergence of Independent Black Churches, 1760–1840.* New York, 1973.

Murphy, Larry G., J. Gordon Melton, and Gary L. Ward, eds. *Encyclopedia of African American Religions.* New York, 1993.

Pinn, Ann H., and Anthony B. Pinn. *Fortress Introduction to Black Church History.* Minneapolis, Minn., 2002.

Richardson, Harry V. *Dark Salvation: The Story of Methodism as It Developed among Blacks in America.* Garden City, N.Y., 1976.

JAMES ANTHONY NOEL (2005)

ALL-FATHER. Nineteenth-century reports on southeastern Australia showed a widespread belief in a male spirit who transcended others in this part of the continent. Known by diverse names, including Baiame, Bunjil, Daramulun, Kohin, and Munganngaua, he was said to live in the sky (although earlier he had been on earth). The Aborigines credited him with great achievements—laying down laws, instituting man-making ceremonies, shaping the earth, and teaching the arts of life. The amateur anthropologist A. W. Howitt (1830–1908), who collected much of the data on the topic, saw through differences in name and detail to underlying resemblances in the various tribal conceptions and suggested that this spirit be identified by the term *All-Father.* Howitt denied the being's divinity, while others voiced the suspicion that such a spirit must reflect Christian influence on the Aborigines. The extent of the area over which beliefs in the All-Father were known made this implausible even then (although it is likely that some of the descriptions were colored by Christianity). Since the 1940s a high degree of circumstantial probability has been lent to the All-Father's authenticity by reports of an All-Mother from northern Australia. Evidently Aborigines have had no difficulty in conceiving of a spirit who stands above the social order in the sense of having the same relation to all persons—for obscure reasons this being is male and paternal in some regions, female and maternal in others.

Howitt's denial of the All-Father's divinity appears to have rested on the absence of worship and, perhaps more subtly, on the absence of the elevated properties ideally ascribed to the Christian God. Yet in his *Native Tribes of South-East Asia* (1904), he readily admitted the All-Father to be supernatural, and he propounded a theory of his genesis as an otherworldly embodiment of a tribal headman—"full of knowledge and tribal wisdom, and all-powerful in magic, of which he is the source, with virtues, failings and passions, such as the aborigines regard them" (pp. 500–501).

More rewarding to consider than questions of definition is the All-Father's role in Aboriginal life (in the past, that is, for the belief is almost certainly now moribund). Here scholars are especially indebted to Howitt and his younger contemporary Robert Hamilton Mathews (1841–1918), also an amateur anthropologist. All southeastern Aborigines knew something of the All-Father, but deeper knowledge was revealed to those who went through the man-making ceremonies. An old Theddora woman told Howitt that the spirit came down with a noise like thunder when boys were initiated. The ceremonies themselves were, for most men, the main avenue of knowledge about the All-Father. Not only were they said to have been instituted by him, but they included many symbolic references to him, and sometimes the fiction of an actual encounter with him was maintained. The Wiradthuri people's Burbung, for example, was an initiation cermony that was supposed to have been set up by the All-Father after he slew a lesser spirit who used to kill and eat some of the boys whom the All-Father took for tooth avulsion (the man-making operation). Having put the monster's voice in the trees, the All-Father found that he could reproduce it in a bull-roarer. He told the leading men that from then on they should initiate boys and use bull-roarers. Women and children were to continue to believe that the monster destroyed the boys and then restored them to life.

The All-Father's appearance was shown by images made of him in this and other ceremonies. In a Burbung attended by Mathews in 1893 a figure of a man was molded from earth to represent the All-Father. Lying face down with arms outflung, the figure had tripped and fallen while chasing an emu he had speared. The figure was 6.6 meters long, 1.7 meters across, and 0.5 meters at the highest point. The anthropomorphic conception is also confirmed by rock engravings and by outlines cut into trees.

An even more esoteric communication between human and supernatural (one which even the most knowledgeable men seemed to regard as literal and not merely symbolic or fictional) took place in the making of magicians. It was believed in at least parts of southeastern Australia that the All-Father played an essential part in this process, which itself was a foundation of the moral and political order. Postulants appeared before the All-Father (no doubt in dream or trance state), were shown how to use quartz crystal for magical purposes, and had this and other objects "sung" into their bodies by him. A Wiradthuri man who underwent the experience described the All-Father to Howitt as "a very great old man with a long beard . . . from his shoulders extended two great quartz crystals to the sky above him" (Howitt, 1904, p. 408).

SEE ALSO Australian Indigenous Religions, overview article.

BIBLIOGRAPHY

The most important single source for the All-Father's role in magic, cosmology, and ritual is A. W. Howitt's *The Native Tribes of South-East Australia* (London, 1904). He collected many observations by others as well as recording his own. For the heated debate over the All-Father's significance and authenticity, the most accessible source is Mircea Eliade's *Australian Religions: An Introduction* (Ithaca, N.Y., 1973), which gives valuable bibliographical references to the ethnographic and polemical literature. My own work, *The Australian Aborigines: A Portrait of Their Society* (London, 1972), puts the All-Father beliefs and the associated man-making ceremonies in a wider Australian mythical and ritual context. Ernest A. Worms's "Australische eingeborenen Religionen," in Hans Nevermann, Ernest A. Worms, and Helmut Petri's *Die Religionen der Südsee und Australiens* (Stuttgart, 1968), pp. 125–322, may also be consulted with advantage, especially for its stimulating linguistic explorations.

KENNETH MADDOCK (1987)

ALL FOOLS' DAY. The first day of April, known as All Fools' Day or April Fools' Day, is traditionally marked by the custom of playing jokes (usually on friends) and engaging in frivolous activities. It stands as one of the few spring festivals in Christian Europe unaffected by the date of the celebration of Easter. All Fools' Day should not be confused with the Feast of Fools, the medieval mock-religious festival involving status reversals and parodies of the official church by low-level cathedral functionaries and others (held on or about the Feast of the Circumcision, January 1). April Fools' Day activities, however, are related in spirit to this once-licensed kind of revelry. The actual origins of April Fools' practices and their connection to the first of April are unknown. The day and its traditions appear to reflect some of the festive characteristics of such non-Christian religious celebrations as the Hilaria of ancient Rome (March 25) and the Holi festival of India (ending March 31). Traditional celebrations related to the vernal equinox and to the arrival of spring in the Northern Hemisphere, as well as that season's playful and often fickle weather, may also have contributed to the timing and persistence of April Fools' customs.

The development of All Fools' Day has been the subject of much popular speculation. The day has been seen as commemorating the wanderings from place to place of the raven and dove Noah sent from the ark to search for day land after the biblical flood. It has also been thought to memorialize in an irreverent way the transfer of Jesus from the jurisdiction of one governmental or religious figure to another in the last hours before his crucifixion. In either case, the events in question were believed to have occurred on or near the first of April. An intriguing explanation for April Fools' Day customs in France, on the other hand, concerns confusion over the change in the date for the observance of the New Year. Those who recognized March 25 as the beginning of their year (a number of different dates were used to mark this occasion in medieval Europe) culminated their eight-day celebration of this event on April 1. When in 1564 Charles IX changed the official date to January 1, some people either resisted the change or failed to remember when the year was to begin. This confusion led to the practice of exchanging false greetings for the first of the year on the old day of its observance (April 1) and of sending false gifts, as a joke, to those who expected the customary holiday presents on that day. Thus some scholars believe that jests of all sorts soon came to be associated with this date. The term *poisson d'avril*, literally translated as "an April fish," is still used to describe the foolish victim of an All Fools' Day prank.

The custom of "April fooling," known and practiced in many European countries, was brought by English settlers to the United States of America. There, any person of any age or rank is susceptible to being made a fool on April first; tradition demands, however, that these jokes take place only within the twelve-hour period from midnight to noon (with the rest of the day reserved, no doubt, for apologies). Today, the practice is usually observed by children, although some adults continue to perpetrate both simple and complex jests and hoaxes on unsuspecting individuals on this day.

BIBLIOGRAPHY

Little worthwhile scholarly work has been done on the subject of All Fools' Day. A valuable English antiquarian source of information on the day's customs is *The Book of Days*, 2 vols., edited by Robert Chambers (1862–1864; Philadelphia, 1914). A more contemporary reflection on April Fools' Day traditions, especially in Great Britain, can be found in Christina Hole's *British Folk Customs* (London, 1976). Hertha Wolf-Beranek's "Zum Aprilscherz in den Sudetenländern," *Zeitschrift für Volkskunde* 64 (1968): 223–227, provides a short but useful summary of the changes that have taken place, in European usage, in the term describing individuals who are fooled on April 1. Catherine H. Ainsworth's "April Fools' Day," in volume 1 of her *American Calendar Customs* (Buffalo, N.Y., 1979), inadequately explains the origins of the observance, but her collected accounts of the day as celebrated in the United States are informative.

New Sources

Aveni, Anthony. *The Book of the Year: A Brief History of Our Seasonal Holidays.* New York, 2003.

Farrell, James J. "April Fool's Day." *Clergy Journal* 77 (April 2001): 12.

LEONARD NORMAN PRIMIANO (1987)
Revised Bibliography

ALMSGIVING may be defined as unilateral gifts to the poor or the religious. In its purest form, the gift of alms is given gratuitously without expectation of return, and is in this sense "free." Almsgiving thus stands apart from reciprocal gifts, which forge human relationships of solidarity by principles of give-and-take. Moreover, alms are praiseworthy when given voluntarily, out of the free will and generosity of the donor; yet almsgiving is often configured as a binding religious duty. Deliberation on almsgiving raises intriguing questions about whether purely gratuitous charity is possible, or whether it is always at bottom motivated by considerations of reciprocity, spiritual reward, or simply the fulfillment of obligations. Reflections on almsgiving have also stimulated considerations of the plight of the poor and how to best serve their needs.

A Free Gift? For some, gifts should be given freely and disinterestedly by the donor, yet should simultaneously inspire reciprocation by the recipient. The Roman philosopher Seneca (4 BCE–65 CE) praised the graciousness of the unconditional gift, even while enjoining the recipient to respond with gratitude and, in turn, future service. This view of gift giving as a form of gracious exchange finds modern expression in studies of gift behavior inspired by Marcel Mauss's classic *The Gift* (1923). Noting that in many tribal societies, social cohesion is made possible through the back-and-forth flow of gifts, Mauss saw the gift as a circuit or loop entailing three obligations: to give, to receive, and to reciprocate. Mauss and his followers were skeptical of the free gift because it appears to be free of social obligations; in not eliciting a return it interrupts the mutuality on which social solidarity rests, leaving asymmetry and imbalance.

Others have doubted whether a gift can truly be free of any expectation whatsoever. While it may not result in direct material recompense by the recipient, every gift returns some benefit to the giver, whether that benefit arrives in the form of enhanced social prestige, a position of dominance over the recipient, or merely a sense of self-congratulation.

Amid these interpretations of the gift, we find religious ideologies proposing that not only are free gifts possible, they are highly commendable. Alms are aimed in two directions: to the poor and dispossessed and to religious professionals living in voluntary poverty, such as priests, monastics, renouncers, or the institutions that support them. Such beneficiaries are little expected to make a direct return on the gifts offered. The resulting asymmetry is part of what make such gifts laudable: they appear to be made without calculation or anticipation of return.

Yet, the absence of direct reciprocity from the recipient may not always entail that the giver be entirely free of interest. Almsgiving may bear the imprint of an older sacrificial order that in many traditions it supplanted: explicit bartering with the gods is replaced by more implicit arrangements. Almsgiving gratifies the cosmic order, which in turn grants further bounty. A donor might legitimately engage in almsgiving as a form of merit-making, with an eye fixed on future meritorious rewards bestowed, for example, through the causality of *karma* in the religions originating in South Asia, or in the form of God's blessings in the Western monotheisms. Almsgiving may thus be regarded as a spiritual investment wherein sacrifices and good deeds in this life are amply rewarded in the hereafter. Almsgiving may also be motivated by a desire for atonement; here the gift may balance the karmic "bank account" by offsetting bad deeds, or offer reparations and expiation for sins committed.

At the same time, within religious traditions there occurs frequent discussion on whether such calculations are appropriate. For some, almsgiving is a purely magnanimous act, a complete and genuine expression of compassion for the poor, esteem for the religious, contempt for worldly goods, or devotion and gratitude to God. Many South Asian theorists posit almsgiving (*dāna*) as a gesture toward the recipient in which either esteem or compassion—rather than interest in merit—prevails. Simultaneously, *dāna* is an act of renunciation, of loosening one's attachments to material possessions. Hindu discourses on *dāna*, for example, rate gifts made to worthy *brahmans* out of a sense either of rightness (*dharmadāna*) or relinquishment (*tyāgadāna*), as estimable above all gifts. Certain Theravāda Buddhist texts assert that the ideal generous intention is entirely suffused with esteem toward the monastic community or compassion toward the needy. Mahāyāna Buddhism, which Jacques Gernet has described as by its nature "antieconomic" and "avid for the incommensurable" (1995, p. 241), regards lavish unilateral and disinterested generosity as a supreme moral and religious achievement.

In the Western religions—Judaism, Christianity, and Islam—almsgiving is a declaration of devotion and gratitude to God. It thus expresses intentions of the highest order, aimed not so much toward the earthly recipient as the divine one. The Christian Gospels make such sentiment explicit when Jesus declares that "what is done for the least of my brethren, that is done unto me" (*Mt.* 25:40). Judaism and Islam too find God present in the recipient; a Talmudic passage states that one who gives to the poor receives "the face of the Presence of God" (Avery-Peck, 1999, p. 54), and the Islamic scholar al-Ghazālī's eleventh-century *On the Mysteries of Almsgiving* asserts that the poor recipient "has made his hand a substitute for that of God" (Faris, 1966, p. 36). Moreover, for all these traditions, since God has given all that one possesses, almsgiving is merely furthering God's work of distributing the bountiful creation. It purifies the donor of stinginess and gives lie to the pretension of human autonomy. Almsgiving is not a matter of self-aggrandizement, but rather of humility and purification.

One of the most poignant ruptures in theologies of calculated giving occurred within Christianity through the Protestant Reformation. In *The Gift in Sixteenth-Century France* (2000), Natalie Zemon Davis suggests that in a "profound sense, the religious reformations of the sixteenth century were a quarrel about gifts" (p. 100). Reformers were offended by the Mass as a sacrifice and source of grace, priests trafficking in indulgences, and gifts edging, in their view, toward heretical reciprocity with God. For reformer John Calvin (1509–1564), since God gives utterly gratuitously, grace cannot be won by pious acts. All gifts can only be free and unidirectional, flowing "downward from the Lord and outward from us" (Davis, 2000, p. 118).

A Voluntary Obligation? Covenantal theologies depict almsgiving as a binding human obligation to God. In the

Torah, God commands the Israelites to "open wide your hand to your brother, to the needy and to the poor, in the land" (*Dt.* 15:11). The practice of *zakāt,* prescribed as one of the five pillars of Islam, makes almsgiving obligatory for every Muslim; in some Muslim countries it is enforced as a legal obligation. In addition to legal sanctions, severe public opprobrium may attach itself to those who resist almsgiving, enforcing charity by the mandate of social pressure.

Ritual obligations also call forth gifts. Entry into ritual spaces often entails passing through the gates of charity. The ritual calendars in many of the world's religious traditions build ritual almsgiving into festival occasions; the hungry know a meal may always be had during Lent and Easter, the Jewish holiday of Purim, the Buddhist celebration of Vesak, and the Muslim Īd al-Aḍḥā. They might also gather at sacred sites where pilgrims are compelled to be free with alms: supplicants await at the banks of the Ganges in Vārāṇasī to offer themselves as auspicious occasions for pilgrims' devotion. Institutionalized ritual practices, such as the passing of the collection plate during the weekly service, ingrain routine patterns of giving.

Where conceived as an obligation compelled by external demands, the element of voluntarism may be obscured. Only in granting the deed an element of free will can it exhibit the appropriate spirit of generosity. Paradoxically, it may be that gifts can be simultaneously obliged and voluntary. Religious discourses on almsgiving often detect nuances in intention that are explored in rankings of gifts. The twelfth-century Jewish theologian Maimonides' eight degrees of charity capture many of the subtleties of almsgiving that allow for gracious intentions within the context of carrying out duties. At the highest level, the donor strengthens the poor Jew, putting him beyond a condition of dependence; next best is the anonymous gift where neither the donor nor the recipient knows the other; after this comes the gift where the donor knows the recipient, but the recipient does not know who the donor is; then, the gift where the recipient knows the donor, but the donor does not know the recipient; then the gift of one who gives before being asked; then the gift of one who has been asked; then the gift of less than is fitting, but given gladly; and lastly, the gift given morosely.

An intriguing counterpart to Maimonides' eight degrees and another list that detects nuances in the donor's intentionality may be found the eight duties of almsgiving outlined by al-Ghazālī, which explore the mysteries of both *zakāt* and voluntary giving (*ṣadaqah*). These duties include understanding why *zakāt* is obligatory, respecting the time and etiquette of paying *zakāt,* giving in secrecy, giving in public (in order to provide an example for others), refraining from taunting or reproaching the beneficiary, belittling the gift (in order to guard against self-congratulation and vanity), giving what is best and dear to the donor, and seeking out particularly worthy recipients (within the prescribed categories of recipients of *zakāt*). Here too we find sensitivities that ennoble the fulfillment of duty.

It is noteworthy that both Maimonides and al-Ghazālī recognize anonymous giving, especially when we notice covert giving in other traditions, such as the secret gift (*gupta-dāna*) admired in South Asian traditions, and Matthew's instruction that in giving "do not let your left hand know what your right hand is doing, so that your alms may be in secret" (*Mt.* 6:3). The secret gift spares the recipient disgrace and arrests the donor's vanity. Yet even while hidden, this most meritorious gift does not go unseen or unrewarded by God, nor by the workings of *karma.*

Crucial considerations in grasping the voluntary nature of almsgiving concern socioeconomic realities and the possibility that unilateral giving, especially in class-stratified societies, may be an imperative placed on the rich by the social pressure of the poor. Acts of charity maintain the status quo by legitimizing the wealth of the haves while softening (but seldom fundamentally altering) the lot of the have-nots (see Bowie, 1998). Jean Starobinski (1994) has suggested that both largesse and charity may always contain an element of darkness in that they expose inequalities without eradicating them. Religious ideologies celebrating charity may be merely giving a religious and moral gloss to what is in fact driven by forces of class appeasement.

Where Do Alms Go? Alms are received in different ways by strangers, neighbors, monks, nuns, holy men and women, the displaced, and the poor. Alms may engender affection and gratitude or they might give rise to humiliation and resentment. Some recent fieldwork studies in India have revealed considerable ambivalence for those on the receiving end of certain types of gifts that bring "poison" and dependency with them (Raheja, 1988; Parry, 1994). In some contexts, recipients may resent the paternalism of those who seek the recipients' moral betterment through charity. Conversely, the poor may distrust the gift that traps them in dependency and degradation, given by those who accept the condition of poverty as part of the created order or as a necessary backdrop for the expression of their good deeds.

Also important is to consider the trajectory of alms that enrich institutions and transform societies. For example, almsgiving practices associated with the arrival of Buddhism in China stimulated the development of an advanced economy through the accumulation of great wealth by monastic institutions. Monastic riches were not hoarded, but were in turn transformed into productive capital that was then redistributed to the poor or deployed for the purposes of conversion and propagation, magnifying Buddhism's reach. Through investing in what came to be called the "Inexhaustible Treasures"—inexhaustible in that they increase wealth and in turn dispense it in every direction—the pious donor could become a *bodhisattva* perfecting infinite generosity (see Gernet, 1995). No political, social, or economic institution in Tang dynasty China remained unaffected by these developments.

Gifts in the modern world too have the potential to transform or constrain the lives of individuals as well as effect great historical change. In modern contexts of tremendous global economic disparities, almsgiving may play a crucial role in rectifying the gross injustices and exploitations of the world. Yet the free, unilateral gift does not arrive without complications. Even when given with the noblest of intentions, alms take different courses as they reach the recipient, sometimes leading to help and self-determination, other times to a labyrinth of dependence. A central question from a modern perspective concerns how best to channel human charitable impulses not merely to offer relief, but to effectively dismantle social and economic structures that create oppression and poverty in the first place.

SEE ALSO Charity; Hospitality; Merit, overview article; Zakāt.

BIBLIOGRAPHY

Seneca's *De Beneficiis*, translated by John Cooper and J. F. Procopé in *Moral and Political Essays* (New York, 1995), offers a nuanced appreciation of the intricacies of the gift. For Maimonides' eight degrees of charity, see Isadore Twersky, ed., *A Maimonides Reader* (New York, 1972), pp. 134–139; for al-Ghazālī's book on almsgiving in the *Iḥyā' ʿulūm al-dīn,* see Nabih Amin Faris, trans., *The Mysteries of Almsgiving* (Beirut, 1966). A thorough overview of Jewish almsgiving can be found in Alan Avery-Peck's entry "Charity in Judaism" in *The Encyclopedia of Judaism* (New York, 1999), vol. 1, pp. 50–63. See P. V. Kane's chapter on *dāna* for Hindu textual reflections on the gift in *History of Dharmashastra* (Poona, India, 1975), pp. 837–888; and *Ethics, Wealth, and Salvation: A Study in Buddhist Social Ethics*, edited by Russell Sizemore and Donald Swearer (Columbia, S.C., 1990), for several chapters on Buddhist *dāna.* Superb historical explorations of almsgiving include Natalie Zemon Davis's *The Gift in Sixteenth-Century France* (Madison, Wis., 2000); Jean Starobinski's *Largesse* (Paris, 1994), translated by Jane Marie Todd (Chicago, 1997); and Jacques Gernet's *Buddhism in Chinese Society: An Economic History from the Fifth to the Tenth Centuries*, translated by Franciscus Verellen (New York, 1995). Social sciences approaches stimulated by Mauss's *The Gift: The Form and Reason for Exchange in Archaic Societies*, translated by W. D. Halls (London and New York, 1990), and particularly fascinating when explored in contemporary South Asia include Gloria Raheja's *The Poison in the Gift: Ritual, Prestation, and the Dominant Caste in a North Indian Village* (Chicago, 1988) and Jonathan Parry's *Death in Banaras* (Cambridge, U.K., 1994). For a clear-eyed study of the social and economic pressures bearing on almsgiving in rural Buddhist Thailand, see Kathleen Bowie's "The Alchemy of Charity: Of Class and Buddhism in Northern Thailand," *American Anthropologist* 100, no. 2 (1998): 469–481. Finally, for a useful anthology with both secular and religious writings on charity and philanthropy, see Amy Kass, ed., *The Perfect Gift: The Philanthropic Imagination in Poetry and Prose* (Bloomington, Ind., 2002).

MARIA HEIM (2005)

ALPHABETS.

This article concerns lore, mystical beliefs, and magical practices involving the alphabet and its letters in the civilizations and religious traditions that use them. The term *alphabet* generally refers to those scripts derived from the original Phoenician *aleph-bet* that have roughly one sign and only one sign for every phoneme, or at least, as in Phoenician, Hebrew, and Arabic, every consonant phoneme. Logographic writing such as Chinese, and syllabaries such as the Maya "glyphs" (largely deciphered in recent decades), Japanese katakana and hiragana, Indian devanāgarī, and the Ethiopian "geʾez" are therefore excluded from the following discussions, even though the last two derive ultimately from the Phoenician script. However, Near Eastern precursors of the alphabet, such as cuneiform and Egyptian hieroglyphics and their offshoots, will be discussed.

ORIGIN OF WRITING. The beginnings of writing can be traced back to the fourth millennium BCE and earlier in Mesopotamia and in Kurdistan, the Zagros Mountains, and the Iranian plateau to the east and north. Subsequently, the idea of writing (however different the forms it took in each area) spread eastward to the Indus Valley and China, and westward to Egypt, Anatolia, and Minoan Crete. Though the earliest uses of writing appear to have been economic—the recording of mundane trade transactions—it quickly became so central to civilized life that every aspect of human endeavor was written down, from the deeds of kings and priestly rituals to the most sacred myths of the people.

MYTHS OF ORIGIN. Myths soon evolved in literate cultures, attributing to gods or heroes the origin of writing and its transmission to human beings. In Mesopotamia, the cradle of writing, Nabu (Nebo)—son of Marduk, king of the Babylonian pantheon—was credited with the invention of writing, which he used to record the fates of men. This notion of the function of writing, represented in the *Book of Daniel* 5:5–28 (cf. the English expressions *hand of fate* and *handwriting on the wall*), is still alive today in the Middle East and the Balkans.

According to Egyptian mythology, the god ḏhwtj (Thoth) discovered writing. This attribution is known to the West through Plato (*Phaidros* 274c) and was accepted even by the church, as proved by the floor mosaic in Siena Cathedral, which depicts Hermes Trismegistos (Thoth) giving writing to the Egyptians. Titles of this divinity include *sš* (scribe) and *nb sš.w* (lord of writing); he was naturally patron of scribes. Perhaps because the pictographic appearance of the hieroglyphic script (actually a consonantal system with some logograms) facilitated the belief that word and thing were essentially identical, writing was closely linked to magic in ancient Egypt, and Thoth was the god of sorcery as well. He was reputedly the author of the Hermetic corpus (first to third century CE), which influenced Christians, Jews, and Muslims alike in the Middle Ages and Renaissance.

The Bible (*Ex.* 31:18; 32:15–16) has God himself inscribe the two stone Tablets of the Law that he gives to Moses with the "writing of God." If this is a memory of the Sinaitic script, possible ancestor of the Phoenician alphabet, Yahweh may figure here as the inventor of writing. Later, the

Paleo-Hebrew script acquired sanctity; some scrolls from Qumran, though written in Square Aramaic letters, write the tetragammaton (*YHWH*) in Paleo-Hebrew. Postbiblical Jewish tradition often refers to Adam or Enoch as discoverer of the alphabet, magic, alchemy, and astrology.

In the Qurʾān also, writing is provided a divine association. God begins his revelation when Gabriel orders Muḥammad to recite from writings the angel has brought down with him from heaven (*sūrah* 96): "Recite thou! For thy Lord is the most Beneficent, / who hath taught the use of the pen— / Hath taught Man that which he knoweth not." Shanawānī (c. 1610 CE) specifically states that God created the alphabet and revealed it to Adam.

The Greeks generally did not attribute their alphabet to deities; most were aware of its foreign, and often of its specifically Phoenician, origin. Herodotos, perhaps following Hekataios, states that "the Phoenicians who came with Kadmos . . . introduced the Greeks to many skills and, what is more, to the alphabet, which I believe had not previously existed among the Hellenes" (5.58). As for writing in general, some sought the source in Egypt: Antikleides names the early pharoah Menes (first dynasty) as *heuretēs* (discoverer), and Plato assigns to Thoth the same role. (Plato, who rebels against the materialism of the pre-Socratics, becomes, significantly, the first Greek to make a *daimōn* invent writing, though he tells his Egyptian tale to denigrate the invention and probably does not believe it himself.) Under Near Eastern or Egyptian influence, some Greeks attributed writing to the three Fates (cf. Nabu) or to Hermes (cf. Thoth), but these authors are Hellenistic or later.

In Norse tradition, Óðinn (Odin), King of the Gods—known as Woden to Angles and Saxons and Wotan to the Germans—is the discoverer, though not the inventor, of the runic alphabet. The runes are endowed with supernatural power and Óðinn/Woden, like Mercury, Hermes, Thoth, and Nabu, is a god of magic. This is the reason Mercury's day (cf., French, *mercredi*, Spanish, *miercoles*) in English is *Wednesday*, from *Woden's day*.

Christian traditions attribute a number of national alphabets to saints and missionaries. Wulfila (Ulfilas) devised a script for Gothic and used it for his translation of the Bible into that tongue. Saints Cyril and Methodios are usually credited with the creation of Cyrillic, named for the former, which they used for their rendering of the Scriptures into Slavonic, but some scholars believe that the saints actually designed Glagolithic, a rival early Slavonic script. Saint Mesrob Mašt'oç (Mesrop Mashdotz) invented not one, but three scripts: one for his native Armenian, still in use today; one for Georgian; and one for the extinct Alwan (Albanian), a Caucasian language once spoken in modern Azerbaijan.

ROOTS OF MYSTICAL SPECULATION. Mystical speculation on the alphabet and its letters stems principally from two sources. The first is the Near East and Egypt—for magic, mainly the latter. The second is the Pythagorean tradition of Magna Graecia, where the western Greeks tended to reject Ionian rationalism.

Pythagoras founded his religious-philosophical school at Krotona in southern Italy around 531 BCE. The complex system he taught gave a central place to numbers (expressed either by dots or by letters of the alphabet); these he believed to underlie the phenomenal universe. Confirming him in this conviction was his discovery that the principal intervals of the musical scale could be expressed by arithmetic ratios. From him or his school probably derives the seven-note scale that is still used today and is still noted after the Greek fashion with letters (*A, B, C, D, E, F, G*). Later thinkers connected the seven tones with the seven known "planets" (hence the expression *music of the spheres*), the seven days of the week (named for the deified "planets"), and the seven vowels of the Greek alphabet (Α, Ε, Η, Ι, Ο, Υ, Ω); all these came to play an important role in magic and mysticism.

Pythagoras strongly influenced Plato, who spent much time in Syracuse with the Pythagorean Archytas of Tarentum (Taranto). Plato popularized Pythagorean ideas such as mind-body dualism and reincarnation and prepared the intellectual ground for letter and number mysticism. A generation later, the conquests of Alexander brought the Pythagorean-Platonic strain in Greek thought face to face with the philosophies and religions of the East, rife with speculation concerning writing. The subsequent Hellenistic and Roman periods are the formative eras for letter mysticism of all kinds.

LETTER MYSTICISM. Letter mysticism includes several kinds of speculations associated with the alphabet. These conjectures are associated with the shapes of the letters; the significance of the various vowels, consonants, and syllables as well as the enigmas connected to the alphabetic system as a whole. These include the number of letters in the alphabet; the nexus between the letters and the constellations; alphabetic numerology; and symbolic characteristics of the letters.

Shapes of letters. Speculation about the shapes of the letters has existed since very early times. In the Greek system Pythagoras himself is said to have used the upsilon (Υ) to symbolize the initially similar, but ultimately radically divergent, paths of virtuous and wicked lives. Proklos in his *scholia* on Plato's *Timaios* (3.225) therefore calls upsilon the *gramma philosophōn* (philosopher's letter); in the Middle Ages, "ad Pythagorae literae bivium pervenire" ("to come to the crossroads of Pythagoras's letter") became proverbial for "coming to a moral crux." Similarly, the psi (Ψ) on an Attic relief may represent the golden mean followed by the philosopher, who avoids extremes on either side.

Epsilon (Ε), if turned on its back (Ш), resembles a scale, and thus represents justice. This, too, may be ultimately Pythagorean, especially since Ε=5 in the Milesian system; it is midway between alpha (Α=1) and theta (Θ=9) and therefore signifies balance. With this may be connected the famous Delphic E about which Plutarch wrote an essay.

The early Christians, too, saw religious significance in the shapes of the Greek letters. Alpha (A) and delta (Δ), each with three lines, represent the Trinity. Tau (T) is recognizable as the cross, as that inveterate skeptic Lucian (c. 117–c. 180 CE) had already pointed out (*Letters at Law* 61). Theta (Θ) is the world (round with an equator). Thus Isidore of Seville (c. 560–636) was combining Christian with Pythagorean symbolism when he declared that five letters are mystical: ΑΘΤΥΩ (for Ω, see below).

Such speculation is also found in Jewish tradition: in the Zohar (part of the Qabbalah), the letter *he'* (ה) is called *heikhal* ("palace, temple") because its shape suggests one.

Vowels and consonants. By the time of Alexander the Great (356–323 BCE), the Ionian alphabet, with its seven vowels, had spread throughout the Greek world. Athens had adopted it in 403–402 BCE. These vowels were soon the center of much mystical speculation, in good part because they numbered seven, which also designated the seven known "planets." Vowels were thought to possess enormous power and were used on Coptic and Greek papyri from Egypt to invoke the gods. Certain combinations of vowels were deemed so potent that they could create gods. The first, middle, and last characters in the vowel series—A, I, Ω—were also the first three letters of ΑΙΩΝ. Moving iota into first position, we have ΙΑΩ, identified with *Yahu*, a short form of the all-powerful name *Yahweh*. The magical *Eighth Book of Moses* says that the name ΙΑΩ is so mighty that God came into existence from its echo. Fuller forms are ΙΑΕΩ, ΙΗΩΥΟ, and ΙΕΟΥΩΗΙ (this last has all seven vowels). One repeated formula is ΤΟΝ ΙΑΩ ΣΑΒΑΩΘ ΤΟΝ ΑΔΟΝΑΙ, where ΙΑΩ (*Sabaoth*, "hosts"), and ΑΔΟΝΑΙ (*Adonai*, "my lord"), are well-known epithets of Yahweh. ΣΑΒΑΩΘ was etymologized by vowel mystics as *šäba' ʿōt* (bad Hebrew for "seven letters," i.e., the seven in the Greek alphabet). Probably A and Ω (*Rev.* 1:8f.) were meant as the first and last of all letters, though Clement of Alexandria (c. 150–215) believed that the vowel series were meant. Given the importance of the number seven in the *Book of Revelation*, that most mystical of New Testament books, he may have been right.

The seven vowels often were equated with the seven planetary spheres; Clement added that the vowels are the sounds of the planets, hence the A and Ω of *Revelation*. When Hyginus (*Fabulae* 277) attributed the invention of the vowels to the Fates, he was thinking of the planets' role in astrological determinations of individual fates.

The consonants play a much smaller role in magic and mysticism than do vowels. If the seven vowels in the Greek alphabet corresponded to seven planets, then perhaps the seventeen consonants represented the twelve signs of the zodiac plus the five elements. The names of the five elements, ΑΗΡ (air), ΥΔΩΡ (water), ΠΥΡ (fire), ΑΙΘΗΡ (ether), and ΓΗ (earth), were spelled with exactly five consonants (ΓΔΘΠΡ) and five vowels (ΑΗΙΥΩ). The twenty-four letters of the Greek alphabet were assigned in pairs to the twelve signs of the zodiac (Aries: ΑΝ; Taurus: ΒΞ; Gemini: ΓΟ; etc.); these were then read as numerals and formed the basis for complex arithmetic and geometrical calculations of horoscopes.

Syllables. On the walls of an archaic Etruscan tomb, an inscription (IG XIV 2420) lists letters of the Greek alphabet and under them, syllables consisting of a consonant plus a vowel: *MA, MI, ME, MY, NA*, etc. (Etruscan lacks *O*). Some have seen this as an echo of Aegean syllabaries from the Bronze Age (e.g., Linear A, B), which were similarly of consonant-plus-vowel type; others consider the inscription to be a magical incantation. Certainly magic papyri from Hellenistic and Roman Egypt (e.g., Leiden Papyrus Y) such syllables as incantations: Α, ΒΑ, ΓΑ, and so forth; Ε, ΒΕ, ΓΕ, and so on. Marcellus Empiricus (10.70), a medical writer of the fourth and fifth centuries, recommends such a set of syllables (ΨΑ, ΨΕ, etc.) to stop bleeding. The Etruscans may have originated the magical use of syllables or inherited it from the Aegean syllabaries; Etruscan refugees from Roman conquest could have introduced them to Egypt. (Compare the Etruscan book of rituals—and perhaps magic formulas—found on the wrappings of the famous Zagreb Mummy.)

The whole alphabet. The number of letters in the alphabet was widely held to be significant. Early Christian writers, following Jewish originals, saw the twenty-two letters of the Hebrew alphabet as representing the twenty-two creations of God, the twenty-two books of the Old Testament, the twenty-two virtues of Christ, and the twenty-two thousand cattle of Solomon (*1 Kgs.* 8:63; *2 Chr.* 18.5). The twenty-four letters of the Greek alphabet corresponded to the twenty-four hours of the day and night, which in turn are double the number of months in the year. Alexandrian scholars divided the *Iliad* and the *Odyssey* into twenty-four books each, with each represented by a Greek letter. It might seem far-fetched to link this with solar symbolism, but some have compared the 350 cattle of Helios, the sun god (*Odyssey* 12.127–130) to the 365 days of the solar year. Alexander of Aphrodisias, commenting on Aristotle, suggests that the twenty-four letters express the total of the twelve signs of the zodiac, the eight spheres (seven planets plus Earth), and the four elements (excluding ether).

The close link between the alphabet and the cosmos is well illustrated by the semantic field of the Greek word *stoicheion*; it means "element, sound, letter of the alphabet; astrological sign; proposition in geometry; number." The Latin equivalent, *elementum*, may derive from the letter names *L, M, N* plus the suffix *-tum*. Everything had a name and a number, so the universe was built of letters as well as physical elements. The alphabet contained all the letters necessary to spell and utter all the names, known or unknown, of all the deities in the universe, and thus to possess power over them.

Since the alphabet was endowed with such enormous power, its first and last letters could be thought of as containing and encapsulating that power. The Hebrew word אוֹת (*ot*) means both "sign, token, divine portent" and "letter of the alphabet"; significantly, it begins with alef, the first letter of the alphabet, and ends with taw, the last. The alphabet came to represent the whole universe, and *ot* came to signify "name of God" or "God." One magical papyrus (Leiden Papyrus 5) refers to ΑΩΘ, "before which every god falls down and every *daimōn* cringes"; ΑΩΘ transcribes אוֹת, while also comprising the first letter of both Hebrew and Greek alphabets (Α/א) plus the last of each (Ω and Θ=ת). The statement "I am the Alpha and the Omega, the beginning and the end" of *Revelation* 1:8, 21:6, and 22:13 should probably be understood in this light.

Gematria, or numerology. The word *gematria,* used to allude to the numerical significance of letters, comes from the Hebrew *gemaṭriyyah,* or *gimaṭriyyah,* derived from the Greek *geōmetria* (geometry), mirroring the origins of this occult discipline. Though there are cuneiform parallels, the use of alphabetic signs as numerals is a Greek invention. The archaic epichoric alphabet of Miletos had twenty-seven letters: the familiar twenty-four plus *digamma,* or *wau* (ϛ, representing /w/); *qoppa* (Ϙ, representing /q/); and *sampi* (ϡ, or Ͳ, representing /ts/). It lent itself to serving as a numerical syatem, with Α–Θ standing for numerals 1–9, Ι–Ϙ for 10–90, and Ρ–ϡ for 100–900. Other numbers were expressed by the additive principle ΙΑ=11, ΙΒ=12, ΡΝΖ=100+50+7=157; 1000=͵Α, 2000=͵Β, and so on (the strokes are later additions). This Milesian system became dominant in the Hellenistic period and was applied to the Hebrew, Coptic, and Arabic alphabets, even though it fit them less well because they did not have exactly twenty-seven letters.

With this additive principle, names and words could be read as numbers. The Pythagoreans argued that every man, animal, plant, and city had its mystical number (*psēphos;* pl. *psēphoi*), which determined the course of its existence. It was a small step to identify this *psēphos* with the sum of the letter-numerals in that name or word. This system of arithmomancy spread rapidly in the Hellenistic period and plays a vital part in Egyptian and Jewish religious practice and later in Christianity and Islam.

The *psēphoi* played an important role in both religious and secular life. The *Sibylline Oracles* (8.148) predicted that Rome would last 948 years; this is the *psēphos* of ΡΩΜΗ. The great Gnostic *aiōn* Abraxas may owe the exact form of his name to its *psēphos*: 365. In the second and third centuries CE, Romans identified Mithra, the Persian god of light, with their Sol Invictus (Invincible Sun), patron deity of the army. Contributing to this syncretism is the *psēphos* of ΜΕΙΘΡΑΣ=365.

Even fragments of words were added up and considered to be significant. Apion of Alexandria (first century CE) thought that the first two letters of the *Iliad,* ΜΗ *(*ΝΙΝ*)*=48, represented the forty-eight total books of the *Iliad* and *Odyssey* together. The Gnostic Valentinus saw in the first two letters of Jesus' name, ΙΗ*(*ΣΟΥΣ*)*=18, a reflection of the eighteen *aiōnes,* the emanations of Divinity central to Gnosticism. The *Epistle to Barnabas* (9.8) explains the 318 servants of Abraham (*Gn.* 14:14) as the ΙΗ=18 of the ΙΗΣΟΥΣ plus Τ (the Cross)=300.

The formulation of *isopsēphoi* (two or more words with the same numerological value) became a central numerological practice. It was believed that, should the *psēphoi* of two words be equal, the words themselves must have a similar significance. A favorite Byzantine *isopsēphos* was ΘΕΟΣ (God)=ΑΓΑΘΟΣ (good)=ΑΓΙΟΣ (holy)=284. Suetonius (69–after 122 CE), author of *The Lives of the Twelve Caesars,* records a Roman political *isopsēphos,* ΝΕΡΩΝ=1005=ΙΔΙΑΝ ΜΗΤΕΡΑ ΑΠΕΚΤΕΙΝΕ (killed his own mother), directed against the matricide emperor Nero. A sexual *isopsēphos* was offered by the poet Straton (second century CE): ΠΡΩΚΤΟΣ (rectum)=1570=ΧΡΥΣΟΣ (gold).

To make more *isopsēphoi,* Jewish arithmomancers introduced elaborate variations. One gives each letter the sum of the Milesian values of the letters in its name (e.g., אלפ=80+30+1=111). Another reckons א–ט=1–9, י–צ=1–9, and ק–ת=1–4; therefore יהוה (Yahweh)=טוב (*ṭob,* "good")=17.

No numerological mystery has held more fascination than the "number of the beast" of the Christian apocalypse. *Revelation* 13:18 exhorts the wise to "calculate [*psēphisatō*] the number of the beast, for it is the number of a man [*arithmos . . . anthrōpou*]." This can only mean that the number 666 (616 and 646 are manuscript variants) is the *psēphos* of a man's name. *Revelation* 17:9 shows that the beast is Rome (7 heads = 7 hills), so the man must be an emperor. ΓΑΙΟΣ ΚΑΙΣΑΡ (Gaius Caesar "Caligula," r. 37–41 CE) fits 616 perfectly; and for 666 there are several candidates. Nero's name in Greek (ΝΕΡΩΝ ΚΑΙΣΑΡ=Nero Caesar, r. 54–68) [mis]spelled in Hebrew נרון קסר, totals 666 ("Caesar" should be קיסר). Titus (ΤΕΙΤΟΣ) took Jerusalem in 70 CE, destroying the Temple; identify him as a Titan, and we have ΤΕΙΤΑΝ=666. Marcus Cocceius Nerva (r. 96–98), first of the Five Good Emperors, seems an unlikely candidate for "the beast"—unless he was considered *Nero redivivus*—but Μ. ΝΕΡΟΥΑ and Κ*(*ΑΙΣΑΡ*)* Κ*(*ΟΚΚΕΙΟΣ*)* ΝΕΡΟΥΑ both =666. The equation ουλπιος (for Emperor Marcus Ulpius Traianus, r. 98–117)=666 must be rejected; it depends on final small sigma (ς)=6, but neither –ς nor ς=6 are attested before the high Middle Ages. The true solution to this riddle has not been established, though Μ. ΝΕΡΟΥΑ as Nero revived fits best with the traditional date for the composition of *Revelations.*

It is noteworthy that the *psēphos* of ΙΗΣΟΥΣ is 888=4 x 222; 666=3 x 222. While 222=2 x 111 (cf. alef=111 above), 3+4=7; three, four, and especially seven pervade *Revelation.* Thus the sum of the *psēphoi* of Christ and antichrist, divided by 222, equals seven.

LATER NUMEROLOGICAL SPECULATION. Numerological speculation has continued to this day. The Gnostic Marcus's complex system of numerology and other occult uses of the alphabet had wide influence in the Middle Ages, especially

The Numerical Values of Greek, Hebrew, and Arabic Letters According to the Milesian System

Greek

	Letter	Name	Transliteration
1	α	alpha	a
2	β	beta	b
3	γ	gamma	g
4	δ	delta	d
5	ε	epsilon	e
6	ς	digamma	w
7	ζ	zeta	z
8	η	eta	ē
9	θ	theta	th
10	ι	iota	i
20	κ	kappa	k
30	λ	lamda	l
40	μ	mu	m
50	ν	nu	n
60	ξ	xi	x
70	ο	omicron	o
80	π	pi	p
90	ϙ	qoppa	q
100	ρ	rho	r
200	σ	sigma	s
300	τ	tau	t
400	υ	upsilon	u
500	φ	phi	ph
600	χ	chi	ch
700	ψ	psi	ps
800	ω	omega	ō
900	ϡ	sampi	ts

Hebrew

	Letter	Name	Transliteration
1	א	alef	-or'
2	בּ	beit	b
	ב	veit	v
3	ג	gimel	g
4	ד	dalet	d
5	ה	he'	h
6	ו	wāw	w
7	ז	zavin	z
8	ח	ḥeit	ḥ
9	ט	ṭeit	ṭ
10	י	yud	y
20	כּ	kaf	k
	כ	khaf	kh
30	ל	lamed	l
40	מ	mem	m
50	נ	nun	n
60	ס	samekh	s
70	ע	'ayin	'
80	פּ	pe'	p
	פ	fe'	f
90	צ	tsadi	ts
100	ק	quf	q
200	ר	reish	r
300	שׁ	shin	sh
	שׂ	sin	ś
400	ת	tav	t

Arabic

	Letter	Name	Transliteration
1	ا	alif	'
2	ب	bā'	b
400	ت	tā'	t
500	ث	thā'	th
3	ج	jīm	j
8	ح	ḥā'	ḥ
600	خ	khā'	kh
4	د	dal	d
700	ذ	dhāl	dh
200	ر	rā'	r
7	ز	zā'	z
60	س	sīn	s
300	ش	shīn	sh
90	ص	ṣād	ṣ
800	ض	ḍād	ḍ
9	ط	ṭā'	ṭ
900	ظ	ẓā'	ẓ
70	ع	'ayn	'
1000	غ	ghayn	gh
80	ف	fā'	f
100	ق	qāf	q
20	ك	kāf	k
30	ل	lām	l
40	م	mīm	m
50	ن	nūn	n
5	ه	hā'	h
6	و	waw	w
10	ي	yā'	y

among Jews and Muslims. In medieval Judaism numerology flourished, and the Ḥasidim cultivate it in present times as well. Numerology also played a prominent role in medieval Islam, as for example in the *Haft Paykar* of the Persian poet Niẓāmī. When used as numbers, the Arabic letters were arranged in the traditional order (Arabic *ʾabjad*) familiar from Hebrew and Greek, and their values followed the Milesian system. The usual order of the Arabic alphabet is based on sound and letter shape. In the West, a different system was used (*A*=1, *B*=2 . . . *Y*=25, *Z*=26), but psephological speculation thrived there, too. One whose destiny was influenced by it was Napoleon Bonaparte (1769–1821); long before he attained power, he discovered that *BONAPART(E)*=82=*BOURBON* and therefore believed that he would one day rule France.

***Temurah*, Acronyms, and Acrostics.** The significance given to letters led to the devising of alphabetic ciphers; examples are *temurah* (simple substitution ciphers), acronyms, and acrostics.

A largely Jewish practice, *temurah* (exchange) is found in the Bible but was most highly developed by the Qabbalists. Letters of the alphabet are represented by other letters according to a definite scheme. The *ʾatbaš* (אתבש) exchanges the first letter א for the last ת, the second ב for the penultimate ש, and so on. The results are significant: ששך=*ŠŠK*, "oppressed," for בבל=*BBL* (Babel) (*Jer.* 25:26), and לב קמי=*LB QMY*, "heart of my enemy," for כשׂדים=*KSDYM*, "Chaldaeans" (*Jer.* 51:1) are early and well-known examples. The variant *ʾalbam* switches the first letter (א) with the twelfth (ל), the second (ב) with the thirteenth (מ), and so on. *Ziruf,* or *gilgul,* involves anagrams of single words; there were, for example, twelve possible permutations *(haviyyot)* of יהוה, the tetragrammaton *YHWH.*

An acronym is a word each of whose letters is the first letter of another word; the words represented by the acronym usually form a title or phrase. Hellenistic Alexandrines thought the designations of the five districts of their city Α, Β, Γ, Δ, Ε (i.e., *A, B, C, D, E,* or 1, 2, 3, 4, 5) represented ΑΛΕΞΑΝΔΡΟΣ ΒΑΣΙΛΕΥΣ ΓΕΝΟΣ ΔΙΟΣ ΕΚΤΙΣΕΝ ("Alexander, king, [of the] race of Zeus, founded [it]"). Jews saw in the sobriquet of the great liberator Yehudah ha-Makkabi (Maccabee, from Aramaic *makkabā,* "hammer,")—spelled *MKBY*—an acronym of the phrase in *Exodus* 15: 11 "Mi Kamokah Ba-elim, Yahweh?" ("Who among the gods is like thee, Yahweh?"). The most famous acronym is the Greek word ΙΧΘΥΣ (fish), standing for ΙΗΣΟΥΣ ΧΡΙΣΥΟΣ ΘΕΟΥ ΥΙΟΣ ΣΩΤΗΡ (Jesus Christ, Son of God, Savior). This meaning is probably secondary; the original idea is a reference to *Matthew* 4:19: "I shall make you fishers of men."

Acrostics begin each line or verse of a poem with the successive letters of the alphabet. The oldest examples are in *Jeremiah* 1–4, but acrostic poems occur elsewhere in the Bible and are frequent in Jewish and Christian writings throughout late antiquity and the Middle Ages.

ISLAMIC SPECULATION INVOLVING LETTERS. Qurʾanic verses are often preceded by unexplained letters (e.g., *ʾalif, lām, mīm,* before *sūrah* 2), a phenomenon about which there has naturally been much speculation and to which mystical meaning has often been attached. The seven letters absent from *sūrah* 1 have special sanctity and are connected with the seven major names of God, seven angels, seven kings of the *jinn,* seven days of the week, and the seven planets. Shanawānī noted that both the Bible and the Qurʾān begin with the letter *B.* A mystical thirteenth-century Ṣūfī text holds that all God's secrets are hidden in the Qurʾān, the entire meaning of which is contained in that letter, ب *(bā=B),* and specifically in the dot underneath it.

Offshoots of Islam carried such speculations further, particularly in Persia and Turkey. Faḍl Allāh of Astarābād (late fourteenth century), founder of the Ḥurūfī sect (from *ḥurūf,* pl. of *ḥarf,* "letter of the alphabet"), taught that God reveals himself to the world through the thirty-two letters of the Persian alphabet; the totality of these letters—and their numerical sum—is God himself manifest. The Bektāshiyyah, a dervish order prominent in Ottoman Turkey, adopted Ḥurūfī letter mysticism as a basic tenet. In the nineteenth century, the founders of the Bahāʾī faith gave an important place to alphabet mysticism and numerology.

The importance of the alphabet to mysticism and occult science may have weakened in modern times, but alphabets remain closely associated with religion. Roman Catholic bishops still trace the alphabet on church floors during consecration rites, and Jews and Muslims adorn their temples with writings from their scriptures. Until recently, non-Arab Muslim peoples all used the Arabic alphabet for their languages, no matter how badly it suited them phonetically. Similarly, Yiddish, originating in a Middle High German dialect, and Ladino Spanish are written in Hebrew letters because their speakers are Jewish. Slavic peoples use Latin letters where Roman Catholic Christianity took root, but Cyrillic, a development of Byzantine Greek script, in areas where Orthodoxy triumphed. In nations of the former Yugoslavia, the language formerly known as Serbo-Croatian is written in the Latin alphabet by Catholic Croats and called Croatian; in Cyrillic by Orthodox Serbs and called Serbian; and formerly in Arabic script, but today in Latin, by Bosnian Muslims and called Bosnian. Since the breakup of the Soviet Union in 1991, although most Central Asian republics are replacing the Cyrillic script with the Latin, Tajikistan, the most strongly Muslim republic, announced plans to go back to the Arabo-Persian alphabet. Even in a secular age, the religious associations of writing are still apparent.

SEE ALSO Astrology; Hermes Trismegistos; Names and Naming; Numbers, overview article.

BIBLIOGRAPHY

Franz Dornseiff's *Das Alphabet in Mystik und Magie* (1922; Leipzig, 1975) remains the definitive work on the alphabet in mysticism and magic. Every aspect of the question is discussed in thorough and rational fashion. In addition to a corpus of *abecedaria* ("Corpus der ABC–Denkmäler"), Dornseiff provides a section of "Additions and Corrections" that is rich in fascinating information. Dornseiff's book serves as the basis of most works on the topic. Alfred Bertholet's *Die Macht der Schrift in Glauben und Aberglauben* (Berlin, 1949) should also be consulted for its general treatment of the subject.

The origin of writing in the ancient Near East is treated by Denise Schmandt-Besserat in "The Earliest Precursor of Writing," *Scientific American* 238 (1978): 50–59, and in "Reckoning before Writing," *Archaeology* 32 (May–June 1979): 22–31.

A lucid account of the Milesian system of alphabetic numerals is given in Herbert Weir Smyth's incomparable *Greek Grammar* (1916; rev. ed., Cambridge, Mass., 1956); pages 102–104 and 347–348 are especially helpful. Peter Friesenhahn's *Hellenistische Wortzahlenmystik im Neuen Testament* (1935; Amsterdam, 1979) is a thorough, although overenthusiastic, attempt to find *psēphoi and isopsēphoi* everywhere in the Greek text of the New Testament, using the system A=1, B=2, . . . Ω=24, instead of the Milesian. Vincent Foster Hopper offers a competent exploration of numerical symbolism of the period, including gematria, in *Medieval Number Symbolism* (New York, 1938). For an example of current popular literature on numerology, look at Martin Gardner's *The Incredible Dr. Matrix* (New York, 1976), which is interesting but, unlike many works on the topic that repeat wild speculations with passionate conviction, does not take itself too seriously.

Concerning aspects of the alphabet in Judaism and Islam, articles in the *Encyclopedia Judaica* (Jerusalem, 1971) and the *Encyclopedia of Islam,* new ed. (Leiden, 1960–) are very informative, especially Gershom Scholem's "Gematria" and Samuel Abba Horodezky's "Alphabet, Hebrew, in Midrash, Talmud, and Kabbalah" in the former and, to a lesser extent, G. Weil's "Abd̲jad" in the latter. These encyclopedias are especially valuable to the English-speaking reader, for serious literature on religious and occult uses of the alphabet in that language is scarce. Georg Krotkoff illustrates the uses of letter and number mysticism in the Islamic Middle Ages in his analysis of the *Haft Paykar* by the Persian poet Niẓāmī in "Colour and Number in the *Haft Paykar*" in *Logos Islamikos: Studia Islamica in honorem Georgii Michaelis Wickens* (Toronto, 1984).

For Norse beliefs about the runes, see Lee M. Hollander, *The Poetic Edda* (Austin, Tex., 1999), especially the *Sigrdrífumál,* verses 6–22. Regarding the translator saints and their alphabets, consult the relevant sections of Hans Jensen, *Sign, Symbol, and Script* (New York, 1969). On the current status of alphabets—and other writing systems—in the world, a helpful guide is Kenneth Katzner, *The Languages of the World* (London and New York, 2002).

JON-CHRISTIAN BILLIGMEIER (1987 AND 2005)
PAMELA J. BURNHAM (2005)

ALTAR. The English word *altar,* meaning "a raised structure on which sacrifices are offered to a deity," derives from the Latin *altare* ("altar") and may be related to *altus* ("high"). This ancient meaning has been further verified by the corresponding Classical Greek term *bōmos* (raised platform, stand, base, altar with a base, i.e., the foundation of the sacrifice). The Latin *altaria* is, in all likelihood, related to the verb *adolere* ("to worship"; originally, "to burn, to cause to go up in smoke or odor"), so that the word has come to signify a "place of fire" or "sacrificial hearth."

THE CLASSICAL WORLD AND ANCIENT NEAR EAST. The above etymology implies both burnt offerings and incense. Nowhere—neither in ancient Greece or Rome nor anywhere else—is the altar necessarily associated with a temple. It is important to distinguish between house altars and public altars, as well as between stationary and portable altars. Both classical antiquity and the ancient Near East offer a rich variety of altars having diverse uses. Attempts at systematization have resulted in a clear understanding of the basic functions of the altar.

Greeks and Romans made careful distinctions between different altar forms: the raised altar site where sacrifices to the heavenly gods were performed; the pit (Gr., *bothros;* Lat., *mundus*) that was dug to receive the offerings to the deities of the underworld; and the level ground where gifts to the earth gods were deposited. The altar was a symbol of the unseen presence of the gods and was therefore considered a sacred spot. Used as a table, it invited the god to partake of the offering; used as a throne it bade the god take his place. The shape of the hearth reflected the transformation of the sacrifice, through fire, into matter appropriate for the spiritual world. It also reflected the role of the hearth as the hallowed and central place both within the family and in society. The altar could also take the form of a burial mound in which the hole or duct that drained the sacrificial blood to the interred bodies within corresponded to the pit formerly used in sacrifices to the dead. Homer uses the word to mean "fireplace," indicating that burnt offerings and an ash altar had been part of the cult of the dead.

The above differentiations and functions apply to altars in general, regardless of how they were constructed or shaped within different cultures and religions: whether boulders, mounds, or piles of rocks; the stepped altars of the Akkadians and Cretans; the sacrificial tables of the Minoans; the sacred hearth of the *megaron,* the male gathering room of ancient Greece and the prototype of the temple; the retables of the Mycenaean pit or cupola graves; or the table and grave altars of the Christian cult of the dead (Fauth, 1964). In a Pawnee house, a wealth of cosmic symbols surround the buffalo skull displayed on an earthen platform—a raised place that Western scholars commonly refer to as an altar (Weltfish, 1965, pp. 63, 66f., 266; cf. Reichard, 1950, pp. xxxv, 334).

Egyptian ritual worship included both portable and stationary altars. The former had no sacred function but were simply cult accessories such as tables or stands used for holding a tray of food, an incense bowl, or a libation cup (according to the type of sacrifice involved). Such portable altars were kept in great numbers in the temple stores. Most of the extant stationary altars were used in the sun temples. These altars were surrounded by a low wall indicating the special sacred nature of their place during sun rites that were devoid of imagery. A large obelisk further underscored the importance of the place in the ancient temples dedicated to Re. Monuments of that size could only be contained in the courtyard of an ordinary temple ("the place of sacrifice"), whereas the holiest of holies, which was inside the temple and harbored the cult image, had to make do with a portable sacrificial table (Bonnet, 1952, pp. 14f.).

HINDUISM. The Sanskrit word *vedi* refers to "an elevated piece of ground serving as a sacrificial altar" or "a clay sacrificial altar." It is synonymous with *pīṭha* ("seat, throne"), an altar stand or pedestal with places for several idols, each backed with a *prabhāvalī,* or "halo" (Liebert, 1976, p. 334). *Vedi* may also designate a shallow trench constructed especially for offerings.

The nomadic Indo-Aryans who invaded India around 1500 BCE carried with them a portable fire altar drawn on a chariot (*ratha*) and protected by a canopy that marked the holiness of the shrine. This eternally burning fire on a rolling base was eventually replaced by fires kindled for the occasion by rubbing sticks together. In the case of domestic sacrifices, the head of the family made the fire in the home hearth (*āyatana*). For communal offerings, a fire was made on a specially consecrated spot (*sthaṇḍila*).

There were no temples during the Vedic period, but a sacrificial hall (*yāgaśālā*) could be erected on holy ground that had first been thoroughly leveled. It consisted of a framework of poles covered with thatching. The sacred area, which like the domestic hearth was called *āyatana*, included subsidiary enclosures and a sacrificial stake (*yūpa*) to which the victim was tied. This stake, which represented the cosmic tree, constituted an intermediate station between the divine world and life on earth. The *vedi* was constructed either inside or outside the sacrificial hall, as a mound of bricks or as a shallow pit where the sacred fires were lit. Burnt sacrifices and libations were offered to the gods who were supposed to attend the ceremonies, sitting on sacred grass (*kuśa*) spread over part of the altar or on its sides. The *vedi* was constructed so as to be narrower in the middle and was likened to a female torso with a womb (Walker, 1968, vol. 1, p. 30).

The *śrauta* sacrifice, performed by priests, was founded on Vedic *śruti* ("heard") revelation; it is the subject of much discussion, especially in *Śatapatha Brāhmaṇa*. The practice calls for three different fire altars arranged around the *vedi*, which serves to hold oblations and sacrificial utensils not in use. The circular *gārhapatya* altar located to the west symbolizes the earth and its fire; it holds the "fire belonging to the lord of the house" that is used for preparing the sacrificial food. The quadrilateral *āhavanīya* altar to the east represents the sky with its four directions. It usually holds "the fire of offering." The semicircular *dakṣiṇā*, or southern altar, symbolizes the atmosphere between the heavens and the earth. It wards off hostile spirits and transmits the offering to the ancestors. The fire god Agni is thus present on all three altars in three different manifestations—as terrestrial, celestial, and aerial fire—uniting the three worlds on one sacred plane. The omnipresent Agni, as all gods in one, provides the link between heaven and earth by conveying the food cooked on earthly fire to the heavenly fire, the sun.

All sacrificial rites are said to be included in and summed up by the stratification of the *agnicaya* (fireplace) or the *uttaravedi* (high altar) to the north with its rich symbolism. It represents the rejuvenation of the exhausted creator god Prajāpati, "the lord of offspring," and hence of all the cosmos, his body. The Agnicayana sacrifice re-creates the cyclic rhythm of the universe: from birth or coming into being to death or annihilation, at which point life begins anew. The sacrificial ceremonies thus serve a triple purpose: at the same time they restore Prajāpati himself, the universe, and the master of the offering (*yajamāna*).

The fire altar in this case is constructed of five layers of bricks, 10,800 in number (one for every hour of the Hindu year). The creator god represents the year with its five seasons. The five layers also symbolize the five regions of the universe. The basic notion behind these cosmic representations is of Prajāpati himself: his hair, skin, flesh, bone, and marrow, as well as another pentad: the god's spiritual self together with the senses. The fire, taken from the *āhavanīya* altar to the *uttaravedi*, lifts the master of the offering to heaven, making him immortal. His spiritual flight is sometimes symbolized by an altar built in the shape of a flying bird. He thus manifests himself simultaneously in time, space, and creation/creator (Gonda, 1960, pp. 141, 190ff.; Hopkins, pp. 18f.).

The Agnicayana ritual may still be studied in India as a living tradition. Its principles, as manifested in the Vāstupuruṣamaṇḍala, a diagram of the incarnation of Puruṣa (Primordial Man), are found in the building symbolism of the Hindu temple (Gonda, 1960, p. 328; cf. Eliade, 1958, secs. 142, 154, 171; 1978, secs. 76ff.).

ISRAELITE RELIGION AND EARLY JUDAISM. The Hebrew term for altar is *mizbeaḥ* ("a place of sacrificial slaughter"), which is derived from *zabah* ("to slaughter as a sacrifice"). In time, the animal slaughter came to be performed beside, not on, the altar. Other kinds of oblations offered on the altar were grain, wine, and incense. The altar sometimes served a nonsacrificial function as witness (*Jos.* 22:26ff.) or refuge (*1 Kgs.* 1:50f.) for most crimes except murder.

The altars, if not made from natural or rough-hewn rocks, were constructed from unhewn stone, earth, or metal. The tabernacle, or portable desert sanctuary of the Israelites, had a bronze-plated altar for burnt offerings in the court and a gold-plated incense altar used within the tent. Both of these altars were constructed of wood, and each was fitted with four rings and two poles for carrying. The altar for burnt offerings was hollow, like its Assyrian counterpart, to make it lighter. Both had horns on all four corners, offering refuge to anyone who grasped them.

The description of the altars in King Solomon's temple (the First Temple) is incomplete (cf. *1 Kgs.* 6ff.; *2 Chr.* 4:1). Two hundred years later Ahaz replaced the sacrificial altar of Solomon with a copy of a Damascene altar (*2 Kgs.* 16:10ff.) that resembled an Akkadian temple tower not only in its storied structure but also in references to the top as "the mountain of God."

Ezekiel's vision of the altar of the new temple may be directly modeled on that of Ahaz, unless it refers to the postexilic altar dating from 515 BCE or is a free construction. Ezekiel calls the incense altar "the table that is before the Lord" (*Ez.* 41:22). The Temple Scroll of the Qumran texts from the beginning of our own era contains a detailed description of the true Temple and its rites, presented as the original revelation of God to Moses that was never realized. Unfortunately, the text dealing with the altar is badly damaged (Maier, 1978, pp. 67, 76).

The function of the Israelite altar was essentially the same as in other sanctuaries of the ancient Near East but with some important differences. While sacrifices were still referred to as "the bread of your God" (*Lv.* 22:25) and "a pleasing odor to the Lord" (*Lv.* 1:17), the notion of actually feeding Yahveh was not implied. This ancient pagan idea has acquired with the passage of time a strictly metaphorical meaning, as in later references to "the Lord's table" (e.g. *Mal.* 1:7). Furthermore, the altars of Yahveh could be erected only in the Promised Land.

The altar itself was sanctified in extensive consecration rites culminating in a theophany described in *Leviticus* 9:23–24: "The glory of the Lord appeared to all the people. Fire came out from before the Lord and consumed the whole-offering and the fatty parts on the altar. And all the people saw, and they shouted and fell on their faces." When, at a later stage in history, only the name of God was believed to dwell in the sanctuary, no theophany could occur. The altar nevertheless represented the place where heaven and earth met, the place from which prayers ascended to God—even in foreign battles, provided that the worshipers turned toward the sacred land, the sacred city, and the Temple (*1 Kgs.* 8:44, 8:48).

The general prohibition against blood was also related to the sacrificial altar. Blood represented the life of the animal that must return to its creator. Thus the slaughter of an ox, a goat, or a sheep had to be undertaken at the altar as an offering to God, lest it be regarded merely as the taking of life (*Lv.* 17:3ff.; cf. *Dt.* 12:13ff.). The altar was the "divinely-appointed instrument of effecting expiation for taking animal life" (Milgrom and Lerner, 1971, col. 765). The sanctity of the altar forbade stepping on it and required that the priests wear breeches to cover their nakedness (*Ex.* 20:26, 28:42f.). Talmudic sources maintain the distinction between the sacrificial bronze altar in the Temple court and the golden incense altar in the sanctuary by referring to them as "outer" and "inner" altars.

Iron could not be used in the construction of an altar, according to rabbinical literature, since the iron sword represented disaster while the altar was a symbol of atonement and peace between Israel and God. The word *mizbeaḥ* resembles four other words meaning "removes evil decrees," "sustains," "endears," "atones." The four consonants of *mizbeaḥ* are sometimes also interpreted as the initial letters of four words meaning "forgiveness," "justification," "blessing," "life." Both the terminology and the legends associated with the altar have given rise to countless metaphors.

Abraham's binding of Isaac on the altar in the land of Moriah is considered the supreme example of self-sacrifice in obedience to God's will, and the symbol of Jewish martyrdom throughout the ages. Abraham himself was, from this point of view, the first person to prepare for martyrdom, and his offering was the last of the ten trials to which he was exposed. According to Jewish tradition, the Temple was later built on that very spot (Jacobs, 1971, cols. 480f.); hence the expression "Whoever is buried in the land of Israel is as if he were buried beneath the altar." Already in *Exodus* 25:9 and 25:40 we read of a heavenly pattern for the tabernacle and its furniture. Earlier still, the Sumerian king Gudea (fl. c. 2144–c. 2124 BCE) had built a temple in Lagash in accordance with a divinely inspired plan. Rabbinical sources have further developed this correspondence: the archangel Mikha'el, serving as high priest, is described as celebrating a heavenly rite on the altar before God, offering the souls of the saints who after death have found rest under the heavenly altar (Kohler, 1901, p. 467; cf. *Rv.* 6:9).

The Jewish table has been looked upon as a kind of altar ever since the destruction of the Second Temple by the Romans. The saying "Now that there is no altar, a man's table atones for him" helps explain many of the table customs in *halakhah* (Milgrom and Lerner, 1971, cols. 767ff.).

CHRISTIANITY. Paul contrasted the Christian service with the pagan sacrificial meal by stating that we cannot partake of the Lord's table and the devil's table at the same time (*1 Cor.* 10:21). He thus distinguished between pagan sacrificial altars and the table at which Christ celebrated the last supper with his disciples. The New Testament constitutes the dividing point between Judaism and Christianity: Christ has, once and for all, made the full and sufficient sacrifice of himself (*Heb.* 8–10). The terminology of the sacrifice is used figuratively in reference to the dedication of Christian life (*Rom.* 12:1) and to the mission of Paul himself (*Phil.* 2:17).

The early church was thus able to refer to the Eucharist as *thusia*, (Gr., "sacrifice"). The table at which it was celebrated was the *thusiastērion* ("place of sacrifice"), the term for altar first used in the Septuagint. The commonly used term among the Christians was *trapeza* ("table"). We find the term *bōmos* used throughout the Bible to designate the altars of the pagan gods (Behm, 1964–1976 p. 182).

Construction of separate rooms for the divine service was a rather late development owing to the persecutions of the first few centuries. The early Christians used portable tables that possessed no special sacred or ritual connotations for the eucharistic meals. This did not change until around 200 CE, when the altar became stationary and was sanctified by a special anointment with oil (*muron*). Under Constantine, Christianity became first a tolerated and later a favored religion, resulting in a rapid rise in church construction.

The Western church eventually settled on the Latin term *altare* ("a raised place") since it corresponded not only to the sacrificial altars of the Temple-centered Israelite religion but also to the various non-Christian cults of the Roman world. The Christians differentiated their altars from pagan ones by using the terms *altare* and *mensa* instead of *ara*, and by referring to their altar in the singular, reserving the plural *altaria* for pagan places of sacrifice. As late as the fourth century, Christian apologists listed the specific characteristics of Christianity: there were no temples, no altars, and no sacrificial rites, that is, in the pagan sense (see Stuiber, 1978, p. 309).

Following the adoption of the altar by the early Christian churches, its sacred nature became increasingly emphasized. It was the foundation of the elements of the Eucharist, and the special presence of Christ was expressed in the epiclesis of the eucharistic liturgy. A rich symbolism could therefore develop. The altar could be seen as a symbol of the heavenly throne or of Christ himself: the altar is made of stone, just as Christ is the cornerstone (*Mt.* 21:42). It also could be his cross or his grave. The martyr cult of the period lent yet another symbolic dimension to the altar: it was shaped like a sarcophagus, on top of which the communion table was placed. The statement in *Revelation* that the prophet sees under the altar the souls of those who were martyred for the Word legitimized the practice of incorporating relics in the altar. This latter development may be illustrated by Saint Peter's Basilica in Rome. Excavations have shown that a small funeral monument was erected on the simple earthen tomb of the apostle Peter around 150 CE. The altar in Constantine's fourth-century basilica and later the main altar of the sixteenth-century cathedral were centered on top of the original tomb. During the construction of the former, the bones of Peter were wrapped in a gold-embroidered purple cloth and deposited in a marble niche. On the wall an unknown hand has carved the following words in fourth-century Greek: "Peter inside." An altar of this kind was also referred to as *confessio* ("witness") after the witness to the faith or the martyr buried there.

During the Middle Ages a document giving the year of dedication was often placed along with the main relic in a hollow place in the top of the altar. This was covered with a stone and referred to as a *sepulcrum* ("grave"). In conjunction with the dedication ceremony it was customary to chisel a cross in each corner and one in the middle of the stone top.

The Middle Ages added little that was new to the symbolism of the altar but rather served to reiterate and sum up the thinking of the church fathers on the subject. The greatest popular preacher of the German Middle Ages, Berthold von Regensburg (c. 1220–1272), provides a good summary of the Christological interpretation:

> The altar manifests Christ. It is built of stone, anointed in a holy way; it stands in an exalted place and serves as a container for the relics of the saints. So is Christ too a rock (*1 Cor.* 10:4); anointed with the Holy Ghost (*Ps.* 44:3); the head of the whole church (*Col.* 1:18), in him the life and glory of the saints lie hidden (*Col.* 3:3). To the extent that it is sacrificed on the altar, it signifies the cross on which Christ offered himself, not only for our sins but for the sins of the whole world. (quoted in Maurer, 1969, p. 36)

After the Reformation, with its opposition to relic worship and to the conception of the Mass as a sacrifice, it was primarily the Eucharist of the early church that came to be associated with the altar table. The reformers emphasized the importance of the true and pure preaching of the word of God, with the result that the pulpit gained a more prominent position, sometimes at the expense of the altar.

The altar also came to be relegated to a secondary role within the Roman Catholic Church during the Middle Ages, when the increasingly opulent ornamentation of screens, paintings, and sculptures was introduced. This development was furthered during the Renaissance and the Baroque era, when the focus increasingly shifted to the sacramental presence of Christ in the Eucharist.

SEE ALSO Agni; Fire; Hestia; Sacrifice; Shrines; Stones.

BIBLIOGRAPHY

Behm, Johannes. "Thuō, thusia, thusiastērion." In *Theological Dictionary of the New Testament*, edited by Gerhard Kittel and Gerhard Friedrich, vol. 3. Grand Rapids, Mich., 1966. A standard work; the supplementary bibliography published in 1979 contains only works on sacrifice.

Bonnet, Hans. "Altar." *Reallexikon der ägyptischen Religionsgeschichte*, pp. 14–17. Berlin, 1952.

Eliade, Mircea. *Patterns in Comparative Religion.* New York, 1958.

Eliade, Mircea. *A History of Religious Ideas*, vol. 1, *From the Stone Age to the Eleusinian Mysteries.* Chicago, 1978.

Fauth, Wolfgang. "Altar." In *Der Kleine Pauly*, vol. 1, cols. 279–281. Stuttgart, 1964. Although brief, refers to the authors of classical antiquity.

Galling, Kurt. "Altar." In *Interpreter's Dictionary of the Bible*, vol. 1, pp. 96–100. A German Old Testament scholar summarizes his important contributions to the discussion of the altar in the ancient Near East.

Gonda, Jan. *Die Religionen Indiens*, vol. 1, *Veda und älterer Hinduismus* (1960). 2d rev. ed. Stuttgart, 1978. By the leading Dutch Indologist.

Gray, Louis H., et al. "Altar." In *Encyclopaedia of Religion and Ethics*, edited by James Hastings, vol. 1. Edinburgh, 1908. Although largely outdated, some sections are still useful (e.g., Christian, Greek).

Hopkins, Thomas J. *The Hindu Religious Tradition.* Belmont, Calif., 1971.

Jacobs, Louis. "Akedah." In *Encyclopaedia Judaica*, vol. 2, cols. 480–487. Jerusalem, 1971.

Kirsch, Johann P., and Theodor Klauser. "Altar: Christlich." In *Reallexikon für Antike und Christentum*, edited by Theodor Klauser, vol. 1, cols. 334–354. Stuttgart, 1950. Well documented, with a lengthy bibliography.

Kohler, Kaufmann, and George A. Barton. "Altar." In *Jewish Encyclopedia*, edited by Isidore Singer, vol. 1, pp. 464–469. New York, 1901. Relates Jewish to Christian material.

Liebert, Gösta. *Iconographic Dictionary of the Indian Religions: Hinduism, Buddhism, Jainism.* Leiden, 1976. Definitions with references to literature.

Maier, Johann. *Die Tempelrolle vom Toten Meer.* Munich, 1978. Translates and comments upon the Hebrew text.

Maurer, Gerd J. *Der Altar aber ist Christus: Zur symbolischen Bedeutung des christlichen Altares in der Geschichte.* Sankt Augustin, West Germany, 1969. A popular but good survey.

Meyer, Jeffrey F. *Peking as a Sacred City.* Taipei, 1976. Cosmic symbolism of various altars.

Milgrom, Jacob, and Bialik M. Lerner. "Altar." In *Encyclopaedia Judaica*, vol. 2, cols. 760–771. Jerusalem, 1971. Stresses Israelite uniqueness.

Reichard, Gladys A. *Navaho Religion: A Study of Symbolism* (1950). 2 vols. Princeton, 1974. A classic.

Staal, Frits, ed. *Agni: The Vedic Ritual of the Fire Altar.* 2 vols. Berkeley, 1983. Collective work of specialists on Indology.

Stuiber, Alfred. "Altar: Alte Kirche." In *Theologische Realenzyklopedie,* edited by Gerhard Krause and Gerhard Muller, vol. 2, pp. 308–318. Berlin, 1978. A fine piece by a well-known patrologist, with an exhaustive bibliography. The preceding section contains a short introduction from the point of view of comparative religion.

Walker, George B. *Hindu World: An Encyclopedic Survey of Hinduism.* 2 vols. New York, 1968. Rather general, without references, and based on a sometimes antiquated literature.

Weltfish, Gene. *The Lost Universe: Pawnee Life and Culture* (1965). Lincoln, Neb., 1977. Based on many years of fieldwork and linguistic training.

Yavis, Constantine G. *Greek Altars: Origins and Typology.* Saint Louis, 1949.

Ziehen, Ludwig. "Altar: Griechisch-Römisch." In *Reallexikon für Antike und Christentum,* edited by Theodor Klauser, vol. 1, cols. 310–329. Stuttgart, 1950. Well documented, with a lengthy bibliography.

CARL-MARTIN EDSMAN (1987)
Translated from Swedish by Kjersti Board

ĀLVĀRS. The Ālvārs are a group of Hindu religious poets of South India. Their name in Tamil means "sages" or "saints." As devotees of Māl, a deity who combines attributes of the Kṛṣṇa of the *Bhagavadgītā* and earlier Purāṇas with those of Viṣṇu and Nārāyaṇa, they differ from a second, contemporary group of poets, the Śaiva Nāyaṉārs. Yet in other respects both groups are closely related and together must be regarded as responsible for the formation of a devotional, vernacular Hinduism.

The only reliable source on the Ālvārs is the corpus of their own poetry, which the semilegendary Nāthamuni compiled in the early tenth century CE (and which was somewhat modified in the twelfth century). This corpus is known as the *Nālāyira-divya-prabandham* (Sacred poetic collection of four thousand); "four thousand" refers to the total number of stanzas. The *Prabandham* consists of twenty-three separate works, arranged in four books (in imitation of the four Vedas), among which the *Tiruvāymoli* by "Caṭakōpaṉ" (as the poet calls himself) is the longest and most important. This compilation and the preservation of the poems were among the achievements of Śrī Vaiṣṇavism. This Viṣṇu-devoted religious movement, which was led by brahmans and oriented itself toward Brahmanical values, had its beginnings in South India during the tenth century and assumed its classic expression in the eleventh and twelfth centuries. In fact, the movement looked back upon the vernacular Ālvārs as its spiritual ancestors. Consequently, Śrī Vaiṣṇavism produced an Ālvār hagiography, institutionalizing these saints and the *Prabandham* itself, and commented and reflected on it through an enormous exegetical literature in heavily sanskritized Tamil. The poets are envisaged here as incarnations of Viṣṇu's heavenly weapons and companions many thousands of years ago, and their life stories are punctuated by miraculous events inevitably interpreted as expressions of Śrī Vaiṣṇava religious ideals and thought.

While a critical appreciation of the *Prabandham* independently from the Śrī Vaiṣṇava tradition has only just begun, the picture thus revealed is very different, though no less colorful. Traditionally, twelve Ālvārs are listed, but in the *Prabandham* only eleven works bear a poet's name (yielding a total of seven different authors), while the remaining twelve works are anonymous. These seven poets provide information in their verses from which we can infer that two were brahman temple priests, Viṭṭucittaṉ (or Periyālvār in familiar Śrī Vaiṣṇava parlance) and Toṇṭaraṭippoṭi (Bhaktāṅghrireṇu); one a brahman woman, Kōtai (Āṇṭāḷ, "the lady"); two chieftains; Kulacekaran (almost certainly not the author of the *Mukundamālā*) and Kalikaṉri (Tirumaṅkai-ālvār, a "robber knight" in hagiography); one a regional landlord, Caṭakōpaṉ (Nammālvār); and one a bard, Maturakavi. According to legend, the remaining five poets were all male low-caste bards and yogins. Geographical references in the poems cover most of what is today Kerala and Tamil Nadu, along with the southern part of Andhra Pradesh. The period from the sixth to the tenth century CE is the most likely one for the composition of the poems in the *Prabandham.*

Against the background of the *bhakti yoga* as found in the *Bhagavadgītā,* that of Vedānta, Pāñcarātra, and Vaikhānasa ritualism, of earlier folk Kṛṣṇaism and sophisticated secular Tamil culture, the Ālvārs evolved a form of religion with intense emotive flavor. Māl (also known as Tirumāl, Māyōṉ, Perumāl, etc.), who is the object of this devotion, manifests himself on earth in three different modes. There are his mythical exploits, many of them known from stories of the classical *avatāras,* especially the amorous Kṛṣṇa. Then there are his incarnations in the statues of numerous South Indian temples (approximately ninety-five such shrines are mentioned by the poets), and finally there is his dwelling within the hearts of his devotees. These three modes provide the emotional and intellectual stimuli that gave rise to Tamil songs and poems (which in turn were intended as further stimuli). The characteristics of eroticism and ecstatic drive, which were subdued in the terse earlier anonymous poems, reached their culmination when Nammalvar drew on Tamil secular love poetry and transformed it into a novel type of mystical literature. Later Ālvārs such as Āṇṭāḷ, Kalikaṉri, and Viṭṭucittaṉ developed this genre further and gave it new shape in the form of folk songs and children's songs. The *Prabandham* contains no systematic theology or philosophy, but its general orientation of thought is in the direction of Śrī Vaiṣṇavism. This latter school, however, had little scope for an ecstatic form of devotion. It was the *Bhāgavata Purāṇa* (a South Indian text of about the tenth century CE, by an unknown author) that adopted the Ālvārs devotion and gave it a Sanskrit mold, in fact by translating or paraphrasing poems of the Ālvārs.

Śrī Vaiṣṇavism was affected in many ways by its Āḻvār heritage; through the *Bhāgavata Purāṇa,* these poets also exercised an enormous influence on Hinduism generally. But the sophistication and often extreme complexity of the nonbrahman poets, and the cultivation of simpler folk genres by brahman Āḻvārs speak against any notion of them as leaders of a rebellion by the oppressed, exploited masses, or as leaders of a movement in favor of simple theistic faith and against the teachings of the Upaniṣads. The antagonism they express is directed against Buddhists and Jains, Śaivas, folk religious practices, and occasionally against a Brahmanical establishment.

SEE ALSO Śaivism, article on Nāyaṉārs; Śrī Vaiṣṇavas.

BIBLIOGRAPHY

Most of the popularly available information on the Āḻvārs is directly or indirectly derived from J. S. M. Hooper's *Hymns of the Āḻvārs* (New York, 1929), a slender work that is now outdated. Samples of Nammāḻvār's poetry, in attractive English translation, are found in *Hymns for the Drowning: Poems for Viṣṇu by Nammāḻvār,* translated by A. K. Ramanujan (Princeton, 1981). For a detailed study of the Āḻvārs, their background and treatment in the *Bhāgavata Purāṇa,* see my book *Viraha-Bhakti: The Early History of Kṛṣṇa Devotion in South India* (Oxford, 1983). An illustration of how Śrī Vaiṣṇavism dealt with its Āḻvār heritage is found in my essay "The Tamil Veda of a *Śūdra* Saint," in *Contributions to South Asian Studies,* edited by Gopal Krishna (Delhi, 1979), vol. 1, pp. 29–87.

New Sources

Dehejia, Vidya. *Slaves of the Lord: The Path of the Tamil Saints.* New Delhi, 1988.

Srinivasa Chari, S. M. *Philosophy and Theistic Mysticism of the Alvars.* Delhi, 1997.

FRIEDHELM E. HARDY (1987)
Revised Bibliography

AMATERASU ŌMIKAMI is the supreme deity in Japanese mythology and the ancestor goddess of the imperial family. Amaterasu was born when the creator god Izanagi washed his left eye. According to the *Nihongi,* Izanagi then said, "Do thou, Amaterasu Ōmikami, rule the High Celestial Plain." The *Nihongi* further states that her grandson, Amatsuhiko Hiko-hononinigi no Mikoto, descended to the earth and that one of his descendants, Jimmu (Kamu-yamato-iwarehiko), acceded to the throne as the first emperor of Japan in 660 BCE. This explanation, however, has been challenged by modern historians because, among other things, no central government capable of controlling local leaders existed at that time.

The word *amaterasu* literally means "shining in heaven," and *ōmikami* means "great goddess." Therefore, Chamberlain's "heaven-shining-great-august-deity" is a more accurate translation of *amaterasu ōmikami* than the more common "sun goddess." The *Nihongi* states that her earlier name was Amaterasu Ōhirume no Muchi. *Muchi* is a suffix used for a respected person or a deity. According to Origuchi, *ōhirume* means "wife of the sun," not the sun itself. In Japanese, *hi* means "spirit" as well as "sun," and *me* means "woman" as well as "wife." Some confusion has resulted from this problem of multiple meanings. It seems that originally the name of this deity meant "great spirit woman," but later the *hi* was misinterpreted as "the sun," and eventually this deity came to be called the sun goddess. While hundreds of rituals have been retained at the Ise shrine where Amaterasu has been deified, none of them is related to the sun. This fact supports the above statement that *amaterasu* did not mean "sun goddess."

No doubt the most dramatic event in Japanese mythology was Amaterasu's retreat into the Rock Cave of Heaven, precipitated by the behavior of Susano-o, her younger brother. First, he broke down the division of the rice fields laid out by Amaterasu, filled up the ditches, and strewed excrement in the palace. While she was sitting in her weaving hall overseeing the weaving of the deities' garments, he broke a hole in the roof, and through it let fall a piebald horse that he had flayed. The woman weaving the heavenly garments was so alarmed by this sight that she struck her genitals against the shuttle and died. Terrified, Amaterasu hid herself in the Rock Cave of Heaven, and the heavenly world became dark. Eight hundred myriad deities gathered to lure Amaterasu out of the cave. Among them, Ame no Uzume, a female deity, played the most important role: "She became divinely possessed, exposed her breasts, and pushed her skirtband down to her genitals. Then the heavenly world shook as the eight hundred myriad deities laughed at once." Her curiosity aroused, Amaterasu opened the door of the Rock Cave of Heaven and came out.

While the *Kojiki* states that the woman who was weaving the garments was struck in the genitals, the *Nihongi* says that Amaterasu herself was injured, without specifying how. The *Nihongi* also does not mention the details of the activities of Ame no Uzume. Probably because of Confucian influences, the editors of the *Nihongi* moderated the sexual material in the original texts. Nevertheless, the basic motif of this myth is the termination of reproduction through destruction of the female genital organs and the reappearance of the female, which suggests the resumption of reproduction. This myth would have almost certainly been accompanied by a ritual celebrating the advent of spring, the season of rebirth in nature. After the rebirth in spring, Amaterasu carefully watches the development of the agricultural activities as the guardian of the crop until the autumn.

Amaterasu is closely linked in Japanese mythology with mirrors. She is said to have given a precious bronze mirror to Ame no Oshiho-mimi, saying: "My child, let it be as if thou wert looking on me." This mirror, according to the *Nihongi,* was then passed from emperor to emperor as one of the Three Imperial Regalia, symbols of imperial legitimacy.

Hundreds of bronze mirrors have been found at early tombs in western Japan, and the *Sanguo zhi* (History of Three Kingdoms), a Chinese dynastic history, states that in 239 the Japanese queen was given one hundred mirrors because they were her favorite objects. These accounts suggest that mirrors were extremely important religious objects for the early Japanese. Early peoples, including the Japanese of ancient times, regarded mirrors with awe and often believed that the reflection in the mirror was the spirit of the person. In this way, the tradition of mirrors as objects of worship was established. It then became linked with the earlier "spirit woman" worship, and finally the mirror came to be regarded as Amaterasu herself.

SEE ALSO Izanagi and Izanami; Japanese Religions, article on Mythic Themes; Susano-o no Mikoto.

BIBLIOGRAPHY

Aston, W. G., trans. *Nihongi: Chronicles of Japan from the Earliest Times to A.D. 697* (1896). Reprint, 2 vols. in 1, Tokyo, 1972.

Chamberlain, Basil Hall, trans. *Kojiki: Records of Ancient Matters* (1882). 2d ed. With annotations by W. G. Aston. Tokyo, 1932; reprint, Rutland, Vt., and Tokyo, 1982.

Kakubayashi Fumio, "A Study of the Historical Developments of the Yayoi Period with Special Reference to Japanese-Korean Relations." Ph.D. diss., University of Queensland, 1980.

Matsumoto Nobuhiro. *Essai sur la mythologie japonaise.* Paris, 1928.

Origuchi Shinobu. *Origuchi Shinobu zenshu,* vols. 1–3. Tokyo, 1975.

Philippi, Donald L., trans. *Kojiki.* Princeton, 1969.

KAKUBAYASHI FUMIO (1987 AND 2005)

AMAZONIAN QUECHUA RELIGIONS.

Persistent confusion permeates the comparative study of the religious beliefs and practices of the peoples of Upper Amazonian rain forests that abut the foothills of the Andes Mountains. This is because Quechua-speaking peoples of that region and Quechua-speaking people of the Andes share a religious complex, which, in turn, is also shared with Jivaroan-speaking and Zaparoan-speaking peoples of the Upper Amazonian region. This article deals with some commonalities of Quechua and Jivaroan religious concepts. The Quechua language has long been associated with the Andes Mountains and with the Inca conquest of the Central Andean peoples radiating out of Cuzco in the late fifteenth century. Jivaroan peoples have long been associated with the Upper Amazonian rain forests and with resistance to Inca conquest, and, thereby, to the permeation of the conquest religion borne by the Inca northward to what is now Colombia and southward into what, today, is Bolivia.

In Ecuador and Peru, Jivaroan and Quechua-speaking peoples of the Upper Amazonian rain forest share not only many core beliefs but also variants of the same terms for these beliefs, even though their languages are completely unrelated. The specific people referred to here are the Canelos Quichua and the Achuar Jivaroans of Ecuador. (*Quichua,* pronounced *Kichua,* is one proper spelling of the name for speakers of northern Quechua dialects.) The Canelos Quichua inhabit the region drained by the Bobonaza and Curaray Rivers and the regions that radiate out of urban Puyo, Ecuador. The Achuar discussed here are those who inhabit the regions of the Copataza, Capahuari, and Conanbo Rivers and also those who live in the vicinity of urban Puyo, including those living on the Llushín River. Many Achuar and Canelos Quichua people intermarry. Many of the Achuar are fluent in Canelos Quichua and in Spanish, and many of the Canelos Quichua are fluent in Achuar and in Spanish. Cultural congeners who speak Jivaroan include the Aguaruna, Huambisa, and Achuar (including Maina-Achuar) of Peru; the Shuar of Ecuador; and the Murato Candoshi and Shapra Candoshi of Peru. The two latter Candoan-speaking people may or may not speak Jivaroan, but their cultural and religious systems are virtually the same as the Jivaroans and Canelos Quichua. Zaparoans of Peru and Ecuador (including Andoa-Shimigae, Záparo, Iquitos, and Arabela) also share this religious complex, though there is no known linguistic relationship between Zaparoan, Jivaroan, and Quechua languages. The Quijos Quichua and Napo Quichua of Ecuador, the Inga of Colombia, and the Napo Quichua of Peru also share segments of this complex.

The history of the Canelos Quichua intertwines with the history of Catholic mission expansion in a manner distinct from the history of the Achuar. Nonetheless, the primary streams of traditional culture and the primary emphases of contemporary ethnic affiliation that constitute modern Canelos Quichua culture stem from Achuar, Zaparoan, early Canelos Quichua, and Quijos Quichua peoples. The Canelos Quichua, in myriad ways, provide ample evidence by which to refute the spurious but pervasive dichotomy made by many scholars between cultural orientations and religious-cosmological structures of the "Andean," or highland, regions and the "Amazonian," or lowland, regions of western South America.

Control of power and recognition of the devastating consequences of its release are fundamental to Canelos Quichua and Achuar Jivaroan cultures. Concepts of such control are embedded in a paradigm centered on knowledgeable ones: shamans for men, potters for women. Strong shamans and master potters continuously increase their knowledge of spirit forces that exert control in human affairs. Spirit forces configure—especially for the Canelos Quichua—into three dominant images: Amasanga, forest spirit master; Nunkwi, spirit master of garden dynamics and of pottery clay; and Tsunki, spirit master of water, or the hydrosphere. Whereas Tsunki and Nunkwi are dominant images in all or most of the aforementioned cultures, Amasanga is specific to the cosmogony of the people addressed in this article.

The concepts of these dominant spirit beings (*supai*), each with a soul (*aya*) and life force (*causai*), evoke mythic and legendary imagery to illuminate the known and unknown cosmos and to relate cosmic networks of souls, spirits, beings, forces, and events to contemporary and past quotidian life. Each dominant image evokes and indexes a myriad of spirit beings specific to various natural and supernatural domains. For example, imagery of Amasanga not only evokes the spirits of thunder and lightning above and within the rain-forest canopy but also the spirit of the mighty trees that dominate sectors of the forest.

The imagery of Amasanga (called Amasank in Achuar) also includes principles of transformation, called *tucuna* in Canelos Quichua. For example, for a given group of Canelos Quichua speakers, Amasanga represents the master spirit force of their own territory. One powerful transformation of Amasanga is that of the feared spirit Jurijuri (called Jirijri in Achuar). Jurijuri is the master of monkeys. All monkeys are associated with other peoples. But Jurijuri is not a "separate" spirit, he/she is a transformation of Amasanga, a transformation from "ours," who protects, to "theirs," who harms. Jurijuri spirits dwell in hillside caves and move under the forest's surface. As the shaman of the forest, Amasanga sits on an iguanid or tortoise seat of power; his/her corporeal manifestation is the black jaguar, and he appears in humanlike form in deep purple garb wearing a red and yellow toucan headdress.

Tsunki evokes spirits of the water world—the entire hydrosphere of airborne and undersoil moisture—which must be kept under spirit or human control if catastrophe is to be avoided. Tsunki is chthonic in association with dwelling sites under rivers or lakes; aquatic in association with waterfalls, rapids, and whirlpools of rivers and with quiet lakes; celestial and radiating in association with the rainbow and, tenuously, with the sun. As first shaman, Tsunki sits on the Amazon turtle (*charapa*) as his seat of power; his/her corporeal manifestation is the mighty anaconda (*amarun* in Quichua, *panki* in Jivaroan). He sometimes appears as one dressed in rainbow colors, or as a naked white man. (Anaconda symbolism permeates the cosmography of power in the rain-forest territories of Upper Amazonia, Central Amazonia, the Northwest Amazon, the Guianas, and beyond.)

Nunkwi is associated with feminine dynamics of undersoil and leaf-mat-root-fungi systems by day, and with growth and renewed fecundity of manioc (cassava) by night. Her corporeal manifestation is the black coral snake with mouth too small to bite. She may appear to women as one garbed in deep purple who dances with hopping steps while tossing her hair to and fro.

Knowledge (*yachana*), which is fundamental to the control of power, derives from ancient cultural mythology and historical legend. It is shaped by strong shamans and by master potters to resonate with immediate historical events and current activities. Knowledge of the cosmos (bound to the concept *yachana*, "to know, to learn") provides the basis by which knowledge from the experiential world (bound to the concepts *ricsina*, "to experience, to perceive, to comprehend," and *yuyana* or *yuyarina*, "to think, to reflect") is shaped by all individuals. Such shaping is bound to another concept, *muscuna* ("to dream, to perceive"). *Muscuna* and *yachana* are, in turn, closely associated with the spirit-master images Amasanga and Nunkwi, both of which are thought to be from datura (*Datura suaveolens*), a narcotic plant of the nightshade family.

When a man or woman ingests datura (called *huanduj* in Quichua, *maikua* in Jivaroan), he or she "perceives" and "knows" human self, human soul, human substance, others, spirits, and all entities and beings in existence. Domains and boundaries that are part of everyday life dissolve in a datura trip as the questing individual enters mythic time-space, called *unai* in Canelos Quichua. Reincorporation into the world of humans, souls, spirits, and beings takes place through reordering by the individual of the relationships previously characterized in his or her life. For example, after taking datura the individual may "know" that someone he thought was his trading partner and true kin is, in this newly found reality, an enemy who seeks to harm him. Accordingly, the domains of kinship and trade are reordered by the individual, who now "sees" the entire kinship network and relations of trade in a new light. Such reordering of domains spreads to other domains, as well. For example, if an individual now perceives another as his enemy rather than his friend, then the powerful shaman who is father or uncle to the new-found enemy becomes a major threat to the health of the questing individual's kinship system, rather than, as previously thought, one of its buttressing ancestors. As the individual continues to reorder the relationships within such domains as kinship, economics, and shamanic protection and harm, his thought patterns and convictions continue to branch out to others both near and far, extending the effects of domain reordering further and further.

A successful datura trip gives the questing individual a sense of power. This sense is derived from knowledge of control of spirit, soul, life force, body, and visionary or imagined features of cosmic beings and events in mythic time-space, and in various past times. For example, a Jivaroan seeks the vision of an ancient being (*arutam*) in such quests and may acquire, thereby, a second soul that "locks in" his own immortal soul. If a person correctly perceives the image-vision, the lock-in mechanism prevents his death, so long as he tells no one of the vision of the acquired soul. Such a lock-in of one's soul gives to others in association with the individual a sense of pending power that must be controlled.

As a questing individual and his or her immediate associates seek to control the power rising from the datura experience, they maintain a sense of religious community in the face of, or in the midst of, possible chaos. To the extent that a person speaks of, or otherwise releases, such newly acquired power, he or she loses control of the knowledge manifest in a successful quest; the results of such release and consequent loss can be devastating. For example, increased shamanic activity aimed at harming those perceived to be enemies, and/or physical violence against such enemies, may erupt from such a release. This eruption causes social and political upheaval that can alter quotidian life and cosmic networks sufficiently to produce a historical marker.

Knowledge derived from cultural mythology and historical legend is fundamental to Quichua and Jivaroan senses of "ours" and "others.'" Figure 1 illustrates how, from Canelos Quichua perspectives, knowledge of "our" culture is juxtaposed to knowledge from "other" cultures. Here the *yachaj*, or more properly *sinchi yachaj* (*uwishin* in Achuar) has attained a level of control such that he is sufficiently strong to balance his knowledge with his visions, to relate his visions to cultural knowledge, and to relate his thoughts and reflections to his knowledge and his visions. He acquires the ability to cure by sucking out magical substances (*tsintsak*) and to harm others by blowing projectiles into them. Shamanic performances take place at night, while the shaman is in self-induced trance aided by *ayahuasca* (soul vine). Among the Canelos Quichua the soul vine is *Banisteriopsis caapi*. Juice from the vine is brewed with the leaves of another *Banisteriopsis* vine, or with *Psychotria viridis* leaves, to produce the chemical bonding necessary for visionary experience. The shaman, seated on a turtle seat of power, is visited by spirits as he—the shaman—visits spirits seated on their seats of power.

To know more about that which is within, the shaman must increasingly know more about that which is without. The shaman becomes a *paradigm manipulator*. His knowledge of the cosmos and his perceptions derived therefrom are stronger than the knowledge and perceptions embodied in other minds and psyches. He moves into a shaman's class (*yachaj sami*) of humans, which parallels a similar class of spirits. He continuously reproduces cultural knowledge, continuously transforms that very knowledge, and imbues it with novel insights. He also maintains the contrast between "our culture" and "other cultures" (from Quichua and Jivaroan perspectives) while transcending the very boundaries that he enforces.

The work of the shaman must, in part, be based on his experience with other peoples who speak other languages; this kind of contact gives the shaman "other-speech knowledge." The shaman maintains Canelos Quichua and/or Achuar paradigms while expanding the paradigms by drawing from his knowledge of other cultures. The shaman controls the process of syncretism. In this control lies the interface between cultural continuity (or reproduction) and cultural change (or transformation).

Among the Canelos Quichua, master potters, all of whom are women, do the same thing. Working with designs that signal the anaconda, the Amazonian turtle, the tortoise, and the iguanid—all representing imagery of shamanic power—master potters produce an array of decorated ceramic containers for storing and drinking manioc porridge. The

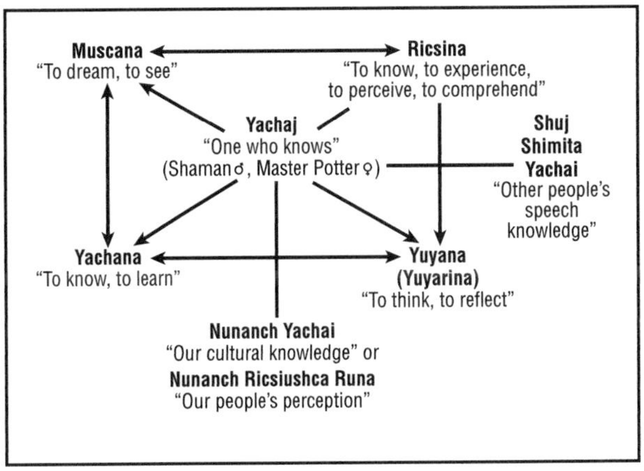

FIGURE 1. Canelos Quichua perspectives on "our" culture and "other" cultures.

designs on the containers link cosmic networks to quotidian events, the general to the specific, the ancient to the present, the mysterious to the mundane. A female paradigm-manipulator may, in Canelos Quichua, be called *sinchi muscuj huarmi* ("strong image-shaping woman"), or even *yachaj huarmi* ("woman who knows").

Among the Canelos Quichua, every master potter is related closely to a strong shaman. In some cases the shaman is a father, in some cases a father-in-law. In many cases there is a complex of shamanic males and master-potter females. Cultural transmission is parallel: female paradigm-manipulators pass their skills to women, male paradigm-manipulators transmit to men. But men and women are conversant with the alter-gender paradigm and, upon the death of a strong shaman, a wife may assume the shamanic activities of her deceased husband.

Male shamanic performance and female ceramic manufacture draw in a parallel way on certain concepts that are fundamental to religious convictions and insights. One of these is that everything is sentient and that, accordingly, everything has a soul (*aya*). Another is that differential power imbues various objects in manners relatively analogous to the ways by which differential power of humans vis-à-vis one another is organized. Inasmuch as power is shaped and organized into various hierarchies by different humans, human groups, spirits, and beings, there is no single power-pyramid; rather, there are many overlapping and interfacing power-pyramids through which humans, spirits, beings, and the souls of each may move.

Another fundamental concept of Canelos Quichua and Achuar Jivaroan religion is that all life exists on different planes of existence at the same time. For example, in the thought of the Canelos Quichua, *unai* refers to mythic time-space. In *unai* everything was (or is) human, and people (like those in present time-space) crawled on their hands and knees like babes and spoke only in a two-tone hum: $^{mm}{}_{mm}{}^{mm}{}_{mm}$. One enters different planes of existence through dreams associated with sleep, through insight, through conscious imagery constructed deliberately or accidentally, through imagery induced by the ingestion of *Banisteriopsis* or datura hallucinogens, through shamanic instruction, through fatigue, through accident or by shamanic (human or spirit) design, and recently by drinking alcohol. In the transformation from *unai* to ancient times, spirits, animals, trees, celestial bodies, colors—everything—underwent reformulation to something other than human. Today, in the worldview of the Canelos Quichua, it is not altogether certain that people speaking other languages emerged fully "human" from *unai.*

The sentient power of breath (*samai,* in Canelos Quichua) is another key Jivaroan and Quichua religious concept; the powers embodied in breath must be carefully controlled. In the transformation from *unai* to ancient times, once-human beings blew on one another and on other beings and spirits, causing them to "stay that way," to be as human beings know and perceive them today. Male shamans breathe gently onto polished stones to "see" whether the stone "lives." Female potters breathe on their pottery-burnishing stones for the same purpose. A strong shaman must have the inner ability to sing his shaman's song well enough to control the spirit defenses needed to thwart incoming shamanic projectiles from rival shamans, which all shamanic songs invoke. Similarly, a master potter must control the breath of fire that releases the souls imparted to, and the spirits associated with, her ceramics, or retribution from the imparted and subsequently liberated souls may result. A man must also control the sounds of spirits that come from *unai* to pass outward on his breath when he plays a flute or musical bow, while women control analogous sounds that come to them from *unai* when they sing songs. The specific knowledge of songs comes to them from other forebear women in other times and places.

Male/female parallelism in cultural transmission is enacted annually by the Canelos Quichua in a ceremony that expands the universe to include all spirits, souls, beings, and people. Enactment takes place only in hamlets with a Catholic church or chapel, where the chaotic and destructive merger of "outside" foreigner's force and "inside" native power may merge. All facets of Canelos Quichua cosmology are enacted as, for three days and nights, celebrants pass back and forth from the male festival house (ritual enclosure of the Moon) to the female festival house (ritual enclosure of Moon's sister-lover, the whippoorwill-like potoo). The ceremony ends with a powerful and palpable ritual reversal. In this enactment, which the Canelos Quichua call Dominario (from the Spanish word *dominar,* "to control"), the mighty anaconda is brought from the water to move on the land.

In Canelos Quichua thought, the anaconda (*amarun,* or *amaru,* as in the Andes) only comes on land to devour humans. In the Dominario, the anaconda, corporeal representative of master-spirit Tsunki, is borne on the back of four men who represent jaguars, corporeal representatives of Amasanga. Instead of controlling Tsunki's domain (the hydrosphere), Amasanga releases it. Instead of the externally imposed social control (*dominario*) represented by the church, indigenous power becomes an embodied apotheosis of stylized resistance. As the Dominario begins, an outsider, downriver (deeper Amazonian), powerful shaman gently plays a combination of flute and drum associated with Andean masked ceremonies. The melody itself is a skillful blend of his private Amazonian shaman's song (*taquina*) and a public Andean ceremonial melodic motif. As the four men come forth bearing a bamboo pole with four copal fires burning within it (the stylized anaconda brought from the water), festival participants begin dancing through arches constructed for the Catholic mission. Then the transformation, called *tucuna,* begins. The pole, as *amarun* (anaconda), Tsunki's corporeal form, is carried in a lurching, going-out-of-control manner. It becomes destructive; the bearers and the pole crash right into and through the church, slamming, falling, rising again, running, frightening everyone, going completely out of control while still in a cultural domain characterized by Catholic mission control, or domination.

Acting against such domination within a domain of domination, the festival reaches a crescendo that is, quite literally, terrifying to the participants. Women dance with their hair flying to and fro, their sideways motion being the analog of the male-performed two-tone hum of shamanic chanting that evokes the imagery of mythic time-space (*unai*). Men beat snare drums, circling and circling while producing a resonating pulse-tremolo signifying Amasanga's rumble of approaching thunder. All souls and spirits and beings are indiscriminately summoned. As escalating chaos reigns, the church is said to be destroyed in one great transformation of the world of forest and garden and earth and mire into an encompassing, rushing, surging, eastward-flowing sea. When performing this event, the Canelos Quichua say that they fear *tucurina,* which derives from *tucuna* ("transformation"), and means "ending everything." The concept of *tucurina* is one of the most powerful ones in Canelos Quichua thought, particularly when applied reflexively to one's own group. It means, in this sense, that to truly destroy the dominating authority of the church by the invocation of the ultimate power of Tsunki, as devouring anaconda, the Canelos Quicha may also destroy themselves, embedded as they are—in a revelatory manner through the vehicle of this ritual—in that very domination.

The festival sketched here embodies and syncretizes many elements of Andean and Amazonian symbolism, as well as wide-flung Catholic and indigenous symbolism. The controlled analysis of its structure and enactment in terms of Andean/Amazonian religions and Christian/animistic religions should take the comparative study of religion far toward dissolving such rigid polarities by establishing new, more productive bases for deep and meaningful comparative understanding.

BIBLIOGRAPHY

Bottasso B., Juan. *Los Shuar y las misiones: Entre la hostilidad y el diálogo.* Quito, 1982. An accurate portrayal of the historical relationships between the Shuar Jivaroans of Ecuador and the Salesian mission.

Brown, Michael Forbes. "Magic and Meaning in the World of the Aguaruna Jivaro of Peru." Ph.D. diss., University of Michigan, 1981. A highly readable doctoral dissertation that seeks to understand the cosmology of the Aguaruna together with the ecological imagery that such a cosmology organizes.

Chumap Lucía, Aurelio, and Manuel García-Rendueles. *"Duik Múun . . .": Universo mítico de los Aguaruna.* 2 vols. Lima, 1979. A splendid two-volume rendition of Aguaruna mythology.

Harner, Michael J. *The Jívaro: People of the Sacred Waterfalls.* 2d ed., rev. Berkeley, 1983. Pioneering ethnography of the Ecuadorian Shuar with an easy-to-read description and analysis of the famous *arutam* (ancient image) and *tsantsa* (human trophy head) complex.

Karsten, Rafael. *The Head-Hunters of Western Amazonas: The Life and Culture of the Jibaro Indians of Eastern Ecuador and Peru.* Helsinki, 1935. A weighty tome that deals with the Canelos Quichua, the Achuar, and the Shuar of Ecuador. Oscillations between firsthand data and speculations are disconcerting, as is the excessive lumping together of data apparently gleaned from bilingual Achuar-Canelos Quichua at Canelos and other Bobonaza River sites with those from a non-Jivaroan informant in Sucúa about the Shuar. This book must be used with care, and information in it must be cross-checked against other sources.

"Mundo Shuar." Quito, 1976–. Series F is devoted to monograph-length publications on key Shuar images, including *Arutam* (no. 1) and *Tsunki* (no. 2), and on shamanism, as in *El Uwishin* (no. 3).

Reeve, Mary-Elizabeth. "Identity as Process: The Meaning of Runapura for Quichua Speakers of the Curaray River, Eastern Ecuador." Ph.D. diss., University of Illinois at Urbana-Champaign, 1985. The history and identity system of the Canelos Quichua of the Curaray River region are portrayed from indigenous and Catholic mission perspectives. Convincingly demonstrates close relationships between Canelos Quichua, Zaparoan, and Achuar cultures and identity systems, as well as the striking parallels between Andean Quechua and Canelos Quichua social structure and ritual enactment.

Taylor, Anne-Christine. "God-Wealth: The Achuar and the Missions." In *Cultural Transformations and Ethnicity in Modern Ecuador,* edited by Norman E. Whitten, Jr., pp. 647–676. Urbana, Ill., 1981. A sensitive portrayal of Achuar cosmological transformations in the face of radical social, economic, and political change.

Whitten, Dorothea S. "Ancient Tradition in a Contemporary Context: Canelos Quichua Ceramics and Symbolism." In *Cultural Transformations and Ethnicity in Modern Ecuador,* edited by Norman E. Whitten, Jr., pp. 749–775. Urbana, Ill., 1981. A penetrating look at the symbolism embedded in Canelos Quichua ceramics not only in terms of traditional cosmology but also by reference to radical social change.

Whitten, Dorothea S., and Norman E. Whitten, Jr. *Our Beauty, Our Knowledge: The Expressive Culture of the Canelos Quichua of Ecuador.* Urbana, Ill., 1985. Script of a thirty-minute video documentation of the key concepts set forth in this article, thoroughly and dramatically illustrated through Canelos Quichua art and music.

Whitten, Norman E., Jr., with the assistance of Marcelo Na-ranjo, Marcelo Santi Simbaña, and Dorothea S. Whitten. *Sacha Runa: Ethnicity and Adaptation of Ecuadorian Jungle Quichua.* Urbana, Ill., 1976. Definitive ethnography of the Canelos Quichua culture area based on modern techniques of description and analysis.

Whitten, Norman E., Jr. *Sicuanga Runa: The Other Side of Development in Amazonian Ecuador.* Urbana, Ill., 1985. Deals extensively with the cosmological underpinnings of remarkable endurance in Canelos Quichua culture. Relationships between women's art and male shamanic performance profusely illustrated by over 150 plates, drawings, photographs, and other illustrations.

New Sources

Harrison, Regina. *Signs, Songs, and Memory in the Andes: Translating Quechua Language and Culture.* Austin, Tex., 1989.

Hess, David J. *Spirits and Scientists: Ideology, Spiritism, and Brazilian Culture.* University Park, Pa, 1991.

Hill, Jonathan, ed. *Rethinking History and Myth: Indigenous South American Perspectives on the Past.* Champaign, Ill., 1988.

Mills, Kenneth. *Idolatry and Its Enemies: Colonial Andean Religion and Extirpation, 1640–1750.* Princeton, 1997.

Skar, Sarah Lund. *Lives Together—Worlds Apart: Quechua Colonization in Jungles and City.* Oslo, 1994.

Thomson, Sinclair. *We Alone Will Rule: Native Andean Politics in the Age of Insurgency.* Madison, 2003.

Urban, Greg. *A Discourse-Centered Approach to Culture: Native South American Myths and Rituals.* Austin, Tex., 1991.

Urban, Greg, and Joel Sherzer, eds. *Nation-States and Indians in Latin America.* Austin, 1991.

NORMAN E. WHITTEN, JR. (1987)
Revised Bibliography

AMAZONS

SEE GENDER AND RELIGION, *ARTICLE ON* GENDER AND ANCIENT MEDITERRANEAN RELIGIONS

AMBEDKAR, B. R.

AMBEDKAR, B. R. (1891–1956), statesman, writer, reformer, and creator of a new Buddhist movement in India; member of an untouchable caste. Bhimrao Ramji Ambedkar, affectionately known as Babasaheb, was born in Mhow (now Mahu), India, where his father was headmaster of an army normal school. A member of the untouchable caste of *mahārs* of Maharashtra, who traditionally worked as village menials, Ambedkar lived at a time when his outstanding personal capabilities, in conjunction with a strong sentiment for reform then emerging among caste Hindus and the beginnings of a movement for rights within his own caste, could effect extraordinary progress and change in the status of untouchables. In his early years he suffered prejudice in school, but was also aided in his education by caste Hindu reformers. K. A. Keluskar encouraged him in his studies when the family moved to Bombay, and gave him a copy of his book in Marathi on the life of the Buddha. Two non-brahman princes, the Gaikwad of Baroda and Shahu Chhatrapati of Kolhapur, helped finance his education, which eventually included a Ph.D. from Columbia University in New York, a D.Sc. from the University of London, and the title of barrister from Grey's Inn in London.

In 1917 Ambedkar returned to Bombay for a three-year period in the midst of his education abroad. During this time he participated in two conferences for the Depressed Classes, testified to the Government Franchise Commission on the rights of untouchables, and began a newspaper entitled *Mūknayāk* (The voice of the mute). All three activities—conferences to organize and inspire, attempts to use the parliamentary process for political and social rights, and educational work—were to become hallmarks of his lifelong efforts at reform. Upon his return permanently to India in 1923, Ambedkar earned a living from teaching and law but spent a major part of his energies on building a movement among untouchables and creating political and social opportunities for them, chiefly through pressure on government. He made efforts to secure religious rights such as participation in public festivals, temple entry, Vedic wedding rituals, and the wearing of the sacred thread, but these ended in 1935 when he declared that although he was born a Hindu he would not die a Hindu, and that untouchables could be free only outside the Hindu religion. Earlier, at a conference called at Mahad, a small town south of Bombay, he had burned those portions of the classic Hindu law book, the *Manusmṛti,* that discriminated against low castes.

His unshakable faith in parliamentary democracy led Ambedkar to testify at every opportunity before the commissions that investigated the furthering of democratization in British India. The prominence he gained in these lengthy and sophisticated statements resulted in his being named a representative to the Round Table conferences in London in 1930 and 1931. Faced there with the demands of Muslims, Sikhs, and other minorities for separate electorates, he began to advocate separate electorates for untouchables also. This led him into direct opposition with Mohandas K. Gandhi, who fasted in prison in Poona against such separation of untouchables from the main Hindu body of voters. Although the Poona Pact of 1932 brought about a compromise with Gandhi consisting of an exchange of separate electorates for more reserved seats for the Depressed Classes, Ambedkar continued to regard Gandhi's belief in a "change of heart," rather than legal measures, as a deterrent to real change, as a cure for untouchability. His 1945 book, *What Congress and Gandhi Have Done to the Untouchables,* indicted the Gandhian form of paternalism.

During the British governmental reforms of the mid-1930s, Ambedkar founded the Independent Labour Party in opposition to the Indian National Congress. The year 1937 brought eleven Scheduled Castes (so called because the government placed untouchable castes on a schedule to receive representation in parliamentary bodies and government employment) into the Bombay Legislative Assembly. Although Ambedkar was to found two other political parties, the Scheduled Castes Federation in 1942 and the Republican Party in 1956, he never again achieved such a large number of seats.

Ambedkar himself was able to effect legislation guaranteeing rights for untouchables as well as measures affecting all India in the appointed positions of Labour member in the viceroy's executive council (1942–1946) and as minister for law in India's first independent ministry (1947–1951). He was also chairman of the Drafting Committee of the Constitution (1947–1948), hailed as the "modern Manu." Among the tenets of the Indian constitution is one outlawing the practice of untouchability, a tribute to the work of both Ambedkar and Gandhi.

Underlying Ambedkar's social and political work was a constant effort to educate his people. The newspapers *Bahishkrit Bhārat* (Excluded India), *Janata* (People), and *Prabuddha Bhārat* (Awakened India) succeeded *Mūknayāk* and were widely circulated in spite of an extremely low literacy rate among the Untouchables. A modest beginning of building hostels so that untouchable children could attend government schools in towns culminated in the People's Education Society, which opened Siddharth College in Bombay in 1946 and Milind College in Aurangabad in 1951. The society runs two dozen institutions in the early twenty-first century and in 1982 laid the foundation stone for Dr. Ambedkar College in Poona. The stress on literacy and learning also encouraged creative writing, and since Ambedkar's death the movement called Dalit Sahitya ("the literature of the oppressed") has become an important new facet of Marathi literature and has influenced similar schools of literature in oher languages. Dalit writers pay tribute to Ambedkar as their chief inspiration and ascribe to the Buddhist conversion movement that he set in motion shortly before his death their sense of freedom from the psychological bonds of untouchability.

Although Ambedkar's interest in Buddhism was evident all his life, he did not convert until October 14, 1956, less than two months before his death on December 6. The ceremony, held at Nagpur, was witnessed by more than half a million people, and in the conversion movement that followed, more than six million people, most of them from former untouchable castes, declared themselves Buddhists. In his talks and in his book *The Buddha and His Dhamma,* Ambedkar stressed a rational, humanitarian, egalitarian Buddhism drawn chiefly from Pali texts. Hindu beliefs and practices and any supernatural Buddhist ideas were eliminated from the Buddhism propounded by Ambedkar. He himself, however, was regarded as the savior of the untouchables and came to be held by many as a *bodhisattva.* In the years since his death, dozens of Buddhist *vihārās* (temple compounds) have been built across the face of the state of Maharashtra, and hundreds of books have been written on Buddhist faith and practice, chiefly in Marathi.

Ambedkar's fame as an emancipator has grown constantly since his death. His statue can be found in almost every city and many villages in India and generally he is shown carrying a copy of the constitution of India. His birth day, conversion day, and death day are observed by millions and the Buddhist conversion movement continues to grow.

See Also Gandhi, Mohandas.

Bibliography

Works by Ambedkar

The Buddha and His Dhamma. Bombay, 1957. Ambedkar's basic presentation of Buddhist stories and tenets. The volume has also appeared in Hindi and Marathi.

Dr. Babasaheb Ambedkar Writings and Speeches. 18 vols. to date. Compiled and edited by Vasant Moon. Bombay, 1979–. Volume 1 contains "Castes in India" (pp. 3–22) and "Annihilation of Caste" (pp. 23–96), first published in 1917 and 1936, respectively, which represent Ambedkar's preconversion thought on the genesis and removal of caste.

The Untouchables. 2d ed. Shravasti, 1969. Ambedkar's thesis that the untouchables had been Buddhists, isolated and despised when India returned to Hinduism.

What Congress and Gandhi Have Done to the Untouchables. 2d ed. Bombay, 1946. Ambedkar's most thorough indictment of the failure of Congress to deal realistically with the problems of untouchability.

Works about Ambedkar

Ahir, D. C. *Buddhism* Vol. 6 in *India: 50 Years of Independence: 1947–97.* Delhi, 1998. Hundreds of books and pamphlets in Marathi and Hindi have been produced by Ambedkar's Buddhist conversion movement, but D. C. Ahir is the only convert who writes extensively in English.

Keer, Dhananjay. *Dr. Ambedkar: Life and Mission.* Bombay, 1954, with many reprints. The most basic life of Ambedkar available in English, always kept in print.

Moon, Vasant. *Growing Up Untouchable.* Lanham, Maryland, 2001. An autobiography that tells of the importance of Ambedkar to untouchables.

Queen, Christopher S., "Dr. Ambedkar and the Hermeneutics of Buddhist Liberation" in *Engaged Buddhism: Buddhist Liberation Movements in Asia,* edited by Christopher S. Queen and Sallie B. King. Albany, 1996.

Zelliot, Eleanor. *From Untouchable to Dalit: Essays on the Ambedkar Movement.* 3d ed. New Delhi, 2001.

Eleanor Zelliot (1987 and 2005)

AMBROSE (c. 339–397), church father, bishop, theologian, and Christian saint. Ambrose is distinguished by being the first Latin church father to have been born and reared in the Christian faith. His life mirrors the social, political, and religious tensions of the Constantinian era. His fame rests largely on his work as churchman and practical administrator. A son of the praetorian prefect of Gaul, Ambrose was educated in Roman law, which he practiced as governor of Emilia-Liguria in Milan before being called to a Christian bishopric by popular demand in 374. He brought the confidence of his social class and training in Roman rhetoric to his ecclesiastical duties. Although he underwent instruction and baptism only after being named bishop, Ambrose contributed significantly to the settlement of Nicene orthodoxy, especially concerning the doctrines of Christ and the Holy Spirit, while imparting moral-ascetical instruction and vigorously defending the church's moral-spiritual authority in relations with the state. Ambrose's life, recorded by his contemporary biographer Paulinus, was one of simplicity and austerity. A popular and powerful figure in Milan, which in his time was the center of Western Roman rule, Ambrose was "court theologian" to a series of notable figures, including the emperors Valentinian I (364–375), Gratian (375–383), and Valentinian II (383–392) as well as Theodosius (379–395, sole ruler of the empire 392–395). In his political dealings Ambrose effectively appealed to Roman legal structures and symbols while invoking the symbolic and sacramental power of the new faith.

Having begun his formal theological training at age thirty-four, Ambrose produced a series of notable works that reflect his active life amid the stresses of the age. He was more a consolidator and a creative transmitter than an original intellect. His chief models were Philo Judaeus and Origen on exegetical, dogmatic, and ascetical teachings and Cicero on morals. Although an important transmission of Neoplatonic thought occurs in his sermons (which deeply impressed Augustine), his Platonizing insight is more evident in spiritual and allegorical interpretations of scripture than in strict philosophical arguments.

Major exegetical works include *Hexaemeron,* six books on the creation epic of the Old Testament; *On Paradise; On Cain and Abel; On Isaac and the Soul;* a meditation on Psalm 118; and a lengthy commentary on Luke, which arose largely from sermons. A series of works in defense of the ideal of chastity characterizes Ambrose's rigoristic moral thought in an age of rampant self-indulgence. These include *On Virginity, To Sister Marcellina on Virginity, On Widows,* and *Exhortation to Virginity.* Ambrose never worked out a formal Mariology, but he resolutely championed devotion to the Virgin Mary. His best-known moral work, *On the Duties of the Clergy* (386), is a lightly but significantly reworked moral handbook for clergy that is modeled on Cicero's *On Duties.* Much debated as a key instrument for transmission of classical Greco-Roman culture, this work is the first comprehensive ethical treatise by a Christian writer. Ambrose's main dogmatic works are *On Faith* and *On the Holy Spirit,* both of which mediate and defend Nicene orthodoxy to the Western world and mark its full victory over the Arian heresy. Two other theological writings, *On the Sacraments* and *On Penance,* arose directly from catechetical needs.

Ambrose had a large impact on his contemporaries through his person and his exercise of church office. He championed what was virtually a monastic clergy under his spiritual direction. In defending the new order of Christian life against lingering influences of a dying paganism, Ambrose was without compromise. His removal of the pagan altar of victory from the Senate house symbolizes this tendency. Ambrose's dedication to Christian primacy is also demonstrated by his sanctioning of the burning of a synagogue in Callinicum by Christians, a deed that he zealously defended when Theodosius initially required the Christians to rebuild it.

In his admiration for Cicero's *On Duties,* Ambrose assumes a place in company with Luther, Melanchthon, Hume, Kant, and Frederick the Great, all of whom recognized in Cicero's work a common, practical Stoic wisdom that lies at the heart of Western humanistic thought. This Stoicism took seriously the ability to pattern a life after one's own nature. The notion of "the fitting" (*decorum*) loomed large as an aspect of the classical virtue of moderation. Ambrose christianized classical ideals, defending the four cardinal virtues (wisdom, fortitude, and justice, in addition to moderation) and the classical "just war" theory, and he perpetuated a Ciceronic way of resolving the clash between duty and expediency by appealing to moral (in his case, biblical) examples.

Like Augustine, Jerome, and Gregory I, Ambrose is considered one of the four major doctors of the Latin-speaking church and a towering figure of the age. From 374 until his death in 397 he held undisputed sway over affairs of the Latin church through the force of his personality and his courage, as seen during the repeated crises between church and state. His most celebrated appeal to ecclesiastical interests in dealing with the state, his humbling of Theodosius when the emperor, in a fit of rage, ordered a massacre of seven thousand citizens as a reprisal for unrest in Thessalonica, echoes the Old Testament prophet Nathan's rebuke of King David. Ambrose's actions provided a momentous precedent for later church-state relations.

Church tradition remembers Ambrose as a founder of Latin hymnody. A number of well-known hymns (e.g., *Aeterne rerum conditor, Deus Creator omnium*) reflect his poetic skill and indicate something of his contribution to the life of liturgy and worship. His effectiveness in acting on practical moral concerns, as seen in the writing on duties and his sermons on behalf of the oppressed (e.g., *On Naboth*), set an enduring pattern for church engagement in public life. Whether it was Ambrose's moral concerns, his platonizing, his elevated scriptural interpretations, or his vital strength of character that led to the conversion in 387 of Augustine of Hippo cannot be easily determined. Ambrose's influence lived on in Augustine, his greatest convert and a figure who never forgot the work and example of the bishop of Milan, even while towering over his mentor intellectually.

BIBLIOGRAPHY

Texts of Ambrose in *Patrologia Latina,* vols. 14 and 15, edited by J. P. Migne (Paris, 1845), are being superseded by those in "Corpus Christianorum, Series Latina." Of the several volumes that are planned, only volume 14, *Sancti Ambrosii Medio-lanensis Opera* (Turnhout, 1957), containing his exposition of *Luke* and fragments on *Isaiah,* has appeared to date. English translations of works and letters are found in *Some of the Principal Works of Saint Ambrose,* "The Nicene and Post-Nicene Fathers," 2d series, vol. 10 (1896; reprint, Grand Rapids, Mich., 1955), and in "Fathers of the Church," vols. 26, 42, 44, and 65 (1954–1972). The contemporary biography by Paulinus, a classic among "lives of the saints," is printed in *The Western Fathers,* edited by F. R. Hoare (New York, 1954), while the comprehensive modern biography is the two-volume work by Frederick H. Dudden, *The Life and Times of Saint Ambrose* (Oxford, 1935). The work of Hans von Campenhausen, *Ambrosius von Mailand als Kirchenpolitiker* (Berlin, 1929), is still the formative study of Ambrose's activities as church politician; Campenhausen's vivid interpretation is restated in his biographical portrait, "Ambrose," chapter 4 of *The Fathers of the Latin Church* (London, 1964). For an account of "middle Stoic" influences and their significance in Western thought, see my "Ambrose's 'On the Duties of the Clergy': A Study of Its Setting, Content, and Significance in the Light of Its Stoic and Ciceronian Sources" (Ph.D. diss., Union Theological Seminary, 1968). Ernst Dassmann's *Die Frömmigkeit des Kirchenvaters Ambrosius von Mailand* (Münster, 1965) constitutes a well-balanced, chronologically arranged study of Ambrose's mystical theology and biblical interpretations.

RICHARD CROUTER (1987)

AMEER ALI, SYED (1849–1928), Indian Muslim historian, jurist, and politician. Ameer Ali was born in Chinsura, Bengal, a suburb of Calcutta. His family spoke Urdu, having migrated from Avadh shortly before his birth to join a small community of fellow Shīʿī Muslims of Iranian descent. Ameer Ali never had any significant contact with Bengali or substantial training in Arabic; his education was in English, supplemented with Persian and Urdu. He was also greatly influenced by Sayyid Karāmat ʿAli (1796–1876), a family friend who had written an Urdu treatise in the rationalistic Muʿtazili tradition of Shīʿī scholasticism. After receiving degrees in law and history from Calcutta University in 1868, he went to London on a government scholarship and qualified as a barrister in 1873. From 1890 to 1904 he was a judge of the Calcutta High Court, after which he retired to England, where he served from 1909 until his death as a member of the Judicial Committee of the Royal Privy Council.

During Ameer Ali's student years in England he wrote *The Critical Examination of the Life and Teachings of Mohammad* (1872), the first version of what in three subsequent revisions was to become famous as *The Spirit of Islam.* More than an apologetic response to Christian polemics and the challenge of nineteenth-century empiricism, as in the writings of Sayyid Ahmad Khan, *The Spirit of Islam* (1922) portrays Islam as a dynamic force, the ultimate generator of "religious progress among mankind" (p. xix). Ameer Ali sees "the achievement of Mohammad in the moral world" in terms of the traditional concept of his role as last of the prophets, the culmination and synthesis of all previous religious discoveries. But he also argues that the initial revelation of Islam is a continually creative "spirit," the source of the ongoing progress of universal human understanding and moral sensibility. Ameer Ali attributes "the present stagnation of the Mussulman communities" to an unwillingness to allow the inspiration of Islam to guide private judgment, to adapt the universal teachings of the Prophet to "the necessities of this world of progress with its ever-changing social and moral phenomena" (pp. 182–183). At the same time, he insists that inspiration be constrained by rationalism and warns against "vulgar mysticism," which "unsettles the mind and weakens the foundations of society and paralyses human energy" (pp. 477–478).

As a major figure in the development of "Anglo-Muhammadan Law," that is, the adaptation of Islamic ethical and legal principles to British judicial institutions and procedures, Ameer Ali made similar arguments for a continually adaptive reading of scriptural sources in the light of "changed circumstances." On this basis he argued against polygamy and female seclusion. In making these interpretations, he claimed for himself, as well as for the non-Muslim judges of the British courts, the right to override traditional Muslim authorities.

Throughout his adult life Ameer Ali was an active political publicist and organizer on behalf of what he deemed to be a homogeneous Indian Muslim community. In 1878 he founded the National Muhammadan Association, the first All-Indian Muslim political organization, with over fifty far-flung branches. He was instrumental in formulating constitutional arrangements for separate Muslim electorates and weighted political representation, on the grounds that Muslims had once ruled India. In 1924 he joined the Aga Khan in appealing to the Turkish Republic to maintain the caliphate, an intervention that Kemal Atatürk took as sufficient grounds for its final abolition. Ameer Ali defended the Sunni institution of the Ottoman caliphate as a "pontifical" headship of a world Muslim polity, but he remained ultimately committed to the "apostolic" Shīʿī imamate—a contrast between democratic consensus "however obtained" and those truly qualified on the basis of intrinsic superiority (see his *Mahommedan Law,* 1912 ed., vol. 1, p. 6). His strong advocacy of British rule in India and opposition to Indian nationalism, especially insofar as it consigned Muslims to minority status, were founded on similar antidemocratic principles.

Except for some minor writings in Urdu, Ameer Ali wrote in English for a British public and, only secondarily, for English-educated Muslims. Although treated with contempt by Islamic scholars, his ideas and style have played a significant part in shoring up the self-confidence of Muslims not only in South Asia but throughout the Islamic world.

BIBLIOGRAPHY

In addition to *The Spirit of Islam: A History of the Evolution and Ideals of Islam,* rev. ed. (1922; reprint, London, 1974), which centers on the life of Muhammad, Ameer Ali's other major works are *A Short History of the Saracens,* rev. ed. (London, 1921), and *Mahommedan Law,* 2 vols., 5th ed., edited by Raja Said Akbar Khan (Lahore, 1976). K. K. Aziz's *Ameer Ali: His Life and Work* (Lahore, 1968) reprints many of his writings, including the "Memoirs," and contains a useful bibliography.

DAVID LELYVELD (1987)

AME NO KOYANE is one of the four deities (*kami*) enshrined at Kasuga Shrine in Nara. The deities worshiped at Kasuga Shrine, who were venerated by the Fujiwara (formerly, Nakatomi) clan, include Takemikazuchi no Mikoto, Iwainushi no Mikoto (Futsunushi no Mikoto), and Ame no Koyane no Mikoto and his wife, ancestral *kami* of the Fujiwara clan.

According to a myth recorded in the *Nihonshoki,* Takemikazuchi and Iwainushi were commanded by Amaterasu Ōmikami (the sun goddess and the ancestral *kami* of Japan's imperial house) to descend from the Heavenly Plain to earth and subjugate the Japanese domain. At the descent of Ninigi no Mikoto, a grandson of the sun goddess, Ame no Koyane was directed by Amaterasu to thenceforth attend and protect her descendants (*tennō*), who were to live in the palace hall with the sacred mirror (*yata no kagami*), one of her divine regalia, and to worship it. By enshrining the four *kami* mentioned in the above myth at their clan-shrine at Kasuga, the Fujiwara attained religious authority to receive supreme political power at the imperial court.

By the end of the Heian period the entities enshrined at Ise (Amaterasu), Hachiman (Hachiman), and Kasuga (the four deities mentioned above) Shrines came to be referred to as the "*kami* of the three shrines" (*sanja no kami*) as a sign of special respect. During the Muromachi period the "three shrine oracle" (*sanja ta-kusen*) was popularly venerated. Ame no Koyane's prestige as a mythic figure was enhanced during the thirteenth century with the publication of the *Gukanshō,* an interpretive history of Japan by the Tendai abbot Jien, himself a member of the Fujiwara line. The *Gukanshō,* marrying certain eschatological notions found in Buddhist scripture with the myths of the founding the Japanese state, declared that during the so-called era of the True law (*shōbō*), Amaterasu had formulated a system of government in which there was direct administration by the *tennō,* but that in the subsequent eras of human history other forms of political organization had been sanctioned by her. During the era of the

Counterfeit Law (*zōbō*), Amaterasu had collaborated with Ame no Koyane to create the regent-chancellor system, in which the *tennō* was assisted by a regent from the Fujiwara clan (the descendants of Ame no Koyane herself). For the era of the Latter Days of the Law (*mappō*), the *Gukanshō* continues, when human institutions have degenerated from their original integrity, Amaterasu consulted with Ame no Koyane and Hachiman to establish the regent-shogun system (combining the institutions of regent and shogun), in which the *tennō* is assisted by the regent-shogun of the Fujiwara clan, the descendants of Ame no Koyane.

Thus, until the end of World War II Ame no Koyane served as a legitimizer of the imperial system. Kasuga Shrine, which honors her, was accordingly revered by the imperial house and protected by the majesty and power of the state.

SEE ALSO Amaterasu Ōmikami; Japanese Religions, articles on Religious Documents, The Study of Myths; Jien; Mappō.

BIBLIOGRAPHY

Brown, Delmer, M., and Ishida Ichirō, eds. *The Future and the Past: A Translation and Study of the Gukanshō, an Interpretive History of Japan Written in 1219.* Berkeley, 1979.

Ishida Ichirō. *Shintō shisōshū.* Tokyo, 1970.

Ishida Ichirō. *Kami to Nihon bunka.* Tokyo, 1983.

ISHIDA ICHIRŌ (1987)
Translated from Japanese by Jenine Heaton

AMESHA SPENTAS. In the Zoroastrian tradition, the Amesha Spentas (Av.; MPers., Amahraspandān), or "beneficent immortals,"are an important group of entities surrounding Ahura Mazdā and figuring significantly in the *Gāthās.* From one point of view, they are aspects of divinity; from another they are personifications of abstract concepts. They do not exist independently but find their *raison d'être* in a system of interrelations and correlations among themselves. Since the divine is mirrored in the corporeal world, they gradually assumed, in theological speculations, correspondences with material elements as well. This explains the later, Manichaean use of *amahraspandān* to refer to the five luminous elements: ether, wind, light, water, and fire. The collective name of the Amesha Spentas and their definiton as a set of six or seven immortals (if the two spirits Spenta Mainyu and Ahura Mazdā are included) is found in the non-Gathic Avesta, in which the adjectives *amesha* ("immortal") and *spenta* ("beneficent") are sometimes used to describe various entities. The words do not, however, occur in the *Gāthās* (Narten, 1982).

The entities positively identified as Amesha Spentas are a well-defined group: Vohu Manah ("good thought"), Asha Vahishta ("best truth"), Khshathra Vairya ("desirable power"), Spenta Ārmaiti ("beneficent devotion"), Haurvatāt ("wholeness" or "health"), and Ameretāt ("immortality" or "life"). Many of these notions are present in Vedic religion. Thus Zarathushtra (Zoroaster), in developing his doctrine, was following a tendency, already present in the older Indo-European tradition, toward the spiritualization of abstract concepts that, according to the Indo-European tripartite ideology, corresponded to functional divinities (Dumézil, 1945; Duchesne-Guillemin, 1962; Widengren, 1965; et al.). Zarathushtra, however, took this tendency in a new and original direction. The *Bundahishn* (Book of primordial creation; ninth century CE) gives us a picture of correspondences between the Amahraspandān and the elements: cattle correspond to Vohu Manah, fire to Asha, metal to Khshathra, earth to Ārmaiti, and water and plants to Haurvatāt and Ameretāt.

Vohu Manah is simultaneously divine and human; through "good thought" humans recognize divinity and divinity indicates to them the way, the goal, and their origins. It is, then, an intermediary between the divine and the human. Asha is the Iranian equivalent of the Indian Ṛta ("truth") and personifies the cosmic, social, ritual, and moral order. Ārmaiti is humankind's devotion to divinity, their receptive and obedient behavior. Khshathra is the power that comes to a person from his or her state of union *(maga)* with divinity—a special power used to conquer the malefic forces and establish the rule of Ahura Mazdā. Haurvatāt and Ameretāt are the drink and food of divinity (offerings are made to them of various kinds of drink and plants) and of humans, for whom they represent a reward for a correctly lived life of good thoughts, good words, and good actions.

BIBLIOGRAPHY

de Jong, Albert. *Traditions of the Magi. Zoroastrianism in Greek and Latin Literature.* Leiden, 1997.

Duchesne-Guillemin, Jacques. *The Western Response to Zoroaster.* Oxford, 1958.

Duchesne-Guillemin, Jacques. *La religion de l'Iran ancien.* Paris, 1962.

Dumézil, Georges. *Naissance d'Archanges.* Paris, 1945.

Geiger, Bernhard. *Die Ameša Spentas: Ihr Wesen und ihre ursprüngliche Bedeuntung.* Vienna, 1916.

Gershevitch, Ilya. "Zoroaster's Own Contribution." *Journal of Near Eastern Studies* 23 (1964): 12–38.

Gershevitch, Ilya, trans. and ed. *The Avestan Hymn to Mithra.* Cambridge, 1959.

Gray, Louis H. *The Foundations of the Iranian Religions.* Bombay, 1930.

Kellens, Jean. *Le panthéon de l'Avesta ancien.* Wiesbaden, 1994.

Lommel, Herman. "Die Elemente im Verhältnis zu den Ameša Spenta's." In *Feschrift für Ad. E. Jensen,* vol. 1, edited by Eike Haberland et al., pp. 365–377. Munich, 1964.

Narten, J. *Die Ameṣa Spentas im Awesta.* Wiesbaden, 1982.

Nyberg, H. S. *Irans forntida religioner.* Stockholm, 1937. Translated as *Die Religionen des alten Iran* (1938; 2d ed., Uppsala, 1966).

Schlerath, Bernfried. "Die Gathas des Zarathustra." *Orientalistische Literaturzeitung* 57 (1962): 565–589.

Thieme, Paul. "Die vedischen Āditya und die zarathustrischen Ameša Spenta." In *Zarathustra,* "Wege der Forschung," no. 169, edited by Bernfried Schlerath, pp. 397–412. Darmstadt, 1970.

Widengren, Geo. *Die Religionen Irans.* Stuttgart, 1965. Translated as *Les religions de l'Iran* (Paris, 1968).

GHERARDO GNOLI (1987)
Translated from Italian by Roger DeGaris

AMITĀBHA

AMITĀBHA ("immeasurable light"), or Amitāyus ("immeasurable lifespan"), are the Sanskrit names of a Buddha who in Mahāyāna Buddhism is represented as the supernatural ruler of "the Land of Bliss" (Sukhāvatī), a paradise-like world in the western part of the universe. According to the doctrine associated with his name and commonly called Amidism (from the Japanese form, Amida), he is a superhuman savior who, by the force of his "original vow," has created an ideal world into which all those who surrender to his saving power are reborn, to stay there until they reach *nirvāṇa.* In India and Central Asia, the complex of beliefs centered on Amitābha never appears to have given rise to a distinct sect within Mahāyāna Buddhism. In East Asia, however, the cult of Amitābha (Chin., Emituo; Kor., Amit'a; Jpn., Amida) eventually led to a characteristic form of popular Buddhism, especially as manifested in the various sects and movements known collectively as Pure Land (Chin., *jingtu;* Kor., *chongt'o;* Jpn., *jōdo*).

ORIGIN AND EARLY DEVELOPMENT. The figure of Amitābha belongs wholly to the Mahāyāna tradition, for he is nowhere mentioned in the Theravāda canon. The religious lore connected with Amitābha and Sukhāvatī contains a number of elements common to Mahāyāna Buddhism as a whole: the idea that in the universe there are many regions in which "extraterrestrial" buddhas are active; the belief that some of these Buddha worlds are regions of great beauty and spiritual bliss, as a result of the karmic merit accumulated by the Buddha in the course of past lives; and the conviction that pious believers can be reborn there to listen to his teachings. In this general context, Amitābha and his Buddha world in the west are mentioned a number of times in early Mahāyāna scriptures, where, however, he is not singled out for special worship. At the same time, the figure of Amitābha and the cult specifically rendered to him show a number of features that are so far removed from Indian Mahāyāna that several scholars have sought their origin outside India, in the northwestern borderlands where Buddhism was exposed to strong Iranian influence. There its rise was probably also stimulated by the popularity of eschatological ideas around the beginning of the common era. There was a belief that the world had degenerated to a point where humanity could no longer be delivered by its own effort and must rely on faith and on devotion to a powerful savior in order to be released from sin and suffering. A similar idea, that of the "last phase of the Doctrine," was to play an important role in the development of Amidism in China and Japan.

Amitābha devotionalism is based on a few rather short scriptures of two types: one concerning Amitābha's spiritual career, the glories of the western Buddha world, and the promise of rebirth in that region, the other devoted to the technique of "visualization" of Amitābha by a process of mental concentration performed before an icon that represents the Buddha in his paradise. The first Chinese translation of an Amitābha scripture dates from the first part of the third century CE. This scripture already contains the story of the Buddha Amitābha's original resolution to save all beings. A famous episode that has remained the basic theme of Amidist soteriology, this tale recounts how, many aeons ago, the monk Dharmākara, the being destined to become the Buddha Amitābha, had pronounced a series of forty-eight vows and declared that he would not realize Buddhahood unless he could fulfill all these vows by the force of his own karmic merit, to be accumulated in future lives. He vowed to create a Buddha world of unparallelled splendor and to open it to all beings who sincerely believe in his saving power and express their faith by the invocation of his holy name. With the exception of the gravest sinners, all beings may enter that realm of ethereal beauty and spiritual bliss, where even the birds sing hymns in praise of the Doctrine. Sincere faith is especially important at the moment of death: To the one who at his death surrenders to Amitābha's grace, the Buddha himself will appear, and his soul (a basically non-Buddhist notion) will be transported to Sukhāvatī, there to be born from the bud of a supernatural lotus flower. In some of these scriptures, Amitābha is already represented as forming a triad with the two powerful *bodhisattvas* who in later iconography are his constant acolytes—Avalokiteśvara (Chin., Guanyin, since the tenth century mostly represented as a female *bodhisattva*) and Mahāsthāmaprāpta; these two represent the two main aspects of his being, mercy and wisdom. From the late fourth century onward, the cult of Amitābha, with its characteristic features (devotionalism; "visualization"; beatific visions at the moment of death; invocation of the Buddha's name), is attested in Chinese sources, but it is generally combined with other Buddhist beliefs and practices. It was only in the sixth century that Pure Land Buddhism became established as a distinct religious movement.

EARLY PURE LAND BUDDHISM IN CHINA. Pure Land Buddhism as founded by Tanluan (c. 488–c. 554) and elaborated by Daochuo (562–645) and Shandao (613–681) must be viewed against the background of eschatological beliefs concerning "the final phase of the Doctrine" (Chin., *mofa;* Jpn., *mappō*). These were widespread in sixth-century China, particularly after the severe persecution of Buddhism in the years 574–578. *Mofa* thought implied an extremely pessimistic view of society as made up of a world of sinners, a degenerate clergy, and a tyrannical government—in other words, a situation in which it was impossible to practice the doctrine to its full extent and complexity. Instead of individual effort to reach the ideal of saintliness and enlightenment and the arduous task of studying the complicated teachings of the

Buddhist scriptures, humankind needed a simple way to salvation, and if humans were unable to tread it alone, the power of the Buddha's compassion would be there to help them.

The rise of Pure Land Buddhism was no doubt also stimulated by indigenous Daoist thought. Since early times, Sukhāvatī appears to have been associated with one of the Daoist terrestrial paradises, also located in the far west. This was the fabulous Kunlun mountain where Xi Wang Mu, the divine Queen Mother of the West, ruled over a population of immortals. Furthermore, both the repeated invocation of the esoteric name of a deity and the visualization of supernatural beings were well-known Daoist practices. It was no coincidence that the founder of the Pure Land movement, Tanluan, had been deeply interested in Daoism before he became a Buddhist.

By the middle of the Tang dynasty (eighth century), Amidism had become a powerful movement, as is attested by the popularity of Amidist literature and the innumerable icons and votive inscriptions devoted to the Buddha of the western paradise. In spite of the simplicity of its message, it attracted followers from all classes, including the cultured elite of courtiers and scholar-officials.

Later Developments in China: Ritualization and Syncretism. The basic expression of faith and devotion in Pure Land Buddhism consisted of mental concentration on Amitābha's saving power and on the mercy of the *bodhisattva* Guanyin, who in due course became as prominent as the Buddha himself. This was accompanied by the unceasing repetition of the formula "Homage to the Buddha Amitābha" (Skt., "Namo Amitābha-buddhāya"; Chin., "Namu Emituofo"; Jpn., "Namu Amida Butsu"), sometimes up to a hundred thousand times a day. However, in spite of its doctrinal simplicity, Amidism in China developed an elaborate and characteristic liturgy, with hymn singing, the chanting of spells, collective prayer, and penitential ceremonies that in many variations have continued until the present.

In iconography, Amidism gave rise to a special type of religious art that takes as its basic theme an extremely elaborate representation of Amitābha and his acolytes in the splendor of the western paradise. As may be expected, Pure Land devotionalism appealed to the lay public, and the collective activities of lay believers, both male and female, often in the form of pious societies or congregations organized for common prayer and the performance of good works, always have played an important role. Over time a tendency developed to supplement the simple message of Pure Land Buddhism with a philosophical superstructure borrowed from other, more sophisticated systems of Buddhist thought such as the "One Vehicle" doctrine of the *Lotus Sūtra,* the esoteric symbolism of Tantric Buddhism, and Chan (Jpn., Zen) intuitionism. In late imperial times, Chan-Pure Land syncretism could be found in most Chinese monasteries. The Chan ideal of inner enlightenment, attained through the realization of one's own "Buddha nature," was combined with the cult of Amitābha, resulting in the beliefs that the true Pure Land is to be found within oneself and that the formula of the Holy Name can be used as a theme (Chin., *gongan;* Jpn., *kōan*) in Chan meditation.

Amidism in Korea and Japan. Following the official adoption of Buddhism as the state religion by the Korean kingdom of Silla (528 CE), the various schools of Chinese Buddhism, including the Pure Land sect, were introduced into Korea, where they reached their highest development in the seventh and eighth centuries. From Korea, Amidism soon reached Japan; it is known to have been expounded at the Japanese court before the middle of the seventh century. However, as in China, Japanese Amidism only slowly became a distinct sect. As a sectarian movement, it clearly showed the characteristics of a popular, almost protestant, reaction to the more sophisticated and aristocratic doctrines and institutions of the established sects, and, once more, this reaction was largely inspired by eschatological beliefs concerning the "final stage of the Doctrine."

In the eleventh and twelfth centuries, the popularity of Amidism rose with the activities of popular preachers such as Genshin (942–1017) and Kūya (Kōya), the "saint of the marketplace," both of whom preached the principles of "relying on the strength of the Other One" (*tariki*) and the invocation of the Sacred Name (*nembutsu*). In the late twelfth century the Jōdo sect was formally established by Genshin's disciple Hōnen (1133–1212), who attracted a huge following from all classes in spite of growing resistance on the part of the Buddhist establishment. In Hōnen's Pure Land devotionalism, centered on the idea that salvation can be reached by *nembutsu* while everything else may be left to Amitābha's saving grace, there is found already the tendency toward extreme reductionism that would culminate in the True Jōdo sect (Jōdo Shinshū) founded by the great reformer Shinran (1173–1263). According to Shinran, Amitābha's "original vow" implied that salvation was open to all sincere believers. Thus not *nembutsu* but faith must be the basis of religious life. Humanity can only be redeemed by a single and total act of surrender to Amitābha's grace; the invocation of his name is not a means by which to achieve salvation, but rather a constant expression of gratitude for the gift of faith from Amitābha. Amitābha's all-embracing grace erases all distinctions, including even the distinction between "own effort" (*jiriki*) and "relying upon the Other One" (*tariki*). Shinran also stressed the fact that Amitābha is the only Buddha who should be worshiped. All other Buddhist teachings and practices are secondary, or even irrelevant. Because there must be no separation between religion and ordinary life, even the principle of celibacy is rejected. Like their founder who described his own status as being "neither priest nor layman," Shinshū priests may marry. It is in this extremely reduced and "congregational" form that Amidism has become the most widespread variety of Buddhism in Japan. At present, the Jōdo and Jōdo Shinshū sects (the latter in two main branches) together have a following of about twenty million.

See Also Celestial Buddhas and Bodhisattvas; Daochuo; Genshin; Hōnen; Iconography, article on Buddhist Iconography; Ippen; Jingtu; Jōdo Shinshū; Jōdoshu; Nianfo; Pure and Impure Lands; Shandao; Shinran; Tanluan; Worship and Devotional Life, article on Buddhist Devotional Life in East Asia; Xiwangmu.

Bibliography

The basic scriptures of Amidism have been published in an English translation in the series "Sacred Books of the East," vol. 49 (1894; reprint, New York, 1969). These are two versions of the *Sukhāvatīvyūha,* both translated from Sanskrit by F. Max Müller, and the Scripture of the Visualization of Amitābha, *Guan wuliangshoufo jing,* translated from Chinese by Takakusu Junjiro. See also Fujita Kotatsu's invaluable study, *Genshi jōdo shisō no kenkyū* (Tokyo, 1970). The most comprehensive treatment of Amitābha is to be found in volume 2 of Henri de Lubac's *Aspects du bouddhisme* (Paris, 1955), translated by George Lamb as *Aspects of Buddhism* (New York, 1963). For a possible Iranian influence on the cult of Amitābha and Avalokiteśvara, see Marie-Thérèse de Mallman's *Introduction à l'étude d'Avalokiteçvara* (Paris, 1948). The early history of Pure Land Buddhism is summarized in Kenneth Chen's *Buddhism in China* (1964; reprint, Princeton, N. J., 1972), pp. 338–350. For Amidism in Japan (Jōdo and Jōdo Shinshū), see Harper H. Coates and Ryūgaku Ishizuka's *Hōnen, the Buddhist Saint,* 5 vols. (Kyoto, 1949), and A. Bloom's *Shinran's Gospel of Pure Grace* (Tucson, Ariz., 1965).

New Sources

Aoki, A. *Kenkoin Amida Nyoraizo zonai nonyuhin shiryo.* Kyoto, 1999.

Kainuma, Y. "Kaikei and Early Kamakura Buddhism: A Study of theAn'amiyo Amida Form." Ph.D. diss., University of California, Los Angeles, 1994.

Kaneko, Daiei, and W. S. Yokoyama."Rennyo the Restorer." *Eastern Buddhist* 31, no. 1 (1998): 1–11.

Payne, R. K., and K. K. Tanaka. *Approaching the Land of Bliss: Religious Praxis in the Cult of Amitabha.* Honolulu, 2004.

Schopen, Gregory. "The Inscription on the Kusan Image of Amitabha and the Character of the Early Mahayana in India." *Journal of the International Association of Buddhist Studies* 10, no. 2 (1987): 99–137.

Erik Zürcher (1987)
Revised Bibliography

AMOGHAVAJRA

AMOGHAVAJRA (705–774), known to the Chinese as Bukong or, more fully, as Bukongjin'gang; propagator of Zhenyan Buddhism. Apparently born of a North Indian *brahman* family, Amoghavajra became the disciple of the Vajrayāna master Vajrabodhi at fifteen and traveled with him to Śrīvijaya and then on to China in 720. Like other Zhenyan masters, Amoghavajra is credited with wide learning in the Buddhist tradition and is thought to have especially excelled at the study of Vinaya (monastic discipline). According to one account, Amoghavajra wished to learn the "Three Mysteries" and the method of the "five divisions" of the *Sarvatathāgatatattvasaṃgraha,* but Vajrabodhi was reluctant to instruct him. Thus, Amoghavajra made plans to return to India to seek the teachings from another master, but before he could announce his plans Vajrabodhi dreamed of Amoghavajra's departure and relented. After Vajrabodhi's death in 732 Amoghavajra made a pilgrimage to India and Sri Lanka, where he made further studies in the Vajrayāna. He returned ladened with texts and spent much of his life in the Da Xingshan Temple, translating and performing rites for members of the imperial family.

After the death of Vajrabodhi and his own return from India Amoghavajra set about furthering the influence of the Zhenyan school. Under the patronage of the emperor Xuanzong (r. 713–756) he met with a modicum of success. But under Suzong (r. 756–763) and Daizong (r. 763–779), Amoghavajra led the Zhenyan school to wide popularity and great power. Amoghavajra was both friend and teacher to Daizong; under his patronage he established a Vajrayana headquarters on Mount Wutai and instituted a variety of public rites for the welfare of the emperor and the state. Amoghavajra retranslated the *Sarvatathāgatatattvasaṃgraha* (T.D. no. 865), which had been partially translated by his own teacher, Vajrabodhi. He outlined the larger *Vajrosṇisa,* of which the *Sarvatathāgatatattvasaṃgraha* is the first part, in his *Shibahuizhigui* (Outlines of the essentials of the eighteen assemblies; T.D. no. 869). Amoghavajra produced volumes of translations of Esoteric scriptures and rites as well as new Esoteric versions of old scriptures, such as the *Prajñāpāramitā Sūtra for Humane Kings Who Wish to Protect Their States* (T.D. no. 246). His output as a translator was second only to that of the Chinese pilgrim Xuanzang (596–664). Amoghavajra's public preeminence is chronicled in a collection of his memorials to the throne and other documents, the *Biaozhiji* (T.D. no. 2120), assembled by his disciple Yuanzhao.

Amoghavajra was repeatedly honored by the emperor and courtiers, who built him temples and sponsored Esoteric rites. He was appointed Guoshi, "Teacher of the Realm," and had free access to the emperor's private chapel. He was even enfeoffed as a duke shortly before his death in 774. No monk in Chinese history, either before or since, has wielded such immense power.

Amoghavajra promoted the *Tattvasaṃgraha* as the fast way to enlightenment, but he also taught the techniques of the *Mahāvairocana Sūtra.* Indeed, it was either Amoghavajra or his immediate disciples who paired the teachings and the maṇḍalas of the two texts, a pairing that marks Zhenyan and its Japanese offspring, Shingon, as a distinctive branch of the Vajrayāna.

Through his astute use of Esoteric rites and "powers" *(siddhi),* Amoghavajra led the Zhenyan school to a unique position in Chinese religious history. In doing so, Amoghavajra enhanced the dimension of Vajrayāna practice both as a path to enlightenment and as the best way to promote the goals of the state. Like Śubhākarasiṃha and Vajrabodhi—and, indeed, like Padmasambhava, who later missionized Tibet—Amoghavajra sought to demonstrate that the practice of enlightenment entailed the exercise of *siddhi,* or wondrous salvific powers.

SEE ALSO Mahāsiddhas; Zhenyan.

BIBLIOGRAPHY

A carefully annotated translation of the standard biography of Amoghavajra, as well as notes on other sources for his life, can be found in Zhou Yiliang's "Tantrism in China," *Harvard Journal of Asiatic Studies* 8 (March 1945): 241–332.

New Sources

Amoghavajra, and Charles D. Orzech. "The Legend of the Iron Stupa." In *Buddhism in Practice,* edited by Donald S. Lopez, Jr., pp. 314–317. Princeton, 1995.

Hunter, Harriet. "A Late Heian Period Reinterpretation of the Rishukyo Mandara." *Japanese Religions* 27, no. 1 (2002): 69–98.

CHARLES D. ORZECH (1987)
Revised Bibliography

AMORAIM. The Aramaic word *amora'im* (sg., *amora'*), meaning "speakers," generally refers to those masters who in explaining and applying the earlier teachings of the Palestinian tannaim (c. 70–200 CE) contained in the Mishnah (and in its related collections, such as the Tosefta), made rabbinic Judaism into a wider social movement. Occasionally the term may denote the individual who repeated a rabbi's statement. The significance of the amoraim lies in what they accomplished in their own day and in the impact on later generations of Jews of the collection of their teachings in the *gemara'* (which combined with the Mishnah is the Talmud) and in the Midrash.

The amoraim are conventionally divided into generations demarcated by the life span of several prominent teachers: three to five generations of Babylonian and Palestinian masters (c. 220–375) and two or three longer additional Babylonian generations (375–460/500). Recently scholars have suggested that Ashi (375–424/7) should be considered the last of the amoraim proper, after whom (to 500) flourished those authorities who generally taught anonymously. Following the enumeration of Moshe Beer (*Amora'ei Bavel,* Ramat Gan, 1974), the amoraim cited in the two Talmuds number 773 masters: 371 in Palestine and 402 in Babylonia, or 74 masters per generation in Palestine and 57 in Babylonia with a generation spanning approximately thirty-one to thirty-five years. Hardly a mass movement in their own right, they formed an elite group that was able to influence Jewry at large.

According to Jacob Neusner (1966–1970) and David M. Goodblatt (1975), the amoraim, aided by a band of students, eventually transformed Jewish society by presenting the ideal that all should become rabbis, masters of God's Torah, which contains the key to health and happiness. Their devotion to Torah study brought them great respect, and since they were believed to be able to help the common folk and intercede with God, they were seen as holy men. Their influence was reinforced by their roles as judges and community administrators, especially in Babylonia, as collectors of charity, and as teachers who were responsive, for example, to the social and economic crisis that affected the third-century eastern Mediterranean Roman world.

The amoraim continued as a group longer in Babylonia than in Palestine, expanding and redacting the Babylonian *gemara'* into the fifth century, at a time when their rabbinical colleagues in Palestine, where the Jerusalem Talmud was already closed, were apparently primarily engaged in transmitting and redacting Midrashic teachings and possibly developing practical halakhic guides. Thus the amoraim creatively applied the scriptural and tannaitic tradition to differing Babylonian and Palestinian post-Mishnaic contexts—one a pagan Persian world and the other a pagan and then Christian Roman world, the one in the Diaspora and the other in the Holy Land. Although still valuing cultic notions, amoraim in both lands were able to dissociate ideas and institutions from the Temple; for example, separating features of the Passover evening celebration from its origins as a sacrificial ritual meal, they emphasized the symbolic significance of the protocol especially in terms of freedom and liberation. A comparable variation is discernible in the attempts to bolster the practice of saying blessings before eating food with the argument that the omission of a blessing constitutes a sin. While the tannaim, by drawing on the idea of trespass against the Temple cult, suggested that the individual would be performing the sin of sacrilege against the Lord, the amoraim first defined the terms so that they might be meaningful to those who had not experienced the Temple cult and then revised the metaphors, speaking of robbing the Holy One and the congregation of Israel (B.T., *Ber.* 35a–b). Responsive to the nation's political situation, the amoraim amplified traditional redemptive motifs, though they held that these hopes for divine intervention were contingent on human deeds. They thus asserted that the divine redemption celebrated during Passover took place because the people had merited it and thereby taught contemporary Jews awaiting an eventual redemption that they too must become worthy.

The emphasis on the study of Torah and on the importance of personal action and fulfillment of the commandments caused the amoraim to stress love of one's neighbor and the importance of law, order, and justice. Likewise, in responding to contemporary intellectual challenges, they drew on, yet transformed, many Hellenistic ideas, such as those concerning astrology and notions of an afterlife, and customs, such as in popular modes of taking oaths and vows. To be sure, rabbis differed on small and sometimes larger matters, but since rabbinic teachings were constantly revised in the process of transmission to make them address more directly whatever contemporary issue seemed most pressing, their original nuances often became obfuscated. Because the teachings were given a literary framework when woven together and fashioned into the larger whole of the *gemara'*, they appeared to form part of a collective effort.

The advances in the efforts of Talmudic criticism to unravel what happened to the teachings during the processes of transmission and redaction (e.g., of David Weiss Halivni) should enable a more accurate recognition of the fundamental form of a teaching and the meanings it gained in subsequent generations. This should further enable scholars to analyze the distinct amoraic approaches and thus surpass the important though highly selective earlier work of scholars from Wilhelm Bacher to E. E. Urbach.

The amoraic heritage came to be transmitted through the text of the Talmud: because the Talmud became the central book of study in later Judaism, its literary and methodological traits rival its substantive content in importance. The Talmud's process of inquiry inculcates a critical intellectual approach that uses the mind to evaluate the significance and appropriateness of ideas. This outlook characterizes Torah study as an encounter with the divine—an act of ongoing revelation—so that reason, reflection, and rational discourse are the means both to approach life and to imitate God, hence to become holy. Amoraic biblical exposition, or *midrash,* which makes use of the imaginative faculty, also inculcates these traits, for even interpretations and homilies are grounded in scripture and must often withstand a process of questioning and challenge. Both the Talmudic and the Midrashic literature inculcated later generations with the value of study and critical thinking, supplementing the substantive rabbinic teachings on human action, social order, compassion, and justice.

SEE ALSO Abbahu; Abbaye; Ashi; El'azar ben Pedat; Huna'; Midrash and Aggadah; Rabbah bar Nahmani; Rabbinic Judaism in Late Antiquity; Rav; Rava'; Shemu'el the Amora; Shim'on ben Laqish; Talmud; Yehoshu'a ben Levi; Yehudah bar Yeḥezqe'l; Yoḥanan bar Nappaha'.

BIBLIOGRAPHY

Analytical bibliographic information can be found in my article "An Annotated Bibliographical Guide to the Palestinian Talmud" and David M. Goodblatt's "The Babylonian Talmud," both in *Aufstieg und Niedergang der römischen Welt,* vol. 2.19.2 (Berlin and New York, 1979), pp. 139–256, 257–336, and both reprinted in *The Study of Ancient Judaism,* edited by Jacob Neusner, vol. 2, *The Palestinian and Babylonian Talmuds* (New York, 1981). Note in particular Saul Lieberman's *Greek in Jewish Palestine,* 2d ed. (New York, 1965), and *Texts and Studies* (New York, 1974); Jacob Neusner's *A History of the Jews in Babylonia,* 5 vols. (Leiden, 1966–1970), which treats comprehensively the rabbinic sources from the perspective of their late antique social, religious, and historical context; E. E. Urbach's *The Sages,* 2 vols., 2d enl. ed. (Jerusalem, 1979), which remains useful despite its insufficient differentiation between sources; and David M. Goodblatt's *Rabbinic Instruction in Sasanian Babylonia* (Leiden, 1975), a model study on the institutions of teaching. See also Jacob Neusner's *Judaism in Society* (Chicago, 1984), a study of the self-images of Palestinian amoraim; my *The Origins of the Seder* (Berkeley, Calif., 1984); and David Weiss Halivni's *Midrash, Mishnah, and Gemara* (Cambridge, Mass., 1986).

New Sources

Bader, Gershom. *The Encyclopedia of Talmudic Sages.* Translated by Solomon Katz. Northvale, N.J., 1988.

Berger, Michael S. *Rabbinic Authority.* New York, 1998.

Breuer, Yohanan. "On the Hebrew Dialect of the 'Amora'im' in the Babylonian Talmud." *Scripta Hierosolymitana* 37 (1998): 129–150.

Kalmin, Richard Lee. *Sages, Stories, Authors, and Editors in Rabbinic Babylonia.* Brown Judaic studies, no. 300. Atlanta, 1994.

Kalmin, Richard Lee. *The Sage in Jewish Society in Late Antiquity.* New York, 1999.

BARUCH M. BOKSER (1987)
Revised Bibliography

AMOS (fl. eighth century BCE) is considered the first classical prophet, the first whose words are preserved in writing, the biblical *Book of Amos.* Whereas other books of the Hebrew Bible such as *Samuel* and *Kings* contain numerous indirect prose reports of earlier prophets' activities, the books of the classical prophets, beginning with Amos, focus on the prophets' words, usually recorded in poetic form.

As a rule, the early prophets addressed a specific person, often the king himself, while the classical prophets addressed a wide audience. Hence they were not merely God's messengers but also speakers, or orators. The call for justice, which earlier had been directed primarily toward the king (by Nathan to David, by Elijah to Ahab) was now directed toward the rulers and the social elite and was in the form of a public address. It has been suggested that the development of this prophetic oratorical style is connected with the Assyrians' use of propaganda (see Rabshakeh's speech in *2 Kings* 18:28–35 [citations herein follow the English version]).

HISTORICAL CONTEXT. As the superscription to the *Book of Amos* (1:1) reveals, Amos prophesied during the reign of Jeroboam II (787/6–747/6 BCE). The superscription also states that he was active "two years before the earthquake" (see also *Zec.* 14:5), which, by means of the archaeological evidence at Hazor, has been dated to 760 BCE. Jeroboam's forty-year reign was a period of political stability, military success, and economic prosperity. The biblical historiographer (*2 Kgs.* 14:23–29; cf. *2 Kgs.* 13:24–25) reports on Jeroboam's territorial expansions and the strength of his kingdom.

Nevertheless, this period of prosperity had apparently created severe social tensions. Although the social elite, who prospered, were content, the people of the land, the small farmers, suffered greatly from the upper classes' pursuit of luxury (for the social structure, see *2 Kings* 24:14). It may be that the sudden increase in the standard of living resulted in greater taxation, which led to further oppression of the poor, who then became even poorer (see *Am.* 1:6–7a, 3:9, 4:1–2, 5:11, 6:4–6, 8:4–6).

AMOS'S BACKGROUND AND MESSAGE. The social inequities and oppression of the time precipitated Amos's protest and call for justice. The prophet's concern, however, was not merely social injustice but religious practice as well. Amos saw the religious practices of the elite as mirroring their perpetuation of social injustice, as indicated in his accusation in 2:7–8, and he labels the religious behavior of the leaders meaningless (4:4ff., 5:4–6, 5:21–27, 8:10).

The question arises: what does Amos's sharp criticism of the cult and its ritual mean? Does he intend to deny the efficacy of cultic worship? Is he opposed to the cult of specific shrines, such as Bethel and Gilgal? Is he calling for another type of worship (cf. 5:16)? In responding to these questions, scholars have intensively investigated Amos's social background. Who was he? The superscription refers to him as one of the *noqdim,* "shepherds" (sg. *noqed*), and this remark is echoed (though in another term, *boqer*) in 7:14. But in the Bible *noqed* does not refer to a simple shepherd; Mesha, king of Moab, bore the same title (*2 Kgs.* 3:4). Attention has been called to a Ugaritic text in which *nqd* is parallel to *khn* ("priest"), which may suggest that Amos himself was from a priestly family.

Amos definitely does not repudiate the cult, but calls for his audience to approach God. In his vision in 9:1, Amos reports that "I saw my Lord standing by the altar" (JPS). That is, God revealed himself to the prophet in the cultic center that is God's house. Amos's repeated reproach, "yet you did not return to Me" (*Am.* 4:6, 4:8, 4:10, 4:11) and his demand to "seek Me" (5:4, 5:14), which has a cultic connotation (cf. *1 Sm.* 9:9), may be understood as a call for purification of the worship. It can also be argued that Amos felt that the cultic centers of Bethel and Gilgal should cease to function as God's temples because their worshipers had demonstrated their insincerity through their pursuit of luxury and pleasure. Thus, Amos does not call for totally abstract worship and does not oppose the cult in principle. He harshly criticizes, however, the shrines that legitimate social oppression and thus the existence of religious hypocrisy.

Furthermore, the leaders toward whom Amos directs his criticism seem to be devoted worshipers (8:5). One may assume that the political and economic success of the state was taken by the ruling class as a sign of God's protection of Israel. In essence, the cult that assured its worshipers of the stability of their way of life served as religious protection for the social elite. Amos attacks this self-serving belief, pointing out that daily deeds and social justice are inseparable from the cult and, in fact, dominate God's demands of his worshipers.

Amos attacks as well the common belief that God's function is merely to save and protect his people. There was an expectation that there would be a sign, by means of revelation, of God's victories over Israel's enemies. Amos rejects this and argues that "the day of the Lord is darkness, and not light" (*Am.* 5:18–20); the day will be one of punishment, not salvation. Introducing the idea of God's punishment, he connects it with social crimes and the corruption of ritual. Amos is rooted in the sacred traditions of Israel (e.g., *Am.* 2:9–10, 3:1, 4:10, 4:11, 5:25, 9:7), and mentions them as proof of God's past and continuing involvement with Israel; but he emphasizes that this involvement is only in response to Israel's social and moral behavior.

In his autobiographical account, Amos mentions his occupation as a dresser of sycamore trees (7:14). This is a trade that required travel, especially since Tekoa, Amos's hometown (located about 8 miles [12.9 km] south of Jerusalem), is in an area where the sycamore does not grow (cf. *1 Kgs.* 10:27). Amos's travels may shed light on his broad education and deep knowledge of world affairs (see 1:2–2:16), as well as his contacts with the northern kingdom of Israel. It has also been suggested that Amos's Tekoa was somewhere in the north, which might explain his prophetic activity there; however, no evidence of a northern Tekoa has been found.

Sociologically, one must realize that many prophets (e.g., Amos, Micah, Jeremiah) came from the periphery to preach against urban centers. Villages and small towns preserved a traditional, clear view of the world. Cities, such as Samaria, were centers (especially during Amos's time) of prosperity, new developments, and social change. Social research reveals that it is not unusual for a visitor from a traditional area to be incensed by the breaking of traditional conventions in the city. Thus the changes that defied his traditional views kindled in Amos the fire of criticism and the desire to punish the evildoers.

LITERARY STYLE AND STRUCTURE. There have been many discussions of Amos's language. Although he was the first literary prophet, his style is well developed. Does this mean that Amos followed a specific literary tradition, and if so, which? This question should not be of great concern to the modern reader, since in antiquity there was not a significant difference between an oral address and a written speech. Both genres were designed stylistically to be heard, not read silently by an individual reader. Thus Amos did not start a new written tradition but continued a well-developed tradition of oratory.

An analysis of Amos's style reveals impressive literary variations. He employs the conventional prophetic patterns of speech, such as "Thus says the Lord" (e.g., 1:3, 1:6, 1:9, 1:11, etc.); the prophetic formula for a conclusion, "Says the Lord" (2:3, 2:16); and the prophetic verdict, "Therefore" (3:2). He uses specific conventions of the wisdom literature, for example, the formula 3 x 4 (repeated in chaps. 1–2), comparisons, and rhetorical questions (3:3–8), the latter two reflecting secular language. He also employs ritualistic language, such as the hymn (4:13, 5:8–9, 9:5–6) and the lament (e.g., 5:2; see also 5:16–18, 6:1). Amos reveals himself to be a great poet, a master of language with creative skills who knows how to use various modes of speech effectively. His objective is to appeal to his audience. Thus, for instance, in 3:3–6 and 3:8 he utilizes a series of rhetorical questions, a most effective device since its function is to emphasize, and it is stronger than a direct statement. Amos's use of figurative language enables him to describe the disaster he encounters in concrete terms; see, for example, his use of simile in 2:13 and 3:12.

The *Book of Amos* is divided into four main parts: (1) the superscription plus the chain of oracles against the nations, including Judah and Israel (1:1–2:16); (2) a series of speeches (chaps. 3–6); (3) the vision accounts (7:1–3, 7:4–6, 7:7–9; 8:1ff., 9:1ff.); and (4) a prophecy of salvation (9:11–15). It has been suggested that the first three visions are Amos's call and should be placed at the beginning of the book. In the vision (8:1ff.) of the basket of summer fruit (*keluv qayits*), the word *summer* (*qayits*) is a pun on the word for "destruction" (*qets*), which symbolizes the end of Israel. This wordplay may shed light on the psychology of prophetic revelation, in which the viewing of an object of daily life is interpreted in a vision or dream as a symbol. The series of vision accounts is interrupted by a biographical account (7:10–17), which reports on the conflict between Amaziah, priest of Bethel, and Amos, in which the priest demands that Amos go to Judah. In response to the question of why this account was inserted among the visions, scholars have suggested that the conclusion of Amos's attack on Amaziah, "Israel shall surely go into exile away from its land" (7:17), corresponds to the vision "The end has come upon my people Israel" (8:2) and that an editor, who some forty years later witnessed the exile of the priest of Bethel and his people by the Assyrians, inserted his account of this event as a sign of prophetic fulfillment.

Nineteenth-century scholarship assigned most of the material in the *Book of Amos* to Amos himself (except, perhaps, the prophecy of comfort at the end of the book). Current scholarship, however, is more skeptical and suggests a lengthy and complex redactional history. It has long been argued that the book's conclusion (9:11–15), a prophecy of comfort focusing on the house of David (and not on the northern kingdom or its rulers), reflects a later period. The prophecy against Judah in 2:4–5, which is foreign in its context, is also considered to be late. Recent scholarship has been attempting to organize the editorial layers in order according to the occurrence of political developments. Wolff has suggested that six stages of redaction took place, with the first three stages in the eighth century: the collection of the oracles in chapters 3–6 (the words of Amos himself); the incorporation of the oracles directed against the nations at the beginning of the book and the visions at the end of the book; and the insertion of the prose account of the Bethel episode. In the fourth stage, in the time of Josiah, the doxologies (hymns) were added, as well as an elaboration of Amos's critique of Bethel and the local cult corresponding to Josiah's reform (cf. *2 Kgs.* 23:15). Later there was a fifth, Deuteronomistic, redaction, which occurred in the exilic period and added the oracles against Tyre (1:9–10), Edom (1:11–12), and Judah (2:4–5). Finally, there was a postexilic redaction that added themes of salvation and eschatology so that the book would conclude on a positive note. Another suggestion, by Coote, is that the *Book of Amos* is the product of three stages of redaction: (1) the words of judgment by Amos delivered against the ruling class; (2) the period of Judah's reform, which added oracles of reinterpretation concerning the possibility of repentance; and (3) another series of reinterpretations for Judahites who were in exile or who had returned to the homeland.

These theories of redactional history are nonetheless speculative, since they consider certain thematic developments or changes in the genre of prophetic speech to be indications of later accretions. They assume that changed historical conditions led to new theological interpretations. This notion of systematic change and reinterpretation may be challenged, however, in light of Amos's intention to appeal to his audience, which required stylistic and emphatic variety as well as sensitivity to the audience's mood. He may sometimes have called for repentance or perhaps delivered an oracle of salvation based upon his overall religious worldview. Still, this does not mean that Amos was the sole author of the entire book. There may have been specific insertions (e.g., 5:13), which, however, do not imply a systematic editorial process.

BIBLIOGRAPHY

Coote, R. B. *Amos among the Prophets.* Philadelphia, 1981.

Kapelrud, Arvid S. *Central Ideas in Amos.* 2d ed. Oslo, 1961.

Mays, James Luther. *Amos: A Commentary.* Philadelphia, 1969.

Wolff, Hans Walter. *Joel and Amos.* Edited by Dean McBride and translated by Waldemar Janzen. Philadelphia, 1977.

New Sources

Hasel, Gerhard F. *Understanding the Book of Amos: Basic Issues in Current Interpretations.* Grand Rapids, Mich., 1991.

Hayes, John Haralson. *Amos, the Eighth-Century Prophet: His Times and His Preaching.* Nashville, 1988.

Polley, Max E. *Amos and the Davidic Empire: A Socio-historical Approach.* New York, 1989.

Rosenbaum, Stanley Ned. *Amos of Israel: A New Interpretation.* [Louvain, Belgium] Macon, Ga., 1990.

Watts, John D. W. *Vision and Prophecy in Amos.* Macon, Ga., 1997.

YEHOSHUA GITAY (1987)
Revised Bibliography

AMULETS AND TALISMANS. An amulet is an object, supposedly charged with magical power, that is carried on the person or displayed in a house, barn, or place of business in order to ward off misadventure, disease, or the assaults of malign beings, demonic or human. A talisman is an object similarly used to enhance a person's potentialities and fortunes. Amulets and talismans are two sides of the same coin. The former are designed to repel what is baneful; the latter, to impel what is beneficial. The employment of both (which is universal) rests on the belief that the inherent quality of a thing can be transmitted to human beings by contact.

The choice of objects used as amulets and talismans is determined by several different criteria. They may be (1) of unusual form, such as perforated stones; (2) rare, such as four-leaved clovers; (3) medicinal herbs or flowers, such as mugwort (thought to ease childbirth) or various kinds of febrifuges; (4) parts of animals exemplifying certain characteristics (for example, of a hare for swiftness or a bull for strength), or deemed potent in protecting from attacks by those animals; (5) relics of holy or heroic persons, or even dust from their graves, regarded as imbued with those persons' "numinous" charisma; (6) figurines of gods and goddesses; (7) models of common objects to which a symbolic significance is attributed, such as miniature ladders exemplifying the means of the soul's ascent to heaven; (8) exotic objects of foreign provenience, which are held to contain powers not normally available in a given society. The color of an object may also be decisive, on the basis of "like affects like"; a red stone, for instance, may be thought to relieve bloody flux or menstrual disorders and a yellow stone, to ward off jaundice. Ubiquitous also are models of the male and female genitalia, to increase procreation and sexual pleasure, and threads, to bind evil spirits.

Nor is it only in material things that magical power is thought to reside. Since, in primitive thought, the name of a person is not a mere verbal appellation but an essential component of his being (like his shadow or voice), that of a god or demon written on a slip or engraved on a gem or a medallion can serve as an effective amulet or talisman. Similarly, a text relating some feat or special benefit, especially the discomfiture of a demon, dragon, or monster, associated in traditional myth and folklore with a god or hero, may be regarded as charged with the power that accomplished that deed, so that to carry such a text on one's person transmits that power and perpetuates it. Scrolls or scripts containing excerpts from scriptures accepted as divinely inspired and therefore instinct with the divine essence, or (in medieval Christian usage) copies of letters said to have fallen from heaven are likewise favored.

Sometimes, however—especially when an amulet is directed against human rather than demonic enemies—the procedure adopted is not to enlist the influence and charisma of gods or "numinous" objects but to scare potential attackers by exhibiting in houses statuettes or figurines of monstrous, terrifying creatures. The Babylonians, for instance, fashioned models of the head and body of the grim demon Pazuzu, and one form of Greek amulet was the head of a gorgon whose eye could petrify would-be assailants.

Of salient importance is the material out of which an amulet or talisman is made, since the magic power is inherent in, not merely associated with, the object itself. Gems have to be of substances and colors believed to convey qualities efficacious for particular needs and written texts have to be inscribed on specified skins and in special inks or pigments.

Amulets and talismans borne on the person take the form of ornaments—brooches, lockets, pendants, seals, and sachets. Indeed, it is maintained by several authorities that what came eventually to be mere decorations were originally designed for protection.

A cardinal feature of amulets in many cultures is that they are esoteric and although, to be sure, they are often exhibited in full view on the walls of rooms and buildings, when they are carried on the person it is often a requirement that they must not be revealed to anyone except to the one who uses them on a specific occasion, to the magicians who make and dispense them, and to the hostile beings against whom they are directed. For this reason they are commonly concealed in the clothing or tucked away in bags or small cases. Moreover, in the case of written texts, they frequently employ cryptic alphabets or are couched in gibberish (known as *ephesia grammata*—perhaps a distortion of *aphasia grammata,* i.e., "unutterable letters"), supposed to be the scripts and languages of gods and demons. (These can sometimes be identified as genuine ancient scripts and tongues garbled in the course of the ages.) Signs of the zodiac and conventional symbols of constellations and metals also appear, because such signs are, like names, part and parcel of what they represent and because the inherent properties of constellations and metals are believed to control human fate and fortune. Common too are permutations of letters spelling out in esoteric fashion the words of the text. Thus (to use English equivalents) *z* will substitute for *a, y* for *b,* and so forth. In much the same way, the initial or final letters of words in a scriptural verse will be used instead of writing it out in full, and in alphabetical systems (like Hebrew) where each letter also possesses a numerical value (i.e., $a = 1$, $b = 2$, etc.), a combination of letters that add up to the same total as those of the word intended—a device known as gematria (probably a distortion of the Greek *grammateia*)—is employed. (The Library of Congress possesses the manuscript of a complete Hebrew Bible so written as a manual for the preparation of amulets!) A further device is the use of magical squares, each vertical column and each horizonal line of which adds up to the same sum, and all of them together spelling by gematria the name of God or of a protective angel.

The esoteric character of amuletic texts, it may be added, is matched in oral spells by having them recited in a whisper or crooned in a low voice. Indeed, this is the primary meaning of the term *incantation.*

Written amulets frequently express their numinous character by beginning with the words "In the name of [this or that god]" (e.g., the Arabic Bismillah, "In the name of

God, the Merciful, the Compassionate") and by being interspersed with religious signs (e.g., the cross, swastika, or shield of David), and their efficacy is increased by marks or letters (*ss* or *kh*) indicating that their recitation is to be accompanied by hissing and spitting to ward off demons. They also feature strings of vowel letters standing cryptically for the powers of angels or planets. Sometimes too the power of a written amulet is conveyed not simply by wearing it but by immersing it in water that is then drunk.

Amulets and talismans seem to have been in use even in prehistoric times, for cowrie shells, celts, arrowheads, and stones buried with the dead (a practice surviving throughout the ages) were evidently intended to protect them in the afterworld. Amuletic too were the pictures of eyes painted on prehistoric walls and monuments; these represented the providential vigilance of benevolent gods or spirits, countering the evil eye of the malevolent demons.

It is obviously impossible in the space of this article to describe in detail the whole host of amulets and talismans current all over the world. We shall therefore confine ourselves to representative examples of the principal types drawn from various cultures ancient and modern.

Historically, the oldest amulets came from Egypt. Dating as far back as the fourth millennium BCE, these take the form of images and figurines made of faience, feldspar, carnelian, obsidian, jasper, and the like wrapped in the bandages that swathed mummies. Each limb of the corpse had its appropriate amulet, usually placed over it. In addition to figurines of gods and goddesses there are miniature hearts, eyes of Horus, frogs, ladders, and steps. The eyes of Horus (usually a pair), made of gold, silver, lapis lazuli, hematite, or porcelain, represented the all-powerful might and watchfulness of that god and were worn also by the living to bring health and protection. The frog, emblematic of teeming abundance, symbolized life in the broadest sense, including resurrection of the body. The miniature ladder stood for the means of ascent to heaven. Miniature ladders are still set up beside graves by the Mangors of Nepal, and a ladder made of dough was traditionally placed next to coffins in some parts of Russia. One recalls also Jacob's ladder in the Bible (*Gn.* 28:12) and the reference to the same notion in Dante's *Paradiso* (21.25ff.)

Ubiquitous also was the familiar *ankh*. What it actually portrays is uncertain; some say it represents a combination of the male and female genitalia and hence (eternal) life. It was carried also in the right hand of deities, where, of course, it was not amuletic but a symbol of immortality. Scarabs (a species of beetle) were also interred with the dead. This particular type of beetle, one that continually rolls pellets of dung until they become larger and larger, symbolizes the process of continuous creation.

Mention should be made also of the so-called Horus *cippi*, stelae or plaques inscribed with legends of that god and portraying him standing on, or beside, serpents he had vanquished. A Canaanite version of this myth has recently been recognized in a Canaanite magical text from Ras Shamra (Ugarit) in northern Syria. The *cippi* were displayed to ward off malign spirits.

Other ancient Near Eastern amulets, common among the Babylonians, Assyrians, Canaanites, and Hittites, take the form of cylinder seals, usually made of diorite or hematite, engraved with mythological scenes depicting the discomfiture of demonic monsters by gods or the vanquishing of the formidable Huwawa, guardian of the sacred forest of cedars, by the heroes Gilgamesh and Enkidu. Sometimes, too, pictures of men supplicating gods, the beneficent sun rising between mountains, or a goddess bountifully pouring water from two jugs are featured. In interpreting these "mythological" amulets it is important to bear in mind that the scenes depicted may be simply mythologizations of general principles. Thus the goddess who pours water may be simply an illustration of bountiful profusion. Often, indeed, the basic meaning may be elicited by matching the glyptic portrayal with a corresponding verbal metaphor.

Another popular Mesopotamian and Canaanite amulet was a plaque portraying the ravages and eventual dispatch of a demonic hag or wolf who stole newborn babes. This has analogues in many parts of the world, for example, in Armenia, Ethiopia, and the Balkans, and especially in a Jewish charm, the so-called *Kimpezettl* (a Yiddish distortion of the German *Kindbettzettel*, "childbirth note"), in which the beldam is identified with Lilith.

Despite the monotheistic orientation of the writers of the Old Testament, amulets seem to have been used by the masses in ancient Israel. The prophet Isaiah castigates women who wore charms (3:20), and a silver amulet inscribed with the words of the Priestly Blessing (*Nm.* 6:24–27) and purportedly dating to the sixth century BCE has been found in Palestine. On the other hand, a figurative reference to amulets in *Deuteronomy* 6:8 was later taken literally and led to the modern Jewish practise of affixing to doorposts a small cylinder (*mezuzah*) containing excerpts from the Pentateuch and of wearing phylacteries (*tefillin*) on the brow and arm at morning prayer.

More modern Jewish amulets are the hexagram, fancifully termed the shield, not star, of David. This, however, is simply a Judaized version of a magical symbol of disputed meaning that is widely used elsewhere. Its counterpart is the equally universal pentagram, known to Jews as the seal of Solomon. Common too are metal amulets in the shape of the divine hand (likewise fairly universal), often engraved with the letter *h*, an abbreviation of Je*H*ovah. A favorite written amulet is a strip of paper on which is inscribed the legend "Abracadabra" (variously interpreted) in a series of lines, each of which has one more letter cut off at the end, so that the whole forms an inverted triangle ending with the single letter *a*. In recent times a further popular amulet is a golden pendant or brooch shaped in the form of the letters of the Hebrew word *ḥai* ("life, living").

Of special interest is a class of gems or semiprecious stones (sard, beryl, chalcedony, onyx, etc.) found mainly in Egypt of the Greco-Roman period (but later also in other lands), featuring fantastic images—often part human and part animal—of Egyptian and other gods accompanied by magical inscriptions such as the mysterious "Ablalhanalba," which is said to be a distorted palindrome of the Hebrew phrase "Av lanu [Aram., *lan*] attah," "Thou art a father to us." Prominent among the deities depicted is a certain Abraxas (or Abrasax), who is an important figure in the teachings of the Gnostics. These have therefore been termed Gnostic amulets, but the attribution is increasingly questioned by modern scholars. When these amulets came to be current in Christian circles the mysterious name *Ablalhanalba* was explained as equivalent by gematria to *Jesus.*

In many countries, written amulets are more common than any other. Among Muslims, for instance, the most popular type is a small case containing excerpts from the Qurʾān or a list of the ninety-nine epithets of God. The Copts use pictures illustrating the defeat of a monster by Saint George of Lydda, and the Ethiopians, scrolls relating the praises of the Virgin Mary, or grotesque representations of the divine eye or face. This, however, by no means precludes the use of ornamental amulets. Christians most often carry miniature crosses or crucifixes, but equally common is the written legend "Sator Arepo," which is really "Paternoster" spelled cryptically.

The Japanese use, besides relics, two forms of amulet that deserve mention. One of these is an image, painted on pillows, of an animal who swallows bad dreams. The other amulet is a pair of dead sardines affixed to a stick of holly at the entrance to a house to keep away noxious spirits at the annual festival of Setsubun. (This finds a parallel in the use of garlic elsewhere.)

The use of colors in amulets is influenced also in medieval magic by the belief that they carry the charisma of the sun, moon, and the seven planets. Thus, yellow stones (amber, topaz) bear the "influence" of the sun; whitish stones (diamond, mother-of-pearl), of the moon; red stones (ruby), of Mars; green stones (emerald), of Venus; black stones (jet, onyx, obsidian), of Saturn; and so forth. Moreover, each stone "controlled" a specific condition. Agate, in Italy, is deemed efficacious against the evil eye, and in Syria against intestinal disorders. Crystal cures dropsy and toothache; diamond neutralizes poisons and also averts thunderstorms. Furthermore, gems promote human passions and affections. Beryl gives hope; carbuncle, energy and assurance; ruby, love; and of coral it is said that it fades when a friend dies. There is also a stone for every month, and these are often featured in brooches inscribed with zodiacal signs portraying a person's horoscope.

Lastly, with regard to the use of exotic objects as amulets and talismans, a curious fact is worth mentioning. Many years ago the present writer had occasion to examine a number of ceremonial costumes worn by African shamans and found that several of them included a pouch worn on the breast. Opening these, he discovered that their contents consisted mainly of European hairpins, scissors, cigarette butts, London omnibus tickets, and similar foreign paraphernalia deemed magical.

Like myths and popular tales, the actual forms of amulets migrate from one culture to another as the result of trade relations, conquests, importation of captives, intermarriage, voyages, and the like, but new meanings are then read into them in order to accommodate them to the beliefs and traditional lore of those who adopt them. Thus (as we have said) the hexagram became to Jews the shield of David, the cross to Christians a symbol of Christ, and the dung-rolling beetle (heper) to the Egyptians the emblem of the creator god Hepera and the pellet as the orb of the sun that he rolled across the sky. It is necessary, therefore, in interpreting these vehicles of magic, to get behind such particular local explanations of them and to attempt to recover their underlying, subliminal significance. This approach, however, is inevitably fraught with the perils of subjectivism and has led, indeed, to any number of psychological fantasies and absurdities. But *abusus non tollit usum;* a spurious coin does not invalidate currency, and the basic nature of amulets will never be understood unless the attempt is made to do so.

SEE ALSO Images; Relics; Stones.

BIBLIOGRAPHY

For English readers the most serviceable survey and discussion is E. A. W. Budge's *Amulets and Talismans* (reprint, New Hyde Park, N.Y., 1961), originally entitled *Amulets and Superstitions.* Useful also is Frederick Thomas Elworthy's *The Evil Eye* (New York, 1970), although this work tends at times to go too far afield and to indulge in untenable theories. C. W. King's *The Gnostics and Their Remains, Ancient and Mediaeval,* 2d ed. (London, 1881), gives a good survey of the "Abrascas" and kindred amulets, but it is a bit antiquated in its interpretations. Arabic amulets are treated fully in Edward W. Lane's classic *An Account of the Manners and Customs of the Modern Egyptians,* 5th ed. (New York, 1973), and in Edmond Doutté's *Magie et religion dans l'Afrique du Nord* (Algiers, 1909). Jewish amulets are discussed in Joshua Trachtenberg's *Jewish Magic and Superstition* (1939; New York, 1982).

New Sources

Blair, Nancy. *Amulets of the Goddess: Oracle of Ancient Wisdom.* Oakland, Calif., 1993.

Fulghum, Mary Margaret. "Coins Used as Amulets in Late Antiquity." In *Between Magic and Religion.* See pages 139–147. Lanham, Mass., 2001.

Leland, Charles Godfrey. *Etruscan Roman Remains and the Old Religion: Gods, Goblins, Divination and Amulets* (1892). London and New York, 2002.

Tambiah, Stanley J. *Buddhist Saints of the Forest and the Cult of Amulets.* Cambridge, U.K., 1984.

Wardwell, Allen. *Tangible Visions: Northwest Coast Indian Shamanism and Its Art.* New York, 1996.

THEODOR H. GASTER (1987)
Revised Bibliography

AMUN was originally one of the eight primordial gods of Hermopolis in Middle Egypt. Together with his consort Amaunet, Amun represented the precreation chthonic aspect of "hiddenness." This pair, with the three other pairs comprising the Hermopolitan ogdoad, produced the egg from which the creator god came forth.

In the Middle Kingdom (2050–1756 BCE), when a Theban family took the throne of Egypt their local god, Montu, a war god, became assimilated with Amun and also with Min, the ithyphallic fertility god of Coptos, Thebes' neighbor and ally. This new, all-powerful, anthropomorphic god also incorporated the attributes of his predecessor, Re, the chief god of the Egyptian pantheon in the later Old Kingdom (2686–2181 BCE). Amun-Re, "king of the gods," who was sometimes represented as a ram-headed sun god, had as his consort Mut ("mother"); their son, Khonsu, was the local moon god.

The cult center and chief temple of Amun-Re, at Karnak in the Theban nome of Upper Egypt, was begun in the Middle Kingdom and was added to and greatly enlarged through the next two thousand years. This cult temple became the religious center of Egypt; it benefited greatly from the victorious campaigns of New Kingdom pharaohs (1567–1160 BCE) and eventually was controlled by a family of priests who also became kings of Egypt in the twenty-first dynasty.

Henotheistic hymns to Amun-Re were very near to the tone of Akhenaton's hymn to Aton. The so-called Amarna Revolution that Akhenaton fostered seems to have been as much a political move against the growing power of the priesthood of Amun as a religious move to supplant Amun-Re, though the reaction to Akhenaton's changes appeared as a condemnation of heresy.

The chief festivals of Amun-Re included the Opet Feast and the Beautiful Feast of the Valley. In the former the image of the god in his shrine was carried in procession on a bark between Karnak and the Luxor temple, which was known as the Southern Harem. For the Feast of the Valley, the statue of the god was ferried to the west bank of the Nile for visits at several of the royal mortuary temples and shrines in this vast Theban necropolis.

To the south of Egypt, in Nubia, devotion to Amun was at least as fervent as it was in Egypt during the Late Period. When Piye (Piankhy) conquered Egypt (c. 750 BCE) he intended to set things right for Amun in his native land. He even left his own daughter to serve as Divine Adoratress of Amun at Karnak. Some of the largest additions to the Karnak temple were made during the last native dynasties, and important additions were made by the Greek rulers after Alexander's conquest.

SEE ALSO Akhenaton.

BIBLIOGRAPHY

Otto, Eberhard. *Osiris und Amun: Kult und heilige Stätten.* Munich, 1966. Translated by Kate B. Griffiths as *Ancient Egyptian Art: The Cult of Osiris and Amon* (New York, 1967).

Sethe, Kurt H. *Amon und die acht Urgötter von Hermopolis: Eine Untersuchung über Ursprung und Wesen des ägyptischen Götterkonigs.* Berlin, 1929.

LEONARD H. LESKO (1987)

AN is the head of the Sumerian pantheon. In the initial stages of the writing system his name was represented graphically by a star, which the writers interpreted as either the actual name of the god, as the sky, or as an element indicating the divine essence (the general name to indicate god). If it was intended to emphasize the divine nature of a character, the name was prefixed with the sign of *an.* This determinative does not predate the god An, however, so that it is sometimes difficult to decide whether writers are referring to the god or the sky. The relationship between the god An and the sky has been interpreted in different ways. For some scholars An is identical with the sky; for others they are two distinct entities. The absence of the determinative before his name means, furthermore, that it is impossible to know for certain whether or not An is mentioned in the earliest list of gods, the *List of Fara* (c. 2600 BCE). This begins by mentioning *AN,* which could be understood as an element indicating divinity or as the god An whom the others follow. Scholars hold different opinions on this matter.

The Akkadian equivalent of the god An is Anu. In the earliest sources this name indicates the head of the Assyro-Babylonian pantheon, a position subsequently occupied by Marduk among the Babylonians and by Ashur among the Assyrians. In later texts he is represented by the divine number $^{d}60$, the largest number of the sexagesimal Mesopotamian system. The abstract, encompassing all the essential characteristics of Anu's role, is denoted in Akkadian texts by the term *anūtu* and only bestowed upon other gods in order to stress their particular relative importance.

The laudatory epithets of An/Anu place particular emphasis upon his position as the god and ruler of the skies, the father of the gods and supreme creator of the world, the first and most important of the cosmic triad consisting of Anu, Enlil, and Enki/Ea. An/Anu determines fate along with them. It is An/Anu who retains the original divine ordinances—the *me,* and he holds the archetypal royal insignia, which he grants to the chosen sovereign. It is not mere chance that literary texts often assert that the power of kingship descends (or descended) from the sky. According to the Code of Hammurabi, as a member of the triad, An/Anu supports the king in the exercise of power and represents part of the divine protection of curses turned upon those who break or revoke laws passed by the sovereign.

Both Sumerian and Akkadian sources constantly stress the superiority of the supreme triad, even when Marduk is elevated to head of the Akkadian pantheon. The latter did not depose the three great gods, but rather, according to the *Enuma elish,* it was they who elevated the young Marduk and chose him as their leader. The other gods revolved around this triad and their tasks were closely defined and constantly directed by the assembly of the gods, presided over by An. This divine trio devised and carried out the plans that govern heaven and earth, the microcosmos and macrocosmos—"When the gods Anu, Enlil, and Ea planned heaven and earth" (astrological series *Enuma, Anu, Enlil,* thirteenth century BCE)—and they were also in charge of omens.

Epigraphic sources frequently mention the statue of An/Anu, although as with many other gods, his exact representation is unclear. There has been some discussion as to whether he appears among relief figures of the neo-Assyrian period (probably from the reign of Sennacherib, c. 704–681 BCE) from Maltai (around 40 kilometers north of Mosul). These include a god represented standing and on the *mushhushshu* dragon, holding a rope and a hoop in his left hand. Some scholars regard this as An, others Enlil, but the fact that An is mentioned much more often than Enlil in the list of cult statues drawn up in the reign of Sennacherib certainly supports the idea that it is indeed An. The Kudurru of the Kassite period (thirteenth–eleventh centuries BCE) portray the symbol of Anu as a headdress with horns. This originally indicated generic divine status.

Understanding his role in Sumerian theo-cosmogony is complex. It is clear from diverse sources that he is a first principle, together with the earth (as well the Kur, the cosmic mountain from which every form of life originated, and the abyssal regions).

According to Jan van Dijk, who retraces the existence of two Sumerian theo-cosmongonies on the basis of the god lists from the theological schools of Nippur and Eridu, the god An did not exist *ab aeterno.* According to the theology of Nippur, before heaven and earth came into being, there existed a undeveloped world, called *uru-ul-la,* an "ancient city" that contained "life" in hidden form. The Numina who produced An (the sky), Ki (the earth), and Nammu (the flowing waters) lived here. In contrast, the school of Eridu proposed a dualist first principle, Abzu (the sweet waters) and Tiamat (the salt waters), which produced the sky, the earth, and the flowing waters.

The Sumerian literary texts relate that the earth and sky were directly connected in primordial times. Only after their separation—apparently brought about by An, regarded as the sky yet at the same time distinct from it—and their subsequent union did the actual cosmic process itself begin, bringing about the birth of life on earth, along with the birth of some of the gods who were regarded as their children, such as Enlil, Enki/Ea, Inanna, and Nergal. There is no complete list of the children of An/Anu, but the lists differ, just as he has different wives. In the Sumerian religion, Ki, Ninhursag, Urash, and Nammu are mentioned, while in Assyro-Babylonian versions, the wife of An/Anu is Antu, a name analogous to his own, but also Ishtar. The lists reflect the diverse pantheons of the cities, or their different national histories, or, ultimately, the historical development of the various kingdoms that came one after another in the Fertile Crescent.

According to a Sumerian theo-cosmogonic tradition expressed in the *Song of the Hoe,* Enlil separated the sky and the earth, and An took the sky for himself, while Enlil took the earth. It has been proposed that the tool used to effect this separation was the hoe, but this is not universally accepted (Wilcke, 1972/1975, p. 36). If it were so, it would be possible to make comparisons with the Hittite version of the *Song of Ullikummi* (c. 1200 BCE, belonging to the so-called Kumarbi cycle) and with the Greek *Theogony* of Hesiod. In the current state of scholarship, such theories do not seem tenable, since the hoe appears to have been created by Enlil not to separate the earth and sky, but to allow the creation of the human race and as a working tool for humankind, to whom it had been given. In contrast to the Sumerian texts, in the Akkadian work *Atrahasis* (1800 BCE onwards) the origin of the allocation of the sky to the god An came about via the "casting of lots" by An, Enlil, and Enki.

Still, in the realm of theo-cosmogony, the Akkadian documents, especially the god lists, provide various lists of Anu's ancestors. The two most famous are the *TCL XV* from the Old Babylonian period (nineteenth to sixteenth centuries BCE) and *An=Anum* from Babylon, which was edited during various periods from the Old Babylonian onwards. The latter opens with a list of twenty-one divine couples, "fathers and mothers of Anu," with the following section devoted to the ancestors of Enlil (forty-two in all). *TCL XV,* after a list of fourteen pairs of divine ancestors, mentions Anu, several of his epithets, and his court. Four ancestors of An also occur in the Babylonian poem *Enuma elish:* Lahmu and Lahamu, and Anshar and Kishar. Of these, only Anshar (but with the name Alla) is also mentioned in the short version, edited in Akkadian, concerning the birth of the worm.

The reference in *An=Anum* to the god A-la-la—one of the ancestors of Anu, as well as the theomachy described in *Enuma elish,* indicates that the latter work may have been linked with Hesiod's *Theogony* and the Hittite theogony known as the *Kingship in Heaven.* The Hittite text tells of a struggle for divine succession as follows: Alalu r Anu r Kumarbir the storm god. Anu is not regarded as the son of Alalu, however, while in the *An=Anum* list he is listed among Alalu's twenty-four ancestors. Furthermore, according to the Hittite text, Alalu is the father of Kumarbi, the god who castrated and overthrew Anu. Diverging from the Hittite poem, the *Enuma elish* does not describe a single removal or overthrow, in that Anu is here portrayed as the first ancestor of a divine generation that will emerge victorious in the struggle against the primordial gods, headed first by Apsu and then by Tiamat.

Only in the theological commentaries of the Achaemenid (seventh to fourth centuries BCE) and Greek periods (fourth century BCE) do the principal gods of the pantheon, including Anu, meet a violent end at the hands of Bēl-Marduk. In contrast, in the Seleucid period (fourth to first centuries BCE), Anu, Enlil, and Ea return to the head of the pantheon.

Only in two Sumerian works is the appearance of humankind upon the earth attributed to An, namely in the prologue of the *Hymn to Eengurra* and in the *Sumerian King List.* In the latter, An re-creates humankind after the flood and in conjunction with Enlil.

An/Anu was the poliad god of the city of Uruk, the seat of his main sanctuary, Eanna (house of heaven). He was also honored in other cities, such as Lagash, Ur, Dilbat, Kish, Ashur, and Nippur. It has been debated whether his cult was already in evidence during the age of Fara; it has been documented from the third millennium BCE. Even if changing events led to a diminution of its importance, though never to its complete oblivion, An's cult nonetheless remained strong until the Seleucid era. Documents of this period describe in detail his cult and the ritual of the New Year's festival of Akītu.

As far as personal theophoric names are concerned, it is difficult to retrace An's name with certainty, since it is difficult to determine whether the sign *AN* represents the sky or the god. Nonetheless, it has been found in Sumerian, Akkadian, and Aramaic theophoric sources, as well as in Hittite, Hurrite, and Ugaritic ones. As far as Sumeria is concerned, it is worth recalling that many sovereigns of the first dynasty of Lagash had the sign *AN* contained within their names. Besides, an analysis of these theophoric names shows that the god has an active role in the sphere of kingship (Bauer, 1998, pp. 514–515). This aspect brings us to the problem of the so-called inactivity of An/Anu. In the current state of scholarship, An/Anu does not seem to fall into such a category, since he has a cult, is mentioned in personal names, and is also in evidence outside of Mesopotamia. Although there is a lack of documented hymns and prayers addressed to him, he plays a full, active, and central part in the myths, even if contemporary scholars do not associate them with him. His presence is constantly seen at all the worldly events in which the gods intervene, so that he cannot be defined as an abstract and elusive god. It should also be mentioned that in a prayer for the king (RS 79.025) found at Ugarit and Emar and written in Sumerian, in the section "Blessing of Gods with their Special Gift," Anu and his gift are invoked: "May Anu satiate you (the king) with opulence of life!"

Because of his supposed inactivity, An has been likened to the Hittite god of the same name, to the Greek Uranus, and to the Ugaritic El. An shares various aspects with the Semitic El: their names contain the idea of god and the abstract shows the essential aspects of their function. Both are regarded, albeit in different ways, as the father and king of the gods, they are both the final divine court of appeal, and they both preside over the assembly of the gods. This last point is standard in Mesopotamia among the Hittites, at Ugarit, in the Bible, and in Greece (Burkert, 1999, pp. 26–27). An, as the sky, may be linked with similar cosmic entities in the Near East, in Anatolia, and in Greece, but their roles are not absolutely comparable with An's, even if in some cases they are considered divine, receive offerings, govern treaties, and are associated with swearing oaths.

SEE ALSO Mesopotamian Religions, overview article; Sky, article on Myths and Symbolism.

BIBLIOGRAPHY

Bauer, Josef. "Der vorsargonische Abschnitt der mesopotamischen Geschichte." In *Mesopotamien: Späturuk-Zeit und Früdynastische Zeit,* edited by Joseph Bauer, Robert K. Englund, and Manfred Krebernik, pp. 431–585. Fribourg, Switzerland, 1998.

Beaulieu, Paul-Alain. "Antiquarian Theology in Seleucid Uruk." *Acta sumerologica* 14 (1992): 45–75.

Black, Jeremy, and Anthony Green. *Gods, Demons, and Symbols of Ancient Mesopotamia: An Illustrated Dictionary.* London, 1992. See pages 30, 102–103.

Burkert, Walter. *Da Omero ai Magi: La tradizione orientale nella cultura Greca.* Venice, 1999.

Casadio, Giovanni. "A ciascuno il suo: Otium e negotium del dio supremo dalla Siria alla Mesopotamia." *Studi e Materiali di Storia delle Religioni* 58 (1992): 59–78.

Cliffort, Richard. *Creation Accounts in the Ancient Near East and in the Bible.* Washington, D.C., 1994.

Hutter, Manfred. "Heaven." In *Dictionary of Deities and Demons in the Bible,* edited by Karel van der Toorn, Bob Becking, and Pieter van der Horst, pp. 739–742. Leiden, 1995.

Lambert, William. "Göttergenealogie." In *Reallexikon der Assyriologie,* edited by Ernest Weidner and Wolfram von Soden, vol. 3, pp. 469–470. Berlin, 1957/1971.

Lambert, William. "Götterlisten." In *Reallexikon der Assyriologie,* edited by Ernest Weidner and Wolfram von Soden, vol. 3, pp. 473–479. Berlin, 1957/1971.

Litke, Richard. *A Reconstruction of the Assyro-Babylonian God-Lists, An: dA-nu-um and An: Anu sha ameli.* New Haven, Conn., 1998.

Pettinato, Giovanni. *Mitologia sumerica.* Turin, Italy, 2002.

Pettinato Giovanni. *Mitologia accadica.* Turin, Italy, 2003.

Tallqvist, Knut. *Akkadische Götterepitheta.* Helsinki, 1938, see pages 251–254; reprint, New York, 1974.

van Dijk, Jan. "Le motif cosmique dans la pensée sumérienne." *Acta orientalia* 28, nos. 1–2 (1964): 1–59.

Wilcke, Claus. "Hacke." In *Reallexikon der Assyriologie,* edited by Dietz Otto Ezdard, vol. 4, pp. 33–38. Berlin, 1972/1975.

SILVIA MARIA CHIODI (2005)
Translated from Italian by Paul Ellis

ANABAPTISM. *Anabaptist* comes from the Greek word meaning "rebaptizer." It was never used by the Anabaptists, for whom baptism signified the external witness of an inner faith covenant of the believer with God through Jesus Christ. Baptism was always administered in the name of the Trinity, usually by pouring water, but sometimes by sprinkling or immersion.

The Anabaptist movement had multiple origins. An earlier view saw it primarily as an effort on the part of Conrad Grebel (c. 1498–1526), Felix Mantz (c. 1498–1527), and other co-workers of Huldrych Zwingli (1484–1531), the Zurich reformer, to complete the reformation of the church. Researchers are now aware, however, of additional influences in bringing the movement to birth. These include peasant unrest brought on by social and economic injustice; the rhetoric of the fiery German peasant leader Thomas Müntzer (1488?–1525); the writings of Martin Luther (1483–1546) and, especially, Andreas Karlstadt (1480–1541); the influence of late medieval mysticism and asceticism; and the dynamics of reform in specific monasteries. Anabaptism arose as a radical reform movement out of the economic, social, political, and religious situation in early sixteenth-century Europe.

Anabaptism began formally in Zollikon, near Zurich, on January 21, 1525, when Grebel, Mantz, Georg Blaurock (c. 1492–1529), and others baptized each other on confession of faith, thus forming a separatist congregation. This event, however, was preceded by debates with Zwingli and the Zurich city council, beginning in 1523, over the nature of desired reforms. On issues like abolition of the Mass, dietary regulations, the authority of scripture over tradition, and the veneration of relics, these first Anabaptists were in complete agreement with Zwingli. Nor was infant baptism, which they believed to be contrary to scripture, a critical issue, although it had great implications for the nature of the church. The ultimate break with Zwingli concerned the authority of the city council (the state) over the church, which Zwingli affirmed and his disciples denied. The immediate and final event that precipitated the first baptismal ceremony was a decree issued by the city council demanding the baptism of all infants within eight days, on pain of banishment of the persons involved.

The (Swiss) Brethren, as the new group preferred to be called, found strong support among the people, not so much on the issue of baptism but in the Brethren's anticlericalism, their desire for local congregational autonomy, their rejection of excessive taxation, and their involvement in small Bible-study groups and other practices that met apparent spiritual needs of the people. As a result, the movement grew rapidly, and with its growth there was increasingly severe persecution. Mantz became one of the first martyrs when he was drowned in the Limmat River at Zurich in January 1527.

In 1530, Melchior Hofmann (c. 1495–1543), a widely traveled Lutheran preacher with chiliastic tendencies, came to Strasbourg, where his contacts must have included not only Swiss Brethren but also spiritualists and other "free spirits," as well as the major Strasbourg reformers Martin Bucer (1491–1551) and Wolfgang Capito (1478–1541). Hofmann left the city the same year, under the duress of the reformers and the city council, because of an inclination to Anabaptism, although it is not clear whether he himself received believers' baptism. On arrival in the northern city of Emden he soon attracted a large following, in part at least because of his apocalyptic message of the imminent return of Christ; and in a short time more than three hundred persons had been baptized. Selected leaders were ordained, and they in turn ordained others to help bring in the Kingdom.

Hofmann was pacifistic, content to await God's own time, but others armed themselves to bring in the Kingdom by force. In May 1530 there was an abortive attempt to take the city of Amsterdam. Other incidents followed. In 1534 the city of Münster in Westphalia was declared to be the New Jerusalem and fell under the control of the Melchiorites, though Hofmann himself had returned to Strasbourg and lay in prison there. In 1535 Münster fell before the onslaught of the regional bishop's troops, and most of its inhabitants were killed. The Münster episode was in large part responsible for the centuries-long designation of Anabaptism as violent and revolutionary. It was also in response to these events that Menno Simons left his nearby Roman Catholic parish and, after going underground for a time of reflection and writing, emerged as the primary leader of peaceful Anabaptism.

Meanwhile, the Swiss and South German Brethren grew in numbers even as persecution increased. As a result, many migrated to other areas, particularly Austria and Moravia. As refugees arrived, a sharing of goods with them seemed both practical and biblical. This practice began in 1529, and by 1533 it had become normative for many in the area under the leadership of Jacob Hutter (d. 1536), who made it a central article of faith. Those who followed this group became known as Hutterian Brethren, or Hutterites. Numerous congregations also emerged in south-central Germany under the leadership of Hans Hut (d. 1527), Hans Denk (c. 1500–1527), Pilgram Marpeck (d. 1556), the more radical Melchior Rink (c. 1494–1545), and others.

The variety of centers from which Anabaptists emerged and the various influences upon them make it difficult to talk about one all-encompassing faith to which all confessed. There was a great deal of pluralism. Nevertheless, there was in all the sixteenth-century Anabaptists a common core of beliefs by which they recognized one another and that in time became normative. The elements of this core came from their statements of faith, the testimony of martyrs, court records, hymns, letters, records of disputations held with authorities and others, and the writings of major leaders. The extent to which the ideals of these affirmations of faith were practiced in daily life, or were simply held as embodying an ideal vision, also varied from person to person.

In September 1524, Grebel and his friends wrote to Luther, Karlstadt, and Müntzer to seek counsel. Only the two letters to Müntzer are extant. In them several emphases are already clear: the primary authority of the scriptures; the Lord's Supper conceived as a memorial and a sign of love among believers; the importance of redemptive church discipline according to *Matthew* 18:15–18; the belief that baptism must follow a personal profession of faith and that it is a sign of such faith rather than a saving sacrament; the belief that children are saved by the redemptive work of the second Adam, Christ; a conviction that weapons of violence have no place among Christians; and the belief that the church is called to be a suffering church.

In 1527 the Anabaptists convened a conference at Schleitheim, on the Swiss-German border. The death of many early leaders led to some discontinuity with their thought and spirit. A more separatist-sectarian view emerged. Seven articles constituted the "Brotherly Union," as it was called, a statement summarizing the central issues of faith in which the framers of the statement differed from the "false brethren." Who these brethren were is not clear. The prime mover at the meeting and the author of the articles was Michael Sattler (c. 1490–1527), a former Benedictine monk from Saint Peter's monastery near Freiburg, Germany. In addition to most of the above emphases, three others were added: a radical church-world dualism that asserted complete separation of believers from all others; the importance of church order and the necessity of pastoral leadership as discerned by the congregation; and rejection of the oath as an affirmation of truth.

The other documents mentioned above amplify but do not add significant new doctrinal affirmations to the two early statements from Grebel's letter and the Brotherly Union. The primacy of the New Testament over the Old Testament is affirmed, as well as the doctrine of separation that naturally excludes participation in civil or political office. Simons stressed that the church, as the bride of Christ, must be pure; he also stressed the importance of witness and mission, which most Anabaptists took for granted as a part of discipleship. Dirk Philips (1504–1568) affirmed the ordinance of foot washing. In their verbal and written statements, most Anabaptists confirmed their intention of restoring the church to its early New Testament pattern and practice.

SEE ALSO Mennonites; Müntzer, Thomas; Simons, Menno.

BIBLIOGRAPHY

The standard reference work in English is *The Mennonite Encyclopedia,* 4 vols. (Scottdale, Pa., 1955–1959). A helpful bibliographical tool is *A Bibliography of Anabaptism, 1520–1630,* compiled by Hans J. Hillerbrand (Elkhart, Ind., 1962). In the area of historiography, James M. Stayer's "The Anabaptists," in *Reformation Europe: A Guide to Research,* edited by Steven Ozment (Saint Louis, 1982), pp. 135–159, indicates the direction of present research generally. Walter Klaassen has edited a convenient collection of source translations on most Anabaptist theological themes in his *Anabaptism in Outline* (Scottdale, Pa., 1981). For all of this literature, George H. Williams's massive *The Radical Reformation* (Philadelphia, 1962) provides an indispensable contextual framework, as does his edited volume *Spiritual and Anabaptist Writers,* "Library of Christian Classics," vol. 25 (Philadelphia, 1957). In *The Believers' Church: The History and Character of Radical Protestantism* (New York, 1968), Donald F. Durnbaugh places the various movements within Anabaptism into a narrower and more definitive context.

CORNELIUS J. DYCK (1987)

ANĀHITĀ. Along with Mithra and Ahura Mazdā, Anāhitā is one of the major divinities of ancient Iran. Her cult grew from the Achaemenid to the Parthian period and extended beyond Iran during the rule of the Sasanids. In Armenia and in Asia Minor it flourished near Persian communities and was spread through the syncretic and eclectic activities of the Magi. As the Iranian great goddess, Anāhitā has multivalent characteristics: she is the divinity of royalty, of war, and of fertility, with which she is especially associated (Dumézil, 1947).

As Herodotos testifies, Anāhitā was of foreign origin, Assyrian and Arab. This is confirmed by the fact that her cult was not aniconic: according to Berossus, Artaxerxes II (404–359 BCE) proclaimed the cult of the goddess throughout the empire, erecting statues of her. The Mesopotamian Ishtar, the divinity of the planet Venus, and the Elamite Nanā certainly exerted a strong influence on her development.

Anāhitā is an amalgam of an Iranian or Indo-Iranian divinity, the spirit of the waters that run down from the mythical Mount Harā, and the great goddess of Near Eastern tradition. Perhaps originally named *Harahvatī ("rich in waters"), she is analogous to the Indian goddess Sarasvatī (Lommel, 1954). The Avesta mentions the *yazata* Aredvī Sūrā Anāhitā—a name comprising three designations that reflect her multivalent character: "moist, strong, immaculate"—to whom the important hymn "of the waters" (*Yashts* 5) is dedicated. Achaemenid inscriptions, beginning with Artaxerxes II, invoke Anāhitā along with Mithra and Ahura Mazdā. Classical sources, especially Strabo, document the importance of the goddess's cult in the Parthian period. She had many Greek interpretations: from Aphrodite Ourania to Hestia, from Artemis to Athena.

Anāhitā gained in importance with the accession of the Sasanids, linked by tradition to the goddess's sanctuary at Stakhr, in Fārs. According to various sources at our disposal (Syriac, Armenian, and Arabic), the warlike character and regal nature of the great goddess are prominent under Sasanid rule. She appeared at the sovereigns' investiture (Göbl, 1960) and played a major role, not inferior to that of Ōhrmazd himself, as royal divinity, the source and protector of sovereignty.

SEE ALSO Sarasvatī.

Bibliography

Boyce, Mary. "Bībī Shahrbānū and the Lady of Pārs." *Bulletin of the School of Oriental and African Studies* 30 (1967): 30–44.

Boyce, Mary. "Iconoclasm among the Zoroastrians." In *Christianity, Judaism and Other Greco-Roman Cults,* edited by Jacob Neusner, vol. 4, pp. 93–111. Leiden, 1975.

Boyce, Mary. *A History of Zoroastrianism,* vol. 2. Leiden, 1982.

Boyce, Mary, and Frantz Grenet. *A History of Zoroastrianism,* vol. 3. Leiden, 1991.

Chaumont, Marie-Louise. "Le culte d'Anāhitā à Staxr et les premiers Sassanides." *Revue de l'histoire des religions* 153 (1958): 154–175.

Chaumont, Marie-Louise. "Le culte de la déesse Anāhitā (Anahit) dans la religion des monarques d'Iran et d'Arménie au premier siècle de notre ère." *Journal asiatique* 253 (1965): 167–181.

de Jong, Albert. *Traditions of the Magi: Zoroastrianism in Greek and Latin Literature.* Leiden, 1997.

Dumézil, Georges. *Tarpeia.* Paris, 1947.

Gnoli, Gherardo. "Politica religiosa e concezione della regalità sotto i Sassanidi." In *La Persia nel Medioevo,* pp. 225–253. Rome, 1971.

Gnoli, Gherardo. "Politica religiosa e concezione della regalità sotto gli Achemenidi." In *Gururājamañjarikā: Studi in onore di Giuseppe Tucci,* pp. 23–88. Naples, 1974.

Göbl, Robert. "Investitur im sasanidischen Iran und ihre numismatische Bezeugung." *Wiener Zeitschrift für die Kunde des Morgenlandes (Festschrift Herbert W. Duda)* 56 (1960): 36–51.

Gray, Louis H. *The Foundations of the Iranian Religions.* Bombay, 1930.

Hoffmann, Georg, ed. *Auszüge aus syrischen Akten persischer Märtyrer.* Leipzig, 1880.

Lommel, Herman. "Anāhitā-Sarasvatī." In *Asiatica: Festschrift Friedrich Weller,* pp. 404–413. Leipzig, 1954.

Ringbom, Lars I. *Zur Ikonographie der Göttin Ardvi Sura Anāhitā.* Turku, 1957.

Shepherd, Dorothy G. "The Iconography of Anāhitā." *Berytus* 28 (1980): 47–86.

Wikander, Stig. *Feuerpriester in Kleinasien und Iran.* Lund, 1946.

Gherardo Gnoli (1987)
Translated from Italian by Roger DeGaris

ANALYTIC PHILOSOPHY. In a broad sense, the practice of seeking better understanding through the analysis (i.e., the breaking down and restatement) of complex, obscure, or problematic linguistic expressions has been present within philosophy from its pre-Socratic origins to the present. More narrowly considered, analytic philosophy ("linguistic analysis") is a style of philosophizing originating within twentieth-century English-language philosophy and drawing much of its inspiration from the later thought of Ludwig Wittgenstein (1889–1951).

The remote ancestry of analytic philosophy is well illustrated in the dialogues of Plato, where Socrates is shown to be concerned with delineating the meaning of key concepts like "piety," "justice," or "soul." In the *Phaedo,* Socrates, in one of his last moments with his disciples, is shown teasing Crito about the corrupting power of familiar but misleading language. Crito has asked how Socrates should be buried. Socrates points out that one should not confuse the person designated "Socrates" with his body and thus should not speak of burying a "you," a person. Unanalyzed speech, as in this case, Socrates warns, can lead to unreflective materialism in thought and life. A major strand or concern in the rest of the history of Western philosophy can be read in a similar light, as overt or covert analysis of language.

The more immediate origins of analytic philosophy, however, lie in the reaction of British philosophers at the beginning of the twentieth century against the then-dominant Hegelianism of such thinkers as F. H. Bradley (1846–1924), who placed all emphasis on finding meaning in the "whole" rather than any partial expressions and thus placed in jeopardy, it was feared, all finite human understanding. Leaders in the attempt to counter the exaggerated stress on "synthesis" with clarifying analyses of philosophical obscurities were G. E. Moore (1873–1958) and Bertrand Russell (1872–1970). Moore, appealing to "common sense" arguments, provided detailed ordinary language analyses of such important terms as "good" and what it means to have "certain knowledge" of something. Russell, on the other hand, offered more technical translations, using the symbolic logic he had created with Alfred North Whitehead to express, for instance, his "theory of definite descriptions" as a means of analyzing problematic sentences about nonexistent but still meaningful entities (like "Hamlet" or "the present king of France") and thereby of removing puzzlements and paradoxes.

To this philosophical context Ludwig Wittgenstein, a former student of Russell's, returned in 1929, to Cambridge from Vienna, fresh from conversations with members of the Vienna Circle, with whom he had helped to develop the logical rule ("the verification principle of meaning") that the meaning of all nontautological statements is to be identified with the method of their sensory verification. Wittgenstein's *Tractatus logico-philosophicus* (completed in 1918 and first published in 1921) had carried to its limit the quest for a powerful and simple formalization of ideal language, rooting all factual meaning in basic propositions naming atomic facts. These ultimate simples had later been identified with sensory observations by the radical empiricists of the Vienna Circle in the creation of logical positivism. Now Wittgenstein began to have misgivings, not only about the empirical interpretation given to his more general theory of language but also about the theory itself. In its simplicity lay its great power, but its application in logical positivism showed also its oversimplicity when compared to the many actual uses of human language—for instance, in asking, thanking, cursing, greeting, praying. The assertion of sensorily verifiable fact, Wittgenstein saw, is only one among a vast range of functions of language. Such a function is doubtless of great importance in natural science and in ordinary life, but even such an important function hardly begins to exhaust the richness of speech.

Wittgenstein's subsequent meditations on the limitations of his own *Tractatus* and on the rich complexity of language, published posthumously in 1953 as *Philosophical Investigations* (henceforth abbreviated as *PI*), were enormously influential, particularly after World War II. Philosophically puzzling expressions, Wittgenstein contends, did not need verification so much as analysis of their use. In the use would be found the meaning. "Look at the sentence as an instrument," he advises, "and at its sense as its employment" (*PI*, 421). In this way philosophical confusions can be eliminated by the method of returning a puzzling expression to its origins in ordinary use. "The confusions which occupy us arise when language is like an engine idling, not when it is doing work" (*PI*, 132). This method will not involve the application of a single procrustean technique, like the verification principle, but a generally open attitude toward the various uses that language may be given. Thus philosophical method will be fitted to each occasion. "There is not *a* philosophical method, though there are indeed methods, like different therapies" (*PI*, 133). Wittgenstein liked and repeated his therapeutic analogy: "The philosopher's treatment of a question is like the treatment of an illness" (*PI*, 255).

The application of this style of philosophical analysis to theological and religious speech differs in tenor depending on whether the assumption is made that theological discourse is, ipso facto, an "idling" form of language or whether it is capable of "doing work." If the former, then the "therapy" called for might be termed "eliminative analysis." If the latter, however, then the point of analysis will be to show what sort or sorts of "work" constitute the meaning of theological utterances. These, which might be termed "illuminative analyses," further divide according to the range of functions found.

For the most part the philosophical climate created by linguistic analysis is not hospitable to eliminative analysis. Such an enterprise would bear too much resemblance to the pugnacious days of logical positivism. Indeed, most attempts to show that a "systematic misuse of language" necessarily infects theological talk, and that people should not talk that way, rest on verificationist assumptions. On the other hand, "illuminative" analysis can be perceived by believers as no less threatening than eliminative analysis if the linguistic functions identified are too meager to accord with the user's own sense of the dignity or importance—or intent—of the speech-act involved. The logical positivists themselves had granted at least that the utterances of religious people perform the function of expressing or evoking emotion. The shift to linguistic analysis from logical positivism called for penetration. As Wittgenstein himself said: "What am I believing in when I believe that men have souls? What am I believing in, when I believe that this substance contains two carbon rings? In both cases there is a picture in the foreground, but the sense lies far in the background; that is, the application of the picture is not easy to survey" (*PI*, 422).

One answer attempting to penetrate beyond the logical positivist's analysis of religious utterance as merely emotive was offered in 1955 by R. B. Braithwaite (b. 1900) after his conversion to Christianity. Though remaining a philosophical empiricist, and on such grounds finding it impossible to affirm the doctrines of his religion in a traditional sense of belief, Braithwaite suggested that Christian speech can in fact function otherwise, by making and supporting ethical commitments to the "agapeistic" way of life. Images of Christian love (agapē) are vividly presented in the sacred writings, all of which, he claimed, refer to or reduce to the love commandment. Uttering words from these writings is not like asserting a matter of fact—though the form of the words may suggest this—but is committing oneself to a way of life authoritatively pictured in these stories. Such is the legitimate "work" of religious speech, which thus supplies the needed "application of the picture."

Braithwaite's analysis, though not widely accepted as adequate to the full functioning of Christian language, showed how a more flexible approach to "how we do things with words" could be applied to the theological context. The highly regarded Oxford philosopher J. L. Austin (1911–1960) further spurred such attempts with his stress on the "performative" significance of language. His influence brought much attention to the fact that sometimes we are not so much describing the world as performing in it when we speak: making promises, uttering commands, taking oaths, naming, bidding at auctions, pronouncing marriage vows, accepting invitations, and the like. In Canada, Donald Evans (b. 1927) offered a detailed account of religious speech, demonstrating the logic of "self-involvement" as performative.

To such analyses were added others aiming to show how the belief-statements of theology might also play an important role, though not, of course, in making simple empirical claims. R. M. Hare (1919–2002), in Oxford, provided an analysis of religious belief-statements as "bliks," or unshakable preconditions for seeing the world in a certain way. Some "bliks" might be insane, as in delusional paranoia, but others might be both sane and essential, as in the conviction that the world is causally bound together in a regular way. Neither kind is falsifiable, like an empirical hypothesis, but either may function to shape a world-picture within which particular empirical observations make sense in one way or another. Likewise John Wisdom (1904–1993), at Cambridge, stressed the way in which certain utterances, though not themselves factual, may direct attention to patterns in the facts that otherwise might be missed. A metaphor of the Taj Mahal, applied to a woman's hat, could change not the facts but the way the facts were seen; the metaphor of the world as a garden could have a similar effect in directing attention to patterns among the facts of everyday life as well as in influencing attitudes toward them.

Such analyses of the heuristic power of theological images, especially if they are taken (as with Wisdom) as illuminating or (with Hare) as potentially sane or insane, go far toward reestablishing theological discourse, with regard to at least one aspect of its "work," as making claims that could be supported or attacked in normative ways. That such claims are often in fact intended by religious believers had long been evident to any analyst who might care to ask (or to participate in) the community of religious-language users; but, perhaps because of the legacy of logical positivism's animosity to metaphysics, some analytical philosophers were slow to shake the curious supposition that analyses of linguistic use might proceed as though the intentions of the primary users could be ignored or corrected. Genuine analysis aims at revealing, not changing, what the user is doing with words.

A linguistic philosophy that is not tied to an a priori supposition that certain functions of speech, such as metaphysical ones, are "impossible" will be hospitable to all the various sorts of "work" that are done by religious utterances. These will include, among others, factual claims (e.g., "The Shroud of Turin dates from early in the first millennium AD"), historical claims (e.g., "Ramses III was the pharaoh of the Exodus"), poetic utterances (e.g., "My yoke is easy, and my burden is light"), ethical prescriptions (e.g., "Turn the other cheek"), parables, folk tales, and complex theoretical doctrines. Several functions may be performed by a single type of utterance. Telling the parable of the prodigal son under certain circumstances, for example, may involve at the same time the act of self-commitment to a way of life, the receiving of emotional support, the expression of remorse and hope for personal forgiveness, and the affirmation of a doctrine of God's nature. Standing in church and reciting an ancient creed, on the other hand, may sometimes function more as a ritual of group-membership and reverence for continuity with the past than as an assertion. Part of the work of linguistic philosophy as applied to religion is to clarify the subtle differences between these functions and to help the users themselves see more clearly the range of lively possibilities afforded by their speech.

At least in some important cases, as we have seen, religious discourse makes claims and bears resemblances to other putatively referential speech. This was acknowledged by Wittgenstein in the passage (*PI*, 422), cited above, in which he compared belief in the soul with belief in carbon rings. In both cases a model, or a "picture," must be connected by indirect means to a sense that lies "far in the background." Another part of the work of linguistic philosophy, therefore, is to trace the similarities and differences between such puzzling cases. Perhaps the vivid poetical "pictures" of religious first-order discourse provide conceptual parallels to the scientific models "in the foreground" that interpret theoretical concepts functioning to unify and illuminate experience. If so, the range of relevant data to be organized is typically much broader for religious concepts, since scientific concepts—though often less open to observational verification or falsification than the logical positivists had claimed—are always kept deliberately close to some specifiable observational domain. This is typically not the case with the "omnirelevant" concepts of theology. Another key difference is that the sacred stories, myths, and "pictures" of religious thinking play a more important, historically and valuationally primary, role in the discourse of religious communities than do models in scientific discourse. Both considerations help one understand why religious concepts are not used to make readily falsifiable claims. At the same time, however, such considerations show that theological theory based on the imagery of primary religious speech may function to aid in efforts of conceptual synthesis, the attempt to hold together a unifying world-picture that is both theoretically intelligible and framed in terms of sacred values.

Linguistic analysis is not merely "about language," then, as one unfortunate misconception would have it. The aim of analytic philosophy pursued in the spirit of the later Wittgenstein is to illuminate the varied functions of speech and the many meanings of "meaning." Its efforts are spent in allowing whatever is said to be said more effectively and with greater awareness for both speaker and listener. Like all philosophy, it is engaged in the serious exercise of consciousness-raising. This does not entail, of course, that analytic philosophy must somehow "oppose" movements toward conceptual synthesis. All of metaphysics and much of science are engaged in conceptual synthesis. Just as analysis is identifiable from the beginning as a major strand or concern in Western philosophy, so also is the quest for synthesis found in all periods. Mature analytic philosophy recognizes that analysis and synthesis need one another as poles in never-ceasing interaction. Overweening claims on behalf of synthesis helped to stimulate analytic philosophy early in the twentieth century, but similar overweening attitudes, though sometimes unfortunately encountered today, have no proper place among the analysts who themselves have become dominant in English-speaking philosophy.

For theologians, as for simple religious believers, then, there is nothing to fear and much to be gained from analytical philosophy. Properly construed, linguistic analysis claims only at lifting to clarity and self-awareness the complex and powerful human acts of speech. Sometimes, no doubt, self-awareness may lead some persons in good conscience to a questioning of hitherto unreflective uses of speech, perhaps to a restatement, perhaps even to abandonment. At other times self-awareness may allow for ever more meaningful reaffirmations. Analytic philosophy is not a doctrine either in favor of or opposed to religious belief or metaphysical thinking. Its prime objective is, in the Socratic mood, the prevention of intellectual confusion due to language and the consequent "corruption of the soul."

See Also Logical Positivism; Socrates; Wittgenstein, Ludwig.

BIBLIOGRAPHY

The indispensable book for understanding analytic philosophy is Ludwig Wittgenstein's *Philosophical Investigations*, 2d ed. (Oxford, 1968); it is a posthumously published compilation of Wittgenstein's thoughts from various years after 1929, many of which (part 1) were prepared by him for publication in 1945 but were not actually brought out at that time. For a useful aid to the understanding of Wittgenstein's philosophy and the *Investigations*, see part 2 of George Pitcher's *The Philosophy of Wittgenstein* (Englewood Cliffs, N. J., 1964). A succinct history of the transition to analytic philosophy can be found in J. O. Urmson's *Philosophical Analysis: Its Development between the Two World Wars* (Oxford, 1956). Good examples of the analytical style on general topics are represented in J. L. Austin's *How to Do Things with Words*, 2d ed., edited by J. O. Urmson (Cambridge, Mass., 1975), and Gilbert Ryle's *Dilemmas* (1954; reprint, Cambridge, 1966). Specifically directed to cosmological and religious issues, the book *Metaphysical Beliefs* (London, 1957), by Stephen Toulmin, Ronald W. Hepburn, and Alasdair MacIntyre, offers three rather extended treatments, all with a critical stance. Tending to show the use of analysis in defense of religious concerns are the essays in *Faith and Logic: Oxford Essays in Philosophical Theology*, edited by Basil Mitchell (London, 1957). The application of performative analysis to theological questions is shown in Donald D. Evans's *The Logic of Self-Involvement: A Philosophical Study of Everyday Language with Special Reference to the Christian Use of Language about God as Creator* (London, 1963). A treatment of the emergence of analytic philosophy from logical positivism and the possibilities for constructive theological applications of functional rather than verificational analysis may be found in my *Language, Logic and God* (New York, 1961).

New Sources

Badious, Alain, Oliver Feltham, and Justin Clemens, eds. *Infinite Thought: Truth and the Return to Philosophy*. New York, 2003.

Dejnozka, Jan. *The Ontology of the Analytic Tradition and Its Origins: Realism and Identity in Frege, Russell, Wittgenstein, and Quine*. Lanham, Md., 1996.

Heck, Richard, Jr., and Michael Dummett, eds. *Language, Thought, and Logic: Essays in Honour of Michael Dennett*. Oxford, 1998.

Levine, Michael P. "Contemporary Christian Analytic Philosophy of Religion: Biblical Fundamentalism, Terrible Solutions to a Horrible Problem, and Hearing God." *International Journal for Philosophy of Religion* 48 (October 2000): 89–119.

Prado, C. G., ed. *A House Divided: Comparing Analytical and Continental Philosophy*. Amherst, N.Y., 2003.

Schneewind, J. B. "Recovering the Pastness of the Past." *Journal of Religious Ethics* 28 (June 2000): 285–294.

Smith, Quentin. *Ethical and Religious Thought in Analytic Philosophy of Language*. New Haven, 1998.

FREDERICK FERRÉ (1987)
Revised Bibliography

ANAMNESIS.

The close tie of philosophical inquiry with theological and religious thinking points to a wide realm of meaning to which the term *anamnesis* ("recollection") could be applied. In many ways anthropogonic and cosmogonic theories everywhere can be interpreted as recollections of a communal group about its origins, the origins of the universe, the existing world, and the role of humankind in it. We find mythical tales of this kind in social groups everywhere, along with related ritual action. Both forms of recollection, the recital and the dramatic performance and re-creation of events in the beginning of time, can be seen as forms of the mythology of remembering. In order to be able to use the term *anamnesis* for such commemorative and re-creative acts, a careful analysis of the connotations of recollection in Plato's philosophical system is indispensable.

PLATO'S EPISTEMOLOGY OF REMEMBERING AND ITS THEOLOGICAL BASIS. Plato's doctrine about the nature of the soul and its connection to the notion of the realm of ideal forms are both intertwined with the key concept of recollection. The Greek term *anamnēsis* achieves its specific meaning of "recollection" in the dialogues of Plato as that particular faculty of the soul that enables it to remember those things that it has seen when residing in the realm of eternal forms or Ideas; it is, as Plato formulates this vision, "recollection of the things formerly seen by our soul when it traveled in the divine company" (*Phaedrus* 249b). However, through repeated incarnations in new bodies (metempsychosis, "soul migration," or, rather, metensomatosis, "reembodiment") the soul forgets most of the things it has seen or contemplated in the divine sphere, as mortal bodies with their imperfections, base desires, and passions dull the sensibilities of the soul that is chained to, and thus takes on a portion of, the nature or characteristics of the material bodies. As Plato puts it through the voice of Socrates in the *Phaedo*, forgetting begins because the soul is "nailed to the body through pleasure and pain" (*Phaedo* 83d).

Thus the true knowledge of the things seen by the soul between different incarnations or materializations in consecutive bodies is never quite lost; it is hidden but still latently there, and it can be regained, recovered, brought to consciousness. It is at this point that the true vocation of the philosopher comes to the fore, because it is through his methodical questioning that the philosopher can recover such eternal truths that are beyond the varied sense experiences and thus lead the intelligent soul away from the world of varied opinions (*doxa*) to that form of true knowledge (*noēsis* or *epistēmē*) that is beyond the empirical world and that concerns the very essence of things, which is eternal, indivisible, and pure, being removed from birth and decay, from becoming, and from the temporal and spatial contingencies of all matter. The philosopher, who in Plato's thought has special abilities and is gifted through his search for eternal truths (a giftedness that, as shall be seen, has specific implications for the forms that the reincarnation of philosophers takes, thus setting him apart from the rest of humankind), can make people aware of their divine ancestry through his method of questioning, the art of midwifery (maieutic art) referred to by Socrates in the *Theaetetus.* Plato starts his reasoning with the analogy of the normal working of our memory when the mind is "pregnant" or "in labor with" a thought that presses to awareness or "birth." The philosopher as midwife merely brings the thoughts to full consciousness; he does not put into the mind anything that was not there already. We therefore do not learn new things about this world from the investigations of existing matter through reflection about sense experiences, arriving at generalizations (as Aristotle would later teach); we only recollect what we always knew.

Plato thus puts humankind in a middle position between the category of all-knowing gods (after all, Zeus had swallowed Metis, intelligence personified, as the theogony of Hesiod relates and as diverse Orphic theogonies were to mythologize about the nature of the gods later) and the category of animals who have souls but do not participate in intelligence. Plato thus also answers the logical dilemma posed first by the Sophists who had maintained that either we know what we are looking for, and thus we do not need to search, or we do not know what we are trying to find and we are therefore doomed to eternal ignorance. Plato rejects the "either-or" of ignorance versus complete knowledge to which humankind would be condemned; he deals in degrees of knowledge. For Plato the device of anamnesis therefore becomes the cornerstone for the two major assertions that he puts forward in the *Phaedo* dialogue: one is the assertion that humankind has the ability to know the essence and form of things in their true reality of divine origin and that there are essences behind the contingent things of the world of the senses; the other is that there is an indivisible soul substance that participates in the divine sphere, a soul that descends from that sphere into embodiment and returns to that divine realm after death.

Before entering into a discussion of the reasoning that Plato employs to prove the existence of the metaphysical, eternal kingdom of forms or ideas, it is useful to remind ourselves of the main aim of his philosophical enterprise. It has often been assumed that the main purpose of Plato was to establish a tightly reasoned scheme for the foundation of knowledge, a knowledge understood as the theoretical justification for science. However, as Romano Guardini (1943) and others have pointed out, Plato does not look for an idealist (or rather realist) epistemology for its own sake. Rather, Plato's whole endeavor is aimed at a reality that goes beyond the knowledge that can be gained through the analysis of material forces. Furthermore, the knowledge he is aiming for is that knowledge that is a virtue, namely wisdom, and this implies the search for the original constitution of things beyond their shifting and variable appearances. The knowledge that is wisdom, being aware of its divine origin or model of which the material representations are but mirror images, would lead ultimately to the virtue that becomes the foundation stone for an ethics of action in this world, namely the knowledge of truth.

What appears at first sight as a specious argument about the reality of generalizations such as those about values or virtues (justice, goodness, truth) that are not tangible in this world of the senses becomes finally a guide for action for those who have achieved the vision of the eternal forms, in particular of the ultimate virtue, wisdom, through divine inspiration. As Plato expresses it in the *Meno,* virtues are not that kind of knowledge that can be taught (as the Sophists had argued) but a knowledge that is inherent in the soul and can be recovered through recollection (these are the implications of the conclusions in *Meno* 98d–e). Knowledge does start with experience, but it does not derive from it, particularly not that knowledge that concerns the virtues. It is rather a knowledge, as Plato puts it, "which we own from our background" (*oikeia epistēmē; Phaedo* 75). We see again that the foundations of such ultimate knowing are put into the sphere of the divine through the still unproved hypothesis about the nature of the soul, its origin and fate before and after death of the earthly body.

Taken from this vantage point, the suggestion put forward by Guardini (that Plato's notion about the immortality of the soul and the concomitant notion that the soul is only passing through the stages of corporeal incarnation in order to arrive at its true home denigrate historicity and the uniqueness of the individual's existence) seems not quite as pronounced when the ethical orientation of Plato is taken into consideration. If a person through recollection can find the insight and vision of the ultimate foundations of virtues, he would, so Plato repeatedly argues, strive to fulfill the requirements of a virtuous life. Besides, as we will see, Plato also holds out different fates for each soul, according to its conduct in this life, in regard to the form and duration of reincarnations.

We thus see that in the dialogues of the middle period (from the *Meno* and *Symposium* to the *Phaedo, Phaedrus,* and *Republic*) the search for the foundations of the knowing subject (the soul with intelligence and possessed with a drive to find its home) as well as of the known things (the objects in the tangible world as well as the generalizations of the mind, namely the virtues), of the subject and object of the epistemological equation, are but the tools for establishing the truth about the reality of the divine sphere and the grounding of subject and object in it. When this has happened and when the total structure of reality is known, action would be informed by this insight. For Plato the proof of the ability and effectiveness of *anamnēsis* as a faculty of the soul and mind of humankind therefore becomes the key for the proof of the kingdom of ideal forms and of ultimate truth.

The focal point, where the argument about the immortality of the soul and its reincarnations is joined to the proof through the notion of *anamnēsis,* occurs in the dialogue that is set around the occasion of the imminent death of Socrates, the *Phaedo.* Socrates has just proved by analogy that the soul is immortal, everlasting, and reincarnated in successive bodies: in much the same way, as the unity of the personality is still there through the various stages of sleep and waking, the soul must be a unifying principle surpassing birth and death. It just participates for a while in the life of mortal matter but discards the body like a worn garment and returns from where it came.

Socrates uses the further analogy that if there were only a movement from birth to death, all life would come to an end. There must be a countermovement from death to life, and this is the reincarnation of the soul after death into new bodies (*Phaedo* 70c–72a). Plato reformulates here insights that were common stock since the teachings of Empedocles and Heraclitus about the impermanence of things, of the constant change of conditions and aggregates, and about the cyclical repetition of natural processes, an impermanence of the world of experience that, however, has an underlying unchanging structure. While Ionian nature philosophy looked for the underlying permanency in the laws of matter, Plato makes the radical change by asserting that what is permanent is the perceiving subject and at the same time the ideal form behind the empirical reality. Since matter is perpetually dying and being reborn in different form, Plato declares that a permanent reality can only be an immaterial one that is only accessible to pure thought.

It is now up to Plato, through the words of Socrates, to prove these assertions. Kebes, one of the dialogue partners, gives him the entry by referring to Socrates' often-used adage that "learning is nothing but remembering" (*Phaedo* 72e). This refers to the previous experiment, where Socrates had an untutored slave arrive at the proof of a Pythagorean mathematical paradigm (*Meno* 82ff.). The objects of mathematics are similar to the moral forms, the virtues, and it is indeed these that Plato recognizes as having the necessary attributes. As Cornford pointed out, this implies that memory, which contains such knowledge, cannot be a personal or individual memory but must by necessity be an impersonal memory: all individuals can potentially arrive at the same truth, the only difference being to which extent the latent knowledge has been recovered (Cornford, 1952, p. 56). This might imply that Plato's notion of the soul as perceiving agent is akin to the Hindu proposition (of the Upaniṣads) that the *ātman* (personal soul) and *brahman* (universal soul) are identical. As shall be shown, there are some reservations with this view, as Plato also has recourse to the myth of retribution after death and to the karmic notion of the influence of the conduct in the present lifetime upon the form of reincarnation, as extolled in the *Phaedrus.*

Before embarking upon that discussion, I shall return to the *Phaedo,* where Socrates now resumes his proof about the latent memory of the soul: he states that our ability to discern equal things (and contrasts as well) presupposes the idea of equality itself (or of sameness and difference). In the same way as there is no empirical equivalent to a geometrical form (as proved in the *Meno*), there are no two things in our empirical world that are exactly the same. But the sight of approximately equal things revives the thought of perfect equality, the knowledge of which must be inborn, be previous to sense experience (*Phaedo* 75c–76d). This part of the discussion of anamnesis ends in the assertion that the essence of the soul is of the same kind as the essence of the object of thought processes, the idea. True knowledge surpasses the empirical in two ways: from its object, it is the idea; from its subject, it is the pure thought of the soul, both being non-empirical, immortal, indivisible, and indestructible (*Phaedo* 79a–c).

GNOSTICISM, MANICHAEISM, SUFISM, AND QABBALAH. Plato's thought system underwent various modifications in the following centuries that cannot be followed here in a systematic manner. Under the impact of Oriental religions and influenced by Christian soteriology, Hellenistic thinking brought forth a number of doctrines that occupied themselves much with the question of the nature of the soul and its relation to the body as well as with its fate after death. These various doctrines, which in the first few centuries after the beginning of the Common era were considered by the Church Fathers as a dangerous challenge to Christian orthodoxy, are generally labeled the Gnostic movement. The aim of this many-sided movement of speculative thought was cogently summed up in the following statement: gnosis is "the knowledge of who we were, what we have become, where we were, into what place we have been thrown . . . what is birth, what is rebirth" (Clement, *Excerpta ex Theodoto* 78.2).

Although the term *gnōsis* connotes "knowledge," the Gnostics meant by it not the intellectual process but rather wisdom gained through mystical insight or enlightenment by an immediate vision of truth. For the Gnostics, this knowledge was designed to help to liberate as well as to redeem mankind from its confinement in a material world. For those men who possessed the knowledge of the true nature of the world and of the soul, the knowledge itself is the redeeming factor, or as one of the tractates found at Nag Hammadi expressed it, if anyone has gnosis, he knows from where he comes and where he goes, and, so the *Gospel of Truth* continues, "he knows like someone who was drunk and has become sober from his drunkenness, and, restored again to himself, has again set his own in order." The same text refers to ignorance as forgetfulness and annihilation. The Gnostics believed that there were three diverse classes of people: the elect (the pneumatics or "spirituals") had divine inspiration; a second class were the psychics, who possessed soul but as yet no insight; the third class, the carnal ones, were beyond redemption.

Without delving deeper into the often contradictory tales of cosmogony and anthropogony that the diverse Gnostic schools developed, the basic doctrine is one of the fall of parts of the light through error, variously attributed, into the world of matter and coming to rest in primordial man. The whole soteriology of the Gnostic movements is then concerned with the reascent of the light to its original source. However, the soul, which is the light particle lost in the world of matter, cannot achieve this ascent unaided, because she is drunken or asleep, as the abundant metaphorical images put it. To this purpose the godhead sends out the redeemer, identified with Christ in Christian circles.

It is the prerogative of the adherent of the Gnostic movement to be awakened, to have insight into the process of the fall of the light and the redemption attempt of Christ. However, he has to prove his mettle in the fight in this world, in his fight with matter, in particular against the snares and traps of bodily passions. The purpose of all the ascetic practices with which Gnosticism abounds is the training of the spiritual or pneumatic aspects of oneself for the final ascent to the divine light (Gr. *plērōma*). One of the major doctrines of most Gnostic schools was the strong reliance on self-redemption through the insight that the soul of the elect had gained through instant revelation. It seems clear from the sources that the concept of self-redemption of the man of superior knowledge and the redemption through a helper, the redeemer sent by the deity, remained one of the points of contention between different Gnostic schools (and remains also a problem for modern research into Gnosticism).

The mythology of remembering, waking up from sleep or drunkenness, is put into different terms in the doctrines of the Manichaeans, who start from the primordial dualism of two forces, light and darkness, spirit and matter (due to Iranian-Zoroastrian influence, no doubt; see Widengren, 1961). Matter in this system desires to engulf the light, and after succeeding in the battle, light has to send out various messengers and emissaries or mercenaries who, however, get trapped by the forces of darkness. One of these emissaries is primordial man, Adam, who, when put into sleep or unconsciousness by engulfing matter, is wakened by a call from above. Here the strategies of light are finally victorious, as matter that has partaken of light and thus has the powers of light, its own enemy "ingested," as it were, is defeated from inside. But before this plan of light can succeed, matter has established its rule by creating the figure of libido or concupiscence, which through constant copulation binds the light particles to bodies (the cannibalistic and sexual stigmata that remain with humankind as reminders of their beastly descent from demonic powers). But light now sends out further emissaries to free the divine spark that is indestructibly present in Adam and humankind from the world of demons by reminding Adam and humankind of their own true essence (see Widengren, 1961; Puech, 1937).

Although the Manichaean system appears generally more clear in its exposition than other Gnostic movements, all of them are often intellectually and ritually contradictory; they remained hybrid systems due to their tendency of syncretistic merging of various religious and cultural traditions, ranging from Greek philosophy, Jewish biblical traditions, Christian eschatology, and Persian dualism (a variability reflected in the many languages in which the documents of these traditions have come down to us, from Greek to Uighur, Coptic, and Chinese). All Gnostic traditions are artificial mythologies and are a far cry from the intellectual enterprise of Plato. This was clearly perceived by the late follower of Plato, Plotinus (third century CE), for whom the world was, if not perfect, at least beautiful, and man a complete vessel, though needing perfection. The whole atmosphere of the doctrine of forgetting of the Gnostics seems often contrived and complicated as well as convoluted beyond logical needs and far indeed from the splendid vision of the power of the mind as taught by Plato, for whom the world with its beauty of bodies was after all the instigator of the drive of Eros to strive for perfection.

A far more consistent religious principle arose with the emergence of Islamic mysticism, or Sufism (*taṣaw-wuf*), in the eighth century. The original core of Sufism is the asceticism of a life in poverty through which man is better able to meditate on the Qurʾān and so to draw near to God through prayer or repetitive chanting of religious formulas. (This process is called *dhikr*, lit., "remembrance.") The formulas were accompanied by a variety of rules about body posture and breathing techniques. All these techniques aim to empty the mind so that it can be filled with the presence of God.

For most of Islamic history, the Ṣūfīs were anathema to orthodox theology, as they stressed inner qualities more than outer action, the practical example more than strict adherence to the letter of the law propounded by theologians, and the spirit of the principles of Islam more than the strict observance of ritual.

This tendency led to statements that outraged traditionalists, such as that of al-Ḥallāj, crucified in 922, who proclaimed: "I am the truth." In the same spirit, Ibn al-ʿArabī, whose work influenced the later development of Qabbalah considerably, once stated: "My heart has become capable of every form . . . a temple for idols, and the pilgrim's kaaba, and the tables of the Torah and the book of the Qurʾān. I follow the religion of love" (trans. Reynold A. Nicholson). While al-ʿArabī's statement may be interpreted as simple universalism or pantheism, in connection with the disdaining of bookish knowledge, sayings of this kind are more akin to the jolting of the mind as practiced by Daoists and Zen Buddhists, who also seek through the disorientation of habitual thinking to open the mind to ultimate truth. It is in this vein that we have to take the following statement by Abū Saʿīd of Nishapur: "Books, ye are excellent guides, but it is absurd to trouble about a guide after the goal has been reached"; or again, "I practiced recollection [*dhikr*] uninterruptedly . . . only after all these trials do we realize self-conceit" (Nicholson, 1921, pp. 15, 21). Such utterances of paradox align the Ṣūfīs squarely with the Greek Cynics; their varied expressions of the yearning for unification with the divine through love show their Platonic affinity.

The techniques of *dhikr* were intended to induce a form of ecstasy or trance in which the soul would then be able to conduct a dialogue with God (the final aim of "the search for the real [*al-Ḥaqq*]," as al-Ghazālī called it). As an alternative there exists the technique of *fikr*, meaning contemplation and reflection. The whole idea of recollection appears most clearly in poetic formulations such as the following by Ibn al-Fāriḍ (1181–1235): "In memory of the Beloved we quaffed a vintage that made us drunk before the creation of the vine." The commentator Nābulusī says that this means nothing but that the soul was intoxicated with the wine of divine love during its existence before the creation of the body (Nicholson, 1921, pp. 184ff.). Ṣūfī brotherhoods can be differentiated as to their final aim: some aim for *ilhāmīyah*, or inspiration by God, others for *ittiḥādīyah*, the mystical union with God.

Many Ṣūfīs were definite adherents of a theory of transmigration of souls (*tanāsukh*), though there were exceptions. The doctrine of metempsychosis was also adhered to by other Muslim groups, such as the Nuṣayrīyah, the Kurds, and the Druze, as was reported by the historian of religion al-Shahrastānī, from Khorasan (1076–1153). The Ṣūfīs adhered to the theory of the transmigration of souls because they believed that before the creation of bodies the souls were illuminated by divine light; therefore affinal souls can smell each another out, as was formulated by Abū Saʿīd (Nicholson, 1921, p. 56). This notion appears clearly also in the poetry of Ibn al-Fāriḍ, who like many other Ṣūfī mystics accords great importance and proof for the preexistence of the soul to dream states: "In dreams the soul knows itself as it was in the state of preexistence" (v. 669), or again, "In the world of reminiscence the soul has her ancient knowledge" (v. 759; Nicholson, 1921, pp. 265).

In any case, the aim of the Ṣūfī is the unification with God and a cessation of transmigration and, by total absorption into the deity, the extinction of existence (*fanāʿ*). Some of the most evocative lines of poetry combining the idea of *fanāʿ* with that of *tanāsukh* have come down to us from Jalāl al-Dīn Rūmī, who founded the Mevlevī order in Konya in the late thirteenth century: "I died as mineral and became a plant, I died as plant and rose to animal." This poem ends in the rapt cry "Oh, let me not exist!" (*The Ascending Soul*, trans. Nicholson, 1964, p. 103).

The mystical tendencies of Islamic Sufism—such as its emotional and inner devotion to the divine agency, contemplative and prayerful, together with a strong ethical orientation that could almost be labeled pietist—passed relatively early into the developing Jewish Qabbalah. One of the most influential works in this connection was the *Ḥovot ha-levavot* (Duties of the heart) by Baḥye ibn Paquda in 1080, translated into Hebrew in 1161. The underlying theme of this work finds its strongest expression in the later Lurianic movement as well as in the Hasidic tradition in Spain and in central and eastern Europe. For Paquda there are two kinds of duty: one that relates to the body and that concerns man's overt actions, and the other that relates to the heart and concerns man's inner life. To the first belong the ethical commands of the Torah, the observance of the Sabbath, prayer, and charity. To the latter belong the belief in the existence and singleness of God, the fear and love of him as well as the trust in him.

Paquda warned against overemphasis on the duties of the body, thus advocating a countermovement against halakhic orthodoxy. The aim of life is spiritual perfection and ultimate union and communion with God. The way to this is through the ten gates, such as sincerity of purpose, humility, repentance, self-examination, asceticism, and love of God. In accordance with Platonic principles, the soul is of celestial origin, placed into material bodies where it begins to forget its nature and mission. The soul receives great help from the intellect, since in it all the duties of the heart are grounded. There has to be a perfect correspondence of behavior and conscience. Paquda is far from advocating asceticism but opts for the middle way: live in temperance but fulfill your duties in social life (see Scholem, 1954, 1965).

There are considerable differences between Sufism and Qabbalah, in particular in regard to the strong reliance on exegesis among Jewish thinkers and in regard to the downplaying of ascetic practices. However, Qabbalah took some notions of metempsychosis, which play a great role in the later movement in Safad, from Sufism. Early Qabbalah of the twelfth century is more restrictive in the use of the term: it uses the notion of *gilgul* or *haʾataqah* ("transference") as a translation of the Arabic *tanāsukh* (which in turn is also a translation of the Stoic concept of *aposakatastasis*) for certain, mostly sexual, offenses. The decisive turn occurs in the sixteenth century, when a system of moral causes and physical effects, similar to the Hindu *karman*, takes root. The other very specific Jewish notion concerns the metaphorical equivalence of the exile of the soul from its divine spiritual abode and the exile of the chosen people from its homeland.

Behind the Jewish idea of transmigration stands the doctrine of the creation of the world as a series of emanations from the godhead (Ein Sof), which is symbolized by the ten *sefirot* that contain as vessels the divine light. In particular the tenth *sefirah*, the female Shekhinah, is responsible for receiving and distributing the divine light-essence to earth. It is through man's sinful nature and his fall from grace that the energy flow was interrupted, leading to disharmony as well as evil in the world. The deed is traced to primordial man, Adam Qadmon, whose fall brought about the breaking of the vessels, so that the divine essence became dispersed in innumerable fragments as light particles, which are contaminated with matter (the closeness to some Gnostic notions is noticeable). This basic system was further elaborated by the Palestinian qabbalist Isaac Luria (1534–1572) but also flourished in Italy.

It is with the thirteenth-century founder of Ashkenazic Hasidism, Elʿazar of Worms, that we find one of the strongest reminiscences of the doctrine of transmigration and Platonic *anamnēsis*. In an interpretation of the *Midrash on the Creation of the Child*, he expostulates that after the guardian angel has given the newborn child a tap on the upper lip, it forgets all the infinite knowledge it had acquired before its birth in the celestial house of learning. And why does the child forget? asks Elʿazar. Because, he answers, if the child did not forget, the course of the world would drive it mad in the light of what it knows from its former existence in divine grace. (The relation to Job is evident.)

The whole purpose of man's existence on earth is the restoration of the ideal order and the collection of the pure divine light in the vessels. Salvation thus means nothing but restitution or reintegration of the original whole (*tiqqun*). In Lurianic Qabbalah, transmigration, as for some Ṣūfī brotherhoods, is not just a result of evil or of the sinful nature of man, but it is actually one chance, a boon, to achieve the goal of self-emancipation, defined here as being freed from transmigration. The souls of the emancipated ones then wait, each in its blessed house, to be reunited with the soul of Adam, the first man.

However, and here we also get a unique variation of the theme of transmigration and redemption, while the purpose of reincarnation is always purification or atonement for the sins of mankind, the role of the suffering of the righteous is of the greatest importance, because they help with the restoration of the universe. Here the universal effect of good deeds and thoughts, of a devout life in the pietist sense, is combined with the ancient notion of the efficacy of ritual to restore the proper functioning of universal forces and energies. The notion of metempsychosis, also called "impregnation" (*'ibbur* in early Qabbalah), is taken to its furthest extent when it is stated that a soul, in particular that of an ethically advanced person, can enter, even temporarily, another man's body and thus help his soul come closer to perfection. The universe can only be restored to its original purity when all people have reached perfection. In spite of this seemingly unified system, we find in Qabbalah the same major splits of interpretation as in the Ṣūfī tradition. Two basic aims are given as the highest goal for the life of man: Maimonides advocates the knowledge of God, while his son opts for union with God. We thus find in all traditions so far discussed the same split between knowledge and devotion as the main aims of life.

AUSTRALIAN ABORIGINAL BELIEFS IN RITUAL ACTION AND REBIRTH PROCESSES. In most systems discussed so far we find a tendency to identify the realm of the spirit with the notion of essence or form, abstracted from all material discrete reality: the bodies of humans and other animate beings are perceived as prisons for the divine element, life force, or soul. Matter is thus seen as inimical to the soul's attainment of its true state, in which it is a part of, or is united with, the godhead.

The religious systems of the Australian Aborigines developed a different, almost diametrically opposed, notion. Here the divine element is embodied in a diversity of material objects, ranging from features of the geographical landscape to such items as bull-roarers. Man himself is a divine being and agent, either as an individual or as a member of a social group; and particular social groups as much as particular individuals are identified or correlated with features in the landscape. The social groups such as clans are themselves sacred corporations in perpetuity. The sacred nature of material items such as bull-roarers is made clear through their use: they are efficacious for the continued fertility of all nature, including humankind, because they are thought of as endowed with the power of the culture heroes of the Dreaming.

In a similar fashion, the whole earth and all its features, such as rocks, indentations, but especially waterholes, are considered sacred substances or emanations of the creative thoughts of the ancestral heroes and divinities. The creator ancestors walked the earth in primordial times and created every animate and inanimate object through externalizing, objectifying, and materializing their thoughts in the act of dreaming. Man is the paramount agent who either through ceremonies or dreaming guarantees the continuation of these creative acts.

Aboriginal religious thought thus perceives a very intimate relation between man and environment in what has become known as a totemic thought system, where each individual and each group becomes closely linked to a feature of the external world (landscape, plants, animals). While these features of the external world are the self-manifestations of the creator deities of the Dreaming, man has to identify through ritual and through dreaming with these features and internalize them. The continuation of the visible reality depends on the meticulous performance of rites at the ceremonial centers of the diverse totemic ancestor beings; individuals and groups are thus (as reincarnations of the supernatural beings) guardians and connective links to the eternal order that, though once established in its final form, needs the constant renewal in the present. This belief explains also the frequent handling of sacred objects (for which the Aranda term *tjurunga* has become synonymous) by young initiates, who through this action try to keep in touch with the essence of that being of which they are the spiritual double themselves (see Elkin, 1954, p. 186).

There exists in Aboriginal thinking no clear delineation between eternity and temporality, between now and the past: the eternal order is not only the basis for the re-creation through ritual in the present, as laid down by the law of the ancestor deities, but is inseparably linked with the present through the sacred agency of humankind, which carries within its individuals and groups the spark of life derived from the original creative beings through constant reincarnations. In short, in ritual action, eternity is here and now and merging with the present. The cosmic dimension of the maintenance of the world through ritual finds its correlate in the notion of the constant reincarnation of a personal soul-entity. In most Aboriginal systems of thought the spiritual essence enters man through dreaming at a totemic center. These totemic centers are the places into which the ancestor spirits disappeared when they had finished creation and to which the souls of the dead depart and become deposited, there to await rebirth. When a man sleeps at such a place, the spiritual essence or soul that has been deposited in these centers enters him through dreaming, and the male transfers the new soul to his female partner during procreation.

The self-identification of the living persons and groups of Aboriginal society with the ancestors and their spiritual essence is thus achieved through dreaming at the very places where the divine entities externalized and materialized their own thoughts in dreaming in very concrete and substantial form. This identity of substance of the living world and of man is often expressed by Aborigines when they refer to the sacred totemic places as "my dreaming there." Thus dreaming, life essence or soul, and the supreme creator deities are sometimes called by the same term. This self-identification of the individual and of groups with the externalizations of the ancestral heroes, be they features of the landscape or living creatures in nature, is expressed through the concept of the birth and rebirth at particular centers and, more pointedly, through initiation rituals. The aim of initiation rituals is not only to remind the young initiand of the significance of the sacred landscape but even more to teach him his own lost knowledge, to actually make him aware of his own sacredness (females are in some parts of Australia considered sacred by nature).

As each individual represents the reborn ancestor, he is thus learning what he always actually knew but forgot when he rested in the spirit places after death in his last incarnation. As T. G. H. Strehlow put it about the understanding of this process among the Aranda: "At the time of birth the totemic ancestor who has undergone re-incarnation is totally unaware of his former glorious existence. For him the preceding months have been a 'sleep and forgetting.' If he is born as a boy, the old men will later on initiate him and reintroduce him into the ancient ceremonies which he himself had instituted in his previous extence" (Strehlow, 1947, p. 93).

We would scarcely find anywhere else a stronger resemblance to the Platonic notion of *anamnēsis*, yet in Australian Aboriginal thought the living human is even more pronouncedly part of the divine, being, if not the divinity, at least the ancestor hero. When a grown adult performs the increase ceremonies as laid down by the ancestor deities, he is reperforming his own law, for he, in his former incarnation as ancestor, had a part in devising the law.

It is from this vantage point that the merging of the present and the past—of concrete reality and actions within it with the original and therefore not only past but ever-present essential foundations of reality—can be understood. As Strehlow has it: "The whole countryside is his living, age-old family tree. The story of his own totemic ancestor is to the native the account of his own doings at the beginning of time, at the dim dawn of life, when the world as he knows it now was being shaped and moulded by all-powerful hands. He himself has played a part in that first glorious adventure, a part smaller or greater according to the original rank of the ancestor of whom he is the present re-incarnated form" (ibid., pp. 30–31).

At death the immortal part of the human reincarnation returns to the abode of the primordial state, either beyond the sea, in the sky, or under the ground. While the belief in reincarnation is general and widespread among Australian Aborigines, the rebirth is perceived not as that of a previous particular human personality but as one of primordial existence as creative agent. There exists no retribution for activities in this life, though the ancestor heroes were not without fault or blame. But even their deeds that are wrong by the standards they laid down themselves are not judged in an afterlife, nor do they influence reincarnation.

However, present Aborigines realize and express the idea that their ancestor deities may sometimes have gone wrong and may sometimes have been killed for their wrongdoing by the original incarnations of present-day people. Although killed, these ancestor heroes did not die in spirit; as the Berndts note, they remain part of the "Eternal Dreaming stream" (Berndt and Berndt, 1977, p. 418). The religious systems of all Aboriginal groups seem to be what W. E. H. Stanner once called an "affirmation of life" (see Stanner, 1959–1963). There is certainly no trace of asceticism or denial of the body to be found in Aboriginal beliefs. There is no need for such abasement, for the divine eternity is concretely realized in material form in this world and can always be made present through ritual action.

The comparison with the Platonic system of recollection cannot be fully developed (see also Eliade, 1973, pp. 58–59). Yet one point is worth emphasizing: for Aborigines, the manifestations of the ancestor heroes of the Dreaming, such as features of the landscape, become the outward sign to recall the deeds of these ancestors. This comes close to Plato's notion about the efficacy of objects of beauty to arouse in humans the desire of Eros to attain absolute beauty, the desire to attain something that one lacks, in particular to attain immortality.

It might not be too farfetched to extend this philosophical interpretation to the mytho-ritualistic identification that the Aborigine intends when handling sacred objects, performing the ancient sacred increase rituals or learning about his oneness with the Dreaming and its objects or emanations. This, and more, is revealed to the Aborigine in the long drawn-out process of initiation and achievement of adulthood and is regularly made clear in ritual action, when each participant becomes an ancestor. Each, too, will thereby re-create the universe, but none will attempt to change it. The ritual recollection of the Australian Aborigines and of other tribal societies is replaced in Plato's system by the philosopher through the *daimōn* of Eros. Both forms of recollection seem to share the same aim: through ritual the paradigmatic model is repeated over and over again and made present and efficacious forever; through the drive of Eros the philosopher aims at gaining what he has not yet obtained, namely, immortality and divine status. Both Eros and ritual action are creative.

A member of the Murinbata once said to Stanner: "White man got no dreaming, him go 'nother way. White man, him go different. Him go road belong himself." Our comparison about the notion of recollection from Platonic *anamnēsis* to Aboriginal beliefs in reincarnation and remembering of their own divine status has shown that a reminder of our own roots might instill in us a sense of humility. Were we to recollect our Platonic heritage, we might perceive the Australian Aborigine as a related soul. We might realize that Europe since ancient times has been working toward the same goal as the Aborigines: only our methods differ.

See Also Dhikr; Dreaming, The; Exile; Knowledge and Ignorance; Soul.

Bibliography

The most lucid treatment of recollection in the framework of the whole of Plato's middle dialogues is found in F. M. Cornford's *Principium Sapientiae: The Origins of Greek Philosophical Thought*, edited by W. K. C. Guthrie (Cambridge, U.K., 1952). A careful reading, line by line, of the *Phaedo* is given by Romano Guardini in *Der Tod des Sokrates* (Berlin, 1943), translated as *The Death of Socrates: An Interpretation of the Platonic Dialogues* (Cleveland, 1948). The problem of Plato's notion of beauty in the context of European art theory is developed by Ernesto Grassi in *Die Theorie des Schönen in der Antike* (Cologne, 1962). For pre-Platonic ideas about soul migration, three authors make a strong case for the existence of Orphic and Pythagorean cult doctrines to be found in Platonic writings: W. K. C. Guthrie, in *Orpheus and Greek Religion* (1935: 2d ed., rev., London, 1952); E. R. Dodds, the most skeptical of the three, in *The Greeks and the Irrational* (Berkeley, 1951); and Ivan M. Linforth, in *The Arts of Orpheus* (1941; reprint, New York, 1973). A balanced account of Pythagorean-Orphic practices and a meticulous source criticism can be found in Walter Burkert's *Lore and Science in Ancient Pythagoreanism* (Cambridge, Mass., 1972).

Many of the Platonic and pre-Platonic ideas of soul migration have been traced back to shamanistic practices by Karl Meuli in his now-classic interpretation "Scythica," *Hermes* 70 (1935): 121–176; his line of thought is taken up by Walter Burkert in "Gōes: Zum griechischen 'Schamanismus,'" *Rheinisches Museum für Philologie* 105 (1962): 36–55, and by Mircea Eliade in *Myth and Reality* (New York, 1963). For an anthropological notion of possession states and the Greek evidence, see my essay "Individual and Collective Possession: The Shaman as Primeval Healer and Artist in Modern Japan and Ancient Greece," in *Under the Shade of a Coolibah Tree*, edited by Richard A. Hutch and Peter G. Fenner (Lanham, Md., 1984), pp. 279–321. For the extant sources, Erwin Rohde's *Psyche* (Leipzig, 1894; Eng. trans., London, 1925) is still useful and readable. The interpretations in Jane Ellen Harrison's *Prolegomena to the Study of Greek Religion* (Cambridge, U.K., 1903) now appear dated and marred by a too literal application of Frazerian anthropology. For the importance of Mnemosyne, the well-known dictionary of myths of antiquity by W. H. Roscher, *Ausführliches Lexikon der griechischen und römischen Mythologie* (Leipzig, 1897–1909), vol. 3, is still indispensable.

On Gnosticism, the most understandable survey of the sources, with an excellent bibliography and a history of research, remains Kurt Rudolph's *Die Gnosis* (Göttingen, 1977; Eng. trans., San Francisco, 1983). A full introduction, which opened the way for many new interpretations, such as the separation of a Hellenistic from an Iranian stream of Gnosticism, is presented by Hans Jonas in *Gnosis und spätantiker Geist*, 2 vols. (Göttingen, 1934–1954; vol. 1, 3d ed., 1964; vol. 2, 2d ed., 1966).

The variety of influences on Gnosticism is excellently shown by Gilles Quispel in *Gnostic Studies*, vol. 1 (Istanbul, 1974). A stimulating work, although often theoretically speculative, is Richard Reitzenstein's *Die hellenistischen Mysterienreligionen*, 3d ed. (Leipzig, 1927; Eng. trans., Pittsburgh, 1978). The Manichaean variant of the Gnostic movements is traced to their Iranian roots by Geo Widengren in *Mani und der Manichäismus* (Stuttgart, 1961; Eng. trans., New York, 1965). For a survey discussion on the Manichaean soteriology in the light of the Turfan fragments, see H. C. Puech's "Erlosung im Manichaismus," in *Eranos Jahrbuch 1936* (Zurich, 1937).

On Ṣūfī movements, the works of Reynold A. Nicholson are classics. His *Studies in Islamic Mysticism* (1921; Cambridge, U.K., 1976) and *Personality in Sufism* (Cambridge, U.K., 1923) offer interpretations fully embedding the sectarian development in a linguistic and cultural analysis of the whole of Islam; his *Rumi, Poet and Mystic, 1207–1273*, 3d ed. (London, 1964), displays his skill in poetic translation.

On Qabbalah in its various extensions in Spain, Safad, Italy, and central Europe, the most profound interpretation is that of Gershom Scholem, set forth in his *Major Trends in Jewish Mysticism*, 3d rev. ed. (Jerusalem, 1954), and *Jewish Gnosticism, Merkabah Mysticism, and Talmudic Tradition*, 2d ed. (New York, 1965).

The earliest comprehensive work on Australian Aboriginal religion is A. P. Elkin's *The Australian Aborigines* (1938; 3d ed., Sydney, 1954). A more recent survey is Ronald M. Berndt and Catherine H. Berndt's *The World of the First Australians*, 2d ed. (Sydney, 1977). On particular Aboriginal concepts in various regions, T. G. H. Strehlow's *Aranda Traditions* (Melbourne, 1947) is a classic of exposition. W. E. H. Stanner's "On Aboriginal Religion," *Oceania* 30–34 (1959–1963), in seven parts, is also valuable. A complete survey of Aboriginal religious beliefs, with a cross-cultural phenomenological orientation, is provided by Mircea Eliade's *Australian Religions* (Ithaca, N. Y., 1973).

On ritual processes, an easy introduction is given by Paul Radin in *Primitive Religion* (New York, 1937). A more recent structural approach can be found in Victor Turner's *The Ritual Process: Structure and Anti-Structure* (Chicago, 1969). The application of the notion of anamnesis to an epistemology of cultural translation has been undertaken by Hans P. Duerr in his *Traumzeit* (Frankfurt, 1978).

New Sources

Michèle Simondon, *La mémoire et l'oubli dans la pensée grecque* (Paris, 1982) and Giovanni Pugliese Carratelli, "Mnemosyne e l'Immortalità," *Archivio di Filosofia* 51 (1983), 71–79, reprinted in *Tra Cadmo e Orfeo* (Bologna, 1990), 379–389 deal with the Greek idea of memory.

On Platonic and Pythagoric theories of anamnesis see also: C. E. Huber, *Anamnesis bei Plato* (Munich, 1964); Domnic Scott, "Platonic Anamnesis Revisited." *Classical Quarterly* 37 (1987): 346–366; Theodor Ebert, *Sokrates als Pythagoreer und die Anamnesis in Platons Phaidon* (Stuttgart, 1994).

For similar theories in Gnosticism, concerning memory, fate, reincarnation and salvation as return to the self, see Aldo Magris, *La logica del pensiero gnostico* (Brescia, 1997), pp. 333–429.

On Sufism and Islamic mysticism see some of the numerous works by Annemarie Schimmel, *Mystical Dimensions of Islam* (Chapel Hill, 1975); *Sufi Literature* (New York. 1975); *Triumphal Sun: A Study of the Works of Jalaloddin Rumi* (London, 1978); *Muhammad Iqbal: prophetischer Poet und Philosoph* (Munich, 1989); *I Am Wind, You Are Fire: The Life and Work of Rumi* (Boston, 1992); *The Secrets of Creative Love: The Work of Muhammad Iqbal* (Wimbledon, 1998); *Gesang und Ekstase: Sufi-Texte des indischen Islam* (Munich, 1999); *Sufismus: Eine Einführung in die islamische Mystik* (Munich, 2000).

Avicenna's doctrine of illumination, which follows the Neoplatonic development of anamnesis, is outlined by Herbert A. Davidson, *Alfarabi, Avicenna, and Averroes on Intellect: Their Cosmologies, Theories of the Active Intellect, and Theories of Human Intellect* (New York, 1992).

See also: Henry Corbin, *The Man of Light in Iranian Sufism,* translated by Nancy Pearson (Boulder, 1978). Timothy J.Gianotti, *Al-Ghazālī's Unspeakable Doctrine of the Soul: Unveiling the Esoteric Psychology and Eschatology of the Ihyā,* (Leiden, 2001). Suhraward, *The Philosophy of Illumination* (Hiqmat al-ishrāq), translation and comment by John Walbridge and Hossein Ziai (Provo, Utah, 1999). John Walbridge, *The Wisdom of the Mystic East: Suhrawardī and Platonic Orientalism* (Albany, 2001).

KLAUS-PETER KÖPPING (1987)
Revised Bibliography

ʿANAN BEN DAVID (fl. Baghdad, second half of the eighth century CE), titular founder of the Karaites, a Jewish sect. According to a rabbinic-Jewish (Rabbinite) tradition cited first by the twelfth-century Karaite author Eliyyahu ben Avraham, ʿAnan was rejected for the position of exilarch (secular head of the Jewish community in Iraq and its representative before the Muslim caliph's court) on the ground of heretical tendencies. When the office went to his younger brother Ḥananyah, ʿAnan's followers (styled Ananites, or ʿĀnānīyah in Arabic) declared him their own exilarch. Since this action amounted to open defiance of the caliph's customary right to confirm a newly elected exilarch, ʿAnan was cast into prison and faced execution. A Muslim fellow-prisoner (according to Jewish sources, Abū Ḥanīfah, the founder of the Ḥanafī school of Muslim jurisprudence) advised him to bribe his way before the caliph and then to plead that the Ananites were a religious denomination distinct from the Rabbinites and were therefore entitled to have their own exilarch. ʿAnan followed this advice, was acquitted, and was set free.

The historicity of this account is open to challenge, however. Opposition to postbiblical, or Talmudic, tradition (so-called oral law, distinct from written law in the Old Testament) and the cry "Back to the Bible!" antedated ʿAnan by several centuries, and for the period immediately before him, the names of some leaders of such antitraditionalist movements have been preserved. These movements were found mostly in the outlying provinces of the Muslim Empire, among Jewish communities apparently composed to a considerable degree of emigrants from metropolitan Iraq; they belonged to the poorer classes of artisans and farm laborers and felt themselves sorely oppressed by the rabbinic religious and secular bureaucracy, which overburdened them with special taxes imposed for its own maintenance.

What seems to be certain is that ʿAnan was a man of aristocratic Rabbinite descent and of considerable learning and that he was the first to lend these two prestigious qualifications to the contemporary sectarian leadership. He was also apparently the first to compose a comprehensive scholarly code of sectarian (nonrabbinic) law based formally only on the Bible. This was written in Aramaic, the language of much of the Talmud, but is known under the Hebrew title *Sefer ha-mitsvot* (Book of precepts). Only fragments of this work have been discovered so far. Containing concise formulations of law, but no polemics against rabbinic dogma or law, they reveal ʿAnan as a rigorous and ascetic teacher rather than an ambitious seeker after secular power.

That ʿAnan was influenced to some extent by earlier antitraditionalist teachings seems fairly certain, although this influence should not be exaggerated. He was a self-assured and independent thinker. Later Karaite scholars disagreed with him on many points of law and chided him for what they considered his excessive borrowing from rabbinic law. His predilection for the analogical method in deducing new rules from the biblical text may indicate some influence from Muslim jurisprudence.

Later accounts credit ʿAnan with a work on the transmigration of souls and state that he regarded Jesus and Muḥammad as inspired prophets sent to their respective nations, but these are not supported by any reliable evidence.

The Ananites, never numerous, were eventually absorbed by the Karaites. ʿAnan's direct male descendants bore the honorific title of prince (*nasi*ʾ) and were treated accordingly by the Karaites, but they apparently wielded little actual power and, with one or two exceptions, did not distinguish themselves as scholars.

SEE ALSO Karaites.

BIBLIOGRAPHY

Nemoy, Leon. "Al-Qirqisānī's Account of the Jewish Sects and Christianity." *Hebrew Union College Annual* 7 (1930): 317–397. For al-Qirqisānī's summary of Ananite teachings, see pages 383–386.

Nemoy, Leon. "Anan ben David: A Reappraisal of the Historical Data." In *Semitic Studies in Memory of Immanuel Löw,* edited by Alexander Scheiber, pp. 239–248. Budapest, 1947. Reprinted in *Karaite Studies,* edited by Philip Birnbaum (New York, 1971).

Nemoy, Leon. *Karaite Anthology.* New Haven, 1952. See especially pages 3–20, 51–52, and 395. Includes a list of published fragments of the *Book of Precepts*. The fragment published by Sokolov was reprinted by Zvi Harkavy, with English translation by Leon Nemoy, in the *Jewish Quarterly Review* 66 (October 1975): 109–119.

Poznanski, Samuel. "Anan et ses écrits." *Revue des études juives* 44/45 (1902).

New Sources

Ben-Shammai, Haggai. "Between Ananites and Karaites: Observations on Early Medieval Jewish Sectarianism." In *Studies in Muslim-Jewish Relations*, edited by Ronald L. Nettler, vol. 1, pp. 19–29. Chur, Switzerland, 1993.

Cook, Michael. "Anan and Islam: The Origins of Karaite Scripturalism." *JSAI* 9 (1987): 161–182.

Margolies, Morris B. *Twenty/Twenty: Jewish Visionaries through Two Thousand Years*. Northvale, N.J., 2000.

LEON NEMOY (1987)
Revised Bibliography

ĀNANDAMAYĪ MĀ (the bliss-permeated Mother, 1896–1982) was a leading Hindu spiritual master in twentieth-century India. She was regarded a divine manifestation by her disciples, who came from all strata of the Indian society and from around the world. A number of them were well-known scholars, artists, as well as social and political leaders, including Indira Gandhi (1917–1984), the former prime minister of India. At the core of Ānandamayī Mā's teaching was the identity of the individual Self (*ātman*) with the Absolute (*brahman*) and the unity of all existence. She recommended a fundamental reorientation of life in order to realize one's identity with the Absolute. While these precepts have long been a part of Hindu philosophical thought, what drew people to her was her powerful yet gracious presence that seemed to bear a living testimony to them. The course of her life seemed to flow from a deep spiritual awareness that often led her to deviate from the norms of contemporary Hindu society. Her life, like lives of many Hindu women saints, was marked by enigma and paradoxes.

Ānandamayī Mā was born to a devout but poor *brahman* couple, Bipin Bihari Bhattacharya and Mokshada Devi, in the village of Kheora in East Bengal (now Bangladesh) and was given the name Nirmala Sundari (the one of taintless beauty). She was indeed very beautiful. Even as a child, she surprised elders by going into trancelike states during sessions of devotional singing and showing deep affinity with animals and trees. As was customary at the time, after receiving little formal education, Nirmala was married to Ramani Mohan Chakravarti at the age of twelve. When she joined her husband five years later, she excelled in performing household duties, but declined to have a physical relationship. Instead, she asked permission to engage in spiritual exercises (*sādhanā*) every night after finishing her domestic work.

Nirmala had had no formal training in spiritual matters, yet various yogic postures and the states of mind (*bhāvas*) associated with them seemed to come effortlessly to her as she followed her spiritual impulse, which she called *kheyāla*. One night, she initiated herself onto the meditative path in a unique manner: She played the roles of both the *gurū* and the disciple, establishing nondifferentiation between the two. A few months later she initiated her husband and became his *gurū*, inverting the norm for Hindu women of the time. During this period of her intense *sādhanā* (1918–1924), she was often found in ecstatic states, viewed by some as signs of mental disturbance. With her husband's support, however, she continued her practice.

By 1924, when her husband accepted a job on the Shahbag estates in Dhaka, she had attracted a considerable following. Her husband welcomed in their home crowds of people, including scholars and professionals who were amazed at Nirmala's succinct answers to their complex philosophical queries. Here, Nirmala also led worship ceremonies (*pūjā*) for the goddess Kālī, departing from the tradition by excluding animal sacrifice. From 1926 Nirmala came to be called Ānandamayī Mā by her disciples, for they saw her in a state of constant bliss. They built a small *āśrama* (retreat center) near Dhaka that became the first of the thirty established before the end of her life. Around the same time she began to refer to herself as "this body," indicating detachment from it, and declared that her true self was unchanging.

From the early 1930s until her passing away in 1982, like a Hindu renunciant, she ceaselessly traveled across India imparting spiritual guidance to a wide range of people. She was, however, not a traditional renunciate. Her husband, now called Bholānāth, accompanied her until his death in 1938. During his last illness, Ānandamayī Mā served him as a devoted wife, but continued her work after his death. Through example and conversations in everyday language she taught her followers to make Self-realization the main goal of life. She did not prescribe a specific method for all for the attainment of this goal and recognized that each individual had to follow the path suitable for him- or herself. The only spiritual program that she guided yearly was a weeklong retreat in one of her *āśramas* that emphasized self-restraint and meditation. Her femininity imparted a grace and gentleness to her spiritual mentoring that touched everyone who came to her.

Ānandamayī Mā did not recognize sectarian, religious caste, or gender differences at the level of the Self. She blessed and guided all who approached her. Her followers included Hindus across caste boundaries, non-Hindus, and a large number of women who found her especially inspirational. She, however, did not intervene in the working of her *āśramas*, where the administrators followed purity/pollution rules that mark the Hindu caste system. For this, she was criticized by some as the *gurū* of the elite and the high caste. Some remark that her teaching did not emphasize charitable work, even though schools, hospitals, and veterinary clinics were and still are run by her *āśramas*. Others explain that in Ānandamayī Mā's inherently spiritual view, the solution to human suffering had to be sought through spiritual advancement. This would lead people to see others as a part of the self. Charity would not be needed then. Ānandamayī Mā is recognized as a mystic of rare spiritual insight in India. Holding together the roles of wife, renunciate, and spiritual guide in a seamless manner, her life pointed out the possibilities for spiritual life that are open for women in the Hindu milieu despite the restrictive norms set for them by the orthodoxy.

SEE ALSO Guru.

BIBLIOGRAPHY

Banerjee, Shyamananda. *A Mystic Sage: Ma Anandamayi.* Calcutta, 1973.

Chaudhuri, Narayan. *That Compassionate Touch of Ma Anandamayee.* Delhi, 1980.

Ganguli, Anil. *Anandamayi Ma: The Mother Bliss-Incarnate.* Calcutta, 1983.

Hallstrom, Lisa Lassell. *Mother of Bliss: Ānandamayī Mā (1896–1982).* New York, 1999.

Kaviraj, Gopinath, ed. *Mother as Seen by Her Devotees.* 2d ed. Varanasi, India, 1976.

Lannoy, Richard. *Anandamayi: Her Life and Wisdom.* Shaftesbury, UK, 1996.

Lipski, Alexander. *The Life and Teaching of 'Srī Ānandamayī Mā.* Delhi, 1977.

Maschmann, Melita. *Encountering Bliss: Journey through India with Ānandamayī Mā.* Translated by Shridhar B. Shrotri. Delhi, 2002.

Mukerji, Bithika. *From the Life of Anandamayi Ma.* 2 vols. Calcutta, 1980–1981; 2d ed., 1996.

NEELIMA SHUKLA-BHATT (2005)

ANAT. The maiden Anat (*btlt ʿnt*) is a West Semitic or Canaanite warrior-goddess known for her violent temperament and volatile emotions. Although her name and cult are attested from the late third millennium BCE to the fourth century BCE, Anat plays a prominent role only in the Late Bronze Age mythological texts from the Syrian city of Ugarit (modern-day Ras Shamra). These poetic narratives, written in an alphabetic cuneiform script, depict Anat as a fierce and impetuous goddess who delights in bloodshed. As a hunter and protector of wild animals, Anat also functions as a "Mistress of Animals" in Canaanite tradition. Anat's primary epithet in Ugaritic sources is *btlt* (maiden), which identifies her as an adolescent female, a girl of marriageable age. Iconographic representations from Egypt and Syria-Palestine depict the goddess as young and nubile, with small breasts and a thin body. Called "the loveliest of the sisters of Baal," Anat is also a player of the lyre and singer of love songs in Ugaritic narrative. Although female, the adolescent goddess engages in the traditionally masculine pursuits of warfare, hunting, and political intrigue.

Earlier studies often assume that Anat is Baal's consort. More recent studies by Peggy Day and Neal Walls, however, argue that the extant Ugaritic texts never depict her as sexually active. While some scholars have erroneously identified Anat with the cow that mates with and bears an heir for Baal, the Ugaritic narratives clearly distinguish between Anat and Baal's cow. As his devoted sister, Anat actively supports Baal's quest for kingship among the gods. She serves as a diplomatic intermediary in securing the support of El, her elderly father, for the establishment of his royal palace. The warrior Anat boasts of having vanquished many of Baal's foes, including Yamm (the Canaanite primordial sea), the Twisting Serpent, and the Seven-Headed Dragon. Whether or not Anat is the consort of Baal, the maiden goddess maintains her autonomy and independence from male control. She lives in her own palace on her sacred mountain *Inbb* rather than in the household of her father, brother, or consort. Ugaritic poetry venerates Anat as the "Mistress of Kingship, Mistress of Dominion, and Mistress of the High Heavens." The meaning of her epithet *ybmt limm* remains uncertain, but it most likely refers to her position within the pantheon's kinship structure.

Anat displays her malevolent aggression in two encounters with El, in which she threatens to drag him from his throne "to the ground like a lamb" for slaughter. She promises to smash his skull and to make his "gray hair run with blood and his gray beard with gore" unless he agrees to her demands. El's response to his belligerent daughter seems more indulgent than fearful, "I know, my daughter, that you are incorrigible, and that among the goddesses there is no rancor like yours." While El apparently denies her request in one text, in the other he yields to her rash demands, "Depart, my daughter; haughty is your heart. Take what is in your mind, carry out [what] is in your breast. Whoever hinders you will be destroyed." El's words are perhaps reflected in an eighth-century Akkadian text that praises Anat, "whose heroism among the goddesses has no equal."

Another famous scene from Ugaritic myth depicts Anat's bloodthirsty nature as she gleefully slaughters armies of human warriors. Delighting in the carnage of battle, Anat "wades in their blood up to her thighs." She adorns herself by placing her enemies' severed heads on a garland around her neck and their severed hands on a belt around her waist before she exultantly wades into the gore of battle a second time. Possibly a description of ritual cannibalism, this grisly scene clearly portrays the murderous quality of Anat's martial enthusiasm.

In contrast with her warlike attributes, Anat is also portrayed in Ugaritic myth as a compassionate goddess who pathetically grieves the death of her brother: "Like the heart of a cow for its calf, like the heart of a ewe for its lamb, such is the heart of Anat for Baal." On hearing of his death, Anat scours the earth in search of her slain brother's corpse, which she then buries with elaborate funerary sacrifices and mourning rites. Anat "gashes her cheeks and her chin" in a heartfelt display of ritual bloodletting. She then humbly entreats Mot, the Ugaritic god of death, to return her brother to her. After her diplomatic efforts have failed, however, Anat reverts to her more characteristic mode and viciously attacks Mot: "She seizes divine Mot; with a blade she splits him, with a sieve she winnows him, with fire she burns him, and with mill-stones she grinds him." Anat scatters his pulverized remains in a field for the birds to consume. This scene of utter annihilation demonstrates Anat's impulsive ferocity, but it also leads to Baal's restoration as ruler of the earth. Although the text is broken at this point, it is clear that Baal returns to power, bringing his fertilizing rains to the thirsty fields in a renewal of natural fecundity. The maiden Anat's hostile actions are thus crucial to the balance of cosmic power and the continuation of life on the earth in Ugaritic myth.

Anat's passionate disposition takes on a more sinister quality in the Ugaritic epic of Aqhat. In a scene that is perhaps related to Hellenistic accounts of Artemis and the Babylonian account of Ishtar's failed seduction of Gilgamesh, Anat attempts to wrest a divinely crafted bow from the young hero Aqhat. He disdains her offer of gold, silver, and immortality in exchange for the composite bow and insolently informs her that females are not meant to be warriors. Seeking revenge for the insult, Anat eventually has her henchman murder Aqhat. The bow, however, is lost, and Anat tearfully regrets her impulsive actions in killing the young man, an injustice that causes drought and famine in the land. The conclusion to this epic has yet to be recovered.

Anat was introduced into Egypt during the Hyksos period (c. 1650–1550 BCE) and became a patron goddess of the Ramesside era (c. 1295–1069 BCE) as the "Mistress of the Heavens," a martial goddess who gives victory in battle. Aramaic texts from the fifth-century BCE Jewish community in Elephantine, Egypt, refer to Anat-Bethel (*ʿntbytʾl*) and Anat-Yahu (*ʿntyhw*), which some scholars interpret as references to the goddess Anat as the consort of the gods Bethel ("House of God") and Yahweh, respectively. Other scholars translate the word *ʿnt* as "providence" or "sign" and understand it as the cultic hypostasis of the male deity rather than the appearance of Anat in the syncretistic Jewish literature. Anat-Bethel also appears in the list of divine witnesses to the seventh-century Assyrian treaty between King Baal of Tyre and Esarhaddon. Hellenistic sources sometimes equate Anat with the virgin warrior Athena, as in a fourth-century BCE bilingual inscription in Phoenician and Greek from Lapethos on Cyprus. Later traditions often identify Anat with other Canaanite goddesses, such as Astarte and Atargatis-Derketo.

See Also Baal.

Bibliography

Cornelius, Izak. "Anat and Qudshu as the 'Mistress of Animals': Aspects of the Iconography of the Canaanite Goddesses." *Studi Epigrafici e Linguistici* 10 (1993): 21–45.

Day, Peggy L. "Anat: Ugarit's 'Mistress of Animals.'" *Journal of Near Eastern Studies* 51 (1992): 181–190.

Day, Peggy L. "Why Is Anat a Warrior and a Hunter?" In *The Bible and the Politics of Exegesis: Essays in Honor of Norman K. Gottwalk on His Sixty-fifth Birthday,* edited by David Jobling, Peggy L. Day, and Gerald T. Sheppard. Cleveland, 1992.

Day, Peggy L. "Anat." In *Dictionary of Deities and Demons in the Bible.* 2d ed. Edited by Karel van der Toorn, Bob Becking, and Pieter W. van der Horst, pp. 36–43. Leiden, 1999. An excellent overview with bibliography.

Parker, Simon B., ed. *Ugaritic Narrative Poetry.* Atlanta, 1997. Excellent and accessible English translations of the Ugaritic mythological texts.

Walls, Neal H. *The Goddess Anat in Ugaritic Myth.* Atlanta, 1992.

Neal H. Walls (2005)

ANCESTORS

This entry consists of the following articles:

ANCESTOR WORSHIP
MYTHIC ANCESTORS
BALTIC CULT OF ANCESTORS

ANCESTORS: ANCESTOR WORSHIP

The term *ancestor worship* designates rites and beliefs concerning deceased kinsmen. Rites of ancestor worship include personal devotions, domestic rites, the ancestral rites of a kinship group such as a lineage, periodic rites on the death day of the deceased, and annual rites for collectivity of ancestors. Generally excluded from the category are rites for the dead having no specific reference to kinsmen, and beliefs about the dead in general that lack any special reference to kinship.

General Characteristics and Research Problems. Ancestor worship has attracted the enduring interest of scholars in many areas of the study of religion. In the late nineteenth century, it was identified as the most basic form of all religion, and subsequent studies of the subject in specific areas have provided a stimulating point of access to related problems of religion, society, and culture.

The worship of ancestors is closely linked to cosmology and worldview, to ideas of the soul and the afterlife, and to a society's regulation of inheritance and succession. In East Asia ancestor worship is found combined with the practice of Buddhism, and ancestral rites compose a major part of the practice of Confucianism. It is generally acknowledged that ancestor worship functions to uphold the authority of elders, to support social control, and to foster conservative and traditionalist attitudes. In addition, ancestor worship is clearly linked to an ethic of filial piety and obedience to elders.

The institution of ancestor worship is properly regarded as a religious practice, not as a religion in itself. It is generally carried out by kinship groups and seldom has a priesthood separable from them. It is limited to the practice of the ethnic group; there is no attempt to proselytize outsiders. Its ethical dimension primarily refers to the proper conduct of family or kinship relations. It does not have formal doctrine as such; where texts exist, these are mainly liturgical manuals. In most cases ancestor worship is not the only religious practice of a society; rather, it exists as part of a more comprehensive religious system.

The meaning of *worship* in *ancestor worship* is problematic. Ancestor worship takes a variety of forms in different areas, and its attitudinal characteristics vary accordingly. The ancestors may be regarded as possessing power equivalent to that of a deity and hence may be accorded cult status and considered able to influence society to the same extent as its deities. Typically, the conception of ancestors is strongly influenced by ideas of other supernaturals in the society's religious system. Ancestors may be prayed to as having the power to grant boons or allay misfortune, but their effectiveness is regarded as naturally limited by the bonds of kinship. Thus, a member of a certain lineage prays only to the ancestors of that lineage; it would be regarded as nonsensical to pray to ancestors of any other lineage. Accordingly, members of other lineages are excluded from the ancestral rites of kinship groups of which they are not members. The religious attitudes involved in the worship of ancestors include filial piety, respect, sympathy, and sometimes, fear.

The rites of death, including funerary and mortuary rituals, are regarded as falling within the purview of ancestor worship only when memorial rites beyond the period of death and disposition of the corpse are carried out as a regular function of a kinship group. Thus, the funerary rites and occasional memorials common in Europe and the United States are not regarded as evidence of ancestor worship. However, when ancestors are collectively and regularly accorded cult status by their descendants, acting as members of a kinship group, such practices are regarded as ancestor worship.

Dead or stillborn children, miscarriages, and abortions are generally conceptually distinguished from ancestors. For the most part these exceptional deaths are accorded very abbreviated funeral rites, if any, and they generally receive little memorial ritual. Like those who die in youth before marriage, their fate is regarded as especially pitiable and as a source of possible harm to the living.

The study of ancestor worship involves several different questions. How are the ancestors viewed in relation to their descendants? Is ancestor worship in some sense a reflection of actual relations between fathers and sons? In what circumstances are the ancestors viewed as capable of harming their descendants, and is the ancestors' benevolence or malevolence linked to descendants' sense of guilt toward them? What can be learned about relations of jural authority from studies of ancestor worship? What is the character of domestic rites? These often seem to reflect a feeling that the dead are still "living" in some sense, that they can be contacted and their advice sought. Studies in this area illumine attitudes toward death and reveal a very general perception that the dead gradually lose their individual characteristics and merge into an impersonal collectivity. A recent topic of research concerns the differing attitudes of women and men toward ancestors.

Ancestor Worship in the History of the Study of Religion. In *Principles of Sociology* (1877) Herbert Spencer wrote that "ancestor worship is the root of every religion." According to his view, the cult of heroes originated in the deification of an ancestor, and in fact all deities originate by an analogous process. Spencer's euhemerist theory rested on the idea, familiar in the scholarship of his day, that religion as a whole has a common origin from which its many forms derive. Knowledge of this original form would provide the key to understanding all subsequent developments.

Somewhat earlier Fustel de Coulanges wrote in *La cité antique* (1864) that the ancient societies of Greece and Rome were founded upon ancestor worship. Furthermore, when the beliefs and practices of ancestor worship were weakened, society as a whole was entirely transformed. In the view of de Coulanges, Greece and Rome were founded upon a common belief in the soul's continued existence after the body's death. The family that continued to worship its ancestors became society's basic unit, expanding gradually to the clan divisions of gens, phratry, and tribe. Eventually cities were founded, governed as quasi-religious associations by patrician families.

In *Totem and Taboo* (1913), Sigmund Freud postulated that the belief that the living can be harmed by the dead serves to reduce guilt experienced toward the dead. That is, in kinship relations characterized by conscious affection there is inevitably a measure of hostility; however, this hostility conflicts with the conscious ideal of affectionate relations and hence must be repressed. Repressed hostility is then projected onto the dead and takes the form of the belief that the dead are malevolent and can harm the living.

Meyer Fortes considerably refined Freud's hypothesis on the basis of African material. In *Oedipus and Job in West African Religion* (1959), Fortes found that among the Tallensi belief in the continued authority of ancestors, rather than fear of them, is the principle means of alleviating guilt arising from repressed hostility.

Among the Tallensi relations between fathers and sons are affectionate, but, because a son cannot attain full jural authority until his father's death, sons bear a latent resentment of their fathers. However, this resentment does not manifest itself as belief in the malevolence of the dead. Instead, the Tallensi believe that the authority of the father is granted to him by his ancestors, who demand from the son continued subordination. Thus the function of ancestor worship is to reinforce the general, positive valuation of the authority of elders, quite apart from the individual personality of any specific ancestor. A related function is to place a positive value upon subordination of the desires of the individual to the collective authority of tribal elders. This value is useful in ensuring the continued solidarity of the group.

In *Death, Property, and the Ancestors* (1966), Jack Goody studied ancestor worship among the LoDagaa of West Africa. Property to be inherited by descendants is not distributed until the death of the father. Prevented from commanding the full possession of this property, a son experiences a subconscious wish for the father's death. Repression of this guilt takes the form of the belief that the dead have eternal rights to the property they formerly held. In order to enjoy those rights, the dead must receive sacrifices from the living. If sacrifices are not forthcoming, the ancestors will afflict their descendants with sickness and misfortune. Thus beliefs concerning ancestral affliction are inextricably linked to social issues of inheritance and succession.

In "Gods, Ghosts, and Ancestors," Arthur Wolf (1974) shows how Chinese concepts of a variety of supernatural beings closely correspond to social reality. In particular, the conception of ancestors replicates perceptions of parents, elders, and other kin. This is not to say that the living and dead are not distinguished, but that the same relations of authority and obedience are found among the living and in their rites for their ancestors.

Ancestor Worship in Practice. This section describes the practice of ancestor worship in various cultural areas and in relation to several religious traditions.

Africa. Ancestor worship normally forms only one aspect of an African people's religion. A person without descendants cannot become an ancestor, and in order to achieve ancestorhood, proper burial, with rites appropriate to the person's status, is necessary. After an interval following death, a deceased person who becomes an ancestor is no longer perceived as an individual. Personal characteristics disappear from the awareness of the living, and only the value of the ancestor as a moral exemplar remains. Ancestors are believed to be capable of intervening in human affairs, but only in the defined area of their authority, that is, among their descendants.

In an important study of African ancestor worship, Max Gluckman (1937) established the distinction between ancestor worship and the cult of the dead. Ancestors represent positive moral forces who can cause or prevent misfortune and who require that their descendants observe a moral code. The cult of the dead, on the other hand, is not exclusively directed to deceased kinsmen, but to the spirits of the dead in general. Here spirits are prayed to for the achievement of amoral or antisocial ends, whereas ancestors can be petitioned only for ends that are in accord with basic social principles.

Among the Edo the deceased is believed to progress through the spirit world on a course that parallels the progress of his son and other successors. Events in this world are punctuated by rites and are believed to have a counterpart in the spirit world. Thus it may be twenty years before a spirit is finally merged into the collective dead and descendants can receive their full complement of authority. In this sense the ancestors continue to exert authority over their descendants long after death. Until that authority ceases, the son must perform rites as prescribed and behave in approved ways.

Among the Ewe of Ghana, ancestor worship is an important focal point of the whole society. It is the basis of the entire religious system and a point of reference for the conceptualization of all social relations. The Ewe believe that the human being has two souls. Before birth the being resides in the spirit world; it comes into this world when it finds a mother, and it returns to the spirit world at death. This cycle of movement through the realms is perpetual. The ancestors are invoked with libations on all ceremonial occasions. Rites range from simple, personal libations to complicated rituals involving an entire lineage. During a ritual, the soul of the ancestor returns to be fed through the ceremonial stool that serves as its shrine. In addition to individual stools, there is a lineage stool for lineage ancestors that is kept wrapped in silks or velvet.

The studies of Igor Kopytoff (1971) on the Suku of Zaire raise the question of the appropriateness of the term *ancestor worship*. The Suku have no term that can be translated as "ancestor"; they make no terminological distinction between the dead and the living. A single set of principles regulates relations between seniors and juniors. The dividing line between living and dead does not affect those principles. Thus it may be said among the Suku ancestor worship is an extension of lineage relations between elders and their juniors. Furthermore, lineages must be considered as communities of both living and dead. The powers attributed to ancestors can only be seen as a projection of the powers of living elders. In this sense the term *ancestor worship* can be misleading.

Melanesia. Ancestors are one of many types of spirits recognized by Melanesian tribal peoples. Regarding the role of ancestor worship in tribal life, Roy A. Rappaport's study *Pigs for the Ancestors* (1977) presents an innovative approach not seen in the study of ancestor worship in other areas. Among the highland Tsembaga, ancestral ritual is part of a complex ecological system in which a balanced cycle of abundance and scarcity is regulated. Yam gardens are threatened by the unhindered growth of the pig population, and human beings must supplement their starch-based diet with protein. Propelling this cycle is a belief that pigs must be sacrificed to the ancestors in great numbers. These sacrifices provide the Tsembaga with protein in great quantity. Pigs sacrificed when someone dies or in connection with intertribal warfare supplement the ordinary diet of yams, which is adequate for ordinary activity but not for periods of stress. Thus ancestor worship plays a vital role in the ecological balance of the tribe in its environment.

India. Ancestor worship in India takes a variety of forms, depending upon the area and the ethnic group concerned; however, providing food for the dead is a basic and widespread practice. Orthodox Hindu practice centers on an annual rite between August and September that includes offering sacred rice balls (*piṇḍa*) to the ancestors. The *Laws of Manu* includes specific instructions for ancestral offerings. Descendants provide a feast for the *brahmans,* and the merit of this act is transferred to the ancestors. The feast itself is called the Śrāddha. The form of this rite varies depending on whether it is observed during a funeral or in subsequent, annual observances. Texts prescribe ritual purifications and preparations in detail.

Buddhism. Based on a canonical story, the All Souls Festival, or Avalambana, is observed throughout Southeast and East Asia. The story concerns one of the Buddha's disciples, Maudgalyāyana, known for skill in meditation and supranormal powers. The mother of Maudgalyāyana appeared to her son in a dream and revealed to him that she was suffering innumerable tortures in the blackest hell because of her *karman.* Through magic Maudgalyāyana visited his mother in hell, but his power was of no avail in securing her release. Eventually the Buddha instructed him to convene an assembly of the priesthood, which then would recite sūtras and transfer the merit of those rites to ancestors. In other words, descendants must utilize the mediation of the priesthood in order to benefit ancestors. The result is an annual festival, traditionally observed on the day of the full moon of the eighth lunar month. At this festival special sūtra recitations and offering rites for the ancestors are held in Buddhist temples, and domestic rites differing in each country are performed. In addition to rites for ancestors, observances for the "hungry ghosts" and for spirits who have died leaving no descendants are performed.

Although one of the key concepts in early Indian Buddhism was the idea of no-soul (*anātman*), in fact the idea of a soul is widely accepted in East Asia. The idea of rebirth in human, heavenly, and subhuman forms is found combined with the idea that an eternal soul rests in an ancestral tablet or inhabits a world of the dead. The contradictions involved in this complex of ideas are not generally addressed as problematic by those who hold them.

In East Asia today the performance of ancestral and funeral ritual provides the Buddhist clergy with one of its greatest sources of revenue, a tendency particularly marked in Japan. The Buddhist clergy is typically employed to recite sūtras for the dead and to enshrine ancestral tablets in temples.

Shamanism. Throughout East Asia ancestor worship is found in close association with shamanistic practices. Shamanism in East Asia today consists in large part of mediumistic communications in which the shaman enters a trance and divines the present condition of a client's ancestors. These practices are based on the folk notion that if a person suffers from an unusual or seemingly unwarranted affliction, the ancestors may be the cause. If the ancestors are suffering, if they are displeased with their descendants' conduct, or if they are offered inappropriate or insufficient ritual, they may cause some harm to come to their descendants. However, it is only rarely that this belief is straightforwardly expressed as the proposition that ancestors willfully, malevolently afflict their descendants.

Chinese ancestor worship. An important component at work in the metaphysics of Chinese ancestor cults is indigenous theories of the soul. First of all, since Zhou times (c. 1123–221 BCE) the idea of the soul as the pale, ghostly shadow of a man has been a perduring notion found in popular stories. These apparitions are called *gui,* meaning demons, devils, and ghosts, as opposed to *shen,* the benevolent spirits of ancestors (a word used also to refer to all deities).

Together with this idea of the ghostly soul there developed a conception of the soul in terms of yin and yang. According to this theory, the yin portion of the soul, called *po,* may turn into a *gui* and cause misfortune if descendants do not perform proper ancestral rites. If the *po* is satisfactorily placated, however, it will rest peacefully. Meanwhile, the yang portion of the soul, called *hun,* associated with *shen,* will bless and protect descendants and their families. Thus Chinese ancestral rites have been motivated simultaneously by the fear of the vengeful dead and by the hope for ancestral blessings.

Chinese ancestor worship can be seen as two separate cults: one that expresses the unity of a lineage of lineage-segment, the so-called hall cult, and another directed to the recently deceased members of a household, the domestic cult. Lineage observances center upon an ancestral hall in which tablets representing lineage ancestors are enshrined and worshiped by descendants in a Confucian mode. Domestic rites center upon daily offerings at a home altar. Lineage ritual tends to formality and the expression of sentiments of obedience to the authority of ancestors and elders as a group, whereas domestic ritual focuses upon the expression of individual sentiments and continued relations between descendants and particular deceased individuals.

Chinese ancestor worship is closely linked to property inheritance; every deceased individual must receive offerings from at least one descendant who will provide him with sustenance in the next life. However, a specific person is only required to worship those ancestors from whom he has received property.

Confucianism. Confucianism lays heavy emphasis upon the correct practice of ancestral ritual. Special attention is given to minute details concerning the content and arrangement of offerings, proper dress, gesture and posture, and the order of precedence in appearing before ancestral altars. According to the *Book of Family Ritual* of the neo-Confucian scholar Zhu Xi, the *Zhuzi jiali,* commemoration of ancestors became primarily a responsibility of eldest sons, and women were excluded from officiating roles in the celebration of rites.

The highest virtue in Confucian doctrine is filial piety, quintessentially expressed in the worship of ancestors. When Buddhism was first introduced to China, one of Confucianism's strongest arguments against it was the assertion that Buddhism was in essence opposed to filial piety and was likely to disrupt the practice of ancestor worship. If sons took the tonsure and failed to perform ancestral rites, then not only would spirits in the other world suffer from lack of ritual attention but social relations in society would also be undermined.

In traditional Chinese society gravesites are located through a geomancer. Based upon the idea that an ideal confluence of "winds and waters" (*feng-shui*) benefits the dead and their descendants, a geomancer seeks a site in which the burial urn can be nestled in the curve of rolling hills and near running water. This combination of cosmic forces is believed to benefit the dead and to facilitate their progress in the other world. Lineages compete fiercely with one another for these scarce resources and may even forcibly remove unprotected urns so that new ones may occupy auspicious sites.

Korea. In Korea women and men hold quite different images of ancestors. A woman marries away from her natal village and enters her husband's household under the authority of his mother and father. The wife's relations with her husband's kin are expected to be characterized by strife and competition. Her membership in the husband's lineage is tenuous and is never fully acknowledged in ritual until her death. Because women's relation to the lineage is strained in these ways, they hold more negative views of the ancestors than do men. Women's negative conceptions are expressed in the idea that ancestors maliciously harm their descendants by afflicting them with disease and misfortune. Men worship ancestors in Confucian rites from which women are excluded, while women perform rites for ancestors in a shamanic mode, utilizing widespread networks of shamans, most of whom are women. This gender-based bifurcation in ancestor worship is a special characteristic of Korean tradition.

Japan. Since the Tokugawa period (1600–1868) Japanese ancestor worship has mainly been carried out in a Buddhist mode, though Shintō rites also exist. As in China, ancestral ritual reflects relations of authority and inheritance, but instead of lineage rites, rites are performed by main and branch households of the traditional family system, the *ie.* Branch families (*bunke*) accept the ritual centrality of the main household (*honke*) by participating in its rites in a subordinate status. The *honke* does not reciprocate. In addition to *honke-bunke* rites, domestic rites performed before a Buddhist altar are a prominent feature of Japanese ancestral worship.

In *Ancestor Worship in Contemporary Japan* (1973) Robert Smith demonstrates that sympathy often provokes the Japanese to enshrine the tablets of entirely unrelated persons in their own domestic altars. They may also keep duplicate tablets out of personal attachment to a deceased person and with no feeling that sanctions will be forthcoming if they fail to do so. Thus, in addition to its reflection of kinship relations, ancestor worship becomes a means of expressing affection.

The "new religions" of Japan are a group of several hundred associations that have appeared in the nineteenth and twentieth centuries. Whether their doctrine is derived from Shintō or Buddhism, most reserve a special place for ancestor worship in some form. Reiyukai Kyodan (Association of Friends of the Spirits) represents a rare example of a religious group in which worship of ancestors is the main focus of individual and collective rites. Reverence for ancestors in the new religions and in Japanese society in general is closely linked to social and political conservatism and to a traditionalist preference for the social mores of the past.

SEE ALSO Afterlife, article on Chinese Concepts; Domestic Observances, article on Chinese Practices; Family; Genealogy; Soul, article on Chinese Concepts.

BIBLIOGRAPHY

Ahern, Emily. *The Cult of the Dead in a Chinese Village.* Stanford, Calif., 1973. A comprehensive study of ancestor worship in Taiwan that clarifies the relation between lineage and domestic observances.

Blacker, Carmen. *The Catalpa Bow.* London, 1975. An evocative study of shamanistic and ancestral practices in Japanese folk religion.

Freedman, Maurice. *Lineage Organization in Southeastern China* (1958). London, 1965. An anthropological study of lineage organization that establishes the distinction between hall and domestic ancestral cults and includes valuable material on geomancy.

Gluckman, Max. "Mortuary Customs and the Belief in Survival after Death among the South-Eastern Bantu." *Bantu Studies* 11 (June 1937): 117–136.

Groot, J. J. M. de. *The Religious System of China* (1892). 6 vols. Taipei, 1967. A comprehensive study of Chinese religions with rich data on ancestor worship, principally from Amoy.

Hardacre, Helen. *Lay Buddhism in Contemporary Japan: Reiyukai Kyodan.* Princeton, 1984. A study of a new religion of Japan with special reference to ancestor worship.

Janelli, Dawnhee Yim, and Roger L. Janelli. *Ancestor Worship in Korean Society.* Stanford, Calif., 1982. A study of Korean ancestor worship with special reference to gender differences in belief and practice.

Jordan, David K. *Gods, Ghosts, and Ancestors: The Folk Religion of a Taiwanese Village.* Chicago, 1969. A study of ancestor worship and related phenomena, especially spirit marriage, in Taiwan.

Kopytoff, Igor. "Ancestors as Elders in Africa." *Africa* 41 (April 1971): 129–142.

Newell, William H., ed. *Ancestors.* The Hague, 1976. A useful collection of essays on aspects of ancestor worship, especially in Africa and Japan.

Takeda Choshu. *Sosen suhai.* Tokyo, 1971. A study of Japanese ancestor worship with special reference to Buddhism.

Wolf, Arthur P. "Gods, Ghosts, and Ancestors." In his *Religion and Ritual in Chinese Society,* pp. 131–182. Stanford, Calif., 1974.

Xu, Francis L. K. *Under the Ancestors' Shadow.* New York, 1948. A classic study of Chinese ancestor worship.

Yanagita Kunio. *Senzo no hanashi.* Tokyo, 1946. Translated by F. H. Mayer and Ishiwara Yasuyo as *About Our Ancestors* (Tokyo, 1970). A folkloristic view of Japanese ancestor worship and its place in Japanese culture.

New Sources

Friesen, Steven J. *Ancestors in Post-Contact Religion: Roots, Ruptures, and Modernity's Memory.* Cambridge, Mass., 2001.

Lee, Kwang Kyu. "The Concept of Ancestors and Ancestor Worship in Korea." *Asian Folklore Studies* 43, no. 2 (1984): 199–214.

HELEN HARDACRE (1987)
Revised Bibliography

ANCESTORS: MYTHIC ANCESTORS

Cosmogonic myths are narratives that depict the creation of the world by divine beings. In many cosmogonic myths a supreme being or high god creates the world, after which other divine beings come into being, who in the form of culture heroes or other types of gods reveal the realm of the sacred, death, sexuality, sacred geography, and the methods of food production. The narrative of the cosmogonic myth moves from the initial creation of the world to the revelation of the archetypal actions and gestures of divine beings and culture heroes, thus describing a sacred history of primordial times. These divine beings and culture heroes form the ancestral lineages of the human race. The situation of the human race is based upon the activities, adventures, discoveries, and disappearance of these first creative ancestors, who appeared in sacred history.

PRIMORDIAL RUPTURES. In the Mesopotamian myth *Enuma elish,* a tension develops between the first creators and their offspring. This tension leads to a rupture in the initial creation and a struggle between its gods and their offspring. In the ensuing battle, the foundation is established for human existence. In the *Enuma elish,* the god Marduk is the leader of the offspring who fight Tiamat, the mother. In the battle Tiamat is slain, and her body becomes the earth on which human beings live. Certain archetypes for human existence are established as a result of this battle: the cooperation between the offspring gods becomes a model for cooperative enterprise among human beings, which the death of Tiamat affirms. In the biblical myth of the *Book of Genesis,* Adam and Eve live in Paradise with the creator god. When they sin they become the archetypal ancestors of the human community, for they now must experience sexuality, birth, labor, and death, the universal lot of all human beings.

A Dogon myth from West Africa describes a similar situation. The god Amma began creation by first forming a cosmic egg, in which the embryos of twin deities matured; they were to become perfect beings. One of the twins became impatient and decided to leave the egg before maturation. In so doing it tore out part of the placenta and fell to what is now the earth, creating a place of habitation from the torn placenta of the egg. This was an incomplete creation, however, and Amma, to rectify the situation, sacrificed the other twin. Even with this sacrifice, the creation could not be made perfect. Instead of creating perfect beings who were both androgynous and amphibious, Amma was forced to compromise. Thus, humans are not androgynous but rather composed of two sexes; they are not amphibious but essentially terrestrial; they do not live continuously in a perfect state of illumination (composed of equal parts of dark and light), as was the original intention of Amma, but in two alternating modes of full light and darkness. In addition to this, the opposing natures of the obedient and the malevolent twin, who are the ancestors of all human beings on earth, define modes of life throughout the universe.

In myths of this kind we are able to recognize what Mircea Eliade (1969) identified as two forms of primordiality. There is, first of all, the primordiality defined by the great creator deities who brought the world into being. Their creativity is inaccessible to ordinary human beings and they appear remote and unconcerned with the human condition. There is another primordiality that can be recognized in the tension and rupture between the creator deities and other deities who enter upon adventures and exploits that define the archetypal modes for human existence. Through these activities, the creator deities bring the sacred into the existential modes of human existence and are seen as the ancestors of human beings.

In some cultures, the cosmogonic myths make no reference to great creator deities. The narrative begins with the second primordiality and the action is that of the culture hero, whose actions create the human condition. Among the Kwakiutl Indians of North America, the culture hero is Transformer and comes upon the scene as a human being living in a human family. Whenever he discovers human deceit or error, he transforms the human being into a bird or other animal, thus filling the landscape with the food supply necessary for human existence. In this manner Transformer sets the rules for the production and consumption of food and for reincarnation (to ensure a continuous supply of food). Prior to the actions of Transformer there is no order in the cosmos. After his participation in the production of the food supply, all other forms of order—within the family, society, and so on—come into being. The chiefs of the segmented social units *(numaym)* are each related to an animal ancestor. In fact, following upon the transformation of humans into animals, the Kwakiutl believe that animals and spirits lead lives that are exactly equivalent to those of human beings. Animals are considered to be human beings who are wearing masks and costumes created by their animal forms.

The second primordiality also dominates the myth of what Adolf E. Jensen (1963) has called "cultivator cultures." In a myth cited from the Indonesian island of Ceram, he describes a type of deity referred to by the indigenous peoples as a *dema* deity. The activity of these deities goes back to the end of the first primordial period. They sometimes possess human form and at other times animal form. The decisive event in their lives is the killing of one *dema* deity by another, which establishes the human condition. Before the death of the *dema,* the human condition is not characterized by sexual differentiation or death; it is only after the death of the *dema* that these aspects come into existence. The *dema* come at the end of primordial time and are thus the first of all human ancestors. Through the death of the *dema,* human beings are accepted again within their community. In myths of this kind the ancestors are gods, heroes, or divine beings, who through their actions make possible and render meaningful the human condition as it is, with all of its possibilities and limitations, and it is through them that the human condition possesses a divine presence.

Ancestors not only set forth the general and universal human condition; they are also the founders of clans, families, moieties, and other segments of the human community. N. D. Fustel de Coulanges's classic work *The Ancient City* (1901) describes how ancient Greek and Roman families were founded by ancestors who were heroes or divine beings. The family cult was at once the basis for the order and maintenance of the family and a cult of the ancestor. Similar notions are present among Australian Aborigines, where each totemic group has its own totemic ancestor who controls the food supply and is the basis for authority and marriages among the groups. In almost the same manner, the Tucano Indians of Colombia understand their origins as arising from mythical ancestors, the Desána, who revealed all the forms of nature and modes of being to the human community.

An exemplary expression of the cult of ancestors is found in Chinese religions. It is the duty of Chinese sons to provide for and revere their parents in this life and the life after death; this is a relationship of reciprocity. The household is composed of the living and the dead; the ancestors provide and sustain the foundations of spiritual order upon which the family is based, while the living keep the family in motion. The living are always under the tacit judgment of their ancestors, on account of which they attempt to conduct their lives in an honorable manner.

THE FOUNDING OF CITIES. Not only do divine ancestors and culture heroes form the lineages of families and totemic groups, they are equally present at the beginnings of almost every city foundation in ancient and traditional cultures. Cain in the biblical story is the culture hero who founds the city of Enoch; Romulus is the founder of Rome; Quetzalcoatl, of Tollan. In Southeast Asia, the founding of states and kingship follow the archetypes of the Hindu god Indra.

The founding of a city may be a response to the experience of a hierophany. Hierophanies of space, or ceremonial centers, are revelations of the sacred meaning of space itself. The divine beings or culture heroes who found cities derive their power from such sacred ceremonial centers. In some cases, a sacrifice is necessary to appease the gods of the location; thus, many of the myths involving the founding of cities relate a story of twins, one of whom is killed or sacrificed, as in the case of Cain's slaying of Abel, or Romulus's murder of Remus. In one of the mythological cycles of Quetzalcoatl, for example, a magical combat takes place in which Quetzalcoatl kills his uncle.

The ancestors as founders of a city establish the archetypes for all domesticated space. The normalization of activities in the space of the city, whether in terms of family structures or the public meanings of space, are guaranteed by the founding ancestor. All other establishments or reestablishments of cities will follow the model of the archetypal gestures of the founding ancestor of the city. The ruler of the city represents and symbolizes the presence of the divine ancestor, and elaborate rituals of rulership take place at certain temporal intervals to commemorate and reestablish the founding gestures.

DEATH. In some myths death enters the world because of an action, inaction, or quarrel among the creator deities. They may have simply forgotten to tell human beings whether they were immortal or not, or the creator deity allows death to enter the world. In a myth from Madagascar two gods create human beings: the earth god forms them from wood and clay, the god of heaven gives them life. Human beings die so that they may return to the origins of their being.

In most mythic scenarios, however, death is the result of a sacred history that introduces the second meaning of primordiality. Through ignorance, interdiction, or violence, a break is made by the divine offspring from the creator deity, and in this rupture is the origin of death. The origin of the abode of the dead is equally located in this event, for, in the mythic scenarios, the rupture creates divisions in space among which a place of the dead comes into being. For example, in the Dogon myth mentioned above, the placenta of the god Amma is the earth, and at death one returns to the earth which was the original stuff of creation.

Funerary rituals are very important, for they assure that the dead will arrive in the correct manner at the abode of the ancestors. The souls of the dead must be instructed and led on the right path lest they become lost. At death the deceased is vulnerable and subject to the attack of malevolent spirits. Funerary rituals prescribe the correct behavior and route to be taken by the dead to the land of the ancestors.

SEE ALSO Animals; Archetypes; Center of the World; Cities; Cosmogony; Culture Heroes; Death; Deus Otiosus; Fall, The; Funeral Rites; Totemism.

BIBLIOGRAPHY

A general discussion of cosmogonic myths can be found in my *Alpha: The Myths of Creation* (New York, 1963). For Mircea Eliade's discussion of the two types of primordiality, see "Cosmogonic Myth and Sacred History," in his *The Quest* (Chicago, 1969). For ancient Near Eastern myths, see *Ancient Near Eastern Texts relating to the Old Testament,* 3d ed., edited by J. B. Pritchard (Princeton, 1969). N. D. Fustel de Coulanges's *The Ancient City* (1901), 12th ed. (Baltimore, 1980), remains the best general introduction to Greek and Roman religion dealing with the meaning of ancestors. Joseph Rykwert's *The Idea of a Town* (Princeton, 1976) is a brilliant discussion of the myths and rituals of the founding of Rome. Paul Wheatley's *The Pivot of the Four Quarters* (Chicago, 1971) is the best work on the meaning of the ceremonial center as the basis for the founding of cities. Robert Heine-Geldern's "Conceptions of State and Kingship in Southeast Asia," *Far Eastern Quarterly* 2 (November 1942): 15–30, describes state and urban foundation in Southeast Asia. Davíd Carrasco presents the full cycle of the myths, histories, and city foundations of Quetzalcoatl in *Quetzalcoatl and the Irony of Empire* (Chicago, 1982). For the Tucano Indians of Colombia, see Gerardo Reichel-Dolmatoff's *Amazonian Cosmos* (Chicago, 1971). Adolf E. Jensen's *Myth and Cult among Primitive Peoples* (Chicago, 1963), is the best general work on the religious meaning of culture heroes and *dema* deities. For China, see Raymond Dawson's *The Chinese Experience* (London, 1978). Dominique Zahan's *The Religion, Spirituality, and Thought of Traditional Africa* (Chicago, 1979) places the meaning of ancestors within the general structures of African religions. Hans Abrahamsson's *The Origin of Death* (Uppsala, 1951), is still the best study of the myths of death in Africa. For the ancestors of the Dinka, a cattle-raising people in Africa, see Godfrey Lienhardt's *Divinity and Experience: The Religion of the Dinka* (Oxford, 1961). Jack Goody's *Death, Property and the Ancestors* (Stanford, 1962) is a detailed study of death and funerary rituals among the LoDagaa of West Africa. Stanley Wallens's *Feasting with Cannibals* (Princeton, 1981) is a study of the meaning of ancestors among the Kwakiutl.

CHARLES H. LONG (1987)

ANCESTORS: BALTIC CULT OF ANCESTORS

Despite the cultural and historical similarities between the Baltic peoples of Latvia and Lithuania, several different approaches to research on Baltic religion have developed. Lithuanian scholars, who consider relics of the cult of ancestors as part of their pre-Christian world, have primarily studied written sources, drawing as well on archaeological, linguistic, folklore, and ethnographic data. By contrast, in reconstructing the Latvian religious tradition, Latvian scholars have looked to not only the previously mentioned sources, but they have leaned heavily on information found in a specific folklore genre, that of poetic quatrains called *dainas,* the majority of which are intended to be sung. *Dainas* have a specific formulaic structure and are characterized by a high level of abstraction, as well as a functional realism. These characteristics allowed strata of archaic, cultural, and historical information to survive up to the time when *dainas* were first written down during the second half of the nineteenth century. In these quatrains are found such religious beings from the pre-Christian era as the mother of the shades, the mother of graves, the mother of sand, and the mother of the earth, complete with elaborate character portraits and descriptions of their respective spheres of influence.

Few in-depth studies have been done either in Latvia or Lithuania on the question of ancestor worship. With the exception of a number of monographs, the most significant work in this field consists of isolated references within descriptive and analytical works on Baltic religion and cultural traditions regarding family feasts and calendar festivities. The most important work on pre-Christian Baltic religion continues to be Marija Gimbutas's *The Balts* (1963) and Wilhelm Mannhardt's *Letto-Preussische Götterlehre* (Latvian-Prussian mythology, 1936), in which Mannhardt analyzes works by various authors.

LATVIA. The pre–World War II era is considered the most productive period in research on pre-Christian Baltic religion and the cult of ancestors. The most important studies to come out of this period were by Pēteris Šmits, Mārtiņš Bruņenieks, Kārlis Straubergs, and Ludvigs Adamovičs. Šmits, in his 1918 study *Latviešu mitoloģija* (Latvian mythology), considers ancestor worship as a particularly important building block in the worldview of humanity. With that in mind, he describes Latvian mourning practices, the concept of an afterlife, and the religious images that link humans to the world of the dead, and he compares these to traditions of other cultures. Mārtiņš Bruņenieks, in his comparative study *Senlatviešu reliģiskais pasaules uzskats* (Ancient Latvian religious views of the world, 1937), applies the animism theory to analyze the Baltic cult of ancestors and compares it to the religious beliefs of other peoples, such as the Babylonians, the Egyptians, and the Greeks. In *Senlatviešu reliģija agrīnā dzelzs laikmetā* (The religion of ancient Latvians in the early Iron Age, 1930), Adamovičs devotes special sections to ancestor worship, examining archeological materials, written historical records from the thirteenth century on, documented accounts, ethnographic descriptions and folklore texts, and folk beliefs and songs recorded in the nineteenth century.

Eduards Šturms analyzes burial practices of the Baltic peoples in *Chroniku un senrakstu ziņas par baltu tautu bēŗu parašām* (Information on Baltic burial practices sourced from chronicles and ancient texts, 1938), using historical sources from the thirteenth, fourteenth, and first half of the fifteenth century. Using archaeological data, Šturms separates out distinct Baltic peoples consisting of Prussians, Curonians, Zhemaits, and Aukshtaitians, and he describes their burial practices. In *Lettisk folktro om de döda* (Latvian folk beliefs about the dead, 1949), Kārlis Straubergs looks at burial practices and the Baltic concept of the afterlife within the context of ancestor worship by other European nations. Similar aspects of the Latvian ancestor cult are discussed in other works by the same author. For example, Straubergs deals exclusively with this topic in his essay "Hanovijs par dvēseļu kultu pie latviešiem" (Hanovijs on the cult of the dead among Latvians, 1925). Straubergs also includes material on the cult of ancestors within the larger context of Latvian sacral issues in books like *Pār deviņi novadiņi* (Across the country, 1995) and in his collection of essays, *Latvju kultūra* (Latvian culture, 1948).

Osvalds Līdaks's *Latviešu svētki: Latviešu svinamās dienas* (Latvian feasts: Latvian calendar festivities, 1940s/1991) describes, based on Latvian folklore material, annual Latvian celebrations, including those linked to the cult of ancestors. Haralds Biezais's *Germanische und Baltische Religion*

(German and Baltic religion, 1975) offers an in-depth analysis of the Baltic and Latvian view of the world, including a discussion of the cult of ancestors and related deities.

Among later works that include some references to ancestor worship, Edīte Olupe's *Latviešu gadskārtu ieražas* (Latvian calendar festivity traditions, 1992) contains a segment describing season-based ancestor worship. In a doctoral thesis titled "Priekšstati par mirušo pasauli latviešu bēru tautasdziesmās" (Concepts of the world of the dead in Latvian burial folksongs, 1992) Guntis Pakalns charts the location of the world of the dead in the binary world model as described in Latvian mythological concepts. The unique features of Latvian burial practices and afterlife concepts as reflected in Latvian folklore have also been examined by Janīna Kursīte in *Latviešu folklora mītu spogulī* (Latvian folklore in the mirror of mythology, 1996) and *Mītiskais folklorā, literatūrā, mākslā* (The mythical in folklore, literature, and art, 1999). Kursīte has also delved into the semantics of two Latvian religious beings associated with the worship of ancestors: Zemes māte (the mother of the earth) and Veļu māte (the mother of the shades). Additionally, an analysis of the comparative Latvian and Lithuanian traditions of the feeding of dead souls and the development of those traditions over time can be found in Rūta Muktupāvela's essay "Ubagu mielošana: Žēlsirdība vai kontraktuālā darbība"(The feeding of beggars: Charity or contractual act, 1997).

LITHUANIA. In Lithuania, Jonas Basanavičius was one of the first scholars to do a comparative analysis of the Baltic perspective and beliefs on life after death. In *Iš gyvenimo vėlių ir velnių* (From the lives of dead souls and devils, 1903) Basanavičius begins his study of an extensive folklore collection by examining Baltic (Prussian, Latvian, and Lithuanian) ancestral culture. The book contains information on burial and remembrance practices from the ninth to the nineteenth centuries, drawn from historical sources as well as from archaeological digs of the late nineteenth century. Jonas Balys's *Dvasios ir žmonės: Liaudies sakmės* (Dead souls and people: Folk tales, 1951) and *Mirtis ir laidotuvės* (Death and burial, 1981) cite and comment on Lithuanian folktales and beliefs recorded before World War II about the dead and life after death, including descriptions of the tradition of feeding the dead.

For an analysis of ancestor worship as it pertains to concepts of a chthonic world in traditional culture, an excellent source is Norbertas Vėlius's *Chtoniškasis lietuvių mitologijos pasaulis* (The chthonic world in Lithuanian mythology, 1987). This study is particularly useful for its extensive research data on the Baltic cult of ancestors. The same is true of Vėlius's fundamental work *Baltų Religijos ir mitologijos šaltiniai* (Baltic religious and mythological sources, 1996/2001), which has become more and more valued in modern research. Gintaras Beresnevičius's *Dausos* (The world of the shades, 1990), analyzes individual elements in Baltic afterlife concepts through symbolic images found in folklore related to death and the dead. Also worthy of mention is Beresnevičius's article "Protėvių kultas: Vėlių maitinimas" (Ancestor worship: Feeding of the dead, 1996), in which he interprets the semantics of the Lithuanian cult of ancestors and the factors behind its development based on historical, archaeological, ethnographic, and folklore material. Arūnas Vaicekauskas's "Nekrokultas kalendorinėse apeigose" (Calendar festivity customs of the cult of ancestors, 1999) emphasizes that at the end of the nineteenth century and the beginning of the twentieth century the cult of ancestors was an integral part of agricultural rituals; its followers viewed it as inseparable from nature and the concept of life and death as a unified whole. Daiva Vaitkevičienė and Vykintas Vaitkevičius's "Mirtis, laidotuvės ir atminai" (Death, burial, and prayers for the souls of the dead, 1998) provides an analysis, based on archeological and historical sources, of ancestor cult characteristics, and also interprets mythological and religious concepts reflected in Lithuanian ethnography.

THE CULT OF ANCESTORS AT THE TURN OF THE TWENTY-FIRST CENTURY. Socially significant forms of ancestor worship, both in Latvia and Lithuania, fit into Christian-oriented beliefs and religious practices and are influenced by the traditions of all denominations. In Lithuania, ancestor worship coincides with the Catholic calendar, according to which November 2 is Vėlinės, a day devoted to the remembrance of the dead and designated as a national holiday. On this day Lithuanians light candles, place flowers on graves, and attend special church services dedicated to the departed. Within the family the dead are also remembered on Christmas Eve in a festival called Kūčios, named for a ritual meal of sprouted grains and honey. Even today the mistress of the household will leave a portion of the Christmas feast on the table all night to feed the souls of the dead.

The Latvian Dead Souls Remembrance Day falls on the last Sunday in November, but it has not been designated a national holiday. However, Latvians, unlike Lithuanians, continue to celebrate Kapu svētki (literally, "graveyard celebration," with the meaning of "celebration of ancestral burial places"), which includes features of ancestor worship. This celebration typically takes place in the second half of summer or at the beginning of autumn. During the celebration, hymns are sung at the graveyard and ministers hold a service and bless the graves. Loved ones and relatives of the dead usually attend the service in great numbers, and following the official ceremony they meet in a relative's home or even behind the graveyard wall to partake of a special meal. Remembering the departed and their good deeds, the celebrants drink beer or spirits. In many cases this celebration is the only time during the year when all the extended members of a family congregate in one place.

Elements of the cult of ancestors can be found in some contemporary religious systems, such as Dievturība (literally, "religion of those who keep their God") in Latvia and Romuva in Lithuania, both of which developed in the twentieth century. The ideology of these religious movements is based on an attempt to reconstruct the pre-Christian view of the world that included worship of ancient Baltic deities. Followers of these movements call on the authority of ancestors in life's critical moments, and with the help of ritual practices and offerings ask for their benevolence.

The Baltic Cult of Ancestors in a Cultural and Historical Context. Ancestor worship in the Baltics has survived in the tradition of Indo-European farming cultures, as evidenced specifically in the view that the dead continue to be present among the living, at least for a short period, or that after death they periodically leave the netherworld to "return home to take a look," according to the folklorist Vaitkevičienė (1998). The visiting dead seemingly have the power to affect the well-being of the community of the living, and to punish violations or disrespectful behavior towards the order of things as defined by the ancestors.

There are various cultural and historical reasons—low population density, single-family farms, and the presence of xenophobic elements in the traditional culture—why, after the official introduction of Christianity into the Baltics, it functioned rather formally. As recently as the twentieth century, ethnologists in Latvia and Lithuania recorded original eyewitness accounts of practices that do not fit into the official Christian system of practices regarding honoring the dead and that are considered remnants of the Baltic cult of ancestors.

The Baltics were converted to Christianity relatively late: Latvia in the thirteenth century and Lithuania at the turn of the fifteenth century. The representatives of this new religion—missionaries, monks, and travelers from Christian Europe—observed, recorded, and interpreted local religious practices within the context of their own experience in the Baltic milieu. In its directives and edicts, the Christian Church recorded practices that it unequivocally considered pagan and therefore candidates for eradication. For example, it is written in the Riga District Council Statutes (*Statuta Provincialia Concilii Rigensis*) of 1428:

> Up to the present time, certain peasants in this country stubbornly maintain their archaic pagan customs, often holding feasts in the graveyard for their departed ancestors and friends, leaving them food and drink, in the belief that this will bring them peace. Sincerely hoping to destroy other such signs of paganism as well as this one, we order the lords and vassals of this land, particularly the leaders of the church, to make a special effort to threaten and punish these people for such destructive Godless evil. (Vėlius, 1996, p. 614)

Proof that the Christian church did not have an easy time destroying these "archaic pagan customs" can be found in seventeenth-century records of church visitations, which admit that Latvian peasants continued to feed the souls of the dead and that they could not "be dissuaded" from this practice (Šmits, 1941, 325220).

Honoring the Dead according to the Traditional Calendar. There are special words in the Baltic languages to refer to the dead: in Latvian, *velis*; in Lithuanian, *vėlė.* Both words, according to linguists, originated in the common Indo-European root-form **wel-*, which has several meanings, including "to wound" or "to kill." Many special names that can be traced back to the seasonal remembrance period honoring the cult of ancestors have survived in the Latvian language; examples include: Dieviņi, Pauri, Iļģi, and Veļi (different local names for the souls of the dead); and Tēvu dienas, Iļģu laiks, and Vecļaužu dienas (names for the festival commemorating the dead). For Lithuanians, even the name of their festival honoring the dead has survived to the present time: Vėlinės, originating in the word *vėlė.* Another name for the festival, Ilgės, is mentioned in written historical sources, and Lithuanian dialects include various names for the celebration, such as Diedai, Stalai, Uždūšinės, Ažinkai, and Šermenia.

The cult of ancestors in the lives of the Balts cannot be separated from the seasonal cycle because the ancestor cult is linked to the beliefs of a farming culture and the influence of the dead on fertility and productivity. Thus, in one way or another, the themes of ancestor worship, or at minimum their remembrance, show up in all endeavors associated with agrarian rites. Moreover, the dominant seasons in the cycle of ancestor worship were primarily autumn and winter. Thus, in Latvia the period of the dead was generally considered to be from September 29 (Saint Michael's Day) to October 29 (Simjuda's Day, a folk composite of the words Simon and Judas), or even up to November 10 (Saint Martin's Day). In some places only one night, from November 1 to 2, was dedicated to honoring the dead. Likewise, in Lithuania most rituals relating to ancestor worship took place in autumn, particularly in October and the beginning of November. Such rituals were also practiced at Christmas. For both Latvians and Lithuanians these were considered to be among the most important celebrations. Already in the fifteenth century, the historian Jan Długosz wrote in his *Historia Polonica* (History of Poland) that the annual October celebrations with their offerings to the souls of the departed were very important and could not be ignored. Latvians of the seventeenth century thought them no less significant, believing that "if one does not honor the dead, one will not have a good year but rather will experience a poor harvest and hunger" (Šmits, 1941, 32520).

Feeding of the Dead. Evidently in ancient times in the Baltic milieu, the cult of ancestors had not become standardized into one coherent system; hence, a great variety of ritual forms existed. Ethnographic material indicates that within a single era ancestor worship could take place either in a graveyard, in a birch grove considered to be sacred, or at the foot of big rocks or trees. Frequently the worship also took place in living quarters or farm buildings, such as a barn, granary, or bathhouse. Ritual practices were harmonized with local traditions, and, despite variations in such rituals, historical and ethnographic material allows them to be categorized into specific activities that were considered dominant in the Baltic cult of ancestors.

One of the important expressions of ancestor worship was the feeding of dead souls, a fully developed and logical outcome of traditional culture that aimed to harmonize and reconcile the world of the living with the netherworld, to maintain morality standards, and to guarantee the survival of existing lifestyle patterns. The dead souls feast was accompanied by prayer, calling out of the names of departed ancestors, and an invitation for them to cleanse themselves in the bathhouse. Frequently the event also included fire rituals. At times the meal was simply taken to the graveyard, bathhouse, barn, or granary and left there for the night. In the morning the mistress of the house would see if the food had been touched in order to learn whether the dead had a benevolent or malevolent relationship with the living. The feeding of dead souls constituted a contractual activity whereby the living remembered, honored, and looked after the departed, who in turn were responsible for a good harvest, productivity, and the well-being of the living, protecting them from cataclysms of nature and other undesirable events. According to traditional views, the departed had the ability to accomplish these feats because they existed in a sacral dimension that was superior to the profane. People believed that if the dead did not adequately fulfill their responsibilities, they could be punished: "The master of the house opened the door and taking up a whip struck all those places where he thought a dead soul sat. . .and thinking that he had sufficiently skinned them all, went to the doorway and said 'Now you can leave, but don't even think of repeating your performance of previous years.'" (Šmits, 1941, 32541).

According to the folklorist Jonas Balys, documented ethnographic accounts indicate that the peasants prepared special dishes to take to the graveyard and leave at the graves of their relatives. The worship of the dead was particularly impressive in Lithuania, even as recently as the nineteenth century. Relatives would gather, and led by the oldest member of the family they would go together to the graveyard, bringing food and drink and singing special hymns in honor of the dead. At the cemetery the family elder would point in all directions of the compass and call out all the names of the dead that he could remember. Then the family members would pour, again in all directions, beer, home-made spirits, mead, and milk, and they would place bread, meat, and other foods on the graves.

Information on graveyard feasts honoring the dead in Latvia can be found in written sources dating back to the fifteenth century. Seventeenth-century church visitation records include a reference to food, eggs, and beer being left on graves in the region of Vidzeme, with a written request asking: "Old folks, please help our barley and rye to grow well, and our horses and farm animals grow strong!" (Šmits, 1941, 32523). If the ancestor worship took place in the farmhouse or in a farm outbuilding, then one of the first things the worshipers did was to invite the dead souls in. When the mistress of the house had set the table, the master lit candles or kindling and called the dead ancestors by name, asking them to come dine and drink. The farmers of Vidzeme, hoping to receive especially benevolent treatment from the dead, saddled their horses and rode to the graveyard or to the nearest tavern in order to bring back the dead souls so that they could partake of the prepared feast.

The purpose of lighting candles or kindling at the beginning of the feast was "to provide the dead souls with better lighting for dining" (Šmits, 1941, 32545), so that "the dead souls can see their food" (Balys, 1993, p. 286). If the food was left in the barn or granary, lit candles or kindling was also left behind. According to nineteenth-century accounts, this custom sometimes caused fires, but the practice continued, regardless. The candles and kindling were also lit at the end of the feast to send the dead souls back to their graves. If the ancestors dined in the graveyard, certain rituals associated with fire were practiced as well. In the southern region of Lithuania that meant actually building a bonfire.

According to Vaitkevičienė, prior to the feast of the dead the worshipers thought it important to cleanse themselves and to heat up the bathhouse for the anticipated visitors from the netherworld, laying out clean linens and shirts for them. In the Kurzeme region of Latvia the custom was to leave a pail of milk, clean water, and a clean towel each night so that "the dead souls who were walking about that night could wash themselves" (Šmits, 1941, 32535, 32540, 32558).

One can also find in both Latvian and Lithuanian ethnographic accounts the practice of "pouring off" (Latvian, *noliešana*). This custom referred to the pouring of a first drink or the throwing of the first or best morsel from the feast under the table, behind the stove, into a corner of the room, or into the hearth. The practice is also mentioned in historical sources, such as Długosz's *Historia Polonica,* as well as the sixteenth-century *De diis Samagitarum caeterorumque Sarmatarum et falsorum Christianorum* (About gods of Samogitians, other Sarmats, and false Christians) by Jan Łasicki. From the 1593 *Annuae Litterae Societatis Jesu* (Annual Jesuit report) we learn that the Zhemaits, the inhabitants of the western part of Lithuania, were in the habit of throwing the first morsel of food under the table, thereby "sending it off to the dead" (Vėlius, 2001, p. 618).

In the Zemgale region of Latvia, records show that the first morsel of food was intended for the deity of horses, the deity of the barn, and other spirits who lived behind the stove, in the piles of stones of collapsed buildings, or in big old trees with rotted hollows. The master of the house himself hid the first morsel of every dish in various places "so that no one would see or notice it" (Šmits, 1941, 32546). Similar practices also existed in the Vidzeme region of Latvia.

The relevance and persistence of this practice of leaving food morsels is evident in the following account recorded in 1996 in western Lithuania: "During the entire sacred feast period meat is served but the diners remain standing and do not sit. The whole family stands and then the food is served and the first spoonful is poured under the table. One spoonful. A second. A third. And only then the people eat for the food poured under the table is for the dead" (Vaitkevičienė, 1998, p. 255).

In the nineteenth century another important custom developed as part of the ritual associated with ancestor worship. Even though food intended for the dead continued to be taken to graveyards well into the twentieth century, people also started giving it to beggars. In Dzūkija, the southwestern region of Lithuania, prior to every holy day and every day of remembrance for the dead the mistress of the house baked beggar's bread called *dziedu duona.* In the morning, after breakfast, prayers, and various other remembrance rituals, she put four loaves of this bread in a basket, along with porridge, meat, and other food items; then, instead of taking them to the graveyard, she took them to church and distributed them to beggars. In return, the beggars would promise to pray for the dead and also for a good harvest and a lot of honey in the coming year. Similar accounts in other regions of Lithuania encourage scholars to conclude that the functions of the ancient ancestor cult were slowly transferred to beggars. In the nineteenth and early twentieth century, beggars were considered in the traditional culture as the dregs of society, but also, like departed ancestors, as intermediaries between this world and the netherworld.

FOOD AND LIBATIONS SERVED AT THE DEAD SOULS FEAST. The remembrance of the dead celebrations typically took place in autumn, after the harvesting was completed. The feast for the dead souls was prepared using certain grains and meat from animals raised and slaughtered on the farm. An enormous variety of food and drink was included in the feast, ranging from common milk products, such as cheese and butter, to more unusual items made from hemp and poppy seeds. Baked goods were common feast items, and included *plāceņi* or *pīrāgi,* types of buns and filled pastries made from newly harvested grains. Often the dead would be offered legumes, such as peas and beans. In Latvia the dead dined on *grūsli* or *pītes,* little round dumplings made of cooked peas, beans, and potatoes mixed with finely chopped hemp seeds.

Lithuanians, during the autumn and winter calendar festivities, made, and still make, tiny rye and wheat dumplings called *kleckučiai,* which were eaten accompanied by hemp or poppy milk. This milk was prepared from seeds that were roasted, crushed, and mixed with sugared water. It was considered important during the feast to partake of the meat dishes, along with offering them to dead souls and beggars. The meat could be homegrown fowl, pork, or beef. A much valued meat, especially on Saint Martin's Day, was rooster, as well as pork with sauerkraut and blood sausage. Soup made from fatty meat, grits, flour, and potatoes was also highly regarded in Lithuania. In addition, milk and honey are often mentioned as part of the dead souls feast in both Latvia and Lithuania. As for alcoholic drinks, beer, mead, and homemade spirits were all specially prepared and taken to the graveyard as part of the celebration.

RELIGIOUS ICONS ASSOCIATED WITH THE CULT OF ANCESTORS. The religious aspect of the cult of ancestors is reflected in concrete icons or images whose responsibilities coincided with those accredited to ancestors, namely, benevolence, fertility, and productivity. In describing the fifteenth-century dead soul festivities of the Zhemaits, Długosz writes that on October 1 throughout the western region of Lithuania, people celebrated "a great festival" during which they made offerings to their pagan gods, including first and foremost the god they called Perkuno (*Deo lingua eorum appellato Perkuno*). Their hope was that through these offerings they would strengthen their ties with their ancestors (Vėlius, 1996, p. 560).

Various Baltic deities and spirits mentioned by the following folklorists deserve further scholarly research since their function or role has not yet been fully determined. Alexander Guagnini describes sixteenth-century autumn festivities during which the first morsels of food were offered to the god Ziemiennik with the words "*Haec tibi o Ziemiennik deus*" (This is for you, oh God Ziemiennik), (Vėlius, 2001, p. 471). Jan Łasicki confirms that offerings were made to the god Ziemiennik during the festivities of Ilģi (Vėlius, 1996, p. 596). Łasicki refers to the god of dead souls as Vielona, to whom offerings were made during the feast of dead souls (Vėlius, 2001, p. 595). Matthäus Prätorius considers the deity representing dead souls to be a goddess by the name of Žeminėlė (Mannhardt, 1936, p. 62). The Jesuit Petrus Culesius, in his account of a dead souls remembrance day in the Rezekne area in the seventeenth century, mentions Lelo Deves and Zemes Deves (Straubergs, 1939, p. 777). And Latvian researchers of folklore, such as Šmits and Kursīte, associate non-Christian deities with the world of the dead, including Zemes māte and Veļu māte, as well as Rūšu māte (the mother of rusty earth), Kapu māte (the mother of graves), and Smilšu māte (the mother of sand).

BIBLIOGRAPHY

Adamovičs, Ludvigs. *Senlatviešu reliģija agrīnā dzelzs laikmetā.* Riga, Latvia, 1930.

Balys, Jonas. *Dvasios ir žmonės: Liaudies sakmės.* Bloomington, Ind., 1951.

Balys, Jonas. *Mirtis ir laidotuvės.* Silver Spring, Md., 1981.

Balys, Jonas. *Lietuvių kalendorinės šventės.* Vilnius, 1993.

Basanavičius, Jonas. *Iš gyvenimo vėlių ir velnių.* Vilnius and Chicago, 1903.

Beresnevičius, Gintaras. *Dausos.* Vilnius, 1990.

Beresnevičius, Gintaras. "Protėvių kultas: Vėlių maitinimas." *Liaudes Kultūra* 1 (1996): 14–16.

Biezais, Haralds. *Germanische und Baltische Religion.* Stuttgart, 1975.

Bruņenieks, Mārtiņš. *Senlatviešu reliģiskais pasaules uzskats.* Riga, Latvia, 1937.

Dundulienė, Pranė. *Lietuvos etnologija.* Vilnius, 1991.

Gimbutas, Marija. *The Balts.* New York, 1963.

Greimas, Algirdas Julijus. *Tautos atminties beieškant.* Vilnius and Chicago, 1990.

Karulis, Konstantīns. *Latviešu etimoloģijas vārdnīca.* 2 vols. Riga, Latvia, 1992.

Kursīte, Janīna. *Latviešu folklora mītu spogulī.* Riga, Latvia, 1996.

Kursīte, Janīna. *Mītiskais folklorā, literatūrā, mākslā.* Riga, Latvia, 1999.

Līdaks, Osvalds. *Latviešu svētki: Latviešu svinamās dienas.* Vilnius, 1991.

Mannhardt, Wilhelm. *Letto-Preussische Götterlehre.* Riga, Latvia, 1936.

Muktupāvela, Rūta. "Ubagu mielošana: Žēlsirdība vai kontraktuālā darbība?" *Karogs* 6 (1997): 147–157.

Olupe, Edīte. *Latviešu gadskārtu ieražas.* Riga, Latvia, 1992.

Pakalns, Guntis. "Priekšstati par mirušo pasauli latviešu bēru tautasdziesmās." Ph.D. diss., 1992, Institute of Literature, Folklore and Art of the Latvian Academy of Sciences.

Šmits, Pēteris. *Latviešu mitoloģija.* Moscow, 1918.

Šmits, Pēteris, ed. *Latviešu tautas ticējumi.* 4 vols. Riga, Latvia, 1941.

Straubergs, Kārlis. "Hanovijs par dvēseļu kultu pie latviešiem." *Izglītības ministrijas mēnešraksts* 5 (1925): 492–500.

Straubergs, Kārlis. *Latviešu buŗamie vārdi.* Riga, Latvia, 1939.

Straubergs, Kārlis. *Latvju kultūra.* Esslingen, Germany, 1948.

Straubergs, Kārlis. *Lettisk folktro om de döda.* Stockholm, 1949.

Straubergs, Kārlis. *Pār deviņi novadiņi.* Riga, Latvia, 1995.

Šturms, Eduards. *Chroniku un senrakstu ziņas par baltu tautu bēŗu parašām.* Riga, Latvia, 1938.

Vaicekauskas, Arūna. "Nekrokultas kalendorinėse apeigose." *Darbai ir Dienos* 11, no. 20 (1999): 131–155.

Vaitkevičienė, Daiva, and Vykintas Vaitkevičius. "Mirtis, laidotuvės ir atminai." *Tautosakos darbai* 9, no. 16 (1998): 204–261.

Vėlius, Norbertas. *Chtoniškasis lietuvių mitologijos pasaulis.* Vilnius, 1987.

Vėlius, Norbertas, ed. *Baltų religijos ir mitologijos šaltiniai.* Vilnius, 1996 (vol. 1), 2001 (vol. 2).

Vyšniauskaitė, Angelė. *Mūsų metai ir šventės.* Kaunas, Lithuania, 1993.

Rūta Muktupāvela (2005)
Translated by Margita Gailītis and Vija Kostoff

ANCHOR. While the anchor has had some currency in various cultures as a symbol relating to the sea and to virtues like constancy and hope, its religious significance became paramount only with the growth of Christianity. In fact, the anchor as we know it and as the object early Christians turned into a symbol did not appear until well into Roman times; the Greeks used an anchor that was essentially an arrangement of sandbags.

Both the appearance and the function of the anchor played a role in its development as a religious symbol. Early Christians saw in it an allegorical and disguised form of the cross. Its function became metaphorical in the New Testament in *Hebrews* 6:19: "We have this as a sure and steadfast anchor of the soul, a hope that enters into the inner shrine behind the curtain where Jesus has gone as a forerunner on our behalf."

Signifying steadfastness and hope, the anchor became one of the commonest symbols in the catacombs and on early Christian jewelry and seal stones. It was also associated with other symbols, as, for example, in the anchor cross, which combined the two shapes to make one that showed the Christian's hope firmly joined to Christ.

The anchor also appeared with the letters alpha and omega to represent eternal hope, and with the fish to signify, again, hope in Christ. In combination with the dolphin, the anchor came to mean the Christian soul or the church guided by Christ. The speedy dolphin was represented with the anchor to illustrate Augustine's motto *Festina lente* ("Make haste slowly").

Another early, if odd, use of the symbol was to identify Clement of Rome, a church father and one of the earliest bishops of Rome. Legend relates that Clement's persecutors tied an anchor around his neck and tossed him into the sea. The prayers of his followers made the waters withdraw, revealing a small temple where his body was found. Clement was frequently portrayed with an anchor around his neck or beside him.

The anchor was popular as a symbol until the medieval period, at which time it largely disappeared. When it reappeared it was, for example, as a symbol of Nicholas of Myra, because of his patronage of sailors, and as the attribute of hope, one of the seven virtues in Renaissance art.

Other, more exotic, ideas grew up around the symbol in some forms of magic and mysticism. Evelyn Jobes (1961) describes the bottom of the anchor as a crescent moon (ark, boat, nave, vulva, yoni, or female principle), in which is placed the mast (lingam, phallus, or male principle), around which the serpent (fertility, life) entwines itself. With the crossbeam, the parts add up to the mystic number four, and the anchor thus also symbolizes the four quarters of the universe, as well as both the sun and the world's center. The entire symbol expresses the idea of androgyny and of the union that results in new life. Finally, Ad de Vries (1978) ascribes to Freud the concept of the anchor as a combination of the cross (the body of Christ rising) and the crescent (Mary), the whole representing life.

Bibliography

The anchor is included in almost any book of Christian symbols. An example is *Signs and Symbols in Christian Art* by George W. Ferguson (Oxford, 1954). More far-ranging interpretations can be found in the following: *Dictionary of Mythology, Folklore and Symbols* by Evelyn Jobes (Metuchen, N.J., 1961); *Dictionary of Symbols and Imagery*, rev. ed., by Ad de Vries (New York, 1978); and *Dictionnaire des symboles* by Jean Chevalier and Alain Gheerbrant (Paris, 1982).

Elaine Magalis (1987)

ANDRAE, TOR (1885–1946), historian of religions and bishop of the Swedish church. Tor J. E. Andrae was born on July 9, 1885 into a Protestant minister's family in Hevna. After finishing school in Linköping, he began to study humanities at Uppsala in 1903 and eventually became proficient in Hebrew as well as Arabic. His degree in humanities completed, he turned to theology, obtained his candidacy in 1909, and was, like each of his three older brothers, consecrated a minister of the church. During his theological studies, Andrae was deeply influenced by Nathan Söderblom, who suggested that he study the Prophet of Islam and who was instrumental in shaping his scholarly career. Andrae, interested in religious psychology, turned to the problem of Muḥammad's response to the divine call that made him a prophet; in his first steps into Arabic literature, he was guided by Ignácz Goldziher. The young theologian, who served the church first in Delsbo and then in Gamla Uppsala, was enabled to spend some time in 1915 in Berlin reading Arabic manuscripts. The result of his intense studies was his book *Die person Muhammeds in lehre und glauben seiner gemeinde* (Stockholm, 1918). For the first time, the development of the veneration of Muḥammad in Muslim piety and mystical theory was shown with convincing clarity. Andrae's mastery of the sources is evident, and the book remains to this day the best, and virtually unique, contribution to the important problem of how and why Muḥammad grew from "a servant to whom revelation came" into the Perfect Man and axis of the universe.

Andrae was awarded the Th.D. in 1921, and his writings and sermons of the early twenties show his deep concern for the Swedish church, which seemed to him to embody the Christian ideal of a religious community. He always emphasized that Christianity is the most perfect religion, a conclusion that, he admitted, cannot be proved by scientific methods but is to be experienced as a result of one's personal search for truth.

In the fall of 1923, Andrae was invited to lecture on the history of religions at the University of Stockholm. His lectures about the psychology of mystical experience, which presented a broad survey of unusual experiences on all levels of religion, were published as *Mystikens psykologi* in 1926. In the same year appeared *Der Ursprung des Islams und das Christentum,* a study that takes up one of Andrae's favorite themes, the strong influence of Syrian Christianity on the formation of early Islam. This influence, he pointed out, is also palpable in early Islamic pietistic trends ("Zuhd und Mönchtum," *Le monde oriental,* 1931). In his inaugural lecture as professor in Stockholm in 1927, Andrae dealt with the history of religions and the crisis of religions, discussing the extent to which the difference between the believer and the nonbeliever exists throughout history, an issue that led him later to write on the "problem of religious propensity" (*Die Frage der religiösen Anlage,* Uppsala, 1932). In his lectures Andrae rejected the purely evolutionist trend in the history of religions and stressed the fact that primitive religions as we know them now are not to be confused with the original religions.

In 1929 Andrae became professor of religious studies in Uppsala, and during the following years some of his best-known books were published. Chief among these was *Muhammed: Hans liv och hans tro* (Muḥammad: The man and his faith; Stockholm, 1930). This book, which has been translated into several languages, was highly admired for its sensitive psychological approach to the Prophet of Islam, and it is still a standard work. In 1931 the death of Archbishop Söderblom, Andrae's master and friend, caused him to write a fine, deeply felt biography of Söderblom (Uppsala, 1931).

The following year Andrae was elected into the Swedish Academy and, as inspector of the Olaus-Petri-Stiftelse, had the opportunity of inviting leading historians of religion to Uppsala in the following years. His monograph on the Swedish theologian and polyhistor Georg Wallin (d. 1760) shows him as a historian of high rank. For a brief period in 1936 Andrae served as minister of ecclesiastic affairs in the Swedish government and was elected bishop in his home province, Linköping, where he spent the last nine years of his life. He died in January 1946 after expressing his firm faith in God and in eternal life in his last broadcast sermon on New Year's Eve 1946.

For all his deep-rooted love for the Swedish church and his Christian faith, Andrae was able to appreciate foreign religions as well. He was particularly interested in showing that Islam, so often maligned as a purely legalist religion of military uniformity, knows the secret of divine grace very well, because God has revealed himself in Islam as in all other religions (a Söderblomian idea). Andrae's booklet *I myrtenträdgården* (In the garden of myrtles) was published posthumously in 1947; it sketches the early development of the Ṣūfī movement with insight and love. Fascinating are Andrae's studies *Det osynligas värld* (Uppsala, 1934), in which he deals with the problem of immortality and eternal life and holds that, if eternal life is real life, it cannot be static but must imply a continuing development of the spirit—ideas known from Lotze and Eucken and expressed in 1928 by Muhammad Iqbal, the Indo-Muslim philosopher. Andrae's conviction of an unending life after death was a result of the dynamism of his own religion, a dynamism that led him also to dislike all forms of gnostic religions, which, he felt, were too intellectualistic.

Andrae's books are fruits of a deep study of the sources, combined with a fine understanding of the psychological roots of religious experience, coupled with respect for the religious personality. Besides, they are stylistically perfect. His contributions to the study of Islam, particularly to a better understanding of the spiritual role of the Prophet in the Muslim community, and his intense work for the Swedish church are the two most outstanding facets of his life and work.

BIBLIOGRAPHY

Muhammed: The Man and His Faith, translated by Theophil Menzel (1936; reprint, New York, 1956), is the only one of Andrae's books currently available in English. A translation of his studies on early Sufism, *I myrtenträdgården,* is a desideratum. Among German translations are *Mohammed: Sein Leben und sein Glaube* (Göttingen, 1932); *Die letzten Dinge* (Leipzig, 1940), a translation of *Det osynligas värld* by Hans Heinrich Schaeder, with a good biographical sketch; *Islamische Mystiker* (Stuttgart, 1960), a translation of *I myrtenträdgården* by Helmhart Kanus-Credé; and Andrae's biography of Söderblom, translated by E. Groening and A. Volkein (Berlin, 1938). A full account of Andrae's life and work has been given by Geo Widengren in *Tor Andrae* (Uppsala, 1947).

ANNEMARIE SCHIMMEL (1987)

ANDROCENTRISM refers to cultural perspectives where the male is generically taken to be the norm of humanness. Androcentrism originates from a male monopoly on cultural leadership and the shaping and transmission of culture. In religion this means that males monopolize priestly and teaching roles of religion and exclude women both from the exercise of these roles and from the education that such roles require. Thus women are prevented from bringing their own experience and point of view to the shaping of the official public culture of religion, however much they may participate in the religion as consumers of the public cult or in auxiliary cults restricted to women. The official public definition of the religion in terms of law, cult, and symbol is defined both without female participation and in such a way as to justify their exclusion.

Women's exclusion from the learning and shaping of the cult and symbol system also means that they do not participate in the processes by which a religion remembers and transmits its traditions. As a result, religions or religious practices that do not exclude women are forgotten or are remembered in a way that makes this participation appear deviant. Androcentric religious culture makes woman the "other"; woman's silence and absence are normative. Consequently, her presence is remarked upon only to reinforce her otherness, either by definitions of "woman's place" or by remonstrances against women who are deemed to have "gotten out of their place."

Androcentric culture also translates the dialectics of human existence—superiority/inferiority, right/left, light/darkness, active/passive, life/death, reason/feeling, and so forth—into androcentric gender symbolism. In this gender symbolism the female is always the "other": inferior in relation to superior, weaker in relation to stronger, negative in relation to positive. Even when the qualities assigned to women are positive, such as love or altruism, these are defined in such a way as to be supplemental or auxiliary to a male-centered definition of the self. The female becomes the unconscious that completes the conscious, the affectivity that completes rationality. Thus, despite the appearance of balance in such gender complementarity, the female is always relative and complementary to the male, rather than herself the one who is complemented or completed in her own right.

Androcentrism must be seen as a pervasive influence on all religious cultures, having shaped either those religious cultures themselves or the way they have developed or the way they have been reported upon and studied, or in many cases all three. The fact that this influence has remained largely unnoticed is itself an expression of its pervasiveness. It has been so pervasive and normative that it itself has not even been noticeable, since one cannot notice a given point of view unless another point of view is also possible.

Androcentrism pervades all aspects of the religious culture—its view of human nature, its definitions of good and evil, its creation stories, its images of the divine, its laws, rituals, polity, and practices of worship. One could illustrate this from many religions, but in this essay the illustrations will be drawn from the Judeo-Christian tradition. In this tradition, although the two creation stories in the *Book of Genesis,* chapters 1 and 2, offer alternative possibilities, religious anthropology has in fact been drawn from the second. Here the male is the norm, the one created first; woman is created second and taken by God from man's rib. This is a very peculiar story, since it reverses the actual experience of human birth, in which both males and females are born from the female. By making a male God the midwife of the birth of the female from the side of the male, it defines woman's place as auxiliary and secondary to the male. So normative is this assumption that few Christians even notice the oddness of the story, its reversal of actual human birth.

This place of woman as secondary and auxiliary to the male has been evident in all classical Christian anthropology. Christian anthropology operates within a dualistic framework that sets the good human self, created in the "image of God," in tension with an evil self that has lost or diminished its originally good human nature and positive relation to God. Although the *Genesis* 1 story defines both male and female equally as possessing the image of God, all classical Christian anthropology has regarded the male as the normative image of God in such a way as to make woman the image of either the lower or the fallen part of the self. While it is never denied that women possess some relationship to the image of God, they are seen as related to that image only under and through their relationship to the male, rather than in their own right. In themselves, women are said to image the body that is to be ruled over by the mind, or else the sin-prone part of the self that causes sin and the Fall.

This androcentric definition of humanity is evident in Augustine's treatise on the Trinity (*De Trinitate* 7.7.10):

> How then did the apostle tell us that man is the image of God and therefore he is forbidden to cover his head, but that the woman is not so and therefore she is commanded to cover hers? Unless forsooth according to that which I have said already when I was treating of

> the nature of the human mind, that the woman, together with her own husband, is the image of God, so that the whole substance may be one image, but when she is referred to separately in her quality as a helpmeet, which regards the woman alone, then she is not the image of God, but as regards the male alone, he is the image of God as fully and completely as when the woman too is joined to him in one.

Deeply embedded in this Christian definition of female subordinate and auxiliary existence is the story of female primacy in sin. Although the story of Eve's role in the expulsion from Paradise is by no means a normative story for the Old Testament or even for the Christian Gospels, through the Pauline tradition it assumed normative status for defining the human predicament in such a way that not only all Christian theology but the Bible itself is read with this presupposition. Female primacy in sin is the underside of woman's subordination in the divinely ordained nature of things: things got out of hand for humanity and its relationship to God in the beginning because woman got out of hand. Woman acting on her own initiative caused sin to come into the world and Adam to be expelled from Paradise. He is punished by the alienation of his work, but she is punished by the alienation of her humanity. She must now bring forth children in sorrow and be under the subjugation of her husband.

This story operates to justify female subordination in society and religion. This status of subordination had now been redoubled and reinforced as divine punishment for an original sin of acting on her own. Any efforts of women to act on their own, rather than as auxiliaries in a male-defined social order, can then be seen as new evidence of sinful female propensities—propensities that are to be repressed by reference to this original sin that caused everything to go awry. Woman acting on her own initiative can only do evil and cause chaos. She can never do good by herself, but only when she restricts herself to obedient response to male commands.

The androcentric presuppositions of the Christian view of creation and sin are maintained also in the definitions of salvation. The redeemer, the Messiah, the manifestation of God in the flesh, appears in male form. This maleness of the Christian redeemer could be regarded as a historical or cultural accident, similar to the fact that he is Jewish and appears in a particular time and place. These particularities in no way limit his ability to represent universal humanity. Yet Christian theology has in fact typically treated Jesus' maleness differently from his Jewishness, so as to make that maleness ontologically necessary to his ability to represent God. For Thomas Aquinas, the maleness of Jesus flows directly from the fact that the male is the normative or "perfect" expression of the human species, while woman is nonnormative and defective. Thus to represent the fullness of human nature, it is necessary that Jesus be male. Here we see clearly the androcentric presupposition whereby the male possesses a generic humanity that is both complete in itself and capable of encompassing the representation of woman as well, while the woman cannot even represent herself, much less the male, as a human being.

This androcentric definition of Christology or the necessary maleness of the incarnation points in two directions. On the one side, it reveals the presumed maleness of God. On the other side, it excludes women from the priesthood and from representation of Christ's and God's divine authority in church leadership. Although Christian theology does not claim that God is in a literal sense male, there is an overwhelming bias in Christian theology, itself derived from its parent religion Judaism, to image God in male form. Male roles are seen as representing authority and rule, initiation and power. Since God is by definition the absolute expression of these roles of initiation, power, and sovereignty, only male metaphors are apppropriate for him. Female metaphors can be used only for what is ruled over, created by, or acted upon by God; they cannot signify what acts, rules, or has autonomous power.

This gender dualism of God and creation as male and female is evident in biblical as well as Christian symbolism. Although female theological metaphors are not absent from the Bible and Christian cult and theology, these primarily either symbolize creaturely subordination to God or else point to evil or negative traits that separate the human from God. Christian symbolism of the female thus splits into two forms, the good feminine and the bad female. The good feminine represents creaturely existence totally submissive to divine initiative, self-abnegating of any pride or activity of its own. Typically, this is also expressed as "purity" or suppression of sexuality. The Virgin Mary represents the apogee of this ideal. The feminine is also used in both Judaism and Christianity to image the elect people in relationship to God. The covenant relationship to God is imaged along the lines of a patriarchal marriage, with Israel or the church as bride in relation to the bridegroom.

Influenced by ascetic spirituality, Christianity emphasizes the virginal character of the church not only in her espousal to her Lord, but also in her birthing of the people of God. Christian baptism is imaged as a new birth that transforms and negates the sinfulness of birth through the female. Actual birth destroys virginity and brings forth sinful offspring, while through baptism the church remains virginal and brings forth virginal offspring. This baptism symbolism illustrates another typical trait of androcentric patriarchal religion: the extent to which its symbols and rituals duplicate female biological and social roles—conception, birth, suckling, feeding—but in such a way as to negate these roles in their female form, while elevating them to a higher spiritual plane through the male cultic monopoly on these activities.

Female symbolism in Christianity also symbolizes the soul and its passive reception of divine initiative, as well as creation itself or the earth as the object of God's creative work. In *Proverbs* and the wisdom tradition feminine roles are in the same way ascribed to God. This continues in Judaism in concepts such as the divine Shekhinah, or divine presence. Some minority traditions in Christianity have also imaged the Holy Spirit as female or revived the wisdom tradition to speak of God as having a feminine side. But in all versions of this notion of divine androgyny, the feminine roles or aspects of God are thought of as secondary and auxiliary to a male-centered divine fatherhood. Wisdom is seen as a secondary and dependent principle that comes forth from the divine father to mediate his laws and actions to creation. Thus she is often pictured as resembling the family mother who mediates the commands of the father to the children. Thus even these minor instances of feminine imagery for God do not fundamentally break out of the androcentric patriarchal symbolism that allows the "good feminine" to image only that which is secondary and auxiliary to a male-centered ultimacy.

Female participation in Christian redemption has also been biased by androcentric anthropology. In the ascetic traditions of Christian spirituality, the holy woman is defined as transcending not only her bodily temptations but also her female nature: she is said to have become "virile" and "manly." This peculiar formulation is found in gnosticism (see logion 114 of the *Gospel of Thomas*), but also in orthodox Christian asceticism (see Leander of Seville's preface to his *Institutes on Virginity*). It derives from an assumed analogy between maleness and spirituality (or rationality), and between femaleness and corporeality or the passions. Asceticism restores the male in his spiritual manliness, but is possible for woman only by transcending her "female weakness." This notion suggested to many early Christian women that asceticism might be the route to female emancipation. But the church tradition, as defined by male leadership, hastened to add that the true spirituality of woman is expressed only through the most total submission to male authority, especially ecclesiastical authority.

In the Protestant tradition, where spirituality is reincorporated into a familial context, woman's piety is seen as expressible only through submission to her husband, as well as to church and civil authority (as long as these public authorities are of the correct Christian sect). Thus, Christian redemption does not set woman free, but rather forgives her for her original sin of insubordination by displaying her as voluntarily submissive to male authority.

Nevertheless, Christian androcentrism remains deeply suspicious that all women, even holy women, conceal tendencies to insubordination. When these tendencies come out in the open and are asserted unrepentantly, woman becomes witch or handmaid of the devil. When she is crushed or suppressed, as she should be, woman—even if holy—remains Eve, the punished woman put back in her place. Thus Mary, image of the ideal woman as totally submissive and purged of any sexual or willful traits, in effect remains an unattainable ideal for real women, an ideal by which all women are judged and found lacking.

All the androcentric presuppositions discussed come together in the exclusion of woman from ecclesiastical leadership as priest, teacher, or minister. The identification of male authority and divine authority excludes women from being able to represent God or speak as the voice of God. As a person who cannot act autonomously or as an authority in her own right, she cannot exercise such authority in human society generally, much less in the church, the restored human society. As one deficient in moral self-control and rationality, she is incapable of teaching and of spiritual government.

Despite these pervasive androcentric assumptions of Christian theology, Christianity, as practiced, has been much more ambivalent. Androcentrism has partially shaped the practice of biblical and Christian religion, in the sense of actual exclusion of women from leadership and the indoctrination of an androcentric piety accepted as normative by women as well as men. But there have also been many instances of female religious power that are by no means contained by these definitions: prophetesses in both Old and New Testaments; female teachers, apostles, and local leaders in the New Testament; and holy women, healers, charismatics, and mystics who were by no means as submissive to male authority as these theories demand. Learned Christian women have studied scripture, founded religious orders and movements that they led in their own name, and written religious treatises of all kinds to express their religious experience and teachings. Yet, the evidence for this alternative history has only begun to be discovered in recent times, as the presuppositions of androcentrism itself are challenged by female religious scholars.

The final expression of androcentrism lies in its command of the transmission of tradition. Tradition is continually rewritten to conform to androcentric presuppositions. Alternative realities are erased from memory, or they are preserved in such a way as to deny them public authority. Religiously powerful women are defined in the tradition in such a way as to make them conform to male definitions of submission or else to be remembered in pejorative ways that allow this memory to function only as a caveat against female religious leadership. Thus, in the *Revelation to John,* a female prophet who is the leader of a community rivaling those of the prophet John is termed "Jezebel," the name by which Old Testament androcentrism rejected a queen who worshiped other gods. As long as it is impossible to imagine that Jezebel's gods might have been expressions of the divine as authentic as those of Elijah (or that the Jezebel of the *Revelation to John* was as authentic a prophet as John), androcentric readings of the Judeo-Christian tradition remain intact.

SEE ALSO God, article on God in Postbiblical Christianity; Women's Studies.

BIBLIOGRAPHY

Baer, Richard. *Philo's Use of the Categories of Male and Female.* Leiden, 1970.

Børresen, Kari E. *Subordination and Equivalence: The Nature and Role of Women in Augustine and Aquinas.* Washington, D.C., 1968.

Davies, Stevan L. *The Revolt of the Widows: The Social World of the Apocryphal Acts.* Carbondale, Ill., 1980.

Laeuchli, Samuel. *Power and Sexuality: The Emergence of Canon Law at the Synod of Elvira.* Philadelphia, 1972.

Rogers, Katherine. *The Troublesome Helpmate: A History of Misogyny in Literature.* Seattle, 1966.

Ruether, Rosemary Radford, ed. *Religion and Sexism: Images of Women in the Jewish and Christian Traditions.* New York, 1974.

Ruether, Rosemary Radford. *Sexism and God-Talk: Toward a Feminist Theology.* Boston, 1983.

Ruether, Rosemary Radford, and Eleanor McLaughlin, eds. *Women of Spirit: Female Leadership in the Jewish and Christian Traditions.* New York, 1979.

Schüssler-Fiorenza, Elisabeth. *In Memory of Her: A Feminist Theological Reconstruction of Christian Origins.* New York, 1983.

Wemple, Suzanne Fonay. *Women in Frankish Society: Marriage and the Cloister, 500–900 A.D.* Philadelphia, 1981.

ROSEMARY RADFORD RUETHER (1987)

ANDROGYNES. The androgyne (from the Greek *andros,* "man," and *gune,* "woman") is a creature that is half male and half female. In mythology, such a creature is usually a god and is sometimes called a hermaphrodite, after Hermaphroditus, son of Hermes and Aphrodite, who is said to have grown together with the nymph Salmacis (Ovid, *Metamorphoses* 4.347–388). In religious parlance, androgyny is a much more comprehensive and abstract concept than is implied by the literal image of a creature simultaneously male and female in physical form. To say that God is androgynous is very different from saying that God is an androgyne. But if we limit ourselves to the relatively narrow interpretation of the bisexual god, usually a creator, we are still dealing with a very broad and important religious concept.

It is often said that androgynes are universal, or even archetypal. This is not true. It has been demonstrated that the androgyne is confined in its distribution either to areas formerly of the early "high civilizations" or to areas affected by influences from these centers. Nevertheless, this distribution does extend over a very wide area indeed, testifying to the great appeal of the image. The myth of the splitting apart of a bisexual creator is implicit in the Hebrew myth told in *Genesis* and is explicit in related texts from ancient Mesopotamia; it appears throughout the ancient Indo-European world and in the myths of Australian Aborigines, African tribes, North American and South American Indians, and Pacific islanders; and it is an important theme in medieval and Romantic European literature. Yet many religions, particularly "primitive religions," have managed to survive without it, and it has very different meanings for many of the cultures in which it does appear. (See Baumann, 1955, p. 9; Kluckhohn, 1960, p. 52; Campbell, 1983, map on p. 142.)

One might attempt to construct a taxonomy of androgynes in various ways. Beginning with the visual image, androgynes may be horizontal (with breasts above and a phallus below) or, more often, vertical (with one side, usually the left, bearing a breast and half of a vagina and the other side bearing half of a phallus). One may also distinguish "good" and "bad" androgynes in two different senses: morally acceptable and symbolically successful. In the first sense, it must be noted that although androgynes are popularly supposed to stand for a kind of equality and balance between the sexes, since they are technically half male and half female, they more often represent a desirable or undesirable distortion of the male-female relationship or a tension based on an unequal distribution of power. Thus in some societies, divine or ritual androgynes play positive social roles, affirming culturally acceptable values, while others are despised as symbols of an undesirable blurring of categories.

In the second sense, androgynes may be regarded as "good," in the sense of symbolically successful, when the image presents a convincing fusion of the two polarities and as "bad" when the graft fails to "take" visually or philosophically—that is, when it is a mere juxtaposition of opposites rather than a true fusion. "Bad" androgynes often turn out, on closer inspection, to be not true androgynes but pseudo-androgynes, creatures with some sort of equivocal or ambiguous sexuality that disqualifies them from inclusion in the ranks of the straightforwardly male or female. These liminal figures include the eunuch, the transvestite (or sexual masquerader), the figure who undergoes a sex change or exchanges his sex with that of a person of the opposite sex, the pregnant male, the alternating androgyne (queen for a day, king for a day), and male-female twins.

Perhaps the most important way in which androgynes may be split into two groups, as it were, is in terms of their way of coming into existence. Some are the result of the fusing of separates, male and female; others are born in a fused form and subsequently split into a male and a female. In orthodox mythologies of creation, chaos is negative, something that must be transcended before life can begin; distinctions must therefore be made—male distinguished from female, one social class from another. This corresponds to the Freudian belief that the desire to return to undifferentiated chaos, to return to the womb or the oceanic feeling, is a wish for death, for Thanatos (though it has been demonstrated that this is a facile and incorrect interpretation of the wish to return to chaos; see Eliade, 1965, p. 119). In the mythology of mysticism, however, chaos is positive; the desire to merge back into chaos is the goal of human existence, the supreme integration toward which one strives. In many rituals, too, androgyny is "a symbolic restoration of 'Chaos,' of the undifferentiated unity that preceded the Creation, and this return to the homogeneous takes the form of a supreme regeneration, a prodigious increase of power" (ibid., pp. 114, 199, 122). The mystic striving toward positive chaos is a clear parallel to the Jungian integration of the individual, for it celebrates the merging of two apparently separate entities (the self and God) that are in fact one. Thus, fusing androgynes may be viewed as instances of positive, Jungian chaos, and splitting androgynes may be viewed as instances of negative, Freudian chaos. Let us consider these two types separately.

THE SPLITTING ANDROGYNE. The more dominant of the two types is the splitting androgyne, which appears in a variety of cultures, both Indo-European and "primitive." A few examples taken from very many will have to suffice to establish the general pattern.

Greek. Plato depicts Aristophanes as the author of a complex myth of the primeval androgyne:

> In the ancient times there were three kinds of beings, each with four legs and four arms: male, female, and androgynous. They grew too powerful and conspired against the gods, and so Zeus sliced them in two. The parts derived from the whole males are the ancestors of those men who tend to homosexuality and pederasty; the parts derived from the whole females are the ancestors of women who incline to be lesbians. The androgynes, who are nowadays regarded with scorn, gave rise to men who are woman-lovers and adulterers, and to women who are man-lovers and adulteresses. (*Symposium* 189e–191e)

The androgyne is explicitly denigrated in this myth, not only in the statement of reproach for its present-day physical manifestations but in the implication that creatures derived from it are excessively lustful; the splitting of the androgyne is responsible for the fact that we expend (and, by implication, waste) so much time and trouble trying to get back together again.

Judaic. No account of the myths of androgyny can fail to mention *Genesis,* though we shall discuss the myth of Adam and Eve at greater length in the context of European myths. The *midrash* on *Genesis* 1:27 explicitly states that when God created the first man he created him androgynous; thus Adam gave birth to Eve. If man be made in the image of God, the creator himself would be an androgyne, although there is nothing explicit about this in the text of *Genesis* itself. It is, however, interesting to note that *Genesis* (2:24) does attribute to the origin of Eve from Adam the fact that, just as Plato noted in the same context, men and women have ever since sought to unite physically.

Indian. The earliest of all Indo-European androgynes, Sky-Earth (Dyāvā-Pṛthivī in the *Ṛgveda*) is a splitting androgyne: the first cosmogonic act is to separate the two halves. In the Upaniṣads, Prajāpati, the Lord of Creatures, becomes a more explicit androgyne:

> In the beginning this world was Soul [*ātman*] alone, in the form of Purusa [the Man]. He had no joy, and desired a second. Now he was as large as a woman and a man in a close embrace, and so he caused his self to fall into two pieces, which became a husband and wife. Therefore it is said, "Oneself is like a half-fragment." He copulated with her and produced human beings. But then she thought, "How can he copulate with me when he has just produced me from himself? I will hide." She became a cow; he became a bull, copulated with her, and produced cattle. She became a mare; he a stallion. . . . Thus were born all pairs there are, even down to the ants. (*Bṛhadāraṇyaka Upaniṣad* 1.4.3–4)

The splitting of the androgyne is here tied directly to the more general, and nonsexual, splitting of the primeval man, Puruṣa; androgyny is seen as a variant of sacrificial dismemberment. In other Indo-European myths, too, the primordial dismemberment is not of a man but of an androgyne. The incestuous implications of androgynous splitting and procreation are here made explicit; they continue to pose a moral problem for later Indian variants of this myth, in which the role of the primeval androgyne is played by Brahmā, and then by Śiva (cf. *Liṅga Purāṇa* 1.70).

North American. The Navajo say that First Man and First Woman had five sets of twins; the last four sets were each composed of a boy and a girl, but the first pair were barren hermaphrodites (Long, 1963, p. 53). The last four sets procreated, but the first set were the first people to die, and "she" (i.e., the female hermaphrodite of the pair) went to the underworld to become associated with the dead and the devils in the lower world (Spencer, 1947, p. 98). The male hermaphrodite simply dies; the female androgyne becomes the devil. Both are barren. Among the tribes of the Northwest Coast, too, mythic hermaphrodite dwarfs are killers, banished not to the underworld but to the moon (Boas, 1895, vol. 23, pt. 3, p. 53). Among the Zuni, however, one does find a central and positive androgynous creator, named Awonawilona ("he-she"; Stevenson, 1887, pp. 23, 37), an early precursor of nonsexist language and a powerful mythological figure.

African. Sudanese and Dogon art depicts horizontal androgynes, with breasts as well as penises. These figures may represent the primeval state of androgyny: man the way God made him, before the intervention of society made possible the perpetuation of the human race through the reduction of dangerously complete creatures to more manageable and useful halves. At birth every Dogon child has both a female soul and a male soul; at puberty every child undergoes ritual circumcision or clitoridectomy in order to remove the androgyny with which he or she is born.

> In so far as the child retains the prepuce or the clitoris—characteristics of the sex opposite to its own apparent sex—its masculinity and femininity are equally potent. It is not right, therefore, to compare an uncircumcised boy to a woman: he is, like an unexcised girl, both male and female. If this uncertainty as to his sex were to continue, he would never have any inclination for procreation. (Griaule, 1965, pp. 156–158)

The Dogon divine androgyne is a true androgyne, a creative figure containing both male and female physical and psychical elements; but it must be transformed into a human androgyne manqué, a figure whose complete nature has been defaced both physically and psychically. God may be an androgyne; but man must not.

The Fusing Androgyne. The fusing type of androgyne is originally created as a male and female in isolation and must fuse in order to create. The separate components are barren; only the androgyne is creative (in contrast with the splitting androgyne, which is creative only when the male and female parts have separated). The most common variant of the theme of the fusing androgyne is the Two-in-One or hierogamy (i.e., sacred marriage). In broader theological terms, this symbolizes the merging of complementary opposites—the *conjunctio oppositorum* (Eliade, 1965, pp. 103–125). But the more straightforward form of the fusing androgyne, in which the male and female partners each give up one half of their bodies to fuse into a single being, half male and half female, is relatively rare.

Indian. All early myths of the androgynous Śiva are myths of splitting androgynes; medieval Sanskrit texts and folk traditions, however, describe a fusing androgyne that arose when, out of passion, gratitude, or some other emotion, Śiva embraced Pārvatī so closely that their bodies fused into one. According to one account, Śiva was a beggar, but one day he smoked so much hashish that he could not go out on his usual rounds; Pārvatī begged in his place, and when she returned she fed him with the food she had collected, which so pleased Śiva that he embraced her violently and became one with her.

On another occasion, Pārvatī became jealous of Śiva's infatuation with another woman and left him. Śiva came to her and said, "You are the oblation and I am the fire; I am the sun and you are the moon. Therefore you should not cause a separation between us, as if we were distinct people." And as he said this, Śiva caused her to enter the side of his own body, as if she were hiding there in embarrassment, and their paired bodies became one, because of their love (*Skanda Purāṇa* 1.3.2.18–21).

Elsewhere, it is cynically remarked that Pārvatī took over half of Śiva's body in order to curb his philandering with other women. But the quintessentially fused Saiva androgyne is the so-called *Śiva-liṅga*, or phallus, which is, in fact, almost always accompanied by the yoni, the symbol of the Goddess's sexual organ, and as such is an iconic, though not anthropomorphic, androgyne: the male is surrounded by the female, in a representation of sexual union.

North American. A more complex candidate for androgyny is the notorious North American trickster. Even though primarily male, he not only masquerades as a female but actually gives birth to children. He normally keeps his detached phallus in a box and is thus self-castrating (like many Greek androgynes); in order to have sexual intercourse, he removes the phallus from the box and sends it to the woman. What his character represents, however, is a coincidence of opposites far more general than androgyny: it is primeval chaos, in which the basic social, moral, sexual, and even gross physical distinctions are yet unmade (Radin, 1956). The trickster is thus androgynously creative and psychologically "full," but the bitter humor with which he is depicted and the tragedy that follows upon his creative enterprises produce a sardonic vision of theological "wholeness" and a satire on human sexual integration. This aspect of his nature has led many scholars to identify him as a devil rather than a god, but this is not a useful distinction in dealing with a character who is morally so protean as the androgyne.

The Problem of the Androgyne: Getting Together. From the preceding survey, selective and sketchy though it is, it becomes apparent that most cultures have felt more comfortable with the concept of the splitting androgyne than with that of the fusing androgyne. Androgyny is thus not always a symbol of perfect union and balance. Many myths point out that the permanently fused androgyne is, technically, the one creature in the world who is certain to be unable to copulate. As Alan Watts has remarked, the androgyne symbolizes a state "in which the erotic no longer has to be sought or pursued, because it is always present in its totality" (Watts, 1963, pp. 204–205). Yet the androgyne may also imply that the greatest longing may be felt in complete union, when satiation is so near and yet so far; water, water everywhere, nor any drop to drink. Thus the androgyne may symbolize satiation without desire or desire without satiation.

Western androgynes, which are usually fused rather than splitting, are often unsuccessful. Many visual images of medieval androgynes that express complicated alchemical and occult concepts are ludicrous to the eye. Maurice Henry has produced a brilliant and hilarious series of cartoon androgynes who can neither fuse nor split and who are at last driven to saw themselves apart so that they can come together. A far more horrible sort of cartoon is Goya's *Disorderly Folly, Also Known as Disparate Matrimonial*, depicting a married couple grotesquely joined together back to back, like Siamese twins.

In our day, androgyny has once again become trendy, particularly in feminist and homosexual circles; but we are still not truly comfortable with the *physical* androgyne. Michel Foucault has pointed out, in his introduction to the memoirs of Herculine Barbin, a nineteenth-century French hermaphrodite, the ironic contrast between the Romantic *idea* of androgyny and the barbarism with which an actual androgyne was treated. This dichotomy can best be understood in the context of the history of modern European and Christian responses to the androgyne, a subject to which we now turn.

European Mysticism and Esotericism. The Judeo-Christian myth and theology of the androgyny of the primal man were successfully reinterpreted and revalorized by Jakob Boehme (1575–1624). For this great mystic and theosophist, Adam's sleep represents the first fall: Adam separated himself from the divine world and "imagined himself" immersed in nature, by which act he lowered himself and became earthly. The appearance of the sexes is a direct consequence of this first fall. According to certain of Boehme's followers, on seeing the animals copulate Adam was disturbed by desire and

God gave him sex to avoid worse (texts in Benz, 1955, pp. 60–66). Another fundamental idea of Boehme, Gichtel, and other theosophists was that Sophia, the divine virgin, was originally part of the primal man. When he attempted to dominate her, the virgin separated herself from him. According to Gottfried Arnold (1666–1714), it was carnal desire that caused the primal being to lose this "occult bride." But even in his present fallen state, when a man loves a woman he always secretly desires this celestial virgin. Boehme compared the break-up of Adam's androgynous nature to Christ's crucifixion (texts in Benz, 1955, pp. 125ff).

Jakob Boehme probably borrowed the idea of the androgyne not from Qabbalah but from alchemy; indeed, he makes use of alchemical terms. Actually, one of the names of the "philosophers' stone" was Rebis (lit., "two things"), the "double being," or the Hermetic androgyne. Rebis was born as a result of the union of Sol and Luna or, in alchemical terms, of sulfur and mercury (Eliade, 1965, pp. 102ff).

The androgyne as the primal and final perfection became extremely popular with the theosophists of the eighteenth century, from Friedrich C. Oetinger (1702–1782) and Karl von Eckartshausen (1752–1803) to Michael Hahn (1758–1819), Pierre-Simon Ballanche (1776–1847), and their disciples (cf. Faivre, 1973, pp. 67ff.). Boehme was the principal source of inspiration, either directly or through Franz von Baader (1765–1841). According to Baader, the androgyne had existed at the beginning (Adam) and will be again at the end of time. Baader borrowed from Boehme the conception of Adam's first fall, the sleep in which his celestial companion was separated from him. But, thanks to Christ, man will again become an androgyne, like the angels.

Baader wrote that "the aim of marriage as a sacrament is the restoration of the celestial or angelic image of man as he should be." Sexual love should not be confused with the instinct for reproduction; its true function is "to help man and woman to integrate internally the complete human image, that is to say the divine and original image." Baader considered that a theology presenting "sin as a disintegration of man, and the redemption and resurrection as his reintegration" would conquer all other theologies (see the texts reproduced by Benz, 1955, pp. 219ff).

To the German Romantics the androgyne was the perfect, "total" human being of the future. J. W. Ritter (1776–1810), a well-known doctor and friend of Novalis, sketched in his *Nachlass eines jungen Physikers* a whole philosophy of the androgyne. For Ritter the man of the future would be, like Christ, an androgyne. "Eve," he wrote, "was engendered by man without the aid of woman; Christ was engendered by woman without the aid of man; the androgyne will be born of the two. But the husband and wife will be fused together in a single flesh." The body that is to be born will then be immortal. Describing the new humanity of the future, Ritter uses alchemical language, a sign that alchemy was one of the German Romantics' sources for their revival of the myth of the androgyne.

Wilhelm von Humboldt took up the same subject in his youthful *Über die männliche und weibliche Form,* in which he dwells particularly on the divine androgyne. Friedrich Schlegel, too, envisaged the ideal of the androgyne in his essay "Über die Diotima," in which he attacks the value attached to an exclusively masculine or feminine character, a value produced, he charges, only by education and modern custom. The goal toward which the human race should strive, he believed, is a progressive reintegration of the sexes, ending in androgyny (Eliade, 1965, pp. 98ff).

From Balzac to Aleister Crowley. Balzac's *Séraphita* is undoubtedly the most attractive of his fantastic novels. Not because of the Swedenborgian theories with which it is imbued but because Balzac here succeeded in presenting with unparalleled force a fundamental theme of archaic anthropology: the androgyne considered as the exemplary image of the perfect man. Let us recall the novel's subject and setting. In a castle on the edge of the village of Jarvis, near the Stromfjord, lived a strange being of moving and melancholy beauty. Like certain other Balzac characters, he seemed to hide a terrible secret, an impenetrable mystery. But here it is not a secret to be compared with that of Vautrin, the master criminal who figures in several other Balzac novels. The character in *Séraphita* is not a man eaten up by his own destiny and in conflict with society. He is a being different in quality from the rest of mankind, and his mystery depends not on certain dark episodes in his past but on the nature of his own being. This mysterious personage loves and is loved by Minna, who sees him as a man, Séraphitus, and is also loved by Wilfred, in whose eyes he seems to be a woman, Séraphita.

This perfect androgyne was born of parents who had been disciples of Swedenborg. Although he has never left his own fjord, never opened a book, never spoken to any learned person or practiced any art, Séraphitus-Séraphita displays considerable erudition; his mental faculties surpass those of mortal men. Balzac describes with moving simplicity the nature of this androgyne, his solitary life and ecstasies in contemplation. All this is patently based on Swedenborg's doctrine, for the novel was primarily written to illustrate and comment on the Swedenborgian theories of the perfect man. But Balzac's androgyne hardly belongs to the earth. His spiritual life is entirely directed toward heaven. Séraphitus-Séraphita lives only to purify himself—and to love. Although Balzac does not expressly say so, one realizes that Séraphitus-Séraphita cannot leave the earth before he has known love. This is perhaps the last and most precious virtue: for two people of opposite sex to love really and jointly. Seraphic love no doubt, but not an abstract or generalized love all the same. Balzac's androgyne loves two well-individualized beings; he remains therefore in the concrete world of life. He is not an angel come down to earth; he is a perfect man, a complete being.

Séraphita (1834–1835) is the last great work of nineteenth-century European literature that has the myth of the androgyne as its central theme. Toward the end of the century, other writers—notably the so-called *décadents*—returned to the subject, but their works are mediocre if not frankly bad. One may mention as a curiosity Péladan's *L'androgyne* (1891), the eighth volume in a series of twenty novels entitled *La décadence latine.* In 1910 Péladan treated the subject again in his brochure *De l'androgyne* (in the series "Les idées et les formes"), which is not entirely without interest, despite its confusion of facts and its aberrations. The entire work of Péladan—whom no one has the courage to read today—seems to be dominated by the androgyne motif. Anatole France wrote that Péladan was "haunted by the idea of the hermaphrodite, which inspires all his books." But Péladan's whole production—like that of his contemporaries and models, Swinburne, Baudelaire, Huysmans—belongs to quite a different category from *Séraphita.* Péladan's heroes are perfect only in sensuality; the metaphysical significance of the perfect man had been degraded and finally lost in the second half of the nineteenth century.

French and English *décadents* have occasionally returned to the theme of the androgyne (cf. Mario Praz, 1951), but always in the form of a morbid or even satanic hermaphroditism (as did Aleister Crowley, for example). As in all the great spiritual crises of Europe, here once again we meet the degradation of the symbol. When the mind is no longer capable of perceiving the metaphysical significance of a symbol, it is understood at levels that become increasingly coarse. The androgyne has been understood by *décadent* writers simply as a hermaphrodite in whom both sexes exist anatomically and physiologically. They have been concerned not with a wholeness resulting from the fusion of the sexes but with a superabundance of erotic possibilities. Their subject has not been the appearance of a new type of humanity, in which the fusion of the sexes produces a new, unpolarized consciousness, but a self-styled sensual perfection, resulting from the active presence of both sexes in one.

This idea of the hermaphrodite has probably been encouraged by the study of certain ancient sculptures. But *décadent* writers have been unaware that the hermaphrodite represented in antiquity an ideal condition that men endeavored to achieve spiritually by means of rites; they have not known that if a child showed at birth any signs of hermaphroditism, it was killed by its own parents. In other words, the ancients considered an actual, anatomical hermaphrodite an aberration of nature or a sign of the gods' anger, and they consequently destroyed it out of hand. Only the ritual androgyne provided a model, because it implied not an augmentation of anatomical organs but, symbolically, the union of the magico-religious powers belonging to both sexes.

SOME MODERN CHRISTIAN THEOLOGIES. In a youthful writing, *The Meaning of the Creative Act* (1916), Nikolai Berdiaev took up again the old *theologoumenon;* he proclaimed with vigor that the perfect man of the future will be androgynous, as Christ was (Eliade, 1965, p. 103, n. 5). An important ideological contribution was *Die Gnosis des Christentums*, by Georg Koepgen, published in Salzburg in 1939, with the episcopal imprimatur (but afterward placed on the index). The work gained a certain popularity after C. G. Jung discussed it in his *Mysterium Coniunctionis.* According to Koepgen, "In the person of Jesus the male is united with the female. . . . If men and women can come together as equals in Christian worship, this has more than an accidental significance: it is the fulfillment of the androgyny that was made manifest in Christ" (*Die Gnosis*, p. 316). With regard to *Revelation* 14:4 ("Those are they that were not defiled with women; for they are virgins"), Koepgen asserts:

> Here the new androgynous form of existence becomes visible. Christianity is neither male nor female, it is male-female in the sense that the male paired with the female in Jesus' soul. In Jesus the tension and polaristic strife of sex are resolved in an androgynous unity. And the Church, as his heir, has taken this over from him: she too is androgynous. (ibid., p. 31)

As regards her constitution, the church is "hierarchically masculine, yet her soul is thoroughly feminine." "The virgin priest . . . fulfills in his soul the androgynous unity of male and female; he renders visible again the psychic dimension which Christ showed us for the first time when he revealed the 'manly virginity' of his soul" (ibid., p. 319; noted by Jung, 1963, pp. 373ff.). As Jung remarks, for Koepgen not only Christ is androgynous but the church as well. In the last analysis, any Christian is predestined to become an androgyne.

SEE ALSO Feminine Sacrality; Gender Roles; Indian Religions, article on Mythic Themes; Masculine Sacrality; Tricksters.

BIBLIOGRAPHY

The classic study of androgynes remains Hermann Baumann's *Das doppelte Geschlecht: Ethnologische Studien zur Bisexualität in Ritus und Mythos* (Berlin, 1955), though one awaits with interest the promised volume on hermaphroditism scheduled to appear in Michel Foucault's *History of Sexuality.* The present article is based in large part upon two published works by the joint authors: Mircea Eliade's *The Two and the One* (*Mephistopheles and the Androgyne*) (Chicago, 1965) and Wendy Doniger O'Flaherty's *Women, Androgynes, and Other Mythical Beasts* (Chicago, 1980). Three other useful surveys with material on androgyny are Alan Watts's *The Two Hands of God: The Myths of Polarity* (New York, 1963), Joseph Campbell's *Historical Atlas of World Mythology*, vol. 1 (New York, 1983), and Clyde Kluckhohn's "Recurrent Themes in Myths and Mythmaking," in Henry A. Murray's *Myth and Mythmaking* (New York, 1960), pp. 46–60.

The material on North American and African androgynes in this article has been taken from Franz Boas's *Indianische Sagen von der Nord-Pacifischen Küste Amerikas* (Berlin, 1895); Charles H. Long's *Alpha: The Myths of Creation* (New York, 1963); Marcel Griaule's *Conversations with Ogotemmêli: An Introduction to Dogon Religious Ideas* (London, 1965); Paul Radin's *The Trickster: A Study in American Indian Mythology*

(1956; New York, 1969); Katherine Spencer's *Reflections of Social Life in the Navaho Origin Myth* (Albuquerque, 1947); and Matilda Coxe Stevenson's *The Religious Life of the Zuñi Child*, Annual Report of the Bureau of American Ethnology, no. 5 (Washington, D.C., 1887).

For further material on Greek androgynes, see Luc Brisson's *Le mythe de Tirésias* (Leiden, 1976) and his "Aspects politiques de la bisexualité: L'histoire de Polycrite," in *Hommages à Maarten J. Vermaseren*, edited by Margaret B. de Beer and T. A. Elridge (Leiden, 1978), pp. 80–122; and Michel Meslin's "Agdistis ou l'androgynie malséante," in volume 2 of the Vermaseren festschrift, pp. 765–776. For Indian androgynes, besides O'Flaherty's work cited, see also Adalbert J. Gail's "Die zweigeschlechtliche Gottheit in Indien," *Kunsthistorisches Jahrbuch Graz* 17 (1981): 7–19, and Marguerite E. Adiceam's "Les images de Śiva dans l'Inde du Sud," part 5, "Harihara," and part 6, "Ardhanarisvara," *Arts asiatiques* 13 (1966): 83–98 and 17 (1968): 143–164.

For European androgynes, see Maurice Henry's *The Thirty-Two Positions of the Androgyne* (New York, 1963); Ernst Benz's *Adam: Der Mythus des Urmenschen* (Munich, 1955), an excellent anthology of the most significant texts; Antoine Faivre's *L'esotérisme au dix-huitième siècle* (Paris, 1973), a concise and learned introduction to a difficult subject; C. G. Jung's *Mysterium Coniunctionis*, 2d ed. (Princeton, 1970); and Mario Praz's *The Romantic Agony*, 2d ed. (Oxford, 1951).

New Sources

Feuerstein, Günther. *Androgynos: das Mann-Weibliche in Kunst und Architektur.* Stuttgart, 1997.

Zolla, Elémire. "L'androgino: l'umana nostalgia dell'interezza." *Arte e immaginazione* (1989).

WENDY DONIGER (1987)
MIRCEA ELIADE (1987)
Revised Bibliography

ANESAKI MASAHARU (1873–1949) is known as the founder of religious studies in modern Japan. Through his "Introduction to Religious Studies" lectures at Tokyo Imperial University and the publication of his book *General Introduction to Religious Studies* (1900), Anesaki established a new form of the academic study of religion in Japan. Thereafter he became a professor and occupied the chair of religious studies (established in 1905) at the Imperial University. He later became chairman of the Japanese Religious Studies Association. Anesaki's life itself reflects the development of religious studies in Japan before the outbreak of World War II.

Anesaki's early ideas concerning religious studies were expressed in his *General Introduction to Religious Studies.* He thought that the subject of religious studies should be constituted into three areas: religious psychology, religious ethics, and religious sociology. His main goal was to comprehend religion as an expression of the human desire for the infinite. From this point of view, all religious phenomena can be understood equally as one, while the same humanistic psychological processes lay behind the differences in religions. Anesaki's psychological ideas were influenced by C. P. Tiele and William Starbuck, and by Wilhelm Bender and Benjamin Kidd in terms of irrational human desires.

In early modern Japan, there was no unified conception of a "religion" behind religions, or even of "Buddhism" behind Buddhist sects. It was only in the modern era, with the arrival of Christianity and the formation of a nation-state, that the category of "religion" emerged in academic and legal discourse in discussions concerning how to regulate the relationship between Christianity, Buddhism, and Shintō, and between the different sects in each religion, in order to create and then support a Westernized nation-state. Anesaki provided a discursive framework for "religion" that could bring all religious phenomena into one and the same category: namely, the sui generis "religion." Furthermore, by interpreting religious categories as a psychological dimension of the human mind, Anesaki relocated the things concerned with the other world (e.g., God, heaven, and hell) into worldly civil society. Therefore, it may be said that Anesaki's idea of religious studies provided the Japanese people with a national identity that transcended individual beliefs by interpreting the category of "religion" as referring to the psychological interiority that members of a society need to support a nation-state. In this, Anesaki was influenced by his nationalist teacher Inoue Tesujirō, a famous scholar who emphasized the importance of national values, and by Raphael von Koeber, who argued that much of the individual's interior life could not be reduced to rational terms.

In response, religious studies as envisioned by Anesaki granted the sphere of individual consciousness priority of uniqueness. This promised a way to guarantee the protection of individual religious freedom from the power of the state. At the same time, it included the possibility of connecting this interiority with enthusiastic nationalism, which had grown after the separation of the church and state in Japan. In fact, when the government appointed Anesaki a member of an investigative committee for religious institutions, he criticized the intervention of the state into matters of religious beliefs. At the same time, however, at a meeting held in 1912 consisting of Christians, Buddhists, and Shintōists, he took the lead in advocating that religious groups support the Japanese government. Anesaki was known as a follower of Nichiren, whom Anesaki believed was the ideal prophet who had connected religious devotion to belief in the nation-state.

In this sense, his admiration during the latter half of his life for Prince Shōtoku is worthy of note. Throughout his life, Anesaki thought of the emperor as a religious figure who existed as the center of the Japanese people's interiority. Prince Shōtoku was an imperial prince in antiquity and a noted exponent of the *Lotus Sūtra.* This form of Buddhism sought to save all people who could be saved. Here, one can see a close relationship drawn between religion and national identity. As such, Anesaki's vision derived more from the early modern Japanese social and political climate than from modern Western thought, where the separation of church and state was the ideal. In fact, Anesaki was born into a family working for a Buddhist temple. His ancestors had worked as servants of the imperial family in Kyoto from the early modern period. Thus, though Anesaki's vision of religious studies as a field was developed under the strong influence of Western thought, it included native elements that cannot be reduced to modern Western concepts.

In addition, his study of Japanese religious history is worthy of note. He cast a great deal of light on some aspects of Japanese religious history, including the religious personalities of Nichiren and Prince Shōtoku, Buddhist art, and the "hidden Christians" (*kakure kirishitan*). Interestingly, these works were first written in English and later translated into Japanese. It was while he was a visiting professor at Harvard University from 1913 to 1915 that he started to study Japanese religious history in earnest. This was during World War I, and he was exposed to the Yellow Peril campaign in the United States. As a result, he felt that the Japanese needed to explain their cultural character to Westerners in order to be understood. For him, religion was an essential common matter among people that informed the Japanese core character. Thus, he began to study Japanese religious history in English. This provided him with a framework to describe "Japanese" religious history as a unified concept. As a result, people could describe Japanese religious history as occurring within a circumstantial space where various religions had interacted with each other. However, the question of whether it is possible to write about Japanese religious history as a whole is today still a difficult problem for scholars. Anesaki's Japanese religious history has also lost some of its significance because many scholars today question the utility of the very concept of "Japanese religious history."

Nevertheless, Anesaki's attempt to describe Japanese religious history deserves respect and should be reevaluated as the first attempt to portray Japanese identity through a comparison with the West. Anesaki's role in establishing the field of religious studies contributed to the establishment of the idea of representing "Japanese religious history" itself. His works, incorporating both this notion of "religion" and "Japanese religious history," represented an important response to the cultural and political conflicts raised within Japanese society by the overwhelming influence of the West. From this perspective, Anesaki's publications on religious studies provide us with highly interesting material that can be used to analyze the reactions of members of the Japanese elite undergoing Westernization during the late nineteenth and early twentieth centuries.

BIBLIOGRAPHY

Collected Works in Japanese

Anesaki Masaharu Shū. 9 vols. Tokyo, 2002.

Kaitei Anesaki Masaharu chosakushu. 10 vols. Tokyo, 1976, 1982.

Waga shogai. Tokyo, 1951; reprint, 1993. His autobiography.

Works by Anesaki in English

Buddhist Art in Its Relation to Buddhist Ideals, with Special Reference to Buddhism in Japan. Boston, 1915.

Nichiren, the Buddhist Prophet. Cambridge, Mass., 1916.

The Religious and Social Problems of the Orient. New York, 1923.

A Concordance to the History of Kirishitan Missions. Tokyo, 1930.

History of Japanese Religion: With Special Reference to the Social and Moral Life of the Nation. London, 1930.

Art, Life, and Nature in Japan. Boston, 1933.

Prince Shōtoku, the Sage Statesman, and His Mahasattva Ideal. Tokyo, 1948.

Secondary Works

Isomae Jun'ichi. *Hidetaka Fukasawa, Kindai Nihon niokeru Chishikijin to Shukyo: Anesaki masahu no Kiseki.* Tokyo, 2002.

Isomae Jun'ichi. "The Discursive Position of Religious Studies in Japan: Masaharu Anesaki and the Origins of Religious Studies." *Method and Theory in the Study of Religion* 14, no. 2 (2002): 21–46.

Suzuki Norihisa. *Meiji Shukyo Shicho: Shukyogaku Kotohajime.* Tokyo, 1979.

ISOMAE JUN'ICHI (2005)

ANGELS. An introductory overview of the term "angel" in a historical and religious context necessitates a preliminary discussion of the limits and context of this word, which has become deeply entrenched in Western culture. If it is correct that the word "angel" applies to ranks of spiritual or heavenly beings which serve as intermediaries between the earthly and divine worlds, it would be appropriate to restrict the scope of an investigation to cultural situations that are most generally associated with monotheistic theological ideas—Judaism, Christianity, Islam—or else to religions with strongly monotheistic leanings, albeit with a mythological framework and large number of gods in a secondary role, such as Zoroastrianism. Religious movements such as Gnosticism, Manichaeism, and Mandaeism, which have common cultural links with both the monotheistic Judeo-Christian spirituality, and the diverse world of Greek, Hellenistic, and late antiquity culture, should also be examined. Soteriological and eschatological ideas expressed in Neoplatonic and hermetic circles should also be considered in any discussion, as should influences produced from links with alchemy, astrology, divination, and magic. Of the latter group, in which angelology centered on a belief in the need for salvation in this world or the next, a whole range of exorcistic, prophylactic, and therapeutic attitudes arose which in some cases led to misunderstanding of the original function of angels and its being reduced to superstitious observance.

From here proceeds a geographical summary which ranges from the classical world to the eastern Mediterranean, its environs, the Middle East, and India. Even Central Asia, when some Manichaeistic angelological ideas are taken into account, is also relevant to the summary. The attempt by Ananda Kentish Coomaraswamy to interpret Vedic and Hindu gods in terms of opposition between "Angels" and "Titans" seems misleading, and is the product of outstanding scholarship which has applied the Western category of "angel" to the Hindu mythological heritage, identifying angels with gods (*daeva*) as opposed to *ahura* (demons, titans), with interesting if somewhat speculative and intellectually over-elaborate results. The etymological parallels between the Greek word *aggelos* and the Sanskrit *an.giras,* are rather different, however, since the word denotes a group of priest-singers who occupy an intermediary position in the Vedic cult, as their name shows, but are not to be identified with angels in the metaphysical or theological sense with which we are concerned.

CLASSICAL WORLD. The Greek *aggelos* and the Latin *angelus* form a lexical and conceptual basis which has passed into the vocabulary of the majority of European languages. The "god-angels" of funerary inscriptions should be seen as divine epithets, personifications of the divine which humankind can gain access to and perceive: for example, angels of the underworld, representing the qualities of gods such as Hermes, Hekate, Pluto, and Persephone; or the angels of Neoplatonic thinking, which are invoked by magicians as divine emanations and representations. These appear to humans as "visible gods" with specific characteristics (creative angels, generative angels, savior angels), which humankind can propitiate with sympathetic magic, even if their presence is not always benign when they are invoked. Both Porphyry and Iamblichus discuss the problem of how someone unskilled can conjure up malignant, demoniac spirits. The link with Hermes shows their position as intermediaries between the world of the living and the dead. Etymologically speaking, they are "messengers" or heralds involved with communications between different worlds and in particular with a psychopompic role in beliefs concerning the afterlife. One example is the *angelus bonus* in the mysteries of Sabazios, who wears the crown of immortality and introduces the dead person into the assembly of the Blest. Their intermediary role involves accompanying the soul at the moment it comes into existence, when the soul descends and crosses the planetary spheres, taking in a varying degree of heavenly influences which will determine the character of the person as yet unborn. Thus they are the soul's guardian angels throughout its earthly life and its custodians (*phulakes*) until it returns to heaven, when the angels are responsible for its purification, breaking the links of the soul with the world of matter at the moment of its death.

The close connection between angels and souls in beliefs concerning immortality demonstrates a commonality between these two ideas, since the best souls become angels: hence the explanation, in terms of conduct, that a person who has been trained in spiritual perfection becomes in essence similar to the angels. This explains the addition of the word "angel" to the name of the deceased in funeral inscriptions, setting down the good fortune of immortality which may be the fate of the deceased. In hermetic Gnostic belief, the final outcome involved the ascent to heaven of the soul of the mystic after death, and transformation into one of the most important angels of the Ogdoad and of the fixed stars, which stand before God and contemplate him, rejoicing in the arrival of the soul and singing hymns of praise to the Father.

ZOROASTRIANISM. Angels are a fundamental part of Iranian thinking and its perception of the divine in terms of ideas and concepts—morality, thought and life—as personified not in mythological stories but in intermediate figures assisting the supreme god Ahura Mazdā with the order and maintenance of the cosmos. The religious history of Zoroastrian Iran has shown interesting ideas concerning angels since the earliest part of the Avesta, containing songs (*Gāthā*) attributed to Zoroaster himself, in which Ahura Mazdā is accompanied by an entourage of spiritual beings called the *Amesha Spentas* (the Beneficent Immortals) who are similar to angels. They are subordinate to a supreme god and lack a distinct mythology, in contrast to the gods celebrated in the Avestic hymns (*Yasht*). The actual names of these angelic beings—Good Thinking (Vohu Manah), Right Mindedness (Ārmaiti), Harmony (Asha), Power (Xshathra), Wholeness (Haurvatat) and Immortality (Ameretat)—illustrate that they represent abstract metaphysical concepts, vaguely personified only by their names. They may intercede in the sacrificial exchange between heaven and earth, to grant the person performing it the favor of the divine world, spiritual energy, and powers such as strength, youth, wealth, vigor, physical well-being and immortality. Within the psychology of Zoroastrian ritual the *Amesha Spentas* thus symbolize the many different states of the person making the sacrifice. They fulfill important role in angelic mediation, and facilitate a person's communion with the divine via a particular kind of consciousness and visionary experience.

This important intermediary function would remain a constant within Zoroastrianism, and can be found in the Pahlavi texts of the Sassanid period, which refer to a mysticism based upon angelic internalization being achieved in the inmost consciousness. For example, it is advised to join with Good Thinking, in its purely spiritual form, to make it welcome, and hence enjoy spiritual benefits. The angelic strain existing within Zoroastrian from its philosophical beginnings may be clearly seen from the angelizing process to which its mythology was subject, something which continued in the Sassanid period with the recommendation of various philosophers to "make a home for the gods within the body." In this instance the gods (*yazdān*) rather than mythological deities appear as spiritual personifications, similar to angelic spiritual beings and subject to the supreme god, which are realized in the heart of the faithful by means of ethical and moral virtue and sacrifice. Further interesting angelic qualities may be seen in elements such as fire, a medium *par excellence,* since indeed it is actually called "messenger" (*dūta*). Fire plays an essential part in worship and is treated with special reverence—to the extent that it is styled the "son" of Ahura Mazdā—and is a living symbol. The heat and light energy which rises upwards conveys offerings on high, in the same way as the Vedic god of fire, Agni, also does. It is not a matter of chance that some scholars link Agni with *an.giras,* which is etymologically related to the Greek *aggelos.*

A further kind of angel may be traced in the Fravashi, guardian spirits of society and the individual, from particularly mythological treatises which depict them as angels of the heavenly host and dressed in helmets with armor and iron weapons. They group in battalions, advancing with standards unfurled, coming to the aid of those who call upon them against demons, and descend from heaven like birds with fine wings.

MESOPOTAMIA. In Mesopotamia there were a number of angelological ideas which would be transmitted to monotheistic religions, especially their role as intermediaries and personal guardians of human beings. The "messenger" idea, indicated by the term *sukkal,* refers to a whole group of figures—such as Nuska and Kakka—which are connected with the most important gods and acted as messengers and intermediaries of the heavenly court. Marduk had Nabu as his *sukkal,* while Anu and Inanna had Papsukkal and Mummu. This role should be seen as a reflection of the Mesopotamian court culture, which would have an enormous influence upon the religious and political ideas of the Near East and the world of Hellenistic and late antiquity. The role of protective spirits is fulfilled by the *shedu* and *lamassu,* guardian spirits depicted on house doorposts, who accompany human beings when they leave the dwelling. The *karibu* (an Akkadian term meaning "one who prays") are spirits of intercession and blessing, represented with hands outstretched in prayer, in both human and animal form (body of a bull or lion, wings of an eagle). The representation in animal form of these spirits and *karibu* (from which the name "cherubim" is derived), depicted with two or three pairs of wings, influenced the angelic iconography of Judaism, Christianity, and Islam.

JUDAISM. In Judaism, the similarity between the Mesopotamian *karibu* and the Hebrew *kerub* is for the most part only linguistic, since the biblical *kerub* is not a deity, has no mythology of its own, and is merely a minister of the one, omnipotent God. In the Old Testament *mal'āk,* from the root *l'k* "to send," may refer to someone who carries news or messages and who looks after the interests of the sender, acting as a spy, an observer, or a negotiator. This role as messenger is clearly shown in the Vulgate with a distinction between *nuntius* (human messenger) and *angelus* (divine messenger).

In connection with Jhwh, the *mal'ak Jhwh* is the angel of Yahweh with particular duties and the divine representative who conveys God's words or deeds on earth. He intervenes directly in the life of humankind, and is a personal heavenly being at the center of particular events who proclaims salvation (*Jgs.* 13), rescues from danger and distress (*Gn.* 19, Exod. 14:19) watches over man on his travels (*Ps.* 91:11), conveys an instruction to a prophet (*Zec.* 1:9), and even causes devastation and destruction, as for example when the people are punished for the sins of David (*1 Chr.* 21:15).

The history of post-exile Judaism contains interesting cultural adaptations from Persian angelology. Similarly there arose a demonology which seems to have been influenced by Iranian and Semitic currents of thought, such as the name of the demon Asmodeus in *The Book of Tobit,* derived from the name of the Zoroastrian god of anger, Aeshmadaeva. In apocalyptic writing (*The Book of Enoch*), an elaborate belief system is set out regarding fallen angels who have become inferior to humans as a punishment for relations with women and for having revealed to humankind the secrets of the world. This hidden knowledge is revealed to Enoch by an angel that accompanies him and interprets his visions (*angelus interpres*); the same thing also happens to Levi (*Testaments of the Twelve Patriarchs*). Angels are positively described in the writings of Qumran, according to a level of participation and communion with them by individual sect members: warrior angels stand alongside the Essene community in the eschatological war, fulfilling an important role as intermediaries revealing heavenly secrets, on the basis of the level of purity required for carrying out priestly worship. Common knowledge about angels in late antiquity aroused the fear of rabbis that it might overshadow the unity and supremacy of the Lord God, since in a number of passages in the Talmud it is advised to call upon God in case of misfortune and not the angels Mika'el or Gavri'el.

In the Jewish mysticism of the Qabbalah, angelology is developed starting from the episode of the struggle between Jacob and the angel (*Gn.* 32: 27); in addition to other speculation on the first chapter of Genesis, there is commentary on the first chapter of Ezekiel (*ma'aseh merkavah,* or work of the chariot), the basis for the ideas regarding the vision of God's chariot, the throne of His Glory (*Kabod*), in which God is conveyed by Cherubim (*Chayyoth*), winged creatures in the form of humans, bulls, lions, and eagles. In *Hekhaloth* literature, which is based on Old Testament Apocrypha and the *Book of Enoch,* angels are guardians of the gates of the heavenly palace, beings who sing the praises of God and admit anyone who is worthy, accompanying him into the presence of God; they could also, however, punish humans by inflicting madness and death upon anyone who did not invoke them properly and who had not reached a sufficient degree of purity to attain the vision of the *merkavah.* Only minimal study of the Torah allowed one to reach the level of rectitude and purity necessary to distinguish true angels from unclean spirits.

In Medieval mysticism and amongst the Hasidim we find the angel Metatron. This figure was connected with the angels known as the "Princes of the Face," who may gaze upon the face of God. Metatron had an important role in esoteric Jewish doctrine—which subsequently passed into popular religious belief—as an angel who defends Israel in the heavenly judgment of Yom Kippur, and carries the prayers of the faithful before the throne of God. According to popular Jewish legend, angels presided over certain natural phenomena:

Yurkemi is the prince of hail,
Ridyah, of rain;
Rahav, of the sea;
and Laylah, of birth and death.

CHRISTIANITY. Christianity accepted and redeveloped aspects of Old Testament angelology according to its new requirements. Angels intervene in the central events involving the coming of the Messiah: Gabriel is the angel of the Annunciation, while an angelic star, a celestial symbol of power, acts as a heavenly sign guiding the Wise Men who have come to Palestine from the East in search of the Redeemer. Paul's letter to the Colossians (1:16, 2:10) lists the angelic hierarchy: Thrones, Dominations, Principalities, and Powers. It also sets down a central tenet of Christianity, which would determine later theological disputes (*Col.* 2:18): namely, that care should be taken to avoid idolatry and the worship of angels.

The Council of Laodicea in 336 (Canon 35) proscribed the invocation and adoration of angels. Patristic efforts concentrated on limiting the mythological and poetic developments of Judaic and Gnostic angelology and emphasized the role of angels as intermediaries in the action of salvation and their role as servants. The very iconography which avoided depicting them with wings in early centuries—these would appear at the end of the fourth century—was driven by the need to avoid confusing them with winged pagan gods, such as statues of Nike (Victory).

In the sixth-century work of Dionysius the Areopagite, Neoplatonic and Christian ideas are put together to create an angelic hierarchy of three sets of three, grouped according to their closeness to God: Seraphim, Cherubim, and Thrones; Dominations, Powers, and Virtues; and Principalities, Archangels, and Angels. These became well-known designations during the Middle Ages.

ISLAM. According to Islam, anyone who denies the existence of angels denies the word of God and the Prophet and is regarded as an unbeliever. Allah created angels with two, three, or four pairs of wings, the number varying according to the speed with which they carried out divine commands. Angels support God's throne, they are beside him, they praise and adore him, and they will sound the trumpet at the end of the world; they are infinite in number. Some are noted for carrying out particular tasks, such as Munkar and Nakir, who are responsible for judgment after death; Malik is the guardian of hell; Ridwan the guardian of paradise. Among the more important angels, Gabriel occupies the leading place in terms of angelic power, Michael is a messenger and intermediary, Israfil is the angel of the end of the world, and Azrail is the angel of death, not mentioned by name in the Qurʾān. The angels Harut and Marut, on the other hand, reflect Zoroastrian angelological ideas and are regarded as fallen angels who reveal to humankind the secrets of magic; they are punished for falling in love with mortal women.

The angel Gabriel occupies an important position in Islam for the audible revelation of the divine words. These spoken words are the only ones to have divine sanction, and are thus superior to anything visual. Angels can be distinguished from the simple spirits (*jinn*) of popular religion; "faithful spirit" (*rūḥ*) does mean angel in various passages of the Qurʾān. According to tradition, Muḥammad was visited by the angel Gabriel, who revealed to him his role as Messenger, enjoining him to preach while he was resting in the cave where he had gone for a spiritual retreat. While Muḥammad was sleeping, the angel Gabriel approached him with a silk cloth covered in writing, which he repeatedly commanded him to read; within this he bound Muḥammad so tightly that he was almost suffocated. Muḥammad woke up, left the cave and saw Gabriel as a man with wings. Gabriel also features in a version of the story of Muḥammad's ecstatic ascent to heaven (*Miʿrāj*) as the angel who guides him up the stairway which brings him into the presence of Allah.

In the realm of eschatology still, two angels called Munkar and Nakir question the dead person immediately after his death and if he does not answer correctly, they will torture his body in the grave. There is another tradition concerning the childhood of Muḥammad, in which angels also play a part in inaugurating the spiritual career of the future Prophet in circumstances rather similar to certain bloody shamanistic practices. As a four-year-old child, Muḥammad was seized and thrown to the ground by two angels, who opened his chest, drew a drop of blood from his heart, and washed his insides with melted snow that they carried in a golden cup.

There are elaborate angelologies to be found in Islamic philosophical and religious writings. In Avicenna, from a first intelligence emerge a large variety of intermediate spiritual beings called the ten cherubic intelligences (*Angeli intellectuales*) or celestial Souls (*Angeli caelestes*). In the philosophy of Sohrawardi there is a complex and well-developed angelology which contains elements of Neoplatonic and Zoroastrian influence: from a Light of Glory emerges an emanation of beings of light, led by the archangel Bahman, equivalent to the Avestic Vohu Manah. All sensible and material reality is created and controlled by a particular type of archangel. These archangels occupy a *mundus imaginalis* between the physical and spiritual worlds and can be perceived by the sage by means of imagination.

In the more extreme forms of Shīʿī Islam, such as Ismāʿīlīs, there are enduring Gnostic Hellenistic and Zoroastrian ideas; the divine can be made manifest in the world via angels who can take on a concrete physical form in members of the Ismāʿīlīte hierarchy. According to the beliefs of the Yezidi, incorrectly called "devil-worshippers," God created the world but the task of looking after it was entrusted to seven divine angels; among these the peacock angel (*Malak Taʾus*) is the symbol of immortality and the sun, the supreme angel, and active essence of God, who has declined in power but who weeps and cries tears of sorrow, which put out the fires of hell.

GNOSTICISM AND MANICHAEISM. In classical gnosis we find a variety of angelological ideas, including angels who create the world and rule it badly by fighting each other (Simon Magus), with a role not unlike the Demiurge. In this case the angels are usurpers of power (in the philosophy of Carpocrates, Menander, Saturninus and Basilides), against whom the act of salvation is directed, and therefore ignorant powers that have forgotten their subordinate place in the hierarchy of spiritual beings and are thus in the grip of envy and greed; these beings include the Jewish god who was responsible for creation. The Gnostic elect must therefore despise and free themselves from these powers that control the world, and train their souls to avoid the snares of these ruling powers that block their progress to the celestial planes. In its most positive interpretation, the soul of the elect could directly correspond with the angel that was his transcendental real self, the eternal prototype of which the soul was an earthly reflection, image (*eikon*), and part (*meros*). The angel could also be a heavenly messenger who reveals mysteries and awakens knowledge in humankind. Objects for personal use such as "Gnostic jewels" reveal aspects of a Hellenistic, Hermetic syncretism, which blend Christian and pagan elements: along with a Iaô (Yahweh) and Abrasax they call upon generic Faustian "powers" (*dynameis*). In other cases the jewels have the image of a manifold deity Hermes-Phosphoros-Michael, with inscriptions on the body referring to Yahweh, the archangels, and magic spells; these objects were used as seals so that the soul would pass over the cosmic planes and eventually reach the spiritual realm. Other images depict Olympian gods with the name of an angel inscribed alongside: Hermes (with his caduceus wand) and Michael; Iuppiter (armed with lightning and with the eagle) and Satoviel; and Diana (with bow, arrows and a crown) and Gabriel.

In a Gnostic religion such as Mandaeism, the priest is the earthly representative of messengers and angels (*uthrê*, literally "riches") who live in the world of light. These spiritual beings surround the supreme god and grant benefits on humankind, such as baptism, a gift of the divine beings of light to Adam and an important ritual which allows the soul to ascend to heaven. One important type of Mandaean exorcistic text inscribed on cups sets out magic spells used to neutralize demons and *liliths;* not just gods but also angels are invoked who can bless, set free, ward off, and destroy.

In Manichaeism too, there are also important angelological ideas: the angel of Mani is his spiritual twin (*syzygos*) who talks to him and provides him with instruction on the Gnostic mysteries. The *syzygos* thus reveals to him things that have been hidden, raises him up, and takes him to unknown and indescribable places. Protected from childhood in the baptismal community by guardian angels and divine powers, Mani grows up and eventually meets his "Twin" (Narjamig in Iranian texts, in Arabic al-Tawm in the *Fihrist* of an-Nadim) who enlightens him and encourages him in his missionary vocation. The Twin protects him spiritually against the snares of Greed (Az) and Evil (Ahrmen).

Angelic apparitions can be found in the myth of Manichaean cosmogony: during the first emanation, after the Mother of Life has produced Primordial Man, an angel emitting light called Nahashbat appears before him with a crown in his hand. There are also angelic presences that provide rewards, fine garments, the diadem, and the crown of light to the soul after death, when the soul of the Elect is escorted by gods and angels, who protect it against demons, until it meets its light image. In the universal eschatology of judgment day, Jesus will chair the court, surrounded by the Elect who have become angels. Concerning this angelic court, we have the evidence of Augustine of Hippo (354–430) who speaks of ranks of angels (*cohortes angelorum*), which make up the divine entourage in the paradise that is the Kingdom of Light. In his work, the *Book of Giants*, Mani retells the story of the fall of the angels (from the first book of Enoch), combining it with other narrative material. The Egregoroi, for example, who are attracted to women and marry them, become demons imprisoned in the world from which the race of giants originated, and are defeated by the archangels Raphael, Michael, Gabriel, and Istrael, as well as by Uriel and Fanuel.

MEDIEVAL, MODERN, AND CONTEMPORARY IDEAS. In late antiquity and the early Middle Ages, there continued to be reservations about the role of angels. In the seventh century, Pope Gregory I specified that the name angel should refer to their role and not their nature (*nomen est officii non naturae*). Based upon a passage of *Ezekiel* (28:13) concerning jewels, Gregory theorized a set of links between precious stones and angels according to their essence and spiritual clarity (Sardonyx, Topaz, and Jasper; Crisolite, Onyx, and Beryl; and Sapphire, Ruby, and Emerald).

During the Middle Ages, the work of Thomas Aquinas (1225–1274) and Bonaventure marked the high point of the success of Dionysius the Areopagite in scholastic philosophy. After the Lateran Council of 746, the cult was restricted to the three archangels, thus establishing the preeminence of Michael (soldier angel and protector), Raphael (guardian angel and healer), and Gabriel (the angel of the Annunciation); as a result of the addition of the epithet "Saint," these angels became humanized and Michael in particular was the subject of a popular cult and devotion with the establishment of shrines that spread his veneration throughout Europe. Michael's protective warlike qualities were appreciated by "barbarian" nations—among them the Celts, Germans, Slavs, and Baltic peoples—who gradually converted to the Christian faith. The cult of Saint Michael resulted in a pilgrimage route known as the "way of angels," which linked Normandy's Mont Saint-Michel with San Michele della Chiusa in Piedmont, Italy and San Michele del Gargano in Puglia, Italy.

The heretical and dualist ideological ideas of religious movements such as the Bogomils and Cathars reworked the story of the fallen angel, Satan. According to the Cathars, the devil created the human body by imprisoning an angel of light; this soul has an angelic nature which longs to return to heaven, but is condemned to be continually reborn in bodily form until it discovers the truth. Every angel/soul therefore has an individual spirit (*Spiritus sanctus*); the Virgin Mary herself was regarded as an angel in order to justify, from a docetic perspective, the immaterial nature of the body of the Savior. In the Encratite anthropology of the Bogomils, imitating the angel-eunuchs who live in heaven was a way of attaining, via asceticism, the detachment and sublimation of sexuality required to strive against materialism and reproductive instincts.

In medieval Grail epics, angels appear in a variety of situations as beings who impart stories of the Grail to hermits in visions. The Grail itself was originally a precious stone, an emerald, which fell to earth from the crown of Lucifer during the battle between the good and bad angels. In this battle, caused by Lucifer's rebellion, a number of so-called neutral angels did not take part and they became the guardian angels of the Grail. Four angels support the throne on which Joseph of Arimathea is seated, and this quartet carries two candles, the crimson silk, and lance to be placed above the Grail which is used to catch the drops of the blood of Christ.

The Renaissance, with its rediscovery of Neoplatonic theurgy and magic, witnessed a reformulation of various angelological and demonological ideas. These had been inherited from such ancient philosophers as Iamblichus, Proclus, and Psellus, and spread until the time of the philosopher Giordano Bruno (1548–1600). After him there was a gradual censorship by the Counter-Reformation of the *phantasia* of Renaissance pagan imagination. In the works of Marsilio Ficino (1433–1499) the idea of philosophy is seen as a mystery initiation, consisting of meditations and visions intended to raise the mind to the plane of angels, demons and planets. Pico della Mirandola asserted that elements of Christian angelology are also present, tinged with Platonism and qabbalism. In the natural philosophy of Paracelsus, magic allows control of the world of heavenly, astral, and earthly intelligence as well as the elemental demons connected with the four elements. For Henricus Cornelius Agrippa, the basic angelological hierarchy was divided into four categories of angel:

of Fire (Seraphim, Virtues, Powers);

of Air (Dominations, Principalities);

of Water (Thrones, Archangels);

and of Earth (Cherubim).

A system of angel and demon intelligence was linked to the seven planets and to graphic signs and pentacles used in performing magical ceremonies. Angels were also connected to signs of the zodiac, the four winds, and the four cardinal points of the compass. There were angels that describe the functions and powers of God (Vision, Strength, Virtue, Glory), while three good demons protect humankind by acting as guardian angels.

In the modern age there have been individuals and secret societies with universalist, utopian systems, such as the Rosicrucians, who were interested in the ideas of theosophy and alchemy. Illustrations in alchemical writings from the fifteenth century (*Opera Chemica*) attributed to Raimondo Lullo represent the biblical episode of Tobit and Raphael, the healing angel, and hint that the alchemical Great Work of the philosopher should always take place under the guidance of heavenly powers so as not to stray into darkness. In the work of Jakob Boehme (1575–1624), angels intervene in the alchemical work of the Magus and their revelation determines the success of the work. An account by Johann Georg Gichtel depicts the battle of Saint Michael with the Dragon, symbolizing the struggle between the forces of Love and Anger and between Light and Darkness. In Elizabethan England there was a kind of angelic spiritualism, particularly illustrated by the magus John Dee. Dee may have inspired both the character of Prospero, the master of the sprite Ariel in Shakespeare's *The Tempest,* as well as the title character in Gustav Meyrink's 1927 novel *The Angel of the West Window.* Dee claimed to have been visited by the angel Uriel, who brought him a gift of a magic crystal to enable the magus to communicate with him via a supposed language of angels.

During the seventeenth and eighteenth centuries spiritualism and evocation of angels was widespread: in the writings of the Lutheran theologian Emanuel Swedenborg (1688–1772) the universe has a spiritual structure and the human microcosm is the image of the divine macrocosm; angels allowed communion with the divine which could be known via visionary experiences. This theosophy influenced not only philosophers but also artists and writers like William Blake (1757–1827), who put forward ideas concerning angels in both his engravings and his poetic works. Swedenborg was identified with an angel in Blake's *Marriage of Hell and Heaven,* while the "Four Zoas" in Blake's poetry are angelic and devil images of the four elements. Angelic influence in romantic and spiritualist imagination was marked in Pre-Raphaelite and Impressionist art. Twentieth-century occult movements, like the Hermetic Order of the Golden Dawn, practiced a version of angelic spiritualism and provided visionary and poetic inspiration. One of its most famous members was William Butler Yeats (1865–1939); another famous member of an esoteric brotherhood, the magician Aleister Crowley (1875–1947), carried out ritual "magick" ceremonies by calling upon an angelic being named Aiwass. In other cases the subject of angels was the source of philosophical ruminations from the great artistic and cultural figures of the twentieth century, including Gershom Scholem, Walter Benjamin, Paul Klee, and Rainer Maria Rilke. Angels have also become subject matter for mass-media interpretations, perhaps most notably by German filmmaker Wim Wender's 1987 classic *Wings of Desire.* Also bearing mention are the spiritualist and irrational New Age movements and kinds of recollective possession and contacts with spirit guides via mediumistic channeling experiments.

See Also Demons; Fravashis; Satan.

BIBLIOGRAPHY

Anges et Démons: Actes du Colloque de Liège et de Louvain-la-Neuve, 25-26 Novembre 1987, edited by Julien Ries & Henri Limet, Louvain-la-Neuve, Belgium, 1989. See pages 383–398.

Bussagli, Marco. *Storia degli Angeli: Racconto di Immagini e di Idee.* Milan, 1991.

Cacciari, Massimo. *L'angelo necessario,* 2d ed. Milan, 1998. Translated as *The Necessary Angels* (New York, 1994).

Coomaraswamy, Ananda Kentish. "Angels and Titans." *Journal of American Oriental Society* 55 (1935): 373–419.

Corbin, Henri. *Le paradoxe du monothéisme.* Paris, 1981.

Couliano, Ioan. *Eros et magie à la renaissance: 1484.* Paris, 1984.

Couliano, Ioan. *Les gnoses dualistes d'occident.* Paris, 1989.

Cumont, Franz. "Les anges du paganisme." *Revue de l'histoire des religions* 36 (1915): 159–182.

Génies, Anges et Démons Egypt-Babylon-Israël-Islam-Peuples Altaïque-Inde-Birmanic-Asie du sud-Est-Tibet-Chine. Paris, 1971.

Leclercq, Henri. "Anges." In *Dictionnaire d'archéologie chrétienne et de liturgie,* edited by Fernand Cabrol and Henri Leclercq, Vol. 1/2, cols. 2080–2161. Paris, 1907.

Maier, S.A. "Angel." In *Dictionary of Deities and Demons in the Bible,* edited by Karel van der Toorn, Bob Becking, and Pieter W. van der Horst, pp. 81–90. New York, 1995.

Montgomery, A. James. *Aramaic Incantation Texts from Nippur.* Philadelphia, 1913.

Pettinato, Giovanni. *Angeli e Demoni a Babilonia: Magia e Mito nelle Antiche Civiltà Mesopotamiche.* Milan, Italy, 2001.

Piras, Andrea. "Messaggeri e inviati nello zoroastrismo." *Avallon* 42 (1997): 17–33.

The Intellectual Heritage of Assyria and Babylonia in East and West. A Searchable Database of the Legacy of Ancient Mesopotamia to Later Civilizations: entry "Angels." Available from http://www.aakkl.helsinki.fi/melammu/.

ANDREA PIRAS (2005)
Translated from Italian by Paul Ellis

ANGLICANISM.

ANGLICANISM. Anglicanism, also called the Anglican Communion, is a federation of autonomous national and regional churches that are in full intercommunion through the archbishop of Canterbury of the Church of England. Anglican churches share a tradition of doctrine, polity, and liturgy stemming from the English Reformation of the sixteenth century. Often classified as Protestant, they also claim a Catholic heritage of faith and order from the ancient, undivided church.

EARLY HISTORY. The endeavor to hold together in a comprehensive middle way (*via media*) the tensions of its Protestant and Catholic elements is characteristic of Anglicanism. This tradition is a legacy of the English Reformation, which was essentially an act of state, not a popular movement. Without the coercive power of the state Anglicanism might have died aborning. The long reign of Queen Elizabeth I (r. 1558–1603) ensured its survival.

Like her father, Henry VIII (r. 1509–1547), Elizabeth was determined to rule both church and state. The Act of Supremacy of 1559 changed Henry's title of "supreme head in earth of the Church of England" (1534) to that of "supreme governor." Elizabeth had no intention of submitting England to papal authority, which her sister, Mary I (r. 1553–1558), had restored. She was equally adamant against agitation for a presbyterian form of church government that would dispense with the royal supremacy, the episcopacy, and the liturgy.

The two editions of *The Book of Common Prayer* authorized in 1549 and 1552 under Edward VI (r. 1547–1553) were chiefly the work of Archbishop Thomas Cranmer of Canterbury (1533–1556), whom Queen Mary had burned as a heretic. Both books were Protestant in doctrine, but many ceremonies and ornaments from the Latin rites that were retained in 1549 were eliminated in 1552. Elizabeth preferred the 1549 prayer book. Parliament would accept only that of 1552, but the queen succeeded in making a few substantial changes in it. Pejorative references to the bishop of Rome were omitted. The 1,549 words of administration at Communion were added. Those additions clearly identified the consecrated bread and wine with the body and blood of Christ. Elizabeth eliminated a rubric stating that kneeling to receive Communion did not imply adoration of "any real and essential presence there being of Christ's natural flesh and blood," but she was unable to enforce a new rubric restoring the ornaments of the church as they had been specified in the second year of Edward VI's reign.

Many episcopal sees, including Canterbury, were vacant at Elizabeth's accession. Most of Mary's bishops were deprived of their offices for refusing to accept the new settlement. Careful to maintain the episcopal succession, Elizabeth chose Matthew Parker, a moderate reformer and a friend and admirer of Cranmer, to be archbishop of Canterbury. He was consecrated on December 17, 1559, by two bishops from Henry's time and two from Edward's. Vacant sees were filled with the queen's supporters.

In 1571 Parliament approved the Thirty-nine Articles, the only official confessional statement of Anglicanism, which are still included in most editions of the prayer book. They are not a complete system of doctrine but point out differences from Roman Catholicism and Anabaptism and indicate nuanced agreement with Lutheran and Reformed positions. The queen added in Article 20 the statement "The Church hath power to decree Rites and Ceremonies."

Elizabeth's settlement remains the foundation of Anglicanism. It affirms the status of the canonical scriptures as the final arbiter in all matters of doctrine and as containing all matters necessary to salvation. Traditions of the ancient church and teachings of the early Church Fathers, unless contrary to scripture, are treasured. The dogmatic decisions of the first four ecumenical councils on the Trinity and the Incarnation are accepted. Anglican liturgies regularly use the

Apostles' and Nicene creeds and in some places the Athanasian Creed (*Quicunque vult*).

THEOLOGY AND CHURCH GOVERNMENT. Today most Anglicans accept modern methods of literary and historical criticism of the scriptures and other religious documents. Anglicanism has never had a dominant theologian such as Thomas Aquinas, Martin Luther, or John Calvin. The apologetic work of Richard Hooker (1554–1600), *Of the Laws of Ecclesiastical Polity,* is still influential with its appeal to scripture, church tradition, reason, and experience. Anglican theology tends to be biblical, pastoral, and apologetic rather than dogmatic or confessional.

The Anglican polity is episcopal and preserves the ordained orders of bishops, presbyter-priests, and deacons that go back to apostolic times. There is no official doctrine of episcopacy. Some Anglicans consider it essential; others feel it is needed for the proper ordering or fullness of a truly catholic church. In negotiations for unity or intercommunion with other churches Anglicans insist that an unbroken succession of bishops, together with the other two orders, be maintained.

All Anglican churches are constitutionally governed, with each church having its own canons for executive and legislative authorities. Bishops, the clergy, and the laity participate in all synodical decision making, but a consensus of these orders, voting separately, is necessary for decisions about major doctrinal, liturgical, or canonical matters. Outside England bishops generally are elected by a synod of the diocese in which they will serve, subject to confirmation by other bishops and representative clergy and laity from each diocese.

The Church of England is the only contemporary Anglican church that is state-established. The archbishop of Canterbury has a primacy of honor among all Anglican bishops but has no jurisdiction outside his own diocese and province. The British Crown, after appropriate consultations, nominates the English bishops, who then are elected by their respective cathedral chapters. Parliament retains final control over doctrine and liturgy, but the Synodical Government Measure of 1969 gave the English church the freedom to order its internal life through a general synod of bishops, clergy, and laity.

In addition to the episcopate, Anglicanism is bonded by a common liturgy that is contained in various recensions of *The Book of Common Prayer* and is based on either the Elizabethan version of 1559 or that of 1549. Use of the prayer book is prescribed in all Anglican churches. With the Bible and a hymnal, it provides everything needed for the churches' rites and ceremonies. The prayer book has been in continuous use since the sixteenth century except for the years of the English Commonwealth (1645–1660), when it was proscribed for public and private use. It is the only vernacular liturgy of the Reformation period still in use.

The prayer-book formularies, many of them derived from the ancient church, are a principal source of doctrine and a primary basis of the spirituality of both the clergy and the laity. The daily and Sunday liturgies are set within the framework of the traditional seasons of the Christian year and the fixed feasts of Christ and the saints. The sacraments of baptism and the Lord's Supper (also called Holy Communion or Eucharist) generally are considered necessary to salvation.

Valid baptism is by water "in the Name of the Father, and of the Son, and of the Holy Spirit." When they reach a competent age, persons who were baptized in infancy are expected to reaffirm the baptismal promises made by their parents or sponsors, at which time they receive confirmation by a bishop. The Eucharist, with invariable elements of bread and wine, consecrated by a thanksgiving prayer that includes Christ's "words of institution" at the last supper, is a memorial of Christ's once-for-all redemptive acts in which Christ is objectively present and effectually received in faith.

CHURCHES OUTSIDE ENGLAND. For almost three centuries the expansion of Anglicanism was hindered by the Church of England's lack of an overall missionary strategy and its concept of a church that must be established by the state and sufficiently endowed. Within the British Isles the Church in Wales, whose roots go back to the ancient church in Roman Britain, was part of the province of Canterbury from the Norman Conquest of 1066 until its disestablishment and disendowment (the political actions that made the church independent of the government, and self-supporting) in 1920. It now uses Welsh as well as English in its liturgy.

The English Reformation was rejected by 90 percent of the people in Ireland, yet not until 1870 was the (Anglican) Church of Ireland disestablished and largely disendowed. Four Anglican dioceses now straddle the border between Northern Ireland and the Republic of Ireland. Old enmities between the Irish church and its predominant Roman Catholic neighbor have diminished.

The Reformation in Scotland was predominantly presbyterian. A precarious Anglican episcopate was maintained by the Stuart sovereigns. For its loyalty to James II and his male descendants after their deposition by Parliament, the Scottish Episcopal Church was disestablished in 1689 and subjected to penal laws between 1715 and 1792. Yet it maintained its episcopal succession, revised its liturgy, and in 1784 consecrated its first American bishop, Samuel Seabury of Connecticut (1729–1797).

Beginning in Virginia in 1607, the English church came to be established in the American colonies from Maryland southward and in New York City. Except in Virginia Anglicans were outnumbered in the colonies by religious dissidents and refugees. The bishop of London exercised general supervision, yet no bishop visited America during the colonial period.

After a brief visit to Maryland the Reverend Thomas Bray (1658–1730) founded in 1701 the voluntary Society for the Propagation of the Gospel in Foreign Parts (SPG).

The Archbishops of Canterbury

Name	Made a Bishop	Years as Archbishop
Augustine	597	601-604
Laurentius	604	604-619
Mellitus	604	619-624
Justus	604	624-627
Honorius		627-653
Deusdedit		655-664
Theodore of Tarsus		668-690
Beorhtweald		693-731
Tatwine		731-734
Nothelm		735-739
Cuthbeorht	736	740-760
Breguwine		761-764
Jænbeorht		765-792
Æthelheard		793-805
Wulfred		805-832
Feologild		805-832
Ceolnoth		833-870
Æthelred		870-889
Plegmund		890-914
Æthelhelm	909	914-923
Wulfhelm	914	923-942
Oda	923	942-958
Ælfsige	951	942-959
Beorhthelm	956	959-dep. 959
Dunstn	957	960-988
Æthelgar	980	988-990
Sigeric	985	990-994
Ælfric	990	995-1005
Ælfheah (Alphege)	984	1005-1012 [martyred]
Lyfing	999	1013-1020
Æthelnoth		1020-1038
Eadsige	1035	1038-1050
Robert of Jumièges	1044	1051-exp. 1052; d. 1070
Stigand	1043	1052-dep. 1070; d. 1072
Lanfranc		1070-1089
Anselm		1093-1109
Ralph d'Escures	1108	1114-1122
William de Corbeil		1123-1136
Theobald		1139-1161
Thomas Becket		1162-1170
Richard (of Dover)		1174-1184
Baldwin	1180	1185-1190
Hubert Walter	1189	1193-1205
Stephen Langton		1207-1228
Richard le Grant		1229-1231
Edmund Rich		1234-1240
Boniface of Savoy		1245-1270
Robert Kilwardby		1273-1278
John Pecham (Peckham)		1279-1292
Robert Winchelsey		1294-1313
Walter Reynolds	1308	1313-1327
Simon Mepeham		1328-1333
John Stratford	1323	1333-1348
Thomas Bradwardine		1349
Simon Islip		1349-1366
Simon Langham	1362	1366-res. 1368
William Whittlesey	1362	1368-1374
Simon Sudbury	1362	1375-1381
William Courtenay	1370	1381-1396
Thomas arundel	1374	1396-trans. 1397
Roger Walden		1398-depr. 1399; d. 1406
Thomas Arundel		rest. 1399-1414
Henry Chichele	1408	1414-1443
John Stafford	1425	1443-1452
John Kemp	1419	1452-1454
Thomas Bourchier	1435	1454-1486
John Morton	1479	1486-1500
Henry Dean	1496	1501-1503
William Warham	1502	1503-1532
Thomas Cranmer		1533-1556
Reginald Pole		1556-1558
Matthew Parker		1559-1575
Edmund Grindal	1559	1576-1583
John Whitgift	1577	1583-1604
Richard Bancroft	1597	1604-1610
George Abbot	1609	1611-1633
William Laud	1621	1633-1645
William Juxon	1633	1660-1663
Gilbert Sheldon	1660	1663-1677
William Sancroft		1678-depr. 1691; d. 1693
John Tillotson		1691-1694
Thomas Tenison	1692	1695-1715
William Wake	1705	1716-1737
John Potter	1715	1737-1747
Thomas Herring	1738	1747-1757
Matthew Hutton	1743	1757-1758
Thomas Secker	735	1758-1768
Frederick Cornwallis	1750	1768-1783
John Moore	1775	1783-1805
Charles Manners Sutton	1792	1805-1828
William Howley	1813	1828-1848
John Bird Sumner	1828	1848-1862
Charles Thomas Longley	1836	1862-1868
Archibald Campbell Tait	1856	1868-1882
Edward White Benson	1877	1883-1896
Frederick Temple	1869	1896-1902
Randall Thomas Davidson	1891	1903-ret. 1928; d. 1930
Cosmo Gordon Lang	1901	1928-ret. 1942; d. 1944
William Temple	1921	1942-1944
Geoffrey Francis Fisher	1932	1945-ret. 1961; d. 1972
Arthur Michael Ramsey	1952	1961-ret. 1974
Frederick Donald Coggan	1956	1974-ret. 1980
Robert Alexander Kennedy Runcie	1970	1980-1991
George Carey	1987	1991-2002
Rowan Williams	1992	2003-

TABLE 1. For those consecrated as bishop prior to becoming Archbishop of Canterbury, the year of consecration is noted. Abbreviations: d. = died; dep. = deposed; depr. = deprived; exp. = expelled; res. = resigned; rest. = restored; ret. = retired; trans. = translated to another see.

Until the American Revolution the SPG sent more than three hundred missionaries into the colonies. The revolution undid those accomplishments, with the Anglican clergy and laity becoming divided between American patriots and loyalists to the British Crown.

With independence, all SPG support was withdrawn. A large proportion of the clergy and laity had left for England or Canada. There were no more establishments, and in Virginia disendowment followed. The remaining clergy and laity, both patriots and loyalists, began to organize in state conventions. The consecration of Bishop Seabury for Connecticut by Scottish bishops, who were considered schismatic by the Church of England, spurred the English bishops to obtain an act of Parliament in June 1786 that enabled them to consecrate American bishops without the customary oaths of obedience to the royal supremacy and the archbishop of Canterbury. Three Americans were so consecrated: for Pennsylvania and New York in 1787 and for Virginia in 1790.

Under the leadership of Bishop William White of Pennsylvania (1748–1836) and Bishop Seabury, a national church that was formed at a general convention in 1789 adopted a constitution, canons, and a revised prayer book. By the General Convention in 1835 the Episcopal Church was strong enough to establish a concerted missionary strategy, and it organized the Domestic and Foreign Missionary Society, which to this day includes all its baptized members. A bishop was chosen to organize dioceses on the western frontier, and a bishop was resident in China in 1844 and in Japan in 1874. Liberia received its first bishop in 1851.

In England evangelical Anglicans, influenced by the revival movement of the Wesleys, in the late eighteenth century formed the Church Missionary Society, whose aims were comparable to those of the SPG. Later other voluntary missionary societies with special areas of interest arose. The Church of England was slow, however, in providing bishops for its burgeoning missions overseas, and voluntary societies could not provide them legally since bishops can be appointed only by the church, not by voluntary societies, even if they are affiliated with the church. Canada received its first bishop in 1787, followed by India in 1814, the West Indies in 1824, Australia in 1836, New Zealand in 1841, and South Africa in 1847.

Conflicts, Congresses, and Interfaith Dialogue. By the 1860s two internal conflicts were disturbing many Anglican churches: the emergence in some churches of modern biblical criticism and the rise of ritual and ceremonial practices influenced by the Tractarian (or Oxford) Movement of the 1830s and 1840s, which emphasized the Catholic heritage of Anglicanism. At the request of the Canadian bishops and with the counsel of his own convocation, Archbishop Longley of Canterbury invited all Anglican bishops to meet at his palace at Lambeth in London in 1867 for common consultation and encouragement. Seventy-six bishops attended. The success of that meeting led to similar Lambeth Conferences at approximately ten-year intervals except when the two world wars intervened.

The encyclical letters, resolutions, and reports of these conferences have no legislative, but only advisory, authority. They deal with internal Anglican affairs, ecumenical relations, and important social and ethical issues. The 1958 conference was the first to invite representative observers from other churches, both eastern and western, to attend. Anglican congresses in Minneapolis (1954) and Toronto (1964) of bishops and clergy and lay delegates from most of the Anglican dioceses, along with congresses in Lambeth (1958 and 1968), opened the way to new structures of Anglican intercommunication.

In 1960 the first Anglican executive officer, serving under the archbishop of Canterbury, was chosen. His duties were to visit and assess the problems of the various Anglican churches and promote communication and common strategy for missionary work among them. In 1971 the Anglican Consultative Council came into being, and the Anglican executive officer became its secretary general. The council meets every two or three years in different parts of the Anglican world. The archbishop of Canterbury is its president, but the council elects its own chairperson; to date three of the chairs have been laypersons. Members consist of representative bishops, clergy, and laity of the several Anglican churches. Its concerns are much the same as those of the Lambeth Conferences, and like them it has no legislative authority.

Anglicanism is strongly involved in endeavors for Christian unity. The 1888 Lambeth Conference proposed a fourfold basis for negotiations: the scriptures as "the rule and ultimate standard of faith"; the Apostles' and Nicene creeds as "sufficient statement of the Christian faith"; the sacraments of baptism and the Supper of the Lord as instituted by Christ; and "the Historic Episcopate, locally adapted . . . to the varying needs of nations and peoples." This "Lambeth Quadrilateral" has been constantly reaffirmed.

The Episcopal Church under the leadership of Bishop Charles Henry Brent (1862–1929) planned the first World Conference on Faith and Order at Lausanne in 1927, over which Brent presided. Delegates from more than a hundred Protestant and Eastern Orthodox churches attended. This movement became part of the World Council of Churches, constituted in 1948.

At Bonn in 1931 the Anglican Communion entered into an agreement with the Old Catholic churches of the Union of Utrecht (1889) for full intercommunion, which stated that this does "not require from either Communion the acceptance of all doctrinal opinion, sacramental devotion, or liturgical practice characteristic of the other, but implies that each believes the other to hold all the essentials of the Christian Faith." This concordat has been the basis of all intercommunion with non-Anglican Episcopal episcopal churches, which Anglicans call the Wider Episcopal Fellowship.

A member of this fellowship is the Philippine Independent Catholic Church, which split from the Roman Catholic Church in 1902 and in 1948 requested and received from the Episcopal Church the historical episcopal succession. In 1961 full intercommunion was established, and in 1965 the Philippine church became a member of the confederation of Old Catholic churches. A unique development began when Anglican dioceses joined with other Protestant churches in forming the Church of South India in 1947, with Anglicans providing the historical episcopate. The churches of North India, Pakistan, and (after national independence) Bangladesh subsequently were formed on the same basis. Intercommunion also has been established with the ancient Mar Thoma Syrian Church of Malabar in India.

Serious efforts to achieve the future reunion of Anglicanism with the Roman Catholic Church began with an official visit of Archbishop Ramsey of Canterbury with Pope Paul VI in March 1966. A joint preparatory commission in 1967 and 1968 sorted major theological issues for dialogue and made recommendations for areas of cooperation. Between 1970 and 1981 the Anglican-Roman Catholic International Commission published substantial agreements on eucharistic doctrine, ministry, and ordination and two agreements on authority in the church. Those agreements were gathered, with some elucidations, in the commission's *Final Report* (1982). When Pope John Paul II visited Britain in 1982, he and Archbishop Runcie signed the "Common Declaration" at Canterbury Cathedral on June 29 for a new commission to study further theological issues, pastoral problems, and practical steps for "the next stage" toward unity.

Anglican-Lutheran international dialogues took place between 1970 and 1972. The ensuing report has been influential in an official Lutheran-Episcopal dialogue in the United States. In September 1982 three Lutheran bodies, in the process of uniting, agreed with the Episcopal Church to celebrate an interim shared Eucharist on specified occasions as a step toward closer unity in doctrine, liturgy, and ministry. Moves toward ecumenism between the the Church of England and other European denominations and between the American Episcopal Church and other denominations continued throughout the 1980s and 1990s.

Such dialogues recall expectations voiced in the encyclical letter of the 1948 Lambeth Conference that, no doubt, was influenced by the formation of the Church of South India the year before:

> Reunion of any part of our Communion with other denominations in its own area must make the resulting Church no longer simply Anglican, but something more comprehensive. . . . The Anglican Communion would be merged in a much larger Communion of National or Regional Churches, in full communion with one another, united in all the terms of what is known as the Lambeth Quadrilateral.

In addition to developments related to the ecumenical movement, a significant change in the Anglican Communion during the twentieth and twenty-first centuries has been its growth in African and Asian countries. Whereas there are currently about 26,000,000 Anglicans in England; 2,400,000 in the United States; about 4,000,000 in Australia, Aotearoa/New Zealand, and Polynesia; and about 700,000 in Canada, the real growth of Anglican churches has occurred elsewhere. There are over 41,500,000 Anglicans in Africa, with Nigeria alone accounting for 17,500,000. Indeed, the independence of African countries that was won after World War II led to an increased rate of conversion to Anglican churches even in areas that had never been colonies of Britain. The leadership and clergy of African Anglican churches are also indigenous in a way they were not before the collapse of nineteenth- and twentieth-century colonialism. At the 1998 Lambeth Conference bishops from Africa and Asia (224 and 95, respectively) outnumbered those from Europe, the United States, and Canada combined (316). A resolution affirming traditional disapproval of homosexually active clergy passed largely because of support from African bishops.

Current differences of opinion on ethical issues in the Anglican Communion, especially those related to the ordination of women and the morality of homosexuality, often reflect geographical differences. The General Convention of the Episcopal Church (U.S.A.) first allowed the ordination of women in 1976, an event that was prompted by two instances of retired bishops ordaining female deacons to the priesthood without official approval on July 29, 1974, in Philadelphia and on September 7, 1975, in Washington, D.C. The first female Episcopal bishop, Barbara Harris, was elected in 1989. The General Synod of the Church of England voted in favor of allowing the ordination of women on November 11, 1992; in 1975 it had narrowly voted that it had "no fundamental objections" to women's ordination.

However, these developments have not met with approval throughout the Anglican Communion, with the churches and bishops in Africa and Asia notably opposed to such changes. In 1998 the Eames Commission, the Archbishop of Canterbury's Commission on Communion and Women in the Episcopate, reported that no ordination of women to any clerical office was at that time allowed in the provinces of Central Africa, Jerusalem and the Middle East, Korea, Melanesia, Nigeria, Papua New Guinea, South East Asia, and Tanzania. Other provinces allow women's ordination to the deaconate but not to the priesthood. Only a few provinces allow women's ordination as both deacons and priests and allow the election of a woman as bishop.

Similarly, there has been disagreement about the morality of same-sex unions and the ordination of openly gay or lesbian Christians to the priesthood. When the Episcopal Church in the United States allowed the election of an openly gay man as bishop of Vermont in 2003, that event caused much controversy within and among Anglican communions, with the most vociferous disapproval being voiced by African bishops.

Since its beginning as a national, Protestant church in England in the sixteenth century, the Anglican communion has grown into a worldwide, diverse federation of churches bound together by a respect for a common tradition of doctrine, liturgy, and polity. The different churches draw on a past that includes both Protestant and Catholic elements. The loosely structured, federated nature of the communion may frustrate some attempts at greater unity and conformity, but it also may enable survival, and perhaps even flourishing, of the church in an increasingly international world.

SEE ALSO Cranmer, Thomas; Hooker, Richard.

BIBLIOGRAPHY

For official church documents and reports, see the *Official Report of the Lambeth Conference* for 1988 (London) and 1998 (Harrisburg, Pa.). See also the *Official Year Book of the Church of England,* published each year. For surveys of Anglicanism with a bibliography, see J. W. C. Wand, *Anglicanism in History and Today* (London, 1961); Stephen C. Neill, *Anglicanism,* 3d ed. (Baltimore, 1965). See also Hugh Gerard Gibson Herklots, *Frontiers of the Church: The Making of the Anglican Communion* (London, 1961); Paul D. L. Avis, *Church, State, and Establishment* (London, 2001); Paul D. L. Avis, *Anglican Understanding of the Church: An Introduction* (London, 2000); Christopher Webber, *Welcome to the Episcopal Church: An Introduction to its History, Faith, and Worship* (Harrisburg, Pa., 1999); Andrew Wingate, et al., eds., *Anglicanism: A Global Communion* (London, 1998).

On *The Book of Common Prayer,* including its texts and sources (1549–1662), see Frank E. Brightman, *The English Rite,* 2d ed., 2 vols. (London, 1921); Geoffrey J. Cuming, *A History of Anglican Liturgy,* 2d ed. (London, 1980). For Anglican worship from an ecumenical and artistic perspective, see Horton Davies, *Worship and Theology in England,* 5 vols. (Princeton, N.J., 1961–1975). For Anglican–Roman Catholic relations, see Bernard Pawley and Margaret Pawley, *Rome and Canterbury through Four Centuries: A Study of the Relations between the Church of Rome and the Anglican Churches, 1530–1973,* with a large bibliography and an American epilogue by Arthur A. Vogel (New York, 1975).

On recent developments regarding the ordination of women, see Pamela W. Darling, *New Wine: The Story of Women Transforming Leadership and Power in the Episcopal Church* (Cambridge, Mass., 1994); Susan Dowell and Jane Williams, *Bread, Wine and Women: The Ordination Debate in the Church of England* (London, 1994).

MASSEY H. SHEPHERD, JR. (1987)
DALE B. MARTIN (2005)

ANI LOCHEN (c. 1865–1951) came to achieve the most treasured status of Tibetan culture, that of a religious master, and her devotees regard her as an emanation (*sprul sku*) of the the famous eleventh-century *yoginī* Machig Labdron. An exceptional autobiography, written during her last years, provides insight into her spiritual achievements, as well as the more mundane aspects of the life of female religious specialists in Tibet during the mid-nineteenth to the mid-twentieth centuries.

In her youth Ani Lochen was an itinerant *yoginī;* in midlife she was ordained a nun (*a ne*); and in her mature years she became a famous lama (*bla ma*). Ani Lochen was addressed as *rinpoche* (precious), a title reserved for high lamas and only exceptionally used for female masters. In premodern Tibet, thousands of male yogins, *rinpoches,* and learned monks competed for attention and support, and it is highly remarkable that a woman of humble origins was able to rise from poverty, physical and psychological abuse, and ethnic, social, and gender discrimination to become a treasured teacher of Tibetan Buddhism.

At the turn of the twentieth century, Ani Lochen established one of the largest and most famous nunneries in Tibet, Shug gseb (Shugseb), at the mountain Gangri Thokar south of Lhasa. Organized as a mountain hermitage, Shug gseb became the refuge of three hundred *yoginīs* and nuns, who practiced meditation and yoga in caves and cells scattered on the hillside above the convent. Apart from periods of strict seclusion, Ani Lochen's door was always open—even during the night—for nuns in need of advice and instruction. At Shug gseb the routines of meditation were broken only when famous teachers visited, for common rituals on special days, and for the daily duties of monastic living.

Ani Lochen came to embody important cultural and religious impulses from all of Tibet, stretching from Amdo and Kham in the east, where her main teachers came from, to the holy mountain Kailash in the west, which she visited twice. She also spent years meditating in caves in the Himalayas in Nepal. Ani Lochen received her training from masters of the "old school" of Tibetan Buddhism (Rnying ma [Nyingma] pa), which traces its spiritual ancestry back to ancient sources of Buddhist wisdom, yoga, and meditation disseminated in Tibet during the ninth century, possibly earlier. Ani Lochen combined learning from several Tibetan Buddhist schools and continued an eclectic tradition *(ris med)* transferred to her by her main teacher Pema Gyatso (d. c. 1889), himself a personal disciple of the great yogin Shabkar (1781–1851) from Amdo in northeastern Tibet.

During Ani Lochen's lifetime, Shug gseb became a vibrant and active religious community attracting many well-known yogins and scholars. One of the greatest scholars and adepts in Tibetan history, Klong chen Rab 'byams pa (Longchen Rabjampa,1308–1363), wrote his main works on Buddhist philosophy in a cave near Ani Lochen's convent, thus making the mountain an important site of pilgrimage. Among religious masters and important persons visiting Shug gseb during Ani Lochen's days were Rva sgreng rin po che (Reting Rinpoche, (1912–1947), the regent of Tibet; Si tu chos kyi rgya mtsho (Situ Chokyi Gyatso, 1880–1925), the abbot of Kah thog (Kathok) Monastery in Kham; the king of Gling tshangs (Lingtsang, Kham); Rang byung Rig pa'i rdo rje (Rangchung Rigpe Dorje, 1924–1981), the sixteenth Karma pa; and the father of the fourteenth Dalai

Lama. Among Ani Lochen's teachers were also such "crazy" *siddhas* as the tenth 'Khrul zhig rin po che (Trulshig Rinpoche, d. 1920s) and Stag lung Ma sprul Rin po che (Taklung Matrul Rinpoche, 1916–1976), who employed unconventional means to reach the Buddhist goal of enlightenment.

When Ani Lochen and her religious companions arrived in Lhasa around 1880—after years of wandering in the Himalayas—people were amazed to see such a group of yogins and *yoginīs*, their hair long and matted, their cotton robes in rags. In Lhasa word spread quickly of this remarkable *yoginī*, and soon the aristocracy—particularly the women—took her to their hearts. She was invited to noble mansions like that of the Lha klu (Lalu) family to read sūtras; she was ordained a nun on the terrace of Rag shag (Ragshag) House, and she became the house-lama of Lady Bshag byang (Shagjang) in E-yul. Counted among her devout disciples and supporters were some of the most influential families in Lhasa: the Phreng ring (Taring), the Nga phod (Ngaphö), the Spang mda' tshang (Pangda Tsang), the Ka shod (Kapshö), the 'Brang stod (Drang Tö), the Ragshag, the Lcog bkras (Chogdre), the Kun bzang rtse (Kunsangtse), the Pha la (Phala), the Hor khang (Horkang), and the Sne do (Nedo). Lady Nedo (b. 1917) recalled the following:

> I had heard much about Jetsun [Venerable] Rinpoche in Lhasa, but didn't really have faith in her. But in 1948 I stayed at her nunnery for more than a month. At Shugseb there were people from all walks of life: nobles and businessmen, peasants and nomads. They came from Lhasa and from different villages in the vicinity: from Western Tibet (Ngari), Shigatse, Lhoka and Kham. I even saw Bhutanese there. The pilgrims gathered in [the] monastery kitchen and in the assembly-hall. Jetsun Lochen told the nuns to feed them all. Since her private quarter was so small, the devotees had to wait in line to receive her blessings and advice. She treated everyone alike, making no distinction between high and low. Jetsun Lochen would say, "*yar shog, yar shog*"—"come in, come in!" I was invited one day into her private room at the time of her morning toilette. I had heard that Jetsun Lochen liked French perfume, and I offered her a small blue bottle of expensive perfume which I bought in Lhasa [the perfume was labeled *Evening in Paris* and was popular among the noble ladies in Lhasa at the time]. Jetsun Lochen was so old—she could not move or walk. When the nuns lifted her naked body—like one does a baby—her legs remained in cross-legged position. When they tried to stretch them out, her legs immediately resumed the meditation position—there were even bumps on them marked by years of sitting like this. The nuns changed Jetsun Lochen's diapers made of soft wool, and even after days and nights in meditation, the urine did not smell bad at all. I had never seen anything like this—suddenly I had great faith in Jetsun Rinpoche. I thought, "She is the real Machig Labdron and the real Tārā [goddess of compassion]!" I still have faith in her—it has not changed since then. (Nedo, 1999)

In the traditional (pre-1950) Tibetan context, female religious specialists were few in number, and even fewer were famous. They did not have important clerical positions, they were generally not in demand by laypeople, and they were poor. Ani Lochen was an exceptional woman in Tibet—one who painstakingly pursued her spiritual quest, and who was able, through the practice of yoga and meditation, and with the help of generous support from her devotees, to become the spiritual master of thousands of disciples. Even at present, Ani Lochen's death is ritually commemorated on the thirteenth day of the month by nuns and *yoginīs*, but also by monks and yogins at rDeng rgyal Ri khrod (Dengyel Hermitage, built near the cave of another famous *yoginī*, the eighth-century Ye shes mtsho rgyal), at Zangs ri mKhar dmar (Sangri Kharmar, the residence of Machig Labdron during the latter part of her life), and of course, at Shug gseb.

See Also Nuns, article on Buddhist Nuns.

Bibliography

Primary Sources

Shortly before Ani Lochen's death, devotees requested that she tell the story of her life. The nun Gen Tinley wrote the draft, and the autobiography was edited by Dawa Dorje. Then it was carved on woodblocks and printed. The copy used as the main source here was reproduced from a tracing of a print from woodblocks by Sonam Topgay Kazi and published in 281 folios in the Ngagyur Nyingmay Sungrab series, vol. 22 (Gangtok, Sikkim, 1975): *Autobiography of the Shug gseb rje btsun rig 'dzin chos nyid bzang mo.* About half of the text consists of spiritual songs presumably composed by the editor Dawa Dorje. A new 320-page edition, edited by Lobsang Tsering, was published by the Tibetan People's Publishing House in Lhasa in 1997: *Shug gseb rje btsun sku zhabs kyi rnam thar.*

Secondary Literature

Havnevik, Hanna. "On Pilgrimage for Forty Years in the Himalayas: The Female Lama Jetsun Lochen Rinpoche's (1865–1951) Quest for Sacred Sites." In *Pilgrimage in Tibet*, edited by Alex McKay, pp. 85–107. Richmond, U.K., 1998.

Havnevik, Hanna. "The Life of Jetsun Lochen Rinpoche (1865–1951) as Told in Her Autobiography." *Acta Humaniora* 50. Ph.D. diss., University of Oslo, 1999.

Horkang, Sonam Pelbar. "Shug gseb rje btsun rin po che rig 'dzin chos dbyings bzang mo'i rnam thar mdor bsdus." *Bod ljongs Zhib jug* 1 (1989): 124–133. Sonam Pelbar Horkang is the younger brother of Lady Nedo, whose reminiscences of Ani Lochen are quoted above.

Nedo, Tsering Yudron. Interview by Tseyang Changopa in Lady Nedo's home in Lhasa, May 20, 1999.

Hanna Havnevik (2005)

ANIMALS. According to one prominent definition of the term *animal*, religion is both created for and practiced by animals, since humans are, in modern biological terms at least, incontrovertibly members of the animal family. But what of other animals, ranging from the simplest of creatures to domesticated work partners to large-brained, extravagantly wild creatures who exhibit emotional and intelligent lives in community? What part have these beings had in human religious life and belief?

Renewal of an Ancient Inquiry. At the very end of the twentieth century, scholars of religion renewed and deepened the ancient inquiry into other living beings' place in religious traditions as a whole. As a result, twenty-first-century scholarship on religion and animals continues to develop in a wide-ranging, inclusive, and interdisciplinary manner. It is now clearer than ever that the earth's nonhuman life-forms have, from ancient times, had a remarkable presence in religious beliefs, practices, images, and ethics. Engagement with these other lives ranges from the belief that some are divinities who bring blessings into the world to the conviction that the animals are merely unintelligent objects created by a divine power expressly for humans use.

Other biological beings' presence in the religious imagination has been neither static nor simple. Ivar Paulson observes that with the development of agriculture and animal domestication, "much of the earlier numinous power and holiness experienced by the hunter in his encounter with the game was lost" (1964, p. 213). This altered, nonspiritual status is carried through in the 1994 Catholic description of the place of nonhuman lives in the believer's world: "Animals, like plants and inanimate things, are by nature destined for the common good of past, present, and future humanity" (*Catechism of the Catholic Church,* par. 2,415, p. 516).

The story of religion and animals goes well beyond accounts of their divinity on the one hand or subservience on the other. Held at times to be individuals in every sense that humans are individuals, and even ancestors, family, clan members, or separate nations, the life-forms outside the human species have regularly engaged humans at multiple levels, and thus at many times and places energized religious sensibilities dramatically.

A range of issues. Contemporary scholarship on the intersection of religious sensibilities and nonhuman animals undertakes the daunting task of engaging the entire gamut of humanity's complex relationships with other biological lives. Beyond the familiar tradition of using animals for food and other material needs, nonhuman creatures have served as fellow travelers, communal society members and workers, and, often, intermediaries between the pyhysical world and the supernatural realm. For many peoples, kinship with nonhumans has been maintained through dreaming and waking visions, as well as ritual ceremonies in which interspecies bonds are honored.

Many religious traditions have attempted to analyze the essence not only of human lives, but of the relationship between human and nonhuman lives and even the nature of nonhuman animals' daily and existential realities. The historical Buddha is quoted on this subject often, as in this passage from the *Majjhima Nikāya*: "Men are indeed a tangle, whereas animals are a simple matter. " The tendency of religious traditions to pass judgement on the value of animals' lives has had a profound impact on human thinking about the earth and its other inhabitants. The historian of biology Ernst Mayr argues that Christianity has profoundly influenced biological matters because Christianity "abolished free thinking" by making "the word of God . . . the measure of all things" (1982, p. 307). Mayr believed that Christianity was responsible for establishing Western culture's controlling assumptions about the important notion of species, and that a crucial change in the Christian worldview occurred during the Reformation, by which species came to be seen as unalterably static rather than subject to development and change: "The fixity and complete constancy of species now became a firm dogma . . . [because a] literal interpretation of *Genesis* required the belief in the individual creation of every species of plants and animals on the days prior to Adam's creation" (p. 255).

Mayr's comments reflect the interest that many disciplines outside religious studies and theology have in the role religious traditions have played in developing many basic assumptions about nonhuman lives. Interest is also spurred by the recognition that although religions' relationships with animals are ancient, many religious traditions have, over time, narrowed their already minimal appreciation of nonhuman creatures. In the Western cultural tradition, for example, studies of animals by Christian theologians and interested believers have declined in the last few centuries. Nonhuman animals have been broadly dismissed in Western culture's secular circles through various developments since the seventeenth century in philosophy (for example, Descartes's thesis that other living beings are more like clocks than like humans) and scientific experimentation (particularly powerful in the late nineteenth and throughout the twentieth century).

In the latter half of the twentieth century, the place of food animals and laboratory animals in industrialized countries became increasingly that of a mere resource, even as dogs and cats were more and more frequently included as family members. Wild animals held an ambiguous position: sometimes thought of as pests or recreational hunting targets; sometimes as representatives of the natural world's power and majesty.

The forms of religion dominant in most societies where animal research and food production became key industries were amenable to such uses. In addition, religious institutions remained, on the whole, silent regarding environmental and habitat damage. As a result, in many ways religious institutions, like secular institutions, failed to notice or take seriously humans' profound and destructive impact on nonhuman lives.

Renewal, and even deepening, of the ancient inquiry into animals' place in religion occurred in response to this increasing crisis, and for independent reasons as well. Inquiries outside religious circles about nonhuman lives produced remarkable information that revealed some nonhuman animals to be decidedly more complex than Western culture and science held them to be. The findings of various biological sciences, for example, provided grounds for a more respectful evaluation of various animals' complex lives. When such details were noticed and taken seriously, the resulting openness had the potential to re-create ancient religious understandings about the human community with other lives. Additionally, the interfaith dialogue tradition of the second half of the twentieth century revealed deep concerns for the ethical dimensions of human interactions with other animals and highlighted religions such as Jainism and Buddhism that did not share the Western anthropocentric agenda.

The religions of the world have had, and will continue to have, a major impact on the way their adherents, as well as the secular world, look at the realities and moral responsibilities of the human interaction with other animals. Believers, religious leaders, scientists, and scholars of religion now have a much keener awareness of how engagement with other animals will reverberate in a multitude of issues.

Sources of complexity. Many of the issues surrounding religion's interaction with animals—ethical matters, symbolism, rituals—are, when considered individually, extraordinarily complex. Over the millennia, religious traditions have produced an astonishing variety of beliefs, factual claims, symbols, and actions on many everyday subjects. Even if the frame of reference is only a single tradition, views of nonhuman animals can, across time and place, be in significant tension.

Further complexities stem from living beings' significant differences from one another. Some are mentally, socially, and individually extremely simple; others are mentally and socially complex and so enigmatic that we may not be able to understand their lives at all. Ignorance of the features of other animals' lives has often led to crass oversimplifications both within and outside of religion. Such coarse caricatures are encouraged by the way humans talk about other living beings, for upon careful examination much human discourse about other animals is revealed to rely upon profoundly inaccurate descriptions of their lives.

Religious institutions, as enduring cultural and ethical traditions, have often been the primary source of answers to a fundamental question: "Which living beings really should matter to me and my community?" The field of religion and animals attempts to assess the many ways in which religious traditions formulate answers to this question, and, in their cultural milieux and beyond, to influence how living beings outside the human species have been understood and treated.

The Role of Inherited Perspectives. The influence of traditional religious doctrines has caused many believers' perspectives on nonhuman animals to be dominated by something other than a careful engagement with the animals themselves. Sometimes inherited preconceptions have taken the form of dismissive generalizations found in documents held to be revealed. Sometimes a one-dimensional sketch of a few local animals has operated as a definitive assessment of all nonhuman animals' nature, abilities, and moral significance.

At other times, positive but inaccurate stories have operated similarly to obscure the actual realities of the local nonhuman animals. Custom and tradition that underlie inflexible claims about animals can present severe problems for historians, theologians, and believers who wish to engage evidence that contradicts, in letter or spirit, a heritage of views that is inadequate or misleading when assessing empirical realities.

Animals as Symbols. Religious art, writing, dance, and oral traditions abound with images of the world's nonhuman living beings. Some are connected in one way or another to the animals portrayed, but many are not closely related to the animals whose images are used. Some studies of religion and animals have been confined solely to the study of such images, thus ignoring the actual biological beings themselves.

Stanley Walens observes that misinterpretations of animal symbols have plagued both anthropological and religious studies: "The tendency of Western scholars to ascribe to a particular animal symbol the meaning it has in Western culture is one of the fundamental errors of Western comparative theology." Scholars now recognize that the alleged simplicity of early and indigenous religions was more a by-product of the "coarse analytic methods of researchers and of the inability of the outsiders to capture the depth and complexity by which people in tribal societies are able to metaphorize themselves and their world" (Walens, 1987, p. 293).

Caution is thus in order when dealing with symbols that use nonhuman animal images, for as Walens notes, "The capable scholar must look very skeptically at the record of animal beliefs in pre-Christian societies" (p. 294). In particular, the scholar must also be careful of purporting to talk about "animals" when what is being discussed are animal images that work primarily, even exclusively, to convey some feature of human complexity rather than any information about the nonhuman beings whose images are being employed for human-centered purposes.

Ethical Concerns. Religion has traditionally been the cradle of humans' ability to exercise concerns for "others," a category that has historically included both humans and nonhumans. The study of religion and animals has been greatly complicated by the fact that some religious traditions insist that the universe of morally considerable beings includes all living beings, while others have had, ethically speaking, a pronounced human-centered bias, asserting that humans are the only living beings that really matter. While these competing claims differ radically in how far human concern should reach outside the human species, they share the conviction that humans are characterized by a profound ethical ability to care for others. Central questions in the study of religion and animals are thus these inherently ethical queries: "Who have the others been?" and "Who might the others be?"

Treatment of Other Animals. Because most religious traditions embrace the insight that actions speak more loudly about what one really believes than do words, any assessment of a religion's view of animals must be represented, at least in part, by some account of how it actually treats other living beings. If a religion features images of bulls in its temples but allows cattle to be treated with brutality in the world outside the temple, this gives us an important insight into their underlying beliefs. Another religion may prohibit the harsh treatment or killing of cattle but include no images of the animal in its worship, rituals, or material culture. The former may leave artifacts that suggest bulls were important, but daily life in the latter suggests a more respectful engagement with cattle. Each religion engages with cattle in its own way. A careful analysis can provide much information about underlying social values.

Linked Oppressions. Religious traditions often suggest that when a human harms another living being, the actor and even other humans are desensitized, so that they may subsequently do even more harm (Thomas Aquinas made this argument, as did Immanuel Kant). This insight has been one of the classic justifications for traditions prohibiting cruelty to animals. Contemporary sociologists and law enforcement officials advance a modern version of this idea based on evidence that certain instances of human-on-human oppression, such as domestic violence, are psychologically linked with violence to nonhuman animals. A related insight is advanced by the Oxford historian Keith Thomas, who suggests that in western Europe the domestication of animals "generated a more authoritarian attitude" and "became the archetypal pattern for other kinds of social subordination" (1983, p. 46). The study of religion and animals can, when it addresses the idea that oppression of one kind of living being leads to the oppression of other kinds of living beings, be closely tied to social justice concerns that now are common features of religious institutions.

Transmission of Views about Animals. As carriers of a culture's worldviews, religious traditions are ancient educators in cultural, ethical, social, ecological, intellectual, and political matters. In this role, religious traditions quite naturally have transmitted from generation to generation views of nonhuman animals, for the latter are inevitably around and with us in our local communities. As suggested by Ernst Mayr, these views affect the most basic human ideas about animals' nature, as well as their place in, or exclusion from, human communities.

This feature of religion is always a highly contextualized piece in any religious tradition's larger puzzle, and an essential task in the study of religion and animals is to discover how a particular human community's engagement with the local world plays in its larger worldviews and lifeways.

Previous Scholarship on Religion and Animals. Greek and Roman thinkers were heir to a remarkable tradition of vigorous debate regarding whether nonhuman animals possessed mental and social abilities, including language, senses of justice and morality, and even reason. Richard Sorabji concludes that Augustine was the pivotal figure in shutting down the vibrant debate in the Hellenistic world about the specific abilities of nonhuman animals. The result was a broad dismissal in the cultural tradition and, in particular, its religious institutions regarding other animals' significance. Since the time of Augustine, the vast majority of scholarship in the Western intellectual tradition has gone forward on the assumption that humans alone are intellectually complex, capable of emotional depth and commitment, characterized by social connections and personality development, and able to develop the kinds of autonomy that moral beings intuitively respect.

This dismissal of animals, long a centerpiece in academic curricula and pedagogy, is now in tension with the rich information developed in the life sciences about animals' mental, social, and emotional complexities. Even so, academic expression in the twenty-first century, including religious studies and theology, continues to reflect the anthropocentric bias of the Western tradition.

Believers' engagement with nonhuman lives is an ongoing challenge for religious pedagogy. Sociological studies reveal that ethical concern for nonhuman animals' welfare continue to have a place, subordinated though it may be at times, in the complex Jewish, Christian, and Islamic traditions as they carry their ancient ethical insights forward. Francis of Assisi and Albert Schweitzer are cited regularly as examples of believers with a profound concern for other animals. Influential figures like Rūmi, Maimonides, Ibn Taymīyah, and Isaac Bashevis Singer also included animal-friendly themes in their works, and Augustine's fellow Christians, including Ambrose of Milan, Basil of Caesarea, Martin Luther, John Calvin, John Wesley, Karl Barth, Paul Tillich, Pierre Teilhard de Chardin, and Thomas Berry, have in creative ways reflected their tradition's capacities for seeing and caring about living beings beyond their own species.

It is thus misleading to suggest that all who have thought about religion and animal issues have, naturally and obviously, dismissed nonhuman animals in the manner of the mainstream Western intellectual tradition that remains dominant today. The recent emergence of a more systematic and open-minded treatment of nonhuman animals in the doctrines, rituals, experiences, ethics, myths, social realities, and ecological perspectives of religious traditions suggests that when a clearer picture is drawn, it will be a rich tapestry of alternatives for interacting with the earth's nonhuman beings.

Institutionalized Religious Views: A Survey of World Religions. Anthropocentric biases continue to dominate many modern religious institutions' discourse generally, and their official pronouncements and conceptual generalities reflect the prevailing assumption that humans alone are the appropriate subjects of human ethics. Mainstream religious institutions have generally failed to challenge the frequently cruel way animals are treated in modern industrialized societies. There have been some challenges, mostly from indigenous traditions and those of the Indian subcontinent.

A survey of the views of nonhuman animals that dominate major religious traditions reveals that traditional and mainstream religious institutions have, on the whole, accepted not only humans' domestication of some animals for food and work, but also deprecated nonhuman animals generally and scorned the value of careful engagement with other animals' day-to-day realities. Such a survey also shows, however, that various subtraditions and prominent figures within the larger tradition often have questioned whether core values of the overall tradition aren't violated by both subordination and facile dismissals of nonhuman animals. It is not uncommon, then, for some part of religious traditions to have engaged nonhuman beings in some fuller way such that even if their place is not front and center in institutional pronouncements, ritual, or traditional language, nonhuman animals remain present and relevant to some believers' spiritual and ethical lives.

Hinduism. The Hindu tradition offers an immense range of views about the living beings who share our ecological community. Two general beliefs dominate Hindu conceptions of the human relationship to other animals. First, human beings, recognized to be in a continuum with life, are considered the paradigm of what biological life should be—thus one often finds the hierarchical claim that human status is above that of any other animal. Second, belief in reincarnation, a hallmark of most Hindus' beliefs, includes the notion that any living being's current position in the cycle of life is a deserved position because it has been determined by the strict law of *karma.*

These two beliefs have resulted in an ambivalent view of animals. On the positive side, animals are understood to have souls and be worthy of ethical consideration; the notion of nonharming, or *ahiṃsā,* for example, applies to them. On the negative side, all of the earth's numerous nonhuman animals are understood to be inferior to any human. According to the *sanatana dharma,* the eternal law and moral structure of the universe, all living beings, human and nonhuman, are born into that station in life for which their past *karma* has fitted them. Humans who in past lives acted immorally are destined to be born as nonhuman—an inferior life because animals' lives are thought of as particularly unhappy, at least compared to human existence.

The ambivalence toward nonhuman life is negative in the recurring implicit and explicit scorn shown to animals (as well as to lower-caste humans). The positive side appears in the tradition's remarkable ethical sensitivity to other animals as beings who should not be killed. Many Hindu scriptures include the injunction that one should treat other animals exactly like one's own children. Central religious texts, such as the *Ṛgveda* and *Atharvaveda,* hold that the earth was not created for humans alone, but for other creatures as well. Daily life in India, especially at the village level, provides many examples of coexistence with other animals, the best known of which is the sacred cow. There are, however, many examples of mistreatment as well.

Humans, even if Hindus believe them to have a privileged place in the hierarchy, are also believed to have special obligations to all living beings. This ethical claim is often buttressed by the close association of many Hindu deities with specific animal forms. Rāma and Kṛṣṇa were thought to have reincarnated as a monkey and a cow. Ganesh, an elephant-headed god, and Hanuman, the monkey god, have long been worshiped widely in India.

Historically, around 500 BCE the animal sacrifice that dominated the ritual life of the brahminical tradition was challenged by Buddhists and Jains as cruel and unethical. This challenge had a great effect on the later Hindu views of the morality of intentionally sacrificing other animals, and *ahiṃsā,* the historically important emphasis on nonviolence, has now become a central feature of the tradition.

Buddhism. Buddhist ideas about nonhuman animals share many features with Hindu views, because both reflect cultural assumptions that dominated the religions of the Indian subcontinent. For example, all animals, human and otherwise, are viewed as fellow voyagers in *saṃsāra* (the cycle of death and rebirth). Compassion toward other animals has often produced expressions of concern for other living beings in Buddhist literature that lead many believers and scholars to claim that Buddhism takes a kind, sympathetic view toward nonhuman lives.

Alongside this very visible feature of the Buddhist tradition, however, sit complicating features, for in important ways Buddhism has a negative view of nonhuman animals' existence and abilities. Buddhist thinking groups all nonhuman animals into a single realm or category, which in the hierarchical social structure that dominated the Indian subcontinent meant that other forms of life were inferior to the human realm. Hence, the very fact that a being is born as any animal other than human is thought of negatively.

The animal world is viewed as an unhappy place—as the historical Buddha said in the *Majjhima Nikāya,* "so many are the anguishes of animal birth." Birth at a "subhuman" level in the Buddhist hierarchy is conceived to be the direct result of less-than-ideal conduct. A human who violates moral norms is constantly threatened with punishment in the next life as a lower animal. Nonhuman animals are regularly described by Buddhists as so simple, relative to humans, that their lives are easily understood by the superior human intellect. Buddhist scriptures characterize animals as pests who are in competition with their human superiors.

Even though these factors lead to descriptions of animals in the Buddhist scriptures that seem fundamentally negative, these views are moderated by central ethical commitments. The First Precept states that a Buddhist will refrain from killing any life forms. Some portions of the tradition, though not all, emphasize vegetarianism as a means to this end. The well-known *bodhisattva*'s vow to refrain from entering *nirvāṇa* until all beings are saved reflects one prominent feature of the Buddhist tradition's deep concern for beings outside the human species.

Buddhist engagement with other animals, then, is a mixture of the tradition's heavy investment in hierarchical thinking and a strong ethical commitment to the value of life in all its forms. Despite all its avowed respect for nonhuman lives, however, the tradition has never emphasized seeing other animals in terms of their own realities. This leads to a dismissive prejudgment of animal life, which is undermined by careful engagement with animals' actual lives.

The Abrahamic traditions. Just as the religions of the Indian subcontinent share many common assumptions, the views dominating the Abrahamic traditions also have important assumptions in common. Judaism, Christianity, and Islam are dominated in many essential respects by what amounts to ethical anthropocentrism, that is, a pronounced tendency to focus on the members of the human species as if they alone should be the object of ethical and moral protection. It is a fundamental article of faith in the Abrahamic traditions that the world was designed by a divine creator who elevated the human species above all other forms of life. This human-centeredness, which manifests itself in a tendency to justify practices that harm other animals, is, however (as in the Indian subcontinent traditions), moderated at critical points, as when sacrificial rules mandate that the victim's death be brought about as quickly as possible.

Judaism. Ideas about nonhuman animals are not simple in the Judaic tradition, in part because the Hebrew Bible contains diverse and even contradictory views of humans in relation to other living beings. A prominent model focuses on the importance of keeping humans safe from dangerous animals. A more utopian vision is that of peace with and among wild animals, which can also function as a metaphor for cosmic and social peace among humans. Of these two views, the first dominates, for human interests are characteristically seen in Judaism as far more important than animals' interests. Richard Bauckham has noted that the idea that humans need "peace from evil animals" is an "ancient tendency" stemming from the Jewish tradition's decision to see "wild animals primarily as threats to human life" (1994, p. 8).

Philo Judaeus, a first-century Jewish historian, employed an image of a continuous warfare by the animals against humankind. This negative image of animals who are not under human control is contrasted with the tranquillity of humans' relationship with, and domination of, domesticated animals. There is some irony in this view, for the notion that wild animals are evil, a common biblical theme, is rooted in the belief that disorder in nature stems from archetypal wrongs committed by human ancestors and the unfaithfulness of Israel.

Alongside the Hebrew Bible's dominant view that wild animals are evil is the countervailing notion that other animals were created by God, who is proud of them (as expressed in various passages in *Job*) and daily feeds them. Living under God's reign, other living beings at times appear as examples of right order, in great contrast to humans. Many provisions, such as the law codes (*Exodus* 22–23 and 34, *Leviticus* 22 and 25, and *Deuteronomy* 14–26) recognize the welfare of other animals, at least to some extent. Such provisions are limited, however, primarily to: (1) the welfare of domestic animals, that is, those that work for or produce benefits for humans, and (2) restrictions on how sacrificial animals could be killed.

Although scholars such as Stephen Webb argue that the practice of animal sacrifice benefited nonhuman animals in general, the practice raises complex issues, for animal sacrifice functioned as an institutionalized means of atoning for human violations of moral rules or purity taboos. The fact that nonhuman beings suffer because of human wrongs is, of course, related to the human evaluation of human and nonhuman lives. Why only those animals useful to humans were chosen for sacrifice is worth further inquiry into the role that anthropomorphism and anthropocentrism play in the general practice of animal sacrifice.

Judaism arose in geographical areas that afforded believers only limited exposure to the most complex nonhuman animals (such as elephants, chimpanzees, whales, and dolphins), a fact that may account for its sometimes one-dimensional view of nonhuman lives. Jewish materials, nonetheless, particularly by virtue of the body of traditional Jewish law that concerns itself with animal welfare known as *tsa'ar ba'alei chayim,* provides a basis for arguing that care for other animals of all kinds is mandated by the core values and insights of the tradition.

Nonhuman forms of life are mentioned in some of the covenants found in the Hebrew Bible, including the covenant with Noah in *Genesis* 9:9–16. Some theologians, such as Andrew Linzey, who argues that Christians have a theological duty to protect nonhuman animals, make a great deal of this in their works. Others have argued that the larger context, including the preceding set of verses (*Genesis* 9:1–7), which mentions that "the dread of you should be upon every beast" and "every moving thing that lives shall be food for you" radically qualifies the significance of nonhuman animals' inclusion in the covenant established in *Genesis* 9:9–16 and reflects that other animals are "in the subordinate relationship to humankind which has already been set forth in Genesis" (Murray, 1992, pp. 33–34).

Yet even if humans are conceived in the Jewish tradition as separate from the rest of life in critically important ways, an important sense of connection remains by virtue of the number of specific animals mentioned and observations about the variety of life these suggest. The early Hebrews noticed and appreciated the extraordinary diversity and interconnectedness of human and nonhuman beings.

Christianity. The Christian tradition inherited and developed the Hebrew vision of humans as distinct from all other animals. Some believe the Christian tradition narrowed this heritage by its handling of the biblical claim that all humans, and only humans, are made in the image of God and have been given dominion over the earth. Some early proponents of Christianity, including Origen and Augustine, asserted that part of Christianity's basic message is a fundamental, radical division between human animals and all other animals. In important ways, this has led to the exclusion of all other animals' interests when they are in conflict with even minor, unnecessary human interests.

Historically, the expression and development of Christian views of animals reflects ties to both Hebrew and Greek sources. Early Christians borrowed from them their fundamental cultural assumptions. The result over time was an amalgam in which connections to nonhuman animals were subordinated to human superiority. Ultimately, humans came to be seen as distinct in every relevant way from other animals, and therefore ontologically superior to the rest of creation.

This led prominent sects within Christianity to persistently refuse to examine other animals' realities. The extent of the denial can be seen in the comment made by Pope Pius IX (r. 1846–1878) to English antivivisectionist Anna Kingsford: "Madame, humankind has no duties to the animals." Pius IX backed this up by "vigorously" opposing the establishment of a society for the protection of animals in Rome.

Christianity faces a basic challenge from the developing body of knowledge about nonhuman animals. Based on data from the biological sciences and an appreciation of indigenous cultures' respectful engagement with life outside our species, many people now argue that at least some nonhuman life-forms are proper objects of human morality. It remains to be seen whether the Christian tradition (or any religious tradition) will finds ways to integrate new factual information into its views of nonhuman creatures.

Islam. Islamic views often reflect the Abrahamic emphasis on humans as the centerpiece of a created universe, but Islam also shows a countervailing recognition of the moral dimension of the very existence of other animals. Even though the Qurʾān frequently asserts that other animals have been placed on Earth solely for the benefit of humans, how humans treat other animals, who are deemed creatures of Allāh, also plays an important role in the tradition. The Qurʾān and other central writings of Islam reflect numerous ways in which believers have recognized that other animals have their own importance. For example, *sūrah* 6:38 states that other animals have their own communities: "There is not an animal in the earth, nor a flying creature on two wings, but they are communities like unto you." Muḥammad himself commented, "Whoever is kind to the creatures of Allāh, is kind to himself." He also compared the doing of good or bad deeds to other animals to similar acts done to humans.

The result is that there are both negative and positive views of other animals at the center of the complex Islamic tradition. As with Judaism, the ritualized slaughter of animals for food (*dhabh*) reflects the basic belief that humans are divinely appointed representatives of Allāh (*Khalīfa,* often translated as "vice regent" or "steward"). This is one version of the claim that other animals, even if not on earth solely for human use, are subordinate to humans and in special instances ordained for human use.

Although humans are, in the Islamic tradition, the centerpiece of creation, and thus the most important living beings, ethical sensibilities regarding other animals are still prominent, as in the rules governing the humane killing of sacrificial animals. Thus, the Islamic tradition provides moral space, as it were, for the view that other animals have an integrity and inherent value of their own.

THE ANIMAL PRESENCE OUTSIDE THE WORLD RELIGIONS. Views of the place of animals in human lives are far different outside the mainstream religions. Native or indigenous traditions worldwide often reflect a spiritual kinship with many kinds of nonhuman living beings. John Neihardt begins the now famous account *Black Elk Speaks: Being the Life Story of a Holy Man of the Oglala Sioux* (1932) with observations about sharing and kinship with other animals: "It is the story of all life that is holy and is good to tell, and of us two-leggeds sharing in it with the four-leggeds and the wings of the air and all green things; for these are children of one mother and their father is one Spirit" (p. 1).

Communication with specific kinds of animals, often mammals or birds known to be highly social and intelligent, such as dolphins or ravens, are often found in nature-oriented spiritual traditions. Most show a deep concern for and connection with nonhuman animals as fellow beings or even as individuals not unlike humans. Many contemporary nature-oriented religions, which tend to be decentralized and to give primacy to individual experience, emphasize nonhuman animals. Relatedly, respected members of contemporary scientific communities, such as primatologist Jane Goodall and cognitive ethologist Marc Bekoff, have emphasized the relevance to human spiritual quests of studying and understanding animal behaviour. Noticing and taking nonhuman animals seriously is also evident in the Chinese folk, Daoist, and Confucian traditions, Japanese Shintō, the Jain tradition of India, Sikhism, and many other religious traditions that offer profound insights into the importance and ethical dimensions of the human connection with other natural beings.

CONCLUSION. Considering the seemingly simple question of how the two important topics of religion and animals intersect raises many possibilities. One of these is a deeper understanding of religious traditions' roles in shaping human concepts of, discourse about, and ethical engagements with the Earth and its nonhuman inhabitants. The religious component of a human interaction with other animals can offer significant personal value as well. An increasing number of theologians, ethicists, philosophers, poets, and scholars from many disciplines have echoed Thomas Berry's insight: "Indeed we cannot be truly ourselves in any adequate manner without all our companion beings throughout the earth. This larger community constitutes our greater self" (Berry, 2005).

SEE ALSO Anthropomorphism; Bears; Birds; Cats; Elephants; Evolution, article on Evolutionism; Fish; Horses; Lady of the Animals; Lord of the Animals; Monsters; Rabbits; Sacrifice; Snakes; Totemism; Tricksters, overview article.

BIBLIOGRAPHY

Ascione, Frank R., and Phil Arkow, eds. *Child Abuse, Domestic Violence, and Animal Abuse: Linking the Circles of Compassion for Prevention and Intervention.* West Lafayette, Ind., 1999.

Bauckham, Richard. "Jesus and the Wild Animals (*Mark* 1:13): A Christological Image for an Ecological Age." In *Jesus of Nazareth: Lord and Christ,* edited by Joel B. Green and Max Turner. Grand Rapids, Mich., 1994.

Berry, Thomas. "Loneliness and Presence." In *A Communion of Subjects: Animals in Religion, Science, and Ethics,* edited by Paul Waldau and Kimberley Patton. Chicago, 2005.

Catechism of the Catholic Church. London, 1994.

Chalmers, Robert. *Further Dialogues of the Buddha, Translated from the Pali of the Majjhima Nikàya by Lord Chalmers.* 2 vols. Delhi, 1988.

Deen, Samarrai, and Mawil Y. Izzi. "Islamic Environmental Ethics, Law, and Society." In *Ethics of Environment and Development: Global Challenge, International Response,* edited by J. Ronald Engel and Joan Gibb Engel. London, 1990.

Gaffney, James. "The Relevance of Animal Experimentation to Roman Catholic Ethical Methodology." In *Animal Sacrifices: Religious Perspectives on the Use of Animals in Science,* edited by Tom Regan. Philadelphia, 1986.

Goodall, Jane, with Phillip Berman. *Reason for Hope: A Spiritual Journey.* New York, 1999.

Goodall, Jane, and Bekoff, Marc. *The Ten Trusts: What We Must Do to Care for the Animals We Love.* San Francisco, 2002.

Harrod, Howard L. *Renewing the World: Plains Indian Religion and Morality.* Tucson, Ariz., 1987.

Hillman, James. "Interview with Thomas Moore." *Parabola* 8, no. 2 (1983): 49–53.

Linzey, Andrew. *Christianity and the Rights of Animals.* New York, 1987.

Linzey, Andrew. *Animal Theology.* Chicago, 1994.

Masri, B. A. *Animals in Islam.* Petersfield, U.K., 1989.

Mayr, Ernst. *The Growth of Biological Thought: Diversity, Evolution, and Inheritance.* New York, 1982.

Murray, Robert. *The Cosmic Covenant: Biblical Themes of Justice, Peace, and the Integrity of Creation.* London, 1992.

Neihardt, John G. *Black Elk Speaks: Being the Life Story of a Holy Man of the Oglala Sioux.* New York, 1932.

Paulson, Ivar. "The Animal Guardian: A Critical and Synthetic Review." *History of Religions* 3, no. 2 (1964): 202–219.

Regan, Tom, ed. *Animal Sacrifices: Religious Perspectives on the Use of Animals in Science.* Philadelphia, 1986.

Sorabji, Richard. *Animal Minds and Human Morals: The Origins of the Western Debate.* Ithaca, N.Y., 1993.

Thomas, Keith. *Man and the Natural World: Changing Attitudes in England 1500–1800.* New York., 1983.

Waldau, Paul. "Buddhism and Animals Rights." In *Contemporary Buddhist Ethics,* edited by Damien Keown. Richmond, U.K., 2000.

Waldau, Paul. *The Specter of Speciesism: Buddhist and Christian Views of Animals.* New York, 2001.

Waldau, Paul, ed. "Religion and Animals." *Society and Animals* 8, no. 3 (2000).

Walens, Stanley. "Animals." In *The Encyclopedia of Religion,* edited by Mircea Eliade, vol 1. New York, 1987.

Webb, Stephen H. *On God and Dogs: A Christian Theology of Compassion for Animals.* New York, 1997.

PAUL WALDAU (2005)

ANIMISM AND ANIMATISM. The term *animism* properly refers to a theory set forth by the English scholar E. B. Tylor (1832–1917), one of the founders of modern anthropology, in order to account for the origin and development of religion. Tylor's theory was in general harmony with the dominant evolutionistic views of his age, as represented by the naturalist Charles Robert Darwin (1809–1882) and the social philosopher Herbert Spencer (1820–1903). Darwin and Spencer both viewed the development of the natural and social world as a movement from lower to higher forms, from the simple to the complex.

The distinctiveness of Tylor's theory was its assumption that the earliest form of religion was characterized by human ideas concerning a plurality of spirits and ghosts. In this he differed from Spencer, who had posited atheism at the beginning of human culture, although both followed the common pattern of their evolutionistic contemporaries in deriving a most archaic form of religion from humanity's rational reflections on the world of nature and on itself.

Inevitably, each theory of the most archaic form of religion led to speculations on still earlier stages or other hypothetical beginnings. One supposed earlier stage that was widely accepted among scholars was linked to the name of R. R. Marett (1866–1943), best known for his *The Threshold of Religion* (1909). Marett, who first launched his own theory in 1900, saw it as an extension of Tylor's and for that reason spoke of preanimism, or animatism. This hypothetical earliest stage of "prereligion" was also known as dynamism, a term introduced by the French anthropologist Arnold van Gennep in his *Les rites de passage* (1909). The term *dynamism* (from the Greek *dunamis,* "power, energy") suggests the presence of a power that is not, or is not necessarily, individualized. It is still somehow homogeneous, not yet differentiated as it is in the stage of animism. Marett himself made the comparison with electricity. His term *animatism,* like *dynamism,* points to a thing, situation, or state of affairs that is enlivened or animated, but not in any individual, soul-like manner.

The theories of animism and animatism are difficult to take seriously in the present time, given the psychological sophistication that has come to be taken for granted in intellectual circles since Freud. Assuredly, Tylor's theory of successive stages and the production of ever higher religious forms by the human mind is far too unwieldy to account for the phenomena history offers. As early as 1887, sixteen years after Tylor published his influential work *Primitive Culture,* the Dutch historian of religions P. D. Chantepie de la Saussaye expressed his reservations in his famous *Lehrbuch der Religionsgeschichte.* He grouped Tylor together with other evolutionists who, in his opinion, tried too hard to apply a mechanical worldview to historical, social, cultural, and religious facts. However, even though Chantepie de la Saussaye found support for his criticism in F. Max Müller, the famous Indologist and historian of religions, and in the philosophies of the German thinkers Eduard von Hartmann (1842–1906) and R. H. Lotze (1817–1881), he was far from rejecting the theory of animism altogether. The influence of Tylor and the other evolutionists pervaded the age.

At the present time one might feel inclined to dismiss the subjects of animism and animatism as irrelevant for scholarship, were it not for three considerations. In the first place, Tylor's theory in particular has had a firm hold on scholarship for some seventy or eighty years and still turns up in some circles today as if it were authoritative. Second, animism can be seen as a twentieth-century name given to a type of theory that has been influential throughout the history of intellectual dealings with religion. Third, animism, with its progeny, illustrates in a clear fashion the nineteenth-century obsession with origins, and this subject falls squarely within the interest of the history of religions, for in the final analysis the obsession with origins of ultimate human orientations is itself a religious phenomenon.

THE THEORY, ITS IMPACT, AND ITS INADEQUACIES. Turning to the first of the three reasons why animism is still worthy of attention, one should look more closely at the theory Tylor developed. The theory owed not a little of its appeal to Tylor's superb style of writing. He reflected on the diverse mass of ethnological data that reached his desk, tried to account for it by imagining what might have happened in the minds of early man, and presented his findings in vivid colors in perfect harmony with the prevailing ideas and sentiments of his time.

The "noble savage," unspoiled by education, had been popularized by Jean-Jacques Rousseau, and the image of the child's growth was invoked by Lessing in his *Die Erziehung des Menschengeschlechts* (1780) to explain the historical development or "education" of the human race. In Tylor's *Primitive Culture* (1871), however, the poetic simile was presented as science. Tylor argued for a strict, scientific analogy between the primitive human and the child and its mentality. His formulation gave the analogy new force, as if it could be relied on as an established fact, and it would be taken up again several decades later by the French philosopher Lucien Lévy-Bruhl (1857–1939) and the Dutch phenomenologist Gerardus van der Leeuw (1890–1959).

Tylor's evolutionism did not lose touch with all religious sentiment, however. Tylor was a Quaker, and in the spirit of his age he associated the evolution of humans with the natural process of growth and with a general increase in human understanding and responsibility. The English anthropologist E. E. Evans-Pritchard has suggested that a good many of the anthropologists who theorized on "primitive religion," from the latter half of the nineteenth century to the present, were really preparing a means to attack Christianity, while they despised the primitive religions they studied as a mass of illusions. Such an assessment of Tylor would be unfair. Tylor's evolutionism was in fact more akin to that of Nathan Söderblom (1866–1931), the Swedish Lutheran archbishop and historian of religions, who saw Christianity as the most perfect image of the goal toward which all religous evolution headed. Together with this essentially religious, apologetic motive, however, Tylor's view of primitives also shared something of the vision of Rudyard Kipling (1865–1936), the English poet laureate who celebrated the British empire's responsibility to "carry the white man's burden" and lead the way for the savages, even when the latter failed to understand the nobility of that task or went so far as to rebel against their benefactors. This side of Tylor's theory of evolution shows it to be the product of British imperialism and colonialism. Both elements, the religious tenor and the nationalism, intermingle in Tylor's work.

Tylor proposed the term *animism* for the study of "the deep-lying doctrine of Spiritual Beings, which embodies the very essence of Spiritualistic as opposed to Materialistic philosophy." He called his concept a minimum definition of religion. He would have preferred the term "spiritualism" for his theory if that term had not come into use (especially in his day) to designate groups with extreme views on supernatural phenomena. It is not unfair to say that Tylor's interest in "ghosts" and "souls," in spite of its outstanding quality and distinctiveness, is still part of the intellectual fashions of his time, a time in which the most famous ghost story of all Western literary history, Charles Dickens's *A Christmas Carol* (first published in 1843), attained an unprecedented success.

Tylor was fascinated with the reflections that he believed to be fundamental to early man, whom he believed to be represented by the "savages" of the present. These reflections, he thought, arose from the experience of death and dying, and from dreams and dreaming. What happens when life leaves a body? Where does one's life, one's dying breath, go? The primitive observed what happened and refused to accept death as final. Moreover, in a dream one would see the deceased alive, moving, speaking. For the primitive, the dreamworld would not be less real than the waking state. In reflections such as these on the spirits of the dead and the ghosts perceived in dreams, Tylor saw the first forms of a religious signature.

Tylor did not at all plan his work as a work of speculation. On the contrary, he did his utmost to be fair to all evidence. Although the experiences of death and dreams seemed to explain many ideas among tribal peoples, he recognized the existence of traditions concerning a great many other "spirits," especially spirits of nature, of woods, lakes, and so on. The spirits of the dead, nevertheless, remained for Tylor the earliest phenomena that could have triggered humans' minds in the formation of religion.

Spirits could take on a truly independent existence, according to his theory, and the manifold traditions from all over the world confirmed it. Nothing seemed more natural than the slow development from low to high, from a plurality of spirits on to a polytheistic system, a hierarchy among nature spirits, and ultimately some form of monotheism. Some elements in his scheme of development had had their predecessors, as in the ideas of the philosopher David Hume (1711–1776) concerning the gradual development of religion leading from polytheism toward monotheism, but the mass of evidence drawn from history and from among contemporary tribal traditions gave Tylor's theory the impressive scientific persuasiveness that a more empirically inclined age desired.

The same tendencies that raised Zeus to his supreme place among the Olympians and elevated the Indian deity Brahma above the rank of mighty nature spirits are visible according to Tylor in the formation of the Great Spirit among North American Indians and have further analogies in the processes at work among the tribesmen on the Chota Nagpur plateau of India, as well as among the peoples of Ethiopia. In general, developments taking place on the "lower level of mythic religion" are confirmed in higher, more intellectual traditions, such as those of Greece and China, and are finally reinforced by the spread of Christianity. It then becomes the ongoing task of systematic theology to develop and define the figure of the supreme deity, whether he is called the God of Heaven, the Sun, or the Great Spirit.

This final building block in Tylor's theory is not a mere ornament but the finishing touch to an architectonic system. Tylor was quite consciously trying to give substance to the traditional, formal Christian-theological concept of natural religion. He called the theory of the soul "one principal part of a system of religious philosophy that unites, in an unbroken line of mental connexion, the savage fetish-worshipper and the civilized Christian."

The completeness of Tylor's theory should not be allowed to conceal a certain ambiguity in its details, however, an ambiguity that is more a characteristic of the scholarship of his time than a personal weakness. Although he wished to show that primitive religion was rational, that it arose from unmistakable observations, nevertheless he judged these observations to be inadequate in themselves. Although logical deductions were drawn from these observations, he believed these deductions were faulty. And although the "savages" managed to construct a natural philosophy, as a philosophy it remained crude. Tylor thus stressed the rational element in primitive religion and at the same time referred to that religion as "this farrago of nonsense." The classification necessary to science was basic to it, yet it went wrong when the magician mistakenly inferred that things that are like have a mystical link between them, thereby mistaking an ideal connection for a real one, a subjective one for an objective one (Evans-Pritchard).

Since the middle of the twentieth century the knowledge of prehistory has increased so much as to make one objection to Tylor's theory evident at once: his theory of "animism" as the original form of religion has not found any historical confirmation. Moreover, the key ingredients of his theory are limited to hypothetical considerations ascribed to the mind of very distant, primordial men, and the chances that those men used the same sort of logic or lived in circumstances calling for positivistic concerns of the sort that Tylor took for granted are remote. At present, prehistorians, historians, and anthropologists would agree that Tylor's theory has very little bearing on anything they would consider a religious phenomenon.

In the history of scholarship, among the first objections raised against Tylor's animism were those that appealed to a theory of preanimism or dynamism. However, as already noted, Marett, who was the first to speak of preanimism (in 1900), thought not of rejecting but rather of extending Tylor's reasoning, and of making a space for a stage in which ideas concerning a life-force had not yet been differentiated into the notion of independent spirits. Marett actually goes so far as to compare the supposed impersonal power with electricity. The comparison is characteristic of the times and had great appeal when some big cities, such as New York, had begun to look like forests of poles for electrical wiring. The idea of a mysterious force, alive and yet homogeneous, not yet individualized, was at once popular. The same objections that can be raised against animism can be raised against preanimism as well. Both theories attribute a modern, mechanical, and positivistic concern to early man. Nor has historical evidence for dynamism as the origin of religion been forthcoming. Marett's theory leaned in part on work done by R. H. Codrington in the Pacific (*The Melanesians,* 1895). The key conception was *mana,* a Melanesian idea that in Marett's opinion could be identified with notions of other "primitives" (such as *wakan* among the Lakota, *orenda* among the Iroquois, *manitou* among the Algonquin). It seemed as if *mana* could provide an improved, even an adequate minimum definition of religion, namely, "supernatural power." Other scholars extended Marett's line of reasoning and found traces of the same original conception in the *brah-*

man of the Hindus and in both the *numen* and the *imperium* of the Romans.

Anthropologists have since pointed out, however, that even in Codrington's descriptions, *mana* cannot often be properly interpreted as "impersonal power." The term occurs as a rule in a far more complex context, as do words such as "the sacred" or "magic" with ourselves. Moreover, even when the term *mana* conveys the notion "power," it is always the power of a spirit or some other agent; hence Marett's insistence on its impersonal character is not convincing. In addition, it is now known that notions of an "impersonal power" do not occur among peoples that are culturally least advanced and who would represent a truly "primitive" stage in an evolutionary process. Contrary to what the theory would require, they do not occur among the most archaic gatherers and hunters but rather in much more developed societies such as those on the cultural level of nomadic cattle breeders with intricate patriarchal kinship systems.

The main objection against the sort of preanimistic theory designed by Marett, as in the case of Tylor's animism, remains philosophical in nature. The theories of animism and preanimism suffer from the problem of reading one's mental assumptions into the data without sufficient critical analysis. Marett's formula of a "supernatural power" as a minimum definition of religion is eloquent. The adjective *supernatural,* which has dominated the anthropological vocabulary for a long time in endeavors to delineate religion, implies a natural world that is known, on top of which the unknown or rather the not-yet-known or perhaps altogether illusory dimension elevates itself. The real quality of this unknown or illusory upper story escapes not so much one's mind as that of "the primitives." Hence the latter create for themselves strange conceptions and thereby indulge in a strange ("childish") habit from which the investigator is free.

Animism and preanimism are both concepts to which the rule formulated by the philosopher Henri Bergson (in 1903) fully applies: concepts, especially if they are simple, have the disadvantage of being in reality symbols for the object they symbolize and demand no effort on one's part. The very concept of "the primitives" is itself an abstraction for an enormous, variegated group of human traditions. The theories make them into an object and single out the idea of "spirits" or "power" to suggest an even more concise concept. In the process the illusion that the people studied and the modern investigator represent two altogether different groups of mankind (an illusion that always lurks in the background in humanistic and social studies) threatens to become permanent. Such a dichotomy was generally considered valid throughout the period of colonization by Western nations during which Tylor and Marett did their work. The attitude that was then prevalent explains how for several generations, in the best of intellectual circles, the term *animist* became a synonym for what a former age would have called "pagan." The term had the advantage of a certain scientific ring. Thus, in missionary surveys and elsewhere one can occasionally still read, for instance, that Burma's population consists mainly of Buddhists, Muslims, and Animists. Tylor's theory has had such an impact as to suggest that animism is in fact a religion, whereas in fact it was never more than a theory about religion. One cannot reproach Tylor for this popular revamping of his ideas, and yet the philosophical assumptions of the theory carried this potential danger with them.

Animism in the History of Scholarship. As a theory in religion, Tylor's animism does not stand in total isolation, in spite of its splendor, influence, and popularity. Ideas concerning a creative human imagination conjuring up superhuman figures are ancient. Of special relevance is the idea of the dead as the nucleus around which a world of spiritual beings could have been built up. The name of the Greek Euhemerus (third century BCE) is inseparable from the theory that bears his name, "euhemerism." According to this theory, the gods were originally no more than human rulers who were later elevated to the status of gods by subsequent generations because of the benefits they bestowed on mankind. The theory endured well into the eighteenth century, yet Augustine of Hippo and other early Christian thinkers, who were quite familiar with it in its classical form, gave it a new twist. In Christian thought a distinction unknown to Classical Greece was made between true and false religion. Thus whereas formerly the gods owed their divinity to the benefits they had bestowed on man, now the idea was introduced that their superhuman state was the result of their stupendous vices and evil deeds; not their radiant kingship, but their mere humanity came to be emphasized; not veneration, but fear was the proper human response to their acts, not adoration, but propitiation. They were demonic rather than divine. This new interpretation of euhemerism agreed very well with another pre-Christian idea, as expressed by the Roman author Statius (c. 40–96 CE): "Primus in orbe deos fecit timor" ("The first reason in the world for the existence of the gods was fear").

Neither in antiquity nor in the Middle Ages did anyone posit human reflection on death or any other single idea as the cause of religion. Such a theoretical attempt to find a single principle at the origin of religion did not really occur until the end of the eighteenth century, and full-fledged reductionistic theories were not developed until the nineteenth century. However, with regard to this topic, two eighteenth-century names stand out. David Hume's *The Natural History of Religion* (1757) can be read as a prelude to nineteenth-century evolutionistic schemes of religion. Hume posited a plurality of gods at the beginning of human religious history and a monotheistic system at its culmination. The other name is that of the French magistrate and Enlightenment scholar Charles de Brosses (1709–1777). De Brosses is of interest not only for his idea of an evolving religiousness but also for notions that resemble Tylor's animism and Marett's preanimism. In 1757 de Brosses wrote an essay, *Du culte des dieux fétiches* (The Cult of the Fetish Gods), that dealt with the similarity between the religion of ancient Egypt and that of contemporary sub-Saharan Africa. The Académie des Inscriptions, to which de Brosses had submitted his work, considered it too daring and published it only anonymously in 1760. Most remarkably, de Brosses used the term *fetishism* in a very wide sense, to describe the original common form of all religion, and precisely this comprehensiveness makes it resemble Tylor's animism.

Fetishism in de Brosses's vocabulary included the cult of animals and plants as well as inanimate objects. This first crude form of religion would have been uniform in humanity's earliest state of existence, again like Tylor's animism. Evolutionist *avant la date,* the Frenchman posited the idea of a subsequent development of the human mind by degrees "from the lower to the higher." Unlike his fellow *philosophes,* who in their zeal sought to show a purely natural religion at the root of all later development, de Brosses pointed to idols in ancient Egypt that were partially formed in the shape of animals. Ahead of his time in this respect, he was actually guided more than his contemporaries by empirical evidence. Evidence showed that the origin of religion could only be found in savage expressions, and that is precisely what his "fetishism" tried to explain. (The word *fetish* was borrowed from the Portuguese for "amulet" or "charm." That the intellectual climate of the nineteenth century was indeed affected by the work of de Brosses is clear from the fact that Auguste Comte, the principal philosopher of positivism, in developing his "law of the three states" through which mankind supposedly passed—the "theological," the "metaphysical," and the "positive"—drew on him to articulate the first (theological) state. Through Comte, de Brosses thus became a source for the socioreligious evolutionism of the century of Darwin and Tylor.

Even when all "influences" and all earlier ideas concerning worship of the dead are listed, however, the origin of the complete evolutionistic systems of the nineteenth century is still not fully explained. This point must be emphasized especially with respect to euhemerism, for contrary to widely held scholarly opinion, the explanatory intent of euhemeristic ideas before the eighteenth century was quite limited. Early euhemerism, although speaking of gods as originally human beings, was primarily a narrative device that allowed people like Snorri Sturluson (1178–1241), the Icelandic scholar, to weave together biblical accounts, the Homeric story about Troy, and traditions concerning the gods of the ancient pagan North.

By contrast, the theories of Tylor, and likewise those of Herbert Spencer, did not merely combine, arrange, or rearrange myths but posited a causal explanation for the phenomenon of religion in general. Thus theories concerning "the dead" as a factor in the formation of religion, although most clearly originating with euhemerism, may be clearly divided into three very different groups: (1) a first group illustrated by Euhemerus himself, who was a narrator, a "novelist," and who told a story concerning the gratitude of people to royal benefactors who came to be adored and thereby lifted onto a celestial plane (notably, in Euhemerus's story, Kronos, Ouranos, and Zeus); (2) Augustine and all other early Christian theologians, who did not regard the pagan gods as nonexistent but made use of euhemeristic ideas to explain them as mere human beings who had become demonic in character and were remembered and placated because of their evil deeds; and (3) the theories of Tylor and Spencer, positing one principal cause for the development of religion and finding that cause located primarily in rational human reflections concerning the departed souls.

ANIMISM AND THE OBSESSION WITH ORIGINS. The distance that separates us from "typical" nineteenth-century views allows us to perceive the peculiar fascination with origins that then dominated scholarship, not merely in the study of life forms (in the famous work of Darwin), but especially in the social, historical, and religious studies of the time. Theories about the primal form of religion abounded. Atheism and ancestor worship (Spencer), preanimism (Marett), totemism (employed by the sociologist Émile Durkheim, 1858–1917, the Old Testament scholar W. Robertson Smith, 1846–1894, and others), a first parricide (Sigmund Freud, 1856–1939), a primal monotheism (the ethnologist Wilhelm Schmidt, 1868–1954), magic (the English folklorist and classicist James G. Frazer, 1845–1941)—all vied with animism. All aimed to provide the best explanation for the origins of religion.

It is true that more recent times have added to the list of supposed "causes"; particularly influential has been the idea that religion originated in the use of intoxicants, which as a subject demanded attention in the wake of medical and pharmaceutical studies and an increase in the use of drugs in and since the 1950s. However, these more recent speculations have not seriously engaged historians and anthropologists. The striking feature of the earlier theories is precisely that reputable scholars did take them seriously and, as in the case of animism, came to rely on them as on a well-established law.

The generally shared worldview that encouraged such lines of inquiry requires special attention. It was a commonly and uncritically held assumption during the nineteenth century that knowledge concerning the origin of something was the only essential knowledge of it. This preoccupation with the knowledge of origins can be explained in various ways; it can itself be shown to have had several different historical origins. The tradition in the history of philosophy that led to Hegel, and through him to most of the nineteenth century, was certainly the most powerful. The wave of philosophical materialism, multifarious as it was, was also of great significance and explains the overwhelming interest in the mechanisms of causality operative in biology, society, and religion. From the point of view of the historian of religions, however, a specifically religious structure can be detected in the nineteenth-century fascination with origins, a structure that was no less evident in evolutionistic scholars who thought of themselves as "areligious" or "antireligious" than it was in consciously religious adherents.

The most easily traceable roots of the nineteenth-century obsession with origins, viewed as a peculiarly religious structure, can be found in the first period of modern history, which saw the beginnings of all modern scientific inquiry. The famous Renaissance thinkers Marsilio Ficino (1433–1499) and Giordano Bruno (1548–1600) were not at all exceptional in their time in regarding the newly rediscovered Hermetic writings as some sort of primordial revelation (Frances A. Yates, Mircea Eliade). Ancient Egypt, to which their origin was (erroneously) attributed, was traditionally considered to be the cradle of everything truly archaic (a tradition already attested in the Greek historian Herodotus in the sixth century BCE). Renaissance men of the most diverse backgrounds were convinced of the extraordinary significance of these supposedly pre-Mosaic Hermetic writings. This odd enthusiasm, though explicable to some extent by the ignorance of the true history of the Hermetic corpus, can also be understood as an urge to find true origins beyond any limited and known tradition.

The function of the Hermetic writings among the learned in the Renaissance can be compared to the function of cosmogonic myths in all archaic religious traditions (Eliade). They provided a manner of positing an irrefutable, unshakable reality, a primordial revelation, first in time and significance. The mysterious quality of the meaning of the Hermetic writings was not a drawback but rather an enhancement. Giordano Bruno was certain that his understanding of their real meaning allowed him to grasp the significance of Corpernicus's discoveries better than Copernicus himself, because he saw that the primordial revelation, obscure to many, was here confirmed.

Doubts concerning the truth of Christianity, and certainly concerning its traditionally conceived truths, had their place in the intellectual climate of the Renaissance. Nor were similar doubts at all hard to find in the nineteenth century, even if one recognizes that in Tylor, more than in most of his fellow evolutionists, a religious motivation played its part. In a perfectly sober survey of the great figures of anthropology and the history of religions, including Tylor, Marett, Lang, Frazer, and Robertson Smith, it is easy to detect an attitude that came to view religion as a lost cause (David Bidney). However, the climate of erudition and science that developed in the nineteenth century also provided a new sense of an "ultimate reality" or, at the very least, a dependable epistemological framework within which all religious phenomena could be placed, each with its limited value and historical limitations. It is true that this "ultimate reality" turned out to be very limited in its turn, but it is also true that even at the time of Tylor and Marett, and all their fellow scholars, the "ultimate" concern for origins and evolution demanded constant exegesis, exactly as did the Hermetic corpus in the Renaissance, which thereby did not undermine its value, but confirmed it.

The principal epistemological problem of Tylor's evolutionism, as well as other cultural and religious evolutionisms (as in the circles of the Religionsgeschichtliche Schule, centered in Germany) was not that it did not recognize its own religious structure, for such recognition as a rule does not occur until the following generation. Rather, the principal problem was that the object of study, the religious traditions of humankind, was mutilated by reducing it to an object on a dissecting table. In the process every religious structure evaporated. The knowledge of religion as basically "animistic" or "preanimistic" is knowledge as power, but this power is destructive. A tradition that is understood reveals itself as a movement in which one generation can pass on its "power" over life and human orientation to the next, as something that gives life. The weakness of animism and related theoretical constructs is the weakness visible in all "emaciation in learning and science" (van der Leeuw) resulting from an unjustifiable objectification. The evolutionisms, of which Tylor's became the most popular and influential, in the end failed epistemologically, in a way analogous to the political failure of the empires in which they were born, and to which they were related.

See Also Cosmogony; Demons; Dynamism; Evolution, article on Evolutionism; Fetishism; Ghosts; Numen; Power; Preanimism; Supernatural, The.

Bibliography

Henri Bergson's *An Introduction to Metaphysics,* translated by T. E. Hulme (New York, 1949), is a most helpful discussion for understanding the limited value of concepts, easily applicable to a concept such as animism. David Bidney's "The Concept of Value in Modern Anthropology," in *Anthropology Today: Selections,* edited by Sol Tax (Chicago, 1962), approaches the same subject from an anthropological point of view. For Euhemerus and the history of euhemerism in Western intellectual history, see my "In Defense of Euhemerus," in *Myth and Law among the Indo-Europeans,* edited by Jaan Puhvel (Berkeley, 1970). Henry Duméry's *Phenomenology and Religion: Structures of the Christian Institution* (Berkeley, 1975) contains an appendix with a survey of the history of the philosophy of religion, clearly showing the fundamental shift from the classical era to the Christian era.

A very extensive discussion of the intellectual problems in the interpretation of "primitive" religions is Wilhelm Dupré's *Religion in Primitive Cultures: A Study in Ethnophilosophy* (The Hague, 1975). Émile Durkheim's *The Elementary Forms of the Religious Life* (1915; New York, 1961) is not only important as a study centering on totemism as an early rival to animism as a theory on origins but remains one of the most articulate works in theoretical problems concerning origins and functions of religion in primitive religions in general. Mircea Eliade's *Shamanism: Archaic Techniques of Ecstasy,* rev. & enl. ed. (New York, 1964), presents elaborate and precisely documented information on spirits and their functions in the most ancient traditions. Of special value for the subject of the fascination with origins in the study of religion is the same author's *The Quest: History and Meaning in Religion* (Chicago, 1969).

E. E. Evans-Pritchard's *Theories of Primitive Religion* (Oxford, 1965), in spite of its date of publication, deals almost exclusively with theories of the nineteenth century and their immediate aftermath. Burton Feldman and Robert D. Richardson's *The Rise of Modern Mythology, 1680–1860* (Bloomington, Ind., 1972), though not covering Tylor and more recent theoreticians, is an indispensable reference work for the entire intellectual history concerning religion leading up to them. Among the most readable works that deal largely with theories in a critical manner is Adolf E. Jensen's *Myth and Cult among Primitive Peoples,* translated by Marianna Tax Choldin and Wolfgang Weeissleder (Chicago, 1963). Gerardus van der Leeuw's *Levensvormen* (Amsterdam, 1948) contains an essay on the process of "emaciation" of science, and one on the nature of history; both are of immediate relevance to a critical evaluation of theories such as animism.

The same author's famous work *Religion in Essence and Manifestation,* 2 vols., translated by J. E. Turner (1938; reprint, Gloucester, Mass., 1967), has as its starting point the author's own conception of power in religion. R. R. Marett's "Pre-Animistic Religion," *Folklore* 11 (1900): 162–182, and *The Threshold of Religion,* 3d ed. (London, 1915), present the original formulation of preanimism. Wilhelm E. Mühlmann's *Geschichte der Anthropologie,* 2d ed. (Frankfurt, 1968), presents the history of anthropology in the widest context of philosophy and history. A much more concise, but helpful discussion of the discipline is given in T. K. Penniman's *A Hundred Years of Anthropology* (New York, 1974). E. B. Tylor's work on animism, *Primitive Culture,* vol. 1, *The Origins of Culture,* vol. 2, *Religion in Primitive Culture* (London, 1871), is accessible in many reprints (e.g., New York, 1970). Jan de Vries's *Perspectives in the History of Religions* (Berkeley, 1977) contains critical assessments of the evolutionists' views of religion.

New Sources

Barnhart, Joe E. "Anthropomorphism." In *Modern Spiritualities: An Inquiry,* edited by Laurence Brown, Bernard C. Farr, and R. Joseph Hoffmann, pp. 171–178. Amherst, N.Y., 1997.

Stringer, Martin D. "Rethinking Animism: Thoughts from the Infancy of Our Discipline." *Journal of the Royal Anthropological Institute* 5, no. 4 (December 1999): 541–556.

KEES W. BOLLE (1987)
Revised Bibliography

ANISHINAABE RELIGIOUS TRADITIONS.

The Anishinaabe (A-ni-shi-naa-bay; pl. Anishinaabe or Anishinaabeg) occupy an area roughly described by the Great Lakes. To the north, they can be found in the Canadian province of Ontario. In the United States, their home territory includes parts of Michigan, Wisconsin, and Minnesota. Other branches can be found in outlying areas, such as Manitoba and North Dakota. There are many names by which the Anishinaabe are known, the most common being Ojibwe (Ojibwa, Ojibway) and Chippewa. In Canada, the term Saulteaux can also be found. Some Anishinaabe view their nation as consisting of the "three fires," the Ojibwe, Ottawa (Odawa), and Potawatomi. Anishinaabe is thought of as the most traditional name, and its usage is starting to become more widespread and common. Like many native societies, the Anishinaabe are traditionally organized by clans, or *dodaims,* from which the English term *totem* is derived.

The migration story of the Anishinaabe holds that the people originally lived around the Gulf of Saint Lawrence in Canada. Sometime in the late 1500s, however, the Anishinaabe began to move west. There are several accounts of how this migration began. Most commonly, it is thought that an epidemic originally spurred the migration. However, it is also said that a sacred megis shell appeared before the people to lead them west. They were to stop for a period of time at various points when the shell showed itself, and finish the migration when the shell appeared for the last time. The route of the migration included stopping points at current-day Montreal and Lake Nipissing in Canada, Sault Ste. Marie in Michigan, and Madeline Island in the Apostle Island group in Lake Superior in northern Wisconsin. Madeline Island was the last place at which the shell showed itself, establishing that location as one of the most sacred places for the Anishinaabe. The migration continued, however, and the Anishinaabe eventually established outposts in Minnesota and as far west as Turtle Mountain in North Dakota. Other Anishinaabe moved along the north shore of Lake Superior and into Manitoba.

Anishinaabe cosmology pictures a layered universe filled with "other-than-human" agents. The layers consist of the underwater realm, the land, and the sky. Living beings are thought to be controlled by what are sometimes referred to as the "masters of the species." That is, each species of living beings has a *manitou (manito, manidoo),* or spirit, which controls the presence and movements of representatives of that species on earth. The master can dispense or withhold blessings as it sees fit. However, individual representatives of the species also have a certain degree of autonomy.

Within the layered universe, one particularly important dynamic is that which exists between the Thunderers and Michibizhii. The Thunderers are generally imagined as large birds of prey. Michibizhii, or Messhepeshu, has various incarnations. He is sometimes pictured as a snake-like creature, but he can also appear as more cat-like, or even as a combination of the two. He is the leader of the fish, reptile, and amphibian *manitous.* While not entirely hostile toward humans, he is very powerful, and that power must be carefully respected. For example, it is not uncommon for Anishinaabe to sprinkle tobacco over the water when venturing out by boat in order to appease him. It is thought that the Thunderers prey on Michibizhii, hunting him with lightning bolts. Not ever being able to destroy the *manitou* completely, their eternal battle is reenacted with every summer thunderstorm.

Another significant being is the *windigo,* a giant, cannibal ice skeleton who roams the woods in the winter, preying on human beings. Under conditions of starvation, human beings could also become, or turn, *windigo.* When an individual turned into a cannibal in this manner, it was thought there was no hope of cure, and the only option was to kill the affected person. The last known case of so-called *windigo* psychosis occurred in Canada in the early twentieth century.

One of the most important aspects of Anishinaabe morality involves maintaining good relations with other humans and "other-than-human" agents. Maintaining respect for all living things is a core value by which the Anishinaabe live. Sometimes the relationships are individual in nature; other times the relationships are more corporate. Usually, maintaining good relationships will take the form of giving thanks or asking for blessings. Many of these relationships are with animals or natural forces, but it should under no circumstances be thought that the Anishinaabe worship nature. In the past, the custom was to thank an animal for sacrificing its life and to treat the animal as an honored guest so that its individual spirit would make a favorable report back to the master of the species, thus ensuring the continued pity and blessings of the master. Maintaining good relations can take other forms, however. After killing a deer, for example, it is taught that part of the liver should be left with the entrails as a gift for the wolves, whom the Anishinaabe hold very close to their hearts.

Human life is regulated by its own moral system, which is referred to as *bimaadiziwin,* or the "Good Life." The Good Life is oriented toward achieving a long and healthy existence. The teaching of *bimaadiziwn* operates at many levels. On a simple day-to-day basis, they suggest such actions as rising and retiring with the sun. *Bimaadiziwin* governs human relations as well, stressing the type of conduct appropriate between individuals and the manner in which social life is to be conducted. *Bimaadiziwin* also covers the relationship with the broader environment. So, for example, it teaches the necessity of respecting all life, from the smallest insects on up. *Bimaadiziwin,* however, does not exist as a definitive body of law. Instead, it is left up to the individual to develop an understanding of *bimaadiziwin* through careful attention to its teachings wherever they can be found. Because of this the term is quite complex and can apply variously to a religious blessing, a moral teaching, a value system, or a goal in life.

Humor is an important part of the worldview of the Anishinaabe, who believe that maintaining a sense of humor is a critical part of life. This perspective leads to certain thinking patterns and modes of conduct, and it informs everything from complex conceptual schemes to situation ethics, patterns of social integration, and attitudes of forgiveness or pragmatism, which include complex conceptual schemes, situational ethics, patterns of social integration, attitudes of forgiveness, and a pragmatic approach to life. The root of the comic vision of the Anishinaabe is found in their sacred stories, most especially those involving Nanabush.

Nanabush is the cultural hero of the Anishinaabe, and he is often thought of as a trickster figure. He is known by many names, including Nanabush, Nanapush, Nanabozho, Manabush, Manabozho, and Wenabozho. Tales about Nanabush are told only during the winter and it is considered a severe breech of Anishinaabe etiquette and spiritually dangerous to discuss him out of season. Traditionally, it was thought his father was the West Wind, and he is commonly paired with a twin brother, Flint. His mother died in childbirth while giving birth to Flint, so Nanabush was raised by his grandmother, or Nokomis in the Anishinaabe language. In the present day, some religious leaders teach that Nanabush is the son of God, and that while God sent Jesus to instruct Europeans, He sent Nanabush to teach Indian people.

While not all Anishinaabe myths involve Nanabush, he is a central figure in traditional lore, and so will form the nexus of the discussion of Anishinaabe sacred stories here. As with many trickster figures, Nanabush is not thought to have created the world, but rather to have shaped life into its current configuration. He is thus credited with having named the different aspects of creation and with having determined their present form. Nanabush was also responsible for the creation of human beings, to whom he brought the various accoutrements of civilization, such as fire and music. Earlier in human history, the Anishinaabe believe, giant cannibals and other monsters roamed the earth. Nanabush was responsible for destroying them.

However, in true trickster fashion, Nanabush was also responsible for introducing greed, gluttony, selfishness, laziness, and other base behaviors. However, the Anishinaabe do not fault Nanabush for being morally decrepit or evil as a result. Instead, they point to the shortcomings of Nanabush as a way of explaining human behavior. Nanabush served as the model for and creator of human conduct. Thus, whenever he did anything stupid, he said to himself, "There's another foolish thing my aunts and uncles [human beings] can do." So, being able to attribute less than noble acts to Nanabush allows the Anishinaabe to exercise forgiveness in regard to their own weaknesses.

Eventually, Nanabush left this world, and it is now commonly thought that he stands in the Northwest sky next to his father, the West Wind. The Northwest wind is thus a reminder of Nanabush to the Anishinaabe. Some believe he will one day return to help restore Anishinaabe culture.

In the peopled universe of the Anishinaabe, access to the sacred was achieved through vision quests. In traditional society, the quest had to occur before the supplicant reached puberty. It should be borne in mind that the word for "vision" in Anishinaabe also has the nuance of deep thought. So, children were primed for the vision quest in being directed by their parents to spend time the woods thinking about life and absorbing the environment. Vision quests could last anywhere from four to eight days, during which time the condition of the faster was carefully monitored. Children were admonished to not seek too much spiritual strength by fasting for overly long periods of time. They were also told they could reject visions. Thus, weaker "spiritual guides"—that is, beings who visited them during visions—were to be shunned in favor of stronger beings. Children not successful in the spiritual quest were thought to lack direction in life.

For those who were successful, it was customary not to reveal the identity of the spirit guide. Doing so could result in severe retribution from the guide. At the start of the twenty-first century, the practice of the vision quest continues among some Anishinaabe, and instances of individuals past the time of puberty going on the vision quest occur.

Spiritual power gained in the vision quest is further developed in the Midewiwin, or "Grand Medicine Society." The Midewiwin is often thought of as the traditional religion of the Anishinaabe. The rites and teachings surrounding the Midewiwin are secret, however, and modern-day Anishinaabe are reluctant to discuss the Society. For this reason, the remarks here will be kept to a minimum. The Midewiwin is a medicine society. Priests are known as *Midé,* and there are either four or eight degrees of initiation, depending on the local tradition. Along with the teaching of traditional lore, instruction in healing is provided, particularly concerning the use of herbs. In the past, it was not uncommon for the Midewiwin to handle funerals as well.

In traditional thinking, the land of the ancestors is thought to lie to the west. Upon death, the soul begins a four-day journey. Each day along the path the soul encounters a different temptation in the form of berries. The list of these temptations varies, but strawberries, blueberries, raspberries, and gooseberries are commonly mentioned. A soul being guided along the path of the dead is admonished to not stop and eat. Doing so will result in one being permanently stuck in that location. Once having passed those temptations, the soul reaches a river across which is a slippery log, difficult to cross. Traditionally, this was not conceived of as a test of moral character or judgment of one's actions in life. However, those not able to cross the log were thought to be swept away into oblivion. After safely crossing the river, one could join the ancestors.

The religious landscape of the Anishinaabe was altered with the arrival of Europeans on these shores, of course. However, it should in no way be thought that the Anishinaabe were passive victims or unthinking recipients of religious conversion. Many Anishinaabe kept to the old ways, and those who converted adapted Christianity to fit their own worldview. As Michael D. McNally has shown in detail, the introduction of Anishinaabe religiosity into Christian forms is most evident in the singing of hymns. For example, the texts of Anishinaabe hymns reflect the many ways in which life in this world is privileged over salvation in the next. Other aspects of Anishinaabe culture are reflected in hymn-singing as well, such as the importance of silence. Hymns are sung very slowly, which exaggerates and gives meaning to the pauses between sounds. Also, since the hymns are sung in the Anishinaabe language, hymn-singing is one means by which the language is being kept alive. So, in its Nativist form, Christianity among the Anishinaabe expresses the traditional worldview and culture in some ways.

There is a belief among the Anishinaabe that after the appearance of Europeans, an historical phase consisting of seven "fires," or eras began, each with its own characteristics. The "sixth fire" is a time of great loss and struggle. The "seventh fire" is a time of recovery of lost traditions. Many Anishinaabe believe that the "seventh fire" has been lit. And, indeed, there is a resurgence of Anishinaabe culture underway. Of course, it must be acknowledged that expressions of religion among the Anishinaabe today are quite varied. Some Anishinaabe are fully assimilated into mainstream culture, while others are deeply rooted in Anishinaabe language and tradition. Many Anishinaabe fall in between these two extremes. The cultural movement, though, is toward a return to traditions. Thus, while Anishinaabe religion, culture, and worldview are certain to continue to undergo changes, it appears the "seventh fire" will continue to burn.

SEE ALSO Cosmology, article on Indigenous North and Mesoamerican Cosmologies; Native American Christianities; North American Indian Religions, overview articles.

BIBLIOGRAPHY

Two good introductory books on Anishinaabe religion are Frances Densmore's *Chippewa Customs* (1929; reprint, St. Paul, Minn., 1979) and Christopher Vecsey's *Traditional Ojibwa Religion and Its Historical Changes* (Philadelphia, 1983). However, Vecsey's conclusions about the collapse of Anishinaabe culture need to be viewed with caution in light of the resurgence of the traditions of the people over the last several decades.

In the current age, the Anishinaabe are starting to write about their religion and worldview. Basil Johnston is a well-known and authoritative author on the Anishinaabe. His books include: *The Manitous: The Spiritual World of the Ojibway* (New York, 1995), *Ojibway Ceremonies* (Lincoln, Neb., 1982), and *Ojibway Heritage* (Lincoln, Neb., 1976). Winona LaDuke is an internationally recognized Anishinaabe leader and activist. She has written on *bimaadiziwin* in "White Earth: A Lifeway in the Forest," included in a book edited by her: *All Our Relations: Native Struggles for Land and Life,* pp. 115–134 (Cambridge, Mass., 1999). Edward Benton-Banai is a spiritual leader from Madeline Island. His version of certain Anishinaabe sacred stories appears in his book for children, *The Mishomis Book: The Voice of the Ojibway* (St. Paul, Minn., 1988). Ann M. Dunn is a storyteller from the Leech Lake reservation in Minnesota. Her books include *When Beaver Was Very Great: Stories to Live By* (Mount Horeb, Wis., 1995).

Modern scholars are doing a better job than some of their predecessors at representing the Anishinaabe, especially as a living tradition. Two of the best are Michael D. McNally and Theresa S. Smith; see McNally's *Ojibwe Singers: Hymns, Grief, and a Native Culture in Motion* (Oxford, 2000) and Smith's *The Island of the Anishinaabeg: Thunderers and Water Monsters in the Traditional Ojibwe Life-World* (Moscow, Idaho, 1995).

This author's work focuses on cultural interpretation, and deals especially with the manner in which Anishinaabe religion is surviving the impact of colonialism; see Lawrence W. Gross's "Bimaadiziwin, or the 'Good Life,' as a Unifying Concept of Anishinaabe Religion," *American Indian Culture and Re-*

search Journal 26, no. 1 (2002): 15–32; "Cultural Sovereignty and Native American Hermeneutics in the Interpretation of the Sacred Stories of the Anishinaabe," *Wicazo-Sa Review* 18, no. 2 (Fall 2003): 127–134; and "The Comic Vision of Anishinaabe Culture and Religion," *American Indian Quarterly* 26, no. 3 (Summer 2003): 436–459.

A good treatment of the Anishinaabe worldview can be found in Rupert Ross's *Dancing with a Ghost: Exploring Indian Reality* (St. Louis, Mo., 1992).

Selwyn Dewdney's *The Sacred Scrolls of the Southern Ojibway* (Toronto, 1975) provides the most thorough investigation of the birch-bark scrolls used by the Anishinaabe to record their history and teaching. His observations on deviant scrolls, however, should be read with caution. For more sacred stories and an academic interpretation of their meaning, consult Thomas W. Overholt and J. Baird Callicott's *Clothed-in-Fur, and Other Tales: An Introduction to an Ojibwa World View* (Lanham, Md., 1982).

M. Inez Hilger was a Catholic nun who worked with the Anishinaabe for a number of years. Her works provide insights into the everyday life of the Anishinaabe, including religious beliefs; see her *Chippewa Child Life and Its Cultural Background* (Washington, D.C., 1951; reprint, St. Paul, Minn., 1992) and *Chippewa Families: A Social Study of White Earth Reservation, 1938* (Washington, D.C., 1939; reprint, St. Paul, Minn., 1998).

The works of two earlier scholars of the Anishinaabe, A. Irving Hallowell and Ruth Landes, must be read with caution. Evidence of an anti-Anishinaabe bias can sometimes be found in their writing. So, while their ethnographic observations are useful, some of their conclusions are suspect. However, they have made major contributions to the field, so their works must be included here. Hallowell's *Culture and Experience* (Philadelphia, 1955; reprint, Prospect Heights, Ill., 1988) is a collection of essays, and his "Ojibwa Ontology, Behavior, and World View," in *Culture in History: Essays in Honor of Paul Radin*, edited by Stanley Diamond, pp. 19–52 (New York, 1960), is one of the most classic treatments of the Anishinaabe. Landes's works include *Ojibwa Religion and the Midéwiwin* (Madison, Wis., 1968), *The Ojibwa Woman* (New York, 1938; reprint, Lincoln, Neb., 1997), and *Ojibwa Sociology* (New York, 1937; reprint, 1969).

One of the best ethnographic descriptions of the Midewiwin can be found in W. J. Hoffman's "The Midé'wiwin or 'Grand Medicine Society' of the Ojibwa," in the *Seventh Annual Report of the Bureau of Ethnology, 1885–1886,* edited by J. W. Powell, pp. 143–300 (Washington, D.C., 1891).

William Warren was an Anishinaabe well versed in the tradition and history of his people. His history of the Ojibwe includes discussions of Anishinaabe religion; see his *History of the Ojibway People* (St. Paul, Minn., 1885; reprint, 1984). The German traveler, Johann Kohl, provided a detailed discussion of his visit to the Anishinaabe in the 1850s, and his work remains a valuable resource; see his *Kitchi-Gami: Life among the Lake Superior Ojibway,* translated by Lascelles Wraxall (London, 1860; reprint, St. Paul, Minn., 1985).

The works of Henry Rowe Schoolcraft need to be addressed because of their enduring legacy. His so-called Algic research on the Anishinaabe and other woodland nations should only be used with extreme caution, and his works are not recommended, nor will they be listed here. Schoolcraft mixed Anishinaabe, Iroquois, other woodland Indian, and non-Indian myths, religions, and cultures; committed errors in his analyses and conclusions; falsified material; and invented evidence. Thus, unless one is well versed in the sacred stories and other traditions of woodland nations, it is better to avoid his work.

LAWRENCE W. GROSS (2005)

ANNWN. The Celtic otherworld is known in Welsh as *Annwn* or *Annwfn*, variously analyzed as connoting "non-world," "within-world," or "very deep." There is no formal description of this world in Welsh, and allusions in medieval Welsh texts and folklore suggest that it had many aspects. Its identification in medieval times with Hell and in modern folklore with fairyland is, of course, secondary. It is sometimes located below ground and is entered by subterranean tunnels, or it may be below the waters of a lake. Both concepts occur in medieval texts and in recent folktales. In the "Four Branches" of the *Mabinogi* (c. 1060–1120), the medieval Welsh collection of mythological tales, Annwn is conceived of as a world adjacent to the natural world, between which there are no boundaries but an awareness of a new dimension. Thus the hero Pwyll travels from his own land of Dyfed in southwestern Wales to Annwn along roads which should logically have been familiar to him. In other cases the act of sitting upon a mound or hill opens the way to traffic from one world to the other.

Two poems in the thirteenth-century *Book of Taliesin* portray Annwn, although not under that name, as an island. One of these, the so-called *Spoils of Annwfn*, refers to an attack on the otherworld by Arthur from which only seven of his retinue return and uses a variety of names for the otherworld, probably indicating different aspects—for example, Caer ("fortress"), Sidi (perhaps from the Irish *sídh*, "mound"), Caer Feddwid (perhaps "drunkenness"), and Caer Wydr ("glass"). This last name recalls an account in the ninth-century *Historia Brittonum* said to have been written by one Nennius, which tells of an attack by sea upon a glass tower. Since both texts refer to silent sentinels, it may be assumed that the otherworld is the land of the dead. It is never viewed as a land of torment, however. The other poem in the *Book of Taliesin* describes it as being free of sickness and old age and flowing with wine.

In the Second Branch of the *Mabinogi*, the timeless world of forgetful bliss underlies the feasts and sojourn of Brân's followers at Harlech and the island of Gwales, and this motif is common in modern folktales. The birds of Rhiannon, whose song heard over the water lulls the living to sleep, are doubtless from this otherworld. Annwn has its own kingdoms, and its rulers may call upon mortals to aid them, as Arawn, king of Annwn, summons Pwyll in the First Branch.

Most commonly Gwynn ap Nudd, not Arawn, is known as king of the otherworld. He has this role in the eleventh-century story *Culhwch and Olwen* and in the sixteenth-century *Life of Saint Collen.* In modern folklore he is king of the fairies, but he has a more sinister role as leader of the Wild Hunt, the hounds of which are known as Cwn Annwn ("dogs of Annwn").

BIBLIOGRAPHY

A good popular discussion is provided in Proinsias Mac Cana's *Celtic Mythology* (London, 1983), especially useful in this context because it cites Irish examples of these otherworld concepts. Patrick Sims-Williams extends the discussion in "Some Celtic Otherworld Terms," in A. T. E. Matonis and Daniel Melia, eds., *Celtic Language, Celtic Culture* (Van Nuys, Calif., 1990), pp. 57–81. John Rhys's *Celtic Folklore: Welsh and Manx*, 2 vols. in 1(1901; reprint, London,1980) gives folklore examples, as does T. Gwynn Jones, *Welsh Folklore and Folk Custom* (reprint, Cambridge,1979). Marged Haycock edits and discusses the "Spoils of Annwn" poem in " 'Preideu Annwn' and the Figure of Taliesin," *Studia Celtica* 18/19 (1983–84): 52–78.

BRYNLEY F. ROBERTS (1987 AND 2005)

ANSELM (c. 1033–1109), Benedictine theologian, doctor of the church, archbishop of Canterbury, and Christian saint. Anselm is best known for an ontological argument for the existence of God that is still debated and for his opposition to the English kings William Rufus (William II) and Henry I on matters of ecclesiastical rights.

Born of a wealthy Lombard family in the Alpine village of Aosta in Piedmont, northern Italy, Anselm received his earliest education first from a relative and then from the local Benedictines. After the death of his mother in 1056, he gave up his patrimony and crossed the Alps with a companion in search of learning. In 1059 he made his way to the Benedictine abbey of Bec in Normandy (founded around 1039 by the abbot Herluin), where the learned and famous Lanfranc, a fellow Lombard from Pavia, taught. During the following year, at the age of twenty-seven, Anselm was persuaded to enter the abbey and begin a life of intense prayer and study. Three years later, when Lanfranc was chosen to be abbot of Saint Stephen's in Caen, Anselm succeeded him as prior and teacher. On the death of Herluin in August 1078, the community pleaded with Anselm to become their abbot, and he was consecrated in 1079. Within his first year as abbot he visited England on business for the monastery and took time to visit Lanfranc, who had been induced by William the Conqueror to accept the archbishopric of Canterbury in 1070. About the year 1070, when he was thirty-seven years old, Anselm began his writing career. Most of his works were begun, and almost all of them were published, at the request of his monks as an aid to understanding and defending the teachings of faith or expressing devotion.

When Lanfranc died in May 1089, the new king William Rufus refused to name a successor, claiming all revenues of Canterbury and other monasteries for his military campaigns. William eventually consented to appoint Anselm, who reluctantly was invested as abbot by the king on March 6, 1093, and consecrated bishop on December 5. Over the next four years tension mounted between king and archbishop over William's refusal to repair churches, to acknowledge Urban II as pope, and to give up his claim to lay investiture of the clergy. Refused permission to leave the realm, Anselm blatantly left England in November 1097 to see the pope, whereupon the king confiscated all church property belonging to Anselm and annulled all his transactions. During his first exile (1097–1100), Anselm was well received by the pope, completed his best-known work, *Cur Deus homo* (Why the God-Man), addressed the Council of Bari on the procession of the Holy Spirit (later published as *De processione Spiritus Sancti*), visited the abbey of Cluny, and wrote *De conceptu virginali et peccato originali* (On Virginal Conception and Original Sin).

On the death of William on August 2, 1100, Henry I was crowned king, succeeding his brother; the king and a number of barons invited Anselm to return to England. Henry, however, insisted that Anselm be reinvested and pay homage for his see. When Anselm refused, it was agreed that the case would be presented to the new pope, Paschal II. In Rome the king's envoy claimed that Henry would never submit to the loss of the right to invest the clergy, and the pope was equally adamant that he do so. On the journey back to England, Anselm was informed by the envoy that he would not be welcome in England unless he recognized all rights claimed by the king. Anselm's second exile (1103–1106) ended in a compromise reached in Normandy between the king and the archbishop: Henry relented on the issue of lay investiture of the clergy, and Anselm allowed payment by an English bishop for temporalities of his see. Relative peace was restored, and Anselm composed his most significant work, *De concordia praescientiae et praedestinationis et gratiae Dei cum libero arbitrio* (On the Harmony between God's Foreknowledge, Predestination, Grace, and Free Choice). During Lent of 1109, Anselm became seriously ill and died on Wednesday of Holy Week, April 21, 1109.

WRITINGS AND DOCTRINE. Just as Anselm was always able to give "reasons" for the rectitude of his actions, so as a theologian he was always ready to give "justifying reasons" (*rationes necessariae*) for the faith and hope that was in him (1 Pt. 3:15). In his writings, he touched on the whole Roman Catholic teaching found in scripture and the Fathers without adducing the authority of the scriptures to establish his conclusions. He tried instead to convince his readers "by rational arguments," by which he meant the reasonableness of his conclusions. When Lanfranc, who was not enthusiastic about Anselm's writing, suggested that scripture be quoted as an authority, Anselm replied that all his own statements could be supported by the Bible or Augustine and that he was only doing what Augustine had done in his *De Trinitate,* but more briefly (Epistle 1.68). Indeed, Anselm's writings are so thoroughly Augustinian in spirit and Boethian in logic that he can rightly be called "the father of Scholasticism."

Asked to explain his reflections of God's nature and attributes, Anselm compiled a book without a title, which he began to refer to as *Exemplum meditandi de ratione fidei* (An Example of Meditating on the Rationale of Faith). When the work was readied for publication around 1076, Anselm renamed it *Monologion de ratione fidei,* meaning a monologue or soliloquy on reasons for the faith. Anselm's work, like the Apostles' Creed, started with the existence of God, and then considered the Trinity, the life of Christ, and the "four last things." Although Anselm in the *Monologion* speaks as a believer, he argues that God must exist because (1) the grades of goodness in nature require an all-perfect good, (2) everything that exists requires a cause, and ultimately one supreme cause, and (3) the hierarchy of more or less perfect beings, since they cannot be infinite in number, requires an infinitely perfect being superior to all and inferior to none. From this all-perfect being, Anselm argued to all the truths of the Catholic faith.

Soon afterward he wondered whether he could show by a single, brief argument "what we believe and preach about God . . . that he is what we believe him to be," and he completed a second treatise on the same material by 1078. When Anselm came to give it a title, he called it *Fides quaerens intellectum* (Faith Seeking Insight), then simply *Proslogion* (Address), because it is addressed either to himself or to God in prayer. This single brief argument presented in chapters 2 through 4 is original, startling, and undoubtedly the most famous of all Anselm's contributions to religious thought.

The argument may be summarized thus: According to our faith, God is that being than which no greater can be thought. Even the fool, on hearing the phrase "that than which no greater can be thought," understands what he hears, and what he understands is in the understanding. But "that than which no greater can be thought" cannot exist in the understanding alone, for what exists in reality as well as in understanding would be greater than what exists in understanding alone. Therefore, "that than which no greater can be thought" must exist in reality, or it would at the same time be and not be "that than which no greater can be thought." Hence God exists in reality. Even the fool who says in his heart, "There is no God" (Ps. 14:1), would have to admit that God necessarily exists in reality as well as in his understanding.

Almost immediately this ontological argument, as Kant was to call it, was criticized politely but very insistently by Gaunilo, a monk of the abbey of Marmoutier in his *Liber pro insipiente* (For the Fool); Anselm replied to this in his *Liber apologeticus.* Thereafter Anselm requested that both these works be appended to his *Proslogion* in all future copies. In defense of the fool, Gaunilo raised two main objections: first, there is no distinct idea of God from which to infer his existence; second, one cannot rely on existence in thought to prove existence outside thought, for although one can conceive the idea of the most perfect of all blessed islands, it does not follow that that blessed island also exists in reality. To which Anselm replied: passing from existence in thought to existence in reality is possible and necessary only when it is a question of the greatest being one can conceive. Whatever exists except God alone can be thought of as not existing. Over the centuries there have always been thinkers to take up the argument and refashion it or reject it. Bonaventure, Duns Scotus, Descartes, Leibniz, and Hegel took it up, whereas Thomas Aquinas, Locke, and Kant followed Gaunilo in rejecting it, each for different reasons.

Between 1080 and 1085 Anselm wrote *De grammatico,* a useful introduction to logic, and *De veritate,* a thorough analysis of different kinds of truth, namely, truth in God as truth itself (cause of all truth), truth in things produced by God (ontological), and truth in the mind (logical) and in the will (moral), both measured by reality. During this same period he wrote *De libero arbitrio,* a work on the true nature of freedom, particularly regarding morality. True freedom for Anselm isnot the ability to choose evil (sin) but the ability to choose different kinds of good as means to a worthy end. This led to his *De concordia gratiae Dei cum libero arbitrio* (1107–1108), an influential work that harmonized God's foreknowledge and grace with human freedom. Anselm's most important theological work was *Cur Deus homo* (1097–1100), followed by *De conceptu virginali,* a treatise on "necessary reasons" why God became sinless man by a virgin and died on the cross to redeem fallen humanity from sin.

The case for Anselm's canonization was presented to Rome around 1163 by Thomas à Becket when he was archbishop of Canterbury, but there is no record of the proceedings. However, a calendar from Christ Church, Canterbury, before 1170 mentions the transfer of the relics of "Saint Anselm the Archbishop" on April 7 and his feast day on April 21. He was declared a doctor of the church by Pope Clement XI in 1720.

BIBLIOGRAPHY

The first satisfactory edition of Anselm's complete works was by Gabrielis Gerberon, *Opera omnia* (1675), reprinted in *Patrologia Latina,* edited by J.-P. Migne, vols. 158 and 159 (Paris, 1863–1865). A critical edition was published by F. S. Schmitt, *S. Anselmi opera omnia,* 5 vols. (Seckau, 1938–1942; reprinted and a sixth volume added, Edinburgh, 1946–1961). The chief sources for Anselm's life are the *Historia novorum* and the *Vita Anselmi* by his chaplain and disciple, Eadmer, edited by Martin Rule (London, 1884); see also Migne's *Patrologia Latina,* vol. 159 (Paris, 1865). The best modern biography and study is Richard W. Southern's *Saint Anselm and His Biographer: A Study of Monastic Life and Thought, 1059–1130* (Cambridge, 1963). A good exposition of Anselm's philosophical doctrine can be found in Étienne Gilson's *History of Christian Philosophy in the Middle Ages* (New York, 1955), pp. 128–139, with good bibliography, pp. 616–619.

JAMES A. WEISHEIPL (1987)

ANTHESTERIA (blossoming rites) was the new-wine festival of the god Dionysos as celebrated at Athens and in cities of Ionia (on the Aegean Islands and the coast of Anatolia). The first of the new wine was opened and drunk in the month that takes its name from the festival, Anthesterion (February). It was a moment of anxiety and relief, of superstitious fear and joyous thanksgiving. At Athens, where the festival program is best known, Anthesteria lasted three days, from the eleventh through the thirteenth of the month. Wine was first distributed to everyone, tasted and tried by everyone on command, and finally used for general festivity. Each day was fondly named for the kind of vessel that typified the day's activity: Pithoigia (jar-opening), Choes, (jugs), and Chytroi, (pots).

On the first day, Pithoigia, the wine was drawn from the large clay "jars" sunk in the ground, where it had fermented since the vintage, and was carried in skins or amphorae to households throughout the countryside and the city and to public buildings in the old city center, the original Agora, just east of the Akropolis. When Athens grew larger, wine and the jugs of the second day were sold at a special market.

At the same time Dionysos was welcomed with joyous ceremony. His effigy was conveyed through the streets in a wagon fitted out like a ship, as if he had just arrived from overseas. Celebrants costumed as satyrs joined him in the wagon, playing pipes. The procession went its merry way to the city center, to the official quarters of the Basileus "king," the chief magistrate whose title was handed down from an earlier day. Here the wife of the Basileus was presented to the god in a symbolic "meeting and marriage."

The life of Dionysos as expressed in myth and ritual runs parallel to the growth and maturation cycle of vine and wine. He is born at the pruning of the vines, a helpless frightened babe nursed by women in the hills. But now, at the moment for opening the wine, he is imagined as an exulting, impetuous young man. Stories tell how he once arrived in one city or another and was resisted, only to demonstrate his overwhelming power. Within each city a ritual marriage celebrates the consummation of his manhood, which is reflected in the famous myth of Ariadne, a royal woman yearning on the seashore, taken by Dionysos.

On the second day, Choes, drinking contests were staged at the city center and in the households as a means of implicating everyone, all at once, in the magic peril of the new wine. At a trumpet signal, each contestant sought to drain his own *chous*, a three-liter jug of neat wine (wine that was not mixed with water). The individual jugs and the neat wine were in contrast to the usual style of social drinking in which the company was served from a large mixing bowl with cups of wine uniformly watered in agreed-upon proportion. The festival custom was explained by the story that Athens, always a haven for the persecuted, had once harbored the fugitive Orestes, son of Agamemnon, after he killed his mother Klytaimnestra, and on this one day kept all the drinkers separate so that blood pollution would not spread.

When the contests were over, households settled down to eat and drink in comfort. Boys in their second year had a special role. They were crowned with flowers and given smaller jugs of wine so that they could join the celebration. Hundreds of these little jugs have survived, with painted scenes of children crawling on the floor, playing with wagon-wheels and other toys, and also mimicking adult ceremonies. It was another way to glorify the new wine. The wine, if we take it back to the pruning of the vines nearly two years before, was of the same age as the boys. Ritual in the vineyards was conducted on a matching two-year cycle. "Blossoming rites," the festival name, refers both to the completion of the cycle and to the crowning of the boys.

At day's end many people still had not finished their wine, so they wreathed the jugs and carried the remnants to the sanctuary of Dionysos in an area of springs beside the river Ilissos, called "the Marshes." The wine was collected and poured over the head of a young he-goat, which was then sacrificed to Dionysos. Sacrifice in its various forms had the effect of reinforcing some part of nature with the vigor of animals. In being soaked with wine, the he-goat was directed to the corresponding part of nature, the domain of Dionysos. The sanctuary was opened just once a year, on Anthesterion 12, for this all-important sacrifice.

The third day, Chytroi, was again devoted to the use of wine, but more sociably, and indeed publicly, with song and dance and masking. *Chytros* denotes the vessel in which the wine was now mixed with water—a large "pot." A mixing bowl in general is called *krater*, and some of the handsomest Athenian vases are of this kind. The festival shape however always remained much simpler—it is a *chytros*, though modern experts have adopted another conventional name, *stamnos*. Vases of this shape have also survived, and the painted scenes show women mixing the wine in just such vases and ladling it into cups and dancing with tambourines and castanets. At the center is an impromptu image of Dionysos, a wooden pillar surmounted by a bearded mask and draped with a long robe, so that the god is present among his worshipers. *Chytroi* or *stamnoi* were placed at the Marshes among the springs, and filled with wine and fresh cold water, and the hangovers from the day before were soon cured. Then the worshipers set out through the streets, singing or shouting in praise of Dionysos.

Their destination was the south side of the Akropolis—the lower slope and the ground in front—which eventually became the marble theater of Dionysos and its orchestra or dancing-place. Performers called *ithyphalloi* (with-erect-phallus) formed choruses and competed in song and dance. They too were robed and masked to look like reeling drunkards; and they too had paraded through the streets behind a carved and painted phallus pole from which they took their name. The exuberant masking is a precursor of Attic drama in its developed forms of satyr play, comedy, and tragedy, which came to be performed during other festivals of Dionysos at the same locale.

There was revelry in the Attic countryside as well. Amid the general disorder, girls went out freely (as they did not at other times) and amused themselves by riding on swings hung from trees. This sportive conduct was another kind of license appropriate to the occasion and was known by two standard names: *aletis* (roaming) and *aiora* (swinging). The country celebration gave rise to its own tale of origin, covering all three days. An old rustic named Ikarios was visited by the god Dionysos and became the first to learn how to make wine. Going round on his wagon, he distributed skins of wine to the country people, and they first drank it neat and were stupefied, then drank it with water and were sexually excited. Thinking it a harmful drug, they killed Ikarios. His daughter Erigone (Child-of-the-morning) went out at dawn to search for the body and, when she found it, hanged herself from a tree. Thus did she "roam" and "swing."

The story was told by the Hellenistic scholar and poet Eratosthenes, who in the fashion of his time pointed to constellations that attest it, Bootes ("ox-driver," i.e., Ikarios) and Virgo (Erigone). In another story that explains the same ritual (as often happens), the suicidal girl, still named Erigone, is the daughter of Klytaimnestra's paramour Aigisthos, also murdered by Orestes. She had followed Orestes to Athens in the vain hope that he would be tried and condemned for the murders. One of these stories, more likely the latter, was brought to the stage by Sophocles in a lost tragedy titled *Erigone.*

Such was Athens' version of the Anthesteria. Ionia celebrated in much the same way. At Ephesos and Smyrna the pageant of the ship-wagon, with its train of revelers, was especially renowned. At Kolophon the poet Theodoros wrote songs of remarkable lewdness for women to sing at the "roaming" (they have not survived). The festival continued under Roman rule. Mark Antony was hailed as the "New Dionysos," and when he arrived at Ephesos in early 41 BCE he was led through the city by a costumed train of satyrs and bacchants. It was likewise in Ephesos that Saint Timothy, the companion of Saint Paul, was allegedly martyred in 97 CE when he fell into the hands of the revelers. Like many pagan festivals, the Anthesteria died out in the third century CE.

OTHER FESTIVALS OF DIONYSOS. Whereas the new-wine festival marked the end of the growth and maturation cycle, another standard festival of Dionysos came at the beginning, at the pruning of the vines in winter. At Athens and in Ionia it was called Lenaia, and the corresponding month was Lenaion (January). The name is taken from the *lenai,* women who reveled on the hills where the vines were mostly grown. *Bakchai,* "bacchants," and *maenads* (meaning "mad ones," cognate with "mania") are other terms for these women. (Male celebrants, such as the maskers at the new-wine festival, are *bakchoi).*

The women's conduct in the hills was alternately tender and furious, a strange reversal that typifies the myths of Dionysos. They made a show of cherishing a baby, crooning and dandling and even suckling. This was a magic means of reviving the withered and ravaged vines. But they also ran and howled and flung about, and they beat the ground with a *thyrsos,* a rod festooned with ivy or pinecones, winter's tokens of new growth. This too was a magic means of stimulating nature, like a rain dance. Vase paintings often depict the women in their wildness. They slice and scatter small animals, a drastic form of sacrifice—nature was again reinforced with animal vigor. Myth equates the animal victims with human ones. There is in fact a magic or mystic unity that embraces the god, the worshipers, the victims, and life in nature. Bakchos (Bacchus) is another name for Dionysos himself, and *bakchos* another term for the fertilizing rod.

Myths of Dionysos dwell on all these features. They tell how nymphs were nursing the baby god, or how royal women were nursing offspring, until they were either routed or transformed by some intruder and the happy scene changed to savagery. The baby is threatened, or even torn and scattered, like the small animals. In the charter myth of Orphic societies the baby Dionysos is torn to pieces, only to be strangely reborn. Euripides' *Bacchae,* the most famous literary treatment, varies the pattern by substituting for the babies a youthful and untried king who is torn by his mother and other women.

Every Greek city had its own calendar of months named for local festivals, and the months named for the two festivals of Dionysos are among the commonest of all. In early days, every community produced wine as a dietary staple and worshipped the wine god zealously. The other two main branches of the Greek stock, Aeolian and Dorian, differed from the Ionian but agreed with each other in the naming of festivals and months. The new-wine festival was *Agerrania* (gathering rites); that is, the occasion for collecting wine and assembling people. The new-growth festival was *Theodaisia* (god-dividing rites), a name that identified the god with both the vines as they were pruned and the animal victims as they were scattered.

SEE ALSO Dionysos.

BIBLIOGRAPHY

Among festivals of Dionysos, the Anthesteria has been the subject of persistent misunderstanding, with consequences also for the nature of the god. It began with the commentators of late antiquity, who were called upon to explain the many references to the festival in classical literature, especially in the works of the comic poet Aristophanes. The word *chytros* occurring in the name of the third day was unfamiliar to them, and they equated this masculine form, meaning "a large pot," with the feminine form *chytra* (a small pot), which happened to be employed in a distinctive ritual of another kind—the offering of a mixture of boiled seeds to underworld powers. So the third day, which was in fact the liveliest of all, was said to be a somber placation of the dead, as if the mood had changed abruptly. Other evidence was made to fit this theory. There was a famous line from a play that had become a proverb: "Out of the house, you Carians; the Anthesteria is over!" The Carians were slaves who were ordered back to work after the holiday. For Carians a different word was substituted, *keres*, meaning "evil spirits," which makes it appear that they had been conjured up during the festival.

On this outlook the Anthesteria became a curious amalgam of gaiety and gloom. The same contradiction was found in the nature of Dionysos, thought to be the lord of souls who at once brings new life and ecstasy and rules over the dead. It was indeed a fertile misunderstanding, propagated by two acute and influential writers on Greek religion, Erwin Rohde, the friend of Friedrich Nietzsche, in his book *Psyche* (1894), translated by W. B. Hillis (London and New York, 1925), and Jane Harrison, the leading voice of the Cambridge school of ritualists. Thereafter, Walter F. Otto, in *Dionysos: Myth and Cult* (1933), translated by Robert B. Palmer (Bloomington, Ind., 1965), described a god of polar opposites, of boundless vitality and all-consuming destruction. As an avowed variation, Karl Kerényi, in *Dionysos: Archetypal Image of Indestructible Life* (Princeton, 1976), spoke of "infinite life and limited life." The dark side is emphasized but also somewhat attenuated by Parisian structuralists as a strangeness or otherness or, by Marcel Detienne, *Dionysos at Large*, translated by Arthur Goldhammer (Cambridge, Mass., 1989), as a sudden disruptive force. These larger views, important as they are to the history of religion, have the effect of distorting Dionysos's function in Greek society as the god of wine.

Although the festivals were focused on this function, they too have been reinterpreted. Walter Burkert, "Greek Tragedy and Sacrificial Ritual," *Greek, Roman, and Byzantine Studies* 7 (1966): 87–121, regards the goat sacrifice of Dionysos's festivals as a way of acting out, and atoning for, the ancient and necessary human impulse to aggression. In the chapter "Anthesteria" of *Homo Necans: The Anthropology of Ancient Greek Sacrificial Ritual and Myth* (Berkeley, 1983), pp. 213–247, Burkert argues that the use of wine was assimilated to sacrifice and killing as a guilty consumption of other life; the *keres* of the third day are masked figures representing demons whose onslaught embodies the guilty feeling. Jan Bremmer, *The Early Greek Concept of the Soul* (Princeton, 1983), pp. 109–122, assigns the Anthesteria to the general category of festivals of license and disorder; the Carians are outsiders who burst into the community in order to be driven off. The picture of the festival given above is fully argued by Noel Robertson, "Athens' Festival of the New Wine," *Harvard Studies in Classical Philology* 95 (1993): 197–250. For the other festivals of the vine and wine cycle, see Robertson, "Orphic Mysteries and Dionysiac Ritual," in *Greek Mysteries: The Archaeology and Ritual of Ancient Greek Secret Cults*, edited by Michael B. Cosmopoulos (London, 2003), pp. 218–240. In "The Magic Properties of Female Age-groups in Greek Ritual," *Ancient World* 26 (1995): 193–203, Robertson illustrates the similarity of women's roles in promoting both staple crops—wine and grain—at festivals of Dionysos and Demeter.

The two kinds of vase distinctive of the Anthesteria, the *chous* of the second day and the *chytros* or *stamnos* of the third, have often been studied separately. Richard Hamilton, *Choes and Anthesteria: Athenian Iconography and Ritual* (Ann Arbor, Mich., 1992), tabulates the childhood toys and treats depicted on *chous* vases and arranges them in statistical groups, which are taken to reflect the adult activities of the festival. Françoise Frontisi-Ducroux, *Le dieu-masque: Une figure de Dionysos d'Athènes* (Paris, 1991), interprets the *stamnos* vases in a structuralist mode, not as festival scenes but as an expressive collage of ritual and mythical motifs. It is remarkable that these Athenian vases were mostly used and admired far from Athens. The *chous* vases were exported to all parts of the Greek world, where local customs were not necessarily the same. The *stamnos* vases were made exclusively for Etruria, a prosperous non-Greek area that had its own new-wine festival and gave women much freedom. Thus the vases evoke an ideal celebration for everyone, and they might be compared to Christmas cards with tableaux of Dickensian London.

Dionysos's festivals gave a customary or institutional form to unruly, even frenzied behavior. Albert Henrichs, "Greek Maenadism from Olympias to Messalina," *Harvard Studies in Classical Philology* 82 (1978): 121–160, traces the appearances of declared maenads at different places. Henrichs also, in "Changing Dionysiac Identities," in *Jewish and Christian Self-Definition*, vol. 3: *Self-Definition in the Graeco-Roman World*, edited by Ben F. Meyer and E. P. Sanders (London, 1982), pp. 137–160, provides examples of private associations named for Dionysos and his ritual, among them mere drinking clubs, which sought to reproduce an intense communal feeling. Susan G. Cole, "Procession and Celebration at the Dionysia," in *Theater and Society in the Classical World*, edited by Ruth Scodel (Ann Arbor, Mich., 1993), pp. 25–38, documents the official status of obscene language and display.

Since Dionysos's festivals are reflected in a great many myths, and the myths are firmly located in different Greek cities, it is possible to distinguish both local patterns and historical changes. The most famous myths belong to Boeotia and the northeastern Peloponnesus, the heartland of Mycenaean (late Bronze Age) civilization. Viticulture and its religion started here but afterwards declined and flourished more in other regions. Giovanni Casadio treats several of the early centers and the history of their festivals in *Storia del culto di Dioniso in Argolide* (Rome, 1994) and *Il vino dell' animo: Storia del culto di Dioniso a Corinto, Sicione, Trezene* (Rome, 1999).

NOEL ROBERTSON (2005)

ANTHONY OF PADUA (1195?–1231), born Ferdinand de Bulhoes; Franciscan preacher, miracle worker, and saint. Born in Lisbon, Portugal, Ferdinand de Bulhoes entered the monastery of the Canons Regular of Saint Augustine while still an adolescent. He was ordained a priest at the monastery of his order in Coimbra in 1219. Inspired by the martyrdom of Franciscan missionaries in Morocco, he left the monastery to join the Friars Minor in 1220, taking the religious name of Anthony. After an abortive attempt at mission work in Morocco, Anthony went to Italy, where he participated in the general chapter of the Franciscans at Assisi (1221) and, presumably, met Francis of Assisi. In 1223 Anthony was appointed lector in theology at the Franciscan house of studies in Bologna. A letter from Francis, of disputed authenticity, ratified that position as long as such study did not "extinguish the spirit of prayer and devotion."

By 1226 Anthony had been appointed the Franciscan minister for the Emilia (a region in northern Italy) and served as a Franciscan delegate to the Vatican. In that same year he received permission from Pope Gregory IX to relinquish all offices in order to devote his life to preaching, for which he had demonstrated great flair. For the rest of his brief life, Anthony traveled through the region around Padua as an incessant preacher of reform and as an obdurate opponent of heresy. In 1231 he died at Padua; Gregory IX canonized him the following year at solemn ceremonies in the Cathedral of Spoleto. In 1946 Pius XII named him a doctor of the church.

The only surviving authentic writings of Anthony are two series of sermons, one for Sundays (*Sermones domenicales*) and one for various feast days of the liturgical year (*Sermones in solemnitatibus sanctorum*). From these writings scholars have attempted to reconstruct the saint's theological vision.

Anthony's theology was shaped both by his use of the sermon and by his stated desire to combat the twin heresies of the Cathari and the dissident evangelical sects like the Waldensians. He emphasized the incarnational themes of theology, the need for interior conversion, and a return to the sacraments, especially the sacrament of penance, as a sign of reconciliation with the church. The framework of his sermons was most typically constructed by harmonizing the scriptural texts of the liturgy celebrated on the day he preached. While the sermons were meant for general consumption they still reflect considerable learning, in both theological and mystical literature.

Anthony's mysticism was influenced heavily by Augustine of Hippo and the twelfth-century exegete Richard of Saint-Victor; he shows no direct dependence on the writings of Dionysius the Areopagite. His scriptural exegesis, based on the traditional fourfold sense of scripture, leans heavily toward the moral sense of the text, which he uses both to exhort to virtue and to warn against the reigning heresies of the time. His focus, typically Franciscan, on the humanity of Jesus led to an emphasis on the healing virtue of the wounds of Christ. Some have seen in the sermons of Anthony the beginnings of the devotion to the Heart of Jesus, a devotional *figura* that would blossom fully only in late medieval piety. His series of sermons on the Virgin Mary constitute a brief compendium of Mariology; his name was invoked by Pius XII as one of the doctors who held the doctrine of the bodily assumption of Mary into heaven, a doctrine defined by the pontiff in 1950.

While Anthony's contemporaries praised his deep knowledge of scripture and his power as an apologist and preacher, posterity best remembers the saint as a thaumaturge. Celebrated in art and narrated in legend, his miracles have the simple charm associated with early Franciscan charisma. The center of Anthony's cult is the Basilica of Il Santo in Padua, which incorporates the old Church of Santa Maria Materdomini where Anthony was originally buried. One of Donatello's famous bronze panels at the basilica depicts an unbeliever's donkey, which, to the evident discomfiture of its owner, is venerating the Eucharist held by Anthony. The popular fourteenth-century Italian anthology of Franciscan stories known as the *Fioretti* (Little Flowers) reflects Anthony's importance in the estimation of the early Franciscans by associating him with the stories of Francis and his earliest companions. The *Fioretti* tells of Anthony preaching to the fish near Rimini after the heretics of the city refused to hear him. The literary similarity of that story to the one of Francis preaching to the birds is patent.

In the centuries after his death the cult of Saint Anthony developed with an intensity second only to that of Francis himself. From that popular devotionalism springs both some common beliefs (a prayer to Saint Anthony will retrieve lost articles) and charitable practices, such as the collection of alms for the poor under the rubric of "Saint Anthony's bread."

The iconography of Saint Anthony has had considerable development over the centuries. The earliest representation of the saint is very much like that of the early pictures of Francis: a young man dressed in a poor habit with a young and unbearded face. He is often shown with an open book in his left hand, while holding in the other a tongue of fire. The latter symbol was most likely borrowed from the iconography of Anthony the Abbot.

By the fifteenth century Anthony is shown with a flowering lily branch in his hand (a symbol of purity) and a book (a symbol of his theological acumen), as the statue by Jacopo Sansovino (in the Church of San Petronio in Bologna) and another in Padua attributed to Donatello attest. By the end of the fifteenth century Anthony, under the influence of popular miracle stories, is often depicted carrying the Christ Child in his arms. This theme became extremely popular in the post-Reformation period, as evidenced in paintings by Esteban Murillo and José Ribera. One variation of this theme is Anthony Van Dyck's Brera altarpiece of the Virgin extending the child Jesus to the expectant arms of the saint. Anthony's role as a theologian and antiheretical apologist is not often depicted in art but he does appear, along with the other doctors of the church, in the Brizio Chapel of the Cathedral of Orvieto in a large work by Luca Signorelli.

BIBLIOGRAPHY

The standard, if deficient, edition of the sermons of the saint is *Sermones Sancti Antonii Patavini,* 3 vols. in 1, edited by Antonio M. Locatelli (Padua, 1895–1913). Sophronius Clasen's *Saint Anthony: Doctor of the Gospel* (Chicago, 1961) is a work by a noted Franciscan scholar. The article "Antonio di Padova," in the *Bibliotheca Sanctorum,* vol. 1 (Rome, 1960), pp. 156–188, is a generally reliable, if somewhat pious, study of the saint's life, doctrine, iconography, and place in folklore.

LAWRENCE S. CUNNINGHAM (1987)

ANTHROPOLOGY, ETHNOLOGY, AND RELIGION. In his classic discussion of "the sick soul" in *The Varieties of Religious Experience* (1902), William James observes that "philosophic theism has always shown a tendency to become pantheistic and monistic, and to consider the world as one unit of absolute fact." In contrast, popular or practical theism has "ever been more or less frankly pluralistic, not to say polytheistic, and shown itself perfectly well satisfied with a universe composed of many original principles." While James ultimately deems the divine principle supreme and the rest subordinate, his immediate sympathies lie with less absolute "practicalities," and he situates analyses of religious experience within the felt tension between theistic monism and the pluralism of actual populations. In many respects the anthropological study of religion has sustained and enlarged upon these sympathies.

Anthropology's traditional concentration on nonliterate societies has shaped its approach to religious practice and belief in general. But ethnological theory has seldom been confined to so-called primitive peoples, tribal groups, or even "marginalized" peoples discredited by a dominant religious establishment. Ethnographers have long addressed religious contexts evolved from what Karl Jaspers called "the Axial Age," marked by world-rejecting beliefs in either a transcendental realm or an abstractly negative realm distinct from the worldly or mundane. Anthropologists encounter the entire range of religious values in ideal and implementation at every scale of society and state and all manner of sect, renunciation, and commodification. Still, when addressing cultural circumstances of world religions, anthropologists often emphasize practitioners' more immediate experience—from spirit cults to ancestor worship to everyday cure and money-mediated expenditure. Such transmundane concerns can qualify those transcendental doctrines or ethical canons (paramount for historians of religion) professed by priests, monks, scribes, and kindred specialists.

METHODOLOGICAL FOUNDATIONS. The contemporary anthropology of religion stems from diverse theoretical persuasions: Émile Durkheim's view of religious "social facts," which brackets issues of truth versus error; Max Weber's ideal types of sweeping processes behind religious, economic, and bureaucratic reformisms; Marxist and Freudian explorations of ideological and expressive behavior. The task of retranslating works by such seminal figures keeps them salient today. For example, Stephen Kalberg's 2002 translation of Weber's *Protestant Ethic and the Spirit of Capitalism* (1904–1905) foregrounds its comparative rhetorical power, and Durkheim's *Elementary Forms of Religious Life* (1912) finds renewed life in Karen Field's spirited rendition (1995); her introduction illuminates how Australian evidence pushed Durkheim's writing toward reflexive interpretations. Steven Lukes's biography of Durkheim (1973) also evokes his dramatic nondogmatism when addressing the Union des Libres Penseurs et de Libres Croyants in 1914: Durkheim urged each party (believers and freethinkers) heuristically to exchange ideals—to act in "organic solidarity" as totemic moieties each to each. Durkheim's impromptu and charismatic speech on this occasion produced effervescent outbursts of applause among customarily staid listeners. Lukes calls this episode "the nearest Durkheim ever came to [Weber's] principle of *Verstehen*" (p. 515).

What Talal Asad (1993), following Michel Foucault, has called the "genealogies of religion" extend to anthropological approaches to religions as well. Many anthropologists attempt phenomenological and hermeneutic interpretations of religious life and sacred symbols or semiotic analysis of communication codes; they apply complex models of social interaction, ritual speech, mythic order and transgression, cosmological archetypes, and historical forces of scapegoating, sacrifice, oppression, and revolution. Religion appears in mechanisms of socialization and in dialectical processes of change; its manifest and latent patterns underlie both consensus and transformation, both integration and subversion.

Rival definitions of religion characterize anthropological efforts. Such scholars as Melford E. Spiro retain a notion of the superhuman and rebuke Durkheim for diluting religion to whatever is ritually "set apart." Others, such as Clifford Geertz, deflect issues of superhuman, supernatural, or holy content, defining religion generally as a set of powerful symbols conjoined to rhetorics of persuasion that are uniquely realistic to adherents and apparent in their moods, motivation, and conceptions. Some working definitions support Mircea Eliade's sense of a distinctive *homo religiosus;* others pose religion as a basically compensatory reaction to mundane deprivation, suffering, or violence. Regardless, anthropologists explore sacred values across domains of illness and cure, aesthetics, law, politics, economy, philosophy, sexuality, ethics, warfare, play, sport, and the many kinds of classifications and performances that both organize and challenge cultural systems of knowledge and affect.

Like its topics and boundaries, vexed issues in the anthropology of religion keep expanding. Is the discipline's task explanatory, requiring so-called objectivity, or is it interpretive, inviting multiple, nonaligned empathies? Is one's goal to bundle religious usages into tidy symptoms of basic human drives, or is it to unravel, even transvalue, such usages through informed readings of cultural and historical contexts, ritual activity and speech, priestly texts, and contested commentaries generated in the name of *religio?* Does evidence of religious activity reduce to neuroscientific bases, or does conveying religious experience enact a reflexivity that keeps trumping its own grasp? And are such alternatives necessarily mutually exclusive?

Even scholars committed to nonpartisan research may question whether comparison can ever be neutral; critical inquiry has intensified into dilemmas of "value-freedom" versus *Verstehen* in the Weberian sense. Any approach to religion may necessarily entail preconceptions that qualify, under certain definitions, as themselves religious (one kind of reflexivity). On the more practical side, research on active religions is often declared off-limits, either by adherents of those religions or by agents of the governments seeking to control them. For these and other reasons, the discipline's findings and the discipline itself remain controversial. Difficult obstacles and opportunities pervade comparative studies of religions, including "secularism" (Asad, 2003); refusals of so-called religion may demonstrate qualities that some scholars (e.g., Durkheim) might call "religious," rather in the manner of renunciation.

One introductory work informed by a coherent view of religion is James L. Peacock and A. Thomas Kirsch's textbook *The Human Direction* (1980), which employs Robert N. Bellah's Parsonian framework of evolving roles in religious and political differentiations. Another is John Bowen's *Religions in Practice* (2002), which uses Pierre Bourdieu's notions of extrastructural, nonformal norms; religions are crossings of cultural boundaries: local, national, and transnational. Scholarly consensus in the anthropology of religions remains inevitably agonistic, a quality captured in William A. Lessa and Evon Z. Vogt's *Reader in Comparative Religion* (1979). That venerable volume's repeatedly updated vintage and vanguard articles have yielded to such worthy successors as Michael Lambek's *Reader in the Anthropology of Religion* (2002), with more emphasis on state politics, assertive "fundamentalisms" (Christian, Islamic, etc.), and diverse religious diasporas.

METHODOLOGICAL CRITIQUES. As the anthropology of religion proceeds, it properly intensifies its retrospection. One can better appreciate current trends by reconsidering the emergence of specialized scholarship on so-called primitive religions.

Fallacies in nineteenth-century quests for the origins of religion, taken as a distinct category of human experience, have been often noted. E. E. Evans-Pritchard's succinct *Theories of Primitive Religion* (1965) enumerates now-rejected studies on the stages of the religious impulse in humans, proposed in different combinations and sequences by successive evolutionist scholars. Besides monotheism we find fetishism, manism, nature-mythism, animism, totemism, dynamism, magism, polytheism, and certain psychological states (p. 104). Although certain such complexes may be real enough—one thinks particularly of shamanism—none demonstrably existed as a distinct stage in a progression either toward religious sagacity or beyond it into "mature" scientific objectivity. Efforts to correlate religious types and socioeconomic levels—for example, the shamans of flexibly structured hunter-gatherer societies versus the priests and prophets of stratified civilizations—have yielded to less monolithic schemes more attentive to evidence of coexisting religious specializations enacted as divination, prophecy, calendrical ceremonies, and many blends of magic, sorcery, and thaumaturgy. For example, contemporary research on shamanic practices by Piers Vitebsky (1995) addresses both the Sora of tribal India and the Sakha (once Yakut) of Siberia. Sora today are abandoning ritual dialogues with the dead, becoming Baptist, and going psychologistic; in contrast, post-Soviet Sakha (sitting on rich mineral deposits) are dressing long-suppressed shamanic ways in New Age merchandizing and global environmentalism. Such transformations and rekindlings of "jungle and tundra shamanism" inflect community/cosmopolitan borderlands and agitate forces of both reformism and commercialism, of both reinvented tradition and the Internet.

In 1962 Claude Lévi-Strauss published a critique of the history of abstracting "totemism," construed broadly as analogies between social divisions and categories of the natural surroundings. His was a particularly spirited critique of the vain pursuit of origins. Evans-Pritchard, again, captures the flavor of prejudicial dichotomies that often, but not inevitably, favored Europeans: "We are rational, primitive peoples [are] prelogical, living in a world of dreams and make-believe, of mystery and awe; we are capitalists, they communists; we are monogamous, they promiscuous; we are monotheists, they fetishists, animists, pre-animists or what have you, and so on" (1965, p. 105). Similar stereotypes could adorn antievolutionist arguments as well, such as Alfred Russel Wallace's *Natural Selection and Tropical Nature* (1891), in which Wallace's spiritist sympathies inclined him to excuse the human species from evolutionary processes: "Natural selection could only have endowed savage man with a brain a few degrees superior to that of an ape, whereas he actually possesses one very little inferior to that of a philosopher" (p. 202). Wallace thus managed to offend everyone—"savage man," the ape, the philosopher, and the evolutionists alike. His awkward rationalization nicely illustrates the invidious comparisons across types, species, and specialized roles that characterized many nineteenth-century attitudes.

The twentieth century brought vigorous responses to social Darwinism, eugenics movements, and other theories of qualitative divisions in the human species. Franz Boas and his followers in the United States, Durkheimians in France, and some diffusionists and functionalists in Britain and elsewhere exposed false evolutionist schemes of myth, magic, and religion. Scholars today continue to debunk "awe theories" that can be illustrated with A. H. Keane's article "Ethnology" in the *Encyclopaedia of Religion and Ethics* (vol. 5, 1912). Keane recapitulates notions of psycholatry, nature worship, the priority of magic, and primitive confusion between the unclean and the holy—common subjects of debate among rivalrous philologists, mythologists, and ethnologists, including F. Max Müller, Andrew Lang, W. Robertson Smith, E. B. Tylor, and James G. Frazer. Keane repeats theories of the concept of independent soul, according to which the soul extends from one's "own person" to one's fellows, then to animals, plants, and finally to the organized world, itemized rather breathlessly as follows: "Such conspicuous and lifelike objects as the raging torrent, the rolling seas, snowy peaks, frowning crests, steep rocky walls, gloomy gorges, dark woods, trees, crags, clouds, storms, lightning, tornadoes, heavenly bodies, until all nature becomes animated and everything personified and endowed with a living soul" (p. 526). Such dubious theories of religious origins and their metaphorical extensions at least reveal symbolic classifications implicit in Europeans' own views of nature and, unfortunately, of human cultures as well.

HISTORICAL REVALUATIONS. Anthropologists today are willing to assess neglected intricacies of dated works, despite their errors. Books by early professional anthropologists and the founding figures of Indology, comparative mythology, and folklore up to 1860 (surveyed in Feldman and Richardson, 1972), while riddled with false explanations, also managed to involve readers in the unfamiliar, the inexplicable, even the forbidden. Narrative strategies and discursive devices of bygone scholarship gain fresh resonance in such pathbreaking studies as Michael West's *Transcendental Wordplay* (2000).

In the anthropology of religion proper, even Evans-Pritchard's sometimes-dismissive historical synopses could reassess aspects of R. R. Marett and A. E. Crawley, as well as Lucien Lévy-Bruhl's controversial ideas of prelogical mentality. In the history of the anthropology of religion, the way has thus been cleared for serious rereading, rather than mere revisionism; a more anthropological attitude toward anthropology's past has emerged (Stocking, 1987). There is evident dissatisfaction with a "use and abuse" self-legitimating history; old stereotypes of disciplinary progress are now shaken, sometimes gently, sometimes violently. Less readily does the field's past divide in positivistic fashion into "before Malinowski" or "before Boas," versus "after." The sustained field research and systematic models of language and social organization established as modern anthropological standards remain definitive developments, but it is not certain that conceptual breakthroughs coordinated data-gathering. The field's history does not conform to a "maturation model," if only because anthropologists of religion—both the bookish and the fieldworking variety—do not exist in isolation from other disciplines and experiences. James G. Frazer's *The Golden Bough* (1890), for example, was a successor to the work of Gibbon and Ruskin as much as to that of Tylor; ideas of scapegoats and the durability of liturgy-like rites reflected Frazer's endeavors in folklore and religious and cultural history as much as in ethnology.

Less seemingly literary scholars as well—including the Bronislaw Malinowski of *Magic, Science and Religion, and Other Essays* (1952) and the Robert H. Lowie of the somewhat perfunctory *Primitive Religion* (1948)—were influenced by diverse disciplines and styles of writing. Lowie cast his last musings on Plains Indian and Pueblo religions more like Ruth Benedict's style of contrastive integration in *Patterns of Culture* (1934). Lowie's posthumously published essay, "Religion in Human Life" (in Murphy, 1972), expressed wariness of easy secularism in ironic tonalities perhaps redolent of Weber's "Beruf" (cited by Lowie in 1948): "One day it occurred to me that both the Indians and the hardy souls who were trying to convert them to Christianity had some inner strength that I lacked. Nor was I unique in this lack." Lowie next wonders "how many scientists would undergo for their science the years of poverty that the priests and ministers willingly accepted for their religion." His reflexive ruminations implicate the very "science" that he strives to practice: "I have known anthropologists who accorded a benevolent understanding to the Hopi but denied it to Catholics, Mormons, Buddhists or Mohammadans [sic]. This dichotomy of viewpoint strikes me as ridiculous and completely unscientific" (Murphy, 1972, pp. 160–161).

Such intricate sensibilities of complicated scholars are often neglected in standardized histories of "progress" in dominant methods. New-sounding themes may not have been so new after all; old paradigms could be discarded before they were exhausted, along with worthy figures. Durkheim's circle, for example, closed ranks to exclude scholars less committed to the "socio-logic." Durkheimians were in turn neglected after their hybrid expertise in ethnology, sociology, history, and comparative philology (particularly Sanskrit) was overshadowed by the fieldwork imperative, particularly in the United States and among British functionalists. Certain British scholars as well were consequently "marginalized."

An interesting case is R. R. Marett. His nonevolutionist entry, "Primitive Religion," in volume 23 of the *Encyclopaedia Britannica* (1911), is nearly contemporaneous with Keane's article "Ethnology," although conventional histories often imply that scholarship advanced beyond evolutionism monolithically. The *Britannica* format in effect contrasted "primitive religion" (with cross-references to "Animism," "Fetishism," "Magic," "Mythology," "Prayer," "Ritual," "Sacrifice," and "Totemism") with "higher religion." Marett's discussion, however, does not broach origins; rather it catalogs categories of "the sacred," providing representative examples of what are called its "activity," "exploitation," and "results." Marett adopts a trusted anthropological convention (perhaps traceable to Latin Christendom's methodical incorporation of select practices and lexemes from pagans it aimed to convert) in which modes of the sacred are aligned with exotic counterparts. *Sacred* can imply "forbidden" (as in the Latin, *sacer,* whence the English word is derived; as well as in the Polynesian, *tabu*), "mysterious" (Siouan, *wakan*), "secret" (Aranda, *tjurunga*), "potent" (Melanesian, *mana*; Huron, *orenda*), "animate" (as in the phenomenon labeled *animism*), or "ancient" (Aranda, *alcheringa,* "the Dreaming"). This constellation of North American Indian, Oceanic, and Australian Aboriginal terms indexes, as it were, the variable universality of the sacred.

Under "results," Marett considers what were later called religion's functions, including education, government, maintenance of food supply, reinforcement of kinship and family bonds, enhanced sexuality, and integrated personalities. Marett's "exploitation" covers dimensions of ritual process and ceremonial celebration; he cites cases of acquisition, concentration, induction (including sacrifice), renovation, demission, prophylactic insulation, and "direction," suggestive of an ethos or those "moods" later signaled by Geertz. He even addresses transformative properties of religion that return secular government and aristocratic traditions to a more primitive, democratic spirit. "Everyone," notes Marett, "has his modicum of innate *mana*" (*Encyclopaedia Britannica*, 1911, vol. 23, p. 67). His "abuse of the sacred" merges religion with individualized resistance; by "activity" Marett intends general motivations and meanings of the sacred: fecundity, transmissibility (parallel to Frazer's notion of contagion), and finally ambiguity and relativity, both apparently construed positively.

Marett clearly anticipates such successors as Victor Turner, who expands Arnold van Gennep's "rites of passage" to include ritual performances that consolidate structure with antistructure and coordinate themes of liminality or periodic involvement with regenerative in-between states. That the views of Marett (whose shortcomings are here de-emphasized) anticipate later theories is obscured by his casual jargon. Like Arthur M. Hocart, he retained interpretive terms borrowed from European or Indo-European religious traditions. Although Marett's "sacraments of simple folk" or Hocart's Hindu, Fiji, and Australian "sacraments" in fact approximate liminal rites for celebrating changes in office or social state, their rubrics ran counter to fashions for more technical-sounding coinages in theory and method.

These few examples illustrate a key development: illusions of a simple heritage of influence and unpoliticized progress—out of darkness into light—of an anthropology of religion are being dispelled. Interest in "primitive religion" stemmed from ideas of exoticism once pervading European conceptualizations of cultural differences that Europeans sought to subjugate. The anthropology of religion, even when centered on fieldwork results and organized by the conviction that ritual and belief have direct social consequences, has never proceeded in a simple developmental line insulated from the broad history of ideas of otherness, charged with philosophical and political implications. Errors and prejudices of past scholarship must be corrected, of course; but the cultural and historical values that sustained that work also deserve anthropological interpretation. A scholar content to denounce predecessors' denunciations of primitive superstition risks committing the very sin decried, effectively dismissing "anthropology-then" as primitive.

Thus, the anthropology of religion grows more mindful of its own involvement in the paradoxes it investigates. Consider, for example, philosopher Ludwig Wittgenstein's notations (1979) on his copy of a condensed edition of Frazer's *The Golden Bough*: "Here, purging magic has itself the character of magic" ("Das Ausschalten der Magie hat hier den Charakter der Magie selbst"). Yet Frazer delivered his own ambivalent suggestions that primitive superstitions underlie civilization's basic tenets (of political authority, private property, and truth) as midnight lectures styled after the strange rites they disclosed. Frazer, not devoid of romantic irony (particularly in *Psyche's Task*, 1909), was conceivably sensitive to paradoxes that Wittgenstein would later inscribe in somewhat superior fashion in the margins of Frazer's book. Regardless, Wittgenstein's own *Philosophical Investigations* (1953) may imply that even purging the purging of magic (as when Wittgenstein corrects Frazer) has "the character of magic" as well. The history of scholarship may itself pulse to cyclic rhythms conjoining victims and redemption—rhythms redolent of widely distributed and recurring patterns of ritual practice.

Reassessments of Frazer's immense corpus confirm his self-awareness of such echoes and emulations. Robert Fraser's *The Making of the Golden Bough* (1990) argues persuasively: "For, if in Robertson Smith a ruthless evangelical honesty contrives to undermine the sanctity of the biblical text, in Frazer the idealistic premises of Humean empiricism turn in on themselves to make doubt itself an impossibility." And he concludes incisively: "To the end Frazer remained sceptical, even of his own sceptism" (p. 209). Such themes, still fertile today, reverberate back to Frazer's earliest work on Plato and on immortality as "the death of death." The late Jean Pouillon formulated a connected insight (possibly in accord with Durkheim's relational sense of sacred/profane distinctions): "C'est l'incroyant qui croit que le croyant croit" ("It is the unbeliever who believes that the believer believes") (Izard and Smith, 1982, p. 2). This kind of paradoxical (and sometimes dialectical) "doubling"—death of death, belief in unbelief—continues to infuse varieties of interpretation at the conjunctions of disciplines that concern us here.

Trends and Prospects. A review by Clifford Geertz (1968) of the anthropological study of religion remains a valuable point of departure for surveying subsequent developments. Geertz discusses psychodynamic frameworks based on Sigmund Freud, on theories of culture and personality following Clyde Kluckhohn, and on socio-psychological components of Malinowski's functionalism. One persistent issue concerns whether beliefs and rites exist to "reduce ambiguity" (a functionalist notion) or to harness it, thus generating sustained worlds of semantic, emotive, and intellectual values. The latter view is held by diverse scholars disenchanted with functionalist assumptions that religion bolsters "society"—equated with a machinelike or an organism-like system of reinforcements that vent pressure built up by anything dysfunctional or indigestible, like so much steam or gas.

Some studies pursue possibilities of universal patterns linking ritual and neurosis (anticipating today's interest in neuroscience). Others seek less to discover whether all peoples harbor, say, an Oedipal complex than whether certain rituals serve purposes analogous to Western psychotherapies.

Sudhir Kakar (1982), for example, has compared Muslim and Hindu curative, shamanic, and Tantric techniques to psychotherapeutic devices—demonological constructions resemble Freudian idioms—but India, he stipulates, does not share the West's tradition of introspection. Contextual investigations of parallels between Western and Asian psychodynamics include works by Gananath Obeyesekere and Bruce Kapferer on Sri Lanka, by Robert A. Paul on Nepal and Tibet, and by Sherry Ortner on Nepal. Ideas of Freud, Carl Jung, and such part-Boasians as Ruth Benedict and Paul Radin remain pertinent in analyzing therapeutic narrative and ritual styles coordinated with worldviews of disease and its cure.

A second area reviewed by Geertz—sociological approaches—merges with interpretations of symbolic forms that dominated postwar research. Durkheim's view of religion's social foundation remains central. Durkheim never " explained away" religion as some sort of mass delusion; rather he linked religious rites and ideas to the fact that any society is both divided and coherent, both subcategorized and at least periodically "in unison." Durkheim's *Elementary Forms of Religious Life* continued his earlier emphases on varieties of the division of labor; on categories implicit in ritual objects, cosmography, and mythic tales; and on the compartmentalized tasks and specialized knowledge that enrich every social order. For Durkheim's school, a "tribe" was "international," composed of segments occasionally congregated in ritual gatherings but for other purposes dispersed. Totemic rites and ceremonies of competitive gift exchange do not simply reinforce something already existent; rather they constitute an additional axis of interrelations. This view of religion and society is less "consensualist" than certain translators, followers, and critics have suggested.

Another major source of social theory is Max Weber's work on emergent charismatic figures. Weberians and compatible anthropologists study religious change; they investigate how routinization, secularization, modernization, and related disenchantments proceed; they question whether particular religions are inimical to certain kinds of economic or political rationalization. Assumptions that modernization is inevitably accompanied by secularization have been shaken by evidence of purifying revivals (Protestant, Buddhist, Islamic, etc.) in societies where market forces and commercialization are intensifying, and by the place of religion in racial and ethnic self-assertions. All boundaries between modernities, postmodernities, and premodernities are being relentlessly questioned. One may recall that for Weber, capitalism (and so-called secularization) developed through a displacement of rationalized techniques from otherworldly monasticism into this-worldly routines. Reform movements and "enlightenments" may reflect less a defeat of the religious sector than the elimination of a distinction between otherworldly and in-worldly roles and institutions.

Some anthropologists question certain implications of both Durkheim and Weber, declaring any conjunction of "religion" and "church" (or churchlike entities) too "corporate" a notion, too tied to politics of legitimation. Like the Hegelian "state" (or its Marxist inversions) these constructions require contesting epistemologically in the manner of Foucault on dispersed "power" or Georges Bataille on radical "expenditure" (*dépense*). Some alternative approaches regard religious activity as a subversive strain of individuation or as a decentering or randomizing of values that appear to cohere because of ideological or political forces overlooked by scholars in search of cultural integration. Nevertheless, prominent bodies of work of the postwar generation of such anthropologists as Victor Turner, Claude Lévi-Strauss, Louis Dumont, Clifford Geertz, and Mary Douglas remain indebted to Durkheim and Weber in particular. A subsequent generation has drawn on Antonio Gramsci, Frantz Fanon, and other theorists who stress colonialist and postcolonialist contexts of history's "hegemonies" (Asad, 1993; Taussig, 1987; John and Jean. Comaroff, 1991/1997).

One favored prognosis of the mid-1960s has not materialized: a full-blown anthropological theory of religion, combining historical, psychological, sociological, and semantic or cultural dimensions. The interrelations, contradictions, and dissonance of data, contexts, events, and interpretive methods have multiplied to an extent that may impede any imaginable synthesis (unless in the name of neuroscience). What has emerged instead will be examined below. Some who once anticipated the unified approach deem the present "confusion" a crisis. Others, Geertz foremost among them, mindful of William James's "many original principles," find a pluralist profusion of issues and aims to be warranted by the complexity of religious realities that anthropology desires to illuminate.

Many recent works analyze religious experience as somehow dialectical. Others examine religious life as negotiated through arts of rhetoric or social tropes stressed by such literary theorists as Kenneth Burke. Some investigate religion by focusing on its language-like codes, continual reformulation, even when not caught up in the dynamic trends (e.g., millenarian and messianic movements, cargo cults), or revitalizations that punctuate religious history or a particular group's sense of that history. Just as tradition is now recognized as being continually reinvented, so convictions of timelessness are themselves created as a temporal process. Anthropologists, moreover, are increasingly attentive to dissent and hidden alternatives neglected when scholars take for granted divisions of peoples into "cultures" conceived of as consensual creeds. Circumstances once deemed degraded and therefore marginal to anthropology's central concerns—such as missionary efforts, competing brands of religious authority, covert cults, hybrid creeds (syncretism), and tourism—are being carefully inspected. Religious rivalry, blends, borrowings, and commercialization have shaped the historical and contemporary experience of much of the world's population, including tribespeople and traditional-seeming peoples. Anthropology now addresses radically commoditized spiritisms, multimedia fundamentalisms, religious observances as "show business," and high-tech modes of religious solidarity and schism (Hess, 1991; Harding, 2000; Fardon, 1995; Boon, 1999; Blank, 2001).

What could be called "religion on the move" need not be reactionary or compensatory. In his opus on Bwiti religion and other Fang cults in the Gabon Republic, James W. Fernandez discloses the capacity of an emergent religious culture "to create its own realities" (1982). He also warns against exaggerating the coherence of Bwiti cosmology—its practitioners' intellectual achievement is more subtle (p. 570). Such flexibility of cosmological categories is also demonstrated in Obeyesekere's work (1984) on Sri Lanka's cult of the goddess Pattini. He traces a changing pantheon over space and time, where shifting deities coordinate the specialized roles of priests, monks, and healers, and articulate factions within both Buddhism and Hinduism, between the two, and between Buddhism and Hinduism and outsiders. Obeyesekere elsewhere stresses convoluted connections among H. P. Blavatsky and Henry Steel Olcott's Theosophical Society, Rational Buddhism, and exportable schools of meditative discipline. Mark Juergensmeyer calls such formations "global religions," yet includes Roland Robertson's important caveat: "Antiglobal movements have inexorably become part of the globalization process itself" (Juergensmeyer, 2003, p. 115).

Plays of oppositions in religious identities resemble mythic fields of contrast in Hindu texts illuminated by Wendy Doniger O'Flaherty, whose early works in philology incorporated Lévi-Strauss's views on dialectical variations among neighboring myths and rituals. Studies that once delineated apparently stable cosmologies—such as the Dogon depicted by Marcel Griaule, or the Ngaju Dyaks depicted by Hans Schärer—are being reassessed to detect what led informants or their interrogators to attribute fixity to their categories. Although religion is not timeless, it can be made to seem so, whether by its devotees or by scholars keen on recapturing something original. Other research that contextualized and historicized religious cosmologies includes Alfonso Ortiz's studies of the Tewa Pueblo and Gerardo Reichel-Dolmatoff's works on the Amazonian Desána. In related developments, the adequacy of notions of belief, couched in pat generalizations such as "People *X* believe thus and so," have received serious critical scrutiny (Needham, 1972; Izard and Smith, 1982).

Advances in ethnographic knowledge of religion and ritual practice, coupled with consideration of the political and philosophical implications of both collecting and cataloging that knowledge, have continued in every region. Complexities in religious contexts and in power structures behind texts and ceremonies make anthropologists now wary of designating their studies "the religion of" any particular place. Such a title can seem too synthetic or overgeneralized, although works such as Geertz's influential *The Religion of Java* (1960) deal with political tensions, economic factions, and conflicting theodicies (in Weberian fashion) as much as they deal with religious integration.

Methodological Accommodations. Concern with religious transformations has renewed interest in many classic topics: rituals of sacrifice; nostalgia for lost pasts; memory and historical trauma (Holocaust, AIDS, terrorism); utopian visions; charismatic leaders, curers, and performers; life histories of individual practitioners; purity or pollution codes; trickster motifs; clowning and ritual inversions; witchcraft and sorcery; and left-hand and right-hand magic. Following the suggestions of Marcel Mauss, magic, freed from connotations of irrationality or error, becomes something like an enacted subjunctive mood, a "would that it were" outlined in special syllables and objects, a grammatical category "danced out" in speech and *materia.* Less corporate forms of worship and restriction, such as prayer, private taboos, chant and trance, hallucinogenic quests, religious techniques of the body, and meditation are being investigated either as evidence of deviation (allowable improvisations along culturally constrained lines) or as possibilities of free play that escape surveillance by local authority. Whatever else religion might involve across cultures, it entails speaking or silencing and sometimes writing; persuading, classifying, and acting out; arranging boundaries (periodically permeable), interrelating arts, and formulating logical and ethical codes; manipulating peers, rivals, inferiors, and superiors; possibly suffering, perhaps escaping, and negating as well as affirming. And all such practices may be less naïve or credulous than reflexive and rhetorical. Mauss's "magic," again, implies a "foreignness" at home to itself: "There are magical systems which are perfectly conscious of their diversity and refer to it with special words and metaphors" (1972, p. 60).

Anthropologists have thus adapted insights from sociolinguistics, philosophies of translation, literary theory, rhetoric, structuralism and post-structuralism, performance studies, folklore, political theory, gender analysis, and other areas to augment the generality and specificity, and sometimes the obscurity, of their descriptions and comparisons. Fruitful exchanges between anthropology and literary criticism may blur the boundaries of these pursuits. Marxism, psychoanalysis, semiotics, and deconstruction offer a larger sense of literature than did traditional canonical approaches. Such scholars as Raymond Williams, Julia Kristeva, Michel de Certeau, Tzvetan Todorov, Jonathan Culler, and followers of Walter Benjamin, Jacques Lacan, and Mikhail Bakhtin manage accommodations between theories of literary production and theories of culture. Models of "the text" advanced by Paul Ricoeur have helped change the way scholars look at ritual activity, manuals of religious practice, documents of historical conquest, and even the notion of culture itself. Just as texts are never read neutrally, cultures appear never to be crossed innocently, according to anthropologists who apply the metaphor of reading to what ethnographers do. Intricate properties of "literariness"—nonstop paradox, writing and its philosophical effacement, and continuous intertextuality—are disclosed in many cultural and religious usages, marked by trickster-like play between rules, their transgressions, and other subtle subversions, including profusive "abjection" (Bernstein, 1992). The documentation of cross-cultural encounters at the heart of anthropology may run parallel—stylistically as well as epistemologically—to the history of literary discourse, particularly the novel and genres of satire. Challenges to any positivistic sense of ethnography that downplays such parallels have multiplied in anthropological accounts of religion, aesthetic performance, and varieties of oral and written enactments.

Many methods and issues in the anthropology of religion have converged with scholarship in the history of popular religion, the sociology of marginal religions, and the analysis of systematic differences among orthodoxies, heterodoxies, and heresies. Historians of witchcraft, for example, now resemble anthropologists of the past; and anthropologists are less content with synchronic methods, even as heuristic devices. Ethnographers document not just Kwakiutl, Nuer, and Ndembu, but Quakers, Pentecostals (both Protestant and Catholic), Primitive Baptists, and televangelists. Structuralist techniques for analyzing oral mythologies are turned toward scripture; and approaches from biblical exegesis, typological analysis, and hermeneutics are now adapted by anthropologists to all kinds of cultures and "consumer rites" (Schmidt, 1995) wherever markets flourish. Accordingly, controversies grow "curiouser and curiouser."

Long-term directions of religious change have sometimes turned on the violent suppression of heterodoxies. Moreover, the modern anthropological record is distorted by colonialist and nationalist efforts to consolidate standardized, controllable creeds and confessions. Philological and ethnographic enterprises themselves can be in league with forces of centralization—a theme of many feminist and Marxist accounts; hence the growing concern with alternative forms of religious authority and leadership, often female-mediated ones. Researchers increasingly consider who profits and who suffers when thaumaturgical beliefs lapse. What are the consequences when new forms of knowledge compete with conventions that tie physical, psychic, and spiritual prosperity and well-being to concrete ritual practice in delicate balances of interlocking sympathies, risky equilibriums, sacred and dangerous affinities, and various periodic cycles? In Asia, Africa, the Americas, Oceania, and in Europe as well, many studies of peasantries, regional cultures, and commercial networks stress domestic rituals and local confessions resistant to one or another politico-religious hegemony. Examples include work on popular vestiges of European hermetism revealed by historian Frances A. Yates and on spiritism in both Europe and its colonies. Similarly, anthropologists studying South and Southeast Asia have accentuated spheres of sustained ritual, such as Tantrism, that serve as source-pools of symbols and practice used to set apart rival orthodoxies and competing sects over time (Boon, 1990).

After 1968, provocative works, such as Edward Said's influential *Orientalism* (1975), implicated comparative studies, including anthropology, with forces of colonialist oppression that continue in the contemporary organization of knowledge and power. Many cultures, religions, and ethnic groups—once scrutinized exclusively by ethnographers from the outside—now produce their own scholars or send select members abroad for anthropological training. Efforts to expand ethnological enfranchisement, to extend "voice" to the once silenced, and to reverse or overthrow interpreter/interpreted inequalities continue, controversially. Some commentators proclaim victory over an earlier anthropology's parasitism, a condition that benefited only the outside observer; others declare continuity with ethnography's traditional task of presenting marginalized peoples and inscribing, across cultures and languages, evidence of the unwritten (preliterate social life, ritual praxis, religious action, and heterodoxy). And subaltern and postcolonial theorists remain wary of lingering divisions into first-, second-, and third-world, where more agency seems to adhere to the first (and to "the West"), including the very style of theoretical critique here at stake.

The fact that areas once subjected to ethnography now often subject themselves to ethnography tends not to quell but to reinvigorate ideological disputes. Some national governments, averse to admitting foreign anthropologists (whose presence, they feel, implies "primitive" subjects) may nevertheless send scholars abroad for training and require them to return to perform research. Obstacles abound for "third-world" scholars who might wish to practice ethnography elsewhere than home, particularly if they desire gainful employment there. This power-saturated situation impedes realization of a fully comparative anthropology, especially in sensitive areas of religion often declared off limits. Home-grown ethnographers, of course, may be "outsiders" to the peasant, tribal, or minority populations they often study, even if they share language and ethnicity. Educated "natives" whose researches are sponsored by a dominant government will likely be regarded with as much suspicion (including class suspicion) as were the colonial agents or the foreign freelance fieldworkers of yore.

Finally, What Arjun Appadurai, James Fergusson, Emily Martin, and others call today's "flows"—virtual border-straddling in transnational sites and spaces—keep blurring distinctions among local, regional, and global connections and sharpening senses of diasporic identities, stateless persons, homeless circumstances, and "fluid" flexibilities of identity and property. Both before and since the attacks on the World Trade Center and the Pentagon on September 11, 2001, ever-expanding surveillance technologies threaten intrusion; even noble technical measures to protect subjects and respect human rights may impede the informality of encounter (and situational "trust") that the anthropology of religion may require, both ethnographically and theoretically.

Anthropological description and interpretation can only be seen as inherently political. Classic distinctions between foreign observers and observed natives of an area have assumed subtler guises; polities today internalize the division between knower and known. (Actually, certain forms of colonialism prefigured subtle polarities as well—Hannoum, 2001; Boon, 1990.)

Promising Approaches and Possible Futures. Recourses exist for anyone understandably daunted by the plethora of theories, methods, descriptions, and reevaluations of the discipline's findings and legitimacy. One might concentrate on a particular topic, such as death rites, restored to prominence by anthropologists, social historians, ethicists, and others. Research on mortuary practices may avoid drawbacks to defining religion in the abstract. What cultures do to and with their bodies before, during, and after funerals pertains to religious processes of continuity and schism, as relations among the living are rearticulated with reference to the dead (Bloch and Parry, 1982; Huntington and Metcalf, 1991; Panourgia, 1995; Lock, 2002).

Another recourse is to assess histories of representing and contesting religious identities in particular locales or regions or in global expanses. One might explore the burgeoning research on ritual values and contradictions in Papua New Guinea, where some areas were opened to sustained contact only after 1930 (Herdt, 1992; Knauft, 2002). Or one might examine a repeated restudied culture, such as Bali, Indonesia, with rival sectors of sacred authority in convoluted ties with the colonialist, nationalist, and transnationalist history of political and commercial forces in the region, including the military and tourism (Boon, 1990; Howe, 2001). One could track exploding coverage of anthropological approaches to Islam, noting interdisciplinary disputes about responsible treatment in ideologically charged circumstances (Geertz, 2003; Hammoudi, 1993; Bowen, 2002; Rosen, 2002).

Alternatively, one might consider complex projects by key interdisciplinary scholars. Examples include efforts by anthropologists to augment Georges Dumézil's views of the tripartite basis of Indo-European ideals of authority and continuity (Littleton, 1980), and ethnographic work extending R. Gordon Wasson's monumental endeavors on hallucinogenic rites involving fly agaric in both Asia and the New World (La Barre, 1970). Also compelling are efforts to consolidate approaches in religion, medical anthropology, science studies, and issues of alternative modernities and new technologies of subjectivity (by Arthur Kleinman, Byron Good, Veena Das, Nancy Scheper-Hughes, Thomas Csordas, and others), along with renewed attention to religion and the emotions (by Karl Heider, Umi Wikan, and others), including specific cultural and political circumstances of "religion against the self" (Nabokov, 1992). The lifeworks of certain figures—for example, Louis Dumont, Mary Douglas, Victor Turner, Clifford Geertz, and Stanley Tambiah—are themselves immense projects that keep anthropology and religious studies deeply intertwined. Dumont's contributions ranged over South Indian ethnography, the comparative study of hierarchy and reciprocity, and the sources of Western political economy. He set Hindu and European values into controversial juxtaposition and established terms of debates still raging (see Dirks, 2002) concerning notions of caste versus ideological individualism. Dumont's later work (1982) traces a Christian pedigree of so-called modernity (and of the West's own hierarchies) with a critical-comparative scope worthy of Weber—unusual in anthropology after functionalism (Boon, 1999).

Two trends deserve special emphasis. The first is neuroscientific studies, including resurgent interest in the neurophysiological parameters of religious "behavior" and the neuropsychological aspects of religious "cognition." Pascal Boyer's provocative titles—*The Naturalness of Religious Ideas* (1994), *Religion Explained* (2001)—have attracted attention to such pursuits. Certain "cognitive theory" (e.g., Konner, 2002) seeks biological constraints; it may seek to clarify phenomena of synesthesia (intersensory sensitivities prevalent in much religious, artistic, and poetic experience) by genetic mutations that create dense neural connections in supposedly specialized brains. Such work hopes to "explain" general and figurative experience (e.g., anyone's synesthesia) by the isolable and clinical (diagnostic "synesthetes"). Refined computerized methods are often advocated to resolve issues that may date back to the Culture and Personality school. This trend's more psychological side (represented by such scholars as Richard Schweder and Bradd Shore) emphasizes religious and cultural diversity along with evolutionary psychology; practitioners anticipate advancing inquiry into "the human mind" in ways foreshadowed by Gregory Bateson, who was intent on how biology and meaning might meet (if they can).

Biology-minded frameworks range from research on "the neurology of joy through brain-reward systems" (Diener and Suh, 2000) to the "affective neuroscience" of Jaak Panksepp. Culturally minded scholars (e.g., Roy D'Andrade, Tanya Luhrman) also recommend paying more than lip service to "bedrock commonalities" of cultures (meaning coevolved neurophysiology). Investigations in this mode speak of "religious acquisition," cognitive schemata, mental models, scripts, memory stores, and similar notions inspired by information theory wedded to ideas of "rationality" (Dan Sperber). Boyer's polemics reproach cultural relativists for shoving universals outside anthropology's proper subject matter; he likens them to chefs interested in differences in diet but not "in the way the gut works" (2001, p. 440). The science Boyer proposes would clarify "gut-workings" (to extend the metaphor) by devising "a different mode of data-gathering" including "constrained experimental studies" into religious symbolism as "rigorously cognitive" (1993, p 42). Again, earlier debates and long-term disciplinary divides are being revitalized, rather like a religious movement.

The second trend of note is the increased attention to reflexivity in interpretation and everyday practice alike. Excruciating self-consciousness about description and translation—fraught with epistemological and political doubts—stamps much contemporary work in anthropology and religion. Ample precedents exist in the scholarship of Bateson, Lévi-Strauss, Ruth Benedict, Clifford Geertz, and even Frazer, Durkheim, and William James (as suggested above). Feminist emphasis on gendered experience and representation has been crucial, along with the linguist turn and various rhetorical twists (Burke, Paul de Man, Richard Rorty) in theories and anti-theories (deconstructions) of interpretive life. Prominent critical writers—Judith Butler, Slavoj Zizek, Homi Bhabha, Henry Gates, and many more—champion awareness of all positionalities in any communicative act or deceptive dodge. Another important nexus of influence has been interdisciplinary historians of religion, such as Wendy Doniger O'Flaherty, Davíd Carrasco, Carolyn Bynum, Catherine Bell, and Bruce Lincoln.

Bell joins those anthropologists who regard ritual practice as itself theoretical and reflexive: a "semantic framework" whose very repetition is "not static, but repetition with a difference" (1992, p. 220). And Lincoln, like many ethnographers, considers "discursive formations" to be agentive rather than merely reactive. Concentrated reflexivity is manifest in Amy Hollywood's work on "sensible ecstasy" stressing "performativity, citationality, and ritualization" in so-called mystical practices; she combines insights from Butler's "Excitable Speech" with issues of "meta-indexicality" as advanced by anthropological linguist Benjamin Lee. This truly is high theory: intense and difficult.

Reflexivity rules in more anecdotal dimensions of anthropology and religion as well. A review article by Judy Rosenthal and Adam Lutzker ("The Unheimlich Manoeuvre," 2001) nicely indicates this transdisciplinary state of affairs. The piece stages a collaborative dialogue concerning three books about commercialized fundamentalism in U.S. religion and movements of apocalyptic violence internationally (Harding, 2000; Hall et al., 2000; Crapanzano, 2000). Conflicted stances of the authors toward their subjects is matched by ambivalence and anxiety of the reviewers—one is a former member of Jehovah's Witnesses turned superb ethnographer of West African vodou; the other is a "secular leftist" worried about complicitous "dogmatism within the secular project." Attuned, then, equally to "Vodou literalism" and Jerry Falwell's literalism, the reviewers are wary of both secularisms and fundamentalisms. They expect unremitting reflexivity from all concerned, including themselves: "Because I criticize Crapanzano for not putting his subject position in question, it is only fair to put mine on the line" (p. 921).

This passionate review, critically focused on various literalisms, may well pertain to the neuroscientific projects mentioned above, which themselves suggest a resurgent "literalism" in emergent theoretical persuasion. Regardless, taken together, the two trends—neuroscience, intent on "hardwired" universals; and reflexivity, which construes so-called "science" otherwise—confirm that the anthropology of religion remains diverse, possibly boundless, and agonistic. As the discipline (or antidiscipline) strives to become ever more inclusive, it remains devoted to understanding religious differences. Earlier aspirations to contain any culture's "belief" in an ethnographic monograph have faded away. Nor can fieldwork results be insulated from vast issues in phenomenological, existential, hermeneutic, pragmatist, structuralist, deconstructive, politicized, "scientized," or "humanized" study of religious practice and commentary. Bold ideas in the comparative history of religions must heed actual contradictions—what Edmund Leach once termed the "dialectics of practical religion"—lived out in religious hinterlands, beyond the margins of rival orthodoxies, and in religious centers as well.

The anthropology of religion thus inhabits our difficult age—whether we consider it postmodern, new millennial, increasingly terrorist, globalist, or neo-imperial. For such interpretive pursuits in such times, there is nowhere left to hide. What Clifford Geertz has called "The World in Pieces" (2000, p. 218) pertains even to the pieces themselves: the pieces (including religions) are in pieces. As William James foresaw in his postscript to *The Varieties of Religious Experience*, a sort of polytheism has, in truth, returned upon us—and keeps returning, possibly endlessly, possibly not.

See Also Consciousness, States of; Culture; Evolution, article on Evolutionism; Psychology, article on Psychology of Religion; Shamanism; Sociology, article on Sociology of Religion; Structuralism; Study of Religion.

Bibliography

Asad, Talal. *Genealogies of Religion: Discipline and Reasons of Power in Christianity and Islam.* Baltimore, 1993.

Asad, Talal. *Formations of the Secular: Christianity, Islam, Modernity.* Stanford, Calif., 2003.

Bataille, Georges. *Theory of Religion.* Translated by Robert Hurley. New York, 1989.

Bauman, Richard. *Let Your Words Be Few: Symbolism of Speaking and Silence among Seventeenth-Century Quakers.* Cambridge, UK, 1983. A study of ritual and restraint that approaches from folklore, sociolinguistics, and social interaction.

Bell, Catherine. *Ritual Theory, Ritual Practice.* Oxford, 1992.

Bernstein, Michael A. *Bitter Carnival: Ressentiment and the Abject Hero.* Princeton, 1992.

Blank, Jonah. *Mullahs on the Mainframe: Islam and Modernity among the Duadi Bohras.* Chicago, 2001.

Bloch, Maurice, and Jonathan Parry, eds. *Death and the Regeneration of Life.* Cambridge, UK, 1982. A wide-ranging collection that responds to works by Jack Goody, Edmund Leach, Mary Douglas, and many others.

Boon, James A. *Other Tribes, Other Scribes: Symbolic Anthropology in the Comparative Study of Cultures, Histories, Religions, and Texts.* Cambridge, UK, 1982. Interrelates the anthropology of religion, semiotics and literature, and the history of ideas and institutions.

Boon, James A. *Affinities and Extremes: Crisscrossing the Bittersweet Ethnology of East Indies History, Hindu-Balinese Culture, and Indo-European Allure.* Chicago, 1990.

Boon, James A. *Verging on Extra-Vagance: Anthropology, History, Religion, Literature, Arts. . .Showbiz.* Princeton, 1999.

Bowen, John R. *Muslims through Discourse: Religion and Ritual in Gayo Society.* Princeton, 1993.

Bowen, John R. *Religions in Practice: An Approach to the Anthropology of Religion.* 2d ed. Boston, 2002.

Boyer, Pascal. *The Naturalness of Religious Ideas: A Cognitive Theory of Religion.* Berkeley, 1994.

Boyer, Pascal. *Religion Explained: The Evolutionary Origins of Religious Thought.* New York, 2001.

Boyer, Pascal, ed. *Cognitive Aspects of Religious Symbolism.* Cambridge, UK, 1993.

Comaroff, John L., and Jean Comaroff. *Of Revelation and Revolution.* 2 vols. Chicago, 1991/1997.

Crapanzano, Vincent. *Serving the Word: Literalism in America from the Pulpit to the Bench.* New York, 2000.

Csordas, Thomas J. *Language, Charisma, and Creativity: The Ritual Life of a Religious Movement.* Berkeley, 1997.

Diener, Ed, and Eunkook Suh. *Culture and Subjective Well-Being.* Cambridge, Mass., 2000.

Dirks, Nicholas B. *Castes of Mind: Colonialism and the Making of Modern India.* Princeton, 2001.

Dumont, Louis. *Homo Hierarchicus: The Caste System and its Implications.* Rev. ed. Translated by Mark Sainsbury, Louis Dumont, and Basia Gulati. Chicago, 1980.

Dumont, Louis. "A Modified View of Our Origins: The Christian Beginnings of Modern Individualism." *Religion* 12 (1982): 1–27.

Eliade, Mircea. *The Forge and the Crucible.* 2d ed. Chicago, 1978. A comparative survey of alchemical and hermetic constructions and related heterodoxies, with appendices on Jung, Frances A. Yates, and others.

Evans-Pritchard, E. E. *Theories of Primitive Religion.* Oxford, 1965.

Fabian, Johannes. "Six Theses Regarding the Anthropology of African Religious Movements." *Religion* 11 (1981): 109–126. Challenges orthodox assumptions about the confines of religion. Studies by Fabian, T. O. Beidelman, Ivan Karp, and others have rethought African "systems of thought" and religion.

Fardon, Richard. *Counterworks: Managing the Diversity of Knowledges.* London, 1995.

Feldman, Burton, and Robert D. Richardson. *The Rise of Modern Mythology, 1680–1860.* Bloomington, Ind., 1972.

Fernandez, James W. *Bwiti: An Ethnography of the Religious Imagination in Africa.* Princeton, 1982.

Fraser, Robert. *The Making of the Golden Bough: The Origins and Growth of an Argument.* New York, 1990.

Geertz, Clifford. "Religion: Anthropological Study." In *International Encyclopedia of the Social Sciences,* edited by David Sills, vol. 13. New York, 1968.

Geertz, Clifford. "Religion as a Cultural System." In *The Interpretation of Cultures: Selected Essays.* New York, 1973. Extraordinarily influential work.

Geertz, Clifford. *Available Light: Anthropological Reflections on Philosophical Topics.* Princeton, 2000.

Geertz, Clifford. "Which Way to Mecca?" *New York Review of Books* 17 (July 3, 2003).

Hall, John R., with Philip D. Schuyler and Sylvaine Trinh. *Apocalypse Observed: Religious Movements and Violence in North America, Europe, and Japan.* London, 2000.

Hammoudi, Abdellah. *The Victim and Its Masks: An Essay on Sacrifice and Masquerade in the Maghreb.* Chicago, 1993.

Hannoum, Abdelmajid. *Colonial Histories, Post-Colonial Memories: The Legend of the Kahina, a North African Heroine.* Portsmouth, N.H., 2001.

Harding, Susan Friend. *The Book of Jerry Falwell: Fundamentalist Language and Politics.* Princeton, 2000.

Hefner, Robert W. *Conversion to Christianity: Historical and Anthropological Perspective on a Great Transformation.* Berkeley, 1993.

Herdt, Gilbert, ed. *Ritualized Homosexuality in Melanesia.* Rev. ed. Berkeley, 1992.

Hess, David J. *Spirits and Scientists: Ideology, Spiritism, and Brazilian Culture.* University Park, Pa., 1991.

Howe, Leo. *Hinduism and Hierarchy in Bali.* Santa Fe, N.Mex., 2001.

Huntington, Richard, and Peter Metcalf. *Celebrations of Death: The Anthropology of Mortuary Ritual.* 2d ed. Cambridge, UK, 1991. Accessibly reviews ideas of Robert Hertz, Arnold van Gennep, Victor Turner, Clifford Geertz, and others; cases from Indonesia, Madagascar, European history, and the modern United States.

Hyde, Lewis. *The Gift: Imagination and the Erotic Life of Property.* New York, 1983. Consolidates Mauss's theories of magic and exchange with a poetics of creativity.

Izard, Michel, and Pierre Smith, eds. *Between Belief and Transgression: Structuralist Essays in Religion, History, and Myth.* Translated by John Leavitt. Chicago, 1982. Relates the anthropology of religion to Lévi-Strauss's studies of kinship and myth and to studies of classic Greek myth by Jean-Pierre Vernant, Marcel Detienne, and others.

Juergensmeyer, Mark, ed. *Global Religions: An Introduction.* Oxford, 2003.

Kakar, Sudhir. *Shamans, Mystics, and Doctors: A Psychological Inquiry into India and Its Healing Traditions.* New York, 1982.

Keane, A. H. "Ethnology." In *Encyclopaedia of Religion and Ethics,* vol. 5, edited by James Hastings with John A. Selbie et al. Edinburgh and New York, 1912.

Keyes, Charles F., and E. Valentine Daniel. *Karma: An Anthropological Inquiry.* Berkeley, 1983. The articles coordinate issues in the anthropology of religion, the history of religions, and philology.

Knauft, Bruce M. *Exchanging the Past: A Rainforest World of Before and After.* Chicago, 2002.

Konner, Melvin. *The Tangled Wing: Biological Constraints on the Human Spirit.* 2d ed. New York, 2002.

La Barre, Weston. "Review of *Soma: Divine Mushroom of Immortality*" by R. Gordon Wasson. *American Anthropologist* 72 (1970): 368–373.

Lambek, Michael, ed. *A Reader in the Anthropology of Religion.* Malden, Mass., 2002.

Lessa, William A., and Evon Z. Vogt, eds. *Reader in Comparative Religion: An Anthropological Approach.* 4th ed. New York, 1979.

Lévi-Strauss, Claude. *Totemism.* Translated by Rodney Needham. Boston, 1963. An impeccable rethinking of totemism—always "so-called."

Littleton, C. Scott. *The New Comparative Mythology: An Anthropological Assessment of the Theories of Georges Dumézil.* 3d ed. Berkeley, 1980.

Lock, Margaret. *Twice Dead: Organ Transplants and the Reinvention of Death.* Berkeley, 2002.

Lukes, Steven. *Émile Durkheim, His Life and Work: A Historical and Critical Study.* London, 1973.

Lutzker, Adam, and Judy Rosenthal. "The Unheimlich Manoeuvre." *American Ethnologist* 28, no. 4 (2001): 507–523.

Marett, R. R. "Primitive Religion." In *Encyclopaedia Britannica: A Dictionary of Arts, Sciences, Literature, and General Information,* vol. 23. Cambridge, UK, and New York, 1911.

Mauss, Marcel. *A General Theory of Magic.* Translated by Robert Brain. New York, 1972.

Murphy, Robert F. *Robert H. Lowie.* New York, 1972.

Nabokov, Isabelle. *Religion against the Self.* New York, 2000.

Needham, Rodney. *Belief, Language, and Experience.* Chicago, 1972.

Obeyesekere, Gananath. *The Cult of the Goddess Pattini.* Chicago, 1984. An ethnographic and historical study addressing the sociology and psychology of religion.

Obeyesekere, Gananath. *Imagining Karma: Ethical Transformation in Amerindian, Buddhist, and Greek Rebirth.* Berkeley, 2002.

O'Keefe, Daniel Lawrence. *Stolen Lightning: The Social Theory of Magic.* New York, 1982. An exhaustive survey, studiously positivistic, of every conceivable hypothesis purporting to explain magic, religion, and the occult.

Panourgia, Neni. *Fragments of Death, Fables of Identity: An Athenian Anthropography.* Madison, Wis., 1995.

Peacock, James L., and A. Thomas Kirsch. *The Human Direction: An Evolutionary Approach to Social and Cultural Anthropology.* 3d ed. Englewood Cliffs, N.J., 1980.

Peacock, James L., and Ruel W. Tyson Jr. *Pilgrims of Paradox: Calvinism and Experience among the Primitive Baptists of the Blue Ridge.* Washington, D.C., 1989.

Rappaport, Roy A. *Ritual and Religion in the Making of Humanity.* Cambridge, UK, 1999.

Rosen, Lawrence. *The Justice of Islam.* New York, 2000.

Schmidt, Leigh E. *Consumer Rites: The Buying and Selling of American Holidays.* Princeton, 1995.

Spiro, Melford E. "Religion: Problems of Definition and Explanation." In *Anthropological Approaches to the Study of Religion,* edited by Michael P. Banton, pp. 85–125. New York, 1966.

Stocking, George W., Jr. *Victorian Anthropology.* New York, 1987.

Taussig, Michael. *Shamanism, Colonialism, and the Wild Man: A Study in Terror and Healing.* Chicago, 1987.

Taussig, Michael T. *The Magic of the State.* New York, 1997.

Turner, Victor. *Dramas, Fields, and Metaphors: Symbolic Action in Human Society.* Ithaca, N.Y., 1974. A pivotal collection bridging Turner's Ndembu ethnography and his comparative work in performance.

Wallace, Alfred Russel. *Natural Selection and Tropical Nature: Essays on Descriptive and Theoretical Biology.* New ed. with corrections and additions. New York, 1891.

West, Michael. *Transcendental Wordplay: America's Romantic Punsters and the Search for the Language of Nature.* Athens, Ohio, 2000.

Wittgenstein, Ludwig. *Remarks on Frazer's Golden Bough.* Edited and revised by Rush Rhees and translated by A. C. Miles. Retford, U.K., 1979.

JAMES A. BOON (1987 AND 2005)

ANTHROPOMORPHISM, from the Greek *anthrōpos* ("human being") and *morphē* ("form"), is a modern term, attested since the eighteenth century, denoting the practically universal tendency to form religious concepts and ideas and, on a more basic level, to experience the divine, or the "numinous" (the term is used here as a convenient shorthand, without necessarily implying commitment to Rudolf Otto's theories), in the categories and shapes most readily available to human thinking—namely, the human ones. The idea has a long history in Western thought. Ancient Greek, including patristic, literature referred (contemptuously) to "anthropomorphites," meaning people holding anthropomorphic ideas of the divine. This term was also used in Latin by Augustine to refer to those who because of their "carnal thought imagine God in the image of corruptible man" (*Patrologia Latina* 42.39), and, under his influence, it continued to be used by authors as late as Leibniz in the seventeenth century.

DEFINITIONS AND DISTINCTIONS. In a more general sense, anthropomorphism can be defined as the description of nonmaterial, "spiritual" entities in physical, and specifically human, form. The idea of human form is an essential part of the definition, since otherwise one would have to deal with representations and manifestations of the divine in all possible material forms. Of course, sharp distinctions are often arbitrary and even misleading, especially since in many religious cultures, the gods often assume, both in mythology and in iconography, animal form (which is, strictly speaking, theriomorphism); mixed, hybrid, semianimal-semihuman form (which is, strictly speaking, therianthropism); or "unrealistic," wildly imaginative, or even grotesque forms. Deities may be conceived as wholly or partly animal, as were Hathor and Anubis, the cow goddess and jackal god in ancient Egyptian religion, or they may have animal *avatāras,* as does Viṣṇu, who appears as fish, tortoise, man-lion, and boar. Gods and goddesses may have multiple heads or arms, as does Brahma; goddesses may be many-breasted, as was the great goddess of Ephesus (Artemis); or they may be represented with ferociously "demonic" forms of face or figure and with nonnatural combinations of body parts, as are androgynes and some tricksters. Indian and ancient Egyptian religions, among others, provide a plethora of examples. Resorting once more to Otto's terminology, one could argue that it is precisely the nonhuman quality of theriomorphic or therianthropic representations that enables them to function as symbols of the numinous as the "wholly other."

While the phenomenon of anthropomorphism proper has been a central problem in the history of religions, theology, and religious philosophy (in terms of criticism of religion as well as of religion's internal struggles for a better self-understanding of its own symbolism), the transition from theriomorphism to anthropomorphism (according to the evolutionary view current until some decades ago) has often been viewed as marking a definite progress. Thus Hegel, in *Lectures on the Philosophy of History,* praised Greek religion because its anthropomorphism signified that "man, as that which is truly spiritual, constitutes that which is genuinely true in the Greek gods." Elsewhere, in *Lectures on Aesthetics,* Hegel adds that Christianity is superior to Greek religion because it has taken anthropomorphism a decisive step farther: God is not merely the humanly shaped ideal of beauty and art but a "real, singular, individual, wholly God and wholly man, that has entered into the totality of the conditions of existence." This stands in marked contrast to the views of the German poet Schiller (1759–1805), who considered Christianity as inferior to Greek religion: "When the gods were more human, men were more divine" (The Gods of Greece). One hardly need add that in medieval polemics both Islam and Judaism condemned Christianity not only for its "polytheism" (meaning the doctrine of the Trinity) but also for its anthropomorphism.

A distinction is frequently made between physical anthropomorphism (anthropomorphism proper) and mental or psychological anthropomorphism, also called anthropopathism (i.e., not human form or shape but human feelings: love, hate, desire, anger, etc.). Thus, while there are only faint traces of anthropomorphism proper in the Hebrew scriptures (Old Testament), God is described as loving, taking pity, forgiving, being angry and wroth (at sinners and evildoers), and avenging himself upon his enemies. Even when theological thinking progressively divests the deity of the "cruder" forms of physical and mental anthropomorphism, some irreducible elements remain. For example, certain types of theology of history (*Heilsgeschichte*) imply that God "has a plan" for his creation or for humankind. In fact, religion is often expressed in terms of humanity's duty to serve the achievement of this divine plan and purpose. The ultimate residual anthropomorphism, however, is the theistic notion of God as personal, in contrast to an impersonal conception of the divine. Also, verbal imagery, no matter how metaphorical it is supposed to be, preserves this basic anthropomorphism: God is father, mother, lover, king, shepherd, judge. Verbal and iconic imagery can be very different things even when both are anthropomorphic. Thus Buddhism is an essentially metaphysical religion, yet Buddhist temples (Theravada no less than Mahayana) can be full to the bursting point with anthropomorphic images. Shinto mythology, on the other hand, is as anthropomorphic as can be, but a Shinto shrine (at least if uncontaminated by Buddhist influence) is as empty of statues and images as a mosque or a synagogue.

Another important distinction has to be made between what may be called primary and secondary anthropomorphism. The former reflects a simple, naive, uncritical (or precritical) level of immediate, concrete, "massive," and mythological imagination. The latter is more dogmatic and deliberate. It is fundamentalist in the sense that anthropomorphic assertions are made and defended not because they reflect the immediate level of religious consciousness but because they reflect a dogmatic position: holy scriptures or canonical traditions use anthropological language, hence this language has to be literally accepted and believed in. Many discussions in the history of Muslim theology have to be seen in the light of this distinction.

Theological and Philosophical Implications. A survey of all the instances of anthropomorphism in the world's religions would be tantamount to a survey of the mythologies and religious iconography of the world. This article will be limited to a brief review of the theological and philosophical implications of anthropomorphism, and even these will be surveyed mainly in the history of Western thought, not because analogous developments are lacking elsewhere, but because in the history of Western thought the problem has been dealt with more systematically and consistently. Western religious history also exhibits a very interesting special case, namely Christianity (cf. the dictum of Hegel cited above), since Christ is considered as more than just another divine *avatāra,* or manifestation, and hence the doctrine of the incarnation poses the problem of anthropology in its widest sense—that is, the doctrine of the nature of man and its relation to the divine—and in a very special way. But even aside from incarnation, the "personalist" element in theistic religion remains, as has been seen, an irreducible anthropomorphism. This situation was well defined by the German Old Testament scholar and theologian Bernhard Duhm when he said that the real problem for biblical religion was how to get rid not of anthropomorphism but "physiomorphism" in its representation of God.

Most religions start with straightforward and naive anthropomorphic ideas of the divine (gods, goddesses) and even in their more highly developed stages do not greatly mind that the simple folk maintain their "primitive" ideas, although the spiritual élite may consider anthropological imagery crude and substitute for it a more sophisticated language. Physical and anthropomorphic imagery is then explained (or explained away) as a symbolic reference to certain qualities of the divine that, in their turn, may later have to be further transcended by an even more spiritual understanding.

Anthropomorphism and the Criticism of Religion. The expression "criticism of religion" has to be understood on several levels. It need not necessarily be atheistic or irreligious. The expression merely signifies that religious representations and statements (whether primitive, popular, traditional, or otherwise normative) are criticized because of their allegedly crude and, at times, immoral character. This criticism can come from the outside—from philosophy, for example—or from inside—that is, when religious consciousness becomes more sophisticated, refined, and self-critical (often under the impact of philosophy from outside). Among the earliest and best-known examples of this tendency is the Greek author Xenophanes (fifth century BCE), of whose writings only fragments have been preserved. He ironically notes that Ethiopians represent the gods as black, Thracians depict them as blue-eyed and red-haired, and "if oxen and horses . . . had hands and could paint," their images of gods would depict oxen and horses. Xenophanes thus anticipates the modern atheistic inversion of the Old Testament account of creation, to the effect that men create gods in their own image. He also attacks anthropopathism: "Homer and Hesiod attribute to the gods what among men would be considered reprehensible: stealing, adultery, and deceit." Yet Xenophanes was far from irreligious. He speaks of one God "who neither in shape . . . nor in thought" resembles anything human. He has no eyes and no ears, but himself is "wholly eye, wholly spirit, wholly ear."

Plato, too, objects to the all too human conception of the gods. For this reason he would also ban traditional Homeric mythology from his ideal republic, "no matter whether [these stories have] a hidden sense or not" (*Republic* 377–378). But the fact that Plato mentions the possibility of a hidden sense indicates one of the roads that religious thinking and apologetic would take in response to the critical challenge. This critical challenge, it must be reiterated, is not antireligious; it is, rather, a religious trend toward self-purification by purging itself of elements considered to be primitive and crude. The same tendency is in evidence in many parts of the Old Testament, and not only in the second of the Ten Commandments. It gathers strength, under the influence of Hellenistic philosophy, in, for example, the Targums (the Aramaic translations of the Old Testament), which, in their wish to eliminate all anthropomorphism, substitute for Hebrew phrases meaning "and God appeared unto," "God spoke," "God saw," "the hand of God," and so on such alternative phrases as "the glory of God appeared," "the power of God," and the like.

This "first purgation," however, does not solve the problem of mental anthropomorphism. When the sixteenth-century French essayist Montaigne wrote that "we may use words like Power, Truth, Justice, but we cannot conceive the thing itself. . . . None of our qualities can be attributed to the Divine Being without tainting it with our imperfection" (*Essais* 2.12), he merely summed up what Muslim, Jewish, and Christian philosophers had already discussed in the Middle Ages. Their problem, like Montaigne's, was not the objectionable character of physical and of certain moral attributes, but the admissibility of attributes as such. The great twelfth-century Jewish philosopher Moses Maimonides (Mosheh ben Maimon), like the Muslim philosophers who had preceded him, taught with uncompromising radicalism that no positive attributes whatever can be predicated of God. It should come as no surprise that most of the efforts of Maimonides, who besides being a great philosopher was also a leading rabbinic authority, should be devoted to explaining away the many anthropomorphisms in the Bible. Once one embarks on this radical road, the next question becomes inevitable: is not "being" or "existence" also a human concept, and is not the definition of God as pure or absolute being also an anthropromorphism, although perhaps a very rarefied one?

Two main tendencies can be distinguished in response to this challenge. The one leads to a cessation of speech ("mystical silence"); the other to a more sophisticated theology based on an analysis of human consciousness.

MYSTICISM. The most radical method that religious consciousness can adopt to purge itself of anthropomorphism is the assertion that no adequate statements about the divine are possible in human language. In the West this tradition goes back to the Neoplatonic mystical theologian known as Dionysius the Areopagite (fifth century CE), who introduced into Christian terminology the "hidden godhead" and the "divine darkness." This tradition was transmitted to the Latin West by John Scottus Eriugena (ninth century CE), from whom it passed to Eckhart and the Rhineland mystics and to such English figures as Walter Hilton and the author of *The Cloud of Unknowing,* and influenced later mystics (Jakob Boehme, Angelus Silesius) and even nonmystical, "mainline" theologians. Thomas Aquinas gave a place in his system to this *theologia negativa,* and Martin Luther thought highly of the mystical tract known as the *Theologia Deutsch.*

The challenge of anthropomorphism, or to be more precise, the critical reflection as to how to meet this challenge, thus turns out to be an important factor in the development of mysticism. But this radical mystical "purging" of language ultimately links up with agnostic and even nonreligious criticism. The central text in this respect is David Hume's *Dialogues concerning Natural Religion* (1779), written in the form of a conversation between three interlocutors: a skeptic, a Christian close to the mystical tradition, and a theist. The Christian mystic asserts that the divine essence, attributes, and manner of existence are a mystery to humans. The skeptic agrees, but admits the legitimacy of anthropological attributes (wisdom, thought, intention), because human beings simply do not have at their disposal any other form of expression. He merely warns against the mistake of assuming any similarity between one's words and the divine qualities. In other words, the mystical and the skeptical, even agnostic, criticisms of anthropomorphism tend to converge. The theist speaker is not slow to seize on this point. His theism is of a more sophisticated kind; it has absorbed and integrated the anti-anthropomorphic critique. But if all ideas about the divine are by definition totally incorrect and misleading, then religion and theology necessarily and automatically cease to be of any interest whatever. A spiritual being of which nothing can be predicated (no will, no emotion, no love) is, in actual fact, no spirit at all. Hume's argument that mysticism (including pantheism) and atheism ultimately converge has had far-reaching influence. Nineteenth-century philosophical atheism took up Hume's argument and used the critique of anthropomorphism as well as the dead end to which it leads as leverage for the shift from theology to anthropology: the essence of God is, in fact, nothing but one's projection, on a celestial screen, of the essence of human. Thus concluded, for example, Ludwig Feuerbach (1804–1872).

OTHER ATTITUDES TOWARD ANTHROPOMORPHISM. Aside from mysticism, Christian thought has responded in two ways to criticisms of anthropomorphism. The traditional, standard form of theistic theology tries on the one hand to purge from religion the kind of anthropomorphism that invites facile criticism and strives on the other hand to avoid the kind of radical "purging" that leads either to mystical silence or to atheism. The alternative is to speak of God, unapologetically and with a certain robust courage, knowing full well that such speech is valid "by analogy" only. The subject is one of the most complex in the history of theology. For the purpose of this article, it must suffice to point to the existence of this middle way, without going into technical details or analyzing the different types of "theology of analogy": analogy of attribution, mainly known in the form of "analogy of being" (*analogia entis*), a central concept in official Roman Catholic theology; analogy of proportionality; analogy of faith (opposed by the Protestant theologian Karl Barth to the Roman Catholic concept of *analogia entis*); analogy of relation; and so on. The theology of analogy uses a distinction made by the Muslim Aristotelian philospher Ibn Rushd (Averroës) between univocal, equivocal, and analogous predication. The former two were rejected by the Fourth Lateran Council (1215) of the Roman Catholic church, which espoused "analogy."

Another, and typically modern, method of evading the problem of anthropomorphism is the view that holds all religious statements to be statements about one's religious consciousness. The father of this theory, in the history of Western thought, is the nineteenth-century German Protestant theologian Friedrich Schleiermacher. In the last resort, this view, too, represents a shift from theology to anthropology (as Feuerbach was quick to point out), with the difference that for Schleiermacher this shift serves religious understanding, whereas for Feuerbach it serves the radical critique of religion as such. Schleiermacher's insights are still operative in Rudolf Bultmann's program of "demythologizing" the gospel. According to Bultmann, all statements about God's concrete acts should be interpreted "existentially," except the notion of God acting (i.e., his saving intervention in human existence). The non-Bultmannian will, of course, ask why one should stop short at this particular anthropomorphism. This theology of religious consciousness has been condemned as heretical by both the Roman Catholic church (see the papal encyclical *Pascendi,* 1907) and Protestant orthodoxy (e.g., Karl Barth).

CONCLUSION. This article, although it focuses on the history of Western thought, is intended to give a coherent picture of the kind of problems generated by anthropomorphism. Similar phenomena, though less systematically elaborated, can be found in other religious traditions, for example, in the Vedantic impersonalist conception of the Absolute, which considers personalist theism and *bhakti* devotion as a lower form of religion. Mahāyāna Buddhism possesses a highly developed anthropomorphic and semianthropomorphic pantheon, but these figures are symbolic images to be transcended on the higher levels of meditation. Altogether, Eastern religions make greater allowance for differences in the levels of religious understanding between different kinds and conditions of humans. Some medieval Muslim theologians too advocated the (near-heretical) doctrine of "double truth," reminiscent of the Indian distinction between samvrti (conventional truth) and paramartha satya (absolute truth). Similarly, a more simple language and imagery, adapted to the capacities of the less mature and less advanced, is justified by Buddhists as *upāya* ("skillful means" for teaching the truth). Even Zen Buddhists in their daily practice worship statues of Buddhas and *bodhisattvas,* although theoretically they aspire to absolute nothingness and are taught to "kill the Buddha" if they encounter him as an obstacle on the way. A Hindu analogy would be the distinction between saguna and nirguna (i.e., the "qualified" versus the "unqualified" Absolute). The Upaniṣadic neti, neti, or Nāgārjuna's "eightfold negation" could be adduced as Indian instances of a "negative theology." The religious, as distinct from the philosophical, problem could be summarized in the simple question: Can one pray to a nonanthropomorphic deity?

SEE ALSO Animals; Therianthropism.

BIBLIOGRAPHY

Jevons, Frank B. "Anthropomorphism." In *Encyclopaedia of Religion and Ethics,* edited by James Hastings, vol. 1. Edinburgh, 1908.

Jevons, Frank B. "Anthropomorphismus." In *Reallexikon für Antike und Christentum,* vol. 1. Stuttgart, 1950.

Leeuw, Gerardus van der. *Religion in Essence and Manifestation* (1938). 2 vols. Gloucester, Mass., 1967. See the index, s. v. *Anthropomorphism.*

Zimmer, Heinrich. *Myths and Symbols in Indian Art and Civilization.* Edited by Joseph Campbell. New York, 1946.

For articles related to anthropomorphism in Islam, see "Tashbih" and "Muʿtazila" in *The Encyclopaedia of Islam* (Leiden, 1913–1938) and "Hashwiyya," "Karramiyya," "Ibn Hazm," and "Ibn Tamiyya" in *The Encyclopaedia of Islam,* new ed. (Leiden, 1960–).

New Sources

Barnhart, Joe E. "Anthropomorphism." In *Modern Spiritualities: An Inquiry,* edited by Laurence Brown, Bernard C. Farr, and R. Joseph Hoffmann. pp. 171–178. Amherst, N.Y., 1997.

Bekoff, Marc. "The Evolution of Animal Play, Emotions, and Social Morality: On Science, Theology, Spirituality, Personhood, and Love." *Zygon* 36, no. 4 (2001): 615–655.

Ferré, Frederick. "In Praise of Anthropomorphism." *International Journal for Philosophy of Religion* 16 no. 3, (1984): 203–212.

Guthrie, Stewart Elliott. *Faces in the Clouds: A New Theory of Religion.* New York, 1993.

Insole, Christopher J. "Anthropomorphism and the Apophatic God." *Modern Theology* 17, no. 4 (2001): 475–483.

Schoen, Edward L. "Anthropomorphic Concepts of God." *Religious Studies* 26 (1990): 123–139.

Yonan, Edward A. "Religion as Anthropomorphism: A New Theory that Invites Definitional and Epistemic Scrutiny." *Religion* 25 (1995): 31–34.

R. J. Zwi Werblowsky (1987)
Revised Bibliography

ANTHROPOSOPHY ("knowledge of the human being" or "human wisdom"), is the name that Rudolf Steiner (1861–1925), the Austrian philosopher-educator-esotericist, gave to his teachings and to the spiritual practice he recommended as an antidote to modern Western materialistic consciousness. Steiner also referred to his teaching as spiritual science, signaling what he considered to be the empirical character of his research concerning the spiritual world. As a spiritual movement, primarily Western but intended for all of humanity, anthroposophy is continuous with the Rosicrucian stream of the Christian esoteric tradition.

Early History and Teachings. In 1902 Steiner assumed the position of leader of the Berlin lodge of the Theosophical Society, but the centrality of Christ in his teachings, in contrast to the theosophical emphasis on Hindu and Buddhist spiritual teachers, made it inevitable that he eventually would feel the need to separate from that society, which he did in 1912. Steiner's followers, most of whom had been members of the Theosophical Society, followed Steiner when he broke with Annie Besant (then president of the society) and founded the Anthroposophical Society in 1912. Although both Rudolf Steiner and anthroposophy can be seen to have evolved from the Theosophical Society, especially if one compares the writings of H. P. Blavatsky with the early esoteric writings of Steiner (e.g., *An Outline of Esoteric Science* of 1909), it is more accurate to say that anthroposophy is continuous with the entire Western esoteric tradition, especially the esoteric teachings of Egypt, Greece, Johannine Christianity, and Rosicrucianism.

Steiner's most succinct characterization of anthroposophy appears in the opening paragraphs of *Anthroposophical Leading Thoughts*, which he wrote in 1924, during the last months of his life:

1. Anthroposophy is a path of knowing (thinking) to guide the spiritual in the human being to the spiritual in the universe. It arises as a need of the heart, of the life of feeling; and it can be justified only inasmuch as it can satisfy this inner need.
2. Anthroposophy is communicated knowledge that is gained in a spiritual way. For at the very frontier where the knowledge derived from sense-perception ceases, there is opened through the human soul itself the further outlook into the spiritual world. (Steiner, 1973, p. 13)

From his first systematic work, *The Philosophy of Freedom* (1984), until his last writings and lectures in 1924 Steiner sought to exemplify, and to enable others to attain, spiritual, or sense-free, knowledge. Anthroposophy may be understood as the discipline of seeing the inner, or spiritual, core of every reality, even realities that seem to be grossly material. Although it ordinarily is understood as a teaching, anthroposophy is essentially a discipline by which to see directly into the spiritual world. Steiner reportedly was able to track the souls of the deceased and read the "Akashic Record," which can be thought of as a transcript of human and cosmic history that is available to accomplished psychics and spiritual seers.

Steiner consistently urged spiritual seekers to eschew the cultivation of revelations received while unconscious and instead develop the capacity for conscious esoteric research. In this respect, anthroposophy has an emphasis different from that of contemporary teachings and practices that rely primarily on dreams, mediumship, channeling, and hypnosis. Steiner's emphasis on the cultivation of higher thinking capacities is different as well from reliance on revelations of ancient wisdom to Blavatsky and to several other first-generation leaders of the Theosophical Society by mahatmas, or discarnate Himalayan teachers.

One of the key claims of Steiner's spiritual science is that knowledge of the higher, or spiritual, world is made possible by the core of the self that he refers to as "Spirit," "Ego," or "I." According to Steiner, each of the four levels of knowledge corresponds to a level of the human being. Sensory perception is made possible by the physical body; imaginative knowledge, by the etheric body; inspirational knowledge, by the soul, or astral body; and intuitive (or spiritual) knowledge, by the I, Ego, or Spirit.

One of the reasons anthroposophy is difficult to summarize is that Steiner prescribes methods for growth on all levels of apprehension or, correspondingly, intended for the development of each of the four levels of the human being. Techniques for the increase of knowledge and the transformation of human beings include the study of natural science, projective geometry, sculpture, and painting as well as speech formation, music, eurythmy (an artistic method of movement to sound), interpersonal relations, the experience of scriptures, and religious rituals. Steiner worked in these and other endeavors as a way of to demonstrate the varied possibilities for the cultivation of imaginative, inspirational, and intuitive knowledge.

According to Steiner, the supersensible knowledge that lies behind his discoveries and disclosures is a distinctive capacity of the present age just as, earlier, the thinking capacity of the classical Greek philosophers and early Christian thinkers was significantly different from that of more ancient seers, whether the *rsis* of India, Moses, or Homer. In Steiner's elaborate account of the evolution of consciousness thinking has evolved in direct relation to the devolution of clairvoyance. Steiner attempted to show that the supersensible mode of perception he espoused combines conscious thinking with a spiritual or intuitive grasp akin to the clairvoyance characteristic of ancient times. At the center of this double evolution Steiner saw the descent of the Christ, which made possible a reversal of a downward, materialistic trend in favor of an ascent toward an increasingly free, spiritual mode of thinking.

Steiner conducted esoteric research into the afterlife of significant individuals and the secrets of life between death and rebirth. He spoke of Christ as the Lord of Karma. He also gave many lectures on the role of great spiritual beings such as Moses, Zoroaster, Krishna, Buddha, Plato, Socrates, the figures in the New Testament, Saint Francis, and Christian Rosenkreutz in the evolution of human consciousness. In more than a dozen lecture cycles from 1909 to 1913 Steiner disclosed his research on those figures, particularly concerning Krishna, Buddha, and Christ, working collaboratively in the spiritual world on behalf of the evolution of humanity. He also lectured on a topic of significance in light of the current trend toward ecological devastation: the reappearance, beginning in the twentieth century, of the resurrected Christ in the etheric envelope of the earth.

LATER DEVELOPMENTS. Although few if any of Steiner's thousands of followers have attained the kind of supersensible perception he exhibited, they have applied his spiritual discipline and insights creatively. Among the works arising from Steiner's teachings have been the biodynamic method of soil cultivation, anthroposophically extended medicine, and the Waldorf School movement, currently the largest nonsectarian independent school system in the world. Anthroposophists are also responsible for the Camphill movement, which consists of villages for children and adults who require special mental and emotional care. Drawing on Steiner's lectures on the arts and on his suggestions to artists with whom he collaborated, Anthroposophical artists have brought Steiner's artistic methods to bear on the visual and performing arts, especially painting, sculpture, architecture, speech, drama, and eurythmy.

Steiner intended spiritual science to supersede religion, but in response to a request from Protestant pastors and seminarians for help in fostering Christian renewal, he generated the sacramental forms and organizational structure of the Christian Community, a modern church that is not formally allied with the Anthroposophical Society but is part of the same Johannine esoteric Christian stream and clearly draws its inspiration and much of its teaching from Steiner's spiritual life and research.

At the Christmas Foundation Meeting in 1923, in addition to establishing the Anthroposophical Society as a resource for anyone wishing to gain a basic knowledge of the supersensible, Steiner established the School of Spiritual Science for members of the Anthroposophical Society who were willing to commit themselves to represent anthroposophy or spiritual science in and to the world. Members of the School of Spiritual Science, which Steiner intended to have nine classes but lived to found only the first class, strive to develop imagination, inspiration, and intuition in fields such as mathematics, medicine, pedagogy, agriculture, the social sciences, the visual arts, and the performing arts. Research in those fields is centered in the Goetheanum in Dornach, Switzerland, but also is conducted by members of the School of Spiritual Science working alone and in groups throughout the world. The publication of books and periodicals and the holding of conferences to explore research in these fields demonstrate the continuing vitality of Steiner's esoteric teaching and method of research.

In the 1930s and 1940s conflicts between European countries adversely affected the working of the Anthroposophical Society. In recent decades the influence of Rudolf Steiner's teachings and the practice of anthroposophy seem to have been limited by a conservative tendency among some anthroposophists.

Subsequent anthroposophical researchers and authors include Christopher Bamford, Owen Barfield, Bernard Lievegoed, Robert McDermott, Robert Powell, Mary Carolyn (M.C.) Richards, Robert Sardello, Douglas Sloan, Edward Reaugh Smith, Valentin Tomberg, Andrew Welburn, and Arthur Zajonc. Endeavors such as biodynamic agriculture, Waldorf education, and anthroposophical medicine stand out as creative examples of thinking, feeling, and willing that advance the effort to (re)join the material and spiritual dimensions of human consciousness.

SEE ALSO Besant, Annie; Blavatsky, H. P.; Rosicrucians; Steiner, Rudolf; Theosophical Society.

BIBLIOGRAPHY

Steiner's published writings total more than 350 volumes, most of which consist of cycles of lectures. More than two hundred of these works and another several hundred on anthroposophy, including all the titles listed below, are published by Anthroposophical Press/Steiner Books, Great Barrington, Mass., and are available from http://www.Anthropress.org.

Foundational Books

Steiner, Rudolf. *Theosophy: An Introduction to the Spiritual Processes in Human Life and in the Cosmos.* Translated by Catherine E. Creeger, Hudson, N.Y., 1994.

Steiner, Rudolf. *How to Know Higher Worlds: A Modern Path of Initiation.* Translated by Christopher Bamford, Hudson, N.Y., 1995.

Steiner, Rudolf. *Intuitive Thinking as a Spiritual Path: A Philosophy of Freedom.* Translated by Michael Lipson, Hudson, N.Y., 1995.

Steiner Rudolf. *An Outline of Esoteric Science.* Translated by Catherine E. Creeger, Hudson, N.Y., 1997.

Introductions

Bamford, Christopher, ed., intro. *Spiritualism, Madame Blavatsky, and Theosophy: An Eyewitness View of Occult History,* Great Barrington, Mass., 2001.

Bamford, Christopher, ed., intro. *What Is Anthroposophy?* Great Barrington, Mass., 2002.

Lipson, Michael. *Stairway to Surprise: Six Steps to a Creative Life,* Great Barrington, Mass., 2002.

ROBERT A. MCDERMOTT (1987 AND 2005)

ANTICHRIST. The final opponent of good, known as Antichrist, has haunted Christianity since its beginnings. With roots in Hellenistic Judaism, and an Islamic echo in the figure of al-Dajjāl, the Antichrist myth has had a potent influence on belief, theology, art, literature, and politics.

The name *Antichrist* occurs in the New Testament only in the Johannine letters (1 Jn. 2:18, 2:22, 4:3; 2 Jn. 7), but the figure of a final enemy appears in several New Testament books. *Second Thessalonians* contains a description of "the rebel, the lost one" who is now "restrained" but who will lead the "great revolt," enthrone himself in the sanctuary of the temple, and be slain by Christ at the Parousia (2:1–12). The apocalyptic discourse found in the synoptic Gospels (*Mk.* 13, *Mt.* 24–25, *Lk.* 21) speaks of the "abomination of desolation" to be set up in the holy place (*Mk.* 13:14, *Mt.* 24:15) and the appearance of false Christs and false prophets (*Mk.* 13:5–6, 13:21–23; *Mt.* 24:4–5, 24:23–24; *Lk.* 21:8). The *Book of Revelation* contains symbolic portrayals of Antichrist figures under the guise of two beasts—one arising from the sea (or abyss) with seven heads and ten horns (11:7, 13:1–10, 17:3–18, 19:19–21), whose number is 666 (13:18), the other coming from the land as the servant of the former monster (13:11–17, 16:13, 19:19–21).

It is evident that the early Christians made use of traditions regarding eschatological opponents that depended upon Jewish apocalyptic and earlier prophetic traditions (e.g., Gog and Magog in Ez 38–39). The *Book of Daniel* is the source for both the "abomination of desolation" (9:27, 11:31, 12:11) and for the beasts described in *Revelation* (7:1–9, 7:15–27). Other Jewish texts contain speculation about an evil angel named Beliar who functions as God's final adversary (e.g., *Testament of Levi* 3.3, 18.2; *Sibylline Oracles* 3.63–3.74). Modern research has uncovered similar concerns about eschatological foes in the Qumran community (e.g., *War Rule* 17.6 and the fragments known as 4 Q 186). Late Jewish apocalyptic seems to be the source of physical descriptions of Antichrist (e.g., *Apocalypse of Elijah* 3.14–3.18) that were also used by Christians. Belief in a final opponent of the Messiah survived in later Judaism in the legendary descriptions of the persecuting king Armilus (e.g., in *Sefer Zerubbabel).*

Various explanations have been given for the origin of Antichrist. Wilhelm Bousset advanced a mythological interpretation that saw Antichrist as a projection into the end time of the monster of chaos who had warred against the creator god in Near Eastern cosmogonies. R. H. Charles argued that Antichrist originated from the interaction of three traditions: individual and collective notions of an eschatological enemy based upon political events, the mythic figure of Beliar, and the growth of the Nero myth.

The evidence indicates that belief in Antichrist arose through the interaction of ancient myths and current political situations. The desecration of the Temple by the Seleucid king Antiochus IV (167 BCE) and his savage persecution of the Jews were shocking events that called out for universalistic interpretations based on archetypal myths (*Dn.* 8:9–14). Subsequent persecutors of Jews and Christian were also given mythological stature, and their stories in turn further shaped the legendary narratives. The most important of these persecutors was the Roman emperor Nero (54–68). Building on the confusion surrounding the death of Nero, legends about a returning (or later resurrected) Nero who would function as an ultimate enemy influenced contemporary Christian and Jewish texts (e.g., *Rv.* 13, 17; *Ascension of Isaiah* 4.1–4.4; *Sibylline Oracles* 3.63–3.74, 4.119–4.150, 5). Another historical figure whose legendary history became intertwined with Antichrist was Simon Magus (*Acts* 8:9–13).

Christian thinkers of the second and third centuries tried to weave the diverse traditions concerning Antichrist into a coherent picture. Was he to be one or many? A human person or a demon? Jewish or Roman in origin? A false teacher (a pseudomessiah) or an imperial persecutor? The Antichrist legend developed as the reverse side of the growing Christology of the early church, speculation on the person and prerogatives of Christ encouraging attention to his eschatological opposite. In the early third century, Hippolytus of Rome wrote a treatise, *On Christ and the Antichrist,* that gave a handy summary of belief and legend. Some of his successors (e.g., Commodianus, Lactantius, Sulpicius Severus) deal with the variety of traditions about Antichrist by distinguishing between two final enemies: a Roman persecutor, for which Nero was the prototype, and a false Jewish messiah born of the tribe of Dan who would rebuild the Temple at Jerusalem.

Antichrist myths continued to flourish after the conversion of the Roman empire to Christianity. Building upon the description of many Antichrists in the New Testament letters of John, the Donatist exegete Tyconius (d. 390?) stressed a moralizing view of the final enemy as the aggregate body of evildoers within the church. This tradition was handed on to the Middle Ages by Pope Gregory I (d. 604). Corporate views of the Antichrist, including those that focused on heretics, Muslims, or Jews, were common in the Middle Ages, but evil individuals within or without Christianity were still often identified with Antichrist or his immediate predecessor.

Christian beliefs about Antichrist, especially those originating in Syria, were the source for Islamic legends regarding a final eschatological foe, called al-Dajjāl ("the deceiver"). Although al-Dajjāl does not appear in the Qurʾān, traditions appeared early concerning this monstrous figure who was to be manifested shortly before the end, lead the faithful astray, and be slain either by Jesus or by the Mahdi.

The Christian monk Adso's *Letter on the Antichrist* (c. 950), written on the model of a saint's life, depicts the final enemy as a combination of both a pseudo-Christ and a persecuting tyrant, a depiction that was to remain standard in Latin Christianity for centuries. The twelfth-century renewal of apocalyptic thought was rich in speculation on Antichrist. In Germany, the first and greatest of the medieval Antichrist dramas, *Ludus de Antichristo,* appeared, while in Italy, Joachim of Fiore (d. 1202) wove both corporate and individual views of Antichrist together into his new apocalyptic schema.

In the later Middle Ages, the view of Adso, passed on by writers such as Hugh of Strassburg and John of Paris, remained popular and in the fifteenth century was illustrated in a remarkable series of block books. The Joachite tradition looked forward to a struggle between one or more spiritual popes (*pastores angelici*), who would try to reform the church, and their opponents, evil popes introduced by force or schism who were identified with Antichrist or his predecessors. In Peter Olivi's Franciscan Joachitism, there are dual final Antichrists: the papal *Antichristus mysticus* and the *Antichristus magnus,* a persecuting emperor (sometimes identified with a reborn Frederick II). Fueled by the Avignon papacy, the schism of 1378–1417, and the general failure of the papacy to reform the church, such beliefs were widespread in the fourteenth and fifteenth centuries. John Wyclif and the Hussites sharpened the identification of the papacy with Antichrist. It is no surprise that Martin Luther and other reformers seized upon Antichrist rhetoric in the battle against Rome.

Reformation identification of the papacy with Antichrist (e.g., Smalcaldic Articles 2.4) went beyond most late medieval views in its total rejection of the papal office and in its insistence upon a renewed corporate interpretation that identified the institution of the papacy, and not individual popes, with Antichrist. Some reformers also held double-Antichrist views coupling the Turks with the papacy. The strength of the corporate view may have been the source of the widening of Antichrist rhetoric that marked the sixteenth- and seventeenth-century Reformation debates, especially in England, where *Antichrist* became a term of opprobrium that could be used against any institution or group.

It is tempting to think that this inflation of rhetoric, together with Enlightenment criticism of religion, stifled belief in Antichrist, but the last enemy's ability to serve as a symbol of evil has given the figure a singular longevity. Historical figures, like Napoleon I and Mussolini, have been seen as Antichrist, as have such movements as the French Revolution, socialism, and communism. Friedrich Nietzsche's adoption of the role of Antichrist and his use of the title for this most violent attack on Christianity and bourgeois morality are well known. No less significant are the uses of the myth by some of the Russian writers of the nineteenth century, such as Fedor Dostoevskii, Vladimir Solovʾev, and Dmitrii Merezhkovskii. Belief in an individual final Antichrist continues in popular culture, and Fundamentalist Christianity, but for other Christians the Antichrist has become a symbol of the evil in the human heart.

BIBLIOGRAPHY

Bousset, Wilhelm. *The Antichrist Legend.* London, 1896. A classic work.

Emmerson, Richard K. *Antichrist in the Middle Ages.* Seattle, 1981. Deals primarily with the Adsonian tradition.

Jenks, Gregory. *The Origins and Early Development of the Antichrist Myth.* Berlin, 1991.

McGinn, Bernard. *Antichrist: Two Thousand Years of the Human Fascination with Evil.* 2d edition, New York, 2000. The most complete account.

Malvenda, Tomás. *De Antichristo libri undecim.* Rome, 1604. An extensive survey of the traditional materials.

Preuss, Hans. *Die Vorstellungen vom Antichrist im späteren mittelaalter, bei Luther und in der Konfessionellen Polemik.* Leipzig, 1906. Unsurpassed for its period.

Wright, Rosemary Muir. *Art and Antichrist in Medieval Europe.* Manchester, 1995.

BERNARD MCGINN (1987 AND 2005)

ANTICULT MOVEMENTS are the complementary reverse side of the coin to new religious movements (NRMs). Anticult movements may be focused on one group, as was the nineteenth-century anti-Catholic Know-Nothing Party or the various anti-Mormon efforts. Anticult movements may also be more inclusive in their focus, as with the nativist antiblack, anti-Catholic, and anti-Semitic Ku Klux Klan of the twentieth century. In modern terms, most anticult movements are multidimensional and espouse a dislike (and often a nonunderstanding) of nontraditional religions. This opposition includes the belief that NRMs are subversive of revered social institutions, the prediction of imminent danger from such groups, and claims that such groups do not "legitimately" attract willing converts but rather employ beguiling means to build a slavelike membership base. Anticult groups often make appeals to civic values and patriotism to justify their opposition to NRMs. Historians show that such countermovements, either secular or sacred in their oppositional thrusts, are a sociological consequence of resentment toward incipient or spreading religious pluralism in North America, Europe, and even Asia (in particular, Japan and the Peoples Republic of China).

THE MODERN NORTH AMERICAN ANTICULT MOVEMENT. While sectarian opposition and competition among religious groups seems to be ubiquitous, the most recent wave of secular anticult groups (*cult* being the pejorative label for a myriad of publicly unpopular NRMs, such as the Unification

Church, the International Society for Krishna Consciousness, and the Church of Scientology International) began in North America during the late 1960s and early 1970s. At this time there were a variety of cultural factors that combined to allow persons, particularly young adults, the opportunity to experiment and "dabble" in exotic alternative religions. These factors included the end to the American military draft for males, the disillusionment of some with the Vietnam War, various social reform movements, and the actions in 1965 to rescind older twentieth-century alien restriction laws that facilitated the immigration of *gurūs*, swamis, and other teachers from Asia into the United States.

North America became the springboard for the export of a secular template of anticultism to Europe, as well as to Israel and various South American countries. For many years North America has been home to a religious wing of the anticult movement that has opposed NRMs as promoting false doctrine and that produces a largely conservative Christian apologetic literature. It is the secular wing of the anticult movement, however, with its emphasis on the presumed social-psychological dynamics of conversion, retention, and removal of NRM members, that has garnered the most public attention and legal controversy.

The secular anticult movement has always been a loose network of organizations, some aimed at individual NRMs and others opposing a broader array of groups. There has also always been a laissez-faire understanding of just what constitutes a "cult" or "destructive cult," though there have been numerous failed attempts by anticult spokespersons to arrive at a precise definition. A large part of the latter problem is that so many NRMs (cults and sects) possess characteristics of more established churches and denominations, from charismatic leadership to wealth and elitist dogmas.

The first organization in the modern secular anticult movement was Free the Children of God, which was established in Denver in 1971 in response to high-pressure recruitment of teenagers and young adults by the Children of God (later renamed the Family). Free the Children of God also objected to the Children of God's migratory communal lifestyle. Other local anticult groups, largely made up of relatives of young persons who joined such unconventional religious groups in lieu of pursuing more conventional career and family trajectories, spontaneously arose across the United States. As these anticult groups gradually discovered each other, they began communicating and making common cause. Soon these organizations, many quite small, began arranging joint conferences, and they eventually made attempts to coalesce into national organizations. The first national (and largest) anticult group was the California-based Citizens Freedom Foundation, formed in 1974; this group was renamed the Cult Awareness Network and relocated to Chicago in 1985.

In 1979 a second national organization, the American Family Foundation, emerged out of the Citizens Freedom Foundation. Comparing the two, the Cult Awareness Network was more activist and public-relations-oriented, including (as is now known indisputably from the group's records) not only endorsing coercive "interventions" called *deprogrammings* to remove legal adults from NRMs, but also serving as a clearinghouse to connect desperate aggrieved families with deprogrammers. The American Family Foundation, on the other hand, functioned entirely as a repository for information on NRMs, sponsoring white paper reports and conferences, publishing a professional journal, lobbying for anti-NRM legislation, and seeking to attract degreed professionals, academic or otherwise, to support its cause.

Working sometimes in parallel, sometimes in concert with the Cult Awareness Network and the American Family Foundation, have been several other groups and individuals. First, there has been a small but highly visible coterie of coercive deprogrammers, who later, due to negative publicity from civil libertarians, relabeled themselves "exit counselors" or "thought reform specialists." Most have not been professionally trained in any behavioral science; instead, they act in maverick, entrepreneurial fashion to "retrieve" NRM members on a fee-for-service basis and attempt to convince them to renounce their unconventional allegiances. Second, there has existed a small but vocal network of mental health and behavioral science professionals who have enjoyed a good deal of publicity as spokespersons for the anticult movement, presenting themselves to the media as experts on the controversy and providing counseling and rehabilitation services to exiting NRM members. Third, there have been voluntary groups, usually short-lived, of former NRM members who offered transition support to other former NRM members as they readjusted to secular society.

What both the national organizations and the smaller groups have held in common is a fundamental assumption that NRMs use a subtle but nevertheless powerful "mind control" method to recruit and retain members. Anticult activists thus interpret NRM membership as the end result of manipulative practices that undermine individual capacity for voluntary thought and action, practices that are popularly known as *brainwashing*. This assumption became tempered by the late 1980s, as seen in anticult conference presentations and in its literature, as mainstream psychiatric, psychological, and sociological research across a host of NRMs demonstrated the mind control thesis as too simple a model for explaining human influence processes.

NRMs fought against anticult groups and deprogrammers with their own professional apologists, conferences, sympathetic literature, publicity campaigns, and lawsuits. Although anticult groups won the battle in the public imagination by discrediting many NRMs, the NRMs won the legal battles through libel lawsuits and other litigation against deprogrammers (who often failed in their deprogramming attempts). One result was that the Cult Awareness Network was driven into bankruptcy in 1995 after a series of punitive suits, the most important of which concerned deprogramming referrals.

The North American anticult movement's failure to mobilize governmental and regulatory agency sanctions, except occasionally at the local level, to support its cause of "exposing" and putting an end to what it considered outrageous NRM behavior, has been coupled with an inability to forge an alliance with religious-based opposition to NRMs. The religious countercult movement, which dislikes the term *anticult*, has always emphasized voluntary exit of NRM members and a return to "true doctrines," an approach incompatible with coercive deprogrammings. The secular anticult wing, on the other hand, has always claimed that it is not concerned with religion, but only opposes mind-control practices. Moreover, in various secular anticult documents, one can perceive a distinct antipathy to religion, in particular to conservative high-demand religious groups.

Still, at the very time that the Cult Awareness Network was being damaged by legal entanglements and the entire anticult movement was being marginalized as a credible force in the United States, its leaders were acting as missionaries to export their ideology to other countries. They promulgated it at conferences, through correspondence, and at personal meetings with government officials and grassroots anticult groups in Canada, Belgium, Denmark, Italy, Germany, France, and England. The Cult Awareness Network, now defunct, and the American Family Foundation, still active in 2004, were recipients of inquiries for information concerning possible affiliation with smaller anticult groups in various parts of the world, including Africa (e.g., South Africa, Nigeria), Asia (e.g., the Philippines), Eastern Europe (e.g., Russia), South America (e.g., Argentina), and the People's Republic of China. For a time, at least, the discredited ideology of the North American anticult movement has been accepted to justify the potential exercise of political and other institutional sanctions abroad. Anticult movements appear to be a staple in pluralistic, globalizing societies to the same extent as new religious movements.

SEE ALSO Brainwashing (Debate); Cults and Sects; Deprogramming; Law and Religion, article on Law and New Religious Movements.

BIBLIOGRAPHY

Billington, Ray Allen. *The Protestant Crusade, 1800–1860: A Study of the Origins of American Nativism.* New York, 1938.

Bromley, David G., and James T. Richardson, eds. *The Brainwashing/Deprogramming Controversy: Sociological, Psychological, Legal, and Historical Perspectives.* Lewiston, N.Y., 1984.

Bromley, David G., and Anson Shupe. "New Religions and Countermovements." In *The Handbook on Cults and Sects in America*, edited by David B. Bromley and Jeffrey K. Hadden, pp. 177–198. Greenwich, Conn., 1993.

Davis, D. B. "Some Themes of Counter-Subversion." *Mississippi Valley Historical Review* 67 (1960): 205–224.

Jenkins, Philip. *Mystics and Messiahs: Cults and New Religions in American History.* New York, 2000.

Melton, J. Gordon. *Encyclopedic Handbook of Cults in America.* Rev. ed. New York, 1992.

Shupe, Anson, and David G. Bromley. *The New Vigilantes: Deprogrammers, Anti-cultists, and the New Religions.* Beverly Hills, Calif., 1980.

Shupe, Anson, and David G. Bromley. "Social Responses to Cults." In *The Sacred in a Secular Age: Toward Revision in the Scientific Study of Religion*, edited by Phillip E. Hammond, pp. 58–72. Berkeley, Calif., 1985.

Shupe, Anson, and David G. Bromley. *Anti-Cult Movements in Cross Cultural Perspective.* New York, 1994.

Singer, Margaret Thaler, with Janja Lalich. *Cults in Our Midst.* San Francisco, 1995.

Zablocki, Benjamin, and Thomas Robbins, eds. *Misunderstanding Cults: Searching for Objectivity in a Controversial Field.* Toronto, 2001.

ANSON SHUPE (2005)

ANTI-SEMITISM. The term *anti-Semitism* is relatively recent, coined only at the end of the nineteenth century, when it became the identifying symbol of an innovative anti-Jewish political platform that projected the Jews as an alien element in European society. The term was intended to encompass the entire spectrum of contemporary and historic anti-Jewish thinking and behavior and to convey a sense of the monolithic quality of all anti-Jewish thinking and behavior. Use of the innovative term spread quickly among adherents of the new political program and among their opponents as well. Subsequently, the term has been widely utilized as a synonym for all or at least most anti-Jewish attitudes and actions.

The present survey will accept popular usage of the term anti-Semitism as synonymous with historic and early twenty-first-century anti-Jewish attitudes and actions. It will, however, dissent from any sense of the monolithic quality of anti-Jewish thinking. This survey will insist instead that evolving anti-Jewish themes must be seen in context, that is, against the backdrop of their particular time and place. At the same time, this survey will acknowledge common and recurrent motifs in anti-Jewish thinking over the ages. It will suggest that the recurrence of these motifs can be traced in part to the tendency of the Jews over the ages to emerge as discordant elements in a variety of societies; it will further suggest that, once anti-Jewish motifs have been generated, they have often become staples of popular wisdom and folklore, thus resurfacing in later and often radically altered contexts.

EARLY ANTIQUITY. Our evidence for Jewish life and also for anti-Jewish attitudes and actions in early antiquity comes largely from the biblical corpus, with its attendant problems, and—to a limited extent—from the ever-increasing body of ancient Near Eastern artifacts and texts uncovered by archaeologists. From this fragmentary data, it would seem that the frictions between Israelites and Judeans and their neighbors involved relatively normal tensions between rival polities. Wars were common in Canaan, with the Israelites and Judeans sometimes the aggressors and sometimes on the defensive. Anti-Israelite and anti-Judean sentiment seems to have been associated with the shifting political constellations of the ancient Near East.

The biblical corpus and the texts from the ancient Near East both note that the Israelites and Judeans—especially the latter—made their way beyond the confines of their kingdoms and settled in other lands, sometimes on their own initiative and sometimes forcibly. These sources suggest that the migrating Judeans brought into their new habitations innovative problems flowing from the incongruities between Judean religion and the larger polytheistic environment, as the Judeans insisted on one deity only and rejected alternative divinities. Two of the later books of the Hebrew Bible—the books of *Daniel* (*Dn.* 1-6) and *Esther*—portray both admiration and animosity on the part of Persians in the face of Judean unwillingness to worship the gods of their empire. While the tone of both books is folkloric, Judean monotheism might well have touched off hostility as a result of its innovative religious norms, perceived as threatening to the established religio-political order. These biblical stories have created a subsequent sense—among Jews and non-Jews alike—of animosity aroused by Jewish distinctiveness, in this case devotion to monotheistic ideals.

The Greco-Roman World. During the fourth pre-Christian century, the Near East was invaded from the west by the Greek forces of Alexander the Great (356–323 BCE), which profoundly disrupted Near Eastern civilization. All segments of that ancient civilization, Jews included, had to come to grips with a new political order and a new culture. Anti-Jewish sentiment eventually emerged, resulting from the intersection of Jewish religious commitments and non-Jewish political concerns. The harsh decrees of the Seleucid king Antiochus III (242–187 BCE) have been interpreted as an effort on his part to suppress what he perceived as dangerous Jewish rebelliousness rooted in commitment to the Jerusalem Temple and the religious dictates of Jewish tradition. The Seleucid ruler seems to have been convinced that only by attacking the Jewish religious system itself could he successfully repress Jewish rebelliousness.

This same combination manifested itself under Roman rule in Palestine as well. For the Romans, Palestine—perched at the eastern end of the Mediterranean Sea—was of utmost strategic significance and had to be maintained under Roman control. While portions of the Jewish population were quite amenable to Roman overlordship, other Jews were deeply opposed to Roman rule. Twice, the Jews erupted in revolt, and twice the revolts were crushed. Roman hostility seems to have been rooted in simple political considerations, although these eventuated in attacks on the Jewish faith. At the close of the first revolt in the year 70 CE, the Jerusalem Temple was destroyed; at the close of the second revolt in 135, key elements of Jewish tradition were banned by the Roman authorities. Once again, anti-Jewish actions seem to have been fueled by political considerations.

All through late antiquity, significant numbers of Jews lived outside Palestine, in an eastern diaspora centered in Mesopotamia and in a western diaspora spread throughout the Mediterranean Basin. The same Roman authorities that attacked Jewish religion in the aftermath of the rebellions in Palestine were quite generous in recognizing the special religious needs flowing from the demands of monotheism, and Jews were regularly exempted from problematic imperial obligations. In the Roman diaspora, a different kind of tension emerged, the tension between ethnic and religious minorities jockeying for position with their Roman rulers. Competition and contention seems to have developed, for example, between the large Jewish community of Roman Alexandria and the Greek population of that same great city. This contention escalated recurrently into violence.

Judaism seems to have both attracted and repelled the diverse populations that made up the Roman Empire. The attraction and the repulsion were stimulated by the special beliefs of the Jews and their zealous commitment to this belief system and its moral demands. Especially distressing to many Roman observers was the attraction of Judaism to some of their contemporaries and the implications of that attraction for loyalty to the traditional pillars of Roman civilization. Sharp expression of this distaste for Jews and Judaism can be found in Tacitus (c. 55–120), who bemoans the fact that Romans attracted to Judaism thereby sunder all the normal ties of Roman society—their loyalty to state, cult, and family.

Early Christianity. Most students of anti-Semitism agree that, with the birth and development of Christianity, new, more intense, and more persistent anti-Jewish thinking and behavior emerged. While earlier anti-Jewish sentiment involved relatively normal political, ethnic, and religious strife and dissipated quickly, Christian anti-Jewish sentiment has proven far more intense and enduring. Scholars have struggled to explain the intensity and longevity of this Christian anti-Jewish sentiment, especially in the wake of World War II and the Holocaust.

Paul, whose writings form the earliest stratum of the New Testament, was intensely concerned with and highly ambivalent toward Judaism and the Jewish matrix out of which Jesus had emerged. For Paul (d. between 62 and 68), the Jews were God's first chosen people and would someday be fully reunited with their deity. However, the magnitude of Jewish sinfulness was overwhelming and necessitated divine rejection of the Jewish people and their replacement with new bearers of the divine-human covenant. The Pauline portrait of sinful Jews had enormous impact on the early crystallization of Christian thought.

While the complex development of early Christianity can no longer be reconstructed, the end product of this complex development—the post-Pauline four gospels—set the course for subsequent Christian thinking, including its views of the Jews. Although these alternative accounts of the birth, activities, crucifixion, and resurrection of Jesus differ in some details, they are unanimous in identifying the Jews as Jesus' sole and implacable adversaries and by imputing to the Jews full responsibility for his death. To be sure, the Romans ruled Palestine; crucifixion was a Roman punishment; and the crucifixion of Jesus is depicted by the gospels as administered by the Romans. Nonetheless, the gospels impute ultimate responsibility for the crucifixion of Jesus to the Jews, who purportedly demanded it and would accept no alternative proposed by the Roman governor.

In the frictions that preceded the birth of Christianity, anti-Jewish thinking was localized, rooted in political and practical circumstances, and generally evanescent. Christian views of the Jews, as crystallized in Christian Scripture and in the authoritative writings of the Church Fathers, lost any semblance of temporality; they were projected as timeless, meaningful for Christians—indeed all of humanity—over the ages. Portrayed as oppositional, blind to the truth, malevolent to the point of murderousness, and rejected by God, Jews took on a central role in the Christian myth and in the Christian sense of cosmic reality.

As Christianity ascended to power in the Roman Empire, its leaders had to assess their stance toward non-Christians, Jews included, from a new vantage point, that of power. Jews were recognized as a legitimate religious community, with rights to security and exercise of their religious tradition. Once again, the Jews were thrust into a position of uniqueness. Now, they were the sole legitimate non-Christian grouping in what was intended to become eventually a thoroughly Christianized society. The theological underpinnings of Jewish legitimacy were fully formulated by Augustine (354–430), whose doctrine of toleration of the Jews remained authoritative over the ages. Yet, upon close inspection, this Augustinian doctrine, intended to safeguard Judaism and the Jews, reflects many of the negative themes bequeathed from earlier Christian history.

While Augustine identified a number of grounds for toleration of the Jews, two predominate, with both pointing to the utility of the Jews in the Christian scheme of things. The first argument asserts that Jews bear witness to Christian truth by proclaiming the validity of the Hebrew Bible—in Christian terms the Old Testament—as divine revelation. Thus, in advancing their case, Christians can comfortably cite the testimony of their Jewish opponents. To be sure, the Jews do not comprehend the revelation to which they attest. Thus, while insisting on Jewish rights, Augustine powerfully reinforced the earlier imagery of the Jews as failing to grasp the truth vouchsafed to them by God.

The second Augustinian argument for toleration of the Jews is likewise simultaneously protective and demeaning. According to this second argument, Jews offer Christianity—and indeed the world—incontrovertible evidence for the working of human sin and divine punishment. In the Christian view, Jesus' Jewish contemporaries sinned by rejecting him and occasioning his death. This sin immediately set in motion God's rejection of the Jews, his destruction of their sanctuary and sacred city at the hands of the Romans, and his decree of exile and degradation for their heirs. Christians are precluded from harming Jews, for God himself has already imposed their punishment. The sequence of Jewish sin and divinely ordained punishment is illuminating, useful for Christians and indeed all of humanity to contemplate.

The Middle Ages. During the first half of the Middle Ages (seventh through eleventh and twelfth centuries), the Jewish population in Christendom was relatively sparse. The overwhelming majority of Jews lived in the realm of Islam. With the arousal of western Christendom in the eleventh century and its rapid growth and expansion, increasing numbers of Jews were absorbed into Christian territories, either through conquest of formerly Muslim lands or through immigration. With this growth in the number of Jews with whom medieval Christians had genuine contact, ecclesiastical policies concerning the Jews had to expand, and Christian imagery of Jews took a number of new and negative turns.

Ecclesiastical policies were aimed by and large at obviating any kind of harm that the Jews might cause to the Christian host majority. Concerns included the possibilities of Jews blaspheming Christianity, influencing Christian neighbors religiously, and—from the twelfth century on—inflicting damage through business and banking activity. The policy focus on potential Jewish harmfulness served to heighten perceptions of the Jews as hostile. These perceptions were much exacerbated by the emergence of crusading as a church-sponsored initiative in the eleventh century. Exhilarated animosity toward the external enemies of Christendom tended to draw negative attention to the Jews, perceived as the unique internal enemy.

The combination of traditional Gospel imagery, ecclesiastical policies, and crusading fervor served to occasion a series of negative turns in the imagery of the Jews. The first of these involved transformation of the alleged Jewish responsibility for the crucifixion of Jesus into perceptions of medieval Jews as murderously hostile to Jesus' followers. This notion of murderous Jewish malevolence first surfaced in the middle decades of the twelfth century. In 1144 the mutilated body of a young tanner named William was found outside the English town of Norwich. According to a slightly later account, the townspeople of Norwich were divided in their reactions. Some were immediately convinced that the Jews of Norwich had surely done the bloody deed; others rejected the allegation. Likewise, in 1147 in Würzburg, discovery of a dismembered body led to the conviction among some burghers that their town's Jews had committed the murder. In both instances, the killings were allegedly motivated by historic Jewish hatred of Christ and Christianity. In Würzburg, those convinced of Jewish guilt transformed the dead Christian into a martyr and venerated his remains until the local bishop intervened. In Norwich, many of the town's Christians viewed William as a martyr and transformed his grave into a shrine, at which miracles were quickly reported.

In the Norwich case, an important new motif of purported Jewish hatred for Christianity emerged. In the face of ongoing dispute among the Christians of Norwich as to the sanctity of the lad, a late-arriving cleric undertook to make the case for William's sainthood. This case involved three critical elements: a blessed and pure childhood; a martyr's death; and the production of miracles at the gravesite. Of these three elements, the second was decisive, and the chronicler Thomas of Monmouth made an elaborate case for the martyrdom of William, depicting in graphic detail alleged Jewish torture of the young tanner and eventual murder via crucifixion. Thomas portrayed the Jews of Norwich as imitating precisely their Jerusalem ancestors, thus eliminating any doubt as to William's status as martyr.

Over the remaining decades of the twelfth century and on into the thirteenth, further imaginative embellishments grounded in the basic image of the Jews as murderously hostile proliferated. These included the claims that Jews were committed to reconstituting their ancient sacrificial system through the murder of Christians, that Jews killed Christians in order to utilize their blood for Jewish ritual, and that Jews sought to gain possession of host wafers in order to subject them to torture and suffering. During the devastating mid-fourteenth-century bubonic plague, the imagery of murderous Jewish animosity eventuated in the popular conviction that Jews had poisoned the wells of Europe and thus brought about the plague. Thousands of Jews lost their lives in the resultant violence.

A second negative turn in Christian imagery of Jews resulted from the combination of the sense of Jewish hostility and malevolence and a new Jewish economic specialization that developed during the twelfth century. As the vitalization of western Christendom accelerated, European society keenly felt the need for enhanced flow of capital. Both Christian and Jewish understandings of *Deuteronomy* 23:20–21 forbade their adherents from taking interest from or giving interest to fellow Christians or fellow Jews. However, traditional readings of these verses allowed the taking and giving of interest across denominational lines. As the need for capital became more pressing, Jews found it increasingly advantageous to use their special circumstances to enter the banking business. To be sure, bankers have never been popular, and Jewish involvement in such business combined with traditional imagery of Jewish hostility toward Christ, Christianity, and Christians to create the perception that moneylending became another vehicle through which Jews sought to inflict harm on Christian society.

Yet a third negative turn in Christian imagery of the Jews involved the conviction that Jewish acts of malevolence were hardly individual and local. Rather, it was claimed that Jews, scattered throughout the world as part of their divinely imposed punishment, utilized their wide-ranging Jewish network for inflicting harm throughout Christendom. Thomas of Monmouth, for example, indicated that a convert from Judaism to Christianity had reliably informed him that the murder in Norwich in 1144 was by no means an isolated deed undertaken by a small band of local Jews. Rather, an international Jewish conspiracy lay behind the Norwich event, with that particular town selected for that particular year. Regularly, it was asserted, the international Jewish conspirators met and selected the site for the annual anti-Christian crime.

A final turn in anti-Jewish perception emerged in the wake of large-scale conversion of Jews during the violence that swept across the Iberian Peninsula in 1391. In much traditional ecclesiastical thinking, baptism thoroughly altered the nature of the convert, meaning that Jews lost their inherently negative characteristics through acceptance of Christianity. However, traditional thinking was complex, with some voices suggesting that in fact inherited Jewish characteristics could not be totally effaced by baptism. Prior to the fourteenth century, this uncertainty remained unresolved and an interesting theoretical issue only. With the conversion of tens of thousands of Iberian Jews, this theoretical issue quickly assumed practical significance. What emerged was a form of racist thinking, with many Old Christians convinced that their New Christian neighbors had lost none of their prior Jewish infirmities. Clarification of genealogical lines and proof of blood purity became preoccupations of Spanish society, with numerous groups, both ecclesiastical and lay, denying membership to applicants whose lineage was tainted by Jewish ancestry.

By the end of the Middle Ages, as western Christendom stood on the threshold of major change, anti-Jewish imagery had proliferated and hardened into widely shared beliefs regarding Jewish otherness, Jewish hostility toward Christianity and Christians, and Jewish harmfulness. The central organs of the Roman Catholic Church regularly repudiated many of the radical anti-Jewish canards, while at the same time continuing to purvey the more traditional themes of Jewish otherness and enmity. The entire spectrum of anti-Jewish motifs, including the most radical, became staples of European folk thinking.

The Reformation. Much of the Reformation's energy was directed at dismantling the authoritarian centralization of the Roman Catholic Church. Thus, the tendency toward fragmentation is pronounced, and scholars regularly speak of a number of reformations. Once more, however, our interest lies with the broad stratum of folk conviction common to many of the diverse strands of Reformation thinking.

Since so much of Reformation thinking is oriented toward change, it is reasonable to anticipate that some of this change might have involved improved treatment and imagery of the Jews. During the Reformation, there were indeed signs of more positive imagery of the Jews, which flowed largely from two directions. Some of the reformers, Martin Luther (1483–1546) for example, used the issue of the Jews as a cudgel with which to beat the Roman Catholic Church, arguing that its harsh policies and the anti-Jewish imagery it projected turned the Jews into enemies. More sympathetic perception and treatment of Jews would surely win them over to Christianity. Additionally, the suffering of some of the reform groups transformed the meaning of persecution from divine punishment to divine testing. Persecuted Protestants viewed Jewish suffering and Jewish perseverance in a positive light.

However, the Reformation did not improve overall perceptions of the Jews. Martin Luther himself, disappointed in the Jewish failure to respond to his earlier ameliorative statements, expressed bitterness toward Jews in his later writings and supported extreme anti-Jewish measures. Urging the need to "prayerfully and reverentially practice a merciful severity," Luther proposed the following steps:

1. total destruction of synagogues;
2. parallel destruction of Jewish homes;
3. prohibition of Jewish literature;
4. prohibition of rabbinic teaching;
5. revocation of all travel rights;
6. prohibition of Jewish usury; and
7. forcible labor for the Jews.

Lurking beyond all these specific measures lay the possibility of expulsion of the Jews from all German lands. Luther couched his extreme recommendations in the most vituperative and demeaning terms. However, in neither the program nor the rhetoric does Luther break new ground. The imagery upon which he built his program and which he reinforced with his harsh language is identifiably a legacy of the later Middle Ages. What makes the Luther program and imagery especially striking was the potential that the Reformation had for change; instead, a number of its leading figures reinforced the most negative elements in medieval perceptions of Judaism and the Jews.

The Enlightenment. The Enlightenment as well was grounded in a profound desire for innovation, with the attendant promise of significant alterations in policy and thinking vis-à-vis the Jews. Once again, there were changes, in this case more far-reaching policy changes than had emerged from the Reformation. At the same time, the new order entailed its own dangers. Moreover, folkloric stereotypes survived into the new environment and continued to affect the European majority in both overt and subtle ways.

One of the major stimuli to Enlightenment change was accelerating despair over the toll taken by post-Reformation religious warfare. Thinkers like John Locke (1632–1704) began to ask whether there might not be a reasonable alternative to the ceaseless struggle for religio-political domination. Might it not be possible to fashion a society within which men and women would be free to practice a variety of religious confessions while belonging to a nondenominational civil society? A second major stimulus in the move toward the Enlightenment was the rapid advance of Western science, suggesting new paradigms for knowledge and raising serious doubts with respect to traditional religious scholarship and theology. This new knowledge further diminished the standing of the various Christian churches and further encouraged creation of a secular sphere of societal life, grounded in reason, in which all might participate.

Once again, the new thinking had complex implications for the Jews. On the one hand, criticism of prior ecclesiastical legacies—whether rooted in moral or intellectual considerations—often highlighted maltreatment of the Jews and called for changes. At the same time, Judaism was seen as the precursor to and the source of the ills and cruelties of Christianity. The turn away from Christian sources and the revival of Greco-Roman classics reintroduced non-Christian anti-Jewish themes appropriate to the new anticlerical mood of Enlightenment thinking. Most important, the popular stereotypes created during the Middle Ages continued to affect imagery of the Jews, who were perceived as separatist, malevolent, and harmful. Many of the leading Enlightenment thinkers, especially Voltaire (1694–1778)—perhaps the most influential of all—expressed intense anti-Jewish sentiments.

The social ideals of the Enlightenment reached their realization in the two revolutions of the later eighteenth century. In the earlier of the two, the American Revolution, Jewish presence in the fledgling United States was too small to occasion a serious debate about Jewish rights. These rights simply emerged as part of a broad commitment to human liberty. In the French Revolution, the situation was quite different, with pockets of Jewish population stirring considerable controversy as to the appropriateness of the Jews for citizenship in the new society. What quickly came to the fore were arguments for and against granting rights to Jews. For proponents of Jewish rights, Jewish infirmities—fully acknowledged—were simply the result of prior circumstances. Elimination of the restrictive circumstances would quickly eventuate in the emergence of healthy Jewish citizens of France. For opponents, the infirmities of Jewish life included political loyalty to the Jewish world and a concomitant lack of political loyalty to France, cultural depravity and an inability to comprehend French civilization, and economic predispositions damaging to French society. It is not difficult to see in these negative views remnants of the realities of pre-modern Jewish life in Europe and prior anti-Jewish imageries.

Ultimately, the proponents of Jewish citizenship in France won out, but the victory was predicated on an assumption of change in Jewish behavior and mentality. This made the Jews in France—and eventually elsewhere in Europe where the battle for Jewish rights was fought and won—subject to incessant scrutiny and judgment. Jews were criticized from a number of directions. On the one hand, adherents of their emancipation found fault with them for failure to integrate sufficiently into the new order; at the same time, opponents of the new order saw the Jews as the instigators, beneficiaries, and exploiters of radical and deleterious change.

Nineteenth- and Twentieth-Century Nationalism and Anti-Semitism. As the new Europe and its recently enfranchised Jews made their way into the nineteenth and then twentieth century, the accelerating nationalisms of the period resulted in a renewed sense of the Jews as different and hostile. Once again, Jews were thrust into a situation of uniqueness, this time as a unique foreign element in coalescing national states. This perception of Jewish distinctiveness resulted in part from the real residue of premodern European life, and in other part it involved the reactivation of earlier anti-Jewish perceptions. In this new setting, many of the older images of Jewish hostility and harmfulness resurfaced.

In 1879 Wilhelm Marr entitled his most important anti-Jewish work *The Victory of Jewry over Christendom.* Marr was hardly a religious traditionalist; rather, he wrote of the victory of the Jewish people over the German folk. Marr's work reflects a strong sense of the Jews as a different people; a conviction that this different people was committed to struggle against the German-Christian world; and that one of the major tools in this struggle was economic. It is not difficult to see in these assumptions many of the major motifs in medieval anti-Jewish thinking.

In the subsequent and influential *Protocols of the Elders of Zion,* these three convictions are reasserted in striking ways. To them is added the sense of an international Jewish conspiracy aimed at subverting the Christian world, in part through manipulation of finance, in part through the techniques of democracy, and in part through the mass media. Here again, earlier anti-Jewish motifs resurface in terms appropriate to radically altered circumstances.

Some late-nineteenth- and twentieth-century anti-Semites pushed the new term in a more focused direction, influenced by anthropological thinking of the period. For such anti-Semites, the key to understanding the Jews lay in clarifying the racial dimensions of the issue. Framing the issue of the Jews in racial terms was useful in the altered circumstances of the nineteenth and twentieth centuries, in which many Jews had successfully amalgamated into European society and were no longer readily distinguishable from their neighbors in social and religious terms. Racial categorization was intended to remove all doubt and to permit identification of Jews on allegedly scientific grounds. Moreover, racial thinking was also meant to highlight the innovativeness of the new movement and to efface any sense of age-old religiously inspired anti-Jewish thinking. To be sure, such racial conceptualization—as we have seen—had roots in the later centuries of the Middle Ages.

Adolf Hitler (1889–1945) was deeply affected by the anti-Semitic thinking of the nineteenth century and became its most effective twentieth-century proponent and propagandist. In *Mein Kampf* (2 vols., 1925–1927), he claims to have been initially opposed to the teachings of the nineteenth-century anti-Semites, portraying himself as only slowly awakening to the realities of Jewish distinctiveness and malevolence. Subsequent to this awakening—he claims—he saw the Jewish danger in its true proportions. Hitler made this insight a cornerstone of his political program, utilizing anti-Semitism as an effective tool in mobilizing German society toward achievement of his overall vision. He took anti-Semitic thinking to new extremes in the program of genocidal destruction of the entire Jewish people that he eventually espoused. The zeal with which destruction of European Jewry was pursued even during the closing days of World War II, when German defeat was inevitable, reflects the radical nature of the anti-Semitic element within Nazi thinking.

Post–World War II and the New Anti-Semitism. As the horror of the Holocaust became clear, Western societies and thinkers were appalled and undertook serious examination of the roots of anti-Semitic thinking. This effort involved Jews, on the one hand, and diverse Christian communities, on the other. Especially noteworthy was the effort on the part of numerous Christian denominations to examine the Christian roots of anti-Semitism and to eliminate—to the extent possible—the religious foundations of anti-Jewish thinking. Anti-Semitism was widely condemned and became a term of opprobrium. "Anti-Semite," a designation once embraced publicly by many, became a label to be avoided at all costs.

However, post–World War II realities created new conflicts into which Judaism and the Jews were absorbed. The creation of the State of Israel in a thoroughly Islamic sphere, the wide-ranging rejection of prior Western colonialism, and accelerating liberal espousal of postcolonial thinking have combined to create new anti-Jewish sentiment, diversely perceived in different quarters. For some, anti-Israel sentiment involves rational and moral recoiling from the injustices imposed on Palestinians. Other observers see in this recoiling the activation of traditional anti-Jewish motifs, earlier absent in the Islamic sphere.

The premodern world of Islam was quite different from premodern Christendom. The most obvious difference is the variety of populations encompassed within the world of premodern Islam, which was a rich mélange of racial, ethnic, and religious communities. Within this complex human tapestry, the Jews were by no means obvious as lone dissenters, as they had been earlier in the world of polytheism or subsequently in most of medieval Christendom. While occasionally invoking the ire of the prophet Muḥammad (c. 570–632) and his later followers, the Jews played no special role in the essential Muslim myth as the Jews did in the Christian myth. The *dhimmi* peoples, defined as those with a revealed religious faith, were accorded basic rights to security and religious identity in Islamic society and included Christians, Jews, and Zoroastrians. Lack of uniqueness ameliorated considerably the circumstances of Jews in the medieval world of Islam.

In the post–World War II period, however, the Jewish-Zionist enterprise did take on elements of uniqueness: it was projected as the sole Western effort at recolonization within the Islamic sphere. This perception has triggered intense antipathy for Zionism and its Jewish supporters, often viewed as indistinguishable, and has resulted in the revival of harshly negative imagery spawned in the altogether different sphere of medieval Christendom. Popular Muslim writing and journalism now regularly introduce themes such as ritual murder, Jewish manipulation of finance, and worldwide Jewish conspiracy, themes taken over with little difficulty from an entirely different ambience. Once again, these themes have proven flexible, readily transferable from milieu to milieu.

REFLECTIONS. Despite the sense in early and medieval Christian circles and in modern racial circles that Jewish nature—and hence anti-Jewish sentiment as well—is fixed and immutable, in fact anti-Jewish perceptions over the ages were very much set in specific contexts of time and place. Changing contexts conditioned the emergence and intensity of anti-Jewish motifs and affected the content of these motifs as well. To be sure, review of the history of anti-Semitism suggests considerable repetition of themes, attributable to two factors. First, it was the fate of the Jews to become a unique minority in a number of settings—initially as monotheists in a polytheistic world, then as the only legitimate non-Christian group in Christianized society, and later as the unique foreign element in nationalistic societies and the Western element in an Islamic postcolonial milieu. The sense of Jewish uniqueness was not always negative; Jewish distinctiveness evoked complex reactions of admiration, anxiety, and distaste. The negative responses, however, played a considerable role in historic anti-Jewish sentiment. Moreover, as Christianity evolved, it created a powerful myth that placed the Jews in a central position of opposition, animosity, and harmfulness. During the Middle Ages, these core Christian notions were transformed into potent popular perceptions of Jewish malevolence and harmfulness. These popular motifs survived as a key element in the folklore of European societies, resurfacing recurrently during the modern period in a variety of new settings, including the Enlightenment, nineteenth- and twentieth-century European nationalisms, and the postcolonialist developing nations.

BIBLIOGRAPHY

The fullest survey of anti-Semitism is Léon Poliakov, *The History of Anti-Semitism,* translated by Richard Howard et al., 4 vols. (New York, 1965–1985). The best one-volume survey is Robert S. Wistrich, *Antisemitism: The Longest Hatred* (London, 1991). For anti-Jewish sentiment in Greco-Roman civilization, see Louis Feldman, *Jew and Gentile in the Ancient World* (Princeton, N.J., 1993), and Peter Schafer, *Judeophobia: Attitudes toward the Jews in the Ancient World* (Cambridge, Mass., 1997). For overviews of Christian anti-Jewish thinking, see Jules Isaac, *The Teaching of Contempt,* translated by Helen Weaver (New York, 1964); Rosemary Radford Ruether, *Faith and Fratricide: The Theological Roots of Anti-Semitism* (New York, 1974); William Nicholls, *Christian Anti-Semitism: A History of Hate* (Northvale, N.J., 1993); and James Carroll, *Constantine's Sword: The Church and the Jews* (Boston, 2001). Much effort has been extended to identifying anti-Jewish motifs in early Christianity. See John Gager, *The Origins of Anti-Semitism: Attitudes toward Judaism in Pagan and Christian Antiquity* (New York, 1983); Craig A. Evans and Donald A. Hagner, eds., *Anti-Semitism and Early Christianity: Issues of Polemic and Faith* (Minneapolis, Minn., 1993); and William R. Farmer, ed., *Anti-Judaism and the Gospels* (Harrisburg, Pa., 1999).

Considerable attention has focused on anti-Jewish thinking in twelfth-century western Christendom. See Gavin I. Langmuir, *History, Religion, and Antisemitism* (Berkeley, Calif., 1991); Anna Sapir Abulafia, *Christians and Jews in the Twelfth-Century Renaissance* (London, 1995); Robert Chazan, *Medieval Stereotypes and Modern Antisemitism* (Berkeley, Calif., 1996); and Jeremy Cohen, *Living Letters of the Law* (Berkeley, Calif., 2000). For anti-Jewish motifs in the Reformation, see Heiko A. Oberman, *The Roots of Anti-Semitism in the Age of Renaissance and Reformation,* translated by James I. Porter (Philadelphia, 1981), and Frank E. Manuel, *The Broken Staff: Judaism through Christian Eyes* (Cambridge, Mass., 1992). For the Enlightenment, see Arthur Hertzberg, *The French Enlightenment and the Jews: The Origins of Modern Anti-Semitism* (New York, 1968); Manuel, *The Broken Staff* (cited above); and Adam Sutcliffe, *Judaism and Enlightenment* (New York, 2003). Useful surveys of nineteenth-century anti-Semitism include Jacob Katz, *From Prejudice to Destruction: 1700–1933* (Cambridge, Mass., 1980), and Albert S. Lindeman, *Esau's Tears: Modern Anti-Semitism and the Rise of the Jews* (Cambridge, Mass., 1997). For the New Anti-Semitism, see Bernard Lewis, *Semites and Anti-Semites: An Inquiry into Conflict and Prejudice* (New York, 1986).

ALAN DAVIES (1987)
ROBERT CHAZAN (2005)

ANUBIS. The Egyptians represented the god Anubis as a black jackal (a wild dog?) crouching "on his belly," or as a man with a jackal's or dog's head. *Anubis* is the Greek form of his Egyptian name, *Anpu*; the meaning of the latter is uncertain. The cult of Anubis originated in Middle Egypt, in the seventeenth province (nome), where his worship was centered. The province's town of Hardai, which had a dog cemetery in its environs, was called Kunopolis (Cynopolis) by the Greeks. But the cult was spread all over the country.

Anubis is one of the oldest funerary deities. Originally a destroyer of corpses, he was reshaped by theologians as the embalmer of gods and men. To Anubis was entrusted the mummification of Osiris (the ruler of the dead) and his followers, and the guardianship of their burials. Later Egyptian texts referred to Anubis as the son of Osiris—the product of a relationship between Osiris and his sister Nephthys.

In funeral ceremonies, the role of Anubis as promoter of the revival of the dead was performed by a priest-embalmer. Thus their earlier enemy had become their powerful ally. During the New Kingdom and later periods, a figure of the recumbent god usually appeared atop the "mystery chests" containing the prepared viscera of the dead. In this way Anubis, "he who is over the mystery," fulfilled his duty as keeper of the internal organs that he had resuscitated.

Anubis tended not only the physical well-being of the dead but their moral nature as well. He played a prominent part in the judgment hall of the hereafter. As "magistrate of the court" he examined the deceased, whom he permitted to leave the hall if the outcome was satisfactory. He continued to be the "conductor of souls" (Gr., *psuchopompos*) in the cult and mysteries of Isis during Hellenistic and Roman times. Anubis was closely associated with the pharaoh, not only after his death but at his birth as well.

BIBLIOGRAPHY

Altenmüller, Brigitte. "Anubis." In *Lexikon der Ägyptologie,* edited by Wolfgang Helck and Eberhard Otto. Wiesbaden, 1975.

DuQuense, Terence. *Jackal at the Shaman's Gate.* Thame Oxon, 1991. Anubis Lord of Ro-Setawe.

DuQuense, Terence. *At the Court of Osiris.* London, 1994. Anubis and judgment.

Grenier, Jean-Claude. *Anubis alexandrin et romain.* Leiden, 1977. Anubis in the Greco-Roman period.

Heerma van Voss, Matthieu. *Een mysteriekist ontsluierd.* Leiden, 1969. Anubis and the "mystery chest."

Heerma van Voss, Matthieu. *Anoebis en de demonen.* Leiden, 1978. Anubis as "magistrate of the court."

Leclant, Jean. "Anubis." In *Lexicon Iconographicum Mythologiae Classicae,* edited by John Boardman et al. Zürich, 1981. Anubis in the classical world.

M. HEERMA VAN VOSS (1987 AND 2005)

ANUM SEE AN

APACHE RELIGIOUS TRADITIONS.

The Lipan Apaches are one of the Apache tribes of the American Southwest outlined in the general Apache entry. Of all Apaches, the Lipans ranged the farthest east, even as far as the Mississippi River. The Lipans primarily hunted buffalo until it was no longer possible due to the near eradication of bison. During the nineteenth century the Lipans ranged over all of Texas, most of New Mexico, and adjacent areas of Mexico. Between 1680 and 1730, Apache buffalo hunters ranged Colorado, Kansas, Nebraska, and Oklahoma. The extent of Lipan Apache territory meant that some bands were not in contact with others and that frequent interaction with outside groups led to variations in Lipan material culture and worldviews. Lipan Apache leadership was inestimably important in the emergence of traditions that have been heavily drawn upon in the religious use of peyote. Lipan relations with indigenous peoples south of their range were key in their adoption of the religious use of peyote and Lipan relations with buffalo hunters in the north were integral to the transmission of peyote religion to American Indian tribes in New Mexico and Oklahoma.

LIPAN APACHE BUFFALO HUNTERS: ORIGINS AND MIGRATIONS. Lipan oral tradition from New Mexico states that the first Lipan tipi was put up far to the north (Begay, 2003) and oral tradition among the Texas Lipans states that the people came from northern origins (Romero Jr., 2000). In 1940 Morris Opler, while documenting Lipan oral tradition, recorded claims of a northern origin for Lipans and accounts of an exodus out of the forest and onto the plains. However, Lipan oral tradition in New Mexico holds strongly to a belief in an origin in the Sierra Madre Mountains of Chihuahua (Begay, 2003), from whence emerged 'Isánáklésh, a divine being whose face is stained white. This belief is one of the pillars of Apache creation stories on the Mescalero Apache Indian reservation and is still central to the women's coming-of-age ceremony, the Fire Ceremony. Despite differences as to whether Lipan origins lie in the north or south, there is agreement that from quite early on Lipans lived as buffalo hunters on the northern plains. This conforms to the view of linguists that the Athapaskan language had its origins in northern Canada and Alaska.

Linguistic, archaeological, and historical evidence shows that Lipan Apache origins are embedded in a buffalo-hunting tradition that spanned North America for over 11,000 years and that was characterized by tipi rings, buffalo kill sites, bow and arrow technology, and burned rock middens on the Great Plains. Between 1450 and 1725, Lipan ancestors occupied a massive territorial homeland that spanned the buffalo plains of Texas, eastern New Mexico, southern Colorado, Oklahoma, Kansas, and Nebraska. Before the European invasion, Apache buffalo hunters participated in trade networks that included the pueblos of the Southwest and the Caddoan Plains villages. Later, this system was disrupted by pressure from Spanish colonialists and by the enmeshment of Apache buffalo hunters in patterns of violence and slavery that culminated in the 1680 Pueblo Revolt in New Mexico. These changes resulted in Apache buffalo hunters becoming mounted hunters and rangers who forged anticolonial alliances with indigenous peoples of south Texas and northeastern Mexico, alliances that produced specific forms of cultural affiliation. However, the Lipans eventually left Texas and Mexico to join the Mescaleros and Chiracahuas in New Mexico. At Mescalero, Lipan religion was maintained as part of everyday life on the reservation.

LIPAN RELIGION ON THE MESCALERO APACHE RESERVATION. According to Meredith Begay, a medicine woman from the Mescalero Apache Reservation with Lipan, Mescalero, and Chiracahua lineage, Apache religion is based on a spiritual sense by which Apaches live with respect. Begay referred to this as a sixth sense that directs Lipans to treat the sacred in a specifically Apache way. Importantly, Lipans should seek to understand the stories told about the way people act and the way that people should act, and conduct themselves accordingly. All Apaches carry this spiritual respect for the Creator, the Four Directions, Mother Earth, and "certain deities in the sky like the north star, the sun, the moon and some of the other stars that are there" (Begay, 2004). These deities take care of humans and so must be revered. The desire to build correct relations in accordance with the stories provides direction for Lipan life and a means by which Lipans cultivate knowledge and the power to heal. It is through this alignment of the stories with personal vision and action that medicine is acquired. Medicine is intended for the good of one's family and tribe, and when a person pursues and utilizes such power for personal gain at the expense of others, this is understood as witchcraft or the misuse of power.

The Lipan account of the creation of the earth involves the prophets Killer-of-Enemies and his brother Child of Water, as well as their mother 'Isánáklésh, also known as Changing Woman. 'Isánáklésh's part in the creation story is the model for the girls' puberty ceremony that is common to all Apaches. Special ceremonies such as this are times when families are called upon to bring their medicine in the form of songs and the spiritual work of ceremonial preparation and participation. However, sacred narratives are not just ceremonial guideposts, they are integral to teaching basic understandings of Lipan life.

For example, Child of Water represents the "right hand" and loving way, whereas the Killer-of-Enemies symbolizes the "left hand," which is not so loving. Child of Water provides refuge and salvation for people and animals, whereas Killer-of-Enemies changes animals from destroyers and killers of people to providers of meat and clothing by making sacred agreements between animals and people. Mrs. Begay explained that in a blessing for Daniel Romero Castro III, who was about to be sent to Iraq, she made sure, because she knew he might be going to the desert, to "talk to the snake, to the scorpion, to the spiders, to any other living creatures that wanna, . . . uh, be mean. . . . I ask them please look at him with the right hand."

Lipan oral traditions and the rituals and games associated with them not only instruct Lipans on how to behave, they also explain a system of correspondences between human and animal behaviors and attitudes that is rooted in the time when animals spoke and acted like people. The Moccasin Game reflects the way that the sun first broke free and lit up the earth after a Lipan gambling game. The game is played with a "buffalo shoe," which is the ball that is above the buffalo's heel. Four holes are dug into the ground, songs are sung for every animal and bird, and one person hides the ball. Players form two teams and all night long bet on who will find the ball. The center of the Yucca flower is used to keep count. Mrs. Begay explained its importance:

> Before the Shoe [Moccasin] Game the world was dark, it was completely dark. . . . So, what happened is that, the big animals, they could see in the dark, and that the small animals, they could not see in the dark. The only time they saw was when the lightning struck . . . and they were getting killed by the big animals. So, they got together, both sides, and said we'll have a Shoe Game and whoever wins will rule the earth. If the big animals win it can be dark and if the small people win they call it daylight. . . . That's when the Game started; they started to hide the ball (buffalo shoe), and the last one to find it was a small animal and that's when the sun came out. The big animals got mad and started fighting. The Giant was the last to die. And then the Giant who died, he fell . . . [there are] four mountains there where he fell. Everybody in that Shoe Game, whatever they do, is still with them today. However, they paid with themselves; everything they was changed since the minute that the sun got turned and it stayed with them. . . . [Before,] they could understand one another, they could talk to the plants, rocks and everything—that stopped right there. (2004)

During the Moccasin Game, all of the animals did crazy things that changed them forever. For example, when the fight broke out in the morning, the bear put his feet on backwards and the snake—which at that time had many legs, like a centipede—gambled away all his limbs. Coyote was already up to his tricks. While the other animals were trying to win for their respective teams, Coyote was sneaking around in the back, switching sides all night long, trying to get on the winning side. This vacillating attitude and behavior stayed with him and is a central element of Lipan Coyote Stories that admonish people, especially men, for selfish and irresponsible behavior. In addition to providing spiritual knowledge and warnings about the consequences of bad behavior, the stories also provide positive role models that exemplify proper leadership, participation, and etiquette in everyday life. Lipan leaders are constantly reminded of the necessity for proper conduct and the dangers of transgression. Similarly, other family and social roles are defined in the stories and Lipans are strongly encouraged to fulfill these roles by exhibiting proper behavior and respecting important taboos.

Important to the Lipan spiritual life are medicines that fulfill both spiritual and medical needs. Preparation for the religious work of blessing and healing includes the gathering of medicine. Medicine in this sense is part of a system of kinship relations that a Lipan has with celestial, elemental, animal, and plant beings that are corresponded with and called upon through the correct arrangement of words, actions, and objects. For example, Apaches are supposed to always carry cattail pollen in case they have a vision or other similar experience and must bless both themselves and the place in which the sacred event occurred. Thus, the simple act of carrying a pollen bag and knowing how to make a pollen blessing are ways in which Apaches manifest their respect for the sacred.

Pollen is a central part of Lipan religious life. According to Begay, "pollen is used because it is so light and so fine that it brought light to us. So pollen is used for blessing anything. An Apache never goes anywhere without pollen, they always carry it in a bag" (2004). Other important medicines include tobacco, sage, osha, the eagle feather, and ashes from a clean wood fire. Begay comments, "cigarette smoke, tobacco, is part of our religion . . . [and] the sage medicine from burning the sage, smudging and all that." She also refers to the importance of herbal medicines, such as *Hi'eechida,* known in Mexico as *Tuchupate,* and in English as osha, bear root, or hot root. Ashes can help people with *Son on di kou,* a state of anxiety or trauma often accompanied by nightmares and sleepwalking. According to Begay, *Son on di kou* occurs to people "cause they saw somethin' crazy, or they did something crazy during the day, or something scared them so bad that they get up that night and they walk around" (2004). But, as in all blessing and healing, 99 percent is in the mind and spirit and only 1 percent comes from outside.

It is important to understand the Lipan conception of the dead. Zelda Yazza, Mrs. Begay's daughter, comments in unpublished notes: "Dead people go to the other side of the river within four days after they die. When they go over there they join with those other people and become enemies. This is why it is traditionally important to bury people within four days." This belief has much to do with Lipan avoidance and even fear of the dead. However, this attitude has been altered over time by Christian beliefs and practices.

LIPAN APACHE RELIGIOUS USE OF PEYOTE. By the middle of the eighteenth century, Spanish documents attribute the religious use of peyote to Apache buffalo hunters, within the context of their reputation as a key pivot in anticolonial action and warfare. Indigenous people living in missions near the peyote gardens, from present-day Coahuila through Nuevo León and into Tamaulipas, form an important foundation of the use of peyote in *mitotes* (a term used by Spanish chroniclers to refer to Native American spiritual gatherings and festivities). Father Juan Larios, who in 1673 established a mission just south of the Lomería de los Peyotes (Peyote Hills) near Villa Unión, Coahuila, identified the local hills as gardens from which Indians would harvest peyote for their *mitote* and ceremonials (Steck, 1932). In 1674 San Bernardino de la Candela was founded for Catujano, Milijae, and Tilijai Indians, known for their *mitotes* (Wade, 1998). Alonso de León described the *mitote* as the most common and frequent pastime for the indigenous people of northeastern Mexico. León reported that indigenous people collected peyote and gathered around a fire to sing vocables (words with no linguistic meaning), shake small gourds filled with stones gathered from ant mounds, dance, and hold giveaways in the morning (León, Chapa, and Zamora, 1961, p. 24). All of these practices are traditions in the Native American Church.

The association of Mission Indians in northeastern Mexico with peyote and *mitote* provides key evidence that helps explain how Lipan Apaches adopted the religious use of peyote. Lipan oral tradition identifies the Carrizo Nation as the source of the rite that includes the religious use of peyote. Historical documents show that by 1755 Carrizo groups had ties to the Apache anticolonial alliance, lived within neighboring missions, and are reported to have engaged in the religious use of peyote with Apaches and Lipans. On April 14, 1770, Father Lorenzo de la Peña reported that Apaches and Julimeños held a *mitote* with peyote at Mission Peyote. In 1828 Jean Berlandier reported that the coastal peoples, Tonkawas, and Lipans still used peyote in their feasts. Almost fifty years later, Frederick Buckelew reported that the Lipan Apaches had shared a *mitote* with the Kickapoo in 1865.

After 1865 the religious use of peyote began to expand outside of Texas, leading eventually to the formation of the Native American Church. The widespread adoption of the religious use of peyote via the influence of Comanche Chief Quanah Parker, who had learned a form peyote ceremonial from the Lipan Apaches, is well known. The Quahadis Comanches, led by Quanah Parker, learned of *Wok-wave* (as Comanches call peyote) from the Lipan Apaches sometime before 1878. Kiowa-Apache and Arapaho oral tradition agree with this understanding. Nelson Big Bow, a Kiowa, stated, "Quanah Parker brought Lipan Apache from Mescalero to run *Peyote* meetings." These Lipans were identified as Chivato, Pinero, and Escaona and were brought to Cache, Oklahoma, by Quanah Parker. In addition to the Native American Church's religious use of peyote, there is evidence of the survival of the religious use of peyote among the Cuelgahen Nde Lipan Apaches at Three Rivers, Texas.

Santos Peralez Castro, interviewed in 1999, recalled a *mitote* held in 1956 that included the religious use of peyote:

> I remember my dad and mom calling it a *miyote [mitote]*, it was a green cactus. I remember my mom and dad would invite their friends over, my mom used to cook lots of stuff. Before the invited got there, they would get a lot of corn, they used a lot of corn and we all would grind it and make tamales and tortillas from the corn and she would cook beans and rice. The friends used to make a circle and a big fire and they used to make a circle around the fire and all their friends were in the circle. All the friends used to make a circle, all the grown-ups would make the circle. They would all smoke this big pipe and pass it around the circle to smoke it and after they smoked it they would pass a small basket and eat the peyote and they eat all night and would continue all night, singing and dancing till the next day. I remember the kids were not allowed in the circle and we would sleep all night and then wake up the next morning to eat, I remember.

CONCLUSION. As with most indigenous American religions, Lipan spiritual life is not relegated to church or holidays, but is part of a respectful way of life that is prescribed in the oral tradition and that guides proper relations with and behavior toward both sacred objects and deities and one's family and tribe.

SEE ALSO North American Indians, article on Indians of the Southwest.

BIBLIOGRAPHY

Begay, Meredith. Interview by Enrique Maestas. Digital recording. Mescalero, N. Mex., November 15, 2003.

Begay, Meredith. Interview by Enrique Maestas. Tape recording. Mescalero, N. Mex., April 8, 2004.

Castro, Santiago Castro. "Castro Oral History." Tape recording. San Antonio, Tex., April 1995.

Castro, Santos Peralez. "Family Oral History with Santos Castro." Tape recording. Corcoran, Calif., April 12, 1999.

León, Alonso de, Juan Bautsita Chapa, and Fernando Sánchez Zamora. *Historia de Nuevo León, con noticias sobre Coahuila,*

Tamaulipas, Texas, y Nuevo México. Monterrey, Mexico, 1961.

Maestas, Enrique. "Culture and History of Native American Peoples of South Texas." Ph.D. diss., University of Texas, Austin, 2003.

Opler, Morris. "The Use of Peyote by the Carrizo and Lipan Apache Tribes." *American Anthropologist* 40, no. 2 (1938): 271–285.

Opler, Morris. *Myths and Legends of the Lipan Apache Indians.* American Indian Folklore Society Memoir 36. New York, 1940.

Romero, Daniel Castro, Jr. Interview by Enrique Maestas. Tape recording. San Antonio, Tex., October 5, 2000.

Salinas, Martin. *Indians of the Rio Grande Delta: Their Role in the History of Southern Texas and Northeastern Mexico.* Austin, Tex., 1990.

Sjoberg, Andrée. "Lipan Apache Culture in Historical Perspective." *Southwestern Journal of Anthropology* 9, no. 1 (Spring 1953): 76–98.

Stewart, Omer C. "Origin of the Peyote Religion in the United States." *Plains Anthropologist* 19, no. 64 (1974): 211–223.

ENRIQUE MAESTAS (2005)

APHRODITE. Aphrodite's name is closely related to ideas of sex, love, pleasure, and beauty. To evaluate the relevance of this minimal definition in the goddess's own cultural context, it is necessary to investigate both Greek literature carrying myths and Greek cult practice. Even if each of these fields has its own language, they act as mirrors of each other.

SOME LITERARY EVIDENCE. The most ancient Greek texts present two traditions of Aphrodite's birth. According to Hesiod *(Theogony* 188–206), she was born from the severed genitals of the Sky god, Uranus, which were thrown to the Sea god, Pontos. Aphrodite is the first anthropomorphic goddess to emerge in the cosmogonic process after the first physical entities, such as Earth, Sky, Mountains, and so on. Eros (Love), whose presence at the world's very beginning promotes union and reproduction, submits to the goddess as soon as she appears. Hesiod explains the name *Aphrodite* by the marine and seminal foam *(aphros)* from which she grows, and he defines her divine power as the field of seduction and deception.

According to Homer, Aphrodite is the daughter of Zeus and Dione, and she is concerned with the "works of marriage" (*Ilias* 5, 429). From a cosmogonic point of view, the difference between Hesiod and Homer is important. On the one hand, Aphrodite belongs to the earlier generation of deities, before Zeus himself. On the other hand, she is placed under the paternal authority of Zeus. However, her sphere of intervention remains the same: sexuality legitimated by society (with marriage), as well as its destructive aspect (the rape of Helen by Paris, presented as a reward offered by Aphrodite, is at the core of the Trojan War). The fifth *Homeric Hymn* offers another example of such ambivalence. The hymn first praises Aphrodite as the goddess who makes all the gods (even Zeus) mingle with mortal women. This uncontrolled power, which confuses divine and human levels, is dangerous for the cosmic order. To avoid this potential disturbance, Zeus makes the goddess lie with a mortal, Anchises, and she gives birth to a child, Aeneas. At this moment of the theogonic process, Aphrodite truly becomes a daughter of Zeus.

On the classical Athenian stage, tragedy illustrates how necessary it is to submit to sexual union—and to what extent the goddess's anger can be disastrous to the human who refuses this destiny. Hippolytos's fate in Euripides's homonymous play perfectly fits this important aspect of the human condition: because he despises sexual union and marriage, the young hero insults a mighty goddess and must die. A fragment of Aeschylus's *Danaids* (fr. 44 Radt), quoting a monologue of Aphrodite, presents with sexual imagery the sky irrigating the earth to bring forth for mortals the pasturage of sheep and cereals. This watery union is explicitly presented as Aphrodite's work. As goddess of sexuality, her field of manifestation includes fecundity and fertility in close connection, but it would be inadequate to interpret the Greek Aphrodite only as a mother goddess or a fertility goddess. Fertility is part of this field as an extension, of which the cultic manifestations are difficult to discern. From Sappho to Lucrece, poetry celebrates the power of love, the impact of beauty, and the force of desire, closely connecting them with Aphrodite's sphere. Ares, Hephaestus, Hermes, Dionysos, and Adonis are at various times given as her lovers.

CULTS. Aphrodite's cults extend widely over the Greek world, but her temples and festivals cannot compete with those of other great feminine divinities, such as Hera, Demeter, or Artemis. Aphrodite was worshiped above all as presiding over sexuality. Thus, in many cities, girls about to be married made sacrifices to Aphrodite so that their first sexual experience might be propitious (Diod. Sic. 5, 73, 2; Plutarchus *Mor.* 264b; Pausanias 2, 32, 7; 34, 12). This is the particular sphere of Aphrodite, compared with other goddesses involved in marriage: Hera protects its legal status, Demeter favors reproduction, and Artemis patronizes defloration and pregnancy and protects unborn children and infants.

But sexuality is much broader than marriage. Aphrodite protects all forms of sexual union—in or outside marriage; hetero- or homosexual; or with concubines, courtesans *(hetairai)*, or prostitutes *(pornai)*. These women are well attested in different festivals in honor of Aphrodite, separated or not from "respectable" matrons (Alexis, fr. 253 Kock = Athenaeus 13, 574b–c). The city of Corinth was particularly known for the beauty and luxurious living of its courtesans, who revered the local Aphrodite (Pindar, fr. 122 Snell-Maehler). It is unlikely, however, that her sanctuary on Acrocorinth was the location of an institutionalized form of what is generally called "sacred prostitution." The only source for this practice is the geographer Strabo (first century BCE; 8,

6, 21 [C378–379]), but he places it in a vague past time and is certainly influenced by practices of this type that have been documented in Asia Minor, his native country. Herodotus, who mentions a similar practice in several parts of the Mediterranean area, does not say anything in regard to Corinth. Even if the argument *ex silentio* is always difficult to use, it invites caution. Some indigenous cults that *interpretatio graeca* translates into Aphrodite cults in Asia Minor (Tralles), in Italy (Gravisca, Locri) or Sicily (Eryx), have been associated with this kind of sacred prostitution. Without systematically rejecting this view, it has to be evaluated with caution.

In Hesiodic *Theogony,* Harmony is the daughter of Aphrodite (Love) and Ares (War). In the same vein, Aphrodite is closely connected with the Charites, or the "Graces," personifications of *charis,* (grace and charm). Such symbolic associations encompass the goddess's associations with civic harmony, concord, and order. Since the fifth century BCE at least, magistrates honored her in their official capacity at the end of services. Two interpretations, which are not incompatible, can be proposed: on the one hand, these officials thank the goddess for the harmonious performance of their duties; on the other hand, these *aphrodisia* mark the return from duty to the pleasures of private life. Such dedications can associate the goddess Peitho (Persuasion) with Aphrodite.

This civic aspect of Aphrodite's sphere is also attested to by the *epiklesis* (cultic qualification) Pandemos. It means "she of all the people" and declares the goddess to be responsible for political concord and civic inclusiveness. In Athens, the goddess was worshiped with Peitho, and her epithet was explained by the myth of Theseus, who had unified all the Attic demes in one city (Pausanias 1, 22, 3). A third-century BCE Athenian inscription describes an official procession for Aphrodite Pandemos (where it is tempting to imagine the participation of "all the people") and the cathartic sacrifice of a dove, her sacred animal, in her temple (*Inscriptiones Graecae* II^2 659 = *Lois sacrées des cités grecques* no. 39). In Plato's *Symposium* (180 d–e), Aphrodite Pandemos appears in opposition to Aphrodite Urania as the goddess who protects, respectively, vulgar heterosexual love and spiritual love between males. This philosophical fantasy will become very popular, but it contradicts what is documented for both cults. Pandemos does not mean "vulgar love" in the cult (even if comic poets associate the cult's foundation with funds received from public brothels, [Athenaios 13, 569d–e]), and the Athenian cult of Urania is deeply rooted in heterosexual love and marriage (*Supplementum Epigraphicum Graecum* 41, 182; Pausanias 1, 27, 3).

On the island of Cos, Aphrodite was worshiped as Pandamos (the Doric form of Pandemos), just as in Athens, but also as Pontia (she of the sea). This joint cult is known from two inscriptions referring to the sale of the priesthood (Parker, 2002). Both aspects are reflected in the worshipers' quality and obligations. All women who marry on the island, citizen women, illegitimate women, and metics, have to offer a sacrifice to the goddess within a year: a good summary of sexual and inclusive divine functionality. On the other hand, sea-traders also have to honor the goddess, "she of the sea," with sacrifice or cash payment. Such an association with the sea is widely attested in the Mediterranean era by epithets like Euploia (she who gives good sailing) or Limenia (she of the shore). One way to explain this refers to the peculiar birth of the goddess from the sea foam. Another refers to her general power to calm and to dissolve disorder, be it human or natural.

Two last aspects of Aphrodite's cults are the "black" side and the "armed" side. In some places, Aphrodite bears the epithet *Melainis* (the black one) (Pausanias 2, 2, 4; 9, 27, 5; 8, 6, 5), which could possibly show her power on the "black earth" and humus, as well as on the shades of the night, the favorite time for sexual relations. According to Pausanias, there were statues showing an armed Aphrodite, particularly in Sparta (3, 15, 10; 3, 23, 1). The Spartan upbringing of girls was very martial, and it is not surprising to see the goddess of femaleness being given male attire there, but the actual examples of this scarcely permit the interpretation of Aphrodite as a war goddess, except in connection with a protective role, such as she had at Corinth.

From a structuralist perspective, her association with Ares has more to do with a wish to bring opposites together than with a similarity of function. But a historical perspective for studying Aphrodite's cults and persona leads to another interpretation. Aphrodite is not attested in the Mycenaean Linear B texts, and the Greeks themselves made the goddess arrive from the Levantine coast, or even Assyria, via Cyprus through the Phoenician agency (Herodotus 1, 105; Pausanias 1, 14, 7). The Sumerian Innana, Akkadian Ishtar, and Phoenician Astarte share many significant characteristics with Aphrodite. Indeed, all are "Queens of Heaven" (Urania), connected with sexuality, birds, war, and, in the case of Astarte, seafaring. As early as Homer, Aphrodite is called Kupris (the Cypriote), and her main sanctuaries belong to the island—in Paphos, where her tripartite shrine dates from the twelfth century BCE onward and where she is called Paphia or Wanassa (the Queen) in Myceneaen Greek; in Amathous, where she is called Kupria; and in Kition, with a clearly Phoenician cult.

Today, the theory of Aphrodite's oriental origin, dated early in the first millennium, is largely accepted, and Indo-European or indigenous points of view do not have enough support in the evidence at hand. But the ways of Aphrodite's arrival are very difficult to discern with certainty, in spite of the positive conclusions of Stephanie Lynn Budin (2003). The iconography of the frontally naked "goddess" that reaches Mediterranean sanctuaries in the Geometric and early Archaic periods could have been an important medium for the conceptualization of a goddess concerned with sexuality at a time when local Greek pantheons were in development. The iconography of a nude goddess then disappears for two centuries, returning with the Aphrodite of Praxiteles in the mid-fourth century BCE. Such a masterpiece opens the road to the Hellenistic and Roman representations of the nude Aphrodite-Venus that inhabit Western museums and imaginations.

SEE ALSO Goddess Worship, overview article; Hierodouleia; Venus.

BIBLIOGRAPHY

Ammerman, Rebecca Miller. *The Sanctuary of Santa Venera at Paestum II: The Votive Terracottas.* Ann Arbor, Mich., 2002. See pages 26–98 for a discussion of the "naked goddess."

Boedeker, Deborah Dickmann. *Aphrodite's Entry into Greek Epic.* Leiden, 1974.

Böhm, Stephanie. *Die "Nackte Göttin": Zur Ikonographie und Deutung unbekleideter weiblicher Figuren in der frühgriechischen Kunst.* Mainz, Germany, 1990.

Bonnet, Corinne. *Astarté: Dossier documentaire et perspectives historiques.* Rome, 1996.

Budin, Stephanie Lynn. *The Origin of Aphrodite.* Bethesda, Md., 2003.

Delivorrias, Angelos. "Aphrodite." In *Lexicon Iconographicum Mythologiae Classicae,* vol. 2, pp. 2–151. Zurich, 1984.

Farnell, Lewis R. *The Cults of the Greek States,* vol. 2, pp. 618–761. Oxford, 1896. Still a useful reference work, full of ancient sources.

Flemberg, Johan. *Venus Armata: Studien zur bewaffneten Aphrodite in der griechisch-römischen Kunst.* Stockholm, 1991.

Friedrich, Paul. *The Meaning of Aphrodite.* Chicago, 1978.

Graf, Fritz. "Aphrodite." In *Dictionary of Deities and Demons in the Bible* (DDD), edited by Karel van der Toorn, Bob Becking, and Pieter W. van der Horst, pp. 118–125. Leiden, 1995.

Parker, Robert. "The Cult of Aphrodite Pandamos and Pontia at Cos." In *Kykeon: Studies in Honour of H.S. Versnel,* edited by H. F.J. Horstmanshoff, H. W. Singor, F. T. van Straten, and J. H. M. Strubbe, pp. 143–160. Leiden, 2002.

Pirenne-Delforge, Vinciane. *L'Aphrodite grecque. Contribution à l'étude de ses cultes et de sa personnalité dans le panthéon archaïque et classique.* Liège, Belgium, 1994.

Pirenne-Delforge, Vinciane. "La genèse de l'Aphrodite grecque: le dossier crétois." In *La questione delle influenze vicino-orientali sulla religione greca,* edited by Sergio Ribichini, Maria Rocchi, and Paolo Xella, pp. 169–187. Rome, 2001.

Rudhardt, Jean. *Le rôle d'Eros et d'Aphrodite dans les cosmogonies grecques.* Paris, 1986.

VINCIANE PIRENNE-DELFORGE (2005)

APOCALYPSE

This entry consists of the following articles:

APOCALYPSE: AN OVERVIEW

Apocalypse, as the name of a literary genre, is derived from the *Apocalypse of John,* or *Book of Revelation,* in the New Testament. The word itself means "revelation," but it is reserved for revelations of a particular kind: mysterious revelations that are mediated or explained by a supernatural figure, usually an angel. They disclose a transcendent world of supernatural powers and an eschatological scenario, or view of the last things, that includes the judgment of the dead. Apocalyptic revelations are not exclusively concerned with the future. They may also be concerned with cosmology, including the geography of the heavens and nether regions, as well as history, primordial times, and the end times. The judgment of the dead, however, is a constant and pivotal feature, since all the revelations have human destiny as their ultimate focus. The great majority of these writings are pseudonymous: the recipient of the revelation is identified as a famous ancient person, such as Enoch or Daniel. (The *Book of Revelation* is an exception in this regard.) The ascription to a famous person added to the authority of the works, which were in any case presented as divine revelation.

The *Book of Revelation* (about 90 CE) is the earliest work that calls itself an *apocalypse* (*Rv.* 1:1), and even there the word may be meant in the general sense of "revelation." The usage as a genre label became common from the second century on, and numerous Christian compositions are so titled (e.g., the *Apocalypse of Peter,* the *Apocalypse of Paul).* The *Cologne Mani Codex* (fifth century) refers to the apocalypses of Adam, Sethel, Enosh, Shem, and Enoch. The title is found in some Jewish apocalypses from the late first century CE (e.g., *2 Baruch* and *3 Baruch*), but may have been added by later scribes. The ancient usage is not entirely reliable. The title was never added to some major apocalypses (e.g., those contained in *1 Enoch*) and it is occasionally found in works of a different genre (e.g., the *Apocalypse of Moses,* which is a variant of the *Life of Adam and Eve*).

THE JEWISH APOCALYPSES. The genre is older than the title and is well attested in Judaism from the third century BCE on. The Christian apocalypses, beginning with the *Book of Revelation,* are modeled more or less directly on Jewish prototypes. The Jewish apocalypses are of two main types. The better known of these might be described as historical apocalypses. They are found in the *Book of Daniel* (the only apocalypse in the Hebrew scriptures), *4 Ezra, 2 Baruch,* and some sections of *1 Enoch.* In these apocalypses, the revelation is given in allegorical visions, interpreted by an angel. The content is primarily historical and is given in the form of an extended prophecy. History is divided into a set number of periods and, most importantly, is coming to an end. The finale may include the national and political restoration of Israel, but the emphasis is on the replacement of the present world order by one that is radically new. In its most extreme form the eschatology of this type of apocalypse envisages the end of the world, as, for example, in *4 Ezra* 7, where the creation is returned to primeval silence for seven days. These apocalypses often had their origin in a historical crisis. The *Book* *of Daniel* and some sections of *1 Enoch* were written in response to the persecution of the Jews by Antiochus Epiphanes that led to the Maccabean revolt (c. 168 BCE). *4 Ezra* and *2 Baruch* were written in the aftermath of the Jewish war against Rome and the destruction of Jerusalem.

The second type of Jewish apocalypse is the otherworldly journey. In the earliest example of this type, the "Book of the Watchers" in *1 Enoch* (third century BCE), Enoch ascends to the presence of God. Angels then take him on a tour that ranges over the whole earth to the ends of the universe. More characteristic of this type is the ascent of the visionary through a numbered series of heavens. The standard number of heavens was seven, although three (in the *Testament of Levi*) and five (in *3 Baruch*) are also attested. More mystical in orientation, these apocalypses often include a vision of the throne of God. The eschatology of these works is focused more on personal afterlife than on cosmic transformation, but they may also predict a general judgment.

These two types of apocalypse are not wholly discrete. The *Apocalypse of Abraham,* an ascent-type apocalypse from the late first century CE, contains a brief overview of history in set periods. The *Similitudes of Enoch,* a Jewish work of the mid-first century CE, combines allegorical visions with an ascent and is largely concerned with political and social abuses. Both types are found in the collection of writings known as *1 Enoch,* which is known in full only in Geez (Ethiopic) translations, but is now attested in Aramaic fragments from the Dead Sea Scrolls, which date to the second century CE.

If apocalypse is conceived as a literary genre, in the manner described above, then the primary corpus consists of Jewish and Christian texts that date from the Hellenistic period to the early Middle Ages, although some instances can also be found in other traditions. The importance of apocalypse in the history of religion, however, is not confined to the instances of the literary genre. The kinds of ideas that find their classic expression in apocalypses like *Revelation* can also occur in other works, whether they are represented as revelations or not. This analogous phenomenon is called *apocalypticism,* or sometimes *apocalyptic.* So, for example, in ancient Judaism, the "Community Rule" in the Dead Sea Scrolls describes a world divided between the forces of light and darkness, where history is divided into periods and there will be a final judgment when God will put an end to wickedness. This view of the world is clearly influenced by the apocalypses of *Enoch* and *Daniel,* and is similar to the typical content of apocalyptic revelations, but it is not presented in the form of a vision or other revelation. It is simply presented as dogmatic teaching.

Again, early Christianity is often said to be "an apocalyptic movement," although the only apocalypse in the New Testament (*Revelation*) is one of the latest writings in the corpus. The Gospels and the Pauline epistles share basic features of the apocalypses, especially the expectation of judgment from heaven followed by the resurrection and judgment of the dead, so that we may speak of a common worldview. In modern colloquial usage, the word *apocalypse* is often associated with the end of the world, or with some great catastrophe. This analogous usage of the word *apocalyptic* is inevitably imprecise, as resemblance is a matter of degree. In the Western world, the case for this broader usage is strengthened by the pervasive influence of the literary apocalypses, especially the *Book of Revelation.* The expectation of an "end" of history, or of a new era of radical change, has been enormously important in Christian tradition, but also in Judaism and Islam, and while it is often the subject of a vision or a revelation it can also be communicated in many other ways. Moreover, these ideas have also been appropriated by secular culture.

Analogous ideas and movements can also be found in many other cultures. One thinks, for example, of the cargo cults of Melanesia or the Ghost Dance of the American Indians in the late nineteenth century (although in the latter case there was some influence of Christian ideas). The historical type of apocalypticism is difficult to distinguish from *millennialism,* a term that is itself derived from the expectation of a thousand-year reign in *Revelation* 20, but which has come to mean the expectation of radical change and a utopian future. Strictly speaking, apocalypticism should imply a claim of supernatural revelation, which may or may not be the case with millennial expectation. Also related to apocalypticism is *messianism,* or the expectation of a messiah or savior figure. This term also derives from Jewish and Christian tradition, and originally referred to the restoration of native kingship in Judea. Some apocalypses accord a central role to a messiah (e.g., Christ in *Revelation,* or the Jewish messiah in *4 Ezra*). The earliest Jewish apocalypses, however, in *1 Enoch* and *Daniel,* have no place for a human messiah. Conversely, a messiah may be expected to restore the political order on earth, rather than bring about the kind of cosmic upheaval described in the apocalypses. Messianism and apocalypticism, then, overlap, but the two categories are not identical.

ORIGINS OF THE GENRE. This genre appears relatively late in Judaism, and its origins remain obscure. Several key apocalyptic motifs can be found at much earlier times in the ancient Middle East and in the eastern Mediterranean world. Many ancient myths describe a climactic battle in which a good god defeats the forces of chaos. This battle is sometimes associated with the creation of the world, as in the Babylonian *Enuma elish,* where the god Marduk defeats and kills the primeval monster Tiamat. In Canaanite tradition, the fertility god Baal defeats the primordial sea, Yamm. These ancient myths are echoed in the climactic battles in apocalypses such as *Daniel* and *Revelation,* but the conflict is projected into the future.

Descriptions of journeys to the heavens or the netherworld were fairly common in antiquity. Examples can be found as early as book 11 of Homer's *Odyssey.* A whole tradition of such revelations can be found in Greek and Roman philosophical texts (e.g., the "Myth of Er" in Plato's *Republic,* book 10; Cicero's *Somnium Scipionis* in the last book of his *Republic*), in what would seem to be a secondary use of the genre. The Greek material exercised some influence on the Jewish journey-type apocalypses and on the Christian development of the genre, but it was not a primary model. There are also traditions of ascent to heaven and descent to the netherworld in Babylonian tradition, although they are sparsely attested. Especially noteworthy here is a "Vision of the Netherworld" from the seventh century BCE, in which a man descends to the netherworld in a dream vision. The ascent of the soul after death was an important motif in Persian eschatology from early times. The only Persian example of a thoroughgoing ascent-type apocalypse is the ninth-century CE *Book of Arda Viraf,* or *Ardā Wirāz Nāmag,* but there seems to have been a native Persian tradition of heavenly ascent. These ascent traditions (Greek, Babylonian, and Persian) were independent of each other, but all may have influenced the Jewish and Christian apocalypses to some degree. The judgment of the dead, a central apocalyptic motif, is widely attested in ancient Egypt. We can scarcely speak of an apocalyptic tradition in Egypt, however, although there are several predictions of times of chaos, and there are some oracles from the Hellenistic period about the restoration of native Egyptian rule (most notably, the *Potter's Oracle*) that bear some similarity to the historical apocalypses.

Apart from the Jewish and Christian apocalypses, the most important apocalyptic tradition in antiquity is undoubtedly the Persian. This tradition is found primarily in the Pahlavi literature that was compiled in the late Sassanian and early Islamic periods (sixth to twelfth centuries CE). This literature is priestly in character, and it provides compendia of authoritative teaching. It does not preserve independent literary revelations or apocalypses such as are found in Jewish and Christian literature, with the arguable exception of the *Bahman Yasht,* which describes a vision of Zoroaster in which the branches of a tree represent the periods of history. One of the most important of these compilations is the *Bundahishn,* which deals with cosmogony and cosmology and has important sections treating eschatology. Another is the *Dēnkard,* which contains, among other things, a systematic description of the apocalyptic events from the fall of the Sassanian empire to the restoration of the world. Other important Persian writings for this subject include the *Wizīdagīhā ī Zādspram* (Selections of Zādspram, a late ninth-century author) and the *Dādestān ī Dēnīg* (compiled by a brother of Zādspram). The latter composition contains questions and answers on such topics as the resurrection and the renewal of the world. Also cast in the form of question and answer is the *Dādestān ī Mēnōg ī Xrad* (Judgments of the spirit of wisdom) in which a fictive figure called Dānāg (literally, "wise, knowing") addresses questions to the Spirit of Wisdom. Some of these questions concern eschatological matters.

These traditions may be described as apocalyptic because they share some of the characteristic features of the historical apocalypses, such as the division of history into a set number of periods, the final destruction of evil, and a restoration of the world that involves the resurrection of the dead. The most complete account is found in the *Bundahishn.* From the beginning, there were two cosmic spirits of light and darkness. The decisive battle between them is postponed for nine thousand years, and during that time they share the sovereignty. The nine thousand years is divided into three ages of three thousand years each. At the completion of the last period, evil is eliminated, the dead are resurrected, and the world is restored. The last three thousand years is divided into three millennia with similar characteristics. The first begins with the appearance of Zoroaster. Each of the others also starts with a savior figure, Ušēdar and Ušedarmāh. Each millennium ends with trials and tribulations. The final savior, who ushers in the restoration, is Sōšans. Two other messianic figures, Kay Wahrām and Pišyōtan appear at the end of the millennium of Zoroaster.

There is endless debate as to the antiquity of these traditions. The Pahlavi literature was compiled from the sixth to twelfth centuries CE, but it certainly preserves older traditions. The *Bahman Yasht* is a commentary on a lost book of the Avesta, which is itself of uncertain date. Some key apocalyptic motifs, such as the final battle between the forces of good and evil in the end-time, and the judgment of the soul after death, are found already in the *Gāthās,* the hymns of Zoroaster, which may date to as early as 1000 BCE. Belief in a savior figure and in the resurrection of the dead was developed already in the Avesta. Important glimpses of early Persian beliefs are provided by an account preserved by Plutarch (*On Isis and Osiris* 47, attributed to Theopompus, who lived in the fourth century BCE), and by the *Oracle of Hystaspes,* a pre-Christian Persian work that is cited in Latin by Lactantius. Both of these sources mention the division of history into periods and the resurrection of the dead. Plutarch recounts the original opposition of the two spirits of light and darkness. This dualistic view of the world seems to have influenced a Jewish sect of the first century BCE, whose views are reflected in the Dead Sea Scrolls. Nonetheless, the dating of Persian traditions is fraught with difficulty and remains controversial. It is clear that there was a native Persian tradition of considerable antiquity, which had a view of history that is quite similar to what we find in Jewish and Christian apocalypses of the historical type. Notable points of affinity include predeterminism, periodization, the importance attached to millennia, the role of savior figures, and the hope for resurrection. Most of these features (with the exception of savior figures) were novel in Judaism in the Hellenistic period. Nonetheless, it remains unclear whether the development of the apocalyptic genre in Judaism was due in any significant way to Persian influence, because of the difficulty of dating the Persian materials.

The Genre in Christianity. Apocalypticism in the broader sense was a major factor in the rise and spread of Christianity. While the intentions and self-understanding of Jesus of Nazareth are a matter of endless debate, he is portrayed in the Gospels as an apocalyptic prophet, who predicted that the "Son of man" would come on the clouds of heaven to save the elect and judge the wicked. (See, for example, *Mark* 13; the title "Son of Man" alludes to a vision in *Daniel* 7.) After Jesus' death, his followers quickly came to believe that he had risen from the dead, and that this, in the words of Paul, was the first fruit of the general resurrection. Paul told his followers that Jesus would return on the clouds while some of them were still alive. This expectation lent urgency to his attempt to spread the Christian gospel to the end of the earth.

The apocalyptic genre declined in Judaism after the first century CE, although heavenly ascents continued to play an important part in the Jewish mystical tradition. By contrast, the genre flourished in Christianity. The *Book of Revelation* in the New Testament has its closest analogies with the *Book of Daniel* and the historical apocalypses, but it is exceptional in not being pseudonymous. The convention of pseudonymity was quickly adopted, however, and apocalypses of Peter, Paul, and others proliferated into the Middle Ages. These apocalypses were primarily, but not exclusively, of the ascent type, and were mystical rather than political in their orientation. The expectation of cosmic change depicted in the *Book of Revelation* was viewed with suspicion by church authorities, although the main outline was incorporated in Christian dogma. The church fathers tended to interpret apocalyptic symbols with reference to the present. Augustine of Hippo (354–430 CE) interpreted the thousand-year reign of *Revelation* 20 as referring to the time of the church, and held that the first resurrection is spiritual and takes place in this life. This line of interpretation was widely influential, and defused the role of apocalyptic expectation in the mainline church.

A distinctive variant of the use of apocalypses in the Christian tradition can be seen in the Gnostic codices found at Nag Hammadi in Egypt in 1945, which date from about 400 CE. The corpus includes apocalypses of Adam, Peter, Paul, and James. The Gnostic apocalypses differ from the Jewish and Christian ones in their emphasis on salvation in the present through *gnōsis,* or saving knowledge, and their lack of interest in cosmic transformation, although some Gnostic apocalypses envision the destruction of this world. The Gnostic apocalypses also are distinctive in their emphasis on the spoken word. Often the revelations take the form of dialogues or discourses, rather than visions. The origin and fall of humanity is a prominent theme. The most important transformation of the genre, however, lies in the focus on the present rather than the future as the time of salvation.

The mystically oriented ascent-type apocalypse continued to exist in Christianity quite apart from Gnosticism and left an imprint on world literature in Dante's *Commedia.* The historical type of apocalypticism was more widely influential in the Middle Ages. Apocalyptic expectations played a role in launching the Crusades. A crucial figure in medieval apocalypticism was Joachim of Fiore, a twelfth-century abbot who looked for a new age of the Holy Spirit, to be ushered in by the defeat of the antichrist. Historical apocalypticism merges easily into millenarianism, where the emphasis is less on supernatural revelation than on the coming utopian age. Apocalyptic expectations of the overthrow of the present world order fueled radical Christian movements in the late Middle Ages, notably Franciscan dissidents and early reformers such as John Wyclif (late fourteenth century) and his followers, the Lollards. These radicals often viewed the papacy as the antichrist. Apocalyptic hopes also provided the ideology that inspired a whole series of peasant revolts, and there was an outpouring of apocalyptic prophecies in connection with the Reformation. In Germany the radical preaching of Thomas Müntzer culminated in the Peasants' Revolt in 1525, and the Anabaptists established the New Jerusalem in Münster, under a messianic "king," John of Leyden (1534). In England, a century later, the Puritan revolutionaries saw themselves as "the saints of the Most High," who were mentioned in the *Book of Daniel,* while Gerrard Winstanley, and the Diggers and Levellers whom he inspired, drew on the *Book of Revelation* to advance a more radically egalitarian view of Christianity.

The Puritans brought their apocalyptic beliefs with them to North America, and inaugurated a tradition of studying biblical prophecy with a view to discerning the signs of the end-time. While interest in apocalyptic timetables was prominent in American Protestantism from the seventeenth century onward, it was given a boost in the early nineteenth century by a Church of Ireland minister, John Nelson Darby (1800–1882), who developed a system of "dispensational premillennialism." History was divided into a series of distinct stages or dispensations, in each of which God dealt with humankind in different ways. The millennium, or thousand-year reign, was not the time of the church but was still to come. Darby rejected any form of historicist interpretation and held that the last events of prophetic significance occurred in the time of Jesus. Darby's followers developed into the sect of the Plymouth Brethern, but he was widely influential among evangelical Protestants. One of his most distinctive beliefs was in the rapture, when believers would be caught up to meet the Lord in the air (see *1 Thess.* 4:16–18). Dispensational premillennialism was popularized in the early twentieth century by the Scofield Reference Bible, which provided prophetic interpretations for the entire King James Bible.

The most colorful episode in American apocalyptic tradition occurred in the 1840s. A farmer named William Miller, from upstate New York, calculated, on the basis of the book of *Daniel,* that the second coming of Christ would occur in 1843. When that year ended uneventfully, some of his followers recalculated the date as October 22, 1844. They assembled in expectation, and suffered a crushing disappointment. That scenario has been replayed many times by small groups on the fringes of American Protestantism. Nonetheless, this kind of literal interpretation of apocalyptic prophecy continues to flourish at the beginning of the twenty-first century. The Millerites eventually evolved into the Seventh-day Adventist Church, under the leader of a visionary and prolific writer, Ellen G. White (1827–1915).

The emergence of a modern Pentecostal movement in the early twentieth century gave another boost to fundamentalist apocalyptic interpretation. In the latter part of the twentieth century, dispensational premillennialist interpretation was popularized by such writers as Hal Lindsey, whose best-seller, *The Late Great Planet Earth* (1973), sold millions of copies. Unlike Darby, Lindsey readily identified prophetic allusions to contemporary events, and even suggested that the rapture might come in 1981. Since the 1980s, this kind of apocalyptic interpretation has become identified with the religious right wing in American politics, particularly through the activism of such people as Pat Robertson and Jerry Falwell. It also continues to thrive on the fringes. The Branch Davidians who died in the conflagration in Waco, Texas, in 1993, were a heretical offshoot of the Seventh-day Adventists and spiritual descendants of the Millerites, with their own apocalyptic prophet, David Koresh. There has also been a revival of apocalyptic and messianic expectations in some circles within Judaism, inspired by the rebirth of the land of Israel after the disaster of the Holocaust.

Apocalyptic Traditions in Islam. Apocalyptic expectations played a significant role in Islam from the beginning. These expectations include the resurrection of the dead, the day of judgment and salvation, and damnation in the end-time. They also include preparatory events leading to the resurrection, including the coming of the *mahdī* (an Islamic messiah). Already in the Qurʾān, there are several references to "the Hour," which is the time of calamity that precedes the resurrection. There is considerable interest in the signs of the end. These ideas were influenced by Jewish, Christian, and Persian traditions. Jesus retains an important role in the eschatological scenario: he will return to Jerusalem and kill the antichrist. Much more apocalyptic material entered Islam after the death of the Prophet, and it grew in popularity in times of war. By the Middle Ages there was a developed science for the calculation of the predetermined future, which involved astrology. These predictions are not typically presented as visionary revelations, in the manner of the Jewish and Christian apocalypses, but rather as teachings, in the manner of the Persian tradition. There have been numerous movements in the history of Islam that have employed apocalyptic or messianic rhetoric to proclaim the dawn of a new era. There was an upsurge of such rhetoric in connection with Islamic fundamentalism in the late twentieth and early twenty-first centuries.

Modern Adaptations of Apocalypticism. The terms *apocalypse* and *apocalyptic* are used widely and loosely in modern culture, often in ways that have little in common with the ancient apocalypses. Continuity is clearest in the case of fundamentalist Christians who look for literal fulfillment of the biblical prophecies, and try to identify the signs of the times in current political events. There are also secular groups (such as survivalist movements in the American west) that believe that a cosmic disaster and a change of world order is imminent. These people often cling to what Michael Barkun has called "spurned knowledge" (ideas that are rejected or despised by the society at large) and consequently see themselves as a persecuted minority. They are characterized by a kind of esotericism, or insider-belief, that bears some analogy to the revelations of the ancient apocalypses. There is some justification for calling such groups apocalyptic, admittedly in an attenuated sense. More questionable is the widespread use of the term *apocalyptic* in connection with modern literature. The English poet William Blake (1757–1827) made extensive use of the *Book of Revelation,* but he looked for a revelation initiated not by God but by humans, which would entail a change in our perception of the world. Some critics, however, use the term *apocalyptic* for any "revelation" or transformation of perception, even if there is no use of traditional apocalyptic imagery. In contemporary literature, the writing that has most in common with ancient apocalypses is science fiction, insofar as it is an imaginative exploration of worlds that are outside normal human experience. But here again the analogy is limited, as science fiction is not presented as revelation and lacks the religious and instructional dimensions of the ancient apocalypses.

See Also Ascension; Biblical Literature, articles on Apocrypha and Pseudepigrapha, New Testament; Eschatology, overview article; Judgment of the Dead; Millenarianism, overview article.

Bibliography

For a comprehensive survey of apocalypticism in Judaism, Christianity, and Islam, from ancient to modern times, see John J. Collins, Bernard McGinn, and Stephen Stein, eds., *The Encyclopedia of Apocalypticism,* vol. 1, *The Origins of Apocalypticism in Judaism and Christianity;* vol. 2, *Apocalypticism in Western History and Culture;* vol. 3, *Apocalypticism in the Modern Period and the Contemporary Age* (New York, 1998), condensed into one volume as *The History of Apocalypticism* (New York, 2003). The first volume includes articles on the ancient Middle Eastern, Persian, and Greco-Roman apocalypticism. Less comprehensive but representative is Abbas Amanat and Magnus T. Bernhardsson, eds., *Imagining the End: Visions of Apocalypse from the Ancient Middle East to Modern America* (London, 2002).

An overview of apocalyptic writing as a genre in antiquity can be found in *Apocalypse: The Morphology of a Genre,* a special issue of *Semeia* 14 (1979). This volume contains essays on material from various cultures: Jewish (John J. Collins), Christian (Adela Yarbro Collins), Gnostic (Francis T. Fallon), Greco-Roman (Harold W. Attridge), rabbinic/later Jewish (Anthony J. Saldarini), and Persian (John J. Collins); it also includes extensive bibliographies. Essays on apocalypses and related material from several ancient cultures can be found in *Apocalypticism in the Mediterranean World and the Near East,* edited by David Hellholm (Tübingen, Germany, 1983). Other studies of the ancient apocalypses include Christopher Rowland's *The Open Heaven: A Study of Apocalyptic in Judaism and Early Christianity* (New York, 1982) and John J. Collins's *The Apocalyptic Imagination: An Introduction to Jewish Apocalyptic Literature,* 2d ed. (Grand Rapids, Mich., 1998). The influence of the apocalypses on Jewish mysticism is explored by Ithamar Gruenwald in *Apocalyptic and Merkavah Mysticism* (Leiden, 1980). The later Jewish tradition is discussed in several works by Gershom Scholem; see especially *The Messianic Idea in Judaism and Other Essays on Jewish Spirituality* (New York, 1971) and *Jewish Gnosticism, Merkabah Mysticism, and Talmudic Tradition,* 2d ed. (New York, 1965).

The roots of apocalyptic traditions in the ancient world, especially in Persia, are explored by Norman Cohn, *Cosmos, Chaos, and the World to Come: The Ancient Roots of Apocalyptic Faith,* 2d ed. (New Haven, 2001). Ancient traditions about the judgment of the dead, especially in Egypt, are described by J. Gwyn Griffiths, *The Divine Verdict: A Study of Divine Judgment in the Ancient Religions* (Leiden, 1991). For relevant Mesopotamian traditions, especially the "Vision of the Netherworld," see Helge S. Kvanvig, *Roots of Apocalyptic: The Mesopotamian Background of the Enoch Figure and of the Son of Man* (Neukirchen, Germany, 1988). Apocalyptic traditions from Hellenistic Egypt are discussed in A. Blasius and B. U. Schipper, eds., *Apokalyptik und Ägypten* (Leuven, Belgium, 2002). Comprehensive overviews of Persian apocalypticism are provided by Anders Hultgård, "Persian Apocalypticism" in *The Encyclopedia of Apocalypticism,* vol. 1, pp. 39–83, and Philip G. Kreyenbroek, "Millennialism and Eschatology in the Zoroastrian Tradition" in Amanat and Bernhardsson, eds., *Imagining the End,* pp. 33–55.

For the medieval Christian material, see especially Norman Cohn, *The Pursuit of the Millennium* (New York, 1970) and Bernard McGinn's studies: *Visions of the End: Apocalyptic Traditions in the Middle Ages* (New York, 1979); *Apocalyptic Spirituality: Treatises and Letters of Lactantius, Adso of Montieren-Der, Joachim of Fiore, the Franciscan Spirituals, Savonarola* (New York, 1979); and *The Antichrist: Two Thousand Years of the Human Fascination with Evil* (San Francisco, 1994). For apocalyptic traditions in modern America, see Paul Boyer, *When Time Shall Be No More: Prophecy Belief in Modern American Culture* (Cambridge, Mass., 1992).

On apocalypticism in Islamic tradition see Saïd Amir Arjomand, "Islamic Apocalypticism in the Classic Period" in *The Encyclopedia of Apocalypticism,* vol. 2, pp. 238–283; Abbas Amanat, "The Resurgence of Apocalyptic in Modern Islam" in *The Encyclopedia of Apocalypticism,* vol. 2, pp. 230–264. On the resurgence of apocalypticism in modern Judaism, see Aviezer Ravitzky, *Messianism, Zionism, and Jewish Religious Radicalism* (Chicago, 1996).

On modern adaptations of apocalypticism see the essays in *The Encyclopedia of Apocalypticism,* vol. 3, especially the essays of Stephen O'Leary, "Popular Culture and Apocalypticism" (pp. 392–426) and Michael Barkun, "Politics and Apocalypticism" (pp. 442–460).

For examples of scholarly application of the notion of apocalypse to a much broader range of religious traditions, see Jonathan Z. Smith's "A Pearl of Great Price and a Cargo of Yams," *History of Religions* 16 (1976): 1–19, which examines the applicability of apocalyptic and Gnostic patterns of revelation to the Babylonian Akitu festival and a cargo cult in the Moluccas. See also Bruce Lincoln's article "'The Earth Becomes Flat': A Study of Apocalyptic Imagery," *Comparative Studies in Society and History* 25 (January 1983): 136–153, which begins with a consideration of Plutarch and the Iranian *Bundahishn* and compares these with Chinese and Japanese materials, as well as with colonial rebellions. On the Ghost Dance and analogous phenomena, see Weston La Barre, *The Ghost Dance: Origins of Religion* (New York, 1970).

JOHN J. COLLINS (1987 AND 2005)

APOCALYPSE: JEWISH APOCALYPTICISM TO THE RABBINIC PERIOD

The genre "apocalypse" first appears in Judaism in the Hellenistic period. The early apocalypses are of two types. One type, attested in *Daniel,* the Animal Apocalypse and the Apocalypse of Weeks, provides an overview of the course of history and may be dubbed the "historical" type. The other, typified by the Book of the Watchers in *1 Enoch* 1–36, describes an otherworldly journey and is primarily a description of places outside the normal range of human experience.

THE EARLIEST APOCALYPSES. The *Book of Daniel* (164 BCE) provides the only example of the genre in the Hebrew Bible. The earliest noncanonical apocalypses are found in *1 Enoch.* This is a collection of five books fully preserved only in Ethiopic, but four of the five books are attested in Aramaic in the Dead Sea Scrolls. The earliest copies date to the second century BCE. Some of the books of *Enoch* (The Book of the Watchers, *1 Enoch* 1–36, and the Astronomical Book, *1 Enoch* 72–82) are likely to date from the third century BCE, whereas others (the Animal Apocalypse, *1 Enoch* 83–90 and the Apocalypse of Weeks, *1 Enoch* 93:1–10 and 91:11–17) are roughly contemporary with the *Book of Daniel.*

THE HISTORICAL APOCALYPSES. In *Daniel* 7–8 the revelation takes the form of symbolic visions. In chapter 7, Daniel sees four beasts rising from the sea. Then he sees a judgment scene in which a white-headed "Ancient of Days" condemns the beasts and confers the kingdom on "one like a son of man" who comes on the clouds of heaven. This vision is explained to Daniel by an angel. The beasts represent four kings or kingdoms. The final kingdom is ruled not only by the "one like a son of man" but also by "the holy ones of the Most High" and "the people of the holy ones of the Most High." (The interpretation of the "one like a son of man" and of "the holy ones of the Most High" is disputed. Most probably, the former is the archangel Michael, who is explicitly identified as the "prince" of Israel in chapters 10 to 12, and the holy ones are the angelic host). In *Daniel* 8, the vision concerns a he-goat, which defeats a ram. Then one of its horns rises up against the heavenly host and disrupts the cult. The angel explains that the ram, which has two horns, represents the kings of Media and Persia, whereas the goat is the king of Greece. The rebellious horn represents an arrogant king who will succeed for a time but will suddenly be broken, "not by human hands." In *Daniel* 9, the revelation is triggered by a prophecy of Jeremiah that Jerusalem would be desolate for seventy years. An angel explains to Daniel that this really means seventy weeks of years, or 490 years. Finally, chapters 10 to 12 contain a lengthy prediction about kings and wars that is a thinly disguised overview of Hellenistic history and the wars between the Ptolemies of Egypt and the Seleucids of Syria. This account culminates in a persecution of "the holy covenant" by an arrogant king who exalts himself above every god. This king meets a sudden end, however. Then follows the resurrection of the dead, when the righteous martyrs are exalted in glory and their enemies are condemned to everlasting disgrace.

The recipient of these visions, Daniel, was supposedly one of the captives taken to Babylon by King Nebuchadnezzar of Babylon in 597 BCE. In fact, he is a fictitious character, whose legendary exploits are recounted in *Daniel* 1–6. His revelations concern the course of history from the Babylonian era forward. The four kingdoms portrayed as beasts from the sea in chapter 7 are identified by other references in the book as Babylon, Media, Persia, and Greece. The climax of the revelations relates to the persecution of the Jews by King Antiochus Epiphanes of Syria from 168 to 164 BCE. The historical references in *Daniel* 10–12 can be verified down to the time of persecution, but the king did not die in the manner predicted in *Daniel* 11:40–45. Already in antiquity, critics inferred that the *Book of Daniel* was not written in the Babylonian period, but in the time of persecution, before the actual death of Antiochus Epiphanes became known in Jerusalem. The lengthy predictions are *ex eventu*, or prophecy after the fact. The accuracy of these predictions helps reassure the reader that the part still unfulfilled (the end of the persecution and the resurrection) is also reliable. The purpose of the revelations is to assure the persecuted Jews that their deliverance is at hand. The reassurance is supported by several claims of authority: the revelation is given by an angel to a famous ancient figure, and much of it could already be verified at the time the book was actually written. It is essential to an apocalypse that the revelation is "out of this world." It reveals a hidden reality no one could know without such revelation.

The historical apocalypses in *1 Enoch* are less colorful than in *Daniel* but exhibit a similar logic. In this case the recipient is more ancient than Daniel. Enoch supposedly lived before the Flood. According to *Genesis*, Enoch did not die but was taken up to heaven (*Gn.* 5:24). He was therefore exceptionally well qualified to convey revelation to humanity. Living before the Flood, Enoch is able to "predict" the entire course of history, from before the Flood to the crisis of the Hellenistic age. The Animal Apocalypse recounts a symbolic dream in which the human actors are symbolized as animals, as was also the case in *Daniel* 7–8. The Apocalypse of Weeks is an instruction of Enoch to his children, based on what he had seen in the heavenly books. In this case history is divided into periods that are called weeks (compare *Daniel* 9). The wicked are defeated at the end of the seventh week. In the tenth week there is a cosmic judgment when the first heaven will pass away and a new heaven will appear. In the Animal Apocalypse, God descends to earth for the judgment, and it is followed by the resurrection of the dead. Both of these apocalypses, like *Daniel*, culminate in the Hellenistic period. The Animal Apocalypse alludes clearly to the persecution in the time of Antiochus Epiphanes and to the Maccabean revolt. It is apparent that the conflict of this period was a major factor evoking this kind of apocalypse.

THE SOURCES OF HISTORICAL APOCALYPTICISM. There is evident continuity between this kind of apocalypse and biblical prophecy. From the eighth century BCE onward, Hebrew prophets had visions that related to historical events, and that foretold divine intervention for judgment. These visions were often symbolic. For example, Amos saw a basket of dried fruit, symbolizing the coming end of Israel (*Am.* 8:1–2). After the Babylonian exile there were some significant changes in the nature of prophecy. The visions of Zechariah (520 BCE) are interpreted by an angel, like the later visions of Daniel. Many oracles from this period proclaim a radical change, not only in the fortunes of Israel but in the conditions of human life. An addition to the *Book of Isaiah* (*Is.* 65:17) declares that the Lord will create a new heaven and a new earth. The Book of Joel speaks of the Day of the Lord as a day of cosmic judgment (*Jl.* 3–4). *Isaiah* 24–27 say that God will destroy death forever (*Is.* 25:8) and kill Leviathan, the sea–dragon (*Is.* 27:1). Because of the similarity of these themes to those found later in *Daniel* and the *Book of Revelation,* many scholars refer to these chapters as "the Apocalypse of Isaiah." In these and other postexilic oracles an increased use of mythic imagery describes the coming judgment. Ancient Near Eastern creation myths often described a battle between the creator god and a chaos monster (e.g., the Babylonian *Enuma Elish*). In postexilic prophecy, and also in the apocalyptic literature, this battle is projected into the future. The symbolism of the sea–dragon Leviathan also underlies the beasts that arise from the sea in *Daniel* 7 and the seven–headed beast in *Revelation* 18. The late prophetic texts also resemble the apocalypses insofar as both depict the current situation as desperate and both look for God to change radically the conditions of human existence.

Despite these similarities, however, there are also significant differences between the late prophetic texts and the apocalypses. The prophetic oracles either are attributed to the actual prophets who delivered them (Zechariah, Joel) or are anonymous additions to other prophetic books, such as *Isaiah.* The apocalypses, in contrast, are pseudonymous: they are attributed to famous ancient figures such as Enoch and Daniel. It is unlikely that the actual authors concealed their identity for fear of persecution; rather, the name of the ancient figure was probably thought to enhance the authority of the writing. The interpreting angel appears in *Zechariah,* but not otherwise in the prophetic writings. The apocalypses often divide history into periods (e.g., four kingdoms, ten weeks). The most important difference, however, is in the expectation about the last things, or eschatology. Whereas all these texts expect the restoration of Israel, the apocalypses also expect the resurrection and judgment of the individual dead. Even *Isaiah* 24–27, which say that God will swallow up death, expect neither the resurrection nor judgment of the individual dead. It is in the apocalypses of *Daniel* and *Enoch* that the resurrection and judgment of individuals first appeared in Jewish tradition. This new belief entailed a profound shift in value systems. Prior to this, "salvation" was to live a long life and see one's children's children. Now the goal of life was to live with the angels in heaven. Consequently, it made sense to let oneself be killed in time of persecution rather than break the law. The apocalyptic belief in resurrection would be crucially important for the origin of Christianity.The apocalypses are sometimes seen as an outgrowth of wisdom tradition rather than prophecy. Enoch and Daniel are presented as wise men rather than as prophets, and the apocalypses place great emphasis on understanding. Nonetheless, the content of the apocalypses bears little similarity to that of the wisdom books. Jewish wisdom was traditionally very this-worldly and practical.

The apocalypses deal with heavenly mysteries. It seems likely, however, that the authors of the apocalypses were learned people (in their fashion), although their kind of learning was traditional and not scientific. The apocalypses are not popular folk literature, but rather the works of literate scribes. It is possible but difficult to prove that the historical apocalypses were indebted to Persian models. Typical features of the apocalypses, such as the periodization of history and the belief in resurrection, are also prominent in the Persian apocalyptic tradition. The Persian material, however, is notoriously difficult to date, and so its relation to the Jewish tradition remains controversial.

THE OTHERWORLDLY JOURNEY. The second type of apocalypse is the otherworldly journey. The Book of the Watchers in *1 Enoch* 1–36 is an early example, although somewhat atypical. This book elaborates upon a brief and enigmatic story in *Genesis* 6 about the sons of God who married the daughters of men. In *Genesis,* God reacts by limiting the lifespan of human beings to 120 years. Shortly afterwards, the wickedness of humankind is so great that God sends the Flood, but this is not directly related to the descent of the sons of God in *Genesis.* The Book of the Watchers makes the connection explicit. The Watchers are fallen angels. Their descent is an act of rebellion. They are guilty not only of sexual sin but also of improper revelation and of spreading violence on earth. Eventually God decrees that they should be destroyed and imprisoned under the earth. This story provides a different paradigm for the origin of evil from the more familiar story of Adam and Eve. Here sin does not arise because of human disobedience but is imported into the world by supernatural agents.

Enoch is introduced into this story as a righteous scribe who is asked to intercede for the Watchers. The intercession is not successful, but it provides an occasion for an ascent to heaven. Enoch is taken up on the clouds and brought into the presence of the Most High. He sees the inner chambers of the heavenly temple. Then he is taken on a tour to the ends of the earth, guided by an angel. He is shown such places as the storehouses of the winds and the places where the dead are kept to await judgment. He is also shown the place prepared for the judgment in the middle of the earth.

Traditions about ascents to heaven and descents to the netherworld can be found in many traditions in the ancient world. The closest analogy to Enoch is provided by the legendary Mesopotamian king Enmeduranki, who was taken up to heaven and shown the tablets of heaven, and who became founder of a guild of diviners. It is likely that the earliest stages of the Enoch tradition developed in the Babylonian Diaspora. The Astronomical Book (*1 Enoch* 72–82) is indebted to Babylonian astronomy, but of a rather archaic sort. In the Book of the Watchers, a clear contrast exists between the Watchers, who were heavenly but descended to earth and consequently perished, and Enoch, the human being who ascended to heaven to live forever with the angels. The implication is that one should aspire to live a heavenly, spiritual, life.

Unlike *Daniel* or the historical apocalypses, the Book of the Watchers does not seem to have originated in a time of persecution. Some scholars read the story of the Watchers as an allegory for the spread of Greek culture in the Near East, which often conflicted with native traditions. Others think the Watchers represent the priests of the Hellenistic period who were thought to have fallen from their state of holiness. The story is not directly allegorical in the manner of the symbolic visions of Daniel. Most basically, however, it seems to represent a conflict of cultures. After the Watchers descended to earth, the world was changed. The sense seems to be that the new developments in the Near East in the Hellenistic period defiled the world, and the reaction of the pious, represented by Enoch, is to withdraw by ascending to heaven, if only in their imagination, to live with the angels. This goal would be fully realized after death. In the meantime, the example of Enoch encouraged a tendency to mysticism that would be developed in later Jewish tradition.

Later Jewish mystics had techniques by which they could "descend to the chariot" or initiate visionary experience. It is noteworthy that both Daniel and Enoch describe certain practices that induce their visions. Daniel fasts for three weeks and does not anoint himself (*Dn.* 10:2–3). Enoch sits by the water and reads a petition aloud until he falls asleep (*1 Enoch* 13:7). In the later apocalypse of *4 Ezra,* Ezra eats the flower of the field and has a wonderful vision (*4 Ezr.* 9:26). Similar practices are known to induce visions in other cultures. The difficulty in the case of the Jewish texts is that all these visionaries are pseudonymous, so there is no way of knowing if the experiences attributed to them were the experiences of the actual authors. Nonetheless, it appears that the authors were familiar with the practices of the visionaries, and the possibility that they themselves practiced such techniques remains intriguing.

The Spread of Apocalypticism. The corpus of Jewish apocalypses from the pre-Christian period is quite small, but characteristic themes and ideas of this literature became widespread and also appear in other genres. For example, the Sibylline Oracles, written in Greek hexameters in the Jewish Diaspora, share many features of the historical apocalypses, especially the long overview of history in the guise of prophecy and the division into periods. The earliest Jewish Sibylline Oracles derive from Egypt in the second century BCE. These oracles look for a restoration of the Jewish people around Jerusalem. The fourth book of Sibylline Oracles, from the late first century CE, is thought to have been composed in Syria or Palestine, and has a more strongly apocalyptic character. This oracle concludes with a cosmic conflagration and the resurrection of the dead. The genre of testament, or deathbed instruction, also typically involves an overview of history in the guise of prophecy. The Testaments of the Twelve Patriarchs contain the main corpus of testaments, including much material of Jewish origin, but they were clearly edited by Christians in their final form, and their value for the study of Judaism is controversial. It should be noted that the Apocalypse of Weeks in *1 Enoch* can be construed as a testament, as it is presented as an instruction by Enoch to his children rather than a direct account of the revelation.

The main evidence for the influence of apocalyptic beliefs outside the apocalypses in pre–rabbinic Judaism is found in the Dead Sea Scrolls, which are thought to constitute the library of a sectarian movement, most probably the Essenes. The Scrolls include multiple copies of the apocalypses of *Daniel* and *Enoch*. These were not products of the sectarian movement itself, but part of the larger corpus of Jewish literature in its library. They also contain several fragmentary works, mostly in Aramaic, that are clearly related to the apocalypses, but whose genre is difficult to determine because of their fragmentary state. These include at least two works in the name of Daniel that are distinct from the biblical book, each of which contains a prediction of the course of history and an eschatological conclusion (4Q243–244; 4Q245). Other possible apocalypses include a vision that foresees the coming of a figure who is called "Son of God," (most probably the messiah, 4Q246) and a vision in which someone sees four trees, representing four kingdoms (4Q552–553). Because the main sectarian texts are all in Hebrew, some scholars think that this Aramaic literature is part of the wider Jewish literature of the time.

It is not clear that the sect represented by the Scrolls actually composed new writings in the form of apocalypses. The clearly sectarian writings use different genres: rule books, biblical commentaries, and hymns. But some of these writings are profoundly influenced by apocalyptic ideas. In the Community Rule (1QS) a treatise on creation and eschatology is inserted in columns 3 and 4 before the actual rules and regulations. According to this treatise, when God created humanity he also created two spirits, of light and darkness. The spirits are viewed both as dispositions that people share and as angelic/demonic powers that inspire the dispositions. All humanity is divided between these spirits and will remain so until the predetermined time when God will put an end to iniquity. This view of history is more sharply dualistic than anything else in Jewish tradition, and it is clearly indebted to Zoroastrianism. It resembles the apocalypses, however, in the attempt to give a comprehensive account of history, the division into periods, and the expectation of a final judgment. The final denouement of history is addressed directly in the Rule of the War, which prescribes preparations for a final war between the Children of Light and the Children of Darkness, in which the Children of Light will be led by the archangel Michael and the Children of Darkness by Belial (another name for Satan) The sectarian scrolls express a consistent belief that the righteous will enjoy a beatific afterlife, whereas the wicked are damned to everlasting fire. (They do not express a belief in resurrection: the spirits or souls of the dead go directly to their reward or punishment.) The most distinctive belief in these scrolls, however, is that the righteous do not have to wait until after death to enjoy their reward. Already in their community life, they enjoy the fellowship with the angels that is the destiny of the righteous after death in the apocalypses. This belief is expressed especially in the hymns of the community.

The fact that the sectarians did not express these beliefs in the form of apocalyptic visions is related to the structure of authority in their community. The primary mediator of revelation is the Teacher, the person who gave the movement its distinctive character. He in turn based his teachings on the interpretation of the Torah. The sectarians, then, did not need to base their revelations on the authority of *Enoch* or *Daniel*. The role filled by these figures in the apocalypses was now filled by the Teacher and his interpretations.

Apart from the Dead Sea Scrolls there is very little literature from Israel from around the turn of the era (200 BCE to 200 CE). The historian Josephus wrote of various prophets and would–be messiahs in the first century CE who hoped for divine intervention to restore a Judean kingdom. The career of Jesus of Nazareth belongs in this context. While the aims of the historical Jesus are very controversial, he is portrayed in the Gospels as an apocalyptic prophet who prophesied that the Son of man would come on the clouds of heaven, as foretold in *Daniel* 7. After Jesus' death, his followers believed he was risen again and would return as the Son of man. We have no way of knowing just how widespread such ideas were in the first century CE, but they were evidently current.

The Later Historical Apocalypses. Most of the surviving historical apocalypses are clustered around two great historical crises: the persecution by Antiochus Epiphanes from 168 to 164 BCE and the destruction of Jerusalem by the Romans in 70 CE. The Similitudes of Enoch (*1 Enoch* 37–71), probably dating from the first half of the first century CE, provide one exception. This apocalypse adapts both types of apocalypse discussed, in that Enoch is taken up to heaven and sees his visions there, but he is not given a tour, and there is no description of a journey. The visions are clearly indebted to *Daniel*, especially *Daniel* 7, but there is no overview of history such as we find in the other historical apocalypses. Much of the interest of this apocalypse centers on a figure called "that Son of Man," who is clearly modeled on the "one like a son of man" in *Daniel* 7. The figure from the Similitudes of Enoch is depicted as a kind of super-angel who is the heavenly patron of the righteous on earth. At the end of the Similitudes, Enoch is taken up to heaven again and told, "you are the Son of Man who has righteousness." There is no indication in the earlier chapters that Enoch and the Son of Man are one and the same. It may be that the passage identifying Enoch with the Son of Man is a secondary addition. It is also possible that Enoch is being told that he is "a righteous man," like the Son of Man, rather than identified with him. Throughout the Similitudes there is emphasis on the correspondence between the righteous in heaven and the righteous on earth, with the implication that the human righteous are elevated to join their heavenly counterparts when they die. Some scholars have suspected that the Similitudes, which are not found in the Dead Sea Scrolls, are of later Christian origin, but it is inconceivable that a Christian author would have failed to identify Jesus as the Son of Man.

Two of the longest Jewish apocalyptic texts were composed in the years after the destruction of Jerusalem. These are *4 Ezra* (= *2 Esdras* 3–14) and *2 Baruch* (Syriac). These apocalypses differ from the older apocalypses in *Daniel* and *Enoch* insofar as they engage the question of theodicy. Both are ostensibly reflections on the first destruction of Jerusalem (by the Babylonians), but there is little doubt that the works were actually written after the second destruction. *4 Ezra* begins with a series of dialogues between Ezra and an angel. In each case, Ezra complains bitterly about the destruction, and the angel responds by telling him God knows best and everything will be resolved in due time. Ezra does not seem to be convinced. Then he has a vision in which he sees a woman transformed into a city, representing Jerusalem. The immediacy of the vision seems to persuade where the words of the angel did not. Ezra then sees two other visions that follow the typical conventions of the historical apocalypse. (Both are influenced by *Daniel*.) In the end, Ezra is inspired to restore the Law, which had been burnt, but also to write out seventy other books that contain the secret of wisdom. *2 Baruch* has a similar view of the future but lacks the skeptical questioning of divine justice that distinguishes *4 Ezra*. Both of these apocalypses give a prominent place to the messiah, a figure who was not represented at all in the early apocalypses of *Enoch* and *Daniel*.

The Later Otherworldly Journeys. The subgenre "otherworldly journey" is attested primarily in the early centuries of the Common Era. Whereas Enoch was taken on a tour of the ends of the earth, the later visionaries are typically taken up through a series of heavens. The classic number is seven, but other numbers are also attested (three, seven, ten). Besides the ascent of Enoch to the divine throne, there is an ascent of Levi attested in a fragmentary Aramaic text from the Dead Sea Scrolls. *3 Baruch,* written in Greek, comes from the period after the destruction of the Temple. In this case there is no attempt to address the problem of theodicy. Baruch is told to stop worrying about the fate of Jerusalem and to contemplate instead the mysteries of God. This somewhat detached view of the fate of Jerusalem was probably more feasible for a Jew who lived in Egypt, as the author of *3 Baruch* apparently did, than for someone who lived in the land of Israel. Another major account of an ascent through the heavens is ascribed to Enoch in a text only preserved in Slavonic (*2 Enoch*), but it is thought to have been written in Greek at the beginning of the era, most probably in Egypt. These ascent texts show little concern for history, although one apocalypse, the Apocalypse of Abraham, combines a heavenly journey with a brief historical review.

The Rabbis and Apocalypticism. Judaism in the ancient world changed radically at the end of the first century CE because of a series of Jewish revolts against Rome that were crushed mercilessly. Jerusalem was destroyed. The once flourishing Jewish community in Egypt was virtually wiped out. The rabbis who salvaged Jewish traditions in Palestine were understandably cautious and avoided anything that might seem to encourage revolution and rebellion by predicting that God would intervene to overthrow the enemies of Israel. The great compilations of Jewish law, the Mishnah and the Talmud, have scarcely a glimmer of apocalyptic hope. The tradition of historical apocalypticism died out in Judaism for several centuries.

The tradition of the otherworldly journey, however, was taken over and adapted by Jewish mystics. Continuity with the earlier apocalypses is most clearly evident in the text known as *Sefer heikhalot*, or *3 Enoch*. This complex text cites Rabbi Ishmael, from the early second century CE, but was probably compiled in the fifth or sixth century CE. The most intriguing feature of this text is the figure of Metatron, a kind of super-angel and even called "the lesser YHWH." Amazingly, this figure is identified as none other than Enoch, taken up to heaven and exalted. *3 Enoch,* appears to continue the tradition found at the end of the *Similitudes,* that Enoch was taken up to heaven and either identified or closely associated with a heavenly being. The Jewish mystical tradition, of which *3 Enoch* is part, continued to flourish down to the Middle Ages.

Bibliography

Charlesworth, James H., ed. *The Old Testament Pseudepigrapha,* vol. 1. *Apocalyptic Literature and Testaments.* New York, 1983. The major nonbiblical apocalyptic texts in English translation.

Collins, John J. *Daniel: A Commentary on the Book of Daniel.* Minneapolis, 1993.

Collins, John J. *Apocalypticism in the Dead Sea Scrolls.* London, 1997.

Collins, John J. *The Apocalyptic Imagination.* 2d ed. Grand Rapids, Mich., 1998. Standard introduction to the Jewish apocalypses.

Collins, John J., ed. *The Encyclopedia of Apocalypticism*, vol. 1, *The Origins of Apocalypticism in Judaism and Christianity*. New York, 1998. Contains essays on various aspects of Jewish apocalypticism, including the Dead Sea Scrolls, messianism, and mysticism.

Gruenwald, Ithamar. *Apocalyptic and Merkavah Mysticism*. Leiden, the Netherlands, 1980. Shows the continuity between the apocalyptic literature and later Jewish mysticism.

Hanson, Paul D. *The Dawn of Apocalyptic*. Philadelphia, 1975. Stimulating study of postexilic prophecy as early apocalypticism.

Himmelfarb, Martha. *Ascent to Heaven in Jewish and Christian Apocalypses*. New York, 1993. Careful study of the ascent apocalypses.

Nickelsburg, George W. E. 1 Enoch *1: A Commentary on the Book of* 1 Enoch, *Chapters 1–36; 81–108*. Minneapolis, 2001. Detailed commentary on 1 *Enoch*.

Rowland, Christopher. *The Open Heaven. A Study of Apocalyptic in Judaism and Early Christianity*. New York, 1982. Emphasizes the mystical aspects of the apocalypses.

Sacchi, Paolo. *Jewish Apocalyptic and its History*. Sheffield, U.K., 1997. Finds the root idea of apocalypticism in the sin of the Watchers in *1 Enoch*.

Stone, Michael E. *Fourth Ezra. A Commentary on the Book of Fourth Ezra*. Minneapolis, 1990. Detailed commentary on *4 Ezra*.

VanderKam, James C. *Enoch and the Growth of an Apocalyptic Tradition*. Washington, D.C., 1984. Discusses the Babylonian models for the figure of Enoch.

JOHN J. COLLINS (2005)

APOCALYPSE: MEDIEVAL JEWISH APOCALYPTIC LITERATURE

While the Talmudic and Midrashic literature of late antiquity appropriated various elements of the classical apocalyptic of the intertestamental period, it did so in an unsystematic and fragmentary fashion. Apocalyptic themes competed for attention amidst a wide range of contrasting views on eschatological matters in rabbinic literature. The early decades of the seventh century, however, witnessed the reemergence of a full-fledged apocalyptic literature in Hebrew. Produced primarily between the seventh and tenth centuries in the Land of Israel and the Near East, these generally brief but fascinating treatises exhibit a rather clearly recognizable set of messianic preoccupations and literary themes.

This literature may be illustrated by reference to one of the most important and influential of these works, *Sefer Zerubbavel* (Book of Zerubbabel). Composed in Hebrew in the early part of the seventh century, probably shortly before the rise of Islam, the *Sefer Zerubbavel* may have been written within the context of the military victories achieved by the Byzantine emperor Heraclius against the Persians in the year 629. These historical events no doubt incited speculation concerning the conditions under which the final messianic battles would be waged and their ultimate outcome.

As is characteristic of apocalyptic literature, the book is pseudepigraphically ascribed to a biblical figure, in this case to Zerubbabel, the last ruler of Judaea from the House of David, whose name is associated with the attempts to rebuild the Temple in Jerusalem following the Babylonian exile. He is presented as the beneficiary of a series of auditions and visions. The angel Michael (or Metatron as he is also called here) reveals himself to Zerubbabel and leads him to Rome, where he encounters a "bruised and despised man" in the marketplace. The latter turns out to be the Messiah, son of David, named here Menaḥem ben ʿAmmiʾel. The Messiah informs Zerubbabel that he is waiting in Rome until the time is ripe for his appearance. Michael then proceeds to relate to Zerubbabel the events that will lead up to the End of Days.

Zerubbabel is informed that the forerunner of the Messiah, son of David, the Messiah, son of Joseph, identified as Neḥemyah ben Ḥushiʾel, will gather all of the Jews to Jerusalem, where they will dwell for four years and where they will practice the ancient sacrifices. In the fifth year the king of Persia will rise over Israel, but a woman who accompanies Neḥemyah, Hephzibah, mother of the Messiah, son of David, will successfully resist the enemy with the help of a "rod of salvation" that she possesses.

Following these events Zerubbabel is shown a marble statue in Rome of a beautiful woman; he is told that Satan will cohabit with this woman, who will thereupon give birth to Armilus, a cruel tyrant who will achieve dominion over the whole world. Armilus (whose name may be derived from Romulus, founder of Rome) will then come to Jerusalem with nine other kings, over whom he will rule. He will wage war against Israel, slaying Neḥemyah ben Ḥushiʾel and driving the survivors of Israel into the desert. Suddenly, however, on the eve of the festival of Passover, the Messiah son of David will appear in the desert to redeem the Jewish people. Angered by the scorn and disbelief with which he is greeted by the elders of the community, he will shed his tattered clothes for "garments of vengeance" (*Is.* 59:17) and go up to Jerusalem, where he will prove his identity by conquering Armilus and the forces of evil. As with much of this literature, this book does not describe the messianic age itself, but focuses on the developments leading up to it.

The *Sefer Zerubbavel* became extremely popular and widely influential. The characters and events depicted in this work provided the basis for a considerable variety of apocalyptic texts over the next several centuries, including the final section of *Midrash Vayoshaʿ*, the *Secrets of Rabbi Shimʿon bar Yoḥai*, the *Prayer of Shimʿon bar Yoḥʿai*, apocalyptic poems by Elʿazar Kallir, and the eighth chapter of Saʿadyah Gaon's important philosophical treatise, the *Book of Beliefs and Opinions*.

The messianic speculation found in these and other works is characterized by several distinctive features, which, when taken together, provide a shape to Jewish medieval apocalyptic literature. There is, for example, a preoccupation with the political vicissitudes of great empires; historical upheavals are regarded as bearing momentous messianic significance. There is, moreover, a concern for the broad march of history, of which contemporary events are but a part, leading up to the final tribulations and vindication of the people of Israel. In the apocalyptic literature, redemption is not a matter for theoretical speculation but a process that has already begun, whose culmination is relatively imminent and whose timing can be calculated. A related feature of this literature is the sense that historical and messianic events have a life of their own, independent of the behavior of human beings. There is an inevitability to the force of events with little regard for the choices that Israel might make, such as to repent and gain God's favor. Nor do the authors of these texts indulge in theorizing about why events unfold as they do, other than the obvious fact that righteousness is destined to win over evil.

From a literary point of view, the apocalyptic treatises are, like their themes, extravagant. They revel in fantastic descriptions of their heroes and antiheroes, richly narrating the events that they reveal, and often regard their protagonists as symbols for the cosmic forces of good and evil. Another feature of apocalyptic literature is its revelatory character; knowledge of heavenly secrets and mysteries not attainable through ordinary means are revealed, typically by angels who serve as messengers from on high.

In subsequent centuries various authors wrote under the influence of these early medieval apocalyptic texts. The sixteenth century, in particular, witnessed an explosion in Mediterranean regions of messianic writing that had strong overtones of apocalypticism. In the wake of the calamitous expulsion of Jewry from Spain and Portugal in the last decade of the fifteenth century, messianic calculation and eschatological ferment were widespread, especially among the Jewish communities of the Mediterranean. Apocalyptically oriented writings of this period include, among others, the extensive and highly influential works of Isaac Abravanel (1437–1508), whose interpretation of the *Book of Daniel* led him to calculate the year 1503 as the beginning of the messianic age; the anonymously authored *Kaf ha-Qetoret* (Spoonful of incense; c. 1500), which interprets the Psalms as battle hymns for the final apocalyptic wars; the treatises of a Jerusalem rabbi and qabbalist, Avraham ben Eli'ezer ha-Levi (c. 1460–after 1528); and the work of Shelomoh Molkho (c. 1501–1532).

Medieval apocalyptic literature had at least two important historical consequences. First, it played a highly significant role in shaping the vision that Jews had concerning the events leading up to the End of Days. Most rationalist thinkers, exemplified best by Moses Maimonides (1135/8–1204), opposed the apocalyptic conception that the eschaton would be accompanied by cataclysmic events and that the messianic era would differ radically from the established natural order. But despite such reservations on the part of philosophical rationalists, apocalyptic visions and themes occupied a prominent place in the medieval Jewish imagination. Second, apocalyptic literature developed in a religious climate that also gave rise to a variety of short-lived messianic movements. Their connection to apocalypticism may be seen in the militant activism, the penchant for identifying signs of the messianic age, and the consuming interest in international events that typically characterized these movements. Particularly between the seventh and twelfth centuries, especially under Muslim rule in the Near East and Spain, a number of small movements emerged. In the seventeenth century the most significant messianic movement in Judaism since the birth of Christianity came into existence—Shabbateanism. Centered around the figure of a Turkish Jew, Shabbetai Tsevi (1626–1676), the movement, which stirred intense messianic turmoil throughout the Near East and Europe, incorporated within it elements of apocalypticism. Various Shabbatean apocalypses were written (some of which included enlarged and revised versions of *Sefer Zerubbavel)* and employed for the purposes of confirming the messiahship of Shabbetai Tsevi and justifying his antinomian behavior.

See Also Messianism, article on Jewish Messianism; Shabbetai Tsevi.

Bibliography

The most important collection of primary sources for medieval Jewish apocalyptic literature is *Midreshei ge'ulah,* in Hebrew, edited by Yehudah Even-Shemu'el (Jerusalem, 1954). This volume also contains excellent bibliographical information. A somewhat dated but still useful overview of this literature in English is Abba Hillel Silver's *A History of Messianic Speculation in Israel from the First through the Seventeenth Centuries* (New York, 1927), especially part 1, chapter 2. Concerning the apocalyptic tendencies of the Shabbatean movement, see Gershom Scholem's *Sabbatai Sevi: The Mystical Messiah, 1626–1676* (Princeton, 1973).

New Sources

Cook, Stephen L. *Prophecy and Apocalypticism: The Postexilic Social Setting.* Minneapolis, 1995.

Himmelfarb, Martha. *Ascent to Heaven in Jewish and Christian Apocalypses.* New York, 1993.

Sacchi, Paolo. *Jewish Apocalyptic and Its History.* London, 1996.

Stuckenbruck, Loren. "The 'Angels' and 'Giants' of *Genesis* 6:1–4 in Second and Third Century BCE Jewish Interpretation: Reflections on the Posture of Early Apocalyptic Traditions." *Dead Sea Discoveries* 7 (November 2000): 354–377.

VanderKam, James C., and William Adler. *The Jewish Apocalyptic Heritage in Early Christianity.* Minneapolis, 1996.

Lawrence Fine (1987)
Revised Bibliography

APOCATASTASIS.

The oldest known usage of the Greek word *apokatastasis* (whence the English *apocatastasis*) dates from the fourth century BCE: it is found in Aristotle (*Magna Moralia* 2.7.1204b), where it refers to the restoration of a being to its natural state. During the Hellenistic age it developed a cosmological and astrological meaning, variations of which can be detected (but with a very different concept of time) in Gnostic systems and even in Christian theology, whether orthodox or heterodox, especially in the theology of Origen.

MEDICAL, MORAL, AND JURIDICAL MEANING. Plato employed the verb *kathistanai* in the sense of to "reestablish" to a normal state following a temporary physical alteration (*Philebus* 42d). The prefix *apo-* in *apokathistanai* seems to reinforce the idea of an integral reestablishment to the original situation. Such is the return of the sick person to health (Hippocrates, 1258f.; Aretaeus, 9.22). The verb has this meaning in the Gospels in the context of the hand made better by Christ (*Mt.* 12:13; *Mk.* 3:5, *Lk.* 6:10). There are Hellenistic references to the apocatastasis, or "resetting," of a joint. In a psychological sense, the same meaning is present (with nuances that are hard to specify) in magical papyri and in the so-called Mithraic Liturgy. Origen (*Against Celsus* 2.24) uses the verb in his commentary on *Job* 5:18 ("For he wounds, but he binds up; he smites, but his hands heal") in one of several expositions where he compares the divine instruction on salvation to a method of therapy. The shift to a spiritual acceptation is evident, for example, in Philo Judaeus (*Who Is the Heir* 293), where "the perfect apocatastasis of the soul" confirms the philosophical healing that follows the two stages of infancy, first unformed and then corrupt. The soul recovers the health of its primitive state after a series of disturbances.

In a sociopolitical context, apocatastasis may signify a reestablishment of civil peace (Polybius, 4.23. l), or of an individual into his family (Polybius, 3.99.6), or the restoration of his rights (readmission of a soldier into an army, restoration of an exiled citizen to his prerogatives, etc.). Thus the verb *apokathistanai* is applied to the return of the Jews to the Holy Land after the captivity of Babylon (*Jer.* 15:9) as well as to the expression of messianic and eschatological hopes. Yet the noun form is not found in the Septuagint.

ASTRAL APOCATASTASIS AND THE GREAT YEAR. The popularity and development of astrology influenced the cosmological systems of Hellenistic philosophy starting at the end of the fourth century BCE. Apocatastasis here refers to the periodic return of the stars to their initial position, and the duration of the cycle amounts to a "Great Year." Plato defines the matter without using the word in the *Timaeus* (39d), where he talks of the eight spheres. Eudemius attributed to the Pythagoreans a theory of eternal return, but the Great Year of Oenopides and Philolaus involves only the sun. That of Aristotle, who calls it the "complete year," takes into account the seven planets: it also includes a "great winter" (with a flood) and a "great summer" (with a conflagration). Yet one could trace back to Heraclitus the principle of universal palingenesis periodically renewing the cosmos by fire, as well as the setting of the length of the Great Year at 10,800 years (this latter point is still in dispute). The astronomic teaching on the apocatastasis was refined by the Stoics, who identified it with the sidereal Great Year concluded either by a *kataklusmos* (flood) or by an *ekpurosis* (conflagration). Cicero defined it (with Aristotle) as the restoration of the seven planets to their point of departure, and sometimes as the return of all the stars (including the fixed ones) to their initial position. The estimates of its length varied considerably, ranging from 2,484 years (Aristarchus); to 10,800 years (Heraclitus); 12,954 years (Cicero); 15,000 years (Macrobius); 300,000 years (Firmicus Maternus), and up to 3,600,000 years (Cassandra). Diogenes of Babylon multiplied Heraclitus's Great Year by 365.

The Neoplatonist Proclus attributes the doctrines of apocatastasis to the "Assyrians," in other words to the astrologers or "Chaldeans." However, Hellenistic astrology also drew from Egyptian traditions. The 36,525 books that Manetho (285–247 BCE) attributed to Hermes Trismegistos represent the amount of 25 zodiac periods of 1,461 years each, that is, probably one Great Year (Gundel and Gundel, 1966). The texts of Hermes Trismegistos make reference to the apocatastasis (*Hermetica* 8.17, 11.2; *Asklepios* 13). In the first century BCE, the neo-Pythagorean Nigidius Figulus perhaps conceived the palingenetic cycle as being a great cosmic week crowned by the reign of Apollo. Whence the celebrated verses of Vergil's Fourth Eclogue: "A great order is born out of the fullness of ages . . . now your Apollo reigns." The return of Apollo corresponds to that of the Golden Age. The noun *apocatastasis* (as well as the verb from which it derives) always evoked the restoration of the old order. It often implied a "nostalgia for origins." It is no accident that, in the scheme of the Mithraic mysteries, the last of the "doors" is made out of gold and corresponds to the sun, since the order of these planetary doors is that of a week in reverse; there is the presupposition of a backward progression to the beginning of time. In the teaching of the Stoics, this new beginning is seen as having to repeat itself indefinitely, following a constant periodicity that rules out of chance, disorder, and freedom. During the imperial age, the Roman mystique of *renovatio* rested upon the same basic concept (Turcan, 1981, pp. 22ff.).

GNOSTIC APOCATASTASES. In Gnosticism, apocatastasis also corresponds to a restoration of order, but in a spiritual and eschatological way from the perspective of a history of salvation that is fundamentally foreign to the Stoics' "eternal return." The Christ of the Valentinians "restores" the soul to the Pleroma. Heracleon interprets the wages of the reaper (*Jn.* 4:36) as being the salvation of souls and their "apocatastasis" into eternal life (Origen, *Commentary on the Gospel of John* 13.46.299). The Valentinian Wisdom (Sophia) is reintegrated through apocatastasis to the Pleroma, as Enthumesis will also be. The female *aiōn* Achamoth awaits the return of the Savior so that he might "restore" her syzygy. For Marcus, the universal restoration coincides with a return to unity. All these systems tell the story of a restoration of an order disturbed by thought.

The concept of the followers of Basilides is difficult indeed to elucidate, since they imagine at the beginning of all things not a Pleroma but nonbeing. Given this premise, there is no talk about a restoration to an initial state, even less to the truly primitive state of nothingness. However, for the Basilidians the salvation that leads men to God amounts to no less than a reestablishment of order (Hippolytus, *Philosophuma* 7.27.4). Like the Stoics, Basilides linked apocatastasis to astral revolutions: the coming of the Savior was to coincide "with the return of the hours to their point of departure." (ibid., 6.1). Yet this soteriological process is historical: it unfolds within linear rather than cyclical time. The Basilidian apocatastasis is not regressive but rather progressive and definitive. Some other Gnostics integrated astral apocatastasis into their systems: the Manichaeans seem to have conceived of a Great Year of 12,000 years with a final conflagration.

CHRISTIAN APOCATASTASIS. In the New Testament, the first evidence of the noun *apocatastasis* used in an eschatological sense is found in *Acts of the Apostles* 3:21: Peter states that heaven must keep Jesus "till the universal apocatastasis comes." According to André Méhat (1956, p. 209), this would mean the "definitive achievement" of what God has promised through his prophets and would indicate the notion of accomplishment and fulfillment. In the Gospels, *Matthew* 17:11 and *Mark* 9:2 speak of Elijah as the one who will "reestablish" everything, and *Malachi* 3:23 (of which the evangelists could not help but think) speaks of the day when Yahveh will "restore" hearts and lead them back to him. Apocatastasis thus represents the salvation of creation reconciled with God, that is, a true return to an original state. The verb has this meaning for Theophilus of Antioch (*To Autolycus* 2.17). For both Tatian (*Address to the Greeks* 6.2) and Irenaeus (*Against Heresies* 5.3.2) apocatastasis is equivalent to resurrection and points without any ambiguity to a restoration of man in God. In Clement of Alexandria, the precise meaning of the word is not always clear, but this much may be said: apocatastasis appears as a return to God that is the result of a recovered purity of heart consequent to absorption in certain "Gnostic" teachings; it is a conception not unlike that found in the *Book of Malachi* in the Hebrew scriptures (Old Testament).

It is in Origen that the doctrine of apocatastasis finds its most remarkable expression. In *Against Celsus* 7.3, where he mentions the "restoration of true piety toward God," Origen implicitly refers to *Malachi.* Elsewhere (*Commentary on the Gospel of John* 10.42.291), the word involves the reestablishment of the Jewish people after the captivity, yet as an anticipatory image of the return to the heavenly fatherland. Origen's originality consisted in his having conceived apocatastasis as being universal (including the redemption even of the devil or the annihilation of all evil) and as a return of souls to their pure spirituality. This final incorporality is rejected by Gregory of Nyssa, who nonetheless insists upon apocatastasis as a restoration to the original state. Didymus the Blind and Evagrios of Pontus were condemned at the same time as Origen by the Council of Constantinople (553) for having professed the doctrine of universal apocatastasis and the restoration of incorporeal souls. Yet there is still discussion concerning this principal aspect of Origen's eschatology. Astronomical theories and Greek cosmology seem also to have inspired the Greek bishop Synesius of Cyrene, a convert from Neoplatonism. Yet Tatian (*Address to the Greeks* 6. 2) had already emphasized what fundamentally set Christian apocatastasis apart: it depends upon God (and not upon sidereal revolutions) and is completed once and for all at the end of time, without being repeated indefinitely.

SEE ALSO Ages of the World; Golden Age.

BIBLIOGRAPHY

Bouché-Leclercq, Auguste. *L'astrologie grecque* (1899). Brussels, 1963.

Carcopino, J. *Virgile et le mystère de la quatrième eglogue.* Paris, 1943.

Crouzel, Henri. "Différences entre les ressuscités selon Origène," *Jahrbuch für Antike und Christentum* 9, supp., *Gedenkschrift für A. Stuiber* (1982): 107–116.

Daniélou, Jean. "L'apocatastase chez saint Grégoire de Nysse." *Recherches de science religieuse* (1940): 328ff.

Daniélou, Jean. *Platonisme et théologie mystique.* Paris, 1944.

Daniélou, Jean. *Origen.* Translated by Walter Mitchell. New York, 1955.

Faye, E. de. *Origène: Sa vie, son œuvre, sa pensée.* Paris, 1923–1928.

Gundel, Wilhelm, and Hans Georg Gundel. *Astrologumena.* Wiesbaden, 1966.

Hoven, R. *Stoïcisme et stoïciens face au problème de l'audelà.* Paris, 1971.

Lenz, Chr. "Apokatastasis." *Reallexikon für Antike und Christentum* 1 (1950): 510–516.

Méhat, André. " 'Apocastastase,' Origène, Clément d'Alexandrie, *Act.* 3, 21." *Vigiliae Christianae* 10 (November 1956): 196–214.

Méhat, André. "Apokatastasis chez Basilide." In *Mélanges d'histoire des religions offerts à Henri-Charles Puech,* pp. 365–373. Paris, 1974.

Müller, G. "Origenes und die Apokatastasis." *Theologische Zeitschrift* 14 (1958): 174–190.

Mussner, Franz, and J. Loosen. "Apokatastasis." In *Lexikon für Theologie und Kirche,* vol. 1, pp. 708ff. Berlin, 1957.

Siniscalco, P. "I significati di 'restituere' e 'restitutio' in Tertulliano." *Atti della Accademia delle Scienza di Torino* 93 (1958–1959): 1–45.

Siniscalco, P. "Apokatastasis nella letteratura cristiana fino a Ireneo." *Studia Patristica* 3 (1961): 380–396.

Turcan, Robert. *Mithras platonicus: Recherches sur l'hellénisation philosophique de Mithra.* Leiden, 1975.

Turcan, Robert. "Rome éternelle et les conceptions grécoromaines de l'éternité: Da Roma alla terza Roma." *Seminario internazionale* (April 1981): 7–30.

New Sources

Charalambos, Apostolopoulos. *Phaedo Christianus. Studien zur Verbindung und Abwägung des Verhältnisses zwischen dem platonischen "Phaidon" und dem Dialog Gregor von Nyssa "Über die Seele und die Auferstehung."* Bern, 1986.

Crouzel, Henri. "L'apocatastase chez Origène." In *Origeniana Quarta. Die Referate des 4. Internationalen Origeneskongresses (Innsbruck, 2.–6. September 1985)*, edited by Lothar Lies, pp. 282–290. Innsbruck, 1987.

Kettler, F. H. "Neue Beobachtungen zur Apokatastasislehre des Origenes." In *Origeniana secunda. Second colloque international des études origéniennes (Bari, 20–23 septembre 1977)*, edited by Henri Crouzel and Antonio Quacquarelli, pp. 339–348. Rome, 1980.

Kretzenbacher, Leopold. *Versöhnung im Jenseits. Zur Widerspiegelung des Apokatastasis-Denkens in Glaube, Hochdichtung und Legende.* Munich, 1971.

Maturi, Giorgio. "Apokatastasis e anastasis in Gregorio di Nissa." *Studi e Materiali di Storia delle Religioni* 24 (2000): 227–240.

Sachs, John R. "Apocatastasis in Patristic Theology." *Theological Studies* 54 (1993): 617–640.

Salmona, Bruno. "Origene e Gregorio di Nissa sulla resurrezione dei corpi e l'apocatastasi." *Augustinianum* 18 (1978): 383–388.

van Laak, Werner. *Allversöhnung: die Lehre von der Apokatastasis: ihre Grundlegung durch Origenes und ihre Bewertung in der gegenwärtigen Theologie bei Karl Barth und Hans Urs von Balthasar.* Sinzig, Germany, 1990.

von Stritzky, Maria Barbara. "Die Bedeutung der Phaidrosinterpretation für die Apokatastasislehre des Origenes." *Vigiliae Christianae* 31 (1977): 282–297.

ROBERT TURCAN (1987)
Translated from French by Paul C. Duggan
Revised Bibliography

APOCRYPHA SEE BIBLICAL LITERATURE, *ARTICLE ON* APOCRYPHA AND PSEUDEPIGRAPHA

APOLLINARIS OF LAODICEA

APOLLINARIS OF LAODICEA (c. 310–c. 390), Christian bishop and heretic. Apollinaris was born in Laodicea. He admired Greek philosophy and literature, to the dismay of Bishop Theodotus, who asked him to repent. After finishing his studies, he became a teacher of classical literature, combining exceptional erudition, admirable rhetorical ability, and excellent theological education.

Apollinaris gained the affection and the admiration of the church because he reacted vigorously against the emperor Julian the Apostate, who by decree forbade the Christians to teach and use Greek Classical literature. Apollinaris rewrote much of the Bible in an attractive Greek Classical form. In order to provide the Classical methodology for Christian youth, he composed Platonic dialogues from gospel material and paraphrased *Psalms* in hexameters. Using the prose style of ancient Greek writers (such as Euripides), he wrote lives of saints as well as beautiful Christian poetry, for private use as well as for liturgical purposes. Unfortunately, from all this splendid production, nothing survived.

Apollinaris was an uncompromising supporter of the doctrine of Nicaea. He fought and wrote against Origen, Arius, the Arian bishop Eunomius, Marcellus of Ancyra, and others. He enjoyed for a long period of time the respect and affection of the great Fathers of the fourth century, including Athanasius, Basil of Caesarea, and Gregory of Nazianzus (Gregory the Theologian) who called the Apollinarian controversy a "brotherly dispute." His prestige is testified by the fact that he was elected orthodox bishop of Laodicea in 360, having the trust of the Nicene community at large.

Most of Apollinaris's writings have been lost. Quasten in his *Patrology* (vol. 3, pp. 377ff.) divides Apollinaris's writings into exegetical works, apologetic works, polemical works, dogmatic works, poetry, and correspondence with Basil of Caesarea. Among the exegetical works were "innumerable volumes on the Holy Scriptures" (cf. Jerome, *On Famous Men* 104). Among the apologetic works were his thirty books against the Neoplatonist Porphyry and his work *The Truth,* against Julian.

One of the most brilliant theologians of his time, Apollinaris faced the most difficult question of the fourth century: how divinity and humanity could be united in the one person of Jesus Christ. Influenced by Platonic, Aristotelian, and Stoic philosophical understandings of human nature, he tried to apply their method, in an original and syncretistic way, in interpreting the New Testament and in defending the Nicene faith against the heresies of the times, especially Arianism. Thus, he rejected the Arian conception of the incarnation of Christ, which he thought diminished the importance of both God and humanity in Jesus Christ.

Apollinaris believed that a complete entity, one *phusis,* or nature, cannot be changed or destroyed. A human, in its total existence as body, soul, and spirit (*nous,* or intellect), can be called one *phusis.* In Christ, union of a complete human nature with the complete divine nature is impossible, for neither nature can be destroyed (the Stoic understanding of mixture). In other words, two complete natures could not produce the one nature of Jesus.

Apollinaris suggested, instead, the "trichotomist" view of humanity. He approached *1 Corinthians* 15:45 and *1 Thessalonians* 5:23 as meaning that the flesh of Jesus Christ was composed of body, the irrational animal soul, and instead of the intellect, the Logos itself: thus his famous expression "One incarnate nature of the God the Logos" (found in his letter to the bishops exiled at Diocaesarea). For Apollinaris, Christ, having God as his spirit, or intellect, together with soul and body, is rightly called "the human being from heaven" (Norris, 1980, p. 108). In explaining his thesis, Apollinaris writes: "Therefore, the human race is saved not by the assumption of an intellect and of a whole human being but by the assumption of flesh, whose nature it is to be ruled. What was needed was unchangeable Intellect which did not fall under the dominion of the flesh on account of its weakness of understanding but which adapted the flesh to itself without force" (ibid., p. 109).

Apollinaris's acceptance of the full union of the humanity and divinity of Christ in one person, the Logos, did not contradict the dogmatic position of the orthodox Fathers. His great fallacy was the reduction of the humanity of Christ to a body without a rational soul, thus concluding that in Christ there was not a full human nature and that excluded human nature from the fruits of salvation in Jesus Christ. In the end, Apollinaris's Christ was God, to be sure, "enfleshed," but not incarnated.

The orthodox concept of the *theanthropos,* that is, God and human, is missing from the christological structure of Apollinaris. By eliminating the biblical and patristic emphasis on the full humanity of Christ—with full and complete human body, soul, and mental and intellectual capacity—Apollinaris made impossible humanity's full union with the Logos and thus the scope and extent of humanity's salvation. Gregory refuted the thesis of Apollinaris with his devastating statement: "If anyone has put his trust in [Christ] as a man without a human mind, he is really bereft of mind, and quite unworthy of salvation. For that which he has not assumed he has not healed; but that which is united to his Godhead is also saved" (*To Cledonius against Apollinarius,* letter 101).

Apollinaris's heresy, Apollinarianism, is considered the first important christological heresy of the fourth century. Until 374, when Jerome became his pupil in Antioch, Apollinaris's deviation from the orthodox doctrine had not become well known. Basil finally realized the depth and repercussions of Apollinaris's heresy and asked for his condemnation. Gregory wrote his two famous letters to Cledonius against the heresy, and Gregory of Nyssa (c. 385) attacked Apollinaris in his *Antirrheticus.* Pope Damasus I condemned him in Rome (c. 374–380). Finally the teaching of Apollinaris was officially condemned in 381 by the Council of Constantinople.

BIBLIOGRAPHY

Grillmeier, Aloys. *Christ in Christian Tradition,* vol. 1. 2d rev. ed. London, 1975. Includes a bibliography.

Hubner, Reinhard. "Gotteserkenntnis durch die Inkarnation Gottes: Zu einer neuen Interpretation der Christologie des Apollinaris von Laodicea." *Kleronomia* (Thessaloniki) 4 (1972): 131–161.

Leitzmann, Hans, ed. *Apollinaris von Laodicea und seine Schule* (1904). Reprint, Tübingen, 1970. Still the classic edition of original texts.

Mühlenberg, Ekkehard. *Appollinaris von Laodicea.* Göttingen, 1969.

Norris, Richard A., Jr., ed. and trans. *The Christological Controversy.* Philadelphia, 1980.

Prestige, G. L. *St. Basil the Great and Apollinaris of Laodicea.* London, 1956.

Quasten, Johannes. *Patrology,* vol. 3. Utrecht, 1953. Includes a full bibliography on Apollinaris on pages 377–383.

Raven, Charles E. *Apollinarianism.* Cambridge, 1923.

Riedmatten, Henri de. "Some Neglected Aspects of Apollinarist Christology." *Dominican Studies* 1 (1948): 239–260.

Torrance, Thomas F. "The Mind of Christ in Worship: The Problem in the Liturgy." In his *Theology in Reconciliation,* pp. 139–215. London, 1975.

Wolfson, Harry A. "Philosophical Implications of Arianism and Apollinarianism." *Dumbarton Oaks Papers* 12 (1958): 3–28.

Wolfson, Harry A. *The Philosophy of the Church Fathers.* 3d ed. Cambridge, Mass., 1970.

Young, Frances M. *From Nicaea to Chalcedon.* Philadelphia, 1983.

GEORGE S. BEBIS (1987)

APOLLO, the son of Zeus and Leto and the twin brother of Artemis, is the Greek god whom the European tradition already associated with the aesthetic splendor and brilliance of Greece before Johann Jakob Winckelmann (1717–1768), the founder of Greek art history, regarded the Belvedere Apollo (a Roman copy of a fourth-century Greek original that shows Apollo as a youthful archer) as the most perfect embodiment of Greek aesthetics and Greek gods. Apollo's image as a beautiful and permanently young man significantly contributed to this modern evaluation, as did Apollo's identification with the sun. His darker sides, expressed through his deathly mastery of archery, were eclipsed in this modern reception. In Greek myth, Apollo is the favorite son of Zeus but has relatively few independent stories; he is connected either with young men and women, or with specific sanctuaries such as Delos or Delphi. In Greek religion, Apollo was the protector of young males and presided over divination, healing, and the complex of music and dance (Greek, *molpē*), whereas Etruscan and Roman religion embraced him almost exclusively as a healer.

THE ETYMOLOGY OF APOLLO. Almost uniquely among the twelve Olympian gods, Apollo's name does not appear in the Mycenaean Bronze Age texts; these texts only preserve a god called Paiawon, presumably an early form of Apollo's later epithet "Paian." In Homer and Hesiod, however (that is, in the late eighth or early seventh centuries BCE), Apollo's mythical and religious roles are firmly established, presumably developing and spreading during the intervening Dark Ages of the eleventh through the ninth centuries BCE.

Among the many competing modern etymologies of his name, the derivation from the Doric *apella,* "association of the free male citizen" (Burkert, 1975, pp. 1–12), has found the most adherence; the marginality of the Dorians in the Greek Bronze Age and their immigration into most of Southern Greece—from the Peloponnese to the islands of Crete and Rhodes—explains Apollo's absence in the Bronze Age, as well as his position in the early Iron Age and his function as the protector of the young warriors and their institutions based on common song and dance. That the month Apellaios is the first month in Delphi points to a connection between the New Year's festival, citizens' associations, and the introduction of the young warriors into society through their display of song and dance; it is, however, impossible to derive all functions of Apollo from this or any other homogeneous ritual complex.

APOLLO IN DELOUS AND DELPHI. In early Greek poetry, Apollo's mythical and cultic personality is fully established.

Born on the island of Delos (*Homeric Hymn to Apollo*, 25–178 [seventh century BCE]) against the will of Hera, Apollo's birth founds and legitimates the great renown of the Delian sanctuary—the central sanctuary for the cities of archaic Ionia—and a sacred island for all of Greece in later times (see Callimachus, *Hymn* 4). Apollo's main monument on the island was an altar made from the horns of sacrificial goats. The monument stood next to the palm tree that lent support to Leto when giving birth (*Odyssey* 6,162–163). (Such altars are attested to in other Apolline sanctuaries as well.) His birthday, on the seventh day of an unstated month (Hesiod, *Works and Days* 771), was the day most festivals of Apollo were held—the seventh day of a given month—yet they could also fall on the first day of a month (Apollo *Noumēnios*, "He of the New Moon").

Apollo's first youthful exploit is the killing of the snake Pytho and the foundation of his other main sanctuary, the oracular shrine of Delphi (*Homeric Hymn to Apollo*, vs. 214–544; *Iliad* 9.404–405), by far the most important oracular shrine in archaic and classical Greece. In order to punish the sacrilegious arrogance of the Greek leaders in Troy, Apollo sends a plague into their camp (*Iliad* 1.44–52); the plague is then healed through a sumptuous sacrifice, purificatory rites, and the singing and dancing of a paean by the "young men of the Achaeans" (*Iliad* 1.313–474). Apollo had caused the plague by shooting animals and men with his arrows, and thus his archery is an image for the deadly power of the illness. Much later, an image of the archer Apollo, erected in a city gate, was thought to avert disease and evil from the city. His arrows were believed to send swift and unexpected death to men in the same way that Artemis's arrows could kill women. Yet Apollo is also considered the patron god of real archers.

One of Apollo's other attributes is his playing of the lyre. The *Homeric Hymn to Hermes* (sixth century BCE) narrates how Hermes made the first lyre out of the shell of a tortoise and gave it to his older brother Apollo. The same *Hymn* makes it clear that divination, to know the "mind of Zeus," is Apollo's prerogative alone (vs. 471–472).

Most Panhellenic sanctuaries of Apollo were major oracular shrines (Delos is the one exception). Alongside Delphi, the sanctuaries in Didyma near Miletus and Clarus near Colophon in Western Asia Minor were already important in archaic Greece; they remained famous to the end of pagan antiquity. The Greco-Egyptian Magical Papyri refer to Clarian and Pythian Apollo as conferring private oracular dreams (Papyri Graecae Magicse II .130, fourth century CE), and the *Tübingen Theosophy,* a sixth century Christian treatise, still cites Clarian oracles to support the thesis of a pagan preknowledge of Christian theology. The ritual forms of divination differed from sanctuary to sanctuary, although they all had a medium prophesy in an altered state of consciousness; in Clarus and Didyma, the water of a sacred spring provoked ecstasy in a priest (Clarus) or priestess (Didyma), whereas in later sources the Delphian Pythia was said to prophesy under the influence of mephitic gases. Apollo also attracted noninstitutionalized divination: both the sibyl and the Trojan seer Cassandra were said to be his lovers.

APOLLO'S CULTIC ROLES. The cults in individual cities stress other aspects of Apollo, especially his connection with young men (ephebes) and male citizens on the one hand, and with his power for healing on the other.

Apollo the Healer (*Iētros, Oulios*) is mainly attested to in the Greek East from the sixth to the fourth centuries BCE. Slowly, however, this function was taken over by Apollo's son Asclepius, with whom he shared many important healing sanctuaries—such as Epidaurus or Kos. Although official documents from these sanctuaries stress the coexistence of both deities, private worship focused solely on Asclepius. Asclepian healing focuses on incubation and dream oracles. It can be seen as specialized form of Apolline divination, and Apollo himself could be called *iatromantis,* the "healing seer," and had close ties to the mythical seer and healer Melampus. As a healer, Apollo had already been adopted by the Etruscans and Romans prior to the fifth century BCE. Apollo Medicus (Healer) was introduced in Rome to heal a plague in 431 BCE (Livy 4.25.3). The sanctuary survived the introduction of the Greek Asculapius in 293 BCE and was restored under Augustus.

More generally, Apollo was seen as a divinity that kept away evil (averter, *apotropaios*). Together with his sister Artemis, he guarded the city gates, and in a crisis, an image of the archer Apollo could defend a city against disease. Private houses were protected by simple stone pillars that were taken as Apolline symbols (*agyieus*). In the cities of the Greek East and in Athens, the Apolline festival Thargelia was a festival of purification. The Athenians celebrated it on Thargelion 6 and 7 (the penultimate month of the year), and, as in some Ionian cities, they performed among other rites a scapegoat ritual (*pharmakos*) in order to cleanse the city before the period of reversal that leads to the Athenian New Year.

But at least as important as these functions is Apollo's connection with the young men of the city, connections already visible in the derivation of his name from *apella* and so fundamental as to shape Apollo's iconography as an eternally young man (ephebe), complete with an ephebe's long hair and adolescent body. The Spartans performed several Apolline festivals in which the young men were central: the Gymnopaidia (Naked dances), which had their ritual center in the singing and dancing of young male choruses; the Karneia—the main festival of many Doric cities—were entirely organized by the young citizens; and the Hyacinthia—the main Spartan festival—featured as its etiological myth the story of how Apollo killed his adolescent lover Hyacinthus with the mistaken throw of a discus. Although the ritual combined grief for Hyacinthus with dance performances of boys and young men, the iconography of Apollo turned him into an archaic warrior who was depicted with shield and lance.

Yet the complex of dancing and singing of all-male groups—called *molpē* by the Greeks—is in archaic Greece noted well beyond the world of the Doric cities. Apollo enters this complex there as well. Perhaps the most prominent group in which Apollo figures is with the *molpoi* of archaic Miletus—an aristocratic cult group whose leader was, at the same time, the supreme official of the city. These Milesian *molpoi* were associated with the cult of Apollo Delphinios and, to some degree, with oracular Apollo in Didyma. When the Milesians founded their colony of Olbia in the Black Sea, they introduced the same institution, and it is in institutions like these—with a common meal as well as common dancing and singing—that musical Apollo finds his origin and social relevance.

Among the later developments of Apollo's image, two have to be singled out: his identification with the sun, and the opposition between Apollo and Dionysos. The identification with the sun and with Helios is first attested in the early fifth century BCE but becomes important only much later, especially in astrology where Apollo represented the "planet" sun and his sister Artemis the "planet" moon; astrological iconography transmits this into the European Middle Ages, whereas Apollo as sun is common in mythical allegories both in late antiquity and in the European Renaissance and Baroque epochs.

The opposition between Apollo and Dionysus has its cultic root in Delphi where Dionysus reigned during Apollo's absence in winter, and where Dionysos was even said to have his grave. The opposition gained sharper contours when Augustus (63 BCE–14 CE) presented himself and his personal god Apollo to his antagonist Marc Anthony (82–30 BCE), who stylized himself as the New Dionysus. Whereas Dionysus stood for all the decadent pleasures of the East, Apollo represented the purity and clarity of the order that Augustus restored and put under the patronage of an Apollo whose temple had become part of his house on the Palatine. Another point of view, from the early nineteenth century, describes how musical history made use of the same opposition in which Dionysus represented ecstatic music whereas Apollo represented serene, well-ordered tunes. From musical theory Friedrich Nietzsche (1844–1900) would develop the opposition between the two gods as the basic feature of Greek tragedy.

SEE ALSO Artemis; Delphi; Dionysos; Divination, article on Greek and Roman Divination; Hera; Hesiod; Homer; Muses; Oracles; Pythagoras; Sun.

BIBLIOGRAPHY

Most of the ancient texts cited above are available in critical editions with English translations in the Loeb Classical Library.

Bentz, Martin, and Dieter Steinbauer. "Neues zum Aplu-Kult in Etrurien." *Archäologischer Anzeiger* (2001): 69–78.

Boyancé, Pierre. "L'Apollon solaire." In *Mélanges d'archéologie, d'épigraphie et d'histoire offerts à Jean Carcopino.* pp. 149–170. Paris, 1966.

Burkert, Walter. "Apellai und Apollon." *Rheinisches Museum* 118 (1975): 1–21.

Detienne, Marcel. *Apollon le couteau à la main: Une approche expérimentale du polythéisme grec.* Paris, 1998.

Dumézil, Georges. "Apollo Medicus." In *Apollon sonore et autres essais:Vingt-cinq esquisses de mythologie,* pp. 36–42. Paris, 1982.

Fontenrose, Joseph. *The Delphic Oracle: Its Responses and Operations.* Berkeley, Calif., 1978.

Fontenrose, Joseph. *Didyma: Apollo's Oracle, Cult, and Companions.* Berkeley, Calif., 1988.

Gagé, Jean. *Apollon Romain: Essai sur le culte d'Apollon et le dévelopement du "ritus graecus" à Rome des origines à Auguste.* Paris, 1955.

Pettersson, Michael. *Cults of Apollo at Sparta: The Hyakinthia, the Gymnopaidia and the Karneia.* Stockholm, 1992.

Solomon, Joe, ed. *Apollo: Origins and Influences.* Tucson, Ariz., 1994.

von Reibnitz, Barbara. "Apollinisch–Dionysisch." In *Ästhetische Grundbegriffe,* vol. 1, pp. 246–271. Stuttgart, Germany, 2000.

Zeitlin, Froma I. "Apollo and Dionysos: Starting from Birth." In *Kykeon: Studies in Honour of H. S. Versnel,* edited by H. F. J. Horstmanshoff, et al. pp. 193–218. Leiden, Netherlands, 2002.

FRITZ GRAF (2005)

APOLOGETICS. [*This entry, which is restricted to consideration of monotheistic religions, places religious apologetics in comparative perspective and examines the difference between apologetics and polemics.*]

Apologetics is other-directed communication of religious belief that makes assertions about knowing and serving God. It represents the content of a particular faith in an essentially intellectualist fashion and, like a national boundary, acts as a membrane for the exchange of ideas. The content of apologetics is based in the revelation of God, but its format is based in culture. Apologetics often is other-directed insofar as it presupposes, at least apparently, an audience external to the faith it represents. Furthermore, it communicates by virtue of patterns of thought and language common to speaker and hearer, which leads the apologist to employ terminology, styles of thought, and ideas familiar to the hearer.

Despite the fact that the audience addressed in religious apologies is often presumed to be outside the faith, apologetic literature often has been most popular within the confines of the religious community for which it speaks rather than among the critics to whom it is nominally addressed. The adoption of an addressant serves as a powerful rhetorical device that helps promote the clarification of ideas. This inclination toward refinement of thought makes apologetics as much a strategy in the forging of an orthodox system of belief as a genre of testimony to nonbelievers. Any religion, monotheistic or otherwise, might adopt an apologetic posture under circumstances in which it perceives the need to defend itself against misunderstanding, criticism, discrimination, or oppression, but the pattern of religious apology that will be examined here emerged from the engagement of unitary conceptions of God with the culture of Greco-Roman polytheism during the first several centuries of the common era.

Defense of Monotheism. In Greco-Roman culture, whose intellectual foundations were buttressed by polytheistic beliefs and practices, monotheism was judged to be both blasphemous and incredible. Jewish thinkers as early as the third century BCE, followed by Christian and Muslim thinkers in early periods of the development of doctrines of Christian and Islamic beliefs, made use of the intellectual apparatus provided by Hellenistic philosophy to explain and defend systematically the foundations of belief in one God. A well-known model for the reasoned defense of belief and practice was Socrates' address before the Athenian court in 399 BCE, which is preserved in Plato's *Apology.* The Greek word *apologia,* meaning "speech in defense," refers to an oral and literary genre known throughout the ancient Mediterranean world. When Socrates was accused of demonstrating impiety toward the ancestral gods of his state and of corrupting the morals of Athenian youth through adherence to unusual beliefs, he argued his case against ignorance and unenlightened authority by means of reason. Although he failed to convince a majority of jurors that his pursuit of wisdom, which had made him a critic of prevailing religious belief, was based in truth, his effort became a model for future apologists. Biblical monotheists subsequently employed established patterns of philosophical argumentation that owed much to Greek philosophy and the example of Socrates to account for the superiority of their positions on faith. They, too, sought to expose what to their way of thinking were the inconsistencies, errors, and even absurdities of polytheism. Furthermore, the Hebrew legacy of truth they represented bore a rational coherence attractive to the Hellenistic way of thinking.

The tradition of justice, divine providence, and the sharp rejection of idolatry emphasized by the Hebrew prophets resounds in Josephus Flavius's treatise known as *Against Apion.* Composed in Greek in the first century CE, Josephus's response to Apion's criticisms of the Jews asserts the antiquity of the Jewish faith according to patterns of Greek historiography, celebrates the biblical God as lawgiver, and denounces polytheistic religions as immoral and irrational. "I would therefore boldly maintain that we have introduced to the rest of the world a very large number of very beautiful ideas. What greater beauty than inviolable piety? What higher justice than obedience?" (2.293). Striving to assure the right of Jews living under Roman domination to refuse participation in local cults, Josephus indicts the polytheists for ignoring the true nature of God and for appealing licentiously to the public taste. On the other hand, he praises the virtue and purity of the law of Moses and recalls the sensible wisdom of Plato. As the Jewish philosopher Philo Judaeus (d. 50 CE) had done before him, Josephus affirmed a compatibility between biblical faith and the higher morality of Greek philosophy, claiming with bold historicity that the Greek philosophers were among the first imitators of Mosaic law.

The Talmud records disputations between learned rabbis and Roman authorities over the veracity of Jewish ideas and freedom of worship. Beginning in the second century CE, Christians also exercised a strenuous apologetic effort to explain the foundations of their emerging beliefs and to defend themselves against oppression and popular slander. Because Christians would not serve the gods legitimated by Roman authority, they were held to be atheistic and seditious elements of the population. Moreover, the emerging forms of Christian worship and the way of living Christianity promoted among disenfranchised elements of society were viewed suspiciously by the state, eliciting charges of cannibalism and incest. Christian response was defensive, but also, on the model of Josephus, not without an offensive thrust. The defenders of Christianity claimed that the Roman state religion was absurd idolatry, and they offered in its place a simple moral appeal bearing resemblance to Stoic ideals.

Beginning with Quadratus, who wrote in Athens during the reign of Hadrian (117–138), and Aristides, and followed by, among others, Justin Martyr, Tatian, Athenagoras, Melito of Sardis, Theophilus of Antioch, Tertullian, the anonymous author of *To Diognetus,* Clement of Alexandria, Origen, and Augustine of Hippo (the last of early Christianity's great apologists), written defenses of the young and growing religion proliferated, often in the form of open letters addressed to critics of Christianity or to the emperor in Rome. Much of what must have been a large body of literature has been lost. The arguments in defense of Christian faith and its forms of worship followed methods of reasoning borrowed selectively from Platonism and its influential variations, from Stoicism, and from Skepticism.

Generally, early Christian apologetics had more influence among other Christian thinkers than among non-Christians. The legacy of this prodigious literary output can be located, therefore, in the development of the philosophical foundations of subsequent doctrines of God and of teachings concerning the incarnation and resurrection of Jesus Christ. Although these apologies reveal compatibilities with current philosophical thought, their practical importance for Christianity lay in their role of helping to define an emerging orthodoxy that found itself in growing competition with gnosticism and Marcionism for the religious allegiance of gentiles. The New Testament itself includes appeals to non-Christians that are apologetic in tone, although no full-fledged apologetic writings are identified before those of the second-century apologists.

The engagement of biblical faith with sophisticated Greek philosophy is evidenced clearly in early Christian apologetic literature. But although the function of apologetics as intellectual discourse was primary, it should not be overlooked that the apologetic spirit displayed in these writings cooperated intimately with other than solely intellectual religious motives; before the official sanction of Christianity by the Roman emperor in the fourth century, Christian apologists also display a commitment to mission and conversion. The effectiveness of the Christian appeal to conversion was indebted to the formulation of an intellectual foundation of belief, but it also owed its success to the conviction won by martyrdom. Justin Martyr (d. 163/5), in the opening sections of his first apology, evokes the memory of Socrates and embarks upon an argument "required" by reason that proves the case for Christianity as the storehouse of divine providence. The success of his reasoning may be disputed, but the proof of religious conviction gained by martyrdom, which he discusses in the twelfth chapter of his second apology, invokes a form of assertion beyond the realm of dispute: "I myself, too," he says, "when I was delighting in the doctrines of Plato, and heard the Christians slandered, and saw them fearless of death, and of all other things which are counted fearful, perceived that it was impossible that they could be living in wickedness and pleasure." Like many others before and after him, Justin, through his death as through his writings, was to bear proof of the claims made by his newly adopted faith.

In the sixth century of the common era, the prophet Muḥammad's recitation of God's word radicalized monotheism in ways unfamiliar to Jewish and Christian monotheists. The Qurʾān, like the New Testament before it, reflects the emergent competitive relation into which the family members of biblical religion were to come: "The Jews say, 'The Christians stand not on anything'; the Christians say, 'The Jews stand not on anything'; yet they recite the Book. So too the ignorant [i.e., the Gentiles] say the like of them" (2:107).

As had postbiblical Christian faith five centuries earlier, post-Qurʾanic Islamic faith eventually also underwent a period of formulation and defense of beliefs under the powerful influence of Hellenistic philosophy, which, along with the rich legacy of Indian medicine and mathematics and of Persian literature, provided new dimensions of thought to an expanding Arab world. In the second century of Islam, theological doctrines began to emerge alongside the current traditions of the Prophet. Confronted from within with degradations of the faith and from without by non-Muslim critics armed with the tools of reasoning developed in Greek and Persian philosophy, some Muslim scholars embraced a speculative theology (*ʿilm al-kalām*) for assistance in proclaiming the Prophet's revelation. Adherents to this practice of speculative theology were originally called *mutakallimūn*, and although their school was condemned in 848 CE by the caliph al-Mutawakkil, the philosophical traditions introduced into the expression of Islamic faith by thinkers such as Abū al-Hudhayl al-ʿAllāf (d. 849) and al-Naẓẓām (d. 846) left an ongoing mark that survived in the moderate Ashʿarī school of subsequent decades.

Originally endorsed by the court, the Muʿtazilah defended Islamic beliefs by demonstrating that there was nothing in Qurʾanic faith that contradicted reason. In addition to making claims for the unity of God, the prophethood of Muḥammad, and the validity of the Qurʾān, apologists for Islam began to formulate a cosmology that elaborated an Islamic picture of the universe. The earliest speculative Islamic theology of the Muʿtazilah, however, while it was basically Qurʾanic and sought to defend the Prophet's revelation, inclined in such a degree toward intellectualism and the presumption that truth could be demonstrated by reason that even its moderate mutations continued to give offense to the orthodox. What began as an effort to preserve the philosophical wisdom of the past, a prodigious effort that eventuated in an extensive program of translation into Arabic of the works of Aristotle and other Greek philosophers, placed Greek thought so determinatively at the center of Islamic thought that the Islamic philosophical tradition was rejected by Islamic theology.

The conflict between reason and revelation, witnessed early in the foundation of Islamic beliefs, has its counterparts throughout the histories of biblical religions. This conflict reflects a characteristic element of apologetics derived from its employment of reason as a tool of religious expression, namely the potential of apologists to give offense to the community of believers for whom they speak, or mean to. Because apologetics customarily turns outward and borrows its modes of expression from a prevailing culture, it opens itself to criticism from within. Philo Judaeus and Josephus (d. around 100 CE) were viewed with suspicion by other Jews of their day and later centuries, as were Moses Maimonides (d. 1204), Barukh Spinoza (d. 1677), and Moses Mendelssohn (d. 1786). The Latin church father Tertullian, even as he benefited from his knowledge of ancient philosophy, was to become famous for his view that the church has as much to do with the philosophical academy as a Christian with a heretic. Familiarity with philosophy has been viewed by many of the orthodox as a pollution of biblical faith and has weighed heavily against many thinkers in the church's struggle to define its parameters of acceptable belief. Modern advocates of Christianity's reasonableness such as Vladimir Solov'ev (d. 1900), Maurice Blondel (d. 1949), and Paul Tillich (d. 1965), who chose to employ patterns of philosophical discourse appropriate to their intelligence of God's word, suffered the mistrust of their coreligionists, as have modern Jewish thinkers such as Franz Rosenzweig (d. 1929) and Martin Buber (d. 1965).

Apologetics rankles, despite its dedication to God's revelation, because it occupies a place on the boundaries of belief. It employs forms of expression that depend in part upon intellectual and cultural transformations occurring outside the confines of particular traditions of belief, and it uses language that is not wholly natural to the sacred language it interprets. The culture, however, is not merely a challenge but also a promise to the apologetic motive of religious thinkers, because it presents the possibility of a new form of a normative content, a renewed account of God's being and will.

Fundamental Theology. The view of religious apologetics given above—namely, that it emerged historically as a defense of monotheism—bespeaks the empirical circumstances of one age and (more or less) one culture: the Hellenistic. In the longer religious histories of the Middle East, North Africa, Europe, and elsewhere the confrontation of monotheism with nonmonotheistic systems of belief was eclipsed by confrontations between various interpretations of monotheism, both in the struggle for orthodoxy within each of the dominant monotheisms and in the broader encounter of these monotheistic faiths with one another. Under these competitive circumstances, the effort to clarify the fundamentals of belief no longer referred to the basic propositions of monotheism alone but also to the elements of each particular tradition. This gave rise to a distinction in function between apologetics and polemics, which, although it exists in theory, does not always occur in practice.

The Protestant theologian Friedrich Schleiermacher (d. 1834) in his analysis of the discipline of theology, *Brief Outline on the Study of Theology*, distinguishes between the apologetic and the polemical sides of philosophical theology. Although they are closely related, he finds that apologetics aims to make truth recognizable; polemics, on the other hand, aims to expose deviations from truth (secs. 39 and 40). Determination of where the exposure of error ends, however, and where the proclamation of truth begins (and vice versa) depends upon the breadth of one's religious understanding. Is it apologetic or polemical for Christian scripture to proclaim Jesus of Nazareth the Messiah of Jewish expectation? Is it apologetic or polemical for Muḥammad, reflecting Christian controversies about the doctrine of the Trinity, to implicate polytheism in that Christian doctrine about God by declaring, "In the Name of God, the Merciful, the Compassionate / Say: 'He is God, One, / God, the Everlasting Refuge, / who has not begotten, and has not been begotten, / and equal to Him is not any one'" (*sūrah* 112)? Is it revelation or offense for Paul of Tarsus, as apostle of Christ, to proclaim to the people of Athens that his God is the God they worship at their altar dedicated "To the Unknown God" (*Acts* 17:23)? Truth informs each of these claims, and in each claim a defense of truth is made; but in the act of defending belief an offensive position is taken that is polemical as well as apologetic, because it exposes purported deviation from the truth at the same time as it recognizes truth. The outward-looking proclamation and the inward-looking critique are bound together.

Religious apologetics can be defined usefully in modern terms as the laying out of the fundamentals of religious belief. It is an orienting rather than refining branch of religious expression. The language it employs, though aptly described as "reasoning," will differ according to context. Patterns of reasoned discourse are themselves the subject of much philosophical debate, and, therefore, it is not possible to say with assurance what forms apologetics as a religious phenomenon will take.

In the intellectual history of the West, the dominance of Christian religion made the fundamentals of Christian belief as self-evident as those of polytheism and the state cult had been in the ancient Roman world. Roman Catholic apologetic writings against Muslims in the Middle Ages (e.g., Thomas Aquinas's *Summa contra gentiles*) and against non-Catholic Christians during and after the Protestant Reformation concentrated on particulars of Christian belief. After the European Enlightenment, however, a shift occurred with respect to the issues at stake in founding religious belief. No longer a matter of belief in many gods rather than one, or of one monotheism as distinct from another, the very reasonableness of belief itself was called into question in the intellectual discourse of Western culture, and countless defenses of Christianity were penned that argued for the very validity of religion and the reality of the supernatural.

By striving to make religion comprehensible in the intellectual and cultural environment it inhabits, apologetics, according to J.-B. Metz, recognizes that part of its essence is "to share the questioning and problems of the world in which it lives." But what constitutes "the world" for Jews, Christians, and Muslims, however unified advancing technologies of communication may make it seem, differs radically depending upon historical contingencies. For many Christians, for example, the virtues and validities of Judaism and Islam remain quite alien. The situation described by Syed Ameer Ali (d. 1928), the Indian modernist, in the preface to his *The Spirit of Islam* (1890) is not at all inappropriate a century later, nor is Ali's message at all unlike that of Josephus in addressing the Romans about Jewish religion: Islam's "great work in the uplifting of humanity," says Ali, "is either ignored or not appreciated; nor are its rationale, its ideals and its aspirations properly understood."

It would be unnecessarily limiting to presume that the preeminent form of apologetics, the treatise, remains the only medium for enhancing the comprehensibility of religious belief and for laying out its fundamentals. The censors of post-Reformation Europe were not unaware of the power of visual images in the competition between Catholicism and Protestantism. What the introduction of electronic media into parts of the world largely untouched by literacy will mean to efforts to give reasonable foundations to religious belief can only be surmised and not explored at all in this context. It can be said, however, that the sensitivities with which apologists for religion respond to their world will determine the vitality of their expressions of belief.

Philo sought the compatibility of biblical religion with ancient wisdom; al-Naẓẓām strove to preserve his faith from misconception through reliance on reason; Maimonides aimed to guide the perplexed with the help of Aristotle; Tillich diagnosed the human predicament in search of God's cure; for a significant number of theologians, the responsibility of the rich for the poor has become not merely a topic of contemporary theology but its point of departure, its foundation. As the concerns that provoke fundamental expressions of belief change, so too do religious responses to them. Leitmotifs of "too Greek," "too philosophical," "too intellectual," "too psychological," "too Marxist"—and their many variations, both theological and ideological—will remain part of the chorus of religious apologetics as long as apologetics remains a lively element of religious ideas.

SEE ALSO Agnostos Theos; Dialogue of Religions; Enlightenment, The; Falsafah; Heresy; Kalām; Martyrdom; Philosophy; Polemics; World's Parliament of Religions.

BIBLIOGRAPHY

A broad comparative history of religious apologetics does not exist, but useful introductory surveys of the apologetics of particular traditions can be found in specialized encyclopedias. For Jewish apologetics, see "Apologetics," in the *Encyclopaedia Judaica,* vol. 3 (Jerusalem, 1971). Josephus's *Against Apion* is available in Greek and in English translation by Henry St. John Thackeray in *Josephus,* vol. 1, "Loeb Classical Library" (Cambridge, Mass., 1956). For Christian apologetics, see "Apologetik," *Theologische Realenzyklopädie* (Berlin, 1978), an extensive three-part survey from the early church to the twentieth century, with excellent bibliographies. Johannes-Baptist Metz's "Apologetics," in *Sacramentum Mundi: An Encyclopedia of Theology,* vol. 1 (London, 1968), provides a good analysis of the role of apologetics in Roman Catholicism. The texts of Justin Martyr's apologies have been translated by A. Cleveland Coxe in *The Ante-Nicene Fathers,* vol. 1 (Washington, D.C., 1948). Friedrich Schleiermacher's *Brief Outline on the Study of Theology* has been translated by Terrence N. Tice (Richmond, Va., 1970). For Islamic apologetics, see H. S. Nyberg's "al-Mu'tazila," in the *Shorter Encyclopaedia of Islam* (Leiden, 1974), and Marshall G. S. Hodgson's *The Venture of Islam: Conscience and History in a World Civilization,* vol. 1, *The Classical Age of Islam* (Chicago, 1974), especially pages 437–442. Syed Ameer Ali's *The Spirit of Islam: A History of the Evolution and Ideals of Islam with a Life of the Prophet* (1890; London, 1974) is an excellent example of an apologetic spirit at work. Robert M. Grant examines Greco-Roman religious thought relative to monotheism in *Gods and the One God* (Philadelphia, 1986).

New Sources

Bloom, John. "Is Fulfilled Prophecy of Value for Scholarly Apologetics?" *Theological Research Exchange Network (TREN)*: Conference Papers, 1997, 1–15.

Clausen, Matthias. "Proclamation and Communication: Apologetics after Barth." *International Journal of Systematic Theology* 1 (July 1999): 204–221.

Edwards, Mark, Martin Goodman, and Simon Price, eds. *Apologetics in the Roman Empire: Pagans, Jews and Christians.* New York, 1999.

Gruen, Erich. *Heritage and Hellenism: The Resurrection of Jewish Tradition.* Berkeley, 1998.

McDermott, Gerald. *Jonathan Edwards Confronts the Gods: Christian Theology, Enlightenment Religion, and Non-Christian Faith.* New York, 2000.

Nichols, Stephen. "Contemporary Apologetics and the Nature of Truth." *Theological Research Exchange Network (TREN)*: Conference Papers, 1999, 1–8.

Shank, Michael. *"Unless You Believe, You Shall Not Understand": Logic, University and Society in Late Medieval Vienna.* Princeton, 1999.

Van Inwagen, Peter. *The Possibility of Resurrection and Other Essays in Christian Apologetics.* Boulder, Colo., 1997.

PAUL BERNABEO (1987)
Revised Bibliography

APOPHATISM SEE LANGUAGE, *ARTICLE ON* BUDDHIST VIEWS OF LANGUAGE; THEOLOGY, *ARTICLE ON* CHRISTIAN THEOLOGY; VIA NEGATIVA

APOSTASY is derived from the Greek *apostasia,* a secondary form of *apostasis,* originally denoting insurrection or secession (*Acts* 5:37). In the sense of "rebellion against God" it had already been used in the Septuagint (*Jos.* 22:22). The Christians of the third century definitely fixed its usage to the meaning of abandonment of Christianity for another religion, especially paganism (Cyprian, *Epistula* 57.3.1). The Christian usage of the term provides its essential elements: apostasy occurs in public and not in private, and apostates abandon an exclusive and institutionalized religion for another. In this sense apostasy is subject to specific historical conditions. It occurs when different religions compete with each other in one public arena. This essay will distinguish three aspects: occurrences of apostasy; legal sanctions with regard to apostates; and expectations of an apocalyptic desertion of the true religion at the end time.

APOSTASY IN JEWISH RITUAL LAW. Clear instances of apostasy are first found in Hellenistic Judaea. The very notion of *hellenismos* was coined for the conflict that occurred in the Jewish community under Antiochus IV Epiphanes of Syria (r. 176–165 BCE). It began when the Jewish high priest Jason "abolished the constitution based on laws and introduced new customs contrary to these laws" (*2 Mc.* 4:11). He founded a gymnasium and an institution for training *ephēboi,* or young men. Everyone who passed could then be enrolled in the register of citizens of Antiochea, the new name for Jerusalem (*2 Mc.* 4:9). A "passion for Hellenism" and "an influx of foreign customs" swept over the country (*2 Mc.* 4:13). The Maccabean adversaries of the *hellenismos* fought in their turn for the *iudaismos (2 Mc.* 2:21). The struggle between these two adversaries intensified in 167 BCE, when the next Jewish high priest, Menelaus, succeeded in convincing the Seleucid ruler "to compel the Jews to abandon their fathers' religion" (Josephus Flavius, *Jewish Antiquities* 12.384), and the ruler ordered the abandonment of the Jewish law (*1 Mc.* 1:44–53, *2 Mc.* 6:1ff.). At first, abandonment of the Jewish law occurred without any oppression by the rulers, and spontaneous apostasy recurred sporadically in later times. Well known is the case of the nephew of the Jewish philosopher Philo, Tiberius Alexander, a politician serving in the Roman state, "who did not stand by the practices of his people" (Josephus, *Antiquities* 20.100). There are also some instances of Alexandrian Jews adopting Greek philosophy. For the sake of political alliances with pagans, Jews were willing to abandon circumcision, food rules, and Sabbath laws. Intermarriage with pagans and shifting intellectual interests were among the reasons for their deviation from ancestral practices (Feldman, 1993, pp. 79–83).

The *Book of Daniel,* written between 167 and 163 BCE, made Jewish apostasy part of the apocalyptic drama. At the end of time, it stated, there will be Jews abandoning the holy covenant (*Dn.* 11:30). The pre-Maccabean *Apocalypse of Weeks* clung to the same idea: "After that in the seventh week an apostate generation shall arise, its deeds shall be many and all of them criminal" (*1 En.* 93:9). Apostasy is assessed not only in religious terms but also in moral and political ones. Abandonment of belief is near to treason and crime. Similarly, treason is rejected for religious reasons. When the historian Josephus Flavius, as commander of Galilean insurgents, was suspected of treason in 66 CE, his chief adversary told the people: "If you cannot, for your own sakes, citizens, detest Josephus, fix your eyes on the ancestral laws *(patrioi nomoi),* which your commander-in-chief intended to betray, and for their sakes hate the crime and punish the audacious criminal" (Josephus, *The Life* 135). The Jewish notion of the martyr reflects the same set of beliefs from a different perspective: due to his loyalty to the ancestral laws, the martyr is assured of resurrection to life (*2 Mc.* 7:14). His death is at the same time "an example of high-mindedness and a memory of virtue" (*2 Mc.* 6:31). If religion and citizenship are fused, the apostate who abandons the religion of his ancestors is regarded as a traitor. He is virtually the domestic ally of the external enemy.

Apostasy needed to be legally regulated. Since the first century BCE Jewish communities outside Israel were established as recognized associations either under Roman law or under the law of independent cities. Their communities were recognized as "collegia"—the Latin notion for these associations—or as "politeuma" and practiced internal jurisdiction. Jews who were responsible for civic unrest could be tried and punished by the officials of these bodies. The conflicts between Jews and Christians therefore affected legal issues. Paul was portrayed by Jewish opponents as teaching apostasy from Moses (*Acts* 21:21). When Paul complained: "Five times I have received from the Jews the forty lashes minus one" (*2 Cor.* 11: 24), he refers to a punishment, inflicted by Jewish authorities according to their ancestral laws (*Dt.* 25:2). What Paul experienced as a persecution was from a different point of view, as E. P. Sanders rightly noticed, as a legal prosecution (Sanders, 1986, p. 86).

Apostasy was subject of religious reflection. "Whole Israel has a share in the world to come. . . . And these don't have a share in the world to come: whoever says, 'There is no resurrection of the dead in the Torah' and 'There is no Torah from heaven,' and the Epicurean" (*San.* 10:1). The apostate is denied salvation by the Pharisees. About 100 CE the twelfth prayer of the so-called eighteen benedictions was expanded with the *birkat haminim* ("the blessing over the heretics"). The oldest wording of that prayer is found in a version discovered in the Cario Geniza: "And for apostates let there be no hope; and may the insolent kingdom be quickly uprooted, in our days. And may Nazarenes [Christians] and the Minim [heretics] perish quickly; and may they be erased from the Book of life" (Schürer, 1979, pp.454–463). This amplification implies that apostates had earlier been cursed in Jewish divine service. Since the Babylonian recension of the prayer does not mention either the Nazarenes or the Minim, it is a matter of controversy whether the early form of the prayer actually refered to Christians at all. Later Christian literature corroborates that after the fall of the temple Jews cursed Christians in the synagogues. Justin, in his *Dialogue with Trypho,* relates that Jews were cursing in their synagogues those that believe in Christ (16, 4). But only after the third century CE did the rabbis possess the legal power to expel dissidents from Judaism; previously this power rested with the local Jewish communities.

The *Gospel of John,* which originated in Asia Minor, mentions several times the expulsion of Christians from synagogues (9:22, 12:42, 16:2–3). The Jewish communities of Asia Minor and other parts of the Roman Empire had been granted the privilege to form associations *(sunodos)* of their own in accordance with their ancestral laws and to decide on their own affairs and settle controversies. In the *Gospel of John,* the term *sunagogē* refers also to the community as a whole and not to a building. A Jewish community could withdraw the membership from Christian apostates in its *politeuma.*

Apostasy in Greek and Roman Public Cults. Conversion was unknown in Greek and Roman religions because exclusivity was alien to them. There were, however, limits of tolerance. These limits were reached when public citizens abandoned their ancestral religion or refused to participate in the common civic cults. Even as early as the time of Livy (59 BCE–17 CE), he could report with indignation that in the crisis of the Second Punic War (218–210) "not only in secret and within the walls of private houses Roman rites were abandoned, but in public places also, and in the Forum and on the Capitoline, there was a crowd of women who were following the custom of the fathers neither in their sacrifices nor in prayers of the gods" (Livy, *History of Rome,* 25.1.7). With the Christian mission, abandonment of the *mos maiorum* (the ancestral custom) became much more frequent. In his First Letter to the Corinthians, Paul advised the Gentile Christians not to participate in pagan temple meals (*1 Cor.* 8:10–12, 10:19ff.). The Christian apologists sustained this rejection of pagan cults.

The pagan reproaches addressed to Christians diverged from East to West. In the Greek East, the Christians were accused of godlessness *(atheotes).* The accusation is attested for the first time by Justin Martyr in *1 Apology* 6.1 (written between 150–155 CE) and in the *Martyrdom of Polycarp* 3 (shortly after 156 CE). In the Latin West, the Christians were accused of "abandoning the religion of their ancestors" *(christiani qui parentum suorum reliquerant sectam).* In his edict of tolerance (311 CE), Galerius gave this abandonment as reason for the persecution. Christians should be forced to acknowledge the ancestral religion, he argued (Lactantius, *De mortibus persecutorum* 34). The reproach of having left the *mos Romanorum* ("way of the Romans") had already been uttered earlier in the acts of Scillitan martyrs.

In general, the pagan cults did not expel members who adhered to rival cults or philosophical circles. But often the gods of pagan cults were officially recognized by the civic authorities and ranked, in Rome, for example, with the *di publici populi Romani* (the public gods of the Roman nation). Every citizen had the duty to respect these civic gods. The Christians refusing to do so were not only suspected of *superstitio,* but also of political disloyalty. The first important critic of ancient Christianity, the Middle Platonic philosopher Celsus, accused the Christians of insurrection *(stasis)* against the community (Origen, *Against Celsus* 3.5). One hundred years later, about 270 CE, Porphyry renewed this criticism. The Christians are atheists, he wrote, "because they abandoned the ancestral gods, on which the existence of every nation and every city is based" (transmitted by Eusebius in his *Praeparatio evangelica* 1.2.2). Other pagan critics called for action. In the writings of Dio Cassius, Maecenas says to Augustus: "Venerate the Divine everywhere and totally according to the ancestral customs and compel the others to do the same" (*Roman History,* 52.36). The general persecutions of Christians since Decius (r. 249–251 CE) met the demands of such a program. The same holds true for the edict of Diocletian against the Manichaeans (297 CE). It states: "It is the most serious crime to reject what once for all has been arranged and established by the ancestors" (*Mosaicarum et Romanorum legum collatio* 15.3.2f.). In sum, apostasy only became a problem for pagan society when its ancestral customs were rejected. The limits of tolerance were mainly political ones.

Apostasy in the Christian Church. Christianity found its adherents among Jews and pagans. But these new Christians did not always resolutely abandon their old religious loyalties. Until the time of the Bar Kokhba revolt (132–135 CE) there were Christians who followed Jewish ritual law painstakingly (e.g., *Gal.* 2:11–14). Other Christians continued to participate in pagan temple meals (e.g., *1 Cor.* 8:10). Paul, in his First Letter to the Corinthians, addressed their risk of falling away (*1 Cor.* 10:20–21), but did not regard this practice as apostasy per se (Oropeza, 2002, p. 223). Only when the church had separated itself from Jewish-Christians and Gnostics did this evaluation change. Apostasy then became a clear-cut issue. The Neoplatonic philosopher Ammonius Saccas is said to have been a Christian who apostatized (Eusebius, *Church History* 6.19.9f.). The most noted apostate to paganism was the emperor Julian the Apostate (361–363 CE). Committed to Neoplatonism, he thwarted the church's aims by every means in his power, short of actual persecution, and resumed the reproach directed against Christians for despising ancestral beliefs. Furthermore, he sustained pagan temples and attempted to reform them.

The notion of an apocalyptic desertion migrated from Jewish beliefs into the writings of the early Christian authors. In his Second Letter to the Thessalonians, Paul maintains that the coming of the Lord cannot take place "if not at first comes the apostasy and reveals himself the man of lawlessness the son of perdition" (*2 Thes.* 2:3). The synoptic apocalypse in the *Gospel of Mark* expects that at the end of time many will be lead astray and betray each other (*Mk.* 13:5–12). But the early Christian conception of an apocalyptic apostasy differed from the above-mentioned Jewish one. Early Christians were less anxious about apostasy to foreign religions than the Jews of the Maccabean era had been. They were far more anxious about teachers of a false doctrine. The First Letter to Timothy explicitly states that the apostasy at the end of time is due to Gnostic heretics. And the First Letter of John points out that the last hour has come because false prophets and teachers have arisen from the community, fulfilling the prophecy of the coming of the antichrist. Interesting parallels can be detected in some Jewish literature which appeared contemporaneously with these Christian texts. Passages originating from Qumran speak about the teacher of lies who has not obeyed the teacher of justice. At the ascension of Isaiah, one passage asserts, all men in this world will believe in Belial, the antichrist.

From the third century on, the term *apostasy* referred exclusively to apostasy to paganism. Cyprian used the term to describe Christians who had returned to paganism in the time of the persecution by Decius, a move Cyprian equated with heresy (*Epistula* 57.3). In the ancient church the corresponding notion to apostasy became perseverance. Genuine faith was endangered by three kinds of threat: sedition and vices; heresy; and persecution. Originally, however, apostasy had been conceived as an internal fission of the community due to false prophets and teachers. Here the Jewish and Christian views of apostasy diverge. The apostate abandoning Christian belief is not an ally of the external enemy, but the follower of an internal adversary. For this reason, the law of the early church in regard to apostasy was severe. Apostasy was an inexpiable offense. After baptism there could be no forgiveness of this sin.

Only long after the persecution of Decius was readmission of the *lapsi* ("the fallen") allowed (Cyprian, *Epistula* 57). After the conversion of Constantine (d. 337), apostasy became a civil offense punishable by law. Edicts in the Theodosian Code, composed in 438 CE, testify to this severity. "Those Christians who have become pagans shall be deprived of the power and right to make testaments and every testament of such decedent . . . shall be rescinded by the annulment of its foundation" (381 CE CTh 16, 7,1). It is important to note that an edict of 383 CE explicitly mentions Manichaeism in the same context as pagan temples and Jewish rites. Christians simply carried on the persecution of Manichaeans started by Diocletian in 297 CE. The Manichaean teachers were to be punished, the attendants of their assemblies to become infamous, and their houses and habitations in which the doctrine was taught to be expropriated by the fiscal agents of the government. Two edicts promulgated in 391 CE directed that all persons having betrayed the holy faith shall be segregated from the community of all men, shall not have testamentary capacity, shall not inherit, shall forfeit their position and status, and shall be branded with perpetual infamy (CTh 16,7,4). The Code of Justinian (534 CE) treated the apostate as a criminal (CJ 1, 7). Due to the fact that the code became a major source for later canonical law and the Western legal tradition, the law remained effective until citizenship and religious affiliation were separated by the constitutions of modern states.

Under modern political conditions the phenomenon of apostasy did not vanish, but changed profoundly. In the latter half of the twentieth century, religious communities arose in the United States that challenged the value of family relations and private property and replaced them by a utopian communal order. In some cases, external opposition to such groups was vehement. Concerned relatives mobilized media, politicians, and law-enforcement officials against the evil of these "cults." Apostates of the disputed communities joined with opponents to become principal witnesses for the allegation that only by mental coercion ("brainwashing") had they joined such groups. These apostates fulfilled a crucial role in the violence that exploded in the cases of Peoples Temple in Jonestown, Guyana, in 1978 and of the Branch Davidians, a sect of the Seventh-day Adventists, in the Texas town of Waco in 1993 (Bromley, 1998, pp. 9–10).

APOSTASY IN THE ISLAMIC COMMUNITY. The Arabic word *murtadd* denotes the apostate, and the terms *irtidad* or *riddah* denote apostasy. Qurʾanic texts referring to apostasy threaten the apostate with punishment in the other world. The "wrath of God" will fall upon him, "except he has been forced, while his heart has been found in the belief" (*sūrah* 16:106). A similar idea is put forward by *sūrah* 3:82–89: those who apostatize are the true evildoers. Their reward will be the curse of God, angels, and men. They will be condemned to hell "except those who afterward return and mend their ways. God is compassionate and ready to forgive" (*sūrah* 3:89). These early Islamic texts are less severe than the canonical and Imperial laws and the later Islamic ones.

There are also in Islam some scarce references to an apocalyptic apostasy. Occasionally the apocalyptic scenarios concerning the rise of the *mahdī*, or Islamic Messiah, provide for an antichrist called *al-dajjāl.* This word, not found in the Qurʾān, is borrowed from the Aramaic language. The Syriac version uses *daggala* to translate the *pseudochristoi* of *Matthew* 24:24. Al-dajjal, who will rule for a limited period, shall lead the crowds astray.

Later Islamic jurisprudence elaborated on the meaning of apostasy. As Yohanan Friedmann shows, it covered not just a retraction of the confession of faith, but also vilifying the Prophet, impugning the honor of his mother, denying the Qurʾān or parts of it, rejecting manifest commandments as the five pillars, and making licit well-known prohibitions (2003, pp. 121–159). If these transgressions are due to a person's ignorance, the person should be apprised. If the person persists, he or she becomes an unbeliever. Their legal status is different from those who had never joined Islam. The apostate lacks "religion" and is not entitled to participate in such religious actions as marriage or slaughtering for food. While in the Qurʾān apostasy was punished in the hereafter, later the sanction was transferred into this world. Mālik ibn Anas (d. 796), founder of the Mālikī school, transmitted the following as a sentence of the Prophet: "Whoever changes his religion, kill him." But there was dissent among the *ʿulamāʾ* over the particulars: was it applicable to women as well as men, and to Muslim by conversion as well as by birth? There was further debate regarding whether in each case an effort should be made to bring the apostate to repentance before execution. Mālik ibn Anas held the view that such efforts should be restricted only to those who bluntly abandoned Islam. Those who turned tacitly to *zindiqs* ("heretics") should be killed immediately. Efforts to bring them to repentance are useless, for the sincerity of their repentance cannot be recognized because they have been infidels in secret before, while they confessed in public to be followers of Islam. The reference to *zindiqs* is instructive. The Middle Persian term *zandik,* from which the Arabic *zindiq* is derived, derives in turn from *Zand* (the commentary of the Avesta text) and refers to Manichaean and Mazdean heresy. As early as the reign of Bahram II (276–293 CE), the chief of the Zoroastrian clergy, Kardēr, had ordered followers to persecute Christians and *zindiqs*. In the same way as Christians adhered to the laws taken by pagan emperors against the Manichaeans, so the Islamic conquerors carried on the pre-Islamic persecutions of the *zindiqs*. The prototype of the apostate was the heretic. The numerous persecutions of members of the Bahāʾī religion in Iran since 1852 testify to the severity of this Islamic law. The apostates must be killed, their property confiscated, and their marriages annulled.

Islamic apostasy did not vanish in contemporary times. Since apostasy was defined so broadly, it covered many forms of blasphemy. A Muslim could even become an apostate unintentionally, as was the case with author Salman Rushdie. In his 1988 English-language novel *The Satanic Verses,* he used vulgar terminology in passages about Muḥammad and his wives. The title of his novel was actually a reference to a tradition which held that some verses of the Qurʾān may have been inspired by Satan (*sūrah* 22:52; 53, 19–22). This reference seemed to cast doubt on the belief that the entire Qurʾān was the verbal utterance of God. Though Rushdie's novel was written for a post-Christian Western audience, it stirred tremendous wrath among Muslims worldwide. South Africa, India, and Pakistan banned the book's sale in their countries due to their substantial Muslim populations, but in Great Britain it was sold freely. Though British Muslims demanded: "Freedom of speech, yes! Freedom to insult no!," the British authorities declined to apply a blasphemy statute against the book. The most dire consequence came in early 1989, when Iran's leader, the Ayatollah Khomeini, issued a *fatwa* against Rushdie. Khomeini declared to the world's Muslim population that *The Satanic Verses* was against Islam, the Prophet, and the Qur'ān, and sentenced Rushdie to death. The *fatwa* also included any publishers of editions of the book who were aware of its content. Khomeini called upon zealous Muslims to execute them quickly (Ruthven, 1990, p. 112). Though Khomeini went with this ruling far beyond the competence of an Islamic cleric, it took years before the *fatwa* was retracted in 2001 by Iran's president. Another well-known case concerns the Egyptian scholar Nasr Hamid Abū Zayd. Since Abū Zayd reportedly refuted the Qur'ān as the word of God, he was declared an apostate and forcibly divorced from his wife (Dupret, 2003, pp. 137–138).

SEE ALSO Expulsion; Heresy, overview article.

BIBLIOGRAPHY

Bromley, David G., ed. *The Politics of Religious Apostasy. The Role of Apostates in the Transformation of Religious Movements.* Westport, Conn., 1998.

Cassius, Dio. *Roman History.* 9 vols. With an English translation by Earnest Cary on the basis of the version of Herbert Baldwin Foster. Cambridge, Mass., 2000.

Codex Iustinianus. Edited by Paul Krüger. Corpus Iuris Civilis. Band 2. Berlin, 1929.

Codex Theodosianus: Theodosiani libri XVI cum Constitutionibus Sirmondianis et Leges novellae ad Theodosianum pertinentes. Edited by Theodor Mommsen and Paulus M. Meyer. Berlin, 1904.

Codex Theodosianus. Translated by Clyde Pharr. Princeton, N.J., 1952.

Collatio legum Romanorum et Mosaicorum. Edited with translation and notes by Moses Hyamson. Oxford, 1913.

Cyprianus. *Correspondence.* 2 vols. Edited by L. Bayard. Paris 1961–1962.

Dupret, Baudouin. "A Return to the Shariah? Egyptian Judges and Referring to Islam." In *Modernizing Islam: Religion in the Public Sphere in the Middle East and Europe,* edited by John L. Esposito and François Burgat, pp. 125–143. London, 2003.

Eusebius. *Praeparatio evangelica.* Edited by K. Mras. 1954–1956.

Feldman, Louis H. *Jew and Gentile in the Ancient World. Attitudes and Interactions from Alexander to Justinian.* Princeton, N.J., 1993.

Forkman, Göran. *The Limits of the Religious Community: Expulsion from the Religious Community within the Qumran Sect, within Rabbinic Judaism, and within Primitive Christianity.* Lund, Sweden, 1972. An investigation into the attitude of three Jewish groups toward expulsion.

Frend, W. H. C. *Martyrdom and Persecution in the Early Church: A Study of a Conflict from the Maccabees to Donatus.* Oxford, 1965. A comprehensive historical investigation into the notion of martyrdom and the reaction of ancient political society to Jewish and Christian exclusiveness.

Friedmann, Yohanan. *Tolerance and Coercion in Islam. Interfaith Relations in the Muslim Tradition.* Cambridge, U.K., 2003.

Josephus, Flavius. *The Life.* Edited and translated by H.St. J. Thackeray. Cambridge, Mass., 1926.

Josephus, Flavius. *Jewish Antiquities.* Edited and translated by H.St. J. Thackeray and Ralph Marcus. Cambridge, Mass., 1930–1963.

Lanctatius. *On the Manner in Which Persecutors Died* (de mortibus persecutorum), vol 7: *Ante-Nicene Fathers.* 1994, pp. 301–322.

Livy. *History of Rome* (Ab urbe condita). 14 vols. Cambridge, Mass., 1919–1959.

Maier, Johann. *Jüdische Auseinandersetzung mit dem Christentum in der Antike.* Darmstadt, Germany, 1982. A collection and interpretation of Jewish texts testifying to the frictions between Jews and Christians in ancient history.

Menasce, Jean-Pierre de. "Problèmes des Mazdéens dans l'Iran musulman." In *Festschrift für Wilhelm Eilers,* edited by Gernot Wiessner, pp. 220–230. Wiesbaden, Germany, 1967. A study into relevant Zoroastrian material concerning the apostasy to Islam.

Nock, Arthur Darby. *Conversion: The Old and New in Religion from Alexander the Great to Augustine of Hippo.* Oxford, 1933. A famous study tracing the rise of the idea of conversion and exclusiveness in Greek and Roman thought.

Oropeza, Brisio Javier. *Paul and Apostasy: Eschatology, Perseverance, and Falling Away in the Corinthian Congregation.* Tübingen, Germany, 2002.

Ruthven, Malise. *A Satanic Affair: Salman Rushdie and the Wrath of Islam.* London, 1990.

Sanders, E. P. "Paul on the Law, His Opponents, and the Jewish People in Philippians 3 and 2 Corinthians 11." In *Anti-Judaism in Early Christianity,* edited by Peter Richardson, vol. 1: *Paul and the Gospels.* Waterloo, Ont., 1986, pp. 75–90.

Schürer, Emil. *The History of the Jewish People in the Age of Jesus Christ (175 B.C.-A.D. 135),* vol. 2. Revised and edited by Geza Vermes, Fergus Millar, and Matthew Black. Edinburgh, 1979.

Vajda, Georges. "Die zindiqs im Gebiet des Islam zu Beginn der Abbasidenzeit" (1938). In *Der Manichäismus,* edited by Geo Widengren, pp. 418–463. Darmstadt, Germany, 1977. A valuable collection of sources on groups regarded as heretical by the Zoroastrian church and still existing in Islamic times.

H. G. KIPPENBERG (1987 AND 2005)

APOSTLES. The word *apostle* is known mainly from the Christian religion as a title of a religious leader, especially in early Christianity. The origin of the word, the concept for which it stands, and its specific expressions in various religious traditions are far more complex than is usually assumed. The term itself is derived from the Greek *apostolos* (Heb., *shaliaḥ;* Lat., *apostolus*) and means "messenger," "envoy," either in a secular or a religious sense (messenger of a deity).

The basic concept of the messenger is simple: "Everyone who is sent by someone is an apostle of the one who sent him" (Origen, *In Ioannem* 32.17). This can refer to the legal and administrative institution of envoys and ambassadors as well as to highly theological expressions of messengers sent by a deity into the world to bring a message of salvation. Concrete expressions of both these concepts are influenced by different cultural and religious presuppositions. Although these presuppositions exercise continuous influence even in different religious traditions, there is room for specialized developments.

"At present the question as to the origin and the idea of the apostolate is one of the most intricate and difficult problems of New Testament scholarship." This statement was first made by Erich Haupt in 1896 and was reiterated by twentieth-century scholars, in spite of numerous studies on the subject. The main causes for the problem are the limited sources, in particular from the earliest stages of the development in primitive Christianity, and the confusion caused by the several expressions of a basic concept found as early as the New Testament itself.

The New Testament sources show an advanced stage, not the beginning, of the development of the concept of apostleship. In fact, the New Testament contains several different and competing expressions of the concept that have begun to merge with one another. This state of affairs is also bound up with the definition of apostleship, which was in dispute as early as the time of Paul.

Apostles as Missionaries. A number of New Testament passages refer to apostles as traveling missionaries. Their title and function is described, for example, in *2 Corinthians* 8:23 (cf. *Phil.* 2:25) as "envoys of the churches." These envoys were elected or appointed by the people they were supposed to represent (cf. *2 Cor.* 8:6, 8:16–23). This process of appointment does not necessarily exclude divine intervention (cf. *Acts* 13:1–3). Apparently, the early Christian mission was carried out to a large extent by these missionary apostles, some of whom may have been women, although the evidence for women is uncertain. The task of these apostles included preaching the gospel and administering the newly founded churches, but no clear job description is found in the New Testament (cf. *1 Cor.* 9:5, 12:28; *2 Cor.* 11:13; *Rom.* 16:1–23; see also *Didache* 11.3–11.6).

Jesus' Disciples as Apostles. A more specialized concept of *apostle* is mentioned in *Galatians* 1:17, 1:19, and *1 Corinthians* 9:5 (cf. *1 Cor.* 15:7), where the former disciples of Jesus are called apostles. Apparently this title was given to those disciples who had experienced a vision of the risen Christ (*1 Cor.* 9:1, 15:3–8), but the situation is unclear because in the decisive passage, *1 Corinthians* 15:3–7, concepts that were originally different have been merged: *1 Corinthians* 15:5 names Cephas and the Twelve, *1 Corinthians* 15:7 names James "and all the apostles" as the recipients of the visions, while *1 Corinthians* 15:6 speaks of the "five hundred brothers" without calling them disciples of Jesus or apostles. Some New Testament writers, especially Luke, identify the disciples of Jesus (or apostles) with "the Twelve," originally a different leadership institution (*Mk.* 3:16–19, *Mt.* 10:2–4, *Lk.* 6:14–16, *Acts* 1:13, and, differently, *1 Cor.* 15:5). The names of the disciples who were counted among the Twelve differ to some extent in the tradition (cf. *Acts* 6:2; *Mk.* 14:10 and parallels, 14:43 and parallels; *Jn.* 6:71, 12:4, 20:24). When Luke, author of *Luke* and *Acts,* limits the Twelve to the disciples of the historical Jesus, he in effect denies the title of apostle to Paul (except *Acts* 14:4 and 14:14, where Paul and Barnabas, from an older source, are called apostles). Luke also refers to the twelve apostles as the leaders of the Jerusalem church (e.g., *Acts* 4:35–37, 5:2, 5:27–32), an assignment that conflicts with their role as missionaries. In *Acts* 1:21–22, Luke states what for him, and no doubt for others in early Christianity, are the criteria for apostleship: an apostle is "one of the men who have been our companions during all the time when the Lord Jesus went in and out among us, beginning with the baptism of John until the day when he was taken up from us, a witness of his resurrection together with us." However, these criteria are a later construction, designed to limit the concept to those who were eyewitnesses (*Lk.* 1:2) and thus to curtail the increasing confusion about the nature and authority of apostles.

Paul the Apostle. The origin of Paul's apostleship is still as puzzling as it was in early Christianity. If the criteria of *Acts* 1:21–22 are applied, Paul does not qualify as an apostle. In fact, Paul's claim to apostleship was disputed in much of early Christianity (*1 Cor.* 9:2, 15:9–10). At the beginning of his Christian career, Paul worked as a missionary apostle with his mentor Barnabas (*Acts* 9:27, 13:1–3, 14:4, 14:14; cf. *Gal.* 1:15–2:14). However, the title used by Paul in his letters, "called apostle of Christ Jesus" (*1 Cor.* 1:1), expresses an understanding of his own apostleship different from the understanding of Luke. Despite the evidence provided by Paul, the origin and background of this title are to some extent still a mystery. Since Paul did not qualify under the normal definition, his own title presupposes a critical reinterpretation and redefinition of the entire concept of apostleship. In his earliest letter, *1 Thessalonians,* Paul does not use the title. It appears first in the prescript of *Galatians* (1:1): "Paul, apostle not from men nor through [a] man but through Jesus Christ and God the Father who raised him from the dead" (cf. *1 Cor.* 1:1, *2 Cor.* 1:1, *Rom.* 1:1–7). This new title became the standard in the Pauline churches (*Col.* 1:1; *Eph.* 1:1; *1 Tm.* 1:1, 2:7; *2 Tm.* 1:1, 1:11; *Ti.* 1:1).

By this redefinition Paul in effect claimed to be more than an ordinary missionary apostle; he claimed the same rank and authority as the former disciples of Jesus (cf. *Gal.* 1:17; *1 Cor.* 9:1–5, 15:1–10), indeed, a higher authority. His letters testify, however, that he encountered considerable difficulties obtaining recognition that his apostolic authority was legitimate. His claim seems to have initiated bitter controversy about the question of who were the true and who were the false apostles (cf. *2 Cor.* 11:13). Paul's apostleship was accepted fully only after his death as a martyr, when Peter and Paul came to be regarded as the great founder figures of early Christian history. Jewish Christianity, however, never recognized Paul as a legitimate apostle.

Paul's claim to be the "apostle of the Gentiles" (*Rom.* 11:13; cf. *Rom.* 1:5–7, 1:13–15) implied that he had a unique position in the church. Sent out by the risen Christ, who had appeared to him and appointed him (*Gal.* 1:15–16), he served as Christ's messenger, representative, and imitator on earth in an almost exclusive sense (for the concept of *mimetes,* or "imitator," see *1 Thessalonians* 1:6, 2:14 and *1 Corinthians* 4:16, 11:1). His assignment was not only to spread the gospel and found churches; his entire physical and spiritual existence was to become an epiphany of the crucified and resurrected Christ (cf. *Gal.* 6:17; *2 Cor.* 2:14–5:21, 13:3–4; *Phil.* 3:10). Paul's apostolic office had a firm position in the history of salvation as well as in the redemption of the cosmos. At the Last Judgment, he expected to serve as the representative of his churches before the judgment seat of Christ (*2 Cor.* 11:2; cf. *1 Cor.* 1:8; *1 Thes.* 2:10, 5:23; *Phil.* 2:15; also *Col.* 1:22, *Eph.* 5:27).

Paul's concept of apostleship emerged from intensive struggle in the early church. In this struggle his own theological ideas about apostleship underwent profound changes. This process was also informed by other notions. Geo Widengren has shown that Paul's concept of apostle has its closest parallels, and most probably antecedents, in Syriac Gnosticism. In the study *Der Apostel Paulus und die sokratische Tradition,* this article's author has shown that Paul was deeply influenced by the Socratic tradition, in which Socrates figured as a messenger sent by the deity. Thus Paul's concept of apostleship is a highly complex and composite creation that reflects the struggles of his own career as well as early Christianity's conflicts about the legitimacy and authority of its leadership.

LISTS OF EARLY CHRISTIAN APOSTLES. The struggle about the apostolic authority is reflected also in the lists of the apostles, which differ to a considerable degree. *Mark* 3:16–19, *Luke* 6:14–16, and *Acts* 1:13–26 give diverse accounts. The history of the lists of apostles continues in the second century, sometimes reflecting the differing interests of Christian groups. Confusion about who was and was not an apostle is found in other parts of the New Testament as well. Was James, "the brother of the Lord" (*Gal.* 1:19), an apostle? While Barnabas is called apostle, together with Paul, in *Acts* 14:4 and 14:14, Paul never calls him by this name (cf. *Gal.* 2:1–10, 2:13; *1 Cor.* 9:6). Does he want to avoid any reference to an earlier concept of apostleship (cf. *Acts* 15:36–40, *Gal.* 2:13)? On the other hand, Paul speaks of missionary apostles when the difference between them and him is clear.

CHRIST AS APOSTLE. Christ is called an apostle only once in the New Testament: "Jesus, the apostle and high priest of our confession" (*Heb.* 3:1). This Christological concept is late, but it may have older roots. There is a peculiar situation in the Fourth Gospel, where Christ is never called apostle but functions as a messenger from God (cf., however, *John* 13:16: "Truly, truly I say to you, a slave is not greater than his master, nor is an apostle greater than the one who sent him"). Christ's entire mission is described by the technical term *apostello* ("send"). He is the Logos and Son of God who was sent by God the Father into this world (*Jn.* 1:6, 3:17, 3:34, 5:36–38, 6:29, 6:57, 10:36, 17:3, 17:8, 17:18, 17:21, 17:23, 20:21; cf. *1 Jn.* 4:9, 4:10, 4:14). He in turn sends out his own disciples (*Jn.* 4:38, 17:18), the Twelve, who are, however, not called apostles (*Jn.* 6:67, 6:70, 6:71, 20:24). It appears that the title of apostle has been avoided by the Fourth Gospel. Because the similarity between the Johannine Christology and the Pauline concept of apostle is so strong, the answer to the question of why the Fourth Gospel is not interested in the title of apostle may have something to do with the still unexplained relationship between Pauline and Johannine Christianity. The Christological concept of apostle is found later, in the second century, in Justin Martyr (*1 Apology* 12.9, 63.5) and subsequently in patristic sources.

MANI AND MUḤAMMAD AS APOSTLES. Mani, founder of the third-century movement of Manichaeism, called by his followers "apostle of Jesus Christ," "apostle of light," and "father of all apostles," was believed to be the last of a series of apostles. Mani conceived his apostleship in strongly Pauline terms, but made fuller use of an older prototype. Widengren has shown the roots of this prototype in Syriac Gnosticism. In heterodox Jewish Christianity, the still mysterious figure of Elchasai seems to represent a similar type. It appears that the Manichaeans drew their concept of the apostleship of Mani not only from Paul but also from a broader spectrum of ideas, perhaps the same spectrum that informed Paul when he formulated his concept of apostleship.

Muḥammad called himself "apostle of God" (*rasūl Allāh*). As such, he occupied a unique position between God and the faithful and considered himself the "last messenger of God." According to the Qurʾān Muḥammad is the bringer of light, illuminating the scriptures for the enlightened (5:18, 9:32–33). On the other hand, Muḥammad can call others by the same title, "apostle of God." Later this function seems to have influenced the figure of the imam.

SEE ALSO Jesus; Mani; Manichaeism; Muḥammad; Paul the Apostle.

BIBLIOGRAPHY

Agnew, Francis H. "On the Origin of the Term *Apostolos.*" *Catholic Biblical Quarterly* 38 (January 1976): 49–53.

Agnew, Francis H. "The Origin of the New Testament Apostle-Concept: A Review of Research." *Journal of Biblical Literature* 105 (1986): 75–96.

Betz, Hans Dieter. *Der Apostel Paulus und die sokratische Tradition.* Tübingen, 1972.

Betz, Hans Dieter. *Galatians.* Philadelphia, 1979.

Betz, Hans Dieter. "Gottmensch II: Griechisch-römische Antike und Urchristentum." In *Reallexikon für Antike und Christentum,* vol. 12. Stuttgart, 1982.

Bühner, Jan-Adolf. "*Apostolos,* Gesandter, Apostel." In *Exegetisches Wörterbuch zum Neuen Testament,* vol. 1. Stuttgart, 1980.

Hennecke, Edgar. *New Testament Apocrypha.* 2 vols. Edited by Wilhelm Schneemelcher. Philadelphia, 1963–1965. See especially volume 2, pp. 25–87, with important surveys of the evidence in the early church.

Klein, Günter. *Die Zwölf Apostel.* Göttingen, 1961.

Lampe, G. W. H., ed. *A Patristic Greek Lexicon.* Oxford, 1961. See pages 211–214, and the index, s.v. *apostolos.*

Lüdemann, Gerd. *Paulus, der Heidenapostel.* 2 vols. Göttingen, 1980–1983. Volume 1 deals with the chronology of Paul's life, volume 2 with the anti-Pauline opposition. Volume 1 has been translated by F. Stanley Jones as *Paul, Apostle to the Gentiles* (Philadelphia, 1984).

Rengstorf, Karl Heinrich. *"Apostello, apostolos"* (1933). In *Theological Dictionary of the New Testament.* Grand Rapids, Mich., 1964.

Roloff, Jürgen. "Apostel/Apostolat/Apostolizität, I. Neues Testament." In *Theologische Realenzyklopädie,* vol. 3. Berlin, 1978.

Schmithals, Walter. *The Office of the Apostle in the Early Church.* Nashville, 1969.

Schoeps, Hans Joachim. *Paul: The Theology of the Apostle in the Light of Jewish Religious History.* Philadelphia, 1961.

Schüssler-Fiorenza, Elisabeth. *In Memory of Her: A Feminist Theological Reconstruction of Christian Origins.* New York, 1983, pp. 160–204.

Widengren, Geo. *Muhammad, the Apostle of God, and His Ascension.* Uppsala, 1955.

Widengren, Geo. *Religionsphänomenologie.* Berlin, 1969. See the index, s.v. *Apostel, Ausgesandter.*

New Sources

Brock, Ann. *Mary Magdalene: The First Apostle; The Struggle for Authenticity.* Cambridge, Mass., 2003.

Brown, Peter Robert Lamont. *The Body and Society: Men, Women, and Sexual Renunciation in Early Christianity.* New York, 1988.

Donfried, Karl P. Paul. *Thessalonica, and Early Christianity.* Grand Rapids, Mich., 2002.

Keck, Leonard. *Paul and His Letters.* Philadelphia, 1988.

King, Karen L. *The Gospel of Mary of Magdala.* Santa Rosa, Calif., 2003.

Meeks, Wayne. *The First Urban Christians: The Social World of the Apostle Paul.* New Haven, Conn., 2003.

Robinson, James M., and Richard Smith, eds. *The Nag Hammadi Library in English.* 3d ed., San Francisco, 1988.

Wiarda, Timothy. *Peter in the Gospels.* Tübingen, 2000.

HANS DIETER BETZ (1987)
Revised Bibliography

APOTHEOSIS

APOTHEOSIS is the conferring, through official, ritual, or iconographic means, of the status of a god upon a mortal person. The Greek verb *apotheoun* appears first in the writings of the historian Polybius, which date from the second century BCE. The noun *apotheōsis* is found for the first time in Cicero, though it may have existed already in the classical Greek world. It is during the Hellenistic epoch, however, that *apotheōsis* takes on new forms that display the stamp of the Roman cult of emperors and of the dead.

ORIGINS. Even though the immortal and blessed condition of the gods differentiates them radically from human nature, the Greeks regarded as "divine" (*theios*) the person whose outstanding qualities set him or her individually apart from the commonplace. The heroization of founders of cities or of benefactors and peacemakers assured them posthumously a kind of official cult. Recipients of such honor included Brasidas, Miltiades, Gelon and Hiero I of Syracuse, Theron, and Timoleon. However, if genius, virtue, and political or military success embody divine potential in exceptional men, it is especially so while they are living. Consequently, there is no need to wait for their death before heaping upon them such homage as is accorded the gods (*isotheoi timai*), yet without identifying them with deities. Such was the case with Lysander after the victory of Aegospotami in 405 BCE: dedicated to him were statues, altars, chants, and sacred games that raised him to the status of the Olympians.

Aristotle grants that superiority in valor or virtue secures for certain people the honor of being counted among the gods (*Nicomachean Ethics* 7.1.2). The Hellenistic ideology of the savior-sovereign, beneficent and *euergetēs* (benefactor), derives directly from this concept. The Stoics would apply it generally to people who excelled in services rendered. It was the *virtus* (braveness) of civilizing heroes that earned apotheosis for Herakles, for the Dioscuri, and for Dionysos. Philosophers, wise men, and miracle workers (among them Pythagoras and Empedocles, and later Plato, Epicurus, and a number of others) were regarded as god-men, benefactors of humanity. The case of the young Gnostic Epiphanes, adored as a god after his death for being the founder of the Carpocratian sect, exhibits the same process.

ALEXANDER, THE DIADOCHI, AND HELLENISTIC ROYALTY. In dedicating funeral solemnities, of which some elements (particularly eagles) prefigure certain aspects of imperial Roman apotheosis, to the memory of his friend Hephaestion, Alexander established a cult for him, ordering that sacrifice be made to him "as to a god of the highest order" (Diodorus Siculus, 17.114–115). His funeral pyre with five levels presaged the *rogus consecrationis* (funeral pyre) of the Caesars. It has been suggested that it was Alexander who proposed to the Diadochi (successors) the plan for his own posthumous consecration. Indeed, the tomb of the conquering Macedonian became the site of a cult at Alexandria that corresponded to that of the hero *ktistēs,* or "founder." However, the Ptolemies made of it a state cult that deified the dead king by allotting to him the service of a namesake priest. Like the Olympians, Alexander was to be honored fully as a god. (His name was not preceded by the title *theos,* which fundamentally differentiated him from the Lagides kings.) When the first of the Ptolemies died, his son dedicated a temple to him as a "savior-god." The first of the Seleucids was similarly deified in 280 BCE by Antiochus I. The divinization of dead queens and kings, which was connected with the cult of Alexander by following the categories of Greek mythology, was legitimized by proclaiming that Arsinoë had been borne away by the Dioscuri, Ptolemy II by Zeus, and Berenice by

Aphrodite. This representation of divine abductions would long survive in funerary imagery.

The posthumous deification of sovereigns that developed during the third century BCE coincides both chronologically and ideologically with the success of euhemerism. In a revolutionary book entitled *Sacred Scripture,* Euhemeros of Messene declared that religions derive from the homage rendered to beneficent kings or to civilizing conquerors. It is the epoch that witnessed the popularization of the myth of Dionysos roaming through Asia for the purpose of propagating the use of wine and also of spreading, like Alexander, Hellenic culture. Yet parallel (or correlative) to this concept of the hero-*euergetēs,* there is affirmed the idea of the living god, incarnate in the active person of the sovereign. Already in 324 BCE, Alexander had laid claim to this deification: it involved a political idea, that of the unity of a universal and cosmopolitan empire in need of a religious foundation in the person of the king himself, as was later the case in the persons of the Caesars. In Egypt the process took root in the local practice of identifying the pharaoh with Horus and of adoring him as the "son of Re." The Greeks compared the Ptolemies to Zeus, Dionysos, Apollo, Hermes, and Poseidon, and their wives to Hera, Aphrodite, Isis, and Demeter. In the same way, Antiochus I was compared to Zeus Nikator, and his son to Apollo Soter. The notion was also entertained of the reincarnation of this or that deity in the person of the sovereign: Ptolemy XIII and Mithradates VI Eupator were each regarded as a "new Dionysos." Alexander too had been a "new Dionysos," a "new Herakles."

Like the Lagides, the kings of Syria and Pergamum instituted a dynastic cult alongside local cults of sovereign founders of cities. Each satrapy had its own high priest for the royal cult, just as during the Roman era each province would have its own *archiereus* for the imperial cult. This divinization was sanctioned through appeal to genealogy: the Lagides descended from Herakles or from Dionysos. There was no hesitation in proclaiming Demetrios Poliorcetes as the "son of Poseidon and Aphrodite." The epodic hymn that the Athenians sang to him in 307 BCE serves as a revealing document of the new conception of deities: "You, we see you here present, not as an idol of wood or stone, but really here." The apotheosis of living beings, visible or "epiphanous," appeared as one consequence (among others) of the decline of the rule of the cities and of the cults entwined with them. The erosion of belief in the traditional gods benefited the ideology, indeed the theology, of the leader as savior and peacemaker, as effective and direct protector of the people who needed him. The same phenomenon repeated and expanded itself three centuries later to the advantage of the Roman emperors.

THE ROMAN WORLD. Motifs like those discussed above early permeated Roman culture, together with the diffusion of Hellenistic influences (a poem such as Callimachus's *Lock of Berenice* was imitated by Catullus in the first century BCE). In particular, the idea of the divinity of humans gained much support from Stoicism. It was also a tenet of Pythagoreans, since their doctrine of the immortality of the soul included the ascent of the soul to the stars after death.

In Roman religion, the dead, as the *manes,* were collectively and indiscriminately deified, the "sacrifices" offered to them having the purpose of helping them rest quietly under the ground. But from the second century BCE onward, this cult tended to coincide with a kind of heroization of impressive individuals, such as some members of the Scipionic family. The sarcophagus that contained the remains of Scipio Barbatus had the shape of a monumental altar, which attests to the deceased being a *deus parens* (Saladino, 1970, pp. 24 ff.). Even the poet Ennius, whose activity was patronized by the Scipios, asserts that "one man shall be raised to the heavens" (*Annals* 1.54, Skutsch); while some considered immortality something that a few may obtain after ascending to the heavens (Lactantius, *Divinae institutiones* 1.18; Cicero, *De republica,* frag. 6). Cicero, who is largely influenced by Pythagorean and Stoic trends, likewise says that Romulus became a god through his deeds and virtue (*De republica* 2.17), and Scipio is told to rise to the stars by pursuing justice and piety (Cicero, *De republica* 6.16; *Tusculanae disputationes* 1. 43). Scipio is also the main character in the last section of Cicero's dialogue on the state, which deals with the notion of astral immortality—promised to meritorious statesmen, in conformity with the Hellenistic ideology of the hero-*euergetēs.* The same writer first attests the Greek word *apotheōsis* with reference to the posthumous divinization with which he attempted to honor his daughter Tullia (*Epistles to Atticus* 1.16.13).

"Private" examples of apotheoses are the privileged object of altar-shaped tombs, which entered into widespread usage in the first century BCE. Their ornamentation is also significant, particularly the eagles of apotheosis, thought to bear the soul of the deceased to heaven, like the eagle of Zeus that abducted Ganymede. In freeing the spiritual person from his or her carnal shell, the funeral pyre served to aid ascension to the ethereal realm of the gods. A fortiori, being struck by lightning was a measure of apotheosis, as the myths of Semele, Herakles, and Asklepios show. Scenes of military life and hunting, as well as intellectual activity, also symbolized heroization through *virtus.* Finally, untimely deaths were thought to assure the apotheosis of those whom the Greeks called *ahōroi* (those who die untimely deaths).

CAESAR AND AUGUSTUS: A "TRANSITIONAL" PHASE. The deification of Romulus, the founder of Rome (who after his ascension to heaven was worshiped under the name Quirinus), traces back to Ennius, but it was greatly elaborated and became a topical image in the Augustan age (Livy 1.16.1–3; 1.40.3). Other mythical heroes of divine offspring, such as Aeneas and Hercules, were worshiped as gods. Their apotheosis served as a prototype for the divinization of Julius Caesar and, later, Augustus.

Two years after his murder in 44 BCE, the senate stated the official consecration of Caesar. It was a crucial development that provided a partial model for later imperial deifications. However, divine honors were offered to Caesar even during his lifetime, together with a solemn public funeral and the addition of a day to the calendar on which prayers should be addressed to him. The famous comet that appeared in July during the games held in memory of Caesar was believed to be his soul. This comet indicated that he had attained the heights of heaven and was a god with his own place among the stars.

Such themes are echoed in contemporary literature: in the *Eclogues* and especially the *Aeneid*, Vergil, by displaying numerous references to astral imagery, emphasizes the Golden Age and the divinity of Augustus, to whom divinity is bestowed by an encomiastic homage pronounced by Anchises in a prophetic passage at the end of the sixth book. An analogous motif of Hellenistic ascendance, the *catasterismos* (transformation into a star) concludes Ovid's *Metamorphoses* and shows Pythagorean patterns in dealing with Caesar's apotheosis. Ovid also offers a comparison between Romulus and Augustus and a striking account of the apotheosis of Romulus in his calendar. A contemporary poem, the *Consolation to Livia* (255–258) explicitly compares the imperial funeral pyre to that of Hercules. The idea of the emperor being counted among the stars even recurs in Germanicus, who includes in his astronomical poem a reference to the Capricorn, Augustus's birth sign, which is now his heavenly seat. These numerous literary references illustrate how many factors, including personal charisma, paved the way for the cultic veneration of emperors and a sacralization of their role. It must be noted that even though the Hellenistic kings and the Caesars had been themselves adored while alive (Cassius Dio 51.20.7 traces the official institution of the cult of the living *princeps* back to 29 BCE), it is possible to speak of true apotheosis only posthumously.

IMPERIAL APOTHEOSIS. The apotheosis ritual is perhaps the most significant innovation in religious practice during the transition from the Republic to the Empire. It is strictly related to the cult of the emperors, which raises many exegetical problems, since it varied in its forms or rituals according to the different regions of the Roman Empire or to the different epochs.

This ceremony was an important part of the symbolism that defined the imperial house and became rooted in Roman tradition. In addition, the building of a great temple to the new god aimed to make this status more evident in stone and marble. Such a *consecratio* (the official Latin term for an imperial apotheosis), whose artful ritual was developed from the funeral ritual of aristocratic families, was inaugurated after the death of Augustus in 14 CE. From Augustus to Constantine the Great (d. 337), thirty-six emperors and twenty-seven members of their families were bestowed with an apotheosis and received the title of *divus,* a term which differred from *deus* insofar as it was employed only for divinized humans. Political meanings were implied in the deification: on one hand, it was a fitting end for a good emperor; on the other hand, the granting of deification allowed the senate to obtain a sort of authority for the emperor (the refusal to deify Tiberius is noteworthy). The senate continued to play a formal role in apotheosis, although this role became increasingly reduced, especially in the second and third centuries. At the same time, by supervising the deification of his predecessor, the new emperor confirmed his rightful role and emphasized his own piety. In this sense, consecration can be considered a rite of passage because it involves the transmission of authority to a new ruler.

Many sources, both iconographic and literary, preserve accounts of apotheosis rituals. Along with inscriptions (which record the official formulas), coins and cameos, and even the vault of the Arch of Titus, display the distinctive signs of the apotheosis ritual such as the pyre and the eagle. Moreover, imposing monuments are still preserved in Rome, including Hadrian's mausoleum, the Castel Sant'Angelo, the Temple of Antoninus Pius and Faustina in the Forum (now the Church of Lorenzo in Miranda), and the sole surviving raised relief on the pedestal of the column of Antoninus Pius. This relief displays the *decrusio* (the army's ritual encirclement of the bier) and, more significantly, in a Roman setting (note the Campus Martius, identified by the Egyptian obelisk set up by Augustus, two personifications of Roma, a seated armed female, and the River Tiber in the foreground), the apotheosis of the emperor and of his wife, carried away by the spirit of eternity (*Aiōn*) on its wings. The third-century Greek historians Cassius Dio and Herodian, who record the funerals of Augustus, Pertinax (193), and Septimius Severus's (211), offer further detailed accounts of the ceremony.

Among the literary sources, Seneca's prosimetric satire, *Apocolocyntōsis divii Claudii*, contains a parody of Claudius's funeral and deification, decreed after his murder in 54 CE: the title, an evident *jeu de mots* with *apotheōsis*, has been understood as "metamorphosis into a gourd," an allusion to Claudius's stupidity. Rather than a polemic against the recent institution of apotheosis, the work must be considered a direct attack against Claudius, which at the same time possessed a political function: to make Claudius an example to Nero of how not to govern. Such ironic patterns or "reversal" elements induced scholars to suggest a link with the winter festival of the *Saturnalia*, which probably was also the occasion for delivering it.

According to the ritual, an immense four-tiered pyre would be built upon the Field of Mars. This *rogus consecrationis* was constructed of planks enclosing combustible materials and was elaborately decorated on the outside with costly embroidered fabrics adorned with gold, paintings, embossments, and garlands. A funeral pallet bore the cadaver of the new *divus*, covered with spices, fragrant fruits, and perfume essences. Around the pyre the priests and horseman would move in a circle. There was also a procession representing famous persons of the past, the nations of the Roman Empire, the guilds of different trades, and the senatorian order. A speech was made in honor of the dead emperor, whose body or wax image was on a bier. The new emperor would then take a torch to kindle the pyre, and everyone participating would do the same. Finally, from the top of the pyre an eagle would take flight as if bearing the soul of the deceased Caesar to the heavenly Olympus. After the ceremony, a witness would attest to having seen the consecrated prince soar into the air, and there was no lack of omens portending the apotheosis. Thereafter, the deceased would be entitled to a cult served by a priestly corps comprising members of the imperial family.

The ceremonial was maintained throughout the centuries and the increasing importance of the pyre became even more striking in the light of changing patterns of burial for the population. The extension of the Empire and of the powers of the emperor sacralized his function, and indeed his person and that of the empress, and they were compared in word and picture to the divinities of the traditional pantheon. However, an evolution in the worship of the emperor and in the external features of the apotheosis can be outlined. These features increased as a result of cultural contacts with Eastern countries (in particular, Persia), so that from the Antonine age onward such attributes as the radiant nimbus, which symbolized the divine glory conferred on the king, became common in iconography.

Among the relatives of the emperors honored with an apotheosis, an important example is provided by Antinous, the young boy beloved by the emperor Hadrian, whose death in Egypt raised controversial interpretations. It is not certain whether he fell accidentally into the Nile or whether his life was offered in sacrifice in a sort of *devotio* for Hadrian's safety. The emperor honored him by founding a city named Antinoopolis near the place where the boy was drowned. An apparition of a new star, as in the case of Caesar, was also reported. The deified Antinous was identified with or portrayed as various Greek gods (Hermes, Dionysos, and others) and explicitly merged with Osiris, not only because of the way he died but because his death took place on the anniversary of Osiris's drowning. The deification of Antinous also recalled the Egyptian custom of according divine honors to persons drowned in the Nile. The cult of Antinous soon spread, especially in his birthplace of Bithynia, and it is variously recorded on epigraphs and statues. However, the emperor came under ridicule, especially after his sister Paulina died and he did not immediately accord her any honors. The case of Antinous, together with that of Livia, Augustus's wife, in the fourth century, was condemned by the Christian poet Prudentius (*Against Symmachus* 1.245 ff.).

After the conversion of Constantine to Christianity in 312, apotheosis became incompatible with the new religion and was denounced by many fathers of the church because it implied the worship of dead people as gods. Constantine was probably the first emperor to be inhumed and the first for whom a pyre was not erected. Yet coins of consecration were nonetheless struck upon his death; these depicted the emperor in a chariot, extending his hand toward the hand of God emerging from the sky. In any case, the title *divus* did not imply apotheosis for the Christians, and Constantine's biographer Eusebius of Caesarea clearly states that Constantine enjoyed a Christian immortality. The artful funeral of Constantine constituted a model for a subsequent elaboration of the Byzantine ceremonies for dead emperors, as is depicted in the *Liber de caeremoniis* and in panegyric poetry.

See Also Deification; Emperor's Cult.

Bibliography

Alföldi, Andreas. "La divinisation de César dans la politique d'Antoine et d'Octavien entre 44 et 40 avant J. C." *Revue numismatique* 15 (1973): 99–128.

Bickermann, Elias. "Die römische Kaiserapotheose." *Archiv f. Religions Wissenschaft* 27 (1929): 1–34.

Bickerman, Elias, Willem den Boer, et al. *Le culte des souverains dans l'empire romain.* Geneva, 1973.

Bömer, Franz. "Über die Himmelserscheinung nach dem Tode Caesars." *Bonner Jahrbücher* 152 (1952): 27–40.

Bonamente, Giorgio. "L'apoteosi degli imperatori romani nell'Historia Augusta." *Miscellanea Greca e Romana* 15 (1990): 257–308.

Bosworth, A. Brian. "Augustus, the *Res Gestae,* and Hellenistic Theories of Apotheosis." *Journal of Roman Studies* 89 (1999): 1–18.

Boyancé, Pierre. "L'apothéose de Tullia." *Revue des études anciennes* 46 (1944): 179–184.

Cracco Ruggini, Lellia. "Apoteosi e politica senatoria nel IV s. D.C. Il dittico dei Symmachi al British Museum." *Rivista storica Italiana* 89 (1977): 425–489.

Cumont, Franz. *Lux Perpetua.* Paris, 1948.

Davies, Penelope J. E. *Death and the Emperor: Roman Funerary Monuments from Augustus to Marcus Aurelius.* Cambridge, U.K., 2000.

Eitrem, Samson. "Zur Apotheose." *Symbolae Osloenses* 10 (1932): 31–56, and 11 (1933): 11–34.

Fishwick, Duncan. "The Deification of Claudius." *Classical Quarterly* 52, no. 1 (2002): 341–349.

Hazzard, Richard A. "Theos Epiphanes: Crisis and Response." *Harvard Theological Review* 88 (1995): 415–536.

Kleiner, Diana E. E., and Fred S. Kleiner. "The Apotheosis of Antoninus and Faustina." *Rendiconti della pontificia accademia di archeologia* 51–52 (1978–1980): 389–400.

Lambert, Royston. *Beloved and God: The Story of Hadrian and Antinous.* London, 1984.

L'Orange, Hans Peter. *Apotheosis in Ancient Portraiture.* Oslo, 1947; reprint, New Rochelle, N.Y., 1982.

Melearts, Henri, ed. "Le culte du souverain dans l'Égypte ptolémaïque au IIIe siècle avant notre ère." *Actes du colloque international, Brussels, 10 mai 1995.* Leuven, 1998.

Price, Simon. "From Noble Funerals to Divine Cult: The Consecration of Roman Emperors." In *Rituals of Royalty: Power and Ceremonial in Traditional Societies,* edited by David Cannadine and Simon Price, pp. 56–105. London, 1987.

Saladino, V. *Der Sarkophag des Lucius Cornelius Scipio Barbatus.* Würzburg, Germany, 1970.

Seneca. *Apocolocyntosis.* Edited by Patricia T. Eden. Cambridge, U.K., 1984.

Small, Alistair, ed. *Subject and Ruler: The Cult of the Ruling Power in Classical Antiquity.* Papers presented at a conference held in the University of Alberta on April 13–15, 1994, to celebrate the 65th anniversary of Duncan Fishwick. Ann Arbor, Mich., 1996.

Strong, Eugénie Sellers. *Apotheosis and Afterlife: Three Lectures on Certain Phases of Art and Religion in the Roman Empire.* London, 1915.

Taeger, Fritz. *Charisma: Studien zur Geschichte des antiken Herrscherkultes.* 2 vols. Stuttgart, Germany, 1957–1960.

Turcan, Robert. "Origine et sens de l'inhumation à l'époque impériale." *Revue des études anciennes* 60 (1958): 323–347.

Turcan, Robert. "Le piédestal de la colonne antonine." *Revue archéologique* (1975): 305–318.

Turcan, Robert. "Le culte impérial au troisième siècle." In *Aufstieg und Niedergang der römischen Welt* 2, no. 16.2 (1978): 996–1084.

Vogel, Lise. *The Column of Antoninus Pius.* Cambridge, Mass., 1973.

Voisin, Jean-Louis. "Antinoüs varius, multiplex, multiformis." In *L'Afrique, la Gaule, la réligion à l'epoque romaine: Mélanges à la mémoire de Marcel Le Glay,* edited by Yann Le Bohec, pp. 730–741. Brussels, 1994.

Wardle, David. "Deus or Divus: The Genesis of Roman Terminology for Deified Emperors and a Philosopher's Contribution." In *Philosophy and Power in the Graeco-Roman World: Essays in Honour of Miriam Griffin,* edited by Gillian Clark and Tessa Rajak, pp. 181–191. Oxford, 2002.

Weinreich, Otto. "Antikes Gottmenschtum." *Neues Jahrbücher für Wissenschaft und Jugendbildung* 2 (1926): 633–651.

Weinstock, Stefan. *Divus Julius.* Oxford, U.K., 1971.

Wilcken, Ulrich. "Zur Entstehung des hellenistischen Königskultes." *Sitzungsberichte der Preussischen Akademie der Wissenschaften: Philosophisch historische Klasse* (1938): 298–321.

Williams, Mary Frances. "The *Sidus Iulium,* the Divinity of Men, and the Golden Age in Virgil's *Aeneid.*" *Leeds International Classical Studies* 2, no. 1 (2003). Available from www.leeds.ac.uk/classics/lics/2003/200301.pdf.

Wrede, Henning. *Consecratio in formam deorum: Vergöttlichte Privatpersonen in der römischen Kaiserzeit.* Mainz, Germany, 1981.

Robert Turcan (1987)
Chiara Ombretta Tommasi (2005)

APPARITIONS See GHOSTS; HIEROPHANY; VISIONS

'AQEDAH See ISAAC

'AQĪDAH See CREEDS, *ARTICLE ON* ISLAMIC CREEDS

'AQIVA' BEN YOSEF

'AQIVA' BEN YOSEF (c. 50–c. 135 CE), Palestinian tanna. 'Aqiva' lived during the time of the transformation of Palestinian Judaism from a religion centered on the Temple of Jerusalem to one focused on the study of Torah, the totality of God's revelation to Moses and the Jewish people. 'Aqiva' was born shortly before the destruction of the Temple in 70 CE and died during the Bar Kokhba Revolt (132–135), the Jews' last attempt to wrest freedom from the Romans. Described as a poor shepherd, 'Aqiva', encouraged by his wife, supposedly began his rabbinic studies at the age of forty and learned the alphabet together with his young son (*Avot de-Rabbi Natan* 6; B.T., *Ket.* 62b–63a, *Ned.* 50a).

The influence of 'Aqiva' touched all areas of rabbinic thought and all levels of rabbinic lore. The Talmud relates that

> the anonymous statements in the Mishnah [the earliest collection of rabbinic teachings] should be attributed to Me'ir, the anonymous statements in the Tosefta [a document that parallels the Mishnah but that did not achieve its official status] should be attributed to Neḥemyah, the anonymous statements in *Sifra'* [an early collection of exegetical statements on *Leviticus*] should be attributed to Yehudah, the anonymous statements in *Sifrei* [an early collection of exegetical comments on *Numbers* and *Deuteronomy*] should be attributed to Shim'on, and all of them are according to the opinion of 'Aqiva'. (B.T., *San.* 86a)

The major sages after 'Aqiva' traced their intellectual heritage back to him. Even the patriarch Gamli'el of Yavneh acquiesced to the knowledge of 'Aqiva' (B.T., *Ber.* 27b–28a), and the greatest patriarch, Yehudah ha-Nasi', studied with the five major pupils of 'Aqiva' (B.T., *Meg.* 20a). Even Moses is said to have asked God why he revealed the Torah through him if he had such a one as 'Aqiva' (B.T., *Men.* 29b).

Scholars such as Jacob Brull, Jacob Zuri, and Zacharias Frankel attribute to 'Aqiva' a central role in the codification of the Mishnah; however, Jacob Neusner and his students have raised serious questions about the traditional view of how the Mishnah came into being and the role of 'Aqiva' in that process. Compilation of the early *midrashim* (collections of exegetical statements) by 'Aqiva' also has been the subject of scholarly debate since the time of David Hoffmann (late nineteenth century) and Chanoch Albeck.

The traditional picture of 'Aqiva' as a biblical exegete goes beyond the assigning of particular early collections of exegetical statements to him. It is commonly claimed that 'Aqiva' represents a major trend in early rabbinic biblical commentary (Heschel, 1962). He is said to have followed an imaginative and creative form of biblical exegesis and to have derived his comments from every aspect of the biblical text, including the shapes of the letters (B.T., *Men.* 29b) and the peculiarities of biblical Hebrew, such as the repetition of words and phrases and the appearance of certain prepositions, conjunctions, and adverbs (B.T., *Ḥag.* 12a, *Shav.* 26a; *Gn. Rab.* 1.14, 22.2, 53.20). The exegetical activity of ʿAqivaʾ is often contrasted to that of Yishmaʿeʾl ben Elishaʿ, who is said to have followed a more rational approach to the biblical text. For example, the repetition of "a man, a man" in *Leviticus* 22:4 led ʿAqivaʾ to conclude that the uncircumcised were included in the prohibition against eating the Passover sacrifice, while Yishmaʿeʾl proved this point by a citation of *Leviticus* 22:10 and *Exodus* 12:45 (*Sifraʾ*, Emor 4.18). However, recent work on the exegetical traditions of Yishmaʿeʾl and ʿAqivaʾ (Porton, 1976–1982) has demonstrated that the methods used by these two rabbis were more similar than most scholars have thought.

Just as the rabbinic tradition assigned ʿAqivaʾ a prominent place in the compilations of the legal and exegetical collections, so it assigned him a pivotal role in the formation of the mystical texts of Judaism. He is included, along with Ben ʿAzzʾai, Elishaʿ ben Avuyah, and Ben Zomaʾ, among those "who entered the garden," which is taken as a reference to mystical teachings, and he alone is said to have "left in peace" (B.T., *Ḥag.* 14b and parallels). His importance in the mystical tradition is seen in the attribution of sayings to him in the Heikhalot literature (collections of visions of those who traveled through God's palace) and by the attribution of *Heikhalot zuṭratti* to him.

ʿAqivaʾ did not limit himself to the sphere of the intellect. He was pictured as being actively involved in the Bar Kokhba Revolt. In fact, ʿAqivaʾ is normally said to have claimed that Bar Kokhba was the Messiah and to have been the major rabbinical supporter of the uprising (J.T., *Taʿan.* 68d). The rabbinic texts claim that he suffered a martyr's death at the hands of the Romans during the revolt (B.T., *Ber.* 61b). However, Peter Schafer has raised serious objections to the scholarly consensus concerning the revolt and the role of ʿAqivaʾ in it.

Although recent scholarship has challenged many of the details regarding the life of ʿAqivaʾ that are found in rabbinic texts, it does not detract from the impression he made on his contemporaries and on subsequent generations. The picture we find in the documents of ancient Judaism is one of an extraordinary talent. He is described as affecting every aspect of rabbinic thought—legal, exegetical, mystical, and even philosophical. "Man has free will," ʿAqivaʾ is reported to have said, "but all is foreseen by God" (*Avot* 3.16). His rise from poverty to greatness must have been an inspiration to many—so much so that he was placed at the center of the important historical and intellectual events of his time.

SEE ALSO Tannaim.

BIBLIOGRAPHY

For traditional views of ʿAqivaʾ, see the *Encyclopedia of Talmudic and Geonic Literature,* edited by Mordechai Margalioth (Tel Aviv, 1945), vol. 2, pp. 725–731; Aaron Hyman's *Toledot tannaʾim veamoraʾim* (1910; reprint, Jerusalem, 1964), vol. 3, pp. 988–1008; Harry Freedman's "Akiva," in *Encyclopaedia Judaica* (Jerusalem, 1971), vol. 2, cols. 492–498; and the wholly uncritical study by Louis Finkelstein, *Akiba: Scholar, Saint and Martyr* (Philadelphia, 1934). Charles Primus deals with a small portion of the Akivan corpus in *Aqiva's Contributions to the Law of Zeraʿim* (Leiden, 1977), and I have dealt with the traditions of ʿAqivaʾ that occur with those of Yishmaʿeʾl ben Elishaʿ in my four-volume study *The Traditions of Rabbi Ishmael* (Leiden, 1976–1982). Abraham Joshua Heschel discusses the traditional distinctions between Yishmaʿeʾl and ʿAqivaʾ as biblical exegetes in the introduction to his *Theology of Ancient Judaism,* 2 vols. (New York, 1962), while my analysis in my fourth volume on Yishmaʿeʾl challenges the traditional picture. On the problem of rabbinic biography, see William S. Green's "What's in a Name? The Problematic of Rabbinic 'Biography,'" in his *Approaches to Ancient Judaism* (Missoula, Mont., 1978), vol. 1, pp. 77–96.

New Sources

Edwards, Laurence L. "Rabbi Akiba's Crowns: Postmodern Discourse and the Cost of Rabbinic Reading." *Judaism* 49 (2000): 417–435.

Ilan, Tal. "'Daughters of Israel, Weep for Rabbi Ishmael:' The Schools of Rabbi Akiva and Rabbi Ishmael on Women." *Nashim* 4 (2001): 15–34.

Levey, Samson H. "Akiba—Sage in Search of the Messiah: A Closer Look." *Judaism* 41 (1992): 334–345.

GARY G. PORTON (1987)
Revised Bibliography

AQUINAS, THOMAS SEE THOMAS AQUINAS

ARABIAN RELIGIONS.

The advent of Islam in the seventh century of the common era marked a clear division in the political and religious history of Arabia. In the eyes of Muslim authors, pre-Islamic time is viewed as the Jāhilīyah ("age of ignorance"), a term applied to pre-Islamic history within and without Arabia. From a religious standpoint, this term corresponds especially to the polytheistic beliefs and rituals that to a large extent characterized religious life in Arabia.

In addition to polytheism, Judaism and Christianity were practiced in Arabia in pre-Islamic times. The second Abyssinian invasion of South Arabia in 525 was prompted by—among other factors—the anti-Christian excesses of Dhū Nuwās, the Jewish Ḥimyarī ruler. A Jewish colony had long been established at Yathrib (Medina) when Muḥammad emigrated there from Mecca in 622. There is no archaeological evidence that Zoroastrianism had been practiced among pre-Islamic Arabs, but Sasanid rule over the area from circa 575 to 628 must have resulted in the practice of this religion within the Persian garrisons in South Arabia. Muslim sources also mention the *Majūs of Bahrein* (i.e., the Zoroastrians of Eastern Arabia), particularly in commenting on Qurʾān 9:29.

Historical Background. Known in antiquity as Arabia Felix, South Arabia was a fertile area with elaborate waterworks that supported the rise of a number of states in pre-Islamic times: Maʿīn (the Minaeans), Saba (the land of Sheba), Qatabān, and Hadhramaut. These later formed the Ḥimyarī kingdom (capital, Ẓafār), which fell to the Abyssinians in 525. The Sabaeans were mentioned in the annals of Assyrian kings as far back as the eighth century BCE, and the peoples of Arabia Felix were known to classical writers as early as the end of the fourth century BCE. Strabo preserved an excerpt from Eratosthenes that mentions Minaeans, Sabaeans, Qatabānians, and Hadhramautis, and he himself gave an account of the expedition of Aelius Gallus into the area in 24 BCE. References to these peoples are also found in the anonymous *Periplus of the Erythraean Sea* (between c. 95 and 130 CE) and in the works of Pliny (c. 77 CE) and Ptolemy (c. 150 CE).

This region, known as the land of incense, maintained an active trade with Egypt, Abyssinia, and India. The *Periplus* mentions the South Arabian ports of Okēlis, Kanē, and Muza as the main trading places for Egyptian cloth and wine, African ivory, and Indian spices. Saba and Hadhramaut are mentioned in the Bible; the former gained fame as the land of Sheba, whose queen paid a visit to King Solomon in Jerusalem and is described in the Bible as "having a great retinue and camels bearing spices and very much gold and precious stones" (*2 Chr.* 9:1–12). Excavations in 1955–1956 and 1960 of the sites of Yeha and Melazo (in Ethiopia) that yielded a number of Sabaean inscriptions revealed that by the fifth century BCE Sabaean immigrants had established themselves in northeastern Ethiopia.

The capitals of the South Arabian states were Qarnaw (Maʿīn), Timnaʿ (Qatabān), Shabwa (Hadhramaut), and Ṣirwāḥ and Maʾrib (the two capitals of Saba). Some scholars date the rise of the first South Arabian state as far back as 1200 BCE, but the chronology of the rise and fall of these states is not yet well established. Except in Maʿīn, the rulers of these states bore the theocratic title of *mukarrib* ("priest-king"). With the consolidation and expansion of the Sabaean state, this title changed to *malik* ("king").

Although Mecca was not a capital city, it was an important economic center, linking trade routes from South Arabia with the great cities of Syria and Iraq. It was also an important religious center for the tribes of the Hejaz (western Arabia). Later, this area became the cradle of Islam, a monotheistic religion that was to eradicate all traces of paganism. We are told by al-Azraqī that as many as 360 idols were destroyed in Mecca following its capture by the prophet Muḥammad and his supporters in 630.

In the northern Hejaz, a Minaean colony flourished in al-ʿUlā. Farther north, from Madāʾin Ṣāliḥ to Petra, are the temples and rock-cut funerary monuments of the Nabateans, Arabs whose kingdom existed from the first century BCE until its fall to the Romans in 106 CE. Another North Arabian kingdom was founded around the Syrian city of Tadmor (Palmyra) and is known for its role in fending off Sasanid expansion into the area. It reached its zenith from about the middle of the second century CE to 272, when it was annexed by the Romans following the defeat of its queen, Zenobia.

Religion. South Arabian religion was dominated by astral worship. Each people worshiped its own moon god: Wadd (the Minaeans), ʿAmm (the Qatabānians), Sīn (the Hadhramautis), and Ilumquh (or Almaqah, the Sabaeans). Other lunar deities are mentioned in a number of South Arabian inscriptions, but the consensus among specialists is that they represented a particular aspect or function of each of the aforementioned moon gods, and were not distinct deities. Thus Hawbas could be invoked along with Ilumquh, Anbay or Warakh with ʿAmm, Hawl with Sīn, and Naḥasṭāb with Wadd. The specific features of each of these gods is still a matter for discussion: Gonzague Ryckmans (1951) considers that Hawbas represented the "ebb and flow" aspect of the moon god, and Hawl that of "recurrence," and that the meaning of the name *Anbay* was "spokesman." The nature of Naḥasṭāb is not clear, but Albert Jamme (1947) thinks that he was probably a moon god.

The solar deity was worshiped as a goddess and is mentioned mostly with a number of attributes beginning with the word *dhāt* ("endowed with, possessing"). The different names under which she appears are generally viewed as reflecting aspects of the sun according to seasonal changes: Dhāt Ḥimyam ("the blazing one") and Dhāt Baʿdān ("the faraway one") in Sabaean inscriptions. Among the Hadhramautis, she is known as Shams ("sun"). Occasionally, she is associated with the name of a local temple: Dhāt Nashq and Dhāt Ẓahrān, in some Minaean and Qatabānian inscriptions.

The third major South Arabian divinity was ʿAthtar, the male equivalent of the stellar deity Venus. He is considered by most scholars to be the god of irrigation, and he appears in inscriptions under the common name of ʿAthtar but more often with an epithet or in a construct denoting a location: ʿAthtar Shārqan ("ʿAthtar of the east"), ʿAthtar Shāriq ("ʿAthtar rising from the east"), and ʿAthtar Dhū Qabḍim ("ʿAthtar, lord of Qabd"). The invocation of ʿAthtar before the other deities is common, especially in the concluding formulas of votive inscriptions.

The triad of moon god, sun god, and ʿAthtar worshiped by the Sabaeans of Arabia is also encountered in Sabaean inscriptions found in Ethiopia. An inscription from the site of Melazo (a few miles southeast of Aksum) mentions Ilumquh next to Hawbas; another is dedicated to ʿAthtar (ʿAstar) alone, and a third to ʿAstar, Hawbas, Ilumquh, Dhāt Ḥimyam, and Dhāt Baʿdān (see A. J. Drewes, "Les inscriptions de Melazo," *Annales d'Éthiopie* 3, 1959, pp. 83–99).

A lack of dated inscriptions impedes a better understanding of the religious evolution of South Arabia. In the extant inscriptions, a host of deities are mentioned individually or in combination with one or more members of the triad. Their nature and position in the pantheon remain very sketchy, however, because of the disparity and wide variety of these "secondary" deities. Some of the deities, with their probable meanings, are Balw ("death, misfortune"), Dhū Samāwī ("lord of the sky [heaven]"), Ḥalfān ("oath, contract"), Ḥalīm ("the wise one"), Nasr ("eagle"), Raḥman ("the compassionate one"), and Samīʿ ("the one who listens").

The temple formed the cult center among the sedentary settlements in this part of the peninsula. Each temple had a keeper, whose functions have not been clarified but who is thought to have assumed certain religious duties; the term *sacerdotal* is inappropriate here owing to our present lack of knowledge of the subject. Among South Arabian temples, two are well known: the temple of Ḥuraydah (Hureidha) in Hadhramaut, dedicated to Sīn, the local moon god, and the temple of ʿAwwām (Ḥaram Bilqīs) in Maʾrib, dedicated to Ilumquh, the Sabaean moon god. The remains indicate that these were elaborate structures consisting of a large courtyard and several partitions for cultic purposes.

The Hejaz. The nomadic way of life and the tribal organization left their impact: the multitude of deities worshiped in the Hejaz were tribal deities. Each tribe had its own god or goddess, represented generally in the form of a baetyl, a sacred stone. The mobility of nomadic life led to the adoption of suitable cultic practices. Thus, the members of a tribe could worship their deity anywhere by investing any form of stone with the divine. This "substitute" was referred to as a *nuṣub* (pl., *anṣāb*, Qurʾān 5:90). Although the cult of baetyls was the most important religious feature, there are a few examples of the veneration of trees and spirits. The Muslim author al-Azraqī noted that the Quraysh tribe worshiped Dhāt Anwāṭ, a "huge green tree" located at Ḥunayn, on the road from Mecca to Taif. Al-ʿUzzā, the major goddess of the same tribe, was believed to have been incarnated in a cluster of three acacia trees in the Ḥurāḍ Valley, on the road from Mecca to Medina. The presence of these trees along seasonal migratory tracks led to their worship. As for jinn (spirits), a number of sources, including the Qurʾān (6:100–101), indicate that they were worshiped by Arabs in pre-Islamic times. According to Ibn al-Kalbī (trans. Faris, 1952, p. 29), the clan of Banū Mulayḥ of the Khuzāʿa tribe was notable for jinn worship.

Three tribal deities were preeminent in Central Arabia. These were Manāt, Allāt, and Al-ʿUzzā, the three goddesses mentioned in the Qurʾān (53:19–22). The most ancient of these was Manāt, who was worshiped by the Azd tribe and whose sanctuary was at Qudayd, on the Red Sea, near Mecca. The cult of Manāt was also popular in North Arabia, where the name of this deity appears in inscriptions in its archaic form, *Manawat*. In Palmyra, she was associated with the ancient god Bel Hamon; "the inscriptions presumably define her personality as that of a goddess who appropriates gifts to her worshippers and presides over chance and luck" (Teixidor, 1979, p. 17). A Nabatean inscription from the tomb of Kam Kam (Cantineau, vol. 2, 1932, p. 26) invokes Manāt and Allāt together with Dushara, the Nabatean sun god.

Allāt was the goddess of the Thaqif tribe but was also revered by the Quraysh. Her sanctuary was at Taif and was, in the words of Ibn al-Kalbī, "a square stone." As was the case for Manāt, her cult spread to North Arabia, where she was featured as the warrior goddess. A temple was dedicated to her at Palmyra and also at Ṣalḥad (Ṣarḥad), in the Hauran region of Syria. G. A. Cooke (1903, p. 253) believes that her cult was introduced into the Hauran by the Nabateans following their capture of Damascus in 85 BCE.

Al-ʿUzzā was the goddess of the Quraysh tribe, and her cult originated later than the cults of Manāt and Allāt. She was incarnated, as mentioned above, in three trees in the Ḥurāḍ Valley, where a sanctuary was dedicated to her. In North Arabia, her cult was not so extensive as those of Allāt and Manāt.

Two deities, Isāf (male) and Nāʾilah (female), seem to have been of South Arabian origin; they were worshiped as a couple. We are told by Ibn al-Kalbī and al-Azraqī that their images were placed in the proximity of the Kaʿbah and were worshiped by the Khuzāʿa and Quraysh tribes. The legend surrounding this couple states that they were originally two persons from the Jurhum tribe in Yemen who fornicated in the Kaʿbah and as a result were turned to stone.

Five other deities, all of South Arabian provenance, are mentioned in the Qurʾān (71:23–24): Wadd, Suwāʿ, Yaghūth, Yaʿāq, and Nasr. Of these, Wadd was the "national" god of the Minaeans. Suwāʿ and Nasr are mentioned by Ibn al-Kalbī (1952, pp. 8–11) and appear in a few inscriptions. According to al-Shahrastānī, Yaghūth and Yaʿāq were worshiped in Yemen.

Hubal, the most important deity of Mecca, was a god of great complexity. Unlike the deities cited above, Hubal does not seem to have been of local origin. He was a late addition to the deities worshiped in the Hejaz and is not mentioned at all in the Qurʾān despite the preeminence of his cult in Mecca. The majority of Muslim authors describe him as a carnelian red statue with a broken right arm, a limb that the Quraysh tribe repaired in gold. They state that this statue was brought from Syria (according to al-Azraqī, from Mesopotamia) by ʿAmr ibn Luḥayy; from a passage of al-Shahrastānī it may be deduced that this occurred no earlier than the middle of the third century CE. The statue was placed in the Kaʿbah and was worshiped as a god by the Arabs of the Hejaz, especially by the Quraysh tribe. It was this god who was invoked by Abū Sufyān, a leader of the Quraysh, during the battle of Uḥud against Muḥammad and his followers. The legend surrounding Hubal shows him as the god of rain and a warrior god. Toward the end of the pre-Islamic era he emerged especially as an intertribal warrior god worshiped by the Quraysh and the allied tribes of the Kināna and Tihāma.

The astral character of the cult was prominent among the South Arabians and also among the Palmyrenes and Nabateans. However, it is not certain that this was so among the tribes of the Hejaz. A number of Qurʾanic passages, especially "Adore not the sun and the moon, but adore God who created them" (41:37), and information gathered from literary sources indicate the existence of the "worship of stars" in pre-Islamic Arabia in general. These references, however, are vague and insufficient for the identification of astral deities worshiped by the tribes of the Hejaz. There, religion was marked by the preeminence of tribal deities, a feature reflecting the nomadic way of desert life. These deities and their sacred places were as mobile as nomadic life itself, as demonstrated by the worship of *anṣāb* (baetyls). The number of stone-built sanctuaries was small, and, if the Kaʿbah was a prototype, they reflected the simplicity of nomadic life.

Cultic practices. It is not known whether specific rituals, such as prayers, were prescribed, and our knowledge of cultic practices is limited to the yields of excavations, including inscriptions, and to the occasional accounts of medieval Muslim authors.

Offerings were the most common cultic practice. The worshipers offered a few valuables in recognition of the deity's care or support. Thus, a wealthy Minaean merchant made an offering of money to ʿAthtar Dhū Qabḍim, a Sabaean dedicated a gold camel to Dhū Samāwī, and another, a gold statue to ʿAthtar Dhū Ḍibān. Offerings could also consist of public works, such as a water cistern or a tower. This practice was common in the Hejaz as well, with variations from one deity to another. The offerings could include a portion of the harvest, money, jewelry, or gold. Several accounts mention that worshipers gave money or camels to the keeper (*sādin*) of the Kaʿbah when consulting Hubal for an oracle, while Ibn Hishām mentions that money, jewelry, gold, and onyx were found in the sanctuary of Allāt upon its destruction in Islamic times.

Animal sacrifice, especially of sheep and camels, was most common in Arabia, and is corroborated by a number of votive inscriptions from South Arabia. The 1937–1938 excavation by Gertrude Caton Thompson of the temple of Sīn in Ḥurayḍah revealed partitions that contained a number of shrines with sacrificial altars in their middle, as well as remains of animal bones. This cultic practice was widespread in the Hejaz, and it is often mentioned in early Muslim sources. Ibn al-Kalbī (1952, pp. 16–17) recounts that the prophet Muḥammad said he made, in pre-Islamic times, an offering to Al-ʿUzzā consisting of a dust-colored sheep. Another passage from Ibn al-Kalbī (p. 18) implies that the flesh of the sacrificial animal was divided among those who were present at this occasion.

The sacrifice of humans was nonexistent. The Qurʾān (81:8–9) notes the rare practice of *waʾd al-banāt* (the burial alive of infant daughters), but this should not be viewed as a form of human sacrifice (cf. 16:58–59).

Offerings of incense and fragrances were common in South Arabia, but not in the Hejaz. Incense burners were found among the remains of the temple and tombs of Ḥurayḍah, in the tombs of Timnaʿ (Qatabān), and in the Sabaean tombs excavated at Yeha (Ethiopia).

The belief in some form of an afterlife was widespread among the Arabs. Archaeological evidence from the abovementioned excavations (which took place in 1937–1938, 1951, and 1960, respectively) tends to support this view: the excavations brought to light artifacts consisting of pottery, jewelry (mostly beads), incense burners, and a few tools and utensils. These objects were placed in the tombs for future use by the dead. Until very recently, no trace of mummification was found in South Arabian necropolises, but the discovery, at the end of 1983, of two tombs near Sanʿa (the capital of Yemen) containing five mummies will certainly lead to a reassessment of South Arabian sepulchral practices.

BIBLIOGRAPHY

Scholarly investigation of pre-Islamic religion in South Arabia (Yemen and Hadhramaut) gained impetus toward the end of the nineteenth century through the pioneering epigraphic works of Joseph Halévy and Eduard Glaser. Our knowledge of the antiquities of the area was expanded in the twentieth century through the efforts of scholars such as Yaḥyā al-Nāmī, Ahmed Fakhry, William F. Albright, Frank P. Albright, Gonzague Ryckmans, Jacques Ryckmans, H. St. John Philby, Wendell Phillips, Gertrude Caton Thompson, Jacqueline Pirenne, and Albert Jamme, to mention only a few. As a result of their work, thousands of South Arabian epigraphic texts have come to light. The French Académie des Inscriptions et Belles-lettres devoted the fourth part of its "Corpus Inscriptionum Semiticarum" to Ḥimyarī and Sabaean inscriptions. Three volumes of text and three of illustrations were published between 1889 and 1931. Another set of inscriptions was published from 1928 to 1938 by the Commission du "Corpus Inscriptionum Semiticarum" in volumes 5 to 7 of the "Répertoire d'épigraphie sémitique" (RES). These two series form the largest collections of South Arabian texts.

Next to the epigraphic sources, our knowledge of pre-Islamic religious life in Arabia is drawn from sparse Qurʾanic references and their commentaries, and from literary and historical works of early Muslim authors such as Ibn Isḥāq (d. 768), Ibn al-Kalbī (d. 819 or 821/2), al-Wāqidī (d. 823), Ibn Hishām (d. 833), Ibn Saʿd (d. 845), al-Azraqī (d. 858?), al-Ṭabarī (d. 923), and al-Shahrastānī (d. 1153). Except for the Qurʾān, these sources were not contemporaneous with the rise of Islam. One of the earliest known works was a biography of the prophet Muḥammad, *Sīrat rasūl Allāh*, by Ibn Isḥāq, as compiled by Ibn Hishām; an interval of about a century and a half separates it from the beginning of the new religion. Because of their retrospective view of events, these works naturally lack systematic information about pre-Islamic religions on the peninsula.

The only known work treating solely the topic of religion in pre-Islamic Arabia is the *Kitāb al-aṣnām* of Ibn al-Kalbī, a native of al-Kūfa, in Iraq. This work was known, prior to its publication in 1914, primarily through extensive quotations by

Yāqūt al-Ḥamawī (d. 1225) in his geographical dictionary, *Mu'jam al-buldān.* Ibn al-Kalbī's work has been translated into English by Nabih A. Faris as *The Book of Idols* (Princeton, 1952). The interesting feature of Ibn al-Kalbī's work is its listing of idols and some brief information regarding rituals and tribal idol worship. The *Akhbār Makkah* (History of Mecca) of al-Azraqī is another important source, to which should be added the works of al-Hamdānī (d. 945), a native of San'a, in Yemen. These are *Ṣifat jazīrat al-'arab* (a description of the Arabian peninsula) and *Kitāb al-iklīl,* of which only parts 8 and 10 are known. Part 8 has been translated by Nabih A. Faris as *The Antiquities of South Arabia* (1938; reprint, Westport, Conn., 1981).

Early works pertaining to Arabian religions are listed in volume 2, part 1, of RES. Later works are numerous; the reader may consult the bibliographies of recent monographs, and articles in relevant journals, especially *Muséon,* the *Bulletin of the American Schools of Oriental Research* (*BASOR*), *Syria, Annales d'Éthiopie,* and the *Comptes-rendus de l'Académie des Inscriptions et Belles-lettres.* Also valuable is the bibliography compiled by Youakim Moubarac in *Les études d'épigraphie sud-sémitique et la naissance de l'Islam: Éléments de bibliographie et lignes de recherches* (Paris, 1957).

No single work offers comprehensive coverage of pre-Islamic Arabian religions. The following selected works deal with particular aspects.

Albright, Frank P., and Richard LeBaron Bowen. *Archaeological Discoveries in South Arabia.* Baltimore, 1958.

'Alī, Jawad. *Al-mufaṣṣal fī tārīkh al-'arab qabl al-islām.* 10 vols. Beirut, 1968–1969.

Anfray, Francis. "Une campagne de fouilles à Yĕvā." *Annales d'Éthiopie* 5 (1963): 171–192.

Blakely, Jeffrey A., and Abdu O. Ghaleb. "Sanaa: 2300-Year-Old Mummies Discovered." *American Schools of Oriental Research Newsletter* 35 (July 1984): 6–8.

Cantineau, Jean. *Le nabatéen.* 2 vols. Paris, 1930–1932.

Cleveland, Ray L. *An Ancient South Arabian Necropolis.* Baltimore, 1965.

Cooke, G. A. *A Text-Book of North-Semitic Inscriptions.* Oxford, 1903.

Drewes, A. J. *Inscriptions de l'Éthiopie antique.* Leiden, 1962.

Drijvers, Han J. W. *The Religion of Palmyra.* Leiden, 1976.

Fahd, Toufic. *Le panthéon de l'Arabie centrale à la veille de l'Hégire.* Paris, 1968.

Gibb, H. A. R. "Pre-Islamic Monotheism in Arabia." *Harvard Theological Review* 55 (1962): 269–280.

Hammond, Philip C. *The Nabataeans: Their History, Culture, and Archaeology.* Göteborg, Sweden, 1973.

Hommel, Fritz. "Arabia." In *The Encyclopaedia of Islam.* Leiden, 1913–1938.

Jamme, Albert. "Le panthéon sudarabe préislamique." *Muséon* 60 (1947): 57–147.

Montgomery, James A. *Arabia and the Bible* (1934). Reprint, New York, 1969. With a Prolegomenon by Gus W. Van Beck.

Müller, Walter W. *Südarabien im Altertum.* Rahden, 2001.

Philby, H. St. John. *The Background of Islam.* Alexandria, 1947.

Phillips, Wendell. *Qatabān and Sheba.* New York, 1955.

Ryckmans, Gonzague. *Les noms propres sud-sémitiques.* 3 vols. Louvain, 1934–1935.

Ryckmans, Gonzague. "Les inscriptions monothéistes sabéennes." In *Miscellanea Historica in Honorem Alberti De Meyer,* vol. 1. Louvain, 1946.

Ryckmans, Gonzague. *Les religions arabes préislamiques.* 2d ed. Louvain, 1951.

Ryckmans, Jacques. *L'institution monarchique en Arabie méridionale avant l'Islam.* Louvain, 1951.

Teixidor, Javier. *The Pantheon of Palmyra.* Leiden, 1979.

Watt, W. Montgomery. "Belief in a 'High God' in Pre-Islamic Mecca." *Journal of Semitic Studies* 16 (1971): 35–40.

ADEL ALLOUCHE (1987 AND 2005)

ARAMEAN RELIGION. When the Arameans first appeared in the ancient Near East is not known. The early attestations of *Aram* as a place-name—in an inscription of Naram-Sin of Akkad at the end of the third millennium BCE, in the Mari texts of the eighteenth century BCE, and at Ugarit in the fourteenth century BCE—cannot be taken as a proof of the early existence of an independent ethnic group, even though during the first millennium some of the Aramean kings styled themselves "king of Aram." The Arameans are characterized by their names and their dialects, the novelty of which strikes the historian as he compares them with the preexistent Akkadian names and language used in Mesopotamia.

In the second half of the eleventh century the Arameans are known to have gained control of large areas of the Syrian desert and thus of its caravan routes. They succeeded in forming in northern Syria and around Damascus major confederacies in which dialects of Aramaic were spoken and written. The Aramean states spread over the great bend of the Euphrates, on the upper and lower Habor, and in the northern Syrian hinterland at Samal, Arpad, Aleppo, and Hama. Some information about the Arameans comes from biblical sources, which state that David defeated Hadadezer of Aram-Zobah (near modern Hama), whose political influence had reached as far south as Ammon in Transjordan (*2 Sm.* 8:3, 10:6), or that the continuous disputes between Judah and Israel helped the rise of Damascus as an Aramean power in Syria (Malamat, 1973, pp. 141–144). The Assyrians could not allow a threat to their hegemony in the Near East, however, so Ashurnasirpal II (r. 883–859 BCE) and Shalmaneser III (r. 858–824 BCE) subdued the Aramean states in northern Syria, and Tiglathpileser III (r. 744–727 BCE) reduced Damascus to an Assyrian province.

Yet even defeated, the Arameans maintained the prestige of their language, and the gods they called on in treaties and religious inscriptions became the gods of the whole of Syria and remained so up to the first centuries CE. The massive arrival under the Persians (sixth century BCE) and the

Greeks (fourth century) of Arab tribes into southern Palestine, the Hauran, Damascus, the Syrian desert, and even northern Syria did not disrupt the traditional ways of living and praying because the newcomers adopted the culture and the language of the Arameans. Any analysis of the Aramean religion must therefore take into consideration all the inscriptions written in Aramaic, from the earliest ones of the ninth century BCE down to those of the first three centuries CE (the latter are written in Syriac, a cognate language of Aramaic, and still reflect the influence of the ancient pagan cults of northern Syria).

The Cults of Hadad and Sin. A bilingual inscription (in Akkadian and Aramaic) found in 1979 at Tell Fekhariye, near Tell Halaf, on the border between Syria and Turkey, records the gratitude of Hadadyisi, ruler of Sikanu and Guzanu, to Hadad of Sikanu. Both the script and the historical context date the life-size statue of the ruler on which the text is engraved to the first part of the ninth century BCE. This is the earliest, most important text in Aramaic ever found, and the mention of the god Hadad (in Akkadian, Adad) becomes of paramount interest to the history of his cult among the Arameans. Hadad is praised in both languages in a formula that is often used to praise Adad in Akkadian inscriptions from Mesopotamia. The god is styled "the inspector of the waters of heaven and earth"; the one "who pours richness and dispenses pastureland and moisty fields to all countries." Hadad is the one "who provides the gods, his brothers, with quietness and sustenance." He, the great lord of Sikanu, is "a merciful god," a deity whose almighty providence ranks him above other gods and makes him for humans a storm god and a weather god.

Although Adad's minor position in the Mesopotamian pantheon does not compare with his counterpart's preeminence in northern Syria and among the Arameans in general, his name appears as a theophorous element in some Semitic personal names of the pre-Sargonic period; after the reigns of Sargon of Akkad (late third millennium BCE) and his grandson Naram-Sin, the first Semitic rulers to establish an empire in the Mesopotamian lands, such theophorous names became very frequent. The element *Addu* (Adad/Hadad) occurs frequently in personal names from the Syro-Mesopotamian area. Letters from Mari, on the middle Euphrates, reveal the popularity of the god at the beginning of the second millennium BCE.

A colossal statue of Hadad was found in 1890 in a village to the northeast of Zinjirli (Turkey). According to the inscription carved on the monument, it had been erected by King Panamu of Yady (Samal, in the Zinjirli region) to acknowledge that his royal power derived from Hadad. Although Panamu was not a Semite, he gave his son a Semitic name, Barsur, and extolled Semitic gods in his inscription: besides Hadad the text lists El, the high god adored at Ugarit and in pre-Israelite Canaan; Reshef, the ancient Syrian god of pestilence and the underworld, but also of well-being (identified with Nergal in Mesopotamia and with Apollo by the Greeks); and Rakib-El, whose name can be interpreted as "charioteer of El," thus becoming a suitable epithet for the moon god, since the crescent of the moon can easily be imagined as a boat navigating across the skies. (The plausibility of this interpretation is heightened by the inscription's mention of Shamash, the sun god, right after Rakif-El, as if the intention was to show that the two celestial bodies formed Hadad's cortege.)

Panamu's dynasty is known from another Aramaic inscription, one written on the statue that King Barrakib erected to his father, Panamu II. The monarch recounted in it his father's political career and how Hadad saved him from the curse that had fallen on his dynastic family. Following the religious traditions of the family, Barrakib invoked Hadad together with Rakib-El, the dynastic god of the kings of Samal, and Shamash. A few years later he had another inscription carved alongside a relief that represented him in Assyrian dress. The monarch asserted that "because of my father's righteousness and my own righteousness, my lord Rakif-El and my lord Tiglathpileser seated me upon my father's throne." On a relief from Harran, in northwestern Mesopotamia, the same ruler proclaimed his faith in the moon god by declaring that his lord is the *baal* ("lord") of Harran.

At Harran the *baal* was the moon god known by the name Sin, which is a late development of the Mesopotamian name Suen. The Akkadians seem to have been responsible for introducing the name of the moon god into southern Sumer, where Suen was identified with the moon god Nanna, the city god of Ur (Roberts, 1972, p. 50), from whence the cult probably traveled to Harran with the Aramean nomads. The cult of the moon god attained high prominence at Harran and throughout the Syro-Mesopotamian region. But the Aramaic inscriptions portray the miscellaneous character of religious life in these lands: the funerary stelae of two priests of the moon god recovered in 1891 at Nerab (southeast of Aleppo), dated to the seventh century BCE, reveal that the priests bore Akkadian theophorous names of Sin but worshiped the moon god under his West Semitic name, Sahar.

The devotion of the Aramean population to the moon god (under whatever name) became a distinctive feature of the religiosity of northern Syria, especially when the area came under Babylonian rule after the destruction of the Assyrian Empire. At the end of the seventh century, Nabopolassar (r. 625–605 BCE) and Nebuchadrezzar (r. 604–562 BCE) settled Babylonians in the various countries they conquered. The cult knew a glorious period under Nabonidus, the last king of Babylon (r. 556–539 BCE), for he rebuilt Ehulhul, the sanctuary of Sin at Harran, which had been destroyed by the Medes in 610 BCE as they crushed the Assyrian remnant of the city (Lambert, 1972, p. 58). In the words of Nabonidus himself and of his mother, the priestess of the god at the sanctuary, Sin was "the king of the gods." Except for the Assyrian king Ashurbanipal (r. 668–627 BCE), who had himself crowned at Harran, and Nabonidus, no Assyro-Babylonian king is known to have given the lord of Harran this epithet, which was usually given to the gods Ashur and Marduk (Levy, 1945–1946, pp. 417–418).

It is likely that there were close religious links between the Arameans of the province of Harran and the Arab tribes of Dedan and Teima in northern Arabia, for one of the sources relating the conquest of the Aramean states by the Assyrian king Adadnirari II (r. 911–891 BCE) mentions the presence of three Temanite *shaykhs* in the area. The prolonged and probably religiously motivated stay of Nabonidus at Teima (Lambert, 1972, p. 60) could not but strengthen these links. The Aramaic inscription of the sixth century BCE found at Teima attest to this to some extent, for bull heads were frequently recovered with the inscriptions, and this seems to suggest the existence of a cult of the moon among the Aramaic-speaking population of the Arabian desert (Teixidor, 1977, pp. 71–75).

ASSOCIATIONS OF GODS. The very few inscriptions that provide information about the Aramean religion during the eighth, seventh, and sixth centuries BCE record only the religious feelings of the ruling class. No indication of what the religious life of the commoners might have been is ever found. In the final analysis the study of the ancient Near Eastern religion comes down to a listing of divine names, with occasional glimpses as to what a given deity must have meant in concrete terms to an individual. Associations of gods of various origins are frequent in the epigraphic texts, but these were probably the result of political confederacies in which different tribes or groups would invoke their respective gods in order to warrant their mutual commitments. In this respect (1) the stele of Zakkur and (2) the treaties concluded by Matiel, an Aramean king of Arpad, deserve special attention.

1. Zakkur was king of Hamath and Luath in the region of modern-day Hama. Hostilities in this northern part of Syria reached a dramatic point at the beginning of the eighth century. The inscription informs us that Zakkur, a usurper, erected the stele for Ilwer, his god, and to express appreciation for Beelshamen's help in delivering him from his many Aramean enemies. The inscription states that Zakkur lifted his hands to the god Beelshamen, and "Beelshamen spoke to me through seers and messengers, and Beelshamen said to me: Fear not, because it was I who made you king" (Gibson, 1975, pp. 8–9). If this was so, it is not clear why the stele was erected to Ilwer and not to Beelshamen. The two gods are mentioned a second time together, along with Shamash and Sahar, on the right face of the stele. *Ilwer* is the Aramaic spelling of the ancient Mesopotamian name *Ilmer*, a storm god who came to be assimilated into Hadad. *Beelshamen* (in Phoenician, *Baalshamim*), on the other hand, is an epithet, meaning "lord of the heavens," that was used in the ancient Near Eastern inscriptions to name the supreme god of any local pantheon. Prior to Greco-Roman times, however, Hadad and Beelshamen/Baalshamim were worshiped by different ethnic groups: Hadad by the Arameans in the Syrian hinterland, and Baalshamim by the Phoenicians on the Mediterranean coast. In Zakkur's inscription, the association of the Phoenician god of heavens to Ilwer/Hadad could have been intended as a political move in order to gain to Zakkur's side the alliance of some western people.
2. Treaties concluded by Aramean rulers indirectly point to the active role that the gods played in daily life, since the gods are always invoked to witness the treaties, and their divine curses are called on should there be any violation of the clauses. Matiel, the Aramean king of Beit Gusi (of which Arpad, some nineteen miles north of Aleppo, was the capital), concluded a treaty with Ashurnirari V (r. 754–745 BCE). To ensure it against possible violations, the Assyrian king summoned the gods to curse Matiel "should he sin against the treaty." Sin and Hadad were called on in a particular manner:

> May the great Lord Sin who dwells in Harran, clothe Mati'ilu, his sons, his officials, and the people of his land in leprosy as in a cloak so that they have to roam the open country, and may he have no mercy on them. . . . May Hadad put an end to Mati'ilu, his land and the people of his land through hunger, want, and famine, so that they eat the flesh of their sons and daughters and it taste as good to them as the flesh of spring lambs. May they be deprived of Adad's thunder so that rain be denied to them. Let dust be their food, pitch their ointment, donkey's urine their drink, rushes their clothing, let their sleeping place be in the corners [of walls]. (Reiner, in Pritchard, 1969, p. 533)

LATE ARAMEAN RELIGION. Exposed to Assyro-Babylonian influences and in continuous contact with the Canaanite traditions, the Arameans amalgamated cults and beliefs that were not distinctly their own. The disparateness of the Aramean religion is best observed in the fifth-century-BCE texts from Egypt (Memphis, Elephantine, and Aswān), where, beside Jewish and Aramean mercenaries, an Aramaic-speaking populace of deportees, refugees, and merchants settled with their families during the Persian period. This motley community worshiped a host of deities among whom the inscriptions single out the god Nabu and the goddess Banit from Babylon, and the Aramean deities Bethel, Anat-Bethel, and Malkat-Shemen ("queen of heaven"). The god Bethel appears in the names of two other no less popular deities, Eshembethel ("name of Bethel") and Herembethel ("sanctuary of Bethel"; the element *herem* is related to the Arabic *ḥaram*, "sacred precinct," the temple thus being deified and made a new hypostasis of Bethel).

In the eclectic society of Egypt under the Persians, when Greeks, Cilicians, Phoenicians, Jews, and Syrians lived together, the religious syncretism cherished by the Asiatics is most manifest in those documents that record oaths sworn by Jews in the name of Egyptian and Aramean gods (in addition to the oaths taken by Yahveh) and in the Aramean personal names that reveal the worship of Bel, Shamash, Nergal, and Atar along with the Egyptian deities. yet nothing is known about the religion of the Arameans living in Egypt. The historian must wait until Greco-Roman times to benefit from the overall picture that Semitic and Greek inscriptions provide for the study of the Syrian religion. In general, religion in the Near East was not subject to the challenge of speculative and critical thought that influenced the daily life in Greece at this time, for the inscriptions do not reflect the impact of new fashions.

Under the Seleucid occupation, in the fourth century BCE, the Syro-Phoenician religion seems more coherent, and the cult of the supreme god, whatever its name (Baal, Bel, Hadad, Beelshamen), appears to have been unified, probably after the cult of Zeus was brought in by the new monarchs. From Kafr Yassif, near Ptolemaïs (modern-day Acre), comes a limestone tablet of the second century BCE bearing a Greek inscription that reads as follows: "To Hadad and Atargatis, the gods who listen to prayer. Diodotus the son of Neoptolemos, on behalf of himself and Philista, his wife, and the children, has dedicated the altar in fulfillment of a vow." At this time Hadad concealed his identity under different names: at Heliopolis (modern-day Baalbek) he became Jupiter Heliopolitanus; at Dura-Europos, Zeus Kurios. At eṭ-Ṭayyibe, near Palmyra, the title *Zeus megistos keraunios*, applied to Beelshamen in a Greco-Palmyrene inscription of 134 CE, reveals one of the best-known epithets of Hadad, "the thunderer," a traditional description of the god's mastery over rain and vegetation. This is expressed differently in the Hauran by the title *Zeus epikarpios*, "the bringer of fruits," to be found on a Greek altar from Bostra.

The acceptance of a god of the heavens led the Syro-Phoenician clergy to couch the belief in this god's supremacy in a new theological notion, that of *caelus aeternus* ("eternal heavens"). The cosmic deity was supposed to preside over the course of the stars and, accordingly, was represented in the iconography as escorted by two acolytes, the sun and the moon. Palmyra offers a good example of this theological development. In 32 CE, at the same time as a cult was inaugurated at the temple of Bel, who was the national god of that city and the surrounding country, Palmyrene inscriptions present Beelshamen as "lord of the world." The lack of archaeological and epigraphic evidence does not permit a full understanding of these two important cults at Palmyra. It is tempting to stress, however, the importance that liturgical processions like the one held at Babylon on the occasion of the New Year might have had for the unification of the two cults. The presence of the temples of Bel and Beelshamen ought to be taken as a sign that these two cults were the result of the coexistence of two originally independent ethnic groups in the city (Teixidor, 1977, pp. 113–114, 136–137).

The commercial activity of Palmyra, lying on one of the main routes of the caravan trade, offered a propitious atmosphere for syncretistic cultic forms. At the same time Palmyra's social structures, organized in a tribal manner, imposed patterns on the entire religious life of the city. The importance of the god Yarhibol is illustrative of the role played by his worshipers, who settled in the neighborhood of the spring of Efca about the beginning of the second millennium BCE. Yarhibol's authority, exercised by means of oracles, transcended the territory of Efca: the god bore witness for some individuals, attested oaths, and allotted lands to temples and individuals. His civic responsibilities were never diminished throughout the entire history of Palmyra (Teixidor, 1979, pp. 29–32). Another tribal group worshiped Aglibol as a moon god, and Malakbel ("angel of Bel") as the sun god. To the Palmyrenes living in Rome, Malakbel was Sol Sanctissimus ("most sacred sun"). At Rome the cult of the sun reached its climax under the Syrian emperor Elagabalus (Heliogabalus). The heliolatry propagated by him succeeded in merging the cult of the emperors with that of Sol Invictus ("invincible sun"), and in 274 CE, under Aurelian, the cult of the sun became a state religion. These religious fashions came into the western Mediterranean from Syria and were transformed by the Roman philosophers; thus the sun became the ever-present image of the intelligible God (Teixidor, 1977, pp. 48–51).

Female deities were prominent in the Aramean pantheons, but their role in the religious life is not always clear, for their personal features are often blurred in the iconography. Atargatis was the Aramean goddess *par excellence*. Nowhere did her cult excel more than at Hierapolis (modern-day Membidj). According to Lucian (*De dea Syria* 33.47–49), statues of Hadad and Atargatis were carried in procession to the sea twice a year. People then came to the holy city from the whole of Syria and Arabia, and even from beyond the Euphrates. In a relief from Dura-Europos, Atargatis and her consort are seated side by side, but Atargatis, flanked by her lions, is larger than Hadad. Hadad's attribute, the bull, is represented in a considerable smaller scale than are the lions. As was the case at Hierapolis, the supremacy of the weather god was overshadowed by the popularity of his female partner. A major representation of the goddess can be seen today at Palmyra on a colossal limestone beam in the temple of Bel. On it Bel is shown in his chariot charging a monster. The combat is witnessed by six deities, one of whom is Atargatis. She is identified by the fish at her feet, an artistic tradition linked to Ascalon, where Atargatis was portrayed as a mermaid (Teixidor, 1979, pp. 73, 74, 76).

During Greco-Roman times the Arab goddess Allat assumed some of the features of other female deities: in Palmyrene iconography she appears both as a Greek Athena and as the Syrian Atargatis. Her sanctuary at Palmyra, excavated in the 1970s, is located in the neighborhood of the temple of Beelshamen, and this fact lends a special character to the city's western quarter, in which Arab tribes settled during the second century BCE. A Greek inscription recently found in this area equates Allat with Artemis (Teixidor, 1979, pp. 53–62). This multiform presence of Allat underlines the formidable impact of the Arab tribes on the Aramaic-speaking peoples of the Near East. Aramean traditions persisted, however. The region of Edessa (modern-day Urfa), called Osrhoene by the Greeks, was ruled by a dynasty of Arab origin from about 132 BCE, but it remained open to cultural influences from Palmyra, Jerusalem, and Adiabene. Notwithstanding the presence of Macedonian colonists and several centuries of commercial activity with the West and the Far East, traditional cults survived. At the beginning of the modern era, Sumatar Harabesi, about twenty-five miles northeast of Harran, became a religious center primarily devoted to the cult of Sin (Drijvers, 1980, pp. 122–128).

PRESENCE OF THE SUPERNATURAL. The inspection of the entrails of sacrificial animals for divinatory purposes was much in favor in Mesopotamia, as is emphasized by its omen collections, and this technique of communication with the supernatural forces was certainly spread over Syria and Palestine (Oppenheim, 1977, pp. 213–217; cf. *2 Kgs.* 16:15). On the other hand, message dreams and oracles must have become an essential feature of Aramean religious life, for in the meager body of Aramaic inscriptions we read about Panamu erecting a statue to Hadad at the god's request and about Zakkur being comforted by Beelshamen through seers and messengers. During Greco-Roman times, occasional texts written in the Aramaic dialects of Palmyra, Hatra (near Mossul), and Sumatar Harabesi (at nearby Urfa, in Turkey) refer too to temples and statues erected by individuals upon the deities' request.

AFTERLIFE. Although the Aramaic texts of all periods mention the names of various deities and occasionally convey the prayers that individuals addressed to them, the epigraphic material rarely supplies any evidence of a belief in an afterlife. Funerary texts do stress the inviolability of the tomb, but this is a universal human concern: the fine epitaph of one of the priests of Nerab in the early seventh century BCE is a good example of this concern:

> Si'-gabbari, priest of Sahar in Nerab. This is his image. Because of my righteousness before him he gave me a good name and prolonged my days. In the day I died my mouth was not bereft of words, and with my eyes I gazed upon the children of the fourth generation: they wept for me and were deeply distraught. They did not lay with me any vessel of silver or bronze: with my shroud they laid me, lest my sarcophagus be plundered in the future. Whoever you are who do wrong and rob me, may Sahar and Nikkal and Nushk cause him to die a miserable death and may his posterity perish! (Teixidor, 1979, pp. 45–46)

The royal inscription of Panamu I of Yady that is carved on the statue of Hadad asks the son who should grasp the scepter and sit on Panamu's throne to do sacrifice to Hadad. It says: "May the soul of Panamu eat with thee, and may the soul of Panamu drink with thee." But this text is not characteristic. The Cilician region of which Panamu was king was never a land of Semites, and consequently the Aramaic inscription may express convictions that are not Semitic. Neither the Aramaic texts from Egypt nor the Palmyrene inscriptions disclose their authors' views on death and afterlife. This silence is especially striking at Palmyra, where hundreds of funerary inscriptions give the name of the deceased in a terse, almost stereotyped manner, and the historian is inclined to conclude that the Palmyrenes did not have any concern whatever for the afterlife.

SEE ALSO Adad; Nanna.

BIBLIOGRAPHY

Abou-Assaf, Ali, Pierre Bordeuil, and Alan R. Millard. *La statue de Tell Fekherye et son inscription bilingue assyro-araméenne.* Recherche sur les civilisations, études assyriologiques, no. 7. Paris, 1982.

Drijvers, Han J. W. *Cults and Beliefs at Edessa.* Études préliminaires aux religions orientales dans l'empire romain, vol. 82. Leiden, 1980.

Dupont-Sommer, André. *Les Araméens.* Paris, 1949.

Gibson, John C. L. *Aramaic Inscriptions,* vol. 2 of *Textbook of Syrian Semitic Inscriptions.* Oxford, 1975.

Greenfield, Jonas C. "The Zakir Inscription and the Danklied." In *Proceedings of the Fifth World Congress of Jewish Studies,* vol. 1. Jerusalem, 1971.

Greenfield, Jonas C. "Aramaic Studies and the Bible." In *Vetus Testamentum Supplement,* vol. 32, *Congress Volume; Vienna 1980.* Leiden, 1981.

Grelot, Pierre. *Documents araméens d'Égypte.* Littératures anciennes du Proche-Orient, vol. 5. Paris, 1972.

Lambert, W. G. "Nabonidus in Arabia." In *Proceedings of the Fifth Seminar for Arabian Studies, Held at the Oriental Institute, Oxford, 22nd and 23rd September 1971.* London, 1972.

Levy, Julius. "The Late Assyro-Babylonian Cult of the Moon and Its Culmination at the Time of Nabonidus." *Hebrew Union College Annual* 19 (1945–1946): 405–489.

Malamat, Abraham. "The Aramaeans." In *Peoples of Old Testament Times,* edited by D. J. Wiseman. Oxford, 1973.

Oppenheim, A. Leo. *Ancient Mesopotamia: Portrait of a Dead Civilization.* Rev. ed. Chicago, 1977.

Porten, Bezalel. *Archives from Elephantine: The Life of an Ancient Jewish Military Colony.* Berkeley, 1968.

Pritchard, J. B., ed. *The Ancient Near East: Supplementary Texts and Pictures relating to the Old Testament.* Princeton, 1969.

Roberts, J. J. M. *The Earliest Semitic Pantheon: A Study of the Semitic Deities Attested in Mesopotamia before Ur III.* Baltimore and London, 1972.

Teixidor, Javier. *The Pagan God: Popular Religion in the Greco-Roman Near East.* Princeton, 1977.

Teixidor, Javiere. *The Pantheon of Palmyra.* Études préliminaires aux religions orientales dans l'empire romain, vol. 79. Leiden, 1979.

New Sources

Brinktrine, J. A. "Notes on Arameans and Chaldeans in South Babylonia in the early 7th cent. BC." *Orientalia* 46 (1977): 304–325.

Catastini, Alessandro. *Profeti e tradizione.* Pisa, 1990.

Collart, Paul, and Jacques Vicari. *Le sanctuaire de Baalshamîn à Palmyre.* 2 vols. Rome, 1969.

Dirven, Lucinda. "The Nature of the Trade Connection between Dura-Europos and Palmyra." *Aram* 8 (1996): 39–54.

Dirven, Lucinda. *The Palmyrenes of Dura-Europos.* Leiden, 1999.

Drijvers, Han J. W. "Afterlife and Funerary Symbolism in Palmyrene Religion." In *La soteriologia dei culti orientali nell'impero romano. Atti del Colloquio Internazionale (Roma 24–28 Settembre 1979)*, edited by Ugo Bianchi and Maarten J. Vermaseren, pp. 709–733. Leiden, 1982.

Dunant, Christiane, and Rolf A. Stucky. *Le sanctuaire de Baalshamîn à Palmyre*, vol. 4. Rome, 2000.

Feldtkeller, Andreas. "Synkretismus und Pluralismus am Beispiel von Palmyra." *Zeitschrift für Religions- und Geistesgeschichte* 48 (1996): 20–38.

Fitzmyer, Joseph A., et al. *An Aramaic Bibliography.* Baltimore, 1992.

Fleming, Daniel E. *The Installation of Baal's High Priestess at Emar: A Window on Ancient Syrian Religion.* Atlanta, 1992.

Frey, Martin. *Untersuchungen zur Religion und zur Religionspolitik des Kaisers Elagabal.* Stuttgart, 1989.

Gawlikowski, Michel. *Aus dem syrischen Götterhimmel. Zur Ikonographie der palmyrenischer Götter.* Mainz, 1981.

Gawlikowski, Michel. "Les dieux de Palmyre." In *Aufstieg und Niedergang der Römischen Welt* 2.18.4, pp. 2605–2658. Berlin and New York, 1990.

Haider, Peter, Manfred Hutter, and Sigfried Kreuzer. *Religionsgeschichte Syriens.* Stuttgart, 1996.

Hoftijzer, Jacob. *Religio Aramaica.* Leiden, 1968.

Kaizer, Ted. *The Religious Life of Palmyra.* Stuttgart, 2002.

Kippenberg, Hans-Georg. *Garizim und Synagoge. Traditionsgeschichtliche Untersuchungen zur samaritanischen Religion der aramäischen Periode.* Berlin, 1971.

Kleiner, Gerhard. "Baalbek und Palmyra." *Damaszener Mitteilungen, hrsg. von dem Deutschen Archäologischen Institut (Station Damaskus)* 4 (1989): 191–203.

Lipinski, Edward. "Aram et Israël du x au VIII s. av. n.è." *Acta antiqua Academiae Scientiarum Hungaricae* 27 (1979): 49–102.

Lipinski, Edward. *Studies in Aramaic Inscriptions and Onomastics*, vol. 2. Leuven, 1994.

Lipinski, Edward. *The Arameans. Their Ancient History, Culture, Religion.* Leuven, 2000.

Lipinski, Edward, ed. *State and Temple Economy in the Ancient Near East.* Leuven, 1979.

Millar, Fergus. *The Roman Near East.* Cambridge, Mass., and London, 1993.

Naveh, Joseph. *Amulets and Magic Bowls: Aramaic Incantations of Late Antiquity.* Jerusalem, 1985.

Parlasca, Klaus. "Die Stadtgöttin Palmyras." *Bonner Jahrbücher* 184 (1984): 167–176.

Sader, Hélène. *Les Etates araméens de Syrie depuis leur fondation jusqu' à leur transformation en provinces assyriennes.* Beirut, 1987.

Schmidt-Colinet, Andreas, ed. *Palmyra.* Mainz, 1995.

Schwarz, Gunther. *'Und Jesus Sprach'. Untersuchungen zur aramaeischen Urgestalt der Worte Jesu.* Stuttgart, 1987.

Segal, Judah Benzion. *Edessa, the Blessed City.* Oxford, 1970.

Sokoloff, Michael, ed. *Arameans, Aramaic, and the Aramaic Literary Tradition.* Ramat-Gan, Israel, 1983.

Tarrier, Dominique. "Banquets rituels en Palmyrène et en Nabatène." *Aram* 7 (1995): 165–182.

Teixidor, Javier. "Cultes d'Asie Mineure et de Thrace à Palmyre." *Semitica* 32 (1982): 97–100.

Tubach, Jürgen. *Im Schatten des Sonnengottes. Der Sonnenkult in Edessa, Harran und Hatra am Vorabend der christlichen Mission.* Wiesbaden, 1985.

See also the various monographic issues of *Aram*, a scientific journal, concerned with all aspects of Syro-Mesopotamian cultures.

JAVIER TEIXIDOR (1987)
Revised Bibliography

ĀRANYAKAS SEE BRĀHMAṆAS AND ĀRAṆYAKAS

ARARBANEL, ISAAC SEE ABRAVANEL, ISAAC

ARCHAEOLOGY AND RELIGION. Even in contemporary circumstances, with living informants and known histories, the analysis of religion presents formidable obstacles to the scholar. It follows that the exploration of prehistoric religious ideas and institutions is even more difficult. The archaeologist must cope with the partial evidence, mute artifacts, and immature methodologies that are available. Given these barriers, it is not surprising that over the past century archaeology and the study of religion have maintained a close but uneasy relationship. Yet both of these broad intellectual endeavors have evolved slowly into more systematic disciplines, and their relationship has matured into a mutually supportive one.

HISTORICAL PERSPECTIVE. Archaeology, the study of past cultures from their material remains, is a mongrel discipline, and only a few of its many heritages are respectable. The beginnings of archaeology included looting for the collection of antiquities, searches for lost biblical tribes, and excavations to verify claims of national, racial, or ethnic superiority. The evolution of archaeology as a scholarly field took distinctly different paths in different world regions, and its relationship with the study of religion varied accordingly.

Protohistoric archaeology. In the Near East and the Mediterranean, the nineteenth-century decipherment of the Egyptian hieroglyphs, Mesopotamian cuneiform, and other ancient scripts began the legitimate tradition of Old World archaeology. Classical and biblical archaeology, Egyptology, and much of Mesopotamian archaeology generally have been very concerned with the discovery of new texts, the verification and refinement of the information presented in the existing historical corpus, and the extension of an understanding of the historical periods into the immediately preceding prehistoric epochs. This aspect of archaeology—as a supplement to textual scholarship—was, and remains, an important element in the study of religion. It is certainly the most important aspect of archaeology for exploring the origins of the major Old World religious traditions. Excavations have unearthed many of the tablets, scrolls, and inscriptions that form the corpus of textual materials on the origins and nature of the religions of the ancient Near East. This contribution of archaeology to the study of religion continues, as demonstrated by the impact on biblical studies of recent discoveries of early texts during such excavations as those at Ugarit and Ebla in Syria.

However, excavations at other sites—Jericho in Palestine, Ur and Uruk in Mesopotamia, and Nimrud and Nineveh in Assyria—have also yielded the material remains of these ancient cultures and the broader context of early cult and ritual. Such excavations have provided a direct view of the material culture of religious life—temples, shrines, images, and artifacts. The earlier levels at these sites have also revealed the evolution of religion leading into the historical periods. Structure foundations, early tombs, the strata of tells, and their associated artifacts allow researchers to trace the prehistoric development of rituals and cults, mortuary practices, and multifunctional temple complexes in ancient Palestine, Egypt, and Sumer.

Pre-Columbian archaeology. In the New World, archaeology and the study of religion also started from a historical base. The Spanish conquest and colonization of Mexico and Peru left a legacy of historical description by the conquistadors, inquisitors, and bureaucrats who administered the conquered empires, kingdoms, and tribes of the American Indians. The descriptions from contact and colonial periods throughout the Americas were rich in their coverage of pre-Columbian religion, because it was of particular concern to the missionaries and bureaucrats who were the primary historians and ethnographers of American cultures. In addition to these European texts, a number of native bark and deerskin folding books (codices) survived the colonial era and provided an indigenous perspective on the pre-Columbian culture. Scholars of this combined historical and ethnographic corpus, ethnohistorians such as Eduard Seler, began the tradition of studies of pre-Columbian religion.

By the beginning of the twentieth century, the gradual and continuing decipherment of the hieroglyphs of the Maya civilization of Mexico and Central America led such scholars as Sylvanus G. Morley back into the archaeological exploration of the gods and rites of earlier periods. In the first half of the twentieth century archaeological excavations worked back from the rich ethnohistorical record to uncover the art, iconography, and glyphic texts of earlier pre-Columbian religions. Interpretations relied heavily on later ethnographical and historical records, a methodology referred to as the "direct-historical approach" to archaeology. The earlier form and context of Indian religion was elucidated by extensive excavations at the great prehistoric urban and ceremonial centers of the New World: ancient Maya centers such as Copán in Honduras and Chichén Itzá in the Yucatán, as well as imperial capitals such as that of the Aztec at Tenochtitlán (now Mexico City) and the Inca capital at Cuzco, Peru.

As pre-Columbian research progressed, it enriched the cross-cultural study of religion. The limits of previous concepts of religious behavior were stretched by consideration of the nature and scale of Aztec human sacrifice, Inca ancestor worship, and Maya fascination with astronomical lore and calendric ritual. Explorations of all these phenomena involved a combination of colonial history, epigraphic research, and direct-historical field archaeology.

Prehistoric archaeology. Because of the combination of historical and archaeological approaches, the high civilizations of the Near East, the Mediterranean, Mesoamerica, and Peru initially provided the most information of the greatest reliability for studies of cross-cultural variation in religious behavior and of the history of religious traditions. Yet it was the archaeology of less politically complex societies in North America and Europe that led to most of the methodological and theoretical insights of this century. These breakthroughs eventually allowed the discipline to transcend its dependence on textual evidence and the direct-historical approach. Perhaps it was the weakness of the historical record for these areas that led to more innovative approaches. Alternatively, it may have been that the less complex structure of many of these societies—egalitarian bands, tribes, and chiefdoms—made them more amenable to cross-cultural analogy and comparison, because most ethnographically studied societies were at these levels.

Whatever the impetus may have been, the use of ethnographic analogy and anthropological comparison was widespread in interpretations of the archaeological record in North America. By the 1940s and 1950s Walter Taylor, Julian H. Steward, and others were advocating an even closer association between anthropology and archaeology and their use in interpreting the artifactual remains of ancient societies. Steward emphasized that cultures were not just collections of traits but integrated systems adapted to their environments. He stressed that human culture, like any other system, was patterned and that these patterns were reflected in the nature and location of sites and in the distribution and types of ancient artifacts.

The ideas of Steward and "culture ecologists" like him led to new approaches to the archaeological reconstruction of ancient cultures. In the 1950s, in Peru, Gordon Willey first applied the method known as "settlement-pattern studies," that is, the analysis of site distribution and variation, to reconstruct the nature and evolution of prehistoric societies. In Europe, Graham Clarke used culture ecology to identify ancient subsistence and economic systems accurately. These new approaches to interpretation were further strengthened by technical breakthroughs such as the radiocarbon and tree-ring dating methods, and by improved field techniques, which could now recover such trace remains as preserved human feces (coprolites) and microscopic fossil pollen.

Religion, unfortunately, was initially ignored by these progressive developments in archaeology. The growing theoretical and methodological sophistication of archaeology had its roots firmly in culture ecology and other materialist approaches. Some influential thinkers, such as Leslie White, explicitly argued that religion was of no importance in cultural evolution, that it was "epiphenomenal." Others, such as Steward, felt that while religion was essential to the core of cultural behavior, it was, unfortunately, inscrutable to archaeological analysis. While many archaeologists believed that all aspects of culture left patterns in the archaeological record, they also felt that the patterning in religious behavior was too complex, idiosyncratic, or obscure to be accurately perceived. Thus, throughout the period of transformation in archaeology in the 1940s and 1950s, the archaeology of religion progressed systematically only in those regions and periods that could be related to historically known religions. Analysis of fully prehistoric ideology was left to those who were willing to apply unsystematic and subjective interpretations, often drawn from popular psychology, to ancient architecture, artifacts, or art.

The "New Archaeology." It took a second revolution in archaeological interpretation, beginning in the 1960s, to bring modern archaeology and the study of religion together as collaborative disciplines. Lewis R. Binford in the Americas and David Clarke in Britain were among the archaeologists who began to argue that the capabilities of archaeology could be broadened through the use of analogy to ethnographic societies and, above all, through computer-assisted statistical approaches. In a series of controversial papers and texts, these self-designated New Archaeologists decried the complacency of conventional archaeological methodology, especially its reluctance to explore the nature of ancient societies beyond questions of chronology and subsistence. Binford argued that hypotheses concerning the nature of ancient social or even religious systems could be drawn from ethnographic comparisons and could then be verified or discredited by vigorous statistical examination of the patterning in the archaeological remains. These new approaches and greater ambitions for archaeology were tested, generally verified, and refined by studies of the Indians of the southwestern United States and ethnoarchaeological studies of the Inuit (Eskimo) of the Arctic, the !Kung San of southern Africa, and the Aborigines of Australia.

While there was never an explicit, universal acceptance of the new approaches, they were gradually, perhaps unconsciously, absorbed into many branches of archaeology, including research on prehistoric religion. Numerous studies of fully prehistoric ideological systems began in this period. Gerald Hawkins and Alexander Thom began computer-assisted studies of the patterning and astronomical alignments of Stonehenge and other megalithic constructions of Bronze Age and Neolithic Europe (c. 4000–1800 BCE). These researches gave rise to the subdiscipline of archaeoastronomy, research on the ancients' concern with astronomy and astrology, and this concern's reflection in architecture and settlement patterns. Studies of the patterning and placement of markings, images, and art of the Stone Age were begun by scholars such as Alexander Marshack, André Leroi-Gourhan, and Peter J. Ucko. All of these studies drew upon statistical assessment and analogy to ethnographically known peoples in order to elucidate the structure of Stone Age religion.

Such researches demonstrated that early prehistoric religion was amenable to archaeological interpretation. Current research has continued and expanded the scrutiny of archaeological patterns for material reflections of ancient religious behavior. Studies by John Fritz, Joyce Marcus, and Evon Z. Vogt, to name a few, have examined the structure of ideological conceptions as reflected in architecture and site placement in the Anasazi culture of New Mexico (c. 600–1300 CE) and the ancient Maya civilization of Guatemala (c. 300–900 CE). Central-place theory and other forms of locational analysis have been used to study site placement in regional landscapes, in order to deduce how worldviews might have affected the selection and relative importance of ceremonial centers and shrines.

Religion and evolutionary theory. The ambitions of contemporary archaeological methodology to decipher ancient belief systems, though still struggling, have led to a renewed interest in the role of religion in the evolution of human culture. For the first half of the twentieth century, economic, Marxist, and ecological theory dominated studies of the prehistoric development of civilizations. In retrospect it is now clear that this materialist bias was inevitable, given the methodological limitations of archaeology. With the conviction that prehistoric religious systems were beyond scientific analysis, theoretical assessment of cultural change and development had naturally turned to other factors. However, the new methodological concerns resulted in a resurgence of interest in the role of ideology in prehistoric change. In the 1970s archaeologists from diverse theoretical backgrounds began to call for a new look at religion's impact on the rise and fall of civilizations. Archaeologists have responded in recent publications, discussing the general evolutionary role of ancient religion as well as the specific effects of ideology on the formation and reinforcement of early state polities.

This revived interest in the role of religion in the evolution of culture has led to new theoretical perspectives even in the archaeology of the great protohistoric civilizations. Most archaeologists of late prehistoric Mesopotamia, for example, no longer turn exclusively to the effects of irrigation or demographic pressure for the causes of state formation. For decades, historical and anthropological scholars, including Mircea Eliade and Paul Wheatley, have argued that the ceremonial center was the nucleus of the early city. Anthropological archaeologists have turned again to such perspectives in their examination of earlier prehistoric developments.

For example, a series of researches have examined patterns of pottery distribution of the northern Mesopotamian Halaf and Samarran cultures (c. 5500–4500 BCE). The identified patterns of intersite similarity and difference in design-element distributions have been seen to reflect the territories of early chiefdoms. The distinctive styles of the chiefdoms are also seen as indications of the integration and communication provided by early ceremonial centers and their religious rituals. In these interpretations the early ceremonial center is related archaeologically to a presumed function of reinforcement of collective identity, a role seen as critical in the evolution of later, more complex societies. Thus, the theoretical perspectives of thinkers such as Émile Durkheim, Max Weber, and Eliade, too long alien to archaeology, have been returned to field research and interpretation. In the process religious behavior has been incorporated into anthropological assessments of prehistoric cultural evolution.

In discussing the later period of the formation of humankind's first civilization, ancient Sumer, archaeologists continue to emphasize the importance of irrigation, demographics, trade, and warfare in the genesis of urban society. However, they also incorporate ideology into the evolutionary equation—and not merely as a Marxist, after-the-fact legitimation of political authority. For example, Robert M. Adams, in *Heartland of Cities* (1981), takes a holistic perspective on the origins of the state in Mesopotamia. He sees early city-states and their proto-urban antecedents as centers of security in all senses: subsistence security because of their role in irrigation, storage of surplus, and trade; defensive security provided by a large nucleated population; and spiritual security and identity in the form of the temple. The ceremonial centers of Ubaid times (4500–3500 BCE) evolved into the urban centers of Uruk times (3500–3100 BCE) because they became central places servicing the full range of economic, social, and spiritual needs. The temple-dominated economies of such centers were also preadapted to legitimate the state political authority that emerged in later periods.

Similarly, perspectives on cultural evolution in the New World have begun to reincorporate religion into interpretations of the rise and fall of civilizations. Kent V. Flannery and Robert Drennan have argued that religion and ritual were vital to the formation of early complex pre-Columbian societies such as the Olmec civilization of Mexico. Geoffrey W. Conrad and the author of this article have presented reinterpretations of the importance and nature of such religious phenomena as the Inca worship of royal mummies and the Aztec central cult of mass human sacrifice. These new perspectives argue that such cults helped to drive the explosive expansion of both the Inca Empire of Peru (1438–1532) and the Aztec hegemony in Mexico (1428–1519). Indeed, they contend that due to religious and political institutionalization the cults became irreversible forces that destabilized these pre-Columbian empires and predisposed them to swift disintegration.

So, in both the Old World and the Americas archaeologists have rediscovered the study of religion. Appropriate methodologies for the study of prehistoric religion have been suggested and continue to be explored. Meanwhile, theoretical models for prehistoric cultural evolution have reincorporated the study of religion into considerations of social change. In turn, these researches and interpretations in archaeology have broadened the temporal and geographic range of information available to scholars of comparative religion. The future holds even more promise as methodologies improve, theory becomes more sophisticated, and the symbiotic relationship of these two disciplines grows.

RECENT CONTRIBUTIONS. The historical development of the relationship between archaeology and religion involved a sequence of important projects, discoveries, and theoretical breakthroughs. However, there also have been many contributions by archaeology to the study of religion in particular regions and periods. Here it is only possible to cite a few of the noteworthy finds.

Paleolithic religion. The archaeology of religion in the Paleolithic period, the Old Stone Age, is one area in which new methodologies and concerns have led to surprising discoveries. It is now possible to say with certainty that *homo religiosus* predates *Homo sapiens* by a considerable period.

Humanity's ancestor of a million to a hundred thousand years ago, *Homo erectus,* had an average cranial capacity of about two-thirds that of modern humans. Yet *Homo erectus* left traces of possible religious or ritual behavior. This evidence includes finds of ocher earth pigments (perhaps for body painting) at Terra Amata in France and the discovery of *Homo erectus* skull remains at the Zhoukoudian cave in China that may indicate ritual cannibalism. These data can be contested, being based only on analogy to ethnographically known belief systems. There can be no question, however, about the rich spiritual life of Neanderthal humans, *Homo sapiens neanderthalensis.* Beginning about one hundred thousand years ago, this robust early form of *Homo sapiens* devoted considerable energy to the burial of the dead, as shown by excavation of Neanderthal cemeteries in France, Germany, and the Near East. Ritual treatments include the use of red ocher, sometimes grave goods, and, in at least one instance, offerings of flowers.

In the Upper Paleolithic period, beginning about thirty-five thousand years ago, anatomically modern *Homo sapiens* appeared, and made a quantum leap in art and religious imagery. New statistical approaches to patterning in the archaeological record have been applied to generate specific hypotheses on the spectacular cave paintings, portable art, and complex, enigmatic markings characteristic of the late epoch of the Stone Age. Ucko, Andrée Rosenfeld, and other anthropologists have turned to the ethnography of contemporary hunting and gathering societies for analogies. Their interpretations emphasize hunting magic, totemism, and shamanism. Leroi-Gourhan uses statistical assessment of patterning in the forms and distributions of specific images in the caves. He has produced a structural, almost linguistic, analysis of message and meaning in Paleolithic art. Marshack also turns to statistical assessment in his work on the markings and iconographs of the Paleolithic. However, he concludes that the complex symbolic system was concerned with lunar cycles and other calendric patterns, as well as with fertility and sympathetic magic. Taken together, recent archaeological studies constitute a considerable corpus on the fully prehistoric belief systems of early humankind.

The early Near East. In the Near East, the heartland of many of the world's major religions, the contribution of archaeology to the study of the origins of these traditions extends back to the seventh and eighth millennia BCE. Excavations by Kathleen M. Kenyon in preceramic Jericho and finds at related sites (e.g., Beidha, Ain Ghazal, Tell Ramad) have revealed burial practices and iconography emphasizing skull worship. James Mellaart's excavations in seventh-millennium levels at Çatal Hüyük, Anatolia, have uncovered elaborate religious imagery in shrines with plaster sculptures and artwork incorporating the skulls of bulls. Continuity of some iconographic elements, including bullhead designs, suggests that these earliest Neolithic religions may have influenced the later cults of the northern Mesopotamian Halaf and Samarran chiefdoms. In turn, excavations at ceremonial centers of these chiefdoms, such as Tell es-Sawwan, indicate that they greatly influenced the temple complexes of the Ubaid culture, the first phase of the Sumerian civilization in southern Mesopotamia. Thus, recent evidence suggests a continuous evolution of religious systems leading to the historical Near Eastern religions.

Archaeological research since the 1930s has unearthed a wealth of data on the religion of the later high civilization of Mesopotamia, and at early Sumerian centers such as Eridu, Uruk, Ur, and Tepe Gawra. This evidence has permitted detailed characterization and dating of the development of Sumerian temple architecture, art, and iconography, as well as the changing cultural context of religion and ritual. Concerning later, historical periods (after 3000 BCE), the excavations at Ur in the 1930s and 1940s by C. Leonard Woolley provided a clear glimpse of Sumerian elite life and state religion in that city-state's temple complexes and royal cemetery. Twentieth-century excavations sponsored by British, French, German, and American institutions at Ur, Uruk, Mari, Babylon, Nineveh, and other Mesopotamian sites have also recovered thousands of tablets. From the recovered texts and inscriptions, the epigraphers Samuel Noah Kramer and Thorkild Jacobsen have reconstructed the nature of theology, ritual, and myth in ancient Sumer, Akkad, and Babylon. Meanwhile, the excavations and tablets of Nuzi, Susa, Mari, and other sites have provided evidence on the identity and cults of the surrounding, previously shadowy, historical peoples—the Hurrians, the Elamites, and the kingdom of Mari.

Perhaps the most important and unexpected discovery of recent years came from excavations by an Italian team at Tell Mardikh, in Syria. In 1975 they found a royal archive of over fifteen thousand tablets, detailing the history and culture of the third-millennium kingdom of Ebla. The ongoing decipherment of the Ebla tablets is revolutionizing current understanding of early Near Eastern history and religion. These texts have provided a new perspective on the ancient Near East and promise to provide a closer view of the origins of the religious systems of later times.

Biblical archaeology. One beneficiary of these discoveries of early kingdoms in adjacent regions has been biblical archaeology. At Ras Shamra in Syria, Claude F.-A. Schaeffer directed excavations, uncovering the ancient city of Ugarit and thousands of Ugaritic tablets. These texts have had a profound impact on biblical studies, because they detail the nature of second-millennium Canaanite religion and society. Meanwhile, progress in biblical archaeology in Palestine itself has been substantial and steady. Literally hundreds of sites relating to the Old Testament period have been excavated in the past half-century, including such important sites as Jericho, Jerusalem, Megiddo, Tel Dan, Gezer, Shechem (modern-day Nablus), Lachish, and Samaria.

One should not overlook the contributions of archaeology to the historical study of religions of later times in the Near East. Archaeology has provided a richer context of material evidence to check, refine, and extend the historical record on religion in ancient Egypt, early Islam, and early Christianity. Furthermore, many of the actual historical and religious texts have been recovered by systematic archaeological excavations, including most of the Dead Sea Scrolls and numerous papyrus texts in Egypt. The recent excavations and discoveries at Nag Hammadi in Egypt illustrate the close interplay between religious textual studies and archaeology. Archaeologists returned there in the 1970s to excavate areas in a zone where Gnostic texts had been fortuitously discovered decades earlier. These ongoing excavations are establishing the material context of these important documents.

China and India. In the study of the religious systems of Asia, archaeology has been traditionally limited to a supplementary role. Excavations have recovered texts and inscriptions and have confirmed or refined the interpretations of historical scholarship. The bronzes, oracle bones, bamboo tablets, and other inscriptions so critical to the study of early Chinese religion have been recovered in large numbers by the systematic, albeit largely atheoretical, archaeology of modern China. Excavations at the Shang tombs at Anyang (c. 1400 BCE) and the mortuary complex of the first emperor (200 BCE) have revealed the spectacular nature of early Chinese religion and its critical role in polity and power. Indeed, new theoretical perspectives by historical scholars, such as David Keightley, have argued that the genesis of China's first states and the form of its early theology are inseparable.

Modern anthropological archaeology has only just begun in China. Yet already more methodologically rigorous approaches to prehistoric and protohistoric periods are beginning to challenge traditional interpretations. In a series of works K. C. Zhang has compared texts with archaeological evidence and datings to show that the early Xia, Shang, and Zhou dynasties may have been largely contemporaneous polities rather than a linear sequence of dynasties. Such broad reconsiderations of chronology and history will require parallel rethinking of the history of early state religion in China. Recent archaeological contributions to the study of early Chinese religion also include evidence on belief systems in the Neolithic Yangshao (4000–2500 BCE) and Longshan (2500–1800 BCE) periods. He Bingdi and other Chinese archaeologists have argued that iconography, settlement layouts, and even domestic architecture in these village societies reflect uniquely regional views on cosmology, ancestor worship, and fertility. While largely based on analogy to later religions, such interpretations show the potential of future archaeological research.

The archaeology of the Indus Valley civilization (2400–1800 BCE) of Pakistan and India is another field in which evidence and analogy can be used to project intriguing, but still uncertain, connections with historical religions. In this case, the architecture, art, and iconography of Mohenjo-Daro, Harappa, Lothal, and other cities of the Indus Valley civilization have been carefully compared to the Vedic texts on early Hindu ritual and belief. General conceptual parallels have been inferred from the archaeological evidence, such as concerns with bathing and the ritual use of water, or the probable existence of a rigid, castelike social organization. Archaeologists and Vedic scholars have also noted many quite specific shared traits between Indus Valley artifacts, glyphs, or iconography and historical descriptions of Aryan culture in the Vedas, for example, the form of incense burners, the lotus sitting position, and possible prototypes of specific deities. Such interpretations are complicated by growing evidence that the Indus Valley civilization was created by a racially and linguistically Dravidian, rather than Aryan, people. Nonetheless, the archaeology of the region does seem to point to Indus Valley culture for the origins of many aspects of the Hindu tradition.

The Mediterranean and Europe. Archaeological research in Greece and Egypt has always been dominated by textual and historical studies. As in biblical studies the archaeologist has provided texts and inscriptions as well as evidence on the broader material context of early religion. This contribution of assistance to epigraphic research often has been of great significance. For example, the excavations of the sacred capital at Amarna, in Egypt, have uncovered iconography, architecture, and texts that vastly expand existing views on the religion of Egypt and adjacent cultures in the fourteenth century BCE.

Archaeological research has also pushed back the chronological limits of the knowledge of religion in ancient Egypt and Greece. In Egypt current understanding of the antiquity and evolution of religion has been extended by the excavation of Neolithic cemeteries and of late predynastic mastaba tombs, the mudbrick antecedents of the pyramids. In the Aegean and Balkans, recent excavations have established a chronological and cultural context for the study of religion, including ample evidence concerning Mycenaean and Minoan religion and even earlier (third and fourth millennia BCE) shrines, funerary practices, and religious icons. Marija Gimbutas and other archaeologists have carried interpretations on religion back to the earliest Neolithic developments in eastern Europe in the seventh millennium BCE. Gimbutas has synthesized the evidence from excavations of shrines, burials, and figurine iconography to reconstruct the general form, specific deities, and development of the indigenous cults of Old Europe. While still highly speculative in nature, such contributions demonstrate the growing potential of archaeology for the study of fully prehistoric religious systems.

The prehistoric archaeology of western Europe has been transformed in recent years by new approaches, including the studies already mentioned on Paleolithic religion and on astronomical patterning in Neolithic and Bronze Age megalithic shrines. Of even greater significance has been a revolution in chronology and evolutionary interpretation led by Colin Renfrew and other British archaeologists. In the 1960s the correction of errors in the radiocarbon dating method produced new chronological alignments for all of European prehistory, redating the beginning of megaliths in northern Europe to before 3500 BCE. It is now clear that these and other spectacular manifestations of early European religion can no longer be defined historically or interpreted iconographically in terms of influences or parallels with the Aegean world. As a result, the study of religion and cultural development in prehistoric Europe has turned to the new approaches and ethnographic perspectives popular in American archaeology. European and American prehistoric studies have entered an exciting period of cross-fertilization in anthropological concepts and archaeological methods.

The Americas. In the New World methodological and theoretical assessments have enriched the traditional ethnohistorical and direct-historical approaches to the study of pre-Columbian religion. Prehistoric cultures from diverse regions, such as the Mississippian peoples of the southeastern United States (c. 1000–1500), the Pueblo cultures of the Southwest (300–1300), and the Moche civilization of Peru (200 BCE–600 CE), have been studied by systematic statistical analysis of patterning in their archaeological remains. In the search for patterns, settlement distribution, grave goods, architectural alignments, distribution of design elements on potsherds, and many other potential reflections of ancient social groups, political divisions, and belief systems have been examined. These studies, along with broader theoretical assessments, have led to a tremendous increase in understanding prehistoric religion in the New World and its interrelationship with the political and social evolution of pre-Columbian tribes, chiefdoms, and states.

These new approaches also hold the prospect of resolving long-standing issues in the study of pre-Columbian religion. Since the 1950s George Kubler and other scholars have warned against the general practice of simply imposing the historically known meaning of contact-period religious artifacts and art onto the evidence from earlier periods. Kubler has pointed out that, over the centuries, shifts or even complete disjunctions in the meaning of religious symbols may have occurred. Systematic approaches to patterning in the record may provide methods of testing ethnohistorically presumed meanings through study of the distribution and association of artifacts and images.

New archaeological discoveries and new approaches to interpretation are also challenging long-standing opinions on specific aspects of pre-Columbian religious studies. For example, many scholars studying the religions of the high civilizations of Mesoamerica and Peru have begun to doubt the utility of seeking specific identities or referents for individual deities. Instead, they are analyzing art and iconography for evidence of concepts and structures in pre-Columbian belief systems. The results have shown that pre-Columbian religions were as laden with sexual symbolism, manifold godheads, and structural complexities as the religions of East Asia. Archaeological research is also discovering unexpected aspects of pre-Columbian religions—for example, the importance of ancestor worship among the ancient Classic Maya civilization of Central America (300–900 CE) and the shamanistic nature of the religion of the early Olmec culture in Mexico (1300–600 BCE).

Prospects. Beyond the small sample cited here, archaeology has contributed to the study of religion in virtually every world region and period. The archaeology of Japan, Southwest Asia, Australia, sub-Saharan Africa, Central Asia, and other zones has involved extensive excavation and interpretation of the material evidence of religious behavior. As archaeological research broadens in geographical range and further develops its methodological tools, it will become an even more important aspect of the study of religion. It will continue to extend the breadth and depth of scholars' search for variations, connections, structural similarities, and cognitive parallels in human religious systems.

SEE ALSO Cities; Prehistoric Religions, article on Old Europe.

BIBLIOGRAPHY

A good general history of archaeology in the Old World is Glyn E. Daniel's *A Short History of Archaeology* (London, 1981), and for the New World see Gordon R. Willey and Jeremy A. Sabloff's *A History of American Archaeology,* 2d ed. (London, 1981). An important presentation of the new, anthropological approaches to archaeology is Lewis R. Binford's *An Archaeological Perspective* (New York, 1972). Recent works exemplifying the integration of religion into archaeological approaches to cultural evolution are *Ideology, Power, and Prehistory,* edited by Daniel Miller and Christopher Tilley (Cambridge, 1984), and *Religion and Empire* by Geoffrey W. Conrad and myself (Cambridge, 1984). For innovative syntheses of Paleolithic archaeology and religion, see Peter J. Ucko and Andrée Rosenfeld's *Palaeolithic Cave Art* (New York, 1967); André Leroi-Gourhan's *The Dawn of European Art* (Cambridge, 1982); and Alexander Marshack's *The Roots of Civilization* (New York, 1972). A good regional review of archaeology in the Near East is Charles L. Redman's *The Rise of Civilization* (San Francisco, 1978). For later periods and biblical archaeology see Howard F. Vos's *Archaeology in Bible Lands* (Chicago, 1977). Kwangzhi Zhang's *Shang Civilization* (New Haven, 1980) includes consideration of early Chinese religion, while Zhang's *The Archaeology of Ancient China,* 3d ed. (New Haven, Conn., 1977), is the definitive general synthesis. A review of evidence on the Indus Valley civilization and Vedic parallels is given in the first chapters of Arun Bhattacharjee's *History of Ancient India* (New Delhi, 1979). *The Goddesses and Gods of Old Europe, 6500–3500 B.C.,* by Marija Gimbutas (Berkeley, Calif., 1982) is a notable study of archaeological evidence on early European religion and an excellent example of the integration of archaeology, iconographic analysis, and the study of religion. For the Americas, traditional regional syntheses of art, archaeology, and religions can be found in *The Handbook of Middle American Indians,* 16 vols., edited by Robert Wauchope (Austin, 1964–1976), and *The Handbook of South American Indians,* 7 vols., edited by Julian H. Steward (Washington, 1946–1959). For broader structural and conceptual approaches to the nature of pre-Columbian religion, see Miguel León-Portilla's *Time and Reality in the Thought of the Maya* (Boston, 1973); my own *Viracocha* (Cambridge, Mass., 1981); and especially Eva Hunt's *The Transformation of the Hummingbird* (Ithaca, N.Y., 1977).

ARTHUR ANDREW DEMAREST (1987)

ARCHETYPES. The English word *archetype* derives from a Greek word that is prominent in the writings of religious thinkers during the Hellenistic period. In modern times, the term has been used to refer to fundamental structures in the human psyche as well as in religious life. In either sense, an archetype is a pattern that determines human experience (whether on a conscious or an unconscious level) and makes itself felt as something both vital and holy.

THE MEANING OF ARCHETYPE. The Greek compound derives from the combined meaning of two words, *tupos* and *archē,* both of which have double referents. *Tupos* refers both to a physical blow and to the concrete manifestation of its impact. Hence, the seal and its imprint are both *tupoi.* Further, the relation between any form and its derivative forms is indicated by this term. For example, the cast that molds the statue and the statue itself are both *tupoi,* as is the mold that is placed around a fruit by a grower in order to shape it as it grows. Internal and invisible molding is also a kind of *tupos* as in biological generation: the child is the *tupos* of its parent. Finally, as in the English cognate, *type, tupos* comes to signify any character or nature that is shared by numerous, related phenomena with the result that they appear to have been cast from the same mold: for example, the eucalyptus is a type of tree.

The nominal prefix *archē* refers to what is first or original, both in a temporal and in an ontological sense. As such, it may indicate equally the heavenly powers that govern the cosmos, the ruler of a realm, or the vital organs that empower life in the body.

Together, these two Greek words make up *to archētupon,* or "the archetype," a term that was not so commonly used as either of its components but that does appear with some frequency in the rather esoteric writings of certain Hellenistic religious philosophers. Already in *De opificio mundi* (1.69), the Jewish theologian Philo Judaeus refers to the archetype as the *imago dei* ("god-image") residing in and molding humanity in the likeness of God.

Later, Irenaeus uses the term when, in his lengthy treatise attacking the so-called Christian heretics (*Against Heresies* 2.7.5), he recounts a Valentinian version of the cosmogony. According to the Valentinians, a group of gnostic Christians, the world was not created by God out of nothing, but rather it was the fabrication of a demiurge, who copied directly or indirectly (depending on the version) an archetypal world (the Pleroma) that existed outside himself. In this view, the Demiurge creates in the manner of a mechanic who builds a robot that simulates, but does not replicate, a living model.

A third use of *to archētupon* during the Hellenistic period is found in the writings of the Platonic mystic Plotinus. He intuited a divine realm of which the creation was a mere reflection. Plotinus reminds his reader to observe the regularity and order exhibited by the natural world. This harmonious state of affairs, he claims, depends on a higher reality for its laws of being. The phenomenological realm does not truly exist, according to Plotinus, but appears at the boundaries between true being, that is, the One, and the void external to it. Plotinus's cosmogony thus presents a third use of the imagery associated with the term *archetype.* At work here is neither Philo's idea of an inner force (inspiration) nor the Valentinian concept of the craftsman basing his creation on a model (imitation), but rather the metaphor of reflection that depicts an emptiness upon which is cast—as if upon a mirror—the form of a divine but transcendent reality.

For all three philosophers, the word *archetupon* is used to depict a cosmogonic principle. Common to all three belief systems is the conviction that the creation of the cosmos, including the creation of man, depends on the preexistence of a transcendental reality.

During the twentieth century, the word *archetype* has been rehabilitated by the historian of religions Mircea Eliade and the depth psychologist C. G. Jung. Eliade, in his study of the religions of humankind, uses the term to name the sacred paradigms that are expressed in myth and articulated in ritual. For Jung, the concept of the archetype can also be applied to the dynamic structures of the unconscious that determine individual patterns of experience and behavior.

ELIADE'S UNDERSTANDING OF THE ARCHETYPES. In his preface to the 1959 edition of *Cosmos and History,* Eliade explains that, for him, the terms *exemplary model, paradigm,* and *archetype* are synonymous. For the member of tribal and traditional cultures, the archetypes provide the models of his institutions and the norms of his various categories of behavior. They constitute a sacred reality that was revealed to humankind at the beginning of time. Consequently, the archetypal patterns are regarded as having a supernatural or transcendent origin.

The sacred and the profane. These observations provide the basis for Eliade's description of the way in which a religious person distinguishes two separate modes of being in the world: the sacred and the profane. The member of a tribal or traditional society may be called *homo religiosus* ("religious human") precisely because he or she perceives both a transcendent model (or archetype) and a mundane reality that is capable of being molded to correspond to the transcendent model. Furthermore, he or she experiences the transcendent model as holy, that is, as manifesting absolute power and value. In fact, it is the sacred quality of the archetype that compels him to orient his life around it. Finally, the sacred is recognized as such because it appears to humans within the profane setting of everyday events. This is the hierophany ("appearance of the sacred"), that is, when the supernatural makes itself felt in all its numinosity in contrast to the natural order.

The hierophany. The appearance of the sacred may take on any form. It may be perceptible by way of the senses: God in the form of a white buffalo or in the magnificence of a roaring waterfall. The sacred may appear to humans by way of a dream, as in Jacob's dream of the angels of the Lord descending and ascending upon the ladder between heaven and earth (*Gn.* 28:12). Or the hierophany may be envisioned by way of the imagination, as, for example, the visions of Muḥammad, Black Elk, and Teresa of Ávila. The sacred reality makes itself known to the consciousness of humans by whatever means are available to it.

Orientation. The consequence of an encounter with the sacred, states Eliade, is the desire to remain in relation to it, to orient one's life around it in order to be filled continually with the sense of being and meaning that it evokes. In this sense, the hierophany creates a new order of things. No longer do space and time make up a homogeneous continuum; one moment, or one place, has become touched by the sacred, and from that time on, it will provide a means of connecting the two realms, a center that mediates sacred and profane experience.

This connection may be strengthened in many ways. Jacob set up an altar in the place where he had the dream. Religious people may build their homes, villages, or cities on a sacred site. They may practice a way of life revealed to them by means of a hierophany. Any action may become sacred if it is enacted in imitation of the way the gods have acted. Human life itself becomes assimilated to the sacred paradigm and becomes sanctified insofar as it shares in the numinous quality of the timeless archetype.

A modern example of an orientation governed by an archetype is the ritual Eucharist. In the Mass, the Christian repeats a series of actions that were performed *in illo tempore,* that is, for the Christian, in the beginning of a new age, at a time when God in the person of Christ still walked the earth. By reenacting the last supper, the Christian re-creates that sacred time and shares in its sanctity.

The spirituality that is inherent in this form of religion is not otherworldly. The people do not seek to escape this world for another (celestial or unknown) world. Instead, their actions are directed at making profane existence over into a replica of the archetypal world that has been revealed to them. They seek to realize paradise on earth. For *homo religiosus,* the limits inherent in temporal existence (decay, impermanence, and death) are transcended by imitating and incarnating the eternal patterns. In this way, they abolish time. Guided by the archetype, they experience the greatest freedom of their nature: they become like one of the gods.

Value of the history of religions. Modern humans may regard themselves as free precisely because they no longer seek to emulate a divine paradigm and see themselves, instead, as an unconditioned agent of history (unbound to external models). This is, of course, the inheritance of the Enlightenment, according to which progress is possible only after detachment from the so-called superstitions of the past in order to follow the dictates of a pure reason. In Eliade's view, one may be fully secularized, yet still be the product of a religious inheritance. Self-understanding requires an examination of that inheritance. Eliade suggests, further, that knowledge and the understanding of the religions of one's ancestors can be a source of meaning and value.

In addition, the archetypal themes that influenced our ancestors are still alive for modern people, both consciously and unconsciously. For instance, the difficulties of life can be regarded as obstacles to fulfillment or, interpreted against the archetypal theme of initiation, aspects of an ordeal that may lead to growth and, ultimately, transformation. Exile from one's homeland can be a source of bitterness and regret, or, viewed in light of mythical paradigm, the path of the hero such as Parzival, Odysseus, or even Moses, to name a few for whom the journey brought with it rewards unobtainable to those who remained at home.

Furthermore, in Eliade's view, the archetypal patterns linger on in the unconscious of modern individuals, serving as themes that motivate and guide them. On a collective level, the search for eternal life seems to underlie much of the science of modern medicine. On the individual level, the person may play out an unconsciously motivated role that has a recognizable mythical form: the hero, the sacred marriage, the wise old woman, the eternal child. The paradigms appear in numerous constellations with varied force at different times, even during the life of the individual. The insight that governs *homo religiosus,* an insight that Eliade elucidates, is this: There is a difference between the possession of happiness or wealth or power or success, on the one hand, and the realization in one's own life of an archetypal pattern. For the religious person, salvation can never be possessed but must always be embodied.

The Meaning of Archetype in Jung's Psychology. Many people have pointed out the difficulty of presenting a systematic analysis of C. G. Jung's theory of archetypes. This is perhaps a direct result of his method: As a physician, Jung discovered the existence of the archetypal reality through an examination of the subjective experiences of his patients and himself. Therefore, his theory was constantly growing in response to his clinical work. His contribution to a general theory of archetypes lies along the same lines of Philo's thought; like Philo, Jung emphasizes the presence of divine images within humans, directing and influencing human development.

At the Eranos seminars in Ascona, Jung and Eliade were able to discuss and compare their ideas on archetypes. As a psychologist knowledgeable in the study of religion, Jung knew and accepted the concepts of Eliade—archetype as transcendent model, the nature of hierophany, and so forth—but, in addition, for Jung, the archetype was also active in determining the inner life of humans in both its spiritual and material dimensions.

Instinct. The archetype is most concretely viewed as instinct. Jung states that the archetype

> is not meant to denote an inherited idea, but rather an inherited mode of psychic functioning, corresponding to the inborn way in which the chick emerges from the egg, the bird builds its nest, a certain kind of wasp stings the motor ganglion of the caterpillar, and eels find their way to the Bermudas. In other words, it is a pattern of behavior. This aspect of the archetype is the biological one. (quoted in Jacobi, 1959, p. 43)

However, the instinctual life of the body is unconscious. It is felt indirectly through drives and compulsions as well as through images that arise spontaneously in dreams and fantasy. It is the imagination that serves to mediate the subjective experience of instinct to the ego. Instinct clothes itself in images taken from everyday experience. The archetypal nature of instinct appears in the numinous quality of many of these images, that is, they have the power to compel one absolutely.

This is not to suggest that, for Jung, the archetype is nothing but instinct. On the contrary, it is the transcendent model that is recognized as having a directive force in the lives of individual persons even on the biological level. In fact, Jung suggests that *instinct* and *spirit* are simply two different names for the same reality seen from opposing perspectives. What looks like instinct to the outsider is experienced as spirit on the subjective level of inner life. The appearance of the archetypal pattern at different levels of human experience in varying forms is described as projection.

Projection. Employing Eliade's term, Jung might say that the hierophany, or appearance, of the archetype may take place anywhere, even within the unconscious life of the body. The psychological term *projection* simply points to the mode of appearance and not to the ontological status of the archetype, that is, the archetype does not exist as a projection, but rather it appears in projection. This form of speech recalls the metaphor of Plotinus, that the One is reflected by the outer void. In a similar way, we can imagine the archetype reflected (through being projected) on various planes that support the total human experience: the outer world of sense experience, the inner world of imagination, and the unconscious world of the body. In other words, the gods may appear to humans on top of a holy mountain, within a dream during a rite of incubation, or even as a bodily compulsion. Still, the transcendent nature of the archetype is not affected. Here, as in all religious language, we encounter the paradox of transcendence and immanence, each capable of an independent existence requiring the existence of the other.

The Religious Meaning of Archetype. The existence of archetypes cannot be proved, but archetypes can be subjectively experienced. Jung often explained that, as a psychologist, he could not prove the existence of God. Nevertheless, in *Face to Face,* his interview with John Freeman for the BBC, he admits that he has no need of belief in God because he has knowledge based on experience. In *Ordeal by Labyrinth,* a book of conversations with Claude-Henri Rocquet, Eliade insists on the religious content of the archetype.

> If God doesn't exist, then everything is dust and ashes. If there is no absolute to give meaning and value to our existence, then that means existence has no meaning. I know there are philosophers who do think precisely that; but for me, that would be not just pure despair but also a kind of betrayal. Because it isn't true and I know that it isn't true. (Eliade, 1982, p. 67)

Even when employed in the twentieth century by a historian of religions and a psychologist, the ancient term *archetype* retained the religious significance that it had for three religious philosophers during the first centuries of the common era. Referring both to the sacred model and to its appearance within the world of phenomena, the archetype is meaningless in any system of thought that denies the reality of a transcendent principle. In other words, the term suggests a view of creation according to which this world depends for its very nature on some reality outside itself.

See Also See also Hierophany; Iconography; Jung, C. G; Orientation; Transcendence and Immanence.

Bibliography

Eliade, Mircea. *Cosmos and History: The Myth of the Eternal Return.* New York, 1954. A good introduction to the role of archetypes in the religions of traditional cultures.

Eliade, Mircea. *Patterns in Comparative Religion.* New York, 1958. Discussion of archetypal theory throughout.

Eliade, Mircea. *Ordeal by Labyrinth: Conversations with Claude-Henri Rocquet.* Chicago, 1982. The autobiographical material provides a valuable framework for Eliade's theoretical writings.

Jacobi, Jolande. *Complex, Archetype, Symbol in the Psychology of C. G. Jung.* Princeton, 1959. The best introduction to Jung's theory of archetypes, this small volume provides the reader with a guide to Jung's writings on the topic as well as to related material in the works of other analytical psychologists.

New Sources

Henry, James P. "Religious Experience, Archetypes, and the Neurophysiology of Emotions." *Zygon* 21, no. 1 (1986): 47–74.

Laughlin, Charles D., and C. Jason Throop. "Imagination and Reality: On the Relations between Myth, Consciousness, and the Quantum Sea." *Zygon* 36, no. 4 (2001): 709–736.

McCollister, B. "Religion: Intrinsic to the Human Psyche?" *Humanist* 50, no. 1 (1990): 39.

Beverly Moon (1987)
Revised Bibliography

ARCHITECTURE. [*This article presents a thematic overview of religious architecture. Monuments associated with prehistoric religious practices are discussed in* Megalithic Religion; Paleolithic Religion; *and* Prehistoric Religions.]

Architecture may be defined as the art of building, and consequently *religious architecture* refers to those buildings planned to serve religious purposes. These structures can be either very simple or highly complex. They can take the form of a circle of upright stones (megaliths) defining a sacred space or they may spread over acres like the sanctuary at Angkor Wat. They can be of any and every material from the mounds of earth reared over royal tombs to the reinforced concrete and glass of twentieth-century houses of worship.

Yet the practice of religion does not of itself require an architectural setting. Sacrifice can be offered to the gods in the open air on a hilltop; the adherents of Islam can perform their daily prayers in a railroad car or even in the street; the Christian Eucharist can be celebrated in a hospital ward. Nevertheless all the major world religions have buildings especially planned for their use, and these constitute an important source of knowledge about these faiths. They can reveal what is believed about the nature of the gods; they can provide insight into the character of the communities for which they were designed and the cultus celebrated therein.

To comprehend and appreciate the significance of these buildings it is necessary to classify them, but their variety is so great that one single method would be incomplete. Hence several typologies have to be devised if the subject matter is to be covered adequately; indeed it is possible to identify at least four. In the first place, the vocabulary applied to religious buildings can be taken as the basis for the formulation of a typology. This, however, is by no means exhaustive, and so it is essential to move on to a second typology derived from the character or nature ascribed to each building, which may differ depending upon whether it is regarded as a divine dwelling, a center of reference, a monument, or a meeting house. A third typology may be presented by analyzing the functions for which each building provides, including the service of the gods, religious teaching, the manifestation of reverence and devotion, congregational worship, and symbolization. A fourth typology is architectural rather than religious but needs to be noted: this is based upon the categories of path and place. Other factors that should be borne in mind for a complete picture relate to the different materials used, the effect of climate, culture and its expression in different styles, and also the influence of patronage.

CLASSIFICATION ACCORDING TO TERMS USED. The terms used to refer to religious buildings provide a preliminary indication of both their variety and their significance.

Terms that designate a structure as a shelter. These may be further differentiated according to the class of being or thing associated with them.

For gods. The Hebrew *beit Elohim* is to be translated "house of God," while *heikhal*, a loanword from Sumerian through Babylonian (*ekallu*), is used for a very special house or palace. In Greek there is *naos*, from *naio*, "to dwell in," and *kuriakos* ("of the Lord") lies at the origin of both *kirk* and *church*. In Latin there is *aedes sacra*, a "sacred edifice," as well as *domus dei*, a "god's home." *Tabernacle* (Lat., *tabernaculum* from *taberna*, a "hut") has a similar domiciliary connotation. Hinduism has *prāsāda*, or platform of a god, and *devalaya*, a residence of a god, while the Japanese word for shrine is literally "honorable house."

For objects. In English the primary term is *shrine*, derived from *scrinium*, which means a case that contains sacred things. More specifically there is *chapel* from *capella* ("cloak"), referring to the garment of Saint Martin that was venerated in a small building; there is *cathedral*, which shows that the particular church is where the bishop's *cathedra*, or throne, is located. *Pagoda*, which is a deformation of the Sinhala *dagoba*, is a tower containing relics. *Agyari*, a place of fire, is the designation of a Parsi temple in which the sacred flame is kept alight. The Temple of the Sleeping Buddha in Peking characterizes the form of the statue within.

For humans. The Latin *domus ecclesiae* points to the Christian community as the occupant of a building. *Beit hakeneset* in Hebrew and *sunagōgē* in Greek (from *sunagō*, "to gather together"), with *synagogue*, as the English transliteration, denote a place of assembly. The term used by Quakers, *meeting house*, has the same implication.

Terms that indicate the character of a structure. In Greek there is *to hagion*, the place of dread, from *azomai*, "to stand in awe of," and *to hieron*, the "holy place." In Latin *adytum* is a transliteration of the Greek *aduton*, "not to be entered," because it is the holy abode of a divinity. *Templum* is a space cut off; it comes from *tempus*, meaning a "division" or "section," which in turn derives from the Greek *temenos*, referring to an area set apart for a particular purpose such as the service of a god. *Temple* in English has the same etymology, while *sanctuary* (*sanctus*) emphasizes the holiness of the building.

Terms that affirm an association with a person or events. To speak of Saint Paul's Cathedral in London is to declare a link with the apostle. The Süleymaniye Mosque complex in Istanbul commemorates its patron, Sultan Süleyman the Magnificent. The Roman Pantheon, which is Latinized Greek (*pantheion*), was dedicated to "all the gods." The Anastasis in Jerusalem commemorates the resurrection (*anastasis*) of Jesus. *Basilica* denotes a public building with royal (*basileus*) links. The generic term is *marturion* (Lat., *martyrium*), from *martureo*, "to be a witness." Such an edifice is a monument or memorial; the two terms are synonymous—the one from *moneo*, "to remind," and the other from *memor*, "to remember." It therefore preserves or promotes the memory of a person or event; the English Cathedral of Saint Albans, for example, commemorates a martyred saint, and the Church of the Nativity in Bethlehem recalls the birth of Christ.

Terms descriptive of the activity for which a building is used. The Hebrew *devir*, which denotes the holy of holies in the Jerusalem Temple, may suggest an oracle, from a verb meaning to "speak" in which case it is similar to the Latin *fanum*, from *fari*, "to speak," especially of oracles. *Proseuke* (Gr.) and *oratorium* (Lat.), in English *oratory*, or place of prayer, all point to a particular form of religious devotion. *Baptistery* (Gr., *baptizō*, "to dip") specifies ceremonial action, and *mosque* (Arab., *masjid*, "place of prostration" [before God]), the place of an action.

Terms indicative of the shape of the edifice. These relate mainly to funerary architecture: *tholos*, a "dome" or "vault," signifies a round tomb; *tomb* itself comes from *tumulus*, a sepulchral mound; *pyramid* suggests a geometric form and is at the same time the designation of a pharaoh's resting place; *masṭabah* is the Arabic for a bench that describes the shape of a tomb; *stupa*, from the Sanskrit *stupa* (Pali, *thūpa*), signifies a reliquary "mound" or tower; *ziggurat*, from the Babylonian *ziqqurratu*, meaning "mountain peak" or "pinnacle," is descriptive of the superimposed terraces that make up this structure.

TYPOLOGY ACCORDING TO CHARACTER. Granting the unavoidable overlap, four main types may be specified.

Divine dwelling. Taking pride of place, because the majority of terms in use emphasize this particular category, is the structure that is regarded as a divine habitation. Since the chief occupant enjoys divine status, the model is believed to have been provided from above. Gudea, ruler of Lagash in the third millennium BCE, was shown the plans of his temple by the goddess herself. The shrine of Amaterasu, the Japanese sun goddess, was built according to the directions provided by an oracle. Various passages in the Hebrew scriptures (Old Testament) indicate that the Tabernacle and the Temple were considered to have transcendent exemplars. Yahveh's instructions to Moses were to this effect: "Let them make me a sanctuary, that I may dwell in their midst. According to all that I show you concerning the pattern of the tabernacle, and of all its furniture, so you shall make it. . . .

And see that you make them after the pattern for them, which is being shown you on the mountain" (*Ex.* 25:8f., 25:40). Similarly, when David gave the plans of the Temple of Solomon, it is reported: "All this he made clear by the writing from the hand of the Lord concerning it, all the work to be done according to the plan" (*1 Chr.* 28:19). In the *Wisdom of Solomon*, the king is represented as saying that what he has built is "a copy of the holy tabernacle which you did prepare aforehand from the beginning" (9:8). The author of the *Letter to the Hebrews* reproduces the same idea when he describes the Temple and its furniture as "a copy and shadow of the heavenly sanctuary" and as "copies of the heavenly things" (*Heb.* 8:5, 9:23).

The work of the divine architects is frequently held to include not only god-houses but entire cities. Sennacherib received the design of Nineveh drawn in a heavenly script. The New Jerusalem, in the prophet Ezekiel's vision, is described in the greatest detail, with precise dimensions included. The Indian holy city of Banaras is thought to have been not only planned but actually built by Śiva.

Similar ideas are present in Christian thought from the fourth century onward. When large churches came to be built, as distinct from the previous small house-churches, recourse was had to the Old Testament for precedent, since the New Testament provided no guidance. Thus the basilica came to be regarded as an imitation of the Jerusalem Temple: the atrium corresponded to the forecourt, the nave to the holy place *(heikhal)*, and the area round the altar to the holy of holies (*devir*). By the thirteenth century it was normal to consider a Gothic cathedral as an image of the heavenly Jerusalem, a reflection of heaven on earth.

Divine presence. The presence of the god may be represented in a number of ways, most frequently by statues as, for example, in Egyptian, Greek, and Hindu temples, and alternatively by a bas-relief, as at the Temple of Baal in Palmyra. The building is then appropriately called a shrine. The Hebrews, forbidden to have graven images of deity, which were dismissed as idols, took the ark as the center of their devotion and this eventually was regarded as a throne upon which Yahveh sat invisible. Again, mosaics or paintings can be employed, notably in the apses of early Christian basilicas or on the iconostases of Eastern Orthodox churches. But in certain religions, the entire structure is regarded as a revelation of the deity. Greek sanctuaries were so conceived, and to this day Hindu temples are not only places but objects of reverence, evoking the divine.

Precisely because this type of building is regarded as the mundane dwelling of a deity, constructed according to a transcendental blueprint, it is also understood as a meeting place of gods and humans. So the ziggurat of Larsa, in lower Babylonia, was called "the house of the bond between heaven and earth." This link may be physically represented by a sacred object. The Kaʿbah in Mecca, the holiest shrine of Islam, is the symbol of the intersection between the vertical axis of the spirit and the horizontal plane of human existence: a hollow cube of stone, it is the *axis mundi* of Islamic cosmology. In other religions wooden poles or stone pillars fulfill the same function; such were the *asherim* of the Canaanites reported in the Old Testament. The finial of a Buddhist stupa is conceived to be the top of a pillar passing through the whole structure and providing the point of contact between earth and heaven.

The divine is also associated with mountains that rear up into the sky; Olympus in ancient Greece was one such place, and in the myths of the Maasai, Mount Kilimanjaro on the border of Kenya and Tanzania is dubbed the "house of god." This symbolism can be applied to the religious building itself. Each Egyptian temple was believed to represent the primordial hillock, while the Babylonian ziggurats were artificial high places. Hindu temples, such as the one at Ellora, are sometimes called Kailasa, which is the name of Śiva's sacred mountain. Their superstructure is known as the "crest" (*śikhara*) of a hill, and the contours and tiered arrangement of the whole building derive from a desire to suggest the visual effect of a mountain.

Sacred and profane. As noted above, while a religious building can be called a house, it is not any kind of house: there is something special about it, and hence words denoting "great house" or "palace" are used. But its particular distinction derives from the nature of the being who inhabits it and who invests it with something of his or her own character. In most religions the divine is a being apart; his or her habitation must consequently be a building apart, and so it is regarded as a holy place in sharp opposition to profane space.

To speak of the sacred and the profane in this way is to refer to two antithetical entities. The one is potent, full of power, while the other is powerless. They cannot therefore approach one another without losing their proper nature: either the sacred will consume the profane or the profane will contaminate and enfeeble the sacred. The sacred is therefore dangerous. It both attracts and repels human beings—it attracts them because it is the source of power, and it repels them because to encounter it is to be in peril. The sacred is "the wholly other"; it is a reality of an entirely different order from "natural realities." Contacts can only be intermittent and must be strictly regulated by rites, which can have either a positive or a negative character. Among the former are rites of consecration whereby someone or something is introduced into the realm of the holy. The negative takes the form of prohibitions, raising barriers between the two. These rites allow a certain coming and going between the two spheres since they provide the conditions within which intercourse is possible. But any attempt, outside the prescribed limits, to unite sacred and profane brings confusion and disaster.

Underlying all this dualism is the concept of two worlds: a sacred world and a secular world. Two realms of being are envisaged, and this opposition finds its visible expression in holy places. The sacred space, defined by the religious building or precinct, is first of all a means of ensuring the isolation and so the preservation of both the sacred and the profane. The wall that keeps the one out also serves to keep the other in; it is the demarcation line (*temenos, tempus, templum*) between the two worlds. But within the sacred enclosure, the profane world is transcended and hence the existence of the holy place makes it possible for humans to pass from one world to another. The door or gate is then an object of great importance, for it is the means of moving from profane to sacred space. The name *Babylon* itself literally means "gate of the gods," and Jacob at Bethel declared: "This is the gate of heaven." In the same realm of ideas is to be found the royal doors that provide access through the iconostasis to the altar of the Eastern Orthodox church and the "Gates of Paradise," which is the name given by Michelangelo to Lorenzo Ghiberti's sculpted doors at the Florence Baptistery.

The precise location of these holy places is ultimately determined by their association with divine beings. The Nabataean high place at Petra is legitimized by being on a mountain top that, as seen above, has religious connotations. Equally holy were caves, linked in the religious consciousness with the womb, rebirth, the darkness of Hades, initiation rites, and so forth: many a Hindu holy place enshrines a cavern in a cliff. A theophany too constitutes a holy place. David knew where to build the Temple in Jerusalem because of a manifestation at the threshing floor of Araunah (Ornan) the Jebusite. Under the Roman Empire, augurs were consulted, sacrifices offered, and the divine will thereby discovered. The shrine at Monte Sant'Angelo in the Gargano (c. 1076) was built because it was believed that the archangel Michael had visited the place. Similarly the sixteenth-century Church of Our Lady of Guadalupe, near Mexico City, marks the spot where the Virgin Mary presented herself to a peasant. Rites of consecration can act as substitutes if there is a lack of any definite command from above; by their means a space is declared set apart, and the god is besought to take up residence with confidence that the prayer will be answered.

Center of reference. Both individuals and communities require some center of reference for their lives so that amid the vagaries of a changing world there is a pivot that may provide an anchor in the ultimate. Religious buildings can and do constitute such centers to such an extent that the idea of a middle point has been taken quite literally. Every Egyptian temple was considered to be located where creation began and was therefore the navel of the earth. In Jewish thought the selfsame term has been applied to Jerusalem, and the site of the Temple is held to be the place of the original act of creation. In Greek religion it was the shrine of Apollo at Delphi that was declared to be the earth's midpoint. According to Hinduism, Meru is the axial mountain at the center of the universe, and the name *Meru* is also used in Bali for the superstructure of a temple. The main shrine of the Tenrikyo sect of Shintō at Tenrishi marks the cradle of the human race and encloses a sacred column indicating the center of the world.

Within the same ambit of ideas is the view that a religious building may be related to cosmic forces and therefore assist in geomancy. Hence, for example, the monumental structures at Teotihuacán in Mexico are arranged within a vast precinct in such a way as to observe the relations of the earth to the sun. The orientation of Christian churches so that their sanctuary is at the east end is another way of affirming this cosmic link, while the concern of Hindu architects for the proportions and measurements of their designs rests upon the conviction that the universe as a whole has a mathematical basis that must be embodied in every temple.

In Hinduism too the temple plan functions as a *maṇḍala*—a sacred geometrical diagram of the essential structure of the cosmos. This interpretation of religious buildings is widespread in time and space. The "big house" of the Delaware Indians of North America stands for the world: its floor is the earth, the four walls are the four quarters, and the vault is the sky. An identical understanding of Christian churches is to be found as early as the seventh century and is typical of Eastern Orthodox thought; the roof of Saint Sophia in Edessa was compared to the heavens, its mosaic to the firmament, and its arches to the four corners of the earth. Medieval cathedrals in the West, such as the one at Chartres, were similarly regarded as models of the cosmos and as providing foretastes of the heavenly Jerusalem.

Monument or memorial. The essentials of a sacred place are location and spatial demarcation rather than buildings, but when there are edifices, they too serve to locate and spatially demarcate. Their importance is to be found not so much in the specific area as in the events that occurred there and that they bring to remembrance. In other words the locations are mainly associated with notable happenings in the life of a religious founder or with the exploits of gods and goddesses, and they stand as memorials (remembrancers) or monuments (reminders). One of the units in the complex erected by Emperor Constantine in fourth-century Jerusalem was known as the Martyrium, the testimony to or evidence and proof of the reality of Christ's death and resurrection, which were believed to have occurred at that very site. Also in Jerusalem is the Muslim Dome of the Rock, which enshrines the spot whence the prophet Muḥammad is believed to have ascended to heaven, a site already associated in Jewish tradition with Solomon's Temple, the tomb of Adam, and the sacrifice of Isaac. At Bodh Gayā in the state of Bihar, India, the Mahābodhi Temple is situated in front of the bodhi tree under which Gautama attained enlightenment. At Sarnath, near Banaras, a stupa commemorates the Buddha's first sermon delivered in the Deer Park to five ascetics.

Not only founders but also individual followers may be honored in this way. Numerous stupas are monuments to Buddhist sages, and many a martyrium in the days of the early church was set up on the very spot where a martyr (*martus*, "witness") had testified to his faith with his blood. The buildings also serve as shrines to protect their remains and can therefore be classified as tombs. Indeed every tomb that assumes a monumental character is a reminder of the dead, whether in the form of separate memorials to individuals, as found in the Père-Lachaise cemetery in Paris, or of a single edifice to a person representative of many, such as the tomb of the unknown warrior beneath the Arc de Triomphe in the same city.

Many religious buildings that function as memorials enclose space: the pyramids of Giza have within them the burial chambers of pharaohs; the Cenotaph in London, on the other hand, a monument to the dead of two world wars shelters nothing. It corresponds to the second of the four fundamental modes of monumental architecture. First, there is the precinct, which shows the limits of the memorial area and finally develops through a typological series to the stadium. Second is the cairn, which makes the site visible from afar and indicates its importance, the ultimate development of this type is the pyramid. Third is the path that signals a direction and can take the sophisticated form of a colonnaded street, thus dignifying the approach to the main shrine. Fourth, there is the hut that acts as a sacred shelter, with the cathedral as one of its most developed types.

Meetinghouse. A religious building that is regarded as a divine dwelling, or *domus dei*, is a meeting place of heaven and earth, but when it is understood as a meetinghouse, it is more correctly styled a *domus ecclesiae* because it is a building where the people of god assemble. Solomon had been led to question the validity of the temple type when he asked "Will God indeed dwell upon earth?" (*1 Kgs.* 8:27). However, it was not until the birth of Christianity that a full-scale attack was directly launched upon the whole idea of an earthly divine domicile; in the words of Stephen, "The Most High does not dwell in houses made with hands" (*Acts* 7:48). In the light of the later development of Christian thought it is difficult to appreciate how revolutionary this new attitude was.

The early believers committed themselves to an enfleshed god, to one who was no longer apart or afar off but had drawn near; at his sacrificial death the Temple veil had split in two so that the Holy of Holies was no longer fenced off. The living community now became the temple of the divine presence. A new concept of the holy was minted: there can no longer be anything common or profane for Christians (*pro*, "in front of," or outside the *fanum*) since they constitute the *naos* of the Holy Spirit (*1 Cor.* 3:16). The dining room of a private house is a suitable venue for the assembly; the proud boast is that "we have no temples and no altars" (Minucius Felix, c. 200). All this was to change drastically in the fourth century when Christianity became the official religion of the Roman Empire and took over the public functions of the pagan cults. It was not until the Protestant Reformation that the New Testament understanding was given a fresh lease of life when divines such as John Calvin objected to the idea of special holy places. Such a view is not peculiar to Christianity; Judaism has its synagogues for meeting together, and Islam has its mosques, which are equally congregational. If a building as a divine dwelling is at one end of a spectrum, then the meetinghouse is at the other extreme.

Typology according to Function. The different types of building just delineated provide for the fulfillment of certain purposes in that they accommodate religious activities; it is consequently both possible and necessary to specify a second typology according to function, which stems from but also complements the previous typology according to character.

Service of the deities. At home, resident within their temples, the gods require their devotees to perform certain services for them. Perhaps the most striking illustration of need is provided by the toilet ceremonies of ancient Egypt. Each morning the cult image was asperged, censed, anointed, vested, and crowned. At the present day very similar ceremonies are conducted in Hindu temples, where the images are cooled with water in hot weather, anointed, clad in beautiful clothes, and garlanded. During the day it used to be the custom to divert them with the performances of the *devadāsīs*, or temple dancers. At night they are accompanied by a procession to their beds. Food may be provided, from the simple gift of grain in an African village to the hecatombs of Classical Greece. Another normal form of worship is sacrifice, ranging from human victims to a dove or pigeon, from the first fruits of the harvest to shewbread.

Positive and negative functions. The motives for such services can be diverse; sometimes they are prompted by the concern to provide sustenance, while at other times they are to establish communion, to propitiate, to seek favors. Functions now become reciprocal: the service of the gods is expected to obtain a response from the gods, in that they now serve human needs. Two examples, for many, will suffice to illustrate this.

Since the temple is a divine dwelling, to enter its precincts is to come into the presence of the god and so be under his or her protection. As a sacred place, the building is inviolable, and no one can be removed from it by force; to do so would be sacrilege, since a person who is inside the area of holiness has been invested with some of the sacredness inherent in it and thus cannot be touched as long as he or she does not emerge. This is the rationale of sanctuary as it was practiced in the classical world. The most famous case was that of Demosthenes who in 322 BCE sought sanctuary in the Temple of Poseidon on the island of Calauria. When, in the post-Constantine era, church buildings were included in the same class as pagan temples, as specially holy places, it was natural that the idea of sanctuary should also be connected to them. The right of fugitives to remain under the protection of their god became legally recognized and in western Europe continued to be so for centuries; indeed, in England it was not until 1723 that all rights of sanctuary were finally declared null.

The second example of the gods themselves fulfilling a function on behalf of their followers is the practice of incubation. This is a method of obtaining divine favors by passing a length of time in one of their houses, usually sleeping there. Its primary aspect is medical, to obtain a cure, either immediately or after obeying the divine will disclosed in a vision. In the Temple of Ptah at Memphis therapeutic oracles were delivered and various remedies were revealed through dreams to those who slept there. The two principal healing gods in the Greek and Roman pantheons were Asklepios and Sarapis, and there is record of a shrine of the former at Aegae where those who passed the night were restored to health. The apparent success of these two gods ensured their continued popularity, and their cults only fell into disuse when churches replaced their temples as centers of healing believed to be accomplished by Christ through his saints. Among the most successful of the Christian holy men to cure illness were Cosmas and Damian, to whom a church was dedicated in Constantinople. Running this center a close second was the Church of Saint Menas near Alexandria; there some patients stayed for over a year and the church itself was so completely filled with mattresses and couches that they had to overflow into the sacristy. Incubation has had a continuous history down to the present day; in eastern Europe, for example, it can still be witnessed.

These several functions may all be regarded as positive in character, but a corollary of viewing a religious building as a holy place is the requirement for negative rituals to safeguard it by purifying those who wish to enter. Such rituals determine some of the furnishing, and so, for example, the forecourts of mosques have tanks and/or fountains for ablutions. Holy water stoups are to be found just inside the entrance of Roman Catholic churches; baptismal fonts were originally placed either in rooms separate from the main worship area or in entirely distinct buildings. The removal of shoes before entering a Hindu temple, of hats before going into a Christian church—all of these testify to the seriousness of entering a holy place. Many religious buildings have guardians to protect their entrances. The giant figures in the royal complex at Bangkok, the bull Nandin in the temples of Śiva, the scenes of the Last Judgment in the tympana over the west doors into medieval cathedrals—these are but a few examples.

Determination of form. The interior disposition of those religious buildings conceived to be divine dwellings is very much determined by the forms of the services offered. Where, for example, processions are a habitual feature of the ceremonial, then corridors for circumambulation have to be designed, as in the complex of Horus at Idfu; this also explains the labyrinthine character of many Hindu temples. When a statue is only to be seen by a special priesthood and has to be shielded from profane gaze, an inner chamber is created, often entirely dark, to protect humankind from the brilliant light of the divine presence, and this sanctuary may be protected itself by a series of surrounding rooms or courtyards. Where there are sacrifices, altars are needed, but these are frequently outside the shrine so that the individual worshiper can actually witness what the priest is doing with his or her gift. Classical Greek temples sheltered statues of the tutelary deities, but the all-important altars were outside; on the Athenian Akropolis, for example, it was in front of the Parthenon. Sometimes altars can themselves be architectural in character: the Altar of Zeus of Pergamum (c. 180 BCE), now in Berlin, has a crepidoma measuring 36.44 by 34.20 meters, and the Altar of Hieron II (276–222 BCE) at Syracuse is some 200 meters long and 27 wide.

Conveyance of revelation and teaching. As a center of reference, a religious building may accommodate activities that convey meaning, guidance, and instruction in the faith. Many Babylonian temples, for example, were sources of divination and even had a full complement of soothsayers, exorcists, and astrologers. Daoist temples equally are resorted to for divinatory purposes. The oracle was consulted at Delphi, to instance the greatest focus of this activity in the ancient world. The Jewish Temple in Jerusalem had cultic prophets on its staff.

Where a sacred book is central to a religion, provision for its reading and exposition has to be made. In synagogues there has to be a shrine for the Torah and a desk from which to comment on the text. In Christian churches there are lecterns for the Bible and pulpits for the sermon. Islam has its stands for the Qurʾān, and its *minbar* is the equivalent of the Christian pulpit, although the shape differs in that it is a miniature flight of stairs rising away from the congregation whom the preacher faces down the steps. Sikh worship concentrates on the reading of the Granth, which is accompanied by prayers and exposition. In these ways religious buildings function as centers of meaning.

Manifestation of reverence and celebration of festivals. The religious building as memorial, it will be recalled, often contains relics of religious founders or particularly saintly people. Reverence for these can be shown by visitation, sometimes to offer thanks for benefits received and sometimes to petition for help. Those who seek healing go in great numbers to the shrine of Our Lady of Lourdes to bathe in the sacred spring. In this and similar instances the designs of the buildings are affected by the need to accommodate the sick for short or long stays. In the Muslim world the virtue of a saint is believed to be available to those who follow him (or her) or touch some object associated with him. If he be dead, then his tomb, which is his memorial, becomes a center of his supernatural power (*barakah*) and attracts many visitors. Pilgrimages are one of the forms that these visits may take. So too Hindus travel to Hardwar (North India), which displays a footprint of Viṣṇu in stone. Jains go to Mount Abu, also in India, where the last *tīrthaṅkara* (guide), named Mahavira, spent the thirty-seventh year of his life. Buddhists go to Adam's Peak in Sri Lanka, where there is a footprint of Gautama; adherents of Islam make the *ḥājj* to Mecca, and indeed it is one of the five duties of Islam. Christians have their holy places in Israel and Jordan or visit the catacombs in Rome.

Festivals are the celebrations of the births or deaths of saints, and they commemorate key events in the sacred history of a religion. For Jews, to celebrate Passover in Jerusalem is a traditional goal. For Christians, too, there is a certain fittingness in observing Christmas, the Feast of the Nativity, in Bethlehem itself. Religious buildings then function as centers for such celebrations.

Congregational worship. It is important, if this particular category is to be appreciated, to distinguish it clearly, despite some overlap, from the service of the deities described above, with which it can easily be confused. The essential difference can be made plain by applying the term *cult* to the first function and reserving *worship* for this fourth one. The basic understanding of *cult* is evident from its etymology. It derives from *colere*, which means "to till the ground" and hence to take care of, or attend to, with the aim that the object of attention should bear fruit or produce some benefit. Next it signifies "to honor" and finally "to worship." The cultus is therefore a cultivating of the gods, a cherishing of them, seeing to their needs; it is the bestowal of labor upon them and the manifestation of regard toward them. There is more than a hint of doing something to obtain a favor, as in the phrase "to cultivate someone's acquaintance." Cultus stems from the human side, whereas worship, as it is used here to describe this fourth function, is from the side of the gods. Not only are they the ones who provide the form and matter of worship, but through it they come to encounter their community.

Worship of this kind is characterized as congregational to differentiate it further from cultus, which is primarily individualistic. Worship then is meeting: the religious building is the meeting house. What takes place is not an activity aimed at or on behalf of the gods; the gods take the initiative. Hence worship is a memorial celebration of the saving deeds of the gods, and by it the people are created and renewed again and again. So, in Christian terms, the Body of Christ (the Christian community) progressively becomes what it is by feeding upon the sacramental body of Christ. Worship fosters community identity, and hence in the chapels of Christian monasteries the seating frequently faces inward, thus promoting a family atmosphere.

The precise interior disposition of a building will also depend upon the particular understanding or form of the communal rite. Religions that center on a book of revelation, such as Judaism, Islam, and Sikhism, require auditoria. Protestantism, concentrating upon the word of God, similarly tends to arrange its congregations in rows suitable for an audience (*audientes*, a group of "hearers"). Roman Catholicism, with its greater emphasis on the Mass, stresses the visual dominance of the altar, which is now no longer outside the building, as with Roman and Greek exemplars, but inside.

If the act of worship is understood to be conducted by a professional hierarchy on behalf of the community as a whole, then some separation is likely, ranging from the Eastern Orthodox iconostasis at one extreme to communion rails at others. Where there is no sharp differentiation of role, as in Islam (since the imam is simply a prayer leader and is in no sense an ordained minister), the space is not partitioned; instead there is lateral disposition, with the worshipers shoulder to shoulder facing toward Mecca.

SYMBOLIZATION. On whatever basis a typology of religious buildings may be constructed and whatever purposes they may serve, there is one overall function that must be considered: symbolization. Each building proclaims certain beliefs about the deities to whom it is dedicated. One has only to contrast a Gothic cathedral with a Quaker meeting house to appreciate this. The former in all its grandeur speaks of a god who is high and lifted up, remote, awesome in majesty, fearful in judgment, demanding obeisance; the latter in all its simplicity witnesses to a being who is to be known in the midst of life, who is not separate, whose dwelling is with humankind, offering fellowship. The one speaks of power and might, the other of self-emptying and servanthood.

Sometimes the symbolism is intellectually apprehended before it is given visible form, and then it needs interpretation. Baptism, for example, is a sacrament of dying and rising with Christ. A detached baptistery may be hexagonal or octagonal: in the former case it refers to the sixth day of the week, Friday, on which Jesus died and in the latter, to the eighth day, or the first day of a new week when he rose from the dead. The dome, surmounting many a baptistery, is also a habitual feature of Byzantine churches and Muslim mosques, and as the baldachin or canopy it can enshrine any holy object or complete a memorial structure. Its popularity derives from its ideological context: it is a representation of the transcendental realm, an image of heaven. It is a not-inappropriate roofing for tombs, and many baptisteries took the shape of contemporary burial edifices precisely because of the meaning of the purificatory rite. Different parts of a building can have their own messages: towers declare heavenly aspirations; monumental doorways can impress with regal authority. Sculpture, painting, mosaic can and do fulfill a symbolic function. Gargoyles ward off evil spirits; paintings recall events or persons in sacred history; Christ as *creator mundi* holds his worshipers within his downward gaze. The handling of light is frequently symbolic. In a mosque it testifies to God as the light of heaven and earth; in Gothic architecture it is a basic constituent and is regarded as a manifestation of the glory of God.

ARCHITECTURAL TYPES. There is yet another typology to be reviewed that applies to all buildings whatever their function, and religious buildings are no exception. This is a dual typology that divides structures into the categories of path and place. For a path to be identifiable, it must have (1) strong edges, (2) continuity, (3) directionality, (4) recognizable landmarks, (5) a sharp terminal, and (6) end-from-end distinction. For a place to be identifiable, it must be (1) concentrated in form with pronounced borders, (2) a readily comprehensible shape, (3) limited in size, (4) a focus for gathering, (5) capable of being experienced as an inside in contrast to a surrounding exterior, and (6) largely nondirectional.

The application of these types to religious buildings can be briefly illustrated by contrasting a basilica and a centralized mosque. A basilica is a path leading toward the altar; every detail of the design confirms this. The nave, framed by aisles, has firm edges; there is continuity provided by floor patterns and advancing rows of columns, which themselves indicate a direction—everything points toward the holy table framed in a triumphal arch and backed by the embracing shape of the apse. For a pilgrim people, for those who have here no abiding city, such a royal road is obviously very appropriate. A centralized mosque, on the other hand such as those designed by Sinan in Istanbul, suggests no movement, it is a place, a point of reference and gathering, it is concentrated. Once within, there is no incentive to leave and every enticement to stay. Embodying perfect equipoise, it promotes contemplation; it is indeed embracing architecture. Its spaciousness expresses not the specificity of the Christian doctrine of the incarnation but the omnipresence of the divine; it manifests *tawhid*, which is the metaphysical doctrine of the divine unity as the source and culmination of all diversity.

The difference then between basilica and mosque is not stylistic; they are distinct architectural types, which in these two instances correspond to each religion's self-understanding. This circumstance does not, however, provide support for the nineteenth-century theory that every religion develops its own supreme architectural form to best express its ethos and spirit. The character of any building at any epoch is affected by many factors: technical aptitude, climate, availability of materials, function, and so on. Patronage has also played an important role. The Temple in Jerusalem, for example, was in origin Solomon's royal chapel, and indeed, not a few English medieval churches were on the estates of local lords, who regarded them as their own possessions. One effect of this influence was the monumentalization of many religious buildings: they were designed to display the power and authority not only of a heavenly being but of an earthly ruler. In this way many a Mughal mosque in India proclaimed the might of the ruling house. Royal, princely, and ducal boxes and galleries were inserted, and in western Europe the well-to-do could provide for their continued well-being by constructing private chantry chapels within existing parish churches. Communal patronage was not necessarily less concerned with outward show. Civic pride and congregational piety can result in costly programs.

Yet the study of the architecture of the world religions is not just a part of social history; it is an important element in understanding the religious traditions themselves. Since cult or worship is at the heart of any faith, and such an activity can only be studied and appreciated fully within its own special setting, it would be an abstraction to concentrate upon texts alone. Moreover, the symbolic function of architectural forms is in itself an additional source of knowledge to be taken into account.

Throughout the ages human beings have found meaning and succor in sacred places enshrined in their religious buildings. In a secularized society there still survives a need for centers of reference, meeting places, and memorials, but they then become associated with national figures and national identity. The Kremlin wall where leaders of the Russian Revolution are buried, together with Lenin's tomb, constitute one such place for Russian citizens. The Lincoln Memorial in Washington has a spacious chamber containing a seated statue and having the words of the Gettysburg and the Second Inaugural addresses incised on its walls; both president and texts have important contributions to make to United States identity. The White House in Washington and Buckingham Palace in London are seen as the dwellings of those who have about them a semidivine aura. The birthplaces or museums containing souvenirs (relics) of film and pop stars become centers of pilgrimage. A monument to Egypt's first president, Gamal Abdel Nasser, overlooks the Aswan Dam on the Nile. The former concentration camp at Dachau has become a memorial of the Nazi Holocaust. At the same time temples, cathedrals, mosques, and the like continue to be built: sacred sites, whether overtly religious or not, are a continuing feature of the human scene.

See Also Axis Mundi; Banaras; Basilica, Cathedral, and Church; Biblical Temple; Circle; Circumambulation; Cities; Cosmology; Jerusalem; Ka'bah; Labyrinth; Monastery; Mosque, article on Architectural Aspects; Orientation; Pilgrimage; Portals; Procession; Pyramids; Relics; Sacred Space; Shrines; Synagogue; Temple; Tombs; Towers; Worship and Devotional Life.

Bibliography

Arnheim, Rudolf. *The Dynamics of Architectural Form.* Berkeley, 1977.

Davies, J. G. *The Secular Use of Church Buildings.* London, 1968.

Davies, J. G. *Temples, Churches and Mosques: A Guide to the Appreciation of Religious Architecture.* New York, 1982.

Eliade, Mircea. *The Sacred and the Profane.* New York, 1959.

Grabar, André. *Martyrium: Recherches sur le culte des reliques et l'art chrétien antique* (1946). 2 vols. Reprint, London, 1972.

Smith, Baldwin. *The Dome: A Study in the History of Ideas* (1950). Reprint, Princeton, 1978.

Turner, Harold W. *From Temple to Meeting House: The Phenomenology and Theology of Places of Worship.* The Hague, 1979.

New Sources

Arnheim, Rudolf. *The Split and the Structure: Twenty-eight Essays.* Berkeley, 1996.

Downey, Susan B. *Mesopotamian Religious Architecture: Alexander through the Parthians.* Princeton, 1988.

Humphrey, Caroline, and Piers Vitebsky. *Sacred Architecture.* Boston, 1997.

Jones, Lindsay. *The Hermeneutics of Sacred Architecture: Experience, Interpretation, Comparison.* 2 vols. Cambridge, Mass., 2000.

Lawlor, Anthony. *The Temple in the House: Finding the Sacred in Everyday Architecture.* New York, 1994.

Pearman, Hugh. *Contemporary World Architecture.* London, 1998.

Petruccioli, Attilio, and Khalil K. Priani. *Understanding Islamic Architecture.* London, 2002.

Richer, Jean. *Sacred Geography of the Ancient Greeks: Astrological Symbolism in Art, Architecture, and Landscape.* Albany, N.Y., 1994.

Scully, Vincent J. *Architecture: The Natural and the Manmade.* New York, 1991.

Taylor, Mark C. *Disfiguring: Art, Architecture, Religion.* Chicago, 1992.

Williams, Peter W. *Houses of God: Region, Religion, and Architecture in the United States.* Urbana, Ill., 1997.

J. G. Davies (1987)
Revised Bibliography

ARCTIC RELIGIONS

This entry consists of the following articles:

ARCTIC RELIGIONS: AN OVERVIEW

Arctic religions may be treated together, as constituting a more or less unified entity, for two reasons. First, these religions are practiced by peoples situated in the polar North, who mostly live on the tundra (permanently frozen ground) and partly in the taiga (the northern coniferous forest belt that stretches around the world); like their cultures in general, the religions of these peoples reflect to no little extent the impact of the severe natural environment. Second, the whole Arctic zone constitutes a marginal area and an archaic residue of the old hunting culture and hunting religion; whereas in the south the waves of Neolithic agriculture and animal husbandry inundated the originally Paleolithic hunting culture, the latter was preserved in the high north, where no cultivation of the ground was possible.

There was also a diffusion of ideas from west to east, and vice versa, within the Arctic area. This diffusion mostly took place in the boreal zone in the Old World, whereas in the New World there was little contact between Arctic groups and their Asian brethren.

Although interior change and later intrusion of world religions (such as Christianity and Buddhism) partly altered the ancient religious structures, their basic foundations and major features persisted until modern times in Siberia and North America. Only the systematic atheistic drive from 1930 onward managed to overthrow the old religions in the Soviet areas.

Ethnic and Cultural Survey. The tribes and peoples of the Arctic culture area belong to several linguistic families. All of them, with the exceptions of some Paleosiberian peoples and the Inuit, are also represented in cultures south of the high Arctic zone. In the following survey, names of peoples will be given as they are authorized today by their respective governments and by the peoples themselves. Their earlier names, used up to the 1930s or later and still popularly used, will be mentioned in parentheses. The main sources of subsistence will also be noted.

1. The Uralic language family. In Scandinavia, in Finland, and on the Kola Peninsula, the Arctic tundra and coast and the northern interior woodland are inhabited by the Sami (Lapps). Most of them are fishing people, but in the mountain regions and in parts of the woodland areas reindeer breeding is a common way of life. East of Lake Onega live the Komi (Zyrians), who are reindeer breeders as well, and the Samoyeds. The latter are divided into two main groups, who move extensively over the tundra with their reindeer herds: the Nentsy (Yuraks), from the Northern Dvina River to the Ural Mountains, and the Nganasani (Tavgi), from the Ob River to Cape Chelyuskin. Along the lower parts of the Ob and Irtysh rivers live two Ugric peoples (related to the Hungarians), the Khanty (Ostiaks) and the Mansi (Voguls), who practice some reindeer breeding but who are mostly fishermen and hunters.

2. The Tunguz language family. The wide areas from west of the Yenisei River to the Anadyr River in the east and from the tundra in the north to the Sayan Mountains in the south are the country of the dispersed Tunguz tribes: the Evenki, west of the Lena River, and the Eveny, east of it. Their typical habitat is the taiga, where they subsist as reindeer breeders on a limited scale.

3. The Turkic language family. The numerous Yakuts on the Lena River and farther east combine reindeer breeding with horse breeding. Their language is also spoken by the Dolgans in the Taimyr Peninsula area, a group of earlier Tunguz tribes.

4. The Yukagir. Now almost extinct, the Yukagir, a group that may be related to the Finno-Ugric peoples, once covered a large area east of the Lena. They were hunters and fishermen until the seventeenth century, when they turned into reindeer-breeding nomads.

5. The Paleosiberian language family. The Chukchi, on the Chukchi Peninsula, and the Koriak and the Itelmen (Kamchadal), on the Kamchatka Peninsula, make up the Paleosiberian language family. The inland Chukchi are reindeer breeders; the coastal Chukchi, the Koriak, and the Itelmen are ocean fishermen.

The economy of the people of the Arctic culture was founded on reindeer breeding, hunting, and fishing in the Old World, and only on hunting and fishing in the New World. Wintertime hunting was carried out on skis in the western parts of the area and on snowshoes in eastern Siberia and among the woodland Indians of Canada. Sledges (as well as toboggans in the New World) were used for transportation in the winter, and animal-skin boats and occasionally bark canoes in the summer. Animal-skin clothes and fur moccasins constituted the dress. The dwellings were mostly conical skin tents, although more southern groups substituted bark tents in the summer. Round or rectangular semisubterranean houses, sometimes covered with sod, occurred among the river- and coast-dwelling peoples. The social organization was simple in the north, with small, usually bilateral groups. In the south there were clan systems with tendencies toward totemism and more complicated political structures.

Common Religious Elements. Against this harmonious background, it is not surprising that a wide range of religious phenomena are spread out over most of the region, usually as a combined result of ecological and historical factors. The available data bear out Robert H. Lowie's observation that the whole Arctic area constitutes one gigantic entirety from the angle of religious belief. One may make a certain reservation for the New World Arctic area, however, because both archaeologically and ethnologically the Inuit lack several common circumpolar features, and the same holds for their religion.

The main characteristics of Arctic religions are the special relationships of people to animals and the elaboration of shamanism. While the latter feature probably owes its special appearance to developments among peoples farther south such as the Tunguz and the Yakuts, there is a remarkable emphasis on shamanism, from the Sami in the west to the Inuit in the east, that seems aboriginal. Indeed, it is possible that the strain of the Arctic climate has stimulated strong religious forms of reaction, just as it has provoked the psychic reactions known as Arctic hysteria. No such explanation can be given for the hypertrophic extension of animal ceremonialism. It has its roots, of course, in ancient Eurasian hunting rituals, but its prolific occurrence in the Arctic probably has to do with the necessary dependence on an animal diet in these barren regions.

The spiritual universe. According to the religious beliefs of the Arctic peoples, the whole world is filled with spirits: Mountains, trees, and other landmarks have their spirits, and animals have their spirit masters. It is among all these spirits that shamans find their supernatural helpers and guardians. However, such human-spirit relationships could also occur among common people, as the evidence shows among the Sami and North American Indians, and there are obvious tendencies in the same direction among the Chukchi, as their "general shamanizing" (that is, when everybody tries to handle the shamanic drum and fall into ecstasy) testifies. The multifarious world of spirits may have something to do with the fact that the figure of a supreme being is so often diffuse. There is, it seems, a pattern of spiritualism here that defies all more personal expression of higher theistic concepts.

Supreme power. The inclination to conceive the highest supernatural being or beings more as nonpersonal power than personal figure or figures is generally part of Arctic religions and particularly characteristic of the Samoyeds, the Paleosiberian tribes, and the Inuit. The Sami constitute a great exception, but their high-god beliefs have been heavily influenced by Scandinavian and Finnish as well as Christian religious concepts.

A characteristic, somewhat impersonal power concept of the Samoyeds is Num. The word stands for both a deity and the sky. Num is an inclusive concept since it can denote both the highest spirit—the chief spirit or high god—and spirits through which the high god expresses its being, for instance, the spirits of thunder or of the rainbow. Similarly, the Khanty's semipersonal, highest power, Num-Turem, makes himself known to humans by speaking in the thunder or the storm. The Inuit believe in a rather nebulous supreme being called Sila (or Silap Inua, Hila, etc.), mostly rendered in English as "the lord of the air" (or the weather, or the world). This being is only partly thought of in truly personal terms and, at least among the Central Inuit, it is vested with an uncertain sexual affiliation.

It would seem that the personal character of the supreme being is more apparent among the northern Tunguz and Yakuts. Thus, the highest god of the Evenki, while sometimes represented by the sun, is clearly anthropomorphic.

The vague character of the supreme being of most Arctic groups may to some extent reflect their elementary social organization or the apparent infinity of their tundra world. There is no doubt, however, that this being stands at the apex of the religious pantheon in northern Siberia. The Samoyeds, for instance, think that he lives in heaven, and they sacrifice white reindeer to him on high mountains, particularly in the spring when there is thunder in the air. In northern Siberia there is a close connection between the world pillar and the high god.

In the Arctic area of the Old World, the worldview is dominated by the belief in several heavens over each other and several underworlds under each other, usually seven among the Ugric peoples and nine among the Altaic peoples, such as the Yakuts. Sometimes the sky is portrayed as a tent with holes through which the heavenly light shines down (the holes are the stars). Sometimes the Milky Way is thought of as the backbone of the sky (a concept shared by North American Indians) or as a river in the landscape of the sky. As among the Tunguz, the world pillar or world tree is believed to penetrate all levels, from the underground to the sky. On the whole, the three-leveled division of the world into a sky world, the earth, and the underworld is a typical Arctic feature.

Other spirits and divinities. Next to the supreme being, the most important spirits of the upper world are the Sun, the Moon, and the thunder spirits. The Sun is often related to the high god (as among the Tunguz), and the Moon can represent the mistress of the dead or, among some Inuit, the mistress of the sea animals (who is herself, secondarily, a mistress of the dead). Among the western Inuit, the moon god rules over the weather (he makes snowstorms) and the animals. The thunder spirits are portrayed as birds, particularly among the eastern Siberian peoples, the Inuit, and the North American Indians. Among the Samoyeds the thunder is supposed to be caused by ducks or by manlike beings, unless it represents the voice of the supreme being.

The surface of the earth is the habitat of a large crowd of spirits—some rule the animal species, some are spirits of the woods, lakes, and mountains (among Eurasian Arctic groups), and some are dangerous ogres, giants, and dwarfs. The Inuit in particular offer a variety of this last class of beings. Of immense importance are the masters of the animals. First, there are the guardians of the species, which are usually represented in the forms of the animals they protect; and second, there is the general lord of the animals, who is mostly conceived in the disguise of the dominant animal, be it the walrus (as among the Chukchi), the pike (as among the Khanty), or the reindeer (as among the Nentsy). In the Inuit area, the mother of the seals and of other water beings, called Sedna or Nuliayuk, is the dominant deity. The walrus mother of the Chukchi is probably related to her. The master or mistress of the animals is a most important divinity to these hunting and fishing peoples, who pray to this being to release the animals or to receive its permission to hunt them. When taboos have been broken, the master of the animals prohibits people from killing them. A primary task of Yukagir and Inuit shamans is to intervene in such cases by visiting the offended spirit and trying to propitiate it.

Such spirits have been thought to reflect a feudal social order. However, similar masters of the animals are found in places where such a social system has not existed, for instance, in North America. They seem to belong to a very ancient heritage.

The mistress of the game may be a variation of the mother-goddess complex. The old Paleolithic mother goddess, a divinity of birth and fertility, has been preserved among these northern peoples, partly as a mistress responsible for the game, partly as a birth goddess. Thus, among the Samoyeds and Ugric peoples she appears as Mother Earth and the birth goddess, among the Yakuts as a birth goddess, and among the Tunguz as the mother of the reindeer and the guardian of home and family. The Tunguz, and possibly also the Chukchi, know her also as a spirit of fire who protects the tent and its inhabitants, that is, the family. She then receives meat offerings in the fire. In some cases, as among the Sami, the tasks of the mother goddess are divided between several female divinities. Throughout the Eurasian Arctic, the mother goddesses have connections with the door of dwellings and are supposed to live under the ground. The Inuit have no particular birth goddess, but Sedna, the mistress of the sea animals, is in her unclean states a prototype of the woman who is ritually unclean, particularly when pregnant or giving birth. The birth goddess is primarily the protectress of women, and in some tribes female spirits are inherited from mother to daughter.

Cultic Practices. Characteristic of the cultic complexes among Arctic peoples is the simple development of ritual forms and the use of cultic objects—such as crude sculptures in wood and peculiarly formed stones—as symbolic receivers of offerings. The relationships between the sacrificers and these objects varies from veneration to coercive magic.

Sacrifices. Throughout the Arctic the supernatural powers have received offerings of some sort. Sacrifices are particularly important in Eurasia, whereas the Inuit have been less indulgent in this practice. In some dangerous places the Inuit offer pieces of blubber or flesh to the residing powers. Presents decorating sacred stones are supposed to give good hunting. However, the Inuit resort a good deal to magic—to spells, talismans, and amulets—to attain the same results. In the Arctic Old World, on the other hand, there is more religious supplication in ritual attitudes.

The most common offerings in northern Eurasia are simple pieces of tobacco and meat and, on more important occasions, the sacrifices of whole reindeer. The Sami, for instance, made offerings of tobacco to ensure good fishing when passing sacred rocks in a boat and of reindeer to the gods and local spiritual rulers when particular reasons demanded so. Such reasons could be the occurrence of a disease, the spread of a reindeer pestilence, the wish for the increase of the reindeer herds, and so on. The Samoyeds and other Arctic peoples of Siberia also evince these various attitudes to sacrifices, except that they also slaughter dogs. Both the Sami and the Samoyeds also consecrate animals to spiritual powers without killing them. Both tie a picture of the master of the fishes to the sacrifice given to this spirit. The northern Tunguz regularly perform sacrifices for the different masters of the animals.

The shaman often acts as the ceremonial leader, or sacrificial priest, at the larger offerings, particularly when his peculiar knowledge of the spirits is needed for the correct conduction of the ceremonies. Some ritual occasions are great annual ceremonies in which the shaman has a central function. To this category belongs the Samoyed ceremony held at the return of the sun after the polar winter night. It includes dancing (by shaman and common people alike), healing, and divination. Another such ceremony occurs among the Tunguz and is concerned with the revivification of nature in the spring, the growth and increase of the animals, and luck with future hunting. This ceremony is also connected with general shamanizing and the installment of new shamans.

Cultic images. The stone cult is prominent everywhere. Among the Saami, strangely formed stones, called *seite,* are connected with spirits that control the animals in the vicinity or the fish in water where the stone stands. The Samoyeds make offerings to similar stone gods, as do the Khanty, the Mansi, the Tunguz, and the Inuit. In some reports the stones seem, at least momentarily, identical with the spirits, but otherwise the general idea is that the stone represents the spirit or serves as its abode. The stone cult is a very important feature of Sami religion. The Sami, like the Samoyeds, the Khanty, and the Mansi, smeared the mouths of the stone idols with blood from the reindeer sacrificed to them.

The same form of offering occurs among the Tunguz and the Yakuts in their cult of the master of the forests. This spirit is represented by a carved human figure on the trunk of a living tree. Other northern peoples, such as the Sami, have made similar carvings on trees to symbolize spirits.

The most common custom, however, was to make crude wooden sculptures of the spirits. Such spirit figures occur all the way from Lapland to Alaska. Throughout northern Eurasia they are surprisingly similar—pointed at the top, usually without limbs, and occasionally decorated with cross marks on the body. The Khanty and the Samoyeds dress up these spirit images. Some wooden idols are set outside, often in groups at the same place; others are occasionally stationed outside but are mostly kept in the sacred corner of the house or tent.

Wooden figures also occur in Siberian shamanism among the Tunguz and the Dolgans. For these peoples, the figures symbolize the shaman's helping spirits and the world pole or world tree. A line of seven or nine pillars represents the lower sky worlds, where the shaman's soul or guardian spirit rests on the way to heaven. These images are often used for just one shamanic séance and are then discarded.

Animal ceremonialism. Much of the cultic life centers on animal ceremonialism, that is, the rituals accorded the slain game. Several animal species are shown a ceremonial courtesy after hunting; for example, their bones are buried in anatomical order. All over the area, a special complex of rites surrounds the treatment of the dead bear.

Particular attention is given to the way in which the bear's body is brought home. It is carried in procession, often with patches on its eyes so it cannot see its slayers and take revenge on them. It is brought into the tent through a sacred entrance at the back. Such sacred doors or openings occur in dwellings throughout northern Eurasia. A festive meal is arranged, and the men who have killed the bear assure it of their innocence and blame others. The bear is admonished to observe the respect and kindness with which it is treated and to tell the bears in the world of the spirits about this treatment so that more bears will allow themselves to be slain. Afterward, the bones of the bear are carefully buried and its skull is placed in a tree or on a pole. The aims of the ceremony are obviously to persuade more animals of the same species to be killed. The size and ferocity of the bear probably induced its traditionally special treatment.

Paleosiberian peoples and Alaska Inuit paid similar attention to the whale. The Inuit celebrated the dead whale ritually for five days, a period corresponding to the mourning period for a dead person. The Alaska Inuit also had a bladder festival in December, at which the bladders of the seals that had been slain during the year were restored to the sea. The Inuit, like the Finno-Ugric peoples, make a clear distinction between what belongs to land and what belongs to water: the bones of land animals are deposited in or on the earth; the bones and bladders of fish and sea animals are put in the water.

Ceremonies are held not only for food-giving animals but also for animals that are feared. The Koriak feast the slain wolf and dance in its honor, at the same time asking the supreme being not to make the wolf angry. A reindeer sacrifice to the same god is a humble appeal to him not to send wolves into the reindeer herds.

The persistent concern with animals and hunting is reflected in the host of hunting taboos, and in rock drawings that have "life lines" drawn between the mouths and the hearts of the depicted animals, possibly suggesting the animals' souls.

Shamanism and soul beliefs. Since the shamanism of the Arctic peoples is discussed elsewhere, only a few critical remarks will be made here. It seems that the extreme development of shamanistic ritual farther to the south in Siberia is somewhat attenuated in the northern Arctic. On the other hand, in the Arctic the intensity of the shaman's ecstatic trance is certainly not weaker, but is in fact stronger, than it is in Siberia. North and south are also remarkably different in regard to the conception of the soul basic to shamanism. As always where true shamanism operates, there is a dualism between the free soul that acts during dream and trance and that represents humans in an extracorporeal form and the one or several body souls that keep individuals alive and conscious during their waking hours. It is typically the shaman's free soul that, in a trance, tries to rescue a sick person's soul (of either type), which has left its body and gone to the land of the dead and possibly reached this place. This is indeed the conception of the soul and disease among the Arctic peoples. However, among the more southerly Tunguz and Yakuts, the soul types are more intricate, and the soul sent out by the shaman is commonly a body soul. Therein lies the obvious and basic difference between Arctic and other Siberian peoples.

There are other differences as well. The idea of the shaman being possessed during a trance is well developed in southern Siberia and the American Northwest Coast culture, but it is not so frequent among the Arctic peoples. On the other hand, Shaking Tent ceremonies, in which the shaman is tied up and covered by blankets, calls upon spirits for information, and then breaks free from the bonds, can be found among the Samoyeds, the Yakuts, and the Inuit (and northern Algonquians in North America). Iconographic representations of what seem to be double-headed assistant spirits occur all over the Arctic. Divination by lifting weights is common among the Sami, the Tunguz, and the Inuit, and divination by scapulimancy has been recorded in northern Siberia, in China, and among the Algonquian-speaking Indians of northeastern North America. It is less certain that the chief guardian spirit of the Yakuts and Dolgans, the animal mother, is derived from northern influences. Other items of possibly Arctic and ultimately Paleolithic origins such as the shaman's drum (and the drawings on it) are hardly conducive to more secure conclusions.

Afterlife. Unlike most other hunting peoples, the peoples in the North generally believe that the realm of the dead is situated in the underworld. The Khanty think that the world of shades extends close to the mouth of the Ob River; it is characterized by cold, eternal darkness, hunger, and silence. The Tunguz view of the underworld is more optimistic. The people there live in birchbark tents, hunt, fish, and tend to their reindeer in the woods. The Central and Eastern Inuit realm of the dead is identical with Sedna's place at the bottom of the sea. It is not bright, but endurable. The rule in most places is that only those who have suffered a violent death go to heaven; among the Chukchi and Inuit these fortunate beings make their appearance in the aurora borealis. Often, the underworld is conceived to be contrary to our world in every respect; for instance, while it is night in the underworld it is day on earth.

There are traces of evidence among the Paleosiberian peoples that they once believed in two lands of the dead, one underground and the other in heaven or at the horizon. Such pieces of information may be interpreted as testimony of a conception of afterlife that was originally more sky-oriented, overlayered by later influences from the south.

Myths. Several myths and legends have a remarkable distribution along the Arctic coast, such as those of the "bear wife" and "the resuscitation of the animal with the missing member." Many myths of more southerly origin have been integrated with local mythological patterns, such as the myths of the "earth diver" and the Flood. Quite a few tales are star myths, legends of the first shamans, or narratives of supernatural animals. A widely distributed myth tells about the cosmic stag, or elk, represented in the night sky as the Great Bear. He steals the sun but is deprived of it by a hare who restores the heavenly light to humankind. Among the Tunguz, this tale is connected with the spring ceremonies described above.

The Paleosiberian peoples share with North American Indians the idea of a culture hero and trickster. His name is Raven, or Big Raven among the Northwest Indians, and he appears as human or as a bird. Among the Koriak, Big Raven formed the earth, brought light to it, and created all the animals. He is humanity's ancestor and the first shaman. He is the most prominent divinity (although there is a vague, otiose sky god, identical with dawn, who also represents the universe). At the same time Big Raven is a most obscene trickster, and he dominates mythology.

History of Arctic Religions. Because of the absence of reliable written sources, not much is known of the religious developments in the Arctic. However, certain clues can be obtained through the study of the ethnic history of the area.

As stated before, the cultures of the Arctic area are remnants of a Paleolithic hunting culture at the northern fringe of three continents. They preserve hunting customs and religious ideas that have disappeared or become transformed in the southern pastoral and agricultural societies. The Finno-Ugric peoples and the Paleosiberian peoples have best preserved their archaic heritage. The Inuit represent a later cultural phase with roots in the circum-Pacific fishing cultures. Their original connections to the Old World are reflected in the way animals are depicted in their art, ultimately inspired by Eurasian steppe art some two to three thousand years ago. The Inuit belong ecologically, but only in part historically, to the Arctic hunting culture. They therefore deviate considerably from the other Arctic peoples in their religious structure. On the other hand, the Pacific fishing culture has had an important impact on Paleosiberian culture and religion.

At the other end of the Arctic, the Sami were heavily influenced by their Scandinavian neighbors, first through old Nordic religion, later by Christianity. Reindeer-breeding nomadism developed in Christian times and has not palpably changed Saami religion.

In the Siberian Arctic, changes were brought about by influences from the south. First, both material culture and religion were affected by cultural waves from the Near East and China; the subterranean location of the realm of the dead may partly be a result of this impact. Second, with the move of the Tunguz and Yakuts toward the north, a major cultural shift took place in the Arctic. The Tunguz, coming from the Baikal area, slowly supplanted or incorporated Paleosiberian tribes, such as the Yukagir. They were probably the main instigators of the diffusion of reindeer breeding (reindeer-breeding nomadism with large herds apparently did not develop until the eighteenth century). The introduction of reindeer breeding in the Arctic did not change traditional religions palpably, but some new spirits, such as the master of the tame reindeer, were incorporated. The continued dependence on hunting and fishing may have impeded the development of a purely nomadic religion. On the other hand, the Tunguz peoples were probably instrumental in spreading the intense form of shamanism in the north, a form that had been influenced by Buddhist ideas and Tibetan ecstatic practices.

This southern influence was strengthened with the arrival of the horse-tending Yakuts from Mongolia during the medieval centuries. The Yakuts who followed the Lena Valley to the north replaced some of the dispersed Tunguz groups and partly absorbed the original population. The Tunguz and Yakut influx created in the north what has been called "the Siberian gap," a void between the more ancient Finno-Ugric cultures in the west and the Paleosiberian cultures in the east. This void is easily observable in the religious context where Tunguz and Yakut thought and practice represent more complex and developed forms.

See Also Bears; Ecology and Religion; Inuit Religious Traditions; Sami Religion; Samoyed Religion; Shamanism.

Bibliography

The concept of an Arctic cultural area was first used by Artur Byhan in his *Die Polarvölker* (Leipzig, 1909). An archaeological survey of the area can be found in Guterm Gjessing's

Circumpolar Stone Age (Copenhagen, 1944). The general features of some Arctic cultures are briefly presented in Nelson H. H. Graburn and B. Stephen Strong's *Circumpolar Peoples: An Anthropological Perspective* (Pacific Palisades, Calif., 1973). This work has also excellent bibliographic references. Various questions related to Arctic culture are discussed in *Circumpolar Problems,* edited by Gösta Berg (Oxford, 1973), and in the serial *Arctic Anthropology* (Madison, Wis., 1962–).

The Siberian Arctic peoples and their cultures are described in *The Peoples of Siberia,* edited by M. G. Levin and L. P. Potapov (Chicago, 1964), and in Gustav Ränk's "Völker und Kulturen Nordeurasiens," in *Handbuch der Kulturgeschichte,* edited by Eugen Thurnher (Frankfurt, 1968).

Arctic religions as a separate entity have hitherto only been described in one major article, Ivar Paulson's "Les religions des peuples arctiques," in *Histoire des religions,* vol. 3, edited by Henri-Charles Puech (Paris, 1976). Arctic religions are part of presentations of northern religions in *Mythology of All Races,* vol. 4, *Finno-Ugric, Siberian* (Boston, 1927), by Uno Holmberg (later Harva); in *Die religiösen Vorstellungen der altaischen Völker* (Helsinki, 1938), by the same author; and in *Les religions arctiques et finnoises* (Paris, 1965), by Ivar Paulson, Karl Jettmar, and me. Much material pertaining to Arctic religions is given in Mircea Eliade's *Shamanism: Archaic Techniques of Ecstasy,* rev. & enl. ed. (New York, 1964); *Studies in Siberian Shamanism,* edited by Henry N. Michael (Toronto, 1963); *Popular Beliefs and Folklore Tradition in Siberia,* edited by Vilmos Diószegi (The Hague, 1968); *Shamanism in Siberia,* edited by Vilmos Diószegi and Mihály Hoppál (Budapest, 1978); and *Shamanism in Eurasia,* 2 vols., edited by Mihály Hoppál (Göttingen, 1984). Although somewhat dated, M. A. Czaplicka's classic work, *Aboriginal Siberia* (Oxford, 1914), is still valuable from the religio-historical point of view.

There is an analysis of the diffusion of Arctic religious traits in my "North American Indian Religions in a Circumpolar Perspective," in *North American Indian Studies,* edited by Pieter Hovens (Göttingen, 1981), as well as in an earlier article by Robert H. Lowie, "Religious Ideas and Practices of the Eurasiatic and North American Areas," in *Essays Presented to C. G. Seligman,* edited by E. E. Evans-Pritchard et al. (London, 1934). There are several papers on selected aspects of Arctic religions, such as A. Irving Hallowell's "Bear Ceremonialism in the Northern Hemisphere," *American Anthropologist* 28 (1926): 1–175; Uno Holmberg's "Über die Jagdriten der nördlichen Völker Asiens und Europas," *Journal de la Société Finno-Ougrienne* (Helsinki) 41 (1926): 1–53; Eveline Lot-Falck's *Les rites de chasse chez les peuples sibériens* (Paris, 1953); Balaji Mundkur's "The Bicephalous 'Animal Style' in Northern Eurasian Religious Art and Its Western Hemispheric Analogues," *Current Anthropology* 25 (August–October 1984): 451–482; Gudmund Hatt's *Asiatic Influences in American Folklore* (Copenhagen, 1949); and Gustav Ränk's *Die heilige Hinterecke im Hauskult der Völker Nordosteuropas und Nordasiens* (Helsinki, 1949). This last work deals with the sacred corner in Arctic homes.

Åke Hultkrantz (1987)

ARCTIC RELIGIONS: HISTORY OF STUDY

Arctic religions have been explored by scholars from many countries, though primarily from the countries where these religions are practiced: Denmark (the Inuit of Greenland); Norway, Sweden, and Finland (the Sami); Russia and the former Soviet republics (the northern Eurasian peoples); and the United States and Canada (the Inuit and northernmost American Indians). This has meant that several research traditions and research premises have been involved. For a long time the study of Arctic religions was a subordinated part of the ethnographic research on peoples and cultures, and in many places, particularly in the former Soviet republics, it still is. Until the end of the nineteenth century, descriptions of Arctic religions were encapsulated in travel reports and tribal monographs, but since that time particular issues of Arctic religions, such as shamanism, have been debated. However, conscious attention to connections between various Arctic religions was missing from scholarship until the beginning of the twentieth century.

The Development of Circumpolar Studies. The exploration of Siberian and Canadian Arctic cultures at the turn of the century made scholars aware of their great similarities. Since this was the time when geographic environmentalism swayed high—and the Arctic is known for its extreme climate—Arctic cultures were readily given an environmentalist interpretation. The pioneer of this approach, Artur Byhan, author of the classic *Die Polarvölker* (1909), brought together pertinent religious materials from all over the Arctic and referred many religious manifestations to the pressures and inspiration of the Arctic environment. He certainly did not make a real analysis of the mechanisms implied, but he presented cultural and religious data in their environmental context.

Other scholars followed suit. In the writings of Waldemar Bogoraz, M. A. Czaplicka, Kai Birket-Smith, Daryll Forde, and Åke Ohlmarks, different shades of an environmentalist interpretation of Arctic religions are represented. In a modified, ecological form, I have substantiated the environmental impact on these religions.

Most ethnologists and anthropologists, however, have favored a cultural-historical analysis in which all the Arctic cultures belong together, either as a common field of diffusion or as an archaic residue. This approach originated with the American anthropologist Franz Boas, who compared Paleosiberian and Northwest American Indian mythologies. His speculations resulted in the assumption of a direct communication between North America and North Asia. This perspective was expanded by Austrian and Danish diffusionists.

Wilhelm Schmidt, the dominating figure of the so-called Vienna culture-circle school, accepted the idea of an Arctic "primeval culture" (*Urkultur*) that, although somewhat faded, has been preserved to some extent among Samoyeds, Koriak, and Caribou Inuit. Schmidt also found shared religious elements among some North American "primeval peoples" (*Urvölker*) and the Arctic peoples, such as the "earth-diver" myth, the association of the high god with the rainbow, the dualism between thunder spirits and water spirits, and the sacred fire. He therefore postulated the existence of a continuous Arctic-North American primeval culture in which religious ideas and customs were formed in the same mold.

While Schmidt's general scheme of historical developments has been discredited, his reconstruction of an Arctic cultural and religious area rests on solid ground. The research of Danish ethnologists, in particular Gudmund Hatt and Kai Birket-Smith, revealed an interconnection between all Arctic cultures in a circumpolar round. Hatt has shown distributions of myths and folk tales over, primarily, the Siberian and North American Arctic regions. Robert H. Lowie, Francis Lee Utley, and I have suggested historical connections in the religious and mythological field, some of them joining the Saami with the inhabitants of northernmost North America. Archaeologists have also contributed to the investigations of the spreading of religious ideas in the Arctic zone: Gutorm Gjessing, for instance, has illuminated the Arctic rock-drawing panels by comparing eastern and western Arctic traits (such as the so-called life line).

All these historical investigations have followed the diffusionist approach. Very little has been done along the other line of historical approach, the study of common heritage. A. Irving Hallowell has, certainly, suggested the possibility that bear ceremonialism originated within the larger Eurasian Paleolithic hunting culture. Its circumpolar distribution would thus, at least partly, be a leftover from a once more extended context. Indeed, not only the Arctic but also all North and South American hunting cultures show evidence of their status as remnants of this old basic culture, as Boas and, in particular, Erland Nordenskiöld demonstrated. As observed by Mircea Eliade, the outlines of one and the same shamanistic complex are found from Alaska to Tierra del Fuego. Everyone who compares Mapuche shamanism in Chile with Siberian shamanism will notice obvious parallels. Seen in this perspective American hunting religions are an extension of Arctic religions.

Some scholars have tried to discern major changes in the development of Arctic religions. If earlier evolutionist theories are excluded, this discussion has been connected with the interpretation of animal ceremonialism and shamanism. The ceremonies associated with the bones of the slain animals have mostly been identified as burial and rejuvenation rites. Some authors, however, have expressed other opinions. For example, Alexander Gahs and Wilhelm Schmidt have interpreted these bone rites as offerings (*Primitialopfer*) to the supreme being or to its manifestations in other supernatural beings, such as the master of the animals. Although this opinion is not shared by other scholars, there is no doubt that some animal rituals, namely those associated with the reindeer, have a clear sacrificial character among the Samoyeds, the Tunguz, and the Koriak; the Tunguz, for instance, make reindeer sacrifices to the spirits of the woods. Karl Meuli, therefore, considered that a change had taken place from the animal ceremonialism of the hunting culture to the sacrificial ideology of reindeer-breeding nomadism; the animal, surrounded by revivification rites, was transformed into a sacrifice to the powers. At the same time, bear ceremonialism lingered on and had a firm grip in all nomadic cultures of the North, as shown by Hans-Joachim Paproth's investigations.

PARTICULAR AREAL STUDIES. Most authors have concentrated their efforts on the study of subfields or tribes within the Arctic area. They have, from their particular points of departure, often reached conclusions that refer to the whole circumpolar zone or large parts thereof; but their real intentions have mostly been to reveal the religious systems or specific traits of these systems. It is possible to distinguish three main Arctic regions of exploration, usually (but not always) treated as separate from each other. They will be called here the Sami field, the northern Eurasian field, and the Inuit field.

The Sami field. The scientific analyses of Sami religion on the basis of older sources (there were few vestiges left in the nineteenth century besides folkloric materials) began late in the nineteenth century. This was the time when such scholars as J. A. Friis, Gustaf von Düben, Johan Fritzner, and others began to systematize Sami religious ideas. The interest in the possible contributions that Sami religion could make to our understanding of Scandinavian religion, a perspective introduced by Fritzner, was later continued by such men as Axel Olrik, Kaarle Krohn, and Wolf von Unwerth. The underlying idea was that Sami religion was inspired to a large extent by Scandinavian thought and retained Old Scandinavian religious features. In the 1920s the pendulum swung, and Sami religion began to be considered in the light of Finno-Ugric and Arctic religious ideas and cults. Uno Holmberg (later Harva) and Björn Collinder guided this new perspective. Since then a host of writers, including Ernst Manker, Ernst Emsheimer, Gustav Ränk, T. I. Itkonen, Olof Pettersson, Hans Mebius, Nils Storå, and Louise Bäckman, have tried to coordinate Sami religion with other Arctic and northern Eurasian religions.

The northern Eurasian field. The first accounts of the "primitive" peoples of the Russian empire and their religious customs date from the seventeenth and eighteenth centuries. More systematic studies were undertaken in the nineteenth century when the Finnish-speaking peoples were investigated by Mathias Alexander Castrén; the Mansi by Bernhardt Munkácsi; the Samoyeds by Castrén, Otto Finsch, and V. V. Radlov; the Yakuts by W. L. Sieroszewski and Radlov; and the Eveny (an eastern Tunguz tribe) by Leopold von Schrenk. These accounts are all classic and still authoritative. The only treatises that compared aspects of various cultures dealt with the bear ceremonial complex (N. M. Yadrintzeff) and shamanism.

The beginning of the twentieth century saw the continued publication of tribal monographs. Waldemar Bogoraz and Waldemar Jochelson, respectively, published excellent studies of the Chukchi and Koriak that contain important chapters on religious life. Jochelson also wrote a book on what was preserved of Yukagir religion. In the same way, Leo Sternberg advanced our knowledge of the religious customs of the Amur and Sakhalin tribes. Finnish scholars continued the interest in Arctic peoples that had started with Castrén: Toivo Lehtisalo and Kai Donner visited the Samoyeds and K. F. Karjalainen visited the Khanty (Ostiaks).

During the postrevolutionary era, Soviet scholars made several tribal ethnographic investigations of considerable importance, although one-sidedly Marxist and evolutionist in outlook. Religious issues, shamanism in particular, have been discussed from this programmatic point of view. Unfortunately, few works have been translated into Western languages. Among the more prominent contributors to the study of religious themes are N. A. Alekseev (on the Yakuts), A. F. Anisimov (on the Tunguz), A. A. Popov (on the Samoyeds and Yakuts), E. D. Prokofeva (on the Samoyeds), and G. M. Vasilevich (on the Tunguz).

If shamanism is excluded, Soviet authors may be generally said to have neglected comparative studies of religion. There are some papers on such topics as mother-goddess worship and totemism, and Dimitri K. Zelenin's book-length work on *ongons,* that is, idols that portray animals or human beings, is a major comparative treatise. These investigations, however, are exceptions. I. S. Gurvich comments on the paucity of Soviet-era papers in this genre in an article (1979) on ethnographic parallels in the Arctic.

The basic surveys of Finno-Ugric and northern Siberian religions have been composed by non-Russian scholars, such as M. A. Czaplicka, Uno Holmberg Harva, Wilhelm Schmidt, Ivar Paulson, and Gustav Ränk. Other comparative studies have been written by Adolf Friedrich (on beliefs about bones and skeletons), Alexander Gahs (on bones as offerings), Eveline Lot-Falck (on hunting rituals), Josef Haekel (on the cult of idols and totemism), Gustav Ränk (on the house and family cults), Ivar Paulson (on concepts of the soul, masters of the animals, bone rites, and house idols), Horst Nachtigall (on burial customs), and Ivan A. Lopatin (on cult of the dead). The Soviet papers previously referred to should also be mentioned: Zelenin's study of idols, A. M. Zolotarev's writings on totemism, and Anisimov's discussion of cosmology.

The particular religious connections between northern Siberian and North American Arctic and Northwest Coast cultures were illuminated at the turn of the century by the Jesup Expedition, sponsored by the American Museum of Natural History in New York, with Boas as the director and Bogoraz and Jochelson as Russian members. This intercontinental ethnological problem, which included the question of religio-historical relations, received less attention among Russian scholars after the Russian Revolution of 1917.

The Inuit field. The Danes had already secured important information on the Greenland Inuit in the eighteenth century. Danish scholarship in the field started in the nineteenth century when Gustav Holm and H. Rink described, in particular, the East Greenland Inuit religion. At the other end of the Inuit area, in southern Alaska (at that time part of the Russian empire), the Finn H. J. Holmberg noted down Inuit and Indian religious ideas about the same time. Toward the end of the nineteenth century, American anthropological research entered the scene with Franz Boas, who wrote a monograph on the Central Inuit, and A. L. Kroeber, who described the Inuit of Smith Sound.

The twentieth century saw a rich scholarship on Inuit religion, most of it directed from Copenhagen. Knud Rasmussen covered the whole Inuit area with his insightful analyses of Inuit religious thinking, but first of all the Greenland, Central, and Polar Inuit. William Thalbitzer wrote on beliefs, myths, and cults of the Greenlanders, Erik Holtved on the Polar Inuit, and Kai Birket-Smith on the Caribou Inuit and the Chugach of Alaska. Among American scholars, Diamond Jenness, who described the Copper Inuit, and Margaret Lantis, who analyzed the ceremonialism of the Alaska Inuit, were prominent. As pointed out before, the Danish scholars were occupied with investigating circumpolar trait diffusions, using the Inuit traits as their point of departure.

BIBLIOGRAPHY

An early environmental interpretation of circumpolar religions will be found in M. A. Czaplicka's "The Influence of Environment upon the Religious Ideas and Practices of the Aborigines of Northern Asia," *Folklore* 25 (March 1914): 34–54. A later collocation based on religio-ecological analysis is my "Type of Religion in the Arctic Hunting Cultures," in *Hunting and Fishing,* edited by Harald Hvarfner (Lulea, 1965).

Methodological approaches to the distribution and history of religious traits in the area have been discussed in articles mentioned in the bibliography of the overview article on Arctic religions. In addition, there are short comprehensive surveys such as Waldemar Bogoraz's "Elements of the Culture of the Circumpolar Zone," *American Anthropologist* 31 (October–December 1929): 579–601, and Gudmund Hatt's "North American and Eurasian Culture Connections," in *Proceedings of the Fifth Pacific Science Congress* (Toronto, 1934). See also I. S. Gurvich's study, cited below.

Studies of religious change have been presented by, for instance, Wilhelm Schmidt, *Der Ursprung der Gottesidee,* vols. 3 and 6 (Münster, 1931 and 1935), and Karl Meuli, "Griechische Opferbräuche," in *Phyllobolia für Peter von der Mühll zum 60. Geburtstage,* by Olof Gigon et al. (Basel, 1946). On the development of the bear ceremony, see Hans-Joachim *Paproth's Studien über das Bärenzeremoniell,* vol. 1 (Uppsala, 1976).

Summary reports of the scholarly publications on Sami religion and folklore up to 1950 were issued in the *Journal of the Royal Anthropological Institute* in the 1950s: Knut Bergsland and Reidar Christiansen's "Norwegian Research on the Language and Folklore of the Lapps" (vol. 80, 1950), and my "Swedish Research on the Religion and Folklore of the Lapps" (vol. 85, 1955). Later books and articles on the subject are annotated in Louise Bäckman's and my *Studies in Lapp Shamanism* (Stockholm, 1978).

There is no similar survey of scholarly contributions in tsarist and Soviet Russia, except the studies of shamanism. Some points of view on Soviet studies are presented in I. S. Gurvich's "An Ethnographic Study of Cultural Parallels among the Aboriginal Populations of Northern Asia and Northern North America," *Arctic Anthropology* 16 (1979): 32–38. The comprehensive areal works by Uno Holmberg Harva and Ivar Paulson contain some introductory remarks, but no more. The student has to go to the separate books and articles, most of them published in Russian, but some in western European languages: this applies, of course, first of all to the works of scholars residing in western Europe and America. No collocation of all this scholarship has ever been done.

The same applies to the split publications on Inuit religion. The total research contribution has not yet been evaluated. See, however, the short introduction to the subject by Ivar Paulson, Karl Jettmar, and me in *Les religions arctiques et finnoises* (Paris, 1965), pp. 346f.

ÅKE HULTKRANTZ (1987)

ARHAT.

ARHAT. The Sanskrit term *arhat* (Pali, *arahant*) derives from the root *arh (arhati)* and literally means "worthy" or "deserving." The term is especially important in Theravāda Buddhism, where it denotes the highest state of spiritual development, but it also has pre-Buddhist and non-Buddhist applications.

HISTORY AND DEVELOPMENT OF THE TERM. In Vedic and non-Vedic contexts, the noun *arhat* and the verb *arhati* applied generally to persons or gods whose particular status earned for them the characterization of "worthy" or "deserving of merit." The terms also denoted "being able to do," or "being capable of doing." For example, in *Ṛgveda* 1.94.1 Agni is addressed in a song of praise as "the worthy one" (*arhat*). The term *arhat* does not appear in the Upaniṣads, but the verb *arhati* occurs there five times with the sense of "being able." The ten occurrences of the verb in the *Bhagavadgītā* convey a similar general meaning.

In the Jain *sūtras* the term is often used in a sense closer to that found in Buddhist writings. Here the arhat is described as one who is free from desire, hatred, and delusion, who knows everything, and who is endowed with miraculous powers. While these characterizations are consistent with the Buddhist use of the term, it should be noted that the Jains applied the word exclusively to the *tīrthaṃkaras* or revealers of religion, whereas in Buddhism arhatship is an ideal to be attained by all serious religious strivers, especially monks and nuns.

In the Pali scriptures of Theravāda Buddhism *arahant/arahati* shares with Vedic, Hindu, and Jain sources the same general meanings "worthy, able, fit." In a more specific usage, but one that is not yet part of the most prevalent formulas found in the Sutta and Vinaya Piṭakas, the term is applied to those who have supernatural powers or who practice austerities.

PLACE IN BUDDHIST SOTERIOLOGY. In its most typical usage in Theravāda Buddhism, however, the term *arahant* signifies persons who have reached the goal of enlightenment or *nibbāna* (Skt., *nirvāṇa*). In the Pali canon the *arahant* emerges not simply as the revealer of the religion or the person worthy of receiving gifts but as one who has attained freedom of mind and heart, has overcome desire and passion, has come to true knowledge and insight, has crossed over the flood (of *saṃsāra*) and gone beyond (*pāragata*), has destroyed the *āsavas* (deadly attachments to the world), is versed in the threefold knowledge (*tevijja*) of past, present, and future, has achieved the thirty-seven factors of enlightenment, and who has attained *nibbāna.*

In the Vinaya, the concept of the *arahant* appears to be connected with the concept of *uttarimanussa* ("further being, superhuman being"). Here, the *arahant* is said to possess one or more of the four trance states (*jhāna*), one or more of the four stages of sanctification, mastery of the threefold knowledge and the sixfold knowledge (*chaḷabhiññā*), which includes knowledge of previous rebirths, and to have achieved the destruction of the *āsavas,* or "cankers." Indeed, it may be that the notion of *uttarimanussa* constitutes the earliest beginning of a more elaborated and refined concept designated by the term *arahant.*

It is in the Nikāyas, however, that the concept of the *arahant* achieves its mature form. In the first volume of the *Dīgha Nikāya* ten of the thirteen *suttas* deal almost entirely with this theme; the other three are indirectly related to it. In these texts arhatship is extolled as the highest of social ranks, the only form of sacrifice worth making, the best asceticism, and the true form of *brahmacariya* (Skt., *brahmacarya*). Clearly, the term *arahant* signifies the Buddhist transvaluation of terms applied to the most worthwhile aspects of life. In the *Majjhima Nikāya* the *arahant* is said to recognize things as they really are, to have eliminated the *āsavas*, to be far removed from evil, and to be beyond birth, decay, and death.

There are several *arahant* formulas in the Pali Tipitaka. Perhaps the best known is the following:

> Rebirth has been destroyed. The higher life has been fulfilled. What had to be done has been accomplished. After this present life there will be no beyond. (*Dīgha Nikāya* 1.84 and elsewhere)

Other formulas emphasize the attainment of the emancipation of mind, the transcendence of rebirth, the realization of *jhanic* states, knowledge of the Four Truths, the overcoming of the *āsavas*, and the gaining of salvation and perfect knowledge. The term also appears in the formulaic phrase characterizing the Buddha: "A Tathagata arises in the world, an *arahant,* a fully enlightened one perfect in knowledge and conduct, a wellfarer, a world-knower, unsurpassed driver of men to be driven, a teacher of *devas* [gods] and mankind, A Buddha, an Exalted One."

Arhatship figures prominently into the Theravāda notion that the salvific journey is a gradual path (*magga*) in which one moves from the condition of ordinary worldly attachments governed by ignorant sense desires to a state of liberation characterized by utter equanimity and the knowledge of things as they are. As Buddhagosa put it in his *Visuddhimagga* (Path of purification), the classic synopsis of Theravāda doctrine, the *arahant* has completed all of the purities derived through the observance of the moral precepts (*sīla*), meditational practice (*jhāna*), and the purity of knowledge (*paññā-visuddhi*). The sine qua non of this path is meditation, which leads to extraordinary cognitive states and stages of consciousness (*jhāna*) and, allegedly, to the acquisition of various supernormal "powers" (*iddhi*). These attainments became fundamental to the cult of saints, an important aspect of popular Theravāda Buddhist practice. This popular aspect of arhatship has not always been easy to reconcile with the classical notion, which emphasizes the acquisition of what Buddhaghosa refers to as the "analytical knowledges," for example, the analysis of reality in terms of its conditioned and co-arising nature (*paṭicca-samuppāda;* Skt., *pratītya-samutpāda*).

Both the Therāvada *Kathavātthu* (Points of controversy) and Vasumitra's *Samayabhedoparacanacakra* (History of the schisms, a Sarvāstivāda work) give ample evidence that during the first few centuries following the death of the Buddha there were frequent disputes within the order concerning the nature and attributes of the arhat. The greatest challenge to the arhat ideal, however, came from the Mahāyāna tradition, which proclaimed the career of the *bodhisattva* to be superior to that of the arhat. Texts such as the *Saddharmapuṇḍarīka* and *Vimalakīrti Sūtras* criticize the arhat for pursuing, in their view, an unacceptably self-centered soteriological path.

The Arhat as Cult Figure. In popular Buddhism the arhat has become a figure endowed with magical and apotropaic powers. In Myanmar, the *arahant* Shin Thiwali (Pali, Sivali), declared by the Buddha to be the foremost recipient of gifts among his disciples, is believed to bring prosperity and good fortune to those who petition him. The *arahant* Upagupta, who tamed Māra and converted him to Buddhism, is thought to have the power to prevent storms and floods as well as other kinds of physical violence and unwanted chaos. Customarily, Buddhist festivals in Myanmar and northern Thailand are initiated by an offering to Upagupta in order to guarantee the success of the event. In Myanmar, offerings are made to the Buddha and the eight *arahants* (Sāriputta, Moggallāna, Ānanda, Revata, Upāli, Koṇḍañña, Rāhula, and Gavampati) as part of a long-life engendering ceremony in which each *arahant* is associated with one of the eight days of the Myanmar week and with a special planet. Piṇḍola Bhāradvāja, one of the sixteen great arhats (Chin., *luohan*), was particularly venerated as the guardian saint of monasteries' refectories in China and Japan (where he is known as Binzuru), and was also worshiped as a popular healing saint.

The arhat, as one who has realized the *summum bonum* of the spiritual path, is worshiped on the popular level as a field of merit (*puṇy akṣetra*) and source of magical, protective power. Some, such as Upagupta and Piṇḍola, became in effect protective deities believed to have the power to prevent violence and illness. Offerings to their images or symbolic representations of their presence constitute cultic practice in both domestic and public rituals. However, arhats other than those associated with the Buddha during his lifetime or the sixteen arhats enumerated in Nandimitra's *Record of the Abiding of the Dharma* (T.D. no. 2030) have served as sources of power. Claims of arhatship are continuously being made on behalf of holy monks in countries such as Sri Lanka, Myanmar, and Thailand. Devoted laypersons seek them out for boons and wear protective amulets bearing their image or charred remains of their hair or robe. They may be venerated as wizards (Burm., *weikza*) with magical skills in alchemy, trance, and the like. Elaborate hagiographies tell of extraordinary natural signs announcing their birth and detail careers characterized by the performance of miraculous deeds. Their monasteries, in turn, may become holy pilgrimage centers both during and after their lifetime.

In short, the arhat embodies one of the fundamental tensions in the Buddhist tradition between the ideal of enlightenment and equanimity and the extraordinary magical power concomitant with this attainment. This tension, while present in the texts, is further heightened in the light of popular Buddhist attitudes and practices regarding the figure of the arhat.

See Also Bodhisattva Path; Mahāsiddhas; Nirvāṇa; Perfectibility; Soteriology; Tīrthaṃkaras.

Bibliography

The classic study of the *arahant* in the Theravāda tradition is I. B. Horner's *The Early Buddhist Theory of Man Perfected* (London, 1936). In more recent years both historians of religion and anthropologists have studied the Buddhist saint. Nathan Katz has compared the *arahant* concept in the Sutta Piṭaka to the concepts of the *bodhisattva* and *mahāsiddha* in the Mahāyāna and Tantrayāna traditions in his book, *Buddhist Images of Human Perfection* (New Delhi, 1982). George D. Bond's "The Problems of 'Sainthood' in the Theravāda Buddhist Tradition," in *Sainthood in World Religions,* edited by George Bond and Richard Kieckhefer (Berkeley, Calif., 1984), provides a general analysis of the Theravāda *arahant* while Michael Carrithers's *The Forest Monks of Sri Lanka* (New York, 1983), and Stanley J. Tambiah's *The Buddhist Saints of the Forest and the Cult of Amulets* (Cambridge, U.K., 1984) offer anthropological analyses of the Theravāda saint in the contexts of modern Sri Lanka and Thailand, respectively. John S. Strong provides a reminder that the arhat receives approbation in the Mahāyāna as well as the Therāvada tradition in "The Legend of the Lion-Roarers: A Study of the Buddhist Arhat Piṇḍola Bhāradvāja," *Numen* 26 (June 1979): 50–87.

New Sources

Buswell, Robert E., and Robert M. Gimello. *Paths to Liberation: The Marga and Its Transformation in Buddhist Thought.* Honolulu, 1992.

Dhaky, M. A. *Arhat Parsva and Dharanendra Nexus.* Delhi, 1997.

Mehta, T. U., and A. K. Singh. *The Path of Arhat: A Religious Democracy.* Varanasi, 1993.

Nattier, Janice J., and Charles S. Prebish. "Mahasamghika Origins: The Beginnings of Buddhist Sectarianism." *History of Religions* 16 (1977): 237–272.

Swearer, Donald K. "The Arhat." In *Buddhism and Asian History,* edited by Joseph Mitsuo Kitagawa and Mark D. Cummings. See pages 361–364. New York, 1989.

DONALD K. SWEARER (1987)
Revised Bibliography

ARIANISM is the heretical doctrine promulgated by the Christian Alexandrian priest Arius (c. 250–336) that asserted the radical primacy of the Father over the Son. Three distinct streams of influence merged in the sea of doctrinal upheaval of Christianity in the fourth century: (1) the theological system developed by Arius himself, which was his private and pastoral accomplishment; (2) the moderate and conservative Origenism of the majority of Eastern bishops who found themselves in consonance with Arius's own Origenian background; and (3) the political initiatives of these bishops against Alexander of Alexandria. The complex state of church affairs arising from the confluence of these three streams has become known as the Arian controversy.

Without Arius the controversy would never have existed. Paradoxically, however, the Alexandrian priest contributed more to the name of the crisis than to the shaping of its doctrinal issues. In Arius's thought, certain trends of Alexandrian theology, formulated by Origen a few generations earlier, reached their ultimate consequences. Arius's concept of the Christian godhead was monarchic, that is, it held that the first and unique absolute principle of divinity is the Father. Consequently, any other divine reality was considered by him as secondary to the Father. He applied this view first of all to the Logos, the Word of God, the Son who becomes the instrument of the divine plan of creation and salvation. The Son, being bound to the decision of the Father in the very process of his own generation as the Son, is not eternal in the same sense as the Father is eternal; more important, he is not eternal because only the Father is ungenerated. On the other hand, being the instrument of the fulfillment of the Father's will, the Son is by nature linked with the divine creation. He is, so to speak, the first transcendent creature, the principle of all things. Arius developed several Origenian insights in a way that led him finally to contradict Origen's notion of the godhead. In the course of his systematic inquiry, he not only urges traditional forms of trinitarian subordinationism, he pleads also for a radical dissimilarity among the Father, the Son, and the Holy Spirit.

It is not easy to garner an authentic picture of Arius's teachings on the incarnation of the Word and his interpretation of the gospel narratives. His main opponents, Alexander of Alexandria and Athanasius, have transmitted no direct evidence from Arius on these points; one must deduce Arius's conceptions from what his opponents denounce and refute in their anti-Arian writings. Arius's teachings on incarnation were probably traditional and reflective of Origen's christological legacy. Arius, like Origen, advocated that Christians should imitate the Son's asceticism and contemplate the mystery of his kenosis, which involved the Son even in the experience of death. The final glorification means that the risen Christ earned the right to be recognized in his divine rank as the Son of God. It has been suggested that Arius conceived of Jesus as being without a human soul, the Logos himself taking its place, but there is no support for this thesis in Arius's own writings.

Underlying the whole of Arius's thought is a philosophical perspective that guarantees the uniqueness of his system among the Origenian-type theologies current in the Greek-speaking churches of the first half of the fourth century. Arius's writings show a passionate concern for the radical transcendency of the first principle in the godhead, and he interprets the Christian notion of the Son in light of a rigorous, metaphysical deduction about the nature of the Son as proceeding from the first principle, his Father. Sharing the metaphysical concerns of Plotinus in *Ennead* 5 but using the Christian categories of Father and Son, Arius develops his view of God and the world only in regard to the origination of the second principle of the godhead, without regard to the teaching of the New Testament on the full divinity of Christ.

This underlying point of view seems to have shaped Arius's thought more than anything else. It was for this reason that he remained relatively isolated in the theological scene of his time, before as well as after his condemnation in Nicaea in 325. The misunderstandings to which his system led are best exemplified by the public statements against him by Alexander of Alexandria and Athanasius. Even the Eastern bishops, who for a time became his main supporters, ignored the merits of his rigorous logic and rejected his conclusions concerning the nature of the Son.

The Eastern bishops contributed in their own way to the controversy by their conservative politics. What Athanasius and other supporters of the Nicene Creed denounced as Arianism in the thought and the writings of certain Eastern bishops basically amounted to the Eastern bishops' opposition to the term *homoousios* ("same substance"), which had been canonized at Nicaea, and their preference for more biblical, more traditional, and often more or less subordinationist formulations, in the tradition of Origen.

The main party of bishops was called Homoeans, from *homoios,* meaning "similar" rather than "same," because they stressed the similitude of the Son to the Father in biblical terms, without dogmatic precision. The most prominent figures among the so-called Semi-Arians actually reverted to Nicene orthodoxy after the death of Emperor Constantius II (337–361). A true Arianism, which radicalized the rationalistic theology of Arius, recurred only once, in Alexandria, from about 355 to 366, with Aetios and Eunomios as its leaders.

Not only bishops, clerics, and church communities but emperors also may be called Arians during the struggles of the fourth century. Constantine, however, was never called Arian, even though he allowed the pro-Arian bishops to protect Arius during his lifetime. His son and successor, Constantius II, following in his father's footsteps, became an Arian in the eyes of the pro-Nicene bishops who were persecuted under his reign; it is difficult, however, to discern a precise theological motivation in the religious concerns of Constantius's complex personality. The emperor Valens (364–378) supported the pro-Arian majority of bishops in the East without true personal conviction. Arianism, transmitted to the Teutonic tribes, survived in the West until the sixth century.

BIBLIOGRAPHY

A general survey on the nature and origins of Arianism can be found in Jaroslav Pelikan's *The Emergence of the Catholic Tradition, 100–600,* vol. 1 of *The Christian Tradition: A History of the Development of Doctrine* (Chicago, 1971). Thomas A. Kopecek's *A History of Neo-Arianism,* 2 vols., "Patristic Monograph Series," no. 8 (Cambridge, Mass., 1979), as well as Robert C. Gregg and Dennis E. Groh's *Early Arianism: A View of Salvation* (Philadelphia, 1981), are useful introductions to specific aspects of Arianism. A survey of current research is provided in *Arianism: Historical and Theological Reassessments,* edited by Robert C. Gregg (Philadelphia, 1985).

CHARLES KANNENGIESSER (1987)

ARISTOTELIANISM is a school and style of philosophy that flourished throughout the Middle Ages in four languages and over three continents and that persists even now. Aristotle's school, the Lyceum, continued after his death under the leadership of his students, most notably Theophrastus (c. 371–c. 286 BCE). The vigor and brilliance of the Aristotelian legacy diminished after Theophrastus and were revived only after several centuries, but the editing of Aristotle's writings under the supervision of Andronicus of Rhodes was accomplished around 30 BCE in Rome. The work of Andronicus laid the literary foundations of the philosophical tradition of Aristotelianism. The philosophical, as distinct from the philological, study and development of Aristotelian philosophy owes much to Alexander of Aphrodisias (fl. 200 CE). His commentaries on Aristotle's *Metaphysics* and *On the Soul* became classics and were studied carefully by later Muslim and Jewish philosophers. Another important ancient commentator was Themistius (fl. fourth century CE) in Constantinople, whose paraphrase of book 12 of Aristotle's *Metaphysics* became a classic treatise in natural theology and was translated into Arabic, Hebrew, and Latin. Beginning in the fifth century, extremely valuable and influential commentaries on Aristotle's works were written by a group of scholar-philosophers who were more influenced by Plato and Plotinus than by Aristotle himself. Although most of these commentators were non-Christian, for instance, Simplicius (fl. sixth century), some were Christian, notably John Philoponus (fl. sixth century).

The transmission of the Aristotelian legacy to the Semitic world was begun by Syriac-speaking Christian thinkers who, living in or near the Byzantine empire, knew Greek and translated Aristotle's works either into Syriac first and then into Arabic or into Arabic directly. To some extent Aristotelian ideas had already filtered into the work of the Greek Church Fathers before becoming "semiticized" later on. In several Greek Christian theological texts we find some use of such Aristotelian terms as *ousia* (substance)—which in turn entered into Latin theological literature as *substantia.* Yet the Aristotelian philosophical influence on patristic literature was not so great as the Platonic and was generally confined to some of his logical writings, which were incorporated into the early medieval Greek and Latin educational program. Most of Aristotle's writings, especially the scientific, were either unknown or ignored in the West until they were translated from Arabic several centuries later.

By the ninth century a distinctive intellectual tradition had emerged in the Muslim world. Its practitioners, the *falāsifah* ("philosophers"), were set off from and opposed to the *mutakallimūn* ("theologians"). These Muslim philosophers, the first of whom was probably al-Kindī (803–873), attempted to assimilate the Greek philosophical tradition as they knew it and to formulate a conception of Islam as a religion in philosophical terms. The most notable of these philosophers were al-Fārābī (870–950), Ibn Sīnā (980–1037; known in the Latin-speaking world as Avicenna), and Ibn Rushd (1126–1198; Averroës). Each represented a further development and refinement of Aristotle's philosophy, with increasing liberation from the Plotinian supplements and interpretations that had accumulated along the way. This incorporation of Aristotle into the "house of Islam" did not pass unchallenged, and at times the Islamic opposition to Aristotelian philosophy was quite strong.

Once Arabicized, Aristotle's writings began to spread into other languages. Since the majority of medieval Jewry was living in the Muslim world and speaking and writing Arabic, the Arabic translations of Aristotle eventually became part of the Jewish philosophical tradition, which, although small, comprised a continuous series of notable thinkers throughout the Middle Ages. By the middle of the twelfth century, Aristotle had so thoroughly captivated the Jewish philosophical world that the earlier Neoplatonic writers were not only eclipsed but almost obliterated. From Maimonides (1135/8–1204) on, Jewish philosophical and theological literature was dominated by Aristotle. As in Islam, Jewish thinkers in the twelfth and thirteenth centuries, such as Yitsḥaq Albalag and Mosheh Narboni, absorbed Aristotle's ideas. Critical response was sometimes moderate and sometimes severe and thoroughgoing. Nevertheless, Aristotle's influence was still prominent in Jewish thought throughout the Renaissance, diminishing only in the seventeenth century.

The Latinizing of Aristotle occurred both early and late. In the sixth century the Roman writer and civil servant Boethius translated some of Aristotle's logical treatises into Latin; but these first fruits were to be the only works of Aristotle available in the Latin world until the late twelfth century. Because of this lack the Latin philosophical world of the Middle Ages was for several centuries relatively "dark," while the Arabic-Hebrew world was "enlightened." This cultural gap was, however, to vanish. Initially Aristotle's works were rendered into Latin from Arabic or Hebrew along with the commentaries of Ibn Sīnā and Ibn Rushd; later Latin translations were made directly from the Greek, although these were less common until the fifteenth century. By the middle of the thirteenth century, Thomas Aquinas (1225–1274) had virtually the entire Aristotelian corpus at his disposal and was thus able to do for the Christian world what Maimonides and Ibn Rushd had tried to do for their coreligionists: establish a philosophical interpretation of the religious beliefs of Judaism, Christianity, and Islam within the general conceptual framework of Aristotle's philosophy.

Subsequent Christian theologians and philosophers continued Thomas's work by writing commentaries upon Aristotle's treatises and composing philosophical books in which Aristotle's ideas were either expanded or criticized. By the thirteenth century Aristotle was referred to in Arabic, Hebrew, and Latin as "the Philosopher." His writings constituted almost the entire philosophical library and curriculum of the medieval world until the fifteenth century, when signs of a Platonic revival begin to surface in Renaissance Italy. But even in the sixteenth and seventeenth centuries, such thinkers as Giordano Bruno (1548–1600) and Galileo (1564–1642) suffered because of the power of the Aristotelian professors and theologians at Italian universities.

INFLUENCE OF ARISTOTELIANISM. Perhaps the most attractive feature of Aristotle's philosophy is its comprehensiveness. It is not just that Aristotle wrote on every topic from astronomy to zoology but more that what he did write added up to an integrated system of thought that made good sense out of ordinary human experience. Aristotle's philosophy begins with logic, and the first translations of Aristotle were the Latin versions of several of his logical treatises. Logic was to be a steady interest of medieval philosophers, who, in Latin, Arabic, and Hebrew, continued to develop, refine, and supplement Aristotelian logic as a topic-neutral discipline.

In most medieval curricula the subject studied after logic was natural science, an area of pervasive interest to Aristotle, who wrote treatises in both the physical and the biological sciences. In addition to his separate studies in the special sciences, Aristotle developed his scientific views into a general theory of nature, a "philosophy of nature." The medievals took Aristotle's general cosmological scheme for granted and usually adopted its main principles. The Aristotelian cosmos is a well-ordered physical system in which natural processes follow regular patterns and determinate goals. Aristotle's doctrine of natural teleology was a medieval commonplace. The same is true with respect to his doctrine of finitism. The medievals shared his general prejudice against the infinite and believed with him that the world is a "closed" system: finite in size and in the number of individuals contained within it.

Aristotle's philosophy of nature was also attractive to the medieval mind because it allowed for theology. His theory of celestial motion provides the premises for a proof for the existence of a deity; indeed, Aristotle himself gives such a proof, one that was developed by medieval philosophers and theologians through the thirteenth century. Eventually, Aristotle's own natural theology, sketched out in *Metaphysics* 12, became the philosophical paradigm according to which many medieval thinkers developed their own theories of divine attributes. Further, Aristotle's theory of celestial motion allowed for a plurality of "unmoved movers" of the heavenly spheres, although one of them—God—was regarded as primary. Medieval philosophers took this doctrine even further and, under the influence of Plotinian themes, developed a cosmology within which various levels and kinds of cosmic intellects, or powers, devoid of matter, function within the universe. Aristotle's cosmos became to the medieval mind a richly diversified scale of being, some of whose rungs were occupied by intellectual forces that were inferior to the supreme mind, God, but superior to all embodied souls or animate beings, such as humans, dogs, and roses. At this point a marriage between Aristotle and Plotinus had been arranged, one that the biblical doctrine of angels either motivated or could easily be fitted into. The biblical angels were indeed identified by al-Fārābī and Maimonides as Aristotle's separate, unmoved movers. In this context we have really a marriage among three partners: Aristotle, Plotinus, and scripture.

One Aristotelian idea that proved to be troublesome, however, was the thesis of the eternity of the world. After all, what could be more clear or explicit than *Genesis* 1:1: "In the beginning God created the heavens and the earth"? Throughout the Middle Ages, Muslim, Jewish, and Christian thinkers wrestled with what appeared to be an irreconcilable conflict between Aristotle and scripture on this fundamental cosmological doctrine. Various solutions were proposed, some veering toward Aristotle, others toward scripture. Of the former variety was the view of the Muslim philosophers who developed a doctrine of eternal creation, whereby the universe eternally emanates from God, its first and ultimate cause. Others, like Levi ben Gershom, or Gersonides (1288–1344), a French-Jewish philosopher and astronomer, criticized and rejected the Aristotelian eternity thesis altogether and defended the biblical doctrine of creation. But at this point the creationist camp split: some advocated the idea, an "absurdity" to the Greeks, that God created the world *ex nihilo;* others, a small minority including Gersonides, adopted the Platonic suggestion of a divine sculptor crafting the world out of formless, uncreated matter (see Gersonides' *The Wars of the Lord* 6.1.17). Some thinkers, however, believed that this question was not philosophically decidable and that one had to appeal to revelation for the correct answer. This cosmological agnosticism was advocated by Thomas Aquinas and was accepted by many Christian theologians thereafter (*Summa theologiae* 1.46.2).

The question of creation proved to have more than just cosmological implications. Inseparably bound up with it was the issue of miracles and divine omnipotence. Maimonides welded the link between these questions quite tightly: the affirmation of the world's eternity implied strict determinism, which rules out, he claimed, the possibility of miracles (see his *The Guide of the Perplexed* 2.25). In turn, the denial of miracles implies a serious restriction on God's omnipotence. By the end of the thirteenth century some of the more "irreconcilable" philosophical and scientific theses of Aristotle and the Muslim philosophers were condemned as heretical and false by Stephen Tempier, bishop of Paris. Aristotle's doctrine of the eternity of the universe was equated with a curtailment of God's infinite power.

A number of modern scholars have maintained that although the 1277 condemnation by Stephen Tempier superficially looks like theological interference with philosophical inquiry, it really was not. Instead, these scholars claim, thinkers were thus liberated from their Aristotelian fetters and were free to pursue lines of thought, particularly scientific hypotheses, that previously had not been open to them and that were ultimately to replace Aristotelian physics. Whether or not the condemnation itself led to a more critical approach to Aristotelian natural philosophy is difficult to determine. What is undoubtedly true is that from the fourteenth century on there was a growing dissatisfaction with some of the more important ideas in Aristotle's cosmology and physics. That this critique took place in the Jewish philosophical orbit too suggests that it was not so much Stephen Tempier who stimulated the critical spirit as the continuous close study of Aristotle's ideas by independent-minded philosophers and theologians. Gersonides, living far from Paris, criticized Aristotle's major principle of mechanics, the theorem that every moving body is moved by an external mover. With the rejection of this physical principle, the argument for the existence of God as the first unmoved mover fails.

Perhaps the most thoroughgoing and profound premodern critique of Aristotelian natural philosophy was developed by the Spanish-Jewish theologian Ḥasdai Crescas (1340–1420). Wanting to undermine the whole medieval Aristotelian tradition in Jewish theology, Crescas correctly focused his efforts upon the basic physical theorems of Aristotle. One by one these cornerstones crumble under Crescas's acute criticisms. Why can't there be an actual infinite? Why can't there be a vacuum? Do the heavenly bodies need to be continuously moved by external, incorporeal unmoved movers? Why can't there be a successive series or even a simultaneous plurality of worlds? These and other questions eventually led Crescas to reject the whole Aristotelian physical system. In its place he suggested an actually infinite universe in which the heavenly bodies move according to their own inherent motion, without unmoved movers. Such a universe, Crescas insisted, manifests God's infinite power.

Another persisting perplexity that the medievals inherited from Aristotle had to do with his psychology. Aristotle's obscure, indeed mysterious remarks about "the intellect that makes all things" and "the intellect that becomes all things" (*On the Soul* 3.5) turned out to be one of the most commented-upon passages in his entire corpus. His somewhat parenthetical comment that the former intellect might be immortal and eternal aggravated the matter and opened up a can of philosophical and theological worms. What did Aristotle mean by an active mind and a passive mind? Where are these intellects? Are they immanent within the human mind or transcendent? How do these different intellectual functions work? Wherein lies the immortality of the intellect? These were only a few of the questions that were to vex Aristotle's commentators and medieval disciples.

Alexander of Aphrodisias made several important terminological and conceptual clarifications of this passage. Dubbing the active intellectual part the "agent intellect" (*nous poiētikos*) and the passive part the "material intellect" (*nous hulikos*), he went on to claim that the former is a unique, transcendent incorporeal power identical with God, whereas the latter is a corporeal disposition of the human body. The agent intellect is the active cause in human cognition; the material intellect is the receptive, or passive, capacity to acquire knowledge. Finally, the mature human intellect perfected by its accumulated cognitions is the "acquired intellect" (*nous epiktētos*). It is this last member of this cognitive trio that Alexander suggests might be immortal. Jewish, Christian, and Muslim thinkers agreed that the agent intellect was not only the primary active cause in human intellection but also a major factor in prophecy. The prophet is a person whose intellect is so perfect that he is eligible to receive a special "overflow" from the agent intellect that makes him the recipient of divine information, which he conveys to other people. The ordinary religious believer refers to the agent intellect as an angel, since scripture, written in the language of ordinary people, depicts the agent intellect figuratively so as to give the reader some idea of how prophecy is given.

A number of Parisian philosophers, following Ibn Rushd's conclusion that agent intellect and material intellect are virtually and actually one, could not quite reconcile that view with their religious belief in individual immortality. Thus emerged the notorious doctrine of the double truth, according to which what is taught by divine revelation may not be compatible with what is taught by sound philosophy. Throughout the late thirteenth century the Latin philosophical-theological scene was obsessed with this issue, until the "Latin Averroists" were finally suppressed. In this battle to "protect the faith" Thomas Aquinas wrote a polemical essay against the Averroists. According to him, the agent intellect is not a unique transcendent power but is immanent in each human mind, which is as a whole a substance capable of independent existence. Individual immortality is thereby ensured (*Summa theologiae* 1.75, 76, 79, and *On the Unicity of the Intellect: Against the Averroists*).

Despite the various criticisms made of these different aspects of Aristotle's doctrines, his influence remained strong throughout the Middle Ages and even in the Renaissance. Galileo's frequent sarcastic and mordant criticisms of the "simple-minded" Aristotelian professors, who prefer to look at the heavens in their books rather than through the telescope, testify to the still-living tradition of Aristotelian thought in the seventeenth century.

Aristotelianism was influential in the twentieth century in Roman Catholic theological circles and in university faculties. Recently, however, the Aristotelian imprint upon Christian theology has begun to seem either foreign or obsolete to theologians who look to modern philosophers for inspiration. Nevertheless, Aristotle's metaphysical ideas and vocabulary persist and are defended or at least employed by some contemporary Anglo-American philosophers, such as P. F. Strawson, who consider him to be one of the more suggestive thinkers in the classical tradition of Western philosophy.

SEE ALSO Attributes of God; Falsafah; Humanism; Logic; Neoplatonism; Nominalism; Proofs for the Existence of God; Scholasticism; Science and Religion; Soul; Theology.

BIBLIOGRAPHY

Copleston, Frederick C. *A History of Philosophy*, vols. 2 & 3, *Medieval Philosophy.* London, 1946. The most comprehensive survey of medieval philosophy in English.

Crombie, Alistair C. *Medieval and Early Modern Science.* 2d rev. ed. 2 vols. New York, 1959. Very good on the medieval reception and development of the Aristotelian scientific legacy.

Düring, Ingemar. *Aristotle in the Ancient Biographical Tradition.* Stockholm, 1957.

Guttman, Julius. *Philosophies of Judaism.* New York, 1964. Part 2 includes an excellent discussion of Jewish Aristotelianism.

Peters, F. E. *Aristotle and the Arabs.* New York, 1968. A most useful account of the transmission of Aristotle to the Arab-speaking world.

Randall, John Herman, Jr. *Aristotle.* New York, 1960. A suggestive monograph showing the relationship of Aristotle to Dewey and modern science.

Sorabji, Richard. *Times, Creation, and the Continuum.* Ithaca, N.Y., 1983. A fine philosophical and historical study of basic topics in Aristotle's philosophy.

New Sources

Badawi, Abdurrahman. *La transmission de la philosophie grecque au monde arabe.* Paris, 1968.

Barnes, Jonathan, ed. *The Cambridge Companion to Aristotle.* Cambridge, U.K., and New York, 1995. Blumenthal, Henry, and Howard Robinson, eds. *Aristotle and the later tradition.* Oxford, 1991.

D'Ancona Costa, Cristina. "Commenting on Aristotle: from late antiquity to the Arab Aristotelianism." In *Der Kommentar in Antike und Mittelalter. Beiträge zu seiner Erforschung*, edited by Wilhelm Geerlings and Christian Schluz, pp. 201–251. Leiden-Boston-Köln, 2002.

Davidson, Herbert A. "Alfarabi and Avicenna on the active intellect." *Viator* 3 (1972): 109–178.

Davidson, Herbert A. *Alfarabi, Avicenna, and Averroes on Intellect: Their Cosmologies, Theories of the Active Intellect, and Theories of Human Intellect.* New York, 1992.

Donini, Pier Luigi. *Tre studi sull'aristotelismo nel secondo secolo d.c.* Torino, 1974.

Donini, Pier Luigi. *Le scuole, l'anima, l'impero.* Torino, 1983.

Endress, Gerhard, Jan Aertsen, and Klaus Braun, eds. *Averroes and the Aristotelian Tradition.* Leiden-Boston, 1999.

Theophrastus of Eresus. *Sources for His Life, Writings, Thought and Influence*, edited and translated by W. W. Fortenbaugh, P. M. Huby, Robert W. Sharples and Dimitri Gutas, together with A. D. Barker, J. J. Keaney, D. C. Mirhady, David Sedley, and M. G. Sollenberger, Part One. Leiden-New York-Cologne, 1992.

Garfagnini Gian Carlo. *Aristotelismo e Scolastica.* Torino, 1979. Genequand, Charles. *Ibn Rushd Metaphysics.* Leiden, 1984.

Gutas, Dimitri. *Avicenna and the Aristotelian Tradition.* Leiden, 1988. Gutas, Dimitri. *Greek Philosophers in the Arabic Tradition.* Aldershot, 2001.

Gutas, Dimitri. *Greek Thought, Arabic Culture: The Graeco-Arabic Translation Movement in Baghdad and Early 'Abbāsid Society.* London, 1998.

Hadot, Ilsetraut. *Le problème du néoplatonisme alexandrin. Hiéroclès et Simplicius.* Paris, 1978.

Irmscher, Joachim. "Die spätantiken Aristoteleskommentatoren in ihrer geschichtlichen Umwelt." In *Romanitas-Christianitas. Untersuchungen zur Geschichte und Literatur der römischen Kaiserzeit. Johannes Straub zum 70. Geburtstag am 18. Oktober 1982 gewidmet*, edited by Gerhard Wirth, pp. 411–425. Berlin, 1982.

Lauth, Bernhard. *Formallogische Untersuchungen zu Aristoteles und Thomas von Aquin.* Munich, 1988.

Lee, Tae-Soo. *Die griechische Tradition der aristotelischen Syllogistik in der Spätantike. Eine Untersuchung über die Kommentare zu den Analytica priora von Alexander Aphrodisiensis, Ammonius und Philoponus.* Göttingen, 1984.

Luna, Concetta. *Trois études sur la tradition des commentaires anciens à la Métaphysique d'Aristote.* Leiden, 2001.

Lutz-Bachmann, Matthias, ed. *Ontologie und Theologie: Beiträge zum Problem der Metaphysik bei Aristoteles und Thomas von Aquin.* Frankfurt, 1988.

Mansion, Suzanne. *Études aristotéliciennes. Recueil d'articles.* Louvain-la-Neuve, 1984.

Menne, Albert, and Niels Offenberger. *Zur modernen Deutung der aristotelischen Logik*, vol. 1. Hildesheim, 1982.

Moraux, Paul. *Der Aristotelismus bei den Griechen; von Andronikos bis Alexander von Aphrodisias*, vol. 2. Berlin, 1984.

Moraux, Paul. *Le commentaire d'Alexandre d'Aphrodise aux Seconds analytiques d'Aristote.* Berlin, 1979.

Motte, André, and Joseph Denooz, eds. *Aristotelica secunda: Mélanges offerts à Christian Rutten.* Liège, 1995.

Petersen, Peter. *Geschichte der aristotelischen Philosophie im protestantischen Deutschland.* Leipzig, 1921 (reprinted Stuttgart-Bad Cannstatt, 1964).

Piaia, Gregorio, ed. *La presenza dell'aristotelismo padovano nella filosofia della prima modernità: Atti del Colloquio internazionale in memoria di Charles B. Schmitt,* Padova, 4–6 settembre 2000. Rome, 2002.

Pines, Salomo. *The Collected Works. Studies in Arabic Versions of Greek Texts and in Medieval Science.* Leiden, 1986.

Pozzo, Riccardo, ed. *The Impact of Aristotelianism on Modern Philosophy. Washington DC, 2004. Renaissance readings of the Corpus Aristotelicum. Proceedings of the conference held in Copenhagen 23 – 25 april 1998,* ed. by Marianne Pade. Copenhagen, 2001.

Rohls, Jan. *Wilhelm von Auvergne und der mittelalterliche Aristotelismus. Gottesbegriff und aristotelische Philosophie zwischen Augustin und Thomas von Aquin.* Munich, 1980.

Schmitt, Charles. *John Case and Aristotelianism in Renaissance England.* Kingston, Ont., 1983.

Seidl, Horst. "Remarques sur la doctrine aristotélicienne de l'essence et son développement chez saint Thomas d'Aquin." *Revue de Philosophie Ancienne* 14 (1996): 39–55.

Sharples, Robert W. "Alexander of Aphrodisias. Scholasticism and innovation." In *Aufstieg und Niedergand der Römischen Welt* 2.36.2, pp. 1176–1243. Berlin-New York, 1987.

Sharples, Robert W. "Aristotelian Tradition after Aristotle." In *Traditions of Theolgy. Studies in Hellenistic theology. Its background and Aftermath,* ed. by Dorothea Frede and André Laks, pp. 1–40. Leiden, 2002.

Sharples, Robert W., ed. *Whose Aristotle? Whose Aristotelianism?,* Aldershot, 2001.

Sharples, Robert W. *Alexander of Aphrodisias on Fate.* London, 1983.

Sorabji, Richard, ed. *Aristotle and After.* London, 1997.

Sorabji, Richard, ed. *Aristotle Transformed: The Ancient Commentators and Their Influence.* Ithaca, 1990.

Sorabji, Richard, ed. *Philoponus and the Rejection of Aristotelian Science.* Ithaca, 1987.

Sorabji, Richard. *Necessity, Cause, and Blame. Perspectives on Aristotle's Theory.* Ithaca, 1980.

Steel, Carlos. "Des commentaires d'Aristote par Thémistius." *Revue Philosophique de Louvain* 71 (1973): 669–680.

Tommasi, Francesco V. "Franz Albert Aepinus, l'aristotelismo tedesco e Kant. Un contributo per la comprensione della filosofia critica tra metafisica ed epistemologia." *Archivio di filosofia* 71 (2003): 333–358).

Verbeke, Gérard. *D'Aristote à Thomas d'Aquin: antécédents de la pensée moderne.* Leuven, 1990. Watt, John W. "From Themistius to al-Farabi." *Rhetorica* 13 (1995): 17–41.

Weidmann, H. *Metaphysik und Sprache. Eine sprachphilosophische Untersuchung zu Thomas von Aquin und Aristoteles.* Freiburg, 1975.

Wiesner, Jürgen, ed. *Aristoteles. Werk und Wirkung. Paul Moraux Gewidmet,* Berlin, 1987.

Wisnovsky, Robert. *Avicenna's Metaphysics in Context.* Ithaca, 2003.

Zimmermann, Albert. *Ontologie oder Metaphysik? Die Diskussion über den Gegenstand der Metaphysik im 13. und 14. Jahrhundert.* Leiden, 1965.

SEYMOUR FELDMAN (1987)
Revised Bibliography

ARISTOTLE

ARISTOTLE (384–322 BCE), along with Plato, was the greatest philosopher of antiquity. His influence on Western philosophical and scientific culture has been enormous, and even in the twenty-first century in many fields of knowledge (metaphysics, logic, ethics, biology, and psychology) the name of Aristotle represents an important point of reference.

LIFE AND WORKS. Aristotle was born in the city of Stagira in northern Greece and at the age of seventeen moved to Athens, where for about twenty years he attended the Academy, the school founded by Plato. There he obtained an extensive and liberal education, ranging from logic to natural philosophy, from metaphysics to astronomy. From 360 BCE onward he held regular courses and seminars within the Academy. After the death of Plato in 348 BCE, Aristotle left Athens and the Academy, traveling to Atarneus, Assus, and Mytilene and then to Pella, where he was the tutor of Alexander the Great, the future ruler of Greece, for about three years. During this period Aristotle concentrated his efforts on the study of biology and zoology and produced his scientific works. From 335 BCE he was once again back in Athens, where he founded the Lyceum, a school that rivaled the institution established by Plato and headed at that time by Xenocrates. The composition or definitive arrangement of Aristotle's major scholarly works may be dated to this period of teaching at the Lyceum.

The writings of Aristotle are traditionally divided into two groups: those intended for publication, the so-called exoteric works (*exoterikoi logoi*), and those written for internal use in the school and thus termed acroamatic (from *akroasis,* what is heard, thus heard in a lesson) or esoteric. The first group includes dialogues, such as the *Protrepticus* (an exhortation to philosophy), *On Philosophy,* and *Eudemus,* as well as doctrinal and polemical works, such as *On the Good* and *On Ideas*; the second includes the major treatises written for his school, such as *Metaphysics, Physics, On the Heaven, Nicomachean Ethics, Eudemian Ethics, On the Soul, Rhetorics, Poetics,* the works on biology and zoology (*On the Parts of Animals, The History of Animals*), and the works of logic (*Categories, Topics, Analytics*). By a quirk of fate only those works not intended for publication, that is, the acroamatic or esoteric texts, still exist, whereas none of the works published by Aristotle has survived. Knowledge of these relies upon quotations from later writers.

THE THEOLOGY OF THE YOUNG ARISTOTLE. In the twentieth century there were a number of studies concerning the so-called theology of the young Aristotle. In the dialogue *On Philosophy,* Aristotle probably alluded to two divinities, one cosmic, represented by the heavens (alive and composed of ether), the other metacosmic, in all probability represented by the unmoved prime mover, "Thought of Thought." In any case it seems certain that he laid down a clear order of importance between the two divinities, making the metacosmic divinity, that is the prime mover, superior to the heavens, whose very movement depended upon the unmoved mover. In the *Eudemus* he developed a theory of the soul, even if it is unclear whether in this dialogue Aristotle supported a radical dualism between body and soul like that of Plato or presented the idea of the soul as a form and function of the body just as in the work *On the Soul.* The *Protrepticus* finally contained proof of the superiority of the contemplative or speculative life, that is to say the truly philosophical way of life. The latter was considered divine, because it reveals man as like God, who is Thought, that is pure contemplative activity. The *Protrepticus* also contained an important argument in support of the unavoidable nature of philosophy, because even the rejection of the same requires its use in argument and thus "playing philosophy."

NATURE AND ITS PRINCIPLES. The starting point of Aristotle's philosophical thinking can be identified in the rejection of the theory of the forms put forward by Plato. Even during the years he spent at the Academy, Aristotle distanced himself from the theories of his teacher. Moving from a systematic analysis of language, especially predicative language, Aristotle singled out the primary meaning of being, upon which everything else somehow depends. This first meaning is represented by the category of substance (*ousia*), which in its purest form is identified with the particular individual. In order to be able to describe a particular reality as old (quality), as 170 centimeters tall (quantity), as in the Lyceum (place), as married to Xanthippe (relation) one must recognize the existence of an individual, in this case Socrates, all these attributes pertain to or are inherent in him. In its fullest meaning therefore being is not that of ideas, that is, of universals, but rather of substances, namely particular individuals or things (Socrates, a dog, the computer used to type these words).

The concept of substance expressed in the *Categories* is presumed in the analysis of the principles and causes of nature (*physis*) developed in the first two books of the *Physics.* Here too Aristotle starts by rejecting the Platonic theory of forms, especially the claim that the causes of the existence of sense objects may be seen in forms. According to Aristotle the common condition of all natural reality consists of motion, namely in the fact that all natural beings are subject to processes of reproduction and decay, of alteration, modification, and movement, and that they contain within themselves the cause of this change. Platonic forms, which are unmoved and separate, cannot in fact be the causes of natural reality because they are not able to explain the essential characteristic of the latter, namely that they are subject to movement (kinesis) and change *(metabolē).*

In his study of the principles of motion, Aristotle begins by recognizing, in common with many of his predecessors, that they are represented by opposites (love and strife, thick and thin, night and day). Because they do not, however, intersect with each other, it is necessary to recognize a third principle. Furthermore in order to talk about becoming, something must become, and in particular there is a certain reality that remains constant during the process of becoming. Aristotle thus divides any natural event into three constituent parts: the start is characterized by the absence or lack (*steresis*) of the form the object is to attain; the end in which the reality concerned takes on the form (*eidos*) with which the process ends or is fulfilled; and a third element that remains unchanged during the process and provides its unitary aspect, that is, the subject or underlying substrate (*hypokeimenon*). If the event to be described is the process of Socrates growing old, the *steresis* is Socrates when he is not old, the form is Socrates when he is old, and the underlying substrate or subject is Socrates himself.

It is important to understand that according to the Aristotelian concept the principles of becoming are not things but rather aspects of the things, points of view through which it is possible to analyze the mechanisms of change (*Physics,* I). A similar function is elaborated upon from the concepts of potentiality (*dynamis*) and actuality (*energeia, entelecheia*). These make natural processes intelligible and can be considered the realization of an already existing potentiality. Aristotle thus introduces the dimension of finalism and teleology into the analysis of the nature of becoming. Being and becoming of things may be analyzed from a causal perspective, because knowledge is the knowledge of cause (*aitia*). According to Aristotle there are four kinds of cause: material cause, that is, the matter (*hyle*) from which something is made; formal cause, that is, its form (*eidos*) and its organizing principle; efficient cause, that is, the moving principle (*to kinoun*); and final cause, that is, the purpose (telos) why something is what it is or an event takes place (*Physics,* II).

The kind of motion characteristic of natural realities also depends upon the elements of which they are composed. Those that belong to the sublunar world are made of four traditional elements (earth, air, fire, and water). That is to say they are subject to decay and naturally inclined to move in straight lines. Heavenly bodies, meaning the stars, are made of a fifth element, the well-known ether, which is the reason for their incorruptibility and the circular motion they have.

"FIRST PHILOSOPHY." Aristotle called physics "second philosophy" to distinguish it from "first philosophy," that is, from the branch of study that has been given the name "metaphysics" by Western tradition. "First philosophy" (*prote philosophia*) can be distinguished from physics on two grounds: (a) the universality of its object, which is not a single aspect of being but rather the study of "being as such," and (b) on account of the value and elevated nature of this object, which is ontologically superior to the realities of the physical world. In modern philosophy these two have been given the names *metaphysica generalis* (or ontology) and *metaphysica specialis* (or theology). Thus a philosopher such as Martin Heidegger held Aristotle responsible for founding ontotheology, namely Western metaphysics. Studies have shown nonetheless Aristotle's first philosophy was neither one thing nor the other. Rather, it was essentially a theory of substance because substance is the most important of the meanings of being. Being can be spoken of with many meanings (*to on pollachōs legetai*), but all relate to one principal meaning, that of substance (*Metaphysics,* IV). This idea has been called *focal meaning,* because it regards the meanings of being on the basis of the relationship with one unique principal meaning (*pros hen* Relation). The task of first philosophy is also to investigate what belongs to being as such, that is, its common attributes, such as unity and multiplicity, identity and diversity (medieval transcendentals). Furthermore it should also study the principle common to all demonstrations and therefore to all being: the principle of noncontradiction. This cannot be proved directly (because it is the basis of every proof), but it can be dialectically demonstrated that it is impossible to refute (*Metaphysics,* IV).

First philosophy is transformed into a theory of substance (*Metaphysics,* VII–IX), because substance is the first meaning of being. For Aristotle substance is the specific individual composed of form and matter. Yet still more substance is the form (*eidos*) that determines the being-as-it-is of a particular matter. In this sense substance as form or essence is the cause of being of the individual (*Metaphysics,* VII). In contrast to the Platonic forms, the Aristotelian substances-forms are not universal but rather individual, that is, they belong individually to the things of which they are forms. Form is therefore the organizing principle of matter. In terms of definition the forms of individuals of the same species are identical, but in numerical terms each individual has its own form. In the case of living beings the form is the soul, which represents the organizing vital principle of the body (*On the Soul,* I–II). Contrary to Plato, Aristotle considers the soul inseparable from the body, even if he does concede the possibility that part of it, the famous active intellect (*nous poietikos*), is independent of the body—arising in it from outside—and perhaps immortal (*On the Soul,* III). In any case the active intellect is not the unmoved prime mover, as Alexander of Aphrodisia thought.

The most famous idea of Aristotle is in Book XII of the *Metaphysics* and concerns the "immovable prime mover." This probably dates back to his youth and is not easy to reconcile with subsequent teachings. The observation of the eternity of motion and time caused Aristotle to postulate the existence of eternal principles, which are the cause of the eternal nature of physical motion. The latter finds its most elevated expression in the motion of the heavens. Aristotle observes that the cause of eternal motion must be an active and unmoved reality, otherwise it would itself require a principle and so on ad infinitum. Since the highest and most noble activity consists of thought (*noēsis*), this principle must be identified with thought and in precise terms with the thought of the most elevated object, that is, itself. The principle of motion must be "thought of thought" (*noēsis noēseōs*). Aristotle calls this being God (*theos*) as well as living an eternal and perfect life like the gods. The traditional interpretation attributes final causality to the unmoved mover. He moves the first heaven, that is the heaven of fixed stars, in which he is loved. This is possible because the heavens (or the celestial spheres) are given a soul, which longs for and loves the immovable mover, and via their circular motion the heavens try to imitate the absolute immobility of the latter as far as possible. In the twentieth century there was a new interpretation, according to which the unmoved mover does not move as a final cause but rather as a cause of motion, that is, efficient. He moves in the same way as the soul, except that the unmoved mover is transcendent with regard to the heavens, whereas the soul is immanent to what moves.

In Book VI of the *Metaphysics,* Aristotle attempts to bring together the two perspectives of "first philosophy," namely its universality and the value of its object. He asserts that "first philosophy" is first because its object consists of unmoved substances and is thus also universal, and its task will be to investigate being as such and its characteristics.

Ethics and Politics: Happiness. Physics, "first philosophy," and mathematics are theoretical sciences; their aim is in essence a dispassionate knowledge of reality. For Aristotle beside theoretical exist practical disciplines, that is, directed toward action (praxis). These comprise the fields of ethics (relating to individual moral action) and politics (concerning the action of the community). The ultimate aim of action is, according to Aristotle, the attainment of happiness (*eudaimonia*) (*Nicomachean Ethics,* I). For human beings the condition of happiness corresponds to the fulfillment of the highest form of life, that is, the one related to the highest function of the soul. The rational soul has two parts, the calculating part (*logistikon*) and the scientific part (*epistemonikon*). A particular virtue corresponds to each of these: respectively practical wisdom (*phronesis*) and theoretical wisdom (*sophia*). Both are dianoetic virtues, that is, they concern thought (*dianoia*) (*Nicomachean Ethics,* VI). Because a part of the soul had to do with the emotions and passions, it is necessary to recognize corresponding virtues here. This means the famous ethical virtues of courage, temperance, and liberality. Each of these represents the golden mean between two extremes, excess and deficiency (*Nicomachean Ethics,* II). Of the two dianoetic virtues, *sophia* concerns those aspects of reality that cannot be other than they are, that is, what is essential: it represents a kind of theoretical reason. When they achieve the highest form of life, contemplation, human beings are similar to God, who is, however, greater, because he lives eternally in that single state that people may only attain for a limited time (*Nicomachean Ethics,* X).

Phronesis, on the other hand, deals with those things that can be other than they are, that is, contingent reality: in this sense it represents practical reasoning. According to Aristotle the supreme practical virtue, *phronesis,* consists in the ability to establish suitable means to achieve determined ends. However, the latter seem to be set outside the deliberative dimension of practical philosophy. The identification of ends depends upon an act of the will (*boulesis*), which is independent of *phronesis.* For Aristotle indeed the determination of the ends of praxis by the will belongs to the realm of inclinations and desire, which are not subject to practical reasoning. This position has led some contemporary interpreters to charge Aristotelian ethics with making conservative assumptions, as it does not seem to possess rational criteria to legitimize the selection of the ends of action and risks basing the scope of ends on accepted prevalent values in a particular society. This discussion belongs to the so-called re-establishment of practical philosophy.

"Man is by nature a political animal" (*Politics,* III) is a statement that inicates that the social aspect is essential for the attainment of well-being. The two basic units of social life are the family and the state, that is the polis. The family consists of not only husband, wife, and children but also the slaves and the household generally (*oikos*) and its property. To Aristotle women were naturally subordinate to men, children to their father, and slaves to their master. The purpose of the family was the preservation of the human species and property. The states have different kinds of constitutions, depending upon whether they are governed by an individual, a restricted group, or the entire citizen body. The first of these is a monarchy, the second an aristocracy, and the third a *politeia,* that is, the positive form of democracy. Each of these three kinds of constitutions also has a debased form, which occurs when those who govern do so in their own interest rather than that of the citizens as a whole. These are tyranny, oligarchy, and debased democracy, that is, rule by demagogues.

Bibliography

Works by Aristotle

Works. Vols. 1–23. London and Cambridge, Mass., 1938–.

The Complete Works of Aristotle: The Revised Oxford Translation. 2 vols., edited by Jonathan Barnes. Princeton, N.J., 1984.

Studies

General surveys

Barnes, Jonathan, ed. *The Cambridge Companion to Aristotle.* Cambridge, U.K.,1995.

Berti, Enrico, ed. *Aristotele.* Rome and Bari, Italy, 1997.

Jaeger, Werner. *Aristotle: Fundamentals of the History of His Development.* Oxford, 1934.

Kraut, Richard. *Aristotle.* Oxford, 2002.

Lear, Jonathan. *Aristotle, the Desire to Understand.* Cambridge, U.K., 1988.

Lloyd, Geoffrey E. R. *Aristotle: The Growth and Structure of His Thought.* London, 1968.

Young Aristotle

Berti, Enrico. *La filosofia del primo Aristotele.* 2d ed. Milan, 1997.

Bos, Abraham P. *Cosmic and Meta-Cosmic Theology in Aristotle's Lost Dialogues.* Leiden, 1989.

Chroust, Anton Hermann. *Aristotle: New Light on His Life and on Some of His Lost Works.* 2 vols. London, 1973.

Dumoulin, Bertrand. *Recherches sur le premier Aristote.* Paris, 1981.

Philosophy of nature

Lang, Helen S. *The Order of Nature in Aristotle's Physics.* Cambridge, U.K., 1998.

Sorabji, Richard. *Necessity, Cause, and Blame: Perspectives in Aristotle's Theory.* Ithaca, N.Y., 1980.

Sorabji, Richard. *Matter, Space, and Motion.* Ithaca, N.Y., 1988.

Wieland, Wolfang. *Die aristotelische Physik.* Göttingen, Germany, 1970.

Metaphysics, epistemology, and psychology

Aubenque, Pierre. *Le problème de l'être chez Aristote.* Paris, 1962.

David, Charles. *Aristotle on Meaning and Essence.* Oxford, 2000.

Frede, Michael, and Charles David, eds. *Aristotle's Metaphysics Lambda.* Oxford, 2000.

Furth, Montgomery. *Substance, Form, and Psyche.* Cambridge, U.K., 1988.

Irwin, Terence. *Aristotle's First Principles.* Oxford, 1988.

Reale, Giovanni. *The Concept of First Philosophy and the Unity of the Metaphysics of Aristotle.* Albany, N.Y., 1980.

Scaltsas, Theodor, Charles David, and Marie-Luise Gill, eds. *Unity, Identity, and Explanation in Aristotle's Metaphysics.* Oxford, 1994.

Shields, Christopher. *Order in Multiplicity: Homonymy in the Philosophy of Aristotle.* Oxford, 1999.

Spellman, Lynne. *Substance and Separation in Aristotle.* Cambridge, U.K., 1995.

Ethics and politics

Anagnostopoulos, Georgios. *Aristotle on the Goals and Exactness of Ethics.* Berkeley, Calif., 1994.

Annas, Julia. *The Morality of Happiness.* New York, 1993.

Broadie, Sarah. *Ethics with Aristotle.* New York, 1991.

Miller, Fred D. *Nature, Justice, and Rights in Aristotle's Politics.* Oxford, 1995.

Nussbaum, Martha C. *The Fragility of Goodness: Luck and Ethics in Greek Tragedy and Philosophy.* Cambridge, U.K., 1986.

Sauvé Meyer, Susan. *Aristotle on Moral Responsibility.* Oxford, 1993.

Seymour Feldman (1987)
Franco Ferrari (2005)
Translated from Italian by Paul Ellis

ARJUNA. Of the Pāṇḍavas, the five sons of Pāṇḍu in the *Mahābhārata,* Arjuna is the third oldest, or "middle" Pāṇḍava. He is the youngest son of Kuntī, mother of the three oldest brothers. All five are only putatively Pāṇḍu's sons, for each had been sired by a god whom the mother invoked in consultation with Pāṇḍu, who had been cursed not to have sexual relations on pain of death. Unbeknownst to the Pāṇḍavas, there is also a sixth brother, Karṇa, whom Kuntī had abandoned in her youth. Arjuna is the son of Indra, king of the gods, and Karṇa is the son of the sun god Sūrya.

For Arjuna's conception, Pāṇḍu performs special *tapas* (ascetic acts) to gain Indra's cooperation in siring his best son. At the infant's birth, a heavenly voice announces his glory and forecasts his success, predicting that he will perform three sacrifices. Arjuna rather than his eldest known brother, Yudhiṣṭhira, will be the chief sacrificer (*yajamāna*) in the sacrificial acts that connect the story. Thus, one of Arjuna's names is Kirīṭin ("the crowned one"). Furthermore, it will be through Arjuna's son Abhimanyu that the royal lineage will continue. But the Pāṇḍavas will also act in concert, presenting a refracted image of the ideal king and sacrificer.

Arjuna, his brothers, and their cousins the Kauravas study weaponry with the brahman Droṇa. Arjuna becomes his best pupil and receives instruction in using the doomsday weapon of Śiva—the Brahmaśiras, or "Head of Brahmā." But when it comes time to display his prowess in a tournament, Arjuna is matched by his unknown brother Karṇa, who from this point on becomes the champion of the Kauravas.

Deepening dimensions of Arjuna's role are now conveyed in three episodes: the marriage of Draupadī, Arjuna's sojourn in the forest, and the burning of Khāṇḍdava Forest. In the first episode, he succeeds where all others have failed in an archery feat that wins him the hand of the fire-born Draupadī, incarnation of the goddess Śri (Prosperity), who in her dark aspect as Kṛṣṇa ("black lady") is also the epic's personification of the goddess of destruction. Although Draupadī soon weds all five Pāṇḍavas, Arjuna remains her favorite. Next, because of his violation of an agreement among the brothers never to intrude when any one of them is alone with Draupadī, Arjuna is banished for twelve years. He is supposed to be a celibate (*brahmacārin*), but he nonetheless contracts three additional marriages during this period, the last to his cross-cousin Kṛṣṇa's sister Subhadrā. She will bear him Abhimanyu. Arjuna then consolidates his relation with Kṛṣṇa and they destroy Khāṇdava Forest, each on a separate chariot, to sate the god Agni (Fire). Here one learns that in former lives Arjuna and Kṛṣṇa were the *ṛṣis* Nara ("man," perhaps also "soul," or *puruṣa*) and Nārāyaṇa (a cosmic form of Visnu). Furthermore, this passage introduces them as "the two Kṛṣṇas," a foreshadowing of the war in which they will be known as "the two Kṛṣṇas on one chariot," especially in reference to their chariot duel with Arjuna's brother Karṇa.

Thus Kṛṣṇa shares his name not only with the goddess Draupadī-Kṛṣṇa, but with Arjuna. *Arjuna* itself means "silver" or "white," and the name *Kṛṣṇa* evokes opposite dimensions. The name they share links all three in the destructive tasks they must undertake to inaugurate the "sacrifice of battle."

In the two episodes in which Arjuna next figures prominently, he prepares himself for battle in ways that show deepening connections with the destructive Śiva. During the Pāṇḍavas' exile after the disastrous dice match with the Kauravas, Arjuna performs *tapas* to Śiva until the god appears to grant Arjuna's use of the doomsday weapon. Śiva's touch permits Arjuna to ascend to heaven, where he is further instructed by Indra. Later, when the Pāṇḍavas disguise themselves in their thirteenth year of exile, Arjuna becomes a eunuch dancing instructor, recalling myths of Śiva's castration and his lordship of the dance. In battle, Arjuna will "dance" on his chariot and will see Śiva before him bearing a lance and carrying out the actual destruction of his foes.

Arjuna's most crucial scene, however, is that described in the *Bhagavadgītā*. Poised on his chariot to begin the war, with Kṛṣṇa now his charioteer, he is overcome with compassion for his foes and refuses to fight. Kṛṣṇa unveils Arjuna's true warrior calling and reveals his own "omniform" as Visnu in the destructive form of Time. Arjuna's role is to be the instrument of a destruction that will occur anyway. In submitting to Kṛṣṇa's teaching, Arjuna becomes the ideal *bhakta*, or devotee. This pivotal epic figure thus represents the ideal king and sacrificer, the principal husband of the incarnation of the Goddess, the son of Indra and protégé of Śiva, and the companion and ideal devotee of the *avatāra*.

See Also Bhagavadgītā; Mahābhārata.

Bibliography

For the foundational studies, see two works by Georges Dumézil: *Mythe et épopée:*, vol. 1, *L'idéologie des trois fonctions dans les épopées des peuples indo-européens* (Paris, 1968), and *The Destiny of the Warrior*, translated by Alf Hiltebeital (Chicago, 1969). For further extension of Dumézil's insights applied to the Hindu context, see Madeleine Biardeau's "Études de mythologie hindoue, Chap. II, Bhakti et avatāra," *Bulletin de l'École Française d'Extrême Orient* 63 (1976): 111–263 and 65 (1978): 87–238; Alf Hiltebeitel's "Śiva, the Goddess, and the Disguises of the Pāṇḍavas and Draupadī," *History of Religions* 20 (1980): 147–174; and Jacques Scheuer's *Śiva dans le Mahābhārata* (Paris, 1982).

New Sources

Katz, Ruth Cecily. *Arjuna in the Mahabharata: Where Krishna Is, There Is Victory (Studies in Comparative Religion)*. Columbia, SC, 1989.

Alf Hiltebeitel (1987)
Revised Bibliography

ARMENIAN CHURCH.

According to legend, the apostles Thaddeus and Bartholomew were the original evangelizers of Armenia. Reliable historical data indicate that there were bishops in western Armenia during the third century, principally in Ashtishat in the province of Taron. Eusebius of Caesarea mentions "brethren in Armenia of whom Merozanes was the bishop"; Dionysius of Alexandria wrote a letter on repentance to Merozanes in 251. There are scattered stories of Armenian martyrs during the third century, but records are meager and mostly questionable.

Historical Development of the Church in Armenia. The cultural contacts of the Armenians with the Greeks in the west and the Syrians in the south and the missionary outreach of important Christian centers in Caesarea and Edessa facilitated the introduction of the Christian religion into Armenia, which was a kingdom under Roman protectorate. Following the Edict of Toleration issued in 313 by Emperor Constantine at Milan, the king of Armenia, Tiridates III (298–330), and his courtiers were converted and baptized by Gregory the Illuminator, the apostle of Armenia. Armenia became in 314 the first nation with Christianity as its established state religion.

Following the king's baptism, Gregory traveled to Caesarea (Cappadocia) in the fall of 314 and was consecrated by Metropolitan Leontius as the first catholicos, or chief bishop, of the Armenian church. Gregory's consecration marked the farthest extension of the Christian church in northeast Asia Minor from its base in Caesarea, where Gregory himself had been raised and educated. The formal conversion of Armenia reinforced its political and cultural ties with the Roman world.

On his return, Gregory was installed as catholicos by Bishop Peter of Sebaste; he then proceeded to the royal city of Vagarshapat, which became the catholicate of the Armenian church. The city was renamed Echmiadzin ("descent of the Only-begotten") in celebration of the vision in which Gregory saw Christ strike the ground three times with a golden hammer and show the form of the cathedral to be built.

Gregory's son succeeded him in 325 as catholicos and was one of the bishops who participated in the Council of Nicaea convened in the same year. A number of Gregory's descendants followed him as catholicos, in accordance with a hereditary system reflecting the feudal society of the time. Only in the fifth century did the office become elective.

The first Armenian church council was called in Ashtishat in about 354 by Catholicos Nersēs I. Following the example of his contemporaries, Basil of Caesarea and Eustathius of Sebaste, Nersēs had the council enact rules for moral discipline and for the establishment of monastic and charitable institutions in the country.

The Armenian church was originally formed as an eastern province connected with the see of Caesarea. Later, as the authority of Caesarea waned and Greater Armenia was divided between Rome and Persia in 387, the Armenian church pursued an independent course. Catholicos Sahak I acceded to the catholicate in 389 without reference to the see of Caesarea. At the Council of Shahapivan in 444, Sahak's successor, Hovsep I, was confirmed as catholicos, thereby affirming the autonomy of the Armenian church.

After the partition of Armenia, the church posed an enduring political problem for the Persians. For about three hundred years the latter never ceased to exert pressure on the Armenians to break their religious and cultural ties with the Greeks. The new religion from the west, now flourishing in Armenia, so alarmed Yazkert II of Persia (r.438–457) that he issued an edict bidding the Armenians to renounce their faith and embrace Mazdaism. After an unsuccessful revolt, in which the Armenian hero Vartan Mamikonian was killed in battle, the resistance continued and a second revolt in 481 forced King Firuz to declare full recognition of freedom of religion for Armenians.

The fifth century is considered the golden age in the history of the Armenian people and its church. The leadership of Catholicos Sahak I and the missionary and literary labors of Mesrop Mashtotsʿ gave rise to the Christian culture of the Armenian people. Complete translation was made of the Scriptures as well as of the more important liturgical and theological writings of the eminent church fathers.

The catholicate moved many times with the shifts of the center of political power in the nation. In 484, it moved to Duin, where it remained until 901. An even more significant move was made with the establishment in 1116 of the catholicate in Cilicia, where the Armenian princes had settled and founded principalities and later a kingdom (1080–1375). The see was returned to its original site at Echmiadzin in 1441.

There have been a number of jurisdictional schisms in the history of the church. The longest of these began in 1113 when a schismatic catholicos, David, was installed on the island of Alʾthamar in the province of Van. He opposed the lawful incumbent, Gregory, whose seat was then located outside Armenian territory. David tried and failed to exercise jurisdiction over Greater Armenia in the northeast. The last incumbent of Alʾthamar died in 1895 without a successor.

A more serious and still unresolved division came about in 1441 when the see, then in Cilicia, was returned to Echmiadzin by the decision of a church assembly. Despite the fact that the Armenian kingdom of Cilicia had fallen to the Mamluks of Egypt in 1375, and there was no reason to maintain the center of the church away from its original location, the incumbent of the see (in the city of Sis) refused to comply. The Cilician catholicate has retained its independent existence. Following World War I, its seat was moved from Sis to Antelias, Lebanon.

As early as the twelfth century, Armenians came into contact with the Latin church through close cultural and political ties with the Crusaders. Aided by the missionary activities of Franciscans and Dominicans, a Latinizing movement gained ground among liberal elements in the church. Although this movement—of varying strength—lasted for about four hundred years, it did not result in any significant secession to Rome. Only in 1831, under a new Ottoman policy toward Christian minorities, was an Armenian Rite Catholic Church within the Roman communion legally recognized. The catholicate of Armenian Catholics is located in Beirut, Lebanon.

In 1830, American Protestants began their missionary activity in Asia Minor. In 1846, the Ottoman government legally recognized the separate status of an Armenian Protestant community. Continued affiliation of Armenian evangelicals with American missionary organizations has been another source of Western influence. Schools and colleges have been established and the Bible translated into the modern vernacular.

It should be noted that the early divisions within the church did not arise on dogmatic grounds. They were caused primarily by the resistance of secular rulers to the presence within their territories of a church community dependent on an authority beyond their frontiers and influence. Complete secessions on dogmatic grounds have occurred only in the nineteenth century with the formation of Armenian Roman Catholic and Protestant Evangelical church communities.

The nineteenth century brought important changes to the juridical status of the church after Russia took eastern Armenia from the Persians in 1828. The tsar issued a statute that was accepted by the ruling catholicos even though it reduced his power by creating a standing synod of bishops tightly controlled by the government.

In 1863 in western Armenia the church received a constitution for the management of its own affairs as part of the Ottoman civil code. The constitution provided for a national assembly with the Armenian patriarch of Constantinople as its president. The assembly had two administrative councils, religious and civil. This development was in keeping with the long-standing Ottoman policy of giving leaders of Christian minorities jurisdiction over their own internal affairs, inasmuch as Christians could not be made subject to the Qur'anic law. This system ended after World War I.

MODERN DEVELOPMENTS. The catholicos of all Armenians, residing at Echmiadzin in Armenia, remains the supreme head of the Armenian church. Outside Armenia, each established church community, whether under Echmiadzin or another jurisdiction, has its own form of regulations or bylaws, adapted to local political or cultural conditions. By and large, these regulations are formed on the principle of conciliarity; lay participation at all levels of administration is common.

The ecclesiastical jurisdiction of the catholicos in Echmiadzin extends over twenty dioceses: Armenia South, Armenia North, Tbilisi, Baku, Moscow, Bucharest, Sofia, Baghdad, Calcutta, Sydney, Cairo, Vienna, Paris, London, New York, Los Angeles, Toronto, Buenos Aires, Istanbul, and Jerusalem. The catholicos of the Armenians of Cilicia in Antelias, Lebanon, presides over four dioceses: Beirut, Aleppo, Damascus, and Nicosia. In the 1950s, for political reasons, the dioceses of Tehran, Athens, and the two newly created dioceses of New York and Los Angeles, paralleling those under Echmiadzin, came under the jurisdiction of the catholicos of Cilicia. The legitimacy of these changes of jurisdiction is a matter of continuing dispute.

There are Armenian patriarchates established in Jerusalem and Istanbul. Each of these comprises only one local diocese. The patriarch of Jerusalem is one of the three custodians of Christian holy places in and around Jerusalem. The patriarch of Istanbul, once the administrator of the entire Armenian "nation" in the Ottoman Empire, now controls only the diocese of Istanbul itself and a number of small struggling parishes in the interior of Turkey. At present the patriarchate does not have a written constitution and is governed by the patriarch on the basis of established customs and practices.

Liturgy. The prototype of the Divine Liturgy, or Eucharist, has been the liturgy of Basil of Caesarea, which was translated into Armenian in the fifth century. Later this liturgy gave way to the Byzantine liturgy of Chrysostom. During the period of the Crusades, however, Latin influence brought about some minor changes in the ceremonials and vestments. Since the tenth century, the form of the liturgy has remained constant with the exception of the addition of the Last Gospel (*Jn.* 1:1–15) at the end of the Eucharist.

The use of unleavened bread and unmixed red wine was already established during the seventh century. Communion is given in both elements, with the communicant standing. The sacrament is reserved but not ceremonially venerated. At the conclusion of the Eucharist, fragments of thin unleavened bread, simply blessed, are distributed to those not receiving Communion.

Seven offices, including Nocturn, Matins, Prime, Midday office, Vespers, Peace, and Compline, comprise the liturgy of the canonical hours. There are other occasional offices such as the Penitential, the Memorial, the Processional, and the Adoration of the Church. In the fourteenth century, the principal sacraments were counted as seven following Latin custom: baptism, chrismation, Eucharist, penance, ordination, marriage, and anointing. The church does not practice extreme unction as it is known in the Latin rite. Baptism, ordinarily of infants, is administered by immersion; chrismation (confirmation) and then Communion follow immediately after baptism. This sacrament of initiation conforms to the practice of the other Eastern churches.

Fasting calls for abstention from all animal foods. Apart from the forty days of Lent, there are ten weekly fasts of five days each. Wednesdays and Fridays are fast days, except during the fifty days following Easter.

About 360 saints (including groups of saints under collective names) are recognized in the directory of feasts. Of these, 100 are biblical, 100 are Armenian, and 160 are non-Armenian belonging to the first five centuries of the Christian era. Gregory of Datev (early fifteenth century) is the last of the saints formally recognized by the church. The Holy Virgin has a unique position as foremost among the saints and is venerated extensively in liturgical worship.

The directory of feasts is arranged on the septenary principle. Each liturgical observance falls on a day in the week, numbered in the series of weeks following the Sunday nearest to the anchor date of one of the four periods of the annual liturgical cycle. Easter moves on a range of thirty-five days; the first Sunday of Advent and the feasts of the Assumption and Exaltation move on a range of seven days. Seven feasts commemorating episodes in the life of the Virgin Mary are observed on fixed dates. Dominical feasts fall on Sundays.

Clergy. There are three major orders of the clergy, according to the tradition of all ancient churches: deacon, priest, and bishop. "Archbishop" is an honorary title conferred by the catholicos. Parish priests are ordinarily chosen from among married men; marriage after ordination is not allowed, although several exceptions have been made since the 1940s. Bishops are chosen from among the celibate clergy. Widowed priests may be promoted to the episcopate. Clergy are trained in seminaries at Echmiadzin, Jerusalem, and Antelias.

Doctrine. Of the seven ecumenical councils, the Armenian church, in company with the Coptic and the Syrian Orthodox churches, acknowledges the first three: Nicaea (325) against Arianism; Constantinople (381) against Apollinarianism; and Ephesus (431) against Nestorianism. It does not accept the fourth, Chalcedon, and has made no pronouncements about the remaining three. It should be noted, however, that the church condemns Eutychianism, does not agree with the doctrine of two wills in the one person of Christ, and holds to the veneration of icons. The Armenian church reveres and follows the teachings of all the leading church fathers of the first five centuries of the common era, with the exception of Pope Leo I.

The Council of Chalcedon (451) caused an intense and lasting controversy in Eastern Christendom about the relation of divinity and humanity in the person of Christ. Of the two parties for or against Chalcedon in the Armenian church, the latter prevailed at a council in 607. Nevertheless, ambivalence over the problem of the natures of Christ continued in the church down to the fourteenth century. Since then the church has held the doctrine that "one is the nature of the Word of God incarnate." The dispute on this matter of dogma has reflected the contest between those who sought political advantage from the West and those who stood for national independence. From Constantine to the last emperor of Byzantium, unity of faith was considered concomitant to the unity of the empire. Consequently, for non-Greek churches of the East that unity meant submission to Byzantium, where the emperor was the effective head of the church and the dogmatic decrees of the general councils promulgated by the emperors were enforceable by law on pain of exile.

During the second half of the twelfth century, the great catholicos Nersēs of Cla, "the Graceful," maintained that there was no contradiction between the Chalcedonian teaching of "two natures" and the teaching of the "one nature." Shortly thereafter, a synod convened by Catholicos Gregory IV and attended by thirty-three bishops stated in a declaration to the emperor and patriarch of Constantinople: "We confess, in agreement with you, the theory of the dual nature of the ineffable oneness of Christ." Significantly, the synod did not refer to the Council of Chalcedon itself. Later synods in the fourteenth century affirmed formal reunion with Rome but were ineffectual because there was no representation from the area of Greater Armenia in the northeast and especially because the faithful were not in sympathy with such a move.

Creeds. The Nicene-Constantinopolitan Creed is recited in the liturgy every Sunday. There is also a somewhat longer creed, introduced during the fourteenth century and used after confession of sins by a penitent. It refers to the Cyrilian formula mentioned above: "One is the nature of the incarnate Word of God." A short creed is recited at the beginning of the sacrament of baptism.

Canon law. The canons of the church, contained in the *Book of Canons*, are grouped in three sections. The first is the codex formed by John of Odzun in 725. It brings together various legislations—"apostolic," postapostolic, and conciliar—as well as decretals of Greek and Armenian church fathers. The second section, from the eighth to the twelfth centuries, consists of later conciliar canons and decretals of church fathers. A less extensive third section, added in the twelfth century, deals with matters of civil law.

SEE ALSO Armenian Religion; Gregory of Datev; Gregory the Illuminator; Mashtots', Mesrop; Nersēs of Cla; Nersēs the Great; Sahak Parthev.

BIBLIOGRAPHY

The one outstanding and comprehensive history of the Armenian church is by Mal'achia Ormanian, *Azgapatowm* (History of the nation), 3 vols. (1912–1927; reprint, Beirut, 1959–1961), which uses primary sources extensively. A similar but older work is that by Michael Chamchean, *Patmut'iwn Hayots*, 3 vols. (Venice, 1784–1786). An abridged edition has been translated into English by Johannes Audell as *History of Armenia*, 2 vols. (Calcutta, 1827). There are also three smaller histories of the Armenian church titled *Patmut'iwn hay ekeghets' woy:* those by Melchisedek Muratean (Jerusalem, 1872), Abraham Zaminean (Nor Nakhijevan, 1908), and Kevork Mesrop (Istanbul, 1913–1914). Other studies in Armenian church history are either topical or periodic. However, ecclesiastical material is often incorporated into secular histories. Important among these are Jacques de Morgan's *Histoire du peuple arménien: Depuis les temps les plus reculés de ses annales jusqu'à nos jours* (Paris, 1919), translated by Ernest F. Barry as *The History of the Armenian People: From the Remotest Times to the Present Day* (Boston, 1965); François Tournebize's *Histoire politique et religieuse de l'Arménie* (Paris, 1910); and René Grousset's *Histoire de l'Arménien des origins à 1071* (Paris, 1947).

TIRAN NERSOYAN (1987)

ARMENIAN RELIGION.

The Armenians' remotest ancestors immigrated to Anatolia in the mid-second millennium BCE. Related to speakers of the Thraco-Phrygian languages of the Indo-European family, they probably brought with them a religion akin to that of the proto-Greeks, adopting also elements of the cultures of Asianic peoples such as the Hittites, from whose name the Armenian word *hay* ("Armenian") may be derived. Thus, the Armenian divinity Tork' is the Hittite Tarḫundas, and the Armenian word now used for "God," *Astuac*, may have been the name of an Asianic deity, although its etymology remains hypothetical. The Armenian word *di-kʿ* ("god[s]") is an Indo-European cognate to the Latin *deus.*

The Armenians were at first concentrated in the area of Van (Urartean Biaina), a city on the southeastern shore of Lake Van, in eastern Anatolia, and in the Sasun region, a mountainous district to the west of the lake. The Armenian god Vahagn (Av., Verethraghna; cf. Sogdian *Vashaghn*), whose cult centered in the area of present-day Muş, appears to have assimilated the dragon-slaying exploits of the Urartean Teisheba, a weather god. An Urartean "gate of God" in the rock of Van was consecrated to Mher (Av., Mithra) and is still known in the living epic of Sasun as *Mheri duṛn* ("gate of Mher"), preserving the Urartean usage.

Although Herodotos in the fifth century BCE still recalled the Armenians as Phrygian colonists of Phrygian-like speech, they had been conquered twice—first by the Medes about 583 BCE, then by the Persians under Cyrus II the Great—and had assimilated elements of the conquering cultures. After the conquest of Cyrus, the faith of the Iranian prophet Zarathushtra (Zoroaster) was to exercise the primary influence upon the Armenian religion; indeed, Zoroaster was believed by Clement of Alexandria and other classical writers to have been identical with Err, the son of Armenios of the *Republic* of Plato. Strabo (*Geography* 11.13.9, 11.14.6) declared that the Armenians and the Medes performed the same religious rites, those "of the Persians," the Medes having been also the source of the way of life (*ethē*) of the Persians themselves. Like the Armenian language, which retains its ancient and distinct character while preserving a preponderance of Northwestern Iranian loanwords of the pre-Sasanid period, the ancient religion of the Armenians apparently retained distinct local features, although the great majority of its religious terms and practices belong to the Zoroastrianism of Arsacid Iran and earlier periods.

Ahura Mazdā (OPers., Ahuramazda), creator god of Zoroastrianism, was worshiped by the Armenians as Aramazd, the Parthian form of his name. The principal cult center of Aramazd, the "father of all" (Agathangelos, para. 785), was a temple in Ani, Daranaghi, where the necropolis of the Armenian Arsacids was also located. (Later, the center of the cult shifted to the royal capital at Bagawan, to the east.) The shrine of Barshamin (Sem., Baʿal Shamin, "the lord of heaven") was established at Tʿordan, a village near Ani, probably to indicate that the Semitic god was seen to resemble the Iranian creator god. A similar reformist trend toward monotheism based on an Iranian model is seen in the inscriptions of Arebsun in nearby Cappadocia, probably of the late Achaemenid period, in which is described in Aramaic the marriage to Bel (Baal) of the "religion of Mazdā-worship" (OPers., *dainâ mazdayasnīsh*).

According to Movsēs Khorenatsʿi, Mazhan, the brother of King Artashēs I (Gr., Artaxias; early second century BCE), served as the priest of Aramazd, while the noble families (*nakharars*) served the lesser divinities of whom Aramazd was regarded as the maker; the Vah(n)unis, for instance, may even derive their name from Vahagn, whom they served. According to foreign writers, the most popular of these lesser divinities was Anahit (Gr., Anaitis; OIran., Anāhitā), and it is she who seems to be shown in the mass-produced terracotta votive figurines found at Artaxata and other ancient Armenian sites, with one or several male children clinging to her matronly robes, like the scenes of Cybele and the infant Attis. The Armenian Nanē (Pth., *Nanai; Gr., Nanaia) seems to have been a goddess of almost identical character, except that Anahit, as in Iran, was also a goddess of the waters, which Nanē probably was not. Another Armenian goddess, Astghik ("little star"), consort of Vahagn, seems to be identical with Astarte.

Armenian and pre-Sasanid Iranian temples often contained cult statues—such shrines were called in Armenian *bagins* ("places of the god")—but it seems that, with or without images, all Armenian temples had fire altars, called *atrushans* (like *bagīn*, a Middle Iranian loanword), so that the major Zoroastrian rites might be consecrated there. A place for fire, and its light, was a focal point of worship and cultic life.

The chief shrine of Vahagn stood at Ashtishat ("rich in *yashts*" ["acts of worship"]), the place later consecrated to Saint John the Baptist by Gregory the Illuminator as the earliest see of the Armenian church. Vahagn is described in a fragment of a hymn preserved by Khorenatsʿi (1.31) as "sun-eyed" and "fiery-haired," attributes found in the Avesta and later applied in Christian Armenia to Mary and to seraphs. From various sources it appears that Vahagn was regarded as a sun god, perhaps acquiring this feature from Mihr (Mithra), who is closely associated with the sun in Zoroastrianism. There is oblique evidence of a conflict between devotees of the two gods in Armenia. Nonetheless, the Armenian word for a pagan temple, *mehean*, containing the name of Mithra, indicates the god's great importance, and it is noteworthy that this term for a Zoroastrian place of rites is very similar to, but much earlier than, the Persian *dar-i Mihr* (with which the Armenian *Mheri duṛn*, mentioned above, is indeed identical).

Among the other gods, the Armenians worshiped Tir (MIran., Tīr), chief of the scribal art and keeper of celestial records, including, some believed, those of human destiny. He survives in modern Armenian folklore as the Grogh ("writer"); a clairvoyant is called *Groghi gzir* ("deputy of the Grogh"). Spandaramet (MIran., Spandārmad; Av., Spenta Ārmaiti), goddess of the earth, was also venerated. (Her name is rendered as "Dionysos" in the fifth-century Armenian translation of the biblical books of the Maccabees.) Another form of the same name, *sandaramet*, sometimes pluralized with *–kʿ* or shortened to *sandarkʿ* (cf. Cappadocian *Sondara*), is Southwestern Iranian and may reflect pre-Zoroastrian beliefs, for it is a common noun used in Armenian texts to refer simply to the underworld. Torkʿ of Anggh (Ingila), treated by Khorenatsʿi as a legendary and fearsome hero, is an Asianic divinity equated with Nergal in the Armenian translation of the Bible. There was an Armenian royal necropolis at Anggh, so it seems that Tork' was regarded as a divinity of the underworld. Two of the Zoroastrian Amesha Spentas, Haurvatāt ("health") and Ameretat ("long life"), often paired, gave their name to a flower (see Agathangelos, para. 643), which Armenian maidens pluck in silence on Ascension Eve (talking at meals is believed by Zoroastrians to offend the two divinities).

Ancient Armenians celebrated the Iranian New Year, Nawasard (OPers., *Navasarda), which was consecrated to Aramazd. A midwinter feast of fire, Ahekan (OPers., *Athrākana), still survives with its rituals intact in Christianity as Tearnendaṛaj, the Feast of the Presentation of the Lord to the Temple. The old month-name of Mehekan preserves the memory of Mihragān, the feast of Mithra, and Anahit seems to have received special reverence on Vardavaṛ, a feast of roses and of the waters. At year's end, Hrotits' (from Avestan *Fravashayō*) commemorated the holy spirits of the departed, leading Agathangelos (para. 16) to accuse the Armenians of being *uruapashtk'* ("worshipers of souls").

Although monotheistic in its regard for Ahura Mazdā as the creator of all that is good in heaven and earth, Zoroastrianism postulates a cosmic dualism in which the Lord Wisdom (Av., Ahura Mazdā; Pahl., Ōhrmazd) strives against an inferior but independent adversary, the Hostile Spirit (Av., Angra Mainyu; Pahl., Ahriman). The name of the latter is found in two forms in Armenian, *Arhmn* and *Haramani*, and Armenian words for evil people and noxious creatures (e.g., *druzhan*, "betrayer"; *kakhard*, "witch"; *gazan*, "beast") are often of Iranian origin and reflect a dualistic attitude. The Zoroastrian ethical habits of cleanliness, reverence for fire and light, and steadfast cheer in the battle against evil seem to have been fully integrated into Armenian Christianity, which reveres God as *hrashap'ar* in some hymns, an epithet combining the two characteristically Mazdean features of *frasha-* ("visibly miraculous") and *khvarenah* ("divine glory") in loanwords from Middle Iranian.

Gregory the Illuminator, son of an Armenian Arsacid *nakharar* named Sūrēn Pahlav, converted King Tiridates to Christianity in the second decade of the fourth century. Armies were sent to destroy the old temples, and churches were built over the ruins. The *k'rmapets*, or high priests, resisted with main force this military imposition of a new creed, and many Armenian *nakharars* joined the fifth-century Sasanid king Yazdegerd II in his campaign to reconvert the Armenians to Zoroastrianism. But the iconoclastic state church of southwestern Iran differed too greatly from the old faith to appeal to many Armenians, and the translation of scripture into Armenian with the newly invented alphabet of Mesrop Mashtots' made the patriarchs and the saints "Armenian-speaking" (*hayerēnakhaws*), as Koriwn wrote. Christianity triumphed over all but a small sect, the Arewordik' ("children of the sun"), who were said by medieval writers to follow the teachings of "the magus Zoroaster," worshiping the sun and exposing rather than burying the dead. A very few adherents of the sect may have been alive at the time of the 1915 holocaust, when traditional Armenian society was obliterated.

SEE ALSO Armenian Church.

BIBLIOGRAPHY

Abeghian, Manuk. *Der armenische Volksglaube*. Leipzig, 1899. Reprinted with an Armenian translation in his *Erker*, vol. 7 (Yerevan, 1975).

Alishan, Lerond. *Hin hawatk' kam het'anosakan krōnk' Hayots'*. Venice, 1910.

Ananikian, Mardiros H. "Armenian Mythology." In *The Mythology of All Races*, vol. 7, edited by J. A. MacCulloch, pp. 5–100. Boston, 1925.

Gelzer, Heinrich. "Zur armenischen Götterlehre." *Berichte der königlichen sächsischen Gesellschaft der Wissenschaften* (Leipzig) 48 (1896): 99–148. Translated into Armenian by Y. T'orosean (Venice, 1897).

Russell, J. R. *Zoroastrianism in Armenia*. Cambridge, Mass., 1987.

New Sources

Hovannisian, Richard G. *The Armenian People from Ancient to Modern Times: The Dynastic Periods: From Antiquity to the Fourteenth Century*. New York, 1997.

Kochakian, Garabed. *Art in The Armenian Church: Origins and Teaching*. New Rochelle, N.Y., 1995.

Matthews, Thomas F., and Roger S. Wieck, eds. *Treasures in Heaven: Armenian Art, Religion, and Society*. New York, 1998.

Salt, Jeremy. *Imperialism, Evangelism and the Ottoman Armenians 1878–1896*. London, 1993.

Thomson, Robert W. *Studies in Armenian Literature and Christianity*. Brookfield, Vt., 1994.

J. R. RUSSELL (1987)
Revised Bibliography

ARMINIUS, JACOBUS

ARMINIUS, JACOBUS (1559/60–1609), latinized name of Jacob Harmenszoon, Dutch Reformed theologian remembered chiefly for his criticisms of Calvinist views of predestination. Arminius taught that human salvation is due entirely to the grace of God in Christ, whereby fallen humankind is enabled to respond in freedom to the divine call. He proposed a universal "sufficient" grace in place of Calvin's limited "effective" grace. Further, he denied a predestination of particular persons to salvation on the basis of God's secret will, but he affirmed a particular predestination on the basis of God's foreknowledge of human free choices. For much that has come to be known as Arminianism, the central issue is "free will" versus "election."

Arminius was born to well-to-do parents in Oudewater, Holland. He lost his parents while young and was educated under the influence of Dutch biblical humanism. University studies at Marburg (1575) and Leiden (1576–1581) did not seem to have moved him to a strict Calvinism.

With support from Amsterdam merchants, he began theological studies in Geneva, where one of his teachers was Theodore Beza (1519–1605). Arminius and Beza clashed. Arminius studied for a time at Basel, but he returned to Geneva to finish his studies, after which he went to Amsterdam to become that city's first native Dutch clergyman (he was inducted into the Dutch Reformed ministry in 1588). At the time the question of predestination was raging, and Arminius came under fire for refusing to defend any of the Calvinist options and for interpreting *Romans* 7 and *Romans* 9 in a manner different from Calvin. He was sustained in his office and position by the Amsterdam merchant-oligarchy, to which he was allied by blood and marriage.

The same humanistic laity supported him in his call to be a professor of theology in Leiden (1603), where he soon incurred the enmity of his colleague Franciscus Gomarus (1563–1641) and other ardent Calvinists. Theological issues were intertwined with political issues, the Arminians siding with the civil official Johan van Oldenbarneveldt (1547–1619), who favored a truce with Spain, and the Calvinists with the military leader Maurice of Nassau (1567–1625), who wanted to press for war. Arminius died in the midst of the conflict, in 1609.

Arminius's cause was taken up by the Remonstrants, so called from their *Remonstrance* of 1610 that presented the Arminian doctrines of salvation, but power shifted to the Calvinists and Maurice. The Synod of Dort (1618–1619) deposed the Arminians, and Oldenbarneveldt was executed. By the 1630s, however, the Remonstrants had regrouped to form a new denomination, the Remonstrant Brotherhood, which maintained a scholarly, liberal, and progressive emphasis into the twentieth century. Hugo Grotius (1583–1645), Simon Episcopius (1583–1643), Philippus van Limborch (1633–1712), and C. P. Tiele (1830–1902) were among its noted adherents and scholars.

In England, under James I and Charles I, Anglican opponents of Calvinist Puritanism came to be known as Arminians, and Arminianism became allied with the religious and political doctrines of Archbishop William Laud (1573–1645) and was the main line of theology in the Church of England. Non-Anglican Arminianism appeared in the teachings of the General Baptists, often tending toward Unitarianism.

In the eighteenth century, however, John Wesley (1703–1791) and his brother Charles (1707–1788), by their preaching and hymnody, spread a new evangelical Arminianism throughout Britain. John Wesley, even when visiting Holland, made no common cause with the Remonstrants, who by this time were heavily influenced by the Enlightenment.

Dissent from Calvinism in New England was called "Arminianism," but it did not get its impetus from Arminius. American Methodism did, however, and John Wesley's *The Arminian Magazine* (1778) was printed on both sides of the Atlantic, as were English editions of Arminius. Wesleyan evangelical Arminianism spread with Methodism across North America in the nineteenth century to the extent that American culture has been designated as "Arminian." There are links from this pervasive Arminian spirit to movements as diverse as frontier revivalism, communitarian perfectionism, the Holiness movement, political and theological individualism, and theological liberalism.

BIBLIOGRAPHY

The most recent edition of Arminius's writings is *The Works of James Arminius,* 3 vols., translated by James Nichols and William R. Bagnall (1853; reprint, Grand Rapids, Mich., 1956). For a modern treatment of Arminius, giving attention to political, economic, and social contexts of his life and thought, see my *Arminius: A Study in the Dutch Reformation,* 2d ed. (Grand Rapids, Mich., 1985). For important interpretive essays on early Dutch Arminianism, see G. J. Hoenderdaal's "Arminius en Episcopius," *Nederlands Archief voor Kerkgeschiedenis,* n.s. 60 (1980): 203–235; and John Platt's *Reformed Thought and Scholasticism: The Arguments for the Existence of God in Dutch Theology, 1575–1650* (Leiden, 1982). A. W. Harrison's *Arminianism* (London, 1937) remains a useful survey of Arminianism in England.

CARL BANGS (1987)

ART AND RELIGION is a discrete field of multidisciplinary study that attends to the creative interplay between image and meaning making as religious activities. More general usage of the term signifies investigations into the role, place, or experience of art in religion(s).

As a mode of creative expression, communication, and self-definition, art is a primordial facet of human existence and constitutive factor in the evolution of religion. Through visible expression and form, art imparts meaning and value to anthropic aspirations, encounters, and narratives, and simultaneously orients the human within the horizon of a community, world, and cosmos. Thereby, art renders the human situation—origin, existence, death, and afterlife—comprehensible through visual representations. As a stimulus for creativity and culture, religion is the spiritual impulse that conjoins humanity with divinity through spiritual experience, ceremony, and mythology. Art and religion converge through ritual practice and presentation of sacred narrative, thereby affecting "an experience of the numinous" (Otto, 1923). Enigmatically, art can recognize and project the essence and significance of a spiritual experience through form, thereby engendering a tangible record that informs the initiation or repetition of the original spiritual moment. Commensurately, art employs visual archetypes and idealizations on the journey to truth and beauty, thereby proffering visions of the sacred and models to follow on the path to salvation. As visible religion, art communicates religious beliefs, customs, and values through iconography and depictions of the human body. The foundational principle for the interconnections between art and religion is the reciprocity between image making and meaning making as creative correspondence of humanity with divinity.

The intimacy between art and religion has prevailed beyond historical convolutions, transformations, and permutations in global cultural and religious values. Unimaginably arduous to label with a universal standard, the intercommunion between art and religion has endured proliferation, diversification, and diminution through world cultures and religions. Nonetheless, this impossible regularization or definition of art and religion in any form, communal or universal, may be interpreted as appropriate to as amorphous an entity as art and religion is, and reflects its fundamental heuristic and multivalent nature. From their inexplicable differences within individual cultures to their inherent and unconscious manifestations in the human psyche, the numerous conjunctures between art and religion persist even unto their camouflaged survival in the secular societies of the twentieth and twenty-first centuries.

OVERVIEW. Art has power in the anthropological sense of *mana.* This troublesome and distinctive characteristic of art, and commensurately of images and imagery, is evidenced through the power to evoke or affect the human capacity to *feel.* The distinguishing human ability to feel, to have feelings, extends beyond simple emotion to the capacity and sensitivity that are elemental to the human capability to interpret and to reason. This connection between art and feeling is privileged by the naming of the philosophy of beauty as "aesthetics." The English word *aesthetic* is derived from the Greek root *aisthetikos,* meaning "to be sensitive" in the etymological context of "coming to know through the senses." Conversely, an anaesthetic prohibits the human ability to have feeling. The universality of this association of art as an affector of emotions and sensitivities, and a connective to religion, is evidenced in Bharata Muni's treatises on art. His comprehension of *rasa* as levels of human consciousness educed by art in which the aesthetic merges into the spiritual for artist and viewer is crucial to the Hindu tenet of the indivisibility of art and religion. This aptitude to effectuate feeling, either as emotions or sensitivities, is an elementary motive in the intellectual "fear of art" that led to the denial of the visual both as a prime response to the epistemological question and as primary evidence in the study of history.

The authoritative preference, at least in the West, is for the primacy of the text, that is, of the word over the image. Historians of religion reputedly advocate the unconscious act of selection between the image and the word by every religious tradition with appropriate cultural consequences. Religions, like Hinduism and Eastern Christianity, which favor the primacy of the image are differentiated as sacramental, creative, and intuitive in linguistic and cultural attitudes from those religions, such as Protestant Christianity and Judaism, preferring the primacy of the word and labeled as legalistic, pragmatic, and rational in language and cultural reception. Further, the study of religion, particularly in the West, has been predicated upon the authority of the written text, or a series of texts, not upon the image. The disciplined reading of these canons encompasses exegesis as the fundament for study, debate, and interpretation. A hegemony of texts, canons, and scriptures—that is, the written word—results in the incorporation of art simply as illustration for explication and dissemination of textual themes.

Late twentieth- and early twenty-first century publications in religious studies reveal interest in the inclusion of new themes, foci, and methodologies, given the insights toward religion accessible through a variety of new disciplinary fields interested in the religious dimensions of art, most specifically material culture, popular culture, and visual culture. These new styles of analysis incorporate "activities," including worship, personal piety, public rituals, and all styles and levels of art, in unison with intellectual interpretation of the canon to provide broader comprehension of religion. Although recognized as a contributor to religious meaning and orientation, the partnership of art and religion remains a complex enigma. Art as an object to be both analyzed and experienced is recognized as empowering artist and viewer in transcending the quotidian existential and the rational in a temporary communion with the sacred, the experience of which is so singular as to incite the desire for repetition emphasizing the ritual character of art.

Art is simultaneously an objective and a subjective event—the object being seen and the effect of the process of seeing. This exchange between art and religion, in coordination with the fundamental reality of its heuristic and mutually beneficial mien, challenges the logocentricity of traditional, especially Western, scholarship and cultural values, which normatively dissociates religion from art. This Enlightenment principle of the separation of the experience of art from the intellectual analysis of religion parallels the transfer of religious meaning from institutional to non-institutional environments. The intellectual divorce of the academic study of religion from the practice of religion, and from the experience of art, is analogous to the separation of the academic study of art history from the creating and encountering of art.

THE PRACTICE AND THE STUDY OF ART AND RELIGION. The position of art—whether in the broadest frame of religious studies, or a specific category such as church history or history of Buddhism—locates a useful parallel in traditional distinctions between the study of religion and the practice of religion. Applicable to art as well as to religion, this dichotomy exceeds the categories of objectivity and subjectivity, for "the doing of" religion (or art) is physically and intellectually distinct from "the thinking about" religion (or art). The telling distinctions here include recognition of class, gender, and ethnicity as well as education and the revelation of the privileging of the study of religion, and of art and religion, as a Western scholarly phenomenon. The practice of religion is primarily sited in worship and religious education, or catechesis, in which art either iconographically or figuratively envisions established narratives to transmit religious ideas and practices, to convey religious truths and practices, and to promote worship individually and communally.

Historically, Western scholars, especially those intrigued by religious art, or what they may have identified as the interconnections between art and religion, emphasized the primary role that art played in religious practice, for example, an altarpiece or a bronze sculpture of Śiva Nataraja, and were unaware the fact that this mode of study could be read as restrictive, exclusivist, and parochial. Further interpretive difficulties arose as these scholars—including theologians like Roger Hazelton (1967) and Paul Tillich (1987) and art historians such as Jane Daggett Dillenberger (1986/1998) and Timothy Verdon (1984)—were committed members of the religious communities whose art was being examined. This style of scholarly investigations is better identified as theology and art, not art and religion. The significance of both the choice of category names and the order of their arrangement—that is, art and religion as distinct from religion and art—announces more than the focus of intellectual attention.

Traditionally the academic study of religion has been distinguished by the suspension of personal faith commitments so that the scholarly deciphering and evaluation of art and religion encourages the innocent eye to be open to the multivalent meanings and influences of art upon religion, and of religion on art, without prejudgment or prejudice. This is not to suggest that the work of art is neutral or benign, for art is neither conceived nor executed in a vacuum. The significance of art, regardless of medium or critical appraisal, is its cultural embeddedness by which it enables reflection on past cultural histories, connection with contemporary cultural attitudes, and projection of emerging cultural values. The fundamental ambiguity in the reading or perception of art attests to its heuristic and multivalent nature.

Art, especially religious art, is the external expression of the artist's personal vision, and under normal circumstances, a work of religious art, whether identified as Christian, Jain, or Aboriginal, is initiated from an identifiable faith commitment and communicates in the vernacular of that faith community. For example, the sixteenth-century German artist Mathias Grünewald depicts in his magisterial *Isenheim Altarpiece* (1515: Musée d'Unterlinden, Colmar) a series of significant biblical episodes in the life of Jesus of Nazareth for the hospice at the Antonite Monastery in Colmar. Grünewald included specific visual cues so that members of that religious community could "read" his meaning, and other Christians familiar with either the biblical narratives or the liturgical celebrations of Christmas and Easter could access this work of art. *The Isenheim Altarpiece* operates as visual theology within a clearly defined religious tradition reflecting its religious practices and beliefs. Concurrently, the "outsider," visitor, or curious can see this artwork as an invitation to or initiation into a particular religious vocabulary and landscape of religious vision.

Traditionally, for scholars of religious studies, especially in the West, the "voice of authority" has been a canon—a series of written texts including a sacred scripture, commentaries on that scripture, and doctrinal or conciliar decrees. However the "reality" of religion is more complicated given the transmutations and permutations of history, geographic expansion, and the constant presence of the human element, especially the collective of believers, many of whom were illiterate, thereby unschooled in the finer points of textual exegesis and theological ruminations. A religion to be apprehended and comprehended fully by both the faith community and researchers requires the display of its multiple dimensions from iconography to canon, from theological tome to devotional prayers. Such a coordination of the elite and the mundane reconstructs the meaning of religion as texts are accessible to the literate, whereas art ranging generically from icons to devotional hymns to liturgical dance to folk art, poetry, and morality tales proffers an inclusive and comprehensive reading of fourteenth-century Western Christianity in coordination with the "authoritative texts."

Critical Questions. Regardless of methodological approach or religion investigated, art and religion inquiries have been initiated from two critical, oftentimes implicit, questions—"what makes art religious?" and "how is religion artistic?" Since the 1970s, scholarship in art and religion has incorporated several other critical questions into the modes of approach in both research and publications. These critical questions affected the direction of study and interpretation process. Primary among these critical questions is the issue of the "starting point" for an art and religion investigation. The choices range from an individual work of art or a group of works, to one artist or a group (school) of artists, to a specific historical or religious event, to a new religious doctrine or a singular iconographic motif. The second critical question is what art is to be studied. Each investigator develops a set of criteria to discern art as high or low, art as popular culture, art as material culture, and art as an element of visual culture. The crucial decision is whether the focus of study is a traditionally defined work of art or from one of the domains of art such as folk art, photography, or popular culture. The third critical question is that of procedure, for example, examination from a specific historical question such as that of the process of secularization, the meaning of Christian art as the "Bible of the poor," or the implications of political power and authority for religious art. The fourth critical question has been formed by the academic recognition of "the marginalized"—those previously little investigated groups including women, racial and ethnic minorities, classes, and gender—whose art has reformulated traditional art historical categories not simply by introducing new iconographies or styles but by the very nature of their understandings of art and religion in their respective societies and cultures.

With the advent of the new century, scholarship in art and religion has formulated new critical questions arising from both contemporary events and a growing global recognition of the broader ethical and societal responsibilities for cultural heritage. The recent loss of works of religious art through natural disasters, war, and violent acts of iconoclasm has focused attention on the role of religion in fomenting or silencing acts of destruction, whether initiated by environmental neglect or military activity. Further analysis as to religious meaning and cultural value of the works selected for destruction is a topic for new studies from the perspective of art and religion. The related critical question for art and religion study is that of the complex ethical and moral issue of the "theft" or transfer of art from one country to another on the grounds of protection or military conquest, and the potential for repatriation. Another new critical question, which may be related to the primary question of "what makes art religious?" and which simultaneously impinges upon the ethical quagmire of ownership, is the collecting and display of religious art in institutional environments such as public museums and special exhibitions, thereby in sites and for uses distinct from those sacred criteria for which it was created, and perhaps consecrated.

The Nature of the Relationship(s). The oftentimes controversial and amorphous interconnections between art and religion proffer five distinctive relationships that can be categorized as distinguished by power (Apostolos-Cappadona, 1996) and that extend beyond *mana* to include economic, gendered, political, societal, and religious concepts of power. The first is authoritarian, in which art is subject to religion. The authoritarian relationship permits no place for artistic creativity, individuality, or originality; rather, art and artists are controlled by the higher authority as art becomes visual propaganda. The second relationship is that of opposition, in which both art and religion are equal powers, and while neither is dominated or subservient to the other, there is a constant struggle to subjugate the other. The third relationship is one of mutuality when these two "equals" inhabit the same cultural environment in a symbiotic union of inspired nurture. The fourth relationship is separatist, as each operates independent of and without regard for the other, as in an iconoclastic religious environment or a secular culture. The fifth relationship is unified, so that their individual identities become so completely blended into a single entity it is impossible to discern what is art from what is religion.

As a corollary to, if not a result of, the fact that there is no universally agreed upon definition of either art or religion, none of the major world religions have a historically consistent attitude toward art. These cultural and geographic variations even within one religion such as Islam and Buddhism confirm that any or all of these five relationships between art and religion exist either simultaneously or in a chronological progression in one religious tradition. In his now classic *Sacred and Profane Beauty: The Holy in Art* (2005 [1963]), Gerardus van der Leeuw (1890–1950) considered the nature of the arts in relation to religion and specifically identified Christianity as a religious locus in which all five relationships between art and religion can be identified.

Religious Attitudes Toward Art. Every religious tradition has an attitude toward art, and thereby toward image. Some are formalized in written canons, hierarchy, dogma, creeds, and liturgy, while others are predicated upon oral tradition, ritual, and mythology. The fundamental modes of religious attitudes toward art are iconic (advocacy), aniconic (acceptance), and iconoclastic (denial or rejection). The iconic attitude locates the image in representational or anthropomorphic figures of identifiable and known reality, as evidenced in the Byzantine icons of Mary as *Theotokos* or Jesus Christ as the Pantocrator. Taken to its extreme, however, the iconic religious attitude treads lightly upon idolatry. The aniconic attitude defines the image as a symbolic or allusive presentation of sacred reality, exemplified in nonrepresentational images to facilitate contemplation, devotion, and worship, as evidenced in the elegant calligraphy of illuminated Islamic manuscripts or the Śiva *liṅga.* Taken to its extreme, the aniconic religious attitude verges on total abstraction and thereby the complete absence of forms. The iconoclastic attitude rejects totally images and imagery in any media, style, or form, as exemplified in the otherwise imageless environment of Jewish synagogues and many Protestant churches. Taken to its extreme, the iconoclastic attitude is violent destruction of all images and imagery, sacred and secular.

Although these three religious attitudes toward art can be delineated, it is rare in the history of any religious tradition to operate without some variation in its attitude(s). As with all theories and constructs in art and religion, there is a coexistence of multiple religious attitudes toward images either in a historic process of evolution or simultaneously so that patterns develop: iconic to iconoclastic to iconic; iconic to iconoclastic; iconic to aniconic; aniconic to iconoclastic; or aniconic to iconic. Buddhism is one of several world religions that has had these three religious attitudes toward art in its history. Initially aniconic, Hinduism slowly assimilated image into worship and devotional practice, eventually establishing a complex religious iconography composed of representational and symbolic elements. The operative principle is that as each world religion evolves, its fundamental attitude toward art is similarly transformed. Certain religions such as Christianity and Buddhism have espoused a variety of attitudes toward image. Earliest Buddhist teaching was aniconic, while Zen Buddhism is iconoclastic. However, contacts with other cultures, including Hellenism, and expansion into other geographic regions caused Buddhism's initial aniconicism to evolve into a bifurcation of the iconic and iconoclastic religious attitudes. This Buddhist dichotomy is illustrated in the use of iconic and aniconic forms in those *maṇḍalas* that are ceremonially created and then ritually destroyed. Further, a fundamental ambiguity exists within several world religions as the hierarchy affirms the proscriptions or prescriptions pronounced in written texts, dogmas, or creeds, while the praxis of the collective of believers venerates an unconsecrated but nonetheless miraculous image.

The Veneration of Art. Images are either inherently venerable or become sacralized through an act or ceremony of consecration. The primary classification of natively venerable images is those singular sacred images known as *acheiropoietai* (from the Greek for "not made by hands"). Believers recognize these particular images as divinely inspired and divinely created as they are discovered either fully formed in nature, including the *acheiropoietai* images of Buddha, Śiva, or the Black Madonna of Montserrat, or those *acheiropoietai* reported to have "fallen" from the heavens to the earth like the iron *thokchaks* in Tibet and the Black Stone in Mecca. A second mode of *acheiropoietai* are those formed by direct divine imprint on cloth, such as the legendary Mandylion of Edessa and the Christian scriptural Veil of Veronica. A third mode of *acheiropoietai* are contemporary portraits of sacred persons created in their lifetimes by an artist who may also have been a holy person; for example, the icons of the *Theotokos and Child* painted by Luke the Evangelist and the sandalwood images of the Buddha reputed to have been carved in his actual presence.

A second category of sacred image meriting adoration and respect is the miraculous image that receives gifts and votives regularly from devotees. Miraculous images such as the Black Madonnas of Spain, Italy, France, and Switzerland, or Ganeśa, the Hindu "remover of obstacles," exhibit their sacrality by performing miracles, especially miraculous healings of otherwise inexplicable illnesses, bodily ailments, and physical disabilities; the dissipation of obstacles; and the conception and birth of healthy children to previously barren women. To evidence reassurance or perhaps to foretell impending disaster, some miraculous images produce a sign such as a glowing light, aromatic scents, streams of oil or blood, or tears as those of the renowned twelfth-century icon of the *Theotokos of Vladimir.* Other miraculous images such as the icon of the *Theotokos Hodegetria* of Constantinople were known for responding to prayers of protection from invading armies or natural disasters, so the preservation of the city or the conditions for a good harvest witnessed the inherent sacrality of the image.

Rituals of consecration performed by holy periods, or ecclesiastical hierarchs, affirmed venerability through the ceremonial imbuing of diving energy so that the image is worthy of adoration and respect. Consecration ceremonies range from the ancient Egyptian "Opening of the Mouth" ritual to the Hindu "Installation of Breath" rite in which the image was brought to life through the initiation of breath to the Zen Buddhist rite in which the eyes of the image are completed. Representative of that living dichotomy between the collective of believers and the religious hierarchy are images accepted as miraculous and venerable by the former prior to any formal ecclesiastical approval or consecration ceremony, as with a manifestation of the Bodhisattva Avalokiteśvara or an icon of *Theotokos Treheroussa.*

Following the ceremonies of consecration, sacred images garner specific forms of behavior and reception from believers. Often the simple viewing of the sacred image is an efficacious ritual, as witnessed through the ceremonial acts of elaborate ornamentation and dressing of sacred images in Hinduism and Roman Catholicism. The practice of offering delicate edibles, lit lamps, aromatic incense, beeswax candles, fresh flowers, and objects precious to the believer to the sacred image occurs either on significant feast days or upon the fulfillment of an intercessory plea. Sacred images are oftentimes anointed with consecrated liquids ranging from precious oils to holy water to melted butter—as a rite of cleansing and honor. The secularization of this ritual is practiced in the consecration of monarchs with precious oils and holy water. Devotees may follow prescribed patterns of posture and gestures to embody their acts of veneration, such as offering prayers from positions of prostration or the kissing of the sacred image with the intoning of prayers. Furthermore, the religious practice of ritual processions, which concurrently display and honor the sacred image, extend the ritualized boundaries of sacred energy and blessing throughout the processing areas.

Religious Categories for Art. Art has performed a variety of roles in the environments, rituals, and teachings of world religions, from devotional objects to divinely inspired works to communicators of sacred knowledge. Through pedagogy, devotions, and contemplation, art has nurtured the development and establishment of religious identity for both individual believers and the larger collective community. One of the normative and primary rationales for art in the context of religion is "to teach the faith" by means of symbolic and representational depictions of the major sacred narratives and tenets. This pedagogical, or didactic, aspect of art in religion is identified as "visual theology." Representational art can provide visible models for appropriate behavior, dress, postures, gestures, and modes of liturgical actions, and symbolic and representational liturgical objects of beautiful design and proportions can enhance the religious ceremonies. This liturgical, sacramental, or ritualistic dimension of art in religion is labeled "visual liturgy." Whether symbolic or representational, works of art that induce prayer or evoke personal devotions are identified as "visual contemplation." Art that offers spiritual orientation as the symbols and images facilitate the devotee into an experience of transcendence or momentary encounter with the sacred are categorized as "visual mysticism." The symbolic vocabulary of motifs, images, or signs that transfer religious meaning and theological tenets in a mode accessible only to the initiated is the art of "visual codes." Art that enhances through design and patterning the religious environment or the experience of spiritual encounter for the believer is identified as "visual decoration." The art of any of the world's religions can also be a combination of any or all of these categories so that one work can be symbolic and mystical or didactic and liturgical. Nonetheless, there are always works of art that are difficult, if not impossible to categorize, such as the Muqarnas, or stalactite decoration of Islamic architecture, which some scholars and believers identify as beautiful form and others interpret as the multiplicity of God's unity.

Art as Religious Communication. As a multivalent communicator of meaning and value, art can be defined as religious art on account of its theme, subject matter, or iconography, ranging from a scriptural narrative to a sacred portrait to a holy image created within the prescriptions of a particular faith. Religious art incorporates signs and symbols accessible to the initiated who have learned to read the iconography while recognizable as beautiful form to the uninitiated, such as the carved reliefs covering the interior and exterior walls of the Khandarīya Mahādeva Temple in Khajurano or multiple panels on Mathias Grünewald's *Isenheim Altarpiece.*

Art may be characterized as religious art by its function. The fundamental function of most religious art is as religious pedagogy to illustrate bodily postures and gestures or a story or dogma of a religious tradition, as do visual symbols and representational imagery. Beautiful ceremonial objects that priests or religious officials employ in a sacramental manner or as part of a religious ceremony, such as illustrated holy books, candelabra, or chalices, have a clearly identifiable religious function. Visual art, for example, the wall frescoes depicting yoga postures at Ajantā in western India or the Byzantine mosaics portraying the sacrament of baptism on the ceilings of the Orthodox Baptistry in Ravenna, have simultaneous liturgical and pedagogical functions. Other works of art such as Yoruban masks and Navajo sand paintings have a function as ritual art.

The positioning or site of a work of art—on an altar or inside a temple—signifies it as religious art. Religious edifices differ in architectural style and function from religion to religion and country to country; however, ecclesiastical, monastic, ritual, and sacred locations include temples, synagogues, cathedrals, monasteries, and mosques as well as tombs and shrines. Oftentimes, patrons, whether individuals, royalty, religious hierarchs, or monastic communities, commission works of art, including but not limited to altarpieces or stained-glass windows, for a specific location. An artist's comprehension of the scale and siting of the work of art from the time of the commission permits design according to the spatial environment, as with Hubert and Jan van Eyck's *Ghent Altarpiece* (1432). Other works of art, for example, the sculpture of Athena in the Parthenon or the monumental Buddha at Kamakura, are identified as religious art as their function determines their placement.

Commissions for works of art either for placement or use within a religious environment—whether temple, mosque, monastery, synagogue, or church—or for a religious activity—ecclesiastical, liturgical, sacramental, devotional, contemplative, or catechetical—qualify art as religious art. Patronage of religious art may be the result of a special devotion, a healing, a response to an intercessory plea, or to assuage divine anger. Throughout the religions of the world, patrons of religious art have included laypeople as well as monastics and religious, the court and aristocracy as well as the lower classes.

The artist as the creator of art has a significant role to play in the characterizing of art as religious art. The definition of the artist and of the artist's spirituality varies from religion to religion. The characteristics and categories by which the artist is defined include descriptions of the relationship between artist and art, between art and personal spirituality, and ultimately, between the aesthetic and spiritual experiences, and are delineated in distinctive fashions within each world religion and culture. For example, art discloses the character and thereby the spirituality of the artist, according to Daoist and Confucian aesthetics, while an intimacy between artist, art, and spirituality is presumed by Hindu aesthetics, as art is spiritual and the spiritual is expressed through the arts. However, the distinction between artist and art, whereby a nonbeliever could create works for a religious community or environment, is the modern Western position. Traditionally, even in the West, the normative pattern was that the artist was a believer and practicing member of a religious community for whom the creation of art was a spiritual path. The making of religious art was, then, a form of religious ritual that began with an act, or period, of spiritual cleansing, including intense prayer, abstinence from sexual relations, and fasting. Further a complex but carefully defined rubric of forms, symbols, colors, and motifs was followed; each religious image was a codebook and "earned" the appellation "religious art." In the making of *maṇḍalas* the Buddhist monk followed such ritual procedures and codified rules as did the Eastern Orthodox Christian monk who "wrote" icons and the Navajo shaman who created the healing image through sand paintings.

Religious Responses to Art. The response to religious art is predicated upon individual faith, pronounced dogma, religious attitudes toward the image, and aesthetic quality projected by the work of art. The operative principle should be that as the embodiment of the sacred, a religious image provides for immediate and permanent access to the deity. Such a response, however, would require the believer's receptivity to the power of images and the primacy of sacred nature. The practical reality is that even one work of religious art can garner a diversity of responses, each of which is dependent upon the believer's preconceptions regarding religious encounter and the image. As an example of this multiplicity of response to one image, consider that of Śiva Nataraja, the divine dancer who creates and destroys the universe with each footstep. Śiva is invited to enter an image of himself at the beginning of ritual prayer or ceremonies; his presence may be perpetual or fleeting, although the physical image endures through the work of art. Throughout the ritual both Śiva and his sacred energy reside within the image but depart when the ritual comes to a close. The image remains as a visual aid for personal devotion and prayer and as a visual remembrance of the god's activity so that Śiva's sacred presence is known even in his absence. The artistic rendering of Śiva Nataraja functions as a visual reminder of the divinity's existence rather than an embodiment or temporary receptacle of the sacred; it thereby becomes a centering point for meditation, prayer, ritual, or religious experience. For many devotees, such an image is simply the point of initiation toward their individual "goal" to transcend materiality and to ascend to a mystical state of imageless union with the divine. Other believers find such an image to be simply a pedagogical object but not relevant for personal prayer, devotions, or mystical experiences. For an iconoclast, such an image of Śiva Nataraja should be denied, if not destroyed, as much out of a fear of idolatry as a simple distrust of images.

What is most significant in the human response to religious art is that even a minimal response provides an entry into the experience of or participation in divine power and energy. Works of religious art, for believers, are not simply material objects but mediators of spiritual energies. Simultaneously as efficacious location and a distancing from devotees, sacred space is created by the presence of a religious image. Recognized as a religious image in many religions, the human body is identified as a reflection of the divine bodies of the gods and goddesses in Classical Greece and as an object of glorification in certain Hindu sects and African traditions. Thereby, the response of the human body to religious art provides an aesthetic channel for devotions, contemplation, prayer, and worship.

A Preliminary History of the Field. As a discrete field of study, art and religion has no singular historic event or scholar to recognize as its formal beginning or founder. From the beginnings of scholarly discourse, critical and academic discussions of art or religion impinged each upon the territory of the other, as reflected in the initial pages of this entry. As an identifiable formal topic, however, the study of art and religion was initiated with the virtual plethora of mid-nineteenth-century publications on Christian art that emerged from the pens of a diverse group of predominantly self-trained writers beginning with Alexis-François Rio (1797–1874), *De la poésie Chrétienne* (1837); Adolphe Napoléon Didron (1806–1867), *Iconographie Chrétienne* (1843); Lord Lindsay Alexander (1812–1880), *Sketches of the History of Christian Art* (1847); and Anna Brownell [Murphy] Jameson (1794–1860), *Sacred and Legendary Art* (1848). These publications, especially Jameson's books and serialized texts, which built upon her renown as an author of museum guidebooks, inaugurated a genre dedicated to the appreciation of Christian art as an exemplar of moral values and good taste. Nonetheless, these texts situated the paintings and sculptures discussed within their historical contexts, carefully described any stylistic or technical innovations, and explained the "lost language" of Christian signs and symbols. Apparently, there was a charisma for Christian art at this time throughout Western Europe and America, as witnessed by the establishment of a variety of art movements—the Academy of St. Luke in Rome, the Pre-Raphaelite Brotherhood in London, and the Nazarenes in Vienna—dedicated to the reunification of art and religion as epitomized in the medieval synthesis.

Cultural and language shifts beginning with the Renaissance were formative on this nineteenth-century movement, as the concept of art was transformed from craft and that of the artist to individual creator. These terms were further clarified with the Enlightenment and the Romantic movement, as the Renaissance cult of the artist as an individual, and perhaps a genius, matured into common vocabulary. The German Romantic philosophers, including J.G. Fichte (1762-1814), Friedrich W.J. Schelling (1775-1854), and August Wilhelm Schlegel (1767-1845), built upon the foundations of subjectivity introduced by Immanuel Kant (1724–1804) and the spiritual in art of Johann Wolfgang von Goethe (1749-1832). Other philosophical and theological influences from Friedrich Schleiermacher (1768–1834) to Charles Baudelaire (1821–1867) to Ralph Waldo Emerson (1803–1882) to John Ruskin (1819–1900) corroborated this transformation toward a spiritualizing of art and toward the establishment of an academic discourse identifiable as art and religion. This genre of Christian art initiated by Rio, Lindsay, and Jameson was quickly expanded by a variety of ministers, artists, and educators predominantly from England, France, Germany, and then the United States. Their publications included travel diaries, behavior manuals, gift books and annuals, and treatises on the history and symbolism of Christian art; and this genre flourished into the early twentieth century, as witnessed by the popular books of Estelle Hurll, *The Madonna in Art* (1897) and Clara Erskine Clement Waters, *Saints in Art* (1899).

Concurrently, the academic study of religion, especially as the history of religions, began to surface in the German university system, while an assortment of cultural events, including the artistic modes of Orientalism and Japonisme in the nineteenth century and the fascination with *le primtif* in the early twentieth century, the Christian missions into China and Japan, the Chicago World's Fair, the Parliament of World Religions, and the phenomenon of theosophy created a cultural climate of intellectual and popular interest in other religions, particularly Hinduism and Buddhism. Nonetheless, the lens was Western—so a Western perception of Hinduism or Buddhism as both a religion and a culture. Western scholars and commensurately Western scholarship has privileged this field of study. Students of religion and artists learned about the aesthetics and art of "the other." As the academic study of art history was being organized in several European universities, the recognition of the need to learn about religion was mandatory for the research and discussion of Christian art, and later of the arts of India, China, and Japan. From its earliest moment, then, art and religion was a multicultural and multireligious form of discourse.

Further developments in the study of art and religion resulted from the breadth of vision among a select group of religion scholars: Rudolf Otto (1869–1937), Gerardus van der Leeuw (1890–1950), Mircea Eliade (1907–1986), and Suzuki Daisetz (1870–1966); art historian Ananda K. Coomaraswamy (1877–1947); and theologian Paul Tillich

(1886–1965). Of this magisterial group, the phenomenologist of religion, Rudolph Otto, and the historian of religions, Mircea Eliade, contributed most significantly to the development of the discrete field of study known as art and religion. In his now classic *The Idea of the Holy,* Otto identified the connectives between art and religion. Beyond normative language and rational description, religious experience is initiated by the nonrational modes of communication and sensory perceptions provided by art. Despite his silence on any comparison between aesthetic and religious experience, or the commonalities between religion and artistic creativity, Otto points to the critical importance of the experience of art as a moment of the silence, awe, wonder, and fear encountered before the numinous.

Eliade describes the visualizing of the otherwise invisible sacred through art in a variety of forms and styles in *Symbolism, the Sacred, and the Arts* (1994 [1985]). Art is a conduit to the sacred and a human activity permitting the possibility for involvement with divinity/ies. Art is essential to the proper performance of religious ceremonies and rituals. Eliade interpreted art as embedded in the human universal consciousness and in all world cultures and emerging in the artistic visioning and reinterpretation of symbols and images even in the secular art of the twentieth century. Coomaraswamy sought for the commonalities between the spiritual art of East and West, but perhaps his most significant contributions came during his tenure as curator of Asian Art at the Museum of Fine Arts in Boston, where he introduced the concept of "spiritual art" into the vocabulary of curators, museum displays, and special exhibitions. He furthered the definition of spiritual art when he supervised the acceptance of several of Alfred Stieglitz's (1864-1946) photographs as works of art—the first photographs ever to enter a museum or gallery collection under the rubric of art—into the museum's collection. Van der Leeuw proposed a phenomenology of art and religion in his *Sacred and Profane Beauty: The Holy in Art,* in which he described how all the arts—dance, drama, poetry, painting and sculpture, architecture, and music—signaled and manifested the presence of the sacred. His is the only text to expand the discussion comparatively among the arts.

Tillich is to be credited with relating contemporary Christian theology with twentieth-century art. His efforts to see and to discuss the connectives between contemporary works of art with both religious and secular themes to the classic masterpieces of Christian art, and as venue for discussing theological issues, opened the door to the serious consideration of the spirituality of modern art. Suzuki's significance to the study of art and religion was his masterful text *Zen and Japanese Culture* (1970 [1938]), in which he introduced his interpretation of the Zen aesthetic to the West. However, his famed lectures on Zen and Zen aesthetics at Columbia University in the 1950s opened the eyes and the minds of many of New York's most promising and creative artists, including musician John Cage (1912–1992), choreographers Martha Graham (1914-1999) and Merce Cunningham (b. 1919), and the painters and sculptors who became known as the Abstract Expressionists, including Jackson Pollock (1912-1956) and Mark Rothko (1903-1970), to an alternate way of envisioning and experiencing the sacred, and to the spirituality of art.

Similarly, a quick survey of the academic field of art history and of the influence of several prominent art historians such as Charles Rufus Morey, Émile Mâle, Erwin Panofsky, and Meyer Schapiro would provide critical moments in the evolution of the field of art and religion. Panofsky's work in deciphering iconography from iconology may be one of the most crucial art historical contributions to the study of art and religion prior to Freedberg's "response theory." Iconography was a carefully detailed method of analysis of the symbolic vocabulary delineated within an image, while iconology was an explanation of an image or art form within the context of the culture—social, political, religious, and engendered—that produced it.

Methods and Methodologies. The amorphous nature of the relationship between art and religion as both a topic of investigation and a field of study is paralleled by the oftentimes perceived "flexible" methodologies employed by specialists. The breadth of methodological approaches, technical languages, and questions investigated continue to expand in tandem with the study of religion. The lacuna of a single or even commonly accepted "core" methodology is irksome at best. The diverse technical vocabularies and methodologies include but are not limited to art history, iconography and iconology, cultural history, church history, ethics, history of religion, ritual studies, comparative religions, and theology. The primary characteristic of art and religion that defies its definition as a normative field of study is that it is fundamentally a multidisciplinary field that is broad in its subject matter, geographic sweep, world religions foci, and technical language.

From its possible "official" beginnings in the mid-nineteenth century into the twenty-first century, art and religion has traversed a variety of methodological formulae and vocabularies, beginning with art history, iconography and symbolism, history of religion, cultural history, theology, philosophy, phenomenology, and iconology, while the foci of a new generation of scholars in the 1970s incorporated the principles and lenses to expand the borders of art and religion into the questions raised by the emerging categories of "the marginalized" and feminism into the 1980s issues of the body and class. The reception of art historian David Freedberg's groundbreaking study, *The Power of Images* (1989), defined and traced the history of "response theory," which provided art and religion with an affirmation of its interest in the human, or worshiper's, experience of art. Beginning with the late 1980s, specialized studies with methodologies and languages for material culture, popular culture, performance and display, visual culture, and museum studies were incorporated, sometimes tangentially, into art and religion.

These additional disciplinary approaches and topical interests may be interpreted as diffusing the field of art and religion that much more broadly. However, the reality is twofold: oftentimes these new approaches or fields give a "name" such as Freedberg's "response theory" to an attitude, theme, or subject of art and religion research and investigation; and secondly, the fundamental nature of art and religion is to be inclusive, and to that end, it is a metaphor for religious studies. Nonetheless, it is reasonable to consider whether art and religion as a field without a methodology is an academic nomad or a valid but discrete field of study.

The methodological lacuna for art and religion may be problematic, especially in any attempt to defend its existence as a field of study. However, the range of disciplinary methods and topics ranging from art history to cultural studies to theology to gender studies and beyond has created a multilayered syntax for the research, writing, and discussions of art and religion. Among the fundamental topics for investigation have been the historical relationships between art and religion(s); religious attitudes toward image (or icon or idol); religious attitudes toward the veneration of images; the symbolism of gender in religious art; changing cultural attitudes toward religion and the effect(s) upon art; changing cultural values toward art and the implications for religion; and the visual evidence for cultural shifts in understanding of gender and the body. Further, the normative pattern has been that specialists in art and religion operate with the methodological formulae and vocabulary in which they were first trained, and expand, transform, and re-form these in the process of research and writing about art and religion.

From the nineteenth-century "establishment" of art and religion as a focus of study, there are three identifiable investigative categories related directly to the initial or primary lens in which a scholar of art and religion is initially trained: art history, theology, and history of religion. Further, these categorizations to the point of origin within the research—that is, the category of "art-centered investigations"—proceed from art as a primary document; "religion-centered investigations" advance from the religious impulse; and the "art-and-religions-centered investigations" emerge from the comparative study of traditions.

Art-centered investigations begin with a fascination with or spotlight on art, particularly a specific work of art. Critical in this mode of analysis are the topics of the origin of the work of art, the "reading" of the signs and symbols, and recognition of the cultural and historic context as formative in the shaping of the artist and the artistic vision. Scholars who operate from this category of "art-centered investigations" are predominantly art historians, art critics, and aestheticians who typically analyze the art and religion of one faith tradition, as evidenced by Hisamatsu Shin'ichi's (1889–1980) study of Zen Buddhist art (1982), André Grabar's (1896–1990) texts on Christian art and iconography (1968), and Stella Kramrisch's (1898–1993) work on Hindu art and architecture (1946 and 1965). Students involved in research on Byzantine, medieval, and Renaissance art will quickly learn that the art of those historical epochs is undisputedly difficult to decipher without some study of the history and theology. The texts on Christian art by Émile Mâle (1984), Erwin Panofsky (1953 and 1972), and Otto von Simson (1956) evidenced a careful interweaving of theology, scripture, and church history as connectors in the visual codes in the individual artworks analyzed. During the late 1960s the formal academic concern for the creative process corresponded with more than a comparative analysis of the aesthetic and the spiritual experience. Rather, fascination grew with the code of visual vocabulary and the mode by which images communicate ideas, as seen in the 1969 and 1974 texts of Rudolf Arnheim (b. 1904) and the 1971 text by Martin Heidegger (1889–1976).

Religion-centered investigations emerge from a fascination with or a devotion to the theological impulse or religious character of art. Central to this mode of examination are the topics of the affect of theology or religion on the making and symbolic content of a work of art, and of the cultural interplay between artists and the theological postures of prevalent themes. Scholars who participate within the frame of "religion-centered investigations" include art historians, church historians, and theologians who typically engage in the study of art and religion from the perspective of one faith tradition, as witnessed by Jane Daggett Dillenberger's books on the style and content of Christian art (1965), John Dillenberger's texts on Christian art in the context of church history and theology (1988 and 1999), and John W. Dixon's studies of the theological impulse in Christian art (1978 and 1996). The creative process for the artist as an act of religious communication of ideas is evidenced in the "religion-centered investigations" of Jacques Maritain's (1882–1973) 1978 work and Nicholas Wolterstorff's 1980 study.

Religions-and-art-centered investigations proceed with comparative analyses of at least two religious traditions, with art as the focal point. The process of comparative readings of the same work of art determines the universality of art and of the religious impulse. Comparative studies of symbols and images extend beyond syntax and vocabulary to witness the creative impulse of imagination as it shapes new worlds and formulates new understandings of the human and of the world, which cannot be achieved through language or reason. Scholars operating within the "religions-and-art-centered" investigations include art historians, historians of religion, and aestheticians who share a passion for comparative study and the desire to learn the vocabulary of signs and symbols, such as Titus Burckhardt's (1908–1984) comparative analyses of Hindu, Christian, and Islamic art (1967 and 1987), Coomaraswamy's studies of Christian and Hindu art and religion (1943), and S. G. F. Brandon's (1907–1971) books on comparative rituals and iconography (1975). Also within this category is a place for the art of world religions to be evaluated with reference to the energy and power of art to fascinate and communicate through emotive codes and images, as discussed by André Malraux (1953 and 1960) and F. S. C. Northrop (1946).

The interpretative critiques raised by those scholars representing "the marginalized" transferred attention from the traditional art being studied to the nature and intent of the questions being asked. Initially, feminism wielded vast influence in transforming scholarly foci and the methodological formulae. The incorporation of feminist concerns, motifs, methods, and vocabulary in art and religion is evidenced by the work of Margaret R. Miles (1985) and Celia Rabinovitch (2002). Scholarly interest in the process of seeing, the relationship between art and religious vision on all levels of society, and the role of seeing in the process of making art is emphasized in the new disciplinary visual culture studies by Colleen McDannell (1995) and David Morgan (1998 and 2005). An important reference is the special exhibitions and their catalogues and books, which have begun to focus on issues related to the art and religion of the so-called Third World in the work of Rosemary Crumlin (1988 and 1991), Thomas B. F. Cummings, and Kenneth Mills (1997). The writing and discussions of two art historians—David Freedberg (1989) on response theory and James Elkins (2001) on the interconnections of optics/vision, human emotions, and religious meaning in art—have greatly advanced the studies of art and religion.

New Considerations. As scholars engaged in the study of art and religion continue their perennial quest to answer the critical questions "what makes art religious?" and "how is religious artistic?", the analytic methods, subjects, and vocabulary have responded by crossing over into the borders of new disciplines, such as visual culture, and the new critical gauntlets of technology, globalization, and secularization. Technology transformed the definition, experience, and study of art with the nineteenth-century invention of the camera, as photography challenged painting into new directions. The contemporary challenges of technology include the advent of computer art, virtual reality, and an environment in which one merely needs to press the right button to encounter masterpieces of art on the websites of major museums. The computer becomes then a mediator between art and the viewer, between art and artist, and between human consciousness and the projection of reality.

The challenge of globalization coincides with religious pluralism as the dominance of Western cultural and religious values appears to be ending as the symbolism and visual codes of Western art are being synthesized with those from other cultural and religious heritages. A new visual vocabulary is emerging from the confluence of religious traditions. Interwoven into this new fabric of the global and pluralistic world are the questions raised about the moral and ethical policies of collecting and exhibiting the sacred art of other cultures, and the issue of repatriation. Multiple considerations related to the presentation and display of sacred art in a secular or institutionalized setting are significant topics for the study of art and religion, including the issues of function, consecration, and response. Furthermore, and perhaps more significant, globalism and pluralism should assist in erasing the privileged status of Western scholars and Western art within the boundaries of art and religion. Comparative studies of specific artistic images or motifs might prove to be a positive venue to examine the commonalities and the differences and even the possibility of reformulating the basic vocabulary and issues of this discrete field of study.

Another way to consider this serious concern of the presentation of sacred art is the growing awareness that the "objects" being studied are being analyzed, researched, and encountered outside of their original placement and purpose. Thus, to be inclusive, our analysis must extend to the consideration, if not reconstruction, of the physical space in which the work was originally sited, its function (devotional, liturgical, ceremonial, ritual), and the experience of encountering the work for the first time in its "home" place.

Art is an imaged reflection, prophecy, and witness to human experience and religious values as well as an expression of culture. The topic of art and religion continues to entice consideration and to adapt itself to the transformations and permutations of scholarly concerns. The call continues among a new generation of young scholars to define the field and to adopt a methodology. The field of study identified as art and religion continues to survive despite its lack of a recognized methodology or academic vocabulary. Art, like religion, defies categorization and universal definition. Art and religion are inexorably interconnected throughout human history and human creativity.

Bibliography

Reference Works

Apostolos-Cappadona, Diane. *Dictionary of Christian Art.* New York, 1994.

Apostolos-Cappadona, Diane. *Dictionary of Women in Religious Art.* New York, 1998 (1996).

Becker, Udo, ed. *The Continuum Encyclopedia of Symbols.* New York, 1994.

Bell, Robert E. *Dictionary of Classical Mythology: Symbols, Attributes, and Associations.* Los Angeles, 1982.

Bernen, Robert, and Satia Bernen. *Myth and Religion in European Painting, 1270–1700: The Stories as the Artists Knew Them.* New York, 1973.

Biedermann, Hans. *Dictionary of Symbolism: Cultural Icons and the Meanings behind Them.* Translated by James Hulbert. Cleveland, Ohio, 1994.

Cirlot, J. E., *Dictionary of Symbols.* Translated by Jack Sage. New York, 1972.

Cooper, J. C. *An International Encyclopedia of Traditional Symbols.* London, 1978.

Encyclopedia of Archetypal Symbolism. 2 vols. Boston, 1991–1997.

Ferguson, George. *Signs and Symbols in Christian Art.* New York, 1954.

Goodenough, Erwin. *Jewish Symbols in the Greco-Roman World.* 13 vols. New York, 1953–1968.

Hall, James. *Dictionary of Signs and Symbols in Art.* New York, 1979.

Hall, James. *Illustrated Dictionary of Symbols in Eastern and Western Art.* San Francisco, 1994.

Herder Dictionary of Symbols. Translated by Boris Mathews. London, 1993.

Metford, J. C. J. *Dictionary of Christian Lore and Legend.* London, 1983.

Moore, Albert C. *Iconography of World Religions: An Introduction.* Philadelphia, 1977.

Murray, Peter, and Linda Murray. *The Oxford Companion to Christian Art and Architecture.* Oxford, 1996.

Promey, Sally. "The 'Return' of Religion in the Scholarship of American Art." *The Art Bulletin* 85, no. 3 (2003): 581–604.

Roberts, Helene, ed. *Encyclopedia of Comparative Iconography.* 2 vols. Chicago, 1998.

Unterman, Alan. *A Dictionary of Jewish Lore and Legend.* London, 1991.

Van der Waal, Henri. *Iconoclass: An Iconographic Classification System.* Amsterdam, 1973–1985.

Theories of Religion and Art

Adams, Doug. *Transcendence with the Human Body in Art: George Segal, Stephen DeStaebler, Jasper Johns, and Christo.* New York, 1991.

Adams, Doug, and Diane Apostolos-Cappadona, eds. *Art as Religious Studies.* Eugene, Ore., 2002 (1987).

Adams, Doug, and Diane Apostolos-Cappadona, eds. *Dance as Religious Studies.* Eugene, Ore., 2001 (1990).

Apostolos-Cappadona, Diane. "To Create a New Universe: Mircea Eliade on Modern Art." *Cross Currents* 33, no. 4 (1983): 408–419.

Apostolos-Cappadona, Diane. "Picasso's *Guernica* as Mythic Iconoclasm: An Eliadean Reading of Modern Art." In *Myth and Method,* edited by Wendy Doniger and Laurie Patton, pp. 327–351. Charlottesville, Va., 1996.

Apostolos-Cappadona, Diane. "Religion and Art." In *Dictionary of Art,* edited by Jane Shoaf Turner, vol. 26, pp. 137–142. New York, 1996.

Apostolos-Cappadona, Diane. "Religion and Sacred Space." In *The Religion Factor: An Introduction to How Religion Matters,* edited by Jacob Neusner and William Scott Green, pp. 213–226. Louisville, Ky., 1996.

Apostolos-Cappadona, Diane. "Art." In *Encyclopedia of Women and World Religions,* edited by Serenity Young, vol. 1, pp. 61–65. New York, 1999.

Apostolos-Cappadona, Diane. "Arts, Architecture, and Religion." In *The Blackwell Companion to the Study of Religion,* edited by Robert Segal. Oxford, 2005.

Apostolos-Cappadona, Diane, ed. *Art, Creativity, and the Sacred: An Anthology in Religion and Art.* New York, 1995 (1984).

Apostolos-Cappadona, Diane, and Lucinda Ebersole, eds. *Women, Creativity, and the Arts: Critical and Autobiographical Perspectives.* New York, 1995.

Arnheim, Rudolf. *Visual Thinking.* Berkeley, Calif., 1969.

Arnheim, Rudolf. *Art and Visual Perception: A Psychology of the Creative Eye.* Berkeley, Calif., 1974.

Barasch, Moshe. *Giotto and the Language of Gesture.* New York, 1987.

Barasch, Moshe. *Icon: Studies in the History of an Idea.* New York, 1992.

Belting, Hans. *Likeness and Presence: A History of the Image Before the Era of Art.* Chicago, 1994.

Berdyaev, Nicholas. *The Meaning of the Creative Act.* New York, 1962.

Bowlam, David, and James K. Henderson. *Art and Belief.* New York, 1970.

Brandon, S. G. F. *Man and God in Art and Ritual: A Study of Iconography, Architecture and Ritual Action as Primary Evidence of Religious Belief and Practice.* New York, 1975.

Burckhardt, Titus. *Sacred Art in East and West.* London, 1967.

Burckhardt, Titus. *Mirror of the Intellect: Essays on Traditional Science and Sacred Art.* Edited by William Stoddard. Albany, N.Y., 1987.

Burckhardt, Titus. *The Essential Titus Burckhardt.* Edited by William Stoddard. Bloomington, Ind., 2002.

Coomaraswamy, Ananda K. *Christian and Oriental Philosophy of Art.* New York, 1956 (1943).

Coomaraswamy, Ananda K. *Traditional Art and Symbolism.* Edited by Roger Lipsey. Princeton, N.J., 1986 (1977).

Cort, John E. "Art, Religion, and Material Culture: Some Reflections on Method." *Journal of the American Academy of Religion* 64, no. 3 (1996): 613–632.

Crumlin, Rosemary, ed. *Beyond Belief: Modern Art and the Religious Imagination.* Melbourne, Australia, 1998. Exhibition catalogue.

Dixon, John W. "Art as the Making of the World: Outline of Method in the Criticism of Religion and Art." *Journal of the American Academy of Religion* 51, no. 1 (1983): 15–36.

Dixon, John W. "Reckonings on Religion and Art." *Anglican Theological Review* 74, no. 2 (1992): 267–275.

Dixon, John W. "What Makes Religious Art Religious?" *Cross Currents* (spring 1993): 5–25.

Eliade, Mircea. *Symbolism, the Sacred, and the Arts.* Edited by Diane Apostolos-Cappadona. New York, 1992 (1985).

Elkins, James. *Pictures and Tears: A History of People Who Have Cried in Front of Paintings.* New York, 2001.

Freedberg, David. *Iconoclasts and Their Motives.* Maarssen, Netherlands, 1985.

Freedberg, David. *The Power of Images: Studies in the History and Theory of Response.* Chicago, 1989.

Gutmann, Joseph, ed. *The Temple of Solomon: Archaeological Fact and Medieval Tradition in Christian, Islamic and Jewish Art.* Missoula, Mont., 1976.

Gutmann, Joseph, ed. *The Image and the Word: Confrontations in Judaism, Christianity, and Islam.* Missoula, Mont., 1977.

Heidegger, Martin. *Poetry, Language, Thought.* Translated by Albert Hofstader. New York, 1971.

Hinnells, John R. "Religion and the Arts." In *Turning Points in Religious Studies: Essays in Honour of Geoffrey Parrinder,* edited by Ursula King. Edinburgh, 1990.

Hunter, Howard, ed. *Humanities, Religion, and the Arts Tomorrow.* New York, 1972.

Kandinsky, Wassily. *Concerning the Spiritual in Art, and Painting in Particular.* New York, 1977 (1914).

Laeuchli, Samuel. *Religion and Art in Conflict: Introduction to a Cross-Disciplinary Task.* Philadelphia, 1980.

Lipsey, Roger. *An Art of Our Own: The Spiritual in 20th-Century Art.* Boulder, Colo., 1989.

Malraux, André. *The Voices of Silence.* Translated by Stuart Gilbert. Garden City, N.J., 1953.

Malraux, André. *The Metamorphosis of the Gods.* Translated by Stuart Gilbert. Garden City, N.J., 1960.

Maritain, Jacques. *Creative Intuition in Art and Poetry.* Princeton, N.J., 1978.

Martin, James A. *Beauty and Holiness: The Dialogue Between Aesthetics and Religion.* Princeton, N.J., 1990.

Martland, Thomas R. *Religion as Art.* Albany, N.Y., 1981.

Mazur, Eric Michael, ed. *Art and the Religious Impulse.* Lewisburg, Pa., 2002.

Morgan, David. *Visual Piety: A History and Theory of Popular Religious Images.* Berkeley, Calif., 1998.

Morgan, David. "Toward a Modern Historiography of Art and Religion." In *Reluctant Partners: Art and Religion in Dialogue,* edited by Ena Giurescu Heller, pp. 16–47. New York, 2004.

Morgan, David. *Religious Visual Culture in Theory and Practice.* Berkeley, Calif., 2005.

Morgan, David, and Sally Promey, eds. *The Visual Culture of American Religions.* Berkeley, Calif., 2001.

Northrop, F.S.C. *The Meeting of East and West.* New York, 1946.

Otto, Rudolf. *The Idea of the Holy.* Translated by John W. Harvey. Oxford, 1923.

Pfeiffer, John E. *The Creative Explosion: An Inquiry into the Origins of Art and Religion.* New York, 1982.

Plate, S. Brent, ed. *Religion, Art, and Visual Culture: A Cross-Cultural Reader.* New York, 2002.

Plate, S. Brent. "The State of the Arts and Religion: Some Thoughts on the Future of a Field." In *Reluctant Partners: Art and Religion in Dialogue,* edited by Ena Giurescu Heller, pp. 48–65. New York, 2004.

Pointon, Marcia, and Paul Binski, eds. *The Image in the Ancient and Early Christian Worlds.* Oxford, 1994.

Rabinovitch, Celia. *Surrealism and the Sacred: Power, Eros, and the Occult in Modern Art.* Boulder, Colo., 2002.

Rosenblum, Robert. *Modern Painting and the Northern Romantic Tradition: Friedrich to Rothko.* New York, 1975.

Taylor, Mark C. *Disfiguring: Art, Architecture, Religion.* Chicago, 1992.

Tuchman, Maurice, Judi Freeman, and Carel Blotkamp, eds. *The Spiritual in Art: Abstract Painting, 1890–1985.* Los Angeles, 1986. Exhibition catalogue.

Van der Leeuw, Gerardus. *Sacred and Profane Beauty: The Holy in Art.* Translated by David E. Green. New York, 2005 (1963 [1932]). Reprint edition.

Weiss, Paul. *Religion and Art.* Milwaukee, Wis., 1963.

Wuthnow, Robert. *Creative Spirituality: The Way of the Artist.* Berkeley, Calif., 2001.

Wuthnow, Robert. *All in Sync: How Music and Art Are Revitalizing American Religion.* Berkeley, Calif., 2003.

African Art and Religion

Hackett, Rosalind I. J. *Art and Religion in Africa.* London, 1996.

Thompson, Robert Farris. *African Art in Motion.* Berkeley, Calif., 1974.

Thompson, Robert Farris. *Flash of the Spirit: African and Afro-American Art and Philosophy.* New York, 1984 (1983).

Pacific Art and Religion

Crumlin, Rosemary. *Images of Religion in Australian Art.* Kensington, Australia, 1988.

Crumlin, Rosemary, ed. *Aboriginal Art and Spirituality.* North Blackburn, Victoria, Australia, 1991.

Moore, Albert C. *Arts in the Religions of the Pacific.* London, 1997.

Hindu Art and Religion

Coomaraswamy, Ananda K. *The Transformation of Nature in Art.* New York, 1956 (1934).

Coomaraswamy, Ananda K. *The Dance of Shiva: Fourteen Indian Essays,* rev. ed. New York, 1957.

Davis, Richard. *Lives of Indian Images.* Princeton, N.J., 1997.

Eck, Diana. *Darsan: Seeing the Divine Image in India.* New York, 1998 (1981).

Kramrisch, Stella. *The Hindu Temple.* Calcutta, India, 1946.

Kramrisch, Stella. *The Art of India: Traditions of Indian Sculpture, Painting and Architecture.* London, 1965.

Kramrisch, Stella. *Manifestations of Śiva.* Philadelphia, 1981. Exhibition catalogue.

Kramrisch, Stella. *Exploring India's Sacred Art: Selected Essays by Stella Kramrisch,* edited by Barbara Stoller Miller. Philadelphia, 1983.

Larson, Gerald J., Pratapaditya Pal, and Rebecca P. Gowen. *In Her Image: The Great Goddess in Indian Asiat and the Madonna in Christian Culture.* Santa Barbara, Calif., 1980. Exhibition catalogue.

Zimmer, Heinrich. *Myths and Symbols in Indian Art and Culture.* Princeton, N.J., 1974 (1946).

Buddhist Art and Religion

Hisamatsu, Shin'ichi. *Zen and the Fine Arts.* Translated by Gishin Tokiwa. Tokyo, 1982.

Pilgrim, Richard B. *Buddhism and the Arts of Japan.* New York, 1998 (1993).

Suzuki, Daisetz T. *Zen and Japanese Culture.* Princeton, N.J., 1970 (1938).

Classical Mediterranean Art and Religion

Gardner, Ernest. *Religion and Art in Ancient Greece.* Port Washington, N.Y., 1969 (1910).

Gordon, R. L. *Images and Values in the Graeco-Roman World: Studies in Mithraism and Religious Art.* Aldershot, U.K., 1996.

Rosenzweig, Rachel. *Worshipping Aphrodite: Art and Cult in Classical Athens.* Ann Arbor, Mich., 2004.

Scully, Vincent. *The Earth, the Temple, and the Gods.* New Haven, Conn., 1982.

Jewish Art and Religion

Bronstein, Leo. *Kabbalah and Art.* New Brunswick, N.J., 1997 (1980).

Mann, Vivian. *Jewish Texts on the Visual Arts.* Cambridge, U.K., 2000.

Mayer, Leo A. *Bibliography of Jewish Art.* New York, 1967.

Narkiss, Bezalel, ed. *Journal of Jewish Art* (volumes 1–5, Spertus College; volumes 6 *ff.*, Center for Jewish Art, Hebrew University, Jerusalem).

Christian Art and Religion

Apostolos-Cappadona, Diane. *The Spirit and the Vision: The Influence of Christian Romanticism on the Development of 19th-century American Art.* New York, 1995.

Apostolos-Cappadona, Diane. "Painting," "Sculpture," and "Symbol." In *Christianity: A Complete Guide,* edited by John Bowden. London, 2005.

Bailey, Gauvin A. *Art on the Jesuit Missions in Asia and Latin America, 1542–1773.* Toronto, 1999.

Brown, Frank Burch. *Religious Aesthetics: A Theological Study of Meaning and Making.* Princeton, N.J., 1989.

Brown, Frank Burch. *Good Taste, Bad Taste, and Christian Taste: Aesthetics in Religious Life.* New York, 2000.

Coulton, G. G. *Art and the Reformation.* New York, 1958.

Damian, Carol. *The Virgin of the Andes: Art and Ritual in Colonial Cuzco.* Miami Beach, Fla., 1995.

Dewhurst, C. Kurt, Betty MacDowell, and Marsha MacDowell. *Religious Folk Art in America: Reflections of Faith.* New York, 1983. Exhibition catalogue.

Dillenberger, Jane. *Secular Art with Sacred Themes.* Nashville, Tenn., 1969.

Dillenberger, Jane. *Style and Content in Christian Art.* New York, 1986 (1965).

Dillenberger, Jane. *Image and Spirit in Sacred and Secular Art.* Edited by Diane Apostolos-Cappadona. New York, 1990.

Dillenberger, Jane. *The Religious Art of Andy Warhol.* New York, 1998.

Dillenberger, Jane, and John Dillenberger. *Perceptions of the Spirit in Twentieth-Century American Art.* Indianapolis, Ind., 1977. Exhibition catalogue.

Dillenberger, Jane, and Joshua C. Taylor. *The Hand and the Spirit: Religious Art in America, 1700–1900.* Berkeley, Calif., 1972. Exhibition catalogue.

Dillenberger, John. *A Theology of Artistic Sensibilities: The Visual Arts and the Church.* New York, 1986.

Dillenberger, John. *The Visual Arts and Christianity in America: From the Colonial Period to the Present.* New York, 1989 (1988).

Dillenberger, John. *Images and Relics: Theological Perceptions and Visual Images in Sixteenth-Century Europe.* New York, 1999.

Dixon, John W. *Nature and Grace in Art.* Chapel Hill, N.C., 1964.

Dixon, John W. *Art and the Theological Imagination.* New York, 1978.

Dixon, John W. *The Physiology of Faith: A Theory of Theological Relativity.* San Francisco, 1979.

Dixon, John W. *The Christ of Michelangelo: An Essay on Carnal Spirituality.* Atlanta, 1994.

Dixon, John W. *Images of Truth: Religion and the Art of Seeing.* Atlanta, 1996.

Finney, Paul Corby. *The Invisible God: The Earliest Christians on Art.* New York, 1994.

Freedberg, David. *Iconoclasm and Painting in the Revolt of the Netherlands, 1566–1609.* New York, 1988.

Gambone, Robert L. *Art and Popular Religion in Evangelical America, 1915–1940.* Knoxville, Tenn., 1989.

Grabar, André. *Christian Iconography: A Study of Its Origins.* Princeton, N.J., 1968.

Hazelton, Roger. *A Theological Approach to Art.* Nashville, Tenn., 1967.

Hirn, Yrjö. *The Sacred Shrine: A Study of the Poetry and Art of the Catholic Church.* Boston, 1957.

Mâle, Emile. *Religious Art in France, the Thirteenth Century: A Study of Medieval Iconography and Its Sources.* Princeton, N.J., 1984.

Mathews, Thomas F. *The Clash of Gods: A Reinterpretation of Early Christian Art.* Princeton, N.J., 1993.

McDannell, Colleen. *Material Christianity: Religion and Popular Culture in America.* New Haven, Conn., 1995.

Miles, Margaret R. *Image as Insight: Visual Understanding in Western Christianity and Secular Culture.* Boston, 1985.

Mills, Kenneth. *Idolatry and Its Enemies: Colonial Andes Religion and Extirpation, 1640-1730.* Princeton, N.J., 1997.

Morey, Charles Rufus. *Early Christian Art,* 2d ed. Princeton, N.J., 1953 (1935).

Morgan, David. *Protestants and Pictures: Religion, Visual Culture, and the Age of American Mass Production.* New York, 1999.

Panofsky, Erwin. *Early Netherlandish Painting, Its Origins and Character.* Cambridge, Mass., 1953.

Panofsky, Erwin. *Studies in Iconology: Humanistic Themes in the Art of the Renaissance.* New York, 1972.

Pattison, George. *Art, Modernity, and Faith: Towards a Theology of Art.* New York, 1991.

Promey, Sally M. *Painting Religion in Public: John Singer Sargent's Triumph of Religion at the Boston Public Library.* Princeton, N.J., 1999.

Rombold, Günter, and Horst Schwebel. *Christus in der Kunst des 20, Jahrhunderts.* Basel, Switzerland, 1983. Exhibition catalogue.

Schapiro, Meyer. *Late Antique, Early Christian, and Medieval Art.* New York, 1979.

Schwebel, Horst and Heinz-Ulrich Schmidt. *Die Andere Eva: Wandlungen eines biblischen Frauenbildes.* Menden, Germany, 1985.

Steinberg, Leo. *The Sexuality of Christ in Renaissance Art and in Modern Oblivion.* Chicago, 1996.

Steinberg, Leo. *Leonardo's Incessant Last Supper.* New York, 2001.

Tillich, Paul. *On Art and Architecture.* Edited by Jane Dillenberger and John Dillenberger. New York, 1987.

Verdon, Timothy, and John Dally, eds. *Monasticism and the Arts.* Syracuse, N.Y., 1984.

Von Simson, Otto. *The Gothic Cathedral.* London, 1956.

Warner, Marina. *Alone of All Her Sex: The Myth and the Cult of the Virgin Mary.* New York, 1976.

Wolterstorff, Nicholas. *Art in Action: Toward a Christian Aesthetic.* Grand Rapids, Mich., 1980.

Islamic Art and Religion

Blair, Sheila S., and Jonathan M. Bloom. *The Art and Architecture of Islam, 1250–1800.* New Haven, Conn., 1995.

Blair, Sheila S., and Jonathan M. Bloom. *Islamic Arts.* London, 1997.

Burckhardt, Titus, and Roland Michaud. *Art of Islam: Language and Meaning.* London, 1976.

Grabar, Oleg. *The Formation of Islamic Art.* New Haven, Conn., 1973.

Grabar, Oleg. *The Shape of the Holy: Early Islamic Jerusalem.* Princeton, N.J., 1996.

Rice, David Talbott. *Islamic Art.* New York, 1965.

DIANE APOSTOLOS-CAPPADONA (2005)

ARTEMIS in Greek mythology is the daughter of Zeus and Leto and the twin sister of Apollo. In Greek religion she is concerned with the transitions of birth and growing up of both genders, as well as with the death of women and with the spaces outside the cities and the human activities in them—especially hunting and warfare. In the Greek East she is also a city goddess. Her equivalents in Anatolia and the Near East were the Phrygian Cybele and the Persian Anahita. The Romans identified Artemis with Diana, whereas the Etruscans accepted her under her Greek name as "Artume(s)." She is known as "Artimus" in Lydia, and as "Ertemi" in Lycia; she had many local sanctuaries all over Anatolia. The Greek goddess entered both the Lycian and Lydian pantheon under her Greek name, and numerous local goddesses all over Anatolia were hellenized as Artemis.

EARLY ARTEMIS. Her name defies etymology. She is most likely referred to in the inscriptions from the Bronze Age Pylus (Linear B), although her functions are unclear. She is also referenced in Hyampolis (Boeotia), a sanctuary that in the first millennium BCE belonged to Artemis and Apollo goes back to the later Bronze Age; however it is unclear whether this attests to her cult at this early age.

The mythology and religious roles of Artemis are fully established in early Greek poetry. Homer and Hesiod (late sixth to early seventh centuries BCE) know her as the daughter of Zeus and Leto, where together with her mother and her brother Apollo, she takes the side of the Trojans against the Greeks (*Iliad* 20.479–513) (although she is a rather inept fighter). Homeric poetry narrates some of her myths: how she took revenge on the Calydonian king Oineus for neglecting her sacrifice (*Iliad* 9.533–540) and on the Theban queen Niobe for slighting her mother (*Iliad* 24.603–609), as well as how—in an idiosyncratic form—she killed Orion, the lover of Eos (*Odyssey* 5.121), and Ariadne on the behest of Dionysos (*Odyssey* 11.324).

The *Homeric Hymn to Aphrodite* (seventh and sixth centuries BCE) provides a catalogue of Artemis's functions, which include archery and hunting in the mountains, playing the lyre, girls' dancing and ritual shouting in her sacred groves; and "the city of just men"—that is, her political and civic functions (vv. 17–20). Epic poetry reflects these aspects. The hunt, the main human activity in the wilderness beyond the city space, is important. Artemis is the "Lady of Animals" (*potnia thērōn, Iliad* 21.470) and protects the good hunter and punishes the bad one, such as Orion or Actaeon. In the company of her nymphs, Artemis hunts boars and stags, but she also relaxes with dance and play (*Odyssey* 6.102–109). The nymphs, the mythical projection of the nubile girls with whom Artemis is often connected, share her space during their transitional rites. Like these nymphs, Artemis, too, is a virgin; but unlike her, these maidens (*korai*) will lose their virginity (the chorus of "resounding Artemis" and her *korai* provokes erotic conquests).

Hunting means killing, and the huntress Artemis also kills humans—and not only in revenge. Her unfailing arrows were believed to cause the death from disease of women of every age and station. The invisible arrow of Artemis also explained unexpected female death (*Odyssey* 11.172). Hera, the protectress of married women, once called Artemis "a women's lioness" (*Iliad* 21.483).

The *Homeric Hymn to Apollo* (seventh century BCE) alludes to her birth in Ortygia (vs. 16). The passage separates Ortygia from Delus, where some later texts locate her birth, usually on the sixth day of the month Thargelion—Artemis has to be older than her twin brother, with whose birth she assisted on the seventh day of Thargelion. In most calendars, the festivals of Artemis are celebrated on the sixth day of any month, while Apollo's is celebrated on the seventh. The temple of Artemis on Delus dates to about 700 BCE and is almost two centuries older than the first temple of Apollo, who was Delus's main divinity; its cult focused on the "Altar of Horns."

The Greeks knew of another place called Ortygia, in a lonely river valley outside the city of Ephesus, Artemis's main city in the ancient world. The local myth told how Leto fled to this sacred grove to give birth to her daughter. In order to protect mother and baby from being pursued by Hera, armed demons—the Kouretes—performed a noisy armed dance around the newly born goddess (Strabo, *Geography* 14.1.20). This explained the religious and political role of a body of leading male citizens connected with the political center of Ephesus, the "sacred Kouretes."

ARTEMIS, HUNTING, AND WARFARE. In the documentation on later Greek religion, the roles of Artemis become further varied. Public cult rarely documents Artemis the huntress, although individual hunters dedicate the heads, antlers, or hides of their prey to Artemis, as they also do to Pan, another god of wild nature with whom she sometimes interacts. A late oracle from Didyma even prescribes sacrifices to Artemis in order to gain her help against Pan's wrath (Eusebius, *Prae-*

paratio Evangelica 7.5). Since fishing is another form of hunting, fishermen, as well, dedicate portions of their catch to Artemis. Images often represent Artemis as a huntress with a short dress, high boots, a bow, and a quiver or a couple of hunting spears; at times she'll appear with a female deer at her side; this is as common on Attic vase paintings as in Classical and post-Classical sculpture.

To the Greeks, warfare and hunting were closely connected. Hunting was training for war, and in several Greek states, Artemis was also connected with warfare. Before a battle, the Spartans offered a sacrifice to Artemis Agrotera (The Wild One) (Xenophon, *Hellenica* 4.2.20). The Athenians celebrated the victory of Marathon with an annual sacrifice to Artemis and Enyalios, a god of war often identified with Ares (Aristotle, *State of Athens* 58.1). Artemis Tauropolos, a goddess connected with groups of young warriors—and perhaps also with bull's masks—is the protectress of the Macedonian army and of the armies of the successors of Alexander the Great (356–323 BCE). In these roles, then, Artemis appears as the female goddess at the center of a group of male warriors and citizens, as does the Anatolian Cybele.

ARTEMIS AND YOUNG MEN. Artemis's protection and patronage of young men is part of this same function of hunting and warfare. However, her patronage here is often expressed in cruel rites.

In the sanctuary of Artemis Tauropolos in Attic Halai Araphenides, where young men performed armed dances, a young man's throat would be ritually cut until he bled. Myth explained this as a substitution for Orestes' sacrifice to the cruel Artemis of the Taurians. The rites in the Spartan sanctuary of Artemis Orthia were even more spectacular, rousing the interest of Greek and Roman visitors and scholars. The Spartans flogged a young man at the altar of Artemis until he bled. While this took place, her priestess assisted with the act, carrying a small image of the goddess. If the beating was not hard enough, the image the priestess carried grew heavier. This ritual was thought to replace a human sacrifice, although it developed from a contest among young males in which one group tried to steal cheese from Artemis's altar while a second group tried to prevent the theft.

Several statues of a priestess with a small, archaic-looking image belong to another sanctuary of Artemis Orthia, in the city of Messene. The Spartan image was said to be identical with the image in Artemis's sanctuary among the Taurians, located at the northern shore of the Black Sea. (Iphigenia and Orestes brought this image to Greece.) At some point in the ritual, the image was bound into the boughs of a *lygos* bush (a willow), hence the name Artemis *Lygodesme* (Bound in Willow) (Pausanias, *Description of Greece* 3.16.11).

In another local ritual from Tyndaris in Sicily, the same Taurian image was wrapped in a bundle of wood (*phakelos,* hence Artemis Phakelitis) and carried in a procession. According to a Spartan myth, the Taurian image drove the Spartans who found it mad. In the city of Pellene another small image of Artemis was carried around the walls of the besieged city in order to instill madness in the attackers, whereas in the Peloponnesian city Lousoi yet another Artemis (Hemerasia, the Tameress) could heal madness. Cruelty, madness, divine protection, and the world of young warriors seem to blend into one complex that expressed itself in a small image of Artemis that looked, in a native reading, old and foreign.

Several Greek cities performed yet another ritual that indigenous interpreters connected with warfare, with hunting, or with human sacrifice. In his *Description,* Pausanias gives an elaborate account of the contemporary festival (mid-second century CE) of Artemis Laphria in city of Patras: on a large pyre surrounded by a wooden palisade, the priests burned alive a large number of wild animals, including bears and stags (7.18.8–11). The ritual and the image of the goddess were said to have been transferred to Patras from the town of Calydon, where Artemis possessed an important sanctuary in the archaic period. A comparable ritual is confirmed in the cult of Artemis Laphria in Hyampolis in which the etiological myth derived from a war, while a fire ritual of Artemis Tauropolos in Phocaea was said to culminate in a human sacrifice.

ARTEMIS AND YOUNG WOMEN. Artemis was at least as important for young girls and women as she was for young men. A chorus of girls dancing for Artemis was common, especially in the Peloponnese; the girls often performed in sanctuaries situated far outside the cities, often in the mountains or in swampy regions. There, Artemis was Limnatis or Limnaia ("Lady of the Lake"; Pausanias, 4.4.2; 2.7.6) from the grove's position near a lake, or Kedreatis ("Lady of the Cedar Tree"; Pausanias, 8.13.2) and Karyatis ("She of the Hazelnut Tree"; Pausanias, 3.10.7) from the prominent trees of a sacred grove. None of this material, however, points to Frazerian tree cult in the service of Artemis.

Young Athenian girls spent some time in the secluded sanctuary of Artemis Brauronia on the East coast of Attica, far away from any city. The archaeological finds from the sanctuary attest to dancing of choruses, running contests of naked girls, and the use of bear masks. Local mythology explains that the cult was instituted to appease Artemis; she was angry because the Athenians had killed her sacred bear. Myth and cult also recall the story of Callisto, a nymph whom Artemis turned into a bear to punish her for her loss of virginity. Callisto would give birth to Arcas, the founder of Arcadia, who, as a hunter, unwittingly shot his bear mother. This story combines the topic of girls in the service of Artemis with the male topics of bear hunt and the foundation of a state. Callisto's name, the "Most Beautiful Girl," also refers to beauty contests that were sometimes connected with choruses of girls.

As a patroness of nubile girls, Artemis does not only protect their virginity as long as necessary; she also presides over the birth of their children once these girls become married women. Before their weddings, brides dedicated their toys to her, sometimes providing sacrifice to her during the wedding ritual. More often, Artemis was called Lochia (Lady of Birth) or was identified with the birth-goddess Eileithyia. Iphigenia, who shared the sanctuary of Brauron with the goddess, received the clothing of women who had died while giving birth.

OTHER ROLES. It was only in the Greek East that Artemis was also the protectress of cities, primarily in Ephesus. The Ephesian sanctuary became her main sanctuary during the Archaic Age. Shortly after 600 BCE, king Croesus of neighboring Lydia contributed to the construction of a splendid temple. The New Testament account of Paul's visit in Ephesus (*Acts* 19.23–48) demonstrates the importance of her cult and the religious fervor of the Ephesians. During the Hellenistic and imperial epochs, many Greek and Anatolian cities took over the cult of Ephesian Artemis, sometimes with mysteries. The official cult image of Ephesus represented the goddess with two burning torches. Yet the Ephesians also had another image, the one of a many-breasted (*multimamma*) Artemis that is preserved in several ancient copies and whose explanation is still uncertain—its iconography seems to follow archaic Anatolian iconography that has nothing do to with female breasts.

Artemis played a similar role in the Anatolian cities of Perge, where her image followed a comparable iconography. Her role was much the same in Magnesia, on the Maeander; here Artemis Leukophryene became prominent because of an epiphany in the third century BCE.

The poet Aeschylus identified Artemis with the moon, as he identified Apollo with the sun. Later, these identifications became commonplace, especially in Roman literature. During the imperial epoch, Artemis (often as a moon goddess) was identified with a large number of other goddesses, especially with Hekate and Isis, thus giving her some importance in magic, as well.

SEE ALSO Apollo; Dionysos; Divination, article on Greek and Roman Divination; Greek Religion; Hera; Homer; Soul, article on Greek and Hellenistic Concepts.

BIBLIOGRAPHY

Most of the ancient texts cited above are available in critical editions with English translations in the Loeb Classical Library. No comprehensive scholarly treatment of Artemis is available. The following books and articles treat specific aspects of the goddess:

Bammer, Anton. *Das Heiligtum der Artemis von Ephesos.* Vienna, 1984.

Brulotte, E. L. "Artemis: Her Peloponnesian Abodes and Cults." In *Peloponnesian Sanctuaries and Cults: Proceedings of the Ninth International Symposium at the Swedish Institute at Athens, 11–13 June 1994,* edited by Robin Hägg, pp. 179–182. Stockholm, 2002.

Bruns, Gerda. *Artemis die Jägerin.* Berlin, 1929.

Calame, Claude. *Les choeurs des jeunes filles en Grèce archaïque.* I: *Morphologie, fonction religieuse et sociale.* Rome, 1977. Translated as *Choruses of Young Women in Ancient Greece: Their Morphology, Religious Role, and Social Functions.* Translated by Derek Collins and Janice Orion. Lanham, Md., 1997.

Christou, Chryssanthos. *Potnia Theron.* Thessaloniki, Greece, 1968.

Cole, Susan Guettel. "Domesticating Artemis." In *The Sacred and the Feminine in Ancient Greece,* edited by Sue Blundell and Margaret Williamson, pp. 27–43. London, 1998.

Dawkins, R. M. *The Sanctuary of Artemis Orthia at Sparta.* London, 1929.

Fleischer, Robert. *Artemis von Ephesos und verwandte Kultstatuen aus Anatolien und Syrien.* Leiden, 1973.

Galvano, Albino. *Artemis Efesia.* Turin, Italy, 1990.

Gentili, Bruno and Franca Perusino, eds. *Le orse di Brauron. Un rituale di iniziazione femminile nel santuario di Artemide.* Pisa, Italy, 2002.

Vernant, Jean-Pierre. *Figures, Tables, Masques,* pp. 137–207. Paris, 1990.

FRITZ GRAF (2005)

ARTHUR, traditionally known as a sixth-century king of the Britons. Discussion of the origins of Arthur is of long standing. He is the hero or, later, the central figure of a large body of literature, much of it cyclic, in most western European languages but most especially in the medieval forms of French, German, English, and Welsh. He is consistently portrayed as a British ruler, and there is no doubt that his origins are to be sought in early Welsh sources and, to a lesser extent, in Breton and Cornish literature.

The evidence for Arthur's historical existence is meager and difficult to evaluate. Chapter 56 of the ninth-century *Historia Brittonum,* usually attributed to "Nennius," places him in the context of the first period of the attacks on Britain by the Germanic invaders, in the second half of the fifth century, and lists twelve of his famous victories. The chronicle now known as *Annales Cambriae* notes under the year 518 the Battle of Badon, as an Arthurian victory, probably the same as that which closes the Nennian list, and under 539 the Battle of Camlan, in which Arthur and Medrawd fell (Medrawd, Geoffrey of Monmouth's Modred, is the rebellious nephew of Arthur whose abduction of Guenevere led to the catastrophic final Battle of Camlan). The Nennian notes and the chronicle entries probably derive from the same northern British source of the eighth century and are the earliest testimony to a historical Arthur. The places referred to in the list of battles cannot be securely located, and not all are to be associated with Arthur; but the list probably represents the remnant of a pre-ninth-century Welsh poem that contained a catalog of some of Arthur's traditional victories. Together with a eulogistic reference to Arthur in another Welsh poem, *Gododdin,* from northern Britain, these early allusions suggest the development of a fifth-century British leader into a popular heroic figure celebrated in song. (The

Gododdin reference cannot be dated more securely than to the sixth to eleventh century.) The British author Gildas, however, writing about 540, does not name Arthur, although he celebrates the Battle of Badon; nor do other major historical sources, such as *The Anglo-Saxon Chronicle* or Bede, refer to him, so that some doubt as to his historical existence must remain.

Stories of Arthur, like many other northern British heroic legends, were relocated in early medieval Wales and achieved great popularity even before the arrival of the Normans in the eleventh century opened the way for this material to become a major component in the chivalric literatures of western Europe. Welsh poems from before 1100, *mirabilia* recounted in the *Historia Brittonum*, and material in some saints' lives of the eleventh and twelfth centuries all testify to a variety of tales being told about Arthur and to the fact that the hero was beginning to attract to himself legends and heroes from other cycles. Nineteenth-century scholars attempted to interpret this material in terms of solar mythology and the mythological type of the culture hero; though this approach is discredited in view of the nature of the historical evidence, it may yet be necessary to see Arthur, if not as a mythological figure, at least as one of fictional, folkloric origins. In Nennius's *mirabilia* Arthur and his dog Cabal hunt the boar Porcum Troit, a story more fully developed in the eleventh-century Welsh tale *Culhwch and Olwen*, and stories of Arthur in this latter source have already become associated with topographical features. Poems in the *Black Book of Carmarthen* and the *Book of Taliesin*, manuscripts from the thirteenth century, portray Arthur as the leader of a band of renowned warriors, Cei and Bedwyr foremost among them, who fight with monsters, hags, and giants and who carry out a disastrous expedition against the otherworld to free a prisoner. The twelfth-century *Life of Saint Gildas* contains the story of the abduction of Arthur's wife by Melwas and her imprisonment in the Glass Island, euhemerized as Glastonbury. These are the elements, together with some personal names, which seem to represent the earliest stratum of the Arthurian legend and which reappear in contemporary terms throughout its later forms.

There is more than one tradition of Arthur's end besides that of his death at Camlan. One that is attested early is his removal to the Isle of Avalon to be healed of his wounds and to await the call to return. At the end of the twelfth century the monks of Glastonbury claimed to have discovered the graves of Arthur and his wife at their abbey, but this seems never to have found popular acceptance. Arthur's role as the awaited hero remained a political force throughout the Middle Ages among the Celtic peoples of Wales, Cornwall, and Brittany. The later stages of his legend as the chivalrous king who was head of the Round Table and instigator of the search for the Holy Grail belong to the realm of literary history.

BIBLIOGRAPHY

Good surveys of individual Arthurian topics will be found in R. S. Loomis's *Arthurian Literature in the Middle Ages* (Oxford, 1959), where K. H. Jackson writes on the Arthur of history and of the early Welsh sources. The best survey of the earliest material is Thomas Jones's, "The Early Evolution of the Legend of Arthur," *Nottingham Medieval Studies* 8 (1964): 3–21.

All aspects of medieval Welsh literature relating to Arthur are discussed in a collaborative volume edited by Rachel Bromwich, A. O. H. Jarman, Brynley F. Roberts, *The Arthur of the Welsh* (Cardiff, 1991). Other volumes in this series (Arthurian literature in the Middle Ages) are: W. J. Barron, editor, *The Arthur of the English* (2001), W. J. Jackson and others, editors, *The Arthur of the Germans* (2000). J. B. Coe and S. Young, *The Celtic Sources for the Arthurian Legend* (Felinfach, 1995) is a useful and dependable compendium. O. J. Padel, *Arthur in Medieval Welsh Literature* (Cardiff, 2000) and again "The Nature of Arthur," *Cambridge Medieval Celtic Studies* 17 (1994): 1–31, bring many new and challenging insights to the material. A. O. H. Jarman describes the Welsh poetry in "The Delineation of Arthur in Early Welsh Verse" in *An Arthurian Tapestry*, edited by Ernest K. Varty (Glasgow, 1951), while Rachel Bromwich discusses the question of the development of the legend in two articles, "Concepts of Arthur," *Studia Celtica* 10/11 (1975–1976): 163–181, and "Celtic Elements in Arthurian Romance: A General Survey," in *The Legend of Arthur in the Middle Ages*, edited by P. B. Grout and others (Woodbridge, 1983). Rachel Bromwich's *Trioedd Ynys Prydein: The Welsh Triads*, 2d ed. (Cardiff, 1978) is a fund of information on Arthurian themes and characters. Jean Markale, *King of the Celts: Arthurian Legend and Celtic Traadition* (Rochester, 1994). Marged Haycock, "Preiddeu Annwn and the Figure of Taliesin," *Studia Celtica* 18/19 (1983–1984): 52–78. Melville Richards, "Arthurian Onomastics," *Transactions of the Honourable Society of Cymmrodorion* (1969): 250–269; Patrick K. Ford, "On the Significance of Some Arthurian Names in Welsh," *Bulletin of the Board of Celtic Studies* 30 (1983): 268–273.

BRYNLEY F. ROBERTS (1987 AND 2005)

ARTIFICIAL INTELLIGENCE (AI) is the field within computer science that seeks to explain and to emulate, through mechanical or computational processes, some or all aspects of human intelligence. Included among these aspects of intelligence are the ability to interact with the environment through sensory means and the ability to make decisions in unforeseen circumstances without human intervention. Typical areas of research in AI include the playing of games such as checkers or chess, natural language understanding and synthesis, computer vision, problem solving, machine learning, and robotics.

The above is a general description of the field; there is no agreed-upon definition of artificial intelligence, primarily because there is little agreement as to what constitutes intelligence. Interpretations of what it means to say an agent is intelligent vary, yet most can be categorized in one of three ways. Intelligence can be thought of as a quality, an individually held property that is separable from all other properties of the human person. Intelligence is also seen in the functions one performs, in one's actions or the ability to carry out certain tasks. Finally, some researchers see intelligence as something primarily acquired and demonstrated through relationship with other intelligent beings. Each of these understandings of intelligence has been used as the basis of an approach to developing computer programs with intelligent characteristics.

First Attempts: Symbolic AI. The field of AI is considered to have its origin in the publication of Alan Turing's paper "Computing Machinery and Intelligence" (1950). John McCarthy coined the term *artificial intelligence* six years later at a summer conference at Dartmouth College in New Hampshire. The earliest approach to AI is called *symbolic* or *classical AI*, which is predicated on the hypothesis that every process in which either a human being or a machine engages can be expressed by a string of symbols that is modifiable according to a limited set of rules that can be logically defined. Just as geometers begin with a finite set of axioms and primitive objects such as points, so symbolicists, following such rationalist philosophers as Ludwig Wittgenstein and Alfred North Whitehead, predicated that human thought is represented in the mind by concepts that can be broken down into basic rules and primitive objects. Simple concepts or objects are directly expressed by a single symbol, while more complex ideas are the product of many symbols, combined by certain rules. For a symbolicist, any patternable kind of matter can thus represent intelligent thought.

Symbolic AI met with immediate success in areas in which problems could be easily described using a small set of objects that operate in a limited domain in a highly rule-based manner, such as games. The game of chess takes place in a world where the only objects are thirty-two pieces moving on a sixty-four-square board according to a limited number of rules. The limited options this world provides give the computer the potential to look far ahead, examining all possible moves and countermoves, looking for a sequence that will leave its pieces in the most advantageous position. Other successes for symbolic AI occurred rapidly in similarly restricted domains, such as medical diagnosis, mineral prospecting, chemical analysis, and mathematical theorem proving. These early successes led to a number of remarkably optimistic predictions of the prospects for symbolic AI.

Symbolic AI faltered, however, not on difficult problems like passing a calculus exam, but on the easy things a two-year-old child can do, such as recognizing a face in various settings or understanding a simple story. McCarthy labels symbolic programs as brittle because they crack or break down at the edges; they cannot function outside or near the edges of their domain of expertise since they lack knowledge outside of that domain, knowledge that most human "experts" possess in the form of what is often called common sense. Humans make use of general knowledge, millions of things we know and apply to a situation, both consciously and subconsciously. Should such a set exist, it is now clear to AI researchers that the set of primitive facts necessary for representing human knowledge is exceedingly large.

Another critique of symbolic AI, advanced by Terry Winograd and Fernando Flores (*Understanding Computers and Cognition,* 1986), is that human intelligence may not be a process of symbol manipulation; humans do not carry mental models around in their heads. When a human being learns to ride a bicycle, he or she does not do so by calculating equations of trajectory or force. Hubert Dreyfus makes a similar argument in *Mind over Machine* (1986); he suggests that experts do not arrive at their solutions to problems through the application of rules or the manipulation of symbols, but rather use intuition, acquired through multiple experiences in the real world. He describes symbolic AI as a "degenerating research project," by which he means that, while promising at first, it has produced fewer results as time has progressed and is likely to be abandoned should other alternatives become available. His prediction has proven to be fairly accurate. By 2000 the once dominant symbolic approach had been all but abandoned in AI, with only one major ongoing project, Douglas Lenat's Cyc project. Lenat hopes to overcome the general knowledge problem by providing an extremely large base of primitive facts. Lenat plans to combine this large database with the ability to communicate in a natural language, hoping that once enough information is entered into Cyc, the computer will be able to continue the learning process on its own, through conversation, reading, and applying logical rules to detect patterns or inconsistencies in the data Cyc is given. Initially conceived in 1984 as a ten-year initiative, Cyc has yet to show convincing evidence of extended independent learning.

Symbolic AI is not completely dead, however. The primacy of primitive objects representable by some system of encoding is a basic assumption underlying the worldview that everything can be thought of in terms of information, a view that has been advanced by several physicists, including Freeman Dyson, Frank Tipler, and Stephen Wolfram.

Functional or Weak AI. In 1980, John Searle, in the paper "Minds, Brains, and Programs," introduced a division of the field of AI into "strong" and "weak" AI. Strong AI denoted the attempt to develop a full humanlike intelligence, while weak AI denoted the use of AI techniques to either better understand human reasoning or to solve more limited problems. Although there was little progress in developing a strong AI through symbolic programming methods, the attempt to program computers to carry out limited human functions has been quite successful. Much of what is currently labeled AI research follows a functional model, applying particular programming techniques, such as knowledge engineering, fuzzy logic, genetic algorithms, neural networking, heuristic searching, and machine learning via statistical methods, to practical problems. This view sees AI as advanced computing. It produces working programs that can take over certain human tasks, especially in situations where there is limited human control, or where the knowledge needed to solve a problem cannot be fully anticipated by human programmers. Such programs are used in manufacturing operations, transportation, education, financial markets, "smart" buildings, and even household appliances.

For a functional AI, there need be no quality labeled "intelligence" that is shared by humans and computers. All computers need do is perform a task that requires intelligence for a human to perform. It is also unnecessary, in functional AI, to model a program after the thought processes that humans use. If results are what matter, then it is possible to exploit the speed and storage capabilities of the digital computer while ignoring parts of human thought that are not understood or easily modeled, such as intuition. This is, in fact, what was done in designing the chess-playing program Deep Blue, which beat the reigning world champion, Garry Kasparov, in 1997. Deep Blue does not attempt to mimic the thought of a human chess player. Instead, it capitalizes on the strengths of the computer by examining an extremely large number of moves, more than any human could possibly examine.

There are two problems with functional AI. The first is the difficulty of determining what falls into the category of AI and what is simply a normal computer application. A definition of AI that includes any program that accomplishes some function normally done by a human being would encompass virtually all computer programs. Even among computer scientists there is little agreement as to what sorts of programs fall under the rubric of AI. Once an application is mastered, there is a tendency to no longer define that application as AI. For example, while game playing is one of the classical fields of AI, Deep Blue's design team emphatically stated that Deep Blue was not artificial intelligence, since it used standard programming and parallel processing techniques that were in no way designed to mimic human thought. The implication here is that merely programming a computer to complete a human task is not AI if the computer does not complete the task in the same way a human would.

For a functional approach to result in a full humanlike intelligence it would be necessary not only to specify which functions make up intelligence, but also to make sure those functions are suitably congruent with one another. Functional AI programs are rarely designed to be compatible with other programs—each uses different techniques and methods, the sum of which is unlikely to capture the whole of human intelligence. Many in the AI community are also dissatisfied with a collection of task-oriented programs. The building of a general, humanlike intelligence, as difficult a goal as it may seem, remains the vision.

A Relational Approach. A third approach to AI builds on the assumption that intelligence is acquired, held, and demonstrated only through relationships with other intelligent agents. In "Computing Machinery and Intelligence," Turing addresses the question of which functions are essential for intelligence with a proposal for what has come to be the generally accepted test for machine intelligence. A human interrogator is connected by terminal to two subjects, one a human and the other a machine. If the interrogator fails as often as he or she succeeds in determining which is the human and which the machine, the machine could be considered intelligent. The Turing Test is based, not on the completion of any particular task or the solution of any particular problems by the machine, but on the machine's ability to relate to a human being in conversation. Discourse is unique among human activities in that it subsumes all other activities within itself. Turing predicted that by the year 2000 there would be computers that could fool an interrogator at least 30 percent of the time. This, like most predictions in AI, was overly optimistic. No computer has yet come close to passing the Turing Test.

The Turing Test uses relational discourse to demonstrate intelligence. However, Turing also notes the importance of being in relationship for the acquisition of knowledge or intelligence. He estimates that the programming of background knowledge needed for a restricted form of the game would take, at a minimum, three hundred person-years to complete. This is assuming that one could identify the appropriate knowledge set at the outset. Turing suggests, rather than trying to imitate an adult mind, that one construct a mind that simulates that of a child. Such a mind, when given an appropriate education, would learn and develop into an adult mind. One AI researcher taking this approach is Rodney Brooks of the Massachusetts Institute of Technology (MIT), whose robotics lab has constructed several machines, the most famous of which are named Cog and Kismet, that represent a new direction in AI in that embodiedness is crucial to their design. Their programming is distributed among the various physical parts; each joint has a small processor that controls movement of that joint. These processors are linked with faster processors that allow for interaction between joints and for movement of the robot as a whole. Cog and Kismet are no longer minds in a box, but embodied systems that depend on interaction within a complex environment. They are designed to learn those tasks associated with newborns, such as eye-hand coordination, object grasping, face recognition, and basic emotional responses, through social interaction with a team of researchers. Although they have developed such abilities as tracking moving objects with the eyes or withdrawing an arm when touched, Brooks's project has so far been no more successful than Lenat's Cyc in producing a machine that could interact with humans on the level of the Turing Test. However Brooks's work represents a movement toward Turing's opinion that intelligence is socially acquired and demonstrated.

The Turing Test makes no assumptions as to how the computer would arrive at its answers; there need be no similarity in internal functioning between the computer and the human brain. However, an area of AI that shows some promise is that of neural networks, systems of circuitry that reproduce the patterns of neurons found in the brain. Current neural nets are limited, however. The human brain has billions of neurons and researchers have yet to understand both how these neurons are connected and how the various neurotransmitting chemicals in the brain function. Despite these limitations, neural nets have reproduced interesting behaviors in areas such as speech or image recognition, natural-language processing, and learning. Some researchers (e.g., Hans Moravec, Raymond Kurzweil) look to neural net research as a way to reverse engineer the brain. They hope that once scientists have the capability of designing nets with a complexity equal to that of the brain, they will find that the nets have the same power as the brain and will develop consciousness as an emergent property. Kurzweil posits that such mechanical brains, when programmed with a given person's memories and talents, could form a new path to immortality, while Moravec holds out hopes that such machines might some day become our evolutionary children, capable of greater abilities than humans currently demonstrate.

AI in Science Fiction. While some advances have been made, a truly intelligent computer currently remains in the realm of speculation. Though researchers have continually projected that intelligent computers are imminent, progress in AI has been limited. Computers with intentionality and self-consciousness, with fully human reasoning skills or the ability to be in relationship, exist only in the realm of dreams and desires, a realm explored in fiction and fantasy.

The artificially intelligent computer in science fiction story and film is not a prop, but a character, one that has become a staple since the mid-1950s. These characters are embodied in a variety of physical forms, ranging from the wholly mechanical (computers and robots), to the partially mechanical (cyborgs), to the completely biological (androids). A general trend from the 1950s to the 1990s has been to depict intelligent computers in an increasingly anthropomorphic way. The robots and computers of early films, such as Maria in *Metropolis* (1926), Robby in *Forbidden Planet* (1956), Hal in *2001: A Space Odyssey* (1968), or R2D2 and C3PO in *Star Wars* (1977), were clearly constructs of metal. On the other hand, early science fiction stories, such as Isaac Asimov's *I, Robot* (1950), explored the question of how one might distinguish between robots that looked human and actual human beings. Films and stories since the 1980s, such as *Blade Runner* (1982), *The Terminator* series (1984–2002), and *A.I.: Artificial Intelligence* (2001), depict machines with both mechanical and biological parts that are, at least superficially, practically indistinguishable from human beings.

Fiction that features AI can be classified in two general categories. The first comprises cautionary tales that explore the consequences of creating technology for the purposes of taking over human functions. In these stories the initial impulses for creating an artificial intelligence are noble: to preserve the wisdom of a race (*Forbidden Planet*), to avoid nuclear war (*Colossus: The Forbin Project,* 1970), or to advance human knowledge (*2001: A Space Odyssey*). The human characters suppose that they are completely in control, only to find that they have, in the end, abdicated too much responsibility to something that is ultimately "other" to the human species. The second category comprises tales of wish fulfillment (*Star Wars; I, Robot*) in which the robots are not noted for their superior intelligence or capabilities but for the cheerful assistance and companionship they give their human masters. The computers in these stories are rooted in a relational rather than a functional view of human intelligence.

Religious and Ethical Implications. Many researchers in AI are committed physicalists and believe that the design of a truly intelligent machine will vindicate their belief that human beings are nothing but biological machines. Few would consider religious questions to be of import to their work. (One exception to this stance has been the robotics laboratory at MIT, which included a religious adviser, Anne Foerst, as part of the research team developing the robot Cog.) However, the assumptions that human beings are merely information-processing machines and that artifacts that are nonbiological can be genuinely intelligent have both anthropological and eschatological implications.

The most important questions raised by AI research are anthropological ones. What does it mean to be human? At what point would replacing some or all of our biological parts with mechanical components violate our integrity as human beings? Is our relationship to God contingent on our biological nature? What is the relationship of the soul to consciousness or intelligence? These questions are raised by the search for an artificial intelligence, irrespective of whether or not that search is ever successful.

Should that search be successful, ethical problems arise. What rights would an intelligent robot have? Would these be the same rights as a human being? Should an artificial intelligence be held to the same standards of moral responsibility as human beings? Should a robot be baptized or take part in other sacramental or covenantal acts? How one answers such questions depends largely on what one sees as central to our nature as human beings—mind, body, function, or relationship. Once again, whether AI becomes a reality or not, the debate over questions such as these is helpful in clarifying the principles on which our view of humanity rests.

AI also raises a set of ethical issues relevant to the search itself. In a controversial article in *Wired* (2000) Bill Joy, chief scientist at Sun Microsystems, warns that self-replicating robots and advances in nanotechnology could result, as soon as 2030, in a computer technology that may replace our species. Moravec of the AI lab at Carnegie Mellon University pushes the time back to 2040 but agrees that robots will displace humans from essential roles and could threaten our existence as a species. Joy calls for research in the possibly convergent fields of artificial intelligence, nanotechnology, and biotechnology to be suspended until researchers have greater certainty that such research would in no way threaten future human lives. On a lesser scale, the amount of responsibility the human community wishes to invest in autonomous or semi-autonomous machines remains a question.

The view of human identity as the information in one's brain has led several researchers to posit a new cybernetic form for human immortality. In *The Age of Spiritual Machines* (1999), Kurzweil predicts that by the end of the twenty-first century artificial intelligence will have resulted in effective immortality for humans. He expects that the merger of human and machine-based intelligences will have progressed to the point where most conscious entities will no longer have a permanent physical presence, but will move between mechanically enhanced bodies and machines in such a way that one's life expectancy will be indefinitely extended. Kurzweil is not the sole holder of this expectation, though he may be among the more optimistic in his timeline. Physicists Dyson and Tipler suggest a future in which human identity is located in the information that makes up the thoughts, memories, and experiences of each person. In *The Physics of Immortality: Modern Cosmology, God, and the Resurrection of the Dead* (1994), Tipler conjectures that the universe will cease to expand and at some point end in a contraction that he calls the "omega point." Tipler sees the omega point as the coalescence of all information, including the information that has made up every person who ever lived. This point can thus be seen as corresponding to the omniscient and omnipotent God referred to in many different religious traditions. At such a point, the information making up any given individual could be reinstantiated, resulting in a form of resurrection for that person, a cybernetic immortality. Cybernetic immortality provides one avenue for belief in a manner of human continuance that does not violate the assumption of a material basis for all existence. It is thus compatible with the most rigorous scientific theories of the natural world. However, cybernetic immortality is based on the assumptions that thoughts and memories define the human person and that consciousness is an emergent property of the complexity of the human brain. In other words, human beings are basically biological machines whose unique identity is found in the patterns that arise and are stored in the neuronal structures of the brain. If these patterns could be replicated, as in sophisticated computer technology, the defining characteristics of the person would be preserved. Such a view is not necessarily compatible with the anthropologies of most religions.

SEE ALSO Cybernetics.

BIBLIOGRAPHY

Daniel Crevier's *AI: The Tumultuous History of the Search for Artificial Intelligence* (New York, 1993) provides a clear history of the first forty years of AI research. A more critical view of the field can be found in Hubert Dreyfus's *Mind over Machine: The Power of Human Intuition and Expertise in the Era of the Computer* (New York, 1986). Another classic critique of AI is Terry Winograd and Fernando Flores, *Understanding Computers and Cognition: A New Foundation for Design* (Reading, Mass., 1986). *Mind Design II: Philosophy, Psychology, Artificial Intelligence*, edited by John Haugeland, 2d ed. (Cambridge, Mass., 1997) is a compilation of a variety of seminal papers on AI, including Turing's 1950 paper and John Searle's famous "Chinese Room" paper. *HAL's Legacy: 2001's Computer as Dream and Reality*, edited by David Stork (Cambridge, Mass., 1997), includes a good variety of papers examining the state of the various subfields that made up AI at the end of the twentieth century.

Turning from the history of the field to prognostications of its future, *Mind Children: The Future of Robot and Human Intelligence* (Cambridge, Mass., 1988) by Hans Moravec suggests that computers will be the next stage in human evolution, while Raymond Kurzweil, in *The Age of Spiritual Machines* (New York, 1999), posits a future in which human beings and computers merge. A good overview of films dealing with AI can be found in J. P. Telotte's *Replications: A Robotic History of the Science Fiction Film* (Urbana, Ill., 1995); fictional portrayals of AI are discussed in Patricia Warrick's *The Cybernetic Imagination in Science Fiction* (Cambridge, Mass., 1980). For theological implications, see Noreen L. Herzfeld, *In Our Image: Artificial Intelligence and the Human Spirit* (Minneapolis, 2002).

NOREEN L. HERZFELD (2005)

ARVAL BROTHERS.

The college of Arval Brothers (Collegium Fratrum Arvalium), a Roman religious fraternity of great antiquity, was restored in about 28 BCE by the future emperor Augustus. It is known from a few references in literary works and, chiefly, from a famous collection of about 240 fragments of official records on marble that represent fifty-five different years and cover the period from 21 BCE to 241 or even 304 CE.

Usually numbering twelve and presided over by an annually elected leader (*magister*) with a *flamen* (priest, i. e., one of the brothers) to assist him, the Arval Brothers met in Rome or in the sacred grove of the goddess Dia. In Rome, depending more or less on the sovereign, the college took part in regular public worship (*vota*, votive sacrifices on the occasion of political or dynastic events). The brothers also celebrated rites connected with their own liturgy, a liturgy that culminated in the festival of the goddess Dia. This festival was a movable one, and during the first part of January the brotherhood determined the days of the festival for that year. It was usually celebrated on May 17, 19, and 20 if the year was an odd-numbered one and on May 27, 29, and 30 if the year was even-numbered.

The festival of the goddess Dia lasted three days. The first day was celebrated in Rome, in the house of the president of the brotherhood, and consisted of a banquet eaten in the presence of the goddess during which the priests passed from hand to hand dried and green ears of grain as well as loaves of bread crowned with laurel.

On the second day the brotherhood went to the sacred grove of the goddess Dia at the fifth milestone on the Via

Campana, on the boundary of the *ager Romanus antiquus* ("ancient Roman soil"), where her shrine stood next to a temple to Fors Fortuna. Here, in the morning, the president offered Dia two sacrifices: young sows in expiation of possible faults and a cow to do her honor. The brothers then ate a sacrificial meal. Afterward they donned the wreaths made from ears of grain that were their mark and at midday entered the shrine of Dia. In front of and inside the shrine they performed a second, complex series of rites that is still obscure to us in many respects. First they sacrificed a ewe lamb to Dia; then they once again passed the dried and green ears of grain from hand to hand and offered a meal to the "mother of the *lares*" by throwing down in front of the temple *ollae* (vessels of sundried clay) that contained a grain porridge. Then, behind closed doors, the priests performed a solemn dance (*tripudium*) and sang the famous *Carmen Arvale,* a hymn of great antiquity that is known to us from an inscription of 218 CE. A sacrificial banquet, chariot races, and another banquet in Rome concluded the second day. On the third day the Arval Brothers held a further banquet in the home of their president and handed around the ears of grain one last time.

The rites of the festival were addressed to Dia, goddess of "the sunlit sky"; she was asked to favor the proper ripening of the grain, symbolized in the rite by the continuity between green grain and grain that had become fully ripe. The *Carmen Arvale,* on the other hand, was addressed to Mars as defender of landed property and of the *ager Romanus.* A possibly late interpretation connects the Arval Brothers with Acca Larentia, the supposed nurse of Romulus and Remus, and thus associates them with the story of Romulus; this is consistent with the hypothesis that the Arval rites go back to the end of the period of the kings (sixth century BCE).

SEE ALSO Dea Dia; Flamen.

BIBLIOGRAPHY

Henzen, Wilhelm, ed. *Acta fratrum Arvalium quae supersunt.* Berlin, 1874.

Olshausen, Eckart. "'Über die römischen Ackerbrüder': Geschichte eines Kultes." In *Aufstieg und Niedergang der römischen Welt,* vol. 2.16.7, pp. 820–832. Berlin and New York, 1978. Includes a bibliography.

Scheid, John, *Romulus et ses frères. Le collège des frères arvales, modèle du culte public dans la Rome des empereurs.* Bibliothèque des Écoles Françaises d'Athènes et de Rome, vol. 275. Rome, 1990.

Scheid, John, *Commentarii fratrum arvalium qui supersunt. Les copies épigraphiques des protocoles annuels de la confrérie arvale (21 av.–304 ap. J.-C.).* Collection Roma antica, vol. 4. Rome, 1998.

Syme, Ronald. *Some Arval Brethren.* New York, 1980.

JOHN SCHEID (1987 AND 2005)
Translated from French by Matthew J. O'Connell

ĀRYADEVA, often called simply Deva (Tib., 'Phagspa-lha); an important Buddhist dialectician, linked with several other names such as Kāṇadeva, Nīlanetra, Piṅgalanetra, Piṅgalacakṣuḥ, and Karṇaripa, although the identification with some of these is doubtful. In China, he is known both by the transcription of his name, Tibo or Tiboluo (Jpn., Daiba or Daibara), and by the translation of his name, Cheng-t'ien, (Jpn., Shōten).

Scholars have identified at least two Āryadevas. The first, who will be referred to as "Āryadeva I," was a Madhyamaka (Mādhyamika) dialectician, the most eminent disciple of Nāgārjuna, who lived between the third and fourth centuries CE. The second, "Āryadeva II," was a Tantric master whose date has been variously proposed as in the seventh to tenth centuries (most probably at the beginning of the eighth century), because he cites the *Madhyamakahṛdayakārikā* of Bhāvaviveka (500–570) and the *Tarkajvālā,* its autocommentary, in his *Madhyamakabhṛamaghāta,* and because verse 31 of his *Jñānasārasamuccaya* is cited in the *Tattvasaṃgrahapañjikā* of Kamalaśīla (740–795).

Biographies are available in Chinese sources (T.D. no. 2048; see also T.D. no. 2058, chap. 6), in Tibetan materials (Bu ston, Tāranātha, etc.), and partially but most genuinely in Sanskrit documents (Candrakīrti's *Catuḥśatakaṭīkā,* the *Mañjuśrīmūlakalpa,* etc.). If the Chinese sources are concerned solely with Āryadeva I, the Tibetan ones in general combine and do not adequately distinguish between the two Āryadevas. Both traditions confuse history and legend, and now it is almost impossible to separate them. However, if one singles out only the most plausible elements, the two individuals can be described as follows. Āryadeva I was born in Sri Lanka (Sinhaladvīpa) as the son of a king but abandoned his glorious career and went to South India. After traveling throughout India, he met Nāgārjuna at Pāṭaliputra and became his disciple. He showed his talent in debate and converted many Brahmanic adherents to Buddhism. He is called Kāṇadeva ("One-eyed Deva") because he offered his eye to a non-Buddhist woman (according to Tāranātha), to a tree goddess (according to Bu ston), to a woman (according to the *Caturaśīti-siddha-pavṛtti,* or *Biography of the Eighty-four Siddhas*), or to a golden statue of Maheśvara (according to the Chinese sources).

Āryadeva II studied alchemy at Nālandā under the Tantric Nāgārjuna, who was a disciple of Saraha and founder of the 'Phags-lugs lineage of the *Guhyasamāja Tantra.* The story of offering one eye is related about him also, but this might be an interpolation from the biography of Āryadeva I.

All of the texts ascribed to Āryadeva in the Chinese canon and most of the texts so ascribed in the Madhyamaka section of the Tibetan canon can be considered as the works of Āryadeva I. The most famous is his *Catuḥśataka* (Derge edition of the Tibetan Tripiṭaka 3846, hereafter cited as D.; Bejing edition of the Tripiṭaka 5246, hereafter cited as B.; T. D. no. 1570 [the second half only], see also T.D. no. 1517), which consists of sixteen chapters, the first eight being concerned with the preparation of those who practice the path and the last eight explaining the insubstantiality of all *dharmas*. The *Śatakaśāstra,* a so-called abridged version of the *Catuḥśataka* available only in Kumārajīva's translation (T. D. no. 1569), and the *Akṣaraśataka* (T.D. no. 1572), said to be composed by Nāgārjuna in Tibetan versions (D. 3834, B. 5234), are especially noteworthy as the works of Āryadeva I.

On the other hand, all the works ascribed to Āryadeva in the Tantric section of the Tibetan canon are unquestionably attributed to Āryadeva II. The most important and well-known texts among them are the *Cittaviśuddhiprakaraṇa* (D. 1804, B. 2669), a Sanskrit version of which was edited by P. B. Patel (Calcutta, 1949); the *Caryāmelāpakapradīpa* (D. 1803, B. 2668); and the *Pradīpoddyotana-nāma-ṭīkā* (D. 1794, B. 2659). There are also some texts in the Madhyamaka section of the Tibetan canon that can, on the basis of their contents, be attributed to Āryadeva II: the *Madhyamakabhṛamaghāta* (D. 3850, B. 5250), most of which simply consists of extracts from the *Madhyamakahṛdaya* and the *Tarkajvālā* of Bhāvaviveka; the *Jñānasārasamuccaya* (D. 385l, B. 5251), a *siddhānta* text exposing the philosophical tenets of non-Buddhist and Buddhist schools; and the *Skhalitapramathanayuktihetusiddhi* (D. 3847, B. 5247), consisting of non-Buddhist objections and Buddhist answers.

The *Hastavālaprakarana* (D. 3844, B. 5244 and 5248; see also autocommentary, D. 3845, B. 5245 and 5249), attributed to Āryadeva in its Tibetan versions, is now considered to be a work of Dignāga, as indicated in the Chinese version (T.D. nos. 1620, 1621). If the identification of Piṅgalanetra (Chin., Qingmu) with Āryadeva is correct, Āryadeva I also composed a commentary on the *Mūlamadhyamakakārikā* (T.D. no. 1564).

SEE ALSO Mādhyamika.

BIBLIOGRAPHY

Lamotte, Étienne. *Le traité de la grande vertu de sagesse,* vol. 3. Louvain, 1970. See especially pages 1370–1375.

Lindtner, Christian. "Adversaria Buddhica." *Wiener Zeitschrift für die Kunde Südasiens* 26 (1982): 167–194. See page 173, note 21.

Robinson, James B. *Buddha's Lions: The Lives of the Eighty-four Siddhas.* Berkeley, Calif., 1979.

Ruegg, David S. *The Literature of the Madhyamaka School of Philosophy in India.* Wiesbaden, 1981.

New Sources

Aryadeva, Candrakirti, and Karen Lang. "Aryadeva and Candrakirti on Self and Selfishness." In *Buddhism in Practice,* edited by Donald S. Lopez, Jr., pp. 380–398. Princeton, 1995.

Jong, J. W. de. "Materials for the Study of Aryadeva, Dharmapala and Candrakirti: The Catuhsataka of Aryadeva." *Indo Iranian Journal* 36 (1993): 150–153.

McClintock, Sara. "Knowing All through Knowing One: Mystical Communion or Logical Trick in the Tattvasamgraha and Tattvasamgrahapanjika." *Journal of the International Association of Buddhist Studies* 23, no. 2 (2000): 225–244.

MIMAKI KATSUMI (1987)
Revised Bibliography

ĀRYA SAMĀJ. The Ārya Samāj ("society of honorable ones") is a modern Hindu reform movement founded in Bombay, India, in 1875 by Dayananda Sarasvati (1824–1883), advocating Hindu renewal by a return to Vedic religion. The basic principles of the Ārya Samāj were developed by its founder, Dayananda, a Gujarati brahman who became a *saṃnyāsin* ("renunciant") in 1847 and spent the rest of his life in religious quest. From 1847 to 1860 Dayananda lived as a wandering yogin searching for personal salvation, and later, after three years of Sanskrit study in Mathura with his guru, he worked as a reformer seeking to revive Hinduism.

Dayananda's sense of what Hinduism needed was gradually shaped by his guru, by debates with sectarian pandits in the western areas of Uttar Pradesh, and by discussions of religious issues with members of the Brāhmo Samāj and a variety of Hindu scholars and intellectuals in Calcutta. By the time he founded the Ārya Samāj on April 10, 1875, he had written a statement of doctrinal principles that was published two months later as *Satyārth prakāś.* A handbook on the daily Five Great Sacrifices, the *Pañcamahāyajñavidhi,* was published later in 1875, and a manual on the family life cycle rituals, *Saṃskārvidhi,* was published in 1877. Although these publications contained Vedic quotations in Sanskrit, the works themselves were composed in Hindi to make them accessible to the widest possible audience. Dayananda revised each of these basic guides over the next few years; as the mature product of his thinking, the revised editions were Dayananda's lasting legacy to the Ārya Samāj.

The central element in Dayananda's position was his belief in the truth of the Vedas. His guru had convinced him that the only true writings were those of the *ṛṣis* ("seers") who flourished before the composition of the *Mahābhārata* and that all subsequent scriptures contained false sectarian views, but Dayananda had to arrive at his own understanding of the line between truth and falsehood. He had lost his faith in image worship as a youth and was an active opponent of Vaiṣṇava sectarianism after 1863, but it took longer to reject the worship of Śiva and even longer to abandon the *advaita* ("nondualistic") philosophy of the Upaniṣads. By the second edition of *Satyārth prakāś,* however, he had decided that neither the Upaniṣads nor the Vedic ritual texts, the Brāhmaṇas, had the authority of revelation; this was an honor due only to the collections of Vedic hymns, (i.e., the four *mantra saṃhitās* of the *Ṛgveda, Sāmaveda, Yajurveda,* and *Atharvaveda*), because they alone were directly revealed by God to the *ṛṣis*. True religion, that is Aryan religion, must thus be based only on the hymns, which convey eternal knowledge of the one true God.

The religion that Dayananda established on this base was derived from Vedic sources, but its particular features were his own creation. Although a brahman by birth, Dayananda, rejected Brahmanic control of Vedic religion. He insisted that Vedic knowledge should be available to everyone, including women and members of the traditionally impure *śūdra* castes. Membership in the Ārya Samāj was open to any person of good character who accepted its beliefs, and the Vedic rituals Dayananda prescribed could be performed by any Ārya, or member of the movement. Caste was irrelevant, since the same *dharma* (duties) applied to all: to perform Vedic rituals, to study and propagate Vedic knowledge, and to promote social well-being.

The theology that Dayananda bequeathed to the Ārya Samāj was as innovative as his social reform program and his attitude toward Vedic knowledge. He was convinced that the Vedic hymns proved the existence of a single supreme God. God is not, however, the only reality; rather, God is eternally coexistent with the *jīvas* (conscious and responsible human selves) and with *prakṛti* (the unconscious material world). In their ignorance, the *jīvas* bind themselves to rebirth in the world by their *karman* (actions). God cannot release the *jīvas* from responsiblity for their deeds, but in his mercy he has revealed the Vedas to guide the *jīvas* to *mokṣa* (freedom from rebirth and union with God). However, since the cause of *mokṣa* is finite human action, *mokṣa* itself must be finite, and the *jīvas* must eventually be reborn into the world. Each *jīva*, according to Dayananda, is thus eternally active, moving from worldly involvement to freedom in God's bliss and then back again into the world.

Dayananda's views were rejected by every branch of Hindu orthodoxy, most vehemently by orthodox brahmans. In Bombay, though, Dayananda found a group of progressive Hindus led by members of several merchant castes who were eager to adopt his teachings and to organize, in 1875, the first chapter of the Ārya Samāj. The second important chapter, and the leading chapter from that point on, was founded in Lahore in 1877, led by a rising elite also predominantly from the merchant castes. The simple set of membership rules developed by the Lahore chapter was adopted by new chapters that sprang up rapidly elsewhere in the Punjab and in western Uttar Pradesh. Dayananda's emphasis on individual responsiblity and full religious participation appealed to the merchants and professionals who joined, and they in turn proved to be excellent organizers. Dayananda gave each chapter full responsibility for its affairs within the general rules, so that when he died in 1883 the Ārya Samāj was not only a self-sustaining movement, but it was able to begin active expansion in new directions.

The Dayanand Anglo-Vedic school was established in Lahore in 1886 and became a college in 1889, providing a model for an extensive system of schools and colleges. The practice of *śuddhi*, or reconversion by purification initiated by Dayananda on an individual basis, was expanded into a movement to reconvert Hindus who had become Christians or Muslims. Āryas were active in social reform programs and in the Indian nationalist movement, the more militant helping to form the Hindu Mahāsabhā party. The partition of India in 1947 placed Lahore and other centers in the Punjab within Pakistan, but the organization recovered from the loss to remain a significant force for Hindu education and social causes. With chapters in almost every city and town in northern India and with an estimated membership of over one million, it has proved to be the most successful of the nineteenth-century reform movements.

SEE ALSO Brāhmo Samāj; Dayananda Sarasvati.

BIBLIOGRAPHY

There is much less literature in English on the Ārya Samāj than on other nineteenth-century movements such as the Brāhmo Samāj and Ramakrishna Mission, partly because most of the movement's own publications are in Hindi and partly because Westerners (and westernized Indians) have been less attracted by it. The best general treatment of the movement by a member, though now dated, is the nationalist leader Lala Lajpat Rai's *The Ārya Samāj* (London, 1915). An early Western critique that reflects Christian resentment of the movement's militant Hinduism is found in J. N. Farquhar's *Modern Religious Movements in India* (New York, 1915), pp. 101–129. For the founder's autobiography up to 1875, supplemented by a statement of his basic doctrines, a chronology of his life, and an annotated list of his publications, see *Autobiography of Swami Dayanand Saraswati*, edited by K. C. Yadav (New Delhi, 1976). The most scholarly and authoritative study of the founder and the early movement is J. T. F. Jordens' *Dayānanda Sa-rasvatī, His Life and Ideas* (Delhi, 1978). A more detailed study of the Ārya Samāj's development in the region of its greatest early strength is Kenneth W. Jones's *Ārya Dharm: Hindu Consciousness in Nineteenth-Century Punjab* (Berkeley, 1976). A survey of the movement's main developments up to 1947 is provided by Kenneth W. Jones's's, "The Ārya Samāj in British India," in *Religion in Modern India*, edited by Robert D. Baird, (New Delhi, 1981), pp. 27–54.

New Sources

Llewellyn, J. S. *The Ārya Samāj as a Fundamentalist Movement: A Study in Comparative Fundamentalism.* New Delhi, 1993.

Prakash, Satya. *Speeches, Writings, and Addresses by Svami Satya Prakash Sarasvati.* Delhi, 1987.

THOMAS J. HOPKINS (1987)
Revised Bibliography

ASAHNTI RELIGION SEE AKAN RELIGION

ASAṄGA (c. 315–390 CE) was the founder of the Yogācāra school of Mahāyāna Buddhism in India. Asaṅga was born as a son of a *brahman* in Puruṣapura (Peshawar in Pakistan). His younger brother was the famous Yogācāra thinker Vasubandhu. Originally Asaṅga belonged to the Mahīśāsaka school of Hīnayāna Buddhism, but later converted to the Mahāyāna. According to Paramārtha's biography of Vasubandhu, Asaṅga's conversion took place after an ascent to Tuṣita Heaven, where he received religious instruction from Maitreya, a *bodhisattva* who is worshiped as the future Buddha. Later, Asaṅga composed a treatise dealing with the seventeen stages (*bhūmi*) of *yoga* practice based on the teachings he had received from Maitreya. The same account is recorded by Xuanzang in his *Da Tang xiyu ji.* As there exist some Yogācāra treatises that are traditionally ascribed to Maitreya(nātha), some scholars have assumed that the *bodhisattva* Maitreya, to whom Asaṅga is said to have owed his knowledge of the Yogācāra system, was really a historical person. The opinion of modern scholarship remains divided on this issue. In his old age, Asaṅga is reported to have converted his brother Vasubandhu, previously an exponent of the Hīnayāna teachings, to Mahāyāna. Asaṅga continued a life of religious scholarship in the vicinity of Ayodhya until his death at the age of seventy-five.

The most important of Asaṅga's many treatises are (1) *Abhidharmasamuccaya,* a brief explanation from the Yogācāra viewpoint of the elements constituting phenomenal existence; (2) *Xianyang shengjiao lun* (**Āryadeśanāvikhyāpana*), an abridgment of the *Yogācārabhūmi;* and (3) *Mahāyānasaṃgraha,* a comprehensive work on the Yogācāra doctrines and practices. Asaṅga's works are characterized by a detailed analysis of psychological phenomena inherited from the Abhidharma literature of the Hīnayāna schools. The *Mahāyānasaṃgraha,* in which Asaṅga gives a systematic exposition of the fundamental tenets of the Yogācāra school, comprises ten chapters dealing respectively with the following subjects: (1) *ālaya-vijñāna,* (2) three natures of beings (*trisvabhāva*), (3) the realization of the truth of representation-only (*vijñaptimātra*), (4) six kinds of perfection (*pāramitā*), (5) ten *bodhisattva* stages (*bhūmi*), (6) moral conducts (*śīla*), (7) meditative concentration (*samādhi*), (8) non-discriminative knowledge (*nirvikalpa-jñāna*), (9) the transformation of the base of existence (*āśraya-parāvṛtti*) and the state of "*nirvāṇa* without abode" (*apratiṣṭhita-nirvāṇa*), and (10) the three bodies of the Buddha. The first two chapters are concerned with the object to be learned (*jñeya*), chapters 3 to 8, the learning and the practice leading to the attainment of Buddhahood, and chapters 9 to 10, the result of learning and practice. Asaṅga's basic thoughts are presented in the first two chapters.

The first chapter treats the doctrine of *ālaya-vijñāna* in full detail. The term *ālaya-vijñāna* occurs in earlier works such as the *Saṃdhinirmocana Sūtra* and the *Yogācārabhūmi,* but there is no mention of it in the treatises attributed to Maitreya. The *ālaya-vijñāna* is a subliminal consciousness in which the impressions (*vāsanās*) of past experiences are preserved as the seeds (*bījas*) of future experiences. The "consciousness-in-activity" (*pravṛtti-vijñāna*), that is, the six kinds of sensory and mental consciousness, is produced from the seeds preserved in the *ālaya-vijñāna.* When the *pravṛtti-vijñāna* functions, it leaves its impression in the *ālaya-vijñāna.* This impression becomes the seed of a future consciousness-in-activity. According to the Yogācāras, a human being is nothing other than the stream of consciousness thus formed by the mutual dependence of the *ālaya-vijñāna* and the consciousness-in-activity. Asaṅga admits that besides the six kinds of consciousness there is the "I-consciousness" called *manas* (or *kliṣṭa-manas*), whereby the *ālaya-vijñāna* is wrongly conceived of as a real self (*ātman*). However, the classical theory of eightfold consciousness is not explicitly advocated by him.

The second chapter of the *Mahāyānasaṃgraha* is devoted to the elucidation of the so-called three-nature doctrine, which maintains that all beings possess an "imagined nature" (*parikalpita-svabhāva*), a "dependent nature" (*paratantra-svabhāva*) and a "consummated nature" (*pariniṣpanna-svabhāva).* The image of an object that appears in a stream of consciousness is of dependent nature precisely because the image is dependent for its origination upon the impressions of past experiences preserved in the *ālaya-vijñāna.* The object fictively superimposed upon it is of imagined nature, while the *absence* of the superimposed object, that is, the object as devoid (*śūnya*) of reality, is of consummated nature. This doctrine is also found expounded in earlier Yogācāra works, but Asaṅga sets forth an original view that the imagined and the consummated natures are two divisions or two aspects of the dependent nature.

The *Mahāyānasaṃgraha* was translated into Chinese by Paramārtha (499–567), and became the basic text of the newly formed Shelun sect (abbreviated from the Chinese name for the *Mahāyānasaṃgraha*, the *She dasheng lun*). This sect suffered a decline following the establishment of the Faxiang sect by Kuiji, a disciple of Xuanzang (596–664), who recognized the transmission of the Yogācāra teachings of Dharmapāla (530–561) as authoritative.

SEE ALSO Ālaya-vijñāna; Maitreya; Vasubandhu; Vijñānabhikṣu; Yogācāra.

BIBLIOGRAPHY

Frauwallner, Erich. *Die Philosophie des Buddhismus.* 3d rev. ed. Berlin, 1969. A brief explanation of Asaṅga's philosophical ideas and a German translation of some important portions of the *Mahāyānasaṃgraha* are given on pages 326–350.

Lamotte, Étienne. *La somme du Grand Véhicule d'Asaṅga* (*Mahāyānasaṃgraha*); vol. 1, *Version tibétaine et chinoise* (*Hsüan-tsang*); vol. 2, *Traduction et commentaire.* Louvain, 1938–1939. In the footnotes of the translation many passages of the commentaries by Vasubandhu and Asvabhāva are translated from Chinese.

Nagao Gadjin. *Shōdaijōron: Wayaku to chūkai,* vol. 1. Tokyo, 1982. The translation is based on the Tibetan version. A Chinese translation by Xuanzang is printed above the Japanese translation. The Tibetan text with a reconstituted Sanskrit text is also appended. Volume 1 covers up to the end of Chapter 2.

New Sources

Hopkins, Jeffrey. "A Tibetan Contribution on the Question of Mind-Only in the Early Yogic Practice School." *Journal of Indian Philosophy* 20 (1992): 275–343.

Keenan, John P. "Asanga's Understanding of Madhyamika: Notes on the Shung-chung-lun." *Journal of the International Association of Buddhist Studies* 12, no. 1 (1989): 93–107.

Prets, Ernst. "The Structure of Sadhana in the Abhidharmasamuccaya." *Wiener Zeitschrift fur die Kunde Sudasiens und Archiv fur indische Philosophie* 38 (1994): 337–350.

HATTORI MASAAKI (1987)
Revised Bibliography

ASBURY, FRANCIS (1745–1816), chief architect of American Methodism. Raised on the fringes of Birmingham in England's "Black Country," where the industrial revolution was beginning, Asbury became a lay preacher at eighteen, eager "to live to God, and to bring others to do so." In 1766 he was admitted as one of John Wesley's itinerant preachers, and in 1771 he was chosen as one of the second pair of volunteers to serve in America. Asbury proved a tough and dedicated pioneer, a stable and influential leader in the manner of Wesley, whose writings saturated his mind. During the Revolutionary War he endeared himself to native-born Methodists by his refusal to return to England, and he restrained those who wanted to break away from Wesley. In 1784 Wesley named the absent Asbury a member of the "legal hundred" to administer British Methodism after Wesley's death, and he also appointed him to receive ordination as "superintendent," or bishop without pomp, at the hands of Thomas Coke. Asbury refused such ordination without the summoning of a conference of his colleagues, who thereupon elected him to that office.

At first Asbury and Coke jointly administered the new Methodist Episcopal Church, but Coke's frequent absences from America increasingly left authority in the hands of Asbury, who was in any case much more fully identified with the American preachers and laity. Asbury was noteworthy for his own tireless travels, both in settled areas and along the expanding frontiers, and his constant recruiting and nurturing of native preachers. He maintained that Methodism would succeed in its mission only through the retention of a disciplined itinerant system and an authoritative but sacrificial episcopacy such as his own. His preachers accepted his discipline because they recognized in him the true marks of the apostle of American Methodism.

SEE ALSO Methodist Churches.

BIBLIOGRAPHY

The Journal and Letters of Francis Asbury, 3 vols., edited by Elmer T. Clark and Jacob S. Payton (London and Nashville, 1958), is an authoritative collection of annotated autobiographical materials. No first-rate biography exists, although L. C. Rudolph's *Francis Asbury* (Nashville, 1966) is useful. Additional insights can be gained from chapters 7 and 8 of my book *From Wesley to Asbury: Studies in Early American Methodism* (Durham, 1976).

FRANK BAKER (1987)

ASCENSION. In many purely literary works the theme of a heavenly journey is employed only for adventure's sake, but according to the majority of religious traditions, an ascent to heaven represents a journey into divine realms where the soul, living or dead, reaps many rewards. The result of such a journey is not only a transcendent vision or spiritual knowledge, but the possibility of divinization or assimilation with the gods. Rituals of ascent involve the living person becoming initiated into a new, sacred status.

Many cultures record ways that such a journey can be made (via, for example, a mountain path, a ladder, a tree, a rope, or even a cobweb). Some cultures also offer the further possibility of magical flight. The theme of the celestial ladder has been developed in monotheistic religions from *Genesis* 28:12, which describes Jacob's dream of a ladder reaching up to heaven upon which angels ascend and descend. Similarly, Muḥammad saw a ladder with angels in the temple in Jerusalem, and some Christian mystics, in particular John Klimakos (seventh century), used the ladder as a symbol to represent the phases of spiritual ascent. Likewise, from East Asia to the Americas, from ancient Greece to Israel, the ascent of a mountain is considered a privileged means by which one can enter into the presence of God.

Because the theme of ascension has been variously developed in different cultures, it is difficult to ascertain the relationship among the religious ambits where ascension is attested and where it often involves the quest for origins and possible reciprocal influences. Scholars have tried to trace the ascension theme back to a precise milieu, be it Iranian, Greek, Jewish, or shamanistic; psychological approaches have also been attempted. However, rather than looking for origins, it is important to compare the different testimonies so as to establish interferences or cross-cultural contacts, as well as universal typologies.

APOCALYPSE AND ECSTASY. Some general patterns can be ascertained, comprehensive of different and more complex features, such as otherworldly journeys or the descent (followed by a glorious ascent) of a supermundane entity, with the subsequent redemption or *ascensus* of the soul of those who receive revelation. Accounts of heavenly journeys share many features with apocalyptic literature, whose definition owes much to J. J. Collins's research. Apocalypse is, in fact, considered a literary genre in which the narrative framework features a revelation mediated to a human recipient because of his or her merits toward the divine realms. A topical pattern in apocalyptic literature is thus the extramundane journey, performed—bodily or spiritually—with a celestial or angelic guide who discloses a transcendent reality involving both eschatological salvation and revelation of a supernatural world.

Ascension is often linked to ecstasy, or separation of the soul from the body. This is explained as a transcendent state of awareness (trance), or as a psychogenic reaction according to the dictates of the visionary's mind. Such a state is seen as an expression of the conscious and unconscious desires of the ecstatic person, or even as a condition of psychic dissociation. In fact, the literal Greek term *ekstasis* means to escape from one's own rational and definite position. In this sense, ecstasy has the same aims as mysticism: to transcend the assumed limits of personality. In yoga, ecstatic techniques are somewhat different; the cosmic layers are experienced as a number of internal "principles," and the journey to the other world is considered a journey within oneself *(enstasy)*. Analogous schemes of a passage from objectification to interiorization have also been applied to late antiquity, and particularly to inner experiences in Neoplatonic and Christian mysticism.

SHAMANISM. Rituals in shamanistic culture are universally considered examples of objective ecstatic performance, especially after Mircea Eliade's investigations. The recurrent and central idea of "flight" or "riding" in reference to shamans is simply the figurative expression for ecstasy, which is controlled throughout shamanistic rituals in conformity with traditional prescriptions. The shaman is, by means of ecstasy, allowed to experience primordial time and to reach planes accessible to ordinary people only through death. Although a competent shaman can control ecstasy voluntarily, others receive the god's commands in dreams or visions, or by the use of hallucinogenic mushrooms (such as the fly agaric) and narcotics. The mental states that result from sensory overload and emotional arousal require great physical and mental exertion, which is achieved through dancing, drumming, and singing. Furthermore, every aspect of the behavior and paraphernalia of the shaman is oriented toward one principal goal—the journey to heaven or the netherworld. This journey is performed before the eyes of those who engage the shaman for practical purposes, and it is accompanied by such purificatory acts as frenetic drumming or the frenzied imitation of a bird call.

The ecstatic experiences that determine the shaman's vocation involve the traditional scheme of an initiation ceremony: suffering, death, and resurrection. The direct link that the shaman has with the supernatural world is not forged without difficulty or pain; the initiation into the otherworld is experienced as an upheaval that involves the destruction of the whole person by spirits, followed by a kind of resurrection as a new being who exists in both the mundane and the spiritual world. Visions are tied to an internal transformation and a spiritual mission. Ascent to the sky and dialogue with the gods, as well as descent to the underworld and conversation with spirits and the souls of dead shamans, are fixed patterns of this ritual. For example, the birch tree (in central and northern Asian shamanism), or, in different traditions, other trees around which the ceremony often develops, symbolizes the "world tree," and the steps of the ritual represent the various heavens through which the shaman must pass on his or her ecstatic journey to the highest heaven. It is probable that the cosmological schema implied in this ritual has an oriental origin, since the religious ideas of the ancient Near East penetrated far into Central and North Asia and contributed considerably to the features of Central Asian and Siberian shamanism.

IRAN. When the theory of the so-called *Himmelsreise der Seele* (ascent of the soul to heaven) was developed at the beginning of the twentieth century by the representatives of the *Religionsgeschichtliche Schule* (by Wilhelm Bousset in particular, followed by other scholars, such as Richard Reitzenstein, Franz Cumont, Joseph Kroll, Rudolf Bultmann, and Geo Widengren), they sought the origins of this doctrine in Iranian religion. They inferred from eschatological Middle-Persian or Pahlavi texts that belief in the ascent of the soul, as well as Gnostic dualism, originated in ancient Iran and was propagated in late antiquity by means of the mysteries of Mithra.

Although some have questioned whether Zoroaster acted as a "shaman," arguing that his ecstatic journeys may not be the product of a merely artificial practice, ecstatic experiences induced by hallucinogens are attested in pre-Zoroastrian Iran. A narcotic drink called *haoma* (Sanskrit, *soma*) was used to obtain visionary experiences, along with a sort of release or separation of the soul, as well as physical sleep. Zoroastrian reform, which was directed against wild ecstasy, fits into a wider Indo-Iranian mysticism that insists on inner vision and the mind's light, and came to be a theological contemplation of the fire. The so called younger Avestan priests reintroduced the cultic veneration of *haoma* and the use of exhilarants. Two such exhilarants have been identified as extractions from henbane and hemp, both called *bang* in Middle Persian (Avestan, *bangha*; Sanskrit, *bhang*).

It seems likely that ancient ecstatic or initiatory experiences developed into ritualistic practices, so that a voyage in an extraordinary dimension or a vision of spiritual realms became a symbolic representation or a devotional liturgy. It is in the context of such a historical development, rather than in a supposed evolution of Gathic spirituality, that scholars can recognize the relative antiquity (at least in its tenets) of the *Ardā Wirāz Nāmag* (Book of the righteous Virāz), which cannot be simply regarded as a late product from post-Sasanian times.

The *Ardā Wirāz Nāmag,* a well-known Pahlavi text probably written in the ninth century, is one of the preeminent sources for knowledge about the eschatological doctrines of ancient Iranian religion. The text describes Virāz's journey to the otherworld, and aims at demonstrating the efficacy of Zoroastrianism through its emphasis on ethical and moral teachings and its vivid description of rewards and punishments. In this sense it may be considered a catechetical work, but far from being a literary device, it represents a religious propagandistic document in the post-Sasanian age, when Mazdaism was under attack. Scholars have demonstrated how the term *ardā* (Avestan, *ashavan*; Sanskrit, *rtvān*) is related to eschatology in signifying a spiritual knowledge reached by the initiated or a condition of beatitude postmortem. After an introductory section, the *Ardā Wirāz Nāmag* describes how the soul of the pious protagonist Virāz flows out of his body, reaches the Mount of the Law at the center of the earth, and then crosses the Chinvat bridge that leads to the otherworld. Here Virāz first sees the souls of righteous people performing good deeds and observing religious precepts; then hell is revealed, with its terrible chastisements that conformably correspond to the faults of the souls found there. The text ends with the glorious and radiant vision of Ohrmadz (chap. 101 ff.). A similar narrative of a vision followed by conversion is attributed to Vishtasp, the prince who protected Zarathushtra, and is contained in a late collection of texts (*Dēnkard* 7, 4, 85).

Many motifs in these accounts are already attested in Zoroastrian literature: for example, the bridge, which could be large or narrow depending on the protagonist's behavior during life; the encounter with the *daēna* (Pahlavi, *dēn*), a sort of "double" soul depicted as a wonderful girl; and the three heavens—consisting of *humata* ("fair thoughts," the stars), *hūkhta* ("fair words," the moon); and *hvarshta* ("fair deeds," the sun)—to which the *anagra raoca,* the layer of the "lights without beginning," must be adjoined. The three heavens reflect the old Avestan order, mythical rather than astronomical, linked to a sort of religious gradation of fiery purity and brightness as one ascends from earth to heaven. The origin of later schemes comprising six or seven spheres is connected with the six *Amesha Spentas,* or with the planetary order of Greek origin (the five known planets plus the sun and the moon). It is worth noting that in Greece the planetary order was liable to vary; therefore we speak of a Chaldaean or an Egyptian order.

More ancient (third century) and more conservative in their description are the four inscriptions drawn up by the famous fanatical high priest Kirdīr (or Kērdēr or Kartīr, according to different transliterations), the grey eminence of King Shāpūr and his successors. Although they are preserved in slightly different versions, they all refer to Kirdīr's experience and should be seen as more than a literary device or an "initiatory myth." Kirdīr's experience is deeply rooted in the culture of the Magi and in Mazdaism. Eschatological motifs also recur in these inscriptions: the *daēna,* the bridge, the balance where the soul is judged, the throne, and a probable vision of hell. Moreover, the complex anthropology described in these texts resembles shamanistic culture in its description of the state of apparent death, otherworldly journeys, such expressions as "bony body" and "bony soul," and such themes as the duplication of the soul or demons who are at the head of limbs. As a result, scholars have inferred that shamanistic practices existed in ancient Iran. It should be noted that Ossetic mythology shares similar patterns, which may be explained by cultural contacts with Persia.

Even though scholars possess only late documents concerning Iranian eschatology, and even though the resolute—and sometimes disputed—position held by the representatives of the *Religionsgeschichtliche Schule* must in some cases be qualified (e.g., in considering Mesopotamian borrowings), it is nevertheless true that in the second half of the first millennium BCE the Greeks were acquainted with the initiatory and mystical-ecstatic aspects of Iranian religious doctrines. Zoroaster's *katabasis* was so well known that Plato identified him with Er, son of Armenios, in the tenth book of his *Republic,* as well as with Aristeas. The ancient Greeks appear to have been interested in such themes as ecstasy or *enthousiasmos* (divine possession), and they were especially interested in the immortality of the soul and doctrines concerning its status after death, already professed by the Magi, as recorded by Eudemos of Rhodes (fourth century BCE), who also offers accounts on Zalmoxis or Abaris.

ANCIENT GREECE. In Greece, belief and practice concerning catalepsy and the flight of the soul were widespread, and existed apart from the belief in Dionysos, the ecstatic divinity par excellence. Karl Meuli, Eric R. Dodds, and others have argued that Mediterranean religions exhibit a pattern of prophecy and heavenly ascension that has much in common with shamanism. Such features are shared by the so-called *iatromanteis* (from *iatros* [healer], and *mantis* [seer]), Greek medicine men and oracles connected with a divinity (interpreted as Apollo) who dwelled in Hyperborea, the mysterious land of the north. To the category of *iatromanteis* belonged such notable personalities as Empedocles and Pythagoras and, perhaps less influential but no less typical for this religious complex, Abaris, Aristeas of Proconnesus, Bakis, Epimenides of Crete, and Hermotimos of Clazomenae. Some of these were reported either to fly or to free their souls and leave their bodies in a state of catalepsy. It would be brash to say that their catalepsy was induced by hallucinogenic substances, even if a plant called *alimos* (literally, "hungerless"), which probably contained an alkaloid, is mentioned in their biographies. The soul of Aristeas, taking the form of a raven, was said to travel as far as Hyperborea; the soul of Epimenides, to converse with the gods; and the soul of Hermotimos, to visit faraway places and record local events. A similar account reports the loss of Hermotimos's soul from the body after his death, which permitted him to condemn his wicked wife and his enemies.

Although the pre-Socratic philosophers and the poet Pindar were acquainted with beliefs concerning the immortality of the soul and its consequent elevation to heaven, the cataleptic separation between body and soul, during which the soul was supposed to have supernatural experiences, was resumed by Plato in the apocalypse of Er in the tenth book of *The Republic.* Er, son of Armenios of Pamphylia (Asia Minor), was wounded in a battle and appeared to be dead. His catalepsy lasted twelve days, until the very moment his body was going to be burned. Er then came back to life and reported all the secrets of the afterlife that had been revealed to his soul.

Plato's pupil Heracleides Ponticus (fourth century BCE) took direct inspiration from the *iatromanteis.* In his lost dialogues he was concerned with catalepsy and its treatment, and in one of these (*Abaris,* or "On things in hell"), Heracleides introduced a fictitious character, Empedotimos (derived from *Empedocles* and *Hermotimos*). Some scholars have attributed to Heracleides an important innovation in Greek eschatology, namely the complete suppression of any subterrestrial place for punishment of the dead. Other scholars have claimed that the spread of celestial eschatology was due to the influence of Pythagoreanism and Stoicism, and indeed, Stoicism might have played an important role in the transformation of Hellenistic eschatology. It is worth noting that the Latin writer Cicero (first century BCE) ends his Platonic work, titled *Republic,* with an account of Scipio's dream, wherein the hero was granted an ascent throughout the heavens and a vision of the Blesseds. This well-known account became the object of allegorical interpretation during late antiquity, and the Neoplatonist Macrobius wrote an extensive commentary on it at the end of the fourth century.

Hellenistic World. By the end of the first century CE, the idea of an underground Hades was no longer fashionable, so in rearranging the great eschatological Platonic myths, Plutarch's ambition was to give a "modern" version of them in order to meet the intellectual exigencies of the time. Plutarch offers interesting details about catalepsy and incubation in his dialogue *On Socrates' Daemon,* based on traditions concerning the famous oracular cave of Trophonius at Lebadea, near Chaeronea. If Lamprias, Plutarch's brother, was a priest of that sanctuary, Plutarch may have had access to the wooden tablets on which those consulting the oracle were supposed to write down their experiences. The hero of this apocalypse is Timarch, whose soul leaves his body and visits the heavenly Hades, remaining below the sphere of the moon, which is only the first among the seven planetary spheres. Here, as well as in the dialogue *On the Face in the Moon,* the moon is the receptacle of souls that are freed of their bodies, with the exception of those that fall again into the circle of transmigration *(metensōmatōsis).* The earth represents the lowest and meanest point of the universe. Another important myth is contained in the dialogue *On the Delayed Revenge of the God,* which resumes many elements of the apocalypse of Er. The dishonest Aridaeus of Soloi, after having experienced a cataleptic state and after his soul has watched the judgment of the dead and witnessed the painful lot of the sinners, changes his attitude, becomes a pious man, and begins calling himself Thespesius ("godly").

Late Hellenism was dominated by an obsession with human liberation from the world and out of the world, in, or beyond, the heavenly spheres. This is reflected, for example, in the Gnostic systems of the second and third centuries CE and in their polemic against astrology. The seven "planets" themselves, the signs, the decans, and the degrees of the zodiac are often represented as evil archons, or heavenly rulers. These are extremely important for the embodiment and disembodiment of the individual soul. The heavenly ascent of the soul through the spheres is therefore considered a central tenet of Gnosticism. The techniques that are intended to assure the Gnostic's soul a safe passage through the spheres of the hostile archons up to the *plērōma* (fullness) of the godhead actually form the most important part of *gnosis.*

One of the first testimonies for the Gnostic theory of the embodiment and disembodiment of the soul is the doctrine of Basilides, who was active in Alexandria around 120 CE, and of his son Isidorus, according to whom the transcendental spirit of human beings is temporarily attached to a soul. During its descent, the planetary vices attack the soul and stick to it in the form of concretions of "appendages" *(prosartēmata).*

The technical expression *antimimon pneuma,* or "counterfeit spirit" (sometimes *antikeimenon,* or "evil spirit"), occurs for the first time in the *Apocryphon of John,* one of the oldest surviving Gnostic treatises, extant in Coptic translations. Some scholars claim that the *Apocryphon of John* predates even Basilides, whose theory of the *prosartēmata* is based on the *antimimon pneuma* doctrine. In fact, the *antimimon pneuma* is an appended spirit, an intermediary between the soul and the material body. The soul itself is a creation of the evil heavenly archons (i.e., the seven "planets") or, to be more precise, of the seven attributes forming conjunctions (syzygies) together with the archons.

The formation of the *antimimon pneuma* is more explicitly stated in the *Pistis Sophia,* also preserved in Coptic. The "counterfeit spirit" derives directly from the archons of the *heimarmenē,* or astral destiny, which are the seven "planets." The *antimimon pneuma* follows the soul in all its reincarnations *(metabolai)* and is itself a cause of reincarnation. The goal of Gnostic mysteries is to free the soul from bondage to the *antimimon pneuma.* On the basis of the planetary order in chapter 136 of *Pistis Sophia* and in other texts of late antiquity, it seems likely that this doctrine derives from the Hermetic astrological treatise *Panaretos,* which includes a discussion of the degrees *(klēroi)* or positions *(loci)* of the planets; that is, the coordinates within the horoscope of nativity, where each planet is supposed to confer its principal qualities upon the subject. However, Gnostics mention only the negative qualities or vices derived from the planetary influence.

The doctrine of *antimimon pneuma* became influential in Hermetism, where it merged with the idea of the soul's descent into the world and its return to heaven. During its descent through the planetary spheres, the soul acquired from each planet the dominant vice ascribed to it in astrology, while during its ascent, those concretions were put off (*Poimandres* 25–26). The ascent of the soul in Gnosticism could be much more complicated, and the ritual performances or "mysteries" intended to assure the soul an easy passage through the archons differed widely, although they presented some fixed patterns, such as learning by heart magical names or invocations. Some Sethian treatises from Nag-Hammadi *(Zostrianos, Allogenes, The Three Steles of Seth),* where the path of ascent shows Platonic nuances, prelude the life-intellect-being triad later developed by Plotinus.

It should also be noted that the same motif of secret names or watchwords and seals indispensable for passing through the heavenly customs is also described in magic literature and in the Jewish mysticism of the *merkavah.* An important example is the famous *Mithrasliturgie* (*Papyri Grae-*

cae Magicae VI, 475–824), which describes how to gain immortality by an elevation process.

The second-century Platonic writer Celsus (attested by Origen, *Contra Celsum* 6, 22 ff.) ascribed to the Persian god Mithra, whose veneration increased during late antiquity and who was reshaped to suit the changed religious attitude of Hellenism, a ritual object consisting of a ladder with seven steps or "gates" *(klimax heptapylos),* representing the planets. Similar objects are also depicted in Mithraic temples. According to Celsus, this object symbolized the passage of the adept's soul through the planetary spheres, which could be accomplished in concomitance of the *magnus annus* of Plato's doctrine (*Timaeus* 39d). This interpretation raises some difficulties, however, since the steps are arranged according to the order of the days of the planetary week, which is explained by Celsus in accordance with the musical theory of the *tetrachordon.* Celsus linked this doctrine to a related diagram ascribed to the Gnostic sect of the Ophites. Some interpreters have argued that these steps and their associated rituals represent a meditative technique to obtain inner knowledge of the self, and the steps are thus structured as an interior journey.

In Hellenistic culture a relationship was established between the seven "planets" and the levels that the soul had to transverse in its heavenly ascent. It can thus be maintained that, as far as the mysteries of late antiquity are concerned, their divinities, in some cases traditionally connected with the earth and the underworld Hades, are transported entirely to heaven, where they are supposed to receive the souls of their adepts after death. Moreover, Gnostic polemics against astrology gave rise to the formation of the influential theory of the passage of the soul through the spheres, fashionable among Neoplatonists from the third to the sixteenth century CE. It is impossible to state whether Neoplatonists (e.g., Porphyry, Proclus, and Macrobius) took this theory from Numenius of Apamea or from the Gnostic-Hermetic tradition. It should also be noted that the Christian writer Arnobius, at the beginning of the fourth century, directed his polemic against a group of Neoplatonic mystics who maintained the doctrines of the Chaldaean Oracles, attributing to them formulas and other means for transporting their clients to heaven.

The embodiment *(ensōmatōsis)* of the soul entails a descent from the top of the cosmos to the bottom, through the planetary spheres that confer certain characteristic features upon the soul. Disembodiment is the reverse of this process. In late Neoplatonism, which borrowed this doctrine from Chaldaean theurgy, the ethereal body that enveloped the soul and that was formed by planetary qualities was its "vehicle" *(ochēma).* Sometimes this "vehicle" was distinguished from others that were meant to serve as intermediaries between the soul and the material body, according to a theory of Aristotle that was influential in Greco-Roman and Arabic medicine. The theory of the passage of the soul through the spheres was taken over from Macrobius by medieval medicine and psychology. Through the works of Marsilio Ficino (1433–1499), it became one of the most widespread doctrines from the time of the Renaissance down to the end of the sixteenth century and even into the seventeenth.

Another interesting Latin document preserving a description of an initiatory ascension is *De Nuptiis,* written in the fifth century by Martianus Capella. Despite the far-fetched and heterogeneous material collected in *De Nuptiis* (the author aimed at offering an encyclopedia of the seven liberal arts), its allegorical stamp emerges from the first two books and is testified by commentaries written during the Middle Ages. The hierogamy between Philology, allegory of human knowledge, and Mercury is prepared by a complicated ritual and by Philology's ascent throughout the seven spheres in order to purify herself from earthly filth. Chaldaean and Neoplatonic borrowings are palpable.

JUDAISM AND EARLY CHRISTIAN LITERATURE. The heavenly journey is a constant pattern in Jewish and, later, Christian apocalypses. Apart from the Scriptural references (*Gen.* 5:24; 2 *Kgs.* 2:11; *Sir.* 44:16; 48:9; *Ez.* 1; and *Dn.* 7:13, important for later interpretations), among the Old Testament Pseudepigrapha there are numerous texts describing both an elective ascension of patriarchs (Abraham, Enoch, Isaac, Jacob, Levi, Moses, and Shem) or prophets (Baruch, Esdra, Isaiah, Elijah, and Ezekiel), and the granting of a vision.

Extensive and detailed accounts of ascensions begin with *1 Enoch,* the oldest parts of which were completed at the end of the third century BCE. Enoch's adventures are recounted in this text in much more detail than in the Bible. Written originally in Aramaic (fragments were discovered among the Dead Sea Scrolls), *1 Enoch* is fully preserved only in an Ethiopian translation that is based on a Greek version. No less than five works, written over a period of centuries, are included in this collection. The book of *2 Enoch,* which seems originally to have been written in Greek, survives only in a translation into Old Church Slavonic. Much of the material in it probably dates back to the early centuries CE, although its final form appears to be the result of a long process of transmission. According to this work, Enoch ascended to heaven and was given a tour of the celestial realm, where he was transformed into an angelic being when he came before the throne of God. This is the background of the story narrated in *3 Enoch,* which begins with the ascent of R. Ishmael to the seventh heaven and his encounter with God and the angels. One of them, Metatron, reveals that he was once the man Enoch, but he was taken to heaven in a fiery chariot as a witness to the generation of the flood. After having been challenged by the angels, he was finally enthroned by God.

The voyage through seven or three heavens became a commonplace of Jewish apocalyptic literature with the *Testaments of the Twelve Patriarchs* (second century BCE). Seven is the prevailing number in the mystical tradition related to the *merkavah,* the chariot carrying God's throne in the famous vision of Ezekiel. Under the name *ma'aseh merkavah* ("work of the chariot"), this form of speculation goes back to the Pharisees of the Second Temple. From the second or third to the sixth century CE, *merkavah* mysticism is mainly expressed through hekhalotic literature (from *hekhal,* "heavenly palace"), represented by various groups of testimonies of different dates. Jewish magic, as recorded in, for example, the *Sefer ha-razim* (sixth or seventh century CE), was also concerned with the vision of seven heavens, which was fundamental to *merkavah* mysticism and hekhalotic literature. The related writings contain the revelation of seven "heavenly palaces," which the adept was supposed to attain after strenuous preparation. In Jewish mysticism, the seven heavens are never associated with the seven planets. Some scholars have argued that both the Second Temple apocalypses and hekhalot literature are fictitious or clearly literary events, while others have underlined patterns kindred to shamanism.

The same basic ecstatic experience is reflected in Christian accounts of celestial elevation, including Paul's and the enigmatic and indirect autobiographical account in *2 Corinthians* (12:2 ff.). This reference to visions and revelations of the Lord may suggest either that Paul's opponents, against whom the epistle is directed, boasted of such experiences, or that they decried his apostolic title because it was based on a "vision." It is interesting to note that the Hellenic writer Lucian (second century CE) caricatured Christianity by describing "the Galilean. . .who went by air into the third heaven" (*Philopatris* 12).

A long section of the early Christian apocryphal text *Ascensio Isaiae* (dating back to the second century CE, probably to Syrian ambit, and preserved in different fragmentary versions of varying length and chronology) contains an apocalyptic account. In this text, the prophet Isaiah, helped by an angel, rises to the seventh heaven, where he can contemplate the preexistent Christ together with the Holy Spirit, and the coming of Christ in the world. *Ascensio Isaiae* puts into evidence not only eschatological themes, but also attempts at enucleating a complex Christology, sometimes pervaded with Gnostic or dualistic features. The link between ascension and the manifestation of God's glory *(kavod)* was inherited by many other apocryphal Christian texts, including, for example, the Gnosticizing *Gospel of Thomas.*

Any inquiry concerning heavenly journeys in ancient Christianity cannot omit consideration of the ascension of Christ, considered dogma from the earliest times and the earliest credo formulas. Its account is recorded by Luke both in the *Gospel* and in the proemial section of the *Acts;* only the Markan appendix contains something parallel (16:19). This double reference—which can be considered a climax to the latter part of the *Gospel of Luke,* from chapter 9 (the transfiguration)—makes it clear that one has to reckon with this ascension account as the crucial marker that distinguishes the period of the church from that of Jesus. The term *ascension* has a different meaning in this case, since it does not simply refer to a motion upward through the "heavens" but also involves the notion that the ascended Christ joins his heavenly Father in "glory," and the disciples behold Jesus in this state. Nevertheless, all scholars have emphasized how Christ's ascension sums up the tradition of biblical heavenly ascensions, explaining his role as both redeemer and mediator between God and humans.

The early tradition that Luke makes use of is otherwise expressed in terms of Jesus' "exaltation" (e.g., in the pre-Pauline formulation echoed in *Philippians* 2:9). However this belief is partly an attempt to define more clearly the relation between the living Jesus who died on the cross and the risen Lord who appeared to the apostles by explaining, for example, where the "life" of Jesus had been during the three days following his death. While Paul shows no awareness of the problem, the question was bound to arise eventually, and the answer depended on the view taken about the relation between soul and body. According to the Pauline view, the resurrection was the passage from earth to heaven, or it was identical to the ascension, but the views of Luke and John, which the early church adopted, held that the resurrection was a temporary restoration of Jesus' intercourse with the disciples on earth, which ended with the ascension.

ISLAM. The most famous example of an ascension in Islamic culture is the *Miʿrāj,* or ascent of the prophet Muḥammad, developed and expanded from an enigmatic hint in the Qurʾān (17:1). This account is preserved in various Arabic texts from the eighth and ninth centuries CE, as well as in medieval Latin versions. Accompanied by the archangel Gabriel, the Prophet is transported to Jerusalem and then to heaven either on Burāq (a sort of winged horse with a peacock's tail) or in a tree growing with vertiginous speed up to the sky.

Other accounts of heavenly journeys are recorded in Arabic literature (in turn influenced by Persia), some of them equally characterized by the common denominator of Gnostic trends and by a mythic and symbolic geography (what Henry Corbin called the *mundus imaginalis*). A precursor of the grail legend is recognizable in the account of the visionary Kay Khosraw in Firdawsī's *Book of the Kings* from the late tenth century. In addition, the *Si Murg* describes the journey of thirty birds toward their king, the Phoenix (*Simurgh*), through seven dreadful valleys. At the end they realize that the Phoenix is nothing more than themselves, with a wordplay on the title, expressing at the same time one of the principal Gnostic tenets—that divinity dwells in the inner self. Furthermore, the allegorical works by the Gnostic philosopher Suhrawardī Maqtūl (d. 1191), written in a style similar to Avicenna's tales, feature the leitmotiv of the soul's redemption from its corporeal bonds and the laud to its true homeland, *na-kaja-abad* (place without space).

Also important is the *Seir al-ʾIbad ilà ʿl-Maʿad* (Journey of the servants of God toward the reign of the goals), a poem written in the twelfth century by Sanāʾī. The purpose of the journey that is described in this poem is to reach the "Supreme Goal" through a progressive divinization, which is described in the introductory section, with the exhortation to forsake the "bony body." The spiritual guide is represented by the Intellect (*ʿAql*), disguised as an old man. The traveler ascends through the four elements first, a place ruled by the passions and death, then it reaches a hell in which the sovereign is represented as a whale. Finally, after passing through eternal Time's crystal gate, the traveler rises to the planets, symbolizing the vices (an inheritance from the Mazdean tradition), as far as the ninth sphere. The ninth sphere represents the World Soul, in conformity with the strong emanationism pervading the poem. Although the narrator is inclined to stop his ascent at this point, the Intellect persuades him to continue. The final section is the most gnosticly marked, since there is an overlap or identification between the storyteller and his Intellect, in order to accomplish divinization.

MEDIEVAL CHRISTIANITY AND DANTE. Late Hellenistic Christian apocalypses continued to play an important role during the Middle Ages. The Latin *Vision of Esdra*, transmitted in a tenth-century manuscript, was extremely influential. From the twelfth century, which was particularly productive of revelations, three works are most important: the *Vision of Alberic* (1127), written by a monk of Montecassino, possibly influenced by the Miʿrāj legends, transmitted by Constantine the African (1020–1087), a translator from Arabic who spent the last years of his life in that monastery; the *Vision of Tundal* (1149); and the *Purgatory of Saint Patrick* (1189), which is similar to ancient Irish models and to the Latin legend of Saint Brendan's life (ninth century).

The most important account of a heavenly ascension in Western culture is considered to be Dante Alighieri's epic poem *The Divine Comedy*, written in the early 1300s. *The Divine Comedy* is not only a literary masterpiece, it is also a summation of medieval philosophical and religious ideas, in which different sources seem to flow together. For example, the Christian apocalyptic tradition involving Paul's experience (*2 Cor.* 12:2–4) is explicitly asserted in the *Inferno* (2:28 ff.) and *Paradiso* (1:74 ff.). Classical reminiscences also appear, including Aeneas's catabasis, which derives from the sixth book of Vergil's *Aeneid.* The poet uses these two models to insert himself into a line of exemplary people who are worthy of seeing the celestial realms, even if he always remarks that providential action operated by divine grace in offering to a human the possibility of ascending to supernatural spheres. Moreover, after Miguel Asín Palacios's seminal suggestions (partly questioned), scholars have begun looking for traces of Islamic descriptions from the Miʿrāj in the *Commedia.* This hypothesis is highly probable, since translated versions of the so-called *Liber scalae* circulated in Europe during the thirteenth century, and one of them had been arranged by a Tuscan dignitary, Bonaventura da Siena, as Enrico Cerulli has demonstrated. If Dante employed such heterogeneous sources, this may be considered the clearest—and the most important—example of an osmotic interaction (sometimes not free from polemic) between Arabic and European culture in the Middle Ages, an interaction that lasted until the sixteenth century. Dante may also have been inspired by the Arabic philosophical apocalypses described above, even though these were radically different in their purpose: Whereas the latter were deeply influenced by Gnostic ideas and praised the role of intellect, Dante's guide in his pilgrimage is Beatrice, who symbolizes Christian love after the defeat of human reason (represented by Vergil). It should be noted that Gnostic interpretations of Beatrice have been put forward, but these are not convincing.

Such a majestic text has been the object of manifold interpretations due to its difficulty and its elaborate literary frame. In the final part (*cantica*) of *The Divine Comedy,* the narrator, after having passed through hell and purgatory with Beatrice, rises to the heavenly spheres, where he is granted a vision of the Virgin Mary and God. In his description of the universe Dante follows Ptolemaic astronomical conceptions in which the earth is stationary and central, with the seven planets revolving around it at various speeds. Beyond these are the spheres of the fixed stars and the material heavens, the last of which is called the Crystalline, or the Primum Mobile, because the other heavens derive their slower motions from its infinite speed. In Dante's universe, the grace of God increases as one moves into the higher and higher heavens. Nine angelic orders rule and control the heavenly spheres, which influence human life and character. The various souls are described according to the corresponding predominant character of their earthly lives. When the Blesseds crowd, they vary their voices and sounds into a sweet and exultant harmony.

Dante and Beatrice reach the heaven of the Moon first, they then travel to the heaven of Mercury, and then the third heaven (ruled by Venus), where lovers dwell. A whirling light glows in the heaven of the Sun, whose inhabitants are philosophers and theologians, such as Thomas Aquinas and Bonaventure, as well as Siger de Brabant. The heaven of Mars is trimmed with a white gleaming cross, while in the heaven of Jupiter the spirits (rulers and sovereigns) form a gigantic eagle, symbolizing imperial power. In the next heaven, that of Saturn, Dante is faced with a great golden ladder upon whose steps manifold splendid lights (the contemplative spirits) ascend and descend. From here Dante can look back toward the earth, which appears to him in all its paltriness. As soon as he arrives in the heaven of the fixed stars, Dante is presented with a procession of the triumph of Christ, while at the same time he is examined by the saints in order to rise toward the ninth heaven and finally to the Empyrean, which exists outside of time and space, pervaded by eternal intellectual light and holy love, and where angels and saints live, their blessedness consisting of an eternal vision of God. The thrones of the saints and the biblical figures (Eve, Rachel, Sarah, Rebecca, Judith, Adam, Moses, Saint Peter, Saint John, Saint Francis, Saint Augustine, Saint Lucy, as well as Beatrice) sit there in ranked order, with the Virgin sitting at their radiant peak. In the end, Saint Bernard begins a prayer to the Virgin so that the poet can preserve the blessedness he saw. She deigns to look down at him and the light of God shines down on Dante, granting him the beatific vision and the ultimate salvation.

See Also Afterlife, overview article; Apotheosis; Flight; Gnosticism; Miʿrāj; Shamanism, overview article.

Bibliography

The classic study devoted to the ascension of the soul is Wilhelm Bousset, "Die Himmelsreise der Seele" in *Archiv für Religionswissenschaft* 4 (1901): 136–169; the same view is shared by Karl Hönn, *Studien zur Geschichte der Himmelfahrt im klassischen Altertum* (Mannheim, Germany, 1910). Among the scholarly production influenced by this critical trend, it is worth mentioning Eduard Norden's impressive commentary on the sixth book of the *Aeneid* (P. Vergilius Maro, *Aeneis Buch VI,* Leipzig and Berlin, 1903; 3d ed., 1934), which, especially in the introductory section, deals with apocalyptic and eschatological literature from Empedocles to the Middle Ages. Important methodological remarks on the subject are provided by Carsten Colpe, "Die 'Himmelsreise der Seele' ausserhalb und innerhalb der Gnosis" in *Le Origini dello Gnosticismo,* edited by Ugo Bianchi (Leiden, 1967), pp. 429–445; see also Colpe's "Die 'Himmelsreise der Seele' als philosophie- und religionsgeschichtliche Problem" in *Festschrift für Joseph Klein,* edited by Erich Fries (Göttingen, 1967), pp. 85–104.

Two books by Ioan Petru Culianu, *Psychanodia: A Survey of the Evidence concerning the Ascension of the Soul and Its Relevance,* vol. 1 (Leiden, 1983), and *Expériences de l'extase: Extase, ascension, et récit visionnaire de l'hellénisme au Moyen Age* (Paris, 1984), offer detailed commentary on Judaic, Christian, and Islamic literature from ancient Greece through the Middle Ages, as well as a scholarly history marked by a strong criticism of the *Religionsgeschichtliche Schule* view. Fascinating, but not strictly scientific, is Elémire Zolla, *Lo stupore infantile* (Milan, 1994), pp. 77–91 and 111–120. See also Ioan Petru Culianu, *Out of this World. Otherwordly Journeys from Gilgamesh to Albert Einstein* (Boston and London, 1991, 2001).

Among the manifold contributions on apocalyptic literature and its distinctive patterns and purposes, see David Hellholm, ed., *Apocalypticism in the Mediterranean World and the Near-East: Proceedings of the International Colloquium on Apocalypticism, Uppsala, Aug. 12–17, 1979,* 2d ed. (Tübingen, 1989), and Claire Kappler, ed., *Apocalypses et voyages dans l'au-delà* (Paris, 1987). See also the synthesis by John J. Collins, *The Apocalyptic Imagination: An Introduction to the Jewish Matrix of Christianity* (New York, 1984).

The best single book on shamanism and related ecstatic phenomena in different religious contexts remains Mircea Eliade's *Shamanism: Archaic Techniques of Ecstasy,* translated by Willard R. Trask (New York, 1964); on yoga techniques viewed in a broad historico-religious scope see Eliade's *Yoga: Immortality and Freedom,* 2d ed., translated by Willard R. Trask (Princeton, 1969). On related themes see Alexander Golitzin, "'Earthly Angels and Heavenly Men': Nicetas Stethatos, the Old Testament Pseudepigrapha, and the Tradition of 'Interiorized Apocalyptic' in Eastern Christian Ascetical and Mystical Literature" in *Dumbarton Oak Papers* 55 (2001): 125–153.

On *ecstasis* induced by hallucinogens in ancient Iran see David S. Flattery and Martin Schwartz, *Haoma and Harmaline: The Botanical Identity of the Indo-Iranian Sacred Hallucinogen "Soma" and Its Legacy in Religion, Language, and Middle Eastern Folklore* (Berkeley, 1989). For Iranian apocalypticism, Philippe Gignoux has translated and written a commentary on the *Ardā Wirāz Nāmag* in *Le livre d'Ardā Vīrāz* (Paris, 1984), as has Fereydun Vahman in *Ardā Wirāz Nāmag: The Iranian "Divina Commedia"* (London, 1986). On Kirdīr's inscriptions, see Philippe Gignoux, *Les quatre inscriptions du Mage Kirdīr, Texte et Concordances* (Paris, 1991), as well as Gignoux's many contributions on Iranian eschatology and shamanistic features. On the same theme there is also an important paper by Gherardo Gnoli, "Asšavan: Contributo allo studio del Libro di Arda Viraz" in *Iranica* (Naples, 1979), pp. 387–452. Antonio Panaino's "Uranographia Iranica I: The Three Heavens in the Zoroastrian Tradition and the Mesopotamian Background" in *Au carrefour des religions: Mélanges offerts à Philippe Gignoux,* edited by Rika Gyselen (Bures sur Yvette, France, 1995), pp. 205–225, deals with the threefold division of universe and planetary order.

On the Greek *iatromanteis* and their relationships to shamanism see Karl Meuli, "Scythica," in *Hermes* 70 (1935): 121–176; as well as chapter 5 of Eric R. Dodds, *The Greeks and the Irrational* (Berkeley, 1951). On Shamanic features in Greek oracular practice, see Pierre Bonnechere, *Trophonios de Lébadée: cultes et mythes d'une cité béotienne au miroir de la mentalité antique* (Leiden, 2003).

The magnificient book by Franz Cumont, *Lux Perpetua* (Paris, 1949), deals with eschatology and the otherworld in the Hellenistic age. Plutarch's eschatology is investigated by Frederick Brenk, *In Mist Apparelled: Religious Themes in Plutarch's Moralia and Lives* (Leiden, 1977). On the mysteries of Mithra and their relationship to the ascent of the soul, see Robert Turcan, *Mithras platonicus: Recherches sur l'hellénisation philosophique de Mithra* (Leiden, 1975), and Bernd Witte, *Das Ophitendiagramm nach Origens' Contra Celsum* 6: 22–38 (Altenberge, Germany, 1993). On Macrobius and the passage of the soul through the spheres, a good survey is Jacques Flamant's *Macrobe et le néo-platonisme latin, à la fin du quatrième siècle* (Leiden, 1977). The survival of this doctrine during the Renaissance is investigated by Daniel P. Walker, *Spiritual and Demonic Magic: From Ficino to Campanella* (London, 1958), and Ioan Petru Culianu, "Magia spirituale e magia demonica nel Rinascimento" in *Rivista di storia e letteratura religiosa* 17 (1981): 360–408.

The classic book on magic literature is Albrecht Dieterich, *Eine Mithrasliturgie,* 3d ed. (Leipzig, 1923), which must be supplemented by Hans-Dieter Betz, *Gottesbegegnung und Menschwerdung: Zur religionsgeschichtlichen und theologischen Bedeutung der Mithrasliturgie* (PGM IV, 475–820) (Berlin and New York, 2001). See also Betz's English translation and commentary, *The Mithras Liturgy* (Tübingen, 2003).

Good surveys of the Jewish mysticism of the *merkavah* are Gershom Scholem, *Jewish Gnosticism, Merkavah Mysticism, and Talmudic Tradition* (New York, 1960; 2d ed., 1965), and Ithamar Gruenwald, *Apocalyptic and Merkavah Mysticism* (Leiden, 1980). See also Peter Schäfer, *The Hidden and Manifest God: Some Major Themes in Early Jewish Mysticism,* translated by Aubrey Pomerance (Albany, N.Y., 1992); Martha Himmelfarb, *Ascent to Heaven in Jewish and Christian Apocalypses* (Oxford, 1993); and James R. Davila, "Shamanic Initiatory Death and Resurrection in the Hekhalot Literature" in Paul Mirecki and Marvin Meyer, eds., *Magic and*

Ritual in the Ancient World (Leiden, 2002), pp. 283–302, together with his monograph *Descenders to the Chariot: The People behind the Hekhalot Literature* (Leiden 2001). See also James H. Charlesworth, ed., *Old Testament Pseudepigrapha* (Garden City, N.Y., 1983).

Contributions on how Christianity developed the ascension theme are offered by Alan F. Segal, "Heavenly Ascent in Hellenistic Judaism, Early Christianity and Their Environment" in *Aufstieg und Niedergand der Römischen Welt* II, 23, 2 (Berlin and New York, 1980), pp. 1333–1394; and James D. Tabor, *Things Unutterable: Paul's Ascent to Paradise in its Graeco-Roman, Judaic, and Early Christian Context* (New York, 1986). Further bibliographical references can be found in Joseph A. Fitzmeyer, *The Gospel According to Luke* (Anchor Bible 28–28A; New York, 1981); and Karin Wilcke, *Christi Himmelfahrt. Ihre Darstellung in der Europäische Literatur von der Spätantike bis zum ausgehenden Mittelalter* (Heidelberg, 1991). A critical edition and commentary of the *Ascensio Isaiae* is provided by Paolo Bettiolo, Alda Kossova, Claudio Leonardi, Enrico Norelli, and Lorenzo Perrone (Turnhout, Belgium, 1995; CCSA 7–8). See also Enrico Norelli, *L'Ascensione di Isaia: Studi su un apocrifo al crocevia dei cristianesimi* (Bologna, 1994), and April De Conick, *Seek to See Him: Ascent and Vision Mysticism in the Gospel of Thomas* (Leiden, 1996).

The relationships between Persian and Arabic religious literature are investigated by Henry Corbin, *Corps spirituel et terre céleste: De l'Iran mazdéen à l'Iran shi'ite,* 2d ed. (Paris, 1979); on the same subject see also Alessandro Bausani, *Persia religiosa: Da Zaratustra a Bahā'u'llāh,* 2d ed. (Cosenza, Italy, 1999), available in *English as Religion in Iran: From Zoroaster to Baha'ullah,* translated by J. M. Marchesi (New York, 2000). On the Mi'rāj see Geo Widengren, *Muhammad: The Apostle of God and His Ascension* (Uppsala, Sweden, 1955).

A good survey of the most important medieval visions and apocalypses is given in Sir John D. Seymour, *Irish Visions of the Other-World* (London, 1930), and Jacques Le Goff, *La naissance du Purgatoire* (Paris, 1981), available in English as *The Birth of Purgatory,* translated by Arthur Goldhammer (London, 1984). On Dante's *Commedia* see Charles S. Singleton, *Journey to Beatrice* (Dante Studies 2; Cambridge, Mass., 1958). A detailed commentary is offered by Anna Maria Chiavacci Leonardi in a new edition of the *Commedia* (Milan, 1997). In English see Charles Singleton's commentary in the Princeton translation (1970–1975). Dante's knowledge of Islamic sources is discussed in Miguel Asín Palacios, *La escatologia musulmana en la Divina comedia, seguida de la historia y crítica de una polémica,* 2d ed. (Madrid, 1943)—the first edition of this work was translated by Harold Sunderland as *Islam and the Divine Comedy* (London, 1926). Asín Palacios's views were reconsidered and corrected by Enrico Cerulli, *Il "Libro della Scala" e la questione delle fonti arabo-spagnole della Divina Commedia* (Vatican City, 1949), and *Nuove ricerche sul "Libro della Scala" e la conoscenza dell'Islam in Occidente* (Vatican City, 1972).

CHIARA OMBRETTA TOMMASI (2005)

ASCETICISM.

ASCETICISM. The word *asceticism* is derived from the Greek noun *askēsis,* meaning "exercise, practice, training." The Greek athlete, for example, subjected himself to systematic exercise or training in order to attain a goal of physical fitness. In time, however, the word began to assume philosophical, spiritual, and ethical implications: one could "exercise" and "train" not only the body in the pursuit of a physical goal but also—systematically and rigorously—the will, the mind, and the soul so as to attain a more virtuous life or a higher spiritual state.

Although the modern word *asceticism* has eluded any universally accepted definition, the term, when used in a religious context, may be defined as a voluntary, sustained, and at least partially systematic program of self-discipline and self-denial in which immediate, sensual, or profane gratifications are renounced in order to attain a higher spiritual state or a more thorough absorption in the sacred. Because religious man (*homo religiosus*) seeks a transcendent state, asceticism—in either rudimentary or developed form—is virtually universal in world religion.

ORIGINS OF ASCETICISM. The origins of asceticism are found in primitive or archaic society, that is, in prehistory. Many of the major ascetic forms such as fasting, sexual continence, and seclusion appear universally among present-day primitives or nonliterate peoples. The purpose of such prohibitions or taboos is very frequently to escape or avoid the influence of demonic powers. There is, for example, a prevalent belief in primitive societies that evil forces may enter the body while one is eating. To avoid this, one fasts for certain periods or abstains from certain foods altogether. The objective of primitive prohibitions may also be purification. In preparation for ritual activities of a particularly sacred nature, such as initiation, marriage, or sacrifice, participants rid themselves of impurity by engaging in often austere acts of self-denial. Such purity is particularly necessary if one is to approach the gods. To a lesser degree, one may also use austerities as a form of penance to atone for transgressions, thus averting the wrath of a deity. Certain practices, particularly fasting and seclusion, are also employed to induce visions or vivid dreams. Among American Indians, for example, such techniques are used during puberty initiations to evoke a revelation in dream or a vision of the youth's guardian spirit.

Although the origins of asceticism may be found in primitive society, it is often argued that asceticism per se exists there only in rudimentary form or not at all. One's position on this issue depends almost entirely upon how one defines asceticism, thus making the issue less soluble but also less critical. It should be observed, however, that such ascetic forms as fasting, seclusion, infliction of pain, and even bodily mutilation have a far more compulsory, less voluntary character in preliterate than in literate societies. The ordeals associated with puberty rites, for example, are more or less imposed. Further, the austerities to which the primitive submits rarely demonstrate a systematic and sustained program of ascetic behavior, when compared with comprehensive systems such as yoga or monastic life. Also, a preponderant number of primitive austerities, acts of self-denial, and taboos have as their sole intent the avoidance of evil, so it is questionable whether they should even be labeled asceticism. But since in almost all societies asceticism is elitist, being meant for the few, a developed asceticism in primitive society should be sought among such sacral specialists as the shaman. Although the shaman is often "compelled" by higher powers to assume his role, the rigors of shamanic life are hardly imposed from without in the usual sense. Seclusion, fasting, sexual continence, and endless vigils are part of a sustained self-discipline calculated to generate visions, bring communion with spirits, and penetrate sacred realms.

FORMS AND OBJECTIVES OF ASCETICISM. Viewed cross-culturally, the variety of ascetic forms is limited. Virtually universal are (1) fasting, (2) sexual continence, (3) poverty, under which may be included begging, (4) seclusion or isolation, and (5) self-inflicted pain, either physical (through such means as whipping, burning, or lacerating) or mental (e.g., contemplation of a judgment day, of existence in hell, or of the horrors associated with transmigration). More difficult to define, but perhaps also more significant, is what may be termed an "inner asceticism," consisting essentially of spiritual rather than physical discipline. Such asceticism involves not detachment from or renunciation of any specific worldly pleasure but rather detachment from or renunciation of the world per se. It is reflected in the biblical attitude of being "in the world, but not of it," or in the *Bhagavadgītā*'s "renunciation in action, rather than renunciation of action." It appears in almost every major religion yet has no equivalent in primitive thought. In addition to the universal forms indicated, specific note must also be made of that set of practices or techniques (e.g., specific postures, chanting, breathing techniques) that make up the yogic and meditative complex indigenous to the Indian subcontinent. Yoga, although an asceticism of the body, is an inner asceticism as well.

Asceticism in classical and modern religion is generally rooted in a developed and well-articulated philosophical or theological system. Such a system provides the rationale or justification for ascetic activity. It is helpful to consider the objectives of asceticism from the perspective of these systems, whether theistic or nontheistic.

Virtually all theistic traditions develop a mystical movement wherein the individual, through an ascetic program, seeks a personal union with the deity. This desire for personal experience of the deity may be seen as a reaction against doctrinal abstraction or ethical formalism. Even theistic traditions such as Judaism, Christianity, and Islam, in which the gap between creator and creature is perceived to be unbridgeable, have produced ascetics in pursuit of such mystic union: the eleventh-century Jewish mystic Baḥye ibn Paquda; Johannes Eckhart (d. 1327 CE) and Johannes Tauler (d. 1361 CE) in medieval Christianity; and the entire Ṣūfī movement in Islam. Because the mystic seeks to bridge the gap between man and God, the effort has often been perceived as audacious from the perspective of theistic orthodoxy. Virtually all mystics in a theistic tradition, therefore, make it clear that the state of apparent union with the deity is only momentary and, at best, a foretaste of that salvation yet to come. The Ṣūfī, like many mystics in theism, does not claim to be equal to God, but rather to be extinguished or lost in him.

In nontheistic traditions this thirst for the ultimate through mystical experience takes on varied forms. It is frequently a quest for the true or essential self, which is perceived to be identical with the ground or foundation of all creation. The Hindu yogin employs the sophisticated techniques of Yoga to realize that his *ātman*, or permanent self, is one with *brahman*, the unchanging foundation of all. The *Yoga Sūtra* of Patañjali (first century CE) describes breathing and meditative techniques, which, when coupled with sexual continence, fasting, bodily postures, and other disciplines, permit the individual to move "inward and downward" until his true essence is "perceived." Similarly, the meditative techniques of Zen Buddhism permit the practitioner to realize the Buddha nature within himself.

Experiential knowledge of the true self in nontheistic traditions is frequently related to the liberation of the self from the sorrows and illusions of this phenomenal world. According to the Hindu philosopher Śaṇkara (788–820 CE), the body and personality with which we habitually identify ourselves are revealed to be no more than *māyā*, or illusion. Our suffering and bondage are rooted in ignorance, which ascetic-meditative effort gradually dispels through the mystical knowledge that it produces. The Jain monk, through the most rigorous of ascetic techniques involving total passivity and detachment from the world, seeks to purify and eventually liberate his true self (*jīva*) from the material defilements that most actions produce. Although Theravāda Buddhism denies the existence of any permanent self, its objective is, like that of the Indian traditions, liberation from the round of worldly suffering. An ascetic life of monastic simplicity and celibacy, an ascetic program of detachment, and a meditative effort to cultivate a selfless state lead the Theravāda monk to realization of *nirvāṇa*—"extinction" or "liberation."

Unlike the theistic systems, in which a mystical experience generated through ascetic activity can never grant salvation, nontheistic systems frequently equate such an experience or realization with salvation itself. Awareness of one's *ātman* in Hinduism or of one's *puruṣa* in Sāṃkhya (i.e., a philosophical system associated with traditional Yoga) or of one's Buddha nature in Zen *is* enlightenment or salvation. Unlike the theistic religions, nontheistic systems frequently affirm that salvation is attainable here on earth. One becomes "liberated in life" as in Tantrism, or one realizes, as in Zen, that one was never bound.

In both theistic and nontheistic systems asceticism may be seen as a meritorious form of behavior, a good work, or a laudable course of action felt to ensure or facilitate a preferred condition after death. Self-denial is considered to be a way of earning posthumous reward. In theistic traditions such as Catholicism, Śaivism, and Vaiṣṇavism, such activity has often been thought to ensure or facilitate salvation in a way that mysticism cannot. A monastic life of self-denial, for example, in which one is secluded from the temptations of the flesh, could be esteemed as a more perfect life than one lived in the world. Despite its prevalence, however, this effort to earn one's own salvation has frequently appeared problematic and even pretentious in theistic traditions, given their emphasis upon salvation as a gift of the deity. In nontheistic traditions ascetic works are logically more appropriate. Through self-denial, for example, one can burn out bad *karman* (the effect of past deeds) and improve one's future state in the ongoing round of transmigration. In nontheistic systems, however, ascetic works divorced from knowledge or realization can never generate salvation itself, but only some lesser objective.

In both theistic and nontheistic systems, acts of self-denial—particularly self-inflicted pain—may serve as a form of penance for previous misdeeds. Hindu law books such as the *Mānava Dharmaśāstra* (composed between 200 BCE and 100 CE) detail numerous activities of this kind to atone for transgressions, so that the penitent can avoid torment in either the next life or an intermediate hell. In the theistic traditions of Islam and medieval Christianity, activities such as self-flagellation were often employed. In nontheistic systems these practices function mechanistically to overcome the negative consequences of evil deeds, whereas in theistic traditions they are performed in order to warrant the forgiveness of a personal god. Because its objective is merely forgiveness, in theistic systems asceticism as a form of penance has enjoyed a less problematic rationale than has asceticism as a way of achieving salvation itself. This is particularly true when ascetic acts are seen as an *expression* of repentance rather than as a means of earning it.

Most evident in Catholicism, but confined neither to it nor to theistic traditions in general, is the use of asceticism, particularly self-inflicted pain, as a means of experiencing or reexperiencing the sufferings of either a deity or a human paradigm (i.e., a model individual). Nontheistic Jainism produced ascetics whose acts of self-denial took as their model the activities of Jain saints (*tīrthaṅkaras*) such as Pārśva or Mahāvīra. The Hindu hero Bhīṣma was so pierced by arrows during the great battle described in the *Bhagavdgītā* that, supported by their shafts, he lay parallel to the ground. This event forms the model for the well-known bed of nails employed by some Indian holy men. In Catholic Christianity the imitation of Christ's suffering is raised to a level of mystical significance. Suffering not only as Christ suffered but *with* him has become a means of mystical union with the deity. In this regard, suffering became virtually an end in itself, taking on soteriological significance.

Viewed cross-culturally, a given ascetic form may have different, even opposite objectives. In primitive society, for example, self-flagellation or scourging is intended primarily to drive away demonic powers that have attached themselves to the individual. In Christianity, however, the same activity—once prevalent in Italy, the Rhineland, and Mexico—was intended to produce pain, thereby bringing the ascetic into mystical union with the suffering Christ. Likewise, fasting in Christianity often has sought to produce pain, either as penance or, again, as a way of identifying with the suffering deity.

In Yoga, however, the purpose of fasting is quite different. The objective is not to cause but to alleviate discomfort. By fasting, the yogin conditions his body so he can go for prolonged periods not only without food but, more important, without the thought of food. Fasting is therefore a technique through which the yogin becomes oblivious of his body and is thus able to direct all his mental energies toward meditation. Similarly, the many other forms of self-discipline found in Yoga—the postures and sexual continence, for instance—are to be seen less as privation than as techniques to redirect energies toward a meditative end.

Yoga itself, however, as an ascetic form, has different objectives. In most of Upanisadic Hinduism its purpose is to realize the unity of one's permanent self, or *ātman*, with the unchanging foundation of the universe, or *brahman*. In Theravāda Buddhism its goal is to realize that there is no permanent self, while in the Sāṃkhya system it seeks to realize that the true self is ideally in a state of total isolation from the phenomenal world of flux.

In virtually every religious tradition, meditation or contemplation takes place in some degree of seclusion. Anthony (d. 356 CE) and other Christian saints lived for prolonged periods alone in the African desert. The early Buddhists likened themselves to rhinos who wandered alone, far from the haunts of men, and Daoist recluses sought to commune with nature beyond the reach of civilization and its distractions. But again, the goals of such secluded exercises are varied. The Daoist seeks harmony with nature and therewith serenity and joy. The Theravāda Buddhist seeks to realize that nature is transient and thus a source of sorrow. Saint Anthony, somewhat like a Tibetan Buddhist, went forth to confront demonic powers in their own ominous haunts.

CROSS-CULTURAL ISSUES. Although universal, asceticism is far more prevalent in certain traditions than in others. Classical Jainism, early and Tibetan Buddhism, early Christianity, and various branches of Hinduism are heavily ascetic, whereas Confucianism, Shinto, Zoroatrianism, and Israelite religion are not.

World-rejection. Although it is narrow to suggest that only traditions that postulate an evident dualism between soul and body or God and world or matter and spirit produce ascetic activity, it is nonetheless fair to suggest that dualistic philosophies are inclined both to justify and generate a dramatic and developed asceticism. Jain asceticism, for example, is rooted in the dualism between spirit and matter and the need for purging the former of the latter. Much Hellenistic Christian asceticism, particularly self-inflicted pain, was rooted in a dualism between spirit and flesh in which the body was perceived as evil. The ascetic efforts of the

Theravāda Buddhist are rooted in the dualism between *saṃsāra*, bondage in the round of transmigration, and *nirvāṇa*, or liberation.

Although dualistic traditions, with the exception of Zoroastrianism, lend themselves well to ascetic activity, it would be wrong to conclude that asceticism necessarily involves a denigration of this world, the material realm, or the body. Although some ascetic traditions are otherworldly, many others are not. The Tantric tradition of Hinduism and its Buddhist equivalent, the Vajrayāna, are clearly ascetic, employing various yogic and meditative techniques. Yet the worldly realm, including the body and its passions, is not denigrated by them. The body, in fact, is seen as a means toward salvation, a servant of the spirit requiring nurture, even praise. Similarly, those in a Zen or Daoist monastery exhibit many ascetic traits, yet are far more inclined to rejoice in and affirm this world than to reject it.

The most complete repudiation of world-rejection may be found in what the German sociologist Max Weber (1864–1920) termed "inner-worldly asceticism," which abandons specific ascetic activities as well as monastic life to attain salvation in the midst of worldly activity. Although it exists to a limited degree in various religions, the most thoroughgoing expression of inner-worldly asceticism appears in the reformed traditions of Protestantism. A disciplined, methodical, controlled—in short, ascetic—pursuit of one's vocation in the world came to be seen as both service to God and confirmation of one's salvation.

Asceticism and normal behavior. Although the ascetic need not renounce the world per se, he desires the sacred and therefore rarely accepts life as it is given. Seeking to transcend the normal or the natural, he rejects the given in favor of the possible. For this reason the ascetic frequently does the opposite of what human nature or social custom may dictate. In Yoga this practice is explicitly referred to as "going against the current." The yogin does not sit as natural man sits, breathe as natural man breathes, eat as natural man eats. Ascetic behavior not only deviates from the norm, it very frequently seeks an extreme. Viewed cross-culturally, however, these extremes may be diametrically opposed. The ascetic, for example, may shave his head completely, as do most Buddhist monks; or he may never cut his hair at all, as is the case with many Hindu holy men. The ascetic may wear very distinctive clothing, as does the Roman Catholic priest, or he may wear no clothing at all, as do the "sky-clad" (Digambara) monks of Jainism.

Some ascetics constantly wander, as did Mahavira, the founder-reformer of Jainism, who to avoid permanent ties remained no more than one night in any village. Other ascetics, however, restrict their movement dramatically, living, as did many Christians, in cells so small that they could hardly move. The ascetic may also differentiate himself either by remaining perpetually silent or by chanting and reciting continually. The ascetic may nurture, cleanse, or purify his body inordinately, or not only neglect his body but abuse it in countless ways. The ascetic may overcome the human norm either by abstaining from sex or by making sex a significant part of his ascetic routine. In "left-handed" Tantrism, for example, sexual intercourse affords a ritual procedure—indeed, a technique, which, when coupled with meditation, is used to alter consciousness. The activity is dramatically ascetic, as no ejaculation is permitted; the semen is withheld or "returned" at the last moment. By so returning his semen, the Tantric too "goes against the current," transcending normal or profane activity.

According to almost every religious tradition, ascetics, because of their activity, develop magical powers or miraculous abilities. Although often recognized as an obstacle to higher spiritual goals, such reported powers play an important role at the popular level. Muslim fakirs who walk unharmed on burning coals, Indian yogins who levitate, Christian saints who miraculously heal, Tibetan lamas who read minds, Buddhist monks who remember past lives, Chinese Daoists who live forever, and primitive shamans who fly—these are but a few examples.

The psychology of asceticism. Despite the fact that all religions condemn extreme forms of asceticism, pathological excesses have appeared in every tradition. Examples are multiple, from the recluses who avoid all human contact to the individuals who receive ecstatic pleasure from the most aberrant forms of self-inflicted pain. But despite these aberrations, it would be misguided to seek the heart of asceticism or its primary psychological impetus in neuroses or psychoses. Yogic meditation, Christian monasticism, and Zen technique exemplify the major advances made by asceticism, both Eastern and Western, in self-understanding and the effort to lift repression and make the unconscious conscious. The psychological heart of asceticism seems to lie in a reaction against the purely theoretical, the doctrinal, or the abstract. Above all, the ascetic wishes to know through experience.

SEE ALSO Fasting; Meditation; Monasticism, article on Christian Monasticism; Mortification; Mystical Union in Judaism, Christianity, and Islam; Ordeal; Samnyasa; Spiritual Discipline; Tapas.

BIBLIOGRAPHY

Few works provide a detailed overview of the subject. "Asceticism," an extensive entry in volume 2 of the *Encyclopedia of Religion and Ethics*, edited by James Hastings (Edinburgh, 1909), contains thirteen articles. Although still useful, this survey is dated, particularly in its methodological approach. A more readable overview, although also dated and written from a clearly Christian perspective, is Oscar Hardman's *The Ideals of Asceticism: An Essay in the Comparative Study of Religion* (New York, 1924).

Many works deal with asceticism in specific religious traditions. Outstanding is Mircea Eliade's *Yoga: Immortality and Freedom*, 2d ed. (Princeton, 1969), which discusses a wide range of ascetic practices in India and Tibet. A classic collection of information and observation, readable if not always credible, is John Campbell Oman's *The Mystics, Ascetics, and Saints of India: A Study of Sadhvism* (London, 1903). Sukumar Dutt's *Buddhist Monks and Monasteries of India: Their History and Their Contribution to Indian Culture* (London, 1962) is excellent, though only one of several related works by the author. D. T. Suzuki's *The Training of a Zen Buddhist Monk* (Kyoto, 1934) is a classic by Zen's most famous representative in the West. For the Christian tradition, Walter Nigg's *Vom Geheimnis der Mönche* (Zurich, 1953), translated by Mary Ilford as *Warriors of God* (New York, 1959), is a very readable, often insightful account of the ascetic saints, particularly those who founded religious orders. Owen Chadwick, in *Western Asceticism* (London, 1958), has selected and edited a collection of very useful primary source materials also representative of the Roman Catholic tradition. The various essays by Max Weber on the social psychology of asceticism, translated and edited by Hans H. Gerth and C. Wright Mills in *From Max Weber: Essays in Sociology* (Oxford, 1958), are pioneering and perceptive. J. Moussaieff Masson's "The Psychology of the Ascetic," *Journal of Asian Studies* 35 (August 1976): 611–625, is a one-sided but interesting article that sees the ascetic as essentially psychotic.

New Sources

Bianchi, Ugo. "Askese. 1. Religionsgeschichtlich." In *Lexikon für Theologie und Kirche,* vol. 1. Freiburg, Germany, 1994, pp. 1074–1077.

Bianchi, Ugo (ed.). *La tradizione dell'enkrateia. Motivazioni ontologiche e protologiche.* Rome, 1985. A collection of seminal studies on ascetic doctrines and practices in Early Christianity and its environment, including an introduction important from the methodological point of view.

Brown, Peter. *The Body and Society. Men, Women, and Sexual Renunciation in Early Christianity.* New York, 1988. An immensely learned book ranging over six centuries of Mediterranean history and based on a clear anthropological vision. Very full bibliography of primary and secondary sources.

Bynum, Caroline Walker. *Holy Feast and Holy Fast. The Religious Significance of Food to Medieval Women.* Berkeley and Los Angeles, 1987. Innovative.

Cantalamessa, Raniero, ed. *Etica sessuale e matrimonio nel cristianesimo delle origini.* Milano, 1976.

Clark, Elisabeth A. *Ascetic Piety and Women's Faith. Essays on Late Ancient Christianity.* New York and Toronto, 1986. A collection of ground-breaking essays by a prominent scholar of Christian asceticism.

Fischer, Klaus. *Erotik und Askese.* Cologne, Germany, 1979. Erotic scenarios in Indian religious art as forms of asceticism.

Rousselle, Aline. *Porneia. De la maîtrise du corps à la privation sensorielle.* Paris, 1983. A pioneering research.

Verardi, Giovanni. "The Buddhists, the Gnostics and the Antinomistic Society, or the Arabian Sea in the First-Second Century AD." *Annali Istituto Orientale Napoli* 57 (1997): 323–346. A very stimulating comparison between Gnostic and Buddhist ascetic models.

Vööbus, Arthur. *A History of Asceticism in the Syrian Orient.* Louvain, 1958. The basic reference work.

WALTER O. KAELBER (1987)
Revised Bibliography

ASCLEPIUS SEE ASKLEPIOS

ASHʿARĪ, AL-

ASHʿARĪ, AL- (AH 260–324/874–935 CE), more fully Abū al- Ḥasan ʿAlī ibn Ismāʿīl ibn Abī Bishr Isḥāq; Muslim theologian and founder of the tradition of Muslim theology known as Ashʿarīyah. He is commonly referred to by his followers as the Master, Abū al-Ḥasan, and he is sometimes referred to by his opponents as Ibn Abī Bishr.

LIFE AND WORKS. Very little is known concerning al-Ashʿarī's life. He was for some time an adherent of the Muʿtazilī school and a disciple of al-Jubbāʾī (d. 915), but at some point, probably prior to 909, he rejected the teachings of the Muʿtazilah in favor of the more conservative dogma of the traditionalists (*ahl al-ḥadīth*). He renounced the Muʿtazilah publicly during the Friday prayer service in the congregational mosque of Basra and thereafter wrote extensively against the doctrines of his erstwhile fellows and in defense of his new position, for which he had become quite well known by 912/3. Sometime later he moved to Baghdad, where he remained until the end of his life.

Some hundred works are attributed to al-Ashʿarī in the medieval sources (see McCarthy, 1953, pp. 211–230), of which no more than the following six seem to have survived:

(1) *Maqālāt al-Islāmīyīn* (Theological Opinions of the Muslims) is a lengthy work setting forth the diverse opinions of Muslim religious thinkers; its two separate (and largely repetitious) parts likely represent two originally distinct works, the first of which may have been substantially complete prior to al-Ashʿarī's conversion.

(2) His *Risālah ilā ahl al-thaghr bi-Bāb al-Abwāb* (Epistle to the People of the Frontier at Bāb al-Abwāb [Darband]) is a brief compendium of his teachings, composed shortly after his conversion.

(3) *Al-lumaʿ* (The Concise Remarks) is a short, general compendium or summa that was evidently the most popular, if not the most important, of al-Ashʿarī's theological writings; commentaries were written on the *Lumaʿ* by al-Bāqillānī (d. 1013) and Ibn Fūrak (d. 1015) and a refutation of it, *Naqd al-Lumaʿ* (Critique of the Concise Remarks), by the Muʿtazili *qāḍi* ("judge") Abd al-Jabbār al-Hamadānī (d. 1024). The evidence of direct citations of the *Lumaʿ* made by al-Ashʿarī's followers seems to indicate that there were originally two recensions of the work, of which the one available at present is the shorter.

(4) *Al-īmān* (Belief) is a short work on the nature of belief.

(5) *Al-ibānah ʿan uṣūl al-diyānah* (The Clear Statement on the Fundamental Elements of the Faith) is a polemical and apologetic exposition of basic dogma, ostensibly written against the Muʿtazilah and the followers of Jahm ibn Ṣafwān (d. 745), but its formally traditionalist style suggests that this work was composed as a kind of apolo-

gy to justify al-Ashʿarī's own orthodoxy after the Ḥanābilah refused to recognize him as an adherent of traditionalist doctrine.

(6) *Al-ḥathth ʿalā al-baḥth* (The Exhortation to Investigation) is a polemical apology for the use of speculative reasoning and formal terminology in theological discussion directed against the radical traditionalists. Most likely composed later than the *Ibānah,* this work has been published several times under the title *Istiḥsān al-khawḍ fī ʿilm al-kalām* (The Vindication of the Science of *Kalām*), but the correct title, given in Ibn ʿAsakir's and Ibn Farḥūn's lists of al-Ashʿarī's writings, appears in a recently discovered copy of the work.

A number of other works are quoted with some frequency by later followers of the school of al-Ashʿarī, among them his commentary on the Qurʾān, perhaps originally composed before his conversion; *Al-mūjiz* (The Epitome); *Al-ʿamad fī al-ruʾyah* (The Pillars concering [God's] Visibility), a work on the visibility of God; *Iḍāḥ al-burhān* (The Clarification of Demonstration); and *Al-ajwibah al-miṣrīyah* (The Egyptian Responsa), as well as various *majālis* or *amālī,* notes or minutes taken from his lectures.

Though it is clear that al-Ashʿarī converted from Muʿtazilī theology to a more conservative, "orthodox" doctrine that he himself identified with that of the traditionalists, the precise nature of this conversion and the character of his teaching have always been the subject of much debate. It is obvious that he changed his adherence from one basic set of dogmatic theses to another, shifting, for example, from the Muʿtazilī thesis that since God is altogether incorporeal he cannot be seen, to one that God is somehow visible and will be visibly manifest to the blessed in the next life. Yet al-Ashʿarī's claim that he taught the doctrine of the traditionalists was vehemently rejected by the more conservative of them, particularly the Ḥanābilah, whose approbation and support he had expected to receive but who looked upon him as an unreconstructed rationalist. Hostility between the Ḥanābilah and the followers of al-Ashʿarī continued unabated for many centuries, sometimes erupting into civil disturbances, and the polemic and counterpolemic of later supporters and opponents of Ashʿarī doctrine tended to obscure the basic issues somewhat, as current attitudes were often projected backward onto the founder himself. Against Ḥanbalī accusations that al-Ashʿarī had changed some of his views but not his basic attitude, some later apologists, most notably Ibn ʿAsākir (d. 1176) and al-Subkī (d. 1370), depict al-Ashʿarī as a wholehearted traditionalist. Most of those who taught or supported al-Ashʿarī's doctrine, such as the Shafiʿī *qāḍi* and jurisconsult Abū al-Maʿālī ʿAzīzī ibn ʿAbd al-Malik (d. 1100) in his apology against the Ḥanbalī extremists, held that al-Ashʿarī taught a doctrine intermediate between the rationalizing theology of the Muʿtazilah and the anthropomorphizing fundamentalism of the radical traditionalists. It is this "middle way" that is witnessed in al-Ashʿarī's own writings and in those of most of the theologians who held allegiance to his school. This is also the view of most modern scholars, although a few have tended to adopt one or the other of the more extreme views.

From the works available, two points are clear. First of all, not only did al-Ashʿarī give up the characteristic dogmas of Muʿtazilī doctrine, but also, in taking the revelation (Qurʾān and *sunnah*) and the consensus of the Muslims as the primary foundations and criteria of basic dogma, he rejected the basic attitude of al-Jubbāʾī's school, namely that autonomous reason is the primary and, in most instances, the original and definitive source and judge of what is true in theology. Second, after his conversion, he continued to express, explain, and argue theological theses in the formal language of *kalām* theology in such a way as to give them logical coherence and a degree of conceptual clarity. The first stance set him at irreconcilable odds with his erstwhile fellows among the Muʿtazilah, while the second made him unacceptable to the radical traditionalists. It is thus that when he wrote the *Ibānah* to demonstrate his orthodoxy to the Ḥanābilah, al-Barbahārī (d. 941), one of the most widely respected Ḥanbalī teachers of the day, rejected the work out of hand because in it al-Ashʿarī had not repudiated *kalām* reasoning, nor had he said anything incompatible with his own *kalām* analyses.

Basic Teachings. In its basic elements, the doctrine of al-Ashʿarī is not wholly new. A beginning had been made several generations earlier toward the formation of a conservative, non-Muʿtazilī *kalām,* but its progress had been arrested in the aftermath of the mihnah as a result of the ascendancy of traditionalist anti-intellectualism during and immediately after the reign of the caliph al-Mutawakkil (847–861). Al-Ashʿarī appropriated or adapted a number of elements from various earlier theologians. To a large extent his teaching follows and develops that of Ibn Kullāb (d. 855), who is regarded by later Ashʿarī theologians as one of their own fellows (*aṣḥab*). Al-Ashʿarī's theory of human action, however, is based on a distinction previously formulated by Ḍirār ibn ʿAmr (d. 815) and al-Najjār (d. toward the middle of the ninth century), while some of his discussion of the divine names probably depends upon al-Jubbāʾī. His doctrine on the Qurʾān regarding the distinction between the recitation and the copy on the one hand and the text as the articulate meaning that is read and understood on the other, though based on Ibn Kullāb, is regarded as original by later authorities. While al-Ashʿarī's teaching can be viewed on one level as a synthesis and adaptation of elements already present in one form or another but not hitherto assembled into a single system, it is nonetheless true that out of these elements he constructed a new, conceptually integrated whole of his own.

According to al-Ashʿarī, the Qurʾān and the teaching of the Prophet present a reasoned exposition of the contingency of the world and its dependence upon the deliberate action of a transcendent creator, which, though not expressed in formal language, is complete and rationally probative. Thus, in contrast to the Muʿtazilah, he holds that theological inquiry is not originated autonomously by the mind but is provoked by the claims of a prophet, and that it is because of the rational validity of the prophet Muḥammad's basic teaching that one must accept the entire revelation, including those dogmas that cannot be inferred on purely rational grounds (for example, that God will be visible in the next life), and submit unconditionally to the divine law. Undertaking such theological inquiry is morally obligatory not for any psychological or intellectual reason, but because God has commanded it, and the command is known only in the revelation. With regard to the revelation itself, al-Ashʿarī stands in significant contrast to his followers insofar as he does not employ in any of the works that are available to us the common *kalām* proof for the existence of God, the basic form of which is found in Chrysostom and other patristic writers, but, rather, prefers an argument based entirely and directly on the text of the Qurʾān.

In his discussion of the nature of God and of creatures, al-Ashʿarī employs a formal method based on the Arab grammarians' analysis of predicative sentences. He holds that predications are divided into three categories: (1) those that assert the existence of only the subject itself *(al-nafs, nafs al-mawṣūf)*; (2) those that assert the existence of an "attribute" *(ṣifah, maʿnā)* distinct from the "self" of the subject as such; and (3) those that assert the existence of an action *(fiʿl)* done by the subject. Since "knows" is not synonymous with "exists," the former must, when said of God, imply the existence of a cognition that is somewhat distinct from his essential being *(al-nafs)*. Following a common tradition, al-Ashʿarī holds that God has seven basic "essential attributes": the ability to act (*al-quadrah*), cognition, volition, life, speech, sight, and hearing. Since "perdures" (*bāq*) is not synonymous with "exists," he adds to this list a distinct attribute of "perdurance" (*al-baqāʾ*). On the basis of the revelation al-Ashʿarī also includes as eternal attributes God's hand(s) and face, which are neither understood anthropomorphically as bodily members nor reduced metaphorically to his self or to one of the seven basic eternal attributes. None of these attributes can be fully comprehended and explained by human understanding; each is distinct from the others and from God's "self," though it is true neither that they are identical with God's self nor that they are other than it.

Al-Ashʿarī's view of creation is basically occasionalistic. Whatever exists and is not eternal, God creates, and its existence is his action. Among those events that take place in individuals, however, they distinguish those events that are simply undergone from those that they do intentionally. The former are God's acts alone; the latter occur through an ability to act (*bi-qudrah*) created in a person at the moment the act occurs and are formally referred to as *kasb* or *iktisāb* ("performance" or "doing"; these terms are commonly, but misleadingly, rendered by "acquisition"). What God wills, and only what he wills, comes to exist. Because he is subject to no rule his acts are just and ethically good as such. The objects of God's will are not coextensive with those of his command. The ethical values (*aḥkām*) of human actions are grounded unconditionally in God's command, license, and prohibition, and as God has already informed humanity, he will punish and/or reward individuals in the next life according to their obedience and disobedience in this life. There is no intrinsic relationship between humans' actions and their status in the life to come; God does and will do what he wills, and what he wills is just by definition.

METHOD. Although al-Ashʿarī did work out a comprehensive and coherent theology, he seems to have deliberately restricted the scope of his theological reasoning, which does not go much beyond the presentation of his fundamental theses in such a way that the propositions formally asserted are logically unambivalent on the basis of a rigid set of definitions and principles, and even these are not always explained and even less often argued in the texts. Rational arguments for individual theses are set forth in their most elementary form, sometimes in the form of a Qurʾān citation and, again, on the basis of presuppositions that, even if stated, are not argued. Where argument is based on the authority of scripture, or where a citation of the Qurʾān alludes to and encapsulates a rational argument, the formal principles of the underlying exegesis are presumed known and accepted. Since countertheses and the arguments that support them are logically incompatible with the definitions and principles employed by al-Ashʿarī, they are usually disposed of in a purely formal way. Al-Ashʿarī's surviving dogmatic works are few and quite brief. For some questions, they can be supplemented by citations found in the works of his successors, but even though the later Ashʿarī theologians had access to a large number of his writings, they are unable to state his position on a number of important issues. In some instances they do know Ibn Kullāb's teaching (for example, on whether or not God's essential attributes are denumerable), but sometimes the sources themselves explicitly recognize that what they offer as the teaching of al-Ashʿarī is merely an inference or conjecture. It appears, then, that on a number of questions al-Ashʿarī either refused to commit himself or had not carried his inquiry beyond an elementary level. His fundamental aim seems to have been simply to present the basic sense and truth of the primary Islamic dogmas so that they could be thematically possessed and appropriated in an unambiguous form and to distinguish them from heresy and unbelief in such a way that the error of the latter would be clearly understood and displayed.

LATER INFLUENCE. How rapidly and how widely al-Ashʿarī's theology was adopted by orthodox Muslims has been a matter of debate, as has the question of its ultimate significance in the religious and intellectual history of Sunnī Islam. Its early importance is witnessed by the treatment al-Ashʿarī receives in Ibn al-Nadīm's bio-bibliographical encyclopedia, *Al-fihrist* (The Catalog), composed in 987–988, and in *Al-fiṣal fī al-milal* (Judgments on the Sects), a heresiographical work by the Ẓāhirī jurist and philosopher Ibn Ḥazm of Cordova (d. 1064). Certainly by the latter half of the eleventh century Ashʿarī theology was upheld by the leading Shāfiʿī jurisconsults, and for the historian Ibn Khaldūn (d. 1406) it represents the mainstream of orthodox *kalām.* A number of Ṣūfīs, beginning already with several of the disciples of al-Ḥallāj (d. 922), were Ashʿarī in systematic theology, employing *kalām* as a kind of conceptual, dogmatic foundation to their mystical thought, and others, such as al-Kalābādhī (d. 990), though not strictly Ashʿarī in dogma, were influenced by Ashʿarī teaching. Again, although the school of al-Māturīdī (d. 944) always maintained its theological distinctiveness, Ashʿarī influence appears in some of their works. Similarly, the influence of Ashʿarī language and concepts can be detected even in some later Ḥanbalī *ʿaqīdahs* (outlines of basic doctrine), and in at least one case, the *Muʿtamad fī uṣūl al-dīn* (The Foundation concerning the Basic Doctrines) of the Ḥanbalī *qāḍi* Abū Yaʿlā al-Farrāʾ (d. 1066), several formulations are taken over directly from the theological writings of al-Bāqillānī, a leading Ashʿarī theologian of the preceding generation.

BIBLIOGRAPHY

Translations of works by al-Ashʿarī

Klein, Walter C., trans. *Al-ibānah ʿan uṣūl ad-diyānah* (The eucidation of Islam's foundation). New Haven, 1940. Includes an introduction and notes by the translator.

McCarthy, Richard J., trans. *The Theology of al-Ashʿarī.* Beirut, 1953. Contains both text and translation of *Al-lumaʿ* and *Al-ḥathth ʿalā al-baḥth* (under title *Istiḥsān al-khawḍ fī ʿilm al-kalām*), together with a translation of early biographical sources and of Ibn ʿAsakir's apology against the Ḥanābilah and list of works attributed to al-Ashʿarī.

Spitta, Wilhelm, trans. *Zur Geschichte Abū l-Ḥasan al-Ašʿarī's.* Leipzig, 1870. This study, now outdated, contains a translation of *Al-īmān* (pp. 101–104).

Works about al-Ashʿarī

Allard, Michel. "En quoi consiste l'opposition faite à al-Ashʿarī par ses contemporains ḥanbalites?" *Revue des études islamiques* 28 (1960): 93-105.

Allard, Michel. *Le problème des attributs divins dans la doctrine d'al-Ašʿarī et de ses premiers grands disciples.* Beirut, 1965. This book contains the most thorough and balanced discussion of the problem of al-Ashʿarī's biography and of the authenticity of the extant works.

Frank, R. M. "The Structure of Created Causality according to al-Ašʿarī: An Analysis of *Kitâb al-Lumaʿ,* §§ 82–184." *Studia Islamica* 25 (1966): 13–75.

Frank, R. M. "Al-Ašʿarī's Conception of the Nature and Role of Speculative Reasoning in Theology." In *Proceedings of the Sixth Congress of Arabic and Islamic Studies,* edited by Frithiof Rundgren. Stockholm, 1975. An analysis of the first section of the *Epistle to the People of the Frontier.*

Frank, R. M. "Al-Ashʿarī's *al-Ḥathth ʿalā l-Baḥth.*" *Mélanges de l'Institut Dominicain d'Études Orientales* 18 (1985).

Frank, R. M. "Elements in the Development of the Teaching of al-Ashʿarī." *Le muséon* 98 (1985).

Makdisi, George. "Ashʿarī and the Ashʿarītes in Islamic Religious History." *Studia Islamica* 17 (1962): 37–80; 18 (1963): 19–39. Basing his analysis wholly upon the polemical and apologetic works of al-Ashʿarī and his followers, the author denies the authenticity of *Al-ḥathth ʿalā al-baḥth* and sees al-Ashʿarī as basically a traditionalist.

Rubio, Luciano. "Los Ašʿaríes, teólogos especulativos, Mutakállimes, del Islam." *Ciudad de Dios* 190 (1977): 535–577. An account of several major themes, chiefly causality and action, as presented in the writings of al-Ashʿarī.

R. M. FRANK (1987)

ASHʿARĪYAH.

ASHʿARĪYAH. The theological doctrine of the Ashʿarīyah, the followers of al-Ashʿarī, is commonly regarded as the most important single school of systematic theology in orthodox Islam. The school and its members are commonly referred to in Arabic as *al-Ashʿarīyah* and its members often as *al-ashāʿirah* (the "Ashʿarīs"). Ashʿarī masters during the tenth and eleventh centuries CE most commonly refer to themselves and the school as *ahl al-ḥaqq* ("those who teach the true doctrine") or *ahl al-sunnah wa-al-jamāʿah* ("the adherents of the *sunnah* and the consensus [of the Muslim community]") and sometimes as *ahl al-taḥqīq* ("those whose doctrine is conceptually clear and verified"). It should be noted, however, that other groups, including some opponents of the Ashʿarīyah, use the same expressions, and the first two in particular, to describe themselves. Ashʿarīyah is not, as such, identified with any single juridical tradition (*madhhab*); most Ashʿarī theologians were Shāfiʿī, and some were famous as teachers of Shafiʿi law, but a large number of them were Mālikī, the most famous being the Mālikī *qāḍi* ("judge") al-Bāqillānī.

The history of the school can be divided into two clearly distinguishable periods, the division falling about the beginning of the twelfth century CE. The first period, often referred to as that of classical Ashʿarī theology, is characterized by the formal language, analysis, and argumentation of the Basran *kalām* employed by al-Ashʿarī himself, while the second is characterized by the language, concepts, and formal logic of philosophy *(falsafah),* that is, of the Islamic continuation of Greek philosophy. The school received strong official support under the Seljuk vizier Niẓām al-Mulk (d. 1092), with many of its masters appointed to chairs of the Shāfiʿī law in the colleges (*madrasahs*) that he founded. Many scholars identify the acme of the school with the great Ashʿarī masters of this period. Many, most notably Georges C. Anawati and Louis Gardet, have seen the introduction and adaptation of Aristotelian logic and concepts as analogous to the *via nova* of Western Scholastic theology and accordingly hold that the Ashʿarī thinking of the later period is more sophisticated and more truly theological than that of the earlier period.

PRINCIPAL FIGURES. There is very little concrete data concerning the teaching of al-Ashʿarī's immediate disciples. Abū Bakr al-Qaffāl al-Shāshī, Abū al-Ḥasan al-Bāhilī, and Abū Ṣahl al-Saʿlūkī are regularly cited in the theological writings of later Ashʿarī thinkers, but the only theological work by one of his direct disciples that is known to have survived is the *Taʾwīl al-āyāt al-mushkilah* (The Interpretation of Difficult Verses) of Abū al-Ḥasan al-Ṭabarī. In formulation and conception this work appears to follow the teaching of al-Ashʿarī rigidly: the proof for the contingency of the world and the existence of God, for example, is not the one universally employed by the Ashʿarīyah of succeeding generations, but depends directly on al-Ashʿarī's *Al-lumaʿ* (The Concise Remarks). The most important of al-Ashʿarī's immediate disciples, however, was certainly al-Bāhilī; although al-Qaffāl's student al-Ḥalīmī (d. 1012) is cited with some frequency by later authorities, it is three students of al-Bāhilī who dominate Ashʿarī thinking in the next two generations. These are the *qāḍi* Abū Bakr al-Bāqillānī (d. 1013), Abū Bakr ibn Fūrak (d. 1015), and Abū Isḥāq al-Isfaraʾini (d. 1027).

Several of al-Bāqillānī's theological writings have survived and are published: two compendia of moderate length, *Al-tamhīd* (The Introduction) and *Al-inṣāf* (The Equitable View), and a major work on the miraculous character of the Qurʾān, *Iʿjāz al-Qurʾān* (The Inimitability of the Qurʾān). Of his longest and most important work, *Hidāyat al-mustarshidīn* (The Guidance of Those Who Seek to Be Guided Aright), however, only a part, yet unpublished, of the section on prophecy is presently known. A number of important works that are commonly cited appear not to have survived at all, among them a tract on the ontology of attributes and predicates entitled *Mā yuʿallal wa-mā lā yuʿallal* (What Is Founded in an *ʿIllah* and What Is Not) and *Al-naqḍ al-kabīr* (The Major Critique), which is perhaps a longer recension of his *Naqḍ Al-naqḍ* (The Critique of *The Critique*), a work written in response to the *Naqḍ Al-lumaʿ* (The Critique of [al-Ashʿarī's] *Al-lumaʿ*) composed by the great Muʿtazilī master ʿAbd al-Jabbār (d. 1024). Ibn Fūrak's *Bayān taʾwīl mushkil al-ḥadīth* (The Clear Interpretation of Difficult Traditions) was very popular in later times and survives in many copies, but among his dogmatic writings only a few short works, none of them published, are known to have survived. (The lengthy *Uṣūl al-din* [Basic Doctrines] contained in the Ayasofya collection of Istanbul and attributed to him in several European handbooks is by his grandson.) Of al-Isfarāʾīnī's writings, only one short compendium (*ʿaqīdah*), yet unpublished, is known to have survived, although a large number of theological works are cited by later Ashʿarī writers, among them *Al-jāmiʿ* (The *Summa*), *Al-mukhtaṣar* (The Abridged Compendium), *Al-wasf wa-al-ṣifah* (Predications and Attributes), and *Al-asmāʾ wa-al-ṣifāt* (The Names and Attributes [of God]).

Among the Ashʿarīyah of succeeding generations, the principal figures—some of whose theological works are available and in part published—are ʿAbd al-Qāhir al-Baghdādī (d. 1037), who studied with al-Isfarāʾīnī; Abū Bakr al-Bayhaqī (d. 1056), best known as a traditionist and jurisconsult; Abū al-Qāsim al-Qushayrī (d. 1072), a student of both Ibn Fūrak and al- Isfarāʾīnī, renowned as a teacher and writer on Sufism; his student Abū Saʿd al-Mutawallī (d. 1086), best known as a jurisconsult, and Abū Bakr al-Fūraki (d. 1094), a grandson of Ibn Fūrak and son-in-law of al-Qushayrī. None of the theological writings of Abū al-Qāsim Isfarāʾīnī (d. 1060) have survived, though his commentary on the *Mukhtaṣar* of Abū Isḥāq al-Isfarāʾīnī is often cited along with others of his works. His disciple Abū al-Maʿālī al-Juwaynī (d. 1085), known as Imām al-Ḥaramayn (Imam of the Holy Cities, that is, Mecca and Medina, to which he was forced to flee for a time), was not only one of the foremost Muslim theologians of any period but also the leading Shāfiʿī legist of his age.

A number of al-Juwaynī's dogmatic works have survived and are published; most important his *Irshād* (Guidance), the *Risālah al-niẓāmīyah* (The Short Tract for Niẓām [al-Mulk], twice published under the title *Al-ʿaqidah al-niẓāmīyah*), and *Al-shāmil fī uṣūl al-din* (The Complete Compendium of the Basic Doctrines), which is a very extensive exposition (*taḥrīr*) of al-Bāqillānī's commentary on al-Ashʿarī's *Al-lumaʿ*. A significant portion of *Al-shāmil* is preserved, and the substance of the remainder survives in an abridgement of some two hundred folios by an unknown author, entitled *Al-kāmil fī ikhtiṣār Al-shāmil* (The Perfect Abridgement of *Al-shāmil*). Although the second major period of Ashʿarī theology, already foreshadowed in some of al-Juwaynī's work, is inaugurated by his most famous student, al-Ghazālī, several of his disciples continued to pursue *kalām* in the traditional form, and their surviving works are of great importance as sources for current understanding of the development of the school in the classical period. These are the *Uṣūl al-dīn* (Basic Doctrines) by al-Kiyāʾ al-Harāsī (d. 1110), a highly respected jurisconsult, and *Al-ghunyah fī al-kalām* (Sufficiency in *Kalām*) by Abū al-Qāsim al-Anṣārī (d. 1118), of whose commentary on the *Irshād* of al-Juwaynī a significant fragment is also preserved.

Doctrines and Methods of the Classical Period. The school of al-Ashʿarī universally holds that the sources of theological knowledge are, in order of priority, the Qurʾān, the *sunnah*, the consensus of the Muslim community, and human reason, and their basic teaching varies little from one master to another during the classical period. God's being is eternal (*qadīm*) and unconditioned; in his "self" (*nafs, dhāt*) and in his "essential attributes" (*ṣifāt al-nafs*), his nonexistence is impossible. Every being other than God and his essential attributes exists as an action of his that is finite, corporeal, and temporal, and therefore altogether unlike him. Temporal beings are referred to as God's "attributes of action" (*ṣifāt afʿālihi*), since it is they that are asserted to exist when any predicate of action such as "creates" or "sustains" is said of him.

Though questioning the denumerability of the "essential attributes" of God, the Ashʿarīyah all recognize seven principal ones: life, cognition, volition, the ability to act, sight, hearing, and speaking. They hold these to be real (*thābitah*) and distinguishable, as what is asserted by "wills" is distinct from what is asserted by "knows," and so forth; they are neither simply identical with God's "self" nor are they other than it, since "other" implies separability and therefore contingency. The objects of his ability to create are infinite and are known to him as such. What he knows will be, he wills to be, and nothing comes to be that he does not will; whatever comes to be, comes to be through his ability to act when and as his will determines.

As God is one, so each of his essential attributes is one: he knows an infinity of objects in a single, eternal cognition and wills the existence of an indefinite number of beings in a single, eternal volition. Since he has neither needs nor desires, he cannot be said to act for a motive or reason. Neither his acts nor his commands can be rationalized; since he is the absolute Lord of creation, they are right and just *(ʿadl)* simply because they are his, independently of any apparent good or harm they may constitute or cause with respect to any creature.

God makes himself known to the believer in a special way in the Qurʾān, and one of the issues most vehemently contested between the Ashʿarīyah and their opponents, both the Muʿtazilah and the Hanābilah, is the validity and sense of the thesis "the Qurʾān is the uncreated speech of God." According to the Ashʿarī analysis, "speech" or "speaking" (*kalām*) refers to an interior intention that is materially signified and expressed by spoken, written, and remembered expressions *(ḥurūf)*. God's eternal attribute of speaking is one and undivided: it becomes differentiated into statements, commands, and so on in its material articulation in a particular language by means of which it is revealed and manifested. Thus the believer's recitation (*qirāʾah*) of the Qurʾān, like the written copy, is created, but what is recited (*maqrūʾ*), that is, the intention made present and understood, is the uncreated speaking of God.

The Qurʾān is miraculous not merely because it foretold and foretells future events, but in a unique way because of the sublimity of its rhetorical expression. According to the Ashʿarīyah God is properly described only by those expressions "by which he has described himself," that is, those given in the Qurʾān and in the tradition. Although God's being is beyond the grasp of human intelligence, these predicates, known as "his most beautiful names" (*asmāʾuhu al-ḥusnā*), are known to be true and adequate. The Ashʿarīyah analyze them systematically, first, in order to reduce them referentially to God's "self," to one of his essential attributes, or to one of his "attributes of action," and second, to examine their specific connotations. That God is in some real sense visible they hold to be rationally demonstrable; that he will be seen by the believers in the next life is known only by revelation.

Ontological bases of Ashʿarī thought. According to the Ashʿarī theologians of the classical period, the world consists of two kinds of primary entities: atoms, which are conjoined to form bodies, and the entitative "attributes" or "accidents" that reside in these atoms, each of which contains a single discrete instance of each class *(jins)* of accident or its contrary. The atoms perdure through many instants, but the "accidents," since they exist for only an instant, are continually created anew by God. Events are the coming to be of entities, and since God causes the existence of every entity, the causation of one event by another *(tawallud)* is denied. The system is thus fundamentally occasionalistic, and the interrelationships between distinct entities as they exist separately in temporal succession are little discussed as such in the available texts.

Events that are properly described as human actions (*aksāb*) are defined as those that are the immediate objects of a "created ability to act" *(qudrah muḥdathah)* and are limited to those events that take place in the agent as and insofar as they are intended by the agent. As entities they are ascribed to God, as his action; under other descriptions they qualify the part, and only the part, of the agent in which they occur and are so ascribed to him as his action. The human agent is properly said to be able to perform the act he or she performs only at the moment it is actually performed; only at this instant does God create in the human the ability to perform it. On this basis the Ashʿarī theologians are accused of holding that individuals are in some instances commanded by God to do what they are not able to do (*taklīf mā lā yuṭāq*). Though this is formally true, appropriate distinctions are made between an agent's not being able to do something (*ghayr qādir*) and being unable (*ʿājiz*) to do it, and accordingly between voluntary omission (*tark*) and involuntary omission. This analysis of human actions was radically opposed by the Muʿtazilah, who considered it to be deterministic. Viewed from the standpoint of the Ashʿarī school, however, the issue is not one of freedom and determinism, but of whether or not any event can occur independently of God's will and action.

In fact, the question of determinism is treated ambivalently in most of the texts that survived. Those events that occur regularly as the apparent consequences of human actions are not considered as true effects of the basic act, but are created by God occasionalistically according to the consistency of the "convention" (*ʿādah*) that he freely follows in ordering material events. Miracles are events that God has created with a radical departure from the sequence in which he usually makes things happen, in order to verify the divine origin of a prophet's message. Belief (*īmān*) is essentially the assent (*taṣdīq*) of the believer to the truth of God's message transmitted by the prophet, and one in whom this assent occurs is by definition a believer (*muʾmin*). The assent requires, but is distinct from, cognition and entails, but is distinct from, the performance of what God commands. God commands the belief of the unbeliever but does not will it (otherwise the unbeliever would believe). The obedience of the believers is neither the cause nor the necessary condition of their reward in the life to come; it is simply a criterion arbitrarily decreed by God.

Ashʿarī methods. The Ashʿarī school disapproves of *taqlīd,* the unreflecting assent to religious dogmas by simple acquiescence to recognized authority. They hold that, at least on a basic level, the believers ought to know the sense and coherence of what they hold to be true and should rationally understand the validity of its foundation in the Qurʾān and the teaching of the Prophet. According to the traditionalist method, creedal and theological statements are established and verified through the collection of a consistent body of citations from the Qurʾān, the Prophet, and recognized authorities among the first generations of Muslims, so that any deviant thesis can be excluded on grounds of contextual incompatibility with these canonical sources. By contrast, the Ashʿarī method proceeds to a formal, logical, and conceptual analysis of the terms of each thesis on the basis of a rigid set of definitions and distinctions, axioms and principles, which both explain the elementary sense and foundation of the thesis and exclude any counterthesis as unfounded or inconsistent in some respect.

Among the most conspicuous aspects of the Ashʿarī texts are the formalism that dominates both their expression and their intention and the narrow delimitation of topics as defined by the particular thesis. Since the Ashʿarīyah, unlike the Muʿtazilah, did not consider it necessary to found their theology autonomously on philosophical reasoning, the theoretical principles and implications of their doctrine are not extensively set forth in the texts. One begins from and always returns to the basic definitions and distinctions, which are presented and argued in what often appears to be a rather peremptory manner. Even where positions are argued at great length in terms of a variety of questions and against a number of counterpositions, as in al-Juwaynī's *Al-shāmil,* the discussion of the basic issue seldom advances much beyond its original statement. Consequently, and especially given the limited sources currently available, for a number of important questions it is extremely difficult to interpret what is explicitly presented within the broader implications of the question. For this reason, the Ashʿarī *kalām* of the classical period has been considered chiefly a dialectic exercise and one that is mostly, if not entirely, apologetic in character. The formal disputation (*munāẓarah*) was from the outset a central element in the study and cultivation of the religious sciences in Islam, and as in the case of Western Scholasticism, it largely determined the literary expression of Muslim theology.

A number of leading Ashʿarī theologians wrote works on dialectics *(jadal).* Although the form of their presentation is often dialectical, few if any classical Ashʿarī works are dialectically apologetic in the strict sense of the term, for both the question and the argument are always presented and elaborated within the narrow context of the formal and theoretical presuppositions of the school's own doctrine, not those presupposed by the counterthesis or any other that might presumably be acceptable to both disputants. Even so, their Muslim opponents, at first chiefly the Muʿtazilah and later the Karrāmīyah, had a significant catalytic effect on the development of Ashʿarī theology in the classical period: They were not simply a source of countertheses that had to be dealt with, but were also significant figures within the religious and intellectual milieu, and as such were, along with the Ḥanābilah, competitors for the allegiance of the Muslim community and in some cases for patronage too.

Philosophical problems. It was apparently under pressure from the Muʿtazilī school of Basra, then approaching its zenith, that Ashʿarī theology made rapid advances in sophistication toward the beginning of the eleventh century. Concepts that had remained somewhat vague or inadequately elaborated in the work of al-Ashʿarī and his immediate disciples underwent revision and redefinition, while principles and constructs that had not been sufficiently thought through were redefined and the system as a whole brought into more rigorous coherence. In the process, a certain diversity of teaching became apparent in the works of the leading masters. The distinction between the necessarily existent (the eternal) and the contingent (*al-muḥdath,* the temporal) was fundamental.

Beyond this, most of the Ashʿarī theologians of the classical period understood being univocally, to the extent that terms meaning "entity" *(shayʾ, dhāt, mawjūd)* were applied to the atoms and their accidental properties alike. The Ashʿarīyah of this period were basically nominalists. God determines the various kinds of beings, creating each with its distinctive characteristics; the names of the classes or kinds of things by which their individual instances are called are given originally in God's instruction *(tawqīf),* not by human convention. The basic adjectival or descriptive terms that ascribe distinct or accidental properties to things are derived from the names of those properties, as *ʿālim* (knows) is derived from *ʿilm* (cognition) to describe a subject in which a cognition exists.

The question of what qualifications or predicates of a being are or are not grounded (*muʿallalah*) in distinct properties was the subject of considerable discussion. Because the foundation of the system lay in its analytic formalism, problems inevitably arose concerning the universality of many terms. These were especially acute since they held that terms that name both human and divine attributes (*life, cognition, volition,* for example) are basically univocal, while asserting at the same time that God and his eternal attributes are wholly unlike created beings and so belong to no class (*jins*) of entities: It is known that these terms name God's attributes truly and adequately because they are used by God in the Qurʾān. Formulations to the effect that God's will, for example, "is a volition unlike volitions" stated but did not adequately resolve the problem.

Following a formula found already in al-Ashʿarī, Ibn Fūrak and others held that things simply "deserve" (*istaḥaqqa*) to be called by the terms that describe them properly and truly. Any subject in which there exists a cognition, for example, "deserves" to be described by the expression *knows,* and the cognition is, in each case, the reason or cause of the predication *(ʿillat al-waṣf);* what they have in common (*jāmiʿ*) is this cause or reason. What any two cognitions, on the other hand, have in common is simply that they deserve to be named by the expression *cognition.* Some authorities will speak of their having the same "particular characteristics" (*khawāṣṣ, khaṣaʾiṣ*). Al-Bāqillānī, however, adapting a concept from his Muʿtazilī contemporaries, posits the reality of non-entitative attributes or "states" (*aḥwāl*) of things, which are the referential or ontological basis of the universality of descriptive terms. In this way, every cognition, whether created or uncreated (eternal), is qualified by a state of "being a cognition" (*ʿilmīyah*), and every subject in which there exists a cognition is qualified by a state of "being cognizant" (*ʿālimīyah*). Similarly a human action *(kasb)* is qualified by a state of being a human action (*kasbīyah*). Among the Ashʿarī masters of the classical period, only al-Juwaynī accepted and defended al-Bāqillānī's concept of "states."

There were a number of other difficulties and differences among the Ashʿarī theologians of the period, though these are less clearly presented in the available sources. The school agreed, for example, that God is able to create an infinite number of individuals belonging to any given class of beings, but did not agree as to whether or not he is able to create an infinity of classes other than those he has actually created. The question of whether, and in what way, God's will is general or particular with regard to its objects was debated, but exactly how the problem was treated by the various authors remains unclear. Likewise, al-Juwaynī, and he alone, it would seem, held that God's knowledge of creatures is general and not particular, but again the available sources do not provide an adequate view of his thought on the question. Though the same basic distinctions are made with regard to the createdness of human actions, and the same set of basic propositions are formally maintained by all authorities, there are differences concerning the way the concrete relationships between the elements involved in human actions are understood. Some, among them al-Juwaynī, hold that the relationship between the created ability to act and its object is simply intentional. The antecedent or concomitant actuality of motivation and volition is seldom discussed in the available texts, since it is not formally pertinent, given the way the basic question of the createdness of human actions is posed and treated. The most conspicuous deviation from the normal form of the school's teaching in this period is found in al-Juwaynī's *Risālah* (or *ʿAqīdah*) dedicated to Niẓām al-Mulk. Although he maintains the basic theological dogmas of the school, the way in which they are presented and explained is new and, in the case of some major elements, irreconcilable not only with the teaching of his predecessors but also with that of his own major theological writings. In many respects the work anticipates the fundamental trend of the following period.

LATER ASHʿARĪYAH. With the rapidly increasing assimilation of ancient and Hellenistic learning, both scientific and philosophical, and its integration into the intellectual life of Islam, the change in both language and conceptualization that characterizes the second major period of Ashʿarī theology was inevitable: the urgent need of Sunnī orthodoxy to counter the growing influence of Ismaʿīlī gnosticism and of the philosophers (*falāsifah*), particularly the Neoplatonism of Ibn Sīnā (Avicenna), made it imperative. The three most creative theologians of this period were al-Ghazālī (d. 1111), al-Shahrastānī (d. 1153), a student of Abū al-Qāsim al-Anṣāri, and Fakhr al-Dīn al-Rāzī (d. 1209). The major Ashʿarī texts surviving from this period are more numerous and also more diverse than those of the earlier school, since many of them, especially those of al-Ghazālī and al-Rāzī, enjoyed great popularity over the centuries, while the earlier works, rapidly outdated, became progressively more remote in concept and expression. The apologetic and polemic of the Ashʿarī theologians of this period engage their rationalistic opponents directly, not merely in their own language, but on purely rational grounds, as in al-Ghazālī's famous refutation of Ibn Sīnā's philosophy, *Tahāfut al-falāsifah* (The Incoherence of the Philosophers), and in al-Shahrastānī's *Muṣāraʿat al-falāsifah* (Wrestling the Philosophers Down). Where the formal and theoretical principles of their doctrine were not much discussed in the texts of the classical period, they are now set forth in extensive detail.

The general attitudes of the three great masters of the period and the character of their thought manifest significant differences, however. Al-Ghazālī's view of the nature and value of formal, systematic theology, in particular, was not shared by other Ashʿarī thinkers either before or after him. In the wake of intellectual and religious crises, he became convinced that the only valid and certain knowledge of God is given in direct mystical experience. As a result, where the common Ashʿarī tradition held that systematic theology furnishes a sound and valuable, if not essential, conceptual foundation for one's belief, al-Ghazālī insists that it is wholly inadequate. Since it cannot be grounded in autonomous human reason, moreover, it is at best founded in *taqlīd* and, he concludes, has no valid function other than as a dialectical apologetic. He did, however, produce two *kalām* compendia in the traditional form, the *Iqtiṣād fī al-iʿtiqād* (The Just Mean in Belief) and the *Qawāʿid al-ʿaqāʾid* (Foundations of the Creeds, which is book 2 of the first part of his *Iḥyāʾ ʿulūm al-dīn* [The Vitalization of the Religious Sciences]). While these works by no means embody his entire theology, they are demonstrative of his dogmatic thought as it relates to the Ashʿarī tradition.

In these works, as in al-Shahrastānī's *Nihāyat al-iqdām fī ʿilm al-kalām* (The Furthermost Steps in the Science of *Kalām*), one sees not so much a sudden and radical break with the past as an effort to rethink and recast the basic dogmas within an expanded theoretical framework, one that required and produced a definite, and ultimately definitive, movement away from the rigid kind of analysis and close restriction of topics that had characterized the school since its foundation. The traditional formulation of the basic dogmatic theses is thus consistently maintained, but the exposition and argumentation of most of them is in many respects new and often impressive.

Against what they regard as an impoverished conception of God's being held by the *falāsifah,* al-Ghazālī and al-Shahrastānī set forth an understanding of the traditional seven essential attributes that, in taking them more as aspects of God's "essence" than as distinct properties, is somewhat analogous to the position of the Muʿtazilī school of Basra. The relation between God's eternal power, knowledge, and will and their temporal objects is more thoroughly and explicitly explored than in earlier Ashʿarī texts and in different, more Aristotelian terms. God's speaking is conceived in terms akin to cognition, with all modalities of interior speech tending to be reduced to propositions. The attribute of "perdurance" (*al-baqāʾ*), previously rejected by a number of Ashʿarī masters, is considered simply as a negative concept ("perdures" = "does not cease to exist") by al-Ghazālī, who explicitly rejects the earlier conception of the ontological grounding of attributes.

Where the classical doctrine of the school had held that all beings other than God are corporeal, the Ashʿarī theologians now recognize the existence of a host of "spirits" (*arwāḥ*) belonging to the "upper world" (*al-ʿālam al-aʿlā*). The atomistic conception of material bodies continues to be stated in much the same terms as before, but on another level, living beings tend to be talked of not as mere composites of atoms and their discrete "accidents," but as beings having a real, essential unity. The conception of God as the sole cause of the existence of every contingent being is maintained, though now discussed and argued with somewhat different terminology, as is the thesis of the createdness of human actions, which continues to be set forth on the basis of the same set of distinctions as in the texts of the classical period. The occasionalistic language that characterizes classical Ashʿarī writing is formally retained, but its radical tone is to some extent mitigated and the function of secondary causes plainly recognized.

The adoption of Aristotelian psychology is of signal importance. The changing perspective of the Ashʿarī *kalām* is perhaps most conspicuously exemplified in al-Ghazālī's discussion of what is morally good and bad, right and wrong. The traditional Ashʿarī conception of ethical valuations in terms of obligation based in God's unconditioned command, license, and prohibition he rationalizes through a sort of utilitarianism of virtue: one ought always to act for his own ultimate good (that is, that to be achieved in the next life), and this is uniquely made known in God's revelation. He accounts for good (*ḥasan*) and bad (*qabīḥ*) not directly in what is commanded and forbidden but, harmonizing Ṣūfī teaching with an Aristotelian notion of virtue, in terms of ends (*aghrāḍ*), where moral perfection is measured by one's nearness to God.

If in their *kalām* works al-Ghazālī and al-Shahrastānī seem to have harmonized or juxtaposed disparate conceptual frameworks in a synthetic unity, this is not the case with al-Rāzī, who maintained a profound commitment to the Muslim philosophical tradition. He wrote extensively on philosophy (as well as on medicine and other sciences), and in his principal *kalām* works, *Maʿālim uṣūl al-dīn* (The Landmarks of Fundamental Doctrine) and the much longer *Kitāb al-arbaʿīn fī uṣūl al-dīn* (The Forty [Questions] concerning Fundamental Doctrine), as also in his monumental commentary on the Qurʾān, one finds Ashʿarī theology almost fully adapted to the conceptual universe of the philosophical tradition. Indeed, it seems possible that in some places al-Rāzī may follow his philosophical sources (chiefly Ibn Sīnā) so far as to compromise one or more of the fundamental theological tenets of the school. The number and diversity of his works are so great, however, that with the present state of knowledge it is not possible to come to a firm assessment of his thought.

After al-Rāzī, Ashʿarī theology is continued chiefly in a series of manuals eclectically dependent upon the great writers of the past. The most famous of these, *Al-mawāqif fī uṣūl al-dīn* (The Stages in Fundamental Doctrine) of ʿAḍud al-Dīn al-Ījī (d. 1355), has continued to serve as a textbook on theology to the present day. Among the various commentaries written on it, the most important and widely used is that of al-Jurjānī (d. 1413), and together with this text the *Mawāqif* has gone through a large number of printed editions since the early nineteenth century.

Because of the differences in language and conceptualization between the Ashʿarī theology of the classical period and that of later times, especially after al-Rāzī, it is impossible to define or characterize the tradition in terms of a single way of conceiving, formulating, and dealing with theological and metaphysical problems. The original success of Ashʿarī theology stemmed from the kind of coherent balance it achieved between rational understanding and a religious sense that was rooted in a basically conservative reading of the Qurʾān and the *sunnah.* Its development followed the religious and intellectual evolution of Sunnī Islam. The unity of the school lies largely in its common adherence to a basic set of theses, which sets it apart from other Muslim schools of speculative theology, such as the Māturīdīyah, on the one hand, and in its conceptual rationalization of these theses, which sets it apart from the more rigid traditionalists, on the other. Above all, it is the tradition's sense of its own continuity, beginning with the immediate disciples of al-Ashʿarī, that allows it to be identified by itself and others as Ashʿarī.

SEE ALSO Ashʿarī, al-; Attributes of God, article on Islamic Concepts; Falsafah; Free Will and Predestination, article on Islamic Concepts; Ghazālī, Abu Hamid al-; Iʿjāz; Ījī, ʿAdud al-Din al-; Kalām; Occasionalism.

BIBLIOGRAPHY

Sources

Ess, Joseph van. *Die Erkenntnislehre des ʿAdudaddin al-Īcī, Übersetzung und Kommentar des ersten Buches seiner Mawāqif.*

Wiesbaden, 1966. The extensive commentary here presents a vast amount of valuable material on the history of a large number of questions treated by the Ashʿarīyah and other Muslim theologians from the earliest period.

Frank, R. M. "Two Short Dogmatic Works of Abū l-Qāsim al-Qushayrī: 'Lumaʿ fī l-iʿtiqād.'" *Mélanges de l'Institut Dominicain d'Études Orientales* 15 (1982): 53–74.

Frank, R. M. "Al-Fuṣūl fī l-uṣūl: Part Two." *Mélanges de l'Institut Dominicain d'Études Orientales* 16 (1983): 59–94.

Kholeif, Fathalla. *A Study on Fakhr al-Dīn al-Rāzī and His Controversies in Transoxiana.* Beirut, 1966. Contains text and translation of al-Rāzī's *Munāẓarat fī-mā warāʾ al-nahr* together with a somewhat superficial commentary.

Klopfer, Helmut, ed. and trans. *Das Dogma des Imâm al-Ḥaramain al-Djuwainī und sein Werk al-ʿAqīdat an-niẓâmīya.* Cairo, 1958. A very brief discussion of al-Juwaynī's teaching followed by the translation of the Nizamian creed.

Köbert, Raimund. *Bayān muškil al-aḥadīt des Ibn Fūrak, Auswahl nach den Handschriften in Leipzig, Leiden, London und dem Vatikan.* Analecta Orientalia, vol. 22. Rome, 1941. Although it does not contain the entire text, this edition and translation of Ibn Fūrak's *Interpretation of Difficult Traditions* does have the author's preface (omitted in Eastern editions of the work!), which is of considerable importance for understanding the principles of Ashʿarī theology and exegesis in the period.

Luciani, J.-D., ed. and trans. *El-Irchâd par l'Imâm El-Harameïn.* Paris, 1938.

McCarthy, Richard J. *Freedom and Fulfillment: An Annotated Translation of al-Ghazālī's al-Munqidh min al-Ḍalāl and Other Relevant Works of al-Ghazālī.* Boston, 1980. Al-Ghazālī is one of the most studied and translated of Muslim religious writers; this work contains a fulsome discussion of his personality and thought and an excellent critical bibliography in which studies on al-Ghazālī and translations of his other works are listed and evaluated.

Commentaries

Allard, Michel. *Le problème des attributs divins dans la doctrine d'al-Ašʿarī et de ses premiers grands disciples.* Beirut, 1965. A detailed study of the texts and teaching of al-Bāqillānī, al-Baghdādī, al-Bayhaqī, and al-Juwaynī; a valuable work.

Bouman, J. *Le conflit autour du Coran et la solution d'al-Bâqillânī.* Amsterdam, 1959.

Frank, R. M. "Moral Obligation in Classical Muslim Theology." *Journal of Religious Ethics* 11 (1983): 204–233. A general analysis of the theology of moral action in classical Ashʿarī thought.

Frank, R. M. "Bodies and Atoms: The Ashʿarīte Analysis." In *Medieval Islamic Thought: Studies in Honor of George F. Hourani,* edited by M. E. Marmura, pp. 39–53. Toronto, 1984. A study of several basic concepts and their development during the period of the classical Ashʿarīyah.

Gardet, Louis, and Georges C. Anawati. *Introduction à la théologie musulmane* (1948). 2d ed. Paris, 1970. Still the best introduction to the general topic and to the role and character of Ashʿarī theology in Islam.

Gimaret, Daniel. *Théories de l'acte humain en théologie musulmane.* Études musulmanes, vol. 24. Paris, 1980. Contains a detailed account of the teaching of al-Ashʿarī and the most important Ashʿarī thinkers into the sixteenth century CE, together with translations and paraphrases of portions of a number of important works.

Hourani, George F. "A Revised Chronology of Ghazālī's Writings." *Journal of the American Oriental Society* 104 (1984): 289–302.

Jabre, Farid. *La notion de la 'Maʿrifa' chez Ghazali.* Beirut, 1958. A study of al-Ghazālī's understanding of the nature of religious knowledge and human knowledge of God.

Rubio, Luciano. "Los Asʿaríes, teólogos especulativos, Mutakállimes, del Islam." *Ciudad de Dios* 190 (1977): 577–605; 192 (1979): 355–391; 193 (1980): 47–83. An account, without much analysis, of the teaching of al-Bāqillānī, al-Juwaynī, and al-Ghazālī concerning creation and human action.

Watt, W. Montgomery. "The Authenticity of the Works Attributed to al-Ghazālī." *Journal of the Royal Asiatic Society* (1952): 24–45.

Watt, W. Montgomery. *The Formative Period of Islamic Thought.* Edinburgh, 1973. More a study of the period than of theology. An excellent introduction to the historical context of classical Ashʿarī thought.

R. M. FRANK (1987)

ASHERAH SEE ATHIRAT

ASHER BEN YEḤI'EL

ASHER BEN YEḤI'EL (c. 1250–1327), known as Rabbenu ("our teacher") Asher or as R'oSH, the acronym of that epithet; Talmudist and rabbinic legal authority. Born and educated in Germany, Asher was the leading disciple of the outstanding German rabbinic scholar of his age, Me'ir ben Barukh of Rothenburg. The turbulence disrupting German Jewish life impelled him to emigrate in 1303. He eventually settled in Toledo; that a man of such alien background was accepted as head of the Toledo rabbinical court reflects the power of his learning and his personality.

In Spain, Asher was immediately embroiled in a Kulturkampf over the study of philosophy. The product of an exclusively Talmud-centered curriculum, he did not fully understand all the issues involved (he declined to answer a legal query concerning the astrolabe because, he said, "It is an instrument with which I am not familiar"). Asher hesitated to support the ban promulgated by Shelomoh ben Avraham Adret proscribing the study of Greek philosophy until age twenty-five, because this implied that such study was permissible later, and he believed it should be prohibited throughout life. He ultimately endorsed the ban to ensure that failure to do so would not be misunderstood as support for philosophy. His was the most conservative position taken by any major protagonist in the conflict.

Asher's legal works, which emerged from intensive study of the Talmud, are of three kinds: (1) commentaries on two orders of the Mishnah and several Talmudic tractates; (2) *to-*

safot, brief excursuses on specific problems in the Talmudic text, which brought together recent German and Spanish insights; and (3) a codification called *Pisqei ha-R'osh.* Following the order of the Talmud and covering most of its tractates, *Pisqei ha-R'osh* integrated the Talmudic argument with decisions of post-Talmudic authorities to arrive at the operative law. Asher condemned the practice of rendering legal decisions based on Maimonides' *Mishneh Torah* by those not expert in the Talmudic sources.

Asher's *responsa,* or replies to legal questions, are among the more important and influential of this genre. He was frequently called upon to interpret communal ordinances and their relationship to classical Jewish law, and to decide which local Spanish customs should be honored (e.g., the use of capital or corporal punishment in cases of blasphemy or informing) and which should be opposed. *Responsum* 55 moves from the specific issue, concerning a wife's right to dispose of her assets as she desired through a will, to a significant debate over general principles of jurisprudence. Asher rejected the use of philology, philosophical logic, and commonsense argumentation in order to defend the integrity of the halakhic decision-making process, insisting that philosophy and Torah are "two opposites, irreconcilable, that will never dwell together."

A bridge between the great rabbinic centers of Germany and of Spain, Asher and his sons had a lasting impact on the development of Jewish law. One son, Yehdah, succeeded him as rabbi in Toledo; another, Ya'aqov, used his father's legal oeuvre as the basis for his own magnum opus, the *Arba'ah ṭurim,* a code of operative Jewish law with a new structure independent of the Talmud and earlier codes, which became the basis for Yosef Karo's *Shulḥan 'arukh.*

Bibliography

The most detailed bio-bibliographical monograph on Asher, his disciples, and his descendants is Alfred Freimann's "Ascher b. Jechiel, Sein Leben und Wirken, " *Jahrbuch der jüdisch-literarischen Gesellschaft* 12 (1918): 237–317, and "Die Ascheriden, 1267–1391," *Jahrbuch der jüdisch-literarischen Gesellschaft* 13 (1920): 142–254. Yitzhak F. Baer assessed Asher's communal leadership at Toledo in Historical context in *A History of the Jews in Christian Spain,* vol. 1 (Philadelphia, 1961), pp. 316–325. A provocative analysis of the jurisprudential issues in *responsum* 55 is provided in J. L. Teicher's "Laws of Reason and Laws of Religion: A Conflict in Toledo Jewry in the Fourteenth Century," in *Essays and Studies Presented to Stanley Arthur Cook,* edited by D. Winton Thomas (London, 1950), pp. 83–94. More technical treatment of the Talmudic writings is available in Hebrew: see Haim Chernowitz's *Toledot ha-posqim,* vol. 2 (New York, 1947), pp. 144–160; E. E. Urbach's *Ba'alei ha-tosafot,* 4th ed. (Jerusalem, 1980), vol. 2, pp. 586–599; and a superb index to the subjects and sources of the *responsa, Mafteaḥ ha-she'elot ve-ha-teshuvot: Shu"t ha-R'osh* (Jerusalem, 1965), by Menahem Elon.

New Sources

Gutwirth, Eleazar. "Asher b. Yehiel e Israel Israeli: actitudes hispano-judías hacia el árabe." *Creencias y culturas* (1998): 97–111.

Ta-Shma, Israel Moses. "Between East and West: Rabbi Asher b. Yehi'el and His Son Rabbi Ya'akov." In *Studies in Medieval Jewish History and Literature,* vol. 3, edited by Isadore Twersky and Jay M. Harris, pp. 179–196. Cambridge, Mass., 2000.

Washofsky, Mark R. "Asher ben Yehiel and the 'Mishneh Torah' of Maimonides: A New Look at Some Old Evidence." *AJMT* III (1988): 147–157.

Marc Saperstein (1987)
Revised Bibliography

ASHES are the irreducible dry residue of fire. They may be burnt offerings, such as the cremation of a human body, the sacrificial burning of an animal, or the ritual burning of a plant. Ashes have religious significance as the substance remaining after the divine living energy of sacred fire has departed from a living being or has acted to purge, purify, destroy, volatilize, punish, consume, sublimate, or extract the essence of some created thing. Ashes variously manifest and represent the residue or effect of sacred fire in its manifold creative and negating functions. As hierophanies of power and as sacred symbols, ashes are connected with rites of penitence, mourning, sacrifice, fertility, purification, healing, and divination.

In certain myths dealing with origins, ashes are the material from which things are made. For example, the San depict the Milky Way as being made of ashes, as do the Macoví, for whom the Milky Way is made of the ashes of the Celestial Tree. In Aztec myth humankind itself is made of ashes. Likewise, participants in the Ash Wednesday rite of the Roman Catholic Church are reminded penitentially that they are but the stuff of ashes: "Memento, homo, quia cinis es; in cinerem reverteris."

Ashes, together with any other residue left once the sacrificial fire has extracted the living essence of an offering, are manifestations of sacred renunciation. In certain spiritual disciplines, the rubbing of ashes on the body represents the renunciation or burning up of energic or libidinal attachments to life for the sake of spiritual development or enlightenment. For example, in Hindu mythology the god Śiva, the divine paradigm of yogins, burns up all the other gods with a glance from his third eye, which possesses the vision that penetrates to the essential nullity of all forms. Śiva then rubs the gods' ashes on his body. The yogins rub the ashes of the sacred fire on their bodies as a symbol of having sublimated the fiery power of procreation or lust (*kāma*). The whiteness of the ashes is referred to as the glow of the ashes of the yogins' semen.

Ashes, by connection with the cleansing power of the divine fiery energy, have the power to purify. For example, in the Red Heifer ritual of the Hebrews the ashes of the sacrificed animal's body are mixed with water and sprinkled on a person who is ritually unclean from contact with a corpse. Ritual cleanliness is also achieved by the *brahmans* in India by rubbing the body with ashes or bathing it in ashes before performing religious rites.

Covering one's clothes and body in ashes is a part of various rituals of mourning, humiliation, and atonement. Wearing ashes exteriorizes or manifests spiritual states of loss, sorrow, emptiness, or worthlessness before the divine power. For example, in the Arunta tribe the widow of the deceased covers herself during mourning rites in the ashes of her husband. In the Bible Job humbles himself before Yahveh, saying, "I knew you then only by hearsay; but now, having seen you with my own eyes, I retract all I have said, and in dust and ashes I repent" (*Jb.* 42:5f.).

The pattern, or tendency, of fiery divine life-forces is interpreted by means of the pattern of ashes made during divinatory rites. The Maya Indians in Yucatán, for example, use this type of oracle to determine the particular divinity responsible for a child's life. Possibly the idea behind this practice is similar to the idea of various North American Indian peoples who regard the life patterns in the palm and fingertips of a person's hand as traces of the divine energy ordinarily manifested as wind or breath.

Finally, ashes as the residue of life manifest the fiery divine life-force itself and are used in fertility rites to stimulate the life energy of crops and flocks. Thus in many European rites, such as those celebrated at Easter and on Saint John's Day, a human figure of straw representing the vegetation spirit is burned, and the ashes are scattered on the fields to stimulate the growth of crops. Likewise, in ancient Rome, the ashes from sacred fires of animal sacrifices were fed to flocks in order to stimulate their fertility and their production of milk.

BIBLIOGRAPHY

Further discussion can be found in W. Brede Kristensen's *The Meaning of Religion: Lectures in the Phenomenology of Religion* (The Hague, 1960).

RICHARD W. THURN (1987)

ASHI (c. 352–424/7), the leading sixth-generation Babylonian amora. A student of Kahana, Ashi was reputedly based in the city of Mata Meḥasya for sixty years. He served as judge of a local Jewish court and as community administrator, positions that enabled him to implement rabbinic law in many areas; he expounded scripture and taught oral law to disciples, whom he trained in his court, and to other Jews at large, whom he tried to persuade to follow rabbinic norms. His reported ability to enforce Sabbath and other laws previously not widely enforced by rabbis suggests that he had greater impact on Jewry than his predecessors. Disciples and colleagues in particular revered him and believed that he was respected by the exilarch (the lay Jewish leadership sponsored by the Persian government) and even in the court of the Persian king.

A Talmudic account mentions that Ashi ordered a crumbling synagogue to be pulled down but had his bed put into it to ensure that it be completely rebuilt (B.T., *B.B.* 3b). This story suggests not only a belief in his power but also the means to which he had to resort to activate the community. The dictum that he "combined Torah and greatness" conveys the rabbinic view that he took over prerogatives of, and even instructed, the exilarch. But this is inconsistent with sources that depict rabbis as solicitous of the exilarch's staff. In actuality, the exilarch may have brought his circles closer to the rabbis but, in the process, used them to bolster his own power.

It is as a teacher that Ashi is especially remembered. He extended rabbinic law to cover more refined issues in diverse areas from the liturgy to civil law and addressed personal ethics such as the importance of humility. As the dictum "Ashi and Rabina' are the end of *hora'ah* [instruction]" notes, Ashi marked a turning point in intellectual development. The statement is usually held to mean that Ashi redacted the Talmud, although later editors may have restructured the discussions. In recent scholarship, Ashi is seen as not a redactor but the last named master who employed categorical statements, which later anonymous masters (between 427 and 500) expanded and wove into elaborate arguments and which final savoraic editors revamped and restructured. This new assessment credits Ashi with considerable impact, since it implies that rabbis after Ashi believed they could not teach independently but only rework earlier thinking.

SEE ALSO Amoraim; Talmud.

BIBLIOGRAPHY

A comprehensive treatment and bibliography of Ashi and his teachings can be found in Jacob Neusner's *A History of the Jews in Babylonia*, 5 vols. (Leiden, 1966–1970), esp. vol. 5. Ashi's mode of teaching is discussed in David M. Goodblatt's *Rabbinic Instruction in Sasanian Babylonia* (Leiden, 1975). His role in the formation of the *gemara'* is discussed in Goodblatt's "The Babylonian Talmud," in *Aufstieg und Niedergang der römischen Welt*, vol. 2.19.2 (Berlin and New York, 1979), pp. 292, 308–318, reprinted in *The Study of Ancient Judaism*, edited by Jacob Neusner, vol. 2, *The Palestinian and Babylonian Talmuds* (New York, 1981); and in David Weiss Halivni's *Midrash, Mishnah, and Gemara* (Cambridge, Mass., 1986).

New Sources

Kalmin, Richard Lee. "The Post-Rav Ashi Amoraim—Transition or Continuity? A Study of the Role of the Final Generations of Amoraim in the Redaction of the Talmud." *AJS Review* 11 (1986): 157–187.

BARUCH M. BOKSER (1987)
Revised Bibliography

ASHKENAZIC HASIDISM. In the late twelfth century, the Jewish communities of Mainz, Worms, and Speyer saw the emergence of a Jewish pietistic circle characterized by its own leadership and distinctive religious outlook. For almost a hundred years, the Jewish Pietists of medieval Germany (*ḥasidei Ashkenaz*) constituted a small elite of religious thinkers who, along with their followers, developed and sought to carry out novel responses to a variety of social and religious problems.

Pietistic texts were written by three members of the same circle who were also part of the Qalonimos family. Tracing their origins to northern Italy, the Qalonimides claimed to be descendants of the founding family of Mainz Jewry in Carolingian times and bearers of distinctive ancient mystical traditions. The three major figures in this group were Shemuʾel, son of Qalonimos the Elder of Speyer, known as "the pietist, the holy, and the prophet" (fl. mid-twelfth century); his younger son, Yehudah, known as "the pietist" (d. 1217); and Yehudah's disciple and cousin, Elʿazar, son of Yehudah of Worms, who called himself "the insignificant" (d. 1230?).

In their pietistic writings, Shemuʾel, Yehudah, and Elʿazar developed in detail the contours of a distinctive perception of the ideal Jewish way of life, which they thought must be followed for the individual Jew to attain salvation in the afterlife. This shared personal eschatology, or vision of the ideal way for the individual to behave, was attached to the ancient biblical and classical rabbinic term *ḥasid,* which had denoted, at various times, those who are loyal or faithful to God (e.g., *Ps.* 31:24, 37:28–29) or someone who is punctilious in observing the religious commandments of Judaism and who even forgoes that to which he is entitled (e.g., *Avot* 5.10).

The German-Jewish Pietists built their own understanding of *ḥasid,* or "Pietist," upon the cumulative foundation of earlier meanings but moved in new directions as well. Their worldview was grounded in the idea that God's will is only partially revealed in the words of the Pentateuch, or the Torah, given to the prophet Moses at Mount Sinai. God's will requires of the truly faithful and punctilious Jew, that is, of the *ḥasid,* a search for a hidden and infinitely demanding additional *torah,* which God encoded in the words of scripture. He did this, moreover, to enable the Pietist to earn additional reward in the afterlife by searching for it and fulfilling it as best he can.

The difficult task of discovering the hidden will of God is part of a central concept in Pietism. The Pietists maintained that life consists of a divinely ordained trial by which the pietist's loyalty to God is continually tested in all he does, thinks, and feels. The source of the trial is a person's passions, such as sexual attraction to persons other than a spouse or the drive for personal honor and adulation in this world. The pietistic authors refer to these urges as the "evil impulse" (*yetser ha-raʿ*), a term from classical rabbinic theology. Sometimes associated with the tempter or the accuser (Satan) in the *Book of Job* (e.g., 1:6–12), the Pietist's trial by passions is part of God's plan to reward the successful Pietist who resists them. As Shemuʾel says, "Is not the evil impulse good for man? If it did not dominate him, what reward would he earn for acting virtuously?" (*Sefer ha-yirʾah,* or *Book of the Fear of God,* para. 2). God's reward for the Pietists derives not only from their struggle to search scripture for God's hidden commandments but also from their continuous resistance of the evil impulse. That effort, in turn, involves a constant self-examination of one's motives and feelings. As such, German Hasidism constitutes one of several contemporary developments in the spiritualization of ancient Judaism which led to new modes of piety. Along with Maimonidean religious philosophy, theosophical mysticism, or Qabbalah, and the scholastic legal achievement of the glossators of the Talmud, German-Jewish Pietism permanently reshaped classical Judaism into traditional Judaism, which lasted down to the modern period.

One result of the fact that the Pietist's life requires resistance to all kinds of temptations of the flesh and ego was the tendency toward asceticism. Grounded in the authors' focus on maximizing otherworldly reward by resisting temptations in this world, the Pietists are told to avoid all illicit physical or psychological pleasure during their life. For this reason, Pietists should not play with their children or benefit from any social honors. Yehudah the Pietist even goes so far as to prohibit authors from writing their own name in the introduction to books they have written. Their children might take pride in their parents' work, and this "enjoyment" in this world will deprive them of some of their reward in the next one.

The centrality in the pietistic ideal of viewing life as a continuous divine trial probably was a reaction, at least in part, to the traumatic memory of acts of suicidal Jewish martyrdom which took place in the same Rhineland towns in the spring of 1096. In the wake of the First Crusade hundreds of Jews, including many of the intellectual elite of Mainz and Worms, were either killed for not converting to Christianity on the spot or else martyred themselves in acts of ritualized socioreligious polemic. Rather than be defiled by the "impurity" of Christians, whom the Jews at that time regarded as idolators, many men and women created a boundary between themselves and their enemy by taking their own lives. In so doing, they acted as though they were Temple sacrifices or holy things which only the holy, or other Jews, could touch. By killing their own families and then themselves, they sought to keep ritual pollution in check. The Hebrew chronicles that describe these events indicate that the crusader mob never reached Jerusalem. By picturing the Jewish martyrs as Temple sacrifices, the chroniclers indicate that the Jews of Mainz in effect erected their own symbolic version of the Temple of Jerusalem and by so doing affirmed their absolute loyalty and faithfulness to God and Judaism through the ultimate sacrifice of having to give their lives.

In the pietistic writings of the Qalonimides are found echoes of the trauma of 1096. Not only is the life of the Pietist a trial, as were the events of that year, but the need to resist the evil impulse is compared to the willingness to be martyred if necessary. In fact, the authors assume that their readers would willingly sacrifice their lives if Christians were to threaten them with the penalty of death for not converting: "If you were living at a time of religious persecution, you would endure tortures or death for the sake of the Holy One, blessed be He. . . . You certainly should endure this [trial] which is not as severe but is only [resisting] your evil impulse which strongly urges you to sin" (*Sefer ha-yirʾah,* para. 2).

The conception that the Pietist's life was a trial that should be resisted might have led to the conclusion that temptations were to be sought out and fought off. This possibility was discussed but was considered very risky. The struggle between the Pietist who tries to live on the boundary, nearly sinning while resisting temptation, is illustrated in Yehudah the Pietist's major work about Pietism, *Sefer hasidim* (Book of the Pietists). There Yehudah illustrates the pietistic ideal in hundreds of exempla, or moralistic tales, about Pietists and the Jewish communities in which they lived among Christians and other Jews who were not Pietists. In one of his most celebrated tales, he describes a Pietist who comes close to sinning by risking his own life in order to affirm his loyalty to God.

Yehudah tells of a Pietist who used to torture himself in the summer by lying down on the ground among fleas and in the winter by placing his feet in a container filled with water until they froze. A friend challenged his extremes of self-punishment by quoting a classic proof-text against suicide (*Gn.* 9:5). The Pietist answered that he was only atoning for his sins.

After the Pietist died, one of his students sought to find out if his teacher was being rewarded or punished for undergoing such extreme penances. In a dream, the Pietist takes the student to Paradise and tells him that his place is high up and that the student will only attain such a high place if he continues to perform acts of virtue. This vision convinced the student that his master was not being punished for flirting with the prohibition of committing suicide (*Sefer ḥasidim,* ed. Wistinetzki, para. 1556).

THE SOCIORELIGIOUS PROGRAM. While all three Qalonimides shared a common vision regarding a personal eschatology, there were major ways in which Yehudah differed with Shemuʾel and other ways in which Elʿazar disagreed with Yehudah. Since only one tract by Shemuʾel has survived, *Sefer ha-yirʾah,* it is impossible to know many of his religious ideas, but from a comparison of that work with Yehudah's *Sefer ḥasidim,* Yehudah emerges as an important innovator in several respects. Above all, he developed a social, as well as a personal, program for the Pietist. In the process of defining his socioreligious understanding of the demands of Pietism, Yehudah focuses on Jews who were not Pietists and criticized communal leaders or rabbis who permitted or condoned social abuses. He accuses them of ignoring justice and of taking advantage of the poor.

In addition to presenting Pietism as having a social as well as a personal dimension, Yehudah defines a new social context for the Pietists themselves. While Shemuʾel's work is addressed to the individual Pietist, Yehudah takes for granted that Pietists are organized as a fellowship distinct from other Jews who are not Pietists. Moreover, he views this sectarian fellowship as a subcommunity of Jews who are led not by non-Pietist communal elders but by their own religious leaders, charismatic figures called sages (*ḥakhamim*). Thus the social world presupposed in Yehudah's *Sefer ḥasidim* consists of three groups: pietistic Jews, nonpietistic Jews, and Christians. For Yehudah, unlike Shemuʾel, a Jew may be rich or poor, scholarly or ignorant, powerful or common, but the only distinction that matters is between being a Pietist and not.

The exclusivistic character of Yehudah's Pietists was not absolute: a non-Pietist could become a Pietist by undergoing an initiation ceremony of atonement. For this purpose, Yehudah's *Sefer ḥasidim* includes a penitential manual that he designed for the sage who now functions as a confessor and dispenser of penances. This elaborate penitential ritual serves the sectarian functions of disciplining Pietists who temporarily lapse and enabling non-Pietists to "enter," or be initiated into pietism by means of a penitential rite of passage. A Pietist or would-be Pietist approaches a sage, confesses his sins to him, and receives from the sage an appropriate penance to perform.

Although the door to Pietism was open for others, the Pietists generally appeared to other Jews as a self-righteous elite. It is not surprising, then, that they experienced a great deal of antagonism from other Jews. By insisting that only Pietists should serve as cantors in the synagogue, or be scribes, or be considered proper spouses for themselves or their children, or be eligible to receive charity, they made themselves extremely unpopular. And so to be a Pietist was to be the butt of jokes, the target of ridicule, and the victim of intemperate hostility.

In view of their high regard for themselves, one might have expected the Pietists to try to take over the Jewish communities in which they lived. In fact, in Yehudah's writings there are signs of three political strategies by which they sought to implement their programmatic vision of the perfect Jewish society. Two of these strategies failed: They could not take over the leadership of the communities for long, and they failed to maintain at least one attempt to create a utopian commune of Pietists living in splendid isolation apart from other Jews. A third approach, however, is characteristic of the Pietists who are described in *Sefer ḥasidim.* Groups tried to live in, but not with, the rest of the Jewish community while struggling to retain their fellowship and resist being absorbed or even influenced by the nonpietistic majority. Not surprisingly, even this compromise form of sectarianism was short-lived, so much so that it left barely any trace outside of Yehudah's own writings.

Although Jews resisted Yehudah's radical program of forming a sectarian fellowship, they were able to remain Pietists as individuals thanks to Elʿazar of Worm's translation of Pietism back into a personalist idiom. In marked contrast to the sectarian and political orientation of *Sefer ḥasidim,* Elʿazar's writings, like Shemuʾel's, are addressed to the individual Pietist or Jew, not to organized subgroups of Pietists and their sages. There is not even a hint in Elʿazar's writings that he thought of sages except as a failure. Thus unlike the penitential in *Sefer ḥasidim,* which was designed for the use of the sage as confessor, Elʿazar's private penitentials enable sinners to learn by themselves which penances to undergo simply by reading the manual. He even tells his readers that his manuals were necessary because Jews were too embarrassed to approach another Jew and confess their sins to him.

By articulating a nonsectarian, personalist formulation of Pietism in the wake of Yehudah's failed attempt to effect a social as well as personal religious revival, Elʿazar was a conservative spokesman for a pre–*Sefer ḥasidim* form of German-Jewish Pietism. But Elʿazar was himself resourceful in adapting and salvaging the shared vision and values of the pietistic ideal. He institutionalized it by incorporating it into his book of German-Jewish customary law, *Sefer ha-roqeaḥ.* In so doing, Elʿazar "normalized" an innovative expression of Judaism by bringing it into the mainstream of rabbinic legal precedents. Ironically, the penances which Yehudah, a critic of the nonpietistic rabbinic and communal elite, devised for new members of the pietistic fellowship, were later implemented by rabbinic leaders themselves, thanks to Elʿazar's including them in his book of religious law. Elʿazar thus transformed and preserved the values and many of the customs first advanced by the Pietists and blended them into his compendium of earlier German-Jewish tradition. This enabled pietism to become a critical part of "ordinary" European Jewish piety throughout the succeeding centuries.

THEOLOGICAL AND MYSTICAL WORKS. Thanks to Yehudah's stricture that authors should not mention their own names in the books they write, there is no explicit internal evidence about Yehudah's own writings. Nevertheless, it is reasonably clear from early attributions and quotations that he wrote not only the major collection of pietistic thought, *Sefer ḥasidim,* but also several books of esoteric lore. Thus Joseph Dan has posited, with good reason, that Yehudah probably is the author of several still unpublished esoteric works found, for example, in Oxford, Bodleian Library, Hebrew Manuscript Oppenheim 540 (Neubauer no. 1567). In these writings, many of which Elʿazar edited under the title *Sodei razayyaʾ* (Esoteric secrets), Yehudah deals with the problem of anthropomorphism in an original way. Although unaware of most of the medieval Jewish philosophical tradition, which was being translated then from Arabic into Hebrew, Yehudah did have a "paraphrased" version of the tenth-century Jewish philosophical work by Saʿadyah Gaon, *Emunot ve-deʿot* (The book of beliefs and opinions). There Saʿadyah posits that God is one and that all concrete imagery in the Bible and rabbinic lore which seems to refer to God himself actually refers to a created aspect of God, the divine glory, or *kavod.*

Yehudah the Pietist maintained the distinction between God's oneness and a *kavod,* but he argued that the *Kavod* was itself a twofold emanation of God and not a created being. In separate tracts, Yehudah discussed the implications for the practical religious life of this theological distinction. Particularly at stake was the question as to which aspect of God the Pietist should concentrate on when he prays. Yehudah insisted that the Pietist must think only of the upper, hidden "face" of the glory, not of the lower "face," which is revealed in images to the prophets. To think of the latter would be idolatry. Moreover, Yehudah wrote that the Pietists should pray slowly, in a drawn out or deliberate style (*be-meshekh*), in order to permit time to think about elaborately worked out word and number associations attached to the words of the liturgy. Several versions of these mystical prayer commentaries exist, although none has been published. Other parts of Elʿazar's *Sodei razayyaʾ* deal with manipulations of the Hebrew alphabet and of the divine names to achieve mystical results, including the fabrication of a homunculus or *gōlem.*

One genre which expressed the Qalonimides' theology about anthropomorphism did find its way not only into print but even into the standard prayerbook. The Songs of Divine Oneness *(shirei yiḥud)* extol God himself as being beyond any attributes. Complementing these prayers is the equally mystical Song of Divine Glory *(shir ha-kavod),* an intensely evocative expression of the Pietist's yearning to see God's glory, based on *Exodus* 33:18ff., *Song of Songs* 5:11ff., and the Babylonian Talmud, *Berakhot* 7a.

Apart from the library of esoteric, theological, and mystical texts which can be ascribed with varying degrees of probability to Shemuʾel, Yehudah, and Elʿazar, other works contain some divergent ideas and themes and have been ascribed to mainly anonymous subgroups. Of these writings, mention should be made of *Sefer ha-ḥayyim* (The book of life) and *Sefer ha-navon* (The book of the discerning). Of the few known authors outside the Qalonimide circle and their descendants, the most fascinating is Elḥanan, son of Yaqar, who atypically knew Latin and made use of Christian works in his esoteric commentaries and text in the late thirteenth century.

Although some of the esoteric writings associated with German-Jewish thinkers consist of exegetical speculations about God, many others deal with mystical experience and practice and are derived from ancient Jewish mystical traditions. It is significant that the Qalonimides preserved, studied, and elaborated much of the late ancient and early medieval Palestinian and Babylonian mystical texts about the divine chariot (*merkavah*), based on *Ezekiel,* chapters 1 and 10, and on the ascent through the heavenly palaces (*heikhalot*). Their writings about manipulating the divine name in the form of permutations of the Hebrew alphabet to achieve mystical and magical goals, decidedly influenced later Jewish mysticism in Spain. Thus, their mystical and esoteric writings and their expression of ascetic Pietism contributed to the Jewish mystical tradition and, more generally, to the distinctive fabric of traditional Jewish piety.

BIBLIOGRAPHY

The most comprehensive treatment of the pietistic movement and its worldview is my book *Piety and Society: The Jewish Pietists of Medieval Germany* (Leiden, 1981). Important, stimulating, and profound earlier studies are Yitzhak F. Baer's "Ha-megamah ha-datit ha-ḥervratt shel 'Sefer ḥasidim,'" *Zion* 3 (1937): 1–50 and Haym Soloveitchik's "Three Themes in the *Sefer Ḥasidim*," *AJS Review* 1 (1976): 311–357.

Concerning the Pietists' esoteric doctrines, the best study is Joseph Dan's *Torat ha-sod shel ḥasidut Ashkenaz* (Jerusalem, 1968). Gershom Scholem expressed his views on this subject in the chapter "Hasidism in Medieval Germany" in his book *Major Trends in Jewish Mysticism* (1941; reprint, New York, 1961), pp. 79–118. An important essay on the Pietists' innovative prayer commentary is Joseph Dan's "The Emergence of Mystical Prayer," in *Studies in Jewish Mysticism*, edited by Joseph Dan and Frank Talmage (Cambridge, Mass., 1982), pp. 85–120.

New Sources

Alexander, Tamar. "Dream Narratives in 'Sefer Hasidim.'" *Trumah* 12 (2002): 65–78.

Chazan, Robert. "The Early Development of Hasidut Ashkenaz." *JQR* 75 (1985): 199–211.

Dan, Joseph. *Hasidut ashkenaz be-toldot ha-mahashavah ha-yehudit* (Ashkenazi Hasidism in the History of the Jewish Thought). Tel-Aviv, 1991.

Dan, Joseph. *Jewish Mysticism and Jewish Ethics.* 2d ed. Seattle, 1986; Northvale, N.J., 1996.

Fishman, Talya."The Penitential System of Hasidei Ashkenaz and the Problem of Cultural Boundaries." *JJTP* 8 (1999): 201–229.

Kanarfogel, Ephraim. *Jewish Education and Society in the High Middle Ages.* Detroit, 1992.

Soloveitchik, Haym. "Piety, Pietism and German Pietism: 'Sefer Hasidim I' and the Influence of 'Hasidei Ashkenaz.'" *Jewish Quarterly Review* 92 (2002): 455–493.

IVAN G. MARCUS (1987)
Revised Bibliography

ASHOKA SEE AŚOKA

ASHRAM. The term *ashram* or *ās'rama* is derived from the Sanskrit root *śram,* meaning "intense exertion." It refers to both the mode of life associated with religious striving and the abode of those so engaged.

As a mode or way of life specified for twice-born Hindus (usually male), the ashramic ideal set forth four stages of development: being a student *(brahmacārin)* devoted to one's teacher; a householder *(gṛhastha)* with obligations to family, priests, and deities; a hermit *(vanaprastha)* who, with or without his wife, retreats from material concerns; and finally a renouncer *(sannyasin)* who forsakes all possessions in order to contemplate the eternal and, like the hermit, pursue *mokṣa* (spiritual liberation).

A clear delineation of this four-fold system can be traced to the Upaniṣads (cf. *Jābāla Upaniṣad* 4), which are believed to have been composed by *ṛṣis* (seers) in forest hermitages that were likewise called ashrams. The latter became places where young students and older seekers would come to "sit down near" *(upa-ni-ṣad)* a respected teacher *(gurū)* who would serve as their spiritual guide. Because the ancient Hindu teacher insisted on oral transmission, the *gurū-śiṣya* (teacher-disciple) relationship became central. Ashram life was simple and no distinctions were made between rich and poor or between castes. It seems, however, that only boys were sent to study outside the home, and thus the ashramic system of education contributed to a gap in learning between the sexes. Besides study, students would perform chores for their *gurū,* including begging for alms from wealthy residents. It was common for rulers and other wealthy individuals to support the establishment of these educational centers.

"Graduation" was marked by social expectations as well as a ceremonial bath. In the *Taittirīya Upaniṣad* (1:11:1) we read that, upon completing their initial *brahmacarya* stage of learning, students were exhorted by their teachers to "speak the truth," "practice virtue *(dharma),*" and not neglect their studies or obligations to teachers, gods, and ancestors.

Over the centuries, ashrams became centers of pilgrimage, as people were drawn to one *gurū* or another, and to their legacies. As the spiritual magnetism of these *gurūs* came to attract Jains and Buddhists as well as Hindus, the forest retreats gradually lost their sectarian character.

REVIVAL OF HINDU ASHRAMS IN MODERN INDIA. Revival of the ashram mode of life in the early twentieth century can be attributed to neo-Hindu movements and, more specifically, to Hindu Reformers like Narendranath Datta, known as Vivekananda (1863–1902), Rabindranath Tagore (1861–1941), Mahatma Mohandas Karamchand Gandhi (1869–1948), Sri Aurobindo Ghose (1872–1950) and his disciple Mira Richard, known as "the Mother" (d. 1973), and Śivānanda (1887–1963).

Each of these early reformers was open to the West but, as Indian nationalists, they were also critical of British colonialism and Christianity's apparent link to it. They selected aspects of Western Christian ideas and culture that could be incorporated into the religious and philosophical traditions being retrieved from ancient Hinduism. This blending gave rise to creative institutions that identified themselves with one or more of the three traditional spiritual paths or *mārgas,* namely the path of selfless action and social service *(karma-mārga);* the path of ritual and devotional practices *(bhakti-mārga)*; and the path stressing contemplative union with God *(jñāna-mārga).*

This modern ashram movement attracted support and followers from the West as well as the East and, in this way, it provided an ecumenical model of spiritual renewal, in addition to advancing the cause of nationalism by stressing Indian identity, advocating independence in political and economic life, and countering claims of Western superiority.

One of the earliest and most enduring manifestations of the renewal of ashram life can be seen in the Ramakrishna Mission and Ramakrishna Order founded in Calcutta by Vivekananda in 1897 and 1899 respectively. Named after Vivekananda's *gurū,* Ramakrishna, who died in 1886, this mission was the first to be successful in the West. Today it has more than eighty centers in India and some twenty others abroad dedicated to education, social welfare, and the spread of Upaniṣadic thought. The order combines the Hindu tradition of renunciation *(saṃnyāsa)* and selfless service *(karma yoga)* with Christian models of organized monastic life. In 1954 a separate, independent women's branch named after Ramakrishna's wife, Śrī Śāradā Devī, was opened.

While the early period of the Ramakrishna movement follows the classic pattern of disciples gathering around a charismatic figure, later developments exemplify the way in which movements become institutionalized and routinized, such that loyalty once focused on a *gurū* is redirected to the organization itself.

Śāntiniketan (Abode of Peace) Ashram, originally founded in 1863 by Devendranath Tagore in a rural part of Bengal, was refounded in 1901 by his son, Rabindranath Tagore. This ashram provided a setting for the blending together of Indian and Western traditions and values, a cross-pollination that led to the restoration of the tradition of disciples living with their teachers, a rejection of caste distinctions, and the development of a communal life-style lived in harmony with nature. Today, what remains of Tagore's project is attached to Viśva Bhārata University.

In 1915 Mahatma Gandhi initiated the Satyāgraha (Truth-force) Ashram near Ahmedabad, Gujarat. It was moved three years later to Sabarmati. For Gandhi, it was essential that political and economic progress be rooted in religion, which he understood as a liberating force of truth and love. These ashrams were envisioned as training centers for persons of all classes, castes, and creeds who were committed to personal and national liberation. To make them accessible, he had situated them in the midst of towns and villages rather than in forests. He sought to combine the three *mārgas* and drew on both popular and Vedantic expressions of the Hindu tradition. A second ashram, Sevāgrām, was established near Wardha in Maharashtra under the guidance of Vinoba Bhave (1895–1982), who was especially concerned with advancing women's liberation.

Later, in 1959, Vinoba established the Brahmā Vidyā Mandir Ashram, also near Wardha, for women disciples, who were responsible for its day to day running. Its *raison d'être* was to empower women in the service of national unity. Both here and at the nearby Sevāgrām Ashram, followers lived according to the eleven principles formulated by Gandhi. These included five observances drawn from the moral prerequisites set down in Patañjali's *Yoga Sūtra*: *ahiṃsā* (nonviolence and love), *satya* (truth-seeking), *asteya* (simple living), *aparigraha* (minimizing possessions), and *brahmacarya* (celibacy). The six additional observances called for *sharir ashram* (manual labor), *asvāda* (restricted consumption), *sarva bhaya barjana* (fearlessness born of taking refuge in the Lord), *swadeshi* (solidarity with one's country, especially its poorest inhabitants), *sarvadharma samatva* (a respect for all religious traditions), and *sparsha bhāva* (rejection of untouchability).

The largest, most organized, and most commercialized of the modern ashrams is the Aurobindo Ashram located in Pondicherry, Tamil Nadu. Established in 1926, this spiritual retreat has some 2,000 members, many from the West, and is dedicated to the integration of the *jñāna* and *karma mārgas.* Its goal has been to develop an "Integral Yoga" that will allow Hindu spirituality to engage the contemporary world and its ideas. Prior to his death in 1950, Aurobindo transferred his authority to a disciple known as "the Mother." Under her leadership the ashram expanded and, to this day, she is the one who is regarded as its dominant symbolic *gurū.*

Swami Śivānanda, founder of the Śivānanda Ashram (1932), served his nation in several ways. Besides supporting social service programs, his creation of the Divine Life Society enabled him to gain a following for Vedantic teachings at home and abroad. His ashram, with its commitment to contemplation and its openness to seekers of all faiths, had a significant influence on the Catholic ashram movement, which was likewise driven by nationalist and anticolonial sentiments.

THE CHRISTIAN ASHRAM MOVEMENT. If the neo-Hindu reform movement involved in reviving ashram life can be seen as a creative response to the challenges posed by both British colonialism and Western Christian imperialism, the Christian ashram movement should be seen as a creative response, by some Indian Christians and foreign missionaries living in India, to challenges posed by existing forms of institutional Christianity that tended to alienate their followers from the rich cultural heritage of India. In other words, Christian ashram movements were the products of a new religious consciousness that recognized the colonial structures embedded in Christian institutions and responded by creating communal spaces where more authentic indigenous expressions of the faith could be developed.

Protestant Christians took the lead in this move to indigenize and inculturate Christianity. At a meeting of the National Missionary Society in 1912, Charles F. Andrews, a Christian minister who collaborated with Gandhi, put forth a proposal to establish ashrams to accomplish evangelical and social goals. In 1921 Savarirayan Jesudason and E. Forrester Paton established the first major Christian ashram, named Christukula, in Tiruppatur, Tamil Nadu. The founders of this and other Protestant retreats drew their inspiration from Hindu reformers like Gandhi, who is known to have stayed at Christukula. Protestant centers borrowed from the *bhakti* tradition, taking from it its melodies, instruments, vernacular phrasing, and democratic outreach to all castes. Gandhi-like, they emphasized social work, education, and health programs and took clear stands against colonialism. In the late 1940s, after independence, an Inter-Ashram Fellowship was formed.

Although it is not usually recognized as such, the Bethany Ashram, founded by Orthodox Syrians, was in fact the first Christian ashram to be established. It was founded in 1918 in what is now Kerala with the goal of drawing on the traditions of *bhakti* yoga and *jñāna* yoga in order to revitalize Orthodox Syrian spirituality in a way that would reflect its ties to Indian culture and the goals of nationalism. Today the Orthodox Syrian Church has a number of autonomous celibate communities with monks wearing the ochre-colored (*kavi*-colored) robes of Hindu renunciates and following a vegetarian diet, but because little else remains of Hindu forms, the term *ashram* seems to be nominal.

Among Catholics, a proposal to combine Christian monastic practice with elements of Hindu ashram life was made as early as 1891 by a *brahman* Bengali convert, but it was met with incomprehension. It was not until the time of the Second Vatican Council (1962–1965) that the seeds of inculturation were sown and institutional support for a Catholic ashram movement was made available by the Catholic Bishops Conference of India. That said, the need for Catholic ashrams had already been anticipated by two individuals: a French diocesan priest named Jules Monchanin and Henri le Saux, a French Benedictine who took the name Abhishiktānanda. Together they formed the first Catholic retreat center, Saccidānanda Ashram, also known as Shāntivānam (Forest of Peace), in 1950. Although Europeans, these pioneers were steeped in Hindu spirituality and they were committed to an Indianization of Christianity in order to Christianize Indians.

In Shāntivānam, inculturation led nuns and monks to adopt the *kavi*-colored robes of Hindu renunciates and to use Sanskritic names. New residents are welcomed with *dīkṣā*, a ritual of initiation, practice yoga, and follow a vegetarian diet. The chapel is built like a typical South Indian temple, an *OM* is inscribed over the entrance to the sanctuary and its altar has the shape of an inverted lotus. During the liturgy verses, from the Upaniṣads and the bible are read. Atop a *gopuram* ("tower") are statues of Paul, Mary, and Benedict, carved in poses reminiscent of Hindu temple *mūrtis* (images) and Jesus is regarded the *Sat* (true) *gurū*.

It should be noted that such attempts at inculturation were met with suspicion and criticism by many in the Hindu community who regarded the linking of evangelization and Indianization as a stealth form of Christian imperialism. Sīta Ram Goel's work *Catholic Ashrams: Sannyasins or Swindlers?*, published in 1995, exemplifies this response.

In the decades following Vatican II, a noticeable shift occurred. Ashram pioneers like Ignatius Hirudayam, SJ, in Madras, Sisters Vandana Mataji and Sara Grant in Pune, and Bede Griffiths, OSB, who took over leadership of Shāntivānam, stressed the ecumenical dimension of their communities. Their goal was to create a prayerful climate where "otherness" was valued and where participants in interfaith encounters and collaborations would be mutually challenged and enriched.

Marks of True Ashrams: A Consensus. As the ashram movement of Hindus and Christians enters into the twenty-first century, a consensus seems to have emerged regarding the requirements of genuine ashrams, that they be open to people of all creeds, castes, cultures, and countries; include women, whether in separated or mixed communities; address social inequalities; be responsive to the needs of those who do not belong to the ashram's denomination or sect; challenge such divisive elements as communalism, fanaticism, and fundamentalism; protect the environment; treasure the pluriform spiritual heritage of India; and contribute to national integration.

See Also Aurobindo Ghose; Gandhi, Mohandas; Gurū; Hinduism; Ramakrishna; Sādhus and Sādhvīs; Saṃnyāsa; Śāradā Devī; Tagore, Rabindranath; Vivekananda.

Bibliography

Amaladoss, Michael. "Ashrams and Social Justice." *Word and Worship* 15 (1982): 205–214.

Dhavamony, Mariasusai. "Monasticism: Hindu and Christian." *Bulletin Secretarius pro non Christianis* 37, no. 131 (1978): 40–53.

Gandhi, M. K. *An Autobiography: The Story of My Experiments with Truth.* Translated by Mahadev Desai. London, 1949.

Griffiths, Bede. *Christian Ashram: Essays towards a Hindu-Christian Dialogue.* London, 1966.

Hallstrom, Lisa Lassell. *Mother of Bliss: Ānandamayī Mā (1896–1982).* Oxford, 1999.

Jesudason, Savarirayan. *Ashrams, Ancient and Modern: Their Aims and Ideals.* Vellore, India, 1937.

Kane, Pandurang Vaman. *History of Dharma Sastra: Ancient and Medieval Religious and Civil Law.* Vol. 2, part 1. Pune, India, 1941.

Mataji, Vandana. *Christian Ashrams: A Movement with a Future?* Delhi, 1993.

Miller, David M., and Dorothy C. Wertz. *Hindu Monastic Life: The Monks and Monasteries of Bhubarneswar.* New Delhi, 1996.

Olivelle, Patrick. *The Asrama System: The History and Hermeneutics of a Religious Institution.* Oxford and New York, 1993.

Ralston, Helen. *Christian Ashrams: A New Religious Movement in Contemporary India.* Lewiston, N.Y., 1987. Provides an insightful survey of Hindu and Christian ashrams.

Selva, Raj J. "Adapting Hindu Imagery: A Critical Look at Ritual Experiments in an Indian Catholic Ashram." *Journal of Ecumenical Studies* 37, nos. 3–4 (Summer/Fall 2000): 333–351.

Vandana. *Gurus, Ashrams, and Christians.* Madras, India, 1978.

Williams, George M. "The Ramakrishna Movement: A Study in Religious Change." In *Religion in Modern India,* edited by Robert D. Baird, pp. 55–79. New Delhi, 1981.

JUDITH G. MARTIN (2005)

ASHTART SEE ASTARTE

ASHUR was the national god of Assyria; his name is that of the city-state of Ashur (or Assur). The characteristics of this god are very different from those of the other divinities of the Sumerian-Akkadian pantheon. There is some speculation that Ashur was formerly recorded in a list of divine names of the middle of the third millennium BCE (Mander, 1986, p. 69). However, in the earliest confirmed documents (twentieth to nineteenth centuries BCE), it is the god who appears as the real lord of his city, whereas the Assyrian sovereign was nothing more than Ashur's chief priest and manager of the city on his behalf. The god Ashur personifies the homonymous city (similar conditions are documented in High Mesopotamia, Syria, Anatolia, and the Diyala region, but are neither so frequent nor so relevant) as a possible expression of the holiness of the place near present-day Shirqat, where an imposing spur was the spot of the ancient city (it is to be remarked that the praises that were addressed to the towns or temples of the gods in southern Mesopotamia were intended as allusions to the "glory" of the god who there manifested himself: a completely different phenomenon). This peculiar origin is probably the reason for his marked difference with the other gods of the Mesopotamian pantheon. Ashur lacks family relations, no epithet is attributed to him, nor does he show clear connections with the world of the cosmic natural powers. He is praised in no hymns, nor is he ever engaged in incantations, and no mythological poem about him is known. His images are not anthropomorphic but only symbolic icons.

TRANSFORMATION OF ASHUR. From the beginning of the second millennium BCE, however, Ashur began to transform from a *numen loci* (divine presence of the place) into a *deus persona* (god person). The first step in this gradual passage was the combining of the god Ashur with the weather-god Adad (fifteenth century BCE), an evident resonance of the Syrian tradition in which El and Baal were the divinities at the head of the pantheon. Even the position of the king in respect to the god slowly changed. Shamshi-Adad I (1812–1780 BCE), a usurper who led the first moment of the Assyrian expansion assumed the title of "king." However, it was not until the time of Adad-nirari I (1305–1274 BCE) that the god ordered his king to undertake wars of conquest, an errand that the above-mentioned sovereign strove at his utmost to accomplish, thus beginning the second moment of the Assyrian expansionism. The process of strengthening the monarchy led—under his successor Salmanassar I (1273–1244 BCE)—to the nomination of the king and of his dynasty by the god. Times were mature for a turning point, and under Tukulti-Ninurta I (1243–1207 BCE) Ashur was identified with the Sumerian-Babylonian king of the gods, Enlil, and even his wife, Ninlil, was considered to be the wife of Ashur (Ninlil was called *Mullissu* in Assyria) and the city of Ashur became the holy center of Assyria, just as the city of Nippur—the see of Enlil—was for Babylonia. Ashur was therefore the indisputable king of the gods and the only god tied to a people by means of such a significant linkage. Due to this exclusive linkage, the Assyrian people believed they were invested with the mission to conquer the world, and they thus considered themselves almost an elected people.

ASHUR AND THE SARGONIDS. A further phase of the god Ashur's history took place under the Sargonids who wanted him to overcome Marduk, the city-god of Babylon, when the latter replaced Enlil as king of the gods. The usurper Sargon II (founder of the Sargonids; r. 721–705 BCE) developed the theology of Ashur in order to attribute to him an *omnipotentia divina,* thus designating him as the divine power from which both men and gods depended (both having been created from that power). To that aim Sargon II introduced the identification of Ashur with An-shar. An-shar was a primordial god mentioned in *Enuma elish,* the poem of Marduk's exaltation to the lordship over the gods and the universe, probably composed around the eleventh century BCE. In it, An-shar plays the role of progenitor of the gods having just issued from the fresh and salted waters (Apsu and Tiamat, respectively) when the cosmic gate of the universe was generated (cf. W. G. Lambert, "The Pair Lahmu-Lahamu in Cosmology," *Orientalia* 54 (1985), pp. 189–201). This identification made the god's generational preeminence possible: Ashur/An-shar was the first-born among all the gods (and therefore was their principle); he was Marduk's ancestor, being indeed three generations older. Marduk was Ea's son and An's grandson, the latter having been generated by An-shar. An-shar was mentioned in texts before the *Enuma elish* was composed (it is one of the earliest elements that were absorbed and refashioned in the poem)—his name is found in the earliest Mesopotamian tradition in lists of primeval gods, and one of these lists is that of Enlil's ancestors. The identification with An-shar was therefore an extraordinary success and meant the acquisition of a position of absolute priority for a god like Ashur, who was not even included in the main Mesopotamian religious tradition, which did not include him in its pantheon.

Sargon II's son, Sennacherib (r. 704–681 BCE), further developed this theology by combining it with basic elements of the Sumerian-Babylonian religious thought, which he conveniently adopted. His struggle against Babylon eventually led him to destroy that city in 689 BCE, a policy mirroring his theological reform intended to nullify Marduk by replacing him with Ashur. The king went even further with the elimination from worship in Assyria of the cults of the South (even that of the very important son of Marduk, Nabû). In this context, by increasing An-shar's characteristics, the god Ashur becomes *deus summus omnipotens* and *creator absolutus.* From these attributes it consequently resulted that he alone could determine the destinies of the universe and—this is particularly crucial to the understanding of his position—that he was "the creator of himself," as an Assyrian text states.

In this context the *akitu* ceremony was moved to the city of Ashur. When performing the ceremony, the god Ashur was seen to fight against Tiamat, a deed that Marduk accomplished in *Enuma elish.* This overlapping is not to be considered as a merely outrageous behavior but rather as a traditional theological explanation of defeat. Babylon had been destroyed because Marduk had abandoned it as a direct consequence of its presumed impious acts. The son and successor of Sennacherib, Esarhaddon (r. 680–669 BCE), explicitly mentioned this concept when, in inverting the course of his father's policy, he rebuilt Babylon and reestablished the cults in the restored temples. In any case, he by no means repudiated his predecessors theology of Ashur.

Simo Parpola has presented a theory of the monotheism of Ashur: it was a reality limited to an elite and not to the whole population. Ashur, as "metaphysical universe of light, goodness, wisdom and eternal life" (2000, pp. 165–209) was considered to be the "intermediate entity between existence and non-existence" (with reference to the creative nonexistence). The gods were hypostasis of his almightiness, of the "powers and attributes of God" (i.e., Ashur). Parpola compares them to the Jewish and Christian archangels; he recalls furthermore the Elohim in the Bible (a possible Assyrian influence) as the designation of a transcendent god. To support his thesis, Parpola quoted not only textual and iconographic data, but also onomastic data—for example, the personal names Gabbbu-ilani-Ashur, which means "Ashur is all the gods"; Ilani-aha-iddina (= "God [literally: the gods] gave [singular] a brother"); and that of King Esarhaddon (the Assyrian form of which is Ashur-aha-iddina, "Ashur gave a brother"). Analogous forms are well known, which were defined, if not as "monotheism," at least as "sophisticated polytheism." In some texts the gods were denoted as particular aspects of Marduk (Lambert, 1975). The image of Ashur, especially as he is outlined in the Sargonid period, is very close to this theology of Marduk. In the ancient Near East a form of monotheism had formerly appeared: it was the reform of the god Aton, which the pharaoh Ekhnaton had wanted in the fourteenth century BCE (Assmann, 1997). Raffaele Pettazzoni, in his *L'Essere Supremo nelle religioni primitive* (1957, pp. 156–162) warned researchers to start from known elements in order to disclose unknown ones—and the known elements are the historical monotheisms. Now all of them are seen to share common features: a prophet or reformer preaching a new religion that is precisely monotheistic and that considers *omnes dii gentium daemonia* (all the Gentile gods are demons). Such a revolution is not recorded in Assyria, so—assuming Pettazzoni's nomenclature—one cannot speak of a monotheism in Assyria (the case of Aton is, however, to be included in this class) but rather of a theology of the Supreme Being.

SEE ALSO Akitu; Enuma Elish; Marduk.

BIBLIOGRAPHY

Assmann, Jan. *Moses the Egyptian: The Memory of Egypt in Western Monotheism.* Cambridge, Mass., 1997. See chapter 2.

Fales, Frederick Mario. *L'impero assiro.* Rome and Bari, 2001.

Lambert, W. G. "The Historical Development of the Mesopotamian Pantheon: A Study in Sophisticated Polytheism." In *Unity and Diversity,* edited by H. Goedicke and J. J. M. Roberts, pp. 191–200. Baltimore and London, 1975.

Lambert, W. G. "The God Ashshur." *Iraq* 45 (1983): 82–86.

Livingstone, A. "Assur." In *Dictionary of Deities and Demons in the Bible,* edited by K. van der Toorn et al., pp. 108–109. Leiden, Boston, and Cologne, 1999.

Mander, Pietro. *Il pantheon di Abu-Salabikh.* Naples, 1986.

Mayer, W. "Der Gott Assur und die Erben Assyriens." In *Religion und Gesellschaft,* edited by Rainer Albertz and Susanne Otto, pp. 15–23. Münster, 1997.

Parpola, Simo. "Monotheism in Ancient Assyria." In *One God or Many? Concepts of Divinity in the Ancient World,* edited by Barbara N. Porter, pp. 165–209. Chebeague, Maine, 2000.

Pettazzoni, Raffaele. *L'Essere Supremo nelle religioni primitive.* Turin, 1957.

Tallqvist, Knud Leonard. *Der assyrische Gott.* Helsinki, 1932.

Vera Chamaza, G. W. *Die Omnipotenz Ashshur's.* Münster, 2002.

TIKVA FRYMER-KENSKY (1987)
PIETRO MANDER (2005)

ʿĀSHŪRĀʾ

ʿĀSHŪRĀʾ is the tenth day of Muḥarram, the first month of the Muslim calendar. Its general significance as a fast day for Muslims derives from the rites of the Jewish Yom Kippur (Day of Atonement). The Arabic term *ʿāshūrāʾ* is based on the Hebrew word *ʿasor* with the Aramaic determinative ending.

Scholars are not agreed as to the exact day on which ʿĀshūrāʾ was observed in early Islam. Early *ḥadīth* tradition seems to indicate that the day possessed special sanctity in Arab society even before Islam. Thus the Jewish rite, which the Prophet observed in Medina in 622 CE, only helped an already established Arab tradition to acquire religious content and hence greater prestige. The Jewish character was soon obscured, however, through its incorporation into the Muslim calendar and its observance as a Muslim fast day. With the institution of the fast of Ramadan in the second year of the Hijrah, ʿĀshūrāʾ became a voluntary fast.

THE MARTYRDOM OF ḤUSAYN. For over thirteen centuries the Shīʿī community has observed the day of ʿĀshūrāʾ as a day of mourning. On the tenth of Muḥarram 61 AH (October 10, 680) Ḥusayn ibn ʿAlī, the grandson of the Prophet and third imam of the Shīʿī Muslims, fell in battle on the plain of Karbala, a small town on the banks of the Euphrates in Iraq. Muʿāwiyah, the first Ummayad caliph, had died in the spring of the same year and was succeeded by his son Yazīd. This hereditary appointment met with strong opposition in many quarters of the Muslim community, which was already torn by conflict and dissension. Among the dissenting groups was the party (*shīʿah*) of ʿAlī.

The events leading to Ḥusayn's death, which were subsequently elaborated and greatly embellished, helped to heighten the drama of suffering and martyrdom. With his family and a small following, Ḥusayn encamped in Karbala on the second day of Muḥarram. During the week of his fruitless negotiations with ʿUmar ibn Saʿd, the Iraqi governor's representative, Ḥusayn and his family were denied access to the Euphrates. The thirst of the women and children and their pathetic entreaties for water provided one of the major themes of suffering and heroism for the drama of Karbala. In the fateful battle between Ḥusayn's small band of less than one hundred and the four-thousand strong army of ʿUbayd Allāh ibn Ziyād, governor of Iraq, Ḥusayn and nearly all his followers fell. The women and children were carried captive first to ʿUbayd Allāh ibn Ziyād in Kufa, and from there to Damascus, where Yazīd received them kindly and at their own request sent them back to Medina.

ʿĀSHŪRĀʾ IN SHĪʿĪ PIETY. The death of Ḥusayn produced an immediate reaction in the Muslim community, especially in Iraq. It is reported in al-Majlisī's *Biḥār al-anwār* (vol. 45, pp. 108–115) that when the people of Kufa saw the head of the martyred imam and the pitiful state of the captives they began to beat their breasts in remorse for their betrayal of the grandson of the Prophet and son and heir of ʿAlī. This reaction produced an important movement known as al-Tawwābīn (the Repenters), which nurtured a spirit of revenge for the blood of Ḥusayn and provided fertile soil for the new ʿĀshūrāʾ cult. ʿAlī Zayn al-ʿĀbidīn, the only surviving son of Ḥusayn, was proclaimed fourth imam by a large segment of the Shīʿī community. His house in Medina and those of subsequent imams became important centers for the growth of the ʿĀshūrāʾ celebration, where commemorative services (*majālis al-ʿazāʾ*) were held. At first, these consisted of recounting the tragedy of Karbala and reflecting on its meaning and reciting elegies (*marāthī*) in memory of the martyred imam. Soon, the shrines of the imams became important places of pilgrimage (*ziyārah*), where the pious continue to this day to hold their memorial services.

During Ummayad rule (680–750) the ʿĀshūrāʾ cult grew in secret. But under the Abbasids (750–1258), who came to power on the wave of pro-Alid revolts, it was encouraged, and by the beginning of the fourth century AH (tenth century CE) public commemorations were marked by a professional mourner (*nāʾiḥ*), who chanted elegies and led the faithful in the dirge for the martyred imam and his followers.

In 962, under the patronage of the Buyids (an Iranian dynasty with deep Shīʿī sympathies that held power in Iraq and Iran from 932 to 1055), ʿĀshūrāʾ was declared a day of public mourning in Baghdad. Processions filled the streets, markets were closed, and shops were draped in black. Special edifices called *ḥusaynīyāt* were built to house the ʿĀshūrāʾ celebrations. By the end of the third century AH such buildings were common in Cairo, Aleppo, and many Iranian cities.

The greatest impetus for the development of the ʿĀshūrāʾ celebration as a popular religious and artistic phenomenon came with the rise of the Safavid dynasty in Iran in 1501. The Safavids adopted Shiism as Iran's state religion and worked tirelessly to consolidate and propagate it. It was during their rule that the literary genre known as *taʿziyah* (passion play) was highly developed and popularized. From Iran the ʿĀshūrāʾ celebration spread first to the Indian subcontinent and from there to other areas influenced by Iranian language and culture.

Some scholars have postulated a direct relation between the ʿĀshūrāʾ celebration and the ancient rites of Tammuz and Adonis, but the extent of such influence can never be determined. The fact that Ḥusayn died on the very spot where they were observed may simply be a historical coincidence, and it is perhaps more plausible that parallels between these two phenomena are due to human psychology and the need to express strong emotions through a common form of myth and ritual.

SEE ALSO Taʿziyah.

BIBLIOGRAPHY

My *Redemptive Suffering in Islam: A Study of the Devotional Aspects of ʿĀshūrāʾ in Twelver Shīʿism* (The Hague, 1978) is the most comprehensive work to date in English dealing with the rise and meaning of the ʿĀshūrāʾ cult and its earliest written sources. Gustave E. von Grunebaum's *Muhammadan Festivals* (New York, 1951) discusses ʿĀshūrāʾ in the context of other Muslim festivals. Charles Virolleaud's *Le théâtre persan, ou Le drame de Kerbéla* (Paris, 1950) provides a comprehensive study of the ʿĀshūrāʾ celebrations and the passion plays associated with them.

MAHMOUD M. AYOUB (1987)

ASKLEPIOS, also known as Asklapios (Gr.) and Aesculapius (Lat.), was the ancient Greek god of healing. The etymology of the name *Asklepios* is uncertain, but it may derive from *ēpiotēs,* meaning "gentleness."

ORIGIN OF THE CULT. Asklepios's cult seems to have originated at Tricca (modern Trikkala in Thessaly), where he must have been consulted as a *hērōs iatros* ("hero physician"). Though excavated, his site there has yielded no further information about his cult. From Tricca, Asklepios traveled in the form of a baby in swaddling clothes to Titane on the Peloponnese. His fame as a healer grew, and he came to settle at nearby Epidaurus. There he ranked already as a god and was recognized by the state cult (as was also the case later in Kos,

Athens, Rome, and Pergamum). Epidaurus maintained the cult and the rites associated with it; furthermore, the city founded numerous sanctuaries elsewhere that were dedicated to the god. Two hundred are known to have existed throughout the Greco-Roman world. Migrations of the cult were always effected by transporting one of Asklepios's sacred snakes from the sanctuary in Epidaurus. The snake was the god in his theriomorphic manifestation, for Asklepios was an essentially chthonic deity (one having origins in the earth), as his epithets "snake" and "dog" amply testify. The snake embodies the capacity for renewal of life and rebirth in health, whereas the dog, with its reliable instinct for following a scent, represents a healthy invulnerability to both illusion and sham. Asklepios probably inherited his dog aspect from his father Apollo Kunegetes ("patron of dogs").

MYTHOLOGY. Asklepios was apparently more successful than other mortal healers such as Amphiaraos or Trophonios. Nevertheless, knowledge about these two figures is invaluable in our reconstruction of the cult of Asklepios. After proving himself a healer of extraordinary success, serving for instance as *genius loci* ("guardian spirit") at the oracle of Tricca and curing the most hopeless illnesses, Asklepios went so far as to resurrect the dead, a display of pride or hubris that greatly angered Zeus. Zeus then cast a thunderbolt at the physician, but instead of killing him, the shock rendered him immortal by way of apotheosis.

The history of the divine Asklepios is found in both Pindar's *Pythian Ode* and Ovid's *Metamorphoses* 11, in which the mortal woman Coronis becomes pregnant with Asklepios, fathered by Apollo. She wants to marry one Ischys in order to legitimatize the birth of the child, but Apollo gets jealous and causes her to be burned to death. While the mother dies on a funeral pyre, Apollo rescues his child by means of a Caesarean section, and entrusts the infant to the centaur Chiron. Chiron teaches the child the art of healing, and Asklepios grows into his role as a god-man (*theios anēr*). Additional knowledge about the healer is derived, for the most part, from tales about the cures he effected, especially through the process called incubation.

INCUBATION. The cult of Asklepios is hardly documented, whereas literary evidence of his cures is abundant. Extant are more than seventy case histories from the sanctuaries at Epidaurus, Kos, and the Tiber Island at Rome. Edited with care by priests, the texts have been carved on stone slabs, or stelae. Each gives the identity of the patient, the diagnosis of the illness, and the dream experienced during incubation in the holy precincts. The dream was believed to have been the therapeutic experience resulting in the cure.

Upon arriving in the *hieron*, the sacred precinct, the patient was lodged in a guest house and came under the care of the priests. A series of lustrations for purification, followed by sacrifices, were performed by the patient as preparation for the ritual cure. Baths, in particular cold baths, were always required of the patients. Abundant springs existed in the sanctuaries of Asklepios, but because they were cold rather than warm or mineral baths, the Asklepieia never degenerated into mere spas for pleasure.

The preferred sacrificial animal was the cock, as witnessed by Plato (*Phaedo* 118a), who tells how Socrates, having taken his lethal drink, asks his friends to offer a cock to Asklepios for having cured him of the sickness of life. The patient reported his dreams to the priest and, as soon as he had a propitious dream, was taken the following night to the *abaton* (or *aduton*), that is, to the "place forbidden to the 'unbidden' ones." There the patient had to lie on a cot, or *klinē* (from which our word *clinic* derives), in order to await the healing experience, which came either during sleep or while he was yet awake from excitement, in other words, by means of a dream or a vision. During this night the patient nearly always had a decisive dream; called the *enupnion enarges* ("effective dream"), it was considered to constitute the cure. Indeed, a patient not healed at this time was deemed incurable. A small offering of thanksgiving was required at this point; should the patient forget, the god would surely send a relapse.

We learn a great deal more about the god Asklepios through the records (*iamata*) of the healing dreams themselves. If the god manifested himself, he appeared as a tall, bearded man with a white cloak (much like the modern physician) and a serpent staff (the emblem of the healer even today), possibly accompanied by a dog. He was often accompanied as well by his wife or daughters: Hygieia ("health," whence our word *hygiene*), Panakeia ("panacea"), Iaso ("healing"), and Epione ("the gentle-handed"). The serpent, the dog, or Asklepios himself by means of his *digitus medicinalis* ("healing finger") would touch the diseased part of the incubant's body and disappear.

Such is the pattern of the typical miraculous cure, but many variations were witnessed. Some of the dreams were prophetic (revealing the location of lost property, or the mending of a broken object, for instance), and showed Asklepios to be the true son of Apollo, the god of prophecy. Additional cases are known, however, where the god refused to effect an immediate cure and instead prescribed a specific therapy: the taking of cold baths, attending the theater, making music (analogous to Socrates' daemon), or writing poetry (as in the case of Aelius Aristides). In yet other cases, he prescribed a certain medicine or applied shock therapy. Rumor had it that Hippocrates learned his art of medicine from the dreams of the patients of the Asklepieion at Kos, the activity of which he tried nevertheless to suppress in favor of his so-called scientific method. After Hippocrates' death, however, the Asklepieion was further enlarged, and theurgic medicine flourished there all the more, with the result that the Hippocratic physicians, claiming a scientific tradition, were unable to eliminate the cult altogether. Thus, a period followed during which physicians and priests coexisted in the treatment of disease to the benefit of the patients.

HISTORY. On account of his spectacular successes in healing, Asklepios soon became the most popular deity of the Hellenistic world. His shrines multiplied until no large settlement existed without one. Well over two hundred shrines are known today, and still more are being discovered from time to time. The radius of this explosion was considerable: even today it is possible to find his snakes (*elaphē longissima*) at the German spa Schlangenbad ("snake bath"). With the rise of Christianity, Asklepios, because of his gentleness and willingness to aid suffering people, came into rather serious competition with Christ, so that the Christian bishops, Theophilus in particular, found themselves compelled to eradicate his temples.

At this point, it may be useful to examine the history of the Asklepieion on the Tiber Island in Rome. In 291 BCE a devastating plague ravaged Latium, and neither medicine nor sacrifice had any effect. The Roman authorities sent a delegation to Epidaurus to ask Asklepios for help. The god accepted their invitation and boarded the Roman boat in the guise of a huge snake. When the boat arrived at Ostia and was being drawn up the river Tiber, the snake jumped onto an island (Isola Tiberina) and insisted on dwelling there. A temple was built and dedicated to Asklepios, and the plague subsided.

This Asklepieion flourished for centuries, and the island was enclosed with slabs of travertine (a light-colored limestone) in the shape of a ship, the stern of which was adorned with a portrait of Asklepios and his serpent staff. Later, an Egyptian obelisk was erected in the middle of the island to represent the ship's mast. The temple has since been turned into a Christian church, San Bartolomeo, which is still adorned by fourteen splendid columns from the Hellenistic temple. In front of the altar is a deep well that contains the water of life so indispensable to Asklepios. Still more striking is the fact that, to this day, the Tiber Island remains a center of healing: the hospital of the Fatebenefratelli, the best of all the clinics in modern Rome, is located right across from the church.

COMPARATIVE RELIGION. Emma J. and Ludwig Edelstein (1945) have tried to reconstruct the cult of Asklepios from carefully collected testimonies; their attempt remains unconvincing, however, because they failed to develop a comparative point of view. It is important to take note of comparable heroes or deities connected with the ritual practice of incubation: Amphiaraos, Trophonios, Sarapis, and Imhotep, to name a few. In every instance the cure is regarded as a mystery, and the rites leading to the cure become models for the ritual components of the mystery cults. The oracles and healing cults were always found in sacred groves, were entered by means of a descent into the earth, and included a sacred well for purificatory baths. An analogy may be noted to the worship of Mithra, which took place *inter nemora et fontes* ("among groves and springs") and whose incubants regarded themselves as prisoners of the deity in a state of sacred detention *(katochē)*. Aristides called the literary works that he owed to Asklepios *hieroi logoi* ("sacred words"), the technical expression reserved for mystery texts. Here also we discover the symbolism of the ritual bridal chamber (*thalamos*) and the sacred marriage (*hieros gamos*) that later became central in both Gnosticism and Christian mysticism (especially in the writings of Origen). The paraphernalia surrounding the cult of incubation guaranteed the people of the ancient world a restoration of health and wealth by restoring the harmony of body and soul (*soma kai psuche*), the disturbance of which was understood to be the source of any illness, a notion present already in Plato's *Symposium* (186d).

The Tiber Island is only one example of the assimilation into Christianity of an important religious phenomenon belonging to one of its closest neighbors. In modern Greece, moreover, and in the Balkans, there are still numerous churches where people go to sleep in order to receive beneficial dreams. Most of these belong to the Panagia Pege ("all-hallowed fountain") taken over from Asklepios's consort, Hygieia. Each one has its own well or is situated close by a river.

ARCHAEOLOGY. Because the Christian bishops were so thorough in destroying the temples of Asklepios, architectural remains are very scanty. However, three things associated with the shrines are worth noting: the theater, the rotunda, and numerous statues. Drama and music were essential elements in the treatments of Asklepios. The theater at Epidaurus is the largest and finest of the ancient world. The rotunda there was the most beautiful and most expensive building of antiquity and was under construction for twenty-one years. Its foundation is a classical labyrinth, and the cupola is covered with Pausias's paintings of Sober Drunkenness (*methē nēphalias*) and Eros, the latter having thrown away his bow and arrows to hold instead the lyre. We can only guess at the function of this building. Several of the statues of Asklepios have been preserved, and the best one (from the Tiber Island) is now in the Museo Nazionale in Naples. Reliefs illustrating memorable dream events from the *abaton* are also on view there. The statues of Asklepios are often accompanied by the dwarfish figure of Telesphoros ("bringer of the goal"), a hooded boy who is associated with mystery cults like the one at Eleusis. From Pausanias we know that Asklepios was eventually assimilated into the Eleusinia.

SEE ALSO Dreams; Healing and Medicine; Sleep.

BIBLIOGRAPHY

Aristides. *The Complete Works.* 2 vols. Edited and translated by Charles A. Behr. Leiden, 1981.

Deubner, Otfried. *Das Asklepieion von Pergamon: Kurze vorläufige Beschreibung.* Berlin, 1938.

Edelstein, Emma J., and Ludwig Edelstein. *Asclepius: A Collection and Interpretation of the Testimonies.* 2 vols. Baltimore, 1945.

Herzog, Rudolf. *Die Wunderheilungen von Epidauros: Ein Beitrag zur Geschichte der Medizin und der Religion.* Leipzig, 1931.

Kerényi, Károly. *Asklepios: Archetypal Image of the Physician's Existence.* New York, 1959.

Meier, C. A. *Ancient Incubation and Modern Psychotherapy.* Evanston, Ill., 1967.

New Sources

Aelius Aristide. *Discours Sacrés. Rêve, religion, médicine au IIe siècle apr. J.Chr.*, introduction and translation by André-Jean Festugière, notes by Henry-Dominique Saffrey, preface by Jacques Le Goff. Paris, 1986.

Aleshire, Sara B. *The Athenian Asklepieion. The People, their Dedications and the Inventories.* Amsterdam, 1989.

Aleshire, Sara B. *Asklepios at Athens. Epigraphic and Prosopographic Essays on the Athenian Healing Cults.* Amsterdam, 1991.

Benedun, Christa. "Asklepius: der homerische Arzt und der Gott von Epidauros." *Rheinisches Museum* 133 (1990): 210–226.

Benedum, Christa. "Betrachtungen zu Asklepios und dem Aesculapius der Römer." *Würzburger Jahrbücher für die Altertumswissenschaft. Neue Folge* 25 (2001): 187–297.

Clinton, Kevin. "The Epidauria and the Arrival of Asclepius in Athens." In *Ancient Greek Cult Practice from the Epigraphical Evidence: Proceedings of the Second International Seminar on Ancient Greek Cult, Organized by the Swedish Institute at Athens, 22–24 Nov. 1991*, edited by Robin Hägg, pp. 17–34. Stockholm, 1994.

Den Boeft, Jan. "Christ and Asklepios." *Euphrosyne* 25 (1997): 337–342.

Festugière, André-Jean. *Personal Religion among the Greeks.* Berkeley-Los Angeles, 1954. See chapter 6, pp. 85–104 ("Popular Piety: Aelius Aristeides and Asclepius").

Graf, Fritz. "Heiligtum und Ritual. Das Beispiel der griechisch-römischen Asklepeion." In *Le sanctuaire grec*, edited by Albert Schachter and Jean Bingen, pp. 159–199. Vandeouvres-Genève, 1992.

Guarducci, Margherita. "L'isola tiberina e la sua tradizione ospitaliera." In *Scritti scelti sulla religione greca e romana e sul cristianesimo*, pp. 180–197. Leiden, 1993.

Habicht, Christian. *Die Inschriften des Asklepieion.* Berlin, 1969.

Leglay, Marcel. "Hadrien et l'Asklépieion de Pergame." *Bulletin de Correspondance Hellénique* 100 (1976): 347–372.

Musial, Danuta. *Le développement du culte d'Esculape au mond romain.* Toruń, Poland, 1992.

Ruttimann, R. J. *Asclepius and Jesus: The Form, Character and Status of the Asclepius Cult in the Second Century CE and its Influence on Early Christianity.* Ann Arbor, 1990.

Schäfer, Daniel. "Traum und Wunderheilung im Asklepios-Kult und in der griechisch-römischen Medizin." In *Heilkunde und Hochkultur. 1. Geburt, Seuche und Traumdeutungen in den antiken Zivilisationen des Mittelmeerraumes*, edited by Axel Karenberg and Christian Leitz, pp. 259–274. Münster, 2000.

C. A. MEIER (1987)
Revised Bibliography

ASMĀʾ AL-ḤUSNĀ, AL- SEE ATTRIBUTES OF GOD, *ARTICLE ON* ISLAMIC CONCEPTS

AŚOKA (Skt.; Pali and Prakrit, Asoka), the third and most powerful of the Mauryan emperors who once dominated the Indian subcontinent (fourth to third centuries BCE), figures centrally in historical as well as legendary accounts of the early Buddhist community's transformation into a world religion. Aśoka's landmark reign (c. 270–230 BCE) laid important structural foundations for subsequent south Asian imperial formation and corresponding transregional Buddhist networks, while his memory has continued to inspire and shape Buddhist practices and politics into modern times.

Scholars possess invaluable evidence for reconstruction of Aśokan history in the form of proclamations issued in Aśoka's own voice and inscribed on rocks, stone slabs, and ornate carved pillars that have survived in scattered places throughout what was once Aśoka's empire, spreading from central India to the Northwest Frontier province of Pakistan. These inscriptions, which are the oldest surviving south Asian written documents of any kind, were composed in the vernacular language (*prakrit*) of Magadha (northeast Indian), where Aśoka lived and ruled, modified as appropriate in the various regions where they were inscribed or erected (one of them also appeared in Aramaic and Greek). Aśoka intended them to be read aloud, announcing his policies, laws, decisions, and especially his religio-political philosophy to all his subjects in a language they could understand.

The central conception underlying the philosophy of these inscriptions is *dharma* (Skt.; Pali, *dhamma*; Prakrit, *dhaṃma*) or "righteousness," through which Aśoka claimed to rule. The question of whether this *dharma* should be taken as a secular philosophy of Aśoka's own invention or equated with the specifically Buddhist usage of that term (to mean "doctrine," "truth," "the Buddha's words") is much debated and unresolved, as is the question, given his generous support of non-Buddhist (Brahmanical, Jain, and Ājīvika) as well as Buddhist practitioners, whether he was genuinely or exclusively Buddhist in personal practice. But it is certain that at least after the eighth year of his reign Aśoka strongly supported, and gained support from, the teachings and practices of the Buddha's followers, and later legendary accounts celebrate him primarily as a paradigmatic supporter of Buddhist monks and institutions.

Aśoka states that his commitment to *dharma* was wrought in the regret he felt at the suffering he caused by conquering Kaliṅga, in eastern India (modern Orissa and eastern Andhra Pradesh), during his eighth year. Henceforth, he pursued "conquest by righteousness" (Prakrit, *dhaṃmavijaya*) and, after his thirteenth year, administered the empire through "righteous ministers" (Prakrit, *dhaṃmamahāmāta*), effecting laws and policies that, as mentioned, reflected Aśoka's piety and sincerity (or, as some scholars have argued, his shrewd self-presentation). In personal practice, he tells us, he became a Buddhist lay devotee (*upāsaka*) in his eighth regnal year but only began to strenuously exert himself eighteen months later. His inscriptions (and other archaeological evidence) testify to that effort: he constructed stupas and gave other financial support for monks and monasteries, intervened in monastic disputes (and recommended which texts monks, nuns, and fellow laypeople ought to study), and made pilgrimages to sites of significance in the Buddha's life.

The Buddhist spirit behind Aśoka's *dharma* is also manifest. His inscriptions recommend kindness to all creatures including plants (he tried to eliminate all killing of animals, birds, and fish in his dominions, and protected and planted forests and medicinal herbs even outside his own domains); respectfulness and obedience (toward parents, elders, teachers, Brahmins, and mendicants, and royal authority); liberality, truthfulness, impartiality, frugality and lack of acquisitiveness, and reverence and faith; avoidance of violence, cruelty, anger, arrogance, hastiness, laziness, and jealousy; and similar "righteous virtues" (Prakrit, *dhaṃmaguna*), which left an indelible mark on south Asian religions even outside the Buddhist context. Though the Mauryan dynasty did not long outlast Aśoka himself, his hope that his "sons, grandsons, and great-grandsons will increase [his] practice of *dharma* until the end of a universal aeon" did come true in this and several additional ways, and Aśoka's life and deeds remained foundational for subsequent South Asian and Buddhist political and religious history.

First, Aśoka's own imperial strategies were appropriated and developed by his post-Mauryan successors, effectively constituting Aśoka's empire as the one that all subsequent kings struggled to remake for themselves. Aśoka inherited an already sizeable kingdom in northeastern India from his father, Bimbisāra (c. 298–270 BCE), and his grandfather, dynastic founder Candragupta Maurya (c. 322–298 BCE), whose court was visited by ambassadors of Alexander the Great (providing a synchronism with Western chronology upon which much of ancient Indian history is still dated). But, ruling from his capital at modern Patna in northern Bihar, Aśoka was the first known Indian king of any dynasty to expand the empire to embrace the whole subcontinent (except, in Aśoka's case, the modern Tamil Nadu, Kerala, southern Karnataka, Assam, and Bangladesh), and he pushed its borders northwest into what is now eastern Afghanistan. He maintained diplomatic relations even farther afield, sending embassies to rulers in the far south and Sri Lanka, and also throughout the eastern Hellenistic world, which established Aśoka among the most powerful monarchs of his day. More important than military conquest in this expansion—especially after his eighth year—were Aśoka's innovative strategies for displaying and maintaining his imperial overlordship, always in the context of his proclamation of the *dharma*.

One of the most important imperial strategies, whose significance is often overlooked by scholars, was the practice itself of erecting stone inscriptions, which must have involved considerable mobilization of resources—Aśoka's pillar capitals rank with India's earliest and most treasured art; the technology of preparing and inscribing the various surfaces is sophisticated; and the attempt to broadcast the same messages in a local idiom which thereby functioned as a *lingua franca* across such a wide expanse of territory demonstrates enormous internal organization and vision—and was unprecedented in Indian history (it has been argued that Aśoka imitated Persian and Hellenistic predecessors). But the practice allowed Aśoka to physically and permanently mark his authority over the different regions whose submission he won, to address the subjects of these regions directly (and lovingly), and to make them feel sheltered by his single royal umbrella. This practice of inscribing decisions, donations, and eulogies in stone, and simultaneously landmarking key sites in important monarchs' territories, became a *sine qua non* of subsequent south Asian political formation, especially at the imperial level. The vast corpus of south Asian epigraphs that today constitute the most important primary evidence for south Asian history literally continued Aśoka's discourse in stone for more than two millennia; for more than five centuries after Aśoka this lithic discourse even continued to use essentially his same alphabet and language.

Similarly, a number of key Buddhist sites Aśoka constructed or visited—such as Sāñcī, Sārnāth, Amarāvatī, Bhārhut, Lumbinī, Bodh Gayā, and Kusinārā—continued to be developed and improved by influential Buddhist monks, nuns, and wealthy laypeople, including a string of Aśoka's imperial successors, for more than five hundred years after his death. These sites were subsequently transformed into Hindu sites or reclaimed by Buddhists beginning in the late nineteenth century; these remain important places of worship even today. In like fashion, even after Hindu disciplinary orders had come to dominate the ideology of Indian imperial formation beginning in the third century CE, numerous additional Aśokan imperial strategies—with widely divergent content—persisted into modern times, including engaging in imperial processions to the various regions and holding festivals and conspicuous displays in them, summoning kings and other representatives of those regions to the imperial court, constructing public works such as roadside rests and wells, centralizing the administration of outlying regions, making laws, employing royal symbols and epithets, practicing public and much-publicized charity to the poor and religious mendicants, freeing prisoners, adjudicating sectarian disputes, and facilitating transregional diplomacy, trade, and intellectual and artistic exchange, especially through the employment of a universal language.

In addition to the imperial strategies that Aśoka himself employed, talking about Aśoka—and claiming to be his legitimate successor—became an important post-Aśokan imperial strategy in its own right. Aśoka's founder status in the imperial struggles that concerned later kings made claims about his life and legacy politically and religiously significant, quite apart from their correspondence or lack of correspondence to the historical Aśoka. These claims developed in communities of monks and nuns favored by strong kings, and were textualized as the famous legends of Aśoka, a second important means by which he continued to impact political and religious thinking long after his inscriptions had become illegible antiques. Two basic recensions are especially well known. One was preserved in the northern Buddhist traditions of Kashmir, Central Asia, and later East Asia and is epitomized by the *Aśokāvadāna* of the *Divyāvadāna* collection, composed in Buddhist Sanskrit in about the first century CE, then translated into Chinese and Tibetan. The other was preserved in the Sri Lankan and Southeast Asian *vaṃsa* or chronicle traditions, which originated in central India, were codified in Pali in Sri Lanka, and were also transmitted through vernacular literatures in the region. But contradictions and disagreements about the details abound, even within these two main lines of transmission and especially between them, while scattered evidence in the accounts of Chinese pilgrims to India, as well as additional texts preserved in the Chinese *tripṭaka* and the Tibetan historical annals, indicate that this pan-Buddhist discourse about Aśoka was much wider and more varied still. The accounts of Chinese pilgrims make clear that claimed associations with Aśoka still mapped most of Buddhist Asia even in their day (fourth to seventh centuries CE); they relate their multiple versions of the Aśoka legend in the context of places he was remembered to have visited or stupas he was remembered to have constructed, many of them far beyond Aśoka's own reach. In Sri Lanka, Nepal, and Southeast Asia such associations have persisted into modern times.

Despite the wide variation among them, all the extant versions of the Aśoka legend share a basic narrative structure, which in places bears partial affinity to the historical Aśoka known through the inscriptions. These legends all maintain that Aśoka was originally a cruel king who experienced a transformation into Dharmāśoka ("Righteous Aśoka") after being pleased (Skt., *prasāda*; Pali, *pasāda)* by the Buddha's *dharma*. Aśoka created a great Buddhist empire, ceremonially abdicated power to the *saṃgha*, and landmarked it by the construction of stupas and the performance of Buddhist liturgies (the northern Buddhist versions focus upon festivals held every fifth year; the southern Buddhist versions highlight constant bodhi tree worship). He also sponsored a recitation of the *dharma*, which was headed up by a favored patriarch, who then effected the dissemination of that *dharma* and with it Aśoka's imperial legacy to all of Asia in general and especially to some favored region that had been predicted by the Buddha himself to be of extraordinary significance during later history; a close kinsman of Aśoka's played some special role in this paradigmatic sequence of events. But within this detailed basic agreement the texts disagree furiously about when Aśoka lived, which teachings of the Buddha effected Aśoka's transformation (and served as the basis of his imperial power), which regions were directly embraced by Aśoka, which specific stupas he built, which liturgies he performed, which recitation of the *dharma* he sponsored, the identity of his favored monk, the location of the privileged region predicted to be of significance in later history, the name of the kinsman and his relationship to Aśoka, and the nature of the role this kinsman played in the king's transformation.

The scholars who first deciphered the Aśokan inscriptions in the 1830s already knew these legends, and relied upon them for vocabulary and syntax, as well as for numerous "facts" left out of the inscriptions, beginning with details about Aśoka's ancestry and youth; at least four queens, two sons, and a daughter who are unknown in the inscriptions (wherein are mentioned a queen and her son unknown in the legends); various specifics of his conversion and religious practice; and his old age and death. But given the disagreements among the different versions, this required scholars to privilege one over the others, generating a number of influential theories about which version was in fact the earliest or most authentic, and attacks on the others as derivative or fabricated. Beginning with the work of Vincent Smith at the turn of the twentieth century, however, scholars grew more cautious about using the legends as historical sources; their sometimes great distance from the time of Aśoka himself, the various miraculous, supernatural or otherwise difficult-to-believe aspects they contain, and especially their disagreement over details with each other and with the inscriptions, led many scholars following Smith to dismiss all of them as having any relevance to the historical study of Aśoka. Other scholars continued to treat them, at best, as colorful footnotes to the hard evidence of the inscriptions.

While divorcing the legends from the inscriptions was no doubt crucial for the reconstruction of Aśokan history proper, in the later twentieth century scholars returned to them with more fruitful questions than what facts about Aśoka they can provide. John Strong has shown that in the time of the Chinese pilgrims (fourth to seventh centuries CE) Aśokan pillars were still remembered as Aśokan, but could no longer be read; the information the pilgrims gathered was all based on the legends, even when it was presented to them as a reading of some inscription. By the fourteenth century even the association with Aśoka had been lost; now-dominant Hindus and Muslims were providing alternative legendary accounts of the pillars (and had reduced Aśoka to a mere name in their lists of Mauryan kings). Thus for most of history the Aśoka known and admired by Buddhists has been the Aśoka of the legends, not the inscriptions.

In one sense these legends about Aśoka can be read as post-Aśokan political ideology, privileging the authority of an empire-building Buddhist king and the monks most closely associated with him to command Aśoka's imperial space. The questions engendered by this discourse were simultaneously questions about the then-present, an actual interregnal Buddhist world that all Buddhists agreed to frame according to the Aśokan legacy. Arguments about when Aśoka lived, who that patriarch was, where he established the center of the Buddhist world and what lineage he represented, were simultaneously arguments that this (not that) is the true center of the Buddhist world, the true lineage from the Buddha, correct practice, correct doctrine. The debate raged over details because Buddhists (especially Buddhist kings and courtiers) in different regions, and even within the same region, had different ambitions as regards the "this," the particular hierarchical constellation of Buddhist polities and schools to which any particular version of the Aśoka legend committed them.

But in another sense these legends were more than political posturing; they could be championed in a politically significant way only to the extent that they were believed to paint the truest picture of an Aśoka who was admired and revered as paradigmatic across the Buddhist world. There is plentiful evidence that in India, central Asia, Sri Lanka and Southeast Asia, and even China various powerful Buddhist kings directly modeled themselves after the legendary Aśoka, either explicitly (as in their inscriptions or official chronicles) or implicitly, through their imitation of his paradigmatic activities in the legends, such as stupa construction; bodhi worship; gift-giving; the convening of festivals, conferences, and recitations of the *dharma*; and integrity and personal piety. Taking Aśoka as exemplary of proper Buddhist kingship was so common in premodern Theravāda Buddhist kingdoms in modern Myanmar, Thailand, and Sri Lanka, in fact, that scholars have theorized a specifically Aśokan model of kingship, social order, and imperial formation that has even been invoked by contemporary politicians in these regions to a variety of political and personal ends.

Outside politics altogether, aspects of these legends of Aśoka, especially those popularized in vernacular literature (and art), have inspired generations of Buddhists in a variety of ways. Individual monks associated in these legends with Aśoka and the Aśokan dissemination of the *dharma* have been worshiped throughout the Buddhist world. Pilgrimage in honor of Aśoka's son Mahinda (who according to the southern recension of the Aśoka legend brought the religion to Sri Lanka at the conclusion of the Third Council convened by Aśoka's favorite patriarch, Moggaliputtatissa) remains one of the most important annual Sinhala Buddhist festivals. There is premodern Burmese evidence of veneration of Sona and Uttara, who according to the southern recension brought the religion to that land, and likewise of Madhyantika in Kashmir. A wide variety of religious practices surrounding Upagupta, Aśoka's favorite patriarch according to the northern recension of the Aśoka legend, were once widespread in the northern Buddhist world and survive in contemporary Burma and northern Thailand. Stories about Aśoka's conduct as king, and that of his queens, have been invoked as both positive and negative paradigms for then-present royal conduct; as an exemplar of religious giving (*dāna*) more generally, Aśoka is virtually unexcelled in Buddhist hagiography. Stories about Aśoka's past-life deeds and their consequences in the present have also enjoyed this more general religious significance in Buddhist countries.

The post-1830s Orientalist project of reconstructing "the historical Aśoka" has opened yet another avenue through which that ancient Indian emperor's influence continues to be felt today, for he emerged there as a model of virtues worth imitating universally, even outside the cultural and religious context to which both the historical and the legendary Aśokas belonged. These virtues include globalism, religious tolerance and interfaith dialogue, diplomacy over violence, support for the poor, commitment to truth and liberty, personal integrity, and environmentalism. This "Great Man" Aśoka—who has been compared with Constantine, Marcus Aurelius, Charlemagne, Alexander the Great, Napoleon Bonaparte, Saint Paul, and V. I. Lenin, among many others—has been lauded by twentieth-century luminaries including H. G. Wells, who said "the name of Aśoka shines, and shines almost alone, a star" among all the great monarchs of history, and Jawaharlal Nehru, for whom Aśoka exemplified the sort of secular federalism that India adopted at independence (an Aśokan pillar capital with four lions constitutes India's official seal). Aśoka is ubiquitous in academic and popular accounts of Indian and Buddhist history ranging from scholarly monographs to comic books.

See Also Cakravartin; Missions, article on Buddhist Missions; Saṃgha, article on Saṃgha and Society in South and Southeast Asia.

Bibliography

Primary and secondary sources for the study of Aśoka abound even in English and other European languages, and especially in Asian languages. A good basic reference for readers of English is Ananda W. P. Guruge, *Asoka: A Definitive Biography* (Colombo, Sri Lanka, 1993), a massive tome that surveys virtually all the primary sources for the study of Aśoka, including Prakrit (and Greek and Aramaic) texts and English translations of all the known inscriptions and discussions and lengthy translated quotations from Pali, Sanskrit, Chinese, and Tibetan legendary materials; this volume also reviews and gives an extensive bibliography of English and other European-language secondary scholarship about Aśoka, and provides Guruge's own judgments on various points debated by scholars of "the historical Aśoka" in the form of a chronological biography that weaves together inscriptional and legendary material into a believable if not uncontestable narrative. A more precise and critical general historical study of the extant sources for Aśoka, his Indian successors, and the legends of Aśoka is Étienne Lamotte, *History of Indian Buddhism, from the Origins to the Śaka Era*, translated by Sara Webb-Boin (Louvain-la-Neuve, Belgium, 1988), especially chap. 3. The now classic study of "the historical Aśoka" is Vincent A. Smith, *Aśoka: The Buddhist Emperor of India* (Oxford, 1901), while the most acclaimed work in the genre remains Romila Thapar, *Aśoka and the Decline of the Mauryas* (Oxford, 1963; 2d ed., 1973), which together with Guruge and Lamotte provide good points of entry into the larger discourse on the topic.

For texts and translations of the Aśokan inscriptions complete with plates and a text-critical apparatus, readers can consult E. Hultzsch, ed., *Corpus Inscriptionum Indicarum*, Vol. 1: *Inscriptions of Asoka, New Edition* (Oxford, 1925). Wilhelm Geiger, trans., *The Mahāvaṃsa, or the Great Chronicle of Ceylon* (London, 1901), chaps. 5 and 25, contains the most polished version of the southern recension of the Aśoka legend available in English, dating to about 460 CE; Hermann Oldenberg, ed. and trans., *The Dīpavaṃsa: An Ancient Buddhist Historical Record* (London, 1879), dating to the early fourth century CE, contains less refined textual fragments (1:24–28; 5:55–59; 5:82; 5:100–102; all of chaps. 6–8; 11:12–16:41; 17:80–109) that are probably closer translations of the now-lost and considerably more ancient sources used also by the author of *Mahāvaṃsa.* The *Aśokāvadāna* of the northern recension has been masterfully translated by John S. Strong, *The Legend of King Aśoka* (Princeton, 1983); Strong also provides an important discussion of textual interpretation, the history of the *Avadāna* collection, and the political and religious dimensions of the Aśokan paradigm contained in that text. Jean Pryzluski, *The Legend of Emperor Aśoka in Indian and Chinese Texts,* translated by Dilip Kumar Biswas (Calcutta, 1967), also includes an English rendering (inferior to Strong's) of Pryzluski's excellent French translation of *Aśokāvadāna (La legende de l'Empereur Aśoka [Aśoka-Avadāna] dans les textes Indien et Chinois* [Paris, 1923]), but more importantly makes accessible to English readers Pryzluski's pioneering work on the Kausambian and Mathuran roots of the Kashmiri version of the text as it exists today, and his arguments for its comparative antiquity vis-à-vis the southern recension. The authenticity of the southern recension is championed in the introduction to Geiger's translation of *Mahāvaṃsa.* Jonathan Walters has examined textual and archaeological evidence for its composition within the first century after Aśoka's death: "Mapping Sāñchi in a Whole Buddhist World," in C. Witanachchi, ed., *Lily De Silva Felicitation Volume* (Peradeniya, Sri Lanka, 2002), chap. 1. Ronald Inden, Jonathan Walters, and Daud Ali, *Querying the Medieval: Texts and the History of Practices in South Asia* (Oxford, 2000), chap. 3, contains a critical study of the primary sources in the southern recension, and an appendix that details early Orientalist readings of them vis-à-vis the Aśokan inscriptions. English translations of primary Tibetan texts that contain versions of the Aśoka legend are Lama Chimpa Alaka Chattopadhyaya, trans., *Tāranātha's History of Buddhism in India* (Delhi, 1990), especially chaps. 6–8; and George N. Roerich, trans., *The Blue Annals* (Delhi, 1976), especially pp. 23–35. Original texts of the travels of Chinese pilgrims Faxian and Xuanzang, replete with differing versions of the Aśoka legend and important evidence for reconstructing Aśoka's significance to Buddhists across Asia in that period can be found in the much-reprinted but still readable (and usefully indexed) Samuel Beal, trans., *Si Yu Ki: Buddhist Records of the Western World* (London, 1884; Delhi, 1981). The surveys by Guruge and Lamotte will lead readers to additional, as yet untranslated Pali, Sanskrit, Tibetan, Khotanese, and Chinese primary texts of relevance.

Three collections of essays edited by Bardwell L. Smith have proven seminal in more recent scholarship that treats the legends of Aśoka as sources for understanding his paradigmatic significance to later Buddhists rather than as sources for historical reconstruction of his own period: *The Two Wheels of Dhamma: Essays on the Theravada Tradition in India and Ceylon* (Chambersburg, Pa., 1972), and *Religion and Legitimation of Power in Sri Lanka* and *Religion and Legitimation of Power in Thailand, Laos, and Burma* (both Chambersburg, Pa., 1978). Stanley J. Tambiah, *World Conqueror and World Renouncer: A Study of Buddhism and Polity in Thailand against a Historical Background* (Cambridge, UK, 1976) is a monograph-length treatment of how the Aśokan paradigm was played out in actual political and religious practices and ideology in premodern Thailand. John C. Holt, *The Religious World of Kīrti Śrī: Buddhism, Art, and Politics in Late Medieval Sri Lanka* (New York and Oxford, 1996), examines the same question within the thicket of colonial (eighteenth-century) Sri Lanka. John S. Strong, *The Legend and Cult of Upagupta: Sanskrit Buddhism in North India and Southeast Asia* (Princeton, 1992) is an important study of the transmission of stories from the northern recension about the figure who represents its "favored patriarch of Aśoka," and their co-existence with the corresponding (and contradictory) claims of the southern recension, as well as a whole range of religious practices surrounding Upagupta in Burma and northern Thailand. Jonathan Walters's *Finding Buddhists in Global History* (Washington, D.C., 1998), especially chap. 3, theorizes in general terms the pan-Buddhist significance of debates about Aśoka in post-Aśokan Buddhist history. A valuable collection of essays that represent historicist as well as history of religions approaches to the study of Aśoka is Anuradha Seneviratne, ed., *King Aśoka and Buddhism: Historical and Literary Studies* (Kandy, Sri Lanka, 1994). For a new study of Aśoka's queens see John S. Strong, "Toward a Theory of Buddhist Queenship: The Legend of Asandhimittā," in John C. Holt, Jacob N. Kinnard, and Jonathan S. Walters, eds., *Constituting Communities: Theravāda Buddhism and the Religious Cultures of South and Southeast Asia* (Albany, N.Y., 2003), pp. 41–55.

JONATHAN S. WALTERS (2005)

ASSASSINS. The disparaging term *assassins,* originating in the Arabic *ḥashīshīyah* (users of hashish, *Cannabis sativa*), has been used to designate the followers of the Nizārī Ismāʿīlī branch of Islam. In its original form, from about the twelfth century onward, the name was used by those hostile to the movement to stigmatize the Ismāʿīlīyah of Syria for their alleged use of the drug. The designation, as well as a growing legend about the group, was subsequently transmitted to Europe by Western chroniclers of the Crusades and travelers such as Marco Polo. The legend portrayed the Nizārī Ismāʿīlīyah as a religious "order of assassins" ruled by the diabolical "Old Man of the Mountain," who incited them to murder through the use of drugs and the creation of an illusory sense of paradise. Reinforced by early Western scholarship, the term and the distorted view of the Nizārī Ismāʿīlīyah became general, until disproved by modern research.

HISTORICAL DEVELOPMENT. The Nizārī branch of the Ismāʿīlīyah had its origin in a succession dispute following the death of the Fatimid Ismāʿīlī imam al-Mustanṣir in 1094. Those who gave their allegiance to Nizār, al-Mustanṣir's eldest son, as the designated successor and imam organized themselves locally in various parts of Iran and Syria by building on and extending the groundwork already laid there during the Fatimid period.

Particularly in Iran, the Nizārīyah faced markedly changed circumstances, owing to the presence of the powerful, militantly Sunnī Turkish dynasty of the Seljuks. In addition to the hostility prevailing in political and military spheres, the Nizārī Ismāʿīlīyah, like their predecessors under the Fatimids, became the object of theological and intellectual attacks, the most significant one being that of the Sunnī theologian al-Ghazālī (d. 1111). This climate of threat accentuated a sense of isolation and prompted direct political and military action by the Nizārīyah against leaders of the Seljuk state, which in turn caused popular Sunnī feeling to harden further against them.

The focal point of the Nizārī Ismāʿīlī movement was the fortress of Alamut in the Elburz Mountains of northern Iran. This fortress, captured by the famous Ismāʿīlī leader Ḥasan-i Ṣabbāḥ in 1090, now became the center for a number of growing strongholds that were established through military and diplomatic means. In time, these centers became part of a network in Iran as well as in Syria. According to Nizārī tradition, Ḥasan acted as the representative of the imam and organized the various settlements. This process of consolidation provided a basis for what was to become a Nizārī Ismāʿīlī state incorporating both Iranian and Syrian strongholds and ruled from Alamut by Ismāʿīlī imams descended from Nizār, who assumed actual control after the initial period of establishment. Though under constant threat, the state thrived for more than 150 years, when confrontation with the expanding Mongol power led to its downfall, the demolition of its principal strongholds, and a general and widespread massacre of the Ismāʿīlīyah.

The history of the Nizārī Ismāʿīlīyah following the destruction of their state and the dispersal of their leaders in Iran and elsewhere is little known. In Syria, as in Iran, they continued to survive persecution. The Nizārī sources speak of an uninterrupted succession of imams in different parts of Iran and, in the fifteenth century, the emergence of new activity that led to a further growth of the Nizārī Ismāʿīlīyah in parts of India and Central Asia. In modern times, the community has witnessed a remarkable resurgence under its imams, Sulṭān Muḥammad Shāh, Aga Khan III (1877–1957) and the present imam, Shāh Karīm Aga Khan (1957–), both of whom have also played a major role in promoting development activities in Muslim and Third World countries. The Ismāʿīlīyah are currently found in various countries in Asia, Africa, the Middle East, and the West.

TEACHINGS. While still articulating the Shiʿi Ismāʿīlī vision of Islam developed under the Fatimids, the Nizārīyah laid particular emphasis on the principle of *taʿlīm,* authoritative teaching, and on the cosmic and metaphysical significance of the imam, whose role it was to impart that teaching. These fundamental notions acquired a more immediate relevance in conditions calling for greater discipline and obedience. Unfortunately, few Ismāʿīlī sources of the period have survived, and it is often difficult on the basis of available materials to gauge the precise significance of doctrinal development.

One religious event highlighted in the sources that came to have particular doctrinal consequence was the *qiyāmah.* Although it appeared to outsiders as a declaration of reform, it was essentially an affirmation of a religious impetus present in Ismāʿīlī doctrine from the beginning. Providing the culmination of Ismāʿīlī sacred history, the event marked the primacy of the spiritual and inner meaning of religious acts. The outward performance of ritual elaborated in the *sharīʿah,* or religious law, was not abrogated as is generally thought; as Henry Corbin, the noted French scholar of esoteric forms of Islam, has pointed out, the Ismāʿīlīyah affirm positive religion in order to inspire believers to exceed it. The symbolic meaning of the *qiyāmah* was this affirmation of the esoteric basis of Ismāʿīlī thought, the public proclamation of which came to represent a contrast with the *sharīʿah*-mindedness of those scholars of other schools who had developed a different synthesis of Islam.

The doctrine also projected a spiritual basis for the nature of the imam and for the inner transformation effected in the being of individual followers as they sought to acquire this understanding. Naṣīr al-Dīn Ṭūsī (d. 1274), the noted Shīʿī scholar, was one of those attracted by the intellectual milieu of the Ismāʿīlī state and during his stay there became an exponent of Ismāʿīlī doctrine. Within the esoteric perspective, according to his works, the physical bond between imam and follower was to be transcended by the development of a spiritual bond, so that in addition to acceptance of the historical and formal aspect of the imam's role, the believer would also be led to a recognition of the *ha-aiqah,* the aspect of Islam that, in the Ismāʿīlī view, complemented the *shariʿah* and constituted the highest level of reality in Islam.

The goal of religious life offered to the individual Ismāʿīlī by this vision was a continuing quest for inner transformation and a graduation to successively higher levels of spiritual growth and understanding. In the period following the fall of Alamūt, the inward, personal search for religious meaning would lead to increasing interaction between Ismāʿīlī doctrine and some of the principles of Sufism.

SEE ALSO Aga Khan; Imamate; Shiism, article on Ismāʿīlīyah.

BIBLIOGRAPHY

The standard modern work on the Nizārī Ismāʿīlī state is Marshall G. S. Hodgson's *The Order of Assassins: The Struggle of the Early Nizari Ismāīlis against the Islamic World* (1955; reprint, New York, 1980), of which an excellent summation will be found in his article entitled "The Ismāʿīlī State," in *The Cambridge History of Iran,* vol. 5, edited by J. A. Boyle (Cambridge, Mass., 1968), pp. 422–482. The legend and its transmission are discussed in Bernard Lewis's *The Assassins: A Radical Sect in Islam* (London, 1967) and in an unpublished paper by Amin Haji, "The Term 'Assassin' and Its Transmission in Muslim and European Sources" (Institute of Ismaili Studies, London, 1984). Henry Corbin's work on the Ismāʿīlīyah represents the most perceptive analysis of its esoteric dimension; articles relevant to Nizārī teachings are contained in his *Cyclical Time and Ismāʿīlī Gnosis* (London, 1983). Naṣīr al-Dīn Ṭūsī's *Taṣawwurāt* has been edited and translated by W. Ivanow as *Rawdatu't-Taslim, Commonly Called Taṣawwurāt* (Leiden, 1950). For the Ismāʿīlīyah in general, see the various essays in *Ismāʿīlī Contributions to Islamic Culture,* edited by Seyyed Hossein Nasr (Tehran, 1977).

AZIM NANJI (1987)

ASSOCIATION FOR RESEARCH AND ENLIGHTENMENT (ARE) is a nonprofit corporation whose mission is to spread the transformative insights that derive from the psychic readings of Edgar Cayce (1877–1945). ARE's headquarters are in Virginia Beach, Virginia, but its outreach is global. The association sponsors conferences and educational activities around the world on such topics as dreams, reincarnation, lost civilizations, psychic development, personal spirituality, *qigong, feng-shui,* and holistic health. ARE also supports the Cayce/Reilly School of Massotherapy, Atlantic University, an online bookstore, a retreat/camp for children and adults, and a library that houses an impressive collection of books and films on all aspects of personal spirituality and psychic research. It would not be an overstatement to say that ARE, during its seventy-five years of existence, has been one of America's most influential purveyors of the combination of beliefs and practices commonly known to scholars as New Age spirituality. ARE's successful adaptation to changing currents in spiritual and therapeutic practice between the mid-1960s and 2000 is a remarkable story of a new religious movement that struggled for survival during its founding generation only to flourish during a later period of cultural upheaval.

ARE's origins lie in the life and work of Cayce, a native of rural Kentucky whose experiments in self-hypnosis led him to a career as a psychic healer. The experiments came about during a period of ill health that rendered Cayce almost incapable of speech. A doctor from New York, one of many specialists consulted by Cayce's family, suggested that Cayce diagnose his own condition while in a hypnotic trance. The diagnosis and treatment that Cayce prescribed in this trance state resulted in the complete cure of his condition. After a national paper published an article about the cure, Cayce began receiving requests for psychic "readings" from people with health problems. Cayce would hypnotize himself and view the ill person clairvoyantly. He would then dictate a diagnosis and a treatment regimen that often included folk remedies such as castor oil, massage, and herbal compresses. The successful outcome of many of these cases made Cayce a nationally known spiritual healer.

In 1923, a Theosophist named Arthur Lammers met with Cayce and suggested that he also give readings into the past lives and "karmic" conditions of his patients. Soon Cayce was giving both health readings and "life" readings that mentioned subjects such as reincarnation, the lost continent of Atlantis, crystal healing, spiritual development, meditation, psychic development, prophecy, imminent earth changes, the past lives of Jesus, and the Essene community. These subjects and practices would become staples of the New Age movement during the second half of the twentieth century.

Cayce's notoriety also attracted the attention of two businessmen, Morton and Edwin Blumenthal, who persuaded the psychic to use his "gift" to find oil and mineral deposits and to devote his efforts exclusively to clairvoyant activities. In 1927, Cayce and his supporters created the Association of National Investigators (ANI) to conduct research into the alternative healing information delivered through his health readings. The following year, ANI built a thirty-bedroom hospital in Virginia Beach, where patients could come to be treated with the holistic Cayce remedies. Atlantic University, a private liberal arts college staffed by faculty sympathetic to Cayce's work, opened in 1930 in Virginia Beach. Only a year later, when ANI's financial backers sustained heavy losses during the Great Depression, the hospital and university were closed.

Cayce's inner core of supporters met during 1931 to discuss strategies for salvaging ANI's work. They decided to incorporate the ARE as a philanthropic organization dedicated to supporting Cayce's clairvoyant readings and research into psychic development. Part of this support included the hiring of a trained stenographer to record verbatim transcripts of the readings. ARE grew slowly between 1931 and 1945, and its primary service was a newsletter that it published to contributing members. Interest in Cayce's work was rekindled during the early 1940s following publication of Thomas Sugrue's sympathetic biography of Cayce, *There Is a River,* and of a *Coronet* magazine article detailing Cayce's work. A flood of new members joined ARE and Cayce was besieged with requests for readings. Cayce's health began to decline in 1944 and he died in 1945. Many of ARE's members left the association when they realized Cayce would no longer be available for readings, and the organization hovered on the brink of collapse. It was the efforts of Cayce's eldest son, Hugh Lynn Cayce (1907–1982), that prevented the dissolution of the association. A trained psychologist, Hugh Lynn Cayce had created small ARE study groups around the country during the 1930s and organized annual meetings for ARE before going off to serve in World War II. He now set about to preserve his father's legacy for future generations and to make the readings available to an international audience.

The younger Cayce lectured annually throughout the United States, visiting college campuses, churches, radio programs, retreats, and conferences. He also took legal measures to secure the Cayce family's guardianship of the reading archives. The legal entity he established in 1946, the Edgar Cayce Foundation, microfilmed and cross-indexed the readings by subject matter so that they might be of use to researchers. Another initiative undertaken by Hugh Lynn Cayce was to create relationships with universities and hospitals engaged in cutting-edge research in areas such as psycho-archaeology, parapsychology, and alternative healing therapies. As part of this research initiative, Cayce created a clinic where trained psychologists and physicians could test his father's medical readings. To address the opposition ARE faced from fundamentalist churches, Cayce stressed the scientific and nonsectarian nature of ARE's work and invited mainstream ministers to address the association's national and regional conferences. Cayce also established the ARE Press, which began a successful effort to publish books and other educational materials that focused on the various topics covered by the readings. Finally, the younger Cayce reached out to New Age forerunner groups such as Unity, Divine Science, the Rosicrucians, the Theosophical Society, and the Arcane School by lecturing at their centers on topics ranging from psychic development and positive thinking to dreams and ancient cultures.

These initiatives paid off during the 1960s, when the association's membership grew from 2,500 members and 90 study groups in the early part of the decade to 12,000 members and 1,023 study groups by 1970. By 1974, the ARE Press had printed nine million books and pamphlets. ARE's staff increased from fifteen employees in 1960 to eighty-three by 1970. Demographically, the association's membership began to reflect the spiritual seekers of the youth counterculture and also included growing numbers of humanistic psychologists, alternative health practitioners, and prisoners.

New kinds of ARE workshops, seminars, and programs reflected these changes in demography. These included Asilomar Workshop and Camp weeks in Monterrey, California, where entire families attended sessions on psychic development, holistic medicine, reincarnation, and meditation, as well as an ARE youth camp in rural Virginia. Cayce drew young people to Virginia Beach by offering research grants to high school and college students who wished to use the ARE library to research term papers on clairvoyance, dream interpretation, extrasensory perception (ESP), and reincarnation. ARE-sponsored lecturers also hit the college circuit during this decade, making the Cayce material accessible to a new generation of young people. Prominent psychological researchers Jean Houston and Stanley Krippner joined such noted figures as Marcus Bach of Unity, nutritionist Adelle Davis, psychic investigators Joan Grant and Ruth Montgomery and popular writer Jess Stearn for lectures on such topics as "Psychedelic and Meditative Explorations of the Potential of the Human Mind" and "Expanding Your Awareness." Stearn's 1967 biography, *Edgar Cayce: The Sleeping Prophet,* drew a large new audience to ARE's work.

The nexus of ARE's membership during this period was the Cayce study groups, which were overseen by a national board of trustees and local councils (composed of several study groups in one city). Two small books, *A Search for God, Part I* and *Part II,* guided discussions on topics such as prayer, meditation, and healing. The purpose of the discussion groups was to test and apply the precepts found in the Cayce material. Participants believed that a field of mental and spiritual energy was created through their fellowship, which accelerated each member's spiritual growth.

The beliefs of ARE members can be articulated as five major principles. First, spiritual growth and the development of psychic ability can be achieved without crash breakthroughs using drugs or risky psychotherapeutic group work. Second, all persons enter physical incarnation to learn certain soul lessons. Third, authentic spiritual development needs the support of a group of fellow seekers. Fourth, conventional rituals and dogmas can be an impediment to spiritual progress. Finally, the best leadership for study groups comes from the "master within" rather than human leaders or *gurus.* For the most part, the egalitarian, inner-directed, and dogma-free ethos of ARE study groups helped them to avoid the pitfalls of charismatic leadership that plagued other alternative spirituality groups of this era.

During the 1970s and 1980s, ARE continued to expand, reaching a membership of 32,000 by 1981. Study groups were established in Canada, England, Ireland, Australia, Mexico, and New Zealand and numbered 1,784. The association's 146 employees oversaw as many as twenty-four international lectures, workshops, and conferences a month. A one million dollar Edgar Cayce Memorial Library was completed in 1975 next to the national headquarters in Virginia Beach. This facility houses the association's fully cross-indexed files of the transcripts of readings and a collection of over 30,000 books on psychic phenomena and spiritual growth. By the early 1980s, over 45,000 visitors were using the library's facilities annually.

During this time ARE became a determined and influential purveyor of New Age goods, services, and ideas. For example, the phenomenon of "channeling" material from disembodied spiritual entities meshed well with the association's focus on personal development of psychic abilities and with the mode through which Cayce's readings had been received. Prominent New Age channelers such as Judy Skutch, Paul Solomon, and Kevin Ryerson had either been ARE members or had studied the Cayce materials before beginning their independent careers. In addition, ARE was an early promoter of research into lost civilizations such as Lemuria and Atlantis and into such ancient mysteries as the Dead Sea Scrolls and the Great Pyramid complex at Giza, Egypt.

The New Age movement's interest in holistic healing and bodywork has been reflected in ARE's annual symposia on alternative medicine and its research into osteopathy, chiropractic treatment, and physiotherapy. In 1981, an ARE-sponsored clinic of physiotherapy began employing a staff of osteopaths, nurses, and massage therapists, and in 1987, the Cayce/Reilly School of Massotherapy was created. To date, this school has trained more than 750 individuals from forty-five states and thirteen countries in concepts of holistic bodywork found in the Cayce readings. These concepts include Cayce/Reilly Massage, a style of Swedish massage developed by Dr. Harold J. Reilly from information in the readings. The school prepares its students for careers in massage therapy by offering classes in anatomy and physiology, advanced massage techniques, and business ethics.

In line with the New Age movement's ideals of spiritual community building, ARE in the late 1970s established a clearinghouse for information on the creation of intentional spiritual communities. The association also held conferences on community building that featured speakers such as Findhorn's Peter Caddy, and created a kindergarten using concepts from alternative educational systems like Waldorf and Montessori.

The once defunct Atlantic University reactivated its charter in 1972. Initially, the school sponsored intensive summer study sessions on various topics related to the Cayce legacy. The school also attempted to arrange for their courses on dream interpretation, meditation, and alternative healing to count for credit toward degrees at fully accredited universities. In fall 1985, Atlantic University reopened as a graduate school offering a degree in the developing field of transpersonal studies. The university received a provisional license from the State Council on Higher Education in Virginia in 1989 and was subsequently licensed to confer the degree of master of arts in transpersonal studies. In 2001, the school's continuing education program gained accreditation from the International Association for Continuing Education and Training.

ARE's leadership now rests with Charles Thomas Cayce (b. 1942), Hugh Lynn Cayce's son. Because of his training as a child psychologist, Charles Thomas Cayce has championed research into children's education and humanistic psychology during his tenure. From its humble beginnings, ARE has grown into a global network that sponsors numerous conferences and educational activities related to the Cayce legacy. Edgar Cayce Centers exist in over twenty-five nations, and outreach occurs in more than eighty countries. The association remains true to its original mission to disseminate the Cayce material through all available technologies and modalities. This entails ARE's publication of over three hundred books and pamphlets and the release of the Cayce readings on CD-ROM.

See Also Cayce, Edgar; New Age Movement.

Bibliography

Bro, Harmon. "Miracle Man of Virginia Beach." *Coronet* (September 1943).

Carter, Mary Ellen. *My Years with Edgar Cayce: The Personal Story of Gladys Davis Turner.* New York, 1972.

Cayce, Hugh Lynn. *Venture Inward: Edgar Cayce's Story and the Mysteries of the Unconscious Mind.* New York, 1964; reprint, Virginia Beach, Va., 1996.

Furst, Jeffery. *Edgar Cayce's Story of Jesus.* New York, 1968.

Lucas, Phillip C. "The Association of Research and Enlightenment: Saved by the New Age." In *America's Alternative Religions,* edited by Timothy Miller. Albany, N.Y., 1995.

Niemark, Anne E. *With This Gift: The Story of Edgar Cayce.* New York, 1978.

Stearn, Jess. *Edgar Cayce: The Sleeping Prophet.* New York, 1967.

Sugrue, Thomas. *There Is a River: The Story of Edgar Cayce.* New York, 1942; rev. ed., 1945.

Phillip Charles Lucas (2005)

ASSYRIAN RELIGION See MESOPOTAMIAN RELIGIONS

ASTARTE

ASTARTE was a Syro–Palestinian goddess widely attested throughout the Mediterranean Levant. References to her first appear in texts from Syria in the third millennium BCE (at Ebla and perhaps Early Dynastic Mari), and increase in the second millennium BCE (at Emar and Ugarit). Her cult was imported to Egypt in the latter half of the second millennium. From the first millennium BCE on, worship of Astarte spread via the Phoenicians from their coastal cities (e.g., Sidon, Tyre, and Byblos) to Cyprus, Carthage and North Africa, Italy, Malta, Spain, and Greece. She appears in the Hebrew Bible/Old Testament mostly in the role of a generic Canaanite goddess.

Astartē is the Greek form of the deity's name, but the earliest form in the third millennium, *Ashtart* (from *Aštarta*), ultimately reflects the feminine of Semitic Ashtar/Athtar, a Venus deity. The name of the goddess Ishtar also derives from Ashtar, but hers kept the masculine form without a *-t* ending, and she became the popular goddess of love, war, and the planet Venus in Mesopotamia, whereas Astarte became a leading deity in western Syria. One may thus infer that Astarte was, as Ashtar and Ishtar, astralized. However, her nature and features varied in the different regions and periods in which her cult prospered, and they seem to have also included associations with love and fertility, war, maritime activities, royal patronage, and more.

In Syria and Phoenicia. In the texts from Ugarit, the name of the goddess is spelled *ʿṯtrt,* probably vocalized as *ʿAthtart*(*u*). She is prominent among the gods in Ugaritic offering and ritual texts, but appears less often in mythic or literary texts, where the goddesses Asherah and Anat outshine her. She is occasionally mentioned together with Anat. For example, both have famed beauty in the Keret epic (*KTU* 1.14.iii.41–42); they prepare food for a feast and go hunting together in the *marziḫu*-banquet text (*KTU* 1.114.9–14, 22–23); they are paired together in the lists of deities invoked in serpent charms (*KTU* 1.100.20, 1.107.14); and in the Baal epic they both try to dissuade Baal from killing the sea-god Yamm's messengers (*KTU* 1.2.i.40–42). Scholars have often assumed that Astarte and Anat were consorts of Baal, but neither is ever explicitly identified as such at Ugarit. Astarte is called *šm bʿl,* "name-of-*Baʿlu,*" at least once (as well as in a later Phoenician text); but this may merely suggest that she could be seen as a hypostasis of Baal, and not necessarily a consort. Another epithet for Astarte at Ugarit is "Astarte of the field" (*ʿ ṯtrt šd)*, perhaps hinting at an association with animal fertility. At Mari, Astarte was perhaps the spouse of the river-god, and at Emar she had an extensive cult alongside the god Baal. Her names or epithets at Emar include "Astarte of battle," "Astarte of the city," and "Astarte of the mountain."

Astarte was a leading goddess across the Phoenician world, and her name in Phoenician (*ʿštrt*, pronounced ʿAshtart), occurs as a theophoric element in hundreds of first millennium BCE personal names. She was the chief goddess of Sidon and was worshiped alongside Baal and Eshmun; inscriptions on the fifth-century sarcophagi of the Sidonian king Tabnit (*KAI* 13) and his son Eshmunazar (*KAI* 14) refer to two royal priests of Astarte (Tabnit's father and Tabnit), as well as a royal priestess (Tabnit's wife, queen Immi–ashtart, "My mother is Astarte"), and *KAI* 14 mentions several shrines devoted to her. At Tyre she was worshiped alongside Melqart and Baal-shamem, and she appears with those deities and others as a witness in the Assyrian king Esarhaddon's treaty with Tyre in the seventh century. In the Kition tariff inscription from Cyprus (*KAI* 37A), which lists expenditures for her temple there, Astarte is called "the holy Queen." Another standard title for her in other Phoenician or Punic texts is *rbt* (Lady).

In Philo of Byblos's *Phoenician History* (c. 100 CE, partially preserved in Eusebius's *Praeparatio evangelica*), which Philo claims to be a Greek translation of a work written by a native Phoenician called Sanchuniathon, Astarte is the daughter of Ouranos along with two sisters who are sent to kill Kronos, who instead takes them as his wives. Kronos has seven daughters by Astarte, called the Titanids or Artemids, and two male children, called Desire and Love (*PE* 1.10.22–24). In addition, *Praeparatio evangelica* 1.10.31–32 states that "greatest Astarte" and Zeus Demarous (Baal Hadad) ruled "over the land with the consent of Kronos," and that Astarte wore a bull's head on her head as an emblem of kingship. As a testament to her astral features, Philo adds that Astarte found a fallen star (*astera*) and consecrated it in Tyre. He concludes, "the Phoenicians say that Astarte is Aphrodite."

IN EGYPT. Astarte was one of many imported Asian deities from the New Kingdom to the Late Period (Egyptian *ʿsṯrt, ʿ sṯrt, isṯrt*). She is called *nbt pt*, "Lady of Heaven," in many New Kingdom texts, and she appears often in iconography depicted as a goddess of war with a shield and spear or a bow and arrow, sometimes on horseback. She is the military patron of eighteenth- and nineteenth-dynasty pharaohs Amenhotep II, Thutmose IV, Rameses II, and Rameses III. In the "Contendings of Horus and Seth," Astarte and Anat are presented as the daughters of Re and the wives of Seth–Baal. "Astarte and the Sea" is a paraphrase of the Canaanite myth in which Baal (Seth in the Egyptian version) with Astarte's help defeats the Sea (Yamm), who wished to exact tribute from the gods and to take Astarte as his wife.

IN THE BIBLE. The goddess's name occurs nine times in the Masoretic Text of the Hebrew Bible/Old Testament. The singular form of the name, *ʿAštōret*, occurs three times. In *1 Kings* 11:5, Solomon is said to worship Astarte of the Sidonians and Milcom of the Ammonites, and in verse 33, Chemosh of Moab. *2 Kings* 23:13 states that Josiah defiled the high places built by Solomon for the same three deities. The singular form *ʿAštōret* was probably given its vowels in order to echo those of the word *bōšet* (shame), a word often used in the Bible in place of the name of Baal (see *Hosiah* 9:10 and *Jeremiah* 11:13, for example, or *2 Samuel* 2:8 where Ishboshet [*ʾîšbōšet*, "man of shame"] occurs, instead of Ishbaal, *[ʾîšbaʿal])*. The plural form *ʿAštārôt* appears six times in deuteronomistic passages condemning the worship of foreign gods. *Judges* 10:6, *1 Samuel* 7:4, and *1 Samuel* 12:10 all condemn worship of "the Baals (*bĕʿālîm*) and the Astartes" (a set expression similar to the Akkadian *ilāni u ištarāti*, meaning "gods and goddesses" generically); whereas it is "the foreign gods . . . and the Astartes" in *1 Samuel* 7:3, and "the Baal (sing.) and the Astartes (pl.)" in *Judges* 2:13. The final instance of plural *ʿAštārôt* is in *1 Samuel* 31:10, where perhaps the singular was originally meant. There, the armor of the fallen king Saul is taken by the Philistines to the temple of "Astartes," and his body is fastened to the wall in Beth–Shean.

Astarte's name is used as a plural abstract in an expression found in *Deuteronomy* 7:13; 28:4, 18, 51: *ʿaštĕrôt ṣōʾnekā* (the increase of your flock), which occurs alongside *šĕgar ʾălāpêkā* (the offspring of your cattle). Both phrases reflect vestiges of beliefs about fertility and the gods; *Šgr* is a deity at Ugarit and is paired with Ashtar in the Balaam text from Deir ʿAlla, I.16. The so-called Queen of Heaven, whose worship is detested in *Jeremiah* 7:18; 44:17–19, 25, may be Astarte, although cases have also been made for other Canaanite goddesses or the Mesopotamian Ishtar. Astarte's cult in the fourth-century BCE Kition tariff text likely involved offerings of cakes as did that of the Queen of Heaven in Jeremiah (but that was true for Ishtar's cult as well). Astarte also appears as a place-name in the Bible–Ashtaroth or Ashtaroth–Qarnaim (Astarte of the [two] horns; see, for example, *Gn.* 14:5), as at Ugarit and elsewhere.

The so-called Astarte clay plaques from the Late Bronze and Early Iron Ages portraying naked females with emphasized sexual organs are not to be explicitly identified with the goddess Astarte. They are usually uninscribed and the associated traits might fit with any of several goddesses, or may even depict human women.

The continued pairing of Astarte with Anat throughout the Levant eventually ended in their coalescence in the form of the goddess Atargatis, worshiped in Syria in the Hellenistic and Roman periods. The Greek name Atargatis (*ʿtrʿth* or *ʾtrʿtʾ* in Aramaic) is a compound of *ʿAṯtar* (cf. other forms of Astarte's name) and *ʿAttaʾ* (an aramaizing form of Anat). The *De dea syria* attributed to Lucian of Samosata in the second century CE describes the cult of the Syrian goddess at

Hierapolis. However, Astarte probably remained a separate goddess alongside Atargatis for a while.

BIBLIOGRAPHY

For editions of Ugaritic texts (KTU), see M. Dietrich, O. Loretz, and J. Sanmartín, *The Cuneiform Alphabetic Texts from Ugarit, Ras Ibn Hani and Other Places (KTU)* (Münster, Germany, 1995). For editions of Northwest Semitic inscriptions (KAI), see H. Donner and W. Röllig, *Kanaanäische und aramäische Inschriften (KAI), I–III* (2d ed., Wiesbaden, 1966–1969).

On Astarte herself, see C. Bonnet, *Astarté: Dossier documentaire et perspectives historiques* (Rome, 1996); W. Heimpel, "A Catalog of Near Eastern Venus Deities," *Syro–Mesopotamian Studies* 4, no. 3 (1982): 59–72; J. Leclant, "Astarté à cheval d'après les représentations égyptiennes," *Syria* 37 (1960): 1–67; N. Wyatt, "Astarte," in *Dictionary of Deities and Demons in the Bible*, (2d ed., edited by K. van der Toorn and others), pp. 109–114 (Leiden, 1999).

For a recent edition with commentary of *De dea syria*, see Lucian, *On the Syrian Goddess*, edited by J. L. Lightfoot (Oxford, 2003). For Philo's Phoenician history, see Philo of Byblos, *The Phoenician History*, edited by H. W. Attridge and R. A. Oden, Jr. (Washington, D.C., 1981).

On Astarte in the Northwest Semitic pantheon, see J. Day, *Yahweh and the Gods and Goddesses of Canaan*, pages 128–150 (Sheffield, U.K., 2000); E. Lipiński, *Dieux et déesses de l'univers phénicien et punique* (Louvain, 1995). On the iconography of ancient Near Eastern goddesses, see U. Winter, *Frau und Göttin: Exegetische und ikonographische Studien zum weiblichen Gottesbild im Alten Israel und in dessen Umwelt* (Freiburg, Germany, 1983).

TAWNY L. HOLM (2005)

ASTRAL MYTHOLOGY SEE SKY, *ARTICLE ON* THE HEAVENS AS HIEROPHANY

ASTROLOGY.

When astrology, a product of Hellenistic civilization, appeared at the end of the third century BCE, its origins were ascribed to the revelations of the Egyptian god Hermes (Thoth). However, its practitioners were usually called "Chaldeans," a formula devoid of any actual historical reference to Mesopotamia. Hellenistic astrology was actually a combination of Chaldean and Egyptian astral religion and Greek astronomy and methods of computation. Even though Hellenistic astrology and the astrology of late antiquity took on the features of different local traditions when exported to India, China, or Islamic countries, their basic ingredients are, in all places, Greek science and Chaldean and Egyptian astral lore.

The actual contribution of the latter to Greek astrology is debatable, for the Chaldean and Egyptian traditions were widely divergent on some points. However, the idea of two malefic planets—Mars and Saturn—is genuinely Chaldean; genuinely Egyptian, but no older than the third century BCE (although based on a more ancient doctrine of the *chronokratores*, the "rulers of time") is the invention of the thirty-six decans of the zodiac. The latter was called *zōidiakos* (from *zōidion*, "carved figure") by the fifth-century Greeks, after the shapes of figures that they imagined were in the heavenly constellations. One of the oldest astrological treatises, a Hellenistic compilation dating from the second century BCE, is also said to be Egyptian in origin. It is attributed to the mythical Egyptian pharoah Nechepsos as well as to the priest Petosiris, who may be the same as the Petosiris whose mummy was found in a fourth-century BCE tomb discovered at Eshumen in Upper Egypt.

Eudoxus of Cnidus (408–355 BCE), the father of Greek astronomy, was also versed in the principles of universal and meteorological astrology. The great astronomer Hipparchus (fl. 146–127 BCE) studied the correspondences of planetary signs with the people and the geographic features of the earth; he was also acquainted with astral melothesy (the study of the correspondences between the human body and planets, signs, and decans) and Hermetic astrology.

Hermetic lay astrology was concerned with the study of universal astrology (*genika*), world periods and cycles (*apokatastaseis*), planetary lots (*klēroi*), and the horoscope of the world traced according to the position of the planets in the signs at the time the earth was formed (*thema mundi*). It was also concerned with the interpretation of signs as manifested in the omens given by thunder (*brontologia*) and the prognoses given at the New Year (*apotelesmata*). In addition, Hermetic astrology involved the study of correspondences between astral phenomena and the human body or material objects, as in the study of individual or medical (iatrological) astrology; astrological medicine (*iatromathēmatika*), based on a complicated astral melothesy; and the study of the correspondences between stars, precious stones, plants, and metals. Most of the texts of Hermetic astrology are no longer extant, but they were frequently quoted by writers of late antiquity and the Renaissance.

The development of astrology was decisively influenced by the great astronomer Ptolemy (Claudius Ptolemaeus, c. 100–178 CE), the author of the *Apotelesmatika* (also known as *Tetrabiblos* or *Quadripartitum*), who made popular the pseudepigraphon *Karpos*, or *Centiloquium*. Other important astrologers of late antiquity were Vettius Valens, author of the *Anthologeuon biblia* (written between 152 and 188 CE), and Firmicus Maternus, who wrote the *Matheseos libri VIII* around 335, before he became a Christian.

After the closing of the philosophical school of Athens in 529 CE, several Greek scholars emigrated to Persia, where they were granted asylum by the emperor Khosrow I (531–579). There they translated several Greek texts, some of which were astrological treatises, into Pahlavi (Middle Persian). These treatises were later translated from Pahlavi into Arabic by Abū Maʿshar (787–886), known also as Albumasar, a scholar in the court of the caliph al-Maʾmūn of Baghdad. Many texts entered the corpus of Arabic works on astrology through Persia: the Arab Masala (c. 770–820), in his compilation of a catalog of books on astrology, listed forty-six titles of Persian provenance. By around 750 CE the Arabs had developed a considerable interest in astrology. Arabic translations of astrological texts greatly influenced the thought of the late Middle Ages and the Renaissance.

Greek astrology reached India between the first and third centuries CE, introduced possibly by a Buddhist monk. The most important Indian astrologer was the sixth-century philosopher Varāhamihira, the author of astrological treatises and of the *Pañca-siddhāntikā*, a work that contained what was then known of Indian, Egyptian, Greek, and Roman astronomy. However, Indian astrology, despite its subsequent development and later influence, was unoriginal. Chinese astrology may have derived from Indian astrology, but it is based primarily on an impressive indigenous system of correspondences between the microcosm and macrocosm.

The role of astrology in the cultural and political life of Europe from the fifteenth to eighteenth centuries is only partially known. Astrology had a prominent place in Renaissance science, but it gradually lost this position when the church disassociated itself from astrology at the end of the sixteenth century during the Reformation. Only the names of a few of the greatest astrologers of the Renaissance are still known today: Johann Müller (known as Regiomontanus), Guido Bonato of Forli, and Luca Gaurico, bishop of Civitate (Naples), who worked for Catherine de Médicis.

Some astrologers who are almost unknown today were once famous for having prophesied public events. Their predictions were associated with the theory suggesting the universal influence of Great Conjunctions of planets and signs upon religious and political matters. This theory dates to antiquity and was much discussed by the Arab thinkers al-Kindi and Abū Maʿshar. One of the best-known prophesies stated that Luther and the Reformation were the consequences of the conjunction of the superior planets Jupiter and Saturn in Scorpio during November of 1484. Interpreting this conjunction, Johann Lichtenberger predicted that a German reformer would be born who would become a monk and would have another monk as a counselor. The prediction was later rediscovered and associated with Luther (b. 1483) and Philipp Melanchthon.

During the sixteenth century, the theory of conjunctions played an important role in the works of Cyprianus von Leowitz and of the Englishman Richard Harvey. At the beginning of the seventeenth century, the theory was used by Johannes Kepler in his astrological calculations concerning a star that had appeared in 1604. On the basis of the appearance of this nova, Kepler claimed to be able to calculate the precise date of the nativity of Jesus Christ, who, because he was a great prophet, was to have been born at the time of a Great Conjunction. His birth was also to have been announced by a nova, the star of the Magi. These calculations fostered the hope that a general reformation of faith would change the deplorable conditions of contemporary humanity. This hope was also expressed by the followers of Johann Valentin Andreae (1586–1654), the author of the Rosicrucian manifestos. The dates of the last two Great Conjunctions figure importantly in the apocryphal history of the founder of the Rosicrucian order.

Astrological predictions were feared by the authorities for their possible deleterious political consequences. Astrology was often condemned or suppressed during antiquity and the Renaissance. For example, to counteract the effect of the prophecy concerning the church reformer born under the 1484 conjunction, Innocent VIII issued the bull *Summis desiderantes affectibus*, which had some effect on the great witch craze of the sixteenth and seventeenth centuries. Eventually astrology was officially condemned by the church at the end of the sixteenth century, as a consequence of other disastrous predictions. However, the liberal trends at the beginning of the seventeenth century were in great measure dependent upon astrological predictions. Astrology seems to continue to exert a certain influence on the political and cultural life of modern Europe, although it is much less influential than it was during the fifteenth to seventeenth centuries.

Confutations of astrology have a common pattern, which usually consists of denying the possibility that the stars could influence human affairs. Some of these confutations are famous, such as those of Girolamo Savonarola, Giovanni Pico della Mirandola, and John Calvin. Although Pico's *Disputationes astrologiam adversus divinatricem* was left unprinted because of his sudden death in 1494, it is very possible that this semiofficial treatise was meant to put forth the antiastrological policies of Innocent VIII and his successor, and to obtain for Pico a full pardon for his past errors and prepare the way for a high ecclesiastical career.

The Methods of Astrology. Greek astrology was based on Greek astronomy, which was abstruse and difficult to practice. This is one of the principal reasons why many of the authors of astrological treatises in antiquity and late antiquity made inadvertent mistakes in astrological formulations that were by their very nature almost impossible to apply. Another reason for the varied and even contradictory astrological systems of late antiquity was the weight of tradition. Traditionally complex numerical systems of astrology were inevitably altered in their transmission and were rarely interpreted in the same way by any two different authors. For example, the numerical systems of specific astrological tables could be interpreted in various ways: the *horia* (*fines, termini*), or portions of a sign distributed among the five planets; the tables of *hupsōmata*, or "exaltations" of the planets in different signs; the tables of *tapeinōmata* (*deiectiones*), or "depressions" of the planets; the tables of the so-called *partes vacuae* or *vacantes*, the "empty spaces" of the zodiac; and so on. Ptolemy tried to eliminate discrepancies among different traditions by replacing corrupt or unintelligible traditions with numerical series linked by logical, arithmetical operations.

Astrology superimposes two different complex systems: that of the heavens and that of the collective and individual destinies of the human beings on earth. Through the observation of the heavens (and the interpretation of those observations according to a framework of theoretical, nonobservational assumptions), these systems attempt to account for the changes within the human system, which are otherwise unpredictable, unobservable, and unsystematic. It is true that from a scientific viewpoint there is no real connection between the two systems, and thus Greek astrology has been perceived as an attempt to give mathematical justification to absurd theoretical assumptions. However, instead of emphasizing the arbitrary nature and incorrect theoretical basis of astrology, one might consider its contributions from a psychological point of view. The choice of an analogous system for human fate reflects a deep insight into the transience and singularity of human lives and human events.

Astrological systems are multiple-choice systems based on several informational operators that are capable of accounting for an almost unrestricted number of operations. This astrological "computer program" was used to store information in the memory by several mnemotechnical systems.

The first operator in the zodiac, or wheel, composed of the twelve constellations (more or less arbitrary groups of stars) through which the planets circulate. In addition to these constellations, there are several others that are not in the path of the planets; as extrazodiacal signs (*paranatellonta*) that rise together with the signs of the zodiac, they can also figure in astrological computations and analyses. Beginning from the sign rising at the spring equinox, the twelve constellations are the Ram (*Krios*, Aries), the Bull (*Tauros*, Taurus), the Twins (*Didumoi*, Gemini), the Crab (*Karkinos*, Cancer), the Lion (*Leōn*, Leo), the Virgin (*Parthenos*, Virgo), the Scales (*Zugos*, Libra), the Scorpion (*Skorpios*, Scorpio), the Archer (*Toxotēs*, Sagittarius), the Goat (*Aigokerōs*, Capricorn), the Waterbearer (*Hudrochoos*, Aquarius), and the Fish (*Ichthues*, Pisces). The twelve signs of the zodiac are further grouped into triangles according to their form, sex, quality (cold, warm, wet, or dry), and the element to which they belong. Thus Aries, Leo, and Sagittarius constitute the fire triangle; Taurus, Virgo, and Capricorn, the earth triangle; Gemini, Libra, and Aquarius, the air triangle; and Cancer, Scorpio, and Pisces, the water triangle.

Each of the twelve signs occupies 30 degrees of a 360-degree circle. Each sign is further divided into three decans (*dekanoi*) of 10 degrees each; they are sometimes divided into single degrees (*monomoiriai*). To each sign are assigned constant features according to its element, quality, sex, shape, and position. The zodiac revolves on an ideal plane divided into *topoi* ("places" or "houses"). There are two systems of *topoi*: (1) a system of eight houses (*oktōtopos*), which is described only by Marcus Manilius and Firmicus Maternus, and (2) a more general system of twelve houses (*dōdekatopos*). The twelve houses are life (*vita*), wealth (*lucrum*), brothers and sisters (*fratres*), parents (*parentes*), sons (*filii*), health (*valetudo*), marriage (*nuptiae*), death (*mors*), travels (*peregrinationes*), honors (*honores*), friends (*amici*), and enemies (*inimici*). According to a medieval mnemonic couplet, these are

> Vita, lucrum, fratres, genitor, nati, valetudo Uxor,
> mors, pietas, regnum benefactaque, carcer.

The revolution of the zodiac within the houses makes possible many significant combinations; however, the great variability of the system is due to the movements of the planets. According to the geocentric system, there are seven "planets," arranged according to their distance from the earth and by the length of their respective revolutions: the moon, Mercury, Venus, the sun, Mars, Jupiter, and Saturn. These were further classified according to sex and quality. Mars and Saturn were specifically designated as "malefics," a feature inherited from Babylonian astrology.

Ptolemy stated that the planets have two kinds of "aspects": (1) the aspect determined both by their positions in the zodiac and by their positions relative to one another and (2) the aspect determined only by their positions relative to one another. The most important position of the first aspect is the so-called *idioprosōpos*, the position of a planet when it is located at the same circular distance from the sun and moon that its domicile is from the domiciles of the sun and moon. The domiciles (*oikoi*) are the signs ruled by each planet. The sun and moon each rule only one sign, Leo and Cancer, respectively; the other planets each rule two signs. Mercury rules Gemini and Virgo; Venus, Taurus and Libra; Mars, Aries and Scorpio; Jupiter, Sagittarius and Pisces; and Saturn, Capricorn and Aquarius. In addition to the domiciles, each planet has an "exaltation" at a special place in one sign, and a "depression" (or "exile") in another.

Of the second kind of aspect, Ptolemy cites only two positions: the *sunaphē*, "contact," or *kollēēsis*, "sticking" (Lat., *contactus*, *coniunctio*, *applicatio*, or *glutinatio*), positions that occur when two planets meet on the same meridian. The conjunction is followed by a separation or *aporroia* (Lat., *defluxio*). Several other positions were successively added to these two, but they were not based on the relative positions of planets but on their *aktinobolia* (*emissio radiorum*), or power to emit rays. When these rays meet under certain conditions they form "figures" (*schēmata*), called *adspectus* in Latin because of the way the planets are "looking" (*adspicio*) at one another. The term *aktinobolia* itself was usually employed to indicate a negative aspect in which a planet could be "blocked" or "sieged" (Gr., *perischesis* or *emperischesis*; Lat., *detentio* or *obsidio*, etc.). While conjunction with the malefic planets is usually maleficent, there are two aspects that are always benefic (120° and 60°) and two others (opposition, or 180°, and square, or 90°) that are always negative.

Signs, decans, and planets are said to rule both the zones of the earth and the human body. The correspondences between them are classified according to astrological chorography, or the distribution of the sidereal influences of the *oikoumenē*, and melothesy, or the doctrine of the correspondences between stars and the human body. There are three kinds of melothesy, which consider the influence of the signs, decans, or planets respectively. The seven planets are ascribed correspondences with metals, stones, plants, and animals. These are used in astrological medicine, or *iatromathēmatikē*, a complicated science of ascribing drugs or other remedies according to the momentary position and influence of the planets, especially the moon.

Astrological predictions are of two kinds: (1) general or catholic (*katholikos*, "universal") predictions, which are based on portentous events such as eclipses, comets, meteors, Great Conjunctions, the aurora borealis, and so on; and (2) particular, or genethliac, predictions, which are concerned with the position and influence of the stars at one's birth. The astrologer draws a "birth theme" (Lat., *thema*, or *diathema tēs geneseōs*; Lat., *constellatio*) by determining first the *hōroskopos* (Lat., *ascendens*), or "indicator," of the sign or planet rising at the eastern horizon at the precise moment of the client's birth. After the ascendant, three other points are determined on the zodiac: the zenith (Gr., *mesouranēma*; Lat., *medium coelum*), the nadir (Gr., *antimesouranēma* or *hupogeion*; Lat., *imum caelum*), and the western horizon (Gr., *dusis*; Lat., *occasus*).

The meridian line is not perpendicular to the horizon line, and thus the problem of the "ascensions" *(anaphorai)* of each sign is not a simple one; their oblique ascension, according to the real inclination of the zodiac, has to be translated on the equatorial plane, and their angular speed depends on the latitude of the geographic location where the calculations are made. During antiquity, tables were drawn for "seven climates" or latitudes. The astrologer is supposed to calculate with accuracy the ascensions of the signs and planets, and to exhaust, on a birth theme, all possible combinations of the constituents of the system.

SEE ALSO Divination; Occultism; Sky, article on The Heavens as Hierophany.

BIBLIOGRAPHY

The best work on Greek and Roman astrology is Auguste Bouché-Leclercq's *L'astrologie grecque* (Paris, 1899). It should be supplemented now with Wilhelm Gundel and Hans Georg Gundel's *Astrologumena: Die astrologische Literatur in der Antike und ihre Geschichte,* "Sudhoffs Archiv," no. 6 (Wiesbaden, 1966). The latter also contains valuable information on the history of astrology outside Greece and Rome. An excellent popular work on astrology is Wilhelm Gundel's *Sternglaube, Sternreligion und Sternorakel: Aus der Geschichte der Astrologie,* 2d ed. (Heidelberg, 1959). Another valuable popular work is Franz Johannes Boll and Carl Bezold's *Sternglaube und Sterndeutung: Die Geschichte und das Wesen der Astrologie,* edited by Wilhelm Gundel (Leipzig, 1926).

Numerous original Greek astrological works have been collected in the *Catalogus codicum astrologorum graecorum,* edited by Franz Cumont and Franz Johannes Boll (Brussels, 1898–).

There is no catalog of Renaissance works on astrology. Some general information is provided in Wayne Shumaker's *The Occult Sciences in the Renaissance* (Berkeley, 1972). Some details on Renaissance astrology are found in Will-Erich Peuckert's *Astrologie* (Stuttgart, 1960).

Information on Renaissance astrology can also be found in the writings of little-known astrologers such as Richard Argentine, Lucio Bellanti, Petrus Buccius, Joachim Camerarius, Johann Clario, A. Couillard, Claude Dariot, L. Digges, John Eschuid, Oger Ferrier of Toulouse, Thomas Finck, Oronce Fine, Giovanni Maria Fiornovelli, Jacques Fontaine, Marcus Frytschius, Alonso de Fuentes, W. Fulke, Giovanni Paolo Gallucci, Jean Ganivet, J. Garcaeus, A. P. Gasser, Francesco Giuntini, Bernardo de Granollachs of Barcelona, Joseph Grünbeck, J. Guido, A Guillermin, Richard Harvey, Jacob Koebel, Edmond Le Maistre, Cyprianus von Leowitz, Johann Lichtenberger, R. Lindenberg, G. Marstallerus, Giacomo Marzari, Antoine Mizauld, Sebastian Münster, V. Nabod, Paolo Nicoletto of Venice, Augustinus Niphus, Caspar Peucer, Alessandro Piccolomini, Annibale Raimondo, Henricus Rantzovius (governor of Holstein and owner of a 7,000-volume library), Gregorius Reisch, J. F. Ringelbergius of Anvers, Cornelius Scepperus, Johann Schöner, Jac. Schonheintsz, Joh. Stadius, Joh. Taisnier, Georg Taunstetter-Collimitus, Johannes Virdung of Hasfurt, et al.

For works discussing theories of Great Conjunctions, see Abū Maʿshar's *De Magnis Conjunctionibus Annorum revolutionibus ac eorum perfectionibus octo continens tractatus* (Venice, 1515), Johann Lichtenberger's *Prognosticatio Latina Anno LXXXIII/1483 ad magnam coniunctionem Saturni et Jovis quae fuit anno LXXXIIII/1484 ac eclipsis solis anni sequentis sc. LXXXV/1485 confecta ac nunc de nouo emendata* (Moguntiae, 1492); Cyprianus von Leowitz's *De Conjunctionibus magnis insignibus superiorum planetarum, Solis defectionibus et Cometis* (1564); and Richard Harvey's *An Astrological Discourse upon the great and notable Conjunction of the two superior planets, Saturn and Jupiter, which shall happen the 28th day of April, 1583* (London, 1583).

IOAN PETRU CULIANU (1987)

ASTRONOMY SEE ETHNOASTRONOMY

AŚVINS SEE TWINS

ATAHUALLPA (c. 1502–1533) was the thirteenth ruler of the Inca Empire and the last to preside over it before its conquest by the Spanish. Present-day Andean people envision Atahuallpa as a messiah. In poetry, drama, and legend, he is associated with both autochthonous and Roman Catholic beliefs. His symbolic identity transcends his historical identity.

Historically, Atahuallpa was neither the noblest nor the last of the Inca rulers. He was the son of Huayna Capac (r. 1493–1527), the eleventh Inca (the title given to heads of the empire). The heir to the throne was not Atahuallpa but his brother Huascar (r. 1527–1532), who, at Huayna

Capac's request, let Atahuallpa rule over the empire's northern half, from Quito to Jauja. Three years later, in 1530, Atahuallpa defeated Huascar in a civil war that left the Inca empire so debilitated that it was easily occupied by Spanish forces under Francisco Pizarro in 1532. Pizarro captured Atahuallpa, who tried in vain to form an alliance with Pizarro to buttress his title. To avoid being burned at the stake, Atahuallpa agreed to be baptized as a Christian, although he previously had refused to accept conversion. Nevertheless, he was put to death by strangulation on August 28, 1533.

To stifle Quechua (Inca) rebellions in 1535, Pizarro made Atahuallpa's son, Manco II, the Inca ruler. Manco resisted Spanish rule until his death in 1545. Subsequent Inca rulers—Sayri Tupac (r. 1545–1557), Tito Cusi Yupanqui (r. 1557–1569), and Tupac Amarú (r. 1569–1572)—prolonged this resistance for forty years. The conquest officially ended in 1572 with the execution of Tupac Amarú, although Indian revolts continued. Because of his capitulation, Atahuallpa was ignominious, but as personal memories of him began to fade he became a tragic and redemptive figure who stands at the crossroads of Inca and Spanish culture.

The seventeenth-century Peruvian poet Garcilaso de la Vega reflects the soul of a conquered people in his *Royal Commentaries of the Inca* (1609; Eng. tr., 1961). Garcilaso, himself the son of a Spanish conquistador and an Inca princess who was the niece of Huayna Capac, describes Atahuallpa as a traitor. Garcilaso quotes a citizen of the Inca capital, Cuzco, as saying, "Atahuallpa destroyed our empire and committed every crime against the Incas. Give that man to me and even if he be dead I will eat him raw, without seasoning!"

Garcilaso also depicts Atahuallpa as a symbol of the lack of communication between Indians and Spaniards. At the first meeting between Atahuallpa's retinue and Pizarro's troops in 1532, the Inca was confronted by a priest, Vicente de Valverde, to whom he said, "You claim that Christ is God, but how can he be dead? We worship the Sun and Moon, which are immortal! By what authority do you say that God created the universe?"

"The Bible!" Valverde replied, handing his copy to Atahuallpa. The Inca placed the book to his ear, shook it, and replied, "It is silent?" He threw it to the ground, and at this Valverde ordered the Spanish troops to kill the Indians. Garcilaso's irony is that Valverde represented peace but brought destruction, whereas Atahuallpa represented civil war but sought reconciliation.

During the colonial (1532–1826) and republican (1826–present) periods, Atahuallpa came to symbolize the conquered people, and his death came to signify the disruption of nature caused by the conquest. This is poignantly illustrated in a poem, *A Eulogy to Atahuallpa,* written in the sixteenth century by an unknown author:

> A black rainbow covers Cuzco, tight like a bow. . . .
>
> Hail hits our heads; rivers flow with blood;
> The days are black and the nights are white.
>
> Our hearts are overwhelmed because Atahuallpa is dead,
> The shadow who protects us from the sun. . . .
>
> Spaniards became rich with your gold.
> Yet their hearts rotted with greed, power, and violence.
> Atahuallpa, you embraced and gave them all,
> But they beheaded you. . . .
>
> Today, may your heart support our sinful ways.
> (trans. by Bastien, from Arguedas, 1957)

According to the present-day belief system of the Quechua peoples, the conquest destroyed harmony between the Inca and his subjects, between Indian and Spaniard, and between heaven and earth. Harmony, it is believed, will be restored by the resurrection of Atahuallpa, which is represented in a popular dance drama, *The Death of Atahuallpa,* performed annually in the Bolivian cities of Kanata and Oruro. In Oruro the drama is performed on the Sunday and Monday of Carnival. The actors playing Atahuallpa and the Inca princesses stand across the central plaza from those playing Pizarro and his soldiers. Atahuallpa debates with his diviner about ominous prophecies and the divinity of the conquistadors. Pizarro captures, tricks, and executes Atahuallpa. As a finale, a choir of Inca princesses chants, "Eternal Lord, make arise the all-powerful and youthful Inca Atahuallpa!" Clowns then bring Atahuallpa back to life. In Kanata a similar drama is performed during a fiesta dedicated to Jesus. Like Christ, Atahuallpa suffers trial and execution and is resurrected. Actors dressed as Inca princesses dedicate the drama to the Blessed Mother and march in procession carrying a statue of Jesus. Finally, they enact the capture, trial, death, and resurrection of Atahuallpa.

These actors transform Atahuallpa and Jesus into a composite symbolic figure who is acceptable to both the conquerors and the conquered and who promises the regeneration of a harmonious culture in a future age. The archetypal imagery of death and rebirth forms a common denominator between the Atahuallpa of the Inca and the Jesus of the Spanish. However, the drama separates Atahuallpa and Jesus from negative historical associations: Atahuallpa is not remembered as a traitor and tyrant, and Jesus is dissociated from the Catholic colonial heritage.

The rebirth of Atahuallpa is also expressed in the legends surrounding the figure of Inkarri (whose name is a Quechua corruption of the Spanish *Inca rey* [Inca king]) that are found throughout the Andes. According to these legends, the father of Inkarri is the Sun. Inkarri has abundant gold. His head is buried somewhere in Cuzco. His body is slowly being regenerated, growing from the head down. When Inkarri's body is complete, he will return to judge the world. Although the Inkarri legends portend the return of the Inca in general, they are also associated with Atahuallpa. Traditional Andeans believe that Atahuallpa's head is also buried in Cuzco, where his body, too, is being regenerated by the forces of Pachamama (Mother Earth), a major deity in the Andes. When he is regenerated, Atahuallpa will emerge from

Lake Titicaca. During the messianic age that follows, he will judge all who have upset nature, culture, and society.

Ethnohistorically, Atahuallpa has thus become a symbol combining Inca ideas of earthly and cosmic rebirth with Christian beliefs about the death, resurrection, and second coming of Christ. Christian beliefs, however, are secondary to the association of Atahuallpa with the earth as the center of a regenerative cycle from birth to death to renewed life. This more basic process provides cosmic meaning for the tyranny initiated by the conquest.

As the twenty-first century begins, the rivalry and fratricide between the two brothers Atahuallpa and Huascar still functions as a foundation myth for the existence of Ecuador, which descends from Atahuallpa, and Peru, which descends from Huascar. Their rivalry was the start of the rivalry between the two nations. This is the most important thing about Atahuallpa from the perspective of the modern nations. Hence the story of Atahuallpa is partisan depending on which nation one belongs to. In short, Atahuallpa is a symbolic figure with multiple meanings evoked for varying religious beliefs, political parties, and national identities that have changed since the conquest.

See Also Manco Capac and Mama Ocllo.

Bibliography

Four chronicles of early colonial times refer to events in the life of Atahuallpa. The most reliable is by Felipe Guamán Poma de Ayala (1526–1614). He describes the contact between Atahuallpa and the Spaniards in folios 378 to 391 of *El primer nueva corónica y buen gobierno* (1613), edited by John V. Murra and Rolena Adorno, translation from Quechua and textual analysis by Jorge L. Urioste, 3 vols. (Mexico City, 1980). Guamán Poma bases his account on testimonies by his father and others who were adults at the time of the conquest. The second chronicle was dictated by Tito Cusi Yupanqui, who ruled as Inca from 1557 to 1569; it was published as *Relación de la conquista del Peru y hechos del Inca Manco II* (Lima, 1916). The nephew of Atahuallpa, Tito Cusi faithfully reflects the Inca viewpoint and eloquently points out the injustices perpetrated by the Spaniards. The third chronicle, *Relación de antiguedades desde reyno del Peru,* written by Juan de Santa Cruz Pachacuti Yamqui at the beginning of the seventeenth century, appears in *Historia de los incas y relación de su gobierno,* edited by Horacio H. Urteaga (Lima, 1927). Much shorter than that by Guamán Poma, this chronicle contains information about Andean beliefs and cosmology and includes a map of the Andeans' universe. Atahuallpa is unfavorably depicted as the killer of Huascar and his wife and child. The fourth chronicle, *Commentarios reales de los Incas,* written by Garcilaso de la Vega in 1609, appears in *The Incas: Commentaries of the Inca Garcilaso de la Vega 1539–1616* (New York, 1961), translated by Maria Jolas from the critical, annotated edition by Alain Gheerbrant (1959). Educated in the classical tradition, Garcilaso wrote in a humanistic style that embellished Inca traditions and criticized the Spaniards for their betrayal of Christian culture.

The poem "A Eulogy to Atahuallpa" was translated by José María Arguedas in *Apu Inqa Atahuallpaman* (Lima, 1957). Jesús Lara presents a complete translation of an early version of the folk drama of Oruro in *Tragedía del fin de Atawallpa* (Cochabamba, Bolivia, 1957). Several scholars have analyzed the drama: Miguel León-Portilla compares Atahuallpa with Mexico's Moctezuma II—they were both products of millenarian cultures and believed that Pizarro and Cortés were returning deities—in *El reverso de la conquista* (Tabasco, Mexico, 1964). Along similar lines, Nathan Wachtel, in *The Vision of the Vanquished: The Spanish Conquest of Peru through Indian Eyes, 1530–1570* (New York, 1977), interprets the drama from a structuralist perspective: the conquest brought disharmony, Atahuallpa brings harmony, and the drama reveals these contradictions. Clemente Hernando-Balmori has written a profound study of this drama in *La Conquista de los españoles: Drama indígena bilingue quechua-castellano* (Tucumán, Argentina, 1955). He interprets it in the context of Inca drama and Andean cognitive patterns.

A useful source for articles about Andean messianism is an anthology edited by Juan Ossio Acuña, *Ideología messianica del mundo andino* (Lima, 1973). This includes twenty-two articles on messianic movements in past and present Andean history, including José María Arguedas's interpretation of the Inkarri legends, "El mito de Inkarri y las tres humanidades."

A compendium of studies on the overthrow of the Inca Empire can be found in *Transatlantic Encounters: Europeans and Andeans in the Sixteenth Century* (Los Angeles, 1991), edited by Kenneth Andrien and Rolena Adorno, and in the article by Vicente Cantarino, "Conquista en el Nuevo Mundo," published in *Civilización y Cultura de España* (Englewood Cliffs, N.J., 1995), edited by Steve Debow.

Joseph W. Bastien (1987 and 2005)

ATESHGAH.

ATESHGAH. A Zoroastrian term still used in New Persian, *ateshgah, or ātashgāh* (also pronounced *āteshgāh*), originally meant "place of the fire" or, technically, "fire precinct." It derives from Middle Persian or Pahlavi *ātakhshgāh,* reflecting an Old Persian and Avestan nominative singular *ātarsh* (fire), plus Old Persian *gāthu* and Avestan *gātu, gātav* (place, space). The Avestan and Old Persian term *ātar-* produced the Middle Persian and New Persian word *ātur* or *ādur* (fire) as well. Consequently *āturgāh* and *ādurgāh* also have been used to denote places or precincts in which fires burn. A fire that burns in an *ateshgah* is regarded as *spēnāg* (holy) and is utilized for Mazdean or Zoroastrian rituals. It did not and does not have to be a constantly burning fire, or one of the highest ritual rank, nor be tended solely by the Zoroastrian magi or clergy. In practice, an *ateshgah* did not even have to be within an enclosed building but could be an outdoor precinct.

Another designation used in conjunction with *ateshgah* is New Persian *ātashkada* (also pronounced *āteshkade,* "room of the fire, house of the fire"), commonly translated as "fire temple," deriving from Middle Persian *ātakhshkadag* and *kadag ī ātakhsh,* originating from Old Persian and Avestan *ātarsh* plus Old Persian **katha* and Avestan *kata* (room, small house). Usage indicates this term has consistently been utilized to denote a building which housed one or more ateshgah. By the fifteenth century CE, as attested in the *Persian Revāyats* (Treatises 2.18), Zoroastrians in Iran were using the phrases *dar-i mehr* and *dar be-mehr,* both meaning "court of Mithra," as equivalents of other terms for temples that enclosed *ateshgah.* Mithra (later Mihr, Mehr), as the minor Zoroastrian divinity of contracts and covenants, was believed to traverse the sky with "the radiant fire of liturgical glory before him" (*Yasht,* "Devotional Poem" 10.127). So that spirit's association with fire resulted in devotees' naming fire temples after him. The phrases *dar-i mehr* and *dar be-mehr* remain popular into the twenty-first century among Zoroastrians in Iran, India, and even the United States and Canada for referring to their current, functional fire temples. Yet another word for a fire temple building, namely *agīārī,* commonly rendered as *agiary,* arose among the Parsis (Persians) or Zoroastrians of India through the translation of *ātashākada* into the Gujarati language in premodern times.

Within a fire precinct of a fire temple, a fire is placed in a receptacle. That vessel has consistently been designated in New Persian as an *ātashdān,* usually translated as "fire altar," from Middle Persian *ātakhshdān* and Parthian **ātarōshan,* preserved in Armenian as *atrushan.* It was rendered into Greek as *bōmos* (altar). The Iranian term reflects an Old Persian and Avestan nominative singular *ātarsh* plus *stāna* (place). The Parsis call the fire holder an *āfrīnagānyu* or *afargānyu* (place for blessings), based on a loanword from New Persian into Gujarati.

HISTORY. Fire precincts seem to have been utilized by pre-Zoroastrian or early Zoroastrian devotees in Central Asian Bronze Age communities (c. 2100–1750 BCE) such as at Togolok 21. Archaeological excavation at the Median citadel of Tepe Nush-e Jan (c. mid-eighth century–sixth century BCE) has revealed two fire precincts with square, raised, mud brick altars. Excavations at the contemporaneous Median city of Hagmatāna (Ecbatana, later Hamadan) produced a small open-sided pavilionlike chamber with four columns supporting a domed ceiling that seems to be a precursor of fire precinct architecture later popular in Sassanian times. Among the earliest precincts for holy flames during the Achaemenian Empire (550–331 BCE) is the open air one at Pasargadae. It contains two hollow white limestone plinths aligned north to south, with the southern one having stairs attached. Reliefs carved above tombs of subsequent Achaemenian rulers indicate the king or a magus climbed to the top of the southern plinth, faced the northern plinth, which bore a fire altar with flame, and performed devotions.

The *Vidēvdād* (Code to ward off evil spirits, 8.81–96), a Young Avestan text codified under the Parthian regime (238 BCE–224 CE), provides the first scriptural reference to the creation of a holy fire of the highest ritual grade—*ādar warahrān* in Parthian, *ātakhsh wahrām* in Middle Persian, and *ātash bahrām,* "fire of Verethraghna (Vərəthraghna) or Wahrām" (the divinity of victory), in New Persian and Parsi Gujarati. Each such fire was said to blaze within a *dāityāgātu* (fixed place or appropriate precinct), called *dādgāh* in Middle Persian, which apparently was another term for an *ateshgah.* It is created by a purification and fusion of flames that had been used for sixteen different functions. The same text noted that holy fires should be kept free from impurities and tended with care, and that magi should perform all such rites while wearing a *paitidāna* (Middle Persian *padām,* New Persian *panām,* Parsi Gujarati *padān*), or "mouth and nose mask," so as not to pollute the flames with breath (*Vidēvdād* 8.73–74, 18.1).

Establishment of the three most famous *ādar warahrān* of antiquity seems to date to mid-Achaemenian times at the earliest and mid-Parthian times at the latest. Possibly relocated more than once, their fire temples continued to be funded, staffed, and well maintained in Sassanian times (224–651 CE). Ādur Farrōbay, considered the *ādar warahrān* of clergy and nobility, may have always been enthroned in Fārs at the site of Kariyan. Ādur Gushnasp, linked to rulers as the *ādar warahrān* of warriors, seems to have been originally established within a fire temple in Media (Kurdistan). Under the early Sassanians during the third century CE, it was moved to the site of Takht-e Sulayman southeast of Lake Urmiya (later in Iranian Azerbaijan). Ādur Burzēnmihr, regarded as the holy fire of farmers and pastoralists, seems to have been burned within a fire temple on a mountain called Revand northwest of Nishapur in Parthia (later Khurāsān), as noted by the ninth-century CE magus Zādspram (*Wizīdagīhā,* "Selections" 3.85).

Three ritual grades of fire were standardized by the Sassanian magi, and those ranks are still retained by Zoroastrians: *ātakhsh wahrām, ātakhsh ādarān* (fire of fires), or simply *ādarān,* and *ādurōg ī dādgāh* (small fire in a fixed place), or simply *dādgāh.* Only *ātakhsh wahrām* had to burn constantly. Flames of the *ādarān* and *dādgāh* grades would periodically be allowed to burn out. Forming a hall or portico whose four sides were open, the *chahār tāq* (four arches)—or four columns supporting a *gumbad* ("domed roof," a term that eventually came to serve as an alternate for *chahār tāq*)—became the quintessential architectural form for fire precincts. The *chahār tāq* usually was situated inside a fire temple and within it a holy fire burned upon a fire altar. That style is seen in ruins at locales such as Tepe-Mill near Tehran; Qala-ye Dokhtar near Qom; Kazerun and Mil-e Naqara Hana in Fārs province; Isfahan and Neyzar in central Iran, near Kermān city; and between Mashhad and Torbat-e Haydariya in Khurāsān.

As Iranians adopted other faiths, the *ateshgah* became a symbol of the old order that had to be changed. So in Armenia, Zoroastrian fire precincts were transformed into Christian churches at locales like Ejmiacin and Dvin after 300. The process gained momentum with the spread of Islam between the eight and thirteenth centuries. Most fire precincts were either transformed into mosques, destroyed, or abandoned. The *chahār tāq* style with its domed roof passed into Muslim religious architecture as domed mosques. Notable examples of *ateshgah* providing the infrastructure for a medieval Muslim *masjid-e jāmi*ʿ (congregational mosque) are at the cities of Urmiya, Qazvin, Yazd, Naʾin, Isfahan, Natanz, Kermān, Nishapur, and Bukhara.

MODERN USES. Now, as in premodern times, holy fires—especially those of the *ātash bahrām* and *ātash ādarān* ranks—usually burn in altars on stone platforms upon tiled floors, within a *pāwī* (pure space), surrounded by *kash* or *kish* (separatory furrows) inscribed on the floor of a fire precinct that is often modeled after the medieval *chahār tāq*. A few of several such fire temples functioning in Iran can be mentioned. The *ātash bahrām* named Ādur Farrōbay burns in a modern temple at Yazd. The *ātash bahrām* called Ādur Anāhīd, originally the fire of Persian royal families, is housed at a temple in the town of Ardakan of the Sharifabad area in Yazd. The capital city, Tehran, has an *ādarān* flame in the Bhika Bahram fire temple. The city of Kermān has the Banu Rostam Farrokh fire precinct, opened in 1924 to house an *ādarān* flame, plus a more modern fire temple within the same compound. Due to state pressure, access to fire temples in Iran is available to members of all faiths, who are requested but not required to cover their heads and remove footwear as signs of respect for the fires.

The largest number of Zoroastrian fire precincts is found in India. In about 941, some five years after their arrival in Gujarat on the west coast of India, the Parsis established an *ātash bahrām* named Irān Shāh, which now blazes in an ornate fire temple at Udvada and is the focus of pilgrimage by devout Zoroastrians. There are seven other highest-level fires, each with its own temple, including the Bhagarsath Anjuman *ātash bahrām* at Navsari, established in 1765. At the start of the twenty-first century, there are eighty-two fire temples in India housing *ādarān* flames (pronounced *ādariān* in Parsi Gujarati). Additionally, sixty fire temples with only *dādgāh* flames are supported by Zoroastrian communities there. Those Parsis do not permit nonbelievers or converts to enter fire temples. Devotees, who must possess Zoroastrian paternity, are required to don prayer caps or scarves and perform the *pādyāb,* or purification, and *kustī,* or holy cord rites, before worship.

As Zoroastrians dispersed globally, their praxes relating to fire went with them. The community in Pakistan worships at two fire temples with *ādarān* fires in Karachi, one with a *dādgāh* in Lahore, and another with a *dādgāh* in Quetta—all dating from the nineteenth century. Devotees living in Sri Lanka (earlier called Ceylon) have worshiped at an endowed fire temple with a *dādgāh* at the city of Colombo since 1927. Only individuals born from Zoroastrian fathers are permitted to worship—after donning caps or scarves, purifying themselves, and retying the cord—at fire temples in Pakistan and Sri Lanka. Zoroastrians in Hong Kong have the Pherozeshaw Kawasji Pavri Memorial Prayer Hall with a *dādgāh* flame on the sixth floor of a modern multipurpose steel and glass building. The community in England can attend religious services at two centers in London—Zoroastrian House, opened in 1969, and the Zartoshty Brothers Hall, dedicated in 2001, both housing *dādgāh* fires. Zoroastrians in Australia at Sydney (1994), Canada at Toronto (1980) and Vancouver (1986), and the United States in the suburbs of New York City (1977, relocated in 2001), Washington, D.C. (1990), Chicago (1983), Houston (1998), San Jose (1992), and Los Angeles (1985) utilize temples containing fires of the *dādgāh* level. Access to fire temples in Europe and North America is granted to persons of all faiths, with the fire often—but not always—burning within a fire precinct separated from the congregation by glass panels.

Each fire is intended to serve as an icon through which worship is directed toward Ahura Mazdā (later Ōhrmazd) the creator deity or god of Zoroastrians. Women abstain from visiting fire temples when menstruating and immediately after childbirth for reasons of ritual purity. At fire temples, laity offer fragrant firewood and incense as fuel for the fire. Facing the *ateshgah* while standing, or occasionally seated or kneeling, they quietly recite prayers such as those for the *gāh* (period or time) of day or night, the *Ahuna Vairya* (*Ahunawar,* "As is the lord"), and the *Ashem Vohū* (Order is good). The central ritual surrounding fires in *ateshgah* is termed *Bōy* ([Offering of] Incense), conducted five times at the beginning of each period of the day by a magus. The presence of *dādgāh* fires is required for a range of other rituals, including the *Yasna* (worship), *Vidēvdād* or *Vendidād* (Code to ward off evil spirits), *Āfrīnagān* (Blessings), *Farokhshī* (All souls), and *Jashan* (Thanksgiving service).

SEE ALSO Parsis; Zoroastrianism.

BIBLIOGRAPHY

Boucharlat, Rene. "Chahar Taq et temple du feu sasanide: quelques remarques." In *De l'Indus aux Balkans: Recueil à la mémoire de Jean Deshayes,* edited by J.-L. Huot et al., pp. 461–478. Paris, 1985.

Boyce, Mary. "On the Fire Temples of Kerman." *Acta Orientalia* 30 (1966): 51–72.

Boyce, Mary. "On the Sacred Fires of the Zoroastrians." *Bulletin of the School of Oriental and African Studies* 31 (1968): 52–68.

Boyce, Mary. "On the Zoroastrian Temple Cult of Fire." *Journal of the American Oriental Society* 95 (1975): 454–465.

Boyce, Mary. *A Persian Stronghold of Zoroastrianism.* Oxford, 1977; reprint, Lanham, Md., 1989.

Boyd, James W., and Firoze M. Kotwal. "Worship in a Zoroastrian Fire Temple." *Indo-Iranian Journal* 26 (1983): 293–318.

Choksy, Jamsheed K. *Purity and Pollution in Zoroastrianism: Triumph over Evil.* Austin, Tex., 1989.

Choksy, Jamsheed K. *Conflict and Cooperation: Zoroastrian Subalterns and Muslim Elites in Medieval Iranian Society.* New York, 1997.

Choksy, Jamsheed K. "To Cut-Off, Purify, and Make Whole: Historiographical and Ecclesiastical Conceptions of Ritual

Space." *Journal of the American Oriental Society* 123 (2003): 21–41.

Darrow, William R. "Keeping the Waters Dry: The Semiotics of Fire and Water in the Zoroastrian Yasna." *Journal of the American Academy of Religion* 56 (1988): 417–442.

Dastur, Faroukh, and Firoza Punthaky Mistree. "Fire Temples and Other Sacred Precincts in Iran and India." In *A Zoroastrian Tapestry: Art, Religion, and Culture*, edited by Pheroza J. Godrej and Firoza Punthaky Mistree, pp. 301–323. Bombay, 2002.

Eilers, Wilhelm. "Herd und Feuerstätte in Iran." *Innsbrucker Beiträge zur Sprachwissenschaft* 12 (1974): 307–338.

Erdmann, Kurt. *Das iranische Feuerheiligtum.* Leipzig, Germany, 1941.

Giara, Marzban J. *Global Directory of Zoroastrian Fire Temples.* 2d ed. Mumbai, India, 2002.

Godard, André. "Les monuments du feu." *Athār-é Īrān* 3 (1938): 7–80.

Gropp, Gerd. "Funktion des Feuertempels der Zoroastrier." *Archäologische Mitteilungen aus Iran,* 2 (1969): 147–175.

Houtkamp, J. "Some Remarks on Fire Altars of the Achaemenid Period." In *La religion iranienne à l'époque achéménide: Actes du Colloque de Liège 11 décembre 1987,* edited by Jean Kellens, pp. 23–48. Ghent, Belgium, 1991.

Huff, Dietrich. "Sasanian Chahār Tāqs in Fars." In *Proceedings of the Third Annual Symposium of Archaeological Research in Iran, 1974,* pp. 243–254. Tehran, Iran, 1975.

Keall, Edward J. "Archaeology and the Fire Temple." In *Iranian Civilization,* edited by C. J. Adams, pp. 15–22. Montreal, 1973.

Kotwal, Firoze M. "Some Observations on the History of the Parsi Dar-i Mihrs." *Bulletin of the School of Oriental and African Studies* 37 (1974): 664–669.

Leslie, Donald D. "Persian Temples in T'ang China." *Monumenta Serica* 35 (1981–1983): 275–303.

Menasce, Jean de. *Feux et fondations pieuses dans le droit sassanide.* Paris, 1964.

Modi, Jivanji J. *The Religious Ceremonies and Customs of the Parsees.* 2d ed. Bombay, 1937.

Moorey, Peter Roger Stuart. "Aspects of Worship and Rituals on Achaemenid Seals." *Archäologische Mitteilungen aus Iran* 6 (1979): 218–226.

Schippmann, Klaus. *Die iranischen Feuerheiligtümer.* Berlin, 1971.

Stronach, David. "On the Evolution of the Early Iranian Fire Temple." In *Papers in Honour of Professor Mary Boyce, Acta Iranica,* vol. 24, pp. 606–627. Leiden, 1985.

Tirmidhi, B. M. "Zoroastrians and Their Fire Temples in Iran and Adjoining Countries from the 9th to the 14th Centuries as Gleaned from the Arabic Geographical Works." *Islamic Culture* 24 (1950): 271–284.

Wikander, Stig. *Feuerpriester in Kleinasien und Iran.* Lund, Sweden, 1946.

Yamamoto, Yumiko. "The Zoroastrian Temple Cult of Fire in Archaeology and Literature." *Orient* 15 (1979): 19–53 and 17 (1981): 67–104.

JAMSHEED K. CHOKSY (2005)

ATHANASIUS (c. 298–373), bishop of Alexandria, theologian, church father, and saint. Athanasius was born around the year 300, perhaps in 298, according to a chronicle composed soon after his death and preserved in Syriac. Later Coptic legends locate Athanasius's birthplace in Upper Egypt, but these claims seem to contradict his genuinely Greek education. In his youth he may have visited Christian monks in the desert areas near Alexandria. The Alexandrian bishop Alexander (311–328) ordained him as a deacon at the time of the fateful dispute with Arius, and in the spring of 325 Athanasius accompanied the bishop to the imperial Council of Nicaea, where Arianism was solemnly condemned as a heresy. Elected by a small minority of the Egyptian clergy and by the Alexandrian laity as the successor of Alexander in the summer of 328, the young Athanasius, not yet in his thirties, faced a critical situation.

More than half of the many bishops subordinated to the jurisdiction of the Alexandrian pope had recognized the authority of the schismatic bishop Meletios of Lycopolis in Upper Egypt. Soon after the episcopal election of Athanasius, the Meletians built up a common front against him in supporting Arius and his friends. They were encouraged to do so by a coalition of bishops from the eastern provinces of the empire under the leadership of Bishop Eusebius of Nicomedia, who was hostile to the Alexandrian see for political reasons. Athanasius was exposed to attacks from all sides in imposing without compromise the decrees of Nicaea, which condemned the Arian heresy and regulated strictly the readmission of Meletians into the Catholic church. He hoped for a time to consolidate his precarious position by rallying the monastic groups in the deserts of Egypt and the Coptic communities along the Nile Valley. Between 328 and 334 his pastoral visits reached the border of modern Sudan and the western parts of Libya. But in 335 the Synod of Tyre, organized by the anti-Alexandrian and pro-Arian party, succeeded in driving Athanasius out of office. As it was invested with imperial power like the Council of Nicaea ten years earlier, this synod made questionable the very legitimacy of Athanasius as a bishop.

Athanasius was exiled by Emperor Constantine on November 7, 335. Only after Constantine's death on May 22, 337, could Athanasius return to Alexandria. But his legitimacy was still rejected by the Eastern bishops, who had gained the favor of Constantius II, Constantine's son and successor in the East. In 338 Athanasius again found himself driven from Alexandria. In dramatic circumstances he fled to Rome, where he was welcomed by Bishop Julius I and rehabilitated by his local synod. In 342 a broader synod, convoked in Serdica (modern-day Sofia) by the emperor of the West, Constantius's brother, Constans I, ratified this recognition of Athanasius as legitimate bishop of Alexandria.

Only in October 346 could the exiled bishop regain his see, but not without Constans's heavy political pressure on his younger brother Constantius in the East. Athanasius's fulfillment of his pastoral duties in Alexandria, from 346 to

356, became increasingly difficult after Constans was murdered by a usurper in 350. As sole ruler of the whole empire, Constantius tried to work out a unified religious policy. However, this policy was unacceptable to Athanasius, because it interfered in the realm of the church's dogma as canonized in Nicaea in 325. In fact, Constantius, influenced by a conservative majority of bishops in the East, rejected the creed of Nicaea. He organized a vast subversive campaign in the West and the East against Athanasius, as the main supporter of Nicaea. Outlawed and sought by the emperor's secret police, Athanasius vanished, remaining in the desert from February 356 until November 361, hidden by the monks but very active in the clandestine administration of his diocese. Exile under Constantius's successor, Julian (361–363), proved less disruptive. Finally, under Emperor Valens (364–378), Athanasius was exiled for only a few months. On February 1, 366, he was fully recognized and was reinstalled in his office, where he remained until his death in early May 373.

Fifteen years and ten months of exile had not damaged Athanasius's popular links with the Alexandrian church, or with Coptic monastic circles. The mature energies of this dominant figure revealed themselves in an even more efficient way during his repeated exiles. At the time of his first exile, Athanasius completed a compilation of older notes and gave them the form of an apologetic treatise. In doing so, he added to a first work, *Against the Heathen,* a second apology, *On the Incarnation of the Word,* with a deeply renewed view of Alexandrian Christology. In the early stage of his second exile, in Rome, Athanasius finished his principal dogmatic work, entitled *Discourse against the Arians,* originally in one or two books. During his third exile, among the monks, he dictated important historical, dogmatic, and apologetic works, especially his *Letters to Serapion concerning the Divinity of the Holy Spirit,* the apology *On the Synods of Rimini and Seleucia,* and *Life of Anthony.*

Through these works Athanasius entered into dialogue with various pro-Nicene theological parties, among them the group of Basil of Ancyra. Their reconciliation was celebrated at the Synod of Alexandria in the summer of 362.

Athanasius's theology remains strikingly coherent throughout his writings. It focuses on the incarnation of God in Christ as the central principle of Christian theology. The Trinity is truly known only in light of the gospel message. The incarnate Son of God operates in divinizing humankind, which is saved by the Son from death and corruption in conjunction with its own godlikeness. The mystery of Christ, revealed by the New Testament, is actualized in the life of the church, in its official creed, in baptism, in the Eucharist, and in the religious improvement of its members.

The literary and doctrinal legacy of Athanasius was decisive through the Cappadocian fathers in the East and Ambrose of Milan in the West. His doctrine on the salvific incarnation of Christ has shaped subsequent Christian traditions. During his lifetime, Athanasius was acclaimed by Basil of Caesarea, among others—and after his death, universally—as champion of the church's dogmatic freedom against the state's political administration.

Bibliography

The writings of Athanasius are available in English translations such as *Select Works and Letters,* translated and edited by Archibald Robertson, "A Select Library of Nicene and Post-Nicene Fathers of the Christian Church," 2d series, vol. 4 (New York, 1892); *The Life of Anthony,* translated by Robert T. Meyer, "Ancient Christian Writers," vol. 10 (Westminster, Md., 1950); *Life of Saint Anthony,* translated by Mary Emily Keenan, "The Fathers of the Church," vol. 15 (New York, 1952); and *Contra gentes and De incarnatione,* translated and edited by Robert W. Thomson (Oxford, 1971). The Athanasian doctrine on Christ is developed in Aloys Grillmeier's *Christ in Christian Tradition,* 2d ed., rev. (Atlanta, 1975). My critical study on Athanasius's career as a bishop and a writer, *Athanase d'Alexandrie: Évêque et écrivain* (Paris, 1983), offers a new evaluation.

Charles Kannengiesser (1987)

ATHAPASKAN RELIGIOUS TRADITIONS

This entry consists of the following articles:

AN OVERVIEW
ATHAPASKAN CONCEPTS OF WIND AND POWER

ATHAPASKAN RELIGIOUS TRADITIONS: AN OVERVIEW

The Athapaskan-speaking (alternative spellings include Athabascan, Athabaskan, and Athapascan) nations of Alaska, Canada, the Pacific Northwest, and the American Southwest can be sorted into three broad cultural areas: the Northern Athapaskans, the Southern Athapaskans of the American Southwest, and the Athapaskans of the Pacific Northwest. Religious traditions in each of these areas vary markedly from each other. In general, the Northern Athapaskan religious traditions follow culturally scripted theories of ever-watchful spirit forces whose primary relationship with human beings centers on hunting and other subsistence issues. By contrast, the Southern Athapaskan religious traditions of the American Southwest focus on patterns reinforcing social harmony. The Athapaskan religious traditions of the Pacific Northwest fall into two general categories: subsistence-based traditions poised in complex social structures, and millenarian traditions that followed the arrival of European immigrants. Sacred stories, concepts of the numinous, and cultural practices, ritual activities, and concepts of leadership align themselves within these cultural areas.

Northern Athapaskan Religious Traditions. Northern Athapaskan nations are divided by the Canadian–United States border. Eleven of the twenty-nine Northern Athapaskan nations extend across the interior rivers of Alaska, while the rest occupy much of Canada's subarctic interior and western regions. Numerous sacred stories fall into cultural patterns in roughly three large geographic zones: (1) those nearest the northwest-coast cultural region, who include the Dena'ina, Ahtna, Tahltan, and Tagish; (2) those of the interior Alaskan Tanana and Yukon riverways (Gwich'in, Han, Koyukon, Holikachuk, Deg Hit'an, Tanana, Tanacross, and Upper Tanana); and (3) northern Canadian Athapaskan nations, including the Dogrib, Hare, Sekani, and Kaska.

The Athapaskans nearest the northwest-coast cultural region tell stories closely reflecting their historical links with the coastal Tlingit and Haida, nations with whom they have long established family and trading connections. Raven is a key element in these stories, always serving in its capacity as trickster and harbinger of change. Many of the key animal species depicted in stories of this region, such as Wolf, Whale, Seagull, and Eagle, reflect kinship group names or euphemisms for trading partners from the northwest coast. The development of shamanic power serves as a key component of oral narratives, underlying all Northern Athapaskan religious traditions.

Among the interior Athapaskans, the most important of these stories includes a pantheon of narratives about a mythical traveler, sometimes accompanied by his younger brother. Through feats of unexplained powers or humorous accidents the traveler populates the world with animals and plants. Significant species, such as ducks, mink, foxes, and wolves, are featured in their own narratives, while less important species take supportive roles. Here, too, Raven serves as the catalytic trickster figure whose actions often reverse or galvanize new lifeways among the creatures introduced by the traveler. Another important narrative from the Alaskan interior is commonly called "The Blind Man and the Loon," a sacred story with links to Inupiat stories in the north and Algonkian stories in the south. These myths, always an expression of the tellers' subsistence needs and the precarious impact of weather and environmental catastrophes, enclose humanity in a framework of spirits ever weighing human judgment, moral behavior, and mental attitudes.

Canadian Athapaskan sacred stories also feature a mythological heroic man, but rather than moving from area to area in a methodical way to populate the natural environment, the Canadian Dené hero interacts with his wife in constant tension with enemies from other areas. Translated into English as "The Man without Fire," stories about the northern Canadian Athapaskan hero narrate exploits about saving his wife from kidnapping and avenging his brother's murder.

Northern Athapaskans situate their concepts of the supernatural, humanity, and related worldviews in sacred stories. Where human populations are small and widely separated, the spiritual world dominates all activity, and ethical decisions emerge from good rapport with the natural world rather than human relations. Scarcity of food predicates the importance of sharing everything. Throughout the Alaskan Athapaskan community, clan-based feasts (usually called potlatches) serve as the primary institution for marking life-cycle events and redistribution of goods. The needs of the group submerge individual aspirations in an ethos of survival. Likewise, Northern Athapaskan individuals who manage to display appropriate self-sacrifice, personal strength, and devotion to the group emerge as great leaders. While a few women have filled such roles, Northern Athapaskan cultures generally allow primacy to men in leadership and authority.

Since the arrival of Euro-Americans, Christianity has replaced most Athapaskan religious traditions with the exception of the potlatch. Some features of the potlatch have been enhanced by American and Canadian trade goods, such as woolen blankets, rifles, and bolts of cotton cloth, each of which play an important role in the festivities, particularly as gifts. While the Anglican and Catholic faiths now predominate in Canada, Alaska's Christian sects follow the pattern established in 1885 by Sheldon Jackson, who asked twelve denominations to preside over loosely defined geographic areas in Alaska as missionaries, and also to provide education, medical aid, and orphanages.

SOUTHERN ATHAPASKANS OF THE AMERICAN SOUTHWEST. Two Athapaskan peoples, the Diné and the Apache, prevail in the American Southwest in terms of population and land holdings. They are unique among Athapaskans because of their agricultural subsistence base (primarily corn) and herding. The Diné, or Navajo, with the largest Native American population in the United States (298,197 in the 2001 census) and one of the largest North American territories (over 27,000 square miles in the states of Utah, Colorado, Arizona, and New Mexico) also predominate in terms of the amount of scholarly research into their religious traditions.

Navajo traditions. *Diné bahane,'* popularly known as the Navajo creation story, forms the paradigmatic core of all Diné religious, philosophical, medical, and artistic traditions. *Diné bahane'* narrates four emergences of human beings into new worlds, each replete with its own benefits and sources of trouble. The fourth and present world, like the three previous worlds, revolves around dualistic relations between male and female, harmony and chaos, and sky and earth. Changing Woman, the most important of the Diné pantheon of deities, represents the renewal of life as the core of the earth and its seasons. Other Diné deities include First Man, First Woman, and Monster Slayer, all of whom are described and explained in *Diné bahane'.*

Gender relations dominate the narrative themes in *Diné bahane',* along with discussion of linguistic styles, artistic styles, and daily work activities, all emphasizing the importance of social roles in Diné society, in contrast to the dominance of subsistence values in the Northern Athapaskan regions. Diné environmental conditions, while harsh, nonetheless have provided reliable food and shelter over the centuries, allowing the Diné to focus on their relations to each other as well as to the land. *Diné bahane'* provides a metaphoric explanation for the importance of the four mountains held sacred by the Diné: Blanca Peak in Colorado, Mount Taylor in New Mexico, San Francisco Peaks in Arizona, and Hesperus Peak in Colorado. According to sacred narrative, the Diné are never to leave the precincts of these four sacred mountains.

The hogan, or dwelling, reveals the cosmological significance of the four sacred mountains by its configuration and spatial orientation. Each part of the hogan represents structures of the universe, with the floor corresponding to the earth as well as to female power, and the round roof reflecting the sky and male power. Many religious ceremonies take place in the hogan.

The Diné make use of many ritual ceremonies, of which the blessingway is the most important and performed most frequently. A two-day ceremony, the blessingway brings peace, beauty, and protection so one may achieve a long and harmonious life. During a blessingway, *Diné bahane'* is recited in its entirety.

Although balanced gender relations form a core religious and social value in Diné life, from the smallest elements of daily hegemony to the largest, men dominate in the household, as ritual leaders, and in their communities, as well as in national affairs.

Apache traditions. Apachean religious traditions are in some ways similar to those of the Diné, particularly in terms of the central deity, White Clay Woman, also known as Changing Woman, or 'Isánáklésh in the Mescalero language. Like the Diné's Changing Woman, 'Isánáklésh is considered to be the earth and all of its seasons and changes, as well as representing female power. Her counterpart, Usen, also called Life Giver, represents male power and appropriate leadership. The Apachean peoples of the American Southwest include the Jicarilla, Chiricahua, White Mountain, San Carlos, Mescalero, and Kiowa-Apache, many still living on reservations across the Southwest.

The women's puberty rite continues to be the most important Apache religious ceremony. Since precolonial times Apache people have celebrated a woman's first menses through what is now a four-day event in which the young woman is sponsored by a prominent religious leader (usually female) and an equally prestigious male singer, who are expected to instruct her in the sacred arts of becoming an adult Apache woman. The ceremonial activities include long hours of dancing, running at dawn toward 'Isánáklésh, and finally a blessing by all of her family and kin with the use of sacred cattail pollen.

Colonial history has left the Apaches with little reservation land, but fierce reputations as warriors. Geronimo and Lozen stand out in Apache history as paradigms of the sacred power of Usen. Lozen, a late-nineteenth-century Apache woman who fought with her brother and his warriors against the U.S. government, earned a reputation for having the power to locate the enemy and possessed the male powers of Usen rather than the female powers of 'Isánáklésh. Unlike most Apache women, Lozen took a prominent position in Apache leadership because of her legendary visionary and prophetic abilities. After Geronimo's defeat and the Apaches' internment on reservations, Apache religious and leadership styles changed to suit American demands for conversion to Christianity (although some follow Apache religious traditions even today) and secular elections.

Athapaskans of the Pacific Northwest. The Athapaskans of the Pacific Northwest area, unlike other Athapaskan peoples, live near rugged coastal areas in Oregon and northern California. These Athapaskan nations include the Tolowa, Hupa, Mattole, Nongatl, Sinkyone, Lassik, Wailaki, and Kato. These Athapaskan nations competed for territory with Algonkian and Hokan peoples in precolonial times. Of these, the Hupa are the largest group, numbering around two thousand in the twentieth century. Their traditional subsistence resources have been salmon, acorns, and trade. Like most of the nations of this area, Athapaskan and otherwise, the aboriginal societies were hierarchical and wealthy enough to have community leaders whose primary occupations entailed conducting ritual procedures and redistributing goods.

Sacred stories and songs, although spoken in their own languages, blended thematically with those of neighboring nations. In addition to ceremonies related directly to subsistence efforts, such as the Acorn Feast and the ceremonies to honor the first salmon of the spring salmon run, some of the Pacific Northwest Athapaskan ceremonials, such as the Jump Dance, initiate young men into what Alfred Kroeber (1907) referred to as secret societies, groups which inaugurated them into the socioeconomic and political system. (Some of the nations are now bringing back female initiation ceremonies as well.) Other ceremonials centered on protection from earthquakes and mud slides, common environmental disasters in this area.

Postcolonial religious traditions of the late nineteenth and early twentieth centuries include the Shaker religion, originated in 1882 by Joe Slocum and his wife, Mary, of Puget Sound after Mr. Slocum recovered from a near-death experience. The Shaker religion came to northern California in 1926. Termed a revitalization movement or millenarian religion, the Slocums' revelations encouraged Native peoples throughout the northwest Pacific coast to rediscover the individual rapport with spirit forces found in earlier traditions, in a mode much like the Prophet Dance of Washington and the Plateau area.

The Shaker religion incorporates a mixture of precolonial Native American shamanic traditions with Christian practices. By contrast, another revitalization tradition in the Pacific Northwest area, labeled the World Renewal System by Kroeber (1949), emphasizes a return to the environmental rites of northern California's precolonial era. The Hupa version includes six traditional rites: the Acorn Feast, First Salmon Ceremony, Fish Dam Ceremony, First Eel Ceremony, the Jump Dance, and the Deerskin Dance.

Early studies on Athapaskan religious traditions began in the American Southwest in the late nineteenth century, and have continued to the present era with increasing involvement by Athapaskan scholars. Most significant among these are Gladys Reichard's work on Navajo religion, Inés Talamantez's research on Apache female initiations and religious traditions, Émile Petitot's transcriptions and translations of Canadian Dené oral narratives, Cornelius Osgood's contributions on Ingalik (now referred to as Deg Hit'an) cosmology, Jules Jetté's transcriptions of Koyukon religious traditions, Kroeber's enthographies of the California Indians, and Richard Keeling's ethnomusicological work with the Hupa.

BIBLIOGRAPHY

Basso, Keith H. *Western Apache Witchcraft.* Tucson, Ariz., 1969.

Beck, Peggy V., Anna Lee Walters, and Nia Francisco. *The Sacred: Ways of Knowledge, Sources of Life.* Tsaile, Ariz., 1996.

Buckley, Thomas. "The Shaker Church and the Indian Way in Native Northwestern California." In *Native American Spirituality: A Critical Reader,* edited by Lee Irwin, pp. 256–269. Lincoln, Neb., 2000.

Fast, Phyllis Ann. *Northern Athabascan Survival: Women, Community and the Future.* Lincoln, Neb., 2002.

Heizer, Robert F., and Albert B. Elsasser. *The Natural World of the California Indians.* Berkeley, Calif., 1980.

Jetté, Jules. "On the Medicine-Men of the Ten'a." *Journal of the Royal Anthropological Institute of Great Britain and Ireland* 37 (1907): 157–188.

Jetté, Jules. "On the Superstitions of the Ten'a Indians (Middle Part of the Yukon Valley, Alaska)." *Anthropos* 6 (1911): 95–108, 241–259, 602–723.

Keeling, Richard. *Cry for Luck: Sacred Song and Speech among the Yurok, Hupa, and Karok Indians of Northwestern California.* Berkeley, Calif., 1992.

Kroeber, Alfred L. "The Religion of the Indians of California." *American Archaeology and Ethnology* 4, no. 6 (1907).

Kroeber, Alfred L., and Edward W. Gifford. "World Renewal: A Cult System of Native Northwest California." *University of California Anthropological Records* 21, no. 1 (1949): 1–210.

Nelson, Richard K. *Make Prayers to the Raven: A Koyukon View of the Northern Forest.* Chicago, 1983.

Osgood, Cornelius. "Ingalik Mental Culture." *Yale University Publications in Anthropology* 56 (1959).

Petitot, Émile. *Traditions indiennes du Canada nord-ouest* (1886). Paris, 1967.

Reichard, Gladys A. *Navajo Religion: A Study of Symbolism.* Princeton, N.J., 1950.

Ridington, Robin. *Trail to Heaven: Knowledge and Narrative in a Northern Native Community.* Iowa City, Iowa, 1988.

Ridington, Robin. "Voice, Representation, and Dialogue." In *Native American Spirituality: A Critical Reader,* edited by Lee Irwin, pp. 97–120. Lincoln, Neb., 2000.

Slobodin, Richard. "Without Fire: A Kutchin Tale of Warfare, Survival, and Vengeance." In *Northern Athapaskan Conference 1971,* vol. 1, edited by A. McFadyen Clark, pp. 259–301. Ottawa, 1975.

Slobodin, Richard. "Kutchin." In *Handbook of North American Indians,* vol. 6, *Subarctic,* edited by June Helm, pp. 514–532. Washington, D.C., 1981.

Witherspoon, Gary. *Language and Art in the Navajo Universe.* Ann Arbor, Mich., 1977.

Youst, Lionel, and William R. Seaburg. *Coquelle Thompson, Athabascan Witness: A Cultural Biography.* Norman, Okla., 2002.

Zolbrod, Paul G. *Diné bahane': The Navajo Creation Story.* Albuquerque, N.Mex., 1984.

PHYLLIS ANN FAST (2005)

ATHAPASKAN RELIGIOUS TRADITIONS: ATHAPASKAN CONCEPTS OF WIND AND POWER

The views of the Athapaskan-speaking Native American peoples of North America about the source of the powers of life, movement, thought, and the supernatural abilities of human beings, animals, and other elements of the natural world have been a matter of debate among cultural anthropologists. This article will provide a brief review of the diverse interpretations, and it will seek to show that the different views can be partially reconciled based upon relatively new understandings of Athapaskan conceptions of the nature and sources of power.

In *Holy Wind in Navajo Philosophy,* James Kale McNeley presents evidence that in the Navajo view the atmosphere or air itself is endowed with the powers of life, movement, thought, and communication, and provides such powers to all living things. The atmosphere so conceived, with powers that are not acknowledged in Western culture, is hereafter referred to as Wind, a gloss of the Navajo term *níłch'i.*

The Navajo, along with the Apachean peoples of New Mexico and Arizona, make up the Southern Athapaskan segment of the speakers of Athapaskan languages, while the Northern Athapaskans consist of two groups, the Athapaskans of western Canada and interior Alaska, and Athapaskans of the Pacific Northwest. Richard Perry found clusters of culture traits that are widely shared among Northern and Southern Athapaskan groups, including the view that all objects in nature are alive and sapient and the belief that personal power can be acquired through dreams. It therefore seems likely that conceptions of the ontological source of such life and power are also shared among these groups.

McNeley observes that the Navajo term *níłch'i diyinii* (holy wind) refers to the natural air or wind, albeit endowed with life-giving powers. This all-pervasive Wind is conceived by the Navajo to enter into and give life and other powers to all aspects of the natural world, including such elements as the earth, sky, sun, moon, and things on the earth's surface. Such natural phenomena, having been endowed with Winds by which they live and think, are equipped to provide guidance and instruction to the Navajo by means of Little Winds that are sent by these holy ones to influence human thought and conduct. From another perspective, each living being may be said to participate in the powers of an all-encompassing and unitary Wind.

Conceptions of the role of Wind that are similar to Navajo beliefs are found in accounts of Apachean culture. Morris Opler cites the belief that, just as a human being is created from natural elements, the supernatural powers send Wind into the bodies of human beings to render them animate. Natural phenomena are also regarded as being animate, and they communicate with humans by means of Wind that carries messages to them. The whirlwind as a messenger for the supernaturals is a recurring theme in the religious traditions of the Jicarilla Apache.

In earlier descriptions of Northern Athapaskan cultures, the view is commonly expressed that each animal or natural object is individually animated by a spirit or soul that dwells within it. Cornelius Osgood described this belief among the Ingalik. John Honigman sometimes alternatively referred to such an animating force as "soul" or "wind," reporting that the power to perform a shamanistic vision quest represented a portion of the animal's "wind (or soul)" passing into the dreamer to enhance the latter's natural ability (Honigman, 1954, p. 105), while the Kaska view is that a shaman effected cures "with the aid of the power that resided in his soul or wind" (p. 111). Honigman's account left unresolved the critical ontological question of whether the Athapaskan concept should be interpreted as reference to a strictly spiritual phenomenon or as a reference to a natural element that has some special qualities.

However, as David M. Smith notes, there is some evidence that the use of the word *soul* may be traced to the influence of missionaries, and diverse ethnographers (including Honigman himself) have elsewhere favored the term *wind* in interpreting the indigenous concept in stating that a sorcerer might try to steal his victim's "wind." According to J. Alden Mason, "the Yellowknife shamans drum and sing for wind when such is needed for their journeys" (Mason, 1946, p. 39). There are also references to wind as a force pervading the natural world comparable to the Navajo concept: Mason cites an old Slave Indian who referred to "the wind which is the spirit of all and pervades everything" (p. 38). This is similar to other ethnographic accounts that present Athapaskan conceptions of an all-pervading life force.

Some accounts of Athapaskan culture cite a belief in magical or mysterious power without identifying that power. June Helm writes that Franz Boas characterized the fundamental concept in the religions of North America as the belief in magic powers, "the wonderful qualities which are believed to exist in objects, animals, men, spirits, or deities, and which are superior to the natural qualities of man" (Helm, 2000, p. 272). A Northern Athapaskan term for such power, *inkonze,* also connotes a powerful form of knowledge that encompasses both practical knowledge and what Smith calls "supraempirical" knowledge acquired through dreams and visions of animals. The superior power and knowledge attributed to animals has given rise to efforts to acquire that power, including beliefs in the possibility of transformation between human and animals forms.

Smith suggests that dualistic assumptions underlying Western thought confounded earlier attempts to understand Athapaskan religious concepts, and he advocates instead the monistic view that one's relationship with a helping animal is with the entire animal, body and spirit. Similarly, McNeley asserts that the Navajo conceive of supernatural power as being a characteristic of natural elements, including Wind. What is common to both conceptions is that elements of the natural world have powers that we in the Western world do not acknowledge but which Athapaskans do, and which they seek to access for their own benefit.

Smith compares *inkonze* with the Omaha concept *wakonda.* Based on James R. Walker's data, McNeley has suggested that, for the Dakota, *wakonda* refers to an unseen power in which the Dakota participate by means of Skan (Great Spirit), just as the Navajo term *diyinii* (holy ones), refers to unseen powers in which the Navajo participate through the agency of Wind. The combined evidence suggests that, for Athapaskans, Wind is conceived of as a natural element that is empowered to give life, thought, and movement and to establish and sustain human contact with other natural elements that have powers of their own.

SEE ALSO Navajo Religious Traditions; North American Indians, article on Indians of the Southwest.

BIBLIOGRAPHY

Helm, June. *The People of Denendah.* Iowa City, Iowa, 2000.

Honigman, John J. *The Kaska Indians: An Ethnographic Reconstruction.* New Haven, Conn., 1954.

Mason, J. Alden. *Notes on the Indians of the Great Slave Lake Area.* New Haven, Conn., 1946.

McNeley, James Kale. *The Navajo Theory of Life and Behavior.* Ph.D. diss., University of Hawaii, 1975.

McNeley, James Kale. *Holy Wind in Navajo Philosophy.* Tucson, 1981.

Opler, Morris Edward. *Myths and Tales of the Jicarilla Apache Indians.* New York, 1938.

Osgood, Cornelius. *Ingalik Social Culture.* New Haven, Conn., 1958.

Perry, Richard J. *Western Apache Heritage.* Austin, Tex., 1991.

Smith, David M. "An Athapaskan Way of Knowing: Chipewyan Ontology." *American Ethnologist* 25, no. 3 (1998): 412–432.

Walker, James R. *The Sun Dance and Other Ceremonies of the Oglala Division of the Teton Dakota.* New York, 1917.

JAMES KALE MCNELEY (2005)

ATHEISM. The term *atheism* is employed in a variety of ways. For the purpose of the present survey atheism is the doctrine that God does not exist, that belief in the existence of God is a false belief. The word *God* here refers to a divine being regarded as the independent creator of the world, a being superlatively powerful, wise, and good. The focus of the present study is on atheism occurring within a context of thought normally called "religious."

Rudiments in Ancient and Primitive Religion. Already in the writings of Cicero (c. 106–43 BCE), the question was raised whether there might be some "wild and primitive peoples" who possess no idea of gods of any kind. The view of David Hume in his *Natural History of Religion* (1757) was that polytheism, in his view the earliest religion of humankind, was devoid of a belief in God. According to most nineteenth-century anthropological theories, the belief in God was a late development in the evolution of religious ideas. Contemporary ethnographic research supports the view that a belief in a supreme creator is, at least, a pervasive feature of the religion of many primitive peoples.

The complete absence of the idea of God would not qualify as atheism as it has here been defined, but the role of the supreme being among primitive peoples is instructive for an understanding of religious forms of atheism as they occur under other cultural conditions. Where primitive religion includes the belief in a supreme being, the creator of all that exists, this being is not always the center of religious life and worship. In the traditional religion of many African peoples the most common acts of worship are directed toward spiritual beings known as the living-dead. These are individuals of the community who have died, but whose influence is still profoundly felt by the living. In some cases God is approached directly only when the living-dead have failed, or in cases of severe distress. Where a belief in the supreme being occurs among primitive peoples, the possibility of atheism is remote, for like other conceptions among such societies the supreme being is not so much a belief, in the sense of a credal affirmation that might be rejected, as an integral component of a total conception of reality through which experience is ordered.

The first step toward religious atheism occurs in the context of religious thought in which a variety of beings, each believed to be supreme, or in which a variety of conceptions of the supreme being, appear concurrently and compete. The earliest documents of the Hindu religious tradition, the Vedas (c. 900 BCE), refer to a variety of gods who preside over various powers of nature and are often practically identified with them. In the *Ṛgveda* any one of these diverse gods can stand out as supreme when he is the object of praise. In this context no god of the Vedas is more often praised than Indra, the king of the gods. It is interesting, then, that among the hymns that praise him are also found passages that ridicule his reputed power and that cast doubt upon his existence.

Such doubt is hardly representative of the praises sung to Indra. Yet it is significant that this kind of skepticism is included in the most authoritative of Hindu scriptures. It seems to arise concurrently with new ways of conceiving the divine expressed among some of the late hymns of the *Ṛgveda.* Here, beside the hymns to the nature gods, one finds reference to an unknown god who has encompassed all created things. Here are found hymns to Viśvakarma, the father who made all. And here is found that One wherein abide all existing things, that One which, before all existing things appeared, "breathed windless" by its own inherent power. In these late hymns is also found reference to an impersonal order to the universe, a law (*ṛta*) to which even the highest gods are subject or which by their power they uphold.

The possibility of conceiving of the ultimate source of the universe not as a god, but as something quite impersonal, is also reflected in the early Upaniṣads (c. 700–600 BCE), the concluding portions of the Vedas. The Upaniṣads are the repository of diverse currents of thought, but the quest that pervades them is for that supreme object of knowledge in which all that has being has its ultimate ground. The Upaniṣads refer to this reality, called *brahman,* in two significantly differing ways. On the one hand, the Upaniṣads speak of *brahman* as having qualities (*saguṇa*). In this context it is the ultimate cause, the true creator of all that is, the personal God, the Lord (Īśvara) of the Universe, and the supreme object of worship. On the other hand, they speak of *brahman* as beyond qualities (*nirguṇa*). No concepts are adequate to describe it. The most that one can say about it is by way of negation. With such opposing conceptions, the possibility emerges of a rejection of the existence of God that is nevertheless religious.

The possibility of conceiving of the ultimate as something other than a god, even the highest of gods, can be seen in the writings of other civilizations as well. In the Chinese classics and in inscriptions of the Shang dynasty in China (c. 1750–1100 BCE), are found frequent reference to a supreme ruler in heaven known as Shangdi. This god is not known as creator, but he was undoubtedly a personal being, a divine supervisor over human society, whose decrees determine the course of events on earth. At about the time the Shang dynasty was supplanted by the Zhou (c. 1100 BCE) the name *T'ien* appeared alongside of *Shang-ti* as a designation for the supreme ruler in heaven. But the word *tian,* meaning both "heaven" and "sky," gradually lost the connotation of a personal being and came to suggest the more universal conception of a cosmic rule that impartially determines the affairs of men on earth by their conformity to a moral order. Closely related to *tian,* the ultimate ordering principle of things, was the completely impersonal Dao, literally "way" or "road." By extension it means the way to go, the truth, the normative ethical standard by which to govern human life. In the famous *Dao de jing,* ascribed to Lanzhou (sixth century BCE), it is the metaphysical principle that governs the world. It cannot be described in words, but can be dimly perceived within the intricate balance of nature. It is the law or order of nature identified with nature itself. It is not understood as God or as a god.

Classical Forms in Eastern Religious Thought. Skepticism about the existence of a god, even the king of gods, and the emergence of impersonal conceptions of the ultimate ground of the universe is not yet atheism, as defined above. Such conceptions have yet to advance arguments that belief in God is a false belief. Such arguments begin to appear where emerging theistic conceptions of God and impersonal conceptions of the absolute source and rule of the world confront one another as philosophical options over an extended period of time.

Ancient China. In ancient China the personal concept of a supreme ruler in heaven seems gradually to have been replaced by the impersonal idea of *tian* often associated with the concept of Dao. For Confucius (551–479 BCE), the most influential of ancient Chinese minds, obedience to the will of heaven is simply the practice of the moral law. By following the rules of duty and protocol handed down from the sage kings of the distant past, one lives in harmony with the moral order that governs the heavens and the life of the earth below. Confucius acknowledged the value of religious ceremonies and endorsed the veneration of ancestors, but he saw the will of Heaven operating by a kind of inherent providence. A person who has sinned against Heaven (*tian*) has no god to pray to at all.

Opposing the views of some of the early followers of Confucius, Mozi (c. 468–390 BCE) attributed to Heaven more anthropomorphic properties. He held that Heaven loves the world and desires that all human beings should relate to one another in undifferentiated love and mutual aid. Because he ascribed to Heaven such qualities as love and desire, some have suggested that Mozi's understanding of Heaven approximates the Western conception of God. Yet, as with Confucius, the providential care that Mozi sees in the working of Heaven is administered to man through the natural order of things.

By attributing love to the rule of Heaven, Mozi wished to offer an alternative to the fatalistic views of some of the disciples of Confucius. In this effort he also acknowledged the real activity of the dead and of spirits in the daily lives of human beings and therefore justified on more than ceremonial grounds the religious practices that pertained to them. In contrast to this, Xunzi (298–238 BCE) argued that Heaven is no more than a designation for the natural process through which good is rewarded and evil punished and upon which religious acts can have no effect. Because Xunzi denied the existence of supernatural agents, including the popular gods and the spirits of the dead, he might be called an atheist. But the issue that separates the thought of Xunzi from that of Mozi is an issue very different from the question of the existence of God. What divides them is whether one can ascribe personlike qualities to the ordering law of the universe that both of them presume to exist.

Strictly speaking, there was no precise equivalent in Chinese thought to the concept of God before the idea was introduced to China by the Jesuits in the sixteenth century. In the absence of this conception, the atheism of ancient China can hardly be more than implied. It was in India, where both theistic notions of the source and governance of the universe and impersonal conceptions of the ultimate ground were able to challenge one another, that explicit forms of religious atheism emerged.

God in classical Indian philosophy. The early Upaniṣads form the intellectual background for both the heterodox and the orthodox schools of Indian philosophy that began to develop around the sixth century BCE. These groups of schools are distinguished not on the basis of any specific doctrine but according to whether they affirm (*āstika*) or do not affirm (*nāstika*) the authority of the Vedas. Of the heterodox schools, those that do not affirm the authority of the Vedas, the Cārvāka and the Jains are explicitly atheistic. In Buddhism, the third of the heterodox schools, atheism is implied. Of the six orthodox schools (*darśanas*), Sāṃkhya, probably the oldest, is atheistic. It is associated closely with the Yoga (meditation) school, which affirms the existence of God. Between the sixth and tenth centuries CE, the Nyāya (logic) school became associated with the Vaiśeṣika (atomist) school, and together they developed forceful arguments to prove the existence of God, while the Pūrva Mīmāṃsā attacked and rejected such arguments. Its sister school, the Uttara Mīmāṃsā, better known as Vedānta, acknowledged that arguments for the existence of God have persuasive power at the level of everyday truth but held that at the higher level of religious knowledge the supreme being is really an illusion.

It was argued by the Nyāya school that objects made of parts are invariably the effect of a cause. Because the world as a whole is made of parts, the world must be the effect of a causal agent, and this causal agent is God (Īśvara). To this line of argument it could be objected that the world is so different from other effects that one cannot infer a cause to the world as a whole. The Nyāya, however, replied that a valid inference can be drawn from the concomitance of two things without limiting the inference to the peculiarities of the concomitance observed. Otherwise, if one had observed only small amounts of smoke (say from cigarettes), one could infer only the existence of small amounts of fire. On this "principle of concomitance," the conclusion should be that if a smaller effect has a cause, then the largest of effects must also have a cause. This, it is held, is the invisible and bodiless but infinitely wise and benevolent creator.

A related argument states that since objects characterized by order and design, such as garments, buildings, and devices, are invariably the products of intelligent beings, it follows on the principle of concomitance that the world, which displays the same characteristics, must also be the work of an intelligent being. Further, orthodox Hindu philosophies shared the affirmation of a moral order by which the voluntary actions of persons are rewarded with good or evil in this or a future life. For some exponents of the Nyāya and the Yoga schools, this view implies the existence of God, who as the ultimate arbiter apportions the appropriate reward. In Indian thought there is found no specific effort to infer the existence of God from the fact that the idea of God exists in the mind. There are, however, arguments that try to show, on the assumption that he exists, that he is superlatively powerful and wise. It was noted by some early exponents of the Yoga school that qualities like intelligence and power are found among finite beings in variations of degree. Since the degrees of perfection of any quality represent a continuum of degrees, the qualities of wisdom and power must find their highest degree in an omniscient and omnipotent being.

Heterodox Indian thought. Of the heterodox Indian schools, the Cārvāka represents the most radical departure from the tenor of religious thought in the Upaniṣads. It holds that the Vedas are the work of knaves and fools, and it rejects all sources of knowledge other than the senses. With this, it rejects the principles of inference upon which the Nyāya-Vaiśeṣika school depends to demonstrate the existence of God. The Cārvāka holds that the visible world alone exists, that the only heaven is that to be found in the wearing of beautiful clothing, in the company of young women, and in the enjoyment of delicious food. The only sovereign is the king. The only hell to be avoided is the difficulties of the present life. The only liberation is death; and that is to be avoided as long as humanly possible.

One could hardly call the Cārvāka a system of religious life and thought unless one saw a religious motivation behind its prodigious effort to liberate its adherents from the sophistry and abuse of the religious setting in which it arose. The exponents of the Cārvāka reject the doctrine of the soul and with it the ideas of *karman* and rebirth. They reject all forms of religious asceticism and hold that religious rites are incapable of any effect. By contrast, the Jains endorse an intensely ascetic path to the release of the soul (*jīva*) from an otherwise endless cycle of rebirth. According to the Jains, the soul, by nature, is eternal, perfectly blissful, and omniscient. Yet in consequence of accumulated *karman,* conceived as a subtle material substance, all but liberated souls are ensnared in a limiting material body.

The Jains depict the cosmos as uncreated and eternal. They therefore require no doctrine of God in order to explain its existence. Their points against theistic ideas are expressed in differing versions of arguments developed over centuries of dispute. Space permits mention of only a few. (1) If the world is held to be an effect from the mere fact that it is made of parts, then space must also be considered an effect. Yet the Naiyāyikas (the adherents of Nyāya-Vaiśeṣika theism) insist that space is eternal. (2) It cannot be held that the world is an *ex nihilo* effect because the Naiyāyikas also hold that the world is composed of eternal atoms. (3) If the view that the world is an effect means that the world is subject to change, then God too is an effect since he must undergo change by having created the world. (4) But even if it is granted that the world has the nature of an effect, it does not follow that the cause must be an intelligent one. (5) And even if it is granted that the creator is an intelligent being, it is impossible to see how this agent could create except by means of a body. (6) And if the possibility of a bodiless creator is admitted there remains the problem of his motive. If one says that God created from self-interest or need, one has admitted that God was lacking in some perfection. He could not have created out of compassion, for prior to the creation there were no beings to have compassion upon. If he created out of inherent goodness then the world should be perfectly good. If he created out of whim, then the world would have no purpose, and this the Naiyāyikas deny. If he created simply out of his nature, it would be as reasonable to say that the world is the effect of nature itself.

To the argument from design, the Jains reply (7) that if a beehive, or an anthill, is the work of a multitude of beings, there is no apparent reason why the world should not have been the work of a committee of gods. To arguments from moral order, the Jains raise the question whether God is arbitrary in the rewards he gives. (8) If God makes a gift of happiness to those he simply chooses, he is guilty of favoritism. (9) If he rewards precisely in accord with the merit of each individual, then he himself is subject to a moral law beyond him.

In its earliest period, Buddhist thought is less polemical than that of the Jains in its attitude toward belief in God. Yet here as well theistic ideas are found wanting. By nature Buddhism is a path of intense self-reliance, explicitly rejecting the religious system of the Vedas that seeks the favor of the gods. In the Pali canon, the earliest of Buddhist scriptures, the Buddha ridicules the claim of the brahmans to possession of a way to union with a perfect being who has never been seen and who is beyond human knowledge. This, he says, is like the man who claims to love the most beautiful woman in this or another country and desires to make her his own but knows not her name, her caste, where she lives, or what she looks like.

Unlike the Jains, who accept the reality of the material world, the Buddhists hold that all that can be said to have being is but part of a succession of impermanent phenomena, call *dharmas*. To this way of thinking, the idea of a changeless God is clearly out of place. Later Buddhist writers like Vasubandhu and Yaśomitra (fourth to fifth century CE) argue that if God is the sole cause of all that exists, then, given the cause, all existing things should have been created at once. On the hypothesis that the world is a flux of phenomena, it could never have been the effect of a single, ultimate cause. Buddhism, moreover, holds that the succession of *dharmas* is governed by an immutable law expressed in the doctrine of dependent origination (*pratītya-samutpāda*). The arising of one phenomenon is dependent upon the occurrence of others. Since this law is held to apply without exception, it admits of no room for an uncaused cause.

Among the Buddhist criticisms of theistic belief, there are also found questions about the motive of God's creative act. If he created out of his own good pleasure, then he must take delight in the suffering of his creatures. But it also holds that if God is the ultimate cause of all that occurs, then every performance of every person is ultimately a performance of God. If this is true, it removes from the individual person all responsibility for his actions and finally removes all meaning from the ideas of right and wrong.

Orthodox Hindu philosophy. Acceptance of the authority of the Vedas does not imply theistic belief. While the Nyāya-Vaiśeṣika school regards the Vedas as having been created by God, the Sāṃkhya and the Mīmāṃsā schools hold that the Vedas are such that they require no creator. For the Sāṃkhya school the universe consists of two distinct realities: soul (*puruṣa*) and matter (*prakṛti*). Neither of them can be identified with God, and neither requires God as cause, governor, or designer. The soul is pure consciousness, devoid of qualities of any kind. But in its ambiguous association with the body it is unconscious of its freedom and independence and falsely identifies itself with one or another aspect of material reality. *Prakṛti* is the primordial ground from which the universe has evolved. It is composed of three fundamental qualities or kinds of substance (*guṇas*), like a rope composed of three differing strands. Before the emergence of the universe the chaotic distribution of the three qualities had produced a state of static equilibrium. Subsequently, upon a cosmic disturbance, an unequal aggregation of these qualities proceeded gradually to bring forth all the material realities in the universe.

According to the Yoga school, this disturbance in the primordial equilibrium of *prakṛti* was an effect of the will of God. The Sāṃkhya hold it was not. Rather, *prakṛti*, in the Sāṃkhya view, evolves by its own inherent teleology, providing the *puruṣa* the conditions necessary for its liberation (*mukti*). To the view of the Yoga school that this sort of teleology points to the existence of a God, the Sāṃkhya school replies that *prakṛti* is capable in itself of this kind of purpose just as milk, though it is devoid of intelligence, is capable of providing nourishment for the calf. A minority within the Sāṃkhya school hold that the existence of God is simply incapable of proof. The majority hold that belief in God is a mistaken belief. If he is perfect he cannot have created out of selfishness, and he could not have created out of kindness, for his creatures are most unhappy.

The Mīmāṃsā school holds the Vedas to be authoritative, but not as created or revealed by God. The Vedas, rather, are the expression in words—sacred words—of the eternal, ritual, and moral order of the world. The Mīmāṃsā supports the performance of sacrifice to a variety of gods. Yet it holds that it is not the gods as such but the potential (*apūrva*) energy generated in the performance of the ritual that delivers the heavenly reward, and it explains the creation stories in the Vedas as merely underlining the importance of the ritual action to which these stories pertain.

The Mīmāṃsā shares with the Jains the view that the world is eternal, rendering superfluous the idea of God as the ultimate cause. In the work of the founder of the Mīmāṃsā school, Jaimini (second century CE), there is found no specific reference to the doctrine of God. Later exponents, such as Kumārila and Prabhākara (eighth century CE), advance definite arguments to refute theistic views. It is held by Kumārila that in order to establish that God created the world it would be necessary to provide authoritative testimony. But in the nature of the case no witnesses are available. The view that God revealed the truth of his creative act is without avail, because it would still be necessary to establish the veracity of his claim. Kumārila also objects to the Nyāya-Vaiśeṣika view that God created the world out of atoms but has established the varieties of happiness and unhappiness of finite beings in the world in accordance with their merit. If the distribution of happiness and unhappiness can be explained on the basis of the merit of individual souls, then it is unnecessary to attribute this to God. Other arguments of the Mīmāṃsā school are that if God is a material substance he is incapable of being affected by the qualities of merit or demerit of immaterial souls. If he is a spiritual being it is impossible that he could have acted as cause upon the material atoms that compose the world. If God is the explanation for the existence of the world it is impossible to see how he could also be, as he is in the Nyāya-Vaiśeṣika view, the destroyer. To these objections the Mīmāṃsā add others familiar among other atheistic schools. It is impossible to think of God as having a body, since this body would require a creator as well, yet it is impossible to see him as creating anything without one. And to these are added again the question of the motivation of God.

Like the Mīmāṃsā, Śaṅkara (788–820 CE), the founder of the Advaita (or nondualist) school of Vedānta, regards the Vedas as eternal and uncreated. Yet Śaṅkara's interest is not in the ritual injunctions that the Vedas prescribe but in the meaning of those sections of the Upaniṣads that refer to that pure Self that pervades all existing things, the knowledge of which is the ultimate truth. Śaṅkara, like the Sāṃkhya school and the Jains, affirms the existence of the soul. But unlike them he holds that souls are not a plurality of beings but One. What seems to be a variety of souls is but the illusory manifestation of this One, like a candle flame seen through a broken lens. He also holds that the variety perceived among objects of experience is also like an illusion. In the final analysis there is no material world and no God. There is but one ultimate reality called *brahman*.

The study of those sections of the Vedas (the *Jñānakāṇḍa*) that pertain to this truth should be restricted, according to Śaṅkara, to persons who are beyond the desire for earthly or even for heavenly rewards. Those sections of the Vedas (the *Karmakāṇḍa*) that pertain to ritual action he recommends to persons less advanced. In the light of this distinction Śaṅkara admits of two differing levels of truth. To say that the world of empirical experience is illusory is not to say that it is completely false. Rather, it begins and moves within the error that identifies the self with the body, the senses, or the objects of sense. It proceeds under the assumption that the knower is an object within the material world. From the standpoint of the absolute truth this kind of knowledge is seen as illusion, on the analogy of illusions encountered in the mundane world. In the world of empirical experience, reality is understood in terms of time, space, and cause. As such it presents a cohesive picture manifesting a measure of order and design. In the light of this, Śaṅkara argues that on the level of mundane experience the world is appropriately seen as an effect, and that from this effect it is reasonable to infer a cause. He also holds that the evident design and adaptation of the world, as seen from this perspective, is sufficient to infer an intelligent being who has fashioned it like a potter makes a pot from clay. And, in accordance with the view of God as lord of the moral order, Śaṅkara argues that the law of *karman* in itself is insufficient for the just administration of rewards of good and evil.

While Śaṅkara offers these arguments as serious considerations, he acknowledges that the existence of God is not amenable to proof and turns finally to the authority of the Vedas. Any proof for the existence of God is bound to be formulated within the context of a false duality in which the ultimate is seen as acting as cause upon the objects of name and form. The difficulties in proving the existence of God, then, are presumably resolved in the higher knowledge in which appearances like God and world finally give way to the perfect truth.

Atheism and Religious Thought in Western Philosophy. Religious forms of atheism in India appeared in a context in which differing conceptions of deity and of the ultimate source and order of the universe were each capable of supporting an integrated system of religious thought and action. Early periods of Western thought manifested similarly differing conceptions of deity and of the ultimate ground of all that exists. But just as Chinese intellectual history came to be dominated by the impersonal conception of the natural order of the world, so the personal conception of deity gradually achieved ascendency in the West. While alternative conceptions of deity continued as minor currents of Western thought, the possibility of an atheistic form of religious thought received new attention with the criticism of the philosophical doctrine of God by secular thought.

Ancient Greece. The religion of ancient Greece depicted in the poetry of Homer (eighth century BCE) revolved around a pantheon of gods presided over by the sky god Zeus, who was seen not as a creator but as the upholder of moral order. The gods, here associated with various aspects of the universe, are represented as superhuman immortal beings endowed with human passions, frequently behaving in undignified and amoral ways. Nevertheless, the worship of these gods in temples and other holy places, especially by means of sacrifice, constituted the state religion of Greece throughout the classical period. While there was no precise conception of God in ancient Greece, philosophical criticisms of the gods of popular belief are of interest because of their similarity to arguments later brought against theism and because of the alternative conceptions of the divine they often put in their place. The denial of these gods was a gradual development, finally expressed in uncompromising terms only around 300 BCE.

Xenophanes (c. 570–475 BCE) attacked the anthropomorphic and amoral representations of the gods in the poetry of Homer. He suggested that if animals could draw and paint, they too would represent gods in their image. As the counterpart of his rejection of the gods of the poets, he held a philosophical idea of a higher divine being who must be one, eternal, and unchangeable. There is evidence both for and against the view that he identified this being with the universe as a whole.

The development of Ionic naturalism (c. fifth century BCE) presented a challenge to traditional belief, because it offered natural explanations for phenomena that had been accounted for on the basis of belief in the gods. Naturalistic theories, however, often accommodated belief in the gods or in some conception of the divine. According to Democritus (c. 460–370 BCE), the world and all that occurs within it is but the modification in shape and arrangement of the eternal atoms of which all things are composed. Within this view such events as thunder and lightning popularly ascribed to Zeus are explained in natural terms. At the same time Democritus held that fire is the divine soul-substance that accounts for the life of the body and constitutes the soul of the world. Anaxagoras (c. 499–427 BCE), on the other hand, was accused of impiety and was required to leave Athens, not for an explicit denial of the popular gods, but for his teaching that the heavenly bodies are purely natural objects, that the sun is a red-hot stone and the moon made of earth.

Among the Sophists (c. third to fourth century BCE) criticism of the gods was based on the distinction drawn between law, or human convention (*nomos*), and nature (*phusis*). Ideas associated with public worship were assigned to the former category. They were seen as relative to human society and in some cases as the product of the purely human imagination. With the advent of Sophistic thought, criticism of the gods became more visible, because it occurred not simply in the context of a naturalistic theory that left public worship undisturbed but also in the context of higher education. On the other hand, because their fortunes depended largely upon public acceptance, the Sophists did not always extend their criticism of human convention to an outright denial of the gods. Protagoras (c. 485–420 BCE), the best known of the Sophists, was tried and outlawed in Athens for asserting that he could say of the gods "neither that they exist nor that they do not exist." He, however, is, as far as is known, the first to raise the question of the existence of the gods as a question for which an uncompromising negative answer might be given.

Proceeding further along Sophistic lines, Prodicus of Ceos, a younger contemporary of Protagoras, sought to explain the existence of the popular belief in gods. Observing that Homer occasionally used the name of Hephaistos instead of "fire," he inferred that the gods had originally been associated with things that man requires for his existence. In explaining the origin of popular belief, he did not, however, explicitly repudiate the existence of the gods or the divinity of the sun or moon. The earliest expression of thoroughly atheistic belief in ancient Greece appears in a fragment of satirical drama by Critias, a contemporary and acquaintance of Socrates. In this work the character Sisyphus articulates the view that at its origin humanity was devoid of social organization. Subsequently, men made laws to prevent mere power from prevailing over right. The enforcement of law thus prevented observable evil. Then a wise man conceived of making the people believe that there are gods to police their secret deeds and thoughts. It is not known, however, whether the speech of the dramatic character Sisyphus expresses the view of Critias himself. Thinking along a similar line, Euhemerus (c. 300 BCE) argued that the gods had once been kings and rulers who had become the objects of worship because of the improvements in civilization they had bestowed upon their subjects. Yet he too seems to have held that the heavenly bodies are real and eternal gods.

While many philosophers of this period rejected certain of the gods of popular belief, they also often affirmed the divinity of the celestial bodies and developed alternative ideas of the divine, sometimes in pantheistic or vaguely monotheistic terms. Theodorus of Cyrene (c. 300 BCE), on the other hand, seems to have rejected all such ideas. Diogenes Laertius and Cicero both observe that he did not accept the existence of any god.

Early Christianity. Contemporary research on Christian origins suggests that early Christianity did not unanimously appropriate the view of God set forth in the Hebrew scriptures. A pervading theme of the gnostic literature that circulated widely in early Christian communities is that the world is an untoward environment. It is not the work of an omnipotent and benevolent being but the result of a divine fault. Its creator is unworthy of the religious devotion of man and an obstacle to the religious goal of liberation from the present evil world. The ultimate reality, on the other hand, is not to be thought of as a God at all. It is referred to as the unknown One, the unfathomable, the incomprehensible. Occasionally, this reality is spoken of paradoxically as the One that exists in nonbeing existence. Although by the fourth century, gnosticism was condemned as unorthodox by a majority of Christian churches, it is undeniable that it represented for its adherents a religious way of life.

The emergence of the Western conception of God. Despite the pervasiveness of gnostic ideas in the first centuries of the Christian era, the biblical image of God as father and creator received the stamp of orthodox Christian teaching. The idea that God as creator of the world can be known by means of reason is expressed in the New Testament (*Rom.* 1:18–23, *Acts* 17:23) and becomes a persistent theme in Christian theology from the time of the apologists of the second and third centuries. The speculative theologians of Alexandria (Athanasius, Didymus, Cyril) all hold that although God in himself is beyond comprehension, he can be known through the creation and through the human soul, which was created in his image. In the works of Augustine of Hippo (384–430 CE) one finds support for the belief in the existence of God from a variety of facts of experience. With the emergence of Scholasticism, such ideas were developed into rational proofs for the existence of God that were intended to stand to reason without appeal to revelation. According to Anselm of Canterbury (1033–1109), God is that than which nothing more perfect can be thought. From the fact that an existent being is more perfect than a purely imaginary object, it follows that God must exist.

Thomas Aquinas (1228–1274) rejected Anselm's proof but under the influence of Aristotle's metaphysics elaborated the famous five ways by which the existence of God can be known. According to Thomas, (1) the facts that there is motion in the universe and that everything in motion derives its motion from something else show that there must be an unmoved mover. Secondary movers move only when they are moved by something else. (2) From the fact that all events have an efficient cause, Thomas infers that there must be a substantial agent that is its own cause. If the chain of efficient causes goes on forever, there would be no first efficient cause and therefore no effect. (3) From the fact of contingent and corruptible things about us, Thomas proceeds to the fact that there must be a being that exists by its own very nature, a necessary being. (4) Because the highest degree of any quality observed in any finite thing is always the cause of that quality in anything in which that quality is found, the gradations in goodness, beauty, and truth in objects of experience imply that all being and goodness in the universe must have their source in one who is the perfect being. (5) Finally, from the orderly character of natural events there must be a general order to the universe, and this universal order points to the existence of an intelligent agent who has ordered all things. Following Thomas, other arguments were offered in support of belief in such a God. Among the most influential of these were the arguments of René Descartes (1591–1650), who attempted to demonstrate the existence of God from the presence of the idea of God in the mind.

The attack upon theism. Since the seventeenth century this conception of God and the arguments that claimed to demonstrate his existence have been subject to persistent attack. In the first place, because Thomas took the physics of Aristotle as the basis for his understanding of cause and motion, his arguments were less capable of supporting theistic belief once Aristotle's views on these matters were supplanted by those of Isaac Newton (1642–1727). For Aristotle, an explanation is required both for the initiation and for the continuance of change. The first mover of Thomas, since it is taken as both initiating and continuing change, supports the view of God both as creator and governor of the universe. Newton's first law of motion, on the other hand, holds that a body will remain at rest or in continuous motion in the same direction unless it is subject to a contravening force. When the idea was developed by Pierre-Simon de Laplace (1749–1827) that the world is a regular and perfectly determinate system, the idea of God as the source of its movement was rendered superfluous. Moreover, once the idea of the universe as a perfect system was established, eternal existence could be attributed to the material world, as in the work of Paul-Henri d'Holbach (1723–1789). Theistic arguments were further eroded by the view articulated by David Hume (1711–1776) that cause itself is but an immanent habit of thought and not a necessary relation between substances or events. With this the possibility of inferring the existence of God from any classical form of a causal argument was undermined.

Influenced by Hume and others, Immanuel Kant (1724–1804), in his famous *Critique of Pure Reason* (1781), gathered the substance of various arguments for the existence of God into three. (1) The ontological argument proceeds from the idea of God to the existence of God. It holds that this idea is such that the nonexistence of God would not be possible. (2) The cosmological argument proceeds from the fact of the existence of the world to the existence of God as the sufficient reason or the ultimate cause of its being. (3) The physico-theological argument proceeds from the evident order, adaptation, or purposefulness of the world to the existence of an intelligent being who made it.

None of these arguments, in the view of Kant, is adequate to prove the existence of God. The ontological argument treats existence as though it could be the property of an idea. The cosmological argument posits the first cause only to avoid an infinite chain of causal relations. And it presupposes the validity of the ontological argument in its use of the category of a necessary being as the first cause. The physico-theological argument presupposes the validity of the first two, but even if accepted could prove only the existence of a designer or architect of the universe and not a creator.

Such speculative reasoning fails, according to Kant, because it depends upon the illegitimate use of the concepts of the pure theoretical reason that individuals employ in their apprehension of spatial and temporal objects to extend their knowledge beyond the reach of sensuous experience. Kant denies, however, that this analysis should lead to the conclusion that God does not exist. In his *Critique of Practical Reason* (1778), he argues that it is in the domain of moral action that religious ideas have their real significance, and it is here that belief in God can be justified on rational grounds. The substance of his argument is that it is necessary to postulate freedom, immortality, and God in order to live reasonably according to the "moral law within."

It was precisely the transposition of religious ideas from the realm of metaphysics to the realm of practical reason, the idea of belief in God as the support for moral action, that attracted the most violent assault upon theistic ideas in the following generation. Its significance for the nineteenth century is indicated in the view of Ludwig Feuerbach (1804–1872), who argues (1) that religion is the "dream of man," in which he projects his own infinite nature as a being beyond himself and then perceives himself as the object of this projected being; (2) that such a being, as "a contradiction to reason and morality," is quite inadequate to support a genuine human community; and (3) that a new philosophy based upon the being of man must unmask the essential nature of religion, which is to alienate man from himself, and replace theology with the humanistic underpinning for an ethically legitimate order.

Karl Marx (1818–1883) concurred in the judgment that religion is a symptom of alienation. But he argued that a merely intellectual liberation from religion would be unable to bring about the kind of human community that Feuerbach had envisioned. Religion, he argued, is an instrument of economic control. By its construction of an illusory happiness religion presents an obstacle to the liberation of the alienated worker from economic exploitation in the real, that is the material, world. Later in the century Friedrich Nietzsche (1844–1900) articulated a view of the moral significance of theistic faith very different from that of Marx. Yet it is no less hostile to theistic belief. The God of the Judeo-Christian tradition, he held, is the support of a slave morality. God was the instrument of the weak in inflicting a bad conscience upon the powerful and healthy and thus undermining their vitality and love of life. The success of this strategy has brought Western civilization to the brink of a nihilism that signals both the imminent death of God and the dawning of a new day in which Christian morality will be left behind.

In the twentieth century a new challenge to theism arose from the effort of philosophers to develop a criterion to distinguish between meaningful and meaningless language. In order to make sense, it was held, a statement has to be capable of empirical verification. Because statements about God cannot be shown to be true or false by methods of empirical testing, they seem to be without claim to cognitive standing. With this and further developments, the challenge to religious thought was no longer to the justification of theistic belief but to the status of the expression of theistic belief as meaningful language. The threat was not to its intellectual support but to its claim to belong to the domain of serious philosophical dispute.

The twentieth century. To the attack upon theism since the seventeenth century, theologians in the twentieth century responded in a variety of ways. These responses can be discussed as two opposing types: (1) those who continued to affirm the existence of God as the superlatively wise, powerful, and benevolent creator of the world and (2) those who did not affirm the existence of such a God or who even openly deny it. It is within this latter group that the most recent forms of religious atheism are found. The first type includes the revival of scholasticism in Roman Catholic and Anglican theological circles, which was accorded official ecclesiastical support during the First Vatican Council (1870). Among the most influential of these theists were Reginald Marie Garrigou-Lagrange (1877–1964), Jacques Maritain (1882–1973), and Étienne Gilson (1884–1978). Central to this response was a reaffirmation of metaphysics and of the importance of natural theology, at least in the sense of a rational structuring of the truths received through revelation and a clarification of these truths in terms of ordinary experience.

A second movement that belongs to this type, neoorthodoxy, dominated Protestant thought during the first half of the twentieth century, especially after World War I. Rejecting the prevalent themes of nineteenth-century Protestant thought, neoorthodoxy rediscovered the personal God of the Bible and the Protestant reformers. It repudiated efforts to find God through human effort, and instead affirmed that he is to be known through his revelation attested in sacred scripture and by means of the obedience of faith. The God of Karl Barth (1886–1968), the most influential exponent of this movement, is a God who exists, who lives, and who has made himself known through mighty acts in history of which the Bible is witness.

Around the turn of the twentieth century, the significance of change or process in the works of William James (1842–1910), Henri Bergson (1859–1941), Samuel Alexander (1859–1938), and others, together with a widespread criticism of the absolute determinism of Laplace, provided the context for new efforts toward a doctrine of God in the thought of such figures as Alfred North Whitehead (1861–1947), Henry Nelson Wieman (1884–1975), and Charles Hartshorne (1897–2000). Claiming independence from what it saw as the static theism of both the Thomistic and neoorthodox traditions, it conceived God as a limited being who is subject to "becoming" in time as natural "process" unfolds. God, in this view, fulfills his own being, as the force for progress, in and through the ordering of the world.

A reply to the attack upon theism very different from all of these was developed in the thought of Paul Tillich (1886–1965). It centers upon his view of faith as a state of "being concerned ultimately." This view of faith, according to Tillich, transcends the three fundamental kinds of theism that have been the object of secular attack. (1) "Empty theism" is the affirmation of God employed by politicians and dictators to produce the impression that they are moral and worthy of trust. Its use of the idea of God exploits the traditional and psychological connotations of the word without any specification of what is meant. (2) Theism as "divine-human encounter" found in the Bible and among the reformers is the immediate certainty of divine forgiveness that is independent of moral, intellectual, or religious preconditions. Its power is evident in the capacity of such a personal image of God, supported by scripture and personal experience, to defeat the anxiety of guilt and condemnation, fate and death. Yet given the doubt prevailing in the present age, the experience of divine forgiveness is subject to psychological explanation, and the idea of sin appears relative at best and meaningless at worst. (3) "Theological theism" tries by means of the various proofs for the existence of God to transform the divine-human encounter into a doctrine about two different beings that have existence independent of one another. This, however, can establish the existence of God only as a being beside others and bound to the subject-object structure of reality. Under the gaze of such a being of infinite knowledge and power the alienated human being is deprived of freedom and creativity. Against this kind of theism, says Tillich, the atheism of the nineteenth century was a justified response.

What Tillich calls "absolute faith," on the other hand, accepts and affirms despair and in so doing finds meaning within the disintegration of meaning itself. In "absolute faith" the depth and power of being is revealed in which the negation of being is embraced. Its object is the "God beyond God," the God who appears when the God of theism has disappeared in the anxiety of meaninglessness and doubt. This God is not a being but the ground of Being itself.

In an effort towards a radical recasting of the fundamental categories of theology, Bishop John A. T. Robinson (1919–1983) of Woolwich, England, employed a number of Tillich's insights together with some of the more famous ideas of Dietrich Bonhoeffer (1906–1945) and Rudolf Bultmann (1884–1976). Writing in 1963, he affirmed, with Bultmann, that the Bible assumes a cosmology in which God is a being "up there." The Christian who is heir to the Copernican revolution tends to translate such categories into terms compatible with the modern view of the world. When one speaks of God "up there," one really means the God "out there." This he thinks, is poor translation, for there are no vacant spaces in the universe in which God could really be said to reside. Robinson is willing to concede that the skies are empty, and that humanity, as Bonhoeffer had said, has come of age. The divine transcendence, he argues, is to be confronted not in the "beyond" or in the "height" but in the infinite and inexhaustible "depth" or "ground" of being revealed in the midst of life.

Neither Tillich nor Robinson referred to their thought as atheistic. Tillich suggested, however, that to understand God as the depth of being practically requires one to forget everything traditional that one has learned about God, and perhaps even the word itself. Robinson stated that he did not yet have a name for the kind of religious thinking he wanted to bring about. In the United States, on the other hand, reflection of a similar sort was given a name that gained it an instant vogue: the theology of the death of God.

The "death of God" theology was a heterogeneous movement encompassing a variety of issues upon which its members often disagreed. Besides the question of God, it was concerned with a variety of forms of alienation within the Christian community, with the significance of the secular world and its intellectual norms, and with the significance for theology of the person and work of Jesus. The movement received its name from the title of a work published in 1961 by Gabriel Vahanian that announced the death of God as a cultural fact, the fact acknowledged by Bonhoeffer and Robinson that modern man functions intellectually and socially without God as a working hypothesis. This cultural fact, for Vahanian, implies a loss of the sense of transcendence and the substitution of a radically immanentist perspective in dealing with questions of human existence. That the death of God has occurred as a cultural fact in no way implies for him, however, that God himself has ceased to exist. God is, and remains, infinite and wholly other, still calling humanity to existential and cultural conversion. Vahanian's concern is for a transfiguration of culture in which the living God is freed from the false images that have reified him.

Vahanian's view of the reality of God sets him clearly apart from other persons associated with the death of God. For Paul M. Van Buren, writing in 1965, the issue for theology is how the modern Christian, who is in fact a secular being, can understand faith in a secular way. Taking his method from the philosophical tradition known as language analysis, he argues that not only the God of theism but also any other conception of God has been rendered meaningless to the modern mind. He concludes that when the language of Christian faith is sorted out, the gospel can be interpreted as the expression of a historical perspective concerning Jesus that has wide-ranging empirical consequences for the ethical existence of the Christian.

For William Hamilton, writing at about the same time, the death of God means the loss of the God of theism and the loss of "real transcendence." His response is a new understanding of Protestantism that liberates it from religion—from, that is, any system of thought or action in which God is seen as fulfilling any sort of need or as solving any human problem, even the problem of the loss of God. Hamilton's Protestant is a person without God, without faith in God, but also a person in protest against release or escape from the world by means of the sacred. He is a person led into the affairs of the world and into solidarity with his neighbor, in whom he encounters Jesus and where alone he can become Jesus to the world.

In the thought of Vahanian, Van Buren, and Hamilton, the death of God is a metaphor. In the work of Thomas J. J. Altizer, on the other hand, the death of God is to be taken literally. In a work published in 1967 he seems to be saying both that God did once exist and that he really did cease to exist. He believes that the death of God is decisive for theology because in it God has reconciled himself with the world. God, the sovereign and transcendent Lord of the Christian tradition, has taken the form of a servant and entered the world through Christ. With this, the realm of the transcendent and supernatural has become empty and God has died. With the death of God, humans are liberated from fears and inhibitions imposed upon them by an awesome mystery beyond.

The view of these thinkers that belief in God is impossible, unnecessary, or wrong, has apparently not caused them to believe that they are disqualified as theologians. To this extent they stand alongside other forms of religious atheism encountered in the history of religious thought. It has certainly been objected by other theologians that the "death of God" theology does not authentically represent the Christian tradition. For the present it is sufficient that the death of God represents a controversy of significant dimensions in the record of Christian thought and that its influence continues to affect the development of theology in the early twenty-first century.

CONCLUSIONS. The forms of atheism that appear throughout the history of religions represent an important resource for the interpretation of twenty-first century religious thought. Much of the reasoning behind the rejection of popular religion in ancient Greece or theism in India can be compared with the reasoning behind the rejection of theism in the West. The naturalism of ancient Greek and classical Indian philosophy invites comparison with naturalism in the West, the atheism of the Sophists with that of nineteenth-century Europe. The widespread secularistic mood in contemporary society bears comparison with the secularism of late Greek and Roman antiquity. And the ethical preoccupation of some exponents of the death of God invites comparison with the ethical practicality of the philosophies of ancient China. The major forms of religious atheism are perhaps less distinguished by the traditions they belong to than by affinities in inner structure.

From the present survey it is possible to conclude that doubt about the existence of God does not in itself imply the end of piety, ethics, or spirituality. Elaborate systems of ethical religious thought and action have been based both on the view that God does and that God does not exist. The question that arises from the present survey is not whether it is possible to speak any longer about God but whether it is necessary to do so. The question whether it is possible for modern philosophy or theology to develop a compelling system of religious thought and action that rejects belief in God will be addressed more effectively as the dimensions of the question that emerge in differing historical situations are compared.

SEE ALSO Doubt and Belief; Naturalism.

BIBLIOGRAPHY

The idea that civilization begins at a stage at which the concept of God is absent is developed by David Hume in *The Natural History of Religion* (1757), edited by H. E. Root (Stanford, Calif., 1957). A similar view is developed by John Lubbock in *The Origin of Civilisation and the Primitive Condition of Man* (1870), edited by Peter Rivière (Chicago, 1978). An excellent contemporary study of the significance of God in traditional African religion is John S. Mbiti's *Concepts of God in Africa* (New York, 1970). See also Ake Hultkrantz's *Belief and Worship in Native North America* (Syracuse, N.Y., 1981). Both of these works contain excellent bibliographies. The question whether native peoples are without a concept of God has received new interest in light of John Nance's *The Gentle Tasaday* (New York, 1975).

The most thorough work on the classical philosophies of India remains Surendranath Dasgupta's *A History of Indian Philosophy*, 5 vols. (Cambridge, 1922–1955). Nikunja Vihari Banerjee's *The Spirit of Indian Philosophy* (New Delhi, 1974) is a thoroughly readable introduction containing a useful discussion of arguments for and against the existence of God in Indian thought. Ninian Smart's *Doctrine and Argument in*

Indian Philosophy (London, 1964) presents the substance of Indian metaphysics in language accessible to the Western reader. It contains also a useful glossary and bibliography. More specialized studies include Kewal Krishnan Mittal's *Materialism in Indian Thought* (Delhi, 1974); Dale Riepe's *The Naturalistic Tradition in Indian Thought* (Seattle, 1961); and Helmuth von Glasenapp's *Buddhism: A Non-Theistic Religion* (New York, 1966). A useful selection of relevant original texts is presented in translation in *A Source Book in Indian Philosophy,* edited by Sarvepalli Radhakrishnan and Charles A. Moore (Princeton, N.J., 1957). A concise introduction to Chinese thought is presented in Fung Youlan's *A Short History of Chinese Philosophy* (New York, 1948), which offers a short bibliography.

Relevant works on ancient Greek material include Roy K. Hack's *God in Greek Philosophy* (Princeton, N. J., 1931), which contains a selected bibliography, and Anders B. Drachmann's *Atheism in Pagan Antiquity* (1922; Chicago, 1977), which provides extensive notes. For a scholarly treatment of the concept of God in ancient Israel, see William F. Albright's *Yahweh and the Gods of Canaan* (London, 1968) and Harold H. Rowley's *The Faith of Israel: Aspects of Old Testament Thought* (London, 1956). Elaine H. Pagels's *The Gnostic Gospels* (New York, 1979) is an introduction to gnostic Christian literature based on the recent discoveries at Nag Hammadi, Egypt. The development of theism, from Augustine to its criticism through the nineteenth century, is thoroughly discussed in Frederick C. Copleston's *A History of Philosophy,* 8 vols. (New York, 1946–1966). A concise introduction to the development of the Christian idea of God is found in the article "God" in *The Oxford Dictionary of the Christian Church,* 2d ed., edited by Frank Leslie Cross and Elizabeth A. Livingston (London, 1974), which contains a useful bibliography. For a thorough discussion of contemporary developments in theology, including the theology of the "death of God," see Langdon Gilkey's *Naming the Whirlwind: The Renewal of God-language* (Indianapolis, 1969).

Finally, a useful reference work is *The Encyclopedia of Unbelief,* 2 vols., edited by Gordon Stein (New York, 1985). Although clearly focused on the West, it includes a broad range of articles on various forms of unbelief in most parts of the world.

GEORGE ALFRED JAMES (1987 AND 2005)

ATHENA (or *Athenaia,* Ionian *Athenaie,* epic *Athene;* in the Roman world, she corresponds to *Menerva/Minerva*) was the Greek goddess of war, the arts, and feminine works. According to the *Homeric Hymn to Aphrodite* (5.8–15) she "has no pleasure in the works of golden Aphrodite, but delights in war and the works of Ares; she first taught human craftsmen how to build chariots and work the bronze, but she too teaches young girls in the house, putting in their mind knowledge of splendid art" (compare *Iliad* 5.733–737, where, in arming herself for war, the goddess takes off the splendid robe she had made with her own hands). These diverse aspects of her nature manifest themselves in her iconography: according to Apollodorus (*Bibl.* 3.12.3), the Palladion, the extremely ancient wooden statue of the goddess that had famously fallen from the sky and was venerated in Ilion, portrayed her with a spear in her right hand and a distaff and spindle in the left. These two aspects may be reconciled under the capacity for rational organization. Both in war and in craft the goddess refrains from excess and impulsivity, and she privileges rational, intelligent preparation. As such she is indeed a goddess of the arts of war and of creative intelligence, and a protectress of the city, closely tied to its social organization.

Athena is certainly a very ancient divinity: it is possible to recognize in her a pre-Hellenic protectress of the Mycenaean citadel atop the Acropolis. An *atana potinija* is attested in the dative, together with Enyalios, Paiaon, Poseidaon, and the Erinyes in a linear B text from Knossos. The interpretation commonly accepted, even though by no means certain, is "mistress of (place-name) Athana." Athena is indeed unique among Greek gods in being connected, via her name, with a specific city, Athens. This connection is underlined by the fact that in early Attic inscriptions her name appears in the adjectival form, *Athenaia* (the Athenian goddess), as in the Homeric formula, *Pallas Athenaie.* However, the linguistic relation between place and goddess is difficult to define; if the Athenians, both in myth (the gift of the olive tree, the birth of Erichthonios) and in cult (the Panathenaia festival), stressed their privileged relation with the goddess, in Panhellenic mythology she shows no special interest in Athens or in Athenian heroes. Thus, according to Pindar (*Olympian* 7.34–53), the Rhodians believed Athena to be particularly associated with their island. In many Greek cities she appears as *Polias* or *Poliouchos,* citadel and city-goddess (this is also true of Troy: legend had it that until her Palladion had been stolen from the city, it would not fall); very often her temples are on the central, fortified hill of the city.

Athena's emblems are the owl (*glaux,* compare her epithet *glaukōpis,* "bright-eyed"), and the snake, living among the rocks of the Athenian Acropolis (Herodotos VIII 41.2–3). These have been taken by some modern scholars as signs of the close connection between her, the Minoan snake goddess, and the Mycenaean palace goddess. Athena's main weapon in battle is the aegis (as the name implies, a goat-skin): when she raises it, panic overtakes her enemies. On it, she wears the petrifying head of the Gorgon.

Her centrality in the Greek pantheon is expressed by her closeness to Zeus. The story of her birth (an Oriental motif, which finds a parallel in the Hittite myth of Kumarbi) forcefully underlines the strong relationship between the two divinities. Zeus, after having received the power to rule among the gods, married the Okeanid Metis, the "most knowing of the gods and men" (Hesiod, frag. 343.15; *Theogony* 886–900); then, in order to avoid being overthrown by a more powerful son, he swallowed her. Some time later, Zeus gave birth from his head to a grown-up and fully armed goddess, Athena. Other versions have Zeus call on Hephaistos to help relieve him of labor pains. Hephaistos with his ax split Zeus's head open, and out of it, in full armor and with a war song on her lips, sprang Athena. This is the version usually depicted on Attic vases.

Zeus's courageous, self-confident, clear-eyed daughter became his favorite child, the only one to carry his aegis and thunderbolt. She in turn revered him and boasted of being the child of him alone, of being motherless (thus in *Homeric Hymn* 28; similarly, in another passage of Hesiod's *Theogony* 924–929, the birth of Athena from Zeus is paralleled by the story of Hera giving birth alone, out of anger against Zeus, to Hephaistos). Athena and Zeus share exclusively between them the cult epithet *Polias*/*Polieus*. At Sparta, the *rhētra* attributed to Lycurgus mentioned a Zeus *Syllanios* and an Athena *Syllania* (the meaning of this term is unknown). The unique relationship between Athena and Zeus finds its best literary expression in Aeschylus (*Eumenides* 736–738): Athena appears there as the great reconciler between men and gods, and, because of her peculiar birth, between male and female. At a deeper level, however, it can be claimed that by her refusal of marriage the goddess paradoxically destabilizes the patriarchal and civilized order that she apparently champions.

The most frequent among her other epithets are *Tritogeneia*, which may allude to the circumstances of her birth, even if the precise meaning of the term is disputed, and *Pallas*. One of the ancient explanations for the latter is that Pallas was a childhood friend whom Athena inadvertently killed during a fencing match. Athena erected a wooden image, a *palladium*, to commemorate her foster sister, an image that came to represent Athena herself in her role as protectress of the polis. Of this Palladium, originally situated in Troy, many cities boasted of possessing an exemplar (Athens, Argos, and Rome, among others). According to another version, Pallas was a giant and an adversary of Athena in the Gigantomachy, out of whose skin the goddess made herself the aegis (a local, Athenian variant of the Gigantomachy myth has Theseus fighting against a rival king Pallas and his fifty sons). Yet others interpreted Pallas as "the one who dances," or "who brandishes weapons" (Euripides, *Ion* 209–211; Plato, *Cratylos* 406d–407a), or *pallas* simply as "maiden" (Strabo, 17.1.46, with the approval of modern etymological dictionaries). Particularly important in fifth-century Athenian ideology is the goddess's connection with victory: as Athena *Nikē* she had a priestess and a temple at the gate of the Acropolis.

Athena's central concern is the wellbeing of the community. As Aelius Aristides (*Or.* 37.13) puts it, "Cities are the gifts of Athena." As a patron of civic institutions, she has a role in the socialization of youths of both sexes. Thus, in Athens, in her quality of *Phratria*, the goddess is, together with Zeus *Phratrios*, the patroness of the Apaturia festival, in which young men were introduced into the phratry; these were the gods that defined Athenian citizenship. The ephebes took their oath in the sanctuary of Aglauros, one of the three daughters of Kekrops, regarded as the first priestess of Athena; among the principal divinities invoked were Ares and Atena *Areia*. Every year, they escorted Pallas (so report the epigraphic texts, with a striking personification: the wooden Palladium must have been intended) to Phalerum and to the sea for a ritual cleansing (the occasion of this ritual is disputed: it may have been the Plynteria). Conversely, an Athena *Apaturia* is attested at Troizen, to whom young girls offered their girdle before their wedding.

More generally, the goddess nurtures the children on whom the city's future depends and encourages its citizens in the arts and crafts so integral to civilized existence. Her foundational role in Athens is clearly expressed by the story of her victory over Poseidon through the gift of the sacred olive tree, and in the connected local Athenian myth of the birth of Erichthonios. According to the legend, Hephaistos tried to rape the goddess; she flew, and in his pursuit, his semen fell on her thigh. The goddess in wiping it off threw it to the ground, and the earth gave birth to the boy Erechtheus/Erichthonios, whom Athena raised (already attested in *Iliad* 2.547–551). She then gave him over to the care of the daughters of snake-tailed Kekrops, the autochthonous king of Athens, warning them not to open the chest in which the boy lay. They however opened the chest, and, overcome with madness at what they saw, threw themselves down the cliff of the Acropolis. Erichthonios later became king of Athens, and instituted the Panathenaia; the story of the Kekropids was remembered in the rite of the Arrhēphoria. Two (or four) young girls of noble family, aged between seven and eleven, were chosen annually by the *archon basileus* to serve Athena *Polias* on the Acropolis. At the end of their year, at night, the *arrhēphoroi* were given covered baskets, which they had to carry down to the temple of Aphrodite "in the garden." There they were given something else that they had to bring back to the Acropolis. The meaning of this ceremony is disputed (transition or fertility ritual), but it has clearly to do with the story of the daughters of Kekrops, since the *arrhēphoroi* are said to accomplish their duties in regard to Athena *Polias* and Pandrosos, one of the Kekropids. The myth encapsulates Athena's care for Athens, and more generally for the raising and education of both boys and girls, as well as the Athenians' rootedness in their landscape.

Athenian maidens and women wove a peplos for Athena; the loom for the weaving was set up by the priestess of Athena *Polias* and the *arrhēphoroi* at the Chalkeia. The peplos (embroidered with scenes from the Gigantomachy, and thus once again exposing the other side of the deity) was offered to the goddess nine months later at the Panathenaia, her most important festival at Athens. At this same festival male citizens competed in contests reserved for Athenians which, just as the Panathenaic procession, stressed the force and the sense of common identity of the polity. There were also contests open to foreigners; the prizes for the quadrennial contests of the Great Panathenaia were the so-called Panathenaic amphoras, filled with olive oil from the sacred olive trees and bearing on one side the image of the fully armed, striding Athena *Promachos*.

Athena is particularly identified with the womanly arts of spinning and weaving, and is often called, in this connection, *Erganē* (the maker). As such, she also protects carpenters, metalworkers and more generally artisans: "Be on your way, all people who work with your hands, you who entreat Zeus' daughter, *Erganē* of the terrible eyes, with baskets placed before her, and by the anvil with the heavy hammer" (Sophocles, frag. 844 Radt).

Like many spinning goddesses, Athena is a virgin; at Athens, she is addressed as "the" *parthenos.* Yet her virginity implies no withdrawal from involvement with males, but rather an easy companionship undisturbed by sexual tension. Loyal and resourceful, she is a friendly mentor to many of the heroes of Greek mythology—Perseus, Bellerophon, Herakles, and above all Odysseus, whose skeptical prudence and practical cunning so resemble her own. Although in late classical times the goddess came to be regarded as a personification of wisdom in the abstract, her *mētis* ("wisdom") is rather common sense and the technical and artistic skillfulness she encouraged in her protégés. She is *glaukōpis,* bright-eyed, like her emblem the owl. At least until the end of the fifth century, Athena was not seen as a contemplative being, but rather as "spirited immediacy, redeeming spiritual presence, swift action." At least until the end of the fifth century, Athena was not seen as a contemplative being, but rather, as Walter F. Otto memorably put it, a "Göttin der nähe" ("goddess of nearness"), "spirited immediacy, redeeming spiritual presence, swift action."

SEE ALSO Goddess Worship, overview article.

BIBLIOGRAPHY

Athena is an important presence in Homer's *Iliad* and *Odyssey*; Aeschylus's *Eumenides* is the other most important ancient source. The goddess is frequently invoked in drama: for instance in Euripides' *Children of Heracles* 748–783 and in Aristophanes' *Knights* 581–594. A somewhat darker aspect of her nature emerges from Sophocles' *Ajax.* Callimachus in his *Hymn* 5 illustrates a ritual in honor of the Argive Athena; for the perception of the goddess at the time of the second sophistic, see Aelius Aristides' *Hymn to Athena* (*Or.* 37).

Modern scholarly treatments include Lewis R. Farnell, *The Cults of the Greek States,* Vol. 1 (1896; New Rochelle, N.Y., 1977), pp. 258–320; Walter F. Otto, *Die Götter Griechenlands: Das Bild des Göttlichen im Spiegel des griechischen Geistes* (Bonn, Germany, 1929), translated by Moses Hadas as *The Homeric Gods: The Spiritual Significance of Greek Religion* (New York, 1954), pp. 43–60; Ulrich von Wilamowitz-Moellendorff, *Der Glaube der Hellenen* (Berlin, 1931–1932), Vol. 1: pp. 234–237, Vol. 2: pp. 162–168; Károly Kerényi, *Die Jungfrau und Mutter der Griechischen Religion: Eine Studie über Pallas Athene* (Zurich, 1952), translated by Murray Stein as *Athene: Virgin and Mother in Greek Religion* (Dallas, Tex., 1978); Martin P. Nilsson, *The Minoan-Mycenean Religion and Its Survival in Greek Religion,* 2d rev. ed. (Lund, Sweden, 1950), pp. 485–501; Walter Burkert, *Griechische Religion der archaischen und klassischen Epoche* (Stuttgart and Berlin, 1977), rev. ed., translated by J. Raffan as *Greek Religion: Archaic and Classical* (Cambridge, Mass., 1985), pp. 139–143; Robert T. C. Parker, "Athena," in *The Oxford Classical Dictionary,* 3d ed., edited by Simon Hornblower and Antony Spawforth (Oxford and New York, 1996), pp. 201–202; and Fritz Graf, "Athena," in *Der neue Pauly,* Vol. 2 (Stuttgart, Germany, 1997), pp. 160–166.

On her importance in Athens see specifically C. John Herington, *Athena Parthenos and Athena Polias: A Study in the Religion of Periclean Athens* (Manchester, UK, 1955), and his "Athena in Athenian Literature and Cult," in G. T. W. Hooker, ed., *Parthenos and Parthenon, Greece and Rome,* Suppl. 10 (Oxford, 1963), pp. 61–73; Nicole Loraux, *Les enfants d'Athena* (Paris, 1981), translated by Caroline Levine as *The Children of Athena: Athenian Ideas about Citizenship and the Division between the Sexes* (Princeton, N.J., 1993); Jenifer Neils, ed., *Goddess and Polis: The Panathenaic Festival in Ancient Athens* (Princeton, N.J., 1992); and Jenifer Neils, ed., *Worshipping Athena: Panathenaia and Parthenon* (Madison, Wis., 1996). The goddess's connection with Athenian democracy is explored by Irmgard Kasper-Butz, *Die Göttin Athena im klassischen Athen: Athena als Repräsentantin des demokratischen Staates* (Frankfurt am Main, Germany, 1990). The most complete discussion of Attic rituals for Athena is still Ludwig Deubner, *Attische Feste* (Berlin, 1932), pp. 9–39.

Specific aspects are explored in Susan Deacy and Alexandra Villing, eds., *Athena in the Classical World* (Leiden, Netherlands, 2001), which also provides an extensive bibliography. In a series of articles, Noel Robertson proposes a global reinterpretation of rituals for Athena: see in particular "Athena as Weather Goddess: The *Aigis* in Myth and Ritual," in Deacy and Villing, eds., *Athena in the Classical World* (Leiden, Netherlands, 2001), pp. 29–55, and "Athena and Early Greek Society: Palladium Shrines and Promontory Shrines," in Matthew Dillon, ed., *Religion in the Ancient World: New Themes and Approaches* (Amsterdam, 1996), pp. 383–475. In this same volume, Daniel Geagan, "Who Was Athena?" pp. 145–164, charts the development of the cult of Athena in Athens across a wide chronological period. On the cult of Athena at Troy/Ilion, see Alexandra Villing, "Athena as Ergane and Promachos: The Iconography of Athena in Archaic East Greece," in Nick Fisher and Hans van Wees, eds., *Archaic Greece: New Approaches and New Evidence* (London, 1998), pp. 147–168. Her role as a goddess of *mētis* and practical cunning is examined in Marcel Detienne and Jean-Pierre Vernant, *Les ruses de l'intelligence: La mêtis des Grecs* (Paris, 1974), translated by Janet Lloyd as *Cunning Intelligence in Greek Culture and Society* (Hassocks, U.K., 1978; Chicago, 1991). A wealth of material on the diverse aspects of the cult of Athena in the Greek world is to be found in Gerhard Jöhrens, *Der Athenahymnus des Ailios Aristeides* (Bonn, Germany, 1981).

A detailed survey of the iconography is offered by Paul Demargne and Hélène Cassimatis, "Athena," in *Lexicon iconographicum mythologiae classicae,* Vol. 2.1 (Zurich and Munich, 1984), pp. 955–1044.

CHRISTINE DOWNING (1987)
PAOLA CECCARELLI (2005)

ATHENAGORAS, Christian apologist, flourished in Athens during the second half of the second century. Only one of his writings has been transmitted to posterity, *Legatio,* or *Presbeia,* which he composed between 176 and 180. He was a professional philosopher and, from the time of his conversion, a teacher of Christian doctrine. His apology in defense of the Christians could have been published as early as September 176 when the co-emperors Marcus Aurelius and his son Commodus visited Athens. More probably it was written after the anonymous letter from Gaul describing the persecution of Lyons in 177 became known in Greece, since the same expressions are used in both documents for the second and the third of the three main charges addressed against the Christians at that time: "Atheism, Thyestean banquets, and Oedipean unions" (3.1).

Legatio responds at length to the popular accusations against the Christians charging them with atheism and immorality. Athenagoras introduces the Christian doctrine of God with the help of an abundance of comparative quotations, from Homer to contemporary Middle Platonists. He stresses the absolute power of the creator and the creator's care for the world. He presents the Christian ethic as uncompromising. His doctrine of God culminates in trinitarian theology, but he avoids the doctrine of the incarnation. In his ethics he relies on the philosophical tradition of Stoicism. Thus, in assuming the correctness of many of the religious views of paganism, Athenagoras's philosophical theology rests on the sincere hope of a reconciliation between the church and the empire.

A treatise entitled *On the Resurrection,* traditionally attributed to Athenagoras, must be considered inauthentic. Its views on the general resurrection of the dead in the last days are best understood against the background of the debate over Origen's doctrine concerning resurrected bodies. This debate generated treatises of that sort only near the end of the third century. Differences in style are also discernible in comparison with *Legatio.*

Athenagoras remained virtually unknown by the later Christian generations in the ancient church. Only Methodius of Olympus, in the early fourth century, alludes to *Legatio* and identifies its author. In the tenth century, Arethas, archbishop of Caesarea in Cappadocia, rediscovered the Athenian Christian philosopher of the second century and his apology.

BIBLIOGRAPHY

A substantial introduction to the work and the apologetics of Athenagoras can be found in Wilhelm R. Schoedel's edition of *Legatio and De Resurrectione* (Oxford, 1972). The tenth-century copy of *Legatio* made by Arethas's secretary has been preserved (Paris Codex 451).

CHARLES KANNENGIESSER (1987)

ATHIRAT, called Ashiratum or Ashratum in Old Babylonian texts, was a West Semitic goddess, worshiped in Syria in the second millennium BCE and still widely attested in southern Arabia in the mid-first millennium BCE and later. The Old Babylonian spellings of her name—with and without the internal vowel *i*—show that this vowel was short and could be elided. This is confirmed by the spellings *Abdi-Ashirtu* and *Abdi-Ashratu* of the name of the famous Amorite chieftain in the Amarna correspondence from the fourteenth century BCE. The divine name was thus formed on the active participle of *ʾṯr,* "to walk" or "to tread on." Hence it was rightly explained as "walker" or "trampler."

SUN GODDESS. Ashiratum was the consort of Amurrum, as Babylonians were calling the chief deity of the western nomads, the Amorites, and her realm was the steppe. The proper name Ashratum-ummi, "Athirat is my mother," shows how she was regarded by her worshipers. Later mythological texts from Ugarit indicate that she was the mother of the gods. The Gracious Gods Dawn and Sunset, as well as the heir of King Keret in the Ugaritic epic are supposed to suck the milk of Athirat. Since Amurrum was in fact a moon god, his consort was most likely a sun goddess or a particular aspect of the solar deity. This is corroborated to a certain extent by her role in southern Arabia where her name is borne by the spouse of the masculine lunar deity, which was called by different names and bynames. Athirat was the consort of ʿAmm, the main god of Qataban, who despite some doubts seems to have been a lunar deity. The situation is somewhat complicated because the sun goddess is also mentioned with the Quarter-of-the-Moon, a particular aspect of the moon god.

A territory of the kingdom of Qataban, called Dhu-Athirat, was dedicated to her and she was worshiped in a temple together with Wadd, certainly the moon god of the kingdoms of Maʿin and Awsan. A month in the calendar of Maʿin bore her name, Dhu-Athirat, obviously because a major festival was celebrated during that period in her honor. The sun goddess received in southern Arabia a number of epithets, and the name of Athirat is likely to have alluded initially to the solar disk "treading on" the vault of heaven from the east to the west. The image of the sun padding in the skies occurs also in the biblical *Psalms* 19:6, where the sun is said "to run along a road." As the female member of the great South Arabian triad of upper deities, she was regarded as the mother of the young stellar god Athtar. This explains her role in Ugaritic mythological texts, where she nominates Athtar as the successor of Baal immediately after Baal's death.

Her worship spread to northern Arabia, where she is mentioned in the fifth century BCE among the three "gods of Taima": Ṣalm zi Maḥram, Sin-egalla, and Ashira, written in Aramaic script with *shin* and without the final *t,* dropped in the current pronunciation. The first deity is the sacred standing stone of the sanctuary, the second is the "moon god of the palace," and Ashira is likely to be his consort, the sun goddess. Her name appears also as a theophorous element in a few North Arabian proper names.

CONSORT OF EL. In Syria, Athirat appears in the mythological texts from Ugarit and in a myth preserved in a Hittite adaptation. She is the consort of the resting chief god El and the mother of the gods. In the Hittite text, she appears as the wife of Elkunirsha, a transcription of the Semitic title "El, the owner of the earth." At Ugarit, she is not identified with the sun goddess Shapash, but her title of "Lady walking on the sea," *rbt atrt ym*, still seems to allude to the sun setting in the west, on the Mediterranean sea. Her servant, "the fisherman of Athirat," is called "Holy passer," *qdš(-w-)amrr*, and he is supposed to traverse the sea in order to reach Caphtor, which is Crete. He may have been the boatman of the sun goddess, who sails every night on the ocean of the netherworld. This episode of the myth is not preserved, but its existence is implied by the *Midrash Tehillim* 19:11 and the *Yalkut Shimoni* II, §676, where reference is made to the Sun's ship.

In a phonetically atypical text from Ugarit, apparently written in another dialect, Athirat is referred to in parallel with the moon god Yaraḥ. This seems to imply that she is the consort of the lunar deity, most likely the sun goddess. Another text from Ugarit, known conventionally as the *Poem of the Gracious Gods*, mentions Athirat and the sun goddess Shapash in parallel. In view of this poetic device Athirat might be identical there with Shapash, but the badly damaged passage does not allow a firm conclusion. It seems at any rate that at some point Athirat became a deity distinct from the sun goddess, although she kept some of the goddess's characteristics.

The goddess is not attested in Canaan, either in the Amorite proper names of the *Egyptian Execration Texts* or in letters from Tell Taanak, where her name has been read by mistake. As far as we know, the worship of Athirat did not reach Egypt. Neither are there any traces of her cult in the Syro-Phoenician realm after the collapse of the Bronze Age civilization in the early twelfth century BCE.

HOLY SITES. In some quarters, the Akkadian noun *aširtu*, Phoenician *ʾšrt*, used also in the Philistine city of Ekron, Aramaic *ʾtrt*, and Hebrew *ʾašērāh*, all meaning "holy place," were confused with the name of the goddess Athirat. This confusion provoked a considerable secondary literature, inspired by the Hebrew epigraphic mention of "Yahweh and his *asherah*," the latter being regarded as the consort of Yahweh. Engaging often in speculations of a recondite kind, this approach displays a remarkable neglect of ancient written sources and of rules of Hebrew grammar, while no evidence is offered that, for instance, female pillar figurines in clay are statuettes of a goddess Asherah.

The occasional Hebrew spelling *ʾšyrh*, followed in the *Targums Onqelos* and *Jonathan*, shows that the noun in question does not follow the same nominal pattern as the name of the goddess Athirat: it is a passive derivative of the root *ʾṯr*, designating a site "trodden on," thus a place. The context of the noun in the available sources always indicates that a holy site is meant. The masculine passive derivative *Ashur* of the same root had a similar meaning, as it indicated the sacred hill on which the capital city of Assyria was built, but it became the name of a particular deity. No similar evolution can be observed in the case of *asherah*, since the occasional use of the definite article, the often occurring plural—generally with the masculine ending *-īm*—and the use of *asherah* with the pronominal suffix show that the word remained a common noun in Hebrew.

At least in the northwest Semitic realm, a holy site called *asherah* was connected with the presence of trees. *Deuteronomy* 16:21 prohibits one to "plant an *asherah* of any kind of tree," while *Judges* 6:25 orders Gideon to "cut down the *asherah*," which consisted of several trees. The text speaks explicitly of "the trees of the *asherah*," which had to provide fuel for the sacrifice of a bullock, and Gideon needed ten servants to cut them down (*Jgs.* 6:26–27). The *asherah* could thus be a grove of quite a considerable size, and not a simple pole.

The injunction of *Exodus* 34:13 uses the plural *asherim* to designate the sacred groves that must be cut down. The expression "Yahweh and his *asherah*," occurring in Hebrew inscriptions from Khirbet el-Qom and Kuntillet Ajrud, indicates that those were sites where Yahweh was worshiped. The unique biblical text referring to a Baal's *asherah* is *1 Kings* 18:19, where "the four hundred prophets of the *asherah*" are ministrants of Baal's shrine. However, the expression may be a later intrusion, since it is asterized in Origen's *Hexapla*. The formula of *Exodus* 34:13 is repeated with variants in several texts. The *asherim* must be cut down, as indicated in *2 Kings* 18:4 and 23:14, hacked down, as stated in *Deuteronomy* 7:5 and *2 Chronicles* 14:12, 31:1, or simply burnt, as required in *Deuteronomy* 12:3 and *2 Kings* 23:15. They can also be uprooted, as indicated in *Micah* 5:13.

All these texts use a traditional terminology, coined in a period when the *asherah* was a grove of trees popularly regarded as a sacred site. The *Temple Scroll* 51:20, written about 160 BCE, repeats the biblical prohibition of "planting *asherot*" and "erecting standing-stones." It alludes obviously to sacred groves with symbols of the deity, while using the more recent plural *asherot* instead of *asherim*. It is not surprising that the Greek version of the Bible, made in Alexandria in the third and second centuries BCE, usually translates *asherah* by *alsos*, "sacred grove," or by *dendera*, "trees." Similarly, the Latin Vulgate version uses the terms *lucus* or *nemus*, both with the same meaning. Philon of Alexandria (c. 30 BCE–45 CE) notes in his work *On the Special Laws* I 74 that there was no *alsos* in the Temple of Jerusalem, at least in his time. And Flavius Josephus, in his work *Against Apion* I 199, quotes Hecataeus of Abdera, a Hellenistic writer from the early third century BCE, who expressly states that the Temple had no sacred plants, obviously referring to the *asherah* or *alsos*, well attested in heathen sanctuaries.

In the monarchic period, the *asherah* could be a chapel or shrine like in Assyro-Babylonian texts, in which *ashirtu* appears as a sacral building or a particular place in a sanctuary. It was "built" (*2 Kgs.* 14:23), "set up" (*2 Kgs.* 17:10), or "restored" (*2 Chr.* 33:19). As a holy place, it is associated with chapels, altars, and hill shrines, or is mentioned in antithetical parallel with "the house of Yahweh," as in *2 Chronicles* 24:18. These texts do not make any reference to a grove or tree.

According to *Jeremiah* 17:2, *1 Kings* 14:23, and *2 Kings* 17:10, *asherim* were erected on heights, by old spreading trees. One can note that such shrines find analogies even in modern Palestine, were they are known as the tombs of saints or *welis*, erected on hilltops, near a venerated tree. *Asherim* existed also in cities. Towards the end of the tenth century BCE, according to *1 Kings* 15:13 and *2 Chronicles* 15:16, queen mother Maaka had made a *mipleṣet* for the *asherah* of Jerusalem. This was probably a phallic stele, a symbol of human and agricultural fertility. It may have signified the presence of Yahweh, like the idol or emblem (*pesel*) that King Manasseh placed in the Temple according to *2 Kings* 21:7: "and he put in the temple the idol of the *asherah* that he had made." That *asherah* with its idol remained in the Temple complex until the reform of King Josiah. The narrative of *2 Kings* 23:6–7 specifies that Josiah took it away and pulled down the annexes of the Temple, "where women were weaving for the *asherah*," probably adorned with carpets and draperies. A famous *asherah*, which stood in Samaria under Jehoahaz, is alluded to in *2 Kings* 13:6—probably the one made by Ahab, as reported in *1 Kings* 16:33.

Sanctuaries are also meant in Aramaic and Phoenician inscriptions. The Phoenician ostracon from Akko, dating to the fifth century BCE, mentions "the overseer of the *ashirat*," and an inscription from Umm el-Amed is a dedication "to Astarte in the *ashirat* of the gods of Hammon," the ancient name of the town, south of Tyre. The allusions to offerings brought "to the *ashirat*" of Ekron parallel the offering made "to the *maqom*," a general term designating a holy place. The earliest Aramaic attestation of *ashirat* appears on one of the inscriptions from Sefire, in northern Syria, dating to the mid-eighth century BCE. The latest one, supposed to date from the period between the fourth and the sixth or seventh centuries CE, occurs in a Judeo-Aramaic incantation inscribed on a magic bowl, found in Mesopotamia. It curses "the *ashirat* of the king of the demons," *ʾšrt mlkʾ d-šydy*. In all these texts, *ashirat* can be translated simply by "sanctuary," "shrine," or "sacred precinct." Nothing indicates that the presence of a sacred tree is implied.

However, a single tree may indeed characterize a holy site. The Aramaic inscription from Sardis, dating from the mid-fourth century BCE, mentions "the tree of the holy place," in Aramaic *atīrtā*, a variant spelling of *ashirta*. According to *Genesis* 21:3, Abraham planted a sacred tree at Beersheba and invoked "the everlasting God." The sacred oak or terebinth of Mamre was famous in the time of Flavius Josephus, who mentions it twice, in *The Jewish War* IV 533 and in *Jewish Antiquities* I 186. It was later a haunt of "angels," as the fifth-century church historian Sozomen writes, and Constantine the Great was obliged to put down the heathenish cult. Rabbi Simeon ben Eleazar, active in the second century CE, mentions three other *asherot* in Palestine: the evergreen carob of Kfar Qasem, the carob of Kfar Pigsha, and the evergreen sycamore, growing among the pine trees on Mount Carmel.

The first *asherah*, probably located on the southwestern rim of the Samarian Hills, was apparently famous for oracles, as the name *qasem*, "divination," suggests. Already *Genesis* 12:6 mentions the "terebinth of the teacher" at Shechem, evidently an ancient sacred tree from which oracles were obtained, and *Judges* 9:37 refers to the "terebinth of the diviners," most likely the same sacred tree. It may also be identical with the "tree of the standing-stone" in *Judges* 9:6. This symbol of the divinity was placed under the tree, thus manifesting the sacred character of the site, which was certainly an *asherah*, defined in the Mishnah as "any tree under which is an idol." At the same time, the mention of the standing-stone expressed the difference between the sacred tree or grove and the divine occupant. This distinction was not always clearly drawn and it is quite intelligible that prayers could be addressed to the occupant and to his abode, for instance "to Yahweh and to his *asherah*," or even to the sole abode of the divinity, becoming a deity in its own right, like the Aramean gods Bethel, "God's house," and Turmasgad, "Mountain of worship." The only remote possibility of understanding *asherah* in a similar way occurs in *Judges* 3:7, where the Israelites are accused by the Deuteronomistic historian of having served "the Baals and the *asherot*." However, the parallel passages of *Judges* 2:13 and 10:6, and *1 Samuel* 7:4 and 12:10 mention "the Baals and the *Ashtarot*." Two Hebrew manuscripts and the Latin Vulgate version, made directly on the Hebrew text, read *Ashtarot* as well in *Judges* 3:7, instead of *asherot*. The latter reading should therefore be regarded as a scribal error.

Summing up, the Hebrew word *asherah* designates a holy site, a sanctuary, especially one marked by the presence of a sacred grove or green tree. It has no relation whatsoever to the goddess Athirat. There is a quite consistent and uninterrupted tradition, from biblical to Mishnaic times and the Middle Ages, in the understanding of this Hebrew word. Maimonides writes in *Mishneh Torah* (I 75b: 2–3): "A tree that was planted, from the outset, for the purpose of being worshipped, is forbidden to be used. This is the *asherah*, mentioned in the Torah."

BIBLIOGRAPHY

The present entry updates Edward Lipiński's contribution "The Goddess A̱tirat in Ancient Arabia, in Babylon, and in Ugarit," in *Orientalia Lovaniensia. Periodica* 3 (Louvain, Belgium, 1972), pp. 101–119. A study of the topic in early rabbinic literature is provided by Mireille Hadas-Lebel, "Le paganisme à travers les sources rabbiniques des IIe et IIIe siècles: Contribution à l'étude du syncrétisme dans l'empire romain," in *Aufstieg und Niedergang der römischen Welt* II: *Principat*, edited by Hildegard Temporini and Wolfgang Haase, vol. 19/2 (Berlin and New York, 1979), pp. 397–485, in particular pp. 409–412. For South Arabia, one can refer to François Bron, "Notes sur le culte d'Athirat en Arabie du sud préislamique," in *Études sémitiques et samaritaines offertes à Jean Margain*, edited by Christian Bernard Amphoux, Albert Frey, and Ursula Schattner-Rieser (Lausanne, Switzerland, 1998), pp. 75–79. Further studies dealing with speculations about *asherah* as Yahweh's consort include Saul M. Olyan, *Asherah and the Cult of Yahweh in Israel* (Atlanta, 1988); Steve Wiggins, *A Reassessment of 'Asherah': A Study according to the Textual Sources of the First Two Millennia B.C.E.* (Kevelaer and Neukirchen-Vluyn, Germany, 1993); Christian Frevel, *Aschera und der Ausschliesslichkeitsanspruch YHWH's: Beiträge zu literarischen, religionsgeschichtlichen, und ikonographischen Aspekte der Aschera: Diskussion* (Weinheim, Germany, 1995); Tilde Binger, *Asherah: Goddesses in Ugarit, Israel, and the Old Testament* (Sheffield, U.K., 1997); Paolo Merlo, *La dea Ašratum-Aṯiratu-Ašera* (Rome, 1998); Judith M. Hadley, *The Cult of Asherah in Ancient Israel and Judah: Evidence for a Hebrew Goddess* (New York and Cambridge, U.K., 2000); and W. Wyatt, "Asherah," in *Dictionary of Deities and Demons in the Bible*, edited by Karel van der Toorn, Bob Becking, and Pieter W. van der Horst, 2d ed. (Leiden and Grand Rapids, Mich., 1999), pp. 99–105.

EDWARD LIPIŃSKI (2005)

ATĪŚA. Indian scholar-monk regarded as a reformer of Tantric practices and founder of the Buddhist "path literature" in Tibet. Atīśa (more properly Atiśa) was invited to Tibet by Byang chub'od under the advice of Ye shes 'od to revive Buddhism after Glan dar ma's (d. 842) persecution of the religion. He is also variously known as Śrī Atīśa, Dīpaṃkararakṣita, Dīpaṃkara Śrījñāna, and Śrī Dīpaṃkarajñānapada in Sanskrit, and Jo bo rje Dpal ldan, Mar me mdzad Dpal ye shes, and Dpal ldan Atīśa in Tibetan.

The dates of Atīśa vary—some accounts give as his dates 980–1052, others as 982–1054; in any case, he lived for seventy-two years. Some sources claim that he was born at Vikramapura, Dacca (East Pakistan); others claim him to be a native of Bhagalpur (Bihar); still others claim that he was the son of a king of Zahor, a country noted for Tantrism. His father was Kalāyṇaśrī, the king of Bengal, and his mother was Padmaprabhā. Recent studies tend to confirm that Atīśa was born in Bengal, was a member of a family with some royal blood, and lived from 980 to 1052. Accounts of his life can be found in the Tibetan historical literature (*chos 'byun*) and the extensive biographical literature (*rnam thar*).

Atīśa's first religious encounter came at an early age, when he had a vision of the Vajrayāna goddess Tārā, who remained his tutelary deity throughout his life and to whom he was especially devoted. He sought a monk's career and studied at Nālandā. At the age of thirty-one, he went to Suvarṇadvīpa (Sumatra?), where he studied under Dharmapāla for twelve years. Upon his return to India he became steward of the Buddhist college Vikramaśīla, from which he left for Tibet in 1040 as the result of an invitation from Nag tsho (b. 1011), who had been sent to the college for this purpose. After a year in Nepal Atīśa arrived in Gu ge in 1042; from there he traveled to central Tibet, and finally to the Snar thang (Narthang) Monastery, where he died.

Atīśa's activities in Tibet centered in and around western Tibet at the beginning, but after a few years he began to travel extensively. Within a short time he gained great fame for his scholarly abilities and for the bold stand he took in favor of religious reform in Tibet. He was not, however, accepted by everyone; 'Brog mi (992–1074) and Mar pa (1012–1096) are said to have avoided meeting him, and even Rin chen bzang po, who impressed Atīśa on their first meeting, was not always in accord with him, although he finally submitted to Atīśa and acknowledged his superiority. It is related that on his visit to the Bsam yas Monastery, Atīśa discovered Tantras that did not exist in India.

Atīśa's mission in Tibet was to restore monastic order and discipline. In 1057 he founded the monastery of Rwa sgreng. His *Bodhipathapradīpa* (Tib., *Byang chub lam gyi sgron ma*), written for the Tibetans as a manifesto of Buddhist reform, became the basis for the Lam Rim ("stages of the path") teachings of Tsong kha pa (1357–1419).

Atīśa worked on many translations of the various Prajñāpāramitā Sūtras. He also must be credited for his important work on reckoning dates by a method in which the well-known cycle of twelve animals is complemented by the five elements, thus resulting in a sexagenary cycle. According to this work, the first year of the first cycle of sixty years is 1027 CE; all other dates, past and future, are derived from this year. Although Atīśa was instrumental in reviving Buddhism in Tibet, his influence did not seem to last too far beyond his lifetime.

SEE ALSO Buddhism, Schools of, article on Tibetan and Mongolian Buddhism.

BIBLIOGRAPHY

Chang Ke-ch'iang. "Atīśa." In *Encyclopaedia of Buddhism*, edited by G. P. Malalasekera, vol. 2, fasc. 2. Colombo, 1967. A good summary of his life and work. Includes lists of Atīśa's writings on the Tantras, the Prajñāpāramitā literature, and the Mādhyamika literature as well as lists of his commentaries and translations.

Chattopadhyaya, Alaka. *Atīśa and Tibet* (1967). Reprint, Berkeley, Calif., 1981. An up-to-date study, including valuable appendices on biographical materials; the works of Dīpaṃkara; selected writings of Dīpaṃkara, with Sanskrit restoration of the *Bodhipathapradīpa* and photostat reproductions of the manuscript containing the *Sayings of Atīśa;* and the Tibetan sexagenarian cycle.

Das, Sarat Chandra. *Indian Pandits in the Land of Snow* (1893). Reprint, Calcutta, 1965. Four lectures by S. C. Das on his own research on Atīśa based upon Sanskrit, Pali, Tibetan, and Chinese sources.

New Sources

Brom ston, Rgyal bai byun gnas. *Jo-bo rje lha gcig dpal ldan A ti sa'i rnam thar bla ma'i yon tan chos kyi 'byun gnas sogs Bka' gdams rin po che'i glegs bam.* Zi lin, 1993.

Brom ston, Rgyal bai byun gnas, and Hubert Decleer. "Atisa's Journey to Tibet." In *Religions of Tibet in Practice,* edited by Donald S. Lopez, Jr., pp. 157–177. Princeton, 1997.

Decleer, Hubert. "Atisa's Journey to Sumatra." In *Buddhism in Practice,* edited by Donald S. Lopez, Jr., pp 532–540. Princeton, 1995.

LESLIE S. KAWAMURA (1987)
Revised Bibliography

ATONEMENT

This entry consists of the following articles:

JEWISH CONCEPTS
CHRISTIAN CONCEPTS

ATONEMENT: JEWISH CONCEPTS

Jewish conceptions of atonement consist of various strands reflecting the plurality of connotations of the Hebrew term *kipper* ("to make atonement"). Etymologically, the biblical term may mean (1) "covering up" (*Ex.* 25:17, *Lv.* 16:2), (2) "purging" or "wiping off" (Is. 27:9, Jer. 18:23), or (3) "ransoming" (*Ex.* 30:12, *Nm.* 35:31–32). Correspondingly, atonement may represent (1) the process of covering up sins to forestall retribution, (2) a form of catharsis that decontaminates individuals from impurities induced by sinful behavior, or (3) expiatory or propiatory acts designed to avert divine wrath and bring about reconciliation by redressing the imbalance caused by offenses against the deity.

Although the term *kipper* is also employed in the Torah (Pentateuch) with reference to the removal of ritual impurity, there is no suggestion whatsoever that the rites themselves are endowed with magical power. The desired results of expiation or purification are not viewed as the effect caused by the performance of rites. Atonement can only be granted by God; it is not the direct effect of any human action (see, for example, *Leviticus* 16:30).

Confession is specifically mandated by the Torah in conjunction with the expiatory rites performed by the high priest on the Day of Atonement as well as with the sacrifice called the *asham* (guilt offering). Rabbinic Judaism construes this latter requirement as paradigmatic for all types of sacrifices offered with the intent to secure forgiveness, expiation, or atonement for sins. Unless preceded by confession, any *ḥaṭ'at* (sin offering) or *asham* would be stigmatized as "a sacrifice of the wicked which is an abomination" (B.T., *Shav.* 12b).

REPENTANCE. Although the Torah refers only to confession, the rabbis of the Mishnah, Talmud and Midrashic works cite various biblical verses from the rest of the Hebrew Bible to interpret this formal requirement in a much broader sense. The act of confession is construed as verbalization of an internal process of *teshuvah,* the act of "turning" that involves not only remorse but a sincere effort to make reparation and the resolve to mend ways. The very possibility of *teshuvah* as the re-creation of the human self presupposes freedom of the will. Judaism maintains that human beings have the capacity to extricate themselves from the causal nexus and determine freely their conduct.

For all the emphasis upon *teshuvah*—the psychological transformation of the self wrought by human effort—one essential component of the traditional view is the notion that divine mercy is necessary to heal or redeem man from the dire aftereffects of sin. Because any transgression of a divine commandment through sins of omission or commission constitutes an offense against God and damages a person's relationship with the Creator, divine grace is required to achieve full atonement. It is for this reason that prayers for atonement are an integral part of the *teshuvah* process. There are, however, sins of such severity that *teshuvah* by itself cannot completely remove the stains of guilt. According to the classical formulation of the second-century tanna Rabbi Yishma'el:

> He who transgressed a positive commandment and repented, is forgiven before he has moved from his place: as it is said, "Return, O backsliding children" [*Jer.* 3:14]. He who has transgressed a negative commandment and repented, repentance merely suspends [punishment] and only the Day of Atonement secures atonement. As it is said: "For on this day shall atonement be made for you . . . from all your sins" [*Lv.* 16:30]. He who has violated a law punishable by extirpation or capital punishment and has repented, repentance and the Day of Atonement suspend and only suffering completes the atonement, as it is said: "Then will I visit their transgression with the rod and their iniquity with strokes" [*Ps.* 89:33]. But he who has been guilty of the desecration of the divine name, repentance is incapable of suspending punishment, the Day of Atonement cannot secure atonement, and suffering cannot complete it, but all of them together suspend the punishment and only death completes atonement, as it is said: "And the Lord of hosts revealed himself in my ears. Surely, this iniquity shall not be expiated till you die" [*Is.* 12:14]. (B.T., *Yoma'* 86a)

EXPIATION AND GRACE. The rabbinic tenet that "the dead require atonement" (*Sifrei Shoftim* 210) is further evidence that atonement is not merely a function of repentance. Repentance is only feasible for the living, yet Judaism encourages practices such as offering of charity, prayer, or Torah study in behalf of the deceased. Significantly, vicarious expiatory significance is attributed to the death of the high priest (J.T., *Yoma'* 7.3) or that of the righteous (B.T., *Mo'ed Q.* 28a). Similarly, according to a number of tannaitic opinions, the occurrence of the Day of Atonement in itself, and especially the performance of the rites of the scapegoat, may expiate some sins even of the nonrepentant (B.T., *Yoma'* 65b). It should, however, be noted that Menaḥem Me'iri (1249–1306/1310), a prominent French-Jewish authority, categorically rejects the possibility of atonement in the absence of at least minimal repentance (*Ḥibbur hateshuvah* 2.13). But while Jewish theology attributes expiatory efficacy to fasting, charity, and other cultic or ritual practices and for that matter to death and suffering, overriding importance is attached to catharsis. Significantly, tractate *Yoma'* 8.9 of the Mishnah concludes with ʿAqiva' ben Yosef's exclamation, "How happy are you Israelites! Before whom do you cleanse yourselves, and who cleanses you? Your father who is in Heaven."

Proper atonement calls for human initiative in returning to God, who will respond by completing the process of purification, ultimately leading to the reintegration of the fragmented human self and resulting in the restoration of a wholesome relationship between man and God. According to a Talmudic opinion, repentance is a necessary condition of the messianic redemption, In qabbalistic thought, repentance is not only deemed indispensable to national redemption but acquires metaphysical significance as a preeminent aspect of the process of *tiqqun ʿolam* ("mending the world")—the returning of the alienated creation to its Creator.

See Also Ashkenazic Hasidism; Biblical Temple; Hasidism, overview article; Ro'sh ha-Shanah and Yom Kippur.

BIBLIOGRAPHY

Studies in Sin and Atonement in the Rabbinic Literature of the First Century by Adolf Büchler (Oxford, 1928) is a pioneering but somewhat dated exposition of rabbinic conceptions of atonement. A thorough analysis of biblical conceptions in the light of recent research may be found in Herbert Chanan Brichto's "On Slaughter and Sacrifice, Blood and Atonement," *Hebrew Union College Annual* 47 (1976): 19–55. Two pieces by Jacob Milgrom, "Kipper" and "Repentance," in the *Encyclopaedia Judaica* (Jerusalem, 1971), are very useful as introductions to biblical and postbiblical conceptions of atonement. A phenomenological study of Jewish conceptions of atonement and repentance by preeminent philosopher and authority on Jewish law is Joseph Ber Soloveitchik's *ʿAl hateshuvah,* edited by Pinchas H. Peli (Jerusalem, 1974). This work has been recently translated into English by Pinchas H. Peli as *Soloveitchik: On Repentance* (Ramsey, N.J., 1984).

New Sources

Althann, Robert. "Atonement and Reconciliation in Psalms 3, 6 and 83." *JNSL* 25 (1999): 75–82.

Bautch, Richard J. *Developments in Genre between Post-Exilic Penitential Prayers and the Psalms of Communal Lament.* Academia Biblica, no. 7. Atlanta, 2003.

Douglas, Mary. "Atonement in Leviticus." *Jewish Studies Quarterly* 1, no. 2 (1993–1994): 109–130.

Grayston, Kenneth. "Atonement and Martyrdom." In *Early Christian Thought in Its Jewish Context,* edited by John Barclay and John Sweet, pp. 250–263. Cambridge, 1996.

Neusner, Jacob. "Sin, Repentance, Atonement and Resurrection: The Perspective of Rabbinic Theology on the Views of James 1–2 and Paul in *Romans* 3–4." *Annali di Storia dell'Esegesi* 18 (2001): 409–431.

Walter S. Wurzburger (1987)
Revised Bibliography

ATONEMENT: CHRISTIAN CONCEPTS

According to its linguistic origins atonement (at-one-ment) means "the condition of or resulting from being at one." It is one of the few English words that have become theological terms. The word occurs many times in the Old Testament, and this usage has influenced the New Testament and subsequent tradition. Its appearance in the Authorized (King James) Version as the translation of *katallagē* in *Romans* 5:11 ("through our Lord Jesus Christ, by whom we have now received the atonement") consolidated its theological use. The Revised Standard Version, however, and nearly all modern versions translate *katallagē* as "reconciliation," leaving the New Testament in English now without the word *atonement.* In contemporary theological usage *atonement* has come to mean the process by which reconciliation with God is accomplished through the death of Christ. Its earlier usage tended to have as well the wider meaning of the end sought through the atoning process, as in reconciliation, redemption (in older Roman Catholic writing), and salvation (in Protestant orthodoxy).

Old Testament Background. The Hebrew root for atonement is *kpr,* which probably means "to cover" or perhaps "to wipe away." The Greek equivalent is *hilaskethai* and its derivatives. The system of sacrifice that was practiced by the Israelites was regarded as an institution graciously provided by God and had atonement as its aim. Its rationale may be seen in *Leviticus* 17:11: "it is the blood that makes atonement, by reason of the life." On the solemn yearly Day of Atonement the high priest went into the holy of holies to the covering over the ark, the mercy seat (*kaporet, hilastērion*), where God was believed to appear and announce forgiveness of sins to his people.

Some scholars would translate *hilastērion* in *Romans* 3:25 ("whom God set forth to be a *hilastērion*") simply as "mercy seat." Their feeling is that Paul meant to assert that the cross of Christ is now the place where God shows his saving mercy. Most translators, however, render the word in this context as either "propitiation" or "expiation," depending on whether they want to suggest that God's wrath must first be satisfied before he will forgive human sinfulness or locate the block to restored relationships not primarily in God but in the alienation that is created by the sin itself and is acted upon directly by Christ's atoning action. Strongly divergent theories of atonement were constructed later on the basis of this debate.

The prophets constantly warned against any automatic assumption that sacrifice of itself would provide forgiveness; they preached that God desires mercy and repentance (*Is.* 1:10–17). The ritual system of sacrifice was spiritualized in the Old Testament in the prophetic view of a new covenant to replace the original, Mosaic covenant (*Jer.* 31:31) and was personalized in the actions of the suffering servant of Yahveh (*Is.* 53) sent by God to become an *asham* ("guilt-offering") and to bear the sins of many in a redemptive act of self-oblation.

New Testament Foundation. The associations of atonement with animal sacrifice, the offering of incense, and payments of money disappeared in the New Testament except as vivid metaphors for elucidating the atoning life, death, and resurrection of Jesus Christ and, especially, the "once for all" (*Heb.* 10:10) event of Calvary. When Christians say that the cross is the crucial point of the early preaching of the gospel, they do not so much make a pun as testify that the Atonement, whatever else it has done, has changed the language. It was probably inevitable that sacrificial language would be emphasized in describing the Atonement simply because the contemporary institution of sacrifice was well known to the early Christians (as it is not today) and because the actual penal process of crucifixion with its attendant shedding of blood suggested at once the religious ritual of sacrifice.

The Gospels and Jesus' Teaching. By parable and by direct discourse Jesus taught forgiveness of sins, relating God's forgiveness to forgivingness between people. Controversy swirled around Jesus' authoritative absolutions, a situation that perhaps more than any other raised for his Jewish hearers the question of his divine status or blasphemy. He regarded his death as likely not simply because many prophets had been martyred for the unpopularity of their message but because he saw it as controlled in some way by a divine must, as a decisive part of his mission to inaugurate the kingdom of God: "For the Son of man also came not to be served but to serve, and to give his life as a ransom (*lutron*) for many" (*Mk.* 10:45). Later questions about the various agencies to whom the ransom would be paid were to determine variant forms of the Greek theories of atonement. The image of a ransom is commercial, indicating the price needed to buy a slave's freedom. Conjoined with the phrase "for many," which may invoke the sacrificial image of the servant in *Isaiah* who will deliver many from their sins, use of the word ransom points out the costliness of reconciliation.

A second saying attributed to Jesus in the Marcan tradition of the last supper also casts light on the pervasive problem of the divine must: "This is my blood of the covenant, which is poured out for many" (*Mk.* 14:24). This language is reminiscent of the previous saying about ransom, here with an emphasis on a new covenant, such as was foreshadowed in *Jeremiah,* and recalling God's liberation of the Israelites from Egypt. Paul could say, "Christ our passover is sacrificed for us." To the Markan saying about the "blood of the covenant which is poured out for many" Matthew added, "for the forgiveness of sins" (*Mt.* 26:28), making explicit that the atoning action is because of sin.

John developed the image of "the Lamb of God who takes away the sin of the world" (*Jn.* 1:29, 1:36). There are other references to the lamb in the *Book of Revelation,* such as *Revelation* 13:8, "the Lamb slain from the foundation of the world" (Authorized Version). This disputed translation became a justification for subsequent interpretations of the Atonement that regarded the event at Calvary not as an isolated incident but as the sacramental expression of the eternal reality of God's suffering love for humanity. The *Letter to the Hebrews* expands the image of sacrifice, making it the basis for the most sustained theory of the Atonement to be found in the New Testament. The theological question for all theories of sacrifice is whether Christ's death was itself the decisive sacrifice to God or whether the wealth of sacrificial images employed in New Testament literature is simply a way of demonstrating that what was sought through the Old Testament system of sacrifice has, in fact, been completely and finally accomplished in the life and death of Christ.

Paul on the Atonement. Paul is the earliest written source for the dimensions of atonement in apostolic preaching: "For I delivered to you as of first importance what I also received, that Christ died for our sins in accordance with the scriptures" (*1 Cor.* 15:3). He used the images of Christ the victor over sin, wrath, the demons, and death, and also used the illustration of the law court. For Paul the atoning death and resurrection went beyond the merely human dimensions of salvation to include the world of spirits and of nature itself in its groaning and travail (*Rom.* 8:19–23).

Paul grasped the moral dilemma in all thought about the Atonement: How can a God of holiness and righteousness accept sinners without either destroying his holiness or sentimentalizing his love by an immoral indifference to evil? As a former Pharisee, Paul naturally used legal language to describe faith in Christ. He used the language of the law court provisionally, only to introduce the paradox of grace: God does not ultimately, in Christ, deal with humanity along the lines of retributive justice, which a human judge is obliged by oath to dispense. The revelation of God's righteousness "has been manifested apart from law" (*Rom.* 3:21). Expositions of the vicarious and representative work of Christ have been constructed from the penal implications of such Pauline texts as "For our sake he made him to be sin who knew no sin, so that in him we might become the righteousness of God" (*2 Cor.* 5:21). The problem with such expositions, however, is that they tend to subject God's gracious love to the necessities of a law court. The gospel according to Paul is that God actually does what no human judge should do: God in a revolutionary way actually accepts sinners. Jesus had taught a love of this quality and actualized it by associating with outcasts, sinners, the despised, and the victims of power and injustice in his society until its religious and political forces crucified him.

There is no single New Testament doctrine of the Atonement—there is simply a collection of images and metaphors with some preliminary analysis and reflection from which subsequent tradition built its systematic doctrines and theories. The New Testament asserts that God was in Christ reconciling the world to himself in such a way that the act resembled a military victory, a king establishing his power, a judge and prisoner in a law court, a great ritual sacrifice before priest and altar, the payment of ransom for war prisoners or the payment of a redemption for a slave's freedom, the admission to responsible sonship within a family, and more. Tradition has tried to decide what parts of this picture should be taken literally and what parts metaphorically and has developed extended rationales, added new images according to the conditions of different eras and cultures, and established cross-relationships with other Christian doctrines of the Trinity, the Incarnation, the church, and the sacraments. Often it has tried to make one theory of the Atonement dominant over the others.

A Typology of Atonement Theories. Gustaf Aulén in his classic *Christus Victor* (1930) suggested three basic types of atonement theory: the classical type, the Latin type, and the subjective type. Combining these with additional categories from R. S. Franks's definitive *History of the Doctrine of the Work of Christ* (1918) yields the following typology:

(1) *Classical type:* Greek, patristic, Christus Victor, ransom, Eastern.

(2) *Anselmian type:* Latin, objective, transactional, Western.

(3) *Reformation type:* penal, objective, juridical, governmental, transactional.

(4) *Moral-influence type:* Abelardian, subjective, exemplary, modern.

(5) Other types are sacrificial, mystical, psychological, incarnational, and eucharistic in character.

This scheme is regarded as approximate and as bearing historic names that are sometimes not simply descriptive but are slanted by their supporters' claims or their detractors' criticisms. This article will select only a few of the most significant theories for analysis.

Classical theories of atonement. Aulén looked behind the dramatic mythology of the Greek fathers to find the theme of Christus Victor, a view that he claimed integrates ideas of the Incarnation, Atonement, and resurrection into a unified concept of salvation. Ragnar Leivestad in *Christ the Conqueror: Ideas of Conflict and Victory in the New Testament* (1954) supplemented Aulén by describing Christ's struggle with the demons and Satan in his work, teaching, and, especially, healing. Aulén rooted his description in Paul's writings, carried it through the Eastern and Western fathers before Anselm, and found it expressed again in Martin Luther's buoyant feeling of being on the winning side. One version of the theory had the devil unjustly in possession of humanity; another affirmed the justice of the devil's hold; still another claimed that although the devil had no rights, God graciously withheld from forcibly stripping him of his gains. Special strategies against the devil were the mousetrap (the humanity of Christ as bait to hide his divinity) and Augustine's fishhook play. In addition to the Christus Victor theme there are in patristic theology the views of Christ as the bearer of incorruption (expounded by Athanasius in the fourth century), the revealer of truth and model of humanity, the physician of humanity, and the sacrificial victim (expounded by Gregory of Nazianzus, also in the fourth century). The contrast between the church's official dogma of the Incarnation as developed through the Council of Chalcedon (451) and the unofficial status of atonement theories has often been pointed out, but the difference can be easily exaggerated since the criterion for Christological decision was usually how the proposed understanding of Christ's person would effect the salvation of humanity. There is growing agreement that the work of Christ and the person of Christ must be integrated: Christ does what he is and is what he does.

Anselmian theories of atonement. *Cur deus homo* (Why the God-man?), written by Anselm, archbishop of Canterbury, in about 1097, is the single most influential book on the Atonement. Anselm criticized all ransom-to-the-devil theories by turning them upside down and asserting that the ransom, which Anselm called "satisfaction," must be paid to God. Debate has gathered around the influence that feudalism and the ancient Teutonic customs of blood money had on Anselm, but the vital center of the Anselmian theory is a rationalization about satisfaction, which, together with contrition and confession, constitutes the three parts of the Latin sacrament of penance. Even the sacrificial images are reinterpreted in terms of satisfaction as their rationale. Since sin derogated from the honor of God and must be infinite in offense because it is against God, either punishment or the payment of an infinite satisfaction is required. Such a satisfaction finite humans should but cannot pay. The answer to this dilemma becomes the God-man, whom Anselm described as bound by simple duty to lead a life of obedience but who, having lived a life of sinlessness, is not justly subject to the claim of death. Therefore Christ's death alone possessed the superfluous merit that made it an adequate satisfaction for the sins of humankind. There have been many criticisms of Anselm: that his confidence in reason is too great to explain mystery; that he quantified sin mathematically rather than personalizing it; that he concentrated so much on Christ's death that Jesus' life of sacrificial love is emptied, along with the resurrection, of significance. The overarching objection is that rigid procedures according to legal justice demote God's love to a secondary place. Later medieval modification of Anselm (e.g., Thomas Aquinas in the thirteenth century) stressed acceptance by God rather than strict necessity as the ground for atonement. A penitential system of indulgences managed by the church grew up around the doctrines of Christ's superfluous merits.

Reformation theories of atonement. The Reformation opted for Anselm's unused alternative of punishment. John Calvin in the sixteenth century emphasized Christ's vicarious and substitutionary endurance of God's punishment on behalf of humankind or of the elect. The dominance of Anselmian analysis in Reformation orthodoxy and the Counter-Reformation can be demonstrated by showing that for the Roman Catholic the Atonement continued to be the basis for the ecclesiastical apparatus that mediated salvation while for the Protestant, looking at the Atonement through the doctrine of justification by faith, it became the reason for rejecting that whole apparatus as unnecessary.

Hugo Grotius (1583–1645) substituted for the juridical image of a judge dispensing retributive justice the political image of a governor concerned for the public good and able to pardon humanity safely because of the deterrent effect of Christ's death. This governmental or rectoral theory Jonathan Edwards introduced into Calvinist thought in America in the eighteenth century.

Moral-influence theories. Theories of moral influence describe the Atonement as something accomplished in the hearts and minds of those who respond to Jesus' message and example of love—"love answers love's appeal" was the phrase used by Peter Abelard in the twelfth century to summarize this moral influence. The strength of this view lies in its primary emphasis upon the love of God rather than on God's wrath or justice. The intrinsic weakness of such theories lies in the widespread perception that such declarations by themselves have little power to free the sinner when they alone are seen as constituting the sum total of atonement rather than part of a total atoning activity initiated and carried through by Christ's action.

Horace Bushnell in *Vicarious Sacrifice* (1866), writing at the time of the American Civil War, took his illustrations of the Atonement from family relationships, friendship, and patriotism. Albrecht Ritschl in *Justification and Reconciliation* (originally published in 1870–1874 in German) expanded the responding agent from the individual only to a group. He stressed Jesus' reconciling love and faithfulness unto death as inspiring a community of ethical response in history. J. McLeod Campbell in *Nature of the Atonement* (1856) emphasized vicarious penitence. Robert C. Moberly in *Atonement and Personality* (1901) provided a broad view of the work of Christ as the perfect penitent by conceiving Christ's incarnating and atoning activity as continuing through the church and the sacraments in the power of the Holy Spirit.

Twentieth-century theories of atonement. The theology of Karl Barth redirected thought to the objectivity of the Atonement, and Dietrich Bonhoeffer and Dorothee Sölle developed the theme of Christ as representative. In a rehabilitation of the penal theory Leonard Hodgson in *The Doctrine of the Atonement* (New York, 1951) argued that in Jesus Christ the punisher and the punished are one. Anglicans and especially Roman Catholics under the influence of liturgical and biblical renewal, the return to patristic sources, and the impact of Vatican II have turned away from Jean Rivière's hitherto dominant claim (made early in the twentieth century) that Anselm's concept of satisfaction adequately expressed the meaning of sacrifice and toward the restoration of sacrificial language, both in liturgy and in theology.

Few doctrines of Christian faith have produced more theories than the doctrine of atonement, a fact that testifies to the witness of scripture, in which Christ's death is given decisive reconciling power and meaning, but no one theory or family of theories is presented as alone authoritative. The doctrine of atonement is the Christian answer to the human questions about ignorance, suffering, death, and sin, but always the alienation caused by sin is considered more basic than the three other evils. Christ "has broken down the dividing wall of hostility . . . so making peace and . . . [reconciling] us both to God in one body through the cross" (*Eph.* 2:14–16). Atonement as an expression of the mystery of God remains the reality at the core; interpretations of the how and the why of the process multiply as images and metaphors expand into theory and become in turn ancillary or dominant only to dissolve in changing cultural configurations and reappear later in new shapes and relationships. In the current period the classical type of Christus Victor has been increasingly able to attract as satellites the Anselmian and the moral-influence theories. Perhaps the next development lies with a reformulation of the sacrificial theory, which, fortified by the use of liturgy and having come abreast of new understandings of sacrifice in the comparative history of religions, may for a time become a new primary center in its own right.

BIBLIOGRAPHY

Anselm. *Why God Became Man and The Virgin Conception and Original Sin.* Translated with introduction and notes by Joseph M. Colleran. Albany, N.Y., 1969. An accessible and surprisingly readable edition of the most influential book on the Atonement.

Aulén, Gustaf. *Christus Victor: An Historical Study of the Three Main Types of the Idea of the Atonement.* Translated by A. G. Herbert. 1931; reprint, London, 1945. Already a classic in its own right, Aulén's work, which appeared originally in 1930 in Swedish, presents the classic view of the Atonement articulately and with the conviction that the Latin and subjective types are destined to become its satellites.

Barth, Karl. *Church Dogmatics IV: The Doctrine of Reconciliation.* 3 vols. in 4. Translated by G. W. Bromiley. Edinburgh, 1956–1962. Within the larger Barthian corpus these writings on reconciliation and atonement constitute a summa of some 2,600 pages, with impressive interpretations of scripture and footnotes on the history of doctrine.

Dillistone, Frederick W. *The Christian Understanding of Atonement.* Philadelphia, 1968. A comprehensive book analyzing alienation as a problem in human life, with contemporary illustrations from literature, history, psychology, anthropology, and philosophy.

Franks, Robert S. *The Work of Christ: A Historical Study of Christian Doctrine.* New York, 1962. This is a later edition, in one volume, of Franks's earlier definitive work *A History of the Doctrine of the Work of Christ,* 2 vols. (London, 1918).

Leivestad, Ragnar. *Christ the Conqueror: Ideas of Conflict and Victory in the New Testament.* London, 1954. An impressive documentation of the New Testament origins of Aulén's earlier thesis about the classic theory of the Atonement.

Masure, Eugene. *The Christian Sacrifice: The Sacrifice of Christ Our Head.* London, 1944. A point of transition in Roman Catholic writing on the Atonement from the older Anselmian rationale for sacrifice to the new theology on sacrifice that is drawn from scriptural, patristic, and liturgical renewal prior to Vatican II.

Sölle, Dorothee. *Christ the Representative.* London, 1967. A sustained analysis of the kind of representative office that Christ performs, much influenced by Dietrich Bonhoeffer's thought and the Christological title "the man for us."

Taylor, Vincent. *Jesus and His Sacrifice* (1937). Reprint, London, 1951. A helpful study of the passion sayings in the Gospels in the light of the Old Testament and from the perspective of form-criticism. Together with Taylor's later works *The Atonement in New Testament Teaching,* 2d ed. (London, 1946), and *Forgiveness and Reconciliation,* 2d ed. (London, 1952), this book constitutes part of an important trilogy, with an emphasis on a sacrificial understanding of the Atonement.

Wolf, William J. *No Cross, No Crown: A Study of the Atonement.* New York, 1957. A historical survey of the chief theories of atonement and their problems, followed by chapters on deliverance from guilt, justification, sanctification, the atoning God, and the atoning life; an attempt to reformulate an understanding of the Atonement.

New Sources

Bartlett, Anthony W. *Cross Purposes: The Violent History of Christian Atonement.* Harrisburg, Pa., 2001.

Boff, Leonardo. *Passion of the Christ, Passion of the World.* Translated by Robert R. Barr. Maryknoll, N.Y., 1987.

Brock, Rita Nakashima. *Journeys by Heart: A Christological Erotic Power.* New York, 1988.

Dudley, Martin, and Geoffrey Rowell, eds. *Confession and Absolution.* London, 1990.

Gunton, Colin E., ed. *The Theology of Reconciliation.* London, 2003.

Weaver, J. Denny. *The Nonviolent Atonement.* Grand Rapids, Mich., 2001.

Wheeler, David L. "A Relational View of the Atonement." *Theology and Religion,* vol. 54. New York, 1989.

WILLIAM J. WOLF (1987)
Revised Bibliography

ATRAHASIS

ATRAHASIS. Atrahasis, "the surpassingly wise," is the name of the Mesopotamian hero of the Flood in the myth of the same name (corresponding to the biblical Noah), recorded in Assyro-Babylonian literature from the Old Babylonian period up until the New Babylonian period. In Sumerian his name is Ziusudra (which becomes Xisuthros in Berossus), whereas in the *Epic of Gilgamesh* he is called Utanapishtim—meaning, respectively, the one who "has a long life" and the one who "has found life."

The Sumerian pantheon, which was accepted and assimilated by the Semitic Babylonians, had a pyramid structure, with the god An, the sky, at its head, sharing power with his two sons Enlil and Enki, all having clearly defined areas of responsibility. An controlled the sky, Enlil the earth, and Enki the ocean depths. In practice, whether because Enlil was god of the earth or because his priests at Nippur were a particularly powerful social grouping, it was Enlil who gave Sumerian sovereigns their royal power. Enki had nothing to do with the Sumerian kingship, so his son Marduk was cut off from the decision-making process of which Enlil was in charge.

The Babylonian priests showed their bitterness here. The antagonism been Enlil and Enki was well known, so some scholars have thought the two gods may represent two different religions, a chthonic one and a heavenly one, fused in the Sumerian religious system. In their writings, the Babylonians emphasized the rivalry between the two gods, naturally favoring Enki, demonstrating not so much the worthless nature of Enlil but certainly his lack of wisdom and his ill-will toward the human race.

THE *ATRAHASIS* STORY. This is the theme of the poem *Atrahasis,* one of the masterpieces of Babylonian religious literature. Atrahasis is the hero of the Flood, a worshiper of Enki, who is told of the intended catastrophic fate for humankind proposed by Enlil. Three tablets describe the build-up, the catastrophe itself, and the aftermath of the Flood. The first tablet, describing the situation before the Flood in the world of gods and people, is particularly revealing; the story of the Flood itself is also known from a Sumerian poem and from Tablet 11 of the *Epic of Gilgamesh.*

The outlook displayed in the first part of the poem is entirely a product of Semitic Babylonian thought. The gods have been allocated various tasks and functions and then have assigned the lesser gods the task of working the land to produce the food that is needed. However, the effort required is too great, and the lesser gods are unable to bear the hard work this onerous task requires. So they rebel, embarking on the first strike in the history of the world. When the greater gods gather in assembly, summoned by Enlil, the god of the earth, the lesser gods make it clear that they do not intend to work anymore because this work requires too much effort.

The wise Enki next proposes to create humankind to carry out the work and provide sustenance for the gods. After describing the way the human race was created, the writer recounts the new situation. Humankind has multiplied, and the human clamor is rising heavenward more and more loudly because the work the lesser gods had refused to carry out is equally onerous for humans. An impromptu assembly of the gods is convened, and Enlil's proposal to punish the arrogance of humankind, first with plague, then with famine, and finally with flood, is accepted. However, the punishments prove worthless because Enki intervenes on behalf of humankind on all three occasions.

The moment for the final drastic decision draws near. Enlil proposes to finish off the human race with the Flood. The discussion has been heated, and Enki does not agree with what is proposed, considering it unjust and senseless. But the will of the majority prevails, and thus the plan for the Flood is approved. Enki, however, will save humankind by revealing the impending tragedy to Atrahasis and telling him to build an ark. From this point the narrative does not differ greatly from previously known accounts. The one new feature is a phrase the writer uses, momentarily becoming personally involved in the dramatic events to condemn the decision of Enlil as "an evil act, a wicked deed towards mankind" (Tav., II.viii.5).

This is not the place to start a discussion on the ethical values of the Babylonian world but simply to emphasize the hostile and critical attitude of the author toward Enlil, the head of the Sumerian pantheon, in contrast with the repeated demonstrations of devotion and gratitude to Enki, the father of Marduk. The latter is not mentioned in the Atrahasis myth. Indeed he plays no active part in the myths of earlier Sumerian literature or Babylonian literature of the first period.

The Atrahasis myth, an entirely Assyro-Babylonian creation, is the high point of Semitic thought on the divine world and human reality, from the origins of the world to the present time, through various stages of existence, such as the Flood and the new creation. The text has a long history. Created in the Old Babylonian period, it is also recorded in the Middle Babylonian period, then with significant changes in the neo-Assyrian period, and finally in the neo-Babylonian period. It should be stressed that, although the original outline of the work has undergone significant external changes, it has features that readily lead to the conclusion that there were different versions of the myth in the neo-Assyrian period. It should not be forgotten that the myth has a long editorial history, existing in documented form for over thirteen hundred years.

As regards the structure of the myth, the scheme of the Old Babylonian version shows that the three tablets copied by the scribe Ku Aja may be divided into three clear sections. The first tablet deals with the situation in the world of gods before the creation of humankind. The divine pantheon is still Sumerian and is subdivided into two groups, the Anunnaki and the Igigi—the greater and the lesser gods. The problem troubling the gods is how to deal with the lesser gods, who have rebelled after forty years and refuse to put up with the burden of hard work. When the greater gods understand the extent of the revolt and the just reason behind it, they decide to make arrangements to create a substitute for the gods, so the creation of the first human beings, a new species entrusted with the task of working and providing food for the gods, is undertaken by the god of wisdom Ea with the help of the mother goddess Mami.

In the second tablet, humankind begins to multiply, carrying out the assigned task, and puts up with the burden of working for over six hundred years. When also exhausted, humankind resorts to the same weapons employed by the lesser gods, namely causing a commotion and going on strike. The gods are unable to accept humanity's rebellion from the established order, and they decide to punish it. Three times they inflict various woes upon the human race, but on each occasion the human race is saved through the kindly intervention of Ea.

The final act of the tragedy is approaching. The gods, particularly Enlil, the ruler of the earth, cannot accept the insubordination of the creatures that they have made, so they decide to punish the whole of humankind. The gods meet in assembly and swear an oath to accept a unanimous decision and not to frustrate it by their actions. They all go along with the new decision except for Ea, who reveals what is going to happen to Atrahasis in a dream and at the same time encourages him to build a boat to save himself.

In the third tablet, the hero of the universal Flood, Atrahasis, builds a boat that will not be submerged by the waters but will save him, his family, and various types of animals. When the Flood is over, there is a furious argument among the most powerful gods, especially Enlil and Ea, following which the hero of the Flood is raised to the status of a god. Humankind will have to put up with serious hardships, such as illnesses, which will always be with them in this vale of tears.

Other Documents. Preceding the Akkadian myth of Atrahasis is the document that contains the oldest version of the Sumerian Flood, already mentioned in *Sumerian King List.* It predates the Assyro-Babylonian version of the *Atrahasis* poem by more than a century, but it is completely fragmentary. The events preceding the Flood are described, starting from the observation that the human race in primordial times was not doing well, hence the need to create the Sumerians and allow them to raise livestock, then the gift of kingship and agriculture. In the antediluvian period, however, the kings chosen were not human but actually gods, and the five locations of the kingship are taken from the information provided by the *Sumerian King List.*

When the text resumes after a lacuna, some of the gods seem perplexed by the decision that has been taken. At this point the hero of the Flood, the king Ziusudra, according to a plan, receives advance warning of the forthcoming catastrophe. The passage concerning the construction of the ship has been lost. When the text resumes, there is a description of the storm, which lasts for seven days and seven nights. At the end of the Flood, Ziusudra disembarks from the ship and offers sacrifice to the gods. The final part of the story describes the decision of the gods to grant immortality to Ziusudra and his wife because they have been the means by which the human race has been saved.

Alexander Polyhistor, an ancient Greek historian, gives a description of the Flood as set down by the above writer (the *Babiloniaka* of Berosus, a Chaldean priest). After the death of Otiartes, his son Xisuthros ruled for eighteen *Sares* (one *saros* corresponds to 3,600 "human" years), and under his rule came the great Flood. Polyhistor set out the details:

> Chronos . . . had appeared to him in a dream (he is called by some "the father of Aramazad" and by others "time") and told him that on the eleventh day of the month of Daisios (that is Mareri) humanity would be destroyed by the Flood. He had ordered him to bury the earliest writings, the most recent and those written in between, in the city of the sun of Sippar to build a ship and to go aboard, with his parents and his closest

> friends, to stock up with food and drink, to bring on board the wild beasts and birds and animals too, and to be ready to set off with all this gear. Xisuthros had asked where he would have to sail in the ship. He had been given the answer: to the gods and to pray for the salvation of mankind (or: to pray to the gods). He took care to build the ship, which was 15 stadia in length and 2 stadia in width. Prepared, forewarned about everything, after he had received his instructions, he took his wife, his children and his closest friends aboard. When the flood rose and then rapidly subsided again, Xisuthros had sent out some birds, which had found no food and nowhere to settle. They had returned back to the ship. After a few days he had sent more birds and they had returned to the boat a second time, with muddied clay on their claws. He released the birds a third time and they did not return to the ship. Xisuthros knew that the earth had reappeared and the surface was now accessible. He opened a section of the roof and saw that the ship had come to land on a mountain. He then disembarked . . . and prayed on dry land. He raised an altar and sacrificed to the gods. Then he vanished from sight. . . . Those who had remained on board . . . then disembarked too. They wandered round shouting his name loudly, looking for him. Xisuthros was nowhere to be seen. There was a voice from the air, explaining that they should fear God, and that he had been carried up to heaven to the abode of the gods, because of his piety. . . . He gave orders to return to Babylon . . . to dig in the city of Sippar, to retrieve the books hidden there and give them to the human race. . . . When they heard all this, they sacrificed to the gods and they went on foot to Babylon. (Troiani, 1984, p. 45)

A wisdom text, titled by scholars "The Ballad of Ancient Heroes," has survived via copies from Mesopotamia and Syria. In this text the vanity of human life is stressed because it does not endure forever. The text refers to previous kings, in particular to those famous for the lengths of their reign and for the feats they have accomplished. The end of the document differs according to the sources, but the essential point is to stress once more the futility of earthly existence: it is the very rule of human existence to prefer joy to silence, light rather than death.

> The life of the human race has not been made to endure forever; . . . some men have been swept away: Where is Alulu, the king who ruled for 36,000 years? Where is Etana, the king who ascended to heaven? Where is Gilgamesh, who tried to find life, like Ziusudra? (Alster, 1990, p. 23)

The myth of Atrahasis in Assyrian literature has received due attention, as can be seen from the bibliography on the subject. An essential theme is the meaning of the first line, "When the gods were men," which the Neo-Assyrian editor has interpreted as "When the gods were like men," precisely as certain modern translators have attempted to explain, avoiding the historical religious problem caused by the Babylonian writer. Another theme concerns the name of the god who was killed and with whose blood humankind was created, made from clay and the blood of "We, the god who has intelligence," which allows humans to have *etemmu* (life spirit). The reason for the flood is explained by Giovanni Pettinato and Wolfram von Soden as a "rebellion" like that of the Igigi, whereas others (including William L. Moran and A. D. Kilmer) interpret it literally as "uproar." Veronika Afanasieva has collated the various interpretations. Another theme is the new creation after the Flood, which foresees the existence of illnesses, intended to prevent the overpopulation of the earth.

SEE ALSO Flood, The; Noah.

BIBLIOGRAPHY

Afanasieva, Veronika. "Der irdische Lärm des Menschen (nochmals zum Atramhasis-Epos)." *Zeitschrift für Assyriologie und Vorderasiatischen Archäologie* 86 (1996): 89–96.

Bottéro, Jean. "La création de l'homme et sa nature dans le Poème d'Atrahasis." In *Societies and Languages of the Ancient Near East,* edited by M. A. Dandamayev, pp. 23–32. Warminster, U.K., 1982.

Frymer-Kensky, Tikva. "The Atrahasis Epic and Its Significance for Our Understanding of *Genesis* 1–9." *Biblical Archeologist* 40 (December 1977): 147–155.

Kilmer, A. D. "The Mesopotamian Concept of Overpopulation and Its Solution as Reflected in the Mythology." *Orientalia* 41 (1972): 160–177.

Lambert, W. G., and Alan R. Millard. *Atra-Ḫasīs: The Babylonian Story of the Flood.* Oxford, 1969.

Moran, William L. "The Creation of Man in *Atrahasis* I 192–248." *Bulletin of American Schools of Oriental Research* 200 (December 1970): 48–56.

Moran, William L. "*Atrahasis,* the Babylonian Story of the Flood." *Biblica* 52 (1971): 51–61.

Oden, Robert A., Jr. "Divine Aspirations in *Atrahasis* and *Genesis* 1–11." *Zeitschrift für die alttestamentliche Wissenschaft* 93 (1981): 197–216.

Pettinato, Giovanni. "Die Bestrafung des Menschengeschlechts durch die Sintflut." *Orientalia* 37 (1968): 165–200.

Shehata, Dahlia. *Annotierte Bibliographie zum altbabylonischen Atramæasis-Mythos.* Göttinger Arbeitshefte zur Altorientalische Literatur 3. Göttingen, Germany, 2001.

Soden, Wolfram von. "Der Mesch bescheidet sich nicht: Überlegungen zu Schöpfungserzählungen in Babynien und Israel." In *Symbolae Biblicae et Mesopotamicae Francisco Mario Theodoro de Liagre Böhl dedicatae,* edited by M. A. Beck and A. A. Kampen, pp. 349–358. Leiden, 1973.

GIOVANNI PETTINATO (2005)
Translated from Italian by Paul Ellis

ʿAṬṬĀR, FARĪD AL-DĪN (c. 1158–1229 CE) was the most important Ṣūfī poet of the twelfth century, the central figure in the famous trio of Persian Ṣūfī poets beginning with Sanāʾī (d. 1131) and culminating in Jalāl al-Dīn Rūmī (d. 1273).

LIFE AND WORKS. Almost nothing of ʿAṭṭār's life is known except that he was a druggist (*ʿaṭṭār* means "perfumer") by profession and worked in a pharmacy in a local bazaar in Nīshāpūr, and that he died in 1221 or 1229 during a massacre when the Mongols attacked the city. He lived most of his life in Nīshāpūr, which was the administrative capital of Khurāsān in northern Iran and one of the most important intellectual centers in the Islamic world, to which students from all over the Middle East and India flocked to study. One of the few personal details we may gather from his own works is that ʿAṭṭār was far more involved in frequenting the company of local ascetics and Ṣūfīs than in keeping the society of his peers in the medical profession and the marketplace. "From early childhood, seemingly without cause, I was drawn to this particular group [the Ṣūfīs]," he confesses, "and my heart was tossed in waves of affection for them and their books were a constant source of delight for me" (ʿAṭṭār, 1993, p. 8).

More a passionate Ṣūfī poet than a dry theorist of mysticism, ʿAṭṭār composed one prose work and six important works of poetry. His major prose work (in Persian) was the monumental compendium of biographies of the famous Ṣūfīs, *Tadhkirat al-awliyāʾ* (Memoirs of the Saints). His most famous epic poem is the *Conference of the Birds (Manṭiq al-ṭayr),* modeled on the *Treatise on the Birds,* which was composed half a century earlier by another Ṣūfī master, Aḥmad Ghazālī (d. 1126), founder of the "school of love" in Sufism. The poem describes seven valleys representing stages on the Ṣūfī path—Search, Love, Gnosis, Trust in God, Unity, Bewilderment, and Annihilation—which the birds traverse, recognizing at last that they themselves are the Sīmurgh, the deity or divine phoenix they have been seeking. The epic has been adapted to musical and theatrical compositions in the West several times, and its stories are often illustrated in Persian miniature painting. ʿAṭṭār's *Book of Adversity (Muṣībat-nāma)* recounts the Ṣūfī path in other terms, following the voyage of a single pilgrim's tormented soul through the mineral, vegetable, animal, human, and angelic realms. Asking questions along the way, he appeals in turn to forty different cosmic or mythical beings for help, until at last he is directed to the Prophet Muḥammad, who gives him the answers he needs to set him on the right road. ʿAṭṭār's emotional expressions of longing for God in this book are very appealing. ʿAṭṭār's *Divine Book (Ilāhī-nāma)* relates story of a king who asks his six sons what they most desire. They all ask for worldly things, and the king exposes their vanity in a series of anecdotes. The *Book of Mysteries (Asrār-nāma)* is another important poem of ʿAṭṭār's; it concerns twelve of the mystical principles of Sufism, and deeply affected later authors of Ṣūfī epics such as Rūmī and Shabistarī (d. 1320).The *Book of Selections (Mukhtār-nāma)* is a collection of more than 2,000 quatrains *(rubāʿī)* arranged in fifty chapters according to various mystical themes, and his *Collected Poems (Dīwān)* contains some 10,000 couplets, which are notable for their depiction of visionary landscapes and heartrending evocations of the agonies and ecstasies of the *via mystica.* The *Book of Khusraw (Khusraw-nāma),* the story of a romance between a Byzantine princess and a Persian prince, with almost no mystical content, has been attributed to ʿAṭṭār, but Muhammad Riḍā Shafāʾī-Kadkanī has rejected the attribution on convincing stylistic, linguistic, and historical grounds (Shafāʾī-Kadkanī, 1996, pp. xxxiv–lix).

ʿAṭṭār's works had such an impact on both the Ṣūfī community and the literate public at large that his fame soared soon after his death. He was so widely imitated that today there are some twenty-three works once attributed to ʿAṭṭār that have been proven by modern scholars to be spurious or of doubtful authenticity (De Blois, 1994). If we take merely the works that are unquestionably his, however, comprising a good 45,000 lines, ʿAṭṭār's achievement is still monumental.

MYSTICAL THEOLOGY AND SUFISM. The most important aspect of ʿAṭṭār's thought lies in the fact that all of his works are devoted to Sufism *(taṣawwuf).* Concerning his spiritual master(s) in Sufism, we know for certain that ʿAṭṭār was acquainted with a certain Imām Aḥmad Khwārī, a disciple of Majd al-Dīn Baghdādī (d. 1219), who was one of the authorized deputies of Najm al-Dīn Kubrā (d. 1221), founder of the Kubrawiyya Ṣūfī Order—ʿAṭṭār himself informs us of this relationship (Shafāʾī-Kadkanī, 1999, p. 71; Shafāʾī-Kadkanī, 1996, p. 26, n. 1). Almost two centuries after ʿAṭṭār's death, Ibn Bazzāz (d. 1391) in his *Ṣafwat al-safāʾ* (*The Purity of Spiritual Serenity*). cites a certain Ṣūfī poet named Shakar as his teacher, as well as someone else called Majd al-Din Kākulī (Ibn Bazzāz, 1997, p. 771) who had been his master in "experiential and speculative mysticism" (p. 51). Arguments have been advanced (by Shafāʾī-Kadkanī, 1999, pp. 72–79) on the basis of a single statement by the fifteenth-century biographer Faṣīḥ-i Khwāfī (in *Mujmal-i Faṣīḥī,* completed in 1441–1442) that ʿAṭṭār's master in Sufism was in fact Jamāl al-Dīn Muḥammad al-Nughundarī al-Tūsī, the lineage of whose initiatic chain *(silsila)* Khwāfī traced directly, by five links, to the great Ṣūfī mystic Abū Saʿīd ibn Abīʾl-Khayr (d. 1049), the founder of institutional Sufism and the first to codify and record the rules for Ṣūfī novices. However, both Ibn Bazzāz's and Khwāfī's claims are completely speculative, based on sources composed centuries after the poet's death that are uncorroborated by any earlier authors. Hence, all that can be stated with any certitude about his Ṣūfī master and order is that ʿAṭṭār was *probably* affiliated to the Kubrawiyya.

ʿAṭṭār is distinguished in the Persian-speaking Muslim world for his provocative and radical theology of love, and many of the verses of his epics and sonnets are cited independently of their poems as maxims in their own right. These pithy, paradoxical statements are known by heart throughout Iran, Afghanistan, Tajikistan, and wherever Persian is spoken or understood, such as in the lands of the Indo-Pakistani subcontinent. "Anyone who firmly sets his step down in love rises beyond the realm of faith and infidelity," he writes. In fact, the literary edifice of the symbolic poetics of mediæval Persian Sufism was to a large degree established on the foundations of ʿAṭṭār's bold "religion-of-love" poetry, which deliberately celebrates the so-called infidel wild-man's *(qalandar)* "religion of love" as the poet's personal ethic.

ʿAṭṭār's lyrical poetry, and much of his epic poetry, is pervaded by and subject to the influence of the strange, paradoxical utterances of Bāyazīd Bisṭāmī (d. 875) and the ecstatic sayings of Manṣūr al-Ḥallāj (d. 922). At the same time, ʿAṭṭār's love of the Prophet Muḥammad, expressed in glowing terms, penetrates and animates his verse; in many long sections of the preambles and epilogues of his poems he praised the Prophet with symbols such as light, the rose, the beloved, and the soul to demonstrate Muḥammad's central position in Islam. Although his passionate commitment to Islam reflects his own intense piety, faith, and reverence in the classical Islamic ideals, ʿAṭṭār's lyrical Ṣūfī vision is the virtual antithesis of contemporary Islamic religious fundamentalist thought, his lyrics evoking "a powerful statement of the role of esotericism in making possible the crossing of the frontiers of religious universes" (Nasr, 1987, p. 107).

ʿAṭṭār often expressed perplexity about the ultimate questions of existence. He was liberal and preached tolerance of other religions. His complaints about social injustice, poverty, tyranny, and the pain of disease and death, usually voiced in his verse by the so-called *ʿuqalāyi majānīn,* the "wise crazy men," have a philosophical tone. His high-minded exaltation of the suffering of Love-Passion *(dard)* as not only the essence of man, but the essence of God-consciousness, is typified in innumerable classic poetic aphorisms, such as "To the religious his religion; to the heretic his heresy. For ʿAṭṭār's heart but an ounce of your pain suffices." Such poetic dicta sketch the contours of the symbolic erotics of a Ṣūfī piety beyond conventionally designated religious boundaries, whether these are theologically labelled as being in a "devout Muslim form" or a "heretical Christian form," both of which are veils, says ʿAṭṭār, before the *visio dei.*

SEE ALSO Poetry, article on Islamic Poetry; Rūmī, Jalāl al-Dīn.

BIBLIOGRAPHY

ʿAṭṭār's *Ilāhī-nāma* has been translated and annotated by John A. Boyle as The *Ilāhīnāma,* or *Book of God* (Manchester, U.K., 1976). The translation includes an excellent introduction by Annemarie Schimmel. *Muṣībat-nāma* has been translated by Isabelle de Gastines as *Le livre d'épreuve: Musibatnama* (Paris, 1981), also with an introduction by Annemarie Schimmel. A. J. Arberry's *Muslim Saints and Mystics* (London, 1964) is a selection from *Tadhkirat al-awliyāʾ* (ed. Muhammad Istiʿlāmi, Tehran 1993, p. 8) rendered into graceful Victorian-style English prose; the new contemporary translation of the entire work by Paul Losensky (New York, 2005) is a scholarly achievement that is highly recommended. An excellent verse rendering of *Manṭiq al-ṭayr* is *The Conference of the Birds,* translated by Dick Davis and Afkham Darbandi (New York, 1984), whereas a more scholarly, though less readable, translation (but with excellent notes) is Peter Avery's *The Speech of the Birds* (Cambridge, U.K., 1998).

The basic, monumental work on ʿAṭṭār's mysticism is Helmut Ritter's *Das Meer der Seele: Mensch, Welt, und Gott in den Geschichten des Farīduddīn ʿAṭṭār* (Leiden, 1955), translated into English by John O'Kane as *The Ocean of the Soul: Men, the World, and God in the Stories of Farīd al-Dīn ʿAṭṭār* (Leiden, Netherlands, 2003), which has a 125-page analytic index compiled by Bernd Radtke and updated to include contemporary studies on the poet; the German original is also translated into Persian by ʾAbbās Zaryāb-khūʾī, Mihr-āfāq Bāybardī, as *Daryā-yi jān: sayrī dar ārāʾyi u aḥwāl-i Shaykh Farid al-Dīn ʿAṭṭār Nīshābūrī* (Tehran, 1998). Ritter analyzes his main poems, tracing every idea to its origin and showing its development in Islam. Ritter's article "Farīd al-Din Muhammad ibn Ibrāhīm" in *The Encyclopaedia of Islam* (Leiden, 1960), contains detailed biographical data, listing the poet's works, their editions, and important studies. An excellent overview of his life, works, and thought is also given in B. Reinert's article "ʿAṭṭār, Sheikh Farīd al-Dīn" in *Encyclopædia Iranica* (London and New York, 1985).

Badīʿ al-Zamān Furūzānfar placed ʿAṭṭār research on a more solid basis, superseding earlier biographical expositions with his *Sharḥ-i aḥvāl va naqd va taḥlīl-i athar-i Shaykh Farīd al-Dīn ʿAṭṭār* (Tehran, 1961), which includes an analysis of the three main poems. Muḥammad Riḍā Shafāʾī-Kadkanī's biographical study of the poet in his *Zabūr-i pārsī: nigāhī bi zindagī u ghazalhā-yi ʿAṭṭār* (Tehran, 1999) has somewhat revised and updated Furūzānfar's study by offering fresh insight into the local history of his biography, framing it within the twelfth-century Persian Ṣūfī tradition in Nīshāpūr, recalculating ʿAṭṭār's birth and death dates, and reappraising his authentic works, thus significantly changing our understanding of the poet's life, works, spiritual milieu, and literary background.

The following works in Persian also provide important biographical information on the poet: *Mukhtār-nāma: majmu ʿa-yi rubāʿiyyāt athar-i Farīd al-Dīn-i ʿAṭṭār-i Nayshābūrī,* edited with an introduction by M.R. Shaf ā'ī-Kadkānī (Tehran, 1996), and Ibn Bazzāz, *Ṣafwat al-ṣafā',* edited by Ghulām Riḍā Ṭabāṭabāʾī Majd, (Tehran, 1997).

F. De Blois's lengthy study of the poet in his *Persian Literature: A Bio-bibliographical Survey,* vol. 5, part 2: *Poetry ca. A.D. 1100–1225* (London, 1994) contains the most recent survey and study of the manuscripts of all his major works, along with original insights into their authenticity and valuable information on his life.The critical heritage of the ʿAṭṭār industry over the past century in Iran now has its own bibliography in ʿAlī Mīr Anṣārī's *Kitābshināsī-yi Shaykh Farīd al-Dīn ʿAṭṭār Nayshābūri,* (Tehran, 1995), including most of the key scholarly articles and studies on his life and thought and editions of ʿAṭṭār's works.

Studies on specific aspects of ʿAṭṭār's life and thought include ʿAbd al-Ḥusayn Zarrīnkūb, *Sudā-yi bāl-i sīmurgh: darbāra-yi zindagī va andīsha-yi ʿAṭṭār* (Tehran, 1999), which places ʿAṭṭār's life and works in the context of earlier Persian literature. Taqī Pūrnāmdāriyān's *Dīdār bā sīmurgh: haft maqāla dar ʿirfān u shiʿr u andīshahā-yi ʿAṭṭār* (Tehran, 1995) is a ground-breaking study of ʿAṭṭār's aesthetics, Ṣūfī symbolism, and his relationship to Peripateric philosophy. Riḍā Ashrafzāda's *Tajallī-yi ramz u rawāyat dar shirʿr-i ʿAṭṭār Nayshābūrī* (Tehran, 1994) provides an original survey of ʿAṭṭār's narrative techniques, characters, and symbolism, and Pūrān Shajīʿī''s *Jahānbīnī-yi ʿAṭṭār* (Tehran, 1994) discusses most of the key themes (of theology, mysticism, ethics, erotic theory) of his world view. Of the good literary studies, mention should be made of *ʿAṭṭār: Concordance and Lexical Repertories of 1000 Lines,* complied by Daniela Meneghini Correale and Valentina Zanoll (Venice, 1993), and S. H. Nasr, "The Flight of Birds to Union: Meditations upon ʿAṭṭār's *Mantiq al-tayr,*" in S. H. Nasr, *Islamic Art and Spirituality* (Suffolk, U.K., 1987). Leonard Lewisohn and Christopher Shackle (eds.), *The Art of Spiritual Flight: Farid al-Dīn ʿAṭṭār and the Persian Sufi Tradition* (London, 2005) presents the most recent survey of ʿAṭṭār's thought and poetry in light of contemporary scholarship.

LEONARD LEWISOHN (2005)

ATTENTION.

ATTENTION. The subject of attention has until recently been largely confined to the domain of experimental psychology. Researchers have sought to measure and explain such things as the selective capacity of attention, its range and span, the number of objects that it can appreciate simultaneously, and the muscle contractions associated with attentional efforts. Such work has been carried on amid considerable disagreement over basic definitions of the phenomenon of attention itself.

ATTENTION AS A RELIGIOUS PHENOMENON. In more recent years, however, the subject of attention has begun to generate significant interest among students of religion. Increasing study of the various spiritual disciplines in human religious traditions has indicated that attention plays a central role therein. Specifically, attention appears to be a *sine qua non* and common denominator of many of the forms of mental prayer and meditation found in the traditions. To further suggest that this is so and to discuss the nature and significance of contemplative attention are the central tasks of this article.

The investigation of the religious phenomenon of attention has been led by a small number of Western psychologists uncomfortable with the assumptions about human nature reigning in their field. Many have been influenced by Asian wisdom traditions and their promise of extraordinary psychological development, culminating in "liberation," "enlightenment," or "self-realization." If these traditions contained even a grain of truth, these explorers seemed to reason, then Western psychology's estimation of human potential was absurdly low. That Asian wisdom offered well-defined procedures through which its claims might be explored and validated greatly increased the interest shown them by these empirically trained psychologists. Broadly speaking, this was the beginning of a new investigation into the psychotransformative factors of humman contemplative life, an investigation that, although initially rooted in Asian traditions, has begun to extend into Western religious traditions as well. The widely applicable yet tradition-neutral concept of attention has been central to this work.

ATTENTION IN THE TRADITIONS. Practices that strengthen the capacity for concentration or attention play a role in most great religious traditions. The importance of developing attention is most readily seen in the great traditions that arose in India, namely Hinduism and Buddhism. From the Upanisadic seers down to the present day there is in India an unbroken tradition of humanity's attempt to yoke itself (body and mind) to ultimate reality. Yoga takes on many forms, but its essential psychological form is the practice of one-pointed attention or concentration (*citta-ekāgratā*). Whether by fixing the attention on a mantra or on the flow of the breath or on some other object, the attempt to quiet the automatized activities of the mind through concentrated attention is the first step and continuing theme of Hindu psychospiritual yoga.

It could hardly be otherwise for the traditions that stemmed from Gautama Buddha. The *samatha* and *vipassanā* forms of meditation in the Theravada tradition require as their root and anchor an ever increasing ability to attend, to hold one's attention fast without relinquishing it to the various psychological forces that tend to scatter it. *Samatha* is the cultivation of one-pointed attention and is the common starting point for all major types of Buddhist meditation. *Vipassanā* meditation consists in the deployment of the concentrated attention developed in *samatha* from point to point within the organism, with the intent of understanding certain Buddhist doctrines at subtle experiential levels. Though the attention sought in *vipassanā* meditation is not one-pointed in the sense of being fixed on a single object, it remains a highly concentrated and directed form of attention, the very antithesis of dispersed mental wandering. Likewise, the Tibetan practice of visualization, which is attempted only after preparatory training in *samatha,* is a way of developing the mind's ability to remain steadfastly attentive by requiring it to construct elaborate sacred images upon the screen of consciousness. The two practices central to the Zen tradition, *kōan* and *zazen,* have as their common denominator the practice of sustained, vigilant attention. Moreover, the major contemplative schools of Buddhism stress the virtue of mindfulness, the quality of being present, aware, and, in a word, attentive.

By the fourth century BCE the ancient Daoists had already developed methods of meditation and trance induction. They were called *zuowang* and *zuochan* and were fundamentally a training in concentration by the fixation of attention on the breath. How much the origin of these practices owed to Indian influence is not known.

When one turns to the three great Western monotheisms, the phenomenon of attention is not so starkly visible. Nevertheless it is there. Broadly speaking, spiritual disciplines in the monotheisms are not so fully developed as their cousins in the East. Still, these monotheisms contain profound mystical dimensions, and it is there one must look for the practice of attention.

The actual practices and methods of Jewish mystical prayer are difficult to determine. Qabbalist scholar Aryeh Kaplan states that "some three thousand Kabbalah texts exist in print, and . . . the vast majority deal with theoretical Kabbalah" (*Meditation and Kabbalah,* New York, 1982, p. 1). There are also monumental problems of translation and interpretation. References to method can, however, be found intermittently in the ancient Talmudic texts, quite frequently in the works of Avraham Abulafia and some of his contemporaries, in the Safad qabbalists of the sixteenth century, in the works of Isaac Luria, and in the Hasidic texts. The key terms are *hitbodedut* ("meditation"), *hitboded* ("to meditate"), and *kavvanah* ("concentration, attention, intention"). The first two come from a root meaning "to be secluded." They often point beyond mere physical seclusion, however, to the seclusion beyond the discursive activity of the mind attained through concentration. *Kavvanah* likewise refers to a concentrative or attentive form of prayer capable of inducing an altered, "higher" state of consciousness. For the Jewish mystical tradition as a whole, mantralike repetitions of sacred liturgical words seem to be the central vehicles for the training of attention, but references to concentration upon mental images, letter designs, and color and light visualizations can also be found in the texts. Concentrative exercises are also linked with bodily movements and the movement of the breath. Some of the exercises prescribed by the thirteenth-century Abulafia involve long, complex series of instructions and seem to require massive attentive capability to perform without distraction. In this they seem akin to the Tibetan Buddhist practice of elaborate visualization.

In the Christian world is found the Eastern Orthodox "Prayer of the Heart," or "Jesus Prayer," a Christian *mantra* that contemplatives repeat in order to recollect themselves and to unify attention, thereby opening their hearts to the divine presence. The bulk of contemplative texts in the Roman Catholic tradition, like those of the Judaic tradition, are concerned with theory and doctrine rather than specifics of method. In the early Middle Ages one can find references to contemplation as a seeking for God in stillness, repose, and tranquillity, but the specificity ends here. The late Middle Ages witnessed among contemplatives the growth of a prayer form called *lectio divina,* or meditative reading of the scriptures. Cistercian monk Thomas Keating describes *lectio divina* as the cultivation of a "capacity to listen at ever deepening levels of inward attention" (*America,* April 8, 1978). Ladders of progress in mystical prayer abound at this time, but one is hard pressed to find any advice on how to climb them. Practical mysticism comes more fully into bloom with the arrival of Teresa of Ávila and John of the Cross in the sixteenth century. In the opinion of Jacques Maritain, the latter remains the prototypical practitioner of the Roman Catholic mystical way, *the* mystical doctor and psychologist of the contemplative life *par excellence.* And John's way was the way of inner silence, of nondiscursive prayer, of states of mind brought about by what he called "peaceful loving attention unto God." Lately an attempt has been made to popularize this kind of contemplative attention in the "centering prayer," another *mantra*-like technique, for focusing attention and quieting the mind, similar to the Jesus Prayer of Eastern Orthodoxy.

In the world of Islam there are the contemplative practices of both silent and vocal *dhikr,* again a *mantra*-like repetition, usually of the names of God, aimed at harnessing the will and its power of attention. Javad Nurbakhsh, spiritual head of the Nimatullahi order of Sufis, writes that *dhikr* (Pers., *zikr*) "is the total and uncompromised attention to God" (*In the Paradise of the Sufis,* New York, 1979, p. 32). The purpose of *zikr,* the remembrance of the divine name, "is to create a 'unity of attention'. Until this is attained the disciple will be attentive to the various attachments of the self. Therefore, the disciple should try to incline his or her scattered attention to the all encompassing point of Unity" (ibid., p. 20). A more generic term for the kind of meditative attention achieved in *dhikr* is *murāqabah. Murāqabah* is described as a "concentration of one's attention upon God," as the "presence of heart with God," "the involvement of the (human) spirit (*rūḥ*) in God's breath" and the "concentrating of one's whole being upon God" (ibid., p. 72). *Murāqabah,* the Ṣūfīs say, is not only a human activity but a divine one as well: it is because God is constantly attentive to humans that they should be constantly attentive to him.

Two men who have drawn on the traditions listed above and whose eclectic writings have had a significant impact among those interested in self-transformation are G. I. Gurdjieff and Jiddu Krishnamurti. Crucial to the Gurdjieff work is the exercise of "self-remembering," fundamentally an attempt to develop sustained, undistracted, observational attention both outwardly toward experience and, at the same time, inwardly toward the experiencer. This particular aspect of the Gurdjieff work is very similar to the "bare attention" exercises of Buddhist *vipassanā* meditation. Krishnamurti teaches that the practice fundamental to psychological transformation is "choiceless awareness." It is, again, the cultivation of sustained, observational, nonreactive attention to inner and outer experience. In isolation from the rest of Krishnamurti's teaching, this form of attention does not differ significantly from either that of the Gurdjieff work or Buddhist "bare attention."

The preceding survey is not to be understood as implying that the training of attention is the same in every tradition or that it occupies the same relative importance within the various traditions. Quite to the contrary, attention is in these traditions developed in a variety of ways, to varying degrees of depth, within strikingly different contexts, and to apparently different ends. Given the diverse group of contemplative phenomena to which the word *attention* applies, the central task of this article, a general and synthetic account of the nature and significance of contemplative attention, is fraught with difficulty. Needless to say, the following analysis can only be expected to apply "more or less" to the various specific traditions, yet it does claim to indicate the general outlines of something common to them all. Moreover, such a synthetic account is not in vain, for despite the differentiating factors surrounding the training of attention in the various traditions, there seem to be some unitive factors as well. Summarily, the traditions mentioned above conform in the understanding that the human mind in its ordinary state is somehow fragmented, unfree, and given to dispersion. Within each tradition there has evolved at least some kind of practice leading to mental stability, unity, control, and integration. Furthermore, in each tradition is discovered the assumption that such psychological transformation can make reality and truth experientially more accessible.

The Nature of Contemplative Attention. Attention is, of course, a concept that occurs outside the domain of religious praxis. It is part of the vocabulary of everyday mental functioning, and even there it seems to be overworked, a single, blunt term for a wide variety of mental states. The temptation to think of it as one thing should be resisted. It is better to think of it as a spectrum that reaches from the virtual absence of attention, as in sheer daydreaming and mechanically determined mental flux, to acutely active alertness. Though contemplative practices themselves admit of a wide variation, the quality of attention that they require and at which they aim resides at the upper end of the spectrum. The varieties of contemplative attention, in other words, resemble each other more than any one of them resembles that uneven and intermittent phenomenon of ordinary mental functioning that is usually called attention. Some further notion of the relative difference between ordinary kinds of attention and the kinds of attention at which contemplative practices aim must be developed to avoid confusion.

Ordinary attention may be described as discursive, intermittent, and passive. It moves incessantly from object to object, its intensity "flickers," often succumbing to mental wandering, and it is reactive, or "passive," in relation to some sequence of external objects or to the autonomous stream of consciousness. Take, for example, the act in which the reader is currently engaged. The reader is following this exposition closely, attempting to understand it. Surely this is attention rather than inattention. The contemplative would agree. But he would suggest that this attention is discursive, and largely passive. In this particular case, these words are doing the discursing for the reader's attention, leading it from place to place. Moreover, it is highly likely that, while reading, the reader's attention will have wandered a surprising number of times, pulled down one associational path or another by autonomous psychic fluctuations. Even if the reader now turned away from this article and turned inward to work out a chain of reasoning, it is likely to be done in a state of predominantly passive attention, for such creative activity largely involves a sorting out of what the automatic activity of the psyche presents. Only in the most disciplined and highly concentrated feats of thought is passivity reduced to a minimum and the gap between ordinary and contemplative attention closed. However, the intellective modes just mentioned are hardly characteristic of the run of ordinary mentation. There, the discursive, intermittent, and passive qualities of attention are fully evident. In ordinary mentation, attention is not a quality of mind that one brings to experience, but something that occurs, rather haphazardly, as one's organism becomes momentarily more interested in some inner or outer sequence of phenomena. Ordinary attention comes and goes without one's consent; it is not something one *does,* but something that *happens* to an individual. For most people most of the time, "attention" is stimulated, conditioned, and led by mobilizations of energy along the habit-pathways within an individual so that when it confronts its object it is always faced, as it were, by a *fait accompli.*

The attention at which contemplative exercises aim, then, may be distinguished not only from sheer inattention but from ordinary discursive attention as well. Contemplative attention is relatively nondiscursive, sustained, and uncapitulatingly alert. In the majority of contemplative exercises, an effort is made to prevent attention from being diffused centrifugally; rather, the effort is to consolidate it centripetally and to maintain its sharpness. This article shall use the word *concentrative* to name attentional efforts having these characteristics. Contemplative exercises thus aim at concentrative attention, but also at something that has no counterpart in ordinary mentation and can be properly understood only in reference to the attempt to establish concentrative attention. It may be called nonreactive or receptive attention. Concentration and nonreactivity (or receptivity) are the prime distinguishing characteristics of contemplative attention, and both must be kept in mind in order to understand the psychospiritual significance of attentional training.

Some literature on the psychology of meditation has used the terms *concentrative* and *receptive* to name exclusive categories of attentional practice. This can be misleading, however, as contemplative practices seem universally to share a "concentrative" element. Rather, the true categorical distinction is between focalized and defocalized attention. For example, the classical Yoga system of Patañjali requires an extreme focalization of attention on a single point or object for the purposes of absorption of enstasis. In contrast, Soto Zen's *shikantaza* prescribes a *de*focalized attention to the entire screen of consciousness with the proviso that one attend to what arises without reaction or discursive elaboration. But "focalized" and "defocalized" do not translate into "concentrative" and "receptive" for the simple reason that defocalization does not imply a lack of those qualities I have named "concentrative." Contemplative attention may be defocalized, open to the flow of mental contents, but it does not think about them or get carried away by them. It is, in fact, a "nonthinking," that is, themeless and nondiscursive attention, even though defocalized, and the directive for attention to remain acutely alert and sustained applies fully. Without these concentrative qualities, the description of defocalized meditation would be a description of daydreaming. Furthermore, even the purest form of defocalized meditation, Soto Zen's *shikantaza,* is, according to some Zen teachers, too difficult for beginners. To practice it fruitfully requires that a student already have a well-developed attentive ability derived from preliminary training in one-pointed attention to the movement of breath, a *koan,* or some other object. In other words, even the purest form of so-called receptive meditation has roots in focalized, concentrative efforts.

Although focalization and defocalization refer to actual distinctions in the deployment of attention found in contemplative exercises, this distinction is of secondary importance. Of primary importance is the discovery that contemplative practices universally require the aspirant to develop an attentional capacity that, unlike his or her ordinary attention, is relatively nondiscursive, uncapitulatingly alert, and sustained. It is in this sense that contemplative efforts from qabbalistic repetitions of the divine name to Theravada Buddhists' bare attention have a common concentrative element.

Of equal importance is the common receptive or nonreactive element. It stems from unavoidable failure in the attempt to maintain concentrative attention. No one attains attentive equipoise for the mere wishing, and the problem arises regarding what is to be done when distractions occur. Concentrative work is constantly interrupted by autonomous mobilizations of psychic energies that dissolve the unity of attention and carry it away on a stream of associations. What then? There are only two choices: to react with frustration and judgment (in which case one has unwittingly slipped into the very egocentric perspective from which contemplative exercises are trying to extricate one) or simply to observe the distraction nonreactively, to note it, accept it, and then gently bring the mind back to its concentrated mode. Contemplative traditions clearly tend to encourage the latter choice. The theistic constant of "acceptance of God's will," the Christian doctrine of *apatheia* ("indifference"), Buddhist *upekkha* ("equanimity"), Hindu *karmayoga* (acting without seeking the fruits of action), and Daoist *weiwuwei* ("the inaction of action")—all of these, when brought to bear on contemplative exercises, encourage the attitude of nonreactivity. To be nonreactively attentive is, for theistic contemplatives, to bring no new sinful self-willfulness to the practice of contemplation; for nontheistic contemplatives it is to bring no new *karman* to a process meant to dissolve it.

Given the fact that the deep-seated habit patterns of the psyche will repeatedly overpower an inchoate concentrative ability and assuming that the practitioner will repeatedly attempt to establish active, concentrative attention, his constant companions in all of this are impartiality, equanimity, and nonreactive acceptance. When concentrated attention falters, one is to be a nonreactive witness to what has arisen. Whatever emerges in the mind is observed and allowed to pass without being elaborated upon or reacted to. Images, thoughts, and feelings arise because of the automatism of deeply embedded psychological structures, but their lure is not taken. They are not allowed to steal attention and send it floundering down a stream of associations. One establishes and reestablishes concentrated attention, but when it is interrupted one learns to disidentify with the contents of consciousness, to maintain a choiceless, nonreactive awareness, and to quiet the ego with its preferences.

Should this description appear distinctly Asian and raise doubts regarding its relevance to contemplative prayer practices in the monotheisms, consider, by way of balance, this passage from *Your Word Is Fire* (1977), a work on Hasidic prayer:

> Any teaching that places such great emphasis on total concentration in prayer must . . . deal with the question of distraction. What is a person to do when alien thoughts enter his mind and lead him away from prayer? . . . The Baal Shem Tov . . . spoke against the attempts of his contemporaries to . . . do battle with distracting thoughts. . . . He taught that each distraction may become a ladder by which one may ascend to a new level of devotion. . . . God [is] present in that moment of distraction! And only he who truly knows that God is present in *all* things, including those thoughts he seeks to flee, can be a leader of prayer. (pp. 15–16)

Concentration and nonreactivity are thus to be conceived as different but complementary modes of attention, which, it may be conjectured, occur in different and constantly changing ratios across the wide variety of contemplative, attentional practices. In tandem they allow the practitioner progressively to achieve disidentification from the conditioned mental flow and thus to observe that flow objectively and impartially. The dynamics and import of this process can now be discussed.

SIGNIFICANCE OF ATTENTIONAL EXERCISES. The datum against which the significance of attentional exercises is to be understood is the relatively ceaseless and autonomous profusion of mental contents in ordinary conscious experience. Ordinary states of human consciousness may be said to be relatively noisy and dispersed, and the religious traditions that contain attentional exercises do so based on a belief that even ordinary mental turbulence is antithetical to the quiet clarity, recollection, and self-possession needed to understand and appreciate reality in subtler than usual ways. Most spiritual traditions thus contain some notion or other of the false consciousness, or false self, which when overcome, rendered transparent, or otherwise transcended, allows the self-manifesting quality of truth to disclose itself. It may be said, therefore, that the central significance of attentional exercises is to release the human being from bondage to the machinations of the false self. And just as one might attempt to explain an eraser by referring first to what it erases, an explanation of the significance of contemplative attention is best begun with a notion of the false self that it combats.

Human beings experience a persistent need to preserve and expand their being, and thus every person, from birth, undertakes what may be called a self-project. Everyone longs to be special, to be a center of importance and value, to possess life's fullness even unto immortality, and everyone spends energy in pursuit of those things that, according to his or her level of understanding, will fulfill these longings. According to many contemplative traditions, such longing is grounded in a profound truth: ultimately, one shares in the undying life of the ultimately real. Unfortunately, however, the ego transcendence that contemplative traditions prescribe is usually rejected in favor of endless vain attempts to expand the ego in the external world through possession, projection, and gratification.

From the beginning, then, the self-project determines an indiviudual's appropriation of experience in two ways. One is through desire for and attachment to any loci of thought or experience that affirm the self and enhance its will to be. The other is by defense against or aversion for those loci of thought or experience that negate the self and impress upon it its contingency and dispensability. The lineaments of personality are built up in these ways. The psyche becomes a multidimensional webwork of likes and dislikes, desires and aversions, both gross and subtle, that manifest personality in the same way that black and white dots can create the illusion of a face. Time and repetition harden parts of the webwork into iron necessity. With increasing automatism, experiences both internal and external are evaluated according to whether they affirm or negate the self-project. The self-project gradually unfolds into an egocentric system in which beliefs, feelings, perceptions, experiences, and behaviors are automatically viewed and assessed around one's sense of value and worth as an individual. By the time a human being is old enough even to begin to take an objective view of the self-project, he or she is hopelessly enmeshed in it. Predispositions have become so implicit and unconscious that the ego has little chance of recognizing the extent to which its psychological life is already determined. One automatically limits, selects, organizes, and interprets experience according to the demands of one's self-project. The chronic quality of this self-centeredness and the distance it creates between the person and reality is the basis for the common psychological wisdom behind, for example, the Christian's insistence of the "originality" of sin, the Buddhist's notion of the beginninglessness of ignorance, or the Muslim's belief about the recalcitrant quality of *ghaflah,* the forgetfulness of God.

The false self can thus be understood as a metaphor for psychic automatism, that is, automatic, egocentric, habit-determined patterns of thought, emotive reaction and assessment, and imaginary activity that filter and distort reality and skew behavior, according to the needs of the self-project. Having hardened into relatively permanent psychological "structures," these predispositional patterns may be conceived as constantly feeding on available psychic energy, dissolving it into the endless associational flotsam in the stream of consciousness. Energy that would otherwise be manifested as the delight of open and present-centered awareness is inexorably drawn to these structures and there disintegrates into the image-films and commentaries—the "noise"—that suffuse ordinary consciousness. As psychologist Charles Tart sees it, "there is a fluctuating but generally large drain on awareness energy at all times by the multitude of automated, interacting structures whose operation constitutes personality" (*States of Consciousness,* New York, 1975, p. 23). The psychic machinery runs by itself, ever exacerbating one's slavery to conditioning, and, moment to moment, steals attention from the real present and blows it like fluffy spores of milkweed down the lanes of the past or up the streets of the future. The imaginative-emotive distraction is so constant that it becomes accepted as normal. It is seen not as the drain of energy and loss of being it actually is but as the natural state of affairs.

What allows the self-aggravating automatism of the false self to function unchecked is, in a word, *identification.* Every desire, every feeling, every thought, as Gurdjieff once put it, says "I." As long as one is unconsciously and automatically identifying with the changing contents of consciousness, one never suspects that one's true nature remains hidden. If spiritual freedom means anything, however, it means first and foremost a freedom from such automatic identification. Contemplative traditions affirm in one metaphor or another that one's true identity lies not in the changing contents of consciousness but in a deeper layer of the self, mind, or soul. To reach this deeper layer one must slowly disentangle oneself from automatic identification with the contents of consciousness. That is, in order for the self to realize the *telos* adumbrated for it in the doctrines and images of the contemplative tradition to which it belongs, it is necessary to cut beneath psychological noise, to disidentify with it so as to understand it objectively rather than be entangled in it, and, ultimately, to dismantle the very habit-formed structures that ceaselessly produce it.

Once automatism and identification are understood to be the sustainers of the false self, one is in a position to understand the psychotransformative power of concentrated, nonreactive attention. For whether a person is a Muslim repeating the names of God or a Theravada Buddhist practicing bare attention, he or she is, to one degree or another, cultivating the disidentification that leads to the deautomatization of the false self.

The mere act of trying to hold the mind to a single point, an act with which higher forms of meditation begin, teaches the beginner in a radically concrete and experiential way, that he or she has little or no control over the mental flow. All attentional training starts with this failure. This is the first great step in the work of objectifying the mental flow, that is, of seeing it not as something that "I" am doing but something that is simply happening. Without this realization no progress can be made, for one must first know one is in prison in order to work intelligently to escape. Thus, when the Christian is asked to concentrate his attention solely upon God, when the Muslim attempts to link his attention solely to the names of God, when the Tibetan Buddhist attempts with massive attention to construct elaborate images of Tara on the screen of consciousness, the first lesson these practitioners learn is that they *cannot* do it. Ordinary mentation is freshly understood to be foreign to the deepest reality of one's being. The more regularly this is seen the clearer it becomes that one is *not* one's thoughts, and the more profoundly one understands the distinction between consciousness as such and the contents of consciousness. Objectification of the contents of consciousness and disidentification with them are natural outcomes.

At the same time that a contemplative learns that mental flow is not the same as identity, what one deeply is, he or she understands that neither is it the ultimate reality he or she seeks to know. The theocentric contemplative is reminded that God cannot be captured within a construct of consciousness and that, as John of the Cross says, God does not fit into an occupied heart. The Zen Buddhist understands that the *kōan* whose solution may reveal the Buddha nature cannot be solved by an intellectual construct. Not surprisingly, the metaphor of self-emptying spans contemplative traditions. The lesson everywhere reveals that mental flow can neither be identical with nor contain the reality-source one seeks. The aspirant is thus doubly disposed to disvalue the incessant discursion of the mind, to disidentify and detach himself or herself from it. Increasing objectification of mental contents enhances human ability to assess motivation and impulses *before* they are translated into action, thus permitting increasing freedom from impulsive behavior. One can imagine the pace of life slackening and one's behavior becoming smoother and more deliberate. Attention becomes less a slave to external stimuli and more consolidated within.

As attentional training progresses and detachment from the automatized flow of mental contents is achieved, the coiled springs responsible for that very automatism begin to unwind. In other words, disidentification leads to deautomatization.

A single elaboration must suffice. The incessant discursion of the mind may be conceived as the result of the useless consumption of energy by the overlearned structures or patterns of the psyche. Associational thought-sequences that seem virtually unending are a common pattern of such consumption. An increasingly quiet and disidentified attention could catch associational sequences in their beginnings and thus forestall the automatic stimulation of still other sequences and some of the behavior that flows impulsively therefrom. The integrity of the automatized processes, however, depends upon reinforcement through repetition. Forestalling associational sequences and interrupting habitual behavior would weaken that integrity. Unwholesome impulses caught by attention would be deprived of a chance to bear fruit in action or associational elaboration. Attention—or presence, or mindfulness—may thus be conceived as depriving predispositional patterns of their diet.

Contemplative attentional exercises are, in other words, strategies of starvation. Every moment that available energy is consolidated in concentrative and nonreactive attention is a moment when automatized processes cannot replenish themselves. In the dynamic world of the psyche, there is no stasis: if automatisms do not grow more strongly solidified, they begin to weaken and dissolve. When deprived of the nutriment formerly afforded to them by distracted states of mind, the automatized processes of the mind begin to disintegrate. Contemplative attention practiced over a long period of time may dissolve and uproot even the most recalcitrant pockets of psychological automatism, allowing consciousness to recollect the ontic freedom and clarity that are its birthright.

Deautomatization, then, is a psychological, tradition-neutral term that describes an essential aspect of the process of spiritual liberation, the freeing of oneself from bondage to the false self. It names, furthermore, a gradual, long-term process of transformation, a process within which discrete mystical experiences reach fruition and without which they are destined to fade into ineffectual memories.

By upsetting normal functioning, attentional work is bound to evoke eruptions from the unconscious. Recognition of unconscious contents and insight into their meaning, without, however, fascinated fixation upon them, is a necessary step in the process. A part of attentional work, then, is like the therapeutic process in depth psychology: its purpose is to reclaim and reintegrate parts of the unconscious for the self. But attentional work is unlike depth-psychological work in another, crucial respect. For while the contemplative recognizes the contents of the unconscious as belonging to the self, he or she simultaneously sees that self (or is exhorted by tradition to see it) objectively, remaining cognizant of the fact that attachment to it or identification with it will continue to prevent truth from disclosing itself in its fullness.

Ideally, then, long coursing in attentional exercises increases the mind's ability to conserve and rechannel energy, to spend less of it on the useless imaginative-emotive elaboration of desire and anxiety characteristic of ordinary mentation. Ideas, emotions, and images continue to arise autonomously in the mind, but the attentive mind, the emptying mind, is less easily caught up in spasmodic reactions to them, less easily yanked into the past or flung into the future by them. Emotions and impressions begin to be experienced in their "purity"; they "leave no tracks," as the Zen saying goes. Energy formerly spent in emotive reactions, ego defense, fantasy, and fear now becomes the very delight of present-centeredness and a reservoir of compassion. As the psychic habit patterns of the former person are deautomatized, new patterns are formed in alignment with his or her strengthening intention-toward-awakening. Deautomatizing attention and reconstitutive *in*tention lead to a new reticulation of the predispositional structures of consciousness, to a new ecology of mind. By emptying the self of unconscious compulsions and reactive patterns built up over time by the self-project, the contemplative discovers a new life of receptivity, internal freedom, and clarity. Impartial observation of one's existential situation becomes increasingly acute. Intuition is awakened. Freed of the bonds of fear and desire, one begins to taste primordial, ontic freedom. Released into the present, one knows that intersection of time and eternity where reality is, where divinity dwells.

THE IMPORTANCE OF TRADITION. Having thus far focused on the nature and practice of contemplative attention, this article has deliberately ignored the myriad contexts within which it may be practiced. Here, then, is an attempt to adjust the balance by a few concluding remarks on the importance of spiritual tradition.

First, it should be clear that the function of contemplative work is largely destructive. The accoutrements of a spiritual tradition provide a protective and constructive framework within which destructive work can proceed. The more seriously the foundations of the false self are undermined by the practice of attention, the fiercer become the storms of protest from within. The "dying" that occurs during contemplative work can cause internal shocks and reactions so profound that only the deep contours of a tradition can absorb them and turn them to creative effect. The support of a tradition hundreds of years old—rich in symbolism, metaphysical and psychological maps, and the accumulated experience of thousands of past wayfarers—and the guidance of an experienced teacher are indispensable. A "new age" movement that wishes to champion contemplative technique but jettison the traditional context in which it was originally lodged seems likely to be either very superficial or very dangerous or both.

Second, tradition stresses and a spiritual community supports, in a way that a mere technique cannot, the importance of morality as a *sine qua non* foundation and necessary ongoing accompaniment to the inner work. Without the rectification of external conduct, inner work cannot proceed far. One would be hard pressed to find a single exception to this rule in the great traditions.

Finally, human transformation is effected not solely by isolated bouts of intense attentional training; such training must be linked to ordinary life by an intentionality that makes every aspect of life a part of the spiritual work. The contemplative opus, in other words, is hardly limited to formal periods of attentional practice. Ordinary activity and formal contemplative practice must reinforce each other and between them sustain the continuity of practice that alone can awaken the mind and help it realize the *telos* adumbrated for it in the images and concepts of the tradition to which it belongs. And it is precisely the traditions' *teloi* that, by evoking the aspirant's intentionality, provide this continuity.

A spiritual *telos* evokes in the aspirant an overarching aim that fuses the activities of ordinary life and the periods of attentional practice into a continuous line, a "praying without ceasing." So fused, life becomes the "willing of one thing," a Kierkegaardian phrase for "purity of heart" or mature faith. Hubert Benoit calls this state of being "total attention," though a better rendering might be "attention to the totality." When attention is "total" one becomes increasingly aware not only of what one is doing but why one is doing it. One becomes increasingly able to grasp the universal context of one's smallest action, able to see the farthest object toward which one's action in this moment tends. When the intention-toward-awakening becomes so pervasive, attention so "total," and willing so unified, the continuity of praxis leading to deep personal transformation is achieved. Attentional exercises, then, are hardly meant to be practiced in isolation. Their effectiveness requires not only long practice but also the support of a community, the guidance of tradition, the tranquillity effected by moral purification, and, finally, the continuity of practice that allows the power of will, indispensable to the transformative work, to be fully born.

SEE ALSO Meditation; Spiritual Discipline.

BIBLIOGRAPHY

Articles

A classic source for the study of attention is William James, "Attention," in *The Principles of Psychology, vol. 1* [orig. pub. 1890] (Cambridge: Harvard University Press, 1981). One of the best sources of reflection on the phenomenon of attention in religious meditation and its role in psychological transformation is the *Journal of Transpersonal Psychology* (Stanford, Calif., 1969–). Among the entries most helpful in preparation of this article to which one could turn for elaboration of many points here left undeveloped are John Welwood's "Meditation and the Unconscious: A New Perspective," *Journal of Transpersonal Psychology* 9 (1977): 1–26; Michael C. Washburn's "Observations Relevant to a Unified Theory of Meditation," *Journal of Transpersonal Psychology* 10 (1978):45–65; and Ken Wilber's "A Developmental View of Consciousness," *Journal of Transpersonal Psychology* 11 (1979): 1–22. Another seminal article and the one to which I am indebted for the concept of deautomatization is Arthur I. Deikman's "Deautomatization and the Mystic Experience," originally appearing in *Psychiatry* 29 (1966): 324–338, and now more accessibly in *Understanding Mysticism* ed. Richard Woods (Garden City, N.Y.: Doubleday, 1980), 240–260. Prof. Carol Zaleski has made important contributions to the study of the religious significance of attentional practices in "Attention as a Key to Buddhist-Christian Dialogue," *Buddhist-Christian Studies* (1994): 63–80, and "Attending to Attention," in *Faithful Imagining: Essays in Honor of Richard R. Niebuhr* (Atlanta, 1995), which delivers, via footnotes, a bibliographical sketch of psychological, philosophical and religious studies of attention spanning the last two hundred years. Also helpful is noted author Daniel Goleman's brief article, "The Mechanics of Attention," in *Inner Knowing*, ed. Helen Palmer (New York, 1998).

Books

The present study is indebted at many points to Hubert Benoit's *Zen and the Psychology of Transformation* (Rochester, Vt.,

1990, orig. pub. *The Supreme Doctrine* [New York, 1959]), a brilliant if idiosyncratic account of the subtleties of attentional work. P. D. Ouspensky's famed exposition of the ideas of G. I. Gurdjieff in *In Search of the Miraculous* (New York, 1949) offers many provocative suggestions on the function of attention and will in the spiritual life. Because "attentional training" is a technical synonym for meditation, studies of the latter are also highly relevant to the topic at hand. Key works in the field include: Deane Shapiro and Roger Walsh, eds., *Meditation: Classical and Contemporary Perspectives* (New York: Aldine, 1984); *The Meeting of the Ways: Explorations in East-West Psychology,* ed. John Welwood (New York, 1979); K. Wilber, J. Engler, D. Brown, et al., *Transformations of Consciousness: Conventional and Contemplative Perspectives on Development* (Boston, 1986); Michael Washburn, *The Ego and the Dynamic Ground,* 2d revised edition (Albany, N.Y., 1995); Charles Tart, *States of Consciousness* (New York, 1975); and Daniel Goleman, *The Varieties of the Meditative Experience* (New York, 1977). Most of the articles and books mentioned here contain excellent bibliographies for those interested in pursuing matters still further. A book not necessarily sympathetic to the concerns of the present article but extremely helpful in understanding the dynamics of the false self and the universal psychological dimensions of the human predicament is Ernest Becker's *Denial of Death* (New York, 1973).

PHILIP NOVAK (1987 AND 2005)

ATTIS SEE CYBELE; DYING AND RISING GODS

ISBN 0-02-865734-9